Proceedings of the

15th European Conference on Innovation and Entrepreneurship

a Virtual Conference

Supported by

Università degli Studi Internazionali di Roma (UNINT)

Edited by

Prof. Alessandro De Nisco

16-18 September 2020

Review Process

Papers submitted to this conference have been double-blind peer reviewed before final acceptance to the conference. Initially, abstracts were reviewed for relevance and accessibility and successful authors were invited to submit full papers. Many thanks to the reviewers who helped ensure the quality of all the submissions.

Ethics and Publication Malpractice Policy

ACIL adheres to a strict ethics and publication malpractice policy for all publications – details of which can be found here:
http://www.academic-conferences.org/policies/ethics-policy-for-publishing-in-the-conference-proceedings-of-academic-conferences-and-publishing-international-limited/

Self-Archiving and Paper Repositories

We actively encourage authors of papers in ACIL conference proceedings and journals to upload their published papers to university repositories and research bodies such as ResearchGate and Academic.edu. Full reference to the original publication should be provided.

Conference Proceedings

The Conference Proceedings is a book published with an ISBN and ISSN. The proceedings have been submitted to a number of accreditation, citation and indexing bodies including Thomson ISI Web of Science and Elsevier Scopus.

Author affiliation details in these proceedings have been reproduced as supplied by the authors themselves.

The Electronic version of the Conference Proceedings is available to download from DROPBOX https://tinyurl.com/ECIE20 Select Download and then Direct Download to access the Pdf file. Free download is available for conference participants for a period of 2 weeks after the conference.

The Conference Proceedings for this year and previous years can be purchased from http://academic-bookshop.com

e-Book ISBN: 978-1-912764-68-6
e-Book ISSN: 2049-1069
Book version ISBN: 978-1-912764-67-9
Book Version ISSN: 2049-1050

Published by Academic Conferences International Limited

Reading, UK

+44-118-972-4148
www.academic-conferences.org
info@academic-conferences.org

Contents

ECIE Preface

These proceedings represent the work of contributors to the 15th European Conference on Innovation and Entrepreneurship (ECIE 2020), hosted by Università degli Studi Internazionali di Roma (UNINT), Italy on 17-18 September 2020. The Conference Chair is Prof. Alessandro De Nisco and the Programme Chair is Adjunct Professor Emilio Sassone Corsi, both from Università degli Studi Internazionali di Roma (UNINT), Italy.

ECIE is a well-established event on the academic research calendar and now in its 15th year, the key aim remains the opportunity for participants to share ideas and meet the people who hold them. The conference was due to be held at Università degli Studi Internazionali di Roma (UNINT), Italy, but due to the global Covid-19 pandemic it was moved online to be held as a virtual event. The scope of papers will ensure an interesting two days. The subjects covered illustrate the wide range of topics that fall into this important and ever-growing area of research.

The keynote presentation is given by Dr. Kenneth A. Grant, from Ryerson University, Toronto, Canada on the topic of *The Special Case of the University Entrepreneurial Ecosystem.* During the second day of the conference there will be a plenary session entitled NoBORDER INNOVATION – African & European Models of Teaching Entrepreneurship & Innovation.

With an initial submission of 251 abstracts, after the double blind, peer review process there are 92 Academic research papers, 15 PhD research papers, 4 Masters Research papers and 4 work-in-progress papers published in these Conference Proceedings. These papers represent research from Bahrain, Belgium, Brazil, Canada, Czech Republic, Denmark, Egypt, Finland, Germany, Ghana, Greece, India, Indonesia, Iran, Iraq, Ireland, Israel, Italy, Japan, Kazakhstan, Lithuania, Mexico, Nigeria, Norway, Peru, Poland, Portugal, Romania, Russia, Russian Federation, Saudi Arabia, Slovakia, South Africa, South Korea, Sweden, Switzerland, Thailand, The Netherlands, Turkey, UK, USA,

We hope you enjoy the conference.

Prof. Alessandro De Nisco
Università degli Studi Internazionali di Roma (UNINT), Italy
September 2020

ECIE Conference Committee

Biographies

Conference and Programme Chairs

Prof. Alessandro De Nisco is Professor of Management and Marketing at UNINT University, where he is also Dean of the Faculty of Economics and coordinator of the International PhD program in "Intercultural relations and international management". His research interests focus mainly on international management and consumer behavior. Prof De Nisco's research results have been published in leading academic journals, including International Marketing Review, European Management Journal, Journal of Business Research and Managing Service Quality. Moreover, his research has been presented at, and published in the proceedings of, numerous international conferences. He has received 5 best paper awards for his studies in the fields of international management and marketing

Adjunct Professor Emilio Sassone Corsi, is a physicist who teaches "Start up and Business Planning" at UNINT University and "Business Models Innovation" at the University of Rome Tor Vergata. He is an innovative entrepreneur in various sectors that have in common the theme of sustainability. In particular he is CEO of Management Innovation Srl, a financial company that makes scouting and seed capital investments in innovative companies, CEO of Glass to Power SpA, a spin-off of the University of Milan Bicocca that produces transparent photovoltaic windows, CEO of Crypt Security Srl, a company hosted at Tor Vergata University and producing innovative Digital Security products, CEO of Galatea Bio Tech Srl, a spin-off of Bicocca University, engaged in the Bioplastics sector.

Keynote Speaker

A Canadian Scot, **Ken Grant** is currently the Chair of the Department of Entrepreneurship and Strategy in the Ted Rogers School of Management at Ryerson University in Toronto. He holds a DBA from Henley Business School, an MBA from the Schulich School of Business and a BA from the Open University. He is also a Certified Management Consultant and has been a visiting professor at a number of universities in China, Europe and the United Kingdom.

Panellists

Dr. Kevin Koidl, Research Fellow at Trinity College Dublin, expert in Social Technologies, Machine Learning and Natural Language Processing. Dr. Koidl's contribution will centre around aspects of personalised online learning as part of a wider edtech movement. Specifically he will provide insight on how cognitive models of learning evolve within a wider contextual and social context. For this methods leaning on Artificial Intelligence are explored. Overall, his contribution is to provide strategic insight into how a personal learning assistant can create a more globally fair and affordable education.

Dr. Nawtej Dosanjh, Provost at the University of Law (London), Board Member at the London School of Business & Finance. Dr. Dosanjh's contribution will be about designing and transforming educational delivery systems across internationally distributed campuses with widely differing perspectives on entrepreneurship and innovation. His discussion will focus on systems that can be highly personalized and yet rapidly scale to thousands of students, through hybrid face-to-face and online learning.

Dr. Gaidi Faraj, Dean at the African Leadership University, W.E.B Dubois Visiting Scholar at the University of Massachusetts. Dr. Faraj's contribution focuses on teaching innovation, entrepreneurship and futures thinking across the African continent. Specifically he will address how curriculum design in areas of entrepreneurship and innovation at the undergraduate and graduate levels must confront issues of leapfrogging inequality. Harnessing innovation to accelerate entrepreneurial progress emerges as a key component to equipping young Africans in a rapidly-changing world.

Dr. Zukiswa Mthimunye, Professor of Leadership at the Gordon Institute of Business Science, University of Pretoria. Dr. Mthimunye's contribution will focus on the specific role that Leadership Studies plays in positioning students to succeed in areas of entrepreneurship and innovation on the African continent.

Dr. Ying Zhang, Associate Dean and Professor of Entrepreneurship and Innovation at the Rotterdam School of Management, Erasmus University. Dr. Zhang's contribution will focus on equality-based value sharing society, the future of jobs, and the globalization-localization paradox.

Mr. Chidi Afulezi, Faculty of Entrepreneurship & Innovation at the African Leadership University. Mr. Afulezi's contribution centres on applied learning and shifts in pedagogical methods in Africa today. His work across product management, entrepreneurship, and the incubator/accelerator ecosystem on the continent serves as a critical perspective in the discussion of effective outcomes in higher education.

Mini Track Chairs

Erik Arntsen works primarily at the Centre for Entrepreneurship at the University of Agder in Norway, where he has been instrumental in the development, implementation and teaching of a number of studies, courses and programs – both at the master and bachelor level. He has worked in research projects mainly related to entrepreneurship and the installment and start-up of the Centre for Entrepreneurship at the University of Agder. Arntsen was Managing Director of a regional early stage venture fund, Partner and External Evaluator of several international entrepreneurship research projects.

Alexandros Kakouris, MsC, PhD, PhD, is an adjunct lecturer in entrepreneurship and innovation at the University of Peloponnese, at the Hellenic Open University and he is also innovation consultant at the National Observatory of Athens. He holds PhD in Physics, PhD in Entrepreneurship and a MSc in Adult Education. He has been involved in entrepreneurship since 2006 researching educational and learning issues. His special interest concerns fostering entrepreneurship and innovation to science graduates and the support of youth entrepreneurship through teaching and counselling. He also specialises in nascent entrepreneurship, creativity, transformative and experiential learning.

Stefan Lagrosen is a professor of business administration and director of the eHealth Institute at Linnaeus University, Sweden. His research has mainly concerned quality management, particularly in schools and healthcare as well as cultural aspects of quality management. In addition, he has researched work-related health and social media marketing as well as marketing and quality management in the health and fitness industry. He has published a large number of scientific articles and several books in those areas. He is also an experienced educator having taught courses on all levels from basic to doctoral.

Professor Ana Martins is Interim Dean and Head of the Graduate School of Business & Leadership. Her research interests are centred on humanising leadership and organisations.

Professor Isabel Martins is an Associate Professor in Organisational Behaviour. Her research interests address organisational learning, unlearning and knowledge management.

Professor Vannie Naidoo is a full-time academic and researcher. Her research areas include management, service marketing, entrepreneurship, social media, green marketing and sustainability; ICTs in management and education.

Ruslan Pavlov is a senior researcher at the Central Economics and Mathematics Institute of the Russian Academy of Sciences, and post graduated from the same institution. His research interests include the diversification of business and big cycles, as well as the social responsibility of business and social entrepreneurship

Doan Winkel, PhD, is the John J. Kahl, Sr. Chair in Entrepreneurship and the Director of the Edward M. Muldoon Center for Entrepreneurship at John Carroll University. He is the President-Elect of the United States Association for Small Business and Entrepreneurship (USASBE), and a contributing editor for *Entrepreneurship Education & Pedagogy*. He holds a PhD in Organizational Behavior from the University of Wisconsin – Milwaukee. Doan co-founded the Experiential Entrepreneurship Curriculum, which is being used at more than 70 universities to engage students in practicing entrepreneurial skills. His focus is on experiential learning, especially regarding equipping young people with the mindset to think and act entrepreneurially in whatever career path they choose.

Biographies of Contributing Authors

Elisabeth Lise Agerbaek MA is associate Professor in digital development at UCL University College, Odense, Denmark. Current research interests are in the field of university/industry collaboration in relation to robotics, AI and tourism. Other research areas are graphic design and information graphics, because of an entrepreneurial background in design.

Daniel Agyapong is an Associate Professor of Finance and Entrepreneurship at the University of Cape Coast (Ghana). He has 55+ research articles on SME financing and sustainable business. He is involved in African Institute of Transformational Entrepreneurship, Switch Africa Green, Building Bridges Across Continents, and German-African University Partnership Platform for the Development of Entrepreneurs project.

Ali Ahmad is a Senior Fellow of the Higher Education Academy UK, Fellow of Enterprise Educators UK and module leader for Innovation at WMG, University of Warwick. He has a decade of experience in teaching and scholarship in the areas of entrepreneurship and innovation. His works are regularly published in reputable international journals.

Sawsan Al-Husseini is an Assistant Professor and a dean of Institute of Administration - Rusafa at Middle Technical University, Baghdad, Iraq. She received her PhD in management information systems from Plymouth University, UK, in 2014.Her main research areas are innovation, management information systems and education. She has many papers published at national and international journals and conferences.

Wassim J. Aloulou is a professor (Ass.) at the CEAS at IMSIU. He received his PhD. in Management Sciences from the UPMF Grenoble 2, France, and from the FEMS of Sfax, Tunisia in 2008. He is an article editor of Sage Open and has published in journals including EJIM, IJGE, JSBED, JEC, JEEE, JIBED, and MEJM among others.

Dalal Alrubaishi is an Assistant Professor in Entrepreneurship and Family Businesses at the College of Business Administration in Princess Nourah bint Abdulrahman University (PNU), Riyadh, Saudi Arabia. She holds an MBA from Prince Sultan University in Riyadh and a PhD from Royal Holloway, University of London, UK.

Maher Alzyadat is a PhD student in Engineering Management, Department of electronic engineering at the University of York, UK. He holds an MSC in Engineering management, His main research areas are Intrapreneurship and innovation in technology SMEs."

John Amoah is a PhD student at the Tomas Bata University, Zlin Czech Republic at the faculty of Management and Economic Department. He holds a masters degree in Marketing from the Pentecost University of Ghana. His main research area is on SMEs development in developing countries.

Thomas Arctaedius is affiliated professor in entrepreneurship at Royal College of Music in Stockholm, Sweden. He received his PhD in nuclear physics at Stockholm University 1989. His main research areas are early stage start-ups, musical entrepreneurship and entrepreneurship education. He is also an experienced entrepreneur and has started several high-tech companies.

Kaija Arhio, Ph.D. (econ.) working as a principal lecturer at Centria University of Applied Sciences in Ylivieska, Finland. Her background is in engineering (wood technology) and in the field of entrepreneurship research her interests has been focused in networks of small woodworking companies. Nowadays she is teaching entrepreneurship and other business related topics and is involved also in regional projects of entrepreneurship education.

Yuliya Asaturova, PhD (Econ.), Peter the Great Saint-Petersburg Polytechnic University, Russia. Currently employed as associate professor for Higher School of Economics and Engeneering. Presently the research is focused on Financial management, innovative models, digital economy. Yuliya teaches Economics, Financial Management, Financial Analysis, Economics of enterprise.
E-mail: asaturova_yum@spbstu.ru

Natália Augustínová completed her master's degree at the University of Ss. Cyril and Methodius in Trnava, Faculty of Mass Media Communication in 2019. Since that she has been working at the faculty as a full-time doctoral student. She deals with issues of CSR, sustainability and graphic design.

Manuel Luís Au-Yong Oliveira did his post-doctoral studies at the University of Aveiro (2016-2019) with the title "Elements that contribute to organisational competitiveness". Manuel has a PhD in Industrial Engineering and Management, from FEUP (University of Porto, 2012; distinction awarded to the thesis), an MBA from Cardiff Business School (UK, 1993; distinction awarded to the dissertation). Manuel is an Assistant Professor at the University of Aveiro (DEGEIT) where he lectures at the undergraduate, master's and doctoral levels on marketing, innovation, strategy and research methods.

Stratos Baloutsos is a doctoral candidate at AUEB and Business Development Manager at ACEin. His research interests concern entrepreneurship, innovation, and specifically drivers that accelerate start-up within broader innovation ecosystems. He holds a B.Sc. and M.Sc. in Mechanical Engineering and an M.B.A. He is also working on business modelling and commercialization for several EU projects.

Yulia Balycheva, PhD, is a senior research associate of the Central Economics and Mathematics Institute of RAS. Her research areas are the innovative behaviour of firms.

Raphael Bar-El is Professor Emeritus at Ben Gurion University and faculty member of the of the Applied Economics Department at the Sapir Academic College, where he established the specialization of entrepreneurship and innovation. He specializes in regional economic development and innovation policy. He has extensive experience in consultancy in Israel, Brazil and many developing countries.

Gediminas Baublys is a PhD Candidate at Vilnius University, Lithuania. He is focusing his scientific research on the business organization's proactive transformation competence identification and development. His main areas of interest are organizational resilience, sustainability, and agility

Jaroslav Bednárik graduated from the STU in Trnava and he received a PhD degree in 2009. Since 1997, he has been working at University of Ss. Cyril and Methodius in Trnava, Faculty of Mass Media Communication. In 2012 he received the title of Associate Professor. He deals with personal management, sustainable development and CSR.

Marcin Bielicki – research project manager at Poznan University of Economics and Business (Poland) and Fulbright Fellow from Texas Christian University (USA). His research interests are related to entrepreneurship, including above all business pre-incubation and problem-based learning.

Jaroslava Blazkova (Nemcova) is a CSR passionate Director of corporate communication and PhD student at Tomas Bata University. In her work at optics production company Meopta - opitka she focuses on brand, communication, CSR strategy and company culture. Her main research is focused on connections between how companies would like to be perceived and what projects are appropriate to help them achieve this goal.

James Bourne This case study paper looks into the drivers and barriers the successful KT&TT in the PTWEZ, South West Wales. Semi-structured interviews were carried out on key actors in academia, Industry and Government. This also considers this in the context of the Regional Innovation System and the Triple helix model.

Wouter Broekaert, senior researcher at the Center for Sustainable Entrepreneurship (CenSE), has been conducting research on family firms, SMEs and innovation since 2007. He has performed research on topics such as family firms' competitive strategy, strategic change, corporate performance, psychological ownership and corporate financing. His research on innovation focuses on organizational flexibility and open innovation.

Alexandru Ilie Buzatu entrepreneur from Brasov, Romania; PhD student, Academy of Economic Studies Bucharest, Business Administration program. MBA from CNAM Paris and wanted to continue research/studies on business administration. Was accepted at the Academy with a r program on gaining competitive advantage & developing international businesses. Participated at 8 international conferences; published in specialized journals. Research areas are digital transformation, competitive advantage, sustainability, & helping ompanies, mainly from emerging areas, to develop international sustainable businesses with the help of technology.

Ozge Can completed her PhD in Management Studies in Sabanci University, Istanbul. She has been working as a full-time faculty in Yasar University, Izmir since 2013. She also had a researcher position at University of Antwerp, Belgium (2014-2015). She is particularly interested in institutional entrepreneurship, organizational identities andcategorizations, and development of organizational fields

Angelo Cavallo, Ph.D. is Assistant Professor at Politecnico di Milano, Italy. His main research areas include Strategic Management and Entrepreneurship. He has been mainly involved in analyzing business models of digital startups and modeling dynamic and complex systems such as the Entrepreneurial Ecosystem. He is author of journal articles, book chapters and conference proceedings.

Jeroen Coelen is a PhD candidate at Delft University of Technology and lecturer/teacher on entrepreneurship. His research areas are the fundamental building blocks of startups and entrepreneurship education.

Oscarina Conceição is Professor at Polytechnic Institute of Cávado and Ave and researcher at Dinâmia'CET-IUL (Instituto Universitário de Lisboa). She has a PhD in Economics from University of Minho (Braga, Portugal). Her research interests include the following topics: entrepreneurship; academic entrepreneurship; innovation process and their socio-economic effects; knowledge transfer; knowledge and innovation networks.

Elizabeth Conradie is an Innovation Services Manager at Idea Generator Unit, Central University of Technology, Free State, SA. She received her PhD in Molecular Biology from University of Stellenbosch, SA in 2005. She is currently working the field of entrepreneurship and innovation. Her main research areas are new enterprise and intellectual property training developments with an interest in gamification as an educational tool.

Francis Dams lecturer-researcher at the School for Product Development of the Faculty for Design Sciences at Antwerp University, Belgium. He teaches Business Planning, Strategic Management and Project Management in the Master's program in Product Development. He is conducting PhD research about the entrepreneurial propensity of individuals who possess strong entrepreneurial capabilities. He has 25 years of experience in industry and he has dealt with various responsibilities in product development and innovation management.

Stefano D'Angelo is a PhD Candidate researching in the field of Corporate Entrepreneurship. His main research areas include Corporate Entrepreneurship and Digital Entrepreneurship.

Fern Davies is a lecturer of strategy at Swansea University, UK. She received her PhD in business strategy from the School of Management in 2018. Her main research interests centre on SMEs, business ethics and innovation management, particularly in the health and life science sector.

Elli Diakanastasi (MSc, Phd. Candidate) Network and Operations Manager of Athens Center for Entrepreneurship and Innovation. Over decade's worth of experience in entrepreneurship. PhD candidate studying inner workings of entrepreneurial teams and has a Master's in management, product innovation, and entrepreneurship. She is also a founding member of ACEin and an inseparable part of it. In her time there she has coached dozens of teams and taken part in EU funded projects to cultivate and promote entrepreneurial skills and mindset.

Anca Otilia Dodescu. Professor of European Economics and Regional Economics at Faculty of Economic Sciences, University of Oradea, Romania (since 2004), Dean (2004-2011), OECD&European Commission country correspondent for Annual Report on Inclusive Entrepreneurship in Europe (2013-2017), (co-)author of 20 books and 100 scientific papers, manager/expert in 20 EU projects in business support, research interests: inclusive entrepreneurship, regional development.

Yulia A. Dubolazova is an associate professor of economics at Peter the Great St. Petersburg Polytechnic University (SPbPU), Russia. She received his PhD in economics sciences from Peter the Great St. Petersburg Polytechnic University (SPbPU) in 2019. Her main research areas are economics, management, accounting, financial and economical activity of enterprises.

Alice Edwards, MBA is a Ph.D. candidate in Industrial/Organizational Psychology attending Walden University, USA. She founded The CEO Within, LLC, a consulting firm, and co-founded MassInflux LLC, a web and mobile development company. Her main research areas are social capital, education, employees, health and wellbeing, and using technology for process improvement, evaluation, and scalability.

Joan Edwards is a PhD candidate at the Waterford Institute of Technology. Her research focuses on sociotechnical systems and examines the intersection of technology, sociology, and industry. Her work seeks to examine the performative turn in technology and the impact of technological developments on organisations and markets.

Ingunn Elvekrok is an associate professor at The University College of Southeastern-Norway, School of Business. Her research interests include innovation, networks and regional innovation politics, as well as management and tourism studies. She has published in journals such as Regional Studies and Journal of Travel research.

Hadia Fakhreldin is Professor of International Business at the British University in Egypt. She is the Vice Dean for Teaching and Learning at the Faculty of Business, Economics and Political Science. She obtained her B.S.C degree in Economics from the American University in Cairo and her Ph.D. from Cairo University. Her research interest/focus is in the areas of SME development, internationalization, sustainability and cross-cultural management.

Tribowo Rachmat Fauzan, S.T.P. is a graduate student of Master of Science Management (MSM) School of Business and Management, Institut Teknologi Bandung (ITB). He graduated from Universitas Padjadjaran majoring in Food Industrial Technology in 2016. Now he joined Entrepreneurship and Technology Management Research Group under supervision of Wawan Dhewanto, PhD.

Mário Franco is a Professor of Entrepreneurship and SME Administration at the Department of Management and Economics, Beira Interior University, Portugal. He received his PhD in Management from Beira Interior University in 2002. In 1997, he was a doctoral candidate and participated in the European Doctoral Programme in Entrepreneurship and Small Business Management in Spain and Sweden. He is also a member of a Research Center (CEFAGE-UBI) and currently involved in several research projects on SMEs.

Oleg Golichenko has a degree of Doctor of Economic Sciences. He is a chief research associate at the Central Economics and Mathematics Institute of the RAS. He is also a professor at the Moscow Physics and Technique Institute. His research interests are related to investigation of innovation development processes and design of public policy.

Carlos Filipe Vaz Gomes. I was born in 6th of January of 1997, in the city of Guimarães in Portugal. I have a degree in Business Sciences and currently I am a Master's in Business Management and Internationalization student."

Ken Grant is the Chair of the Department of Entrepreneurship and Strategy in the Ted Rogers School of Management at Ryerson University, Toronto. With research interests in entrepreneurial ecosystems, angel investment, youth and diversity issues in entrepreneurship and in pedagogy, he teaches in entrepreneurship, strategy and management consulting.

Allam Hamdan: Professor of Accounting, Dean of college of Business and Finance. Ahlia University. Awarded the First Prize of Al-Owais Creative Award, UAE, 2017; the Second Prize of Rashid bin Humaid Award for Culture and Science, UAE, 2016; the Third Prize of Arab Prize for the Social Sciences and Humanities, Qatar, 2015, and the First Prize of "Durrat Watan", UAE, 2013.

Wayne Hand is currently working for a company operating in Ireland's financial sector. Qualifications include BA in Hospitality Management and MBS in Entrepreneurship and Marketing. Research interests are in the area of entrepreneurship, particularly focusing on the hospitality industry. Wayne is currently working on a project concerning Intrapreneurship and the hospitality industry.

Ata Harandi is a visiting lecturer of strategic management at Tehran University, Iran. He received his Ph.D. in strategic management from Allameh Tabataba'i University in 2018. He is an editor of the eight ISC's Journal and has been involved in organizing 8 international conferences. His main research areas are corporate governance, corporate strategy, and architecture conglomerate organization. He is a lecturer, consulting, supervisor, advisor, and author of strategic management at a corporate level.

Ruth Milagros Haro Merino is an MSc. Innovation Management and Entrepreneurship at the University of Manchester. She is the Coordinator of Innovation for Business programme at the Department of Entrepreneurship Management at the Peruvian University of Applied Sciences. Her research explores the triple-helix model, entrepreneurial skills, and design thinking for social change and development.

Victoria Harrison-Mirauer is an expert innovator with more than 20 years' experience spanning, advertising, marketing, digital transformation and innovation for global blue chips. She spent 7 years based in the UAE leading strategy and digital transformation for the media company and the world famous Formula One. Victoria is the Discipline Lead faculty for Innovation at Hult Ashridge Executive Education. A Cambridge graduate with an MSC in Organisational Psychology she commences her PHD in 2021.

Johanna Haunschild, M.Sc. is senior researcher at Fraunhofer IPK since 2015. She holds a master degree in Industrial Engineering with an emphasis on energy and environmental resources and a bachelor degree in Political Science. She has gathered plenty of work experience in different industry & business sectors. At IPK she is involved in international projects.

Fabian Hecklau, M. Sc., studied industrial engineering at the Otto-von-Guericke University Magdeburg and started working in applied research at Fraunhofer IFF in Magdeburg. Since 2015, he works for Fraunhofer IPK in Berlin and is involved in international research and consulting projects in the field of strategic management of organizations and innovation institutions. He is the head of the Competence Center Innovation Systems & Structures at Fraunhofer IPK since 2020.

Anne Heinze is responsible for entrepreneurship education at University of Applied Sciences HTW Berlin, Germany and develops concepts for how entrepreneurial thinking and acting can be integrated into course curricula. She finished her PhD in the area of cultural entrepreneurship in 2018 at Ludwigsburg University of Education, Germany.

Yusuke Hoshino is an associate professor of Faculty of Business Administration at Musashino University in Japan. He received his Ph.D from Hitotsubashi University. His main research areas are affective engineering, innovation, and business history.

Edson Huamaní Huapaya graduated from Pontifical Catholic University of Peru (PUCP) with BSc Economics, then gained his MSc Economics from Torcuato Di Tella University. He is currently the research coordinator in the Office of Economic Studies in the Ministry of Production of Peru. His main research areas are industrial organization, economic development and public policy evaluation.

Monika Ilves researched the successful strategies for a crowdfunding campaign in her master's thesis after she completed a successful crowdfunding campaign at Kickstarter. Monika graduated with a Master's degree in

Online Communication, is a board member of the SUN scholarship start-up network and connects entrepreneurs. Her main topics are automated marketing, entrepreneurship and innovation for people interested in starting a business.

Blanka Jarolimova is a senior lecturer at Tomas Bata University in Zlin. She graduated from Technical University in Brno, majoring in Management and Economics in 1995. She studied at the Oxford University, UK, where she gained scholarship at ESCP-EAP. For many years, she is also a member of the Chamber of the Tax Advisers of the Czech Republic. Taxation is her main area of research and expertise.

Ekapong Jungcharoensukying got a Thai Government scholarship to pursuit a PhD in Business Information System programme, Cork University Business School, University College Cork (UCC), Ireland. Before receiving this scholarship, he had been teaching in School of Information Technology, King Mongkut's University of Technology Thonburi (KMUTT) in Thailand.

Alexandros Kakouris, MsC, PhD, PhD, adjunct lecturer in entrepreneurship and innovation at University of Peloponnese, at Hellenic Open University and also innovation consultant at National Observatory of Athens. PhD in Physics, PhD in Entrepreneurship and MSc in Adult Education. Been involved in entrepreneurship since 2006 researching educational and learning issues. His special interest concerns fostering entrepreneurship and innovation to science graduates and the support of youth entrepreneurship through teaching and counselling. He also specialises in nascent entrepreneurship, creativity, transformative and experiential learning.

Maria Kamariotou is researcher associate at the Department of Applied Informatics, School of Information Sciences, University of Macedonia, Greece. She graduated from the University of Macedonia with a degree in Applied Informatics Department. She is author and also acts as reviewer for scientific journals and conference proceedings.

Noora Khalid Ali. MSc in Business, Kingdom of Bahrain. Holds a position KKB Bank, Bahrain.

Florian Kidschun is a researcher at Fraunhofer Institute for Production Systems and Design Technology (IPK), Division Corporate Management in Berlin, Germany. He studied Business Engineering at Technical University of Berlin and Dresden. Since joining Fraunhofer in 2015, he conducted international consulting projects in Europe and Brazil with project responsibility on Benchmarking, Strategic Business Development and Best Cost Country Sourcing. The focus of his research lies on the digital transformation of organizations.

Monika Klimontowicz is an Assistant Professor at University of Economics in Katowice, Department of Banking and Financial Markets. Her scientific interests focus on business strategy, banking innovations, creating value for customers, knowledge and intellectual capital, and competition on banking market. She is an author of over 60 scientific publications including 5 monographs. The results of her research are the topic of lectures delivered at the domestic and foreign universities in among others Finland, France, Spain, Portugal, Germany.

Evgenii A. Konnikov PHD, Associate Professor of the Higher School of Engineering and Economics in Peter the Great Saint-Petersburg Polytechnic University (Saint-Petersburg, Russia) since 2014. Research interests: application of the fuzzy logic toolkit to the assessment of complex economic phenomena and systems. Author of 22 publications indexed in Scopus.

Kseniya M. Kozinskaya is a post-graduate student in the Ural Federal University named after the First President of Russia B.N Yeltsin. Also, currently she is a Junior Researcher in the Institute of Economics, the Ural Branch of Russian Academy of Sciences. The field of research interests is institutional economics and social entrepreneurship.

Assel Kurmantayeva is the Development Manager at Civil Society DevelopmentAssociation "ARGO". She holds the Bachelor degree in Economics from the University of Essex and PhD student at Almaty Management University. She participated in the range of international projects run by the university and consulting projects in Kazakhstan form city administration and government on local development.

Alena Kusá, PhD. Professor operates at the University of St. Cyril and Methodius in Trnava, Slovakia. She is a professor and guarantor for media and communication studies. Research and pedagogical activities are focused on communication strategies of companies, consumer behavior, as well as current trends in communication of sustainability and environmental issues.

Stefan Lagrosen is a professor of business administration at Linnaeus University, Sweden. His research mainly concerns quality management, particularly in schools and healthcare as well as work-related health. He has published widely in those areas. In addition, he is an experienced educator, teaching on all levels.

Carla Azevedo Lobo (PhD in Management) is Assistant Professor at the Portucalense University, Oporto, Portugal. Researcher member at REMIT – Research on Economics, Management and Information Technologies. Research interests are: Internationalization and Entrepreneurship. Is the leading researcher of a project on Internationalization financed by Portuguese and European funds (IEcPBI). Reviewer of some International Journals, and has published in several international journals

Ekaterina Malevskaia-Malevich, 1987, Saint-Petersburg, Russia. Field of study: Financial management, Corporate Finance, Enterprise risk management, Bioeconomy, Recyclig, Environmental issues. Education: St.Petersburg State University of Economics (2014 PhD in Economics), St.Petersburg State Polytechnic University, Faculty of Economics and Management, Bachelor and master program, Field of study – Finance.

Hari Mann is a Professor of Strategy, Innovation and Entrepreneurship at Hult International Business School. He holds a doctorate and Masters degree from the London School of Economics. He has collaborated with a wide range of organisations including private and public sector bodies and think tanks such as the British Academy, and the Royal Society of Arts.

Anneli Manninen is Master of Arts, Business Administration and Science. She has long experience in education policy and regional development from municipal, ministerial and employer organizations. She is project manager for Enterprise Development project at Laurea University of Applied Sciences and doctoral student in Estonian Business School.

Jacopo Manotti is a Ph.D. Candidate researching in the field of Strategy and Entrepreneurship. His main topic concern business model innovation in digital firms, both incumbents and startups. He has recently started to pay attention to the phenomena of New Space Economy.

Florinda Matos holds a PhD in Social Sciences, Organizational Behavior Studies from the Technical University of Lisbon. She is a professor in Post-Graduate courses at the ISCTE – IUL. She is a researcher at DINÂMIA'CET – IUL and, presently, she is leading the project "KM3D - Knowledge Management in Additive Manufacturing: Designing New Business Models" in a national consortium, funded by FCT. She is the founder and the president of Intellectual Capital Association (ICAA).

Peter McLuskie is an Assistant Professor and Senior Lecturer in Enterprise and Entrepreneurship at Coventry University's International Centre for Transformational Entrepreneurship (ICTE) and a Fellow of the International Enterprise Educators Programme (IEEP). I have an interest in Enterprise Education and Creative Enterprise and have produced several publications on the pedagogic issues around enterprise and entrepreneurship.

Telma Mendes is an assistant professor in Business Sciences department at the School of Technology and Management (ESTG). She has a degree in Business Sciences and is an effective member of the Certified Accountants Order's. Her current research developed within the Masters' dissertation focuses on strategic management, with a special emphasis on firms' internationalization speed.

Patrícia Monteiro: "Graduated in Business Sciences, finalist in the master of management and internationalization of companies by ESTG P.PORTO. Her dissertation is under the marketing innovation already having an article published in this area. Currently, she works as a marketing consultant.

Chris Moon FRSA FHEA EFEEUK is a multi-award winning ecopreneur with a PhD from Imperial College. Formerly Head of Sustainability at two companies, Chris is judge of the F Factor, National Enterprise Educator Awards, International Innovation and Entrepreneurship Teaching Excellence Awards, and global Green Stories competition. Chris was awarded an Outstanding Teacher Award in 2019.

Anna Murphy is a lecturer at Cork Institute of Technology, Cork, Ireland. She is currently completing her PhD on immigrant food entrepreneurs and entrepreneurial ecosystems at University College Cork, Ireland. Her research interests are artisan food production, immigrant food entrepreneurs and entrepreneurial ecosystems.

Olga S. Nadezhina is a PhD in Economics, associate professor of the Graduate School of Economics, Peter the Great St. Petersburg Polytechnic University, Saint-Petersburg, Russia. She received her PhD in management of national economy (regional economy; labor market, human capital) in 2006. Her main research arears are regional economy, SMB, human capital.

Cecile Nieuwenhuizen, DHET-NRF SARChI Chair in Entrepreneurship Education, University of Johannesburg. Published 28 accredited articles, 52 conference papers with three Best Paper Awards.Total citations, 1219 and h-index of 17. Supervised seven Doctorates and 19 Masters to graduation. External examiner for 19 Doctorates and 29 Masters. Involved in family businesses.

Marcus O'Dair is Associate Dean of Knowledge Exchange and Enterprise at University of the Arts London (UAL). His books include Distributed Creativity, written as researcher in residence at Digital Catapult, and Different Every Time, a Radio 4 book of the week. He has also delivered consultancy for organisations including the British Council and Music Managers Forum, and released a number of acclaimed albums as a musician.

Ruslan Pavlov is a senior researcher at the Central Economics and Mathematics Institute, and post graduated from the same institution. His research interests include the diversification of business within a context of the long waves theory; institutions of social entrepreneurship as factors of social innovations.

Tor Helge Pedersen is an associate professor at Inland Business School, at Inland University College of Applied Sciences, Lillehammer, Norway. He received his PhD in political science from University of Tromsø in 2009. His main research areas are within public administration, organization and innovation.

Mariana Pita is an Invited Assistant,Department of Economics, Management, Industrial Engineering and Tourism (University of Aveiro, Portugal) in the field of entrepreneurship. Currently, completing the on Entrepreneurial Ecosystems. PhD on Public Policy - Innovation Policy on the University of Aveiro

Sergei N. Polbitsyn is the Professor of Entrepreneurship at the Ural Federal University in Russia. His research interests include entrepreneurship, entrepreneurial ecosystems, innovation policies and systems, social and economic development of rural communities.

Suteera Puangpronpitag is an Assistant Professor of Economics from Mahasarakham Business School, Mahasarakham University, Thailand. Her area of expertise is business economics focusing on university engagement and its impacts on regional development. She is specialized in research into collaborative models for practical knowledge exchange, especially the Triple Helix model and knowledge-based entrepreneurship.

Andrey Pushkarev works as a senior lecturer at the Department of Econometrics and Statistics and a junior researcher in UrFU. His research mainly focuses on innovations and productivity of firms in Russia. Apart from that, his scientific interests include agglomeration effects, econometrics and data analysis.

Yahia AF Ragab is a Senior Director at Green Plaza Centre and a visiting staff member in Pharos University in Alexandria, Egypt. He holds a BSc. in Computer Science from Technological University Dublin and a Masters in Management from Trinity College Dublin, Ireland. His research interests include Artificial Intelligence, Internet Of Things (IoT), and Entrepreneurship.

Ranvir S. Rai is an Associate Professor in Innovation and Entrepreneurship at Kristiania University College. He holds a PhD from BI Norwegian Business School. His research interests concern innovation processes, disruptive innovation and use of design thinking as organizational capability. He has published in international journals; such as Information & Management and Service Industries Journal.

Anna Rauhut graduated with a master's degree in technology management at the University of Stuttgart. Since April 2019, Anna Rauhut is a research assistant at the Ferdinand-Steinbeis-Institute of the Steinbeis-Foundation.

She leads the funded research project TREND, which investigates an elaborates methods for digital business model innovation in the crafts sector.

Moritz Philip Recke studied Media Technology and Next Media at Hamburg University of Applied Sciences, conducted entrepreneurship policy research at UNSW Business School in Sydney and focused on entrepreneurial ecosystems, public policy discourse and sociotechnical imaginaries for his PhD. He is a faculty member of the Apple Developer Academy at University of Naples Federico II.

Yevhen Revtiuk is a assistant professor of management at Poznan University of Technology, Poland, and professor of management at Ivano-Frankivsk National Technical University of Oil and Gas, Ukraine. His main research areas are human capital management and entrepreneurial capital.

Nibedita Saha , MBA, Ph.D working at University Institute, Tomas Bata University in Zlin as a Project Manager for EU projects and e-COST Action since 2012 and also associated as Lecturer at Faculty of Management & Economics (FaME). Associated with e-COST Action- CA 15216, CA 18236 and HRS4R Project. She published 33 research articles. https://uni.utb.cz/en/contacts/nibedita-saha-ph-d-mba-2/

Fadhul Salman. MSc in Business, Kingdom of Bahrain. Holds a position KKB Bank, Bahrain.

Silvia Sanasi is a Ph.D. Candidate in strategy, innovation and entrepreneurship at the School of Management of Politecnico di Milano, where she also collaborates as a researcher in the Hi-Tech Startups Observatory. Her research interests encompass experimentation in business model design and innovation, as well as the strategic implications of innovation management and digital platforms.

Juha Saukkonen is a Senior lecturer of Management in JAMK University of Applied Sciences in Finland. He has individually and jointly published in journals and conferences on topics of Foresight, Knowledge Management, Anticipation and Entrepreneurial Learning and Education. He is a guest writer and lecturer on these topics in various universities and organizations abroad.

.

Kim Seok-Soo, Director of Global Entrepreneurs Foundation, Korea. Graduated from Seoul National University Doctoral (Hansung University, Consulting). Professor of Youth Entrepreneurs Academy Samsung Fine Chemicals (R&D). Kolon Industries (Technology Commercialization). The main research areas are SMEs' Performance, Startups & Entrepreneurs, Technology Commercialization, Digital Transformation of SMEs, Global Entrepreneurship

Aman Sharma is a final year student at Indian Institute of Technology - Kharagpur, pursuing a Dual Degree course in Chemical Engineering with Micro specialization in Engineering Entrepreneurship. He has had firsthand product development and strategizing experience during his roles within the strategy and resource management teams at India's largest child relief organization – Child Rights and You (CRY). He actively works in exploring the role of technology in bringing about sustainable positive impact for stakeholders belonging to all the economic strata.

Cristina Sousa is Assistant Professor at Iscte – Instituto Universitário de Lisboa and researcher at REMIT – Research on Economics, Management and Information Technologies and at DINAMIA'CET. Her research interests include: innovation processes and their socio-economic effects; the the dynamics of knowledge and innovation networks; entrepreneurship and new business models; and the transition to sustainable systems.

Gabriela Doina Stănciulescu is a PhD student at Doctoral School of Entrepreneurship, Business Engineering and Management, University "Politehnica" of Bucharest. She has a Bachelor's Degree in Electronics, Telecommunication and Information Technology and a Master's Degree in Entrepreneurship, Business Engineering & Management, obtained within the same university.

Chryssi Stathaki holds a Diploma in Planning and Regional Development and a Master of Science in European Regional Development Studies, both from the University of Thessaly, Greece. She is currently a Researcher and PhD Candidate at the University of Thessaly, Department of Planning and Regional Development.

Christy Suciu - Boise State University. She has written a book called "Design Thinking and Strategy," Suciu and Kaupins. Her research interests include design thinking, innovation, and strategy. She is published in the Academy of Management Learning and Education journal, "The Need for Design Thinking in Business Schools." She is also a design thinking consultant for major global companies.

Nina Szczygiel holds a PhD in Industrial Management and is an assistant professor in the Department of Economics, Management, Industrial Engineering and Tourism at the University of Aveiro, Portugal. Her main research areas are intersectoral, inter-organisational and social networks, integration, and mobility. She is particularly interested in quality of life and well-being in societies, organisations, and individuals.
Daria Telepaeva is a post graduate student of Ural Federal University, Russia. Her main research areas are volunteering at sports events and management of non-profit organizations.

George Teodorescu Univ. Prof. Head of the International Institute for Integral Innovation. Univ.Professor for Integral Innovation , Head of Master Program. Author of Kenotomy. International expert for Higher Education and Consulting in Integral Innovation. Innovation is Hope Projects for Creative Communities: India, South Africa, Peru, Namibia. Conceptualizer. Think tank moderator and keynote speaker

Elena Tkachenko (1969) – the Doctor of Economics, the professor of the Department of the Economy and management of enterprise (St. Petersburg State University Of Economics). Author more than 120 scientific and methodical works, including 10 textbooks and 7 monographs. The sphere of scientific interests –innovations, investments, management of the intellectual capital, Industrial development? finance, regional development

Maria Urbaniec is an Associate Professor at the Department of Entrepreneurship and Innovation of the Cracow University of Economics (Poland). She received her PhD in Economics and her MA in Business Economics from the International Graduate School Zittau at the Technische Universität Dresden (Germany). Her research focuses on entrepreneurship, innovation, sustainability, labour market, industry 4.0.

Marianna Urmínová has been working as a full-time doctoral student at the Faculty of Mass Media Communication in Trnava since 2019. As part of her scientific activities, she focuses mainly on marketing communications in the field of sustainable fashion, consumer behavior, customers and their environmentally oriented preferences.

Thea van der Westhuizen is from the University of KwaZulu-Natal's School of Management, Information Technology and Governance. She is a national convener for Universities South Africa, a body of twenty-six public universities, where she drives academic entrepreneurship development in Learning, Teaching and Research.
Nicole Vaskovits, M. Sc. studied Industrial engineering and management in Magdeburg and Jena (Germany). After her studies, she worked at Autovision GmbH in Wolfsburg as a logistics planner and since 2014, she work as a research associate at the Chair of Materials Handling, Material Flow, Logistics at the Technical University of Munich.

Andreas Walmsley is Associate Professor in Entrepreneurship at the International Centre for Transformational Entrepreneurship, Coventry University. His research revolves around entrepreneurship education, mentoring for entrepreneurship and responsible entrepreneurship. He also continues to publish in the area of employment in the service industries.

Chun Yan (Kelly) Wang studying for a Masters by Research in School of Business at Dundalk Institute of Technology, Ireland. BA in Accounting and Finance and MBS in Entrepreneurship and Marketing. Completed her research dissertation ((2018) entitled "crowdfunding collaborates with traditional funding methods to create a better business financing option--start up entrepreneurs", presented research at International Academy of Management and Business Conference in Lisbon, Portugal 2018. Currently researches use and Adoption of Crowdfunding among Start-up Entrepreneurs in Ireland.

Knut Ingar Westeren has been a Professor of Economics at Nord University in Norway since 2001. He teaches knowledge management, knowledge and competitiveness and public economics at Nord University. He has numerous books and publications dealing with aspects of knowledge and competitiveness, the public sector and regional development.

Birgitte Wraae is Associate Professor in entrepreneurship at UCL University College Denmark. Her current research interests are in the field of entrepreneurship education; the role of the entrepreneurship educator, the student-educator relationship and identity formation of both students and educators.

Stella Xu is lecturer in Enterprises & Entreprenuership at Coventry University, a Fellow of HEA and Chartered member of Chartered Association of Business Schools. She is an MCIM and MCMI with rich industry & consulting experience. Her research areas are Urban sustainability and city branding, Entrepreneurship and Entrepreneurship Education. Her latest publications involve book chapters re E Business leadership, Entrepreneurship Education and blended teaching

Andrey Zaytsev, doctor of economics, professor of Higher School of Economics and Engineering, Peter the Great Saint-Petersburg Polytechnic University, Russia. Author of theory and methodology of rent regulation of economic relations sustainability in agrarian sphere. Research is focused on state regulation of economy, socio-economic development of countries and regions, theory of sustainable development, problems of econometric research, rent diagnostics and regulation, financial investment management, innovative development and intellectual capital management.

Heidi Zhou Zihui is a master student majoring Business in Marketing and Entrepreneurship programme at Dundalk Institute of Technology.

Impact of Interdisciplinary Teaching Practices in an Entrepreneurial Ecosystem

Elisabeth Agerbaek and Birgitte Wraa
UCL – University College, Odense, Denmark
ela@ucl.dk
biwr@ucl.dk
DOI: 10.34190/EIE.20.129

Abstract: This conceptual paper explores how changing educational practices towards interdisciplinary collaboration influences innovation and entrepreneurship processes for both students and educators when involved in a real-life project in cooperation with an external organisation. Recent research in entrepreneurship education suggests that the educational sector plays an important role as an actor in an entrepreneurship ecosystem. The ecosystem's five elements are students, educators, educational institution, community and external organisations (often a company). Furthermore, the entrepreneurship education ecosystem is characterised by the individual participants mutually influencing each other through dialogic relationships. Working with innovation and entrepreneurship processes in education can pose a challenge for educators, who are used to thinking within the traditional learning environment with educators and students as the main participants. There can be a discrepancy between the perception of an innovation and entrepreneurship project within the external organisation and within the educational institution. In the latter, the project will be viewed through the point of view of the different disciplines, in which any education is divided, whereas the project, in the former, will be seen more as a whole. Often projects are part of the teaching in a single discipline only, and the students will have other disciplines at the same time - which are then seen as unrelated. Working with the project in all disciplines will allow students and educators to view the project as a whole, thus mirroring the more holistic view of the external organisation. Our paper will present a didactic approach as well a practical tool for how to facilitate interdisciplinary collaboration as a method to support the educational institution in becoming an important and equal actor in the ecosystem as well as enhancing the transversal skills of the students. This would be of interest to educators who are in the process of planning and executing innovation and entrepreneurship projects involving several educational disciplines.

Keywords: entrepreneurship education ecosystem, transversal skills, interdisciplinary student projects, dialogic relationships, cooperation with companies

1. Introduction

In her exam portfolio a student at UCL - University College, Odense, Denmark writes: "I gained learning ... by helping customers find solutions to current challenges in their company, because of this educations' framework. Some customers find it difficult to define what they want and then they approach us so that we can help them find the most ideal solutions for their business. This is also where this program differs significantly from my former education." The student indicates two characteristics of this 'different' education. One is that the perceived learning derives from solving challenges from external companies, the other that it is the framework of the education that enables this. Without putting too much emphasis on one student's words she describes what this article aims to conceptually examine: When understanding themselves as an integrated part of an entrepreneurial education ecosystem, how can educators support learning through interdisciplinary collaboration?

In this article, we begin by introducing the entrepreneurial education ecosystem and from there move to discuss the impact for the educators and the education framed by the didactical relational model. Finally, we discuss how this can be used as a tool for planning and executing a semester's teaching based on interdisciplinary collaboration.

2. The entrepreneurship education ecosystem

Universities of applied sciences in Denmark is generally known for their collaborative work with both the private and the public sector. Our study is therefore founded in an acceptance of that educational institutions play a vital role in delivering and developing students, so that while they are students they are able to interact with the surrounding society, while at the same time making them ready to act in a job after their studies have been finalized. Brush (2014) describes the educational institutions as 'a complex community and environment where the learning interacts within a blended environment where time, place and space are ever changing' (p. 28). This article would like to argue for and present a method which facilitates how the educators granulate the curriculum of a specific entrepreneurial education by interpreting the learning goal into teaching so it aligns with the goals of external organisation.

The collaborative role can be illustrated by using an entrepreneurship education ecosystem (figure 1) that incorporates each actor alongside learning processes as central element of this interaction (Wraae and Thomsen, 2019, 2018). As such the actors are connected through dialogic relationships to underline how each actor is dependent on each other (Jones and Matlay, 2011). Moreover, and inspired by Bruyat and Julien (2001), the dialogic relationships includes reasoning that a connection between two actors in the system (for instance student and external organisation) can be viewed as a formed system that cannot be separated if our goal is to understand said system.

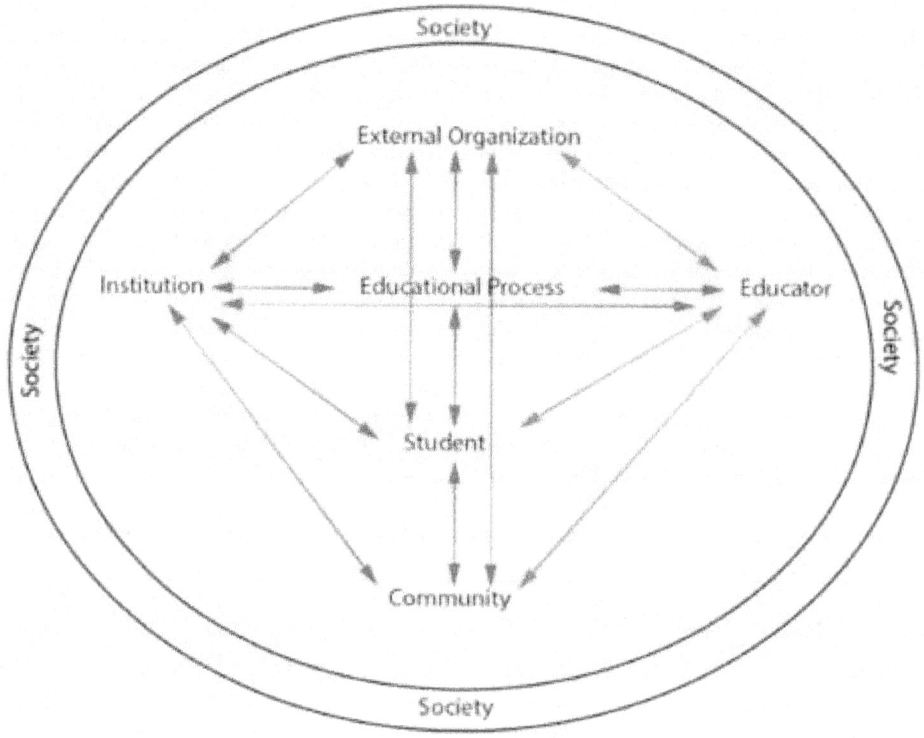

Figure 1: The entrepreneurship education ecosystem. Source: (Wraae and Thomsen, 2019, 2018)

Before zooming in on each actor we look towards Brush's (2014) description of the stakeholders as those that 'are social and human components of the school...all of those involved in the three aspects of entrepreneurship curriculum, co-curricular activities and research' (p. 32). Thus, each stakeholder represents different needs, motivation, and connections which are vital when establishing a productive ecosystem (Brush, 2014). Even though this paper has a wider perspective that the entrepreneurial curriculum entirely, we have applied the above thoughts to all interdisciplinary teaching practices.

Zooming in on the different elements presented in figure 1, we here focus on four of the elements: students, educators, educational institution and the external organisation. Beginning with the students, we perceive them as a diversified group with different backgrounds: 'from where have your students travelled? How different have their life paths been? What differences in prior learning and future aspirations do they hold? Finding answers to these three simple questions will reveal an abundance of diversity' (Jones and Matlay, 2011, p. 695). The represented student diversity is an important factor to take into consideration for the educator when planning and executing teaching. On the other hand, the students are expected to be able to develop different skills, including personal maturity skills (Chang and Rieple, 2013), as an actor in the ecosystem.

The students are enrolled at the educational institution, that bears the responsibility of offering studies, hiring competent educators and having the responsibility of acting with the surrounding society among a lot of other tasks that need to be performed in relation to administering studies. According to Ratten (2017) the educational institution has the role of the changer of mindsets. Furthermore, universities can transform 'the businesses and lives of people in the community' (Ratten, 2017, p. 312). The educational institutions are therefore expected to connect with their surroundings in a quest to offer entrepreneurial activities and to act entrepreneurial (Etzkowitz, 2013)

Moving on to the educators, educators often act in the role of liaison officers as they try to connect students with the external organisations and the community. Also, they act in the role of intermediaries between the educational institution and the students, for instance by delivering information or by interpreting the learning goals into teaching. Fulgence (2015) argues, that the educator acts in a lot of different roles; trainer, a participant in outreach activities and the responsibility for creating a learning environment.

These outreach activities are often in cooperation with the external organisations, which mostly are seen as representing the private companies. However, this element also contains both the public sector and NGOs (Wraae and Thomsen, 2019, 2018). No matter who the external organisations are, they are expected to have a need for and an interest in cooperating in innovative projects.

The above described elements are linked together through educational processes, whether that be delivering useful knowledge, entrepreneurial co-curricular activities (Brush, 2014) or working 'with the individual's capacity to embrace a combination of experience/knowledge and deeper understanding of a life world of uncertainty and complexity (Gibb and Haskins, 2013, pp. 14–15).

3. Planning and executing learning

Illeriis argues, that 'the external conditions of learning are features outside the learner that influence learning possibilities and are involved in the learning processes.' (Illeriis 2009, p. 17). The learning processes are in other words influenced by the educational processes, which may hinder or further the above mentioned 'change of mindset'.

Still following Bruyat and Julien (2001), we argue that the dialogic relationships between institution, educator and student as a formed system, are reflected in and can be transferred to the didactical relational model (Hiim and Hippe 2014) presented in figure 2. It highlights six aspects of this dialogue. In the thinking of the entrepreneurship education ecosystem we add a further actor - the external organisation - which changes the dialogue. This collaboration with external organisations poses didactical challenges for educators, who are used to regarding the educational process as one where educators and students are the only participants.

Founded in Hiim and Hippe (2014) we use their definition of didactics as a 'practical-theoretical planning, completion, evaluation and critical analysis of teaching and learning' (Hiim and Hippe 2014, p. 14).[1]

We use the model to highlight how the entrepreneurship educational ecosystem impacts the didactics. The dialogical relationships in the ecosystem have impact on all of the six categories of the didactical relations. Qvortrup & Keiding (2016) argue that recent discussions tend to focus on a 'methodication of didactics in HE' and thus emphasise the need for a holistic reflection focusing on the relations between and interdependency of the categories.

The category 'pedagogical framework' should be viewed as relationally dependant on the category 'educational content' when this is perceived by the educator as a having an impact on 'possibilities for teachers and students' (Hiim & Hippe 2014). For example, an interpretation of the totality of the learning goals for a specific education as divided into different educational disciplines, in each of which the students achieve specialised competences, can be seen both as a 'pedagogical framework' and as 'educational content'. Viewing the disciplines as educational framework may mean that the educator perceives it as unchangeable, whereas interpreting the disciplines as educational content allows the teachers more leeway for working across disciplines.

[1] We are aware that this is not the common English use of the term didactic as moral education. However, we want to keep the 'nordic' use of didactics as used by Hiim and Hippe (2014).

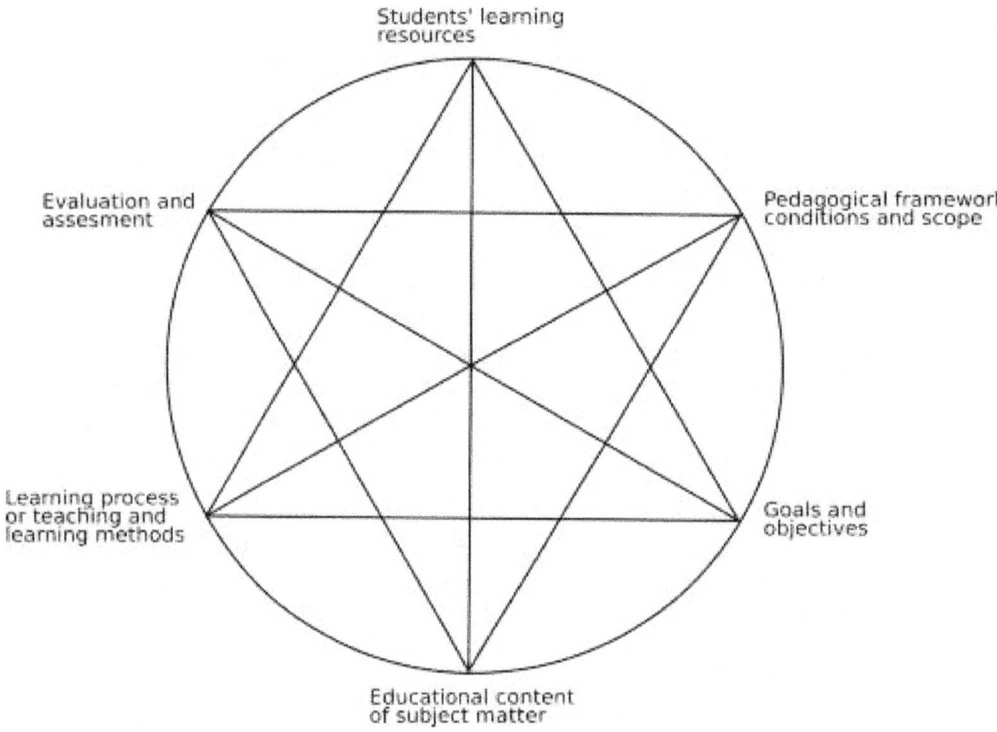

Figure 2: The didactical relational model. Source Hiim and Hippe 2014, p. 114

3.1 Goals and objectives

In Denmark the goals and objectives of an education are described in governmental acts as knowledge, skills and competences, following the Framework of Qualifications for the European Higher Education Area (The Framework of Qualifications 2018), to be met for the student to be perceived as educated. These are further described through a set of disciplines stipulated in a national curriculum.

As a part of the entrepreneurship education ecosystem the external organisation has a non-specialised viewpoint. For this actor the division of the education into several disciplines has little consequence. The external organisation expects the students to work with all the knowledge, skills and competences they possess, no matter how this is taught. In this way, the point of view of the external organisation is more holistic in relation to the students' overall competencies. This actor also evaluates a totality of competences in future employees. Berglund emphasize how an entrepreneurial approach to education has become linked to employability during the last two decades (Berglund 2013).

Following Hafeez and Esmail, Chang (2014) argues that the employability of graduates is closely linked to innovative solutions, and that student's employability 'involves extra efforts to develop their innovation capability by implementing appropriate curricula through strategic partnerships' (Chang 2014, p. 871). Regarding an external organisation as a strategic partner for an education is precisely to make room for innovation by allowing the students to work with a challenge put forward by this partner.

The goal of this industry/university collaboration is not to have the industry challenge be just an "add-on" to the normal teaching. To mirror the more holistic view of the external organisation the educator wants it to frame the totality of learning goals within knowledge, skills and competences that students are supposed to achieve in a specific semester.

3.2 Educational content or subject matter

Hiim and Hippe discuss the merits of regarding the content or subject matter of an education as separated from the teaching methods. Even in traditionally theoretical disciplines they question this separation: 'The question is whether it may not be possible here also to turn towards practical, real-life tasks that can help to structure the content in a meaningful way. This will require a relatively high degree of subject integration, theme teaching and problem-solving learning (Hiim and Hippe 2014, p. 220, authors' translation).

Agerbaek (2016) argues that to use an industry challenge as educational content requires that this challenge is authentic following Pirinen (2009), who explains that: "In this context: the term "authentic" means that all transactions and implementations of learning situations are simultaneously connected to real development cases within the world of work and have a definite value in the value network". Authentic challenges are real unsolved problems for which the external organisation, as well as the educators, does not have a set solution. If the innovation challenge is the educational content, the external organisation should be as unsure of the best result as the students (and educators) are.

Wahlgreen (2016) argues that the students experience the urgency of learning a skill or competence, the shorter the distance is between the learning period and the time when they need said skill to solve a real-life situation. As such, there will be no transfer if the time between learning and the point of application is too long. The benefit of giving the students a challenge from an external organisation as educational content is that they have reason to use theories and methods taught immediately.

In our experience the students understand the interdisciplinary interplay of the disciplines, if the external organisation challenge is brought into all disciplines, so every topic is explained and trained in light of this challenge. Thus, the understanding of different disciplines and the interplay between them can be learned through the work with the external organisation challenge.

3.3 Learning process or teaching and learning methods

The didactical relational thinking implies the educator's main role is that of a counsellor, Hiim and Hippe (2014) writes. This entails putting the student's work, experience and learning at the centre of the learning process. To enable the interdisciplinary understanding of a challenge put forward by the external partner, a team of educators, who teach all the different disciplines of an education in a semester, need to plan the learning process together.

Collaborating in a team of educators on an innovation challenge requires a double understanding. An educator must understand how his or her own discipline can be interpreted in relation to the challenge, as well as understanding how the interdisciplinary interplay may influence each discipline. The coherence and order of each discipline, as well as the overall professional progression should be considered.

3.4 Pedagogical framework conditions and scope

Hiim and Hippe describe the pedagogical framework conditions as preconditions for the teaching. This includes laws and acts but also more concrete organisational preconditions as the number of students in a class or the physical room in which teaching takes place (Hiim & Hippe 2014, p. 168). To integrate industry challenges framework conditions include allowing ample resources for team collaboration among educators as well as liberty to reinterpret learning goals.

Hiim and Hippe also argue that the teacher him/herself can be viewed as a part of the pedagogical framework: 'If we ... choose to regard the teacher as a framework condition, the teacher's qualifications and attitudes towards his or her subject, is perhaps one of the most important factors, which may further or hinder the teaching and learning' (Hiim & Hippe 2014, p. 169, authors' translation). An educator who regards his or her subject or discipline as too separate or unique for it to be involved in interdisciplinary collaboration thus may hinder the integration of an industry challenge into the curriculum. This means that institutional support for this type of collaboration is of the essence.

3.5 Student's learning resources

As already mentioned when we introduced the entrepreneurship education ecosystem, students are a diversified group. Jones and Matlay (2011) sum this up nicely: "Students differ in terms of the commitments they hold towards employment, volunteering and/or other personal commitments. Students differ in terms of their ability to engage in their studies due to the circumstances of their lives, many that lay beyond the responsibility and/or control of their educators. Students differ in terms of their preferred styles of learning." (p. 696). All considerations the educator must work around when planning and executing teaching in general, and in the case of working interdisciplinary consider how to emphasize and strengthen each student with the above in mind.

Hiim and Hippe emphasize that the learning resources of the students are fundamental in the teaching and learning processes, and that the point is to 'get the students to mobilize their own resources' (Hiim and Hippe 2014, p. 147, authors' translation). They argue, that meaning and motivation is related to proximity to reality. 'Teaching that is related to the pupil's real and practical life, is often perceived as meaningful' (Hiim and Hippe 2014, p. 149, authors' translation). Also, they describe how the students' learning resources are in constant evolvement, so they recommend that teachers never cease to adapt to these. This impacts how evaluation and assessment is framed, another of the six categories of the didactical relational model.

3.6 Evaluation and assessment

Besides the more traditional normative assessment methods applied to the traditional teaching we argue, that working interdisciplinary also invites to applying other forms for assessment. Chang and Rieple (2013) suggest to consider introducing reflective accounts that are more in alignment with working with real life projects and thus supports students being able to work with and solve both complicated and unstructured problems. Furthermore, other studies show, that reflective assessment elements heighten the students' understanding of their own learning (Wraae et al., 2018).

Portfolio as an assessment method has been widely acclaimed as a way of enhancing students' reflective practices. Qvortrup et al. (2017) describes three decades of pedagogical discussion surrounding this assessment method. Qvortrup (2006) describes the portfolio as "a particular interface for interaction between the individual student and the teacher, among students, but also between the individual student and the education system". Thus, the portfolio could be seen as an assessment method that supports the dialogical relationships within the entrepreneurial educational ecosystem.

4. Putting the tool into practice

Several ways of adding an innovation challenge to a semester-flow can be envisioned. Firstly, you can have different challenges for each discipline. Secondly, you can work with the challenge as "breaks" between otherwise not directly related teaching in each discipline. Thirdly, you can use the challenge as a frame around all disciplines taught in a specific semester, so each taught discipline relates all topics to finding a solution to the challenge. The three ways are illustrated below:

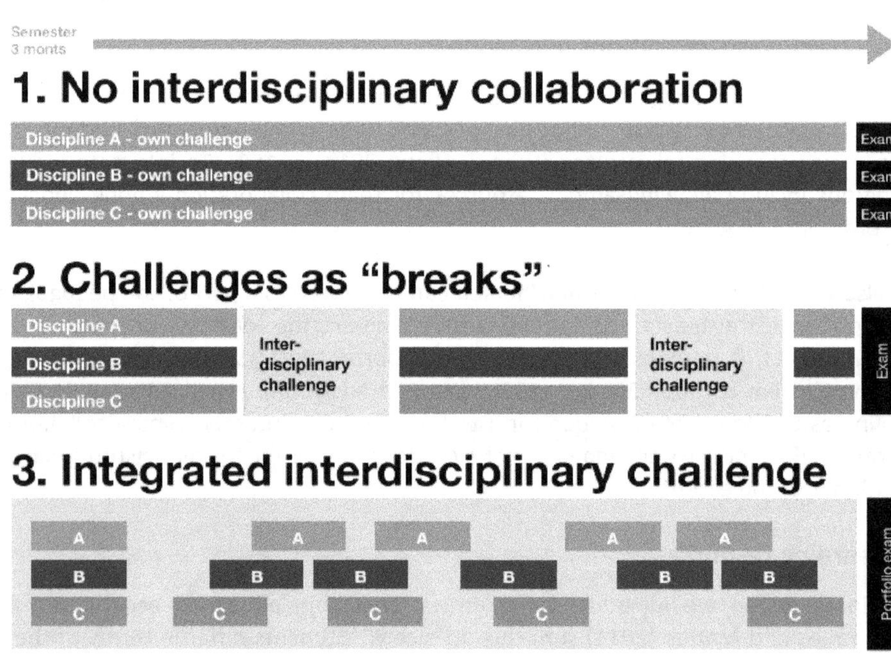

Figure 3: Ways of integrating industry challenges

As discussed above, working with a challenge presented by an external organisation in all disciplines of an education allows students and educators to see this project as a whole and thus reflect the more holistic view of the external organisation. As mentioned this requires extensive interdisciplinary cooperation. In a working paper Agerbaek and Houmøller (2019) suggest a didactical tool to facilitate interdisciplinary collaboration.

The purpose of this tool is to facilitate the educator' understanding of the industry challenge in light of each discipline (e.g. through lesson plans) as illustrated as option three in Figure 3. A, B and C are different disciplines granulated into topics. They are encompassed by the innovation challenge, presented by the external organisation, through the entire semester.

The didactical tool is a semester preparation tool. It entails using a whiteboard, but adding "micro whiteboards" to the mix. Each educator granulates her/his discipline into a number of topics (theories or methods), which he or she writes on various micro whiteboards. This allows an educator to shift the sequence of his/her topics around – by moving the micro whiteboards - while having a dialogue on how these may be relevant to the challenge presented by the external organisation. By the end of this preparation workshop each educator has a sequence of topics that translates directly into a lection plan for the following semester. Together the lection plans of all disciplines translate to a semester plan.

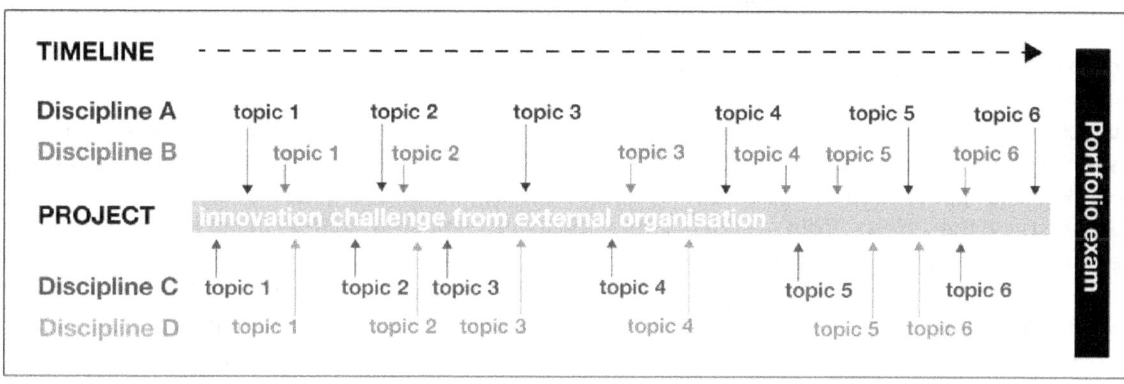

Figure 4: The result of the use of the tool

Figure 4 shows how the granulated topics from each discipline have been moved around for the purpose of being meaningful in relation to the innovation challenge. In the terms of the didactical relational model the learning process is planned in a pedagogical framework of interplay between disciplines. The industry challenge becomes the educational content across disciplines, and the students' learning resources are considered, because of the challenge's proximity to reality. Lastly the assessment method supports reflective practices of the students.

5. Discussion and conclusion

In the above we have presented a didactical approach and a tool for incorporating interdisciplinary projects in the curriculum with the purpose of conceptually examine how educators can support learning through interdisciplinary collaboration. Our understanding of interdisciplinary collaboration is founded in the entrepreneurship education ecosystem (figure 1) and the linkage between students, educators and external organisations through dialogical relationships that benefit them all. The external organisations obtain new aspects on a challenge they struggle with while at the same time they see first-hand the skillset of the students and how these can assist in any given organisation. At the other end of this dialogical relationship the students learn to use learned topics in a mix to solve a given challenge. Moreover, they gain insight into themselves and their own competencies; in other words, into their employability (Chang and Rieple, 2013). The educators act in the role of planners and executors of teaching including acting as liaison officers between the students and external organisations. Working with an external organisation adds to the educator's knowledge about 'real life' challenges and how the correspond to the education. Further, they assist the students in preparing for their future employability. Moreover, the tool presented is setting the stage for educators when they plan an interdisciplinary project. We argue, that the dialogical relationships present in the ecosystem connect to the didactical relational model (Hiim and Hippe 2014). Finally, these elements are to be considered during the planning phase with the model's six elements (figure 2). As such, we show how the educator can move from using the didactical tool in the planning phase and into the practice phase.

The interdisciplinary collaboration as well as incorporating different disciplines to solve a challenge can in itself be viewed as a novelty. Therefore, it should give leave to discuss introducing other assessment methods as a part of this try-out. Chiang and Rieple (2013) argue for assessment methods that includes a reflective element. The students will benefit from such an element threefold. Firstly, reflections add to deeper learning rather than superficial learning (Biggs, 1999). Secondly, reflections assist in creating meaning for the students: ". reflection is a systematic process of self-introspection in order to develop one's meaning and new perspectives about experiences undertaken. While reflecting, the learner may profit from accumulation of previous experiences, use prior knowledge, or be in the process of actual doing, but the final aim of this learning process is to develop knowledge" (Hägg and Kurczewska, 2016, p. 708). Thirdly, reflections aid the students in viewing themselves in an employability perspective. No doubt, we consider the reflective element as crucial for students to understand their own role in the ecosystem both in view of their current students' role as well as how a future role could be like. The employability path could be investigated further, for instance by using the same methodological approach as Chiang and Rieple (2013).

Understanding the students and where they come from is essential for the educator if the educator wants the students to exploit their personal skills in combination with their professional competencies in an interdisciplinary project. For this to happen, the educator must, as proposed by Jones and Matlay (2011), and Hiim and Hippe (2014), understand and accept each student's learning resources to be able to assist each student to put them into use in relation to working with practice.

Our suggested approach could be investigated further. We have argued for the entrepreneurship education ecosystem in an entrepreneurial context, here widely defined. We propose to investigate whether our presented framework can be applied to all educations in an institution of higher education, thereby broadening the concept as well as study the effects from working interdisciplinary compared to executing traditional teaching. Furthermore, we propose to investigate how each actor view their role and perceive their learning in relation to the ecosystem (Wraae & Thomsen, 2019, 2018). This would add new insights into how each actor learns in this context including adding new insights into how we understand the dialogical relationships. We propose a qualitative methodological approach with interviews and observations (Chang and Rieple, 2013). Assuming the students are the centre of our interest, we propose to let students reflect on their learning journeys, for instance by using video clips where the students are allowed to reflect on their own role and learning (Wraae et al., 2020, 2018). This video clip approach could be introduced in the beginning and at the end of the course in order to discover differences.

From a quantitative perspective we propose to use an online survey to all actors about the value of the concept, including questions about learning. Here, we propose to scale the questions using the Lichard scale to measure their attitudes. We suggest an ex-ante/ex-post to measure any differences in the participants' attitude at the start of the interdisciplinary project and again at the end.

References

Agerbaek, Lise & Houmøller, Ellen (2019) *Working Paper: Framing Employ Skills through university/industry cooperation*, UCL, https://www.ucviden.dk/portal/da/publications/framing-employ-skills-through-universityindustry-cooperation(4c3ba489-ab05-4589-a4ad-985909cf1900).html (downloaded 04152020)

Agerbaek, Lise (2016) "What are the right kind of problems to solve in a university/industry collaboration?" in *Proceedings, ICERI2016* pp. 4087-4093

Berglund, Karin (2013), "Fighting against all odds: Entrepreneurship education as employability training". In *Ephemera - Theory & Politics in Organization Vol 13 (4)* pp. 717-735.

Biggs, J., 1999. "What the Student Does: teaching for enhanced learning". *Higher Education Research & Development 18*, 57–75. https://doi.org/10.1080/0729436990180105

Brush, C.G., 2014. "Exploring the Concept of an Entrepreneurship Education Ecosystem", in: Hoskinson, S., Kuratko, D.F. (Eds.), *Innovative Pathways for University Entrepreneurship in the 21st Century, Advances in the Study of Entrepreneurship, Innovation & Economic Growth.* Emerald Group Publishing Limited, Bingley, UK, pp. 25–39. https://doi.org/10.1108/S1048-473620140000024000

Bruyat, C., Julien, P.-A., 2001. "Defining the field of research in entrepreneurship". In *Journal of business venturing 16*, 165–180.

Chang, Chi-Cheng (2014),"An instructional cycle for enhancing innovation-embedded employability", in *Education + Training, Vol. 56 Iss 8/9* pp. 870 - 883 http://dx.doi.org/10.1108/ET-03-2014-0021 (Downloaded 04132020)

Chang, J., Rieple, A., 2013. "Assessing students' entrepreneurial skills development in live projects". In *Journal of Small Business and Enterprise Development 20*, 225–241. https://doi.org/10.1108/14626001311298501

Darsø, Lotte (2009) *Innovation in the Making*, Frederiksberg, Denmark: Samfundslitteratur

Etzkowitz, H., 2013. "Anatomy of the entrepreneurial university". In *Social Science Information 52*, 486–511.

Fulgence, K., 2015. "Assessing the status of entrepreneurship education courses in higher learning institutions: The case of Tanzania education schools". In *Education + Training 57*, 239–258. https://doi.org/10.1108/ET-05-2013-0063

Gibb, A.A., Haskins, G., 2013. "The University of the Future. An Entrepreneurial Stakeholder Learning Organisation?", in: Fayolle, A., Redford, D.T. (Eds.), *Handbook of Research in Entrepreneurial Education Volume 4 –Entrepreneurial University Handbook*. Edward Elgar Publishing Ltd, Cheltenham, UK ; Northampton, MA.

Hägg, G., Kurczewska, A., 2016. "Connecting the dots: A discussion on key concepts in contemporary entrepreneurship education". In *Education + Training 58*, 700–714. https://doi.org/10.1108/ET-12-2015-0115

Hiim, Hilde & Hippe, Else (2014) *Læring gennem oplevelse, forståelse og handling*, Gyldendal

Illeriis, Knus (2009) "A comprehensive understanding of human learning" in Illeriis, Knud (ed) (2009) *Contemporary Theories of Learning*, Routledge, London

Jones, C., Matlay, H., 2011. "Understanding the heterogeneity of entrepreneurship education: going beyond Gartner". In *Education + Training 53*, 692–703. https://doi.org/10.1108/00400911111185026

Pirinen, Rauno (2009) "Action Research in Integrative Action" in *Proceedings of the 8th WSEAS International Conference on EDUCATION and EDUCATIONAL TECHNOLOGY*

Qvortrup, A., Keiding, T. (2016) "The Mistake to Mistake Learning Theory for Didactics" in Qvortrup, A., Wiberg, M., Christensen, G. & Hansbøl, M. (ed.) *On the Definition of Learning*, Odense: University Press of Southern Denmark

Qvortrup, A., Hansen, J., & Christensen, I.-M. (2017). "Portfolio, refleksion og feedback". In *Tidsskriftet Læring Og Medier (LOM), 10 (17).*

Qvortrup, L (2006) *Knowledge. Education and Learning: E-learning in the Knowledge Society,* Samfundslitteratur

Ratten, V., 2017. "Entrepreneurial universities: the role of communities, people and places". In *Journal of Enterprising Communities: People and Places in the Global Economy 11*, 310–315. https://doi.org/10.1108/JEC-03-2017-0021

THE FRAMEWORK OF QUALIFICATIONS FOR THE EUROPEAN HIGHER EDUCATION AREA (2018) http://www.ehea.info/media.ehea.info/file/2018_Paris/77/8/EHEAParis2018_Communique_AppendixIII_952778.pdf (downloaded 04072020)

Wahlgren, B. (2016). "Adult educators' core competences" in *International Review of Education, 62(3)*, 343-353. https://link.springer.com/article/10.1007%2Fs11159-016-9559-4

Wraae, B., Tigerstedt, C., Walmsley, A., 2020. "We had the experience but missed the meaning" – Using reflective videos to enhance entrepreneurial learning. To be published in *Journal of Entrepreneurship Education and Pedagogy*.

Wraae, B., Tigerstedt, C., Kratzer, J., 2018. "Introducing Student Self-assessment as a New Assessment tool in Entrepreneurship Education". In *Journal of Higher Education Theory and Practice 18*.

Wraae, B., Thomsen, J., 2019. "Introducing a New Framework for Understanding Learning in an Entrepreneurship Education Ecosystem". In *Journal of Higher Education Theory and Practice 19*.

Wraae, B., Thomsen, J., 2018. Entrepreneurial Learning in Higher Education Through Ecosystems. Presented at the University - Industry Interaction Conference, London June 19-20 2018.

Transition to Circular Economy: A Strategic Support for Small and Medium Enterprises in the Waste of Electronic and Electronic Equipment Sector

Daniel Agyapong
University of Cape Coast, Ghana
dagyapong@ucc.edu.gh.
DOI: 10.34190/EIE.20.152

Abstract: Agenda 2030 imposes calls on businesses and countries to engage in sustainable consumption and production. This is supported by the emerged view of the circular economy. Proponents of the circular economy argue for businesses to shift from the use of the linear model (take, make and dispose of) to circular business model based on reuse, resource efficiency, sharing economy and closed-loop. This is critical in the pre-production, during production and post-production and consumption of e-waste. Ghana is one of the world's leading recipient of e-waste. The paper focuses on the technical, legal and policy interventions and their impact of e-waste management. Using mixed methods, the paper concludes there are four major impacts of e-waste including social, health, economic and environment. Majority of the SMEs in the e-waste business are unregistered. An avenue for continuous capacity building for the businesses in this sector and investments in technologies could help improve the current works processes of the venture.

Keywords: circular economy, strategic support, SMEs, electronic waste

1. Introduction

The United Nations Sustainable Development Goals 6, 11 and 12 jointly call upon the world to ensure availability and sustainable management of water and sanitation for all; make cities and human settlements inclusive, safe, resilient and sustainable; and ensure sustainable consumption and production patterns. These goals, which form the basis for this paper, impose both ethical and legal responsibility on stakeholders in the electronic and electrical equipment (EEE) sector in their bid to ensure a sustainable economy and environment. Following the Ghana e-waste country report in 2011, there have been concerns about the impact of e-waste. Among the negative concerns raised in the Country Report included its impact on human, aquatic life and plants. Meanwhile, it creates jobs and income for those involved and their families. The waste of electronic and electrical equipment (WEEE) or e-waste are old, used or broken electronic products, nearing their useful life, and disposed of by their original users.

Global e-waste is estimated at 20-50 million tons. About 80% end up in Africa, Asia with Ghana in the list of lead recipient countries (Arora, 2008; Caravanos, Clarke & Lambertson, 2011; Lewis, 2015). It is the fastest growing waste stream in the world. It formed 70% of electrical equipment imported into Ghana. Amoyaw-Osei *et al.*, (2011) reports that WEEE formed 70% of the 215,000 tons of EEE that were imported into Ghana in 2009. The waste-to-resource axiom, espoused in the circular economy argument, points to the fact that e-waste is money in transition but not waste. However, the management of e-waste in Ghana is largely left with the informal sector. The effect has been that these businesses leave the environment in a more deplorable state, exposing it to more health hazards. In transiting into the circular economy, it is required of businesses to adopt sustainable business practices – decoupling economic activity from the consumption of finite resources and designing waste out of the system. To overcome the transitional problems, there was a need for intervention in the way SMEs deal with e-waste and its implications on society.

SMEs' and informal businesses are at the core of WEEE management in Ghana. However, these businesses have employed crude technology in their operations. Thus, exposing society to additional risks from poor handling of this waste. Previous studies including Oteng-Ababio, (2012) and Vasina (2018) have found individual operators in the informal sector are agents of pollution in the e-waste sector. The paper explores two interventions in the e-waste sector. The rest of the paper was divided into four. Part 2 looked at the literature review followed by the research method in part 3. Part 4 contained the discussion and part 5 provides the conclusions and implications.

2. Literature review

The circular economy is a system based on the philosophy that waste is redefined as an economic input, as opposed to a linear economy that emphasized on the take, make and dispose of (Stahel, 2016 and Jørgensen & Pedersen, 2018). It was originally introduced in the work of Boulding, (1966), Pearce and Turner (1989). It was founded on sustainability theory. Society expects businesses to engage in sustainable business practices that minimize waste, reduce harm to human, animals and plants. The theory of sustainability emphasizes meeting the needs of current and future generation. This suggests firms find an alternative usage for the waste they generate; move from the take, make and dispose of (linear economy) to the situation in which they keep the resource in use as long as they can gain the maximum benefit through recycling and regeneration (circular economy). The need for thinking of circular flow benefit stakeholders and the business, especially in times of increasing operating costs. Therefore, the circular economy axiom makes a business case for what used to be waste.

Empirical studies on the circular economy in Ghana have not focused on SMEs in the e-waste sector. This sector has received attention in recent times due to its economic benefits, but adverse environmental impact. Mohanty *et al* (2015) and Balde *et al* (2015) indicated that e-waste offers enormous business opportunities. The Seattle Journal of Environmental Law in 2015 showed that between 121,800 and 201,600 people were employed in this sector in 2014 in Ghana. The economic benefits accrued was between US$ 105m and US$ 268M to the Ghanaian economy. According to ILO (2019), the sector employs over 500,000. Its job creation ability spams from collection through to refurbishment (Forti, Balde & Kuehr, 2018).

Similarly, Mihai *et al* (2019) document the job prospects in the processing of e-waste. The unemployment status of the youth makes the sector an alternative source of livelihood. Oteng-Ababio and Grant (2020) found the activities in the e-waste sector has been largely informal. Furthermore, different fractions of e-waste have been found to contain precious minerals and substances including gold, silver, copper, palladium etc. that offer valuable income stream for the SMEs in the sector (SGS Group, 2014; Balde *et al*, 2014; Agyapong, 2017). Unfortunately, due to poor technology, these SMEs have not been able to fully take advantage of the opportunities in the sector.

Due to the inappropriate handling of e-waste by the 98.8% of the informal sector businesses, it has had a significant negative impact on the soil, air, water and the wellbeing of humans (Mihai *et al.*, 2019; Ongondo *et al.*, 2010). The epic centres of recycling waste like Agbogbloshie in Ghana and Guiyu in China present improper management of e-waste (Parajuly *et al.*, 2019; Kyere *et al.* 2018; He *et al.*, 2017). Forti, Balde and Kuehr (2018) submit backyard recycling using inappropriate technology leads to human health and environmental complications. Alabi, Adeoluwa and Bakare, (2019) indicated that e-waste workers have no or little education. This adversely impacts on their operations. Ghana's e-waste sector is dominated by informal businesses, characterized by poor technology that exposes the workers to health hazards (Mihai *et al.*, 2019). They use low skilled labour, operate in poor, unsafe and unhealthy work environment resulting in very low recovery of valuable materials from the e-waste (Lepawsky, 2018, ILO, 2019). The ILO identifies exposure to social risk as there is often no social security paid. Nwajiuba *et al* (2020) submit among other things barriers to small businesses including lack of finance, lack of innovation, poor technology, taxation and regulations. Besides, the sector is not attractive to investors. Prakash *et al* (2010) suggest that investments into machinery are essential if the total benefit of e-waste is to be realized.

At the national level, interventions have been legislations to reduce its potential harm on the society, key among these legislations includes the introduction of the hazardous and electronic waste control and management Act, (Act 917) and the L12250 of 2016. Act 917 place emphasizes on regulations and extended producer responsibility based on law than from the ethical and corporate social responsibility. There is less emphasis on working to develop technologies and capacities of SMEs in the informal sector involved in e-waste. To bridge the gap, two major interventions have been made with the help of the European Union and Switch African Green initiatives. The paper highlights two cases; the establishment of eco-innovative policy centre for SMEs and the electronic waste management in Ghana projects.

3. Research methods

The paper adopted a sequential embedded design. This method is appropriate because it combines qualitative and quantitative methods in projects of intervention in nature (Morgan, 2014a; Creswell & Clark, 2018 p.41).

The approach was to start with qualitative (before intervention) quantitative (intervention trial) and qualitative (post-intervention) method or stage. The pre-intervention research issues were deduced from the literature. The population of the study constitutes SMEs in the e-waste sector drawn from the two hot spots (Accra and Kumasi) of e-waste in Ghana (Kyere *et al.* 2018). Although the population of the SMEs in the sector is not known, a preliminarily study revealed 2000+ businesses were operating in the project coverage areas (Dagomba Line in Kumasi and Agbogbloshie in Accra, Ghana). The accessible population were those participants involved in the project. In all, there 120 SMEs involved in the project.

The data used was obtained from interviews, observation and interviewer-administered questionnaire. Seventy-eight (78) SMEs responded to the questionnaires. The rest were unavailable during this data collection exercise. Purposive sampling was used to select 48 respondents for an in-depth interview. Those interviewed were the leaders of the various associations and those who have been in the business for more than 10 years. The objective was to understand their perspective about the sector for the period they have operated. The observation part was made during the monitoring and evaluation visits to their company premises. Data were analyzed using the chi-square and paired t-tests. The rest of the analysis was thematically done. The chi-square was used to test goodness-of-fit in classification problems and the paired t-tests were used to analyses the significance level of change in the processes of the operators in the e-waste due to the intervention.

To avoid being implicated in any income and corporate tax issues, operators in this business would often avoid offering information on their activities, including their finance and business processes to third parties. This makes studies in this sector difficult. Therefore, the study used the participants in the two intervention projects mentioned. Participants' identity and business details were kept strictly confidential. Every details of participants' information were obtained through informed consent. Data collection was done at the convenience of the SMEs.

4. Results

4.1 Pre-intervention

The paper explores interventions in the e-waste sector, emphasizing on the business case of the sector. From the initial interaction with the operators, it was observed that the majority of the businesses were unregistered. Furthermore, probe into why these small businesses are not registered revealed that a number of the owner/managers did not understand the rationale for formalizing a business. This was a key skill gap among the owner/managers. In most cases, they did not meet the requirements of the Environmental Protection Agency (EPA) and did not have a tax identification number (TIN). They did not adopt proper e-waste management practices, thus impacting adversely on the environment (Mihai *et al.*, 2019; Ongondo *et al.*, 2010). Meanwhile, they paid some fee to the local authority in the jurisdiction they operate. Thus, they contributed to the income of the local community. However, they barely understood the legal framework of the sector.

During the baseline interview session, it was revealed that those involved in the e-waste business had little knowledge of risk, made no use of personal protective equipment (PPE), fire protection and payment of social security. They also burn in open spaces, dump e-waste in drains and had poor inventory management and did not have EPA permit.

4.2 Post-Intervention

These results emerged after the introduction of the intervention in the sector. Results from the analysis of their legal status, income change and owner/manager's experience showed 72% of them were yet to register their business. About 92% now kept records and experienced income change over the period, indicating the positive impact of the intervention. Their failure to register and formalize their business often prevent them from participating transactions where formal business certificates are required including accessing credit. Li *et al* (2006) submit SMEs in the e-waste are often not registered.

Lack of records keeping would adversely affect decision making and long term planning. As Tagoe, Nyarko and Anuwa-amarh (2005) suggest, records keeping promotes small business success and enhance good investor relations. Lenders and investors access the creditworthiness and business viability using operational and financial records. This implies their inability to access credit may be partly due to their poor record keeping.

Figure 1: SME business characteristics

5. Managing risk

Figure 2 shows an improvement in the use of PPEs from 2015 to 2017. There was an increase in the number of coveralls, boots, hand gloves and standard tool-kits usage. However, the SMEs did not make use of googles and aprons. This means future capacity building should target the use of such PPEs. Overall, the total number of accidents reduced from 247 in 2015 to 118 in 2017. The possible explanation is their willingness to commit financial resources into purchasing of PPEs and their preparedness to adapt to change. The people in this vocation are often reluctant to change from their crude practice after decades of practice. Therefore, it would take time and more education for them to accept any new practice.

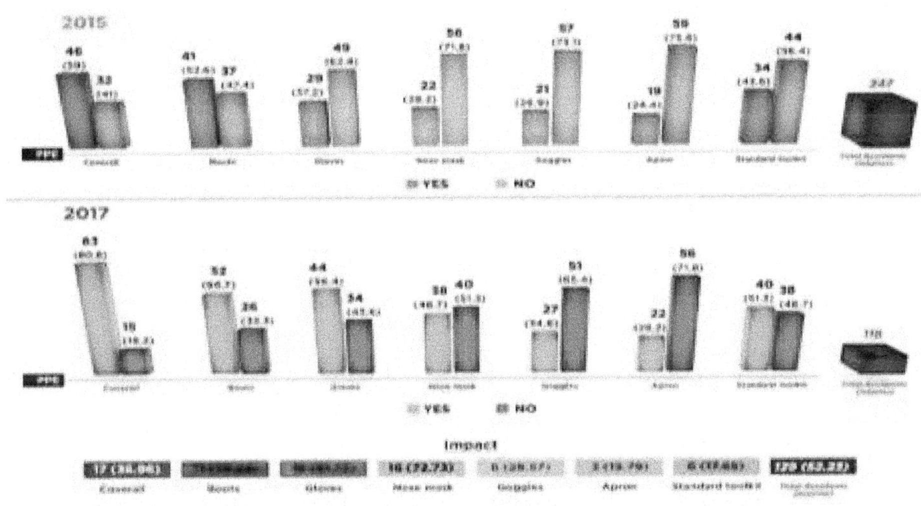

Figure 2: Use of personal protective equipment

6. Estimated income

Figure 3 provides an estimate of the mean values of income and output for SMEs in the e-waste sector. It was observed that items and fractions from computers, LCD/LED TV, and air conditioners attracted the highest value per ton. However, other components parts including plastics and aluminium found in large volumes (daily output) attracted relatively low price/unit due to low demand for such components. The reason is that there was rarely ready market for these parts. The source, the value of the items and markets for the different fractions of e-waste included hazardous substances and components.

Table 1 shows the results for the various paired sample *t-test*. On average, almost all variables experienced a change due to the intervention. The number of people employed by the SMEs increased from 4.87 to 6.5; the size of customers rose from 29.05 to 41.24; monthly income from GHS6,297.05 to GHS19,541.01 and other income from GHS586.67 to GHS782.89. Other variables experienced a reduced size after the intervention. These included the number of injuries, from 3.17 to 1.51 times; the volume of e-waste collected from 18.05 to 15.84 tons, and the volume of e-waste processed from 13.24 to 12.10 tons. Nevertheless, there were no significant changes in the values of the number of new jobs created by the firms. Decreases in the number of e-waste items picked and processed were due to the awareness created on the value of e-waste. Therefore, participants such as repairers and technicians, who previously gave out e-waste now prefer to keep and dismantle it rather than dispose of it as a non-valuable waste.

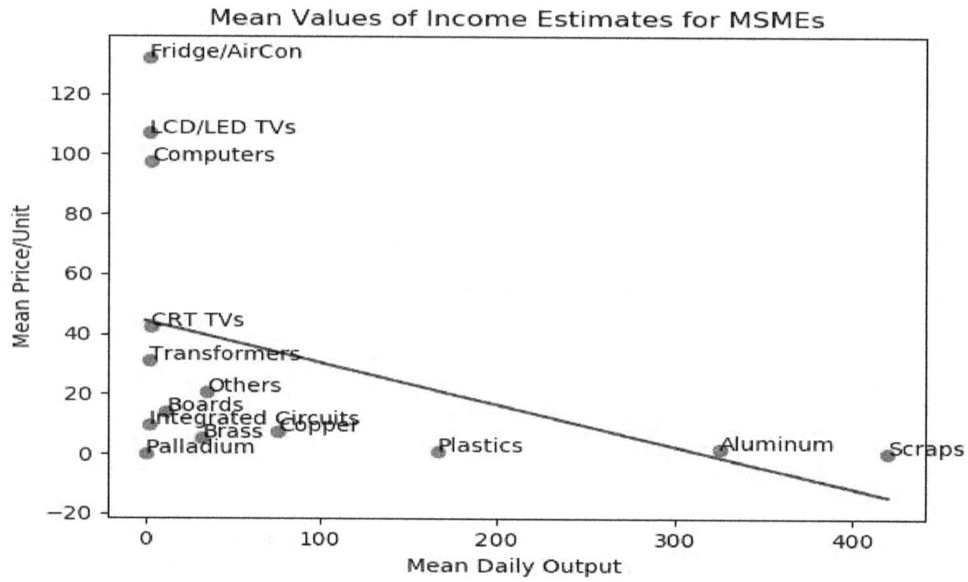

Figure 4: Estimating Income

Table 1: Paired samples statistics

Item	Variables	Mean	N	Std. Deviation	Std. Error Mean
Pair 1	Experience_2014 (years)	11.85	78	7.55	.85
	Experience_2017	13.83	78	7.62	.86
Pair 2	No. of_employees_2014	4.87	78	5.77	.65
	No. of_employees_2017	6.50	78	9.09	1.03
Pair 3	No. of_Injuries_2014	3.17	78	5.16	.58
	No. of_Injuries_2017	1.51	78	2.64	.29
Pair 4	No. of_customers_2014	26.05	78	36.99	4.19
	No. of_customers_2017	41.24	78	59.22	6.71
Pair 5	Vol of e-waste collected in 2014	18.05	78	18.47	2.09
	Vol of e-waste collected in 2017	15.85	78	17.30	1.956
Pair 6	No. of e-waste processed per day in 2014	13.24	78	13.32	1.51
	No. of e-waste processed per day in 2017	12.10	78	11.69	1.32
Pair 7	New_employees_2014 (GHS)	3.21	78	3.04	.34
	New_employees2017	3.63	78	2.39	.27
Pair 8	Monthly_income_2014 (GHS)	6,267.05	78	23,882.85	2,704.20
	Monthly_income_2017	19,541.01	78	30,293.72	3,430.09
Pair 9	Monthly_income_other_sources_2014 (GHS)	586.67	78	1,719.51	194.69
	Monthly_income_other_sources_2017	782.89	78	1824.07	206.54

Furthermore, a paired *t-test* was used to ascertain the significance of these differences between variables. Thus, the null hypothesis "the paired sample means are equal" can neither be accepted nor rejected. From Table 2 we observed the difference in the mean of the number of injuries was significant with a *p-value* of .00. The difference amounted to 1.65 on average. This change was as a result of respondents learning new ways of dismantling e-waste items. Moreover, respondents experienced an increased in the number of customers with an average increase of 15.19 customers. The increased in the number of customers could be attributed to the discovery of the use of the various parts of e-waste.

On revenue, data from the owner/managers showed an increase in revenue. The positive change in revenue could be attributed to the competencies the owner/managers acquired from the capacity building on financial and operations management. The SMEs that participated in the workshop were taught how value could be derived from the various fraction of e-waste they disposed of initially. This reflected in the volumes of e-waste processed daily.

Table 2: Final paired t-test

Item	Variables	Paired Difference			t	df	Sig. (2-tailed)
		Mean	Std. Dev.	Std. Error Mean			
Pair 1	Experience_2014 Experience_2017	-1.99	.34	.04	-51.37	77	.00
Pair 2	No. of employees_2014 No. of employees_2017	-1.63	7.93	.89	-1.81	77	.07
Pair 3	No. of injuries _2014 No. of injuries _2017	1.65	4.06	.46	3.59	77	.00
Pair 4	No. of customers _2014 No. of customers _2017	-15.19	32.91	3.73	-4.08	77	.00
Pair 5	Vol. of e-waste collected _2014 Vol. of e-waste collected _2017	2.21	16.04	1.82	1.21	77	.23
Pair 6	Vol of e-waste processed_2014 Vol of e-waste processed _2017	1.14	11.59	1.31	.87	77	.39
Pair 7	No. of new employees_2014 No. new employees _2017	-.42	3.53	.39	-1.06	77	.29
Pair 8	Monthly_Income_2014 Monthly_Income_2017	-13273.96	39144.75	4432.27	-2.99	77	.00
Pair 9	Other_Sources_2014 Other_Sources_2017	-196.23	354.35	40.12	-4.89	77	.00

7. Managing the environment

The question of their current perception of the environment was posed to them during the interview. Almost all the respondents referred to how the intervention exposed them to the negative effect of burning and dumping e-waste into drains. The majority made particular reference to brominated flame retardants and its ability to cause cancer and stillbirths. They bemoan low awareness level of Ghanaians on e-waste disposal, unsafe dismantling techniques. As one participant puts it:

> *.........I am still alive and working. Before the workshop we had in Kumasi, I was asked by the doctor to stop the scrap work and stay home. He said if I don't stop, I will leave more than a year. He said some chemical from burning wires is affecting my breath. Now we don't burn like we used to do................*

Furthermore, they also revealed that the knowledge acquired on the value of every fraction of e-waste meant they need not burn the remaining fraction of the e-waste they did not need previously. One respondent said:

> *...........We now can make money from all parts of the e-waste. Formerly, we burn the plastics because we did not have buyers for the plastics in the e-waste. We now know where we sell them and how to keep them so we don't harm the environment as we await the buyers to collect them from our premises...................*

Moreover, the respondents recounted how the capacity building exposed them to the technical and legal know-how of the e-waste business. More than 30 respondents indicated that they did not know that their activities were detrimental to the soil, humans and water bodies. The few that indicated they were aware of the impact of their activities, did not have the competencies nor the technology to correct it. They barely understood the role of the EPA. They saw the EPA as a threat to their existence since they only come in to shut down businesses. As one of the owner/managers remarked;

> *".....we have for all this while perceived the work of the EPA as a threat to our business. They only come in to close down your business. We do not have the kind of money they require certification. but now, we know not all our perception was right ....".*

Meanwhile, from the interaction with the SMEs during the interview, it was revealed a number of them hitherto, did not consider registering their businesses. They did not consider it critical to the operation of their business. They found it as time-wasting and expensive. This suggests they did not plan on formalizing their businesses.

They cited cost, time, bureaucracy and lack of documentation as the main barrier to their formalization. As one recounted;

> *"……..they want me to fill some forms I did not understand any part of. But they just handed me the papers………….."*

Nonetheless, thirty-eight (38) respondents of the 48 interviewed had acquired their Tax Identification Number (TIN) and 40 e-waste associations consisting of small associations were formed in eight regions in Ghana.

8. Barriers to e-waste business

Majority of the responses (45) cited financial constraints as the main barriers to the e-waste business. This is followed by information on e-waste (40), technical skills (34), recycling (26) and raw material (15). Assess to finance has been one major constraint to small businesses' growth in the country. Several studies including Hashi (2001), Ullah (2020); Makdissi and Tannous (2020) reports financial constraints and its impact on small firms. Besides, there is no one-stop database for information on e-waste. Information on the informal sector is scarce, unorganized and fragmented. Loukil and Rouached (2020) argue that the absence of a database on the sector makes planning difficult. To further explore the impact of the identified barriers on the businesses in the e-waste sector, a chi-square test was conducted based on predetermined factors from (Prakash *et al,* 2010; Lepawsky, 2018; Leblanc, 2019). The hypothesis was:

> *H_0: The type of business enterprise does not depend on the barriers encountered by the enterprise.*

Table 3. presented the result from the chi-square analysis based on the 78 respondents involved in the intervention. The *Ho* was rejected for all the barriers identified.

Table 3: Chi-Square test of business type and business barriers

Variable	$\chi^2_{0.05}$	df	p-value	Decision
Technical skills	0.200	2	0.905	Failed to reject H_0
Financial constraints	2.940	2	0.230	Failed to reject H_0
Raw materials (e-waste)	3.622	2	0.163	Failed to reject H_0
Information on e-waste	1.528	2	0.466	Failed to reject H_0
Recycling	1.046	2	0.593	Failed to reject H_0

Source: Survey, 2018

Thus, the barriers to the e-waste business are similar across the different business lines. That is, those who collect, dismantle, transport, process and recycle face similar challenges. Prakash *et al* (2010) submit investments into machinery is necessary to realize the full potential of the e-waste business. Access to capital continues to be a major barrier. Nwajiuba *et al* (2020) emphasize on other barriers in the business including poor technology, absence of the right infrastructure and the low skills of employees.

9. Discussion

First was the lessons from the capacity building and environmental awareness. The workshops exposed the SMEs to the risks associated with the e-waste business, especially the acquisition of the right skills and the use of appropriate technologies. The absence of skill due to lack of education might compel the SMEs to use crude methods (Alabi, Adeoluwa & Bakare, 2019). During the capacity-building workshops, the owner/managers had the opportunity to learn about the significant role played by the EPA. It is expected that this would motivate the SMEs to cooperate with the agency in the discharge of their responsibility as regulators of the sector. The interaction with the EPA officials during the capacity building workshops enabled the SMEs to asked the relevant questions and for the officials to understand the perspectives of the owner/managers operating in the sector. For instance, EPA officials took time to explain to the SMEs how could sometimes be agents of pollution (Oteng-Ababio, 2012; Vasina, 2018) in this sector.

Meanwhile, several SMEs did not consider registering their businesses. This supports the view of Li *et al* (2006) who concluded SMEs in the e-waste are mostly unregistered. They regarded registering a business as time-wasting. Entrepreneurs have often cited cost, time, bureaucracy, lack of documentation as barriers to their formalization. Formalization is a means to capture data on small businesses in the country. However, because the owner/managers do not register, it is difficult to have access to data to help plan and execute strategic support for businesses in this sector. Loukil and Rouached (2020) submit that the lack of a database on the sector makes planning challenging.

Next was the business case of e-waste concerning new product development in small firms. Respondents revealed that the workshops on creativity, financial management, record-keeping and operations equipped them with the entrepreneurial skills and proper business practices in the sector. From the interview, respondents indicated they have experienced a positive change in revenue and improved livelihood. Besides, they have experienced improved working conditions due to reduced accidents and the ability to obtain value from virtually all fractions of e-waste. The results imply that the SMEs in the e-waste sector has the potential to create more jobs, increase revenue and make available more materials through recovering and regeneration as part of the circular economy philosophy. Forti, Balde and Kuehr (2018) and others have submitted that the sector has the potential of creating jobs. However, this would require the acquisition and application of technologies to promote sustainable e-waste business among in SMEs.

10. Conclusions and recommendation

The intervention had a positive effect on the activities of the small firms involved in the e-waste business. Thus the intervention yielded results that could be nurtured as we transit into the circular economy. The deduction from previous and this study reveal the sector contains significant business opportunities. It impacts on social, health, economic and environment of the country. However, the majority of the business engaged in the activities in this sector are unregistered. Finance was cited as the major challenge followed by information on the e-waste.

There is a need for continuous capacity building for the owner/managers and entrepreneurs in the sector. This should be supported by investments in technologies to improve the current work processes of the SMEs in the sector. Leveraging on the formal-informal partnership could be useful in this direction. Given the number of years of experience of the owner/managers, such a partnership could help make more business case for e-waste. The circular economy practice suggests activities such as e-waste management provide the opportunity for resource recovery, reuse and regeneration by entrepreneurs. Adequate incentives should be provided to attract private investments and finance in the sector in the entire circular economy space. Incentives could be in the form of tax breaks, issuing circular economy bonds and equities aimed at financing entrepreneurial activities in this space. The transition into circular economy requires investments by investors and into technologies required for the retrieval, recovering, regenerating and re-application of resources at their end-of-life.

In transiting into the circular economy, it is imperative to integrate sustainable consumption, production and the green economy activities into the national development plan. Meanwhile, there should be the institutionalization of mechanisms for coordination and control of activities in the circular economy. Besides, given the volumes of e-waste generated annually in the country, there would be the need for the expansion of capacity of existing renewable energy facilities as we transit into the circular economy. In any of the strategy the country adopts at the transition, particular attention should be paid to the role of entrepreneurs and SMEs operating in this sector. As key players in the sector, key policy and strategy should support SMEs and entrepreneurial activities.

It is expected that the interactions between the EPA and SMEs would promote yield favourable outcomes. It would encourage the SMEs to operate more responsibly and more importantly, cooperate with the regulator in dealing with the numerous environmental challenges stemming from their operations. Meanwhile, as we transit into the circular economy through the adoption of sustainable business practices in the sector, there would be the need for a comprehensive database of the SMEs in the sector. This would in the planning and execution of the strategies to the negative effect of their activities.

11. Suggestion for future research

The study has some limitations that could form the bases for future research. First, the study concentrated on the participants in the two intervention projects. Future studies could expand the scope of this study and look at other operators in other parts of the country. Future studies could measure the size of the effect of SMEs' activities on the environment, income and job creation.

Acknowledgements

The author wishes to acknowledge the contribution of the Switch Africa Green and E-MAGIN projects and Eco-BPC projects. These projects were funded by the European Union.

References

Agyapong, D. (2017). 'Alternatives for Financing Waste Management: Implications for Ghana's Growing Electronic and Electrical Equipment Waste', *Asian Journal of Economics, Business and Accounting*, pp.1-14.

Alabi, O.A., Adeoluwa, Y.M. and Bakare, A.A. (2020). 'Elevated serum Pb, Ni, Cd, and Cr levels and DNA damage in exfoliated buccal cells of teenage scavengers at a major electronic waste dumpsite in Lagos, Nigeria', *Biological Trace Element Research*, 194(1), pp.24-33.

Amoyaw-Osei, Y., Agyekum, O.O., Pwamang, J.A., Mueller, E., Fasko, R. and Schluep, M. (2011). 'Ghana e-waste country assessment' *SBC e-waste Africa Project*, 66, p.111.

Arora, R. (2008). 'Best Practices for e-waste management in developing nations', *Europe Aid Co-operation Office*, pp.1-24.

Balde, C.P., Wang, F., Kuehr, R. and Huisman, J. (2015). *The global e-waste monitor 2014: Quantities, flows and resources. United Nations University Institute for the Advanced Study of Sustainability (UNUIAS).* Scycle, Bonn, Germany, 2014.

Boulding, K. E. (1966). 'The economics of the coming spaceship earth', *Environmental Quality in a Growing Economy. Baltimore*, pp. 3-14.

Caravanos, J., Clarke, E. and Lambertson, C. (2011). 'Assessing the exposure risks and potential health effects from chemical contamination at electronic and electrical recycling and waste site in Accra, Ghana', *Journal of Health and Pollution*, 1(1).

Creswell, J. W., and Clark, V. L. P. (2018). Designing and conducting mixed methods research. Thousand Oaks, CA: Sage Publications.

Forti V., Baldé C.P., Kuehr R. (2018). *E-waste Statistics: Guidelines on Classifications, Reporting and Indicators* (2nd ed.), United Nations University, ViE – SCYCLE, Bonn, Germany.

Hashi, I. (2001). 'Financial and institutional barriers to SME growth in Albania: results of an enterprise survey', *MOST: Economic Policy in Transitional Economies*, 11(3), pp. 221-238.

He, K., Sun, Z., Hu, Y., Zeng, X., Yu, Z. and Cheng, H. (2017). 'Comparison of soil heavy metal pollution caused by e-waste recycling activities and traditional industrial operations', *Environmental Science and Pollution Research*, 24(10), pp. 9387-9398.

ILO (2019*). Decent work in the management of electrical and electronic waste (e-waste)*. GDFEEW/2019, International Labour Organization, International Labour Office, Geneva, Switzerland.

Jørgensen, S. and Pedersen, L. J. T. (2018). *RESTART sustainable business model innovation*, Springer.

Kyere, V. N., Greve, K., Atiemo, S. M., Amoako, D., Aboh, I. K. and Cheabu, B. S. (2018). 'Contamination and health risk assessment of exposure to heavy metals in soils from informal e-waste recycling site in Ghana', *Emerging Science Journal*, 2(6), pp. 428-436.

Leblanc, R. (2019 June) *Electronics waste recycling business opportunities*. Available at: https://www.thebalancesmb.com/opportunities-electronics-recycling-sector-2878174

Lepawsky, J. (2018). *Reassembling rubbish: worlding electronic waste*. MIT Press.

Li, J., Tian, B., Liu, T., Liu, H., Wen, X. and Honda, S. I. (2006). 'Status quo of e-waste management in mainland China', *Journal of Material Cycles and Waste Management*, 8(1), pp. 13-20.

Loukil, F. and Rouached, L. (2020). 'Waste collection criticality index in African cities', *Waste Management*, 103, pp. 187-197.

Makdissi, R. and Tannous, J. (2020). 'Funding Challenges Facing SMEs' Growth in Lebanon', *International Journal of Business and Economics Research*, 9(1), pp. 50.

Mihai, F. C., Gnoni, M. G., Meidiana, C., Ezeah, C. and Elia, V. (2019). 'Waste Electrical and Electronic Equipment (WEEE): Flows, Quantities, and Management—A Global Scenario', In *Electronic Waste Management and Treatment Technology* (pp. 1-34). Butterworth-Heinemann.

Mohanty, S., Vermeersch, E., Hintsa, J., Di Cortemiglia, V. L. and Liddane, M. (2015). *Weaknesses in European e-waste management*, In Operational Excellence in Logistics and Supply Chains: Optimization Methods, Data-driven Approaches and Security Insights. Proceedings of the Hamburg International Conference of Logistics (HICL), Vol. 22 (pp. 535-561). Berlin: epubli GmbH.

Morgan, D. L. (2014a). Integrating Qualitative and Quantitative Methods: A Pragmatic Approach. Thousand Oaks: Sage. Soc. Sci.

Nafea, I., Alharbi, A., Abduh, A., Alharbi, A. and Moussa, R. M. (2019). 'Color shade matching by mobile applications in dental practice: An experimental comparative in-vitro double-blind study', *The Saudi Dental Journal*, 31, S13.

Nwajiuba, C. A., Igwe, P., Binuomote, M. O., Nwajiuba, A. O. and Nwekpa, K. C. (2020). 'The Barriers to High-Growth Enterprises: What Do Businesses in Africa Experience?' *European Journal of Sustainable Development*. EJSD V9N1: 2020.

Ongondo, F.O., Williams, I.D. and Cherrett, T.J. (2010). 'How are WEEE doing? A global review of the management of electrical and electronic wastes', *Waste Management,* 31, pp. 714–730

Oteng-Ababio, M. (2012). *Electronic Waste Management in Ghana - Issues and Practices. Sustainable Development - Authoritative and Leading Edge Content for Environmental Management.*
Oteng-Ababio, M. and Grant, R. (2020). 'E-waste recycling slum in the heart of Accra, Ghana: the dirty secrets', *Handbook of Electronic Waste Management*, pp. 355–376.
Parajuly, K., Kuehr, R., Awasthi, A. K., Fitzpatrick, C., Lepawsky, J., Smith, E., ... and Zeng, X. (2019). Future E-Waste Scenarios.
Pearce, D. W. and Turner, R. K. (1990). *Economics of natural resources and the environment*, JHU Press.
Prakash, S., Manhart, A., Amoyaw-Osei, Y. and Agyekum, O. O. (2010). 'Socio-economic assessment and feasibility study on sustainable e-waste management in Ghana', *Öko-Institut eV in cooperation with Ghana Environmental Protection Agency & Green Advocacy Ghana.*
SAG (2017). *Five projects at a glance. Project Sheet for SWITCH Africa Green (SAG) Programme Ghana.*
SGS Group (2014). *Self-funding E-waste solutions*. SGS Group Management SA.
Stahel, W. R. (2016). The circular economy. *Nature*, *531*(7595), pp. 435-438.
Tagoe, N., Nyarko, E. and Anuwa-Amarh, E. (2005). 'Financial challenges facing urban SMEs under the financial sector liberalization in Ghana', *Journal of small business Management*, 43(3), pp. 331-343.
Ullah, B. (2020). 'Financial constraints, corruption, and SME growth in transition economies', *The Quarterly Review of Economics and Finance*, 75, pp. 120-132.
Vasina, M. (2018). *Health-related practices and perceptions among waste pickers: the case of Mbeubeuss waste dump in Senegal*. Unpublished Dissertation.

Women-Owned Community-Based Enterprises in Developing Countries: *A Critical Reflection on Factors Influencing Robustness*

Ali Ahmad and Dwitya Amry
WMG, University of Warwick, Coventry, UK
ali.ahmad@warwick.ac.uk
d.amry@warwick.ac.uk
DOI: 10.34190/EIE.20.068

Abstract: Developmental work for women's empowerment has a new focus - Community Based Enterprises (CBEs) to facilitate 'successful' women's entrepreneurship. CBEs are touted as mechanisms for inclusive development where women and other marginalized communities are often target beneficiaries. Although successful in creating upward social mobility in the short-term, CBEs tend to dissipate away in the medium-term owing to an array of organizational and contextual "problems" unique to developing countries (DC). This leaves their target beneficiaries in the lurch, which is problematic. Our aim in this paper is to unpack and explain the factors that lead to durable and sustainable women-owned CBEs. We explain 'durability' conditions of women-owned CBEs and as to how these differ between developed versus DCs. This is done through an interrogation of evidence presented in extant literature on women's entrepreneurship. We analyse four previously identified 'conditions' that create CBE durability in a developed country-context for validity in a developing country context. We found that there were other conditions that related to governance, cultural and resource factors that need to be added to the four previously identified conditions when explaining robustness of DC CBEs. This paper contributes to the ongoing debate on how best to design and support CBEs to alleviate poverty at the grassroots level. This will have implications for policymakers and practitioners looking to deliver sustainable socio-economic development through the promotion of women's entrepreneurship.

Keywords: critical analysis, community-based enterprise, developing countries, women's entrepreneurship

1. Introduction

In the last few decades, women's entrepreneurship in developing countries has attracted the attention of academics, development practitioners and policymakers alike. This interest, as Minniti and Naudé (2010) argue, is driven by two factors. First, women's engagement in increased entrepreneurial activities will ultimately lead to job creation and socio-economic development (Haugh & Talwar, 2016; Subramaniam, 2012). If 50% of the world's population is grossly under-represented in new wealth creation activity, future economic growth, sustainability and socio-economic change agendas such as human development can hardly materialize. Second, female led micro and small enterprises (MSEs) have a greater impact on household welfare when compared to male led MSEs (Mayoux, 2002; Haugh & Talwar, 2016). The literature on female-led entrepreneurial ventures provides ample evidence that supporting women entrepreneurs contributes to family welfare and household income while enhancing their participation in economic and community activities (Kasseeah and Tandrayen-Ragoobur, 2016; Hailemariam and Kroon, 2018). Hence, scholars argue that fostering women's entrepreneurship has significant benefits as it not only improves their status in society but creates wider societal impact through enhanced family and community well-being (Haugh & Talwar, 2016).

In the past few decades, to actively promote women's entrepreneurship in the developing world, numerous policies and programs by governments and the civil society have been rolled out (Haugh & Talwar, 2016; Vossenberg, 2013). However, the 'success' of such initiatives has been questioned; women led MSEs in developing countries have not shown robustness. As the GEM report stated: women in DCs start businesses out of necessity, with a high failure rate and a low propensity for growth (Kelley *et al.*, 2017). Although successful initially, with the passage of time, a vast majority of women-led ventures tend to fail (Alarcon & Sato, 2019), leading to the gender gap in entrepreneurship persisting (Vossenberg, 2013; Hailemariam and Kroon, 2018).

We argue that the Community-based enterprise (CBE) as a model of entrepreneurship offers the ideal mechanism for facilitating women's entrepreneurship in a developing country context. CBEs are managed and governed to pursue the economic and social goals of a community to yield sustainable individual and group benefits over the short and long term (Peredo and Chrisman, 2006). Since their work, a growing body of literature has emerged on CBEs that has examined these initiatives in both developed (Van Meerkerk, Kleinhans and Molenveld, 2018) and developing countries (Torri and Martinez, 2014). This literature has illustrated the potential of CBEs to uplift marginalised communities in different geographical and cultural contexts. However, to the best of knowledge, with the exception of Torri (2010) and Torri & Martinez (2014), there is a dearth of literature that focuses on women-only CBEs in developing countries. Hence, our understanding on the emergence and persistence of women-led grassroots initiatives acting as enterprising collectives is rather limited. There is a special need to examine perspectives on enterprising communities in a developing country context and how such perspectives impact the *robustness, durability* and/or *sustainability* of a CBE (Peredo et al., 2015). Such an examination is the prime focus in this paper.

Hence, our aim in this research is to "present a critical reflection on the factors that lead to robustness within women-led CBEs in DCs". This will lead to the development of theoretical propositions for capturing extant understanding on the subject. The paper contributes to the understanding on CBE durability in the context of women's entrepreneurship by highlighting how individual autonomy and agency contribute to social empowerment and, therefore, increased CBE durability. We also show how group membership of a collectively owned enterprise politically empowers women through their participation in collective action.

This paper proceeds as follows. First, we describe our approach and methods of inquiry. We then frame our study in the extant literature related to women's entrepreneurship, social entrepreneurship and community-based entrepreneurship considering how this research complements and diverges from previous research. We consider the context of our study in the broader social entrepreneurship literature, with a specific focus on the intentionality of design within business models. Next, critical reflections are presented along three thematic areas, from which three theoretical propositions are drawn. Finally, we conclude with implications for researchers, policy makers, and practitioners while offering recommendations for future research.

2. Method of Inquiry

Our approach in the proceeding literature review followed a snow-balling method. We started out with generic keywords such as 'women entrepreneurship' and 'community-based enterprise' as stand-alone and limited the literature ring fenced for analysis to the last 10 years. This allowed us to capture the state-of-the-art in theory relevant to the main themes under study. Next, we further restricted literature by looking at results based on combining keywords such as 'women entrepreneurship' with 'developing countries', 'emerging markets' or 'non-industrialised countries' and 'community-based enterprise' with 'durability' and 'robustness'.

We use a theory building approach in achieving our aim. Zahra (2007) argues that theory building in entrepreneurship research allows for contextualising theory into the phenomenon under study. Existing literature on women's entrepreneurship is interrogated and 'durability' factors in developed versus developing country contexts are isolated and analysed for plausibility and relevance. Here, theory building as a method is understood as the reflective practice of analysing how bodies of theory explaining phenomena embedded in a certain context *may* or *may not* apply in other contexts. This is because context deeply matters in entrepreneurship theory building (Yousafzai *et al.*, 2018). Our ambition is to uncover ways through which theoretical propositions derived from an analysis of theoretical perspective could be suitably modified when applied to a comparable but in many ways different context, such as the context of women starting up and doing business in developing vs. developed economies. Additionally, we use a feminist perspective (Vossenberg, 2013) in analysing the literature on CBEs to examine how gender can contribute to sustainability and robustness.

3. Background: Community based enterprise as a means for women's entrepreneurship?

Since the eighties, policymakers in DCs have been promoting women's entrepreneurship (WE) on the premise that at a macro level WE creates employment, improves household welfare and alleviates poverty (Minniti and Naudé, 2010; Langevang *et al.*, 2015) while at the meso and/or micro levels, it empowers women to "confront systematic discrimination or deprivation in the workplace, community and society" (Torri and Martinez, 2014, Pg. 34). Despite this, the gender gap in entrepreneurship persists (Vossenberg, 2013) and high failure rates are reported in women-led MSEs (WMSMEs) (Alarcon and Sato, 2019). One of the often cited reasons for this is that women struggle with work-life balance, frequently prioritising family (Langevang *et al.*, 2015). Thus, a sustainable entrepreneurial solution to women's empowerment remains a challenge.

Haugh and Talwar (2016) proposed that in DCs, emancipatory models of entrepreneurship like CBEs are needed to enable women to achieve empowerment at individual and group levels. Western values of individualism on which most entrepreneurship promotion in DCs has been framed has little relevance. This proposition is in line with the evidence that suggests that women are more likely to engage in *collective* forms of entrepreneurship when compared to their male counterparts (Soto Alarcón and Sato, 2019). In recent years, an emerging body of literature has shown how CBEs have been able to positively influence collective action and contribute to women's empowerment in DCs (Alarcon and Sato, 2019; Haugh & Talwar, 2016; Torrri & Martinez, 2014; Datta & Gailey, 2012, Subramanium, 2011).

In their seminal article, Peredo and Chrisman (2006, pp. 310) define CBEs as a "community acting corporately as both entrepreneur and enterprise in pursuit of the common good". A CBE is, therefore, the result of a process in which the community acts entrepreneurially to pursue both 'economic' and 'social' goals. CBEs emerged as a social innovation in DCs (Handy, Cnaan, Bhat, & Meijs, 2011) to provide novel solutions for poverty alleviation through collective action (Montgomery, Dacin and Dacin, 2012). The 'community' in CBE is viewed as an aggregation of people initially not defined by shared goals or an enterprise but by shared location, accompanied by collective culture and/or ethnicity and other shared relational characteristics such as gender (Peredo and Chrisman, 2006).). Thus, women's entrepreneurship will flourish within a CBE especially in DCs where gender biases are more prevalent, where CBEs' collectivist approach would enable strong internal support mechanisms to take root.

Despite the growth in CBE numbers globally, evidence is limited on their 'durability', especially as models for promoting WE. Although, many CBEs are set up, a large proportion either fail or do not grow – they lack robustness (Meerkerk et al., 2018; Peredo & Chrisman, 2006). A *durable* or *robust* CBE is defined as one "which has sufficient internal capacity to keep its business running, and to realise its objectives, while simultaneously meeting community needs and having external legitimacy (Van Meerkerk et al., 2018, pg. 653). Cases of robust CBEs are very rare.

Some of the reasons behind CBEs' lack of robustness can include the following; *first*, governance challenges owing to hybrid organizational structures (Van Meerkerk et al., 2018). To illustrate, research on 27 CBEs in Europe revealed problems of mission drift over time which negatively daily operations efficiency (Dentoni *et al.*, 2018). This mission drift might mean too much emphasis on the 'social' rather than the 'commercial' (Van Meerkerk, Kleinhans and Molenveld, 2018) creating difficulties in sustaining business operations. On the other hand, leaning too much on the 'commercial' aspects leads to inevitable shifts in social value, internal and external adversity and legitimacy concerns (Dentoni *et al.*, 2018). The *second* factor influencing CBE durability is their internal decision-making processes. CBEs' institutional designs require a participatory and pluralistic form of governance (Torri, 2010; Peredo *et al.*, 2015; Soto Alarcón and Sato, 2019) and this requires high levels of social capital. Research suggests that in participatory forms of governance, conflicts may arise when trust, openness and honesty are absent (Sherwood and Taylor, 2014).

In summary, as CBEs are potentially a viable vehicle for success in WE, there is a need to extend our understanding on their durability. We find that CBE's durability requires an institutional design with a collectivist governance approach, participatory decision making and the need for constant alignment between its organisational mission, social values and external legitimacy. Therefore, CBEs' robustness cannot rely only on business performance, but also on its collective mission and internal and external legitimacy (Somerville and McElwee, 2011).

4. CBE durability conditions in developing countries

We draw upon Van Meerkerk et al's (2018) study on conditions leading to durable CBEs. They highlighted four conditions for durable CBEs: (1) strong social capital; (2) entrepreneurial community leadership; (3) relationships with key institutional players; and, (4) a strong business model. Their analysis of 11 Dutch case studies found that the interplay between (1), (2), and (4) highly influences durability, while (3) was not an imperative aspect within an industrialized country context. In the remainder of this section, we use a feminist perspective to analyse the validity of the above conditions when applied to CBEs in a DC context.

4.1 Strong social capital

Bhatt and Ahmad (2017) showed that social capital is the most important *capital* needed in establishing a new venture in depleted communities that lacked financial and human capital. Social capital refers to resources accessed by an individual through social interactions and networks (Somerville and McElwee, 2011). In the context of CBEs, Peredo and Chrisman (2006) noted that community-based initiatives relied more on social capital in both the initial and operational phases.

Torri and Martinez (2014) highlight that 'gender' can be viewed as *mutuality* leading to a common interest that enhances social capital. In their study situated in Bangladesh, the common interest of women empowerment becomes the underlying foundation of strong social capital when gender-biases were found prevalent. Struggles for gender justice in conditions where high-gender bias exists can be through a 'common vision' driven by empowerment. This common vision then translates into a sense of *mutuality* leading to high social capital.

Thus, social capital viewed through the lens of mutuality is considered an enabling determinant in CBEs' durability. If there is, within a CBE, a vision, mission and value system based on *mutuality* (such as a common gender amongst members), these then create a sense of belonging which positively impacts CBE durability.

4.2 Entrepreneurial community leadership

In industrialized countries, entrepreneurial community leadership is viewed as a major determinant in CBE emergence and governance. McElwee, Smith and Somerville (2018) studied CBE emergence in rural villages within the UK and pointed out the need for *animatorship* - a community leader initiating a movement towards a certain goal. However, collective forms of enterprise such as CBEs require more than just *animatorship.* For robustness, they require an institutional model that adopts pluralistic governance mechanisms as opposed to a unitary orientation (Taylor, 2015), such as *animatorship* by a community leader. This implies that stakeholders (or community members) utilise participatory mechanisms and serve as a society's intermediaries in addressing wider societal needs. Hence, when third sector organisations, like CBEs, adopt pluralistic governance, it leads to better representation of stakeholder needs, increased performance and robustness (Taylor, 2015).

Dentoni et al (2018) suggest that leadership roles within CBEs need to balance their dual missions. Therefore, entrepreneurial community leadership is needed in DC CBEs for building relationships and alliances to acquire external resources (Van Meerkerk et al. 2018). The role of CBE leadership is to pursue and exploit opportunities or to act entrepreneurially, and identify and acquire resources especially in the highly resource-scare environments of DCs (Gofen, 2015; Haugh, 2007). Thus, CBE leadership enables building bridges to access external support to ensure durability.

4.3 Relationships with key institutional players

Research suggests that CBEs in industrialized settings emerge due to *epiphanies* that address community empowerment and 'making the world a better place' (Dentoni et al., 2018), rather than the more specific and deep-rooted community problems prevalent in DCs. In the UK, food enterprises formed a "CBE" to support and empower each other in order to stay competitive and sustainable (Sonnino and Griggs-Trevarthen, 2013). In such cases, collaborations trigger a movement towards a mutual mission.

In order for collaborations to be sustainable, external validity is needed, and this can be achieved through legitimacy with key institutional players such as the government. In such countries, CBEs' service provisions might *overlap* with and *complement* public services which is not viewed as problematic (Bailey, 2012). Strong relationships with the public sector improves CBEs' ability to acquire resources and other forms of governmental support, which in turn affects their durability.

In contrast, in the context of DCs where CBEs might be the only vehicle for public service provision to marginalized communities (Sonnino and Griggs-Trevarthen, 2013), they *compete* with rather than *overlap* with or *complement* existing government-led services (Gofen, 2015) which then affects their ability to acquire public resources such as grants (Van Meerkerk, Kleinhans and Molenveld, 2018). Lack of access to public resources can potentially negatively impact CBE robustness in a DC context.

4.4 Business model

CBEs are hybrid organisations, adhering to the principles of fulfilling social purpose while maintaining a steady surplus to ensure longevity. In the literature, this hybridity is often the source of problems emerging from a weak business model that might be too dependent on voluntary services and public funds (Montgomery, Dacin and Dacin, 2012; Van Meerkerk, Kleinhans and Molenveld, 2018). Thus, CBEs' business models need to focus on the ability to generate a steady revenue stream with surpluses which can then be used to further its mission sustainably (Haugh, 2007; Bailey, 2012). Needless-to-say, the business model must allow the CBE to be self-reliant without dependence on external grants or voluntary funding (Van Meerkerk, Kleinhans and Molenveld, 2018).

Thus, self-reliance to sustain its operations through operational revenue is a challenge to CBE robustness; and this challenge, whether the context is one of a DC or an industrialized economy, can only be overcome with a well thought-out business model.

5. Critical reflections

5.1 Reflections on Van Meerkerk et al.'s (2018) Criteria

It is acknowledged that the conditions set forth by Van Meerkerk et al. (2018) above are generally valid for determining CBE robustness and durability. These conditions should not be viewed as discreet though, rather they are interrelated to one another, and the aggregation of each condition or factor can influence CBE durability. For example, an entrepreneurial community leader might be present, however, they could lack a strong social foundation with the rest of the community. This might then pose a problem in gaining social capital. Social foundations too are context dependant – by geographical proximity, culture, ethnicity, religion and/or gender (Somerville and McElwee, 2011; Delgado-Márquez, Justo and De Castro, 2018).

Studies of CBEs emerging in depleted communities show that the focus of venturing does not lie as much on the 'commercial', but more on the deep-rooted problem being solved. Mahaul, an embroidery venture led by women from a rural community (Haugh and Talwar, 2014) – was about improving WE. Women supporting each other to overcome gender-constraining ideologies. It gave women an opportunity to learn from each other through a network and participation in governance, ensuring that they serve the community. Thus, in DCs, CBE durability will likely depend on how deep-rooted the social problem is, which would then increase social capital to enable members to work towards a mutual mission.

In DCs, for women to effectively participate in CBEs, the designed business model should be embedded in the local context, perhaps one which enables women to participate from home-based micro entrepreneurial ventures to accommodate family commitments with a route out of poverty (Haugh & Talwar, 2016). Although, this would limit their opportunities to sectors like agriculture or handicrafts (Kelley *et al.*, 2017), it would ultimately create opportunities where none existed prior.

5.2 Emergence issues and durability

To understand DC CBE durability we must also consider how such collective forms of organizations emerge in the first place. We find that CBEs in depleted communities emerge due to some form of *animatorship* exogenous to the indigenous community (McElwee, Smith and Somerville, 2018). Resource constrained communities are unable to self-assess opportunities and self-realise initiatives to become self-reliant without initially introduced to the opportunity/problem beforehand. Hence, in the beginning of the entrepreneurial journey, 'animators' contribute and serve as an initial intermediary offering support and guidance such as opportunity identification (McElwee, Smith and Somerville, 2018).

To illustrate the above, Handy et. al (2011) explained the emergence of a CBE whose members are jasmine flower cultivators in coastal Kanartaka, India. They highlight the important role of a Catholic priest who introduced jasmine growing and harvesting to the region (pp. 408). The catholic priest can be considered the initial animator who then handed over the rest of the CBE creation process to the community.

Exogenous intervention, thus, plays a part in the organic emergence of a CBE in a non-western context. However, this intervention is only an initial nudge, which triggers an organic entrepreneurial process of self-mobilisation, capitalising on social foundations and networks throughout the journey. It also shows that participation in CBEs in developing countries might initially focus on economic gains to achieve an equilibrium condition (Peredo and Chrisman, 2006), but it's spill-over effects of community empowerment and social mobilisation take precedence overtime.

5.3 The role of women in CBE durability

We have shown in the previous sections that there are differences in CBEs when explaining the phenomenon from the perspective of industrialized versus non-industrialized contexts. We found numerous studies calling for a new examination of how gender influences CBE emergence and durability (Soto Alarcón and Sato, 2019) .

Generally, women's entrepreneurship is somehow seen as underperforming on the criteria of economic growth and financial gain when compared to entrepreneurship initiated and led by men (Hailemariam and Kroon, 2018). Interventions are usually proposed to provide mitigations for the causes of underperformance. However, it is known that women entrepreneurs add a different and extended value to the new venture creation process, regardless of context – such as championing social spill-over effects on top of monetary gain (Sheikh et al., 2018). Taking women's value-add factors into consideration enables a more nuanced understanding on CBE durability to emerge, especially those CBEs based in non-industrialized contexts and initiated and maintained by women.

Hailemariam and Kroon (2018) wrote about women's entrepreneurship in Ethiopia, highlighting what was considered a "successful" women's enterprise. It is suggested that entrepreneurship success should be determined on the basis of performance on set initial goals. Initial goals can be highly subjective and linked to context; what women might consider as a parameter for "success" can differ from men. Women have higher level extrinsic goals when pursuing an entrepreneurial journey linked to social spill-over effects such as community empowerment, family welfare and self-fulfilment. Women in impoverished contexts, who are married and with limited access to education, engage in entrepreneurial activity for extrinsic goals, as they prioritise other people's (their own families') well-being on top of their own (Hailemariam and Kroon, 2018).

Sheikh et al. (2018) have highlighted that the venture creation process can be differentiated by gender. They and others have highlighted that because of numerous barriers exclusive to women in non-industrialized contexts, they tend to rely much more on social capital (Somerville and McElwee, 2011; Mckeever, Anderson and Jack, 2014) and a strong social foundation (Somerville and McElwee, 2011; Sheikh et al., 2018). Hence, women treat the 'social value' they create as an outcome of their entrepreneurial journey. Such 'value' can include individual value (related to self-empowerment, self-development and self-fulfilment), business value (related to monetary gain and financial success), family value (related to household income and perception on gender roles) and community value (related to community empowerment, women's social mobility and the community perception on women's role) (Sheikh et al., 2018).

Based on the above, it can be surmised that women in non-industrialized settings would be, in a way, predisposed to setting up more robust CBEs. The extended value created as a result of their entrepreneurialism goes beyond individualism and champions collectivism. Thus, as CBE relies on strong social foundations (participation and cooperation) as an asset for sustainability, women's role in CBEs must not be neglected or less prioritised and ought to be better understood when it comes to robust CBE design (Delgado-Márquez, Justo and De Castro, 2018).

6. Discussion

There has not been much research on women-owned and managed CBEs – especially that which looks at issues of durability. In this paper, an attempt has been made to address this gap in knowledge by presenting critical reflections from the evidence present in extant literature. As a result, a new arena for women's entrepreneurship – the CBE - has received reflective treatment, and in doing so the scope of women's entrepreneurship research is somewhat broadened.

Our first theoretical outcome is that gender and cultural aspects need to be carefully deciphered to fully appreciate women's entrepreneurial motivations when pursuing initiatives with an embedded social mission. We concur that feminism in various DC contexts is unique in that it is intrinsically linked to the history of the a particular region which could have had influences from Aryan or Indo European, Greek, Mughal, Colonial British, French, Portuguese and other traditions. Evidence has shown that impoverished women from rural backgrounds have succeeded in pursuing the dual goals of a *social mission* and *commercial sustainability* to a greater extent than their male counterparts. This in turn lead to women-owned CBE longevity. This has been due to unique socio-cultural worldviews that women subscribe to; such as a 'collectivist orientation' and a 'democratic disposition'. Thus, we propose:

P1: *Women-owned CBEs are more robust in a DC context owing to their founders' values relating to collectivism, democracy and the desire to create social spill-over effects.*

A second outcome of our reflection is that *religion* can have a meaningful influence on women's participation in entrepreneurship. Both cultural symbols and religious practices play an important role in indigineous communities (Patel, Kaseke and Midgley, 2012). These values facilitate the fostering of collectivist tendencies and encourages volunteering behaviours. Both of this tendency and behaviour create a strong foundation for social capital, through trust and reciprocity (Patel, Kaseke and Midgley, 2012). Members of CBEs in DCs where cultural and religious symbols and practices remain important, will go above and beyond to ensure that their community prospers. We argue that these cultural and religious values enhance durability as they decreases the risk of 'mission drifts'. In the Subcontinent for example, religion is practiced in a fluid manner where a *collective approach* to entrepreneurship could be influenced by the concept of Vasudeva Kutumbha (Sanskrit terminology that translates as Vishnu's-Vasudeva OR in other words the world is one God's family) OR the importance of compassion from Buddhist principles. Similarly, Islamic teachings can influence the promotion of craftsmanship within a community of artisan women. Gender segregation can be viewed positively if we see how it can galvanize Muslim women to engage in CBE to produce handicrafts, while avoiding male exploitation. Thus, we propose:

P2: *Women embedded in a DC context where collectivist religious tenets are routinely practiced will be more enabled to set up and grow robust CBEs.*

A third outcome from our critical reflections is that the durability of a CBE in a DC context can be maximized by pursuing innovation and in implementing operational and marketing strategies that are embedded in a social mission without the possibility of mission drifts. We believe that both *collaborative innovation* and *inclusiveness* can influence CBEs in DCs to diversity their product portfolio and geographical outreach, which in turn can ensure profitability while creating the intended social impact. The idea is that, by empowering more women to pursue entrepreneurial initiatives, the social mission of CBEs is achieved. While, exponential growth can occur as a result of ongoing engagement of more women. Both these goals can be achieved through features of business models that allow for scalability. This would be contrary to standard approaches to the scaling of business models which are based on process automation of rationalization. Thus, we propose:

P3: *Business model innovation that allows the pursuit of a social mission and facilitates the inclusion of more women members for scaling will add robustness to DC women-owned CBEs.*

We propose the following model to synthesize our findings and highlighting contributions to the discourse.

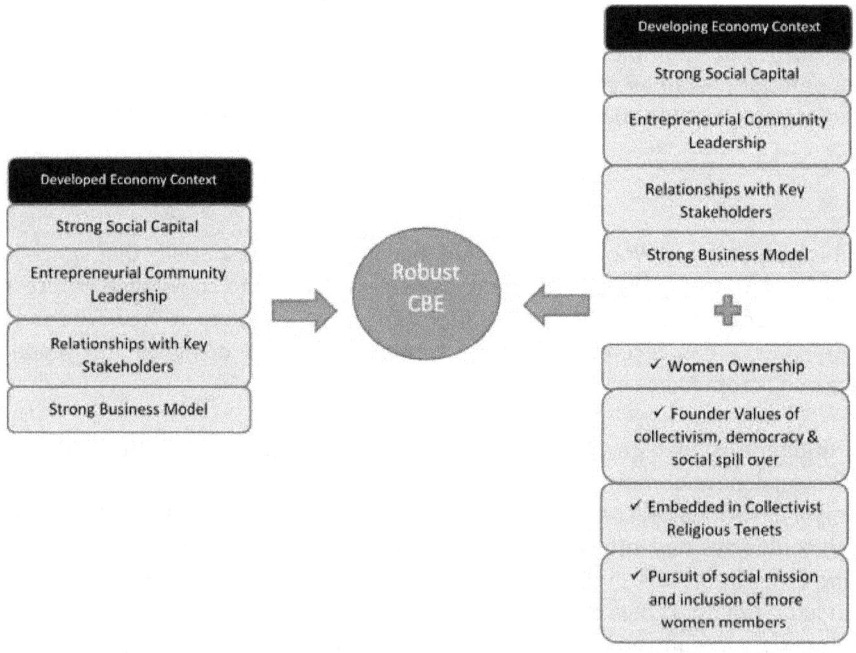

Figure 1: Conditions for CBE robustness: Developing versus developed economy contexts

7. Conclusion

This paper has achieved two major outcomes. First, we have identified a number of ways through which women can be empowered through CBEs. Secondly, we have also outlined the influencing factors of how women-led CBEs can achieve durability in a DC context.

In the first part of our paper, we argued that CBEs are the ideal means for promoting women's entrepreneurship due to several reasons. First, because women in DCs are embedded in conditions of gender imbalance, the communal entrepreneurship model, is perhaps the best means of empowerment and overcoming oppression. Secondly, women entrepreneurs in DCs view success through a different value lens. Monetary gain is not seen as the only indicator of success, but the ability to empower local communities and enhancing family wellbeing are viewed in an equally important light. Thus, the CBE model is ideal in a sense that it allows women to achieve commercial success without compromises to family and community wellbeing. This sociocentric perspective of CBEs in DCs creates a different definition of 'success' when compared to how success is established in a developed country context.

Evidence suggests that women owned CBEs in DCs are overwhelmingly more robust when compared to other ownership models. By critically assessing Van Meerkerk' et al.'s (2018) criteria, we find that in addition to the four identified conditions for CBE durability, there are a number of other 'conditions' which are applicable in a DC context (see Figure 1). These include, *first*, the entrepreneurial opportunity needs to be embedded within the socio-cultural milieu of marginalised women. In DCs, family bearing is considered a women's main priority, therefore, home-based and flexible working arrangements are preferable to enable entrepreneurial activities. Although this might be seen as limiting, the CBE model, as it facilitates the priorities of women in DCs, would represent an opportunity that would not exist otherwise. *Second*, women-led CBEs require a different governance approach, without much dependency on 'animatorship' or 'orchestrated leadership'. In DCs, gender imbalance can create a 'sense of belonging' that would lead to a higher degree of trust. Thus, social capital becomes embedded within the relationships of community members. This in turn promotes longevity as it increases members' accountability in ensuring that *everyone* benefits. *Third*, when women founders engage more women in the ownership of the CBE, it ultimately increases both commercial and social impact.

Further research should examine the characteristics of robust CBEs in DCs, especially those that are owned and managed by women, such as their governance mechanisms and how community participation is achieved for effectiveness and sustainability. To guide such research, we have developed three research propositions, testing these should involve methods such as social network analysis to allow a more embedded understanding of community entrepreneurship by women to emerge. Finally, we also need to understand how durable CBE business models, especially those animated by women, are reliably scaled or replicated in different DC contexts.

References

Bailey, N. (2012) 'The role, organisation and contribution of community enterprise to urban regeneration policy in the UK', Progress in Planning. Elsevier Ltd, 77(1), pp. 1–35.

Bhatt, P. and Ahmad, A. J. (2017) 'Financial social innovation to engage the economically marginalized: insights from an Indian case study', Entrepreneurship and Regional Development. Routledge, 29(5–6), pp. 391–413.

Delgado-Márquez, L., Justo, R. and De Castro, J. O. (2018) 'The influence of gender on social orientation and familyfriendly policies in community-based enterprises in Brazil', in Yousafzai, S., Fayolle, A., and Adam, L. (eds) Women Entrepreneurs and the Myth of 'Underperformance' : A New Look at Women's Entrepreneurship Research. 1st edn, pp. 192–210.

Dentoni, D. et al. (2018) 'Learning "who we are" by doing: Processes of co-constructing prosocial identities in community-based enterprises', Journal of Business Venturing. Elsevier, 33(5), pp. 603–622.

Gofen, A. (2015) 'Citizens' Entrepreneurial Role in Public Service Provision', Public Management Review. Routledge, 17(3), pp. 404–424.

Hailemariam, A. T. and Kroon, B. (2018) 'Redefining success beyond economic growth and wealth generation: the case of Ethiopia', in Yousafzai, S., Fayolle, A., and Adam, L. (eds) Women Entrepreneurs and the Myth of 'Underperformance'. Edward Elgar Publishing, Incorporated, pp. 3–19.

Handy, F. et al. (2011) 'Jasmine growers of coastal Karnataka: Grassroots sustainable community-based enterprise in India', Entrepreneurship and Regional Development, 23(5–6), pp. 405–417.

Haugh, H. (2007) 'Community-Led Social Venture Creation', Entrepreneurship Theory and Practice, (March), pp. 161–182.

Haugh, H. M. and Talwar, A. (2016) 'Linking Social Entrepreneurship and Social Change: The Mediating Role of Empowerment', Journal of Business Ethics. Springer Netherlands, 133(4), pp. 643–658.

Kasseeah, H. and Tandrayen-Ragoobur, V. (2016) 'Ex-garment female workers: a new entrepreneurial community in Mauritius', Journal of Enterprising Communities, 10(1), pp. 33–52.

Kelley, D. J. et al. (2017) Women's Entrepreneurship 2016/2017 Report, Global Entrepreneurship Monitor. London.

Langevang, T. et al. (2015) 'Bounded Entrepreneurial Vitality: The Mixed Embeddedness of Female Entrepreneurship', Economic Geography, 91(4), pp. 449–473.

McElwee, G., Smith, R. and Somerville, P. (2018) 'Conceptualising animation in rural communities: the Village SOS case', Entrepreneurship and Regional Development. Routledge, 30(1–2), pp. 173–198..

Van Meerkerk, I., Kleinhans, R. and Molenveld, A. (2018) 'Exploring the durability of community enterprises: A qualitative comparative analysis', Public Administration, 96(4), pp. 651–667.

Minniti, M. and Naudé, W. (2010) 'What do we know about the patterns and determinants of female entrepreneurship across Countries?', European Journal of Development Research, 22(3), pp. 277–293.

Montgomery, A. W., Dacin, P. A. and Dacin, M. T. (2012) 'Collective Social Entrepreneurship: Collaboratively Shaping Social Good', Journal of Business Ethics, 111(3), pp. 375–388.

Patel, L., Kaseke, E. and Midgley, J. (2012) 'Indigenous Welfare and Community-Based Social Development: Lessons from African Innovations', Journal of Community Practice, 20(1–2), pp. 12–31.

Peredo, A. M. et al. (2015) 'Introduction article: gender perspectives on enterprising communities', Journal of Enterprising Communities, 23(3), pp. 283–286.

Peredo, A. M. and Chrisman, J. J. (2006) 'Toward a theory of community-based enterprise', Academy of Management Review, 31(2), pp. 309–328.

Sheikh, S. et al. (2018) 'Value Creation through Women's Entrepreneurship', in Yousafzai, S., Fayolle, A., and Adam, L. (eds) Women Entrepreneurs and the Myth of 'Underperformance' : A New Look at Women's Entrepreneurship Research. 1st edn. Edward Elgar Publishing, Incorporated, pp. 20–33.

Sherwood, A. and Taylor, K. (2014) 'Unique Expectation of Co-operative Boards: taking on the challenges of the democratic enterprise', The International Journal of Co-Operative Management, 7(1), pp. 29–42.

Somerville, P. and McElwee, G. (2011) 'Situating community enterprise: A theoretical exploration', Entrepreneurship and Regional Development, 23(5–6), pp. 317–330. Sonnino, R. and Griggs-Trevarthen, C. (2013) 'A resilient social economy? Insights from the community food sector in the UK', Entrepreneurship and Regional Development, 25(3–4), pp. 272–292.

Soto Alarcón, J. M. and Sato, C. (2019) 'Enacting peasant moral community economies for sustainable livelihoods: A case of women-led cooperatives in rural Mexico', World Development, 115, pp. 120–131..

Subramaniam, M. (2012) 'Grassroots groups and poor women's empowerment in rural India', International Sociology, 27(1), pp. 72–95.

Taylor, K. (2015) 'Learning from the Co-operative Institutional Model: How to Enhance Organizational Robustness of Third Sector Organizations with More Pluralistic Forms of Governance', Administrative Sciences, 5(3), pp. 148–164.

Torri, M. C. (2010) 'Community-based Enterprises: A Promising Basis towards an Alternative Entrepreneurial Model for Sustainability Enhancing Livelihoods and Promoting Socio-economic Development in Rural India', Journal of Small Business and Entrepreneurship, 23(2), pp. 237–248.

Torri, M. C. and Martinez, A. (2014) 'Women's empowerment and micro-entrepreneurship in India: Constructing a new development paradigm?', Progress in Development Studies, 14(1), pp. 31–48.

Vossenberg, S. (2013) Women Entrepreneurship Promotion in Developing Countries: What explains the gender gap in entrepreneurship and how to close it ? 2013/08. Maastricht.

Zahra, S. A. (2007) 'Contextualizing theory building in entrepreneurship research', Journal of Business Venturing, 22(3), pp. 443–452.

Does Profitability Matter in Determining Entrepreneurial Orientation and Performance of Social Enterprises?

Ghadah Alarifi
College of Business Administration, Princess Nourah bint Abdulrahman University, Riyadh, Kingdom of Saudi Arabia
gaalarifi@pnu.edu.sa
DOI: 10.34190/EIE.20.245

Abstract: Despite the increasing body of literature on social enterprises (SEs), there is a need for more focused research to differentiate between for-profit and not-for-profit SEs. More specifically, literature seems to struggle with apprising entrepreneurial orientation (EO) differences between for-profit and nonprofit SEs. Most of the research focuses on SEs as if they were solely third-sector organizations, and only a handful of studies have included for-profit SEs within their analysis of the phenomena. This research aims to fill that gap by quantitively examining 220 SEs in the Kingdom of Saudi Arabia to check for variances between for-profit and nonprofit SEs. We hypothesize that social for-profit and nonprofit enterprises differ in terms of EO, innovativeness, and performance. Our study contributes to enhancing our knowledge of how EO can explain the success of SEs, as well as assessing if their profiting orientation can enhance or hinder their capacity to create social value while being financially sustainable and innovative.

Keywords: social entrepreneurship, entrepreneurial orientation, performance, social enterprises

1. Introduction

During the past two decades, social enterprises (SEs) have become some of the most successful organizations in terms of social value creation, especially in terms of community empowerment, gender equality, poverty reduction, and job creation (Fitzgerald and Shepherd, 2018; Mendell and Nogales, 2009; Smith, et al., 2010; Smith, Gonin, and Besharov, 2013). SEs escape the conventional logic of traditional businesses (Morris, Webb, and Franklin, 2011; Moss, et al., 2011) and orthodox nonprofit organizations (Johanisová, Crabtree, and Fraňková, 2013) because they are agents of social change that compete within a market economy to provide solutions to social problems instead of producing profit for their owners (Morris, et al., 2011; Stoudt, 2012; Conway Dato-on and Kalakay, 2016). SE success drove an important number of organizations within the third sector to become SEs or create SEs to help them achieve a level of financial sustainability, and several for-profit businesses have shifted toward including social value creation as a central organizational tenet (De Cuyper, 2016; Peng and Liang, 2019).

Despite the growing body of literature on SEs (Bacq and Janssen, 2011; Doherty, Haugh, and Lyon, 2014; Conway Dato-on and Kalakay, 2016; Peng and Liang, 2019), their definition is still nebulous and requires further theorizing, especially concerning their function within the economic system and how to differentiate social from commercial entrepreneurship (Morris, et al., 2011). More specifically, literature seems to struggle with apprising entrepreneurial orientation (EO) differences between for-profit and nonprofit SEs (Gorostiaga, et al., 2019). Most of the research focuses on SEs as if they were solely third-sector organizations (Conway Dato-on and Kalakay, 2016; Gorostiaga, et al., 2019), and only a handful of studies have included for-profit SEs in their analysis of the phenomena (Teles and Schachtebeck, 2019). This research aims to fill that gap by examining differences between for-profit and nonprofit SEs. We hypothesize that for-profit and nonprofit SEs differ in terms of EO, innovativeness, and performance, leading to our research question: Does the profit orientation of SEs determine their level of EO, innovativeness, and performance?

2. Literature review

2.1 Social Enterprise characteristics

SEs are substantially diverse organizations. They diverge in terms of social and commercial goals, business and social practices, organizational forms, and ways to produce positive social impacts and social value. These variations depend on both external factors—such as the local jurisdictional, economic, and political context—and intrinsic characteristics like organizational and individual EO. This vast diversity is a challenge for scholars trying to understand the phenomenon, and it is not uncommon for SEs to be lumped together with other third-sector organizations such as charities, cooperatives, NGOs, developmental agencies, and microfinance banks, among others (Borzaga, Depedri, and Tortia, 2009; Morris, et al., 2011; Conway Dato-on and Kalakay, 2016; Shahriar, Schwarz, and Newman, 2016; Fitzgerald and Shepherd, 2018).

The consensus among scholars and practitioners is that SEs are organizations that use commercial practices to compete within a market economy to instill positive social change (Doherty, et al., 2014; Conway Dato-on and Kalakay, 2016; Peng and Liang, 2019). In that sense, SEs can be seen as hybrid organizations with both commercial and social aims that may be at odds with each other. Additionally, evidence suggests that SEs are more prone to creating long-term sustainable social value (Pieterse, 2010; Johanisová, et al., 2013) because they allow grassroots communities to create sustainable and independent sources of income and social services, empowering communities by making them independent from aid (albeit creating new forms of inequality in the form of organizational structures required to deliver welfare; Nimruji and Kamalika, 2018), and because third-sector organizations can create or use them to be financially sustainable and independent from donors and government funding agendas (Kim Alter, 2010).

Nevertheless, this does not mean that all SEs are successful. On the contrary, there is a high rate of SE failure, especially within developing economies where the institutional context is averse to their success because market resources are limited, government funding is insufficient, legislation is unfavorable, available skilled labor is lacking, and/or social entrepreneurs lack the skills required for long-term survival (Krauss, et al., 2005; Goyal, Sergi, and Kapoor, 2017; Nimruji and Kamalika, 2018; Shin and Park, 2019; Teles and Schachtebeck, 2019). In light of these elements, EO emerges not only as a potential explanation of SE success and failure, but also as a solution to ensure their long-term sustainability—and perhaps even to overcome challenges resulting from inequality (Morris, et al., 2011; Kiruki, 2016; Alsolamy, 2019a; Teles and Schachtebeck, 2019).

2.2 Entrepreneurial orientation

To be successful within a market economy—and even to survive in the long term—a business requires proactive innovation marked by the creation of new products and services and taking risks to exploit opportunities. In other words, being an entrepreneur means maintaining an "entrepreneurial spirit" that allows organizations and leaders to maintain a longstanding engagement in the process of innovation and technological change, rather than holding to rigid structures that prevent change (Schumpeter, 1943; Gorostiaga, et al., 2019). To provide a behavioral and quantified appraisal of this entrepreneurial spirit, Miller (1983) introduced the concept of EO, which today is a well-established concept within behavioral, managerial, and organizational studies.

The idea expands on the nebulous concept of entrepreneurial spirit introduced by Schumpeter (1943), grounded as EO in 1983 by Miller, and operationalized by Covin and Selvin (1989) through a scale that measures attitudes and behaviors (organizational and individual) around three dimensions: innovativeness, proactiveness, and risk-taking. Researchers in organizational and behavioral research use this scale, and each dimension has been heavily expanded and defined during the past three decades (Covin and Slevin, 1991; Morris, et al., 2011; Gorostiaga, et al., 2019). The innovativeness dimension is related to creativity and experimentation and can be defined as the propensity to produce novel ideas and/or to combine existing ideas in innovative ways to create new products, services, processes, and leadership skills (Bridgstock, et al., 2010; Morris et al., 2011; Gorostiaga, et al., 2019; Teles and Schachtebeck, 2019). The proactiveness dimension is related to the capability of an organization to anticipate change rather than simply react to it. It can be defined as the ability to predict future problems and consumer desires and needs to implement change ahead of competing firms or individuals (Morris, et al., 2011; Balta, et al., 2012; Teles and Schachtebeck, 2019). The risk-taking dimension can be defined as the ability to accurately calculate the risk involved and actively commit resources to introducing novel products and services to the market, as well as to implement organizational changes. Risk-taking allows entrepreneurial organizations to increase their aptitudes to seek market opportunities (Balta, et al., 2012; Teles and Schachtebeck, 2019).

Since the introduction of Colvin and Selvin's (1989) three-dimensional model, researchers have expanded the EO dimensions. The most common new dimensions attached to the model are competitive aggressiveness, autonomy (Lumpkin and Dess, 1996), achievement orientation, and learning orientation (Krauss, et al., 2005). However, these added dimensions are still subject to considerable debate. Most EO studies have opted to change them, add new dimensions within the original three-dimensional model, or simply not use them (Rauch, et al., 2009; Abaho, et al., 2017). Additionally, there is increasing debate on how EO's dimensions interact with each other. Rauch et al. (2009) conducted a systematic literature review on the concept, concluding that about

65% of papers understand EO as unidimensional. In other words, most researchers have used EO's dimensions on the assumption that they are deeply interdependent or combined them within a single factor. This situation has changed very little over the past decade (Gorostiaga, et al., 2019)

The consensus suggests that innovativeness, proactiveness, and risk-taking are still the crucial dimensions of EO. Moreover, this study focuses on SEs, where dimensions such as competitive aggressiveness may not be as important as in the commercial sector (Phillips, 2006; Morris, et al., 2011; Tykkylainen, et al., 2016; Abaho, et al., 2017; Alsolamy, 2019b). Therefore, this literature review will make use of Covin and Selvin's (1989) proposed dimensions to assess EO in for-profit and nonprofit SEs.

2.3 Entrepreneurial orientation and the third sector

A growing body of literature makes use of EO within the nonprofit context. These researchers look for behavioral and organizational perspective to explain why some third-sector organizations are successful where others tend to fail. In their research, innovativeness, proactiveness, and risk-taking emerge as important dimensions to explain the performance of third-sector organizations. These studies have found an interesting correlation between higher levels of EO and long-term organization survival, financial sustainability, and efficacy in social value creation (Phillips, 2006; Vickers and Lyon, 2014; Tykkylainen, et al., 2016). However, EO requires some changes before it can be applied to third-sector organizations, given that they prioritize the production of social value and social change over financial goals (Phillips, 2006; Borzaga, et al., 2009; Tykkylainen, et al., 2016; Valentinov, 2015). This implies some organizational and behavioral changes, especially concerning competitiveness and cooperation. While commercial firms engage in hostile competition because their goal is to outcompete other businesses to increase their market share and profits, third-sector organizations tend to cooperate with other organizations to maximize their capacities to generate social value (Morris, et al., 2011; Fitzgerald and Shepherd, 2018).

According to Alarifi, Robson, and Kromidha (2019, p. 88), "there has not been a well-established modified scale of EO in the SE context." Alarifi et al. (2019, p. 88) also pointed out that most "of the studies on EO [within the third sector] have measured either three or four dimensions, but innovativeness, proactiveness, and risk-taking are central to most of the studies." This research, like the present study, does not aim to provide a new EO scale for SEs but rather uses the original three-dimensional model proposed by Covin and Selvin (1989).

Another challenge is related to a widespread tendency to lump under the same label organizations as different as SEs, NGOs, community grassroots organizations, development agencies, social responsibility organizations, and more (Alter, 2010; Morris, et al., 2011; Gorostiaga, et al., 2019). This lack of distinction among organizations may be related to increased overlapping between the private sector and the third sector; most third-sector organizations are cooperating with private-sector companies to create SEs or creating SEs that allow them to obtain direct financing from the market economy (Morris, et al., 2011). However, lumping third-sector SEs together may be detrimental to understanding their hybrid nature because it can lead to overlooking SEs with a for-profit orientation. On this point, managerial literature may benefit from the definitions and differences developed within the field of development studies (Pieterse, 2010) and by practitioners in the third sector.

Despite this tendency to generalize, there is an extant body of literature that differentiates for-profit SEs from nonprofit SEs to explore how EO influences both groups' performance. These studies share certain characteristics: a) they tend to be highly localized, limiting their generalizing potential; b) they all included the three dimensions developed by Covin and Selvin (1989); c) they found a correlation between high levels of innovation and proactiveness and better performance in terms of social value creation, long-term survival, outreach, and social services delivery; and d) institutional context played a key role in SE success.

2.4 Adapting EO scales to a social entrepreneurship context

Morris et al. (2016) proposed one of the most comprehensive attempts to adapt the EO scale to the social entrepreneurship context, supplying an entrepreneurship typology based on the level of social and commercial entrepreneurship that nonprofit organizations may have. Their typology has the potential to explain how commercial entrepreneurship and social entrepreneurship intertwine to create diverse practices within the third-sector context. By exploring social and commercial entrepreneurship as independent factors within the same phenomena, their typology provides a comprehensive picture of EO within nonprofits. It shows the complexity faced by third-sector organizations when they attempt to create novel ways to address social issues while finding and exploiting financial and market opportunities.

Morris et al.'s (2016) typology can be adapted to understand the differences in EO between for-profit and nonprofit SEs, which, as mentioned in the introduction, have been left largely unexplored in scholarship, except for a few studies we will introduce below. Nevertheless, being commercially entrepreneurial does not mean an SE is for-profit. Therefore, this adaptation must be flexible and wide to encompass the vast variety of organizational, commercial, and social arrangements one can find within SEs. For example, Teles and Schachtebeck's (2019) inclusion of the four lenses of SE typology within the Morris et al. (2016) EO model allowed them to gain a complex understanding of South African SEs that included and differentiated between for-profit and nonprofit SEs. There is no unified research framework to understand EO's role within SEs, and because SEs are lumped together with nonprofit organizations, it is difficult to assess differences in EO between for-profit and nonprofit SEs. Nevertheless, there is an extant body of literature that assesses the changes in SEs' EO in terms of their profiting orientation. These early studies have faced some challenges, such as small datasets that were prominently localized, limiting their generalization potential.

In one such study, Teles and Schachtebeck (2019) used a quantitative approach to assess the level of EO within South African SEs and how it helped them navigate a hostile institutional and economic environment. SEs in South Africa tend to have a short lifespan; most disappear within their first year. This is related to a high dependence on inadequate government funding, their struggle to attract and retain skilled and qualified employees, and difficulties in identifying their market target. Teles and Schachtebeck (2019) found significant differences in EO among nonprofit, hybrid, and for-profit SEs. The most relevant difference was related to the risk-taking dimension. Nonprofits were less likely to engage in endeavors that could risk employees'/associates' job security than those enterprises that had a hybrid profiting orientation. This may be explained by the fact that the former tended to be more focused on social than on financial goals.

Likewise, for-profit SEs tended to be more innovative and proactive than nonprofit SEs. This may be related to the need for hybrid SEs and for-profit SEs to innovate in many dimensions: financial, commercial, and social. Nonprofit SEs, however, tended to be more conservative in how they created social value, let alone financial value (Shaw and Allen, 2009; Fedele and Miniaci, 2012; Stoudt, 2012; Teles and Schachtebeck, 2019). As Morris et al. (2016) pointed out, in the nonprofit context, a low level of social innovation is related to a low level of proactiveness, which may provide a partial explanation of why nonprofit SEs tended to be less proactive in the South African context (Teles and Schachtebeck, 2019). However, Teles and Schachtebeck (2019) found no significant statistical difference between the levels of competitive aggressiveness for for-profit and nonprofit SEs. This may be related to the tendency of SEs to cooperate (even among for-profit ones) instead of competing. This is not only related to the fact that their ultimate aim is to create social value but also to the fact that interorganizational collaboration helps them build market legitimacy (Smith, et al., 2010; Stoudt, 2012; Fitzgerald and Shepherd, 2018; Gorostiaga, et al., 2019).

Complementing the case of South Africa, Abaho et al. (2017) observed that in Uganda, SEs with a for-profit business tended to have a higher EO in terms of innovation, risk-taking, and proactiveness. This higher EO allowed these SEs to a) invest more resources in radical and incremental innovation, which led them to grow in terms of beneficiaries, quality of services provided, and positive responses from customers; b) have a better capability to take risks, helping them to grow; and c) be more proactive, acting on innovations and dealing with risks.

Similarly, Alsolamy (2019b) noticed that in Saudi Arabia, EO affects SE innovation capabilities and sustainable competitive advantage. The more EO, the more competitive and innovative an SE is. Alarifi et al.'s (2019) observation on the Saudi SE sector complements Alsolamy's (2019) studies, showing that innovativeness and proactiveness have a positive effect on Saudi SE performance—both for-profit and nonprofit. As in the case of Uganda and South Africa, higher levels of EO can help an SE to survive and even thrive in a context of limited resources (Alarifi, 2018; Alarifi, et al., 2019; Alsolamy, 2019b). These findings also resonate with Kiruki's (2016) study of SEs in Kenya, in which the author found that Kenyan SEs had low levels of EO, especially in terms of proactivity. However, those SEs that showed a higher level of EO had better financial performance and sustainability, as they obtained competitive advantages within the Kenyan context. However, at least in this case, a better EO did not necessarily imply better performance in terms of social value creation. Kiruki's (2016) conclusions are in line with most literature on EO and SEs that suggests that there is conflict between SEs' social and commercial missions, as their social missions can prevent or encourage commercial growth by narrowing their growing paths (Phillips, 2006; Vickers and Lyon, 2014; Tykkylainen, et al., 2016). One example of this phenomenon consists of finding effective financing options, such as crowdfunding, which depends heavily on the social mission of creating actual paths to de-grow as SEs substitute the goal of profit maximization with the goal of social value creation (Morris, et al., 2011; Kickul and Lyons, 2015; Shin and Park, 2019; Guo and Peng, 2020).

The literature suggests that for-profit SEs present higher levels of EO and, therefore, higher rates of financial sustainability and long-term survival. However, EO seems to have positive effects solely over the commercial goals of SEs. In other words, for-profit SEs are more innovative, proactive, effective, and resilient when committing resources to risky endeavors. However, although this may have a positive effect on their financial performance, the evidence does not suggest a positive or negative correlation between EO and social performance.

H1: For-profit SEs have higher EO than nonprofit SEs.

H2: For-profit SEs have higher innovativeness than nonprofit SEs.

H3: For-profit SEs have higher performance than nonprofit SEs.

3. Methods

A quantitative approach was used in this study. Materials used include a questionnaire developed in English and translated into Arabic (and later back-translated along with the answers), and pre-test reviews by three independent scholars, all of whom are bilingual in Arabic and English. SEs received these materials via email, and data were collected via electronic survey.

3.1 Measures

In total, 220 valid questionnaires were received as responses from survey participants for the data analysis. The EO scale used in this study was developed by Covin and Slevin (1989). The performance scale is a four-item scale previously used by Alarifi et al. (2019) that is a subjective measure of social and economic performance. The organizational innovativeness construct was developed by Wang and Ahmed (2004).

3.2 Results and analysis

An independent sample t-test was run to assess the significance of differences in EO, innovativeness, and performance between for-profit and nonprofit SEs (Table 1). The study found significant differences in EO (t (220) = 2.317, p = .021) between for-profit and nonprofit SEs. EO was higher in for-profit SEs (Mean = 4.47, SD = 1.14) in comparison to nonprofit SEs (Mean = 4.12, SD = 1.08). The study found significant differences in innovativeness (t (155.067) = 3.040, p = .003) between for-profit and nonprofit SEs. Innovativeness was higher in for-profit SEs (Mean = 5.70, SD = .67) in comparison to nonprofit SEs (Mean = 5.35, SD = .95). The study also found significant differences in performance (t (220) = 2.28, p = .023) between for-profit and nonprofit SEs, with for-profit SEs showing higher performance (Mean = 5.64, SD = .979) in comparison to nonprofit SEs (Mean = 5.34, SD = .983).

Table 1: Comparing for-profit and non-for-profit social enterprises

Constructs	Groups	Mean	Std. Deviation	Levene's Test for Equality of Variances		t-test for Equality of Means		
				F	Sig.	t	df	Sig. (2-tailed)
Entrepreneurial Orientation	For Profit	4.4798	1.14286	.478	.490	2.317	220	.021
	non-profit	4.1266	1.08849					
Innovation	For Profit	5.7011	.67111	7.762	.006	3.040	155.067	.003
	non-profit	5.3507	.95479					
Performance	For Profit	5.64	0.979	.1606	.689	2.28	220	.023
	non-profit	5.34	0.983					

N: For Profit = 128, Non-Profit = 92

4. Discussion and conclusion

A handful of studies in social entrepreneurship have explored EO in SEs. Their conclusions are generally attuned to a broader analysis of EO within social entrepreneurship contexts, especially regarding the correlation between high levels of EO and good financial sustainability and long-term survival among SEs, and concerning EO's crucial role in the SEs' capacity to survive and thrive within a hostile institutional context. Nevertheless, the evidence does not provide enough data about the relationship between EO and its effects on SEs' social performance. This research found significant differences in EO between for-profit and nonprofit SEs, with EO higher in for-profit SEs. In terms of innovativeness, this study also found significant differences between for-profit and nonprofit SEs, with a higher level of innovativeness in for-profit SEs. This study also found significant differences in performance, which was higher in for-profit SEs in comparison to nonprofit SEs.

This study contributes to enhancing our knowledge of how EO can explain the success of SEs, as well as confirming their profiting orientation can enhance their capacity to create social value while being financially sustainable and independent. EO emerges not only as a potential explanation of the success and failure of SEs, but also as a solution to ensure their long-term sustainability, and perhaps even to overcome challenges posed by inequality

Referencies

Abaho, E., Begumisa, D. B., Aikiriza, F., & Turyasingura, I. (2017). Entrepreneurial Orientation Among Social Enterprises in Uganda. *Business Management Review*, *20*(2), 1–14.

Alarifi, G. (2018). *The Institutional Environment, Entrepreneurial Orientation and Performance of Saudi Social Enterprises Ghadah*. University of London. https://doi.org/10.1109/robot.1994.350900

Alarifi, G., Robson, P., & Kromidha, E. (2019). The Manifestation of Entrepreneurial Orientation in the Social Entrepreneurship Context. *Journal of Social Entrepreneurship*, *10*(3), 307–327. https://doi.org/10.1080/19420676.2018.1541015

Alsolamy, M. Q. (2019a). Exploring the Relationship between Entrepreneurial Orientation, Innovative Capability and Social enterprises Competitive Positioning: Evidence on Social Enterprises in Saudi Arabia.

Alsolamy, M. Q. (2019b). Exploring the Relationship between Entrepreneurial Orientation, Innovative Capability and Social enterprises Competitive Positioning: Evidence on Social Enterprises in Saudi Arabia. *Global Journal of Economics and Business*, *7*(3), 335–347. https://doi.org/10.31559/gjeb2019.7.3.6

Bacq, S., & Janssen, F. (2011). The multiple faces of social entrepreneurship: A review of definitional issues based on geographical and thematic criteria. *Entrepreneurship and Regional Development*, *23*(5–6), 373–403. https://doi.org/10.1080/08985626.2011.577242

Balta, M., Darlington, C., Smith, S. L., & Cornelius, N. (2012). Entrepreneurial orientation and social innovation practices in social enterprises: The rhetoric and reality.

Borzaga, C., Depedri, S., & Tortia, E. C. (2009). The Role of Cooperative and Social Enterprises: A Multifaceted Approach for an Economic Pluralism.

Bridgstock, R., Lettice, F., Özbilgin, M. F., & Tatli, A. (2010). Diversity management for innovation in social enterprises in the UK. *Entrepreneurship and Regional Development*, *22*(6), 557–574.

Conway Dato-on, M., & Kalakay, J. (2016). The winding road of social entrepreneurship definitions: a systematic literature review. *Social Enterprise Journal*, *12*(2), 131–160. https://doi.org/10.1108/sej-06-2015-0016

Covin, J. G., & Slevin, D. P. (1991). A Conceptual Model of Entrepreneurship as Firm Behavior. *Entrepreneurship Theory and Practice*, *16*(1), 7–26. https://doi.org/10.1177/104225879101600102

De Cuyper, L. (2016). Doing Good while Making Profit: Perspectives on Reconciling Multiple Objectives in Social Enterprises. Retrieved from https://spiral.imperial.ac.uk/handle/10044/1/44558

Doherty, B., Haugh, H., & Lyon, F. (2014). Social enterprises as hybrid organizations: A review and research agenda. *International Journal of Management Reviews*, *16*(4), 417–436. https://doi.org/10.1111/ijmr.12028

Fedele, A., & Miniaci, R. (2012). "Stakeholder Orientation" and Capital Structure: Social Enterprises Versus For-Profit Firms in the Italian Social Residential Service Sector.

Fitzgerald, T., & Shepherd, D. (2018). Emerging Structures for Social Enterprises Within Nonprofits: An Institutional Logics Perspective: *Nonprofit and Voluntary Sector Quarterly*, *47*(3), 474–492.

Gorostiaga, A., Aliri, J., Ulacia, I., Soroa, G., Balluerka, N., Aritzeta, A., & Muela, A. (2019). Assessment of entrepreneurial orientation in vocational training students: Development of a new scale and relationships with self-efficacy and personal initiative. *Frontiers in Psychology*, *10*(MAY), 1–10. https://doi.org/10.3389/fpsyg.2019.01125

Goyal, S., Sergi, B. S., & Kapoor, A. (2017). Emerging role of for-profit social enterprises at the base of the pyramid: the case of Selco. *Journal of Management Development*, *36*(1), 97–108. https://doi.org/10.1108/JMD-05-2015-0070

Guo, B., & Peng, S. (2020). Do Nonprofit and For-Profit Social Enterprises Differ in Financing? *VOLUNTAS: International Journal of Voluntary and Nonprofit Organizations*. https://doi.org/10.1007/s11266-020-00218-5

Johanisová, N., Crabtree, T., & Fraňková, E. (2013). Social enterprises and non-market capitals: a path to degrowth? *Journal of Cleaner Production*, *38*, 7–16.

Kickul, J., & Lyons, T. S. (2015). Financing Social Enterprises. *Entrepreneurship Research Journal*, *5*(2), 83–85.

Kim Alter, S. (2010). The Four Lenses Strategic Framework.

Kiruki, L. (2016). The Relationship between Entrepreneurial Orientation and Performance of Social Enterprises in Kenya.

Krauss, S. I., Frese, M., Friedrich, C., & Unger, J. M. (2005). Entrepreneurial orientation: A psychological model of success among southern African small business owners. *European Journal of Work and Organizational Psychology*, *14*(3), 315–344. https://doi.org/10.1080/13594320500170227

Lumpkin, G. T., & Dess, G. G. (1996). Clarifying the Entrepreneurial Orientation Construct and Linking It to Performance. *The Academy of Management Review*, *21*(1), 135–172. https://doi.org/10.2307/258632

Mendell, M., & Nogales, R. (2009). Social Enterprises in OECD Member Countries. *Local Economic and Employment Development*, 89–138.

Miller, D. (1983). The Correlates of Entrepreneurship in Three Types of Firms. *Management Science*, *29*(7), 770–791. https://doi.org/10.1287/mnsc.29.7.770

Morris, M. H., Webb, J. W., & Franklin, R. J. (2011). Understanding the Manifestation of Entrepreneurial Orientation in the Nonprofit Context. *Entrepreneurship Theory and Practice*, *35*(5), 947–971. https://doi.org/10.1111/j.1540-6520.2011.00453.x

Moss, T. W., Short, J. C., Payne, G. T., & Lumpkin, G. T. (2011). Dual identities in social ventures: An exploratory study. *Entrepreneurship: Theory and Practice*, *35*(4), 805–830. https://doi.org/10.1111/j.1540-6520.2010.00372.x

Nimruji, J., & Kamalika, C. (2018). Local geographies of developing country social enterprises. *Social Enterprise Journal*, *14*(3), 367–386. https://doi.org/10.1108/SEJ-11-2016-0051

Peng, X. E., & Liang, C. (2019). Before Nonprofit Organisations Become Social Enterprises. *Voluntas*, *30*(3), 460–474. https://doi.org/10.1007/s11266-018-00071-7

Phillips, M. (2006). Growing pains: the sustainability of social enterprises. *The International Journal of Entrepreneurship and Innovation*, *7*(4), 221–230.

Pieterse, J. N. (2010). *Development Theory. Development Theory: Deconstructions/Reconstructions*. https://doi.org/10.1017/CBO9781107415324.004

Rauch, A., Wiklund, J., Lumpkin, G. T., & Frese, M. (2009). Entrepreneurial orientation and business performance: An assessment of past research and suggestions for the future. *Entrepreneurship: Theory and Practice*, *33*(3), 761–787. https://doi.org/10.1111/j.1540-6520.2009.00308.x

Schumpeter, J. A. (1943). *Capitalism, Socialism and Democracy* (Seventh). Taylor & Francis. Retrieved from https://books.google.com.co/books?id=ytrqJswoRCoC

Shahriar, A. Z. M., Schwarz, S., & Newman, A. H. (2016). Profit orientation of microfinance institutions and provision of financial capital to business start-ups. *International Small Business Journal*, *34*(4), 532–552.

Shaw, S., & Allen, J. B. (2009). " To Be a Business and to Keep Our Humanity " A Critical Management Studies Analysis of the Relationship Between a Funder and Nonprofit Community Organizations. *Nonprofit Management and Leadership*, *20*(3), 83–96. https://doi.org/10.1002/nml

Shin, C., & Park, J. (2019). How Social Entrepreneurs' Value Orientation Affects the Performance of Social Enterprises in Korea: The Mediating Effect of Social Entrepreneurship. *Sustainability*, *11*(19).

Smith, B. R., Knapp, J., Barr, T. F., Stevens, C. E., & Cannatelli, B. L. (2010). Social Enterprises and the Timing of Conception: Organizational Identity Tension, Management, and Marketing. *Journal of Nonprofit & Public Sector Marketing*, *22*(2), 108–134.

Smith, W. K., Gonin, M., & Besharov, M. L. (2013). Managing Social-Business Tensions: A Review and Research Agenda for Social Enterprise. *Business Ethics Quarterly*, *23*(3), 407–442. https://doi.org/10.5840/beq201323327

Stoudt, H. D. (2012). *Entrepreneurial orientation in nonprofit organizations and its effect on the development of social entrepreneurial strategies*. Capella University.

Sudolska, A., & Chodorek, M. (2016). Pro-Innovative Orientation of Polish Social Enterprises: The Empirical Perspective. *International Joint Conference on Knowledge Discovery, Knowledge Engineering and Knowledge Management*.

Teles, D., & Schachtebeck, C. (2019). Entrepreneurial orientation in South African social enterprises. *Entrepreneurial Business and Economics Review*, *7*(3), 83–97. https://doi.org/10.15678/EBER.2019.070305

Tykkylainen, S., Syrjä, P., Puumalainen, K., & Sjögrén, H. (2016). Growth orientation in social enterprises. *International Journal of Entrepreneurial Venturing*, *8*(3), 296–316.

Valentinov, V. (2015). Value devolution in social enterprises: Institutional economics and systems theory perspectives. *Econstor Open Access Articles*, 1126–1133.

Vickers, I., & Lyon, F. (2014). Beyond green niches? Growth strategies of environmentally-motivated social enterprises. *International Small Business Journal*, *32*(4), 449–470.

Wang, C.L. and Ahmed, P.K., 2004. The development and validation of the organisational innovativeness construct using confirmatory factor analysis. European journal of innovation management.

Enhancing Process Innovation Through Social Capital Components: An Empirical Study

Sawasn Al-husseini
Materials Management department, Institute of Administration - Rusafa, Middle Technical University, Baghdad, Iraq
Sawasn.al-husseini@hotmail.com
DOI: 10.34190/EIE.20.207

Abstract: Innovation is considered one of the key capabilities required for organisations to achieve success. Previous studies have claimed that social capital influences innovation capabilities but have not looked at the individual effects of its dimensions (cognitive, relational, and structural. This research seeks to examine the linkage between social capital (structural, relational, and cognitive) and process innovation in the banking sector. A total of 260 usable questionnaires were collected from private banks in Iraq. Structural equation modelling with AMOS v.26 confirmed the importance of social capital in developing innovation in the banking sector. It was revealed that of the three components, relational capital had the greatest effect on process innovation. This research develops some guidelines for researchers as well as managers and provides evidence supporting the use of social capital to enhance process innovation within the banking sector in developing countries, particularly Iraq. The implications of the findings and suggestions for future research are discussed.

Keywords: social capital, innovation, bank, Iraq

1. Introduction

The banking sector is today facing an increasingly challenging period. Global recession, increased competition, globalisation, technological advances, and a demand for improved service quality. In such environments, innovation becomes a fundamental requirement for achieving sustainability, survival, and growth (Bohlmann et al. 2012), which is forcing the banking sector to be not only efficient and effective but also innovative.

To be more effective in innovation, organisations need to focus on how they manage intangibles. Social capital, as a bundle of intangibles, is a critical resource for organisational performance and firms' ability to innovate, create, and sustain competitive advantage (Nahapiet and Ghoshal 1998). Social capital theory is powerful, explaining how organisations can access knowledge resources through relationships. These are the sum of the actual and potential resources embedded within, available through, and derived from, the network of relationships possessed by an individual or social unit (Adler and Kwon 2002). Social capital is a multi-dimensional construct composed of structural (relationship configuration), relational (relationship quality), and cognitive (shared mental models) social capital. From the resource-based view, stronger social interaction ties, trust, and shared goals and visions are critical organisational resources that may increase knowledge sharing, which in turn supports innovation (Wang and Wang 2012).

The banking sector is the most active sector in Iraq's economy, and it plays an active role in the economic development of the country. Financial organisations such as banks require social interaction among their employees to be able to achieve their goals and perform at a high level (Oppong and Pattanayak 2019). The Iraqi banking sector is viewed as one of the major beneficiaries of the government's continuous efforts to diversify its economy to non-oil sectors. It seems to be a complex and highly competitive environment, operating in such a dynamic environment requires bank employees to fully understand all the factors associated with successful innovation in the market.

Previous studies have looked at the relationship between intellectual capital and innovation (Cabrilo and Dahms 2018; Subramaniam and Youndt 2005), however few have touched on the elements of social capital (structural, relational, and cognitive) and their impact on employees' process innovation (Nahapiet and Ghoshal 1998), and there is no consensus on how particular social components are related to organisational innovation (Wang et al. 2016), or which of these components are the most valuable in developing countries, and more specifically Iraq. Since innovation is important in private organisations, including financial organisations (Smith 2009) such as banks, this research aims to examine the impact of three components of social capital, namely structural, relational, and cognitive, on process innovation using the context of Iraqi private banks. The outcomes will be useful for managers and decision-makers of private banks in developing management strategies for innovation that will work best for the sector.

2. Theoretical background

2.1 Social capital

Social capital plays an important role in meeting the needs of organisations and contributes to their survival in today's competitive world. It encourages organisational members to form relationships, communicate with each other, and act together more effectively to achieve organisational goals (Adler and Kwon 2002). Social capital provides an excellent atmosphere for increased employee flexibility in an uncertain environment (Nahapiet and Ghoshal 1998).

Filieri et al.(2014) described social capital as features of social organisations such as networks, norms, and social trust that facilitate coordination and cooperation for mutual benefit. This includes the knowledge embedded in the social relationships and networks among individuals, communities, and society (Wang et al. 2016). It is argued that this capital inheres within the structure of relations of authority, trust, and norms between and among persons (Adler and Kwon 2002).

Prior literature has identified three components of social capital: structural, relational, and cognitive (Nahapiet and Ghoshal 1998). Structural social capital refers to the social interactions and impersonal configuration of linkages among a social group of people. It includes the ties or connections among network members, as well as the overall network configuration, which considers factors such as structural holes, centralisation, and the density of the network (Cabrera and Cabrera 2005). Structural social capital can facilitate the flow of information, enable influences on network members, certify network members' social credentials, reflecting their ability to access resources via social relationships, and reinforce people's identity and aid their recognition as social group members who share similar interests and resources with other members (Wang et al. 2016). Filieri et al. (2014) found that structural social capital had generated controversy regarding its potential for achieving business results such as product innovation or economic profitability.

Relational social capital refers to the assets that are rooted in relationships, such as trust and trustworthiness (Wu et al. 2008). It encompasses the network relationships such as interpersonal trust, the existence of shared norms, and identification with other individuals in the network (Cabrera and Cabrera 2005). Relational social capital is the knowledge that is embedded in the identification, development, and maintenance of external relationships (Joshi et al. 2013). Adler and Kwon (2002) found that relational social capital was the ability of an organisation to interact with a wide range of external stakeholders, such as customers, suppliers, competitors, and trade and industry associations. It provides information about market needs and opportunities, and competitive dynamics, providing a useful external map or guide to how the organisation can improve existing and develop new knowledge (Costa et al. 2014).

Chang and Chuang (2011) noted that cognitive social capital concerns the extent to which people in a social network share a common perspective or understanding. It derives from individuals' perceptions and mental processes, resulting in norms, values, and beliefs that contribute to cooperation. Akhavan and Hosseini (2016) found that this type of social capital was embodied in attributes such as a shared code or paradigm that facilitated a common understanding of collective goals and proper ways of acting in a social system. Cognitive social capital is embedded in properties such as a common language or vision that support a common understanding of shared goals and norms of action in a social setting (Allameh 2018).

2.2 Innovation

Organisations today are increasingly focusing on innovation as a key factor of success and competitive advantage (Tidd and Bessant 2011). Innovative organisations have the capacity to improve individual and organisational performance and solve problems by effecting change and creating opportunities (Schilling 2010). This can provide entry to new markets and enhance the effectiveness of organisations.

Tidd and Bessant (2011) defined innovation as the adoption of new ideas, behaviours, products, systems, processes, policies, and programmes new to an organisation. Previous literature has reported that process innovation is essential for organisations, often determining their success or failure (Gunday et al. 2011). Organisations with greater process innovation capabilities can obtain a better response from the environment and more easily build the capabilities needed to enhance organisational performance (Schilling 2010). Bi et al.

(2006) indicated that process innovation enabled organisations to realise a competitive advantage. It is argued that, through this type of innovation, organisations can reduce the costs of production and become more efficient (Tidd and Bessant 2011).

Gunday et al. (2011) noted that process innovation within the banking environment includes significant changes in production tools, such as equipment, techniques, or software, that transform resources into output, as well as automated voice response systems, computers, faxes, the Internet, the streamlining of the cheque-handling process, and the creation of new methods of service delivery.

2.3 Social capital and innovation

Gunday et al.(2011) indicated that innovation was an important determinant of organisational success and a firm's ability to sustain a competitive advantage. It is the core of business performance as it drives growth and helps address social challenges (Gault 2018). To enhance innovation, organisations require commitment and must encourage communication based on trust among their members (Wang and Wang 2012). Wang et al. (2016) pointed out that social capital could facilitate innovation by supporting ties amongst employees, trust, and group cohesion. Meanwhile, Wu et al. (2008) found that a network structure, that encouraged the members of a network to share knowledge was of greater importance for innovation.

Prior literature has reported that social capital is an antecedent of innovation. For instance, Cabrilo and Dahms (2018) found that structural and relational capital had a positive effect on innovation within Serbian companies. Buenechea-Elberdin (2017) asserted that businesses nowadays have realized that they can gain sustainable innovation through intellectual capital, and that their success largely depends on their ability to manage this valuable asset. Allameh (2018) found that the three elements of social capital (structural, relational, and cognitive) were essential for maintaining an atmosphere of innovation and developing sustainable innovative capabilities in a competitive environment. Similarly, Gu et al. (2013) confirmed that innovation in R&D teams had a positive association with structural, cognitive, and relational capital, through psychological safety. Moreover, social capital can enable employees to reach an agreement on the expected outcomes of new process development, and motivates them to solve problems together, allowing manufacturers to introduce process innovations frequently (Adler and Kwon 2002). Castro and Roldán (2013) indicated that both internal and external relations were important sources of new knowledge and novel ideas and insights, and could therefore accelerate innovation. An empirical study aimed at investigating the impact of the three components of intellectual capital namely (human, social, and organisational) on innovation generation and adoption within chemical industry firms in Thailand revealed that social capital, through individuals and their interrelationships, collaborative networks, and partnerships, had an impact on the adoption of innovation, and suggested that preserved knowledge became a more reliable and effective resource for innovation adoption when individuals discussed and interpreted that knowledge with their networks and partners (Dost et al. 2016). Social capital is important for business networks as it enhances knowledge transfer and innovation (Inkpen and Tsang 2005). Based on the above discussion, the following hypotheses are proposed:

> *H1: Structural social capital has a direct positive effect on process innovation in Iraqi private banking.*
>
> *H2: Relational social capital has a direct positive effect on process innovation in Iraqi private banking.*
>
> *H3: Cognitive social capital has a direct positive effect on process innovation in Iraqi private banking.*

3. Research method

3.1 Sample and data collection

The research used a self-administered questionnaire and the delivery-and-collection method of distribution, with a five-point Likert scale ranging from 1= strongly disagree to 5= strongly agree. To develop the instrument, the researcher asked six Iraqi professors to examine it for face and content validity, and some modifications were made to ensure its suitability to the Iraqi context. The questionnaire was translated into Arabic using the translation back-translation procedure, and then piloted (Saunders et al. 2019).

According to the annual report of the finance ministry, there are twenty-five private banks in Iraq. Employees from the private banks in Iraq were randomly selected to receive the questionnaires and rate social capital and process innovation. Saunders et al. (2019) indicated that this type of sampling was more effective than other methods when the population of the study covered a large geographical area and the researcher could easily access the entire population.

The sample chosen for this research offered some advantages; Banking has been recognised as one of the most competitive and efficient sectors in the Iraqi economy. It is noted that the employees are one of the most important assets of a bank and a source of competitive advantage, because of their expertise, and knowledge creation and sharing activities. Banks need information on how to allocate their intangible resources such as intellectual capital, and how to promote cooperation, trust, and social interactions among organisational members so as to enhance innovation. 500 questionnaires were sent to the twenty-five private banks, of which 260 were returned and found usable for analysis, representing a response rate of 52%.

Table 1 gives the respondents' characteristics (age, gender, marital status, work experience, etc.). There are more female (57%) than male respondents. In terms of age, marital status and work experience, the respondents are distributed across the different categories. In terms of education level, the majority of the respondents (38%) held a Master's degree.

Table 1: Demographic profile of respondents

Characteristic		Frequency	%
Gender	Male	112	43.00
	Female	148	57.00
Age	<29	38	14.61
	30-39	27	10.33
	40-49	35	13.46
	50-59	98	37.60
	>60	62	24.00
Marital status	Single	88	34.00
	Married	138	53.00
	Divorced	14	5.00
	Widowed	20	8.00
Work experience	<10 years	59	22.69
	11-15	35	13.46
	16-20	38	14.62
	21-15	86	33.08
	>26	42	16.15
Education Level	Bachelor's degree	80	30.50
	Master's degree	98	38.00
	PhD	30	11.50
	High school	52	20.00

3.2 Measurements

In this research, social capital was described as the close interpersonal relationships among organisational members. This factor includes three dimensions, namely: structural, relational, and cognitive social capital. Structural social capital was measured by four items, capturing employees' degree of contact with and accessibility to their colleagues. Relational social capital was operationalised as employees' degree of willingness to be vulnerable to the actions of colleagues, again measured using four items. Three items relating to the degree to which an employee shares collective goals, missions, and visions with their colleagues were used to gauge cognitive social capital. These items were adapted from Nahapiet and Ghoshal (1998).

Process innovation was measured using eight items reflecting the use of new approaches in service and delivery, through the development and use of new technology, and the implementing of incentives and reward systems for members of staff. This measurement was developed from Perri (1993) and Daft (1978).

4. Analysis and results

4.1 Measurement model evaluation

The data were analysed using AMOS v.26 to apply structural equation modelling-SEM. AMOS aims to provide the best estimates of the freely varying parameters, based on minimizing a function that indexes how well the model fits. SEM consists of two steps: a measurement model to evaluate the convergent validity of the constructs, and a structural model to test and evaluate the causal relationships between the factors (Hair et al. 2018).

Confirmatory factor analysis-CFA was used to establish construct validity and reliability of the model. The factor loadings and average variance extracted (AVE) are well above the commonly applied threshold of 0.5 (Fornell and Larcker 1981). This also meant that items did not have to be dropped from the initial constructs. Reliability was assessed separately for each dimension included in the model based on composite reliability (CR) and Cronbach's alpha, each of which should exceed 0.7 (Hair et al., 2010). The results shown in Table 2 indicate that the convergent validity and internal reliability were satisfactory, and all factor loadings and the CR and AVE are acceptable and significant.

Table 2: Measurement model and constructs

Factor	Item code	Factor loading	α	AVE	CR
Structural social capital	SSC1	0.811	0.89	0.72	0.90
	SSC2	0.852			
	SSC3	0.753			
	SSC4	0.884			
Relational social capital	RSC5	0.904	0.88	0.70	0.92
	RSC6	0.860			
	RSC7	0.784			
	RSC8	0.856			
Cognitive social capital	CSC9	0.890	0.900	0.73	0.93
	CSC10	0.858			
	CSC11	0.868			
Process innovation	P112	0.821	0.89	0.69	0.89
	PI13	0.833			
	PI14	0.910			
	P115	0.731			
	PI16	0.745			
	PI17	0.843			
	PI18	0.850			
	PI19	0.821			

Following Fornell and Larcker (1981), this research assessed discriminant validity by ensuring that the square root of each AVE was higher than the corresponding correlations between the constructs, as shown in Table 3. All of the constructs were found to be empirically distinct and the discriminant validity was confirmed statistically. Table 3 also displays the descriptive statistics.

Table 3: Discriminant validity and descriptive statistics

Factor	Mean score	S.D	SSC	RSC	CSC	PI
Structural social capital-SSC	3.389	0.978	**0.73**			
Relational social capital-RSC	3.410	0.886	0.532	**0.70**		
Cognitive social capital-CSC	3.371	0.964	0.425	0.430	**0.73**	
Process innovation-PI	3.240	0.889	0.613	0.420	0.450	**0.69**

Note: SD = Standard Deviation, N=260

The research also used the goodness of fit indices to evaluate the measurement model, as shown in Table 4. This included: χ^2/df, the root mean square error of approximation (RMSEA), and incremental fit measurement, which included a normed fit index (NFI), comparative fit index (CFI) and the Tucker-Lewis index (TLI). The results indicate good validity for social capital and process innovation according to the recommended criteria (Hair et al. 2018).

Table 4: Goodness of fit indices

Fit index	χ^2/df	CFI	NFI	TLI	RMSEA
Social capital	1.533	0.982	0.966	0.976	0.042
Process innovation	1.367	0.975	0.942	0.985	0.033
Recommended criteria	≤ 2-5	≥ 0.90	≥ 0.90	≥ 0.90	< 0.05-0.08

4.2 Structural model evaluation

The results from the SEM supported the direct effect of the three components of social capital, namely: structural, relational, and cognitive social capital, on process innovation (0.544). The results are presented in Table 5 and Figure 1 showing that the model fit indices are acceptable. It is found that structural (0.502), relational (0.648), and cognitive social capital (0.534) significantly improve process innovation in Iraqi private banks, which supports H1, H2, and H3.

Table 5: Structural model

Hypothesis	Independent variable	Dependent variable	Estimate
H1	Structural social capital	Process innovation	0.502
H2	Relational social capital	Process innovation	0.648
H3	Cognitive social capital	Process innovation	0.534
H1, H2, H3	Social capital	Process innovation	0.544
Fit indices	χ^2/df=1.421, RMSEA=0.045, NFI=0.968, CFI=0.987, TLI=0.975		

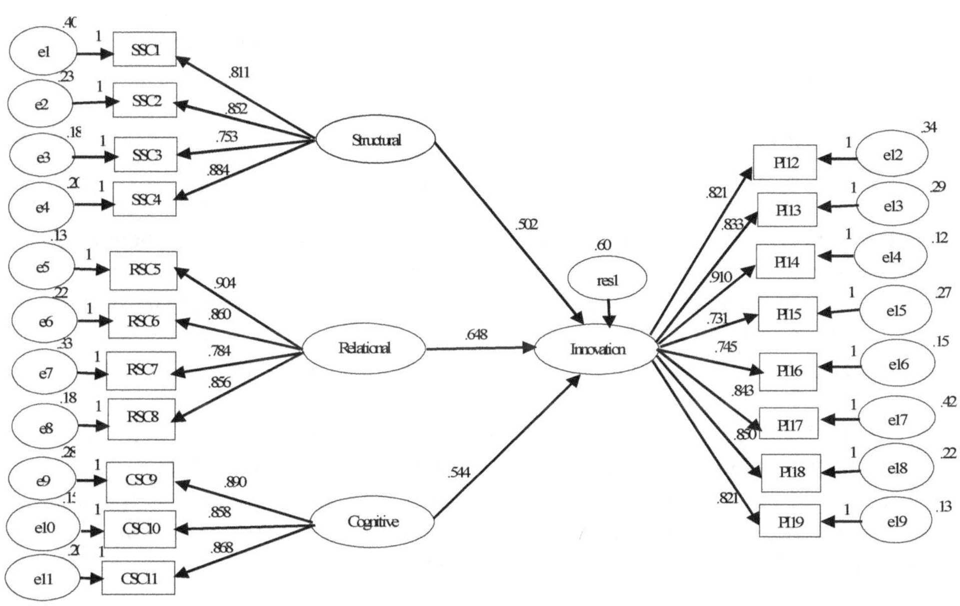

Figure 1: Results of structural model

5. Discussion and Implications of the research

The results of the SEM support the hypothesised relations between social capital and process innovation (*H1, H2 and H3)* in private banking in Iraq. Wang and Wang (2012) found that process innovation was enhanced when organisational members exchanged information, insights, skills, lessons learned, and experiences. According to the resource-based view, social capital is a potentially critical asset in maximising organisational advantage. Where there are high levels of collaboration and good will among organisational members, this is likely to increase knowledge, generate new ideas, and develop new business opportunities, thus facilitating innovation activities. Social capital reflects the knowledge embedded within networks of social relationships. It allows employees to find colleagues who have the knowledge and skills that are critical to solving their problems (Buenechea-Elberdin 2017).

Structural social capital includes social relationships and networks that determine how people communicate with one another. It relates to the social connections or network ties amongst colleagues. Employees can use this type of social capital to obtain job information or access resources in their organisation. Nahapiet and Ghoshal (1998) noted that cooperative relationships among employees played an important role in facilitating the absorption of knowledge. When employees are comfortable discussing problems openly, they are more likely to share knowledge about the latest process developments and analyse it together. Thus, learning takes place, which in turn leads to changes of behaviour and enhanced innovation (Adler and Kwon 2002). The results of this research demonstrate that the employees of private Iraqi banks that were surveyed were willing to cooperate with others, to produce valuable knowledge process innovation (i.e. taking and developing training programmes and adopting new technology). It is suggested that a high degree of social interaction between them will generate and thus lead to the implementation of innovation. This explanation has confirmed that stronger social ties amongst employees in the Iraqi banking sector can affect and enhance the link between social capital and innovation. This is mainly due to the nature of the Arabic culture, and particularly that in Iraq, were a very high score, of 62% has been found for collectivism (Hofstede et al. 2010).

Relational social capital explains the nature of the relationships that members build with each other during periods of interaction. It refers to the development of trust, respect, and friendship that develop among individuals, thereby influencing their behaviour (Nahapiet and Ghoshal 1998). Relational capital also offers influence, control, and power, and produces mutual solidarity, which can increase the chances of co-creation (Adler and Kwon 2002). Chow and Chan (2008) noted that, the key aspect of this dimension was trust, and suggested that trusting relationships would improve organisational members' willingness to exchange and absorb each other's knowledge, thereby leading to greater knowledge sharing. Trust generates security in terms of confidence that partners will not exploit opportunities to steal their colleagues' knowledge. Employees who feel that their relationships involve a high level of trust are not only willing to listen to others but are also able to absorb knowledge from them, and as a result tend to become interested in sharing skills, information, and knowledge.

Cognitive social capital is the collection of characteristics and shared codes or paradigms that are the foundation of the collective goals and appropriate behaviour of a social system (Chang and Chuang 2011). It consists mainly of the principles and procedures required for people to act collectively to achieve common goals in the social system. The results of the current research suggest that shared goals encourage employees to have common responsibilities and goals, which sustain progress in innovative activities in the Iraqi private banking sector. It is indicated that organisational members who share the same ambitions and vision at work, are also enthusiastic about pursuing the collective goals and missions of the whole organisation. As a result, they create new organisational learning, and shape a vision that enables their organisation to be more innovative.

The findings of the current research support the assertions of previous studies that have found that the components of intellectual capital, such as human, structural, and relational capital, can enhance firm performance (Dost et al. 2016; Wang et al. 2018). The findings are also congruent with Wu et al.(2008), who argued that social capital through network ties encourages knowledge sharing among the actors, which in turn enables the creation of new knowledge that will generate innovation.

The research makes a theoretical contribution to the literature on social capital and innovation. Social capital refers to the interaction and collaboration among employees that facilitates knowledge sharing, value creation, and competitive advantage that in turn enhance innovation. The results of this research confirm the importance of the three components of social capital, and of innovation theory, and help to provide a better understanding of the inter-linkages between them. They show that high-quality communication, trust, and confidence among employees causes them to exchange their information more easily, and thus improves social interaction that is important for enhancing the innovation of an organisation.

Through the analysis of the found effects, this paper clarifies specific aspects of social capital (structural, relational, and cognitive) and their impacts on the process innovation carried out by employees. This information can provide managers with ideas about the type of social capital they can use to enhance process innovation among employees, unlike previous studies (Cabrilo and Dahms 2018; Costa et al. 2014) that have not identified specific types of social capital and their effects on innovation, having studied this variable as a single factor.

The research provides support for the resource-based view of social capital and the strength of the role social capital plays in enhancing process innovation. It implies that innovation emerges if social interactions can encourage and create a social culture among employees. In addition, it provides a better understanding of these relationships in the banking environments of developing countries, particularly Iraq, a context that has been neglected in previous studies.

In terms of practical implications, the research could help managers in the banking sector to establish social capital strategies so as to achieve innovation. The results illustrate the importance of three components of social capital namely; structural, relational, and cognitive in Iraq's private banks and show that innovation requires employees to share and generate new knowledge. Therefore, managers should design strategies aimed at encouraging employees to engage in social interaction activities, providing resources for informal groupings, thus spreading trust among the members to facilitate cooperation and knowledge transfer, and also managing a knowledge repository of valuable, acquired knowledge.

6. Conclusions, limitations, and directions for future research

Social capital is recognised a foundation stone of an organisation's competitive advantage. This research aimed to examine the impact of the three components of social capital, namely, structural, relational, and cognitive, on process innovation in Iraqi private banks. In line with previous studies, this research found that social capital is an enabler of process innovation in these banks.

This research has some limitations, and some points will need researching further. First, this study focuses on social capital in the private banking sector in Iraq. Further studies could examine different samples in other industries or countries. This research employed the resource-based view to justify the research model. It is recommended that, in future, actor network theory is used to build an innovations network of the interactions among the components of social capital. Finally, this research tested the effects of social capital on process innovation. Although the elements of social capital explained an acceptable level of the variance in process innovation, future research could analyse intermediate constructs such as leadership style, or knowledge sharing, which may produce better explanations of the development of innovation.

References

Adler, P. S., and Kwon, S. (2002). "Social Capital: Prospects for a New Concept." *Academy of Management Review* Vol. 27, No.1, pp.17–40.

Akhavan, P., and Hosseini, M. (2016). "Social capital, knowledge sharing, and innovation capability: An empirical study of R&D teams in Iran." *Journal of Technology Analysis & Strategic Management*, Vol. 28, No.1, pp.96–113.

Allameh, S., Mohsen (2018). "Antecedents and consequences of intellectual capital:The role of social capital, knowledge sharing and innovation." *Journal of Intellectual Capital*, Vol. 19, No. 5, pp.858-874.

Bi, K., Sun, D., Zheng, R., and Li, B. (2006). "The construction of synergetic development system of product innovation and process innovation in manufacturing enterprises"*Proceeding of the 13th international conference on management science and engineering, ISBN: 7-5603-2355-3, 5-7 october, pp. 628-636.* City: France.

Bohlmann, J., Spanjol, J., Qualls, W., and Rosa , J. (2012). "The interplay of customer and product innovation dynamics: An exploratory study." *Journal of Product Innovation Managemt*, Vol.30, No.2, pp.228–244.

Buenechea-Elberdin, M. (2017). "Structured literature review about intellectual capital and innovation." *Journal of Intellectual Capital*, Vol. 18, No. 2, pp. 262-285.

Cabrera, E. F., and Cabrera, A. (2005). "Fostering knowledge sharing through people management practices." *International Journal of Human Resource Management*, Vol.5, pp.720-735.

Cabrilo, S., and Dahms, S. (2018). "How strategic knowledge management drives intellectual capital to superior innovation and market performance." *Journal of Knowledge Management*, Vol. 22 No. 3, pp. 621-648.

Castro, I., and Roldán, J. L. (2013). "A mediation model between dimensions of social capital." *International Business Review*, Vol. 22 No. 6, pp. 1034-1050.

Chang, H., H., and Chuang, S.-S. (2011). "Social capital and individual motivations on knowledge sharing: Participant involvement as a moderator." *Journal Information & Management*, Vol.48, pp.9–18.

Chow, W. S., and Chan, L. S. (2008). "Social Network, Social Trust and Shared Goals in organizational knowledge sharing." *Information & Management*, Vol.45, No.7, pp.458–465.

Costa, R. V., Fernández, C. F. J., and Dorrego, P. F. (2014). "Critical elements for product innovation at Portuguese innovative SMEs: An intellectual capital perspective " *Knowledge Management Research & Practice*, Vol.12, No.3, pp.322–338.

Daft, R. (1978). "Organizational Innovation." *Academy of Management Journal*, 21(2), 193 - 210.

Dost, M., Badir, Y. F., Ali, Z., and Tariq, A. (2016). "The impact of intellectual capital on innovation generation and adoption." *Journal of Intellectual Capital*, Vol. 17, No. 4, pp. 675-695.

Filieri, R., McNally, R. C., O'Dwyer, M., and O'Malley, L. (2014). "Structural social capital evolution and knowledge transfer: Evidence from an Irish pharmaceutical network." *Industrial Marketing Management*, Vol. 43, No. 3, pp. 429-440.

Fornell, C., and Larcker, D. (1981). "Evaluating Structural Equation Models with Unobservable Variables and Measurement Error." *Journal of Marketing Research* Vol. 18, No. 1 (Feb.), pp. 39-50.

Gault, F. (2018). "Defining and measuring innovation in all sectors of the economy." *Research Policy*, Vol. 47 No. 3, pp. 617-622.

Gu, Q., Wang, G., and Wang, L. (2013). "Social capital and innovation in R&D teams: The mediating roles of psychological safety and learning from mistakes." *R&D Management*, Vol.43, pp.89-102.

Gunday, G., Ulusoy, G., Kilic, K., and Alpkan, L. (2011). "Effects of innovation types on firm performance." *International Journal of Production Economics*, Vol.133, No.2, pp. 662–676.

Hair, J. F., Black, W. C., Babin, B. J., and Anderson, R. E. (2018). *Multivariate Data Analysis, 8th ed., Cengage*, New Jersey, US

Hofstede, G., Hofstede, G., and Minkov, M. (2010). *Cultures and Organizations - Software of the Mind, 3rd ed.*, New York, US: McGraw Hill Companies.

Inkpen, A. C., and Tsang, E. W. (2005). "Social capital, networks and knowledge transfer." *Academy of Management Review*, Vol.30, No.1, pp.146-165.

Joshi, M., Cahill, D., Sidhu, J., and Kansal, M. (2013). "Intellectual capital and financial performance: An evaluation of the Australian financial sector." *Journal of Intellectual Capital*, Vol.14, No.2, pp.264–285.

Nahapiet, J., and Ghoshal, S. (1998). "Social capital, intellectual capital, and the organizational advantage." *Academy of Management Review*, Vol. 23, No. 2, pp. 242-266.

Oppong, G. K., and Pattanayak, J. K. (2019). "Does investing in intellectual capital improve productivity? Panel evidence from commercial banks in India." *Borsa Istanbul Review*, Vol.19, No.3, pp. 219-227.

Perri. (1993). "Innovation by nonprofit organizations: policy and research issues." *Nonprofit Management & Leadership*, Vol. 3, No. 4, pp. 397-414.

Saunders, M. N. K., Lewis, P., and Thornhill, A. (2019). *Research Methods for Business Students, Pearson Education, England*.

Schilling, M. A. (2010). *Strategic management of technological innovation, 3rd ed., New York McGraw-Hill/Irwin*.

Smith, D. (2009). *Exploring Innovation, 2nd ed. London: McGraw-Hill Higher Education*.

Subramaniam, M., and Youndt, M. (2005). "The influence of intellectual capital on the types of innovative capabilities." *Academy of Management Journal*, Vol. 48, No.3, pp.450–463.

Tidd, J., and Bessant, J. (2011). *Managing innovation: Integrating, technological , market and organizational change, 4th ed.*, London: John Wiley & Sons.

Wang, Z., Caib, S., Liangc, H., Wangd, N., and Xiange, E. (2018). "Intellectual capital and firm performance: The mediating role of innovation speed and quality." *The International Journal of Human Resource Management*, https://doi.org/10.1080/09585192.2018.1511611 accessed online (15/11/2019), pp.1-30.

Wang, Z., and Wang, N. (2012). "Knowledge sharing, innovation and firm performance." *Expert Systems with Applications*, Vol. 39, No.10, pp. 8899 - 8908.

Wang, Z., Wang, N., Cao, J., and Ye, X. (2016). "The impact of intellectual capital – knowledge management strategy fit on firm performance " *Management Decision*, Vol. 54,No. 8, pp. 1861-1885.

Wu, W., Chang, M., and Chen, C. (2008). "Promoting innovation through the accumulation of intellectual capital, social capital, and entrepreneurial orientation." *Journal of R&D Management*, Vol.38, No.3, pp.265-277.

The Influence of Perceived Institutional Context Dimensions on Saudi University Students' Entrepreneurial Intentions

Wassim Aloulou
Imam Mohammad Ibn Saud Islamic University, Riyadh, Saudi Arabia
University of Sfax, Tunisia
Wassim.aloulou@gmail.com
DOI: 10.34190/EIE.20.134

Abstract: The purpose of this research is to examine the country institutional profile for encouraging entrepreneurial activity in Saudi Arabia. This research attempts to contribute to a better understanding of how a country's institutional environment (with its dimensions) impacts the entrepreneurial intentions of university students. This research introduces and validates a measure of a country institutional profile for entrepreneurship consisting of regulatory, cognitive, and normative dimensions conceived by Busenitz et al (2000) on a Saudi university students' sample in order to investigate the influence of their perceptions of the institutional context on their entrepreneurial intentions. Data was collected from 287 Saudi university students from several universities located in Riyadh in Saudi Arabia. To analyze the data and test the proposed hypotheses, a confirmatory factor analysis and structural equation modelling (SEM) are applied. Research findings revealed positive and significant relationships between regulative, cognitive and normative dimensions of the institutional environment and students' entrepreneurial intentions. Implications for researchers and practitioners are advanced to help university decision-makers in promoting entrepreneurship and applying adequate policies. Limitations and future research directions are discussed in terms of generalization of findings and potential streams of research in the field.

Keywords: country institutional profile, entrepreneurial intentions, university students, Saudi Arabia

1. Introduction

The Kingdom of Saudi Arabia has undertaken deep transformations in all sectors since the announcement of the vision of the Kingdom of 2030 through its main axes, including "The booming economy, a fruitful opportunity" and its branches "We learn to work", "We support our emerging, small and medium enterprises and productive families" "Reducing the unemployment rate from 11.6% to 7%", "increasing the participation of SMEs in GDP from 20% to 35%" and "increasing the participation of women in the labor market from 22% to 30%" (Saudi Council of Economic and Development Affairs, 2016). Specifically, the approach of the country to innovation and entrepreneurship has become imperative in order to boost the diversification of the economy and create employment for its youths (Alkhaldi, 2018; Aloulou, 2016a; 2017). That's why government reforms, policies and transformations were undertaken in its entrepreneurship and business ecosystem hoping to institute a new culture of entrepreneurship in the Saudi context (universities, corporate settings, workplace...) (Aloulou & AlOthman, 2020).

While there has been substantial research on the role of institutional context for promoting entrepreneurship, small businesses and social entrepreneurship, its impact has rarely been especially within the context of developing economies in the Middle East and more specifically in the KSA (Alkhaldi, 2018). Thus, the purpose of this study is to investigate how perceptions of institutional context' dimensions may influence entrepreneurial intentions (EI hereafter) of Saudi students enrolled in several universities located in Riyadh in Saudi Arabia. Our paper proceeds as follows: Section 2 reviews the literature on institutional context and entrepreneurial intention, and advances the research framework and its hypotheses to be tested. In section 3, we describe the data, variables, and methods we employ in data analyzing and hypothesis testing. In section 4, we present the results of our hypothesis testing. Section 5 discusses our findings and their implications for both scholarship and practice.

2. Theoretical framework and hypotheses

2.1 Institutional context and entrepreneurship

The importance of institutions and their effects on economic development were addressed by several scholars (North, 1990; Scott, 2001). In institutional literature, the emphasize on organizations is concerned with the question of how socially constructed environment shape organizational behaviors and outcomes (Sine & David, 2010). With the work of Douglass North (1990), institutions were defined as any form of constraint that human beings develop to shape human interaction. For him, there was a clear distinction between formal and informal institutions. In fact, he viewed formal institutions as the visible *"rules of the game"* (e.g., constitutional law) and informal institutions as the invisible ones (e.g., norms, values, acceptable behaviors, and codes of conduct). The formal and informal institutions both influence the development of entrepreneurship. Thus, an interplay between the two exists because they interdependent and often evolve together (Veciana & Urbano, 2008). Furthermore, Scott (2001) is credited with a widely accepted typology of formal and informal institutional forces that classifies them into three pillars that were identified to conceptualize institutional environment as consisting of cultural-cognitive, normative and regulative pillars providing stability and meaning in social behaviors. The first pillar "regulatory dimension" (RD hereafter) consists of laws, regulations, and government policies that provide support for new businesses, reduce the risks for individuals starting a new company, and facilitate entrepreneurs' efforts to acquire resources. The second pillar "cognitive dimension" (CD hereafter) consists of the knowledge and skills possessed by the people in a country pertaining to establishing and operating a new business. The third pillar "normative dimension" (ND hereafter) measures the degree to which a country's residents admire entrepreneurial activity and value creative and innovative thinking.

Most scholars emphasize the role of institutional context in affecting entrepreneurship (Veciana & Urbano, 2008; Bruton, et al, 2010; Urbano & Alvarez, 2014; Sine & David, 2010). Several studies argued that these institutional dimensions have impact on entrepreneurial activity at the national level and from the perspective of international comparisons between countries using GEM data or macro-data (Valdez & Richardson, 2013; Gupta et al, 2012, 2014; Urbano & Alvarez, 2014). From an entrepreneurial viewpoint, Bruton et al (2010) argue, that issues such as culture, legal environment, traditions and history as well as economic incentives can have an impact on an industry and in turn on entrepreneurial success. They acknowledged that the institutional perspective can be a powerful tool in explaining entrepreneurial behavior.

There is growing recognition in entrepreneurship research that entrepreneurial behavior can be better understood within its context and especially within institutional one as this context provides individuals with opportunities and sets boundaries for their actions. This context was profiled across several countries in relation to entrepreneurship (Busenitz et al, 2000; Manolova et al, 2008). In fact, Busenitz et al, (2000) conceived a country institutional profile following Kostova (1997) in viewing the regulatory, cognitive, and normative dimensions as conceptually and empirically distinct. They used Kostova (1997) approach as foundation for developing and validating a measure of a country institutional profile for the domain of entrepreneurship in order to explore how and why levels of entrepreneurship vary by country. The instrument was tested and validated with 257 U.S. undergraduate students from a large state university in the Southwest in USA. After them, Manolova et al, (2008) confirmed a validation of Busenitz et al, (2000)' instrument for measuring country institutional profiles for the promotion of entrepreneurship in a sample of 254 business students from three emerging economies: Bulgaria, Hungary, and Latvia. Important differences were found in the three dimensions (regulatory, cognitive, and normative) of the institutional profiles across the three emerging economies, reflecting their idiosyncratic cultural norms and values, traditions, and institutional heritage in promoting entrepreneurship. In examining the influence of institutional dimensions on the probability of becoming an entrepreneur through logistic regression, Urbano & Alvarez (2014) found that a favorable RD, ND and CD increase the probability of being an entrepreneur. Data were obtained from both the GEM and the International Institute for Management and Development for 2008, considering a sample of 30 countries and 36,525 individuals.

Therefore, an institutional perspective on entrepreneurship examines how these institutional pillars of environment shape entrepreneurial processes, intentions and behaviors (Sine & David, 2010). In this study, the influence of institutional environment on students' EIs will be investigated, hereafter, for the validity of instrument used and for the significance of relationships hypothesized.

2.2 Relationship between institutional dimensions and entrepreneurial intention and research hypotheses

EI is an intention toward starting a new business or initiating a new venture. It is considered as a single direct and best predictor of planned behavior and the immediate antecedent of it (Ajzen, 1991). It resumes the motivation and willingness of individual to implement the desired behavior: the higher the intention to undertake this behavior, the higher the probability of performing it.

Several studies investigated the determinants of EI using the theory of planned behaviour of Ajzen (1991) as a well-known and influential theory (for literature review on it, see Aloulou, 2015; 2016a; 2016b; Fayolle & Liñán, 2014; Krueger et al, 2000; Liñán & Chen, 2009; Liñán & Fayolle, 2015; Schlaegel & Koenig, 2014). In Saudi Arabia, found that personal attitudes, social norms and perceived behaviour control have significant effects on EI of university students (Alexandre-Leclair et al, 2013; Aloulou, 2015; 2016a; 2017; Choukir et al, 2019; Redien-Collot et al, 2017).

At the individual level, the influence of institutional dimensions of the environment on EI of university students were investigated using a Busenitz et al, (2000)' Country Institutional Profiling instrument within student sample in different countries (Cypros: Hadjimanolis, 2016; Turkey: Duygulu, 2008; South Korea and United Arab Emirates: Gupta et al., 2012; Brazil, China, India, and Korea: Gupta et al, 2014; Central and Eastern Europe: Manolova et al, 2008; Manolova & Eunni, 2012; South Africa: Urban, 2013b; Norway, Sweden, Finland, UK and the USA: Oftedal et al, 2018). However, little research has been done in Arab World applying the institutional profile survey to four countries for example (Egypt; Kuwait; UAE; and KSA) to explore how entrepreneurship contexts are conducive to entrepreneurship (Farid et al, 2011), or to compare two different developmental states: South Korea and United Arab Emirates (Gupta et al, 2012). This influence also was similarly investigated on social EIs of individuals in previous studies (Hispanish adults in the USA: Abebe, 2012; South-African university students: Urban, 2013a; Urban & Kujinga, 2017; entrepreneurial students of Rajasthan in India: Vyas et al, 2014) or on EIs of academics in China (Ju & Zhou, 2020). Results from different studies suggest that EI is higher when the institutional context (universities, regional context, cultural and social norms or media...) is more favorable (Linan & Fayolle 2015; Engle et al, 2011). The influence of these institutional dimensions differs in weight from country to another. For example, Urban & Kujinga (2017) found that regulatory support has an association with social EI. As Urban (2013b) notes, the individuals' perceptions of the RD, CD and ND of institutional profile are favorable in the context of South Africa. Following this line of reasoning and despite of the existence of some mitigated results (e.g., Hadjimanolis, 2016), it is predicted that the institutional context has a positive effect on EI (Busenitz et al, 2000; Manolova et al, 2008; Manolova & Eunni, 2012). In fact, the research hypotheses are stated as follow:

H1: *The perception of RD of the institutional environment is positively related to EI.*

H2: *The perception of CD of the institutional environment is positively related to EI.*

H3: *The perception of ND of the institutional environment is positively related to EI.*

H4: *Gender is negatively related to entrepreneurial intention.*

H5: *Prior entrepreneurial experience is positively related to entrepreneurial intention.*

The research model and its hypotheses are presented in figure 1.

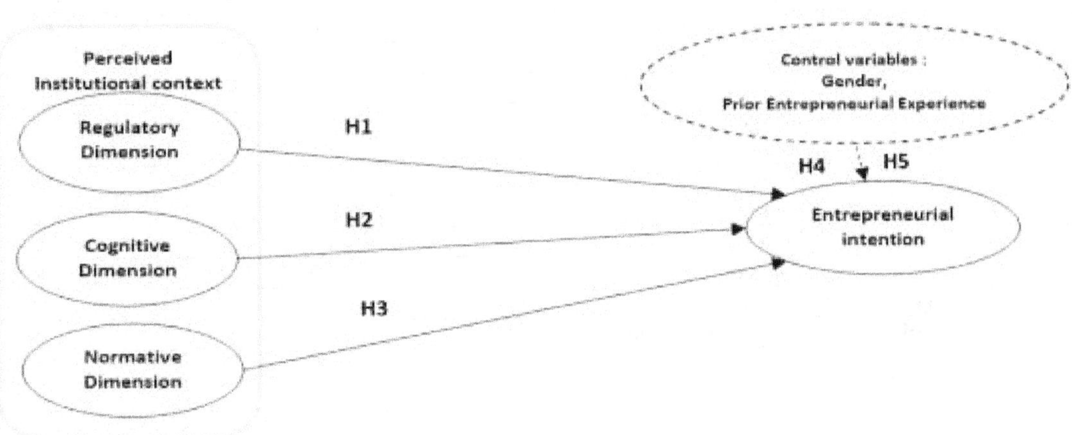

Figure 1: Research model

3. Method

3.1 Participants and data collection

The data in this study were collected from a sample of Saudi students enrolled at universities located in Riyadh, the Capital of Saudi Arabia using online survey method.

Using student sample is fairly common in entrepreneurial career intentions literature (e.g. Krueger et al, 2000; Linan & Chen, 2009). In fact, Abebe (2012) believed that using a student sample is indeed appropriate to empirically examine entrepreneurial career intentions. In particular, recent research has found that young university students (18 – 34 years) show a higher desirability towards starting up a firm in Saudi context (Coduras et al, 2019; Dokhan et al, 2018; de la Vega et al, 2017).

Empirical data for this research were obtained after applying a procedure that help pathways to sample diversity (educational level, specialization, university...) during the summer term in 2019. The fieldwork was carried in June and July 2019. Starting from a sample of 104 students enrolled in entrepreneurship course, questionnaires were administered to them. Then, each one of them is asked to recruit a minimum of three students in his/her network to fill in the online survey and encourage them to come forward and participate in the study in return for course credit (e.g., classmates in other courses in the same college; friends in other colleges in the same university; or from other universities located in Riyadh). The confidentiality of information about respondents were reassured. 377 questionnaires were received and some of them were rejected for redundancy (48) related to the student' ID and email. Only 329 questionnaires were valid. Then after purification of data from outliers, the final sample was made up of 287 usable questionnaires.

3.2 Sample and descriptive statistics

Table 1 reports the descriptive statistics of the Saudi university students' demographics. Sample parameters, which served as control variables (e.g., name of university; specialization; educational year of study; gender; age; occupational status; parents as entrepreneurs; relatives/friends as entrepreneurs; prior entrepreneurial experience; prior entrepreneurial training), rendered a profile, which emerges as: Almost 60.3% of the survey participants were from Imam University. Two third of the sample were men. 13.6% of the sample respondents said to have a prior entrepreneurial experience.

Table 1: Sample characteristics (n = 287)

Variable	Frequency	(%)
University in Riaydh		
Imam University	173	60.3%
King Saud University	65	22.6%
Princess Noura University	20	7.0%
Other university in Riyadh	29	10.1%
Specialisation		
Administrative Sciences (BA, Mkg, HR, MIS)	117	40.7%
Economics, Finance, accounting...	51	17.8%
Applied Sciences	59	20.6%
Humanities, languages and religious sciences	60	20.9%
Educational year		
1st year	23	8.0%
2nd year	56	19.5%
3rd year	73	25.4%
4th year	135	47.0%
Gender		
Male	181	63.1%
Female	106	36.9%
Age (Mean = 22.31 years; SD = 2.039)		
Prior entrepreneurial experience		
Yes	39	13.6%
No	248	86.4%

Source: Author's elaboration

3.3 Measurement of variables

For this study, all items were measured with five-point Likert scales ranging from strongly agree (7) to strongly disagree (1). For *EI,* we adopt the Linan & Chen (2009) scale to measure EI of university students. The scale consisting of six items was tested and validated empirically in two diverse contexts Linan & Chen (2009). Thus, EI1 – EI6 measure the EI construct. For *Institutional dimensions*, we adopt the Busenitz et al, (2000) scale as an appropriate instrument to use in the context of emerging economies and the results of previous studies employing confirmatory factor analysis suggest high reliability, internal consistency, and construct validity (Manolova et al, 2008; Manolova & Eunni, 2012; Urban, 2013a; 2013b; Urban & Kujinga, 2017). Busenitz et al (2000) designed a survey instrument that measures the three dimensions of a country's institutional environment for the promotion of entrepreneurship. The RD was measured with five items (RD1-RD5), the CD with four items (CD1-CD4), and the ND with four items (ND1-ND4). *Control variables* refer to demographic information about respondents and are related to gender and prior entrepreneurial experience. *Gender* was measured as dummy variable with men coded as 0 and with women coded as 1. *Prior entrepreneurial experience* (PEE hereafter) is also measured as a dummy variable: yes (having a PEE) = 1, no (not having a PEE) = 0.

3.4 Analytical strategy

The statistical analysis was made in three parts: the first one, the descriptive analysis was to define the sample characteristics; the second one, the exploratory factor analysis, reliability and validity, and the confirmatory factor analysis were to show the adequacy of measures and fitness of the data to the model (Thompson, 2004); the third one, the structural equation modeling used to examine a set of relationships between independent and dependent variables (Byrne, 2010). The statistical software used was the SPSS version 21 for the exploratory factor analysis (EFA) and related statistical checks and the AMOS version 21 for the confirmatory factor analysis (CFA), structural equation modeling (SEM) (model fit, measurement model and structural model) in order to test the hypothesized effects and simultaneously explain interactions between main variables (Arbuckle, 2012; Byrne, 2010).

3.5 Exploratory factor analysis, reliability and validity

3.5.1 Exploratory factor analysis

Table 2 shows that the measures of the main variables (EI, RD, CD, ND) have loading factors with an explained variance greater than 62.971%. For that, an EFA with Varimax rotation with Kaiser normalization was used to identify items with strong and unique loadings to components identified in the analysis. The factorial contributions of these items (loading) are satisfactory (> 0.5). Cronbach's alpha values ranged from 0.839 to 0.921 for all constructs, which exceeded Nunnally's criterion of 0.7 (Nunnally & Bernstein, 1994). Hence, the scales for all constructs were deemed to exhibit adequate reliability and reflect a good internal coherence. The extracted factors and their items were normally distributed (K-S test of normality was checked for all items). The Kaiser–Meyer–Olkin (KMO) test shows sampling adequacy for each variable to conduct the exploratory factor analysis (KMO was greater than 0.6). Convergent validity can be determined based on three criteria: (1) All factor loadings should be significant and higher than 0.50; (2) The scale composite or construct reliability should exceed 0.70; (3) The average variance extracted (AVE) for each construct should be 0.5 or above (Fornell & Larcker, 1981; Hair et al., 2014; Nunnally & Bernstein, 1994).

Table 2: EFA, % variance, KMO, Cronbach's Alpha and AVE

Construct	# Items	Factor loading	% variance	KMO	Cronbach's Alpha	AVE
Entrepreneurial Intention						
EI	EI1, EI2, EI3, EI4, EI5, EI6	From .748 to .865	67.830%	.887	.904	.678
Institutional context						
Regulatory dimension (RD)	RD1, RD2, RD3, RD4, RD5	From .832 to .917	76.365%	.893	.921	.782
Cognitive dimension (CD)	CD1, CD2, CD3, CD4	From .768 to .870	67.619%	.781	.839	.676
Normative dimension (ND)	ND1, ND2, ND3, ND4	From .831 to .892	73.122%	.785	.877	.731

3.5.2 Reliability and discriminant validity

Discriminant validity indicates the extent to which one construct truly differs from another construct (Hair et al, 2014). If the square root of the AVE estimate for each construct is greater than the correlation between that construct and all other constructs in the model, then discriminant validity is demonstrated (Fornell & Larcker, 1981). Table 3 shows the means, standard deviations and correlations across the main variables. The correlations between the main variables are lower compared to the square root of the AVE of each variable. Discriminant validity is also demonstrated.

Table 3: Mean, S.D., matrix correlation and discriminant validity

Variables	Mean	S.D	Gender	PEE	EI	RD	CD	ND
Gender	.37	.483	**n/a**					
PEE	0.14	.343	-.114	**n/a**				
EI	5.03	1.376	-.059	.136*	**.825**			
RD	5.15	1.358	-.053	.016	.389**	**.942**		
CD	4.27	1.211	.023	.103	.375**	.376**	**.829**	
ND	5.49	1.214	-.015	-.049	.462**	.522**	.356**	**.849**

Notes: * Correlation is significant at $p < 0.05$. ** Correlation is significant at $p < 0.01$.
The **bold values** on the diagonal represent square root of the average variance extracted AVE. n/a not applicable for AVE computation due to single item measures.

3.5.3 Common method variance bias analysis

The common method variance is a serious concern when data are collected from a survey instrument and the variables used in the model refer to perceptual measures of the same individual (Podsakoff et al, 2003). In order to address this issue, we followed the recommendations of Podsakoff & Organ (1986) and Podsakoff et al (2003), and proceeded to include in all the variables (independent, dependent and control) into a factor analysis, and we then extracted five factors with eigenvalues superior to 1.0, which accounted for 70.893 per cent of the variance. The first factor accounted for 19.643 per cent of the variance, while the remaining factors accounted for 51.25% per cent of the variance. We concluded that common method bias was not a problem, as no single factor accounted for the majority of the variance, and the individual factors separated cleanly (Podsakoff et al, 2003).

3.5.4 Confirmatory factor analysis and SEM

According to Hair et al (2014) and Kline (2005), it is appropriate to adopt a two-step approach for SEM: first, assess the measurement model, and second, assess the proposed structural model. A CFA indicated that the measurement model fits the data well. The model fit was assessed using main indices (absolute, relative and parsimonious fit) (for cut-off criteria to accept the model fit; e.g. Hair et al, 2014; Kenny, 2014) for a better fit in accordance with the theory and the logic (Anderson & Gerbing, 1988). Once a satisfactory measurement model was obtained, SEM could be undertaken to test the model containing the hypothesized relations derived from the research literature and depicted in Figure 1.

4. Results

The proposed sets of hypotheses were tested using structural equation modelling (SEM). It was decided through a CFA that the proposed measurement model provided a reasonable fit for the data and permitted the analysis. Figure 2 shows the significant links between variables (independent, dependent and control) and the summary of the model fit.

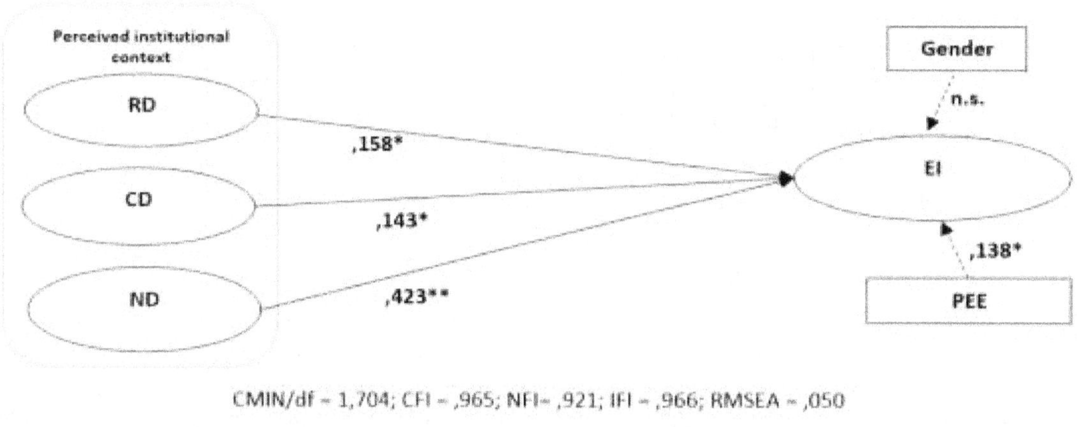

Figure 4: Results of path analysis showing standardized path coefficients

The findings support our hypotheses that stated the positive relationship between institutional dimensions and EI. From Table 4, ND have the higher positive significant relationship with dependent variable ($S.Estimate_{ND}$=,423, $p<0.001$; $S.Estimate_{RD}$=,158, $p<0.05$; ($S.Estimate_{CD}$=,143, $p<0.05$). Only one significant relationship between control variables and EI was found for prior entrepreneurial experience (($S.Estimate_{PEE}$=,138, $p<0.05$). No significant relationship was found between gender and EI.

Table 4: Main results for path relationships

Path relationship	Standardized Estimate	STD. error	t-values	*p*- values	Hypothesis
EntInt <--- RegD	,158*	,079	2,077	,038	H1 Supported
EntInt <--- CogD	,143*	,101	2,096	,036	H2 Supported
EntInt <--- NormaD	,423***	,101	5,247	***	H3 Supported
EntInt <--- gender	-,048	,149	-,901	,367	H4 Not supported
EntInt <--- PriorEntreExper	,138*	,211	2,565	,010	H5 Supported

Notes: S.E.: Standard errors; * p < 0.05, ** p < 0.01, *** p < 0.001.

5. Discussion, implications, limitations and conclusion

The present study adds to the growing knowledge base on the institutional environments in emerging economies. Specifically, it was hypothesized that perceptions of each of the institutional dimensions would be positively and significantly associated with EIs of Saudi university students. On one hand, the findings provide a strong evidence that the country institutional profiling instrument is validated in non-western emerging country (Busenitz et al, 2000; Manolova et al, 2008; Urban, 2013a). On other hand, the findings support previous studies. The normative dimension of institutional context was found to have a strong effect on students' EI relative to the other institutional dimensions. This fact is in congruence with the empirical evidence (e.g., Oftedal et al, 2017). In Saudi Arabia, entrepreneurship is seen as a positive phenomenon, and the social value system admires entrepreneurial activity, risk taking, and creative thinking. This finding is not in contradiction with empirical evidence on this context. In fact, Saudi Arabia is considered as a collectivist country and individuals (students) tend to be influenced by their social system and norms. They make their entrepreneurial career choice based more on social considerations as important parts of people lives than on personal ones (Aloulou, 2016a). Furthermore, the normative dimension has to do with societal values and norms that are acceptable for which individuals follow in society (Valdez & Richardson, 2013; Engle et al, 2011).

Our findings contribute to the entrepreneurial intention literature focusing on institutional perspective in three ways. First, this study has validated the country institutional profiling instrument initially developed in the context of developed countries, then validated in transitional and emergent economies (e.g., Busenitz et al, 2000; Manolova et al, 2008). Second, the assessment of the institutional profile has major implications for public policy measures to provide awareness programs about the regulatory dimensions such as legal reforms, and the required societal knowledge for more favorable entrepreneurial opportunities. Third, the findings of the study show the less influence of cognitive dimension of EI, this may suggest that entrepreneurship educators offer support programs and curriculum to cultivate entrepreneurial skills of their students and help them to improve their self-confidence and subsequently raise their chances to follow an entrepreneurial career.

The limitations of the current research include the cross-sectional data and the non-generalization of the results for other Saudi universities in other Saudi cities. Our study investigated the dimensions of institutional context at country profiling level, future research could measure the narrow impact of the university or social support as part of institutional context on Students' entrepreneurial intentions. Then, future research also could investigate some individual characteristics/dimensions (e.g., such as self-efficacy; perceived desirability, perceived feasibility…) as intervening variables between institutional context and entrepreneurial intentions (Krueger et al, 2000; Díaz-Casero et al, 2012). Future research also could develop an instrument that measure the impacts formal and informal institutional context respectively on entrepreneurial intentions (Engle et al, 2011; García-Rodríguez et al, 2015). Their impacts on EI or behavior deserve further investigation in order to reduce the intention-behavior gap (Aloulou, 2018). Finally, future research could undertake a cross-cultural comparison between Saudi Arabia and other countries in similar regions (GCC, Arab countries, MENA region).

References

Abebe, M. A. (2012), "Social and institutional predictors of entrepreneurial career intention: evidence from Hispanic adults in the US", Journal of Enterprising Culture, Vol 20, No. 1, pp 1-23.

Ajzen, I. (1991). "The theory of planned behavior", Organizational Behavior and Human Decision Processes, Vol 50, No. 2, pp 179–211.

Alkhaldi, T., Cleeve, E., & Brander-Brown, J. (2018). "Formal Institutional Support for Early-Stage Entrepreneurs: Evidence from Saudi Arabia". In European Conference on Innovation and Entrepreneurship, September (pp 903-XIII). Academic Conferences International Limited.

Aloulou, W.J., AlOthman, N., (2020), Saudi Arabia, in Dana, L-P, Palalic, R., Ramadani, V., Entrepreneurship in the Gulf Cooperation Council Region. Evolution and Future Perspectives, World Scientific Publishing. (Forthcoming: https://www.worldscientific.com/worldscibooks/10.1142/q0239.

Aloulou, W.J. (2018), From entrepreneurial intentions to behaviors: wandering in-between and wondering about challenges and avenues, in Brito, S.M. (Ed.), Entrepreneurship – Trends and Challenges, Intech Open Publisher, Chapter 7, pp 105-125.

Aloulou, W., (2017), "Investigating entrepreneurial intentions and behaviors of Saudi Distance Business learners: Main antecedents and mediators", Journal of International Business and Entrepreneurship Development, Special Issue: "Youth and Entrepreneurship Education", Vol 10, No. 3, pp 231-257.

Aloulou, W.J., (2016a), "Predicting entrepreneurial intentions of final year Saudi university business students by applying the theory of planned behavior", Journal of Small Business and Enterprise Development, Vol 23, No. 4, pp 1142-1164.

Aloulou, W.J., (2016b), "Predicting entrepreneurial intentions of freshmen students from EAO modeling and personal background: A Saudi perspective", Journal of Entrepreneurship in Emerging Economies, Vol 8, No. 2, pp 180-203.

Aloulou, W.J. (2015), "Entrepreneurial Intention among Freshmen Students—Application of the Theory of Planned Behaviour in Saudi Context", Journal of Enterprising Culture, Vol 23, No. 04, pp 473-500.

Anderson, J.C. & Gerbing, D.W. (1988), "Some methods for respecifying measurement models to obtain uni-dimensional construct measurement", Journal of Marketing Research, Vol 19, No. 4, pp 120-151.

Arbuckle, J.L. (2012), A IBM® SPSS® AmosTM 21: User's Guide, Amos Development Corporation, Oxford.

Bruton, G. D., Ahlstrom, D., & Li, H.L. (2010), "Institutional theory and entrepreneurship: where are we now and where do we need to move in the future?", Entrepreneurship theory and practice, Vol 34, No. 3, pp 421-440.

Busenitz, L.W., Gomez, C., & Spencer, J.W. (2000), "Country institutional profiles: Unlocking entrepreneurial phenomena", Academy of Management Journal, Vol 43, No. 5, pp 994-1003.

Byrne, M. (2010), Structural Equation Modeling with AMOS: Basic Concepts, Applications and Programming, 2nd edition, Routledge Taylor and Francis Group, New York, NY.

Choukir, J., Aloulou, W.J., Ayadi, F, Mseddi, S., (2019), "Influences of role models and gender on Saudi Arabian freshman students' entrepreneurial intention", International Journal of Gender and Entrepreneurship, Vol 11, No. 2, pp 186-206, https://doi.org/10.1108/IJGE-08-2018-0083

Coduras, A., Dokhan, A., Kelly, D., Roomi, M.A., (2019). Kingdom of Saudi Arabia Report 2018-2019, Available at: https://www.gemconsortium.org/report/kingdom-of-saudi-arabia-report-201819. (Accessed Nov. 16, 2019)

Díaz-Casero, J.C., Ferreira, J.J.M., Hernández Mogollón, R., Raposo, M.L.B, (2012). Influence of institutional environment on entrepreneurial intention: a comparative study of two countries university students. International Entrepreneurship and Management Journal, Vol 8, pp 55-74.

Dokhan, A., Ashri, O.M., Roomi, M.A., & Coduras A., (2018). Kingdom of Saudi Arabia Report 2017-2018, Available at: https://www.gemconsortium.org/report/50079 (Accessed April 16, 2019)

Duygulu, E. (2008). Institutional profiles and entrepreneurship orientation: A case of Turkish graduate students. MPRA Paper. [online]. Accessed February 2, 2015, from http://mpra.ub.uni-muenchen.de/7247/

Engle, R. L., Schlaegel, C., & Dimitriadi, N. (2011), "Institutions and entrepreneurial intent: a cross-country study", Journal of Developmental Entrepreneurship, Vol 16, No. 02, pp 227-250.

Farid, M. I., ElSayed-Elkhouly, S. M., & Barnes, M. J. (2011), "Institutional context for entrepreneurship in Arab countries", International Journal of Sustainable Society, Vol 3, No. 3, pp 292-311.

Fayolle, A., & Liñán, F. (2014), "The future of research on entrepreneurial intentions", Journal of Business Research, Vol 67, No. 5, pp 663-666.

Fornell, C. and Larcker, D.F. (1981), "Evaluating structural equation models with unobservable variables and measurement error", Journal of Marketing Research, Vol 18, No. 1, pp 35-39.

García-Rodríguez, F. J., Gil-Soto, E., Ruiz-Rosa, I., & Sene, P. M. (2015), "Entrepreneurial intentions in diverse development contexts: A cross-cultural comparison between Senegal and Spain", International Entrepreneurship and Management Journal, Vol 11, No. 3, pp 511-527.

Gupta, V. K., Guo, C., Canever, M., Yim, H. R., Sraw, G. K., & Liu, M. (2014), "Institutional environment for entrepreneurship in rapidly emerging major economies: the case of Brazil, China, India, and Korea", International Entrepreneurship and Management Journal, Vol 10, No. 2, pp 367-384.

Gupta, V. K., Yalya, A.A., Sikdar, A., Cha, M-S, (2012), "Institutional environment for entrepreneurship: Evidence from the developmental states of South Korea and United Arab Emirates", Journal of Developmental Entrepreneurship, Vol 17, No. 3, 21p.

Hadjimanolis, A. (2016), "Perceptions of the institutional environment and entrepreneurial intentions in a small peripheral country", International Journal of Entrepreneurship and Small Business, Vol 28, No. 1, pp 20-35.

Hair, J.F., Black, W.C., Babin, B.J., Anderson, R.E. and Tatham, R.L. (2014), Multivariate Data Analysis, Pearson Education Limited, N.J.

Ju, W., & Zhou, X. (2020), "Institutional environment and entrepreneurial intention of academics in China", Social Behavior and Personality: an international journal, Vol 48, No. 4, pp 1-15.

Kenny, D.A. (2014), "Measuring model fit", available at: http://davidakenny.net/cm/fit.htm (accessed 20 February 2017).

Kline, R.B. (2005), Principles and Practice of Structural Equation Modeling, 2nd ed., The Guilford Press, New York, NY.

Kostova, T. (1997), "Country Institutional profiles: concept and measurement", Academy of Management Proceedings, pp 180–184.

Krueger, N., Reilly, M. & Carsrud, A. (2000), "Competing models of entrepreneurial intentions", Journal of Business Venturing, Vol 15, No. 2, pp 411-32.

Liñán, F. and Chen, Y.W. (2009), "Development and cross-cultural application of a specific instrument to measure entrepreneurial intentions", Entrepreneurship Theory and Practice, Vol 33, No. 3, pp 593-617.

Liñán, F., & Fayolle, A. (2015), "A systematic literature review on entrepreneurial intentions: Citation, thematic analyses, and research agenda", International Entrepreneurship and Management Journal, Vol 11, No. 4, pp 907–933.

Manolova, T. S., & Eunni, R. V. (2012), "Institutions and Entrepreneurship in Central And Eastern Europe: A Four-Country Comparison Of University Students' perceptions", 7th International Scientific Conference "Business and Management 2012, May 10-11, Vilnius, Lithuania.

Manolova, T.S., Eunni, R.V., & Gyoshev, B.S. (2008), "Institutional environments for entrepreneurship: Evidence from emerging economies in Eastern Europe", Entrepreneurship Theory and Practice, Vol 32, No. 1, pp 203-218.

North, D. (1990). Institutions, Institutional Change, and Economic Performance, Cambridge University Press, London, UK.

Nunnally, J.C. and Bernstein, I.H. (1994), Psychometric Theory, 3rd edition, McGraw-Hill, New York, NY.

Oftedal, E. M., Iakovleva, T. A., & Foss, L. (2018), "University context matter: An institutional perspective on entrepreneurial intentions of students", Education and Training, Vol 60, No. 7-8, pp 873-890.

Podsakoff, P.M. and Organ, D.W. (1986), "Self-reports in organizational research: problems and prospects", Journal of Management, Vol 12, No. 4, pp 531-544.

Podsakoff, P.M., MacKenzie, S.B., Lee, J. and Podsakoff, N. (2003), "Common method biases in behavioral research: a critical review of the literature and recommended remedies", Journal of Applied Psychology, Vol 88, No. 5, pp 79-903.

Redien-Collot, R., Alexander, L., Aloulou, W., (2017), Saudi women's entrepreneurial intention: The social construction of norms and perception, in Henry, C., Nelson, T., Lewis, K., Routledge Companion of Global Female Entrepreneurship, Routledge Publishing, chapter 4, pp 62-77.

Saudi Council of Economic and Development Affairs (2016), "Saudi vision 2030", 24 April, available at: http://vision2030.gov.sa/download/file/fid/417 (accessed 2 May 2020).

Schlaegel, C., & Koenig, M. (2014), "Determinants of entrepreneurial intent: a meta-analytic test and integration of competing models", Entrepreneurship Theory and Practice, Vol 38, No., 2, pp 291-332.

Scott. W.R. (2001), Institutions and organizations, Sage Publications, Thousand Oaks, CA.

Sine, W. D., & David, R. J. (2010), Institutions and entrepreneurship. In Sine, W.D., & David, R.J, (Eds.), Institutions and Entrepreneurship, Research in the sociology of work, Volume 21, pp 1-26. Emerald Group Publishing Limited.

Thompson, B. (2004). Exploratory and confirmatory factor analysis: Understanding concepts and applications: American Psychological Association.

Urban, B. (2013a), "Social entrepreneurship in an emerging economy: a focus on the institutional environment and SESE", Managing Global Transitions: An International Research Journal, Vol 11, No. 1, pp 3-25.

Urban, B. (2013b), "Influence of the institutional environment on entrepreneurial intentions in an emerging economy", The International Journal of Entrepreneurship and Innovation, Vol 14, No. 3, pp 179-191.

Urban, B. (2018), "The influence of the regulatory, normative and cognitive institutions on entrepreneurial orientation in South Africa", The International Journal of Entrepreneurship and Innovation, 1465750318796721.

Urban, B., & Kujinga, L. (2017), "The institutional environment and social entrepreneurship intentions", International Journal of Entrepreneurial Behavior & Research, Vol 23, No. 4.

Urbano, D., & Alvarez, C. (2014), "Institutional dimensions and entrepreneurial activity: An international study", Small Business Economics, Vol 42, No. 4, pp 703-716.

Valdez, M. E., & Richardson, J. (2013), "Institutional determinants of macro-level entrepreneurship", Entrepreneurship Theory and Practice, Vol 37, No. 5, pp 1149-1175.

Veciana, J. M., & Urbano, D. (2008), "The institutional approach to entrepreneurship research. Introduction", International Entrepreneurship and Management Journal, Vol 4, No. 4, pp 365-379.

de la Vega, I., Roomi, M.A., Ashri, O.M., & Coduras Martinez A. (2017). Kingdom Saudi Arabia Report 2016/17, Global Entrepreneurship Monitor. Available at: https://www.gemconsortium.org/report/49820 (Accessed April 04, 2019).

Vyas, V., Raitani, S., & Mathur, V. K. (2014), "Social entrepreneurship and institutional environment in an emerging economy", International Journal of Social Entrepreneurship and Innovation, Vol 3, No. 2, pp 106-121.

Reputation and Social Relationships for Family Business Continuity

Dalal Alrubaishi
Princess Nourah bint Abdulrahman University, Riyadh, Saudi Arabia
daalrubaishi@pnu.edu.sa
DOI: 10.34190/EIE.20.241

Abstract: The interaction between the family and the business creates unique resources that differentiate family businesses from their counterparts. However, family businesses are homogeneous based on the context where they operate. Drawing on the resource-based view of the firm, we empirically explore the unique resources of family firms in Saudi Arabia, a context emphasising the value of networks and family image. We utilize an interpretive qualitative case study methodology based on 10 Saudi family businesses in a range of industries. Our findings highlight the importance of reputation and social relationships for a family business's competitive advantage. We contribute to the discussions centered on the importance of considering the context when studying family businesses.

Keywords: Family firms, resource-based view, reputation, social relationship, context.

1. Introduction

Family firms are considered the dominant form of organisations around the world (Schulze and Gedajlovic, 2010). They form the backbone of economies, representing an essential source of wealth and employment in both developed and developing countries (La Porta, Lopez-de-Silanes and Shleifer, 1999; Masulis, Pham, and Zein, 2011). Family firms constitute 60%–70% of all organisations in the U.S. and 95% of firms in Asia, the Middle East, Italy and Spain (Kets de Vries, Carlock and Florent-Treacy, 2007). This is also true in Saudi Arabia, where 63% of firms are family businesses, contributing around 32% of the country's GDP (Alrubaishi and Robson, 2019). However, "despite their ubiquity and economic significance, there is a striking absence of research that explains the prevalence, prominence, or even existence of this economic institution" (Schulze and Gedajlovic, 2010, p. 191).

The interaction between family and business systems in these kinds of firms creates a distinctive flavour that can be captured through exploring the special resources of family firms (Habbershon et al, 2003). These special resources in include firm and family social capital (Pearson et al, 2008) as well as firm and family reputation and identity (Zellweger et al, 2010; Carney 2005). While the resource-based view (RBV) theory has been used to understand many different aspects of family businesses, such as innovative capacity (Eddleston et al, 2008) and family business entrepreneurship (Sieger et al, 2011; Zahra et al, 2004), the role of context in the importance and utilisation of resources is absent. Indeed, the effect of the context in which the family business operates has yet to be explored. This is of both theoretical and practical significance because family businesses are not a homogeneous group of organisations. Their heterogeneity stems not only from their governance structure, vision and goals but also from the context in which they operate (Wright et al, 2014). Miller, Le Breton-Miller and Lester (2011) argued that in addition to ownership, social context can have an influence on the strategic decisions of family firms. Indeed, context has an important role in building our knowledge about family firms (Sharma and Chua, 2013). This research provides empirical evidence of the unique resources of family firms based on their context, Saudi Arabia, answering the research question: What are the most important resources for family business continuity in the Saudi context?

We make the following contributions to the literature. First, we acknowledge the influence of the context on family firms (Miller et al, 2011) by providing insights into the influence of the Saudi context in the importance and utilisation of resources in family firms. Second, many studies on family business have been conducted from a Western European and U.S. perspective. By exploring the unique resources of family firms in Saudi Arabia, we respond to calls for family firm research in a non-Western context (Sharma and Chua, 2013).

The paper is structured as follows. Initially, we set out the theoretical framework for the paper, anchored in RBV. The following section presents our research design, methodological rationale and data collection and analysis protocols. This is followed by a summary of the key findings from our research and critical discussion and evaluation of the same. Finally, we conclude by considering the theoretical and practical implications of our arguments.

2. Theoretical framework

2.1 Resource-Based View (RBV)

In strategic management, RBV states that for a firm's resources and capabilities to generate competitive advantage, they must be valuable, rare, imperfectly imitable and Irreplaceable (Barney 1991). The resources of a firm include both tangible and intangible assets, whereas capabilities describe the ability to deploy resources through organisational processes (Amit and Schoemaker, 1993). Capabilities are distinctive competencies that must be built rather than bought (Teece, Pisano and Shuen, 1997). Sustainable competitive advantage is then achieved by accumulating, combining and exploiting those resources and capabilities within the company (Grant 1991). RBV has served as a theoretical base for research in many areas of strategy and management, including human resource management, economics and finance, entrepreneurship, marketing and international business (Barney, Wright and Ketchen, 2001). Drawing on this perspective, Habbershon and Williams (1999) introduced the concept of familiness to facilitate understanding of the competitive advantage and disadvantage of family firms. They defined familiness as "the bundle of resources that are distinctive to a firm as a result of family involvement" (p. 1). Habbershon et al (2003) later proposed a unified system using familiness to explain performance in family firms. They suggested that the resources and capabilities of these kinds of companies, combined with family members and the business, interact to influence company performance. This approach provides a strategic management focus on family firm performance that can help identify the resources and capabilities that make family firms unique organizations. Sirmon and Hitt (2003) took this concept of familiness to develop a resource-management process model based on five unique resources that provide a potential advantage over non-family firms (human capital, social capital, patient capital and survivability capital, in addition to the governance structure attribute). In the same vein, Carney (2005) argued that it is the corporate governance system of family firms that creates the competitive advantage. Building on this notion, Le Breton-Miller and Miller (2006) contended that the governance conditions in family firms tend to promote long-term investments. These investments create competitive advantage because they are hard to imitate in other firms that have a different governance structure. The family-based brand identity has also been found to be a unique family firm resource that enhances their performance (Craig, Dibrell and Davis, 2008).

To foster the development of a strategic management theory of family firms, Chrisman et al (2005) suggested that the most distinctive features of these kinds of firms are family involvement, which can include ownership, management or control, and essence, which is used to denote resources, intentions and behaviour (Sharma and Chua, 2013). In an attempt to construct a theory of family firms by advancing our understanding of the concept of familiness, researchers have argued that this construct is multidimensional and therefore transcends family involvement and essence. Based on the organisational identity theory, Zellweger et al (2010) introduced family firm identity as a component of familiness. This concept was also expanded by Pearson et al (2008), who proposed that familiness should include social capital as a unique resource that arises from the intersection of a family and its business. As Cabrera-Suarez et al (2001) asserted, "The family business's unique features (commitment, shared values, culture, trust, reputation, and so on) give it certain strategic resources and capabilities that could account for its long-term success" (p. 38).

The RBV of a firm provides a solid theoretical base to explain the competitive advantage that family businesses can enjoy over other firms. However, an important weakness of this approach is its implicit assumption that wealth creation is the only goal of family business, thereby ignoring other family noneconomic goals that may be of great importance to family owners such as family well-being and employment of family members (Chrisman et al, 2005). Habbershon and Williams (1999) introduced the concept of "familiness" as a potential source of wealth creation for family firms. Calling for greater consideration to be given to research into noneconomic goals in family firms, Chrisman et al (2003) argued that in addition to wealth creation, familiness may contribute to value creation for a firm. These values may be reflected in the opportunities pursued by firms and in their resource management. This extension of goals in family firms is important because behaviours that are intended to achieve noneconomic goals could directly affect what resources are deployed and how.

2.2 Context

Many studies on family business have been conducted from the U.S. and Western Europe perspective, suggesting that there is a need for research from a broader geographical and cultural base to advance our understanding of family firms (Sharma and Chua, 2013). In developing economies, family firms remain key drivers of innovation and entrepreneurship (Heck, Hoy, Poutziouris and Steier, 2008). Saudi Arabia was chosen as the context of this study because of its growing economy, intense entrepreneurial environment and strong family ties. In Saudi Arabia, social and business life revolves around the family (Davis, Pitts and Cormier, 2000; Field, 1985). A family business in Saudi society is viewed as a lasting legacy for generations to come. As such, this research will illuminate the topic of family business in Saudi Arabia, aiding in understanding family firms in general and potentially helping to explain why family firms continue to be the dominant form of organisation in countries around the world.

Saudi Arabia is the largest economy in the Middle East and North Africa region and one of the 20 largest economies in the world. The majority of registered businesses in the country (63%) are family businesses providing approximately 32% of the country's GDP (Alrubaishi and Robson, 2019). Thus, the survival of these types of organisations is pivotal for the Saudi economy.

In the Gulf Cooperation Council (GCC) area, where Saudi Arabia is the largest estate, "more than in any other area of the world, business is viewed as a way to enhance a family's social standing rather than as an impersonal, wealth-generating, market-driven activity" (Davis et al, 2000, p. 217). Thus, a noneconomic goal is an important factor in family businesses in the GCC area. As such, the maintenance of the family legacy and social status requires the management of the family.

Social and business lives in Saudi Arabia revolve around the family. As such, this research will shed light on family businesses entrepreneurship in Saudi Arabia, helping us understand family firms in general and potentially explaining why family firms continue to be the main form of business organisation around the world.

3. Methodology

3.1 Methods

We utilised a qualitative approach by means of case studies to enable an exploration of the unique resources of family firms in Saudi Arabia that contribute to their continuity. A purposeful sample of family firms was selected based on the following criteria. First, the firm has to be family owned and managed, with at least two family members actively involved in the business, to qualify as a family business. Second, firms should have the intention of intergenerational succession to keep the business in the family. Third, firms in the sample should represent the different industry sectors in an attempt at generalisation to the context. The aforementioned criteria correspond to the definitions of family businesses in the literature (Chrisman et al, 2005).

The final sample constituted 10 family businesses. Generally, the sample size in qualitative research is usually small, with a sample of between 4 and 10 cases being the norm (Eisenhardt, 1989). A total of 20 semi-structured interviews with two family firms' members from each case were conducted. In studying family business, the perspectives of more than one family member are essential in gaining a comprehensive insight into the particular issues under investigation (Sharma, Chrisman and Chua, 2003).

The interview schedule was developed in English, then translated into Arabic and checked for conformance. The interview began with demographic and background questions related to the participant and firm to establish rapport. Afterwards, questions related to the research objectives and variables were asked. Those questions focused on the important resources for family business continuity, financial and non-financial aspects of family firms such as family firm meaning, effect of family influence on strategic decisions and relationships between family members and with other stakeholders.

3.2 Data analysis

All interviews were tape-recorded and transcribed verbatim by the researcher to be closer to the data, which in turn aided understanding and analysis. We utilised matrices analysis (Miles and Huberman, 1994) to explore the unique resources of family firms in Saudi Arabia. This technique is suitable for analysing semi-structured interviews and emphasises the visual display of data analysis.

The first step in analysis was line-by-line coding for each interview. During the coding process, similarities as well as differences among cases were noted. Codes were arranged into matrices and revised and re-revised until a satisfying set of codes that reflected and related to the data was reached. This was done by repeatedly examining data in each cell and going back and forth between the matrices and transcripts. For example, some codes were repetitive or stood for the same concept and thus were merged (e.g., identity and family name; nonfinancial goals and reputation), while other codes were too big and thus were broken down further (eg., relations with employers/customers/suppliers/other firms/government/society). Notes were kept during the revision process to understand the decisions behind creating/modifying codes.

In the second step, a comparative cross-case analysis was conducted to develop categories. Thereafter, a matrix was built for each category where rows represent cases and columns represent codes. In this way, all similarly labelled data were brought together under one column. For clarity, and since the data emerged from interview transcripts, direct quotations were entered into cells (Miles and Huberman, 1994). The last step of analysis was reiterative in moving between codes, categories and the literature to form themes. This process resulted in two themes: reputation and social relationships. These themes emerged from data and are reinforced in the literature. Table 1 illustrates the data structure on how the data moved from codes to categories to themes.

Table 1: Data structure

Codes	Categories	Themes
Statements about: family name; non-financial reputation; personal meaning of business; family meaning of business; fear of loss.	Symbolic capital Family based brand identity Protecting the family name	Reputation
Statements about: relationships with employee; relationships with customers; relationships with suppliers; relationships with other firms; relationships with government; relationships with society; long lasting relationships.	Social capital Relationship with stakeholders Long-term relationships	Social Relationships

The analysis steps were verified by another researcher to ensure the findings' validity and reliability, as well as presenting the research findings to participants, making the different stages of the research transparent and including long extracts from the data text into the findings (Guba and Lincoln, 1994).

The age of the sampled firms ranged between 10 and 40 years, and the number of employees ranged between 23 and 250. The main firms' industries cover construction, general trading, import/export, transportation, services and real estate. All firms operate in Riyadh city, the capital city of Saudi Arabia with 26% of total organisations in the country. The sample is not claimed to be representative of all Saudi family firms. However, it is felt that enough variety is included to allow exploration of the unique resources of family firms in Saudi Arabia. Furthermore, qualitative research is not concerned with generalisability as much as gaining a deeper understanding of the phenomena (Eisenhardt, 1989).

4. Findings and discussion

Two resources emerged as the most important and unique resources of family firms in Saudi Arabia: reputation and social relationship. The themes are illustrated in detail, supported by quotes from respondents and linked to the literature. Further illustrative quotes are presented in Table 3.

4.1 Reputation

Reputational concerns emerged as significant in informing decisions across all 10 family firms. As Company B remarked:

Our reputation is our Capital! We have special privileges from financial institutions and from national and international suppliers, privileges better than that of other bigger companies. This is a base for us, our reputation is a bold line, and specially for my father. My reputation, then my reputation, then my reputation! And that's right, because we are harvesting this now (Company B)

Meanwhile, Company E stressed, 'Our reputation is very, very, very important, both family and business reputation, we have an excellent reputation in the market'. Accordingly, the importance of symbolic and social capital was highlighted in regard to supporting the noneconomic goals in family firms (Bourdieu, 1986). In fact, the accrual of symbolic capital was actually prioritised over financial gains: 'My father used to always say to me: don't be fooled by financial capital, our true capital is our reputation! This saying touched me!' (Company J), whilst Company I remarked, 'Money comes and goes, money is not the goal, what is in your bank account is not the goal. Your goal is your reputation!' Furthermore, the ability to leverage off the family-based brand was deemed crucial as illustrated by the following comment: 'Our reputation is strong in the market, once I say my family name all doors are opened, we can take on credit up to millions, whatever the amount we need, we enjoy more flexibility in negotiations' (Company I).

Family-based brand identity was also associated with continuity and growth of the family business. For example: 'The most important thing for continuity is credibility, reputation, discipline and commitment' (Company C). Furthermore, protecting the family name and reputation was also evident in driving family firms' activities (Tlais, 2015; Zellweger et al, 2013), which is summed up in the following comment: 'All my uncles have family business, each one is working separately but they share the same family name of course, so any fault from any of them is going to harm the whole family!' (Company J). It was evident, therefore, that in the Saudi Arabian context in particular, family pride and reputation are closely tied to the type of work family members perform (Ali and Al-Shakhis, 1989). In such a context, the family firm is seen as an extension of the family, with any reputational damage to the firm spilling over to the whole extended family (Dyer and Whetten 2006). Thus, protecting the family reputation was deemed an important factor in the success of Saudi Arabian family businesses (Davis et al, 2000; Harrison and Roomi, 2015). As Company G remarked,

The best thing about our business is its reputation and being in business for about 50 years now. We are pioneers, I am running a business that is long established, reputation and customers are already built, we have to maintain this reputation by providing the best.

4.2 Social relationships

The accrual of social capital also emerged as important in informing decision making and activities across all 10 family firms. As Company C remarked, 'relationships are the most important thing in business', while Company B commented that 'relations have an important role in the business'. Relationships were even prioritised over financial goals: 'Relations are more important than money, relations are the means to get money!' (Company C). This prioritisation appeared to be heightened within the Saudi Arabia context, as summed up by the following comments: 'Most business dealings rely on relations, take it as a rule, in Saudi Arabia business deals are based on personal relations, and this is the secret of growth' (Company I) and 'Of course relations are part of our life here in Saudi, that is our nature' (Company D). Such relations were built over time, as Company G explained: 'We are the agent for more than 30 companies worldwide, and some of them, we are their agent for more than 40 years, we kept our suppliers by good relations'. Furthermore, such networks were deemed a particular entrepreneurial resource for these family firms (McAdam and Soetanto, 2017). As Company E commented, 'There are no opportunities without relations! We have good relations with our suppliers and they provide us with new opportunities'.

5. Conclusion

In fact, reputation and the leveraging of family-based identity was deemed important as to how the 'enterpriseness' of the family manifested (Watson, 2009). Accordingly, family-based brand identity, a sub-section of familiness, appeared beneficial with regards to market positioning and for the bestowing of trust upon all family firms' activities (Craig et al, 2008; Frank et al, 2016). Given that family businesses are presented as bounded entities (Jack et al, 2005), situated in unique social and business contexts (Cucculelli and Bettinelli, 2016), relations also emerged as a salient factor, especially given that Saudi Arabian culture is characterised by strong kinship and tribal connections (Barakat, 1993; Tlais, 2015).

Because family firms are the dominant form of organizations in the global context, this research supports the wider field of business research. The findings of this study demonstrate the importance of reputation and social relationships to Saudi family firms. This is significant for practitioners and policy makers in understanding and guiding family firms in the country to utilise their resources to achieve a competitive advantage.

This research is not without limitations that provide paths for future research: most notably, the fact that the characteristics of family businesses vary across countries and cultures. Therefore, the potential results of this research may not apply to social and business settings that differ significantly from those in Saudi Arabia. However, the research may be expanded to those countries in the same region with similar social and cultural contexts to Saudi Arabia, especially GCC countries.

References

Ali, A. and Al-Shakhis, M. (1989) "Managerial Beliefs About Work in Two Arab States", *Organization Studies*, Vol 10, No. 2, pp.169-186.

Alrubaishi, D. and Robson, P. (2019) "Innovation in Saudi Family SMEs: The Role of Social Capital and Family Involvement", *International Review of Entrepreneurship*, Vol 17, No. 1, pp. 59-86.

Amit, R. and Schoemaker, P.J. (1993) "Strategic Assets and Organizational Rent", *Strategic Management Journal*, Vol 14, No. 1, pp.33-46.

Anderson, A.R., Jack, S.L. and Dodd, S.D. (2016) "The Role of Family Members in Entrepreneurial Networks: Beyond the Boundaries of the Family Firm", In *Entrepreneurial Process and Social Networks*. Edward Elgar Publishing.

Barakat, H. (1993) *The Arab world: Society, Culture, and State*, University of California Press.

Barney, J. (1991) "Firm Resources and Sustained Competitive Advantage", *Journal of Management*, Vol 17, No. 1, pp.99-120.

Barney, J., Wright, M. and Ketchen Jr, D.J. (2001) "The Resource-Based View of the Firm: Ten Years After 1991", *Journal of Management*, Vol 27, No. 6, pp.625-641.

Bourdieu, P. (1986) "The forms of capital", *Handbook of Theory and Research for the Sociology of Education,* pp. 241-258. New York, Greenwood Press.

Cabrera-Suárez, K., De Saá-Pérez, P. and García-Almeida, D. (2001) " The Succession Process from a Resource-and Knowledge-Based View of the Family Firm", *Family Business Review*, Vol 14, No. 1, pp.37-48.

Carney, M. (2005) "Corporate Governance and Competitive Advantage in Family–Controlled Firms", *Entrepreneurship Theory and Practice*, Vol 29, No. 3, pp.249-265.

Chrisman, J.J., Chua, J.H. and Sharma, P. (2005) "Trends and Directions in the Development of a Strategic Management Theory of the Family Firm", *Entrepreneurship Theory and Practice*, Vol 29, No. 5, pp.555-575.

Chrisman, J.J., Chua, J.H. and Zahra, S.A. (2003) "Creating Wealth in Family Firms through Managing Resources: Comments and Extensions", *Entrepreneurship Theory and Practice*, Vol 27, No. 4, pp.359-365.

Craig, J.B., Dibrell, C. and Davis, P.S. (2008) "Leveraging Family-Based Brand Identity to Enhance Firm Competitiveness and Performance in Family Businesses", *Journal of Small Business Management*, Vol 46, No. 3, pp.351-371.

Cucculelli, M. and Bettinelli, C. (2016) "Corporate Governance in Family Firms, Learning and Reaction to Recession: Evidence from Italy", *Futures*, Vol 75, pp.92-103.

Davis, J.A., Pitts, E.L. and Cormier, K. (2000) "Challenges Facing Family Companies in the Gulf Region", *Family Business Review*, Vol 13, No. 3, pp.217-237.

Dyer Jr, W.G. and Whetten, D.A. (2006) "Family Firms and Social Responsibility: Preliminary Evidence from the S&P 500", *Entrepreneurship Theory and Practice*, Vol 30, No. 6, pp.785-802.

Eddleston, K.A., Kellermanns, F.W. and Sarathy, R. (2008) "Resource Configuration in Family Firms: Linking Resources, Strategic Planning and Technological Opportunities to Performance", *Journal of Management Studies*, Vol 45, No. 1, pp.26-50.

Eisenhardt, K.M. (1989) "Building Theories from Case Study Research", *Academy of Management Review*, Vol 14, No. 4, pp.532-550.

Field, M. (1985) *The Merchants: The Big Business Families of Saudi Arabia and the Gulf States*, Overlook Press.

Florent-Treacy, E. (2007) *Family Business on the Couch: A Psychological Perspective*, John Wiley & Sons.

Frank, H., Kessler, A., Rusch, T., Suess–Reyes, J. and Weismeier–Sammer, D. (2017) "Capturing the Familiness of Family Businesses: Development of the Family Influence Familiness Scale (FIFS)", *Entrepreneurship Theory and Practice*, Vol 41, No. 5, pp.709-742.

Grant, R.M. (1991) "The Resource-Based Theory of Competitive Advantage: Implications for Strategy Formulation", *California Management Review*, Vol 33, No. 3, pp.114-135.

Guba, E.G. and Lincoln, Y.S. (1994) "Competing Paradigms in Qualitative Research", *Handbook of Qualitative Research*, p.105, Sage Publications, Thousand Oaks .

Habbershon, T.G. and Williams, M.L. (1999) "A Resource-Based Framework for Assessing the Strategic Advantages of Family Firms", *Family Business Review*, Vol 12, No. 1, pp.1-25.

Habbershon, T.G., Williams, M. and MacMillan, I.C. (2003) "A Unified Systems Perspective of Family Firm Performance", *Journal of Business Venturing*, Vol 18, No. 4, pp.451-465.

Harrison, P. and Roomi, M.A. (2015) "Entrepreneurial Leadership and Islamic Perceptions: Institutional, Market, and Cultural Approaches", *Research Handbook on Entrepreneurship and Leadership,* Edward Elgar, Cheltenham, UK.

Heck, R.K., Hoy, F., Poutziouris, P.Z. and Steier, L.P. (2008) "Emerging Paths of Family Entrepreneurship Research", *Journal of Small Business Management*, Vol 46, No. 3, pp.317-330.

La Porta, R., Lopez-de-Silanes, F. and Shleifer, A. (1999) "Corporate Ownership around the World", *The Journal of Finance*, Vol 54, No. 2, Pp.471-517.

Le Breton–Miller, I. and Miller, D. (2006) "Why Do Some Family Businesses Out–Compete? Governance, Long–Term Orientations, and Sustainable Capability", *Entrepreneurship Theory and Practice*, Vol 30, No. 6, pp.731-746.

Masulis, R.W., Pham, P.K. and Zein, J. (2011) "Family Business Groups around the World: Financing Advantages, Control Motivations, and Organizational Choices", *The Review of Financial Studies*, Vol 24, no. 11, pp.3556-3600.

Miles, M.B. and Huberman, A.M. (1994) *Qualitative Data Analysis: An Expanded Sourcebook*, Sage.

Miller, D., Le Breton-Miller, I. and Lester, R.H. (2011) "Family and Lone Founder Ownership and Strategic Behaviour: Social Context, Identity, and Institutional Logics", *Journal of Management Studies*, Vol 48, No. 1, pp.1-25.

Pearson, A.W., Carr, J.C. and Shaw, J.C. (2008) "Toward a Theory Of Familiness: A Social Capital Perspective", *Entrepreneurship Theory and Practice*, Vol 32, No. 6, pp.949-969.

Schulze, W.S. and Gedajlovic, E.R. (2010) "Whither Family Business?", *Journal of Management Studies*, Vol 47, No. 2, pp.191-204.

Sharma, P. and Chua, J.H. (2013) "Asian Family Enterprises and Family Business Research", *Asia Pacific Journal of Management*, Vol 30, No. 3, pp.641-656.

Sharma, P., Chrisman, J.J. and Chua, J.H. (2003) "Predictors of Satisfaction with the Succession Process In Family Firms", *Journal of Business Venturing*, Vol 18, No. 5, pp.667-687.

Sieger, P., Zellweger, T., Nason, R.S. and Clinton, E. (2011) "Portfolio Entrepreneurship in Family Firms: A Resource-Based Perspective", *Strategic Entrepreneurship Journal*, Vol 5, No. 4, pp.327-351.

Sirmon, D.G. and Hitt, M.A. (2003) "Managing Resources: Linking Unique Resources, Management, and Wealth Creation in Family Firms", *Entrepreneurship Theory and Practice*, Vol 27, No. 4, pp.339-358.

Teece, D.J., Pisano, G. and Shuen, A. (1997) "Dynamic Capabilities and Strategic Management", *Strategic Management Journal*, Vol 18, No.7, pp.509-533.

Tlaiss, H.A. (2015) "How Islamic Business Ethics Impact Women Entrepreneurs: Insights from Four Arab Middle Eastern Countries", *Journal of Business Ethics*, Vol 129, No. 4, pp.859-877.

Watson, T.J. (2009) "Entrepreneurial Action, Identity Work and the Use of Multiple Discursive Resources: The Case of a Rapidly Changing Family Business", *International Small Business Journal*, Vol 27, No. 3, pp.251-274.

Wright, M., Chrisman, J.J., Chua, J.H. and Steier, L.P. (2014) "Family Enterprise and Context" *Entrepreneurship Theory and Practice*, Vol 38, No. 6, pp.1247-1260.

Zahra, S.A. and Sharma, P. (2004) "Family Business Research: A Strategic Reflection", *Family Business Review*, Vol 17, No. 4, pp.331-346.

Zellweger, T.M., Eddleston, K.A. and Kellermanns, F.W. (2010) "Exploring the Concept of Familiness: Introducing Family Firm Identity", *Journal of Family Business Strategy*, Vol 1, No. 1, pp.54-63.

Zellweger, T.M., Nason, R.S., Nordqvist, M. and Brush, C.G. (2013) "Why Do Family Firms Strive for Nonfinancial Goals? An Organizational Identity Perspective", *Entrepreneurship Theory and practice*, Vol. 37, No. 2, pp.229-248.

How Does Competition by Informal and Formal Firms Affect the Innovation and Productivity Performance in Peru? A CDM Approach

Lourdes Alvarez[1], Edson Huamaní[2] and Yngrid Coronado[2]
[1]Economic and Fiscal Policy Unit, United Nations Environment Programme, Geneva, Switzerland
[2]Economic Department, Pontifical Catholic University of Peru, Lima, Peru
lourdes.alvarez@un.org
ehuamani@pucp.pe
yngrid.coronado@pucp.pe
DOI: 10.34190/EIE.20.145

Abstract: Innovation is one of the main determinants to stimulate productivity. However, incentives to innovate may be affected by the level of competition. In particular, in developing countries, where informality is highly prevalent, formal firms have to face both types of competition: formal and informal. Previous studies have acknowledged a negative impact from competition (*schumpeterian effect*) but also, several recent studies have shown that competition could spur innovation (*escape-competition effect*). Given the importance of informal competition in developing countries, as Peru, where almost three out of four firms are informal and the intensity of investment in R&D+i activities is pretty low, this study aims to evaluate the impact of formal and informal competition, at the industrial level, on the whole innovation process and, expressly, on productivity for Peru. By using a CDM model, this study analyses how the intensity of formal and informal competition affects every stage of the innovation process. The CDM model makes possible to study four interrelated stages of the innovation process: i) the firms' choice to engage with innovation, ii) the amount of resources invested in R&D+i activities, iii) the effects of R&D+i investments on innovation output, and iv) the impacts of innovation outcome on firms' productivity. The model is estimated using firm-level data collected by the Peruvian National Innovation Survey 2018 and the National Business Survey 2018. Our main findings indicate that competition, both formal and informal, affects negatively the decision to engage in innovation. However, the relationship changes throughout the remaining stages of the innovation process. Whereas the informal competition affects negatively the whole innovation process (engage in innovation, intensity of R&D+I activities spending, innovation output and firms' productivity) satisfying the *Schumpeterian theory*; formal competition seems to affect positively the intensity of R&D+i activities spending and also firms' productivity, which can be explained as an *escape-competition effect* within the formal firms. In conclusion, meanwhile it is found that informal competition affects negatively the whole innovation process, formal competition could, instead, encourage formal firms' willingness to invest more in R&D+i activities, increasing their productivity.

Keywords: competition, CDM model, informality, innovation, productivity

1. Introduction

Several empirical studies have demonstrated a positive relationship between the performance of the firm in Research and Development and Innovation (R&D+i) activities, and productivity growth (Hall, 2011; Hall and Jones, 1999; Rouvinen, 2002, Pakes and Griliches, 1980). Nevertheless, literature has emphasized that the execution of R&D+i activities and its spending intensity can be effected by the economic structure of the country.

Particularly, in developing countries, where informality tends to be highly predominant, the economy structure is fractured in two sectors: formal and informal. It means that formal firms not only have to compete with other formal firms, but also with the informal ones. Hence, the innovation process and its impacts on productivity seems to be affected by both types of competition: formal competition and informal competition.

On the one hand, literature recognizes that competition can reduce the incentives to invest in innovation by decreasing the monopoly rents of prospective innovative firms (Schumpeterian effect) but also, several recent studies have shown that competition could spur innovation given the higher returns that firms obtain by their investment given the need to differentiate their products and improve their process in a higher competitive market (escape-competition effect) (Castellacci, 2011).

Moreover, the effect of informality can be negative by diminishing the incentives to investment in innovation given the high levels of entrepreneurial risks (Harris, 2014). In particular, Heredia et al. (2017) find out that the impact of informal competition on the innovation performance of formal firms in emerging economies is negative, which can reinforce the Schumpeterian effect.

In line with that, considering that literature has not delved in the differentiated effects of both types of competition on the whole process of innovation, and expressly, on productivity and that, in Peru, almost three out of four firms are informal (INEI, 2018) and that, even when the propensity to carry out successfully R&D+i activities in the manufacturing sector is high (52.7%), the investment on R&D+i activities respect to sales are still pretty low (1.8%) (ENIM, 2018), this study attempts to delve into how the degree of competition at the industrial level, both formal and informal, can affect the whole innovation process and productivity. To assess this impact, the intensity of formal and informal competition, at the industrial level, is introduced in a CDM model (Crepon, Duguet and Mairesse, 1998) which makes possible to study four interrelated stages of the innovation process: i) the choice of a firm to engage in innovation, ii) the amount of resources to invest in R&D+I activities, iii) the effects of R&D+i investments on innovation output, and iv) the impacts of innovation outcome on firms' productivity.

This article is structure as follow, after the introduction, it is presented a brief literature review. Then, in the third section it is explained the data and methodology applied. The subsequent sections present the results and a discussion of these. The final sections contain the study's main conclusion.

2. Literature review

In order to analyse the relationship between innovation and productivity, Crépon, Duguet and Mairesse (1998) identified in the CDM model a logical framework with three principal interactions around i) the decision to invest in R&D; ii) the R&D spending and its impact on innovation output; and iii) the results of innovation and its effect on productivity. It is worthy to mention that in this study it is considered always the R&D+i activities, also called innovation activities.

In the CDM model, the firms' decision to invest in R&D is influenced, on one hand, by their specific characteristics, such as their size, sector and market share; and, on the other hand, by the business environment, such as the scientific advances and the demand of differentiated products. In that way, those innovative efforts increase the firms' knowledge capital stock and intensify their propensity to innovate through the creation of new products or the adoption of new process. Finally, this innovation output impact on firms' productivity level (see Figure N° 1) (Muinelo-Gallo, 2012).

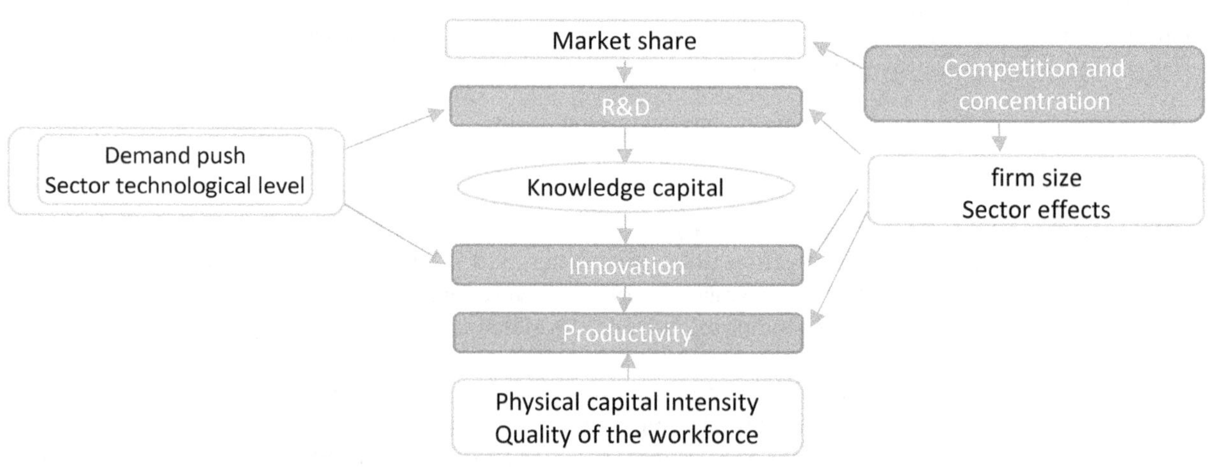

Figure 1: Logical framework of the Crépon, Duguet and Mairesse (1998) Model – CDM Model (adapted from Muinelo-Gallo, 2012)

In the CDM logical framework, the level of competition and concentration in an industry is associated with the sectorial and market share effects that influence each stage of the innovation process. In this context, the literature has shown two types of effects of the competition on innovation.

The Schumpeterian effect: On the one hand, some studies have identified that the higher competition may decrease the monopoly rents of prospective innovative firms, reducing their incentives to engage in R&D activities and innovation (Scherer, 1967; Geroski, 1990; Nickell 1996, Castellaci, 2011; Harris, 2014; Mulkay 2019). Furthermore, the literature recognized that if more monopolistic firms are more active in innovative activities because of less market uncertainty, then competitive pressure could reduce their incentives to invest in R&D (Ahn, 2002) and to commit to innovation. Moreover, Aghion et al. (2015) point out that, in sectors that are not neck and neck, competition may discourage innovation by laggard firms when these firms do not put much weight on becoming a leader and instead mainly look at the short-run extra profit.

The Escape-competition effect: On the opposite side, some studies have shown that higher competition could also spur innovation (Aghion and Howitt, 1998). In that approach, the literature recognize that firms might innovate to survive under the competitive pressure (Porter, 1990). Furthermore, these studies explain that higher competition between companies with "neck-and-neck" technologies increases their incentives to innovate to maintain technological leadership over their rivals (Ahn, 2002, Aghion et al., 2015).

In line with both effects, recent studies have evidenced the existence of an inverted-U shape relationship between the competition intensity and innovation activities (Aghion *et al.*, 2005). In this approach, in low levels of competition, the escape-competition effect is higher and spur innovation. However, if the level of competition is too high, schumpeterian effect incentives to reduce the innovation activity. Actually the effect of competition on innovation depends on the technological state of the sector. In unlevelled sectors, the Schumpeterian effect is at work even if it does not always dominate. But in levelled (neck-and-neck) sectors, the escape-competition effect is the only effect at work. That is, more competition induces neck-and-neck firms to innovate in order to escape from a situation in which competition constrains profits (Aghion *et al.*, 2015). According with recent literature, informality can affect innovation, basically, by two channels (Mendi and Costagna, 2016): i) Since the informal sector tends to required low skills, there are not incentives to encourage the accumulation of human capital, which reduce the innovation practice and ii) due to the fact that informal firms face lower entry costs than formal firms, the number of competitors is too high, which may reduce the incentives to engage in innovation.

Considering the previous theoretical findings, this study aims to evaluate how the degree of competition at the industrial level, both formal and informal, can affect the whole innovation process and productivity. We formulated the two following hypotheses:

> ***H₁:** Formal firms experience the Schumpeterian effect on their innovation process when they face informal competition, because it means dealing with a higher number of firms with less technological intensity.*
>
> ***H₂:** Formal firms experience the Escape-competition effect on their innovation process when they face formal competition, because it means dealing with fewer firms with higher technology intensity.*

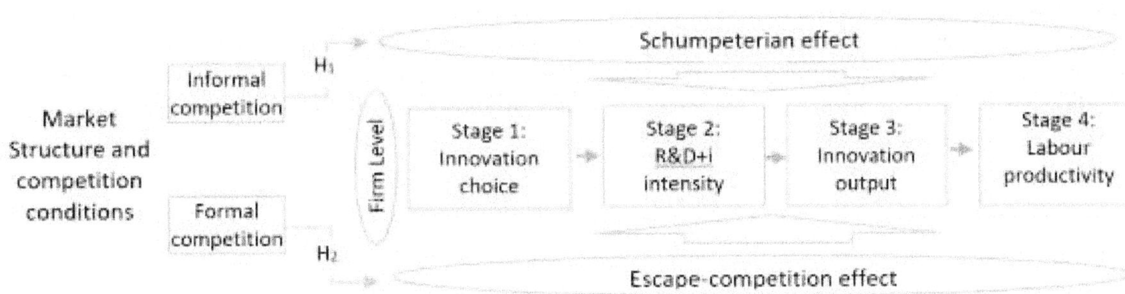

Figure 2: Model and hypotheses

3. Methodology

3.1 Database

The data used in this study came from two surveys with firm-level information: the Peruvian National Innovation Survey 2018 (ENIM) and the National Business Survey 2018 (ENE). The ENIM 2018 database is representative at the national level for manufacturing firms and contains firm level information of innovation activities for the years 2015, 2016, and 2017. The sectoral coverage of the survey was for the manufacturing industry, section C of the International Standard Industrial Classification (ISIC) (Class 1010 to 3320). A total of 1,463 manufacturing firms were interviewed, which is equivalent to 9,894 firms considering the expansion factor.

In this study, the ENIM 2018 information is utilized to identify the innovation process in manufacturing firms and additional firms' specific control characteristics. On the one hand, this database defines nine types of innovation activities: i) Internal R&D, ii) External R&D, iii) Engineering design or creative activities, iv) Marketing and brand value, v) Intellectual Property, vi) Training, vi) Development or acquisition of software, viii) Acquisition of capital goods (including hardware), and ix) Innovation Management. On the other hand, ENIM 2018 consider two types of innovation results: i) in products and ii) in business processes. Likewise, the ENE 2018 database is representative at ISIC-2 digits industrial level. In this study, this source of information is used to identify the level of formal and informal competition at the industrial level. Thereby, the intensity of formal (informal) competition in an industry is defined as the proportion of firms that reported that formal (informal) competition as a relevant obstacle to continue operating.

3.2 CDM model with formal and informal competition

This study is focused on evaluating the impact of formal and informal competition on the whole process of innovation by using a CDM Model. Thus, the model is characterized in four equations that represents i) the firm's decision to invest in innovation activities, ii) the intensity of investment in innovation activities, iii) the knowledge production function (innovation outcome), and iv) the production function (labour productivity transformed by logarithms). Additionally, the formal and informal competition intensity variable are introduced in every function.

The CDM model correct the problem of selection bias and endogeneity in the innovation and productivity process. Therefore, in the first stage, the selection equation (1) describes whether the firm decides to invest in innovation.

$$ID_i = \begin{cases} 1\ si\ ID_i^* = w_i'\alpha + \varepsilon_i > c, \\ 0\ si\ ID_i^* = w_i'\alpha + \varepsilon_i \leq c \end{cases} \quad (1)$$

In equation (1), ID_i is a binary observable variable that represents the investment decision in innovation of the firm 'i'. ID_i is equal to one if the firm invests in innovation activities, and equal to zero otherwise. Likewise, ID_i^* is a latent variable that reveal the preferences of investment decision in innovation of the firms. Thereby, if ID_i^* is above the threshold c, the firm would invest in innovation. Additionally, w is a vector of variables that explain the investment decision in innovation, and includes the formal and informal competition intensity variable. Finally, α is the vector of parameters of interest and ε_i is a normal distributed error term.

In equation (2), the second stage of the CDM model, IE_i is the observed intensity of investment in innovation activities. Likewise, IE_i^* is approximated by means of the logarithm of innovation activities expenditure per worker denoted by IE_i only if firms make (and report) said expenditure. Additionally, zi is a vector of independent variables that affect the effort in innovation, variables. Assuming that the error terms have zero mean, variance $\sigma_\varepsilon^2 = 1$, and correlation coefficient $\rho_{\varepsilon e}$, the system of equations (1) and (2) is estimated using a generalized Tobit model with maximum likelihood.

$$IE_i = \begin{cases} IE_i^* = z_i'\beta + \varepsilon_i\ si\ ID_i = 1 \\ 0\ si\ D_i = 0 \end{cases} \quad (2)$$

In the third stage of the CDM model, equation (3) represents the firms' production function of innovation (or knowledge). Thereby, TI is a dummy variable that equals to one when the company has introduced an innovation, and equals to zero otherwise. Likewise, $IE_i{}^*$ is the prediction of the value of the innovative effort of the company from the previously estimated generalized Tobit equations (2). Thus, x_i is a vector of input variables that affect the knowledge production, which include the formal and informal competition, u_i is an error term and F is a standard normal distribution function.

$$TI_i = F(IE_i^*\gamma + x_i'\delta + u_i) \quad (3)$$

Finally, in equation (4), firms are assumed to adopt a Cobb-Douglas function with constant returns to scale. This function includes the y_i is the firm's labour productivity as dependent variable, and capital per capita (k) and the knowledge input (TI*) estimated in equation (3) as independent variables.

$$y_i = \pi_i k_i + \pi_2 TI_i + v_i \qquad (4)$$

In this study, y_i is the logarithm of sales per worker in the last year of the survey. Similarly, k_i is the logarithm of physical capital per worker in the initial year, and TI_i is the prediction of the knowledge production function and captures the impact of innovation on productivity levels. In addition to these variables, following the studies reviewed, the estimated model incorporates a vector with additional control variables to equation (4), which include the formal and informal competition intensity.

4. Results

4.1 Descriptive statistics: Innovative firms and competition intensity

In Peruvian manufacturing (2015-2017), around 52.7% of companies are innovative firms but the intensity of the investment on innovation activities are still pretty low (ENIM, 2018). On the one hand, the manufacture of petroleum (83.0%), pharmaceuticals (74.4%) and machinery and equipment (73.9%) are the industries with the highest percentage of innovative firms which exceed three-quarters of each industry. On the other hand, the manufacture of non-metallic minerals (4.7%), pharmaceutical products (4.2%) and production of wood (3.8%) are the industries with the highest intensity in investment in innovation activities, but that represents less than 5% of their sales.

Table 1: Innovative behaviour, competition and labour productivity according to manufacturing activity 2018

Div.	Manufacturing sector	Percentage of innovative firms	Investment intensity in innovation activities a/	Labour productivity b/	Informal competition c/	Formal competition c/
10	Foods	51.9%	1.1%	11.9	56.4%	39.9%
11	Drinks	58.8%	0.9%	12.0	47.5%	36.1%
13	Textiles	36.1%	0.7%	11.8	60.7%	43.0%
14	Clothing	48.7%	0.7%	12.0	55.6%	29.3%
15	Leather and related products	65.3%	0.7%	12.0	53.8%	17.3%
16	Wood and derivatives	44.9%	3.8%	11.9	66.0%	32.4%
17	Paper	71.3%	2.0%	11.8	56.9%	50.0%
18	Editing, printing, and recording	42.6%	1.3%	11.8	60.8%	46.6%
19	Petroleum products	83.0%	3.1%	14.1	41.3%	11.4%
20	Chemical substances and products	55.6%	1.6%	12.4	42.9%	41.0%
21	Pharmaceutical products	74.4%	4.2%	12.4	14.8%	44.5%
22	Rubber and plastic	58.6%	2.5%	12.2	52.8%	52.6%
23	Other non-metallic mineral products	49.4%	4.7%	12.0	59.9%	36.5%
24	Common metals	67.4%	0.2%	12.1	44.4%	32.3%
25	Metal products	48.4%	1.7%	11.6	58.2%	28.3%
26	Computer Products	54.0%	1.6%	11.9	27.7%	19.9%
27	Electric equipment	49.6%	0.8%	12.0	50.8%	38.9%
28	Machinery and equipment	73.9%	2.1%	11.7	43.3%	19.2%
29	Motor vehicles	48.7%	1.3%	12.2	63.0%	20.7%
30	Other transport equipment	67.0%	2.7%	12.6	57.5%	27.2%
31	Furniture	65.0%	0.4%	11.6	47.6%	32.3%
32	Other manufacturing industries	65.6%	1.4%	11.8	47.6%	36.9%
33	Machinery and equipment repair	52.7%	3.1%	11.5	55.9%	34.2%
	Total	**52.7%**	**1.8%**	**12.1**	**50.7%**	**33.5%**

a/ The intensity of the investment in innovation activities was obtained by dividing the total spending on these activities, for the period 2015-2017, by the total sales for the same period. The universe considered was the total of manufacturing companies that invested in innovation activities.

b/ Labour productivity is calculated as the logarithm of the following division: sales over the number of workers for the year 2017.

c/ The intensity of competition was calculated by the number of firms in an industry reporting that competition is a relevant obstacle (informal or formal) divided by the total number of firms in the industry.

In Peru, the intensity of informal competition (50.7%) in manufacturing is higher than formal competition (33.5%). The intensity of formal (informal) competition in an industry is defined as the proportion of firms that reported that formal (informal) competition is a relevant obstacle to continue operating. The economic sectors with the highest intensity of informal competition are those related to motor vehicles, leather products, and wood and derivatives. On the contrary, the pharmaceutical products industry presents a greater intensity of formal competition. Finally, highest labour productivity are the ones related to petroleum products, transport equipment and pharmaceuticals products.

4.2 CDM model results

In table 2, the results reveal a significant and negative marginal effect of formal and informal competition on the probability of investing in innovation activities in the Peruvian industry. Thereby, this estimation satisfies the *schumpeterian effect* hypothesis, meaning that the higher level of competition, the lower the probability of investing in innovation activities.

Table 2: Effect of informal and formal competition on the probability of investing in innovation activities

Dependent variable	Probability of investing in innovation activities
Informal competition	**-0.0065*** **
Formal competition	**-0.0048** **
Percentage of qualified employees	0.2221*
Links with research centres / universities	0.5777***
Linking with competitors	0.5574***
Link with technical centres	0.4751***
*** p<0.01, ** p<0.05, * p<0.1	

In table 3, the results reveal a differentiated effect of formal and informal competition on innovative effort. On the one hand, this estimation recognizes that informal competition affects negatively the intensity of investment in innovation activities (*schumpeterian effect*). On the other hand, the formal competition exhibits a positive and significantly effect to the innovative effort (*escape-competition effect*).

Table 3: Effect of informal and formal competition on innovative effort (intensity of investment in innovation activities)

Dependent variable	Innovative effort (intensity of investment in innovation activities)
Informal competition	**-0.022***
Formal competition	**0.024***
Percentage of qualified employees	1.917***
Holding of intellectual property rights	0.776**
Chains with extractive sectors	0.868***
*** p<0.01, ** p<0.05, * p<0.1	

In table 4, the results reveal a significant negative direct effect of formal competition on the probability of obtaining innovation outcome (*schumpeterian effect*). Likewise, the magnitude of the innovative effort, the access to public financing and the size of the firm, associated with the number of workers, significantly increase the probability of achieving an innovative result.

Table 4: Effect of informal and formal competition on the probability of obtaining innovation outcome

Dependent variable	Get innovation results Dichotomous variable (1=innovative firm)
Informal competition	**-0.0011**
Formal competition	**-0.0075*** **
Number of employees (Log)	0.0725***
Access to public financing	0.5009***
Innovative effort (intensity)	0.1775***
*** p<0.01, ** p<0.05, * p<0.1	

In table 5, it is possible to observe that, for the period 2015-2017, considering the effects of competition, innovation and productivity are associated positively. In average, innovation increases in 20.8% - 24.7% labour productivity. This result is in the range of the values reported in the study by Crespi and Zuñiga (2010), identifying the following: Argentina (24%), Chile (60%), Colombia (192%), Panama (165%), and Uruguay (8%).

Otherwise, the results are not entirely conclusive and significant about the direct effect of competition on labour productivity. However, the econometric estimations allow to conjecture that informal competition has a negative impact on labour productivity; meanwhile, formal competition seems to have a positive effect. Indeed, Amin *et. al.* (2019) reported that labour productivity of formal firms that face competition from informal firms is about 75% of the average labour productivity of formal firms that not experience informal competition.

Table 5: Effect of the innovation and the informal and formal competition on labour productivity

Dependent variable	**Labour productivity (1)**	**Labour productivity (2)**	**Labour productivity (3)**	**Labour productivity (4)**
Informal competition	-0.011**	-0.011*	-0.005	-0.007
Formal competition	0.007	0.008*	0.004	0.003
Innovative effort prediction (intensity)			0.208**	0.247***
Introduction of innovation prediction		0.153		-0.287
*** p<0.01, ** p<0.05, * p<0.1				

5. Conclusion

This study was conducted to evaluate how the intensity of formal and informal competition affects every stage of the innovation process. By using a CDM model, the intensity of informal and formal competition, at the industrial level was introduced in every equation representing each stage of the innovation process. Following the provided literature, two hypotheses were tested: i) Formal firms experience the Schumpeterian effect on their innovation process when they face informal competition, because it means dealing with a higher number of firms with less technological intensity and ii) Formal firms experience the Escape-competition effect on their innovation process when they face formal competition, because it means dealing with fewer firms with higher technology intensity.

It is notable that informal competition in the manufacturing sector is more intense than formal competition, on average. Aghion *et al.* (2005) already manifested that the higher number of informal firms with less technological intensity could explain why informal competition does negatively affect the entire innovation process.

Results show that informal competition has a negative effect in the whole innovation process for the manufacturing sector in Peru, that is to say informal competition discourage formal firms to engage with innovation, to invest in R&D+i activities; and as a result, innovation output is null or low that affects negatively firms' productivity. Those findings satisfy the Schumpeterian theory, allowing us to guess that informal competition reinforce the negative effects of competition given the with a higher number of firms with less technological intensity.

Meanwhile, formal competition seems to have a positive impact in the firms' willingness to invest in R&D+i activities and it is associated positively with labour productivity. That result can be explained as an escape-competition effect within the formal firms. Even when the number of formal firms tend to be fewer, the investment intensity in higher technology seems to be greater, which incentives other formal firms to level innovation in order to not lose market share.

References

Aghion, P., Bloom, N., Blundell, R., Griffith, R., Howitt, P., 2005. Competition and innovation: An inverted U relationship. The Quarterly Journal of Economics, Vol. 120, No. 2 (May, 2005), 701-728 http://www.jstor.org/stable/25098750.

Aghion, P. and Howitt, P., 1998. Endogenous Growth Theory. Cambridge, MA: MIT Press.

Aghion, P., Akcigit, U. and Howitt, P., 2015. The Schumpeterian Growth Paradigm. Annual Review of Economics. Vol. 7, p.p. 557-575. https://doi.org/10.1146/annurev-economics-080614-115412

Ahn, S., 2002. Competition, innovation and productivity growth: A review of theory and evidence. OECD Economics Department Working Paper 317. https://doi.org/10.1787/182144868160.

Amin, Mohammad; Ohnsorge, Franziska Lieselotte; Okou, Cedric Iltis Finafa, 2019. Casting a Shadow: Productivity of Formal Firms and Informality (English). Policy Research working paper; no. WPS 8945. Washington, D.C.: World Bank Group.

Castellacci, F., 2011. How does competition affect the relationship between innovation and productivity? Estimation of a CDM model for Norway. Economics of Innovation and New Technology. Economics of Innovation and New Technology 20 (7), 637-658. https://doi.org/10.1080/10438599.2010.516535.

Crepon, B., Duguet, E. and Mairesse, J., 1998. Research, innovation and productivity: An econometric analysis at the firm level. Economics of Innovation and New Technology, 7, (2), 115-158 https://doi.org/10.1080/10438599800000031

Crespi, G., and Zuniga, P. (2012). Innovation and productivity: evidence from six Latin American countries. World Development, Vol. 40 (2), p.p. 273–290. https://doi.org/10.1016/j.worlddev.2011.07.010

Geroski, . P., 1990. Innovation, technological opportunity and market structure. Oxford Economic Papers, 42, (3), 586-602.

Griliches, Z. and Pakes, A., 1980. Patents and R&D at the firm level: A first report. Economics Letters, Vol. 5, (4), 377-381

Hall, B. H., 2011. Innovation and productivity. National Bureau of Economic Research N° 17178, NBER Working Papers. http://www.nber.org/papers/w17178.

Hall, R. and Jones , C., 1999. Why do some countries produce so much more output than others?. The Quarterly Journal of Economics, 114, (1), 83-116.

Harris, J. C., 2014. The confounding influence of urban informality on innovation and production specialisation in production clusters: evidence from Nairobi. African Journal of Science, Technology, Innovation and Development, Vol. 6 (6), p.p. 83-116.

National Institute of Statistics and Informatics (INEI), 2018. Informal production and employment in Peru: satellite account of the informal economy 2007-2017. https://www.inei.gob.pe/media/MenuRecursivo/publicaciones_digitales/Est/Lib1589/libro.pdf

National Innovation Survey (ENIM), 2018. National Institute of Statistics and Informatics (INEI).

National survey of companies (ENE), 2018. National Institute of Statistics and Informatics (INEI).

Mendi, P. and Costamagna, R., 2016. Managing innovation under competitive pressure from informal producers. Technological Forecasting and Social Change, Vol. 114, p.p. 192-202. http://doi.org/10.1016/j.techfore.2016.08.013

Muinelo-Gallo, L., 2012. Modelo estructural de función de producción. Un estudio empírico de la innovación en el sector manufacturero español. Economía Teoría y Práctica N° 36, p.p. 43-82. http://www.scielo.org.mx/scielo.php?script=sci_arttext&pid=S0188-33802012000100003

Mulkay, B. (2019). How does competition affect innovation behaviour in french firms?. Structural Change and Economic Dynamics. Vol. 51, p.p. 237-251. https://doi.org/10.1016/j.strueco.2019.05.003

Nickell, S., 1996. Competition and corporate performance. Journal of Political Economy, Vol. 104, (4), p.p. 724-46. http://dx.doi.org/10.1086/262040

Porter, M., 1990. Competitive Advantage of Nations. Harvard Business Review 68, no. 2, p.p. 73–93.

Rouvine, P., 2002. R&D-productivity dynamics: causality, lags, and dry holes. Journal of Applied Economics. Vol. 5 (1) https://doi.org/10.1080/15140326.2002.12040573

Scherer, F., 1967. Market structure and the employment of scientists and engineers. American Economic Review. Vol. 57, No. 3. https://www.jstor.org/stable/i331434.

A Literature Review on the Impact of Social Media Platforms on Small and Medium Enterprise (SMEs) Development

John Amoah
Tomas Bata University, Zlin, Czech Republic
amoah@utb.cz
DOI: 10.34190/EIE.20.226

Abstract: The paper accesses the impact of social media platforms (networks) on Small and Medium Enterprises (SMEs). The contribution of SMEs to the development of many developed and developing countries cannot be overemphasized in job creation and its significance to the contribution to their Gross Domestic Products (GDPs). Social media has taken dominance in the world and has subsequently introduced a new paradigm in the operations of businesses. The introduction of Smartphone has significantly informed the decisions by SMEs to deploy social media platforms (networks) for their operations. Despite growing interest in this area of research, knowledge gaps still exist, providing opportunities for further research to be conducted. A qualitative approach has been adopted in this research as a methodology, specifically, document analysis. The database of SCOPUS, WoS, and Google Scholar was the source of generating scientific papers via keywords search. The theoretical implication of this paper would add to the existing body of knowledge and contribute to filling the existing research gap in this research area. The results provided by this paper would help SME practitioners to obtain adequate information on the various social media platforms available for them to adopt, and how those platforms can contribute to their success. The study provides the basis for further research since it is purely a literature review.

Keywords: social media, SMEs, platforms (networks)

1. Introduction

Social media has taken dominance in the world and has subsequently introduced a new paradigm in the operations of businesses of Small and Medium Enterprises (SMEs). The contribution of SMEs to the development of many developed and developing countries cannot be overemphasized in job creation and significant contribution to Gross Domestic Products (GDPs)(Kwaku Amoah, 2018; Kumar, 2017).In addition, Kaplan & Haenlein, (2010)has defined social media as a group of internet-based applications that builds on the ideological and technological foundations of Web 2.0 which allows the creation and exchange of user-generated content. For customers or consumers who are on the lookout to obtain product or service information, social media platforms have become a significant source. Most Small and Medium Enterprise now have social media platforms that enable their customers to have access to most of the information they need about their products and services. A study by Darban and Li (2012) where they evaluated the impact of online social networks on the buying behavior of consumers, revealed that social media makes it possible to compare promotions, offers, and services from several businesses to find the best offer.

However, there are several social media outlets that Small and Medium Enterprises have to choose from to enjoy the benefits that social media brings to businesses. Most of the social media platforms used by SMEs include Facebook, LinkedIn, Instagram, and Twitter. Most SMEs at every point in time run promotions on at least, one of these platforms. These social media sites are amongst the popular sites in recent times. Nonetheless, the choice of the type of social media to be adopted by the SME is dependent on the number of individuals who patronize the social media platform, and how accessible the social media platform is (Greenwood, Perrin, &Duggan, 2016). Moreover, Kaplan & Haenlein, (2010) have indicated that social media has the advantage of delivering businesses to end-consumers directly, at a low price and on time. Similarly, social media facilitates two-way communication between individuals and business entities. This provides the opportunity to associate with other people, looping feedback effectively. Also, Georgi & Mink, (2013) disclosed that consumers and customers can interact with one another and retailers on social networking sites. Thus individuals can express freely their concerns and can receive an immediate reply from SMEs. Brand awareness, acquisition of information, purchase behavior, and post-purchase communication and evaluation are stages of consumer decision making processes that are considerably influenced by social media (Mangold and Faulds, 2009). Lee, (2013) conducted a study to describe why, when, and how social media had impacted the buying behavior of consumers. The study employed a quantitative research approach of which empirical data was collected by sending out questionnaires to individuals. Findings from the research revealed that before buying a product, consumers were extremely selective in processing, attending, and selecting information. Further findings indicated that collective feedbacks, particularly, access to word of mouth and customer experiences on social media affected the buying behavior of consumers.

Baruah, (2012) conducted a study on the usefulness of social media as a communication tool and its technology-enabled connections probability. Residents of Guwahati city in the urban areas of North-East India formed the respondents of the study. A sample of 200 respondents consisting of teachers, students, marketing professionals, engineers, and businessmen was included in the study. It was reported that social media technology is a very effective promotional tool since it has the capability of reaching audiences all over the world. Despite growing interest in this area of research, knowledge gaps still exist, providing opportunities for further research to be conducted.

The theoretical implication of this paper would add to the existing body of knowledge and contribute to filling the existing research gap in this research area. The results provided by this paper would help SMEs practitioners to obtain adequate information on the various social media platforms available for them to adopt, and how those platforms can contribute to their success. This paper is structured as follows; the key literature on social media on SMEs is reviewed. Section 3 is followed by the methodology and sources of data for the empirical analysis of social media on SMEs. The limitation and theory of practice are discussed in Section 4 and 5 respectively. The final part gives up with recommendations and suggestions for further research.

2. Literature review

2.1 Profitability/revenue generation

Social media platforms have impacted positively on the financial performance of SMEs and their business and organizational performance(Seiler, Papanagnou, and Scarf, 2020). A study on social media networks or platforms by Apenteng et al., (2020) revealed that there is a positive relationship in terms of profitability or revenue generation through the engagement of Facebook. The publication concluded that revenue generation has been increased by SMEs through this construct. Similarly, Gligor & Bozkurt, (2020) positively expressed that the widespread adoption of social media platforms has consequently increased customer engagement with the firms, leading to improved performance, and affecting the bottom-line through increased revenue generation by the SMEs. The introduction of social media platforms has solved the financial health of Small and Medium enterprises through the maintenance of customer relationship management(Nasir, 2015). Thus, social media is deemed as a key competitive advantage for businesses that seek growth and advancement(Bianchi & Andrews, 2015;)Kuchciak, 2013). For instance, Kuchciak (2013) highlighted that Twitter was used by the Bank of America to provide real-time solutions to customer's problems which resulted in significant improvement in their financial performance. Similar research by Street (2014) also provided that the retail giant, Amazon, through the adoption of Twitter in 2011 supported their business strategy in enhancing interactions between customers and the company. These changes saw significant changes in their financial position.

It thus supposes that these platforms or networks have altered the dynamism of the markets in terms of customer purchase and post-purchase. Extensive research by Odupitan (2017), highlighted that social media platforms such as Facebook, Instagram and Twitter have enhanced many fast-moving consumable goods of the food industry to improve upon their sales targets leading to increased profits. Similarly, Fuentes also agreed that social media platforms like WhatsApp and Facebook have increased the sales margins of most hotels in the hospitality industry of Small and Medium Enterprises after its adoption as a marketing tool. Because of this, we proposed that:

Proposition 1: Social media platforms relate positively to SME's profitability or revenue generation.

2.2 Communication and marketing enhancement

Social media platforms in postmodernism have made consumer and producer relationships very communicative. This factor has caused SMEs to frequently market and communicates with each other without any impediments(Poell, 2017; Ainin *et al.*, 2015)Extensive studies by Kaplan, (2012) about social media outlined that firms now used social media platforms for marketing research to improve upon customer communication, sales promotions or discounts and above all maintain a proper customer relationship with their customers. It was finalized that these social media networks have improved the communication channels of firms. Thus, there is efficiency in solving challenges as compared to the traditional ways of communication by television and radio.

Likewise, Lim et al., (2012) suggested that social media networks have made two- way conversation possible and easier for consumers and SMEs. However, the key functions of marketing departments such as promotion, product distribution, communication, management, and research have become easy to be carried out.

Social media networks have improved marketing strategies for SMEs. Thus, the promotion of products and services online has proven to be efficient and effective(Sokolova& Kefi, 2020). Also, Hwang & Zhang, (2018)outlined that the issue of parasocial relationship which existed between customers and product providers has been eliminated as a result of social media platforms. In this regard, both the customer and provider knows what exists and proceed to establish a more informative and trustworthy relationship than the traditional way of communication. Algharabat et al., (2020) in their publication of investigating the antecedents of customer brand engagement and consumer-based brand equity in social media finalized that three key factors are always factored by firms in marketing and communication enhancement that is consumer involvement, consumer participation, and self-expressive brand. A similar publication by Bianchi & Andrews, (2015)on marketing managers' perspectives on social media also concluded that social media platforms have impacted positively on the marketing practices of SMEs. Further, customer engagement, brand image enhancement, return on investment, and meeting consumer needs through time and place increase with the use of social media. Based on we propose that:

Proposition 2: Social media relates positively to communication and marketing enhancement in SMEs

2.3 Market expansion

Social Media platforms have become the modus operandi that Small and Medium Enterprise are using to expand their marketing accessibility in the 21st century that has influenced the buying behavior of consumers(Fortis et al., 2012). Also, Shao *et al.*, (2016) pointed out that platforms such as Facebook have changed the consumer pattern of consumption hence affecting SMEs positively. Research by Groeger and Buttle, (2016)revealed that social media networks like Facebook, YouTube, and Twitter have impacted positively on the lives of consumers' communication habits of consumption. It is considered that consumers are always in close contact with brands and products by reading, watching, commenting, liking, and sharing causing SMEs to expand their markets to meet the demands of the market. Ainin *et al.*, (2015) also investigated the factors influencing social media by SMEs and concluded that a social media platform like Facebook has impacted positively on the market expansion activities of SMEs because Facebook has now become a popular choice of promoting business. This platform allows communications to go beyond private and evolves into a conversation that is easily followed by many users. Therefore, business owners now fully use Facebook for selling, advertising, and marketing at a relatively cheaper cost. SMEs thus do this promotion by sharing, tagging, messaging, commenting, and notifying.

Small and Medium Enterprises have expanded their market base through the creation of value for the customer, identifying the value stream, creating flow, producing only what is pulled by the customer, and continuous improvement by continuously identifying and eliminating waste (Ghezzi and Cavallo, 2020). In the study of Acquisti and Fong(2020), it is established social networks have created channels for SMEs to facilitate and improve the firm's and consumers' markets. Keegan and Rowley(2017), adds that social networks improve the market linkage of SMEs and their consumers than the traditional marketing channels, centering on the two-way communication or exchange. This has improved their engagement in existing social media conservations to protect their corporate and brand reputation. In response to this, we propose:

Proposition 3: Social media positively influences Market Expansion in SMEs

2.4 Growth and developments

Small and Medium Enterprises have seen tremendous changes in their growth and developments as a result of social media platforms or networks. The growth and development of SMEs have peaked in recent times since these platforms have birthed innovation among firms. Further, it has enabled these firms to modify and adapt their products and services and enhanced new product development(Ghezzi and Cavallo, 2020). In similar literature by Scott and Orlikowski(2012), it was established that social media networks have brought about fair growth and development through online accountability which has been a key part of the processes of Small and Medium enterprises. Thus, social media platforms provide a system for growth and development data generation, which has become a very powerful tool for today's SMEs in its developments by serving its consumers right and at the right time. Therefore we propose that:

Proposition 4: Social media networks or platforms associate positively with growth and development in SMEs

Following the literature review and the corresponding proposition, we conceptualized a framework in figure 1 below:

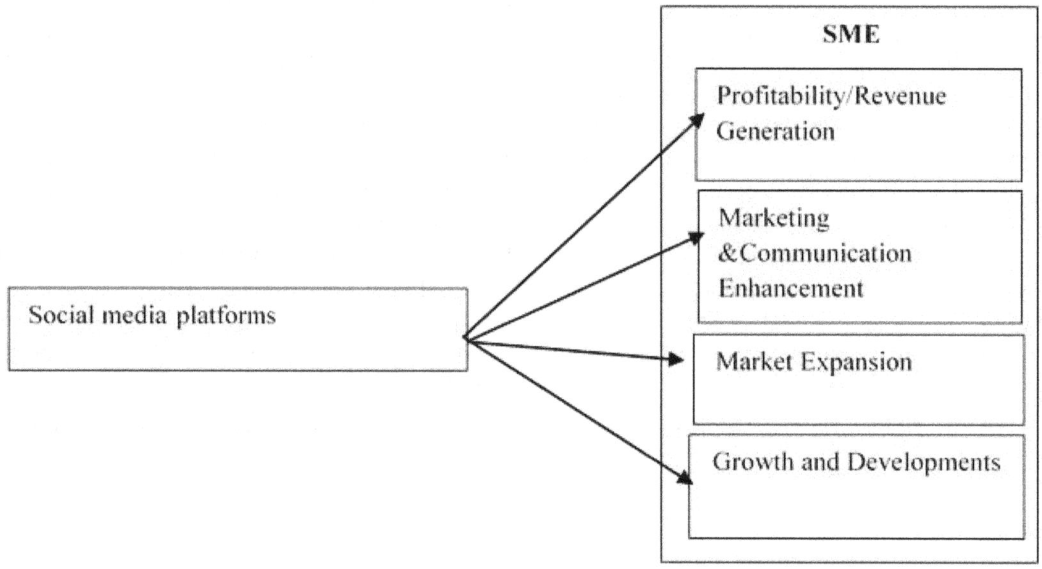

Figure 1: Conceptual model of the study. Source: Author's own

3. Methodology

This paper adopted the qualitative method as the main approach for the work. Document analysis was used as the key technique for this study. Bowen, (2009)defines document analysis by using both printed and electronic materials for reviewing and evaluating documents to arrive at a meaningful conclusion. The adoption of document analysis provided enough grounds for relevant information and contents for this study which also proved positive for this study (Keles, Mccrae and Grealish, 2020; Maharani and Gozali, 2015). Scopus, WoS, and Google Scholar databases were used for searching for information via keywords search using the titles, keywords, and abstracts ranging from 2008 to 2020. Because of the objective in mind, forty one papers were reviewed for the study out of the numerous publications downloaded. All the publications downloaded were published in English.

Also, some information from secondary sources related to the topic was reviewed as part of the method for the research. Other readers and researchers are encouraged to find interest in the research works of ((Tajudeen, Jaafar, and Ainin, 2018; Wardati & Er, 2019; Ainin, Parveen, and Moghavvemi, 2015; Owen, 2014) by conducting a qualitative survey.

4. Limitations of the paper

This study could have been strengthened by including several other popular electronic databases that publish on SMEs to provide a larger base and a holistic view of the dominant issues identified and discussed in this review. Furthermore, articles that we did not have full access to in some databases could not be reviewed as part of this study.

5. Theoretical and practical implications

The topic under discussion has both theoretical and practical implications for research and industry. A significant outcome of this research is to offer knowledge to Small and Medium Enterprises and other industry players on the various social media platforms or networks that are available for their consideration and subsequent adoption which can positively contribute to their success. Secondly, this research establishes that these social media platforms and tools would benefit SMEs in terms of creating meaningful relationships with customers, learning about the audience, improving market intelligence, and discovering new customers. Further, its adoption is likely to ensure instant customer feedback, increase brand awareness, and increase the firms' scope and reach. For SMEs, this research also establishes that social media provides benefits such as increasing sales volume and profitability, improving sourcing for financial assistance, and the maintenance of a solid financial position.

On the other hand, the theoretical implication of this paper would add to the existing body of knowledge and contribute to filling the existing research gap in this research area, and provide insights into the various social media platforms that Small and Medium Enterprise can leverage on for their operations.

6. Suggestions for future research and conclusions

In conclusion, the work established a link between social media platforms and their impacts on Small and Medium enterprises. The researcher has shown that Small and Medium Enterprises can reliably use social media platforms to improve their profitability or revenue generation, communication, and marketing enhancement, market expansion and growth and developments since the use of the traditional way of communication of products and services to customers is becoming obsolete.

Again, there are various reasons why going forward, SMEs must adopt the use of social media platforms especially in developing countries where this phenomenon is emerging, as it can strengthen their base for operations, satisfying customers, and above all improving the financial status or performance.

Because qualitative methodology was used for the study, it therefore, gives room for future suggestions and research. The researcher has proposed a conceptual framework model (Figure 1)showing the relationship between profitability or revenue generation, communication and marketing enhancement, market expansion, and growth and development on SME's platforms or networks. Some literature on media and modernity theory and resource mobilization theory was also reviewed since the entire work is yet to be tested empirically. Moreover, other different approaches can be used for detailed future research on the said topic.

Acknowledgements

This work is supported by Tomas Bata University in Zlin through; IGA/FaME/2019/002. The role of the institutional environment in fostering entrepreneurship.

References

Acquisti, A. and Fong, C. (2020) 'An experiment in hiring discrimination via online social networks', *Management Science*, 66(3), pp. 1005–1024. DOI: 10.1287/mnsc.2018.3269.

Ahmed, I. *et al.* (2013) 'Employee performance evaluation: A fuzzy approach', *International Journal of Productivity and Performance Management*, 62(7), pp. 718–734. DOI: 10.1108/IJPPM-01-2013-0013.

Ainin, S. *et al.* (2015) 'Factors influencing the use of social media by SMEs and its performance outcomes', *Industrial Management and Data Systems*, 115(3), pp. 570–588. DOI: 10.1108/IMDS-07-2014-0205.

Ainin, S., Parveen, F. and Moghavvemi, S. (2015) 'Factors influencing the use of social media by SMEs and its performance outcomes'. DOI: 10.1108/IMDS-07-2014-0205.

Algharabat, R. *et al.* (2020) 'Investigating the antecedents of customer brand engagement and consumer-based brand equity in social media', *Journal of Retailing and Consumer Services*. Elsevier Ltd, 53(October 2018), p. 101767. DOI: 10.1016/j.jretconser.2019.01.016.

Apenteng, B. A. *et al.* (2020) 'Examining the relationship between social media engagement and hospital revenue', *Health Marketing Quarterly*. Routledge, 37(1), pp. 10–21. DOI: 10.1080/07359683.2020.1713575.

Baruah, T. D. (2012) 'Effectiveness of Social Media as a tool of communication and its potential for technology-enabled connections: A micro-level study', *International Journal of Scientific and Research Publications*, 2(5), pp. 1–10. DOI: ISSN 2250-3153.

Bianchi, C. and Andrews, L. (2015) 'Investigating marketing managers' perspectives on social media in Chile', *Journal of Business Research*. Elsevier Inc., 68(12), pp. 2552–2559. DOI: 10.1016/j.jbusres.2015.06.026.

Bowen, G. A. (2009) 'Document analysis as a qualitative research method', *Qualitative Research Journal*, 9(2), pp. 27–40. DOI: 10.3316/QRJ0902027.

Darban, A., and Li, W. 2012. The impact of online social networks on consumers' purchasing decision: The study of food retailers'. *Master, Jonkoping University*.

Fotis, J., Buhalis, D. and Rossides, N. (2012) 'Social Media Use and Impact during the Holiday Travel Planning Process', *Information and Communication Technologies in Tourism 2012*, pp. 13–24. DOI: 10.1007/978-3-7091-1142-02.

Fuentes, I. C. O. (2017) 'Master in hospitality management business plan of repositioning ñaupa house hostel (December).

Greenwood, S., Perrin, A., and Duggan, M., 2016. Social media update 2016. *Pew Research Center, 11*(2).

Georgi, D. and Mink, M. (2013) 'Journal of Retailing and Consumer Services eCCIq : The quality of electronic customer-to-customer interaction', *Journal of Retailing and Consumer Services*. Elsevier, 20(1), pp. 11–19. DOI: 10.1016/j.jretconser.2012.08.002.

Ghezzi, A. and Cavallo, A. (2020) 'Agile Business Model Innovation in Digital Entrepreneurship: Lean Startup Approaches', *Journal of Business Research*. Elsevier, 110(February 2017), pp. 519–537. DOI: 10.1016/j.jbusres.2018.06.013.

Gligor, D. and Bozkurt, S. (2020) 'FsQCA versus regression: The context of customer engagement', *Journal of Retailing and Consumer Services*. Elsevier Ltd, 52(March 2019), p. 101929. DOI: 10.1016/j.jretconser.2019.101929.

Groeger, L. and Buttle, F. (2016) 'preprint - ze złym opisem Deciphering Word-of-Mouth Marketing Campaign Reach.', *Journal of Advertising Research*, 56(4), pp. 368–384. DOI: 10.2501/JAR-2016-000.

Hwang, K. and Zhang, Q. (2018) 'Influence of parasocial relationship between digital celebrities and their followers on followers' purchase and electronic word-of-mouth intentions, and persuasion knowledge', *Computers in Human Behavior*. Elsevier B.V., 87, pp. 155–173. DOI: 10.1016/j.chb.2018.05.029.

Kaplan, A. M. (2012) 'If you love something, let it go mobile: Mobile marketing and mobile social media 4x4', *Business Horizons*. 'Kelley School of Business, Indiana University', 55(2), pp. 129–139. DOI: 10.1016/j.bushor.2011.10.009.

Kaplan, A. M., and Haenlein, M. (2010) 'Users of the world, unite! The challenges and opportunities of Social Media', *Business Horizons*. DOI: 10.1016/j.bushor.2009.09.003.

Keegan, B. J. and Rowley, J. (2017) 'Management Decision Evaluation and decision making in social media marketing', *Management Decision Journal of Research in Interactive Marketing Journal of Small Business and Enterprise Development*, 55(4), pp. 15–31. Available at: https://www.emeraldinsight.com/doi/abs/10.1108/MD-10-2015-

Keles, B., Mccrae, N. and Grealish, A. (2020) 'A systematic review : the influence of social media on depression, anxiety and psychological distress in adolescents', *International Journal of Adolescence and Youth*. Routledge, 25(1), pp. 79–93. DOI: 10.1080/02673843.2019.1590851.

Kuchciak, I. (2013) 'How Social Media will Change the Future of Banking Services', pp. 1–5. DOI: 10.7763/IPEDR.

Kumar, R. (2017) 'Targeted SME Financing and Employment Effects', *Targeted SME Financing and Employment Effects*, (3). DOI: 10.1596/27477.

Kwaku Amoah, S. (2018) 'The Role of Small and Medium Enterprises (SMEs) to Employment in Ghana', *International Journal of Business and Economics Research*, 7(5), p. 151. DOI: 10.11648/j.ijber.20180705.14.

Lee, E. (2013) 'Impacts of Social Media on Consumer Behavior– Decision Making Process', *Bachelor's thesis*, pp. 1–77.

Lim, Y., Chung, Y. and Weaver, P. A. (2012) 'The impact of social media on destination branding: Consumer-generated videos versus destination marketer-generated videos', *Journal of Vacation Marketing*, 18(3), pp. 197–206. DOI: 10.1177/1356766712449366.

Maharani, W., and Gozali, A. A. (2015) 'Collaborative Social Network Analysis and Content-based Approach to Improve the Marketing Strategy of SMEs in Indonesia', *Procedia Computer Science*. Elsevier Masson SAS, 59(Iccsci), pp. 373–381. DOI: 10.1016/j.procs.2015.07.540.

Mangold, W. G. and Faulds, D. J. (2009) 'Social media : The new hybrid element of the promotion mix'. DOI: 10.1016/j.bushor.2009.03.002.

Nasir, S. (2015) *Customer relationship management strategies in the digital era, Customer Relationship Management Strategies in the Digital Era*. DOI: 10.4018/978-1-4666-8231-3.

Odupitan, A. T. (2017) 'Understanding the distribution channels of fast-moving consumable goods (FMCG) of the food industry in Nigeria'.

Owen, G. T. (2014) 'Qualitative methods in higher education policy analysis: Using interviews and document analysis', *Qualitative Report*, 19(26), pp. 1–19.

Öztamur, D., and Karakadılar, İ. S. (2014) 'Exploring the Role of Social Media for SMEs: As a New Marketing Strategy Tool for the Firm Performance Perspective', *Procedia - Social and Behavioral Sciences*, 150, pp. 511–520. DOI: 10.1016/j.sbspro.2014.09.067.

Poell, T. (2017) 'UvA-DARE (Digital Academic Repository) The Affordances of Social Media Platforms', pp. 223–253.

Scott, S. V., and Orlikowski, W. J. (2012) 'Reconfiguring relations of accountability: Materialization of social media in the travel sector', *Accounting, Organizations, and Society*. Elsevier Ltd, 37(1), pp. 26–40. DOI: 10.1016/j.aos.2011.11.005.

Seiler, A., Papanagnou, C. and Scarf, P. (2020) 'On the relationship between financial performance and position of businesses in supply chain networks', *International Journal of Production Economics*. Elsevier B.V., 227, p. 107690. DOI: 10.1016/j.ijpe.2020.107690.

Shao, C. *et al.* (2016) 'Hoaxy: A Platform for Tracking Online Misinformation', pp. 745–750. DOI: 10.1145/2872518.2890098.

Sokolova, K. and Kefi, H. (2020) 'Instagram and YouTube bloggers promote it, why should I buy? How credibility and parasocial interaction influence purchase intentions', *Journal of Retailing and Consumer Services*. Elsevier Ltd, 53(January), p. 101742. DOI: 10.1016/j.jretconser.2019.01.011.

Street, B. (2014) 'Institute of Transport and Logistics Studies Unit of Study Outline', pp. 1–11.

Tajudeen, F. P., Jaafar, N. I. and Ainin, S. (2018) 'Understanding the impact of social media usage among organizations', *Information and Management*. Elsevier B.V., 55(3), pp. 308–321. DOI: 10.1016/j.im.2017.08.004.

Wardati, N. K. and Er, M. (2019) 'The impact of social media usage on the sales process in small and medium enterprises (SMEs): A systematic literature review', *Procedia Computer Science*. Elsevier B.V., 161, pp. 976–983. DOI: 10.1016/j.procs.2019.11.207.

Experiences From University Entrepreneurship Education: Using a Broader Perspective

Thomas Arctaedius[1] and Andreas Nilsson[2] and Karin Hjertzell[1]
[1]Royal College of Music, Academy of Classical Music, Stockholm Sweden
[2]Swedish Center for Digital Innovation
thomas.arctaedius@kmh.se
DOI: 10.34190/EIE.20.120

Abstract: There has been a significant academic increase in the field of entrepreneurship since 2010, this has resulted in dramatic increase of organizational- as well as course initiatives at universities across the globe. There is an ongoing debate regarding suitable ways to teach entrepreneurship spanning between arguments for more theoretical- or more practical approaches. Entangled in higher education uptake of entrepreneurship is also the concept of innovation, and student- and faculty driven innovation initiatives. In this paper, we present experiences from action research engagement in building, scaling and exporting entrepreneurship education and university innovation strategy during a 10 year period. We present data from eight action – reflection cycles. Findings are presented in a discussion format as implications for entrepreneurship course development, and implications for university innovation management. Implications for course development are to i) teach entrepreneurship "as a method", ii) push for interdisciplinary classes, iii) emphasize group projects, and finally iv) use entrepreneurial witnesses. Implications for university innovation strategy are to i) use a broad definition of the concept, ii) own the agenda, iii) nurture early phases of ideas, and finally iv) build the innovation ecosystem.

Keywords: entrepreneurship education, experiences, strategy, higher education, arts

1. Introduction

Over the last years there has been an explosion of entrepreneurship educations. In the United States, the number of entrepreneurship and small business management courses have grown in acceptance at an accelerated pace From the start of entrepreneurship educations approximately 70 years ago, the field has developed to a diverse range of educational opportunities available at almost every university. In Sweden, the number of courses and programs with the term entrepreneurship in the name has risen from 152 fall term 2019 to 219 fall term 2020 (from the Swedish Council for Higher Education website over all course and program in Sweden https://www.antagning.se)

There are many actors urging for the attention of individuals looking to expand their understanding of entrepreneurship and possibly start a business. In addition to the traditional actors such as universities and other education providers, there are commercially driven initiatives associated with sales of products and services to the start-up ventures; this includes offices, legal services, business advice and financing services to name a few. It is common that these services are provided in packages under an "incubation" or "start-up" label. In addition, incumbent organizations engage in various initiatives to increase their level of innovation through Corporate Entrepreneurship (Morris et al 2010). A very interesting contribution about the interplay between entrepreneurship and innovation is provided by McFadzean et al (2005).

It is a complex and extensively debated subject how higher education is best to serve society with regards to the content of their offerings, arguments span from teaching students how to think, (as they will learn the job on the job) all the way to teaching students skills that makes them as "employable" as possible (Knight and Yorke, 2004). The role of higher education in teaching entrepreneurship may be seen from this lens arguing for a more theoretical- or practical approach. Hoppe (2016) gives a solid account for how entrepreneurship has been shifting from "entrepreneurship" to "entrepreneurial learning" to "entrepreneurial culture".

This also impacts the overall strategic approach and view of entrepreneurship and innovation held by the school. What kind of support (if any) should be provided to students and faculty interested in pursuing an entrepreneurial initiative? We are researchers, entrepreneurs and senior managers at higher education and generally agree with a more practice-oriented approach towards entrepreneurship education and innovation strategy.

A few schools stand out as extraordinary successful when output oriented measures e.g. number of patents, number of started companies, turnover of started companies etc. One successful example is Massachusetts

Institute of Technology (MIT), they have a clear strategy how to support and nurture early phases of ideas and team composition all the way from vague student concept to established firm. They have an integrated approach to their alumni strategy. An extensive overview of their approach and impact is provided by Roberts et al (2019).

In this paper, we reflect on experiences from building entrepreneurship education and university innovation strategy in Scandinavia and Eastern Europe between 2009 and 2020. The reflection is done from an action research methodology as proposed by Kemmis et al (2013).

Our investigation is guided by the overall research question:

How can we continuously develop and improve entrepreneurship education and university innovation strategy?

The results of our study are presented as a set of implications for entrepreneurship course development, and university innovation management. The paper is organized as follows: first we provide an introduction the to field and present our research initiative, this is followed by the theoretical section giving an overview of the foundation we base our approach on, this is followed by a method part outlining our action research iterations. The results section details main content of each action – reflection iteration. The paper concludes with a discussion and implications for research and practitioners.

2. Theory

Teachers in entrepreneurship teach based on inspiration from one-, or a combination of three "worlds", beautifully described by Neck and Green (2011). The worlds are called i) The Entrepreneurial world, ii) The process world, and iii) The cognition world.

The Entrepreneurial World idolizes the entrepreneur as a "super person" with extraordinary skills and talent. The role model entrepreneur is almost exclusively a white male, and success is measured on a financial scale. Teaching is conducted in traditional stand and deliver approach complemented by guest speakers following this worlds definition of "successful entrepreneur". Students are taught to Observe, Describe and Measure following basic categorizations.

As the name implies, The Process World teach entrepreneurship as a step-by-step, linear journey from Opportunity identification, Concept development, Resource requirements, Implementation and Exit (Morris, 1998). The approach builds on the notion of planning and prediction. This approach is the most common to teach, courses emphasize on opportunity evaluation, feasibility analysis and business forecasting.

The Cognition World is a refocus on the entrepreneur or the entrepreneur team. The perspective focus on learning, how to "think entrepreneurially" to identify opportunities and comparative advantage. It includes aspects such as the decision to become an entrepreneur, how to handle "gut feelings" but more importantly the dynamics between think – do. The perspective includes use cases and simulations in the classroom and stresses the duality of the decision-making and venture process.

The definition of entrepreneurship has developed over the year from starting out in a business use of the word where economic value creation was in focus emphasising start-ups and risk-taking developing in to adding entrepreneurial activities that encompass a social responsibility by focusing on other types of value creation than economic value.

Entrepreneurship in the arts are unlike many traditional, business-oriented industries, where creative and cultural industries often built up by networks of freelancers and small to medium-sized companies (Creigh-Tyte and Thomas, 2001). These networks are often re-created and transformed, which means that business is often carried out in time-limited projects and contracts. Paul Dimaggio (1981) introduced the term cultural entrepreneurship to his article "Cultural entrepreneurship in nineteenth-century Boston: the creation of an organizational base for high culture in America" where he uses the term to describe a grouping and their work that was behind the emergence by independent cultural institutions. J.C White wrote in his article "Toward a Theory of Arts Entrepreneurship" (2015):

"Arts Entrepreneurship refers to the process of overcoming common challenges and historical barriers to the production, distribution, exhibition and preservation of art."

The concept of entrepreneurship is often interpreted by musicians and artists with a traditional, new business creation approach by associating the concept of creating financial profit and commercial success. This type of association with the concept of entrepreneurship means that for people who value their work based on creativity and artistic success higher than financial gain, entrepreneurship becomes somewhat unattractive and even negative. (Pollard & Wilson, 2013) Many artists believe that "money destroys art" (Beckman, 2007). Such a view of entrepreneurship makes many at art / music colleges and universities negative to entrepreneurship and has difficulty accepting entrepreneurship as a subject at school. Arctaedius and Nilsson presents an interesting start-up case following the digitalization of choir management driven by artist (2019)

3. Method

Action research as a scientific method of inquiry dates back to the 1940s and Kurt Lewins theory of "proceeding in a spiral of steps, each of which is composed of planning, action and the evaluation of the result of action" (Kemmis and McTaggert 1990). Others claim origins back to the Science in education movement of the late nineteenth century (McKernan 1991). In this paper, we follow the broad definition of Action research by McCutcheon and Jung "systemic inquiry that is collective, collaborative, self-reflective, critical and undertaken by participants in the inquiry" (McCutcheon and Jung 1990).

As researchers and teachers, we have a mixed academic background from the scientific disciplines of nuclear physics, information systems and fine arts. We share a passion for entrepreneurship and have started and successfully built several companies in combination with academic work. We find the action research approach suitable when developing entrepreneurship education and university innovation strategy as it enables us to be heavily engaged in driving change and still reflect and draw learning from the context, we engage in.

We are applying a rudimentary approach during a 10-year period iterating between stages of Reflection/Planning and Action. The Reflection/Planning stages comprise of course evaluation and learning workshops, the Action stages comprise of many different activities the main one being execution of courses and dissemination of learning to build larger network.

Below Figure 1 gives an overview of the stages in a timeline, Step A1 – A8 and R1 – R8 are described in chapter Results. As a final step, we conducted an overall reflection iteration (R9) taking the complete journey into consideration.

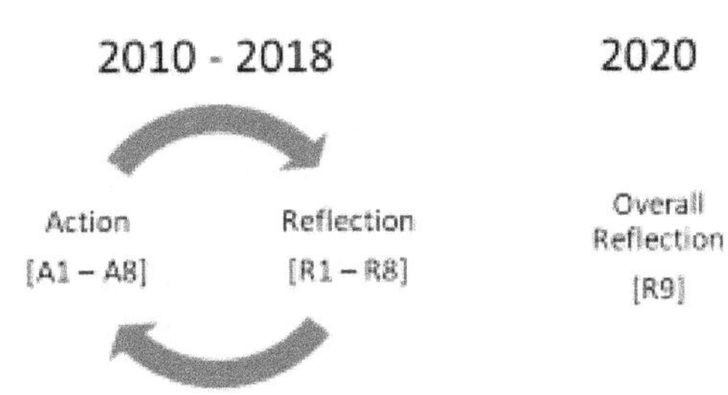

Figure 1: Action - reflection iterations between 2010 and 2020.

4. Results

Our action kicks off during the fall of 2010 when we were put in charge of delivering an entrepreneurship course at Stockholm university at the department of computer science. We came from different scientific disciplines but shared previous entrepreneurial experience and a strong passion to engage in teaching entrepreneurship.

Below account of action, reflection iterations list the main contents:

A1 2010

Development of elective course targeted first year students of game development program at computer Science department at Stockholm University motivated by the fact that the job-situation for game developers was getting increasingly competitive.

The course was developed in collaboration with the university incubator, Stockholm University Innovation. Focus on giving students skills in identifying business opportunities and creating a strong business plan. Course literature was on how to write a business plan and test it

R1 2010

Very positive feedback from students.

Students appears lack ability to understand entrepreneurship from a practical perspective. They have low or no insights into market mechanisms. Students need to meet and talk with more practitioners i.e. "real entrepreneurs".

Challenging but important to have carefully developed practical assignments as part of the course.

As educators, we are missing a forum for thought exchange and course development. Also, we are missing an international perspective.

A2 2011

Updating the course to fit an international target group of students switching language in course from Swedish to English and including a wider student group, not only game-developers. Adding project work in teams to develop a short business plan

Included guest lectures from entrepreneurs every week.

R2 2011

Very successful evaluation of the guest lectures.

How can we provide more international experience and perspective of entrepreneurship?

Many entrepreneurial ventures are triggered within incumbent organizations, does/how does this impact education?

A3 2012

Collaboration with four different universities across Sweden, Ukraine and Georgia backed by funding from Swedish institute enables us to develop the course to be given in a more blended mode type of set-up

Shift in focus from Business plan to using ideas from Lean Start up (Ries 2011) and Business model generation (Osterwalder, Pigneur 2010) Adding the Canvas model to the project work.

Part of the practical work now includes possibility to work with an "intrapreneurship" project.

Performed a study of entrepreneurship education in the Baltic region, including Georgia and Ukraine.Missing engagement from other parts of the university led to increased communication and sharing of results internally.

R3 2012

How can we get more input and help from other parts of the university?

Need to get entrepreneurship on the strategic agenda of the university.

Student project teams with inter-disciplinary representation outperform intra-disciplinary teams.

A push towards the necessity of learning about models, tools, and methods for entrepreneurship rather than "How to become an entrepreneur"

A4 2013

Establishment of international student internship allowing students to have a one-month internship at innovation companies in another country. Pushing students into further inter-disciplinary work and environments.

Remaking the course material based on the "Method World" idea as described by Neck and Green. Results so far summarized in Best practice entrepreneurship education report with funding from Swedish institute.

R4 2013

Lot of attention related to the internship led to some positive publicity and opportunities.

Missing non-commercial aspects of entrepreneurship and how to treat the many different goals and ambitions that entrepreneurs have for starting a company.

New Swedish and EU-level Social innovation strategy shows interest and strength in social entrepreneurship

A5 2014

Collaboration with Center for Social entrepreneurship in Sweden (http://cses.se/) to include parts on social entrepreneurship and factors that are special for social entrepreneurs in way of working. Including new guest from start-ups with other goals of value creation than economic value.

R5 2014

Course and university consolidation period, not a lot of major changes there. Lack of energy and push.

A6 2016

New energy infusion from collaboration project financed by the Swedish institute. The project targeted innovation strategy development on international level and establishment of eco-system of companies surrounding the university capable of facilitating students and ideas at their earliest stage. Visit to MIT and Babson for inspiration and benchmarking.

R6 2016

Lack of support at the earliest stages after idea creation. Existing structures (at the universities) to quickly started with formal processes to protect IP, build prototype etc.

There is no slack, place where the potential entrepreneur can work on refining the idea embryo before it is mature (and good) enough start more formal innovation processes.

A7 2017

Creation of "The room", an actual room where students and faculty meet and in a very open and casual way pitch and work on their ideas in a very informal and uncontrolled manner. A type of open space pre incubator physical space with peer-learning and inspiration. The needs of the idea and the initiator is the guiding principle.

R7 2017

Need to increase the student mix to include not only tech and natural sciences. Lack of true interdisciplinary approach. Many of the student assignments and solutions bare traces of a product from homogeneous thinking, and not much "outside the box". Lack of creativity.

Need from the students and faculty to get support and guidance related to specific technologies gaining massive traction and attention on the market to see if / how it is possible to create companies in this space.

Paper presented at the Nordic Academy of Management conference in Bodö (Arctaedius & Nilsson 2017)

A8 2018

Work with Royal College of Music in Stockholm KMH to develop a version of the course for music student. The work is made together with a project group from different departments at KMH. Interviews with Alumni to gather information on what previous students felt they should have been taught while at KMH. The concept of "artistic core" of individuals is used as a starting point rather than "innovation". The course and other types of entrepreneurial support (Extra-curricular program, coaching etc) is made as an strategic agenda for KMH.

R8 2018

Many challenges internally at KMH to gain acceptance and understanding of entrepreneurship as there is a tension between art and commerce/market. But also, a lot of curiosity and many students signing up for the courses.

The course is decided to be a mandatory course for all students at Royal College of Music.

5. Discussion

This section presents the result of a final overall reflection (R9) comprising the complete timeframe spanning between 2010 – 2018. Our discussion is presented as a set of implications for course development and university innovation strategy.

5.1 Implications for course development

- 1 Teach entrepreneurship as a method

The course is design is heavily influenced by Neck and Green (2011) and the overall "Babson approach" of teaching Entrepreneurship as a method. They argue to go beyond understanding, knowing, and talking to Using, Applying and Acting. Teaching entrepreneurship as a method includes a way of thinking and acting built on a set of assumptions using a portfolio of techniques to encourage creation. Through this approach, the student will practice acting creatively in situations with high uncertainties.

The teaching is based on activities that make entrepreneurship both accessible and transactional using a type of anti-realism in education philosophy – pragmatism. Pragmatism used as synonymous with instrumentalization and experimentalism. This makes the course student and experience centred, with the teachers focusing on empowering the students in fulfilling personal goals. The education pushes for acquisition and modification of knowledge on entrepreneurship tolls and methods.

- 2 Push for interdisciplinary classes/groups

The quality of student projects done in teams are significantly better when teams are not only represented by one gender or one academic discipline. The benefits from mixed and interdisciplinary approaches are of course well known, but still a challenge to achieve. Our experience is that it requires active involvement from course leaders when teams are to be formed. Courses that are given for multidepartment students groups seems to work better than single departments classes (Boni et al 2017, Antal et al 2014) In Stockholm a special organization – Stockholm School of entrepreneurship (https://www.sses.se/) makes it possible to gives courses over five different universities creating very mixed student groups. Letting the teacher be involving in the team composition, it is possible to maximize student learning opportunities in this respect.

- 3 Let students work in groups with innovative/entrepreneurial project

Have the students form project teams around an idea for an innovative project or a start-up. TO allow the group practical work based on learning in the course adds practical understanding to concepts introduced in the course. Activities within the group work gives the students possibilities to apply creativity in the entrepreneurship process using Canvas and prototyping. Which has been shown to be a successful method (Rahm 2019)

One part of the practical assignment for the teams is to formulate a pitch, an attractive and short summary of the general idea. In addition, the students are asked to repeatedly deliver the pitch in front of the class and receive instant feedback.

There are also other ways to get the learning experience and benefit from preparing and conducting pitches, Queensland University encourages post grad student to pitch their research ideas with successful results of reach and relevance (Faff et al 2017).

- 4 Invite entrepreneurial witnesses

By having experienced entrepreneurs of different sorts coming to class and telling their story, the students will hear different versions of what it is like to be an entrepreneur. When possible, use witnesses sharing stories with a connection to theoretical aspects currently covered, as an example, it is good to have a witness with a story related to venture capital when this topic is currently being covered.

Important to have an open mind as to who is an entrepreneur, what is to be determined as a success, and encourage stores that did not end in success, but rather big failures. It is not difficult to invite entrepreneurs to come and share their story, they are usually very open (and love to share their stories).

In addition to learning from the stories, the students also get the chance to expand their view of who and what is a successful entrepreneur to have additional role models to the ones being pushed by the popular media channels (usually a white middle aged man with significant monetary success). Wyrwich et al (2016) presents an interesting study of the importance of entrepreneurship role models and the fear of failure.

5.2 Implications for university innovation strategy

In his book Creating the entrepreneurial university, Clark (1998) describes how universities transform themselves towards becoming Entrepreneurial Universities by five elements: a strengthened steering core; an expanded developmental periphery; a diversified funding base; a stimulated academic heartland; and an integrated entrepreneurial culture. Three of these "pillars" relates directly to what we experienced during our work with establishing entrepreneurship education and support.

Entrepreneurship education and support to entrepreneurial students must be aligned with and supported by university strategies for innovation and development. This is part of what Clark refers to as a "strengthened steering core". The "expanded developmental periphery" involves how to find new and strengthening ways to work with a new periphery of now traditional units. The entrepreneurial culture is about creating a work culture that embraces change.

- 1 Use a broad and modern definition of Innovation and entrepreneurship

To include many different parts of the university and to include students and researchers from the humanities and arts departments, the universities need to use a broad definition of entrepreneurship. The following definition of entrepreneurship, from the Swedish Business Development Agency, allows for many to take interest and be included in the "entrepreneurship world":

Entrepreneurship is a dynamic and social process, where individuals, alone or in co-operation, identify opportunities and do something with them to reshape ideas to practical or aimed activities in social, cultural, or economical contexts. (Berglund & Holmgren, 2013)

- 2 Own the agenda

Universities must take ownership of the entrepreneurship agenda and make strategic decisions on management level on how to develop and use entrepreneurship education and support to strengthen both education and research at the university. This means the involvement into development of an entrepreneurship agenda from both managerial and research levels at the university.

- 3 Nurture early phase ideas

University must nurture early phase ideas and not push them to market prematurely. Within the university ideas that are created from students and researchers are "early" in the sense that they have not been validated towards technology development or market potential. The process of validation and valorized of an idea should be made within the university organization and not pushing students and researcher too early to external organizations or to the market. A positive contribution by the pre-incubator was found by Voisey et al (2013) in a longitudinal study over 10 years.

- 4 Build the innovation ecosystem

University must plan and build conscious relationships with surrounding eco-system of external organizations. The University role is not to develop tech parks or incubators but rather to base on its own agenda and strategic decisions develop partnership with external private and public organizations that can support students and researcher in the development of new commercial ventures. It is crucial that the universities themselves always keep control of these partnership and makes clear rules on how and to what level the external organization can operate inside the universities. A framework for developing a university based innovation eco-system has been described by Cohen Mike (2016)

References

Antal N, Kingman B, Moore D, Streeter D (2014) University wide entrepreneurship education. Innovative Pathways for University Entrepreneurship in the 21st Century, Emerald Group Publishing,

Arctaedius, T., & Nilsson, A. (2017). Sharing Nordic Entrepreneurship Education in Eastern Europe, 24th Nordic Academy of Management conference

Arctaedius, T., & Nilsson, A. (2019). The ScorX Story: Temporal Order of Actions in Early Phase Start-ups. In European Conference on Innovation and Entrepreneurship (pp. 80-XXIII). Academic Conferences International Limited

Cohen Mike (2016) Strategies for Developing University Innovation Ecosystems: An Analysis, Segmentation and Strategic Framework Based on Somewhat Non-Intuitive and Slightly Controversial Findings, les Nouvelles - The Journal of the Licensing Executive Society, September: 184-190.

Gary D. Beckman (2007) "Adventuring" Arts Entrepreneurship Curricula in Higher Education: An Examination of Present Efforts, Obstacles, and Best Practices, The Journal of Arts Management, Law, and Society, 37:2, 87-112

Berglund, K., & Holmgren, C. (2013). Entrepreneurship education in policy and practice. International Journal of Entrepreneurial Venturing, 5(1), 9-27.

Arthur A. Boni , Laurie R. Weingart and Shelley Evenson (2017) Academy of Management Learning & Education Vol. 8, No. 3 Exemplary Contributions Innovation in an Academic Setting: Designing and Leading a Business Through Market-Focused, Interdisciplinary Teams

Carlsson, R. Curtis and Wilmot, W.William. (2006). Innovation - The Five Disciplines for Creating What Customers Want. New York: Crown Business 10: 0-307-33669-7.

Charney, Alberta, and Gary D. Libecap (2000). Impact of entrepreneurship education. Kansas City, MO: Kauffman Center for Entrepreneurial Leadership.

Clark, Burton R. (1998) Creating Entrepreneurial Universities: Organizational Pathways of Transformation. Issues in Higher Education. Elsevier Science Regional Sales, 665 Avenue of the Americas, New York, NY 10010 (paperback: ISBN-0-08-0433545; hardcover: ISBN-0-08-0433421, $27)

Creigh-Tyte A and Thomas B (2001) Employment. In: Selwood S (ed.) The UK Cultural Sector: Profile and Policy Issues. London: Policy Studies Institute, pp. 250–279.

Faff, Robert W., et al. (2017) "Motivating Postgrad Research Students to Pitch Their Ideas: What Have We Learned from'Pitching Research'Competitions at UQ?

Hoppe, M. (2016). Policy and entrepreneurship education. Small Business Economics., 46(1), 13-29. doi:10.1007/s11187-015-9676-7

Jason C. White (2015) Toward a Theory of Arts Entrepreneurship Journal of Arts Entrepreneurship Education, 2015

Kemmis,S., and McTaggert, R., (1990). The Action Research Planner Geelong: Deakin University Press

Kemmis, Stephen, Robin McTaggart, and Rhonda Nixon. (2013) The action research planner: Doing critical participatory action research. Springer Science & Business Media

Knight, P., & Yorke, M. (2004). Learning, curriculum, and employability in higher education. Psychology Press.

McCutcheon,G., and Jurg, B., (1990). Alternative Perspectives on Action Research. Theory into Practice Volume 24, Number 3

McFadzean, Elspeth, Andrew O'Loughlin, and Elizabeth Shaw (2005) Corporate entrepreneurship and innovation part 1: the missing link. European journal of innovation management

McKernan,J., (1991). Curriculum Action Research. A Handbook of Methods and Resources for the Reflective Practitioner London: Kogan Page

Morris, Michael H., Kuratko Donald F., and Covin Jeffrey G. (2010) Corporate entrepreneurship & innovation. Cengage Learning

Morris, Michael H. (1998) Entrepreneurial intensity: Sustainable advantages for individuals, organizations, and societies. Greenwood Publishing Group

Neck, Heidi M., and Patricia G. Greene (2011) Entrepreneurship education: known worlds and new frontiers. Journal of Small Business Management 49.1 (2011): 55-70.

Osterwalder, Alexander, and Yves Pigneur. (2010) Business model generation: a handbook for visionaries, game changers, and challengers. John Wiley & Sons

Dimaggio P (1982), Cultural entrepreneurship in nineteenth-century Boston: the creation of an organizational base for high culture in America, Media, Culture & Society, Volume: 4 issue: 1, page(s): 33-50

Pollard, V., & Wilson, E. (2013). The "Entrepreneurial Mindset" in Creative and Performing Arts Higher Education in Australia. Artivate: A Journal of Entrepreneurship in the Arts, 3(1), 3–22.

Rahm R. (2019) Epistemologies of Entrepreneurship Education: Experiments and Outcomes, Dissertation Stockholm School of Economics 2019

Ries, E. (2011). The lean startup: How today's entrepreneurs use continuous innovation to create radically successful businesses. New York: Crown Business.

Roberts, Edward B., Fiona Murray, and J. Daniel Kim (2019) Entrepreneurship and innovation at MIT: Continuing global growth and impact—an updated report. Foundations and Trends in Entrepreneurship 15.1: 1-55.

Voisey, P., Jones, P., & Thomas, B. (2013). The Pre-Incubator: A Longitudinal Study of 10 Years of University Pre-Incubation in Wales. Industry and Higher Education, 27(5), 349–363. https://doi.org/10.5367/ihe.2013.0168

Wyrwich, Michael, Stuetzer Michael, and Sternberg Rolf (2016) "Entrepreneurial role models, fear of failure, and institutional approval of entrepreneurship: A tale of two regions." Small Business Economics 46.3 467-492.

Innovative Activity as a key Factor in the Formation of Innovative Potential of Enterprises

Yuliya Asaturova and Alexey Kochman
Peter the Great St. Petersburg Polytechnic University, Russia
asaturova_yum@spbstu.ru
4330732@gmail.com
DOI: 10.34190/EIE.20.057

Abstract: Intensifying of innovative activity in entrepreneurship is one of the key factors in the effective market economy. The sustainable development of economic entities in the long term is possible only if the innovation activity builds up, which contributes to the effective neutralization of threats and the instability of the economic environment. However, statistical studies show that the innovative activity of Russian enterprises is currently insufficient due to the lack of financial resources, the high cost of innovations, as well as the insufficient capacity of organizations for innovation. The main objective of the present paper is therefore to determine the role of innovative activity in innovation management, to analyze factors affecting the innovative activity of an enterprise, and to determine conditions conducive to the formation and incensement of the innovative potential of enterprises. The paper explores main provisions of the theory of innovation, clarifies concepts of innovation and innovative activity of enterprises. The concept of innovative activity is defined as a measure of the intensity of innovative performance, manifested in the quantity and speed of the implementation of innovative projects implemented by the company within its innovative potential. The interrelation between building up the innovative potential of the enterprise and the growth of its innovative activity is shown. The sources of financing innovative activity are considered and the main factors that stimulate the innovative activity of enterprises are determined. It is shown that ensuring a stable financial position of the company is one of the decisive conditions for the growth of the innovative potential of the company. The indicators of the financial and economic efficiency of the enterprise that influence the entrepreneurial and innovative activities of the company and improve its innovative potential are identified. Timely controlling and maintaining the required level of selected indicators will lead to an increase in the efficiency of the company's innovation activities. Based on the research results, the main ways to increase the innovative potential of an enterprise are formulated, which determines the relevance of this study.

Keywords: Innovative activity, innovative potential, entrepreneurship, theory of innovation, efficiency

1. Introduction

Creating favorable conditions for innovation in entrepreneurial activity is one of the key factors in the formation of a developed market economy (Steil, Victor and Nelson, 2002). Strategic directions of the development of the Russian Federation for the period up to 2024 set the task of enhancing innovation as the basis for solving socio-economic problems due to breakthrough scientific and technological development. Entering the Russian Federation among the five largest economies in the world requires the effective and sustainable development of entrepreneurship, which provides a significant share of the federal budget revenues (Degtereva, Zaytsev and Kichigin (2019). Sustainable development of economic entities in the long term is possible only if the innovation activity builds up, which contributes to the effective neutralization of threats and instability of the economic environment (Ahlstrom, 2010). However, at present, based on the results of statistical studies, it can be concluded that the innovative activity of Russian enterprises is insufficient. If the proportion of enterprises implementing technological innovations is on average 8-10% in Russia, then in Germany - more than 65%, in Sweden - 50%, in the UK and Portugal - more than 40%. The level of innovative activity of enterprises of industrial production and services in the economy as a whole in recent years has not reached 10% (Rudskaya, Rodionov, 2017). The reasons for this are the lack of financial resources, the high cost of innovations, as well as the insufficient capacity of organizations for innovation.

Activation of innovation is especially relevant for those industries and companies for which it is a prerequisite for sustainable development and growth in their value (Maradana et al, 2017). One of the possible directions of stimulating the innovative activity of economic entities may be to identify instruments for the direct impact of innovation on the value of companies, increase their creditworthiness and investment attractiveness (Bek et al, 2013). To optimize the management of innovative activities and ensure the growth of innovative potential of enterprises, first of all, it is necessary to study the theoretical foundations of the theory of innovations, clarify the concepts of innovative activity and innovative potential of enterprises.

Theoretical and methodological aspects of innovative activity as a category of the theory of innovation have been studied by such scientists as (Schumpeter and Opie, 1983, Mansfield, 1963, Romer, 1990, Zharov, 2018). Research of innovative activity in the business sector was done by (Zaytsev, Degtereva and Dmitriev, 2019, Zabuga and Vaisman, 2017). However, the study of the relationship between innovation, sustainable development and building the innovative potential of companies involved significantly fewer researchers. These include works such are (Kulagina, Mikheenko and Rodionov, 2019, Zaytsev, Kichigin and Kozlov, 2018, Bogdanova et al, 2016).

Also, the relationship of financial position of a company and its innovative activity was not considered sufficiently in literature. Works in this area have descriptive or highly specialized characters (Brealey, Myers and Marcus, 2017, Kudryavtseva et al, 2017). The lack of a unified interpretation of the concept of innovative potential of an enterprise, as well as the luck methods for analyzing factors of its growth, also determines the relevance of the proposed study.

Thus **the main aim of the presented work** is to determine the role and place of innovative activity in innovation management, analysis of factors affecting the increase of innovative activity of enterprises, as well as the determination of conditions conducive to the formation and increase of innovative potential of the enterprise.

Achieving the goal involves solving the following tasks:

- Clarification of the concepts of innovation, innovative activity and innovative potential of enterprises in the framework of the theory of innovation.
- The definition of relationship between the growth of innovative activity of an enterprise and building its innovative potential.
- Analysis of factors that build up the innovative potential of the enterprise and ensure their sustainable development.
- Analysis of sources of financing of innovative activity and determination of ways to stimulate innovative activity of enterprises.
- Identification of key financial and economic indicators, the maintenance of which within the necessary limits will contribute to increasing the investment attractiveness of the company and strengthening its innovative potential.

Clarification of the concepts of innovative activity and innovative potential of enterprises, as well as the definition of the relationship between the growth of innovative activity of an enterprise and the buildup of its innovative potential, determines the scientific novelty and relevance of this study. The theoretical and methodological basis of this study is the fundamental works and applied developments of Russian and foreign authors in the field of innovation theory, sustainable development, financial analysis and statistics. The paper uses analytical research methods based on regulatory models of financial analysis, such as the method of calculating analytical ratios, comparative analysis and factor analysis.

2. Innovative activity and innovative potential of an enterprise as a category of the theory of innovation

Based on the analysis of literary sources, three stages of the formation of the theory of innovation can be distinguished (Dubolazova, Kuporov and Kochman, 2019). In the period 1910-1930 there was the formation of basic, fundamental categories, concepts and ideas. During the years 1940-1960 a significant place in the research was taken by the patterns of innovation and innovative behavior in cycles and crises. A significant contribution to the theory of innovation was made by N.D. Kondratiev, who investigated the macroeconomic causes of the emergence and impact of innovation (Kondratiev, 1989). J.A. Schumpeter (Schumpeter and Opie, 1983) ensured a substantial development of the ideas of its predecessor, examining in detail the relationship of innovation and entrepreneurship, specifically:

- presented innovative activity as an immanent function of entrepreneurship;
- introduced the classification of innovations (innovations in the product and in the process; technological and economic innovations, etc.);
- determined the place and role of innovation in the dynamics of economic cycles;

- substantiated the inevitability of resistance to innovation and overcoming this resistance.

The theory of innovation has its own set of definitions, consisting of both unique and basic concepts of other branches of science (Goldratt and Cox, 1992). The system of its own definitions includes the following definitions: innovation, innovation activity, innovation process, innovation risks and innovation potential. Due to the significant amount of scientific research and publications in the field of the theory of innovations, alternative opinions and approaches, the terminological diversity has not yet been overcome, a unified system of concepts of the theory of innovation has not been developed. Let us consider the most important basic concepts: innovation and innovative activity.

For the purpose of this study, the key concept of which is innovative activity, we will consider definitions used in regulatory documents at the national and international levels. In order to determine the concept of innovation activity, it is necessary to establish the content of two basic categories of the theory of innovation. In Russian practice, the concept of innovation means "A new or significantly improved product (product, service) or process, a new sales method or a new organizational method in business practice, job organization or in external relations" that has been introduced (Federal Law RF, 1996). And innovative activity is interpreted as activity (including scientific, technological, organizational, financial and commercial activities) aimed at implementing innovative projects, as well as creating innovative infrastructure and ensuring its activities».

We can see that the law of the Russian Federation connects innovation with the implementation of innovation projects, while in the recommendations for the collection and analysis of data on innovations used by the countries of the European Union, this definition is interpreted more broadly, allowing for research and development that directly not related to a specific innovation project (Chesbrough, 2003). Such an approach can expand the composition of entities implementing innovations, but it narrows the practice-oriented orientation of innovation. Therefore, in the proposed study, innovation and innovative activity will be understood in the sense of the Federal laws of the Russian Federation. In scientific research the term "innovative activity" in its most general form is understood as the ability of an enterprise to constantly generate innovations. Abramov D.V. defined innovative activity as a dynamic focused "on creation, development in production and marketing of grocery, technological, process, organizational and managerial innovations with the aim of obtaining innovative and active subjects of commercial benefits and competitive advantages" (Abramov, 2016). Bobyrev D.B. offers the definition of innovative activity of an enterprise as a cumulative indicator of its activity, including the intensity and timeliness of innovative actions, the validity and relevance of the methods used, the ability to mobilize the technical and human potential and rationality of the innovation process algorithm in terms of composition and sequence of operations (Bobyrev, 2016).

The team of authors (Rasulev, Trostyansky and Islamova, 2015) defines innovative activity as the level of intensity of the implementation of the innovative potential of an enterprise, by which, in turn, researchers understand a combination of different types of resources (material, technical, financial, intellectual, scientific and technical, and others, necessary for carrying out innovative activities).

We can distinguish a range of studies in which innovative activity is determined both through the intensity of innovative activity and through the degree of realization of innovative potential. For example the team (Kolmykova, Artemiev and Kononova, 2016) believe that innovative activity is a measure of the intensity of innovative practice and the ability to realize innovative potential. Researchers use the concept of "innovative susceptibility" as the ability of a system to absorb various innovations and reflect its degree of adaptation to consumer demands. The analysis and the subsequent generalization of its results allows us to conclude that the definition of innovative potential most often used by authoritative scientists reveals its content as a complex of interrelated resources. Therefore we will define the *innovative potential* that the system possesses as a complex of interconnected resources of the socio-economic system used in the process of innovation. In order to begin innovations, it is necessary that the system is capable of introducing innovations, has adaptive behavior and is able to adapt to the requirements of consumers, that is, have *innovative susceptibility*.

Innovative susceptibility is the reason for initiation of innovative projects, encourages the beginning of innovative practice, the result of which are innovations, i.e. new or significantly improved products (goods, services) or processes introduced, new sales methods or new organizational methods in business practice, organization of workplaces or in external relations. Innovation practice is carried out with different intensities, determined by the number of simultaneously implemented innovation projects, and with different rates of their implementation. This characteristic of innovation is called innovation activity. Therefore, in the future, by innovative activity we will understand the characteristic of innovative practice, manifested in the quantity and speed of implementation of innovative projects implemented by the enterprise within its innovative potential.

Thus, the authors systematize and introduce the following concepts:

Innovative potential — a complex of interconnected resources of the socio-economic system used in the process of innovation.

Innovative susceptibility — the ability of a system to master innovations and adapt to customer needs.

Innovative activity — the degree of intensity of the use of innovative potential, expressed in the quantity and speed of implementation of innovative projects implemented by the subject of innovation practice.

Note that innovative activity determines the measure of the intensity of innovation, which determines the degree of use of innovative potential. Moreover, the innovative potential of the enterprise is considered as a degree of its susceptibility to innovation. High innovative potential and good innovative susceptibility lead to initiation of innovative projects and the implementation of innovative activities (including scientific, technological, organizational, financial and commercial activities) aimed at the implementation of innovative projects, as well as the creation of innovative infrastructure. The growth of innovative activity, in turn, leads to a further accumulation of resources, an increase in the value of the enterprise and, as a result, to a subsequent increase in the innovative potential of the company. The connection between Innovative potential, Innovative susceptibility, Innovative activity is shown in more details in Figure 1.

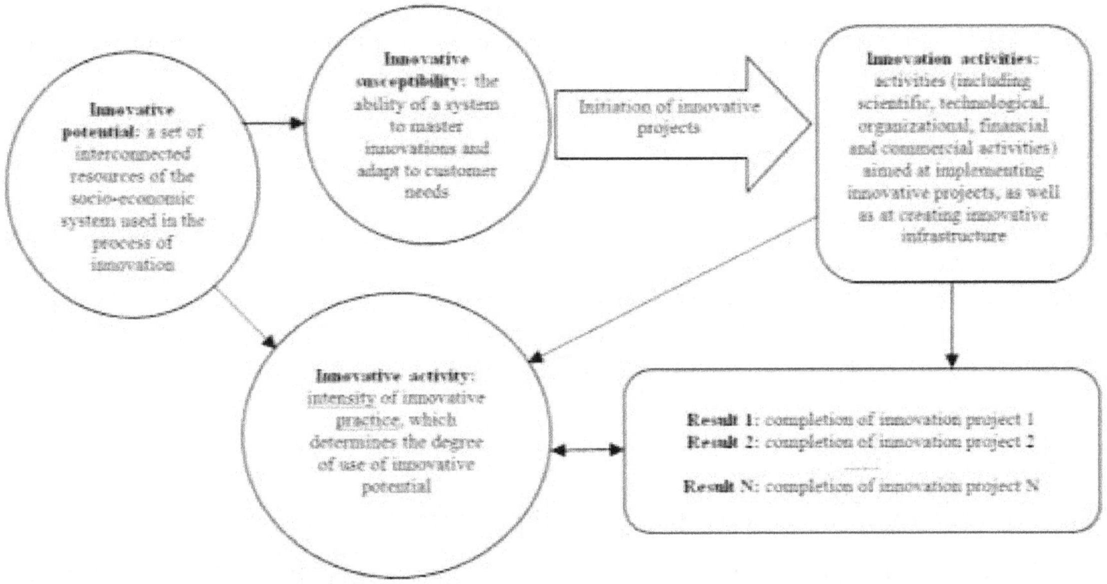

Figure 1: The place of the concept of "innovative activity" in the basic concepts of the theory of innovation

3. Enterprise innovation management

From the position of a systematic approach, innovative activity is an element of a corporate strategy for the development of entrepreneurship (Neff, 2002). The development of an innovative strategy is based on the following parameters: analysis and forecasting of environmental factors, analysis of the internal potential of the company and its corporate strategy (Lee and Saen, 2012).

The analysis of factors of direct and indirect environmental impact is aimed at identifying and formulating probabilistic directions for the development of the scientific and technical potential of companies, identifying competitors in the country and the world, and determining the likelihood of innovative scientific and technical services (Saravia, 2014).

Assessment of the internal resources of enterprises is aimed at identifying the level of innovative potential, that is, the readiness and ability of various structures and business processes to develop and implement innovations at all stages of the production and technological process. One of the important tasks of developing a strategy to stimulate innovative activity is the choice of the object of formation of scientific and technological developments: the creation of a scientific and educational structure as an element of the enterprise or the use of the results of scientific research on the principles of outsourcing (Rudskaya, Rodionov, 2018).

Innovative strategies are implemented in R&D plans and in the investment plans of the company. Management of innovative activity should be implemented on the principles of project management, which implies the determination of financial and time priorities and limitations, detailing the levels of development and implementation, the establishment of responsibility centers, the determination of funding sources for various stages of the innovation life cycle (An, Xu and Zhang, 2018).

The practical implementation of innovation includes the introduction of both direct technological innovations in the production process and the optimization of management functions using the capabilities of digital technologies.

The sources of the formation of innovative potential are scientific research. The most objective qualitative indicator characterizing the effectiveness of innovation is a relative indicator, calculated as the ratio of R&D costs to the company's annual revenue (Biger, Gill and Mathur, 2010).

Stimulation of innovative activity of enterprises is impossible without government incentive measures implemented in the following areas:

- direct state financing of companies through the provision of soft loans, credit guarantees, grants and government contracts for research and development;
- investments in the capital of venture funds and other financial institutions involved in funding innovative projects in a selected area of entrepreneurship (Madrid-Guijarro et al, 2016).

Researchers rightly consider the number of patents received as a characteristic that allows us to evaluate the innovative activity of the subject of innovative activity. Scientist (Voskanyan, 2014) also considers a patent as the most important characteristic of the success of innovation. Despite the fact that the base does not cover all inventions, the most economically valuable of them are calculated." Scientists (Koreysha and Parshina, 2017) on the basis of an econometric analysis proved the direct relationship between the volume of patenting and:

- the number of advanced production technologies developed;
- the volume of innovative products;
- the volume of internal research and development costs for each year individually.

4. Resource constraints and innovative potential at Russian enterprises

An innovation process is a process of transforming scientific knowledge into innovations, which can be represented as a sequential chain of events during which innovations mature from an idea to a specific product, technology or service and are disseminated in practical use (Asaturova and Khvatova, 2019). The possibility of implementing the innovation process is associated with a certain concentration of enterprise resources, the presence of an innovative climate in the country and the internal innovative potential of the enterprise.

An analysis of state statistics data allows us to note that in recent years innovation process at enterprises of Russian Federation is most hindered by economic factors, among which the lack of funds, the high cost of innovations, and economic risk during the implementation of the project are most important. The inability to determine the economic benefits of using innovations, as well as the inadequate potential of organizations for innovation, are also constraining factors for the development of innovative activity of an enterprise (HSE Publishing, 2018).

The problem of lack of finance is constantly under supervision of RF government, active steps are being taken to solve it. Venture and other development funds in the field of innovation are created and supported in the country. However, despite a significant increase in the rating of this factor in recent years, its impact on the innovative activities of modern enterprises is still high. Among the external factors affecting the innovative activity of enterprises, it is necessary to take into account the investment climate in the country, the presence of crisis, current legislation in the investment sphere, the availability of benefits for small and medium-sized enterprises and other favorable conditions for innovative activity. Among internal factors, the most significant is the low innovative potential of the enterprise. The influence of this factor is primarily due to the lack of the necessary resources, qualified staff, and the skills of working with innovative projects at the enterprise. The largest role, from our point of view, in eliminating this drawback, is played by the stable financial position of the enterprise, which significantly affects the possibility of concentration of resources and, as a result, helps to strengthen its innovative potential (Asaturova and Khvatova, 2018).

The presence of factors negatively affecting the innovative activity of the enterprise leads to the presence of restrictions that impede the implementation of the innovative project (Zivaljevic, 2015). The most significant limitations that hinder the strengthening of the company's innovative potential are resource limitations. These restrictions primarily include financial resources, as well as production, technological and labor resources. In the presence of these restrictions, the production or further development of an innovative product is possible only when creating the relationship of minimizing resources with achieving the desired result. To overcome the resource, including financial constraints, it is necessary to increase the level of productivity of the company, which is evaluated by various indicators of business activity and the efficiency of use of enterprise funds (Asaturova and Khvatova, 2019).

The accumulation of profits and increase the profitability of the company will greatly increase the ability of the enterprise to use its own resources to finance innovation. And increasing the solvency and financial stability of a company can contribute to the growth of investment attractiveness of an enterprise and the possibility of using borrowed capital. These indicators were used by the authors when developing a system of key financial and economic indicators that form the innovative potential of the enterprise.

5. Sources of financing innovation and ways to increase the innovation activity of enterprises

The problem of financing innovation is the main factor holding back the innovative development of Russian enterprises. Any innovation and its implementation is associated with investment in innovation. However, as noted above, in the current conditions Russian enterprises have to work in conditions of limited capital. The amount of funds allocated for innovation in the country remains low, while the presence of economic sanctions complement the difficulties in attracting external financing. Enterprises have to withstand fierce competition in attracting capital to finance business and develop innovation. This is especially true for small businesses, while maintaining the entrepreneurial and innovative activity of these companies is of great importance for the development of market competition.

For an enterprise, financial constraints are primarily associated with limiting the ability to attract equity and borrowed capital to finance innovation. Currently, in the context of a reduction in state financing, the main form of borrowed financing for the development of innovative small and medium-sized enterprises is financing through bank loans and other borrowed funds in the financial and credit market.

However, at the moment, the use of bank loans is limited due to high interest rates, and its availability is greatly limited by such parameters as the financial position of the enterprise. Therefore, to ensure the possibility of attracting borrowed financing, it is necessary to increase the investment attractiveness of the enterprise and the level of profitability of its assets.

Self-financing at the expense of the internal funds of the enterprise is one of the main sources of financing the activities of the company in the context of the limited ability to borrow funds. Internal sources of financing primarily include financing of the enterprise from accumulated capital profits, including a reserve fund, depreciation fund of the enterprise and expansion of the share capital of the enterprise. The main limitation for the majority of Russian enterprises according to the survey results is low profitability and, as a result, their lack of net profit as the main internal source of financing (Nikolova, Rodionov and Afanasyeva, 2017).

Thus, under the current conditions of budget financing reduction, the presence of economic sanctions, high interest rates on loans and low profitability of the company's assets, financing of innovative activities of an enterprise is objectively limited. Overcoming these financial constraints is primarily associated with increasing the level of the financial condition of the company. The stable financial position of the enterprise and taking into account such indicators as solvency and financial stability will allow the company to provide a high degree of investment attractiveness to increase the ability to attract borrowed funds. Maintaining a high level of indicators such as profitability and business activity will improve the efficiency of financing innovative activities from the company's own funds.

Key indicators affecting the increase in innovation and investment activity of a company operating in conditions of financial constraints are presented in table 1. The choice of specific indicators from the presented sections depends on the specific conditions of the enterprise. Timely accounting and maintaining the required level of these indicators will increase the ability to raise funds for the enterprise and thereby lead to increased innovative activity of the enterprise.

Table 1: The system of key financial and economic indicators affecting the formation of the innovative potential of the enterprise

Indicator	**Method of calculation**	**Characteristic**
	Profitability indicators	
1. Return on Equity indicator (ROE)	Net Profit / Equity capital * 100 %	Characterizes the efficiency of the equity capital. Promotes the valuation of stock quotes on the exchange.
2. Return on Sales indicator (ROS)	Net Profit / Sales of production * 100 %	Characterizes the profitability of the implementation, estimates the possibility of financing business by profit.
3. Return on Costs indicator (ROC)	Net Profit / Costs * 100 %	Characterizes the level of productivity and cost recovery level.
4. Return on fixed assets indicator	Net Profit / Fixed assets * 100 %	Characterizes the return on property plant and equipment, the efficiency of the use of fixed assets.
	Solvency and financial stability indicators	
1. Current asset ratio indicator (CR)	Working capital / Current Liabilities > 2	It characterizes the ability of pre-acceptance to pay off short-term debts with simultaneous continuation of uninterrupted activity
2. Equity to Total Assets indicator (EtTA)	Equity capital / Total Assets > 0,5	Characterizes the independence of the enterprise from borrowed funds. It is the main criterion for the possibility of borrowing loan capital
3. Financial solidity indicator	(Equity capital + Long-term loan capital) / Total Assets > 0,5	Characterizes the share of capital of long-term use
4. The equity mobility indicator	Net working capital / equity capital * 100 %	Characterizes flexibility in the use of a company's equity capital.
	Business activity indicators	
1. Asset turnover indicators (by types)	Revenues from sales / cost of assets	Characterizes enterprise productivity, resource efficiency, by type
2. The period of assets turnover in days	Number of days per year / asset turnover	Characterizes the duration of one turnover of the assets in days

Using the developed system of indicators in the business practice of the enterprise gives the entrepreneur an opportunity to identify the main shortcomings in the financial and economic activities of the company that negatively affect the innovation process. Correcting these shortcomings can significantly increase the possibility of attracting financial resources to finance innovative projects.

It is necessary to mention that increasing innovation activity not only relates to quantitative investments and achievements. According to the actual report of the "Global Innovation Index" (GII, 2019) assessing the quality, rather than only the quantity of innovation inputs and outputs has become an overarching concern to the global innovation policy community. For example, the GII reports that the Russian Federation is in line with expectations for its level of development. Interestingly, the ranking of middle-income economies in innovation quality indicators remains steady, with China, India, and the Russian Federation in the top 3 positions. A detailed study of the qualitative characteristics that contribute to the growth of innovative activity of the enterprise will represent the directions of further research by the authors.

6. In conclusion

The paper explores the main provisions of the theory of innovation, clarifies the concepts of innovative activity and innovative potential of the enterprise. Based on the results of the work, the main ways to increase the innovative activity of the enterprise and increase its innovative potential are formulated. Upon reaching the goal, the following main results were obtained:

- The concept of innovative activity is defined as a measure of the intensity of the use of innovative potential, expressed in the quantity and speed of implementation of innovative projects implemented by the subject of innovation.
- The concept of the innovative potential of the enterprise as a complex of interconnected resources of the socio-economic system used in the process of innovation is defined. It is noted that innovative potential is characterized by the degree of its susceptibility to innovation.
- The relationship between the growth of innovative activity of the enterprise and the buildup of its innovative potential is shown.
- The external and internal factors affecting the innovative activity of the enterprise are analyzed. It is shown that resource, including financial, restrictions negatively affect the formation of innovative potential in Russian enterprises.
- The sources of financing innovative activities are considered and ways to stimulate the innovative activity of enterprises are identified. It is shown that ensuring a stable financial position of the enterprise, ensuring its creditworthiness and investment attractiveness is one of the decisive conditions for the growth of the innovative potential of the company.
- A system of key financial and economic indicators has been developed that form the innovative potential of the enterprise. It is noted that in order to attract loan capital it is necessary to increase the solvency and financial stability of the company. To mobilize internal sources of financing it is necessary to increase the profitability and business activity of the enterprise. Maintaining the selected indicators within the necessary limits will contribute to increasing the investment attractiveness of the company and strengthening its innovative potential.

Thus, the work shows that in order to enhance innovative activity of the enterprise, it is necessary to increase the investment attractiveness and competitiveness of the company, to monitor the status of key financial indicators. This will allow both to intensify the use of the innovative potential of the company and to accelerate its reproduction.

Acknowledgements

This research work was supported by the Academic Excellence Project 5-100 proposed by Peter the Great St. Petersburg Polytechnic University.

References

Abramov, D.V. (2016) "Possible probable choice of the company's optimal strategy in the context of the global economic crisis and restrictions of economic sanctions", Economics, sociology and law, Vol 4(1), pp 6-13.

Ahlstrom, D. (2010) "Innovation and Growth: How Business Contributes to Society", Academy of Management Perspectives, Vol 24, No. 3, pp 11–24.

Asaturova, Yu. and Khvatova T. (2019) "How constraints influence company innovation processes". In Proceedings of the 14th European Conference on Innovation and Entrepreneurship (ECIE 2019), 29-20 September, Kalamata, Greece, pp 95-103

Asaturova, Yu. and Khvatova, T. (2018) "Innovative activity of enterprises under the condition of financial deficit." Proceedings of the 13th European Conference on Innovation and Entrepreneurship (ECIE 2018), 20-21 September, Aveiro, Portugal, pp 59-67.

An, W., Xu, Y., and Zhang, J. (2018) "Resource constraints, innovation capability and corporate financial fraud in entrepreneurial firms", Chinese Management Studies, Vol. 12 Issue: 1, pp 2-18

Bobyrev, D.B. (2016) "The relationship between innovative activity and the activation of innovative activity of domestic industrial enterprises", Modern science: actual problems and solutions. - No. 4 (26). - S. 101-106.

Bogdanova, N.V., M.A. Naidennaya, Yu.V. Zhirova, O.N. Turkova, T.Yu. Shlapakova. (2016) "Features of managing the innovative potential of industrial enterprises", Current trends in economics and management: a new look. No. 40-1. pp 83-88.

Bek, M.A., Nadezda N. Bek, N.N., Sheresheva, M.Y. and Johnston, W.J. (2013) "Perspectives of SME innovation clusters development in Russia", Journal of Business & Industrial Marketing, Vol 28 (3), pp 240-259

Biger, N., Gill, A. and Mathur N. (2010) "The Relationship between Working Capital Management and Profitability: Evidence from the United States", Business and Economics Journal, Vol 10, pp 1—9.

Brealey, R.A., Myers, S.C. and Marcus, A.J. (2017) "Fundamentals of Corporate Finance", McGraw-Hill Education; 9 edition.

Chesbrough, H.W. (2003) "Open Innovation: The new imperative for creating and profiting from technology", Boston, Harvard Business School Press.

Federal Law RF, 08.23.1996 FZ-No 127 "On Science and Science and Technology Policy"

The Global Innovation Index report (2019) GII 2019

Goldratt, E.M. and Cox, J. (1992) The Goal: A Process of Ongoing Improvement, North River Pr; Revised edition.

Degtereva, V., Zaytsev, A., Kichigin, O (2019) "Rental regulation of the Russian economy as a condition for achieving world leadership", Social, Economic, and Academic Leadership (ICSEAL 2019). Czech Republic, Prague.

Dubolazova, Y.A., Kuporov, Y.Y., Kochman A.V. (2019) "The System of Balanced Development of Innovation Enterprises", Proceedings of 33rd International Business Information Management Association Conference (IBIMA), pp 3818 - 3821.

HSE Publishing (2018). Innovation activity indicators. Statistical Handbook, [online] HSE Publishing, Moscow, https://nangs.org/analytics/vshe-ctatisticheskij-sbornik-indikatory-innovatsionnoj-deyatelnosti-pdf

Kolmykova, T.S., Artemiev, O.G., Kononova, Ya. Sh. (2016) "Current priorities for the formation of feedback between innovative potential and the activity of the economic system", Finance. Control. Innovation. Collection of scientific articles. Kursk, pp. 93-96.

Kondratiev, N.D. (1989) "Large cycles of economic conditions", Problems of economic dynamics. - M.: Economics. pp. 172-226.

Koreysha, Z.A., Parshina, V.S. (2017) The study of patent and innovation as a factor in the economic development of Russia. Issues of innovative economy. V. 7. № 1. pp 31-39.

Kudryavtseva, T.J., Ivanova, E.A., Kozlova, E.A., Skhvediani, A.E. (2017) "Pricing and assessment of competitiveness of innovative medical devices in the context of commercialization strategy. Academy of Strategic Management ", Journal. Volume 16, Special issue 1, pp 110-122.

Kulagina, N.A., Mikheenko, O.V., Rodionov, D.G. (2019) "Technologies for the development of methods for evaluating an innovative system", International Journal of Recent Technology and Engineering. Volume 8, Issue 3, pp. 5083-5091.

Lee, K.H. and Saen, R.F. (2012) "Measuring corporate sustainability management: A data envelopment analysis approach", International Journal of Production Economics, Vol 140, No. 1, pp 219—226.

Madrid-Guijarro, A., García-Pérez-de-Lema, D., and Van Auken, H. (2016). Financing constraints and SME innovation during economic crises, Academia Revista Latinoamericana de Administraci6n, Vol. 29 Issue: 1, pp.84-106.

Mansfield, E. (1963) Size of Firm, Market Structure, and Innovation. The Journal of Political Economy. - Dec. Vol. 71., No. 6. P. 556-576.

Maradana, R.P., Pradha, R.P., Dash, S., Gaurav, K., Jayakumar, M. and Chatterjee, D. (2017) "Does innovation promote economic growth? Evidence from European countries", Journal of Innovation and Entrepreneurship, Vol 13, No.1, pp 1-23.

Neff, C. (2002) Corporate Finance, Innovation, and Strategic Competition, Springer Science & Business Media.

Nikolova, L.V., Rodionov, D.G., Afanasyeva, N.V. (2017). "Impact of globalization on innovation project risks estimation". European Research Studies Journal, 20(2), pp 396-410.

Rasulev, A.F., Trostyansky, D.V., Islamova, O.A. (2015) "Assessment of innovative potential and innovative activity of industrial enterprises", Bulletin of Ufa State Technical University. Science, education, economics. Series: Economics. No2 (12).

Rudskaya, I., Rodionov, D. (2017) "Econometric modeling as a tool for evaluating the performance of regional innovation systems (with regions of the Russian Federation as the example)", Academy of Strategic Management Journal, 16 (Special issue 2).

Rudskaya, I.A., Rodionov, D.G. (2018) "Comprehensive evaluation of Russian regional innovation system performance using a two-stage econometric model", Espacios. Volume39, Issue 4.

Romer, P. M. (1990) "Endogenous technological change", Journal of Political Economy, Vol 98(5), pp 71–102

Saravia, J.A. (2014). "Merger waves and the Austrian business cycle theory", Quarterly Journal of Austrian Economics. Vol. 17, is. 2. pp 179-196.

Schumpeter, J.A. and Opie, R. (1983). "The theory of economic development: an inquiry into profits, capital, credit, interest, and the business cycle". New Brunswick, New Jersey: Transaction Books. ISBN 9780878556984.

Steil, B., Victor, D. G. and Nelson, R. R. (2002) "Technological Innovation and Economics Performance", A Council of Foreign Relations Book. Princeton University Press.

Voskanyan, R.O. (2014) "Features of the formation of a strategy for increasing the value of an innovative company", Bulletin of the Russian University of Economics G.V. Plekhanov. No. 9 (75). S. 37-44.

Zabuga, A.S. and Vaisman, E.D. (2017) "Methodical aspects of the problem of forecasting the competitiveness of innovative products of an industrial enterprise", Nauchno-technicheskie vedomosti SPbPU. Economics, Vol 10, No. 4, pp 155-165.

Zaytsev, A., Kichigin, O. and Kozlov, M. (2018) "Rental analysis of innovation component in resource productivity", IOP Conference Series: Materials Science and Engineering, Volume 497, conference 1. DOI:10.1088/1757-899X/497/1/012064.

Zaytsev, A, Degtereva, V and Dmitriev, N. (2019) "The development of the mathematical apparatus for calculation of the intellectual rent industrial enterprises to achieve innovation leadership", Social, Economic, and Academic Leadership (ICSEAL 2019). Czech Republic, Prague.

Zivaljevic, A. (2015) "Theory of constraints – application in land transportation systems", Management of Environmental Quality: An International Journal, Vol. 26 Issue: 4, pp.505-517.

Zharov, V.S. (2018) "Investment and innovative analysis of the production systems", Nauchno-technicheskie vedomosti SPbSPU. Economic sciences, Vol. 11, No. 6. P. 142–152.

Connecting Startups and Incumbents in University-Driven Innovation Ecosystems: A Look Behind the Curtain

Stratos Baloutsos, Angeliki Karagiannaki and Katerina Pramatari
ELTRUN Research Center, Dept. of Management Science and Technology, Athens University of Economics and Business, Athens, Greece
sbaloutsos@aueb.gr
akaragianaki@aueb.gr
k.pramatari@aueb.gr
DOI: 10.34190/EIE.20.142

Abstract: Entrepreneurship and its connection to the manifestations of innovation has been discussed in academia for quite some time. The last 15 years saw the increasing relevance of open innovation and a rising prominence of so-called ecosystems. As interactions between different stakeholders become more complex, innovation ecosystems are becoming of prime importance. There is a need for further researching how these ecosystems are formed and the factors that can render them successful or failed. The purpose of this article is to present the cases of three university-driven innovation ecosystems, i.e. ecosystems that are formed by established firms and startups under the coordination of a university. These ecosystems are created through an open innovation program aiming to create collaborative schemes by bringing together incumbent firms and startups to accelerate innovation and facilitate a co-creation process. These schemes involved important stakeholders of the local "startup ecosystem" and allowed researchers to observe and discuss how their interactions shape the innovation process. The cases deal with different sectors – airport, food, and finTech – and provide insights on how an ecosystem is formed and how the innovation process is affected by the collaboration of different firms, funds, sponsors, and institutional partners. This work contributes to the current research on how to set up a university-driven scheme and identifies key factors that drive the actors to continue to operate within the ecosystem.

Keywords: innovation ecosystems, university driven innovation, startups, case study

1. Introduction

Entrepreneurship and innovation are two of the most thoroughly researched concepts in business and economics. Entrepreneurship involves recognizing opportunities, creating new value, assuming risks and realising rewards, and may occur in a variety of settings (Beliaeva *et al.*, 2019). Innovation has been a driving force for entrepreneurship whether as a simple invention, a closed innovation research lab, an open innovation system, or an innovation cluster. As knowledge, and consequently innovation, spills over traditional organisation boundaries, entrepreneurial ventures are increasingly affected and forced to adapt their innovation strategy to a broader set of open innovation communities, the so called Innovation Ecosystems (IE) (Dahlander and Gann, 2010; Shaikh and Levina, 2019; Suominen, Seppänen and Dedehayir, 2019).

IEs have been a prominent issue of discussion both in academia and business (Oh *et al.*, 2016; Ritala and Almpanopoulou, 2017). The rise of open innovation practices, the success of the innovation communities, combined with the rising complexity of business environments have shifted a lot of focus on how an IE can be formed and be successful. While the importance of users in the innovation process was established more than 30 years ago by von Hippel (Hippel, 1988), the advent of open communities has highlighted the critical role of communities in the innovation process. Considering the seminal work of Chesbrough on Open Innovation (2003) and its relevance, the ability to identify sustainable and innovative ecosystems is becoming an issue of prime importance for both established and growing companies.

The starting point of this research is, therefore, to contribute to the ongoing discussion around IEs by presenting three different cases of open innovation projects that created IEs. Specifically, this research focuses on university-driven IEs; meaning IEs that are facilitated by a university and involve an established firm (incumbent) and several startups. Within the academic community, the issue of the formation of an IE remains crucial (Ceccagnoli *et al.*, 2012; Dattee et al. 2018). In addition, there is a research gap regarding the factors and KPIs that make an IE successful (Durst and Poutanen, 2013; Oh et al., 2016; Suominen, Seppänen and Dedehayir, 2019). While several strategies for gaining value from ecosystems have been proposed (Hannah and Eisenhardt, 2018), committing to a new ecosystem is still regarded a high risk endeavour (Dattee et al. 2018). To commit to a new ecosystem is more difficult for established firms that may not identify this as a significant added value to their core business. Trying not only to describe the formation of a university-driven IE but also to "look behind the curtain", the specific objectives are:

- to present how a university-driven IE can be setup to bridge the different actors (i.e. incumbents and startups) within an open innovation program;
- to pinpoint key factors that drive the actors involved to form a continuous relationship and to continue to operate within a university-driven IE, thus providing sustainability to the IE in question.

This paper is organized as follows. Section 2 provides a theoretical background on university-driven IEs. Section 3 provides a description of the research design. Section 4 describes the results and Section 5 provides the conclusions, limitations, and future research directions.

2. The university-driven innovation ecosystem

While it is relatively simple to intuitively comprehend what constitutes an IE, many researchers have been discussing IEs in general terms. The first and most widely used definition (Adner, 2006) is one of the most abstract ones. Within this work, we adopt one of the most recent definitions proposed by Granstrand and Holgersson (2020) as: *"the evolving set of actors, activities, and artifacts, and the institutions and relations, including complementary and substitute relations, that are important for the innovative performance of an actor or a population of actors"* (Granstrand and Holgersson, 2020). Based on this definition, we try to define the core elements that constitute the IEs under study, that is an IE under the orchestration of a university as the underlying institution.

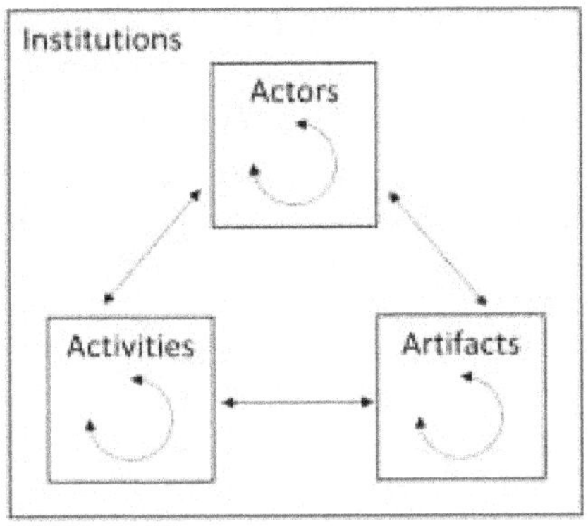

Figure 1: Innovation ecosystem definition

The importance of universities in advancing the innovation process has been generally recognised in the innovation literature (Cooke, Uranga and Etxebarria, 1997; Klofsten and Jones-Evans, 2000; Cohen, Nelson and Walsh, 2002), especially in the context of the entrepreneurial university (Guerrero *et al.*, 2016). Our work expands on this notion. It proposes that utilising a university's position in the broader business ecosystem can facilitate the initiation of an IE by helping to overcome some of the barriers common in such collaborative schemes (e.g. the proverbial "chicken and egg" problem pointed out by Dattee et al. (2018)). It also helps mitigating potential issues that arise when an actor inside an ecosystem has significantly more market power than the rest, a de facto situation in incumbent-startup collaborations.

Based on the above definition, a university-driven IE:

- is formed by *an institution,* specifically a university, that sets the rules and facilitates the innovation process
- involves *actors,* specifically an incumbent and several startups
- performs several *activities* such as the exchange of knowledge and data, the sharing of technological equipment and any facilities
- aims to create common *artifacts* that are co-developed products or services, to address the respective markets.

An adaptation of Figure 1 that conceptualises the IEs in question is shown in Figure 2 (the figure shows only four startups for the sake of brevity). This format is very similar to what is referred to as the hub-based ecosystem where a central stakeholder (i.e. the hub firm) acts as a leader and dictates the governing rules and general direction of the ecosystem (Nambisan and Baron, 2013). However, in these cases, the existence of the university as an orchestrator acts as a differentiating factor that alters many of the qualities of the ecosystem and mitigates several problems. This is in line with the literature arguing the significance of universities in IEs (Etzkowitz and Leydesdorff, 2000; Heaton, Siegel and Teece, 2019).

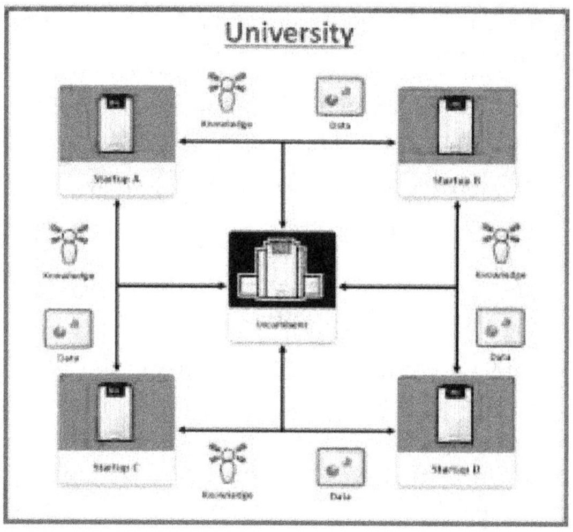

Figure 2: The university-driven ecosystem

3. Research design

This research relies on a multiple-cases design to build theory that is deeply informed by primary data gathered through three qualitative, longitudinal case studies. Given the pre-mature level of a university-driven innovation ecosystem, case research gained respect in this design as it is ideal for answering the "how" and "why" questions (Yin, 2003), allowing for a richer knowledge of non-conceptualized issues. When conducting qualitative research, several stages take place as depicted in Figure 3 (adapted from Murphy et al., 2016): develop initial objective; data collection; the coding process; searching for patterns.

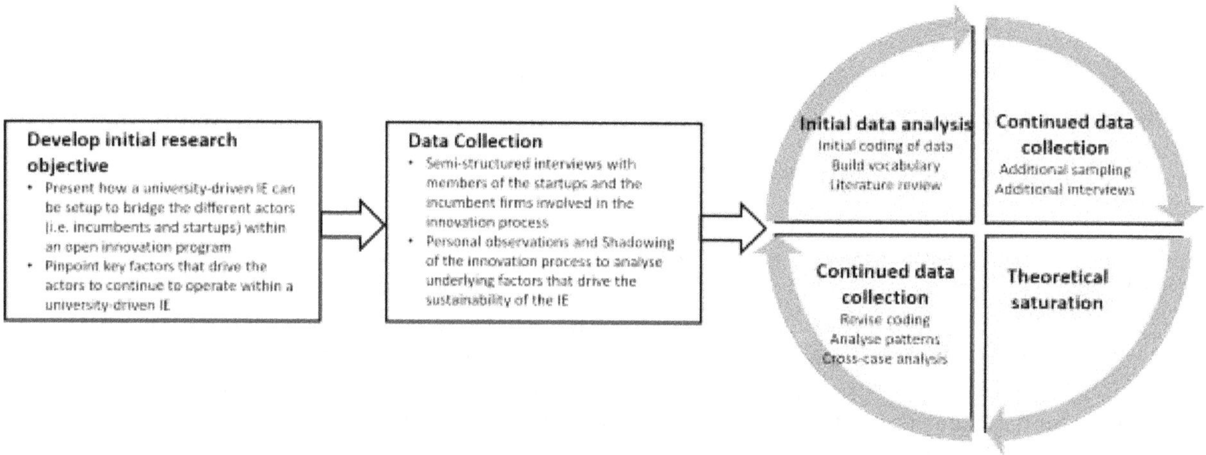

Figure 3: Research design

Data collection. We used the following techniques:

- *Semi-structured interviews* with members of the startups and the incumbent firms involved in the innovation process. This technique is suited to case study data collection, and particularly for exploratory research, as it allows expansive discussion to illuminate factors of importance (Albuam and Oppenheim, 1993; Dennehy and Conboy, 2019).
- *Personal observations and shadowing of the innovation process.* Researchers spent a great deal of time and effort to analyse underlying factors that drive the sustainability of the ecosystem and encourage further collaboration between the actors. This was accomplished by interacting in a day-to-day manner with the incumbent firms and the startups. Based on these observations, the research team was able to gather data about their interactions, collaborations, and general progress throughout the course of the innovation program.

The coding process. To get insights on potential between-subject patterns in the data, which can be a boon for theorizing, we used the principle of constant comparison. In this way, emerging primary data were always viewed through the lens of what has been gathered from the personal observations during the stages of the open innovation process, the semi-structured interviews and the progress reports, as well as existing literature. As a result, during the coding process, we developed some "open codes" using either the vocabulary used by the participants of the IE or "literature-based codes" using vocabulary from the extant literature (Charmaz, 2006). Following the coding process, we moved to emerging categories, a higher level of data abstraction (Glaser, 1978). The most common "codes" were identified and thus we came across some factors that can drive startups and established firms to form a continuous relationship within a university-driven Innovation Ecosystem.

Searching for patterns. Every year that the open innovation programme was active, for each case, interviews were conducted with two key personnel of the incumbent firm and four different startups. This led up to a total of 18 interviews for Case A (3 years), 12 interviews for Case B (two years), and 6 interviews for Case C (one year). These interviews lasted about 30 to 45 minutes. The interviews revolved around the actors' expected knowledge about: (1) factors that hinder or accelerate the successful implementation of the innovation process and (2) issues that drive or discourage continued collaboration. The questions were open-ended in order to allow more freedom of expression in an effort to capture the complexities of operating within an IE more accurately. Over the time frame of our study, we repeatedly reviewed the interviews' material trying to find some patterns.

4. Describing the three open innovation programmes as university -driven IEs

Case A comprises a university-driven IE aiming to activate the startup community to propose a technological innovation that will transform the airport industry. While the initial vision was to innovate the core airport operations, the ecosystem evolved to include several products/services catered to the broader environment and added complementary offerings. Some example artefacts are: an easily adjustable system for detecting foreign objects at airfields; an IoT quantitative recycling performance technology & collection service to disrupt the waste management sector, enabling visualization of measurement data and employee engagement.

Case B comprises a university-driven IE aiming to modernise the customer experience through fintech technologies and help e-commerce and retail industry to stay up to date in a digital environment. Example artefacts created are: an innovative technology which "transforms" physical spaces (e.g. stores, museums) into interactive virtual walkthroughs available for online users to browse and shop; a platform that offers coupons to commuters whose daily route passes through specific points of sales.

Case C comprises a university-driven IE aiming to innovate in the food sector. Some example of artefacts are: valorisation of the organic residues of the coffee in order to generate new products; an analytics platform that gathers transactional data from retail environment.

All three cases represent open innovation programs that are set up using similar principles as university-driven IEs. The university orchestrates the program to ensure trust and collaboration via establishing a transparent and mutually beneficial process. The programs are constructed in consecutive phases: problem identification, idea generation, business model innovation, new prototype design, and implementation support. This structure is based on the steps proposed by West and Bogers (2014) for the open innovation process. This process is important to ensure the alignment of expectations and setup of working channels across different actors in the IE.

In the beginning, the university searches the local entrepreneurial ecosystem to assess the level of maturity of existing startups or research teams. Discussions are held with incumbent firms to involve them in the IE and come up with sets of high-level concepts that would be of interest. The university acts as an intermediary for broadcast search (Jeppesen and Lakhani, 2010). A token monetary prize is decided to attract more startups to collaborate. Another important aspect of this stage is aligning the startups in understanding the business context, identifying business opportunities, and establishing a collaboration context. This is achieved by workshops and meetups which allow actors to familiarise themselves with each other and reinforce the feeling of a shared culture. Team-building exercises support the formulation of teams with complementary skills, including business vision and technical knowledge (Karagiannaki et al., 2018).

As the programs moves forward, the university serves as a facilitator to knowledge transfer and communication between the actors to promote the IE's activities. The university as a central institution can help actors innovate in terms of business model depending on how the co-creation evolves. This is done either by involving its own experts or bringing into the ecosystem expertise from the broader startup ecosystem. This procedure is once again easier to take place with a university present as it acts as a trusted mediator. This way the co-creation process can lead to new products or even a full "pivot" for certain actors.

Finally, as co-designed services start to appear, it is important to ensure a mutually beneficial collaboration by helping actors commercialise their co-creations. Co-creation can lead to decline of interest for some startups especially as the co-developed innovation can sometimes be acquired by the incumbent or allow startup founders to otherwise "exit". Irrespectively, concerning the sustainability of the IE, there is a need of a viable number of startups active and willing to collaborate with each other and the incumbent.

5. Findings and discussion

By analysing the three IEs, a total of 17 factors that drive the sustainability of the ecosystem is identified and consequently the actors' willingness to continue. A summary of the findings can be found Table 1. The factors are categorized based on the type of actor that identified them and their importance that is varied between the different cases. The factors' importance was ranked as high/low or non-applicable (n/a). For the sake of brevity, we opted to omit the interviews, but they are available upon request.

Table 1: Ecosystem sustainability factors by type of actor

Incumbents	Case A	Case B	Case C
Access to Talent	n/a	High	n/a
Acquisition	n/a	High	n/a
Product Co-Creation	High	High	Low
Outwards Exposure	High	High	Low
Innovation Procurement	High	High	High
Intrapreneurial Culture	n/a	Low	High
New Market Expansion	Low	High	High
Startups	**Case A**	**Case B**	**Case C**
Access to Industry Experts	Low	High	High
Customer Acquisition	High	High	High
Outwards Exposure	Low	n/a	n/a
Partnerships/ Joint-Venture	Low	High	Low
Market Knowledge	n/a	High	High
Networking	High	High	Low
Prize Funding	Low	Low	Low
Product/Service Development	Low	High	High
(Pre)Seed Funding	High	High	Low
Time to produce results	Low	Low	Low

5.1 Innovation ecosystem sustainability factors as seen by incumbents

The incumbents identified seven different factors as described in the following paragraphs.

Access to talent refers to the effort to find new people to employ in a firm. This was not explicitly mentioned by the incumbents but in case B there was an effort to absorb talent from the startups to the firm itself. As this only happened in Case B, it can be surmised that it was a firm specific behaviour. Similarly, the incumbent that was more willing to absorb startup staff was also more willing to move forward with the *acquisition* of startups and their solutions when they developed promising products. In the other two cases, both in terms of access to talent and acquisition, the importance was low to non-existent.

Product co-creation refers to the effort to create new products together with the companies involved in the ecosystem. This was high on the list of all the cases, as incumbents were eager early on to develop new innovations by appealing to an innovative ecosystem. However, especially in the Case C as the system was evolving the factor's relevance diminished. This evolution is possibly related to the fact that this sector, i.e. the food industry, requires a lot of resources in terms of time and funds to be devoted to R&D. It also requires a lot of technical expertise for products to be developed and be adopted into the incumbent's supply chain.

Outwards exposure was also important, and incumbents considered it a high priority to demonstrate social responsibility. Case A demonstrated that that exposure was initially a very important driver. However, as the ecosystem matured and the incumbent understood the business value that can be created, exposure became of secondary importance.

Innovation procurement refers to buying new innovations outside of the firm. It is the effort of the established firms that are characterized by incumbent inertia (Lieberman and Montgomery, 1988) to find innovative solutions to their problems that they cannot develop in-house. This was a high priority from the moment the incumbents committed to the IE and remained as such throughout their involvement. Especially when considering complementary solutions that could be used to enhance their core offerings in innovative ways, this was one of the main benefits that the incumbents identified in remaining in the ecosystem.

In some cases, the incumbents were also interested in cultivating entrepreneurial mindset amongst their employees, hence promoting *intrapreneurial culture*. This element was discussed in all cases however it turned out as most relevant in Case C. In all cases the responsible departments wanted to motivate employees to think out of the box and search for new and innovative solutions. Especially in Case C we observed an active effort from the firm's side to involve as many different departments as possible. Also, while the ecosystem was starting to provide results, they involved employees in the ecosystem's activities. We theorise that this happened in part due to the specific personalities that were involved in each case and in part to the industry itself. Actors in the food industry, irrespective of their technological readiness, run traditional operations and are more focused to incremental innovation (Baregheh *et al.*, 2012). Contact with new technologies and disruptive innovation is something out of the ordinary that can be very exciting for people involved in this industry. It is also a harder for them to come in contact with the entrepreneurial ecosystem if they are not actively trying to do so. This, on the other hand, is not the case in fintech where a lot of disruption is happening, and employees are moving across companies sharing knowledge and expertise.

Finally, *new market expansion* was a factor that, while not evident in the beginning and not initially planned, was an indirect result of the incumbents' involvement in the ecosystem. This finding is also supported by the open innovation literature (Chesbrough, 2003) but what we observed in practice was that as new products were developed, that were on the peripheral of the company's main offerings, the company was forced to make the managerial decision to enter a new market, either directly or via a collaborative scheme with a startup, or to abandon the opportunity which usually meant a decline in the interest for future collaborations from the startup side. In some cases, this decision was more complex but in all cases the IE started a discussion about how to address needs in markets that were not the core business of the incumbent.

5.2 Innovation ecosystem sustainability factors as seen by startups

One of the most important elements for startups going into the ecosystem was access to *industry experts*. Their involvement in an ecosystem was deemed crucial to collaborate with people that had unique insights and knowledge. Knowledge that would otherwise be unattainable to an up-and-coming startup. However, the impact these experts had on the startups' value offering largely depended on the sector. For example, in the fintech case this ecosystem provided a lot of knowledge that was crucial for product development and market entry while in the case of airport operations the experts offered a more narrow scope.

A similar reasoning with the "industry experts" factor was evident as startups considered their involvement as an opportunity to gain insights, data, and in-depth *market knowledge*. This possibility constituted a big motivator for startups to join an ecosystem. Especially in the fintech case which involves a complex sector both in terms of regulation and customer acquisition. As the ecosystems evolved the incumbents' involvement and openness to share with the startups either highly motivated or demotivated them to remain active in the ecosystem. Contrary to the other two cases, in the airport operations case, as the ecosystem evolved this became increasingly irrelevant. Most startups were indifferent to learning more about the specific market and rather focussed their attention on other issues.

Another important aspect that retained its relevance throughout the startups' involvement in the ecosystem was *customer acquisition*. Essentially, startups were hoping that their involvement in a broader system would help them attract new customers either in the incumbents themselves, their partner network, or other SMEs that were involved in the process. This factor remained very important and in some cases was a game changer for the startups since they had direct access and exposure to a network of potential customers.

Outwards exposure and publicity outside the ecosystem were not important for both the incumbents and the startups. However, while initially startups considered it a very important factor as time went by this became less relevant for them. A two-sided reason was given for this. On the one hand as incumbents realized that exposure was secondary to the actual value generation, they reduced their effort towards that direction. Since they were the most capable actors to drive publicity, the ecosystem was not exposed as a whole. On the other hand, while this might seem like a loss for the startups, at the same time startups realised that more value could be found inside the ecosystem and through the collaboration they already built and hence outwards exposure became secondary.

The possibility of a *joint venture or partnership* was always a very important factor for the startups. As the ecosystem evolved, we observed several partnerships taking place mainly between an incumbent and a startup. Market relevance was crucial in this process. While specific joint ventures have been discussed, one has yet to come to full fruition. As discussion often take place this is something that startups look forward to and the incumbents have also been positive towards, under the right circumstances.

In every business system, networking is a very powerful tool (Gay, 2014). Throughout their involvement in the ecosystem, startups considered networking as one of the most important factors to remain. The more active the ecosystem was the more networking, making the startups more committed. However, this was sector specific as startups not interested in the core industry of the incumbent were less inclined to pursue networking.

One of the mechanisms to initially engage startups in the ecosystem was *prize funding*. As these ecosystems were built upon an open innovation programme, they were also running in parallel to a competition. The idea was to offer some token prize funding to the startups that showed engagement and progress. This funding was relatively small (up to €5,000) but was seen as an extra incentive. While initially this was considered as an important factor after the continuous collaboration of startups and incumbents the price funding was one of the less motivating factors for a company to continue to operate in the ecosystem.

The IEs offered a unique opportunity to startups to *develop and test their products and services*. These ecosystems allowed startups a chance to test their products, come in contact with the market stakeholders, and validate their offerings. Furthermore, they could develop their products using the facilities and help offered by the other organisations involved (incumbents, startups, and the university itself). This remains a factor of prime importance for them to remain to the ecosystem.

Seed funding is always of central importance for a startup. Startups considered their involvement in the IEs as a way to demonstrate the value of their products and attract VCs. The role of the institution (i.e. the university) here was essential to connect the IE with potential investors to make it more attractive for actors. Several startups remaining over year received venture capital funding afterwards. In hindsight, their involvement allowed them to accelerate their growth and demonstrate that they were capable of navigating a network to create value.

Finally, an unexpected factor that came into play, was the *time to produce results*. Startups were reluctant to continue to operate in the ecosystem if they did not see results for their product quickly enough. The term "quickly enough" is used loosely as it differed a lot across startups. This however meant that if the actors in the ecosystem were not as motivated to work and collaborate it created a demotivation for some startups that wanted to accelerate their innovation. This was not an issue that was reported across startups but rather stressed in certain cases.

6. Conclusion

This study aims to describe a university-driven IE and analyse how actors operating inside it are driven to continue collaborating, thus ensuring the sustainability of the ecosystem. The actors involved identified several factors as critical to continue pursuing the ecosystem activities and creating value adding artifacts. Essentially, the ecosystems proved to be a method of accelerating the maturity of startups and providing incumbents with innovations that would be otherwise unattainable. While these artificial ecosystems were focused on helping internal actors, they eventually drew the attention of stakeholders from the broader startup ecosystem such as venture capitalists and other investors. This is also an important issue for further research as university-driven ecosystems can become the nucleoli around which broader intrapreneurial innovation ecosystems can be formed. Using a university as an orchestrating institution proved important in forming the ecosystems and setting the field for the eventual collaborations between incumbents and startups. It is clear that depending on their sector and size, companies search for different drivers to stay committed in an ecosystem, drivers that while different are not mutually exclusive and are attainable under the right circumstances.

References

Adner, R. (2006) 'Match your innovation strategy to your innovation ecosystem', *Harvard Business Review*, Vol.84, No.4, pp. 98-107

Albuam, G. and Oppenheim, A. N. (1993) 'Questionnaire Design, Interviewing and Attitude Measurement', *Journal of Marketing Research*, Vol.30, No.3, pp.393-395

Baregheh, A. *et al.* (2012) 'Innovation in food sector SMEs', *Journal of Small Business and Enterprise Development*. Vol.19, No.2, pp. 300-321

Beliaeva, T. *et al.* (2019) 'Dynamics of digital entrepreneurship and the innovation ecosystem: A multilevel perspective', *International Journal of Entrepreneurial Behaviour and Research*. Vol.26, No.2, pp. 266-284

Ceccagnoli, M. *et al.* (2012) 'Cocreation of valueina platform ecosystem : the case of enterprise software', *MIS Quarterly*, Vol.36, No.1,pp.263-290.

Chesbrough, H. W. (2003) *The new imperative for creating and profiting from technology*, *Harvard Business Publishing*.

Cohen, W. M., Nelson, R. R. and Walsh, J. P. (2002) 'Links and impacts: The influence of public research on industrial R&D', *Management Science*, Vol.48, No.1

Cooke, P., Uranga, M. G. and Etxebarria, G. (1997) 'Regional innovation systems: Institutional and organisational dimensions', *Research Policy*. Vol.26, No. 4–5, pp.475-491

Dahlander,L. and Gann, M.(2010)'How open is innovation?',*Research Policy*. Vol.39, No.6,pp.699-709

Dattee, B., Alexy, O. and Autio, E. (2018) 'Maneuvering in poor visibility: How firms play the ecosystem game when uncertainty is high', *Academy of Management Journal*. Vol.61, No.2,pp.466-498

Dennehy, D. and Conboy, K. (2019) 'Breaking the flow: a study of contradictions in information systems development (ISD)', *Information Technology and People*. Vol.33,No.2,pp. 477-501

Durst, S. and Poutanen, P. (2013) 'Success factors of innovation ecosystems - Initial insights from a literature review', *CO-CREATE 2013: The Boundary-Crossing Conference on Co- Design in Innovation,* Helsinki.

Etzkowitz, H. and Leydesdorff, L. (2000) 'The dynamics of innovation: From National Systems and "mode 2" to a Triple Helix of university-industry-government relations', *Research Policy*. Vol.29,pp.109-123

Gay, B. (2014) 'Open innovation, networking, and business model dynamics: the two sides', *Journal of Innovation and Entrepreneurship*. Vol.3,No.2

Granstrand, O. and Holgersson, M. (2020) 'Innovation ecosystems: A conceptual review and a new definition', *Technovation*. Vol.90-91

Guerrero, M. *et al.* (2016) 'Entrepreneurial universities: emerging models in the new social and economic landscape', *Small Business Economics*. Vol.47,pp.551–563

Hannah, D. P. and Eisenhardt, K. M. (2018) 'How firms navigate cooperation and competition in nascent ecosystems', *Strategic Management Journal*, Vol.39,No.12

Heaton, S., Siegel, S. and Teece, D. J. (2019) 'Universities and innovation ecosystems: A dynamic capabilities perspective', *Industrial and Corporate Change*. Vol.28, No.4,pp. 921–939

Hippel, E. von (1988) 'The Source of Innovation', *Oxford University Press*.

Jeppesen, L. B. and Lakhani, K. R. (2010) 'Marginality and problem-solving effectiveness in broadcast search', *Organization Science*. Vol.21, No.5,pp.1016-1033

Karagiannaki, A., Trachana, T. and Doukidis, G. (2018) 'Leveraging Digital Entrepreneurship Through Collaboration Between Incumbent Firms and Entrepreneurial Ventures: An Inbound Open Innovation Perspective', *Management Studies*, Vol.6, No.5

Klofsten, M. and Jones-Evans, D. (2000) 'Comparing Academic Entrepreneurship in Europe -The Case of Sweden and Ireland', *Small Business Economics*. Vol14,pp.299–309

Lieberman, M. B. and Montgomery, D. B. (1988) 'First-mover advantages', *Strategic Management Journal*. Vol.9, No.1

Murphy, C., Klotz, A. and Kreiner, G.(2016). 'Blue skies and black boxes: The promise (and practice) of grounded theory in human resource management research', Human Resource Management Review, Vol.27, No.2, pp.291-305

Nambisan, S. and Baron, R. A. (2013) 'Entrepreneurship in innovation ecosystems: Entrepreneurs' self-regulatory processes and their implications for new venture success', *Entrepreneurship: Theory and Practice*. Vol.37,No.5,pp. 071–1097

Oh, S. *et al.* (2016) 'Innovation ecosystems: A critical examination', *Technovation*. Vol.54,No.C,pp.1-6

Ritala, P. and Almpanopoulou, A. (2017) 'In defense of "eco" in innovation ecosystem', *Technovation*. Vol.60–61,pp. 39-42

Shaikh, M. and Levina, N. (2019) 'Selecting an open innovation community as an alliance partner: Looking for healthy communities and ecosystems', *Research Policy*. Vol.48, No.8

Suominen, A., Seppänen, M. and Dedehayir, O. (2019) 'A bibliometric review on innovation systems and ecosystems: a research agenda', *European Journal of Innovation Management*. Vol.22,No.2, pp. 335-360

West, J. and Bogers, M. (2014) 'Leveraging external sources of innovation: A review of research on open innovation', *Journal of Product Innovation Management*. Vol.31,No.4,pp.814-831

Yin, R. K. (2003) 'Case Study Research design and methods'. Sage, Thousand Oaks (CA)

Innovation Activities and Employment Level: An Empirical Assessment of Russian Manufacturing Companies

Yulia Balycheva and Oleg Golichenko
Central Economics and Mathematics Institute of Russian Academy of Sciences (CEMI RAS), Moscow Institute of Physics and Technologies (MIPT), Russia
yulia.balycheva@gmail.com
golichenko@rambler.ru
DOI: 10.34190/EIE.20.043

Abstract: The study analysis the impact of innovation on employment in Russian industry. Because innovation, by nature, has an oppositely directed influence on employment level, the impact of product and process innovations is considered separately. To this end, we study overcompensate and displacement effects. The first one refers to the replacement of labour with technology, and the second one refers to the growth of employment caused by the emergence of product innovation and the corresponding expansion of production. It is found that the growth in costs of process innovation causes a decrease in employment and the increase in innovative production (product innovation) positively affects the level of employment.

Keywords: innovation, employment, labour, industry, Russia

1. Introduction

Even though a steady positive impact of innovation on long-term economic growth has been established, there is still no answer to the question of how innovation processes affect employment levels in the economy. A considerable amount of scientific research is devoted to this problem (Вешкурова et al, 2017; Entorf and Pohlmeier, 1990; Lachenmaier and Rottmann, 2011). The difficulties are largely because innovation, because of its nature, has two impacts on economic employment (Harrison et al, 2014, 2008; Greenan and Guellec, 2011). On the one hand, new technologies replace the use of labor in production processes, and on the other hand, their use leads to increased demand for new products (Moon, 2008; Kwon et al, 2015). The latter encourages firms to expand production, resulting in increased demand for manpower. In other words, innovation, even by releasing labour through displacement effects, can generate additional growth for these resources through the emergence and/or expansion of new products. Therefore, the result is not predetermined and depends on the relationship between the displacement effect and overcompensate effect. Since the theory does not allow to determine this ratio due to the difficulty of predicting the variants of technological development, it is possible to determine how much one of these effects dominates the other only after the application of empirical methods.

From what has just been said, it follows that the displacement and overcompensate effects are generated by different types of innovation: process and product innovation. This is reflected in the different objectives for which firms use these types of innovations (Капелюшников, 2017). Process innovations are designed to improve the production process, in particular, to increase productivity and reduce cost. In a competitive environment, the reduction in the cost of production encourages the producer to reduce the price of the product and thus increases its demand. Growth of demand issue the challenge of expansion of manufacture, i.e. attraction of an additional labour force, if productivity growth does not allow to solve a problem of manufacture expansion completely. That is, along with the displacement effect there is an overcompensate effect (Seidl da Fonseca, 2017). Product innovation has a significant impact on the development of the overcompensate effect. If such innovation is introduced in the existing market, then, by expanding the demand for an improved product, it leads to the expansion of production, i.e. employment growth. When product innovation generates a new market, they trigger additional demand for labour. To meet this demand, it is necessary to either relocate labour from existing markets or involve a new resource that has not yet been used. In the first case, the effect of increasing employment will not work, and in the second case, it might be very significant.

It should also be noted that in some cases process innovations may not cause an overcompensate effect even with significant displacement. In other words, cost reduction may lead to the substitution of labour resources and may not contribute to production expansion (Balycheva ллland Samovoleva, 2019). This situation arises in monopolistic (Vivarelli, 2014) or oligopolistic markets. At the same time, an overcompensate effect arises when a decrease in production costs leads to a decrease in prices and, accordingly, to an increase in demand. It follows from the above that when studying the impact of innovation on employment, the degree of monopolization of markets should be taken into account. The presence of this effect is indirectly reflected in the significant scale of production, which exceeds the amounts needed to achieve optimal productivity and efficiency in the production process. In many activities, large scale production is often associated with the need to optimize the production process. At the same time, however, firms that have reached this level have prerequisites for taking a monopolistic position. One of the indicators of using innovation to strengthen their monopolistic position is the active use of process innovation.

Thus, as a working hypothesis, we can consider that the indicators of the presence of displacement and overcompensate effects are, respectively, the scale of product and process innovation using. These scales, as practice shows, largely depend on the specifics of activities, market structure and the degree of competition. For this reason, this paper looks at the impact of innovation activity on employment changes in the economy, taking into account the type of activity and the type of innovation applied. The impact of product and process innovation on the change in employment levels in different activities is examined separately.

2. Data and methods

The paper uses the data of the Russian Federal State Statistical Service for 2010-2016, published in the collections "Industrial production in Russia, 2016", as well as on the official website of the Unified information system for the Ministry of Education and Science of the Russian Federation.

When building an econometric model, the employment growth rate was used as a dependent variable, taking into account the type of economic activity. To assess the impact of changes in demand for labour caused by the production of old products, the indicator of growth in this output was chosen as an independent variable. In order to assess the impact of innovation activity in the introduction and diffusion of new products, the growth of innovation output was considered. This is a key indicator for assessing the impact of product innovation on employment change (Harrison et al, 2014). An analysis of the impact of process innovation is proposed based on the indicator of unit costs of process innovation. The increase in unit costs of machinery and equipment in the cost of technological innovation is used as an additional indicator to assess the trend towards a renewal of production processes and overall production expansion. To assess the propensity of firms to develop and implement new products and methods of production, the indicator of unit costs for research and development of new products, services and methods of their production in the costs of technological innovation was taken into account. Also, the cost of technological innovation is considered as an independent variable. In the following, indicators will be discussed separately and the main results of the econometric analysis will be presented.

3. General characteristics of employment and innovation in Russian economy

The overall innovative activity of Russian industrial enterprises is low. For most industries, the share of sales of innovative products in all sales is less than 5% and for only a small part of the activities this indicator exceeds 20% (see Fig. 1). This situation is related to high risks and low business interest in the implementation of innovative projects (Balycheva and Golichenko, 2015; Samovoleva and Balycheva, 2018).

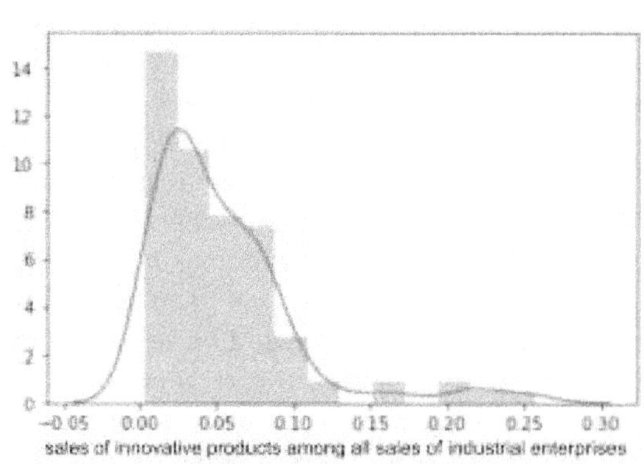

Figure 1: Share of sales of innovative products among all sales of industrial enterprises (2010-2015)

At the same time, most industries are characterized by an increase in the production of innovative products compared to the previous period (see Fig. 2).

Figure 2: Distribution of sales growth of innovative products compared to the previous period (2010-2015)

The low output of innovative products indicates a low tendency of firms to introduce product innovations, which usually lead to higher employment levels. However, companies may be actively involved in the implementation of process innovations to optimize the innovation process and reduce the cost of earlier products. Thus, investments of Russian industrial firms in process innovations are higher than investments in product innovations (see Fig. 3). At the same time, it can be noted that most activities are focused on one type of innovation activity, either companies are engaged in product or process innovations.

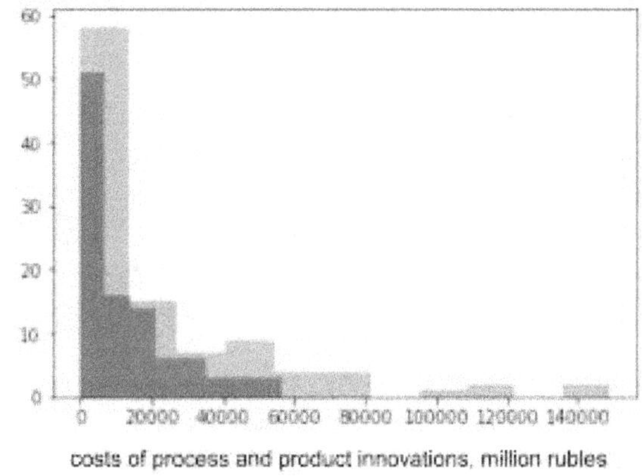

Figure 3: Distribution of costs of process (purple) and product innovations (pink) of Russian industrial enterprises (2010-2015), million rubles

The required number of employees at the enterprise to produce equal value products varies greatly depending on the type of economic activity (see Fig. 4). For example, to produce a unit of production of leather products requires 50 times more manpower than to produce coke and petroleum products.

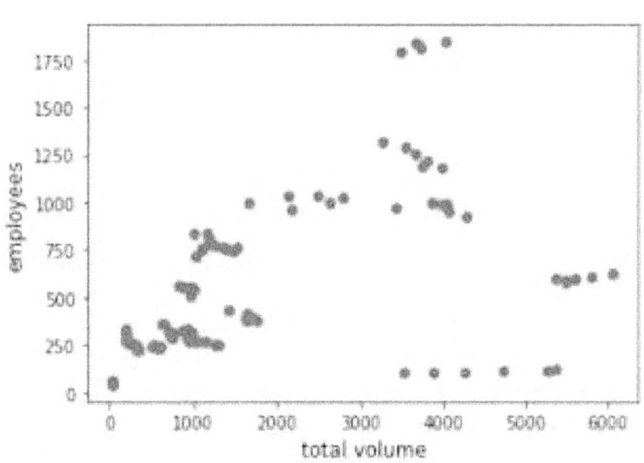

Figure 4: Dependence on the number of employees at Russian industrial enterprises (2010-2015)

A similar situation is observed when considering the dependence of innovative output on pure employment. In some studies, it is proposed to use the hypothesis that the increase in output is equal to the increase in the number of employed in this production to assess the change in employment in the economy as a result of innovation (Harrison et al, 2008). This makes it possible to consider that the increase in demand for the old not innovative products of enterprises, is equal to the increase in the labour resource necessary for its production. As a result, the growth of enterprises engaged in the innovation process can be estimated as the difference between the increase in the overall level of employment in production and the increase in output of non-innovative products. The increase in employment thus calculated can be considered a pure increase in employment. When considering the growth of pure employment and the growth of output of innovative products, there is no obvious linear dependence on them. It can also be noted that the change in pure employment in most cases takes negative values (see Fig. 5), which indirectly indicates the prevalence of the displacement effect.

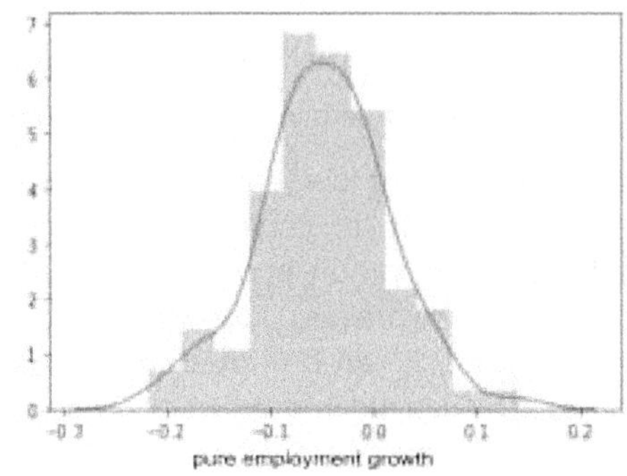

Figure 5: Distribution of pure employment growth of industrial Russian enterprises (2010-2015)

At the same time, the number of employees in research and development units is small; depending on the type of activity, the share of employees engaged in scientific research and development does not exceed 4%. The maximum is observed among high-tech enterprises engaged in the production of electrical equipment, electronic and optical equipment. For these activities, innovation activity is largely based on own research and development to introduce new products through product innovation. As a result, the share of sales of innovative products for this type of activity ranges from 7% to 9%, which is significantly higher than the national average.

The distribution of the number of researchers by type of economic activity is shown in Fig. 6. Thus, for most types of activities, the share of researchers does not exceed 0.4%.

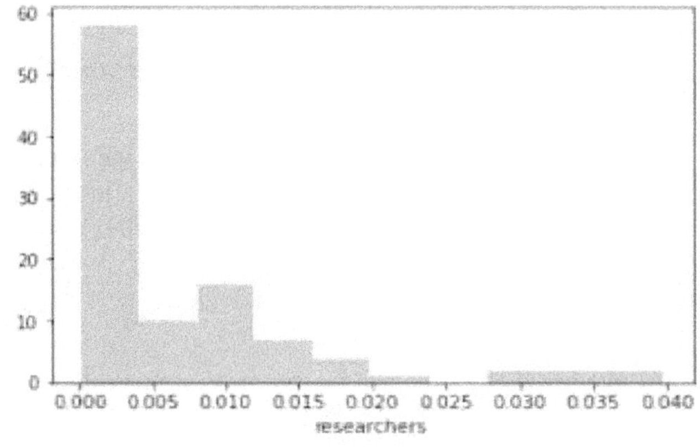

Figure 6: Distribution of the share of researchers in the total number of employees of Russian industrial firms (2010-2015)

Two random forest models were trained for preliminary data analysis and identification of the most significant features. In the first case, the dynamics of the overall change in employment rate is considered as a dependent variable, while in the second case, the change in pure employment rate is considered as a dependent variable. In the first stage, the following variables are considered as attributes: sales of all products, sales of innovative and non-innovative products, costs of product innovation, cost of process innovation, costs of research and development and acquisition of machinery and equipment related to innovation, and the number of researchers. Changes in these indicators and their specific values were also considered. Further, the pairwise correlations of the features in question were analyzed (see Fig. 7).

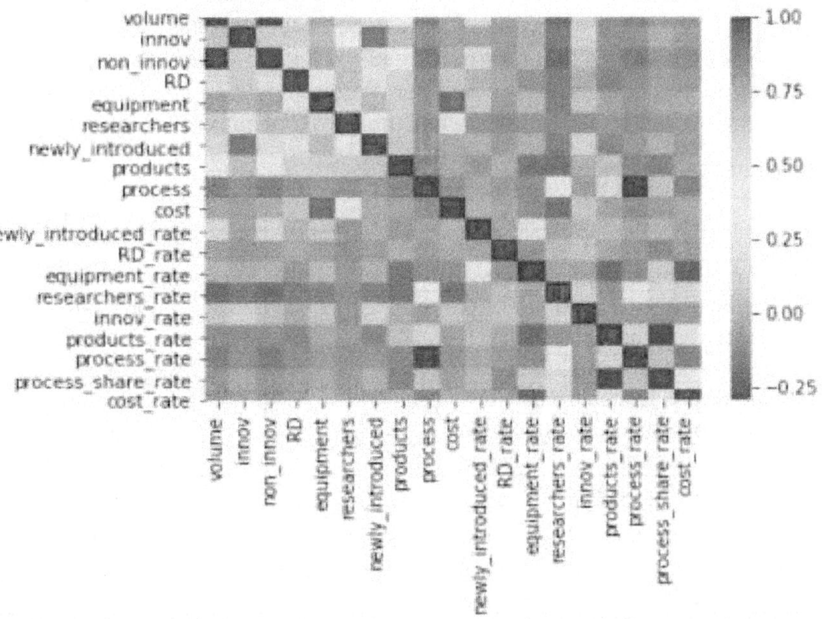

Figure 7: Heatmap of correlation of all considered attributes

Since many indicators are linearly dependent, nine linearly independent features have been selected for further analysis. These were: total volume of all sales, growth in sales of innovative products, growth in sales of newly introduced innovative products, costs of process innovation, growth in research and development costs, growth in costs of product innovation, growth in costs of purchasing machinery and equipment associated with innovation, the number of researchers and growth in the number of researchers. The selected features were considered as independent variables for learning the random forest model. For the first model, the growth rate of total employment calculated as a ratio of the number of employees in the current period to the number of employees in the previous period was considered as a dependent variable. Further, if there was an increase, the indicator was assigned the value +1 if the decrease is 0. When training the model, the whole sample was randomly divided into a training and a test sample, there were 33% of observations in the test sample. For training, 50 random trees were used, with the maximum depth of the tree being 5. An example of one tree is shown in Fig. 8.

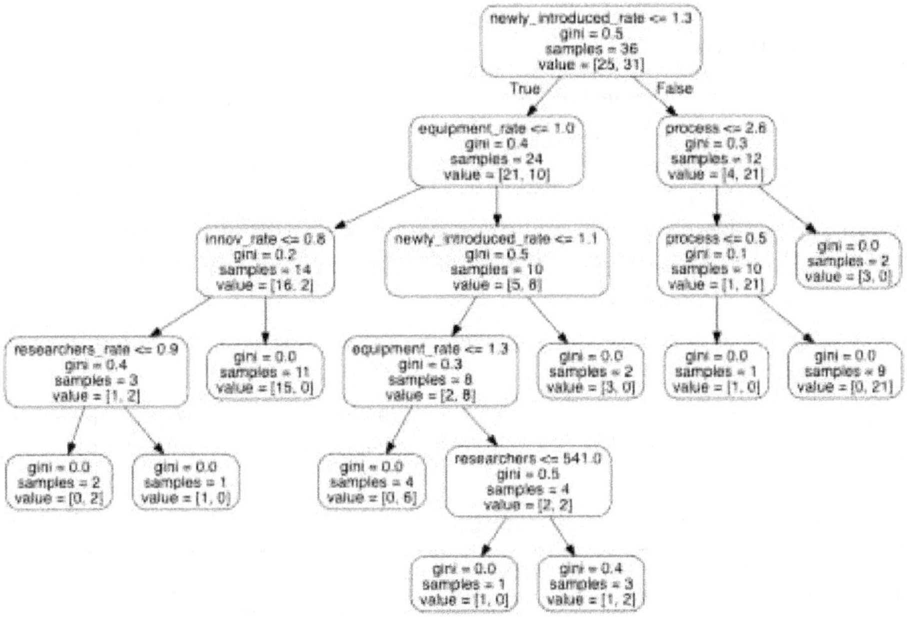

Figure 8: An example of one of fifty random trees used for analysis

After training the model, it was applied on the deferred test sample, the model accuracy was 0.72. Next, the most important indicators for building the tree were selected (see Table 1). It turned out that indicators of sales of all products, growth in sales of newly introduced innovative products and growth in sales of all innovative products were used most often in tree construction. It can be noted that the importance of the indicator in the construction of the tree does not mean that its growth leads to the growth of the dependent variable. This result agrees well with the notion that changes in the number of employed people are most significantly affected by both characteristics of the overall production scale and indicators of changes in innovative output.

Table 1: Importance of indicators in model 1

Indicator	Designation	Importance
Gross sales	volume	0.19
Sales growth of newly introduced innovative products	newly_introduced_rate	0.13
Sales growth of innovative products	innov_rate	0.12
Costs of process innovation	process	0.11
Growth of number of researchers	researchers_rate	0.10
Increased costs of innovation-related machinery and equipment	equipment_rate	0.09
Increased cost of research and development	RD_rate	0.09
Increased costs of product innovation	products_rate	0.08
Number of researchers	researchers	0.07

For the second model, the pure employment change was chosen as a dependent variable, which reflects only the change in employment associated with innovative output. The training was similar to the first model and the accuracy of the second model was 0.86 on test data. The importance of the attributes is shown in Table 2.

Table 2: Importance of indicators in model 1

Indicator	Designation	importance
Increased cost of research and development	RD_rate	0.15
Gross sales	volume	0.14
Costs of process innovation	process	0.14
Sales growth of innovative products	innov_rate	0.13
Increased costs of product innovation	products_rate	0.11
Growth of number of researchers	researchers_rate	0.10
Sales growth of newly introduced innovative products	newly_introduced_rate	0.09
Increased costs of innovation-related machinery and equipment	equipment_rate	0.08
Number of researchers	researchers	0.06

The most significant indicators for dividing the sample into two classes where there was an increase or decrease in employment were indicators of growth in R&D costs, the scale of all production and the cost of process innovation.

4. Employment and output

Most industries are characterized by a decline in employment over the period from 2010 to 2015. The only exceptions are the extractive industry and activities related to the production of coke and petroleum products. Employment in these industries grew by 5% and 12%, respectively (see Table 3). There is also no significant change in the level of utilization of human resources in activities related to the production of electrical equipment, electronic and optical equipment. At the same time, the biggest drop in employment is observed in leather, leather goods and footwear production (23%), pulp and paper production (20%) and textile production (19%).

Table 3: General characteristics of changes in employment and productive activity of enterprises of different types of activities

Type of economic activity	Change of employment level (2010 2015)	Growth in non-innovative output (2010 to 2015)	Growth in innovative output (2010 to 2015)
Extraction of fuel and energy minerals	7,3%	9,7%	47%
Mining of minerals other than fuel and energy resources	0,6%	30,8%	126%
Manufacture of foodstuffs, including beverages and tobacco	-10,0%	22,1%	21%
Textile and garment manufacturing	-19,3%	-2,5%	45%
Manufacture of leather, leather goods and shoes	-22,5%	-21,1%	-18%

Type of economic activity	Change of employment level (2010 2015)	Growth in non-innovative output (2010 to 2015)	Growth in innovative output (2010 to 2015)
Wood processing and production of wood products	-16,4%	28,2%	355%
Pulp and paper production; publishing and printing activities	-20,3%	16,6%	60%
Manufacture of coke and petroleum products	12,0%	38,3%	480%
Chemical industry	-11,1%	24,8%	12%
Manufacture of rubber and plastic products	-4,9%	11,3%	94%
Manufacture of other non-metallic mineral products	-8,7%	14,7%	73%
Metallurgical production and manufacture of finished metal products	-4,5%	21,5%	103%
Manufacture of machinery and equipment	-14,1%	2,4%	-16%
Manufacture of electrical equipment, electronic and optical equipment	0,1%	30,0%	91%
Manufacture of vehicles and equipment	-3,3%	21,1%	79%
Other industries	-14,6%	33,3%	156%
Production and distribution of electricity, gas and water	-2,4%	-5,1%	3%

Despite the decline in employment over the period under study, most industries have seen an increase in non-innovative output and a significant increase in innovative production. Since output was measured in monetary terms, the producer price index by type of economic activity was used to bring the data to one base year.

Conditionally, all the considered activities can be divided into five groups depending on the ratio of labor force growth and non-innovative and innovative output. Thus, the first group includes industries where employment growth is accompanied by both conventional and innovative production. This group includes: mining, production of coconuts and oil products, and production of electrical equipment. There appears to be an expansion of production accompanied by the production of new products and the introduction of new technologies. Thus, for all branches of industry included in this group, there is an increase in the share of newly introduced or significantly improved innovative products in its total volume. There is also an increase in costs of process innovation, which indicates an attempt to improve the production base.

The second group combines industries where a decline in employment is accompanied by an increase in both conventional and innovative products. This group includes food production, wood processing, pulp and paper production, chemical production, rubber and plastic products, metallurgical production, production of other non-metallic mineral products, as well as production of vehicles and other production. It is likely that this group is characterized by the active use of both product and process innovations. At the same time, there is a prevalence of displacement effect and overcompensate effect.

The third group includes activities for which a decline in employment rates occurs against the background of increased innovative output and a decline in conventional output. This group includes textile and garment production and production and distribution of electricity, gas and water. Apparently, the main effect of the decrease in the labor force is caused by the reduction in production, despite some growth in the innovative activity of companies. The fourth group, which includes companies producing machinery and equipment, is characterized by a reduction in employment with the growth of conventional products and a decrease in the production of innovative products. The application of process innovation in this case leads to the substitution of jobs with technology. The fifth group is characterized by a decrease in employment with a decrease in all production activity. This situation is typical for the production of leather, leather goods and shoes. Compression in the industry leads to a reduction in the number of employed people.

5. Impact of innovation activity on changing employment levels

Further, regression analysis will be used to assess in more detail the impact of innovation and production activity on changes in labour use. As mentioned above, employment growth over one year for each activity in question (y) is considered as a dependent variable. The following are considered to be dependent variables: increase in conventional output (x_1), increase in innovative output (x_2), costs of technological innovation (x_3), unit cost of process innovation (x_4), unit costs of research and development of new products, services and production methods, new production processes in costs of technological innovation (x_5), increase in unit costs of machinery and equipment (x_6). The dependency is assumed to be: $y=\alpha_0+\alpha_1x_1+\alpha_2x_2+\alpha_3x_3+\alpha_4x_4+\alpha_5x_5+\alpha_5x_5+\varepsilon$

Table 4: Basic model assessment

	Dependent variable (employment growth rate)
Increase in conventional output (x_1)	0,2*** (0,035)
Increase in innovative output (x_2)	0,008* (0,004)
Costs of technological innovation (x_3)	4,7E-07*** (8,4E-08)
Unit cost of process innovation (x_4)	-0,1** (0,05)
Unit costs of research and development of new products, services and production methods, new production processes (x_5)	0,06** (0,02)
Increase in unit costs of machinery and equipment (x_6)	0,05*** (0,01)
Intercept	0,69*** (0,04)
R^2	0,72
Number of observations	85

Note: Standard errors are indicated in parentheses, "*," * * "and" * * * "indicate the value of the factor at 10, 5 and 1%, respectively.

As a result, it has been found that all factors except the cost of process innovation have a positive impact on employment growth (see Table 2). However, the ratio between innovative and non-innovative output growth rates is 0.04, while the average Russian ratio between innovative and non-innovative output is 4-5%. Thus, the increase in innovative and non-innovative output has the same effect on the growth of the labour force. A positive coefficient at the output growth rate of innovative products means that there is a significant overcompensate effect from product innovation when the growth in production of new products stimulates additional demand for manpower. The conclusion obtained for Russia is similar to the empirical results obtained for other countries, such as Germany (Entorf and Pohlmeier, 1990; Lachenmaier and Rottmann, 2011; Smolny, 1988) , France (Greenan and Guellec, 2011) Great Britain, Spain (Harrison et al, 2008), Italy (Hall et al, 2008), South Korea (Moon, 2008). A negative coefficient for unit costs of process innovation may indicate a displacement effect caused by the introduction of new technologies. This result is also well correlated with other studies (Harrison et al, 2008; Kwon et al, 2015). At the same time, high costs of technological innovation contribute to employment growth. In other words, the positive impact of product innovation compensates for the negative impact on the number of employed process innovation and also provides for their growth. The tendency of firms to develop innovative products, services and production methods in-house is more on the development of a overcompensate effect, rather than a displacement effect. The positive impact of the increase in the cost of acquisition of machinery and equipment associated with the innovative activity of companies is a consequence of the expansion of production and also contributes to the increase in demand for manpower.

6. Conclusions

The study found the impact of different types of innovation on the changing demand for manpower. It found that the growth of innovative products (product innovation) has a positive impact on changing employment levels in the economy. However, the same increase in the volume of innovative and non-innovative production requires an equal increase in the number of people employed to produce innovative and conventional products. This situation may be related to the fact that a large share of the growth of innovative output is occupied by modernized products, the production which does not require significant changes in the production base, i.e., large-scale introduction of process innovations. This means that the expansion of conventional production requires the involvement of new manpower to the same extent as that of innovative production.

The paper also shows that in modern conditions the increase in costs of process innovations in industrial enterprises leads to a significant amount of substitution of labor resources with capital. Unfortunately, the previous result shows that these process innovations are not radical enough to significantly renew production and thus ensure the production of innovative products of high quality (Samovoleva, 2019).

In addition, it should be noted that, depending on the ratio of changes in employment to output of conventional and innovative products, all activities can be roughly divided into five groups. The first group includes industries with increasing employment and output of both innovative and conventional products. This group is characterized by an expansion in production accompanied by the production of new products and the introduction of technologies. The second group is characterized by a decline in employment, accompanied by an increase in the production of both innovative and conventional products. Both product and process innovations are actively used here, with the displacement effect caused by the latter being dominant.

The third group includes activities for which the decline in employment occurs against the background of the growth of innovative output and the decline in the production of conventional products. In this case, the main effect of a decrease in the labour force is due to a reduction in output, despite some innovation activity in the group. The fourth group is characterized by a decrease in employment with the growth of production activity as a whole and a decrease in the volume of innovative products. The application of process innovation in this case can lead to a displacement effect, where jobs are replaced by technology. The fifth group is characterized by lower employment levels with lower overall productive activity. A reduction in the industry's production leads to a reduction in employment. The cumulative effect of all these groups leads to the effects described above.

References

Balycheva, Y., Golichenko, O. (2015) "The innovation process of Russian manufacturing companies", Proceedings of the 10th European Conference on Innovation and Entrepreneurship, ECIE 2015, 2015.

Balycheva, Y., Samovoleva, S. (2019) "Innovative businesses in Russian science cities", ECIE 2019, pp. 110-116.

Entorf, H., Pohlmeier, W. (1990) Innovation, Employment and Export Activity: Evidence From Firm-level Data.

Greenan, N., Guellec, D. (2011) "Technological innovation and employment reallocation", *Labour*, 14 (4), 547–590.

Hall, B.H., Lotti, F., Mairesse. (2008) "Employment, innovation, and productivity: evidence from Italian microdata", *Ind. Corp. Chang.*, 17 (4), 813–839.

Harrison, R., Jamandreu, J., Mairesse, J. (2014) "Does innovation stimulate employment? A firm-level analysis using comparable micro-data from four European countries", *International Journal Ind. Organ*, 35, 29–43.

Harrison, R., Jamandreu, J., Mairesse, J. (2008) "Does Innovation Stimulate Employment? A Firm-level Analysis Using Comparable Micro-data From Four European Countries", *National Bureau of Economic Research*.

Industrial production in Russia (2016), Federal state statistics service.

Kwon, S.J., Park, E., Ohm, J.Y., Yoo, K. (2015) "Innovation Activities and the Creation of New Employment: An Empirical Assessment of South Korea's Manufacturing Industry", *Social Science Information.*

Lachenmaier, S., Rottmann, H. (2011) "Effects of innovation on employment: a dynamic panel analysis", Int. J. Ind. Organ., 29 (2), 210–220.

Moon, S.B., Chun, H.B. (2008) "The effects of innovation activities on employment: evidence from Korean ICT firms", *Korean Journal of Industrial Organization*, 16 (1), 1–24.

Samovoleva, S.A. (2019) "Technological knowledge absorption as a factor of innovation development", *Voprosy Ekonomiki,* (11) pp. 150-158. (In Russ).

Samovoleva, S., Balycheva, Y. (2018), "Absorptive capacity as a factor of firms' innovative behaviour", ECIE 2018, pp. 709-716.

Seidl da Fonseca R. (2017) "The Future of Employment: evaluating the impact of STI foresight exercises", Foresight and STI Governance, vol. 11, no 4, pp.9-22.

Smolny, W. (1988) "Innovations, prices and employment: a theoretical model and an empirical application for West German manufacturing firms" *J. Ind. Econ.,* 46 (3), 359–381.

Vivarelli M.(2014) "Innovation, employment and skills in advanced and developing countries: a survey of economic literature", *Journal of Economics Issues*, 48 (1), pp.123–154.

Вешкурова, А. Б., Пономарев, М.А., Копылова Н.А. (2017) "Влияние экономики инновационного типа на занятость населения", Экономика и управление: проблемы, решения. Т.2, №8., с. 5-11.

Голиченко, О.Г., Балычева, Ю.Е. (2010) "Выбор рыночной стратегии использования интеллектуальной собственности российскими предприятиями", *Экономическая наука современной России,* №4(51), с. 68-82.

Капелюшников, Р. (2017) "Технологический прогресс - пожиратель рабочих мест?", Вопросы экономики, 2017, № 11.

RegTech: Case Studies of Cooperation With Banks in Italy

Luca Battanta, Marco Giorgino, Laura Grassi and Davide Lanfranchi
Politecnico di Milano, Italy
luca.federico.battanta@polimi.it
marco.giorgino@polimi.it
laura.grassi@polimi.it
davide.lanfranchi@polimi.it
DOI: 10.34190/EIE.20.143

Abstract: *Aims*: After the financial crisis financial institutions must comply and manage a huge amount of regulation coming from the EU and Italy. We would like to examine the experiences of technology integration applied to the regulation of the markets and to the compliace, in the banking sector in Italy. Our paper responds to a gap in literature that on the subject of regtech is mainly based on legal, defining arguments and about reviewing the literature on the macro context and the issues generated by the huge amount of regulation. The article will explore three cases of RegTech companies in Italy presenting advantages and criticalities in the adoption of regtech solutions on the Italian market. *Methods/Approach*: Today the literature about case study in RegTech is not proposing any solution of cooperation on the regulatory field in Italy. So we have to fill the gap we find in exploration of literature. An analysis in the field cannot be separated from a preliminary systematic review of the literature on regulatory case studies. We begin our scientific analysis of the subject through a preliminary literature review individuating any case study around RegTech through exploratory case study. Due to the scarcity of papers about case study in RegTech field, we adopt an approach already used for well-studied cases widespread in the FinTech area and an exploratory investigation through in deep interviews following models used in FinTech area and in ERM field. *Results/Findings*: In this article, we will, therefore, propose case studies in the FinTech sector applied to regulatory technology in Italy and we expect to answer the following research questions: We present three RegTech's cases in Italy's financial system exposing the fields of collaboration with financial institutions in RegTech field between incumbents and RegTech industries. We expose also how big I.T. companies, which are providing services for banks, are refocusing and improving compliance through RegTech to provide services linked to compliance, Kyc, Aml, privacy, payments to the incumbents. In conclusion we express topics interested by cooperation between banks and RegTech companies describing the potetial expansion lines. *Implications*: Understand how financial companies through regulatory technology can: Improve risk management and governance in financial institutions. Improve prudential compliance, anti money laundering and customer protection. Reduce the risks of traditional banking business through better knowledge and customer identification and profiling may also offer more favourable terms to companies and lowering compliance costs to shift economic resources towards FinTech's disruptive innovation.

Keywords: regtech, FinTech, finance, innovation, banks, regulation

1. Introduction: The financial environment in which is developed RegTech

After the great financial crisis of 2008, the financial system, in parallel with the rapid emergence of digital technologies in different business models led to the introduction of a new specific regulation for financial sector operators.

In this financial system, in parallel with the rapid emergence of digital technologies, FinTech startups have developed, offering products related to the regulatory sector("The new opportunity," Deloitte 2018.)

In this financial environment for banks is also an emergence because they see augmenting(Cosma et al., 2013) the cost of compliance an activity that does not generate value and revenue, takes money away from innovation, with less financial resources available for innovative services and technologies, to create new services for the customers through FinTech.

For European banks, the industry average cost of compliance is estimated 4% of total revenue average cost of compliance is estimated 4% of total revenue but is expected to rise to 10% by 2022("Compliance costs to more than double by 2022 - Financial News," 2017.).

The Cost of Compliance 2018 Report by Thomson Reuters discovers that 66% of firms expect the cost of senior compliance staff to increase ("COST OF COMPLIANCE", 2018).

For Bain & Co by 2021, that regulatory costs are expected to rise in the world from 4% to 10% of revenue, driven primarily by the sheer volume of regulations("Banking Regtechs to the Rescue?" 2016).

In 2018 thousand RegTech startups are operating around the world, offering most critical solutions for managing regulatory change in the field of AML and KYC, sematic interpretation of the norms, governance, audit, accounting and regulatory reporting platforms ("How RegTech closes the gap between technology and financial services" Bloomberg 2017).

The paper is about what regulation analysis of "RegTech" focusing on the Italian case study on the RegTech market.

We want to analyze characteristics of the actors involved in the Italian market that are spreading RegTech solutions and cooperate with incumbents to decrease costs of compliance and make more efficient to face the regulation. We describe also best practices about this topic applied to the financial industry and the different approaches of cooperation between incumbents and RegTech's startups. The need for adaptation to the new context is particularly relevant for the Italian financial market where banks must comply and help to manage a huge amount of regulation coming from the European Union and national Authorities.

Most of the small number of studies in the scientific literature about regulatory technologies are centred on literature review, law and the macro context (Arner et al., 2016). and about issues generated by the huge amount of the regulation after the great financial crisis. Relevant studies are (Arner et al., 2016), protection of the customers in bank faluire (Baxter, 2016), about the complexity of risk supervisoring in financial istitutions(Anagnostopoulos, 2018a) about supervisory reporting (Kavassalis et al., 2018).

Literature is not today providing a framework of functions and application for the banks for regulatory technology and we have to fill this research gap.

2. Methodology

2.1 The preliminary literature review.

For the research of some academics' papers in the field, we used the following services: Scopus, SSRN, Google Scholar. To identify relevant articles, we conduct a keyword "RegTech case study" in a second step in the over-mentioned databases and over the internet.

The research of definitions of "RegTech" proposed by the consultant was conducted systematically by searching the word "RegTech" on research engines conjointly with the internal research engine of the international websites of the main consultancy firms authorities' papers, along with looking for the references in the consultant and academics articles. We applied as well the following constraints: (1) dating to 15.6.2020 (without any lower time of beginning). (2) available in English.

Once all the papers with the presented methodology have been collected, they were analyzed looking for a case study of "RegTech".

Our literature review in RegTech and FinTech case study, using the Keyword "RegTech case study" and "FinTech case study", shows that few studies have argued about the strategies or the development of a FinTech company. In the field of paper but we don't find any paper or any detailed case.

Only the book "Understanding RegTech for Digital Regulatory Compliance. Disrupting Finance" (Butler; Brien, 2018) has answered positively to our query searched.

The cited case is managed superficially, but the contribute cites advantages noted are the ability to free up regulatory capital due to the better monitoring, as well as automation reducing some of the estimated $70 billion that major financial institutions spend on compliance each year. A key player in RegTech is IBM following their acquisition of Promontory (a 600-staff RegTech), and they now offer a range of AI-driven solutions for reducing RegTech costs, demonstrating the widespread industry interest in the area not just confined to startups. For example, real-time voice conversation analysis to be used to ensure compliance "through a combination of IBM's

Watson AI expertise and Promontory's domain-specific expertise". For (Baxter, 2016) regulators, law makers, entrepreneurs, and investors participate in technology applied within the innovative financial services domain. It is also of interest to bankers who might consider FinTech and strategic partnerships as a prospective, future strategic direction and for (Anagnostopoulos, 2018a) financial inclusion for regulators and for developing countries RegTech has the potential to reshape the way people engage with financial services. One of the key movers of the prospective regulatory transformations is the reimagining of financial infrastructures to include digital identities and blockchain-enabled technologies. (Bhyer et al., 2019).

2.2 The method to find and examine cases

To examine the contemporary phenomenon of RegTech we think to inspire our research from the FinTech's field. In the FinTech field, Pan e Tan and Walsham propose using a qualitative case study research methodology is adopted (Pan and Tan, 2011); (Walsham, 1995).

We have in FinTech and RegTech very diversified and narrow number of cases differences in business in the field so is resulting impossible to apply a quantitative case study approach; instead is compatible with such field. In such way, our paper will develop an illustrative case study about RegTech and the application for incumbents to make the unfamiliar field of regulatory technology more familiar and to give scholars a common language and the first exploration of application studies about the topic in question.

The illustrative case studies were accompanied by Exploratory (or pilot) Case Studies.

We need case studies performed before implementing an investigation to understand the RegTech market and application in Italy. Their basic function is to help identify questions and select types of measurement before the main investigation.

As done in previous case in FinTech (Hung and Luo, 2016) crowdfunding (Lee and Kim, 2015) about and the Erm's topic (Arena et al., 2010) field we organize the extrapolation of relevant concept and the discovery of application and to extrapolate outcomes in the form of lessons learned by practice and the interviewees were identified in conjunction with the CEO and managers, product managers so in our specifical topic the regulatory field division. The first exploratory paper about case study in the FinTech's field, (Hung and Luo, 2016) is the more similar to our intent because it is linked with FinTech companies and collaboration with the banking system. This study aims to identify the strategic considerations in the process of searching for FinTech investment targets.

We decide to collect data primarily through in-depth semi-structured interviews and corroborated by our observation notes, material provided from the entity and secondary data taken from insider and regulatory product managers and legislative counterpart. Case access was negotiated through the company's CEO and the regulatory division responsible, which granted us an immediate "legitimacy and credibility" (Patton, 1990); Since we aim to understand the application of RegTech on regulated actors of the market in Italy to doing this phase of analysis we are inspiring Hung and Luo" Financial Innovation" (2016) because is related to cooperation between banks and FinTech.

For FinTech, there are previous case studies but for RegTech implementation, we have not a referment model so need to think about how to make some use case. We select to analyze the most representative dimensions in our sample and the most involved with the incumbents according to Seawright and Gerring 2008(Seawright and Gerring, 2008), our choice of cases is primarily driven along these dimensions within the population of interest to have a broad view of the phenomenon, for monitoring the regulation, the technological and linguistic interpretation provided by semantic instruments to deliver the correct interpretation of the regulation and for the right application into a financial institution. For individuating company and RegTech usage, we inspire our job to a paper based on the literature review that at the end provided a RegTech definition. Thanks to this definition that we reported below RegTech is involved in "RegTech is the use of technology in the context of regulatory field in compliance, fraud detection, lowering costs to comply to the regulation, KYC, monitoring and managing the risk and reporting anomaly more than existing capabilities" (Battanta et al., 2019)

With these cases study we will analyze collective action and collaboration is important to take innovation in a market like the Italian financial market Interdependencies result from differences between actors in terms of resources, time and money possessed. The cases chosen are focused in fact over Interdependencies may especially trigger collective action as resourceful actors make collaboration attractive for others (Heckathorn, 1993);

RegTech is also connected to Platform Theory.

In the case of banks are the managing of regulatory field and core business of a bank so it is a transversal business through the sector and the distinct characteristics of platforms are relevant the four issues regarding collective interaction for entities and customers.

In the topics of business strategy and management, field utilized the words "industry platform" and define it as "building blocks" (he argues that could be a product, technologies or services) that "act as business ecosystem can develop complementary products, technologies or services"(Gawer, 2009). RegTech is also part of a block applied the financial industry in term of services applied to the regulatory field and compliance.

Also for Walshe e Cropper RegTech is identify as a platform in "Should you be banking on RegTech?"(Walshe and Cropper, 2018)

By mediating interactions between two or more groups of organizations, platforms create network effects (Ballon, 2009); (Evans and Guthrie, 2006); (Rochet and Tirole, 2003).

In the case of banks, RegTech companies, are helping to manage the regulatory field. The banks could focus on the core business and RegTech companies create a transversal business through the financial sector which is the regulatory business. Regtech is complementary to the core business of the bank.

The cases can be viewed as a series of experiments, allowing for replication rather than just sampling(Yin, 1984).

We achieved this with three cases whose findings are replicated across different levels of analysis. In practice, this means that each case is analyzed concerning the framework and the cases. This permits a deeper and richer understanding of the underlying facts and circumstances. This type of empirical grounding gives theory and application that is more likely to be free of the bias of the researcher(Eisenhardt, 1989), and that maintains a close correspondence between the theory that we found and the data available to evaluate it. This is especially important in the early stages of research on a new topic, as RegTech when it is not clear whether the research question is provided by existing theories. In this study, we focus on the technological innovation technologies applied and their cooperation strategies that are being used for entry into the RegTech's market. Following these guidelines chose to map accelerator, consultancy firms and events and acquisition with the keywords "RegTech firms" and in the Italian language.

We found three case in Italy. All three are categorizing themselves as RegTech companies that are involved in lowering costs for a bank and permits the incumbent to be focused in other innovations because RegTech lightens the cost of compliance, that is a huge problem inside the banks.

3. Case analysis and results

3.1 Case one

The first case is Cedacri.

The company makes a revenue of about 350 million euros per year and have 500 employees. As I.T. operator on the Italian market, they are the largest third provider for financial institutions after Accenture and IBM.

Cedacri is the largest Italian-owned company in banking outsourcing services. As far as RegTech application are concerned, they have worked on a data governance information container that ensures quality and traceability of the data and those who decide to join the service may decide to draw on a robust database, being able to extrapolate the different trends and the beliefs of customers.

For Mifid 2 they have developed a native multi-bank system for their shareholder banks and partners that allows the client to be compliant with the regulations but also adapted to different business models in financial institutions. For retail banks they create a technological infrastructure that governs the whole process for the supply chain, for example about financial advisers, they offer a solution to manage requests of customers for the information in all the value chain of the data.

Cedacri has also a certified system and solutions by the rules of Bank of Italy. This allows being interoperable with all banks that use Gateway with an internal Sandbox for PSD2 regulation provided planned and precise testing phases. The Gateway is already in production. The Sandbox allows the check of the legislation and verifies if a request, that is certified by the bank, can return to a third party service provider the information requested based on precise Contracted Service Level and shared with the rules of Bank of Italy.

On GDPR they try to work to make banks compliant with the requests with a complex data governance project to allow banks to extract value from the most interesting data that are provided from customers.

Cedacri proposed is a solution in the market by inserting a concept of compliance then data governance and data quality, the importance of the data collected within a modern and deconstructed structure allows to leap forward with artificial intelligence: "so many talks about it but few realize something" as the managers affirm.

To complete the offer Cedacri has developed also a RegTech solution in the AML field.

On RegTech in AML, they have a market-leading platform where they offer software as Platform as a service. They, therefore, have a platform that handles all AML issues and this platform incorporates all the new AML regulations that come from the Bank of Italy and the ECB.

This is a very important area that is connected to reporting for banks and is useful to give the information to all central authorities; all the data capture part and then creating files in a compliant manner as requested from the certification bodies.

Cedacri is evolved in everything that goes in parallel with the regulations integrated into the open banking process.

All these elements are suitable to create future compliance systems that are based on deconstructed data analyzed in real-time with highly evolved machine learning.

Shareholder banks and customers very different sizes Cedacri provides a data scientist service ad Hoc.

A large bank has its structure to exploit this technology but sometimes needs experts in RegTech that Cedacri provides.

3.2 Case two

Nike was born as a consultancy is a company that was born over twenty years ago (1995) in the field of management consulting and Nike has always taken care of the system of internal controls in the banking and insurance sectors. Nike has over 100 consultants and a revenue of over 6ml.€ in 2018.

The regulation of the financial sector is vastly and fragmented and subject to serveral supervisory Authorithies.

In less than 10 years three full-time lawyers passed to 30 people so with a big expansion of this compliance and RegTech business.

They operate in Italy with an Eu and national vision.

The regulatory manager of Nike finds several issues to apply RegTech in Italy.

The risks are two: the first is that if into the program in machine language is contained something already wrong maybe because of software forced interpretation, it goes to build errors on errors when updating the legislation.

So an initial error in programming the Regulation inside the RegTech's software could generate many errors in future interpretation. To find the original error is very complicated.

This is the second risk is that takes away from human interpretation is something that would be extremely useful but is something is eventually slow to review and to check again.

Today an interpretation result that is 100% reliable in not realistic and to have in production a "ready-to-use solution" is, for the regulatory manager, "how acceptable it is for our end users the margin of error and we really need to get to a margin of error as lower as possible".

Today an issue of banking regulation also Italy is the double language many rules of banking regulation come out in double Italian and English language: a semantic engine reads English and does not read Italian.

If your system reads Italian, it does not match well English.

Big constraints of small and medium-sized national companies are to struggle costs to adapt the regulatory context and for that kind of entities is a cost also to understand which rules these companies have to apply.

Another actual matter is about RegTech connected to Cybersecurity standards in the financial environment in which they are involved.

The job of Nike is to organize a list of rules. They have made a proprietary classification of norms, but it is not an industrial secret.

The system read on the website of the ECB, the European Commission and the Bank of Italy but also technical newspapers about tax rules. The second step is aggregating these sources and going to add, to the Nike cloud system that told the experts in the Nike company and clients how to classify new rules.

The analyzed norm enters into a "rule catalogue". This process is repeated for new regulation. In the catalogue of rules, there are 185 subjects.

The system inserts the rules only if the rules relating and applicable to the client's bank or financial institution.

The proposed solution is applied in small size financial institution but also for the world's leading specialist in big banks.

The regulatory manager shows us that last year detected about 350 regulatory changes and new consultations that impact the financial Italian sector; means more than one working day. All subjects are necessary to be identified and classified, elborated and then sold to customers with the compliance's application of 400-500 pages per day.

They create a kind of network of users (clients) that contributes to the development of the solutions. The more time the software is trained, the more time they spend on machine learning, the more time the solution is used, the more the solutions are refined for the clients.

There are not so many competitors with such a wide offer in Italy declares the regulator manager of Nike.

It is a market issue for RegTech in Italy but this transversality of skills gives to Nike an advantage against competitors.

3.3 Case three

This is the third case a little RegTech startup in Milan that co-operates with banks.

In this context, Txt risk is born, as a "Reg Tech" belonging to the Txt group, which

Realizes innovative and technologically advanced solutions advanced for risk management.

The company was born as T3m, now is a startup in 2018 founded the co-founder of the company, creates a solution compared that are reaching maturity born in a coworking with the third Italian bank and now the solution is in production. They have also an agreement with a branch of Banco Santander group in Italy with several proposals of solutions. For the cofounder comply with regulations with RegTech is more easily with new technologies, that are not confined only in financial industry. The RegTech approach in finance for Txt is the same approach that can be also used for regulating intervention in all regulated sectors to reduce fixed costs and free resources for improving innovation and for the remuneration of the invested capital.

The co founder said his little startup is a pure RegTech, but, in Italy, very few are pure RegTech. Revenue, for the cofounder, will overpass the million next year. They are full in contact Anglo-Saxon environment and the aim to sell also abroad as soon as they consolidate the startup.

The attraction and the push to make business in Regtech descended from EU directives, while in the rest of the world it is global that similar common law concepts are based on principles. The risk approach is a problem for lawyers and the interesting in reading probabilistic models and machine learning had suggested the business idea.

The vision is to read data within the internal and external open data bank including a syntactic and semantic reading of texts, but the most important thing for the co-founder is "where you have to look for data and how to read them". This is very important in certain areas for RegTech as the AML solutions.

The idea was presented also to the Bank of Italy.

Today they are focusing on AML. But they want to extend credit risk fraud and the number of checks can be provided better about controls on risk.

Current costs and solutions of banks, for Txt, have such a high cost of management and licensing that they are no longer sustainable in a competitive environment and need to manage regulation in smarter systems. The entry into force of the new directives on the subject of risk, and the need to be able to measure with bank's exposure is precise and pushes the banks to use new technologies (AI, Big Data, Cognitive Learning, Machine Learning).

The solution, which has a modular structure relating to money destinated to Terrorism, Corruption and Recycling, through the processing of probabilistic models, allows for evaluating and classifying such risks based on regulations of the Bank of Italy.

The manager claims that using his solution there is an increment of efficiency throughout the process risk assessment, thanks to selections of alerts generated from the system. This method allows analyzing only the actual risky situations, with the use of a graphing approach, to reduce evaluation times for each case, while increasing the skills of the analysts. Concrete results are from 60% to 70% reduction of false anomaly alert for practice. This is a big advantage in reducing cost for banks, said the co-founder of Startup.

4. Conclusion

We find several RegTech application with banks in the three cases explained in the article . The most common RegTech applications and the most resquested are: AML, KYC and anti-fraud compliance linked to risk management and cross border operations. Other interesting aspects of cooperation in case one and two are compliance on reporting, privacy, payment directive PSD2 and automatic classification of financial law but this needs bigger entieties and more staff. For banks, better Risk Management about compliance is one of the key elements on which guarantee solidity and confidence from the customers. The entry into force of the new directives on the subject of risk, compliance and the need to be able to measure with precision their exposure, free up resouces banks to the new businesses through FinTech.

As we showed with innovation on AML and KYC, more accurate compliance on risk management, including regulatory compliance, take positive effects on efficiency and so the firm value of financial companies because aligns financing and investment policies, thus reducing costs of external financing and reduces corporate tax burden (Monda et al., 2013) and fines.

We think to predictive analytics models and reporting, the banks can use tools for a reliable assessment to base their funding activities, improving in both the processes decision-making and compliance.

References

Anagnostopoulos, I., 2018. FinTech and regtech: Impact on regulators and banks. J. Econ. Bus. 100, 7–25.

Arena, M., Arnaboldi, M., Azzone, G., 2010. The organizational dynamics of enterprise risk management. Account. Organ. Soc. 35, 659–675.

Arner, D.W., Barberis, J., Buckey, R.P., 2016. FinTech, RegTech, and the reconceptualization of financial regulation. Nw J Intl Bus 37, 371.

Ballon, P., 2009. The platformisation of the European mobile industry. Commun. Strateg. 15.

Banking Regtechs to the Rescue? [WWW Document], 2016. . Bain. URL https://www.bain.com/insights/banking-regtechs-to-the-rescue/ (accessed 4.13.20).

Battanta, L., Giorgino, M., Grassi, L., Lanfranchi, D., 2019. 14th International Forum on Knowledge Asset Dynamics PROCEEDINGS Knowledge Ecosystems and Growth., in: Ifkad. Institute of Knowledge Asset Management (IKAM) Arts for Business Institute ..., pp. 2173–2195.

Baxter, L.G., 2016. Adaptive financial regulation and regtech: a concept article on realistic protection for victims of bank failures. Duke LJ 66, 567.

Bhyer, B.S., Lee, Seyoung, 2019. Banking the Unbanked and Underbanked: RegTech as an Enabler for Financial Inclusion. RegTech Book.

Butler, T., O'Brien, L., 2019. Understanding RegTech for digital regulatory compliance, in: Disrupting Finance. Springer, pp. 85–102.

Compliance costs to more than double by 2022 - Financial News [WWW Document], n.d. URL https://www.fnlondon.com/articles/compliance-costs-to-more-than-double-by-2022-survey-finds-20170427 (accessed 4.13.20).

Cosma, S., Salvadori, G., Schwizer, P., 2013. 12 Too small to be compliant? Financ. Syst. Troubl. Waters Inf. Strateg. Gov. Enhance Perform. Risky Times 219.

COST OF COMPLIANCE 2018: Executive summary and regulatory developments, 2018. . Reuters.

Eisenhardt, K.M., 1989. Building theories from case study research. Acad. Manage. Rev. 14, 532–550.

Evans, L., Guthrie, G., 2006. Incentive regulation of prices when costs are sunk. J. Regul. Econ. 29, 239–264.

Gawer, A., 2009. Platform dynamics and strategies: from products to services. Platf. Mark. Innov. 45, 57.

Heckathorn, D.D., 1993. Collective action and group heterogeneity: voluntary provision versus selective incentives. Am. Sociol. Rev. 329–350.

How RegTech closes the gap between technology and financial services, 2017. . Bloom. Prof. Serv.

Hung, J.-L., Luo, B., 2016. FinTech in Taiwan: a case study of a Bank's strategic planning for an investment in a FinTech company. Financ. Innov. 2, 15.

Kavassalis, P., Stieber, H., Breymann, W., Saxton, K., Gross, F.J., 2018. An innovative RegTech approach to financial risk monitoring and supervisory reporting. J. Risk Finance 19, 39–55. https://doi.org/10.1108/JRF-07-2017-0111

Lee, T., Kim, H.-W., 2015. An exploratory study on FinTech industry in Korea: crowdfunding case, in: 2nd International Conference on Innovative Engineering Technologies (ICIET'2015). Bangkok.

Monda, B., Giorgino, M., Modolin, I., 2013. Rationales for corporate risk management-a critical literature review. Available SSRN 2203546.

Pan, S.L., Tan, B., 2011. Demystifying case research: A structured–pragmatic–situational (SPS) approach to conducting case studies. Inf. Organ. 21, 161–176.

Patton, M.Q., 1990. Qualitative evaluation and research methods. SAGE Publications, inc.

Rochet, J.-C., Tirole, J., 2003. An economic analysis of the determination of interchange fees in payment card systems. Rev. Netw. Econ. 2.

Seawright, J., Gerring, J., 2008. Case selection techniques in case study research: A menu of qualitative and quantitative options. Polit. Res. Q. 61, 294–308.

The new opportunity: RegTech | Deloitte Italy | Financial Services [WWW Document], n.d. . Deloitte Ital. URL https://www2.deloitte.com/it/it/pages/financial-services/articles/the-new-opportunity--regtech---deloitte-italy---financial-servic.html (accessed 4.13.20).

Walsham, G., 1995. Interpretive case studies in IS research: nature and method. Eur. J. Inf. Syst. 4, 74–81.

Walshe, J., Cropper, T., 2018. Should you be banking on RegTech? J. Secur. Oper. Custody 10, 167–175.

Yin, R., 1984. case study research. Beverly Hills. ca: Sage.

Business Pre-Incubators as Structures for Change Toward the Entrepreneurial and Third Generation University

Marcin Bielicki[1] and Blair Stevenson[2]
[1]Poznan University of Economics and Business, Poznan, Poland
[2]Oulu University of Applied Sciences, Oulu, Finland
marcin.bielicki@ue.poznan.pl
blair.stevenson@oamk.fi
DOI: 10.34190/EIE.20.025

Abstract: As business incubation increasingly expands into the domain of universities, the lines between entrepreneurship education, incubation and pre-incubation is blurring. In this way, the process of creating new ventures is increasingly integrated into university studies both as curricular and extra-curricular content. With respect to pre-incubation, higher education studies have expanded such that it is possible to obtain academic credits as a result of participating in pre-incubation projects and programs. This growth in pre-incubation activities necessitates a review of the key indicators of success so as to not only view the number of start-ups generated by universities, but also recognize other potential key outcomes such as personal competence development. The aim of this article is to explore the role of business pre-incubators as they relate to the concepts of the Entrepreneurial University and 3rd Generation University. For this purpose, we conducted interviews with staff involved in the operation of pre-incubators in Belgium, Estonia, Poland and Serbia and collected available documentation describing other pre-incubators located in Europe, Australia and Asia. We analysed data through the lens of existing theories of pre-incubation and the concepts of the Entrepreneurial University and 3rd Generation University. Our findings support that pre-incubators follow two main approaches to supporting entrepreneurship. The first one, emphasized mostly in the concept of the 3rd generation university, is based on technology transfer and the creation of new ventures. The second one, which is a priority in the concept of an entrepreneurial university, focuses on the development of entrepreneurial competences. It can also be noted that while pre-incubators can be used in both concepts, they still face major barriers. These are due to the fact that universities themselves are very resistant to change, including problems with interdisciplinary teaching. This means that even good pathways cannot be used effectively if the whole system is not yet prepared for such a change in education.

Keywords: pre-incubation, 3rd generation university, entrepreneurial university, entrepreneurship

1. Introduction

As economic development has shifted to entrepreneurship, the role of universities in society has also evolved (Audretsch, 2014). Same time universities are under-going a "revolution" (Etzkowitz, 1998; Etzkowitz and Leydesdorff, 2000). This trend has led to the development of two interlinked concepts: an entrepreneurial university and a 3rd generation university. Although both of these concepts explore how the role of universities is evolving, they promote significant differences in our view of academic entrepreneurship. The concept of the 3rd generation university is dominated by an approach focusing on the creation of new businesses based on the commercialization of research and development (R&D) results and knowledge transfer to industry. While the entrepreneurial university concept is based on expanding a university's role in entrepreneurship and that entrepreneurial thinking should be integrated into teaching, learning and conducting research (Kyrö and Mattila, 2012).

Over the last twenty years, the number of pre-incubation programs has grown. While considerable research has been devoted to incubators over that time, the concept of pre-incubation has been rarely recognized or defined comprehensively (Dickson, 2004). Theoretical knowledge of this earliest stage in the incubation process is also rather limited. This poses a challenge especially at a time when the role of pre-incubators is rapidly evolving and pre-incubators have become an integral part of credit studies at some universities (Zeps et al., 2009).

The aim of this article is to define how business pre-incubators act as educational structures in relation to the concepts of 3rd generation university and entrepreneurial university. To do so, documentation available online has been collected from nine current pre-incubators and semi-structured interviews conducted with four pre-incubator staff. Findings were then contrasted with two pre-incubation models: [1] the model developed at the University of Bielefeld; and [2] the LAB studio model, in order to more broadly explore pre-incubations role in university development.

This paper makes two contributions to the entrepreneurship literature. First, we demonstrated how university pre-incubators can be used in various approaches to support academic entrepreneurship, both through the creation of new businesses and the development of entrepreneurial skills. Second, we also pointed out the differences in existing models of pre-incubation.

2. Conceptual frameworks: Entrepreneurial university and 3rd generation university

Entrepreneurial University

The concept of an entrepreneurial university can be traced back to the University Triple Helix Model proposed by Lowe in 1982. The Triple Helix model assumes that the potential for innovation and economic development in a knowledge-based society depends on the role of the university within the process of hybridization of university, industry and state activities in generating new institutional and social forms necessary to create, transfer and apply knowledge (Lowe, 1982).

In the 1990s, the term "entrepreneurial university" was popularized mostly by Clark (1998). Since then, further theoretical models of how an entrepreneurial university functions have emerged within the fourth industrial revolution (Gibb, 2012). In addition to the model proposed by Clark, there are four other models defining an entrepreneurial university (Guerrero, Kirby and Urbano, 2006). Etzkowitz *et al.* (2000) highlight the role of the university in increasingly knowledge-based societies, while Sporn (2001) demonstrates how universities need to adapt their structures to a dynamically changing environment leading traditional universities to transform toward entrepreneurial universities. Etzkowitz (2004) showed the role that universities play in the Triple Helix model such that cooperation between universities, industry and government is key to fostering innovation in knowledge-based society. Kirby (2006) further outlines barriers faced by universities when implementing entrepreneurship and intrapreneurship.

Among the many differences that Kyrö and Mattila (2012) have distinguished as the most important in the context of the role of pre-incubators, one can consider the way entrepreneurship is pe2eceived. In the case of the 3rd generation University, this is understood as a skill, while in the case of the entrepreneurial university, more emphasis is placed on entrepreneurial mindset. This also makes it a priority in the case of the 3rd generation university to create new enterprises and thus to transfer knowledge to the economy, and in the case of the entrepreneurial university, through the development of entrepreneurial competences, the aim is to solve social and economic problems and create welfare.

3rd Generation University

Wissema (2009) highlights the importance of education and research in the changing role of universities in society. He distinguished three generations of universities and points out key features that universities aspiring to be a 3rd generation university should have.

Key features of this concept are the roles of know-how exploitation, creating value, conducting interdisciplinary research, global orientation, and conducting courses and research in English. However, Wissena also stresses the need to transform universities into international centres of technology transfer, which will be able not only to create knowledge, but also to foster the creation of a society made able to solve interdisciplinary problems and adapt quickly to changing environmental conditions.

Both of the concepts above address the changing role of universities. The concept of an entrepreneurial university is directly related to the impact of entrepreneurship on society and the economy, while the 3rd generation university is based on the problems and needs that universities face (Kyrö and Mattila, 2012).

Among the many differences that Kyrö and Mattila (2012) have distinguished as the most important in the context of the role of pre-incubators, one can consider the way entrepreneurship is perceived. In the case of the 3rd generation University, this is understood as a skill, while in the case of the entrepreneurial university, more emphasis is placed on entrepreneurial mindset. This also makes it a priority in the case of the 3rd generation university to create new enterprises and thus to transfer knowledge to the economy, and in the case of the entrepreneurial university, through the development of entrepreneurial competences, the aim is to solve social and economic problems and create welfare.

3. Business pre-incubators

3.1 Bielfield concept of pre-incubation

The first documented university-based, pre-incubator was established in 1997 at the University of Bielefeld in Germany. Since then, the number of pre-incubation programs has grown globally. Pre-incubators aim at founding new enterprises (Wirsing *et al.*, 2002) and are the facilities that supports nascent entrepreneurs and provides conditions to develop and test a fledging business (Dickson, 2004). Additionally, they have been described as a space where market viability of entrepreneurial ideas can be pre-filtered and reduce risks, costs and failures associated with the setup of a new company which may or may not develop. Overall, pre-incubators are the first step in the support process for establishing new ventures. More specifically, this stage is detailed as validating concepts, developing prototypes and building teams with a focus more on consultancy and training (Deutschmann, 2007).

Existing definitions of the pre-incubation process point to two main objectives: 1. to support the start of new enterprises; and 2. to educate potential entrepreneurs. These objectives are achieved by providing appropriate support and conditions in which pre-incubator participants can test and develop their business ideas. Positive impacts from pre-incubators relating to these goals have been recently noted in Germany (Deutschmann, 2007), Wales (Voisey, Jones and Thomas, 2013) and Turkey (Kepenek and Eser, 2016).

Figure 1 visualizes the pre-incubation process as drawn from Wirsing et al (2002) and Kirby (2004).

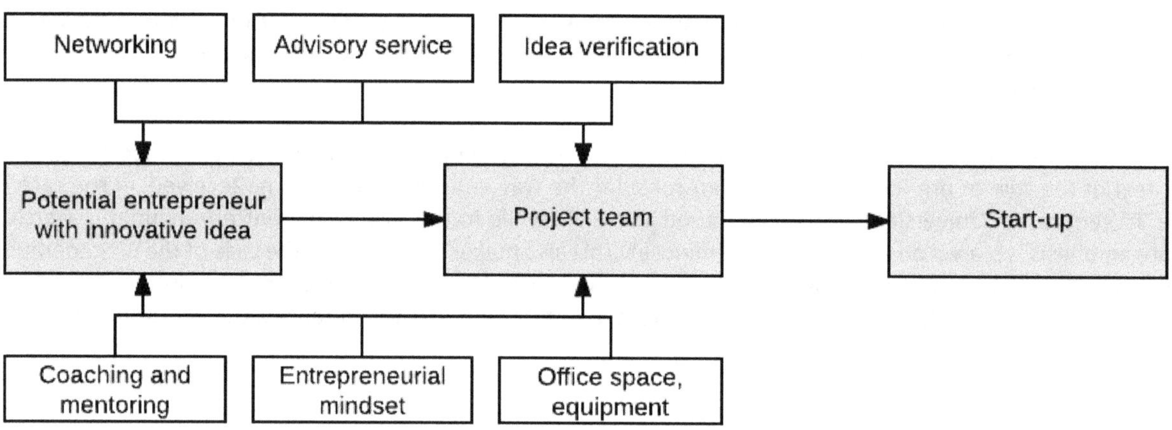

Figure 1: Summary of pre-incubation process as compiled from Wirsing et al. (2002) and Kirby (2004)

The Bielfield concept of pre-incubation aims at "promoting technology-based spin-offs from universities" (Wirsing *et al.*, 2002). In this view, the pre-incubation process usually starts with the initial selection of ideas and their creators and ends when the idea is mature enough to be further developed in the incubator (Wirsing *et al.*, 2002; Hannon, 2004; Deutschmann, 2007).

Ultimately, it is suggested that this approach corresponds to the concept of knowledge transfer and is strongly oriented towards the promotion of entrepreneurship through the creation of new companies.

3.2 LAB studio model

A second concept of pre-incubation that has recently been adopted at various sites internationally is the LAB studio model (Heikkinen and Stevenson, (2015). The concept was created and implemented in 2012 at the Oulu University of Applied Sciences (OUAS), and then adopted within pre-incubators in Slovakia, Belgium, Nepal and Austria. Heikkinen and Stevenson (2015) stated that "the LAB studio model is a multidisciplinary education model aimed at producing skilled professionals, self-directive teams and company start-ups within a certain industry focus".

In this approach, the creation of start-ups is only one of a number of expected outcomes of the model. The model takes a broader approach to entrepreneurship than solely focusing on the transfer of knowledge from universities to business, and emphasizes more the individual development of potential future entrepreneurs. In this context, the authors suggest that this the model is more in line with the concept of an entrepreneurial university rather than the 3rd generation university.

A further difference between these two models is that the LAB studio model often does not require applicants at the recruitment stage to have a business idea. As part of these type of pre-incubation activities, participants are matched into interdisciplinary teams and are presented with real problems from real businesses to solve (Heikkinen and Stevenson, 2015). This process allows participants to focus on problem-based learning and design thinking. It also gives priority to the development of an entrepreneurial mindset, including the acquisition of professional skills such as opportunity recognition and project management.

This focus suggests that the pre-incubation process in this model starts earlier as shown in the figure below.

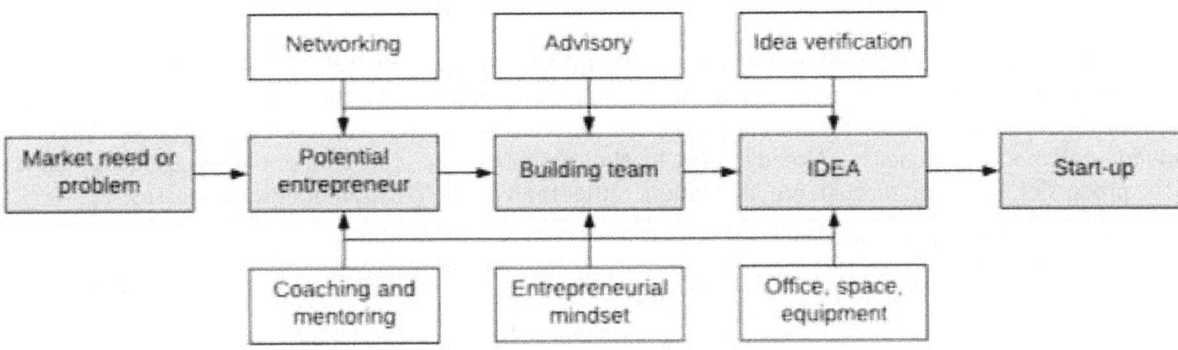

Figure 2: Summary of pre-incubation process as compiled from Heikkinen (2016)

The key differences between these two models are presented in Table 1.

Table 1: Comparison of Bielfield and LAB studio concepts of pre-incubation

Bielfield concept of pre-incubation	LAB studio concept of pre-incubation
Focus on pre-incubated project	Focus on creating entrepreneurs
Offering safe environment for creating start-ups	Fostering, motivating and challenging students to become an entrepreneur
Focused on university – business knowledge transfer	Focused on solving problems existing in local environment
Selecting/expanding teams	Selecting people and creating teams
Venture creation oriented	Education orientation - Part of studies
Focused on risk reduction through legal service, office spaces, advisory	Focused on developing soft and hard skills necessary to become an entrepreneur

4. Method

The study consisted of three stages. In the first stage, we created a list of entities that identify themselves as pre-incubators. We started by creating a database using the keywords "pre-incubator", "pre-incubation" using Google search engine, taking into account only those programs that met the following criteria: the website was available in English, there was at least a short description of what a given pre-incubator offers to applicants and there was no information that the program suspended or terminated its activity. Then, we analysed the materials available on the websites of 15 pre-incubators. All the chosen entities for our study described themselves as "pre-incubator" or "pre-incubation program". Among these pre-incubators, 11 were in Europe, two in Australia, and two in Asia. Representatives were then contacted from all European pre-incubators and four agreed to take part in semi-structured video-conferencing interviews. These four were from Belgium, Estonia, Poland and Serbia. All respondents held managerial positions. All interviews were conducted from November 2019 to March 2020.

In the second stage 4 semi-structured interviews were conducted. The respondents were asked about three areas of operation of their pre-incubator, respectively: [1] the definition and role of pre-incubation, including how success in their organization is understood and measured; [2] key partners, including primarily the degree of integration with the university; [3] barriers and problems in the functioning of their pre-incubator.

5. Results

Analysing how individual pre-incubators describe their programs, two approaches dominate (table 2). The first one focuses on transforming an innovative idea (including even those with a prepared product) into a company, and the most important recurring terms used in the texts of their websites are "*becoming viable companies*", "*development of your idea*", "*improve your business plan*", "*grow your idea*" "*create or improve your business plan*".

This approach shows a very strong focus on the applicant's idea and work on it. Often, already at the recruitment stage, one of the criteria is the presentation of the idea, which will be further developed within the framework of pre-incubation. This trend therefore fits directly into the role of a pre-incubator in line with the concept of the 3rd generation university.

The second approach is oriented towards the participant of the pre-incubator and the development of his entrepreneurial competence. Among the descriptions of the activities of these pre-incubators there are repeated phrases such as "*educate entrepreneurs*", "*self-aware professional*", "*education*", "*learning*", "*provoke, stimulate and motivate students*". Already at the level of describing the programme, there is a clear emphasis on the process of education through pre-incubation, rather than on the creation of new businesses.

Table 2: Self-description of pre-incubators activities

USINE	*"In the pre-incubator young entrepreneurs test the market potential of their products by selling them on national and international markets. Since all business transactions are covered by an insurance of the pre-incubator, financial risks for entrepreneurs are reduced."*
KTH Innovation	*"The KTH Innovation pre-incubator program supports early-stage, tech-based KTH projects with the potential of becoming viable companies."*
PPNT Pre-incubator	*"Together we will develop the support plan for your business idea. Its realization will be supervised by the Tutor, who will determine with you objects and dates of consultancy, individual consultancies with specialists, possible trainings and other services offered under the pre-incubation."*
Greenhouse	*"Climate-KIC offers the Greenhouse pre-incubation programme to starting entrepreneurs who have a climate business idea and the motivation to make it happen.* *You will find tailored workshops, a community of climate entrepreneurs, and the support to further develop your idea and create or improve your business plan."*
SmartStart	*"SmartStart will help you TRANSFORM good ideas into GREAT OPPORTUNITIES. We provide the perfect setting for entrepreneurs to grow ideas into successful businesses. This program goes beyond books and theories, offering hands-on coaching. Entrepreneurs will learn by doing, exploring the operations, funding and marketing needed to launch and grow a business."*
The Hatchery	*"A multi-stream program designed to educate, build and launch the entrepreneurs of the future, from teaching students the essential skills to supporting early stage ventures founded or co-founded by UTS students and recent graduates."*
iDEAlab	*"The core idea behind iDEAlab is to provoke, stimulate and motivate students and young researchers to actively use their intellectual and creative potentials to generate innovative ideas, which are product or service oriented. It is conceived as an open lab that accepts any student from any faculty inside university, fostering cross-disciplinary and cross-university collaboration."*
OAMK LABs	*"Oamk LABs are an innovative and expanding pre-incubator program at Oulu University of Applied Sciences that focus on entrepreneurship and multidisciplinary learning. Growing from our original LAB – Oulu Game LAB – which focuses on the creation of multidisciplinary teams to build prototypes, products and then start-ups targeting the global games industry."*
3iD LABS	*"At 3ID LABS (film), you'll work on a real-life case during a full semester. By the end of this semester, you will be a self-aware professional, ready for the challenges the entrepreneurial world brings."*

Definition and role of pre-incubation

All respondents indicated that the purpose of pre-incubation is to foster entrepreneurship. However, there are differences in approaches to the process itself. We can distinguish the concept according to which the aim of pre-incubation is to bring the idea to the stage when it is ready to incubate ("*help them to come to one point where they are ready to come to the incubator*"), or simply end up creating a company ("*all activities that are designed to prepare teams or individuals to plan and start their own business*"). The second approach indicates that the aim is not to create a business in itself, but to acquire competence ("*It's a hands-on educational program where participants gain knowledge how to start a startup with the supervision of practitioners*"). Furthermore, it was pointed out that even if the programme is built primarily to provide competences, it is very important for the motivation of students to work on a new product/service, even if under a pre-incubation programme these ideas do not reach maturity enough to start an incubation process ("*In pre-incubation we don't have strong enough ideas to start businesses. They will need more time after the program*").

The differences in the level of defining and measuring the success of a pre-incubation program are even more evident. These range from a very strong focus on creating new companies ("*we measure how many companies were established and their survival rate*"), to an approach that gives higher priority to created companies, but the competences and good feedback of the participants is also very important ("*we collect good stories and good examples coming out of our lab*"), and ending with those where the creation of a company is not considered as the ultimate goal, but where the competences acquired by the participants play a major role ("*It's not that we have to establish a company at the end of the program it's more about acquiring competences. It is very much about getting to know about yourself*"; "*Main focus are actually professional competences. It is not about product/company but learning process*"). Unquestionably, in all analysed pre-incubators, both the creation of new companies and acquisition of competences take place, but it is important what is the priority in a given programme.

Key partners, including the role of the pre-incubator in the university structure

Three pre-incubators, in which the respondents worked, were directly connected with the university, one was independent (was dependent indirectly through the technology park). In one of them, it was possible to work full-time, i.e. obtain the credits required to complete a semester only under the pre-incubation programme. In the other two, it was possible to complete the mandatory internship through participation in the programme. The third one was not related to the curriculum at all. Interestingly, the respondents indicated a greater willingness to integrate with courses at the university, but they stressed that the current university structures are not ready for this yet.,

All respondents emphasized that the local environment of the pre-incubator is important, especially: *"industry partners"; "business mentors and investors. They not only provided funding for projects, but also shared very valuable knowledge"; "The most important partners for us are university, local business environment (mentors) and local government"; "local government".*

Existing barriers

Two groups of barriers are particularly visible: human and financial. The first one identifies problems with the involvement of university staff in teaching entrepreneurship ("*we have a problem with professors to involve them to be present with the group and also sometimes their lectures are not covering the newest knowledge in terms of technology*") and access to investors who could both mentor and provide capital ("*the biggest problem was the lack of access to investors*").

Financial barriers are understood here as both the barriers to the development of portfolio companies ("*a lack of micro-financing for innovative ideas on the market*") and the problem of financing the entire pre-incubation project ("*our problem is to ensure financial stability after the end of financing from EU projects*"). This issue is all the more problematic as all pre-incubators have encountered more or less resistance from university/departmental authorities and professors who teach in the traditional way *("the biggest difficulty for the moment which restricted us is the policy of the higher institute itself. In our national educational system there is no place for such as interdisciplinary learning")*.

Despite the dynamic emergence of new concepts such as the university of enterprise and the university of 3rd generation it seems that many universities still resist these changes. The idea of interdisciplinary learning with such a large and important shift away from traditional methods is still a major resistance in the university environment.

As in the case of the University of Entrepreneurship and 3rd generation University, there are significant differences in the approach to entrepreneurship. Functioning pre-incubators often indicate that it is the development of people and not the creation of new businesses that is their primary goal. Regardless of the concept of the university's role, findings suggest that pre-incubators act as a formal pathway to support academic entrepreneurship.

6. Discussion

The goal of the present article was to investigate how business pre-incubators can be used within entrepreneurial university and a third-generation university. In both of these concepts the emphasis is on promoting entrepreneurship, but this is done in a different way. Our aim was to show how pre-incubators, despite these differences, can be adopted in both cases.

Our findings converge with previous findings (Wirsing et al., 2002; Deutschmann, 2007; Voisey, Jones and Thomas, 2013). In addition, they show for the first time that there are two approaches to the creation and operation of pre-incubators. The first one is focused primarily on the transfer of knowledge created at the university and its commercialization through spin-offs. The second one is mainly oriented towards the development of entrepreneurial competence of the programme participants.

Taken together, our findings and the findings of previous studies point towards pre-incubators can be successfully used to support academic entrepreneurship at different levels. However, our results show that there is still considerable resistance from some higher education staff to the wider use of such facilities. Above all, there is a lack of understanding of the new role that universities should play in society. Without more support, it is not possible to implement new instruments effectively.

There is one important limitation of our study – small sample. Pre-incubators are not as popular as incubators or accelerators. Moreover, many entrepreneurship programs, although they fit directly into the definition of a pre-incubator, do not use this term to define their activities. However, we based our results on data available from nine different pre-incubators from three continents. This made it possible to notice at least general trends.

7. Conclusion

In the present article, we investigated how the pre-incubators fit into the new concepts of the university. The literature on pre-incubators identifies them primarily with the model proposed in Bielfield. Our findings show, however, that these entities have evolved significantly.

In conclusion, our findings show that pre-incubators can be used in entrepreneurial university and third generation university. However, it is necessary to better understand how different models of pre-incubation can be used to effectively support entrepreneurship in its various dimensions.

Future research may extend this work by re-defining pre-incubators. As a starting point to addressing the rapid growth of new models, we propose that any revised definition of pre-incubation should expand upon existing descriptions of pre-incubation as becoming an entrepreneur to a conceptualization of pre-incubation as becoming entrepreneurial. In this way, the idea of becoming an entrepreneur focus more on opportunity identification, business development, self-employment, venture creation and growth (Fayolle and Gailly, 2008; QAA, 2018), whereas the vision of becoming entrepreneurial emphasizes personal development, creativity, self-reliance, initiative taking and action orientation (Lackéus, 2015). This means that we should also change the way we evaluate pre-incubation programs. We should use not only such indicators as the number of start-ups created, but also the personal development of the participants. These types of indicators could include potential outcomes to pre-incubation such as personal competence development and increased employment and recruitment of graduates of the programmes.

Acknowledgements

The work was created as a result of a research project No 2018/31/N/HS4/02151 financed by the National Science Centre, Poland.

References

Audretsch, D. B. (2014) „From the entrepreneurial university to the university for the entrepreneurial society", Journal of Technology Transfer, 39(3), ss. 313–321.

Clark, B. R. (1998) Creating Entrepreneurial Universities: Organizational Pathways of Transformation. IAU Press (Advances in Learning and Instruction Series).

Deutschmann, M. (2007) „What difference a «pre» makes: University business preincubators in Germany. A national survey", Lüneburger Beiträge zur Gründungsforschung, 5, ss. 1–12.

Dickson, A. (2004) Pre-incubation and the New Zealand business incubation Industry. Wellington: New Zealand Centre for SME Research.

Etzkowitz, H. (1998) „The norms of entrepreneurial science: cognitive effects of the new university–industry linkages", Research Policy, 27(8), ss. 823–833.

Etzkowitz, H. et al. (2000) „The future of the university and the university of the future: evolution of ivory tower to entrepreneurial paradigm", Research Policy, 29(2), ss. 313–330.

Etzkowitz, H. (2004) „The Evolution of the Entrepreneurial University", Int. J. of Technology and Globalisation, 1, ss. 64–77.

Etzkowitz, H. and Leydesdorff, L. (2000) „The dynamics of innovation: from National Systems and "Mode 2" to a Triple Helix of university–industry–government relations", Research Policy, 29(2), ss. 109–123.

Fayolle, A. and Gailly, B. (2008) „From craft to science", Journal of European Industrial Training, 32(7), ss. 569–593.

Gibb, A. (2012) „Exploring the synergistic potential in entrepreneurial university development: Towards the building of a strategic framework", Annals of Innovation & Entrepreneurship, 3.

Guerrero, M. & Kirby, D. A. and Urbano, D., A Literature Review on Entrepreneurial Universities: An Institutional Approach (2006). Autonomous University of Barcelona, Business Economics Department, Working Paper Series, No. 06/8. Available at SSRN: https://ssrn.com/abstract=1838615

Hannon, P. D. (2004) „A qualitative sense-making classification of business incubation environments", Qualitative Market Research: An International Journal, 7(4), ss. 274–283.

Heikkinen, K-P. & Stevenson, B. (2015). The LAB studio model: Enhancing entrepreneurship skills in higher education. International Journal of Innovation and Learning. Special Issue.

Heikkinen, K. (2016) „Studying the Aspects of Knowledge Creation in the LAB Studio Model", International Journal of Management, Knowledge and Learning, (1), ss. 5–22.

Kepenek, E. B. and Eser, Z. (2016) 'Impact of Pre-incubators on Entrepreneurial Activities in Turkey : Problems, Successes, and Policy Recommendations', TEKPOL Working Paper Series, 08.

Kirby, D. (2004) „Entrepreneurship education and incubators: pre-incubators, incubators and science parks as enterprise laboratories".

Kirby, D. A. (2006) „Creating Entrepreneurial Universities in the UK: Applying Entrepreneurship Theory to Practice", The Journal of Technology Transfer, 31(5), ss. 599–603.

Kyrö, P. and Mattila, J. (2012) „Towards future university by integrating Entrepreneurial and the 3rd Generation University concepts", ss. 1–16. Available at: http://pyk2.aalto.fi/ncsb2012/Kyro.pdf

Lackéus, M. (2015) Entrepreneurship in Education. What, Why, When, How, Entrepreneursjip 360. Background Paper. OECD, ss. 1-36

Lowe, C. U. (1982) „The triple helix - NIH, Industry, and the academic world", Yale Journal of Biology and Medicine, 55(3–4), ss. 239–246.

QAA (2018) Enterprise and entrepreneurship education: Guidance for UK higher education providers, Handbook.

Sporn, B. (2001) „Building Adaptive Universities: Emerging Organisational Forms Based on Experiences of European and US Universities", Tertiary Education and Management, 7, ss. 121–134.

Voisey, P., Jones, P. and Thomas, B. (2013) 'The Pre-Incubator: A Longitudinal Study of 10 Years of University Pre-Incubation in Wales', Industry and Higher Education, 27(5), pp. 349–363.

Wirsing, B. et al. (2002) „Becoming an Entrepreneur for a Trial Period: The Pre-Incubation Experience", The International Journal of Entrepreneurship and Innovation, 3(4), ss. 265–277.

Wissema, J. G. (2009) Towards the third generation university: managing the university in transition. Edward Elgar.

Zeps, V. et al. (2009) 'Pre-Incubation and Incubation in Latvia: Assessment of Some Critical Conditions To Establish Efficient Incubation Cycle', in 4th International Conference Information Society and Modern Business 'The role of regional centers in business development'

Improving Food Transparency Through Innovation and Blockchain Technology

Adriana Botelho[1], Inês Ribeiro Silva[1], Lara Ribeiro[1], Mariana Souto Lopes[1] and Manuel Au-Yong-Oliveira[1,2,3]
[1]Department of Economics, Management, Industrial Engineering and Tourism, University of Aveiro, Portugal
[2]GOVCOPP, Aveiro, Portugal
[3]INESC TEC
adrianacibotelho@ua.pt
inesribeirosilva@ua.pt
lara.ribeiro@ua.pt
marianasouto@ua.pt
mao@ua.pt
DOI: 10.34190/EIE.20.034

Abstract: Due to food contamination scandals worldwide, consumers are becoming increasingly concerned about the origins of the food that they purchase. Producers and retailers have fought their way into providing their customers with information about provenance, logistics, food safety and quality. Do you really know where your food came from? Is it safe? Does it have quality? There has been a growing consumer need to know where food is coming from, where it is processed and the quality of the products. Also, regarding environmental awareness, that consumers increasingly have, questions about the environmental sustainability of their products are posed and need to be answered. The main purpose of this paper was to understand the viability of blockchain in food traceability in Portugal, focusing on the Auchan retail group that has been a pioneer in this area. Auchan is a multinational retail company that has implemented innovative blockchain technology (BCT) in the traceability of a few food products (e.g. poultry, for now). The research question was: Is Blockchain Technology feasible for Food Traceability in Portugal? We also considered whether Auchan's strategy could bring competitive advantage. Hence, we conducted a literature review (collecting articles from the last five years, researched in the Scopus database with the following keywords: blockchain; retail; food traceability; innovation; strategy; transparency; Auchan; technology), as well as online research in order to gather recent data about the Auchan company and updated news about the blockchain technology applications in hypermarkets. Finally, a structured interview was performed (in November 2019) with José Cordeiro (responsible for Product Suppliers at Auchan Retail Portugal). There is no doubt that food traceability is a growing concern. Blockchain is a technology that allows for the information to flow along the supply chain without the interveners being able to change the information that the previous one submitted. Hence, blockchain can help with the transparency and safety of the information about the food when it reaches the final client. BCT has proven to be an important tool in the retail market, improving consumer trust and creating competitive advantage for companies. Auchan has been expanding the technology of TE-FOOD and its blockchain solution; having extended the technology to five countries, namely France, Italy, Spain, Portugal, and Senegal (apart from Vietnam where it was first applied). Consumers can check their products' history using their smartphones by scanning the product QR codes and then get access to authentic data about food quality, logistics and every step taken since the farm to the table. Auchan Retail Portugal is now conducting market studies aiming to implement this technology and by doing so is improving its relationship with customers.

Keywords: blockchain, retail, food traceability, innovation, strategy, transparency, Auchan, technology

1. Introduction

Nowadays, due to food contamination scandals worldwide, consumers have started to be concerned about the origins of the food they purchase. This increased concern has led companies to find ways to provide consumer data. It has also led governments to regulate this information in order to trace food contamination when it happens in a fully globalized world. Aware of these new trends, we decided to perform research about technologies that allow the consumer to access data related to food origin and production and came across Blockchain Technology (BCT). With the advance of technology, information may be at one's fingertips. This study aims to understand how BCT can be used in food traceability. BCT allows digital information to be distributed between each player in a supply chain without the intermediation of a central organization. By verifying and adding data in real-time and not having a central authority – a democratized system – blockchain can increase transparency across a supply chain. This technology carries no transaction cost, being a simple way of passing information from A to B in an automated and safer way. There has been a growing consumer need to know where food is from, where it is processed and regarding food quality. Additionally, as consumers become more aware, questions about the environmental sustainability of their products are posed and need to be answered. In order to correspond to the consumers' needs, BCT has been used to trace transactions to strengthen food management, safety and quality (Spencer, 2019).

Folinas et al. (2006) pointed out that the efficiency of a traceability system depends on the ability to track and trace each individual product and logistics unit, in a way that enables continuous monitoring from primary production until final disposal by the consumer (Tian, 2016). With this technology data collection and analysis becomes cheaper, more reliable and easier to use; and data processing and storage are on the verge of a technological shift contributing to the increase of more retailers and food producers starting their own experiments with blockchain and food traceability (TE-FOOD, 2019a). Auchan, a French retail group, has been expanding TE-FOOD's blockchain solution to improve food view transparency having extended it to five countries, namely France, Italy, Spain, Portugal, and Senegal apart from Vietnam where it was first applied. Auchan consumers can check product histories using their smartphones by scanning the product QR codes and then gaining access to authentic data about food quality, logistics and every step taken since the farm to the table.

This article continues with a literature review regarding BCT and its applications in the retail market, followed by a brief presentation of the Auchan Retail Group's strategy through using blockchain. It also includes the analysis of an interview with the Quality Director of Auchan Retail Portugal, José Cordeiro, regarding the theme.

Our research investigates whether BCT is feasible for food traceability in Portugal.

2. Literature review

In this section, we review the concepts of BCT and food traceability to gain an understanding of how this technology can be applied to improve food traceability, particularly in retail businesses.

2.1 Blockchain technology

In October 2008, one or more individuals, by the pseudonym of Satoshi Nakamoto, released the Bitcoin white paper (Nakamoto, 2019), initially known as "computer money" due to its implementation in the finance sector. Blockchain is a type of database created and shared by multiple nodes connected in a peer-to-peer network (Kuzmanovic, 2019), the technology protocol on which the Bitcoin network relies (Bitcoin, 2019).

Blockchain is a technology that can allow authenticated data communication between each player in a supply chain without the intermediation of a trusted central entity. Each transaction in this system is time stamped and verified by a consensus of a majority of participants in the system.

After blockchain became widely known in the financial industry, the supply and logistics chain also caught on and slowly began to realize the benefits of using this technology in their processes (Petersen, Hackius, & von See, 2018). Material traceability, reduced administrative costs, lower risk of fraud and gray-market trading and better control of outsourced contract manufacturing are some of the values that this technology provides.

2.2 Food traceability

In order to understand better the importance of food traceability, it is important to first clarify what traceability means. According to Olsen and Borit (2013), there wasn't a consensus on the meaning of this word. After analyzing 100 scientific articles they encountered a lot of inconsistencies and a lot of the definitions were not precise as well. After a careful analysis of them, along with dictionary definitions and ISO norms, the authors came up with a definition as complete as possible of the term:

> *"Traceability (n) - The ability to access any or all information relating to that which is under consideration, throughout its entire life cycle, by means of recorded identifications."*
>
> *Olsen and Borit (2013)*

The traceability of food has become a growing issue over the last three decades, which called for the necessity of instruments that allow information about the products to be available. Through product labeling, it is possible to increase cosumer protection, allow the consumer to make its own informed choice, according to preference and even possiblythe the generation of economic rents to producers (Krissoff, Kuchler, Nelson, Perry, & Somwaru, 2004). It is believed that the inaccuracy in the information provided to the consumer, whether it is on the production process, the manufacturing process, the ingredients of the food, along with the food hazards of the 90s, has led to a downfall in consumers' trust (Van Rijswijk & Frewer, 2012; Verbeke & Ward, 2006).

Through traceability processes, it is possible to increase the consumers' confidence, a theory that is confirmed by several studies (Golan, Krissoff, & Kuchler, 2002; Hobbs, Von Bailey, Dickinson, & Haghiri, 2005; Moe, 1998; Resende-Filho & Buhr, 2012).

Roosen et al. (2003) concluded, by surveying consumers of beef in France and Germany, that the origin of the meat was the most important attribute to be considered when choosing what to buy. In the UK, however, the steak color, price, and fat content were the most important attributes.

Also, in the beef industry, Verbeke and Ward conducted a study in Belgium that found that Belgian consumers preferred labeling cues regarding the quality of the product (Loureiro & Umberger, 2007).

Profeta et al. (2012) determined that the origin of the food is an important factor when choosing what to buy for one-fifth of the consumers. However, the authors found that there are "different levels of origin for different group products" (Profeta et al., 2012).

These are just some examples of studies that point out that the traceability of food is an increasingly important matter for consumers in Europe. In Portugal, Figueiredo (2019), studied the habits of consumption in Portugal precisely regarding the strategies of Auchan. Amongst other conclusions, the author found out that the dimension that Portuguese people in 2019 valued most was price. Nevertheless, he also concluded that the second most valued dimension was the quality of the products and that 82% of the respondents were willing to pay a higher price for a product with better quality (Figueiredo, 2019).

2.2.1 Portuguese Law regarding food traceability

The Portuguese Government has implemented the Decree-Law No.26/2016 (Assembleia da República, 2016) ensuring the correct implementation of the Regulation (EU) No 1169/2011 of the European Parliament and of the Council of 25 October 2011 (The European Parliament, 2011). The Regulation aims to attain a high level of information for the consumer regarding the origins of the food, increasing customer support levels and improving quality of life.

The article number 18, point one, of the prior mentioned Regulation states that "The traceability of food, feed, food-producing animals, and any other substance intended to be, or expected to be, incorporated into a food or feed shall be established at all stages of production, processing, and distribution" (The European Parliament, 2011).

2.3 Blockchain technology in the retail business

The way food is produced and consumed has drastically changed over the years. The way we acquire food changed from local, in-season and whole or minimally processed foods to a wide variety spectrum of foods, coming from all over the globe and available every day of the year (Chainvu, 2019).

Like we mentioned earlier, blockchain is a technology that allows for the information to flow along the supply chain without the interveners being able to change the information that the previous one submitted. Hence, blockchain can help with the transparency and safety of the information about the food when it reaches the final client (Kamilaris, Fonts, & Prenafeta-Boldú, 2019).

A recent report about BCT affirms that blockchain in the retail market is expected to grow at a compound annual growth rate of more than 65% (Business Wire, 2019).

In fact, there are some super and hypermarket groups that have already tested and implemented BCT in their supply chains for strict food products. One example is the American multinational retail corporation Walmart. In October 2016, Walmart partnered with IBM to develop two projects: one aimed to trace the origin of mangoes sold in its USA stores and the other to trace pork sold in its China stores. These projects involved the joint work of the Walmart Technology team, IBM group, GS1 (the standards authority in barcodes and labeling) and the suppliers (Hyperledger, 2019).

These pilot projects brought an increase not only to the speed of the traceability process but also in the trust of the consumers. Nowadays, Walmart can trace over 25 products from 5 different suppliers using BCT, including fruits (mangoes and strawberries), leafy greens, meat and poultry (pork and chicken), dairy (yogurt and almond milk) and multi-ingredients products (packaged salads and baby foods). In the near future, the purpose of Walmart is to extend the list of foods traceable with BCT (Hyperledger, 2019).

Like Walmart, other hypermarkets have started the use of BCT in food traceability, examples being Carrefour, Auchan and Albert Heijn (Willemse, 2019). Carrefour can currently trace 20 items including chicken, cheese, eggs, oranges, pork and raw milk. This hypermarket chain stated that the program has increased sales and plans to trace more than 100 products in 2019 (Springwise, 2019).

In the examples above, we often see meat and poultry as part of the list of selected food products companies want to trace. This can be justified by the series of meat scandals that occurred in recent years (e.g. 2013 horse meat scandal, 2008 Irish pork crisis and 2017 Brazil's meat scandal). These situations shed light on the importance of meat safety and reiterate the need for traceability and transparency systems in food supply chains (Sander, Semeijn, & Mahr, 2018).

According to a study from Sander et al. (2018), the meat supply chain stakeholders have different perspectives about the potential of adopting BCT in meat traceability, which might be causing the stagnation on developing these systems. The retail managers interviewed in this study indicated that "consumers have not articulated sufficiently strong demand for a complete traceability and transparency system", being only "price-conscious". The main concern of Government officials was "the financial burden and who will bear the costs of such a supply chain-wide system" and the meat providers can also constitute a barrier because they are "unlikely to have an interest in sharing their information about how their animals have been farmed, slaughtered and processed" (Sander et al., 2018). The authors concluded that implementing a traceability system throughout the entire supply chain requires a change in mindset and should be approached in a holistic and altruistic way, considering transparency and traceability as a requirement and not a choice. The study considers that governments must step in to enforce complete and continuous information sharing across all supply chain actors (Sander et al., 2018).

2.4 The use of blockchain technology and the competitiveness of companies

Blockchain is an emergent technology concept (Petersen et al., 2018) and a ground-breaking innovation which presents a whole new approach to the supply chain area (Tian, 2017). Until recent years, all the traceability systems were built on top of centralized information infrastructures (Caro, Ali, Vecchio, & Giaffreda, 2018). The centralized systems are vulnerable to collapse, monopolistic, asymmetric and opaque and could result in fraud, corruption, tampering and falsifying information (Caro et al., 2018; Tian, 2017). On the other hand, blockchain enables the decentralized and immutable storage of information that has been approved by all connected parties (Petersen et al., 2018; Sander et al., 2018).

As blockchains are fully transparent, they can be used as marketing tools (Galvez, Mejuto, & Simal-Gandara, 2018) and improve a company's image and reputation, boost loyalty among existing customers (Pizzuti & Mirabelli, 2015) and attract new ones (Galvez et al., 2018). Additionally, by making the source of foodborne outbreaks identifiable in only seconds (Petersen et al., 2018), BCT can also help to protect companies' brand images and alleviate the adverse impacts of criticism from the media (Dabbene & Gay, 2011; Galvez et al., 2018).

Despite the hype surrounding blockchain's potential, the literature about this technology in the supply chain management field is in its infancy (Queiroz, Telles, & Bonilla, 2018). In fact, Queiroz et al. (2018) identify blockchains and competitiveness as a research gap and propose the identification of gains in the competitiveness of networks utilizing blockchains as a future study opportunity.

According to Kamilaris et al. (2019), blockchain technology is still being studied by companies and organizations and it is likely that they will perform pilot studies involving blockchain for marketing reasons or for the possibility of competitive advantage in the future.

3. The pilot project developed by Auchan Retail Portugal

3.1 Auchan - brand presentation

Auchan is a French multinational retail group. It was founded in 1961 by *Gérard Mulliez*, in Lille's metropolitan area, *Roubaix*, northern France. It is the 11th largest food retailing group in the world, operating in 17 countries, with over 260.000 employees. Mulliez named the company after the *"Hauts Champs"* (the phonetic resembles Auchan) that was the name of the neighborhood where it first opened.

The first shopping center opened in *Englos,* Lille, 1967, and at the time featured thirty stores, a first in Europe, starting their international expansion in the 80s. In Portugal, the retail group first opened in 1996 with the acquisition of *"Pão de Açúcar"* a Brazilian company, known as Jumbo, the name given by the company to its larger stores (Machado, 2019).

In 2019, the *Auchan Retail Portugal* group officially changed the name of its super and hypermarkets to *Auchan,* making "*an additional investment of 90 million euros, divided into the process of launching the brand and opening new stores*" (Machado, 2019). Since the beginning, the *Auchan* group has had a strong reputation for social responsibility as it developed a management style that aims to increase its customized innovations and services to simplify everyday shopping. Nowadays, consumers are becoming more conscious of what they eat and about the protection of the environment. In order to correspond to that, *Auchan* strives to have the smallest possible footprint to ensure environmental sustainability.

3.2 The important partnership with TE-FOOD

TE-FOOD is a German start-up enterprise that ensures Farm-to-Table food traceability using BCT. Its aim is to increase transparency on a product's history (TE-FOOD, 2019a, 2019b).

In 2017, Auchan partnered up with TE-FOOD in order to change the way people look at their products. The pioneer project was held in Vietnam and the Auchan group is now expanding this technology into the Portuguese, Spanish, Italian and Senegalese markets (Auchan Retail, 2018).

It is being used, for now, only to trace the origins and the whole supply chain of chicken products. However, it is expected to grow into the vegetable market. The consumer can access all the information at the tip of their fingers, by installing a QR code reader. All labels will have a QR code with a description of the process. The various levels of production can only be accessed and changed by their representatives, which means that the Auchan chain is not able to change the information provided by the producers. Thus, the customers benefit from the transparency of the process and a deeper supply chain insight, without having to ask questions (Auchan Retail, 2018).

As stated by José Cordeiro in the interview, Auchan Retail Portugal, like Auchan Vietnam is currently discussing with TE-FOOD the details for implementing the same technology in Portugal.

4. Methodology

The main purpose of this paper was to understand the viability of blockchain in food traceability in Portugal, focusing on the Auchan retail group that has been a pioneer in this area. To explore this possibility, a research question was determined, as stated in the introduction: is Blockchain Technology feasible for Food Traceability in Portugal? In order to answer this question, a literature search was conducted between the months of November and December 2019, collecting articles from the last five years, researched in the Scopus database with the keywords defined above: blockchain; retail; food traceability; innovation; strategy; transparency; Auchan; technology. We also conducted online research in order to gather recent data about the Auchan company and updated news about the blockchain technology applications in hypermarkets. After the literature review, a structured interview was conducted, as it is believed that this qualitative methodology can give the researcher valid, reliable and consistent information about the perspective of the interviewee (Myers, 2009; Pettersen & Durivage, 2008). This interview occurred in November 2019, and was answered by email by José Cordeiro, responsible for Product Suppliers at Auchan Retail Portugal. This paper's main research objectives were to collect more information about Auchan, blockchain technology and how these could help in food traceability.

5. Discussion

It is clear that the use of blockchain in order to trace the origin of food has many advantages. By not allowing the different phases of the supply chain to change the information that each one of them made available, it implies that the transparency and safety of it are also improved. This process tends to increase the trust of consumers in the food that they buy. It is also an important step towards the eradication and treatment of food hazards whenever they occur since blockchain makes it possible to identify the origin of the food and of all of the steps in which the problem may have occurred. In a globalized era, where the products can come from anywhere in the world, a tool like blockchain can prevent food hazards from spreading by allowing people to know where the problem lies and to eradicate it faster. This can also be a reason why meat has been used more often to test technology related to food traceability since the recent scandals involving food hazards have been related to meat. Despite this fact, there seems to be a lack of interest amongst the meat industry towards the implementation of food traceability, caused by factors like implementation costs and suppliers not being open to sharing their information.

Even though it is relatively simple to find evidence of the advantages of blockchain, it is also necessary to evaluate the viability of its implementation. Through the analysis of studies in Europe, it was possible to conclude that food quality is a main concern for European consumers. Nonetheless, in Portugal, there was a study conducted by Figueiredo (2019) at an Auchan store. It hints that the Portuguese people still value price over quality when it comes to food. The quality of the products was, nevertheless, the second most valued dimension. This data can indicate that quality, along with price, is a priority for Portuguese people when buying food. Our interviewee José Cordeiro also stated that, in his opinion, customers are more and more concerned about the origin of their food.

Another dimension that could influence the implementation of BCT for food traceability in Portugal is the law regarding the issue. There is a Decree-Law (Assembleia da República, 2016) in order to implement European Regulations, from 2011, regarding the information that is available about food (The European Parliament, 2011). It states that there should be a way to provide information about the product's origin or production to the competent authorities. However, it does not specifically target the consumer as an entity to whom the information must be provided. Even though it is an important step towards the implementation of technology that allows food traceability, it could be easier if there were newer, consumer-targeted regulations from the Portuguese government that would promote the transparency of the food supply chain to the consumer. José Cordeiro also considers that there is not an urgent need for the Portuguese government to regulate this type of technology since a lot of products already have important information on their labels. For this reason, Blockchain will only increase this level of information, thus becoming a competitive advantage for Auchan. The use of blockchain technology can become a powerful marketing tool for the companies that adopt it, as long as consumers value transparency and food safety. Greater loyalty will be the result.

There are, however, other disadvantages regarding the accessibility to this technology. There is a need for specific processes and a big level of digitalization in order to implement BCT, which may not be available to small producers in the short term. José Cordeiro stated that there is very different software being used to trace products, which makes it difficult for BCT to be implemented.

Albeit, the use of blockchain to trace products in Portugal is possible. It can also be an important tool for companies to market themselves. However, issues regarding the software used by small producers or the lack of interest of big companies in sharing the information may complicate the implementation of this type of technology. Hence, it is suggested that it would be possible to be implemented in Portugal, but it is suggested that its generalized use (instead of only for one product or by one company) could only be possible in the medium to long run.

6. The interview

For this article, we have conducted a structured interview with the Product/Supplier Quality Manager of Auchan Portugal, José Cordeiro. The interview was done by email and focused mainly on the adaptation of Auchan's Blockchain technology to the Portuguese market. The Portuguese supply sector has been facing strong variations, fostering a strategy change by retail companies.

As stated by José Cordeiro, Portuguese consumers are now more interested in knowing more about the origins of the food they buy, which led Auchan to focus more on labeling its products with more specific and relevant information. Even though Portuguese law only states that the food should be correctly labeled and own proper documentation, this strategy has proved to be insufficient for some of the products sold by the retail company, as nowadays the amount of food scandals has increased.

To reverse the lack of trust shown by a high number of consumers and following the strategy adopted by Auchan Vietnam, Auchan Portugal is now conducting market studies aiming to implement Blockchain on food traceability. According to Mr. Cordeiro, Blockchain is a promising technology when it comes to food traceability, considering it combines all information from the genesis of the product up until the final consumer.

According to statistics taken from ANIL (2019), the French group Auchan is the 16th largest retail player in the world, with sales of 58,614 million euros. With the implementation of Blockchain for food traceability in Portugal, where it is a top player, Auchan aims to have an additional competitive advantage and improve its Customer Relationship Management (CRM), as well as having enhanced communication and trust from consumers.

Just like in Vietnam, where food traceability is being monitored by the German start-up TE-FOOD, Mr. Cordeiro confirmed that Auchan Portugal is currently discussing a possible partnership and implementation details with the same company. The fact that TE-FOOD is already monitoring the process, facilitates the transition into a new country.

So far, the biggest setback in implementing new technology for food traceability is the fact that every part of the current supply chain is using different software. Hence the struggle to implement a new one. However, as said by Mr. Cordeiro, it will be a worthwhile effort, considering it will benefit the consumers.

Even though the first product monitored by TE-FOOD in Portugal will be chicken, in the long-term, Auchan's goal is to expand transparency to a wider range of food products, such as vegetables.

Unlike what happened in Vietnam, where the traceability of food arose from a government project, José Cordeiro stated that in Portugal there is no urgent need for the State to implement BCT, considering a lot is being done already in the field of food traceability, following the implementation of the Decree-Law No.26/2016 (Assembleia da República, 2016) that follows the guidelines of the Regulation (EU) No 1169/2011 of the European Parliament and of the Council of 25 October 2011 (The European Parliament, 2011). A lot of food already contains on their label a lot of relevant information for the consumer.

7. Conclusions and suggestions for future research

The present article aims to understand on a deeper level what is the possibility of the use of BCT when tracing food in Portugal. It was necessary to, initially, understand how blockchain works and what are its advantages and disadvantages. It became clear why its use in the food supply chain can be an important step towards consumer information. The consumers' concerns towards the quality of food and traceability in Europe were also researched and some studies in this field were analyzed, as well as one in the Portuguese market. It was possible to assume that Europeans, as well as Portuguese consumers, are more and more concerned about the quality and information of food. The Portuguese law regarding food traceability was also pointed out since it could be an important facilitator of implementation. Although there is a decree-law, it is not very specific or consumer-oriented. By analyzing companies in other countries that have implemented blockchain for food traceability, it was possible to assume that it represents a competitive advantage of these companies. The company that intends to be a pioneer in the implementation of blockchain for traceability purposes in Portugal, Auchan, was also briefly described, as well as the company with which Auchan cooperates in order to implement this process, TE-FOOD. An interview with the Quality Director of Auchan Portugal, José Cordeiro, was conducted in order to understand the advantages and disadvantages of the implementation of blockchain on food traceability in Portugal from his point of view.

After the research, by crossing all the data it is suggested that the implementation is possible and it will represent a competitive advantage for the companies that use BCT. Nevertheless, it will possibly only happen in the medium to long run. It could be important to conduct additional studies, however. Future investigation on types of products on which blockchain could not be applied, as well as alternatives for its traceability, should add important data to the literature. Furthermore, in order to understand the viability of the implementation of blockchain, it would also be relevant to understand to what extent can small and local producers adhere to this type of technology, as well as the interest of Portuguese producers in full disclosure to the consumer with all of the information about their products.

There is no doubt that food traceability is a growing concern amongst European and Portuguese consumers. BCT has proven to be an important tool towards providing customers with the right type of information, but it may be a challenge to implement it. In the future, it is necessary to keep monitoring it in order to understand the consumers' and the companies' responses, as well as to face new challenges that may arise concerning food traceability.

Acknowledgements

This work was financially supported by the research unit on Governance, Competitiveness and Public Policy (UIDB/04058/2020), funded by national funds through FCT - Fundação para a Ciência e a Tecnologia.

References

ANIL (2019). Maiores retalhistas mundiais em Portugal são de origem alemã. Associação Nacional dos Industriais de Lacticínios. 22 January. Retrieved March 14, 2020, from https://www.anilact.pt/info/actual/mercado/item/3073-maiores-grupos-retalhistas-mundiais-em-portugal-sao-de-origem-alema

Assembleia da República (2016). Lei n.° 26/2016 de 22 de agosto. Diário da República, 1.ª série - N.° 160.

Auchan Retail (2018). Food traceability: Auchan Retail is launching blockchain technology internationally, (November), pp.1–4.

Bitcoin (2019). How does Bitcoin work? Retrieved October 30, 2019, from https://bitcoin.org/en/how-it-works

Business Wire (2019). Blockchain in Retail Market Expected Growth of More than 65% During the Forecast Period. Retrieved October 28, 2019, from https://www.businesswire.com/news/home/20191011005186/en/Blockchain-Retail-Market-Expected-Growth-65-Forecast

Caro, M. P., Ali, M. S., Vecchio, M., & Giaffreda, R. (2018). Blockchain-based traceability in Agri-Food supply chain management: A practical implementation. In *2018 IoT Vertical and Topical Summit on Agriculture - Tuscany, IOT Tuscany 2018*. IEEE.

Chainvu (2019). The Ultimate Guide To Blockchain In The Food Supply Chain. Retrieved November 10, 2019, from https://www.chainvu.com/blockchain-food-supply-chain

Dabbene, F., & Gay, P. (2011). Food traceability systems: Performance evaluation and optimization. *Computers and Electronics in Agriculture*, Vol.75(1), pp.139–146.

Figueiredo, F. B. de A. e S. (2019). *Estratégias de resposta da Auchan Retail Portugal aos hábitos de consumo dos portugueses na era do digital*. Universidade Católica Portuguesa.

Folinas, D., Manikas, I., & Manos, B. (2006). Traceability data management for food chains. *British Food Journal*, Vol.108(8), pp.622–633.

Galvez, J. F., Mejuto, J. C., & Simal-Gandara, J. (2018). Future challenges on the use of blockchain for food traceability analysis. *TrAC - Trends in Analytical Chemistry*, Vol.107, pp.222-232.

Golan, E., Krissoff, B., & Kuchler, F. (2002). Traceability for food marketing and food safety: what's the next step? *Agricultural Outlook*, Vol.5, pp.21–25.

Hobbs, J. E., Von Bailey, D., Dickinson, D. L., & Haghiri, M. (2005). Traceability in the Canadian red meat sector: Do consumers care? *Canadian Journal of Agricultural Economics*, Vol.53(1), pp.47–65.

Hyperledger (2019). Case Study: How Walmart brought unprecedented transparency to the food supply chain with Hyperledger Fabric. Retrieved November 4, 2019, from https://www.hyperledger.org/resources/publications/walmart-case-study

Kamilaris, A., Fonts, A., & Prenafeta-Boldú, F. X. (2019). The rise of blockchain technology in agriculture and food supply chains. *Trends in Food Science & Technology*, Vol.91. http://doi.org/10.1016/j.tifs.2019.07.034

Krissoff, B., Kuchler, F., Nelson, K., Perry, J.E., & Somwaru, A. (2004). Country-of-Origin Labeling: Theory and Observation, *Electronic Outlook Report from the Economic Research Service*, January.

Kuzmanovic, A. (2019). Net neutrality: Unexpected solution to blockchain scaling. *Queue*, Vol.17(1), pp.20-78.

Loureiro, M. L., & Umberger, W. J. (2007). A choice experiment model for beef: What US consumer responses tell us about relative preferences for food safety, country-of-origin labeling and traceability. *Food Policy*, Vol.32(4), pp.496-514.

Machado, M. P. (2019). Jumbo e Pão de Açúcar mudam de nome. Agora é só "Auchan." Retrieved November 5, 2019, from https://observador.pt/2019/09/12/jumbo-e-pao-de-acucar-mudam-de-nome-agora-e-so-auchan/

Moe, T. (1998). Traceability in food manufacturing can range from in-house traceability in production plants to traceability in whole or part of the production chain from raw material to consumer. *Trends in Food & Science Technology*, Vol.9(9), pp.211–214.

Myers, M. D. (2009). *Quality Research in Business & Management*. London, UK: SAGE Publications.

Nakamoto, S. (2019). Bitcoin: A Peer-to-Peer Electronic Cash System. Retrieved from https://bitcoin.org/bitcoin.pdf

Olsen, P., & Borit, M. (2013). How to define traceability. *Trends in Food Science and Technology*, Vol.29(2), pp.142–150.
Petersen, M., Hackius, N., & von See, B. (2018). Mapping the sea of opportunities: Blockchain in supply chain and logistics. *It - Information Technology*, Vol.60(5-6), pp.263–271.
Pettersen, N., & Durivage, A. (2008). The Structured Job Related Interview Defined. In *The Structured Interview - Enhancing Staff Selection* (pp. 5–10). Québec, Canada: Presses de l'Université du Quebéc.
Pizzuti, T., & Mirabelli, G. (2015). The Global Track&Trace System for food: General framework and functioning principles. *Journal of Food Engineering*, Vol.159, pp.16-35.
Profeta, A., Balling, R., & Roosen, J. (2012). The relevance of origin information at the point of sale. *Food Quality and Preference*, Vol.26(1), pp.1-11.
Queiroz, M. M., Telles, R., & Bonilla, S. H. (2018). Blockchain and supply chain management integration: a systematic review of the literature, (March).
Resende-Filho, M., & Buhr, B. (2012). Economics of traceability for mitigation of food recall costs. International Association of Agricultural Economists (IAAE) Triennial Conference, Foz do Iguaçu, Brazil, 18-24 August.
Roosen, J., Lusk, J. L., & Fox, J. A. (2003). Consumer demand for and attitudes toward alternative beef labeling strategies in France, Germany, and the UK. *Agribusiness*, Vol.19(1), pp.77–90.
Sander, F., Semeijn, J., & Mahr, D. (2018). The acceptance of blockchain technology in meat traceability and transparency. *British Food Journal*, Vol.120(9), pp.2066–2079.
Spencer, N. (2019). What's next for blockchain in the food industry? Retrieved October 28, 2019, from https://www.foodnavigator.com/Article/2019/09/24/Blockchain-technology-is-improving-food-traceability
Springwise. (2019). Hypermarket tracks products from farm to store with blockchain. Retrieved November 5, 2019, from https://www.springwise.com/retail-innovation-carrefour-blockchain/
TE-FOOD (2019a). Food Traceability Trends to watch in 2019. Retrieved October 28, 2019, from https://medium.com/te-food/food-traceability-trends-to-watch-in-2019-179a00b3b625
TE-FOOD (2019b). TE-FOOD - Farm-to-table food traceability on blockchain. Retrieved November 5, 2019, from https://te-foodint.com/
The European Parliament (2011). Regulation (EU) No 1169/2011 of The European Parliament and The Council of 25 October 2011. *Official Journal of the European Union.*
Tian, F. (2016). An agri-food supply chain traceability system for China based on RFID & blockchain technology. In *2016 13th International Conference on Service Systems and Service Management, ICSSSM 2016*.
Tian, F. (2017). A supply chain traceability system for food safety based on HACCP, blockchain & Internet of things. In *14th International Conference on Services Systems and Services Management, ICSSSM 2017 - Proceedings*.
Van Rijswijk, W., & Frewer, L. J. (2012). Consumer needs and requirements for food and ingredient traceability information. *International Journal of Consumer Studies*, Vol.36(3), pp.282–290.
Verbeke, W., & Ward, R. W. (2006). Consumer interest in information cues denoting quality, traceability and origin: An application of ordered probit models to beef labels. *Food Quality and Preference*, Vol.17(6), pp.453–467.
Willemse, L. (2019). Retail Giants like Walmart, Carrefour and Auchan Adopting Blockchain Technology. Retrieved November 4, 2019, from https://hackernoon.com/retail-giants-like-walmart-carrefour-and-auchan-adopting-blockchain-technology-3e7a48460e8e

Knowledge and Technology Transfer in the Port Talbot Waterfront Enterprise Zone

James Bourne, Gareth Huw Davies and Mike Williams
School of Management, Swansea University, UK
869752@swansea.ac.uk
g.h.davies@swansea.ac.uk
m.d.williams@swansea.ac.uk
DOI: 10.34190/EIE.20.070

Abstract: This case study paper examines the Port Talbot Waterfront Enterprise Zone (PTWEZ) and its efforts to maximise its economic contribution to the region involving knowledge transfer (KT) and technology transfer (TT). This study includes consideration of KT and TT initiatives such as AgorIP. The study highlights literature regarding Regional Innovation Systems (RIS), including specifically KT and TT literature. This paper examines the PTWEZ portfolio and draws insight from semi-structured interviews with key triple helix actors, along with first-hand accounts from PTWEZ stakeholder engagement. Findings from this paper reinforce the importance of KT/TT between PTWEZ entities. The importance of a PTWEZ focal point to support the interactions between PTWEZ, while increasing scope and collaboration with AgorIP and relevant industries such as advanced manufacturing and renewable energy.

Keywords: technology transfer, knowledge transfer, regional innovation systems, triple helix

1. Introduction

There has been increasing interest in the significance of 'knowledge' and its impact on the economy and regional growth. (Cooke, 2002; Asheim et al, 2011; Davies, Roderick, & Williams, 2018). This particularly interests post-industrial regions such as south-west Wales, which have become particularly challenged over recent years. (Pugh, MacKenzie, & Jones-Evans, 2018) which has led to a greater emphasis on creating a knowledge-based economy in the south-west Wales region. Morgan (2001) described the need for this following the decline of the heavy industry markets and inward investment; coinciding with introducing devolution in the UK in 1999. Devolution was then followed by the forming of the Welsh Assembly Government (WAG). WAG embarked on the delivery of new policies focused upon knowledge-based activity. This attracted a notable level of academic interest (Cooke, 2004; Huggins & Strakova, 2012). For example, Pugh et al. (2018) describe problems with the 'Technium' knowledge-based initiative, including not learning from the original Swansea Pilot before expanding the initiative. Davies (2019) built upon the work of Huggins and Kitagawa (2012) to further understanding of this initiative inter alia. This echoed points from Pugh et al. (2018) noting that evaluating the question of time horizons for such initiatives. Besides this, Gibson et al. (2007) provided a more industry perspective issue to this domain, highlighting a lack of deals flow between the private sector and academia. These issues are germane in the region's context's plans, such as the Swansea Bay City Region (SBCR) Internet Coast City Deal (SU, 2017); where it looks to enhance the 'Regional Innovation System' (RIS), as per the concept, was set out by Cooke (1992) to support the economic development of a specific area. This model works with the processes of KT & TT and its importance in the production of knowledge and innovation between academia and industry (Bercovitz and Feldmann 2006; Mowery and Nelson 2004). Perkmann & Walsh (2007) highlighted the need for partnerships to form between academic and industry contexts. This paper will look at the barriers and drivers for the successful localisation of KT&TT in South West Wales. While also provides a mapping of the RIS through the Triple helix model (Leydesdorff & Etzkowitz, 1998).

2. Knowledge transfer – technology transfer

One established definition of 'knowledge' by Drucker (1998) describes it as the catalyst to bring about a potential change to something or somebody, allowing individuals or institutions to improve the capability of operative actions. Ankrah et al., (2013) defines knowledge transfer by "any activities aimed at transferring technology or knowledge to help either the company or university to further pursue its activities"; this adds to the importance of recognising both KT & TT as a collective.

Conversely, there is much discussion about how interchangeable the terms KT and TT are (Gopalakrishnan & Santoro, 2004; Martinelli, Meyer, & Tunzelmann, 2008; Ankrah & Al-Tabbaa, 2015). The two should be a combined activity. Nonaka & Takeuchi (1995) defined knowledge transfer between 'tacit' and 'explicit', which backs the argument of the similarity in definitions.

Battistella et al., (2016) provide an in-depth literature review. This looks into both entities. This literature coincides in the broader context of the University-Industry Engagement, which is an integral part of the academic contribution (Tornatzky & Association, 2000).

A subsequent literature review has been produced which tests the university-industry relationships (Perkmann et al., 2013). The driving catalyst for this relationship to form was through the Bayh-Dole Act in the US (Henderson, Jaffe, & Trajtenberg, 1998). In the UK reports produced by Lambert (2003) and additional government documents by (HOC, 2013, 2017) and regional Welsh Government (WAG, 2004). Where they also challenge the issues highlighted by the academics earlier on.

KT & TT is a two-way process; a succinct exchange between academia and industry (Abreu et al, 2009). Kitagawa and Lightowler (2013) discuss the term 'Knowledge Exchange'. There is a collective agreement that this process is bi-directional; this is contrary to the original belief of a unidirectional process; (Gopalakrishnan & Santoro, 2004; Ulhøi, Neergaard, & Bjerregaard, 2012). Bjørn T Asheim et al. (2011) refers to the mechanisms required for knowledge transfer to take place; including human capital and local labour markets and to improve the understanding of local and non-local sources of knowledge.

In the past two decades, TT between government, academia and industry is considered being of immense importance in enhancing regional economic growth and social development. Known as 'the triple helix model' (Leydesdorff & Etzkowitz, 1998). There is much discussion about how effective this model is in practice and whether it has reached the expectations for innovation, employment and GDP potential (B. T. Asheim & Coenen, 2005; McAdam et al, 2011). It is paramount that this process is developed further to solve these issues; this can be done through including a fourth entity, as described by Carayannis and Campbell (2009), includes the societal based innovation user for the quadruple helix model to exist. This is also supported by Bozeman, Rimes, and Youtie (2015) that discusses how society needs to have some input into the TT process.

In North America and Europe, there has been a significant development in public policy regarding innovation (EC, 2013). Since 2010, the UK has seen a reduced growth in development relative to the USA (OECD, 2016). This has then emphasised the issues for post regional regions, such as South West Wales and its ability to have a production RIS. (Isaksen, Martin, & Trippl, 2018)

3. Port Talbot Waterfront Enterprise Zone (PTWEZ)

The PTWEZ is a government-led industrial zone, made up of three areas; Baglan Energy Park, Port Talbot Docks, and Baglan Industrial Estate. These makeup 120.86 Ha of potential real estate for companies ranging from technology start-up to heavy industry and specialise in advanced manufacturing and materials, energy and environment, and construction. This was formed from a direct response to the decline of the steel industry and Tata Steel. (BW, 2019). Below is an image to highlight the mentioned areas of the PTWEZ as fig. 1.

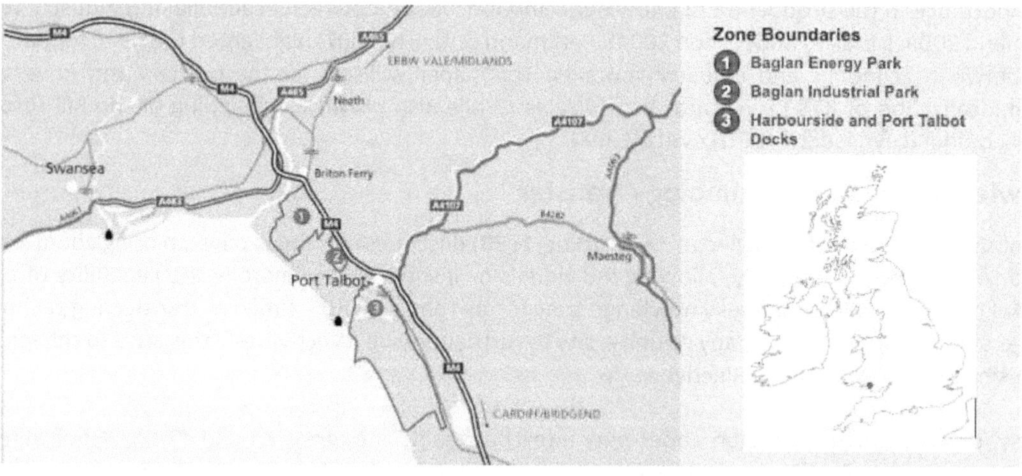

Figure 1: Areas and sites in Port Talbot Waterfront (BW, 2019)

Swansea Bay City Deal announced in January 2020, allocating £58.7 million to the Neath Port Talbot area SBCD (2020) to further the PTWEZ initiative in its ambition for regional economic development. There are 111,900 people employed in the region of Neath Port Talbot according to (WG, 2020). This initiative has recently been associated with the Swansea Bay City Region deal (SU, 2017).

The Welsh Government describes Enterprise zones as: "where we create the best possible conditions for your business to thrive". (WG, 2019) The incentives offered includes infrastructure support and Business rate support; this allows businesses to offset up to a maximum of £55,000 against their business rates incurred during the previous year's financial year or their rates bill paid, whichever is lower. In addition to that, they offer enhanced capital allowance to claim a 100% first-year allowance for capital cost of investment for plant and equipment.

The strategic aims and objectives have been set out by Hatch consulting are as follows;

- "Strengthen and diversify the South Wales economy, building resilience for the longer-term future.
- Stimulate a cluster of advanced manufacturing, energy and engineering companies by providing a well-connected, competitive business environment.
- Work with Welsh Government and other partners to encourage investment and innovation in the steel sector and wider supply chain to ensure a long term future".
- "Champion and facilitate commercialisation of local R&D innovation through investment in property and business to help anchor prototyping, testing and production at PTWEZ.
- Differentiate the commercial market offer and unlock key development sites through investment in infrastructure and buildings to capture business expansion and growth.
- Raise the visibility of the unique development potential of PTWEZ through pro-active marketing".

(Hatch, 2018)

There are however no (SMART) objectives set out in the Hatch Consulting report.

Compared to the strategic plan produced by Business Wales, its aims and objectives provide (SMART) objectives (BW, 2019). Below shows a model set out by Hatch Consulting which briefly summarises the PTWEZ model. fig. 2;

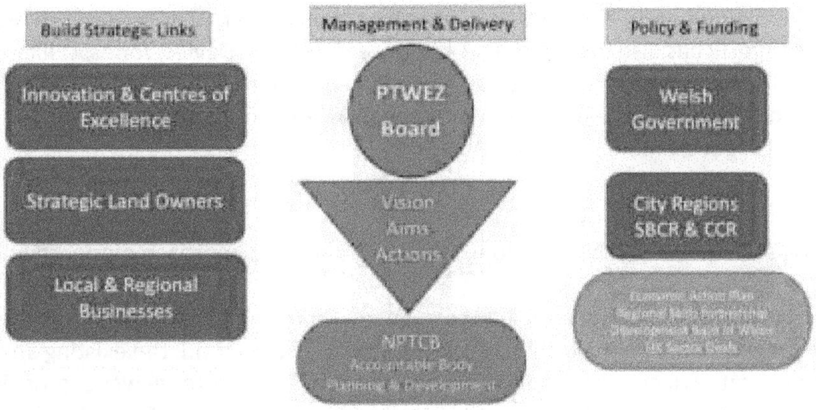

Figure 2: PTWEZ model (Hatch, 2018)

The model above describes its aims and objectives, which are closely coordinated with Welsh and local government. Its policy and funding are closely aligned to the SBCR deal.

Morgan (2015) provides relevant literature on SMART specialisation in the South West region, also a review of a recent initiative 'SPECIFIC' which falls in the PTWEZ zone. (Marques et al, 2019). These strategic aims are closely aligned with the AgorIP university TT initiative in their vision, whereby the two working alongside one another can mutually benefit through aims and objectives. More recently, the PTWEZ have invested 250k into the AgorIP initiative, which was aimed to support "early growth EZ based businesses linked to AgorIP" (BW, 2019)

4. AgorIP

The AgorIP, which is Welsh for 'open'IP. Is an initiative, which was developed in partnership with Welsh Government and industry to commercialise Intellectual Property from university and health board research output. This, similar to the PTWEZ, follows the 'triple helix' model produced by (Leydesdorff & Etzkowitz, 1998). The AgorIP model claims a unique 'zero-waste' approach, whereby it allows these opportunities to progress to give the best opportunities for success (SU, 2016).

The initiative adopts the 'Open Innovation' paradigm originally developed by Chesbrough (2003) and involves targeting KT & TT to occur through the different stages of development. This happened in both existing and/or new markets between different organisations. The AgorIP model is presented below as fig.3;

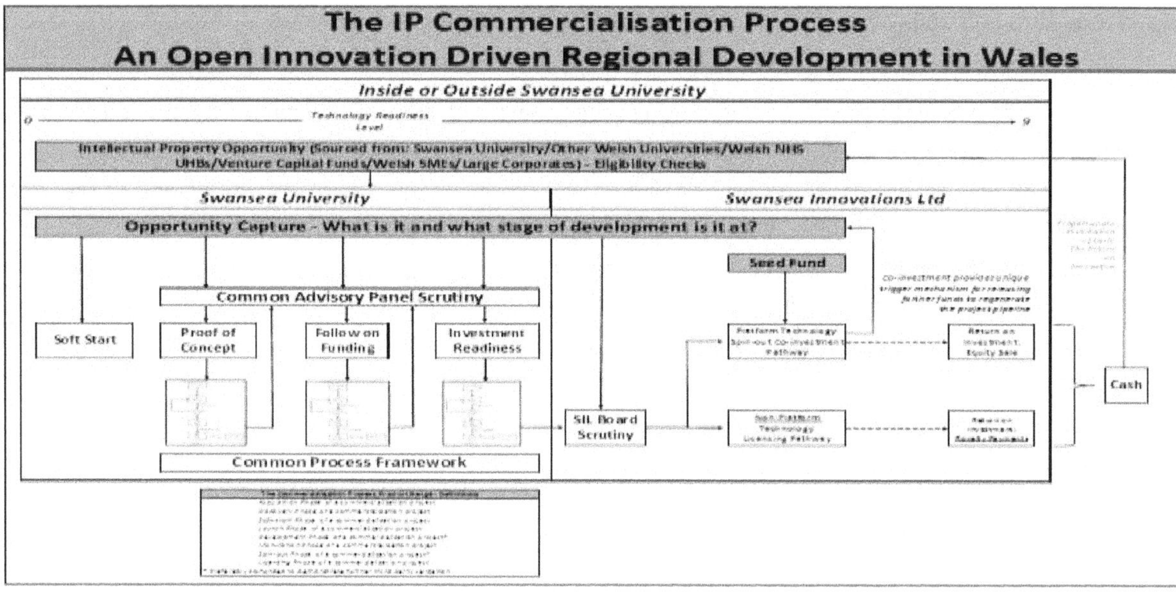

Figure 3: Agor IP model (SU, 2016)

AgorIP involves 5 Technology Transfer Officers (TTO) possessing a multitude of skills including; contract negotiation, market appraisal and project management. The team also provides a wider network of expertise, which allows them to provide potential clients with investment and external sources, such as market research and regulatory advice. AgorIP has also been subject to prior review (G. H. Davies, Jones, Williams, & Joyce, 2019; G. H. Davies et al., 2018). There is an agreement that since the forming of AgorIP, the scope and scale have been widened through this initiative. This is also supported through interest from policymakers in Welsh government HEFCW (2017) and the UK government (RSM, 2018).

5. Approach

The approach for this case study has been developed drawing upon the approach pioneered by Stake (1995).

The research carried out for this paper comprised three parts. This includes the PTWEZ project documentation and portfolio, which provides data on the businesses are within the EZ. Second, the existing analysis of SBCR and PTWEZ project. Primary data collected from semi-structured qualitative interviews; comprising 32 interviews from key actors in the Government, Academia and Industry, which support the 'triple helix' framework (Leydesdorff & Etzkowitz, 1998).

A rapid thematic form of coding was undertaken to synthesise the interviews carried out. Themes and codes identified were then cross-referenced to the PTWEZ project information for the businesses within the PTWEZ.

This will look into how AgorIP can impact on this for the added inclusion of Swansea University, being closely associated with the PTWEZ; the data collected can then act as guidance to both support the TTO at Swansea University and the PTWEZ. This data can also act as a bridge between the two, to open up new avenues for potential KT & TT to take place.

6. Results and discussion

6.1 Academia

Participants from universities cited examples of working with industry, including collaborative research, working as a consultant for an industrial partner, or creation of a university spin-out company. From the interviews carried out, there were proportionately fewer examples described of spins-outs, which could be partly because of the specific experience of the participants.

However, it is important to emphasise that significant spin-outs are a relatively rare phenomenon and can take up to 10-15 years to become financially viable, emphasising that KT & TT can happen through a variety of other ways, such as patenting, licensing, and joint ventures in the more explicit side of transfer, but also 'tacit' forms of movement for this process to happen (Alexander & Childe, 2013).

The structures of universities are so different from industry that it makes it challenging for industry to adapt their timescales do not align proactively, which echoes observation of (Demil & Lecocq, 2010). Industry participants also noted the structural differences between organisations, for example, "you know, that they're structured in such a way that, you know, they just cannot impose that kind of change on the majority of the staff".

There was an agreement to the importance of trust and how it influences relationships in KT & TT (Howard, Steensma, Lyles, & Dhanaraj, 2016) this was supported by the interviews. When exploring participants' experiences with the EZ, few had much experience with the EZ and those that did, with limited impact. It was sometimes believed that the EZ had impractical expectations and that its USP compared to other locations was unclear. This comes back to the importance of SMART specialisation (Foray, David, & Hall, 2009).

6.2 Industry

Views on the effectiveness of universities varied significantly amongst participants. Negative reviews often related to difficulty in finding the individual to help them with their problem. A government official was quoted; "exposing one another to each other".

Academics have agendas, such as publication of papers and securing research grants, which then brings about the debate of the 'publish or patent dilemma' (McAdam et al., 2011). This was also backed by an interview with an industry representative describing this. "We used to say fame and fortune. So they need exposure. They need papers being cited by other researchers and they need their papers to be published in not in high ranking journals and to win awards. And then the fortune is they need to secure research money to keep their research centre going to employ their staff and employ more staff because they will want to grow their research centres".

This is being mainly for academics being measured on this for performance and promotions, rather than upon their collaboration with companies. It was also perceived that that university may, to some extent, be losing sight of their mission and charitable status which should concentrate more on the economic and social development of the region.

There were differing views on proximity being as much of a barrier as is often perceived. Where some did not see this as a barrier where others did, which supports the work by (Malik, 2013). However, when delving deeper into the answers, the overall consensus is that it is required to be in proximity for the initial contact with an individual so that a relationship and trust can be formed. Once this has happened, then the challenge of distance becomes less of a barrier which can add to the literature in this area as this has not been suggested in this way. This was agreed upon, though some individuals highlighting that there will always be the barrier of distance. For example, the distance between London and Swansea was cited as forcing companies to re-locate from the region to increase their chances of receive funding.

6.3 Government

Governments, both national and local, have an important perspective on KT & TT because of their working with both universities and industry. Interviewees echoed the view that the way universities are structured often makes it hard for industry to align their timelines to that of activity within universities (Demil & Lecocq, 2010).

This was described as being because of industry having problems that they need sorting as soon as possible, which does not align with concurrent academic imperatives. However, there were many examples cited of successful relationships between universities and industry, addressing collective problems and contributing to the regional economic development, while also taking into consideration the recent importance of the Future Generations Act, which is described as *"improve the economic, social, environmental and cultural well-being of its area by contributing to the achievement of the well-being goals."* (NAW, 2015)

The main reason for success, which was highlighted through the interviews was where universities are transparent with what they can do to help and are effective in managing the expectations of industry partners and to implement this process appropriately, which is supported in the literature by (De Toni, Nonino, & Pivetta, 2011). Success was also noted as being contributed to by a range of Welsh Government schemes, such as the Strength in Places Fund, Smart Cymru and Open Innovation programmes. There is a limited amount of research that looks into the government side of this process of KT & TT. This paper can then lead to more insight into this point of view.

6.4 Emerging themes

The interviews presented several emerging themes, including;

- Potential for greater collaboration between academia, industry and local and national government institutions, with a focus upon key strengths aligned across industry and academia across the region
- Proximity and frequency of engagement matter in identifying, developing and sustaining collaboration
- Opportunity for a focal point within the Enterprise Zone which would allow for co-location of businesses, universities, funders and related actors to be situated to allow for greater levels of KT.
- Design of appropriated facilities is important for the success of this idea. The characteristics of this will be to have an open plan communal area to allow for the minimal friction flow of knowledge and ideas to pass. Also separation of workspaces and labs for protecting IP and sensitive information.

7. PTWEZ portfolio

The data discussed was got through the Neath Port Talbot County Council, where they have had a first-hand account in bringing in all the new companies into the PTWEZ area. The two sectors predominately In the region are manufacturing and construction industries, both of which support strategic plans set out by (BW, 2019; Hatch, 2018). These 2 sectors make up 108 companies out of the total 217 (49.7%).

Figure 4 provides a breakdown of all the businesses within the PTWEZ.

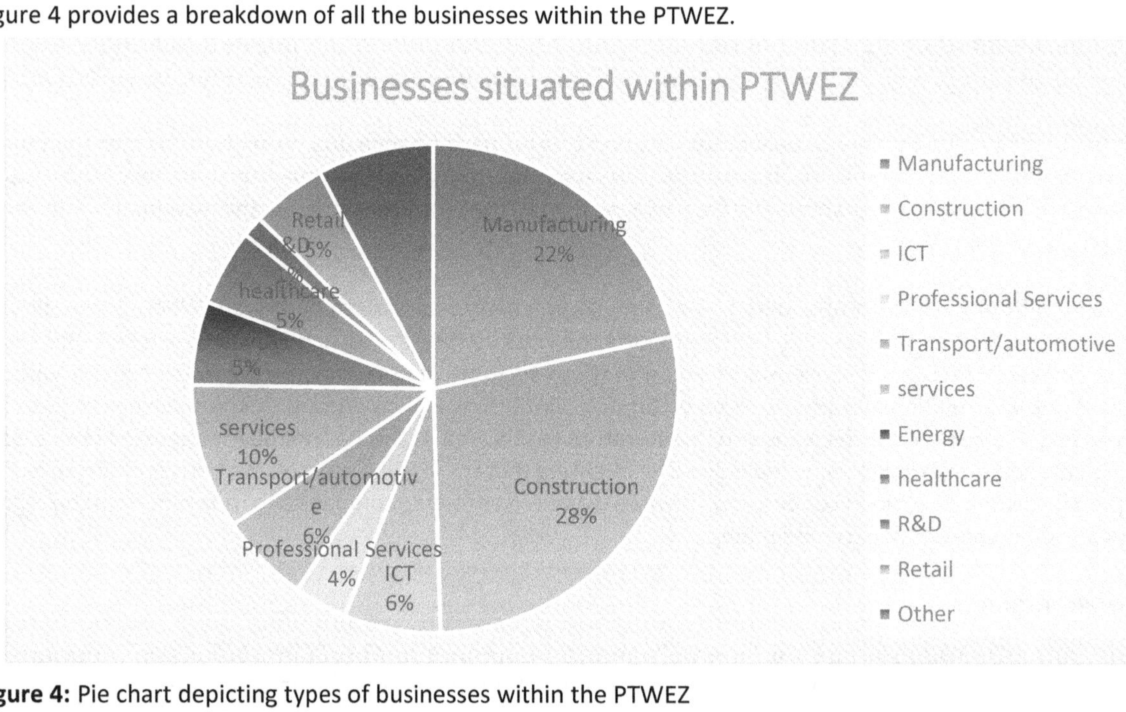

Figure 4: Pie chart depicting types of businesses within the PTWEZ

This is supported by the correct labour force within the area, which echoes observations of (Foray, 2014; Morgan, 2015) SMART specialisation. Recent emphasis has pushed towards Energy and ICT companies forming their clusters. During one interview with a government official, the emergence of an ICT cluster was highlighted in the Port Talbot region; this initiative has recently been associated with the Swansea Bay City Region deal (SU, 2017). Also, energy and renewables have moved recently, which further supports the aims and objectives of the strategic plan.

8. Conclusion

This study has highlighted several well-established issues being apparent within the PTWEZ context; this relates to the theory that follows an increased demand for innovation to be supported by academic institutions (Guerrero et al., 2016). This emphasises the complex nature of KT & TT; this being hard to measure its true impact between unique entities, such as academia, industry, and government. It is important to acknowledge that KT rarely happens quickly, and that there has to be a process and adequate infrastructure in place to allow for this to happen naturally. To facilitate this between Swansea University and the PTWEZ, stakeholders identified the potential for there to be a focal point for ease of communication, between the two parties, which is backed in the literature by (Van Wijk, Jansen, & Lyles, 2008). A good example of a successful model in this area is the 'Sheffield University Enterprise Academy'.

With academia, the participants have the ability, motivation and capacity to facilitate this. Vice versa, academics who do not have an interest in this process, are not obliged to partake. Conversely for practitioners, they need to be directed to the people, due to the individuality of academics and their specialist research. This would be a point for AgorIP to consider in developing interactions between the two parties, as KT & TT is a two-way process.

This case study paper has gained a unique opportunity in gathering data on this EZ and how it can have a direct impact on the region in KT & TT process. This then can add to an additional strand to the literature from this context to provide teachings which then can be translated to other EZs across the UK.

It is important to understand and appreciate that this process can take a long time and all entities should maintain patience; more so for policymakers and critics, for much of the criticism of these initiatives in past years, was because of the premature nature of the evaluation of these KT initiatives and to give it ample time before such evaluation can take place.

The PTWEZ case has highlighted considerations that would be of relevance to regions with similar challenges and contexts, including the opportunity to draw upon well-established learning embedded in concepts such as Smart Specialisation and Open Innovation.

References

Abreu, M., Grinevich, V., Hughes, A., & Kitson, M. (2009). *Knowledge exchange between academics and the business, public and third sectors*: University of Cambridge; Imperial College London.

Alexander, A. T., & Childe, S. J. (2013). Innovation: a knowledge transfer perspective. *Production Planning & Control, 24*(2-3), 208-225.

Ankrah, S., & Al-Tabbaa, O. (2015). Universities-industry collaboration: A systematic review. In *Scand. J. Manag.* (Vol. 31, pp. 387-408).

Ankrah, S., Burgess, T., Grimshaw, P., & Shaw, N. (2013). Asking both university and industry actors about their engagement in knowledge transfer: What single- group studies of motives omit. *Technovation, 33*(2-3), 50-50. doi:10.1016/j.technovation.2012.11.001

Asheim, B. T., Boschma, R., & Cooke, P. (2011). Constructing regional advantage: Platform policies based on related variety and differentiated knowledge bases. *Regional studies, 45*(7), 893-904.

Asheim, B. T., & Coenen, L. (2005). Knowledge bases and regional innovation systems: Comparing Nordic clusters. *Research Policy, 34*(8), 1173-1190. doi:10.1016/j.respol.2005.03.013

Battistella, C., De Toni, A., & Pillon, R. (2016). Inter-organisational technology/knowledge transfer: a framework from critical literature review. *The Journal of Technology Transfer, 41*(5), 1195-1234. doi:10.1007/s10961-015-9418-7

Bozeman, B., Rimes, H., & Youtie, J. (2015). The evolving state-of-the-art in technology transfer research: Revisiting the contingent effectiveness model. *Research Policy, 44*(1), 34-49. doi:10.1016/j.respol.2014.06.008

BW. (2019). *Port Talbot Waterfront Enterprise Zone Strategic Plan 2018 - 2021*. Retrieved from

Carayannis, E. G., & Campbell, D. F. (2009). 'Mode 3'and'Quadruple Helix': toward a 21st century fractal innovation ecosystem. *International Journal of Technology Management, 46*(3-4), 201-234.

Chesbrough, H. W. (2003). *Open innovation: The new imperative for creating and profiting from technology*: Harvard Business Press.

Cooke, P. (1992). Regional innovation systems: competitive regulation in the new Europe. *Geoforum, 23*(3), 365-382.

Cooke, P. (2002). *Knowledge economies: Clusters, learning and cooperative advantage*: Routledge.

Cooke, P. (2004). The regional innovation system in Wales. *Regional Innovation Systems. The Role of Governances in a Globalized World*, 245-263.

Davies, G. (2019). *Reflections on Technium Swansea: Ambition, Learning & Patience* (Vol. 2).

Davies, G. H., Jones, Y., Williams, M., & Joyce, N. (2019). *Sustainable Development Legislation: The Case of the AgorIP Technology Transfer initiative.* Paper presented at the European Conference on Innovation and Entrepreneurship.

Davies, G. H., Roderick, S., & Williams, M. (2018). A sub-regional innovation ecosystem? Life sciences and health in the Swansea Bay City Region. *International Journal of Innovation and Regional Development, 8*(4), 306-321.

De Toni, A. F., Nonino, F., & Pivetta, M. (2011). A model for assessing the coherence of companies' knowledge strategy. *Knowledge Management Research & Practice, 9*(4), 327-341.

Demil, B., & Lecocq, X. (2010). Business Model Evolution: In Search of Dynamic Consistency. *Long range planning, 43*(2), 227-246. doi:10.1016/j.lrp.2010.02.004

Drucker, P. F. (1998). The discipline of innovation. *Leader to Leader, 1998*(9), 13-15. doi:10.1002/ltl.40619980906

EC. (2013). *Guide To Social Innovaiton*. Retrieved from http://s3platform.jrc.ec.europa.eu/documents/20182/84453/Guide_to_Social_Innovation.pdf

Foray, D. (2014). *Smart specialisation: Opportunities and challenges for regional innovation policy*: Routledge.

Foray, D., David, P. A., & Hall, B. (2009). Smart specialisation–the concept. *Knowledge economists policy brief, 9*(85), 100.

Gibson, S., Board, K., Barry, M., & Courtne, I. (2007). Commercialisation in Wales: A Report by the Independent Task and Finish Group. *Independent Review of Publicly Funded Commercialisation Activities in Wales, Cardiff*.

Gopalakrishnan, S., & Santoro, M. D. (2004). Distinguishing between knowledge transfer and technology transfer activities: the role of key organizational factors. *IEEE Transactions on engineering management, 51*(1), 57-69. doi:10.1109/TEM.2003.822461

Guerrero, M., Urbano, D., Fayolle, A., Klofsten, M., & Mian, S. (2016). Entrepreneurial universities: emerging models in the new social and economic landscape. *Small Business Economics, 47*(3), 551-563.

Hatch. (2018). *PORT TALBOT WATERFRONT ENTERPRISE ZONE strategic plan 2018-2021*. Retrieved from

HEFCW. (2017). *Innovation Nation. Higher Education Funding Council for Wales*. Retrieved from

Henderson, R., Jaffe, A. B., & Trajtenberg, M. (1998). Universities as a source of commercial technology: A detailed analysis of university patenting, 1965- 1988. *Rev. Econ. Stat., 80*(1), 119-127.

HOC. (2013). *Bridging the valley of death* House of Commons Retrieved from https://publications.parliament.uk/pa/cm201213/cmselect/cmsctech/348/348.pdf

HOC. (2017). *Managing intellectual property and technology transfer*. House of commons

Howard, M., Steensma, H. K., Lyles, M., & Dhanaraj, C. (2016). Learning to collaborate through collaboration: How allying with expert firms influences collaborative innovation within novice firms. *Strategic Management Journal, 37*(10), 2092-2103.

Huggins, R., & Kitagawa, F. (2012). Regional policy and university knowledge transfer: perspectives from devolved regions in the UK. *Regional studies, 46*(6), 817-832.

Huggins, R., & Strakova, L. (2012). Knowledge-based economic development in emerging regions: policy issues and implications in the Balkan Peninsula. *Regional studies, 46*(7), 961-975.

Isaksen, A., Martin, R., & Trippl, M. (2018). New Avenues for Regional Innovation Systems and Policy. In *New Avenues for Regional Innovation Systems-Theoretical Advances, Empirical Cases and Policy Lessons* (pp. 1-19): Springer.

Kitagawa, F., & Lightowler, C. (2013). Knowledge exchange: A comparison of policies, strategies, and funding incentives in English and Scottish higher education. *Research Evaluation, 22*(1), 1-14. doi:10.1093/reseval/rvs035

Lambert, R. (2003). Lambert review of business-university collaboration. *University of Illinois at Urbana-Champaign's Academy for Entrepreneurial Leadership Historical Research Reference in Entrepreneurship*.

Leydesdorff, L., & Etzkowitz, H. (1998). The Triple Helix as a model for innovation studies. *Science and Public Policy, 25*(3), 195-203. doi:10.1093/spp/25.3.195

Malik, T. H. (2013). National institutional differences and cross-border university- industry knowledge transfer. *Research policy : policy, management and economic studies of science, technology and innovation, 42*(3), 776-787. doi:10.1016/j.respol.2012.09.008

Marques, P., Morgan, K., Healy, A., & Vallance, P. (2019). Spaces of novelty: Can universities play a catalytic role in less developed regions? *Science and Public Policy, 46*(5), 763-771.

Martinelli, A., Meyer, M., & Tunzelmann, N. (2008). Becoming an entrepreneurial university? A case study of knowledge exchange relationships and faculty attitudes in a medium- sized, research- oriented university. *The Journal of Technology Transfer, 33*(3), 259-283. doi:10.1007/s10961-007-9031-5

McAdam, R., Miller, K., McAdam, M., & Teague, S. (2011). The development of University Technology Transfer stakeholder relationships at a regional level: Lessons for the future. *Technovation, 32*(1). doi:10.1016/j.technovation.2011.08.001

Morgan, K. (2001). The new territorial politics: rivalry and justice in post-devolution Britain. *Regional studies, 35*(4), 343-348.

Morgan, K. (2015). Smart Specialisation: Opportunities and Challenges for Regional Innovation Policy. In (Vol. 49, pp. 480-482): Routledge.

NAW. (2015). *Well-being of Future Generatoins (Wales) Act 2015. N. A F. Wales*. Retrieved from

Nonaka, I., & Takeuchi, H. (1995). *The knowledge-creating company: How Japanese companies create the dynamics of innovation*: Oxford university press.

OECD, F. (2016). FDI in Figures. In: Organisation for European Economic Cooperation Paris.

Perkmann, M., Tartari, V., McKelvey, M., Autio, E., Broström, A., D'Este, P., . . . Hughes, A. (2013). Academic engagement and commercialisation: A review of the literature on university–industry relations. *Research Policy, 42*(2), 423-442.

Pugh, R., MacKenzie, N. G., & Jones-Evans, D. (2018). From 'Techniums' to 'emptiums': the failure of a flagship innovation policy in Wales. *Regional studies, 52*(7), 1009-1020.

SBCD. (2020). Regional green light for £58.7 million Neath Port Talbot programme. Retrieved from https://www.swanseabaycitydeal.wales/news/regional-green-light-for-587-million-neath-port-talbot-programme/

SU. (2016). AgorIP business plan. Swansea University.

SU. (2017). Internet Coast: Phase 1: City Deal Proposal Impact Appraisal. V1.26. School of Management.

Tornatzky, L. G., & Association, N. G. (2000). *Building state economies by promoting university-industry technology transfer*: National Governors' Association.

Ulhøi, J., Neergaard, H., & Bjerregaard, T. (2012). Beyond unidirectional knowledge transfer: An empirical study of trust-based university–industry research and technology collaboration. *The International Journal of Entrepreneurship and Innovation, 13*(4), 287-299.

Van Wijk, R., Jansen, J. J., & Lyles, M. A. (2008). Inter-and intra-organizational knowledge transfer: a meta-analytic review and assessment of its antecedents and consequences. *Journal of management Studies, 45*(4), 830-853.

WAG. (2004). *Knowledge Economy Nexus: Role of Higher Education in Wales. Welsh Assembly Government* Retrieved from

WG. (2019). Enterprise Zones Wales. Retrieved from https://businesswales.gov.wales/enterprisezones/

WG. (2020). Employment in the public and private sectors by Welsh local authority and status. *Stats Wales*. Retrieved from https://statswales.gov.wales/Catalogue/Business-Economy-and-Labour-Market/People-and-Work/Employment/Persons-Employed/publicprivatesectoremployment-by-welshlocalauthority-status

Is Innovation in the Hospitality Industry Gender-Biased? A Look at Hotel Managers' Innovation Practices

Filipa Brandão, Zélia Breda and Carlos Costa
DEGEIT – Department of Economics, Management, Industrial Engineering and Tourism of the University of Aveiro, GOVCOPP - Research Unit on Governance, Competitiveness and Public Policies, University of Aveiro, Portugal
filipa.brandao@ua.pt
zelia@ua.pt
ccosta@ua.pt
DOI: 10.34190/EIE.20.220

Abstract: The inclusion of women in economic life is acknowledged as an important source of growth, as women bring added value to business innovation and competitiveness. However, there is little research on the relationship between innovation and gender, because most of the studies focus businesses where women are under-represented, or that are traditionally male-dominated, leading to the dilution of the gender issues in innovation-related research. This paper analyses the dynamics of innovation in the hospitality industry, where women are well represented, following a gender perspective. A sample of 74 hospitality units was analysed. The findings confirm that there are no statistically significant differences between gender and innovativeness. However, gender-based differences can be found. Firms managed by women appear to be more innovative than those managed by men; there are more women as "major innovators"; women are more active in networks at regional and local levels, and establish a higher number of links to create knowledge and new marketing strategies, and to obtain funding. These findings bring important contributions by highlighting the need for further empirical evidence on the specific role of women in innovation in hospitality, both at firm and destination levels. The study of the relation between gender and innovation in sectors where women are widely represented allows identifying potential new businesses and innovation opportunities that may be usually overlooked, fostering creativity, competitiveness, and economic growth.

Keywords: innovation, gender, hospitality industry, tourism

1. Introduction

Gender equality is being viewed increasingly by business groups and development actors as an important plank for long-term economic growth and development. There has been growing interest in the implementation of diversity management approaches, including gender diversity, to maximize innovation and governance within companies (ILO, 2015). Dezsö and Ross (2012: 1072) argue that "female representation in top management brings informational and social diversity benefits to the top management team, enriches the behaviours exhibited by managers throughout the firm, and motivates women in middle management". Female representation in top management improves managerial task performance throughout the firm and should, accordingly, lead to better firm performance. The results of their study show that the positive impact of female representation in top management on firm performance is increasing in a firm's innovation intensity. Innovation is about creating something new and is enhanced by diversity in gender, experiences, perspectives, knowledge, and networks. A balanced gender distribution has a strong effect on the likelihood to innovate and innovative performance of enterprises. Nonetheless, the research field on innovation has yet not embraced fully the issue of gender. By studying innovation with some gender perspective, the innovation field will benefit from this both empirically and theoretically.

Therefore, a search in the Scopus database for scientific papers focusing on this topic was conducted, as performed by Alsos et al. (2013). An initial search for documents containing the word innovation in the title, abstract or keywords returned 412,098 references. Out of these, 13,712 papers were found including the word gender, and, when refining the search results by including the word hospitality, a total of 645 documents remained. The search string "innovation AND gender AND hospitality", used in the title, abstract or keywords, yielded nine documents, none of which specifically related to the topic of study. Thus, it may be concluded that there is little research on the relationship between gender and innovation in the hospitality industry.

To address the identified gap, this paper aims to advance knowledge on the relationship between gender and innovation in the hospitality industry, according to the more comprehensive framework of regional innovation systems. Specifically, it intends to apply a gender perspective on the (i) characterisation of the innovation performance of hospitality firms regarding the types of innovations introduced, the level of novelty and the engagement in activities supporting innovation; (ii) analysis of the patterns of network relationships that lead to innovation; (iii) identification of the knowledge sources that are on the basis of innovation; and (iv) understanding which regional specific factors are most important for innovation. The study of gender and innovation in women-dominated sectors allows identifying potential new businesses and innovation opportunities that may be usually overlooked, thus fostering creativity, competitiveness, and economic growth. The paper is organised as follows: first, the literature on gender and innovation is reviewed, highlighting research gaps and emerging issues; subsequently, the methodology used for the empirical study is described in more detail; and, finally, research findings are reported and discussed, and their implications for further research and applications are highlighted.

2. Gender and innovation in hospitality: Research gaps and emerging issues

"As society becomes more knowledge-intensive, ending any exclusion of women from science and technology becomes more pressing" (Etzkovitz et al., 2000: 4). A higher inclusion of women in the economy as a source of growth has been highly encouraged by several studies and worldwide organisations. However, there is little research and empirical evidence on the relationship between innovation and gender for several reasons. First, due to the concept of innovation, which is, on the one hand, gender-neutral, and, on the other hand, it is more focused on results rather than on the processes leading to innovation, which excludes individuals that innovate and their characteristics. Second, the majority of related studies focus on sectors in which women are under-represented or that are traditionally male-dominated, such as industry and technology-based firms. Additionally, the measurement of innovation is usually based on patents protection of registered designs and trademarks and copyrights, also characteristic of the (male-dominated) product or technological businesses. Finally, the image of an innovator is not compatible with the image of a woman (Blake & Hanson, 2005; Danilda & Thorslund, 2011; Eriksson, 2014; Ljunggren et al., 2010; Nyberg, 2009). Ljunggren et al. (2010) go further to conclude that the innovation concept and research do not take gender into account and that this may have serious implications. In result, the issue of gender becomes diluted and is rarely considered in innovation studies, or women become "invisible" and are often considered to be non-innovative or far less innovative than men (Alsos et al., 2013), or women's innovations are invisible due to the male gender labelling of innovation as a concept (Nyberg, 2009). Subsequently, this brings negative consequences in the access to top management positions and innovation resources, hampering woman's innovative potential. The lack of acknowledgement of women's innovation capacities leads to situations where men-owned businesses continue to attract resources more than women-owned businesses (Ighomereho et al., 2013), which has a clear negative impact on women-owned firms' innovation performance. In consequence, the identification of highly innovative areas and businesses where women can contribute to economic growth becomes constrained, and the vicious circle never ends.

Despite this, Nählinder et al. (2015) and Baldridge and Burnham (1975) found no statistically significant differences between gender and innovativeness. Gratton et al. (2007) demonstrated that teams can be more innovative when they are endowed with gender-diversity, namely 50:50 even proportions of men and women. Dezsö et al. (2012) conclude that women's representation in top management structures has informational and social diversity benefits, enriches managers' behaviours, motivates women in middle management, and improves managerial task performance. The authors' model predicts that female representation in top management increases a firm's innovation intensity, as well as group decision-making, is improved due to gender diversity and to the attributes of women managers. The positive outcomes of involving women in innovation can be optimised in women-dominated industries, such as hospitality and tourism.

The characteristics and dynamics of innovation in hospitality and tourism, as they are based on services, assume distinctive features, and, thus, should be analysed under more comprehensive models. The traditional approaches applied to industry, set on linear and atomistic processes (Rothwell, 1994), are hardly applicable to a systemic, holistic, and inter-organizational sector, such as hospitality and tourism. The changing socio-economic conditions of the last decades led to the evolution of innovation models and practices, from linear to more complex processes based on interactive knowledge creation and sharing, learning and networking (Chaminade & Roberts, 2002), the Regional Innovation Systems (RIS) (Cooke et al., 1998). A RIS can be defined as a system in which *"firms and other organisations are systematically engaged in interactive learning through an institutional milieu characterised by embeddedness"* (Cooke et al., 1998: 1581). There is interaction within public and private interests according to organisational and institutional relationships that lead to the generation, use and dissemination of knowledge. The RIS model and the related concept of innovation may help to overcome the identified limitations of traditional definitions of innovation with relation to gender, as it considers processes, individuals, context, culture, norms, values, the characteristics of the region and the process through which innovation occurs, not only the outcome. This creates a space for women to emerge as important innovators. Moreover, from all the existing models, it appears to be the most suited to tourism and hospitality dynamics, due to its systemic nature and to the importance of regional scope, which are key elements for tourism destinations' management (Brandão et al., 2018).

Despite the existence of studies confirming the positive impact of women in businesses' top management, they are under-represented in hospitality firms in Portugal. There are more men in the overall labour market (66.2% vs. 58.9%) (INE, 2020a). The same uneven distribution is observed in top management positions, with a proportion of 4.5 men against 2.7 women (INE, 2020b). When it comes to the service industry, the percentage of women has been increasing and, at this point, they outnumber men, with 57.2% (INE, 2020a). Tourism industry represents 328,500 jobs in Portugal. Around 58% are occupied by women, which confirms that it is a women-dominated sector (TravelBI, 2020). Despite this, the International Labour Organization (2020) found that, in the worldwide hospitality industry, on average, women account for around 30% of hotel management positions; however, only 26% have a female CEO and 27% a female chairperson on the board of directors.

Although the number of women employed in the hotel industry has risen (Iverson, 2000; Pinar et al., 2011; Purcell, 1996), occupying positions at all levels of the organisational structure, including management, there is still a long way to go. In a study developed by Costa et al. (2012), it was concluded that, in the Portuguese tourism industry, men are more entrepreneurial than women. Amongst tourism graduates, only 10% of women created their own business, against 21.4% of men. These changes in the gender structure of employees bring changes in the general conception of the hotel business (Aykac, 2006; Campos-Soria et al., 2011; Cave & Kilic, 2010; García-Pozo et al, 2012; Iverson, 2000; Pinar et al., 2011). Figueroa-Domecq et al. (2015) conclude that although gender bias is influenced by complex interrelated factors, it stems from the leadership structures, which are dominated by men, who maintain the *status quo* of masculine advantage. Costa et al. (2017) reveal that managerial characteristics associated with women and femininity, such as emotionality, are seen as becoming much desired within tourism management and being progressively incorporated into managerial ideals. Nonetheless, gender roles connecting femininity to caring roles continue their influence. It is, therefore, important to acknowledge the advantages of a contemporary social science approach, which incorporates critical management perspectives to tourism research, highlighting how gendered roles for women and men are enacted and perceived (Mooney, 2020).

3. Methodology

This study aims to identify the dynamics of innovation in hospitality firms, from a gender perspective. To do so, a survey was applied to the population of managers of accommodation businesses in the Portuguese regions of Douro and Aveiro, in a total of 117 establishments. The selection of two distinct regions in different stages of development allows to conduct a comparative analysis and to establish the importance of regional factors to innovation development. The questionnaire was conducted online, in a first stage, and by phone, in a second round, to increase the response rate. Out of these, 74 returned valid responses, which represents a response rate of 63.3%. Data collected regards the firms' innovation performance, namely in terms of the number and types of innovation, and innovation activities, the networks and patterns of cooperation towards innovation, knowledge sources used to innovate and the influence of regional-specific factors for innovation development. All data were analysed to identify the main differences and similarities between men and women. When possible, the Pearson's chi-squared test (X^2) was computed to analyse statistically significant relationships between dependent variables and gender, as well as the Mann-Whitney test to examine the differences in responses of men and women.

4. Results

4.1 The innovation performance of hospitality firms by gender of the manager

Despite being a women-dominated sector, 58.1% of the surveyed managers are men, and only 41.9% are women. Considering a 5% significance level, it can be concluded that there is no statistically significant association between gender and the overall innovation performance. However, it is to be noted that there is a higher number of women managers that are classified as innovators (i.e., that introduced at least one innovation in the last three years) when compared to men (77.4% vs. 74.4%). However, it is to be noted that there is a higher percentage of men stating to have developed every type of innovation, but especially process and organizational. Women are closer to men in product and marketing innovation development (Figure 1).

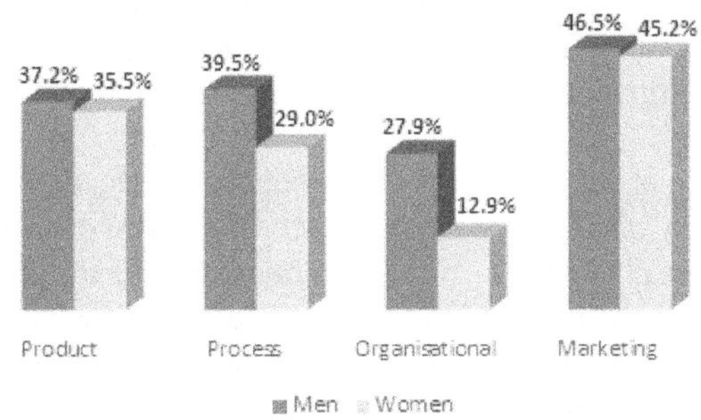

Figure 1: Rate of hospitality managers that developed innovation

A more detailed analysis regarding the intensity of innovation (number of innovation types introduced in the market) demonstrates that more men are developing three and four different types of innovation, while women limit to only one type (Figure 2). There seems to be a slight tendency for men to introduce more innovation types (higher diversity on innovation), although there is no statistical evidence. Further, the dispersion in the innovation levels is higher in men. Except for two women, who are outliers and whose level of innovation is 4, the great part is between level 1 and 3. While at least 31.3% of men have levels 3 and 4, in the case of women, the figure is only 9.7%. The median is 2 in men and women 1.

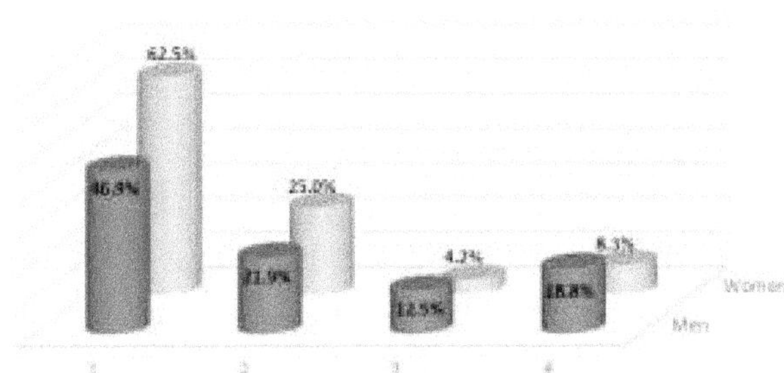

Figure 2: Innovation intensity (number of innovations)

One of the ways of characterising the degree of novelty of new products is to assess whether they are new to the market (major innovators) or new only to the firm (minor innovators). This indicates whether firms and their leaders are risk-takers or followers regarding the innovative process and if innovation is mostly incremental or more radical. Women present a higher percentage of major innovators than men (respectively, 41.7% vs. 23.5%), which may indicate that they are more risk-takers and introduce more solutions that are entirely new to the market.

In what concerns the implementation of activities supporting innovation, no statistical differences were found. However, women outperform men in all types, especially in internal R&D. The exception is the acquisition of external knowledge, where men have a higher percentage (Figure 3).

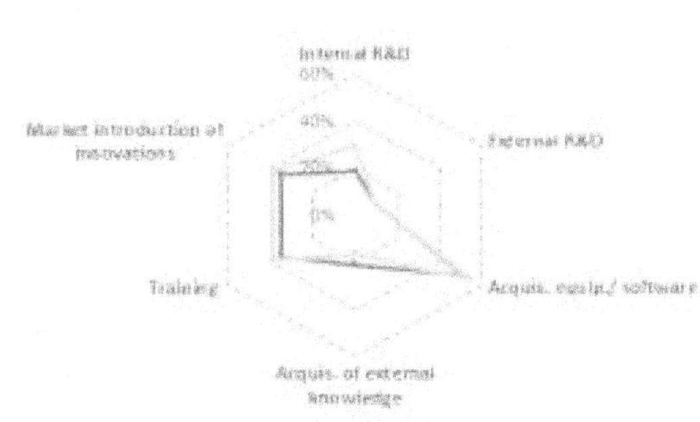

Figure 3: Innovation activities

4.2 Tourism innovation networks: Patterns of cooperation among firms

The lack of access to organisational and inter-organisational networks is increasingly seen as a barrier for women to reach the top (Ragins & Sundstrom, 1989; Ragins & Scandura, 1999). It has been stated that networking opportunities and social capital (or relevant relationships) are key success factors for women's career progression (Bure, 2007). Despite this, women do not seem to be involved in the same informal networks as men, where some of the very important decisions are made outside the traditional workspace. However, even though networks may be part of the problem, as well as the solution in the context of women in innovation, very little research has been published about formal corporate networks of women (Singh et al., 2006). It is acknowledged that innovation takes place in the context of relationships that form a network (Still et al., 2011), and that women are less hierarchical and more cooperative and collaborative than men (Book, 2000). This opens several possibilities for women to be far more represented in networks within the development of innovation. Data collected confirms previous studies that confirm that women's access to formal networks is still low. More men are engaging in innovation networks than women, respectively, 41.9% against 31.7%. Considering that networks and cooperation are key conditions to innovate, this low participation of female hospitality managers in collaborative structures may hamper women's potential.

However, in what concerns cooperation partners (Figure 4), women present a higher quantity and diversity than men. While male hospitality managers mainly choose to cooperate with other accommodation units, rent-a-car and government bodies, women outnumber men in cooperating with restaurants, cultural activities, recreation activities, universities, and training schools. This diversity in the established links brings higher access to distinct resources underlying innovation processes. There are statistically significant differences between the selection of "recreation services" as partners and gender" (p-value = 0,0049). Only 4.7% of men cooperate with them, against 22.6% of hospitality businesses managed by women.

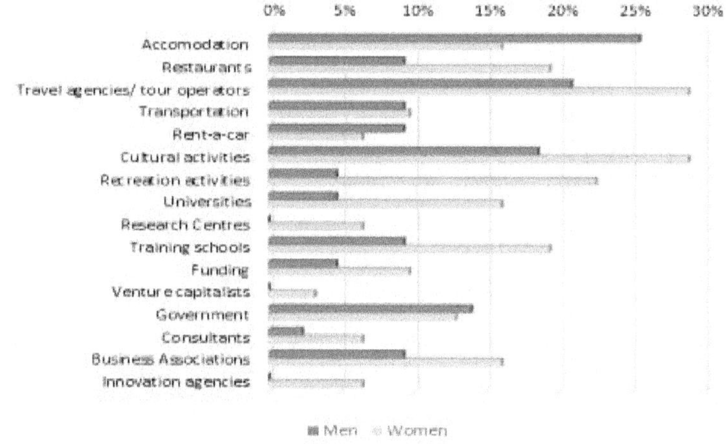

Figure 4: Cooperation partners

Besides the diversity of innovation partners, it is also important to consider the geographical patterns of collaboration to understand the territorial dynamics behind innovation processes. It is known that physical proximity fosters mutual trust, knowledge sharing and collective learning. Still, it has to be combined with links to external (national or international) organisations to assure the access to new and diverse knowledge for innovation, as it becomes obsolete over time (Brandão et al., 2018). Conversely to the type of partners, there is a higher rate of firms managed by women cooperating at all geographical levels. However, women appear to create a higher number of links at the regional level, which confirms the relevance of regional innovation systems' dynamics in this context. Women do privilege internal (regional, local) links (Figure 5). In terms of mean (average links per firm), firms managed by women register a higher number than men, presenting twice as more links at all levels (Figure 6).

Women outnumber men when it comes to specifying the purposes for cooperation towards innovation. This may indicate that they resort more to cooperation partners to develop specific activities that lead to innovation (confirming Book's (2000) findings). Knowledge creation stands out as where the highest difference is shown: 13.3% more firms managed by women engage in knowledge creation within cooperative processes. On average, each firm managed by women has a higher number of links than men for each specific purpose, namely for knowledge creation. Also, knowledge creation, new products and new processes show significant differences between women and men. Cooperation for new marketing strategies is the only purpose where men and women present similar rates (Figure 7).

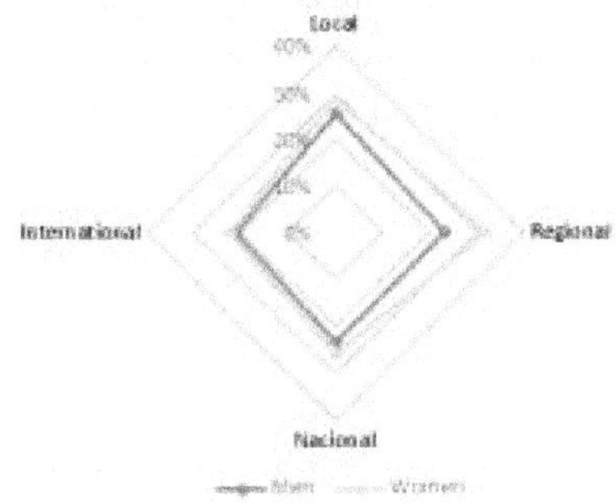

Figure 5: Geographical scope of cooperation

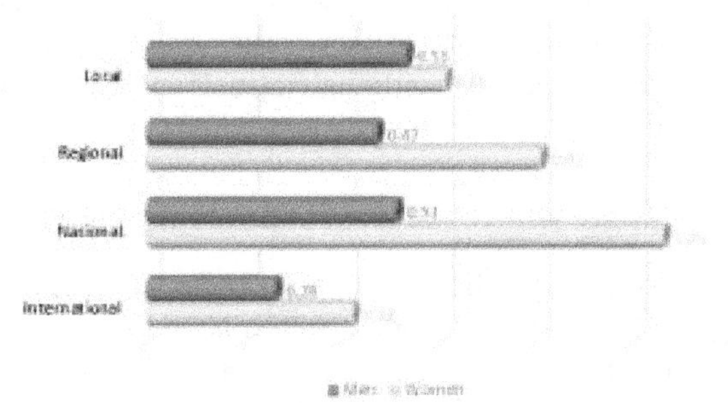

Figure 6: Average number of links per firm, by geographical location

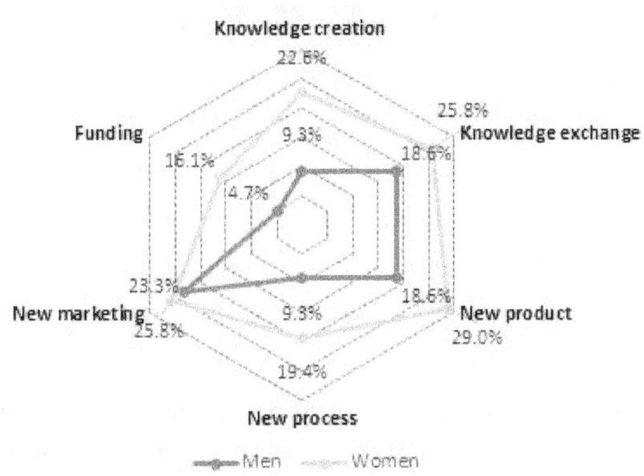

Figure 7: Purpose of cooperation

It was also important to analyse the importance given by the respondents to the role played by the different types of firms and organisations in destination-level innovation. Bearing that in mind, managers were asked to classify their importance on a 5-point scale. Globally, both men and women believe that tourism characteristic activities (accommodation, restaurant, transports, travel agencies, rental services, cultural and recreation activities) play a more relevant role than other organisations (universities, research centres, schools, funding organisations, public agencies, consultants, business associations and innovation agencies), both with a mean of 3.8 for the former and 3.2 for the later. Statistically significant differences were found for the importance granted to:

- (i) Accommodation businesses and their role on regional tourism innovation ($p = 0{,}038 < 0{,}05$): men grant higher importance than women (90.4% of men consider very important or moderately important, against 73% of women);
- (ii) restaurants' role on tourism innovation ($p = 0{,}014 < 0{,}05$): women grant higher importance than men (54.8% of women consider it very important, against 26.8% of men);
- (iii) there are no differences in the average importance attributed by women and men to overall organisations, neither to the group of tourism characteristic activities or other organisations.
- (iv) analysing each type of organisation specifically, Mann-Whitney test informs on the existence of statistically significant differences of gender in the importance attributed to accommodation and restaurants.

4.3 Innovation knowledge sources

The application of the Chi-squared test revealed no association between gender and the variables related to knowledge sources that are the basis of innovation in the hospitality industry, namely R&D, human resources, staff mobility, clients, informal contacts with regional organisations, and globally available information.

However, it may be concluded that men value more the knowledge associated with staff mobility, clients, and globally available information. Women attribute higher importance to knowledge obtained by informal contacts at regional level (confirms their cooperation at regional level), R&D (as they develop it internally, as already mentioned) and knowledge associated to human resources. In terms of geographical and sectoral dynamics, it is seen that men value more knowledge resulting from interaction with international organisations or from other regions, while women, although also involved in external cooperation, are keener on local and regional knowledge.

4.4 Regional specific factors supporting innovation

The Regional Innovation Systems' conceptual framework advocates that besides the processes developed internally to the firms and in external networks, the conditions that exist in the territory are of utmost importance for innovative potential and performance of businesses and organisations. These dynamics are going to influence if they innovate or not, and how innovation-related processes are developed (Edquist, 2006). These conditions are systematised and valued in Figure 8. The application of the Mann-Whitney (U) test informed on the existence of statistically significant differences on:

- (i) regional governance structure fostering innovation ($p = 0{,}01 < 0{,}05$): most women consider it of low importance or high importance, while most men consider it moderately important.
- (ii) human capital ($p = 0{,}008 < 0{,}05$): most women attribute high importance and men consider as moderately.
- (iii) shared values, culture, and norms ($p = 0{,}054 < 0{,}10$): women consider it as very important, while men attribute moderate importance.
- (iv) to a significance level of 5%, Mann-Whitney's test allowed us to conclude that regional governance and human capital show statistically significant differences, and to a significance level of 10%, shared values, culture, and norms.

The most important regional factor is the existence of natural resources for both genders. This makes sense as these resources are the basis for tourism development. The least important is the presence of a cluster and similar organisations.

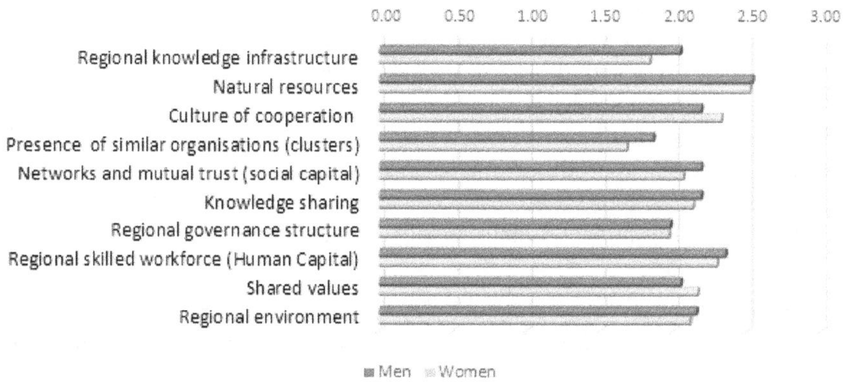

Figure 8: Importance of regional factors to innovation

5. Conclusion

One of the most important conclusions of the study is that hospitality and tourism should be regarded as innovative sectors and, since they are women-dominated, further studies should be conducted to obtain more empirical evidence on the characteristics and differences of innovative practices of men and women in tourism-related businesses. Despite the statistical tests revealing no significant relationship between gender and innovativeness globally, results show that there are more innovative firms managed by women than by men. Despite it, women appear to focus on only one or two types of innovations (product and marketing), while men develop the four types, thus presenting higher diversity. It was also found that there are more women "major innovators". These assume higher risks and are innovation leaders, not followers, as they introduce products that are entirely new to the market. They can, thus, provide a significant contribution to hospitality firms' competitiveness by creating high impact innovations.

In what concerns innovation networks, men appear to be more cooperative, but women present more diverse cooperation partners. This has a positive influence on innovation, as they can access new and diverse knowledge leading to innovation, which increases innovative potential. However, women's engagement in networks needs to be reinforced. Networks provide resources that would otherwise be unavailable, thus, women's reduced participation in networks will limit their access to innovation resources and hamper their potential. It is also concluded that effective regional tourism innovation systems can create collaborative platforms and increase women's participation in innovation networks as well as their links to other firms, government, and academics. Women cooperate more at the regional level, contribute to the strengthening of regional networks, and foster regional tourism innovation. This also indicates that women-developed innovation is more territorially embedded. Female hospitality managers also outperform men in all purposes of cooperation underlying innovation processes. Despite their lower engagement in networks, they are more dynamic in capitalising their connections towards the development of innovation.

In what relates to knowledge sources, since men privilege international links and women prefer the regional level, management teams with gender equality may balance this dynamic and assure access to both internal and external knowledge sources increasing innovation. Women consider human capital as the main source of knowledge leading to innovation in hospitality businesses and, thus, value human resources and skilled workforce more than men. They also develop more internal R&D. Thus, hospitality firms managed by women may present an opportunity to increase the employment rate of tourism graduates and postgraduates.

Further research is needed on gender aspects of innovation at the firm level, focusing on innovation processes with a gender perspective to increase knowledge about how gender influences innovation, including how innovation is defined, which knowledge is regarded relevant to innovation, how innovation is implemented, among other aspects, as also suggested by Ljunggren et al. (2010). It is also suggested that qualitative studies may be developed to assure further and deeper analysis of the phenomenon.

References

Alsos, G. A., Ljunggren, E. & Hytti, U. 2013. Gender And Innovation: State Of The Art And A Research Agenda. *International Journal Of Gender And Entrepreneurship,* 5, 236-256.

Aykac, A. (2006). Linking Scale Of Operation And Labor Transformation On Tourism: Comparative Analysis On Three Turkish Cases. *Anatolia: An International Journal Of Tourism And Hospitality Research, 17*, 257–278. Doi:10.1080/13032917.2006.9687189

Baldridge, J. V. & Burnham, R. A. 1975. Organizational Innovation: Individual, Organizational, And Environmental Impacts. *Administrative Science Quarterly,* 20, 165-176.

Cave, P., & Kilic, S. 2010. The Role Of Women In Tourism Employment With Special Reference To Antalya, Turkey. *Journal Of Hospitality Management And Marketing, 19*, 280–292. Doi:10.1080/19368621003591400

Costa, C., Bakas, F., Breda, Z., & Durão, M. 2017. 'Emotional' Female Managers: How Gendered Roles Influence Tourism Management Discourse. Journal Of Hospitality And Tourism Management, 33, 149-156. Doi: 10.1016/J.Jhtm.2017.09.011

Blake, M. K. & Hanson, S. 2005. Rethinking Innovation: Context And Gender. *Environment And Planning A,* 37, 681-701.

Book, E. W. 2000. *Why The Best Man For The Job Is A Woman.,* New York, Harper Collins.

Brandão, F., Costa, C. & Buhalis, D. 2018. Tourism Innovation Networks: A Regional Approach. *European Journal Of Tourism Research,* 18, 33-56.

Buré, C. 2007. Gender Inland Science, Technology And Innovation Policy: An Overview Of Current Literature And Findings. *Strategic Commissioned Paper For: Innovation, Policy And Science Program Area, International Development Research Centre, Ottawa.*

Campos-Soria, J. A., García-Pozo, A., & Sánchez-Ollero, J. L. 2015. Gender Wage Inequality And Labour Mobility In The Hospitality Sector. *International Journal Of Hospitality Management*,49, 73-82.

Campos-Soria, J. A., Marchante-Mera, A., & Ropero-García, M. A. 2011. Patterns Of Occupational Segregation By Gender In The Hospitality Industry. *International Journal Of Hospitality Management*, 30(1), 91-102.

Chaminade, C. & Roberts, H. 2002. Social Capital As A Mechanism: Connecting Knowledge Within And Across Firms. *Third European Conference On Organizational Knowledge, Learning And Capabilities - Oklc.* Athens, Greece, April 2002.

Cooke, P., Gomez Uranga, M. & Etxebarria, G. 1998. Regional Systems Of Innovation: An Evolutionary Perspective. *Environment And Planning A,* 30, 1563-1584.

Costa, C., Carvalho, I., Caçador, S. & Breda, Z. 2012. Gender And Entrepreneurship In Tourism: An Analysis Of Tourism Graduates' Entrepreneurial Profile. *Journal Of Tourism & Development,* 17/18.

Danilda, I. & Thorslund, J. G. (Eds.) 2011. *Innovation & Gender*: Vinnova, Tillväxtverket & Innovation Norway.

Dezsö, C. L. & Ross, D. G. 2012. Does Female Representation In Top Management Improve Firm Performance? A Panel Data Investigation. *Strategic Management Journal,* 33, 1072-1089.

Edquist, C. 2006. Systems Of Innovation: Perspectives And Challenges. In: Fagerberg, J., Mowery, D. C. & Nelson, R. (Eds.) The Oxford Handbook Of Innovation. Oxford: Oxford University Press.

Eriksson, A. F. 2014. A Gender Perspective As Trigger And Facilitator Of Innovation. *International Journal Of Gender And Entrepreneurship,* 6, 163-180.

Etzkovitz, H., Kemelgor, C. & Uzzi, B. 2000. *Athena Unbound: The Advancement Of Women In Science And Technology,* Cambridge, Cambridge University Press.

Figueroa-Domecq, C., Pritchard, A., Segovia-Pérez, M., Morgan, N., & Villacé-Molinero, T. 2015. Tourism Gender Research: A Critical Accounting. *Annals Of Tourism Research, 52,* 87-103.

García-Pozo, A., Campos-Soria, J. A., Sánchez-Ollero, J. L., & Marchante-Lara, M. 2012. The Regional Wage Gap In The Spanish Hospitality Sector Based On A Gender Perspective. *International Journal Of Hospitality Management, 31,* 266–275. Doi:10.1016/J.Ijhm.2011.06.007

Gratton, L., Kellen, E., Voight, A., Walker, L. & Wolfram, H. 2007. *Innovative Potential: Men And Women In Teams,* London London Business School.

Ighomereho, O. S., Agbalajobi, T. D. & Edegwa, K. S. 2013. Gender Influence On Access To Innovation Resources In Nigeria. *International Journal Of Humanities And Social Science,* 3, 216-227.

Ine. 2020a. *Labour Market Statistics* [Online]. Available: Www.Ine.Pt [Accessed 03/05/2020 2020].

Ine 2020b. *Objectivos De Desenvolvimento Sustentável/ Agenda 2030. Indicadores Para Portugal 2010-2019,* Lisboa, Ine.

Ilo. 2015. *Women In Business And Management. Gaining Momentum. Global Report*, Geneva, International Labour Organization.

Iverson, R. D. 2000. An Event History Analysis Of Employee Turnover: The Case Of Hospital Employees In Australia. *Human Resource Management Review, 9,* 397–418. Doi:10.1016/S1053-4822(99)00027-3

Ljunggren, E., Alsos, G. A., Amble, N., Ervik, R., Kvidal, T. & Wiik, R. 2010. *Gender And Innovation: Learning From Regional Vri-Projects,* Norway, Nordland Research Institute.

Mooney, S. K. 2020. Gender Research In Hospitality And Tourism Management: Time To Change The Guard. International Journal Of Contemporary Hospitality Management, 32(5), 1861-1879. Doi: 10.1108/Ijchm-09-2019-0780

Nählinder, J., Tillmar, M. & Wigren, C. 2015. Towards A Gender-Aware Understanding Of Innovation: A Three-Dimensional Route. *International Journal Of Gender And Entrepreneurship,* 7, 66-86.

Nyberg, A. C. 2009. *Making Ideas Matter: Gender, Technology And Women's Invention.* Phd, Luleå University.

Pinar, M., Mccuddy, M. K., Birkan, I., & Kozakc, M. 2011. Gender Diversity In The Hospitality Industry: An Empirical Study In Turkey, *International Journal Of Hospitality Management*, 30(1), 73-81.

Purcell, K. 1996. The Relationship Between Career And Job Opportunities: Women's Employment In The Hospitality Industry As A Microcosm Of Women's Employment. *Women In Management Review, 11,* 17–24.

Ragins, B. R. & Scandura, T. A. 1999. Burden Or Blessing Expected Costs And Benefits Of Being A Mentor. *Journal Of Organizational Behavior,* 20, 493-509.

Ragins, B. R. & Sundstrom, E. 1989. Gender And Power In Organizations: A Longitudinal Perspective. *Psychological Bulletin,* 105, 51-88.

Rothwell, R. 1994. Towards The Fifth-Generation Innovation Process. *International Marketing Review,* 11, 7-31.

Singh, V., Vinnicombe, S. & Kumra, S. 2006. Women In Formal Corporate Networks: An Organizational Citizenship Perspective. *Women In Management Review,* 21, 458-482.

Still, K., Russell, M. G., Huhtamäki, J., Yu, C. & Rubens, N. 2011. Gender And Innovation: Networks Of Executive Women In Technology-Based Companies. *Proceedings Of The Triple Helix Ix International Conference: Silicon Valley: Global Model Or Unique Anomaly?* Stanford, California, Usa.

Travelbi. 2020. *Employment In Tourism By Gender*. Available: Https://Travelbi.Turismodeportugal.Pt/Pt-Pt/Paginas/Powerbi/Sustentabilidade/Emprego-No-Turismo-Por-Sexo.Aspx [Accessed 04/05/2020].

Family Firms' Goal Priorities and Their Impact on Innovation Propensity

Wouter Broekaert[1,2,3], Bart Henssen[1,2,3] and Johan Lambrecht[1,3]
[1]Center for Sustainable Entrepreneurship (CenSE), Belgium
[2]Odisee University College, Belgium
[3]KU Leuven, Brussels, Belgium
wouter.broekaert@odisee.be
bart.henssen@odisee.be
johan.lambrecht@kuleuven.be
DOI: 10.34190/EIE.20.110

Abstract: Ultimately, every CEO strives to make his company a 'success'. How such success is defined, however, may differ widely from company to company, leading to markedly different approaches to company strategy, organization and innovation. We surveyed 469 Belgian CEOs, both from family and non-family firms, to gauge which company 'success' measures they deem most relevant. Subsequently, we use path analyses to study the relationship between such a priority assessment and the entrepreneurs' short-term intention to innovate. Furthermore, we analyse the impact of family ownership and management on such a relationship. Our findings show that family firms attach more importance to financial success measures than non-family firms but indicate no family firm preference for either value creation or continuity as success measures. Additionally, we find a negative relationship between financial objectives and innovation propensity. Striving for value creation for different stakeholders, on the other hand, is positively related to innovation propensity. We believe our research advances the current literature on family firms and innovation by shedding more light on the underlying reasons for the different innovation profiles of family and non-family firms. As such, our findings can assist managers and policy makers alike in making improved decisions and taking more clearly targeted actions towards stimulating innovation processes. Additionally, our paper responds to the call for more thorough research into the diversity of potential company objectives and its impact on firms' decisions and processes.

Keywords: family firm, company objectives, innovation

1. Introduction

Both in day-to-day practice and in academic research a company's ability to achieve 'success' remains a priority topic. In order to capture or quantify an elusive term as 'success', researchers often resort to a limited number of financial or accounting measures, such as profit, revenue or company growth (Maltz, Shenhar and Reilly 2003). For entrepreneurs however, such measures only represent a small fraction of potential priorities (Daily and Dollinger 1992). While some entrepreneurs indeed prioritize profitability, others may primarily pursue their company's long-term survival, customer loyalty, an outstanding company reputation or various socioemotional wealth targets (Berrone, Cruz and Gomez-Mejia 2012; Holt, Pearson, Carr and Barnett 2017). Moreover, firms may benefit from a multitemporal perspective, i.e. taking into account short- and long-term performance horizons to remain successful (Le Breton-Miller and Miller 2011). Notwithstanding the considerable heterogeneity of firms in general, family firms in particular may differ from their non-family counterparts with regard to their overall objectives, leading to differences in perspective about which performance measures should be prioritized. Thus far, however, the literature offers but few analyses shedding light on how financial company objectives interact with non-financial objectives and how these impact the functioning of family firms (Williams, Pieper, Kellermanns and Astrachan 2018).

In turn, entrepreneurs' priority assessment influences their actions and the strategic course of the company.

The current literature, however, shows a strong focus on company performance indicators as outcomes, while there remains a clear need to study the role of company goals and objectives as determinants and/or benchmarks of performance (Chua, Chrisman, De Massis and Wang 2018; Kotlar, De Massis, Wright and Frattini 2018), as well as determinants of company behaviour (Basco 2017). Specifically, overall company priorities may influence the family firm's propensity to innovate and help explain why some family firms are more willing to accept short-term risks by engaging in innovative activities while others display greater risk aversion and a lower willingness to innovate. As such, we believe the current paper advances the current literature on family firms goals and innovation by shedding more light on the underlying reasons for the different innovation profiles of family and non-family firms.

In the following section we review the existing literature on family firms goals and objectives on the one hand and their innovativeness on the other. Based on our literature overview, we propose research statements regarding the expected relationships between family presence in the company, company objectives and innovation propensity. Section 3 describes the data collection and analysis process and presents some descriptive statistics, while section 4 presents the results from the different path analyses. Finally, we discuss our findings as well as the study's limitations and propose potential avenues for future research.

2. Literature background

2.1 (Family) firm goal diversity

For much of the research literature, various financial performance indicators, like company profits or growth rates, remain the default representatives of company success (Maltz, Shenhar and Reilly 2003). However, for many firms in general and family firms in particular, such an exclusive financial focus is far too myopic. Instead, companies can and do pursue a multitude of different goals and objectives, which means that other outcomes need to be factored in as well before a firm can be considered to be 'successful' or not (Holt, Pearson, Carr and Barnett 2017).

For instance, maintaining long-term strategic and financial control over the family firm and preserving financial independence from external parties can be regarded a top priority for many business families (Ward 1988; Miller and Le Breton-Miller 2005; Thiele 2017). Such a perspective may prompt the family to measure its company's success based on the level of equity ownership within the family (Mullins and Schoar 2016) or on the ratio between internal and external financing as well as between external debt financing and external equity financing (Romano, Tanewski and Smyrnios 2001). Furthermore, family firms' socioemotional wealth considerations, including value creation for the family, family firm continuity and succession potential, are other important goals (Berrone, Cruz and Gomez-Mejia 2012). Other entrepreneurs may primarily measure their success by their ability to maintain a healthy work-life balance (Burlingham 2005).

Additionally, many companies look beyond the owning family's boundaries and adopt a broad perspective by explicitly considering the needs and desires of a wide variety of stakeholders. Hence, the wellbeing of the firm's own employees may be a prime measure of success (Tagiuri and Davis 1992). Family firms in particular may be better equipped to motivate their workforce than non-family firms (Dawson 2012), especially when they are able to sustain an open, warm and respectful organizational culture (Memili, Welsh and Kaciak 2014; Bammens, Notelaers and Van Gils 2015). In addition to the internal stakeholders there are various external groups that may shape a family firm's overall objectives. Hence, some business families may attach great importance to their reputation as a high quality supplier (Tagiuri and Davis 1992), a powerful economic player or even a philanthropist.

In view of the multitude of potential company 'success' measures, a more holistic approach that combines different success measures into broad but distinct categories could yield a more realistic picture of companies' success. Nevertheless, while several family firm goals are similar and may be mutually reinforcing, others may cause conflicts or even counteract each other, leading researchers to propose different categorizations of company objectives. Aparicio, Basco, Iturralde and Maseda (2017) distinguish firm goals inspired by a market, family or community logic. While the market logic leads to financial or customer-oriented goals, the family logic prioritizes family control and wellbeing and the community logic emphasizes business ethics. Similarly, Holt, Pearson, Carr and Barnett (2017) perceive 'business-first' and 'family-first' family firms, giving prominence to commercial versus family goals respectively, with the 'balanced' family firms and their broader stakeholder perspective in between. Additionally, Basco (2017) analyses over 25 potential family firm goals to distil 6 categories, reflecting clearly different temporal (short versus longer term) and stakeholder (family, business and multiple broad stakeholders) priorities.

Therefore we propose the following research statements:

RS 1a. Overall company objectives can be grouped into distinct categories
RS 1b. Family firms and non-family firms prioritize different company objectives

2.2 (Family) firm priorities and innovation

Although several researchers have analysed the differences between family firms and non-family firms when it comes to their innovativeness or their innovation performance, there is no uniform conclusion. While some studies find family firms to be more innovative (e.g. Craig and Dibrell 2006; Ayyagari, Demirgüç-Kunt and Vojislav 2011), others reach the opposite conclusion (e.g. Chin, Chen, Kleinman and Lee 2009; Block, Miller, Jaskiewicz and Spiegel 2013) or find that it in fact depends on the kind of innovation that is analysed (Classen, Carree, Van Gils and Peters 2014). The underlying reasons for the divergence in those research results, however, remain largely unclear. In this paper, we suggest a company's objectives as a useful innovation determinant as those goals are connected to the company's innovation activities (Lengnick-Hall 1992).

One of the other oft-cited determinants of family firms' stance on innovation is the business family's level of risk aversion. Although this can in part be interpreted as a predetermined character trait, it is reasonable to assume it is also strongly connected to the family firm's priority objectives. After all, the uncertainty and risk associated with innovation (Shi 2003), not only pertains to financial but also to reputational risk (Bartholomeusz and Tanewski 2006 in Naldi et al. 2007), both which may have specific implications for family-owned firms (Zellweger 2007; Miller, Le Breton-Miller and Lester 2011) and their level of innovation (Kraus et al. 2012). Moreover, a business family's desire to safeguard non-financial goals, such as family firm continuity and family harmony, may further strengthen such risk aversion (Chen and Hsu 2009).

Lastly, much of the research points to family firms' long-term orientation as an important innovation determinant, where family owners' high and long time commitment to their firm provides an innovation boost (Duran, Kammerlander, Van Essen and Zellweger 2016). Firms that prioritize long-term goals may be more willing to accept short-term risks by engaging in innovative activities (Zellweger 2007; Chrisman and Patel 2012). Moreover, a long-term perspective may in itself be perceived as a unique and valuable resource base for the family firm. After all, taking the time to build and steadily expand a trusted network of business partners and customers not only enhances the company's financial performance but also lays the groundwork for extensive and efficient knowledge sharing and innovation (Sirmon and Hitt 2003; Duran, Kammerlander, Van Essen and Zellweger 2016). On the other hand, a long-term orientation may also impede innovation. Family firms that have flourished under many previous generations may have developed a strong tradition-oriented company culture as well as path dependencies that inhibit the firm's adaptability and innovativeness (Hall, Melin and Nordqvist 2001; Chirico and Salvato 2008; Chirico and Nordqvist 2010). New family generations can find it difficult to step out of their parents' or grandparents' shadow, for fear of endangering the previous generations' legacy or because of moral or financial pressure (Sharma and Irving 2005; Steier and Miller 2010), even when markets and economic circumstances have changed.

In summary, we expect a company's choice of priority objectives to capture important innovation levels, such as risk aversion and long-term orientation. Hence, we propose the following research statement:

RS 2. Different company objectives lead to different levels of innovation propensity

Figure 1 visualizes our full hypothesized model:

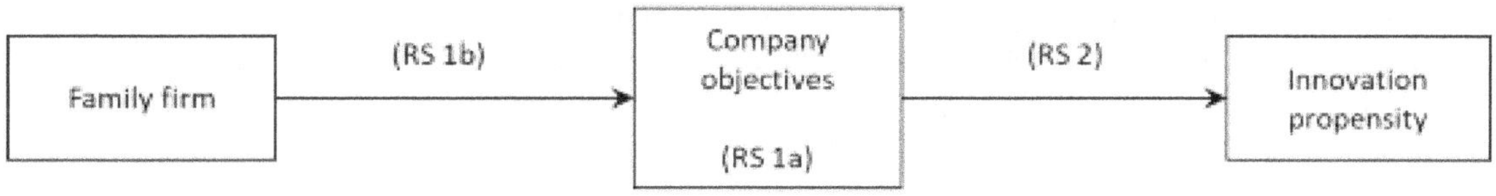

Figure 1: Hypotheses overview

3. Data collection and analysis

3.1 Sample and data collection

During the first half of 2017, we surveyed 469 Belgian CEOs, both from family and non-family firms. Data from these questionnaires were supplemented with data from Bel-first, Bureau van Dijk's extensive national database containing companies' financial statements. After merging the data and eliminating missing values, our final samples contained data on 265 to 270 companies, depending on the dependent variable used.

3.2 Variables and descriptive statistics

Table 1 provides an overview of the descriptive statistics and correlations of our main variables.

3.2.1 Family firm

We label a company as a 'Family firm' when more than half of all shares are owned by the family or when there are family members present in the firm's top management team. As Table 1 shows, our sample contains mostly family firms (84 percent of the sample).

3.2.2 Company objectives

We first asked the respondents to evaluate the suitability of 13 potential measures for their company's success on 5-point Likert scales, with 1 indicating 'Not suitable' and 5 'Very suitable'. The measures are: profit, turnover/sales, equity, liquidity, market share, number of employees, family employment, external reputation, employee loyalty, customer loyalty, company survival, company's financial value, value creation for different stakeholders.

Next, we conducted a factor analysis on those 13 variables, to detect potential components or categories. We opted for a factor analysis with standardized variables and a varimax rotation, as it seems reasonable to assume the existence of several different categories. The analysis suggested 4 components, although some individual items showed low loading values. Hence, we additionally calculated the Cronbach's alpha scores for each of the categories to test whether items in the same component reliably measure that component. When the Cronbach's alpha exceeded 0.7, which was the case for 2 of the components, we retained the suggested category composition.

The first component consistently grouped the success measures 'Profit', 'Equity', 'Liquidity' and 'Company's financial value'. After calculating the mean of the 4 items, we labelled it as an overall company objective of 'Financial success'.

The second component grouped the success measures 'External reputation', 'Employee loyalty', 'Customer loyalty' and 'Company survival'. We calculated the mean of those 4 items and labelled it as an overall company objective of 'Continuity'.

As the remaining 2 components scored considerably lower Cronbach's alpha values, we instead looked at the 5 individual items and opted to include 'Value creation for different stakeholders' as a final and conceptually separate company objective.

The results of our factor analysis allow us to confirm RS 1a, stating that 'Overall company objectives can be grouped into distinct categories'.

3.2.3 Innovation propensity

We use 3 variables to represent the company's innovation propensity with regard to product, process and organizational innovation respectively. Specifically, on a 5-point Likert scale we asked the respondents how strongly they agree that 'During the following year their company will develop product, process or organizational innovation' (1 indicating 'Completely disagree' to 5 signalling 'Completely agree'). We label these variables 'Product innovation', 'Process innovation' and 'Organizational innovation'.

3.2.4 Control variables

Finally, the following control variables were added to our models: the company's age ('Age'), the number of employees in 2016 ('Size') and two binary variables indicating the company's industry ('Manufacturing' or 'Services').

Because of several variables' skewed distribution, we transformed all non-binary variables by taking the logarithm of (1 + variable value) before including them into the analyses.

Table 1: Descriptive statistics and correlations

	Mean (of absolute values)	SD (of absolute values)	Family firm	Financial success	Continuity	Value creation	Product innovation	Process innovation	Organizational innovation	Age	Size
Family firm	0.85	0.36	1								
Financial success	3.41	0.69	0.17**	1							
Continuity	3.97	0.64	-0.02	0.27***	1						
Value creation	3.66	0.90	-0.12	0.12	0.31***	1					
Product innovation	2.71	1.39	0.03	-0.17**	0.10	0.12	1				
Process innovation	2.80	1.37	-0.08	-0.10	0.15*	0.23***	0.79***	1			
Organizational innovation	2.91	1.30	-0.10	-0.06	0.09	0.28***	0.64***	0.76***	1		
Age	38.20	27.47	0.01	0.08	0.07	0.02	0.14*	0.13*	0.10	1	
Size	53.24	145.93	-0.29***	-0.05	0.04	0.14*	0.13*	0.19**	0.16*	0.24***	1

SD: standard deviation. * p < .05; ** p < .01; *** p < .001.

4. Results

We analysed three different path models (one for each of the innovation propensity indicators) through SEM (Structural equation modelling) analysis, using maximum likelihood estimation. As part of the multivariate methods, SEM allows for complex analyses that enable simultaneous testing of multiple relationships among variables (Ullman 2001). Furthermore, SEM analysis yields better and more realistic estimates of variables' indirect effects on other variables and provides a better approach to taking into account the correlation between variables – including between different dependent variables – than univariate statistics (Raykov and Marcoulides 2008). To assess how well the models fit the data we evaluate the standardized root mean squared residual (SRMR), with values below 0.08 considered to indicate a good fit. Furthermore, we look at the coefficient of determination (CD), with values closer to 1 indicating better fit. Our Product innovation model (N=265) yields an SRMR value of 0.057 and a CD value of 0.136, while the Process innovation model (N=267) shows an SRMR value of 0.061 and a CD value of 0.139 and the Organizational innovation model (N=270) yields SRMR and CD values of 0.059 and 0.126 respectively.

Table 2 shows the main path results of the models, using robust standard errors.

Table 2: Path coefficients and (z-Values)

Path from -> to	(1)	(2)	(3)
Direct effects			
Family firm -> Financial success	0.04* (0.01)	0.03* (0.01)	0.03* (0.01)
Family firm -> Continuity	-0.01 (0.01)	-0.01 (0.01)	-0.01 (0.01)
Family firm -> Value creation	-0.02 (0.02)	-0.02 (0.02)	-0.02 (0.02)
Financial success -> Innovation propensity	-0.47*** (0.13)	-0.37** (0.13)	-0.27* (0.12)
Continuity -> Innovation propensity	0.23 (0.19)	0.25 (0.18)	0.1 (0.18)
Value creation -> Innovation propensity	0.19 (0.13)	0.33* (0.13)	0.42** (0.13)
Total effects			
Family firm -> Innovation propensity	-0.02** (0.01)	-0.02** (0.01)	-0.02† (0.01)

(1) Product innovation model, (2) Process innovation model, (3) Organizational innovation model

† p < .10; * p < .05; ** p < .01; *** p < .001.

The results from the path analysis show a significantly positive link between family firms and the professed suitability of financial indicators (i.e. 'Profit', 'Equity', 'Liquidity' and 'Company's financial value') as company success measures. However, we find no relationship between the family nature of a firm and the importance it attaches to continuity objectives ('External reputation', 'Employee loyalty', 'Customer loyalty' and 'Company survival') or value creation for different stakeholders. Therefore, RS 1b ('Family firms and non-family firms prioritize different company objectives') is only partially supported.

With regard to RS 2 ('Different company objectives lead to different levels of innovation propensity'), we find broad confirmation. Companies that primarily focus on financial objectives score significantly lower on innovation propensity for each kind of innovation. The opposite is true for companies aiming for value creation, which is positively linked to both process and organizational innovation propensity but displays no relationship with product innovation propensity. Finally, we find no relationship between continuity objectives and innovation propensity.

Figure 2 visualizes the results of the analyses.

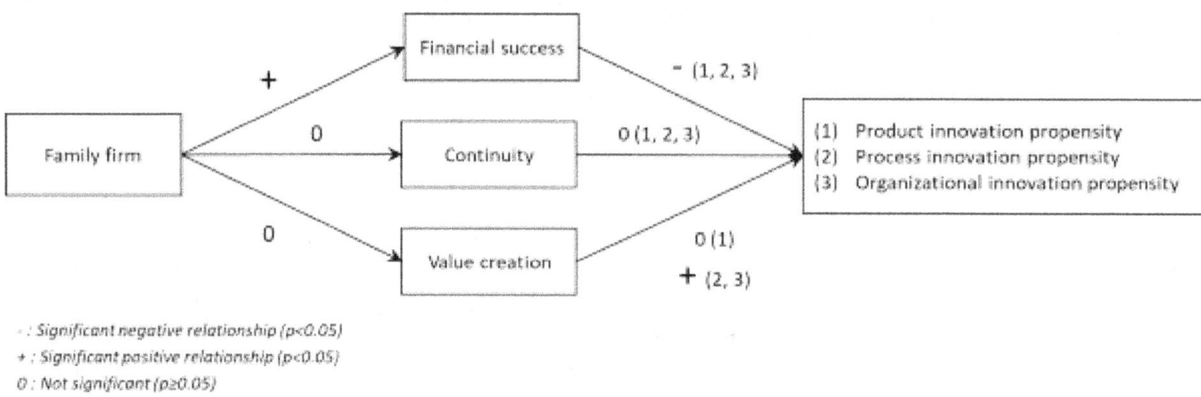

Figure 2: Results overview

As a robustness test, we performed additional path analyses with an alternative family firm variable ('Do you consider your company to be a family firm?'). These analyses yielded in large part similar results to the ones described above.

5. Discussion

Our analysis confirms findings from other research that not every firm sets the same priorities but that instead different companies can and do pursue different objectives. More specifically, our results stress the need to look beyond financial success measures (Daily and Dollinger 1992; Maltz et al. 2003; Williams et al. 2018) and to acknowledge that certain firms can be more oriented towards value creation or continuity instead. As such, we complement earlier studies categorising companies according to the distinct goals they set (e.g. Aparicio et al. 2017; Basco 2017 and Holt et al. 2017).

When we compare family firms' to non-family firms' prioritisation of financial, continuity and value creation success measures, we find some surprising results.

First of all, the family firms in our sample attach more importance to 'hard' financial success measures than non-family firms, while much of the literature assumes the opposite and points to business families' attention to their socio-emotional wealth (Berrone et al. 2012; Holt et al. 2017). Our finding may be linked to the composition of our financial success category, which is comprised of not only shorter-term (i.e. profit and liquidity) but also more structural and longer-term (equity and the company's financial value) indicators. The latter may be especially important for many family firms, given the strong interdependence between the family's wealth and the company's value and the family's desire to retain family control (Ward 1988; Miller and Le Breton-Miller 2005; Thiele 2017). Moreover, it is interesting to note that our results show that family firm CEOs simultaneously attach importance to short-term financial indicators on the one hand and long-term financial indicators on the other, which supports the notion of multitemporality (Le Breton-Miller and Miller 2011).

A second surprise is that our data show no distinct family firm preference for either value creation or continuity as success measures. Especially the latter is interesting, as family firms are typically assumed to have a strong focus on long-term and relational company objectives (Tagiuri and Davis 1992; Berrone et al.2012). However, our finding should not necessarily be interpreted as indications of family firms' lack of long-term vision. Rather, it should caution researchers and family firms against the cliché of the responsible and forward-looking family firm as opposed to the short-sighted non-family firm.

In turn, those overall company objectives influence its strategic decisions. More specifically, our results confirm the importance of company objectives as determinants of innovation propensity.

First of all, we find that an adherence to financial objectives links to a lower innovation propensity. This finding can be seen as supporting that side of the literature that argues that a higher financial risk aversion may impede a company's willingness to engage in innovation. Together with our previous results regarding the higher prominence of financial objectives for family firms, this may help explain the innovative handicap of some family firms.

On the other hand however, we find that striving for value creation for different stakeholders is positively related to innovation propensity. This underlines the importance of explicitly taking into account the interests of different stakeholders when striving for innovation. Hence, it may support the frequent call for more open innovation and for engaging a broader range of innovation partners. Specifically for family firms, it serves as further encouragement to broaden the family's perspective by inviting external advice and experience.

6. Conclusion

We believe our analysis and findings can benefit both family firm managers, researchers and practitioners by providing additional insight into how company or CEO priorities lead to specific actions and to a more innovative company. Moreover, our study advances the current innovation and family firm literature by shedding more light on the underlying reasons for the different innovation profiles of family and non-family firms, especially where the impact of company goals on innovation is concerned. Furthermore, our findings show that, as different firms may have different objectives, it would be ill-advised to take a 'one size fits all' approach towards companies by recommending or stimulating the uniform optimisation of one specific performance outcome like growth or profit. At the same time, we show that differences in priorities between family and non-family firms as they are often assumed by the literature may not always correspond to actual differences in reality, further reinforcing the need to make company goals explicit when analysing family firm behaviour or performance.

Finally, we point to a limitation of our study, related to the composition of our sample. Specifically, the number of non-family firms in our sample is relatively limited. Hence, future research could benefit from more extensive data collection among non-family firms, creating more data diversity within the sample.

References

Aparicio, G., Basco, R., Iturralde, T., and Maseda, A. (2017) "An exploratory study of firm goals in the context of family firms: An institutional logics perspective", Journal of Family Business Strategy, 8 (3), pp. 157-169.

Ayyagari, M., Demirgüç-Kunt, A., and Vojislav, M. (2011) "Firm innovation in emerging markets: The role of finance, governance, and competition", Journal of Financial and Quantitative Analysis, 46 (6), pp. 1545–1580.

Bammens, Y., Notelaers, G. and Van Gils, A. (2015) "Implications of family business employment for employees' innovative work involvement", Family Business Review, 28 (2), pp. 123-144.

Basco, R. (2017) ""Where do you want to take your family firm?" A theoretical and empirical exploratory study of family business goals", Brq-Business Research Quarterly, 20 (1), pp. 28-44.

Berrone, P., Cruz, C. and Gomez-Mejia, L. R. (2012) "Socioemotional wealth in family firms: Theoretical dimensions, assessment approaches, and agenda for future research", Family Business Review, 25 (3), pp. 258-279.

Block, J., Miller, D., Jaskiewicz, P., and Spiegel, F. (2013) "Economic and technological importance of innovations in large family and founder firms: An analysis of patent data", Family Business Review, 26 (2), pp. 180–199.

Burlingham, B. (2005) Small Giants: Companies That Choose to Be Great Instead of Big. New York: Penguin Group.

Chen, H.-L. and Hsu, W.-T. (2009) "Family ownership, board independence, and R&D investment", Family Business Review, 22 (4), pp. 347-362.

Chin, C. L., Chen, Y. J., Kleinman, G., and Lee, P. (2009) "Corporate ownership structure and innovation: Evidence from Taiwan's electronics industry", Journal of Accounting Auditing Finance, 24 (1), pp. 145–175.

Chirico, F. and Nordqvist, M. (2010) "Dynamic capabilities and transgenerational value creation in family firms: The role of organizational culture", International Small Business Journal, 28 (5), pp. 487-504.

Chirico, F. and Salvato, C. (2008) "Knowledge integration and dynamic organizational adaptation in family firms", Family Business Review, 21 (2), pp. 169-181.

Chrisman, J. J. and Patel, P. C. (2012) "Variations in R&D investments of family and nonfamily firms: Behavioral agency and myopic loss aversion perspectives", Academy of Management Journal, 55 (4), pp. 976-997.

Chua, J., Chrisman, J., De Massis, A., and Wang, H. (2018) "Reflections on family firm goals and the assessment of performance", Journal of Family Business Strategy, 9 (2) , pp. 107-113.

Classen, N., Carree, M., Van Gils, A. and Peters, B. (2014) "Innovation in family and non-family SMEs: an exploratory analysis", Small Business Economics, 42 (3), pp. 595-609.

Craig, J. and Dibrell, C. (2006) "The natural environment, innovation, and firm performance: A comparative study", Family Business Review, 19 (4), pp. 275-288.

Daily, C. M. and Dollinger, M. J. (1992) "An empirical examination of ownership structure in family and professionally managed firms", Family Business Review 5 (2), pp. 117-136.

Dawson, A. (2012) "Human capital in family businesses: Focusing on the individual level", Journal of Family Business Strategy, 3 (1), pp.3-11.

Duran, P., Kammerlander, N., Van Essen, M. and Zellweger, T. (2016) "Doing more with less: innovation input and output in family firms", Academy of Management Journal, 59 (4), pp. 1224-1241.

Hall, A., Melin, L. and Nordqvist, M. (2001) "Entrepreneurship as radical change in the family business: Exploring the role of cultural patterns", Family Business Review, 14 (3), pp. 193-208.

Holt, D., Pearson, A., Carr, J., and Barnett, T. (2017) "Family Firm(s) Outcomes Model: Structuring Financial and Nonfinancial Outcomes Across the Family and Firm", Family Business Review, 30 (2) , pp. 182-202.

Kotlar, J., De Massis, A., Wright, M. and Frattini, F. (2018) "Organizational Goals: Antecedents, Formation Processes and Implications for Firm Behavior and Performance", International Journal of Management Reviews, 20, pp. S3-S18.

Kraus, S., Pohjola, M. and Koponen, A. (2012) "Innovation in family firms: an empirical analysis linking organizational and managerial innovation to corporate success", Review of Managerial Science, 6 (3), pp. 265-286.

Le Breton-Miller, I. and Miller, D. (2011) "Commentary: Family Firms and the Advantage of Multitemporality", Entrepreneurship Theory and Practice, 35 (6), pp. 1171–1177.

Lengnick-Hall, C. A. (1992) "Innovation and competitive advantage: What we know and what we need to learn", Journal of Management, 18 (2), pp. 399-429.

Maltz, A. C., Shenhar, A. J. and Reilly, R. R. (2003) "Beyond the balanced scorecard: Refining the search for organizational success measures", Long Range Planning 36, pp. 187-204.

Memili, E., Welsh, D. H. B. and Kaciak, E. (2014) "Organizational Psychological Capital of family franchise firms through the lens of the Leader–Member Exchange Theory", Journal of Leadership & Organizational Studies, 21 (2), pp. 200-209.

Miller, D., Le Breton-Miller, I. and Lester, R.H. (2011) "Family and lone founder ownership and strategic behavior: social context, identity, and institutional logics", Journal of Management Studies, 48 (1), pp. 1-25.

Miller, M. and Le Breton-Miller, I. (2005) Managing for the Long Run: Lessons in Competitive Advantage from Great Family Businesses. Boston: Harvard Business School Press.

Mullins, W. and Schoar, A. (2016) "How do CEOs see their roles? Management philosophies and styles in family and non-family firms", Journal of Financial Economics, 119 (1), pp. 24-43.

Naldi, L., Nordqvist, M., Sjoberg, K. and Wiklund, J. (2007) "Entrepreneurial orientation, risk taking, and performance in family firms", Family Business Review 20 (1), pp. 33-47.

Raykov, T. and Marcoulides, G. A. (2008) An Introduction to Applied Multivariate Analysis. New York: Routledge.

Romano, C. A., Tanewski, G. A. and Smyrnios, K. X. (2001) "Capital structure decision making: A model for family business", Journal of Business Venturing, 16 (3), pp. 285-310.

Sharma, P. and Irving, P. G. (2005). "Four bases of family business successor commitment: Antecedents and consequences", Entrepreneurship Theory and Practice, 29 (1), pp. 13-33.

Shi, C. (2003) "On the trade-off between the future benefits and riskiness of R&D: A bondholders' perspective", Journal of Accounting and Economics, 35 (2), pp. 227–254.

Sirmon, D. G. and Hitt, M. A. (2003) "Managing resources: Linking unique resources, management and wealth creation in family firms", Entrepreneurship Theory and Practice, 27 (4), pp. 339-358.

Steier, L. P. and Miller, D. (2010) "Pre- and post-succession governance philosophies in entrepreneurial family firms", Journal of Family Business Strategy, 1 , pp. 145–154.

Tagiuri, R. and Davis, J. A. (1992) "On the goals of successful family companies", Family Business Review 5 (1), pp. 43-62.

Thiele, F.K. (2017) "Family businesses and non-family equity: Literature review and avenues for future research", Management Review Quarterly, 67 (1), pp.31-63.

Ullman, J. B. (2001) "Structural equation modeling". In Tabachnick, B. G., and Fidell, L. S. (2001) Using Multivariate Statistics, 4th ed. Boston: Pearson, pp. 653-771.

Ward, J. L. (1988) "The special role of strategic planning for family businesses", Family Business Review, I (2), pp. 105-117.

Williams, R. I., Pieper, T. M., Kellermanns, F. W. and Astrachan, J. H. (2018) "Family Firm Goals and Their Effects on Strategy, Family and Organization Behavior: A Review and Research Agenda.", International Journal of Management Reviews 20.S1 (2018), pp. S63-82.

Zellweger, T. M. (2007) "Time horizon, costs of equity capital, and generic investment strategies of firms", Family Business Review, 20 (1), pp. 1–15.

Experimentation and Digitalization: Towards a Brand-New Corporate Entrepreneurship?

Angelo Cavallo, Stefano D'Angelo and Antonio Ghezzi
Politecnico di Milano, Milan, Italy
angelo.cavallo@polimi.it
stefano.dangelo@polimi.it
antonio1.ghezzi@polimi.it
DOI: 10.34190/EIE.20.137

Abstract: This paper explores how experimentation and digitalization may influence corporate entrepreneurship in established companies. Experimentation methods for launching new products and originating new business models for startup company - such as lean startup, design thinking, agile, and (more recently) growth hacking - attracted along the years the favour and appreciation of practitioners as well as a growing attention by entrepreneurship scholars. This has much to do with digitalization. Digital technologies created the conditions for running better experiments in scope and scale, helping entrepreneurs to make decision while reducing related risks. While these considerations intuitively may apply also to entrepreneurial actions in established companies, aka "corporate entrepreneurship", few address such challenge. A pressing and relevant question on this regard is "How experimentation and digitalization are influencing corporate entrepreneurship"?; and more, "are experimentation and digitalization changing known corporate entrepreneurship forms (e.g. corporate venturing, strategic renewal, organizational rejuvenation) till leading towards new forms of corporate entrepreneurship?". Due to the debate's novelty and to the depth of the investigation required to grasp the mechanisms and logics of entrepreneurship in established organizations, we conducted an in-depth single case study based on qualitative interviews and additional triangulated sources related to a system integrator firm. System integrators represents an appropriate research setting since they base their core business on providing digital solutions to other firms, and, they are especially in need to keeping pace with the emerging experimenting approaches to entrepreneurship and the development of emerging technologies, thus representing a suitable case for investigation in accordance with our research questions. Our study shows how experimentation methods and digitalization may enhance corporate entrepreneurship in established firms, shading lights on specific managerial practices employed by the company to orchestrate resources and capabilities. Also, we suggest how our findings may support and further develop the traditional exaptation and effectuation theory applied in corporate entrepreneurship.

Keywords: corporate entrepreneurship, experimentation, digital technologies, digital entrepreneurship, lean startup, agile

1. Introduction

This paper explores how experimentation and digitalization may influence corporate entrepreneurship (CE) in established companies. Literature on experimentation in entrepreneurship is abundant (Kerr et al., 2014, Contigiani and Levinthal, 2019), however there are few studies investigating experimentation methods in established firms despite the clear need for incumbent to look for proper actions to become more "entrepreneurial" (Ireland et al., 2003), the recognized necessity for established organizations for renewal, continual innovation and value creation (Corbett et al., 2013) and the increasing interest in experimentation among managers to understand how enact entrepreneurial process within incumbent firms (Covin and Slevin, 2002). Experimentation methods for launching new products and originating new business models for startup company - such as lean startup (Ries, 2011), design thinking (Brown, 2009), agile (Beck et al., 2001), and more recently growth hacking (Ellis and Brown, 2016) - attracted along the years the favour and appreciation of practitioners as well as a growing attention by entrepreneurship scholars. This has much to do with digitalization. In this context, the large diffusion of digital technologies made entrepreneurial activities more prolific (Arvidsson and Mønsted, 2018), facilitating openness in entrepreneurship, offering more possibilities to experiment and favouring change and recombination (Nambisan et al., 2019). Despite the relevance of the topic, there are yet few critical contributions exploring how the digital technologies may serve to develop and promote entrepreneurship within established organizations.

In view of these arguments, this paper addresses the following overarching question: *"How experimentation and digitalization are influencing corporate entrepreneurship?"* We consider relevant both for theory and practice to analyse how experimentation and digitalization may enhance CE in established companies since: first, there is a significant and unexplored link between CE and digitalization that can open up further investigations about how digitalization can affect CE creating the room for future studies about digital CE (Arvidsson and Mønsted, 2018), second, there is a recognized need for incumbents to enact more entrepreneurial practices based on experimentation to sustain competitive advantage (Covin and Slevin, 2002), third, there is a growing attention from entrepreneurship scholars and practitioners towards experiment-based approaches adopted in established companies that can enhance CE (Hampel et al., 2020).

The research design is based on a single case study. Due to the debate's novelty and to the depth of the investigation required to grasp the mechanisms and logics of entrepreneurship in established organizations, our research question warrants for qualitative research methodology. Specifically, we conducted a single case study based on qualitative interviews and additional triangulated sources related to a system integrator firm. System integrators are appropriate empirical setting since, first, they base their core business on providing digital solutions to other firms, and, they are especially in need to keeping pace with the emerging experimenting approaches to entrepreneurship and the development of emerging technologies, second, system integrator, as core capability leading firms to navigate between technological trajectories and adapting to and influencing an uncertain market context (Iansiti, 1998), has much to do with three key themes in digital entrepreneurship literature (Nambisan et al., 2019), openness, generativity and affordances, that could potentially influence CE. Thus, system integrators represent a suitable case for investigation in accordance with our research question.

The study will provide at least three contributions. First, we assert the critical positive role performed by digital technologies in terms of openness, affordances, and generativity for CE activities. Second, we show how experimentation methods developed around lean entrepreneurship can benefit also established firms. This significantly advances the extant literature on experimentation, which has predominantly focused on startup, lacking any precise characterisation on established companies' peculiarities. Finally, leveraging on a theoretical perspective, we make a significant contribution within CE literature: our findings support and further develop valuable theories employed in CE considering the digital perspective.

2. Literature review

2.1 Corporate entrepreneurship

Recent and more and more studies suggest the centrality and the relevance of entrepreneurship in every organization as a strategic imperative while facing an increasingly competitive and dynamic world (Kuratko, 2017). In this turbulent and uncertain environment, entrepreneurship is a key to sustainable competitive advantage (Morris et al., 2009). Established organizations incapable of embracing entrepreneurial practices are exposed to high risk of failure, since they operate under uncertainty in a constantly changing environment (Ireland et al., 2003). Such entrepreneurial efforts within established companies goes broadly under the name of CE (Wolcott and Lippitz, 2007, Sakhdari, 2016) . Burgelman (1983) provided the first definition of CE as "the process whereby the firms engage in diversification through internal development. Such diversification requires new resource combinations to extend the firm's activities in areas unrelated, or marginally related, to its current domain of competence". While Sharma and Chrisman (1999) delivered one of the most comprehensive definition of CE as "the process whereby an individual or group of individuals, in association with an existing organization, create a new organization or instigate renewal or innovation within that organization." According to the most recent conceptualization of CE (Morris et al., 2011), CE encompasses two main domains: corporate venturing, focused on the creation, addition or investments in new businesses or portions of new businesses via equity investments and strategic entrepreneurship that includes a broad array of entrepreneurial initiatives such as strategic renewal, sustained regeneration, domain redefinition, organizational rejuvenation, and business model reconstruction (Kuratko and Audretsch, 2009). Despite CE can take many forms, it is focused on fostering innovative, risk-taking, and proactive behaviours in established organizations (Morris et al., 2009).

Recently research on CE has expanded and aroused an increasing amount of attention (Kuratko, 2017) due to the need of incumbent companies to achieve and sustain a sustainable competitive advantage in the current uncertain, dynamic and competitive environment. The recognized need for renewal, continual innovation and value creation led practitioners and scholars to consider how entrepreneurial processes might be enacted within established organizations for the purposes of achieving and perpetuating competitive advantage (Covin and Slevin, 2002). Over the past decades, research has shown that organizations undertake CE initiatives for several purposes such as firms revitalization, successful organizational and financial performances, business creation, proactive and risk taking behaviours, innovativeness, strategic renewal and enhanced competitiveness (Tseng and Tseng, 2019). Incumbent companies which exhibit CE are typically perceived as dynamic, flexible entities able to take advantage of new business opportunities (Kuratko et al. 2015). In addition, the large and pervasive diffusion of digital technologies, facilitating and empowering CE (Arfi and Hikkerova, 2019), can contribute to further develop CE literature leveraging on the digital perspective and creating the room for further investigations on digital CE, at the intersection between CE and digital technologies, defined as "the entrepreneurial action by which organization members identify opportunities and pursue them by recombining resources in such a way that the development and scaling of new applications creates potent stepping stones for further action" (Arvidsson and Mønsted, 2018). While the recognized role of CE as an essential success strategy is strongly confirmed in the literature, there are yet few critical contributions exploring how the digital technologies may promote entrepreneurship within established organizations, and our understanding of how CE with digital technology unfolds in organizations is thus limited.

2.2 Digital entrepreneurship

Digital technologies have an extensive and deep impact on how individual and organizations innovate (Enkel et al. 2020). They represent powerful enablers in fuelling entrepreneurial initiatives (Nambisan et al., 2019, Cavallo et al., 2019a) and in potentially shaping entrepreneurial processes and outcomes (von Briel, Davidsson, et al. 2018). Research on digital entrepreneurship, still in its infancy, defined as "the reconciliation of traditional entrepreneurship with the new way of creating and doing business in the digital era" (Le Dinh et al., 2018), at the intersection of digital technologies and entrepreneurship is gaining increasing relevance among scholars and practitioners (Recker and von Briel, 2019).

The emergence of digital technologies has transformed entrepreneurship in significant ways with broad implications (Nambisan et al., 2019). Recent studies on digital entrepreneurship have shown how digital technologies fuel new forms of entrepreneurial initiatives that cross traditional sectoral boundaries, embrace networks, and accelerate the scaling of new ventures (Minola et al., 2017). Others have analysed the ways by which established large companies have tried to redefine themselves and reshape their innovation strategies to respond to the digital transformation (Fitzgerald et al., 2014). Still, other studies (Nambisan, 2017) have investigated how digital technologies transform the nature of uncertainty inherent in entrepreneurship, in terms of both processes and outcomes.

Recker and von Briel (2019) identified three fundamental dimensions of the digital entrepreneurship research: digital technologies as enablers, outcomes, or contexts of entrepreneurship processes. While Nambisan (2017) distinguished three distinct but related elements of digital technologies manifested in entrepreneurship field: digital artefacts, digital platforms, and digital infrastructure. Related to these components, Nambisan and colleagues (2019) identified three key themes in the digital entrepreneurship that could potentially serve as the basis for a future research agenda in CE in the digital age: openness, affordances, and generativity. Concerning openness, digital technologies promote and facilitate openness in varied ways, changing the notion of openness in terms of degree, scale and scope. Digital technologies have transformed the nature of openness in entrepreneurship, in terms of actors, inputs or resources and outcomes. Affordances, defined as "action potential or possibilities or opportunities for action offered by an object, in this case digital technology, in relation to a specific user or, use context, in entrepreneurship" (Nambisan, 2019), enable organizations to reinvent how they create, deliver, and capture value. Generativity refers to the "capacity exhibited by digital technologies to produce unprompted change, through blending or recombination, by large, varied, unaccredited and uncoordinated entities/actors" (Nambisan, 2019). The nature of digital technologies contributes to generative processes (Zittrain, 2006), enabling new functionalities in different market contexts, reshaping existing pathways or opening new pathways to create value.

Despite its contemporary significance, however, limited effort has been made in understanding how digitalization can enhance CE and on theorizing the role of specific aspects of digital technologies in shaping entrepreneurial processes and outcomes within established organisations. The pervasive digitalization create a need for new theorizing in entrepreneurship. In the light of these considerations, a rich opportunity exists for scholars to revise existing theories of CE in the light of digital technologies and to develop new theories of CE in the digital age.

2.3 Experimentation

There is growing interest in business experimentation in the management literature and practice (Felin et al., 2019). Literature on experimentation is extensive (Wiklund and Shepherd, 2011). Scholars have focused on the reasons why entrepreneurs engage in experimentation (Cavallo et al., 2019b). Others have investigated the benefits of experimentation (Cosenz and Noto, 2018). Still, other studies treated the factors influencing experimentation (Foss et al., 2019).

Experimentation became more relevant in the current competitive environment where companies are required to foster their agility to sustain entrepreneurial behaviours (Morris et al., 2009) and in the context of digitalization since digital technologies, as powerful enabling factors, created the conditions for running better experiments in scope and scale, facilitating greater degree of trial and experimentation (Autio et al., 2018). Digital technologies by way of their unique characteristics shape the nature and extent of experimentation and thereby imbue greater variability in the process of experimentation.

Experimentation in entrepreneurship has become the basis for influential approaches to launch new ventures starting from the most diffused lean start-up approach (Ries, 2011). Experimentation methods, such as Agile Software Development (Beck et al., 2001), Scrum (Schwaber, 1997), Customer Development (Blank, 2005), Lean Startup (Ries, 2011), Disciplined Entrepreneurship (Aulet, 2013), Design Thinking (Brown, 2009), Growth Hacking (Ellis and Brown, 2016) and Sprint (Knapp et al., 2016) are only some of the methods that entrepreneurs are growingly adopting to perform experiments and acquire experience and learning within their new ventures. Experimentation as an iterative process to reduce uncertainty, engage stakeholders and promote collective learning at a relatively low cost (Bocken and Snihur, 2019) has diffused also within established companies inspiring a plethora of innovation tools by which established firms can run experiment such as one-off events like hackathons and permanent facilities, such as innovation labs or accelerators. Research (Felin et al., 2019) recognizes that experimentation can benefit also established companies overcoming organizational inertia, driving renewal, spurring continuous innovation, fostering entrepreneurial orientation, stimulating innovation, creativity and growth while maintaining a motivated and productive organization.

While there is a growing literature examining experimentation in start-ups (Balocco et al., 2019) there are few studies investigating the role of experimentation in supporting CE activities despite the increasing interest among managers and the growing literature urging established firms to adopt experimentation (Hampel et al., 2020). It is evident the opportunity for scholars to investigate the growing trend to experiment in established organisations. In addition, despite the growing interest in understanding how digital technologies are reshaping experimentation in entrepreneurship, there are few studies that have investigated how digitalization can influence experimentation in terms of outcomes, process and boundary conditions.

3. Methods

3.1 Industry and case selection

To cope with our research goal, we sought out a system integrator firm for several reasons. First, System Integration, as a core capability leading firms to navigate between technological trajectories, fighting inertia and adapting to and influencing an uncertain market context (Iansiti, 1998) has much to do with CE. Second, system integrators encompass three key themes in digital entrepreneurship (Nambisan, 2019), openness, affordances, and generativity, that could potentially influence valuable theories employed in CE. Third, system integrators represents an appropriate research setting since they base their core business to support digital transformation, and, they are especially in need to keeping pace with the emerging experimenting approaches to entrepreneurship and the development of emerging technologies, thus representing a suitable case for investigation in accordance with our research questions. Multiple reasons led us to the choice of this case. First, this study analyses a system integrator firm that relies on CE to engage in diversification and pursue continual innovation and value creation. Second, this case is based on a digital platform that support the digital transformation, contributing to make organisations dynamic, flexible entities able to take advantage of new business opportunities. Finally, this case shows how experimentation methods are applied in an established firm to stimulate CE. Thus, we deem HN Digee an academically relevant case, consistently with our research question. HN Digee, startup founded in 2019, controlled by Humanativa, is focused on the development of a digital platform, called zoon, specialized in the Intelligent Information Management to support digital transformation.

3.2 Data gathering and data analysis

Data were collected from multiple sources of information. Using different sources of information helps triangulate and validate the data as well as making the results of qualitative research more trustworthy and persuasive (Yin, 2009). Primary source of data were 10 face-to-face interviews with 2 interviewees. As secondary source of data, we collected information from internal and external documents. Our data analysis follows the process described by Gioia and colleagues (2013). The results were analysed and then confirmed by the interviewees to avoid any error or bias and ultimately enhance the correctness of our interpretations.

4. Findings

4.1 Experimentation and corporate entrepreneurship

Experimentation methods, introduced at group level to define a Business Model Canvas and then to identify a validation process, were adopted to implement the CE project and to support continuous innovation. To facilitate the development of the digital platform, a methodological framework, combining the different experimentation methods, has been defined to provide a set of tools for each phase of the development process. Design Thinking has been the first methodology applied to define the problem and to identify early adopters. Then, Agile methodologies, specifically Lean Startup, Design Sprint, Kanban and Scrum, have been adopted to implement the digital platform. Finally, Dev-paradigm Ops was adopted to improve the usability and the functionality of the platform.

Experimentation methods benefit the organization in varied way. First, they allowed to stimulate engagement, second, they share knowledge and skills at group level. Humanativa attributed in fact a synergistic connotation to the project: all the participants of the Innovation Circle, that included the responsible of the line of business of the group were required to contribute in terms of innovative capabilities. Concerning each specific experimentation methods, Lean Startup, represented a valuable tool to test hypotheses continuously, to reduce level of complexity and to validate and measure the learning. Lean Startup introduced two strategic benefits for the entire group: first, it supported the launch of innovative ideas and helped to reduce time and costs, second, it allowed to acquire cultural and methodological elements at group level. As regards Agile development, it allowed to face uncertainty in the product development with the support of an agile transversal team. Agile methodologies, based on weekly sprints, allowed to manage the risk through quality control. Design Sprint were used to share insights, ideate and prototype.

4.2 Digitalization and corporate entrepreneurship

HN Digee, based on a digital platform, is the project of CE of Humanativa. The word itself, Digee, a composite world based on the first letter of Digital and Information and "gee" encourage someone to put more effort into an activity, links digitalization and CE. The vision behind the HN Digee assumes that in order to compete in the digital age, organisations must integrate digital technologies as part of their business model and create value from an intelligent flow of information. In this digital context, where knowledge has a strategic role and competitive advantage is based on the ability to extract value from data, Humanativa believes that organizations need a platform to enhance continual innovation and value creation. The new technological and methodological platform experience, called zoon, aims to satisfy the need to innovate, to adapt and respond to changes in a dynamic environment. Through zoon, it is possible to iterate as the needs of the business change, making organizations as dynamic, flexible entities able to take advantage of new business opportunities when they arise. Zoon, an easy platform for digital business opened to be integrated to the partner ecosystem, is a valuable digital platform to flow intelligently information. The Intelligent Information Management capabilities on which this platform is based are an integral part of the digital transformation challenge of understanding, anticipating and redefining customer experiences.

5. Discussion and conclusion

This study explored how experimentation and digitalization may affect CE. In the current digital context, where knowledge is considered a strategic factor, entrepreneurial activities are required to remain competitive and digital affordances may foster CE, system integration capability, as "key to the broader competitive strategy of the firm" (Hobday, Davies and Prencipe, 2005), facilitate CE practices enabling incumbent to take advantage of new business opportunities and respond to changes (Kuratko et al. 2015). Agile has much to with CE. Embracing Agile methodologies allows the organization to adapt to changes in a dynamic environment (Qumer and Henderson-Sellers, 2006). Agility, defined as the ability to sense and respond to changes and new business opportunities, enacted by exploration-based learning and exploitation-based learning" (Lyytinen & Rose, 2006), seems to be fundamental to pursue sustainable competitive advantage in this changing environment.

Concerning digitalization and CE, this study shows how a system integrator, integrating skills, knowledge and resources, leading firms to navigate between technological trajectories and adapting to an uncertain market context (Iansiti, 1998), influence CE, in terms of generativity (Zittrain, 2006), enabling new functionalities, reshaping existing pathways or opening new ones, in terms of openness (Wareham et al., 2014), facilitating more collective ways of pursuing entrepreneurship (Fischer and Reuber, 2011) and in terms of affordances (Nambisan, 2019), enabling more opportunities to practice experimentation in entrepreneurship. Concerning experimentation and CE, this case reveals how experimentation methods enhance CE in terms of innovativeness and proactiveness (Covin et al., 2019). Lean Startup can support the launch of innovative ideas, stimulating continuous innovation. While Agile methodologies increase the ability to respond to changes in a dynamic environment favouring proactive behaviour.

This study offers value for research in multiple ways. First, we explored how digital technologies affect CE in terms of openness, affordances and generativity creating the room for further investigations on digital CE (Arvidsson and Mønsted, 2018). Second, we significantly advanced the extant literature on experimentation, (Kerr et al., 2014) predominantly focused on startups, shading lights on experimentation methods adopted in established companies opening up further studies about the challenges that firms face in experimentation, and the limits of application of experimentation in established firms. The current research has several implications for practice. First, our findings show how established firms may leverage on experimentation methods to foster CE. Second, we investigated how the digital technologies may develop entrepreneurship within established organizations, increasing our understanding of how corporate entrepreneurship with digital technology unfolds in organizations. We show how digital technologies enhance experimentation in scope and scale as well entrepreneurial process in terms of outcomes, knowledge creation, improved performances and decision-making making CE more prolific and potent.

References

Arfi, W. B., & Hikkerova, L. (2019) "Corporate entrepreneurship, product innovation, and knowledge conversion: the role of digital platforms", Small Business Economics, pp. 1-14.

Arvidsson, V. and Mønsted, T. (2018), "Generating innovation potential: How digital entrepreneurs conceal, sequence, anchor, and propagate new technology", the Journal of strategic information systems, Vol. 27, No. 4, pp.369-383.

Aulet, B. (2013), Disciplined entrepreneurship: 24 steps to a successful startup, John Wiley & Sons.

Autio, E., Nambisan, S., Thomas, L. D., and Wright, M. (2018), "Digital affordances, spatial affordances, and the genesis of entrepreneurial ecosystems", Strategic Entrepreneurship Journal, Vol.12, No.1, pp. 72-95.

Balocco, R., Cavallo, A., Ghezzi, A., & Berbegal-Mirabent, J. (2019) "Lean business models change process in digital entrepreneurship", Business Process Management Journal.

Beck, K., Beedle, M., Van Bennekum, A., Cockburn, A., Cunningham, W., Fowler, M., and Kern, J. (2001), The agile manifesto.

Blank, S. G. (2005) The four steps to the epiphany: Successful strategies for startups, K&S Ranch.

Bocken, N. and Snihur, Y. (2019) "Lean Startup and the Business Model: Experimenting for Novelty and Impact", Long Range Planning.

Brown. T. (2009) Change by Design: How Design Thinking Transforms Organizations and Inspires Innovation, Harper Collins

Burgelman, R. A. (1983) "Corporate entrepreneurship and strategic management: Insights from a process study", Management science, Vol.29, No.12, pp.1349-1364.

Cavallo, A., Ghezzi, A., Dell'Era, C., & Pellizzoni, E. (2019a). "Fostering digital entrepreneurship from startup to scaleup: The role of venture capital funds and angel groups", Technological Forecasting and Social Change, Vol. 145, pp.24-35

Cavallo, A., Ghezzi, A., & Guzmán, B. V. R. (2019b). "Driving internationalization through business model innovation", Multinational Business Revie

Contigiani, A. and Levinthal, D. A. (2019) "Situating the construct of lean start-up: adjacent conversations and possible future directions", Industrial and Corporate Change, Vol. 28, No.3, pp.551-564.

Corbett, A., Covin, J. G., O'Connor, G. C. and Tucci, C. L. (2013) "Corporate entrepreneurship: State-of-the-art research and a future research agenda", Journal of Product Innovation Management, Vol. 30, No. 5, pp. 812-820.

Cosenz, F. and Noto, G. (2018) "Fostering entrepreneurial learning processes through Dynamic Start-up business model simulators", The International Journal of Management Education, Vol.16, No.3, pp.468-482.

Covin, J. and D. Slevin. (2002) "The entrepreneurial imperatives of strategic leadership". In M.A. Hitt, R.D. Ireland, S.M. Camp, and D.L. Sexton (Eds.), Strategic entrepreneurship: Creating a new mindset, pp. 309–327, Blackwell Publishers.

Covin, J. G., and Wales, W. J. (2019). Crafting high-impact entrepreneurial orientation research: Some suggested guidelines.

Ellis, S. and Brown, M. (2016) Hacking Growth: How Today's Fastest-Growing Companies Drive Breakout Success, Random UK, 1st Edition

Enkel, E., Bogers, M. and Chesbrough, H. (2020), "Exploring open innovation in the digital age: A maturity model and future research directions", R&D Management, Vol. 50, No. 1, pp. 161-168.

Felin, T., Gambardella, A., Stern, S. and Zenger, T. (2019) "Lean startup and the business model: Experimentation revisited", Long Range Planning.
Fischer, E. and Reuber, A. R. (2011) Social interaction via new social media:(How) can interactions on Twitter affect effectual thinking and behavior?, Journal of business venturing, Vol. 26, No.1, pp.1-18.
Fitzgerald, M., Kruschwitz, N., Bonnet, D., Welch, M., 2014, "Embracing digital technology: a new strategic imperative", MIT Sloan Management Review, Vol. 55 No.2, 1.
Foss, N. J., Klein, P. G. and Bjørnskov, C. (2019), "The context of entrepreneurial judgment: organizations, markets, and institutions", Journal of Management Studies, Vol. 56, No.6, pp. 1197-1213
Gioia, D. A., Corley, K. G. and Hamilton, A. L. (2013) "Seeking qualitative rigor in inductive research: Notes on the Gioia methodology", Organizational research methods, Vol. 16, No.1, pp.15-31.
Hampel, C., Perkmann, M. and Phillips, N. (2020) "Beyond the lean start-up: experimentation in corporate entrepreneurship and innovation", Innovation, Vol.22, No.1, pp. 1-11.
Hobday, M., Davies, A. and Prencipe, A. (2005), "Systems integration: a core capability of the modern corporation", Industrial and corporate change, Vol.14, No.6, pp.1109-1143.
Iansiti, M. (1998). Technology integration.
Ireland, R. D., Hitt, M. A., & Sirmon, D. G. (2003) "A model of strategic entrepreneurship: The construct and its dimensions. Journal of management", Vol.29, No.6, pp.963-989.
Kerr, W. R., Nanda, R. and Rhodes-Kropf, M. (2014) Entrepreneurship as experimentation, Journal of Economic Perspectives, Vol. 28, No.3, pp.25-48.
Knapp, J., Zeratsky, J., & Kowitz, B. (2016) Sprint: How to solve big problems and test new ideas in just five days, Simon and Schuster.
Kuratko, D. F. (2017) "Corporate entrepreneurship 2.0: research development and future directions", Foundations and Trends in Entrepreneurship, Vol.13, No.6, pp. 441-490.
Kuratko, D. F. and Audretsch, D. B. (2013) "Clarifying the domains of corporate entrepreneurship", International Entrepreneurship and Management Journal, Vol. 9, No. 3, pp. 323-335.
Kuratko, D.F., Hornsby, J.S. and Hayton, J. (2015), "Corporate entrepreneurship: the innovative challenge for a new global economic reality", Small Business Economics, Vol. 45 No. 2, pp. 245-253.
Le Dinh, T., Vu, M.C. and Ayayi, A. (2018), "Towards a living lab for promoting the digital entrepreneurship process", International Journal of Entrepreneurship, Vol. 22 No. 1, pp. 1-17.
Lyytinen, K. and Rose, G. M. (2006) "Information system development agility as organizational learning. European Journal of Information Systems", Vol.15, No.2, pp. 183-199.
Minola, T., Vismara, S., & Hahn, D. (2017) "Screening model for the support of governmental venture capital. The Journal of Technology Transfer", Vol.42, No.1, pp.59-77.
Morris, M. H., van Vuuren, J., Cornwall, J. R. and Scheepers, R. (2009) Properties of balance: A pendulum effect in corporate entrepreneurship, Business Horizons, Vol. 52, No.5, pp.429-440.
Morris, M. H., Kuratko, D. F. and Covin, J. G. (2011) Corporate entrepreneurship & innovation, Boston: Cengage/South-Western/Publishers
Nambisan, S. (2017) "Digital entrepreneurship: Toward a digital technology perspective of entrepreneurship", Entrepreneurship Theory and Practice, Vol. 41,No. 6, pp.1029-1055.
Nambisan, S., Wright, M. and Feldman, M. (2019) "The digital transformation of innovation and entrepreneurship: Progress, challenges and key themes", Research Policy, Vol.48, No.8.
Qumer, A. and Henderson-Sellers, B. (2008) "A framework to support the evaluation, adoption and improvement of agile methods in practice", Journal of systems and software, Vol. 81, No.11, pp. 1899-1919.
Recker, J. and von Briel, F. (2019) "The Future of Digital Entrepreneurship Research: Existing and Emerging Opportunities"
Ries, E. (2011) The lean startup: How today's entrepreneurs use continuous innovation to create radically successful businesses, Crown Books.
Sakhdari, K. (2016) "Corporate entrepreneurship: A review and future research agenda", Technology Innovation Management Review, Vol. 6, No.8.
Schwaber, K. (1997) Scrum development process. In Business object design and implementation (pp. 117-134). Springer, London.
Sharma, P. and Chrisman, S. J. J. (2007) "Toward a reconciliation of the definitional issues in the field of corporate entrepreneurship", In Entrepreneurship, pp. 83-103, Springer, Berlin, Heidelberg.
Tseng, C. and Tseng, C. C. (2019) "Corporate entrepreneurship as a strategic approach for internal innovation performance", Asia Pacific Journal of Innovation and Entrepreneurship.
von Briel, F., Davidsson, P. and Recker, J. (2018) "Digital technologies as external enablers of new venture creation in the IT hardware sector", Entrepreneurship Theory and Practice, Vol. 42, No.1, pp. 47-69.
Wiklund, J., & Shepherd, D. A. (2011) "Where to from here? EO-as-experimentation, failure, and distribution of outcomes", Entrepreneurship Theory and Practice, Vol. 35, No.5, pp.925-946.
Wolcott, R. C., & Lippitz, M. J. (2007) "The four models of corporate entrepreneurship", MIT Sloan management review, Vol. 49, No.1.
Yin, R.K. (2009), "Case study research: Design and methods", Essential Guide to Qualitative Methods in Organizational Research. Applied Social Research Methods Series, Vol. 219.
Zittrain, J. (2006) "The generative Internet", Harv. Law Rev, Vol. 119, No.7, pp.1975–2040.

Business Model Innovation for Sustainability: A System Dynamics Approach

Angelo Cavallo[1], Jacopo Manotti[1], Antonio Ghezzi[1], Habib Sedehi[2] and Andrea Rangone[1]
[1]Department of Management, Economics and Industrial Engineering, Faculty of Management Engineering, Politecnico di Milano, Milan, Italy
[2]LUMSA University - Master School, Rome, Italy
angelo.cavallo@polimi.it
jacopo.manotti@polimi.it
antonio1.ghezzi@polimi.it
habib.sedehi@uniroma1.it
andrea.rangone@polimi.it
DOI: 10.34190/EIE.20.135

Abstract: Recently, sustainability has been gaining momentum both in research and practice. Firms aiming at sustainability purpose have to renew their entire Business Model (BM). Sustainable business model innovation refers to the redesign of the BM's components and the linkages between them to accommodate the adoption of sustainability-based strategies. Extant literature presents valuable contribution, initiating a debate on business model innovation for sustainability. The intersection between the sustainability literature and the business model one is mostly characterized by qualitative studies, highlighting a lack of quantitative research, which could contribute to shed light on the links among micro-dimensions underlying the business model innovation process. Specifically, few studies embrace a system thinking approach, considered appropriate for analyzing a complex and dynamic system such as business model. This study advances the current body of knowledge of business model innovation process for sustainability, by specifically leveraging on system dynamics method. The core mechanism of a sustainable business model is a reinforcing feedback loop between value offering to customers and value captured by the firm and the natural environment. Our study provides a conceptualization of business model innovation process for sustainability through a casual-loop diagram, showing the theoretical interlinks between the different components of the business model.

Keywords: business models, sustainability, system dynamics, systems thinking, business model innovation

1. Introduction

An increased concern regarding the sustainability of the capitalistic economy has been recorded in the last decade, raising attention to possible alternatives and reconfigurations of the actual paradigms in both the industrial systems and the society (Mittelstaedt and Kilbourne, 2008). A crucial role in this transition is covered by media (Brulle et al., 2012), which have the possibility to influence the public opinion regarding delicate issues. For instance, one of the most mainstream manifestations of this concern has been the "Fridays for the Future" movement, a series of events involving millions of people all around the world asking for a more sustainable future, which has been able to raise the interest of United Nations too, which previously published the 17 sustainability development goals in 2015. This growing attention towards the theme has been also received in the academic literature, with an increasing number of scholars from different disciplines who have contributed to the field. Specifically, the business and management community has addressed the phenomenon for a multitude of different perspectives, such as strategy (Cavallo et al., 2020), entrepreneurship and innovation (Adams et al., 2016), with the purpose to analyse whether firms may play a role – and how – in the transition toward a more sustainable paradigm. A recent research (2019) based on a large-scale survey conducted by the worldwide famous consulting firm Accenture Strategy pointed out how "while consumers remain primarily focused on quality and price, 83% believe it's important or extremely important for companies to design products that are meant to be reused or recycled. Nearly three-quarters (72%) of respondents said they're currently buying more environmentally friendly products than they were five years ago, and 81% said they expect to buy more over the next five years.". Consequently, the main challenge for most of the firms in the current future is represented by the adoption and implementation of new strategies aiming at transforming their business model, from its traditional nature to a more sustainable one, aiming at keeping – or even enlarging - their customer base. Some authors have paid attention to the processes of business model innovation, highlighting how the sustainable purpose may represent a relevant driver for that type of innovation (Foss and Saebi, 2017). New and innovative business models have been historically proposed mainly by new ventures and startups (Balocco et al., 2019; Hahn et al., 2019) that, through their strategic flexibility and experimental nature, may overcome some barriers to innovations traditionally associated with incumbents (Trabucchi et al., 2019). Thus, this study conceptualizes the possible interlinks between the different dimensions of the business model of a generic firm that aims at offering a new sustainable value proposition. Specifically, we adopted a systems-thinking perspective, using system dynamics modelling (Forrester, 1961; Sterman, 2000), with the purpose to highlight the transitory and evolutionary process of business model innovation, usually tackled from a too static perspective (Foss and Saebi, 2017). The model allows entrepreneurs to simulate different "what-if" strategies (Sansone et al., 2019), looking at how the different elements of the business model react each other in different scenarios. The contribution of this study is thus two-folded. From one hand, it aims at contributing to the academic literature in business and management, providing a dynamic conceptualization of the business model innovation process in a sustainable-driven context. On the other hand, the study adds a practical tool for strategy-simulation in new ventures, allowing managers and entrepreneurs to assess possible directions ex-ante, often claimed as practical gap many of the studies (Chesbrough, 2010; McGrath, 2010).

2. Theoretical background

2.1 Sustainability

Despite the large attention received in the last years, the concept of sustainability cannot be considered recent. The first work that attempted to describe the impact of human activities on the planet is dated 1948 (Osborne, 1948), followed by other studies particularly in the fermented ideological decades of the sixties and seventies (Carson, 1962; Cole et al., 1973). However, it has been only in 1987 that the idea of sustainable development we have in mind today was conceptualized, in the Brundtland Report for the World Commission on Environment and Development, stating it as "development that meets the needs of the present without compromising the ability of future generations to meet their own needs'". About a decade later, the sustainable development idea gained momentum in the business and management community through the work of Elkington (1997), who firstly proposed the idea of Triple Bottom Line (TBL), highlighting the three dimensions of sustainability today considered pillars of the discipline: environmental, social and economic. This contribution has made the relationship between the managerial community and the sustainable development concept crystallized, recognizing the involvement of firms – and more in general economic agents – to be important drivers of the sustainable transition (Mittelstaedt and Kilbourne, 2008). In the following years, many scholars have contributed to the field presenting their own definition of sustainability management adopting different perspectives or theoretical lenses, resulting in a fragmented and non-cumulated body of knowledge (Adams et al., 2016). Some authors have focused their attention on the environmental cause, introducing definitions of sustainability linked to industrial terms such as eco-efficiency (Whiteman et al., 2013) and green production (Pujari et al., 2003), while others have adopted a social perspective (Peloza, 2009), with – among the others – the idea of responsible innovation (Owen et al., 2013). Some reviews have attempted to provide an overall picture of the sustainability management literature, claiming for a too traditional theoretical and simplistic approach in dealing with the phenomenon, presenting a systemic view to fully capture the complexity of the sustainable transition (Williams et al., 2017). In their review, Adams and colleagues (2016) pointed out four gaps: i) the existing variety of definitions and labels conceptualized so far, ii) the static and dichotomous approach, looking at sustainability as sustainable or non-sustainable as well as an oversimplified input-output process; iii) a general tendency to neglect the social dimension of the phenomenon and iv) the common approach to exclude more recent contributions which place the sustainability literature in a grey area. In the very recent years, the debate on sustainability seems to have shifted more toward the idea of sustainable innovation, with a pronounced emphasis on the possible new products, new processes and new organizational structures that firms may implement with aim to meet stakeholders' expectations (Rennings, 2000). Specifically, the role of small-medium enterprises in dealing with sustainable innovation has been deeply investigated, with Klewitz and Hansen (2014) who proposed a framework highlighting possible strategic sustainable behaviours to drive that type of innovation inside the firm. Following their logical order, the transition may follow a more incremental or more radical approach to firstly overcome barriers and then drive the change toward more sustainable strategies, which see their maximum transformation in the implementation of new sustainable business models. This contribution has been received by many authors who have started to study the sustainable phenomenon through the theoretical lens of the business model, for instance presenting possible sustainable architypes (Bocken et al., 2014) or focusing on the dynamicity of the process through a systemic approach (Abdelkafi and Tauscher, 2016).

2.2 Business model and business model innovation

Today, the business model is considered a consolidated tool at the intersection between strategy and entrepreneurship (Demil et al., 2015), in a theoretical space called strategic entrepreneurship (Ireland et al., 2001), with the double nature to seek for both advantages (a strategic element) and opportunities (an entrepreneurial element) at the same time. Most of the scholars have started to pay attention to the concept of business model at the end of nineties, in the affirmation period of the new economy (Andries et al., 2013). Interestingly, the first studies adopted an incremental perspective to the construct, referring to the different types of business models that the new economy may have required, even if a clear definition of business model was not present before (Timmers, 1998). Thus, it seems that at the beginning the attention was addressed to identify possible innovations for traditional bricks-and-mortar firms to survive and keep competing under the new dynamics brought by the Internet (Mahadevan, 2000). Only in the first years of the new millennium, the business model started to be considered something different from other established strategic models - such as the value chain and the strategic networks (Cavallo et al., 2019)– or economic theories such as the transaction cost economics (Amit and Zott, 2001). Magretta (2002: 6) definetely generalized the construct, defining it as not "the same thing as a strategy, even though many people use the terms interchangeably today. Business models describe, as a system, how the pieces of a business fit together.". This broader definition has been received in the following studies, which have started to use the business model as generic strategic concept, without the coupled association with the Internet anymore (Shafer et al., 2005), being lately re-defined as "the manner by which the enterprise delivers value to customers, entices customers to pay for value, and converts those payments to profit" (Teece, 2010, p.172). Given the increased broadness of the concept at the firm-level, some authors have started to consider the business model as locus of innovation itself, with the possibility to create competitive advantage through its reconfiguration (Amit and Zott, 2012). Thus, undertaking a business model innovation process - referred to as the design and introduction of "novel, non-trivial changes to the key elements of a firm's business model and/or the architecture linking these elements" (Foss and Saebi, 2018, p. 201), now represents an important challenge for whatever type of firm to keep and/or improve its competitive position. It is important to highlight how the innovative process in terms of business model is not a phenomenon limited to already existing companies. Indeed, the literature considers both the innovation referred to a previous status of the same firm's business model and a completely new design for the whole market (Foss et al., 2016; Cavallo, Ghezzi and Guzmán, 2019), with the latter case frequently represented by innovative newcomers such as startups (Cavallo et al., 2019). In the activity to pursue a new business model, Amit and Zott (2015) have identified some drivers to design new architectures, namely i) the goals to create and capture value; ii) the templates of incumbents; iii) stakeholders' activities and iv) environmental constraints. A huge attention has been paid by scholars toward the drivers that may enable business model innovation (de Reuver et al., 2009), from information technologies (Wirtz et al., 2010) to public policies (Teece, 2010), until sustainability (Seelos and Mair, 2007). This last element has been addressed from a multitude of perspectives, mainly linked to its three dimensions outlined by Elkington (1997): economic, social and environmental. If the economic perspective seems to be always taken in consideration, the other two are usually in mutual exclusion in most of the studies. To this extent, an important branch of research has focused on the conceptualization of sustainable business models in low-income markets (e.g. Seelos and Mair, 2007) – also called bottom-of-pyramid (BOP) – while another on the most common archetypes of sustainable business model that firms tend to adopt from an environmental point of view (Bocken et al., 2014, Todeschini et al., 2017, Rosa et al., 2019). However, despite the privileged perspective, the sustainable issue regarding business model has been mainly treated in a qualitative manner, expressing the general immaturity of the discipline in operationalizing the concept of business model (Foss and Saebi, 2017). Few studies attempted to provide scales to capture the intensity of the process of BMI (Clauss, 2017) but further contributions are required. Moreover, the literature largely adopted a static perspective dealing with the business model, focusing on its configurations in punctuated periods in time, without emphasis on the process of evolution between them. Our study aims at contributing to the business model innovation field bridging the sustainable driver and a dynamic perspective of the construct, taking into considerations the relationships between the different dimensions of the business model in the process of change through a system dynamics approach (Forrester, 1961).

2.3 System dynamics

Literature on business models highlighted how a business model's effectiveness and quality is highly dependent by the fit between all its components (Magretta, 2002). All this stress the fact that we are dealing with a "complex system", meaning that even a small change in one of its components interacts with many other components to determine the value of the whole system. This leads to the necessity to adopt a system thinking approach, the perspective widely adopted through the lenses of system dynamics (SD). A SD model requires the definition of a context border line, select the main drivers (variables, parameters, constants) both endogenous and exogenous belonging to the system to include. The graphical result of the qualitative SD analysis is nominated "Causal Loop Diagram" (CLD). A CLD represents the behaviour of a system by showing a collection of connected nodes and the feedback loops created by the connections. A CLD helps visualize how different components (typically variables) in a system are interrelated. One or more of the nodes represent the symptoms of the problem. The rest of the nodes are the causal chains causing the effect of the problem.

A diagram is thus constituted of a set of nodes and edges: nodes represent the variables and edges are the links that represent a connection or a relation between the two variables. A link marked '+' indicates a positive relation while a link marked '–'indicates a negative relation. A positive causal link means the two nodes (variables) change in the same direction, i.e. if the node in which the link starts decreases (increases), the other node also decreases (increases). Similarly, a negative causal link means the two nodes change in opposite directions.

Closed cycles (loops) in the diagram are very important features of CLDs. A closed cycle (loop) is either defined as a reinforcing (amplifying – positive loop) or balancing (stabilizing – negative loop) relation. A positive loop is a cycle in which the effect of a variation in the causal variable propagates through the loop and returns to the variable reinforcing the initial deviation i.e. if a variable increases in a reinforcing loop the effect through the cycle will return an increase to the same variable and vice versa. A balancing loop is the cycle in which the effect of a variation in the causal variable propagates through the loop and returns to the variable a deviation opposite to the initial one. If a variable varies in a reinforcing loop the effect of the change reinforces the initial variation. The effect of the variation will then create another reinforcing effect. Without breaking the loop, the system will be caught in a vicious cycle of circular chain reactions. For this reason, closed loops are considered "decisional" critical features in CLDs.

3. The model

3.1 Model conceptualization

In reference to the system dynamics approach previously introduced, we have developed an aggregated CLD (*see Figure 1*) of our general business model innovation for sustainability which intends to put in evidence the general idea of a dynamic business model for sustainability (Cosenz, Rodirigues & Rosati, 2018) integrated by the suggestions of measuring business model innovation (Clauss, 2017) and the systemic view of the sustainable development goals (Ferri & Sedehi, 2019). The rectangles represent macro-variables, which exhibit connections between each other. Each rectangle has some inputs circles, representing them a higher level of granularity, consistent with the current debate on business models.

As shown in *Figure 1*, a conspicuous number of interlinks and relationships have been mapped among the different components of the business model. Scholars tend to agree regarding the conceptualization of the construct in three macro-building blocks: value creation, value delivery and value capture. With the aim to increase the granularity of the model and the subsequent possibility to act on the single variables, we have decided to further enrich these three dimensions. The value creation concept exhibits links with the blocks of new capabilities, new technological equipment, new partnerships and new processes. It is important to notice the importance of the word "new", referring to a different configuration of these variables compared to a previous status-quo, thus highlighting the intrinsic essence of the business model innovation process at the firm level. These variables might be intended as the inputs leveraged by the firm in the pursuit of building its new value proposition. In strategic management, an important point concerning the value creation is represented by the distinction between key and non-key resources, according to the Resource-based view theory (Barney, 1991). However, we have decided not to adopt this type of difference in the kind of items to be introduced in the model, because of their difficulty in being convincingly operationalized as numbers. The value delivery macro-block shows connections with new offerings, new customers and markets, new channels and new customer relationships. For instance, the model considers whether the firm has enlarged (or reduced) the range of products and services offered (new offers) or whether new customers have been addressed. In terms of value capture, a fundamental role is played by the type of revenue model the specific firm has decided to adopt, defined as the monetization approach by which a firm derives sales from its products (Casadesus-Masanell &

Zhu, 2010). In some cases, the same firm may show different revenue models in relation to different value propositions with the aim to capture as much value as possible, as investigated in some studies (Gassmann et al., 2015). The dual element of the revenue model is represented by the concept of cost structure, intended as the set of cost items the firm face in building its offer. Here the basic distinction is between running costs and fixed costs, usually consequence of different strategies. As shown in the graph, revenue model exhibits a positive relation with value capture because of the increased monetization the block brings to the firm, while the cost instrument has been marked with a red negative relation, because of the reduction in terms of final value achieved by the firm. The interplay between the revenue model and the cost structure exhibits a relevant connection with strategy literature, because of the immediate link with the final financial performance of the company, usually considered the most tangible manifestation of competitive advantage (Mitchell & Coles, 2003). The model highlights how all these consolidated macro-dimensions of the business model may be linked with the three sustainable perspectives introduced by Elkington (1997): economic, social and environmental. Hence, an increasing number of studies have been paying attention at the effects that firms experiencing a business model innovation may have on these aspects, both at the firm level and the societal one. Indeed, authors such as Ludeke-Freund (2010) proved how business model innovation might be increasingly recognized as key to deliver greater societal and environmental sustainability in the industrial system. Bocken and colleagues (2014) qualitatively present eight archetypes of sustainable business models, trying to cluster together common characteristics that may lead to sustainable configurations from a technological, social and organizational point of view. However, the focus is mainly manufacturing oriented, while it may be noticed how other types of sustainable initiatives have gained momentum in service firms too, such as the investments in low-income countries (Yunus et al., 2010) as Corporate Social Responsibility programs, aiming at developing basic services and new social value for the local population. The type of firm implementing those initiatives represents just one element highlighting how the shape of the connections between the different elements may strongly vary according to the context of application. A system-dynamics model might be thus suitable to capture the full complexity of the relationships between these components, with the further possibility to adopt different levels of granularity to effectively show how different decisions at the firm level may represent relevant drivers at both the industrial and societal ones. In order to advance the study, it will be possible to discuss with our main stakeholders (entrepreneurs, managers, …), the objectives of our business model innovation for sustainability, with the aim to gain further insights to include in the model.

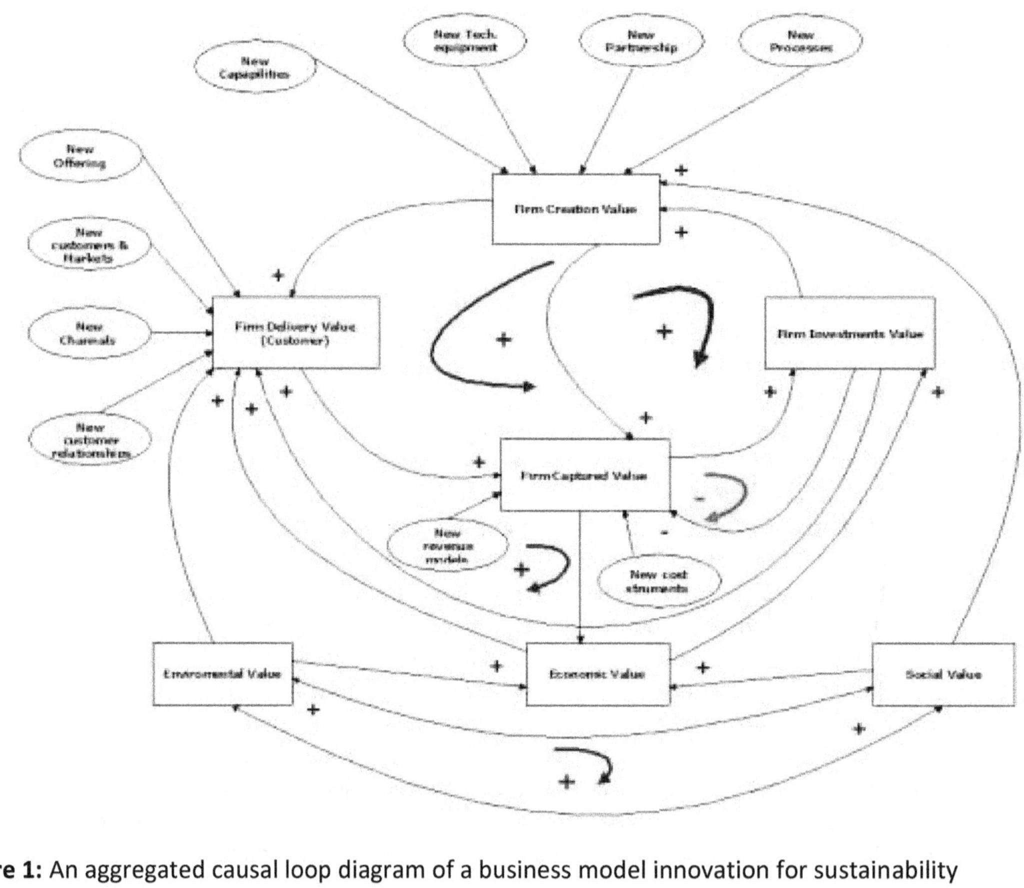

Figure 1: An aggregated causal loop diagram of a business model innovation for sustainability

4. Conclusion

This study highlights the relationships among the different components of the business model and the dimensions of the Triple Bottom Line: economic, social and environmental. The relevance of the model conceptualized in then two-fold. On one hand, it contributes to the extant literature in strategic entrepreneurship, providing a business model mapping which may help in better depicting the causal influences of different building blocks between each other, either comprised the fundamental concepts in sustainability research. On the other hand, the model may be furtherly developed as practical supporting tool for managers aiming at simulating different strategic decisions regarding their firm. In addition, even if not tackled in the study, this conceptualization might be an interesting tool for policymakers too, because of the possibility to look at the possible effects of sustainable incentives on firm's innovation processes and performances, a possible source to leverage on in the design stage of the sustainable-oriented policies.

References

Abdelkafi, N., and Täuscher, K. (2016) Business models for sustainability from a system dynamics perspective. *Organization and Environment*, *29*(1), 74-96.

Adams, R., Jeanrenaud, S., Bessant, J., Denyer, D., and Overy, P. (2016) Sustainability-oriented innovation: A systematic review. *International Journal of Management Reviews*, *18*(2), 180-205.

Amit, R., and Zott, C. (2001) Value creation in e-business. *Strategic management journal*, *22*(6-7), 493-520.

Amit, R., and Zott, C. (2012) Creating value through business model innovation. MIT Sloan Management Review, 53(3), 41-49.

Amit, R., and Zott, C. (2015) Crafting business architecture: The antecedents of business model design. *Strategic Entrepreneurship Journal*, *9*(4), 331-350.

Andries, P., Debackere, K., and Van Looy, B. (2013) Simultaneous experimentation as a learning strategy: Business model development under uncertainty. *Strategic entrepreneurship journal*, *7*(4), 288-310.

Balocco, R., Cavallo, A., Ghezzi, A., and Berbegal-Mirabent, J. (2019) Lean business models change process in digital entrepreneurship. *Business Process Management Journal*.

Barney, J. (1991) Firm resources and sustained competitive advantage. Journal of management, 17(1), 99-120.

Bocken, N. M., Short, S. W., Rana, P., and Evans, S. (2014) A literature and practice review to develop sustainable business model archetypes. *Journal of cleaner production*, *65*, 42-56.

Brulle, R. J., Carmichael, J., and Jenkins, J. C. (2012) Shifting public opinion on climate change: an empirical assessment of factors influencing concern over climate change in the US, 2002–2010. *Climatic change*, *114*(2), 169-188.

Brundtland, G.H. (1987) *Report of the World Commission on Environment and Development: 'Our Common Future'*. New York, NY: United Nations.

Carson, R. (1962) *Silent Spring*. New York, NY: Houghton Mifflin.

Cavallo, A., Ghezzi, A., and Guzmán, B. V. R. (2019) Driving internationalization through business model innovation. *Multinational Business Review*.

Cavallo, A., Ghezzi, A., Dell'Era, C., and Pellizzoni, E. (2019) Fostering digital entrepreneurship from startup to scaleup: The role of venture capital funds and angel groups. *Technological Forecasting and Social Change*, *145*, 24-35.

Cavallo, A., Ghezzi, A., Sanasi, S., & Rangone, A. (2019, September). The Strategic-Value Network Model for Entrepreneurial Ecosystem Assessment. In International Conference on Innovation and Entrepreneurship (pp. 214-XXV). Academic Conferences International Limited.

Cavallo, A., Sanasi, S., Ghezzi, A., & Rangone, A. (2020). Competitive intelligence and strategy formulation: connecting the dots. *Competitiveness Review An International Business Journal.* DOI: 10.1108/CR-01-2020-0009.

Chesbrough, H. (2010) Business model innovation: opportunities and barriers. *Long range planning*, *43*(2-3), 354-363.

Clauss, T. (2017) Measuring business model innovation: conceptualization, scale development, and proof of performance. *RandD Management*, *47*(3), 385-403.

Cole, H., Freeman, C., Jahoda, M. and Pavitt, K. (1973) *Thinking about the Future: A Critique of the Limits to Growth*. London: Chatto and Windus.

Cosenz, F., Rodrigues, V. P., and Rosati, F. (2019) Dynamic business modeling for sustainability: Exploring a system dynamics perspective to develop sustainable business models. *Business Strategy and the Environment*.

de Reuver, M., Bouwman, H., and MacInnes, I. (2009) Business models dynamics for start-ups and innovating e-businesses. *International Journal of Electronic Business*, *7*(3), 269-286.

Demil, B., Lecocq, X., Ricart, J. E., and Zott, C. (2015) Introduction to the SEJ special issue on business models: business models within the domain of strategic entrepreneurship. *Strategic Entrepreneurship Journal*, *9*(1), 1-11.

Elkington, J. (1997) *Cannibals with Forks*. Oxford: Capstone

Ferri, G., and Sedehi, H. (2018) The system view of the sustainable development goals. *Available at SSRN 3287918*.

Forrester, J.W. (1961) Industrial Dynamics. MIT Press, Cambridge, MA.

Foss, N. J., and Saebi, T. (2017) Fifteen years of research on business model innovation: How far have we come, and where should we go?. *Journal of Management*, *43*(1), 200-227.

Foss, N. J., and Saebi, T. (2018) Business models and business model innovation: Between wicked and paradigmatic problems. *Long Range Planning*, *51*(1), 9-21.

"Fridays for Future", official website. Accessible at https://www.fridaysforfuture.org/

Greta Thunberg condemns world leaders in emotional speech at UN https://www.theguardian.com/environment/2019/sep/23/greta-thunberg-speech-un-2019-address.

Hahn, D., Minola, T., & Eddleston, K. A. (2019). How do Scientists Contribute to the Performance of Innovative Start-ups? An Imprinting Perspective on Open Innovation. Journal of Management Studies, 56(5), 895-928.

Ireland, R. D., Hitt, M. A., Camp, S. M., and Sexton, D. L. (2001) Integrating entrepreneurship and strategic management actions to create firm wealth. *Academy of Management Perspectives*, *15*(1), 49-63.

Klewitz, J., and Hansen, E. G. (2014) Sustainability-oriented innovation of SMEs: a systematic review. *Journal of cleaner production*, *65*, 57-75.

Lüdeke-Freund, F. (2010) Towards a conceptual framework of'business models for sustainability'. Knowledge collaboration and learning for sustainable innovation, R. Wever, J. Quist, A. Tukker, J. Woudstra, F. Boons, N. Beute, eds., Delft.

Magretta, J. (2002) Why business models matter. Harvard Business Review, 80(5), 86-87.

Mahadevan, B. (2000) Business models for Internet-based e-commerce: An anatomy. *California management review*, *42*(4), 55-69.

McGrath, R. G. (2010) Business models: A discovery driven approach. *Long range planning*, *43*(2-3), 247-261.

Mittelstaedt, J.D. and Kilbourne,W.E. (2008) Macromarketing perspectives on sustainable consumption. In Ken, T.G., Tukker, A., Vezzoli, C. and Ceschin, F. (eds), *Sustainable Consumption and Production: Framework for Action. 2nd Conference of the Sustainable Consumption Research Exchange (SCORE!) Network*, 10 and 11 March, Halles des Tanneurs, Brussels, Belgium.

More than Half of the Consumers Would Pay More for Sustainable Products Designed to Be Reused or Recycled https://newsroom.accenture.com/news/more-than-half-of-consumers-would-pay-more-for-sustainable-products-designed-to-be-reused-or-recycled-accenture-survey-finds.htm

Osborn, F. (1948) *Our Plundered Planet*. London: Faber and Faber.

Owen, R., Stilgoe, J., Macnaghten, P., Gorman, M., Fisher, E. and Guston, D. (2013) A framework for responsible innovation. In Owen, R., Bessant, J. and Heintz, M. (eds), *Responsible Innovation: Managing the Responsible Emergence of Science and Innovation in Society*. Chichester: John Wiley.

Peloza, J. (2009) The challenge of measuring financial impacts from investments in corporate social performance. *Journal of Management*, 35, pp. 1518–1541.

Pujari, D., Wright, G. and Peattie, K. (2003) Green and competitive: influences on environmental new product development performance. *Journal of Business Research*, 56, pp. 657–671.

Rennings, K. (2000) Redefining innovation—eco-innovation research and the contribution from ecological economics. *Ecological economics*, *32*(2), 319-332.

Rosa, P., Sassanelli, C., & Terzi, S. (2019). Towards Circular Business Models: A systematic literature review on classification frameworks and archetypes. Journal of Cleaner Production, 117696.

Sansone, G., Battaglia, D., Landoni, P., & Paolucci, E. (2019). Academic spinoffs: the role of entrepreneurship education. International Entrepreneurship and Management Journal, 1-31.

Seelos, C., and Mair, J. (2007) Profitable business models and market creation in the context of deep poverty: A strategic view. *Academy of management perspectives*, *21*(4), 49-63.

Shafer, S. M., Smith, H. J., and Linder, J. C. (2005) The power of business models. *Business horizons*, *48*(3), 199-207.

Sterman, J., (2000) Business Dynamics: system Thinking and Modelling for a Complex World. McGraw-Hill, London.

Teece, D. J. (2010) Business models, business strategy and innovation. *Long range planning*, *43*(2-3), 172-194.

Timmers, P. (1998) Business models for electronic markets. *Electronic markets*, *8*(2), 3-8.

Trabucchi, D., Talenti, L., & Buganza, T. (2019). How do big bang disruptors look like? A business model perspective. Technological forecasting and social change, 141, 330-340.

Todeschini, B. V., Cortimiglia, M. N., Callegaro-de-Menezes, D., and Ghezzi, A. (2017) Innovative and sustainable business models in the fashion industry: Entrepreneurial drivers, opportunities, and challenges. *Business Horizons*, *60*(6), 759-7.

Yunus, M., Moingeon, B., and Lehmann-Ortega, L. (2010) Building social business models: Lessons from the Grameen experience. Long range planning, 43(2-3), 308-325.

Whiteman, G., Walker, B. and Perego, P. (2013) Planetary boundaries: ecological foundations for corporate sustainability. *Journal of Management Studies*, 50, pp. 307–336.

Whiteman, G., Walker, B. and Perego, P. (2013) Planetary boundaries: ecological foundations for corporate sustainability. *Journal of Management Studies*, 50, pp. 307–336.

Williams, A., Kennedy, S., Philipp, F., and Whiteman, G. (2017) Systems thinking: A review of sustainability management research. *Journal of Cleaner Production*, *148*, 866-881.

Wirtz, B. W., Schilke, O., and Ullrich, S. (2010) Strategic development of business models: implications of the Web 2.0 for creating value on the internet. *Long range planning*, *43*(2-3), 272-290.

Gaming as an Educational Tool to Teach Entrepreneurial Skills

Elizabeth Conradie[1], Albert Strydom[2] and Ulrich Holzbaur[3]
[1]Idea Generator Unit, Central University of Technology, Free State, South Africa
[2]Department of Management Sciences, Central University of Technology, Free State, South Africa
[3]Department of Management Sciences, Aalen University of Applied Sciences, Aalen, Germany
econradie@cut.ac.za
astrydom@cut.ac.za
ulrich.holzbaur@hs-aalen.de
DOI: 10.34190/EIE.20.115

Abstract: There is a need for entrepreneurial education in South Africa. We present the conceptualization, development, deployment and evaluation of an entrepreneurial game to teach economic principles with a focus on what is needed to establish a sustainable enterprise. The game is structured in seven levels: six levels teach the basic economic principles of an enterprise and one level focus on environmental awareness and sustainability. This facilitated educational game is social interactive and constructed in such a way that participants exchange information with both instructor and other participants, gaining knowledge in a fun way which underlines a critical and reflective method of learning. The aim is to teach entrepreneurial economic principles to a diverse target audience that includes unemployed persons; potential entrepreneurs and those entrepreneurs running small enterprises; students and academics that should be transformed towards entrepreneurship and learners in secondary education. The game design was tested to provide design information for the development of other educational gaming tools to teach similar diverse groups. Results of evaluations of the VALU-E game as an interactive learning system through game playing sessions with learners and students will be presented as well as the adaptations in game development made to enhance participant knowledge exchange. The majority of participants indicated that it was a fun experience and that they gain new decision directed knowledge playing the game. Observations from instructors was that the game taught participants to become more supportive of each other in their group in gaining knowledge due to the competitive nature of this gaming teaching method.

Keywords: competitive gaming, education, entrepreneurial education, economics skills

1. Introduction

Games, as a pedagogic approach, seem to align well with the socio-constructivist educational paradigm (Gibb, 2002). Similarities are that the participant's need for self-determination (Ryan and Deci, 2000) is respected; the dynamics of progression or 'flow' (Wu et al, 2013; Csikszentmihalyi, 1990) within games is applied to ensure pleasure and engagement; it is supportive of cooperative learning (Hattie, 2009; Lee et al, 2011) and provide constructive feedback (Fox et al, 2018; Proulx and Romero, 2016).

The facilitated educational game presented is a social interactive group activity and constructed to exchange information with both instructor and other participants, gaining knowledge in a fun way underlining a critical and reflective method of learning. Smale (2011) proposed game features that facilitate learning: students can take on a new identity, extending commitment of self; interactivity - students perform an action to get feedback; allows to learn from failure; content scaffolded into well-ordered problems and students can learn by doing - prior to being completely competent at a skill. Game play is productive in solving problems and sharing solutions, to develop, to test, and share strategies and can also applied to maintain identities represented through games (Games, Learning, and Society group, 2005/2007).

The aim of the present research is to analyse how entrepreneurial skills and entrepreneurial economic principles can be taught to a diverse target audience that includes unemployed persons; potential entrepreneurs and entrepreneurs running small enterprises; students; academics and learners in secondary education.

For this, we will outline and analyse an educational game that was especially developed for the South African needs and context but which can be easily adapted to other educational settings.

1.1 Gaming in education

Salter (2019) stated that games offer great opportunity for experimenting with playful learning in all disciplines and that games can be effective in small doses without major course redesign. To implement a new teaching method the characteristics of the method should be understand by the facilitators. Gaming is a method applied to transfer knowledge in a fun way which underlines a critical and reflective method of learning. Some games, designed with challenging goals with a point system, consolidate course knowledge while being fun (Chan et al, 2017). In "All Play and No Work" MacKenty (2006) states that, "it's the act of problem solving that makes games so engaging, devoid of challenge or risk of failure, games really aren't all that much fun".

1.2 Gaming as an effective tool in education

Marzano (2010) concluded that "on average, using academic games in the classroom is associated with a 20-percentile point gain in student achievement". Games are a well-known method of training that can claim its roots back to the chess game, used in military and management education (Elgood, 1989).

Pannese and Carlesi (2007) analysed the use of instructional games in training sessions of business professionals and university students in northern Italy concluding that people appreciate this innovative and unconventional training tool more than traditional exercises.

1.2.1 Gaming in entrepreneurship / enterprise education

A need for a basic training in economic skills, entrepreneurs need basic competences and elementary knowledge about the function of an enterprise. Within larger organisations – in industry, administration and academia – economic knowledge and managerial skills are needed to run smaller units efficiently creating an entrepreneurial mindset. The question arises, whether this demand gap can be filled by means of an educational game (Project Proposal: VAL-U game, unpublished). In training future entrepreneurs' educational games should teach decision and risk taking, testing of new ways of problem solving, should allow for failure and navigation an insolvency process (Fox et al, 2018) and working as a team (Krajger et al, 2018). Although educational games are available, a huge demand for entrepreneurial education exists and only few games address this issue.

1.2.2 Facilitated learning – identities, social interaction and simulation

Arguments for facilitated game learning are that non-guided game structure may decrease student engagement and motivation (Taub et al, 2020). Fox et al (2018) stated that as many games do not involve the learner in deeper critical reflection, instructor engagement in the classroom may somewhat alleviate this problem. When presented as a facilitated group activity gaming as educational tool still contains elements of the traditional pedagogy method, as the instructor still plays an authoritative role in the instructional process. Social constructivism is a highly effective method of teaching that all students can benefit from, since collaboration and social interaction are incorporated (Powell and Kalina, 2009).

Gamification as teaching strategy supplement with staging learning scenarios and demonstrations, in a simulated environment to solve problems (Weston, 2019), gives the participants the chance to evaluate their ideas in real world problem solving. Entrepreneurial attributes can be identified. Zulfiqar et al (2019) analysing the influence of business simulation games found that business school students with high uncertainty avoidance are reluctant to take risks.

1.2.3 Educational gaming as a motivation tool to undertake entrepreneurship and to determine challenges

Fellnhofer (2018), utilizing a game prototype adjusted for research purposes (sample size - 41 individuals) find that game elements in entrepreneurship education appear to be adequate instruments for promoting and teaching entrepreneurship to increase entrepreneurial attitudes, intentions and behaviour.

1.3 Entrepreneurship teaching for the previously disadvantaged

In the wake of huge unemployment (Free State Growth and Development Strategy, 2014) coupled with a lack of entrepreneurial skills or entrepreneurial education, training in the Free State and South African context becomes imperative. Similar sentiment exists in Europe. "Establish and run entrepreneurship education schemes for the unemployed to enable them to (re-)enter business life as entrepreneurs based on successful models from a number of European Union (EU) Member States, in partnership with education and training systems as an engagement route into second chance education". Underrepresented within the entrepreneurial population and especially founders of start-ups are young people, women, disabled and/or migrants in Europe (EU 2020 ACTION PLAN Reigniting the entrepreneurial spirit in Europe).

In this study a group of unemployed persons interested in entrepreneurship were invited to participate in gaming sessions. The aim is to transfer entrepreneurial skills to participants via a different methodology in teaching which matches participants' needs.

Conceptualization, development, deployment and evaluation of the game will be presented. The purpose of this article is to provide a theoretical overview of the development process, mechanics of the VAL-U game system, the roll-out and to provide feedback on results achieved during the first phases of implementation.

2. A facilitated educational game for socio-economic development

2.1 Background

The VALU-E Entrepreneurial Board Game is a learning tool aimed at introducing basic entrepreneurial principals through game play. A cooperation of the Aalen University of Applied Sciences with the Management Science Faculty of Central University of Technology, Bloemfontein, Free State (FS) on the aspect of using educational games to foster entrepreneurship and contribute to socio-economic development has led to the conceptualisation of the game (Vogelsang 2008, van den Berg et al 2009, van den Berg 2011). The game was refined after visiting training facilities and small-scale businesses in the Free State Province, South Africa.

The games were used to train CUT students in the Faculty of Management Sciences as Train-the-Trainers in the basics of entrepreneurship. They train members of the community accordingly under the supervision of academic experts – in line with the university strategic drive to become a true entrepreneurial university. Further development and testing took place in the Philippines. The game was assessed positively and some ideas about micro funding also emanated from these activities (Bühr and Rey 2011). In 2017 the basic game Micro-Eco-Nomy, (renamed to VAL-U) was develop into a fully fledge board game, VALU-E® game, by an innovator at the CUT, FS facilitated by the Idea Generator Unit for Innovation and Entrepreneurship Advancement and the Faculty of Management Sciences at CUT. Three hundred students from the CUT, Faculty of Management Sciences participated in the various games incorporated as entrepreneurial classes as course work in 2018. Based on comments and responses of these students during the gaming sessions certain additional activities was added and feedback information was used to refine the physical design of the board.

2.2 Methodology of the game (population and sampling)

Participants in this study consisted of multiple groups of respondents. It includes the following:

- Learners of a local school in Bloemfontein in the age group 17 to 18 years. No sampling was done as the total class group was included in the population. It took place in 2017. Estimated number of learners participating was 45.
- Students in Accounting from the Faculty of Management Sciences at CUT. No sampling was done as the total class group was included in the population. It took place in 2017. Estimated number of 40-45 students participated per session, total of ~ 300 students over a period of 10 months.
- The Management Team of the Faculty of Management Sciences at CUT. No sampling was done as the total management group of 14 was included in the population. It took place in 2018.
- Class groups from various learning programmes in the Faculty of Management Sciences. No sampling was done as the total class group per training session was included in the population. A total of 300 students were involved over a period of 10 months. It took place in 2018 – 2019.
- A group of 15 unemployed people in the Heidedal suburb of the Mangaung Metropolitan area. No sampling was done as all community members who responded positive to the invitation were included in the population. It took place in 2019.

2.3 Target groups

In formal education (school or university) educational games can be the topic of a special course within the curriculum or they can be embedded within courses on special subjects (e.g. business management). As the game is structured in different levels (Table 1), training can be tailored for special courses on entrepreneurship for start-up business owners, potential entrepreneurs, unemployed people to give them skills to start a business, students or learners in secondary education that should be motivated towards entrepreneurship. The aim is to teach entrepreneurial economic principles to a diverse target audience. Testing a fragmented game to accurately address specific skills and determine deficits of the game in a wider landscape with different target groups (Fox et al, 2018) was the aim of this multi-levelled designed game presented to diverse target groups. This diversity also reflects the various challenges of South African economy.

3. Game structure and components

Values and content of economics education covered in games are compiled in Table 1, comparing VAL-U game (Phase 1) to VALU-E game (Phase 2).

Table 1: Comparison of values and content of VAL-U game and VALU-E game

VAL-U game (Phase 1)			VALU-E game (Phase 2)	
Level	**Value aspect**	**Entrepreneurship content**	**Entrepreneurship content**	**Value aspect and *short title***
Six	Entrepreneurial values, sustainable development	Strategic planning, competition, entrepreneurship, Sustainable development, Corporate social responsibility	Sustainable development, Corporate social responsibility, Environmental Awareness	Environmental & Sustainability ***Sustainability***
Five	Adding value to society	Business plan development, forecast and research, 'bringing the plan to action'	Business plan development, Identifying key aspects of the business plan	Adding value ***Business Plan***
Four	Valuing people and culture	Project management, teamwork and leadership, networking, soft skills, culture	Taking individual responsibly, Patience and Perseverance	Decisions making & Planning ***Planning and Management***
Three	Creating value for the market	Marketing and sales, risk management, supply and demand, quality and research, stakeholders	Marketing and Sales, Risk management, Supply & Demand, Quality & Research	Creating value for the market ***Marketing***
Two	Adding monetary value	Accounting, cost analysis, interest and taxes, investment and financing, funding	Accounting, cost analysis, interest & taxes, investment & financing	Adding monetary value ***Accounting***
One	The concept of value creation	Elementary economics: product prize and financial gain, procurement, production and sales	Concept of value creation, elementary economics, product prize and financial gain, procurement & production, strategic decision making, teamwork, risk assessment	The concept of value creation ***Economics***
Start			Leadership and teamwork, company vision and mission	***Ice breaker***

4. Results of practical roll-out for development and implementation assessment

4.1 VAL-U (Phase 1) 2008 – 2016

Following theoretical considerations and practical experiences with educational games, a concept for the first levels of such a game was developed and implemented. At development stage the challenge was to determine relevant skills level of target groups. Phase one was role out for assessment and training session at a day care business, Rocklands, Mangaung, FS, a community-based venture managed on a co-operative basis. The business aimed to sell affordable and quality meals to learners at various schools from the surrounding area. The venture team was made-up of unemployed parents from the community. Small business owners and business suppliers for the mining industry located in Thabong, (Welkom, Lejweleputswa district, FS) were trained in business planning, marketing, risk management, supply and demand, quality, accounting and elementary economics, product prize and financial gain, procurement, production and sales.

Feedback indicated that there is a demand for entrepreneurial skills for small enterprise owners. Additional levels to match the training requirements of the target groups added was to include personal skills development and concepts of value creation (Table 1). Val-U game participants ages were between 15-45 years old. Participants have expressed enthusiasm for the game, with one typical struggling school learner reporting "I would pay for something like this outside of school."

4.2 VALU-E (phase 2) 2017 – 2019

In order to assess the level of knowledge before game exposure, questionnaires were designed for the unemployed study group. It assessed the knowledge about enterprise concepts and their educational background. The questionnaires provided space for suggestions to improve and what participants have learnt during the sessions. Data collection was done with questionnaires and game session assistants provided feedback about their experience. Five different groups took part in evaluation sessions to make improvements to the game: 1) school learners, age group 17 -18 years 2) pre-graduate management sciences students, 3) a university executive committee of the management sciences department to evaluate the difficulty level of games and possible implementation in the curriculum, business studies students, 4) Management and Business Science Students and 5) unemployed members of the community interested in entrepreneurship. No formal feedback was done for school learner groups or small student test groups or executive management group – verbal responses were noted to adjust the games accordingly. Responses with curriculum session implemented for ~ 300 Management Science students was documented for samples groups for these students.

4.2.1 Results

Local school - learners

Outcomes: No formal feedback however the overwhelming response was positive as all learners indicate they want to attend more sessions. Difficulty level of games could easily be adapted by facilitator however a trained assistant for every ten participants was essential and this was implemented.

Small Business & Management Sciences Student Groups

Outcomes: Some of students did not experienced accounting game as 'challenging enough' and an auditing level had to be incorporate to keep interest going. This led to the addition of 'red alert' questions added to ensure interest and discussions going during the game. 'Red alert' questions add to the knowledge gain and was link with concepts taught in formal educational instruction.

Management Sciences Executive group

Outcomes: Positive response after playing three of the levels of the game lead to the approval for the implementation of the VALU-E game for Management Science students hosted at the Idea Gymnasium, CUT to facilitate entrepreneurship education during normal educational programme. Lectures see implementation in the curriculum as possible except for the time factor as session needs 1.5 – 2 hours.

Management and Business Science Students

Outcomes: Most participants indicated it was a fun experience, learning entrepreneurial skills and that they gain new decision directed knowledge playing the game and indicated that playing the game let them feel more confident to do business.

Community Group, Heidedal, Mangaung, FS

Education level: Participants had previous training in business studies – Four participants did business / accounting studies at school level and two participants studied business training at a higher education level.

Entrepreneurship interest: All participants indicate that they would like to own and manage their own business.
Game sessions played: Micro economy and Accounting.

Outcome: Do you feel that you learned something new?
Unedited comments of fourteen participants: "Team work is very important; in business patience is important to succeed & partnership goes a long way; I have to learn to be successful in business you need to take risks; I've learned to stay in one direction, keep going even if it is risky, also to spend money wisely in order to make a profit; learn financial planning on how to run and manage your books; how to work with people; how to manage a business as well as working on a budget; learn that accuracy is very important; learn how to handle the financial aspects in a business; I have learned the difference between skill needed to purchasing a business and to start up a business; accounting and how to manage money in your business; I learned how to make an income and profit; complications of money; how to manage finances."

Outcome: Suggestion on how to improve the session
Unedited comments of some participants: "More sessions; all was well put together; it was very good to learn about business planning; everything was perfect; everything was perfect; no suggestion, everything was perfect; not really – it is good; everything was fine; we need more time to continue."

Outcome: Were you at any point in the game, reminded of a concept that you have previously learned or experienced?

Unedited comments of 15 participants: "You have to double check the figures all the time; had my own business, just learned the importance of it and why certain things didn't work out; business plan is important and to manage your money well; it is very important to manage your business in order to expand the business; a business selling something that I made myself." Seven participants answered that they were not reminded of a concept learned or experienced before.

Assistant facilitator's observations and remarks recorded from unemployed persons interested in entrepreneurship:

Assistant 1 comments: "I have noticed that many of the participants don't know a lot about how to manage your finances on business aspects. The Valu-E game has help them on how to manage their finances and to teach participants how to do accounting. I would recommend that the Valu-E game should be use at high schools for scholars that have Accounting and Business Economics as a subject, to help them get a better understanding of the business industry."

> *Assistant 2 comments: "Participants indicated that this type of a game should be introduced in high schools so that the learners can have a foundation and knowledge of entrepreneurship from a young age. They wish that this type of a game could have been introduced 'back in the days' and maybe then they could have had businesses a long time ago. Specific feedback about games they played was as follow: The accounting game taught them how to be financially responsible by being able to understand the financial statements and how to manage the cash flow and to spend money wisely. They stated that the puzzle game needs focus to play and teamwork. This means that an entrepreneur needs to learn focus and work together as a team with his or her employees to achieve organisational objectives and goals. The micro economy game taught them the importance of having a business and the way of spending and gaining (acquisition) at the same time, because when you spend more, you gain - for a business to grow and being able to take calculated risk within the business."*

5. Summary of results

The game design tested to provide design information for the development of other educational gaming tools resulted in the following suggestions: a trained assistant is needed for every ten to fifth-teen participants for an educational facilitated game; the game can be adapted by a well-trained facilitators and assistants to be an effective educational tool for different educational levels and business experience, the majority of participants indicated it was a fun experience and that they gain new decision directed knowledge playing the game. More sessions were requested and more time to continue playing the game.

Observations from instructors was that the game taught participants to become more supportive of each other in their group in gaining knowledge due to the competitive nature of this gaming teaching method. If incorporated at school level it will create an increase interest in entrepreneurship. By adding competitive game elements in online operating system courses, Lai et al (2012), increased the level of attraction of courses to students, willing to spend time because they want to win, thus fulfilling the purpose of elevating learning motivation.

Educational games foster entrepreneurship however after a first trial of development and roll out, it was observed that the game can be developed and deployed successfully but that there is a need for funding for staff training, further development of the game and materials. Fostering entrepreneurship by offering incentives to the facilitators and student participants (e.g. assessment marks for game sessions to serve as assignments). Resistance to implement gaming as an educational tool is due to the lecture's choice of resources and methods. Preparation time, knowledge of the method, characteristics of the group and incentive from institution (Riccio, Sakata and Carastan, 2000) plays a role.

6. Conclusions

There is a demand for entrepreneurial skills, therefore a demand for methods to teach how to and to change attitudes towards starting a business. In game design the training must match the requirements of the target groups as participants come from different backgrounds with varied profiles of previous education or exposure to business. In a facilitated game the instructor can react on the group dynamics during a session and adapt the game to the specific situation. Observation of assistant facilitators do have value and can improve outcomes during training and providing valuable feedback to improve game development.

Universities' strategic drive to become true entrepreneurial universities is needed to change attitudes towards promoting entrepreneurship / starting a business among students and staff. Curriculum changes implementing entrepreneurial games as education methodology need the buy-in from the institution and staff.

The study shows the needs and requirements for a facilitated educational game for entrepreneurial education and training in the South African context and outlines an adaptive implementation process for such a game. The VALU-E game create interest among participants to start their own business enhancing socio-economic development. Current commercialization of the game is proof that gaming can be both educational and a business venture. Applying new technologies to some of the levels will facilitate access for other target groups that can benefit from this educational multi-level entrepreneurial game.

There is still more demand for systematic research in the effects of educational games on the entrepreneurial skills and sustainability attitudes of participants.

Acknowledgements

The concept development of the educational game system VAL-U (VALues & yoU) is a joint effort of Aalen University of Applied Sciences, Germany and the Central University of Technology (CUT), Bloemfontein, Free State, South Africa. CUT staff members of the Department of Management Science developed the manual under the guidance of Profs Holzbaur and Strydom. Game board design and further development of the VALU-E game was done by Mr Marnus van Zyl. VAL-U game sessions for assessment were facilitated by Dr Edem Agbobli, students of CUT and students of Aalen University of Applied Sciences. VALU-E game sessions for assessment were facilitated by Mr Marnus van Zyl, assisted by Me Laurentia Klassen and Me Itumeleng Mohapi, providing invaluable feedback.

References

Bühr, M. and Rey, S. (2011) MICRO-ECO-NOMY: BWL-Planspiel für Schwellenländer. In Holzbaur, U., Marx, I.: Handlungs- und Erlebnisorientierung in der tertiären Bildung, Aachen: Shaker pp 257 – 268.

Chan, K.Y.G., Tan, S.L., Hew, K.F.T. *et al.* (2017) Knowledge for games, games for knowledge: designing a digital roll-and-move board game for a law of torts class, RPTEL Vol 12, Issue 7 https://doi.org/10.1186/s41039-016-0045-1

Csikszentmihalyi, M. (1990) Flow: The Psychology of Optimal Experience, New York, NY: Harper and Row.

Elgood, C. (1989) Handbook of Management Games, Aldershot: Gower.

Entrepreneurship 2020 Action Plan, Reigniting the entrepreneurial spirit in Europe, COMMUNICATION FROM THE COMMISSION TO THE EUROPEAN PARLIAMENT, THE COUNCIL, THE EUROPEAN ECONOMIC AND SOCIAL COMMITTEE AND THE COMMITTEE OF THE REGIONS.

Fellnhofer, K. (2018) Game-based entrepreneurship education: impact on attitudes, behaviours and intentions. World Review of Entrepreneurship, Management and Sustainable Development, Vol 14 (1/2), pp 205-228.

Fox J., Pittaway L., Uzuegbunam I. (2018) Simulations in Entrepreneurship Education: Serious Games and Learning Through Play, Entrepreneurship Education and Pedagogy Vol 1, Issue 1, pp 61-89.

Free State Growth and Development Strategy (2014) http://app.spisys.gov.za/files/pula/topics/3037832/Provincial_Strategies/Free_State_Province/file_84516279.

Games, Learning, and Society group (2005/2007) https://www.academia.edu/8692640/Proceedings_of_the_Games_Learning_Society_Conference_Vol_3

Gibb, A. (2002) In pursuit of a new enterprise and entrepreneurship paradigm for learning: Creative destruction, new values, new ways of doing things and new combinations of knowledge, International Journal of Management Reviews, Vol 4, Issue 3, pp 213–232.

Hattie, J. (2009) Visible learning: A synthesis of over 800 meta-analyses relating to achievement. London, England: Routledge.

Krajger, I., Lattacher, W. and Schwarz, E. J. (2018) Creating and testing a game-based entrepreneurship education approach. In International conference on interactive collaborative learning (pp. 697–709). Cham: Springer.

Lai, C-H., Lee, T-P., Jong, B-S., *et al.* (2012) A Research on Applying Game-Based Learning to Enhance the Participation of Student. In: Park J., Jeong YS., Park S., Chen HC. (eds) Embedded and Multimedia Computing Technology and Service. Lecture Notes in Electrical Engineering, vol 181. Springer, Dordrecht.

Lee W-C., Huang W-C., Liu Y-C., *et al.* (2011) A Study of Cooperative and Collaborative Online Game-Based Learning Systems. In: Chang M., Hwang WY., Chen MP., Müller W. (eds) Edutainment Technologies. Educational Games and Virtual Reality/Augmented Reality Applications. Edutainment 2011. Lecture Notes in Computer Science, vol 6872. Springer, Berlin, Heidelberg.

MacKenty, B. (2006) All Play and No Work, School Library Journal, Vol 52, pp 46-48.

Marzano, R. J. (2010) Using Games to Enhance Student Achievement. Meeting Students Where They Are, Vol 67, pp 71-72.

Pannese, L. and Carlesi, M. (2007) Games and learning come together to maximize effectiveness: The challenge of bridging the gap, British Journal of Educational Technology, Vol 38, No. 3, pp 438-454.

Powell, K. C. and Kalina, C. J. (2009) Cognitive and social constructivism: Developing tools for an effective classroom. Education, Vol 130, No 2, pp 241-250.

Proulx J-N and Romero, M. (2016) Game and Learning Mechanics Under the Perspective of Self-determination Theory for Supporting Motivation in Digital Game Based Learning. International Conference on Games and Learning Alliance. DOI: 10.1007/978-3-319-40216-1_15

Ryan, R. M., & Deci, E. L. (2000) Self-determination theory and the facilitation of intrinsic motivation, social development and well-being. American Psychologist,55(1), 68–78.

Riccio, E.L., Sakata, M.C.G and Carastan, J. (2000) Teaching – learning methods in accounting education – an empirical research in the Brazillian scenario. Accounting Research in Brazilian Universities. - 1962 - 1999, Caderno de Estudos.

Salter, A. (2019) Why Games? Chronicle of Higher Education, Games in the Classroom. Digital Pedagogy - A Guide for Librarians, Faculty, and Students. https://guides.library.utoronto.ca/

Smale, M. A. (2011) Learning through quests and contests: Games in information literacy instruction, Journal of Library Innovation, Vol 2, No. 2, pp 36-55.

Strydom, A. and Holzbaur, U. (2018) Project Proposal: VAL-U game, unpublished.

Taub, M., Sawyer, R., Smith, A., *et al.* (2020) The agency effect: The impact of student agency on learning, emotions, and problem-solving behaviors in a game-based learning environment. Computers and Education, Vol 147, pp. 103781.

Van den Berg, A. (2011) Fostering Entrepreneurship via Planning Games. In Holzbaur, U., Marx, I.: Handlungs- und Erlebnisorientierung in der tertiären Bildung, Aalen, pp 248 – 256.

Van den Berg, A., Bühr, M., Holzbaur, U., *et al.* (2009) Experiential Methods for Education Entrepreneurs. In: Haubrock, A., Rieg, R. (eds.) Erste Aalener KMU-Konferenz – Beiträge zum Stand der KMU-Forschung. pp 167 – 195.

Vogelgsang, M. (2008) Konzeption und Implementierung eines einfachen und kulturübergreifenden Planspiels zur Einführung in die Grundlagen der Betriebswirtschaft. Diplomarbeit. Aalen: Hochschule Aalen.

Weston, A (2019) Teaching as the Art of Staging: A Scenario-Based College Pedagogy in Action, Sterling, Virginia: Stylus Publishing, LLC.

Wu, T.-C. E., Scott, D. and Yang, C.-C. (2013) Advanced or Addicted? Exploring the Relationship of Recreation Specialization to Flow Experiences and Online Game Addiction, Leisure Sciences Vol 35, Issue 3, pp 203-217.

Zulfiqar, S., Sarwar, B., Aziz, S., *et al.* (2019) An Analysis of Influence of Business Simulation Games on Business School Students' Attitude and Intention Toward Entrepreneurial Activities, Journal of Educational Computing Research, Vol 57, No. 1, pp 106-130.

Estimating the Size of Angel Investment Activity in Canada

Martin Croteau and Kenneth Grant
Ryerson University, Toronto, Canada
m.croteau@ryerson.ca
kagrant@ryerson.ca
DOI: 10.34190/EIE.20.166

Abstract: There is increasing interest in the role of entrepreneurial ecosystems in the creation and development of early stage ventures, with Angel investment seen as a critical component. Angels' investment may have greater impact on new venture formation in Canada than the more frequently publicised investments of VCs, funding many more startups at earlier stages. Measurement of the level of Angel investment in any ecosystem is challenging since investments are informal and are not reported/tracked in any national system unless the angel is part of an angel investment group. However, knowledge of the level of angel activity in an economy is of great importance to policy makers and other analysts. This challenge is recognised and analysed in major economies, where significant efforts have been made to measure the scale of angel investment. Surprisingly, very little data is available about the level of angel investment in Canada, to enable policy decisions and to make comparisons to other jurisdictions, with a lack of knowledge of the numbers of angel investors, the total investment support provided and the number of ventures that receive investment. Using a deductive reasoning approach and survey data from both the demand and supply side of equity investment in Canada, this study provides a conservative estimate of Canadian angel investment to be of the order of $1.4-1.76 billion in 2017.

Keywords: Angel investment, entrepreneurial ecosystem, Canada

1. Introduction

There is increasing interest in how entrepreneurial ecosystems foster the creation and development of early stage ventures. While there is no accepted definition of the "entrepreneurial ecosystem", many suggest a value-chain of resources, from the ideation/networking activities that lead to the birth of new ventures, to the business accelerators/incubators ("BAIs") that feed angel investors ("angels"), to the venture capital ("VC") funds that fuel the ongoing growth of ventures towards maturity. As Mitra (2008) states "The bulk of the responsibility of early stage investment is shouldered by angels."

Angel investment is a critical component of the entrepreneurial ecosystem that supports new ventures. Previous studies (Liu, 2000) have suggested that angel investment may have greater impact on new venture formation and economic development in Canada than the much more frequently publicised investments of VCs. Although it is often suggested that the levels of total investment by Angels and VCs are broadly similar, angels make smaller investments in many more companies than do VCs. In the United States, Entrepreneur Magazine estimated in 2013 that angels invest in 16 times as many startups as do VCs (Entis, 2013) and Mason (2008), drawing on Gaston (1998) and Sohl (2003) claims that Angels are the most important source of equity capital, significantly exceeding the investments of VCs. Thus, their impact on economic development, particularly on employment is likely much higher than that of VC investment. Surprisingly, the impact of angel investment in Canada is unclear, especially when compared to the data available in other jurisdictions. Very little is known, except anecdotally, about the number of angels in Canada, the total investment support they provide and the number of ventures that receive investment.

This lack of data is a major concern. Hechavarria and Ingram (2014) suggest that measures of entrepreneurial activity are very important in evaluating an entrepreneurial ecosystem. A need exists to better inform public policy with respect to the characteristics, practices, patterns and perspectives of Canadian informal investors.

This study provides updated estimates of the scale and impact of angel investment activity in Canada, using data from Statistics Canada's 2018 Survey on Financing and Growth of Small and Medium Enterprises.

2. Previous research

This section provides a brief review of the extant literature on the role of risk capital within entrepreneurial ecosystems, the unique nature of angel investment and previous estimates of angel activity in Canada.

2.1 Entrepreneurial ecosystems

Ketikidis et al. (2017) et al point out that entrepreneurship "can only thrive if equipped with a well-developed ecosystem, with coordination between all relevant stakeholders". In recent years, increasing interest has been given to the concept of an entrepreneurial ecosystem, to such an extent that Brown and Mason (2017) called it "...one of the latest 'fads' in entrepreneurship research".

Spigel and Harrison (2017) defined an entrepreneurial ecosystem as "...a conceptual umbrella for the benefits and resources produced by a cohesive, typically regional, community of entrepreneurs and their supported that help new high-growth ventures form, survive and expand." The term is widely used by policy-makers and practitioners to characterize the resources required by new ventures, and the relationships between these resources. However, the concept lacks conceptual rigour and its theoretical development lags behind policy and practical interest (Speigel and Harrison, 2017, Stam, 2015). Stam (2015) argues that, "the entrepreneurial ecosystem approach speaks directly to practitioners, but its causal depth and evidence base is rather limited." Alvedalen and Boschma (2017) suggested that the concept should further exploit the insights from network theory and should consider the systematic evolution of entrepreneurial ecosystem.

Population ecology and resource dependence theories that govern our understanding of natural ecosystems can also inform our understanding of how entrepreneurial ecosystems function. Carroll (1988) described the population ecology theory of organizations as an ecosystem-level process of selection and replacement, based largely an organization's compatibility to the ecosystem. Ventures compete for financial and human capital much like flora and fauna compete for resources within a natural ecosystem. The munificence of resources within an ecosystem dictates its carrying capacity - the size of the population it can support (Abernethy, 2001). Hence, the density of ventures that can survive within an entrepreneurship ecosystem is moderated by its resource availability through a dynamic process of venture birth and death (Hannan & Freeman, 1988). An increase in resource availability, such as investment capital, may lead to a temporary increase in the rate of new venture creation. However, the increase in the density of new ventures will create greater competition, making it increasingly difficult for new ventures to obtain the resources they need to survive, causing the population of ventures in the ecosystem to level off (Specht, 1993).

Resource dependency theory explains the role of interdependence between organizations on the procurement of resources within an ecosystem (Pfeffer and Salancik, 1978). Access to resources such as investment capital may become a basis of power when the resources required by an organization are controlled by other organizations. New ventures compete for access to capital within an ecosystem through a number of stages, with a new set of stakeholders controlling resource access at each stage.

Initial investment is often provided by the new venture founders themselves, or by friends and family who invest for non-economic reasons (Grant et al, 2018). In some jurisdictions, new ventures may qualify for government grants, loans or equity-based financing. Promising new ventures may be accepted by business accelerators and incubators (BAIs). In addition to any financial and/or in-kind support, BAIs perform a signalling function to potential investors with information on the quality of new ventures (Plummer et al, 2015).

New ventures with the greatest potential become candidates for equity financing. Angel investors are often the earliest source of equity financing (Grant et al. 2018) Ventures that perform well using angel investment may receive follow-on financing from a VC firm. which may continue over several investment rounds, and later-stage rounds may involve a mix of equity and debt instruments. A few ventures that receive equity financing will have a liquidity event providing a return on investment for angels or VCs, either through an Initial Public Offering or the acquisition of the venture (Rowley, 2017)

2.2 Angel investment

Capital availability is a critical resource within entrepreneurial ecosystems. Mason and Brown (2014) state: "Particularly important is a critical mass of seed and start-up investors to provide finance and hands on support." Angel investors are wealthy individuals who invest their own money in new ventures of their choosing (Lerner, Hardymon et al. 2012). Their investment criteria are highly individualized and, unlike VCs, may include both economic and non-economic criteria (Riding, Madill, & Haines, 2007). Compared to VCs, angels also generally invest in earlier stage ventures. Angels often prefer to invest within industries they know well through their own experience (Grant et al, 2018) thus they may provide valuable operational support to new ventures in addition to capital, and may use their professional network to provide access to potential customers or strategic partners.

Angel investment is informal by nature and has traditionally operated with a high-level of discretion, with "lone-wolf" angels investing ad hoc in opportunities presented through their professional networks. Over the last twenty years, more angels have been participating in managed groups (Mason, Botelho et al. 2019). Angel networks are membership-based organizations that aim to streamline access to high-potential investment opportunities, share the burden of conducting due diligence, and provide opportunities for networking and collaboration. As a result, angels increasingly make syndicated investments, with one experienced or knowledgeable angel acting as lead investors, and other angels following (Harrison and Mason 2019). However, many angel investments take place outside of networks and other portals and are inherently difficult, if not impossible, to measure and study (OECD. 2018).

2.3 Angel activity in Canada (500 words)

The National Angel Capital Organization (NACO), Canada's national industry association of angel networks, reports that in the 10-year period from 2010-2019, its members invested more than $1 billion, with a record high of $163 million in 2019 (Mason 2020). The annual gross value added to the Canadian economy by new ventures funded by NACO-affiliated angels over the 7-year period from 2010 to 2016 is estimated at CDN$1.7 billion (Grant, Croteau et al. 2019). However, the detailed data provided by NACO is drawn only from its own Angel group members, representing only one part of the Canadian Angel community.

Venture capital activity has been extensively studied in many jurisdictions due to the availability of reliable data sources. In 2019, Canadian VC firms invested $6.2 billion in 539 ventures, representing an increase of 69% from 2018 (CVCA, 2019). Similar reports on angel activity exist in other jurisdictions. For example, U.S. angel investment was estimated at $24.5 billion in 2015 (UNH Center for Venture Research, 2016), while in the UK it has been estimated to be about 1.5 billion pounds annually (UK Business Angels Association, 2020) In comparison, the level of angel investment activity in Canada in not well understood. Some observers have suggested the total annual angel investment in Canada might significantly exceed CDN$1 billion, but the figure has never been substantiated . Kerr, Lerner and Schoar (2010) found that total angel investment is likely greater than total VC investment in many industrialized countries.

NACO is the only organization that tracks angel investment activity in Canada, but its data is restricted to that provided voluntarily by its members. It remains unclear what proportion of total angel investment in Canada such angel networks represent, let alone what proportion of total investment is represented by angel investment. The most recent estimate of angel activity in Canada was published in 2011 by the Organisation for Economic Co-operation and Development (OECD) using data provided by NACO (Table 1).

Table 1: Estimates of the angel market and comparisons with venture capital (in millions USD)

	"Visible" angel market size (share of total market) in 2009	Estimated size of angel market in 2009	Total VC market in 2009
US	469 (3%)	17,700	18,275
Europe	383 (7%)	5,557	5,309
UK	74 (12%)	624	1,087
Canada	34 (9%)	388	393

**Note: VC market size includes VC investments in all stages.*
Source: OECD based on estimates by the Centre for Venture Research (CVR), EBAN (The European Trade Association for Business Angels, Seed Funds, and other Early Stage Market Players), and Canada's National Angel Capital Organisation (NACO). VC data based on industry statistics by EVCA/PEREP Analytics and PricewaterhouseCoopers/National Venture Capital Association MoneyTree Report and Canada's National Angel Capital Organization.

The OECD (2011) estimated that angel investment in Canada was USD$388 million in 2009, similar in size to the total VC market of USD$393 million. The estimate relies upon an extrapolation from the portion of the "visible" angel market represented by the NACO data (Mason and Harrison 2010). However, the OECD (2011) report provides no information on the source for the assumption that investments through angel groups represent 9% of the total angel market in Canada.

Riding (2008) estimated the number of angel investors in Canada using data from the Statistics Canada's 2002 and 2005 *Survey of Financing of Small and Medium Enterprises,* which asked Canadian business owners about the number and average amount of investments made in unrelated private companies. Riding (2008) conservatively estimated that the market for informal capital in Canada in 2001 was at least CDN$9.64 billion, and that 15,800 Canadian angels invested approximately CDN$1.9 billion in 2004.

Liu (2000) estimated that the total stock of angel investment in Canada could be more than CDN$12 billion and angel activity could be over CDN$3 billion in 1999. However, these estimates lacked rigour and were based largely on anecdotal evidence and the crude assumption that the size of the angel market exceeds that of VC. Farrell Farrell (2000) described several previous estimates of angel activity in Canada, which ranged dramatically between CDN$1 and 20 billion annually.

Given the wide range of estimates, "it seems evident that yet more precise estimates are required" (Riding, 2008, p. 358), ideally using multiple methods.

3. Data and methodology

3.1 Data source

The source of the data used is the *Survey on Financing and Growth of Small and Medium Enterprises* (Statistics Canada, 2020). This survey collects information on the financing activities of Canadian businesses to inform public policy and private sector market analysis. The survey collects data on the types of debt, lease and equity financing that small- and medium-sized enterprises (SMEs) have obtained or have attempted to obtain, and the circumstances that have affected the financing and growth of their businesses.

Initiated by the Task Force on the future of the Canadian Financial Services Sector in 1998 (Mason and Harrison, 2008), the survey was first conducted by Statistics Canada in 2000, and subsequently in 2001, 2004, 2007, 2011, 2014 and 2017. The survey has evolved considerably over time based on the needs and interests of policymakers and private-sector stakeholders. The most recent survey was overseen by a consortium led by Innovation, Science and Economic Development Canada, a federal government department mandated to "foster a growing, competitive and knowledge-based Canadian economy." (Government of Canada, 2020).

The 2017 *Survey on Financing and Growth of Small and Medium Enterprises* used SMEs as its sampling unit. It included a base sample size of 17,323 SMEs out of a total target population of 840,989 SMEs in Canada on the Business Register, a national database of for-profit companies that reported operating activities in the previous year. Companies that represented certain special populations were added from lists provided by other government departments added, increasing the unduplicated size of the sample to 23,527 SMEs.

The reference period for the survey was the 2017 calendar year. Computer-assisted telephone interviews were conducted between February and June 2018. Responding to the survey was voluntary and data are collected directly from the respondents. The response rate to the survey was 59.7%, reducing the likelihood or non-response and selection biases (Riding, 2008). The survey data are an invaluable resource upon which to estimate the size and scope of angel activity in Canada.

3.2 Estimation techniques

Riding (2008) stated that "Collectively, it is understood that business angels invest more funds in more firms than does the formal venture capital industry, particularly with respect to early- stage enterprises. However, it is difficult to obtain precise estimates of business Angel activity," citing the challenges of identifying individual angels and tracking their activities. Despite Wetzel's (1983) conclusion that the number of angels "is unknown and probably unknowable", several methodological approaches have since been used to estimate the size and scope of angel activity, and to overcome the challenges inherent in the imperfect data that are available.

Mason and Harrison (2008) reviewed and categorized several methods available for estimating the informal investment market:

"Playing with Numbers":

This colourful term was used by Wetzel (1987) to describe "broad-brush" and "back-of-the-envelope" (Mason and Harrison, 2008, p. 313) estimates that use simple arithmetic to extrapolate fragments of data from a variety of sources. Such estimates are useful to provide a broad range and a sense of perspective of the scope of angel activity. However, they tie together disparate data using crude assumptions, leading to "quasi-facts" (Wetzel 1986, p. 87) that lack precision and cannot be relied upon. Nevertheless, they have contributed to our understanding angel investing and helped to advance the field of study.

Supply-side Approaches:

Supply-side approaches use data on samples of angel investors to estimate the size of angel activity for the entire population. This approach most often involves surveying the organizations or groups whose members best approximate the conventional profile of angels, which has proved largely ineffective and calls into question the representativeness of the estimates (Mason and Harrison, 2008). Riding and Short (1988) made novel use of the "capture-recapture" method commonly applied in biological ecosystems to predict the total number of angel investors in the Ottawa region based on a limited sample. This method is best suited for estimates within regional ecosystems rather than national-level estimates.

Demand-side Approaches:

Demand-side approaches to estimating angel activity use data from samples of ventures who received angel financing. This approach generally involves surveying small businesses to gather data on how many received angel financing, and the size and frequency of investment. The proportion of ventures with angel financing is then extrapolated to the entire population and multiplied by the average investment size to determine the total size of angel activity. Surveys of small businesses generally suffer from a low response rate, and a relatively small proportion of total small businesses receive angel financing, resulting in very small sample sizes (Mason and Harrison, 2008).

Investment-oriented Approaches:

Investment-side approaches use data from a sample of angel investments to estimate angel activity for the entire population. This approach frequently makes use of data collected by angel networks on the investments made by their members. Since investments through angel networks represent only the "tip of the iceberg" (Mason and Harrison, 2008, p. 323), estimates using this data must rely upon assumptions regarding the proportion of the total market that is made "visible" by angel networks (Harrison and Mason, 2010). Thus, such extrapolated estimates are only as reliable as their underlying assumptions.

McDonald's (2016) review of angel investment data and analysis found that the unit of analysis – investment, business or angel – can have a considerable impact on the interpretation of estimates of angel activity. Businesses were selected as the unit of analysis in this study for two reasons. First, demand-side approaches that make use of data from businesses are the most popular and have been used extensively in previous studies of other jurisdictions. This provides opportunity to incorporate learnings from previous work and creates a basis upon which to compare results with those using similar methods in other jurisdictions. Second, a demand-side estimate of angel activity in Canada has not been undertaken in a generation. Liu's (2000) estimate would be considered "playing with numbers", while Riding (2008) and OECD (2011) used supply-side and investment-oriented approached, respectively. A demand-side estimate would make an important contribution to our understanding of angel activity in Canada.

4. Findings

The survey included several questions that are relevant to the estimation of angel activity in Canada, asking the current owners of the business which sources of finance they used to either start or purchase the business, including financing from angel investors and VCs. The survey also asked if the business sought equity financing in the current year and if so, the value of the equity provided.

The target population of SMEs was categorized by the age of the business, its size in terms of number of employees, as well as its industry and geography. Businesses were considered a start-up if they had been in existence for less than two years. As shown in Table 2, of the base sample of 17,323 SMEs, 1,838 were categorized as startups (10.6%).

Table 2: Population and sample size for business age and size

Category	Population	Sample	Expected SE
Canada	**840,989**	**17,323**	
Age of business			
General population	810,585	15,485	
Start-ups	30,404	1,838	2.1%
Employment category			
1 to 4	487,166	7,379	1.2%
5 to 19*	253,047	4,187	1.5%
20 to 99*	79,213	2,681	2.1%
100 to 499*	11,061	2,318	2.2%

Source: 2017 Survey on Financing and Growth of Small and Medium Enterprises

Although angel investment is generally considered in the context of early-stage startups, the goal of this study was to estimate full scope of angel investment, regardless of characteristics of the investment target. Thus, the estimate of angel activity was not restricted based on the age or the size of the business.

4.1 Estimation of angel activity in Canada

The *2017 Survey on Financing and Growth of Small and Medium Enterprises* asked respondents: "In 2017, did your business seek equity financing?, further specifying that "this could be any request for new or additional financing from an investor, venture capital supplier, angel, members of your co-operative or friend or family member in exchange for a share of the ownership of the business." The results indicate that 0.8% of all SMEs requested equity financing in 2017. As shown in Table 3, the likelihood of seeking equity financing increased with the size of the business – from 0.4% of SMEs with 1-4 employees to 3.5% of those with 100-499 employees.

Table3: Equity financing

All SMEs	Requested equity financing (%)	Total amount of equity provided ($)	Avg. amount of equity provided ($)
1 to 499 employees	0.8	8,448,942,090	1,388,915
1 to 4 employees	0.4	1,366,185,132	776,553
5 to 19 employees	0.9	753,465,971	334,757
20 to 99 employees	2.0	2,871,347,477	1,790,509
100 to 499 employees	3.5	3,457,943,510	7,366,761

Source: 2017 Survey on Financing and Growth of Small and Medium Enterprises

The survey did not ask how many businesses received equity financing among those that sought it out. However, it did ask those that requested equity financing in 2017 to indicate the value of the equity provided. Total equity financing to SMEs in 2017 from all sources was estimated at $8.44 billion. The estimated average equity amount provided in 2017 was $1.38 million. These estimates include equity financing from cooperatives, venture capital firms, angels, and friends and family. Co-operatives represent a minute fraction (0.001%) of the total target population of SMEs in Canada and can be ignored.

In the first step toward isolating total market for angel financing, the VC investment was subtracted. In 2017, the Canadian Venture Capital Association (CVCA) reported 592 investments totaling $3.5 billion (CVCA, 2018). This included venture capital investments in all companies, including an undisclosed number that may not have been SMEs. The CVCA's Venture Capital Canadian Market Overview for 2017 identified fifteen "mega deals" of over $50 million. Examination of the employment data on the companies involved in these large investments found that four had more than 500 employees at the time of investment, totaling $440 million. Although a number of non-SME investments are likely still included in the estimate, the revised total amount of venture capital invested in Canadian SMEs in 2017 was $3.06 billion.

When VC investment is subtracted from the total equity financing to SMEs, the remaining $5.38 billion represents the market for equity financing from informal investors -- friends and family, and angels. Although the *Survey on Financing and Growth of Small and Medium Enterprises* provides no data to help segregating these two distinct sources of informal capital, Riding's (2008) analysis of the *2001 Survey on Financing of Small and Medium Enterprises* provides some guidance. This earlier iteration of the survey asked business owners a series of questions about their investment activity in other businesses, including whether they acted as operators in any of these other businesses and whether they were owned by family or friends.

As shown in Table 4, Riding (2008) used these data to discern four categories of informal investor in Canada and their proportion of the total market for informal financing.

Table 4: Types of informal investor

	Invested in businesses owned by family, friends?		
Acted as operators in investee firms?	Yes	No	Total
Yes	34.7%	37.5%	72.2%
No	14.0%	13.9%	27.8%
Total	48.7%	51.4%	100.0%

Source: Riding (2008), from 2001 Survey on Financing of Small and Medium Enterprises

- 1. Probable angels (13.9%)
- 2. Probable serial entrepreneurs (37.5%)
- 3. Passive love money (14.0%)
- 4. Active love money (34.7%)

Riding (2008) acknowledged that some unknown proportion of business owners in categories 2-4 were also angel investors, hence "the 13.9% of investors who did not invest in firms owned by friends or family and who did not act as operators must be regarded as a very conservative estimate of angel investors within the sampling frame employed for the survey." Riding (2008) used additional data from the 2001 survey on the amount and frequency of informal investments made by business owners and found that "probably angels" made larger and more frequent investments compared with other categories of informal investors. As a result, a minimum of 25% of the informal market is attributable to angels. Following Riding (2008), the conservative estimate of angel equity financing in Canada in 2017 is $1.35 billion ($5.38 billion x .25) with a margin of error of approximately $369 million.[1]

It should be noted that this estimate includes only angel equity financing, and excludes other investment instruments like debt. NACO (2018) reported that 13% of the angel investments made by their members in 2017 were structured as loans.

[1] *The Survey on Financing and Growth of SMEs'* estimates are based on sample results, and are subject to sampling error. Statistics Canada provides a statistical measure of the sampling error associated with a given estimate. The estimate of the total amount of equity provided had a Coefficient of Variation of 27.4%.

Assuming that the NACO data on investment instruments can be extrapolated to the entire population of angels, the size of the angel investment market in Canada in 2017, including equity and debt instruments, is estimated to be between $1.4 billion and $1.76 billion.

5. Discussion

As has been well established, quantifying the level of angel investment in an entrepreneurial ecosystem is extremely challenging, relying on anecdotal evidence and crude assumptions. Despite this, efforts have been made to produce such estimates in a number of national economies. Estimates are very important for those who wish to understand the impact of angels on the entrepreneurial ecosystem and to determine how best to provide support both to angels who provide risk capital and entrepreneurs who need it, particularly those that aspire to high growth.

This study provides the first detailed analysis of the Canadian market for angel financing in nearly a decade, over which period the Canadian entrepreneurial ecosystem has evolved considerably (Startup Genome, 2019). Through deductive reasoning, drawing on demand-side data, supported by the related data provided by CVCA and NACO, has allowed the provision of an estimate range that goes well beyond the "playing with numbers" that Mason and Harrison (2018) used to describe many such efforts.

It would seem reasonable to suggest that the range of $1.4 to 1.76 billion is an under-estimation of the total market for angel financing in Canada given the highly conservative assumptions used to derive it. First, Riding's (2008) definition of "probable angels" (13.8% of informal investors) was chosen to specify an "angel". Riding acknowledged that this definition excludes an unknown number of angels found among other categories of informal investors. Next, the size of the venture capital market was over-estimated since it includes an unknown number of investments in companies with less than 500 employees. Since the estimated size of the angel financing market is derived from subtracting venture capital from the total equity market, an over-estimation of venture capital inevitably leads to an under-estimation of the angel financing market.

6. Conclusions and next steps

This project has developed a current and conservative estimate of the scale of angel investment in Canada. It is the first such estimate done in a decade, using a more rigorous approach than has previously been adopted. Thus, it provides a foundation from which comparisons can be made between Canada and other similar jurisdictions.

Future work will include longitudinal comparative analysis between different national entrepreneurial ecosystems as well as the extension of the model used, to capture better estimates of the local impact of informal angels. In addition, it would be useful to develop better estimates of the number of investments carried out by Canadian angels.

References

Farrell, A. E. (2000). Literature review and industry analysis of informal investment in Canada: A research agenda on angels. Ottawa, Industry Canada

Entis, L. (2013). Where Startup Funding Really Comes From, Entrepreneur Magazine, September 20th, 2013.

Gaston, R. J., (1989). The Scale Of Informal Capital Markets. Small Business Economics. 1: 223-230.

Grant, K. A., et al. (2019). Fact vs. Fiction: The Role of Angel Investment in New Venture Survival. ISPIM Conference Proceedings, The International Society for Professional Innovation Management (ISPIM).

Grant, K.A., Padmanaban, D. & El-Kebbi, A. (2018). The Early Investment Ecosystem for Start-ups in Canada, a Preliminary Study, Kindai Management Review. Vol. 6, 2018

Harrison, R. T. and C. M. Mason (2019). "Venture Capital 20 years on: reflections on the evolution of a field." Venture Capital 21(1): 1-34.

Hechavarria, D. M. & Ingram, A. (2014). A review of the entrepreneurial ecosystem and the entrepreneurial society in the United States: an exploration with the global entrepreneurship Monitor dataset. Journal of Business and Entrepreneurship, 26, 1- 35

Lerner, J., et al. (2012). Venture capital & Private equity: A casebook. Toronto, John Wiley and Sons.

Liu, Y. (2000). "An overview of angel investors in Canada." MFA paper.

Mason, C., et al. (2019). "The changing nature of angel investing: some research implications." Venture Capital **21**(2-3): 177-194.

Mason, C. M. and R. T. Harrison (2010). "Annual report on the business angel market in the United Kingdom: 2008/09." Department for Business Innovation and Skills 2010.

Mason, C. M. and R. T. Harrison (2008). "Measuring business angel investment activity in the United Kingdom: a review of potential data sources." Venture Capital **10**(4): 309-330.

Mitra, S. (2008). Stimulus Package For Entrepreneurs, Forbes Magazine. Retreived from https://www.forbes.com/2008/09/11/mitra-tax-policy-tech-enter-cx_sm_0912mitra.html#8579f8750ab3

Mason, C. M. (2008). *The real venture capitalists: a review of research on business angels*. Retrieved from https://www.strath.ac.uk/rnediafdepartmentslhuntercentrelresearch/worldngpapers/lJMdef

Mason (2020). A Decade of Deals: Annual Report on Angel Investing in Canada. National Angel Capital Organization. Toronto. July, 2020.

OECD (2016), Financing SMEs and Entrepreneurs 2016: An OECD Scoreboard, OECD Publishing, Paris, https://doi.org/10.1787/fin_sme_ent-2016-en.

OECD (2011). Financing high-growth firms: The role of angel investors. Available at SSRN 1983115.

Riding, A. L. and D. M. Short (1988). "On The Estimation of The Investment Potential of Informal Investors: A Capture/Recapture Approach." Journal of Small Business & Entrepreneurship **5**(5): 26-40.

Plummer, L.A., Allison, T.H. & Connolly, B.L. (2015). Better Together? Signaling Interactions in New Venture Pursuit of Initial External Capital. The Academy of Management Journal. June 2015.

Rowley, J. (2017). Here's How Likely Your Startup Is To Get Acquired At Any Stage, Techcrunch, July 17th, 2017, retrieved from https://techcrunch.com/2017/05/17/heres-how-likely-your-startup-is-to-get-acquired-at-any stage/?guccounter=1&guce_referrer=aHR0cHM6Ly93d3cuZ29vZ2xlLmNvbS8&guce_referrer_sig=AQAAAIA5NiXsitG4 2XJKoD0KmTu9J6WdF3VJ0WE_uj-chiV5IWq5LRoJwUiibGbtJb0fiq8LlUPB-5eiUpr2Tar5r34dqtnOC4LpysP-bml7NUFg8gRlzqofVrsT8Av0pV9RnoOWDdaTJ1Qk7E6O1NjepcGtJpyrQifJ7P2t-XbogkJU

Sohl, J.E. (2007). The organisation of the informal venture capital market. In: Handbook of Research on Venture Capital, edited by H. Landström. Edward Elgar, Cheltenham, pp. 347-368

Startup Genome (2017). Global startup ecosystem report 2017. San Francisco. https://startupgenome.com/gser2019.

UK Business Angels Association (2020). Introduction to Angel Investment. Retrieved from https://www.ukbaa.org.uk/services-for-entrepreneurs/support-and-advice/angel-investment-right-business/#:~:text=The%20angel%20investment%20market,-Angel%20investing%20is&text=Whilst%20the%20market%20is%20relatively,in%20early%2Dstage%20businesses%20 annually.

Wetzel Jr, W. E. (1983). "Angels and informal risk capital." Sloan Management Review (pre-1986) 24(4): 23.

Wetzel, W. E. (1986). Informal risk capital: Knowns and unknowns. Cambridge, MA, Ballinger.

An Empirical Study on the Coherence Between Self-Complexity, Entrepreneurial Capability and the Propensity to Step Into Entrepreneurship

Francis Dams[1], Jarl Kampen[1], Alexis Jacoby[1] and Jesse Segers[2,3]
[1]University of Antwerp, Antwerpen, Belgium
[2]Sioo, The Netherlands
[3]Exeter University, UK
francis.dams@uantwerpen.be
jarl.kampen@uantwerpen.be
alexis.jacoby@uantwerpen.be
jessesegers@sioo.nl
DOI: 10.34190/EIE.20.194

Abstract: This study is part of the research that investigates the development of entrepreneurial propensity among individuals with strong entrepreneurial capabilities. We researched quantitatively and empirically whether self-complexity can explain why entrepreneurial capability and entrepreneurial propensity do not seem to go together automatically. We test hypotheses about the relation between self-complexity, career decision difficulty, entrepreneurial propensity and entrepreneurial capability. Contrary to what was hypothesized, the data obtained from 584 respondents showed non-coherence between self-complexity on the one hand and all the other variables on the other hand. We claim the relevance of establishing and documenting these neutral results in view of the question why and how individuals develop the decisions to step into active entrepreneurship. In search for alternative explanations to understand the data we discuss the significant negative correlation in the data between entrepreneurial capability and career decision difficulty on the one hand and the positive correlation between entrepreneurial capability and entrepreneurial propensity on the other hand.

Keywords: entrepreneurial intention, entrepreneurial capabilities, correlation model, self-complexity, career choice

1. Introduction

Policymakers are seeking measures to develop more entrepreneurs with ambitious, high-growth potential, aiming beyond the mere creation of more entrepreneurs (European-Commission, 2013; Stam et al., 2012). Scholars have addressed among other issues the following two questions: firstly, what determines whether an individual decides to step into active entrepreneurship and secondly, what are the characteristics that make an individual more competent to fulfil successfully an entrepreneurial role. Dams and Segers (2018a) refer to the answers to these two questions as the antecedents of Entrepreneurial Propensity and Entrepreneurial Capability. They reviewed the most researched antecedents of these two constructs and concluded that the majority of antecedents can have opposite effects on Entrepreneurial Capability and propensity. This is in line with the conclusion of Bayon, Vaillant, and Lafuente (2015), that objective Entrepreneurial Capability has not shown up as a favorable explanatory variable when modelling entrepreneurial intention and behavior. This is problematic as the capable non-actors of entrepreneurship constitute an unused capacity of economically desired entrepreneurial potential. Models for entrepreneurial intention like the theory of planned behavior (Ajzen, 1991) and the anterior model of the entrepreneurial event by Shapero and Sokol (1982) are well established (Krueger, Reilly, & Carsrud, 2000), however, they do not directly offer an explanation for the paradoxical tension between Entrepreneurial Propensity and Capability. In order to broaden the understanding in this matter Dams and Segers (2018b) proposed theory how Self-Complexity could explain why individuals, who are expected to have the necessary capacities to do well as an active entrepreneur can struggle to develop entrepreneurial intention in the first place. This theory adopts Ibarra's (2005) identity transition theory about voluntary career changes and its application to a career transition into entrepreneurship (Farmer, Yao, & Kung-Mcintyre, 2011; Hoang & Gimeno, 2010). Hoang and Gimeno (2010) have introduced the identity complexity of the founder in this theory and they propose that Self-Complexity has a favorable effect on turning entrepreneurial intention into actual entrepreneurial behavior. Dams and Segers (2018b) acknowledge this role of Self-Complexity but they add that Self-Complexity would hinder the development of entrepreneurial intention in the first place and that Self-Complexity would cohere with Entrepreneurial Capability. Yet, the potentially opposite coherences between Self-Complexity and the development of entrepreneurial intention on the one hand and Entrepreneurial Capability on the other hand have not been examined experimentally. The present study offers a first empirical evaluation to fil that gap.

2. Theory and hypothesis development

In this section we explain in further detail the model and the main constructs used in this theory. We describe step by step how the relations between the constructs are theorized and how this leads to the hypotheses that are tested in the empirical study. Figure 1 depicts the constructs and their hypothesized coherences. We limit ourselves in this study to testing a correlation model, we refrain from including propositions about causality in the path-model as for certain relations alternative causalities can be envisaged. In first instance we want to test whether the correlations that go with the propositions can be established empirically.

Self-Complexity and Career Decision Difficulty

Self-Complexity is defined, as it was originally by Linville (1987), as the degree in which the identity is represented by a greater number of cognitive self-aspects and the degree in which a greater distinction among self-aspects is maintained. Career Decision Difficulty is defined as the difficulty to develop the progression of thoughts by which an individual amalgamates self-knowledge and occupational knowledge to arrive at an occupational choice (Kaur & Singh, 2017; Osipow, Carney, Winer, Yanico, & Koschier, 1987). In order to link Self-Complexity with Career Decision Difficulty, we refer to the identity transition theory for voluntary career changes by Ibarra (2005). She explains that a new active professional self has to be formed in order to initiate career transition behavior. According to Ibarra's identity transition theory, the new active self is developed out of a liminal state in which many future selves are simultaneously present in the mind of the individual, until one alternative self takes the overhand to form the new active self. The suggested dynamics of lifting the liminal state implies that the liminal state is more incessant, when it is more difficult to identify a sufficiently unanimous preferred new self. It seems reasonable to expect that a unanimous preference is less likely to occur when more facets are taken into consideration by the individual, or when the individual evaluates the alternatives at multiple time points in the future or when more alternative possible selves are present (Dams & Segers, 2018b). This is why we propose that Self-Complexity correlates with Career Decision Difficulty, being the difficulty to designate a new active professional self, a difficulty, which stabilizes the status quo in the current career. Research data on this stabilizing effect on the liminal state in the identity transition process, are scarce. However, work by Halberstadt, Niedenthal, and Setterlund (1996) describes negative effects of Self-Complexity on the ease of decision making, in particular in relation to the difficulty to make career decisions, which is in line with the first hypothesis we propose:

Hypothesis 1: Self-Complexity is positively related to Career Decision Difficulty

Career Decision Difficulty and Entrepreneurial Propensity

We defined Entrepreneurial Propensity as how close an individual is to becoming an active entrepreneur (Dams & Segers, 2018a, p. 917): "Qualitatively this dimension ranges from being non-interested, to having different levels of favorable orientations, dispositions, attitudes and desires, and to intending and performing the actual entrepreneurial behavior". Even if the factors and the decision processes that lead an individual to becoming an entrepreneur are not fully understood and it is being debated whether new theories are needed (Ramoglou, Gartner, & Tsang, 2018; Zhao, Seibert, & Hills, 2005), there is consensus that entrepreneurial behavior is planned behavior (Krueger et al., 2000). Consequently, even if developing entrepreneurial intention is not a sufficient condition for an individual to deploy entrepreneurial behavior (van Gelderen, Kautonen, Wincent, & Biniari, 2018), developing entrepreneurial intention is a necessary stage that has to be attained before the actual entrepreneurial behavior can be developed. Entrepreneurial intention we use as defined by Thompson (2009), who reviews the broad use of this construct in entrepreneurial research and proposes the following definition (Thompson, 2009, p. 676):

> *"...individual entrepreneurial intent is perhaps most appropriately and practically defined as a self-acknowledged conviction by a person that they intend to set up a new business venture and consciously plan to do so at some point in the future."*

As reaching entrepreneurial intention on the Entrepreneurial Propensity scale and establishing a new active self in the identity transition process are both necessary steps before entrepreneurial behavior can be developed, we draw a parallel between both theoretical approaches and therefore we propose:

Hypothesis 2: Career Decision Difficulty is negatively related to Entrepreneurial Propensity

Self-Complexity and Entrepreneurial Capability

Dams and Segers (2018a, p. 917) defined Entrepreneurial Capability of an individual as: "the subset of entrepreneurial performance that is fully attributable to the individual even in the absence of any entrepreneurial opportunity, propensity or activity". With respect to the coherence between Self-Complexity and Entrepreneurial Capability no empirical data were found in the entrepreneurship literature. Still, as entrepreneurship is seen as a highly multidisciplinary activity (Jain, 2011; Jain & Ali, 2013; Lazear, 2004; Sexton & Bowman, 1986; Stuart & Abetti, 1990; Zahra, Sapienza, & Davidsson, 2006), we suggest that entrepreneurially capable individuals are not expected to be low on Self-Complexity. Therefore we propose:

Hypothesis 3: Self-Complexity is positively related to Objective Entrepreneurial Capability

We have not found research in the field of entrepreneurship to support this suggestion, however, we found a report in the military context on the positive coherence between Self-Complexity and military leadership (Hannah, Balthazard, Waldman, & Jennings, 2010) and in the field of environmental management we found a report on the positive coherence between capabilities and Self-Complexity (Johnston, 2008).

Entrepreneurial Propensity and Entrepreneurial Capability

Dams and Segers (2018a) reviewed the most researched antecedents of Entrepreneurial Propensity and Capability and they report that nine out of twelve factors can have opposite effects on both constructs and they concluded that an individual who has entrepreneurial capabilities should not be expected to automatically aspire to a career as a founder of a new organization. Therefore we propose that Entrepreneurial Propensity is inversely related to Entrepreneurial Capability:

Hypothesis 4: Objective Entrepreneurial Capability is inversely related to Entrepreneurial Propensity

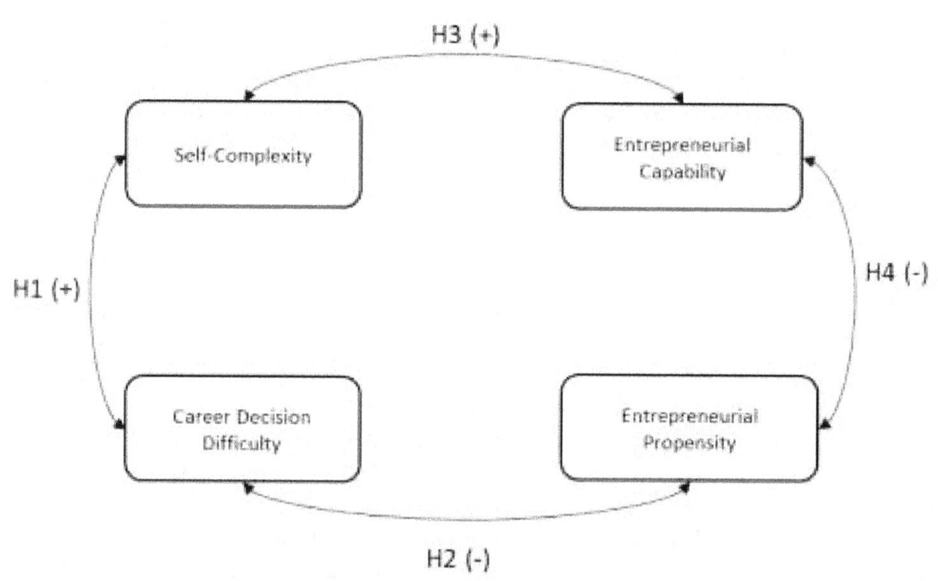

Figure 1: Theoretical model

3. Methodology

3.1 Variables and their operationalization

<u>**Main variables**</u>

***Entrepreneurial Capability*:**

Kyndt and Baert (2015) and Kyndt and Grosemans (2016) describe a study of an instrument, the ENTRE-Spiegel, that measures entrepreneurial competencies by asking the respondents how often they performed a certain behavior. With 48 questions, 11 competencies are measured: 1) Perseverance, 2) Ability to persuade, 3) Building networks, 4) Insight into the market, 5) Risk assessment, 6) Customer orientation, 7) Awareness for potential returns, 8) Taking responsibility, 9) Decisiveness, 10) Seeing opportunities, and 11) Planning for the future. In the current study we use the ENTRE-Spiegel 2.0 to measure the Entrepreneurial Capability construct. The output of the ENTRE-Spiegel 2.0 gives a score on every competency and we use the average as a mono-dimensional measurement of Entrepreneurial Capability which ranges from 1(low capability) to 6(high capability).

Entrepreneurial Propensity:

We have defined Entrepreneurial Propensity on a scale that ranges from being non-interested over developing entrepreneurial intention till the ultimate level where actual entrepreneurial behavior is established. Entrepreneurial Propensity in this study is operationalized with two variables. We measure with a continuous variable the Entrepreneurial Propensity of respondents who did not start a business yet. For this purpose we use the entrepreneurial intent scale developed and tested by Thompson (2009, p. 680). We report the average on a scale between 1(low propensity) and 6(high propensity).

Career Decision Difficulty

For measuring Career Decision Difficulty, we use the Career Decision-Making Difficulties Questionnaire (CDDQ), developed by Gati et al. (1996). They developed this questionnaire to examine empirically their general theoretical taxonomy of career decision-making difficulties. Over the years substantial verification was provided about the validity of the CDDQ (Gati & Saka, 2001; Osipow & Gati, 1998). Being based on a theoretical concept, the CDDQ offers sight on the underlying reasons for a high or low Career Decision Difficulty. The outcome of the questionnaire gives scores on 10 underlying difficulty categories grouped into three major categories and we use the overall average as the overall Career Decision Difficulty score between 1(low Career Decision Difficulty) and 9(high Career Decision Difficulty). The CDDQ was converted from a 44-item paper and pencil version into a 34-item internet based version (Gati & Saka, 2001). It is the 34-item version we use in this study.

Self-Complexity:

Hoang and Gimeno (2010) propose a theory, that assigns effects to the construct of Self-Complexity in the process of developing actual entrepreneurial behavior. The concept of Self-Complexity was defined by (Linville, 1985) as "... a function of two things: the number of aspects that one uses to cognitively organize knowledge about the self, and the degree of relatedness of these aspects". Linville also offers (1985, 1987) a concrete operationalization to measure Self-Complexity: The participants are asked to envisage themselves in as many roles as possible and to assign to every role the traits or characteristics that apply out of a given list of 33 traits. The Self-Complexity is then calculated with the H statistic of Scott (1962) in which the dimensionality of information is quantified:

$$SC = H = \log^2 n - (\Sigma\, n_i \log^2 n_i)/n$$

Since 1985 Self-Complexity has been frequently studied as an explanatory variable for well-being. Rafaeli-Mor and Steinberg (2002) published a review of 70 studies, all using the Self-Complexity metric put forward by Linville (1985), albeit with several variations in the measuring method. The studies use different trait list. They use a different number of traits, ranging from 12 to 80 traits with an average of 36 traits and they use a different fraction of traits with a negative connotation, ranging from 0% to 100%, with an average of 42%. We conclude that there is no reason to deviate from the original method to quantify Self-Complexity as proposed by Linville (1985). No evidence was presented that any of the variants is preferably different from the original one. Therefore we opt for the variant as developed by Linville with 33 traits of which 12 have a negative connotation and we calculate the H statistic to quantify Self-Complexity. We do apply the card sorting technique in an electronic way, respondents get as many screens as they see different roles for themselves. Every screen offers the 33 traits and the respondents are invited to tick the boxes of the traits that apply to the role that is considered on that particular screen. Screens are appended until the respondents do not see any further alternative roles for themselves. We do not force that the respondent provides a title for the self-aspect described on a particular screen. This computer implementation is close to the multipage paper variant as used by Hannah et al. (2010). Shilling and Brown (2015) use an electronic variant with one screen per role, however they ask the respondents to move the applicable traits from one column to another column, which requires more clicks to include or exclude a trait. The latter implementation is a method already introduced and used by Renaud and McConnell (2002) and McConnell et al. (2005).

Demographic variables:

We registered in this study the following demographics: gender, age, level of education and employment status. Level of education was operationalized by asking for the highest diploma they obtained: no diploma, primary education, secondary education, or higher education. Employment status was operationalized with the following categories: unemployed, student, employed, self-employed or retired.

3.2 Sample, data collection and response rates

For this study we have received the Entrepreneurial Capability data registered by the ENTRE-Spiegel 2.0 instrument in the period between August 2015 and October 2018. This sample contains complete Entrepreneurial Capability data of 22032 respondents who live in Flanders. In this sample 7821 respondents gave their consent to be contacted again, once a year, for further scientific research. In this study we contacted the 4000 anterior respondents of the 7821 who gave their consent. These 4000 respondents took the ENTRE-Spiegel 2.0 between August 2015 and December 2016. Between March and May 2019 they were asked to take part in the current study. 584 respondents returned the questionnaire, two reminders were sent to obtain that response rate.

3.3 The analysis plan

The data analysis consists of the frequencies of the demographic variables, the descriptives of the four main variables and the six zero-order bivariate correlation coefficients between the four main variables.

4. Analysis and results

4.1 Demographics

In table 1 we give an overview of the demographic data of the 584 respondents that submitted a questionnaire, it shows that the respondents cover a wide range of the population with respect to age, gender, diploma and professional status. The questionnaire was taken in the Dutch language and most respondents reside in Flanders. These data show that, when the 2019 questionnaire was taken, 197 respondents (33%) were self-employed, whereas a review of the original ENTRE-Spiegel data show that only 27 respondents of the 584 respondents in the current study (5%) were self-employed when they took part in the ENTRE-Spiegel 2.0 in 2015-2016.

4.2 Descriptives and correlations between the main variables

We analyzed the 4 main variables in a correlation analysis. Table 2 shows the descriptives and the bivariate zero-order correlations. Figure 2 shows the relations between the main variables with the zero-order correlation coefficients. The arrows of the non-significant relations are shown with a dashed line.

In the correlation analysis no significant coherence is established between Self-Complexity and any of the other variables. In addition we report a negative correlation coefficient between Career Decision Difficulty and Entrepreneurial Capability (see Table 2). The correlation analysis delivers a positive correlation coefficient between Entrepreneurial Capability and Entrepreneurial Propensity.

Table 1: Demographic properties of the respondents

Demographic Property (2019)	Frequency	Percentage
Gender		
Male	255	43.7
Female	329	56.3
	584	100
Age		
21-30	216	37.0

Demographic Property (2019)	Frequency	Percentage
31-40	133	22.8
41-50	121	20.7
51-60	107	18.3
61-70	7	1.2
	584	100
Educational level		
None	24	4.1
Primary Education	29	5.0
Secondary Education	278	47.6
Higher Education	253	43.3
	584	100
Professional situation		
Student	72	12.3
Unemployed	53	9.1
Employee	258	44.2
Self-employed	195	33.4
Retired	6	1.0
	584	100

Table 2: Main variables descriptives and zero-order correlations

	Descriptives						Zero-order correlations			
Main Variable	n=	Min	Max	Mean	SE	SD	1)	2)	3)	4)
1)Self-Complexity H-Statistic	311	0.44	4.45	1.70	0.045	0.79	-	.09	-.02	.03
2)Career Decision Difficulty	391	1.00	7.31	3.56	0.068	1.35		-	-.33*	-.14*
3)Entrepreneurial Capability	584	2.83	5.91	4.62	0.023	0.55			-	.21*
4)Entrepreneurial Propensity	383	1.00	6.00	3.09	0.066	1.29				-

* Correlation is significant at the 0.05 level (2-tailed).

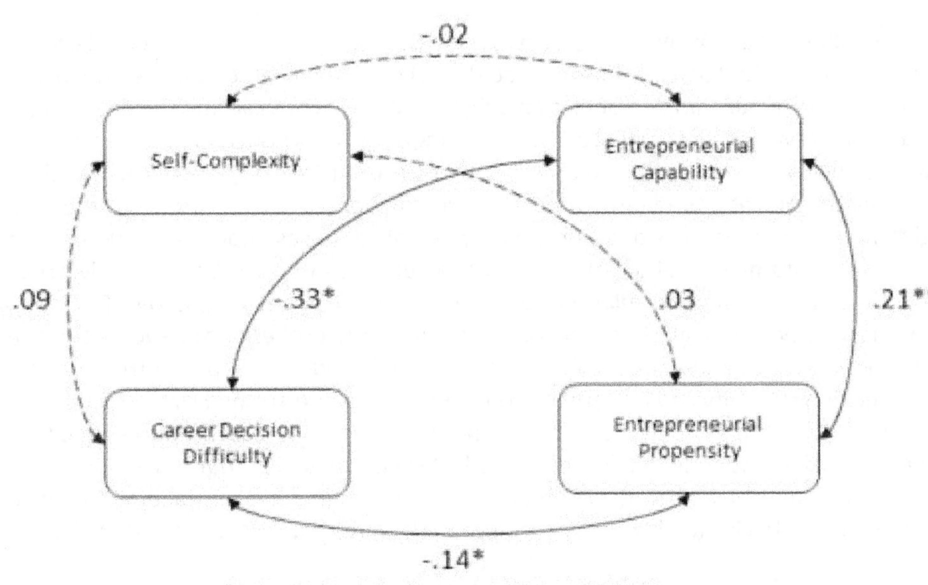

Figure 2: The zero-order correlation coefficients between the main variables

The correlation analysis between Career Decision Difficulty and Entrepreneurial Propensity shows a negative correlation coefficient (Table 2). As both variables have significant correlations with Entrepreneurial Capability we calculated the partial correlation coefficient between Career Decision Difficulty and Entrepreneurial Propensity while controlling for the effect of Entrepreneurial Capability, $r' = -.07$, $p = .30$.

5. Discussion

The data do not provide support for the hypotheses that Self-Complexity explains the paradoxical tension between Entrepreneurial Propensity and Entrepreneurial Capability. Our data show Self-Complexity to be stochastically independent from any of the other main variables, which falsifies hypotheses 1 and 3. This surprising result led us immediately to question the measurement method we applied to measure Self-Complexity. However, our method is fully consistent with its original specification, and the use of the computerized implementation is similar to the one described by McConnell et al. (2005). In the paragraphs further down we will discuss our understanding about these empirical independencies between Self-Complexity on the one hand and Career Decision Difficulty (hypothesis 1) and Entrepreneurial Capability (hypothesis 3) on the other hand.

Firstly we discuss the significant negative correlation we found in our sample population between Entrepreneurial Capability and Career Decision Difficulty. We hypothesized positive coherences with Self-Complexity and therefore we implied that Entrepreneurial Capability would be positively related to Career Decision Difficulty which is falsified by the empirical results (see Table 2). Looking for alternative explanations for this empirical result, we have reviewed the respective 10 and 11 factors out of which both constructs consist as measured. We note decisiveness in general is a factor in Entrepreneurial Capability whereas general indecisiveness is an underlying factor of Career Decision Difficulty. Therefore if no other effects play then general decisiveness can explain the observed negative coherence between Entrepreneurial Capability and Career Decision Difficulty. We proposed an opposite effect if Self-Complexity relates positively with Entrepreneurial Capability (hypothesis 3) and with Career Decision Difficulty (hypothesis 1). We will now further discuss how we interpret the negative empirical results about these two hypotheses.

The 3rd hypothesis was based on the argument that Entrepreneurial Capability is described as a multidisciplinary capability. We theorized that a multidisciplinary profile would go together with Self-Complexity. We found earlier research in other sectors that links Self-Complexity to management and leadership capabilities. As our sample population is not showing any coherence between Entrepreneurial Capability and Self-Complexity and as no other research in the field of entrepreneurship is pointing in that direction, we leave that line of thought. Still, we are not questioning that entrepreneurship is a multidisciplinary and multifaceted endeavor, an endeavor which does not seem to require that the individual possesses a high Self-Complexity .

The 1st hypothesis about the positive relation between Self-Complexity and Career Decision Difficulty is grounded on the proposition that Self-Complexity would stabilize the liminal state as described in Ibarra's (2005) identity transition theory. In our sample population Self-Complexity is not causing the decision process to stall. This is not necessarily revoking the applicability of the identity transition theory to entrepreneurial choice processes. When reviewing the underlying factors of Career Decision Difficulty, there can be other reasons than Self-Complexity why the process, to identify a new sufficiently dominant entrepreneurial self, stalls. Conflicts between the different factors the individuals or their surroundings see as important, lack of information about the self or incomplete information about the alternative future selves can be alternative reasons why the decision process stalls. The negative correlation we observe in the data between Career Decision Difficulty and Entrepreneurial Propensity is not in contradiction with the 2nd hypothesis, however after controlling both variables for the effect of Entrepreneurial Capability the observed and hypothesized negative coherence between Career Decision Difficulty and Entrepreneurial Propensity are explained by the confounding coherence both variables have with Entrepreneurial Capability. The hypothesis was based on the logic that the need to establish entrepreneurial intention on the Entrepreneurial Propensity scale requires a conviction and a decision and that therefore this would be hindered by Career Decision Difficulty. The neutral direct effect between both might indicate that Career Decision Difficulty is not necessarily different for entrepreneurial careers compared to other careers.

The data show a significant positive coherence between Entrepreneurial Capability and Entrepreneurial Propensity. This falsifies the 4th hypothesis which was based on the conclusions of the literature review by Dams and Segers (2018a) who concluded that entrepreneurially capable individuals do not automatically choose for active entrepreneurship. We acknowledge that this hypothesis cannot be withheld. However, as the proportion of shared variance of Entrepreneurial Capability and Entrepreneurial Propensity is at most in the order of 9% (taking the upper limit of the CI), this does not necessarily contradict the conclusions of the literature review on which it was built, and that high Entrepreneurial Capability is not systematically leading to entrepreneurial behavior.

6. Conclusions

We analyzed the answers of 584 respondents in Flanders about their Self-Complexity, their Career Decision Difficulty, their Entrepreneurial Propensity and their Entrepreneurial Capability. No evidence of a relationship of Self-Complexity with Career Decision Difficulty, nor with Objective Entrepreneurial Capability was found. Entrepreneurial Capability correlates positively with Entrepreneurial Propensity and the negative coherence between Career Decision Difficulty and Entrepreneurial Propensity that is observed can be explained by the correlations Entrepreneurial Capability has with both Career Decision Difficulty and Entrepreneurial Propensity. We agree with Van Witteloostuijn (2016) that it is important to share these negative and neutral conclusions with the research community and we propose alternative views to explain the empirical data. We have attempted to explain why Entrepreneurial Capability does not systematically lead to entrepreneurial behavior by including the concept of Self-Complexity in Ibarra's (2005) identity transition theory for voluntary career changes. The empirical results in our sample population do not support that theory, additionally our data indicate that Entrepreneurial Capability is inversely related with Career Decision Difficulty.

7. Outlook

We have not put in question the applicability of the identity transition theory itself. Yet, the question remains how the liminal state is lifted in view of a new entrepreneurial self, in particular in case the actor is entrepreneurially capable. Dams and Segers (2018a) report literature showing that a vast number of aspects play when an individual contemplates an entrepreneurial career change, they illustrate that for 9 out of 12 frequently studied aspects, invers effects are reported between capability and propensity. So if a possible entrepreneurial self always consists of many different aspects that are not expected to point in the same direction, then the complexity that hinders the formation of a sufficiently dominant alternative self might be intrinsically present in any capable entrepreneurial self regardless of the Self-Complexity of the individual as defined by Linville (1985). Therefore an individual decision process about entrepreneurial choice might stall independently of the Self-Complexity of the individual. We understand that high decisiveness can untie this stalling process as an highly decisive individual can more easily grant preference to a less unanimously favored alternative self. Still, in order to understand why entrepreneurially capable individuals do not opt more systematically for active entrepreneurship, we suggest to research and analyze further how capable individuals can be profiled based on the different aspects they consider favorable or unfavorable in view of taking an entrepreneurial choice decision. We suggest to study the degree of complexity of that profile and wonder how in individuals a dominant association of entrepreneurial profile variables forms and activates an entrepreneurial alternative self.

References

Ajzen, I. (1991). The theory of planned behavior. *Organizational behavior and human decision processes, 50*(2), 179-211.

Bayon, M. C., Vaillant, Y., & Lafuente, E. (2015). Initiating nascent entrepreneurial activities: The relative role of perceived and actual entrepreneurial ability. *International Journal of Entrepreneurial Behavior & Research, 21*(1), 27-49.

Dams, F., & Segers, J. (2018a). *Entrepreneurial Capability Versus Entrepreneurial Propensity: Why to Take the Non-Actors Even More Seriously*. Paper presented at the Proceedings of The 13th European Conference on Innovation and Entrepreneurship.

Dams, F., & Segers, J. (2018b). *Identity-Transition into Entrepreneurship: A Two-Phase Theory to Explain the Propensity-Capability Paradox*. Paper presented at the Proceedings of The 13th European Conference on Innovation and Entrepreneurship.

European-Commission. (2013). Entrepreneurship 2020 Action Plan: Reigniting the Entrepreneurial Spirit in Europe. In: European Commission Brussels.

Farmer, S. M., Yao, X., & Kung-Mcintyre, K. (2011). The behavioral impact of entrepreneur identity aspiration and prior entrepreneurial experience. *Entrepreneurship Theory and Practice, 35*(2), 245-273.

Gati, I., Krausz, M., & Osipow, S. H. (1996). A taxonomy of difficulties in career decision making. *Journal of counseling psychology, 43*(4), 510.

Gati, I., & Saka, N. (2001). Internet-based versus paper-and-pencil assessment: Measuring career decision-making difficulties. *Journal of Career Assessment, 9*(4), 397-416.

Halberstadt, J. B., Niedenthal, P. M., & Setterlund, M. B. (1996). Cognitive organization of different tenses of the self mediates affect and decision making. *Striving and feeling: Interactions among goals, affect, and self-regulation*, 123-150.

Hannah, S. T., Balthazard, P., Waldman, D., & Jennings, P. (2010). The neurological basis for leader complexity. *Journal of Applied Psychology (see early version available at: www. bra inmappingforsuccess. com/resources/pdf/Basis-for-Complexity. pdf)*.

Hoang, H., & Gimeno, J. (2010). Becoming a founder: How founder role identity affects entrepreneurial transitions and persistence in founding. *Journal of Business Venturing, 25*(1), 41-53.

Ibarra, H. (2005). Identity transitions: Possible selves, liminality and the dynamics of career change. In *Working paper no. 31/OB, INSEAD*.

Jain, R. (2011). Entrepreneurial Competencies: A Meta-analysis and Comprehensive Conceptualization for Future Research. *Vision: The Journal of Business Perspective, 15*(2), 127-152. doi:10.1177/097226291101500205

Jain, R., & Ali, S. W. (2013). A Review of Facilitators, Barriers and Gateways to Entrepreneurship: Directions for Future Research. *South Asian Journal of Management, 20*(3), 122.

Johnston, K. (2008). Complexity of thinking and levels of self-complexity required to sustainably manage the environment (Unpublished doctoral dissertation). *Australian National University, Canberra, Australia*.

Kaur, P., & Singh, K. (2017). Do chance events have any role in career decision making of undergraduate students? *International Journal in Management & Social Science, 5*(6), 361-375.

Krueger, N. F., Reilly, M. D., & Carsrud, A. L. (2000). Competing models of entrepreneurial intentions. *Journal of Business Venturing, 15*(5), 411-432. doi:Doi 10.1016/S0883-9026(98)00033-0

Kyndt, E., & Baert, H. (2015). Entrepreneurial competencies: Assessment and predictive value for entrepreneurship. *Journal of Vocational Behavior, 90*, 13-25.

Kyndt, E., & Grosemans, I. (2016). Ontwikkeling ENTRE-Spiegel 2.0.

Lazear, E. P. (2004). Balanced skills and entrepreneurship. *American Economic Review, 94*(2), 208-211. doi:Doi 10.1257/0002828041301425

Linville, P. W. (1985). Self-complexity and affective extremity: Don't put all of your eggs in one cognitive basket. *Social cognition, 3*(1), 94-120.

Linville, P. W. (1987). Self-complexity as a cognitive buffer against stress-related illness and depression. *Journal of personality and social psychology, 52*(4), 663.

McConnell, A. R., Renaud, J. M., Dean, K. K., Green, S. P., Lamoreaux, M. J., Hall, C. E., & Rydell, R. J. (2005). Whose self is it anyway? Self-aspect control moderates the relation between self-complexity and well-being. *Journal of Experimental Social Psychology, 41*(1), 1-18.

Osipow, S. H., Carney, C., Winer, J., Yanico, B., & Koschier, M. (1987). The Career decision scale (rev. ed.). *Odessa, FL: Psychological Assessment Resources*.

Osipow, S. H., & Gati, I. (1998). Construct and concurrent validity of the career decision-making difficulties questionnaire. *Journal of Career Assessment, 6*(3), 347-364.

Rafaeli-Mor, E., & Steinberg, J. (2002). Self-complexity and well-being: A review and research synthesis. *Personality and Social Psychology Review, 6*(1), 31-58.

Ramoglou, S., Gartner, W. B., & Tsang, E. W. (2018). *Logic matters: A meta-theoretical analysis of the question of the entrepreneur.* Paper presented at the Academy of Management Proceedings.

Renaud, J. M., & McConnell, A. R. (2002). Organization of the self-concept and the suppression of self-relevant thoughts. *Journal of Experimental Social Psychology, 38*(1), 79-86.

Scott, W. A. (1962). Cognitive complexity and cognitive flexibility. *Sociometry*, 405-414.

Sexton, D. L., & Bowman, N. (1986). The entrepreneur: A capable executive and more. *Journal of Business Venturing, 1*(1), 129-140.

Shapero, A., & Sokol, L. (1982). The social dimensions of entrepreneurship. In *Encyclopedia of entrepreneurship* (pp. 72-90). Englewood Cliffs, N.J. 07632: Prentice-Hall, Inc.

Shilling, A. A., & Brown, C. M. (2015). A cultural examination of self-complexity. *The Journal of Integrated Social Sciences, 5*, 1-26.

Stam, E., Bosma, N., Van Witteloostuijn, A., De Jong, J., Bogaert, S., Edwards, N., & Jaspers, F. (2012). Ambitious entrepreneurship. *A review of the academic literature and new directions for public policy, AWT report, 41*.

Stuart, R. W., & Abetti, P. A. (1990). Impact of entrepreneurial and management experience on early performance. *Journal of Business Venturing, 5*(3), 151-162.

Thompson, E. R. (2009). Individual Entrepreneurial Intent: Construct Clarification and Development of an Internationally Reliable Metric. *Entrepreneurship Theory and Practice, 33*(3), 669-694. doi:10.1111/j.1540-6520.2009.00321.x

van Gelderen, M., Kautonen, T., Wincent, J., & Biniari, M. (2018). Implementation intentions in the entrepreneurial process: concept, empirical findings, and research agenda. *Small Business Economics, 51*(4), 923-941.

Van Witteloostuijn, A. (2016). What happened to Popperian falsification? Publishing neutral and negative findings. *Cross Cultural & Strategic Management, 23*(3), 481-508.

Zahra, S. A., Sapienza, H. J., & Davidsson, P. (2006). Entrepreneurship and dynamic capabilities: a review, model and research agenda*. *Journal of Management Studies, 43*(4), 917-955.

Zhao, H., Seibert, S. E., & Hills, G. E. (2005). The mediating role of self-efficacy in the development of entrepreneurial intentions. *Journal of applied psychology, 90*(6), 1265.

BUCANIER: A Cross-Border Innovation Ecosystem

Fern Davies[1], Thomas Howson[2], Fred Boy[1], Naomi Joyce[2] and Gareth Davies[1]
[1]School of Management, Swansea University, UK
[2]Medical School, Swansea University, UK
f.b.davies@swansea.ac.uk
t.e.howson@swansea.ac.uk
f.a.boy@swansea.ac.uk
n.a.joyce@swansea.ac.uk
g.h.davies@swansea.ac.uk
DOI: 10.34190/EIE.20.069

Abstract: The following paper presents a case study of BUCANIER (Building Clusters and Networks in Innovation Enterprise and Research), an EU funded initiative on the Ireland-Wales Programme. Smart specialisation in regional innovation systems (RIS) has been identified as an approach that can support the competitiveness and economic development of regions. BUCANIER exploits this concept to strengthen the innovation capabilities of small and medium-sized enterprises (SMEs) in three priority sectors: renewable energy, food and drink and life science. A key objective of this is to foster collaboration and knowledge transfer between local government, universities and sector fora as part of a triple-helix approach. Through analysis of the project innovation analytic tool (IAT) (Howson, 2019), this paper analyses the impact of SME interventions, as well as strengths and weaknesses of innovation management at a regional and sectoral level. Through network linkage data, results indicate that BUCANIER has facilitated 301 new connections between 173 stakeholders and the enhancement of both networks and clusters within and across the broader innovation ecosystem.

Keywords: innovation networks, innovation clusters, open innovation, innovation management, small and medium-sized enterprise (SME), entrepreneurship

1. Introduction

BUCANIER is a €2.9 million EU initiative on the Ireland-Wales Programme that aims to support cross-border collaboration in South West Wales and the Eastern Republic of Ireland. A key objective of the programme is to strengthen research, technological development and the innovation capabilities of SMEs, working with local government, universities and industry as part of a triple helix approach (Leyedesdorff & Etkowitz, 1998). The initiatives efforts have been developed to exploit the concept of smart specialisation (Foray, 2014), building upon existing regional strengths in life sciences, food and drink and renewable energy. The focus on these sectors is a direct outcome of the socio-economic analysis carried out by the lead project partners which identifies complementarity in the expertise of both territories.

BUCANIER builds on the innovation framework of INSPIRE (Initiating Pathways for Innovators, Researchers and Entrepreneurs) to support the response of both regions to increase the intensity of knowledge transfer operations, innovation and collaboration in SMEs. This activity is in line with shared priorities of the smart specialisation strategies (Irish Government, 2015; Welsh Government, 2014). The intention is to increase cross-border collaborative research and develop innovation networks and clusters between research institutions and SMEs. Accordingly, the project provides innovation support through workshops, specialist consultancy, networking events and cross-border learning journeys for participant companies, providing bespoke interventions and enhancing absorptive capacity. Transcending the two RIS provides intriguing context, including the noted differences in the role played by Universities (Zhang, Larkin & Lucey, 2017) as central components of BUCANIER.

The following paper provides a case study of BUCANIER, examining the progression of SME innovation projects and their current engagement with the broader innovation ecosystem. Using data drawn from the project innovation analytic tool (IAT) and through elements of social network analysis (SNA), the paper presents innovation practise insight relevant at both participant and programme level. The data drawn from the IAT allows for examination of the project portfolio and identification of individual and cohort level challenges. The SNA data expands on more local and sector specific insight (Davies, Roderick & Williams, 2018), by exploring the number and nature of linkages within and across regions and in supporting the role of BUCANIER. The aims of the paper are therefore twofold: 1) to examine the project portfolio and innovation capabilities of BUCANIER participants and 2) to evaluate if the BUCANIER interventions have contributed to new or enhanced innovation networks and clusters.

2. Literature review

Innovation can be described as "the process by which new ideas are successfully exploited to create economic, social and environmental value" (UK BIS', 2010). There have been numerous attempts to model the innovation process, with the evolutionary development of the concept progressing from a sequential and linear model, to that of open innovation (du Preez & Louw, 2008). Open innovation (Chesbrough, 2003) and the recent introduction of open innovation 2.0 (Curley & Salmelin, 2013) demonstrates a paradigm shift that focuses on collaboration, knowledge and resource sharing as an enabler in the innovation process, with an emphasis on the permeability of organisational boundaries. This not only suggests a free flow of knowledge and ideas between internal and external environments, but the co-creation of innovation with external parties who are embedded within innovation networks, clusters and ecosystems.

However, the process of innovation is complex and can be contextually influenced by actors, knowledge and institutional rules and norms (Tidd, 2001). Accordingly, it is widely accepted that innovation occurs within systems, although these have been categorised from a number of different perspectives. The first is National Innovation Systems (NIS), first developed by Lundvall (1992) and described as "a set of institutions (and actors) whose interactions determine the innovation performance...of national firms" (Nelson, 1993, p. 3). However, Cooke (2001) identified that these do not represent inter-regional variations and suggested the notion of RIS, with Abbey, Davies and Mainwaring (2008) taking this categorisation further to the sub-regional level. RIS allow a degree of autonomy and control over environmental factors that influence the support of innovation and are particularly relevant when elements of government are devolved from central state control.

BUCANIER transcends the two RIS of Ireland and Wales, and aims to embrace the concept of open innovation to "exploit regional diversity, stimulate cooperation across national and regional borders and open up new opportunities" (European Commission, 2010, p. 7). The consideration of BUCANIER in the context of RIS also leads into the more recent concept of smart specialisation (Foray et al, 2009). "Smart specialisation involves businesses, research centres and universities working together to identify a region's most promising areas of specialisation, but also the weaknesses that hamper innovation" (European Commission, 2010, p. 7). This approach within RIS has been identified as suitable to support knowledge-based economic development (Davies et al, 2018). BUCANIER has been developed to exploit the concept of smart specialisation to enhance levels of SME innovation and cross-border collaboration to ensure that knowledge flows more freely across the EU.

BUCANIER's smart specialisation approach includes the specific focus on three priority sectors of renewable energy, food and drink and life science. These sectors align with the economic priorities identified in the *Economic Prioritisation Framework for Welsh European Funds* and the *Ireland Strategic Investment Strategy*. Secondly, the project focuses on improving the innovation capability of SMEs, by increasing the number of knowledge transfer partnerships with research organisations. The need to focus on both SMEs and innovation is relevant for both regions, as identified in the *Citizens Summary Ireland-Wales Co-operation Programme* and the *Regional Policy contributing to smart growth in Europe 2020*. Finally, as Schumpeter (1934) contends, successful innovation requires both technical skills and the knowledge to commercialise the output of technology. However, based on academic discourse and feedback from INSPIRE, the commercialisation process is considered particularly challenging for businesses of all sizes. BUCANIER responds to this with four main pillars of action that aim to strengthen research, technological development and innovation, with a specific focus on bringing new ideas closer to market.

Another aspect of the smart specialisation approach adopted by BUCANIER is the concentration of resources on three existing sectors and focus on innovation networks and clusters (European Commission, 2010). The initiative centres on the development of new, or enhancement of existing networks and clusters of the priority sectors identified above. Networks can be identified as "any collection of actors that pursue repeated, enduring exchange relations with one another" (Podolny & Page, 1998, p. 59) and clusters as "geographic concentrations of industries related by knowledge, skills, inputs, demand and/or other linkages" (Delgado, Porter & Stern, 2016, p. 1). Both are important elements of smart specialisation strategies for regional growth, with recent publications reinforcing the need for cluster-based research to analyse regional comparisons and support policymakers (Delgado et al, 2016). However, the real value for BUCANIER lies in the facilitation of knowledge transfer. By facilitating the successful exchange of knowledge between HE institutions, SMEs and other key actors, BUCANIER promotes the "active exchange of knowledge between organizations, involving measurable and effective knowledge absorption, application and satisfaction by the recipient organization" (Bacon, Williams & Davies, 2019, p. 380).

A further reason for BUCANIER's focus on innovation networks and clusters lies in the development of a cross border, open innovation ecosystem. Open innovation ecosystems involve numerous actors exchanging information for the purpose of co-creation (Radziwon & Bogers, 2018) and are at the core of open innovation activities (Borgers, Chesbrough & Moedas, 2018). Organisations are increasingly turning towards external partnerships to acquire information and in turn, share knowledge across organisational boundaries. The value of such ecosystems is supported by a wealth of research implying that close interaction among divergent organisations can produce a novel recombination of information, leading to greater innovation and learning (Cohen and Levinthal 1990; McEvily and Zaheer 1999). BUCANIER aims to facilitate such interactions to increase innovation, productivity and competitiveness, to ultimately contribute to the economic development and wellbeing of the cross-border region.

In order to support the commercialisation of ideas and competitiveness of firms, good innovation management practise is necessary at an organisational level (Chiesa, Coughlan & Voss, 1996). This can be described as the creation of favourable conditions to support activities associated with the development of novel products, process or services (Tidd & Bessant, 2009). Effective innovation management is related to superior innovation performance (Hidalgo & Albors, 2008), yet a high proportion of businesses report no formal innovation management processes. This is whereby the role of innovation support programmes is particularly important. BUCANIER is part of a wider network of support programmes across the Ireland-Wales region which aim to provide an innovation friendly environment for SMEs, an important aspect of smart specialisation. The programme is tailored to the unique needs of organisations through the use of an IAT, a tool developed by Howson (2019) and used to help practitioners manage innovation management processes, by using a scorecard to benchmark performance against measures of recognised good practise.

3. Methodology

The body of this paper provides preliminary case study information for BUCANIER as part of an ongoing study. The main focus of the data collection is on participating organisations as the principal units of analysis and BUCANIER as the context of the study (Bryman & Bell, 2011). The data collection methods consist of the IAT and network data collated through project documents and participant telephone interviews. All participating organisations of BUCANIER are defined as SMEs or social enterprises that adhere to the European Commission (2016) definition of < 250 employees or ≤ €50m turnover. In terms of geographical reach, the data collection spanned the project region, inclusive of four South West Wales counties and fourteen in the Eastern Republic of Ireland. A prerequisite of the project determines that participants are registered to a postcode within the geographical project boundaries, although the associated network data was not limited to these regions.

Following approval from the Welsh European Funding Office, the IAT scorecard (Howson, 2019) was administered by six project officers to all 126 participants of BUCANIER (72 Wales led and 54 Irish led) upon registration. A third party assessment methodology was utilised that allowed programme staff to engage with participants on a one-to-one basis. Staff were trained to use a broad questioning approach with participants to answer twenty-one questions that translated into the innovation measurement metrics. Ultimately, this created an innovation blueprint for each organisation and a graphical display of the differences between ideal and actual innovation management performance (Chiesa et al, 1996). Importantly, it also identified strengths and weaknesses at organisational and cohort levels at the onset and on conclusion of the project support, allowing for bespoke interventions to be designed and their effectiveness subsequently evaluated. However, for the purposes of this paper, initial IAT findings will be presented from a data set of (n=63) and on a case study basis (n=2).

The preliminary network data for BUCANIER has been collated through numerous methods over the period of the project (March 2017-August 2020). These methods are inclusive of registration details, intervention documents, email logs and telephone interviews (n=39). In order to analyse the data, elements of social network analysis (SNA) were utilised to explore the number, nature and intensity of linkages within and across the BUCANIER regions. SNA can be defined as a distinctive set of methods used for mapping, measuring and analysing the social relationships between people, groups and organisations (Scott, 2000). It is considered appropriate for multi-disciplinary network-based initiatives to recognise the complexity and dynamics of networks and the influence of information flows on behaviour and decisions. The SNA methodology adopted consists of three main stages: (i) describing the set of actors; (ii) characterising the nature and strength of relationships between actors; and (iii) analysing the structure of the systems used to observe the formation or enhancement of networks and clusters.

4. IAT analysis

To examine the project portfolio and innovation management of BUCANIER participants, the following section presents the IAT findings at the start of each intervention. The findings analyse the cohort, regional and sectoral data, as well as presenting two case studies of participating organisations. The available data from the total BUCANIER population represents a sample size of (n=63). 74.6% of this sample constitutes Irish participants and 25.4% Welsh, with 54% representing the food and drink sector, 37% life science and 9% renewable energy. The findings are presented as radar diagrams to provide a visual representation of innovation management performance and are subsequently discussed.

As a cohort, BUCANIER participants evidenced notable strengths in organisational culture, team characteristics, resource input and links with market and industry. However, weaknesses were evident in innovativeness and technology readiness level (TRL) of the innovation, regulatory engagement, market readiness and links with academia (*see Figure 1*).

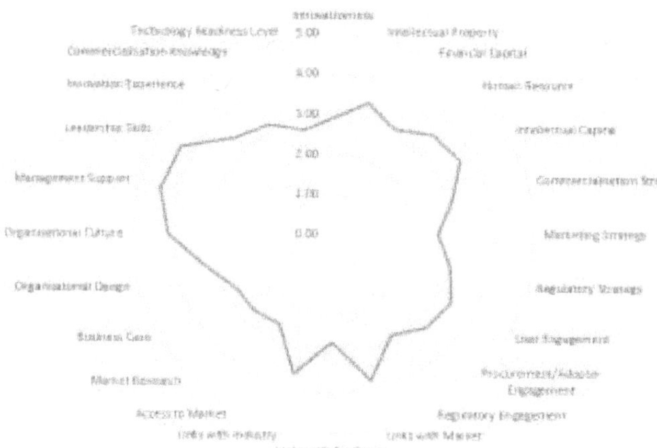

Figure 1: Average results for BUCANIER IAT radars

Innovation strengths of both regions included organisational culture, team characteristics, intellectual capital and links with market and industry. However, a regional strength for Ireland was the acquisition of IP and for Wales, user engagement and innovation experience of the team. Weaknesses for both regions were innovativeness, TRL level, regulatory engagement, marketing strategy and access to market. Particular weaknesses for Ireland included links with academia and market readiness, whereas for Wales these were IP, commercialisation strategy and regulatory strategy *(see Figure 2 below*).

The sectoral findings show the same collective strengths as the regional data. However, food and drink and renewable energy demonstrated particular strength in IP, life science showed strengths in user and adopter engagement and both renewable energy and life science had strong links with industry. Interestingly, renewable energy was the only sector to score high on the innovativeness of their projects. Weaknesses of all sectors include marketing strategies, market readiness and TRL. For food and drink and life science sectors, weaknesses were evident in innovativeness and development of the business case. For food and drink and renewable energy, challenges included links with academia and market research. Both life science and renewable energy sectors faced challenges with financial capital, whilst life science showed weakness in regulatory engagement and renewable energy in availability of HR and commercialisation strategies (*see Figure 3*).

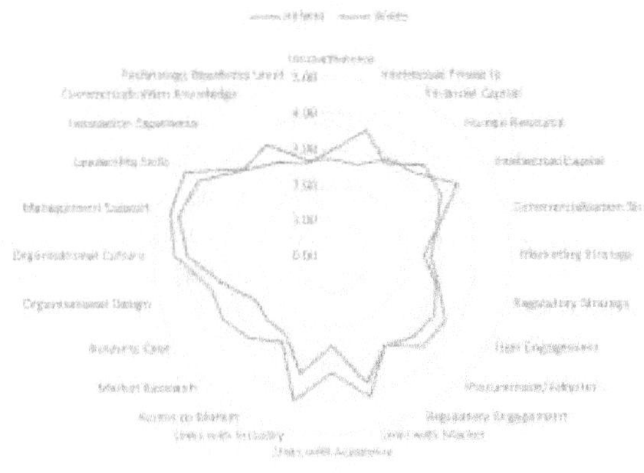

Figure 2: Mean results of IAT (regional)

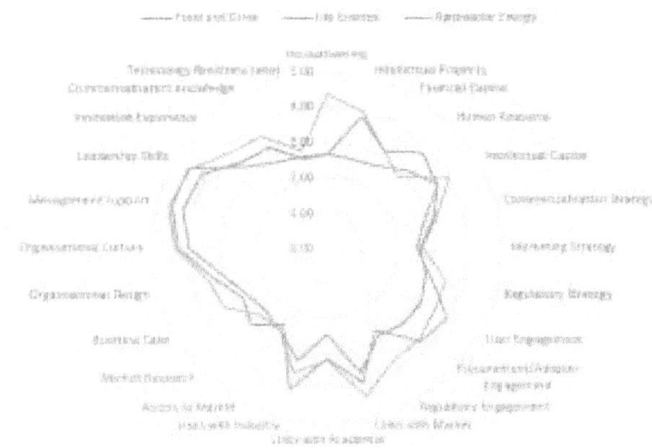

Figure 3: Mean results of IAT (sector)

4.1 BUCANIER case study 1

The following case studies present an innovation blueprint at start and on conclusion of the intervention. *Case Study 1* represents a life science SME developing a novel service for respiratory patients to track their condition. At start of the intervention, the SME possessed adequate levels of financial capital, market research, strong linkages and organisational culture to support the innovation. However, despite a strong innovation strategy, regulatory and marketing strategies were less advanced with a need to develop the business case. The IAT blueprint therefore provided a target area for the BUCANIER intervention. Following 16.5 hours of support in the form of regulatory consultancy and workshop attendance, innovation performance was re-assessed, allowing for evaluation of the programme impact. By examining the innovation blueprints below, *Case Study 1* shows significant improvement to all aspects of their innovation strategy and market readiness, with a notable increase in TRL.

4.2 BUCANIER case study 2

Case Study 2 represents a food and drink SME developing a fermented drinks range. At onset of the intervention, the organisation engaged well with users and industry and had strong organisational and team characteristics to support the development of the innovation. However, preliminary interactions identified a low TRL score and levels of innovativeness, with a need to focus specifically on a regulatory strategy. Following 10 hours of consultancy, product testing and referral, the innovation performance was re-assessed. As evidenced by *Figure 5*, the TRL saw a significant increase, primarily facilitated by the testing and regulatory support. This allowed a subsequent increase in IP consideration and innovativeness of the product range. There were also notable improvements with industry and academia links that are evidenced in the network findings below. Through the increase in TRL levels, both case studies indicate a clear progression towards the commercialisation of their innovation and positive impact from the BUCANIER intervention.

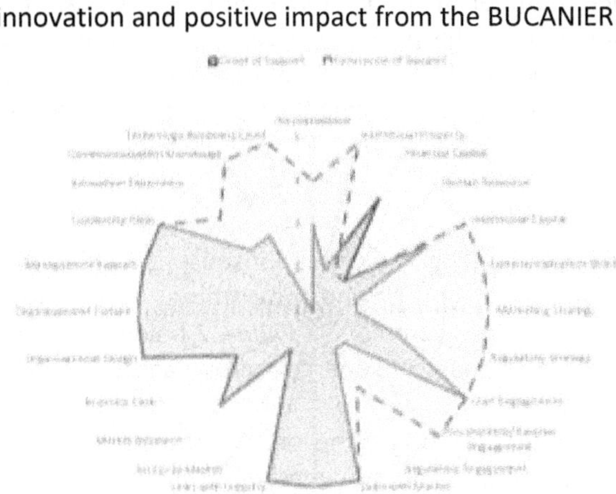

Figure 4: Case study 1

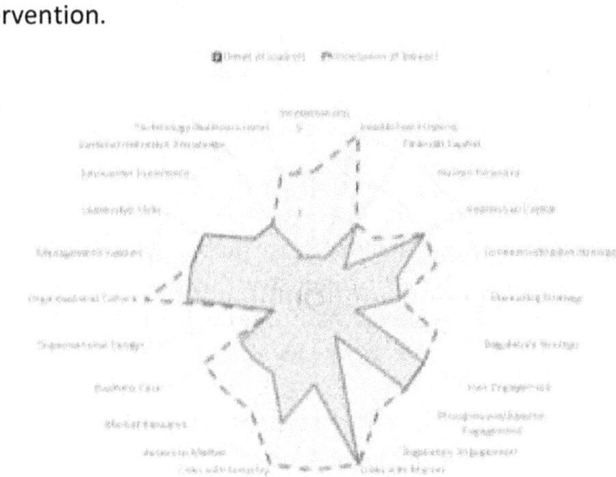

Figure 5: Case study 2

5. Networks analysis

Figure 6 (below) details findings from the BUCANIER network analysis exercise. This provides a visualisation of the emergent network, illustrating the relationships formed between programme participants and wider partners throughout the duration of BUCANIER programme support. In total, 39 BUCANIER participants responded (13 Irish, 26 Welsh), whilst known relationships between participant and lead (partner) organisations were also included. Although only providing an initial snapshot of the BUCANIER network due to the participant response rate, *Figure 6* demonstrates the value added by the BUCANIER programme in supporting the formation of a multi-disciplinary, multi-sectoral, cross-border innovation network.

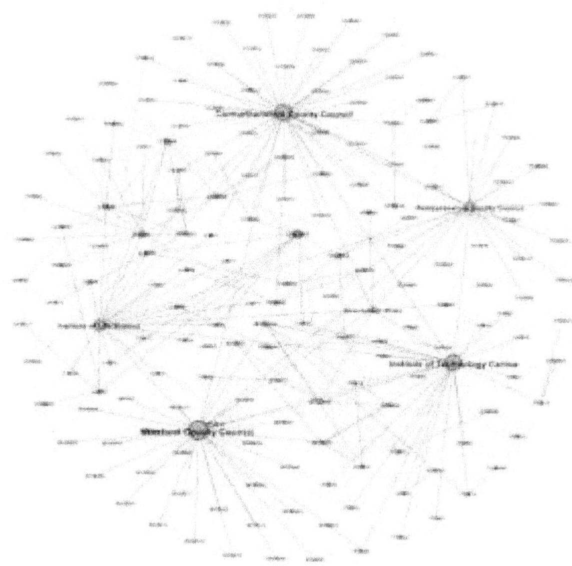

Figure 6: BUCANIER network analysis

Throughout the duration of the programme, 173 stakeholders across private, public and third sectors, formed 301 unique connections or relationships, spanning sectoral boundaries including; food and drink, life science and renewable energy, as well as broader sectoral clusters and supply chains. These relationships varied in both relational type (nature) and relational strength. The nature of relationships reported by participants ranged from business partners and supply chain actors, consultants and regulatory advisors to sources of finance, academic expertise and product testing support. Alongside this multi-functional nature of the BUCANIER network, respondents and programme leads also described a high degree of relational trust between network members, with 72% of participant or programme lead responses reporting repeated dealings between partners.

As anticipated, due to the structure and dynamics of BUCANIER, lead local authority and university partners demonstrated the highest degree of centrality or prominence (number of connections) within the BUCANIER network, which is represented in *Figure 6* by the size of network nodes. This positions programme partners as a major conduit between other members of the triple helix as well as wider ecosystem resources, and affirms their important role in facilitating knowledge transfer, co-ordinating support and managing the highly complex nature of ecosystem dynamics.

6. Cluster analysis

Alongside network analysis data, mapping of BUCANIER participants geographic locations also identifies the presence of a number of industry clusters situated across both Wales and Ireland programme regions. This includes regional clusters associated with both the food and drink (for example see *Figure 7* below) and life science sectors, however low levels of support for clusters within the renewable energy sector was identified.

Although there is reduced evidence to suggest BUCANIER's role in the formation of the identified clusters, insight from geographical mapping, alongside network analysis and participant IAT data, suggests that the programme has enhanced the development and activity of regional clusters through a number of interventions. By acting as a central co-ordinating body, the programme has provided a vehicle to support greater interaction and integration between co-located stakeholders across private, public and third sector institutions. The programme has also provided access to and enhanced engagement with local universities and consultancy services, promoting greater knowledge and resource transfer. Furthermore, as is demonstrated in *Figure 8* below, facilitated by targeted learning journeys, BUCANIER has also linked cross-border innovation clusters, potentially enabling participants to engage more effectively with international markets and counterparts.

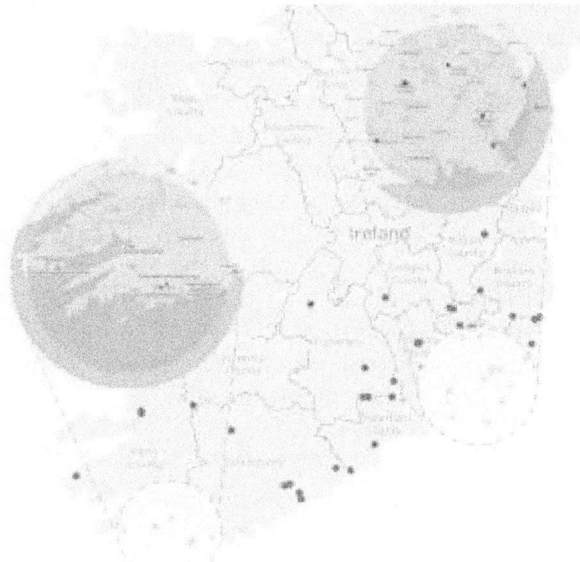

Figure 7: BUCANIER participant location (Ireland) – identifying the presence of two food and drink clusters

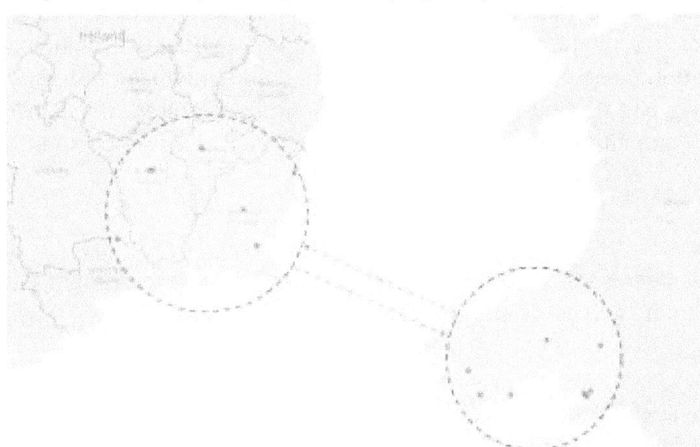

Figure 8: Brewing and distillery clusters (South East Ireland and South West Wales). BUCANIER interventions supported the formation of the cluster

7. Discussion

The above IAT findings represent the innovation capabilities of BUCANIER participants at the start of intervention. It is not feasible to discuss all findings, yet a key theme across the portfolio was low TRL and maturity of technological innovations. This result aligns with the lack of market readiness, of which could be inhibiting progression of the innovation. It would also explain why, despite most businesses having commercialisation strategies, TRL remains low. These findings align with literature that suggests successful innovation requires technical skill *and* knowledge to commercialise outputs (Schumpeter, 1934), of which the latter often presents challenges for SMEs. The case study examples provide preliminary data to identify how BUCANIER has contributed to solving this challenge at a participant level. On both occasions, the innovation blueprint helped to formulate bespoke regulatory interventions that facilitated a subsequent increase in TRL, amongst other measures such as innovativeness.

Regional innovation capabilities currently reside in organisational culture, team characteristics and the intellectual capital of SMEs. However, whilst strengths include market and industry links, there is a lower interaction with academia, particularly in Ireland. Whilst this can be explained by factors such as geographical and sectoral distribution of SMEs, linkages with academia are vital for BUCANIER to embrace the concept of open innovation and to facilitate collaboration and absorptive capacity in SMEs (Chesbrough, 2003). *Case Study*

2 evidences a significant increase in interaction with academia following the BUCANIER intervention. Universities play an important role for economic development in RIS, acting as knowledge hubs (Cooke, 2001). The role of BUCANIER to facilitate trust between SMEs, local authority and academic institutions, as is evidenced in the network findings, is therefore of vital importance to contribute to knowledge transfer success (Bacon et al, 2019) and provides the origins of the BUCANIER innovation ecosystem.

In parallel, the importance of linkages between key actors within the respective innovation ecosystem suggests a criticality in their connection for enduring links between the two RIS (Zhang, Larkin & Lucey, 2017). A positive finding in the network analysis is the relational strength between network members, with 72% of actors reporting repeated dealings. Whilst it is encouraging that the programme partners are a central conduit between members, measures need to be taken to ensure that the strength of ties and ecosystem structure remains beyond the lifecycle of BUCANIER to maintain cross-border collaboration and knowledge transfer. Results also show the involvement of BUCANIER in regional cluster activity between co-located actors in both food and drink and life science sectors across the border. This again is positive, yet there are low levels of support for renewable energy clusters. This could explain the lack of resource inputs at an organisational level and implies a cross-border need to facilitate geographic concentrations of this industry.

8. Conclusion

To conclude, the paper clearly evidences the variation in innovation support needs of participant SMEs. Whilst sample limitations are acknowledged, this preliminary data identifies regional, sectoral and programme strengths and weaknesses, of which can inform regional policy. The two case studies provide initial evidence of the BUCANIER interventions improving the innovation capabilities of SMEs, in particular increasing the TRL and progression towards successful commercialisation. Through network linkage data, results indicate that BUCANIER has facilitated 301 unique connections with 173 stakeholders, spanning across both regional innovation systems and priority sectors, with cluster formation and enhancement occurring within and across the broader innovation ecosystem. Whilst further data collection is required, these insights provide benefit to innovation programmes, practitioners in similar contexts and academics identifying future research opportunities.

Acknowledgements

The BUCANIER project has been supported by the European Regional Development Fund through the Ireland Wales Cooperation Programme and associated partners.

References

Abbey, J., Davies, G., and Mainwaring, L. (2008) "Vorsprung Durch Technium: Towards a System of Innovation in South-West Wales", *Regional Studies,* No. 42, pp 281-293.

Bacon, E., Williams, M. D., and Davies, G. H. (2019) "Recipes for success: Conditions for knowledge transfer across open innovation ecosystems", *International Journal of Information Management,* No. 49, pp 377-387.

Baxter, P., and Jack, S. (2008) "Qualitative case study methodology: Study design and implementation for novice researchers", *The qualitative report*, Vol 13, No. 4, 544-559.

Borgers, M., Chesbrough, H., and Moedas, C. (2018) "Open innovation: Research, practises, and policies", *California Management Review,* Vol 60, No. 2, pp 5-16.

Bryman, A., and Bell, E. (2011). *Business Research Methods* (3rd ed.), New York, Oxford University Press.

Chesbrough, H. W. (2003) *Open innovation: The new imperative for creating and profiting from technology,* Cambridge, Harvard Business School Press.

Chiesa, V., Coughlan, P., and Voss, C. A. (1996) "Development of a technical innovation audit", *Journal of Product Innovation Management*, No. 13, pp 105-136.

Cohen, W. M., and Levinthal, D. A. (1990) "Absorptive capacity: A new perspective on learning and innovation", *Administrative Science Quarterly*, No. 35, pp 128-152.

Cohen, L., Manion, L., and Morrison, K. (2002) Research methods in education. (5th ed.), London, Routledge.

Cooke, P. (2001) "Regional Innovation Systems, Clusters and the Knowledge Economy", *Industrial and Corporate Change*, No. 10, pp 945-974.

Curley, M., and Salmelin, B. (2013) Open Innovation 2.0: A new paradigm, *OISPG White Paper*, pp 1-12.

Davies, G. H., Roderick, S., and Williams, M. (2018) "A sub-regional innovation ecosystem? Life sciences and health in the Swansea Bay City Region", *International Journal of Innovation and Regional Development,* No. 8, pp 182-189.

Delgado, M., Porter, M. E., and Stern, S. (2016) "Defining clusters of related industries", *Journal of Economic Geography*, Vol 16, No. 1, pp 1-38.

du Preez, N. D., and Louw, L. (2008) "A framework for managing the innovation process", Portland International Conference on Management of Engineering & Technology, USA, pp 546-558.

European Commission. (2010) "Regional Policy contributing to smart growth in Europe 2020" [online], https://ec.europa.eu/regional_policy/sources/docoffic/official/communic/smart_growth/comm2010_553_en.pdf [Accessed 21st May. 2020].

European Commission. (2016) "User Guide to the SME Definition" [online], https://ec.europa.eu/growth/smes/business-friendly-environment/sme-definition_en. [Accessed 21st May. 2020].

Foray, D. (2014) "From smart specialisation to smart specialisation policy", *European Journal of Innovation Management,* Vol 17, No. 4, pp 492-507.

Goldkuhl, G. (2012) "Pragmatism vs interpretivism in qualitative information systems research", *European journal of information systems*, Vol 21, No. 2, pp 135-146.

Hidalgo, A., and Albors, J. (2008) "Innovation management techniques and tools: a review from theory and practice", *R&D Management*, Vol 38, No. 2, pp 113-127.

Howson, T. (2019). *"A Tool to Support Life Science and Health Innovation Management*", PhD thesis [forthcoming], Swansea University, Swansea.

Irish Government. (2015) "Innovation 2020" [online], https://dbei.gov.ie/en/Publications/Publication-files/Innovation-2020.pdf [Accessed 21st May. 2020].

Ireland Strategic Investment Fund. (2015) "Investment Strategy" [online], https://isif.ie/uploads/publications/ISIFInvestmentStrategyExecutiveSummaryJuly2015.pdf [Accessed 21st May. 2020].

Ireland-Wales Programme. (2014) "EU Funds: Ireland-Wales Co-operation Programme 2014-2020" [online], file:///F:/Citizens%20Summary%20Ireland-Wales%202014-2020.pdf [Accessed 21st May. 2020].

Leydesdorff, L., and Etzkowitz, H. (1998) "The triple helix as a model for innovation studies", *Science and public policy*, Vol 25, No. 3, pp 195-203.

Lundvall, B. Å. (1992) *National systems of innovation: Toward a theory of innovation and interactive learning*, London, Pinter.

Mackenzie, N., and Knipe, S. (2006) "Research dilemmas: Paradigms, methods and methodology", *Issues in educational research*, Vol 16, No. 2, pp 193-205.

McEvily, B., and Zaheer, A. (1999) "Bridging ties: A source of firm heterogeneity in competitive capabilities", *Strategic management journal*, Vol 20, No. 12, pp 1133-1156.

Nelson, R. R. (1993). *National innovation systems: A comparative analysis*, New York, Oxford University Press.

Podolny, J. M., and Page, K. L. (1998) "Network forms of organization", *Annual review of sociology*, Vol 24, No. 1, pp 57-76.

Radziwon, A., Bogers, M., and Bilberg, A. (2017) "Creating and capturing value in a regional innovation ecosystem: A study of how manufacturing SMEs develop collaborative solutions", *International Journal of Technology Management,* Vol 75, No. 1-4, pp 73-96.

Schumpeter, J. A. (1934) *The Theory of Economic Development*, Boston, Harvard University Press.

Scott, J. (2000) *Social Network Analysis: A Handbook* (2nd ed.), London, Sage Publications.

Tidd, J. (2001) "Innovation management in context: environment, organization and performance", *International journal of management reviews*, No. 3, pp 169-183.

Tidd, J., and Bessant, J. (2009) *Managing innovation: integrating technological, market and organizational change* (4th ed.), Chichester, John Wiley and Sons Ltd.

UK BIS (2010) "Innovation" [online], file:///F:/UK%20Deparment%20for%20Business,%20Innovation%20and%20Skills%202010%20Innovation.pdf [Accessed 21st May. 2020].

Welsh Government. (2015) "The Economic Prioritisation Framework for Welsh European Funds" (Version 3)" [online], https://gov.wales/docs/wefo/publications/150615theeconomicprioritisationframeworkv3.pdf [Accessed 21st May. 2020].

Zhang, Q., Larkin, C., and Lucey, B. M. (2017) "Universities, knowledge exchange and policy: A comparative study of Ireland and the UK", *Science and Public Policy,* No. 44, pp 174-185.

Features of the Investments Effectiveness Evaluating in Innovative Products of Industrial Business System

Daniel Demidenko and Ekaterina Malevskaia-Malevich
Peter the Great Saint-Petersburg Polytechnic University, Russia
demidenko11@rambler.ru,
malevskaia@spbstu.ru
DOI: 10.34190/EIE.20.186

Abstract: The process of transition to an innovative economy causes intensification of enterprises innovative activity in all sectors. One of the most crucial issues nowadays tends to be the effectiveness evaluation of innovation activities. Creating an innovative product requires significant capital expenditures, and to predict the result is a difficult task. Innovative activities are usually characterized by increased risks that must be considered. These and many other features of innovative activity require additional study, despite the significant scientific groundwork on innovative issues. Takin into consideration the limited resources, funds that can be invested in innovative products are also limited, so there is an interest to invest with the greatest impact. If we consider that the market is perfect and the market value of the products corresponds to their consumer value, then the investment of resources in products with the highest market value will be the effective distribution of resources between products. It is widely acknowledged that the effectiveness of investments in innovative products is determined not only by the maximum result achieved under the existing restrictions. Another strategy to consider, which the authors find extremely essential is the possibility of minimizing losses that may arise as a result of the implementation of a number of operational risks specific to the innovation process. In market conditions, the degree of enterprise's efficiency is determined by its profitability. This is a particularly urgent task for enterprises that produce innovative products, which are characterized by a high degree of risk and uncertainty of production conditions, which can be reduced as the use of digitalization methods of the economy increases. For this reason, it is necessary to make wider use of quantitative estimates in economic and financial planning and analysis of the results. Determining the economic efficiency of investments in innovative products, taking into account the characteristics of investment, is the goal of this article.

Keywords: innovative products, investment decisions, cost-effectiveness analysis, innovative specific nature

1. Introduction

One of the most crucial issues nowadays tends to be innovative activity of the enterprises or industrial business systems. Innovative activity of enterprises in their connection to its performance has been much discussed in scientific literature. For example, (Cohen, 2010)) calls it 'Neo-Shumpeterian' studies, that examines the effects of firm size and market concentration upon innovation It is a well-known fact that this type of production activity can be classified as high-risky investment and is referred with uncertainty. (Babkin, 2019, Pupentsova, Livintsova, 2018) This is the reason why the science is responsible for finding relevant methods of effectiveness' evaluation. Takin into account the fact that all resources are limited, funds that can be invested in innovative products are also limited. There appear to be an interest to invest with the greatest impact. (Shvetsova, Rodionova, Epstein, 2018, Konnikov et al., 2019) Much researches show the connection between innovations implement in different fields and the economics efficiency. For example, the study (Camisón & Villar-López, 2014, Guzikova, 2019) describes the connection between the organizational innovation, technological innovation capabilities and firm performance. On the base of empirical data the authors shows that there supposed to be a direct correlation between organizational innovation and overall firm performance. The paper by (Mol & Birkinshaw, 2009) depict the role of management innovation and its connection with firm's effectiveness, which regarding to the authors results does exist. Regardless of numerous researches in this field, the topic is still debating. Determining the economic efficiency of investments in innovative products, taking into account the characteristics of investment, is the goal of this paper.

2. Methods

If we consider that in a perfectly competitive market the market price of the product fully reflects its consumer utility, then purchasing a product on the market will not give the buyer any economic advantages:

3. Product price minus product value is equal to zero

This corresponds to a well-known neo-classical position that "there is no profit in a perfectly competitive market." (Gordon, 1990)

In order to develop production and reduce losses due to non-compliance with the requirements of production conditions in the course of production activities, investments can be made in two directions. Firstly, in the assets of the enterprise or, secondly, in an increase in current production costs, as a result of which an economic effect should be obtained in the form of savings from reducing losses or their complete elimination.

The necessary elements for assessing economic efficiency, especially for innovative enterprises, are: (O'Sullivan, 2000, Levy, 2015, Dvas & Dubolazova, 2018, Degtereva et al., 2020)

- 1) an economic assessment model (an indicator or a system of indicators) of efficiency, quantitative assessment methodology),
- 2) criterion (standard) of efficiency,
- 3) taking into account the "effect of integerness" in assessing economic efficiency,
- 4) the use of the "utility" principle to ensure the comparability of compared strategies for obtaining results.

4. Problem statement and research objective

It is widely acknowledged that determining the market value of the company is the topic of interest for all investors and stockholders. The main question stays the same – is it supposed to be any difference between market and book value of the company, what is it equal to, for what purposes is it used? The presence of this difference may indicate the inaccuracy of the existing financial statements and accounting methods.

On the one hand, the concept of "enterprise's market value" is used to characterize the influence of numerous multidirectional factors on its financial and economic situation. The market value of an entity quoted in the financial market is reflected in the market value of the assets. For enterprises not represented on the financial market (the majority in Russia), the concept of "market value" is conditional. They use calculation methods for assessing market value, the most common of which is the method of "direct capitalization". According to this method, in practice, the determination of market value comes down to dividing the one-period income from investments by the market interest rate, which expresses the price of money in the financial market. Represented formula can be used for the calculation:

$$\frac{result}{interest\ rate} = assets,$$

here it is assumed that any cash flow of income expressing the result of an activity (profit, net cash flow, etc.) can be equivalently represented in the form of a uniform infinite annuity. The interest rate is not a dimensionless quantity, its dimension is equal to:

$$\frac{\frac{MU}{pereod\ of\ time}}{MU} = \frac{1}{pereod\ of\ time} = interest\ rate,$$

it follows that:

$$\frac{\frac{MU}{pereod\ of\ time}}{\frac{1}{pereod\ of\ time}} = MU,$$

it shows that the application of this approach can be obtained by the value of the capitalization of the company assets (expressed in money units).

On the other hand, the capitalization method can be applied in preparing the optimal production plan of innovative products on the enterprise. As it is known, innovative products are characterized by a higher level of added value in comparison with conventional products.

The optimal production plan can be represented as the following optimization task:

$$C_1 \times X_1 + \cdots C_n \times X_n -> max$$

This is the objective function of the integer linear programming optimization problem. An optimal plan should maximize the added value of ongoing projects.

Notation in the formula: control variable $X_i = 0$ or 1, i = 1...n, integers, where 0 - the project is not being implemented, 1 - the project is being implemented, "C_i" is the added cost of producing the i-th product or implementing the project.

In this case, we are talking about the implementation of projects, because, unlike the production of products, each project is implemented once (more than one project is not required), while a different number of products of the same name can be produced and used.

The optimization of the production plan may also have another objective function, for example, maximizing profits from the achieved results of activities: implemented innovative projects or total sales, as well as maximizing the added value of new products. Limitations of the problem (in addition to the previously mentioned restrictions on the number) can also be the production capabilities of the enterprise (or the entire economic system), which determine the realizable size of production and sales, the value added growth (these restrictions can essentially coincide with the objective function):

$$C_1 \times X_1 + \cdots C_n \times X_n \leq M,$$

where M is the acceptable limit for increasing value added or sales. For optimization management problems, one or several resource constraints can coincide with the objective function. Such approaches are described in the scientific economic literature (Novozhilov, 1972, Leont'ev, 1990, Leontief, 1986), but are applicable only for optimization problems in the "classical" formulation (linear programming): for example, "direct" the task is to minimize the consumption of resources, the dual task is to maximize the added value of manufactured products. For optimization problems in a more realistic formulation (integer), this approach cannot be used; these problems can be solved by other methods, for example, the dynamic programming method.

The mechanism of the formation of the economic effect of production costs aimed at reducing losses can be explained using the table below.

Table 1: The formation of the economic effect of production costs aimed at reducing losses

	Useful output	Losses	
		Costs lack	Excessive costs
$O < P$	-	O	-
O=P	P	-	-
O> P	P	-	O-P

Designations in the table: "O" - the value of additional investment in production to prevent production losses; "P" - the expected useful result from the reduction of losses in production.

Production losses are the discrepancy between the actual production result and the planned or expected result. Such a mismatch is a random variable that occurs with a certain probability, so we can say that the deviation of the actual result from the planned one is a risk. In practice, the deviation is expressed by the "product yield" indicator, which reflects the risk of non-receipt of the required quality product at the output of the production process. (Bracio & Szarucki, 2019) The indicator also characterizes the quality of the production process.

This, however, does not mean that production losses will be completely excluded in this production, because instead of previous losses, which we managed to get rid of with the help of targeted production costs, new losses appear, overcoming of which requires new additional costs. It can be seen that the cost of overcoming the losses are always present in the composition of production costs of the enterprise as an integral part of the costs, in many cases quite substantial in size. (Atkeson & Burstein, 2019, Tkachenko, et al., 2019)

The economic effect of additional production costs aimed at overcoming losses can be expressed in the form of the following formula (in the previously adopted notation). The ability to carry out additional production costs is always limited by the available resources of production factors.

Based on the assumption that the market price of a product reflects its value, the economic model of the optimal distribution of limited resources in reducing production losses may be as follows:

$$\mathrm{C}_1 \times \mathrm{X}_1 + \cdots + \mathrm{C}_n \times \mathrm{X}_n -> max$$
$$X_1 \ldots X_n = 1 \text{ or } 0 - \text{integer}$$
$$\mathrm{C}_1 \times \mathrm{X}_1 + \cdots + \mathrm{C}_n \times \mathrm{X}_n \leq L$$

Here $\mathrm{C}_1 \ldots \mathrm{C}_n$ is the market value or price of the product, determined by its market value, X is the control variable, L is the available limit of resources to increase production costs.

Restrictions may be imposed on individual variables, taking into account the specifics of the distribution problems under consideration.

5. Key results

The economic meaning of the task is obvious: the company seeks to attract additional production costs within the program aimed at reducing losses, to increase the output of those products that have the greatest market value.

In the solution of integral distribution problems of this type, losses may also occur during the distribution of limited funds, which can be characterized as "losses due to the whole number". The mechanism of occurrence of these losses, as well as methods for their quantitative determination can be considered using a numerical example.

There are two products $\mathrm{C}_1 = 1\,MU \text{ and } \mathrm{C}_2 = 2\,MU$ with a market price, respectively. (Here and after MU – money units) The total limit of funds for investment in production in order to reduce losses equals 2 MU, it is not enough to purchase two products.

Obviously, the best distribution of the resource limit in this case would be to purchase one unit of the second product (if, as a result of the existing shortcomings of the production process, it is not possible to obtain the product in the required quantity, then loss prevention is the acquisition of missing products of a certain type). The method of determining the best way of allocating scarce costs between the products is the search of all the available and admissible under the terms of distribution costs limit the ways the problem can be shown to obtain this apparent to our simple example the result. Possible distribution options for the limit 2 MU are the following:

- Firstly, all funds of the limit are sent to the production process of product 1, funds are not sent to the production of product 2. In this case, you can "purchase" only one unit of product 1, but since the production of this product requires only 1 MU of the resource, the second allocated money unit is loss (not used). The overall effect of investing under this plan will be (+1 -1 = 0).
- Secondly, all funds of the limit are distributed equally between the first and the second products. In this case, one monetary unit of funds from the allocated limit is sent to the first product (exactly as much as is required for it). One monetary unit remains for the second product, which amounts to losses, because the allocated funds are not enough for this product (since two monetary units are required for the production of the product number two). The total effect for two products will be the following: (+ 1-1 = 0 monetary units).
- Finally, all funds of the limit are sent to the production process of the second product, which means funds are not sent to the production of the first product at all. In this case, you can "purchase" only one unit of the second product, the total effect for the two products together will be equal to the following equation: (0 + 2 = 2 MU).

6. Conclusion

Of the three considered options for allocating the resource of funds, the third option has the highest efficiency, according to which all the funds of the available limit should be invested in the production of the second product; the first product is not considered.

We have obtained a result, which, for our simplest example, was obvious from the very beginning. However, for more complex cases (for example, more products), this method is widely used; on this basis a method for optimizing the effect using "dynamic programming" is built.

To conclude the authors can mention that the development of relevant measurement approaches to determine the innovative effectiveness is crucial today and such tendency will definitely last in the future since innovations are the key elements of sustainable development of the society. Taking into consideration significant scientist's efforts we can state that many questions still are opened and many researches in innovative field are needed to be done in the close future.

7. Discussion

The concept of economic efficiency assessment presented by us essentially considers the issues of a "point estimate" of the effectiveness of investing limited resources in a project / product. In real conditions, we have to solve the problem of evaluating the effectiveness of the process / enterprise or industrial business system. To do this, it is necessary to define a number of basic concepts, principles, methodological approaches and information support elements necessary for evaluation:

The concept of efficiency is wider than the framework of its economic evaluation, but other types of efficiency that are not directly related to the field of economic evaluation are usually related to each other and all together determine the level of economic efficiency. For example, a technical, organizational, or even political decision that requires less cost will not be more cost-effective than other solutions if the costs per unit of the resulting beneficial effect are used as an indicator of efficiency. The principle of performance evaluation is the same for the economy as a whole, industrial business system, the enterprise / organization or individual products: the ratio of the result to the cost of achieving this result. Indicators and criteria for the quantitative assessment of efficiency for all levels stay the same (the economy as a whole, the enterprise, the product).

Acknowledgements

This research work was supported by the Academic Excellence Project 5-100 proposed by Peter the Great St. Petersburg Polytechnic University

References

Atkeson, A., & Burstein, A. (2019). Aggregate implications of innovation policy. Journal of Political Economy, 127(6), 2625-2683.

Babkin, Aleksandr V., et al. "Selection of Tools of Automation of Business Processes of a Manufacturing Enterprise." 2019 International Conference" Quality Management, Transport and Information Security, Information Technologies"(IT&QM&IS). IEEE, 2019.

Benlemlih, M., & Bitar, M. (2018). Corporate social responsibility and investment efficiency. Journal of Business Ethics, 148(3), 647-671.

BODRUNOV, S. (2020). The Concept of Noonomy: Summary of a Prospective Model for Socioeconomic System Organization. DEStech Transactions on Social Science, Education and Human Science, (icesd).

Bracio, K., & Szarucki, M. (2019). Commercialization of innovations through internationalization: a systematic literature review. Business: Theory and Practice, 20, 417-431.

Camisón, C., & Villar-López, A. (2014). Organizational innovation as an enabler of technological innovation capabilities and firm performance. Journal of business research, 67(1), 2891-2902.

Cohen, W. M. (2010). Fifty years of empirical studies of innovative activity and performance. In Handbook of the Economics of Innovation (Vol. 1, pp. 129-213). North-Holland.

Corter, J. E., & Chen, Y. J. (2006). Do investment risk tolerance attitudes predict portfolio risk?. Journal of Business and Psychology, 20(3), 369.

Degtereva, V., Zaytsev, A., & Kichigin, O. (2020, January). Rent Regulation of Russia's Economy as a Condition for Achieving Global Leadership. In 5th International Conference on Social, Economic, and Academic Leadership (ICSEALV 2019) (pp. 68-73). Atlantis Press.

Dvas, G. V., & Dubolazova, Y. A. (2018). Risk assessment and risk management of innovative activity of the enterprise. In Innovation Management and Education Excellence through Vision 2020 (pp. 5650-5653).

Gordon, R. J. (1990). What is new-Keynesian economics? journal of Economic Literature, 28(3), 1115-1171.

Guzikova, L. (2019, December). Construction–industry with increased and uncompensated occupational risk. In IOP Conference Series: Materials Science and Engineering (Vol. 687, No. 5, p. 055071). IOP Publishing.

Karlik, A. E., Platonov, V. V., & Yakovleva, E. A. (2019, October). System Analysis of the Implementation of the Virtual Forms Human-computer Interaction in the Higher Education Sector: Results of the review of the experience of implementation of the virtual forms. In Proceedings of the XI International Scientific Conference Communicative Strategies of the Information Society (pp. 1-6).

Konnikov, E. A., Konnikova, O. A., & Rodionov, D. G. (2019). Impact of 3D-Printing Technologies on the Transformation of Industrial Production in the Arctic Zone. Resources, 8(1), 20.

Leont'ev, V. (1990). Ekonomicheskie esse. Teorii, issledovaniya, fakty i politika. M.: Politizdat, 415.

Leontief, W. (Ed.). (1986). Input-output economics. Oxford University Press.

Levy, H. 2015. Stochastic dominance: Investment decision making under uncertainty. Springer.

Lyukevich, I., & Agranov, A. (2019, March). Correction of originality in cash flow forecasting to assess financial risk. In IOP Conference Series: Materials Science and Engineering (Vol. 497, No. 1, p. 012058). IOP Publishing.

Melnikova, I.Y., Stepanov, I.G. 2008. The model of investment program formation for the enterprise //

Mol, M. J., & Birkinshaw, J. (2009). The sources of management innovation: When firms introduce new management practices. Journal of business research, 62(12), 1269-1280.

Mol, M. J., & Birkinshaw, J. (2009). The sources of management innovation: When firms introduce new management practices. Journal of business research, 62(12), 1269-1280.

Novozhilov, V. V. (1972). Problemy izmereniya zatrat i rezul'tatov pri optimal'nom planirovanii. Nauka.

Nunez, E. C. A., & Dubolazov, V. A. (2018). Labor market and education in the conditions of fourth industrial revolution. Nauchno-tekhnicheskie vedomosti Sankt-Peterburgskogo gosudarstvennogo politekhnicheskogo universiteta. Ekonomicheskie nauki= Scientific and technical statements of St. Petersburg state Polytechnic University. Economics, 11(5), 38-45.

O'Sullivan, M. 2000. The innovative enterprise and corporate governance. Cambridge Journal of Economics, 24(4), pp.393-416.

Olsen, R. A. (1997). Investment risk: The experts' perspective. Financial Analysts Journal, 53(2), 62-66.

Pupentsova, S., Livintsova, M. 2018. Qualimetric assessment of investment attractiveness of the real estate property. Real Estate Management and Valuation,26(2), pp.5-11

Schepinin, V., & Bataev, A. (2019, March). Digitalization of financial sphere: challenger banks efficiency estimation. In IOP Conference Series: Materials Science and Engineering (Vol. 497, No. 1, p. 012051). IOP Publishing.

Shvetsova, O.A., Rodionova, E.A., Epstein, M.Z. 2018.Evaluation of investment projects under uncertainty: Multi-criteria approach using interval data. Entrepreneurship and Sustainability Issues,5(4), pp.914-928

Tkachenko, E., Rogova, E., Bodrunov, S., & Karlik, A. (2019, September). Application of KM Techniques in the Assessment Competences in High-Tech Industries. In European Conference on Knowledge Management (pp. 1023-XXVII). Academic Conferences International Limited.

Vaccaro, I. G., Jansen, J. J., Van Den Bosch, F. A., & Volberda, H. W. (2012). Management innovation and leadership: The moderating role of organizational size. Journal of Management Studies, 49(1), 28-51.

Cross-Countries' Policies Comparison of Supporting Small and Medium-Sized Enterprises During Covid-19 Pandemic

Wawan Dhewanto[1], Elpi Nazmuzzaman[2] and Tribowo Rachmat Fauzan[1]
[1]School of Business and Management, Institut Teknologi Bandung, Bandung, West Java, Indonesia
[2]Faculty of Economics and Business, Universitas Padjadjaran, Sumedang, West Java, Indonesia
w_dhewanto@sbm-itb.ac.id
elpi@unpad.ac.id
tribowo-rachmat@sbm-itb.ac.id
DOI: 10.34190/EIE.20.236

Abstract: Million confirmed cases and over a hundred thousand deaths had taken place globally since the COVID-19 pandemic. Fears of an imminent recession and economic crisis were also provoked. Physical distancing, working-from-home (WFH) and travel bans policies have been implemented to prevent more its adverse effect. One of the significant drawbacks of this pandemic is debilitating the economic activities which caused businesses particularly small and medium-sized enterprises (SMEs) a dramatic drop in the global scale. Due to policies of the government aimed at preventing COVID-19 spread in the country, and thus protecting human health, people 's movement is heavily constrained, and SMEs in different sectors have had to close their doors until additional notification released by the government. Each country may have different policies during this pandemic to cover their business area even they are facing the same problem; thus analysing policies of countries is a needed for countries to learn each other to aid their SMEs sector and will lead to economic recovery. Since COVID-19 is different compared to other natural disasters, the disaster recovery program for business in this pandemic is understudied. We figured out what the response(s) of multiple countries to cover their SMEs ecosystem and what kind of insight that can be extracted through cross-country policy analysis by using qualitative research design with web-based content analysis method generated from secondary data sourcing from international organisations like International Monetary Fund (IMF), World Trade Organization (WTO), official governmental websites, and well-known news websites. The results showed that countries are focusing on giving policies to support SMEs by providing more accessible loan/credit application, direct monetary stimulus and tax deferral. This research could be useful both for the government as the business' regulator and become guides to the business, especially SMEs themselves to recover and helpful in lowering the risk in the future.

Keywords: COVID-19, cross-countries, entrepreneurship, policy, SMEs

1. Introduction

In December 2019, an unexpected incidence of mysterious respiratory disease occurred in Wuhan City, Province of Hubei, China. A novel coronavirus has been recognised by the World Health Organization (WHO) as a potential cause and named as COVID-19 and continue to spread around the world rapidly (Lu, Stratton and Tang, 2020). As of 11.10 am CEST on July 8 2020, 11.635.939 verified cases of COVID-19 had been recorded worldwide to the WHO, including 539.026 fatalities with the USA has the highest confirmed cases for 2.923.432 followed by Brazil which has 1.623.284 confirmed cases and India for 742.417 confirmed cases. For China, as the first source of the virus has 85.366 confirmed cases and for Indonesia has 66.226 confirmed cases with 3.309 deaths (World Health Organization, 2020[a]). This new epidemic of coronavirus pneumonia spread rapidly over time from January 2020 across the continents, and the outbreak has not only a damaging effect on our health but also economic growth (Yue et al. 2020). Several prevention programs have been socialised and actively conducted by the infected countries such as physical distancing or quarantine program. However, quarantine alone will not be enough to deter COVID-19 transmission. The rapid spread is one of the biggest worries in the global effect of this viral infection (Sohrabi et al., 2020). WHO also provides some objectives to response this outbreak which is interrupted transmission from person to person including the reduction of secondary infections among near contacts and workers in health care, avoid amplification transmissions and preventing future global spreading. Multisector collaborations to reduce social and economic impacts also become a priority, and it was proven by many countries which already releasing their responses to minimise the impact of the COVID-19 pandemic (World Health Organization, 2020[b]; International Monetary Fund, 2020).

International Labor Organization (ILO) forecasts that COVID-19 would result in global unemployment increasing from 5,3 to 24,7 million, suggesting that it is particularly difficult for small and mid-sized ventures to support their daily operations. Little scientific research about how this pandemic influences business around countries. The first data comes from polls conducted by OECD (Organization for Economic Co-operation and Development) indicate that enterprises are rapidly deeply distressed and genuinely worried. The surveys found that more than half of companies still expect significant sales declines with enough funds to survive the crisis for only a few months (Organization for Economic Co-operation and Development, 2020[a]). Policymakers along with epidemiologists have a significant role in focusing on the primary prevention aims, e.g. to reduce morbidity and related mortality, avoid an outbreak that overruns health care systems, maintain economic effects within a manageable range, and flatten disease curve to wait for the creation of and delivery of vaccinations and antiviral medicaments. Governments are making challenging choices. As government acts, how citizens respond to advice about how best to avoid dissemination would be as critical. Government communications approaches that educate the public how best to prevent contamination are essential and added help for handling the economic downturn (Anderson, Hesterbeek, Klinkenberg & Hollingsworth, 2020).

Based on this phenomena, our objectives in this research to find what countries' responses through their policies towards the economy in this COVID-19 pandemic. So far, there is still lacking research in an economic impact of COVID-19. This paper would guide to government as policymakers in how to response this pandemic and affected industries in many countries to survive through the pandemic and minimise more losses in the future if a similar disaster happened. This paper reflects on the revival and collapse of SMEs and in particular, the suggestion for an analysis of the revival of SMEs. The following section discusses emerging post-disaster recovery frameworks for SMEs

2. Literature review

A need for the enterprises to provide a disaster response strategy is noticeable in incidents like terrorist threats, blackouts and natural disasters. In general, the plan helps a company address the disruption and lessens potential financial damages. So little preparation, on the other side, will cause problems for a global recovery by growing the number of enterprises who will require catastrophe assistance and increase services disturbance to the local citizens (Flynn, 2007). The rise in the likelihood of a disaster influences the economy by reducing expectations and increasing risks. This elevated uncertainty has a significant effect both on market cycles and asset markets because investors become uncertainty-adverse: drops in stock prices, employment problems, and especially decreases in investment (Gourio, 2012). Throughout the disaster recovery cycle, one of the major components in how enterprises shift in their business operation and survive through the disaster is government policy (Marshall and Schrank, 2014).

Small business and entrepreneurs play a vital role to foster innovation, economic growth and reducing the unemployment rate. In 2014 59.3 million businesses were represented a total of 58.75%, 98.75% were micro-businesses, 1,15% were small, and 0.1% were medium-sized businesses (Organization for Economic Co-operation and Development, 2018). Compared to big corporations, small businesses have sufficient flexibility to rebound from natural disasters. They are therefore crucial for the economy and population of the disaster-influenced area. Hence, it is necessary for us to achieve a deeper comprehension of the recovery of SMEs as regards the recovery of individuals, social-culture, the built environment and government. (Chang; 2010; Marshall and Schrank, 2014).

The SMEs' recovery from disasters is mainly community-oriented. Two separate lenses were used for the group recovery: the recovery of a regional section or the recovery of social-cultural capital. The recovery of essential services such as utilities and infrastructure, housing or state services have been a significant focus of particular geographic areas and, naturally, these 'essentials' are a significant factor in the recovery of families, people, and enterprises dependent on the geographic area. At the other side, the recovery of collective social capital has focused on the recovery of the foundation within the society (Marshall and Schrank, 2014). Webb, Tierney and Dahlhamer (2002) stated that one of the main factor that essentials to business' recovery are previous disaster experience. However, since there are few similar disasters like COVID-19 before, there were few literature reviews to discuss this kind of disaster and the recovery program, particularly for small and medium-sized enterprises. The followings section will be explaining the methodology used to analyse the policies.

3. Methodology

The following research questions will be answered in this paper: What are the policies made by the government each country to support the economy during COVID-19 pandemic? What insights emerge from the government's policies that relevant to economic impact during COVID-19?

To gather empirical data and answer the research questions, we implemented a web-based content review methodology from official government websites each country, international organisation websites that are covering the area of the supporting economy especially SMEs during COVID-19 pandemic (International Monetary Fund / IMF, Organization for Economic Co-operation and Development/ OECD), and official websites of well-known news portal. Countries chosen in this study is based on the member of G-20 (The Group of Twenty) forum. The network of members of the G20 containing 19 economically stable Countries, the Chairman of the EU and representatives of several international organisations (Slaughter, 2012). In 2008 G20 played a significant part in organising international approaches to the global economic meltdown that prevented devastation (Cammack, 2012); therefore the responses of G20 countries are already proven and now needed to mitigate the risk of COVID-19 pandemic towards economy especially SMEs. The web-based content review methodology is the method which use main Internet search engines to find specific information using predetermined keywords (Ndou, Mele and Del Vecchio, 2019). The web-based content analysis was conducted by searching and finding on major Internet's search engines to form policies to maintain the sustainability of small and medium-sized enterprises. In terms of time and cost output, Web-based content methodology is beneficial (Wu et al., 2010). The keywords used for searches are "COVID-19, policy, SME, small business, entrepreneurship". We only listed the policies available in the English language.

4. Findings and discussion

As described above, our main findings focused on how the government's responses to supporting the small and medium-sized enterprises (SMEs) of COVID-19 through its policies. Before we analyse the policies, we provide brief economy situation (GDP/ gross domestic products growth) in G20 countries, as shown in Table 1 to compare the before-after effect of COVID-19 pandemic. As we mentioned in the introduction, Small and Medium-sized Enterprises (SMEs) are one of the significant contributions for economic growth; therefore this can be insightful information for the policy to recover SMEs and the economy itself. Table 2. showed the result of cross-countries' policies with web-based content analysis.

Table 1: GDP growth of G20 countries (Percentage change on the previous quarter) (Adapted from OECD, 2020[b])

COUNTRY	2019				2020
	Q1	**Q2**	**Q3**	**Q4**	**Q1**
ARGENTINA	0.3	-0.7	1	-1	-3.4
AUSTRALIA	0.5	0.6	0.6	0.5	0.3
BRAZIL	0.2	0.5	0.5	0.4	-0.3
CANADA	0.3	0.8	0.3	0.1	-2.1
CHINA	1.4	1.6	1.4	1.5	-9.8
FRANCE	0.5	0.3	0.2	-0.1	-5.3
GERMANY	0.5	-0.2	0.3	-0.1	-2.2
INDIA	1.4	0.9	0.8	0.9	0.7
INDONESIA	1.2	1.3	1.2	1.2	-0.7
ITALY	0.2	0.1	0	-0.2	-5.3
JAPAN	0.6	0.5	0	-1.9	-0.6
MEXICO	0.2	-0.2	-0.2	-0.6	-1.2
RUSSIA	-0.1	0.6	0.5	0.6	0.3
SAUDI ARABIA	-1.3	-0.6	0.3	1.2	-1
SOUTH AFRICA	-0.8	0.8	-0.2	-0.4	-0.3
SOUTH KOREA	-0.3	1.0	0.4	1.3	-1.3
TURKEY	2.1	1.1	0.7	1.9	0.6
UNITED KINGDOM	0.7	-0.2	0.5	0	-2

COUNTRY	2019				2020
	Q1	Q2	Q3	Q4	Q1
UNITED STATES	0.8	0.5	0.5	0.5	-1.3
EUROPEAN UNION	0.6	0.2	0.3	0.1	-3.2

Table 2: Policy comparison of G20 countries

COUNTRY (Source)	POLICY TYPES TO SUPPORT SMALL-MEDIUM ENTERPRISES		
	Financial Aid	Loan Relaxation	Tax Deferral
ARGENTINA (International Monetary Fund, 2020)	Not mentioned	1. "Credit guarantees will be provided to banks' lending to SMEs for the production of foods and essential supplies" 2. "Lower reserve requirements on bank lending to households and SMEs."	Not mentioned
AUSTRALIA (Business Government Australia, 2020)	"The government is providing temporary cash flow support of up to $100,000 for eligibles SMEs that employ staff."	Not mentioned	Not mentioned
BRAZIL (International Monetary Fund, 2020)	Not mentioned	"The five largest banks in the country agreed to consider requests by individuals and SMEs for a 60-day extension of their maturing debt liabilities."	Not mentioned
CANADA (Government of Canada, 2020)	"Canada Emergency Business will provide interest-free loans of up to $40,000 to SMEs."	1. "Export Development Canada (EDC) will guarantee new operating credit and cash flow term loans that financial institutions extend to SMEs, up to $6.25 million" 2. "The Co-Lending Program will bring the Business Development Bank of Canada (BDC) together with financial institutions to co-lend term loans to SMEs for their operational cash flow requirements."	Not mentioned
CHINA (International Monetary Fund, 2020)	Not mentioned	"Expansion of re-lending and re-discounting facilities by RMB 1.8 trillion to support manufacturers of medical supplies and daily necessities micro-, small- and medium-sized firms and the agricultural sector at low-interest rates."	Not mentioned
FRANCE (International Monetary Fund, 2020)	"Direct financial support for affected microenterprises, liberal professions, and independent workers."	"Credit mediation to support renegotiation of SMEs' bank loan."	"Postponement of rent and utility payments for affected microenterprises and SMEs."
GERMANY (International Monetary Fund, 2020)	"€50 billion in grants to small business owners and self-employed persons severely affected by the Covid-19 outbreak."	Not mentioned	"Interest-free tax deferrals until year-end."
INDIA (International Monetary Fund, 2020)	" Introduced regulatory measures to promote credit flow to the retail sector and micro, small, and medium enterprises (MSMEs)"	Not mentioned	Not mentioned

COUNTRY (Source)	POLICY TYPES TO SUPPORT SMALL-MEDIUM ENTERPRISES		
	Financial Aid	Loan Relaxation	Tax Deferral
INDONESIA (Kementerian Koperasi dan Usaha Kecil dan Menengah Republik Indonesia, 2020) (Ministry of Cooperatives and Small and Medium Enterprises of the Republic of Indonesia),	"Direct financial aid for MSMEs (Rp.2 Trillion)"	"Credit restructured program for MSMEs, especially in affected sectors such as tourism and transportation."	"Tax deferral for MSMEs."
ITALY (International Monetary Fund, 2020)	"Grants for SMEs"	"A moratorium on loan repayments for some households and SMEs, including on mortgages and overdrafts; state guarantees on loans to SME."	"Tax deferral for SMEs worth €16 billion (included grants for them)"
JAPAN (The Japan Times, 2020)	"The state-owned Japan Finance Corp. is among entities that will join the program aimed at helping small businesses gain access to financing."	"Extend zero-interest loans with no collateral to small and midsized companies."	Not mentioned
MEXICO (International Monetary Fund, 2020)	"The central bank has opened financing facilities for commercial and development banks (350 billion pesos) to allow them to channel resources to micro, small- and medium-sized enterprises and individuals affected by the COVID-19 pandemic."	Not mentioned	Not mentioned
RUSSIA (International Monetary Fund, 2020)	"Loan guarantee to SMEs and affected industries."	"The interest rate on Central Bank of Russia (CBR) loans aimed at supporting lending to SMEs, including for urgent needs to support and maintain employment was reduced from 4.0 to 3.5 per cent."	"Tax holiday for six months for all taxes (except VAT) for all SMEs in affected sectors."
SAUDI ARABIA (The National, 2020)	" SMEs will get relief from finance costs through a 6bn riyal loan guarantee programme."	"30billion Riyals will be allocated for banks and financing companies to delay loan payments due from SMEs for six months."	Not mentioned
SOUTH AFRICA (International Monetary Fund, 2020)	"Funds are available to assist SMEs under stress, mainly in the tourism and hospitality sectors."	Not mentioned	"Government accelerating reimbursements and tax credits and allow SMEs to defer certain tax liabilities."
SOUTH KOREA (International Monetary Fund, 2020)	"Expanded lending of both state-owned and commercial banks to SMEs "	"Lowering the interest rate to 0.25 per cent (from 0.5-0.75 per cent)"	Not mentioned
TURKEY (International Monetary Fund, 2020)	"Set up a new lending facility for SMEs in the export sector."	Not mentioned	Not mentioned

COUNTRY (Source)	POLICY TYPES TO SUPPORT SMALL-MEDIUM ENTERPRISES		
	Financial Aid	Loan Relaxation	Tax Deferral
UNITED KINGDOM (Government of the United Kingdom, 2020)	1. "Small business grant funding of £10,000 for all business in receipt of small business rate relief or rural rate relief" 2. "Offering loans of up to £5 million for SMEs through the British Business Bank."	Not mentioned	Not mentioned
UNITED STATES (Small Business Administration, 2020)	"Allows SMEs who currently have a business relationship with an SBA (Small Business Administration) Express Lender to access up to $25,000 "	"US government will pay the SMEs' principal and interest of current debt/loans for six months."	Not mentioned
EUROPEAN UNION (Organization for Economic Co-operation and Development, 2020a)	"EUR 1 billion has been provided as a guarantee to the European Investment Fund (part of the European Investment Bank / EIB group) to support SME financing."	Not mentioned	Not mentioned

4.1 Financial aid

Most of the countries find that supporting SMEs can be conducted via direct funding aid which means the priority is to give financial assistance. Some countries also mentioned the amount of financial aid, although the website stated the policies might change over time due to their capacity to support the SMEs. This is in line with the previous study by Liu, Xu & Han (2013) that SMEs recovery during disasters will concentrate on financial support for market regeneration and optimisation, marketing, strategy, funding, human capital and brand survival. Joshi and Nishimura (2016) find that, when public support is available and financial aid equally allocated, citizens are more willing to comply with the government and act according to the government's plans.

4.2 Loan relaxation

Banking industries have been appealed to not cut or withdraw loans during the pandemic and government in many countries also called tax offices to defer the payment to protect multisector industries. For small businesses and more prominent sectors, the most affected sectors are tourism, hospitality and leisure. However, it does not mean that other areas did not affect either because many countries also generalised every industry that damaged by COVID-19 will get financial aid or credit guarantee. Pathak and Ahmad (2016) also mentioned that managing financial resources (personal savings, bank loans, government aid) is the first step to recovery SMEs affected with a natural disaster which is similar with managing SMEs in COVID-19 pandemic. On the other hand, some countries such as Indonesia and South Africa stated that tourism sector is the one who needs to be prioritised to receive aid since the pandemic cause tourists to stay at home due to WHO recommendation to prevent human-to-human contact (World Health Organization, 2020[c]).

4.3 Tax deferral

Compared to financial aid and loan relaxation, the tax deferral segment is relatively less mentioned from the sources. However, it is also necessary to consider the financial impacts of recovery beyond the financial impacts of disaster management on municipal government Damage assessment, emergency demolition, removal of waste, restoration of infrastructure, and planning of the affected areas must be subject to costs. There is often decreased sales owing to delay or deferment concerning these added expenses. Therefore, tax deferral becomes one of the most effective solutions to recover businesses (Lindell and Prater, 2003). Each country has their economic power, and this pandemic will affect it in different level, that could lead to many countries to not mentioned tax deferral/exemption in their program because they want to assess their economic power first after the pandemic is gone. However, both the public and private businesses and the Non-profit organisations, which contribute to social work relevant to disaster and damage prevention should be granted tax exemptions (breaks, waiver, and postponements) (Porfiriev, 2012).

Although SME development could be different in each country, the policies of each state could be similar because they felt the same effect when disaster came in (Liu, Xiu and Han, 2013). This research is useful for supporting the small business that affected by COVID-19 pandemic and also helping governments as the regulator of companies make a proper policy to support the enterprises. The limitation of this research is that there are few studies yet about the implementation of these policies to the business itself. Therefore, for the next researchers could take small businesses' point of view to validate the plans made by the government to support them during the pandemic.

Table 1. show the Economic development from G20 countries indicated by GDP. As we can see from the table, COVID-19 made a significant change to the GDP in Quarter 1 2020 compared to the last Quarter (Quarter 4 2019) or last year (Quarter 1 2019). This pandemic which started at the beginning of 2020 drastically decreasing the countries' income and SMEs have proven as one of the significant parts in increasing the economic growth indicated by the growth of GDP (Beck, Demirguc-Kunt and Levine, 2005). The length of the lockdown or new normal adaptation and of the recovery period was still uncertain at the date of this study. GDP performance in the basic scenario would fall between 3-6 per cent depending on the region (Fernandes, 2020). We expect these policies could have a positive impact on SMEs performance and in the end, increasing GDP.

5. Conclusion

COVID-19, a disease that firstly discovered in China, has become a public enemy not only for human health but also to the economy itself, especially the small business environment. Its rapid spread makes the WHO made a recommendation to minimise direct physical contact, which affects the business and make government in many countries have to respond quickly to prevent any more prominent issues in the future. Government of many countries already released policies to support their economics. The policies are mainly focusing on the financial aspect of recovering affected SMEs. By giving more accessible loan/credit application, direct monetary stimulus and tax deferral, governments hope that both areas could help each other, and the affected business could sustain during COVID-19 pandemic. Since the pandemic is still ongoing at the time this study conducted and the policy itself may change during time depends on the how bad the impact of this pandemic to the SMEs, we are yet to determine which are the best policy to be implemented in each country. Therefore, this can become a future research agenda to determine the policy that suitable the most to recover the SMEs and validate the impact of policies itself to SMEs' performance. Hopefully, the policies become a prove to become a valuable reference for the future disastrous event.

References

Anderson, R. M., Heesterbeek, H., Klinkenberg, D. and Hollingsworth, T. D. (2020) "How will country-based mitigation measures influence the course of the COVID-19 epidemic?". *The Lancet.* DOI:10.1016/s0140-6736(20)30567-5

Beck, T., Demirguc-Kunt, A., & Levine, R. (2005). "SMEs, Growth, and Poverty". *Journal of Economic Growth* vol.10, p199–229 DOI: https://doi.org/10.1007/s10887-005-3533-5

Business Government Australia. (2020). Assistance for affected regions, communities and industries [Online]. Available at: https://www.business.gov.au/Risk-management/Emergency-management/Coronavirus-information-and-support-for-business/Assistance-for-affected-regions-communities-and-industries (Accessed April 12 2020)

Cammack, P. (2012) "The G20, the Crisis, and the Rise of Global Developmental Liberalism". *Third World Quarterly, 33(1), 1–16.* DOI:10.1080/01436597.2012.628110

Chang, S. E. (2010) "Urban disaster recovery: a measurement framework and its application to the 1995 Kobe earthquake". *Disasters, 34(2), 303–327.* DOI:10.1111/j.1467-7717.2009.01130.x

Fernandes, N. "Economic Effects of Coronavirus Outbreak (COVID-19) on the World Economy (March 22, 2020)" [Online]. Available at: http://dx.doi.org/10.2139/ssrn.3557504

Flynn, D. T. (2007) "The impact of disasters on small business disaster planning: a case study". *Disasters, 31(4), 508–515.* DOI:10.1111/j.1467-7717.2007.01022.x

Gourio, F. (2012)" Disaster Risk and Business Cycles". *American Economic Review, 102(6), 2734–2766.* DOI:10.1257/aer.102.6.2734

Government of Canada. (2020). Additional Support for Canadian Businesses from the Economic Impact of COVID-19 [Online]. Available at: https://www.canada.ca/en/department-finance/news/2020/03/additional-support-for-canadian-businesses-from-the-economic-impact-of-covid-19.html (Accessed April 13 2020)

Government of the United Kingdom. (2020). Financial support for businesses during coronavirus (COVID-19) [Online]. Available at: https://www.gov.uk/government/collections/financial-support-for-businesses-during-coronavirus-covid-19 (Accessed April 15 2020)

International Monetary Fund. (2020). POLICY RESPONSES TO COVID-19 [Online]. Available at: https://www.imf.org/en/Topics/imf-and-covid19/Policy-Responses-to-COVID-19 (Accessed: June 13 2020)

Joshi, A. and Nishimura, M. (2016) "Impact of disaster relief policies on the cooperation of residents in a post-disaster housing relocation program: A case study of the 2004 Indian Ocean Tsunami". *International Journal of Disaster Risk Reduction, 19, 258–264.* DOI:10.1016/j.ijdrr.2016.08.018

Kementerian Koperasi dan Usaha Kecil dan Menengah Republik Indonesia. (2020). 8 PROGRAM ANTISIPASI DAMPAK COVID-19 BUAT PELAKU KUMKM [Online]. Available at: http://www.depkop.go.id/read/8-program-antisipasi-dampak-covid-19-buat-pelaku-kumkm (Accesed 29 March 2020)

Lindell, M. K., & Prater, C. S. (2003) "Assessing Community Impacts of Natural Disasters". *Natural Hazards Review, 4(4), 176–185.* DOI:10.1061/(ASCE)1527-6988(2003)4:4(176)

Liu, Z., Xu, J. and Han, B. T. (2013) "Small- and medium-sized enterprise post-disaster reconstruction management patterns and application". *Natural Hazards, 68(2), 809–835.* DOI:10.1007/s11069-013-0657-3

Lu, H., Stratton, C. W. and Tang, Y. (2020) "An outbreak of Pneumonia of Unknown Etiology in Wuhan China: The Mystery and the Miracle". *Journal of Medical Virology.* DOI:10.1002/jmv.25678

Marshall, M. I., & Schrank, H. L. (2014) "Small business disaster recovery: a research framework". *Natural Hazards, 72(2), 597–616.* DOI:10.1007/s11069-013-1025-z

Ndou, V., Mele, G. and Del Vecchio, P. (2019) "Entrepreneurship education in tourism: An investigation among European Universities". *Journal of Hospitality, Leisure, Sport & Tourism Education.* DOI:10.1016/j.jhlste.2018.10.003

Pathak, S. and Ahmad, M. M. (2016) "Flood recovery capacities of the manufacturing SMEs from floods: A case study in Pathumthani province, Thailand". *International Journal of Disaster Risk Reduction, 18, 197–205.* DOI:10.1016/j.ijdrr.2016.07.001

Porfiriev, B. (2012) "Economic issues of disaster and disaster risk reduction policies: International vs. Russian perspectives". *International Journal of Disaster Risk Reduction, 1, 55–61.* DOI:10.1016/j.ijdrr.2012.05.005

Slaughter, S. (2012) "Debating the International Legitimacy of the G20: Global Policymaking and Contemporary International Society". *Global Policy, 4(1), 43–52.* DOI:10.1111/j.1758-5899.2012.00175.x

Small Business Administration. (2020). Coronavirus Relief Options [Online]. Available at: https://www.sba.gov/funding-programs/loans/coronavirus-relief-options

Sohrabi, C., Alsafi, Z., O'Neill, N., Khan, M., Kerwan, A., Al-Jabir, A., ... Agha, R. (2020) "World Health Organization declares Global Emergency: A review of the 2019 Novel Coronavirus (COVID-19)". *International Journal of Surgery.* DOI:10.1016/j.ijsu.2020.02.034

The Japan Times. 2020. Abe unveils zero-interest loan plan for virus-hit small businesses in Japan [Online]. Available at: https://www.japantimes.co.jp/news/2020/03/08/national/politics-diplomacy/shinzo-abe-zero-interest-loan-coronavirus-japan/#.Xoi50YgzbDd (Accessed April 22 2020)

The National. 2020. Saudi Arabia pledges 50bn riyal stimulus package to offset coronavirus impact [Online]. Available at: https://www.thenational.ae/business/economy/saudi-arabia-pledges-50bn-riyal-stimulus-package-to-offset-coronavirus-impact-1.992626 (Accessed April 24 2020)

Organisation for Economic Co-operation and Development. (2018). SME and Entrepreneurship Policy in Indonesia 2018, *OECD Studies on SMEs and Entrepreneurship*, OECD Publishing, Paris [Online]. Available at: https://doi.org/10.1787/9789264306264-en (Accessed: March 20 2020)

Organisation for Economic Co-operation and Development. (2020[a]). Covid-19: SME Policy Responses – OECD [Online]. Available at: http://www.oecd.org/cfe/COVID-19-SME-Policy-Responses.pdf (Accessed: May 15 2020)

Organisation for Economic Co-operation and Development. (2020[b]). G20 GDP growth Quarterly National Accounts [Online]. Available at: https://www.oecd.org/sdd/na/g20-gdp-growth-Q1-2020.pdf

Webb, G. R., Tierney, K. J., & Dahlhamer, J. M. (2002) "Predicting long-term business recovery from disaster: a comparison of the Loma Prieta earthquake and Hurricane Andrew". *Environmental Hazards, 4(2), 45–58.* DOI:10.3763/ehaz.2002.0405

World Health Organization. (2020[a]). WHO Health Emergency Dashboard Coronavirus (COVID-19) [Online]. Available at: https://who.sprinklr.com/ (Accessed: July 8 2020)

World Health Organization. (2020[b]). Novel Coronavirus(2019-Nov): Situation Report - 67, (2020) [Online]. Available at: https://www.who.int/docs/default-source/coronaviruse/situation-reports/20200327-sitrep-67-covid-19.pdf?sfvrsn=b65f68eb_4 (Accesed: 10 May 2020)

World Health Organization. (2020[c]). Novel Coronavirus(2019-nCoV): Situation Report - 80, (2020) [Online]. Available at: https://www.who.int/docs/default-source/coronaviruse/situation-reports/20200409-sitrep-80-covid-19.pdf?sfvrsn=1b685d64_4 (Accesed: 10 May 2020)

Wu, Y.-C. J., Huang, S., Kuo, L. and Wu, W.-H. (2010) "Management Education for Sustainability: A Web-Based Content Analysis". *Academy of Management Learning & Education, 9(3), 520–531.* DOI:10.5465/amle.9.3.zqr520

Yue, X.-G., Shao, X.-F., Li, R. Y. M., Crabbe, M. J. C., Mi, L., Hu, S., ... Dong, K. (2020) "Risk Prediction and Assessment: Duration, Infections, and Death Toll of the COVID-19 and Its Impact on China's Economy". *Journal of Risk and Financial Management, 13(4), 66.* DOI:10.3390/jrfm13040066

Team Dynamics: Entrepreneurship Versus Music. What an Entrepreneurial Team can Learn

Elli Diakanastasi and Angeliki Karagiannaki
Athens University of Economics and Business, Eltrun, E-business Research Center, Greece
diakanastasi@aueb.gr
e.diakanastasi@acein.aueb.gr
akaragianaki@aueb.gr
DOI: 10.34190/EIE.20.123

Abstract: Literature regarding entrepreneurial teams has risen the last decade (Fayolle et al., 2014). Researchers study entrepreneurial teams as a part of a big company, even though an entrepreneurial team usually does not evolve under the context of a large and stable organization. It mostly works and flourish under circumstances of instability, lack of income, uncertainty, innovation, creativity, problem solving. A music band works under the same circumstances. Music bands already have been used as an example in researching how organizations can be more innovative and creative (Kamoche;2003) and some researchers claim that team dynamics of an early stage entrepreneurial team resembles the dynamics of a music band. Using a qualitative approach, entrepreneurial teams and music bands of 3-5 members, where interviewed in order to shed light on team dynamics and team spirit. This empirical research attempts to identify the differences between the two and point out positive aspects of music bands' team spirit. The results extract six variables, 'discussion with the team', 'give space to everyone', 'practice', 'perform as a unity', 'trust', 'everyone acts as a composer/leader' which seems to enhance band's cohesion and performance, as also can help entrepreneurial teams tackle their team dynamics in a way that provides a more efficient outcome.

Keywords: team dynamics, entrepreneurial teams, music bands, interdisciplinary, startups, entrepreneurship, cohesion

1. Introduction

This paper tries to find inspiration from various disciplines in order to ameliorate entrepreneurial team dynamics. As Aldrich (1999) stated 'In non-technology-based populations, some of the knowledge used can be enacted through an arbitrary but creative recombination of existing knowledge. (...) cultural industries – music, theater, the arts, and so forth – spring from new ways of looking at existing knowledge'. After studying the literature review, the researchers found that an entrepreneurial team dynamics' were most common with sports teams' dynamics and small music groups' dynamics (Bartel & Saavedra, 2000). Jazz bands (Oldfather, West. (1994)) have been studied several times in the literature because of the similarities of these teams.

Comparisons revealed that music bands as well as entrepreneurial teams behave as a team and not as a group. If we want to understand the difference, we can set an example. In an aerobics class, there is a group. They listen and follow the trainer and make the same moves synchronized. The main difference with the team is that their actions probably will not affect the other group members because they have a common goal or outcome. That would happen in the case of a team. It is clear that team members behave with the knowledge that their actions will affect the actions of other team members and of the common goal they work for. As Cordery (2004) stated, teamwork is 'the extent to which the members are "truly reliant on each other's actions" and is not to be confused with group work - which does not require a high degree of interdependency unlike a team'. There are many definitions of what a team is, but the researchers prefer to work with the one given by Schjoedt and Kraus pg 515,(2009) regarding entrepreneurial teams:

two or more persons who have an interest, both financial and otherwise, and commitment to a venture's future and success; whose work is interdependent in the pursuit of common goals and venture success; who are considered to be at the executive level with executive responsibility in the early phases of the venture, including founding and pre-start-up; and who are seen as a social entity by themselves and by others.

To further this aim, our article is structured as follows. In the beginning, we review the literature. Method follows and we sum up with a conclusion, research limitations, and directions for future research. Empirically, the research is based on interviews and time spent with the music bands. Using this qualitative data, we explore the factors that could be copied by nascent entrepreneurial teams.

2. Literature review

Research of entrepreneurial teams has received growing recent attention in the last years because of its importance, with extant entrepreneurial literature focused on the upper echelons theory (Hambrick, 2007; Hiebl, 2014; Waldman et al., 2004). Entrepreneurial teams are the base of 79.1 percent of new ventures (Kollmann et al., 2015). However, "even though ETs are now getting the scholarly recognition that they deserve, the overall number of research articles addressing this topic remains reasonably low" (Ben-Hafaïedh, 2017). In the most recent entrepreneurial team literature review we find Klotz et al. (2014) studying intermediary mechanisms that affect how team inputs influences effectiveness. The association amid new venture diversity and performance is under the lens of Zhou and Rosini (2015). The importance of sharing equity from the first steps of team formation to prevent major conflict issues is stressed by Balkin and Swift (2006). This study continues the research around a founding team by taking examples from the music industry.

Ben-Hafaïedh, (2017) quotes there are 'three specific types of outcomes that have proved valuable in examining team effectiveness: (a) the team's production of a high- quality product, be it a physical product, a decision, a plan or other output; (b) the team's contribution to the wellbeing and growth of the team; and (c) the continuing capability of members to work together in the future' (Hackman, 1987; Hackman and Wageman, 2005). This study tried to incorporate these aspects while studying the teams.

In line with the ideas of previous researchers that have searched the meanings of cohesion, fulfillment, conflict and effectiveness in music bands, Pescosolido and Saavedra (2012) claim that 'Cohesion has an instrumental basis. All groups—musical groups, work groups, sports teams, committees—form for a purpose. Even groups that may be considered purely "social" in nature have an instrumental basis for their formation'. Timmons et al. (2004) state that 'Likewise, innumerable metaphors from other parts of life can describe the complex world of the entrepreneur and the entrepreneurial process. From music it is jazz'. In 'Leading entrepreneurial teams: insights from jazz' Ucbasaran et al (2011) emphasizes the concepts of individuality, uncertainty of working conditions, creativity etc. Forbes (2006) points out that we could take examples from such music groups in order to have valuable outcomes for entrepreneurial teams. Bathurst and Ladkin (2012) studied jazz groups to find insights for entrepreneurial leadership.

These and other studies gave us the stimulus to enter this research, and even though we did not replicate the previously reported cases, our results suggest that in most of the studies, jazz music groups were selected as a unit of analysis. Many times, the correlation was with groups in large established organizations. But as Ubscaran et al (2011) state, "Although the link between jazz and management is well established, its absence from entrepreneurship research is notable. We find this surprising given that innovation, creativity and improvisation are central to both jazz music (e.g., Tyler & Tyler, 1990; Hatch, 1997; Weick, 1998) and the entrepreneurial process (e.g. Ward, 2004; Baker, Miner & Eesley, 2003; Hmieleski & Corbett, 2006)".

To take it a step further, the novelty of our study is that it takes as a unit of analysis small music bands from various genres of music (rather than only jazz) and tries to pinpoint patterns of behavior that nascent entrepreneurial teams can adopt for their benefit.

In Table 1, there is a literature review that spurred our interest and motivation for the study.

Table 1: Indicative literature review

Cartwright, P. and Swearing, K., 2020. Group Work: Application and Performance Effectiveness in Musical Ensembles. In *New Leadership in Strategy and Communication* (pp. 329-350). Springer, Cham.	"The creative process of the musician involves two phases, which are described below. The first, the practice phase, is psychologically dynamic and involves specific challenges to the musician's self-experience. It is during the practice stage that the musician is most creative (one exception to this might be the improvisations of jazz musicians). The second phase is that of the public performance, at which time the results of the creative effort are displayed" "we introduce a paradox that underpins plural leadership. Like leadership, music-making begins before any sounds are made or any actions taken. For musicians there is an abiding respect for the tool of his or her trade, the instrument. This respect has developed over many years of personal practice and preparation. Successful performance is not possible without these many hours spent alone grappling with the technical difficulties that the musician confronts when mastering the instrument."

Rabinowitch, T., Cross, I. and Burnard, P., 2012. Musical group interaction, intersubjectivity and merged subjectivity. *Kinesthetic empathy in creative and cultural practices*, pp.109-120.	"Each participant's individual sense that they are experiencing the meaning of the music 'naturally' encourages the perception that the experiences of other participants must be in alignment with their own"
Kamoche, K., Cunha, M.P.E. and Cunha, J.V.D., 2003. Towards a theory of organizational improvisation: Looking beyond the jazz metaphor. *Journal of Management Studies*, *40*(8), pp.2023-2051	"We note, however, that improvisation is not exclusive to jazz. In fact, according to acclaimed guitarist and musical producer Derek Bailey (1992) there is scarcely any musical technique or form that did not originate in improvisation and scarcely any single field in music which has remained unaffected by improvisation. " "Achieving a meaningful performance requires a balance between collaboration and competition. Thus, without seeking to romanticize jazz, we would argue that egotistical behavior must be situated within a context of a collaborative praxis.
Tal-Shmotkin, M. and Gilboa, A., 2013. Do behaviors of string quartet ensembles represent self-managed teams? *Team Performance Management: An International Journal.*	"Typically, the operation of such teams involves designing methods and procedures of work, evaluating performance, making decisions, taking possession of the results, and managing various things for which supervision or management are usually responsible (Attaran and Nguyen, 2000; Polley and Ribbens, 1998). SMTs set their own goals (aligned with their organizational strategy), may prepare their own budget, coordinate with other units, order materials from suppliers, and be responsible for developing skills within the team" "The maintenance of such interpersonal relations requires a culture of transparency of work procedures, mutual encouragement of members in creative and innovative initiatives, and tolerance to different ways of thinking. SMTs"
Ucbasaran, D., Lockett, A. and Humphreys, M., 2011. Leading entrepreneurial teams: insights from jazz. *London: Institute for Small Business and Entrepreneurship.*	"Jazz bands have to deal with these issues whilst having to be highly innovative under conditions of uncertainty. We propose that an empirical examination of the practices of jazz groups and their leaders may reveal valuable theoretical and practical insights into how best to lead entrepreneurial teams in dynamic environments"

3. Method

Working seven years in a university incubator/accelerator, the researchers started pointing out some patterns in the behavior of nascent entrepreneurial teams and the way their in-between team dynamics affect the team's cohesion and the project they work on. As also seen in the literature (e.g., Ucbasaran et al, 2011), nascent entrepreneurial teams work under circumstances of uncertainty, under imbalance and many times zero income for a long time. Their tasks require a lot of creativity, eligibility, innovative ways of thinking and working under pressure. Additionally, both type of teams are formed by people who operate and innovate for their own pleasure, and afterwards market this outcome (Agarwal & Shah, 2014).

For our first goal, we focused on which kind of team to choose. We chose music bands instead of sports teams as a unit of analysis. This is because sports teams always have a coach, with a very distinctive role that guides the team. Whilst music bands and entrepreneurial teams do not always follow that rule.

14 music bands that had between 3-5 members were studied. All the teams had already worked together two years or more. They all self-assessed that they mainly work in harmony and are happy with the outcome. (The researchers wanted contented teams, in order to study what brings them this feeling.) They do not work with a manager.

Table 2: Genre description of music bands studied

Type of music	Number of Band Members
Rock mainly alternative, grunge, progressive	5
Greek post-traditional	4
Fusion rock, tradition, Balkan and reggae	4
Folk, alternative	5
Aggressive Metal	5
Jazz	3
Rock, hard rock, pop rock	4
Rock metal progressive	5
Groovy/Funky	4
Indie	3
Psychedelic reggae	5
Kind of Jazz	4
Pop	4
Indie alternative rock	5

A minimum of two participants per band replied to an open-ended questionnaire, and at least one of them was not the leader (if there was one). The analysts also spent some time during a two years' time with the bands at rehearsals and in live shows. There, unstructured interviews and observation took place. Bands where chosen based on their success both on the result they give out (they have fans, perform lives often and get paid for that) as also their in-between relationships which were described as excellent from all team members. Some of these are also factors of measuring evolution and success of entrepreneurial teams: financial, expansion, and survival indicators (Shah et al., 2019).

Members displayed excellent relationships and a described a sense of happiness and belonging with each other and into their project. That was done in order for the researchers to see what bands do to keep balance and maintain the feeling of fulfillment in order to gather examples that the entrepreneurial teams could use as well.

Moreover, semi-structured interviews were used, with open-ended questions in order to enable an unlimited number of categories to emerge (Marx and Tobias, 2019). The interviews and questionnaire were answered from the bands and from twelve teams from prior research (Diakanastasi et al., 2018) Following theory from Birks et al (2013), who supports that 'if the data that were previously collected are rich enough (e.g., a multi-year ethnographic study), it may allow for strong theory building, following constant comparison and coding approaches'

The questionnaire was adapted from Fairfield et al (2003) to a format that could be answered by music bands and by nascent entrepreneurial teams too. Elements from the original questionnaire which were not relevant to the research's context were erased. We executed an informal content analysis to classify the key words, in order to make a coding of the content. The conclusion was the following key words/phrases: 'discussion with the team', 'give space to everyone', 'practice', 'perform as a unity', 'trust', 'everyone acts as a composer/leader'.

The objective of this study is to pinpoint factors that balance and ameliorate the dynamics of an entrepreneurial team by taking examples from successful (in these points) music bands. Elements of grounded theory were chosen in order to run this research and develop initial question, gather data, and find out patterns and codes in order to build theory (inspired from Murphy, Klotz, & Kreiner, 2017).

The following scheme shows how:

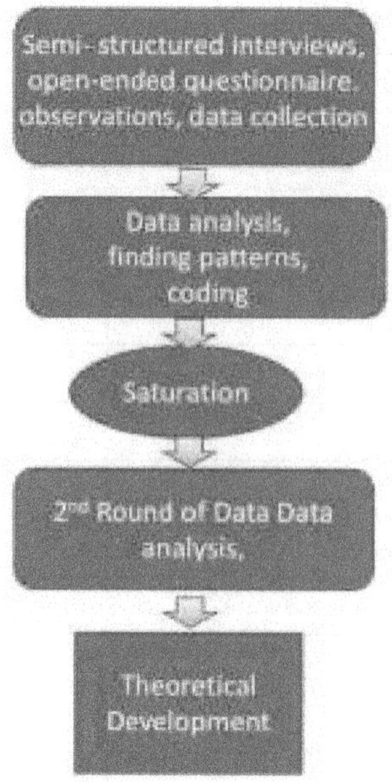

Figure 1: Steps to theoretical development

This research tries to expand theory, not endorse it (Glaser & Strauss, 1967; Strauss, 1987) as 'grounded theory has its emphasis on the socially constructed nature of reality (Goulding 1998), and the aim is to produce interpretations that can explain social phenomenon and provide information of value to those engaged in the behavior under study' (Pettigrew, 2000).

4. Analyzing the codes

We ran a process of tagging the interview text under some categories in order to conclude to a coding scheme which helps as analyze the qualitative data.

'Discussion with the team'

All bands declared that conflicts were solved with discussion and repetition of a given task/music piece. Some also stated that they may vote sometimes and all votes are equal. 'All voices can be heard in our team. There are times that there is a lot of vibration (different opinions), but in the end of the "day" we conclude and in the outside world we have one voice'. This finding is contrary to the findings of Hambrick and Mason, (1984) and the "upper echelon" perspective.

'Practice'

Musicians have the term of "practice". This means to study their pieces and also make some standard exercises alone and some with the band. A lot of practice reduces possibility for problems to occur and almost definitely 'makes easier to find a solution if they appear', reported the music bands. It is worth noticing that in entrepreneurial literature 'practice' is not a term that appears often. 'Most harmony after a lot of practice, less harmony in the beginning' is essential to 'have time to practice all together'.

When the entrepreneurial teams had to respond to this term—although it was not in their everyday vocabulary between them—they understood it as a combination of having experience, studying on your own to solve some problems in your own area and having to work a lot of hours with the rest of the members. The more hours having worked together, the fewer problems there are.

'Give space to everyone'

This term may seem obvious, but it was not for the entrepreneurial teams. For music bands, 'giving space to everyone' meant several things. First of all, to hear everybody's opinion, but mostly to give space to everyone to play their music and shine as a unit. In small bands like the ones that were studied, it is a custom that everybody plays a solo part. The solo is usually played as the last songs of a live concert, and although it keeps a sense of the main song, it usually has a lot of improvisation. A good Improvisation, according to musicians, comes from creativity, passion, technique, lot of practice and a feeling of 'freedom' which they define as 'no critique from the band, only sincere feedback'.

It was noticed from the interviews that entrepreneurial teams didn't have this meaning of "soloing" in their routine. They didn't give the opportunity to team members to also act as units and show their own potential.

'Perform as a unity'

This may seem contradictory from the latter. 'They all try to harmonize to a very good result', 'everyone tries to harmonize with everyone', 'the band is always trying to give new ideas and are contributing to the final shape of the song' and the most explicatory would be 'music works when everybody is playing together, in unity, as opposed to 4-5 different instruments that happen to play at the same time'. This comes really close to the definition of team that this research adopts.

When comparing bands' answers to those of the entrepreneurial teams, it was noticed that this was not self-evident at all. In most of the 15 cases of nascent entrepreneurial teams interviewed, many answered that they didn't care about what the rest of the team do. Especially the IT staff. They just wanted clear tasks to execute.

'Trust'

At first glance this would seem as something obvious coming from a team. Nevertheless, no one coming from the entrepreneurial teams mentioned this word or this meaning. Whilst music bands stated 'we let music happen while trusting each other' and 'we harmonize when there is respect and trust', 'it is a matter of trust to bring out the best of my self'. When there was a mutual feeling of trust, interviewees seemed to feel more comfortable to perform better, but also more called by duty to give their best. 'When I play a melody or my part, each one in the group tries his part quietly till they find the right harmony'.

'Everyone Acts as a Composer/Leader'

Although seven out of twelve bands were a personal project (meaning that the band executes one person's compositions and choosing), everybody had a say as plain performers but also on the orchestration, composing, and performing parts. 'Members act as spectators when they hear a new piece and need to figure out how to play it. Everyone acts as a composer on their side. Everybody puts some effort and their own personality when they perform their part'. 'They all get to say their opinion we're all trying to make the song work. Sometimes the bass player has to compose a bass line or improve a bass line that I've written and sometimes the guitar player would add a riff or play his own solo in a song'.

Adding to all these, there was another factor that may have affected the way the music bands acts, and makes it more stable. This is that they are all on stage during performance. They have all exposure.

In an entrepreneurial team, the end user or the client may never see the people behind the product's service. If they meet someone from the entrepreneurial team, it will most likely be the business developer or a sales person. In the bands we studied, during a live performance they are all in stage, and the 'product' they are selling, is being sold by all of them. They have equal parts of solo performance and interaction.

In order to conclude

Figure 2: Behavioral patterns entrepreneurial teams could copy from music bands

5. Conclusion, limitation and future research

Six variables, 'discussion with the team', 'give space to everyone', 'practice', 'perform as a unity', 'trust', 'everyone acts as a composer/leader' were noted that made a musical team perform better and feel content. Four of them (although they are not the same), could go under a greater umbrella – the meaning of 'team spirit' as given by Silva et al. pg 288, (2014). 'Essentially, team spirit can be viewed as an inter-subjectively shared facility with which individual members of a team can balance opposing tensions in a consistent way, managing to maintain a healthy synthesis between individual and collective needs and expectations, preventing the team from dominating the individuals, as well as specific individuals from capturing the team'.

Music bands members that felt content and functioned well as a group, seems that have the opportunity to feel free to perform, say their opinion, improvise, create, and give feedback in a team environment where they feel secure.

On the other hand this environment has solid structures (clearly set, roles, music pieces, rehearsals, standard performances). It has also three stages of "working". Everyday study, rehearsal and live performance. From our study we conclude that this sense of freedom and flexibility in a structured environment keeps the cohesion and the performance of the team at a high level.

Although entrepreneurship literature is blooming and shows entrepreneurial teams as a stimulant for new venture creation (Cooper & Daily, 1997; Visintin & Pittino, 2014), the most interdisciplinary literature is between organizational psychology and entrepreneurship. The present research grants to this field by proposing a new approach coming from another discipline—music—using qualitative data from a range of musical bands of various size and operating in different genres of music.

Mainly three disciplines – economics, psychology, and sociology – have been used for theorizing and examining entrepreneurial team until now according to Ben-Hafaïedh (2017). The current findings were based on the disciplines of economics, psychology, and literature from musicology writers. The results can serve as stimulus and suggestions for further interdisciplinary research that will address and identify effective behavioral characteristics in musical ensembles in order to apply them to organizations settings.

The present study has several limitations to consider. First of all, the number of the bands. The study was conducted with 14 bands. The interviews did not include recording time in a studio, where processes are different and the producer has a major role.

The fact that the bands were willing to participate in a study like this may show that they are more open minded and extroverted than other musicians.

Because of the lack of time but also the excess resources the study would take, it was decided not to analyze in this paper all the answers the nascent entrepreneurial teams gave. (For further information see Diakanastasi et al, (2018) and limit the study to the factors that could make entrepreneurial teams more effective.)

The limitations of the present studies naturally include that grounded theory may have the problem of generalizability (Goulding 1998; Johnson 1990). Is it really correct to draw conclusions from such a sample where the researcher also has personal contact? On the other hand, it offers opportunities in terms of the in-depth analysis of the phenomenon of interest (Buchanan, 1999; Tsoukas, 2009).

This research beyond its theoretical impact has a practical impact, as can be used by nascent entrepreneurial teams, leaders, founders, accelerators etc. in order to change their perspective and try some of the proposed ways of team work for achieving improved results.

We couldn't agree more with Ben-Hafaïedh (2017): "with acknowledging this view (e.g., Agarwal, 2019), future research may examine how the different elements of the formation process influence advanced phases. Future research may shed light on how initial formation processes can trigger, foster or diminish these compositional and dynamic features over time, and how contextual factors can constrain or shape these relationships at nascent stages of the team'.

Future research can take as a tool a longitudinal approach in order to help us understand how attraction and commitment between the members keep the teams from splitting and keep them running. In this ongoing real time evolutionary study (like this one) we believe can give better results than a retrospective study.

References

Aldrich, H. 1999. *Organizations evolving*. Sage.

Attaran, M. and Nguyen, T.T., 2000. Creating the right structural fit for self-directed teams. *Team Performance Management: An International Journal.*

Agarwal, R. and Shah, S.K., 2014. Knowledge sources of entrepreneurship: Firm formation by academic, user and employee innovators. Research policy, 43(7), pp.1109-1133.

Baker, T., Miner, A. S. and Eesley, D.T., 2003. Improvising firms: Bricolage, account giving and improvisational competencies in the founding process. *Research policy*, *32*(2), pp.255-276.

Balkin, D. and M. Swift (2006), 'Top management team compensation in high-growth technology ventures', Human Resource Management Review, 16 (1), 1–11.

Bartel, C.A. and Saavedra, R., 2000. The collective construction of work group moods. *Administrative Science Quarterly*, *45*(2), pp. 197-231.

Bathurst, R. and Ladkin, D., 2012. Performing leadership: Observations from the world of music. *Administrative Sciences*, *2*(1), pp.99-119.

Ben-Hafaïedh, C., 2017. Entrepreneurial teams research in movement. In Research handbook on entrepreneurial teams. Edward Elgar Publishing.

Birks, David F., Fernadez W., Levina N., Nasirin S. "Grounded theory method in information systems research: its nature, diversity and opportunities." *European Journal of Information Systems* 22.1 (2013): 1-8.

Buchanan D. 1999. The logic of political action: An experiment with the epistemology of the particular. *British Journal of Management 10* (supp. 1): 73–88

Cartwright, P. and Swearing, K., 2020. Group Work: Application and Performance Effectiveness in Musical Ensembles. In *New Leadership in Strategy and Communication* (pp. 329-350). Springer, Cham.

Cordery, J. 2004. Team work. In D. Holman, T.D. Wall, C.W. Clegg, P. Sparrow & A. Howard (Eds.). *The essentials of the new workplace: A guide to the human impact of modern working practices. Chichester: John Wiley*, pp. 99-110.

Cooper, A. C., Daily, C. M. 1997. Entrepreneurial teams. In Sexton, D. L., Smilor, R. W. (Eds.), *Entrepreneurship 2000* (pp. 127-150). Chicago, IL: Upstart Publishing.

Diakanastasi, E., Karagiannaki, A., & Pramatari, K. 2018. Entrepreneurial Team Dynamics and New Venture Creation Process: An Exploratory Study Within a Start-Up Incubator. *SAGE Open*.

Fairfield, Kent D., and Michael B. London. 2003. Tuning into the music of groups: A metaphor for team-based learning in management education. *Journal of Management Education* 27(6): 654-672.

Fayolle A, Liñán, 2014. The future of research on entrepreneurial intentions, *Journal of Business Research* 67 (5), 663-666,

Forbes, D.P., Borchert, P.S., Zellmer–Bruhn, M.E. and Sapienza, H.J., 2006. Entrepreneurial team formation: An exploration of new member addition. *Entrepreneurship Theory and Practice*, *30*(2), pp.225-248.

Glaser, Barney G & Strauss, Anselm L., 1967. The Discovery of Grounded Theory: Strategies for Qualitative Research, Chicago, Aldine Publishing Company,

Goulding, C. 1998. "Grounded Theory: The Missing Methodology on the Interpretivist Agenda." Qualitative Market Research: An International Journal 1(1): 50-57.

Hackman, J.R. (1987), 'The design of work teams', in J.W. Lorsch (ed.), Handbook of Organizational Behavior, Englewood Cliffs, NJ: Prentice- Hall, pp. 315–42.

Hackman, J.R. and R. Wageman (2005), 'A theory of team coaching', Academy of Management Review, 30 (2), 269–87.

Hambrick, Donald C., and Phyllis A. Mason. 1984. Upper echelons: The organization as a reflection of its top managers. *Academy of management review* 9.2: 193-206.

Hambrick, D.C., 2007. Upper echelons theory: An update. The Academy of Management Review Vol. 32, No. 2 (Apr., 2007), pp. 334-343

Hiebl, M.R., 2014. Upper echelons theory in management accounting and control research. Journal of Management Control, 24(3), pp.223-240.

Hmieleski, K.M. and Corbett, A.C., 2006. Proclivity for improvisation as a predictor of entrepreneurial intentions. *Journal of Small Business Management*, *44*(1), pp.45-63.

Kamoche, Ken, Miguel Pina E. Cunha, and Joao Vieira da Cunha. 2003. Towards a theory of organizational improvisation: Looking beyond the jazz metaphor. *Journal of Management Studies* 40.8 2023-2051.

Klotz, A.C., K.M. Hmieleski and B.H. Bradley et al. (2014), 'New venture teams: A review of the literature and roadmap for future research', Journal of Management, 40 (1), 226–55

Kollmann, T., C. Stöckmann and J. Linstaedt et al. (2015), European Startup Monitor 2015, accessed 9 August 2016 at http://europeanstartupmonitor.com/fileadmin/presse/ download/esm 2015.pdf

Marx, Tobias. 2019. Invisible management"–group cohesion in semi-professional music groups."*Miscellanea Anthropologica et Sociologica* 20(2) : 155-172.

Murphy, C., Klotz, A. C., & Kreiner, G. E., 2017. Blue skies and black boxes: The promise (and practice) of grounded theory in human resource management research. *Human Resource Management Review*, *27*(2), 291-305. https://doi.org/10.1016/j.hrmr.2016.08.006

Oldfather P., West J. 1994. Qualitative research as jazz. *Educational researcher* 23.8): 22-26.

Pescosolido, A.T. and Saavedra, R., 2012. Cohesion and sports teams: A review. *Small Group Research*, *43*(6), pp.744-758.

Pettigrew 2000, Ethnography and Grounded Theory: a Happy Marriage? in *NA - Advances in Consumer Research Volume 27,* eds. Stephen J. Hoch and Robert J. Meyer, Provo, UT : Association for Consumer Research, Pages: 256-260.

Polley, D. and Ribbens, B., 1998. Sustaining self-managed teams: a process approach to team wellness. *Team Performance Management: An International Journal*.

Rabinowitch, T., Cross, I. and Burnard, P., 2012. Musical group interaction, intersubjectivity and merged subjectivity. *Kinesthetic empathy in creative and cultural practices*, pp.109-120.

Shah, S. K., Agarwal, R., & Echambadi, R. (2019). Jewels in the crown: Exploring the motivations and team building processes of employee entrepreneurs. Strategic Management Journal, Forthcoming

Schjoedt, Leon, and Sascha Kraus. 2009.Entrepreneurial teams: definition and performance factors. *Management Research News*

Silva, T., Cunha, M.P.E., Clegg, S.R., Neves, P., Rego, A. and Rodrigues, R.A., 2014. Smells like team spirit: Opening a paradoxical black box. *Human Relations*, *67*(3), pp.287-310.

Strauss, Anselm L. 1987. Qualitative analysis for social scientists. *Cambridge university press.*

Tal-Shmotkin, M. and Gilboa, A., 2013. Do behaviors of string quartet ensembles represent self-managed teams? *Team Performance Management: An International Journal*.

Timmons, J.A., Spinelli, S. and Tan, Y., 2004. *New venture creation: Entrepreneurship for the 21st century* (Vol. 6). New York: McGraw-Hill/Irwin.

Tyler, S.A. & Tyler, 1990 M.G. Foreword. In B.P. Keeney, ed. *Improvisational Therapy*. New York, Guilford, 1990, ix-xi. Ucbasaran,

Tsoukas H 2009.Craving for generality and small-N studies: A Wittgensteinian approach towards the epistemology of the particular in organization and management studies. In: Buchanan D and Bryman A (eds) *The Sage Handbook of Organizational Research Methods*. Thousand Oaks, CA: SAGE, 285–301.

Ucbasaran, D., Lockett, A. and Humphreys, M., 2011. Leading entrepreneurial teams: insights from jazz. *London: Institute for Small Business and Entrepreneurship*.

Visintin, F., Pittino, D. 2014. Founding team composition and early performance of university—Based spin-off companies. *Technovation*, 34, 31-43.

Ward, T.B., 2004. Cognition, creativity, and entrepreneurship. *Journal of business venturing*, *19*(2), pp.173-188.

Waldman, D.A., Javidan, M. and Varella, P., 2004. Charismatic leadership at the strategic level: A new application of upper echelons theory. The Leadership Quarterly, 15(3), pp.355-380.

Weick, K.E., 1998. *Introductory essay—Improvisation as a mindset for organizational analysis. Organization science*, *9*(5), pp.543-555.

Zhou, W. and E. Rosini (2015), 'Entrepreneurial team diversity and performance: Toward an integrated model', Entrepreneurship Research Journal, 5 (1), 31–60.

Sharing Economy and its Impact on Society

Yulia Dubolazova
Peter the Great St. Petersburg Polytechnic University (SPbPU), Russia
julia005@mail.ru
DOI: 10.34190/EIE.20.121

Abstract: The article considers the issues of Sharing economy, its future in the context of digitalization of society and the fourth industrial revolution, as well as its impact on the ecosystem, in particular on the environment. The main positive factors of the Sharing economy have been identified: the population receiving additional income using less-used Internet resources. The core point is that participants share their unused resources, which at the same time are necessary for others. These goods and services can be offered at a lower price to the consumer, which leads to lower costs and significant savings; consumers also have more opportunities to choose the necessary goods or services, since the range of suppliers is now not limited only to companies. It requires a continuous increase in the level of competitiveness in the market: now companies must also innovate and improve the quality of their services; the new economy creates additional income for the unemployed, or for those with unpopular specialties, crushed by the crisis, whose skills are difficult to transfer to other activities. But they can still, for example, drive a car, give private lessons or rent out their property. The purpose of the article is to deep study of various organizational forms of the sharing economy, its impact on the ecosystem when it is introduced in various areas of economic activity (in transport, housing, finance, education, energy, tourism, logistics, etc.), the main attention is paid to sharing economy in transport (online taxi service, ride sharing and carpooling, car sharing, etc.), logistics, energy Based on the systematization and analysis of well-known and emerging forms of sharing economy, world experience, the contribution of the sharing economy to solving environmental problems is considered. A number of problems (legal, organizational, economic, social, etc.) has been identified that arise during the introduction of sharing economy and which should increase the effectiveness of its impact on the environment. Recommendations on the elimination of negative consequences are proposed. The processes of digitalization of society and the environment become the prerogative of the global economy and public administration of individual countries, which increases the importance of the problems discussed in the article. The object of the study in the article is sharing economy, its application areas, problems and development prospects in the modern world, its future in the context of digitalization of society and the fourth industrial revolution. The subject of the research in the article is scientific-theoretical, organizational-economic, legal, labor and social problems of sharing economy.

Keywords: green sharing economy, digitalization, organizational and economic problems, sharing logistics, Big Data technology

1. Introduction

In the context of the fourth industrial revolution, under the influence of globalization and the growing digitalization of society the structure of the world economy is changing based on the widespread use of the Internet, information and communication tools, Big Data technology, artificial intelligence, the Internet of things, cloud and other information technologies: many traditional industries lose their significance, new industries are developing rapidly, new organizational forms of business are being introduced, new production and public relationship. In particular, the concept of a sharing economy has appeared. Many experts note sharing economy appearance around 2010, after which it becomes popular in the media, economic and other magazines.

In particular, such authors as Boatsman, R. Richter, K. Sundararajan, A. and a number of others will consider the main points of the study:

First, as noted by the vast majority of authors writing about the sharing economy, the most obvious and at the same time the most basic prerequisite is the presence of the Internet, the possibility of creating online platforms where two parties meet and subsequently exchange. Indeed, before the advent of the World Wide Web, the transaction costs of such an exchange were too high (Henten, A. H. & Windekilde, I. M. 2016).

Secondly, the emergence of the sharing economy made possible the changes in the way of thinking observed today, namely the reorientation towards a more open thinking and lifestyle, concluded by Richter K. and others (Richter, C. Kraus, S. Brem, A. Durst S. & Giselbrecht, C 2017) They concluded that open thinking is necessary on both sides: the consumer and the entrepreneur, and it is expressed in openness to exchange and trust.

Indeed, in order to get into the car with a stranger or to let the person you see for the first time into your apartment, in other words, to be part of the sharing economy, you need a certain trust in strangers, which is not easy to achieve. However, Botsman, R. writes that a sufficient level of such thinking has just been achieved (Botsman, R. & Rogers, R. 2011) Moreover, sharing platforms use special techniques to increase the level of trust in strangers among users, for example, through services for assessing and building reputation, which are now present in most platforms, as stated by Bain & Co partner A. Martynov (Vinogradov. E. 2017)

At the same time, it is obvious that for some services just only trust is not enough, for example, for the provision of medical services, traditional classification as a factor of trust is still needed. Sundararajan, A. proves that the issue of trust has two ways of solving: the first is the already voiced assessment system on the platform, the second – the creation of platforms as self-regulatory organizations, the reorganization of which will take place in a natural way with the help of internal mechanisms. (Sundararajan, A. 2017)

Third, a number of authors write about the changing conditions of life today as a prerequisite for the emergence of sharing and the sharing economy as a business model. They imply the transformation of society, especially the generation of millennials, into more mobile and not tied to either place of residence or place of work. People want to be freer and not dependent on the worries of maintaining property (Richter, C. Kraus, S. Brem, A. Durst, S. & Giselbrecht, C. 2017). Jobs are becoming remote, working time patterns are becoming more flexible, and there is more demand for work-life balance. Young people, for example, claim that they simply have no idea where they will be in the next few years, hence the natural unwillingness to burden themselves with property.

Fourth, the change in human habitat is undoubtedly influencing the emergence of new business models, and urbanization has contributed to the emergence of the sharing economy. Most of the companies in the sharing economy operate in large cities. All the features that stimulate the sharing economy to develop are concentrated here: openness of the population to new solutions, greater anonymity and mobility, higher salaries, better education, lack of space for storing a huge amount of property, better Internet infrastructure. All this contributes to the development of the considered business model (Richter, C. Kraus, S. Brem, A. Durst S. & Giselbrecht, C 2017).

Finally, there is growing concern about environmental problems, and the sharing economy can solve some of them. The depletion of non-renewable natural resources stimulates more efficient use of property, which is already polluting the environment, or at least the awareness of the need for this more efficient use. Moreover, entrepreneurs point to a great opportunity not only to make profits, but also to be able to "do something worthwhile" by helping the environment (Richter, C. Kraus, S. Brem, A. Durst S. & Giselbrecht, C 2017).

2. Statement and description of the research problem

Ecological problems and limited resources also gradually change the attitude towards the consumer culture towards the transition from a consumer society to an SE characterized by the collective use of goods and services. Excessive consumption is the main culprit for serious environmental problems that ultimately cause other problems, in particular the depletion of natural resources.

SE gives the opportunity to use goods and services to those (consumers) who do not need them constantly or if their purchase and operation are unprofitable and expensive, and the owners receive additional income or cover costs. SE has certain advantages: it offers manufacturers new forms of independent work with the possibility of generating additional income, helps reduce unemployment and poverty, creates additional income for the unemployed or for those with unpopular specialties; help reduce age and gender differences, differences in specialties, education, etc.

Goods and services can be offered at a lower price to the consumer, which leads to lower costs and significant savings. Consumers get more opportunities to choose the necessary goods or services, since the range of suppliers is now not limited only to companies. Citizens of different countries are given the opportunity to take advantage of their place of residence. SE significantly enhances both demand and supply, as a result of which the optimal price is determined, which is most suitable for market conditions. The level of competition in the market is increasing: commercial companies should actively innovate and improve the quality of their goods and services. SE virtual platforms allow their users to offer services themselves.

SE increases the level of competition in the market, as a result of which companies must actively innovate, produce new products, reduce prices and improve the quality of services; creates conditions for self-organization and mutual assistance, improving the quality of life; it allows you not only intelligently manage your own property and budget, but also to cultivate respect for the work, time and property of others. Business models based on the principles of SE and electronic platforms lead to the exclusion of intermediaries, reduction of inefficient costs of companies and expenses of the population. Due to more intensive sharing of existing assets without the need to invest in new assets for exactly the same consumption, there will be a reduction in environmental impact.

On the other hand, SE creates certain problems for society: transport organizations and professional drivers lose their earnings, sales from car manufacturers and car dealers fall, tour operators and travel agents go bankrupt, hotel occupancy decreases, crowdfunding and its varieties constitute serious competition to credit organizations, the number of self-employed, freelancers are growing.

Problems arise in the areas of labor relations, social protection of the population, taxation, pensions, security and quality of services, leakage of personal data, professional risks, psychosocial risks and many others.

SE is actively developing; the scope and forms of its application are expanding. The study identified the following key forms of SE: online taxi service (Uber, Yandex and others); ridesharing and carpooling - vehicle sharing; carsharing - short-term car rental; coparking - sharing of parking spaces); short-term rental of private housing around the world (Airbnb and others); coworking - centers for renting a workplace for the necessary time; coliving (community living) - co-existence of a group of people with similar views or life values; crowd funding - people's cooperation on the voluntary pooling of money or other resources; exchange of knowledge and skills in the field of education; in the energy sector - sharing energy from private generators; sharing of free computing power data, SMS; in transport logistics (sharing logistics); food sharing— free distribution of disposable, usable products to the needy; electronic commerce - the purchase and sale of goods between private individuals; home sharing - the provision of free or for a small fee housing in exchange for assistance provided to the homeowner; joint tourism and many others.

In accordance with the stated topic of the article, we consider the impact on the ecosystem of SE in transport and energy. Transport aggregates / services represent one of the most promising market segments based on the shared economy model. The growth of urbanization, the number of citizens and cars leads to the fact that large cities cannot cope with traffic. The complication of traffic, the increase in the number of traffic jams on the city roads, parking problems lead to a decrease in the quality of life, the efficiency of people at work, environmental degradation, etc. (Nunez, E. C. A., & Dubolazov, V. A., 2019).

Transport is one of the main air pollutants. Its share in the total volume of emissions of pollutants into the atmosphere from stationary and mobile sources in Russia is about 40%, which is higher than the share of any other industry. By type of transport, pollutant emissions are distributed as follows: 87% of the total emissions are from road transport, about 8% from the railway, 2% from the road complex, just over 1% from air transport and 2% from river and sea.

The impact of vehicles on the ecosystem is primarily expressed in the pollution of the atmosphere, water bodies and lands, changes in the chemical composition of soils and microflora, in the creation of high levels of noise and vibration, the release of heat into the environment when internal combustion engines work, the alienation of lands for the construction of roads, in the consumption of atmospheric air, oil products and natural gas, water, etc.

The Government of the Russian Federation by order of April 28, 2018 No. 831-r "On Approving the Strategy for the Development of the Automobile Industry of the Russian Federation for the Period until 2025" approved its strategy for the development of the automotive industry until 2025. It defines the goals, priorities and key indicators for the development of the automotive industry. This is, first of all, the electrification of vehicles (the use of electric vehicles), the use of gas motor fuel, increasing the autonomy of cars, the development of telecommunication systems, restricting the entry of cars with a low class of Euro exhaust standards (for example, in Moscow from 2019 the entry of heavy trucks of the Euro class -3 and below has been restricted), the application of new business models for the sharing of vehicles, which include online taxi, ride sharing, carpooling, car sharing, collaboration for vehicles

In Russia, with a lower level of the number of personal cars per 1000 inhabitants compared with developed countries, there will be a faster penetration of SEs in transport. According to expert estimates, the prospects for the development of the Russian market suggest an increase in the share of cars used in car sharing to 10 percent by 2025. In the world, by 2030, the share of passenger cars can reach 9 percent of total sales (10 million common cars, 115 million cars in 2030).

Users in business models of transport sharing (online taxi, ride sharing, carpooling, car sharing, etc.) are attracted by the lower price, less waiting time for the car to be delivered, the ability to place an order and track its execution using the mobile phone application. Confidence in the service increases the ability to evaluate the direct contractor. With the advent of transport aggregators, each driver himself has the opportunity to see incoming orders and, focusing on his own load and proximity of the call, can accept it. This significantly speeds up the process of receipt of the order from the consumer to the direct contractor. In the process of using transport and transport services, a lot of data is accumulated, the use of which can become the basis of new types of business that provide people with comfort and personalization. The model of using transport services instead of owning transport is one of the most promising market segments based on the model of shared economy.

The purpose of the study is to systematize and analyze well-known and emerging forms of SE, primarily in transport and energy, to consider the contribution of SE to solving environmental problems, as well as to understand what organizational, economic and legal issues need to be addressed.

SE helps significantly relieve urban infrastructure (especially transport). Transport services represent one of the most promising market segments based on the model of shared economy. According to analysts, a personal car is used no more than 2 times a day, the time spent on the journey even in a large metropolis is no more than 2 - 3 hours a day. This requires a place where the car will stand idle while it is not in use. In the framework of new business models of SE, a car is used four to ten times more intensively [5] the concept of intellectual mobility can help reduce traffic congestion by up to 30%, carbon emissions by 10%, optimize driving speed by 60% [10], also reduce the territory intended for parking, both public and private. The congestion of city highways will decrease, transport accessibility and the environmental situation will improve, the transparency of the services provided and the safety of passengers will increase.

As a result, the atmosphere is less polluted by emissions, equipment is used more efficiently, the number of cars on city streets is reduced. According to Frost & Sullivan, the spread of car sharing and ride sharing will allow the world to save $ 5.6 billion annually, reduce carbon dioxide emissions by 15% and increase the speed of urban traffic by 60%, reduce the territory intended for parking lots, both public and private.

It is estimated that by 2025 transport units (Yandex taxi, etc.) will occupy 20-50% of the human transportation market (Goldman, 2017). By 2030, 40% of all vehicles will still have individual owners, but the share of their use will be reduced to 5% (Nunez, E. C. A., & Dubolazov, V. A., 2019).

Aggregators / servers appear in transport logistics, providing the possibility of sharing a single vehicle by several companies. The development of a vehicle-sharing business model has led to the spread of Mobility as a service technology (MaaS), which manages real-time multimodal transportation from the start of the route to the destination using different modes of transport (public transport, rent a car, taxi, shuttles on request, etc.) and allowing you to choose the best route according to many criteria (time, cost, user preference, etc.). With the correct construction of logistics processes, the manufacturer can save up to a third of its logistics budget. Keeping your own fleet of vehicles in these conditions is becoming less profitable, therefore, enterprises are increasingly transferring logistics to specialized companies for outsourcing.

Car sharing in several cities and countries is encouraged by the government to reduce the number of cars on the road. The media discusses following issues as supporting the joint use of vehicles: the allocation by the city administration of additional funds to subsidize short-term car rental operators; provision of transport tax benefits; introduction of an environmental tax; provision of free parking within the city; access to lanes for block vehicles; preferential rate for civil liability insurance of the vehicle owner; concession when using paid sections of roads. However, these proposals are not obvious, difficult to implement, require deep study.

For the development of car sharing in large cities, it is advisable to organize fixed free parking places for such cars near metro stations, railway stations, airports, as well as in the central part of the city. For example, in Switzerland, Italy and France, car-sharing companies do not pay for parking, and sometimes their cars are even allowed to use the public transport lanes.

SE affects social issues. So, online taxi, car sharing and ride sharing, especially when providing them with benefits, can cause dissatisfaction with city taxi services and car owners. For example, in Europe, in a number of countries (Belgium, France, Spain, etc.), demonstrations were held against Uber, accusing it of unfair competition, failure to comply with local rules regarding security, taxes and licensing, and a sharp decrease in taxi drivers' earnings. In February 2017, the Brussels Economic Court banned the operation of the Uber service in Belgium. Only drivers with a Brussels license and a luminous taxi signal on the car roof could be engaged in such kind of transportation

There are many problems in transport sharing economy. The legal status of participants and the forms of contractual relations between them are not obvious. The debatable question is what constitutes an aggregator: a provider of information services or transport services like, for example, Uber, Yandex. In first case, the aggregator has an international status, has the right to act in all countries without permits, can be registered in any state, for example, where taxes are less; in the second case - to register only in the country of activity, its activity is under the control of national authorities and may even be prohibited. Aggregators who are information intermediaries, as a general rule, are not responsible to consumers for the quality and terms of the provision of the goods and services offered on their platform.

Aggregators establishing contact between customers and contractors do not always provide adequate security or guarantees regarding the goods and services provided, although there is a possibility for the user to evaluate the contractor, but only after the customer has hired and used the service. Companies that work on the principles of SE, they themselves create a large number of criteria so that users have the opportunity to choose those who can be responsible for the product or service. But even such measures do not provide full guarantees or insurance against accidents, theft, crime or inadequate quality of goods and services. Risks are always present when the community regulates the system of analysis, rating, and feedbacks independently.

Certain information intermediaries are required to comply with statutory requirements. So, drivers registered on the site of the aggregator in the field of road transport must comply with the requirements for licensing their activities, the proper condition of the car, etc. (Nunez, E. C. A., & Dubolazov, V. A., 2019).

There is a lot of debate about what contract should be concluded between the aggregator and the executor - driver: labor or civil law (agency, contracting or the provision of services and performance of work). Due to the lack of labor regulation, people working with the aggregator often have an excessively high pace of work based on their needs, exceeding working hours in many cases without any benefit or protection, without social security. Gradually, in EU countries, transport aggregators are obliged to conclude labor contracts with drivers (such a law, for example, was introduced in France in February 2020).

Sharing economy is a stable global intensively developing organizational and economic model that has firmly entered into life, which is greatly facilitated by the digitalization of society. In recent years, the economy of co-consumption has acquired such a scale that they started talking about it as an alternative to the traditional economy.

By sharing existing assets without having to invest in new ones for exactly the same consumption, there will be a reduction in environmental impact through more stable activities, the exchange of existing assets without the need to invest in something new for the same use, less impact to production.

The ecosystem is particularly affected by the economy of co-consumption in transport. The growth of urbanization, the number of citizens and cars leads to the fact that large cities cannot cope with traffic. The complication of traffic, the increase in the number of traffic jams on the city roads, parking problems lead to a decrease in the quality of life, the efficiency of people at work, environmental degradation, etc. In the framework of business models of sharing economy, cars are used much more intensively, first of all, by reducing the number of vehicles while ensuring the required level of mobility. As a result, the atmosphere is less polluted by emissions, equipment is used more efficiently, and the number of cars on city streets is reduced.

The economy of joint consumption is developing, the scope and forms of its application are expanding.

Summing up some results, it can be argued that a growing number of entrepreneurs are basing their projects on the principles of SE in various industries: transport, housing, travel, energy, money, etc. A business gains access to cheap resources, but at the same time acquires great risks, in particular legal ones. The issue related to taxation also needs to be considered. The state generates or tightens more taxes, but a well-coordinated system for their collection is still lacking. Currently, the efforts of many states are aimed specifically at developing a new tax policy adapted to the economy of the future, including SE. To do this, you need to arrange payment online.

3. Conclusion

Studies have shown the importance and complexity of SE, which contributes to the active informatization of society. The scale and pace of development and penetration into public relations of SEs is striking, which has a significant impact on the incomes of people and organizations, unemployment and employment, competition in the market, on the environment, etc. The newest example concerns the exchange of energy from solar panels installed in private homes. The energy excessively accumulated in the batteries of one house is used by others. Thus, energy has no cost to these communities. With this method of the future, the world will gain greater control and energy savings and better preserve the environment (Richter, C. Kraus, S. Brem, A. Durst S. & Giselbrecht, C 2017.

But this requires the solution of many technical, legal, social, organizational, economic, environmental, behavioral and other problems. Specialists in the field of information systems have a big task to develop aggregators, which should not only allow the consumer to get acquainted with the services provided, their performers and feedback on them, but also conclude contracts for the provision of services between them, charge money and make settlements between participants, calculate and pay taxes, carry out banking operations, etc. State and local authorities must create appropriate infrastructure.

Acknowledgements

We would like to thank the anonymous reviewer for the constructive comments to improve the manuscript.

This research work was supported by the Academic Excellence Project 5- 100 proposed by Peter the Great St. Petersburg Polytechnic University

References

Allen, D. (2015). The sharing economy. Institute of Public Affairs Review: A Quarterly Review of Politics and Public Affairs, The, 67(3), 24.

Armando, N. E. C., & Dubolazov, V. A. (2019). Opportunities and risks of collaborative consumption economy. St. Petersburg State Polytechnical University Journal. Economics, 12(2), 30.

Bataev, A. V. (2017, September). Evaluation the e-learning market in Russia. In 2017 International Conference" Quality Management, Transport and Information Security, Information Technologies"(IT&QM&IS) (pp. 628-633). IEEE.

Botsman, R. Rogers, R. What's Mine is Yours: How Collaborative Consumption is Changing the Way We Live / R. Botsman, R. Rogers. – London: HarperCollinsPublishers, 2011.

Cheng, M. (2016). Sharing economy: A review and agenda for future research. International Journal of Hospitality Management, 57, 60-70.

Edelman, B., Luca, M., & Svirsky, D. (2017). Racial discrimination in the sharing economy: Evidence from a field experiment. American Economic Journal: Applied Economics, 9(2), 1-22.

Daunorienė, A., Drakšaitė, A., Snieška, V., & Valodkienė, G. (2015). Evaluating sustainability of sharing economy business models. Procedia-Social and Behavioral Sciences, 213, 836-841.

Denghua, H. O. U. (2017). On the legal status of network platform under shared economy—taking the online car- hailing as the research object. Tribune of Political Science and Law, 35(1), 157.

Frenken, K., & Schor, J. (2019). Putting the sharing economy into perspective. In A Research Agenda for Sustainable Consumption Governance. Edward Elgar Publishing.

Hamari, J., Sjöklint, M., & Ukkonen, A. (2016). The sharing economy: Why people participate in collaborative consumption. Journal of the association for information science and technology, 67(9), 2047-2059.

Henten, A. H. Windekilde, I. M. Transaction costs and the sharing economy / A. H. Henten, I. M. Windekilde // Emerald Insight INFO. – 2016. Vol. 18 (1).

Jia, Q. S., & Wu, J. (2018). On distributed event-based optimization for shared economy in cyber-physical energy systems. Science China Information Sciences, 61(11), 110203.

Konnikova, O., Konnikov, E., Bozhuk, S., & Pletneva, N. Development of international transport corridors to meet challenges of agriculture.
Kozlov, A., Gutman, S., Rytova, E., & Zaychenko, I. (2017). Human and economic factors of long-distance commuting technology: analysis of Arctic practices. In Advances in Social & Occupational Ergonomics (pp. 409-420). Springer, Cham.
Kozlov, O. A., Rodionov, D. G., & Guzikova, L. A. (2018, January). Information security problems in educational institutions in conditions of network interaction. In 2018 International Conference on Information Networking (ICOIN) (pp. 267-269). IEEE.
Kupriyanovsky, V., Sinyagov, S., Klimov, A., Petrov, A., & Namiot, D. (2017). Digital supply chains and blockchain-based technologies in a shared economy. International Journal of Open Information Technologies, 5(8), 80-95.
Martin, C. J. (2016). The sharing economy: A pathway to sustainability or a nightmarish form of neoliberal capitalism?. Ecological economics, 121, 149-159.
Mednikov, M. D., Sokolitsyna, N. A., Sokolitsyn, A. S., & Semenov, V. P. (2017, May). Game theory model of forming enterprise development strategy in market environment uncertainty. In 2017 XX IEEE International Conference on Soft Computing and Measurements (SCM) (pp. 876-878). IEEE.
Miller, S. R. (2016). First principles for regulating the sharing economy. Harv. J. on Legis., 53, 147.
Nikolova, L.V., Rodionov, D.G., Afanasyeva, N.V. (2017).Impact of globalization on innovation project risks estimation. European Research Studies Journal, Vol 20 №2. pp 396-410
Nunez, E. C. A. (2019). Opportunities and risks of collaborative consumption economy under conditions of digitalization of society. St. Petersburg state polytechnical university journal. Economics, 12(2).
Rodionov, D. G., Kudryavtseva, T. J., & Skhvediani, A. E. (2018). Human development and income inequality as factors of regional economic growth.
Richter, C. Kraus, S. Brem, A. Durst, S. Giselbrecht, C. Digital entrepreneurship: Innovative business models for the sharing economy. / C. Richter, S. Kraus, A. Brem, S. Durst, C. Giselbrecht // Creativity and Innovation Management. – 2017. № 8.
Ristock, H. W. A., te Booij, M., Mezhibovsky, V., Anderson, D., & Petrovykh, Y. (2019). U.S. Patent No. 10,440,185. Washington, DC: U.S. Patent and Trademark Office.
Rudskaya, I. A., & Rodionov, D. (2018). Comprehensive evaluation of Russian regional innovation system performance using a two-stage econometric model. Revista ESPACIOS, 39(04).
Slee, T. (2017). What's yours is mine: Against the sharing economy. Or Books.
Shvab, K. (2016). Chetvertaya promyshlennaya revolyutsiya. Moskva, Rossiya: Eksmo.
Sundararajan, A. (2016). The sharing economy: The end of employment and the rise of crowd-based capitalism. Mit Press.
Schor, J. (2016). Debating the sharing economy. Journal of Self-Governance and Management Economics, 4(3),7-22.
Teece, D., Peteraf, M., & Leih, S. (2016). Dynamic capabilities and organizational agility: Risk, uncertainty, and strategy in the innovation economy. California Management Review, Vol 58 №4. pp 13-35.
Puschmann, T., & Alt, R. (2016). Sharing economy. Business & Information Systems Engineering, 58(1), 93-99.
Vaughan, R., & Daverio, R. (2016). Assessing the size and presence of the collaborative economy in Europe. Publications Office of the European Union.
Vinogradova. E. Joint consumption as a new economic model / E. Vinogradova. URL: http://kp.vedomosti.ru/ (date of access: 23.10.2017)
Velichko, N. Y., Kobersy, I. S., Radina, O. I., Khnikina, T. S., & Ivashhenko, S. A. (2017). Sales promotion in the marketing communications. International Journal of Applied Business and Economic Research, 15(13), 133-142.

Using a Magnifying Glass to Examine Network Formation Among Artisan Entrepreneurs

Ingunn Elvekrok [11] and Anita Ellen Tobiassen[2]
[1]School of Business, University of South-Eastern Norway, Drammen, Norway
[2]Oslo Business School, OsloMet – Oslo Metropolitan University, Norway
ingunn.elvekrok@usn.no
aetobi@oslomet.no
DOI: 10.34190/EIE.20.113

Abstract: This paper explores the formation of a horizontal network between artisan glass-blower studios from the perspective of entrepreneurship. We conducted a longitudinal study following the formation process over four years through different stages from the idea stage to a formal network. The findings show that the network co-ordinator's stamina, the individual members 'expertise and social networks, and the development of trust between network members through regular seminars were important for success. Furthermore, it was vital that the network could preserve artisan entrepreneurs 'mix of artistic and commercial motives to increase their members 'commitment to the network. The glass-blower studios are micro-firms suffering from liabilities of smallness; therefore, they were dependent on various external resources throughout the network-formation process when access to finance was particularly critical.

Keywords: artisan entrepreneurs, micro-firms, horizontal network formation, collaboration, network coordinator, network commitment

1. Introduction

The expansion of creative industries and recognition of their contribution to the economy and society has increased scholarly interest in cultural and artisan entrepreneurs (Luckman, 2015; Ratten & Ferreira, 2017). Artisan entrepreneurs are driven by a mixture of goals related to financial/economic and art/culture/lifestyle factors (Guercini & Cova, 2018; Pagano et al., 2018), often oriented towards the latter (Klamer, 2011). Most have micro-firms, i.e. firms with fewer than ten employees (European Commission, 2014) often suffering from liabilities of smallness (Zahra, 2005).

The literature reveals that some artisan entrepreneurs seek venture growth, innovation and even internationalization (Pret & Cogan, 2019), but they have limited financial and organizational resources to innovate and develop their firms because of their smallness (Guercini & Cova, 2018; Pagano et al., 2018). Research shows that social networks are a means to overcome micro-firm liabilities (Olsen et al., 2012; Pettersen & Tobiassen, 2012). Social capital in the form of vertical and horizontal network relations (i.e. across the supply chain and with competitors and other businesses) can provide artisan entrepreneurs with the resources and innovative ideas necessary to develop and grow their firms (Flanagan et al., 2018; Gundolf et al., 2018; Galloway et al., 2019).

Horizontal social networks between artisan entrepreneurs in the same industry offer potential for growth and increased performance (Kuhn & Galloway, 2015; Galloway et al., 2019). There is scant research on the formation process of horizontal networks in general and among micro-firms and artisan entrepreneurs in the same industry in particular (Fuglsang & Eide, 2013; Pagano et al., 2018; Ratten et al., 2019). Therefore, the aim of this study is to explore the formation of a horizontal network between artisan entrepreneurs, i.e. why, how and what the network develops. Our main focus is on the network-formation process, but to grasp the process it is advantageous to understand the motivation for initiating the network (Kerr & Coviello, 2019). Furthermore, the way in which the process develops may depend on what the network 'brings to the table' for the artisan entrepreneurs, e.g. the form of exchange between network members, such as resources, information or emotional support (Kerr & Coviello, 2019).

The study is grounded in research on artisan entrepreneurship (Pagano et al., 2018; Ratten et al., 2019) and entrepreneurship networks (Lechner & Dowling, 2003; Thorgren et al., 2009; Brink & Svendsen, 2013). The research contributes to the emerging fields of artisan entrepreneurs and network-formation processes.

---

[1]Corresponding author

2. Theoretical approach

Studies on networks in the entrepreneurship literature have focused on why, how and what networks develop (Kerr & Coviello, 2019). These questions are highly interrelated and to understand the process it is vital to understand the motivation for the network formation and what the network develops during the process.

2.1 Why and what: The benefits of networks

Bringing people and businesses together is a necessary but insufficient condition for developing personal ties, trust and commercial co-operation. For this to occur, networking activities and common understanding are also needed (Thorgren et al., 2009; Kerr & Coviello, 2019). Conditions that threaten the network's functionality are disagreements about goals, goal conflicts, short-term thinking and unrealistic expectations (Halme & Fadeeva, 2000). Hence, structural and relational characteristics are important considerations (Elfring & Hulsink, 2007; Hoang & Yi, 2015). Structural characteristics are related to an entrepreneur's position in the network, while relational elements among other factors pertain to the content of exchange between actors in the network, such as resources, information and emotional support (Kerr & Coviello, 2019). Research shows that a network's success is conditional on the anchoring of the participants, and that the actors perceive the participation to have real benefits (Elvekrok et al., 2018). An inactive network fades quickly (Elvekrok et al., 2018).

For artisan micro-firms, time is often consumed on daily operations. Hence, it can be difficult to find time, space and the mental distance needed to rethink and innovate modes of operation, markets and business areas (Elstad & De Paoli, 2014). Horizontal networks are one way to overcome resource limitations of the participating firms through the exchange of knowledge and pooling of resources (Brink & Svendsen, 2013; McAdam et al., 2016). For example, individual members can receive assistance from others on various issues such as legal compliance and technical advice (Weiss, 1987), shared research and development risks and costs (Jost, 2019), and contribute to positive attention and reputation (Olsen et al., 2012; Lin & Lin, 2016). A network can be a catalyst for the development of new ideas, new relationships, new projects and interpersonal exchanges of knowledge and experience (Pittaway et al., 2004; Fritsch & Kauffeld-Monz, 2010). Moreover, horizontal social networks have been found to improve confidence, decision-making and performance in micro-firms (Olsen et al., 2012; Kuhn & Galloway, 2015). However, horizontal networks may entail complexity because the firms are partly competitors and partly collaborators (Bonatto et al., 2017). Hence, artisan entrepreneurs must evaluate the use of resources in relation to the advantages of network membership.

2.2 The network-formation process

The network-formation process is seldom clearly defined and planned by the initiators and participant firms (Lapiedra et al., 2004). Instead, it reflects the effectuation perspective on the entrepreneurial process (Sarasvathy, 2001, 2009; Manning, 2010): First, it requires an entrepreneurial action, where someone initiates the network formation. Next, preparations must be made and the emerging network filled with substance. The third stage is the formalization and institutionalization of the network and finally it is operative. According to effectuation theory, network formation requires the initiators to begin with their available resources, i.e. who they are, what they know and whom they know. Whom they know is particularly relevant in the early phase. By leaving behind the idea that goals of the network are well known beforehand, the network can develop by considering both the individual and collective goals of the participants (Engel et al., 2017). For the network to develop beyond the initial phase, the participants must be willing to share information, skills and resources (Fuller-Love & Thomas, 2004). The ability of participants to build trusting relationships through reciprocal behaviour is a key factor in the depth and richness of the information exchange (Uzzi, 1997). Face-to-face meetings throughout the network-formation process are highly relevant for building trust and may be supported with digital communication (Lapiedra et al., 2004). Thus, for the benefit of participating micro-firms, it is necessary to highlight common interests and develop structures that enforce interaction (Pittaway et al., 2004; Olsen et al., 2012).

The network-development process is bound to involve some unpredictability and goal ambiguity (Engel et al., 2017). Artisans have limited managerial and financial resources for the network-formation process; thus, some support is needed to get the network running (Ratten & Ferreira, 2017; Ratten et al., 2019). The importance of a resourceful network co-ordinator holding the network together by performing the necessary tasks and facilitating progress is documented in the network literature (, Pittaway et al., 2004; Provan et al., 2007; Gausdal & Nilsen, 2011). However, in the end, the network will consist of self-selected entrepreneurial stakeholders willing to make commitment to the network and jointly create its future, reflecting the 'crazy quilt principle' in effectuation theory (Sarasvathy, 2001).

3. Method

3.1 Research design

To explore the process of network formation among artisan entrepreneurs, the study focuses on 'how change processes emerge, develop, grow or terminate over time' (Van de Ven et al., 2007). Hence, the study is based on a four-year longitudinal case study (Eisenhardt, 1989; Yin, 2013). The study is a single case study, where the unit of analysis is 'Norgesglass', an existing network composed by artisan glass-blowers in Norway.[2] Inspired by Czarniawska (1997), a narrative approach is used in the presentation and discussion of the findings. The study is longitudinal and follows the process over four years.

3.2 Data collection

The study was carried out during the period 2016–2020. The data were collected from conversations, observations and document studies. The main source of data is the network reports written by the network co-ordinator and distributed to all participants after each assembly as a part of the common record. The network reports summarize the activities and discussions in each assembly. The reports were written in Norwegian and the quotes were translated into English by the authors. In addition to the account of activities and achievements, the network co-ordinator reflected on what went well and what did not in her writing on the development of the network. The primary data were supplemented with secondary data from sources such as the network website, social media and a members-only Facebook group. The study includes an element of action research (Reason & Bradbury, 2001), as one of the authors participated as an invited speaker in two of the network meetings and administered a survey evaluating the value-creating capacity of the network.

3.3 Data analysis

Data were analysed using an interpretive and explorative approach. Coding of the data followed a thematic analysis, as described by Braun et al. (2019). The initial coding was based on a pre-conception of important themes identified in the theoretical framework. As the interpretation of the data emerged, we analysed patterns in the data, searching for sentiments, categories and themes to be investigated further (Charmaz, 2006; Creswell & Creswell, 2017). The authors performed the data analysis together to strengthen the validity and reliability and reduce potential personal bias throughout the process (Yin, 2013; Hair Jr et al., 2015). Threats to validity were avoided through data triangulation, combining data from interviews, the survey, field notes and the study documents looking for consistent findings.

4. Findings and discussion

4.1 Context

Glass-blowing is a glass-forming technique that involves inflating molten glass into a bubble with the aid of a blowpipe. The general challenges in the industry are the need for expensive and sensitive technical equipment and high energy costs. A furnace requires continuous monitoring and rapid deployment in the event of a technical shutdown. Glass-blower studios have high fixed operating costs related to the smelter.

Currently, there are 37 glass-blower studios scattered throughout Norway (Figure 1). Each glass-blower studio typically consists of the owner/craftsman and several assistants or apprentices. The glass-blowers are highly dedicated to their work with a strong love of the material and the art. Glass-blowing is one of several craft traditions built on knowledge and skills that are important to preserve as a part of a cultural heritage. This however, can be challenging as it is difficult to recruit to the studio glass-blower trade. Geographical distance means opportunities are rare for collegial discussions and knowledge exchange across studios, as well for maintaining the reputation of the craft.

---

[2]'Norgesglass' translates as 'Norwegian Glass'.

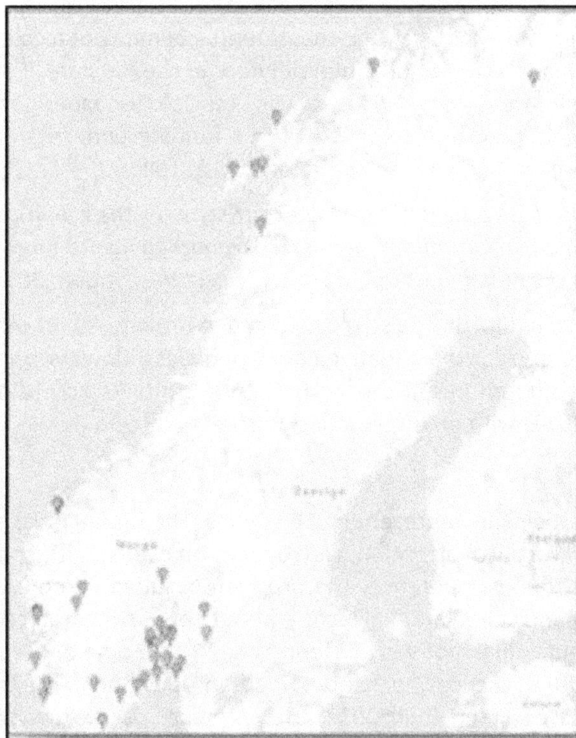

Figure 1: Glass-blower studios in Norway

4.2 The case: Norgesglass—a network of Norwegian glass-blower studios

Norgesglass (NG) is a network of 30 Norwegian glass-blower studios formed by the participating firms during the period 2015–2019. The network is organized through a chosen leader, a geographically distributed resource group and a part-time chief executive officer (CEO). The timeline presented in Figure 2 shows the main assemblies and milestones in the network development from the idea and formation to the present.

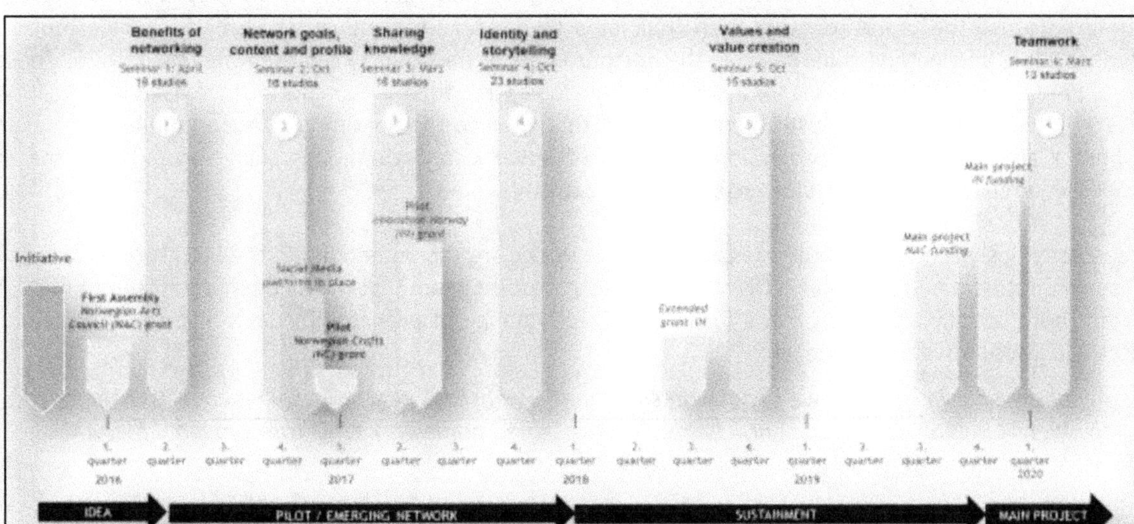

Figure 2: Timeline of activities

4.2.1 The idea and the emergence of a network

Acknowledging various challenges in the industry and the potential benefits of a collaboration, a group of eight glass-blowers in 2015 had the idea to form a horizontal network in the industry. The leaders were a couple, a glass-blower serving as advocate for the group, and his spouse, a sociologist experienced in project management. The initiators approached the Arts Council Norway (ACN) for funding under its program for microbusiness networks in creative industries. The initial purpose was described as follows:

> *The main goal of the project is to help glass-blower artists with their own glass-blower studios' work in Norway by forming a formalized network, strengthening its innovative capacity and competitiveness and thus maintaining its operations. (Project description, 2015)*

The ACN grant made it possible to initiate a first seminar to gauge the interest of other glass-blower studios in joining the network. The target group for the initiative comprised glass-blowers who operated their own glass studio, and invitations were distributed based on the initiators' contacts according to a method similar to snowball sampling (Goodman, 2011) with an effectuation perspective (who do we know?) (Sarasvathy, 2001). In total, 28 studios were contacted.

The first seminar attracted 24 participants representing 18 studios. The seminar was designed with the purpose of being perceived as useful and worthy of attention, with a focus on clarifying the participants' expectations of a network and ways to increase their competence. The program included demonstrations of techniques by a reputed international glass artist and a motivational lecture about network characteristics and benefits, thereby satisfying the artisan entrepreneurs' dual motives (Ratten et al., 2019). Some of the participating glass-blowers contributed by demonstrating their practices, which provided an opportunity for the participants to become familiar with each other's businesses (Olsen et al., 2012). The seminar closed with a world café (Pagliarini, 2006) that give the participants opportunities to voice their opinions and proposals. The feedback on the seminar was positive, and during this first seminar, the network went from an initiative to an emerging network with the project manager appointed as network co-ordinator:

> *We ended up with an action list for the network, with # 1 priorities, as well as a resource group, and each participant wrote down an area in which they could contribute to the network. All in all, I was very happy with the seminar! (co-ordinator, email May 5th, 2016)*

The main action points were to get to know each other, build trusting relations and decide how to establish network continuity, increase competence and increase the visibility of the craft. A closed Facebook group was established to facilitate exchange of information and informal discussions among network members. To increase the craft's visibility, the participants decided to brand the network 'Norgesglass'. By June 2016, the brand had been established with a joint promotion channel on Instagram and Facebook. All glass-blower studios were encouraged to use the brand together with their own to increase the industry's visibility. Furthermore, in September 2016, an elected leader based in the northern part of the country replaced the (capital) Oslo-based leader of the network. This was done for a number of reasons. First, the rural anchoring increased the likelihood of 'fitting in' to the public policy instruments. Second, this reduced the proximity between the leader and the co-ordinator and increased the professionalism of the network, and third, this change could increase the network's legitimacy among glass-blowers all over the country.

Between activities, such as distributed tasks and 'homework', are recommended in the literature as means to increase commitment and legitimacy (Olsen et al., 2012). Despite general acknowledgement of the network as important both socially and as an arena for knowledge exchange, it proved difficult to initiate and continue network activities between assemblies:

> *At the seminar in October, we had a workshop on the website, www.norgesglass.com. To help fill the website with content, the participants were assigned homework. This task proved difficult to implement. (co-ordinator, email February 2017)*

The discrepancy between intentions and actions is not surprising given the studios' smallness and daily workloads. However, one year after the initial assembly, the analysis indicated that membership of the network made a substantial contribution to knowledge exchange between the participants. To illustrate, by February 2017, there were approximately 70 posts on the internal Facebook group concerning practical issues (co-ordinator, email, Feb 2017). Further, collaboration groups on various topics were established, e.g. an apprentice group working on recruitment in a Nordic context. The promotional accounts on Instagram and Facebook had

175 and 111 followers, respectively, and approximately 50 posts from 29 glass artists (Project feedback NAC, 2017). However, funds had run out.

4.2.2 Struggle for sustainment and formalization

By early 2017, the network still awaited a response on a project application to Innovation Norway (IN), a state instrument to support business innovation and growth. Consequently, the upcoming seminar was in danger. Taking an effectuation approach, asking 'who do we know?', a trade organization, Norwegian Crafts (NC), was approached. NC's small grant paid for the program but did not contribute to the required travel grants. However, 16 studios were able to participate, two for the first time. Although this assembly also reaped praise, it became apparent at the seminar that the network had to go from an 'event organizer and a social club' to a more formal arrangement. This was necessary both to prove progress for its members and to prove value and prospects in the public support system. Hence, in December 2017, 21 glass-blowers signed a letter of intent to formalize their membership in the network.

In spite of this, 2018 became a difficult year. The applications for funding were pending far longer than anticipated, which created uncertainty for the future prospects of the collaboration. The activities were kept at a minimum level and the spring seminar had to be postponed. Losing the physical meeting spaces was a setback for the network because these played a significant role in members getting to know each other and developing trusting relationships (Pittaway et al., 2004; Shazi et al., 2015). The co-ordinator attempted to maintain network activity by establishing regional groups and rotating responsibilities for Facebook/Instagram posts. In the end, IN extended the funding and it became possible to hold a seminar in October 2018. However, the money came with conditions imposed by IN: i.e. If the network intended to apply for a main project, some of the allocated funds should be used to conduct an analysis of value creation and market potential of the glass-blower studios.

To respond to this call, a survey was conducted to gain increased insight into the glass-blowers' perspectives and commercial preferences. Based on the survey responses, three avenues were identified by which the network might contribute to profitability (unpublished report, 2019): The first was process innovation, e.g. new ways of working and new ways of solving common challenges. The second was product innovation by fostering creativity in the production of art and by joining forces to compete for major projects at home and abroad (opening new markets). Finally, the third was that collaboration could enhance competitiveness by increasing the visibility of the crafts.

4.2.3 Back on track: Entering the main project

In late 2019, there were two promising announcements. The network had received funding for a three-year main project from ACN and from IN. As a result, the network had the necessary funding to progress to a main project and plan for the coming three-year period.

In 2020, the network is undergoing a new stage of becoming a formal horizontal business network. The network co-ordinator's status has changed from co-ordinator to CEO. The institutionalization of the network is also prominent in the latest post-seminar note to the participants:

> *We must formalize the membership of Norgesglass. We need to investigate and choose modes of operation (...). We must consider a subscription. (Note, seminar 6, 2020, p. 10)*

4.2.4 Discussion

The analysis shows that the network co-ordinator was prominent in the network-formation process. Indeed, in a seminar report, one member were quoted saying *"We need a (name of coordinator) to be on track"* (Note seminar 5, 2018). The co-ordinator had followed the initiative from the very start. Her job was to bind the network together, initiate activities and safeguard the legitimacy and operation of the project to increase commitment to the network by the network members. As the spouse of one of the initiating glass-blowers, she was familiar with the challenges in the industry, and we believe this increased her legitimacy with the network participants.

The resource group is composed of designated regional contacts and resource people, including the network leader. The regional contacts increase the feeling of proximity in the network and co-ordinate collaboration that requires physical proximity. Furthermore, the resource group supports and provides a sounding board for the co-ordinator and leader respectively, thus anchoring their decisions and choice of activities.

The main network activity is the seminars. The seminars have followed the same structure since the start, with the following items on the agenda (Figure 3). Repeating the program structure builds familiarity and a common history, which are important to bind the participants together.

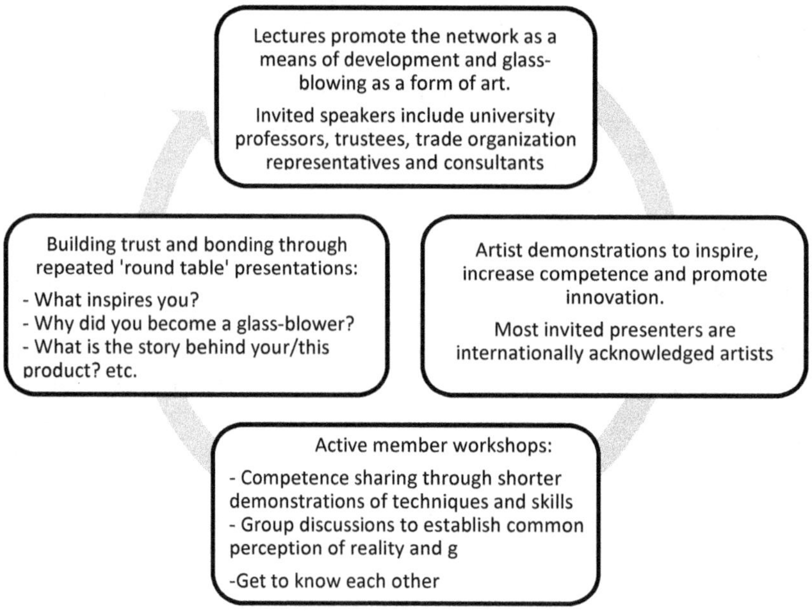

Figure 3: Seminar structure

The network-formation process and network operational development were highly interactive processes. What the network should be was a theme at every assembly, yet the differences from seminar 1 in 2016 to seminar 5 in 2019 were not very large (Table 1).

Table 1: Network goals (unpublished seminar reports 1 and 5)

2016	2019
Increase visibility and reputation	Increase visibility and reputation
Get to know each other, build trust	Exchange knowledge and competence
Focus on common challenges related to production, marketing and competence development	Develop common strategies for cost reduction and economies of scale Develop common recruitment strategies
Initiate collaborative projects	Promote social and professional networking to facilitate development of joint projects
Open new markets, including major projects and international activity	Increase focus on experience-related markets Establish a joint showroom

5. Conclusion

This study contributes to an enriched and a nuanced understanding of the formation of a horizontal network among artisan entrepreneurs. The study follows the formation process over four years from the idea phase to emerging network formation, to sustainment of network and towards a more formal network. The endogenous network was initiated within the industry (Jost, 2019).

The formation process shares some similarities with starting a new business (Zahra, 2005), e.g. because of the considerable uncertainty in the process, such as accessing the financial and organizational resources needed to establish the network. Moreover, it required the interest, ability and commitment of the individual artisan firms to prioritize it. It also shares similarities with an effectual perspective on entrepreneurship (Sarasvathy, 2001, 2009), contradicting the dominant view of network management characterized by the concept of a distributed and collective leadership. The main motivation behind the network formation initiative was not related to the individual initiators' self-interest but to a collective motivation to address the challenges facing the industry as a whole.

The findings indicate that the process of network formation and what it developed were highly intertwined. At an early stage of the process, the entrepreneurs discussed and agreed upon the goals of the network. This bottom-up process increased their commitment to the network and interest in proceeding; with time, the network became a more tightly coupled system (Fuglsang & Eide, 2012). Throughout the process, the participants identified areas for collaboration and their ambitions seemed to increase, and in doing so they found new means (Sarasvathy, 2001). However, the content and goals of the network had to be adapted somewhat to fulfil the requirements of external stakeholders, e.g. public organizations providing financial support, because it was not possible to develop the network without this support. Furthermore, it was important that the network contributed to the entrepreneurs' mixed goals, both artistic and commercial (Pagano et al., 2018). Critical events in the network-formation process concerned gaining access to necessary funding.

The analysis shows that the network co-ordinator played a critical role throughout all stages, and we argue that her role resembles that of an entrepreneur, as she was the main driver and motivator throughout the process. She became involved in the process because she was the wife of one of the network initiators; thus, she was a self-selected stakeholder in the network (Sarasvathy, 2001, 2009). Her enthusiasm and project expertise were critical to move the network forward. The finding of a need for a good project leader is consistent with previous research (Olsen et al., 2012).

References

Bonatto, F., Resende, L. M. M., Pontes, J. & Andrade Junior, P. P. D. (2017). A Measurement Model For Managing Performance Of Horizontal Business Networks And A Research Case, *Production,* 27, E20170051.

Braun, V., Clarke, V., Hayfield, N. & Terry, G. (2019). Thematic Analysis, In Liamputtong P. (Ed.), *Handbook Of Research Methods In Health Social Sciences*, Singapore: Springer, Pp. 843–860.

Brink, T. & Svendsen, G. L. H. (2013). Social Capital Or Waste Of Time? Social Networks, Social Capital And 'Unconventional Alliances' Among Danish Rural Entrepreneurs. *Business And Management Research,* 2, 55–68.

Charmaz, K. (2006). *Constructing Grounded Theory: A Practical Guide Through Qualitative Analysis. London:* Sage.

Creswell, J. W. & Creswell, J. D. (2017). *Research Design: Qualitative, Quantitative, And Mixed Methods Approaches.* London: Sage Publications.

Czarniawska, B. (1997). *A Narrative Approach To Organization Studies*. London: Sage Publications.

Elfring, T. & Hulsink, W. 2007. Networking By Entrepreneurs: Patterns Of Tie—Formation In Emerging Organizations. *Organization Studies,* 28, 1849–1872.

Elstad, B. & De Paoli, D. (2014). *Organisering Og Ledelse Av Kunst Og Kultur*, Cappelen Damm Akademisk.

Elvekrok, I., Veflen, N., Nilsen, E. R. & Gausdal, A. H. (2018). Firm Innovation Benefits From Regional Triple-Helix Networks. *Regional Studies,* 52, 1214–1224.

Engel, Y., Kaandorp, M. & Elfring, T. (2017). Toward A Dynamic Process Model Of Entrepreneurial Networking Under Uncertainty. *Journal Of Business Venturing,* 32, 35–51.

Flanagan, D. J., Lepisto, D. A. & Ofstein, L. F. (2018). Coopetition Among Nascent Craft Breweries: A Value Chain Analysis. *Journal Of Small Business And Enterprise Development*. 25, 2–16.

Fritsch, M. & Kauffeld-Monz, M. (2010). The Impact Of Network Structure On Knowledge Transfer: An Application Of Social Network Analysis In The Context Of Regional Innovation Networks. *The Annals Of Regional Science,* 44, 21 Ff.

Fuglsang, L. & Eide, D. (2013). The Experience Turn As 'Bandwagon': Understanding Network Formation And Innovation As Practice. *European Urban And Regional Studies,* 20, 417–434.

Fuller-Love, N. & Thomas, E. (2004). Networks In Small Manufacturing Firms. *Journal Of Small Business Enterprise Development,* 11, 244–253.

Galloway, T. L., Kuhn, K. M. & Collins-Williams, M. (2019). Competitors As Advisors: Peer Assistance Among Small Business Entrepreneurs. *Long Range Planning*, 101929.

Gausdal, A. H. & Nilsen, E. R. (2011). Orchestrating Innovative Sme Networks. The Case Of "Healthinnovation". *Journal Of The Knowledge Economy,* 2, 586–600.

Goodman, L. A. (2011). Comment: On Respondent-Driven Sampling And Snowball Sampling In Hard-To-Reach Populations And Snowball Sampling Not In Hard-To-Reach Populations. *Sociological Methodology,* 41, 347–353.

Guercini, S. & Cova, B. (2018). Sources Of Unconventional Entrepreneurship: Passion And Consumption. *Journal Of Business Research*, 92, 385 - 391

Gundolf, K., Jaouen, A. & Gast, J. (2018). Motives For Strategic Alliances In Cultural And Creative Industries. *Creativity And Innovation Management,* 27, 148–160.

Hair Jr, J. F., Wolfinbarger, M., Money, A. H., Samouel, P. & Page, M. J. (2015). *Essentials Of Business Research Methods.* New York: Me Sharpe.
Halme, M. & Fadeeva, Z. J. G. M. I. (2000). Small And Medium-Sized Tourism Enterprises In Sustainable Development Networks. *Greener Management International*, 30, 97–114.
Hoang, H. & Yi, A. 2015. Network-Based Research In Entrepreneurship: A Decade In Review. *Foundations And Trends® In Entrepreneurship,* 11, 1–54.
Jost, P.-J. (2019). Endogenous Formation Of Entrepreneurial Networks. *Small Business Economics*, 1-26
Kerr, J. & Coviello, N. (2019). Formation And Constitution Of Effectual Networks: A Systematic Review And Synthesis. *International Journal Of Management Reviews,* 21, 370–397.
Klamer, A. (2011). Cultural Entrepreneurship. *The Review Of Austrian Economics,* 24, 141–156.
Kuhn, K. M. & Galloway, T. L. (2015). With A Little Help From My Competitors: Peer Networking Among Artisan Entrepreneurs. *Entrepreneurship Theory And Practice,* 39, 571–600.
Lapiedra, R., Smithson, S., Alegre, J. & Chiva, R. (2004). Role Of Information Systems On The Business Network-Formation Process: An Empirical Analysis Of The Automotive Sector. *Journal Of Enterprise Information Management*, 17, 219–228.
Lechner, C. & Dowling, M. (2003). Firm Networks: External Relationships As Sources For The Growth And Competitiveness Of Entrepreneurial Firms. *Entrepreneurship And Regional Development,* 15, 1–26.
Luckman, S. (2015). *Craft And The Creative Economy.* London: Palgrave.
Manning, S. (2010). The Strategic Formation Of Project Networks: A Relational Practice Perspective. *Human Relations,* 63, 551–573.
Mcadam, M., Mcadam, R., Dunn, A. & Mccall, C. (2016). Regional Horizontal Networks Within The Sme Agri-Food Sector: An Innovation And Social Network Perspective. *Regional Studies,* 50, 1316–1329.
Olsen, N. V., Elvekrok, I. & Nilsen, E. R. (2012). Drivers Of Food Smes Network Success: 101 Tales From Norway. *Trends In Food Science & Technology* 26, 120–128.
Pagano, A., Petrucci, F. & Bocconcelli, R. (2018). A Business Network Perspective On Unconventional Entrepreneurship: A Case From The Cultural Sector. *Journal Of Business Research,* 92, 455–464.
Pagliarini, R. (2006). The World Café–Shaping Our Futures Through Conversations That Matter. *Journal Of Organizational Change Management*, 19, 266–268.
Pettersen, I. B. & Tobiassen, A. E. (2012). Are Born Globals Really Born Globals? The Case Of Academic Spin-Offs With Long Development Periods. *Journal Of International Entrepreneurship,* 10, 117–141.
Pittaway, L., Robertson, M., Munir, K., Denyer, D. & Neely, A. (2004). Networking And Innovation: A Systematic Review Of The Evidence. *International Journal Of Management Reviews,* 5–6, 137–168.
Pret, T. & Cogan, A. (2019). Artisan Entrepreneurship: A Systematic Literature Review And Research Agenda. *International Journal Of Entrepreneurial Behavior & Research*, 25, 592–614.
Provan, K. G., Fish, A. & Sydow, J. (2007). Interorganizational Networks At The Network Level: A Review Of The Empirical Literature On Whole Networks. *Journal Of Management,* 33, 479–516.
Ratten, V., Costa, C. & Bogers, M. (2019). Artisan, Cultural And Tourism Entrepreneurship. *International Journal Of Entrepreneurial Behavior & Research*, 25, Pp. 582–591.
Ratten, V. & Ferreira, J. J. (2017). Future Research Directions For Cultural Entrepreneurship And Regional Development. *International Journal Of Entrepreneurship And Innovation Management,* 21, 163–169.
Reason, P. & Bradbury, H. (2001). *Handbook Of Action Research: Participative Inquiry And Practice*, Sage.
Sarasvathy, S. D. 2001. Causation And Effectuation: Toward A Theoretical Shift From Economic Inevitability To Entrepreneurial Contingency. *Academy Of Management Review,* 26, 243–263.
Sarasvathy, S. D. (2009). *Effectuation: Elements Of Entrepreneurial Expertise*, Edward Elgar Publishing.
Shazi, R., Gillespie, N. & Steen, J. (2015). Trust As A Predictor Of Innovation Network Ties In Project Teams. *International Journal Of Project Management*, 33, 81–91.
Thorgren, S., Wincent, J. & Örtqvist, D. (2009). Designing Interorganizational Networks For Innovation: An Empirical Examination Of Network Configuration, Formation And Governance. *Journal Of Engineering And Technology Management,* 26, 148–166.
Uzzi, B. (1997). Social Structure And Competition In Interfirm Networks: The Paradox Of Embeddedness. *Administrative Science Quarterly,* 42, 35–67.
Van De Ven, A. H., Sapienza, H. J. & Villanueva, J. (2007). Entrepreneurial Pursuits Of Self-And Collective Interests. *Strategic Entrepreneurship Journal,* 1, 353–370.
Weiss, J. A. (1987). Pathways To Cooperation Among Public Agencies. *Journal Of Policy Analysis And Management,* 7, 94–117.
Yin, R. K. (2013). *Case Study Research: Design And Methods. London:* Sage Publications.
Zahra, S. A. (2005). A Theory Of International New Ventures: A Decade Of Research. *Journal Of International Business Studies,* 36, 20–28.

Social Media use and its Effect on the Performance of MSMEs in Egypt

Hadia Fakhreldin[1], Ahmed Ayman[1] and Rania Miniesy[2]
[1]Department of Business Administration, The British University in Egypt, Egypt
[2]Department of Economics, The British University in Egypt, Egypt
Hadia.Fakhreldin@bue.edu.eg
Ahmed.ayman@bue.edu.eg
RMiniesy@bue.edu.eg
DOI: 10.34190/EIE.20.056

Abstract: Numerous studies have examined the effect of information technology on business, yet a limited number has examined the effect caused by social media, and an even fewer number assessed that effect on micro, small and medium enterprises (MSMEs). This research attempts to fill this gap by focusing on the impact of social media on the performance of MSMEs in an emerging market in the Middle East – Egypt - by adopting the Technology Acceptance Model (TAM) and the Task Technology Fit framework (TTF). Data was collected through questionnaires (383), and then supplemented with in-depth interviews (5) to gain further insights. The structural equation modeling technique was used, and the findings of the statistical analysis provide a better understanding of the antecedents of the social media use and the factors leading to an increased use of it, as well as the positive effect this has on various performance criteria.

Keywords: social media, MSMEs, performance, Egypt

1. Introduction

The development of Information and Communications Technology (ICT) in the last two decades has transformed the communication scale and scope. Social media allows for more interaction between businesses and their customers (Chanthinok, et al., 2015), its use has shown considerable potential in increasing sales, reducing costs, showing higher levels of customer engagement and thus improving customer service, advertising, promotion, branding, searching information, driving traffic to the company website and improving business-to-business relationships, in addition to enhancing relationships with existing customers as well as obtaining new ones through the effect of positive word-of-mouth (Trainor et al, 2014; McCann and Barlow, 2015). Therefore, it is viewed as having a positive effect on business performance (Parveen, et al., 2015), in other words, it enhances the competitiveness of the firms (Ahmad, et al., 2018). Since 2011 and until 2019, several authors have studied the effect of social media on small enterprises and they suggested that ICT facilitates economic competitiveness and sustains long-term economic growth (Crittendena, et al., 2019), therefore, the use of social media has become a strategic priority for most businesses in developed and developing countries. Some studies have investigated the impact of Social Media on the performance of SMEs (Franco, et al., 2016), few scholars have found a positive relationship between social media adoption and general business performance (e.g: Ainin et al., 2015; Ahmad et al, 2018).

This study adopts the technology acceptance model (TAM) and the task technology fit framework (TTF) to observe the impact of social media use on the performance of MSME's in Egypt, an area not adequately explored in academic research (Ahmad, et al., 2018).

2. Background

2.1 ICT theories

ICT is an umbrella term that includes all devices and applications, such as mobile phones, personal computers, and social media applications, which enable individuals to interact with each other in the digital world (Crittendena, et al., 2019). The technology acceptance model (TAM) introduced by Davis (1989), explained the determinants of computer acceptance that are general and capable of explaining user behavior across a broad range of end-user computing technologies and the user population (Rauniar, et al., 2014; Lin and Kim, 2016). TAM suggests that there are different variables that influence the user's decision to whether and how they will use the technology (Nistor, 2019). The theory proposes that an individual's perceptions of a technology's use are the determinants of intentions to adopt the technology and actual adoption behavior. The core concept of the TAM is that the easier a technology is to use, the more beneficial it is to the user (Ritz, et al., 2018). Individuals are more likely to use a new ICT, if they perceive their interaction with the technology to be clear and understandable (Crittendena, et al., 2019).

TAM suggests that the actual use of a new technology depends on the user's attitude towards it (Rauniar, et al., 2014). Behavior is thus predicted using the two main variables describing this attitude, namely the perceived ease of use (Roy, et al., 2014) and the perceived usefulness (Fishbein & Ajzen, 1975). Crittendena et al. (2019) added a "use" variable, which describes the purpose of the use of the ICT and the advantages perceived by the user. Another variable proposed and used by Bianchi et al. (2017) is more complementary, and is referred to as "use capability" and denotes the technological resources or capabilities, which include the infrastructure and the processes, available in the organization and result in turning the information technology into value for the firm (Matikiti, et al., 2012). Therefore, if entrepreneurs understand the benefits of using social media, they will accept and use it to achieve its potential benefits. TAM has proven to be a useful theoretical model in helping understand (Tuyet Mai, et al., 2013) and explain information system acceptance and implementation (Veldeman, et al., 2017).

2.2 Use of social media in Egypt

It was statistically shown that SM plays a major role in the everyday lives of Egyptian Internet users, with Egypt ranking 17th worldwide in terms of audience size and the first in the Arab region (Marzouk, 2016). Egypt holds both the highest number of growth rate and number of users of Facebook in the region, with 41 million users in April 2020 (Clement, 2020). Statista reported that the current number of Instagram users in Egypt surpassed 14 million accounts. Instagram is now considered the top platform for many industries such as fashion, events and travel (Egypt Digital Report, 2017), which is understandable considering that these industries depend on photos more than on detailed information of their product/service. Therefore, businesses cannot afford to ignore the potential business opportunities the social media platforms provide (McCann & Barlow, 2015). Small firms need to develop competitive advantages based on intensive and effective use of information systems, including SM; an essential source of innovation and success in today's market (Hoti, 2015).

2.3 Use of social media and MSME performance

The Task-Technology Fit (TTF) theory proposed by Goodhue and Thompson (1995) pointed out that there is a positive link between technology and performance when the technology utilized is a good fit with the tasks it supports (Agnihotri, et al., 2017). It is important to note, that the TTF focuses on sales as the key performance measure and goal for the technology use and does not take into consideration other variables that can affect the fit (Agnihotri, et al., 2017). It is suggested that the effective usage of social media may be considered as a competitive advantage for businesses, as it clarifies customers' needs through sharing their personal information, and observing their consumer behavior through video posts (Oji, et al., 2017). Therefore, MSMEs embrace social media (Dahnil, et al., 2014), as it raises their competitiveness (McCann and Barlow, 2015) and therefore their performance (Denyer, et al., 2011).

Ahmad et al. (2018) confirmed this by considering several aspects that describe/report performance; increased connectivity, improved customer clientele, improved brand awareness and reputation, reduced communication and marketing cost, increased revenue, creation of competitive advantage. Franco et al. (2016) and Garrido-Moreno & Lockett (2016) suggested that social networks have a positive influence on SME performance; other studies also showed that integrating SM use in SME business operation will improve firm performance (e.g Rapp, et al., 2010; Ghandour, 2018).

2.4 Measuring MSME performance

It is difficult to use a single measure to evaluate performance (Guni, 2016); early studies used quantitative performance measures, such as growth of sales and return on investment (Miller & Toulouse, 1986), lately studies have chosen economic measures of performance when it came to MSMEs, most of which have focused on growth rather than accounting measures or they devised their own performance measures (Gupta & Wales, 2017). The study by Ainin et al. (2015) uses sales transactions, sales volume and number of customers to measure performance, and these will be adopted in this study to evaluate the in-country aspect of MSME performance.

Internationalization is also an indication of positive performance of firms (Pouresmeili, et al., 2018). Buckley & Tian (2017) argue that internationalization can directly lead to better profitability in emerging markets. According to Xu & Meyer (2012), the relation between internationalization and performance is not that direct in emerging countries. Wright et al. (2005) added that research done on MSE or SME internationalization in developed countries may not essentially be relevant to their counterparts in emerging countries as emerging markets have considerably less economic development (Bianchi and Wickramasekera, 2016).

A number of studies have highlighted the positive effect that investment in information technology that supports SM implies better firm performance (Malthouse, et al., 2013; Rapp, et al., 2013). This means that the investment in SM can be regarded as an indication of performance and thus be used as a performance measure. Growth has been also widely used as a measure of performance in both large corporations (Wasiuzzaman & Arumugam, 2013), and SMEs (Ipinnaiye, et al., 2017). However, numerous proxies were used to measure growth, the most common of which is sales growth (Wiklund & Shepherd, 2005); Gupta & Wales (2017) reported 22 different studies that used sales volume increase as a proxy for growth, other researchers measured growth through proxys of growth in market share and increase in productivity (Laitinen, 2002).

Surprisingly, there is limited research on SM adoption and the effect of its usage in the Arab countries (Ahmad, et al., 2018), particularly in Egypt (Marzouk, 2016). This study will use the increase in sales, the increase in followers, the increase in competetive advantage, internationalization, investment in social media and growth and combinations thereof as a proxies for firm performance. It examines the effect of the use of SM on these indicators in Egyptian MSMEs.

3. Hypothesis

H1: The use of SM has a positive and significant effect on the in-country performance (Firmperform) of the MSMEs.

H2: The use of SM has a positive and significant effect on the international performance (Firminterperform) of the MSMEs.

H3: The use of SM has a positive and significant effect on the MSME's intention to internationalize (Internintention)

H4: The use of SM has a positive and significant effect on the investment in SM (InvestinSM).

H5: The use of SM has a positive and significant effect on the growth (Growth) of the MSMEs.

The following figure represents the theoretical framework, which is based on the TTF Theory and the TAM.

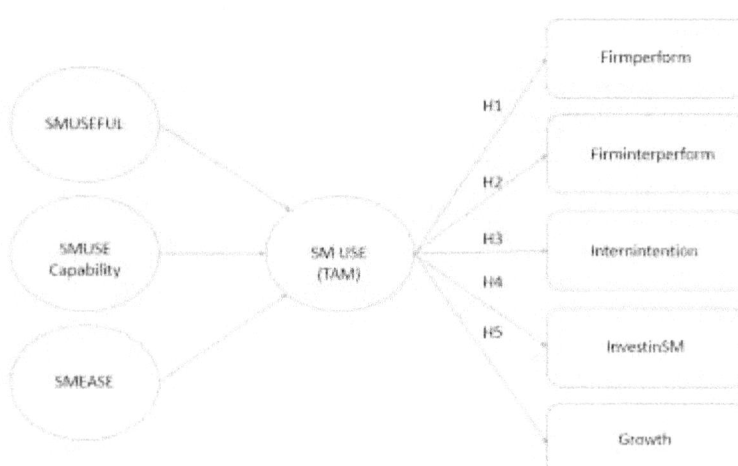

Figure 1: TTF/TAM framework: Social media use & SME performance

4. Methodology

Self-assessment questionnaires are well-regarded in the literature of SMEs (Asamoah, 2014) and overcome the issue of confidentiality ((El-Gohary, 2012), which is a main obstacle in data collection of firm performance in the context of MSMEs (Smits & Mogos, 2013). The MSMEs in this sample were selected based on purposive sampling by focusing on enterprises that have a presence on SM, as well as their willingness to participate in the study (Fraenkel & Wallen, 1996). The main selection criterion was that they had adopted SM for at least 1 year. The questionnaire includes questions to identify the SM platforms used by the MSMEs, the perceived benefits of SM, the effect of SM on the different measures of firm performance, SM platforms used, perceived obstacles of using SM by the firms, and general demographic questions (Rapp et al., 2013; Trainor et al. 2014;). The survey was prepared in English then translated into Arabic; it was then back-translated to English and revisited by the research team to reach highest accuracy (Brislin, 1970). Interviews were conducted as follow-up to gain a deeper understanding of the responses received (McNamara, 1999) and to validate the research findings (Alshenqeeti, 2014).

4.1 Data description

In Egypt, the latest definition of MSMEs was published by the Central Bank of Egypt in 2017. It distinguishes between micro small and medium enterprises, and existing and newly established enterprises. The latter have less than 10 employees and less than 1 million EGP annual sales/revenues, whereas newly established ones have the same number of employees but paid-equity capital of less than 500000 EGP. Lower small, small and medium enterprises have less than 200 employees with annual turnover of EGP between 1-10 million, 10-20 million and 20-100 million respectively for existing firms and paid-equity capital of EGP between 500,000 to EGP 5 million for SMEs newly established enterprises respectively. Although informality predominates private enterprises in Egypt (Kolster, 2016), the focus of this paper is on the formal MSMEs only. A cross-sectional sample of MSMEs in greater Cairo is obtained, as more than 70% of the MSMEs in Egypt are in greater Cairo and the Delta region. The final sample was a multi-industry sample of 383 firms, which ensures the generalization of findings (Alarcón-del-Amo, et al., 2017). All variables that can be verified from independent sources have been confirmed to avoid common method variance (Podsakoff & Organ, 1986), e.g. the Facebook page, the Instagram page, etc. The data was analyzed using SPSS software. Tables 1 through 5 show the main descriptive statistics of the sample studied.

Table 1: Demographics

Age	Older than 38	40.1%
	27 to 38	45.6%
	16 to 26	14.3%
	Younger than 16	0%
Gender	Male	69.7%
	Female	29.3%
Owner nationality	Egyptian	93%
	Other	7%

Table 2: % Use of social media

Digital/social media tool usage	**Percentage**
Website/ E-commerce	16.7%
Facebook	96.9%
Twitter	10.7%
Instagram	37.9%
WhatApp	41.3%
Mobile app	1.6%

Table 3: Nature of social media use

Nature of digital/social media tool use	**Percentage**
Basic information and contacts	81.2%
Product image	83.8%
Product description	64.2%
Prices and promotions	53.8%
E-commerce website	1%
Customer comments	3.1%
Customer orders	8.9%

Table 4: Obstacles facing MSMEs using social media

Main obstacles facing MSMEs using digital/social media	**Percentage**
Time wasted on unrewarding customers	38.1%

Main obstacles facing MSMEs using digital/social media	Percentage
Ideas stolen by competitors	40.2%
High operating cost	16.7%
Negative comments/ feedback	32.9%
Time spent creating and uploading content	7.1%
Online piracy	32.9%
Fake users/spams	7.1%
Lack of customer loyalty	11.8%
Other	20.1%

Table 5: Firm size

Firm size/type	Percentage
Micro	32.3%
Small	39.5%
Medium	28.2%

4.2 Data analysis

A total of 9 indicators are created in this research; each indicator is created by summing the questions which measure this variable. The variables are: SMuseful, SMuse, SMease, TAM USE (sum of SMuseful, SMuse and SMease), these indicators are antecedents of the actual SM use in the MSMEs . Firmperfrom (firm in-country performance), Firminterperform (refers to the same as Firmperform plus international operation), thus it describes the international performance of the firm. InternIntention describes the international entrepreneurial orientation. Growth (growth in sales volume after the use of the various SM platforms). The inter-correlations, means, and standard deviations of the constructs are presented in Table (6).

Table 6: Means, standard deviations, correlations and scale reliability of the variables of sample

	Mean	SD	SM useful	SM use	SM ease	TAM	Firm Perform	FirmInter Perform	Intern intention	Growth	Investin SM
SM useful	3.6356	0.66362	1								
SM use	3.6006	0.89397	.173**	1							
SM ease	3.3324	0.78734	-0.022	.450**	1						
TAM	3.3333	1.61086	.438**	.829**	.743**	1					
Firm Perform	3.5794	1.44654	.624**	0.073	-0.001	.249**	1				
FirmInterPerform	3.2283	1.41175	.658**	0.088	-0.02	.278**	.891**	1			
Internintention	3.4615	0.77493	.480**	0.07	0.063	.266**	.453**	.645**	1		
Growth	3.7232	1.40162	.477**	.158**	0.053	.269**	.274**	.293**	.227**	1	
InvestinSM	3.4615	.77493	.037	.811**	.818**	.872**	.052	.040	.089	.122*	1

* Significance at 0.05 level

** Significant at 0.01 level

A multi-variate statistical analysis is performed in the form of factor analysis to assess the measurement model. The Kaiser-Meyer-Olkin (KMO) test is used to ensure that the factor analysis model is suitably adjusted to the data. The Confirmatory Factor Analysis (CFA) was specified with the 9 constructs (latent variables). All factor loadings were found to be fit (Albright & Park, 2009). As shown in Table (8), the results met the established benchmarks that provide evidence of convergent validity and internal consistency reliability (Fornell and Larcker, 1981). The discriminant validity suggested that all latent variables studied in the conceptual model satisfy the discriminate validity criteria (Fornell and Larcker, 1981). Based on the CFA results, the measurement model is adequate to employ in testing the proposed model through the structural equation modeling (SEM) technique as shown in Table (8), as SEM is an effective multivariate technique that examines the unobserved constructs in proposed relationships and computes the measurement error (Schumacker & Lomax, 2010).

5. Findings/results

The SME in-country performance is positively affected by the use of SM. The relation is significant with a value of 1.68 (Crittendena, et al., 2019). The SMusefulness is the component causing the significant effect on the in-country performance of the firm as a result of the use of SM. The SME international performance is also affected directly and positively by TAM with an estimate of 1.65 at the 5% significance level, where most of the effect is stemming from the usefulness component of the TAM with a value of B of 1.19. When it comes to the effect on the intention to internationalize, the use of SM has a significant direct effect on the intention to internationalize, with a value of 0.17. Although this relation is anticipated in the case of developed countries, it was proposed by Xu & Meyer (2012) and Bianchi & Wickramasekera (2016) that this was not expected in less developed nations. However, the findings of this study support the general international findings. This relation is moderated by the number of branches of the MSME. The relationship between use of SM and the investment in SM is strong and positive. When conducting the linear regression, two components of TAM use, SMuse and SMease have a significant and positive effect on the investment in SM (value of 0.42). The use of SM has a direct and positive effect on the InvestinSM variable, the relationship is negatively moderated by the size of the firm (value of 0.41). Considering growth, there is a positive and significant effect of the use of SM use on growth (value of 0.22. When conducting a linear regression to assess the impact of the SMuseful, SMuse and SMease on Growth, the only significant effect is of the SMuseful component of TAM. The model is significant at the 0.05 level. The use of SM, represented by TAM use has a positive and direct effect on growth (value of 0.215), it has a significant indirect effect on growth through friends and followers (with a value of 0.03). The same relation is moderated by the number of years of SM use (with a value of 0.02).

Table 7: CFA

Variable #	Question	Variable Name/Formulation Question	Communalities	Factor loading	Construct reliability/ Cronbach Alpha	KMO	AVE
1		**SMuseful**			**0.994**	**0.966**	**93.19%**
	Q10	ICT use increase sales volume	0.986	0.993			
	Q11	ICT use increase profits	0.986	0.993			
	Q12	ICT use reduce cost of advertising	0.976	0.988			
	Q13	ICT use reduce cost of customer service	0.978	0.989			
	Q14	ICT use facilitate financial transactions	0.979	0.989			
	Q15	ICT use make it easy to start & manage business	0.982	0.991			
	Q16	ICT use increase market share	0.987	0.993			
	Q17	ICT use make communication more effective	0.723	0.85			
	Q18	ICT use initiates customer relations	0.725	0.851			
	Q19	ICT use increase customer loyalty and retention	0.985	0.992			
	Q20	ICT use increase electronic word of mouth	0.986	0.993			
	Q21	ICT use help expand internationally	0.968	0.984			
	Q23	ICT use improve image of company	0.986	0.993			
	Q24	ICT use increase interactive communication	0.986	0.993			
	Q25	ICT use enhance distribution system	0.698	0.835			
2		**SMuse**			**0.987**	**0.753**	**97.52%**
	Q62	Top-management support is important	0.985	0.992			
	Q63	The allocation of the needed resources is important	0.956	0.978			
	Q64	Employees' knowledge to use technology and social media is important	0.985	0.992			
3		**SMease**			**0.996**	**0.783**	**99.23%**
	Q65	Importance of skilled technical support	0.989	0.995			
	Q66	The government providing enabling technological infrastructure important	0.993	0.997			
4		**TAM USE**			**0.992**	**0.762**	**96.65%**
5		**Firmperform**			**1**	**0.799**	**99.99%**

Variable #	Question	Variable Name/Formulation Question	Communalities	Factor loading	Construct reliability/ Cronbach Alpha	KMO	AVE
	Q40	Sales Volume increased	1	1			
	Q41	Sales Inquiries increased	1	1			
	Q42	Number of Customers increased	1	1			
6		**Firminterperform**			**1**	**0.871**	**99.90%**
	Q40	Sales Volume increased	1	1			
	Q41	Sales Inquiries increased	1	1			
	Q42	Number of Customers increased	1	1			
	Q43	International operations increased	0.997	0.999			
7		**Growth**			**0.899**	**0.711**	**83.50%**
	Q40	Sales Volume increased	1	0.861			
	Q46	Sales Volume increased	0.982	0.939			
8		**Internintention**			**0.693**	**0.5**	**%76.85**
	Q37	I have the intention to go intl in coming 5 years.	0.768	0.877			
	Q38	Internationalization gives competitive advantage	0.768	0.877			
9		**InvestinSM**			**0.991**	**0.881**	**97.53%**
	Q63	The allocation of the needed resources (IT infrastructure, etc,,,) is important	0.943	0.971			
	Q64	Employees' knowledge to use technology and social media is important	0.989	0.994			
	Q65	The company having skilled technical support staff is important	0.989	0.993			
	Q66	The government providing enabling technological infrastructure is important	0.984	0.992			

Table 8: Fitness of the measurement model (n=383) with TAM as independent variable

	NFI	IFI	CFI	RMSEA	Estimate	S.E.	C.R.	P
Performnation	1.00	1.00	1.00	0.05	1.68	0.09	18.78	***
PerformIntern	1.00	1.00	1.00	0.02	1.65	0.08	21.13	***
InternIntention	0.84	0.86	0.93	0.04	0.17	0.04	3.88	***
Investin	0.97	0.97	0.97	0.01	0.04	0.01	31.36	***
Growth	0.81	0.81	0.88	0.01	0.22	0.05	4.21	***

Interviews were conducted with five MSME owners to gain a deeper understanding of the findings. The service companies' entrepreneurs believed that their overall performance improved significantly with their increasing use of SM, mainly Facebook; they also used Instagram and WhatsApp, both had also a website. They elaborated that the website is mostly visited through the links on the Facebook page. When it comes to the MSMEs in the manufacturing sector, they suggested that Facebook is most important. However, it is effectively complemented by Instagram, which is a more appropriate venue for showing their products. An important point they mentioned was, that the use of SM replaced the need to open new branches in other areas. The entrepreneurs added that Facebook, Instagram and WhatsApp constitute an effective combination.

6. Discussion

The findings support that the use of SM has a positive and significant effect on the performance of MSMEs. All five hypotheses are supported, as the use of SM was proven to have a significant effect on the various performance indicators; the in-country performance, the international performance, the MSME's intention to internationalize, the investment in SM and MSME growth. It should be noted that the impact of the "SM usefulness" component has the strongest influence on the performance of the MSME in the cases of firm national performance, firm international performance, internationalization intention, and growth. When it comes to the criterion of investment in social media as an indicator of performance, the "SM use capability" and the "SM ease of use" have the strongest effect on improving the performance of the firm.

The study provides evidence regarding the importance and benefits of SM to MSMEs, which supports the findings of Ahmed et al. (2018) and Tajividi and Karami (2017). Despite the fact that emerging markets in the Middle East are often regarded as a deviation from conventional and established theories of the western world (Bianchi & Wickramasekera, 2016; Lages, et al., 2015), the results of this research seem support the general stream of previous literature (Ainin, et al., 2015; Marzouk, 2016). Building on the TAM, the statistical analysis shows that the significant component in this developed construct is the "usefulness" aspect, which describes the potential benefits that are anticipated with the use of the SM. This is a contribution to theory, proposing that these factors that describe the usefulness of the social media are the true antecedents of it, in the case of MSMEs. These are: potential increase in sales, potential profitability, decrease in advertising and operation costs, increase of market share, customer retention, customer loyalty, brand image, more effective distribution, among other factors that describe the perceived benefits of using SM to an MSME.

The study adds to the research on SM use and its outcomes, as little research has provided a clear analysis of SM as a tool to support the development and growth of MSMEs (Singh & Srivastava, 2019). It provides a better understanding of the factors leading to an increased use of social media and the positive effect this has on various performance criteria. The study is also one of a few that used quantitative methods in researching MSMEs use of SM in developing countries; in contrast to qualitative research methods used in similar cases. It also provides a better understanding of the factors leading to an increased use of social media and the positive effect this has on various performance indicators.

7. Conclusion and recommendations

The findings of the study are timely now with the developments of COVID 19 and the fact that everyone is becoming more connected through the extensive use of ICT. The growing role of SM now is non-presentenced; due to confined movements of people. Therefore, it is expected that MSMEs will grab this opportunity to achieve more growth and development (Dahnil, et al., 2014). The study identified the antecedents that contribute the most to SM use by MSMEs. It confirmed, that SM use has a significant positive effect on the in-country and international performance of these firms, the intention to internationalize, the investment in social media and the growth of the MSME. Therefore, it is important to encourage MSMEs to engage in making the best use of it and invest in it time and effort. Governments whose objective is to enhance the development of MSMEs to drive the economic development of their countries need to make use of this and provide the most-up-to date technology infrastructure to support these firms to reach their optimum performance. Future studies can take a longitudinal approach to investigate SM use, they can also examine other countries in the MENA region and other emerging markets to pursue comparisons and possible generalizations. Furthermore, it would be interesting to compare the different social media tools in terms of their effect on performance. Future studies should examine other indicators of performance, like brand image and customer relation.

Acknowledgements

This study funded partially by a grant from the British University in Egypt (The Young Investigators Research Grant) in 2018

References

Agnihotri, R., Trainor, K. J., Itani, O. S. & Rodriguez, M., 2017. Examining The role of sales-based CRM technology and social media use on post-sale service behaviors in India. KJournal of Business Research, Volume 81, p. 144–154.

Ahmad, Ahmad & Abu Bakar , A. R., 2018. Reflections of entrepreneurs of small and medium-sized enterprises concerning the adoption of social media and its impact on performance outcomes: Evidence from the UAE. Telematics and Informatics, Volume 35, p. 6–17.

Ainin, S. et al., 2015. Factors influencing the use of social media by SMEs and its perfromance outcomes. Industrial Management and Data Systems, 115(3), pp. 570-588.

Alarcón-del-Amo, M.-d.-C., Rialp-Criado, A. & Rialp-Criado, J., 2017. Examining the impact of managerial involvement with social media on exporting firm performance. International Business Review, 27(2), pp. 355-366.

Albright, J. & Park, H. M., 2009. Confirmatory Factor Analysis using Amos, LISREL, Mplus, SAS/STAT CALIS Working paper. The University Information Technology Services (UITS) Center for Statistical and Mathematical Computing, Indiana University.

Alshenqeeti, H., 2014. Interviewing as a Data Collection Method. English Linguistics Research, 3(1), pp. 39-45.

Asamoah, E. S., 2014. Customer based brand equity (CBBE) and the competitive performance of SMEs in Ghana. Journal of Small Business and Enterprise Development, 21(1), pp. 117-131.

Bianchi, C., Glavas, C. & Mathews, S., 2017. SME international perforamnce in Latin America: The role of entrepreneurial and technological capabilities. Journal of Small Business and Enterprise Development, 24(1), pp. 176-195.

Bianchi, C. & Wickramasekera, R., 2016. Antecedents of SME export intensity in a Latin American Market. Journal of Business Research, 69(10), pp. 4368-4376.

Brislin, R. W., 1970. Back-translation for cross-cultural research. Journal of Cross-Cultural Psychology, 1(3), pp. 185-216.

Buckley, P. J. & Tian, X., 2017. Internalization theory and the performance of emerging-market multinational enterprises. International Business Review, 26(5), pp. 976-990.

Chanthinok, K., Ussahawaniti, P. & Jhundra-indra, P., 2015. Social media marketing strategy and marketing outcomes: a conceptual framework. Allied Academies International Conference. Academy of Marketing Studies. Proceedings (Vol. 20, No. 2, p. 82), Jordan Whitney Enterprises, Inc., pp. 35-52.

Clement, J., 2020. Leading countries based on number of Facebook users as of April 2020 (in millions). [Online] Available at: https://www.statista.com/statistics/268136/top-15-countries-based-on-number-of-facebook-users/[Accessed 24 April 2020].

Crittendena, V. I., Crittendenb, W. F. & Ajjanc, H., 2019. Empowering women micro-entrepreneurs in emerging economies: The role of information communications technology. Journal of Business Research, Volume 98, pp. 191-203.

Dahnil, M., Marzuki, K., Langgat, J. & Fabeil, N., 2014. Factors Influencing SMEs Adoption of Social Media Marketing. Procedia - Social and Behavioral Sciences, Volume 148, pp. 119-126.

Davis, F., 1989. Perceived Usefulness, Perceived Ease of Use, and User Acceptance of Information Technology. MIS Quarterly, 13(3), pp. 319-340.

Denyer, D., Parry, E. & Flowers, P., 2011. "Social", "open" and "participative"? Exploring personal experiences and organizational effects of Enterprise2.0 use. Long Range Planning, 44(5-6), pp. 375-396.

Egypt Digital Report, 2017. 2017 Trends Report: The Top Online Statistics in Egypt. [Online] Available at: http://consultyasser.com/egypt-digital-report-2017-top-online-statistics/

El Gendi, Y., 2013. Social Media in Egypt's Transition Period. [Online] Available at: http://schools.aucegypt.edu/huss/pols/Khamasin/Documents/Social%20Media%20in%20Egypt%27s%20Transition%20Period%20-%20Yosra%20El-Gendi.pdf

El-Gohary, H., 2012. Factors affecting E-Marketing adoption and implementation in tourism firms: An empirical investigation of Egyptian small tourism organisations. Tourism Management, 33(5), pp. 1256-1269.

Fishbein, M. & Ajzen, I., 1975. Belief, Attitude, Intention, and Behavior: An Introduction to Theory and Research. 1st ed. Boston, Massachusetts, United States: Addison-Wesley.

Fornell, C. & Larcker, D. F., 1981. Evaluating Structural Equation Models with Unobservable Variables and Measurement Error. Journal of Marketing Research, 18(1), pp. 39-50.

Fraenkel, J. E. & Wallen, N. E., 1996. How to Design and Evaluate Research in Education. New York: McGraw-Hill.

Franco, M., Haase, H. & Pereira, A., 2016. Empirical study about the role of social networks in SME performance. Journal of Systems and Information Technology, 18(4), pp. 383-403.

Garrido-Moreno, A. & Lockett, N., 2016. Social media use in European hotels: benefits and main challenges. Tourism & Management Studies, 12(1), pp. 172-179.

Ghandour, A., 2018. FAHP-based to-do-list for eCommerce websites the case of SMEs in Abu Dhabi. International Journal of Economics and Business Research, 15(1), pp. 52-71.

Goodhue, D. & Thompson, R. L., 1995. Task-Technology Fit and individual performance. MIS Quarterly, Volume 19, pp. 213-236.

Guni, C. N., 2016. General considerations on the meaning and interest of performance measurement. Economics, Management and Financial Markets, 11(1), pp. 310-316.

Gupta, V. K. & Wales, W. J., 2017. Assessing organisational performance within entrepreneurial orientation research: Where have we been and where can we go from here?. The Journal of Entrepreneurship, 26(1), pp. 51-76.

Hoti, E., 2015. The Technological, Organizational And Environmental Framework Of Is Innovation Adaption In Small And Medium Enterprises. Evidence From Research Over The Last 10 Years. International Journal of Business and Management, 3(4), pp. 1-14.

Ipinnaiye, O., Dineen, D. & Lenihan, H., 2017. Drivers of SME performance: a holistic and multivariate approach. Small Business Economics, Volume 48, pp. 883-911.

Lages, C. R., Pfajfar, G. & Shoham, A., 2015. Challenges in conducting and publishing research on the Middle East and Africa in leading journals. International Marketing Review, 32(1), pp. 52-77.

Laitinen, E. K., 2002. A dynamic performance measurement system: evidence from small Finnish technology companies. Scandinavian Journal of Management, 18(1), pp. 65-99.

Lam, H. K. S., Yeung, A. C. L. & Cheng, T. C. E., 2016. The impact of firms' social media initiatives on operational efficiency and innovativeness. Journal of Operations Management, Volume 47-48, pp. 28-43.

Lin, C. & Kim, T., 2016. Predicting user response to sponsored advertising on social media via the technology acceptance model. Computers in Human Behavior, Volume 64, pp. 710-718.
Malthouse, E. C. et al., 2013. Managing Customer Relationships in the social media era: Introducing the social CRM house. Journal of Interactive Marketing, 27(4), pp. 270-280.
Marzouk, W., 2016. Usage and Effectiveness of Social Media Marketing in Egypt: An Organization Perspective. Jordan Journal of Business Administration, 12(1), pp. 209-238.
Mathews, J. A. & Zander, I., 2007. The International Entrepreneurial Dynamics of Accelerated Internationalisation. Journal of International Business Studies, 38(3), pp. 387-403.
Matikiti, R., Mpinganjira, M. & Roberts-Lombard, M., 2012. Application of the Technology Acceptance Model and the Technology–Organisation–Environment Model to examine social media marketing use in the South African tourism industry. South African Journal of Information Management, 20(1), pp. 1-12.
McCann, M. & Barlow, A., 2015. Use and measurement of social media for SMEs. Journal of Small Business and Enterprise Development, 22(2), pp. 273-287.
McNamara, C., 1999. General Guidelines for Conducting Interviews. Minnesota: Authenticity Consulting, LLC.
Miller, D. & Toulouse, J. M., 1986. Chief executive personality and corporate strategy and structure in small firms. Management Science, 32(11), pp. 1389-1409.
Nistor, G., 2019. An extended technology acceptance model for marketing strategies in social media. Review of Economic & Business studies, 12(1), pp. 127-136.
Oji, O., Iwu, C. & Tengeh, R., 2017. Social Media Adoption Challenges of Small Businesses: the Case of Restaurants in the Cape Metropole, South Africa. African Journal of Hospitality, Tourism and Leisure, 6(4), pp. 1-12.
Parveen, F., Jaafar, N. I. & Ainin, S., 2015. Social media and usage and organizational performance: reflections of Malaysian social media managers. Telematics and Innformatics, 32(1), pp. 67-78.
Podsakoff, P. M. & Organ, D. W., 1986. Self-reports in organizational research: Problems and prospects. Journal of Management, 12(4), pp. 531-544.
Pouresmeili, H., Imm, N. S., Sambasivan, M. & Yusof, R., 2018. Degree of Internationalization and Performance: Mediating Role of Innovation and Moderating Role of Knowledge Management System. International Journal of Economics & Management, 12(1), pp. 1-22.
Rapp, A., Beitelspacher, L. S., Grewal, D. & Hughes, D. E., 2013. Understanding social media effects across seller, retailer, and consumer interactions. Journal of the Academy of Marketing Science, 41(5), pp. 547-566.
Rapp, A., Trainor, K. J. & Agnihotri, R., 2010. Performance implications of customer-linking capabilities: Examining the complementary role of customer orientation and CRM technology. Journal of Business Research, 63(11), pp. 1229-1236.
Rauniar, R., Rawski, G., Yang, J. & Johnson, B., 2014. Technology acceptance model (TAM) and social media usage: an empirical study on Facebook. Journal of Enterprise Information Management, 27(1), pp. 6-30.
Ritz, W., Wolf, M. & McQuitty, S., 2018. Digital marketing adoption and success for small businesses: The application of the do-it-yourself and technology acceptance models. Journal of Research in Interactive Marketing, 13(2), pp. 179-203.
Roy, A., Maxwell, L. & Carson, M., 2014. How is Social Media being used by Small and Medium-Sized Enterprises. Journal of Business and Behavioral Sciences, 26(2), pp. 127-137.
Schumacker, R. E. & Lomax, R. G., 2010. A Beginner's Guide to Structural Equation Modeling. 3rd ed. New York: Taylor & Francis Group.
Singh, S. & Srivastava, P., 2019. Social media for outbound leisure travel:a framework based on technology acceptance model. Journal of Tourism Futures, 5(1), pp. 43-61.
Smits, M. & Mogos, S., 2013. The impact of social media on business performance. London, Association for Information System.
Tajvidi, R. & Karami, A., 2017. The effect of social media on firm performance. Computers in Human Behavior, pp. 1-10.
Trainor, K. J., Andzulis, J., Rapp, A. & Agnihotri, R., 2014. Social media technology usage and customer relationship performance: A capabilities-based examination of social CRM. Journal of Business Research, 67(6), pp. 1201-1208.
Tuyet Mai, N., Tuan, N. & Yoshi, T., 2013. Technology Acceptance Model and the paths to online customer loyalty in an emerging market. Trziste / Market, pp. 231-248.
Veldeman, C., Van Praet, E. & Mechant, P., 2017. Social Media Adoption in Business-to-Business: IT and Industrial Companies Compared. International Journal of Business Communication, 54(3), p. 283–305.
Wasiuzzaman, S. & Arumugam, V. C., 2013. Determinants of working capital investment: a study of malaysian public listed firms. Australasian Accounting, Business and Finance Journal, 7(2), pp. 49-69.
Wiklund, J. & Shepherd, D., 2005. Entrepreneurial orientation and small business performance: a configurational approach. Journal of Business Venturing, 20(1), pp. 71-91.
Wright, M., Filatotchev, I., Hoskisson, R. E. & Peng, M. W., 2005. Strategy Research in Emerging Economies: Challenging the Conventional Wisdom. Journal of Management Studies, 42(1), pp. 1-34.
Xu, D. & Meyer, K. E., 2012. Linking Theory and Context: 'Strategy Research in Emerging Economies' after Wright et al. (2005). Journal of Management Studies, 50(7), pp. 1322-1346.

The Impact of Perceptual Variables and Country-Level Culture on Nascent Entrepreneurship

Carlos Gomes, Vítor Braga and Aldina Correia
CIICESI, ESTG /P. PORTO - Center for Innovation and Research in Business Sciences and Information Systems, School of Management and Technology, Polytechnic of Porto, Portugal
8140122@estg.ipp.pt
vbraga@estg.ipp.pt
ic@estg.ipp.pt.
DOI: 10.34190/EIE.20.238

Abstract: There are a lot of policies and stimulus to support entrepreneurship, however they produce different effects on different individuals, justifying why it is important to study the role of individual characteristics and perceptions in this phenomenon. To fill this gap, using GEM APS individual data from 60 countries, this paper investigates the individual characteristics affecting the potential to become a nascent entrepreneur. Following existing literature, we link the decision to start a business with three types of variables: demographic and economic, perceptual and Country-level variables. Our results suggest that all three types of variables are correlated with the choice to become nascent entrepreneur and specifically perceptual and country-effect variables should be included in economic models of entrepreneurial behavior.

Keywords: entrepreneurs behavior, perceptions, opportunities, fear of failure, national environment

1. Introduction

The scientific literature has been paying increasing attention to the phenomenon of entrepreneurship in recent years. There is recognition that entrepreneurship has a positive impact on both national wealth and employment (Acs et al. (2005), Reynolds et al. (2003)).

Based on that growing research, our study follows Arenius and Minniti (2005) paper. First, in the theoretical part, are established a set of variables that influence the choice to become entrepreneur, making possible to create the hypothesis of study. In the empirical part, a “Nascent entrepreneurship (NE)” variable was created, used as dependent variable explained by the three groups of variables: Demographic and economic, Perceptual and Country-effects variables.

Our empirical study used the "GEM 2015 APS GLOBAL INDIVIDUAL DATA” database which has been subject of multivariate analyzes with SPSS. - four logistic regression models were performed.

The objectives of this research are:

- To establish a set of variables that influence the NE,
- To test the variables discussed in the literature,
- To update previous studies on the effect of perceptual variables in NE using recent entrepreneurship data,
- To test if country-effects improve existing models.

This study aims to innovatively contribute to both in the literature and practical perspective, as it follows:

Theoretical implications:

- There are many policies and incentives for NE, however they do not produce the same effects on different individuals, this study fill this gap in the literature studying the role of the perceptual variables in entrepreneurship,
- It determines the variables that should be considered to measure the decision to start a business.

Practical implications:

- This study shows that perceptual variables explain better than the demographic and economic variables the NE,

- Country-effect variables are also important and improve this type of economic models,
- This study can be useful to future entrepreneurs, showing that their perceptions are important, unique and they should consider them before starting a new business instead of focusing only in their demographic and economic characteristics.

2. Literature review and research hypothesis

Studying the NE, Arenius and Minniti's (2005), structure was considered and three types of characteristics were included: Demographic and economic, Perceptual variables and Country-Effects. In the following section we present existing literature for each of these three groups of variables.

2.1 Demographic and economic characteristics

Over the past years, entrepreneurship research has shown mixed outcomes about the role of demographic and economic characteristics, such as age, gender, education, work status and household income on entrepreneurial choices (Parker (2009), Marques (2017)).

Entrepreneurship is widely known as a youth phenomenon (Arenius and Minniti (2005), Levesque and Minniti (2006), Dileo and Pereiro (2019)). Scholars have found that NE is a predominantly male activity (Arenius and Minniti (2005)). Blanchflower and Oswald (1998) and Taylor (1996) have studied the importance of work status and labor markets and have shown that employed individuals are more likely to start new businesses. Higher educational levels have been positively associated to the likelihood of starting a new business by several authors (Bates (1995), Reynolds and White (1997), Delmar and Davidsson (2000), Davidsson and Honig (2003), Arenius and Minniti (2005), Hundt and Sternberg (2016), Klyver et al. (2013), Dileo and Pereiro (2019), Brieger et al. (2020)). Evans and Jovanovic (1989), Kihlstrom and Laffont (1979) and Smallbone and Welter (2001) have shown that entrepreneurial decisions are positively related to individuals' incomes and wealth since the income availability weakens financial constraints.

2.2 Perceptual variables

Empirical entrepreneurship research has increasingly incorporated perceptual variables labeled by various researchers as alertness to opportunities perception, fear of failure, confidence about one's own skills and knowing other entrepreneurs (Arenius and Minitti (2005), Koellinger et al. (2013), Marques (2017)).

An increasing number of scholars agree that opportunity recognition represents the most distinctive and fundamental of entrepreneurial behaviors (Baron (2006), Eckhardt and Shane (2003), Shane and Venkataraman (2000)). Similarly to opportunity recognition, the importance of confidence in one's skills and ability for entrepreneurial behavior is also recognized by the literature (Minniti (2009)).

An individuals' tolerance for risk may also be important for entrepreneurial decisions (Iyigun and Owen (1998), Kihlstrom and Laffont (1979), Wu and Knott (2006)). Shane (2000) explains that the fear of failure is negatively related to the probability of becoming an nascent entrepreneur because the willingness to assume risks is inherent to the entrepreneur (Marques (2017)). Knowing other entrepreneurs should generate positive attitudes toward entrepreneurs in general, by the theory of planned behavior (Ajzen (1991), Brieger et al. (2020)).

2.3 Country-Effects

The importance of country-level (National) culture for entrepreneurship has been established since Hofstede's (1980) contribution. Factors regarding the regional environment gained more importance when scholars (Audretsch and Fritsch (2002), Bade and Nerlinger (2000), Brixy and Grotz (2007), Bosma (2009), Acs and Armington (2004)) tried to explain the individuals' propensity to start a firm or to explain a firm growth. The studies for most of the regions and countries show that irrespective of differences embodied in the individual itself, there are strong regional impacts on an individuals' propensity to be entrepreneur (Brixy et al. (2012)). Feldman (2001) argues that entrepreneurship is primarily a "regional event."

The opinions presented in the literature are tested in the following hypothesis:

Table 1: Hypothesis synthesis and theoretical support

Hypotheses formulated	Theoretical Support
H1a. Older age is negatively related to NE.	Arenius & Minniti (2005), Levesque & Minniti (2006), Hundt & Sternberg (2016), Klyver et al. (2013), Alasadi & Abdelrahim (2008), Arteaga & Lasio (2009), Harada (2003), Kangasharju (2000), Dileo & Pereiro (2019) .
H1b. Men are more likely to become nascent entrepreneur.	Arenius & Minniti (2005), Bosma & Levie (2010), Wagner (2007), Kim (2007), Brush (1992), Marques (2017), Armuña et al. (2020).
H1c. Being in employment is positively related to NE.	Blanchflower & Oswald (1998), Hundt & Sternberg (2016) , Acs et al. (2008), Dileo & Pereiro (2019).
H1d. Higher education level of the entrepreneur has on average a positive effect on NE decisions.	Bates (1995), Reynolds & White (1997), Delmar & Davidsson (2000), Davidsson & Honig (2003), Arenius & Minniti (2005), Hundt & Sternberg (2016), Reynolds et al. (1995), Reynolds (2007), Acs & Armington (2004), Dileo & Pereiro (2019), Brieger et al. (2020) .
H1e. The higher the household income, the higher the propensity to be a nascent entrepreneur.	Evans & Jovanovic (1989), Kihlstrom & Laffont (1979), Smallbone & Welter (2001), Gollier (2002), Guiso et al. (2002,2003), Maula et al. 2005, Bygrave & Hunt (2005), Bygrave & Quill (2006), Mickiewicz et al. (2017), Dileo & Pereiro (2019) .
H2a. The greater opportunities perceptions, the higher the propensity to be a nascent entrepreneur.	Baron (2006), Eckhardt & Shane (2003), Shane (2000), Gaglio & Katz (2001), Eckhardt & Shane (2003), Baron (2004)), Shane & Venkataraman (2000), Minniti (2010), Marques (2017) .
H2b. Higher Confidence in one's skills is positively related to NE.	Minniti (2009), Amit et al. (1993)), Ramos-Rodríguez et al. (2012), Ajzen (1991), Shane (2000), Gaglio and Katz (2001), Eckhardt and Shane (2003), Baron (2004), Koellinger et al. (2007), Minniti (2010).
H2c. The higher fear of failure, the lower the propensity to be a nascent entrepreneur.	Minniti (2009), Amit et al. (1993)), Ramos-Rodríguez et al. (2012), Ajzen (1991), Shane (2000), Gaglio & Katz (2001), Eckhardt & Shane (2003), Baron (2004), Koellinger et al. (2007), Minniti (2010), Entrialgo & Iglesias (2020).
H2d. Knowing other entrepreneurs increases the propensity to be a nascent entrepreneur.	Ajzen (1991), Ramos-Rodríguez et al. (2012), Veciana (2007) , Ellsberg (1961), Tversky & Kahneman (1992), Brieger et al. (2020) .
H3a. Country effects affect the entrepreneurial choices.	Hofstede (1980), Audretsch and Fritsch (2002), Bade and Nerlinger (2000), Brixy and Grotz (2007), Bosma (2009), Acs and Armington (2004), Feldman (2001), Liñán and Fernández (2013), Hundt and Sternberg (2016), Levie et al. (2014), Storr (2012), Gatewood et al. (2009).

3. Methodology

In this study, multivariate statistical analysis tools were applied, with the software SPSS, in order to analyze the questionnaires of the database of the "GEM 2015 APS GLOBAL INDIVIDUAL DATA" project. APS surveys are related to attitudes, activities and aspirations in relation to entrepreneurship. In each country, a standardized survey was administered to a representative sample of adults (18– 64 years old) yielding a cross-country total of 181.281 individuals for the variable under study.

To explore individuals' attitudes in the process of starting a business, respondents were asked: "You are, alone or with others, currently trying to start a new business, including any self-employment or selling any goods or services to others?". Respondents who answered "yes" were asked two additional questions. These questions were used to separate those who were truly committed to a new venture from those thinking about it but not yet committed. These questions inquired (1) "Over the past twelve months have you done anything to help start a new business?" and (2) "Will you personally own all, part, or none of this business?" Only those respondents, who answered "yes" to the first question and "all" or "part" to the second question, were coded as nascent entrepreneurs. A total of 16.580 nascent entrepreneurs were identified in the sample.

In terms of independent variables, the respondents were asked to provide their age and gender, level of education (five levels), income (three levels) and work status (three options). In the logistic regression the first option/level for each question was used as reference of category. The four perceptual variables all have only two options of response being 0=No and 1=Yes.

3.1 Results and discussion

A correlation matrix for the variables was calculated and all the variables have a significant correlation ($p<0.01$) with the dependent variable. About the normality, since the sample is large ($n> 30$), according to Marôco (2010), a normal distribution is assumed. There is no presence of multicollinearity, since the VIFs´ are less than 5 and the Ts´ are higher than 0,1. It is now possible to follow to the logistic regression models.

Table 2: Results of the estimation of a logistic regression

		Model 1		Model 2		Model 3		Model 4	
		Coefficient (std. Error)	Wald	Coefficient	Wald	Coefficient	Wald	Coefficient	Wald
Demographic and economic variables									
Age		-0,022*** (0,001)	916,922	-0,018*** (0,001)	475,525			-0,012*** (0,001)	188,401
Gender		-0,253 *** (0,018)	187,507	-0,080*** (0,021)	14,613			-0,126*** (0,022)	34,372
Work Status	Working		1609,932***		797,019***				878,687***
	Not Working	1,758*** (0,053)	1088,250	1,398*** (0,057)	596,848			1,464*** (0,058)	627,219
	Retired / Student	1,029*** (0,059)	304,954	0,889*** (0,063)	196,293			0,855*** (0,065)	173,940
Education	None		592,681***		215,842***				16,907**
	Some secondary	0,529*** (0,045)	140,377	0,375*** (0,050)	55,283			-0,208*** (0,058)	12,861
	Secondary degree	-0,035 (0,045)	0,626	0,040 (0,050)	0,636			-0,160** (0,055)	8,539
	Post secondary	-0,141*** (0,040)	12,133	-0,072 (0,046)	2,452			-0,159*** (0,049)	10,617
	Grad Exp.	-0,091* (0,040)	5,139	-0,059 (0,046)	1,695			-0,099* (0,048)	4,283
Income	Lowest		433,786***		84,763***				67,335***
	Middle	-0,477*** (0,023)	418,692	-0,227*** (0,026)	76,911			-0,226*** (0,028)	64,238
	Upper	-0,274*** (0,022)	161,806	-0,157*** (0,024)	41,712			-0,135*** (0,026)	27,265
Perceptual Variables									
Opportunity perception				0,729*** (0,021)	1163,017	0,802*** (0,020)	1673,594	0,660*** (0,022)	877,996
Confidence in one's skills				1,543*** (0,029)	2927,334	1,646*** (0,026)	3891,369	1,412*** (0,029)	2297,002
Fear of failure				-0,371*** (0,022)	277,055	-0,369*** (0,021)	2246,423	-0,286*** (0,023)	150,623
Knowing other entrepreneur				0,788*** (0,022)	1328,338	0,940*** (0,020)	322,974	0,792*** (0,023)	1200,509
Model Diagnostics									
Constant		-2,256***	875,302	-4,201***	2231,629	-4,145***	21151,899	-2,043***	294,075

		Model 1		Model 2		Model 3		Model 4	
		(0,076)		(0,089)		(0,029)		(0,119)	
Overall % correct predictions		90,2%		89,3%		89,9%		89,5%	
R^2		0,072		0,229		0,205		0,290	

In the model 1 was used the enter method, including variables measuring the five demographic and economic characteristics. Consistently with the literature, our results suggest that an individuals' demo-economic conditions are very important for understanding the likelihood of being a nascent entrepreneur. The chi-square shows that the overall model is significant at the 0.000 level and it predicts 90,2% of the responses correctly.

Overall, we find that entrepreneurship is as said by Levesque and Minniti (2006), a young man's game. The coefficients of age and gender show a negative and significant relationship with the prevalence of nascent entrepreneurs. Work status results show that unemployed individuals' and students are more likely to be nascent entrepreneurs than employed ones. Analyzing the education, the conclusions are not conclusive since one of the categories is not significant and other is significative only in $p \leq 0{,}05$. Finally, going against the literature, the relationship between NE and higher income is negative.

In Model 2, four perceptual variables are added to the demographic-economic ones. The model is significant and better than Model 1 in explaining the probability of an individual being a nascent entrepreneur, since it displays a higher r^2. In this model, the importance of the demographic-economic characteristics are virtually unchanged. Analyzing the four perceptual variables, all are highly significant. Opportunity perception and Confidence in one's skills are positively and significantly related to be a nascent entrepreneur. The "odds ratio" for the confidence in one's skills variable is 4,68, individuals' who perceive themselves as having the necessary skills are 4,68 times more likely to be nascent entrepreneurs than those who do not.

The fear of failure has a negative and significant impact on being a nascent entrepreneur and finally, knowing other entrepreneurs is positively and significantly related to be a nascent entrepreneur. The "odds ratio" for this variable is 2,2 so individuals' that know other entrepreneurs are 2,2 times more likely to become nascent entrepreneurs.

In Model 3, the logistic regression was produced only with the four perceptual variables. All four are highly significant and comparing the coefficient of these four variables in Model 2 and Model 3 suggests that they are literally equal, and that the addition of demo-economic variables has a minimal effect on them.

Finally, in Model 4, we test the impact of country-effects by using deviation coding. This allows comparing each individual country against the mean for all countries. A dummy for each individual country was constructed (e.g., Portugal = 1 if country is Portugal., otherwise Portugal = 0) and selected USA as the reference country and coded it as -1 on all other country dummies. USA was selected because its nascent prevalence rate is ≈9% which is also the average across all 60 countries in our sample. We then entered all the country dummies at the same time into the regression analysis. In Model 4, 48 of the 60 countries are significant.

Consistently with existing literature (Hofstede et al. (2004)), our results suggest that the macroeconomic environment of some countries are more conducive to entrepreneurial behavior while others penalize it. However, this relationship between cross-country and country specific drivers of entrepreneurial behavior is a very complex variable in entrepreneurship that needs much more work to have solid conclusions.

So, after analyzing the five models, is possible to declare that older individuals are less likely to be entrepreneurs. Attending our results, is more likely that male individuals' became nascent entrepreneurs. The results show that unemployed individuals and students are more likely to be entrepreneurs, this was expected by some authors like Acs et al. (2008). The results about education are not completely solid, since some categories of this variable are not significant to the study, but overall the higher the education the less likely to be a nascent entrepreneur. The final hypothesis regarding demo-economic variables analyses the income and is not in line with the predicted by the literature, the higher the income the less likely to become a nascent entrepreneur.

Analyzing the perceptual variables, the greater the opportunities' perceptions, the higher confidence in one's skills and knowing other entrepreneurs increases the propensity to be a nascent entrepreneur. On the opposite, the higher fear of failure, the lower the propensity to be a nascent entrepreneur. The country-effects affect the choice to become a nascent entrepreneur since the r^2 of the model 4 is the higher than all models.

Only three of the hypotheses formulated in the literature could not be confirmed – those related to education, work status and income. This result may be partially justified by the countries included in our sample, since we used developing countries too, where the level of education and income are normally lower.

4. Conclusions

In terms of literature we can contribute that personal-level variables have a relevant role to play in developing new models to understand the process leading to be a nascent entrepreneur (Liñán and Fayolle (2015), Ruiu and Breschi (2019)). Recent research has shown that even well-known and well-settled models, such as the Theory of Planned Behavior, can be enriched by adding this type of variables (Fayolle and Liñán (2014), Fuller et al. (2018), Entrialgo and Iglesias (2020)).

To achieve the initial goals, binary logistic regression were applied, and it concludes that, across all countries and across genders, that perceptual variables are important to explain the choice of starting a new business.

In terms of demographic and economic variables, the conclusions are that young age and being male is positively correlated with NE. The results about education, income and work status go against the theory, having a job, higher income and higher education are all negatively correlated with NE.

The four perceptual variables are highly correlated with NE, perceiving opportunities, knowing other entrepreneurs and confidence in one's skills are positively correlated with start a new business while fear of failure is negatively related.

Finally the country-effects are also important in NE studies, since the national culture of each country influences both the perceptions of the individuals' as well as the entrepreneurial choices. However It is likely that our study does not include all relevant variables, at the country-effects level, the results of studies like Ramoglou and Tsang (2016) show that demand factors, such as product novelty, market competition and supply factors (Alvarez and Barney (2007, 2010)) are important and related to entrepreneurship.

Differences in the country-effects such as technology, economic development, institutions and culture cause differences in the perceptual variables, so future research about how much these two categories of variables are related is relevant.

The biggest limitation of this paper is that the perceptual variables reflect subjective perceptions rather than objective conditions, a person may consider to have the skills and knowledge to start a new business but, in fact, not being qualified to do so (Minniti (2009)). As a result, they are likely to be biased since distortions in perceptions are common (Cooper et al. (1988), Busenitz and Barney (1997)). These variables are measured only with 2 options, being "yes" or "no" but we cannot guarantee that a "yes" from individual number one is equal to the "yes" of the number two.

So, instead of the Boolean logic in which the values of the variables are usually denoted 1 and 0 like in this case, is suggested to future studies the use of Fuzzy logic, in which the truth values of variables may be any real number between 0 and 1 both inclusive. For that, it is recommended the creation of a questionnaire where the perceptual variables have more hypothesis of response.

Acknowledgements

This work has received funding from FEDER funds through P2020 program and from national funds through FCT - Fundação para a Ciência e a Tecnologia (Portuguese Foundation for Science and Technology) under the project UID/GES/04728/2020

References

Acs, Z. J., & Armington, C. (2004). Employment Growth and Entrepreneurial Activity in Cities. Regional Studies, 38(8), 911-927. doi:10.1080/0034340042000280938

Acs, Z., Arenius, P., Hay, M., & Minniti, M. (2005). Global Entrepreneurship Monitor, 2004 Executive Report. MA, USA/ London, UK: Babson College/London Business School, Babson Park.

Acs, Z., Desai, S., & Hessels, J. (2008). Entrepreneurship, Economic Development and Institutions. Small Business Economics, 31, 219-234. doi:10.1007/s11187-008-9135-9

Ajzen, I. (1991). The Theory of Planned Behavior. Organizational Behavior and Human Decision Processes, 50(2), 179–211. doi:10.1016/0749-5978(91)90020-T

Alasadi, R., & Abdelrahim, A. (2008). Analysis of small business performance in Syria. Education, Business and Society, 1(1), 50-62. doi:10.1108/17537980810861510

Alvarez, S. A., & Barney, J. B. (2007). Discovery and Creation: Alternative Theories of Entrepreneurial Action. Strategic Entrepreneurship Journal, 1, 11-26. doi:10.1002/sej.4

Alvarez, S. A., & Barney, J. B. (2010). Entrepreneurship and Epistemology: The Philosophical Underpinnings of the Study of Entrepreneurial Opportunities. Academy of Management Annals, 4, 557- 583. doi:10.5465/19416520.2010.495521

Amit, R., Glosten, L., & Muller, E. (1993). Challenges to theory development in entrepreneurship research. Journal of Management Studies, 30(5), 815-834. doi:10.1111/j.1467-6486.1993.tb00327.x

Arenius, P., & Minniti, M. (2005). Perceptual Variables and Nascent Entrepreneurship. Small Business Economics, 24, 233-247. doi:10.2307/40229421

Armuña, C., Ramos, S., Juan, J., Feijóo, C., & Arenal, A. (2020). From stand-up to start-up: exploring entrepreneurship competences and STEM women's intention. International Entrepreneurship and Management Journal, 1-24. doi:10.1007/s11365-019-00627-z

Arteaga, M., & Lasio, V. (2009). Empresas dinámicas en Ecuador: factores de éxito y competencias de sus fundadores. Academia Revista Latinoamericana de Administración, 42(6), 1-19. Obtido de https://www.researchgate.net/publication/41805459_Empresas_dinamicas_en_Ecuador_factores_de_exito_y_competencias_de_sus_fundadores

Audretsch, D. B., & Fritsch, M. (2002). Growth Regimes over Time and Space. Regional Studies, 36(2), 113-124. doi:10.1080/00343400220121909

Bade, F.-J., & Nerlinger, E. (2000). Spatial Distribution and Regional Economic Impact of New Technology Based Firms: Empirical Results for West-Germany. Papers in Regional Science, 79, 141-172. doi:10.1007/s101100050041

Baron, R. A. (2004). The Cognitive Perspective: A Valuable Tool for Answering Entrepreneurship's Basic "Why" Questions. Journal of Business Venturing, (19), 221–239. doi:10.1016/S0883-9026(03)00008-9

Baron, R. A. (2006). Opportunity recognition as pattern recognition: How entrepreneurs "Connect the Dots" to identify new business opportunities. The Academy of Management Perspectives, 20, 1. doi:0.5465/amp.2006.19873412

Bates, T. (1995). Self-employment entry across industry groups. Journal of Business Venturing, 10(2), 143-156. doi:10.1016/0883-9026(94)00018-P

Baumol, W. J. (1990). Entrepreneurship: Productive, Unproductive and Destructive. Journal of Political Economy, 98, 893-921. doi:10.2307/2937617

Blanchflower, D., & Oswald, A. (1998). What makes an entrepreneur? Journal of Labor Economics,16(1), 26-60. doi:10.1086/209881

Bosma, N. (2009). The Geography of Entrepreneurial Activity and Regional Economic Development: Multilevel Analyses for Dutch and European Regions. Utrecht University.

Bosma, N., & Levie, J. (2010). Global Entrepreneurship Monitor 2009 Executive Report. Babson College, Universidad del Desarrollo. London Business School, Reykjavík University: Babson Park, MA, Santiago de Chile, Reykjavík, London. Obtido de https://www.researchgate.net/publication/48322611_Global_Entrepreneurship_Monitor_2009_Executive_Report

Brieger, S. A., Bäro, A., Criaco, G., & Terjesen, S. A. (2020). Entrepreneurs' age, institutions, and social value creation goals: A multi-country study. Small Business Economics, 1-29. doi:10.1007/s11187-020-00317-z

Brixy, U., & Grotz, R. (2007). Regional Patterns and Determinants of the Success of New Firms in Western Germany. Entrepreneurship and Regional Development, 19(4), 293-312. doi:10.1080/08985620701275510

Brixy, U., Sternberg, R., & Stüber, H. (2012). The Selectiveness of the Entrepreneurial Process. Journal of Small Business Management, 50(1), 105-131. doi:10.1111/j.1540-627X.2011.00346.x

Brush, C. G. (1992). Research on women business owners: Past trends, a new perspective and future directions. Entrepreneurship Theory and Practice, 16, 5-30. doi:10.1177/104225879201600401

Busenitz, L. W., & Barney, J. B. (1997). Differences between Entrepreneurs and Managers in Large Organizations: Biases and Heuristics and Strategic Decision-Making. Journal of Business Venturing, 12, 9-30. doi:10.1016/S0883-9026(96)00003-1

Bygrave, W. D., & Hunt, S. A. (2005). GEM 2004 Financing Report. Babson College, MA, U.S., and London Business School, London,.

Bygrave, W. D., & Quill, M. (2006). GEM 2006 Financing Report. Babson College, MA, U.S., and London Business School, London,.

Cooper, A. C., Woo, C. Y., & Dunkelberg, W. C. (1988). Entrepreneurs' Perceived Chances for Success. Journal of Business Venturing, 3, 97-108. doi:10.1016/0883-9026(88)90020-1

Davidsson, P., & Honig, B. (2003). The role of social and human capital among nascent entrepreneurs. Journal of Business Venturing, 18(3), 301-331. doi:10.1016/S0883-9026(02)00097-6

Delmar, F., & Davidsson, P. (2000). Where do they come from? Prevalence and characteristics of nascent entrepreneurs. Entrepreneurship & Regional Development: An International Journal, 12(1), 1-23. doi:10.1080/089856200283063

Dileo, I., & Pereiro, T. G. (2019). Assessing the impact of individual and context factors on the entrepreneurial process. A cross-country multilevel approach. International Entrepreneurship and Management Journal, 15, 1393–1441. doi:10.1007/s11365-018-0528-1

Eckhardt, J., & Shane, S. (2003). Opportunities and Entrepreneurship. Journal of Management, 29, 333-349. doi:10.1016/S0149-2063(02)00225-8

Ellsberg, D. (1961). Risk, ambiguity, and the Savage axioms. Quarterly Journal of Economics, 75, 643- 669. doi:10.2307/1884324

Entrialgo, M., & Iglesias, V. (2020). Entrepreneurial Intentions among University Students: The Moderating Role of Creativity. European Management Review, 1-14. doi:10.1111/emre.12386

Evans, D., & Jovanovic, B. (1989). An estimated model of entrepreneurial choice under liquidity constraints. Journal of Political Economy 97, 808-827. doi:10.2307/1832192

Fayolle, A., & Liñán, F. (2014). The future of research on entrepreneurial intentions. Journal of Business Research, 67 (5), 663-666. doi:10.1016/j.jbusres.2013.11.024

Feldman, M. P. (2001). The Entrepreneurial Event Revised: Firm Formation in a Regional Context. Industrial and Corporate Change, 10(4), 861-891. doi:10.1093/icc/10.4.861

Fuller, B., Y. Liu, S. B., Marler, L. E., & Pratt, J. (2018). Examining how the personality, self-efficacy, and anticipatory cognitions of potential entrepreneurs shape their entrepreneurial intentions. Personality and Individual Differences, 125, 120-125. doi:10.1016/j.paid.2018.01.005

Gaglio, C. M., & Katz, J. A. (2001). The Psychological Basis Of Opportunity Identification: Entrepreneurial Alertness. Small Business Economics, 16, 95-111. doi:10.1023/A:1011132102464

Gatewood, E., Brush, C. G., Carter, N. M., Greene, P. G., & Hart, M. M. (2009). Diana: A symbol of women entrepreneurs' hunt for knowledge, money, and the rewards of entrepreneurship. Small Business Economics, 32(2), 129-144. doi:10.1007/s11187-008-9152-8

Gollier, C. (2002). What does the classical theory have to say about household portfolios? In: Jappelli. T. (Ed.), Household Portfolios. MIT Press, Cambridge, MA, 27–54. doi:10.7551/mitpress/3568.003.0005

Guiso, L., Haliassos, M., & Jappelli, T. (2002). Household portfolios: an international comparison. In: Jappelli. T. (Ed.), Household Portfolios. MIT Press, Cambridge, MA, 1-24. Obtido de https://www.researchgate.net/publication/2394284_HOUSEHOLD_PORTFOLIOS_AN_INTERNATIONAL_COMPARISON_Luigi_Guiso_Michael_Haliassos_and_Tullio_Jappelli

Guiso, L., Haliassos, M., & Jappelli, T. (2003). Household stockholding in Europe: where do we stand and where do we go? Economic Policy, 36 (6), 117-164. doi:10.2307/1344655

Harada, N. (2003). Who succeeds as an entrepreneur? An analysis of the post-entry performance of new firms in Japan. Japan and the World Economy,15(2), 211-222. doi:10.1016/S0922-1425(02)00002-6

Hofstede, G. (1980). Culture's Consequences: International Differences in Work-Related Values. Beverly Hills: CA, Sage.

Hofstede, G., Noorderhaven, N., Thurik, A. R., Uhlaner, L. M., Wennekers, A. R., & Wildeman, R. E. (2004). Culture's role in entrepreneurship: Self-employment out of dissatisfaction. In T. E. Brown & J. M. Ulijn (Eds.), Innovation, entrepreneurship and culture. Cheltenham: Edward Elgar.

Hundt, C., & Sternberg, R. (2016). Explaining new firm creation in Europe from a spatial and time perspective: A multilevel analysis based upon data of individuals, regions and countries. Papers in Regional Science 95(2), 223-258. doi:10.1111/pirs.12133

Iyigun, M., & Owen, A. (1998). Risk, entrepreneurship and human capital accumulation. American Economic Review, 88, 454 - 457. doi:10.2307/116966

Kangasharju, A. (2000). Growth of the smallest: determinants of small firm growth during strong macroeconomic fluctuations. International Small Business Journal,19 (1), 28-43. doi:10.1177/0266242600191002

Kihlstrom, R., & Laffont, J. (1979). A general equilibrium entrepreneurial theory of firm formation based on risk aversion. Journal of Political Economy, 87, 719-740. doi: 10.2307/1831005

Kim, G. (2007). The analysis of self-employment levels over the life-cycle. Quarterly Review of Economics and Finance, 47(3), 397. doi:10.1016/j.qref.2006.06.004

Klyver, K., Nielsen, S. L., & Evald, M. R. (2013). Women's self-employment: An act of institutional (dis)integration? A multilevel, cross-country study. Journal of Business Venturing, 28(4), 474–488. doi:10.1016/j.jbusvent.2012.07.002

Koellinger, P., Minniti, M., & Schade, C. (2007). I Think I Can, I Think I Can: Overconfidence and entrepreneurial behavior. Journal of Economic Psychology, 28 (4), 502-527. doi:10.1016/j.joep.2006.11.002

Koellinger, P., Minniti, M., & Schade, C. (2013). Gender Differences in Entrepreneurial Propensity. Oxford Bulletin of Economic Statistics, 75(2), 213-234. doi:10.1111/j.1468-0084.2011.00689.x

Levesque, M., & Minniti, M. (2006). The Effect of Aging on Entrepreneurial Behavior. Journal of Business Venturing, 21(2), 177-194. doi:10.1016/j.jbusvent.2005.04.003

Levie, J., Autio, E., Acs, Z., & Hart, M. (2014). Global Entrepreneurship and Institutions: An Introduction. Small Business Economics, 42, 437-444. doi:10.1007/s11187-013-9516-6

Liñán, F., & Fayolle, A. (2015). A systematic literature review on entrepreneurial intentions: Citation, thematic analyses, and research agenda. International Entrepreneurship and Management Journal,11, 907-933. doi:10.1007/s11365-015-0356-5

Liñán, F., & Fernández, J. R. (2013). Necessity and opportunity entrepreneurship: The mediating effect of culture. Revista de Economía Mundial, 33, 21-47. Obtido de https://www.researchgate.net/publication/235937863_Necessity_and_opportunity_entrepreneurship_The_mediating_effect_of_culture

Marôco, J. (2010). Análise Estatística - Com a Utilização do SPSS (3 ed.). Lisboa: Edições Sílabo.

Marques, H. (2017). The routineness of tasks, gender and culture in entrepreneurship. Socio-Economic Review, 15(4), 1-32. doi:10.1093/ser/mwx017

Maula, M., Autio, E., & Arenius, P. (2005). What drives micro-angel investments? A large sample study of the factors explaining micro-angel investments. Small Business Economics, 25(5), 459-475. doi:10.1007/s11187-004-2278-4

Mickiewicz, T., Nyakudya, F. W., Theodorakopoulos, N., & Hart, M. (2017). Resource endowment and opportunity cost effects along the stages of entrepreneurship. Small Business Economics, 48 (4), 953-976. doi:10.1007/s11187-016-9806-x

Minniti, M. (2009). Gender Issues in Entrepreneurship. Foundations and Trends in Entrepreneurship, 5(7–8), 497-621. doi:10.1561/0300000021

Minniti, M. (2010). Female Entrepreneurship and Economic Activity. The European Journal of Development Research, 22(3), 294–312. doi:10.1057/ejdr.2010.18

Parker, S. C. (2009). The Economics of Entrepreneurship. Cambridge: Cambridge University Press.

Ramoglou, S., & Tsang, E. (2016). A Realist Perspective of Entrepreneurship: Opportunities as Propensities. Academy of Management Review, 41, 410-434. doi:10.5465/amr.2014.0281

Ramos-Rodríguez, A. R., Medina-Garrido, J. A., & Ruiz-Navarro, J. (2012). Determinants of Hotels and Restaurants entrepreneurship: A study using GEM data. International Journal of Hospitality Management, 31 (2), 579-587. doi:10.1016/j.ijhm.2011.08.003

Reynolds, P. D. (2007). New Firm Creation in the United States A PSED I Overview. Foundations and Trends in Entrepreneurship, 3(1), 1-150. doi:10.1561/0300000010

Reynolds, P. D., & White, S. B. (1997). Entrepreneurial processes and outcomes: The influence of ethnicity. In P.D. Reynolds & S. B. White (Eds.), The entrepreneurial process. Westport: Quorum Books.

Reynolds, P. D., Miller, B., & Maki, W. R. (1995). Explaining regional variation in business births and deaths: U.S. 1976–88. Small Business Economics, 7, 389–407. doi:10.1007/BF01302739

Reynolds, P., Bygrave, B., & Hay, M. (2003). Global Entrepreneurship Monitor Report. Kansas City, MO.: E.M. Kauffmann Foundation.

Ruiu, G., & Breschi, M. (2019). The Effect of Aging on the Innovative Behavior of Entrepreneurs. Journal of the Knowledge Economy, 10, 1784–1807. doi:10.1007/s13132-019-00612-5

Shane, S. (2000). Prior Knowledge and the Discovery of Entrepreneurial Opportunities. Organization Science, 11, 448-469. doi:10.1287/orsc.11.4.448.14602

Shane, S., & Venkataraman, S. (2000). The promise of entrepreneurship as a field of research. The Academy of Management Review, 25(1), 217- 226. doi:10.2307/259271

Smallbone, D., & Welter, F. (2001). 'The distinctiveness of entrepreneurship in transition economies. Small Business Economics, 16(4), 249- 262. doi:10.1023/A:1011159216578

Storr, V. (2012). Understanding the Culture of Markets. New York: Routledge.

Taylor, M. (1996). Earnings, independence or unemployment, why become self-employed? Oxford Bulletin of Economics and Statistics, 58(2), 253-265. doi:10.1111/j.1468-0084.1996.mp58002003.x

Tversky, A., & Kahneman, D. (1992). . Advances in prospect theory: Cumulative representation of uncertainty. Journal of Risk and Uncertainty, 5, 297 - 323. doi:10.1007/BF00122574

Veciana, J. (2007). Entrepreneurship as a scientific research programme. Concepts, Theory and Perspective. Springer, 23-71. doi:10.1007/978-3-540-48543-8_2

Wagner, J. (2007). What a Difference a Y Makes—Female and Male Nascent Entrepreneurs in Germany. Small Business Economics, 28(1), 1-21. doi:10.1007/s11187-005-0259-x

Wu, B., & Knott, A. M. (2006). Entrepreneurial risk and market entry. Management Science, 52(9), 1315-1330. doi:10.1287/mnsc.1050.0543

Wyrwich, M., Stuetzer, M., & Sternberg, R. (2016). Entrepreneurial role models, fear of failure, and institutional approval of entrepreneurship: a tale of two regions. Small Business Economics, 46(3), 467–492. doi:10.1007/s11187-015-9695-4

Youth Entrepreneurial Self-Efficacy Towards Technology for Online Business Development

Nolwazi Gumbi and Thea van der Westhuizen[1]
University of KwaZulu-Natal, Durban, South Africa
vanderwesthuizent@ukzn.ac.za
DOI: 10.34190/EIE.20.225

Abstract: Advancing technology has created opportunities for individuals to become online entrepreneurs, a means to combat the triple challenges of unemployment, poverty and inequality. However, business start-ups can be risky and require individuals to have entrepreneurial self-confidence. So, while technology creates opportunities for online businesses, the primary focus of this study seeks to identify how technology influences the development of entrepreneurial self-efficacy (ESE) in South African youth. The study also looks at the importance of entrepreneurship and entrepreneurship education. The literature review mentions the types of digital and technological platforms that the youth can use for online business start-ups. The research approach adopted is quantitative. Data in the form of a questionnaire was collected from eighty honours students at UKZN Westville campus in the School of Management, Information Technology & Governance. The sampling method was convenience sampling. Limitations of this study were geographical, cost and time. The results of this study show that students have significant confidence in business start-ups through the influence of technology. Recommendations are made based on other factors that can help increase the development of entrepreneurial self-efficacy among the youth.

Keywords: entrepreneurial self-efficacy, technology, business start-ups, entrepreneurship education

1. Introduction

In recent years there has been an increased emphasis on policies to create a knowledge-based society. Higher learning institutions play a vital role in creating innovators and entrepreneurs in the current and next generations (Shih & Huang, 2017). The world is changing rapidly due to technology advancements and environment changes. When faced with change, organizations can either adapt to it or ignore it, but it is always best to embrace it (Beato, 2015). The advancement of technology and science cannot be ignored, which is why technology is slowly being integrated within the education system of South Africa. According to Volti (2009: 6), technology is "a system created by humans that uses knowledge and organization to produce objects and techniques for the attainment of specific goals". Technology can also be used to enhance the quality of teaching and learning. Entrepreneurship education focuses on the creation of an entrepreneurial culture. It assists potential student entrepreneurs to identify and pursue business opportunities. The integration of technology is commonly practiced in universities where entrepreneurship education is part of the curriculum. This paper seeks to find the influence of technology on entrepreneurial self-efficacy development for online business start-ups.

2. Motivation and focus of the study

This study is motivated by the increasing rate of youth unemployment in South Africa. Because education is available to everyone, the number of university graduates increases annually. Graduates, however, are faced with a challenge of unemployment. South Africa has one of highest rates of unemployment in the world. The rise of the Fourth Industrial Revolution (4IR) will create a change in the patterns of employment, production and consumption (Global Challenge Insight Report, 2016). Other factors that contribute to youth unemployment include lack of work experience, lack of skills, type of qualification attained, and the low number of internships (Mtero, 2012).

Ndala (2014: 1) states that "educational institutions should provide more relevant forms of education designed to promote self-reliance and responsible entrepreneurial capacity for self-employment and community development to reduce unemployment and to revitalize national development". The intention of this study is to provide an overview of the influence of technology on entrepreneurial self-efficacy and entrepreneurship education. The study also focuses on how entrepreneurship may contribute to the South African youth unemployment problem, and what skills students need if they choose to become entrepreneurs.

[1] Corresponding author: vanderwesthuizent@ukzn.ac.za

According to Ndala (2014: 3), "The TPB states that attitudes, subjective norms and self-efficacy (perceived behavioural control) are antecedents to entrepreneurial intention (EI), which in turn predicts entrepreneurial behaviour". In this study, self-efficacy and attitudes are the focus antecedents to entrepreneurship intention.

In addition, this study also investigates the technological skills of students. The study will analyse the some of the perceptions students have about using technology to facilitate entrepreneurship activities.

3. Background

The history of technology can be seen as the development over time of tools and techniques for doing and making things. One could say that technology is the means by which people manipulate or change their environment. The integration of technology in the education system has the potential to improve entrepreneurship education and training, which is important for economic growth and the development of countries around the world (Ndala, 2014). In order for entrepreneurs to contribute to economic growth and development, they require the knowledge and skills to enable them to identify, evaluate and exploit opportunities. Educational institutions have a key role in developing techniques, methods and processes that will instil in students an entrepreneurial mind-set, and encourage them to be self-employed.

4. Research problems, aim and objectives

Technology changes rapidly. Every sector of government and industry has to adapt to the constant changes that impact on the development and economic growth of a country (Govindasamy, 2013). Peyper (2017) claims that South Africa is not equipped to adapt to a 4IR economy because the country lags in Information Communication and Technology. The challenge of digital inequality limits what people—especially learners—can do. This is exacerbated when they reach higher education institutions. Entrepreneurship education can be hard to facilitate if students are not equipped to handle the technology.

For education to be an effective mechanism in shaping economic growth, the system must keep up with the latest developments in technology. The number of graduates has increased, while the rate of youth unemployment continues to rise. The unemployment rate rose to 27,6% in the first quarter of 2019, from 27,1% in the last quarter of 2018 (Trading Economics, 2019). Youth unemployment increased to 55,2%. Entrepreneurship education is crucial to ensure that students have the knowledge and skills to take advantage of business opportunities and contribute to economic growth.

Government recognises that Youth Entrepreneurship has the potential to boost employment and competitiveness. However, the youth are faced with several challenges, one of which is the entrepreneurial self-confidence to use technology to start up a business. We live in a time when almost every business is a tech business needing to adapt to constant technological changes. Van der Westhuizen and Goyayi (2020) identified some of the problems the youth have with Entrepreneurial Self-Efficacy in using technology:

- Lack of entrepreneurial education: entrepreneurship education is not offered in high schools. The youth could have business ideas and explore entrepreneurial opportunities from their earlier years, but cannot because of insufficient knowledge.
- Young entrepreneurs from underprivileged backgrounds lack digital skills. The use of technology to enhance educational methods and access has increased, but there is a high rate of digital inequality. The lack of digital skills limits the youth from exploring new technologies and acquiring new knowledge.
- Youth entrepreneurship initiatives are generally confounded by their lack of experience and lack of capital. Lack of experience is a barrier to developing the necessary capabilities, and lack of capital limits access to resources such as the latest technology.

To explore these problems, the research aim was set to *investigate the influence of technology on entrepreneurial self-efficacy development for online business start-up.* Four research objectives were set to guide the investigation:

- To determine youths' opportunity identification self-efficacy towards business tech start-up
- To determine youths' relationship self-efficacy towards business tech start-up
- To determine youths' managerial self-efficacy towards business tech start-up
- To determine youths' tolerance self-efficacy towards business tech start-up.

5. Literature review

5.1 Entrepreneurship education in South Africa

The high rate of unemployment has encouraged the country to develop and train learners with skills that will make them entrepreneurs. Umsobomvu (2002:2), quoted in Chimucheka (2014: 405), recommended that "entrepreneurship education be integrated into the school curriculum at all levels so as to build a strong entrepreneurial culture".

Entrepreneurship education was first included in the school curriculum in 2005 in a subject known as Economic and Management Sciences (Du Toit and Gaotlhobogwe, 2018). The main purpose of this subject is to prepare learners for various business and economic environments and develop their financial literacy (Du Toit, 2016). Institutions of higher education do provide entrepreneurial programmes but they are not producing enough entrepreneurs. This could be as a result of the way these programmes are delivered and structured. Urban and Richard (2015) found that the levels of entrepreneurial intentions of students is low across different disciplines, including law and management, commerce, engineering and health sciences.

In 2014, the entrepreneurial activity rate decreased by 34%, with a lack of entrepreneurial education as one of the main factors contributing to this decline (Moodley, 2016).

Entrepreneurship education is a way of changing motives and attitudes that encourage entrepreneurial thinking and responsibility. According to Sowmya *et al* (2010), policy makers believe that education can help attain high levels of entrepreneurial spirit, with the following outcomes:

- Entrepreneurship education provides students with self-confidence and independency (Jwara, 2015). These are important characteristics because through this students believe that they can become successful.
- It helps individuals to broaden their mind-set, become aware of different choices, and provides knowledge and skills that they can use to recognize new business opportunities and take on business ventures.
- Business start-ups can be promoted through entrepreneurship education. Education plays a fundamental role in helping individuals to become familiar with the idea of starting and running their own business at a young age (Heinnovate, 2014).

According to Shinnar *et al* (2014), entrepreneurship education encourages students to participate frequently in different entrepreneurial activities and tasks, thus improving their confidence in doing such tasks and activities in the future. Through doing entrepreneurial assignments, students learn how to analyze the market, formulate a business plan, pitch a business idea, and so on. In doing so, students are able to develop confidence in their ability and enhance their Entrepreneurial Self-Efficacy (Shinnar *et al.,* 2014).

5.2 Entrepreneurial Self-Efficacy (ESE) dimensions

The concept of ESE consists of six dimensions that were developed by De Noble et al (1999). The first of these dimensions is the developing of new market and product opportunities. This dimension involves an individual's belief in their ability to market new goods and services and to identify opportunities. The second dimension is building an innovative environment, which involves an individual's belief in their ability to encourage other people or their team to be innovative and try new ideas. The third dimension is initiating investor relationships, which involves an individual's belief in their ability to create professional relationships and acquire funding for their business. The fourth dimension is defining the core purpose, which involves an individual's belief in their ability to clarify the business's main vision with their team and investors. The fifth dimension is coping with unexpected challenges, which involves an individual's belief in their ability to deal with and tolerate uncertainty and ambiguity. The sixth dimension is developing important human resources. This involves an individual's ability to recruit and keep talented and competent people in the business venture (Setiawan, 2014).

According to Barbosa et al., (2007) there are four task-specific types of Entrepreneurial Self-Efficacy:

- Opportunity-Identification: Self-efficacy perceived by an individual concerning their potential and abilities to identify market opportunities and develop new products. Opportunity recognition explains how organizations and individuals identify new opportunities that were previously unknown to them (Van der

Westhuizen, 2019). In terms of ESE, this refers to confidence in their ability to identify entrepreneurial opportunities in the business environment (Van der Westhuizen, 2016).

- Relationship: Self-efficacy perceived by an individual concerning their ability to build professional relationships with potential investors.
- Managerial: Self-efficacy perceived by an individual concerning their economic and financial management abilities.
- Tolerance: Self-efficacy perceived by an individual concerning their ability to work productively under conditions of pressure, conflict, stress and change.

Chen *et al* (1998) says that Entrepreneurial Self-Efficacy refers to a person's belief in their ability to perform roles and tasks that are aimed at entrepreneurial development. ESE plays an important role in influencing individuals to participate in and develop entrepreneurial behavior and pursue careers in entrepreneurship. Entrepreneurial behavior is viewed as the joining of ideas, resources, and capital with elements of empowerment and creativity (Foote, 2012). In addition, there are three essential elements that are included in the entrepreneurial behavior concept. These three elements are: opportunity recognition, when individuals actively seek and identify needs and resources that are available; initiative, where individuals act upon the opportunities that they have recognized; and risk management, which is the tolerance and assessment of calculated risks (Neto *et al.,* 2017).

5.3 Socio-Economic factors and entrepreneurial self efficacy

Socio-economic factors are the lifestyle components that are used to measure social standing and financial viability that directly affect the degree of financial independence and social privilege. They include income, education, occupation, environment and social status (Das and Jaiswal, 2018). Prabhu and Thomas (2014) state that social factors—like the family's background—directly influence potential entrepreneurs. Gibson and Gibson (2010) found that factors such as gender, race and household income influence student's innovative attitude.

A study conducted by Olanrewaju (2013) showed that demographic factors like the gender and age of students do not influence the youths' entrepreneurial attitudes or intentions. However, the socio-economic status of their parents influenced the interest students have towards entrepreneurship. Family customs, background and beliefs influence a person's entrepreneurial attitude. Family finance or income provided by the family is a great source of financial and social support for young entrepreneurs (Das and Jaiswal, 2018). According to Hallak *et al* (2012) students that have a family business are more confident to run a business successfully.

Gender is also likely to be a factor that affects entrepreneurial attitudes (Van der Westhuizen and Upton, 2017). Harris and Gibson (2008) found that there was an important difference between female and male students, where males showed higher entrepreneurial attitudes than females. Females need the expectation and self-confidence for them to pursue their entrepreneurship aspirations. "Demographic factors such as household income, gender, and race or ethnicity were found to potentially affect the innovative attitude of arts and business students" (Olanrewaju, 2013: 61).

The integration of technology in entrepreneurship education allows for an effective means of technology and knowledge transfer (Kleine *et al.,* 2019). According to Lackeus and Williams Middleton (2015: 52), "Entrepreneurship education utilizing venture creation can be seen to integrate university commercialization activities when collaborating with technology transfer partners". Shih and Huang (2017) mention that higher institutions of education play a significant role in forming the present and future generations of entrepreneurs and innovators. The use of technology in the education system enhances the process of teaching and learning.

5.4 Technology

The rate of technological change and its capabilities has grown immensely over the years, which has given rise to the demand for technology management to increase. According to Cloete (2017), technology is embedded socially and can be linked directly to other social processes and developments like the economy. It is evident, therefore, that there is a link between technology and social developments, because education influences the economy and if the state of teaching and learning within a country is excellent, economic growth increases. Technology is integrated in every industry or sector and yields positive results (Van der Westhuizen and Singh, 2018). The sector that we will focus on in this study is entrepreneurship education.

Technology exists in many forms. Some of the types of technology that exist are tool-making, machine making, production and information technology (Aunger, 2010). In this paper, the focus will be on Information and Communication Technologies (ICT), which can be defined as the technological means of gathering, analysing and transferring information via technology (Ajayi, 2016). For students to be successful in a tech business start-up, it is important that they have the necessary tech and entrepreneurial skills. Some of tech business start-up ideas that they can pursue are blogging, online advertising platforms, digital marketing consultations, web design services, influencer marketing platform, and software and app development services (Pilon, 2019). The way technology has evolved has made it easy for people to become entrepreneurs and do everything "at the tip of their fingers".

5.5 Technological opportunities for online business start-up

Technological growth has allowed potential entrepreneurs to enter the market using technology at a low cost (Van der Westhuizen and Singh, 2018). The strongest contributing factor to this is that businesses can be home-based. Digital platforms can offer potential entrepreneurs new forms of value creation and innovation. The status of digital assets and technology—including levels of investment and connectivity in next-generation technologies such as artificial intelligence and industrial internet—will influence platform scale, generation and growth.

The cloud, mobile and social platforms are three major shifts that exist on the internet landscape, with mobile devices allowing users to always stay connected. More than twenty-two million people in South Africa use smartphones, and this number increases every year (Statistics South Africa, 2019). This usage increases the possibility of people shopping online. Individuals who want to pursue online entrepreneurial ventures can do so through various online business models.

6. Research methodology

The research approach was quantitative using a self-administered questionnaire as the instrument to collect primary data. The instrument gathered information on a) demographics, b) entrepreneurial self-efficacy towards tech start-up, c) opportunity identification self-efficacy, d) relationship self-efficacy, e) managerial self-efficacy, and f) tolerance self-efficacy. A 7-point Likert scale was used in this quantitative study starting at 1, signifying no self-confidence at all, and increasing to 7, signifying complete confidence. A midpoint of 4 signified neither confidence nor lack of confidence in the statements.

The sample population was post-graduate students (honours level) at a public university in South Africa. The non-probability sampling method had a size of N=80.

Data quality control was exercised through conducting a pilot study, and SPSS23 was used to analyse the data.

From the sample, thirty-two (32) were males and forty-eight (48) were females, ranging in age from 21–26 years. Only five respondents were older than 27 years. A diversity of race participated, with fifty-three (53) participants being classified as black, twenty-four (24) as Indian, and three (3) as white.

7. Findings and discussion

7.1 Research Question 1: What is youths' opportunity identification self-efficacy towards business tech start-up?

The Opportunity Identification section consisted of four statements.

The first statement addressed was: *I can recognise a good online opportunity*. The results show that 27.5% of respondents feel that they are completely confident that they can recognise good online opportunities. The results also show that a further 46.25% of the respondents are somewhat confident in recognising opportunities (Likert values 5-6), with 18.75% being neutral. Only 7.5% of the respondents have little self-confidence in this regard.

Statement 2 of Opportunity Identification examined the extent to which respondents thought that they could *confidently come up with new businesses ideas through surfing the internet*. A small percentage (2.5%) are not confident at all in this task (Likert 1). A quarter of the respondents (26.25%) are completely confident (Likert 7) on this statement. Nearly half (48.75%) are somewhat confident in coming up with new ideas from surfing the internet (Likert 5-6).

Statement 3 looked at respondent's confidence levels on the statement: *I can recognise/identify new market opportunities for new products and services on the internet*. Just over two-thirds of the sample (Likert 5-7, 67.9%) expressed confidence in being able to do this, with only 7.7% lacking confidence (Likert 2-3). 24.4% were neutral.

Statement 4 of Opportunity Identification asked if respondents were confident in *identifying potential sources of funding through online searches*. Once again, two-thirds of the respondents (66.25%) expressed confidence in being able to do this, with 18.75% expressing reservations (Likert 1-3). 15% weren't sure (Likert 4).

Schmitt et al (2018: 835) state that "Entrepreneurial self-efficacy acts as a personal resource that helps entrepreneurs to transform increasing perceptions of uncertainty into exploration and opportunity identification". The first section of the research instrument looked at how confident the sample is in identifying opportunities for online business start-up. The average response on the Likert scale to each of the four statements was as follows:

- 1. I can recognise a good online opportunity = 5.41
- 2. I can surf the internet to come up with new business ideas = 5.34
- 3. I can recognise/identify new market opportunities for new products and services on the internet = 5.26
- 4. I can identify new sources of funding through online searches = 5.09

The data indicates that most students are at least somewhat confident of identifying opportunities towards business technology start-up.

A statistical test analysis of the survey data on whether the eighty respondents felt they could recognise good online opportunities indicated that there is significance confidence in their being able to do this, at the 1% ($p<.0005$) level of confidence with $t=9.7$. We may confidently predict, therefore, that this result applies to the general population of students from which this sample of eighty students was drawn.

7.2 Research question 2: What is youths' relationship self-efficacy towards business tech start-up?

Relationship self-efficacy refers to the individuals' perceptions of their ability to create relationships with potential investors. Respondents reacted to four statements which trigger relationship self-efficacy. The same Likert 1-7 scale was applied, with 1 being a complete lack of confidence and 7 being completely confident.

The first statement asked respondents to rate their level of confidence to be able to *persuade others to buy into their idea for product(s) or service(s)*. Respondents were less confident on this statement, with only 56.25% expressing any confidence, compared to 22.5% feeling a lack of confidence. One in five respondents (21.25%) weren't sure either way (Likert 4).

Statement 2 on Relationship Self-efficacy was: *I can work online as a team member on projects where team members live in different countries*. Less than half of the respondents (46.25%) expressed any confidence in being able to do this. Another 23.75% were unsure, and 30% lacked confidence to do this.

Statement 3 asked respondents to rate their confidence to *initiate a conference call with a group of people*. Respondents felt more confident in their ability to carry out this task, with 25% feeling "completely confident" and further 45% feeling at least somewhat confident. Only 18.75% lacked confidence, with 11.25% being unsure.

The fourth statement on Relationship Self-efficacy was: *I can use a mobile device to build online business relationships with others*. Again, there was more confidence expressed here, with 65% responding positively and only 15% expressing a lack of confidence. However, quite a high proportion of 20% sat on the fence at Likert 4.

The next statement asked respondents to rate their confidence on their ability to "*develop and maintain good relationships with potential investors through virtual interaction*". Just over half of the respondents (51.25%)

expressed confidence in doing this. Another 23.75% were unsure (Likert 4), and one respondent in every four (25%) lacked confidence.

Statement 6 tested respondents' confidence in *getting people to agree with them through only seeing them virtually (online)*. Nearly one third (32.9%) lacked confidence to do this, and another 19% were unsure. Only 13.9% were "completely confident", and another 34.2 % somewhat confident.

Overall, the data indicate that there is a slightly lower level of confidence expressed in these statements on Relationship Efficacy compared to Opportunity Identification, as shown by the averaged response rates to each statement:

- 1. I am able to persuade others to buy in to my business idea of a product or service = 4.86
- 2. I can work online as team member on projects where team members live in different countries = 4.43
- 3. I can initiate a conference call with a group of people = 5.16
- 4. I can use a mobile device to build online relationships with others = 5.16
- 5. I can develop and maintain good relationships with potential investors through virtual interaction = 4.58
- 6. I can get pepe to agree with me through only seeing them virtually (online) = 4.39

There is a statistically significant confidence in initiating conference calls with a group of people, and in using mobile devices to build business relationships (M=5.16, t (79) =6.586, p<.0005). There is a lack of confidence in getting people to agree with them through only seeing them online, with the lowest-averaging mean of 4.39, t (78) = 1.937.

7.3 Research question 3: What is youths' managerial self-efficacy towards business tech start-up?

An analysis of the fifteen statements pertaining to managerial self-efficacy shows a high degree of self-confidence amongst the sample. Students responded positively (Likert 5-7) to nearly two-thirds of the statements (62.2%). Respondents lacked confidence in 22.3% of the statements, and responded neutrally (Likert 4) to 15.5% of the statements. The highest levels of confidence were expressed for the following statements:

- I can learn skills that I need through online courses (86.3%, average 6.03)
- I can work productively from anywhere with my laptop (83.9%, average 6.05)
- I can use software or mobile apps to help me accomplish my goals (82.6%, average 5.83)

Respondents were least confident about the following statements:

- I can recruit team members online (43.8%, average 3.99)
- I can develop a working environment that encourages people through blogging (42.6%, average 3.9)
- I am a leader amongst friends in social media networks (38.8%, average 4.14)

Respondents were most unsure (neutral) about the following statement:

- I am able to use business software and social media to develop a new business (32.5%, average 4.77)

7.4 Research Question 4: What is youths' tolerance self-efficacy towards business tech start-up?

Statements related to tolerance self-efficacy showed strong self-confidence, with an overall positive response rate (Likert score 5-7) of 72.5%. Respondents showed an overall lack of confidence (Likert 1-3) on only 16.1% of the statements. Statements to which they reacted most confidently were:

- I can handle whatever comes my way (87.6%, average 6.11)
- If I lose my way, I can find my path using smart phone GPS (87.5%, ave. 6.22)
- I am able to adapt when conditions suddenly change (87.5%, ave. 6.13)

A lack of confidence (Likert 1-3) was shown in the following circumstances:

- I can remain calm when my laptop is giving problems and I have to meet a deadline (37.6%, ave.4.05)
- I could deal efficiently with unexpected technological problems (26.3%. ave. 4.63)

- I can resolve most software problems on my laptop and mobile phone (23.8%, ave. 5.01)

Dealing efficiently with unexpected technological problems was also the statement about which respondents felt most ambivalent/neutral.

7.5 Summary of findings

A literature review shows that entrepreneurship education does indeed develop an entrepreneurial mindset and intention among young people. Furthermore, it is evident that self-confidence can be enhanced through participating in entrepreneurial activities. The researcher found that the socio-economic status of parents, family background, and beliefs influence young peoples' self-confidence to start a business. Self-confidence is higher in individuals that have financial and social support from their families. The results also showed that the respondents are capable of using technology to recognize online opportunities.

Overall, it is concluded that young people are confident that they can use the internet for various entrepreneurial activities. The results showed that the youths' relationship self-efficacy towards business tech start up is above average; the mean for all the statements that address this question was above 4, the midpoint the Likert scale adopted in this quantitative study. Respondents also showed significant confidence in managerial self-efficacy; however, there is a significant lack of confidence in some factors that affect the overall managerial self-efficacy which are discussed in detail in the previous section. The youth showed the highest self-confidence in tolerance self-efficacy compared to the other three questions of this study. This is seen by the mean values which are skewed towards 7, the maximum point in the Likert scale.

8. Conclusion

The research findings indicate that youth perceived themselves to have high levels of entrepreneurial self-efficacy towards starting up a business online and conducting online business. In a post-Covid-19 environment, technological skills and confidence are essential for any entrepreneur. It is worth noting that although the sample may perceive themselves as confident in their abilities, one needs to consider that they completed the instrument from a hypothetical perspective of what it must be like to have an own business, and to be entrepreneurial. Since the sample are still post-graduate students, very few of them have had the opportunity to take entrepreneurial action. One might ask if the findings would have been different if they had had entrepreneurial exposure. A related study conducted at the same public university reported that youths' entrepreneurial self-efficacy tested at a declining rate post-training to familiarise themselves with conducting business online (Van der Westhuizen, 2020). A possible reason for this anomaly might be that the youth do not realise the challenging technical aspects that need to be mastered to create an online business, before the venture can take off. This research concludes by recommending that, for young people to develop realistic entrepreneurial self-efficacy, they should gain more exposure to what it takes to start a business online.

Acknowledgements

This work is based on the research supported in part by the National Research Foundation of South Africa (Grant Numbers: 122002 - Shape).

References

Aunger, R. (2010). What's special about human technology?. Cambridge Journal of Economics, 34(1), pp.115-123.

Barbosa, S. D., Gerhardt, M. W. & Kickul, J. R. 2007. The role of cognitive style and risk preference on entrepreneurial self-efficacy and entrepreneurial intentions. *Journal of Leadership & Organizational Studies,* 13 (4), 86-104.

Beato, I. (2015). Changing World Essay — Science Leadership Academy @ Center City. [Online] Scienceleadership.org. Available at: https://scienceleadership.org/blog/changing_world_essay-2 [Accessed 14 Mar. 2019].

Buchanan, R. (2018). History of technology | Summary & Facts. [online] Encyclopaedia Britannica. Available at: https://www.britannica.com/technology/history-of-technology [Accessed 17 Mar. 2019].

Chen, C.C., Greene, P.G. & Crick, A. (1998). Does Entrepreneurial Self-Efficacy Distinguish Entrepreneurs from Managers. Journal of Business Venturing, 13, 4, (p.p. 295-316).

Chimucheka, Tendai. (2014). Entrepreneurship Education in South Africa. Mediterranean Journal of Social Sciences. 5. 403-416. 10.5901/mjss.2014.v5n2p403.

Cloete, A. L. (2017). Technology and education: Challenges and opportunities. *HTS Theological Studies, 73*(4), 1-7.

Das, S. C., & Jaiswal, A. (2018). Examining Entrepreneurial Self-Efficacy Among University Students: An Empirical Study from Gender Point of View. Journal of Strategic Human Resource Management Volume, 7(2).

De Noble. A.. Jung. D.. and Ehrlich. S. (1999). *Entrepreneurial Self Efficacy: The Development of a Measure and Its*

Du Toit, A., & Gaotlhobogwe, M. (2018). A neglected opportunity: entrepreneurship education in the lower high school curricula for technology in South Africa and Botswana. *African Journal of Research in Mathematics, Science and Technology Education*, *22*(1), 37-47.

Foote, C. (2012).Edu-preneurship: Being more than just a teacher.

Gibson, L. G., & Gibson, R. A. (2010). Entrepreneurial attitudes of arts and business students, {Abstract]. In ICSB 2010, 55th Anniversary, International Council for Small Business, June 24-27,2010, Cincinnati, Ohio: Entrepreneurship: Bridging Global Boundaries, 89.

Gillward, A. (2018). State of ICT in South Africa. Policy Paper no. 5, Series 5: After Access. Cape Town, p.6.

Global Challenge Insight Report. (2016). The Future of Jobs: Employment, Skills and Workforce Strategy for the Fourth Industrial Revolution. World Economic Forum

Govindasamy, P. (2013). Computer literacy, employment and earnings: A cross-sectional study on South Africa using the National Income Dynamics Study 2008. School of Built Environment and Development Studies University of KwaZulu-Natal.

Hallak, R., Assaker, G. & O'Connor, P., (2012). Are family and nonfamily tourism businesses different? An examination of the entrepreneurial self-efficacy-entrepreneurial performance relationship. Journal of Hospitality & Tourism Research

Harris, M., & Gibson, S. G. (2008). Examining the entrepreneurial attitudes of US business students. Education & Training, 50(7), 568-581.

Heinnovate. (2014). The entrepreneurial higher education institution. A review of the concept and its relevance today. (Online). Available

Jones, P., Pickernell, D., Fisher, R., & Netana, C. (2017). A tale of two universities: Graduates perceived value of entrepreneurship education. Education and Training, 59, 689e705.

Jwara, N.C. (2015). The Impact of Higher Education on Entrepreneurial Intentions of Polytechnic Students in South Africa (Doctoral dissertation, University of KwaZulu-Natal, Westville).

Moodley, S. (2017). Creating entrepreneurs in South Africa through education (Doctoral dissertation, University of Pretoria)

Mtero, K. (2012). An Inquiry into the Challenges Faced By Young University Of KwaZulu-Natal Pietermaritzburg Campus Graduates In Their Efforts to Engage In Successful Entrepreneurship.

Ndala, N. (2014). Investigating the provision of entrepreneurship education and training in tertiary education and training institutions in Malawi. PhD. Graduate School of Business and Leadership of the University of KwaZulu-Natal

Neto, R. D. C. A., Rodrigues, V. P., & Panzer, S. (2017). Exploring the relationship between entrepreneurial behavior and teachers' job satisfaction. *Teaching and Teacher Education*, *63*, 254-262.

Nyamunda, J. and van der Westhuizen, T., 2018. Youth Unemployment: The role of Transformative Learning in making the youth explore entrepreneurship. Journal of Contemporary Management, 15(1), pp.314-343.

Olanrewaju, A. K. (2013). Demographics, Entrepreneurial Self-efficacy and Locus of Control as Determinants of Adolescents Entrepreneurial Intention in Ogun State, Nigeria. European Journal of Business and Social Sciences, 1(12), 59-97

Peyper, L. (2017). Africa lags in ICT, not ready for 4th Industrial Revolution - report. [Online] Fin24. Available at: https://www.fin24.com/Tech/africa-lags-in-ict-not-ready-for-4th-industrial-revolution-report-20170507 [Accessed 18 Mar. 2019].

Pilon, A. (2019). 50 High Tech Business Ideas You Can Start Small - Small Business Trends. [online] Small Business Trends. Available at: https://smallbiztrends.com/2017/11/high-tech-business-ideas.html [Accessed 2 Jul. 2019].

Prabhu. A., & Thomas, A. (2014). Influence of parental factors on the entrepreneurial attitude of B school students. International Journal of Research and Development: A Management Review (IJRDMR), 3(1), 35-38

Shih, T., & Huang, Y, Y. (2017). A case study on technology entrepreneurship education at a Taiwanese research university, Asia Pacific Management Review

Shinnar, R.S., Hsu, D.K. and Powell, B.C. (2014). Self-efficacy, entrepreneurial intentions, and gender: Assessing the impact of entrepreneurship education longitudinally. The International Journal of Management Education, 12(3), pp.561-570.

Sowmya, D.V., Majumdar, S. & Gallant, M. (2010), Relevance of education for potential entrepreneurs: An international investigation. Journal of Small Business and Enterprise Development, 17(4), 626-640

Trading Economics (2019). South Africa Youth Unemployment Rate | 2019 | Data | Chart | Calendar. [Online] Available at: https://tradingeconomics.com/south-africa/youth-unemployment-rate [Accessed 12 May 2019].

Umsobomvu Youth Fund. (2002). Entrepreneurship skills development and business support needs of potential and existing young entrepreneurs. Witwatersrand University, South Africa.

Urban, B. & Richard, P. (2015). 'Perseverance among university students as an indicator of entrepreneurial intent', South African Journal of higher Education 29(5), 263–278.

Van der Westhuizen, T., 2016. Developing individual entrepreneurial orientation: a systemic approach through the lens of Theory U. Durban: UKZN Graduate School of Business and Leadership.

Van der Westhuizen, T; Upton, J. 2017. eThekwini Municipality Women Entrepreneurship programme: An assessment. SAIMS Management Research: Science Serving Practice 29:153 -180.

Van der Westhuizen, T. and Singh, T., 2018. Mobile Device Brand Loyalty of Youth: Perceived Value vs. Cybersecurity Choices. In Handbook of Research on Information and Cyber Security in the Fourth Industrial Revolution (pp. 531-545). IGI Global van der Westhuizen, T. and Goyayi, M.J., 2020. The influence of technology on entrepreneurial self-efficacy development for online business start-up in developing nations. The International Journal of Entrepreneurship and Innovation, 21(3), pp.168-177.

Volti, Rudi. (2009). Society and Technological Change. Technology and Culture. 32. 10.2307/3106191.

Identifying the Restrictive Factors of Strategic Plan's Execution of Technology in Order to Modelling

Ata Harandi[1], and Zahra Fatemi[2]
[1]Allameh Tabataba'i University, Tehran, Iran
[2]Tabaran Institute, Mashhad, Iran
Harandi@atu.ac.ir
Fatemi_zahra@yahoo.com
DOI: 10.34190/EIE.20.211

Abstract: The imperfect execution of policies and strategic plans is one of the problems almost all countries face. From the policymaking and strategic plan's knowledge, the main reason for this issue is the deterrent factors for the execution at various levels. The present study uses a qualitative approach based on the philosophy of symbolic interpretation seeking to extract what is and why the model of deterrent factors is the execution of policies and strategic plans of science and technology in Iran. In this concern, the strategy of the classical grounded theory was used through open, axial, and theoretical coding to explain the inductive theory. The data was collected through an unstructured interview with 18 experts, in the field of science and technology policy and through theoretical sampling to reach the theoretical saturation point. After analysis interviews, 165 code was extracted in the open coding stage and classified into 50 key concepts, four categories, and one central theme. In the theoretical coding step, the categories were explained, and the research path was explained. Four key categories: The deterrent factors resulting from the formulation, institutional deterrent factors, cultural and social deterrent factors, and the non-performing factors of promotion have been identified and analyzed as the main categories of the model.

Keywords: science and technology policymaking, strategy execution, policy implementation, deterrent factors of strategy implementation

1. Introduction

National policies and strategic plans are the prospects, orientations, actions, and plans that characterize how governments function in the future. They are often developed to solve a problem and are usually considered as a cycle where problems are recognized as the existing challenges at first. Then, different periods of action were investigated, and the corresponding policies and plans are determined and implemented. Finally, they are evaluated and modified by governments resulting in either success or failure (Somit and Steven, 2003).

Formulation of policies and strategic plans is a complicated, time-consuming, and challenging process, though it is even harder to execute them successfully. The positive effects and consequences of the policy are perceived after its appropriate execution leading to incredible results. In contrast, inappropriate execution of a policy eliminates all hopes for achieving the expected effects of the policy. In the absence of such an ability, varying attractive processes of policymaking will be degraded to an intellectual game level, as the policy will not be able to change the situation without execution. The realities and environmental changes make it harder to enforce policies. These realities are entirely different from the goals and regulations set for achieving them. However, in order to improve the success rate of implementing the policies and plans, we can identify the obstacles via predictive thinking and overcome them. Obstacles are deterrent factors that prevent the use of specific policy tools or limit their execution. All scientific areas encounter obstacles in the successful execution of policies and strategic plans. However, taking the rapid growth rate and changes in the field of science and technology into account, and noting the complex environment surrounding it, it is witnessed that the percentage of execution the policies and strategic plans are deficient (Marsh and Allan, 2010). Whenever vital and critical factors for execution policies and strategic plans are lost, there will be a problem in execution. Thus, each society has its challenges in the strategic planning process, according to its unique circumstances and context (Denhardt and Catlaw, 2014).

Recently, researchers have provided a variety of ways to explore different types of obstacles in the execution of policies and strategic plans and they have attempted to understand, recognize and remove the barriers in the execution of policies (Anderson, 1982; Khalid, 2001; Berg, 2004; Makinde, 2005; Richardson, 2007; Kostka, 2014). In Iran, over the past ten years, the formulation of upstream documents and strategic plans of science and technology has been pursued clumsily. It is imperative that be analysed and pathologically examined so that policymakers and experts can manage it. Unfortunately, despite excessive attention to policymaking and strategic planning, not enough attempt has been made to have a proper model for the execution of the policies.

Accordingly, it is necessary to identify the obstacles and factors hindering the execution of the policies of science and technology in Iran and to take appropriate measures to overcome the deterrent factors. Based on the review of previous studies, the present research realizes it necessary to identify the deterrent factors of execution of the policies and strategic plans of science and technology in Iran for three reasons: 1. Lack of sufficient studies on the execution of policies and strategic plans related to science and technology, concerning the country's context. 2. Excessive attention to the strategic planning of science and technology and lack of a model for its execution. 3. Limited attention to the execution of strategic plans in theoretical studies. The main question this study seeks to answer is: What are the obstacles to executing the policies and strategic plans of science and technology in Iran?

2. Literature review

Elmore highlights the incomplete understanding of problems and challenges, failure to assess the degree of the feasibility of the decisions, inability of executives to carry out the assigned tasks, and the misunderstanding of the strategic plan as the main barriers to implementing the policies (Elmore, 1980). Hawlett, Ramesh, and Perl (2003) categorize the failure factors of macro policies into two groups of internal and external. They recognize a large number of policies, technical difficulties and broad and diverse target groups as internal factors and identified socio-political changes, organizing manner, executive organizations, and resources of political and economic groups, inefficient support and the lack of public support as external factors (Hawlett, Ramesh, and Perl, 2003). Khalid emphasized the role of the main executors and identified the lack of creativity and innovation as the leading causes of failing to implement the policies. He believes that disregarding the benefits of interest groups, the lack of support by citizens, governments' engagement in addressing political concerns, and the lack of coherence between governments' executive plans are other factors hindering the implementation of science and technology policies (Khalid, 2001). Berg highlights the lack of public support for policies and plans as a factor affecting the failure of policy implementation. For the directors, planning and policymaking are more critical than implementation (Berg, 2004). Sometimes the non-implementation of plans and policies is rooted in the compilation phase. If the compilers proceed merely based on unattainable ambitions and without in-depth research and expertise, then a large part of the plan will not be implemented. Lack of a progressive policy, sticking to static policies, planning based on predictability, and disregarding the existing capacities to implement policies are also part of the barriers to implementation and inefficiency of plans and policies (Richardson, 2007).

Strategic planning can indeed offer a systematic, analytic, and deliberate approach to strategy formulation that also provides clarity within and beyond the organization on what its priorities are and how they should be addressed, as well as helps to find the best way to fit with its environment. But there ate some critics on strategic planning, that it is may be ineffective or harmful to organization performance. In other words, the argument that strategic planning, causes to become inflexibility for organizations and nonresponsive to emerging issues or only works in routine, simple organizations is unsupported (George, Walker and Monster, 2019)

It should always be noted that policymaking and strategic planning, especially in the field of science and technology, encounter stakeholders' resistance. The influential participants should be identified and encouraged to cooperate in the implementation of the plan. Therefore, cultural barriers and obstacles to the acceptance of participants and the public, political barriers, legal barriers, institutional barriers, barriers regarding the insufficient knowledge and information, financial and behavioural barriers are all factors that hinder the implementation of science and technology policies (Akreman et al., 2011). Kostka clusters the barriers to policy implementation into two categories of *institutional* barriers and *behavioural, cultural, and social* barriers. The first group includes political and economic incentives, public-private partnerships, financial and political capacity, and the second one includes personal preferences, values, norms, and social pressures (Kostka, 2014).

In the context of Iran, the causes of non-implementation of the policies and restrictive factors are ambiguous and unrealistic targeting, incorrect policy theory, lack of commitment of policymakers to implementation, lack of agreement on policies, unexpected events, lack of time and resources, lack of public support, inadequate technology, conflict of policies with social norms and values, lack of relative independence in executive bodies, lack of clarity of duties of executive departments, Lack of communication and cooperation of executive agencies, Lack of sufficient and appropriate evaluation system (Sharif Zadeh et al., 2013). A significant point in policymaking, and in particular in the case of science and technology, is the formulation of policies based on real-time value. The product life cycle, in the fields of science and technology, is usually fast, and the environment is very agile and turbulent. Value-based and real-time policy making maximizes the opportunities available in the environment (Moghadaspour, DanaeedFard, and Kordnaeehj, 2013).

Specifically, this study research generated a model based on the CGT to formulating plan in strategic sector. the CGT method was selected because of its systematic approach (Allen-Hammer,2018),toward studying the strategic issues with the utilization of emergent ideas to generate an empirically grounded theory that explains the process of policymaking in the area of study.

The CGT method is intended to explain phenomena of and about people's behaviour (Allen-Hammer,2018). Due to its methodological focus, CGT was selected for this research study because it offered a way to explain phenomena that is present, but not understood by those who benefit most from this knowledge, including managers, excusive managers , and various professionals policy makers.

3. Methodology

The present research is a qualitative study. It is a fundamental study in terms of the objective with an exploratory orientation. The strategy used is the classic grounded theory (CGT). Grounded theory (GT) is a structured method that has a flexible methodology. The results of a using GT in study are communicated as a set of concepts, related to each other in an interrelated whole, and expressed in the production of a substantive theory (Chun Tie et al, 2019).

The information was collected through unstructured interviews with the experts of science and technology policymaking in Iran.

Table 1: Methodology

Philosophy	Type of research			Research strategy	Method of data collection	Sample	Sampling method	Sample size
Symbolic	Goal	result	Approach	The classical grounded theory	UnStructured interview	Experts and policymaker in the field of science and technology	Theoretical saturation point	18
	Fundamental	Exploration	Qualitative					

The statistical population of this research includes all experts and policymakers of science and technology. The sampling was done theoretically and by an unstructured interview with 18 people in the research community. Theoretical sampling is a non-random purposeful sampling that assists the researcher in the creation or discovery of theory or concepts whose logical connection with the evolving theory is proven. In the theoretical sampling, events and not necessarily specific documents are sampled, and if a specific document is sampled, the aim is to explore the events. A guide to theoretical sampling is the questions and comparisons that emerge during the analysis, which makes it possible to identify the appropriate categories, characteristics, and dimensions. Sampling continues until the categories reach saturation. Theoretical saturation is a stage in which data is not added to the previous category, and relationships between categories do not change (Khashei and Harandi, 2015). In this study, through using theoretical sampling and until reaching theoretical saturation, 18 experts in the field of policymaking for science and technology were interviewed in an open and semi-structured manner. In order to identify the sample individuals, five characteristics were considered. The individuals entering the interviews had at least three characteristics. These features include:

- Being an associate professor with scientific knowledge in the field of policymaking for science and technology and technology management
- Publishing at least three research papers in authentic journals in the field of policymaking for science and technology and technology management
- Membership in the national strategic planning team in the field of science and technology (such as the comprehensive scientific map of the country, the comprehensive air and space map, and a comprehensive map of the Nanoscale)
- Authorship of at least one book related to policymaking for science and technology
- Fulfilling at least three projects related to policymaking and strategic planning of science and technology.

Then, the interviews were analysed using the CGT strategy. Accordingly, a model encompassing the deterrent factors for implementing the policies and strategic plans of science and technology was designed based on the context of Iran.

In this research, the raw data was collected from an unstructured interview with 18 experts who met the criteria mentioned in the sampling. At the same time, as the interviews were completed, the collected data was analysed and coded. In the next stage, the concept and model categories and the relationship between them were explained in the axial coding process. Finally, in the theoretical coding phase, the narrative of the model was developed.

In order to ensure the validity and reliability of the research, i.e., to test the accuracy of findings from the perspectives of both the researchers and readers of the report, the following measures were taken (Creswell and Miller, 2000):

- Member checking: data analysis process, final model, the final report by interviewees, and participants in the study were reviewed and verified.
- Peer examination: Three professors in the field of technology management and policymaking for science and technology, and two Ph.D. students in strategic management and technology management scrutinized the findings, codes, concepts, and final model. After applying their points, the final model was approved.
- Participatory research: At the same time, interviewees and professors and experts in the field of policymaking for science and technology were requested to assist researchers in the process of data analysis and interpretation, and their valuable contributions were used.

4. Data analysis

4.1 Open coding

Coding is an analytical process used to identify concepts, similarities and conceptual reoccurrences in data. Coding is the pivotal link between collecting or generating data and developing a theory that explains the data (Chun Tie et al, 2019). In this research, 165 initial codes were recorded by the researchers, and appropriate concepts were constructed for each of them. In Table (2), some examples of primary codes are provided.

Table 2: Sample of open coding

No	Interviews Key ntoe	Concepts
P01	In the field of science and technology, usually, the policies and programs developed are not comprehensible and integrated and are not compatible with each other.	Incompatible policies
P12	They are not paid much attention to a real need in science and technology concepts and the development of unsuitable policies and programs.	unsuitable policies
P20	We have a lot of upstream redundancy document in Iran. In such, this volume causes serious and ambiguous hindrances in the direction of their implementation.	Swollen macro documents
P31	In the field of science and technology policymaking, imitation of countries where their local conditions are far from Iran is high, which ignores social preparedness for the implementation of policies and developed programs.	Duplication policies
P47	Programs and policies are retrospective in Iran, which Future research approaches are not attended.	Retrospective policies
P62	In the formulation of goals and priorities, parallel institutions develop goals and priorities inconsistent with each other, and that fits their interests. Such programs are a severe obstacle to the implementation of actions and the realization of goals.	Objectives inconsistent

4.2 Axial coding

In the axial coding stage, by analyzing the codes obtained from the previous stage with the participation of researchers and experts, the concepts, central and peripheral categories, and the final model were developed.

In this phase, 50 concepts were constructed, which were categorized into four categories and one central theme. In Table (3), the axial coding of the research is presented.

Table 3: Axial coding

Main theme	Categories	Concept
deterrent factors in the execution of policies and strategic science and technology	Contradictory factors resulting from the formulation	Incompatible policies
		unsuitable policies
		Unrealistic goals
		Unrealistic goals
		Swollen macro documents
		Duplication policies
		Non-scientific policies
		Inappropriate methodology for planning
		Non-flexible programs
		Retrospective policies
		Not paying attention to national and upstream plans
		Dream politics
		Folk politics
		Non-expert policymakers
		Unrealistic time scheduling
		Parallel programs
		Lack of strategic thinking
	Institutional deterrent factors	Politicians' Political Behaviors
		Ignoring Strategic national interests
		Self-regulation of policy makers
		Lack of strategic control system
		Lack of dynamics of policy enforcers
		Conflicts, Unhealthy Competition and Profitability of the Implementing Entity of Strategies and Programs
		Poor performance guarantee
		Legal barriers to policy implementation
		Lack of incentives
		Lack of feedback system
		Illegitimate policies
		Objectives inconsistent
		Lack of support for senior managers
		Lack of proper motivational system
		Lack of funds
		Insufficient equipment
		Lack of interdisciplinary view among policy makers
		Weak management stability
		Low credit policy
	Socio-cultural deterrent factors	Lack of attention to environmental complexity
		Little attention to stakeholder expectations
		Mismatching stakeholder expectations
		Intervention of values and norms in strategy implementation
		Lack of policy acceptance by stakeholders
		Agency cost
		Little social pressures

Main theme	Categories	Concept
		The lack of a comprehensive look at science and technology
	Promotional preventive factors	Lack of executive instruction
		Lack of adequate knowledge and information
		Sue impressions of politics
		Non-socialization of policies
		Lack of network communication among policy enforcers
		Asymmetry of information

4.3 Theoretical coding

The theoretical coding explains how the categories are related to each other. The preliminary coding graph is usually formed at the time of sorting and integrating the codes. Open coding and axial coding classify, categorize, and split up the data. However, at this stage, through theoretical coding, the categories are associated with each other, and the storyline and theoretical explanations are presented to develop the final model of deterrent factors in implementing the policies and strategic plans of science and technology in Iran. This model is presented in figure (1).

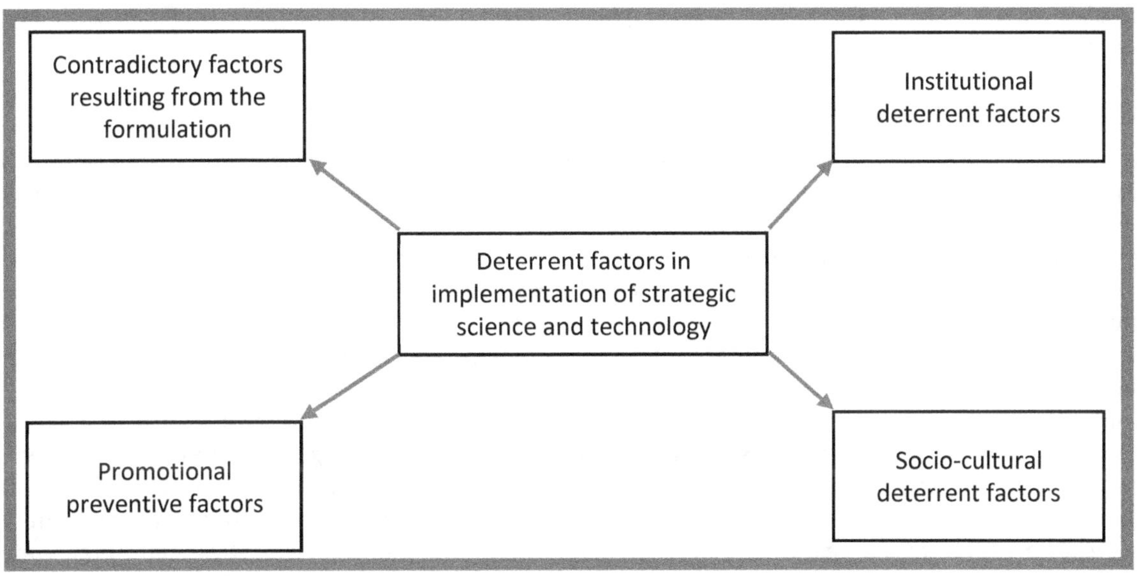

Figure 1: Conceptual model

Based on the review of literature and articles related to the implementation of policies and strategic plans of science and technology in Iran, and after analysing the comments of officials and experts, the factors hindering the implementation of science and technology policies in Iran are classified into four categories: compilation-induced deterrents, institutional deterrents, behavioural and cultural deterrents, and promotive deterrents.

4.3.1 Contradictory factors resulting from the formulation

The primary and critical obstacle in policies and strategic execution in the field of science and technology is rooted in the formulation of policies and plans. In Iran, the policies are usually formed based on old data and previous events, and no future studies are considered in the formulation process. However, in the complex and turbulent field of science and technology, the future is not entirely predictable and is not necessarily similar to the past. This approach to strategic planning and policymaking reduces the effectiveness and efficiency of the policies and strategic plans and lowers their credibility in the execution phase. Another point is that the policies and strategic plans are not consistent and comprehensive. In Iran, each organization, regardless of the plans and macro policies of other peer organizations, compiles policies and plans based on its preferences. As a result, inconsistent and incompatible policies and plans are designed. Naturally, strategic plans in the field of science and technology should be in line with national policies, and they should complement the policies and plans of other organizations. Nevertheless, the lack of enough coordination and attention and taking wilful actions in the process of designing the policies and plans have led to the compilation of inconsistent policies. In order to define the challenges and compile a policy to solve them, the situation must be properly, transparently, and genuinely agreed upon by policymakers, and they should have relative consensus on the favourable situation. Nevertheless, at the moment, the unrealistic perception of the status quo has led to a mismatch in policy formulation. There is a considerable gap in the perception of the status quo among the policymakers, in a way that while some authorities are over-optimistic and formulate idealistic and inappropriate policies, some others are pessimistic and believe that the whole plan will fail. In such circumstances that there is a wide range of understandings, policymaking gets difficult. On the other hand, there is no consensus among policymakers about the desired status of the country, and sometimes there are different and conflicting views on the situation of the country among policymakers and other authorities. The compilation of strategic plans has some technical and political aspects. Strategic planning, as it deals with the allocation of resources and power, is an entirely political process and requires the involvement of influential bodies. When compiling the policies and strategic plans of science and technology in Iran, not all the involved bodies are taken into account. Consequently, their expectations are not identified and managed, and this, naturally, leads to numerous problems and obstacles in the way of the executives of the plans. The lack of sharing knowledge and experience in the field of science and technology is another missing point hindering the implementation of strategic plans in this area. The field of science and technology in Iran requires a knowledge management system that can create a learning circle among policymakers and participants, prevent redundant and repetitive measurements, and stop the formulation of inefficient and unrealistic policies and plans. Policymaking in the field of science and technology requires creative thinking, strategic thinking, prospective thinking, and problem-solving thinking. In the absence of these capabilities among policymakers, the compiled plans will not have high credibility and efficiency at the implementation stage.

4.3.2 Institutional deterrents

As stated, policymaking and strategic planning are political processes since many institutions are involved, and they play a significant role in allocating resources and power. The lack of enough attention, non-accreditation, and political deals are among the main inhibitors of institutional implementation of strategic policies and plans in science and technology. Unfortunately, the executive institutions make their own decisions and actions based on individual and organizational interests, and ignore the macro policies and developed plans. Another point is that the process of strategic management is a psychological process. It is usually witnessed that policies and plans are only communicated after the compilation. In contrast, a strategic plan is made up of innovative initiatives that executives and experts may lack the required expertise and courage to execute them. In Iran, the psychological aspect of strategic planning is often overlooked, and this is one of the main restrictive factors for implementing the plans. Strategic plans require organizing a series of briefings and interpretations of goals, strategies, plans, and actions. Senior executives often spend much time on the formulation of the policies and plans. However, they do not support the execution phase properly and are not so severe at this stage. Effective and efficient execution of strategic plans requires serious support from the senior executives of the organization. The parallel activities of institutions, lack of strong institutional responsibility in the implementation phase, lack of appropriate incentive system, and the use of necessary tools for institutions to implement the policies are among other institutional deterrents.

4.3.3 Cultural and social deterrents

The science and technology area have a turbulent and complex environment. Iranian policymakers and planners usually have a linear and superficial way of thinking and fail to understand these complexities, which are rooted in cultural and social factors. The interference of dominant values and norms in the implementation of policies is another restrictive factor. Iran is a country with multiple subcultures, each of which follows several vital values and norms. Intervention and contradiction of the values and norms hinder the implementation of policies and strategic plans. The execution of policies and strategic plans requires the involvement of mass media, too. If a policy becomes a public discourse in the community, its implementation will be significantly facilitated. The media should step in and turn the country's science and technology policies and plans into a dominant discourse in the community. Personal preferences, lack of social pressures, and rejecting the ideas of other participants are also other cultural and social barriers to the implementation of policies and strategic plans of science and technology.

4.3.4 *Promoter deterrents*

Strategic plans require planning before implementation. It is not possible to enter the implementation phase right after the compilation; instead, it is necessary to design an executive plan, hold briefings and interactive sessions, improve the knowledge of target groups and administrators, answer the possible questions and solve the possible controversies before the start of the execution phase. Unfortunately, this stage and its related circles are ignored, which causes some adverse effects on the implementation of the plans.

5. Conclusion

The full execution of the policies is difficult because many obstacles and impediments cannot be appropriately controlled. However, the critical point is that the more attention is paid to these factors in the processes of making, developing and implementing the policies, the implementation will be more successful, and the effectiveness of the developed policies will be higher. Today, various policies in the field of science and technology have been developed - or are being developed- but theoretical studies that examine the barriers to achieving full implementation of these policies are few. According to the discussions mentioned in this report, we can conclude that:

The lack of awareness among the people of the community, especially the policymakers of science and technology, is a significant barrier to the execution of policies. Most of the time, the planners believe that policies can be implemented through a simple formal letter, but this is not possible in practice. Studies, surveys, and interviews show that the community, especially the elites (whether academic or executive), are not fully aware of the theoretical foundations and contents of these documents, and there have not been many efforts to know those contents as well. The documents above have not been considered as the basis for action. This damage is due to two main reasons: firstly, document developers have not made much effort to engage policymakers as well as experts of each field, and instead emphasize the approach from top to bottom. There have also been some cases in which there was a sense of leadership among document developers, and they tried to enforce and control the implementation instead of holding interactive sessions in each area. The second reason for the damage is the lack of institutionalized scientism in the society, especially among the officials of the administrative system. As a result, there is no systematic thinking in the administrative system, and the managers take action simply based on personal preferences.

Iran suffers from the lack of prioritization in such a way that all the measures mentioned earlier are considered excellent and prioritized. The tendency to include any plan that seems right in the country's documents, regardless of the need to limit the number of goals in the specified periods, has led to an inability to achieve the goals and, consequently, repeating the policies without any improvements. The existing literature on policymaking suggests that the lack of prioritization in upstream documents can confuse policymakers.

Iranian authorities do not consider prospective plans in developing policy documents, and in most cases, they develop the policies simply based on superficial analyses of past studies. The analysis of the processes of compilation and implementation of policy documents on science and technology proves that there is no perspective view in the country's policy system. Therefore, the currently existing challenges of society are not adequately monitored, and there are no proper policies for them.

The policies developed in the field of science and technology in Iran are not in line with the existing contexts and challenges. In order to define the challenges and compile a policy to solve them, the situation must be properly, transparently, and genuinely agreed upon by policymakers, and they should have relative consensus on the favorable situation. However, at the moment, the unrealistic perception of the status quo has led to a mismatch in policy formulation. There is a considerable gap in the perception of the status quo among the policymakers, in a way that while some authorities are over-optimistic and formulate idealistic and inappropriate policies, some others are pessimistic and believe that the whole plan will fail. In such circumstances that there is a wide range of understandings, policymaking gets difficult. On the other hand, there is no consensus among policymakers about the desired status of the country, and sometimes there are different and conflicting views on the situation of the country among policymakers and other authorities.

The authorities involved in the process of policymaking for science and technology act individually, and there is no coherent network among them. Policies can be successful when implemented through interaction and networking among policymakers, which will create mutual learning and sharing of knowledge among them, and also provide a better understanding of the real problems of the society. The study of the process of documentation in Iran shows that those involved in the field are less concerned with this issue and useless interactive mechanisms in policy formulation. So, ignoring the critical role of networking during policy formulation will not pave the way for their successful implementation. Also, analyzing the development process of the existing documents shows that a small group has always been in charge of developing and approving the documents of different contents and functions; also, most of the documents are similar and have the same function. Using an imperative approach, it is not possible to develop documents related to, for example, aerospace, medicinal plants, and stem cells, and expect the community to implement them.

The trust and commitment rate of the policymakers is meager. The lack of consensus among the policymakers and executives has led to a lack of Commitment to the policies in some of the managers. Resultantly, the policies are not regarded as the basis for action. The more complicated issue is that the manifestations of this phenomenon are realized in the long run and are not easily compensated.

The implementation of policies requires interactive discourses. After formulating the policies, it is necessary to explain these policies to the public - and in particular, to the executive body of the state and private institutions and the elites - through interactive sessions. In other words, it is essential to promote the policies tailored to the level of awareness of various layers of the society, so that these policies become a shared perspective for both the operational actors and the public. Promotion and interactive discourse will make national movements towards policy implementation and realization of the prospects. Research in this area suggests that, currently, the policies have discoursed at a minimal level for the community and operators, which would make it impossible to have the necessary sense of Commitment among the executives to make their activities in line with the policies, and move towards the personal preferences of the executives.

Applying the long-term upstream policies (such as the prospectus) on sectoral policies have not been considered seriously among policymakers, and this problem is even getting worse. One of the main problems in policymaking in Iran is the lack of specified and long-term policies. The 20-year vision plan is the only long-term and well-publicized document of the country which has been formulated by the Expediency Discernment Council. As a result, one of the constraints in the country's policy system is the lack of long-term policy governance on sectorial and short-term policies.

There is no multi-sectorial approach in science and technology policy, and most of the organizations have paid attention merely to their interests and replaced policy-orientation with preferences-orientation. In that sense, sometimes the policies are not based on the principles and macro policies of the system, and the plans are not based on these policies. Ultimately, even if the policymakers go through these stages successfully, what is funded and implemented in the end, does not fit into what was initially intended by the policymakers in many respects. In other words, the actual plans which are practically and eventually implemented do not fit into the initial policies in many cases. Incoherence in development, implementation, and evaluation of the policies, the lack of a multi-sectoral approach, and the focus of organizations on their preferences instead of keeping to the orientations of the system are among the reasons for this issue.

There are no systematic and persistent perspectives on strategic and long-term plans in Iran. Policies require long-term planning and monitoring to showcase their effects in the community. Nevertheless, this opportunity has not yet been given to the policy enforcers. Government changes at specific intervals affect the attitudes of the policymakers. Resultantly, the policies which are not stable enough, regardless of the attitudes of the governments, are interrupted and not implemented. For this reason, there is always a need for a fixed body of strategic leadership and policymaking to take responsibility for the policies regardless of any governmental changes.

References

Akerman, J., Gudmundsson, H., Sorensen, C. H., Isaksson, K., Olsen, S., Kessler, F., and Macmillan, J. (2011) "How to manage barriers to formation and implementation of policy packages in transport", In Optic. Optimal Policies for Transport in Combination.

Allen-Hammer, K.(2018) "Demystifying personalizing wellness: a classic grounded theory study", a dissertation for the degree of Doctor of Philosophy in Mind-Body Medicine, Saybrook University

Anderson, J. E. (1982) Cases in public policy-making, Holt McDougal, New York.

Berg, K. (2004) "Implementing Chicago's Plan to Transform Public Housing", In Conference on Chicago Research and Public Policy, Chicago, IL, May, 12.

Brynard, P. (2005) "Policy implementation: Lessons for service delivery", Journal of Public Administration, Vol 40, No.3, pp649-664.

Calista, D. (1994) Policy implementation, Dekker Inc, Marcel.

Chun Tie, Y. , Birks, M., and Francis, K. (2019) "Grounded theory research: A design framework for novice researchers", SAGE Open Medicine, Vol 7,pp1-8.

Creswell, John. W., and Miller, Dana. L. (2000) "Determining validity in qualitative inquiry", Theory in practice, Vol19, No.3, pp124-130.

Denhardt, R. B., and Catlaw, T. J. (2014) Theories of public organization, Cengage learning, Arizona.

Elmore, R. F. (1980). Complexity and Control: What Legislators and Administrators Can Do About Implementing Public Policy? Washington: Institute of Governmental Research, University of Washington.

George, B., Walker. R. M., and Monster., J.(2019) "Does Strategic Planning Improve Organizational Performance? A Meta-Analysis ",Public Administration Review, Vol. 79, No. 6, pp. 810–819.

Howlett, M., Ramesh, M., and Perl, A. (2003) *Studying public policy: Policy cycles and policy subsystems* ,Vol 3. Toronto: Oxford University Press.

Khalid, H. M. (2001) "Policy implementation models: the case of library and documentation services in Pakistan", 1998-2008. New library world, Vol 102, No.3, pp87-92.

Khashei, V., Harandi, A. (2015) "Explaining the strategic control in the weighing industry: Discourse analysis using grounded theory strategy", Strategic Management Studies, Vol22, No.4, pp16-80. (In Persian).

Kostka, G. (2014) *Barriers to the implementation of environmental policies at the local level in China,* s.l.: World Bank.

Makinde, T. (2005) "Problems of policy implementation in developing nations: The Nigerian experience", Journal of Social sciences, Vol 11, No.1, pp63-69.

Marsh, D., and Allan, M. C. (2010) "Toward a framework for establishing policy success", Policy administration, Vol 88, No.2, pp564-583.

Moghadaspour, S., DanaeedFard, H., and Kordnaeehj, A. (2013) "Examining key factors in the failure of some public policies in the GAI: studying tax policies of the country", Management of organization culture, Vol11, No1, pp33-68. (In Persian).

Richardson, W. (2007) "Public policy failure and fiasco in education: perspectives on the British examinations crises of 2000–2002 and other episodes since 1975", Oxford Review of Education, Vol 33, No.2, pp143-160.

Sharifzadeh, F., Alvani, S., Rezaei Manesh, B., and Mokhtar Pirian, M. (2013) "Obstacles to Implementing Cultural Policies of the Country during First to Fourth Development Plans: Examining the Experiences of Cultural Managers", Thought of strategy management, Vol7, No.1, pp33 – 77. (In Persian).

Somit, A., and Peterson,S. (2003) Human nature and public policy: An evolutionary approach ,Springer, London.

Network of Innovation Brokers: Fostering Transnational STI

Johanna Haunschild and Sara Tsog
Fraunhofer Institute for Production Systems and Design Technology, Berlin, Germany
johanna.haunschild@ipk.fraunhofer.de
sara.tsog@ipk.fraunhofer.de
DOI: 10.34190/EIE.20.216

Abstract: The aim of this paper is to propose a hybrid organization that acts as a network of innovation brokers which could enhance the access to new knowledge sources, into new markets and accelerate innovative activities of an economy as a whole. ENRICH is an initiative of EC's Horizon 2020 program that consists of three centres located in Brazil, China and the USA. Its objective is to spur innovative activities and enhance the cooperation in research, technology and entrepreneurship between European Union and the above countries. With the main approach of networking, ENRICH in Brazil, China and the USA aims to become the main hub and contact point of STI actors in the respective countries who wish to collaborate with the EU and vice versa. The paper is a contribution to the development of new business models as well as strategies that aim to effectively foster international collaboration on research, innovation and entrepreneurship. The insights of this article can be of relevance for policy makers that are looking to establish or foster international science, technology, and innovation ecosystems, as well as for academics who are interested in the transnational innovation ecosystems and strategic collaborations. The first and theoretical parts of this paper are based on library resources and recent academic articles. The second portion of the paper presents the European Union Horizon 2020 funded project ENRICH Centres as an example of the proposed hybrid organization.

Keywords: global innovation network taxonomy, international STI co-operation, hybrid organizations, innovation broker, EU & Brazil & China & USA

1. Introduction

Science, technology and innovation (STI) play a key role in a social and economic development. Their capacity lies in the ability to create as well as access knowledge. The world's total knowledge continuously expands. This arises the question where knowledge is being generated and who has access to it. According to the European Commission (EC), more than 70% of knowledge is created outside of Europe and three quarter is produced in G5 countries (United States, Germany, France, Japan and the United Kingdom).

With globalization, the spread of knowledge and technology has been accelerating at a surprising rate, considering that it took more than a millennium for invention of paper to spread to Europe. The increased geographic spread of knowledge was partially due to international cooperation and global innovation networks (GIN). In the first stage, such networks were confined among leading innovative countries and later they were set towards emerging economies as well. To ensure long-term global competitiveness, it is vital for economies to have access to knowledge generated outside own border and gain access to new markets. Effective international cooperation and networking with emerging countries in the area of research, innovation and entrepreneurship is not only valuable for the national economy but it is also necessary to effectively address global societal challenges.

The aim of this paper is to propose a hybrid organization that acts as a network of innovation brokers which could enhance the access to new knowledge sources, into new markets, and accelerate innovative activities of an economy as a whole. The paper seeks to contribute to the development of new business models as well as strategies that aim to effectively foster international collaboration on research, innovation and entrepreneurship by investigating the *European Network of Research and Innovation Centres and Hubs* (ENRICH) which is currently at the final stage of its establishment.

ENRICH is an initiative of EC's Horizon 2020 program that consists of three centres located in Brazil, China and the USA. Its objective is to spur innovative activities and enhance the cooperation in research, technology and entrepreneurship between European Union and the above countries. With the main approach of networking, ENRICH in Brazil, China and the USA aims to become the main hub and contact point of STI actors in the respective countries who wish to collaborate with the EU and vice versa.

The paper is based on both a literature survey and the analysis of the European, Brazilian, Chinese and USA markets and innovations actors compiled prior and during the ENRICH project. It is divided into 6 Sections. The next section succinctly outlines the methodology used in this paper. After reviewing the taxonomy of GINs in Section 3, Section 4 elucidates the drivers and incentives behind the international STI cooperation to provide a comprehension of how thematic priorities are set in order to establish a system of win-win outcome. Then, Section 5 is given over to the concept of innovation brokers along the proposed hybrid organization. The final Section concludes and provides practical implications and further suggestion for investigation.

2. Methodology

The first part of this paper, which presents the taxonomy of GINs and the driving forces of international STI cooperation, was examined using recent literature. This part lays out a conceptual and theoretical basis for the discussion of transnational STI cooperation by providing a clear definition and delimitation of the research topic. When planning a global STI cooperation or collaboration project, it is essential to be able to determine and categorize innovation actors based on their characteristics. It aids to effectively determine the type of the GIN and the roles of the prospective network members in the network structure. Additionally, having knowledge about what drives specific innovation actors to participate in GINs, fosters the acceleration process of cross-border innovative activities. Therefore, for organizations or nation states aiming to foster and promote STI cooperation and collaboration with international innovation actors, it is of importance to be able to implement various methods of investigating the demand of relevant national and international innovation actors in terms of STI internationalization.

The second fragment of this paper presents the ENRICH project as an exemplary case study. The ENRICH project is run on the basis of the action research method (ARM). Prior to the project, the EC and other studies such as FFG (2015) have concluded that nearly 70% of the organizations that have taken part in a survey expressed interest in a STI Joint European Liaison Office (JELO) across the European borders. The majority have shown the most interest in three particular countries – namely, Brazil, China and the USA (FFG, the Australian Research Promotion Agency, 2015). According to O'Leary (2007), the ARM tackles "real-world problems in participatory, collaborative, and cyclical ways in order to produce both knowledge and action". Therefore, after initially identifying a potential problem – a lack of supporting system in the EU international STI collaborative landscape – and its probable causes, the EC under the Horizon 2020 umbrella project has developed a response to the problem by launching the call for the ENRICH project. In the first project phase, ENRICH run an in-depth market analysis of the four economies (EU, Brazil, China, USA) using various business methods. After the initial business model has been outlined, in the next phases a close monitoring has been conducted using an in-house key performance indicators (KPI) specifically designed for the project. By supervising the results of the KPI, ENRICH was able to reflect on its business model and the market development including potential members and customers. This allowed to adjust to any modifications and biases that have been initially overseen or that have occurred over the project years. Based on the results that have been collected over the project duration, this paper proposes a hybrid organization that operates as an innovation brokers.

3. Emergence of GIN and its taxonomy

Over the last decades, economies became more interconnected than ever. An economic behavior of every individual, business and product is linked to an economic behavior of thousands of others around the globe. Production processes became geographically spread as firms have begun to locate various production stages across the globe, resulting in global value chains (GVC). The share of foreign value added grew both in developed and emerging economies. To some extent most countries engage in backward and forward GVC, by either sourcing foreign inputs for export production or providing inputs for foreign partners for their export. Yet, countries with strong backward linkages to GVC tend to have weaker forward linkages to GVC and vice versa (Kowalski *et al.*, 2015). Emergence and further development of GCV made in turn innovation processes more open and geographically spread as well (Wobbe, 2013).

Reports on trade and investment such as (UNCTAD, 2006) show a rising trend of research and development (R&D) investments from high wage countries to emerging economies as well as from emerging countries. Up until the early 1990s, knowledge production was confined within the a few developed countries (e.g. the Triad, Western Europe, Japan, and USA) hence knowledge related foreign direct investments (FDI) were circulating within and between these borders. Branches and controlled subsidiaries of multinational enterprises (MNE) in emerging countries were predominantly trusted with low-skilled tasks, e.g. product and process adaptation into local market conditions (Krishna et al., 2012). During this period, some East Asian countries such as China begun to emulate the high-tech solutions through imitation and reverse-engineering resulting in the development of their local R&D network. As FDI were becoming increasingly ruled by knowledge-seeking strategies, access to foreign knowledge and pool of skilled workers that consisted of returned educational migrants incentivized the Triad and MNEs to invest as well cooperate with the fast developing emerging economies (Ernest *et al.,* 2019). Firms not only produced and sold around the globe but they have also started to innovate globally (Barnard and Chaminade, 2011).

Innovation is indispensable in global competition. National actors are forced to establish links with international innovation domains or tap into global innovation networks with individuals, universities, research institutes and firms in order to access and exploit global value flows, e.g. source knowledge, attract talent, generate ideas, and tackle problems. Firms, for instance draw on a wide spread network of partners that consists of other firms as well as R&D affiliate facilities, resulting in a GIN. GIN is defined as "a globally organized network of complex interactions between firms and non-firm organizations engaged [in the development and/or diffusion of innovation]" (Barnard and Chaminade, 2011). These networks are comprised from various actors such as MNE, high-tech startups, universities, public and private research institutes, venture capitalists and government agencies. Emergence of GINs occurs more organically and is highly preferred as the potential network actors understand and recognize the benefit of tapping into specialized expertise and the gains from specializing. Their objectives nevertheless differ ranging from profit generation, acceleration of growth, efficient way of knowledge generation, access and retaining of tacit knowledge, development and application of solutions to the global problems (Keith and Kamal, 2013).

Just as the GVC, the literature suggests that the phenomenon of GINs was exclusively driven by MNEs from high-wage countries. Barnard and Chaminade (2011) have conducted an empirical analysis challenging this hypothesis by seeking to identify different forms of GINs and the role of various actors of these networks as well as the role of developed and emerging economies in the GINs. They have used firm-level data from various regions of the world (Europe, Brazil, China, India, and South Africa). The authors' hypothesis is based on the assumption that globally organized innovation networks can differ in the degree of their globalness, innovativeness and networkedness. Various combination of these three elements serve as the basic forms of GINs.

Activities of GINs can be restricted within a certain geographical area (e.g. regional) and have internal networks interconnecting the activities of affiliate members. They can be also truly global, on the other hand, and have internal and external or both network directions. External networks set up linkage to foreign actors in order to exploit their knowledge and gain access to local markets and resources (Castellani and Zanfei, 2006). A North-American MNE that establishes a R&D laboratory in Brazil where researchers from Europe use equipment developed in China for innovating a Chemical substance with natural resources from Amazonia is an example of a truly GIN that is internally as well as externally networked and that seeks to produce a novel product. According to (Barnard and Chaminade, 2011) there are five types of firm-based GINs: balanced, global asset exploiters, innovators, networkers and global networkers (Table 1). An extra form of GINs is a network of firms that are innovative and networked enough but have no global reach at all. The majority of firms are somewhat global, innovative and networked and these elements evolve at a similar rate. Second most common type of GINs consists of firms that are not global at all yet are innovative and networked enough. On the other hand, as opposed to the common hypotheses that advocate the importance of MNEs in GINs, highly global, most innovative and strongly networked GINs consist from medium-sized firms.

Table 1: Firm-based taxonomy of GINs (Barnard and Chaminade, 2011)

GIN Type	Description	Main Characteristics
(High-level) Balanced GIN	All elements are in alignment	Mainly medium size companies (between 250-1000); Big enough to handle internationalization without losing capacity to innovate; Mostly located in middle-income countries
Global asset exploiters	Global reach is greater than the extent of innovation or networkedness	Mainly medium size entities; Subsidiaries of MNCs located in high-income countries
Innovators	Firms are relatively more innovative than their global reach or the extent of their networks would suggest	Mainly small firms; Mainly stand-alone firms; Mostly located in high-income countries
Networkers	Strength of networks is greater than global reach or innovativeness	Mainly MNCs; Range of sizes and locations

GIN Type	Description	Main Characteristics
Global networkers	Innovation is not as high as both the globalness and the networkedness. This is the only common combination of two stronger dimensions	Large firms of more than 1000 employees; Can be either headquarters or subsidiaries; Located both in high- and middle-income countries
Domestics	Firms that have no supra-national footprint at all, but are innovative and networked enough to (presumably) survive domestically or locally – this category accounts for the second largest group of firms.	Any size, both economies

4. Incentives of international STI cooperation

It is a travesty to assume that countries chose international STI partners solely based on their STI characteristics. The determining factors of the content and direction of STI collaboration are based on a wide range of rationales. Besides the impact of STI community, world economic development and global production networks primarily influence STI policies which in turn for the most part shape the modern STI co-operation framework. A backstage influence on the choice of international STI partners and STI collaboration patterns have diplomacy, historical cultural ties, development or bilateral aid, linguistic and geopolitical factors (Luukkonen, Persson and Sivertsen, 1992; Arvanitis and Gaillard, 2013).

With the emergence of BRIC countries, the Triad recognized the research and technology capacity of these new players making the FDI in R&D flow out of Triad. Such external developments are multifold. Recent debates over global challenges including climate change and sustainable growth objectives have led to more global research programs by putting increased pressure on the science community but also global society as a whole. As the environmental changes are truly global and are closely linked to economic development of high to low-waged countries, there is no simple one-time solution.

In the analysis of the drivers and incentives of international STI co-operation, EC distinguishes between *narrow STI co-operation paradigm* and *broad research paradigm* (Boekholt *et al.,* 2009). The drivers of the former paradigm aim "to improve the quality, scope and critical mass in research by linking national resources and knowledge in other countries". In the broader paradigm, on the other hand, science and non-science-oriented policy objectives interact with each other so that STI co-operation is instrumentalized to reach other objectives. The motivation behind the narrow paradigm is to "achieve research excellence" and attract or have access to pool of skilled staff. For instance, the demographic development and the lack of MINT (Mathematics, Informatics, Natural Science, and Technology) related professionals in Europe partially shape international STI policies. Nation states strengthen their efforts to attract and retain researchers and highly skilled workers, as globalization has simplified the labor mobility. Hence, as (Boekholt *et al.,* 2009) and Edler and Flanagan (2011) state, the main triggers of reinforced international STI collaborations since the last decade were the following:

- Competitiveness, as it is a magnet for investments;
- Development and bilateral aid R&D collaborations are basic medium for mitigating environmental degradation and tackling global societal issues;
- Maintaining stable diplomatic climate;
- Research excellence on the global STI stage;
- Competition for specialized expertise (e.g. researchers, skilled workers and professionals);
- Building science and technology capability.

The geographical and thematic focus of international research collaboration is defined in a bottom-up approach. Individual researchers and research organizations have the freedom to choose their partnerships and set-up own international strategies. Governments promote and facilitate such approaches by elaborating formal STI frameworks in a following way:

- Setting research funding programs for bilateral and multilateral co-operations and defining the thematic areas;
- Defining and substituting the choice of STI partners on the basis of non-science-related objectives (e.g. cultural ties and fostering diplomacy);
- Gaining broader political benefits;

- Increasing R&D capacity of developing and emerging economies (Chinchilla-Rodríguez *et al.,* 2012).

Considering from the broader paradigm, competitiveness and innovation are the primary drivers of international STI partnerships. Over the recent decades, the choice of national STI priorities has been increasingly focused on strategic national or global problems (Gokhberg, Meissner and Sokolov, 2016).

It is assumed, although not empirically backed-up, that nation states invest substantially into both inward and outward oriented competitiveness strategies out of fear that nationally based industries and human resources might relocate to other countries. The inward oriented strategies focus on gaining an access to foreign knowledge and expertise, whereas the outward one seeks to attract foreign-based firms and FDI.

The selection of STI priority areas in bilateral or multilateral co-operation agendas in the case of Europe are carried out on the basis of substantial and large-scale consultation with leading R&D institutions and other key stakeholders such as industry representatives and government agencies. The final decision on the choice of priority areas is based on several stages that have to approved (OECD, 2010). There are three types of STI priorities (Gassler *et al.,* 2004; Haegeman *et al.,* 2013; Drilhon, 1991; OECD, 2010):

- thematic (fields of science and technology);
- mission-oriented (socio-economic or technological objectives);
- functional (characteristics of national science and innovation system).

Joint priorities in international STI partnerships may be set on the basis of thematic areas (e.g. nanotechnology and bioeconomy), structural issues (human resources and infrastructure), grand challenges (climate change and global viral infections). They can have a more particular or diverse focus, prioritize either traditional or emerging research areas, be focused on basic or applied research, and have various time-lengths. The choices are either based on users' needs, interests of STI community, or broader paradigm of policies (Haegeman *et al.,* 2015).

In numerous developed economies, a methodological tool called *Foresight* was implemented in the design of STI strategies and selection of national and international STI priorities. This tool is a "systematic, participatory, and future-intelligence-gathering and medium to long-term vision building process aimed at present-day decisions and mobilization of joint actions" (Shevchenko and Stukach, 2017). Results of an extensive Foresight project were used for setting the priorities of the Horizon 2020 framework program which "is the financial instrument implementing the Innovation Union, a Europe 2020 flagship initiative aimed at securing Europe's global competitiveness". "By coupling research and innovation, Horizon 2020 is helping to achieve [smart, sustainable and inclusive growth and jobs] with its emphasis on excellent science, industrial leadership and tackling societal challenges. The goal is to ensure Europe produces world-class science, removes barriers to innovation and makes it easier for the public and private sectors to work together in delivering innovation" (EC, 2020).

One of the priorities of the Horizon 2020 strategy is to support inclusive, innovative and reflective societies. Under this program, a project called European Network of Research and Centres and Hubs (ENRICH) was initiated with an aim to encourage a sustainable internationalization of research and business organizations, as well as promote cooperation among EU and Brazilian, Chinese and USA research, innovation and business (R&I&B) organizations.

Next Section will elaborate the ENRICH Centres and its activities as an innovation broker.

5. ENRICH centres: Innovation broker

GINs and network of international R&D activities are well-known phenomenon. Such networks indicate co-operation and collaboration between its members. Innovation brokers, in contrast, are internal or external network actors that link other actors in the network. In corporate world, an innovation broker is defined as "an organization acting as a member of a network of actors in an industrial sector that is focused neither on the generation nor the implementation of innovations, but on enabling other organizations to innovate" (Winch and Courtney, 2007). Network theory states that members play a certain but different role in the network, and one of which acts as a bridge between two or more network members or network externals that otherwise would not be related. In this paper, we propose a hybrid organization ENRICH that acts as an innovation broker. It plays its innovations broking role by coordinating a network of various public and private stakeholders. This includes

R&D&I actors such as MNE, startups, research institutes, and government agencies and non-profits, etc. The capacity to "look cross-sectoral and connect across existing institutes, disciplines, [and] viewpoints" is essential for an innovation broker (ENRD, 2013).

ENRICH is a global network of centres and hubs that promotes internationalisation of European STI. Focusing on knowledge-intensive sectors, ENRICH aims to stimulate collaborative projects.

By the end of the project, which is currently in its final phase, the three ENRICH Centres will be independent entities. It is sought that they will reach financial self-sustainability. Its business model involves both non-profit and for-profit characteristics, as ENRICH operates as a vehicle for promoting and fostering international STI co-operation under the Horizon 2020's program "Europe in a changing world - Inclusive, innovative and reflective societies". This program thread focuses on projects that directly/indirectly address social exclusion, discriminations and various forms of inequalities. It also promotes coherent and effective cooperation with third countries. Therefore, as a hybrid organization, ENRICH has at its core commitment to positive social and environmental changes.

As a network, ENRICH currently offers services to connect European research, technology and business organisations with three global frontrunner innovation markets: Brazil, China and the USA. The ENRICH Services include but are not limited to:

- Connecting European researchers and entrepreneurs with key players in the target countries;
- Linking researchers and entrepreneurs from target countries to innovation influencers in Europe;
- Providing guidance and advice on funding, internationalisation and business acceleration;
- Increasing cooperation in research, innovation and business (R&I&B) between the target countries and European organisations;
- Promoting excellence in business, research and innovation;
- Integrating existing initiatives, projects and networks from Europe and the target markets;
- Offering a wide range of custom-made services to promote and foster STI collaboration.

ENRICH will charge for its services in order to finance its fixed and variable costs. However, it will also apply for grants and funding. Such hybrid behaviour provides means to survive in times when government funding and support are cut-short allowing to earn and accrue capital reserves to support social mission in terms of STI fostering. Hybrids harness the power of capitalism to capture market value and use it for creating social value (California Management Review, 2015). Having a close link to its network members that are geographically dispersed over Europe, Brazil, China and the USA, helps in catalysing innovation through bringing together STI actors and facilitating their interaction. As an independent entity and innovation broker, ENRICH acts as a "facilitator of interaction and innovation systems" (Klerkx and Gildemacher, 2012) on an altruistic basis. Its services allow small and resource-scarce organizations to participate in GINs by breaking down existing barriers to STI co-operation and collaboration.

Adapting further characteristics of innovation brokers, ENRICH can increase their support of small firms and startups and be value to all other STI stakeholders that wish to find international partners, Funding opportunities, internationalize, get to know desired foreign markets and STI landscape.

6. Conclusion

This paper presents the ENRICH Centres as a hybrid organization that acts as an innovation broker. Under the umbrella of Horizon 2020 program framework, the project was initiated to promote and foster international STI cooperation and reinforce the results of other Horizon 2020 projects. As ENRICH Centres represent a certain from of GINs, we have discussed the emergence of GINs and its taxonomy. Innovation actors organized in such networks differ according to the globalness, innovativeness and networkedness. The prevailing notion that mostly MNEs from high-wage economies dictate the intensity, content and direction of GINs does not necessarily hold the truth. Small and medium firms from both developed and emerging countries are more global, more innovative, and more networked. Although there seems to be a synergy in the development of these three indicators.

Afterwards, the paper succinctly outlines the methodology used and elucidates the drivers behind international STI co-operation from a policy-oriented view. Individual firms and organization have the freedom to decide with whom to partner, how to partner and in which area. This Section provides the most common reasons to the recent developments of international STI partnerships. According to the EC, there are two STI co-operation paradigms: narrow and broad. The former is responsible for excellence in research quality, scope and critical mass, whereas in the latter paradigm science and non-science-oriented policy objectives interact with each other so that STI co-operation is instrumentalized to reach other objectives. This could include incentives of tackling global societal challenges, e.g. health hazards or environmental degradation leading to loss of essential biosphere etc. Another instrument from the toolbox of designing and defining the international STI co-operation priorities that has been and still being implemented is the methodology Foresight. Literature suggests that the EU has further specialized in using this tool.

Having elaborated why STI actors participate in international co-operations and how they participate, and what forms of GINs can be formed depending on the network partners and their based locations, the paper continues to introduce the ENRICH Centres in more detail. Since the project is still running, ENRICH Centres haven't reached financial self-sustainability. However, its business model that combines characteristics of a hybrid entity provides some ground to survive even in absence state grants and support. This is certainly not the best case scenario, however having features of a hybrid entity facilitates ENRICH broking independently of others and in an objective way.

In conclusion, it is to note that due to the length and the scope of this paper, this article did not further investigate the theory of innovation brokers and hybrid organizations. It also refrained to provide a detailed representation of the Centres' business model per se. For precise and detailed investigation of the topic, it is suggested to conduct a comparative analysis of similar innovation brokers and run an empirical analysis of the impact of GIN on the objectives of its members, given appropriate data.

References

Arvanitis, R. and J. Gaillard (2013), Research collaboration between Europe and Latin America. Mapping and understanding partnership, EAC éditions des archives contemporaines, Paris.

Barnard, H. and C. Chaminade (2011), "Global Innovation Networks: towards a taxonomy".

Boekholt, P. et al. (2009), "Drivers of International collaboration in research".

California Management Review (2015), Understanding Hybrid Organizations, https://cmr.berkeley.edu/2015/06/hybrid-organizations/, accessed 06 October 2020.

Castellani, D. and A. Zanfei (2006), Multinational firms, innovation and productivity, Edward Elgar Publishing.

Chinchilla-Rodríguez, Z. et al. (2012), "International collaboration in Medical Research in Latin America and the Caribbean (2003-2007)", Journal of the American Society for Information Science and Technology, Vol. 63, No. 11, pp. 2223–2238.

Drilhon, G. (1991), Choosing priorities in science and technology, Organisation for Economic Co-operation and Development, Paris.

EC (2020), What is Horizon 2020? - Horizon 2020 - European Commission, https://ec.europa.eu/programmes/horizon2020/en/what-horizon-2020, accessed 06 October 2020.

Edler, J. and K. Flanagan (2011), "Indicator needs for the internationalisation of science policies", Research Evaluation, Vol. 20, No. 1, pp. 7–17.

ENRD (2013), "Focus Group on Knowledge Transfer & Innovation. Towards Successful Innovation Brokerag: Insights from the 2007-2013 Rural Development Programmes".

Ernest, M. et al. (2019), "Tied in: the Global Network of Local Innovation".

FFG, the Australian Research Promotion Agency (2015), "Operational Feasibility Study for STI Joint European Liaison Offices (STI JELOs) for European Research Organizations in Argentina, Australia, Brazil, Canada, China, Japan, New Zealand, Russia, South Africa and the USA".

Gassler, H. et al. (2004), Priorities in Science and Technology Policy–an international comparison.

Gokhberg, L., D. Meissner and A. Sokolov (2016), Deploying foresight for policy and strategy makers. Creating Opportunities Through Public Policies and Corporate Strategies in Science, Technology and Innovation, Springer International Publishing Switzerland.

Haegeman, K. et al. (2013), "Quantitative and qualitative approaches in Future-oriented Technology Analysis (FTA): From combination to integration?", Technological Forecasting and Social Change, Vol. 80, No. 3, pp. 386–397.

Haegeman, K. et al. (2015), "FTA supporting effective priority setting in multi-lateral research programme cooperation: The case of EU–Russia S&T cooperation", Technological Forecasting and Social Change, Vol. 101, pp. 200–215, www.sciencedirect.com/science/article/pii/S004016251500102X.

Keith, M. and S. Kamal (2013), Global Innovation Networks and their Implications for the Multilateral Trading System, accessed 08 June 2020.

Klerkx, L. and P. Gildemacher (2012), "The role of innovation brokers in the agricultural innovation system", pp. 237–245.
Kowalski, P., J.L. Gonzalez, A. Ragoussis and C. Ugarte (2015), Participation of Developing Countries in Global Value Chains. IMPLICATIONS FOR TRADE AND TRADE-RELATED POLICIES.
Luukkonen, T., O. Persson and G. Sivertsen (1992), "Understanding Patterns of International Scientific Collaboration", Science, Technology, & Human Values, Vol. 17, No. 1, pp. 101–126.
OECD (2010), Priority setting for public research: challenges and opportunities.
O'Leary, Z. (2007), "Action Research", in Z. O'Leary (ed.), The social science jargon buster. The key terms you need to know, Sage Publications, Los Angeles, pp. 1–4.
Shevchenko, Y. and V. Stukach (2017), Foresight in Strategic Planning and Technology Foresight in Kazakhstan: making Decisions about Long-term Investment in Science, International Experience, No. 10, Scholars Journal of Economics, Business and Management (SJEBM).
UNCTAD (2006), World Investment Report 2006: FDI from Developing and Transition Economies. Implications for Development.
Winch, G.M. and R. Courtney (2007), The Organization of Innovation Brokers: An International Review, No. 6.
Wobbe, W. (2013), "Global innovation networks: High Level Economic Expert Group 'Innovation for Growth – i4g'".

Learning Entrepreneurship by Experiencing it: Insights From a Students Communication Design Agency

Anne Heinze
University of Applied Sciences HTW Berlin, Germany
anne.heinze@htw-berlin.de
DOI: 10.34190/EIE.20.021

Abstract: A look at entrepreneurship education research shows that there are basically two types of entrepreneurship courses: First, courses for entrepreneurship and second, courses about entrepreneurship such as lectures, formal seminars, individual essays etc. Most of the latter courses can be characterized as teacher-centric where the student involvement is passive. From a more modern perspective and in order to train entrepreneurship trying, experimenting and learning about one's own experience is crucial. More innovative approaches, such as project based learning, action based learning and experiential learning, therefore, are gradually appearing on the screen. In this context, within the last few years at some universities training firms have been introduced, mostly for students of economics and business. In Germany, due to a lack of legal possibilities training firms at public universities are still a rarity in general and therefore underresearched. Thus, the research question of the present contribution is how informal learning can be structured by instructors using training firms and what effects this has on the preparation of learners for later professional practice and / or self-employment. Therefore, the methodology for this paper is first to review the literature related to entrepreneurial learning in order to better understand the informal learning experience via training firms. Second, the case of a communication design agency for students around the HTW Berlin, a public university of applied sciences is analysed to gain insight into the impact that practice firms can have on entrepreneurship education in general and in particular in non-business subjects. For this purpose, a case study is developed based on interviews, which includes both the perspective of the students and the trainer. Overall, the results will show a best practice example of entrepreneurial training and learning in a university context, which can be useful for those involved in the development of course concepts for entrepreneurship education.

Keywords: entrepreneurship education, informal entrepreneurial teaching, experiential learning, training firms

1. Introduction

Nowadays, researchers assume that entrepreneurial thinking and acting can be achieved particularly well by trying, experimenting and learning about one's own experience. In this understanding, mere informing and learning about entrepreneurship and its components is not enough within entrepreneurship education. This is why, other approaches, such as project based learning, action based learning and experiential learning become more and more important in this context. Generally, these approaches contribute to better prepare alumni for future challenges in their jobs and or self-employment activities.

This paper tries to shed more light on experiential and application-based learning in entrepreneurship education. In this context, training firms offer the opportunity to implement project- and experience-based learning approaches into the curricula of the students. Thus, the research question of the present article is how informal learning can be structured by instructors with the help of training firms and what effects this has on the preparation of the learners for later professional practice and / or self-employment.

First and in order to achieve the research objective mentioned above, the current status of research on entrepreneurship education – with special consideration of modern approaches such as project- and action-based learning as well as experiential learning – is presented. In addition, the informal learning experience through training companies is clarified. Second, the case of a communication design agency for students around University of Applied Sciences HTW Berlin is analysed to gain insights into the impact that practice firms can have on entrepreneurship education in general and in particular in non-business subjects. For this purpose, a case study is developed based on interviews, which includes both the perspective of the students and the trainer. The interviews are conducted according to interview guidelines.

The results shall provide insights into the necessary framework conditions and demands on teachers and learners when implementing a training firm at a public university of applied sciences. All in all, the results will show a best practice example of entrepreneurial training and learning in a university context, which can be useful for those involved in the development of course concepts for entrepreneurship education in academia.

2. Theoretical background

Research on entrepreneurship education has shown that there are basically two types of entrepreneurship courses: First, courses *for* entrepreneurship and second, courses *about* entrepreneurship such as lectures, formal seminars, individual essays etc. (Levie 1999: 3, 18; Manimala and Thomas 2017: 10). Common entrepreneurship courses usually remain with offers in which you learn about entrepreneurship. Most of the latter courses can be characterized as teacher-centric where the student involvement is passive. Such courses are usually offered by the Startup Service Centers at universities on an extracurricular basis (students who take part in these courses generally do not receive credit points for this additional commitment within their studies). But - and that is exactly what such courses are usually not about - entrepreneurship is not linear, but a complex process that cannot be learned through mere content (Linton and Klinton 2019: 1).

However, more modern approaches assume that entrepreneurship can only be achieved by trying, experimenting and learning about one's own experience (Ebbers 2004: 35). This is due to the fact that, according to the newer approaches motivating students to become and / or think as entrepreneurs is key. And you cannot convey motivation by just teaching mere content. In contrast, real life experiences and role playing are more than suitable to achieve this learning goal. In order to promote entrepreneurial thinking and acting, the learning environment must therefore be designed differently and contain, for example, inspiring personalities and successful start-up examples, but also offer opportunities to make the requirements for starting a company tangible. All in all, the learning environment must enable experience in the "real world" as part of a good entrepreneurship education (Pittz 2014: 182). This is why more innovative educational approaches, such as project based learning, action based learning and experiential learning are gradually appearing on the screen in the context of entrepreneurial teaching and learning (Hills et al. 2007: 226). The learning environment of the latter concepts is marked by student-centric contents, experience-based and action-oriented projects and includes, for example, case studies, cooperation with practitioners, simulation exercises, practical workshops, and group projects in general (Levie 1999: 18; Manimala and Thomas 2017: 10).

To further clarify the above-mentioned concepts it can be stated that experiential learning is characterized by the fact that students play an active role in the learning process (Sukavejworakit et al. 2018: 2). Furthermore, experience learning is particularly about the creation of processes with open results (Lackeus and Williams Middleton 2018: 20). For this reason, fixed learning objectives cannot be formulated in advance. The only thing that in this context can be monitored and determined by the trainer are certain framework conditions for the processing and implementation of a project (topics, target groups, deadlines, etc.). "Project based learning places students in realistic contextualized problem-solving learning environments" (Blumenfeldt et al. 1991: 372). The advantage of this approach is that it is interdisciplinary and thus allows a broad view of a topic and its context. In addition, the overall problem as well as the structure are determined by the students themselves. Action based learning, on the other hand, is based on real life experiences, for example in a real-life venture creation environment, but within the protected framework of the respective university. Failure is allowed and widely accepted (Lackeus and Williams Middleton 2018: 28-29). This type of learning environment also applies to training firms, even if they also include aspects of experience-based and project-based learning. The effect of student engagement in training companies as a special method of action learning - and especially of students from non-business subjects - has hardly been analysed in entrepreneurship education research.

Learning concepts can not only be implemented in teaching units that take place at the universities, but can also be used beyond. In this context, a distinction is made between formal and informal learning settings. Formal learning takes place in a formally organized manner at the universities, whereas informal learning can also be undertaken beyond this, for example during an internship, in the new media, in social movements and in leisure activities (Overwien 2009: 23). Many key competences such as social skills or the so-called "soft skills" are increasingly not being formalized, but conveyed in informal learning settings. Incidental learning, i.e. learning without pursuing a specific pre-formulated objective, is also relevant in this context; however, it depends on the student's commitment. Thus, they have to act on their own initiative and take responsibility for their own learning; additionally, a certain proactivity is necessary for this (Overwien 2009: 24). If students are used to formal learning settings, they can easily be overwhelmed by these requirements. Because of this, such settings may not be suitable until later in the course of their studies, or should be based on certain previous experience of the students with self-structured learning formats. To sum up here, informal learning, i.e. learning in real contexts and based on real-life challenges, takes place in different contexts, e.g. in research projects as research-based learning or in the workplace as learning on the job.

In this context, the Finnish team academy approach has gained more importance for entrepreneurship education in academia. Fundamentally, in team academies students work in teams where they learn to do their own businesses with real money and real customers (Fowle and Jussila 2016: 1). The approach has also been adapted for the UK and there at Newcastle Business School of University of Northumbria, for example, consists in a work-based approach to learning which supports a philosophy of 'learning by doing' where participants set up real businesses in teams (Blackwood et al.: 1). In Germany, Bremerhaven University of Applied Sciences has established the Bachelor course „Gründung, Innovation, Führung" where students learn through managing cooperatives, identifying business opportunities for them and developing plans to exploit their businesses. Similar concepts are used at universities by setting up training firms.

However, in Germany, the introduction and sponsorship of a profitable business by publicly financed and state-sponsored universities is difficult. Some of them, within the last years have been introduced by universities, but mostly for students of economics and business. They are often formally maintained by professors who are liable for them with their private assets. The legal restrictions in Germany are probably the reason why, firstly, there are hardly any training firms in general and for students from non-business subjects in particular at German universities and why, secondly, the effects of a possible student engagement in such companies in entrepreneurship education research so far have hardly been researched. The present paper aims to close this gap of research and uses the example of the association "sehen und ernten e.V.", a design agency in students hands in the surroundings of University of Applied Sciences HTW Berlin, which carries out real orders in the design branch, and analyses the impact that practice firms can have on entrepreneurship education in general and in particular in non-business subjects.

3. Methodology

In order to address the research question of the present contribution and, after thoroughly evaluating the current state of research on informal learning in entrepreneurship education a case study on the aforementioned example of the design agency "sehen und ernten e.V." will be carried out. "Sehen und ernten e.V." is a creative agency for conception and design, in which students of communication design come together to work on real orders. It offers students of the University of Applied Sciences HTW Berlin the opportunity to get in touch with the professional world during their studies and to apply what they have already learned during their studies (https://www.sehenundernten.org/, 19.03.2020). The HTW Berlin is the largest public University of Applied Sciences in Berlin and Eastern Germany.

In order to address the main objective of the present paper, the conducted case study aims to answer the research question of how informal learning can be structured by instructors using the concept of training firms, and what effects this has on the preparation of learners for later professional practice and / or self-employment. Therefore, three interviews with first, the instructor of a preliminary tutorial for students interested in participating in the design agency and two more interviews with students attending the course and engaging themselves later on within the design agency were carried out. In the following, the interview guideline will be described in more detail in order to precisely document the qualitative research process (Steinke, 2012: 325).

Each interview was performed using an interview guideline. The guideline for the interview with the instructor of the preliminary tutorial consisted of questions on his own motivation to offer the tutorial at the University of Applied Scienes HTW Berlin, on his background and professional experience as well as pedagogical suitability for the tutorship, on goals and contents of the tutorial including the aspired student skills development, an assessment of whether what has been learned in the tutorial is sufficient for practical implementation in the daily work of the agency, an assessment of whether the gained knowledge from this work has an impact on later professional life and / or self-employment of the students and on the general potential of project courses and student associations in higher education. The questions for the interviews with the two students attending the tutorial and engaging themselves later on within the design agency were the following: Motivation of the students to attend the tutorial, assumed role of the instructor of the tutorial, assessment of their own skill acquisition, assessment of weaknesses or lacking skills of the team, new content or content which was not learned during the respective course of study, biggest personal gain from the tutorial and the work in the agency, assessment of the extent to which the work can prepare them for later professional life and/or self-employed activities, recommendation of this experience to other students and, obstacles with regard to the compatibility of work with their studies.

On the basis of a full transcript of each interview, a qualitative data analysis was performed. The results of the interviews are presented in the next section – first from the point of view of the instructor and then from the perspective of the students – and compared with each other. Building on this, the final section provides insights into the effects that training firms can have on entrepreneurship education in general.

4. Findings

In order to answer the research question of the present paper – which is how informal learning can be structured by instructors using training firms and what effects this has on the preparation of learners for later professional practice and / or self-employment – interviews with a course instructor as well as with students attending his course and engaging themselves later on within a training firm were carried out. Thus, the findings allow insights into the two perspectives of teachers and learners within entrepreneurship education via training firms.

In view of the *instructor perspective*, the results have shown that a certain level of motivation is crucial for teaching entrepreneurship in the context of a training firm. Thus, the interviewed instructor was involved in the firm by himself during his time of studies. The training firm has grown dear to his heart and it is important to him that the firm will continue to exist. He passes this spirit on to his students. In addition to his own involvement in the project and thus his role model function for the students, the instructor also has teaching experience at the university to which the training firm is linked. This seems to be an important key for evaluating the possibilities of cooperation with and the support from the home university. For explanation reasons it should be further clarified here that the design agency analyzed here is not formally part of the university, but was initiated by professors for communication design at the University of Applied Sciences HTW Berlin and has therefore often received orders from the respective professors and / or other university members in the past.

In addition to a good relationship with the home university, industry knowledge is also a crucial aspect that must be imparted to the students as part of the tutorial if not already been acquired during the course of study. Here, too, for explanation reasons I would like to add briefly that the agency was traditionally operated exclusively by students of communication design, but is currently more interdisciplinary – since there are many other tasks to be covered in addition to the actual orders, such as financing, computer technology, personnel recruitment etc. Given the variety of topics and challenges that a student association entails, it is impossible to address all of these aspects as part of a tutorial. It is therefore of crucial importance that the students participating in such an association can bring in additional knowledge from their studies or from their free time or are at least willing to acquire this knowledge on a voluntary basis beyond the tutorial. For example, you need people who are already successfully self-employed, who know how to speak to clients and who at best have already gained some founding know-how. You also need someone to take over the community interface and keep the team together.

Beside self-directed learning, the tutorial can convey the necessary knowledge about association law, business modeling and structuring as well as market analysis and the exchange with former participants and / or other founders for motivation purposes. Despite the contents of the tutorial and a high level of self-motivation of the students participating in the association, it is a challenge to take over the acquisition of orders independently. From the instructor´s perspective, it would therefore be advisable if the students could be accompanied by a mentor, e.g. a professor from the associated university. It is also important that the students manage to take the perspective of their customers and stakeholders. In addition, for the success of the association in general, business management expertise should be represented in the team and not be underestimated. With regard to the team, it is also important to establish a certain level of reliability in order to curb the fluctuation of team members. This is a particular challenge for non-university and voluntary activities in general.

Decisive advantages that students bring with them for their later professional life if they have volunteered in a student association during their studies are for example a high level of practical experience, a good network within the respective industry, knowledge on self-employed activities and relevant experience with team work as well as management experience. All in all, student start-ups offer the possibility to experiment within the safe surroundings of the home university when no real pressure is on the results. In addition, interdisciplinary work is of great relevance when students from different fields of study work together within a student association. This broadens their perspective beyond subject boundaries more than any interdisciplinary project course could.

In view of the *student perspective*, the results have shown that the respective personal motivation plays a major role in the decision to become involved in a student association. Thus, one of the students interviewed was recruited by a friend who was already participating in the tutorial, and another one was motivated by his girlfriend to volunteer. All in all, the students especially highlight the relevance of the preparing tutorial. This is were they gained knowledge on how to run a design agency and some initial management know-how. In addition, the role of the tutor who accompanied them on their way to founding their own association was of crucial importance to them. When they managed the association themselves, they realized that – even if everyone is equally involved in the agency – a clear division of roles is required. The team now has the following roles: a human resources manager who keeps the team together, a finance manager who monitors the finances, and an IT manager who is responsible for the homepage and backend. In addition, the students would want a lawyer in the team who is well versed in association law.

From the students' point of view, the greatest benefit of the engagement in the association is that on the one hand they can find new friends and on the other hand they can get in touch with potential future customers or employers. The involvement in the agency also prepares them for future self-employment. In this way, concepts tested in the agency can later be used to set up their own businesses. Both students interviewed are very interested in becoming self-employed later. One of them has already gained experience as an employee and now sees the advantages of self-employment in flexible working hours and freedom from the decisions of others, especially superiors.

By contrast, the compatibility with the course of study and with the part-time job, which must be pursued in addition to earning money is seen as a challenge. Furthermore, due to time constraints caused by their studies and / or additional jobs, everyone can devote different amounts of time to the design agency. In addition, new members have to be won. A core team of around five people is currently involved in the association, but a size of eight to sixteen would be better, so that not everyone has to be involved in processing an order, but the orders can be divided among them. In the following, from the main findings of the case study some implications for the development of course concepts for entrepreneurship education and especially training firms will be derived.

5. Conclusion

The objective of the present contribution was to find out how informal learning can be structured by instructors with the help of training firms and what effects this has on the preparation of the learners for later professional practice and / or self-employment. The findings of a case study – a communication design agency for students around University of Applied Sciences HTW Berlin – presented in the previous section have given some interesting insights. All in all, it can be said that training firms are a suitable method for informal learning in entrepreneurship education. At the same time, this method requires certain framework conditions and places special demands on teachers and learners, which are presented below.

As the study results have shown, the success of a training company depends to a large extent on the motivation that both – teachers and learners – bring to the company. In this context, trainers can, for example, open the door to possible collaborations and structural support at the home university. Furthermore, the teacher should make contact with a suitable mentor who will provide the founding team with professional support in setting up the company. In order to teach students to also take the perspectives of customers and stakeholders, it would be advisable, for example, to set up an advisory board for the firm with representatives of the respective industry.

The students participating in such an association should bring in industry knowledge and / or management competencies. If not existent, they should at least be willing to acquire this knowledge on a voluntary basis. In view of the variety of tasks, the team additionally must be willing to distribute and assign different roles. To create fairness among all team members, it would be good to set a minimum number of hours per week for the individual engagement of every team member. For student start-ups, since it is a voluntary commitment in addition to studying, a minimum team size should be available in order to ensure the successful flourishing of the company despite time constraints.

To sum up here, the results have shown a best practice example of entrepreneurial training and learning in a university context and the necessary framework condititions, which can be useful for those involved in the development of course concepts for entrepreneurship education. Overall, it can be stated that the advantages of such a commitment clearly outweigh the requirements. All in all, training companies can be seen as an expanded version of volunteering for your own good where the assignments are real but the students are still protected by the home university. This is the case, because in addition to studying, the students receive a high level of practical experience, can build up a good network within the respective branch, acquire knowledge of self-employed activities and management experience and gain relevant experience with teamwork. At the time when they finish their studies, they will already be experienced team workers and will have broadened their perspectives beyond subject boundaries. They furthermore will have made new friends and contacted potential future employers. Other alumni may feel well prepared for self-employment – even if the effects on later professional life and / or self-employment cannot be finally assessed here, since the students interviewed for the case study have not yet completed their studies.

There are some other limitations of the study, which are summarized below. First, the present work is based on a case study that consists of only three interviews. In order to prove the results of the present study, a comparison with the effects of training companies on later career choices and / or self-employment at other universities would be advisable. Since the number of training companies focusing on non-business subjects in German university hands is relatively small, training concepts from other countries could also be included in a further analysis. Second, the interviews showed that the students interviewed here already had an affinity for entrepreneurship. This is probably due to the fact, that engagement in training companies is usually voluntary and out of the studies, and therefore goes hand in hand with a high level of personal motivation. Thus, a larger study with students from different disciplines and with a different level of previous knowledge in entrepreneurship would be interesting in order to gain more insights into the effects that training companies can have on the preparation of learners for later professional practice and / or self-employment.

References

Blackwood, T.; Baty, G.; Dale, B.; Fowle, M.; Hatt, L.; Jussila, N.; Pugalis, L. (2015) "Team Academy Northumbria–Learn to Surprise Yourself", [online], *The Higher Education Academy: Compendium of effective practice in directed independent learning*, http://www.academia.edu/download/41120898/Team_Academy_Northumbria_-_learn_to_surprise_yourself_HEA_Accepted_Peer_Reviewed_Final_Version_Sep_2014.pdf, 06.04.2020.

Blumenfeldt, P. C.; Solowell, E.; Marx, R. W.; Krajcik, J. S.; Guzdial, M.; Palincsar, A. (1991) „Motivating project-based learning: sustaining the doing, supporting the learning", *Educational Psychologist*, 26 (3 &4), pp. 369-398.

Ebbers, I. (2004) *Wirtschaftsdidaktisch geleitete Unternehmenssimulation im Rahmen der Förderung von Existenzgründungen aus Hochschulen*, FGF Entrepreuneurship-Research Monographien: No. 42, Josef Eul Verlag, Köln.

Fowle, M.; Jussila, N. (2016) "The Adoption of a Finnish Learning Model in the UK", [online], *Paper presented at 11th European Conference on Innovation and Entrepreneurship: ECIE 2016*, https://www.researchgate.net/publication/318214562_Team_Academy_The_Adoption_of_a_Finnish_Learning_Model_in_the_UK, 06.04.2020.

Hills, G. E.; Hultman, C. M.; Miles M. P. (2007) "Entrepreneurial marketing and university education", in: Fayolle, A. (ed.) *Handbook of research in entrepreneurship education*, Volume 1, Edward Elgar, Cheltenham and Northampton, pp. 219-229.

Lackéus, M. and Williams Middleton, K. (2018) „Assessing experiential entrepreneurship education: key insights from five methods in use at a venture creation programme", in: Hyams-Ssekasi D, Caldwell EF (eds) *Experiential Learning for Entrepreneurship. Theoretical and Practical Perspectives on Enterprise Education*, Palgrave Macmillan: Cham, pp. 19-50.

Levie, J. (1999) „Entrepreneurship education in higher education in England. A survey.", [online], Research Gate, https://www.researchgate.net/publication/240959715_Enterprise_education_as_pedagogy, 26.03.2020.

Linton, G. and Klinton, M. (2019) „University entrepreneurship education: a design thinking approach to learning", *Jounal of Innovation and Entrepreneurship, 8 (3)*, pp. 1-11.

Manimala, M. J.; Thomas, P. (2017) „Entrepreneurship education: innovations and best practices", in: Manimala, M. J. and Thomas, P. (eds.) *Entrepreneurship education. Experiments with curriculum, pedagogy and target groups*, Springer, Wiesbaden, pp. 3-53.

Overwien, B. (2009) „Informelles Lernen. Definition und Forschungsansätze", in: Brodowski, M.; Devers-Kanoglu, U.; Overwien, B.; Rohs, M.; Salinger, S; Walser M. (eds.) *Informelles Lernen und Bildung für eine nachhaltige Entwicklung. Beiträge aus Theorie und Praxis,* Verlag Barbara Budrich, Opladen & Farmington Hills, pp. 23-34.

Pittz, T (2014) „A model for experiential entrepreneurship education", *Journal of Business and Entrepreneurship, Special Edition on Entrepreneurial Education, Fall 2014, 26 (1)*, pp. 179-192.

Sehen und ernten e.V. – Design Agency (2020), [online], https://www.sehenundernten.org/, 19.03.2020.

Steinke, I. (2012) "Gütekriterien qualitativer Forschung", in Flick, U.; von Kardorff, E.; Steinke, I. (ed.) *Qualitative Forschung. Ein Handbuch. Originalausgabe*, 11th Edition, Reinbek (Hamburg), Rowohlt Taschenbuch Verlag, pp. 319-331.

Sukavejworakit, K; Promsiri, T.; Virasa, T. (2018) "OETEL: An innovative teaching model for entrepreneurship education", *Journal of Entrepreneurship Education, 21 (2)*, pp. 1-6.

Transition of Innovation Context: Text Mining of Newspaper Editorials in Japan

Takashi Hirao[1] and Yusuke Hoshino[2]
[1]Department of Management, Faculty of Contemporary Business, Kyoto Tachibana University, Kyoto, Japan
[2]Department of Accounting and Governance, Faculty of Business Administration, Musashino University, Tokyo, Japan
hirao@tachibana-u.ac.jp
yhoshino@musashino-u.ac.jp
DOI: 10.34190/EIE.20.045

Abstract: This paper aims to elucidate how informal constraints affect formal rules to change institutions through text mining of newspaper editorials that express public opinion on innovation and of official documents of government innovation policies in Japan. By examining Science and Technology Basic Plans that included new innovation policies, this study found that the interaction of informal constraints and formal rules influenced gradual changes in public opinion from negative to positive. Moreover, it is inferable that such a change in public opinion has led to the government's initiative in the hopes of Cabinet approval rating. Consequently, changes in informal constraints also influenced the transition of contents of the Basic Plans. In short, in-house research and development (R&D) reacted swiftly to a shift of formal institutions designed by government, whereas employment practice (called permanent employment) inherent in Japan's labour market did not immediately respond to changes in formal institutional rules. This may suggest the difference in informal constraints based on the underlying cultural and historical factors.

Keywords: national innovation system, informal institution, text mining, newspaper editorial, Japan

1. Introduction

The purpose of this paper is to clarify how public opinion on innovation in Japan has changed through qualitative analysis and text mining of Japanese newspaper editorials.

Previous research has emphasised that the national character of Japan's economic institutions contributed to its economic growth after World War II. For instance, investigating industrial relations in British and Japanese factories, Dore (1973) contrasted the Japanese organizational-oriented system with the British market-oriented system and stressed on the historical peculiarities of Japan's labour market. Anchordoguy (2005) insisted that Japan declined as a result of not implementing a drastic institutional change to protect its communitarian capitalism at the time of the high-tech industry. Focusing on the relationship between government policies and firms' R&D efforts, Odagiri and Goto (1993) depicted the changes in post-war industrial policies and education system to enhance the absorptive capabilities to catch up with the West. Although the role of government policies weakened in funding R&D, active R&D activities in the private sector played an important role in Japan's industrial development. The firm's willingness to invest in R&D depended on the institutional characters such as cross-shareholdings, internal labour market system and long-term supplier relations. Stern (2003) claimed that the nature and degree of cross-shareholdings among industrial and financial institutions in Japan changed because of the financial crisis in the late 1990s. To overcome economic stagnation, Japanese government implemented institutional reforms in science and technology policy since the 1990s. Nagaoka (2009) highlighted four major changes in Japanese innovation policy. First, there was a significant increase in government R&D investment prescribed in the Science and Technology Basic Plans (S&T Basic Plans) starting in 1996 (every five-year plans). The policy aimed to improve national universities and public laboratories accounting for the bulk of scientific and technological research within the Japanese university system and to allocate a large share of the R&D budgets to promote four priority research areas: life science, information and communication, environment and nanotechnology/materials. Second, after 1999, the government encouraged industry–academia collaboration to improve industrial innovations by providing research grants targeting joint research. Third, Japanese policymakers strengthened the intellectual property rights (IPRs) protection to promote technology transfer based on the principle of university ownership of patent rights. More extensive IPR reforms were led by the Intellectual Property Policy Headquarters headed by the prime minister in the 2000s. Fourth, the policy aimed to strengthen international production and use of knowledge following the success of the U.S. innovation policy initiatives in the 1980s. Therefore, this paper aims to explore how national economic institutions change, with a focus on the role of informal institutions. The next section comprises a review of previous literature on institutional changes.

2. Literature review

Research on economic institutions that became a source of national competitive advantages has been categorised as the national innovation system (NIS). To illustrate the differences between countries in innovation performance, Nelson (1993) developed the concept of a NIS, comprising the institutions that support technical innovation that are affected by socioeconomic factors such as the firms, education system, law, politics and government. He argued that a nation's basic institutions such as national education systems and government policies should provide incentives for domestic firms to define the direction of technological development and invest in technological capabilities. He also suggested historical and cultural factors affecting such institutions; however, most research in NIS has basically focused on the changes in the formal rules of economic and social institutions. Conversely, a few studies suggest the role of informal institutional constraints in national economic performance. Focusing on cultural value systems such as collective responsibility, reciprocal obligations and honesty that have existed since pre-industrial Japan, Hill (1995) clarified that such informal constraints played an important role in the decrease in the costs of achieving cooperation and specialisation and, hence, contributed to Japan's competitive advantage in the world economy after World War II. Grzymala-Busse (2010) clarified the process of informal institutions inherited from communist states replaced, undermined and reinforced formal institutions. In terms of the relation between formal and informal constraints affecting institutional change and stability, North (1990) emphasised the effective interaction of formal rules (i.e. constitutions, laws and property rights) and informal constraints (i.e. customs, traditions and codes of behaviour). He suggested that informal constraints arising from culture would not change instantly in response to changes in formal rules because many informal constraints emerge from deep-seated cultural inheritance. Therefore, the continuing tension between the new formal rules and the existing informal constraints has important implications for path dependence of institutions.

With regard to economic policy, the NIS lacks sufficient consideration of the role of informal constraints. As North (1990) emphasised, institutions include both formal and informal constraints; thus, NIS should also include informal constraints in explaining institutional changes. There are several studies that emphasise the importance of informal institutional constraints. However, they are not sufficient to explain the effective interaction of formal and informal institutions because there is a problem with the methodology of analysing informal constraints. As North claimed, although it is difficult to directly observe informal institutional constraints, this paper attempts to explore the indirect evidence of changes in informal constraints by text mining public opinion in newspaper articles, which is reflected in as well as created by media. In this paper, newspaper editorials are considered to reflect public opinion as common knowledge among people at that time, as Neuman et al. (1992) argued that common knowledge was built through interaction between media and audience. According to their theory of media framing, the words in media not only reflect reality but also socially and culturally construct it simultaneously.

In recent years, the progress in Information Technology has led to active research using text mining of newspaper articles. Pollak et al. (2011) described the effectiveness of text mining of newspaper articles to compare ideological differences between local and international media. De Fortuny et al. (2012) stated the effectiveness of positive and negative sentiment analyses of media coverage on political issues with opinion mining in Flemish newspapers.

Therefore, this paper elucidates how Japan's informal constraints to innovation have changed after the 1980s according to changes in the formal rules of innovation policy. This paper aims to tackle this issue through qualitative analysis and text mining of newspaper editorials of *Nihon Keizai Shimbun* (Nikkei newspaper), a Japanese economic newspaper with highest readership among Japanese business persons.

3. Methods

3.1 Data collections

This paper adopted newspaper editorials as data samples for informal institutions, because newspaper editorials reflect the opinion of the publishers and allow for continuous analysis of its trend. Nikkei newspaper was selected as an information source to attempt a time series analysis of the editorials on innovation in Japan.

Searching the Nikkei online database for "innovation" that includes "technological development" as translated words of innovation in Japan presented 728 editorials published from 1981 to 2019. KH Coder (MeCab) extracted 618,292 words from the editorials. Figure 1 shows that the number of the editorials on innovation peaked in the mid-1980s and late 2010s, and that the number of the editorials declined in the late 1980s but has increased gradually since 1996.

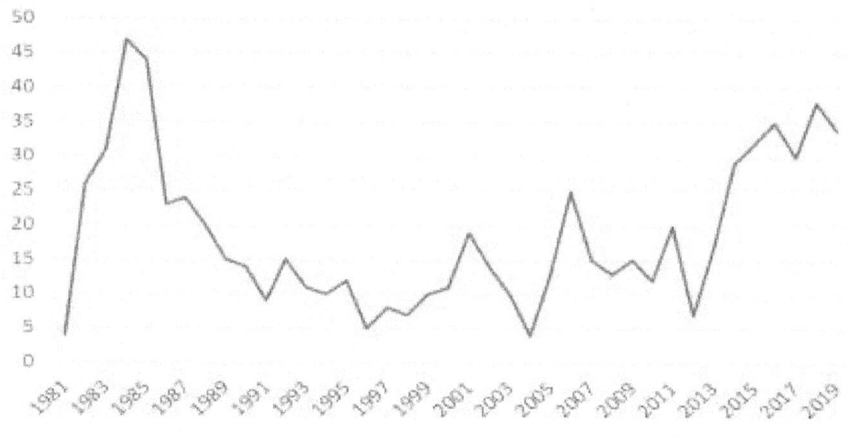

Figure 1: The number of newspaper editorials on innovation

Additionally, this paper used official documents from the S&T Basic Plans as data samples for formal institutions, because the S&T Basic Plans have been updated every five years by Japanese governments and have elaborated on the amount of government R&D investment, basic concepts, key policies and specific measures to promote innovation since 1996. Therefore, the official documents from the S&T Basic Plans can be used to conduct research on changes in formal institutional rules on innovation in Japan. KH Coder (MeCab) extracted 145,694 words from the official documents from first to fifth stages of the S&T Basic Plans from 1996 to 2020.

3.2 Data procedures

In analysing the newspaper editorials, this paper first adopted a sentiment analysis, followed by a hierarchical cluster analysis of words extracted by text mining method. The positive and negative sentiments were evaluated by reading every editorial one by one. While the editorials that expressed the disadvantages of innovation were rated as negative and −1, those that expressed the advantages of innovation were estimated to be positive and 1. Additionally, the editorials that included advantages and disadvantages of innovation were evaluated as neutral and set as 0. In recent years, text mining is widely used as a method to organise unformatted text data according to predetermined rules and to conduct a quantitative analysis, such as correlation, by extracting useful information from a large volume of text. We implemented text mining based on editorials rather than on sentence or paragraph with KH Coder (ver. 3 Alpha) and analysed hierarchical clusters of extracted words. First, words that appeared with a particularly high probability in documents where specific words and codes appeared were listed using a method of Jaccard; second, combinations of words having similar patterns were found by choosing the clustering method of Ward; third, the number of clusters were specified by observing changes in the distance coefficient by cluster agglomeration; and finally, its cluster was labelled by understanding the group of words included in each cluster. Therefore, 56 of the negative sentiment words were classified into seven clusters (see Table 1) and 59 of the positive sentiment words into nine clusters (see Table 2).

Table 1: Negative sentiment words in each cluster extracted from the newspaper editorials

Clusters	Words
industrial relations	unemployment, movement, labour union, annual wage negotiation, wage increase, union and organisation
employment	our country, investigation, labour and management, relation, improvement, employment, advanced age, labour, workshop and living
human resource development	job, human, business, environment, management, manufacturing, industry, change, capability and development
corporate innovation	society, enterprise, technology, innovation, issue, the times and response
economic policy	institution, introduction, government, policy, wage, private, economy and growth
medical insurance reform	health care, insurance, nation, consumption and reform
international economy	finance, international, US, United States, world, Japan, measures, market and influence

Table 2: Positive sentiment words in each cluster extracted from the newspaper editorials

Clusters	Words
employment	labour and employment
institutional reform	regulation, relaxation, institution, finance, reform, private and country
energy policy	electricity, measures, goal and reduction
financial reform	investment, equipment, finance and funds
automotive industry	consumption, business conditions, expansion, automobile, demand and price
service industry	company, market, competition, business, management, communication, utilisation, information and service
corporate innovation	government, industry, enterprise, Japan, technology, innovation, economy, growth, the times, response, issue, society, environment, international, policy and structure
R&D strategy	development, research, field and strategy
globalisation	world, United States, US, domestic, manufacturing, overseas and China

In analysing the S&T Basic Plans, this study conducted a qualitative analysis to extract a trend through the first to fifth S&T Basic Plans by reading each document, followed by a hierarchical cluster analysis of words extracted by text mining. Consequently, 62 of extracted words were classified into 13 clusters (see Table 3).

Table 3: Words in each cluster extracted from the S&T basic plans

Clusters	Words
research and development	technology, science, promotion, research and development
basic plan	basic and plan
economic growth	nation, society, economy, materialisation and development
response to social issues	international, our country, world, issue, response, policy and strategy
corporate innovation	enterprise, innovation and creation
industry–academia collaboration	industry–academia, collaboration, industry, region, construction and relation
institutional reform	system and reform
benefit–cost analysis	institution, fund, competition, evaluation, effect and implementation
practical use	outcome, utilisation, promotion, approach, country, activity, university and facility
human resource development	education, talent, acquisition, support, enrichment, reinforcement and function
national laboratory	national and facility
expected area	improvement, field and expectation
infrastructure development	intellectual, resource, environment, development, infrastructure and information

The next section displays each result, followed by a qualitative discussion on these results in the subsequent section.

4. Results

4.1 The newspaper editorials

Figure 2 shows the result of the sentiments analysis of the newspaper editorials. In the early 1980s, negative editorials outnumbered positive editorials; hence, the result showed negative values. Subsequently, the ratio of positive editorials on innovation in the total editorials has continued to increase. In particular, the trend has gradually become remarkable since 1996, when the first S&T Basic Plan started.

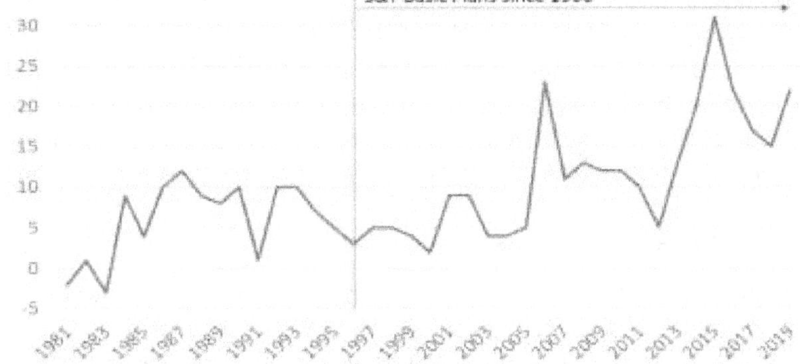

Figure 2: Sentiment analysis of words in the newspaper editorials on innovation

Data for every five years since 1981 have been illustrated in Figure 3; it indicates the trend of the appearance rate of negative words in the editorials by cluster, which shows a decline since the mid-1980s, when there were several negative editorials but an increase again in the late 2010s. The clusters of industrial relations, employment, human resource development and corporate innovation show explicit variations among them.

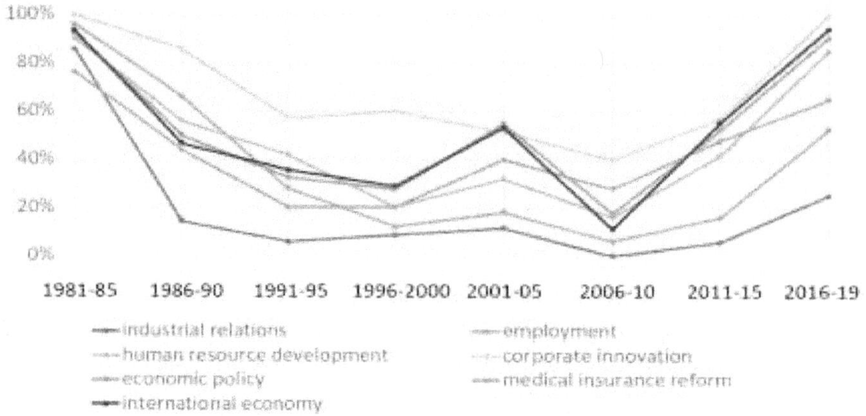

Figure 3: Appearance rate of negative words in the newspaper editorials by cluster

Based on the result of Figure 3, this study conducted a qualitative analysis of discourses of the negative editorials in the clusters where changes in its appearance rate were apparent. Table 4 shows the shift in negative discourses about innovation. The content of the negative discourses in the clusters shifted from rejection to premise of innovation.

Table 4: Shift in negative discourses about innovation in the newspaper editorials

Clusters	Publication Date	Discourses
industrial relations	13/2/1983	'It is important to avoid the deterioration of employment and unemployment caused by technological development'.
	14/8/2017	'There is also the issue that people who have become "in-house unemployment" due to the withdrawal from business in maturity phase has decreased the opportunities to improve their skills through work'.
employment	4/3/1983	'The unions, which have been actively responding to technological development, said that in order to ensure the employment and safety of workers, "the introduction of industrial robots will be carried out on the premise of agreements between labour and management based on the enhancement of beforehand consultations.'
	4/1/2018	'Employment is being threatened by rapid technological development'.
human resource development	17/7/1982	'Compared to young people, middle-aged and elderly workers who have difficulty adapting to new technologies need development of new technologies and new systems that are easy to operate to utilise their abilities and job-rotation respecting the will of the individual'.
	13/2/2018	'Improvement in employees' skills development and infiltration of the performance-based are high-priority themes for labour and management'.
corporate innovation	9/1/1982	'In addition to international friction, advanced technology has the potential to create social friction and tension in Japan'.
	29/8/2016	'What is important is a policy that supports the resurgence of those who are left behind by rapid technological development and changes in the industrial structure'.

Data for every five years since 1981 have been illustrated in Figure 4; it shows the trend of the appearance rate of positive words in the editorials by cluster. It is observed that the positive words in the clusters of energy policy and R&D strategy increased soon after the beginning of the first S&T Basic Plan, and the positive words in the clusters of employment and automotive industry increased after the second S&T Basic Plan.

4.2 The science and technology basic plans

Table 5 shows the overview of the S&T Basic Plans, including R&D budgets and priority policies. The fifth S&T Basic Plan was first formulated by Council for Science, Technology and Innovation (CSTI) headed by the prime minister. The trend indicates that the R&D budgets increased as planned, that the fourth S&T Basic Plan included reconstruction policies from the disaster caused by the Great East Japan Earthquake, and that the focus of the priority policies has shifted from enhancement of basic researches to its development and social application through the division and embodiment of research areas. The fifth S&T Basic Plan report actually addressed "In addition, in the interest of using STI (Science, Technology and Innovation) to address various economic and social issues, initiatives for industry, academia, government and relevant ministries to work together in R&D and social implementations have been advanced, such as the cross-ministerial Strategic Innovation Promotion Program" (The 5th S&T Basic Plan, p.5).

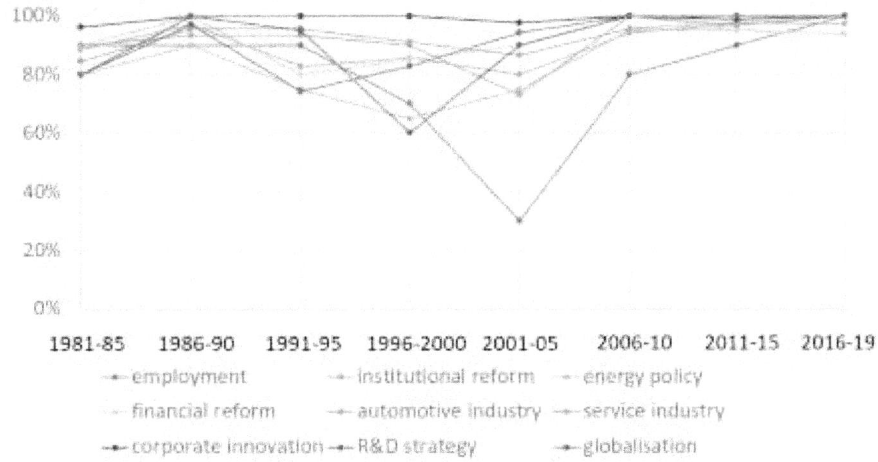

Figure 4: Appearance rate of positive words in the newspaper editorials by cluster

Table 5: Overview of the science and technology basic plans

Basic Plans	R&D Budgets	Priority Policies
1st stage 1996–2000	about 17 trillion yen	Constructing a new R&D system Realisation of a desirable R&D infrastructure (developing and improving the R&D infrastructure) Increase of R&D investment by the government Promotion of learning about S&T and formation of a national consensus
2nd stage 2001–2005	about 24 trillion yen	Strategic priority setting in S&T (life sciences, information and telecommunications, the environmental sciences, nanotechnology and materials science/technology) S&T system reforms to create and utilise excellent results (reinforcement of industrial technology and reform of industry–academia–government collaboration) Internationalisation of S&T activities
3rd stage 2006–2010	about 25 trillion yen	Strategic priority setting in S&T (priority fields: the life sciences, information and telecommunications, environmental sciences and nanotechnology/materials; and fields: energy, MONOZUKURI technology, social infrastructure and frontiers) Reforming the S&T system S&T to be supported by society and the public (promoting proactive participation of the public in S&T)
4th stage 2011–2015	about 25 trillion yen	Realisation of sustainable growth and societal development into the future (reconstruction and revival from the disaster) Key challenges to the priority issues facing Japan Enhancing basic research and human resource development Development of policy created together with society (deepening relationship between society and Science, Technology and Innovation (STI))
5th stage 2016–2020	about 26 trillion yen	Acting to create new value for the development of future industry and social transformation (realising a world-leading 'super smart society' (Society 5.0)) Key challenges to economic and social problems (promoting action from R&D to social implementation for 13 policy-oriented subjects) Developing infrastructure for STI Systematising a virtuous cycle between human resource, wisdom and funds to create innovation Deepening relationship between STI and society, improving functions to promote STI

5. Discussion

This section discusses the interaction of informal constraints and formal rules considering changes in discourses in the newspaper editorials and the transition of contents of the S&T Basic Plans in Japan. The public opinion expressed in the editorials in the 1980s was sceptical and critical of innovation in Figure 2. In particular, the tones of discourses in the editorials warned that innovation would reduce existing jobs. However, the prolonged economic stagnation and the S&T Basic Plans since the late 1990s gradually changed them. Additionally, the social impact of the S&T Basic Plan that focused on improving basic researches with a large budget was significant in Table 5 and, hence, the positive discourses in the clusters of energy and R&D strategies increased immediately in Figure 4. However, it is believed that achievements in basic research are gained over long periods of time and it is difficult to immediately create new industries and jobs. Therefore, the positive discourses in the employment cluster have increased after the focus of the S&T Basic Plan shifted to the development and social implementations of science and technology in Figure 4, because the development and social implementations could create new jobs more than basic researches. Furthermore, it is hypothesised that such a change in public opinion has resulted in the government's initiative in the hope of a Cabinet approval rating. The government that had not made significant progress in *"Abenomics"*, a macroeconomic policy launched by the Abe government in 2013, established CSTI headed by the prime minister in 2014, to promote the creation of innovation by commercialising the fruits of R&D.

6. Conclusions

In conclusion, Japan's informal constraints to innovation changed after the beginning of the S&T Basic Plan in 1996. Moreover, it includes sudden and gradual changes of informal institutional constraints. In other words, R&D practice such as in-house development reacted quickly to a shift of formal institutions designed by the government because changes in formal rules alter the basic incentive structure of an economy. However, employment practice (called permanent employment) that is deep-seated in Japan's labour market did not immediately respond to changes in formal institutional rules because social norms had been providing institutional stability. Therefore, the tone of public opinion on innovation has agreed in principle but disagreed on the details. This might suggest the difference in informal constraints based on the depth of cultural and historical factors that they have inherited. Further, with regard to the impact of informal constraints on institutional changes, first, this paper could quantitatively ascertain changes in informal constraints through text mining of newspaper editorials. Second, the informal institutions were found to be a burden that constrained or delayed institutional changes because Dore and Anchordoguy claimed that Japan's economic institutions could not change because of its cultural inheritance. Third, this paper emphasises the importance of the demand side in the diffusion of innovation. Most textbooks of innovation management focus on the management processes that enable innovation from the viewpoint of the supply side (i.e. Burgelman et al., Tidd et al. and etc.). In restructuring a NIS, however, this paper suggests that it is essential to focus not only on the supply side of innovation such as government policies and corporate R&D strategies but also on its demand side such as traditions, management thought and business practice, as Rogers (1982), who focused on social changes as a terminus for the diffusion of innovation, has argued.

This study requires further research. First, how the institutional change caused by the interaction of informal and formal constraints influences economic performance needs further study. Given that there are several variables that influence economic performance, it is necessary to arrange the variable relationships. Second, it is important to develop a research method for implementing a quantitative analysis of discourses. There are some methods that must be learned with the development of information technologies.

Acknowledgements

This paper is financially supported by JSPS KAKENHI JP16H03653.

References

Anchordoguy, M. (2005) Reprogramming Japan: The High-Tech Crisis under Communitarian Capitalism, Cornell University Press, New York.

Burgelman, R.A., Christensen, C.M. and Wheelwright, S.C. (2004) Strategic Management of Technology and Innovation (fourth edition), McGraw-Hill, New York.

De Fortuny, E.J., De Smedt, T., Martens, D. and Walter, D. (2012) "Media coverage in times of political crisis: A text mining approach", Expert Systems with Applications, Vol.39, No.14, pp.11616-11622.

Dore, R. (1973) British Factory Japanese Factory: The Origins of National Diversity in Industrial Relations, University of California Press, Berkey, Los Angeles, and Oxford.

Grzymala-Busse, A. (2010) "The Best Laid Plans: The Impact of Informal Rules on Formal Institutions in Transitional Regimes", Studies in Comparative International Development, Vol.45, pp.311-333.

Hill, C.W. (1995) "National Institutional Structures, Transaction Cost Economizing and Competitive Advantage: The Case of Japan", Organization Science, Vol.6, No.1, pp.119-131.

Nagaoka, S. (2009) "Reform of Patent System in Japan and Challenges", in National Research Council, 21st century Innovation Systems for Japan and the United States: Lessons from a Decade of Change: Report of a Symposium, The National Academies Press, Washington, D.C., pp.153-168.

Nelson, R.R. ed. (1993) National Innovation Systems: A Competitive Analysis, Oxford University Press, New York.

Neuman, W.R., Just, M.R. and Crigler, A.N. (1992) Common Knowledge: News and the Construction of Political Meaning, the University of Chicago Press, Chicago.

North, D.C. (1990) Institutions, Institutional Change and Economic Performance, Cambridge University Press, New York.

Odagiri, H. and Goto, A. (1993) "The Japanese System of Innovation: Past, Present, and Future", in Nelson, R.R. ed. National Innovation Systems: A Competitive Analysis, Oxford University Press, New York, pp.76-114.

Pollak, S., Coesemans, R., Daelemans, W. and Lavrač, N. (2011) "Detecting contrast patterns in newspaper articles by combining discourse analysis and text mining", Pragmatics, Vol.21, No.4, pp.647-683.

Rogers, E.M. (1982) Diffusion of Innovations, Free Press, New York.

Stern, R.M. ed. (2003) Japan's Economic Recovery: Commercial Policy, Monetary Policy, and Corporate Governance, Edward Elgar Publishing, Massachusetts.

Tidd, J., Bessant J. and Pavitt, K. (2001) Managing Innovation: Integrating Technological, Market and Organizational Change (second edition), John Wiley & Sons, Hoboken.

Slipping Into Service? Exploring Imbrications and Collaborative Boundary Work in an Ambulatory Co-Design Setting

Adeline Hvidsten and Ranvir Rai
Kristiania University College, Oslo, Norway
Adeline.Hvidsten@kristiania.no
Ranvir.Rai@kristiania.no
DOI: 10.34190/EIE.20.103

Abstract: In this paper, we present a qualitative case study of co-design in the ambulatory services of two Norwegian municipalities, following the trial period of the telepresence robot AV1. Norwegian public health care services are facing vast challenges, due to an elderly and more chronically ill population. This means that the sector has to do more with less, and developing more and better technologies has been cast as part of a potential solution However, services are hard to predict and control, and as such there is a need to understand the dynamics happening in design and delivery, or "design as delivery" of services. Drawing on semi-structured interviews we attempt to better understand how seemingly "finished" technologies are co-designed by local users in service delivery. We explore how the concept of imbrications as introduced by Leonardi (2011) can help us understand how human and material agencies are imbricated in a specific context of public health care. More specifically, we shed light on the dynamics between technology and users in the case of the AV1 trial and relate it to the theoretical domain of boundary work. Our study contributes to the growing field of designing for service and encourage further research into how co-design processes shape – and are shaped by – the reconfiguration of existing relationships amongst occupational groups in public services.

Keywords: co-design, imbrication, boundary work, incompleteness, designing for service, health care

1. Introduction

Norwegian public health care is increasingly reliant on developing and integrating new technologies, aimed at improving health for citizens, as well as making health services more sustainable (Ministry of Health and Care Services, 2012). Developing more and better technologies has been argued to provide better treatment, quality, safety, and efficient use of resources in Norwegian health care (Norwegian Directorate of Health, 2015). Often, health care innovations are never implemented into practice (Andreassen, Kjekshus, & Tjora, 2015), and profession-related and industrial characteristics, in addition to governmental resolutions, regulations and laws affects local service provider's ability to adopt and utilize innovations (La Rocca, 2018). Allen (2013, p. 461) recognizes context as key to the success (or otherwise) of health care intervention: novel technologies do not "slip into" practice, but depends on a sensitivity towards the overall work setting. Disregarding the highly professionalized and politically charged nature of health care, with its "interests, conflict, and the role of institutions," means not understanding how innovations become part of daily practice (Nicolini, 2009, p. 2). As a result, health care services face major challenges in adapting innovation and change in knowledge, technology, organization and economy, making the sector extremely relevant for studying innovation processes (Hoholm, La Rocca, & Aanestad, 2018, p. 2).

In this paper, we present the trial of the AV1 robot, which – contrary to what we know about health care innovation – seemed to do just that: in first glance, "slipping into" the ambulatory service of two Norwegian municipalities – without any substantial technological adjustments. However, is it ever so simple? This paper reflects on the implementation and use of a seemingly "inflexible" technology in an ambulatory service setting. Our discussion aims at understanding the role of technologies and explore how the concept of "imbrications" might be useful to understand the co-design of service in a contemporary public service setting. Our findings suggest that when technology is "inflexible" – new routines must accommodate desired changes, in which relationships between occupational groups must be reconfigured, thus realigning existing boundaries as part of the service offering.

The article is organized as follows. Following this introduction, section 2 describes our theoretical framework of reference. Section 3 illustrates our methodology. Section 4 contains our findings, which are discussed and concluded in Section 5.

2. Theory

We apply both contemporary service design theory – from a practice-based perspective; and concepts from organizational studies to theorize the observed phenomenon conducted in our case study.

2.1 The open-endedness of service delivery: co-design in practice

Services are intangible and invisible and co-designed in practice, and as such impossible to control and pre-determine (Meroni & Sangiorgi, 2011). We never know how a particular service interaction will unfold before it has happened. Britton (2017, p. 34) argues that it is time to see co-design as less than a phase or chosen design technique, and more as "the recognition of shared agency or collaboration between those involved in the initial and on-going configuration of the service or product in question" making it "an analytical concept that interrogates the extent to which participants in a design process (including beneficiaries) are able to influence what is being conceived, developed and delivered to their purported benefit(s)". Such an approach also moves the focus of design from "design things", to the generative relationships established in the design process, and the transfer of skills and capacities to users (Björgvinsson, Ehn, & Hillgren, 2012; Britton, 2017; Burns, Cottam, Vanstone, & Winhann, 2006). Indeed, the term "designing" indicates "an ongoing activity to which designers can engage with and affect during their intervention .... Which recalls the existence of pre and post development" (Sangiorgi & Prendiville, 2017, pp. 251-252). Britton (2017) argues, such a perspective on co-design sees the constraint of adaptability or influence/partake in "design-after-design", as a threat to participation.

In terms of users co-designing or re-designing technologies and other artefacts in use though domesticating or re-proposing them is not necessarily a novel idea. We know that artefacts take on different meaning for different people, and in design studies (with influence from Science and Technology Studies) this has been characterized as designs-in-practice (Kimbell, 2009) or design "after design" (Redström, 2008). This means extend the design-process into the arena of use and re-conceptualizes who can and does influence this process. Manzini (2015) argues that everybody can, and does, design. For him, co-design is a process influenced by heterogenous actors at different points in time. However, few studies in the field of designing for service focus on the dynamic relationship between technology and service delivery.

2.1.1 Imbrications between human and material agencies

In organizational studies, a strand of research has focused on the role of technology for organizing through being a constitutive element of routines. Leonardi (2011, p. 514) applies the concepts of *affordances* and *constraints* to explore how what he calls an *imbrication* of human and material agencies produces "either a new routine, or a new technology" in organizations. The concept of affordances has been applied to understand the relationship between environments and occupants – especially concerning form and function (Maier, Fadel, & Battisto, 2009) connecting practice with perception (Fayard & Weeks, 2007). Affordances have been described as relationships between a person and an object, invitations for action: a chair for example affords sitting, but not computing.

Affordances were first introduced by the psychologist Gibson (1966, 1979) in an effort to explain how the material environment of an animal consisted of action possibilities. Krippendorff (1995, p. 10) sees it as such: "Artifacts always afford many meanings [...] the designer can do no more than provide the affordance for users' meaningful involvement". Leonardi (2011) follows a relational approach to affordances suggested by for example Hutchby (2001). He argues that when people interact with technology, they try to unite their own goals with the affordances of the technology (which are relational- and as such unique to the specific person). This means that the person, depending if she sees affordances or constraints, decides how to imbricate human and material agencies. As the relational affordances, constraints are not properties of the technology, but a perception of the individual, and arise due to shifting goals or their own inability to achieve the goal with the technology.

2.1.2 Collaborative boundary work amongst occupational groups

As new technologies are introduced to a service setting , demands of new forms for organizing across disciplines may emerge due to changes in the 'dynamics of practices' (Nicolini, 2006). This is especially relevant for health care settings with its highly professionalized and politically charged nature, thus requiring a sensitivity towards the overall work setting. Consequently, new ways of working in health care not only develop from the specific functioning of a new technology (Barley, 1986), but also from the need to simultaneously meet the requirements of different disciplines and specialties. As such, new or substantially altered practices include efforts across boundaries – often described as "boundary work" (Gieryn, 1983), in which boundaries between different groups are shifted or maintained.

A recent definition from Langley et al., 2019 (p. 4), defines boundary work as: "purposeful individual and collective effort to influence the social, symbolic, material and temporal boundaries, demarcations and distinctions affecting groups, occupations and organizations". The definition provides a processual interpretation, in which boundaries are considered as "continually becoming" (Langley & Tsoukas, 2017) and harmonizes well with our perspective of co-design and open-endedness of service delivery. More specifically, we address collaborative boundary work in this paper, as existing groups develop mutual understanding, negotiate who will do what and utilize boundaries as "junctures" to enable collaboration amongst themselves (Quick & Feldman, 2014). Based on this discussion, we explore how the notion of imbrication can help us conceptualize the dynamic relationship between "finished" technologies and inherently "unfinished" services as co-design in service delivery amongst different occupational groups. Hence, we advance the following research question: How are co-design processes shaped – and shaped by – material artifacts and collaborative boundary work in a public health care setting?

3. Methods

In this section of the paper we introduce the case study, as well as the methods applied in the data collection. We also give a brief overview of the qualitative analysis. The next section presents the findings from the study.

3.1 The AV1 robot

We present a qualitative case study of the trial period of a telepresence robot (AV1) in the ambulatory services of two Norwegian municipalities. AV1 was originally designed for preventing isolation amongst long-term sick children, making it possible for them to participate in school activities and interact with friends via video and audio. In this case study, the robot was introduced to facilitate communication between ambulance personnel and doctors involved in ambulatory settings. Through AV1 and associated tablets, doctors could communicate directly with on-site ambulance personnel, or the patient in need of medical treatment. In this way, doctors could guide ambulance staff through examinations and treatment of the patient, make sure the patient was transferred to the most appropriate place for treatment, and even conduct video consultations directly with the patient. The robot could be carried by ambulance workers, and the doctor could make it turn its head 180 degrees.

3.2 Data collection

This qualitative study addresses the challenges of ambulance workers and doctors during emergency callouts, both with and without AV1, through semi-structured interviews conducted by a team of researchers, including two master students (from Norwegian University of Life Sciences), in autumn 2018. In particular, the study focused on specific efforts in which the respondents applied the AV1 technology to suit their specific needs. Table 1 presents an overview of the research material. 12 interviews were carried out with employees from the two municipalities of Røros and Hotølen, located in the Norwegian county of Trøndelag. Among these, seven were ambulance staff (nurses, paramedics and ambulance workers), two doctors and an intern in the emergency room (all referred to as doctors), one project manager and one section manager for the ambulance. Eight out of twelve informants had first-hand experience with AV1. The project manager, the section manager, as well as two of the ambulance workers had not used the robot first-hand. Interviews were recorded, transcribed in full and translated.

Table 1: Overview of data

Respondents	#
Doctor	2
Intern	1
Ambulance paramedic	2
Ambulance nurse	1
Ambulance personnel	4
Project manager	1
Section manager	1
Total	**12**

3.3 Data analysis

The study generated detailed insights on the challenges facing ambulatory and emergency room services, as well as several aspects related to ongoing process of adjustment between the AV1 technology and practice. The aim of data analysis was to achieve a better understanding of how AV1 was adopted and later re-interpreted in the various ambulatory practices. Data was analyzed through open coding of the interview transcripts, identifying emergent categories (Corbin & Strauss, 1990). Accordingly, various themes that emerged were emphasized. Moreover, specific text segments from the interviews were compared by coding and retrieving data.

As the results are indicative of changes in emerging practice, the findings below are presented as unfolding events transcending occupational boundaries in the ambulatory service.

4. Slipping into service? Findings from the case study

The municipalities in the study were facing a local lack of doctors and were also involved in a project with funding for developing new ICT-solutions. The project leader had seen the AV-1 robot in a TV-commercial, where it was promoted for its original use: connecting long-term sick children with friends and classmates. However, further noticing that is was being tested at the regional hospital, he saw potential for the ambulatory services in his municipality. They contacted the supplier who had not envisioned this use for the robot but was open for the idea. The robot was given new "clothes" in yellow and green, and the words "DOCTOR" (lege) on the front (Figure 1 below).

Figure 1: The AV1 representing "the doctor" in ambulatory service (Photo: Nils Kåre Nesvold)

4.1 Three-way communication

No emergency callouts are identical; however, it is possible to identify some general steps repeated in most callouts. For the ambulance these are the alarm going off, callout, patient retrieval, conferring, transport and evaluation. For the doctor in the emergency, it is the alarm going off, awaiting the assignment, getting updates from the emergency communication center (ECC), the evaluation of the patient and deciding the treatment, registering and the arrival of the patient. This is summarized in Figure 2 below.

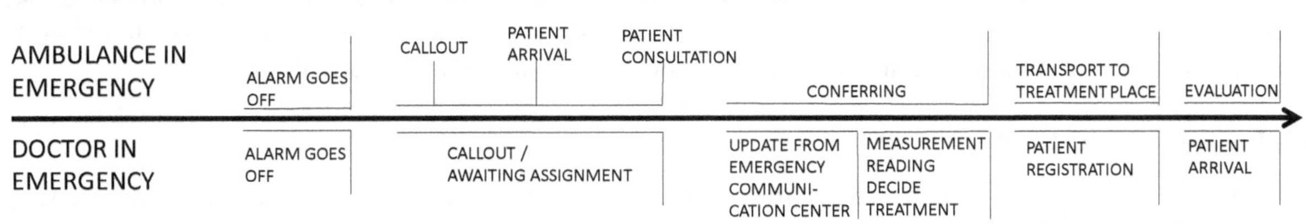

Figure 2: Identified phases in emergency callouts for ambulance and doctors

AV1 was first used in the "conferring phase" (Figure 2), where the location of treatment and decision of further treatment was decided. Ambulance workers communicated with the doctors at the emergency communications center via the emergency communication network (over radio). Whereas over the radio, the communication was two-way, using the AV1, ambulance personnel, physicians and patients could communicate directly using both audio and video.

If it was decided to use AV1, the doctor connected to an application on a tablet and as such see and hear everything the robot saw and heard through the AV1 application. The doctor was then able to speak directly with the ambulance staff and the patient, giving the doctor a better foundation to decide further treatment for the patient. In rural Norway, there are long distances between homes, hospitals and emergency rooms. Ambulance personnel talked about the long travel routes and believed AV1 prevented unnecessary trips on often-icy roads:

if we drive in the direction of the local emergency room (Røros), for the patient to see the doctor, then after the examination he says "No, sorry, here you have to drive to the hospital (St. Olavs)", we have wasted 70-80 km, and it is quite a few minutes' drive in poor winter conditions ... So, if you have the AV1 you might make a faster decision, as the doctor can make the examination using us, and the patient can be driven directly to the hospital.

An ambulance worker said that in the situations where they are inexperienced, the doctor could guide them using the AV1. It was reported that in all the cases where AV1 is used, the doctor has assisted the ambulance staff in conducting examinations. In one situation, the ambulance personnel placed the robot so the doctor could see the face of the patient while putting pressure on his/her stomach: "The doctor could then see how much pain the patient was experiencing. In this situation we ended up driving in the direction of the hospital", an ambulance worker said.

Doctors in the study said that being able to see and talk with the patient makes a pretty big difference from communicating over the emergency radio network, opening the possibilities for better communication between health professionals involved. A doctor describes a situation where "a patient was confused. It was useful to see the patient myself, and it probably influenced what I chose to do in this situation".

4.2 Within the formal requirements

All data exchanged was encrypted, and ongoing video transfers safe from outside retrieval, which meant the robot was approved as communication device in the health sector without any technical redesign. To use the robot, doctors connected via the tablet – the robot was always switched on in the ambulance.

AV1 could not substitute radio communications over the emergency communication network, which recorded and documented the interactions. An ambulance worker stated that "If you call up the ECC [using radio], it actually records. You can go back and examine what has been said. Like, "you said you would give this and that [in reference to medication]". So, it is the foundation." This meant that the AV1 was an add-on, and that even when they used it for communication, they later had to document the conversation on the radio.

Ambulance worker: The problem is that you cannot use the AV1 without the logged radio, because it has to be logged. It does not help that you say, "But the doctor said that...", because the doctors can say that they did not say that. So, we have to use both, and log decisions over the emergency network radio. We did this the last time we used AV1 as well. We made decisions using the AV1, but I called it in and logged it: "Yes, what did you tell me over AV1?" and so forth (ambulance worker).

When the ambulance personnel contacted the doctor, they would jointly decide whether to connect AV1 or use the traditional emergency radio. One upside with using the AV1 is that since a typical consultation would take around 10 minutes, the radio would be free for other emergency calls. And, when they later used the radio to log the consultation decisions were already made, making the use of the radio more efficient.

4.3 Inviting the doctor in

Some informants described that challenges arising from ambulance workers simply explaining and describing what they see, and what utility AV1 brings to those situations where it is difficult to recount and explain the patient's condition. Even though stating that health care professionals understood each other "quite well", a doctor in the study also found that "often the information you get from the ambulance personnel can be a somewhat unspecific, and many times you get a subjective opinion".

However, some ambulance personnel were hesitant to what degree they wanted to "invite" the doctors into the ambulance using video. Some were afraid of being surveilled by doctors. Ambulance personnel reflected that:

There are of course always discussions around "is it not enough to use the radio?" in communication with the doctor. It's the doctor, he is part of the team around the patient, ensuring the best possible care. Many become defensive right away, I believe they afraid of their reputation. It's not enough that *we* say what *we* see to the doctor. People become very defensive. For the better of the patient, I believe that if there so are 10 cameras there, we have a job to do anyway. We are there so that the patient gets the best possible care with the resources we have. A lot of people had that reaction when the AV1 came. Like, "hello, it should be sufficient that we tell them" – it was a big discussion... It's about not being afraid to make mistakes [original verbal emphasis].

When reflection on the usefulness of AV1 for other health care personnel, an ambulance further though that "if doctors get AV1 on their desk in the municipalities, I think there are many doctors who will question their competency. Yes, get defensive..." While some doctors express a trust in what is communicated by the ambulance personnel via phone, seeing the video as a nice supplement, the worries are not completely unwarranted. A doctor in the study stated that "if there are any examinations happening in the ambulance, I can see exactly how they are doing, what kind of examination technique they have, and then I can see if I can trust their assessment or not". However, the doctor further added that this would also allow for "possibly giving advice on how they can do such a study".

For patients, however, ambulance workers believed that the "presence" of the doctor reassured them if they were in a state to notice it: "They thought it was exciting. A bit odd maybe. It is reassuring to have the doctor on the other side of the AV1. The word "doctor" [written on the robot] builds trust. It is a bit like, "oh wow, is (s)he in the car?". So, I sense it makes them feel even more safe". Simultaneously, the often-adult patients found the design a bit weird – the doctor saw them, but they only saw a robot designed to represent a child avatar. One some occasions, patients were asked to speak to the robot but felt more comfortable with speaking with the ambulance personnel instead.

4.4 Transforming the services and routines

Several of the ambulance workers believe that the robot increases the quality of treatment they provide to patients. Doctors can guide them through examinations, which in turn increased the quality of their work. Among other things, it could "provide proper examination, and thus provide better treatment" according to an ambulance worker. The project manager believed that the robot provided a good basis for decision-making, leading to increased quality of work performed and increased safety for the patient.

Indeed, all doctors believed AV1 increased the quality of their basis for decision making, and that patients received safer and better treatment. While some doctors were unsure that if robot would increase the quality of communication between them and the ambulance staff, one of the doctors claimed that:

> *communication is quite straightforward, but once I have seen the patient, I get a lot of information and can clarify questions I want to ask. And it can probably improve communication and give me a better understanding of the situation the patient and the ambulance staff are facing.*

In summary, the benefit of the AV1 was notable, and most ambulance workers and doctors, as well as the project manager, felt secure in being able to get direct feedback on the job that is done correctly or not. Further, all ambulance workers would recommend other municipalities to use AV1. However, certain adaptations of the product were necessary for the municipalities to keep using the solution in the future. The project manager emphasized that it is was necessary that the technology needs several improvements (battery indicator, two-way communication and better sound) to function optimally. However, the project manager was unsure if the producer would make the necessary changes "I think they need to see that there are money in the [health care] system", he says, and also underlines that there is a gap in the market here, if the producer is able to act fast.

5. Discussion and conclusion

Our findings reveal that dealing with "finished" technology – such as AV1 in this case; requires flexible routines amongst occupational groups in order to accommodate and co-design necessary change in practice. The case demonstrates how ambulance personnel and doctors have interacted with the robot, in which they attempt to unite their own goals with the affordances of the technology. Interestingly, the robot facilitated both new action possibilities in terms of collaboration and decision making, whilst simultaneously creating some constraints in terms of communication as well. Consequently, it is clear from the findings that even though the AV1 can "slip into" practice following the formal requirements, it also triggered both positive and negative consequences for the ambulatory setting. As such, imbrication exemplifies the mutual generativity of technologies and practices; and directs our attention towards the agencies involved in changing practice.

By focusing on the boundaries "at work" – our study reveals how various occupational groups attempt to collaborate in new ways. Since the municipalities were not able substantially change the technology itself, it meant that their routines needed to be modified in accordance to the goals within the ambulatory setting. Consequently, the introduction of the telepresence robot triggered to some extend a reconfiguration of the relationship between ambulance personnel and doctors as it required new forms of collaborative work. As mentioned by some of the ambulance workers their voices were now "not sufficient" since the doctors were suddenly digitally present in the ambulatory setting through the robot, thus exposing both competence and practice amongst ambulance staff as an indirect consequence of emerging practice. Such reconfiguration between occupational groups or domains of knowledge is also reflected in prior studies, i. e. the case study of a pharmacy robot implementation by Barret et al. (2012) and the study of new technology in an operating room by Lindberg et al. (2017). Both studies emphasize the role of materiality in which boundaries amongst occupations needed to be realigned to enable collaboration (Langley et al., 2019).

Moreover, our findings illustrate that co-design indeed can be seen as changing practices, not necessarily adjusting the technology, but adjusting it to local practice. Thus, in this case study we see how municipalities exploit the incomplete nature of services by reconfiguring their routines and ways of collaboration. Hence, this study reflects upon the complexity in co-designing improved health care service, with particular attention towards the peculiarities that are evident in an ambulatory service setting. Our study contributes to the growing field of designing for service and to encourage further research into how co-design processes shape – and are shaped by – the reconfiguration of existing relationships amongst occupational groups in public services.

References

Allen, D. (2013). "Understanding Context for Quality Improvement: Artefacts, Affordances and Socio-Material Infrastructure". *Health:, 17*, 460-477.

Andreassen, H. K., Kjekshus, L. E., & Tjora, A. (2015). "Survival of the Project: A Case Study of ICT innovation in Health Care". *Social Science & Medicine, 132*, 62–69.

Barley, S. R. (1986). "Technology as an Occasion for Structuring: Evidence from Observations of CT Scanners and the Social Order of Radiology Departments". *Administrative Science Quarterly, 31*(1), 78-108. doi:10.2307/2392767

Barrett, M., Oborn, E., Orlikowski, W. J., & Yates, J. (2012). "Reconfiguring Boundary Relations: Robotic Innovations in Pharmacy Work". *Organization Science, 23*(5), 1448-1466. doi:10.1287/orsc.1100.0639

Björgvinsson, E., Ehn, P., & Hillgren, P.-A. (2012). "Agonistic Participatory Design: Working with Marginalised Social Movements". *CoDesign, 8*(2-3), 127-144.

Britton, G. M. (2017). *Co-Design and Social Innovation: Connections, Tensions and Opportunities*. New York, New York,London, England: Routledge.

Burns, C., Cottam, H., Vanstone, C., & Winhann, J. (2006). Transformation Design: RED PAPER 02. In. London, UK: Design Council.

Corbin, J. M., & Strauss, A. (1990). "Grounded Theory Research: Procedures, Canons, and Evaluative Criteria". *Qualitative Sociology, 13*(1), 3-21. doi:10.1007/bf00988593

Fayard, A.-L., & Weeks, J. (2007). "Photocopiers and Water-Coolers: The Affordances of Informal Interaction". *Organization Studies, 28*(5), 605-634.

Gibson, *J. J.* (1966). The Senses Considered as Perceptual Systems. In. Boston: Houghton Mifflin.

Gibson, J. J. (1979). The Ecological Approach to Visual Perception. In. Boston: Houghton Mifflin.

Gieryn, T. F. (1983). "Boundary-Work and the Demarcation of Science from Non-Science: Strains and Interests in Professional Ideologies of Scientists". *American Sociological Review, 48*(6), 781-795. doi:10.2307/2095325

Ministry of Health and Care Services. (2012). *Én Innbygger - Én Journal: Digitale Tjenester i Helse- og Omsorgssektoren*. (Meld. St. 9 (2012-2013)). Oslo: Ministry of Health and Care Services

Norwegian Directorate of Health. (2015). *Nasjonale Mål og Prioriteringer på Helse- og Omsorgsområdet i 2015*. (IS-1/2015).

Hoholm, T., La Rocca, A., & Aanestad, M. (2018). "Introduction: Controversies in Healthcare Innovation - Service, Technology and Organization". In T. Hoholm, A. La Rocca, & M. Aanestad (Eds.), *Controversies in Health Care Innovation. Service, Technology and Organization* (pp. 1-17). Oslo: Palgrave Macmillan.

Hutchby, I. (2001). "Technologies, Texts and Affordances". *Sociology, 35*(2), 441-456.

Kimbell, L. (2009). *Beyond Design Thinking: Design-as-Practice and Designs-in-Practice.* Paper presented at the CRESC Conference, Manchester, UK.

Kimbell, L., & Blomberg, J. (2017). "The Object of Service Design". In D. Sangiorgi & A. Prendiville (Eds.), *Designing for Service. Key Issues and New Directions* (pp. 81-92). London: Bloomsbury Academic.

Krippendorff, K. (1995). "Redesigning Design; An Invitation to a Responsible Future". *Departmental Papers (ASC)*, 46.

La Rocca, A. (2018). "Networked Innovation in Healthcare: Literature Review and Research Agenda on the Interplay of Inner and Outer Contexts of Innovation". In T. Hoholm, A. La Rocca, & M. Aanestad (Eds.), *Controversies in Health Care Innovation.Service, Technology and Organization* (pp. 247-277). Oslo: Palgrave Macmillan.

Langley, A., & Tsoukas, H. (2017). *The Sage Handbook of Process Organization Studies*: Sage.

Leonardi, P. M. (2011). "When Flexible Routines Meet Flexible Technologies: Affordance, Constraint, and the Imbrication of Human and Material Agencies". *MIS Quarterly*, 147-167.

Lindberg, K., Walter, L., & Raviola, E. (2017). "Performing Boundary Work: The Emergence of a New Practice in a Hybrid Operating Room". *Social Science & Medicine, 182*, 81-88. doi:10.1016/j.socscimed.2017.04.021

Maier, J. R. A., Fadel, G. M., & Battisto, D. G. (2009). "An Affordance-Based Approach to Architectural Theory, Design, and Practice". *Design Studies, 30*, 393-414. doi:10.1016/j.destud.2009.01.002

Meroni, A., & Sangiorgi, D. (2011). *Design for Services*. Aldershot: Gower.

Nicolini, D. (2006). "The Work to Make Telemedicine Work: A Social and Articulative View". *Soc Sci Med. 62*(11), 2754-2767. doi:10.1016/j.socscimed.2005.11.001

Nicolini, D. (2009). "Medical Innovation as a Process of Translation: a Case from the Field of Telemedicine". *British Journal of Management, 21*, 1011-1026. doi:10.1111/j.1467-8551.2008.00627.x

Quick, K. S., & Feldman, M. S. (2014). "Boundaries as Junctures: Collaborative Boundary Work for Building Efficient Resilience". *Journal of Public Administration Research and Theory, 24*(3), 673-695.

Redström, J. (2008). "RE: Definitions of Use". *Design Studies, 29*(4), 410–423.

Sangiorgi, D., & Prendiville, A. (2017). "Conclusions". In D. Sangiorgi & A. Prendiville (Eds.), *Designing for Service.Key Issues and New Directions* (pp. 251-255). London: Bloomsbury Academic.

Photo: https://nearadio.no/tydal-vil-ha-enda-en-lege/19.18915

Assessing the Impact of Entrepreneurship Education on Entrepreneurial Beliefs and Conceptualizations

Alexandros Kakouris[1], Viviana Molina[2] and Panagiotis Liargovas[1]
[1]Sustainable Development and Entrepreneurship Lab., Department of Economics, University of Peloponnese, Greece
[2]Universidad Autónoma de Manizales, Antigua Estación del Ferrocarril. Manizales, Caldas, Colombia
akakouris@uop.gr
DOI: 10.34190/EIE.20.104

Abstract: One of the least explored domains in entrepreneurship education is the influence of teaching, of various kinds, on the alteration of attitude. This stream of research has been largely based on self-efficacy studies and the Theory of Planned Behaviour aiming to explain the determination of the entrepreneurial intention. Beyond these studies, the recently developed ASKO framework (Ability, Support, Knowledge, Opportunity) employs dialectics to classify entrepreneurial conceptualizations based on beliefs for the success factors of a new business. Four complementary conceptualizations (styles) emerge corresponding to habitual entrepreneurs, social venturing or corporate venturing, self-employment and knowledge-intensive start-ups for growth. Apart from the intention of graduates to establish new firms, the previous conceptualizations inform for the type of venture prospective entrepreneurs are inclined to. Based on entrepreneurship education provided to graduates in the Manizales Más entrepreneurial ecosystem in Colombia, the present study implements the ASKO framework to illustrate and discuss the influence of different instruction and content on perception shifts. The analysis includes the educators' personal beliefs, the teaching approach and the content of the course. Inter-comparisons between different courses and educators are consistently developed and discussed. The results indicate that both the educator's entrepreneurial beliefs (ASKO style) and the content of the course impact the learning outcome. Implications mostly pertain to the effective design of entrepreneurial courses and the assessment of programmes associated with educational policies and economic perspectives.

Keywords: entrepreneurship education, entrepreneurial instruction, entrepreneurial success beliefs, ASKO typology, entrepreneurial ecosystems, Manizales Más

1. Introduction

The encouragement of youth entrepreneurship has nowadays become an imperative demand for economic development and social cohesion. The support of youth entrepreneurs is usually provided through entrepreneurship education in various settings (e.g. Liñán 2007) or through the development of entrepreneurial ecosystems of many forms (e.g. Acs et al. 2017, Isenberg 2010) where prospective or novice entrepreneurs are able to start initiatives from the scratch. Walter and Block (2016) suggest that entrepreneurship education becomes more important for developing countries where youth entrepreneurs are asked to operate in entrepreneurially hostile environments. Nonetheless, the impact of entrepreneurial courses has to be interpreted and assessed more systematically in order to justify the envisaged role of education in these environments. The entrepreneurial ecosystem of Manizales Más in Colombia (Molina and Maya 2018) provides systematic entrepreneurship education as a part of its activity. Hence, the research question for the present study is how different instruction and different educators' beliefs shape the learning outcome within the ecosystem?

'Manizales Más' is a public-private-academic alliance that began with thirteen institutions working together to promote the development of the entrepreneurial ecosystem in the city of Manizales in Colombia. The main goal is to support economic development and to allow business ventures of all sizes and ages to grow more rapidly. Within the main purposes of this ecosystem is knowledgeable and intelligent action to transform the economic conditions of the city (Molina 2017). This structure is operating since 2012 and it has created various programmes that have improved the collaboration amongst diverse agents. Some of these programmes provide an emphasis on education like: *Addventure Más*, *Startup Más*, and *Entrepreneurship Route*. Each of the programmes has different objectives and target audiences. For the present research, data were collected from 'Entrepreneurship Route', a program providing six courses that have become the space for experiential learning. Students are encouraged to create new companies, propose new products, and the most important part, to build a functioning prototype to test their ideas. So far, over 3000 students from different disciplines and six Manizales universities have participated in the courses. Therefore, Manizales Más is a rich source of inclusive entrepreneurship education in Colombia which offers the possibility to study the impact of relevant multi-perspective teaching on learners' entrepreneurial conceptualizations and beliefs and accordingly, on their entrepreneurial attitude.

The present research builds upon the ASKO framework (Kakouris 2018, 2019) which maps the impact of entrepreneurship education, or other interventions, on either personal or collective (i.e. balanced for a group) beliefs for the importance of various entrepreneurial factors regarding the success of a new firm. The research question that triggers the implementation of ASKO is "how two different courses' outcome on personal beliefs can be mapped and compared independently of the specific content and methods followed by the educators?" Beliefs, an under-researched topic in entrepreneurship (Krueger 2007), are known to be cognitive structures which interweave with knowledge in the formation of cognitive schemes. Therefore, they are fundamental structures for the emergence, or alteration, of entrepreneurial conceptualisations that is a crucial learning objective of entrepreneurship education. ASKO beliefs are different than the common entrepreneurial self-efficacy beliefs (e.g. McGee et al 2009, Zhao, Seibert and Hills 2005) which are often measured before and after entrepreneurial instruction. Nonetheless, they can operate in a similar manner, and complementary to self-efficacy (Kakouris 2008, 2011), towards the formation of intentions and, more generally, the influence of the entrepreneurial attitude of trainees. In complement, different ASKO-type ventures are scored by the trainees before and after the semestral courses to examine their consistency with the emergent ASKO representation. Further, entrepreneurial motives (Shane, Locke and Collins 2003) and their change along with entrepreneurial intention (Thompson 2009) are examined. In this way, the analysis becomes more precise by not merely interpreting ASKO shifts but also connecting them with other relevant entrepreneurial constructs affected by the instruction.

The rest of the article is organised as follows. The minimal ASKO configuration is briefly introduced in the following section. Then, the methodology of the empirical research is presented and the results are illustrated and discussed. Conclusions are derived in the last part of the article.

2. The ASKO framework

The ASKO configuration assembles entrepreneurial factors relevant to Ability (A), Support (S), Knowledge (K) and Opportunity (O) in a two dimensional framework (Figure 1).

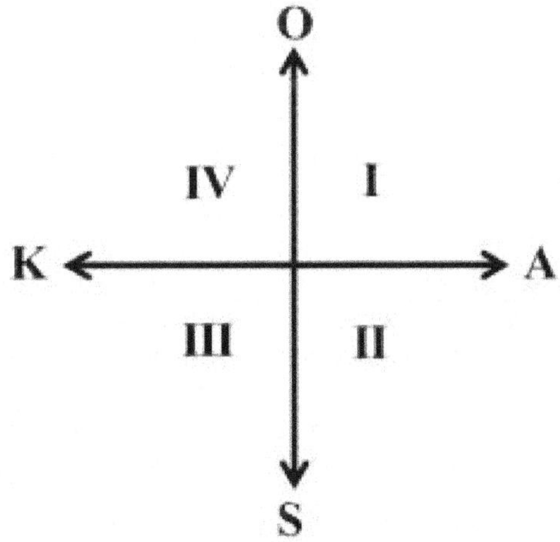

Figure 1: The ASKO framework. Adapted from Kakouris (2019).

The human dimension (A–K) deploys ability and knowledge as dialectically opposed poles of a continuum pertaining to personal resources of an individual in their entrepreneurial decision making. Dialectical opposition implies that the more an individual relies on knowledge the more s/he underestimates ability and the opposite. This does not mean that the individual lacks knowledge or abilities but the ASKO approach and questionnaire seeks the pole that is predominant in her personal entrepreneurial decisions and motivation. Each pole is decomposed in several entrepreneurial factors with variant importance, per individual, for the success of a new business initiative. Certainly, the importance of each pole may be different for different type initiatives, but the ASKO framework seeks a general (trait-like) tendency of the person to respond to entrepreneurial situations. Hence, ASKO aims to describe a personal 'entrepreneurial style' based on personal beliefs for factors which affect the success of new businesses. An analogous description holds for the environmental dimension (O–S) where opportunity is opposed to support both determined by factors rooted to the business environment. Since all these factors are hardly known (or possessed) in real business conditions where the individual responds under time limitations and bounded rationality, the ASKO pattern reveals concisely and with consistency the personal style entrenched to individual's beliefs for business success factors.

According to the four ASKO domains (I-IV) shown in Figure 1, four styles emerge. Domain I represents opportunistic entrepreneurship, a style often pursued by habitual entrepreneurs (McGrath and MacMillan 2000). This type of venturing relies on personal abilities, instead of exact knowledge, which make the individual capable of grasping market opportunities within their window of opportunity. Once abilities are used in combination with available support, instead of striking opportunities, venturing emerges into domain II. This style is representative for enterprising CEOs or social entrepreneurs who need resources at hand to start their ventures. When venturing is relied on possessed (or implicitly acquired) knowledge (or experience), instead of abilities, domain III is representative for deft craftsmen or self-employed who need a sort of support to start, whilst domain IV is representative for knowledge-intensive start-uppers who focus on growth because of the existence of promising opportunities in the market. The latter usually appear in enterprising teams in order to complement the required domain-specific or business knowledge base. The poles of the ASKO framework are very fundamental for any kind of venturing and thus, they are confronted in any entrepreneurial instruction. Therefore, entrepreneurship education can affect one or more of these poles, in different extents, changing the entrepreneurial 'style' of individuals by affecting their entrepreneurial attitude (the mindset). In sum, mapping the ASKO beliefs of trainees for business success factors enables an indirect understanding of their entrepreneurial motivation, decision making and the type of ventures they are inclined to. These individuals are expected to respond to real situations which are coherent to their 'style' and beliefs.

In order to measure the ASKO construct (Kakouris 2008, 2018), a minimal configuration is adopted with eight factors (two per each pole) as shown in Tables 1 and 2. Factors are classified as either 'psychological' or 'marketistic' depend or their subjectivity, i.e. development in the personal framework of the individual, or objectivity, i.e. evidence from market or environmental data.

Table 1: Factors used for the minimal ASKO configuration (Kakouris 2018).

Factors	Ability	Support	Knowledge	Opportunity
Marketistic	Communicating / Networking	Initial capital	Business planning	Market research
Psychological	Tolerance of ambiguity	Partnership	Consulting	Innovation

Table 2: Questionnaire items for factors used in the minimal ASKO configuration of Table 1

1	Initial capital / funding
2	Innovation of the entrepreneurial idea
3	Relevant own-knowledge and planning (i.e., business plan, accounting, SWOT, etc.)
4	Communication own-capacities, interpersonal relationships, socialisation
5	Consultancy (e.g., from business professionals, experts, mentors, accountants, counsellors, etc.)
6	Marketing, megatrends and market-oriented possibilities
7	Partnerships for start-ups (finding partners, allies, consortia, bonding, etc.)
8	Fear tolerance toward failure / tolerance of ambiguity

In response to the ASKO variables, individuals are asked to rank the items of Table 2 in regard to their importance for the success of a new venture. The top item receives the maximum score whilst scores for each pole and dimension are derived through the relevant additions and subtractions. Previous implementations of the minimal ASKO instrument (Bousmpou, Kakouris and Samathrakis 2019, Kakouris 2008, 2011, 2018, Kakouris et al 2019) have shown internal consistency and validity for the construct.

3. Methodology

An online survey was conducted to the trainees of Manizales Más ('Entrepreneurship Route' programme with six courses which provide space for experiential learning) during the academic year 2018-2019. Students of five educators were selected attending the courses shown in Table 3. The online questionnaire was developed in both English and Spanish language in order to facilitate the comprehension of the items. A second questionnaire for the educators was developed and delivered to them after the completion of the courses. In the educators' questionnaire, information about their background, teaching methods and content for their courses were asked beyond the ASKO items.

Table 3: Selected educators and courses. Fourth column shows pre/post matches per course

Edu-cator	Course title (Spanish)	# students	# pre/post responses	
1	Entrepreneurship (Emprendimiento)	34	16	48%
	Finance (Finanzas para emprendedores)	14	10	72%
2	Entrepreneurship (Emprendimiento)	44	22	50%
	Management of new firms (Gerencia de empresas en crecimiento)	9	8	89%
3	Entrepreneurship (Emprendimiento)	18	4	23%
	Entrepreneurial thinking (Espíritu Empresarial)	80	26	33%
4	Entrepreneurship (Emprendimiento)	16	7	44%
5	Entrepreneurship (Emprendimiento)	15	4	27%
	Business management (Gestión empresarial)	15	1	7%

The questionnaire for students was anonymous (exact names and institutional email addresses were not obligatory). It was delivered before the courses' beginning (pre measurement) and it was repeated after the completion of the four to five month training (post measurement). 213 exploitable answers were received before the courses and 152 after them. From the total sample, 98 matches between pre/post measurements were found for the selected courses distributed as shown in Table 3. The analysed responses are representative for the courses taught except the last one (participation < 7%). In order to populate the relevant subgroups and illustrate the ASKO shifts, data from the same educator were grouped. In this case, the emergent pattern is reliable for educators 1-3 and less reliable for educators 4 and 5 due to the small number of respondents. Nonetheless, the result will be shown for completeness reasons.

To examine the type of new venture consistent with the ASKO domains I-IV (Figure 1), the following eight, 7-point Likert items were developed – i.e. two per domain (Table 4).

Table 4: Questionnaire items for different type ventures. 'If you start a new venture...'

ASKO domain	Items
NV I	It would depend on emerging opportunities or market possibilities at hand
	It would be something promising whatever it demands
NV II	I would like it to happen under the auspices of a bigger company
	It would be a social venture dependent on donations and subsidies
NV III	I would rely only on my prior knowledge and experience once supported by others
	I would be self-employed in regard to my specialisation
NV IV	I would use my technological (or other) knowledge to start a business for growth
	It would be something based on new research findings (e.g., a new technology)

Further to ASKO, the students' questionnaire encompassed demographic data such as: gender, age, entrepreneurial experience, work experience and business family. Educational level distinguishes three groups of trainees: undergraduates, postgraduates and lifelong learners. Entrepreneurial intention was measured through six, 5-point Likert items (Agapitou et al 2010, Kakouris 2016) from which a composite index, NASC (from 1 to 7.5), is created where general population with un-crystallised entrepreneurial intention scores around 3, rejectors of entrepreneurship around 2, latent entrepreneurs around 4.5 and nascent entrepreneurs more than 6. Entrepreneurial motivation was measured through six, 7-point items (Shane et al. 2003): MOT 1: Wealth creation (create profits), MOT 2: Need for autonomy (define my own lifestyle), MOT 3: Need for achievement (succeed in something uncertain), MOT 4: Risk-taking propensity (willingness to undertake risks). MOT 5: Following entrepreneurship as a social trend and MOT 6: Other (not specified).

4. Results and discussion

4.1 Overall descriptive statistics and correlations

Results for independent variables show that the sample consists of 46 males (46.9%), 8 postgraduates (8.2%), 33.7% from business families, 20.4% with entrepreneurial experience, 46.9% with work experience. The population is young (mean 21.23 y.o., Table, 5) with high average entrepreneurial intention of 5.07 (Table 5), hence between latent and nascent entrepreneurs. The rest variables of Table 5 show that the sample is motivated by MOT1-MOT4, whilst the less selected new venture items are those of ASKO domain III. T-tests amongst the variables show that those with entrepreneurial experience (who are older) along with males are more entrepreneurially inclined. Those with work experience are older and are motivated by wealth creation (MOT1) and need for achievement (MOT 3) similar to those with entrepreneurial experience. Concerning the ASKO domains, ventures of type I are scored higher by those who have entrepreneurial experience and lower by postgraduates. The last result is sound since postgraduates may like ventures relied on technological or other domain-specific knowledge.

Table 5: Descriptive statistics and correlations between variables

	Descriptive		T-tests and ANOVA					T-test
	MEAN	S.D	Gender	Ed. Level	Fam. Bus.	Entr. Exp.	Work Exp.	Pre/Post
NASC	5.07	1.551	2.482**			4.573***		
AGE	21.23	3.005				2.018*	3.246*	
A–K	-3.28	4.583						
O–S	2.42	3.488						
NV I	4.91	1.099		F=3.133*		2.152*		
NV II	3.66	1.554						
NV III	4.68	1.281						
NV IV	5.56	1.046						
MOT 1	5.33	1.730				3.426**	2.643**	
MOT 2	5.96	1.181						2.205*
MOT 3	5.70	1.589				2.086*	3.034**	
MOT 4	5.30	1.582						
MOT 5	4.21	1.893						
MOT 6	4.47	2.194						

*p<.05, **p<.01, ***p<.001

Table 6: Classification of responses (n=98) into the ASKO domains

ASKO domains	I	II	III	IV
Pre	13 (13.27%)	7 (7.14%)	10 (10.20%)	68 (69.39%)
Post	21 (21.43%)	2 (2.04%)	20 (20.41%)	55 (56.12%)

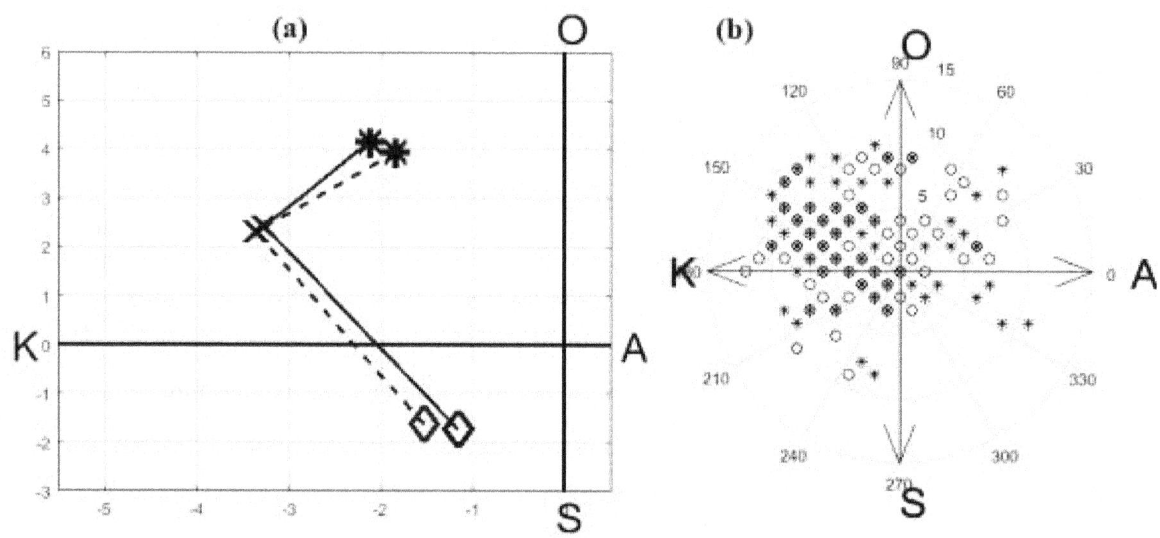

Figure 2: ASKO shifts for the total sample (a) and individuals (b). Solid line in (a) and asterisks in (b) represent the pre measurement whilst dotted line and circles the post one.

T-tests for pre/post measurements show that only MOT 2 (need for autonomy) decreases after the instruction. The overall ASKO variables (Figure 2a) are not significantly affected before and after the courses (p<.8) despite the personal shifts shown in Table 6 and Figure 2b. Thus, assessing only the total sample of trainees one might conclude that the provided education has poor influence on the entrepreneurial beliefs and the entrepreneurial mindsets. However, personal displacements of Table 6 indicate transitions to domains I and III from domains II and IV but the result vanishes, through mutual cancellations, when the amount of shifts (magnitudes of shift vectors) are taken into account in the relevant summation. Not surprisingly (Kakouris 2018), domain IV remains the most populated, before and after the instruction, as technological, knowledge-intensive venturing is highly popular amongst the youth.

Table 7: Spearman correlations amongst the variables

	A		S		K		O		A–K		O–S	
	Pre	Post	Pre	Post	Pre	Post	Pre	Post	Pre	Post	Pre	Post
NASC												
AGE	-.200*	-.296**		.290**						-.180[a]		-.204*
NV I	.215*				-.310**	-.238*			.319**			
NV II						-.171[a]						
NV III					-.181[a]							
NV IV		.199[a]				-.230*				.261*		
MOT 1												
MOT 2												
MOT 3				.216*								
MOT 4												
MOT 5												
MOT 6												

$^{a}p<.1$, $^{*}p<.05$, $^{**}p<.001$

Finally, correlation analysis between the rest variables and the ASKO poles before and after the courses is shown in Table 7. The sample shows a few dependencies before the courses and more after them. The younger rely on ability (the result is amplified in the post measurement) whilst the elderly rely on support after the instruction. New ventures in domain I correlate with ability (the result vanishes in the post measurement), and anti-correlate with knowledge. This is expected due to the nature of the items (Table 4); however, the statistical significance is contracted in the post measurement whilst the statistical significance disappears for the dimension A–K after the courses. Unexpectedly, items of domain III weakly anti-correlate with knowledge but the result vanishes in the post measurement. The result is also unexpected for items of domain IV which correlate with ability and anti-correlate with knowledge after the courses. The statistical significance of A–K is the only one which remains in the ASKO dimensions after the instruction. The finding is contradictory since knowledge-intensive start-ups need certain domain-specific knowledge to succeed. The emergent pattern suggests that the instruction has led a significant part of trainees who rely on ability and opportunity to focus on technological entrepreneurship. Reliance on ability is a feature of intended and usually nascent entrepreneurs; albeit, the acquisition of the technological knowledge is a concern. It is suggested in these cases, the potential or novice entrepreneurs have to carefully elaborate on how they will acquire the demanded knowledge, when they do not possess it themselves, since domain IV is characterised by high competition. Remarkable abilities of networking and leadership may be helpful in the development and growth of technological ventures in this case.

Concerning the motives, only need for achievement (MOT 3) positively correlates with support but only after the instruction. This result is in agreement with remarks of Shane at al. (2003) about McClelland's (1965) achievement, which may not lead to very risky and ambitious initiatives as predefined goals have to be effected. This type of ventures may not need grand opportunities to start but a sort of support in their very beginning.

4.2 ASKO shifts for specific educators and courses

In order to examine how ASKO shifts occurred in specific courses and in connection with the educators' beliefs and techniques, the ASKO traces of five educators and the content taught relevant to each ASKO pole are shown in Figure 3. The respective teaching philosophies (i.e. pedagogies) are shown in Table 8. Collective and individual ASKO shifts per educator are shown in Figure 4. Concerning teaching philosophies, all educators appear to pursue collaborative learning based on personal meaning-making from the instruction. All educators also appear to pursue experiential learning in a high extent, except educator 3. Diversification is observed regarding cognitive methods where educators 2 and 4 appear to pursue cognition and knowledge transfer in a higher extent.

Table 8: Teaching philosophy of each educator

	1	2	3	4	5
Cognitive:	Moderate	High	Moderate	High	Moderate
Experiential:	High	High	Moderate	High	High
Collaborative:	High	High	High	High	High
Constructivist:	High	High	High	High	High

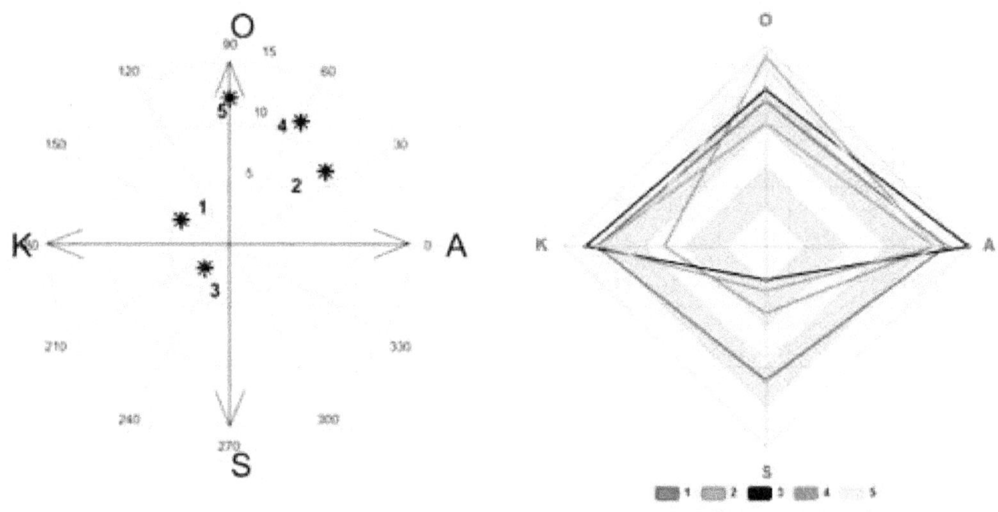

(a) (b)

Figure 3: ASKO traces of five educators (a) and teaching relevant to each ASKO pole (b)

Comparing the ASKO traces, educators 1 and 3 appear close to the origin with a slight reliability on knowledge and on opportunity or support respectively. Educator 1 teaches content relevant to all poles while educator 3 teaches less for support. From the patterns of Figure 4 it appears that dramatical changes have occured in personal frames of reference of trainees in both cases. In the summative result, change for educator 1 is insignificant while educator 3 induces an overall shift towards support. Given that the latter educator teaches less for support but possesses reliability on it, it seems that the personal belief of educator may have prevailed. The result needs a closer examination since the population of 3 is older (22.37), compared to 1 (20.59), and the elderly trainees are found 'attracted' by the importance of support after the courses (Table 7). Thus, it may be the combination (interaction) of the educator's and trainees' beliefs which determined the outcome.

The outcome for educator 2 is notable. The educator clearly falls within domain I and teaches content accordingly. Nonetheless, the induced overall shift appears in the opposite direction (i.e. towards knowledge). This may be attributed to the teaching philosophy of the educator which is significantly cognitive. Focus on knowledge transfer (through lectures, case studies, etc.) can induce this type of shift. The conclusions are different for educator 4 who is of similar style (teaches a bit more about knowledge) but induces an opposite overall shift. However, the latter result is less reliable due to the small number of respondents. The same holds for educator 5 for whom the outcome is shown for completeness. It can be also noted that in all cases (except 5 for which there is lack of data) the horizontal ASKO trace (A–K) lies between -4 and -3 after the instruction. This entails a *post hoc* 'unified' outcome across the courses provided by the ecosystem. In sum, through the current implementation of the ASKO framework not only the overall outcome of education is depicted but also inter-comparisons between entrepreneurial courses, provided by the Manizales Más entrepreneurial ecosystem, are possible. This is a new way to illustrate, and to compare, the impact of education on entrepreneurial beliefs for factors regarding entrepreneurial success and emerging conceptualisations complementary to other types of evaluations. The results are indicative for the method and need further implementations, of an enriched ASKO configuration, to attain deeper understanding for the goals and outcomes of entrepreneurship education especially for the under-researched topic of entrepreneurial beliefs.

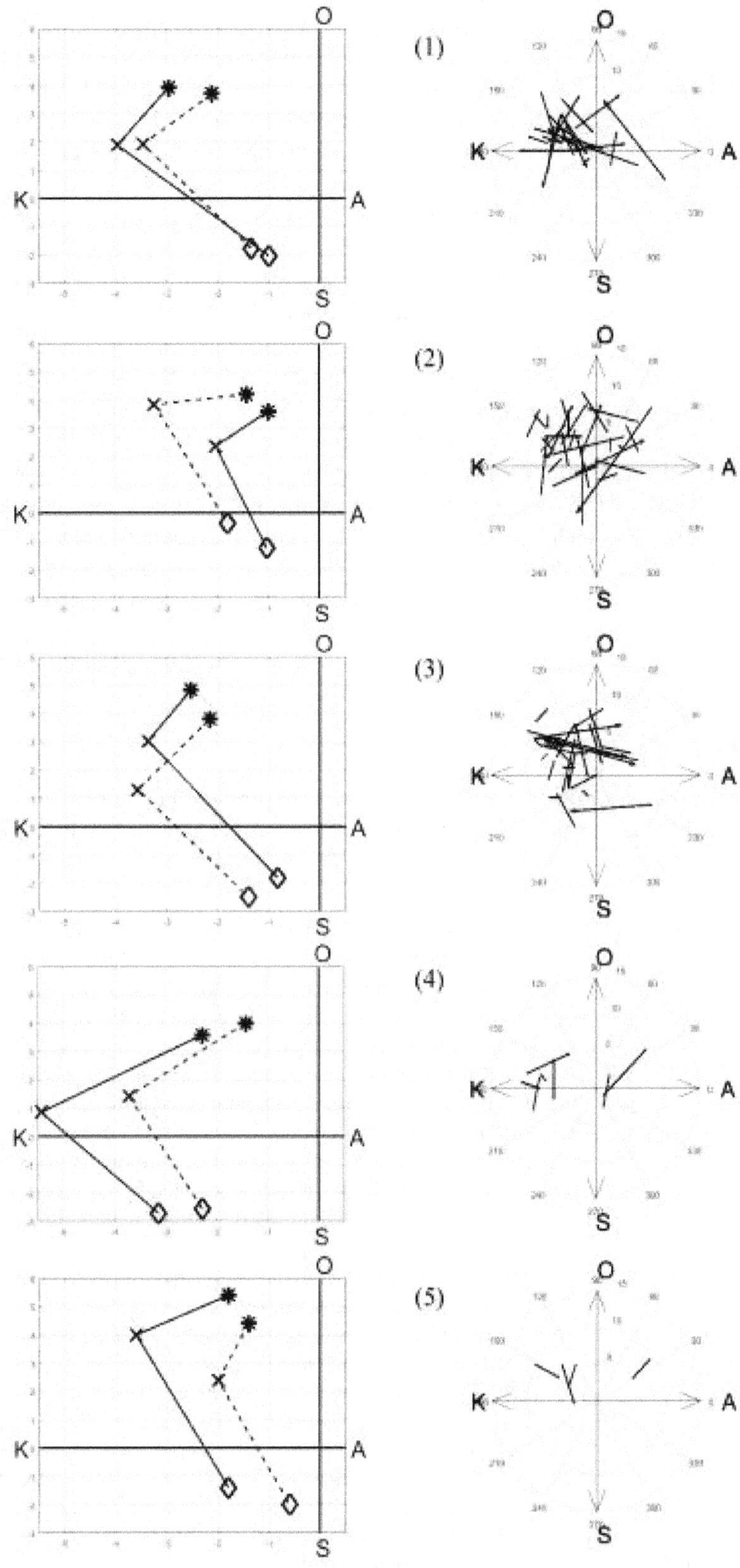

Figure 4: ASKO shifts for the five educators of Figure 3. Left: Pre/solid, Post/dotted, x/total, asterisk/psychological, diamond/marketistic. Right: Individuals' shift vectors

5. Conclusion

The present article aimed to examine the impact of different entrepreneurial courses on trainees' entrepreneurial beliefs and conceptualisations. Based on a dialectical approach to classify the vast majority of entrepreneurial factors into the dialectically opposed poles of Ability, Support, Knowledge and Opportunity (ASKO), results for the overall sample of trainees but also inter-comparisons between different courses are possible. This type of educational evaluation is complementary to others and tends to capture the attitude of trainees (Kakouris and Liargovas 2020) that is important in the instilment of the entrepreneurial mindset. The implementation of ASKO to Manizales Más trainees showed that various personal transformations took place in a way to exhibit the same pre/post summative result. This group of trainees is young and entrepreneurially intended showing reliance to ability prior to the courses. After the instruction, the more elderly rely on the support pole of the environment. Similarly, those who are motivated by the need for achievement rely more on the support pole. Inter-comparisons between courses indicated that educators' beliefs and pedagogies affect the change in ASKO patterns and need to be investigated further.

In accordance with previous research (Kakouris 2018), the majority of youth was found concentrated in the IV ASKO domain considering knowledge and opportunity as pillars for successful entrepreneurship and growth. In the European context, entrepreneurship education and the role of entrepreneurial ecosystems have been essential after the connection of economic development with innovation and endogenous growth (Kakouris, Dermatis and Liargovas 2016). In this sense, much of nowadays entrepreneurship education focuses on the technological domain, especially to digital entrepreneurship, making this topic popular. An analogous focus was revealed in the present sample. Nonetheless, an observed discrepancy, revealed by the ASKO patterns, is that those motivated by technological ventures may underestimate the importance of knowledge as a factor of success. This finding needs further research and adjustment. Conclusively, the present empirical results aimed at illustrating the new method of educational assessment and need to be replicated and extended in future research to retrieve specific suggestions for educators and educational agencies.

Acknowledgements

The authors are grateful to the Laboratory of Sustainable Development and Entrepreneurship (SDE), Department of Economics, University of Peloponnese for financial support towards participating in the conference.

References

Acs, Z.J., Stam, E., Audretsch, D.B., and O'Connor, A. (2017) "The lineages of the entrepreneurial ecosystem approach", *Small Business Economics*, Vol 49, No 1, pp 1-10.

Agapitou, C., Tampouri, S., Bouchoris, P., Georgopoulos, N., and Kakouris, A. (2010) "Exploring underlying beliefs on youth entrepreneurship of higher education graduates in Greece", Paper read at *5th European Conference on Innovation and Entrepreneurship*, edited by A. Kakouris, Academic Conferences Limited, Reading, UK, pp 10–17.

Bousmpou, D., Kakouris, A., and Samathrakis, V. (2019) "Connecting ASKO beliefs and entrepreneurial self-efficacy with entrepreneurial intention", Paper read at 14th European Conference on Innovation and Entrepreneurship, edited by P. Liargovas and A. Kakouris, Academic Conferences Limited., Reading, UK, pp 1245-1249.

Isenberg, D.J. (2010) "How to start an entrepreneurial revolution", *Harvard Business Review*, Vol 88, No 6, pp 40-50.

Kakouris, A. (2011) "On the impact of entrepreneurship education: self-efficacy and shift in perceptions", Paper read at 6th European Conference on Entrepreneurship and Innovation, edited by H. Fulford, Academic Conferences Limited., Reading, UK, pp 504–509.

Kakouris, A. (2016) "Exploring entrepreneurial conceptions, beliefs and intentions of Greek graduates", *International Journal of Entrepreneurial Behavior & Research*, Vol 22, No 1, pp 109–132.

Kakouris, A. (2018) "The ASKO dialectical framework for inter-comparisons between entrepreneurial courses: Empirical results from applications", *Entrepreneurship Education*, Vol 1, No 1/4, pp 41-60.

Kakouris, A. (2019) "The ASKO dialectical framework for entrepreneurial courses construction: theoretical foundation", *Entrepreneurship Education*, Vol 2, No 1/2, pp 51-69.

Kakouris, A. (2008) "On initial implementations of innovation and entrepreneurship courses: a case study for undergraduates at the University of Athens", Paper read at *3rd European Conference on Entrepreneurship and Innovation*, edited by N. Marriot, Academic Conferences Limited., Reading, UK, pp 121-129.

Kakouris, A., Dermatis., Z., and Liargovas, P. (2016) "Educating potential entrepreneurs under the perspective of Europe 2020 plan", *Business and Entrepreneurship Journal*, Vol 5, No 1, pp 7-24.

Kakouris, A., Karagianni M., Molina V., Fleck E., and Pekka-Economou V. (2019) "Classifying entrepreneurial conceptualizations through the ASKO dialectical approach", Paper read at 14th European Conference on Innovation and Entrepreneurship, edited by P. Liargovas and A. Kakouris, Academic Conferences Limited., Reading, UK, pp 488-497.

Kakouris, A., and Liargovas, P. (2020) "On the about/for/through framework of entrepreneurship education: a critical analysis ", *Entrepreneurship Education and Pedagogy*, DOI: 10.1177/2515127420916740

Krueger, N.F. (2007) "What lies beneath? The experiential essence of entrepreneurial thinking", *Entrepreneurship Theory and Practice*, Vol 31, No 1, pp 123-138.

Liñán, F. (2007) "The role of entrepreneurship education in the entrepreneurial process", in Fayolle, A. (Ed.) *Handbook of Research in Entrepreneurship Education*, Edward Elgar, Cheltenham, UK, pp 230-247.

McClelland, D.C. (1965) "N achievement and entrepreneurship: A longitudinal study", *Journal of Personality and Social Psychology*, Vol 1, No 4, pp 389-392.

McGee, J.E., Peterson, M., Mueller, S.L., and Sequeira, J.M. (2009) "Entrepreneurial self-efficacy: refining the measure", *Entrepreneurship Theory and Practice*, Vol 33, No 4, pp 965-988.

McGrath, R.G., and MacMillan, I.C. (2000) *The Entrepreneurial Mindset*, Harvard Business School Press, Boston MA.

Molina, V. (2017) "The Mutualism Relation within the Entrepreneurial Ecosystem", Paper read in ISEA International Symposium on Electronic Art 2017: Bio-Creation & Peace, [online], https://www.researchgate.net/profile/Viviana_Molina/publication/318405479_The_Mutualism_relation_within_entrepreneurial_ecosystem/links/5967eaadaca2728ca6731253/The-Mutualism-relation-within-entrepreneurial-ecosystem.pdf

Molina, V., and Maya, J. (2018) "Successful entrepreneurship ecosystems for regional development: a proposal for their modelling and creation", *International Journal of Innovation and Regional Developmen*t, Vol 8, No 4, pp 322-336.

Shane, S., Locke, E.A., and Collins, C.J. (2003) "Entrepreneurial motivation", *Human Resource Management Review*, Vol 13, No 2, pp 257-279.

Thompson, E.R. (2009) "Individual entrepreneurial intent: Construct clarification and development of an internationally reliable metric", *Entrepreneurship Theory and Practice*, Vol 33, No 3, pp 669-694.

Walter, S.G., and Block, J H. (2016) "Outcomes of entrepreneurship education: An institutional perspective", *Journal of Business Venturing*, Vol 31, No 2, pp 216-233.

Zhao, H., Seibert, S.E., and Hills, G.E. (2005) "The mediating role of self-efficacy in the development of entrepreneurial intentions", *Journal of Applied Psychology*, Vol 90, No 6, pp 1265- 1272.

Stage-Gate and Agile Manufacturing in New Product Development: A State-Of-The Art

Fotis Kitsios and Maria Kamariotou
Department of Applied Informatics, University of Macedonia, Thessaloniki, Greece
kitsios@uom.gr
mkamariotou@uom.edu.gr
DOI: 10.34190/EIE.20.147

Abstract: The purpose of this paper is to conduct a literature review based on Webster's and Watson's (2002) methodology in order to explore the integration of Stage-Gate and Agile Manufacturing in New Product Development. Findings show that many companies have no formal NPD system yet and ad hoc systems provide decision makers with too much discretion which leads to mistakes. Agile software development has been utilized to answer the challenges of software system development in spite of the lack of empirical evidence from academic research. Agile methods are applied within the context of existing Stage-Gate NPD models. The need of developing a NPD software improvement framework which should follow the principles of manufacturing agility frameworks has been stated by researchers. Apparently, such a software product has not been yet fully achieved in practice by large industrial NPD organizations. The contribution of this paper is twofold. First, the structured methodological framework which was used demonstrates how the academic interest in NPD and Agile Manufacturing has evolved over the years and it highlights areas that need further research. Secondly, this literature review can be useful for managers in order to increase the understanding of the complexity of areas regarding NPD, Stage-Gate and Agile software.

Keywords: stage-gate; agile software; agile manufacturing; new product development; innovation strategy

1. Introduction

A complete 100% implementation of a product development process might be a misnomer as all processes are to be both flexible and situational so that they could match the dynamics of technologies, markets, and organizations (O'Connor, 1994). Thus the search for appropriate NPD models or different approaches has become a new emerging topic both for scholars and practitioners resulting from the new disruptive innovation environment which has challenged NPD theory and practice in recent years (Cooper, 2017; Summers and Scherpereel, 2008). As many companies have no formal NPD system yet, ad hoc systems provide decision makers with too much discretion which leads to mistakes. So, some companies have opted for managing NPD within a formal system in an attempt to avoid those mistakes (Summers and Scherpereel, 2008). Yet, a need to adapt Stage-Gate models is pointed out so that higher levels of flexibility and agility can be achieved (Conforto and Amaral, 2016; Ettlie and Elsenbach, 2007).

One of the latest results of research on NPD management is agile NPD, which has recently emerged in an attempt to manage the increasing complexity of the NPD process. The agile methods originate from the software development industry and are being increasingly adapted by research and development industrial companies, amongst others (Sommer et al., 2014).The need of developing a NPD software improvement framework which should follow the principles of manufacturing agility frameworks has been stated by researchers. Apparently, such a software product has not yet been fully achieved in practice by large industrial NPD organisations. It is clear that there is a need for expanding this view in software engineering by adopting applicable key learning by other disciplines (Kettunen, 2009; Sommer et al., 2015). The integration of the agile teams into Stage-Gate software product development has already been investigated by previous studies (Karlstrom and Runeson, 2005).

Software development is almost infinitely divisible and consists of millions of lines of code that can be broken down into one hundred increments of approximately 10.000 lines, each increment yielding a working product. It is more than obvious that physical product development is something much different. The development of a new machine for example, or a new food product, or a polymer cannot be incrementalized. In such a way, therefore the concept of short time-boxed sprints cannot be applied as well (Cooper, 2014). Can agile be integrated with a traditional Stage-Gate model? And can the resulting hybrid model also be used for the development of physical products? (Cooper, 2017; 2016; Cooper and Sommer, 2016). Thus, the purpose of this paper is to conduct a literature review based on Webster's and Watson's (2002) methodology in order to explore the integration of Stage-Gate and Agile Manufacturing in New Product Development.

The structure of the rest of the paper is as follows: Section 2 analyzes the methodology used for conducting the literature review. Then, the results of the analysis of the papers are provided in Section 3. Finally, conclusion and suggestions for future research conclude the paper.

2. Literature review methodology

2.1 Previous literature reviews

Studies were identified using a three-phased literature review methodology, which was suggested by Webster and Watson, (2002), and has been previously used in the field of Computer Engineering and Innovation Management (Berkovich et al., 2011; Jourdan et al., 2008; Kitsios and Kamariotou, 2019a; 2019b; 2016a; 2016b). First, a search of the extant literature reviews was done to select the databases and keywords of the basic search. Then, the backward search was implemented to examine the references of the selected papers and finally the forward search to examine the citations of the selected papers in order to increase their amount. After the selection of the papers, these were classified according to their content.

Previous literature reviews have focused either on agile software development methods either on AM techniques (Gunasekaran, 1999; Heck and Zaidman, 2016; Leite and Braz, 2016). Surveys concerning quality criteria for agile requirements specifications are limited (Ramesh and Devadasan, 2007). Previous researchers have focused on quality aspects of the end product (maintainability, usability) (Heck and Zaidman, 2016). Other studies on agile software development examined the number of articles published on agile software development topics as well as the countries where studies have been conducted. This assessment of the agile literature may serve as a starting point to enable new researchers entering this field to generate advantageous research results on agile software development (Chuang et al., 2014). Furthermore, other studies examined the quality of published papers in agile software manufacturing by studying the number of published papers and the research areas which have been addressed in agile software (Hoda et al., 2017).

2.2 Article selection process

The search was done in Scopus, Science Direct, Web of Science and ABI/INFORM using a combination of the following keywords "stage gate", "agile software" and NPD. Following the inclusion and exclusion criteria by previous literature reviews in this area, papers should be written in English, they should be included in Business Management field or Computer Science or Engineering, they should be published in a journal or in the proceedings of a conference or as a book chapter (Heck and Zaidman, 2016).

Overall, 1087 articles were gathered using keywords in all databases. Then, authors exclude duplicate articles and scanning their titles, 94 articles were relevant with the aim of this paper. Next, examining their abstract, 78 were accepted. A number of studies are rejected because their full text was not accessible. 63 articles were examined according to their full text (Figure 1). In these 63 articles, 17 were added by the backward search. Additionally, 14 more articles were added by the forward search and so a total of 94 articles were revealed.

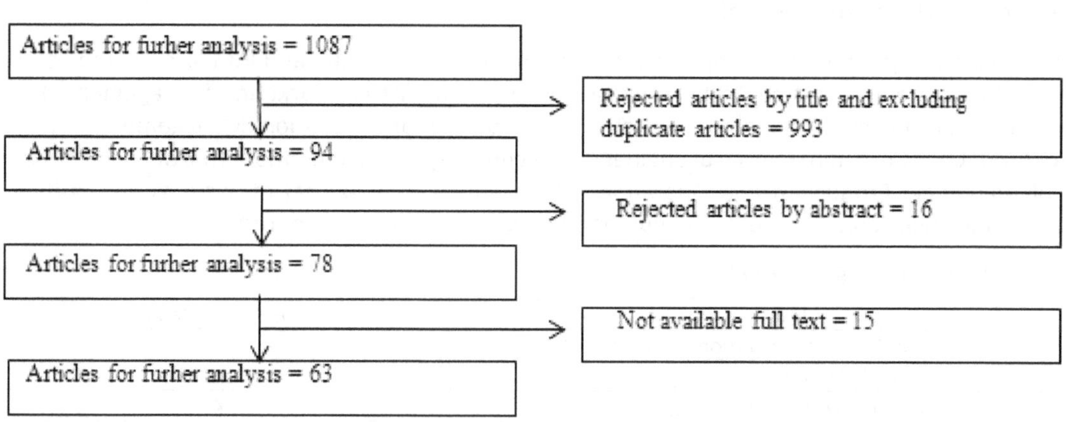

Figure 1: Article selection process

Search was completed when it came to common articles from all databases and different combinations of keywords. Therefore, it was concluded that the critical mass of relevant literature sources had been collected

(Webster and Watson, 2002). Articles were classified to three categories according to their concept. These categories are Stage-Gate, Agile Manufacturing (AM) and NPD.

3. Results

3.1 Number of published articles per year

An open data value network involves the entities which interact in the development of services. These entities, although researchers in Stage-Gate and AM area conducted studies three decades ago, the majority of papers have just been published in the last ten years and particularly in the last five years when researchers started to study the integration of these methods to NPD and NSD (New Service Development) process (Cooper, 2017; 2016; Cooper and Sommer, 2016; Juhola et al., 2014). This is an interesting finding which highlights both the importance of the field and its continuous development. Figure 2 presents a clear increasing trend in the last ten years.

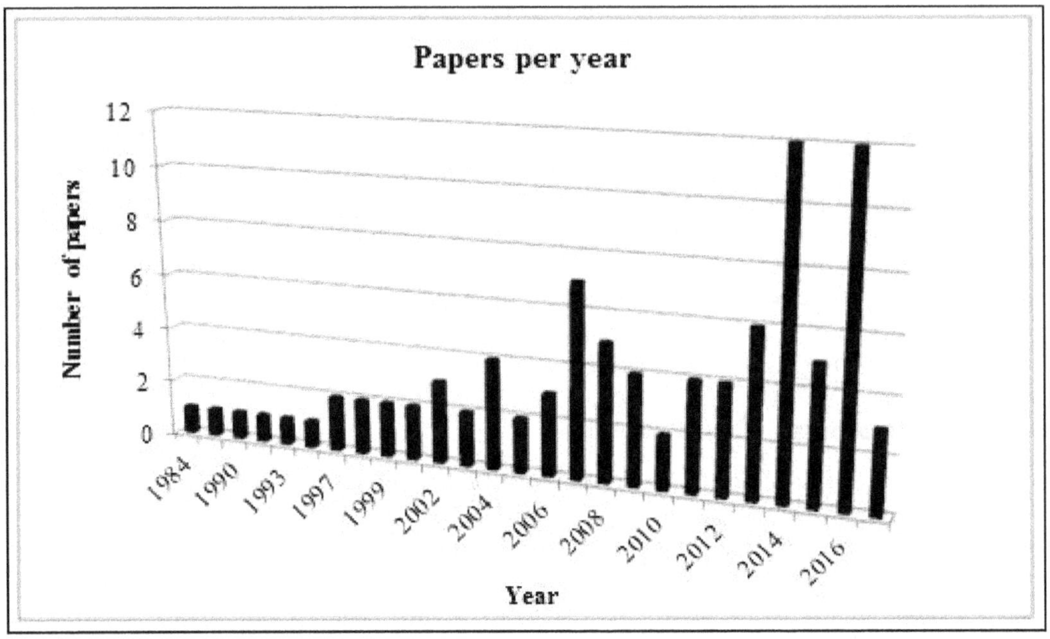

Figure 2: Number of published papers per year

More specifically, the research area of Stage-Gate has appeared since 1984. The highest number of articles was found in 2014 and 2016. The number of articles dropped to the lowest level in the period in 1984-1997, 1998-2001 and 2003, 2005 and 2010.

3.2 Number of articles per journal

The most frequently journals that appeared concerning the Stage-Gate and AM are Journal of Product Innovation Management, Research Technology Management, Industrial Marketing Management, Journal of Manufacturing Technology Management, International Journal of Innovation Management, International Journal of Production Research, Journal of Engineering Technology Management, Journal of Engineering Design, Journal of Marketing, Production and Operations Management, the Journal of Systems and Software and Strategy & Leadership. Table 1 presents the number of published papers per journal.

Table 1: Number of papers per journal

Journal	Number of Papers
Journal of Product Innovation Management	17
Research Technology Management	10
Industrial Marketing Management	4
Journal of Manufacturing Technology Management	3
International Journal of Innovation Management	2
International Journal of Production Research	2
Journal of Engineering Design	2
Journal of Engineering Technology Management	2

Journal	Number of Papers
Journal of Marketing	2
Production and Operations Management	2
Strategy & Leadership	2
The Journal of Systems and Software	2

3.3 Research methods

Although researchers have indicated that several comparative studies between what is known about the agile manufacturing and other approaches that have been applied, as in the case of lean manufacturing, mass customization, among others (Conforto and Amaral, 2016; Leite and Braz, 2016), the most frequently used methods are survey (47,8%) and case studies (25,53%). Figure 3 presents the number of articles per research method.

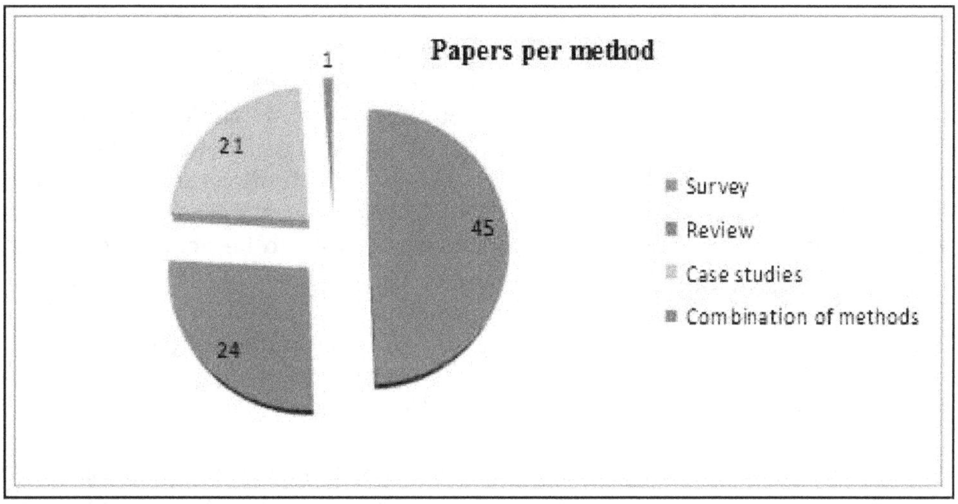

Figure 3: Number of published papers per method

However, empirical studies regarding the implementation of hybrid models combining the Stage-Gate model with AM in NPD are limited. There is a need for empirical studies showing if the combination of Stage-Gate and AM contribute to agility and better project and product development performance (Conforto and Amaral, 2016; Stevens and Dimitriadis, 2005).

4. A research agenda

4.1 Agile manufacturing and Stage Gate integration

The importance of adapting and combining AM practices with more traditional NPD processes (e.g. stage-gates) so as to improve flexibility and response to changes in uncertain and dynamic project management has been shown by recent studies. By eliminating activities that add no value to the product development and by using a minimal set of rules, agile methods can be focused on flexibility. These methods are based on a series of iterative development cycles, promoting self-management and self-discipline attitudes, so as to help the team to be readily responsive to changes. Different approaches, such as iterative development, should be considered by managers so that they could deal with different types of projects. It can be seen from this perspective that AM together with the Stage-Gate approach could be explored as alternatives when dealing with the challenges of managing product development projects in highly dynamic business environments (Conforto and Amaral, 2016).

The idea-to-launch process is broken into a series of five or six discrete stages or phases by the Stage-Gate. These phases begin with the "idea generation" and more to "product launch" and beyond. Stage-Gate is cross-functional, that is, it involves people from marketing, sales and operations together with the technical personnel but when the fact that each stage is a gate where decisions to invest or Go/Kill are made by analyzing whether managers are doing the right, proceeds then such a model is seen as being to linear, too rigid and too planned. For all these reasons is concerned to be unsuitable to deal with today's fast-paced and, more often than not, quickly changing worlds (Cooper, 2016). Thus, questions such as how reductions in particular stage times impact value or whether time reduction efforts should focus on particular stages in the process have to be made (Bendoly and Chao, 2015). Early commitments to large features, long schedules, long feedback loops and the re-planning, which is inherent to traditional product development processes, create inefficiencies and slow the development cycles. Agile offers both greater efficiency and focus, and Stage-Gate provides with a means of coordinating with other development teams and with a communication with functions such as marketing and senior management are of great importance (Cooper, 2016).

4.2 The hybrid model

Models combining the two processes have already been presented by researchers. These models are framework comprising the Stage-Gate model and five dimensions. These dimensions are: (1) phase and project deliverable model (PPDM); (2) project planning and controlling white board (PPCW); (3) weekly activity planning white board (WAPW); (4) project management software (PMS); and (5) simplified performance indicator system (SPIS). With intent to satisfy the requirements of each phase-review milestone (or phase gate) of the product development process, each project phase can have as many iterations as necessary.

The levels of this hybrid model are three. The first one is the Stage-Gate model, represented by for the entire project by the PPDM, its phases, milestones, and macro-deliverables related to the product and technology development phases. The second level has to do with iterative development, also called "sprints" in the Scrum agile method in which the deliverables from the product back login are break down (by the team) into smaller ones, or into tasks and also the order of development is both prioritized and defined during the iterative planning meeting (or sprint planning). There are time-boxed iterations, usually of a 15-day length, during which these tasks are performed. The general set of deliverables and tasks to be performed in each phase are represented by the PPCW which is a physical visual board that evolves during the project life cycle. PPCW could be compared with the product back log described in the Scrum Agile method. As for the third level, this is performed either on a weekly or on daily basis and it bears similarities to the iteration plan or the sprint back log. It is called WAPW and deals with the assignment and performance of daily or weekly tasks. All these three levels provide with information that can be registered in the PMS.

As soon as a new project has begun, the iteration cycles guided by the PPDM (Stage 1) starts by defining the main phases as well as the project deliverables. This is an important element as it aims at guiding the team into the main phases of the product development process. This is why all the main deliverables and documents that are considered as key outputs as for the product and the project that is executed are included in the PPDM. Needless to say that the previously mentioned elements have to be specifically related to the type of project and the particular industry sector.

After the definition of the PPDM and once the team has acquired a broader view of the macro-deliverables in terms of the project, the iterations are collaboratively defined by both the project manager and the team members. At this stage the iteration length, is defined. This length usually is a period of two weeks, that is to say 15 days but that is something basically dependent on the type of project so it can be different when necessary. According to this model the phase length that reflects the characteristics of the project type and of the industry sector is usually longer compared to the iteration length. The PMD is used in the IVPM2 so that project data and information regarding cost, schedule and progress can be documented and also registered, in order to help the team generate reports. These are useful for both the evaluation of the phase review meeting and the iteration performance.

After the PMS (Stage 3) is over, the deliverables must be broken down into activities and tasks that are to be executed during the iteration (sprint). They also have to be placed in the WAPW (Stage 4) so that the work that has to be performed on a weekly basis can be illustrated. During the fifth stage, the performance can be on a weekly or sometimes a daily basis and this procedure is supported by rapid, focused team meeting which are called "stand-ups" or "daily Scrum". In other words, what members need to deliver and what the issues or challenges are, are regularly discussed by the team so that the project manager can proactively address these problems. So, at the next stage (Stage 6) with the help of the PMS the project manager is able to generate performance reports and provide the team with an overview of the project progress. Finally, based on this information, decisions considering the improvement of the process are made, both by the project team and the manager. They also discuss upcoming risks and obstacles in order to plan for the next iteration cycle (Stage 7) (Conforto and Amaral, 2016).

What was found by the researchers though was not only that integration did work with both models having indeed been compatible but also that several major payoffs were yielded by this hybrid approach. The advantages of Stage-Gate have been both well researched and documented (Cooper, 2016; Cooper and Sommer, 2016; Sommer et al., 2015). Although the benefits of the Agile-Stage-Gate hybrid development model are not that well known to hardware developers, manufacturers can benefit greatly from this new approach. What is required by this hybrid method is that the project team should early and cheaply develop a physical or visual project and quickly present it to the customers to get feedback. In contrast, the traditional Stage-Gate methods require that before development begins the problem should be both identified and defined by conducting investigators. So during these early stages, or "homework phases" the project team has to undertake all markets, technical and business assessments so as to be able to define the product and to justify the project financially, while in an agile or hybrid approach requirement do not have to be defined before development but they are gradually established being a part of the solution-finding process. An advantage of this method is that teams are forced to focus on large-finalized lists of requirements or features. Time-boxed sprints, and event time-boxed tasks within sprints, bring a sense of urgency to the development project making project teams commit to certain deliverables at the beginning of each sprint and thus being under pressure to deliver them within the agreed timetable (Cooper, 2016).

The fact that agile method calls for daily meetings provide teams with powerful face-to-face communications which is far more efficient than what can be provided with written documents. Also, fast and continuous feedback given by the customers in terms of a product features support the creation of a more efficient project and subsequently of a better product. The whole procedure leads to cross-functional and more effective teams that have good internal cooperation and communication- both elements frequently cited as the key not only to increased speed to market but also to higher success rates in NPD (Cooper, 2016). Table 2 summarizes the benefits from the integration of these methods.

Table 2: Benefits from the integration of two methods

Benefits	References
Better internal team communication	(Conforto and Amaral, 2016; Cooper, 2016; Cooper and Sommer, 2016; Karlstrom and Runeson, 2005; Schuh et al., 2016)
More efficient planning	
Improved customer feedback	
Clearer resolution of documentation issues	
Improved attitudes	
Contributed to reducing conflicts among customers and project team	

5. Conclusion

In this paper, authors report on a systematic literature review on the implementation of Stage-Gate model and AM in NPD process. Authors devised an overview of the assumptions and theoretical foundations of these methods. Authors also derived recommendations for practitioners that want to integrate them in a hybrid model and a research agenda for academics that highlights the need for further research in this area. In addition, the resulting systematic overview is useful as a reference work for researchers in the field of NPD as well as NSD and helps them identify both related work and new research opportunities in this field.

In general, independencies bring the software product development closer to the AM. In addition, many of the product design principles in AM (e.g. modularity, customization) can be directly applied to the software production. On top of that, enterprise level concepts such as collaboration, core competence management and workforce factors are basically technological independent (Kettunen, 2009). Although it has arisen some case studies there is still a large gap in exploratory studies, it is essential that this gap should be bridged in order to better establish and develop this philosophy. A lack of exploratory scientific research leads to conflicting and even contradictory perspectives of several authors (Conforto and Amaral, 2016; Leite and Braz, 2016).

Despite the great differences between structured and flexible approaches and the fact that literature concerning NPD framework is evolving, yet studies are limited when it comes to understanding the benefits and the limitations that derive from the combination of different practices through approaches that meet current state of technology and product development in today's changing and competitive business environments (Conforto and Amaral, 2016). The added value of this paper is the useful overview of the state of new product development strategies, which highlights issues among Stage-Gate and agile methods research domains, while providing a complete overview of the literature and it is a good starting point for further research. This paper is a bibliometric study that provides a macro picture of a research field, its evolution and connections among studies in order to be a starting point for future research. This literature review may be of interest to academics who are already studying new product development strategies, or researchers who have been introduced to the field but they are interested in examining more specific insights into where current research topics in this literature can be located, and how they may contribute to them. Future researchers could expand this literature review and provide make different bibliometric analyses such as co-author or co-citation (Mircea and Andreescu, 2010).

References

Bendoly, E. and Chao, R. O. (2015) "How Excessive Stage Time Reduction in NPD Negatively Impacts Market Value", *Production and Operations Management,* Vol 25, No. 5, pp. 812–832.

Berkovich, D. I. M., Leimeister, J. M. and Krcmar, H. (2011) "Requirements engineering for product service systems", *Business & Information Systems Engineering,* Vol 53, No. 6, pp. 357-370.

Conforto, E. C. and Amaral, D. C. (2016) "Agile project management and stage-gate model—A hybrid framework for technology-based companies", *Journal of Engineering and Technology Management*, Vol 40, pp. 1-14.

Cooper, R. G. (2017) "Idea-to-Launch Gating Systems: Better, Faster, and More Agile", *Research-Technology Management,* Vol 60, No. 1, pp. 48-52.

Cooper, R. G. (2016) "Agile–Stage-Gate Hybrids", *Research-Technology Management,* Vol 59, No. 1, pp. 21-29.

Cooper, R. G. (2014) "What's Next?: After Stage-Gate", *Research-Technology Management,* Vol 57, No, 1, pp. 20-31.

Cooper, R. G. and Sommer, A. F. (2016) "The Agile–Stage-Gate Hybrid Model: A Promising New Approach and a New Research Opportunity", *Journal of Product Innovation Management*, Vol 33, No. 5, pp. 513-526.

Chuang, S. W., Luor, T. and Lu, H. P. (2014) "Assessment of institutions, scholars, and contributions on agile software development (2001–2012)", *Journal of Systems and Software,* Vol 93, pp. 84-101.

Ettlie, J. E. and Elsenbach, J. M. (2007) "Modified Stage-Gate® Regimes in New Product Development", *Journal of Product Innovation Management*, Vol 24, No. 1, pp. 20-33.

Gunasekaran, A. (1999) "Agile manufacturing: a framework for research and development", *International journal of production economics,* Vol 62, No. 1, pp. 87-105.

Heck, P. and Zaidman, A. (2016) "A systematic literature review on quality criteria for agile requirements specifications", *Software Quality Journal*, pp. 1-34.

Hoda, R., Salleh, N., Grundy, J. and Tee, H. M. (2017) "Systematic literature reviews in agile software development: A tertiary study", *Information and Software Technology,* Vol 85, pp. 60-70.

Jourdan, Z., Rainer, R. K. and Marshall, T. E. (2008) "Business intelligence: An analysis of the literature", *Information Systems Management,* Vol 25, No. 2, pp. 121-131.

Juhola, T., Yip, M. H., Hyrynsalmi, S., Mäkilä, T. and Leppänen, V. (2014) "The connection of the stakeholder cooperation intensity and team agility in software development", *Proceedings of International Conference on Management of Innovation and Technology (ICMIT)*, pp. 199-204. IEEE.

Karlström, D. and Runeson, P. (2006) "Integrating agile software development into stage-gate managed product development", *Empirical Software Engineering*, Vol 11, No. 2, pp. 203-225.

Kettunen, P. (2009) "Adopting key lessons from agile manufacturing to agile software product development—A comparative study", *Technovation*, Vol 29, No. 6, pp. 408-422.

Kitsios, F. and Kamariotou, M. (2019a) "Mapping new service development: a review and synthesis of literature", *The Service Industries Journal* (in press). doi: 10.1080/02642069.2018.1561876.

Kitsios, F. and Kamariotou, M. (2019b) "Service innovation process digitization: areas for exploitation and exploration", *Journal of Hospitality and Tourism Technology* (in press) doi: 10.1108/JHTT-02-2019-0041.

Kitsios, F. and Kamariotou, M. (2016a) "The impact of Information Technology and the alignment between business and service innovation strategy on service innovation performance", *Proceedings of 2016 IEEE International Conference on Industrial Engineering, Management Science and Application (ICIMSA)*, pp. 247-251.

Kitsios, F. and Kamariotou, M. (2016b) "Critical success factors in service innovation strategies: An annotated bibliography on NSD", *Proceedings of British Academy of Management (BAM) Conference 2016,* pp. 1-28.

Leite, M. and Braz, V. (2016) "Agile manufacturing practices for new product development: industrial case studies", *Journal of Manufacturing Technology Management,* Vol 27, No. 4, pp. 560-576.

Mircea, M. and Andreescu, A. I. (2010) "Agile systems development for the management of service oriented organizations", *Proceedings of the 11th International Conference on Computer Systems and Technologies and Workshop for PhD Students in Computing on International Conference on Computer Systems and Technologies*, pp. 341-346. ACM.

O'Connor, P. (1994) "Implementing a stage-gate process: a multi-company perspective", *Journal of Product Innovation Management,* Vol 11, No. 3, pp. 183-200.

Ramesh, G. and Devadasan, S. R. (2007) "Literature review on the agile manufacturing criteria", *Journal of Manufacturing Technology Management,* Vol 18, No. 2, pp. 182-201.

Schuh, G., Schröder, S., Lau, F. and Wetterney, T. (2016) "Next generation hardware development: Requirements and configuration options for the organization of procurement activities in the context of Agile new Product

Development", *Proceedings of Portland International Conference on Management of Engineering and Technology (PICMET)*, pp. 2583-2591, IEEE.

Sommer, A. F., Hedegaard, C., Dukovska-Popovska, I. and Steger-Jensen, K. (2015) "Improved Product Development Performance through Agile/Stage-Gate Hybrids: The Next-Generation Stage-Gate Process?", Research-Technology Management, Vol 58, No. 1, pp. 34-45.

Sommer A. F., Dukovska-Popovska I., Steger-Jensen K. (2014) "Agile Product Development Governance – On Governing the Emerging Scrum/Stage-Gate Hybrids". In: Grabot B., Vallespir B., Gomes S., Bouras A. and Kiritsis D. (Eds.), *Advances in Production Management Systems. Innovative and Knowledge-Based Production Management in a Global-Local World. APMS 2014. IFIP Advances in Information and Communication Technology*, Vol 438, pp. 184-191. Springer, Berlin, Heidelberg.

Stevens, E. and Dimitriadis, S. (2005) "Managing the new service development process: towards a systemic model", *European Journal of Marketing,* Vol 39, No. 1/2, pp. 175-198.

Summers, G. J. and Scherpereel, C. M. (2008) "Decision making in product development: are you outside-in or inside-out?", *Management Decision,* Vol 46, No. 9, pp. 1299-1312.

Webster, J. and Watson, R. T. (2002) "Analyzing the Past to Prepare for the Future: Writing a Literature Review", *MIS Quarterly,* Vol 26, pp. 13-23.

Analysis on the Level of Innovation Development in Almaty

Assel Kurmantayeva, Assel Kalambayeva, Nina Nikiforova, Madina Smykova, Lyaila Zhakypbek
Almaty Management University, Almaty, Kazakhstan
assel.kurmantayeva@gmail.com
a.kalambaeva24@gmail.com
nikiforova1504@yandex.ru
mraisovna@mail.ru
l.zhakypbek@almau.edu.kz
DOI: 10.34190/EIE.20.032

Abstract: Kazakhstan government took the policy on innovative development of the economy, which is needed to diversify the country's economy structure from oil and gas sector. The number of strategic reforms has been implemented since 2010, including the adoption of the State program of industrial-innovative development. It focuses on the development of the manufacturing industry with a concentration of efforts and resources in a limited number of sectors, regional specialization with a cluster approach and effective sector regulation. The article analyses the level of innovation development in Almaty, which is the largest city of the country, and has the most diversified economic structure in the country. However, the level of innovation did not reach the international levels. The authors conducted analysis of innovation activity measurement methods in the world, comparative analysis of innovation activities of cities in Kazakhstan, analysis of the main trends of innovation development in Almaty. The article gives the detailed research on innovation development indicators of the city for 2011-2018 years: innovation financing sources, structural shifts in the sectors and spheres of innovation, the volume of innovative products, innovation level in enterprises and etc. Thus, the authors conducted an analysis of the structure of the economy of Almaty and its industries, and identified the main trends in innovation development in the city; analyzed the international experience of assessing the level of innovation activity and the possibility of its application in the assessment of domestic enterprises; identified factors that affect the innovative activity of enterprises in Almaty in comparison with other cities in Kazakhstan; analyzed the development of innovation in the sectoral context; made assessment on the level of development of the innovative ecosystem of Almaty and determined the degree of its influence on the innovative activity of the city's enterprises. As the result, authors give recommendations on increasing the innovation activity of the city of Almaty. Why is your paper of interest to the conference participants? Use this space to persuade the reviewers why they should select this abstract for the conference: The article might bear interest for researchers, who analyses the development of innovation ecosystem in cities and governments. It can be helpful to make a research on government policies on innovation development, the role of business and government in creating innovative ecosystem.

Keywords: innovation, cities, entrepreneurship, development

1. Introduction

The concept of innovation ecosystem have been reviewed by Durst and Poutanen (2013), and multiple ways of description of the term was described. The approach to think about innovations through ecosystems discussed in academic literature widely. Adner (2006) describe innovation ecosystems as "the collaborative arrangements through which firms combine their individual offerings into a coherent, customer-facing solution". The idea of innovation ecosystem as the idea of thinking on multiple actors were proposed by Rubens et al. (2011) as "creation nets" and "innovation communities" by Wang (2009). Another concept of innovation ecosystem is "Triple\Quadruple Helix" models. Firstly, the concept of "Triple Helix" was introduced by Etzkowitz and Leydesdorff in 1995, when national innovation ecosystem created as the result of intertwine of government, business and academia. The fourth helix as "media-based and culture industries" was suggested by Carayannis & Campbell (2009), and in 2017 the civil society was defined as the fourth helix by by Carayannis & Campbell. In order to benefit from "Quadruple Helix Innovation System Framework" governments should setup mechanisms, procedures, tool which create ecosystem.

The purpose of the research on development of Innovations in Almaty is to identify factors and indicators that influence the development of innovations in the city of Almaty, as well as to develop recommendations for increasing innovation activity, taking into account the specifics of the socio-economic development of the city.

Measuring innovation

The international experience of measuring innovation activity of the country is based on international rankings. The major rankings on measurement of level of innovation activity are The Global Innovation Index, Global Innovation Cities™ Index, The Global Competitiveness Index, Doing Business, Global Financial Centres Index.

The Global Innovation Index (GII) is co-published by Cornell University, INSEAD, and the World Intellectual Property Organization (WIPO, an agency of the United Nation. GII serves as the basis for calculating the Global Innovation Cities ™ Index. The structure of the constituent components of GII is shown in Figure 1.

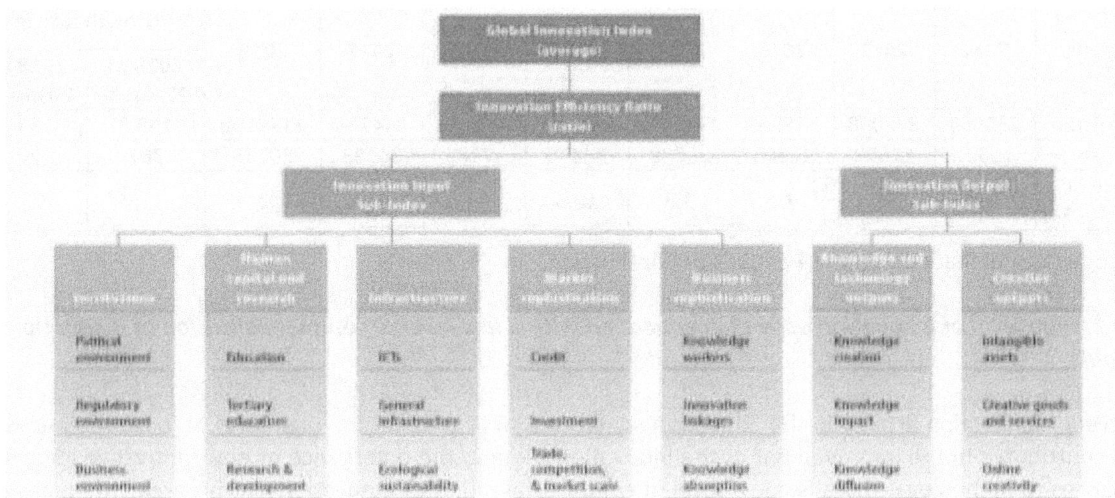

Source: https://www.globalinnovationindex.org/about-gii#framework

Figure 1: The Global Innovation Index components

Kazakhstan is ranked on the 79th place out of 129, scored 31.03 out of 100 in 2019, and ranked 3rd in Central and Southern Asia region. However, moved down five positions compared to 74th position in 2018. Kazakhstan has the weak positions in knowledge and technology outputs (13.20 out of 100), creative outputs (18.4 out of 100).

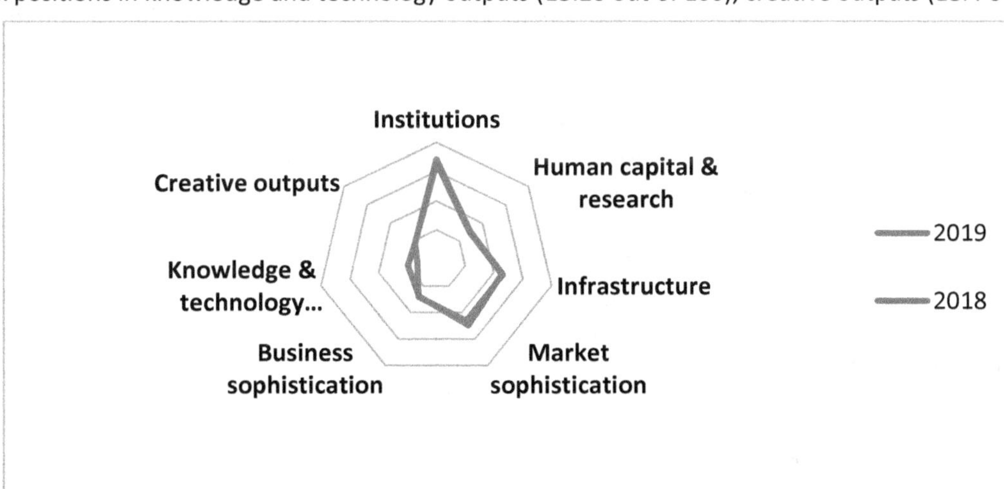

Source: Global Innovation Index Report 2016 (9th Edition)

Figure 2: Kazakhstan in Global Innovation Index (2018-2019)

In general, there is a positive dynamics of Kazakhstan in the ranking and demonstrates fairly high scores in such positions as: ease of business creation, ease of payment of taxes by economic entities and provision of online service of public services, which are usually not typical for developing countries.

2. Analysis of the main trends of innovation development in Almaty

Trend 1. Growth in the volume of manufactured innovative products in Almaty.

Almaty is one of the centers of development and introduction of innovations in the Republic of Kazakhstan. Until 2015 Almaty showed the growth rate of the volume of manufactured innovative products 2.3 times higher than the growth rate of this indicator in general across Kazakhstan (Table 1). However, this tendency slowed down starting from 2013, when the capital of Kazakhstan Nur-Sultan city started to show the growth of innovations, presumably due to activities of newly opened laboratories at Nazarbayev University, launch of Astana Innovation hub and other institutional development centers.

Table 1: Dynamics of growth in the volume of produced innovative products in the Republic of Kazakhstan and Almaty for 2011-2018, KZT million

Regions	2011	2012	2013	2014	2015	2016	2017	2018	Growth rate in	
									2015 to 2011г.,%	2018 to 2014г.,%
Kazakhstan	235963	379006	578263	580386	377196	445776	844735	1179150	159,8	51
Almaty	10601	12579	12505	22088	38876	17186	26183	30228	367	27
Share of Almaty, %	4,5	3,3	2,2	3,8	10,6	4	3	3		

Source: Agency of Statistics of the Republic of Kazakhstan

Trend 2. High level of innovation activity in education with a low level of commercialization of innovations in this field.

The level of innovation activity in the education sphere is 53.7%. Despite the high level of innovation activity, which contributes to the improvement of the innovation climate, the emergence of new innovative ideas and approaches to technology, there is a low level of commercialization of innovations in this area. The measures were taken at the state level, to implement the process of commercialization of innovations: the Law of the Republic of Kazakhstan as of October 31, 2015 No. 381-V "On the commercialization of scientific and / or scientific results" was adopted, and grants were announced for various innovative projects.

With the purpose of activating innovative activity and ensuring the process of commercialization of innovations in the field of education, the universities have begun the process of transforming classical education into an entrepreneurial one, which is aimed at forming entrepreneurial thinking among the teachers and students and acquiring the necessary competencies for the development of innovative projects and their commercialization.

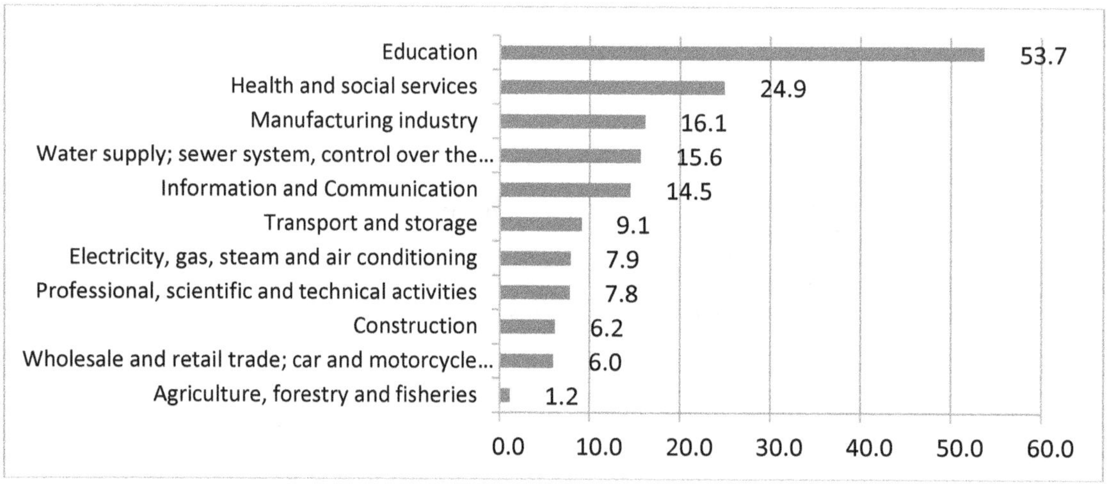

Source: Agency of Statistics of the Republic of Kazakhstan

Figure 3: The level of innovation activity by industry in Almaty in 2018%

Trend 3. Innovation is implemented mainly independently or outsourced.

Enterprises introduce process innovations on their own or jointly with other organizations. Independent innovations are introduced mainly by companies producing food products. Innovation is introduced with the involvement of foreign investors. As can be seen in Figure 4, 36% of enterprises introduce innovation independently, 19% jointly with other organizations, and 37% of enterprises introduce innovations with outsourcing.

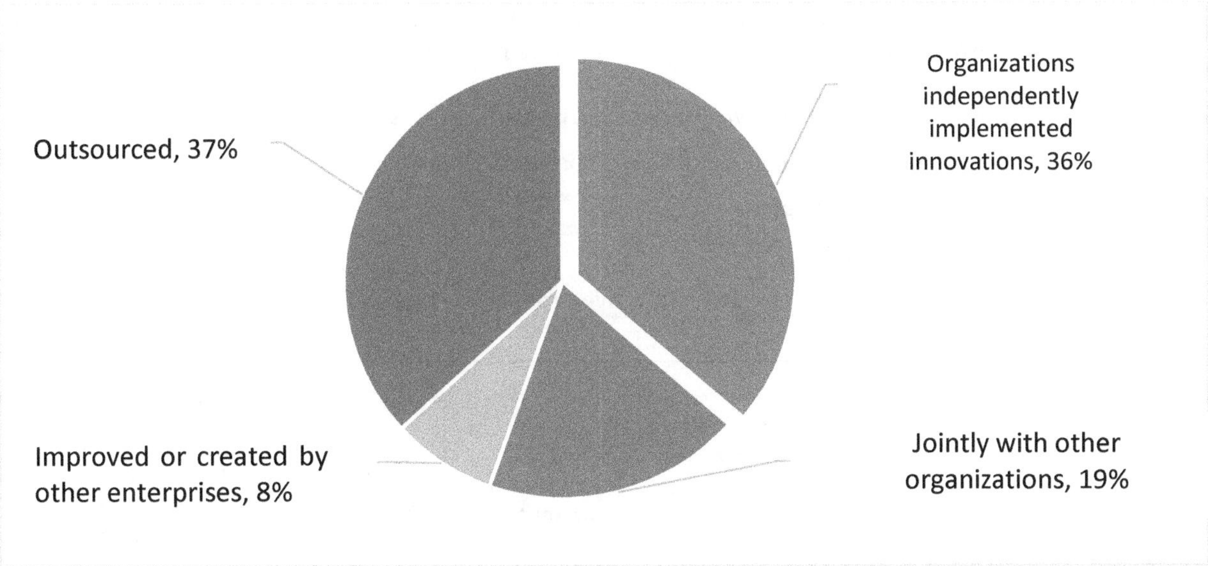

Source: Agency of Statistics of the Republic of Kazakhstan

Figure 4: The share of enterprises that implemented process innovations independently or jointly other organizations in Almaty in 2018,%

Trend 4. The prevalence of process and product innovations.

From the overall 6997 enterprises of Almaty city, only 670 (9,6%) are considered to have innovations. As it can be seen from the data, given in the table 2, enterprises of Almaty mainly introduce process innovations (255 enterprises) and product innovations (202 enterprises). The major share of product and process innovations is related to manufacturing industry (76% and 46%), whereas marketing and organizational innovations are introduced in wholesale and retail trade (74% and 46%). Only 8 enterprises develop and implement all 4 types of innovation (1.2% out of 670). The largest share in process innovation conducted by health and social services industry (20%) and manufacturing industry (18%).

Table 2: The number of enterprises by type of innovation in terms of types of economic activity in Almaty in 2018, million KZT

	Number of enterprises with at least one of four types of innovation	of them				
		product innovation	process innovation	marketing innovation	organizational innovation	all four types of innovation
Wholesale and retail trade	159	36	39	74	46	1
Manufacturing industry	140	76	46	21	34	4
Health and social services	99	17	52	17	51	2
Construction	71	12	3	32	24	-
IT and communication	71	21	33	13	14	-
Transport and warehousing	53	4	29	1	25	-
Professional, scientific and technical activities	46	15	36	11	7	-
Education	22	16	11	2	8	1

Source: Agency of Statistics of the Republic of Kazakhstan

Trend 5. The prevalence of manufactured products over the realized products

In 2018, the city's enterprises produced innovative products for the sum of **30 228** million KZT, while the volume of sold innovative products was **23 646** million KZT or 78% of the volume produced (Table 3).

A comparative analysis of data for 2013 and 2015 showed, that the volume of innovative products produced during these years grew 3,1 times, and the volume of innovative products grew only 2,2 times.

In 2018 almost 22% of innovative products were not sold. The main reasons were:

- not meet the expectations of consumers, not satisfy consumer's demand;
- low level of popularity in the market;
- not competitive in price or quality.

Table 3: The volume of produced and realized innovative products by types of economic activity in Almaty in 2018 (mln. KZT)

			including	
	The amount of innovative products produced	**The amount of innovative products sold**	**new or significantly improved products (services) that are new to the market**	**new or significantly improved products (services) that are new to the organization**
Total	**30 228,40**	**23 646,60**	**11 539,50**	**12 107,10**
Manufacturing industry	x	9 449,40	x	x
Wholesale and retail trade	5 481,90	5 426,10	x	x
Transport and warehousing	3 530,20	x	x	-
Information and communication	8 934,20	5 872,30	x	x
Professional, scientific and technical activities	943,1	1 170,50	733,8	436,8
Education	171,3	134,6	x	x
Health and social services	536,6	x	-	x

Source: Agency of Statistics of the Republic of Kazakhstan

Trend 6. The main source of financing for the company's innovative activity is its own funds and funds from the government budget.

The majority of the innovations are funded by own funds of the companies (47% in 2015 56% in 2018), whereas international investments are not used for innovations. There is a sharp decrease in state budget used for investments from 12 614 mln. KZT in 2015 to 4997 mln. KZT in 2018. 2016 demonstrates the lowest spending on innovations during the period of 2016-2018. From 2017, local budget spending on innovations risen significantly (122 mln. KZT in 2016 to 11 742 mln. KZT in 2017). The main reason for this trend was the decentralization of budgeting system.

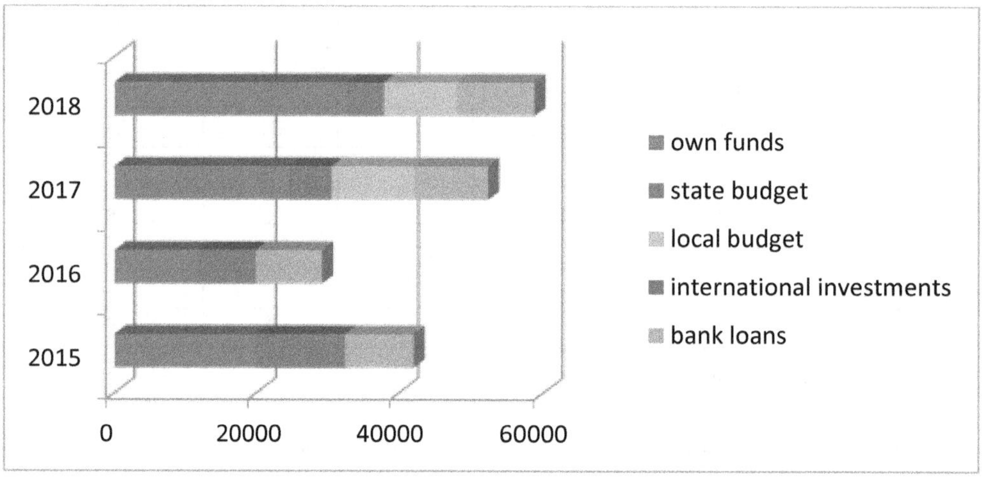

Source: Agency of Statistics of the Republic of Kazakhstan

Figure 5: The amount of innovations funding by the sources in Almaty in 2018, mln. KZT

Trend 7. Lack of demand for innovations is the main reason for the absence of innovations in organizations

39% of companies do not introduce innovations as they assume that there is no demand for innovations, whereas 30% do not have enough funds. Such reasons as "Difficulty in finding partners for innovation", "Lack of skilled staff", "The dominance of existing enterprises in the market", "Lack of market information" have the lowest influence for non-implementation of innovations (Figure 6).

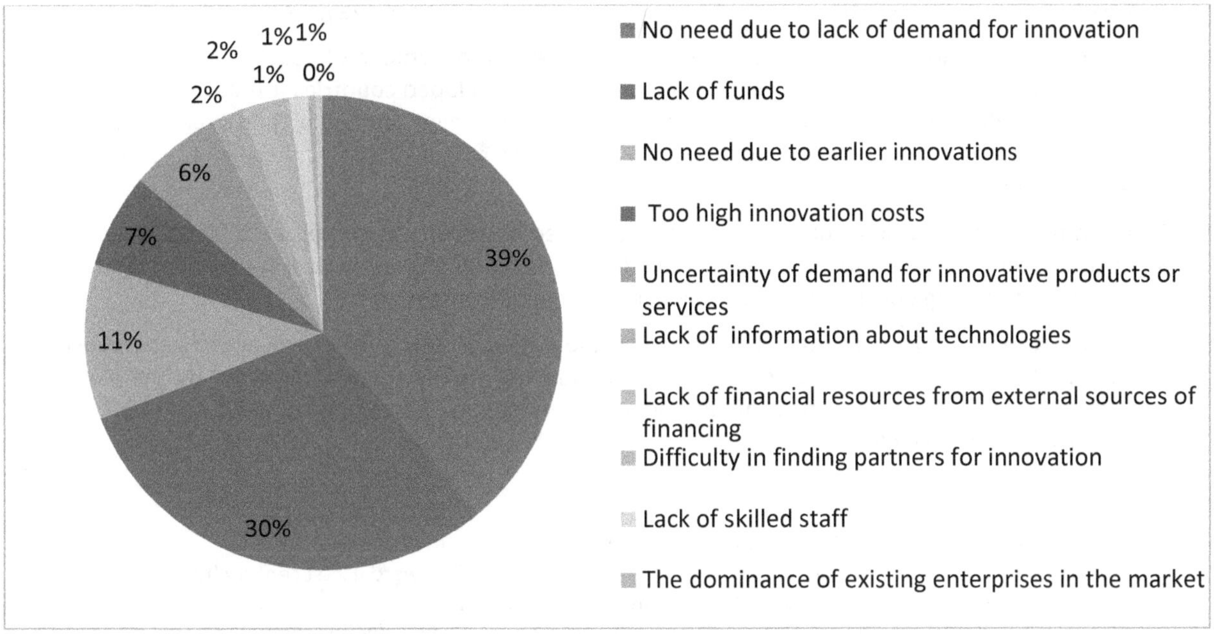

Source: Agency of Statistics of the Republic of Kazakhstan

Figure 6: The reasons for the absence of innovations in organizations in Almaty city 2018, %

3. Conclusion

Almaty is a "rising innovation center" with a limited infrastructure, with a low level of commercialization of innovations. In such circumstances, there is an obvious need for government and local authorities to interfere in the process of creating an infrastructure for the development of innovation. On the other hand, Almaty is a "centrally managed region" in the sphere of innovations. This means that this type of public administration system can provide a coordinated planning system that can lead to a properly structured development of innovation.

A retrospective analysis of scientific and research activities in the field of innovations in Almaty has allowed to draw certain conclusions and identify the main problems. The problems can be divided into strategic and tactical ones.

The main tactical problems in the field of innovative development are the following:

- 1. The equipment and infrastructure for innovative development in Almaty are exhausted and outdated. In universities and companies, the state of the infrastructure of research laboratories is in a decadent state. The situation is exacerbated by the inadequacy of information materials available at university libraries. All these problems are caused by a low level of financing of the innovation infrastructure of Almaty.
- 2. The lack of incentives for the commercialization of inventions by state universities and research institutes adversely affects the relationship between universities and production. The research organization receives an exclusive right only for the use of the invention, but not for its commercialization or obtaining at least part of the revenue from its commercialization.
- 3. Information on the latest achievements in the field of innovation is not available, limited subscriptions to leading scientific databases, specialized research searches and electronic versions of leading scientific journals, which hinders the development of research and the integration of education and research activities.

- 4. Low level of English language, lack of finance for the organization of international symposiums and seminars, as well as participation in foreign exhibitions and conferences does not provide a full and comprehensive development of the city's innovative life.
- 5. The high level of teaching load, about 20-26 hours of classroom work per week, does not allow faculty members to fully engage in research activities. The number of young scientists is decreasing, in particular, those who are engaged in teaching and received a degree of doctors of science. Teams of recognized universities lose their competitiveness in the process of struggling to receive government funding.
- 6. Empirical data show that at present the ratio between the number of researchers, engineers and specialists engaged in development is 25: 4: 1, and in most developed countries it is 1: 2: 4. This indicates that in higher education institutions and research organizations, pilot production and experimental design structures are curtailed everywhere. Commercialization of the results of R&D in these units, respectively, is difficult or impossible.
- 7. In companies, the introduction of innovations, as noted by experts, is complicated by the regulation of standardization processes and licensing documents. The duration of these processes leads to the fact that after all the permitting documents are received, the innovation is obsolete.
- 8. According to World Bank estimates in Kazakhstan, less than one-third of all researchers are involved in the public R& D sector, and RDIs usually receive about 80% of the funding provided by the PWS on a competitive basis. As a result, most of the scientists working in higher educational institutions are not covered by research activities.

References

Agency of Statistics of the Republic of Kazakhstan https://www.stat.gov.kz/

Carayannis, E. G., & Campbell, D. F. J. (2009). "Mode 3" and "Quadruple Helix": toward a 21st century fractal innovation ecosystem. International Journal of Technology Management, 46(3/4), 201.

Carayannis, E.G. (2008) Knowledge-driven creative destruction, or leveraging knowledge for competitive advantage: strategic knowledge arbitrage and serendipity as real options drivers triggered by co-opetition, co-evolution and co-specialization. Journal of Industry and Higher Education, 22, 343–353.

Carayannis, E.G. and Campbell, D.F.J. (2009) "Mode 3" and "Quadruple Helix": toward a 21st century fractal innovation ecosystem. International Journal of Technology Management, 46, 201–234.

Carayannis, Elias G.; Campbell, David F. J. (2006). "'Mode 3': Meaning and implications from a knowledge systems perspective". Knowledge creation, diffusion, and use in innovation networks and knowledge clusters : a comparative systems approach across the United States, Europe, and Asia. Praeger Publishers. pp. 1–25. ISBN 0-313-08323-1. OCLC 70209391.

Etzkowitz, H. and Leydesdorff, L. (2000) 'The dynamics of innovation: from national systems and 'mode 2' to a triple helix of university-industry-government relations', Research Policy, Vol. 29, pp.109–123.

Florida, R. (2004) The Rise of the Creative Class and How It's Transforming Work, Leisure, Community and Everyday Life. New York: Basic Books.

Gibbons M., Limoges C., Nowotny H., Schwartzman S., Scott P., Trow M. (1994) The New Production of Knowledge: The Dynamics of Science and Research in Contemporary Societies. London: SAGE.

Global Trends - 2025: The Transformed World. StopIDCC, Washington DC / 20402-0001. 118 sec. www.dni.gov/nic/NIC_2025_project.html

In Almaty, 21 projects received state support within the framework of the first five-year plan of the Institute for Advanced Studies. - [electronic resource]: http://www.kazpravda.kz/news/ekonomika/v-almati-21-proekt-poluchil-gospodderzhku-v-ramkah-pervoi-pyatiletki-fiir/

The Global Innovation Index. source: https://www.globalinnovationindex.org

The State Program of the Forced Industrial-Innovative Development of the Republic of Kazakhstan for 2010-2014, approved by the Decree of the President of the Republic of Kazakhstan dated March 19, 2010 No. 958.

Examining the Health Effects of an Innovative Collaboration Initiative Aimed at Reducing Social Exclusion

Stefan Lagrosen[1] and Yvonne Lagrosen[2]
[1]Department of Organisation and Entrepreneurship, School of Business and Economics, Linnaeus University, Kalmar, Sweden
[2]Academy for Innovation, Design and Technology, Mälardalen University, Eskilstuna, Sweden
stefan.lagrosen@lnu.se
yvonne.lagrosen@mdh.se
DOI: 10.34190/EIE.20.109

Abstract: While employment levels vary, some people tend to remain far from the labour market. Various efforts are made from different public organisations to enhance their employability. Nevertheless, since their problems are usually complex and multi-dimensional, isolated efforts are usually less successful. In an innovative collaboration initiative in a Swedish municipality, a collaboration unit was formed to co-ordinate the efforts of four organisations: the county council, the municipality, the Swedish public employment service and the Swedish social insurance agency. Various activities are carried out intending to strengthen the clients' overall employability and wellbeing in a holistic way. In previous research, associations between the perceived quality of the organisation people are working in and their reported health status have been identified. However, research into the relationship between the quality of employability enhancing initiatives and client health status is lacking. The purpose of the study is to examine the associations between the health status of people that are excluded from the labour market and the quality of the efforts aimed at increasing their employability. An online questionnaire was developed and answered by 80 participants in the programme. The data was analysed using multivariate statistical methods. Associations between variables measuring health status and experience of the employability enhancing initiatives were examined. The data show that the participants are generally satisfied with the activities of the studied organisation but their self-reported level of health is low. When correlations between the perceived quality of the activity of the initiative and the health status of the clients were measured, few significant associations were found. In contrast, cluster analysis defined four clusters in which the highest reported health scores were found in both the cluster that was most satisfied and the cluster that was least satisfied with the activities. Further research is needed to discover the mechanics behind these results. However, the current study will also be of value for organisations aiming at increasing the employability of people who are far from the labour market.

Keywords: health, quality management, innovation, social exclusion, life style, unemployment

1. Introduction

Notwithstanding temporary changes in employment levels, some people tend to remain far from the labour market with a very low employability. This constitutes a cost for society and often suffering for the people themselves. Various initiatives are taken by different organisations to ameliorate the situation for these people and improve their employability. However, since many organisations are often involved, initiatives sometimes become uncoordinated and lacking in strategic direction. To amend this the organisation Samordningsförbundet (translates approximately as the coordination association) was founded. Their aim is to co-ordinate the efforts of four organisations: the county council, the municipality, the Swedish public employment service and the Swedish social insurance agency. To this end, they carry out different activities and programmes aimed at people that are socially excluded. In the year of study, 2019, they had a special focus on the health of their clients. This is the context in which this study is set.

In previous research, associations have been found between the quality management practices of organisations and the health of their employees (Lagrosen et al., 2006, Lagrosen et al., 2012). However, these studies concerned working people and the practices of the organisations that they work in. No previous study has examined the relationship between the health status of unemployed people and the quality of the efforts made by organisations aiming at helping them.

The purpose of the study is to examine the associations between the health status of people that are excluded from the labour market and the quality of the efforts aimed at increasing their employability.

The remainder of this paper is structured as follows. First, the theoretical concepts that the study is based on, quality management, health and their connection, are discussed in separate chapters. Next, the methodology is described and the findings are presented. On this basis, a discussion and conclusion section follow. Finally, the limitations of the study are considered and avenues for future research are proposed.

2. Quality management

Quality management can be viewed as a system containing values, techniques and tools (Hellsten and Klefsjö, 2000). Furthermore, it has been proposed that these parts can be ascribed to different levels. Our view, is that quality management consists of phenomena on three levels of profundity as illustrated in Figure 1.

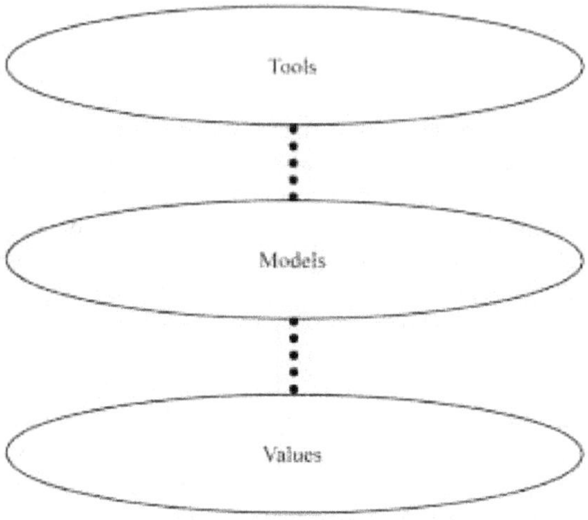

Figure 1: The levels of quality management

In the model, the most superficial level consists of various tools or techniques. These may be decision-aids or statistical tools. They are useful but have a limited impact on the organisation as a whole. On the middle level the different models used in quality management e.g. ISO9000 and the award models are found. They require the organisations to assess all their process and consequently they have a more over-arching effect. Finally, the most profound level contains the values (alternatively called basic principles (Dale et al., 2007) or cornerstones (Bergman and Klefsjö, 2010)) that the organisation espouses. They concern the way of thinking, prioritising and behaving in the organisation. Thus, they are related to culture and they have a substantial effect on the organisation's performance and ways of working. A large number of different values have been proposed but a literature review (Lagrosen, 2006) found the following six to be most common:

- *Customer orientation* – all activities should be focused on satisfying the needs and wants of the customers (internal as well as external).
- *Leadership commitment* – all leaders on all levels should have the quality of the products or services as their main priority and serve as good role models regarding quality.
- *Participation of everybody* – all staff should be engaged in the quest for quality. Quality circles and other types of teamwork should be used to make sure that everybody contributes.
- *Process orientation* – the organisation should be organised around the main processes, not limited by a stiff structure. Important processes should be mapped and process owners should be assigned.
- *Continuous improvement* – the organisation should not contend itself with certain tolerance levels or standards but continually work to become better.
- *Management by fact* – The decisions in the organisation should be based on credible and relevant information.

Quality management initiatives have been used with success by universities for increasing the employability of students (Brits, 2018, Gora et al., 2019). Quality dimensions in different higher education contexts have been investigated (Lee et al., 2016, Dirkse van Schalkwyk and Steenkamp, 2016, Lagrosen et al., 2004). However, we have not been able to find any studies investigating measures aimed at increasing employability for unemployed people, from a quality management perspective.

3. Health

Health can be defined in many different ways. One of the most common definitions, is the one by WHO which states that 'Health is a state of complete physical, mental and social well-being and not merely the absence of disease or infirmity' (WHO, 2006). This definition has been praised for expanding the view of health in a salutogenic (that which creates health) direction and linking it to well-being. Nevertheless, it has also been criticised for being too vague to be measurable. Health can be seen as a state, an experience, a process and a resource. The last alternative is often important as it is frequently the level of our health that enables or limits what we can do in life in terms of work, relationships and leisure activities. An important concept with regard to health is the 'sense of coherence', SOC, which was proposed by Antonovsky as a phenomenon which determines people's ability to maintain good health despite adverse circumstances (Antonovsky, 1987). It contains the dimensions meaningfulness, manageability and comprehensibility. Thus, it concerns whether we can comprehend the occurrences in our lives, if we feel that we can manage them and to which extent we feel that our lives have a greater meaning. Stress is a critical determinant of health, especially in current work-life. In a central model of stress, the demand-control model, the strain that people are subjected to is seen as the relationship between the demands that their work contain and the level to which they can control these demands (Karasek, 1979, Karasek and Theorell, 1990).

In this study, we chose to include the following indices regarding health:

- *Experienced health.* This is an index that was first used in 2004 (Lagrosen, 2004) and has been used in numerous studies since then. It measures the respondents' general well-being, tiredness and frequency of illness.
- *Lack of health as a resource*. In accordance with the discussion above, this index measures the extent to which the respondents are hindered by health problems with regard to their work, study, relationships as well as their general ambitions in life.
- *SOC-variables*. There are elaborated questionnaires measuring sense of coherence. However, since this is only a minor part of this study, we chose to instead only include a simple index containing one item for each of the dimensions: meaningfulness, manageability and comprehensibility.
- *Demand*. In accordance with the demand-control model this variable measures the pressure that the respondents feel regarding time, amount and complexity of tasks etc.

In addition, a single question regarding how often they feel stressed was included.

4. The connection between quality management and health

Many studies have indicated an association between employee health and quality management (Lagrosen, 2004, Lagrosen, 2006, Lagrosen et al., 2006, Lagrosen et al., 2012, Bäckström et al., 2012). The studies have found that the level to which the employees perceive that the quality management values permeate the organisation is correlated with their self-reported health status. In particular, the values leadership commitment and participation of everybody have been shown to be essential (Lagrosen et al., 2010). In this study, the vantage point was the six quality management values presented above. However, customer orientation was judged to be less relevant in this case since the clients are not customers in the normal sense. In addition, the possibilities for the respondents to assess whether the staff of the organisation base their decisions on facts were deemed to be low. Consequently, only the following four values were included in the questionnaire:

- *Participation of everybody.* In this case, the items concerned the clients themselves, if they can influence the way they participate in activities and the activities as a whole.
- *Leadership commitment.* Normally, it is the commitment of the managers that are measured with this index. However, in this organisation all the staff have a kind of leadership role vis-à-vis the clients. Thus, we chose to regard the staff of Samordningsförbundet as leaders and measure the way they support their clients.
- *Process orientation.* This variable is not so different from the one that has been used in studies on employed people. It concerns that the focus is on important activities and that there is always someone who has the responsibility for all processes.

- *Continuous improvements.* This variable concerns whether the activities are improved over time and if the clients are encouraged to participate creatively in the development of the activities.

5. Methodology

Since the purpose is descriptive to its character, a quantitative survey was chosen as methodology. A questionnaire measuring the associations between quality, health and life style, which has been used in several previous studies, was used as a basis. The questionnaire was modified since normally it measures the experiences of employees in an organisation. It consists of several parts aimed at measuring the participants' health, life style and the experience of the quality of the activities of Samordningsförbundet. Normally, the variables were constituted of indices containing three items measured on a five level Likert-type scale with the endpoints 1=Do not agree at all and 5=Agree completely.

The study was carried out in January 2019. The questionnaire was delivered as an online form and filled in by 80 participants. It is not completely clear how many people had the possibility to fill in the questionnaire as the number of people in Samordningsförbundet's activities vary constantly with new people signing in and other people leaving due to having found a work or for other reasons. Thus, the response rate is unfortunately impossible to define exactly. Nonetheless, based on discussions with the manager of the organisation, a conservative estimate would be 200 to 300 people as potential respondents, giving a response rate of somewhere between 26 and 40 percent.

6. Findings

The demographic data regarding the participants are presented in Table 1.

Table 1: Demographic data

Gender		
Female	Male	Other
61.5 %	32.1%	6.4%

Age, years					
19 or younger	20-29	30-39	40-49	50-59	60 or older
2.5%	46.8%	22.8%	13.9%	11.4%	2.5%

Civil status				
Married	Not married but living with partner	Having partner but not living together	Single	Other
7.9%	31.6%	7.9%	51.3%	1.3%

Number of children				
None	One	Two	Three	Four or more
67.1%	7.9%	11.8%	10.5%	2.6%

Thus, the demographic situation of the participants varies considerably. Nevertheless, a majority are young, female, single without children.

Next, the participants' experience of the quality of the activities of Samordningsförbundet and their assessment of their health status were measured. The variables were three-item indices developed from previous research, as described in the previous sections, and the participants were asked to rate their experience on a 5-level Likert type scale with the endpoints 1 = do not agree at all, 5 = agree completely. The results are presented in Table 2.

Table 2: The participants experience of the quality of the activities of Samordningsförbundet and their health status

Variable	**Mean value**	**Std. Dev.**
Participation of everybody	3.43	.87
Leadership commitment	4.13	:89
Process orientation	3.89	.86
Continuous improvements	3.98	.82
Experienced health	2.42	.86
Lack of health as a resource	3.55	1.02
SOC-variables	2.83	.85
Demands	3.55	,75
Stress	3.99	1.06

The experience of the quality of Samordningsförbundets activities is generally good. Ranging between 3.43 and 4.13 on a five-level scale must be considered as high. Nevertheless, particularly concerning participation there is room for improvement. The health variables show a completely different picture. At 2.42 the experienced health level is much lower than what is normally seen in studies on the working population. The same is true for the level of the SOC variables at 2.83. The participants are also often hindered by their lack of health in various ways as can be seen by the fairly high figure of 3.55 on that index. Finally, they experience that there is much stress and high demands. In addition to the figures presented above, several questions regarding life style factors were also included. For instance, it was found that the median sleep duration was 6 hours and many participants suffer from sleeping problems. About 60% do some kind of exercise particularly (48%) walking but also gym-training in groups (16.3%) or individually (21%). Most participants (68%) want to lose weight. The majority do not smoke (59%) and have never used narcotic drugs (63%). In their free time many listen to music, read or paint. These figures were not used in the analysis but may be useful as background information.

In order to investigate the associations between the variables, correlation analysis was carried out. Since normal distribution could not be assumed, Spearman's rho was used. The correlations with experienced health and with lack of health as a resource are presented in Table 3.

Table 3: Correlations

Correlation with Experienced health	**Coefficient**	**Significance**
Participation of everybody	.236*	.043
Leadership commitment	.072	.544
Process orientation	.050	.672
Continuous improvements	.007	.952
Demands	-.415**	.000
Stress	-.409**	.000
SOC variables	.400**	.000
Correlation with lack of health as a resource	**Coefficient**	**Significance**
Participation of everybody	-.142	.229
Leadership commitment	.054	.648
Process orientation	.055	.645
Continuous improvements	.090	.447
Demands	.400**	.000
Stress	-.409**	.000
SOC variables	-.417**	.000

*=significant on the .05 level, **=significant on the .01 level

The results here are also very different from those that have been seen in studies regarding the relationship between quality management values and health in workplace settings. Only participation of everybody is significantly associated with experienced health and none of the quality management variables are significantly associated with lack of health as a resource. On the other hand, Demands and stress were strongly negatively associated and the SOC variables strongly positively associated with experienced health and vice versa regarding lack of health as a resource. This was also expected and in line with previous research. In order, to further investigate the relationships in the material and to find possible classifications among the respondents, cluster analysis was carried out. K-means clustering was chosen and several tests showed that a four-cluster solution gave the most meaningful distribution. The result is presented in Table 4.

Table 4: The cluster analysis

Cluster	**1**	**2**	**3**	**4**
Experienced health	2.70	2.06	3.64	1.86
Lack of health as a resource	3.28	3.67	2.15	4.23
SOC-variables	3.04	2.21	4.03	2.43
Demands	3.35	4.21	2.64	3.89
Stress	3.48	4.75	2.91	4.59
Participation of everybody	3.49	1.92	4.18	3.51
Leadership commitment	4.07	2.33	4.61	4.45
Process orientation	3.68	2.25	4.42	4.26

Cluster	1	2	3	4
Continuous improvement	3.88	2.58	4.42	4.24
Number of participants	23	8	11	32

The clusters were labelled and their characteristics can be summarised as follows:

- *The middle group*. This cluster has intermediate levels on all the variables.
- *The problematics.* The participants in this group are those who are in the worst situation on many accounts. Their health is not good and their health as a resource is much lacking. They have the lowest value on the SOC-variables and the highest experience of demands and stress. They have also the lowest values by far on the quality variables.
- *The copers.* These are the people that manage their life well. They have a high level on the experienced health variable, around the same figure as is expected among the working population. Their health generally serves as a resource, not often hindering them from doing what they want. They also have a high sense of coherence while the demands and stress that they experience is moderate. In addition, they have the highest value on all the quality variables.
- *The unhealthy positives.* This group is interesting. They are actually the most unhealthy of the respondents. Their experienced health is lowest and these are the people whose lack of health means that it gives them most health-related hurdles to what they want to do. In addition, their levels on the SOC-variables is second lowest and they also suffer from high demands and stress. The interesting thing is that despite their poor health, they rate the quality variables highly, almost as high as the previous group.

7. Discussion and conclusions

The data shows that the participants rate the quality variables of Samordningsförbundet highly. This could probably be interpreted to mean that in general they are fairly satisfied with their activities. To what extend this actually does increase their employability is unknown and beyond the scope of this study. It was also shown that their health levels are feeble. These people have problems in life and thus it is of utmost importance to help them becoming more integrated in society. Having a proper employment is an important part of this as it not only gives financial possibilities but also more regular daily routines and increased social interactions. Employability may, however, be difficult, not least since they feel stressed and experience high demands even when they are not working. Helping them to a more healthy lifestyle regarding sleep, exercise, diet, substance use etc. is in this context extraordinarily vital and thus it is a major focus of Samordningsförbundet.

Notwithstanding the finding that the quality variables are rated high, there was basically no significant association between the participants' health levels and their experience of the quality of Samordningsförbundet's activities. This is a bit surprising and in contrast to previous research in which clear associations between the quality variables and employee health is usually found. Nevertheless, the cluster analysis cast additional light on this association, which seems to be exceptionally complex in this context. The most intriguing finding of the cluster analysis was that those who value the quality of Samordningsförbundet's activities highest are both those that have best health and those that have worst health. Thus, there may be an association here that is non-linear. Possibly, the reason is that the staff of the organisation focus most of their energy and time on those clients that have worst health which makes them satisfied while those who have best health manage rather well by themselves. If so, the losers may be those whose health is not bad enough to give them maximum attention from the staff but also not good enough for them to manage without it. With more resources, the organisation would perhaps have been able to focus more also on these groups. Thus, a recommendation would be to assure that organisations such as Samordningsförbundet have sufficient funds to engage all clients.

8. Limitations and suggestions for further research

There are many limitations to this study which means that the results need to be interpreted with some caution. First, it is only a case study of the initiative of one organisation in one country and the possibilities to generalise the findings to other contexts are uncertain. Second, a quantitative survey of the kind used in this study has in itself certain restrictions regarding the depth of the findings. While certain associations can be identified, the mechanics of and reasons for them remain unknown. Third, the response rate was fairly low which means that the actual numbers may be somewhat uncertain. A heuristic non-response analysis was carried out by discussing the demographics of the respondents with the staff which led to the conclusion that the demographics of the respondents are consistent with those of the entire research population. This strengthens the reliability of the findings.

In further research, it would be very interesting to delve deeper into the mechanics of the findings from this study. For instance, knowing how the people in the 'copers' cluster manage their situation so that they can remain in good health would be valuable and contain numerous lessons for the work practices of Samordningsförbundet and other organisations that work with a similar aim. Moreover, examining if the assumption above, that the reason for the high experience of quality by those with the worst health is because they receive more attention, is true, would be very interesting. Obviously, there may be other causes and knowing the characteristics of them would be useful for the further development of the activities. For all these research avenues qualitative methodology should be most useful. Consequently, in-depth qualitative case studies into organisations such as Samordningsförbundet are strongly recommended.

Acknowledgements

The authors wish to acknowledge the staff of Samordningsförbundet for excellent collaboration in this research project.

References

Antonovsky, A. (1987), Unraveling the mystery of health : how people manage stress and stay well. Jossey-Bass: San Fransisco.

Bäckström, I., Eriksson, L. & Lagrosen, Y. (2012), "A health-related quality management approach to evaluating health promotion activities", International Journal of Quality and Service Sciences, Vol. 4 No. 1, pp. 76-85.

Bergman, B. & Klefsjö, B. (2010), Quality from customer needs to customer satisfaction. Studentlitteratur: Lund.

Brits, H. J. (2018), "Assessing employer satisfaction: an attempt to enhance graduate employability at an institution of higher learning", South African Journal of Higher Education, Vol. 32 No. 5, pp. 39-53.

Dale, B. G., van der Viele, T. & van Iwaarden, J. (2007), Managing Quality. Blackvell Publishing: Oxford.

Dirkse van Schalkwyk, R. & Steenkamp, R. J. (2016), "A top management perspective of total quality service dimensions for private higher education institutions in South Africa", South African Business Review, Vol. 20 No. 577-99.

Gora, A. A., Stefan, S. C., Popa, S. C. & Albu, C. F. (2019), "Students' perspective on quality assurance in higher education in the context of sustainability: a PLS-SEM approach", Sustainability, Vol. 11 No. 17, pp.

Hellsten, U. & Klefsjö, B. (2000), "TQM as a management system consisting of values, techniques and tools", The TQM-Magazine, Vol. 12 No. 4, pp. 238-44.

Karasek, R. (1979), "Job demands, job decision latitude and mental strain: Implications for job redesign", Administrative Science Quarterly, Vol. 24 No. 285-307.

Karasek, R. & Theorell, T. (1990), Healthy Work, Stress, Productivity, and the Reconstruction of Working Life. Basic Books: New York.

Lagrosen, S., Seyyed-Hashemi, R. & Leitner, M. (2004), "Examination of the dimensions of quality in higher education", Quality Assurance in Education, Vol. 12 No. 2, pp. 61-69.

Lagrosen, Y. (2004), "Exploring the effects of TQM on employee health", Journal of Management Systems, Vol. 16 No. 3, pp. 1-10.

Lagrosen, Y. (2006), Values and Practices of Quality Management - Health implications and organisational differences. Doctoral Thesis, Chalmers University of Technology: Gothenburg.

Lagrosen, Y., Bäckström, I. & Lagrosen, S. (2006), "Quality management and health - a double connection", International Journal of Quality and Reliability Management, Vol. 24 No. 1, pp. 49-61.

Lagrosen, Y., Bäckström, I. & Lagrosen, S. (2010), "The relationship between quality management and health - exploring the underlying dimensions", International Journal of Productivity and Quality Management, Vol. 5 No. 2, pp. 109-23.

Lagrosen, Y., Bäckström, I. & Wiklund, H. (2012), "Approach for measuring health-related quality management", The TQM Journal, Vol. 24 No. 1, pp. 59-71.

Lee, M. J., Huh, C. & Jones, M. F. (2016), "Investigating quality dimensions of hospitality higher education from student's perspective", Journal of Hospitality & Tourism Education, Vol. 28 No. 2, pp. 95-106.

WHO (2006), Constitution of the World Health Organization. WHO: Geneva.

Entrepreneurship Program Learning: Different Views of Latent, Nascent, Active Entrepreneurs and Abstainers

Stavroula Laspita[1], Ioannis Sitaridis[2], Fotis Kitsios[2] and Katerina Sarri[3]
[1]School of Humanities, Social Sciences and Economics, International Hellenic University, Thermi, Greece
[2]Department of Applied Informatics, University of Macedonia, Thessaloniki, Greece
[3]Department of Balkan, Slavic and Oriental Studies, University of Macedonia, Thessaloniki, Greece
s.laspita@ihu.edu.gr
DOI: 10.34190/EIE.20.125

Abstract: Entrepreneurship education has been discussed in entrepreneurship research as an essential ingredient for the development of entrepreneurial skills and an entrepreneurial mindset among students. Many Universities, all over the world, offer entrepreneurship related courses (either compulsory or elective), among other offerings. The research results regarding the effect of entrepreneurial offerings on student entrepreneurship though, are inconsistent, with some showing a positive and some even showing a negative effect. Additionally, the share of nascent and active entrepreneurs remains relatively low among tertiary students, and only a small share of students would like to become entrepreneurs directly after their studies. The aim of this paper is to assess the perception of Program Learning as an indicator of entrepreneurship offerings effectiveness by different groups of students (active, nascent, dreamers and abstainers) and to identify those that benefit the most out of offerings. We analyze data from 187.492 students in 50 countries of the "Global University Entrepreneurial Spirit Students' Survey" (GUESSS), collected from November 2018 to January 2019. GUESSS is an international research project that focuses on the entrepreneurial intentions and activities of university students across many countries. Results show that active, nascent entrepreneurs and intentional entrepreneurs have greater benefit from university offering, than (non-intentional) abstainers. Also, those who attended compulsory courses as part of their studies explicitly declare to have more benefit than those who attended elective courses. Finally, significant differences are observed between business and engineering students. These results offer valuable insights for the impact of entrepreneurship education to curriculum designers and educators. We propose that entrepreneurship offerings should be redesigned to fit the special needs of different groups of students (intentional, nascent, active entrepreneurs).

Keywords: entrepreneurship education, program learning, career choice

1. Background of the research

Becoming an entrepreneur is among possible career alternatives for University students, while others include paid employment in any form (e.g. employment in a large, medium sized or small company, following an academic career, working in the public sector, etc.) (Sieger, Fueglistaller, Zellweger, & Braun, 2019). The choice to become an entrepreneur, is largely determined by one's entrepreneurial mindset, which is shaped within economic and social environments (Kirby & Ibrahim, 2011). Part of the social environment is the University in which students study and formal Entrepreneurship Education (EE) in Universities can equip students with the necessary skills, aspirations and network for an entrepreneurial career (Bergmann, Geissler, Hundt, & Grave, 2018; Boldureanu, Ionescu, Bercu, Bedrule-Grigoruță, & Boldureanu, 2020; Entrialgo & Iglesias, 2016). Besides compulsory and elective courses in Entrepreneurship, there are also specialized Undergraduate and Postgraduate Entrepreneurship Programs, and an increasing number of students attend these from various disciplines (Kakouris & Liargovas, 2020).

Despite the fact that Universities invest in EE and the fact that there are studies that show a positive effect of the exposure in EE on the selection of an entrepreneurial career, some studies show opposite results (Do Paço, Ferreira, Raposo, Rodrigues, & Dinis, 2015; Marques, Ferreira, Gomes, & Rodrigues, 2012; Oosterbeek, Van Praag, & Ijsselstein, 2010; Sitaridis & Kitsios, 2017). Additionally, the share of nascent and active entrepreneurs remains quite low among tertiary students (Kakouris, 2016; Law & Breznik, 2017; Maresch, Harms, Kailer, & Wimmer-Wurm, 2016). The findings of the Global University Entrepreneurial Spirit Students' Survey (GUESSS), show that the great majority of students do not want to follow an entrepreneurial career path in the short term (Slavtchev, Laspita, & Patzelt, 2012) but they prefer to be employed by firms, regardless if they attend entrepreneurship courses or not (Holienka, Gál, & Kovačičová, 2017; Sarri & Laspita, 2019). These contradicting results show that exposure to general EE may not be enough to aspire different students into becoming entrepreneurs. How different groups of students perceive learning from Entrepreneurship offerings in their Universities may help design specialized Programs for different categories of students.

Students' perceptions of program learning can be used as a measure of entrepreneurship courses effectiveness (Souitaris, Zerbinati, & Al-Laham, 2007). The perceptions of students about courses are often used for course evaluation purposes (Sitaridis & Kitsios, 2019) and can offer a tool to evaluate the students' beliefs regarding the development of abilities and skills during the courses and offerings they attend. Learning from a program can improve students' skills (such as opportunity recognition), knowledge (entrepreneurship specific). It can also provide them access to networks, experience and intuition (Johannisson, 1991; Shepherd & DeTienne, 2005; Souitaris et al., 2007). The comparison of program learning perceptions between different demographic groups, can identify students that benefit the most from these, highlight inefficiencies and help design more effective entrepreneurship programs.

One factor that seems to play an important role on perceptions of Program Learning is students' previous experience. For example, students with a family background in entrepreneurship may be predisposed to entrepreneurship and may have an advantage over other students, since they are more motivated (Fellnhofer, 2017). Further, students, with a prior experience with entrepreneurship, such as nascent or active entrepreneurs, may also benefit the most from entrepreneurship courses. The type of the entrepreneurship course (elective or compulsory), may also have a different impact on students' perceptions of an entrepreneurship career path. For example Karimi, Biemans, Lans, Chizari, and Mulder (2016) found that only elective courses and not compulsory courses significantly increased students' entrepreneurial intention. Lastly, students attending courses in departments of business administration often exhibit a reduced inclination towards entrepreneurship than students of other departments (Franke & Lüthje, 2004; Kakouris, 2016; Law & Breznik, 2017; Maresch et al., 2016; Passoni & Glavam, 2018).

Our research builds upon previous findings and tries to shed light to the following research questions: Are there significant differences in the perceptions of different groups of university students regarding their perceptions on Program Learning offered in their universities? Does the course type affect Program Learning?

The proposed theoretical model for the purposes of this study is illustrated in the following figure **Error! Reference source not found.**. The Program Learning construct is used as the dependent variable, predicted by nascent entrepreneurs, active entrepreneurs, intentional entrepreneurs and abstainers (students with no entrepreneurial intention) as dummy variables.

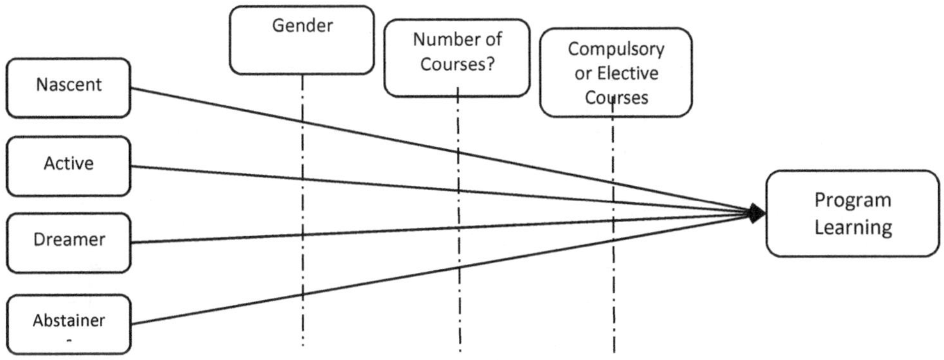

Figure 1: The proposed research model

The structure of the paper is as follows. In the following section the methodology of the study is presented, along with the results. Then the results are discussed and conclusions are drawn. Finally, the limitations of the study are addressed, along with suggestions for future research.

2. Methodology

In order to test the proposed research model, a large sample from the Global University Entrepreneurial Spirit Students'Survey (GUESSS survey) was used. GUESSS is a global research project that focuses on the entrepreneurial intentions and activities of University students, across many countries. Data were gathered by the means of an online questionnaire, during Autumn-Winter 2018, in 54 countries (Sieger et al., 2019). The project is a well-established one in entrepreneurship research (Sieger, Fueglistaller, & Zellweger, 2016; Sieger & Monsen, 2015; Slavtchev et al., 2012; Zellweger, Sieger, & Halter, 2011). The questionnaire is constructed by the research project's core team under the supervision of leading academics in the respective field. Among the objectives of GUESSS is the observation and evaluation of the entrepreneurial activities undertaken by Universities and their respective entrepreneurial spirit as perceived by students (Sarri & Laspita, 2019) .

The sample used for the purpose of this research included only responses with no missing data on the items used. This led us to the inclusion of 50 countries in the final dataset and a final number of N=187.492 responses.

Dummy variables were created for nascent entrepreneurs and active entrepreneurs. Respondents who answered 'yes' to the questionnaire item "Are you currently trying to start your own business / to become self-employed?", were identified as nascent entrepreneurs and individuals who answered 'yes' to the item "Are you already running your own business / are you already self-employed?" were identified as active entrepreneurs. Moreover, in order to distinguish between intentional entrepreneurs (latent) and non-intentional entrepreneurs (abstainers), the entrepreneurial intention scale by Linan and Chen 2009 was used (Cronbach's a= .960). The scale included 6 items (I am ready to do anything to be an entrepreneur, My professional goal is to become an entrepreneur, I will make every effort to start and run my own business, I am determined to create a business in the future, I have very seriously thought of starting a business, I have the strong intention to start a business someday) (Holienka et al., 2017; Kakouris, 2016). To measure Program Learning (PL), participants were asked to indicate the extent to which they agree to five statements about their learning progress during their studies (the courses and offerings... increased my understanding of the attitudes, values and motivations of entrepreneurs; increased my understanding of the actions someone has to take to start a business; enhanced my practical management skills in order to start a business; enhanced my ability to develop networks; enhanced my ability to identify an opportunity) (cronbach's a= .926) (Souitaris et al., 2007). An exploratory factor analysis (EFA) was conducted, for the calculation of factor scores for each construct (entrepreneurial intention and program learning), based on the suggestions of DiStefano, Zhu, and Mindrila (2009). This method is superior to the simple weighted sum score calculation, because it uses a multivariate procedure, taking in account not only correlation between observed variables, but also correlations between latent factors. The EFA resulted in exactly 2 factors, with a 75.6% of total amount of variance explained. All items demonstrated strong communality values and factor loadings on the theoretically corresponding factor. The KMO test (*0.86*) and the significance of the Bartletts's test of sphericity ($\Delta\chi^2=747573.6, sig<0.001$) indicated sampling adequacy of data. Moreover, both factors demonstrated excellent reliability, based on Cronbach's Alpha coefficient values above *0.9*. The results of the factor analysis are summarized in Table 1.

Table 1: Factor analysis

	Communalities		**Factor Loadings**		**Factor Reliability**
	Initial	*Extraction*	*PL*	*EI*	
Program Learning (PL)	.644	.685		.816	.926
	.756	.805		.889	
	.745	.810		.892	
	.609	.560		.765	
	.670	.647		.804	
Entrepreneurial Intention (EI)	.658	.624	.742		.960
	.800	.789	.877		
	.828	.840	.909		
	.859	.894	.958		
	.782	.795	.902		
	.848	.866	.950		
	Extraction Method: Maximum Likelihood.				*Cronbach's Alpha*

Next, we used the factor score for entrepreneurial intention to create dummy variables for intentional entrepreneurs and Abstainers. Cases with EI score equal or greater than zero (EI>=0), were assigned to Dreamers and those cases scoring less than zero (EI<=0), were assigned to Abstainers category.

The descriptive statistics for each group are presented in Table 3. These statistics suggest that a small share of students are active entrepreneurs (11.6%) and nascent entrepreneurs (19%). Larger shares correspond to intentional entrepreneurs (34.9%) and abstainers (34.5%). Moreover, 30% of students were attending Business or related schools, 24% were attending Engineering schools, whereas 37.5% had self-employed parents. Regarding gender differences, both males and females were equally aspiring an entrepreneurial career in terms of intentions, with 34.8% and 35% respectively. However, the picture as far as the gender is concerned changes completely when we look at active and nascent entrepreneurs. The share of female active entrepreneurs (8%) was exactly half the share of males (16%) and the share of nascent female entrepreneurs (16.9%) was smaller than that of male entrepreneurs (21.6%). Moreover, the share of female abstainers was greater (40.1%) compared to the share of male abstainers (27.6%). Finally, the comparison between business students and engineering did not highlight any significant differences. However, business students exhibited more familiarity with the entrepreneurial career option, as their shares in the active category demonstrate a minor prevalence against the share of engineering students. A detailed analysis of participating students by gender, field of studies and age group (among other categories) is given in Table 2.

Table 2: Descriptive statistics

Descriptive statistics					
	All	*Active* (%)	*Nascent* (%)	*Dreamer* (%)	*Abstainer* (%)
All	-	11.6	19.0	34.9	34.5
Male (%)	44.4	16.0	21.6	34.8	27.6
Female (%)	55.2	8.0	16.9	35	40.1
Business (%)	30.0	12.9	21.7	39.0	26.4
Engineering (%)	23.6	10.7	21.0	39.2	29.2
Self Employed Parent (%)	37.5	16.9	22.4	35.4	25.3
16-25 (%)	76.5	9.5	18.6	36.1	35.8
26-35 (%)	15.8	18.0	20.5	30.9	30.6
36-45 (%)	3.8	23.6	21.2	29.0	26.6
46-55 (%)	1.3	23.4	20.8	25.9	30.0
56+ (%)	0.3	34.6	19.3	22.8	23.3

A correlation analysis (in Table 3) was conducted to examine the relation of Program Learning with dummy variables for each group. Program Learning is highly correlated with Active entrepreneurs ($r=.143^{**}$) and Dreamers ($r=.157^{**}$), less correlated with Nascent entrepreneurs ($r=.092^{**}$), whereas Abstainers demonstrate a negative correlation ($r=-.329^{**}$). Following these findings, a nominal variable with four distinct levels, one for each student category, was used as a predictor of Program Learning in one-way ANOVA ($F(3, 187488)=7871.48$, $p=0.000$, $\eta_p^2=.112$). Analysis of variance (ANOVA), is suitable for the statistical analysis of the effect of a nominal predictor on a continuous outcome (Kenny, 1987). The statistical significance of Levene's statistic indicated a violation of homogeneity of variance between groups. In such cases, it is recommended to examine the Welsch test ($F(3,72431.02)=8059.07$, $p=0.000$), which corroborated the existence of means' statistically significant difference between groups. Post-hoc comparisons using a Games-Howell test revealed that the mean Program Learning score of Active entrepreneurs was significantly higher ($M=.395$, $SD=1.00$) than Nascent entrepreneurs ($M=.190$, $SD=.99$), Intentional entrepreneurs ($M=.213$, $SD=.93$) and Abstainers ($M=-.454$, $SD=1.00$), which confirms the correlations' results.

In Figure 2, a graphic representation of the Program Learning mean score for Active, Nascent, Intentional and Abstainer students is shown. Based on the diagram, Active entrepreneurs have gained the greatest benefit from University courses and offerings they have attended, followed by Intentional and Nascent entrepreneurs. On the other hand, Abstainers consider the participation in entrepreneurship courses and offerings a complete waste of time.

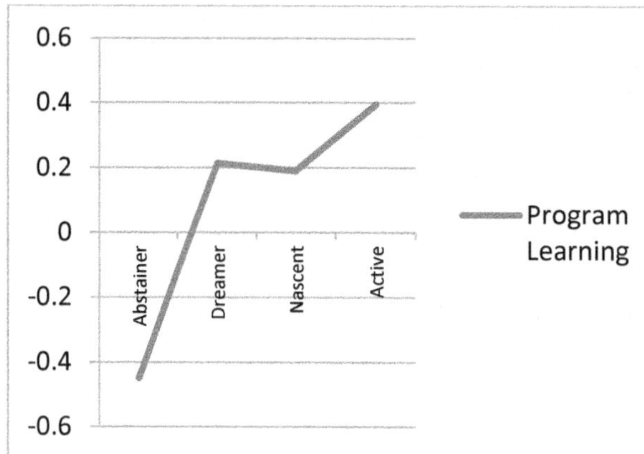

Figure 2: Program learning by student type

Table 3: Correlation analysis

	Active	Nascent	Dreamer	Abstainer	PL	No course*	Compulsory Course**	Elective Course***	Specific Prog****
Active	1	-.175**	-.265**	-.263**	**.143****	-.117**	.085**	.036**	.120**
Nascent	-.175**	1	-.355**	-.351**	.092**	-.098**	.068**	.037**	.038**
Dreamer	-.265**	-.355**	1	-.532**	**.157****	-.069**	.028**	.035**	.004
Abstainer	-.263**	-.351**	-.532**	1	-.329**	.228**	-.142**	-.089**	-.116**
PL	**.143****	**.092****	**.157****	**-.329****	**1**	**-.346****	**.160****	**.189****	**.162****
No course[i]	-.117**	-.098**	-.069**	.228**	**-.346****	1	-.598**	-.536**	-.268**
Compulsory Course[ii]	.085**	.068**	.028**	-.142**	**.160****	-.598**	1	.009**	.023**
Elective Course[iii]	.036**	.037**	.035**	-.089**	**.189****	-.536**	.009**	1	.080**
Specific Program[iv]	.120**	.038**	.004	-.116**	**.162****	-.268**	.023**	.080**	1

All types of entrepreneurship courses exhibit a positive correlation with Program Learning. Elective courses show a higher correlation with Program Learning (*r=.189***) than the other options. This finding was expected, since those who choose to attend an elective course obviously demonstrate a higher interest in entrepreneurship, and this relation is implicitly indicated by the correlation coefficient. However, the measure of correlation is not significantly different than the correlations of the other two course categories examined. On the other hand, Program Learning had a strong and negative correlation with those attended no courses. All in all, these findings suggest that entrepreneurship programs in any form have a positive effect of on students' perception of Program Learning. Next, group comparisons were conducted using an one-way ANOVA test ($F(3, 178905)=7765.14$, $p=0.000$, $\eta_p^2=.115$), in order to highlight explicit group differences. The statistically significance of Levene's statistic indicated a violation of homogeneity of variance between groups. and therefore a Welsch test ($F(3,43405.47)=8296.54$, $p=0.000$), was conducted to confirm thestatistically significant differences of mean scores between groups. Post-hoc comparisons using Games-Howell test have shown that the mean Program Learning score of students with no participation in any university entrepreneurship courses or offerings was significantly lower (*M=-.326, SD=0.97*) than that of the participants of elective courses (*M=.202, SD=.92*), the participants of compulsory courses (*M=.341, SD=.86*) and those attending specific entrepreneurship programs (*M=.641, SD=0.83*). This moderation is clearly shown in Figure 3, representing the differentiation of mean factor scores between the four course categories (Specific Program, Compulsory, Elective and no Course). Based on the diagram, the participants of specific entrepreneurship programs receive the greatest benefit, followed by the participants of compulsory courses and lastly the attendees of elective courses. As indicated in the survey those attending specific programs could also check the compulsory course option, which could probably cause some overlap and can explain the coherence between the means of these two categories. Moreover, the fact that those attending elective courses explicitly declare lower perceptions of Program Learning (expressed in terms of mean value), whereas the implicit measure of correlation is higher, compared to the participants of compulsory courses and specific programs, might indicate that these students are more eager to learn and probably have higher expectations from their courses. Therefore, the effect of Program Learning is clearly moderated by the nature of the course a student participates in (Baron & Kenny, 1986).

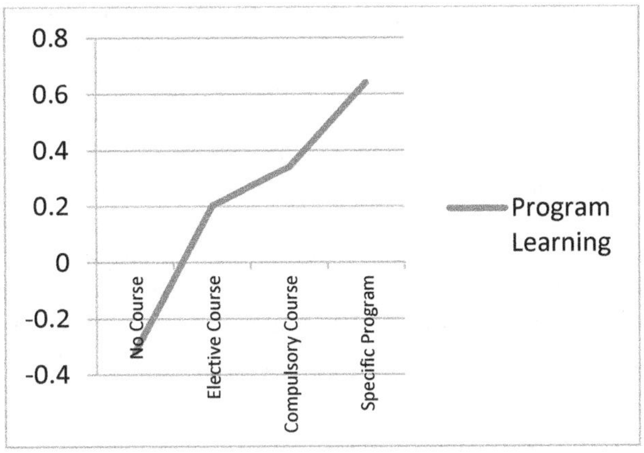

Figure 3: Program learning by course type

3. Discussion and conclusions

The goal of this paper was to gain a better understanding of how active, nascent, intentional entrepreneurs but also abstainers perceive Program Learning from entrepreneurship courses. By doing so we aim to help policy makers and educators to design more effective curriculum for students in different disciplines. We draw data from the GUEESS research project, a global project that focuses on entrepreneurial intentions and activities. Based on data from 187.492 students in 50 countries, our results show the share of nascent and active entrepreneurs remains low among tertiary students, since only 11.6% and 19% of student respectively are actual or nascent entrepreneurs. This result is in accordance with previous studies (Sieger et al., 2016).

Furthermore, contrary to previous research, claiming that business administration students demonstrate reduced preference towards entrepreneurship as a career option, compared to students of other disciplines (Franke & Lüthje, 2004; Kakouris, 2016; Law & Breznik, 2017; Maresch et al., 2016), the findings of the present study indicate that Business students are more inclined to entrepreneurship, at least compared to students from engineering departments. As far as differences observed in the relation of course type and students' perceptions about Program Learning, participants of specific standalone entrepreneurship Programs have the greatest benefit, compared students that attend compulsory or elective courses included in the curriculum of universities in isolation. The later implies that entrepreneurship education should be offered in full time Programs, in postgraduate level for example. Further, courses in entrepreneurship should be incorporated throughout the duration of their studies and not in the form of one or two "isolated" offerings in their curriculum. This result suggests that streams in entrepreneurship and specialized EE programs should be offered by Universities and especially for active and intentional entrepreneurs. In this way students will not only improve their skills and expand their knowledge, but they will also have the opportunity to address their fears and to deal with struggles that they might face in stepping into entrepreneurship, through discussion and mentorship (Sitaridis, 2019; Sitaridis & Kitsios, 2018). Moreover, if Universities wish to cultivate an entrepreneurial mindset to their students and to help them be innovative and creative in any form of employment (paid employment or self-employment), they should expose students to entrepreneurial values through for example field visits, seminars, business idea competitions, etc. (Ahmed, Chandran, & Klobas, 2017; Chen, Greene, & Crick, 1998). In this way they will help students that did not participate in any entrepreneurship related course and did not get any insights about entrepreneurship from the courses included in their curriculum.

The fact that active entrepreneurs are those who benefit most from the Program Learning compared to the other three categories, could be explained by the fact that for these students, it is possible to put immediately into practice the knowledge and skills acquired from the different offerings, like for example enhancing their management skills, having access to networks through the University etc. Intentional entrepreneurs is the group that follows active entrepreneurs, in terms of benefiting from Program Learning. These "aspiring entrepreneurs" are in the "learning process" about entrepreneurship and courses give them the opportunity to develop their idea and their skills, maybe find co-founders, form teams, etc. Furthermore, courses can inspire students and change mindsets (Souitaris et al., 2007). Nascent entrepreneurs also benefit from Program Learning but less than active and intentional entrepreneurs. This may be explained by the fact that entrepreneurship takes place in specific social and spatial context (Bergmann, Hundt, & Sternberg, 2016). In their effort to start a business, students may be caught up in bureaucracy and other procedures in order to start a business (Luo & Junkunc, 2008), which are rarely taught in entrepreneurship courses. For abstainers, taking entrepreneurship courses may be seen as a burden and a waste of their time, in terms of starting a business. However, they may be benefiting from developing entrepreneurial knowledge as life skills (Laspita & Sarri, 2019).

The results of this study offer policymakers, educators and scholars valuable insights on the impact of EE Program Learning. However, a more detailed study of the findings can help in the development of the right tools in order to identify inefficiencies and reveal the causes behind the differences. Furthermore, future research should utilize more advanced methods of analysis, in order to examine causal relations between constructs and validate the significance of the differences observed. Lastly, as our study is built on cross-sectional data, it provides a snapshot of the situation and does not capture potential shifts in intentions. At the same time, our study opens up numerous opportunities for future research that could also address the above-mentioned limitations.

References

Ahmed, T., Chandran, V., & Klobas, J. (2017). Specialized entrepreneurship education: does it really matter? Fresh evidence from Pakistan. *International Journal of Entrepreneurial Behavior & Research*.

Baron, R. M., & Kenny, D. A. (1986). The moderator–mediator variable distinction in social psychological research: Conceptual, strategic, and statistical considerations. *Journal of personality and social psychology, 51*(6), 1173.

Bergmann, H., Geissler, M., Hundt, C., & Grave, B. (2018). The climate for entrepreneurship at higher education institutions. *Research Policy, 47*(4), 700-716.

Bergmann, H., Hundt, C., & Sternberg, R. (2016). What makes student entrepreneurs? On the relevance (and irrelevance) of the university and the regional context for student start-ups. *Small Business Economics, 47*(1), 53-76.

Boldureanu, G., Ionescu, A. M., Bercu, A.-M., Bedrule-Grigoruță, M. V., & Boldureanu, D. (2020). Entrepreneurship Education through Successful Entrepreneurial Models in Higher Education Institutions. *Sustainability, 12*(3), 1267.

Chen, C. C., Greene, P. G., & Crick, A. (1998). Does entrepreneurial self-efficacy distinguish entrepreneurs from managers? *Journal of Business venturing, 13*(4), 295-316.

DiStefano, C., Zhu, M., & Mindrila, D. (2009). Understanding and using factor scores: Considerations for the applied researcher. *Practical Assessment, Research, and Evaluation, 14*(1), 20.

Do Paço, A., Ferreira, J. M., Raposo, M., Rodrigues, R. G., & Dinis, A. (2015). Entrepreneurial intentions: is education enough? *International entrepreneurship and management journal, 11*(1), 57-75.

Entrialgo, M., & Iglesias, V. (2016). The moderating role of entrepreneurship education on the antecedents of entrepreneurial intention. *International entrepreneurship and management journal, 12*(4), 1209-1232.

Fellnhofer, K. (2017). Entrepreneurship education revisited: perceived entrepreneurial role models increase perceived behavioural control. *International journal of learning and change, 9*(3), 260.

Franke, N., & Lüthje, C. (2004). Entrepreneurial intentions of business students—A benchmarking study. *International Journal of Innovation and Technology Management, 1*(03), 269-288.

Holienka, M., Gál, P., & Kovačičová, Z. (2017). Understanding student entrepreneurs: doers, procrastinators, dreamers, and abstainers. *Acta Universitatis Agriculturae et Silviculturae Mendelianae Brunensis, 65*(6), 1935-1944.

Johannisson, B. (1991). University training for entrepreneurship: Swedish approaches. *Entrepreneurship & Regional Development, 3*(1), 67-82.

Kakouris, A. (2016). Exploring entrepreneurial conceptions, beliefs and intentions of Greek graduates. *International Journal of Entrepreneurial Behavior & Research*.

Kakouris, A., & Liargovas, P. (2020). On the About/For/Through Framework of Entrepreneurship Education: A Critical Analysis. *Entrepreneurship Education and Pedagogy*, 2515127420916740.

Karimi, S., Biemans, H. J., Lans, T., Chizari, M., & Mulder, M. (2016). The impact of entrepreneurship education: A study of Iranian students' entrepreneurial intentions and opportunity identification. *Journal of Small Business Management, 54*(1), 187-209.

Kenny, D. A. (1987). *Statistics for the Social and Behavioral Sciences*: Little, Brown.

Kirby, D. A., & Ibrahim, N. (2011). Entrepreneurship education and the creation of an enterprise culture: Provisional results from an experiment in Egypt. *International entrepreneurship and management journal, 7*(2), 181-193.

Laspita, S., & Sarri, K. (2019). *The Attitude of Greek Students towards Entrepreneurship: Latest Data and Recommendations.* Paper presented at the European Conference on Innovation and Entrepreneurship.

Law, K. M., & Breznik, K. (2017). Impacts of innovativeness and attitude on entrepreneurial intention: Among engineering and non-engineering students. *International Journal of Technology and Design Education, 27*(4), 683-700.

Luo, Y., & Junkunc, M. (2008). How private enterprises respond to government bureaucracy in emerging economies: the effects of entrepreneurial type and governance. *Strategic Entrepreneurship Journal, 2*(2), 133-153.

Maresch, D., Harms, R., Kailer, N., & Wimmer-Wurm, B. (2016). The impact of entrepreneurship education on the entrepreneurial intention of students in science and engineering versus business studies university programs. *Technological forecasting and social change, 104*, 172-179.

Marques, C. S., Ferreira, J. J., Gomes, D. N., & Rodrigues, R. G. (2012). Entrepreneurship education: How psychological, demographic and behavioural factors predict the entrepreneurial intention. *Education+ Training, 54*(8-9), 657-672.

Oosterbeek, H., Van Praag, M., & Ijsselstein, A. (2010). The impact of entrepreneurship education on entrepreneurship skills and motivation. *European economic review, 54*(3), 442-454.

Passoni, D., & Glavam, R. B. (2018). Entrepreneurial intention and the effects of entrepreneurial education. *International Journal of Innovation Science*.

Sarri, K., & Laspita, S. (2019). *Greek students' attitude towards entrepreneurship: latest data and insights. Greek Report of the GUESSS Project 2018.* Retrieved from

Shepherd, D. A., & DeTienne, D. R. (2005). Prior knowledge, potential financial reward, and opportunity identification. *Entrepreneurship theory and practice, 29*(1), 91-112.

Sieger, P., Fueglistaller, U., & Zellweger, T. (2016). Student Entrepreneurship 2016: Insights From 50 Countries. St. Gallen/Bern: KMU-HSG/IMU. *International GUESSS Report, 2*(3).

Sieger, P., Fueglistaller, U., Zellweger, T., & Braun, I. (2019). Global Student Entrepreneurship 2018: Insights From 54 Countries. *St. Gallen/Bern: KMU-HSG/IMU.*

Sieger, P., & Monsen, E. (2015). Founder, academic, or employee? A nuanced study of career choice intentions. *Journal of Small Business Management, 53*, 30-57.

Sitaridis, I. (2019). *The Effect of Computer Self-Efficacy on Entrepreneurial Aspirations of Students.* Paper presented at the 2019 IEEE Global Engineering Education Conference (EDUCON).

Sitaridis, I., & Kitsios, F. (2017). Entrepreneurial intentions of information technology students: the theory of planned behaviour, the role of gender and education. *Journal for International Business and Entrepreneurship Development, 10*(3), 316-335.

Sitaridis, I., & Kitsios, F. (2018). *Entrepreneurial intentions in the field of IT: the role of gender typed personality and entrepreneurship education.* Paper presented at the 2018 IEEE Global Engineering Education Conference (EDUCON).

Sitaridis, I., & Kitsios, F. (2019). *Course Experience Evaluation using Importance-Performance Analysis.* Paper presented at the 2019 IEEE Global Engineering Education Conference (EDUCON).

Slavtchev, V., Laspita, S., & Patzelt, H. (2012). *Effects of entrepreneurship education at universities*. Retrieved from

Souitaris, V., Zerbinati, S., & Al-Laham, A. (2007). Do entrepreneurship programmes raise entrepreneurial intention of science and engineering students? The effect of learning, inspiration and resources. *Journal of Business venturing, 22*(4), 566-591.

Zellweger, T., Sieger, P., & Halter, F. (2011). Should I stay or should I go? Career choice intentions of students with family business background. *Journal of business venturing, 26*(5), 521-536.

A Framework for Understanding how Entrepreneurial Accelerator Programmes add Value to the Success of Early Stage Ventures and Corporate Partnerships

Hari Mann[1], Victoria Harrison-Mirauer[1] and Jeremy Bassett[2]
[1]Hult International Business School, Berkhamsted, UK
[2]Co-Cubed, UK
hari.mann@ashridge.hult.edu
DOI: 10.34190/EIE.20.059

Abstract: The challenge of establishing successful corporate partnerships is a well-known issue for many start-up organisations. The corollary to this is the challenge faced by corporate entities in navigating the burgeoning and fast-paced start-up eco-system. Establishing partnerships with larger corporates early in the initial phase of a start-up venture can be of value in accelerating start-up growth. Our findings discuss the role of accelerator programs for early stage ventures in both navigating and accelerating the creation of meaningful corporate partnerships. This paper explores the Co-Cubed accelerator in London and the impact of their acceleration programme on participant organisations. The study explores how start-ups can gain value from connecting with the accelerator programme and associated resources and in what forms this value is created for the corporates and start up organisations participating in the programme. Through a series of primary research interviews, questionnaires, and case studies the research proposes a framework for understanding the success factors in the relationship between accelerator programmes, corporate partners and early stage ventures. The framework shows how such programmes create and develop 'value' between corporates and participant organisations. The research findings highlight the importance of "networks" as a primary source of value gained by early stage ventures from such programmes; demonstrating how start-ups use these networks to develop and gain other resources needed to accelerate growth in the early venture stage. Importantly, these networks are identified as operating both formally and informally. The paper concludes by discussing how research and learning from accelerator programmes can be used to further support successful corporate- early stage venture partnerships covering areas for further academic enquiry.

Keywords: early stage ventures, corporate partnerships, accelerator programmes, value creation, networking

1. Introduction

This research sets out to explore the factors impacting successful value creation between corporates and startups involved in accelerator programmes. Specifically, to identify what aspects of accelerator programmes contribute to the growth and acceleration of member organisations and to value creation between start up participants and corporate entities. By value, we define this as being the resources or activities that have a 'direct' or 'indirect' effect on the growth rate and therefore the growth trajectory of the entrepreneurial venture.(Ulaga, 2003; Anderson et al, 1993)

Our findings indicate that the following are important contributory factors: appropriate selection of startups well-matched to corporate objectives /areas of interest, structured opportunities for formal and informal networking, access to corporate data which is otherwise not publicly available enabling start-ups to identify 'new needs to serve' , (whereby use cases and alternative problem hypotheses can be derived by the startups), participation by corporate decision makers with both the authority to commission further work or progress to contracting, and access to a wider network within the corporate entity, this sits alongside good knowledge of the corporate strategy and intent. The Co-Cubed Accelerator is contract focussed which differs from generic open innovation initiatives and funding competitions. The accelerator structure (cohort driven, time bound and curated) is deemed mutually advantageous as oppose to more general open innovation or competition driven approaches because there is a formal contract at stake for participating entities. For the purposes of this paper, we have focused on this type of accelerator model, contract based initiatives, and the focus is on the value they deliver.

2. Literature review

Peer review literature on accelerators is somewhat limited and fragmented, in part because accelerators are a relatively new phenomenon, with US based Y Combinator starting the trend in the US in 2005. Additionally, there is a degree of conflation in research studies of accelerators and incubators. Both are focused on coaching and developing early stage companies so that they can secure "seed" funding or progress through staged 'funding rounds' and other forms of business financing to scale and grow.

> *"Despite their seemingly similar activities, accelerators are quite different from incubators. However, substantive differences have not been comprehensively documented in the accelerator literature to date". (Roberts and Lall, 2018).*

Alongside this the relative scarcity of peer review literature and longitudinal studies makes the challenge to identify and differentiate accelerator-specific attributes and conducting research (with appropriate validity) more difficult. The literature tends to bias its efforts towards investigating successful outcome for start-ups, rather than taking a more balanced perspectives which seeks to understand corporate accelerators success as an 'exchange' of value for mutual benefit.

The challenges of corporate start-up collaboration have been well noted, both structurally and culturally (Weiblen and Chesbrough, 2015; Kohler, 2016). Given that so much 'know-how' and technology now reside beyond the boundaries of the modern firm however, engaging with entrepreneurial ecosystems through accelerators offers an important access point for corporate innovation. Kohler proposes a 4P framework for designing effective corporate accelerators as part of corporate innovation strategy based on proposition, process, people and place. In *'Bridging the gap',* Kohler identifies the prevalent modes of accelerator collaboration between early stage ventures and corporations as the following; corporate support for pilot projects, the corporate becoming a customer, the corporate becoming a distribution partner, corporate venture investment and corporate acquisition (Kohler, 2016). Importantly, this research also identifies the critical role corporate involvement plays in increasing start-up credibility, conveying, "validation for future customer acquisition" (p351). Kohler's assessment complements Weiblen and Chesbrough's attempts to map the, "ways companies can bridge the gap between themselves and the start-up world", proposing a model to assess corporate accelerators which seeks to, "balance speed and agility against control and strategic direction" (Weiblen and Chesborough 2015). These are important contributions in both illuminating the barriers to collaboration and in proposing a perspective on accelerators that ascribes to them a pivotal bridging role between the corporate and the entrepreneurial eco system (Weiblen and Chesborough 2015).

There is an important body of literature considering government sponsored incubator and accelerator initiatives; this is typically focussed on the role incubators and accelerators play in a city or country innovation 'eco system'. Bliemel and Flores' *Defining and Differentiating Accelerators* (2015) report on the Australian example is a case in point. Like others, they cite the lack of a clear definition of accelerator types as problematic and detrimental to research in the field. They suggest this ambiguity creates the risk of inaccurate conclusions about the ways in which accelerators contribute to regional innovation activity. This study is typical of attempts to contextualise accelerators within a wider entrepreneurial ecosystem, which research is usually situated at the country or regional level.[1]

Having identified the gaps in the literature around accelerators the review of the literature will now consider how accelerator design varies and the type of models that are developed. Typically, an accelerator provides a fixed or short duration program for start-up companies which includes access to resources from workspace to advisors, networking opportunities, and financing options /seed capital. Accelerators often have entry 'criteria' and organised application and selection processes which set them apart from angel investor relations and the informal networks associated with them. Accelerators tend to fall into one of four categories: independent accelerators, corporate accelerators, university accelerators and government accelerators. What differs between types is often the funding models and investment terms, as well as the entry criteria and this accelerator design has become a subject of recent interest to researchers.

To establish a true picture of the breadth of accelerator approaches it is necessary to move beyond the prominent accelerators. Fishback et al, in their review of early stage venture financing models remind us that early stage venture support is in a constant state of flux and renewal (Fishback *et al.*, 2007). More work has been done investigating incubators (independent and corporate) and 'incubatees' than accelerators, however there is much we can learn from the incubator research frameworks (Hackett and Dilts, 2004). This research takes the

---

[1] See Chandra, A., Chao, C.A. (2016). Country context and university affiliation: A comparative study of business incubation in United States and Brazil. *Journal of Technology Management and Innovation*, 11(2), 33–45 (Chandra and Chao, 2016) and Dee, N.J., Livesey, F., Gill, D., Minshall, T. (2011). Research summary: Incubator for growth - *A review of the impact of business incubation on new ventures with high growth potential.* London, UK: NESTA, updated in 2013, Dee, Nicola & Gill, D. & Lacher, R. & Livesey, Finbarr & Minshall, Tim. (2013). *A review of research on the role and effectiveness of business incubation for technology-based start-ups.*(Dee et al., 2013)

view that a small number of 'idols' are determining which start-ups are selected for acceleration and associated financing- the contention is a potentially useful vantage from which to consider our own findings. The point here is the very act of selection itself offers some inherent or initial advantage. (Fishback *et al.*, 2007).

Our research suggests that the process of selection is symbiotic with the process of defining the corporate objective /challenge matchmaking is part science, part judgement on the part of the accelerator team. In the case of Co-Cubed the founder's extensive experience in corporate innovation for a global FMCG means he was well placed to understand and to articulate the corporate objective.

Founders of prominent US-based accelerators like Techstars and Y Combinator are frequently quoted in the press for their views on entrepreneurship and this has support the dominance towards studies of the most prominent programmes. Several research studies have argued for a broadening of scope in relation to accelerator research. Roberts and Lall include the example of *Growth Africa,* which runs accelerators in Kenya, Uganda and Ethopia, "places that bear little resemblance to Silicon Valley" (Roberts and Lall, 2018, p. 4). In their longitudinal study of a German corporate accelerator, Krupp et al cite five success factors including; transparent and aligned goals, an 'independent team of start-up advocates' on the corporate side, an extensive and committed external network, senior leadership backing and tracking longer term performance indicators. While their findings are geographically limited and concerned with a specific sector (telecommunications) this research is extremely valuable in its longitudinal perspective. (Kupp, Marval and Borchers, 2017).

Cohen et al consider the design of accelerator programmes in the US, noting the increasing popularity of accelerators as a model of entrepreneurial innovation and, 'an increasingly important part of entrepreneurial ecosystem (Cohen et al., 2019). While they are able to identify key elements 'common' too many U.S accelerators, (including fixed timeframes, cohort-based approaches providing mentoring and coaching for participants) they also note significant variation in accelerator design. This research seeks to model the connections between accelerator design and start-up outcomes, in an attempt to bring together the disparate research in the field. Importantly Cohen et al note one of the most important, if not the most distinguishing factor between incubators and accelerators as the latter having an elevated focus on 'learning' (Hallen, Cohen and Bingham, 2019). In conclusion, aside from emphasising the favourable impact on start-up funding raised by investor-sponsored accelerators, (over and above their corporate counterparts), this paper highlights the significant implications for research of the lack of an agreed taxonomy of accelerators. Cohen stresses this undermines attempts to understand, quantify and therefore replicate the part played by accelerators across the orchestra of the entrepreneurial ecosystem. Boni and Joseph situate accelerators as one of four models or groups of corporate open innovation approaches, concluding the choices corporates make in terms of extent their open innovation activities evolve based on the degree of an organisation's innovation maturity (Boni and Joseph, 2019). They argue managed accelerator programmes offer a useful option for corporates making early forays into the entrepreneurial ecosystem.

Few studies emphasise the 'soft' side of corporate accelerator collaborations, an exception is Mahmoud-Jouini et al's study of 12 accelerator programmes which suggests two key factors influence accelerator effectiveness; first, a differentiated value proposition for startups based on the capitalization of corporate assets and secondly a specific *process* for managing the relationships between the corporate and start-up participants. Their research highlights the impact of dedicated business developers designated to oversee relationships "to ensure that the interests of both parties converge". (Mahmoud-Jouini, Duvert and Esquirol, 2018)

Much of the literature asks the ostensibly simple question, 'Do Accelerators Work?' in response to challenges from across the innovation field as to their proven efficacy. Hallen et al's (2019) comparative study suggests some timeframes are accelerated for start-up companies as a result of accelerator programmes and demonstrates the importance of interaction and consultation with individuals outside the firm including mentors, peers and customers. (Hallen, Cohen and Bingham, 2019). The central part this networking plays in connecting the start-up and corporate entities is borne out in our research findings. We argue to understand the accelerator programme is to identify outcomes not just for the start-up entity but to uncover areas of mutual benefit. We discuss the role of networking opportunities which are both formal and informal, curated and serendipitous. Hallen et al conclude their study (which includes mixed empirical methods, draws on proprietary data from start-up participants corroborated with auxiliary, publicly available, quantitative datasets), "the practices of early accelerators represent a beneficial and likely replicable form of intervention that may also have relevance for independent entrepreneurs, educational programs, and corporate innovation". The exploration of 'what works' is also central to our study. We attempt however, to broaden the definition of 'what works' by shifting the focus away from prioritising the impact of accelerators on start-up outcomes and instead considering the accelerator model as a processes of value creation.

3. Methodology

The study used a mixed methodology rooted in Grounded Theory (Glaser 2008) in seeking to establish themes and processes concerned with the concept of value exchanged between participants and corporates involved in accelerator programs. Grounded theory allowed for an exploration of the main concern, namely value creation, and associated as processes articulated, described, identified by and valued by participants. The processes which emerged have been formulated into an Accelerator Value framework. The framework suggested offers an explanation of the key principles of value exchange based on thematic evaluation of the qualitative data gathered from three cohorts of participants in Co-Cubed London's accelerator programs. A greater sample size would allow for corresponding qualitative work to further test the findings of this research study. The first program considered concluded in 2017, the last concluded in 2019 which means the data spans three different accelerator program cohorts. We used a broad interpretation of Grounded Theory as "the generation of theories from data" (Glaser in Walsh, Holton et al 2015), taking into account recent scholarship asking for more reflexive, less positivist approaches (Charmaz 2006). It was not possible to augment data from semi- structured interviews with quantitative data due to limited sample size. For future cohorts a blended approach including Action research would help test the robustness of the framework and allow for both ethnographic and observational data capture. This study employed Qualitative research methods included semi- structured in-depth interviews with accelerator participants, followed by transcript coding which enabled the researchers to develop a hypothetical framework to describe value creation concepts in accelerator programs.

4. Research findings

The process whereby accelerators accelerate venture development is multi-faceted, one in which both sides of the relationship transfer, receive and process value. Through our research, we found that varying levels value are both created and added to the organisations involved in the accelerator. This paper does not attempt to understand why these variations occur, rather it focuses on the specific types of value created between the accelerator and the start up.

Of our respondents, 23% indicated that they didn't feel that there had been any relationship of value, and therefore transfer between the accelerator and the start up. These organisations either had very short relationships with the accelerator, of just a few weeks or chose to seek the benefits of the accelerator partnership from other sources. These other sources were either venture capital firms, existing founder networks or alternative programmes of business support based on specific needs.

Of those who responded positively about their relationship with the accelerator (77%), the key areas of value creation offered by participation in the accelerator programme for or 'to' the start ups were those which help to focus the interaction between corporate and start-up. In addition, the efforts designed to ensure relationships and connections could be made quickly were valued most highly. This element of time criticality and the accelerator structure creating urgency and associated speed was deemed particularly helpful, given start-ups often work with limited working capital and at the same time due to their smaller size tend to work in a more agile way.

The findings in the rest of this section focus on the respondents in this later group, based on the following research objectives.

- Objective One: Identify the areas where value is created and added to either the start-up or the corporate via the accelerator program.
- Objective Two: Determine what value, if any, is added by being involved within an accelerator programme.
- Objective Three: What characterized 'success' from the view of the start-up and the corporate organisations involved in the program.

Our research indicated Six dimensions of value creation in the corporate to start up relationship which emerged from our interviews (Fig. 1). In this section, we explore the nature of each of these dimensions and the supporting evidence from this study.

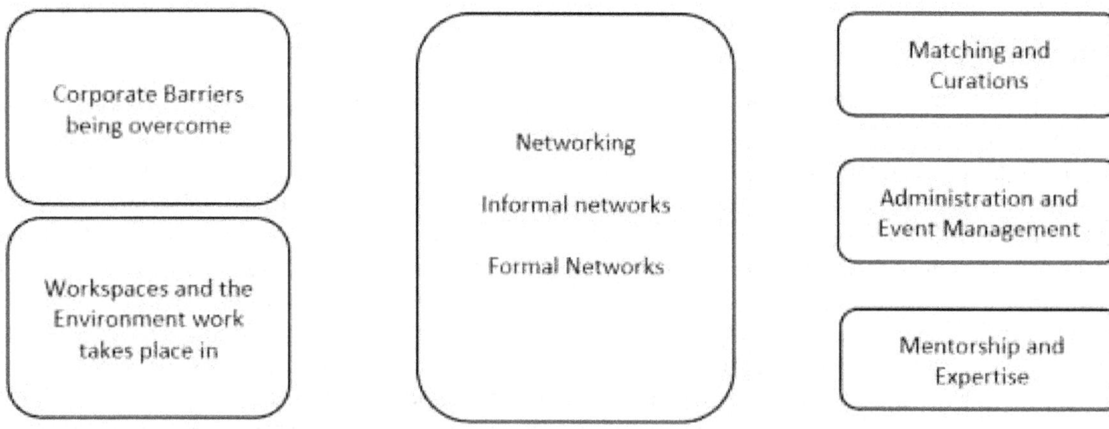

Figure 1: Dimensions of value creation

5. Corporate barriers /speed

Established corporate organisations do not generally open themselves up to agile, entrepreneurial processes; either because they are incumbered by layers of bureaucracy, or because opaque and complex internal decision-making prevents relationships being created. Importantly some of the classic barriers to start-up engagement with the corporate entity such as NDAs and procurement processes are mitigated as a result of the bounded accelerator process. This ability to navigate the corporate entity with inside help was cited as very important by the start-ups in the Co-Cubed accelerator in this study. Start-ups in this research expressed frustration with the lengthy processes synonymous with larger, established entities. They cited the slower speed of response on the corporate side as challenging and a barrier to engagement and contracting. This speed of response is mitigated to an extent by corporate participation in an accelerator programme with structured deadlines and a pacey timescale. The accelerator's role as an intermediator between the corporate and the start up in terms of due diligence is predicated on an aligned shared understanding of each entities potential role and contribution to the other and emphasises the importance of the accelerator in curation, matching and selection- bringing the right start-ups to the right accelerator.

6. Networking both formal and informal

Our research indicated that networking formally and informally was one of the most important areas of value created by participation in the accelerator. Networks were deemed pivotal as they provided access to the resources and services needed by the venture and the entrepreneur. Building a broad network across the corporate entity helped the entrepreneurs to facilitate the speed and ease the friction and /or barriers often experienced outside the accelerator format.

Start-ups cited a series of 'critical incidents' they were able to mitigate and resolve as a direct result of this network building. Examples of these critical incidents for these respondents included; building relations with 'key' customers, service lines /operations and suppliers, access to finance through venture capital and the creation of national supply deals with supermarkets offering new scale.

Fruitful, broad networks are particularly important for incumbent firms working with new technology- these firms rely on access to 'high tech' startup networks alongside collaborations with other corporates, largely because they are increasingly dependent on access to the new technology of other firms and universities and work under a high level of uncertainty related to both technology and markets.

Curated networking events and opportunities created the conditions for informal networking outside the fixed meetings and presentations. These opportunities to establish relationships in the corporate entity are highly valued by the start-up teams hoping to find the right decision makers on the corporate side.

The networking element and its benefits spanned across the venture and individual. For the entrepreneurs this provided connection to a mentor, and the opportunity to build individual networks with like-minded individuals and to develop links that support the strategic objectives of the business (Gulati et al, 2000). Previous studies on in the field of entrepreneurship, (Elfring and Hulsnik, 2007) have emphasised the importance of the network as a key driver of entrepreneurial success and our findings indicated this as the most valuable outcome of value for the venture and the individual entrepreneurs.

7. Workspaces and environment

Those start-ups which located themselves at the provided workspace suggested they benefited more from informal and opportunistic corporate interaction than those start-ups which only joined the co-working environment for specified events and presentations. While colocation is not a necessary success factor, where colocation offers greater opportunities for networking formally and informally and 'ad hoc' meetings with the corporate entity representatives, this proved valuable to the start-ups seeking to identify opportunities and to check back and test out possible ideas informally outside the formal meeting structure.

8. Matching and curation

The initial selection of start-ups invited to join has a material impact on the progress of the accelerator programme, in particular for the corporate entity genuinely seeking new partnerships, acquisition or technology innovation. The skill of the accelerator partner in curation, selection and support for the start-up entities is pivotal. Matching the parties depends on a well-defined corporate brief with requisite buy-in on the corporate side. The value in the accelerator programme is increased where the corporate challenge is central to the organisation's strategic objectives and has corresponding senior level support, rather than being seen as a 'side show' initiative.

9. Administration and event management

The accelerator acts as curator, as mediator and as event manager all of which helps focus the process, taking the administrative and structural burden away from both the corporate and the start-up participant. This administrative function is neglected in previous research but should not be underestimated. Managing diaries and coordinating meetings from outside the corporate entity is both time consuming and challenging for start-ups. Accelerators remove these administrative pain points.

10. Mentorship and expertise

Mentorship takes on several guises as part of an accelerator programme, from the formal introductions and mentoring sessions to informal events and 'founder firesides'. (Deakins et al, 1998). Start-up entities tend to be outbound in actively seeking mentorship from the accelerator network and from the corporate entity itself. The most sophisticated relationships we argue, are those where some reverse mentoring and reciprocal learning takes place with the start-up approach alongside its product or service offer and the entrepreneurial mindset of the start-up founders can be a source of insight and capability building for corporate leaders. Accelerator programmes expose corporate leaders to entrepreneurial thinking and approaches, where senior leaders can work alongside start-ups in this *reciprocal* value exchange rather than the corporate taking a 'dragon's den' or arms' length approach. Intrapreurship has been well documented, as have ways to build a start-up approaches into corporate processes.

11. Towards a research framework to understand accelerator – start up relationships

The primary purpose of this paper and our research objectives is to use our initial findings from this study around corporate accelerators to develop a framework to understand value creation in these relationships. This will support further research into the accelerator model to understand their effectiveness within the growth of entrepreneurial ventures. In doing so, this framework helps to explain ways in which accelerators might derive value for both sides. This research now informs our investigation around how we might view the accelerator, corporate and start up relationship and uncover the value in the transactions we have described above.

This paper develops a framework which allows us to pursue further research with other accelerators to test and validate our findings and enquire more deeply into the ways in which reciprocal value is created and exchanged by means of relationships created through the accelerator model. This research has value in suggesting ways in which these entrepreneurial environments might adapt and evolve to provide a more successful and impactful service, fostering greater and more fruitful entrepreneurial partnerships and collaborations.

In our development of this framework, the key principles derived from the research were centred on the speed of connection, networking, information and knowledge exchange, communication and a goal orientation and alignment. These are now discussed further below.

- Faster connections:
- *The accelerator approach is helpful in accelerating the relationships necessary to ensure contracting progress is made, curation and match making – the right people in the room, tech on the start-up side, decision makers and networkers on the corporate side.*
- Networking is formal and informal:
- *Opportunities for formal and for informal networking- these are equally important, the formal setting ensures a clear agenda, aligned incentives and understanding, the informal meetings provide crucial opportunities for relationship building, widening the contacts as well as the access to expertise on the corporate side, and broadens the scope of opportunity to contract for the start-up.*
- Data and information exchange:
- *This is related to informal networking as data and information shared between the parties during the accelerator process flows both formally and informally. The start-ups, when well networked into the corporate can work with data, otherwise unavailable to them to identify opportunities and new needs to serve. This opportunity creation may not be immediately obvious from the start, and may rely on the corporate opening up, sharing information and strategies informally which the start-up can work with to create new solutions. This was not confined to 'formal' data sharing documentation, but was based on data shared during corporate presentations, meetings and visits; where the start-up corporate networks come into their own sees data and strategy being continually shared and discussed.*
- Communication
- *Communication mattes, both individual and entity to entity. The ability to present /pitch succinctly, to be clear on aligned goals and mutual opportunity and to keep the corporate decision making lines straightforward is useful. (need something here on the end game of the accelerator being hard progress to contract etc not prize money or mentoring etc... or funding, but contracts for work being the most meaningful for growth and scale- ie the corporate becoming a customer at the end of it is the real winner for everyone).*
- Time bound and hard outcome focussed
- *The accelerator design is helpful in mitigating the disconnect between the pace at which corporates typically operate and the pace at which startups typically operate, so a clear, agile, time bound (see Cohen 2019 on common principles of accelerator design)*

These principles provide us with basis from which we developed of a 3 C's ***Accelerator Value Creation*** framework. The framework represents the key ways in which the value is created through accelerator structure between start-up and corporate. The principles of the ***Accelerator Value Creation*** framework centre around *Curation*, namely the organising mechanism and startup selection, *Connection*, the opportunities for and the building of the relationships and the final aspect which drives the success imperative we call, *Commitment*.

12. Development of 3 C's Accelerator Value Creation framework

- ***Curation***-the start up cohort needs to be well selected to appropriately meet a well-defined corporate initiative /objective. This alignment is part of a process we call curation. The accelerator needs to offer clear, time bound activities at pace. This is combined curation; involving who takes part, how well matched the entities are and how well aligned the challenge is. This combined curation is the pivotal part played by the accelerator in bringing these entities together successfully and creating the optimal conditions for collaboration. Curation also pertains to the process and event management aspect of the accelerator, with delivering value on what happens, who takes part, when and where, including the opportunities for fast connections free of administrative burdens.
- ***Connection***- informal and formal networks where data, information are freely exchanged, this connection needs to be transparent, and fluid, with decision makers from the corporate side involved or available /incentivised , environments available to enhance this opportunity for connection.

- ***Commitment*** – both sides committed to (co)-devise hard /tangible /feasible solutions with a view to contracting- vs processes which are billed as competitions and vs wider more amorphous open innovation initiatives which can be 'on going' from the corporate side – Those accelerators which are focused on or aim to complete with hard commitments and contracts offer greater growth and scale potential for the startups and tangible value to the corporate entity.

How Accelerators create value?

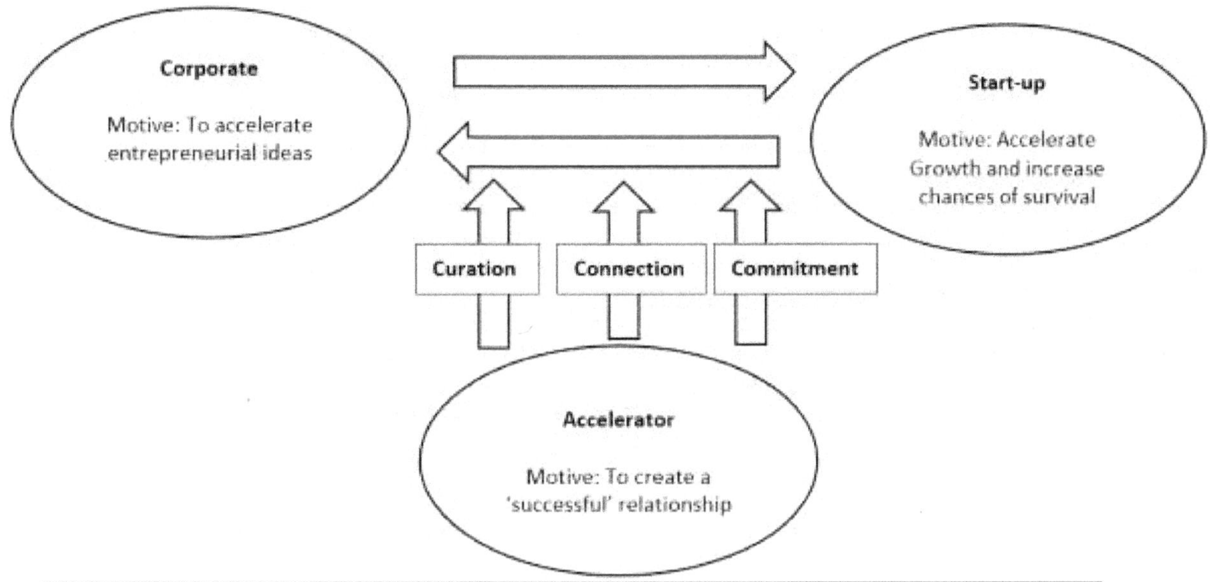

Figure 2: Three C's accelerator value creation framework

13. Uses of this framework

The application of this framework acts as a way of exploring the relationship between start-ups and corporates and furthers our understanding of the ways accelerators support the fruitful exchange and creation of value in the entrepreneurial process. On a practical level, it provides a framework for accelerators and start-ups as well as corporates to use to focus their efforts while developing partnerships. Additionally, it provides the basis of a metric for measurement and success. Our research indicated that for many start-ups and , some new to the process of working with an accelerator, the learning curve they went through varied and this therefore impacted how they received and created the various benefits that can be offered. By understanding what they can expect, how this value can be identified and therefore developed, this framework acts as a tool in the development of the accelerator relationship.

14. Future research and gaps in research

In conclusion, this paper forms the first of our research outputs from this on-going investigation. This is designed to begin an initial discussion of the early findings, and to establish the development of a framework for academic and practical understanding of the accelerator, start up and corporate relationship. Further work may look at how we map this framework across other accelerator programmes and to conduct a longitudinal study of start-ups on exit, at 3 and later 5 years, this would provide data on the longer term impacts of accelerator participation on start-up success.

We would also consider whether different types of accelerator models such as open innovation or funded competitions differ from the model and findings we have discussed. This would be of interest for those working and designing such types of initiatives and for the success of entrepreneurial ventures within them.

References

Anderson, J. C., Jain, D. C., & Chintagunta, P. K. (1993). Customer value assessment in business markets. Journal of Business-to-Business Marketing, 1(1), 3 – 29.

Bassett, Jeremy, April 16 2019 Blog Co-Cubed https://www.co-cubed.com/post/why-corporates-must-involve-everyone-in-innovation

Beauhurst Consulting, *Accelerating the UK* (2018) https://www.beauhurst.com/accelerating-the-uk-report/
Boni, A. A. and Joseph, D. (2019) 'Four Models for Corporate Transformative, Open Innovation', *Journal of Commercial Biotechnology*. ThinkBiotech, LLC, 24(4), pp. 23–31. doi: 10.5912/jcb911.
Chandra, A. and Chao, C.-A. (2016) 'Country Context and University Affiliation: A Comparative Study of Business Incubation in the United States and Brazil', *Journal of technology management & innovation*, 11, pp. 33–45. doi: 10.4067/S0718-27242016000200004.
Charmaz, K. (2011). *Constructing grounded theory: a practical guide through qualitative analysis*. Los Angeles, SAGE.
Cohen, S. *et al.* (2019) 'The design of start-up accelerators', *Research Policy*, 48(7), pp. 1781–1797. doi: 10.1016/j.respol.2019.04.003.
Deakins, David; Graham, Linda; Sullivan, Robert; Whittam, Geoff Journal of Small Business and Enterprise Development, Volume 5, Number 2, 1998, pp. 151-161(11)DOI: https://doi.org/10.1108/EUM0000000006763
Dee, N. *et al.* (2013) 'A review of research on the role and effectiveness of business incubation for technology-based start-ups', in, pp. 113–130.
Elfring, T., & Hulsink, W. (2007). Networking by Entrepreneurs: Patterns of Tie—Formation in Emerging Organizations. Organization Studies, 28(12), 1849–1872. https://doi.org/10.1177/0170840607078719
Fishback, B. *et al.* (2007) 'Finding Business "Idols": A New Model to Accelerate Start-Ups', *SSRN Electronic Journal*. doi: 10.2139/ssrn.1001926.
Glaser, B. G., & Strauss, A. L. (2017). *The discovery of grounded theory: strategies for qualitative research*. https://www.taylorfrancis.com/books/e/9780203793206.
Glaser, B. G. (2005). *The grounded theory perspective III: theoretical coding*. Mill Valey, Sociology Press.
Gulati, R., Nohria, N. and Zaheer, A. (2000), Strategic networks. Strat. Mgmt. J., 21: 203-215. doi:10.1002/(SICI)1097-0266(200003)21:3<203::AID-SMJ102>3.0.CO;2-K
Hackett, S. M. and Dilts, D. M. (2004) 'A Systematic Review of Business Incubation Research', *TheJournal of Technology Transfer*, 29(1), pp. 55–82.doi10.1023/B:JOTT.0000011181.11952.0f.
Hallen, B. L., Cohen, S. and Bingham, C. (2019) *Do Accelerators Work? If So, How?* SSRN Scholarly Paper ID 2719810. Rochester, NY: Social Science Research Network. doi: 10.2139/ssrn.2719810.
Hochberg, Y.V., A. Ljungqvist, Y. Lu. 2007. Whom you know matters: Venture capital networks and investment performance. *Journal of Finance* **62**(1) 251-301.
Kohler, T. (2016) 'Corporate accelerators: Building bridges between corporations and startups', *Business Horizons*, 59(3), pp. 347–357. doi: 10.1016/j.bushor.2016.01.008.
Kupp, M., Marval, M. and Borchers, P. (2017) 'Corporate accelerators: fostering innovation while bringing together startups and large firms', *Journal of Business Strategy*, 38(6), pp. 47–53. doi: 10.1108/JBS-12-2016-0145.
Mahmoud-Jouini, S. B., Duvert, C. and Esquirol, M. (2018) 'Key Factors in Building a Corporate Accelerator Capability', *Research Technology Management*. Routledge, 61(4), pp. 26–33. doi: 10.1080/08956308.2018.1471274.
Miller, P., K. Bound. (2011) *The Startup Factories: The rise of accelerator programmes to support new technology ventures*. NESTA.
Roberts, P. W. and Lall, S. A. (2018) *Observing Acceleration: Uncovering the Effects of Accelerators on Impact-Oriented Entrepreneurs*. Springer.
Ulaga, W. (2003). Capturing value creation in business relationships: A customer perspective. Industrial Marketing Management, 32, 677–693.
Weiblen, T. and Chesbrough, H. W. (2015) 'Engaging with Startups to Enhance Corporate Innovation', *California Management Review*. SAGE Publications Inc, 57(2), pp. 66–90. doi: 10.1525/cmr.2015.57.2.66.

Digital Innovation: A Bibliometric Review and Research Agenda

Jacopo Manotti, Silvia Sanasi, Angelo Cavallo, Antonio Ghezzi and Andrea Rangone
Politecnico di Milano, Milan, Italy
jacopo.manotti@polimi.it
silvia.sanasi@polimi.it
angelo.cavallo@polimi.it
antonio1.ghezzi@polimi.it
andrea.rangone@polimi.it
DOI: 10.34190/EIE.20.116

Abstract: The buzzword "digital innovation" is on everyone's mouth: scholars, firms, governments, research centers, journalists, and even individual citizens, employ it daily to describe a wide range of processes, tools, and practices that characterize everyday activities. This growing interest has led to the accumulation of publications, models, and perspectives within the academic literature dealing with digital innovation. Academic publications on the phenomenon span across very diverse research streams, such as strategic management, organizational studies, information systems, innovation and technology management, and several more. As a consequence, such growth is accompanied by an inherent complexity and fragmentation of the understanding of the digital innovation phenomenon, both from a semantic and a hermeneutic perspective. This study seeks to make clarity in the understanding of digital innovation through a bibliometric literature review. We review the recent digital innovation literature by means of a co-word analysis, aimed at unveiling the structure of the concepts discussed in the scholarly literature and their hierarchy. Findings suggest that the topics debated in extant publications can be ascribed to six themes: (i) digitization; (ii) digital technologies; (iii) design; (iv) digital change; (v) digital business strategy; and (vi) open digital ecosystems. Building on the themes identified, this study highlights a series of relevant opportunities for future research in the digital innovation domain, with a twofold relevance. On the one hand, it provides relevant contributions for scholars, providing them with newly found clarity in understanding the digital innovation phenomenon and the existing themes and discourses, while at the same time suggesting the most promising research avenues for advancing the extant understanding. On the other hand, our findings can provide valuable insights to practitioners, opening up the "black-box" of digital innovation.

Keywords: digital innovation, co-word analysis, digital transformation, digitization, digital business strategy

1. Introduction

Today Digital Innovation is a term widely employed by a multitude of actors, from scholars to journalists, and from managers within firms to individual citizens, with the meaning usually varying according to the context. A survey conducted by the worldwide famous consulting firm Accenture[1] among executives in most diverse industrial sectors, revealed that digital innovation is the first leverage to boost their company's growth, with an expenditure of around 100 billion dollars between 2016 and 2018. This growing interest has led to the accumulation of publications, models, and perspectives within both the academic literature and the practitioner community. However, given the pervasiveness of the topic, publications on the phenomenon span across very diverse research streams, such as strategic management, entrepreneurship, organizational studies, information systems and several more. This multitude of perspectives have often led to the adoption of different units of analysis, as pointed out by Fichman and colleagues (2014), such as product, process and business model. Some scholars have focused more on these specific dimensions, namely the product (Yoo et al., 2010), the process (Brem & Viardot, 2016) and the business model (Bharadwaj et al., 2013), while some reviews have attempted to enrich the comprehension of the digital innovation concept, usually adopting a narrow perspective according to a specific field of interest (Quinton & Simkin, 2016) or a predetermined theoretical lens (Hinings et al., 2018). Thus, given the large diffusion of the concept of Digital Innovation, the growth in terms of contributions has been accompanied by an inherent complexity and fragmentation of the understanding of the phenomenon, both from a semantic and a hermeneutic perspective. This study seeks to make clarity in the broader understanding of digital innovation through a bibliometric literature review, a proven approach to bring order in fragmented bodies of knowledge, as shown by other similar studies (Randhawa et al., 2016). Specifically, the aim will be the one to shed light on the origins of the concept and the relationships between different schools of thought addressing the discipline, in order to provide a comprehensive overview of the DI. A "final corpus" of 2478 documents has been the object of a co-word analysis, showing how the extant DI literature may be reconducted to six clusters: (i) digitization, as the umbrella of prerequisite processes of the DI; (ii) digital technologies, as essential enabler of DI; (iii) design, as the most common architectures in terms of products, services or business models assumed by DI; (iv) digital change, as the shift caused by the DI in society, firms, industries and the most diverse contexts; (v) digital business strategy, as the new direction undertakable by those firms aiming at leveraging DI to create and sustain their competitive advantage; and finally (vi) open digital ecosystems, as structures of generic agents – from single citizens to entire industries - dealing with DI. The relevance of the study is twofold. On the one hand, it provides relevant contributions for scholars, providing them with newly found clarity in understanding the digital innovation phenomenon and the existing themes and discourses, while at the same time suggesting the most promising research avenues for advancing the extant understanding. On the other hand, our findings can provide valuable insights to practitioners, opening up the "black-box" of digital innovation.

2. Data and methods

In the last years, many bibliometric reviews have been published aiming at bringing order in different fields of the literature. In reference to business and management, the focus has been multi-folded, from the possible sources of firm's competitive advantage such as the dynamic capabilities (Vogel & Guttel, 2013) to broader macro-concepts at the system level such as the Circular Economy (D'Amato et al., 2017), to worldwide famous research streams, like Open Innovation (Randhawa et al., 2016) and Design Thinking (Micheli et al., 2019). Bibliometrics use quantitative analysis of empirical data in published literature to study the patterns of publication within a field (De Bellis, 2009) and usually tend to differ between each other because of the techniques used in the analysis, taking the name of co-occurrence techniques. This bibliometric review has been performed by means of a co-word analysis, aiming at shedding light on the structure of the network of the concepts in the literature of digital innovation. For the selection of the documents analyzed, we have relied on the Scopus SciVerse database, with the purpose to consider the vastest and relevant majority of academic contributions to the concept. A co-citation analysis requires as input a "final corpus", a sample of selected documents on which applying the technique. In order to identify the keywords to conduce this selection, we have previously performed a preliminary search of the most relevant terms associated with the words "digital innovation" in the most important sub-streams of the business and management literature. For instance, regarding the branch of strategy, we have bridged two strings, namely "digital innovation strateg*" and "digital business strateg*", following an exploratory search that highlighted the common tendency to refer to the concept in both the ways. Thus, for each sub-field, the most cited article and the most recent one have been identified. The full-text of these documents has been retrieved and then processed in the software T-Lab, a reliable tool in the area of data mining for linguistic-based analyses (Lancia, 2018). The outcome of this procedure has allowed the authors to identify the most common keywords employed in this sample of documents, finally redacting a list of 20 macro-concepts. The list of keywords has been handled to structure the searching query on Scopus, initially returning for 3130 documents, thus refined including only contributions written in English and with the presence of the abstract, leading to an intermediate result of 2883 documents. Another screening was manually executed to check whether the selected contributions effectively showed the search keywords and pertained to the domains of interest, reporting for a final corpus of 2478 documents. To study the connections among the most present keywords in the corpus we performed a multiple correspondence analysis (MCA) through T-Lab software, leveraging on the abstract of each paper identified from the corpus. This analysis highlighted the most co-cited words, accounting for 93 common roots, as well as their relative distance between each other based on the number of co-occurrences. These information allows the generation of six clusters grouping the 93 keywords previously identified. However, the software does not automatically assign a label to these clusters, requiring a manual classification from the authors through the screening of the words grouped together. This procedure pointed out six clusters named as i) Digitization, ii) Digital Technology, iii) Design, iv) Digital Change, v) Digital Business Strategy and finally vi) Open Digital Ecosystem. Hence, with the aim to effectively displaying the six groups, we have made use of NodeXL, a visualization software for bibliometric analyses. This allowed to visualize the different words identified as nodes of a network, enriching the comprehension for the users through the representation of the relationships between the words as lines of different colors according to the strength of their co-occurrence.

3. Results

Figure 1 shows the visual representation of the co-word analysis and the relative clustering aggregation, highlighting six different groups of words pertaining to the macro-concept of Digital Innovation. In particular, the seminal words "Digital" and "Innovation" seem to divide the network in two parts. At first glance, it is possible to observe how the words belonging to Digitisation, Digital Change and Digital Technology take a position closer to the macro-node Digital, while the groups representing Digital Business Strategy and Open Digital Ecosystem appear nearer to the Innovation concept. The Design cluster instead, covers a more widespread position within the whole network. Therefore, looking at dimension of the different nodes (i.e. a proxy of their co-occurrence in the corpus) it is possible to notice how some words may seem more important than others, parameter that have leaded to the assignment of the labels for the different clusters. For instance, the Digital Technology cluster shows how the word "Technology" is much bigger than the others, immediately followed by "IT-techs" and "ICT", with all the remaining nodes of the cluster representing other tech-oriented words, such as "IoT" and "Big Data".

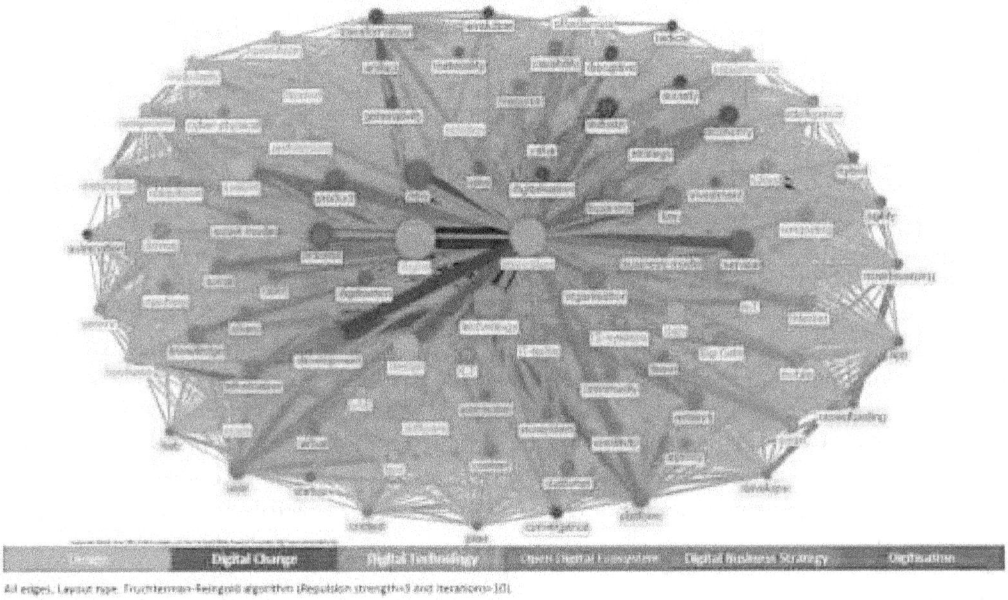

Figure 1: Co-word analysis network map

4. Discussion

Based on the co-word analysis and the relative cluster generation previously described, in this section we critically review the most important aspects covered in the different groups, represented by aggregation of co-occurred words in the sample of the selected articles. With the aim to favour the readability, we have decided to proceed through the separated discussion of the different clusters, namely (i) *digitization*, as the umbrella of prerequisite processes of the DI; (ii) *digital technologies*, as essential enabler of DI; (iii) *design*, as the most common architectures in terms of products, services or business models assumed by DI; (iv) *digital change*, as the shift caused by the DI in society, firms, industries and the most diverse contexts; (v) *digital business strategy*, as the new direction undertakable by those firms aiming at leveraging DI to create and sustain their competitive advantage; and finally (vi) *open digital ecosystems*, as structures of generic agents – from single citizens to entire industries - dealing with DI. In Figure 2 we show the number of keywords associated with each cluster – expressed in percentages – with the aim to provide a further view regarding the concepts related to DI.

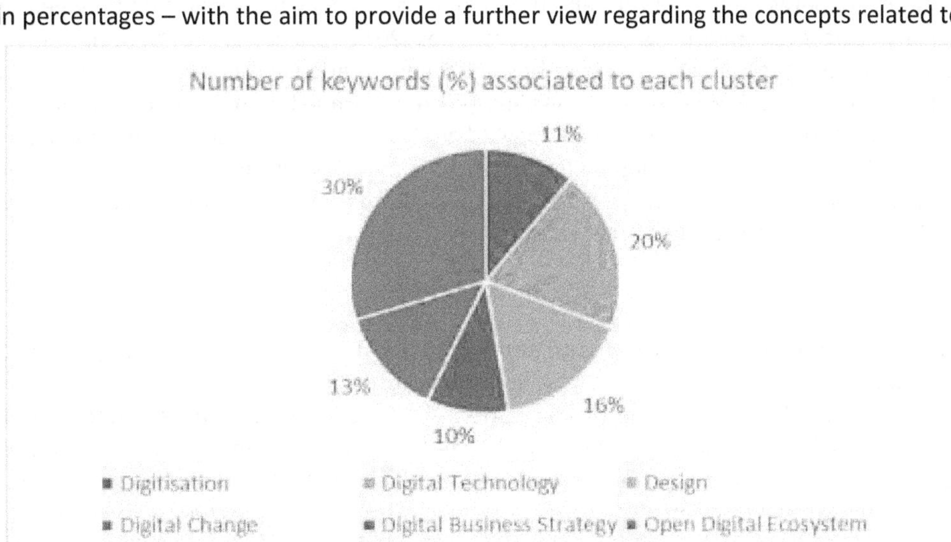

Figure 2: Number of keywords (%) associated to each cluster

4.1 Digitization

The concept of digitization is often associated to the one of Digital Innovation, even if several different definitions in the literature may lead to observe how this particular notion has been approached from a multitude of perspectives. Yoo and colleagues (2010: p. 725) stress the shift from analogic to digital by describing digitisation as "the encoding of analog information into digital format". Bailey et al. (2012) define it by contrasting digitisation and virtuality, arguing that digitisation only enables a "spatial" separation of the people that adopt these digital representations from the original elements of the physical world that have been digitized, while virtuality, instead, can create representations that substitute and stand for the physical phenomena they represent, in such a way that the adopter of the representation does not feel to interact with a physical element at a distance, but uniquely with the virtual representation. Beyond the definitory misalignment, other authors focused their attention on the unit of analysis of the digitization, mainly identified in the i) the process; ii) the product and iii) the business model (Fichman et al., 2010). Similarly, two main approaches deserve importance: the digital product innovation and the digital service innovation. In the former perspective, the attention has been principally focused on the relationship between the intrinsic physical properties of the product and the enabled software-based features acquired through the association with digital technologies (Herterich & Mikusch, 2016), while the latter tends to be more associated with the Servitization research. Some studies here debate on the presence of a materiality going beyond the predefined intangibility of the service, observing how the concept of service might be materialized through the concept of "practice" involving material artifacts, actors and activities that are evidently observable (Yoo, 2013). Another recurrent term related to the one digitisation is generativity. In reference to a generic technology, a generative one is characterized by accessibility, adaptability to different use contexts, ease of mastery, "leverage" (capability to make difficult jobs easier), and can generate new uses that are easy to distribute and are sources of further innovation (Zittrain, 2006).

4.2 Digital technology

An essential component of the process of digitisation is then represented by digital technologies. Through a screening of the extant literature, it seems that the majority of the contributions tend to approach digital technologies as a black-box. The literature favours a perspective focused on the trends of continuous improvement in terms of storage and processing capacities, as well as the increased democratization and pervasiveness of digital devices (Brem & Viardot, 2016). Keeping an evolutionary view of the system, another point that deserves attention is represented by the limited exploration of worldwide digital breakthroughs, often mentioned as marginal references in wider conversations. From a theoretical point of view, an important debate is the one surrounding the concept of technological affordance, the action potentially offered by the digital technology to an adopter having specific purposes and willing to employ the technology in a specific context (Yoo et al., 2012). Importantly, Nambisan and colleagues (2017) shed light on the importance of the context of application of the affordance, a contextual factor that may make it either an enabler or constraint of the innovation. This is strictly linked with the intrinsic features of the digital technology, namely the homogenization of data, the separability between the content and the medium and finally the separation between the function and the form, convincingly summarized by Yoo and colleagues (2010). Particular emphasis has been developed along the direction of this last separation, representing an enabler to add functions without completely redesign the product (Huang et al., 2017), a property also called re-programmability, determining what has been then defined as malleability, or "the ease at which they [digital technologies] can be reconfigured" (Nylén & Holmstrom, 2015). According to Huang and colleagues (2017) this characteristic is one of the critical success factors of digital technologies, because of the possibility to accommodate the user base scaling by continuously adapting the offer through new ways to attract users.

4.3 Design

The main concepts highlighted here are the design of the digital architecture – intended as product or service – and the possible stages of the digital innovation cycle required to develop a new offer. The debate concerning the architecture is mainly divided between product-oriented and service-oriented architectures. The former tends to look at the generic set of commonalities in a digitized product, while the latter insists on the possibility to adopt modular innovations at low marginal cost (Svahn et al., 2009). The discussion regarding the digital innovation cycle seems instead to be more mature, with Fichman and colleagues (2014) presenting a four-stage model made up of phases of discovery, development, diffusion and impact. An important framework frequently associated with these stages is the one of agile development, in the context of digital ventures to rapidly scaling their user base (Huang et al, 2017) or the combination with other methodologies coming from different fields such as the SCRUM (Tate et al., 2018), thought as the development of a product/service divided into short work cadences where a team concentrates on the development of a definite and limited set of requirements.

4.4 Digital change

This cluster is mainly characterized by words revolving around the idea of dynamism caused by DI, the transition from a predefined status-quo to a new position. The subject of this transition often differs according to the perspective adopted by the study: organizational, at the industry level or analysing the whole society. At the organizational level, scholars have paid attention to the development of an internal digital culture, considered an essential enabler to effectively deal with customers. Indeed, customers tend to be more and more described as "digital customers" (Kowalkiewicz et al., 2016) who exhibit new characteristics, such as the omnichannel orientation and the predisposition to exchange opinions and experiences between each other on digital platforms. At the industry level, a crucial concept is the one of disruption, defined as the phenomena leading a newcomer to kick-out the incumbent from its position of industry leadership (Christensen, 1997). An interesting direction of research is represented by scholars who propose strategies for incumbents to mitigate the effects of a digital disruption (Karimi & Walter, 2015), mainly leveraging on a dynamic capabilities' perspective (Vogel & Guttel, 2013). Finally, at the world level, the debate assumes the shape of digital transformation, emphasizing the concepts of speed and scope of change driven by the emergence of new digital infrastructures powered by both startups and incumbents.

4.5 Digital business strategy

Because of the business and managerial orientation of this review, one of the most important aspect highlighted by our analysis is the one of Digital Business Strategy (DBS), defined as "an organizational strategy formulated and executed by leveraging digital resources to create differential value" (Bharadwaj et al., 2013, p. 472). The authors clearly remark the difference between DBS and IT Strategy, stressing three factors: i) the wider domain covered by the DBS within the firm, not restricted to the IT department only; ii) the necessity to concurrently co-formulate the DBS with the more traditional business strategy and finally iii) the role of digital technologies as unlocked source of competitive advantage, beyond optimization and productivity only as outlined in the IT Strategy. Other authors focused instead more on the outputs of DBS, defining it as "a pattern of deliberate competitive actions undertaken by a firm as it competes by offering digitally enabled products or services" (Woodard et al., 2013). Mithas and colleagues (2013) enlarge the perspective of the discussion, introducing the role of contingent factor to DBS. They highlight the effect of industry turbulence, concentration and demand growth on the decisions associated to strategic investments in IT activities, leading to the final action to invest or to outsource. On the opposite side, narrowing the scope of DBS, several contributions tackled the concept of "digital leaders", specifically looking at the desirable skills of a decision-maker to effectively implement a DBS throughout the organization. To this extent, Bennis (2013) highlights the importance to pursue an adaptive capacity, through resilience in adversities, openness to the news and learning from failures. The "functional" view of the "digital leader" has been introduced by Tumbas and colleagues (2017), claiming for the introduction of new professional figure in firms, the Chief Digital Officer (CDO), as the human facilitator of the process of implementation of DBS.

4.6 Open digital ecosystem

This cluster sheds light on the organizing logic under which digital innovation are developed by more agents, both human and technological actors: open digital ecosystems. Definitions privilege different elements, according to the perspective of digital innovation adopted, mainly as digitized artefact developed on a digital platform (like an application/plug-in) or as the service innovation involving also the creation of physical outcomes. In the former case, the ecosystem is made of the digital platform and the human actors involved, whose interaction may lead to develop product innovations such as digitized artifacts (Boudreau, 2012). Conversely, the latter case describes a service ecosystem as an actor-to-actor network in which the members share resources between each other (including knowledge), to co-create value for someone's benefit, focalising on the process and mechanisms by which value is co-created and the ecosystem of relationships among actors evolves over time. The two different views make clear how the structure of the ecosystem represents an important theme, with some authors highlighting the reconfiguration of roles covered by the different actors in the network, such as the involvement of suppliers as peers (Remneland-Wikhamn et al., 2011), pointing out the potential value in the innovation and development of the products and services related to the shared platform.

This introduces the debate about the "degree of openness" that the ecosystem should exhibit, considered an enabler to achieve successful innovations (Sanasi et al., 2020). To this extent, it is possible to report the innovator's position in the innovation ecosystem (Christensen et al., 2005) – discriminating between incumbents and startups – and the degree of transparency of the firm's strategy (Cavallo et al., 2020) within and outside the boundaries of the organization itself (Granados & Gupta, 2013).

5. Implications and future research directions

On the basis of the discussed results, this bibliometric study may provide some eventual suggestions for future research. First, the clusters identified as output of the co-word analysis may represent an interesting source of reflection for both academics and practitioners, an opportunity to have a glance regarding the relationships between different concepts frequently employed in the daily life related to Digital Innovation. Entering in the specific discussion of the co-word analysis, it has been highlighted a limited research in the study of the technical constituents of digital innovation, as well as the link between current technological trends and the successful exploitation within firms. Moreover, future research may contribute to overcome the general tendency to treat the digital technology as a black-box (Magistretti et al., 2020), strengthening the linkages to the theoretical lenses and frameworks already conceptualized. The possible advancement in this direction may represent a starting point to furtherly bridge the communication between academics and practitioners. It is our convinced opinion that academic research in DI should make the effort of addressing topics of interest to managers. Through the identification of the current research topics, this paper represents an opportunity for researchers and managers to check the extent to which both academic research and management practices are keeping the pace with digital innovation. In particular, the academic field seems usually slower in spotting the current hands-on issues indicated as relevant by managers in everyday business life. Hence, although some articles attempted to develop studies with a more practical relevance (e.g. Nylén & Holmström, 2015), we believe that more attention should be spent on this direction.

6. Limitations and contributions

This study certainly presents some limitations due to the research design and to the intrinsic drawbacks of bibliometric methods. For instance, data collection searches have been limited to Scopus platform only, as well as the analysis have been performed on T-Lab and NodeXL software suites. Then, co-word analysis has been performed on the documents' abstract, because of their easier accessibility and processability. The employment of the full text may help to uncover some additional insights. Moreover, the co-word map is a visual simplification of the real representation of the co-occurrences between words. Eventually, co-occurrence methods give higher prominence to nodes strongly related between each other, leading to the possible exclusion of words that individually could be more frequent but that do not have many interrelationships with other words.

Still, the current study provides some contributions. For a growing field like digital innovation, bibliometric studies can afford the complex role to reduce the complexity and the fragmentation faced by scholars who start addressing the field, providing different structures to systematize what is known about the topic and the relevance of the seminal works.

References

Accenture Research. (2018) *How to successfully scale digital innovation to drive growth.* Accessible at https://www.accenture.com/_acnmedia/thought-leadership-assets/pdf/accenture-ixo-hannovermesse-report.pdf

Bailey, D., Leonardi, P. and Barley, S. (2012) The lure of the virtual. *Organization Science,* 23(5), pp. 1485-1504.

Bennis, W. (2013) Leadership in a digital world: Embracing transparency and adaptive capacity. *MIS Quarterly: Management Information Systems,* 37(2), pp. 635-636.

Bharadwaj, A., El Sawy, O. A., Pavlou, P. A., and Venkatraman, N. (2013). Digital business strategy: toward a next generation of insights. *MIS quarterly*, 471-482.

Boudreau, K. (2012) Let a thousand flowers bloom? An early look at large numbers of software app developers and patterns of innovation. *Organization Science,* 23(5), pp. 1409-1427.

Braam, R. R., Moed, H. F. and van Raan, A. F. J. (1991). Mapping of science by combined co-citation and word analysis. I. Structural aspects. *Journal of the American Society for Information Science,* 42(4), pp. 233-251.

Brem, A., and Viardot, E. (2017) Revolution of Innovation Management: The Digital Breakthrough. In *Revolution of Innovation Management* (pp. 1-16). Palgrave Macmillan, London.

Cavallo, A., Sanasi, S., Ghezzi, A., & Rangone, A. (2020). Competitive intelligence and strategy formulation: connecting the dots. *Competitiveness Review: An International Business Journal*.

Christensen, C. (1997) *The innovator's dilemma*. Harvard Business School Press, Cambridge, Mass.

Christensen, J., Olesen, M. and Kjær, J. (2005) The industrial dynamics of Open Innovation - Evidence from the transformation of consumer electronics. *Research Policy,* 34(10), pp. 1533-1549.

D'Amato, D., Droste, N., Allen, B., Kettunen, M., Lähtinen, K., Korhonen, J., Leskinen, P., Matthies, B.D. and Toppinen, A. (2017) Green, circular, bio economy: A comparative analysis of sustainability avenues. *Journal of Cleaner Production*, *168*, 716-734.

De Bellis, N. (2009) *Bibliometrics and citation analysis: from the Science citation index to cybermetrics.* Lanham, Maryland: Scarecrow Press, Inc.

Fichman, R. G., Dos Santos, B. L., and Zheng, Z. (2014) Digital innovation as a fundamental and powerful concept in the information systems curriculum. *MIS quarterly*, *38*(2), 329-A15.

Gmür, M. (2003) Co-citation analysis and the search for invisible colleges: A methodological evaluation. *Scientometrics*, *57*(1), 27-57.

Granados, N. and Gupta, A. (2013) Transparency strategy: Competing with information in a digital world. *MIS Quarterly: Management Information Systems,* 37(2), pp. 637-641.

Herterich, M. and Mikusz, M. (2016) *Looking for a few good concepts and theories for digitized artifacts and digital innovation in a material world.* s.l., ICIS 2016 - 2016 International Conference on Information Systems.

Hinings, B., Gegenhuber, T., and Greenwood, R. (2018) Digital innovation and transformation: An institutional perspective. *Information and Organization*, *28*(1), 52-61.

Huang, J., Henfridsson, O., Liu, M. and Newell, S (2017) Growing on steroids: Rapidly scaling the user base of digital ventures through digital innovaton. *MIS Quarterly: Management Information Systems,* 41(1), pp. 301-314.

Karimi, J. and Walter, Z. (2015) The role of dynamic capabilities in responding to digital disruption: A factor-based study of the newspaper industry. *Journal of Management Information Systems,* 32(1), pp. 39-81.

Kowalkiewicz, M., Safrudin, N. and Schulze, B. (2016) The business consequences of a digitally transformed economy. In: *Shaping the Digital Enterprise: Trends and Use Cases in Digital Innovation and Transformation.* Switzerland: Springer International Publishing, pp. 29-67.

Lancia, F. (2018) *User's Manual T-LAB Plus Tools for Text Analysis 2018.* [Online] Available at: http://www.tlab.it/

Magistretti, S., Dell'Era, C., & Verganti, R. (2020). Searching for the right application: A technology development review and research agenda. *Technological Forecasting and Social Change*, *151*, 119879.

Micheli, P., Wilner, S. J., Bhatti, S. H., Mura, M., and Beverland, M. B. (2019) Doing design thinking: Conceptual review, synthesis, and research agenda. *Journal of Product Innovation Management*, *36*(2), 124-148.

Mithas, S., Tafti, A. and Mitchell, W. (2013) How a firm's competitive environment and digital strategic posture influence digital business strategy. *MIS Quarterly: Management Information Systems,* 37(2), pp. 511-536.

Nambisan, S., Lyytinen, K., Majchrzak, A. and Song, M. (2017) Digital Innovation Management: Reinventing Innovation Management Research in a Digital World. *MIS Quarterly,* 41(1), pp. 223-238.

Nylén, D. and Holmström, J. (2015) Digital innovation strategy: A framework for diagnosing and improving digital product and service innovation. *Business Horizons,* 58(1), pp. 57-67.

Quinton, S., and Simkin, L. (2017) The digital journey: Reflected learnings and emerging challenges. *International Journal of Management Reviews*, *19*(4), 455-472.

Randhawa, K., Wilden, R., and Hohberger, J. (2016) A bibliometric review of open innovation: Setting a research agenda. *Journal of Product Innovation Management*, *33*(6), 750-772.

Remneland-Wikhamn, B., Ljungberg, J., Bergquist, M. and Kuschel, J. (2011) Open innovation, generativity and the supplier as peer: The case of iPhone and Android. *International Journal of Innovation Management,* 15(1), pp. 205-230.

Sanasi, S., Ghezzi, A., Cavallo, A., & Rangone, A. (2020). Making sense of the sharing economy: a business model innovation perspective. *Technology Analysis & Strategic Management*, 1-15.

Svahn, F., Henfridsson, O. and Yoo, Y. (2009) *A threesome dance of agency: Mangling the socio-materiality of technological regimes in digital innovation.* s.l., ICIS 2009 Proceedings - Thirtieth International Conference on Information Systems.

Tate, M., Bongiovanni, I., Kowalkiewicz, M. and Townson, P. (2018) Managing the "Fuzzy front end" of open digital service innovation in the public sector: A methodology. *International Journal of Information Management,* Volume 39, pp. 186-198.

Tumbas, S., Berente, N. and vom Brocke, J. (2017) Three types of chief digital officers and the reasons organizations adopt the role. *MIS Quarterly Executive,* 16(2), pp. 121-134.

Vogel, R., and Güttel, W. H. (2013) The dynamic capability view in strategic management: A bibliometric review. *International Journal of Management Reviews*, *15*(4), 426-446.

Woodard, C., Ramasubbu, N., Tschang, F. and Sambamurthy, V. (2013) Design capital and design moves: The logic of digital business strategy. *MIS Quarterly: Management Information Systems,* 37(2), pp. 537-564.

Yoo, Y. (2013) The tables have turned: How can the information systems field contribute to technology and innovation management research?. *Journal of the Association of Information Systems,* 14(5), pp. 227-236.

Yoo, Y., Henfridsson, O., and Lyytinen, K. (2010) Research commentary—the new organizing logic of digital innovation: an agenda for information systems research. *Information systems research*, *21*(4), 724-735.

Zittrain, J. (2006) The generative Internet. *Harvard Law Review,* 119(7), pp. 1974-2040.

Profitability and Impacts of FabLabs in Portugal

Florinda Matos[1], Miguel Marques[1], Radu Godina[2], Ana Josefa Matos[3] and Pedro Espadinha-Cruz[2]
[1]Lisbon University Institute – ISCTE - DINÂMIA'CET-IUL - Centre for Socioeconomic Change and Territorial Studies, Lisbon, Portugal
[2]UNIDEMI-Research and Development Unit in Mechanical and Industrial Engineering, Faculty of Science and Technology (FCT), Universidade NOVA de Lisboa, Portugal
[3]ICLab - ICAA - Intellectual Capital Association, Santarém, Portugal
florinda.matos@iscte-iul.pt
miguel.tavares.marques@gmail.com
r.godina@fct.unl.pt
anajosefa.matos@icaa.pt
p.espadinha@fct.unl.pt
DOI: 10.34190/EIE.20.163

Abstract: In recent years, new ways of approaching the manufacturing processes have gained importance. The need for greater personalization of goods and the creation of differentiated parts, combined with the urgency to innovate both on the part of companies and consumers, gave rise to the FabLab - fabrication laboratory - concept, which aims to bring together people and technologically advanced tools that are usually expensive and not widely available. FabLabs are spaces that are open to the entire community, allowing their users to become designers and producers of their products. Among the new manufacturing techniques, used in the FabLabs, the concept of additive manufacturing stands out, namely with the use of 3D printers that allow customization and flexibility for low volume productions. This paper presents an exploratory study of the profitability and impacts of FabLabs in Portugal, comparing their management, use and relevance, taking into consideration whether the investment is private or public. In addition, this study aims to highlight the importance of FabLabs as agile places of innovation exploring solutions to problems in the digital society. A quantitative methodology was used based on a questionnaire applied to FabLab managers in Portugal. The study concluded that there are significant differences between FabLabs. Those that received private investment are companies with a larger structure, more demand and higher turnover. On the other hand, companies that are mostly financed by public investment have lower demand. Private FabLabs have a greater focus on organizations that finance them, while public investment based FabLabs' are more concerned about the mission of providing tools to the community, helping to educate the population. This study showed that, in terms of profitability, these organizations are not self-sufficient. The profitability requires a change in people's mindsets, a greater involvement between the organizations and the promotion of curiosity to encourage its use to generate innovation and development.

Keywords: FabLabs, innovation, customization, 3D printers

1. Introduction

The rise of new digital industrial technology, known as Industry 4.0, presents itself as one of the most promising challenges of the next decade. The manufacture of customized physical goods, using additive manufacturing processes, is changing business models, creating new challenges and opportunities to improve productivity and competitiveness, with respect for more sustainable production standards. FabLabs, as laboratories with technological tools that allow work in a "do it yourself" logic, can be very relevant to support companies, especially small businesses that have difficulty accessing these technologies. On the other hand, in poorer communities, these laboratories can contribute to supporting small businesses in the local economy with relevant social contributions (Mikhak *et al.*, 2002; Gershenfeld, 2012). FabLabs have a set of instruments and technologies, the best known of which are 3D printers that allow prototyping and the manufacture of small quantities of products. Also, these laboratories can serve several areas such as education, professional training, and applied research (Troxler and One, 2010; Troxler and Schweikert, 2010). FabLabs present themselves as spaces for the democratization of production since the ease of access, and the prices practised facilitate the inclusion of businesses and people of all origins (Blikstein and Krannich, 2013). According to the FabLabs.io (https://www.FabLabs.io/.) platform, there are more 1,750 FabLabs across the globe. In Portugal, there are presently twenty-one FabLabs, some of them with little activity and practically unknown to the community.

The pandemic crisis of COVID-19 came to show the importance of these laboratories that, in Portugal and other European countries, have placed themselves at the forefront, producing visors and personal protection material needed by professionals most exposed to the virus. This research aims to study the profitability of FabLabs in Portugal, comparing their management, use and relevance, taking into consideration whether the investment is private or public.

2. Literature review

The digital revolution, which began in the 1980s, was firstly based on the use of computers, then on communications and, more recently, it matured to a revolution in the manufacture of physical goods, with the emergence of personal digital manufacturing (Gershenfeld, 2005). It was in the context of the digital revolution of production, based on innovation, differentiation and personalization of articles, that the Fabrication Laboratory concept and the resulting abbreviation FabLab (Troxler and One, 2010; Troxler and Wolf, 2010) emerged, aiming to bring together people and companies with technologically advanced and typically expensive tools that would, otherwise, not have access. The concept appeared at the Center for Bits and Atoms (CBA) of the Massachusetts Institute of Technology (MIT), in the discipline called "How to do almost anything", given by Prof. Neil Gershenfeld.

The FabLab movement is closely related to the Do it Yourself (DIY) movement, very popular in today's society and born from the spirit-maker that characterizes the new generation of workers, the Millennials, and the next generation of workers, the Post-Millennials (Stroud and Brien, 2019). FabLabs include design, digital fabrication and prototyping tools, as well as a wide variety of documentation for the development of applications in the formal and informal educational, environmental and health fields, as well as for economic and social development (Mikhak *et al.*, 2002).

In these laboratories, machines, software, tools and human resources are available to everyone who wants to use their creativity (Rocha, 2011). The objective is for them to use the equipment available, such as 3D printers, to create their artefacts. Personal manufacturing is part of a collaborative process, which implies the cooperation between projects and the shared use of tools in common spaces (Kohtala, 2016). FabLabs share their identity, but each laboratory determines its activities, its key users and its form of revenue, depending on local conditions (Kohtala, 2016).

FabLabs encourage people to participate in the creation of their technological tools in order to find solutions to their problems. The most appropriate computational technologies for development are those that allow people to learn how to use computer-controlled manufacturing tools to build and to make their creations (Mikhak *et al.*, 2002). FabLabs are seen as a new approach to the concept of innovation. Some of the factors that identify them are, among others: the incentive to discovery, with access to digital manufacturing tools; free access to all types of individuals of all ages, disciplines and professions (Troxler and Wolf, 2010), to workshop hours, technical and operational assistance and a global network, among others (Marantos *et al.*, 2017). Therefore, FabLabs are seen as collaborative and creative spaces where creativity and innovation are stimulated (Troxler, 2013; Blikstein, 2014; Walter-Herrmann and Büching, 2014).

Also, to Gershenfeld (2005), FabLabs encourage entrepreneurship and allow young people and adults from all communities to start their own businesses, in order to create solutions to current problems.

According to Gaeiras (2017), director of FabLab Lisboa, there are two significant challenges linked to FabLabs. The first one is in the collection of information on the developed projects, which is still scarce. The second one is in the search for new sources of financing since FabLabs must continually demonstrate that they have a sustainable business model. A study published by Redlich *et al.* (2016) concluded that FabLabs brought new standards of value creation, creativity and innovation as they integrate and empower people of different specialities, professions and ages. These authors presented a study carried out on 75 FabLabs from developed countries and 19 from developing countries, which concluded that:

- Most FabLabs focus more on community building (70%) and education (85%) than on Research and Development (56%);
- 25% of the respondents considered the lack of a communication and collaboration platform as the biggest obstacle, in terms of improving cooperation; and 67% of the respondents indicated that they had external funding from FabLabs;

- 40% indicated that they practised membership fees and 33% of them indicated they were funded through external resources to the projects; 45% of FabLabs in developed countries indicated that membership fees finance them, whereas this number only reached 21% in developing countries. However, it was observed that FabLabs in developing countries are much more successful in acquiring financing for external projects (74% versus 65%). Developed countries are more successful (23% versus 5%) than developed ones. At this point, the differences between FabLabs in developed and developing countries become more evident. FabLabs in developed countries get greater financial support from individuals, while FabLabs in developing countries predominantly require aid from NGOs and institutions to finance their projects.

To Moser and Rice (2016), the development of FabLabs is still recent; thus, many of which are still dependent on public funds or private donations. This author also states that FabLabs can serve as a public good, where the return of the investment is illustrated through innovation and positive effects on local communities. There are, however, FabLabs that charge their users for training and technical support, generating profits. The author also says that revenue generation is not as crucial in developing countries as is in developed countries, where commercial success is imperative. Moser and Rice (2016, p. 20) present a classification of FabLabs according to the number of members and the amount of fees paid:

- 1. Technology Access Centres;
- 2. Training Provider;
- 3. Service Bureau;
- 4. Innovation Hub.

According to this classification, the number of members decreases depending on the payment associated with FabLab. The higher the fees (Innovation Hub), the fewer users attend it. FabLabs with a large number of users are recognized only as centres where individuals can find free technology (Technology Access Centre). Johns and Fab Foundation (2018) analyzed the advantages and disadvantages of public and private financing from FabLabs and concluded that the main advantages of public funding are the fact that the funding usually is non-refundable and there is a possibility to establish partnerships with larger public initiatives, which can boost the FabLab. As the main disadvantage, the authors mention the difficulty in being economically sustainable, resulting in revenues and the need to be financed permanently. For the same authors, private investment has the advantage of allowing sponsorships, consistent earnings from work, and generating good publicity for the organization. The main disadvantage is the investment risk, as it can be difficult to profit from them. Johns and Fab Foundation (2018) also analyzed FabLabs where members pay usage fees, recognizing this form of operation as a way to encourage participation, although challenging to be implemented, considering these organizations have to compete with others that are free. The evolution of FabLabs is associated with the evolution of digital manufacturing. For authors like Gershenfeld (2005), the next digital revolution will be in terms of the production of personalized physical goods, in a context in which 3D printers stand out (Srinivasan and Bassan, 2012; Janssen *et al.*, 2014; Khajavi, Partanen and Holmström, 2014). The authors believe that this technology will revolutionize digital manufacturing and that this revolution is also driven by the resources presented by FabLabs.

3. Research methodology

As previously mentioned, this study presents an exploratory study of the profitability and impacts of FabLabs in Portugal, comparing their management, use and relevance, taking into consideration whether the investment is private or public. The methodology used in this research is quantitative, supported in a semi-structured questionnaire that was developed, tested and applied to a sample composed by the opinion of FabLab managers of all the Portuguese active FabLabs, a total of 21 FabLabs. The questionnaire was divided into 5 distinct sections, using multiple-choice questions and open questions. Section I of the questionnaire aims to characterize FabLab in terms of its geographical location, size, experience and level of training of employees. Section II intends to characterize the socio-economic aspect of FabLab and to understand from the perspective of the manager of each unit which are the strengths, opportunities and critical factors of business success. In the third part of the questionnaire, the investment needed to create and maintain a manufacturing laboratory is quantified, as well as the source of that investment. Section IV explores the opinion of managers in 3D printing technology. Finally, section V contains an open question whose objective is to understand the opinion about the impact that FabLab have on the present and may have on other industries. The 21 Portuguese FabLabs were contacted by email, and the questionnaire was sent by email. The results were obtained between June and July 2019. Of the total number of Portuguese FabLabs contacted, it was only possible to obtain the answer of 11 FabLabs, corresponding to corresponding to approximately 52.4% of FabLabs in Portugal. The low number of responses could be because many of the FabLabs have part-time managers, with very little availability to respond to different requests.

4. Results

4.1 FabLabs characterization

The information collected from the 11 surveys was grouped according to their financing characteristics, giving rise to 3 groups of analysis. Table 1 shows the identification of surveyed FabLabs and the profile can be seen in Table 2.

Table 1: Identification of surveyed FabLabs

FabLab Name	**Geographic Location in Portugal (NUTS II Code):**	**FabLab Age**	**Investment**
Buinho FabLab	Alentejo	Between 2 and 4 years	Private
FabLab EDP	Lisboa and Vale do Tejo	Over 8 years	Private
Lab Aberto	Lisboa and Vale do Tejo	Between 2 and 4 years	Private
OPOLab	Norte	Over 8 years	Private
FabLab Aldeias do Xisto	Centro	Between 4 and 6 years	Public
FabLab Castelo Branco	Centro	Between 2 and 4 years	Public
FabLab Guarda	Centro	Between 4 and 6 years	Public
Vitruvius FabLab	Lisboa and Vale do Tejo	Between 6 and 8 years	Public
FabLab Évora Tech	Alentejo	Between 4 and 6 years	Public and Private
FabLab IPB	Norte	Between 6 and 8 years	Public and Private
FabLab Lisboa	Lisboa and Vale do Tejo	Between 6 and 8 years	Public and Private

Table 2: Identification of surveyed FabLabs

	Type of Investment		
FabLabs Profile	Public	Public and Private	Private
Geographic Location (NUTS II Code)	Centro and Lisboa	Lisboa, Norte and Alentejo	Lisboa, Norte and Alentejo
Dimension (Average Number of Employees)	2	3	5
FabLab Age (Average)	5,0	6,3	5,5
Age of Users	23,5	24,3	24,8

Each of the FabLabs groups (public with 4 Labs, private with 4 Labs and Public-Private with 3 Labs) was analyzed. To facilitate the analysis, a colour table (table 5) was used. This table allows showing in a simple and objective way the level of agreement between the respondents and the different impacts. The different FabLab groups analyzed show some similarities and differences in terms of their profile. The public investment FabLabs are distributed in different areas of Portugal. The Lisbon and Tagus Valley area concentrating the three types of investment: public, private and mixed. Private investment FabLabs have, on average, a larger dimension in terms of workers (five workers), compared to the other groups. Regarding the age of the FabLabs and their users, the values are similar between groups, with private FabLabs attracting a slightly older than average audience.

4.2 FabLabs investment

Regarding the investment made in the different groups of respondents, it can be seen that 50% of public FabLab used European funding, while 67% of public-private FabLab used this type of investment. The average investment required to open a FabLab is similar between the three groups; however, in the public-private FabLabs, the investment is close to thirty thousand euros and in the remaining about thirty-eight thousand euros. Concerning the annual cost of operation, public FabLabs have a lower cost, approximately twenty-four thousand euros, while private ones have the highest costs annually, around thirty-five thousand euros. The investment profile can be seen in Table 3.

Table 3: Investment profile

	Type of Investment		
FabLabs Profile	Public	Public and Private	Private
Financing from European Funds	50%	67%	-
Initial Investment (Average)	38 125	30 833	30 625
Annual Cost	23 750	30 000	28 750

4.3 FabLab economic characterization

The characterization at the economic level, shown in Table 4, points out some differences between the respondents. According to the results obtained, public-private FabLabs are the least dynamic, characterized by having a reduced number of users, with the average expenditure per visit also being lower (15 euros). The average turnover of this group is the lowest, being less than 1,000 euros per year and having grown by 4% per year. The public FabLab, are the ones that have the most demand, presenting a higher value than the others, despite having a low average cost per user (17.5 euros). Turnover is also low, around 8,000 euros, although growth is close to 11% per year. In terms of demand, private FabLabs have values close to the total average of the 3 groups and stand out for being the group that receives the highest value per visitor (23.3 euros). The turnover is also the highest, around 80,000 euros and has an annual growth close to 22%. In all 3 groups the average number of users is low, never exceeding 5 monthly visits.

Table 4: FabLabs economic characterization

	Type of Investment		
Economic Characterization	Public	Public and Private	Private
Number of Users (Monthly)	26,3	16,3	25,8
Number of Monthly Visits (Average per User)	< 5	< 5	Between 5 and 10
Average Spend per Visitor (Euros)	17,5	15	48,75
Business Volume (2018)	7 625	676	74 385
Business Volume Growth (Annual Average)	11%	4%	18%

4.4 Managers' view of FabLabs

To analyze the data collected, it was used the colour scheme shown in Table 5, which is showing the level of agreement between respondents.

Table 5: Color code

Colour Code (Selected the Answer)	
	All (all respondents chose this answer)
	> 65% of respondents
	Mixed (between 35% and 65% of respondents)
	< 35% of respondents
	All Null (no respondents chose this answer)

4.4.1 *Managers' view of FabLabs*

Table 6 shows the impact of FabLabs. Regarding the factors that motivated the emergence of FabLabs, most managers of these organizations indicated "creativity and cooperation". More than 65% of public and private investors chose this option, while all respondents to public-private investment selected it.

Table 6: Impact of FabLabs

		Type of Investment		
Motive	**Of the aspects presented, which ones are most influenced by the emergence of FabLabs?**	**Public**	**Public and Private**	**Private**
	Creativity and cooperation			
	Entrepreneurship, competitiveness, environment and sustainable development			
	The creation of intellectual property			
	Network learning, qualification, vocational training and employment			
	Business generation based on innovation and research			
	Social development and social inclusion			
Critical Success Factors	**What are the critical factors for the success of FabLabs?**	**Public**	**Public and Private**	**Private**
	Price			
	Technology			
	Accessibility			
	Developed know-how			

		Type of Investment		
	Management Quality			
Reasons for Use	**What is the main reason for using FabLabs?**	**Public**	**Public and Private**	**Private**
	Willingness to try new technologies			
	Innovative environment and knowledge sharing			
	Need to create new product prototypes			
	Schoolwork			
	Easy access to the tools available at FabLabs at affordable prices			
Social Impact	**What are the impacts of FabLabs on the social environment?**	**Public**	**Public and Private**	**Private**
	Contributes to the well-being and integration of participants			
	Helps to awaken the interest of younger people in creating products and developing ideas			
	Supports individual development, teaching the best practices for using the available technologies			
	Promotes entrepreneurship			
	Promotes creativity and innovation			
	Facilitates social integration by creating new job opportunities			
Environmental Sustainability	**What is the environmental impact that FabLabs have on the community?**	**Public**	**Public and Private**	**Private**
	Have a positive environmental impact			
	Have a negative environmental impact			

Entrepreneurship, competitiveness, environment, and sustainable development were considered by respondents to be the main drivers of FabLabs. The options "creation of intellectual property" and "development and social inclusion", although they have a considerable percentage (around 35% mostly in all types of investment), do not seem to be the most relevant factors. The generation of business based on innovation and research was also highly regarded by private and public-private investors (more than 65% of respondents). Network learning, vocational training and employment have proved to be of great importance for managers in the private sector (over 65% of respondents) and considerable relevance (about 35% of respondents) for those in the public sector.

4.4.2 Critical factors for the success of FabLabs

Most FabLabs managers of public investment and public-private investment considered the price, the technology, the accessibility and the developed know-how as critical factors for the success of FabLabs.

The private investment FabLabs managers differed in their choices, and approximately half consider that the critical success factors are price and technology, however, accessibility and developed know-how are also mentioned. None of the respondents of the different types of FabLabs chose the "Management Quality" option. For respondents, the quality of management is not a critical factor for the success of a FabLab. Globally, the most chosen critical success factor was the know-how developed, which is matched in the consulted literature.

4.4.3 Motivation for using FabLabs

The FabLabs respondents of public-private investment, considered as the main reason for using these centers the need to create prototypes of new products. Between 35% and 65% of respondents from FabLabs of private investment, considered the innovative environment and knowledge sharing as the main reason. Less than 35% of them also chose to use FabLabs in schoolwork and the desire to try new technologies. The managers of FabLabs public investment chose as their main factor the easy access to the tools available in FabLabs at affordable prices. On a smaller scale, less than 35% of these respondents opted for the need to create prototypes and for the development of schoolwork.

4.4.4 Social impacts of FabLabs

All respondents believe that FabLabs and the fact that they have high-level technology available help to spark the interest of younger people in creating products and developing ideas. All managers of the different types of FabLabs also considered that these laboratories promote entrepreneurship, creativity, innovation and also support individual development, teaching the best practices for using available technologies. With less relevance, the options related to "contribution to the well-being and integration of participants" and "ease of social integration through the creation of new job opportunities" were also considered. The impact of FabLabs on the social environment is one of the main features of this type of laboratory, confirming the literature.

4.4.5 Environmental sustainability of FabLabs

Most of the respondents representing FabLabs believe that FabLabs have a positive environmental impact on the community. Although less than 35% of FabLabs managers in public-private investment consider the FabLabs impact positive, none of the groups of respondents considered this type of laboratory having a negative impact.

4.5 The use of 3D printing technology in FabLabs

4.5.1 Benefits of 3D technology

According to the survey results, all respondents considered that one of the biggest benefits of 3D printing technology is the production of prototypes. Likewise, for more than 65% of respondents, this technology has the main benefit of creating replacement parts for machines and other objects. The creation of models and other marketing samples are also considered relevant by FabLabs managers of public and private investment. The creation of prototypes of pieces of complex geometry was considered as a benefit only by some private investment FabLabs managers, not being considered very relevant.

Table 7 presents the opinion of FabLabs managers regarding the use of 3D technology.

Table 7: 3D printing technology in FabLabs

		Type of Investment		
Benefits of 3D Technology	**Where are the greatest benefits of 3D printing?**	**Public**	**Public and Private**	**Private**
	Prototype production			
	Creating spare parts for machines and other objects			
	Creation of mockups and other marketing samples			
	Production of prototypes and small-scale parts of complex geometry			
Role of 3D Technology	**What role will 3D printing technology play in creating and developing new products?**	**Public**	**Public and Private**	**Private**
	It is a novelty that will not play an important role in the future.			
	Will play a defined role in certain industries			
	Will play a significant role only in certain industries			
	Will play an important role in innovation, development, business and individual life			
3D Massification	**What are the most important points for the development and massification of 3D technologies?**	**Public**	**Public and Private**	**Private**
	Use of sustainable materials			
	User-friendly technologies			
	User education			
	Development of applications that facilitate the process			

4.5.2 Benefits of 3D technology

According to the survey results, all respondents considered that one of the biggest benefits of 3D technology is the production of prototypes. Likewise, for more than 65% of respondents, this technology has the main benefit of creating replacement parts for machines and other objects. The creation of models and other marketing samples are also considered relevant by FabLabs managers of public and private investment. The creation of prototypes of pieces of complex geometry was considered as a benefit only by some private investment FabLabs managers, not being considered very relevant.

4.5.3 Role of 3D technology

Regarding the role that 3D technology plays in the creation and development of new products, all respondents believe that 3D printing will play a relevant role in the creation of new products. Some managers of public-private FabLabs (less than 35%) consider that 3D technology "will have a significant role only in certain industries". The managers of FabLabs for public and private investment considered that 3D technology "will play an important role in innovation, development, business and in individual life".

4.5.4 Massification and 3D technology

Most managers of private investment FabLabs considered that the use of sustainable materials can be one of the most important points for the massification of 3D prinintg technologies. A smaller group of these managers (35%) believe that the ease of use of the technology and the education of users will lead to the use of this technology on a large scale. It was observed that public and public-private investment FabLabs' managers were divided between three options. The first group considered the use of sustainable materials easy to use and the education of users. The second group do not agree with the option of being easy to use, considering that massification may result from the development of applications that facilitate the process.

Thus, it was found that there was no consensus in answer to this question. Respondents differ in their opinions on what is the most important point that will make this type of technology widely used.

4.5.5 Importance of FabLabs

In the final of the research, the respondents were invited to explain the importance of FabLabs for business development. All respondents believe that FabLab will play an essential role in business development, namely because they allow the production of prototypes, more quickly and at a lower cost. Also, respondents consider FabLabs to be important places for transmitting knowledge and adapting to new technologies.

5. Conclusions and recommendations

This exploratory article has provided an overview of FabLabs showing this is a relevant field, where the information is scarce, and that needs to be more studies. As a main conclusion of this study, it was found that there are several differences between the three categories of FabLabs. The FabLabs of private investment have a greater number of workers and a higher volume of business, however, they also have higher costs than the other two groups of FabLabs. On the other hand, public-private FabLabs have lower demand and turnover, which makes them unprofitable. Public FabLabs have greater demand, however, they also have a negative profitability, with a turnover of approximately eight thousand euros per year and operating costs close to twenty-four thousand euros. These differences may be related to the purpose of each laboratory. Thus, private investment FabLab work for private companies that use and finance them. Specifically evaluating the cases of EDP's FabLabs and OPO-LAB, it appears that both were created with a particular purpose of helping in the development of the company's business where they are located, namely by stimulating the development of new companies and innovation.

Regarding FabLabs that are based on public investment, there is a greater focus on the mission of making tools available to the community. In these laboratories, the common user can utilize the tools provided that allow the creation, development, and innovation of prototypes. Without these FabLabs, users with low economic resources would not have access to this type of equipment. Their use is sporadic, except when these FabLabs are physically inserted in higher education institutions, supporting certain academic activities. Finally, the results of this study indicate that these organizations are not profitable and very unlikely to be; however they seem to have a very relevant role in stimulating innovation and entrepreneurship. Especially FabLabs of public and public-private investment have a relevant social role, being crucial for economic development, well-being, quality of life and the correction of inequalities, need to be better known, arousing the interest of many potential users. As the main limitation of this study, we can point out the difficulty in obtaining the answers from the sample of

FabLabs contacted. On the other hand, being a topic still little explored at national level, in the case of laboratories with a very young age, generic conclusions cannot be drawn from this business area.

As a main recommendation, a detailed study of all FabLabs in Portugal is suggested, making it possible to perceive more precisely their importance as facilitators and accelerators of innovation, namely at the level of small businesses.

Acknowledgements

Authors gratefully acknowledge a) the funding of Project project KM3D (PTDC/EME-SIS/32232/2017), supported by through Fundação para a Ciência e Tecnologia, Portugal; b) FCT grant (ref: UIDB/00667/2020 (UNIDEMI)) and d) the FabLabs participating in the case studies.

References

Blikstein, P. (2014) 'Digital Fabrication and `Making' in Education The Democratization of Invention', in *FabLab. transcript Verlag*. doi: 10.14361/transcript.9783839423820.203.

Blikstein, P. and Krannich, D. (2013) 'The Makers' Movement and FabLabs in Education: Experiences, Technologies, and Research', in *Proceedings of the 12th International Conference on Interaction Design and Children*. New York, NY, USA: Association for Computing Machinery (IDC '13), pp. 613–616. doi: 10.1145/2485760.2485884.

Gaeiras, B. (2017) 'FabLab Lisboa: when a Municipality Fosters Grassroots, Technological and Collaborative Innovation', *Field Actions Science Reports - Special Issue: Smart Cities at the Crossroads*, (16), pp. 30–35.

Gershenfeld, N. (2005) Fab: *The Coming Revolution on Your Desktop-from Personal Computers to Personal Fabrication*. New York: Basic Books.

Gershenfeld, N. (2012) 'How to Make Almost Anything - The Digital Fabrication Revolution', *Foreign Affairs*, 91(6), pp. 43–57. Available at: https://www.foreignaffairs.com/articles/2012-09-27/how-make-almost-anything.

Janssen, R. et al. (2014) *TNO: The Impact of 3-D Printing on Supply Chain Management*. Available at: http://3din.nl/wp-content/uploads/2014/02/TNO-Whitepaper-3-D-Printing-and-Supply-Chain-Management-April-2014-web.pdf.

Johns, J. and Fab Foundation (2018) *FabLab Guide – How to set up your lab and maximise its impact*.

Khajavi, S. H., Partanen, J. and Holmström, J. (2014) 'Additive manufacturing in the spare parts supply chain', *Computers in Industry*. Elsevier {BV}, 65(1), pp. 50–63. doi: 10.1016/j.compind.2013.07.008.

Kohtala, C. (2016) 'Making "Making" Critical: How Sustainability is Constituted in Fab Lab Ideology', *The Design Journal*. Informa {UK} Limited, 20(3), pp. 375–394. doi: 10.1080/14606925.2016.1261504.

Marantos, C. et al. (2017) 'FabSpace 2.0: A platform for application and service development based on Earth Observation data', in *Proceedings of 6th International Conference on Modern Circuits and Systems Technologies (MOCAST)*. IEEE. doi: 10.1109/mocast.2017.7937657.

Mikhak, B. et al. (2002) 'Fab Lab: an Alternate Model of Ict for Development', Development by Design (DYD02).

Moser, H. and Rice, C. (2016) Transformative Innovation for International Development - Operationalizing Innovation Ecosystems and Smart Cities for Sustainable Development and Poverty Reduction. Available at: https://csis-prod.s3.amazonaws.com/s3fs-public/publication/160516_Moser_TransformativeInnovation_Web.pdf.

Redlich, T. et al. (2016) 'OpenLabs - Open Source Microfactories Enhancing the FabLab Idea', in *Proceedings of the 49th Hawaii International Conference on System Sciences (HICSS)*. IEEE. doi: 10.1109/hicss.2016.93.

Rocha, J. (2011) FabLabs como ideia, espaço, comunidade e empresa. Available at: https://pt.scribd.com/document/72159679/Relatorio-FabLabs.

Srinivasan, V. and Bassan, J. (2012) '3D Printing and the Future of Manufacturing', in *CSC Leading Edge Forum*.

Stroud, P. and Brien, S. (2019) The Maker Generation - Post-Millennials and the Future They are Fashioning. London. Available at: https://li.com/wp-content/uploads/2018/07/maker_generation.pdf.

Troxler, P. (2013) 'Making the 3rd Industrial Revolution - The Struggle for Polycentric Structures and a New Peer Production Commons in the Fab Lab Community', *Fab Lab: Of Machines, Makers and Inventors*, Cultural and Media Studies, pp. 181–194.

Troxler, P. and One, S. (2010) 'Commons-based Peer-Production of Physical Goods Is there Room for a Hybrid Innovation Ecology? *Fabbing'*, October, pp. 1–23.

Troxler, P. and Schweikert, S. (2010) 'Developing a Business Model for Concurrent Enterprising at the Fab Lab', in *Proceedings of the 2010 IEEE International Technology Management Conference (ICE)*. IEEE. doi: 10.1109/ice.2010.7476996.

Troxler, P. and Wolf, P. (2010) 'Bending the Rules: The Fab Lab Innovation Ecology', in *Practicing Innovation in Times of Discontinuity*. Continuous Innovation Network.

Walter-Herrmann, J. and Büching, C. (eds) (2014) FabLab - Of Machines, Makers and Inventors. Bielefeld: Transcript-Verlag.

Internationalization Speed and Performance Outcomes: A Network Clustering Approach

Telma Mendes, Vítor Braga and Carina Silva
CIICESI - Center for Research and Innovation in Business Sciences and Information Systems, School of Technology and Management (ESTG), Polytechnic Institute of Porto (P. PORTO), Portugal
8140224@estg.ipp.pt
vbraga@estg.ipp.pt
ccs@estg.ipp.pt
DOI: 10.34190/EIE.20.242

Abstract: The relevance of network ties on the firms' competitiveness has been increasingly recognized. However, the attention paid to the networks developed within industrial clusters and their impact on internationalization speed remains largely unexplored and a controversial issue, since the existing studies present mixed results about the nature of this relation. Thus, this study contributes to deepen the knowledge that network clustering exerts on companies' performance, considering the effect of internationalization speed on this relationship. Based on a sample of 1491 Portuguese manufacturing companies, gathered from the CIS database, the results confirm that network clustering has a direct positive impact on clustered firms' performance, and contrary to what was verified in the growth of international sales (scale), the presence in different geographic regions (scope) strengthens this relationship.

Keywords: industrial clusters, network clustering, internationalization speed, performance outcomes

1. Introduction

The speed of internationalization has become an important issue in cross-broader business development (Sadeghi, Rose and Chetty, 2018). It is common to associate the term with a limited temporal perspective, since it only considers the time between firm's inception and internationalization. However, referring to speed only as *time to internationalize* discards the central aspects of firm's internationalization, such as market knowledge and commitment (Chetty, Johanson and Martín Martín 2014).

The powerful instruments that explore the entire network of an industrial cluster remain unexplored (Wei *et al.,* 2019) and the research, to date, has failed on providing clear guidance on *how* specific network interactions influence internationalization (Musteen *et al.,* 2010). In the literature, there is a general assumption that the establishment of network relationships has a positive effect on internationalization speed (Prashantham, 2004; Dubé, Haijuan and Lijun, 2015; Kozma and Sass, 2019), but some authors claim that such interactions does not influence speed (Zucchella, Palamara and Denicolai, 2007; Varma *et al.,* 2016).

Several scholars have been also suggested that a higher internationalization speed enhances firm's performance (Zhou and Wu, 2014; Santhosh, 2019). However, fast-faced international expansion is not risk-free, and companies have no guarantee that this strategy will lead to a better performance (Sadeghi Rose and Chetty, 2018). For these reason, empirical research has reported mixed results about speed-performance link, ranging from a negative (Johanson and Vahlne, 1977; Collins, 1990) to a non-significant effect (Khavul *et al.,* 2010; Hilmersson and Johanson, 2016).

Given this pattern, we propose to shed light on whether network clustering influences performance outcomes, exploring the role played by internationalization speed. The empirical analysis was carried out on a sample of 1491 Portuguese firms obtained from CIS (Community Innovation Survey) database, for the time period between 2012 and 2014. Portugal is predominantly dominated by small and medium-sized firms (SMEs) with higher international orientation (PORDATA, 2020), representing a relevant setting for this study. Our sample includes firms from manufacturing sectors: footwear, textile, chemical and automotive.

The paper is structured as follows. First, we review the literature on the concepts under analysis, exploring the relationship between network clustering, performance outcomes and internationalization speed. The following section describes the sample, data collection and measurements that have been used. Subsequently, we present and discuss the results processed by Structural Equation Modelling (SEM) method. Finally, we introduce our conclusions and their implications for researchers and practitioners.

2. Conceptual framework

2.1 Initial considerations

One of the most recent approaches to territorial agglomeration is linked to industrial clusters described as *"geographic concentration of interconnected companies, suppliers, service providers, firms in related industries, and associated institutions [...] in particular fields that compete but also cooperate"* (Porter, 1998, p. 197); this approach is compatible with the theoretical perspective of industrial clusters as a construct that aggregates geographical and network dimensions.

At the same time, the topic of internationalization speed has emerged as an important issue due to the recent focus on early internationalization driven by globalization (Oviatt and McDougall, 2005). Scanning the literature, it became quite common to differentiate between the *initial speed of entry* (*earliness*) and the *speed that one firm reaches after entering on foreign markets* (*post-entry speed*) (Prashantham and Young, 2011). However, the literature on the concept became complex and, for develop more rigorous studies, there is a need to make further analyses (Casillas and Acedo, 2013).

Considering the relevance of both topics, this article adopts the constructivist perspective of industrial clusters in order to integrate an actor-centered and structural perspective, focusing on the *network dimension* (Johanson and Vahlne, 2009) to explain the international expansion of clustered firms. With regards to internationalization speed, following Zahra and George (2002) the research includes two dimensions: (1) *scale* which captures the level of internationalization that the firm has achieved considering the FSTS growth (ratio between foreign and total sales); and (2) *scope* that comprises the number of countries or, in our case, geographic markets which generates its international sales.

2.2 Research model and hypotheses

The international sales (internationalization scale) are the first dimension of International Entrepreneurship (IE) and one that has received the most attention (Zahra and George, 2002). According to Prashantham (2004), the firms that use their local networks have a higher probability to increase their level of exports and international competitiveness. Following the same line of thought, Boehe (2013) pointed that local ties in an industry association strongly predict the level of international sales. Thus, networks play a significant role in promoting and facilitating clustered firm's internationalization (Dubé, Haijuan and Lijun, 2015).

Additionally, it has been argued that a firm's international experience contributes to its ability for recognize international opportunities (Hohenthal, Johanson and Johanson, 2003). According to Hitt *et al.* (1997) and Himersson (2014), a rapid internationalization can offer cost-based advantages, a more efficient use of available resources, the achievement of scale economies leading, eventually, to a higher market share and financial returns (Oviatt and McDougall, 2005).

In International Business (IB) literature, the role of internationalization scale on performance has not been consistent. While some studies have found a positive relationship (Tallman and Li, 1996; Pangarkar, 2008; Khavul *et al.*, 2010), others revealed a negative effect (Johanson and Vahlne, 1977; Collins, 1990) or even non-significant (Hilmersson, 2014; Hilmersson and Johanson, 2016). Although conflicting findings persist, some scholars suggest that a positive relationship between these two dimensions may exist (Zahra *et al.*, 2000; Qian, 2002).

Hence, searching for business opportunities on international markets is a part of network relationships. Clustered firms that are orientated to develop such relationships exhibit a higher FSTS growth. Likewise, as the companies' internationalization scale increases, new resources are acquired, exerting a positive impact on performance. The above arguments allowed to formulate the following hypotheses:

> ***Hypothesis One:*** *The establishment of network relationships in clustered firms will have a positive impact on FSTS growth.*
>
> ***Hypothesis Two:*** *A higher growth on FSTS will have a positive impact on performance outcomes in agglomeration contexts.*

Despite internationalization scale provides information about the firm's internationalization, some studies suggest the use of other measures incorporating greater multidimensionality (Pla-Barber and Escribá-Esteve, 2006). Therefore, internationalization scope reflects a second dimension of IE (Zahra and George, 2002).

The link between networks and internationalization speed has been examined by a large number of papers (Boehe, 2013; Varma *et al.,* 2016; Kozma and Sass, 2019; Gil-Barragan *et al.,* 2020), but the relationship with internationalization scope has received less attention (Kuivalainen *et al.,* 2007; Felzensztein *et al.,* 2015). Previous research proposes that social networks are able to increase the number of countries that firms are present (Prashantham and Young, 2011).

Recently, Felzensztein *et al.* (2015) showed that having a higher number of networks leads to a more diverse internationalization. The benefits of acquiring strategic resources, beyond national borders, are more pronounced for firms expanding into multiple countries (Mohr and Batsakis, 2017). In this way, a greater geographic diversity increases the likelihood of internationalizing firms obtain critical resources, enabling to catch up the competition and improve their performance (Luo and Tung, 2007).

The relationship between geographical diversification and firm performance has a long history. As Contractor, Kundu and Hsu (2003: 5) stated *"the foundation of international business studies rests on the assumptions that increased multinationality is good for a firm performance"*. Several scholars have supported that internationalization scope positively influences firm's performance (Tallman and Li, 1996; Khavul *et al.,* 2010; Hilmersson, 2014; Hilmersson and Johanson, 2016), while other studies found a negative effect (Collins, 1990; Chang, 2007).

The conflicting findings, it is believed that operating in multiple regions exposes firms to new realities, providing a platform that enables access to several opportunities (Hitt *et al.,* 1997; Zahra *et al.,* 2000). Hence, to exploit new international markets, clustered firms should intensively use their networks in order to overcome resource constraints. In turn, a broader internationalization scope enhances knowledge acquisition and mitigate foreignness liabilities, allowing to attain a better performance. Consistent with most empirical explanations we hypothesize that:

> ***Hypothesis Three:*** *The establishment of network relationships in clustered firms will have a positive impact on geographic diversity.*
>
> ***Hypothesis Four:*** *A higher level of geographic diversity will have a positive impact on performance outcomes in agglomeration contexts.*

Previous research underlines that managerial and social networks have important implications for strategic choice and performance (Cho and Park, 2008; Naudé *et al.,* 2014). The managers' interpersonal ties with top executives in other firms and government agencies help to improve business performance in terms of market share and return on assets (Luo, 2000).

Moreover, the information and resource exchanged within personal networks are believed to enhance firm's financial indicators such as revenue and profitability (Peng and Luo, 2000; Batjargal, 2003). According to Yeoh (2004), personal sources of information and social connections with other network individuals positively relates to the export performance of internationalizing SMEs.

Therefore, the literature recognizes that firms may leverage on network relationships to capture business opportunities in foreign markets, to overcome internationalization barriers and improve competitive advantage (Musteen *et al.,* 2010; Antoldi and Cerrato, 2020). Consistent with previous research, it is expected that firms embedded in industrial clusters will be capable to improve the learning process, reflecting that ability on higher levels of performance. Thus:

> ***Hypothesis Five:*** *The establishment of network relationships in clustered firms will have a positive impact on performance outcomes.*

Based on the literature review, we formulated a model (Figure 1) to test whether network clustering affects performance outcomes, analysing how internationalization speed influences this process. Depending on the acceptance of hypotheses, the model can be purely or partially mediated. In the first case, the influence of network clustering on performance will be mediated by internationalization speed. The second case would entail a direct impact of network clustering on performance, plus an indirect effect through speed.

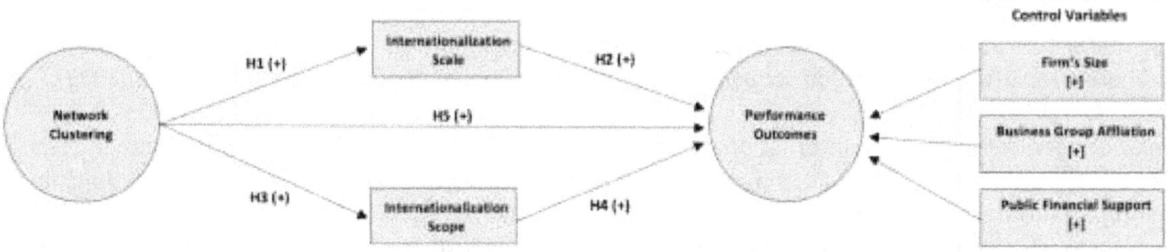

Figure 1: Research model

3. Research methodologies

3.1 Data collection and sample

For accomplish the research goals, we resorted to the IAPMEI website (Agency for Competitiveness and Innovation) to select the Portuguese industrial clusters. Through this preliminary analysis, it was possible to identify 19 clusters. Then, we established contact with these organisations in order to collect additional information.

The initial request was made via email and, later, via telephone. At the end of data collection (October 2019 to February 2020), 17 answers were obtained (89,5% response rate). Subsequently, the statistical information was gathered from the CIS database compiled by DGEEC (General Direction of Statistic for Education and Science). This dataset is based on the CIS questionnaire applied in Portugal between 9th October 2014 and 8th June 2016 (DGEEC, 2016).

Analysing the 17 answers, we concluded that 10 forms returned complete. However, due to limitations of available data and methodological issues, we considered four clusters: (1) Footwear and Fashion; (2) Textile - Technology and Fashion; (3) Petrochemical, Industrial Chemistry and Refining; and (4) Automotive. The research focused on these sectors since they are characterized by a high number of firms with an international orientation and high-quality of product range.

Thus, our sample included all the firms belonging to the clusters aforementioned and that had, at least, one year of international sales. That way, at the data extraction date (June 2020), a sampling of 1491 Portuguese firms was collected from the CIS database, for the time period between 2012-2014.

3.2 Measurements

The key variables are performance outcomes (*target variable)*, network clustering and internationalization speed (*explanatory variables*), firm's size, business group affiliation and public financial support as *control variables*. To operationalize the variables, we conducted a literature review and adapted measures validated in previous studies (Table 1).

Table 1: Theoretical foundation of scales used

Variables	Dimensions and Items	Scale	Theoretical Foundation
Performance Outcomes	3 items divided into two dimensions:		CIS (2014)
	Financial Indicators - 2 items Sales Growth = [(Total Sales 2014 - Total Sales 2012)/Total Sales 2012]. R&D Intensity = [(Internal R&D + External R&D)/Total Sales 2014].	Continuous	Hitt *et al.* (1997); Khavul *et al.* (2010); Zhou and Wu (2014)
	Non-Financial Indicators - 1 item Firm's Innovation: product, process, organizational and marketing innovation.	Ordinal (0-12)	Oslo Manual (OECD, 2005); Zhou and Wu (2014)
	2 items in one dimension:		CIS (2014)

Variables	Dimensions and Items	Scale	Theoretical Foundation
Network Clustering	National Networks - 1 item International Networks - 1 item	Ordinal (0-8) Ordinal (0-11)	Musteen *et al.* (2010); Varma *et al.* (2016); Jankowska and Götz (2017)
Internationalization Speed	2 items divided into two dimensions:		CIS (2014)
	Internationalization Scale: 1 item Growth Rate = [(FSTS 2014 - FSTS 2012)/FSTS 2012].	Continuous	Zahra and George (2002); Khavul *et al.* (2010)
	Internationalization Scope: 1 item Sales or services for European Union (EU) and extra-EU markets.	Discrete	Zahra and George (2002); Maccarini *et al.* (2003)
Control Variables	Firm's Size Number of employees.	Discrete	CIS (2014); Hilmersson (2014); Santhosh (2019)
	Business Group Affliation Dummy Variable.		CIS (2014); Chang and Rhee (2011)
	Public Financial Support Incentives/tax benefits, subsidies, loans or bank guarantees received.	Ordinal (0-3)	Aerts and Schmidt (2008); (CIS (2014)

4. Findings and discussion

We tested our hypotheses using the Partial Least Squares (PLS) that integrates SEM method since the goal was to maximize the explanation of variance (R^2) for performance outcomes in a latent model. According to Chin (1998), this procedure is more robust than a variance-covariance based model for small and medium-sized samples. On the SEM method it is important to analyse:

- Data Adequacy (Chin, 1998).
- Reflective Outer Model (Fornell and Larcker, 1981; Bagozzi and Yi, 1988; Benitez *et al.,* 2019).

The assumptions aforementioned were generally fulfilled, which means that we can proceed with the analysis. In evaluating the structural model, it should be examined the coefficient of determination (R^2), effect size (f^2), and path coefficients with their respective t-values and significance levels (Hair *et al.,* 2012).

The overall approximate model fits (SRMR) is below the recommended threshold of 0,080 (Henseler *et al.,* 2014), being smaller than their corresponding 95% and 99% quantile (Henseler, Hubona and Ray, 2016). Concerning to the path coefficients they range from -0,017 to 0,208, with different significant levels. Moreover, the adjusted R^2 of the target construct decreases from 0,106 to 0,102 when adjusted for the number of variables in the model (Table 2).

Table 2: Structural model evaluation

Relationships	Path Coefficient	t-value	p-value	f^2
Business Group Affiliation → Performance Outcomes	0,075*	2,580	0,005	0,01
Firm's Size → Performance Outcomes	$-0{,}004^{ns}$	0,105	0,458	0,00
Internationalization Scale → Performance Outcomes	$0{,}011^{ns}$	0,366	0,357	0,00
Internationalization Scope → Performance Outcomes	0,095*	2,612	0,005	0,01
Network Clustering → Performance Outcomes	$0{,}208^{+}$	2,330	0,010	0,05
Public Financial Support → Performance Outcomes	0,157**	2,940	0,002	0,03

Network Clustering → Internationalization Scale	-0,017^{ns}	0,960	0,169	0,00
Network Clustering → Internationalization Scope	0,067***	4,099	0,000	0,01
Target Construct	**R^2**		**R^2 Adjusted**	
Performance Outcomes	0,106		0,102	
Model Assessment	**Saturated Model**		**Estimated Model**	
SRMR	0,045		0,046	
Critical Thresholds: at 95%	0,052		0,052	
at 99%	0,056		0,055	
Note: f^2 = effect size; R^2 = construct's explained variance; SRMR = standardized root mean square. t-values thresholds at one-tailed test of alpha = 0,05 and 5000 resamples: t (0,05; 4999) = 1,645; t (0,01, 4999) = 2,327; t (0,005, 4999) = 2,576; t (0,001; 4999) = 3,091. Coefficients significant at p-values: + p < 0,050; * p < 0,010; ** p < 0,005; *** p < 0,001; n.s. Not significant based on t (4999), one-tailed test.				

Table 3: Total and Indirect effects of network clustering and internationalization speed on performance outcomes

Effects	Path Coefficient	t-value	p-value
Specific indirect effects:			
Network Clustering → Internationalization Scale → Performance Outcomes	0,000^{ns}	0,267	0,395
Network Clustering → Internationalization Scope → Performance Outcomes	0,006^{+}	2,286	0,011
Total indirect effects:			
Network Clustering → Performance Outcomes	0,006^{+}	2,239	0,013
Total effects (indirect plus path)			
Network Clustering → Performance Outcomes	0,214*	2,416	0,008
Note: t-values thresholds at one-tailed test of alpha = 0,05 and 5000 resamples: t (0,05; 4999) = 1,645; t (0,01; 4999) = 2,327; t (0,005; 4999) = 2,576; t (0,001; 4999) = 3,091. Coefficients significant at p-values: + p < 0,050; * p < 0,010; **p < 0,005; *** p < 0,001; n.s. Not significant based on t (4999), one-tailed test.			

Our results support some of the hypotheses of this study (Table 2, Figure 2, Table 3). The relationship between network clustering and internationalization speed was partially confirmed. We found no support for H1, which proposed that, the establishment of network relationships in clustered firms had a positive impact on FSTS growth (H1: β = –0,017; p = 0,169). So, the development of network interactions has no overall effect on internationalization scale. In turn, H3 – the establishment of network relationships in clustered firms will have a positive impact on geographic diversity – is supported (H3: β = 0,067; p < 0,001). The findings reveal that agglomerated firms, developing national and international interactions, display a higher geographical diversification (Felzensztein *et al.,* 2015; Mohr and Batsakis, 2017) (beta = + 0,067).

Similarly, the effect of internationalization speed on performance outcomes was partially observed. H2 – a higher growth of FSTS has a positive impact on performance outcomes in agglomeration contexts – was not confirmed (H2: β = 0,011; p = 0,357). Thus, internationalization scale does not influence performance, which is consistent with previous findings (Hilmersson, 2014; Hilmersson and Johanson, 2016). However, H4 – a higher level of geographic diversity has a positive impact on performance outcomes in agglomeration contexts – is supported (H4: β = 0,095; p < 0,01). This means that clustered firms selling for different geographical markets, exhibit a better performance (Khavul *et al.,* 2010; Hilmersson, 2014; Hilmersson and Johanson, 2016) in terms of firm's innovation, R&D intensity and sales growth (beta = + 0,095).

Finally, the results suggest that the development of national and international ties enhances firm's performance (Yeoh, 2004; Musteen *et al.,* 2010) (beta = + 0,208), validating H5. Simultaneously, network clustering also exerts an indirect, mediated effect, through internationalization scope. Given this scenario, we conclude that our model is partially mediated indicating that, a combination of network clustering and geographical diversity, helps improving firms' performance in industrial clusters.

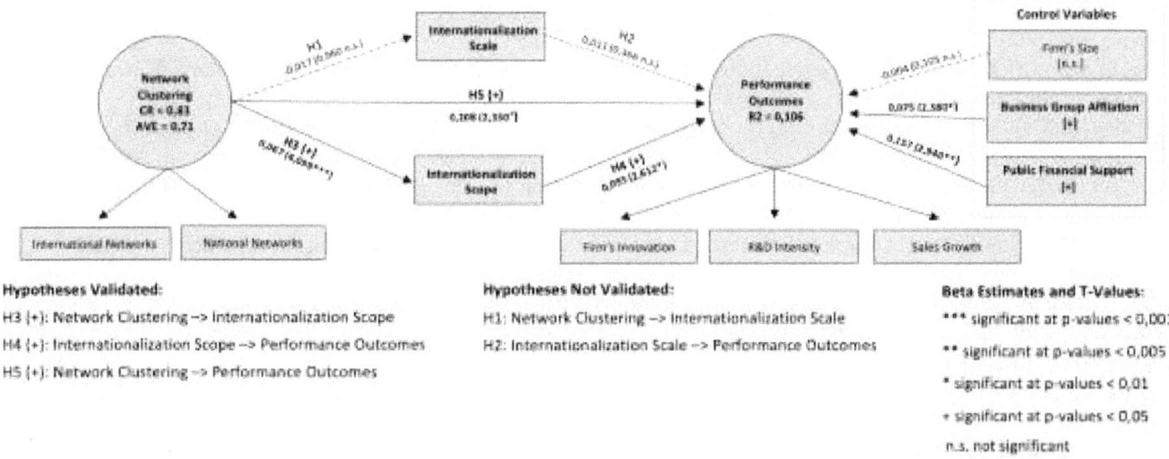

Figure 2: Path analysis

5. Conclusions

This paper contributes to a better understanding of firms' performance considering the analysis of network relations and internationalization speed on industrial clusters. We found that clustered firms display a higher geographical diversity that, in turn, catalyses their innovation, R&D intensity and sales growth. Thus, internationalization scope is one of the channels that translates network clustering into improved performance.

Our theoretical implication is that the resources that are needed to boost a faster international process and enhance short-term performance, are available on industrial clusters due to the network mechanisms established between different actors. In order to secure strategic positioning, particularly when competing in dynamic environment, firms should develop and maintain connections with several partners that provide privileged information to enter in new geographic markets.

The practical implication relates to the need for carefully consider the speed at which firm spread its international activities. Through network clustering, managers of internationalized firms are able to diversify the risks among different countries. Rapid internationalization is a relevant weapon that should be properly managed, since faster may not always be better. Firms' should be aware of the complexities and potential effects of rapid international growth, avoiding blindly fast-paced foreign growth strategies. In particular, for small clustered firms that face financial constraints and limited international experience, managers need to be cautious when decide to speed up their geographical diversification, to avert harming performance.

Our study has some limitations that, in turn, may lead to opportunities for future research. The scope of this research is circumscribed due to its focus on Portuguese firms. Beyond limiting the sample's size and the model explanatory power, raises questions about the generalizability of the results. In future research, efforts should be made to test the external validity of our findings by replicating this research in other contexts. Overall, the database selected to test our predictions has three main constraints: 1) usually, the CIS data are published and available for the community a lot time after being collected; 2) the dataset represents firms in activity between 2012 and 2014; and (3) does not allow to define and empirically measure internationalization speed, taking a long-term perspective. Future research could extend the time period, treating internationalization speed as a multidimensional concept, and testing its influence on firm's performance.

Acknowledgements

CIICESI, ESTG, Polytechnic of Porto. This research has been supported by the FEDER component of the European Structural and Investment Funds, through the P2020 program, and from national funds FCT - Portuguese Foundation for Science and Technology's (Fundação para a Ciência e a Tecnologia) under the project UIDB/04728/2020.

References

Aerts, K. and Schmidt, T. (2008) "Two for the price of one?: Additionality effects of R&D subsidies: A comparison between Flanders and Germany", *Research Policy*, Vol 37, No.5, pp 806-822.

Antoldi, F. and Cerrato, D. (2020) "Trust, Control, and Value Creation in Strategic Networks of SMEs", *Sustainability*, Vol 12, No.5, pp 1-20.

Bagozzi, R. P. and Yi, Y. (1988) "On the evaluation of structural equation models", *Journal of the Academy of Marketing Science*, Vol 16, No. 1, pp 74–94.

Batjargal, B. (2003) "Social capital and entrepreneurial performance in Russia: A longitudinal study", *Organization Studies*, Vol 24, No. 4, pp 535-556.

Benitez, J. *et al.* (2019) "How to perform and report an impactful analysis using partial least squares: Guidelines for confirmatory and explanatory IS research", *Information & Management*, 103168.

Boehe, D. (2013) "Collaborate at home to win abroad: How does access to local network resources influence export behavior?", *Journal of Small Business Management*, Vol 51, No.2, pp 167-182.

Casillas, J. C. and Acedo, F. J. (2013) "Speed in the internationalization process of the firm", *International Journal of Management Reviews*, Vol 15, No.1, pp 15-29.

Chang, J. (2007) "International expansion path, speed, product diversification and performance among emerging-market MNEs: evidence from Asia-Pacific multinational companies", *Asian Business & Management*, Vol 6, No. 4, pp 331-353.

Chang, S. J. and Rhee, J. H. (2011) "Rapid FDI expansion and firm performance", *Journal of International Business Studies*, Vol 42, No.8, pp 979-994.

Chetty, S., Johanson, M. and Martín Martín, O. (2014) "Speed of internationalization: Conceptualization, measurement and validation", *Journal of World Business*, Vol 49, No.4, pp 633- 650.

Chin, W. W. (1998) "The partial least squares approach to structural equation modeling: secondary title", *Methodology for Business and Management. Modern Methods for Business Research*, (April), 295–336.

Cho, N. and Park, Y. (2008) "Determinants of Korean venture performance", *Journal of Entrepreneurship and Venture Studies*, Vol 11, No.1, pp 145-165.

Collins, J. M. (1990) "A market performance comparison of US firms active in domestic, developed and developing countries", *Journal of International Business Studies*, Vol 21, No.2, pp 271-287.

Contractor, F. J., Kundu, S. K. and Hsu, C. C. (2003) "A three-stage theory of international expansion: The link between multinationality and performance in the service sector", *Journal of International Business Studies*, Vol 34, No. 1, pp 5-18.

DGEEC. (2016) "Principais resultados do CIS 2014 – Inquérito Comunitário à Inovação", available at http://www.dgeec.mec.pt/np4/207/%7B$clientServletPath%7D/?newsId=113&fileName=Principais_Resultados_CIS2014_29092016.pdf (accessed 4 May 2020).

Dubé, F. N., Haijuan, Y. and Lijun, H. (2015) "The role of cluster governance in the process of firm internationalization: based on the example of two Malaysian Halal Industrial Parks", *Asia-Pacific Social Science Review*, Vol 15, No. 1, pp 102-115.

Felzensztein, C. *et al.* (2015) "Networks, entrepreneurial orientation, and internationalization scope: evidence from Chilean small and medium enterprises", *Journal of Small Business Management*, Vol 53(sup1), pp 145-160.

Fornell, C. and Larcker, D. F. (1981) "Evaluating structural equation models with unobservable variables and measurement error", *Journal of Marketing Research*, Vol 18, No. 1, pp 39-50.

Gil-Barragan, J. *et al.* (2020) "When do domestic networks cause accelerated internationalization under different decision-making logic?", *European Business Review*, Vol 32, No.2, pp 227-256.

Hair, J. F., Ringle, C. M. and Sarstedt, M. (2011) "PLS-SEM: Indeed a silver bullet", *Journal of Marketing theory and Practice*, Vol 19, No.2, pp 139-152.

Hair, J. F. *et al.* (2012) "The Use of Partial Least Squares Structural Equation Modeling in Strategic Management Research: A Review of Past Practices and Recommendations for Future Applications", *Long Range Planning*, Vol 45, No.5–6, pp 320–340.

Henseler, J. *et al.* (2014) "Common beliefs and reality about PLS: Comments on Rönkkö and Evermann (2013)", *Organizational Research Methods*, Vol *17*, No.2, pp 182-209.

Henseler, J., Hubona, G. and Ray, P. A. (2016) "Using PLS path modeling in new technology research: updated guidelines", *Industrial Management & Data Systems*, Vol 116, No.1, pp 2-20.

Hilmersson, M. (2014) "Small and medium-sized enterprise internationalisation strategy and performance in times of market turbulence", *International Small Business Journal*, Vol 32, No.4, po 386-400.

Hilmersson, M. and Johanson, M. (2016) "Speed of SME internationalization and performance", *Management International Review*, Vol 56, No.1, pp 67-94.

Hitt, M. A. *et al.* (1997) "International diversification: Effects on innovation and firm performance in product-diversified firms", *Academy of Management Journal*, Vol 40, No.4, pp 767-798.

Hohenthal, J., Johanson, J. and Johanson, M. (2003) "Market discovery and the international expansion of the firm", *International Business Review*, Vol 12, No.6, pp 659-672.

IAPMEI. (2019), "Clusters de Competitividade Reconhecidos pelo IAPMEI", available at https://www.iapmei.pt/Paginas/Clusters-de-competitividade-reconhecidos-pelo-IAPM.aspx (accessed 19 October 2019).

Jankowska, B. and Götz, M. (2017) "Internationalization intensity of clusters and their impact on firm internationalization: the case of Poland", *European Planning Studies*, Vol 25, No.6, pp 958-977.

Johanson, J. and Vahlne, J. E. (1977) "The internationalization process of the firm—a model of knowledge development and increasing foreign market commitments", *Journal of International Business Studies*, Vol 8, No.1, pp 23-32.

Johanson, J. and Vahlne, J. E. (2009) "The Uppsala internationalization process model revisited: From liability of foreignness to liability of outsidership", *Journal of International Business Studies*, Vol 40, No.9, pp 1411-1431.

Khavul, S. *et al.* (2010) "Organizational entrainment and international new ventures from emerging markets", *Journal of Business Venturing*, Vol 25, No.1, pp 104-119.

Kozma, M. and Sass, M. (2019) "Hungarian international new ventures–Market selection and the role of networks in early internationalisation", *Society and Economy*, Vol 41, No.1, pp 27-45.

Kuivalainen, O. *et al.* (2007) "Firms' degree of born-globalness, international entrepreneurial orientation and export performance", *Journal of World Business*, Vol 42, No.3, pp 253-267.

Luo, Y. (2000). *Guanxi and Business*, World Scientific: Singapore.

Luo, Y. and Tung, R. L. (2007) "International expansion of emerging market enterprises: A springboard perspective", *Journal of International Business Studies,* Vol.38, pp 481-498.

Maccarini, M.E., *et al.* (2003) *"Internationalisation strategies in italian district-based firms: Theoretical modelling and empirical evidence"* (No. qf0402), Department of Economics, University of Insubria, [online], https://www.eco.uninsubria.it/RePEc/pdf/QF2004_03.pdf.

Mohr, A. and Batsakis, G. (2017) "Internationalization speed and firm performance: A study of the market-seeking expansion of retail MNEs", *Management International Review*, Vol 57, No.2, pp 153-177.

Musteen, M., *et al.* (2010) "The influence of international networks on internationalization speed and performance: A study of Czech SMEs", *Journal of World Business,* Vol 45, No.3, pp 197-205.

Naudé, P. *et al.* (2014) "The influence of network effects on SME performance. Industrial Marketing Management", Vol 43, No.4, pp 630-641.

OECD. (2005) *Oslo manual: Guidelines For Collecting and Interpreting Innovation Data*, *3rd Edition*, OECD publishing.

Oviatt, B. M. and McDougall, P. P. (2005) "Defining international entrepreneurship and modeling the speed of internationalization", *Entrepreneurship Theory and Practice*, Vol 29, No.5, pp 537-553.

Pangarkar, N. (2008) "Internationalization and performance of small-and medium-sized enterprises", *Journal of World Business*, Vol 43, No.4, pp 475-485.

Peng, M. W. and Luo, Y. (2000) "Managerial ties and firm performance in a transition economy: The nature of a micro-macro link", *Academy of Management Journal*, Vol 43, No.3, pp 486-501.

Pla-Barber, J. and Escribá-Esteve, A. (2006) "Accelerated internationalisation: evidence from a late investor country", *International Marketing Review*, Vol 23, No.3, pp 255-278.

PORDATA. (2020) "Pequenas e médias empresas em % do total de empresas: total e por dimensão", available at https://www.pordata.pt/Portugal/Pequenas+e+médias+empresas+em+percentagem+do+total+de+empresas+total+e+por+dimensão-2859 (accessed 11 May 2020).

Porter, M. E. (1998) *"Clusters and the new economics of competition"* (Vol. 76, No. 6, pp. 77-90), Boston: Harvard Business Review, [online], http://marasbiber.com/wp-content/uploads/2018/05/Michael-E.-Porter-Cluster-Reading.pdf.

Prashantham, S. (2004) "Local network relationships and the internationalization of small knowledge-intensive firms", *The Copenhagen Journal of Asian Studies*, Vol 19, pp 5-26.

Prashantham, S. and Young, S. (2011) "Post–entry speed of international new ventures", *Entrepreneurship Theory and Practice*, Vol 35, No.2, pp 275-292.

Qian, G. (2002) "Multinationality, product diversification, and profitability of emerging US small-and medium-sized enterprises", *Journal of Business Venturing*, Vol 17, No.6, pp 611-633.

Sadeghi, A., Rose, E. L. and Chetty, S. (2018) "Disentangling the effects of post-entry speed of internationalisation on export performance of INVs", *International Small Business Journal*, Vol 36, No.7, pp 780-806.

Santhosh, C. (2019) "Earliness of SME internationalization and performance", *Journal of Entrepreneurship in Emerging Economies*, Vol 11, No.4, pp 537-549.

Tallman, S. and Li, J. (1996) "Effects of international diversity and product diversity on the performance of multinational firms", *Academy of Management Journal*, Vol 39, No.1, pp 179-196.

Varma, S. *et al.* (2016) "What Drives Precocity? A Study of Indian Technology-Intensive Firms", *Journal of East-West Business*, Vol 22, No.4, pp 242-269.

Wei, W. *et al.* (2019) "Do Industrial Clusters Still Matter to Trust-Building in the Internet Era? A Network Embeddedness Perspective", *SAGE Open*, Vol 9, No.3, pp 1-12.

Yeoh, P. L. (2004) "International learning: antecedents and performance implications among newly internationalizing companies in an exporting context", *International Marketing Review*, Vol 21, No.4/5, pp 511-535.

Zahra, S. A. and George, G. (2002) "International entrepreneurship: The current status of the field and future research agenda", *Strategic entrepreneurship: Creating a new mindset*, 255-288, [online], http://www2.ufersa.edu.br/portal/view/uploads/setores/65/Zahra%20e%20George,%202002.pdf.

Zahra, S. A. *et al.* (2000) "International expansion by new venture firms: International diversity, mode of market entry, technological learning, and performance", *Academy of Management Journal*, Vol 43, No.5, pp 925-950.

Zhou, L. and Wu, A. (2014) "Earliness of internationalization and performance outcomes: Exploring the moderating effects of venture age and international commitment", *Journal of World Business*, Vol 49, No.1, pp 132-142.

Zucchella, A., Palamara, G. and Denicolai, S. (2007) "The drivers of the early internationalization of the firm", *Journal of World Business*, Vol 42, No.3, pp 268-280.

Equity Crowdfunding as a Socio-Technological Innovation Supporting Entrepreneurship

Krystyna Mitręga-Niestrój and Monika Klimontowicz
University of Economics in Katowice, Department of Banking and Financial Service, Katowice, Poland
krystyna.mitrega-niestroj@ue.katowice.pl
monika.klimontowicz@ue.katowice.pl
DOI: 10.34190/EIE.20.139

Abstract: During the last few decades, the dynamic development of new technology has influenced economies and societies all over the world. Current economic problems such as overregulated economy, the uneven distribution of resources accompanied with the decreasing access to capital, together with the decreasing barriers to entry to different markets, has encouraged both entities and individuals to search new ideas and opportunities as well as innovative sources of financing. As a result, new, innovative financial products and services have appeared on the market. The paper focuses on equity crowdfunding (ECF) and its role in developing individuals' entrepreneurship. The equity crowdfunding seems to be a brilliantly simple mechanism of capital raising that changes the paradigm of capital supply for new business initiatives, for example, start-ups. It influences both sides of the markets. For entities, it is an alternative funding method engaging a group of dispersed investors. For individuals, it gives the opportunity to become micro investors and enter the capital market without professional accreditation. Despite the dynamic development of the equity crowdfunding market, it is still the lack of research analysing its features, advantages and threats for both entities and micro investors as well as its impact on entrepreneurship development. The paper tries to fulfil this gap and find the factors enabling its further adoption and growth. The structure of the paper is as follows. The first section defines equity crowdfunding among other financial innovations and describes its fundraising process and models. The second section includes the characteristic of equity crowdfunding as a source of external financing from the entrepreneurship development perspective. The third section focuses on its role supporting entrepreneurship development with the special attention paid on supporting start-ups in Poland.

Keywords: equity crowdfunding, socio-technological innovations, entrepreneurship funding, start-ups

1. Introduction

During the last few decades, the dynamic development of new technology has influenced economies and societies all over the world. Current economic problems such as overregulated economy, the uneven distribution of resources accompanied with the decreasing access to capital, together with the decreasing barriers to entry to different markets and the emerging of the new economic model - the collaborative economy have encouraged both entities and individuals to search new ideas and opportunities as well as innovative sources of financing. As a result, new, innovative financial products and services have appeared on the market.

The scientific interest in innovations is the result of their importance for entities' development. The scope of the research conducted in many developed countries reflects this interest. The researchers focused on different economies, markets and entities. In the industry, surveys are conducted in three categories: diffusion innovation research, organisational innovativeness research and process theory research.

The research on the diffusion of innovation focused on its determinants such as organisations' characteristic including the type of organisation, leadership style and organisational culture, innovations' features, and external factors influencing innovations' adoption (Rogers, 1962; Zmud, 1982; Damanpour and Gopalakrishnan, 1998; Damanpour and Schneider, 2006).

The surveys focused on an organisational propensity to implement innovations assume that innovations' implementation is (Grover and Goslar, 1993; Subramanian and Nilakanta, 1996):

- the response for chances in organisations' environment,
- the result of strategic initiatives undertaken and promoted by decision-makers,
- beneficial and desirable as they improve an organisation and its performance,
- related to specific organisations' features.

The scientists surveyed the impact of different factors on organisational innovativeness (Vicente et al. 2015; Shuying et al., 2017; Liao et al., 2017; Liu et al., 2018), the impact of organisation's features on effectiveness and performance (Damanpour and Evan, 1990; Anning-Dorson, 2018), the relationship between the innovations, organisational innovativeness, market environment and market position (Gunday et al., 2011; Tepic et al., 2013).

A criticism of organisational innovativeness research led to the development of process theory research. The analysis of these research results enabled to distinguish three generations of models. The first generation - stage models – focused on the process' phases (for example, Ettlie, 1983).

The second generation described the influence of organisational content (strategy, structure, resources, etc.) on the innovation process. Primary, the process was analysed linearly. As the theory was developed, it took interdependencies, interactions and feedbacks into account (Kline and Rosenberg, 1986, p. 640) as well as inspirations and challenges (Rothwell, 1992).

The third generation – the integrated models – abandoned sequencing in favour of simultaneity and interrelations. They noticed the systemic effects, the necessity to cross the organisation's borders, the complexity of stakeholders' interrelations, and, as a result, the need and the importance of a permanent networks' analysis and organisational learning. The research conducted in this field included new types of innovations, new forms of organisations and their behaviour as innovations network, inter-organisational and network learning, inter-organisational cooperation, the selection of partners and network management (Teece, 1996; Dhanaraj and Parkhe, 2006; Ojasalo, 2008; Rampersad et al., 2010).

Open innovations reflect the new organisational forms that cross the entities' borders. Such innovations support new technology development and result from the integration of internal and external ideas, and the pathways to enter the market (Chesbrought, 2003; Saebi and Foss, 2014). The open innovation concept may be treated as the next generation of innovation models (Gassmann et al., 2010). It reflects the virtual networks of entities sharing (via an intranet, extranet and internet) information and knowledge for creating value based on innovations (Tidd et al., 2005; Huizingh, 2011), emergent networks resulting from long-term cooperation (Tidd et al., 2005; Cowan et al., 2007; Rycroft and Kash, 2014), and engineered (designed) networks established for creating and supporting innovations (van Aken and Weggeman, 2000; Tidd et al., 2005; Dhanaraj and Parkhe, 2006).

The paper focuses on the specific open innovation - the equity crowdfunding (ECF), and its role in entrepreneurship development. The equity crowdfunding seems to be a brilliantly simple mechanism of capital raising that changes the paradigm of capital supply for new business initiatives, for example, start-ups. It influences both sides of the markets. For entities, it is an alternative funding method engaging a group of dispersed investors. For individuals, it gives the opportunity to become micro investors and enter the capital market without professional accreditation. The simultaneity of the fundraising process and network interrelations enable analysing the equity crowdfunding as an example of the third generation integrated models. It is a new type of innovation going beyond the framework of Oslo Manual innovations taxonomy that divides innovations into product, process, organisational and market ones (OECD, 2005). It is a socio-technological innovation established as a designed network for creating funds and supporting innovations. Besides, crowdfunding is not only innovation by itself, but it is also a source of innovation and creativity for several levels as products, services, business models, and an incentive for process improvements in established firms. It provides a paradigm shift in the state of science or technology embedded in a product, new R&D resources, and/or new production processes for a firm and new marketplaces for innovations to evolve (Garcia and Cantalone, 2002). According to Leite and Moutinho (2012), it is not a radical innovation as the shift from traditional financing systems has a clear incremental nature, mainly observed at the local of actuation, which is the internet, and at the contributor, that changes from individual to a group. However, it is in the centre of some radical or disruptive discontinuities on both micro- and macro-level, following the Schumpeterian creative destruction notion.

Despite the dynamic development of the equity crowdfunding market, it is still the lack of research analysing its features, advantages and threats for both entities and micro investors as well as its impact on entrepreneurship development. The paper tries to fulfil this gap. The results develop the innovation process theory in the field of third-generation innovation models, present fields of entrepreneurship supported by equity crowdfunding, and give some insights for both sides of the market.

The structure of the paper is as follows. The first section defines equity crowdfunding among other financial innovations and describes its fundraising process and models. The second section includes the characteristic of equity crowdfunding as a source of external financing from the entrepreneurship development perspective. The third section focuses on its role supporting entrepreneurship development with the special attention paid on supporting start-ups in Poland.

The article has a review character which integrates and interprets the existing state of knowledge and available data. It is an initial research stage which may be the foundation for further detailed analysis and future findings. In a view of the initial stage of the research this paper uses the research method based on a literature review. The equity crowdfunding has an emergent character which limits the access to complete information about its development in Poland. The data comes from the available formal and informal reports and internal materials of the Polish crowdfunding platforms

2. The equity crowdfunding – definition, process and models

Equity crowdfunding (also referred to as ECF, investment crowdfunding, crowd-investing or crowd equity) is one of the forms of crowdfunding which, according to the European Commission, is an emerging alternative form of financing that connects those who can give, lend or invest money directly with those who need funding for a specific project. The equity crowdfunding, together with debt-based crowdfunding, belong to so-called investment crowdfunding where investors aim to achieve an economic return. Apart from this, a non-investment crowdfunding exists where investors either seek to support the charity project or receive a non-monetary remuneration (Bradford, 2012) – see Figure 1.

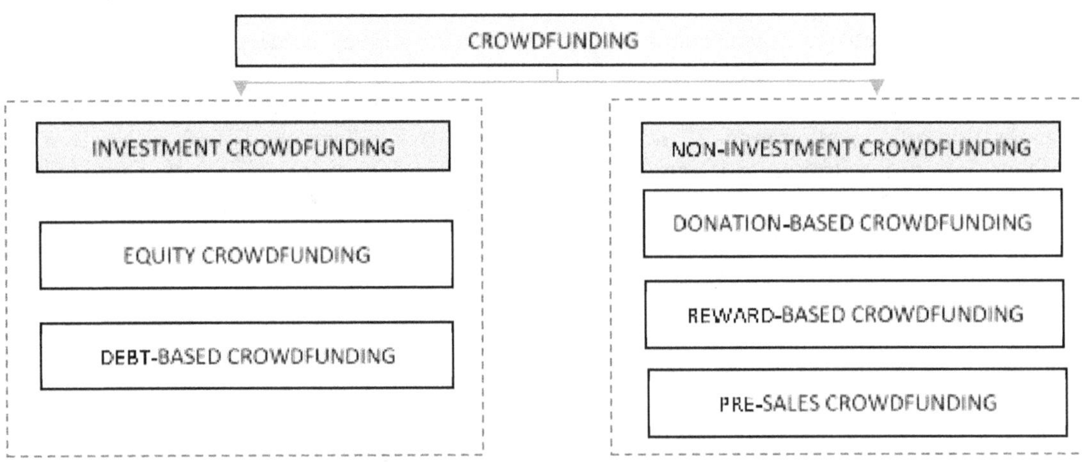

Figure 1: The taxonomy of crowdfunding

In equity crowdfunding entrepreneurs make an open call for funding on the Internet, offering equity or equity-like shares, to attract a large group of investors (Cumming and Johan, 2019). U.S. Securities and Exchange Commission defines this type of crowdfunding as a new and evolving method to raise money using the Internet (SEC, 2014). According to Polish Financial Supervision Authority investment crowdfunding is such an activity where the activities of an entity operating a so-called crowdfunding platform are carried out on behalf of companies raising capital by issuing securities (e.g. shares or bonds). The shares in a limited liability company could also be distributed in this way (UKNF, 2020). Equity crowdfunding is a new way of financing a company - an alternative to bank or stock exchange financing. The equity crowdfunding is also an interesting investment opportunity for micro investors as it enables them to make profits with little capital expenditure and to diversify their investment portfolio into several different crowdfunding projects. The equity crowdfunding market is highly dependent on the legal environment of a country. Moreover, since it involves the sale of securities and is therefore subject to various regulatory problems, it is subject to restrictions in many countries.

The equity crowdfunding process, also referred to as a campaign, includes following basic stages: preparations, planning the pitch, creating the pitch, fundraising, and post-campaign (EU, 2015, pp 25-26).

The first step of crowdfunding campaign includes research on potential crowdfunding platforms, an analysis of their features, rules, terms and legal requirement, creating the timetable and a cost plan, preparing the financial documents required by the platform and starting building the crowd on social media. At this stage, the entity should also analyse the market trends by looking at how much is pledged for current crowdfunding campaigns and what is expected in return. After a successful application to the platform, the business and financial plan must be finalised. The project should present the information concerning the valuation of the business and its logic, financial performance and forecasts, an amount of offered equity with rationale, and an understandable, visually pleasing and engaging description of a business story (idea), product, service, etc. and financials with the links to where to find more information.

Creating the pitch requires a well-designed, informative and appealing website which emphasises to investors the entity's professionalism, the activity on social media, and building the crowd by creating and joining conversations. The effective campaigns usually include a brief video presenting the concept, entity and its team, the performance of the company, and the plan how the gathered money will be spent. This step is significant for further success. It has been shown that campaigns that get above twenty per cent of the target in the first few days are much more likely to succeed (EU, 2015).

The next stage is the continuation of the previous one. It mostly focuses on motivating and encouraging the crowd by sharing and promoting the campaign on social media as well as by talking to journalists, taking part in conferences, trade fairs, etc., and responding to questions, suggestions, and queries.

The post-campaign stage has an administrative character. At this stage, the new company is set-up, a new governance structure and procedures are established, and the returns to investors (as profits, shares, dividends, share buy-back, etc.) are prepared. Depending on the project, the size of the team and time, the stages described above may be more or less complicated.

There are many different models of crowdfunding depending on the regulatory solutions implemented a given country (see Table 1).

Table 1: The models of equity crowdfunding

Equity crowdfunding model	The model characteristic
The profit/revenue sharing model	Entitles the investor to a predetermined share in profits or revenues generated by the start-up or project in a given time, without any ownership rights to the entity whose actions the investor finances
Direct investment in an equity model	In exchange for financial support, the investor becomes a shareholder in an entity already functioning or specially established for the purposes of project implementation
Investor-led (syndicate funding) model	The model provides for an accredited lead investor, ensuring the professionalism of the investment process (it may be a business angel or a venture capital fund), who for example conducts due diligence, negotiates the terms of investment directly
Entrepreneur-led equity crowdfunding	The investments are available for crowd investors; the entity raising funds determines the terms and conditions of the offer
Nominee structure model	The third-party holds the legal title to the shares on behalf of the crowdfunding investor, who is the actual owner. It represents all minority shareholders in relations with the entity in which the investment is made
Participation model	The investor enters into a contractual obligation with a third party, which then invests the capital on behalf of all crowdfunding investors. The title to the shares is in full to a third party, as well as any voting rights
Club model	The platform attracts potential investors as members of a closed "investment club" to avoid the requirements of public offering regulation and investor protection
Cooperative (holding, vehicle) model	The platform creates a special purpose vehicle to raise capital to be invested in a given project
Collective investment model	Various groups of entities participate, including business angels, investing in the development of a company or a specific project relatively small sums
Convertible bonds based model	The bond may be converted into shares according to a specific conversion factor, resulting in the replacement of the debt by equity. Beneficial for companies with large but uncertain growth potential

Source: Authors' work based on EC (2014, pp 6-7, Medzhybovska, 2017, pp 44-45, Kozioł-Nadolna, 2015, Paschen, 2017.

Crowdfunding is still in its early stage of development, and therefore these models might evolve in the future. The most important influence on this process will have regulations and condition of the given economy.

3. The characteristic of equity crowdfunding as a source of external financing enabling entrepreneurship development

Equity crowdfunding provides a unique opportunity for entities in the growth phase, in particular start-ups, which have difficulties in obtaining financing in banks or on the regulated capital market. Nevertheless, it is also used by mature, established companies, not only innovative ones, from various industries. It serves to finance a business activity or a selected part of it, whether strategic or operational, rather than a product or service.

Crowd equity compared to the capital financing of companies that are not listed on regulated markets – venture capital funds, private equity or business angels - is not about establishing a relationship with a single investor, but with a wide range of potential investors (EU, 2015). Besides financing, ECF offers considerable benefits for companies, which is kind of unusual for bank financing, as it confirms the company valuation, prepares for the stock market debut, creates an employee incentive scheme, attracts new customers and business partners, and supports getting publicity and building a community (Beesfund, 2019). It's a public issue of shares - with no prospectus or information memorandum required and could be a remedy for the small number of public offerings on the regulated capital market.

This type of crowdfunding is not only an opportunity to obtain capital for development from many investors. It is also an excellent tool for marketing and promotional purposes, allowing the company to reach a wide range of potential customers. Equity crowdfunding "democratises", opens the complex and hidden world of investing for small investors and for young companies seeking to finance their innovative projects. It is not "just financing", but assigns non-standard roles for participants that is unusual not only for banking financing but also for raising capital on the stock exchange. In crowd equity, one can observe a new type of interaction between entrepreneurs and numerous investors which is enabled by technology and constitutes an innovative environment for financing. The investors, who may be current or future customers of the company, may identify themselves with the undertaking they are financing and even become its 'ambassadors'. What is more, it is not excluded that investors may bring their knowledge, experience, ideas and business contacts to the company, to secure future profits from the investment (Malinowski, 2018). From the investors' perspective, this new form of financing offers direct choice over where to put one's money and a sense of involvement with the project. People who contribute might also get a different perspective on – and more direct contact with – entrepreneurs, which may further promote a culture of entrepreneurship. Additionally, contributors often form a community to back the financed project or might supply non-financial resources in the form of crowd-sourcing (e.g. calls to the public to supply non-monetary contributions to the realisation of a project such as skills, commercial networks, etc.). Equity crowdfunding supports the development of relational capital which emerges between entrepreneurs and investors, also in the long term.

The equity crowdfunding supports different fields of entrepreneurship of both sides of the market – the entities and the investors (see Table 2).

Table 2: The fields of entrepreneurship supported by equity crowdfunding - the perspective of two sides of the market

Entities	Investors
developing the ability to obtain capital from many investors building the business network by establishing a relationship with a wide range of potential investors confirming the company valuation preparing for the stock market debut developing the ability to attracts new customers and business partners developing the capacity to gain and manage the knowledge, experience, ideas and business contacts to the from investors creating an employee incentive scheme supporting getting publicity supporting the commercialisation of innovations	developing investor skills as it gives the opportunity to become micro investors and enter the capital market without professional accreditation building a direct relationship with the entity developing the relational capital in the long-term perspective above-average returns in the medium-term perspective risk diversification

Equity crowdfunding can offer various benefits to a large spectrum of users which is partly explained by its flexibility, and community engagement. It can foster entrepreneurship not only in terms of increased access to finance but also as an additional market testing and marketing tool, which can help entrepreneurs acquiring relevant knowledge of customers and media exposure. No bank financing could give such media interest as an equity crowdfunding action. The experience with crowdfunding campaigns also builds employability skills (Green, 2014), while successful campaigns provide a valuable role model to other 'entrepreneurs to be'. The campaigners collecting funds can include SMEs, start-ups, micro-entrepreneurs, social entrepreneurs, the self-employed, the cultural and creative sectors, public authorities, innovative or environmental projects, public interest bodies, researchers, consumers or the unemployed (EU, 2014).

ECF also has high potential benefits for innovation, research and development, and it could contribute to growth, community development and job creation while financing innovative projects that do not have the level of maturity that traditional financial market sources require. Compared to other types of finance, it can also reduce costs and administrative burden for enterprises, notably SMEs (EU, 2014, p. 5). Equity crowdfunding can support the commercialisation of innovations (Kaliszuk, 2020). Crowd equity is more risky, but also complex for investors than, e.g. debt crowdfunding, and this is mainly due to the specificity of entities that most often look for this type of financing, i.e. start-ups. The high investment risk is obviously to compensate investors for above-average profits. However, it should be noted that equity crowdfunding is a medium-term investment, with an investment period of 3 to 5 years, and is therefore not intended for investors planning to make above-average returns in a short period. Investors may have problems to diversify their investment portfolio with a small number of campaigns available on the platform. In addition, investors must take a due care to familiarise themselves with all available information about the company - including its financial results, business documentation, the project to be financed, etc. (Ferrarini, 2017).

4. The role of equity crowdfunding in supporting entrepreneurship development – the case of Poland

The Polish crowdfunding market is definitely younger and smaller than the Western European ones, but it is developing dynamically and has excellent potential. It is thought to be the main driver of the alternative finance market in Eastern Europe which usually clustered Poland, Czech Republic and Hungary together as Eastern Europe. Poland is on track to become mature alternative finance markets, with a handful of established platforms within their borders. It exhibited the largest growth in this region from €10.2m to € 38.1m (up 272%) in 2015-2016, and from €38.1m to €142m in 2016-2017 (up 274%). (Ziegler et al., 2017, 2018). The share of equity crowdfunding it the total alternative finance market differs among the Eastern Europe countries. Generally, it does not exceed two per cent of the domestic alternative finance market (see Figure 2). It is used in Poland and Czech Republic while not used in Slovakia and Hungary at all. The Polish market is still very small when compared to the biggest European one – the UK equity-based crowdfunding was worth nearly €380m in 2017 (Zang et al., 2018) while in Poland in the years 2015-2017 it was worth €0,18m, €0,9m, €0,76, accordingly (Ziegler et al., 2017, 2018).

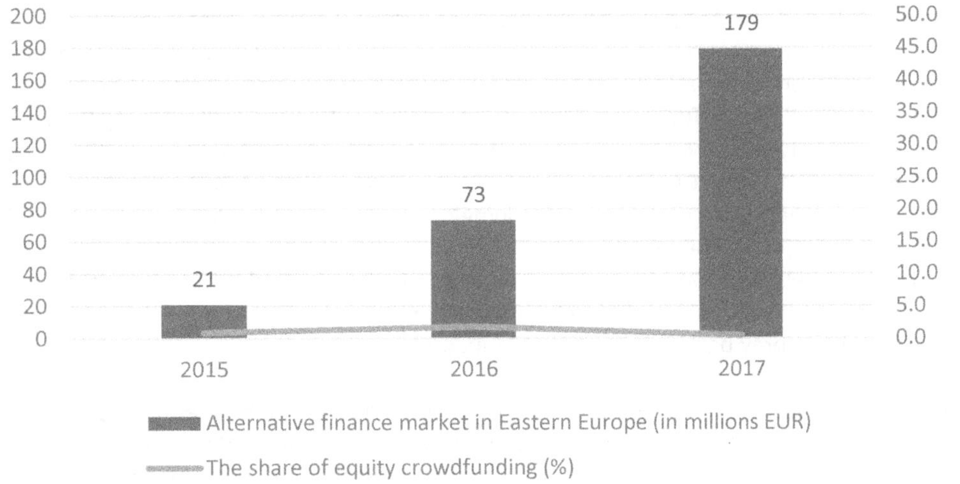

Figure 2: The equity crowdfunding as a part of the alternative finance market (Authors' work based on data retrieved from Ziegler et al., 2017, 2018)

Even though there is still relatively low market share as well as the low awareness of Poles and companies for which ECF could be attractive about this form of investment, ait is the low-cost alternative to bank loans. The year 2019 was a breakthrough for the Polish equity crowdfunding market. The major catalyst for this phenomenon was the change in regulations introducing an increase of the limit of offers of equity crowdfunding from €100,000m to €1m, which made this form of financing more attractive to a broader group of entities (Gemra, 2019). It was the first time in the history that start-ups starting to raise capital through equity crowdfunding platforms were listed on the Warsaw Stock Exchange. Additionally, 50 companies benefited from this method of financing, which in total raised Zl52m. The majority of campaigns were conducted by the most valuable and the oldest market player – Beesfund (27 campaigns). Beesfund was established in 2012 and was the first ECF platform in Poland and the Central and Eastern Europe. It was followed by Crowdway (9 campaigns) and Findfunds (8 campaigns). In 2019 for the first time, investors had the opportunity to make profits by selling their shares to strategic partners of companies or through the Warsaw Stock Exchange (Zgiep, 2020).

Entrepreneurs using equity crowdfunding seek funding from around Zl2.5m. However, most of them did not manage to reach the target amount, so the average raised capital was Zl1.5m (the largest amount so far was Zl4.14m raised by Pinta Barrel Brewing). In the years 2018-2019, companies have attracted a total of 21 thousand investors (provided that one person could invest in many companies). The average value of a single investment was Zl1.7 thous., and a single company engaged on average 0.8 thousand investors.

The crowdfunding is used mainly by technology companies, but also by life-style companies, alcoholic beverages and cosmetics producers, companies related to ecology and sport. Several of the campaigns conducted in the last two years have failed. These were in the minority, but they have common elements - a focus on B2B or a lack of fast-moving products (Maj, 2019).

However, start-ups in Poland are still most willing to finance their activities from their resources, look for an investor or apply for grants. In a survey conducted by the Startup Poland Foundation in 2017, only 2% of Polish start-ups indicated crowdfunding as a source of capital. The demand for financing, particularly the necessity of reducing the equity gap among Polish early-stage companies, is high, and the equity crowdfunding could be an essential countermeasure here (Łukowski and Zygmanowski, 2019). For supporting crowd equity development Warsaw Stock Exchange (WSE) has launched in 2019 the WSE Crowdfunding Partner Programme addressed to brokers who offer crowdfunding and crowd investing services in Poland (GPW, 2019).

In the coming months of 2020, the demand for such type of financing among companies may raise due to first of all by reduced bank financing. The economic crisis triggered by coronavirus pandemia leading to liquidity problems in companies could increase the need for recapitalization. If the campaign were to be used to repay other financial debts, this could pose an additional risk for the whole ECF market, and it would be worth considering whether equity crowdfunding could be used here (Maj, 2020).

5. Conclusion

The equity crowdfunding is currently one of the most innovative forms of entrepreneurship financing. It is a specific kind of open innovation, based on the idea of cooperation, openness and knowledge sharing among entrepreneurs and investors supported by modern technological solutions. The "crowd networks" and social capital plays a significant role in the fundraising process, in selecting ideas and transforming them into successful products or services. This type of crowdfunding assigns new roles to the ECF process participants, uncanny to the traditional bank or stock market financing. It is not uncommon that the investors identify themselves with the project they are financing. A successful crowdfunding campaign entails "building a community" around the company, product or projects. The equity crowdfunding is not only merely the innovation itself, but it contributes to the emergence of innovative solutions, commercializing and diffusing innovations. The equity crowdfunding characteristic and features led to the conclusion that it crosses the borders of commonly applied financial innovations' taxonomy based on the Oslo Manual.

The fundraising process enables the development of entrepreneurial skills of both entities and investors. Among them, from the entities' perspective, the most valuable fields are the ability to develop the business network by establishing a relationship with a wide range of potential investors, the capacity to gain and manage the knowledge, experience, ideas and business contacts to the from investors, and as a result the ability to attract new customers. For investors, the equity crowdfunding gives the opportunity to enter the capital market without professional accreditation and as a result, develop investor skills.

The equity crowdfunding provides a unique opportunity to raise capital also for Polish entrepreneurs, especially young and innovative ones. Therefore, often for those who have difficulties in obtaining bank or stock market financing, especially in conditions of stagnation on the Polish stock market. For entrepreneurs, it is an opportunity for reasonable financial funding from many small investors, and for investors, it is an opportunity for profits, with low capital commitment. The Polish ECF market needs legal regulations that facilitate its development and raising public awareness and understanding of this innovative financing instrument. Although the Polish market is still small, especially in comparison with Western European countries, the potential for growth seems high, even in the current conditions of a pandemic crisis.

References

Anning-Dorson T. (2018), "Innovation and competitive advantage creation. The role of organisational leadership in service firms from emerging markets", *International Marketing Review*, Vol. 35, Iss. 4, pp 580-600.

Beesfund (2019) https://beesfund.com/useruploads/oferta_equity_crowdfunding.pdf

Bradford C. S. (2012) "Crowdfunding and the federal securities laws". *Columbia Business Law Review* 2012(1), pp 14-15.

Chesbrought H. (2003), *Open innovation: The new imperative for creating and profiting from technology*, Harvard Business School Press, Boston

Cowan R., Jonard N., Zimmermann J.B. (2007), "Bilateral collaboration and the emergence of innovation networks", Management *Science*, Vol. 53, Iss. 7, pp 1051-1067.

Cumming D., Johan S. (2019) *Crowdfunding: Fundamental Cases, Facts, and Insights*, Academic Press, p. 213.

Damanpour F., Evan W.M. (1990), *The adoption of innovations over time: Structural characteristic and performance of organizations*, Proceedings of Nacional Decision Science Institute Conference, San Diego

Damanpour F., Gopalakrishnan S. (1998), "Theories of organizational structure and innovation adoption: The role of environment change", *The Journal of Engineering and Technology Management*, Vol. 15, Iss. 1, pp 1-24.

Damanpour F., Schneider M. (2006), "Phases of adoption of innovation in organizations: Effects of environment, organization and top managers", *British Journal of Management*, Vol. 17, Iss. 3, pp 215-236.

Dhanaraj C., Parkhe A. (2006), "Orchestrating innovation networks", *Academy of Management Review*, Vol. 31, Iss. 3, pp 659-669.

Drucker P.F. (1985), *Innovation and entrepreneurship*, Butterworth-Heinemann, Oxford.

Ettlie J.E. (1983), "Organizational policy and innovation among suppliers to the food processing sector", *Academy of Management Journal*, Vol. 26, Iss. 1, pp 27-44.

EU (2014) *Unleashing the potential of crowdfunding in the European Union*, European Commission, Brussels, https://eur-lex.europa.eu/legal-content/EN/TXT/?uri=COM%3A2014%3A0172%3AFIN

EU (2015) *Crowdfunding explained*, European Commission, Brussels, https://op.europa.eu/en/publication-detail/-/publication/d5e626ba-d7c8-11e6-ad7c-01aa75ed71a1/language-en/format-PDF, p. 9, 15.

Ferrarini G. (2017), "Regulating Fintech: Crowdfunding and Beyond", *European Economy. Banks, Regulations, and the Real Sector*, 2017.2, https://european-economy.eu/2017-2/regulating-fintech-crowdfunding-and-beyond/, pp. 121-142.

Garcia R., Calantone R. (2002), "A critical look at technological innovation typology and innovativeness terminology: A literature review", *Journal of Product Innovation Management*, Vol. 19, No. 2, pp 110-132.

Gassmann O., Enkel E., Chesbrought H. (2010), "The future of open innovation", *R&D Management*, Vol. 40, Iss. 3, pp 213-221.

Gemra (2019) "Crowdfunding udziałowy jako forma finansowania rozwoju przedsiębiorstwa", *Kwartalnik Nauk o Przedsiębiorstwie*, nr 3, p. 47.

GPW (2019) *GPW Launches a Crowdfunding Programme for Brokers*, https://www.gpw.pl/news?cmn_id=108991&title=GPW+Launches+a+Crowdfunding+Programme+for+Brokers.

Green A., de Hoyos M., Baenes S.-A., Baldauf B., Behle H. (2014), *Explanatory Research on Internet Work Exchanges and Employability, Analysis and synthesis of quantitative evidence on crowdsourcing for work, funding and volunteers*, Steward J (Ed). JRC Scientific and Policy Report Series, EUR 26423 EN. Institute for Prospective Technological Studies, Joint Research Centre, European Commission, http://ftp.jrc.es/EURdoc/JRC85646.pdf

Grover V., Goslar M.D. (1993), "The initiation, adoption, and implementation of telecommunications technologies in U.S. organizations", *Journal of Management Information System*, Vol. 10, pp 141-163.

Gunday G., Ulusoy G., Kilic K., Alpkan L. (2011), "Effects on innovation types on firm performance", *International Journal of Production Economics*, Vol. 133, pp 662-676.

https://ec.europa.eu/info/business-economy-euro/growth-and-investment/financing-investment/crowdfunding_en.

Huizingh E.K. (2011), "Open innovation: State of the art and future perspective", *Technovation*, Vol. 31, Iss. 1, pp 2-9.

Kaliszuk G. (2020), Emocje warte 29 mld USD – czyli przyszłość crowdfundingu, https://prnews.pl/emocje-warte-29-mld-usd-czyli-przyszlosc-crowdfundingu-450054.

Kline S.J., Rosenberg N. (1986), *An overview of innovation* [in:] R. Landau, N. Rosenberg (red.), *The positive sum strategy: Harnessing technology for economic growth*, National Academy Press, Washington, DC, pp 173-203.

Leite P., Moutinho N. (2012) "Innovation through crowdfunding: a quantitative and qualitative analysis of Kickstarter", *Engineering*, https://www.semanticscholar.org/paper/INNOVATION-THROUGH-CROWDFUNDING%3A-A-QUANTITATIVE-AND-Moutinho-Leite/2ae541505bd849e0da0f0c22988ebcf6c8d29b77

Liao S.-H., Chen C.-C., Hu D.-C., Chung Y.-C., Liu C.-L., (2017), "Assessing the influence of leadership style, organizational learning and organizational innovation", *Leadership & Organization Development Journal*, Vol. 38, Iss. 5, pp 590-609.

Liu Y., Lv D., Ying Y., Arndt F., Wei J. (2018), "Improvisation for innovation: The contingent role of resource and structural factors in explaining innovation capability", *Technovation*, Vol. 74/75, pp 32-41.

Łukowski M., Zygmanowski P. (2019), "The Role of Crowdfunding in Reducing the Equity Gap in Poland", *Ruch Prawniczy, Ekonomiczny i Socjologiczny*, Rok LXXXI – zeszyt 3, p. 199.

Maj S. (2019) *Rynek crowdfundingu w liczbach*, https://www.pb.pl/rynek-crowdfundingu-w-liczbach-969674.

Maj S. (2020) *Tłum może uratować spółki*, https://www.pb.pl/tlum-moze-uratowac-spolki-988132.

Malinowski B. F. (2018) *Crowdfunding udziałowy dla startupów (i nie tylko)*, Warszawa, http://firma.um.warszawa.pl/wp-content/uploads/2018/07/Crowdfunding_udzialowy_dla_startupow_i_nie_tylko_-_Bartosz_Filip_Malinowski.pdf

OECD (2005), *Oslo Manual. Guidelines for collecting and interpreting innovation data*, 3rd edition. OECD, Statistical Office of the European Communities, Luxembourg

Ojasalo J. (2008), "Management of innovation networks: A case study of different approaches", *European Journal of Innovation Management*, Vol. 11, Iss. 1, pp 51-86.

Rampersad G., Quester P., Troshani I. (2010), "Managing innovation networks: Exploratory evidence from ICT, biotechnology and nanotechnology networks", *The Industrial Marketing Management*, Vol. 39, Iss. 5, pp 793-805.

Rogers E.M. (1962), *Diffusion of innovations*, Free Press of Glencoe, New York

Rothwell R. (1992), "Successful industrial innovation: Critical factors for the 1990s", *R&D Management*, Vol. 22, Iss. 3, pp. 221-240.

Rycroft R.W., Kash D.E. (2014), "Self-organizing innovation networks: Implications for globalization", *Technovation*, Vol. 24, Iss. 3, pp 187-197.

Saebi T., Foss N.J. (2014), "Business model for open innovation: Matching heterogeneous open innovation strategy with business model dimensions", *European Management Journal*, Vol. 33(3), pp 201-213.

SAFE (2019) *Survey on Access to Finance of Enterprises*, the European Commission and the European Central Bank, https://ec.europa.eu/growth/access-to-finance/data-surveys_en

SEC (2014) *RE: File Number S7–09–13 – Crowdfunding*, https://www.sec.gov/comments/s7-09-13/s70913-208.pdf

Shuying W., Shuijuan Z., Bobo, L. (2017), "Effect of diversity on top management team to the bank's innovation ability-based on nature of ownership perspective", *Procedia Engineering*, Vol. 174, pp 240-245.

Subramanian A., Nilakanta S. (1996), "Organizational innovativeness: Exploring the relationship between organizational determinants of innovation, types of innovations, and measures of organizational performance", *Omega*, Vol. 24, No. 6, pp 631-647.

Teece D. (1996), "Firm organization, industrial structure, and technological innovation", *Journal of Economic Behavior & Organization*, Vol. 31, Iss. 2, pp 193-224.

Tepic M., Kemp R., Omta O. (2013), "Complexities in innovation management in companies from the European industry: A path model of innovation project performance determinants", *European Journal of Innovation Management*, Vol. 16, Iss. 4, pp 517-550.

Tidd J., Bessant J., Pavitt K. (2005), *Managing innovation. integrated technological, market, and organizational change*, JohnWilley & Sons, Chichester

UKNF (2020) *Stanowisku UKNF dotyczące zasad funkcjonowania tzw. platform crowdfundingu inwestycyjnego*, https://www.knf.gov.pl/knf/pl/komponenty/img/Stanowisko_UKNF_dot_platform_crowdfundingu_inwestycyjnego_69487.pdf, p. 2.

van Aken J.E., Weggeman M.P. (2000), "Managing learning in informal innovation networks: Overcoming the Daphne-dilemma", R&D *Management*, Vol. 30, Iss. 2, pp 139-150.

Vicente M., Abrantes J.L., Teixeira, M.S. (2015), "Measuring innovation capability in exporting firms: The INNOVSCALE", *International Marketing Review*, Vol. 32, Iss. 1, pp 29-51.

Zgiep L. (2020) *Dlaczego warto zainteresować się equity crowdfundingiem w latach dwudziestych XXI wieku?* https://zgiep.com/dlaczego-warto-zainteresowac-sie%CC%A8-equity-crowdfundingiem-w-latach-dwudziestych-xxi-wieku/

Zhang B., Ziegler T., Mammadova L., Johanson D, Gray M., Yerolemou N. (2018) *The 5th UK Alternative Finance Industry Report*, The Cambridge Centre for Alternative Finance, , p.12.

Ziegler T., Shneor R., Garvey K., Wenzlaff K., Yerolomou N., Hao R., Zhang B. (2017), *Shifting ParaExpanding horizons. The 3rd European Alternative Finance Industry Report*, Cambridge Centre for Alternative Finance

Ziegler T., Shneor R., Wenzlaff K., Odorovic A., Johanson D., Hao R., Ryll L. (2018), *Shifting Paradigms. The 4th European Alternative Finance Benchmarking Report*, Cambridge Centre for Alternative Finance

Zmud R.W. (1982), "Diffusion of modern software practices: Influence of centralization and formalization", *Management Science*, Vol. 28, pp 1421-1431.

R&D and Marketing Activities as Factors for Marketing Innovation

Patrícia Monteiro, Aldina Correia and Alexandra Braga
Ciicesi, Estg /P. Porto - Center for Innovation and Research in Business Sciences and Information Systems, School of Management and Technology, Polytechnic of Porto, Felgueiras, Portugal
8150194@estg.ipp.pt
aic@estg.ipp.pt
abraga@estg.ipp.pt
DOI: 10.34190/EIE.20.209

Abstract: Firms that became more successful in producing new and more efficient products or services, need to start thinking more innovatively about new marketing methods (Levitt, 1960). Therefore, Marketing Innovation (MI) appears as an essential factor for the firm's competitiveness. Although MI has been facing an increasing in terms of theoretical and empirical interest, the isolated study of MI remains a gap in the literature. To fill this gap, it was examined the factors that influence MI, using binary logistic regression, to determine the influence of Research and Development (R&D) and Marketing Activities have in MI. The results show that external R&D do not influence MI and empirical support for internal R&D and marketing activities to impact MI positively.

Keywords: marketing innovation, internal R&D, external R&D, marketing activities, logit regression

1. Introduction

Nowadays, firms all around the world are confronted with new challenges in the severely competitive market and changing economic environment. Innovation is essential to stay competitive. It means that, in order to stay and achieve competitive advantage, firms need to develop new strategies to attract more customers (Chuwiruch, Jhundra-Indra and Boonlua, 2015). The Oslo Manual defines Innovation as the *"new or improved product or process (or a combination thereof) that differs significantly from the unit's previous products or processes, and that has been made available to potential users (product) or brought into use by the unit (process)"* (Development and Communities, 2018).

The increasing role of innovations in achieving long-term competitive advantages makes the relevance and significance of the study of innovation, including technological and non-technological innovations. Technological innovations like product and process are just the tip of the iceberg and the study of non-technological innovations lacks the importance too (Birkinshaw, Brannen and Tung, 2011). This sentence tries to explain that technological innovations are the face of innovation, but there is an amount of important work that has been made by non-technological innovations.

Camisón and Villar-López (2011) conclude that the higher use of non-technological innovation, the better is the sustained competitive advantage (SCA) of a firm. In fact, the progress of innovative modern economy requires greater use of the potential of non-technological innovations, particularly promotional ones like MI (Babukh, 2017). Marketing innovation consists a *"new marketing method for a product or service accounting for significant alterations to any of the following elements: product design or packaging, placement, promotion or price establishing criteria"* (Manual, 2005).

Through the analysis of the literature on MI, it was noticed that had taken two directions, the first deals with the importance of marketing innovation in the performance of the firms and the second one with the determinants or factors that influence MI. Regarding the first and most used direction, some studies already prove that MI makes firms more competitive (Naidoo, 2010; Gupta *et al.*, 2016; Ungerman, Dedkova and Gurinova, 2018). Concerning the study of MI and their determinants or factors, it is not usually investigated as an isolated concept. Then, following the research, it was decided to continue one research, which concluded that the factors previously used, although relevant, are insufficient to fully explain MI (Monteiro, Correia and Braga, 2019).

The main goals of this research are:

- To establish a set of factors that support a MI approach;

- To discuss the dimensions of MI;
- To test the factors discussed in the literature;
- To understand the advantages of using some factors to develop MI related to the firms that do not make this type of decision.

This study aims to contribute innovatively both in the literary perspective and in the practical perspective (decision-makers), as follows:

Theoretical implications:

- The main contribution of this paper is to study of marketing innovation isolated, which is little explored in literature, as well as the factors of the innovative capacity of marketing, thus attempting to increase understanding of the subject;
- Numerous studies explore innovation; most of them focus on technological innovations and not in non-technological, such as MI. Medrano-Sáez and Olarte-Pascual (2012) believe that the definition of marketing innovation and their dimensions need to be actualised with the revolution that is currently taking place in marketing, through the possibilities conferred by new technologies. Marketing has been revolutionised by digital transformation and for this reason, we will discuss the actual definitions (most used) and its dimensions;
- The future results of this work are relevant because they expand current knowledge on factors that drive marketing innovation and reveal the specific effects of this type of non-technological innovation.

Practical implications:

- Managers and the remaining collaborators must be aware of the importance of non-technological innovation in terms of MI because it is an essential source of SCA (Berrell *et al.*, 2010);
- Specifically, This study can be useful for decision-makers to understand the advantages of using some factors to develop marketing innovation related to the firms that do not make this type of decision.

2. Literature review and research hypothesis

2.1 Marketing innovation concepts and dimensions

Marketing innovation has been studied for decades; proof of this is the diversity illustrated in Table 1. However, its isolated study is quite recent (Matte, J.; Graebin, 2017). Before introducing the definitions of MI, it is important to point out the definition most widely accepted in the literature and therefore, the most used, which is the OECD definition. This definition will be used in the present study.

Table 1: Marketing Innovation definitions

Literature	Definition
(Levitt, 1960)	Create not new products but new ways of distributing and selling existing products.
(Manual, 2005; Shergill and Nargundkar, 2005; Naidoo, 2010)	The application of a new marketing method which includes significant changes to the product design, placement, promotion or price. Improvements in the marketing mix (4 PS).
(Vorhies and Harker, 2000; Weerawardena, 2003; Lin, Chen and Chiu, 2010)	Market research, price establishing strategy, market segmentation, promotions, sales channels and marketing information systems.
(Chen, 2006)	The development of new marketing tools and methods.
(Utkun and Atılgan, 2010)	An innovative approach in price development, packaging, distribution channels, advertising, customer relations (customer service provided), and store design may bring about marketing innovation.
(Ilić, Ostojić and Damnjanović, 2014)	Marketing innovation involves the use of entirely new marketing strategies, marketing concepts or new marketing methods that have never been applied in the organisation.
(Contò *et al.*, 2015)	Marketing innovation represents the methods or ways in which companies can develop new ways of marketing themselves to potential or existing customers.

Literature	Definition
(Chuwiruch, Jhundra-Indra and Boonlua, 2015)	Marketing innovation strategy is explained as the firm's approach in using new methods for executing a variety of marketing strategies to improve marketing outcomes and to increase marketing performance.
(Babukh, 2017)	Innovative marketing – is the marketing activity of creating and promoting products, services, projects, etc. which have significantly new properties (sustainable competitive advantage).
(Development and Communities, 2018)	New methods for marketing, sales and after-sales support
(Ungerman, Dedkova and Gurinova, 2018)	Marketing innovation is identified as a search for creative and new solutions to problems and needs.

As illustrated in Table 1, marketing innovation is based on dimensions, being 4PS (product design, pricing, promotion and placement) the most used in related studies (Camisón and Villar-López, 2011; Szymańska, 2012; Medrano-Sáez and Olarte-Pascual, 2012; Moreira, Maria Jose Silva, *et al.*, 2012; Moreira, Maria José Silva, *et al.*, 2012; Julia, 2016; Medrano and Olarte-Pascual, 2016; Ros, Garzón and Mas-Tur, 2017; Zastempowski and Glabiszewski, 2017; Ramirez *et al.*, 2018; Rebane, 2018; Mensah and Quaye, 2019; Monteiro, Correia and Braga, 2019).

Zastempowski and Glabiszewski (2017) went further and explained what includes each dimension: 1P- Significantly changes in product or service design/concept or packaging. 2P- New methods of shaping the prices: The purpose of price correction according to demand; Discount system. 3P- New ways in product distribution or sales channels: Franchise; Product licensing; Cold sale; Exclusive dealing; Online sales; Modern concepts of products exposition; Positioning a product in a new market segment and a unique market geographically. 4P- New techniques of product promotion: New media of advertising; New image; New product brands; Loyalty programs (for example loyalty cards); Public relations - taking care of a firm's positive image.

This explanation of each dimension allows us to understand each dimension of MI better. One example of a new method of product distribution or sales channels is the case of "Amazon.com" when with "one-click" online ordering process, have expanded the market for many firms and reduced consumer transaction costs (Chen, 2006). Effectively, MI is the result of a set of changes introduced by firms, influenced by a vast collection of internal and external factors (Moreira, Maria José Silva, *et al.*, 2012). Due to the low number of references to marketing innovation in marketing and business literature, it is interesting to identify and define factors that could influence MI.

2.2 Factors that influence marketing innovation

Marketing innovation can help firms to convert products into profit (Soltani *et al.*, 2015); hence, identify its nature and determinants is essential. There are several factors explaining MI, although the factors that are contributing the most are: the organisational innovation, customer and/or user suggestions, and intellectual property rights and licensing. In the other hand, internationalisation and business size proved to be an obstacle to innovate in marketing (Monteiro, Correia and Braga, 2019). Conclusively, some studies show that other innovations like product, organisational or process, has a positive impact on the propensity to conduct MI (Soltani *et al.*, 2015; Medrano and Olarte-Pascual, 2016; Monteiro, Correia and Braga, 2019). The same happens with the feedback of the customers, Ilić, Ostojić and Damnjanović (2014) points out that listen to the customer suggestions allows the production of "real" products according to the customer needs and desires.

In addition to business characteristics, innovations and consumer, categories like knowledge (e.g. R&D) and marketing (e.g. marketing activities) also have factors that may help in the study of MI. The purpose of open innovation is that innovation cannot be considered as a merely individual act, it depends on the use of internally developed technologies and ideas and external knowledge sources (Doloreux, Turkina and Van Assche, 2019). As a result, Camisón and Villar-López, (2011) note that knowledge-based capabilities are essential for the development of non-technological innovations, like MI.

Starting with internal knowledge, Medrano-Sáez and Olarte-Pascual (2012) conclude that the undertaking of internal R&D is the principal factor of all kinds of marketing innovation and consequently the firms who make significant efforts to carry out internal R&D tasks are also likely to carry out MI. This authors also refer that this type of firms that invest in MI have high turnovers. Other studies go in the same direction (Camisón and Villar-

López, 2011; Moreira, Maria Jose Silva, *et al.*, 2012; Moreira, Maria José Silva, *et al.*, 2012; Julia, 2016). Considering the relevance of internal R&D will be tested the following hypothesis: *H1a. The firms that use the internal acquisition of R&D have a higher propensity to innovate in marketing than other firms.*

In turn, external knowledge can be considered as the acquisition of new and relevant information obtained from external partners and that firm cannot produce internally (Lane and Lubatkin, 1998). The use of external information is vital because complete the work started internally. The relationship with MI and external R&D was studied by some authors, and the results can be divided in two directions: the external R&D has a statistically significant and a positive impact in MI (Doloreux, Turkina and Van Assche, 2019) or external R&D does not have a statistically significant effect on MI (Moreira, Maria Jose Silva, *et al.*, 2012). Considering these directions, the following hypothesis is present: *H1b. The firms that use the external acquisition of R&D have a higher propensity to innovate in marketing than other firms.*

Innovation in marketing is typically from market research, combined with an expertise in advertising, customer management and sales (Grimpe *et al.*, 2017). In Oslo Manual, marketing activities, to improve innovation, including market research and launch advertising (Manual, 2005). The development of market research and launch advertising can be from in-house or outsourcing (Manual, 2005). So, marketing activities are directed linked to the introduction of new products or significantly improved products in the market, helping to differentiate the firm, emphasising that the activities geared primarily through the study of the needs expressed in the market maintain a crucial role in the innovation business process (Moreira, Maria Jose Silva, *et al.*, 2012). The following hypothesis can be studied: *H2. The firms that execute marketing activities have a higher propensity to innovate in marketing than other firms.* Table 2 resume the hypothesis, expected sign and support literature:

Table 2: Hypothesis synthesis and theoretical support

Model Variables	Hypothesis	Expected Sign	Literature
Internal R&D	H1a. The firms that use the internal acquisition of R&D have a higher propensity to innovate in marketing than other firms	+	(Camisón and Villar-López, 2011; Medrano-Sáez and Olarte-Pascual, 2012; Moreira, Maria Jose Silva, *et al.*, 2012; Moreira, Maria José Silva, *et al.*, 2012; Julia, 2016)
External R&D	H1b. The firms that use the external acquisition of R&D have a higher propensity to innovate in marketing than other firms	+/n.s.	(Moreira, Maria Jose Silva, *et al.*, 2012; Moreira, Maria José Silva, *et al.*, 2012; Ramirez *et al.*, 2018; Doloreux, Turkina and Van Assche, 2019)
Marketing Activities	H2. The firms that execute marketing activities have a higher propensity to innovate in marketing than other firms	+	(Moreira, Maria Jose Silva, *et al.*, 2012; Moreira, Maria José Silva, *et al.*, 2012)

Figure 1 presents the proposed model for the study of marketing innovation:

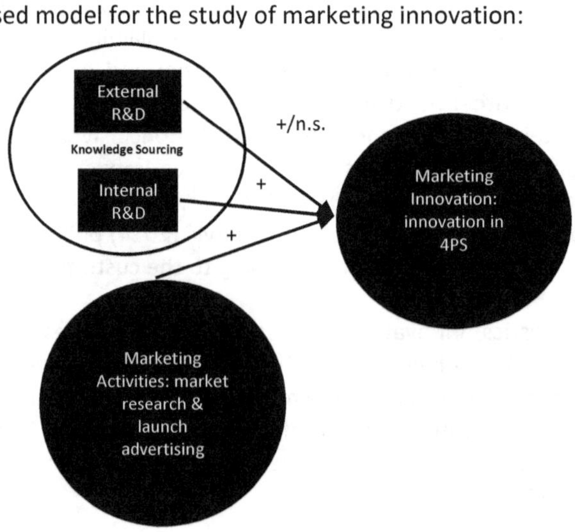

Figure 1: Proposed model for MI

3. Methodology

The database used in this research is the Community Innovation Survey (CIS) 2014. This database covers four types of innovation: product innovation, process innovation, organisational innovation and marketing innovation. Data was collected over the period 2012 to 2014 and got 7 083 valid observations. For the study of our dependent variable: marketing innovation, the following factors are used predetermined by the CIS 2014: R&D activities (internal and external) and marketing activities.

The proxy used to measure the dependent variable (MI) and the independent variables (R&D activities and marketing activities) was developed using the Oslo Manual as a reference (Manual, 2005). So, Table 3 resumes the proxy used:

Table 3: Proxy used to measure the variables - Elaboration based on Oslo Manual (Manual, 2005)

Type	Variables	Acronym	Description	Proxy
Dependent variable	Marketing Innovation	MKT_INNOV	Implementation of a new marketing concept or strategy that differs significantly from the firm's existing marketing methods and which has not been used before.	Both dimensions are proposed as dichotomous variables based on binary data. It takes the value "0" for firms that did not innovate in marketing and the value "1" for those who innovated. CIS consider the variables (MKTDGP (innovation in packaging), MKTPDP (innovation in distribution), MKTPDL (innovation in promotion) and MKTPRI (innovation in price)) for divided in 0 and 1.
Independent variables	Internal R&D	RRDIN	Research and development activities carried out by firms to generate new knowledge or to solve scientific or technical problems (include software developed in-house that meets this requirement).	It takes the value "1" when firms implemented internal R&D activities and "0" if otherwise.
	External R&D	RRDEX	R&D outsourcing (include enterprises firm own group) or to public or private research organisations.	It takes the value "1" when firms implemented external R&D activities and "0" if otherwise.
	Marketing Activities	RMAR	In-house or contracted out activities for the market introduction of your new or significantly improved goods or services, including market research and launch advertising.	It takes the value "1" when firms implemented marketing activities and "0" if not implemented.

Through exploratory data analysis, it was realised that within the 7 083 valid firms, 68.1% did not apply any MI from 2012 to 2014 against 32.8% that involve at least one kind of innovation in marketing (Tables are available under request). Finally, to achieve the study goals, the logistic regression model will be used, because this technique adapts to all types of independent variables and do not require the supposition of multivariate normality (Hair *et al.*, 1999). For the study of the factors that influence MI, this technique is often used (Medrano-Sáez and Olarte-Pascual, 2012; Moreira, Maria Jose Silva, *et al.*, 2012; Moreira, Maria José Silva, *et al.*, 2012; Medrano and Olarte-Pascual, 2016).

3.1 Results and discussion

The assumptions required to perform the binary logistic regression are less when compared to linear regression (e.g.). This happens because there is not a formal requirement for multivariate normality, homoscedasticity or linearity of the independent variables within each category of the dependent variable (Spicer, 2005). However, it is still essential to study the problem of multicollinearity, which relates to very high correlations among the independent variables, since it may affect the reliability of the coefficients (Midi, Sarkar and Rana, 2010). Our model is based on the required assumptions (absence of multicollinearity).

It is important to refer that the conduction of spearman's test and chi-square allowed to draw the same conclusions: significant correlation and weak relationships between independent variables (Tables are available under request). Following these procedures, the model equation (1) was defined under study based on (Moreira, Maria Jose Silva, *et al.*, 2012; Moreira, Maria José Silva, *et al.*, 2012):

$$MKT\_INNOV= \beta 0 + \beta 1RMAR + \beta 2RRDEX + \beta 3RRDIN + \varepsilon i \quad (1)$$

Where: MKT_INNOV = Marketing Innovation; β = coefficients; RMAR = marketing activities; RRDEX = R&D external; RRDIN = R&D internal; εi = residual.

To test if the model adequately fits the data, the Hosmer and Lemeshow test were performed, and the null hypothesis was not rejected (p-value= 0.965 > 0.05). Then it can be concluded that the logistic model is adequate to the data. Complementarily, the percentage of correctly predicted cases by the present model is 63.1% (the cut value is 0.500). Before moving on to the analysis of logistic regression (see Table 4) is critical to note that 12.5 % of MI is explained by the independent variables (marketing activities, internal and external R&D), according to Nagelkerke R square. Table 4 lists the coefficients, the Wald statistic, its significance and the odds ratio (Exp(B)), for the independent variables in this model.

Table 4: Results of the estimation of a logistic regression

Results of the estimation of logistic regression with marketing innovation as a dependent variable					
Factors	**Description**	**B**	**Wald**	**Sig.**	**Exp(B)**
RMAR	Marketing Activities	1.349	265.210	0.000	3.854
RRDEX	External R&D	0.091	1.134	0.287	1.095
RRDIN	Internal R&D	0.226	9.059	0.003	1.254
Constant	Constant	-0.430	72.490	0.000	0.651

There is one variable that is not statistically significant at 5%, specifically "external acquisition of R&D" (p-value= 0.287 > 0.05), so the H1b, was rejected. This result corroborates the study of Moreira, Maria Jose Silva, *et al.*, (2012); Moreira, Maria José Silva, *et al.*, (2012). Oslo Manual, englobe in RRDEX the outsourcing of R&D; when firms excessive R&D activities may lose the control, especially the intellectual property (Bei, Chen and Wu, 2008; Grimpe and Kaiser, 2010) that was proved to be an important factor that influences positively MI (Monteiro, Correia and Braga, 2019). In fact, the acquisition of external R&D can result in the danger of losing knowledge, information and market, but in the most scenarios R&D outsourcing influence positively the innovation (Peri, 2005; Cassiman and Veugelers, 2006; Paula and Silva, 2018). However, in this study, the statistical evidence was not found (neither negative nor positive influence).

On the other side, was discovered that the internal R&D has a positive influence on innovations made in marketing (B=0.226). It is found that firms carrying out internal R&D activity present more likely to innovate in marketing of 1.254 over other firms. The H1a. was supported, the firms that use the internal acquisition of R&D have a higher propensity to innovate in marketing than other firms. For the better comprehension of MI, the choice between internal and external R&D can be obvious: internal R&D has a positive influence when external do not have statistical significance.

The independent variable that presents a more positive influence in MI is marketing activities (B=1.349). So, the firms that invest in marketing activities are more likely to MI of 3.854 over other firms. Consequently, H2 was supported, the firms that execute marketing activities have a higher propensity to innovate in marketing than other firms. This result makes all the sense because the investment in market research and launch advertising is closely related, principally, to the development of new advertising techniques.

4. Conclusions and future research

This research started by identifying the concepts and dimensions of MI. The discussion of MI started early, more appropriately in 1960 with Levit (Levitt, 1960), but only after 2009, this construct gains more importance (Matte, J.; Graebin, 2017). In a broader sense, marketing innovation represents the innovative character of marketing.

Nowadays, the problem is that marketing is not an exact science and this digital transformation era make it difficult to define a current construct of MI. Example of this is that the definition more accepted in the literature is the Oslo Manual concept (with an innovative character in the 4PS of Marketing). This definition approaches more of offline marketing than digital marketing.

Another conclusion of this paper is that many articles use the four marketing dimensions to define MI, but do not explain which they use. This is a problem when a questionnaire is applied to firms since they are not completely clear about what each point encompasses and may interfere with the results. In fact, Medrano-Sáez and Olarte-Pascual (2012) also identified a failure in the perception that firms have about MI, suggesting in future research to find a better definition for the concept of MI. It was also referred that it is not clear what firms understand by marketing innovation. In a methodological perception, Camisón and Villar-López (2011) believe that the existing scales for MI are very limited.

To achieve the initial goals, binary logistic regression was applied, and it concludes that external R&D does not have a significant influence on MI (H1b rejected). Effectively, trough the literature analyses the importance of external R&D can be different, considering the innovation type. In the case of the national study of MI, both our research and Moreira's study (Moreira, Maria Jose Silva, *et al.*, 2012; Moreira, Maria José Silva, *et al.*, 2012) found that there is no statistical influence (positive or negative). When firms use much outsourcing, R&D can lose control and intellectual property rights, which is a factor critical to MI (Monteiro, Correia and Braga, 2019). In the case of MI, the choice between internal and external R&D is simple since unlike external R&D (n.s.), internal R&D has a positive influence. The firms carrying out internal R&D activity are more likely to innovate in marketing rather than other firms. Marketing activities to launch innovation also proved to be vital as it positively influences MI and firms that are carrying out marketing activities present an advantage to innovate in marketing than other firms. So, in this study, the factors that influence MI are internal R&D and marketing activities (H1a and H2 supported).

With this study, part of the main initial goals was achieved. The results show that there is still room for exploring all the factors that explaining MI, since the independent variables only explain 12.5%. Future research may consider actualising the dimensions of MI, also to a digital component. To test this new dimension and understand which factors influence MI in a more recent period, a primary database should be constructed by applying a questionnaire to Portuguese and Spanish companies, thereby achieving a multi-country study. To complete the analyse of MI, we consider essential to specify each dimension in the questionnaire so firms could be aware of what it means. This could prevent a lack of information and unrealistic results.

We propose this future research because we identified some limitations about the database and the measurement of variables. We used CIS 2014 that study the innovation in Portuguese firms in the period of 2012-2014 but marketing is always in mutation, so it is essential to have a more recent approach and results. In the other hand, the variables in CIS 2014 are dummy, which can be a problem to analyse the corporate behaviour, so in future, can be interesting to use a Likert scale.

Acknowledgements

This work has received funding from FEDER funds through P2020 program and from national funds through FCT - Foundation for Science and Technology (Portuguese Foundation for Science and Technology) under the project UID / GES / 04728/2020

References

Babukh, I. (2017) 'COMMERCIALIZATION OF MARKET INNOVATIONS AS EXCLUSIVE TASK OF INNOVATIVE MARKETING.', *Marketing & Management of Innovations*, (3), pp. 15–22. doi: 10.21272/mmi.2017.3-01.

Bei, W., Chen, J. and Wu, Z. (2008) 'The analysis of relationship between R&D outsourcing and firm innovative performance from the perspective of open innovation', *2008 4th IEEE International Conference on Management of Innovation and Technology, Management of Innovation and Technology, 2008. ICMIT 2008. 4th IEEE International Conference on*, p. 1004. doi: 10.1109/ICMIT.2008.4654505.

Berrell, M. *et al.* (2010) 'Sustainable competitive advantage and marketing innovation within firms', *Management Research Review*. Emerald Group Publishing Limited.

Birkinshaw, J., Brannen, M. Y. and Tung, R. L. (2011) 'From a distance and generalizable to up close and grounded: Reclaiming a place for qualitative methods in international business research'. Springer.

Camisón, C. and Villar-López, A. (2011) 'Non-technical innovation: Organizational memory and learning capabilities as antecedent factors with effects on sustained competitive advantage', *Industrial Marketing Management*, 40(8), pp. 1294–1304. doi: 10.1016/j.indmarman.2011.10.001.

Cassiman, B. and Veugelers, R. (2006) 'In search of complementarity in innovation strategy: Internal R&D and external knowledge acquisition', *Management science*. INFORMS, 52(1), pp. 68–82.

Chen, Y. (2006) 'Marketing Innovation', *Journal of Economics & Management Strategy*. John Wiley & Sons, Ltd (10.1111), 15(1), pp. 101–123. doi: 10.1111/j.1530-9134.2006.00093.x.

Chuwiruch, N., Jhundra-Indra, P. and Boonlua, S. (2015) 'MARKETING INNOVATION STRATEGY AND MARKETING PERFORMANCE: A CONCEPTUAL FRAMEWORK.', in *Allied Academies International Conference: Proceedings of the Academy of Marketing Studies (AMS)*, pp. 82–93. Available at: http://search.ebscohost.com/login.aspx?direct=true&db=bth&AN=112686468&site=eds-live.

Contò, F. *et al.* (2015) 'Innovative marketing behaviour determinants in wine SMEs: The case of an Italian wine region', *International Journal of Globalisation and Small Business*, 7, pp. 107–124. doi: 10.1504/IJGSB.2015.071181.

Development, O. for E. C. and and Communities, S. O. of the E. (2018) *Oslo Manual 2018: Guidelines for collecting, reporting and using data on innovation*. OECD publishing.

Doloreux, D., Turkina, E. and Van Assche, A. (2019) 'Innovation type and external knowledge search strategies in KIBS: evidence from Canada.', *Service Business*, 13(3), pp. 509–530. doi: 10.1007/s11628-018-00393-y.

Grimpe, C. *et al.* (2017) 'R&D, Marketing Innovation, and New Product Performance: A Mixed Methods Study', *Journal of Product Innovation Management*, 34(3), pp. 360–383. doi: 10.1111/jpim.12366.

Grimpe, C. and Kaiser, U. (2010) 'Balancing internal and external knowledge acquisition: the gains and pains from R&D outsourcing', *Journal of management studies*. Wiley Online Library, 47(8), pp. 1483–1509.

Gupta, S. *et al.* (2016) 'Marketing innovation: A consequence of competitiveness', *Journal of Business Research*. The Authors, 69(12), pp. 5671–5681. doi: 10.1016/j.jbusres.2016.02.042.

Hair, J. F. *et al.* (1999) *Análisis multivariante*. Prentice Hall Madrid.

Ilić, D., Ostojić, S. and Damnjanović, N. (2014) 'THE IMPORTANCE OF MARKETING INNOVATION IN NEW ECONOMY.', *Singidunum Journal of Applied Sciences*, 11(1), pp. 34–42. doi: 10.5937/sjas11-5015.

Julia, N. (2016) 'Antecedents and outcomes of marketing innovation: An empirical analysis in the hotel industry', *International Journal of Contemporary Hospitality Management*. Edited by D.-M. Gonzalo. Emerald Group Publishing Limited, 28(8), pp. 1554–1576. doi: 10.1108/IJCHM-11-2014-0589.

Lane, P. J. and Lubatkin, M. (1998) 'Relative absorptive capacity and interorganizational learning', *Strategic Management Journal*. John Wiley & Sons, Ltd, 19(5), pp. 461–477. doi: 10.1002/(SICI)1097-0266(199805)19:5<461::AID-SMJ953>3.0.CO;2-L.

Levitt, T. (1960) 'Growth and Profits Through Planned Marketing Innovation.', *Journal of Marketing*, 24(4), pp. 1–8. doi: 10.2307/1248397.

Lin, R.-J., Chen, R.-H. and Chiu, K. (2010) 'Customer Relationship Management and Innovation Capability: An Empirical Study', *Industrial Management and Data Systems*, 110, pp. 111–133. doi: 10.1108/02635571011008434.

Manual, O. (2005) 'The measurement of scientific and technological activities. Proposed guidelines for collecting and interpreting technological innovation data', *Organisation for Economic Co-operation and Development (OECD), 3rd edition.[ONLINE] Available at: http://www. oecd. org/science/inno/2367580. pdf [Accessed 20 February 2018]*.

Matte, J.; Graebin, R. E. (2017) 'Inovação de Marketing na Perspectiva Literária', *Tópicos de Marketing*, 2, p. 258.

Medrano-Sáez, N. and Olarte-Pascual, M. C. (2012) 'Marketing Innovation as an Opportunity in a Situation of Uncertainty: The Spanish Case BT - Soft Computing in Management and Business Economics', in Gil-Lafuente, A. M., Gil-Lafuente, J., and Merigó-Lindahl, J. M. (eds). Berlin, Heidelberg: Springer Berlin Heidelberg, pp. 327–341.

Medrano, N. and Olarte-Pascual, C. (2016) 'An empirical approach to marketing innovation in small and medium retailers: An application to the Spanish sector', *Contemporary Economics*, 10(3Special Issue), pp. 205–216. doi: 10.5709/ce.1897-9254.210.

Mensah, I. and Quaye, D. (2019) 'Marketing innovation and sustainable competitive advantage of manufacturing SMEs in Ghana', *Management Decision*, 57, pp. 1535–1553. doi: 10.1108/MD-08-2017-0784.

Midi, H., Sarkar, S. K. and Rana, S. (2010) 'Collinearity diagnostics of binary logistic regression model', *Journal of Interdisciplinary Mathematics*. Taylor & Francis, 13(3), pp. 253–267. doi: 10.1080/09720502.2010.10700699.

Monteiro, P., Correia, A. and Braga, V. (2019) 'Factors for Marketing Innovation in Portuguese Firms CIS 2014', *Mathematical and Computational Applications* . doi: 10.3390/mca24040099.

Moreira, J., Silva, Maria Jose, *et al.* (2012) 'DRIVERS OF MARKETING INNOVATION IN PORTUGUESE FIRMS', *AMFITEATRU ECONOMIC*, 14(31), pp. 195–206. Available at: http://search.ebscohost.com/login.aspx?direct=true&db=edswss&AN=000300910600014&site=eds-live.

Moreira, J., Silva, Maria José, *et al.* (2012) 'Marketing Innovation: Study of Determinants of Innovation in the Design and Packaging of Goods and Services--Application to Portuguese Firms.', *Contemporary Management Research*, 8(2), pp. 117–129. doi: 10.7903/cmr.11047.

Naidoo, V. (2010) 'Firm Survival Through a Crisis: The Influence of Market Orientation, Marketing Innovation and Business Strategy', *Industrial Marketing Management*, 39, pp. 1311–1320. doi: 10.1016/j.indmarman.2010.02.005.

Paula, F. de O. and Silva, J. F. da (2018) 'Balancing Internal and External R&D Strategies to Improve Innovation and Financial Performance', *BAR-Brazilian Administration Review*. SciELO Brasil, 15(2).

Peri, G. (2005) 'Determinants of knowledge flows and their effect on innovation', *Review of Economics and Statistics*. MIT Press, 87(2), pp. 308–322.

Ramirez, F. J. *et al.* (2018) 'From external information to marketing innovation: the mediating role of product and organizational innovation.', *Journal of Business & Industrial Marketing*, 33(5), pp. 693–705. doi: 10.1108/JBIM-12-2016-0291.

Rebane, T. (2018) 'Complementarities in Performance Between Product Innovation, Marketing Innovation and Cooperation with Clients.', *University of Tartu - Faculty of Economics & Business Administration Working Paper Series*, (113), pp. 3–34. Available at: https://search.ebscohost.com/login.aspx?direct=true&AuthType=ip,cookie,shib,uid&db=bth&AN=133001421&lang=pt-pt&site=eds-live&scope=site.

Ros, S., Garzón, D. and Mas-Tur, A. (2017) 'Entrepreneurial competencies and motivations to enhance marketing innovation in Europe', *Psicology and Marketing*, 34, pp. 1031–1038. doi: 10.1002/mar.21042.

Shergill, G. S. and Nargundkar, R. (2005) 'Market Orientation, Marketing Innovation as Performance Drivers', *Journal of Global Marketing*. Routledge, 19(1), pp. 27–47. doi: 10.1300/J042v19n01_03.

Soltani, S. *et al.* (2015) 'Marketing Innovation in Rural Small Food Industries in Iran.', *Journal of Food Products Marketing*, 21(5), pp. 533–551. doi: 10.1080/10454446.2015.1041196.

Spicer, J. (2005) *Making sense of multivariate data analysis: An intuitive approach*. Sage.

Szymańska, E. (2012) 'MARKETING INNOVATIONS IN TOURIST ENTERPRISES – HOW TO MEASURE THEM AND HOW TO EVALUATE THEM?', *ECONOMICS AND MANAGEMENT*, 17. doi: 10.5755/j01.em.17.3.2131.

Ungerman, O., Dedkova, J. and Gurinova, K. (2018) 'the Impact of Marketing Innovation on the Competitiveness of Enterprises in the Context of Industry 4.0', *Journal of Competitiveness*, 10(2), pp. 132–148. doi: 10.7441/joc.2018.02.09.

Utkun, E. and Atılgan, T. (2010) 'Marketing innovation in the apparel industry: Turkey'. Fibres & Textiles in Eastern Europe 2010.

Vorhies, D. W. and Harker, M. (2000) 'The Capabilities and Perfor Mance Advantages of Market-Driven Firms: An Empirical Investigation', *Australian Journal of Management*. SAGE Publications Ltd, 25(2), pp. 145–171. doi: 10.1177/031289620002500203.

Weerawardena, J. (2003) 'Exploring the role of market learning capability in competitive strategy', *European journal of marketing*. MCB UP Ltd.

ZASTEMPOWSKI, M. and GLABISZEWSKI, W. (2017) 'MARKETING INNOVATIONS OF POLISH SMALL AND MEDIUM ENTERPRISES.', *Scientific Papers of Silesian University of Technology. Organization & Management / Zeszyty Naukowe Politechniki Slaskiej. Seria Organizacji i Zarzadzanie*, (114), pp. 649–661. Available at: http://search.ebscohost.com/login.aspx?direct=true&db=bth&AN=132540227&site=eds-live.

Green Finance for Entrepreneurs: Current Perspectives and Conceptual Model

Christopher Moon[1] and Edward Bace[2]
[1]Department of Management, Leadership and Organisations, Faculty of Professional & Social Sciences, Middlesex University, UK
[2]Department of Accounting and Finance, Faculty of Professional & Social Sciences, Middlesex University, UK
c.moon@mdx.ac.uk
e.bace@mdx.ac.uk
DOI: 10.34190/EIE.20.090

Abstract: Gaining finance is crucial for entrepreneurs. This paper provides an overview of current perspectives on the green finance market and key sources of finance available. We identify the main sources used and the advantages and disadvantages of each for entrepreneurs. Background is provided on the international, European, and UK green finance markets so that entrepreneurs are familiarised with their target market for green finance. Academic papers on green finance tend to focus on the problems faced by entrepreneurs in gaining finance highlighting lack of collateral, uncertainty, complexity, perceptions of higher risk, perceptions of lower scalability, and longer pay-back periods. Nevertheless, Nobel prize winning economist Jeffrey Sachs reminds us that green finance is important as climate change is the world's greatest environmental threat; and that If the current trajectory of global fossil-fuel use continues, the planet's temperature is likely to rise by 4-6 degrees Celsius above its pre-industrial level, be catastrophic for food production, human health, and biodiversity, and threaten communities' survival. We, therefore, focus on the growing opportunities for obtaining green finance and provide positive examples of projects funded. The paper provides a conceptual model of green finance which assists the entrepreneur identify which sources of green finance to target.

Keywords: green finance, green entrepreneurs, green grants, green angels, circular finance

1. Introduction

According to the Green Finance Taskforce (2018) there is a need to accelerate green finance as there has never been a more urgent need for investment to reduce emissions. The universal shift towards a less carbon intensive and more climate-resilient economy carries investment risks and this paper seeks to clarify the green finance landscape for entrepreneurs in order that more informed investment decisions can be made. Academic papers on green finance (e.g. Demirel et al., 2017) tend to focus on the problems faced by entrepreneurs in gaining finance highlighting lack of collateral, uncertainty, complexity, perceptions of higher risk, perceptions of lower scalability, and longer pay-back periods. Building on the position of Nobel Prize winning economist Jeffrey Sachs (Sachs et al. 2019) we focus on the growing opportunities for obtaining green finance and provide positive examples of projects funded.

The Green Finance Taskforce (2018:15) acknowledge that globally the green finance sector is growing but not fast enough. One of the key challenges the taskforce identify is the lack of consistent and comparable data which serves as a barrier to obtaining green finance not least of all as risks are more difficult to identify and quantify in order to assure investment decisions. We clarify this landscape by reviewing the leaders of green finance globally and then use this platform to form a conceptual model of green finance that entrepreneurs can use to guide their decisions. The World Bank (2017) Roadmap on Sustainable Finance assists in navigating the green finance terrain. Our conceptual model additionally provides a heuristic or compass to assist in using any such map.

2. Definitions

The G20 Green Finance Study Group (2016) defined "green finance" as 'financing of investments that provide environmental benefits in the broader context of environmentally sustainable development.' However, this definition does not provide any guidance on sources of green finance or which to select. EC (2017) define "green" in the context of green finance as: green bonds, green lending and green equity investment. However, EC acknowledge there are a number of approaches to defining green within these broad categories, see Table 1.

Table 1: Approaches to defining "green" (EC, 2017)

Approaches to defining "green"						
Instruments	Objectives	Taxonomy	Exclusion criteria	Indicators and Ratings	Process criteria
Objectives	Broad vs. narrow	Common vs. less common objectives, sectors and technologies			Linked / not linked to more detailed taxonomies	
Taxonomies	Detailed vs. general			With/without controversial items		
Exclusions	Based on sectors, technologies or compliance with norms		Working with min. (green) or max. (brown) thresholds		Full or partial exclusions	
Greenness	Binary (green/non-green) vs. degrees of greenness					
ESG	Taken or not taken into consideration for green finance					

Thus, EC (2017) recognise that the landscape of green finance is hard to define and various approaches have been used to help define green finance in terms of specifying the objectives of green finance (e.g. broad vs. narrow), taxonomies of green finance (e.g. detailed vs. general), exclusion criteria (e.g. using min. or max. thresholds), degrees of greenness (e.g. dark green, light green), or corporate governance (e.g. environmental, social, governance standards, ESG).

The Chartered Banker Institute (2018), which launched The Green Finance Certificate as the first global benchmark qualification for the growing Green Finance sector, define green finance more simply as: any financial initiative, process, product or service that is either designed to protect the natural environment or to manage how the environment impacts finance and investment. That is, 'inputs' or 'impacts' [author labels]. However, the CBI (2018) state that most definitions focus on the role of green finance in 'directing' investment towards 'green' sectors with some sectors more universally accepted as 'green' than others. CBI (2018) cite the UNEP Design of a Sustainable Financial System 'flower image' [author description] as useful to show the most commonly included sectors (i.e. the head/face or carpel of the flower) and the least commonly included sectors (i.e. the petals or corolla of the flower). See Figure 1.

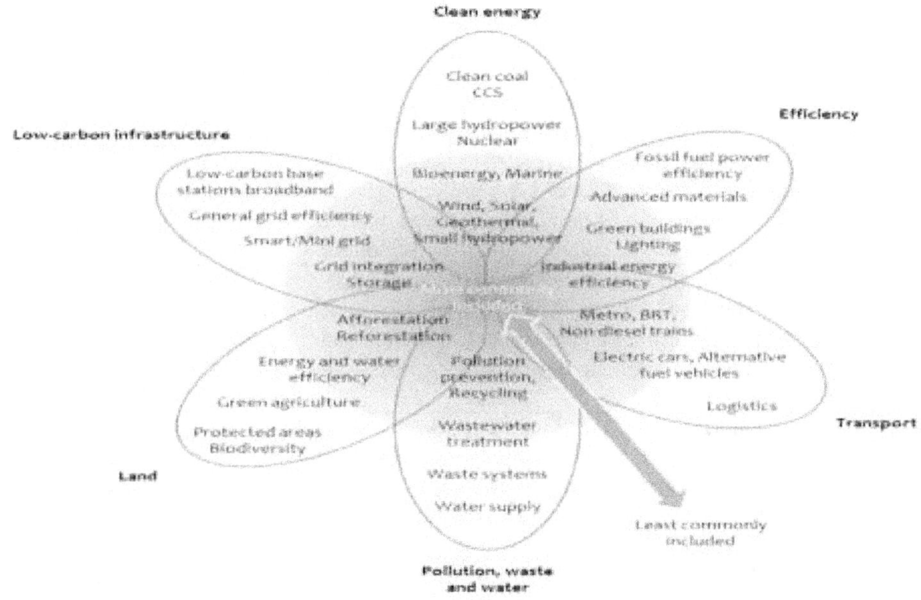

Figure 1: Clusters of categories, UNEP 2016: 8

This image is a useful starting point for recognising the range of categories that could be related to in terms of green finance. However, focussing on specific green industry areas provides specific definitions which can point more clearly to different sources of finance. For example, CBI (2018) provide a table which they relate to three sources of green finance in particular: long-term loans, green mortgages and venture capital. See Table 2.

Table 2: Green Industry Area, Definition (2018: 11-12) and possible source of Green Finance, adapted by the authors

Green Industry Area	Definition	**Green Finance**
Renewable energy	Renewable energy comes from a source that is not depleted when it is used or is naturally replenished within a human timescale. This includes solar, wind, geothermal, tidal, wave, hydroelectric and biomass power.	**Long-term loans** for new renewable energy projects (CBI, 2018)
Energy distribution	Most energy is distributed through a grid (an interconnected network for transmitting power). Green energy distribution tends to focus on the integration of renewable energy into the main grid, distributed generation, microgrids (running separately from the main grid) and smart grids that detect and react to changes in energy usage.	**Green Investment Bank** loan for large scale infrastructure projects (Author insertion). **Crowdfunding** for smaller scale energy projects. (Author insertion)
Energy storage	Renewable energy storage is key to enabling an increase in the take-up and efficiency of renewables. It can include mechanical storage (e.g. pumped water), batteries and thermal energy storage.	**Venture capital** for innovative new storage technologies (CBI, 2018)
Emissions reduction and capture	Emission reduction technologies aim to reduce the carbon dioxide ($CO2$) produced by energy generation, transport and industrial processes. Emissions capture tends to refer to carbon capture and storage (CCS) – technology to capture $CO2$ emissions produced in electricity generation and industrial processes.	**Sovereign green bonds** for large scale projects. (Author insertion)
Energy efficiency	Energy efficiency means reducing the amount of energy that is required to provide a product or service. It is often applied to buildings (domestic, commercial and industrial), appliances and vehicles.	**Green deal** (Author insertion)
Green buildings	Green buildings are designed, built and used in a way that is energy efficient, minimises the use of resources and water, encourages biodiversity and provides a healthy indoor environment.	**Green mortgages** which link repayments to home energy efficiency improvements (CBI, 2018)
Green transport	Green transport minimises $CO2$ and other harmful emissions, uses renewable energy, is energy efficient and supports sustainable communities. The term can refer to public transport systems and infrastructure, as well as to private vehicles.	**Venture Capital** (Author insertion)
Water conservation	Water conservation aims to sustainably manage freshwater resources and to prevent water pollution in nearby lakes, rivers and local watersheds	**Green Deal** (Author insertion)
Pollution control	Pollution control aims to reduce or avoid the release of harmful substances into the environment, including the air, water and soil. Pollution can also be defined by the type of pollutant, including plastic pollution and thermal pollution.	**Green Deal** (Author insertion)
Waste reduction and management	Waste reduction aims to minimise the amount of waste produced by individuals, households and organisations, including through resource efficiency and reuse. Waste management involves the collection, treatment, recycling, re-processing and disposal of waste.	**Venture Capital** (Author insertion)
Biodiversity and habitat protection	Biodiversity protection aims to preserve the full range of ecosystems, species and genepools in the environment – the full variety of life on earth. Habitat protection aims to conserve, protect and restore the natural environments that sustain these plants and animals.	**Green Deal** (Author insertion)
Afforestation / reforestation	Afforestation means the establishment of forests where previously they did not exist, while reforestation means the re-establishment of forests where they previously existed, either through direct planting or through natural growth.	**Green Deal** (Author insertion)

Sources of finance for green entrepreneurs

The above table points to particular sources of green finance that might be more appropriate for different green industry areas (as identified by CBI, 2018). However, most of these green industry areas refer to large scale infrastructure projects requiring significantly high levels of finance and inevitable entail quite complex financing deals. Crowdfunding is a relatively new source of finance which is more appropriate for funding smaller scale projects. However, the amounts funded tend to be relatively small. As UfM (2018) conclude: 'What is missing is a combination of support at different levels and adapted financial tools that allow green start-ups the time and space to develop, test their innovations in the market and develop sustainable business models. In other words, a combination of technical assistance services with getting the business market ready. See Figure 2. This middle space referred to as 'the valley of death' by Achterberg and van Tilberg (2016) is perhaps the most needed for entrepreneurs.

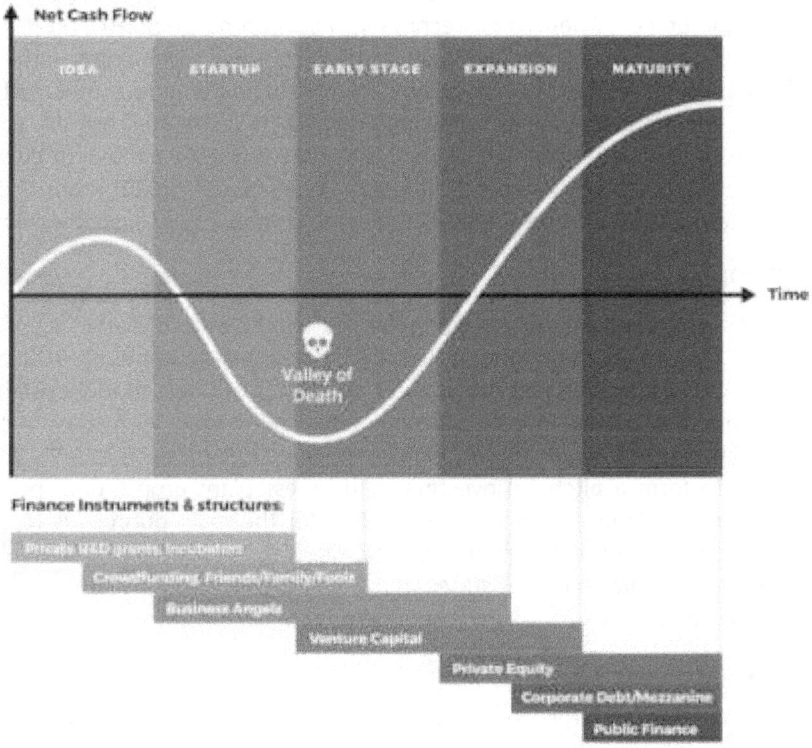

Figure 2: Financing The Valley of Death for circular businesses. Achterberg and van Tilberg (2016)

3. Green grants and awards

Various grants are available to support green projects. For example, #TheSwitchers support programme (2018) was launched in 2017 and provides six grants of €15,000 to the best project in different Mediterranean countries. Each business plan is evaluated as to the level of innovation, the environmental impact, the social impact, the scalability of the project and the sustainability of the business model. Crowdfunding has evolved to include 'donation crowdfunding' where people invest in a cause; 'debt crowdfunding' where investors receive their money back with interest; and equity crowdfunding where investment is exchanged for shares or a small stake in the venture. Crowdcube, Seedrs and Abundance Generation are three prominent crowdfunding platforms.

Other potential awards include through enterprise investment schemes, seed funding schemes, small business funding initiatives, knowledge transfer partnerships and various competitions with significant prize money with the $1m Hult prize being iconic. London-based investment fund The Craftory was only founded in 2018 and has been awarded B Corp certification. The Craftory fund size reaches $375m and offers early-stage and growth capital to consumer brands that it deems to positively impact society and the planet. Beneficiaries have included plastic-free detergent company Dropps and food technology brand NotCo, which is exploring plant-based alternatives for dairy products using artificial intelligence. Craftory is dwared by Blackrock with $7tn in assets and is a founding member of the Task Force on Climate-related Financial Disclosures (TCFD), a signatory to the UN's Principles for Responsible Investment, has joined Climate Action 100+ and states that sustainability should be its new standard for investing.

4. Eco-innovation incubators

Incubators provide a relatively safe haven to test out an application and its commerciality. Experts are normally available to evaluate different aspects of the business and preparing it for further funding. For example, NESTA (2020) in the UK is an independent charity which invests to create positive social and environmental outcomes with a focus on innovation such as cleantech, recycling and energy efficiency. Incubators can also exist in clusters physically or virtually. For example, the Chicago Green Exchange is a public-private partnership designed to house more than one hundred eco-friendly businesses and organizations within a single building originally built in 1914 and is reportedly the largest sustainable business community in the USA. In Berlin Climate-KIC have hosted a Green Garage since 2013 as the first incubator in Germany that exclusively targets climate innovations. The incubator is located in a former industrial site reconstructed and remodelled for business, research and education. Hong Kong established the Science and Technology Parks Corporation (HKSTPC) in May 2001 to offer one-stop support services to technology-based companies including green technology. In the UK, Hertfordshire IQ aims to become the leading place in the UK for businesses operating in modern construction, agri-tech and related digital and environmental technologies following £680,000 investment from the Local Growth Fund. Bristol in the UK is also an active hub for green business. And there has been a move to develop a low carbon industrial centre in the north west of England. Sustainable Workspaces (2020) state they have delivered 65,000sqf of workspace making them Europe's largest collocated community of sustainable businesses.

5. Green business angels

Business angels are part of the most traditional and popular route to finance for early stage start-ups. They can provide finance of approx. £1K to £100K and tend to seek a return on their investment (ROI) in 3-8 years. Angels typically invest in high growth business with an innovative and scalable business model, sustainable competitive advantage or exclusive commercial arrangements, a strong management team with relevant operational/sector experience, past the initial concept stage and an exit in the medium term. The 5 P's framework [author description] can be used to form a pitch to investors or business plan: proposition, people, place, profit, potential. Each of these can be elaborated on in more detail but the main purpose is to be able to explain succinctly the investee green idea in a commercial way. How many specifically green business angels there are is uncertain. The Green Angel Syndicate (2020) states that it is the only angel investment syndicate in the UK specialising in the fight against Climate Change and Global Warming.

6. Public environmental funding

Quite a few municipal governments fund anti-pollution measures, recycling initiatives, combined heat and power schemes, solar energy schemes, green roofs and other green spaces. For example, in the UK there is the London Green Fund and the Waste Resources and Action Programme (WRAP). In Europe there are regional development funds and social funds with green components. The European Green Deal was prioritised by incoming European Commission president Ursula Von der Leyen and will include a Sustainable Europe Investment Plan to incentivise €1 trillion over the next 10 years, and part of the European Investment Bank is to be transformed into "Europe's climate bank" (Gaventa, 2019).

7. Case example

Yasa Motors (2020) in the UK was founded on the principle that small, light electric motors would play a growing role in meeting both the strict emissions targets being set globally in a wide range of industries and the requirement for greater efficiency through electrification. The Company was incorporated in 2009 based on a unique patented motor technology invented by the Company's founder and CTO Dr Tim Woolmer whilst studying for his DPhil at Oxford University. YASA supplies custom and off-the-shelf e-motors and controllers to automotive customers from its headquarters and series production facility near Oxford in the UK. In 2019, YASA announced "Ferrari selects YASA electric motor for SF90 Stradale, the company's first hybrid production series supercar". Further, in 2019 Rolls-Royce unveiled its all-electric YASA powered plane targeting the record books as the first zero-emissions plane with a speed of 300+ MPH (480+ KMH) in late Spring 2020.

YASA was recognised as one of the Sunday Times' best UK small companies to work for in 2020. The independently awarded 3-star accreditation demonstrates the highest level of workplace engagement, ensuring employees are highly valued and feel part of a great team. Critical to the success of YASA has been its funding. Initial support came from Oxford Sciences Innovation (OSI) the venture firm formed in 2015 in partnership with Oxford University to develop its advanced science into new platform companies. £1.5 million was secured from the Regional Growth Fund in the UK and in 2019 the company secured £18m from further VC funding including Inovia Capital which claims to roll up their sleeves to serve founders with dedicated, long-term mentorship, a global talent network, and strategic support for global scale.

8. Conceptual model of green finance

Our conceptual model (see Figure 3) provides a circular economy model of green investment to support new ideas but to ensure that once established green finance is more actively used to perpetuate further ideas and support. The intention is for the government, business and investor communities to more actively recognise critical success factors of green business to create ongoing cycles of green activity, to avoid some of the pitfalls faced as reported by Demirel et al. (2019) and speed up green investment. With the scale and speed of climate change there is a need to more rapidly enact green solutions across all sectors (Sachs et al. 2019) and our model provides a more circular solution to green finance that is simpler and could be made more readily accessible to green entrepreneurs as part of green finance educational programmes.

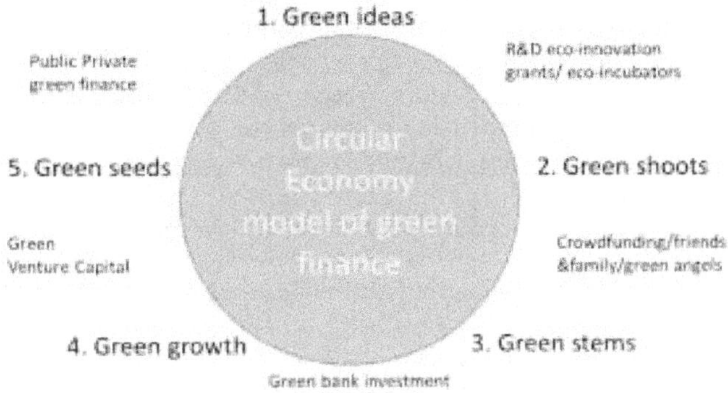

Figure 3: Circular economy model of green finance, author model

9. Discussion

As outlined above, there are different sources of funding suited to different stages of a project. In order to get an idea off the ground, grants and eco-incubators are available, and as green shoots begin to emerge, crowdfunding, friends and business angels can be utilised in order to survive the 'valley of death,' and to build confidence in an idea. Once this critical stage is achieved, there is a prime point of entry for specialised 'green banks,' as project scale and credibility grow. This leads naturally to the next stage. Venture capitalists are becoming increasingly aware of the investment merits of green projects, which contribute to the 'triple bottom line,' not just of profit, but also in terms of environment and sustainability. The example of Yasa given above bears this out. The recent growth in VC firms dedicated to green outcomes is an encouraging development (Ning et al, 2015).

As green stems lengthen and start to produce seeds, various sources of public and private finance open up, and the utility of the circular economy model is that it can be iterative, as refinements are made to original ideas and further opportunities are explored, necessitating some further investment. Retrograde movements can also occur, depending on the nature of refinements and opportunities. The culmination occurs when a project becomes self-sustaining and starts to deliver positive returns to the funders. The virtuous circle of green financing then continues with new off shoot projects which can be funded in part by cash generated from the original initiative. Climate change has become an ever-accelerating phenomenon, and an analogous funding model is needed, not in the traditional sense of growth for growth's sake, but more flexible and adaptable to changing circumstances and circular businesses.

10. Conclusions

Traditional economic models are based on linear economic principles. The green economy needs to adopt circular economy principles more rapidly due to the nature and speed of climate change. This paper highlighted the confusing picture of green finance and the myriad of definitions and concepts. We clarify sources of green finance and provide a new conceptual model based on circular economy principles. Universities are ideally placed to take innovative green solutions to market and YASA Motors UK provides an excellent example of how one company secured different levels of finance at the most appropriate stages of its development. We have applied this learning to form our conceptual model to encourage the growth of green finance and as a catalyst to develop more readily accessible and understandable finance tools for green entrepreneurs.

References

Achterberg, E., and van Tilberg, R., (2016), 6 GUIDELINES TO EMPOWER FINANCIAL DECISION-MAKING IN THE CIRCULAR ECONOMY, www.circle-economy.org.

Chartered Banker Institute (2018), The Green Qualifications Workbook.

Demirel, P., Li, Q. C., Rentocchini, F., & Tamvada, J. P. (2017), Born to be green: New insights into the economics and management of green entrepreneurship. Small Business Economics., 52, 759– 771.

EC (2017a), Eco-innovation, https://ec.europa.eu/environment/ecoap/about-action-plan/union-funding-programmes_en

EC (2017b), Eco-innovation in United Kingdom, https://ec.europa.eu/environment/ecoap/sites/ecoap_stayconnected/files/field/field-country-files/uk_eio_country_profile_2016-2017.pdf

FinanCE (2018), CIRCULAR ECONOMY FINANCE GUIDELINES, ABN AMRO, ING, RABOBANK.

Gaventa, J., (2019), HOW THE EUROPEAN GREEN DEAL WILL SUCCEED OR FAIL, E3G.

G20 Green Finance Study Group (2016), G20 Green Finance Synthesis Report.

Green Angel Syndicate (2020), https://www.greenangelsyndicate.com/

Green Finance Taskforce (2018), Accelerating Green Finance. A report to Government by the Green Finance Taskforce, March 2018. Department for Business, Energy & Industrial Strategy. https://www.gov.uk/government/publications/accelerating-green-finance-green-finance-taskforce-report

NESTA (2020), https://www.nesta.org.uk/

Ning, Y., Wang, W. and Yu. B. (2015), The driving forces of venture capital investments, Small Business Economics, 44(2), 315-344

Sachs, J., Woo, W., Yoshino N. and Taghizaheh-Hesary, F. (2019), Why is green finance important? ADBI Working Paper 917.

Sustainable Workspaces (2020), https://www.sustainableworkspaces.co.uk/

TheSwitchersFund (2017), www.theswitchersfund.eu/en/the-award/

UNEP (2016), DEFINITIONS AND CONCEPTS Background Note, UNEP Inquiry: Design of a Sustainable Financial System, INQUIRY WORKING PAPER 16/13, September 2016.

Union for the Mediterranean (2018), Enabling Access to Finance for Green Entrepreneurs in Southern Mediterranean Countries. Available Options and Potential Innovations. Retrieved from: https://ufmsecretariat.org/wpcontent/uploads/2018/12/UfMSectorialReport_Access-to-financing-for-green-enterpreneurs.pdf

United Nations Environment Programme (2019), SUSTAINABLE FINANCE PROGRESS REPORT, March 2019.

World Bank (2017), Roadmap for a sustainable financial system, http://documents.worldbank.org/curated/en/903601510548466486/Roadmap-for-a-sustainable-financial-system

YASA Motors (2020), Retrieved from: https://www.yasa.com/

Innovation and Social Value Creation of Female Social Entrepreneurs in Africa

Cecile Nieuwenhuizen
University of Johannesburg, South Africa
cecilen@uj.ac.za
DOI: 10.34190/EIE.20.027

Abstract: This paper focuses on social entrepreneurship. This form of entrepreneurship differs from commercial entrepreneurship insofar as it generates social value and impact as opposed to purely profit. A social entrepreneur can be defined as "the most powerful force for good in the world [...]; a person driven by an innovative idea that can help correct an entrenched global problem [through] system-changing solutions that permanently alter existing patterns of activity" (Ashoka.org). Yet the perception is that social entrepreneurs are simply involved in basic upliftment initiatives in deprived communities, more akin to social small businesses. The reality is that many social entrepreneurs are powerful and innovative changemakers. This paper explores the question of who are these dynamic entrepreneurs and what are their innovations which impact the societies in which they operate? Ashoka, an organisation that have pioneered the field of social entrepreneurship since 1980 continuously identify Ashoka Fellows. These are the world's leading social entrepreneurs and their Ashoka profiles provide information for better understanding and appreciation of social entrepreneurs, their innovations and their impact on society. A sample of 143 innovative female social entrepreneurs from Africa was drawn from the Ashoka database of 3,500 Ashoka Fellows worldwide. The keyword 'innovation' was used, yielding representation of social organisations from areas such as Development and Prosperity, Children and Youth, Business and Social Enterprise, Education and Learning, Health and Fitness, Economic Development and Health Care. All of these entrepreneurs had established organisations and had created value in their communities. Using criteria to determine the level of innovation in the organisation to further narrow down the sample, 13 organisations were identified as truly innovative. The research was qualitative, using content analysis to examine the profiles of the 13 social entrepreneurs and to determine the type, level and impact their organisations. This paper contributes a better understanding of female social entrepreneurs in Africa, their innovations and their impact on people, communities and countries. The findings will be valuable for entrepreneurship educators shaping future entrepreneurs as well as stakeholders concerned with the upliftment of communities

Keywords: social entrepreneurship, innovation, social value, impact

1. Introduction

Although there are many, often inconsistent, definitions of social entrepreneurship, three distinguishing characteristics have been identified, differentiating social entrepreneurs from their commercial counterparts: (i) a social mission, (ii) innovation, and (iii) the role of earned income (Lepoutre *et al.* 2013). The first and perhaps the most important distinguishing factor of social entrepreneurship is the social mission of the organisation. This reflects the drive of social entrepreneurs to solve social, environmental or community problems. Social entrepreneurship is therefore a type of entrepreneurship with a primary focus on generating social value and long-term societal change – as opposed to commercial entrepreneurship which is primarily concerned with creating profit. The mission of social organisations thus reflects their aim to do good, to improve their communities and ultimately, the world, by doing business responsibly.

The second distinguishing characteristic of social entrepreneurship is innovation. Social entrepreneurs typically start with an innovative solution to a problem in their immediate community. Such solutions, however, are often relevant at a global scale, namely, developing skills, supporting women or the youth, promoting education and literacy, bettering communities, improving health or creating jobs. Due to their innovative nature, these solutions are often replicated in other communities, countries and sometimes even result in global industries. Social entrepreneurs ensure that their organisations are effective so that their initiatives can be beneficial to more, through the delivery of quality products and services. Their innovations yield better solutions to problems, with higher profits and reduced operational costs in their organisations.

The third distinguishing characteristic of social entrepreneurship is the need to earn an income to ensure the sustainability of the organisation. A study by the Gordon Institute of Business Science (2018) found that for 61% of social organisations, the priority was to achieve their social and environmental objectives, 38% sought a balance between achieving their social and environmental objectives and making a profit whereas only 1% believed that making a profit was their primary objective.

In their comprehensive study, Lepoutre *et al.* (2013) determined the prevalence of the total Social Entrepreneurial Activity (SEA) per country and region of all countries participating in the Global Entrepreneurship Monitor. Total SEA is classified according to nascent, new, established and early-stage social entrepreneurial activity as a percentage of the population. The findings indicate averages of between 1.1% and 4.1% SEA per region. These low levels of SEA indicate the rarity of social entrepreneurs in all countries and regions of the world. This can be explained by the fact that addressing complex and systemic societal problems is a challenging endeavour, often requiring the development of radical new business models with scarce resources (Dacin, Dacin and Matear, 2010).

Africa is affected by a variety of issues that could be addressed by social organisations to ensure the improvement of communities through their innovative business models (Littlewood and Holt, 2015). Entrepreneurial orientation that includes innovative ability is essential for the establishment, sustainability and growth of any organisation. However social organisations often lack entrepreneurial orientation and the ability to be entrepreneurial (Kusa, 2016).

Women play an important role in society, specifically in their contribution to economic welfare as employees, managers, entrepreneurs and leaders. Yet a study conducted by Meyer (2018) reveals that research on female entrepreneurs is limited, there are less female entrepreneurs than males and women are less likely to grow their businesses than men. The study further found that women's motivation to remain in business was independence, work-life balance, the challenge involved, contribution to society and family security.

2. Literature

According to McNeill (2012), the world is evolving into a 'social economy' where social value, social innovation and social entrepreneurship are becoming more important. The focus is therefore shifting to returns that generate social benefit instead of only commercial value. Social entrepreneurs take successful business models and adapt these for the benefit of people, communities, nations and the planet. People have the potential to positively change communities and society as a whole and they do it in creative ways. Schumpeter's (1936) definition of an entrepreneur identifies a person who reconfigures the allocation of available resources, generates value and addresses the social needs of the underprivileged. These actions demonstrate the link between social entrepreneurship and Schumpeter's description of commercial entrepreneurship. They also show how a deeper analysis of Schumpeter's work could stimulate development in social entrepreneurship as he highlights the creative initiative that drives economic development.

In the past, the majority of studies on social entrepreneurship were conducted in developed countries such as the United States and the United Kingdom. However, as awareness of the value created by social organisations has increased, studies are now being done in developing countries (Kusa, 2016:118). The Global Entrepreneurship Monitor report by Herrington, Kew and Kew (2010:99) examined 49 countries and found that the SEA rate ranges between 0.1% and 4.3% of the total population. As alluded to previously, this reflects a minuscule proportion of people involved in SEA.

2.1 Social entrepreneurs

In describing entrepreneurs, Schumpeter (1936) emphasises the ability to create value through innovation by revolutionising methods of production. Drucker (1985) defines entrepreneurs as individuals continuously looking for change, identifying opportunities and exploiting these. According to Dees *et al.* (2001), entrepreneurs are innovative, attuned to opportunities and resourceful in creating value and change. Social entrepreneurs mirror the same characteristics although they are distinguished from commercial entrepreneurs by their social mission.

Austin, Stevenson and Wei-Skillern (2006) identify four variables which differentiate social entrepreneurship from commercial entrepreneurship, namely, (i) market failure, (ii) mission, (iii) resource mobilisation and (iv) performance measurement. These variables create different entrepreneurial opportunities, management approaches and measurement of social and commercial value for the two types of entrepreneurs.

2.2 Types of social organisations

Alter (2007:23) mentions three types of social enterprise: (i) a mission-centric organisation – where the social mission is central to the organisation which is self-financed; (ii) a commercialised organisation – the social mission is central to these organisations but to subsidise it, products and services are sold to generate income; and (iii) social organisations with a focus on income-generation rather than a social mission.

According to a study by the Gordon Institute of Business Science (2018), the main activities of South African social entrepreneurs are as follows: 73% to develop skills, 70% to support the youth, 66% to develop education and literacy, 65% to improve communities, 57% to support women, 57% to improve health, 56% to create jobs, 55% to provide goods for beneficiaries, 49% to protect human rights, 43% to protect the environment and 38% to support the elderly.

2.3 Innovation

Literature stresses the importance of innovation in the successful pursuit of a social entrepreneur's mission (Lepoutre *et al.,* 2013). Schumpeter (1936) was the first to link entrepreneurship with innovation theory and practice. He identified five forms of innovation: (i) innovative products and/or services; (ii) innovative methods of production; (iii) opening up new markets; (iv) identifying and utilising new resources of supply for raw materials or intermediate goods; and (v) carrying out some new organisational form of the industry.

Hamel and Breen (2007) developed a hierarchy of five levels of innovation. Level 1 is operational innovation which involves manufacturing, service delivery and administration processes allowing organisations to become faster, leaner or better. Level 2 is product and service innovation. This can be completely new products, line extensions of products and/or services, new product lines, or the repositioning of products and services. Level 3 is business model innovation through the commercialisation functions of value creation (when customers realise the value of an innovation) and value capture (when the organisation is able to gain from the value a new business model). Level 4 is architectural innovation. This refers to the components of a system and the interaction of these. The focus is on change in the configuration of established systems by linking components innovatively. Lastly, Level 5, the highest level is management innovation which involves processes such as knowledge, strategic, project and performance management in, for example, managing science, allocating capital, technology, intangible assets, capturing employees' wisdom and building global consortiums.

Different levels of social innovation are identified by Weerakoon, McMurray and Douglas (2016:7). These range from Level 1, the most basic to Level 3, the most advanced. Level 1 address basic social demands not catered for by the market and satisfies human needs through the provision of products and services. Level 2 is system innovation which involves changes in social relations. Here blurred economic and social boundaries are addressed through changes in governance, market and sub-systems of society such as institutions and physical infrastructure. Level 3 focuses on systemic change and fundamental change in attitudes and values, strategies and policies as well as organisational structures, processes and delivery systems. The aim of these changes is to reform society to become more participative and increase socio-political capability and access to resources.

According to the Organisation for Economic Co-operation and Development (OECD) (2010:196), social innovation differs from economic innovation insofar as it does not deal with new methods of production or exploits new markets; instead, it seeks to satisfy needs that are not addressed by the market or to create new, more satisfactory ways of inclusion in terms of giving people a place and a role in production. The primary distinction is that the focus of the innovation is on improving the welfare of people and communities through employment, consumption and participation, with the purpose of providing solutions for individual and community problems.

2.4 Social value and impact

A common understanding of 'social impact' is elusive and measures of impact differ between organisations. A number of challenges regarding social impact assessment have been identified. These include conceptual, operational, structural and practical challenges.

There are well established methods to determine and measure the impact of commercial entrepreneurs, notably, price/earnings ratios, financial profit or the traditional bottom line. Social entrepreneurs' creation of social value is more complex and is reflected in the needs of people which have been met. The most important result of a social organisation is sustainable change in the lives of people, preferably at a community level. Just like commercial entrepreneurs, social entrepreneurs must ensure the financial sustainability and efficiency of their organisations. One of the expectations of social entrepreneurs is to ensure clear social outcomes and impact (El Ebrashi, 2013).

A study by Duvnäs *et al.* (2012) found that innovations and innovative orientation characterise successful social organisations, allowing these organisations to remain economically sustainable. It is noted that although the primary aim is not to make a profit for shareholders, profitability is nonetheless important if the organisation is to continue to meet its social objectives. However, Duvnäs *et al.* (2012) indicate the innovations do not necessarily result in profits and that innovation success should be measured in other ways. Thus other performance measures need to be used to determine social impact.

3. Research design

The research design of this study is qualitative. Content analysis using detailed questionnaires was used to examine a sample of innovative female social entrepreneurs.

3.1 Population and sample

The total population of the study was represented by the 3,500 social entrepreneurs listed on the Ashoka database. In line with the objective of the study to determine the innovation and social value creation of female social entrepreneurs in Africa, the population was narrowed down to female Ashoka Fellows in Africa. Through a search of the web page (https://www.ashoka.org/en-za/our-network), 143 women from African countries were identified. These 143 profiles and associated web links to their organisations were reviewed, and with the information from these individual questionnaires were completed on each of the 143 female social entrepreneurs. The questionnaires were analysed to identify those entrepreneurs which met innovation criteria. The criteria was as follows:

- Based on Alter's (2007) three differentiations, the organisation should either have a focused social mission or have a commercialised social mission. It could not be social organisations with a primary mission of income-generation.
- The business idea to create value should represent a type (Schumpeter, 1936) and level of innovation (Hamel and Breen, 2007).
- The impact of the innovation could be determined (El Ebrashi, 2013).

Through this process a sample of 13 innovative social entrepreneurs was identified for inclusion in the study.

3.2 Methodology

The study is qualitative, based on a content analysis of questionnaires which were used to examine the sample of social entrepreneurs and their organisations. The questionnaire used was designed specifically for the study and was informed by literature and personal experience. Data on the 143 profiles was gathered from their web pages and was used to complete sections of the questionnaires on each of the entrepreneurs. The profiles on the Ashoka website are comprehensive and include information on the problems the entrepreneurs identified, their business ideas, their strategies and personal information. In addition, many of the organisations have websites. The questionnaires were evaluated to determine which of the entrepreneurs complied with the criteria of the study. Those identified as relevant were finalised to address the following: personal information on the social entrepreneur including their country of origin and level of education; the focus of their organisation according to Ashoka business categories; their business ideas; the level and type of innovation of the organisation; and the impact of their organisations on society.

3.3 Data analysis

The information in the questionnaires was further analysed to determine trends and insights on innovation and social value creation of the female social entrepreneurs from Africa. The data presented as follows: an overview and descriptive analysis of the types of organisation and representation in the different categories; descriptive analysis of the innovation including the type and level of innovation; descriptive analysis of the impact of the organisation on people, communities and countries.

4. Results

4.1 General information

The most innovative female social entrepreneurs came from four African countries: South Africa (7), Kenya (4), Mozambique (1) and Nigeria (1). All had completed higher education, seven had degrees, three had Honours or specialist degrees such as Architecture, two had Master's degrees and one had a doctorate. Research has proven that successful entrepreneurs often have higher levels of education (Dickson, Solomon, Weaver, 2008). Most of the organisations focused on the business categories Development and Prosperity (6), followed by Education and Learning (3), Health and Fitness (2), Business and Social Enterprise (1) and Children and Youth (1).

4.2 Background of the organisations

The following excerpts from the profiles and websites of the entrepreneurs indicate the types of a businesses included in the sample.

> *"thanks to Florence Wambugu who has, through a variety of scientific and community-based interventions throughout the agricultural value chain, been able to dramatically increase both the food security and incomes of smallholder farms throughout Africa. Florence combines high level scientific research to improve resistance of food crops to disease with effective organization and empowerment of farmers." (Florence Wambugu, African Harvest Biotech Foundation International; https://www.ashoka.org/en-za/fellow/florence-wambugu)*

> *"Dorien Beurskens has developed an affordable way to provide vocational education and training to young people in Southern Africa. She has established training centers that are both learning spaces for students and business hubs for entrepreneurs in the community. Dorien has developed a creative model in which the centres, spaces, equipment and the Young Africa brand are rented to local entrepreneurs who, in turn, train students in their respective fields." (Dorien Beurskema, Young Africa. https://www.ashoka.org/en-za/fellow/dorien-beurskens)*

> *"Knowing the importance of fruit and vegetables to any healthy diet, Claire Reed developed the innovative reel gardening concept to enable South Africans of all ages and backgrounds to take pride in being able to grow their own fruit and vegetables. To do this she ensures food security through home and school-based gardens as an educational tool, through which the joy in growing food is created. Claire realized that schools are the best way to get access to communities and that the success of school fruit and vegetable gardens would be an inspiration to households to start their own gardens." (Claire Reed, Reel Gardening. https://www.ashoka.org/en-za/fellow/claire-reid)*

> *"Tracey has created a comprehensive infrastructure for unemployed mothers and fathers in South African township and peri-urban contexts to start and be successful in generating their own incomes. She does this by first, providing access to best quality merchandise sourced directly from South Africa's top retail companies, which the women and men are able to start trading with. She then puts them through an intensive process, through which she is able to address critical areas of physical, mental and social well-being, through two years of mentorship, life and peer-coaching, and business and technical skills, allowing women and men to take charge of their own growth." (Tracey Chalmers, The Clothing Bank. https://www.ashoka.org/en-za/fellow/tracey-chambers).*

4.3 Quotes on innovations

The following quotes illustrate the innovations of some of the social entrepreneurs as retrieved from their profiles on the Ashoka web page and/or the web pages of their organisations. This is to illustrate the types of innovations of the social entrepreneurs.

> *"Megan is taking the full market approach to significantly reduce the price of sanitary products without compromising on quality by launching her own production process complete with world class R&D. Similarly, she is working at the policy level to remove barriers such as excise duty on women's underwear. She has developed a distribution model that partners with women entrepreneurs in order to tackle the gender and cultural nuances that often interfere with the provision of reproductive health education in conservative societies. All these factors make*

Megan's approach not only new but also potentially disruptive." (Megan Mukuria, Zana Africa Foundation. https://www.ashoka.org/en-za/fellow/megan-mukuria)

"Claire reimagines the food garden as compact, mobile and easy to maintain, with each classroom equipped with its own garden. She links nutrition education to the practical act of taking care of a food garden as well as to the national curriculum, she equips each classroom with its own garden and equip teachers to use it as a teaching tool. She linked the schools to a free App, the Planting Revolution, that guides teachers and learners through the gardening process. Usage of the app is rewarded by free data to learners and teachers." (Claire Reed, Reel Gardening. https://www.ashoka.org/en-za/fellow/claire-reid)

"The artisan craft sector is the second-largest employer in the developing world, yet it is also one of the most marginalized...millions of talented artisans are trapped in micro-economies, unable to earn enough to support their families...Our supply chain innovation uses mobile phones to connect independent artisan entrepreneurs directly to our team and global customers, which allows artisans to receive orders and payment. Through digital banking and accessibility to cell phones, we created a simple, commercially viable way to connect local artisans with the international market and industry. We've coined this system — a virtual factory." (Ella Peinovich, Shop Soko. https://shopsoko.com/)

"Andrea Bolnick is demonstrating a new approach to providing 'dwellings with dignity' to South Africa's most vulnerable. Through active community engagement, Andrea is able to bring about needed renovations to their homes. The result is the effective removal of the threat of fire, flooding, and other general public health concerns that pervade these areas... iKhayalami's areas of focus include: research and development, upgrading of shelters, infrastructural development, community facilities, disaster response and sales to the public to reach more people and lead to sustainability." (Andrea Bolnick, iKhayalami. https://www.ashoka.org/en-za/fellow/andrea-bolnick)

"A new model of hospital care for comatose patients that heeds their rights and needs as well as those of their family members also improving the working conditions and job satisfaction of severely overstretched nursing staff and other hospital personnel. Today, ComaCARE is based in a neurosurgery ward and neuro-ICU in the Groote Schuur Hospital." (Janice Webster, ComaCARE. https://www.ashoka.org/en-za/fellow/janice-webster)

4.4 Form of innovation

The data was analysed to determine the form of innovation (Schumpeter, 1936) of each of the 13 entrepreneurs, as presented in Table 1 below.

Table 1: Form of Innovation

Form of innovation	Number of Participants
1. Introduction of new product or service	Seven of the entrepreneurs had this form of innovation.
2. Introduction of new method of production	One entrepreneur had this form of innovation
3. Opening up a new market	Three entrepreneurs had this form of innovation.
4. Utilising new resources of supply for raw materials or intermediate goods.	One entrepreneur had this type of innovation.
5. Carrying out a new organisational form of the industry.	One entrepreneur had this type of innovation.

4.5 Level of innovation

The data was analysed to determine the level of innovation (Hamel and Breen, 2007) of each of the 13 entrepreneurs, as presented in Table 2 below.

Table 2: Level of Innovation

Level of Innovation	Number of Participants at this level
1. Operational innovation	1
2. Product and service innovation	5
3. Business model innovation	6
4. Architectural innovation	0
5. Management innovation	1

4.6 Impact of the organisation

The organisation, through its innovation, has an impact on people, communities, organisations and countries. Table 3 shows a summary of the most important impacts that these entrepreneurs had on their respective communities.

Table 3: Summary of the most important impacts that these entrepreneurs had on their respective communities

Impact and benefit to:	Short description of impact and benefit
People	Assists 300 million people in Africa by developing vitamin- and iron-rich drought-resistant sorghum. (Florence Wambugu. Africa Harvest Biotech Foundation International) 26,000 youth have graduated from Young Africa in Zimbabwe and Mozambique. About 83% of the graduates in Mozambique have managed to secure employment, either in the formal sector or through self-employment. (Dorien Beurskema. Young Africa) Over 6,000 people participate in more than 360 community yoga classes taught by Africa Yoga Project teachers representing 21 different African countries. More than 400 young people, trained as teachers are earning a living wage by teaching yoga to people who otherwise would not have the opportunity. (Paige Ellenson, Africa Yoga Project.) More than 800 women earn an average profit of $220 per month and 97 men are active with $280 profit per month in their own ventures. Edu-care Centres with 1,193 children educated; 161 jobs created and 30 interns. (Tracey Chambers, The Clothing Bank and The Appliance Bank) Upgrading thousands of homes, expanding Andrea's operations beyond the Western Cape to Johannesburg and Durban. Giving emergency relief to families by providing building materials for upgraded, fire resistant shelters. Creating a place of safety for vulnerable children in informal settlements and upgrading many creches in informal settlements. (Andrea Bolnick, Ikhayalami) MiniChess is an early educational transformation program that makes a significant difference in children's lives at a very early age (4-9 years) using chess as a tool to develop these children's Science, Technology, Engineering & Mathematics (STEM) skills. Thousands of school learners, improve STEM through chess. (Marisa van der Merwe, MiniChess) ComaCARE trains neurosurgery staff, nurses and family members of patients with brain injuries to identify small signs of brain activity and to cultivate those signs into signals for communication. Training modules are offered to nurses working in neurosurgery wards and neuro-ICUs (Janice Webster, ComaCARE). For the leadership and skills training programmes of Generation of Leaders Discovered (GOLD) 17,502 peer leaders were trained; 1,043 job placements and 790 facilitator internships. A total of 54,696 peers and children were reached through the GOLD Programmes. (Sussanah Farr, GOLD youth) Youth for Technology Business (YTB) successfully trained financial literacy skills for over 12,500 women entrepreneurs and their apprentices; software development and coding skills for over 3,500 girls; 3D printing and emerging technology skills for over 2,000 youth; in total trained over 1.6 million youth and women; graduated more than 320,000 youth, with 96% going on to higher education within two years and 55% choosing technology-related fields. The training resulted in the creation and expansion of 14,000 businesses and social franchises. (Njideka Harry, Youth for Technology) Claire links nutrition education to the practical act of taking care of a food garden as well as to the national curriculum, equips classrooms with gardens and teachers to use it as a teaching tool. The project was piloted by Claire in 2300 schools in 2016 impacting 111,000 people. (Claire Reed, Reel Gardening) 2,300 artisans (i.e. make jewellery) who sell their products internationally earn five times more than others for similar work. (Ella Peinovich, Shop Soko) Directly served 2.5 million girls and women with hygiene and sanitary products, winning back 5 million school days and a further 55 million work hours. (Megan Mukuria. Zana Africa.)
Communities	EmpowerNet Clubs – an afterschool girls-only club. (Megan Mukuria. Zana Africa) Over 500,000 farmers in Kenya involved in Africa Harvest make roughly three times more than they had previously. (Florence Wambugu. Africa Harvest Biotech Foundation International) 360 community yoga classes offered. (Paige Elenson. Africa Yoga Project) Developing 832 clothing banks, 97 appliance banks and 31 Grow Educare Centres in communities throughout South Africa. (Tracey Chambers. Clothing Bank) A community upgrading facility fund where upgraded communities will contribute 20% to their upgraded house and 10% to other community development initiatives. (Andrea Bolnick, Ikhayalami) Inspired economic sustainability through business developmemt in 4,500 communities. (Njideka Harry, Youth for Technology)

Impact and benefit to:	Short description of impact and benefit
	2,700 schools and communities reached, 100 0000 metres of seed tapes for home gardening donated; 13 million litres of water saved (Claire Reed, Reel Gardening).
Countries	*Zana Africa:* Kenya *Africa Harvest*: Kenya, offices in South Africa and in the USA, extending to Tanzania, Uganda and other countries in Africa *Young Africa*: Zimbabwe and Mozambique *Africa Yoga:* 21 African countries *Clothing Bank:* South Africa. *Maths Through Mini Chess:* South Africa, Botswana, Ivory Coast, DRC, Kenya, Rwanda, Tanzania, Lesotho, Madagascar, USA, China, Central Asia, New Zealand, Germany *GOLD Youth Training*: South Africa, Zimbabwe, Zambia, Botswana *Youth for Technology:* Nigeria

5. Conclusion

The 10% of innovative organisations, namely 13 of 143 identified for the sample of this study, are aligned with the representation of the populations of all innovative organisations. All the female social entrepreneurs had degrees or postgraduate qualifications that is in line with the general consensus across research that there is a positive and significant relationship between education and entrepreneurial performance (Dickson, Solomon, Weaver, 2008). Through the evaluation and analysis of the 13 social entrepreneurs, it was found that the innovations were primarily the introduction of new products or services (7), followed by the opening up of a new market (3). One entrepreneur was involved in each of the following forms of innovation: introducing a new method of production; utilising a new resource of supply for raw materials or intermediate goods; and carrying out a new organisational form of the industry. Their levels of innovation varied from one at the operational level, five at the product and service innovation level, six at the business model level of innovation and one at the level of management innovation. None of the innovations were at the level of architectural innovation. The impact of these innovative organisations was far-reaching, influencing millions of people. The study proved that innovative social entrepreneurs have a significant impact on the people, communities and countries is which they operate. They are true 'changemakers' and deserve Schumpeter's (1936) accolade of 'true heroes of society'.

References

Alter, K. (2006), "Social Enterprise Typology", [online], http://www. virtueventures.com/setypology/semg.

Ashoka, [online], https://www.ashoka.org/en-za/our-network

Austin, J., Stevenson, H. and Wei-Skillern, J. (2006), "Social and commercial entrepreneurship: Same, different, or both?" *Entrepreneurship Theory and Practice,* Vol 30, No. 1, pp 1-22.

Dacin, P.A., Dacin, M.T. and Matear, M. (2010). "Social entrepreneurship: Why we don't need a new theory and how we move forward from here", *Academy of Management Perspectives*, Vol 24 No. 3, pp 37-57.

Dees, G., Emerson, J. and Economy, P. (eds.). (2001), *Enterprising Non-profits: A Toolkit for Social Entrepreneurs,* John Wiley, New York.

Dickson, P., Solomon, G. and Weaver, K. (2008), "Entrepreneurial selection and success: does education matter?", *Journal of Small Business and Enterprise Development*, Vol. 15 No. 2, pp. 239-258

Drucker, P. (1985), *Entrepreneurship and Innovation*, Heineman, London.

Duvnäs, H., Stenholm, P., Brännback, M. and Carsrud, A. (2012), "What are the outcomes of innovativeness within social entrepreneurship? The relationship between innovative orientation and social enterprise economic performance", *Journal of Strategic Innovation and Sustainability*, Vol. 8, No. 1, pp 68-80.

El Ebrashi, R. (2013), "Social entrepreneurship theory and sustainable social impact", *Social Responsibility Journal*, Vol. 9, No. 2, pp 188-209.

Gordon Institute of Business Science (GIBS). (2018), *Social Enterprises in South Africa: Discovering a vibrant sector,* University of Pretoria, Pretoria.

Hamel, G. and Breen, B. (2007), *The Future of Management*, Harvard Business School Publishing, Boston, MA.

Herrington, M., Kew, J. and Kew, P. (2010) *Tracking entrepreneurship in South Africa: A GEM perspective,* University of Cape Town, Cape Town.

Kusa, R. (2016), "Measuring entrepreneurial orientation in the social context", *Entrepreneurial Business and Economics Review*, Vol 4, No. 3, pp 117-129.

Lepoutre, J., Justo, R., Terjesen, S. and Bosma, N. (2013), "Designing a global standardized methodology for measuring social entrepreneurship activity: The Global Entrepreneurship Monitor social entrepreneurship study", *Small Business Economics,* Vol. 40, No. 3, pp 693-714.

Littlewood, D. and Holt, D. (2015), "Social entrepreneurship in South Africa: Exploring the influence of environment", *Business and Society*, Vol. 57, No. 3, pp 525-561.

McNeill, J. (2012), "Through Schumpeter: Public policy, social innovation and social entrepreneurship", *The International Journal of Sustainability Policy and Practice,* Vol. 8, No. 1, pp 81-94.

Meyer, N. (2018), "Research on female entrepreneurship: Are we doing enough?" *Polish Journal of Management Studies,* Vol. 17, No. 2, pp 158-169.

Organisation for Economic Co-operation and Development (OECD). (2010), "SMEs, Entrepreneurship and Innovation" [online], www.oecd.org/cfe/.

Schumpeter, J. (1936), *The Theory of Economic Development*, Harvard University Press, Cambridge, MA.

Weerakoon, C. McMurray, A. and Douglas, H. (2016), "The Nexus between Social Entrepreneurship and Social Innovation", paper read at the ACERE Conference, Gold Coast, Queensland, Australia.

Business Model Design for the Creative and Cultural Industries: Enterprise Education From the art School

Marcus O'Dair
University of Arts, London, UK
m.odair@arts.ac.uk
DOI: 10.34190/EIE.20.171

Abstract: Business model visualisation has become popular since Osterwalder and Pigneur published their 'business model canvas' in 2010. However, there have been few visualisations specific to the creative and cultural industries, despite the fact that these industries have particular characteristics and perceived lack of business knowledge is a barrier for graduates. This paper presents qualitative and quantitative data from a pilot project carried out in 2019-2020 at University of the Arts London (UAL) with funding from Enterprise Educators UK. The aim was to increase students' understanding of business models, specifically in the context of the art school and the cultural and creative industries. The project had two phases: the first looked at business models as a general concept, the second at the specific business models of graduate entrepreneurs. Core to both phases were three Design students, who created business model visualisations. In the first phase, the Design students tested their visualisation of the business model concept with a focus group of six fellow students. In the second phase, the Design students interviewed three graduate entrepreneurs about their business models, then tested their visualisations of the graduates' business models with a second focus group of five fellow students. While enterprise education is sometimes understood as something done to the art school, this project came from the art school, in that it deployed visualisation, testing and iteration as core methodologies. As well as the principles of design, the project was informed by active learning and 'learning by doing', which is key to effective entrepreneurship education.

Keywords: active learning, art school, enterprise education, business models

1. Introduction: Business modelling and the art school

Teaching entrepreneurship in the art school – where it is often associated with a far-from-celebrated policy shift from public subsidy, associated with the 'arts' or 'cultural industries', towards innovation and growth, associated with the 'creative industries' or 'creative economy' (Hartley et al 2013) – is not the same as teaching it in the business school. The music industry is far from alone in being made up of 'reluctant entrepreneurs' (Haynes and Marshall 2017). Craft makers, for instance, may simply want to 'make a good living' from their practice – and '"good" here refers to a not only financial reward but also operating a business in keeping with their value systems' (Luckman 2018: 324). At the same time, almost one in five graduates (19.85%) from UAL goes on to start a business; this makes UAL the number one university in the UK for graduate start-ups (Hitachi Capital 2020). It is our responsibility, then, to give our students the tools they will need to start a business and give those businesses the best possible chance of survival. The challenge is to introduce entrepreneurial concepts in language and imagery – and aligned to values – that resonate with students studying art, design, fashion, media and performance.

While enterprise education is sometimes understood as something done *to* the art school, this paper concerns a project that came *from* the art school, in that it deployed visualisation, testing and iteration as core methodologies. 17 students and recent graduates were involved in total, all recruited through an open call issued on our in-house recruitment platform, and all were paid for their participation with funding from Enterprise Educators UK. The project had a particular focus on business models, understood here to refer to the ways in which an organisation creates, delivers and captures value (Osterwalder and Pigneur 2010). Much of the literature around business models dates to the dot com boom at the turn of the millennium, and the concept still tends to be associated with technological disruption – for instance, with companies such as Airbnb and Uber. In fact, every business has a business model, whether they realise it or not (Chesbrough 2006), including those in the creative and cultural industries.

The visualisation of business models – by which I mean design-led, visual approaches to understanding how organisations creates, delivers and captures value – has become popular since Osterwalder and Pigneur published their business model canvas in 2010 (Campbell et al 2017, Clark et al 2012, Van Der Pijl et al 2016, Van Wulfen 2014, Young Foundation 2013). Yet only Rodriguez (2016) has created a visualisation specific to the creative and cultural industries – despite the fact that these industries have particular characteristics (Kimbell 2018) and perceived lack of business knowledge is a barrier for graduates in the sector (Smith and Beasley 2011). The emergence of business model visualisation is linked to the rise of so-called 'design thinking'. Yet art schools were engaged in visual communication and idea generation – and emphasising the importance of prototyping, testing, iteration and co-creating with users – long before 'design thinking' was codified by business schools and management gurus. Design needs to be understood as a practice, not simply a set of tools (Hill 2012: 136), and Design students – unlike, for instance, your average management theorist – are deeply engaged in this practice.

As well as principles of design, the project was informed by active learning and 'learning by doing' (Bonwell and Eison 1991), which is a key to effective entrepreneurship education (Siok 2006). However valuable the business model canvas and its variants may be, from an active learning perspective it is even more valuable for students to create and refine their own business model visualisations. The project can be understood as an example of 'business modelling', defined by Rex et al (2018) as 'a heuristic technique organisations use to identify the range of activities and relationships (internal and external) they undertake where different kinds of value are exchanged... a means of enabling practitioners to define their own models which embody their values, objectives and position within the local creative ecosystem.'

2. Project structure

The project began with a workshop to help the three Design students understand the concept of the business model and its possible applications in the cultural and creative industries.

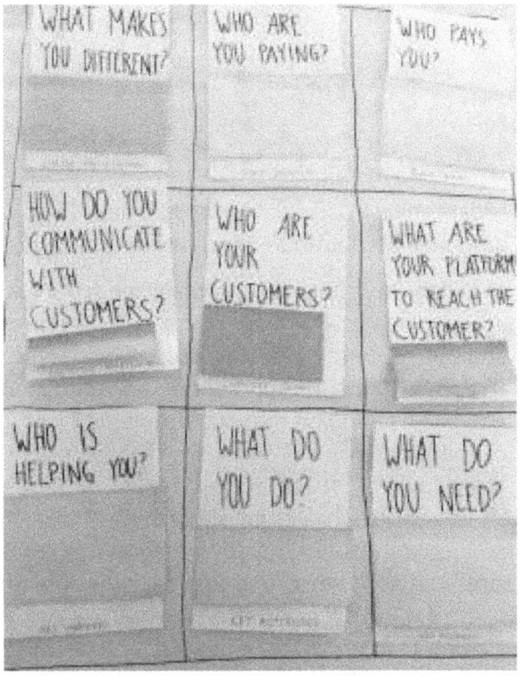

Figure 1: Based on the business model canvas (Osterwalder and Pigneur 2010) available from strategyzer.com. Issued under Creative Commons: Attribution-ShareAlike 3.0 Unported

The Design students then worked collaboratively to develop an initial prototype that visualised the business model as a general concept, using their own words and images (Figure 1), developed from existing canvasses such as the business model canvas (Osterwalder and Pigneur 2010). This was followed by a focus group, in which the Design students tested their prototype visualisation with six of their peers. They also engaged in focus group-style discussion on how the visualisations might be improved. Next, the Design students adapted their visualisation of the generic business model concept in response to the peer feedback (Figure 2). The students re-worked the business model canvas by adding colours to break the nine blocks into themed sections, and changed the fixed piece of paper or PDF into a set of interlocking cards which could be endlessly rearranged. The students also changed some of the language (was 'customer relationship', for instance, the right phrase, or would 'customer experience' or 'customer connection' be more relevant?) and added prompt questions to help students see the relevance to their own practice. Finally, to maximise the sense of interactivity, the students added a layer of acetate on top of each card, allowing users to write on each card and then wipe it clean. The students also created a film and a blog post, explaining how the visualisation had been developed and how it be used by fellow students and graduates.

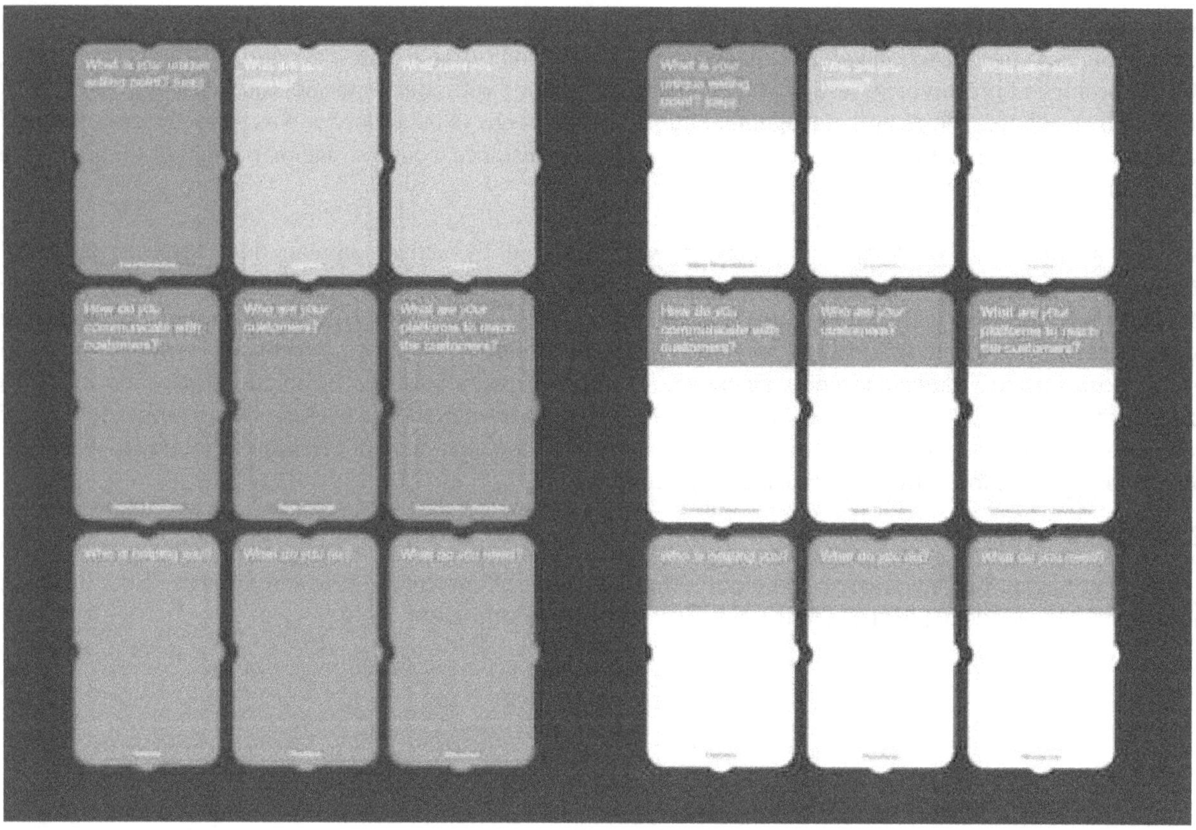

Figure 2: Based on the business model canvas (Osterwalder and Pigneur 2010) available from strategyzer.com. Issued under Creative Commons: Attribution-ShareAlike 3.0 Unported

The second phase of the project, in which the Design students shifted from visualising the business model as a general concept to visualising the business models of specific graduate entrepreneurs, began with a second workshop in which each Design student prepared semi-structured interview questions for an entrepreneur. (These entrepreneurs only graduated in 2019 but all self-identified prior to graduation as committed to setting up their own businesses are they are making good on that commitment. Two work in costume design, while the third works in digital arts with a focus on gaming and virtual reality.) Each Design student then conducted a semi-structured interview with their respective graduate entrepreneurs, with the aim of identifying and then visualising the graduate's business model. Each Design student then visualised the business model of the graduate they interviewed. They then presented those visualisations to the graduates to ensure that the businesses were accurately represented, and modified them in light of feedback.

We then conducted a second focus group to assess the effectiveness of the visualisations of the business models of graduate entrepreneurs. There were five participants rather than six, since one fell ill on the day, but this focus group otherwise worked as the first – expect that, due to the COVID-19 pandemic, it had to be conducted online. Finally, the Design students finalised their visualisations, responding to feedback from the focus group. One graduate business model was visualised as a set of Perspex cards (Figure 3); another as a folded sheet of paper, allowing for the gradual reveal of business model segments (Figure 4); a third as nine circles, using a colour palette specifically chosen to represent the graduate in question (Figure 5). These were released under the same Creative Commons license used by Osterwalder and Pigneur for their business model canvas.

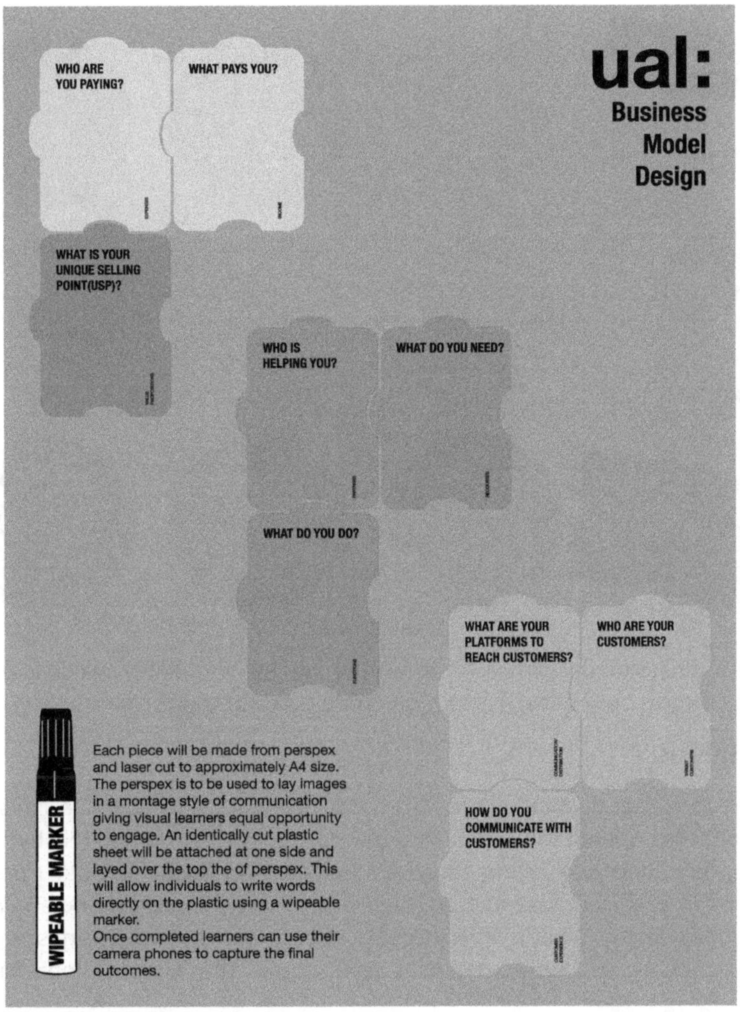

Figure 3: Based on the business model canvas (Osterwalder and Pigneur 2010) available from strategyzer.com. Issued under Creative Commons: Attribution-ShareAlike 3.0 Unported

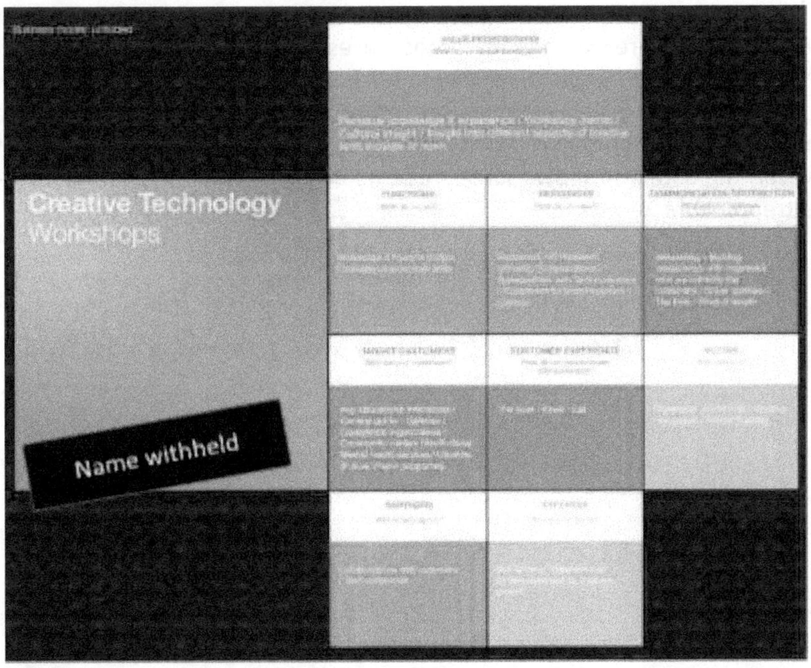

Figure 4: Based on the business model canvas (Osterwalder and Pigneur 2010) available from strategyzer.com. Issued under Creative Commons: Attribution-ShareAlike 3.0 Unported

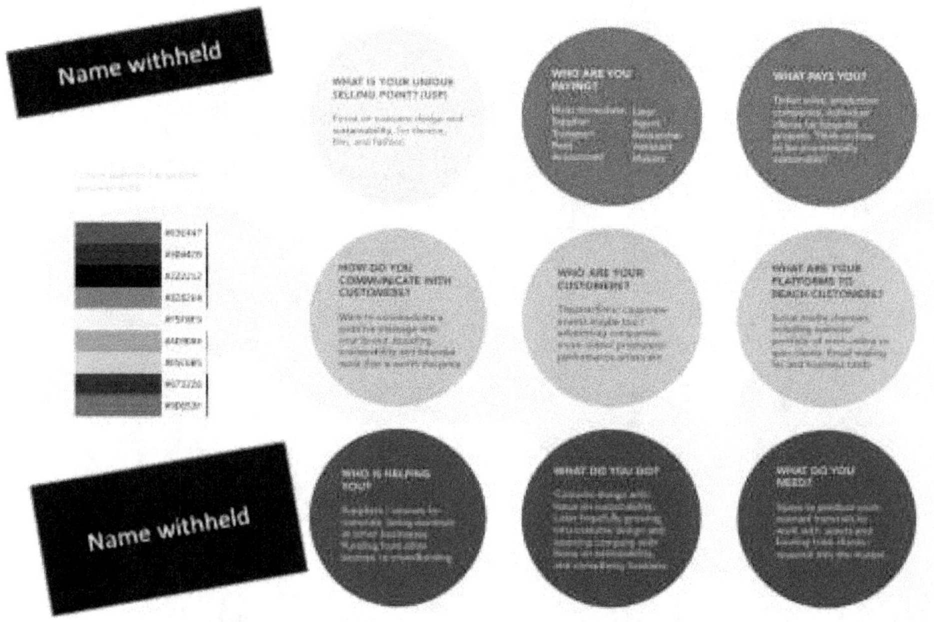

Figure 5: Based on the business model canvas (Osterwalder and Pigneur 2010) available from strategyzer.com. Issued under Creative Commons: Attribution-ShareAlike 3.0 Unported

3. Findings and analysis

The project allowed me to collect qualitative data from the two workshops with Design students and the two focus groups. I also collected quantitative data through questionnaires completed by the 11 students who participated in focus groups and two of the three graduate entrepreneurs. (Data from the third graduate entrepreneur has not been used, because she dropped out during the project.) Analysing this data helps to answer two main questions. Firstly, what did participants already know about business models, and what was their attitude towards them? Secondly, to what extent did the visualisations increase participants' understanding?

4. Initial knowledge of, and attitudes towards, business models

While participants came to the project with differing levels of knowledge, qualitative data from the workshops and focus groups suggests that there was in at least most cases some room for this knowledge to increase. The three Design students suggested in the first workshop, for instance, that business models were in some way related to business plans, but were not able to elaborate much beyond that. One of the graduate entrepreneurs and some participants in each focus group felt that knew what a business model was before the project began (see Figure 6). However, the data also shows some students began with far less confidence – including one of the two graduate entrepreneurs.

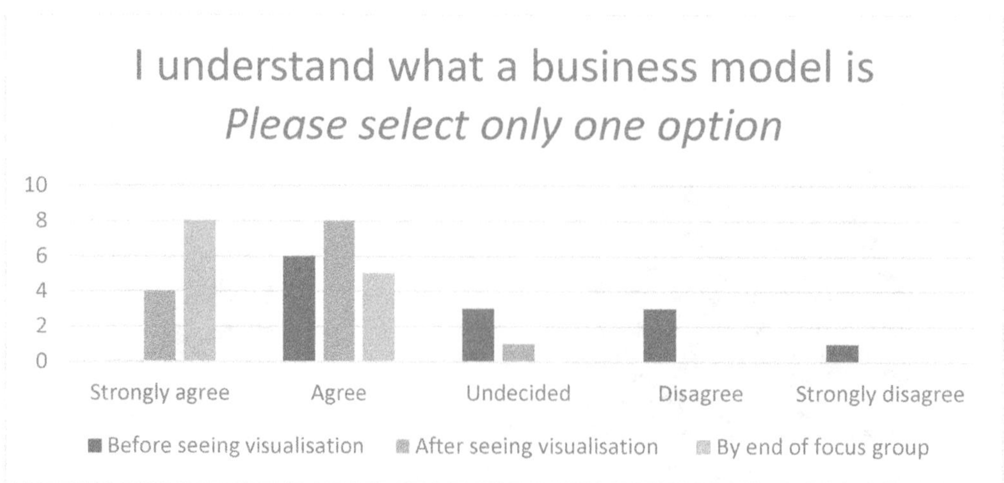

Figure 6: Combined data from the two focus groups and the two graduate entrepreneurs

Quantitative data from interviews with the graduate entrepreneurs and from focus group participants suggests that several participants could already see the relevance of business models to the cultural and creative industries before participating in the project (Figure 7). Again, however, it is noteworthy that even one of the two graduate entrepreneurs came to the project 'undecided' as to whether or not business models were relevant to the cultural and creative industries. Quantitative data from the graduate entrepreneurs and participants in the two focus groups suggests that, while some began with an understanding of the relevance of business models to their own creative practice, this number increased in all three groups after engaging with the project (Figure 8).

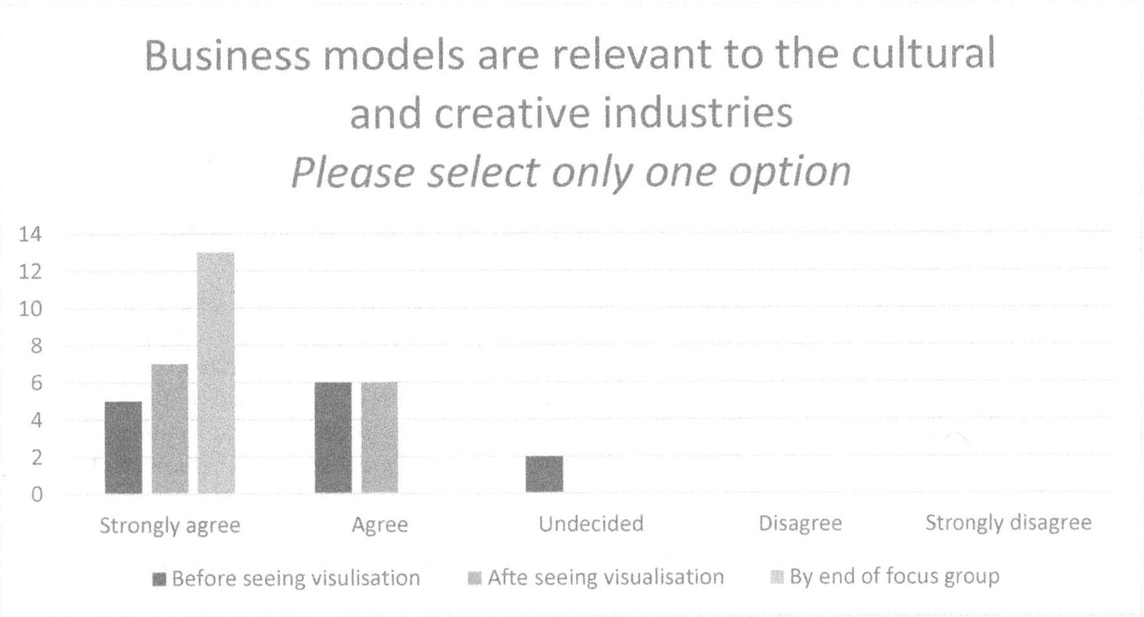

Figure 7: Combined data from the two focus groups and the two graduate entrepreneurs

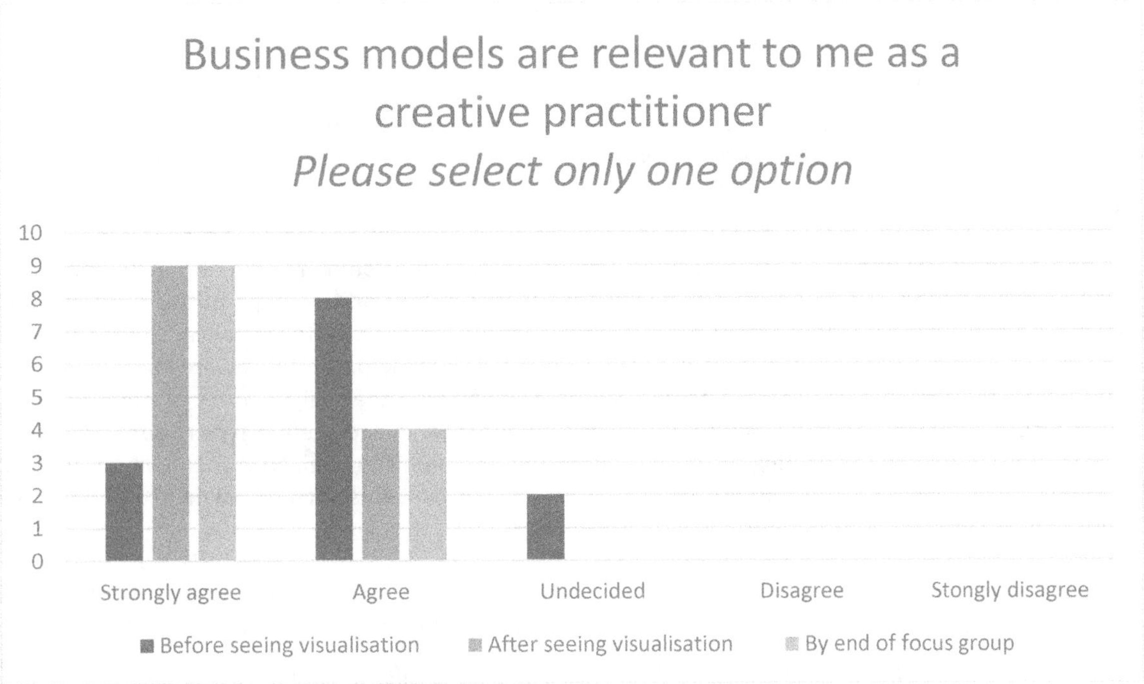

Figure 8: Combined data from the two focus groups and the two graduate entrepreneurs

Qualitative data from the second focus group suggests that some participants began the project sceptical of the very notion of the business model and of entrepreneurship more broadly:

> ***Me:*** *I think we haven't heard from Student K, is that right?*

> ***Participant K:*** *I think it [Participant J's visualisation] is very aesthetically lovely to look at. Um. I struggle with, um, I struggle with, um, like, losing things. And I struggle with... I'm a painter and, speaking of my student cohort, if we were presented this in a lecture, I'm not sure how, I don't know how positively it would be taken. I think that, like, in the art school, if we're talking about, like, trying to get business models to work inside the art school, like, unfortunately, a lot of my experience with painters in my year is, like, we're quite anti-business.*
>
> ***Participant J:*** *Yeah. Yeah.*
>
> ***Participant K:*** *I think it would perhaps be seen as sort of curtailing our creativity to try to fill in boxes like this. Even though it could actually be very helpful, I think you might you have to be aware that some people don't like doing this kind of thing. They see it as very corporate.*
>
> ***Participant J:*** *Definitely. OK, cool...*

As the second focus group continued, the conversation turned to the fact that Participant J had attempted to reflect the identity of the graduate entrepreneur he interviewed in his visualisation of her business model. The mention of 'branding' provoked differing views from participants, some of whom picked up on Participant K's comments quoted above:

> ***Participant A:*** *I think what [Participant K] is saying is really interesting, because whenever I hear the word 'branding', I just go 'agh'. Branding and business, on the one hand, seems to be the antithesis of the art school ethos. That, I think, is a real issue. And maybe we need to find different language around what is ostensibly planning your life. Because there isn't necessarily the scope, I mean even before the situation we're in right now [the COVID-19 pandemic], for every artist to become a business. And I think if you're actually looking at a really practical tool for students about to graduate – it doesn't matter what level they're at, even at PhD level you still have so pay your rent – is that there's a section of this thing, that could maybe not be called a business model, which actually does the practicalities of saying: how much do I need to earn in order to continue my painting practice, and where am I going to earn that from? How many hours do I need to work at the café or the pub while I build this up? So, it's not about saying, it's just that reality check of saying, well, actually, my plan, whatever you want to call it, business model or career path or whatever, is based in reality. How much do I need to earn, how many materials, how much can I produce when I'm only earning this much from working in the café that's going to allow me to buy canvasses...? That is as much part of a business model as.... Anyway, I'll shut up now...*
>
> ***Participant K:*** *I prefer that way more. That seems a much more pragmatic, real, down to earth way of talking about how we can sustain our creative practice. It's when it comes to making myself into a brand, I shut off, I just don't think that way...*

Participants K and, to an extent, A, appear here to be expressing a Romantic or 'art for art's sake' (Caves 2000) perspective, not only assuming a binary opposition between culture and commerce but also assuming that the art school is firmly on the culture side of that divide. (Although it is beyond the scope of this paper, it can be argued, by contrast, that art schools have in fact always been utilitarian; see, for instance, Quinn 2014). The participants' views may to some extent be due to language: at least some participants were more comfortable with 'sustaining their creative practice' than with acknowledging that they might have, or need to have, a business model. Data from the initial workshop suggests that the language used in typical definitions of the business model – for instance, relating to 'value' – does not communicate well to students in an art school context. There was likewise a sense in the first focus group that concepts such as 'value proposition' were difficult to understand.

Not all participants, however, expressed an 'art for art's sake' viewpoint. At least one participant in the second focus group, for instance, disagreed with the views expressed by Participants K and (to an extent) A:

> ***Me:*** *Maybe the phrase 'business model' is a very unhelpful phrase in the art school.* ***Participant H:*** *Part of the purpose of this [project] is to also familiarise artists with the wider world, because a lot of the time artists do have a bohemian, almost, or not realistic, idea of how the world is functioning. So when... it's happened to me more than once. I've taken on a job and the language they are speaking in is not necessarily resonating with me because of my lack of experience. And then it's difficult for me to necessarily execute the thing [I am being paid to do], because I think of things in this individualistic way. Whereas as I feel that the construct of these business models is*

also to align you with the way the rest of the world is speaking in regard to how businesses do work. So, when you do approach your practice, [even though] you have, you know, some kind of qualms with the language that's used, you are able to translate that and understand that this is just basically a universal way of speaking. So, yeah, it is a business model. You don't really want to look at yourself as a business, but that's maybe your own personal way of interpreting it.

Participant J: *Yeah.*

Participant H: *Whereas the things that [Participant J] and [Participant E] and I are designing are to familiarise you with some of these terms on purpose. Because you're going to have to come across them anyway, whether you like it or not. If you're costume designer, you're going to have to speak to some corporation to get a contract, you're going to have to sign something, do you know what I mean, to get that money into your account, to get paid, to get that invoice sorted out. It's quite interesting, as well, there is an element of this that is forcing people, artists, to adjust to the outer world, the world outside your practice, as well.*

Interestingly, even Participant K's objection to branding, and apparent identification with an 'anti-business' viewpoint, was not fixed. Rather, her views appeared to vary according to her various professional identities:

Me: *Maybe I didn't frame it particularly helpfully by telling everyone before we started that this was a business model. Maybe for [Participant K] that's immediately off-putting, before you'd even looked at the model.*

Participant K: *It is and it isn't. I do think of myself as a somewhat business-minded person. Like, I've set up a series of, I set up performance events with a group of my friends, where we charge for tickets, we run a bar, and it is about making money to put back into the events so there's more [money]. And that's the sort of thing where I do think of this as a business, where this kind of model would be useful, would be very useful. [Participant H's model] or [Participant J's model] would be really useful in helping with that. But when I think of my practice as a painter, it doesn't fit with that at all.*

These findings challenge the stereotype of the art school as somehow removed from commercial realities and of art school students as commercially naïve. They also support those scholars who have argued for entrepreneurship education now to be 'owned' by particular areas of the university, such as the business school (Carey and Naudin 2006, Hindle 2007, Jones et al 2012, Rae 2004).

5. Increases in understanding of business models

Qualitative data from the first focus group suggests that the visualisations did help make the concept of the business model more easily comprehensible, for instance through showing that it extended beyond revenue streams to 'back office' functions and communicating with customers. There is a clear sense in the qualitative data, too, that seeing the visualisation of the business model as a general concept, as experienced by those in the first focus group, increased understanding of business models. The subsequent focus group discussion increased this understanding even further. The same pattern – of the visualisations increasing understanding, and that understanding being further increased through subsequent discussion – can be discerned in quantitative data from the entrepreneurs and the second focus group, where discussions concerned the business models of specific business. The quantitative data also suggests that visualisations of specific business models in the cultural and creative industries (as seen by participants in the second focus group) were more useful than visualisations of the concept of a business models as a generic concept (as seen by participants in the first focus group), both in increasing understanding of business models and in showing the relevance of business models to the cultural and creative industries.

In terms of why the visualisations helped to increase understanding of business models, data from the second focus group suggests that participants liked the colours and (even though this focus group had to be conducted online) the fact that the visualisations were intended to be tactile. The following statement, for instance, was made after Participant G praised the tactile nature of the visualisations as helping overcome the 'off-putting' language of business:

Participant H: *The physical aspect is really important. As artists, graphic designers, artists in general, we do work in a very tangible sort of way. Even though you might get this thing on your screen, there's a physical aspect to even getting it to that point. That's a lot of the time what is dismissed in this type of arena, when you're talking about corporate aspects like business: bringing* *this physical aspect where you use images, and moving around blocks, colours. Those things are way more inclusive for everyone, especially in art practice.*

One unexpected finding in the quantitative data is that participants in the first focus group considered business models *less* relevant to the cultural and creative industries after seeing the visualisations than when they started the session, although all 'strongly agreed' about the relevance of business models by the end of the focus group (Figure 7). This is an anomaly. The graduate entrepreneurs clearly found the visualisations helpful, since both 'strongly agreed' with the statement that business models were relevant to the cultural and creative industries even before subsequent discussions. Quantitative data from the second focus group again suggests that the visualisations were very helpful – although in this case participants felt that their understanding was further increased by subsequent focus group discussion. Overall, all 13 participants who submitted quantitative data ended up 'strongly agreeing' with the claim that business models are relevant to the cultural and creative industries.

Members of the first focus group, who saw visualisations of the business model as a general concept, all 'agreed' or 'strongly agreed' that business models were relevant to their own practice after seeing the visualisations; all but one 'strongly agreed' by the end of the subsequent focus group discussion (Figure 8). The graduate entrepreneurs also 'strongly agreed' that business models were relevant to their industries after seeing the visualisations of specific business models. Finally, participants in the second focus group, who tested the visualisations of specific business models, all 'agreed' or 'strongly agreed' that business models were relevant to the cultural and creative industries – although, unexpectedly, the data shows a slight decline in the number who 'strongly agreed' after the subsequent focus group discussion. This again is an anomaly.

The project was not only intended to aid the understanding of focus group participants and the two entrepreneurs: it was also intended to help the three Design students who created the visualisations. Qualitative data from the second workshop suggests that there were improvements in their understanding of business models, apparently linked to the active learning component:

Me: *Do you think that going through all this has helped you understand business models?* ***Participant E:*** *When I look at this, I get it, I completely get it. But when I first looked at the traditional business [model canvas] I was so confused.*

Participant J: *It definitely says something. Taking the business model, which is quite complicated – not even complicated, very, I guess, bland, something that's a bit more corporate – and taking it a step back, just simplifying it, making it into something completely different, but still utilising the same qualities. I think it really does help. Like, I understand it a hell of a lot more than I did before the first session...*

It is illuminating to compare these comments to those made by the Design students in the initial workshop, when they first encountered the original business model canvas:

Participant J: *Oh my god. I hate it.*

Me: *That's so interesting. Why do you hate it?*

Participant J: *It's too boring.*

Participant H: *So boring, like, I'm already falling asleep.*

Participant J: *It needs to be more visual, the blocks, it's too... I don't know...*

These findings support the move away from the business plan to business model that is evident in entrepreneurship education (Jones and Penaluna 2013) but suggest that even the shift to written business models does not go far enough: we need, instead, to consider the importance of visualisation, and to note 'the clear parallels' between the pedagogic approaches associated with design disciplines and the learning outcomes advocated in entrepreneurship education (Penaluna and Penaluna 2009).

6. Conclusion

The sample size was small and not representative of the whole student body: the focus groups were made up of those who responded to an open call, while the two graduate entrepreneurs were approached directly. Any conclusions, then, must be tentative. However, qualitative data from workshops and focus groups, together with quantitative data from questionnaires, does suggest that the practice of 'business modelling' can be productive in an art school context. Several participants appear to have begun the project with little sense of what their own business model as a creative practitioner might be. There was a sense from some participants that the art school was essentially 'anti-business' or the 'antithesis' of business, although others acknowledged the need to familiarise themselves with business concepts. There was also a sense of participants shifting between professional identities, with one participant expressing 'art for art's sake' views in relation to one identity (painter) but self-identifying as 'somewhat business-minded' in relation to another identity (event promoter).

The data also suggests that this approach to teaching concepts related to entrepreneurship, in this case business models, has merit: all 13 participants who submitted quantitative data 'strongly agreed' that business models were relevant to the cultural and creative industries by the end of the project. On the whole, visualisations of specific business models appeared more effective in increasing understanding than visualisations of the business model as a generic concept. The Design students who created the visualisations also experienced an increase in their understanding. One reason for the effectiveness of this approach seems to relate to language: participants were more comfortable with the notion of 'sustaining their creative practice', for instance, than with the idea that they might have a 'business model'. Visual language appears important too: while the Design students found the business model canvas 'boring', focus group participants warmed to the fact that the Design students' visualisations were, by contrast, colourful and (at least intended to be) tactile.

In terms of next steps, there is potential to repeat the exercise with a larger sample, allowing more students and recent graduates to benefit. Repeating the project on a large scale would also generate more data, which would be useful in examining anomalies; these may be related to the small sample size, or flaws in the design of the questionnaire, but further investigation is required. While only the three Design students in this project saw the original business model canvas, it would be possible compare students' responses to the Design students' visualisations to their responses to the original business model canvas through A/B testing. It might be productive to undertake a similar project with a specific emphasis on business models with a 'triple bottom line' of economic growth, social justice and environmental sustainability (Elkington 1997, Honeyman and Jara 2019) or the circular economy (De Angelis 2018). Finally, the pedagogic approach adopted here, combining active learning with visualisation, testing and iteration, could be used to teach other entrepreneurial concepts, for instance cash-flow forecasts.

References

Bonwell C and Eison J (1991) *Active Learning: Creating Excitement in the Classroom* (AEHEERIC Higher Education Report No.1). Washington, D.C.: The George Washington University, School of Education and Human Development. Jossey-Bass

Campbell A, M Gutierrez and M Lancelott (2017) *Operating Model Canvas*. Hertogenbosch: Van Haren

Carey C, Naudin A (2006) Enterprise Curriculum for Creative Industries Students. *Education + Training*. 48(7), 518-531

Caves R (2000) *Creative Industries: Contracts Between Art and Commerce*. Cambridge, Mass.: Harvard University Press

Chesbrough H (2006) *Open Business Models: How to Thrive in the New Innovation Landscape*. Cambridge MA: Harvard Business School Press

Clark T, Osterwalder A and Pigneur, Y (2012) *Business Model You: A One-Page Method for Reinventing Your Career*. Hoboken: Wiley

De Angelis R (2018) *Business Models in the Circular Economy: Concepts, Examples and Theory*. Cham: Palgrave Macmillan

Elkington J (1997) *Cannibals with Forks: The Triple Bottom Line of 21st Century Business*. Oxford: Capstone

Hartley J, Potts J, Cunningham S, Flew T, Keane M and Banks J (2013) *Key Concepts in the Creative Industries*. London: Sage

Haynes J and Marshall L (2018) Reluctant Entrepreneurs: Musicians and Entrepreneurship in the 'New' Music Industry. *The British Journal of Sociology*. 69, 459-482

Hill D (2012) *Dark Matter and Trojan Horses: A Strategic Design Vocabulary*. Moscow: Strelka Press

Hindle K (2007) Teaching Entrepreneurship at University: From Wrong Building to Right Philosophy, in Fayolle, A. (ed.), *Handbook of Research in Entrepreneurship Education*, Edward Elgar, Cheltenham and Northampton, MA, 104-26

Hitachi Capital. 2020. UK University's Students Most Likely to Start or Manage a Business. https://www.hitachicapital.co.uk/business-finance/invoice-finance/invoice-finance-blog/uk-university-s-students-most-likely-to-start-or-manage-a-business/

Honeyman R and Jana T (2019) *The B Corp Handbook: How you can use Business as a Force for Good*. Oakland: Berrett-Koehler

Jones C, Matlay and H Maritz A (2012) Enterprise Education: For All, or Just Some? *Education +Training*, 54: 8/9, 813-824

Jones C, Penaluna A (2013) Moving Beyond the Business Plan in Enterprise Education. *Education +Training*. 55(8/9), 804-814

Kimbell L (2018) *Modelling Shared Value and Mediating Values: Describing Business Models in Performing Arts Organisations and Cultural Venues*. Creative Lenses. https://creativelenses.eu/wp-content/uploads/2019/05/Creative-Lenses-Value-and-Values.pdf

Osterwalder A and Y Pigneur (2010) *Business Model Generation*. Hoboken: Wiley

Penaluna A, Penaluna K (2009) Assessing Creativity: Drawing from The Experience of the UK's Creative Design Educators. *Education + Training*, 51(8/9), 718-732

Quinn M (2014) *Utilitarianism and the Art School in Nineteenth-Century Britain*. London: Pickering and Chatto

Rex B, Kaszynska P and Kimbell L. 2018. *Business Models for Arts and Cultural Organisations: Research Findings from Creative Lenses*. Creative Lenses research report: executive summary. https://ualresearchonline.arts.ac.uk/id/eprint/14392/1/Creative-Lenses-Research-Findings.pdf

Rodriguez J (2016) *To Sell or Not to Sell? An Introduction to Business Models (Innovation) for Arts and Culture Organisations*. https://www.ietm.org/system/files/publications/ietm_business-models_2016.pdf

Siok San Tan C K Frank Ng (2006) A problem based learning approach to entrepreneurship Education. *Education +Training*. 48(6), 416-428

Smith S and Beasley M (2011) Graduate entrepreneurs: intentions, barriers and solutions. *Education + Training*, 53 (8/9), 722-740

Van Der Pijl P, Lokitz J and Solomon L (2016) *Design a Better Business*. Hoboken: Wiley.

Van Wulfen G (2014) *The Innovation Expedition: A Visual Toolkit to Start Innovation*. Amsterdam: BIS

Young Foundation (2013) *The Social Business Model Canvas*. https://youngfoundation.org/social-innovation-investment/introducing-the-social-business-model-canvas-2/

Identifying and Overcoming the Barriers Which Hamper the Development of Social Entrepreneurship

Ruslan Pavlov
Central Economics and Mathematics Institute of the Russian Academy of Sciences, Moscow, Russia
pavlovru@mail.ru
DOI: 10.34190/EIE.20.062

Abstract: Nowadays, the level of development of social entrepreneurship in Russia is rather low. To find out the reasons that led to such state of things, some political measures in Russia and abroad are compared and analyzed. It is stated that in most part the successes of social entrepreneurship in the USA and the UK were determined by the active intervention of the state into the process of development of social entrepreneurship in the form of grants and premiums or by creating a special infrastructure in the form of social stock exchange or microfinance institutions. In Russia such processes were not initiated. Vice versa, neoliberalizm predominates in the political sphere, which, in turn, influenced much the development of social entrepreneurship. So, for instance, the law on social entrepreneurship, which was enacted on first reading, doesn't contain any measures of public support for social enterprises, which hampers much the development of social entrepreneurship. Besides, the wrong definition of social entrepreneurship based on the principles of self-sufficiency and financial sustainability is present in the scientific circles. It is stated that when such phenomena influence the process of determining the strategy of social entrepreneurship in Russia, a confusion, which results in the low level of development of social entrepreneurship, occurs. The findings of the paper are five factors that hamper much the development of social entrepreneurship in Russia. The main result of the paper is the conceptual model of institutions which encourage the development of social entrepreneurship.

Keywords: social entrepreneurship, innovation, neoliberalizm, governmental support

1. Introduction

Social entrepreneurship has become a very popular phenomenon among different scholars nowadays. It presents a great interest not only because of its extraordinary nature, but also due to the paradigm crisis of the neo-liberal economic model, whose features are becoming increasingly evident for the recent times. The events which happened on 17 September 2011, when the protest movement 'Occupy Wall Street' began in Zuccotti Park, were impressionable by their scale and impact. The wave of protest movements all over the world that followed this action showed that the social discontent with economic inequality of people has been growing. According to the Pew Research Center, from 1970 to 2018, the share of aggregate income going to middle-class households fell from 62% to 43%. Over the same period, the share held by upper-income households increased from 29% to 48%. The share flowing to lower-income households inched down from 10% in 1970 to 9% in 2018. These trends in income reflect the growth in economic inequality overall in the U.S. in the decades since 1980 (Horowitz et al., 2020). At the same time the share of economically excluded people is growing steadily, which is evidenced by the recent data on the high rates of unemployment in Portugal and Spain. It is interesting to note that the left movement ideology has attracted lots of new followers which reflects, in particular, in the Marxism revival. 'Why Marx was right?' by T. Eagleton proved to be a bestseller since lots of problems, connected with the system peculiarities of the paradigm crisis being criticized by the contemporary scholars, were efficiently elaborated in the Marxist' terms and some disturbances in the social and economic system resulted from the current trends of the mainstream policy were emphasized against the same disturbances the world economy faced more than a century ago (Eagleton, 2011). Such analogies have become of a great importance allowing for the crisis of methodological tools in the modern economics. Besides, the legitimacy of the left political movement in Europe is increasing, which is evidenced by the victory of the social-democrats at the last parliamentary elections in several European countries. These are, in turn, the signs of poverty growth, labor migration, social exclusion and the failure to solve such problems by means of traditional ways of applying market mechanisms. Such challenge suggests to think about social entrepreneurship as a possible way to mitigate the distortions stated above. It can be viewed not only as an economic or social phenomenon, but also as a political movement, as it challenges the dominating paradigm at all the levels of its pervasion (see, for instance, Nicholls, 2007), forcing the governments to introduce some important radical measures aimed at supporting its development.

2. Methodology of the study

The case study approach is used in this paper. To select the cases for analysis the following criterion is used. Since the majority of social enterprises are not financially sustainable, as the practice suggests, the most clear examples in this respect, which don't comply with the statement of neoliberal economists that social enterprises are financially sustainable, are selected. As a result of using this criterion of such inconsistency between the real practice and the principles of neoliberal theory of social entrepreneurship, four cases, including 2 Russian and 2 foreign social enterprises, were selected. Four cases were selected, because the scope of the paper is limited. The main criterion for choosing the five factors presented in the research was inconsistence of the real practice of social entrepreneurship with the neoliberal theory of social entrepreneurship. That inconsistence can be reflected in each of these factors, which hamper the development of social entrepreneurship.

Since the available literature on social entrepreneurship in Russia also contains some false views on the nature of social entrepreneurship, in this paper we are not going to unfold these existing approaches, but to present a new approach which seems to be better in describing the nature of social enterprises, because it relies upon special cases which were selected in the way presented above. The methodological approach used in the paper is deduction, since we move in studying the main factors that hamper the development of social entrepreneurship from single cases to their generalization.

3. Neoliberal ideology as the main factor, which hampers the development of social entrepreneurship in Russia

Nowadays a social entrepreneurship bill is discussed by the deputies of the Russian parliament. Despite the fact that this bill has been very much waited for by the nation, its last version is imperfect. On the one hand, a variety of different kinds of social entrepreneurship is reflected in this bill, but on the other hand, despite the fact that these entities have the lack of financial sources, the authors of the bill object to including the item of supporting social enterprises by the state into this bill. The authors of the bill are at the same time the authors of the first book on social entrepreneurship in Russia, in which they argue that social enterprises are self-sustainable entities (Moskovskaya, 2011). All these events are happening within the processes of social outsourcing and optimization of the entities of social area, which means that at the high level of the state power the view that the government shouldn't intervene into the economy predominates. This fact significantly hampers the process of development of social entrepreneurship in Russia, because many researchers have already shown that in order to ensure the effective development of social entrepreneurship, the government should intervene into this process. So, for instance, in Great Britain the government actively supports the social enterprises in the form of State initiatives. It is known that every year the UK government spends about 140 billion £ for such initiatives. In the United States a special program with providing grants for supporting social enterprises was launched by B. Obama and it was very successful and led to the intense growth of social entrepreneurship. At the same time in Russia the social entrepreneurship bill doesn't imply any kind of support for social enterprises, such as subsidies or grants. Allowing for the fact that the authors of the bill deliberately leave the item with the State support for the future consideration, it happens that the silence surrounding these problems is the worst response for that, because early attempts of the municipal authorities to provide subsidies to social enterprises will not get the support by the national law. That is due to the neoliberal policy of the Russian government, which is based on the assumption of A. Smith, who stated that the action of invisible hand of the market leads to the best result for the society. Indeed, this policy has already proved its inefficiency, which was evidenced by the economic crisis of 1929-1930 in the USA and the default in 1998 in Russia. The fact that the intervention is needed was proven by the policy of F.D. Roosevelt and the policy of Ye.M. Primakov's government, which restricted significantly the speculations at the stock market. If the government continues to apply the neoliberal policy to the development of social entrepreneurship, then it would be very hard for new social enterprises to survive in these "Spartan" conditions. So, to ensure the stable and prosperous growth of social entrepreneurship, one should get rid of such views, as they can mislead the society and can shape the wrong strategy of development of social enterprises.

4. Three cases of financial instability of social enterprises

The second factor, which hampers the development of social enterprises in Russia is the notion that the principle of self-sustainability and independence from the external sources underlie the essence of social entrepreneurship. This notion is widespread in the Russian political and scientific circles. In order to refute this notion, it is sufficient to present just three examples. The first one is connected with the social enterprise

"Benetech", which can be named as the most progressive social enterprise in the USA. This enterprise was initially named "Arkenstone" and it was engaged in manufacturing a special reading machine for the blind people. Its total amount of financial sources consisted of 33% of its external sources and of 67% of its own income in 2008 (see Figure 1).

The second example is connected with the social enterprise "APOPO" from Mozambique. This enterprise is engaged in landmine and tuberculosis detection, and is a very successive social enterprise, but it always needs some financial support from the external sources. During the period of twenty-one years since its foundation APOPO has developed into a mature organization. 2018 was marked by great progress – not only expanding its existing landmine detection program in Cambodia and securing independent registration in Angola but also enabling it to reach even more tuberculosis patients in Africa with the incredible expansion from 73 partner hospitals in two countries at the beginning of the year to 142 hospitals in three countries at the end of the year. The structure of financial sources of this company is rather diverse. In 2011 96 % in this structure consisted of external sources, such as grants and donations, and only 4% were of its own income (see Figure 2). So, how can we say that the social enterprise is based on self-sustainability? It's a nonsense.

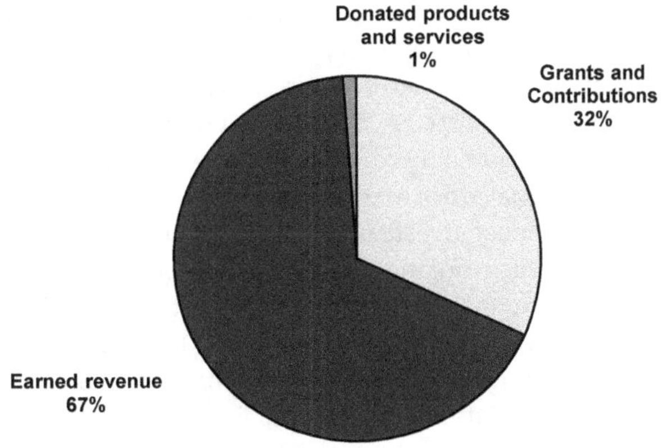

Source: Fruchterman (2008)

Figure 1: Financial sources of Benetech in 2008

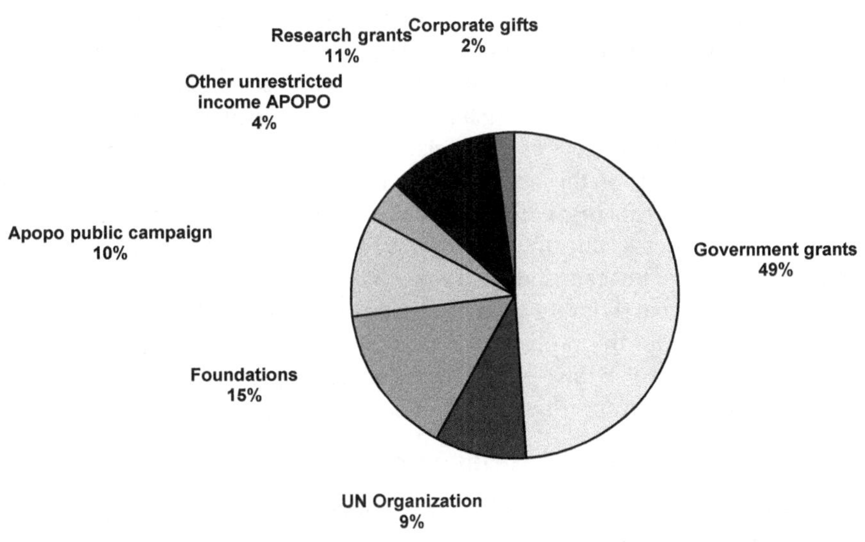

Source: APOPO (2011)

Figure 2: Financial sources of APOPO in 2011

The next case is connected with the well-known Russian social enterprise "Zabavushka". This social enterprise is manufacturing toys for the children, using the folk traditions. It was chosen for analysis, because it contradicts with the neoliberal theory. While the liberals argue that a social enterprise is the unit which is self-sustainable, this enterprise doesn't fit this requirement, because it always is seeking the financial sources and it lacks the necessary resources to hold exhibitions and other important events. So, it succeeded in getting a grant from G. Soros' fund, which amounted to $10 000 and several times it got the support from the local authorities. So, it has a mixed structure of financial sources and though it tries to develop its commercial activity, its scope is not sufficient to cover all the expenses of this social enterprise. So, it is not self-sustainable at all, and we have proved that social enterprises are not financially independent entities, and the above statement stating that social enterprises are self-sustainable is wrong. Thus, the second factor is the wrong statement that social enterprises are self-sustainable and financially independent.

5. The lack of high-quality infrastructure for the development of social entrepreneurship

The third factor is connected with creating the infrastructure for the development of social entrepreneurship in the form of microfinance organizations or in the form of social stock market. Each country has its own peculiarities of development of social entrepreneurship. So, for example, in the USA there is a special infrastructure, which enhances the development of social enterprise, named the Community Development Financial Institutions (CDFIs), which supports the development of microfinance institutions, in the UK there is a social stock exchange which serves as a supplementary source for supporting social enterprises. Indeed, for a long period of time the microfinance organizations in Russia were associated with unscrupulous and unprofessional entities, and as some journalists say, it was a sort of banditry. Even then some deputies from the State Duma initiated the bill aimed at liquidation of microfinance organizations as the criminal ones. Though, that bill wasn't approved. As for the social stock market, nowadays there is a lack of impact investors that form a basis for such stock market. Those impact investors who take part in the meetings at the Impact Hub Moscow are not interested much in creating such organism as the social stock exchange. Maybe the Russian social enterprises are aware that it's rather expensive to have such market, because in the UK the cost of listing at the Alternative Investment Market fees for listing are between £ 300,000 and £ 500,000 even excluding marketing costs (Hartzell, 2007). Besides, the high-quality infrastructure cannot evolve without including the international actors, such as the International Association of Investors in the Social Economy, which was thoroughly investigated by Mendell and Nogales (2009). So, that is also the factor that hampers the development of social entrepreneurship in Russia.

6. The social enterprise "Orto-Lux" as an example of loss-making production

The fourth factor is connected with using false criteria of choosing the best project by the experts of the fund "Our future" in the competition for choosing the best socio-entrepreneurial initiative. This fund offers the zero-interest loans for realizing social projects, and the main criteria, which are used by the experts are the self-sustainability and the novelty of the project, though the common sense proves that one should be guided by such criteria as social need in the project and its social significance. So, for example, the production of orthopedic shoes for the children suffering from cerebral palsy by the social enterprise "Orto-Lux", is a project, which doesn't have any new features and it is not self-sustainable. It is rather loss-making, and it always needs some financial support. One of the loss-making factors of this social enterprise is the absence of the preferential rent rate for social enterprises. The manager of this social enterprise Elena Seliverstova had to sue the Moscow government several times when the special resolution on the preferential rent rate for social enterprises was in effect, and she succeeded in this process, but now, when this resolution has been repealed by the Moscow government, she cannot sue anymore. Instead, she has to pay 300 thousand rubles for the rent for space in a commercial building, which is not a cheap rent rate at all. Such kinds of support as loans of the fund "Our Future", though they are interest-free, don't fit for this project. Though its social significance is so high, that it's very hard to overestimate it. The social need in it is also rather high, which is proved by the high demand for this production. So, the fourth factor is the wrong criterion of self-sustainability used by the fund "Our Future".

7. The lack of governmental support for social enterprises

The fifth factor is the absence of necessary legislation for the development of social entrepreneurship in Russia. Though recently the State Duma has adopted the law on social entrepreneurship in the form of amendments to the law of small and medium sized enterprises (SMEs), we cannot say that the Russian social enterprises can benefit from this law. Indeed, no kinds of financial support for social enterprises are reflected in this law, and this fact makes this law meaningless. At least, two measures of state support are known in other countries.

These are subsidies and participation of social enterprises in the process of public procurement. The subsidies can be used, in particular, for decreasing the rental of premises, which is very high now. For a long time, in Moscow there was a provision, according to which, preferential rental rate was available for the people, willing to launch a social project. Now this provision is repealed, and the social entrepreneurs in Russia have to pay the commercial rental rate, which is much higher than that of preferential one. In order to correct this situation, one should make an amendment in the Federal law, according to which, social enterprises have the right to get the preferential rental rate from the regional authority. Only that way would make this law useful for the social entrepreneurs. On the other hand, we should also allow for the experiment of the UK social enterprises, which suggests that the public procurement is a powerful tool for development of social enterprises. As is known, annually the UK government spends around $140 billion for the public procurement. That fact contributes much to the high rate of early-stage social entrepreneurial activity in Great Britain, which is calculated as a percentage of adult people trying to create a social enterprise within 3.5 years (see Figure 3). So, in order to make this law effective for social enterprises one should set a rate for the social enterprises participating in this process at the level of 25% of the total volume of public procurement in Russia. That would encourage greatly the growth of social entrepreneurship in Russia.

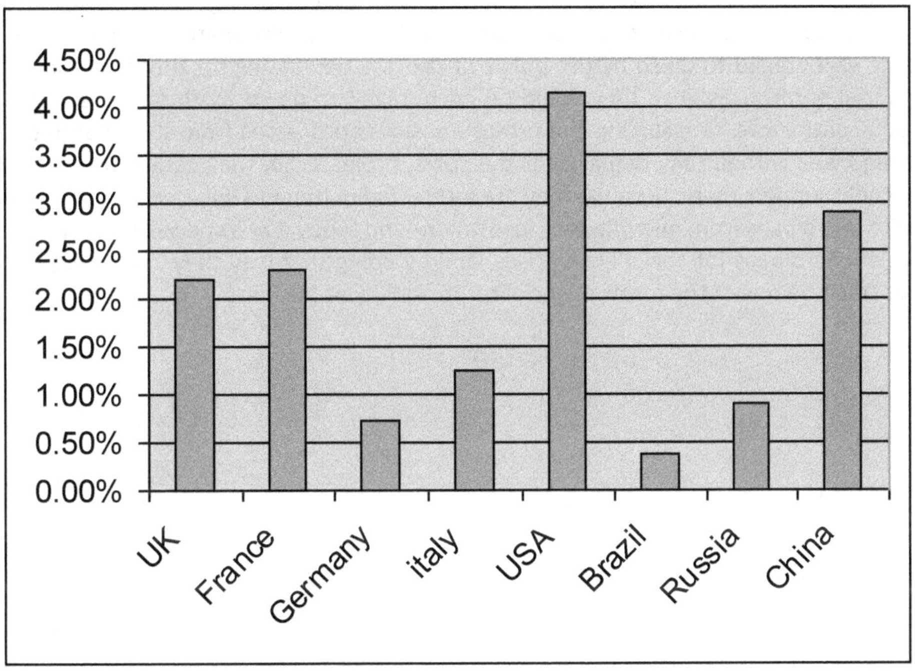

Source: GEM (2009)

Figure 3: Early-stage social entrepreneurial activity (SEA) rate in different countries, 2009

8. A model of interaction between different institutions supporting social enterprises

In this section we provide one of possible models of interaction between different institutions supporting the development of social enterprises. It's necessary to mention such interesting program as Pay for Success which was initiated by B. Obama's Administration in 2009. Indeed, this program was a way of government support of the social entrepreneurship programs, but only those programs which proved to be successful during the process of their realization. Americans have developed programs to tackle seemingly intractable problems, from homelessness to illiteracy, from chronic disease to climate change and more. Some of these services are already proven by rigorous evaluation to be effective; others show tremendous promise to move the needle. But they often are not equipped to make the kind of impact that the U.S. nation needs. Pay for Success (PFS) can be a solution. It tests and advances promising and proven interventions, while providing taxpayer (or other) dollars for successful outcomes for families, individuals, communities, or natural resources. From the other hand, it's necessary to mention such kind of government support as the public procurements which played a major role in strengthening the financial position of the British social enterprises. And the third participant of the support mechanisms of social enterprises at the macro-level are Community Development Financial Institutions (CDFIs). A CDFI is a financial institution that provides credit and financial services to underserved markets and populations, primarily in the USA, but also in the UK. A CDFI may be a community development bank, a community development credit union, a community development loan fund, a community development venture capital fund, a microenterprise development loan fund, or a community development corporation. In 2006 there were approximately 1,250 CDFIs consisting of more than 500 community development loan funds, more than 350 community development banks, more than 290 community development credit unions, more than 80 community development venture capital funds (Wikipedia, 2020).

At the meso-level of mechanisms supporting social enterprises we should mention such institutions as the social stock exchange and microfinance institutions. So, what should be done to enhance the efficiency of the social stock exchange as a new financial tool for supporting social enterprises? First, we should conclude that this instrument should not act as an isolated unit. It should be implemented into the system of different actors supporting social enterprises, along with such potential investors as private sector companies and microfinance institutions (see Figure 3). These actors should interact in such manner that enables a cooperation between them. For instance, microfinance institutions should be encouraged to invest their funds into the social enterprises. They could do it through providing loans for attracting brokers who could find respectable institutional and strategic investors for the social stock exchange. These loans could be repaid from the profits that brokers could get from selling shares. The system would be enhancing by encouraging private sector companies to act in this process. The private sector companies could acquire shares at the social stock exchange, and they could be encouraged to do so by the policy of tax rate decreasing for those companies, who would invest into the social enterprises. Also they could be encouraged to do so by the perspective of using social enterprises as sub-contractors, outsourcing them those business processes from their contract activities that could be performed well without any damage for the social projects. So, they could control them and at the same time they could support them, because they are interested in them as sub-contractors. At the same time they could acquire microloans from microfinance institutions and repay it at a special interest rate that could be higher than that of microloans for social enterprises, and by doing that way they could support microfinance institutions. That could be one of the forms of social responsibility of business.

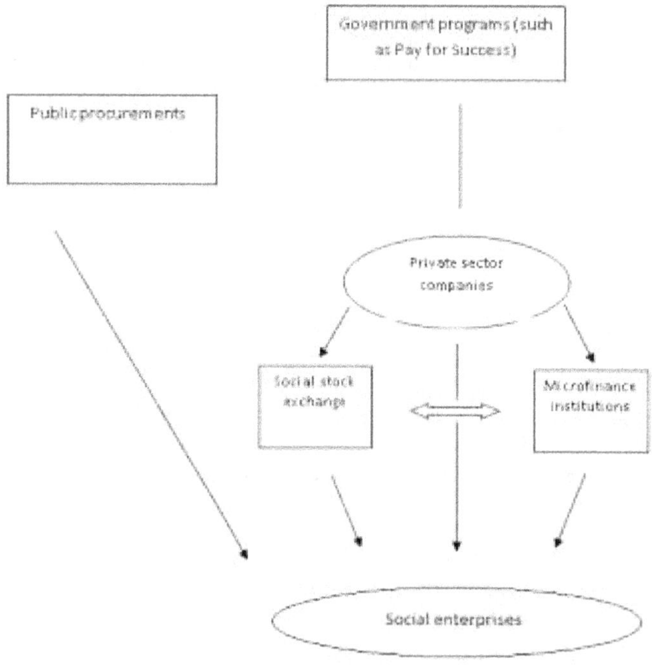

Figure 4: Interaction between different elements of support system for social enterprises

At the same time if the market lacks any necessary investors to maintain its normal performance, microfinance institutions could act as investors themselves, acquiring shares of social enterprises listed at this exchange, and so facilitating the work of this exchange by supporting it. Having much experience in the financial sector services, as well as being successful in raising capital, they could act as a special mutual fund, the funds of which could be spent to acquire shares of social enterprises, and the dividends could be used as micro-loans for other social enterprises being their customers.

The UK social stock exchange acts as a private limited company now, but it should be protected against different ways of takeovers, especially hostile ones. First, the government could protect this financial institute by holding a controlling interest in this exchange as a special social purpose institution. Otherwise it could be captured by the large private companies, and the situation would be similar to the consequences of social outsourcing, when a lot of social entities in the UK were managed by the private business. That led to a disaster in the performance of these entities, because of reducing social costs by new management, which didn't act in line with public interest, but instead was pursuing its own. These cases were highlighted in a special report on social outsourcing in the UK (see Williams, Richardson, 2012). Another measure of securing social stock exchange against any threats of privatizing could be expressed in introducing the asset lock principle, which is often used to protect social enterprises against possible abuses of the private sector.

9. In conclusion

So, we have considered the basic factors, which hamper the process of development of social entrepreneurship in Russia. Indeed, there might be more factors than five, but we have intentionally restricted that amount to analyze deliberately each of them and to derive their negative influence on the development of social enterprises. Each factor is worth of special attention, as each of them presents a barrier, which needs to be overcome, and as the analysis of foreign experience suggests, in the case of getting rid of this barrier, the rate of social entrepreneurship increases significantly. So, for instance, the United Kingdom has got rid of the neoliberal myth concerning the decreased role of the government in the economy. That resulted in the high rate of development of social entrepreneurship in this country. Another example is connected with the USA. In this country the infrastructure for the development of social entrepreneurship exists. It comprises such institutions as Community Development Financial Institutions (CDFIs), which influence greatly the process of growth of social entrepreneurship in this country. So, in order to make social entrepreneurship develop effectively, one should learn from the foreign countries to derive lessons for making an effective strategy of development of social entrepreneurship.

In future we are going to conduct a quantitative research, i.e. to execute the econometric analysis of the impact of social entrepreneurship on the socio-economic development of several countries.

References

APOPO Annual report 2011. [online], www.apopo.org/annual-reports/APOPO_annual_report_2011.pdf

Eagleton, T. (2011) *Why Marx was right,* Yale University Press, London.

Global Entrepreneurial Monitor (2009), [online], www.gemconsortium.org/report/47108

Fruchterman J. (2008) Developing Information Technology to Meet Social Needs. Innovations: Technology, Governance, Globalization, 2008. no. 3 (3), Cambridge: MIT Press, pp. 83-99.

Hartzell, J. (2007) "Creating an ethical stock exchange", [online] Skoll Centre for Social Entrepreneurship, www.sbs.ox.ac.uk/Skoll/Ethical_Stock_Exchange.pdf

Horowitz J.M., Igielnik R., Kochhar R. (2020) Most Americans say there is too much economic inequality in the U.S., but fewer than half call it a top priority, http://www.pewsocialtrends.org/2020/01/09/trends-in-income-and-wealth-inequality

Mendell, M., Nogales, R. (2009) "Social entrepreneurs in OECD member countries: what are the financial streams?" in *The changing boundaries of social enterprises.* Ed. A. Noya, Seoul, Work Together Foundation.

Moskovskaya A.A. (ed.) (2011) Sotsialnoye predprinimatelstvo v Rossii i v mire: praktika i issledovaniya (Social entrepreneurship in Russia and in the world: practice and studies. Higher School of Economics, Moscow.

Nicholls, A. (2007), *What is the Future of Social Enterprise in Ethical Markets?* Office of the Third Sector, London.

Wikipedia (2020) Community Development Financial Institutions, [online], www.en.wikipedia.org/wiki/ Community_development_financial_institution

Williams Z., Richardson C. (2012) The Shadow State. A report about outsourcing of public services, [online], www.socialenterprise.org.uk/uploads/files/2012/12/the_shadow_state_3_dec1.pdf

Organizational Innovation: The Contributions of Joseph A. Schumpeter

Tor Helge Pedersen
Inland University College of Applied Sciences, Lillehammer, Norway
Tor.Helge.Pedersen@inn.no
DOI: 10.34190/EIE.20.131

Abstract: Recent surveys in the field of innovation studies argue that Schumpeter is the most important source of scholarly inspiration (Fagerberg and Verspagen 2009; Martin 2012). In addition, Schumpeter was an early proponent of the term "organizational innovation" (Damanpour and Aravind 2011), and according to Williamson (1983), Schumpeter was one of the initial few economists who recognized the importance of organizational innovation. Even though there has been an increasing interest in Schumpeter's work over the last 30 years, his work on organizational innovation has received less attention. This can be observed in research on organizational innovation where researchers have opted to use other conceptualizations of organizational innovation, probably because Schumpeter is foremost connected to a macro-economic conception of innovation (Ruttan 1959; Damanpour 2014). Motivated by this observation, this paper revisits Schumpeter's work on organizational innovation to explore how he understood this type of innovation and discuss its relevance to organization research today. The theoretical discussion is based on eight of Schumpeter's publications from 1912 to 1949 (approximately 2,400 pages), which focus on organizational innovation. While Schumpeter's understanding of organizational innovation usually held the narrow view that it was a new form of organization of any industry (Schumpeter 1934), the central finding in this paper is that four possible conceptualizations can be identified in Schumpeter's scholarly work. Three of these are clearly about organizational innovation and remain relevant in organization research today. For example, Schumpeter's category of changes in methods of production is both about technological process and organizational process innovation. This category or concept is relevant to understanding the efforts to rationalize production today (i.e. production that exploits new technology). A second example is that new type of organizations (Schumpeter 1939) can also be included in Schumpeter's understanding of organizational innovation. This finding is interesting since Schumpeter's considered new technology (also important today) as possibility for new resource combinations—i.e. for new forms of organization.

Keywords: innovation, organizational innovation, Schumpeter, technology, organization, innovation studies, organization studies

1. Introduction

Organizational innovation can be conceptualized in at least two ways. First, it can be viewed as a novel output and a category in a theory of innovation-driven economic development (Schumpeter 1934). The second (and much more common) conception is that organizational innovation is a specific type of organizational change; it involves "adopting something new to the organization", and this includes ideas, structures, models, technology, products and services (e.g. Hage 1999, p. 599). In other words, this second view proposes that innovation "includes the process of developing and implementing a new idea – whether it is a new technology, product, organizational process or arrangement" (Schroeder et al. 1989, p. 108). This paper discusses the writings of Schumpeter in relation to organizational innovation, including his conceptualization. It investigates how Schumpeter understood organizational innovation, and what relevance his arguments have in organization research today. Several scholars have remarked that organizational innovation has got little attention compared to technological innovation (Williamson 1970, 1983; Edquist, Hommen, and McKelvey 2001), and more recently, scholars have emphasized the possibilities for competitive advantaged and better organizational performance through organizational innovation (Damanpour 2014; Sandidas 2005).

Essentially, Schumpeter's definition of organization innovation is the introduction of a new form of organization to any industry, and this is the concept that he is most widely known for. Furthermore, he saw innovation from the view of the economy as a whole (Penrose 1959); in other words, he held a macro-economic conception of innovation (Ruttan 1959; Romanelli, 1991; Damanpour 2014). Although he stated that, "Technological progress is increasingly becoming the business of teams of trained specialists" (Schumpeter 1942, p. 132), several scholars have highlighted that he did not look inside the firm to identify, for example, the sources and processes of innovation (Ruttan 1959; Freeman 1990), how innovations disrupt the status quo and take place or the content of innovation (Loasby 2007). Rather, he only registered creative destruction or new firms disrupting existing firms (Loasby 2007). Moreover, it has been argued that Schumpeter overlooked or excluded innovations in "the field of business organization" (Chandler and Redlich 1961, p. 23). Finally, Williamson (1970), who advocated for studies of OI, pointed out that Schumpeter (1934; 1942) had used confusing and misleading examples (e.g.

conventional monopoly terms) in his definitions, although his later definition in 1942 came "closer to organizational innovation in the structural sense" (Williamson 1970, p. 176).

Motivated by the situation described above—and partly inspired by Becker, Knudsen and March (2006)—this paper delves into less known writings of Schumpeter. While Becker et al. (2006) based on new knowledge showed that Schumpeter was also interested in the emergence of novelty, this paper focuses on how Schumpeter understood organizational innovation in different writings between 1912 and 1949. This is especially relevant since many (e.g. Williamson 1970, 1983; Sanidas 2005; Loasby 2007) rely predominantly on Schumpeter's most known writings (i.e. Schumpeter 1934; 1942) and thus exclude his 1,095-paged *Business Cycles* and other publications. It is also worth noting that his 255-paged 1934 English edition of *Theory of Economic Development* (TED) has substantial changes compared to the 548-paged original German edition (1912), a fact that has also been stressed by others (e.g. Becker, Knudsen and Swedberg 2012). Finally, although this paper includes a range of Schumpeter's publications (four books and five articles), there are still several publications that are not included, such as his histories of economic analysis and the abridged 1964 version of *Business Cycles*. The remainder of the paper is organized as follows: in Section 2, the Schumpeterian approach is presented; Section 3 presents different conceptualizations of organizational innovation that can be identified in Schumpeter's writings; and Section 4 discusses two of the conceptualizations (e.g. new forms of organization).

2. Elements in the Schumpeterian approach

Schumpeter used the term "organizational innovation" in several places in *Business Cycles* (e.g. Schumpeter 1939, p. 385). Before and after that, he pointed to this concept with both examples and definitions in all of his publications that are included in this review. In 1912, he included it among the examples of what he called "new combinations" (Schumpeter 1912, pp. 158-9). In 1927, he included and exemplified the concept as part of what he henceforth called "innovation", and he defined it as "such changes of the combination of factors of production as cannot be effected by infinitesimal steps or variations on the margin" (Schumpeter 1927, p. 295). While in 1934 he saw innovation as a novel output (e.g. new form of organization of any industry), later, in *Business Cycles,* he defined innovation as setting up a new production function, that is, a new combination of factors of production (technological change), and he explained that this covered "the case of new commodity, as well as those of a new form of organization such as a merger, the opening up a new market, and so on" (Schumpeter 1939, p. 87). He understood innovation as change of economic significance, and he said it "may be directly copied as a whole or in part" (Schumpeter 1939, p. 131).

In Schumpeter's writings, organizational innovation was further conceptualized as one among five categories in innovation-driven economic development. He explained innovation as a source of economic change or business cycles (Schumpeter 1934; 1939). His work is often connected to a macro-economic conception of innovation (Romanelli 1991; Damanpour and Aravind 2011; Damanpour 2014), which considers innovation for its impact on industry or the economy as a whole (Dopfer 2012) and assumes that economic development is driven by the discontinuous emergence of new combinations that replace the old ways of doing things (Schumpeter 1934).

However, in actuality, his framework operates on different levels, including both micro and macro (Santarelli and Pesciarelli 1990) or micro, meso and macro levels (Dopfer 2012). Put simply, the micro level is the entrepreneur that carries out an innovation (entrepreneurial activities) and the emergence of entrepreneurs in clusters. Schumpeter (1934, p. 229) said that entrepreneurs "remove the obstacles for the others". Using the emergence of the motor-car industry as an example, he said that, "the first success will always produce a cluster" (Schumpeter 1935, p. 6). The meso level refers to the swarming of entrepreneurs and followers who imitate the original innovation (Schumpeter 1934; 1935; 1939). Innovations tend to cluster in certain contexts (Schumpeter 1939), because "the appearance of one of few entrepreneurs facilitates the appearance of others" (Schumpeter 1934, p. 228). Finally, this leads to changes, or more specifically, economic impact on specific industries or the economy from within (macro level). For example, Dopfer (2012) argues that the process of creative destruction runs through all levels of micro-meso-macro.

Schumpeter (1934; 1939) separated invention from innovation and emphasized economically relevant effects. Consequently, he has been criticized for paying little attention to the sources and origins of innovation as well as the process of innovation (Solo 1951; Ruttan 1959; Freeman 1990). Although he saw the importance of OI, technological innovation was probably the most important for Schumpeter. He saw technology as a key factor or engine in economic development, and he arrived at the notion that technical change is to be understood as a case of innovation. He used the term technological innovation in only a few places (e.g. Schumpeter 1939, pp. 289, 375), but he stressed in his later book that it is "new technology (...) the new type of organization" that "commands a decisive cost or quality advantage" (Schumpeter 1942, p. 84).

As seen, Schumpeter emphasized the role of the entrepreneur; yet, he also said that every "social environment has its own ways of filling the entrepreneurial function" (Schumpeter 1949, p. 84). In his early writings, he attributed innovation to new men and new firms. In his later writings, he also noticed entrepreneurship in big units in large firms (Schumpeter 1928) or as a "team of trained specialists" in large firms (Schumpeter 1942, p. 132). Finally, even though organizational innovation does not occupy a very large place in Schumpeter's writings, it is mentioned or discussed in most of his publications between 1911 and 1949.

3. The conceptualization of organizational innovation

Four possible conceptualizations of organizational innovation can be identified in Schumpeter's writings.

3.1 New organization of industry

This understanding of organizational innovation can be observed in several places in Schumpeter's writing (1912; 1927; 1934; 1947), and this is the common understanding of OI in innovation research (Fagerberg 2005). For example, Schumpeter used the example of *trust organization form*, and thus, of how the merger movement changed the structure of American industry by creating larger organizations. Later examples can include the market concentration of retailers in larger groupings and the transformation of individual shops into chains or franchises. One possible Norwegian example is the first introduction of the inter-municipal Industrial Estates Corporation in Stavanger in 1968, the year before oil was discovered. This industrial estate later became Forus Industrial Park, which housed many oil companies and approximately 45,000 employees and was important in economic growth and development. Carrying out this idea is arguably an example of carrying out a "reorganization" of industry.

A second example is the corporatization and merger that took place in the Norwegian energy industry. Before the Norwegian Energy Act of 1990, most electricity works were organized as in-house municipal enterprises, municipal departments or inter-municipal associations, and they were often called companies. The new act abolished local monopolies and introduced competition (liberalization). The result was not privatization but rather corporatization and creation of larger regional power companies. Key themes in the advent of this new situation were creation, joint-stock companies, mergers, consolidations and concerns with different subsidiaries.

The third example is the opposite; it is about splitting up so-called cornerstone companies or old state enterprises into smaller firms that carried on under new ownership. This happened in several local communities in Norway since the late 1980s, but the most successful ones were Kongsberg Weapon Factory in 1987 and the Raufoss Ammunition Factories in 2004 (which were turned into 35 independent firms). These examples were a kind of creative destruction; the local transformations created many new firms that were located in the same place, now called industrial parks (and clusters), with different support services being made available to the smaller and larger firms.

3.2 Changes in the methods of production

This category is also called process innovation. It is included as an example of OI based on several examples used by Schumpeter. In most of the highlighted publications, he used examples connected to technology, such as mechanized factories and electrified factories (1942), or to "technological novelties into the production" (1947, p. 153). However, there are places where he also used the example of "Taylorization of work" (Schumpeter 1939, p. 84), thus including the organization of the production process in his model. Edquist et al. (2001), who also built on *Business Cycles,* have suggested dividing this category into the two types: technological process innovations (machines, robots, and IT equipment) and organizational process innovation (new ways to organize business activities, such as production or R & D). This understanding is also supported in later accounts of innovation studies (e.g. Fagerberg 2005). Historical examples of these two types are Henry Ford and the moving assembly line and Frederick Taylor and the rationalization of work. Both of these are also examples of how the technological side and organizational side complemented each other (Sanidas 2005). Both types were important in rationalization before, and both illustrate the interdependence of technology and organization in mass production. More contemporary examples of the organizational process type are just-in-time, TQM, the Toyota

Production System and the principles of lean production. Further, disruptive technologies (e.g. digitalized production technology, robots) today are often not only about production and distribution, but may have consequences for the organizational form. Schumpeter (1939; 1942) describes creative destruction as a competitive process that advances the evolution of new organizational forms in response to the development of new technologies. He considered technological innovation to be the primary factor also in the creation of possibilities for structural change and the possibility for new resource combinations— i.e. for new forms of organization.

3.3 New form of organization

This understanding of OI is found in Schumpeter's later publications (Schumpeter 1939, p. 87; 1942, p. 84), but he does not explicitly define it; instead, he exemplifies it with, for example, the idea of the merger. He explains later that mergers often mean new units of control, new principles of management, new possibilities of industrial research and new technology (Schumpeter 1939, p. 404). Even though Schumpeter does not explicitly define forms of organization, in *Business Cycles*, he describes cases of carrying out new organizational innovations (forms) such as the joint-stock company, chartered companies, trust organization, the holding company and mergers, and he gives several examples, such as the East India Company, Credit Mobilier, Standard Oil, Edison General Electric, and United States Steel Corporation. He also refers to the "setting up of new business organizations such as department stores" (Schumpeter 1939, p. 84). Furthermore, he includes examples of changes in organizational form such as the following: "The fifth Juglar then brought the completion of the organizational innovation that was to set the outstanding example for other industries" (Schumpeter 1939, p 385), namely, Standard Oil. Moreover, he mentions holding companies such as the United States Steel Corporation from 1901.

In contrast, later researchers have further studied new forms and changes in forms as organizational innovation or invention. Chandler (1977) and Williamson (1983) have described economically significant organizational innovations that came after 1840 in the development of the modern corporation, and several of these were changes from existing organizational forms to something new. Chandler (1962) analysed the creation and impact of an OI (the M-form) in four large American firms: Sears Roebuck, DuPont, Standard Oil and General Motors. Later, Padgett (2012) analysed the creation of the partnership systems of Datini and Medici in Renaissance Italy. Put shortly, these examples were both about carrying out new organizational forms and changing existing organizations. This conception also has support from those who only referred to Schumpeter's (1934; 1942) most famous works (e.g. Williamson 1970; Loasby 2007).

3.4 The foundation of a new enterprise

The last possible conception of OI is the most clearly mentioned one in the first German edition of TED. Schumpeter (1912) stated here that the typical case of a new combination was the foundation of a new enterprise. He also said that this represented the organizational, commercial and technical side of the matter. In a later publication, he said that such new firms "generally do not arise out of old ones but start producing beside them" (Schumpeter 1934, p. 66) because incumbent firms have difficulty in giving up old routines, while new firms do not have this problem. In *Business Cycles* he observed so-called modus operandi of innovation, and one was that innovation entailed the construction of a new plant (and equipment) or rebuilding of an old plant (Schumpeter 1939), indicating that this also happened in existing firms. In one of his latest publications, he said that entrepreneurship in the 1800s was often meant to "put into practice a novel method of production by embodying it in a new firm" (Schumpeter 1947, p. 154). In other words, a new firm may involve using a new method of production, or it may be a new type of firm. One example of the latter is illuminated in *Business Cycles*. The Credit Mobilier was set up in 1852 in Paris as a new type of bank that challenged the existing ones in several countries. It was followed by an "outburst" of such banks (Schumpeter 1939, pp. 349-50). These banks were novel, since they combined traditional banking and investment banking, and especially in Germany, they "supplied much of what today would be called venture capital" (Chandler 1990, p. 419). Furthermore, in Scandinavia, there were attempts at establishing such banks (e.g. the Norwegian Credit Bank). These are historical examples; therefore, one can discuss whether this conception should be included in the further discussion as typical for Schumpeter's model of OI. New firms can be introducers of new combinations (Schumpeter 1912; 1934), but only a limited part of new firms is novel in this way.

4. Discussion

As seen above, it is only the fourth example (Section 3.4) that is not necessary to the framework of organizational innovation. Among the other three conceptions of organizational innovation, it is process innovation (of the organizational type) that is easiest to relate to the three levels in a Schumpeterian approach: entrepreneurial activities, swarm of followers imitate and economic impact in society or industry. Entrepreneurial activities include carrying out innovations such as the moving assembly line and later just-in time (Sanidas 2005). The moving assembly line is an example of technological process innovation, while just-in-time is an example of organizational process innovation. Both innovations have had their respective followers and economic impacts. Product innovation and process innovation are the types that have gotten most attention (Williamson 1970; Bruland and Mowery 2005, Sanidas 2005). While product innovation is oriented towards income and growth, process innovation is oriented toward rationalization and cost cutting. Although these examples are older examples, there are several examples today that illustrate the same phenomenon, such as new machines, robots, AI, digitalization, platforms, IT equipment and the principles of lean production. As with mass production and just-in-time, though to a different extent, these changes have also had a swarm of imitators among other entrepreneurs and followers.

Schumpeter also emphasized the importance of economic impact, not just change, as measured by, for example, the "effect of variations in the rate of both technological and organizational changes on economic growth and development" (Ruttan 1959, p. 606). Again, this concerns the macro level, whether it is industry or economy. The economic impact of mass production is well known. When it comes to the just-in-time system, it was an important part of the rapid catch-up of Japanese production to Western productivity levels in the 20th century and that it contributed to the transformation of the global car industry (Fagerberg and Godinho 2005). There is also a connection with organization research today, as it relates to contemporary examples of creating new opportunities with new technology (robots, AI, and so on) in production and distribution.

The two volumes of *Business Cycles* (1939) show that Schumpeter included new organizational forms as part of OI. This is evidenced in several historical examples. There are studies that more or less build on Schumpeter, which have looked at such organizational innovations as for example the M-form (Chandler 1962, 1977; Williamson 1970, 1983). There are others that interpret Schumpeter's conception of OI in this direction (Williamson 1970, 1983; Loasby 2007). Entrepreneurial activities cover both founding new firms and carrying out different innovations. Starting a new firm may also include carrying out an innovation. The earlier mentioned example of Credit Mobilier represented a new type of bank that forced existing ones to follow its example. Schumpeter (1939, pp. 349-50) even talked about the "outburst"—when several other bankers followed—as an example of swarming. Restructuring an organization can involve carrying out an OI. For example, Schumpeter (1939) laid heavy emphasis on the merger movement, and he remarked that mergers in railroads foreshadowed hundreds of other mergers in manufacturing, distribution and retailing (McCraw 2006). Since restructuring may involve carrying out an OI, Chandler's (1962) study of four corporations that created four variants of the M-form could be taken as another example of entrepreneurial activities. Finally, changing an organization may involve establishing new organizational units (Schumpeter 1939, p. 84) such as the internal research lab, which is often mentioned as an important aspect of OI during the second industrial revolution (Bruland and Mowery 2005). This OI is arguably also a new process innovation since the units become part of the business processes such as product development (Edquist et al. 2001).

New forms of organization can be seen in relation to both swarming (meso) and macro-economic levels (economic impact); for example, the aforementioned merger movement resulted in a reshaping of the structure of American industry (Schumpeter 1939). These changes are linked with the execution of a new organization of any industry. Both Chandler (1962) and Williamson (1983) include impact in their discussions. Williamson (1983) remarked that the steel reorganization that Andrew Carnegie carried out benefited both Carnegie and society. Similarly, the organizational innovations that developed the modern corporation in areas such as distribution had economic impact (Chandler 1977; Williamson 1983). Along with new ways of organizing production, these new ways of organizing distribution (Chandler 1990), enabled the United States to forge ahead in the 20th century (Bruland and Mowery 2005).

Finally, both process innovation (organizational process innovation) and organizational innovation are important because they both relate to technological change today as well as in the past (Schumpeter 1939; Chandler 1977), and they are both linked to interdependence between technology and organization (Schumpeter 1939;

Chandler, 1977). Again with the merger example, Schumpeter pointed out that technological innovation could have the following relationship to OI: mergers enable "new types of plant and equipment (...) technology" (Schumpeter 1939, p. 404). Chandler (1977, p. 87) found later that the "swift victory of the railway over the waterway resulted from organizational as well as technological innovation". One the other hand, new technology also enables new organizational forms. The telegraph (invented in 1844) was important in the coordination that enabled the emergence of the large centralized railroad firm (Chandler 1977), and the telephone (1876) enabled firms to physically separate headquarters from field operations. As before, there is new technology today that presents the possibility for new resource combinations as a new form of organization, such as shared services, platform organization and increasing online customer self-service while reducing front offices. Regarding process innovation, interdependence of technological and organizational process innovation occurs when changes in one necessitate changes in the other (Bruland and Mowery 2005).

5. Conclusion

Schumpeter wrote about the great organizational changes in the past that followed, for example, the introduction of railroads, electrification and motorization. His writings are still important in the field of innovation studies today, although OI still receives relatively limited attention. Although Schumpeter did not concentrate on processes inside organizations as part of OI, this paper has argued that his work should be of relevance to varied fields of organization research, especially the field that focuses on the emergence, spread and implementation of new organizational ideas. This paper has shown that at least three conceptions of OI can be connected to Schumpeter. The first, new organization of any industry, is both well-known and still relevant in the contemporary business context (see 3.1). The second, organizational process innovation, is identified through the examples Schumpeter (1939) mentioned around Taylorization of work. At least since Ford (technological process innovation) and Taylor (organizational process innovation), there has been an interdependency of the two types and of later efforts of rationalization of production and other business processes (e.g. robots, information technology and AI, in today's context). The third conception is new forms of organization, which are either embodied in new firms or carried out through reorganization. This is also linked to new technologies, which present many possibilities for resource combinations and new form of organization.

References

Becker, M.C., Knudsen, T. and March, J.G. (2006) "Schumpeter, Winter, and the Sources of Novelty", *Industrial and Corporate Change,* Vol 15, No 2, pp 353–371.

Becker, M.C., Knudsen, T. and Swedberg, R. (2012) "Schumpeter's Theory of Economic Development: 100 Years of Development", *Journal of Evolutionary Economics,* Vol 22, pp 917–933.

Bruland, K. and Mowery, D.C. (2005) "Innovation through Time", 349-379, Fagerberg, J., Mowery, D.C. and Nelson, R.R. (2005) (Eds.) *The Oxford Handbook of Innovations*, Oxford: Oxford University Press.

Chandler, A.D. and Redlich, F. (1961) "Recent Developments in American Business Administration and the Conceptualization", *The Business History Review,* Vol 35, No 1, pp 1–27.

Chandler, A.D. (1962) *Strategy and Structure*, MIT Press, Cambridge MA.

Chandler, A.D. (1977) *The Visible Hand*, Belknap Press, Cambridge MA.

Chandler, A.D. (1990) *Scale and Scope*, Belknap Press, Cambridge, MA.

Damanpour, F. (2014) "Footnotes to Research on Management Innovation", *Organization Studies,* Vol 35, No 9, pp 1265–1285.

Damanpour, F., and Aravind, D. (2012) "Managerial Innovation: Conceptions, Processes, and Antecedents", *Management and Organization Review,* Vol 8, pp 423-454.

Dopfer, K. (2012) "The Origins of Meso Economics: Schumpeter's Legacy and Beyond", *Journal of Evolutionary Economics,* Vol 22, No 1, pp 133–160.

Edquist, C., Hommen, C.L. and McKelvey, M. (2001) *Innovation and Employment: Process Versus Product Innovation*, Edward Elgar, Cheltenham UK.

Fagerberg, J. (2005) "Innovation: A guide to the Literature", in Fagerberg, J., Mowery, D.C. and Nelson, R.R. (Eds) *The Oxford Handbook of Innovations* (pp 1-26), Oxford University Press, Oxford.

Fagerberg, J. and Godinho, M.M. (2005) "Innovation and Catching-Up", in Fagerberg, J., Movery, D.C. and Nelson, R.R. (Eds.) *The Oxford Handbook of Innovation* (pp 514-542), Oxford University Press, Oxford.

Fagerberg, J. and Verspagen, B. (2009) "Innovation Studies – the Emerging Structure of a New Scientific Field", *Research Policy,* Vol 38, pp 218–233.

Freeman, C. (1990) "Schumpeter's *Business Cycles* Revisited", in Heertje, A. and Perlman, M. (Eds.) *Evolving Technology and Market Structure* (pp 17-38), University of Michigan Press, Ann Arbor MI.

Hage, J. (1999) "Organizational Innovation and Organizational Change", *Annual Review of Sociology,* Vol 25, pp 597–622.

Loasby, B.J. (2007). "Firm Organization", in Hanusch, H. and Pyka, A. (Eds) *Elgar Companion to Neo-Schumpeterian Economics* (pp 287-295), Edward Elgar, Cheltenham UK.

Martin, B.R. (2012) "The Evolution of Science Policy and Innovation Studies", *Research Policy,* Vol 41, pp 1219–1239.
McCraw, T.K. (2006) "Schumpeter's *Business Cycles* as Business History", *Business History Review,* Vol 80, pp 231–261.
Padgett, J.F. (2012) "Transposition and Refunctionality: The birth of the Partnership in Renaissance Florence", in Padgett, J.F. and Powell, W.W. (Eds) *The Emergence of Organizations and Markets* (pp 168-207), Princeton University Press, Princeton and Oxford.
Penrose, E. (1959) *The Theory of the Growth of the Firm*, Oxford University Press, Oxford.
Romanelli, E. (1991) "The Evolution of New Organizational Forms", *Annual Review of Sociology,* Vol 17, pp 79–103.
Ruttan, V.W. (1959) "Usher and Schumpeter on Invention, Innovation, and Technological Change", *Quarterly Journal of Economics,* Vol 73, No 4, pp 596–606.
Sanidas, E. (2005) *Organizational Innovations and Economic Growth: Organosis and Growth of Firms, Sectors and Countries*, Edward Elgar, Cheltenham UK.
Santarelli, E. and Pesciarelli, E. (1990) "The Emergence of a Vision: The Development of Schumpeter's Theory of Entrepreneurship", *History of Political Economy,* Vol 22, No 4, pp 677–696.
Schroeder, R.G., Van de Ven, A., Scudder, G.D. and Polley, D. (1989) "The Development of Innovation Ideas", in Van de Ven, A.H. et al (Eds.) *Research on the Management of Innovation: The Minnesota Studies* (pp 107-134), Harper & Row, New York.
Schumpeter, J.A. (1912) *Theorie der Wirtschaftlichen Entwicklung*, Duncker & Humblot, Berlin.
Schumpeter, J.A. (1927) "Explanation of the Business Cycle", *Economica,* Vol 7, pp 286–311.
Schumpeter, J.A. (1928) "The Instability of Capitalism", The *Economic Journal,* Vol 38, pp 361–386.
Schumpeter, J.A. (1934/1983) *Theory of Economic Development*, Transactions Publishers, New Brunswick and London.
Schumpeter, J.A. (1935) "The Analysis of Economic Change", *The Review of Economic Statistics,* Vol 17, No 4, pp 2–10.
Schumpeter, J.A. (1939) *Business Cycles, Vol I-II*, McGraw Hill Company, New York.
Schumpeter, J.A. (1942) *Capitalism, Socialism and Democracy (Second edition 1947),* Harper & Brothers Publishers, New York.
Schumpeter, J.A. (1947) "The Creative Response in Economic History", *The Journal of Economic History,* Vol 7, No 2, pp 149–159.
Schumpeter, J.A. (1949/1967) "Economic Theory and Entrepreneurial History", in Aitken, H.G.J. (Ed.) *Explorations in Enterprise* (pp 45- 64), Harvard University Press, Cambridge MA.
Solo, C.S. (1951) "Innovation in the Capitalist Process: A Critique of Schumpeterian Theory", *The Quarterly journal of Economics,* Vol 65, pp 417–28.
Williamson, O.E. (1970) *Corporate Control and Business Behavior*, Prentice Hall, Englewood Cliffs NJ.
Williamson, O.E. (1975) *Markets and Hierarchies*. Free Press, New York.
Williamson, O.E. (1983) "Organizational Innovation: The Transaction Cost Approach", in Ronen, J. (Ed.) *Entrepreneurship* (pp 101-133), Lexington Books, Lexington, MA.

Participation of Young People in Forming Networks of Social Entrepreneurship's Partners: Case of Ekaterinburg

Maria Pevnaya and Daria Telepaeva
Ural Federal University, Ekaterinburg, Russia
m.v.pevnaya@urfu.ru
daria.telepaeva@urfu.ru
DOI: 10.34190/EIE.20.092

Abstract: Social entrepreneurship in Russia is at the initial stage of its development. As a rule, social enterprises are separate initiatives that have received methodological and organizational support through state programs and financial assistance from private and public funds. Social entrepreneurship is a relatively new mechanism for Russia to solve social problems of certain groups of the population by including them in economic relations. First, young people can be considered as potential initiators of such innovations and social entrepreneurship projects. Secondly, the resource characteristics of the younger generation can help existing projects find their target audience and get information support in social networks, where young people form their own field of communication. The purpose of this article is to study the experience of attracting young people to participate in events to promote social inclusive workshops in a major Russian city. Key research questions: can youth participation form networks of partners, potential and actual consumers of social enterprise products? What is the social effect of such participation on young people and social enterprises? The study was conducted in the non-profit organization "Open city" in Ekaterinburg. The case study method was used to assess youth participation. The following methods were used in the case study: analysis of internal documents of NGOs and open information resources, included monitoring, in-depth interviews with employees of the organization. The report analyzes the project "Ekaterinburg is an Open city", where during the month active citizens came up with fundraising events together with employees of social inclusive workshops and initiative youth. The participation of young people in forming networks of social entrepreneurship's partners is a serious step towards the formation of an effective information field for the non-profit sector of Ekaterinburg. Philanthropy becomes fashionable and popular in certain target audiences. Purposeful work with young influencers through delegating responsibility to young student and community leaders only strengthens the effect of social entrepreneurship projects.

Keywords: Young people, social entrepreneurship, social networks, volunteering, philanthropy

1. Introduction

Social entrepreneurship in modern Russia is at the initial stage of development. The situation looks different in Russian regions. But what it has in common is the development of infrastructure to support social entrepreneurship and search for those initiatives in the non-profit sector that can develop in the direction of social entrepreneurship.

Social enterprises in Russia are individual initiatives that have received methodological and organizational support through state programs, and financial assistance from private and public funds. According to the Russian center for public opinion research, less than 1% of Russian entrepreneurs are engaged in this type of activity. This unpopularity of social entrepreneurship is due to the lack of awareness of the population and potential entrepreneurs about the possibilities of this business, as well as the lack of state regulation of social entrepreneurship in Russia.

For example, in the Sverdlovsk region (a large Russian region where more than 4 300 000 people live), the regional Government's "Center for social innovation" supported only 21 projects in 2019 (SOFP, 2019). 19 of them are being implemented in the capital of the region – a large industrial city (Ekaterinburg) with a population of more than 1 500 000 people (GKS, 2020). According to the private charity fund "Towards change", which helps social entrepreneurs from all over the country to implement innovative ideas, 21 applications for information and financial support were received from the Sverdlovsk region this year (ACE, 2019). This is more than from other regions of the Russian Federation, but still not very much for a territory where 251 organizations are included in the register of socially oriented non-profit organizations, and 184 non-profit organizations received subsidies from the regional budget. In general, with the support of the regional government, non-profit organizations implemented 251 socially significant projects at the expense of subsidies (METD, 2019). It is important to understand the reasons and difficulties that face and stop socially oriented organizations from moving towards social entrepreneurship. It is necessary to study how those who are already moving in this direction are coping with these problems.

Social entrepreneurship is a relatively new mechanism for Russia to solve social problems of certain groups of the population by including them in economic relations (Pavlov, 2015). Firstly, young people in this context can be considered as potential initiators of such innovations and social entrepreneurship projects. Secondly, the resource characteristics of young generation can help existing projects find their target audience and get information support in social networks, where young people form their field of communication.

The purpose of this article is to study the experience of attracting young people to participate in events to promote social inclusive workshops in the major Russian city. Key research questions: can youth participation form networks of partners, potential and actual consumers of social enterprise products? What is the social impact of such participation on young people and social enterprises?

2. Theoretical ideas

Youth participation can be seen as a collective activity that is carried out within the framework of everyday life and aimed at satisfying the public interest. It is localized at the horizontal level, responding to the practice of collective mutual assistance and cooperation (Nikovskaya and Skalaban, 2017). Participation in the context of our research means helping to steer and to form. It can mean working together for a solution or a course of action. Participating doesn't just mean becoming a young activist, it can also mean taking advantage of opportunities that are being offered, like joining groups to learn a new skill (Gozdzik-Ormel, 2008). Through participation in the life of their communities, young people acquire social competence, become aware of their personal effectiveness and learn to set and achieve goals. Participation can lay the foundation for certain youth roles and long-term involvement in local communities (Brennan and Barnett, 2009). Youth participation as a collective co-productive activity with socially significant goals performs an educational function (Suslova, 2016).

Analyzing the potential of youth participation in social entrepreneurship projects, we relied on the theoretical ideas of "co-production" and "co-creation" in the field of public services. This theoretical framework allows us to consider any individual action that directly or indirectly contributes to the effectiveness of any social services, through the prism of the public good, considering the benefits for society and for those who participate in certain social practices, helping professionals from the public or non-profit sector (Brandsen et al, 2018).

Young people as volunteers can be partners in a social enterprise in several roles. Firstly, as co-producers of goods from social workshops, if they work for a non-profit organization and help employees working with people with disabilities in the workplace. They can participate in providing various services to the clients of non-profit organizations. Secondly, young people can realize their co-creativity through fundraising activities. They can initiate and organize various events. Thirdly, young volunteers can help employees create and distribute information content about the organization's activities, projects, and specific products and services that the organization provides. In this role, they reproduce informational content together with employees that helps the non-profit organization to solve its tasks, helps clients of these organizations to learn about it, and helps donors to see real activity when evaluating their social investments. In the implementation of the last one, social networks play an important role, which work well in the public sector and demand in the activities of non-profit organizations (Namisango et al, 2019).

Social media acts as a key mechanism for supporting the relationship between an organization and the population, largely due to the lack of costs for this type of activity and the high popularity of social networks among modern youth. Researchers note that the transfer of information through social networks and other social media can increase the involvement of young people in the practice of civic participation. Government agencies use social media to build virtual networks with socially active citizens, which allows them to be involved at any time, in any place and in any initiative (Meijer, 2012).

In research of participation as a community-oriented activity, the following civic indicators are identified: solving community problems, volunteering in local non-profit organizations, membership in communities and associations and participation in fundraising (Adler and Goggin, 2005). In Russia, youth volunteering in the activities of local non-profit organizations is not widespread, as many students participate in large public pro-government movements, youth and volunteer organizations. However, in recent years, we can find some examples of youth involvement in fundraising and urban projects initiated by non-profit organizations, involving local government and entrepreneurs.

The creation of open creative spaces by non-profit organizations, where citizens realize their co-creativity and co-productivity, is a way of cooperation between the government, entrepreneurs and civil society. Such projects allow building organizational networks where local government often mediates social innovation, at the same time solving problems of scaling and sustainability of civic initiatives (Gasco, 2017). Such projects are not just a platform for meeting between the local authorities and citizens. This is both a visible event in the information space and social activity of citizens, which leaves behind social practices and important results for the community. Various categories of non-profit organizations' clients are involved in the activities of local NPOs supported by the government and commercial enterprises. For example, such participation of migrants develops their communication and professional skills, promotes their employment, and generally contributes to the development of a civic culture and mutual assistance (Tu, 2016).

Despite the fact that many scientists consider social participation as a positive practice, there are researches that show the disadvantages and problems of implementing such social projects (Bouchard, 2016). There are legal issues that affect the regulation of relationship between volunteers and professionals. The problem of provided services' quality is discussed. The danger of a lack of real benefits from the joint production of public goods is highlighted (Dodge, 2013). Social participation of young people in the project of non-profit organization that develops social entrepreneurship as community-based practice can be analyzed as a brief case-study description in an effort to begin to tease out the inputs, outputs, and expected outcomes in one particular example. In particular, it seeks to identify and begin to investigate the range and nature of intermediate outcomes that may be posited to lead to the broader outcomes at the individual and community level that such organizations often seek to effect (Chaskin, 2009).

3. Data and method

The research was conducted in the non-profit organization "Open city" in Ekaterinburg (the capital of the Ural region). "Open city" is an Association of parents who bring up children with autism and other mental disabilities and specialists in the field of pedagogy, science and culture. The organization has been operating since 2015. The main goal is to create the best possible conditions for the life of children with intellectual disabilities in the Sverdlovsk region. The organization works in several areas: inclusion in educational institutions, inclusion in the socio-cultural sphere and sports, and labor inclusion. More than 120 families participate in projects on a regular basis. In 2019, the organization received a state grant and opened social workshops. Social workshops produce souvenirs, which "Open city" sells, thereby ensuring its expenses. Such a social enterprise allows people with autism to adapt in society and master the professional skills of seamstresses, potters, woodworkers, etc.

In this case, we analyzed the implementation of the social project "Ekaterinburg is Open city". This project was initiated by the organization in order for more citizens to learn about the problem of autism, about a specific organization, about its initiatives, including social workshops where people with autism work. The project involved 3 employees of the organization, 5 employees of a non-profit organization that specializes in information support for charity, 18 students as volunteers and 20 schoolchildren who were previously trained as cyber volunteers. During the month, active citizens themselves created and organized fundraising events together with employees of social inclusive workshops. This campaign has identified a target audience: all citizens from 16 to 65 years old who constantly use social networks and actively interested in news and public life. In the Sverdlovsk region, about a million people meet the set parameters: from 16 to 65 years old, constantly use social networks and often visit Ekaterinburg (according to "Target Hunter"). The information that was posted on social networks by the organization's employees and volunteers was aimed at this audience. Announcements about the activities was disseminated via targeted and contextual advertising. Young people actively participated in this project as volunteers.

In the first week of the project a special website for this promotion was launched (https://www.openekaterinburg.com). Its informational support in various social networks has begun. 6 creative fundraising events were organized for the production of souvenirs. All interested citizens could sign up for these master classes and donate any money to the project of social workshops. From the second week of the project, various small fundraising events were initiated by citizens as volunteers, including a lot of young people, as well as various organizations.

A case study method was used to assess youth participation. As part of the case study, we used the analysis of internal documents and open information resources, expert interviews with employees of "Open city" organization and representatives of partner organizations (N=36). We analyzed the content of social enterprise, its structure and resources, and gave a critical assessment of the organization's interaction with partners, volunteers, and real and potential consumers. The article focuses on the direct effects of youth participation in the social project and the long-term indirect effect of developing partnerships between social workshops and other organizations. The research identifies and analyzes the types of partner organizations that have joined the social project "Ekaterinburg is Open city".

4. The results

Within the framework of the project, 35 short-term fundraising charity events were held on various city places in one month. 3000 people were involved in organizing offline events. The project partners were 36 organizations that participated in the organization of fundraising events in this project. The project raised 100,000 rubles in money and about 100,000 rubles as materials for workshops. 52 publications about the project in two social networks of the organization were viewed by 108,651 people. 147 author's posts in social networks were posted by participants of events and volunteers on their own pages, using the hashtag of the project. These posts were reposted 315 times. In total, there were more than 100,000 views. The actions of this project were covered in local media, both in print and electronic versions (ASI, 2019). During the month of the project, 11 publications appeared, with an average of 240,000 views per publication.

Effects of co-production and co-creation of youth participation in the project. Initially, during the organizational planning of this project, young people were involved as assistants who could help in organizing and conducting various events, creating informational materials and posting these materials in social networks, on the website of the project. Their participation in the characteristics of co-production and co-creation can be described in the following forms. Young people contributed to the organization of specific actions, accompanying and assisting employees of the organization. The organization's volunteers actively attracted other volunteers who jointly implemented new fundraising events. Some of the events were held with the participation of employees, some of the events were helped by volunteers who gained some experience in the first week of the project. Additionally, the volunteers helped the organizations that have declared their activities in support of this campaign to raise funds. Some of the volunteers took photos of the events, wrote notes, posted them on the organization's website and social networks, and sent out press releases. Volunteers engaged participants of fundraising events to make posts with the hashtag of the project.

As a result, the participation of young people allowed not only to produce informational content that promotes the project's activities and organization, but also to expand it, making it more diverse due to youth creativity. Young people are better able to use additional features of social networks to create posts and images. We analyzed the number of posts and the variety of content presented in the social network "Vkontakte" for 5 months (2 months before the campaign, one month during the campaign, and 2 months after the end of the project). The data is presented in table 1.

Table 1: Content analysis of the organization's posts in the social network "Vkontakte" for 5 months

Content	Before the campaign (September – October 2019)	During the campaign (November 2019)	After the campaign (December 2019 – January 2020)
The number of posts in total	45	52	63
The number of posts with photos	31	29	44
The number of posts with video	1	10	7
The number of posts with interactive content (audience engagement)	2	13	8

The creation of young people in making information content about the organization and its projects had not only concrete results, but also provided long-term effects. These results include recognition of the organization among citizens, identification of social workshops' product among those people who are predisposed to pro-social behavior, participated in actions, saw information about the project and helped spread this information among their surroundings. After conducting an expert interview with the Director of "Open city" we found an increase in demand for the products of social workshops after the campaign. We analyzed the number of some products sold 2 months before the campaign, and within two months after the end of the project). The data is presented in table 2.

Table 2: The number of products sold before and after the campaign

Product	Before the campaign (September – October 2019)	After the campaign (December 2019 – January 2020)
Toys	36	52
Bijouterie	49	96
Gift packs	21	58

Another delayed result is the trust in this organization from major city shopping malls, exhibition and cultural centers. After this project, the organization constantly conducts its exhibitions and sales in these places. The organization is specially invited to participate in various fairs. We can predict the possibility of long-term interaction of these organizations with social workshops in the future. At the moment, six months after the end of the project, "Open city" constantly conducts its master classes in 3 city locations. We analyzed activity of the organization during the year (6 months before the project and six months after it). The data is presented in table 3.

Table 3: The organization's presence in city locations during the year

Locations	The number of master classes before the campaign	The number of master classes after the campaign
“Mega” shopping mall (traffic – 30,000 people daily)	1	3
“Uspenskiy” shopping mall (traffic – 17,000 people daily)	0	2
Multimedia historical park "Russia is my history" (traffic – 300 people daily)	0	4

The organization's network of partners as a result of the social project. We analyzed 36 organizations that took part in the project “Ekaterinburg is Open city”. It should be noted that the organizers didn’t plan to form a permanent partner network. According to our research, most of the organizations that joined the project received information from young volunteers, or through their involvement in professional community that unite various non-profit organizations. The data is presented in table 4.

Table 4: Answers of partner organizations to the question "How did you find out about the project “Ekaterinburg is open city”? (N=36)

The number of answers	Groups of answers	The most popular answers
25	Posts in social networks	"I saw information on the friends or relatives page" "My friends sent me personally»
11	Posts in specialized groups of social networking for nonprofit organizations	"I am subscribed to the organization's news" "I read news in NGO groups" "My colleagues from other NGOs sent me information"

We identified the types of partner organizations, defined their main goal and expectations for participation in this project. The first type of partner organizations is “creative”. This includes organizations that work directly with children and teenagers and implement various creative programs. This group includes commercial children's development centers, creative studios, as well as state institutions in the socio-cultural sphere. During the project, they held charity workshops for teenagers and their parents, and organized performances. According to the manager and employees, the main goal of this type of partner's participation in the project is to fill their daily work with new content and events.

The second type of partner organizations is “educational”. We have included organizations that work with children and teenagers and implement educational programs. This group includes schools, colleges and universities, public institutions in the socio-cultural sphere and libraries. During the project, they held charity public lectures and round table discussions for teenagers and their parents. The main goal of this type of partner's participation in the project is to diversify educational activities with new formats.

The third type of partner is "solidary". We have included non-profit organizations that solve specific problems of people with disabilities, people with various diseases, and work with foster families and problem children.

These organizations joined the campaign to support the charity initiative with their participation. The fourth type of partner is "service". We have included urban art spaces and cafes, small organizations in the service sector. Charity concerts and performances were held in coffee shops, jazz clubs and city cafes. Beauty salons organized a charity event for their visitors. The purpose of these partners' participation is to support charitable initiatives and provide additional information support for their activities.

According to the results of interviews with the head of "Open city", 10 organizations remained in constant interaction with social workshops. Some organizations are customers of souvenirs. Other organizations help to sell the products of workshops, place exhibition stands. Third-sector partners are invited to hold trade shows at their events or organize collaborative projects.

5. Conclusions and discussion

In this case, we analyzed the inputs, outputs, and expected results of the social project "Ekaterinburg is Open city". We have seen real examples of co-productive practices that have led to concrete direct results that exceed planned targets, as well as results that have long-term value for the organization. Young people naturally expanded the network of those who were informed about this project and involved in through their surroundings, friends, and acquaintances. This effect is an important result for the organization whose audience before this promotion was very specialized and limited, as a rule, to people with autism and specialists who work in this problem field.

The participation of young people in forming networks of social entrepreneurship's partners is a serious step towards the formation of an effective information field for the non-profit sector of large Russian city. Media activity and inclusion of social networks help to involve young people as volunteers who create and organize events, help to cover it in social networks. The concept of co-productive in improving the community allows to discern between different effects: direct results in terms of betterment of the neighborhood and integration of people in their neighborhood, or more indirect effects like empowerment of people, increased social capital and changed attitudes of people towards local government (Brandsen et al, 2018).

In this article, we have considered the direct effects of co-production of youth participation directly in the process of implementing a social project and achieving the results of this project. In addition, we have identified an indirect but long-term effect on the organization. It consists in forming long-term partnerships that are extremely important for the sustainability of social workshops.

Acknowledgements

The reported study was funded by RFBR, project number 20-011-00471 "Social participation of young people in the socio-cultural development of cities in Russia and post-soviet countries: comparative analysis of potential and management models"

References

ACE (2019), *Analytical Center Expert*, [online], http://www.acexpert.ru/articles/socialniy-biznes-pochti-bez-pribili-no-za-ideyu.html

Adler, R.P. and Goggin, J. (2005) "What Do We Mean By "Civic Engagement?", *Journal of Transformative Education*, Vol 3, No. 3, pp 236-253.

ASI (2019), *Agency of Social Information*, [online], https://www.asi.org.ru/news/2019/11/11/ekb-blagotvoritelnaya-aktsiya/.

Bouchard, N. (2016) "The Dark Side of Public Participation: Participative Processes That Legitimize Elected Officials' Value", *Canadian Public Administration*, Vol 59, No. 4, pp 516-537.

Brandsen, T., Steen, T., Verschuere, B. (2018) *Co-Production and Co-Creation: Engaging Citizens in Public Services*, Routledge, New York.

Brennan, M.A. and Barnett, R.V. (2009) "Bridging Community and Youth Development: Exploring Theory, Research, and Application", *Community Development*, Vol 40, No. 4, pp 305-310.

Chaskin, R.J. (2009) "Toward a Theory of Change in Community-Based Practice with Youth: A Case-Study Exploration", *Children and Youth Services Review*, Vol 31, No. 10, pp 1127-1134.

Dodge, J. (2013) "Addressing Democratic and Citizenship Deficits: Lessons from Civil Society?", *Public Administration Review*, Vol 73, No. 1, pp 203-206.

Gasco, M. (2017) "Living Labs: Implementing Open Innovation in the Public Sector", *Government Information Quartely*, Vol 34, No. 1, pp 90-98.

GKS (2020), *Federal State Statistic Service*, [online], https://www.gks.ru/compendium/document/13282.

Gozdzik-Ormel, Z. (2008) *Have Your Say! Manual of the Revised European Charter on the Participation of Young People in Local and Regional Life*, Council of Europe Publishing, Strasbourg.

Meijer, A.J. (2012) "New Media and Coproduction of Safety: An Empirical Analysis of Dutch Practices", *The American Review of Public Administration*, Vol 44, No. 1, pp 17-34.

METD (2019), *Ministry of Economy and Territorial Development of the Sverdlovsk Region,* [online], http://economy.midural.ru/content/reestr-socialno-orientirovannyh-nekommercheskih-organizaciy-poluchateley-gosudarstvennoy-12.

Namisango, F., Kang, K., Rehman, J. (2019) *Generative Nonprofits Will Co-Create Services Using Social Media Platforms*, Yncréa Méditerranée, Toulon.

Nikovskaya, L.I. and Skalaban, I.A. (2017) "Civic Participation: Features of Discourse and Actual Trends of Development", *Polis. Political Studies*, No. 6, pp 43-60.

Pavlov, R.N. (2015) "Strategic Factors of Social Enterprise Development Under the Public Sector Optimization", *St. Petersburg State Polytechnical University Journal. Economics*, Vol 223, No. 4, pp 184-192.

Suslova, S. (2016) "Collective Co-Production in Russian Schools", *Educational Studies Moscow*, No. 4, pp 144-162.

SOFP (2019), *Center for social innovation*, [online], http://social.sofp.ru/#rec47811328.

Tu, X. (2016) "Conditions for the Co-Production of New Immigrant Services in Hong Kong", *International Journal of Public Administration*, Vol 39, No. 13, pp 1067-1076.

Entrepreneurship Education for the Digital Generation: Invention or Transformation?

Sergei Polbitsyn[1], Alexandros Kakouris[2], Aleksei Kliuev[1] and Anna Bagirova[1]
[1]Ural Federal University, Yekaterinburg, Russia
[2] Department of Management Science and Technology, University of Peloponnese, Greece
s.n.polbitsyn@urfu.ru
akakouris@uop.gr
a.k.kluev@urfu.ru
a.p.bagirova@urfu.ru
DOI: 10.34190/EIE.20.037

Abstract: Creation of the digital entrepreneurial ecosystem is becoming one of the main research topics in the field of entrepreneurship. Many researchers believe that such an ecosystem should not be created on the premise of the existing entrepreneurial ecosystem paradigm, but from scratch, based on other, brand new principles and institutions. Scholars purposely include education among the key processes within the digital entrepreneurial ecosystem. Without an appropriate level of education, the digital entrepreneurial ecosystem cannot be developed, and this could be a problem not only for national economies and governments, but global. The emergency of COVID-19 and the associated social distancing is a current alarm for the use of digital ways to respond to both education and entrepreneurship. To assess the ability of the educational system to meet the requirements defined by the digital entrepreneurial ecosystem, we analyzed the existing educational programs in the Russian Federation. Our analysis revealed that entrepreneurial education in Russia is based on traditional, formalized norms and rules, which could negatively affect its adaptation to the requirements of digital entrepreneurship. A short survey shows that the basic supportive processes are not valued yet. To create a viable digital entrepreneurial ecosystem, it is necessary to determine, as in the case of the ecosystem itself, the principles and institutions of its formation. To determine the institutional basis of the educational system of digital entrepreneurship, it is necessary to determine the positions of the main stakeholders, to which we include the entrepreneurs themselves, educators and the state. The present article draws upon previous research on entrepreneurship education in Russian universities to propose how education in the specific environment can respond to the challenge of the digital age to support sustainable digital entrepreneurial ecosystems.

Keywords: digital entrepreneurship, entrepreneurial ecosystem, entrepreneurial education, models of education, Russia

1. Introduction

How could education become a digital entrepreneurship component? We developed the problem of one of our co-authors (Kakouris & Georgiadis, 2016) to demonstrate that in digital entrepreneurship ecosystem education is more vital than even learning for traditional entrepreneurship. More generally, Kakouris and Ketikidis (2012) suggest a triple nexus for innovative entrepreneurship where *learning* is one of its 'poles' while *sources of innovation* and *innovation policies* are the rest two. Apparently, digital innovation refers to a new 'source' of innovation due to the digital disruption (or transformation) of the existing businesses world (Autio, 2017; Weill & Woerner, 2015) while the development of digital entrepreneurial ecosystems refers to the third 'pole' of innovation policies. To identify the proper place of the digital entrepreneurship education we start from the exploration of the land of digital entrepreneurship.

There is no consensus among researchers on how to position or name digital entrepreneurship. "'Internet entrepreneurship' at the inception of the field in 2000–2001 led to e- and cyber entrepreneurship around 2004 and now we seem to have settled on to digital entrepreneurship" (Zaheer, Breyer, & Dumay, 2019).

Digital entrepreneurship is utilizing totally different sales and promotion technologies than traditional entrepreneurship. Digital entrepreneurship is the product of transformation of innovative entrepreneurship (Nambisan, 2017). To develop digital entrepreneurship, "novel institutional arrangements critical for digital transformation: digital organizational forms, digital institutional infrastructures, and digital institutional building blocks" (Hinings, Gegenhuber, & Greenwood, 2018) must be created. This process predominantly encompasses business model innovation (Chesbrough, 2010). (Kraus, Palmer, Kailer, Kallinger, & Spitzer, 2019, p 355) provide different definitions for digital entrepreneurship from which, the one of Hair et al. (2012, p. 2) could serve as a working definition for the present article: "Digital entrepreneurship may be defined as entrepreneurship in which some or all of the entrepreneurial venture takes place digitally instead of in more traditional formats".

To explain digital entrepreneurship researchers must explain the process of transformation, the teachers must teach future digital entrepreneurs how to get transformed to digital, and we may ask the question: *can it be taught, explained by the same words, methods and educational programs as entrepreneurship*? Following (Sussan & Acs, 2017) who presented the digital entrepreneurship as the reinvention of entrepreneurship, based on totally new principles of organization and development, we should admit that the digital entrepreneurship education must be treated as the reinvention of education, based on totally new principles and models as well. The underlying model of digital entrepreneurship could be totally different from typical entrepreneurship and based on sharing as the shortest way to reach the potential customer (Richter, Kraus, Brem, Durst, & Giselbrecht, 2017). This opinion will lead researchers to better understanding that digital entrepreneurship must be judged as totally different type of economic activity and hence methodology of the digital entrepreneurship ecosystem research and development must be unprecedented.

No matter what type of entrepreneurial ecosystem is emerging, the need for teaching entrepreneurs, explaining to them rules of the game, institutes of development is not undervalued. It can be called the common position of the main body of researchers that traditional system of information dissemination, the one that include educational system will not work for digital entrepreneurs (Kraus et al, 2019). Different authors stand on different positions of further development of entrepreneurial education to make it suitable for the digital era. The field of ideas spreads from the modernization of existing system of education (Tolstykh, Vertakova, Shkarupeta, Shishkin, & Krivyakin, 2017) to brand new models based only on open resources (Hilton, 2016) and the team, not focusing on individual education (Warhuus, Tanggaard, Robinson, & Erno, 2017).

For example, the current situation, burdened with coronavirus (COVID-19) pandemic, from one side and opening new opportunities for digital entrepreneurship, from another, the demand for digital entrepreneurial education is flourishing. For instance, the owner of ZOOM videoconferencing platform reported 85% increase in revenue due to the COVID-19 pandemic which led the company to $42bn market value[1]. Early research in the topic indicates that much of entrepreneurship education has moved online (Liguori & Winkler, 2020) and this fact generates certain considerations. The goal of our research is to identify alternative models for the development of digital entrepreneurship education to match them to the requirements of global and national progress. Three research problems need to be answered: to recognize the role of education in the development of digital entrepreneurial ecosystem, to elaborate prospective models of digital entrepreneurial education and to identify appropriate model for digital entrepreneurial education for Russian Federation. The subsequent sections focus on these three research problems.

2. Digital entrepreneurial ecosystem

Digital entrepreneurship emerged from the widespread adoption of ICT which requires reinvention of the company as 'matchmaker' between different groups of customers. According to many scholars, this new type of starting-up needs further research as it significantly differs from traditional startups regarding their customer base. Extant infrastructure is also a precondition for any digital startup. Therefore, digital entrepreneurial ecosystems can be thought as structures able to support and boost business initiatives which aim at identifying and exploiting opportunities within the digital economy. Since this system is a very new concept it is observed undertheorized (Li, Du & Yin, 2017). It lends the 'logic' of entrepreneurial ecosystem which is an older but also underdeveloped theoretical concept (Brown & Mason, 2017; Spigel, 2017).

Sussan and Acs (2017, p. 55) remark that digital entrepreneurial ecosystems are "integrating two well-established concepts: the digital ecosystem [i.e. a self-organized, scalable and sustainable system composed of heterogeneous digital entities and their interrelation] and the entrepreneurial ecosystem". Depend on the roles of infrastructure, institutions, agents and users, the scholars maintain that these systems consist "of four concepts: digital infrastructure governance, digital user citizenship, digital entrepreneurship, and digital marketplace" (p. 55). A better understanding of these fundamental concepts and associated processes (e.g. Song, 2019) will enable the development of digital entrepreneurial ecosystems where digital startups, seen as multisided platforms (i.e. matchmakers), are able to be established and evolve.

---

[1] https://www.theguardian.com/technology/2020/mar/31/zoom-booms-as-demand-for-video-conferencing-tech-grows-in-coronavirus-outbreak

Two main models of digital entrepreneurship can be specified: regional entrepreneurship transferring activities from regional to digital (Feldman & Lowe, 2015) and novel ecosystems, born digital on digital platforms (Nambisan, Siegel, & Kenney, 2018). These models are based on different principles. Digital entrepreneurship, grown from regional roots, contains the genetic code of local entrepreneurship and thus bears specific features that make it different and sometimes peculiar. This type of digital entrepreneurship ecosystem easily complies with regional and national legal systems. The second type of the digital entrepreneurship ecosystem from one side is not so adaptive to regional and national requirements but being born on a digital platform this type of entrepreneurship is easily spreading over regions and countries.

An open problem for digital entrepreneurial ecosystems concerns their organization. Unlike to traditional entrepreneurial ecosystems, digital entrepreneurship ecosystems may not exclusively depend on geographic proximity. Even when their members are spatially neighboring, they utilize much electronic communication and engage in intensive conferences (Li, Du & Yin, 2017). Both bottom-up and top-down organizing can coexist. The way that their members divide and allocate tasks, circulate the information and distribute rewards (Li, Du & Yin, 2017) along with other processes need to be further researched.

It emerges from this brief description that digital entrepreneurial ecosystems significantly vary from the traditional ones. Institutions, infrastructures, actors, stakeholders and their relations may not be clear in these circumstances. The beginning of Uber or AirBnB are indicative examples. Learning, especially technological, has to take place before and during establishing digital businesses. Similar to customary entrepreneurship, the digital one needs to be taught in order to facilitate this type of venturing. Education can be provided at the university level in order to crate nascent digital entrepreneurs who are expected to populate, as users and potentially as agents, digital entrepreneurial ecosystems. This education has to focus on opportunity identification in digital economy, on domain-specific knowledge, and especially on the business models digital companies invent and use. Counseling and informal learning can also be offered to the instituted firms by the ecosystem as part of its support similar to traditional ecosystems' practices. The university, as a key agent (and catalyst) of entrepreneurial ecosystems, can also support the demanded training of the incubated digital startups.

3. Educational approaches for digital entrepreneurship

Digital entrepreneurship is a subset of the, more general, technological entrepreneurship. Hull et al. (2007) recognize three types of digital entrepreneurship: (a) the *mild* one where digital economy processes supplement traditional functions of the company which are dominant, (b) the *moderate* where digitization dominates in marketing and sales along with stakeholders' management and (c) the *extreme* one where all business processes are digital. The degree of digitization of a company is thought beneficial for its expansion: the higher it is the more information for customers and competitors can be gathered and multiple markets can be reached (Hair et al., 2012; Ladeira et al., 2019). The prerequisite for this is the use of technological know-how. The previous features differentiate digital enterprises from the customary ones and their difference has to be clearly depicted in their business models.

In order to inform a model for digital entrepreneurship education, one has to reflect on the different types of traditional entrepreneurship education (Kakouris & Liargovas, 2020; Lackéus, 2015). From the three well-known types (i.e. the about/for/through), we suggest the 'about' and 'for' ones are the more relevant. When in university, students of close disciplines (e.g., informatics, engineering, technology management, etc.) can be taught 'about' digital entrepreneurship. This implies traditional teaching, based on knowledge transfer, for the underlying technologies which enable digital ventures. Knowledge to be transferred can be both domain-specific (ICT) or entrepreneurial (how to identify opportunities and organize resources accordingly). This kind of teaching starts from knowledge and proceeds with skills in order to affect the students' attitude (Kakouris & Liargovas, 2020). It is also fully consistent with teaching in traditional universities where technical disciplines are usually taught. Next to knowledge, skills can also be cultivated in a second stage based on laboratory courses or experiential learning. Besides typical entrepreneurial skills, digital entrepreneurship demands digital skills as well (van Deursen & van Dijk, 2014). How to program and manipulate devices, handle geolocation, collect and study business analytics, conduct digital marketing, communicate in social media with diverse groups, are essential skills, among others, for digital entrepreneurs. Through this traditional teaching (i.e. 'about' digital entrepreneurship), shown in Figure 1a, a positive inclination toward digital venturing can be assumed by the end of the instruction.

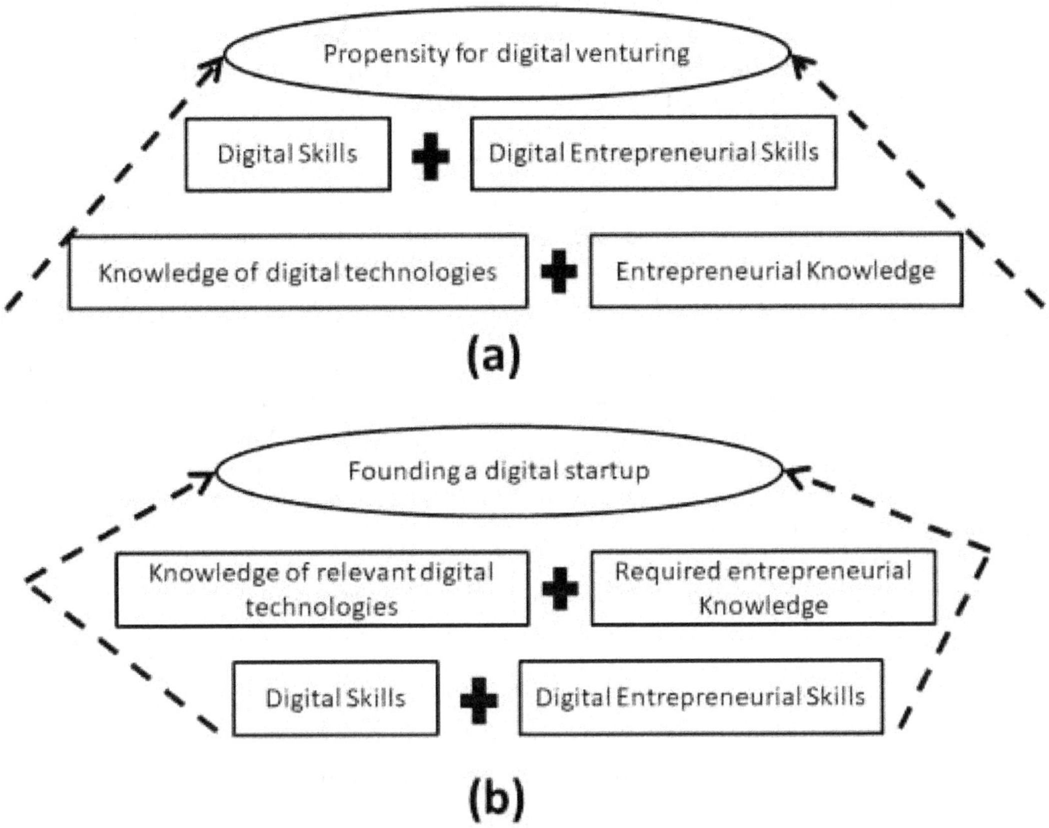

Figure 1: Teaching models: (a) 'about' digital entrepreneurship, (b) 'for' digital entrepreneurship

Unlike the previous traditional teaching, technological startups are based on the competency model of entrepreneurship education (Nabi et al., 2017). According to Kakouris & Liargovas (2020), this model corresponds to teaching 'for' digital entrepreneurship where the goal is not to merely nurture a propensity for digital entrepreneurship (with ambiguous results regarding establishment of new firms) but to create digital startups. In this case the instruction can start from the skill-base of interested individuals, Figure 1b, and to proceed with the demanded knowledge in a second stage. Hence, a scrutinization of the essential core-skillset in the beginning of instruction is appropriate. For example, digital enterprises need to act as 'matchmakers' between different groups (Sussan & Acs, 2017). They also need to perform digital marketing and to invent new business models under uncertainty. Concerning digital skills, individuals who want to engage in digital businesses need to be experienced with social media, internet functions, communication and operations. They also need to tolerate the ambiguity which poor or even absent legislation (or institutions) induces in the sector. Once these essential skills, among others, can be ensured at a required level the instruction proceeds to knowledge acquisition. In the second stage of model (b), only the demanded entrepreneurial knowledge needs to be gained (e.g. business model, digital marketing, business analytics, financing, etc.) and only the relevant to the business idea technological (domain-specific) knowledge to be obtained. The model of Figure 1b may also apply to enterprising teams (action learning) and inform team-matching. It is predominantly based on experiential learning and is more focused toward the establishment of the new firm.

Beyond the education provided in the pre-incubation phase, it was mentioned in the previous section that a digital entrepreneurial ecosystem has to facilitate informal learning for its incubated firms and the rest stakeholders. It is well-documented in relevant studies that learning is a continuous process within these ecosystems since users and agents are in a continuous interaction in order to exploit extant infrastructures, engage in new technologies and identify opportunities. Kakouris & Morselli (2020) discuss different learning theories on which entrepreneurship education can be pedagogically grounded throughout the lifecycle of learners. Apparently, learning within digital entrepreneurial ecosystems is a lifelong learning process that can follow the practices of *legitimate peripheral participation* in communities of practice (Lave & Wenger 2001; Wenger, 2010). Different agents populate the demand and supply sides of a new digital technology around which a common interest is formed. In this way, a series of communities of practice are expected to coexist in the ecosystem (Rae 2017). Intensive conferences observed by Li, Du & Yin (2017) is an example of how digital firms or other stakeholders cooperate and learn from each other. Because of the novelty of the emerging technologies and the business model innovations that take place, this is the only way for novices to learn within these communities of practitioners. The ecosystem, as an entity, has to encourage and facilitate this type of learning.

4. Digital entrepreneurship and education in Russia

Previous research for entrepreneurship education in Russia has shown that Russian universities have a low potential for influencing and supporting innovative entrepreneurship through their activities (Polbitsyn, S., et al., 2020). One of the major persisting challenges for Russian universities as regards entrepreneurial education is the delivery of learning outcomes sought after on the market (Yashin, Klyuev, & Bagirova, 2018). Although there is a growing interest among researchers in entrepreneurship, the problem of educational programs in entrepreneurship is still unexplored (Budyldina, 2018). We attempt to find the factors to prove the proposition that educational programs in digital education are seen by entrepreneurs as a mandatory part of the ecosystem. Digital business is constrained by several factors that can not only reduce the entrepreneurial activities, but also negatively affect the digital entrepreneurial ecosystem. Our research presents a framework for the influence of the rural area indigenes on family business development and is based on socioeconomic and structural forces engaged in family business organizations.

For our research, the following factors were chosen by a group of experts:

- 1. Support of digital business from universities;
- 2. Necessity of educational programs in digital entrepreneurship;
- 3. Necessity for dissemination of information on specific features of digital entrepreneurship;
- 4. Necessity for the special supporting programs for digital entrepreneurs;
- 5. Difficulties in interaction between digital entrepreneurs.

The value of expert-based choice cannot be called flawless and is often questioned by scientists to be subjective and therefore unreliable. However, we decided to base our pilot research on experts' chosen factors pursuing the exercise of more reliable methods in the future.

The questionnaire for the survey was designed as a combination of five point scale (5 - Very Important; 4 – Important; 3 - Moderately Important; 2 - Slightly Important; 1 – Unimportant). This pilot survey serves as an illustration to demonstrate our desire to start the research process.

The questionnaires were distributed during special session in April 2019 as a part of the research conducted by the Ural federal university dedicated to the development of digital entrepreneurship of the Ural region. A sample of 30 respondents among entrepreneurs, who by their words were engaged with digital technologies, was generated. Individual ratings were treated as continuous data (Harpe, 2015). The observed data were analyzed by applying classical tests of hypotheses. We expected that means of all factors, that were chosen as significant, will be not less than 4 ("important") in scoring. One-sample mean comparison test for the 2019 data gave the following results (Table 1).

Table 1: One-sample mean comparison test results

Factors	N	Mean	Standard Error	Standard Deviation	[95% Conf. Interval]		t-value	P value
Support of digital business from universities	30	3.7	.18	.99	3.33	4.07	-1.66	0.05
Necessity of educational programs in digital entrepreneurship	30	3.4	.17	.92	3.36	4.04	-1.80	0.04
Necessity for dissemination of information on specific features of	30	3.2	.14	.77	3.14	3.72	-4.01	0.00

Factors	N	Mean	Standard Error	Standard Deviation	[95% Conf. Interval]		t-value	P value
digital entrepreneurship								
Necessity for the special supporting programs for digital entrepreneurs	30	2.9	.13	.73	2.59	3.132	-8.5	0.00
Difficulties in interaction between digital entrepreneurs	30	2.9	.12	.64	2.69	3.17	-9.13	0.00

The results are unexpected: all factors, that were proposed by experts to be important were not named as very important by respondents.

The survey results are presented graphically on Figure 2. The factor "Difficulties in interaction between digital entrepreneurs" is the most interesting. It was supposed to be one of the main hurdles, but respondents graded it as unimportant or slightly important, responding that there is no rivalry between digital entrepreneurs and no difficulties in interaction.

The factor "Necessity of educational programs in digital entrepreneurship" showed its importance to digital entrepreneurs. However, the problem was identified as the lack of accessible educational programs. Cooperation with universities was suggested as an alternative solution to acquire necessary competence.

When respondents were questioned on "special supporting programs", they demonstrated a lack of understanding of the need to develop not only "digital competences", but also basic entrepreneurial skills.

The answers on information dissemination factor were supplemented with verbal comments from respondents about the dissatisfaction with the capacity of accessible information channels.

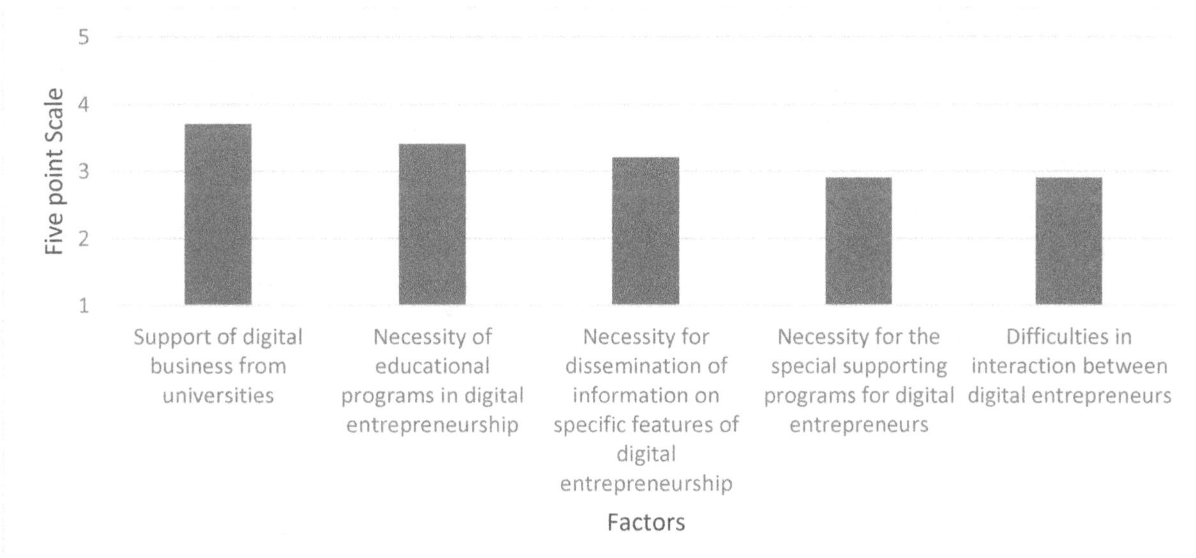

Figure 2: Five point scale of factors restraining the development of digital entrepreneurship in Russia

The described factors serve as the evidence of our hypothesis for the first attempt to identify the role of universities in the development of digital entrepreneurship. We do not argue that our results are comprehensive and overwhelming, but as we said already, it is the first attempt to investigate the digital business and possibilities for relevant education in Russia.

5. Conclusion

This article was aimed to answer one of the most significant problems for educators: do they need to develop the brand new approach to tailor educational programs in digital entrepreneurship or to attempt to adopt the existing programs to the new reality. We examined how entrepreneurship education can meet the needs of digital entrepreneurs and especially the development of digital entrepreneurial ecosystems. Three research problems were tackled: to recognize the role of education in the development of digital entrepreneurial ecosystem, to elaborate prospective models of digital entrepreneurial education and to identify appropriate model for digital entrepreneurial education for Russian Federation.

Present suggestions can be summarized as follows. The digital entrepreneurship education has to focus on opportunity identification in digital economy, on domain-specific knowledge, and especially on the business models digital companies invent and use. Beyond education 'about' digital entrepreneurship offered to graduates in the pre-incubation phase, counseling and informal learning can also be offered to the instituted firms by the ecosystem as part of its support similar to traditional ecosystems' practices. As already suggested, universities, as a key agent (and catalyst) of entrepreneurial ecosystems, can also support the demanded training of the incubated digital startups. Learning within digital entrepreneurial ecosystems is a lifelong learning process that can follow the practices of legitimate peripheral participation in communities of practice. Different agents populate the demand and supply sides of a new digital technology around which a common interest is formed. Because of the novelty of the emerging technologies and the business model innovations that take place, most of them disrupting, this is the only way for novices to learn within these communities of practitioners. The ecosystem, as an entity, has to encourage and facilitate this type of learning.

The main purpose of this study was to identify the readiness of entrepreneurs to see the developing digital entrepreneurship education as a part of the digital entrepreneurial ecosystem in Russia. The analysis of educational environment was specifically analyzed. The Russian economy is in transition, where entrepreneurs are considered to be one of the main contributors to economy prosperity of the country. It was essential to investigate the most critical, most important factors that are influencing the development of the digital entrepreneurship education. The results demonstrated that entrepreneurs regard universities as mandatory element of the digital entrepreneurial ecosystem, able to develop and disseminate necessary knowledge and competences.

From the responses of entrepreneurs, we observed in our study that entrepreneurs do not see hurdles in academic support and the entrepreneurial environment. To their opinion, the core focus of policymakers and educational authorities should be to emphasize digital entrepreneurship and make it a part at all levels of education, from schools to universities. This study is only a piloting study attempting to raise the problems rather than find the final answers. A further study with a larger sample size and a comparison of the cities and genders of the respondents would strengthen this contribution.

This study was limited to Russian universities. Therefore, some of the findings may be region- or country-specific. It would be interesting to compare the intentions of students in different countries. In this way we will investigate the emerging stream of digital entrepreneurship and effective ways to support it.

Acknowledgements

The paper was supported by the Act 211 Government of the Russian Federation, contract № 02.A03.21.0006.

References

Autio, E. (2017). Digitalisation, ecosystems, entrepreneurship and policy. Policy Brief/20/2017. https://www.researchgate.net/profile/Erkko_Autio/publication/321944724_Digitalisation_ecosystems_entrepreneurship_and_policy/links/5a3a5eb5aca2728e698a9498/Digitalisation-ecosystems-entrepreneurship-and-policy.pdf

Brown, R., & Mason, C. (2017). Looking inside the spiky bits: a critical review and conceptualisation of entrepreneurial ecosystems. Small Business Economics, 49(1), 11-30.

Budyldina, N. (2018). Entrepreneurial universities and regional contribution. *International Entrepreneurship and Management Journal, 14*(2), 265-277. doi:10.1007/s11365-018-0500-0

Chesbrough, H. (2010). Business model innovation: opportunities and barriers. Long range planning, 43(2-3), 354-363.

Feldman, M., & Lowe, N. (2015). Triangulating regional economies: Realizing the promise of digital data. Research Policy, 44(9), 1785-1793. doi:10.1016/j.respol.2015.01.015

Hair, N., Wetsch, L. R., Hull, C. E., Perotti, V., & Hung, Y. T. C. (2012). Market orientation in digital entrepreneurship: advantages and challenges in a Web 2.0 networked world. International Journal of Innovation and Technology Management, 9(06), 1250045.

Harpe, S. E. (2015). How to analyze Likert and other rating scale data Currents in Pharmacy Teaching & Learning. *Currents in Pharmacy Teaching and Learning, 7*(6), 836-850. doi:10.1016/j.cptl.2015.08.001

Hilton, J. (2016). Open educational resources and college textbook choices: a review of research on efficacy and perceptions. Etr&D-Educational Technology Research and Development, 64(4), 573-590. doi:10.1007/s11423-016-9434-9

Hinings, B., Gegenhuber, T., & Greenwood, R. (2018). Digital innovation and transformation: An institutional perspective. Information and Organization, 28(1), 52-61. doi:10.1016/j.infoandorg.2018.02.004

Hull, C. E., Caisy Hung, Y. T., Hair, N., Perotti, V., & DeMartino, R. (2007). Taking advantage of digital opportunities: a typology of digital entrepreneurship. International Journal of Networking and Virtual Organisations, 4(3), 290-303.

Kakouris, A., & Georgiadis, P. (2016). Analysing entrepreneurship education: a bibliometric survey pattern. Journal of Global Entrepreneurship Research, 6(1), 6. doi:10.1186/s40497-016-0046-y

Kakouris, A., & Ketikidis, P. (2012). Poles of innovative entrepreneurship: a triple nexus. International Journal of Innovation and Regional Development, 4(3/4), 197-203.

Kakouris, A., & Liargovas, P. (2020), On the about/for/through framework of entrepreneurship education: a critical analysis. Entrepreneurship Education and Pedagogy, doi: 10.1177/2515127420916740

Kakouris, A., & Morselli, D. (2020). Addressing the pre/post-university pedagogy of entrepreneurship coherent with learning theories. In Sawang, S. (Ed.) Entrepreneurship Education: A lifelong learning approach, Springer, forthcoming. doi: 10.1007/978-3-030-48802-4_3

Kraus, S., Palmer, C., Kailer, N., Kallinger, F. L., & Spitzer, J. (2019). Digital entrepreneurship A research agenda on new business models for the twenty-first century. International Journal of Entrepreneurial Behaviour & Research, 25(2), 353-375. doi:10.1108/ijebr-06-2018-0425

Lackéus, M. (2015). Entrepreneurship in education-What, why, when, how. Trento, Italy: Background paper for OECD-LEED. https://www.oecd.org/cfe/leed/BGP_Entrepreneurship-in-Education.pdf

Ladeira, M. J., Ferreira, F. A., Ferreira, J. J., Fang, W., Falcão, P. F., & Rosa, Á. A. (2019). Exploring the determinants of digital entrepreneurship using fuzzy cognitive maps. International Entrepreneurship and Management Journal, 15(4), 1077-1101.

Lave, J., & Wenger, E. (2001). Legitimate peripheral participation in communities of practice. In Clarke, J., Hanson, A., Harrison, R. & Reeve, F. (Eds) Supporting lifelong learning (pp. 121-136). Routledge.

Li, W., Du, W., & Yin, J. (2017). Digital entrepreneurship ecosystem as a new form of organizing: the case of Zhongguancun. Frontiers of Business Research in China, 11(1), 5.

Liguori, E., & Winkler, C. (2020). From Offline to Online: Challenges and Opportunities for Entrepreneurship Education Following the COVID-19 Pandemic. Entrepreneurship Education and Pedagogy. doi: 10.1177%2F2515127420916738

Nabi, G., Liñán, F., Fayolle, A., Krueger, N., & Walmsley, A. (2017). The impact of entrepreneurship education in higher education: A systematic review and research agenda. Academy of Management Learning & Education, 16(2), 277-299.

Nambisan, S. (2017). Digital Entrepreneurship: Toward a Digital Technology Perspective of Entrepreneurship. Entrepreneurship Theory and Practice, 41(6), 1029-1055. doi:10.1111/etap.12254

Nambisan, S., Siegel, D., & Kenney, M. (2018). On open innovation, platforms, and entrepreneurship. Strategic Entrepreneurship Journal, 12(3), 354-368. doi:10.1002/sej.1300

Polbitsyn, S., et al. (2020) Entrepreneurial education in Russian universities: Achievements, reflections and milestones, in P. Jones et al. (Eds.) Contemporary Issues in Entrepreneurship Research, Emerald, forthcoming

Rae, D. (2017), "Entrepreneurial learning: peripherality and connectedness", International Journal of Entrepreneurial Behavior & Research, Vol. 23 No. 3, pp. 486-503.

Richter, C., Kraus, S., Brem, A., Durst, S., & Giselbrecht, C. (2017). Digital entrepreneurship: Innovative business models for the sharing economy. Creativity and Innovation Management, 26(3), 300-310. doi:10.1111/caim.12227

Song, A. K. (2019). The Digital Entrepreneurial Ecosystem—a critique and reconfiguration. Small Business Economics, 53(3), 569-590.

Spigel, B. (2017). The relational organization of entrepreneurial ecosystems. Entrepreneurship Theory and Practice, 41(1), 49-72.

Sussan, F., & Acs, Z. J. (2017). The digital entrepreneurial ecosystem. Small Business Economics, 49(1), 55-73. doi:10.1007/s11187-017-9867-5

Tolstykh, T., Vertakova, Y., Shkarupeta, E., Shishkin, I., & Krivyakin, K. (2017). Assessment of the Impact of Higher Education Development on the Social and Economic Processes in the Region. Sustainable Economic Growth, Education Excellence, and Innovation Management through Vision 2020, Vols I-Vii, 2180-2191.

Van Deursen, A. J., & van Dijk, J. A. (2014). Digital skills: Unlocking the information society. Springer.

Warhuus, J. P., Tanggaard, L., Robinson, S., & Erno, S. M. (2017). From I to We: collaboration in entrepreneurship education and learning? Education and Training, 59(3), 234-249. doi:10.1108/et-08-2015-0077

Weill, P., & Woerner, S. L. (2015). Thriving in an increasingly digital ecosystem. MIT Sloan Management Review, 56(4), 27=34.

Wenger, E. (2010). Communities of practice and social learning systems: the career of a concept. In Blackmore, C. (Ed) Social learning systems and communities of practice (pp. 179-198). Springer.

Yashin, A., Klyuev, A., & Bagirova, A. (2018). DESIGNING ENTREPRENEURIAL EDUCATION IN RUSSIA: HARD AND SOFT SKILLS. *Ekonomski Vjesnik, 31*(2), 261-274.

Zaheer, H., Breyer, Y., & Dumay, J. (2019). Digital entrepreneurship: An interdisciplinary structured literature review and research agenda. Technological Forecasting and Social Change, 148. doi:10.1016/j.techfore.2019.119735

Innovative Entrepreneurship in Local Cross-Country Freight Enterprises in Thailand

Teeraphorn Polhong and Suteera Puangpronpitag
Mahasarakham Business School, Mahasarakham University, Mahasarakham, Thailand
std60010954002@acc.msu.ac.th
suteera.p@acc.msu.ac.th
DOI: 10.34190/EIE.20.159

Abstract: This pager presents an empirical study scrutinizing competitive strategies adopted by local cross-country freight enterprises in a province located in the Special Economic Zone in the Northeast region of Thailand. The opening of the 3rd Thai-Laos Friendship Bridge leads to the need for local business to improve their competitive ability in response to increased competitors and business opportunities attracted by this new cross-country infrastructure. This research is an empirical study conducted in one of the border provinces included in the studied Special Economic Zone named Nakhon Phanom. The research conduct is a multi-site case study with five local freight enterprises observed as the empirical sites. Given the needs of these enterprises to develop enhanced competitive strategies, the study has discovered innovative entrepreneurship elements in the business operation of the studied cases. These elements have significant impacts on the firm's competitive ability. By based on the findings, this paper also theoretically discusses these elements and their effects on three aspects, including inventory strategy, logistic strategy, location strategy. With the study results, this paper can identify the success factors of innovative entrepreneurship in local cross-country freight enterprises. By using the grounded theory, it also theoretically compares the empirical results with innovative entrepreneurial elements identified in the literature and previous studies. The presentation of this paper will contribute to knowledge in the field of innovative entrepreneurship, focusing on how small and local freight businesses can improve their innovation and business management. This knowledge can help to shed light on how small-sized companies can move towards sustainable development in this era of industry 4.0 economy, where innovation and new knowledge is in the central focus.

Keywords: industry 4.0, innovative entrepreneurship, digital economy, knowledge economy, local enterprises

1. Introduction

The current national economic development policy in Thailand is known as the Thailand 4.0 policy. This policy is developed based on the concept of the knowledge-based economy and industry 4.0. The policy recommends innovation and new knowledge as vital success factors for businesses of all sizes, small ones included. To promote its economy, Thailand does not adopt only the notion of industry 4.0 but also the concept of the digital economy as the country seeks to implement digitalization to promote its economic and social development. This paper is interested in the business development of local enterprises in the logistics industry, which is one of the ten targeted industries of the Thailand 4.0 policy (Thailand Board of Investment, 2015).

The paper will present a case study of local cross-country freight enterprises in a border province in the Northeast region of Thailand named Nakhon Phanom. The province is situated in a Thailand's Special Economic Zone near the 3rd Thai-Laos Friendship Bridge that crosses the Mekong River. This bridge is one of the six international bridges linking Thailand to other countries in the region. It has been in use since 2011. In addition to being a Thai-Laos cross border bridge, the 3rd Friendship Bridge is also part of the East-West Economic Corridor (EWEC) of the Greater Mekong Sub-region. It serves international land transportation linking the neighbouring countries, including Thailand, Laos, Vietnam, and the Southern region of China. Since its opening in 2011, it helps to promote the value of international trade passing through the route. Considering the advantages of the location in the Special Economic Zone and the logistic infrastructure, the Thai Government is trying to promote Nakhon Phanom to become the Logistic of Hub of the Greater Mekong Sub-region (Office of Transport and Traffic Policy and Planning, 2015).

The government's promotion implemented in the region has caused a significant increase in business competition in the area; more competitors from outside the region, both domestic and international, have come into the sector (Thailand Board of Investment, 2016). Consistent with the increased number of competitors, there is also an increase in potential domestic and international customers. This expanding market size has brought up the business opportunity for the existing local competitors.

Given the challenges and opportunities for the logistics industry in the area, this paper will examine the business development of local cross-country freight enterprises in Nakhon Phanom province as they try to increase their competitiveness in the industry. Considering the significance of Thailand 4.0 aiming at driving the national economy with innovation, the research question is "how the local cross-country freight enterprises manage their business to acquire innovative entrepreneurship? This question led to the conduct of an empirical study underpinning the presentation of this paper. The research setting was a case study with of Nakorn Phanom province with multiple local cross-country freight enterprises selected as empirical informants.

2. Industry 4.0

Considering the Thailand 4.0 policy and the concept of the digital economy, businesses throughout the country need to develop towards knowledge-based and innovative entrepreneurship. The new knowledge and innovation will help the business organization to add value to their businesses and obtain sustainable competitiveness (Moutinho et al., 2016). Thailand 4.0 recommends the nation to implement new growth engines for its economy comprising three fundamentals as follows (Jones and Pimdee, 2017):

- building economic prosperity through innovation, knowledge, technology, and creativity;
- building social security through equitable distribution of income;
- creating sustainability through environmentally friendly development.

While driving the economy with the 4.0 policy, Thailand identifies ten targeted industrial sectors, with five being recommended as the Thailand 4.0 new S-curve industries. In addition to their own potential to add value to the Thai economies, the government also promotes them to support the advancement of human capital and to facility innovation achievement in other industrial sectors. These industries include robotics, medical hub, biofuels and biochemicals, digital, and aviation and logistics.

3. Digital economy

While promoting the Thailand 4.0 policy, Thailand also implements the concept of the digital economy to its economic and social development, known as Digital Thailand. Digital Thailand is a long-term plan aiming to promote long-term growth and sustainability under the country's 20-year strategy. There are four phases to implement as follows (ONDE, 2019):

- digital foundation (1.5-year plan target), investing and building a foundation for the digital economy transformation;
- digital Thailand (5-year plan target), referring to the national condition that everyone can access and make full use of digital technology;
- Full transformation (10-year plan target), presenting the stage that the country is driven by digital technology and innovation;
- global digital leadership (20-year plan target), targeting the national achievement of becoming a developed country using digital technology to create value in a long-term and sustainable manner.

4. Innovative entrepreneurship

This research lays the concepts of Thailand 4.0 and Digital Thailand as the bounded system of its investigation. To implement the two ideas for business development in Thailand, essential elements of the policy implementation are entrepreneurship and innovation. The combination of entrepreneurship and innovation results in "innovative entrepreneurship" where "entrepreneurs are critical to the innovation process, and the entrepreneurial capacity is a key element in the transfer of knowledge in the commercialization process (Crudu, 2019, p.269). As a result of the review of related literature, the three theoretical concepts bounding the investigation of this paper are industry 4.0, digital economy, and innovative entrepreneurship.

5. Data and method

The empirical setting of the research is a case study of Nakhon Phanom province of Thailand. The province is in the Northeast region of the country. It is situated in Thailand's Special Economic Zone near the 3rd Thai-Laos Friendship Bridge, which is an international bridge that serves international land transportation between Thailand and Laos. By conducting a case study, the researchers consider the contextual conditions of the case setting as significant to the deductive interpretation of the research evidence (Merriam, 2002). The study chooses logistics as the industry of the investigation with local cross-country freight enterprises selected as primary empirical informants. The unit of analysis is a business organization. The business activities and the management strategies of all the studied individual enterprises are in the central focus of the investigation. The aspects of inquiry including elements of innovative entrepreneurship; the components of business strategy and the factors of competitive business performance.

5.1 Methodological stance of the qualitative approach

By considering the three aspects of inquiry identified earlier, the researchers adopted a qualitative approach for their investigation. They opted for qualitative research with no privileges over the quantitative method (Denzin and Lincoln (2008). The essential purpose of carrying out the qualitative study is to understand the complex and detailed management behaviour of local cross-country freight enterprises in Nakhon Phanom province of Thailand. Additionally, statistical findings are not in the central focus of the study. Instead, it seeks to understand the detailing and complex activities of these business organizations. The interpretation of findings uses a deductive approach. The approach helps the understanding of the business management behaviour to emerge from the empirical evidence within the case study boundary rather than being bounded within any preidentified theoretical explanation (Patton, 2002). Therefore, the methodological stance of this research is to make sense of the business management behaviour of local cross-country freight enterprises rather than to measure their management performances.

5.2 Data collection

The data collection instruments are documentary analysis and semi-structured interviews. The documentary analysis helped the researchers to obtain secondary data from public sources, including websites and publications. The data collected at this stage include public profiles of Thailand, the national economic policy, facts and figures of Nakhon Phanom, and the general information of the empirical setting of the case study boundary. The documentary analysis helps the researchers to understand the contextual conditions bounding the interpretation of the case's evidence. Primary research data was collected using semi-structure interviews. The researchers employed purposive sampling as they sampled for the interview informants. As mentioned earlier, the opening of the 3rd Friendship Bridge has significantly caused an increase in competition in the cross-country transportation service business in the area. The researchers, therefore, looked for local cross-country freight enterprises registered the Office of Commercial Affairs of Nakhon Phanom Province with more than ten years of business experience. They aimed at examining how these local companies manage their business before and after the opening of the bridge. This examination would help the researcher understand the impact of the enhanced international infrastructure on the business management of the locals.

Given the selection criteria, five local enterprises were selected. The Interview fieldwork took place from November 2018 to February 2019. The managers of the selected enterprises were interviewed using semi-structured questions.

5.3 Grounded theory analysis

This study aims to scrutinize for elements of innovative entrepreneurship in the business management of the five sampled cross-country freight enterprises. The researchers analysed the data using a grounded theory approach. The use of grounded theory allows the researchers to transform the collected data into the building blocks of a theoretical explanation of the behaviour of the observed organizations to emerge from the collected research data (Glaser, 1992). The contextual conditions of the empirical case were used as part of the case analysis system. Also, throughout the analysis processes, the researchers used the identified related theoretical concepts of industry 4.0 and digital economy as the analysis boundary. The researchers used the grounded theory analysis for constructing a theoretical explanation for the research inquiry into how the local cross-country freight enterprises develop towards innovative entrepreneurship to increase their competitiveness in the industry.

As a result, there were four types of codes developed, including open codes, categories, axial codes, and theoretical codes. The first step was to identify open codes. The open codes are low-inference and do not yet provide a theoretical explanation (Charmaz, 2006). Then, all open codes were classified into categories. This process helped the researchers to synthesize larger segments of data using higher-level concepts (Strauss and Corbin, 1998). Then, there was axial coding, which is the stage of identifying relationships among categories. Finally, there was theoretical coding. This stage delivered hypothetical relationships among categories and axial codes (Glaser, 1992). Table 1 presents all the codes developed through the grounded theory analysis, and Figure 1 shows the eventual theoretical coding.

6. Research findings

The delivery of the research findings of this case study is from the investigation of sampled observed companies having experience ten years and above in the industry. The results show that existing long-term experienced companies in the area are well aware of both increased challenges, business opportunities, and the number of new competitors. As a result, they have been trying to move from traditional business conduct to a more innovative pattern. By doing so, the national economic development concepts of Thailand 4.0 and Digital Thailand have become a significant influence on the business management of local freight enterprises in Nakhon Phanom province. As a result, elements of innovative entrepreneurship are found. These elements are the result of innovative management and the digitalization of the local enterprises. This section presents the research findings.

6.1 Inventory strategy

The studied companies employed modern mobile and digital technology for their inventory management. They purchased digital warehouse management system software to help with the increasing and complex needs of the customers. These customers are from a large variety of business types such as retails, wholesalers, restaurants, supplies shop, constructions, manufacturing. The software helped with the accuracy of inventory management. Additionally, the study shows that local freight companies have moved from using traditional accounting and bookkeeping systems in a family business to a digital transformation of their accounting management; all of the observed companies invested in licensed accounting software. With the use of software, they were able to economically improve their service to meet various financial services required by their customers, such as trade credit, cash management, and insurance. Furthermore, enhanced technology also helped with the customs processes for cross-country customers. The improved inventory strategy created customer trust for their service hence the more recurring customers.

6.2 Transport strategy

In recent days, the cost of using information technology and applications has been lower compared to the last decades. The lower cost of using new technology was a supporting factor for the local freight enterprises in Nakhon Phanom; it helped them to transform from traditional business management into modern business digitalization. With the lower cost of digital technology, these companies were able to upgrade their competitive competency level to measure up with the national and international companies coming to share the market value within the region. These companies used mobile and digital platforms to serve their customers more responsively and more accurately. The platforms in use were the company websites, Line, and Facebook, which they used via both computers and smartphones. By using reliable location sharing service on these platforms, the companies planed their routes more economically based on the correct information of locations of their customers. As a result, with the enhanced transportation technology and integrative digital technology usage, all of the observed companies confirmed that they had lower transportation costs.

Table 1: Initial codes, categories, axial codes and theoretical codes

<table>
<tr><th>Open Codes</th><th>Categories</th><th>Axial codes</th><th>Theoretical Codes</th></tr>
<tr><td>IT services provider
Could systems
Online payment
Mobile payment
QR code</td><td>Inventory management</td><td rowspan="4">Inventory Strategy involves with inventory management, costs of business, inventory expenses and customer services</td><td rowspan="4">Innovative Entrepreneurship of local cross-country freight enterprises is developed with innovative management and digitalization of inventory strategy, transportation strategy, and location strategy</td></tr>
<tr><td>Accounts receivable
Trade credits
Truck maintenance
Vehicle Insurance
Discount
Utilities</td><td>Costs of business</td></tr>
<tr><td>Licensed software
Store room costs
Warehouse costs</td><td>Inventory expenses</td></tr>
<tr><td>Shipment insurance</td><td>Customer services</td></tr>
</table>

Shipment guarantee Customer helplines Staff training costs Marketing mix			
Customer based routes Truck GPS Speed limit	Energy management	Transport Strategy *comprises* energy management, transportation, shipment system, freight management, communication channels and customer relations.	
Check points Truck tracking system	Transportation		
Distribution head office Business partners	Shipment system		
Freight schedule management Vehicle CCTV Route management	Freight management		
Mobile communication Online communication Realtime tracking	Communication channels		
Customer hotlines Advertisement Direct contact Facebook	Customer relations		
Regular customers New customers Potential customers	Customers database		
Customs location Cross border bridge Special Economic zone	Business location	Location Strategy *requires* business location, business partner's locations, customers' locations, transportation systems and transportation infrastructure	
Domestic partners International partners	Business partners' locations		
Regional customers Domestic customers Cross-country customers	Customers' locations		
Land transportation Cross-country bridge Logistics	Transportation systems		
Traffic control Customs duties Law and regulations	Transportation infrastructure		

Source: The authors

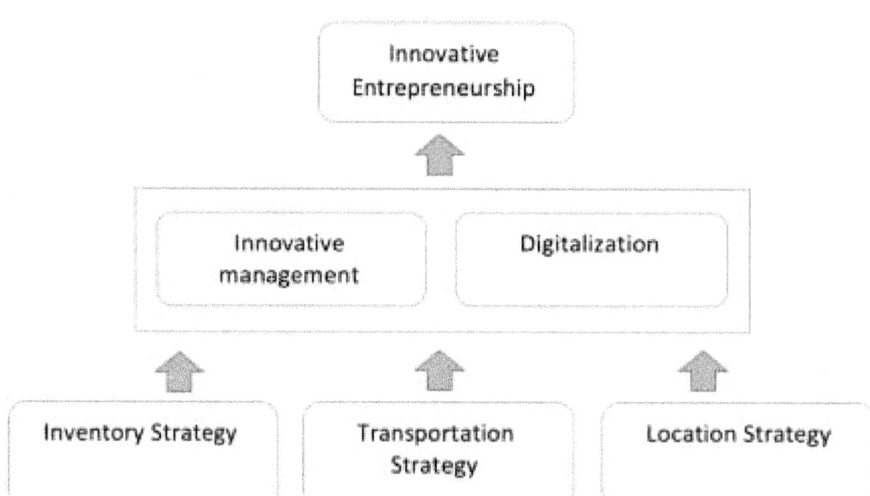

Figure 1: The theoretical coding (developed by the authors)

The studied companies also employed mobile and digital technologies on their freights. These technologies included real-time GPS tracking, vehicle CCTV, mobile communication with the drivers on duty. The innovative transportation management was undertaken for the whole customer service processes, from initial contact with potential customers, a service quotation, route planning, real-time tracking, final delivery to the cross-country destinations, and after-sale services. The reliability and accuracy of transportation service also gave further benefit to the companies as it attracted new customers from word of mouth recommendation from current customers.

6.3 Location strategy

Nakhon Phanom province has become a prime location for international land transportation for two reasons. The first reason is that it is part of an exclusive economic zone of Thailand and the other reason is it is on the route of the East-West Economic Corridor. These two supporting factors make the province a competitive region for logistic industry bringing in more national and international competitors. Research findings show that there were business disadvantages of the locals compared to the newcomers, especially in terms of the company size, capital and resources. Those large firms had integrated systems for air-land-waterway transfer systems and better-trained staff with a higher level of English competency. Despite the identified disadvantages, there were also crucial advantages relating to the long-term personal relationship with regional customers and the location knowledge gained through the long-term business experience in the region. The local companies served well in the part of the market considered not economic worth for the larger companies. This advantage is due to their smaller organisational size of the local that makes these companies more flexible to reach smaller size customers. Modern digital technology helped these companies by enhancing their connections with their customers and business partners, both regional and international.

7. Discussions

The research findings showed increased challenges and opportunities for local cross-country freight enterprises in Nakhon Phanom. These factors led to the effort of these firms trying to improve their competitive ability. Competing in the international logistic industry, these local firms tackled the challenges by implementing new management innovation in three forms, namely inventory strategy, transportation strategy and location strategy. The new improvements are recognized as elements of innovative entrepreneurship discussed in previous studies in the field (Crudu, 2019; Kanellos, 2011). These firms aimed at improving the speed, the accuracy and the reliability of their services. These goals are business success factors of freight companies as identified in a study conducted by Noonoi (2011). While transforming their organization into an innovative company, the local firms employed various digital platforms to facilitate their business including social network applications, websites, GPS tracking system, licensed accosting software and licensed software for warehouse management. Their improvements were in accord with the long-term plan of national policy for Digital Thailand targeting at the digitalization of businesses in all sectors (ONDE, 2019).

Despite their efforts for organizational transformation, empirical evidence showed certain areas of development which the local enterprises required actions of support from public agencies and knowledge sources. First, they needed more supports for new knowledge creation, considering that they had limited resources on undertaking research and development (R&D) to enhance the performance of their business. Second, to increase their competitiveness in serving international customers, they required support for human capital development to improve the work capability and English competency of their staff. Finally, they expected the public to help with creating the links of their service provision to the comprehensive international transportation infrastructures, such as the East-West Economic corridor, the air-land-waterway setups. These identified requirements for supports are considered as the development challenges for not only the local firms but also for Thailand as it is trying to move the countries towards the knowledge-based economy with the concepts of Thailand 4.0 and Digital Thailand.

8. Limitations

This paper has presented research findings and discussions of a case study of a particular area, known as Nakhon Phanom province of Thailand. The contextual conditions of the case study boundary play a significant role in the interpretation of the empirical evidence collected from the case setting. Also, the research employed a qualitative approach for its investigation; the researchers' bias and experiences were inevitably involved with the interpretation of the results.

Despite the limitations, the grounded theory approach allowed the researchers to repetitively revisit the related theories then compared and critically discussed them with the empirical evidence. Therefore, the construction of theoretical explanations of this case study was carefully linked to the existing knowledge in the field. For this reason, the knowledge contribution of this paper may be applied to understand the development of innovative entrepreneurship in the cross-border transportation industry in other settings, especially those with similar geographical, economic and regional contextual conditions to Nakhon Phanom province and the observed enterprises of the study.

9. Conclusions and suggestions for future research

This paper has delivered an empirical case study research into the development of innovative entrepreneurship in local cross-country freight enterprises in a province from the Northeast region of Thailand, named Nakhon Phanom. The researchers chose to study this business sector due to the opening of the 3rd Friendship Bridge, which significantly caused an increase in competition in the cross-country transportation service business in the area. As a result, local transportation enterprises were inevitable in need to improve how to manage their business to survive the competition and to seek for the sustainable development of their organization.

The selected companies included in the case investigation were local companies from within the area with more than ten years of business experience in the industry. The empirical findings show that local companies can compete in an increasingly competitive environment in this era of industry 4.0 by increasing their capacity in creativity and innovation. The essential factors of their competitive ability are the digitalisation and innovative management of three business strategies, including (1) inventory strategy, (2) transportation strategy and (3) location strategy. With this new development, these local companies acquired their innovative entrepreneurship, which is the vital feature of companies in the industry 4.0 economy.

This paper has presented elements of the success factors and challenges for small local freight firms trying to develop toward an industry 4.0 organisation with an added business value and innovation. The empirical evidence, as well as the theoretical discussions of the empirical findings delivered by this paper, are expected to shed light on understanding how small local transportation companies can increase their competitive ability as they face growing competition in the industry. The use of Thailand 4.0 policy follows the idea of the industry 4.0. Industry 4.0 requires business organisations to acquire the new knowledge, the business innovation and the business value added through creativity as the vital elements for development. By doing so, business organisations in the era of industry 4.0 will be able to survive the increased competitions and achieve their sustainable development. This paper has delivered the empirical investigation of success factors and challenges for five selected cross-country freight enterprises for Thailand trying to manage their business following the Thailand 4.0 policy.

The study results and discussions provided in this paper may help to shed light on how small-sized companies can move towards sustainable development in this era of industry 4.0 economy, where innovation and new knowledge is in the central focus. The implementation of the findings may be applied in studies of small business in other regions. Therefore, suggestions for future research are studies in other parts of Thailand or other counties with similar contextual conditions of challenges arisen by cross-border infrastructures and the concepts of industry 4.0 and the digital economy.

Acknowledgements

The conduct of this research project and the paper presentation at the conference received funding from Mahasarakham Business School, Mahasarakham University, Thailand.

References

Charmaz, K. (2000). Grounded theory in the 21st century, in N. K. Denzin and Y. S. Lincoln (eds.), Handbook of qualitative research, 2nd edition, London: Sage, pp. 507–535

Crudu, R. (2019). The Role of Innovative Entrepreneurship in the Economic Development of EU Member Countries. *Journal of Entrepreneurship, Management and Innovation*. 15. 35-60. 10.7341/20191512.

Denzin, N. K. and Lincoln, Y. S. (2008). Introduction: the discipline and practice of qualitative research, in N. K.

Denzin and Y. S. Lincoln (eds.), Strategies of qualitative inquiry, 3rd edition, London: Sage, pp. 1–43.

Glaser, B. G. (1992). Emergence vs forcing: basics of grounded theory analysis, Mill Valley, CA: Sociology Press.

Jones, C., and Pimdee, P. (2017). Innovative ideas: Thailand 4.0 and the fourth industrial revolution. Asian International Journal of Social Sciences, 17(1), 4 – 32.

Kanellos, N., S., (2011). A conceptual framework for analyzing knowledge-based entrepreneurship, in: 2011 International Conference on Integrated Information. Kos, Greece.

Merriam, S. B. (2002). *Qualitative research in practice: examples for discussion and analysis*, 1st edition, San Francisco, CA: Jossey-Bass.

Moutinho, R., Au-Yong-Oliveira, M., Coelho, A., Manso, J.P., (2016). Determinants of knowledge-based entrepreneurship: an exploratory approach. International Entrepreneurship and Management Journal 12, 171–197.

Noonoi, O., (2011). General management factors and management factors of truck transportation entrepreneurs. Master of Management thesis. Burapa Univeristy. Chonburi

Office of the National Digital Economy and Society Commission (ONDE). (2019). Outcome of Preliminary Study of Digital Economy Indicators. Office of the National Digital Economy and Society Commission. Bangkok. Available at https://www.onde.go.th/assets/portals/1/files/ebook/thailand_digital_outlook_en.pdf(Accessed: 12 April 2020)

Office of Transport and Traffic Policy and Planning. (2015). *The potential Assessment and Readiness of Transport Infrastructure and Services in Thailand for ASEAN Economic Community (AEC)*. TransConsult. Bangkok. Available at http://www.otp.go.th/uploads/tiny_uploads/Education_Report/2555/Project2-AEC/ExecutiveENG.pdf. (Accessed: 12 April 2020).

Patton, M. Q. (2002). Qualitative research and evaluation methods, 3rd edition, London: Sage.

Strauss, A. and Corbin, J. (1998). Grounded theory methodology: an overview, in N. K. Denzin and Y. S. Lincoln (eds.), Strategies of qualitative inquiry, London: Sage, pp. 158–183.

Thailand Board of Investment (2015). *A Guide to Investment in the Special Economic Development Zones (SEZ). Office of the Board of Investment. Bangkok*. Available at https://www.boi.go.th/upload/content/BOI-book%202015_20150818_95385.pdf. (Accessed: 12 April 2020).

Thailand Board of Investment (2016). Thailand's Logistics Market Set to Flourish, *Thailand Investment Review*, Vol 26, No. 9, September 2016, pp 5-6.

Regulatory and Supporting Institutions of Social Entrepreneurship in the Digital Society

Evgeny Popov[1], Anna Veretennikova[2] and Kseniya Kozinskaya[2]
[1]Ural Institute of Management of the Russian Presidential Academy of National Economy and Public Administration, Yekaterinburg, Russia
[2]Institute of Economics, the Ural Branch of Russian Academy of Sciences, Yekaterinburg, Russia
epopov@mail.ru
vay_uiec@mail.ru
ksush1@yandex.ru
DOI: 10.34190/EIE.20.107

Abstract: The reasons for the growing interest in social entrepreneurship development, which attracts the attention of the scientific community, government and civil society, are a lack of resources and the growth of social problems in society as well as the new opportunities of economic models that stimulate social entrepreneurship. All this demonstrates the leading role of the institutional environment in the social entrepreneurship development, and the inalienable influence of modern trends on its rapid development. The study is aimed at systematizing the formal institutions of social entrepreneurship worldwide and determining the role of digitalization on its development. At the first stage of the study, the authors identified and systematized the institutions that have the most significant impact on the level of social entrepreneurship development. At this stage, the need for a separate review of the regulatory and supporting institutional environment has been discovered. Within the regulatory institutional environment, we considered legal support institutions and public administration Institutions. Institutions of education, financial and material support, and interaction with markets were investigated as a part of the supportive institutional environment. In the second stage of the study, we used correlation analysis to investigate 23 countries. It lets to determine which of the institutions are more essential for social entrepreneurship development. It is shown that the most important ones are public governance institutions. The analysis of the impact of digitalization on the social entrepreneurship institutional environment shows the possibility of transforming governance institutions and describes examples of digital platforms implementation in the development of interaction between the state, civil society, and social entrepreneurs in the process of solving social problems. Furthermore, the role of shared economy instruments in the development of social entrepreneurship is substantiated. The theoretical significance of the results is the use of institutional analysis for the development of social entrepreneurship. The practical significance consists in demonstrating the role of digitalization for the development of the formal institutional environment.

Keywords: social entrepreneurship, digitalization, institutional environment, governance

1. Introduction

Global trends show social entrepreneurship as a solution to various social problems, such as unemployment, social exclusion, lack of affordable medical care, preschool education, etc. Scientists consider social entrepreneurship as an integral part of the development of the national innovation ecosystem (Suriea and Groenbc 2017) and also an important tool for sustainable economic development (Abdou et al 2014).

A review of academic studies devoted to social entrepreneurship indicates an increase of interest in the phenomenon. Friedman and Desiviglia (2010) note the importance of social entrepreneurship for regional development, Azmat (2013) argues for its positive impact on the economy in developing countries, Yiu et al (2014) show that social entrepreneurship plays an important role in economic development. According to the concept of researcher E. McAnany (2012), social entrepreneurship has significant potential for promoting social change, the development of regional societies, economic growth, poverty reduction, and environmental sustainability.

However, theoretical studies of social entrepreneurship are noticeably lagging behind the practice (Nicholls 2010). The uneven development of the social entrepreneurship activity indicates the presence of unexplored aspects of this phenomenon. One of the promising areas that can clarify the possibilities, patterns, and features of social entrepreneurship development is the study of institutional conditions that affect social entrepreneurship (Lepoutre et al 2013). Thus, there is an interest in applying the institutional approach in the study of social entrepreneurship (Urban and Kujing 2017) In particular, Dacin et al (2002) note that the application of institutional theory to social entrepreneurship practice contributes to the development of both socially-oriented activities and institutional theory.

Furthermore, digitalization processes contribute to the growth of interest in social entrepreneurship, which, on the one hand, facilitate the communication of interested people and help attract new people to the project, reduce the time of social service, on the other, can create new areas for the development of social entrepreneurship.

The spread of digitalization has also affected the system of existing institutions, which play a key role in the development of social entrepreneurship. Digital transformation creates new business opportunities, contributes to a change in the roles of participants in the value chain, and makes fundamental changes in the processes of organizing economic processes, both deleting and creating new links in the chains of reproduction of goods (EIDES, 2019). Thus, the effective institutional environment, as well as digitalization processes, contribute an important role in the rapid transformation of the norms and rules of interaction, including in social entrepreneurship.

The purpose of the research is to analyze and systematize social entrepreneurship formal institutions in the world and determining the digitalization role in its development. As part of the study, the nature of social entrepreneurship was examined, the need for a separate review of regulatory and supporting institutions was substantiated, a correlation analysis of the influence of various factors on the activity of citizens in this area was carried out, the institutions most important for the development of social entrepreneurship were identified, and it was shown how the level of digitalization of institutional environment affects the social entrepreneurship development.

2. Institutional environment of social entrepreneurship

2.1 Social entrepreneurship as an object of institutional analysis

The interest growing to social entrepreneurship in theoretical studies has contributed to the formation of 4 basic research schools: social-innovative (Mair and Marty 2006) social-entrepreneurship (Krimmins and Kiel, 1983; Emerson and Twersky 1996), having roots in the USA; EMES (Stephan et al 2015; Speer, 2001), European school (Dees J., Anderson B., 2006; Popov et al, 2019), and the English school of social entrepreneurship development. The formation of the research schools is based on the experience of developed countries. Developing countries, in turn, undoubtedly have their own individual experience in the social entrepreneurship development, it can be based both on borrowing successful cases from developed countries and demonstrate the choice of a unique development path for this type of activity. That choice takes into account the historical features of economic and social development, as well as a system of formal and informal norms and rules that form the corresponding institutional environment (Singh et al 2017, Mehrotra and Verma 2015). Taking into account not only the national but also the regional level of social entrepreneurship development allows for a more detailed study of this phenomenon, modeling and forecasting its development, as well as creating conditions for increasing its effectiveness (Prochazkova and Noskova 2020).

The dialectics of economic and social, as well as collective and individual goals in the social entrepreneurship implementation, on the one hand, determine the study of the institutional environment in which this type of activity develops; on the other hand, it is the reason for turning to institutional analysis tools, which allows taking into account non-economic incentives for the social entrepreneurship development.

Comparing social and commercial entrepreneurship, it is worth noting the particular importance of the entrepreneur's social mission and its prevalence over the possibility of obtaining commercial benefits (Santos 2012). Hence, the influence on social entrepreneurship of the system of formal and informal rules and norms operating in a particular territory may differ from commercial entrepreneurship.

The activities of public authorities for the development of commercial entrepreneurship can have both a supporting and a restraining effect. However, the development of social entrepreneurship requires special support measures. In order to a deeper study of this issue, it is necessary to consider the institutional environment characteristic of socially oriented activities.

2.2 Regulative and supportive institutions of social entrepreneurship

According to the concept of researchers J. Mair and I. Marty (2006), social entrepreneurship is a process due to the interaction of social entrepreneurs with the environment. B. Urban and L. Kujing (2017) note that the decision to create a new social enterprise is determined by the existing institutional environment that restrains or supports the actions of economic agents.

At the same time, social entrepreneurship initiates processes of institutional change, and directly a social entrepreneur can be considered as an institutional agent (Starnawska, 2017). Starnawska and Brzozowska (2018) also note that focus on the concept of a social entrepreneur as an institutional agent is in line with the structure-agency debate and provides opportunities for discussion on the transformative, change the potential of social entrepreneurship. Moreover, the realization of the role of social entrepreneurship as a transformer of the institutional environment is possible if there are institutions that ensure the development of this type of activity. Thus, we can talk about the inclusion of a social entrepreneur in the cycle of institutional development, where a social entrepreneur allows institutions to move to a new round of development. However, this mechanism will operate with the functioning of an effective institutional environment that stimulates social entrepreneurship. Ensuring its effectiveness requires a more detailed analysis of its impact on social entrepreneurship.

Institutional environment, capable of exerting both direct and indirect influence on the development of social entrepreneurship, is dual. For example, the complexity of regulating the formation of new socially-oriented organizations has a negative impact on this type of activity. The presence of support measures, as well as special conditions for the development of social entrepreneurs, stimulate the activity of society to this type of activity. Thus, the environment is critical for the creation and development of social enterprises.

The primary purpose of institutions in society is to reduce uncertainty by establishing stable structural interactions of individuals. According to North (1990), institutions are human-developed constraints that structure political, economic, and social interactions. According to Williamson (1996), formal institutions can be divided into constitutional and regulatory. Ostrom (1994) calls that phenomenon “constitutional choice” and “collective choice”.

State mechanisms regulate the actions of individuals and determine social norms; therefore, political structures play an important role in perceiving entrepreneurial activity as attractive or unattractive. Later, Scott, studying social entrepreneurship, added "supporting" institutions to Williamson's classification, dividing all the institutions of public entrepreneurs into regulatory, supporting, and cognitive. Regulatory institutions are the most formal and, as a rule, are prescribed in regulatory legal acts. Supported institutions are generally less formal and determine the behavior or actions expected of organizations, specialists, and individuals. Supported institutions are often represented by reputable organizations such as a letter of credit, professional communities, and include other professional standards. Cultural and cognitive institutions are the most informal and widely used rules and beliefs (Scott, 2001). The use of this classification for the analysis of the institutional environment and social enterprises provides a reasonable definition of the rules and norms governing the interaction between economic agents in relation to the implementation of socially oriented activities, as well as stimulating this type of activity. However, it should be noted that the research is based solely on formal institutions.

The regulatory environment refers to "formal rules and incentives that limit and regulate entrepreneurial behavior" and responsible for setting rules, rewards, or punishments (Seelos et al 2011). Since entrepreneurs in emerging markets are facing rapid institutional changes associated with changes in the economic climate, level of state participation, ownership structures, and legislative standards, the regulatory environment has a significant impact on the activities of social entrepreneurs (Peng et al 2009). Silos et al (2011) established that through regulatory factors, control over the processes and results of socially oriented activities is carried out. S. Estrin and B. Urban believe that social and entrepreneurial activity is more successful in the institutional environment with a strong legal system. Based on the analysis of Stefan and Ulaner (2015), the influence of institutional voids, institutional support, and institutional structures on the development of socially-oriented activities revealed that social entrepreneurship is more developed in countries with high government activity in solving social problems of society. Sherir and Lerner (2006) note that state laws affect the environment of organizations, and therefore their success.

A supportive environment plays an important role in determining and forming entrepreneurial results. According to the concept of Silo, the institutional environment through the systematization of norms of behavior creates mechanisms that form the context of social entrepreneurs activities (Seelos et al 2011). Supporting mechanisms arise from social structures and are responsible for the formation of adequate entrepreneurial behavior. These findings were the basis for the analysis of the impact of the institutional environment on social entrepreneurship and made it possible to formulate the null as well as the alternative hypothesis.

> *H0. The formal institutional environment does not affect social entrepreneurship development.*
>
> *H1. Regulative and supportive institutional environment has an impact on the development of social entrepreneurship.*

In analyzing the impact of the institutional environment on social entrepreneurship, we could not avoid to touch upon digitalization processes. The high speed of introducing digital technologies also extends to the system of institutions. The social economy and social enterprises should use digitalization and digital technologies as a lever for economic and social transformations and enhance social impact. Tokarski (European Commission) notes that social innovators and social entrepreneurs should be at the center of digital technologies and introduce new technologies, for example, the blockchain uses an internal approach to decentralization, which can have many consequences for services and create high social added value. The role of public authorities is to ensure that the environment in which enterprises of the social economy operate conforms to them.

Prodanov (2018) was one of the first researchers to raise the question of the relationship between social entrepreneurship and digital transformation, noting that the accelerated development of digital technologies both creates new opportunities for the development of this type of activity and is the cause of growing inequality. Based on the analysis, the scientist identifies possible ways of combining social entrepreneurship and digital technology. However, an equally important condition for establishing the relationship of these phenomena is to determine the impact of specific characteristics of digitalization on social enterprises.

Since digitalization is considered by researchers in two aspects: on the one hand, in the use of new technologies in entrepreneurial activity, in particular in social entrepreneurship, on the other hand, as the impact of digitalization on the institutional environment of social entrepreneurship. All of the above allows us to formulate the following hypothesis:

> *H3. Digitalization of the formal institutional environment has a positive impact on the development of social entrepreneurship.*

3. Methodology

3.1 Data

To assess social entrepreneurship, we used the data presented in the Global Entrepreneurship Monitoring (GEM) report. GEM is global entrepreneurship research conducted by the university association. The share of the population involved in social entrepreneurship was considered as the level of development of this type of activity (GEM, 2015). The analysis of countries by the level of development of social entrepreneurship allowed them to be divided into three groups. The first group included countries with high rates of development of social entrepreneurship: from 6% and above. This group includes Israel, Luxembourg, Australia, USA, Philippines, Norway, and Poland. The second group included countries with average indicators: from 4% to 5.9%. This group included Peru, Colombia, India, Sweden, Switzerland, Uruguay, Estonia, Tunisia, Great Britain, and others (Fig. 1). Countries with the lowest percentage of the population involved in socially-oriented activities belong to the third group. This group includes Romania, Hungary, China, Argentina, Spain, Bulgaria, Iran, and others. This study analyzes the first two groups of countries with rates from 3% in Cameroon to 10.6% in Israel (fig.1).

To test hypotheses, H0 and H1 were considered countries with high and medium level social entrepreneurship development. The total number of observations is 23 countries. For the analysis of institutions affecting on social entrepreneurship we used the information bases of World Bank, The World justice project, World Bank Policy Research, which provided data on the quality of public administration, the human development index, the costs of the social sphere, the index of ease of doing business, the rule of law indicator.

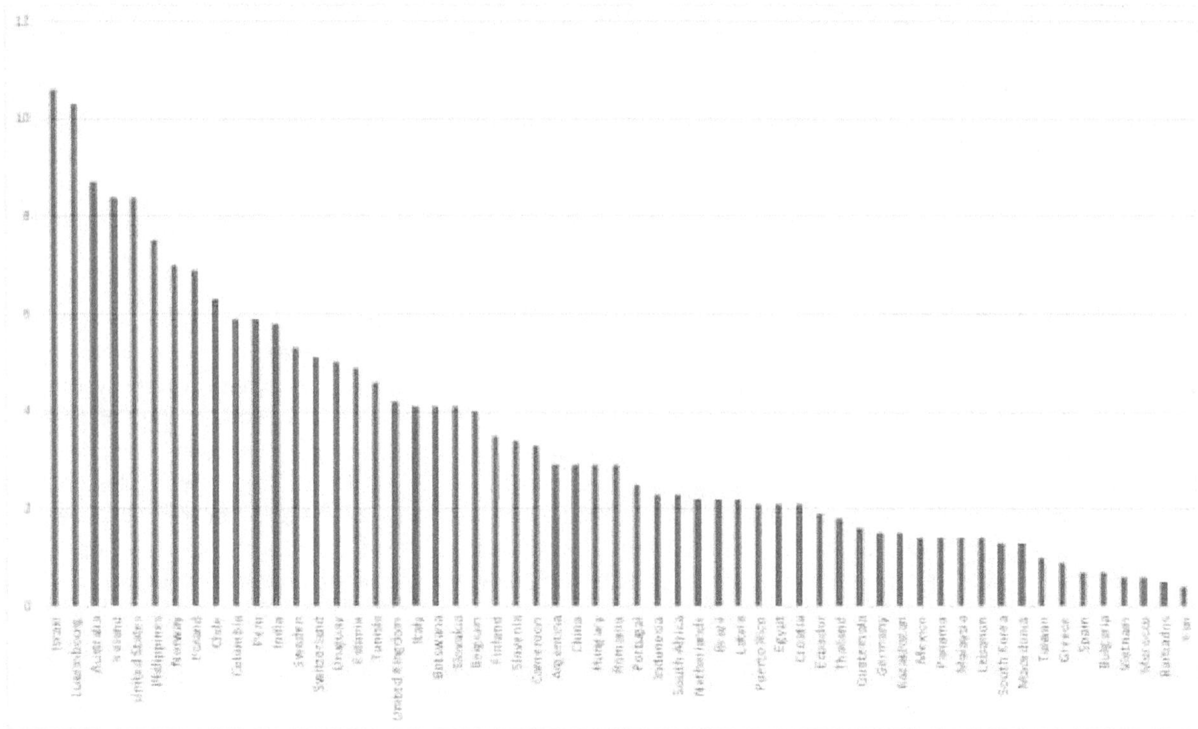

Figure 1: The share of the population involved in social entrepreneurship (GEM, 2015)

In terms of testing hypothesis H2, we turned to the analysis of the European Index of Digital Entrepreneurship Systems (EIDES, 2019). The European Index of Digital Entrepreneurship Systems (EIDES) responds to the need for a tool to better understand and appraise the extent of the digital entrepreneurial institutional environment. This original work attempts to turn the existing index from a tool to measure general framework conditions for entrepreneurship to a tool to framework conditions for digital entrepreneurship. Following the critical review of the ESIS and a discussion of the current transformation of entrepreneurship, this report presents the method adopted to construct the EIDES with the results that the EIDES highlights for the EU 28 countries.

The structure of the revised EIDES encompasses four pillars for the General Framework Conditions (i.e., Culture and Informal Institutions, Formal Institutions, Regulation, and Taxation, Market Conditions, and Physical Infrastructure) and their associated digital counterparts.

In this part of the study, we focused on European countries, which was due to the set of countries covered by EIDES. However, we excluded the countries of Eastern Europe from consideration, due to the entry level of digitalisation of regulatory and supporting institutions in these regions. Thus, at this stage of the study, the sample was limited to 14 observations.

3.2 Methodological design

At the first stage of the study, hypotheses H0 and H1 were tested. The main task of this stage is to determine the institutions of the regulatory environment that have a significant impact on social entrepreneurship development. First of all, institutions, creating the conditions for the development of social entrepreneurship, were systematized, and a list of indicators and indices characterizing the institutional environment in which social entrepreneurs operate was formulated.

As indicators of legal support institutions in countries were used the ease of doing business index (World Bank), based on the study of laws, regulations, and rules related to doing business. To determine the impact of institute of Public Administration on socially oriented activities, the rule of law index (The World justice project) is considered. This indicator reflects the perception of the quality of the rule of law and includes compliance with property rights, the likelihood of the execution of contracts, actions of the police and courts. In addition, an indicator of the quality of public administration (World Bank Policy Research) was used.

To evaluate the institution of social welfare, indices such as social spending as a percentage of GDP (World Bank report) and Human Development Index (UN) as a general indicator of the functioning of formal institutions (Social Expenditure Database).

When testing hypotheses H0 and H1, a correlation analysis was used. It showed the close connection between the level of development of social entrepreneurship and the institutions.

For a more in-depth analysis of the institutional environment of social entrepreneurship, as well as supporting institutions, it was determined that there are norms and rules, various projects that make it possible to judge the functioning or absence of institutions in the countries. This analysis became the basis for forming a list of institutions that directly affect social entrepreneurship development.

In the second stage of the study, using the analysis of European countries as an example were formed the factors describing the level of digitalization of the institutional environment and revealed which of them really affect social entrepreneurship.

Digitalization is intertwined with formal institutions for the formation of entrepreneurship. At the EIDES, the formalization, taxation, and taxation component of digitalization includes several metrics describing digital security and privacy. This pillar also includes proxies that measure how formal institutions and the regulatory environment shape digitization and competition. Reliance also reflects the digitization of public services, with an emphasis on e-government. The modernization and digitization of public services can lead to increased efficiency of public administration, citizens, and enterprises through the provision of high-quality services. The column includes indicators such as: (1) ICT laws (WEF), (2) prevalence of Kaspersky network attacks (Securelist), (3) prevalence of digital threats, such as viruses and malware (Securelist), (4) Software Piracy Rate (WEF), (5) Internet Telephony Competition (WEF) and (6) E Government (United Nations Department of Economic and Social Affairs). The digital counterpart of the Market Conditions (DFC_P3) pillar characterizes the exploitation of online market channels (e.g., e-commerce, e-sales, e-advertisement by households and firms. By adopting digital technology, households and businesses can enhance efficiency, reduce costs, and better engage customers, collaborators, and business partners. Furthermore, the Internet also offers wider access to markets. The digital pillar includes the following six indicators derived from Eurostat and one from Translate.net database: (1) Individuals using the Internet for ordering goods or services, (2) Enterprises having received orders via computer-mediated networks, % of enterprises, (3) Enterprises total turnover from e-commerce, (4) Enterprises having done electronic sales to other countries, (5) Enterprises.

When determining the influence of the presented factors on social entrepreneurship, the indicator of the development of social entrepreneurship given in the Global Entrepreneurship Monitoring (GEM) report, was used as a dependent variable.

Thus, to test hypothesis H2, a regression analysis was carried out and a non-linear model was constructed that shows which of the factors of digitalization of the institutional environment determine the development of social entrepreneurship

4. Results

4.1 Systematization of institutions of social entrepreneurship

As a result of the correlation analysis, it was revealed that the indices that have the most significant correlation dependence on the level of development of social entrepreneurship include: the quality of public administration (r = 0.43) as a characteristic of the executive branch, the human development index (r = 0.42) and costs on the social sphere (r = -0.43), considered as characteristics of social security. At the same time, the correlation was not found with the index of ease of doing business (r = 0.11) and with the rule of law used as a characteristic of the institution of legal support (r = 0.34). In general, we can conclude that the institution of public administration has a direct impact on the formation and development of socially oriented activities.

Regarding to institutions of human capital development, norms were noted with regard to raising awareness of social entrepreneurship, norms of long-term education, exchange of experience, organization and conduct of trainings. Institutions for providing financial and material support characterize the availability and accessibility of grants and consultations in the management of business processes, material infrastructure, support for startups and affordable targeted financial instruments. The functioning of institutions for interacting with the market can be concluded through analysis of support for investment attractiveness, as well as cooperation and access to markets. The legal support institutions that characterize the presence of the Unified State Program for the Development of Social Entrepreneurship, as well as the presence in the legislation of a specialized legal form for the implementation of this type of activity, were analyzed.

It is important to note that most countries with a high or medium level of development of socially oriented activities (USA, Philippines, Australia) have legal forms of social enterprises. In countries such as Ireland, Australia, India, despite the absence of specialized legal forms, Anglo-Saxon law allows the flexible use of existing types of organizations for the implementation of social and entrepreneurial activities.

The analysis also determined the presence of state programs for the development of socially-oriented activities in countries with high rates of development of social entrepreneurship; therefore, it can be concluded that social entrepreneurship development programs have a beneficial effect on social entrepreneurship. In countries such as Luxembourg, Australia, Norway, the Philippines, social entrepreneurship development programs have been adopted at the state level. State programs not only recognize the importance of social entrepreneurship in the economic and social life of the country but also contribute to the phased and systemic development of this area.

Supporting institutions are also quite developed and effective in countries with a high level of social entrepreneurship development (Israel, USA, Australia). Among the supporting institutes, the institute of education, the institutes of providing financial and material support, the institutes of interaction with the markets were identified. Regarding educational institutions, norms were noted with regard to raising awareness of social entrepreneurship, norms of long-term education, exchange of experience, organization, and conduct of training. Institutions for providing financial and material support characterize the availability and accessibility of grants and consulting in the management of business processes, material infrastructure, support for startups, and affordable targeted financial instruments. The functioning of institutions for interacting with the market can be concluded through analysis of support for investment attractiveness, as well as cooperation and access to markets.

Thus, we can conclude that for social entrepreneurship development, not only regulatory institutions are needed, but also comprehensive assistance in the form of supporting institutions.

Thus, hypothesis H0 has been disproved, and hypothesis H1 has been partially confirmed.

4.2 The institutional environment digitalization of social entrepreneurship

In the process of analyzing the influence of independent variables on the level of social entrepreneurship development Y, it was determined that the distribution of random variables for the tested factors and the dependent variable Y is nonlinear. In this regard, the initial data was converted into a nonlinear form, and then a nonlinear regression model was constructed. After eliminating factors that do not have a significant effect, based on testing the hypothesis of the insignificance of the regression coefficients, the dependence of the level of social entrepreneurship on the level of development of physical infrastructure (X3) was established. Thus, a regression model showing the relationship between the dependent variable Y and the independent variable X was presented as follows:

$$Y = e^{-1,31} \times X_3^{\,0,03} \qquad (1)$$

An analysis of the reliability of the results showed that the model is reliable (Fstatistic = 0.021), and also confirms the representativeness of the observations. The determination coefficient R2 = 0.36, which indicates that the spread in the indicators of development of social entrepreneurship by about 36% depends on the indicators selected at the stage of modeling the matrix of pair correlation coefficients. Testing the null hypothesis about the insignificance of the regression coefficients showed that the selected factors have an effect; their regression coefficients are statistically significant. The value of the F-criterion and p demonstrate that the constructed model is significant at the significance level $\alpha = 0.05$. The Darbin-Watson test used to test the model for the presence of autocorrelation of residues (dcalc = 1.95) showed that there is no connection between the residues and they are random.

Thus, the development of social entrepreneurship is affected only by the digitalization indicator of the physical infrastructure, which implies that the H2 hypothesis has also been partially confirmed.

5. Discussion

The analysis of the institutional environment allowed us to systematize the formal institutions affecting social entrepreneurship (Fig. 2).

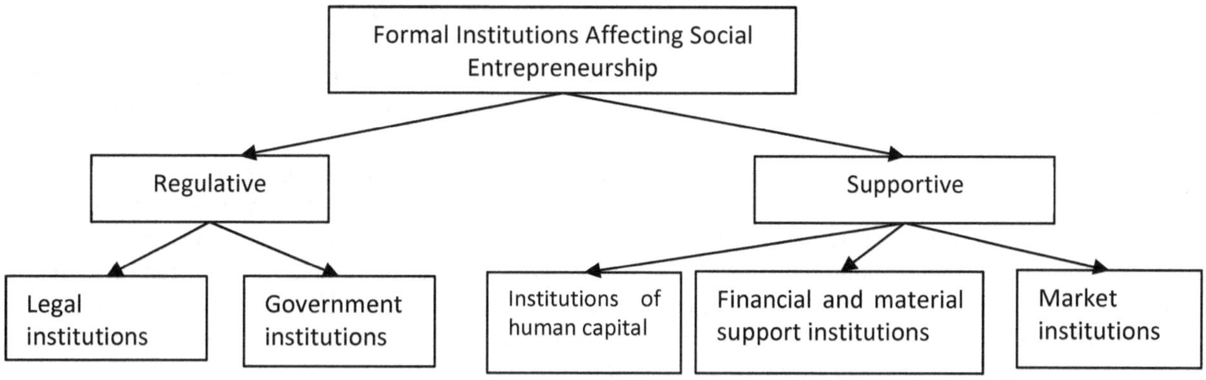

Figure 2: Formal institutions affecting the development of social entrepreneurship

It should be noted that due to economic crises and lack of funds, governments are increasingly refusing to provide social services to their citizens. In this regard, the "free" niche has the opportunity to occupy social entrepreneurs focused on meeting the social needs of society. However, the priority of social goals over economic ones, in this type of activity, requires the development of effective mechanisms for their cooperation with the state. It is important to note that specialized legal forms and state programs for the development of social entrepreneurship open up additional opportunities for access to financial instruments necessary for social entrepreneurs to ensure the financial stability of their enterprises.

Separately, it is necessary to note the role of digital platforms and other digital resources in the development of social entrepreneurship, as shown in the model.

The use of digital platforms as a tool for the development of the regulatory environment is not a new practice and familiar for both developed and developing countries, for example, in the provision of financial and tax reporting or in state registers conducting, etc. There has been particularly strong interest in the development of digital platforms as an element in the development of a supportive environment for social entrepreneurship. In this context, it is necessary to highlight 1) platforms, providing educational resources, as well as information and consulting support for social entrepreneurs; 2) platforms aimed at the development of communications, including in social entrepreneurship; 3) digital platforms, acting as a result of the introduction of innovative ideas in the social sphere with its further capitalization. Platforms of the first group are actively used both at the national and international levels, in particular, the Internet resource Society Profit provides educational courses for social entrepreneurs, and also acts as a platform for the exchange of experience between existing and emerging social entrepreneurs.

The project "Up to youth project" helps to attract young people (graduate students, unemployed graduates or young migrants) and creates the conditions for the development of skills for digital social entrepreneurship. The second group includes digital platforms serving as a platform for communication of individual communities (Researchgate, LinkedIn, etc.), as well as global social networks (Facebook, etc.) as platforms for establishing new connections, finding partners, exchanging information and etc. The third group of digital platforms represents the highest point in the development of social entrepreneurship. As an example, the company Facebook, formed primarily as a non-profit social innovation while having a high level of capitalization at present. According to the 2019 Digital Economy Report prepared by the UN, seven of the world's eighth largest companies in terms of market capitalization use platform business models. However, the development of capitalization opportunities for social enterprises requires a serious transformation of the institutional environment, which involves the transformation of incentives, motives of economic agents, informal institutions in the form of values and traditions, and, above all, the system of state institutions, which can become an important condition for the development of a social economy. The transition to designing such an institutional environment is possible through the development of shared economy projects that transform the traditional patterns of behavior of economic agents, including those related to the reproduction of social goods and services.

6. Conclusion

In the study, with the aim of analyzing and systematizing the formal institutions of social entrepreneurship in the world and determining the role of digitalization in its development, the following results were obtained.

First, approaches to the analysis of social entrepreneurship are disclosed, and the significance of both effective regulatory and supporting institutions in the development of social entrepreneurship is substantiated.

Secondly, on the basis of correlation analysis, as well as identifying the presence or absence of norms and rules governing this type of activity, it is determined by the example of 23 countries which of the institutions are most important for the development of social entrepreneurship. In addition, institutions that have the most significant impact on the level of development of social entrepreneurship are identified and systematized. Within the regulatory institutional environment, legal support institutions and public administration institutions are taken into account; within the framework of a supportive institutional environment - institutions of education, financial and material support, and interaction with markets.

Thirdly, in the course of analyzing the impact of digitalization of institutional environment on social entrepreneurship, the importance of physical infrastructure is determined, which shows the role of digital platforms in the social entrepreneurship development, expands opportunities for communication, access to the acquisition of new skills and resources for implementing social projects.

The findings of the study can be used to develop mechanisms to support social entrepreneurs in the global space.

Acknowledgements

The study was performed as part of the government assignment for the Institute of Economics, Ural Branch of the Russian Academy of Sciences.

References

Abdou, E., Fahmy, A., Greenwald, D., and Nelson J. (2014) "Social Entrepreneurship in the Middle East: Toward Sustainable Development for the Next Generation", The Middle East Youth Initiative Working Paper, 10. Retrieved October 7 (Available at: https://www.brookings.edu/wp-content/uploads/2016/06/04_social_entrepreneurship_es.pdf).

Azmat, F. (2013)"Sustainable Development in Developing Countries: the Role of Social Entrepreneurs", *International Journal of Public Administration*, Vol. 36, No.5, pp 293-304.

Crimmings, J. and Kiel, M. (1983) *Enterprise in the Nonprofit Sector*. Washington, DC: Partners for Livable Places.

Dacin, M., Goodstein, J., and Scott, W. "Institutional theory and institutional changes", *The Academy of Management Journal.* 2002. Vol. 45. No 1. P. 45–57.

Dees, J. and Anderson, B. (2006) "Framing a theory of entrepreneurship: building on two schools of practice and thought", ARNOVA Occasional Paper Series: Research on Social Entrepreneurship: Understanding and Contributing to an Emerging Field, Vol. 1, No. 3, pp 39–66.

Easy of doing business ranking. Available at: http://www.doingbusiness.org/rankings.

Emerson, J. and Twersky, F. (1996*) New social entrepreneurs: the success, challenge and lessons of non-profit enterprise creation*, San Francisco: Roberts Foundation.

Friedman, V. and Desivilya, H. (2010) "Integrating social entrepreneurship and conflict engagement for regional development in divided societies", *Entrepreneurship and Regional Development*. An International Journal, Vol. 22, No. 6, pp 495-514.

GEM 2015 Report on social entrepreneurship. https://www.gemconsortium.org/report/gem-2015-report-onsocial-entrepreneurship, accessed 30 September 2019.

Human Development Reports. Available at: http://hdr.undp.org

Lepoutre, J., Justo, R., Terjesen, S., and Bosma, N. (2013) "Designing a global standardized methodology for measuring social entrepreneurship activity: The Global Entrepreneurship Monitor social entrepreneurship study", *Small Business Economics*, Vol. 40, No. 3, pp 693–714.

Mair, J. and Martí, I. (2006) "Social entrepreneurship research: a source of explanation, prediction, and delight", *Journal of World Business*, No. 41 (1), pp 36–44.

McAnany, E. (2012) "Social Entrepreneurship and Communication for Development and Social Change- Rethinking Innovation", *Nordicom Review*, Vol. 33, pp 205-218.

Mehrota, S., & Verma, S. (2015). An assessment approach for enhancing the organizational performance of social enterprises in India. Journal of Entrepreneurship in Emerging Economies, 7(1), 35-54.

Nicholls, A. (2010) "The legitimacy of social entrepreneurship: Reflexive isomorphism in a pre-paradigmatic field", *Entrepreneurship Theory and Practice*, Vol. 34, No.4, pp 611–633.

North, D. (1990) *Institutions, Institutional Change and Economic Performance*. Cambridge: Cambridge University Press.

Ostrom, E. (1994) "Constituting Social Capital and Collective Action. Journal of Theoretical Politics, Vol. 6, No. 4, pp 527–562.

Peng, M., Sun, S.L., Pinkham, B., and Chen, H. (2009) "The Institution-based View as a Third Leg for Strategy Tripod. *Academy of Management Perspectives*, Vol. 23, No. 3, pp 63–81

Popov, E., Veretennikova, A. and Kozinskaya, K.(2019) "Research schools and stages of social entrepreneurship development in the global space", *Proceedings of 14th European Conference on Innovation and Entrepreneurship, ECIE*, Vol. 2, pp 814-822.

Prochazkova, P., & Noskova, M., (2020). An application of input-output analysis to social enterprises: a case of the Czech Republic. *Journal of Entrepreneurship in Emerging Economies* (DOI: https://doi.org/10.1108/JEEE-08-2019-0114

Prodanov, H. (2018). Social Enterpreneurship And Digital Technologies. *Economic Alternatives*, No.1, pp.123-138

Santos, F. (2012) "A positive theory of social entrepreneurship", *Journal of Business Ethics*, Vol.111, No. 3. pp 335–351

Scott, W.R. (2001) Institutions and organizations. Thousand Oaks, CA, Sage Publ., 280 p

Seelos, C., Mair, J., Battilana, J., and Dacin, T.M. (2011) "The Embeddedness of Social Entrepreneurship: Understanding Variation Across Local Communities", *Research in the Sociology of Organizations*, Vol. 33, No. 4, pp 333–363.

Sharir, M., and Lerner, M. (2006) "Gauging the success of social ventures initiated by individual social entrepreneurs", *Journal of World Business*, Vol.41, No.1, pp 6-20.

Singh, A., Majumdar, S., & Saini, G. (2017). Corporate Social Responsibility and Social Entrepreneurship: An Indian Context. *Journal of Entrepreneurship and Innovation in Emerging Economies*, 3(1), 71–76.

Social Expenditure Database. Available at: http://www.oecd.org/social/expenditure.htm

Society profits. Available at: https://www.societyprofits.eu/about/

Spear, R., Defourny, J., Favreau, L., and Laville, J.-L. (2001) Tackling social exclusion in Europe. *The contribution of the social economy*. Aldershot: Ashgate.

Starnawska, M. (2017). Przedsiębiorczość społeczna w świetle teorii instytucjonalnej – próba przyczynku teoretycznego. *Przedsiębiorczość i Zarządzanie*, No. XVIII(12), pp. 149-160.

Starnawska, M., & Brzozowska, A. (2018). Editorial paper. Social entrepreneurship and social enterprise phenomenon: Antecedents, processes, impact across cultures and contexts. Journal of Entrepreneurship, Management and Innovation, No. 14(2), pp. 3-18. https://doi.org/10.7341/20181421

Stephan, U., Uhlaner L., and Stride C. (2015) "Institutions and social entrepreneurship: the role of institutional voids, institutional support and institutional configurations", *Journal of International Business Studies*, Vol. 46, No. 3, pp 308-331.

Suriea, G. and Groenbc, A. (2017) "The importance of social entrepreneurship in national systems of innovation — An introduction", *Technological Forecasting and Social Change*, 2017, Vol. 121, pp181-183.

The European Index of Digital Entrepreneurship Systems. https://ec.europa.eu/jrc/en/publication/european-index-digitalentrepreneurship-systems, accessed 30 September 2019.

Urban, B. and Kujing, L. (2017) "The institutional environment and social entrepreneurship intentions", *International Journal of entrepreneurial behavior and research*, Vol. 23, No. 4. pp 638-655

Williamson, O. (1985). *The Economic Institutions of Capitalism*, New York: Free Press.

WJP Rule of Law Index. Available at: https://worldjusticeproject.org/our-work/wjp-rule-law-index/wjp-rule-law-index-2016

Yiu, D., Wan, W., Chen, X., and Su J. (2014) "Sentimental Drivers of Social Entrepreneurship: A Study of China's Guangcai (Glorious) ", *Program Management and Organization Review*, Vol. 10, No.1,pp 55–80.

How Does Institutional Environment Affect Innovations in Russia? Beyond Doing Business Rating

Andrey Pushkarev, Karina Nagieva, Natalia Davidson and Oleg Mariev
Ural Federal University, Ekaterinburg, Russia
a.a.pushkarev@urfu.ru
karina.nagieva74a@gmail.com
natalya.davidson@gmail.com
o.s.mariev@urfu.ru
DOI: 10.34190/EIE.20.096

Abstract: The aim of our paper is to assess the impact of human capital on innovation depending on institutional conditions. We use the data from the Business Enterprise Performance Survey (BEEPS) for the period from 2012 to 2014 for 1564 Russian manufacturing firms from 37 regions. In addition to financial and innovative indicators, the survey contains a rich set of institutional indicators. Based on the probit model, we analyze the interaction term between personnel training performed by firms and the institutional indicators that go beyond Doing Business rating. In addition, we include components of Doing Business in the model using principal component analysis and compare the effects of the institutional indicators. Our main hypothesis is that trained employees of firms located in unfavorable institutional conditions experience difficulties in innovation activities. The results show that trained employees contribute less to innovation, when crime, transport and inadequate employee education are serious barriers to firms' activities. Our research shed light on the aspects of business environment not taken into account in Doing Business Index but still affecting business activity. The results will be useful for the local and regional authorities interested in improving the institutional environment in which firms operate, as well as for the business analysts.

Keywords: innovation, institutional environment, human capital, personnel training, Russian regions, Doing Business Index

1. Introduction

In recent years, Russia has made a significant breakthrough, getting into the top 30 of the Doing Business international ranking. However, higher ranking in Doing Business Index did not lead to a surge in investment attractiveness of the country. There has actually been a drop in foreign direct investment, a substantial outflow of qualified personnel, and a competition level was low. A possible reason for such contradiction can be associated with the structure of Doing Business Index. It does not directly take into account, among other things, corruption in the country or regions and insecure business environment. We argue that these factors might be crucial for innovative performance of firms and their survival on the market.

In this regard, *the aim of our paper* is to assess the impact of human capital on innovation, while taking into account institutional conditions that firms operate in. To do this, we use the data from the Business Enterprise Performance Survey (BEEPS) for the period from 2012 to 2014 for 1564 Russian manufacturing firms working in 37 regions. In addition to financial and innovation indicators, the survey contains highly informative data on institutions. Employing probit model, we evaluate the interaction term between human capital and institutional indicators not covered by the Doing Business rating. We also include components of Doing Business index in the model by using principal component analysis and compare the effects of these institutional indicators.

Our *main hypothesis* is that trained employees of firms located in unfavorable institutional conditions experience difficulties in innovation activities. In other words, we assume that institutional environment affects the impact of human capital on innovations. Specifically, unfavorable institutional environment makes it difficult for personnel that received on-the-job training to contribute to innovations.

Doing Business index reflects the ease of doing business in a country or in the regions inside a country. A higher Doing Business rank implies that the regulatory environment is relatively more suitable for establishing and operating a firm. The rankings are calculated based on aggregate scores covering 10 topics. Each topic includes several indicators; equal weight is attributed to each topic. These topics reflect the following 10 aspects of business environment: starting a business, dealing with construction permits, getting electricity, registering property, getting credit, protecting minority investors, paying taxes, trading across borders, enforcing contract, and resolving insolvency. The methodology is constantly being improved; a range of research papers provide foundation for various components of the index (Djankov at el, 2002 etc.).

The current rank of Russia in Doing Business is 28 out of 190, between Austria and Japan. For comparison, the rank of Germany is 22, Canada 23, Rwanda 38, Czech Republic 41, and the Netherlands 42 (Doing Business 2020). In Doing Business 2012 Russia ranked 120 among 183 economies, based on data for Moscow (Doing Business in Russia 2012). The Index shows that business environment in Russia has improved compared to the year 2012. However, it is important to understand, which aspects of business environment actually improved, and which ones did not (Yakovlev, Ivanov, 2018). It raises interest towards the issues captured in the Doing Business Index and those remaining outside of it.

Thus, our research is aimed at analyzing institutional environment in the Russian regions, both the aspects covered by the Doing Business index, and the ones left outside of its scope.

One can interpret the components of the Doing Business index as formal aspects of conducting business activities in a country. These formal aspects are associated in some way with increase in transparency of business and government relations, as well as decrease in red tape and corruption. However, there are also other important aspects of corruption, problems of legal institutions, crime and lack of qualified personnel that are not reflected in the Index.

Another limitation of the Index is that it is calculated only based on Moscow and St. Petersburg data, while it is a common knowledge that these cities are substantially more developed than the other Russian cities and regions. One of the reasons for such uneven development is concentration of political power and financial resources in these cities.

Another reason is that these cities are attractive due to a number of factors, and therefore, highly qualified professionals from other regions and cities are interested to work there. Among the factors making Moscow and St. Petersburg especially attractive are better amenities, high-level universities, headquarters of the leading companies and higher wages. As more professionals come to these cities, they create additional knowledge spillovers and contribute in other ways to development of the cities, this way further increasing their attractiveness.

It is important to study various aspects of business environment in order to understand, which factors are essential for development of business activity and innovations in Russia. There is an on-going discussion that Russian economy needs to be diversified (Lyubimov, 2019). Innovations are important for diversification of economy, while innovative firms are especially affected by business environment (Ayyagari et al, 2014; Srholec, 2011). In our previous research, we have found evidence that external factors, such as economic conditions in the region and quality of human capital affect innovation activivty of firms in Russia (Davidson et al., 2018).

We contribute to a wide field of literature on innovations and business environment in Russia by analyzing the impact of regional institutions on firm level innovation. Specifically, we analyze the impact of such indicators as corruption, crime and employees' educational level on firm's propensity to innovate. Firm level innovation activity is measured as the probability of introducing new products. Our approach allows us to take into account the quality of the existing rules and norms, i.e. institutions, and the level of human capital that enterprises can employ. Moreover, we aim to understand if Doing Business Index is sufficient for estimating institutional environment in Russia, and if not, which other indicators are important.

The paper is structured as follows. The next section is devoted to the existing research. In section 3, the data and methods are discussed. Section 4 is devoted to estimating the impact of institutional environment on the probability to innovate. The last section overviews the implications of the research and concludes the paper.

2. Literature review

The link between institutions and economic development has been established in economics (Easterly, 2008). There are also studies analyzing the relationship among institutions, human capital and development (Acemoglu et al., 2014).

It is also widely discussed that human capital is essential for innovations (Romer, 1986; Carlino, Kerr, 2015; Zemtsov et al, 2016). However, in our opinion, institutional environment is very important for innovation as well, as it can either enhance the innovative output of qualified personnel, or hinder it. Therefore, if government policy is aimed at innovations, development of institutions should be carefully assessed. We contribute to this research area by estimating the impact of institutional environment on the innovation activities performed by qualified personnel.

There are numerous approaches to measuring institutional development in the Russian regions. The same time, correlation between these measures is not uniformly strong, as they tend to reflect different aspects of institutional development (Baranov et al, 2015).

The index that interests us is a well-known indicator of institutional development Doing Business index. This index is useful for understanding institutional environment and tracking its progress across countries and within countries over time. It covers ten essential areas of institutional environment. However, this index does not provide regional level information. It is calculated on a country level, and in case of Russia this calculation is based on two cities: Moscow and St. Petersburg. At the same time, it is obviously impossible to understand the situation in Russia based only on Moscow and St. Petersburg indicators. It is important to use regional level institutional indicators covering as many regions as possible. Only then one can compare institutional development across regions. Moreover, such indicators help to reveal the impact of institutional environment in various regions on firm level innovation. Therefore, we employ institutional indicators from the Business Environment and Enterprise Performance Survey (BEEPS) similar to those from the Doing Business index, as BEEPS indicators are available on the regional level.

Currently institutional environment in Russia is not quite favorable for business and therefore needs to be analyzed and improved (Ausan, 2017; Gurvich, 2017; Yasin, 2014). Doing Business index shows that business environment has improved since recently. However, as we mentioned previously, while this index takes into account some important issues, other essential ones remain outside of its scope (Yakovlev, Ivanov, 2018).

Moreover, if we look at the actual development of business activities, especially in the fields that require innovations the most, we will see that enterprises still face substantial obstacles (Yakovlev, Ivanov, 2018). It is also important to highlight that there is a potential for innovations in Russia, particularly, the level of human capital is relatively high (see Human Development Reports, United Nations Development Programme, UN, 2019). In addition, according to the empirical evidence, investment in R&D and human capital performed during the times of planned economy affects current innovation activities and knowledge-intensive industries location in the Russian regions (Ivanov, 2016; Schweiger, 2018).

To shed more light on these issues, we analyze the indicators of institutional environment similar to those in the Doing Business index and the indicators not covered by this index but frequently mentioned in the literature as important. Then we investigate how these institutional aspects affect the capacity of human capital to contribute to firm-level innovations in various regions of Russia.

As far as human capital is concerned, Capozza and Divella (2018) study human resources as a driver of innovation based on BEEPS V for 29 countries of Eastern Europe and Central Asia. Different kinds of human capital are considered, i.e. higher level of training, industry-specific experience, on-the-job training, involvement and participation at work. Authors study both type of innovation outcomes and the strategies of innovation development. The variable Education is positively and significantly associated with two of the three types of innovation outcome considered: New-to-firm product innovation and New-to-market product innovation. The variable On-the-job training is positively and significantly associated with all the three types of innovation outcome. The variable Participation at work is positively and significantly associated with all the three types of innovation outcome. Across equations, the coefficient of Participation at work is three to four times greater than the coefficient of On-the-job training.

Suna et al (2020) consider how human capital affects firm level innovations in large metropolitan cities and mid-sized cities for the years 2000 and 2002. Authors use patents as a measure of the firm-level innovations, namely patent applications are used as a dependent variable in the econometric estimations. Authors incorporate human capital indicators, as well as R&D and firm characteristics indicators in the proposed models as explanatory variables. They use OLS, Poisson model and Negative Binomial model (due to only 13% of firms applying for patents), IV regression with the number of highly educated workers lagged two years as instrument and estimate zero-inflated negative binomial model. In all cases, results are overall similar. On one hand, positive effects of training of the general manager and the managerial team are observed; on the other hand, average age of the management team has negative effect on the innovation performance in all models.

Another strand of literature that interests us is papers that explore the impact of institutions on innovations. Wang et al (2015) examine the institutional mechanisms through which business groups impact innovation in emerging markets based on hierarchical moderated regression for the dataset of Chinese manufacturing firms for the period of 2005-2007. Authors estimate how inclusion in the business group and state affiliation on different levels, state ownership and 'marketization index' affect firms' innovation performance measured as ratio of new product sales to total sales. Results suggest positive effect of all aforementioned indicators as well as interaction effects between institutional factors and inclusion in the business group: authors find positive effect of the government affiliation, which is increased as the level of the government is increased.

Barbosa and Faria (2011) study the impact of institutional differences on innovations in the European Union, using the Fourth Community Innovation Survey (CIS4) that covers the years from 2002 to 2004 and includes most EU countries. The estimation is conducted on the industrial level for 22 manufacturing industries in 10 EU countries. Authors suggest that by changing the level of competition and affecting the allocation of resources, institutions can play a very important role on innovation activity. As a measures of the institutions authors use: Product market regulation index (OECD), Rigidity of employment index (Doing Business), Credit information index (Doing Business), Indicator of the strength of patent protection. Authors find negative connection between regulation and innovations. They also find negative effects of the intellectual property regulations (IPR) strength, suggesting that in EU these regulations are hindering innovations.

Li (2015) looks at how agglomeration of industries affects innovation output and considers the importance of the institutions based on data of 29 two-digit SIC manufacturing industries in 30 provincial-level Chinese regions in 2009 and OLS model. Positive and robust effect of institutional factors and their interaction effects are found. Rodríguez-Pose and Min (2020) look at how the quality of local government institutions affects the capacity of firms to innovate. They utilize dataset of 2,700 firms with the institutional and socioeconomic characteristics of the 25 cities in China where they operate. Two types of innovation are considered: product and process innovation. For the quality of institutions measures authors use rule of law, government effectiveness, regulatory quality, and control of corruption. Interaction effects between these indicators and time are considered as well. When institutional quality effects are found to be significant they are also found to be positive; the same is true for the interaction effects.

Based on this literature we construct a model that allows us to look into the impact of human capital on innovations in the circumstances defined by the regional institutions.

3. Data and methods

We use the data from the Business Enterprise Performance Survey (BEEPS) for the period from 2012 to 2014 for 1564 Russian manufacturing firms from 37 regions. In addition to financial and innovative indicators, the survey contains a rich set of institutional indicators.

Based on the probit model, we evaluate the interaction term between human capital and the institutional indicators that go beyond Doing Business Index.

As a dependent variable, an innovation activity indicator, we use a dummy variable equal to one, if the company introduced new products, and zero otherwise. As an indicator of human capital, we use a dummy variable that reflects training conducted by the firm. In the literature both this indicator and indicators of employees' educational levels are used (D'Amore et al, 2017; Dostie, 2017). The latter may not be sufficient for Russia, since, on one hand, tertiary education enrollment rate is rather high, and, on the other hand, a lot of university graduates pursue a career in the field different from their specialization. In addition, the knowledge gained at the university does not always reflect the needs of business.

We also include other firm level characteristics, such as age and size of firms, dummy variables for the R&D investment over the past three years and involvement is export operations. The size of firms is determined by the number of employees. Descriptive statistics of the variables are presented in table 1.

Table 1: Descriptive statistics of variables

Variable	Obs	Mean	Std. Dev.	Min	Max
Introduction of new products over last 3 years	1,557	0,374	0,484	0	1
Transport – obstacle to current operations	1,541	0,208	0,406	0	1
Crime - obstacle to current operations	1,530	0,103	0,304	0	1
Inadequately educated workforce – obstacle to current operations	1,544	0,283	0,451	0	1
Corruption – obstacle to current operations	1,467	0,284	0,451	0	1
Formal training	1,549	0,449	0,498	0	1
Age	1,564	28,224	175,745	0	2021
Spending on R&D over last 3 years, dummy variable	1,553	0,187	0,390	0	1
Number of employees	1,564	108,671	478,755	4	11000
Export (dummy)	1,561	0,151	0,358	0	1

Source: authors' calculations based on BEEPS 2012-2014.

Descriptive statistics of variables show that, on average, 37% of industrial firms introduced innovations, 21% of firms experienced difficulties with transportation, 10% of firms – with crime and 28% of firms – with inadequate employee education and corruption. In addition, on average, 45% of firms trained their employees, the average age of firms is 28 years, the average number of employees was 108 people, and 15% of firms, on average, were exporters.

The distribution of innovation and institutional indicators by industries (see Figure 1) shows that, on average, the most innovative industries in the dataset are Food, Chemicals, Machinery and equipment, Electronics, Precision instruments, IT, Communication equipment, etc. In many sectors, corruption is the strongest obstacle to economic activity. In general, firms in all sectors experience barriers related to corruption, inadequate workforce education, crime, and transport.

As our aim is to estimate the effects of factors that are not included in the Doing Business indicator, we need to control for the ones included in this index. The Doing Business Index is constructed from several aggregated indicators, covering different aspects of business operations. Those include starting a business, getting electricity, dealing with construction permits, getting credit, paying taxes, trading across borders and some other. All of them are based on the firm-level surveys and calculated on a country level. Since we consider only the companies working in Russia, and certain regulations are determined on the federal level, some components of the index do not vary across regions. On top of that, it is not clear how exactly the index is constructed and what weight each indicator has. Therefore, we cannot replicate the design of this index on the regional level. Instead, we try to account for the factors used in the Doing Business Index by using principle components analysis.

Essentially, we construct principal components based on several factors available in the Business Enterprise Performance Survey and similar to the ones present in the Doing Business survey. Even though the resulting components are not a precise representation of the Index on a regional level, this approach should allow us to take into account a large number of the relevant factors without inflating the model.

Namely, we use the following indicators to construct principal components: presence of the power outages, issues with transportation across borders, access to land, access to finance, fast operation of courts, share of time management spends on dealing with regulations, high taxes, issues with courts operation, and the share of annual total sales spent on informal payments. Coefficients for the first three principal components are presented in table 2.

These three principal components account for 42% of overall variance of the included variables and should provide a good representation of the factors included in the Doing Business rating. We understand that it is a rather crude method of approximation. However, the choice of the method is determined by the availability of data. There is no available data that would reflect each component of the Doing Business Index on the regional level. Besides, taking all its components separately would pose a threat of significant multicollinearity, as many of them are closely correlated.

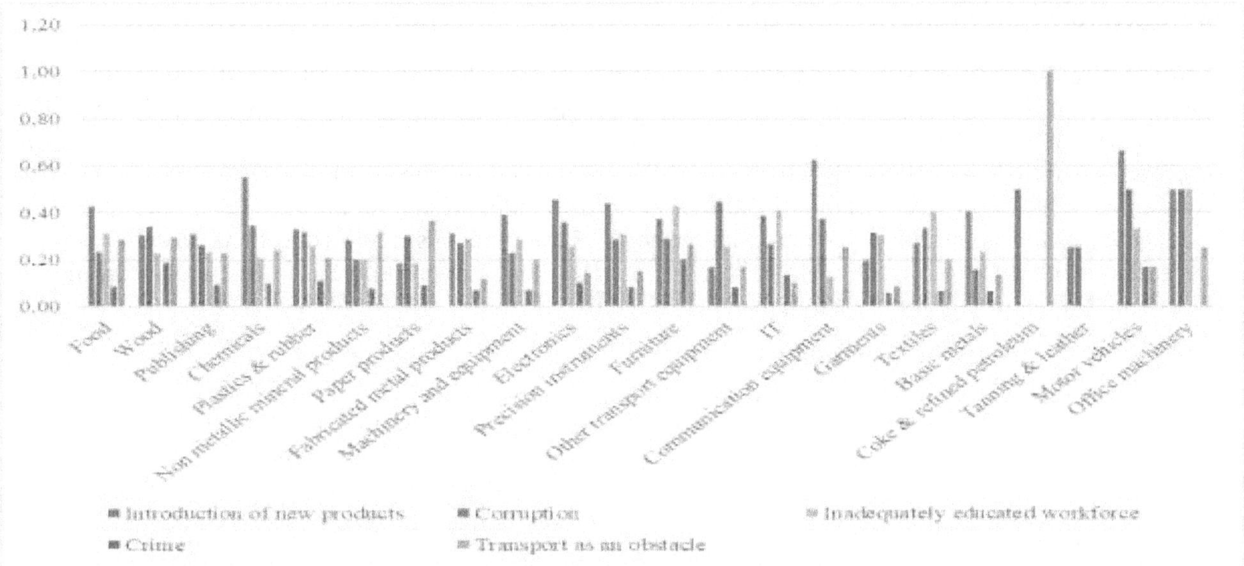

Source: authors' calculations based on BEEPS 2012-2014.

Figure 1: Distribution of innovation and institutional indicators by industries (average values).

Table 2: Rotation coefficients of the first three principle components

	PC1	PC2	PC3
Power outages	-0,02223	-0,4194	-0,01955
Issues with transportation across borders	0,28855	0,510357	-0,02192
Access to land	0,488277	0,098954	0,042993
Access to finance	0,353764	0,411293	0,096313
Fast courts	0,275504	-0,36821	-0,4508
Share of time sent on dealing with regulations	0,25152	-0,09571	0,513842
High Taxes	0,422387	-0,07513	-0,02048
Issue with courts	0,475292	-0,33608	-0,23362
% of annual total sales spent on informal payments	0,095933	-0,34835	0,682469

Source: authors' calculations based on BEEPS 2012-2014.

In the first component, the highest coefficients are assigned to the indicators of the access to land, issues with high taxes and issues with courts. According to this result, we can assume that these factors are the most useful ones for explaining variance in our observations.

Based on the performed analysis, our econometric model contains the interaction term between formal training and selected institutional indicators, firm-level indicators, three first principle components and regional, industrial and location dummies. The final model can be represented as follows:

$$Pr(Innovation)=\alpha_0+\alpha_1 Training_i \times Institutional\ indicators+ \alpha_2\ Firm\text{-}level\ indicators + PCA + Regional\ dummies+ Industry\ dummies + Location\ dummies + \varepsilon_i, \quad (1)$$

where *i* is a firm, *PCA* denotes the principal components. *Pr(Innovation)* is the probability of introducing new products over last 3 years. *Training x Institutional indicators* shows the interaction term between formal training and selected institutional indicators such as corruption, inadequately educated workforce, crime and transportation. *Firm-level indicators* include age, size, export orientation and spending on R&D. Given the measurement of the dependent variable, we evaluate this model using the probit analysis.

In the next section, estimation results are discussed.

4. Results

The results of estimating the probit model are presented in table 3. First, as a base model, we estimate the model without any interaction effects. Essentially, this represents the situation when only the institutional factors present in the Doing Business Index are taken into account using the principal components. Then, we proceed to test the interaction effects between personnel training and the institutional indicators not explicitly considered in the Doing Business rating. Namely, we look at corruption as an obstacle to current operations; inadequacy of the workforce education as an indicator of the problems in the educational systems; crime in general as an obstacle to current operations; insufficient quality of the transport infrastructure, indicating lack of essential infrastructure for the enterprises.

Table 3: Probit model results (marginal effects)

Dependent variable – the probability of introducing new products over last 3 years	Without additional institutional indicators	Corruption – obstacle to current operations	Inadequately educated workforce – obstacle to current operations	Crime – obstacle to current operations	Transport – obstacle to current operations
Formal training programs for permanent full-time employees, dummy-variable	0.0662***				
Corruption X training		0.0954***			
Inadequately educated workforce X training			0.0336		
Crime X training				0.0615	
Transport X training					0.0101
Age, logarithm	-0.00201	0.000861	-0.00335	0.00174	-0.00169
Spending on R&D over last 3 years (dummy variable)	0.310***	0.322***	0.321***	0.314***	0.315***
Number of employees, logarithm	0.0315***	0.0339***	0.0371***	0.0377***	0.0391***
Export (dummy)	0.0689**	0.0693**	0.0667**	0.0643**	0.0692**
Regional, industry, location dummies	Yes	Yes	Yes	Yes	Yes
Three first principal components for taking into account Doing Business indicators	Yes	Yes	Yes	Yes	Yes
Pseudo R2	0.1855	0.1895	0.1805	0.1795	0.1852
Number of observations	1531	1439	1514	1500	1511

Source: authors' calculations based on BEEPS 2012-2014. Notes: *** significant at 1%, ** significant at 5%, * significant at 10%.

Our results show that training of personnel positively and significantly affects innovations. This result is received without taking into account the characteristics of the institutional environment beyond the Doing Business Index. At the same time, this effect does not hold, when additional institutional conditions are accounted for.

For the firms that stated corruption as a barrier, positive effect of personnel training remains significant and becomes even stronger. On one hand, this may indicate that firms are trying to make up for the weakness of the institutional environment by training their employees. On the other hand, organizing a formal training could be accompanied by bureaucratic difficulties for the firms, especially the government-affiliated ones. Thus, bypassing bureaucratic procedures by using corruption schemes may increase the effectiveness of the training process. However, this issue needs further research.

Besides, crime, inadequate education of the workforce, and inadequate transportation system make the effect of employee training insignificant. In other words, for the firms operating in the unfavorable institutional conditions, improvement of human capital does not increase propensity to innovate.

In line with our expectations, the results also show a positive and significant relationship between innovation and the firms' individual characteristics, such as R&D spending, size of the firm, involvement in export, for all specifications of the model. Several industry dummies are significant, suggesting that some industries are inherently more innovative than the others.

Thus, institutional indicators that go beyond Doing Business Index have substantial impact on innovation activity of the company by affecting returns on personnel training. In our opinion, such factors should be taken into account when assessing business environment both at the regional level and at the country level.

5. Conclusion

We performed econometric estimation of the human capital effects on innovation activities in different institutional conditions. Our findings for Russian regions go in line with the previous research for other countries confirming the importance of the institutional environment for positive return on human capital. We also find proof that although the Doing Business Index accounts for very important business environment characteristics, it is not a sufficient measure of regional institutional development.

We found generally positive and significant effect of the personnel training on the innovation activity. This result is valid if only the institutional factors present in the Doing Business survey are considered. However, when interaction effects between training and the other institutional indicators are taken into account we see no significant effect of training in the majority of model specifications. We conclude that favorable institutional environment is essential for contribution of human capital to innovative activities. Namely, the return on the firm's investment into personnel training depends on favorable institutional environment.

Several limitations of the research need to be addressed in the future. First, as it was previously mentioned, our method of accounting for the Doing Business rating is rather crude and can be improved by more careful consideration of the factors included in the original rating. Besides, a different methodology could be applied to calculate their combination. Second, due to the nature of the BEEPS data we can only estimate institutional factors subjectively perceived by the firms' managers and not the objective ones. For example, exactly the same institutional environment can be viewed negatively by one manager and positively by another. Therefore, our results mostly cover perceived quality of institutions.

These results will be especially useful for the local and regional authorities so that they could take steps to improve institutional environment in which firms operate. In addition, the results show that it is useful to supplement Doing Business rating with the other institutional indicators for a more complete picture. This result can be useful for the business analysts.

Acknowledgements

Research was supported by the grant of the Russian Science Foundation № 19-18-00262 "Empirical modelling of balanced technological and socioeconomic development in the Russian regions".

References

Acemoglu, D., Gallego, F. and Robinson, J. (2014) "Institutions, human capital and development", *The Annual Review of Economics,* Vol 6, pp 875-912.

Auzan, A. (2017) Revolutions and evolutions in Russia: In search of a solution to the path dependence problem, *Russian Journal of Economics*, Vol 3, pp 336–347.

Ayyagari, M., Demirguc-Kunt, A. and Maksimovic, V.. (2014) "Bribe Payments and Innovation in Developing Countries: Are Innovating Firms Disproportionately Affected?", *Journal of financial and quantitative analysis*, Vol 49, No. 1, pp 51–75.

Baranov, A., Malkov, E., Polishchuk, L., Rochlitz, M. and Syunyaev, G. (2015) "How (not) to measure Russian regional institutions", *Russian Journal of Economics*, Vol 1(2), pp 154-181, https://doi.org/10.1016/j.ruje.2015.11.005.

Barbosa, N. and Faria, A.P. (2011) "Innovation across Europe: How important are institutional differences?" *Research Policy*, Vol 40, No. 9, pp 1157-1169, https://doi.org/10.1016/j.respol.2011.05.017.

Capozza, Claudia and Divella, Marialuisa. (2018) "Human capital and firms' innovation: evidence from emerging economies", *Economics of Innovation and New Technology*, Vol 28, pp 741-757, http://doi.org/10.1080/10438599.2018.1557426.

Carlino, Gerald and Kerr, William Robert. (2015) "Agglomeration and innovation", *Handbook of regional and urban economics,* Vol 5, pp 349-404.

D'Amore, R., Iorio, R. and Lubrano Lavadera, G. (2017) "Exploring the Relationship between human capital and innovation at the firm level: A study on a sample of European firms", *CELPE Discussion paper 14*.

Davidson N., Mariev O., Pushkarev A. (2018) The Impact of Externalities on the Innovation Activity of Russian Firms. Foresight and STI Governance, vol. 12, no 3, pp. 62–72.

Djankov, S., La Porta, R., Lopez-De-Silanes, F. and Shleifer, A. (2002) "The regulation of entry", *Quarterly Journal of Economics*, Vol CXVII, No. 1.

Dostie, B. (2017) The impact of training on innovation, *Industrial and Labor Relations Review,* Vol 71(1), pp 64-87.

Easterly, W. (2008) Design and Reform of Institutions in LDCs and Transition Economies. Institutions: top down or bottom up?, *American Economic Review: Papers & Proceedings*, Vol *98*(2), pp 95–99.

Gurvich, E. (2017) Institutsional'nye ramki i ekonomitcheskoye razvitiye (Institutional frameworks and economic development). *Obschestvennye nauki i sovremennost (Social Sciences and Modernity)*, Vol 1, pp 20–45. (In Russian).

Ivanov, D. (2016) Human capital and knowledge-intensive industries location: evidence from Soviet legacy in Russia, *The Journal of Economic History*, Vol 76(3), pp 736-768 https://doi.org/10.1017/S0022050716000802.

Li, X. (2015) Specialization, institutions and innovation within China's regional innovation systems, *Technological Forecasting and Social Change*, Vol 100, pp 130-139, https://doi.org/10.1016/j.techfore.2015.06.032.

Lyubimov, I. (2019) "Russia's diversification prospects", *Russian Journal of Economics*, Vol 5, pp 177–198, http://doi.org/10.32609/j.ruje.5.34753.

Rodríguez-Pose, A. and Zhang, M. (2020) "The cost of weak institutions for innovation in China", *Technological Forecasting & Social Change, Technological Forecasting & Social Change*, Vol 153, https://doi.org/10.1016/j.techfore.2020.119937.

Romer, P.M. (1986) Increasing returns and long-run growth, *The Journal of Political Economy*, Vol 94(5), pp 1002–1037.

Schweiger, H., Stepanov, A. and Zacchia, P. (2018) "The long-run effects of R&D place-based policies: evidence from Russian science cities", EBRD Working Paper No. 216

Srholec, M. (2011) "A multilevel analysis of innovation in developing countries", *Industrial and Corporate Change*, Vol 20, No. 6, pp 1539–1569, http://doi.org/10.1093/icc/dtr024.

Sun, X., Li H. and Ghosal, V. (2020) "Firm-level human capital and innovation: Evidence from China", *China Economic Review*, Vol 59, https://doi.org/10.1016/j.chieco.2019.101388.

United Nations Development Programme, (2019) *Human Development Report 2019,* New York, United Nations Development Programme, http://hdr.undp.org/en/content/human-development-index-hdi.

Wang, C., Yi, J., Kafouros, M. and Yan, Y. (2015) "Under what institutional conditions do business groups enhance innovation performance?", *Journal of Business Research*, Vol 68, No. 3, pp 694-702, https://doi.org/10.1016/j.jbusres.2014.08.002.

World Bank, (2012*) Doing Business in Russia 2012 report,* Washington, DC: World Bank, http://www.doingbusiness.org/russia.

World Bank, (2020) *Doing Business 2020,* Washington, DC: World Bank, https://www.doingbusiness.org/content/dam/doingBusiness/pdf/db2020/Doing-Business-2020_rankings.pdf

Yakovlev, A. and Ivanov, D. (2018) "Technical success: why progress of Russia in Doing Business did not help business" (Tecknitcheskiy uspekh: pochemu vzlet Rossii v Doing Business ne pomog biznesu)', [online], RBC, https://www.rbc.ru/opinions/economics/14/11/2018/5bebd6db9a7947c705e43594 . (In Russian).

Yasin, E.G. (2014) *"Cultural influence on Russian modernization"*, Paper read at the XV International conference on economic and social development, Higher School of Economics, Moscow, April.

Zemtsov, S., Muradov, A., Wade, I. and Barinova, V. (2016) "Determinants of Regional Innovation in Russia: Are People or Capital More Important?" *Foresight and STI Governance*, Vol 10(2), pp 29–42.

Science Parks Implementation Framework Proposal

Taiane Quaresma Leite[1], André Luis Silva[2], Joaquim Ramos Silva[3] and Sérgio Evangelista Silva[1]
[1]Institute of Exact Sciences – ICEA, Federal University of Ouro Preto, João Monlevade, Brazil
[2]School of Mines - EM, Federal University of Ouro Preto, Ouro Preto, Brazil
[3]Lisbon School of Economics and Management – ISEG, University of Lisbon, Portugal
tql04@hotamil.com
andre.silva@ufop.edu.br
jrsilva@iseg.ulisboa.pt
sergio.silva@ufop.edu.br
DOI: 10.34190/EIE.20.071

Abstract: Innovation is a key instrument for companies to improve their efficiency and establish a long-term competitive advantage. In this context, Science Parks (SPs) are effective environments to promote new business based on technology and innovation. At the regional level, SPs are important for economic, social, and cultural development. As such, they promote new business and jobs, partnerships with universities and research centres, and attract new technology-based companies (NTBFs), which derive benefits from the spillovers that are generated. However, different regional realities and the varied motivations of the stakeholders explain the diversity among SPs. Accordingly, SPs arise and are governed through the cooperation of different types of stakeholders, such as academic, governmental, entrepreneurial and other agents and entities. Thus, they result from different interests and incentives that converge to their creation. A relevant approach to understand the specific engagement of different stakeholders in the creation of SPs and their respective roles is to study the context and circumstances of their formation. Starting from this point, the objective of this paper is to propose a SPs implementation framework based on cases from two countries – Brazil and Portugal. An investigation was laid down on 4 SPs in Brazil and 4 in Portugal through a comparative analysis methodology. Data collection occurred upon technical visits and, in complementarity, there was a documental approach on government websites, networks and associations and the SPs themselves. The results show that the main prerequisites for the formation of SPs are: a favourable environment with institutional stability, available knowledge, development business space and motivations that converge to a common purpose. As a theoretical contribution, the outcome of the research introduces the SPs implementation framework, emphasizing the main stakeholders and the fundamental prerequisites for their formation and development. As practical implications, the results can guide the design of a favourable institutional environment for the creation of SPs, enhancing the potential to produce good results such as innovation for the involved stakeholders and society, particularly at the level of companies.

Keywords: science parks, technological innovation, NTBFs, startups, public policy

1. Introduction

Innovation is one of the main instruments for technology companies to improve their efficiency and establish a long-term competitive advantage. Science Parks (SPs) have been considered as an effective mechanism for promoting innovation and the development of high-tech companies and industrial clusters in a region or country Lai and Shyu, 2005; Xie et al, 2018). Conversely, SPs are of great importance in the business context of the region in which they carry out their activity (Guadix et al, 2016), and their role can be improved whether they are well located and benefit from local advantages and resources.

Most SPs do not have a mature investment system, so it is often local governments that establish financial institutions to support their foundation and operations. There are two basics ways to create an SP: first, the spontaneous creation that has the support of venture capital (Miao and Hall, 2014); and second, the governmental orientation that is the government-planned regional innovation area dedicated to high technology development (Xie et al, 2018).

In this way, the process of implementation of SPs can be considered relevant for its better performance. Albahari et al (2013) point out through an evaluation study in Italian and Spanish SPs that factors such as the macroeconomic development and the level of development of the innovation system of a country influence the state of development of these environments. In addition, other factors such as the role of the national SPs association, the SPs' business model, internal practices, and the composition of shareholders and managers are relevant points for comparing the development of them (Lamine et al, 2016). Thus, external agents, such as local and regional governments, universities, associations and private entities play important roles for the implementation and management of SPs (Lai and Shyu, 2005; Lamine et al, 2016).

In the literature, research subjects about SPs can be listed as follow: their relationship with established companies (Löfster and Lindelöf 2002, 2003; Schmidt and Balestrin, 2014; Liberati et al, 2015; Albahari et al, 2017), their relationship with universities (Hansson et al, 2005; Albahari et al, 2017) and in some cases there are studies showing the relationship of SPs with external agents such as public service policy (Lai and Shyu, 2005; Sofouli and Vonortas, 2006), national innovation systems (NSI) (Albahari et al, 2013), the concept of public procurement as an integrated innovation policy instrument (Edler and Georghiou, 2007) and the transfer of knowledge of alliances between SPs, governments, agencies and various private sector organizations (Inkpen and Pien, 2006).

Although SPs have been in operation for over 50 years (Vaidyanathan, 2007), to the best of our knowledge, there are not studies that address adequately the environmental and institutional factors necessary to their well succeeded implementation. Also, geographically the largest number of studies are concentrated in Europe and Asia (Henriques et al, 2018). Despite recent studies about SPs in South America (Silva et al, 2020), still there is a need for more studies about these agents in South America (Henriques et al, 2018) and even studies capable of comparing SPs located in different countries and continents. Accounting to the above presented gaps, the aim of this article is to propose a SPs implementation framework useful in different contexts.

This model is based on an empirical study of SPs located in two countries, Brazil in South America, and Portugal, in Europe. Through this qualitative comparative case study, data from 8 SPs from these two countries were obtained and analyzed. Data collection occurred though technical visits, and, in complementarity, there was a documental approach on government websites, networks and associations, and the SPs themselves. The results show that the main prerequisites for the formation of SPs are: a favourable environment with institutional stability, available knowledge, development business space, and complimentary incentives of the several stakeholders involved capable of converting them to the common purpose of creating an SP. This paper is structured as follows: Section 2 explores the theoretical background, Section 3 describes the methodology, and Sections 4 and 5 presents the results and additional findings. Finally, Section 6 states the conclusion.

2. Theoretical background: TPs formation process

SPs have matured in the past three decades in the USA, Canada and Western Europe and have taken root in other South American and Asian countries (Lai and Shyu, 2005; Lamine et al, 2016). An SP is defined as an organization ordered by specialized professionals whose objective is to increase the competitiveness and wealth of their associated businesses and knowledge-based institutions. SPs provide physical support, information and knowledge exchange to develop innovative products and markets, as well as providing a common social environment (Ratinho and Henriques, 2010).

SPs are initiatives that contribute to the creation and growth of new technology-based firms (NTBFs) through value-based services (IASP, 2019). They provide hosted startups with a mix of value-added services, such as physical infrastructure, support services, networking opportunities, access to professional services, capital, university resources, knowledge benefits, public image, and cost savings (Lamine et al, 2016; Albahari et al, 2017). SPs have the role of stimulating economic development by governments through innovation, the creation of new jobs, enhancement of the local image, and creation of NTBFs (Shearmur and Doloreux, 2000), and so its creation must be well prepared, and to have a favourable environment for their development. For universities, SPs promote the dissemination of knowledge that contributes to the development industrial innovations and technology transfer, although the interaction takes time to bear its fruits and requires learning by doing. (Hansson et al, 2005; Albahari et al, 2017; Xie et al, 2018; Silva et al, 2020).

Thus, for the SP environment to grow and become sustainable, the influence of some factors is necessary, such as the presence of: NTBFs, strong and advanced interaction between universities and NTBFs, knowledge endowments, entrepreneurial culture and availability of qualified labor; active partnerships between regional actors, in the form of a triple helix operating with the university, industry, and government, and the presence of facilitators of the innovation process, such as infrastructure, government procurement contracts, research projects, and incentives or subsidies for innovation (Löfster and Lindelöf 2002; Lamine et al, 2016).

In addition, the regional cultural and economic characteristics, government policies, capital market conditions, and other attributes common to a country are factors that make the differences in the SPs implementation process (Lai and Shyu, 2005). In developed countries, SPs are normally created due to the interaction between scientists and innovators and venture capitalists (Xie et al, 2018). In emergent countries, normally, the government plans SPs as a vector of regional innovation for the development of products and services based on high technology (Xie et al., 2018). Local governments are the ones that most value this environment and often establish financial institutions to support startups' operations (Xie et al, 2018). Therefore, the combination of government guidance and market needs, mediated by the firms, particularly NTBFs, plays an important role in the implementation and success of SPs.

Furthermore, the concept of the triple helix is related to the formation and implementation of SPs, as the concept considers that the actions of government agents, universities, and business entities promote innovation (Lamine et al, 2016). Stakeholders have distinct and complementary interests and incentives that contribute to promote or support regional development and innovation (Hansson et al, 2005). In this context, politicians seek economic and regional development through SPs, universities hope that knowledge transfer occurs in SPs to contribute to society, and NTBFs seek in SPs an image, perspective, and partnerships with the university and other companies (Albahari et al, 2017). Non-hosted NTBFs and non-governmental entities and agents are also considered important stakeholders in the SP environment. Non-hosted NTBFs seek partnerships and new products offered in SPs and non-governmental entities and agents collaborate for the growth and development of SPs through social networks, investment and knowledge flow (Morlacchi and Martin, 2009; Silva et al, 2020).

In the literature, some studies approach structural and external factors related to the SPs. Kyoung-Joo and Eun-Young (2018) propose a specialized leadership competency model for public SP leaders. Albahari et al (2013) show that the country's general and environmental macroeconomic conditions provide stability to the purposes of the SPs. Indeed, the country's system, the business model, internal practices, and the composition of shareholders are relevant indicators for the SP assessment.

Despite the above presented studies that approach the structural aspects of the environments of formation of SPs, the literature still needs a more systematical model to permit a better understanding of the necessary pre-requisites for a well succeed formation of these settings. As such, Figure 1 presents a framework based on the main categories related to the formation of SPs, allowing a more systematical and better structuration of a model of formation of these agents. Favorable environment refers to the minimal necessary configuration of the social, economic and technical aspects for a well-succeeded formation of SPs. Catalysts are the agents that will conduct the process of formation of an SP.

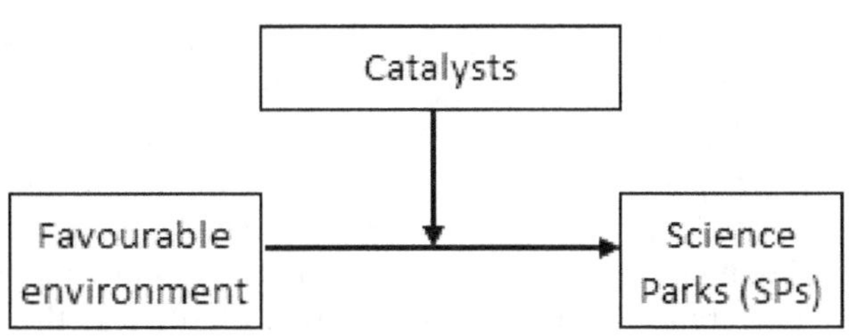

Figure 1: Study analysis

3. Methodology

Our sample consists of 8 SPs, 4 SPs in Brazil (BSP1, BSP2, BSP3, BSP4) and 4 SPs in Portugal (PSP1, PSP2, PSP3, PSP4). The acronym BSP refers to Brazilian SPs and the acronym PSP refers to Portuguese SPs. In general, Brazilian SPs are still very recent structures compared to other developed regions in the world (Schmidt and Balestrin, 2015). The process of the formation of SPs in this country started in the 1990s. There are 43 SPs in operation in this country, 18 of which are in the Southeast (MCTI, 2019). Through the intentional choice, four SPs from this region were investigated because it has a greater economic contribution, a greater number of higher education and research institutions, and a greater contribution of the Brazilian GDP (Gross Domestic Product). Compared with Brazil, the formation of SPs in Portugal is older, starting in 1980s. Currently, there are 17 SPs associated with TecParques (Portuguese Association of Science and Technology Parks). Owing to the four SPs investigated in this region, two of them were the first to start operation in the country, and the other two were chosen due to their proximity to the first, also located in the region that more contributes to the Portuguese GDP.

To explore the implementation structure of the SPs, the collection of the data occurred between June and October 2019 on websites of government networks and associations and on the websites of each SPs, totalizing 98 public documents and data through the websites of the SPs, national and international and governmental associations, totalizing 234 saved webpages. Additionally, two Brazilians SPs were visited in January 2020. The choice of SPs for a visit was due to their time of existence and volume of business, in addition to being geographically close to the researchers. During the visits, information related to the implementation process of each SP was obtained, being recorded with the authorization of the interviewees.

In the coding and analysis of the data the comparative descriptive method was applied. The collected data were processed in a spreadsheet with the aim of identifying the main types of agents that play a role in the formation of SPs. We identified the agents that contributed to the implementation process of each SP, such as government, universities, companies, and other entities. Through the spreadsheet, an analysis was also made of the structural characteristics of SPs that favoured their implementation. Through these data, we identified four groups of prerequisites that classify the essential structural characteristics for the implementation of SPs.

4. Descriptive results

Initially, we identified the main types of agents that played the role of catalysts in the formation of SPs in our sample. Two Brazilian SPs (BSP2 and BSP4) were instituted by the local public university that identified technological relevance and intense technical and scientific production, in addition to being an important anchor for technological, economic, and social development. Therefore, in these cases, the university identified a way of connecting with the business sector for introducing innovation and better functioning. Another Brazilian SP (BSP3) was instituted by a municipal decree, which identified their vocation to be an advanced pole of technological development and innovation. The last Brazilian SP (BSP1) in our sample was established through a partnership between 5 founding partners: university, state government, city hall, business support bodies, and a local industry federation. The SPs of Portugal, in our sample, were created by government initiative. Despite being managed by a specialized association, they aim to stimulate and support the centres of technological innovation, business incubators, and other initiatives associated with economic development, entrepreneurship, innovation, and research. These associations create conditions for the success of the hosted companies and in the use and optimization of the knowledge chain, enhancing the synergies between Universities, R&D Institutions, and Technology-based Companies. They also stimulate entrepreneurship and competitiveness in the Region, based on Innovation and Technology, the closest possible to the companies.

We found that for the implementation of SPs, a favourable environment with essential structural characteristics is necessary. Initially, we identified that the structures or mechanisms of social order, which regulate the behaviour of a set of individuals within a given community, mediating the rules, can be considered a prerequisite for the implementation of SPs in a region. This can be seen in the SPs of our sample, with the presence of public and university policies that promote innovation. For example, in one of the Brazilian cases in the sample, the local government has an innovation law that encourages the creation of environments related to technology and innovation. Another way detected to stimulate the creation of SPs was the presence of a reduction in municipal taxes. Therefore, a stable and favourable institutional environment can be considered relevant to the formation of SPs.

Another characteristic detected as essential for the implementation of SPs is the presence of available knowledge. This was identified through the presence of universities in all SPs, whether as founders or partners. Generally, the presence of universities and research centres aims at the connection with companies in SPs, through agreements and partnerships. Some examples are partnerships with the technology transfer office, with a response centre for the university's skills to be transferred to the market. In addition to the dissemination of events, courses and consultancies that create stronger links and conditions to share knowledge.

Another prerequisite that we verified for the implementation of SPs is the presence of space for business development in the region with the presence of NTBFs with a high capacity for innovation, in addition to the presence of Brazilian business support associations, innovation networks, local industry federations, intellectual property commissions, SP systems and Portuguese associations for coordination and regional development.

Another feature that shows the importance of a business development space is the presence of anchor companies in the aeronautical sector in a Brazilian SP and the partnership with a research support foundation.

Finally, we detected complementary incentives from the various stakeholders involved. For example, government incentives through facilitated credit to reduce the costs of providing services, with emphasis on the European Union, in Portugal, and in Brazil, banks and investment funds, support foundation, funders, partnerships in social programs and municipal tax incentives. Universities encourage the implementation of SP by offering knowledge in the areas of innovation and technology (patents), research, laboratories, and a skilled workforce. Companies have an incentive to absorb the transfer of knowledge and transform them into products and processes for the well-being of society.

With that, we can emphasize that the role of mediators for the implementation of SPs is: public policies to promote economic and social development, the university in search of integration with society, and the company in search of profit and new opportunities. Figure 2 shows the four prerequisites that characterize a favourable environment with the essential structural characteristics and the main catalysts for the implementation of SPs. Table 1 demonstrates fragments of data that prove each prerequisite.

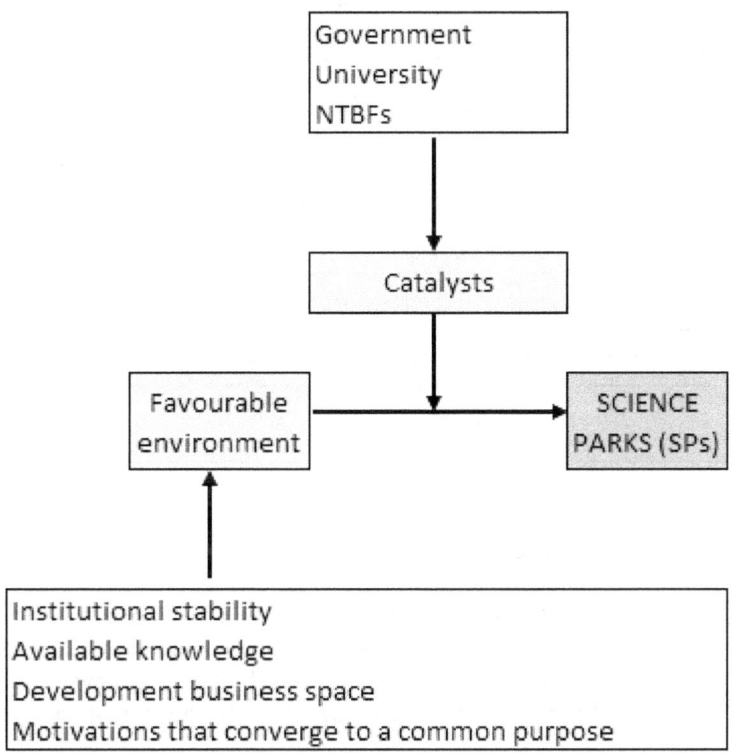

Figure 2: Prerequisites and catalysts for the implementation of SPs

Table 1: Document fragments that prove the prerequisites for implementing SPs

Prerequisites for implementing SPs	Document fragments	Place
Institutional stability	Agency linked to the government that seeks to attract companies to the SP.	BSP1
	The local government has the innovation law.	BSP2
	Presence of a municipal incubator program and an initiative on social entrepreneurship.	BSP3
	It's a member of the Regional System of SPs.	BSP1, BSP2, BSP3, BSP4
	Reduction of municipal taxes.	BSP1, BSP2

Prerequisites for implementing SPs	Document fragments	Place
	Presence of the region's coordination and development commission.	PSP1
	Created by the minister to install startups that originated from research projects in the area of engineering and technology.	PSP2
	Created by government initiative and based on the use and optimization of the knowledge chain.	PSP3
	The local government encourages entrepreneurship and competitiveness in the region, based on innovation and technology.	PSP4
Available knowledge	Presence of universities or research institute.	BSP1, BSP2, BSP3, BSP4, PSP1, PSP2, PSP3, PSP4
	Presence of a technological innovation transfer office.	BSP2
Development business space	Presence of Brazilian business support associations.	BSP1, BSP2
	Intellectual property commission.	BSP2
	Presence of the aeronautical, aerospace and defense industries - sectors of high technological density.	BSP3
	Local federation of industries.	BSP1, BSP2, BSP3, BSP4
	Presence of anchor firms in the aeronautics industry.	BSP3
	Presence of anchor companies in the energy sector.	BSP4
	Presence of technology-based firms.	PSP1, PSP2, PSP3, PSP4
	Coordination and regional development associations.	PSP1, PSP2, PSP3, PSP4
	Innovation networks.	BSP1, BSP2, BSP3, BSP4, PSP1, PSP2, PSP3, PSP4

5. Discussion

The formation of all SPs in our sample is instituted by governmental orientation through local, state governments, public universities, or governmental associations. This fact is consistent with the literature that describes that most SPs do not have a mature investment system, so it is often local governments that establish financial institutions to support operations (Xie et al, 2018). In this type of SP formation, the regional innovation area dedicated to the development of high technology is planned by the local government (Xie et al, 2018). In addition, in most cases, the agents forming SPs subsequently influence the management of the SP.

In addition, the results show that the main prerequisites for the formation of SPs are: favourable environment, with institutional stability, available knowledge, space for business development, and motivations that converge to a common purpose. The institutional stability of the region for the formation of SPs is relevant because through it, they are identified as a social function, which transcends individuals and intentions mediating the rules that govern behaviour.

Another important prerequisite for the SP formation process is the availability of technological, managerial and innovative knowledge, through universities and research centres. The university facilitates companies' access to laboratories, new technologies, patents, professors, researchers and to attract a skilled workforce to occupy jobs.

The availability of space for business development that refers to the presence of technology-based firms in the region is important to support other companies located in SP, absorb the knowledge of universities, and thus contribute to technological development and growth. In addition, there are complementary incentives from the various stakeholders involved for the implementation of SPs, through facilitated credit, tax reduction, public innovation policies, partnerships in social programs, municipal tax incentives, knowledge transfer in the areas of innovation and technology (patents) and qualified labour. In this way, complementary incentives converge towards the common objective of establishing an SP, and thus it also fulfills the mission of boosting entrepreneurship.

Therefore, we propose a framework for implementing SPs (Figure 3) based on cases from two countries, Brazil and Portugal, and we show that the main prerequisites for the formation of SPs are: favourable environment, with institutional stability, available knowledge, space for business development and incentives that converge to a common purpose. That is, for the implementation of an SP, it is necessary to have favourable institutional stability with laws and incentives, usually through public policies. In addition, the availability of available knowledge is necessary through the presence of universities and a research and development centre, as it contributes to the development of new technologies, innovative knowledge, and qualified labour. Another important prerequisite for implementing SPs is the presence of a business development space with the presence of technology-based firms that contribute to transferring the technological knowledge developed to society. Finally, it is important to project the motivations or incentives that each stakeholder involved has, in order to assess whether they are complementary and converge to a common purpose of implementing an SP.

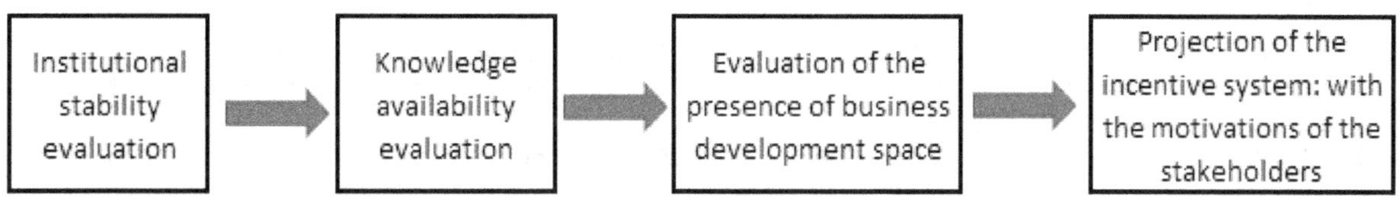

Figure 3: SPs implementation structure

6. Conclusion

Our study sought to understand the involvement of different stakeholders in the creation of SPs and their respective roles. So, different regional realities and the varied motivations of stakeholders explain the diversity among SPs. Our results indicate that different stakeholders' incentives complement each other, and contribute to implementing an SP. In addition, although there are SPs created from private initiatives, we found that the SPs in our sample were created from public government initiatives. The difference is that SPs created from private initiatives exist an interaction between scientists and venture capitalists. In this case, the government provides funding for research institutions to carry out technological innovation and venture capitalists support the commercialization of innovations. In the SPs created by public initiatives are the local governments that most value this environment.

Therefore, our study proposed a structure for implementing SPs based on cases from two countries, Brazil and Portugal. Through a comparative analysis of 4 SPs in Brazil and 4 in Portugal, we discovered that the main prerequisites for the formation of SPs are: favourable environment, institutional stability, available knowledge, space for business development, and motivations that converge to a common purpose. Institutional stability refers to the presence of public support policies which continuity, which support and promote the development of innovation ecosystems, and monitor their evolution. The available knowledge is represented by universities and research centres. The business development space is represented by the presence of associations that collaborate for the best business performance in the region. And finally, the motivations of each stakeholder: the government in search of economic and social development, the university in search of integration with society, and the company in search of profit. Therefore, this structure provides an important model for implementing SPs, particularly if there are favourable conditions for the financing of the commercialization of innovation.

As a theoretical contribution, this article presents the SPs implementation framework highlighting the main prerequisites for the successful implementation of these settings. As practical implications, these results can guide the design of an approach for the creation of SPs, increasing their success probability based on a careful analysis of their stakeholders and their motivations.

The study suffers from some shortcomings which can be addressed in future research. First, our results may have been affected by the choosing of SPs operating only in two countries. Second, this study cannot be statistically generalized to other countries, as each nationality has distinct cultural, economic, and political characteristics that can influence the results. However, the provided prerequisites have a theoretical validity being present in any environment of formation of SPs. Thus, further research on the subject can increase the number of SPs in the sample, including SPs of more countries and even continents. Moreover, other methodological approaches, such as focal groups, can be used to validate and enhance the current model.

Acknowledgements

This study was financed in part by the Coordenação de Aperfeiçoamento de Pessoal de Nível Superior - Brasil (CAPES) - Finance Code 001.

The authors would like to thank Universidade Federal de Ouro Preto and Pró-reitoria de Pesquisa e Pós Graduação (PROPP) to supporting this research.

The authors would also like to thank the National Council for Scientific and Technological Development (CNPq), Brazil, for their financial support.

References

Albahari, A., Catalano, G., & Landoni, P. (5 de 2013). Evaluation of national science park systems: a theoretical framework and its application to the Italian and Spanish systems. Technology Analysis & Strategic Management, 25, 599-614. doi:10.1080/09537325.2013.785508

Albahari, A., Pérez-Canto, S., Barge-Gil, A., & Modrego, A. (3 de 2017). Technology Parks versus Science Parks: Does the university make the difference? Technological Forecasting and Social Change, 116, 13-28. doi:10.1016/j.techfore.2016.11.012

Edler, J., & Georghiou, L. (9 de 2007). Public procurement and innovation—Resurrecting the demand side. Research Policy, 36, 949-963. doi:10.1016/j.respol.2007.03.003

Guadix, J., Carrillo-Castrillo, J., Onieva, L., & Navascués, J. (11 de 2016). Success variables in science and technology parks. Journal of Business Research, 69, 4870-4875. doi:10.1016/j.jbusres.2016.04.045

Hansson, F., Husted, K., & Vestergaard, J. (9 de 2005). Second generation science parks: from structural holes jockeys to social capital catalysts of the knowledge society. Technovation, 25, 1039-1049. doi:10.1016/j.technovation.2004.03.003

Henriques, I. C., Sobreiro, V. A., & Kimura, H. (5 de 2018). Science and technology park: Future challenges. Technology in Society, 53, 144-160. doi:10.1016/j.techsoc.2018.01.009

IASP (2019), International Association of Science Parks and Areas of Innovation. https://www.iasp.ws/. Accessed 13 June 2019.

Inkpen, A. C., & Pien, W. (6 de 2006). An Examination of Collaboration and Knowledge Transfer: China-Singapore Suzhou Industrial Park. Journal of Management Studies, 43, 779-811. doi:10.1111/j.1467-6486.2006.00611.x

Kyoung-Joo, L., & Eun-Young, K. (12 de 2018). A leadership competency model of science and technology parks: the case of Chungbuk Techno Park in Korea. Journal of technology management & innovation, 13, 105-114. doi:10.4067/s0718-27242018000400105

Lai, H.-C., & Shyu, J. Z. (7 de 2005). A comparison of innovation capacity at science parks across the Taiwan Strait: the case of Zhangjiang High-Tech Park and Hsinchu Science-based Industrial Park. Technovation, 25, 805-813. doi:10.1016/j.technovation.2003.11.004

Lamine, W., Mian, S., Fayolle, A., Wright, M., Klofsten, M., & Etzkowitz, H. (12 de 2016). Technology business incubation mechanisms and sustainable regional development. The Journal of Technology Transfer, 43, 1121-1141. doi:10.1007/s10961-016-9537-9

Liberati, D., Marinucci, M., & Tanzi, G. M. (3 de 2015). Science and technology parks in Italy: main features and analysis of their effects on the firms hosted. The Journal of Technology Transfer, 41, 694-729. doi:10.1007/s10961-015-9397-8

Lindelöf, P., & Löfsten, H. (2003). Science Park Location and New Technology-Based Firms in Sweden – Implications for Strategy and Performance. Small Business Economics, 20, 245-258. doi:10.1023/a:1022861823493

Löfsten, H., & Lindelöf, P. (8 de 2002). Science Parks and the growth of new technology-based firms—academic-industry links, innovation and markets. Research Policy, 31, 859-876. doi:10.1016/s0048-7333(01)00153-6

Miao, J. T., & Hall, P. Optical illusion? The growth and development of the optics valley of China. Environment and Planning C: Government and Policy, 32(5), 863–879, 2014.

Morlacchi, P., & Martin, B. R. (5 de 2009). Emerging challenges for science, technology and innovation policy research: A reflexive overview. Research Policy, 38, 571-582. doi:10.1016/j.respol.2009.01.021

Ratinho, T., & Henriques, E. (4 de 2010). The role of science parks and business incubators in converging countries: Evidence from Portugal. Technovation, 30, 278-290. doi:10.1016/j.technovation.2009.09.002

Schmidt, S., & Balestrin, A. (7 de 2014). INOVAÇÃO COLABORATIVA EM AMBIENTES DE PARQUES CIENTÍFICO-TECNOLÓGICOS: PROPOSTA DE UM ESQUEMA TEÓRICO-CONCEITUAL. Review of Administration and Innovation - RAI, 11, 111. doi:10.5773/rai.v11i2.1117

Schmidt, S., & Balestrin, A. (10 de 2015). Brazilian Incubators and Science Parks Resources and R & D Collaboration. Journal of technology management & innovation, 10, 32-43. doi:10.4067/s0718-27242015000300004

Shearmur, R., & Doloreux, D. (6 de 2000). Science Parks: Actors or Reactors? Canadian Science Parks in Their Urban Context. Environment and Planning A: Economy and Space, 32, 1065-1082. doi:10.1068/a32126

Silva, S.; Venancio, A.; Joaquim, S. & Gonçalves, C, 2020. Open innovation in science parks: the role of public policies. Technological Forecasting and Social Change. 151. 1-11. doi:10.1016/j.techfore.2019.119844.

Sofouli, E., & Vonortas, N. S. (8 de 2006). S&T Parks and business incubators in middle-sized countries: the case of greece. The Journal of Technology Transfer, 32, 525-544. doi:10.1007/s10961-005-6031-1

Vaidyanathan, G. (6 de 2007). Technology parks in a developing country: the case of India. The Journal of Technology Transfer, 33, 285-299. doi:10.1007/s10961-007-9041-3

Xie, K., Song, Y., Zhang, W., Hao, J., Liu, Z., & Chen, Y. (10 de 2018). Technological entrepreneurship in science parks: A case study of Wuhan Donghu High-Tech Zone. Technological Forecasting and Social Change, 135, 156-168. doi:10.1016/j.techfore.2018.01.021

Investigating the Status of Egyptian Entrepreneurship in an era of Revolution and Reforms

Yahia Ragab[1], Mohamed Ragab[1] and Sinéad Monaghan[2]
[1]Pharos University, Alexandria, Egypt
[2]Trinity Business School, Trinity College Dublin, Ireland
yahia.af.ragab@pua.edu.eg
mohamed.af.ragab@pua.edu.eg
sinead.monaghan@tcd.ie
DOI: 10.34190/EIE.20.002

Abstract: Amidst the political and economic turmoil of Revolution and Reform, one vital economic driver acted as a bright beacon of light for the country: Entrepreneurship. This exploratory study examines the effects of the Arab Spring on the entrepreneurial ecosystem (EE) in Egypt and assesses its current state by identifying the challenges that entrepreneurs face. The study adopts a qualitative research design employing semi-structured interviews to collect rich data. A total of 18 founders, investors, and venture capitalists (VCs) were interviewed to gain insights from different stakeholders in the Egyptian entrepreneurial ecosystem. The study reveals that the Egyptian EE is yet to reach full development. Regulatory restrictions, cultural limitations, outdated education, insufficient funding, and a limited talent pool were all identified as obstacles that face entrepreneurs in Egypt. The revolution was found only to have a partial role in inducing the Egyptian entrepreneurial spirit, with the primary driver being the rise of entrepreneurship globally. The analysis also reveals that the devaluation of the Egyptian Pound had a more positive than negative effect on the EE. Finally, the findings of the study are summarised, its implications and limitations are presented, and avenues for further research are proposed.

Keywords: entrepreneurship, Egypt, developing countries, entrepreneurial ecosystems, Arab Spring

1. Introduction

The past ten years have been challenging for most countries in the Arab world. At the end of 2010, the people of Tunisia started using social network sites to organise protests against their regime. Twenty-eight days following the start of the protests, the Tunisian people's revolution succeeded in overthrowing the government. The success of the Tunisian Revolution was not only a historic event for Tunisia but also the whole region of the Middle East. This triumph sparked a series of uprisings that swept the region that later became known as *The Arab Spring*. Egypt, an influential and powerful country in the region, was the first country to follow in Tunisia's steps with the *25th of January Revolution*, which resulted in the toppling of President Mubarak's regime, which lasted for almost 30 years. The 25th of January Revolution initiated an era of major political, economic and social reforms in Egypt. A crash in tourism, removal of subsidies, devaluation of the Egyptian Pound, rising energy prices, and high inflation are only a few of the changes that have had profound impacts on Egypt's business environment. However, since the Egyptian Revolution, an increase in entrepreneurial activity in Egypt resulted in Cairo, the capital, being featured in Forbes' list of the top 10 best cities to create a new venture (Guttman, 2015), as well as the production of several start-ups that have been featured in Forbes 30 under 30 (Egyptian Streets, 2018). While Egypt's entrepreneurial ecosystem (EE) is somewhat unique due to the unstable and dynamic environment, it has received little to no attention from scholars in the field of entrepreneurship in developing countries.

The purpose of this paper is to investigate the state of the Egyptian entrepreneurial ecosystem. The structure of this study is as follows: a literature review of entrepreneurial ecosystems, entrepreneurship in developing countries and entrepreneurship in Egypt is presented in the second section. The third section of the study explains the methodology used in conducting the research. In the fourth section, findings are presented and discussed. Finally, the paper concludes the study, and summarises the implication of its main contributions, while also acknowledging limitations, and suggesting possible future directions of research.

2. Literature review

2.1 Entrepreneurial ecosystem

As a key driver of economic growth, entrepreneurship has gained much attention from researchers. It acts as a robust source of employment, as well as a critical driver for innovation, growth and global competitiveness. The most commonly used definition of entrepreneurship is the new venture creation notion. In this context, an entrepreneurial ecosystem (EE) can be thought of as a collection of interdependent components, within a specific geographical space, that function in such a way that enables productive entrepreneurship (Isenberg, 2011). Although there are slightly different conceptualisations of EEs in the literature, most renditions contain elements, which belong to the same six components identified by Isenberg (2011), which are: policy, finance, culture, supports, human capital, and markets.

2.2 Entrepreneurship in developing countries

While a small but growing portion of the literature focuses on start-up activity in developing countries, it remains one of the least research significant economic and social phenomena (Lingelbach *et al.*, 2005). The dictionary defines a developing country as one that "is not yet highly industrialised". Entrepreneurs in such countries operate in an environment that is different and more challenging, domestically and internationally, to the one in which their counterparts are exposed to in developed nations (Sadeghi *et al.*, 2019). There are several crippling factors found in the literature, which hinder developing countries from achieving high industrialisation. Each of these factors falls into one of the six categories identified by Gabriel (2016), listed in Table 1, and described below:

Table 1: Entrepreneurship challenges in developing countries

Challenges	Description	Reference
Financial Challenges	Limited access to formal funding sources and reliance on informal sources	(Lingelbach *et al.*, 2005)
Physical/Technical Challenges	Underdeveloped physical infrastructures and poor logistics	(Kirchgeorg and Winn, 2006)
Challenges Affecting Demand	Lack of property rights laws, low protection against the expropriation of start-up-critical resources	(Khoury and Prasad, 2016)
Knowledge-based Challenges	Lack of research and development and lack of entrepreneurial education	(Amoros and Bosma, 2014)
Governance Challenges	Institutional uncertainty and lack of clear and enforced legislative policies	(Fogel *et al.*, 2006)
Normative Challenges	Presence of corruption, prevalence of informality, and lack of cultural respect for entrepreneurs and integrity	(Amoros and Bosma, 2014)

Adapted from Gabriel (2016)

2.3 Egyptian context

Egypt is one of the most important countries in the Middle East and Africa. Cairo, Egypt's capital city, is the largest city in the region and continent. The country is most famous for its unique ancient Pharaonic history, through which it created one of the earliest and most extraordinary civilisations in history, which left behind two of the Ancient Wonders of The World, the Great Pyramids of Giza and the Lighthouse of Alexandria, as well as many other monuments that attract tourists from the world over. Now considered a developing country, Egypt faces many demographic challenges. According to the World Population Review (2019), Egypt is currently one of the most populous countries in Africa with a growing population of over 100 million, a staggering 52.23% of which are under the age of 25 (as of 2017). The country's illiteracy rate is improving but is still a problem at 20.1% (Zaher, 2017), while the unemployment rate is at 9.9% (Reuters, 2018).

Since the overthrowing of President Mubarak in the 25th of January Revolution in 2011, Egypt has experienced a period of reform, filled with what Bennett and Lemoine (2014) call *VUCA* – volatility, uncertainty, complexity and ambiguity. This period of reform has affected the whole country. One area which was particularly affected by Egypt's unstable political climate in the early 2010s is Egypt's EE. This effect is evident when looking at Egypt's Total Entrepreneurial Activity (TEA), which measures the number of adults who are either trying to create a new venture or who own a business that is less than three and half years old, over the last ten years. According to the Global Entrepreneurship Monitor (GEM), in 2008, Egypt's TEA was 13.10%, which is higher than the current global TEA, 12.30% (GEM, 2018). However, the GEM reports showed a significant decrease in Egypt's TEA in the period coinciding with Egypt's high political unrest. In the period between 2010 to 2015, Egypt's TEA averaged 7.41%, which was at least 5.6% lower than the global average TEA in those years. The 2016 and 2017 reports showed an impressive increase in Egypt's TEA to 14.30% (2% higher than global TEA) and 13.30% (1% higher than the global TEA), respectively.

In 2014, the Egyptian government implemented a transformational reform aimed at bolstering the economy, enhancing the country's business environment, and creating growth opportunities (World Bank, 2018). This plan has left Egypt in a transitional period with many major factors currently affecting its economy. Arguably, the most significant factor is the devaluation of the Egyptian Pound. Boshkov (2019) refers to this as Egypt's "currency crisis". The author explains various factors that resulted in the liberalisation of the Pound including mountains of debt, the 2008 financial crisis, and the increasing cost of food products, which amounts to 45% of the spend of Egypt's middle group. Although the devaluation has cost Egyptians 25% of their money due to high inflation and has dramatically weakened imports, the author highlights benefits of the liberalisation such as an increased GDP and the significant limiting of the black market.

2.4 Entrepreneurship in Egypt

In 2015, Cairo was listed by Forbes as one of the top 10 cities in the world for start-ups (Guttman, 2015). In 2018, 37 Egyptian, innovation-driven start-ups, including *SWVL* and *Wuzzuf*, were on the list of the top 100 start-ups in the Middle East (Forbes Middle East, 2018). Despite having such successful entrepreneurs, however, Egypt is ranked at number 95 on the list of best countries to do business (Forbes, 2018). This is consistent with Mansour *et al.*'s (2018) claims that Egypt's current entrepreneurial boom is a testament to its tech-savvy and multilingual youth rather than the success of the EE. Similarly, Silinevicha *et al.* (2017) concur that while there is much room for improvement, Egypt has seen reasonable growth rates.

The literature surrounding the assessment of the Egyptian EE is small and has not received great attention. Most of the sources in the literature investigate the relationship between entrepreneurship education and entrepreneurship intention, while only a few have assessed the EE in Egypt. Elsayed (2018) is one of the few authors to investigate the effects of the Arab Spring on an aspect of entrepreneurship; however, the author's focus is towards social entrepreneurship as a means to express social freedom following the Arab Spring. Media sources (Solovieva, 2013) and books (Saeed *et al.*, 2015) from the revolutionary period linked the rise in Egyptian entrepreneurship to the events of the Arab Spring, by claiming that these events encouraged the youth to "take matters into their hands".

3. Research methodology

This exploratory study adopted an inductive approach to address the research question. A qualitative method was chosen, as it is more advantageous for the exploration of new topics and for increasing openness for new insights, in comparison to its counterpart, the quantitative method, which is more suited for testing pre-determined hypotheses (Edmondson and McManus, 2007). The study is applied on a cross-sectional time horizon, which is the examination of a particular phenomenon in a specific time period (Saunders and Thornhill, 2009). In order to gain insight into the Egyptian EE, 18 interviews were conducted with a sample of respondents belonging to diverse stakeholder groups (Table 2). Participants were selected using non-probability purposeful sampling, which is best suited for this type of research (Ragab and Arisha, 2018). The interview questions were designed to gauge the status of each of Isenberg's (2011) 6 main components of an entrepreneurial ecosystem: policy, markets, finance, human capital, supports, and culture. Semi-structured interviews allowed a higher degree of flexibility during the interviews; thus, questions varied slightly depending on the background and the replies of the respondent (Greener, 2008). The interviews were transcribed and coded to identify the most salient and emergent themes.

Table 2: Respondents profiles

ID	Type	Job Title	Industry	Firm Size
1	Educator	Lecturer/Executive Manager of Entrepreneurship Centre	Education	N/A
2	Investor	Angel Investor and partner in a major VC firm	N/A	N/A
3	Entrepreneur	Founder/CEO	Fashion	Medium
4	Entrepreneur/Social Entrepreneur	Serial Social Entrepreneur / Partner in VC Firm	Fresh produce, non-profit	Medium
5	Government	Business Support Manager	Technology	N/A
6	Educator/Entrepreneur	Lecturer	Education/Distribution	Large
7	Entrepreneur	Co-founder	Access Control	Large
8	Entrepreneur	Founder	Food Delivery	Small
9	Entrepreneur/Accelerator	Co-founder	FinTech	Small

ID	Type	Job Title	Industry	Firm Size
10	Entrepreneur	Founder	Bakery	Medium
11	Entrepreneur	Founder	Sports Scholarships	Small
12	VC	Value Creation Lead	VC	N/A
13	Entrepreneur	Business Development Director	Mass Transportation	Large
14	Entrepreneur	Founder	Customer Loyalty	Small
15	Angel Investor/VC	Market Research Specialist	Private Equity	N/A
16	Ecosystem Developer	Director of Growth	Start-up Hub	N/A
17	Entrepreneur	Founder/CEO	Medicine	Large
18	Media/Summit Organiser	Head of Content	Media	N/A

4. Findings

This section presents the results of the conducted qualitative study and identifies the key themes which arose from the analysis of the interview data.

4.1 Revolution ramifications

When asked about the effects of the Arab Spring on Egyptian entrepreneurship, mixed responses were received. Replies were mainly split into two opinions. The first and more common view was that the revolution erupted a spirit of self-belief among Egyptian youth that drove them to take matters into their own hands and therefore become entrepreneurs. Interviewee 6 drew on Hofstede's (1984) Cultural Dimensions, by stating that Egyptians went from having a *"collectivistic mentality"* of aspiring to work in large corporates to an *"individualistic mentality"* of wanting to create new ventures independently. The second opinion was that the entrepreneurial revolution was a global phenomenon that was *"inevitably going to happen in Egypt."* Respondents who shared this opinion believed that the idea of the revolution igniting independent business creation was *"a good story at one point... it made it sentimental"* (Interviewee 18).

When focusing on the Egyptian EE, however, there was no doubt among respondents that the revolution had a significant impact, both positive and negative. Interviewee 17 highlighted the vital contribution of the 25th of January Revolution, which started almost entirely on Facebook, in increasing social media usage, especially among the older population, hence creating a wider reach for start-ups. However, Interviewee 17 also acknowledged the adverse effects that the revolution had on investments.

> *"The ecosystem itself in terms of the quality of entrepreneurs and the sheer amount of funding, it actually negatively impacted that, because what happened is that you detained the money from other markets to Egypt, also increasing the risk." (Interviewee 17)*

Similarly, one of the few entrepreneurs to create start-ups before and after 2011, stated:

> *"Of course, investment before the revolution was better, because no one was scared [of the risk]... [Funding] was easier and stronger. After the revolution, investors became very picky." (Interviewee 7)*

4.2 Devaluation: Disastrous or delightful?

The devaluation of the Egyptian Pound is one of the most significant economic changes that followed the revolution. It essentially made the Egyptian currency worth almost a third of what it was against other foreign currencies overnight. While this was a disaster for certain industrial sectors, the subsequent inflation that occurred from this economic change resulted in multiple benefits to the EE. Unsurprisingly, those most affected were importers, or those who operate using imported products, who could no longer afford to import goods at the same capacity. On the other hand, this created a massive demand for high-quality local substitutes. For example, Interviewee 3, who operates in the local fashion industry, saw much higher demand after imported items became out-of-reach for most consumers:

> *"No one's salary tripled in Egypt. Products are five times more expensive. The dollar 3 times, from 5 or 6 Pounds to 18 Pounds... So yes, of course [this has created a demand for products like ours]" (Interviewee 3)*

Founders whose start-ups offer services rather than goods stated they were not necessarily affected by the devaluation of the currency as long as the necessary adjustments in costs and sales are made:

> *"Inflation kind of balances itself out. You need to push your salaries to manage that, but you're also pushing the price ticket, so they balance themselves from a business perspective." (Interviewee 17)*

Interviewee 13, whose start-up operates in the ride-sharing and mass transportation business, claimed that inflation, removal of subsidies, and rising fuel prices work to the company's advantage as consumers become more reluctant to pay the cost of driving when they can save money by using mass transportation services.

4.3 Embryonic ecosystem

The analysis of the data revealed that the Egyptian EE is in an embryonic stage and yet to reach its maturity. This was especially highlighted by those involved in other global or regional EE's. For example, an ecosystem developer stated that the EE is currently at an *"infancy stage"* (Interviewee 16). Similarly, Interviewee 2, who has invested in start-ups operating in various EE's, mentioned that the Egyptian EE is *"twenty years behind Silicon Valley."*

Until recently, there was a lack of support for Egyptian start-ups. The EE had only one or two active VCs and accelerators, the government did not encourage start-up creation, and there were no real success stories that were direct products of the EE. While start-ups still suffer from this lack of support to a certain extent, they now have more opportunities than they previously did, with more active VC firms and accelerators opening annually, more governmental support in the form of incubators, and globally expanding success stories such as *SWVL*. However, the problem remains in the calibre of start-ups, which is yet to catch-up with the growth of available support.

> *"[In Silicon Valley] people are working on data analytics, deep learning, AI and machine learning and stuff like that. Here, everyone is still thinking of making Instacart and 'let's make Tinder for I don't know what...' There are no novel ideas, it's mostly ideas coming from abroad, and there's not a lot of people who execute." (Interviewee 2)*

A lack of corporate start-up partnerships (CSP) is also one of the main reasons behind the EE's limited growth. Egyptian corporations have failed to give start-ups the support required for them to flourish in their respective fields. In some fields such as Financial Technology (*FinTech*), where Egyptian start-ups are required to be backed by official financial organisations, start-ups have suffered. Respondents also pointed out that there have been success stories coming out of Egypt that ended up relocating in order to find more supportive corporate backing.

> *"You have start-ups like Crowd Analyzer, that is a product of Egypt and relocated to Dubai... to find corporates to partner up with them." (Interviewee 18)*

4.4 Funding frustration

Most participants in the study voiced their concerns about the amount of funding available in Egypt. According to Wee Tracker, in 2018, African start-ups raised a total of $725M, of which only $40M were raised in fourth-placed Egypt. To put this into context, the US raised over $150 billion and China over $110 billion in 2018. Of the $40M invested in Egypt, $26M went to 3 start-ups. This left only $14M for the rest of the EE. Of course, these numbers signal that there is not enough funding in the Egyptian EE. Interviewee 16 underlined the consequences of having such meagre numbers by saying:

> *"We need more cash, the cash is [..] going to yield profits, we just need enough cash to invest in a lot of stuff so that you don't have the fear of failure. Because this is a system that is based on almost 90% failure and 10% success. So you need to fail. If you don't have enough money to fail, you're going to miss on the wins, and they're going to happen in other countries." (Interviewee 16)*

When asked about the support available for entrepreneurs, many of the respondents mentioned that there is an increased amount of support available in early stages for entrepreneurs in the form of accelerators, incubators and funding. This is reflected in the small ticket size that VCs often offer. While this support is a significant improvement on the scarce funding available in the past, it only benefits small start-ups and leaves start-ups trying to internationalise and become global at a disadvantage. It is highly unlikely for a start-up in the Egyptian EE to find a fund big enough within Egypt to support its later stages of growth. As a result, such start-ups then begin to search for funding abroad (Interviewee 12). Lack of awareness of the start-up culture in rural or suburban areas of the country, outside of the main cities is also cited as a challenge in this regard. Interviewee 15 elaborates:

> *"I've met wealthy people who still keep their money at home because they haven't heard about angel investing, not because they are stingy." (Interviewee 15)*

4.5 Poor preparation and outdated education

Almost all of the participants of the study expressed their concern towards the level of the education system in Egypt. There was almost no criticism of the standard of technical teaching in the Egyptian education system, in fact, most of the respondents stated that the Egyptian technical graduates, such as engineers or software developers excel in their fields and are in demand from companies abroad. However, educational institutions were criticised for the lack of academic entrepreneurial teaching that has led to culture-wide illiteracy of what entrepreneurship is. The education system was also criticised for its failure to promote innovative thinking among students. Interviewee 5, who is a manager at a well-known governmental accelerator, blamed the tendency of the organisation's applicants, Egyptian entrepreneurs, to copy business models from abroad rather than generating their own ideas on the traditional curriculum that is taught to students in Egyptian schools.

> *"Only 10% maximum [of start-ups] is 'wow', but 90% are things that are copied... [from] abroad or locally... This means that the educational system is not teaching graduates innovation and ideation." (Interviewee 5)*

Respondents censured the inability of Egyptian educational institutions to contribute to the leadership attributes of students. Additionally, they identified a lack of business understanding and professional etiquette displayed by fresh graduates as a significant flaw in products of academic organisations in Egypt.

> *"Whoever studies architectural engineering learns how to design a house, but it doesn't mean he'll be punctual or will know how to talk to a customer... The business side and the business dealings of the technical know-how are absent." (Interviewee 16)*

4.6 Talent trouble

Undoubtedly, a major obstacle cited within the conducted interviews was the recruitment and management of talent within start-ups. Participants complained that they need to filter through large numbers of applications and interviews in order to find suitable candidates for their vacancies yet sometimes are eventually forced to settle for average-calibre talent. This is mainly because, in recent times, the top talent in the country often emigrates to work abroad, a phenomenon known as the *brain drain*. Brain drain was found to be the single biggest threat facing all Egyptian entrepreneurs, particularly high-tech ventures that require high-level software developers. The opportunities abroad are often more attractive for top talent than domestic ones are for several reasons, such as higher pay and a better standard of living. Often, however, immigration means more to these employees than pay; they move abroad to pursue their dreams of working in one of the "blue-chip" companies. Foreign companies welcome Egyptian talent as they are just as skilled as local talent, but cost less. In order for entrepreneurs to convince top talent to remain in Egypt and work for them, they must pay much higher wages than they can afford, particularly in their early stages. The founder of one of the largest start-ups in Egypt, says:

> *"I think the brain drain in Egypt is a very serious situation... I'm talking about the technical talent, the marketing talent, the product talent, the strategy talent, like the really good ones, they leave the country. So you usually end up with not the best talent in the world. You're trying to build a company that has a global presence. That is definitely the major challenge." (Interviewee 17)*

4.7 Cultural complications

A classic cultural challenge in Egypt is the traditional view that self-employment is inferior to employment at large corporations or in the government. Hence, one of the unusual cultural obstacles identified is the unwillingness of parents of university students to allow their children to found start-ups after graduation, as they view this as a waste of time and money compared to traditional and more stable corporate jobs.

> *"Some parents think 'I've invested this much in my son or daughter so I can't afford for them to waste time in a start-up,' even when they can afford it. They think 'Go look for a good and stable job'." (Interviewee 1)*

Cultural problems may also arise with employees who refuse to take instructions from individuals who are of a younger age due to a strong belief in the notion of seniority:

For them it's like 'How is she younger than me and telling me to do things? How dare she give me remarks?' Others think that they don't have to listen to me or they can talk back." (Interviewee 10)

4.8 Regulatory restrictions

Respondents were often critical of the laws and regulations governing business in Egypt. An example is around banking policy:

"Restrictions around like banking policy and the finance policy merging between bringing foreign investments into Egyptian banks can sometimes be very tricky." (Interviewee 4)

Others pointed out regulatory difficulties that are present in the government's policies aimed at aiding small businesses. For example, the government's obligations on banks to offer loans with 5% interest to SMEs was not useful for start-ups because of the legal complications that came with the loan, especially for start-ups who deal with much uncertainty at the beginning (Interviewee 7). Another gap in the Egyptian legal framework that was mentioned is the inadequacy of copyright laws. In the fashion industry, for example, Interviewee 3 shared her experience:

"In 2011, the collection we released was called 'For the Love of Egypt', and it boomed. Everyone bought it. Then it started to get copied in the streets. That's the first problem, royalty rights protection regulations are not sufficient in Egypt. Of course, we didn't really look to fix this problem, because we knew we couldn't do anything to stop street vendors." (Interviewee 3)

4.9 FinTech fervour

One of the most recurring themes in most of the interview responses was the rise of *FinTech* in Egypt. Fintech refers to any technological advancement in the financial sector, such as online payments, blockchain, and internet banking. When it comes to financial services, Egypt has one of the lowest penetration rates in the world, with almost 85% of the population unbanked and relying on cash (Nabil, 2019). Egyptian entrepreneurs see this problem as an opportunity and are currently working diligently towards addressing it. Unfortunately, however, the FinTech sector in Egypt, more so than any other industry, is also significantly inhibited by strict and suffocating laws and regulations that end many start-up ideas before they can start. For example, in Egypt, Blockchain is yet to be legalised. Start-ups are also required to be backed by an official financial organisation, such as a bank or the central bank, and go through a lengthy process in order to gain a license to perform any financial services. An example is in the company founded by Interviewee 9:

"We didn't launch yet, but it's taken us a year just to get a license: to know where to get a license and because the process of the license is long. Now the biggest challenge for us is that no one wants to work with us until they see that we have this license." (Interviewee 9)

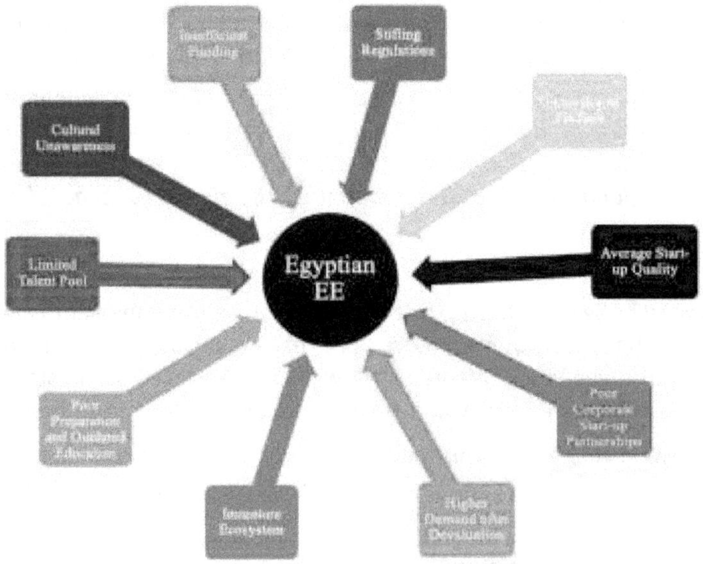

5. Conclusions and implications

Results of this study reveal that the Egyptian EE remains relatively immature and is yet to reach its full potential. Entrepreneurs in the Egyptian EE face a multitude of challenges with the country's policies and regulations, awareness of the start-up culture, accessibility to funding, and available talent pool. It is clear that the majority of the problems are at the root of the EE, stemming from the traditional education system. While the education system has excelled in producing highly skilled technical graduates, who are sought after from multinational companies abroad, it is unsuccessful in preparing graduates to be able to conduct business in a professional manner, as well as to remove the cultural stigmas surrounding self-employment. It is also important to note that regulators share the blame as research has found that an individual's understanding of entrepreneurship is largely dependent on the policies in place (Kurczewska *et al.* 2014). Regulations and policies in Egypt surrounding entrepreneurship, investment, and copyright are mostly unclear, and do not incentivise start-ups to operate within the country. This often drives entrepreneurs to relocate to different geographical locations within the region where the necessary support is available. Regulatory constraints have especially stifled entrepreneurs operating within the FinTech sector. In any EE, the financial technology infrastructure is crucial, as it provides the foundation on which start-ups can make and receive payments. Therefore, confining the development of FinTech impedes the development of the whole ecosystem.

Despite the previous challenges, there have been positive signs of development that indicate that the Egyptian EE is on an upward trend. The EE has seen an unprecedented increase in the number of investors, VCs, and governmental accelerators in recent years. The government has also begun to focus on developing the weak areas of the ecosystem. For example, in an effort towards a cashless economy, the government recently installed more than 7000 ATMs and imposed new laws that require all monetary transactions in governmental services under a certain amount to be paid digitally (Egypt Today, 2019). The EE has also seen increased support from large corporations, which have partnered with multiple accelerators to facilitate the start-up process for new ventures in their relevant fields. Although the revolution had an undeniable effect on encouraging entrepreneurship in Egypt, this study has found that the era of political reform played only a partial role in igniting what was a global and regional trend that was inevitably going to take place in Egypt.

The results of this research have implications on different stakeholders in the Egyptian EE. Policymakers have a lead role to play in advancing the Egyptian EE into a thriving environment that produces successful start-ups. It is integral that they put clear policies in place that mitigate the risk for entrepreneurs and investors, and encourage individuals to take part in the entrepreneurial revolution. It is also imperative that more lenient and up-to-date FinTech laws be imposed in order to develop what is the basis of any EE. Additionally, copyright laws must also be enforced to ensure ethical practice. Start-up founders, on the other hand, should look for funding only from investors or entities who have experience in the industry in which their new venture operates. It is also beneficial for entrepreneurs to take advantage of governmental accelerators that do not require equity from start-ups in order to support them in the early stages. Finally, entrepreneurs must be aware of the scarcity of top talent and be patient in their searches for candidates in order to avoid the difficulties that may arise from hiring average quality human resources. Despite its contribution, the exploratory nature of the study limits its applicability to other contexts, a typical limitation of such kind of work. It is suggested that for future research, a more in-depth analysis be done for each of the entities that constitute an entrepreneurial ecosystem in Egypt.

Acknowledgements

The authors would like to dedicate this paper to the memory of Professor Amr Arisha, an outstanding academic and a dear friend.

References

Amoros, J. E. and Bosma, N. (2014) 'Global entrepreneurship monitor 2013 global report: Fifteen years of assessing entrepreneurship across the globe', Recuperado de http://www. gemconsortium. org/docs/3106/gem-2013-global-report.

Bennett, N. and Lemoine, G. J. (2014) 'What a difference a word makes: Understanding threats to performance in a VUCA world', Business Horizons. Elsevier, 57(3), pp. 311–317.

Boshkov, T. (2019) 'Egypt Currency Crisis: Analysis of the Causes', IJIBM International Journal of Information, Business and Management. Elite Hall Publishing House, 11(1), pp. 1–9.

Economist Intelligence Unit (2016) Egypt takes steps to boost bank lending to SMEs, The Economist. Available at: http://www.eiu.com/industry/article/603842444/egypt-takes-steps-to-boost-bank-lending-to-smes/2016-01-12 (Accessed: 28 March 2019).

Edmondson, A. C. and McManus, S. E. (2007) 'Methodological fit in management field research', Academy of management review. Academy of Management Briarcliff Manor, NY 10510, 32(4), pp. 1246–1264.

Egypt Today (2019) Ministry: E-payment of gov't service fees applicable as of May 1, Egypt Today. Available at: https://www.egypttoday.com/Article/3/67836/Ministry-E-payment-of-gov-t-service-fees-applicable-as (Accessed: 2 July 2019).

Egyptian Streets (2018) Two Egyptians Make Forbes' 30 Under 30 List for 2018, Egyptian Streets. Available at: https://egyptianstreets.com/2018/01/22/two-egyptians-make-forbes-30-under-30-list-for-2018/ (Accessed: 21 June 2019).

Elsayed, Y. (2018) 'At the Intersection of Social Entrepreneurship and Social Movements: The Case of Egypt and the Arab Spring', VOLUNTAS: International Journal of Voluntary and Nonprofit Organizations. Springer, 29(4), pp. 819–831.

Fogel, K. et al. (2006) 'Institutional obstacles to entrepreneurship', Oxford handbook of entrepreneurship. Citeseer.

Forbes Middle East (2018) Top 100 Startups in the Middle East, Forbes Middle East. Available at: https://www.forbesmiddleeast.com/list/top-100-startups-in-the-middle-east-2018 (Accessed: 28 March 2019).

Gabriel, C.-A. (2016) 'What is challenging renewable energy entrepreneurs in developing countries?', Renewable and Sustainable Energy Reviews. Elsevier, 64, pp. 362–371.

GEM (2018) Egypt National Report 2017-2018, GEM. Available at: https://www.gemconsortium.org/country-profile/58 (Accessed: 27 March 2019).

Ghanem, H. (2013) 'The role of micro and small enterprises in Egypt's economic transition (Global Economy & Development Working Paper 55)', Washington, DC: Brookings.

Greener, S. (2008) Business research methods. BookBoon.

Guttman, A. (2015) 10 Top Cities Around The World To Launch Your Startup, Forbes. Available at: https://www.forbes.com/sites/amyguttman/2015/11/29/top-10-cities-in-the-world-to-launch-your-startup-some-may-surprise-you/#a6167cf7e573 (Accessed: 28 March 2019).

Hofstede, G. and Bond, M. H. (1984) 'Hofstede's culture dimensions: An independent validation using Rokeach's value survey', Journal of cross-cultural psychology. Sage Publications Sage CA: Thousand Oaks, CA, 15(4), pp. 417–433.

Isenberg, D. (2011) 'The entrepreneurship ecosystem strategy as a new paradigm for economic policy: Principles for cultivating entrepreneurship', Presentation at the Institute of International and European Affairs.

Khoury, T. A. and Prasad, A. (2016) 'Entrepreneurship amid concurrent institutional constraints in less developed countries', Business & Society. SAGE Publications Sage CA: Los Angeles, CA, 55(7), pp. 934–969.

Kirchgeorg, M. and Winn, M. I. (2006) 'Sustainability marketing for the poorest of the poor', Business Strategy and the Environment. Wiley Online Library, 15(3), pp. 171–184.

Kurczewska, A., Kyrö, P. and Abbas, A. (2014) 'Transformative Capacity of Entrepreneurship Education in Two Different Cultural Settings—Morphogenetic Analysis of Egypt and Finland', Journal of Enterprising Culture. World Scientific, 22(04), pp. 401–435.

Lingelbach, D. C., De La Vina, L. and Asel, P. (2005) 'What's distinctive about growth-oriented entrepreneurship in developing countries?', UTSA College of Business Center for Global Entrepreneurship Working Paper, (1).

Mansour, D. M., Sedita, S. R. and Apa, R. (2018) 'Dynamics of Entrepreneurship in Egypt: Assessing the Entrepreneurial Ecosystem', in Entrepreneurship Ecosystem in the Middle East and North Africa (MENA). Springer, pp. 519–542.

Nabil, Y. (2019) Banking for the unbanked: The growth of fintech in Egypt, Wamda.com. Available at: https://www.wamda.com/2019/05/banking-unbanked-growth-fintech-egypt (Accessed: 30 June 2019).

Ragab, M. A. F. and Arisha, A. (2018) 'Research Methodology in Business: A Starter's Guide'. Dublin Institute of Technology.

Reuters (2018) 'Egypt unemployment rate falls to 9.9 pct in Q2 - CAPMAS', Reuters. Available at: https://www.reuters.com/article/egypt-unemployment/egypt-unemployment-rate-falls-to-9-9-pct-in-q2-capmas-idUSL5N1V61V4.

Sadeghi, V. J. et al. (2019) 'An institution-based view of international entrepreneurship: A comparison of context-based and universal determinants in developing and economically advanced countries', International Business Review. Elsevier, p. 101588.

Saeed, A. et al. (2015) Entrepreneurship in Egypt from Evolution to Revolution. 2nd editio. Cairo: Startology.

Saunders, T. and Thornhill, A. (2009) 'Research Methods for Business Students', Publisher: Financial Times Prentice Hall.

Silinevicha, V., Moussa, H. and Kalinina, K. (2017) 'Entrepreneurship of Eco-system and Its Transformation, Using the Example of Republic of Egypt'.

Solovieva, D. (2013) Egypt's Entrepreneurial Revolution: A Community Of Startups Rises From The Ashes, Fast Company.

World Bank (2018) The World Bank In Egypt, WorldBank.org. Available at: http://www.worldbank.org/en/country/egypt/overview (Accessed: 27 March 2019).

Zaher, H. A. (2017) In Egypt, illiteracy rates down but problem remains, The Arab Weekly. Available at: https://thearabweekly.com/egypt-illiteracy-rates-down-problem-remains#off-canvas (Accessed: 27 March 2019).

Zaki, I. M. and Rashid, N. H. (2016) 'Entrepreneurship impact on economic growth in emerging countries', The Business & Management Review. The Academy of Business and Retail Management (ABRM), 7(2), p. 31.

Institutionalizing Paradox: Contextual Ambidexterity in an Oligopolistic Setting: The Case of a Financial Service Provider

Ranvir Rai and Beniamino Callegari
Kristiania University College, Oslo, Norway
Ranvir.Rai@kristiania.no
Ben.Callegari@kristiania.no
DOI: 10.34190/EIE.20.089

Abstract: Banking and financial industries are increasingly exposed to competition as a result of digitalization, globalization and new global directives. In response, banks are creating new businesses within their existing structures to meet these challenges. In this article, we explore how a specific financial institution is implementing an innovation strategy based on contextual ambidexterity against the backdrop of ongoing digital transformation. Contextual ambidexterity aims towards a comprehensive diffusion of innovative practices among all organizational levels, leading to particularly significant tensions arising within the decision-making process, as employees come to terms with the paradoxical nature of ambidexterity. While our findings confirm that the challenging nature of contextual ambidexterity is maintained in a dynamic perspective, we find evidence for an original managerial supporting strategy, based on leveraging inherited oligopolistic advantage into long-term harmonious structural transformation.

Keywords: organizational ambidexterity, contextual ambidexterity, paradox, innovation management

1. Introduction

The relevance of ambidexterity has long been recognized in the field in organizational studies. Contextual ambidexterity has emerged as a particularly interesting variant, aimed towards the development of organization-wide practices and values supporting the simultaneous pursuit of explorative and exploitative tasks through autonomous decision making. The approach involves most employees to directly confront the tensions and paradox implied by such different, contrasting goals, and to creatively develop their own solutions. It can be considered a high-risk strategy, with potentially high rewards in the form of a profoundly flexible and resilient organizational structure. The main challenge lies in implementing and managing such deep changes.

In our study, we focus on the dynamic issues related to the implementation of contextual ambidexterity. Instead of studying a naturally ambidextrous firm, we focus on a financial firm with a clear inherited bias towards exploitation, currently enduring a long-term transition towards an ambidextrous stance, to be achieved through a contextual ambidexterity strategy. Our objective is to highlight the unique implementation challenges faced by a top-management team using contextual ambidexterity as a tool for strategic change. In particular, our theoretical framework leads us to believe that such situation will lead to the emergence of resources and competence shortages, no matter how rich in both the starting point might be. Our empirical study is focused on exploring the evidence relevant to these hypotheses, and the relative managerial response. We find evidence of a consistent response arising from below, yet sanctioned from the top, of a gradual, careful, and, in the short-term, inefficient, implementation of new practices. Such slow pace, however, is not necessary a failure, but potentially just the symptom of a strategy aiming to leverage oligopolistic advantage into long-term structural realignment.

The article is organized as follows. After this introduction, section 2 describes our theoretical framework of reference. Section 3 illustrates our methodology. Section 4 contains our findings, which are discussed in Section 5. Finally, section 6 concludes.

2. Theory

Following Birkinshaw and Gupta (2013), we conceptualize ambidexterity as the ability to competently and simultaneously pursue two organizationally incompatible objectives, namely the efficient performance of existing routines and the search and development of new ones. Ambidexterity is achieved primarily through managerial capability, as it is to management that most relevant decisions fall. However, as the contextual variety of ambidexterity makes particularly clear, ambidexterity is a multi-level construct, without a single, fixed decisional locus, investing instead the entire business unit and all its members, although under different forms. While autonomy is generally welcomed, it also implies an additional layer of work in the form of decision-making, and an additional source of uncertainty and potential failure to be managed. Neither a single nor a best solution exists. The dynamic nature of organizational capabilities, practices, relations and competitive context, imply not only a large variety of potential approaches, but that their evaluation requires practical experience and a degree of tolerance for failure. The organization needs to be willing and able to commit to novel solutions despite an *a priori* understanding that such solutions might fail, that their failure can only be revealed in the fullness of time, and that the relative costs might be significant. Finally, we see ambidexterity as an interpretative framework of broad applicability, useful to highlight specific tensions arising in organizational practice and development.

While the study of organizational ambidexterity has a long history (Duncan 1976; March 1991; Tushman and O'Reilly 1996), the concept of contextual ambidexterity was introduced to the debate by Gibson and Birkinshaw (2004), as "the behavioral capacity to simultaneously demonstrate alignment and adaptability across an entire business unit. Alignment refers to coherence among all the patterns of activities in the business unit; they are working together toward the same goals. Adaptability refers to the capacity to reconfigure activities in the business unit quickly to meet changing demands in the task environment." (ibid, p.209). In contrast to structural strategies, focused on organizational, task or temporal separation, contextual ambidexterity aims towards diffusing across the whole organization a set of processes or systems allowing individuals to decide autonomously how to allocate resources at their disposal to meet the contrasting goals of alignment and adaptability, exploration and exploitation. While mixed, complementary strategies can be devised, the two categories identify two different approaches to the problem of coordination. Structural ambidexterity pushes the tensions upwards, to be solved by a combination of structures, rules and decisions made by top management. Contextual ambidexterity aims at dissolving the tensions downwards, through the empowerment of lower-level decision making and the diffusion of supporting practices and cultural values.

Consequently, contextual ambidexterity strategies are prone to face unique challenges of implementation (Jansen et al. 2009; De Clerq et al. 2014; Havermans et al. 2015; Lavikka et al 2015). In this study, we aim to focus on the specifically dynamic issues arising from the implementation of a contextual ambidexterity strategy. While all firms eventually face the trade-offs of exploration and exploitation, its relative relevance depends on the characteristics of the markets in which firms operate. Large oligopolistic companies operating in sectors characterized by a relatively low-pace innovation regime might find the issues related to ambidexterity less pressing and challenging than others. Changes in the relevant competitive regime, however, might quickly bring the issue to the fore, forcing top management to devise and implement quick solutions in order to support the necessary substantial internal changes required by the new paradigm. Contextual strategies might appear particularly suited to meet such situations, as their inherent focus is on diffusing practices, values and attitudes supporting both alignment and adaptability across the whole organization. However, the dynamic nature of the situation might lead to the emergence of unique challenges of implementation, as the organization struggle to reconcile new vision and inherited practice, borne out of repeated past success.

Two dynamic problems appear to be particularly relevant. The first is related to resource heterogeneity, a dimension considered problematic for contextual ambidexterity practices (Turner et al., 2013). The qualitative differences between resources create additional complexity for the diffused, autonomous choices implied by contextual ambidexterity. Ongoing change in strategic orientation further compounds the issue by throwing into disarray and making obsolete the resource valuations and allocation procedures developed in the past, creating the possibility for new inefficiencies and tensions, as decentralized decision-making leads to either upsetting choices or prolonged stalls. The second is related to the increased costs of decisional autonomy. The empowerment of lower management and employees can greatly improve day-to-day operational efficiency and increase the organizational ability to recognize and react to uncertainty. However, autonomous decision making requires an environment of diffuse competence and knowledge, supporting and evaluating the numerous decision makers. When dynamic change affects the relevant knowledge base, empowered lower-level decision-makers may lose confidence in their judgment, leading to slower and less effective processes. At the same time, decision quality becomes more difficult to assess contextually, leading to inefficient practices developing and entrenching.

On the basis of this discussion we advance the following hypotheses:

> *H1: The implementation of a contextual ambidexterity strategy in a context of strategic realignment is likely to create tensions related to the control of previously abundant resources.*

> *H2: The implementation of a contextual ambidexterity strategy in a context of strategic realignment is likely to slower the pace and effectiveness of lower-levels decision-making processes.*

Facing these tensions, top management will eventually be facing the decision to either complement the contextual strategy with structural measures, or to revise the process of implementation to meet the emerging challenges. To explore such process, we have performed an in-depth case study on the implementation of a strategy of contextual ambidexterity within a large oligopolistic banking firm during a process of strategic realignment. The case was selected for the following reasons. First of all, the relevance of ambidexterity for service firms such as commercial banks are well known (Jansen et al., 2012; Junni et al., 2013; Faisal Ahammad et al. 2015). Secondly, the firm we studied comes from a long-term dominant position in its main market and has recently embraced a strategic realignment towards a business model more exposed to competitive pressures. Finally, the firm has recently attempted to implement an ambidexterity strategy with a clear, explicit contextual component.

3. Methods

This paper introduces a study of an on-going digital transformation in a large Norwegian bank. More specifically, we examine the issue through a case study of a large financial organization – DNB – currently transitioning from a traditional bank towards a technology-based provider of financial services. In order to explore contextual ambidexterity at DNB, we applied the framework of Lawson and Samson (2001). Building on the idea of ambidextrous organization they propose seven interdependent elements that together comprise organizational innovativeness. These are vision and strategy, harnessing the competence base, organizational intelligence, creativity and idea management, organizational structures and systems, culture and climate, and management of technology. We apply the elements above to synthesize and discuss our empirical findings.

DNB is Norway's largest financial services group and one of the largest in the Nordic region in terms of market capitalization. The bank is a world leader for shipping, has a strong position in the energy sector and seafood industries, reflecting traditional Norwegian economic strengths. As one of the largest financial institutions in the Nordic region, our case company was an excellent exemplar of a company operating under the market institutional logic; this, combined with the company's initiatives to incorporate digital practices in its operations and innovation activities, made DNB a suitable candidate.

The research process has followed the characteristics of "systematic combining," advocated by Dubois and Gadde (2002, 2014). They describe a process of "going 'back and forth' from one type of research activity to another and between empirical observations and theory" (*ibid.*, p. 555), in order to contribute to the development of both. We conducted semi-structured interviews with key stakeholders across operations to gain in-depth insight into organizational members' reasoning and reflections. This allowed us to understand the logic through which they viewed the world (McCracken, 1988). In-depth interviews provide an effective means of obtaining rich insights into the phenomenon of interest, as they provide access to detailed contextual information and individual insight that cannot be obtained from surveys (Gwinner, Gremler and Bitner, 1998).

The interviewees were 12 managers directly involved in the company's innovation projects. They ranged from vice president-level to middle management responsible for strategic innovation initiatives or programs. Interviews were conducted until information redundancy was achieved (Lincoln and Guba, 1985). We used interview guides with a flexible structure of questions, allowing for deviation from the sequence in order to follow interesting lines of inquiry or go deeper into relevant, accidentally appearing, topics. This approach was deemed particularly appropriate to this case study, since the company was undergoing a complex transformation process, leaving many of the respondents to face significant, persistent uncertainty, which showed in their difficulties to engage directly with our questions. The questions covered the company's existing practices at the time of interview, personal experiences with and interpretations of innovation capabilities and tools, processes and resources, culture and values related to innovation initiatives. Interviews lasted for 45 to 60 minutes; they were digitally recorded and transcribed verbatim.

To analyse the data we first carried out open coding of the interview transcripts in order to identify categories. We report the findings from the categories of traditional business division and new business division. Next we applied selective coding (Flick, 2009) to identify further examples and evidence relating to the two categories. Various themes that influenced these capabilities were emphasized. Specific text segments from the interviews were compared by coding and retrieving data. We performed this procedure iteratively, moving back and forth between codes and data until consensus among the researchers emerged.

4. Findings

4.1 Harnessing the competence base

Most interviewees argue that business divisions have abundant operational expertise, but they lack innovation expertise. The reasons are that employees in business departments are usually internally recruited, with most of their work experience having been developed within the bank. Since DNB has only recently developed an innovation focus, with most of the processes still to be fully implemented, few employees have actual experience with innovation management practices.

As one of the informants mentioned:

> *"... you see that the bank makes very good money ... you see changes, you see new technology coming in, new competitors, regulations etc. But we have not seen the big impact of all this yet on the bottom line. DNB has still work to do and we must create a sense of urgency in order to promote the importance of innovation."*
>
> *- Division Director of Innovation Division*

On the other hand, the company has established a new division called "New Business". This division works as a support department for the entire DNB Group, contributing its innovation expertise to other divisions focusing on traditional business areas. The collaboration, however, is more difficult than expected:

> *"... you sit with one foot on the gas and one on the brake. So, then I kind of think it's either go or no go. Either you feel that you are allowed to work with innovation as an employee, or you are one of those who feel that you are hired to make sure things do not go wrong ..."*
>
> *- Division Director of Innovation Division*

Moreover, cross fertilization of competence is hampered by the fact that interdepartmental projects among traditional business divisions are relatively rare. Consequently, collaborative decision-making and resource-sharing procedures remains primarily on an ad-hoc basis, thus inhibiting innovation and the development of innovation capabilities.

4.2 Organizational structures and systems

Several leaders in the business development sections acknowledge that most of their time end up tied into important existing projects, rather than being invested in innovative initiatives. This is partly due to obsolete systems and solutions in need of upgrading and maintenance:

> *"... every area has got its IT resources and resources, and then every business area must prioritize what is prioritized by the business areas that go on" fix the basic and core ", and not so much innovation and ... new innovation projects ... you can't afford because then you have already used up the money for core products."*
>
> *- Division Director Innovation Division*

All managers interviewed described IT resources as scarce and difficult to mobilize, as most of them are tied up in the maintenance of inherited old IT systems. These resources appear to be particularly scarce for innovation departments. As commented by one of the informants:

> *"If we are to do something like that, it costs so much money because we are sitting in a 'technical spaghetti' so we almost give up before we even start."*
>
> *- Section Manager New Business*

4.3 Management of technology

We asked about possibilities for collaborating with external fin-tech companies that can add value to their business by purchasing solutions and incorporating it into their own domain. One of the informants reflected on this:

"The fin-techs are a very good example of where you have companies that have some technology that is much more" cutting edge "than we have, and it will save us a lot of time and money to make the same."

- Division Director Innovation Division

DNB has already established itself on this front by purchasing "Luca Lab" to make their DNB Accounting solution more advanced. In addition, DNB has partnered with "11: FS" to develop a consumer finance solution ("Foundry"). This indicates that DNB has already started to exploit collaboration opportunities to become more competitive with external players. Also, the risk of becoming irrelevant is also part of agenda, as addressed by one of the respondents:

"I don't think we're going to be out-competed, but I probably think the margins within some of our most profitable business models is going to... come under increasing pressure then in the years to come, and that requires us to innovate our existing business models, we need to become more efficient in streamlining our operations."

- Division Director IT Division

4.4 Creativity and idea management

According to some of the informants, another challenge is that a lot of resources – in terms of both worktime and money – are spent on the idea generation and early development phases of new products and services, before any attempt towards validation, resulting in significant sunk costs.

In DNB, there seems to be a increasing focus on testing business concepts and working with new ideas and solutions in a strategic way. As such, they strive to achieve a cultural shift that may underpin collaboration and communication between operations, development and testing. For DNB, this means that employees get appropriate expertise from the right departments when needed, as pointed out by one of the informants:

"So we are really pushing the testing culture in the whole of DNB, building up a testing environment where you can actually test stuff, everyone and I am not talking about Private Market, but that all DNB, IT, everyone is using the same platform, in terms of sharing their learnings."

- Section Manager Person Market

4.5 Organizational intelligence

External relationships are highly prioritized in DNB, which depends on what happens outside their company. In the innovation units, there is a comprehensive collaboration through seminars, universities, large financial organizations and organized hackathons. The differences come from the fact that it is primarily the innovation units that are responsible for this, while the business areas lean on them through internal training and seminars.

4.6 Culture and climate

Through our study we have seen that DNB is on a transformation journey from being a financial institution that has been protected from its environment with little competition, to full competition. This means that DNB must be more forward-looking and be able to embrace failure as part of becoming more innovative. However, such mindset shift is entirely at odds with traditional banking, a business model well-known for its conservative approach and strongly institutionalized aversion to failure.

"The corporate management has stated very clearly that we should move from a culture where we operate 'safely' towards a culture in which it is allowed to fail... we're on a cultural journey that is complex."

- Section manager IT division

Consequently, when new ideas are developed through old practices, challenges and tensions emerge within the organization:

"In the IT division, there has been a culture that has been a bit fear-based, so there are an awful lot of people in the IT division who dare not fail, because there has been no room to fail in the past."

- Section Manager IT division

Everyone we talked to said there is a lot of creativity and idea development in every part of the organization. What appears to be missing, however, is an effective internal process to screen, select and diffuse novel ideas. As pointed out by one of the informants:

> *"... yesterday I was at a meeting where there was someone who had an idea, and a big meeting was set up with many people in high positions, directors here and there, and then it was completely unclear whether there is a problem that this idea actually solves..."*
>
> *- Section Manager IT division*

Also, being a large bank makes it challenging to exploit the perceived creativity due to the numerous criteria to be fulfilled before projects are implemented in the organization.

5. Discussion

Our findings suggest our initial beliefs to be valid. Despite a resource-abundant starting point, the implementation of a contextual ambidexterity strategy in a context of strategic realignment has led to the emergence of scarce resource configurations, namely innovation-management competence and IT resources, creating significant tensions within and between departments as a consequence of attempts toward establishing control (cf. Papachroni et al. 2016). The new strategic aims have also led to a negative re-evaluation of the bureaucratic support structure and its practices, to which some of the disappointing implementation results have been attributed. However, this is only part of the story, as innovative projects that do manage to clear bureaucratic hurdles appear to be inefficiently run, with too much time and too many resources spent in the early developmental phases. Besides being a consequence of the previously mentioned limited innovative competence of lower-level management, it can also be understood as a reflection of the higher uncertainty involved in such projects and, especially, their evaluation. In a context until recently characterized by a particularly fastidious attention to detail and very low tolerance to operative failure, spending significant, and perhaps excessive, amounts of resources on the planning stages is reasonable in light of the need to minimize chances of failures and achieve a justifiable position in case of negative outcomes.

The managerial response has also been largely in line with expectations. Top management have promoted new instruments and practices aimed towards fostering more constructive and effective decision-making, while also incentivizing the collaboration between more and less innovative departments, to support learning and resource-sharing. The search for external partners for the development of new IT solutions also goes in the direction of addressing the suddenly severe shortage of IT resources felt across the whole organization. However, while the response from the top fell largely within our expectations, we were surprised by the reaction from below. Given the significant challenges implied in the restructuring process and the contextual ambidexterity strategy, it appears that the dominant solution adopted by lower-level managers and employees has been to make strategic use of their decisional autonomy to minimize explorative tasks, pouring the vast majorities of resources towards core operative practices instead, thus starving and significantly slowing down the process of wide-spread adoption of the innovation strategy (cf. McNamara and Baden-Fuller 1999; Hill and Birkinshaw 2014).

These results follow directly from the dominant market position held by the firm under study (Davis et al. 2009). While top-management has internalized the need for a long-term shift towards different, more competitive markets, requiring an accompanying internal shift in innovative practices, the operative core of the firm has yet to enter in contact with the new needs and requests of such change, which is mostly yet to be realized. As a result, their focus, their cultural values and their practices remain consistent with the very different requirements maintained by day-to-day operations. This is not a consequence of incompetence, or irrationality, but rather the result of a necessary difference between the timeframe underlying top managerial vision and operative personnel. No matter how well communicated and well understood is the need for long-term change, the enduring inherited practices will necessarily loom large in the mind of those who are tasked with serving two masters. Of those, one is both harsher and more generous than the other. Harsher, because its demands are more clearly defined, their deadlines much shorter and its punishment severe. More generous, because success is also clearer, more commonly perceived and acknowledged, and the rewards well structured. In contrast, the demand to innovate and explore is simultaneously less pressing and less rewarding, leading to the emergence of a strong bias against the allocation of resources to exploration in the context of decision making.

6. Conclusion

Our study has focused on the dynamic aspects of implementation of contextual ambidexterity in a rapidly evolving strategic context. To explore these aspects, we have conducted an in-depth case study of a large established financial firm, currently transitioning from traditional banking to the provision of a wider range of technologically assisted financial services. From a theoretical perspective, we expected a contextual ambidexterity strategy to be hampered by emergent resource scarcity and innovation process failures: these hypotheses have been supported by our empirical evidence. However, the managerial reaction to these challenges was unexpected. From the operational and lower-management levels, the main response has been to limit the resources allocated to innovative projects, and to overemphasize planning and early development stages over more concrete testing strategies, in an attempt to reduce individual exposure to uncertainty and failure. These developments have found a rather meek response from top management, at least so far. While some adjustments and partial amendments have been introduced, evidence of an ongoing learning process, top management remains committed at this time to a contextual ambidexterity strategy and appears content with a slow diffusion of ambidextrous practices and their supporting cultural values throughout the organization.

This is a reflection of the strengths and challenges arising from the firm's inherited dominant market position. The combination of an enduring oligopolistic advantage and a long-term strategic concern for new, more competitive markets, have resulted in a gradual process of transition. On the negative side, this implies that the firm will be slow to evolve, to identify and exploit new opportunities, and will have to rely on external partners to achieve many of its transformative goals. On the positive side, however, a slower pace might be an effective strategy to absorb the inevitable tensions engendered by the pursuit of contextual ambidexterity.

By allowing operational and managerial personnel to gradually enter the murky waters of innovative practices, tolerating partial retreats and slips, the firm is slowly building up the internal innovative competence without which no ambidextrous firm can truly thrive. From a cultural perspective, the tolerance towards slow change goes a long way to credibly signal the increased tolerance towards failure explicitly supporting the contextual ambidexterity strategy currently pursued. The slow pace of implementation can be understood not as a managerial failure, but rather as an intentional managerial strategy, leveraging the enduring, albeit declining, dominant market position to ensure a harmonious long-term transition, at the cost of some missed short-term opportunities lost along the way. Only time will tell. What we can conclude, however, is that the dynamics of contextual ambidexterity implementation are mediated by the relevant market structure, and that inevitable organizational tensions can be effectively diffused through a gradual transformative approach, provided that the firm is in a position to afford such a leisurely pace.

References

Birkinshaw, J., & Gupta, K. (2013). Clarifying the Distinctive Contribution of Ambidexterity to the Field of Organization Studies. *Academy of Management Perspectives*, 27(4), 287-298.

Christensen, C. (2013) *The Innovator's Dilemma: When New Technologies Cause Great Firms to Fail*. Harvard Business Review Press.

Davis, J. P., Eisenhardt, K. M., & Bingham, C. B. (2009). Optimal Structure, Market Dynamism, and the Strategy of Simple Rules. *Administrative Science Quarterly*, 54(3), 413–452.

De Clercq, D., Thongpapanl, N., & Dimov, D. (2014). Contextual Ambidexterity in SMEs: The Roles of Internal and External Rivalry. *Small Business Economics*, 42(1), 191-205.

Dubois, A. and Gadde, L.-E. (2002) 'Systematic Combining: An Abductive Approach to Case Research', *Journal of Business Research*, 55(7), 553–560.

Dubois, A. and Gadde, L.-E. (2014) '"Systematic Combining"—A Decade Later', *Journal of Business Research*, 67(6), 1277–1284.

Duncan, R. B. (1976). The Ambidextrous Organization: Designing Dual Structures for Innovation. *The Management of Organization*, 1(1), 167-188.

Faisal Ahammad, M., Mook Lee, S., Malul, M., & Shoham, A. (2015). Behavioral Ambidexterity: The Impact of Incentive Schemes on Productivity, Motivation, and Performance of Employees in Commercial Banks. *Human Resource Management*, 54(S1), s45-s62.

Flick, U. (2009) *An Introduction to Qualitative Research*. SAGE.

Gibson, C. B., & Birkinshaw, J. (2004). The Antecedents, Consequences, and Mediating Role of Organizational Ambidexterity. *Academy of Management Journal*, 47(2), 209-226.

Gwinner, K. P., Gremler, D. D. and Bitner, M. J. (1998) 'Relational Benefits in Services Industries: The Customer's Perspective', *Journal of the Academy of Marketing Science*, 26(2), 101.

Havermans, L. A., Den Hartog, D. N., Keegan, A., & Uhl-Bien, M. (2015). Exploring the Role of Leadership in Enabling Contextual Ambidexterity. *Human Resource Management*, 54(S1), 179-200.

Hill, S. A., & Birkinshaw, J. (2014). Ambidexterity and Survival in Corporate Venture Units. *Journal of Management*, 40(7), 1899–1931.

Jansen, J. J., Tempelaar, M. P., Van den Bosch, F. A., & Volberda, H. W. (2009). Structural Differentiation and Ambidexterity: The Mediating Role of Integration Mechanisms. *Organization Science*, 20(4), 797-811.

Jansen, J. J., Simsek, Z., & Cao, Q. (2012). Ambidexterity and Performance in Multiunit Contexts: Cross-Level Moderating Effects of Structural and Resource Attributes. *Strategic Management Journal*, 33(11), 1286-1303.

Junni, P., Sarala, R. M., Taras, V., & Tarba, S. Y. (2013). Organizational Ambidexterity and Performance: A Meta-Analysis. *Academy of Management Perspectives*, 27(4), 299-312.

Lavikka, R., Smeds, R., & Jaatinen, M. (2015). A Process for Building Inter-Organizational Contextual Ambidexterity. *Business Process Management Journal*, 21(5), 1140-1161.

Lincoln, Y. S. and Guba, E. G. (1985) *Naturalistic Inquiry*. SAGE.

March, J. G. (1991). Exploration and Exploitation in Organizational Learning. *Organization Science*, 2(1), 71-87.

McCracken, G. (1988) *The Long Interview*. 2455 Teller Road, Newbury Park California 91320 United States of America: SAGE Publications, Inc. doi: 10.4135/9781412986229.

McNamara, P., & Baden-Fuller, C. (1999). Lessons From the Celltech Case: Balancing Knowledge Exploration and Exploitation in Organizational Renewal. *British Journal of Management*, 10(4), 291–307.

Papachroni, A., Heracleous, L., & Paroutis, S. (2016). In Pursuit of Ambidexterity: Managerial Reactions to Innovation–Efficiency Tensions. *Human Relations*, 69(9), 1791-1822.

Turner, N., Swart, J., & Maylor, H. (2013). Mechanisms for Managing Ambidexterity: A Review and Research Agenda. *International Journal of Management Reviews*, 15(3), 317-332.

Tushman, M. L., & O'Reilly III, C. A. (1996). Ambidextrous Organizations: Managing Evolutionary and Revolutionary Change. *California Management Review*, 38(4), 8-29.

Analysis and Evaluation of Business Model Patterns for the Craft Sector

Anna Rauhut, Johannes Votteler and Simon Hiller
Ferdinand-Steinbeis-Institute of the Steinbeis-Foundation, Stuttgart, Germany
anna.rauhut@steinbeis.de
johannes.votteler@gmail.com
simon.hiller@steinbeis.de
DOI: 10.34190/EIE.20.188

Abstract: The German craft sector is an integral part of the German economy. The sector currently accounts for approximately 27 percent of all German businesses and employs around 5.5 million people. With an average capacity utilization rate of 84 percent and revenue indicators close to a previous all-time high, the current economic state of the craft sector is strong. Nonetheless, the sector faces multiple challenges. The businesses are confronted with a shortage of skilled labor, industrial companies capturing customers, the digital transformation, and a dynamic market environment. To sustain its strong economic standing, the craft sector must actively address these issues. One approach is business model innovation (BMI), which has various positive effects that could help to tackle the current challenges. Many business owners in the sector currently lack awareness of the relevance of BMI, and when they are aware have difficulties choosing suitable business models. The current methods for BMI, for example using business model patterns, are perceived to be too complex and thereby met with reluctance. The paper raises the research question of which business models are suited for craft businesses and addresses the need for a BMI method that matches the demands of the craft sector. In the first step, a literature review of existing business model patterns was conducted. Using a qualitative multi-dimensional benefit analysis, three experts evaluated a variety of business model patterns based on five dimensions: level of product adaption, complexity, customer focus, cost, and revenue potential. By compounding a benefit score for each pattern, the patterns were ranked. Out of 60 business model patterns evaluated, 14 patterns were identified to match the requirements of the craft sector.

Keywords: business model innovation, business model pattern, craft sector

1. Introduction

Nationwide, the German craft sector currently accounts for a substantial amount of businesses and ultimately jobs (Anon, 2019). Craft businesses face a series of challenges including a shortage of skilled labor, an increasing competition from enterprises outside the craft sector, and the digital transformation. Markets become increasingly dynamic and customers demand changes (Bauer *et al.*, 2017; Friedl & Glasl, 2018; Rohleder & Schulte, 2017; Stappel, Niegsch & Herborn, 2016; Welzbacher *et al.*, 2015). To secure its competitiveness in the long run, the craft sector needs to recognize and actively address these challenges through innovation. Especially, business model innovation (BMI) is becoming increasingly important, as the competition of product or service innovations is already fierce (Volery & Müller, 2010).

However, BMI is still rarely applied within small and medium-sized enterprises (SME) which also includes the craft sector (Schmeiss & Dopfer, 2017). A variety of obstacles including lack of relevant competencies and limited resources hinder craftsmen from taking action (Bauer *et al.*, 2017; Rauhut, 2020; Stappel, Niegsch & Herborn, 2016; Thomä & Zimmermann, 2016). Workshops conducted within the research project TREND which is founded by the Ministry of Economics, Work and Housing in Baden-Wuerttemberg shows that currently used methods of BMI are perceived to be too complex. The project reveals that BMI methods are required which establish a common understanding of BMI and help generate ideas for innovating business models (Rauhut, 2020). The goal of this research paper is to support craft enterprises by answering the question which business model patterns are suited to the requirements of the craft sector. The conducted research was part of a final thesis within the mentioned TREND project.

2. Related work and background

2.1 Business model

The term business model gained popularity during the 1970s, mainly in connection to business modeling. After 2000, the term was predominantly used in connection with the New Economy and is now widely established in business (Wirtz, 2018). Academic literature includes several different definitions of the term business model as no common definition has yet been agreed to. Analyzing the existing definitions, it is possible to differentiate between two types, those with dimensions and those without.

Definitions without dimensions are offered by Amit and Zott (2001), Teece (2010), and Osterwalder and Pigneur (2010). A common element of these three definitions is the term value. According to Amit and Zott, "a business model depicts the design of transaction content, structure, and governance to create value through the exploitation of business opportunities" (Amit & Zott, 2001). This definition describes how value is created. The definition by Teece states: "The essence of a business model is in defining the manner by which the enterprise delivers value to customers, entices customers to pay for value, and converts those payments to profit" (Teece, 2010). In contrast to Amit and Zott, Teece focuses on the delivery of value for the customer and is thereby more customer centric. The definition by Osterwalder and Pigneur reads, "a business model describes the rationale of how an organization creates, delivers and captures value"(Osterwalder & Pigneur, 2010). Osterwalder and Pigneur utilize the terms value and delivery as used in the other two definitions but add capture.

Definitions that include dimensions are offered by Gassmann et al. (2014), Johnson et al. (2008), and Lindgardt et al. (2009). Gassmann states that "in sum, a business model defines who your customers are, what you are selling, how you produce your offering, and why your business is profitable. Who-what-how-why describes a business model of which the first two (who and what) address its external dimensions and the second two (how and why) address its internal dimensions" (Gassmann, Frankenberger & Csik, 2014). Gassmann defines four dimensions of a business model. Johnson similarly describes four dimensions stating that a business model "consists of four interlocking elements that, taken together, create and deliver value. The most important to get right, by far, is the first. Customer value proposition [...], Profit formula [...], Key resources [...], Key processes [...]"(Johnson, Christensen & Kagermann, 2008). While Johnson mentions the customer value proposition, he does not include the customer group itself into his description of a business model. Lindgardt et al. (2009) defines business models using two overarching elements: value proposition and operating model which each include three sub-elements. For comparative purpose, only the six sub-elements (target segment, offering, value chain, organization, revenue model, cost model) are considered to gain a granular description.

Comparing these three definitions, similarities in the structure of the dimensions become obvious. The dimensions of these definitions are categorized by four over all dimensions: customer group, value proposition, value chain and profit mechanism.

Table 1: Comparison of dimensions used in business model definitions

Dimension/Author	Gassmann (2014)	Johnson (2008)	Lindgardt (2009)
Customer group	Who		Target Segment
Value proposition	What	Customer value proposition	Offering
Value chain	How	Key resources Key processes	Value Chain Organization
Profit mechanism	Value	Profit formula	Revenue Model Cost Model

Business model and strategy are two distinct terms that are often intermixed (Baden-Fuller & Morgan, 2010; Magretta, 2002; Morris, Schindehutte & Allen, 2005; Teece, 2010). To understand which role business models, play in the context of strategy, the terms should be considered separately. Porter defines, "[...] strategy is about being different. It means deliberately choosing a different set of activities to deliver a unique mix of value" (Porter, 1996). While every business automatically operates by a business model, strategy requires a deliberate decision (Casadesus-Masanell & Ricart, 2010). It takes into account an important influence that business models neglect, a firm's competitive environment (Magretta, 2002). To establish sustainable competitive advantages, businesses should thereby define both, a strategy and a business model that fit that strategy (Teece, 2010).

2.2 Business model innovation

BMI generally describes consciously changing an existing business model. Gassmann, takes into account the four dimensions mentioned earlier, and states "innovation of a business model requires modifying at least two of these four dimensions" (Gassmann, Frankenberger & Csik, 2014). This definition is also used to differentiate BMI from process or product innovation, as those would modify only one of the four dimensions.

Setting a focus on BMI has various positive effects on businesses. BMI can help companies build sustainable competitive advantages as business models are perceived to be harder to imitate compared to process or product innovation (Lindgardt *et al.*, 2009; Schallmo & Brecht, 2013; Teece, 2010; Volery & Müller, 2010). In addition, businesses can develop new markets and thereby generate growth (Gassmann, Frankenberger & Csik, 2014; Volery & Müller, 2010). A study by the Boston Consulting Group shows that businesses focusing on BMI outperform those focusing on process or product innovation (Lindgardt *et al.*, 2009). BMI also enables companies to establish partner networks and improves their cost and risk structures (Teece, 2010).

2.3 Business model patterns

One method of BMI is using business model patterns (Remane *et al.*, 2017). These patterns are a standardized way of describing business models that have proven successful in industry (Gassmann, Frankenberger & Csik, 2014; Lassnig *et al.*, 2018; Osterwalder & Pigneur, 2010). They can be used as a source of inspiration for businesses searching for suitable business models. However, simple imitation is not encouraged. It is important to analyze the individual situation of a business and to adapt the patterns accordingly which also may include combining multiple patterns (Gassmann, Frankenberger & Csik, 2014). Various authors offer sets of business model patterns (Fleisch, Weinberger & Wortmann, 2014; Gassmann, Frankenberger & Csik, 2014; Johnson, 2009; Lassnig *et al.*, 2018; Matyssek, 2017; Osterwalder & Pigneur, 2010; Rappa, 2010; Timmers, 1998). The number of patterns and their industry focus varies among sets. Gassmann offers a set of 60 business model patterns, which are subsequently extended by five additional patterns (Gassmann, Frankenberger & Csik, 2015, 2014). The featured patterns are outlined using the business model navigator framework based on Gassmann's four dimensions of a business model mentioned earlier.

2.4 Current situation and challenges of the German craft sector

The craft sector includes a wide range of professions that commonly share characteristics like self-employment, customizable services or products, and professionalized job training (Glasl, Maiwald & Wolf, 2008). In addition, craft businesses are distinct from industrial businesses in that they are predominantly based on manual labor. Craft businesses can be divided into seven trade groups: Main construction trade, building finishing trade, trade for commercial needs, automotive trade, food trade, health care trade, and trade for private needs (German Federal Statistical Office, 2019).

Since, medieval times, the craft sector has evolved into an important pillar of the German economy (Friedl & Glasl, 2018). Over 1 million businesses count towards the sector, approximately 27 percent of all German enterprises. With around 5.5 million people, the craft businesses employ around 12 percent of the German workforce. The gross value added by the craft businesses accounts to approximately 8 percent of the German economy. The average capacity utilization rate as well as the revenue indicators are close to the all-time high from 2018 (Anon, 2019).

Craft sector is facing multiple challenges. Demographic change in Germany results in a shortage of skilled craft labor (Bauer *et al.*, 2017; Friedl & Glasl, 2018; Stappel, Niegsch & Herborn, 2016). Competitors are using innovative business models to gain competitive advantages and enterprises from outside the craft sector are pushing to displace traditional craft businesses (Bauer *et al.*, 2017). The digital transformation changes products, services, processes and communication and requires substantial investments (Rohleder & Schulte, 2017; Welzbacher *et al.*, 2015). Dynamic markets require agile and rapid actions. Customer demands change and the increase in price transparency due to the Internet generates downward pressure (Bauer *et al.*, 2017).

To address the mentioned challenges, BMI is also an option for craft business. There are several potential benefits of BMI when applied in craft businesses. Efficiency-enhancing business models, for example through automation, may relieve employees and reduce the need for skilled workers (Gassmann, Frankenberger & Csik, 2014). Differentiation from the competition by BMI may help craft businesses creating attractive working conditions and thus attracting new skilled workers (Rauhut *et al.*, 2019). Furthermore, building a sustainable competitive advantage enables craft businesses to protect themselves from industrial competitors pushing into the sector (Lindgardt *et al.*, 2009; Schallmo & Brecht, 2013). Digital business models may be an incentive for dealing with the topic of digital transformation and experimenting in one's own company. In addition, strategic flexibility and the improvement of cost and risk structures through BMI can help craftsmen dealing with changes in the market (Schallmo & Brecht, 2013; Teece, 2010).

While the positive effects of BMI are promising, there are multiple obstacles craft businesses need to overcome. Insecurities regarding the profitability and the risk are holding SMEs back (Thomä & Zimmermann, 2016). New technologies and drastic changes are occasionally met with low acceptance or even anxiety (Rauhut *et al.*, 2019). Around 21 percent of businesses in the craft sector complain about a lack of digital expertise among their employees (Rohleder & Schulte, 2017). Furthermore, a shortage of resources hinders the craft businesses to pursue BMI. Due to the currently high capacity utilization, businesses are busy with project execution and thereby hardly find time to invest into strategic topics like BMI (Bauer *et al.*, 2017; Rimpler, 2019). Financial investments associated with BMI are additionally holding craft businesses back (Thomä & Zimmermann, 2016).

3. Methodology

To identify business model patterns that fit the requirements of the craft sector, a multi-dimensional benefit analysis based on Kühnapfel (2019) and Niklas (2014) was conducted. The analysis was executed in seven subsequent steps.

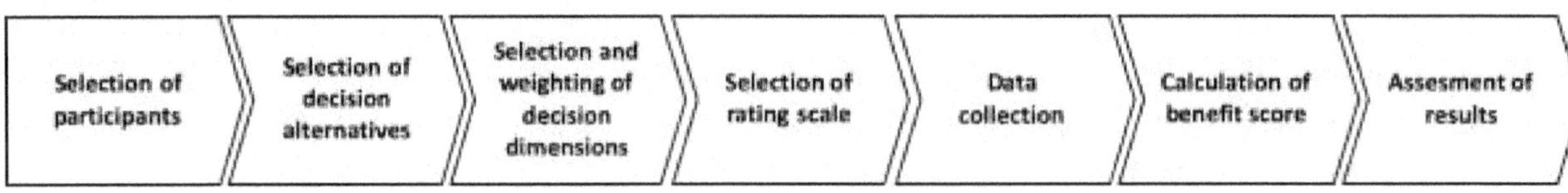

Figure 1: Steps of the multi-dimensional benefit analysis conducted (based on Kühnapfel (2019) and Niklas (2014))

To evaluate the dimension of the multi-dimensional benefit analysis, three experts were interviewed. The respondents were selected based on their practical experience in the field of BMI and in the craft sector.

The business model patterns provided by Gassmann et al. (2015) were selected as decision alternatives for this analysis. The set includes 60 proven patterns from different industries. It is based on the pattern set by Gassmann et al. (2014) which itself is the most exhaustive set available according to an analysis by Remane in 2017 (Remane *et al.*, 2017).

Each decision alternative was rated along five dimensions:

- *1. Level of product adaption*: Level of adaption needed for the existing product or service to fit with the business model
- *2. Customer focus*: Level of customer value generated by the business model
- *3. Complexity*: Level of complexity associated with the implementation and operation of the business model
- *4. Cost*: Cost incurred by the implementation and operation of the business model
- *5. Revenue potential*: Potential revenue generated by the business model

Customer value is often perceived differently by individuals. Therefore, the scope of this study was narrowed to members of Generation Y. This cohort includes people born between 1981 and 2000 and is also referred to as Digital Natives or Millennials. Cohort members can be characterized as mobile, flexible, communicative and demanding (Georg, 2019).

The selection of the five dimensions is based on the four overall dimensions of a business model identified during the literature review. The dimensions are shown in table 2.

Table 2: Mapping of the decision dimensions and the business model dimensions

Dimensions of a business model	Decision-dimensions
Value proposition	Level of product adaption
Customer group	Customer focus
Value chain	Complexity
Profit mechanism	Cost
	Revenue potential

Thereby, all aspects of a business model were included into the decision process. The decision dimensions were weighted equally except for cost and revenue potential which were condensed into a single dimension in order not to overweigh the profit mechanism dimension of a business model.

The rating of the dimensions is based on a bipolar interval scale ranging from 1 to 5 with high rankings being favorable (Raab, Unger & Unger, 2009). Table 3 shows the meaning of the scale rating.

Table 3: Meaning of the scale rating for each dimension

Dimension / scale	1	2	3	4	5
The level of product adaption needed is...	very high	high	intermediate	low	very low
Customer focus is...	very low	low	intermediate	high	very high
Complexity is...	very high	high	intermediate	low	very low
Cost is...	very high	high	intermediate	low	very low
Revenue potential is...	very low	low	intermediate	high	very high

The data collection consists of three expert interviews. During these, the experts rated each of the 60 selected business model patterns using the interval scale and a short qualitative explanation. The individual benefit score of each pattern was compounded after the interviews using multiplication. Multiplication was chosen over addition to increase the impact of negative outliers on the benefit score. For each expert, a provisional benefit score was compounded.

$$Benefit\ score = \frac{PA_1 * CF_1 * CX_1 * \left(\frac{CO_1 * RP_1}{2}\right) + PA_2 * CF_2 * CX_2 * \left(\frac{CO_2 * RP_2}{2}\right) + PA_3 * CF_3 * CX_3 * \left(\frac{CO_3 * RP_3}{2}\right)}{3}$$

PA_n = Level of product adaption score by respondent n
CF_n = Customer focus score by respondent n
CX_n = Complexity score by respondent n
CO_n = Cost score by respondent n
RP_n = Revenue potential score by respondent n

Formula 1: Calculation of the benefit score

The final benefit score of each pattern was calculated using the arithmetic mean of the three provisional scores, illustrated in formula 1.

4. Results

The business model patterns are ranked by their benefit score. The ranking is shown in table 4. Patterns with high benefit scores are more suitable for craft businesses according to the experts interviewed.

Table 4: Extract of the business model pattern ranking

Rank	Business model pattern	Benefit score	Rank	Business model pattern	Benefit score
1	Direct Selling	383	**11**	Aikido	173
2	Customer Loyalty	349	**12**	Experience Selling	173
3	Ultimate Luxury	323	**13**	E-Commerce	172
4	Shop in Shop	317	**14**	Franchising	165
5	Make More of It	307	**15**	Layer Player	148
6	Self-Service	263	**16**	Trash to Cash	144
7	User Design	234	**...**	...	...
8	Subscription	210	**58**	Barter	17
9	Add-on	195	**59**	Two-sided Market	14
10	Cross-selling	176	**60**	Hidden Revenue	10

Towards the top of the ranking, differences between benefit scores are higher compared to the bottom of the ranking. A shift can be observed between the 14th and 15th rank. They show a noticeable benefit score difference of 17 points. While the differences between ranks appear to be even higher than that towards the top of the ranking, there are no such high differences observable after the 15th rank. For this reason, the 14 patterns with the highest benefit score are determined as the most suitable for the craft sector.

It becomes apparent that business model patterns that require digital technology tend to have lower benefit scores and are found towards the bottom of the ranking. An analysis of the decision dimensions reveals that low benefit scores predominately result from the high complexity of new digital technologies as well as the high investment cost associated with those new technologies. An exception from that is the E-Commerce business model pattern, which can be implemented with relatively low complexity and cost and is therefore ranked 13th. In the following table the top-ranked 14 patterns are briefly described and a short fictional example from the craft sector is given.

Table 5: Description and example of 14 patterns

Business model pattern	Description	Craft sector example
Direct Selling	Selling the product or service directly to the customer	Painter not only selling his painting services but also the paint for customers that paint by themselves
Customer Loyalty	Building up a customer loyalty by special offerings or rewards	Bonus point program by doing you service of your house heating by the same craftsmen
Ultimate Luxury	Upgrade of the services or products to ultimate luxury	A specialization of a joiner on luxury doors of mansions
Shop in Shop	Having another selling space in your own shop	Offering painting brands a part of your shop to sell their paint directly
Make More of It	Using capabilities, a company has in a different context	A bakery that teaches baking classes for baking bread at home.
Self-Service	When the customer becomes part of the value chain by serving themselves	A bakery which does self-service checkout for their baked goods so reduce costs for shop men
User Design	Involvement of the customer by designing their own product	A joiner that lets the customer design their own table.
Subscription	Known from magazines or software the subscription pattern charges for a service or product regular	A yearly check up on the roof tile or a regular painting service for the living room.
Add-on	Additionally, service or product to your core service	Selling additional varnish as a carpenter when selling a table.
Cross-selling	Offering complementary services or products while having a focus on your core business	A joiner that sells kitchen might sell cookbooks or recipes to make in that kitchen.
Aikido	Turing the competitors advances against them	Offering a do-it-yourself product that the customer can paint their house by themselves
Experience Selling	Combining the selling of a product with an experience for the customer	A painter that you can paint your own house with and learn from his experience.
E-Commerce	Selling your services online to give the customer a price transparency	Offering services as a carpenter on an online platform
Franchising	Selling a company brand or a special service to other craftsmen within the same sector	Open a new hairdresser shop under the same label

5. Conclusion

The goal of this research was to identify business model patterns that are suited for craft businesses to support the German craft sector in BMI. In the first step, a literature review was conducted to understand the positive effects BMI can have on enterprises, the current challenges in the craft sector, how BMI can help to address these challenges, and what obstacles currently exist.

In the second step, a multi-dimensional benefit analysis was performed via a seven-step process. The goal was to evaluate the suitability of existing business model patterns to the craft sector. In the process, three expert interviews were conducted and a total of 60 business model patterns were analyzed. Based on the calculation of benefit scores, the business model patterns were ranked. 14 patterns were identified to match the requirements of the craft sector best.

The selection of 14 business model patterns are a resource of inspiration, starting point and guideline supporting craft businesses with BMI. The preselected patterns reduce the complexity of the method and save time in comparison to more extensive pattern sets which require the craft businesses to make a preselection themselves. In addition, the five decision dimensions are transparent, can be adjusted to individual requirements, and allow a comparison between patterns.

6. Limitation and outlook

This research paper faces some limitations. Therefore, this research does not claim to be complete and representative. All three experts interviewed for the benefit analysis maintain a professional connection with the Chamber of Crafts of the state of Baden-Württemberg and might thereby share similar views. The small number of respondents as well as the geographical concentration might additionally have negative effects on the accuracy of the results. The decision dimensions chosen are simplified and only represent some of the factors that should be analyzed when choosing a business model. The expert ratings of the five dimensions are based on individual experiences and rough estimations. The actual numbers strongly depend on the individual business and its competitive situation. A content-related limitation is the focus on the 60 business model patterns provided by Gassmann (2015).

Future research in this field should include a more heterogenous group of experts to increase the accuracy of the ratings. Additional decision dimensions, which might also include quantitative data, could be useful to obtain a more coherent assessment of the patterns. Finally, the decision alternatives could be extended by additional patterns.

References

Amit, R. & Zott, C. (2001) Value creation in E-business. *Strategic Management Journal*. [Online] 22 (6–7), 493–520. Available from: doi:10.1002/smj.187.

Baden-Fuller, C. & Morgan, M.S. (2010) Business Models as Models. *Long Range Planning*. [Online] 43 (2–3), 156–171. Available from: doi:10.1016/j.lrp.2010.02.005.

Bauer, J.M., Heinen, E., Müller, K., Haverkamp, K., et al. (2017) *Handwerk 2025: Strategiekonzept und Handlungsfelder für das Handwerk in Baden-Württemberg*. [Online]. Available from: https://www.handwerk-bw.de/fileadmin/media/thema-wirtschaft/struktur-bestandsanalyse-handwerk-2025.pdf [Accessed: 11 February 2020].

Casadesus-Masanell, R. & Ricart, J.E. (2010) From Strategy to Business Models and onto Tactics. *Long Range Planning*. [Online] 43 (2–3), 195–215. Available from: doi:10.1016/j.lrp.2010.01.004.

Fleisch, E., Weinberger, M. & Wortmann, F. (2014) Geschäftsmodelle im Internet der Dinge. *HMD Praxis der Wirtschaftsinformatik*. [Online] 51 (6), 812–826. Available from: doi:10.1365/s40702-014-0083-3.

Friedl, G. & Glasl, M. (2018) *Handwerk als Innovator und gesellschaftlicher Stabilisator*. 39–49.

Gassmann, O., Frankenberger, K. & Csik, M. (2015) *Business Model Pattern Cards*. [Online]. Available from: https://resources.bmilab.com/download-resources-page?submissionGuid=be100c9a-f258-4d2e-92e9-f8db3e9581b8 [Accessed: 17 January 2020].

Gassmann, O., Frankenberger, K. & Csik, M. (2014) *The business model navigator: 55 models that will revolutionise your business*. Harlow, England ; New York, Pearson Education Limited.

Georg, F. (2019) *Die Generation Y und ihre Work-Life-Balance*. Praxisorientierte Personal- und Organisationsforschung Band 23. 1. Auflage. Augsburg, Rainer Hampp Verlag.

German Federal Statistical Office (2019) *Handwerkszählung 2017*.

Glasl, M., Maiwald, B. & Wolf, M. (2008) *Handwerk - Bedeutung, Definition, Abgrenzung*.p.41.

Johnson, M.W. (2009) *Business Model Analogies*. [Online]. Available from: https://www.innosight.com/wp-content/uploads/2016/10/STWS_Business_Model_Analogies.pdf [Accessed: 1 February 2020].

Johnson, M.W., Christensen, C.M. & Kagermann, H. (2008) Reinventing Your Business Model. *harvard business review*. 12.

Kühnapfel, J.B. (2019) *Nutzwertanalysen in Marketing und Vertrieb*. essentials. 2. Auflage 2019. Wiesbaden, Springer Fachmedien Wiesbaden GmbH.

Lassnig, M., Stabauer, P., Breitfuß, G. & Mauthner, K. (2018) Geschäftsmodellinnovationen im Zeitalter von Digitalisierung und Industrie 4.0. *HMD Praxis der Wirtschaftsinformatik*. [Online] 55 (2), 284–296. Available from: doi:10.1365/s40702-018-0402-1.

Lindgardt, Z., Reeves, M., Stalk, G. & Deimler, M.S. (2009) *Business Model Innovation: When the Game gets tough, change the Game*.

Magretta, J. (2002) Why Business Models Matter. *Harvard Business Review*.pp.86–92.

Matyssek, T. (2017) Geschäftsmodelle im Internet der Dinge. In: Andreas Rusnjak, Johanna Anzengruber, Thomas Werani, & Michael Jünger (eds.). *Digitale Transformation von Geschäftsmodellen: Grundlagen, Instrumente und Best Practices*. Schwerpunkt: Business Model Innovation. Wiesbaden, Springer Gabler. pp. 159–178.

Morris, M., Schindehutte, M. & Allen, J. (2005) The entrepreneur's business model: toward a unified perspective. *Journal of Business Research*. [Online] 58 (6), 726–735. Available from: doi:10.1016/j.jbusres.2003.11.001.

Niklas, C. (2014) Mehr Entscheidungssicherheit mit der Nutzwertanalyse. *ProjektMagazin*. 11.

Osterwalder, A. & Pigneur, Y. (2010) *Business model generation: a handbook for visionaries, game changers, and challengers*. Hoboken, NJ, Wiley.

Porter, M.E. (1996) What Is Strategy? *Harvard Business Review*. (November-December 1996).

Raab, G., Unger, A. & Unger, F. (2009) *Methoden der Marketing-Forschung: Grundlagen und Praxisbeispiele*. [Online]. Wiesbaden, Gabler Verlag / GWV Fachverlage, Wiesbaden. Available from: https://doi.org/10.1007/978-3-8349-8230-8 [Accessed: 29 January 2020].

Rappa, M. (2010) *Business Models on the Web*. [Online]. 17 January 2010. Digital Enterprise. Available from: http://www.digitalenterprise.org/models/models.html [Accessed: 3 February 2020].

Rauhut, A. (2020) *Nutzwertanalyse zu Geschäftsmodellen im Handwerk - Experteninterview mit Anna Rauhut, Ferdiand-Steinbeis-Institut.*

Rauhut, A., Hiller, S., Nawroth, G. & Keicher, L. (2019) *TREND-Arbeitspapier*.

Remane, G., Hanelt, A., Tesch, J.F. & Kolbe, L.M. (2017) THE BUSINESS MODEL PATTERN DATABASE — A TOOL FOR SYSTEMATIC BUSINESS MODEL INNOVATION. *International Journal of Innovation Management*. [Online] 21 (01), 1750004. Available from: doi:10.1142/S1363919617500049.

Rimpler, R. (2019) *Konjunkturbericht 2/2019: Konjunkturelles Hoch im Handwerk hält an Aussichten lassen Abkühlung erwarten*.

Rohleder, B. & Schulte, K.-S. (2017) *Zwischen Tradition und Innovation Das Handwerk wird digital Bitkom e.V..pdf*. [Online]. Available from: https://www.bitkom.org/Presse/Presseinformation/Zwischen-Tradition-und-Innovation-brDas-Handwerk-wird-digital.html [Accessed: 28 January 2020].

Schallmo, D. & Brecht, L. (2013) *Geschäftsmodell-Innovation*. Springer Gabler.

Schmeiss, J. & Dopfer, M. (2017) Die digitale Geschäftsmodell-Transformation - Chancen, Risiken und Strategien für den deutschen Mittelstand. *Wissenschaft trifft Praxis*. (8).

Stappel, M., Niegsch, C. & Herborn, A. (2016) *Auf dem Weg zum 'Handwerk 4.0': Schlüsselfunktion für die gesamtwirtschaftlichen Investitionen*. [Online]. p.33. Available from: https://www.dzbank.de/content/dam/dzbank_de/de/library/presselibrary/pdf_dokumente/Handwerk_4_0.pdf [Accessed: 20 January 2020].

Teece, D.J. (2010) Business Models, Business Strategy and Innovation. *Long Range Planning*. [Online] 43 (2–3), 172–194. Available from: doi:10.1016/j.lrp.2009.07.003.

Thomä, J. & Zimmermann, V. (2016) *Innovationshemmnisse in KMU*. [Online]. p.45. Available from: http://dx.doi.org/10.3249/2364-3897-gbh-6 [Accessed: 20 December 2019].

Timmers, P. (1998) Business Models for Electronic Markets. *Electronic Markets*. [Online] 8 (2), 3–8. Available from: doi: 10.1080/10196789800000016.

Volery, T. & Müller, S. (2010) *Business Model Innovation*.

Welzbacher, D.C., Pirk, W., Ostheimer, A., Bartelt, K., et al. (2015) *Digitalisierung der Wertschöpfungs- und Marktprozesse – Herausforderungen und Chancen für das Handwerk –*. 49.

Wirtz, B.W. (2018) *Business Model Management: Design - Instrumente - Erfolgsfaktoren von Geschäftsmodellen*. 4., aktualisierte und überarbeitete Auflage. Wiesbaden, Springer Gabler.

Zentralverband Deutsches Handwerk (ed.) (2019) *Daten und Fakten zum Handwerk im Jahr 2018*. [Online]. Available from: https://www.zdh.de//fileadmin/user_upload/themen/wirtschaft/statistik/kennzahlen/Kennzahlen_2018/Grafiken-Flyer-18-ges.pdf [Accessed: 21 January 2020].

Policy Making Versus Policy Research: The Case of Entrepreneurship Policy in Hamburg

Moritz Philip Recke
Hamburg University of Applied Sciences, Hamburg, Germany
moritz.recke@haw-hamburg.de
DOI: 10.34190/EIE.20.042

Abstract: Public Policy agendas can be aimed at shifting the economic composition of a region. It is common among policy makers to promote entrepreneurship based on the notion that new ventures have impact on economic growth and job creation. This link is highly debated in academic literature and it seems questionable to which extend policy is informed by this debate. This case study explores (dis)connects between regional entrepreneurship policy in the City of Hamburg (Germany) and academic literature. Hamburg has articulated a "Regional Innovation Strategy 2020", which summarises the regional government's general approach towards entrepreneurship. First, this paper reviews and summarizes most salient points of the strategy through which it aims to achieve its goal of stimulating economic growth. Second, this paper reframes relevant features of the strategy from an academic perspective, calling on arguments by Ács & Mueller (2008), Ács et al. (2014), Autio et al. (2007), Autio & Rannikko (2016), Brown & Mawson (2015), Henrekson & Johansson (2009), Shane (2008, 2009) and others. The paper illustrates several disconnects between formulated strategy and literature on entrepreneurship policy and how relevant findings from scientific research have not been considered in the policy formation. Additionally, the paper reveals further deficiencies regarding strategy implementation and proposed metrics. The case study exemplifies challenges in regional policy formation and highlights the need for further research on regional policy discourse to better understand the policy formation process in Hamburg.

Keywords: entrepreneurship policy, innovation policy, policy discourse, policy making, startups

1. Introduction

The City of Hamburg outlined its innovation policy in the regional innovation strategy document "Regionale Innovationsstrategie 2020 der Freien und Hansestadt Hamburg", published in 2014 by Hamburg's Ministry of Economics, Transport and Innovation – BWVI Hamburg (BWVI Hamburg 2014). The overarching strategy aims to further the local economy, its innovative potential and international competitiveness by strengthening networks between industry, university and public sectors and builds on the *Europe 2020 strategy for smart, sustainable and inclusive growth* (European Commission 2010). It displays the common belief among many economic development experts and policy makers that entrepreneurship is linked to economic activity (Acs et al. 2007).

This belief could have been challenged during the policy creation process, but absence of academic literature referenced in the strategy perpetuates isolation between science and practice of entrepreneurship policy. The link between entrepreneurship and regional economic development remains highly disputed within the scientific community. Considering lack of agreement in academia, there might be good reasons for policy makers to deliberately avoid drawing upon this debate. This would imply however, that policy makers are even aware of it. This study will show that omission of academic findings (and debate) on entrepreneurship policy seems rather circumstantial than deliberate.

The study is building on the author' previous research on public policy towards entrepreneurship in Sydney, Australia (Recke & Bliemel 2017, 2018) and his analysis of the entrepreneurial ecosystem in Hamburg and the mediat/IT cluster initiative nextMedia.Hamburg (Recke 2016). The author will briefly introduce Hamburg's regional entrepreneurial ecosystem and present relevant aspects of the regional innovation strategy. Then the strategy is analysed and discussed using Autio & Rannikko's (2016) framework for categorising policy in buffering, bridging and capacity-boosting approaches, Moutinho et al.'s (2015) considerations in regard to Regional Innovation Systems (RIS) and the Triple Helix Approach presented by Ranga & Entzkowitz (2013). Lastly proposed metrics for tracking the policy measures are evaluated.

2. Hamburg's regional entrepreneurial ecosystem

According to KfW Startup Monitor 2015 (Metzger 2015), the City of Hamburg is the second largest location for entrepreneurship in Germany after Berlin. Hamburg had a startup rate of 2.36% for the years 2012-2014 (as opposed to 2,6% in Berlin) and is further closing the gap in recent years. It has been the second largest startup location from 2008-2010 and from 2012 onwards. Many Hamburg based startups have become well established, international corporations such as Innogames, Bigpoint, Goodgame Studios, Jimdo, mytaxi, Statista or XING. Recently funded startups of note include Kreditech and Sonormed. Also, many international internet corporations chose Hamburg for their German headquarters over the years, such as Google, Facebook, Twitter and Yelp (nextMedia.Hamburg 2016).

In accordance with strong growth of the local startup economy in recent years, Hamburg wants to position itself as a leading region for innovation in Europe. Evidently, Hamburg has been a vibrant location for innovative startup activities over past decades. Not only was Hamburg at the epicentre of the dot-com era in Germany, it provides an attractive entrepreneurial ecosystem to aspiring founders. The entrepreneurial ecosystem is advertised as having a very positive dynamic and being integrated in a dense network of support, e.g. in form of accelerator programs, co-working spaces and consulting services by local universities as well as private and public entities (BWVI Hamburg, 2018).

3. Hamburg's regional innovation strategy

Hamburg's regional innovation strategy "Regionale Innovationsstrategie 2020 der Freien und Hansestadt Hamburg" was developed in preparation for securing funding during the European Regional Development Fund (ERDF) subsidy period 2014-2020 (BWVI Hamburg 2014). The document is based on strategic guidelines articulated by the InnovationsAllianz Hamburg, an initiative that started in 2008 and was composed of more than 1000 regional stakeholders from policy, industry and university with the aim to articulate a holistic strategy to secure the region's economic competitiveness and develop Hamburg into one of Europe's leading innovative regions (BWVI Hamburg 2010). Cornerstones of the strategy implementation are divided into areas of innovation climate, education, transfer, subsidies and infrastructure and will be briefly introduced.

Innovation Climate: Measures are meant to nurture an innovative culture, create transparency about relevant contacts and networks as well as consulting services. Marketing activities are supposed to enhance external visibility of Hamburg as an innovative location. Curiosity and spirit of innovation and entrepreneurship are to be strengthened and potential innovators need to be able to access necessary resources quickly and efficiently (BWVI Hamburg 2014). Following operational measures are mentioned without providing any detailed information in regard to objectives, timing or implementation strategy:

- Innovation Portal
- Marketing Hamburg as Innovation Location
- Central Research Information System

Education: Measures are meant to satisfy current and future demand for a skilled workforce in both quantity and quality. In addition, knowledge management and cooperation in education and training are to be nurtured and research activities at local universities are to be intensified. Dual study programs in conjunction with industry training are deemed effective and are to be extended. Future demand for skilled experts needs to be explored and articulated to effectively develop study programs at local universities with special focus on interdisciplinary qualification (BWVI Hamburg 2014). Following operational measures are mentioned without providing any detailed information in regard to objectives, timing or implementation strategy:

- Advanced learning laboratories
- Transparency about setup of advanced learning opportunities
- Enhancement of permeability in education areas
- Intensification of marketing efforts

Transfer: Measures are meant to strengthen cooperation for research & development efforts and to create good surrounding conditions for networks, groups and future initiatives to facilitate transparent and efficient knowledge transfer between industry and research institutes as well as academic studies and training. Complementary knowledge and skills need to be made available in both directions (to and from university and industry) and in a structured manner, improving the chance to utilise knowledge spill over. Small and medium-sized enterprises (SMEs) in particular need to be integrated in cooperation networks. Additionally, conditions for spin-offs created through research at local universities are to be improved (BWVI Hamburg 2014). Following operational measures are mentioned without providing any detailed information in regard to objectives, timing or implementation strategy:

- Innovation Contact Point (Innovations Kontakt Stelle IKS)
- Research meets industry
- Specific network initiatives

Subsidies: Measures are meant to create an efficient subsidy system and means of controlling subsidised innovation projects organised by corporations and research institutes as well as entrepreneurs. The existing subsidy program is to be extended to match evolving demand in both industry and research. Transparency about subsidy programs needs to be improved, double subsidies need to be avoided. Short term options and means of financing for startups as well as small and medium-sized enterprise (SMEs) need to be improved. Used financial means should result in an appropriate contribution to Hamburg's innovative capacities and accelerate the go to market process for innovations. Subsidies are to be targeted at entrepreneurs, corporations, universities and research facilities as well as cooperation between them (see figure. 1). In addition, the subsidy system should provide instruments for consulting, networking, coaching, culture and infrastructure (BWVI Hamburg 2014). Following operational measures are mentioned without providing any detailed information in regard to objectives, timing or implementation strategy:

- Investment funds
- Entrepreneurship aid program InnoRampUp
- Establishment of innovation agency within IFB
- Standard subsidy directives for innovation in Hamburg
- Hamburg consulting standards

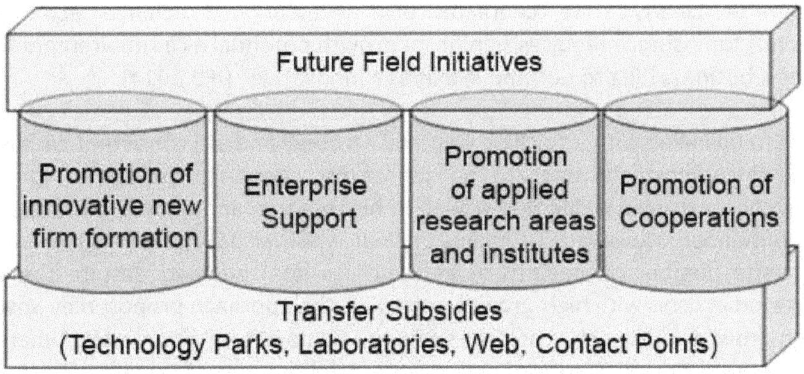

Figure 1: Hamburg subsidy system (BWVI Hamburg 2014)

Infrastructure: Measures are meant to sustain and extend appropriate facilities for practice-oriented research & development and to establish or develop topic specific technology parks for entrepreneurs, young technology-driven companies and research institutions as well as established businesses. Hamburg based corporations and research institutes are to be better connected on a daily basis in order to reduce costs for cooperation (BWVI Hamburg 2014). Following operational measures are mentioned without providing any detailed information in regard to objectives, timing or implementation strategy:

- Research & Innovation parks
- Establishment of Fraunhofer Institute
- Extension of practise-oriented research & development

The specific operational measures outlined in the strategy compose a rather complex policy mix for the various strategic objectives with concrete implementation projects being at different stages of completion. The strategy also lists four established and four young industry clusters that are meant to be developed for the future, namely EEHH [renewable energy], GWHH [healthcare], HKG [creative industry], HAv [Aviation], LIHH [logistics], LSN [life science], MCN [maritime] and nextMedia.Hamburg [media/IT]. The media/IT cluster is considered as one of the established clusters and is attributed with strong connection to entrepreneurial activity and high-growth ventures (BWVI Hamburg 2014).

4. Policy analysis

Quite obviously, the purpose of any public policy agenda towards entrepreneurship is to foster new business formation and prosperous development of new enterprises. In Hamburg, the innovative potential attributed to startups with high-growth dynamics is the main motivator for shaping public policy to nurture these ventures specifically. It is common believe that startups not only have the capacity to transform and reshape industries, but also entail potential to generate economic growth and subsequently create jobs. Taking into consideration various research findings from recent years, it seems that this link is highly disputed among scientists. This calls for a more detailed analysis of outlined strategies for the entrepreneurial ecosystem in Hamburg in respect to arguments presented by the scientific community.

4.1 Policy orientation: Picking winners or supporting various forms of entrepreneurship?

Academic findings have shown that high-growth entrepreneurship affects innovative change and economic growth, while regular forms of entrepreneurship do not (Ács & Mueller 2008, Autio 2005, Henrekson & Johansson 2008, Stam et al. 2009). Subsequently, in order to achieve the goal of generating economic growth, public policy has to address entrepreneurial firm growth specifically. Hamburg stresses the necessity for innovation in its strategy documents (BWVI Hamburg 2014). Technology-driven startups are attributed with having innovative potential to disrupt and reshape entire industries, therefore being an integral part of the city's strategy to manage the ongoing digital transformation within the media/IT cluster in Hamburg (among others). The nextMedia.Hamburg initiative provides information and support and facilitates networking for aspiring entrepreneurs, while entities like Hamburg's Chamber of Commerce assist and consult interested parties on firm formation and financing options. Hamburg's investment and subsidy bank - Hamburgische Investitions- und Förderbank (IFB) - provides specific loan and subsidy programs for innovative new businesses and other publicly supported and privately managed entities provide coaching and financial aid as well. Requirements to access some regional programs clearly state characteristics necessary to achieve economic growth. The Innovationsstarter Fonds for instance requires significant growth potential as a requirement for investment and InnoRampUp requires a business idea to be "above average innovative" (IFB 2014).

These measures seem to be in line with a "picking winners" strategy and are consistent with issues discussed by Shane (2008, 2009). Since most startups are no source for economic growth or job creation, general encouragement of entrepreneurship is deemed flawed in his research and a focus on supporting high- growth ventures only is recommended. However, it remains unclear whether policy makers in Hamburg are aware of this, since increasing the number of startups in general is a goal pursued despite the subsidy programs mentioned being targeted at firms with high-growth potential. The approach proposed by Shane also misses the issue that even a high-growth venture still requires someone to start it - at some point where a venture would not qualify as a high-growth firm and therefore not be supported.

Morris et al. (2015) point out risks for long term economic development if formation of non high-growth ventures is not encouraged as well. They call for a portfolio approach to entrepreneurship policy, differentiating different kinds of ventures, their roles within the economy and different requirements in terms of support, to ensure a healthy economic development. It is concluded that adaptive polices are required to manage dynamics within entrepreneurial ecosystems to ensure economic growth. There are many measures in Hamburg that do not require a specific high-growth approach, such as the BG-Bürgschaft loan guarantee on a regional level, Gründungszuschuss on a federal level or loan programs offered by the KfW that are targeted at startups and young businesses, but do not necessarily require the company to have high-growth potential (Hamburg Chamber of Commerce 2016), calling into question entailed definition of a startup. Also, many types of consulting and support services offered are not limited to innovative ventures but are open to anyone interested. Unfortunately, it does not seem like this is a purposely pursued course by policy makers on a regional or federal level but rather a structure of programs having evolved over many years, still addressing needs articulated at the time of their inception with questionable application for entrepreneurs today. Although being aimed at various target audiences, programs do not seem to cater to fundamentally different types of businesses nor do they seem to be adaptive to changing conditions and requirements. Also, the approach by Morris et al. (2015) calls for consideration of high-growth venture specific requirements in categories such as liberal bankruptcy laws, intellectual property protection, tax write-offs, R&D partnerships, programs to build high-growth management capacity and many others. Potential agendas pursued in Hamburg in this regard remain hidden from reviewed documents. Only current conditions of laws, tax regulation and partnership opportunities are outlined without discussing any need for change in that respect. This calls into question the long-term perspective for surrounding conditions for high-growth entrepreneurs in the regional entrepreneurial ecosystem.

Another issue is Hamburg's strong policy focus on the media/IT . Especially through the nextMedia.Hamburg initiative, the technology-driven media industry is strongly accentuated. Auto et al. (2007) stipulate that rapid growth is expected to occur in technology-push situations and that technology is deemed key for economic success by many policy makers. However, after analysing small and medium-sized enterprise (SME) support initiatives in nine countries, they conclude that investment in technology production and commercialisation does not guarantee success. Additionally, Brown & Mawson (2015) confirm that high-growth ventures are in fact not disproportionally high-tech firms, deeming public policy to support these ventures specifically as ineffective. They recommend a focus on a versatile pool of startups from which high-growth potential startups can emerge. The policy focus on technology-driven startups within the media/IT cluster in Hamburg may therefore not only be ill advised but also contradictory to the objective of generating economic growth and creating jobs, since it might inadvertently exclude companies with vast potential outside of the policy scope.

4.2 Analysis of operational measures to categorise policy efforts

In order to better understand different programs and service offered, entrepreneurship policy can be categorised and classified. Autio & Rannikko (2016) distinguish between buffering, bringing and capacity-boosting approaches. Buffering activities are meant to provide means to protect firms form resource shortness and dependencies as wells as non-monetary benefits such as training, consulting, low cost office space, tax benefits and other privileges. They are aimed at all kinds of entrepreneurship and can be accessed by anyone. Bridging activities are targeted selectively at high-growth ventures using a competitive process. They connect firms with business angels, venture capitalists and other stakeholders through means like networking. Lastly, capacity-boosting activities are meant to nurture innovative capabilities of entrepreneurs. They are available for anyone who applies and do not have a focus on financial components.

The operational measures outlined in Hamburg's regional innovation strategy can be classified in terms of Audio & Rannikko (2016). Most activities and programs focus on capacity-boosting for potential entrepreneurs. High-Growth venture specific activities can be found in certain network activities, such as "Research meets industry" or subsidy programs, such as "Entrepreneurship aid program InnoRampUp", and therefore qualify as bridging policy. Still the majority of subsidy measures outlined rather qualify as buffering policies (see table 1).

Table 1: Classifying measures outlined in Hamburg's regional innovation strategy 2020 in terms of Autio & Rannikko (2016)

Strategic Cornerstone	Operational Measures	Buffering Policy	Bridging Policy	Capacity-Boosting Policy
Innovation Climate	- Innovation Portal - Marketing Hamburg as Innovation Location - Central Research-Information-System			X
Education	- Advanced learning laboratories - Transparency about setup of advanced learning opportunities - Enhance permeability in education areas - Intensification of marketing efforts			X
Transfer	- Innovation Contact Point (IKS) - Research meets Industry - Specific network initiatives		X	
Subsidies	- Investment funds - Entrepreneurship aid program InnoRampUp - Establishment of innovation agency within IFB	X	(X)	

Strategic Cornerstone	Operational Measures	Buffering Policy	Bridging Policy	Capacity-Boosting Policy
	- Standard subsidy directives for innovation in Hamburg - Hamburg consulting standards			
Infrastructure	- Research & Innovation Parks - Establishment of a Fraunhofer Institute - Extension of practice-oriented R&D			X

Although policy approach towards entrepreneurship in Hamburg seems to be largely managed through the nextMedia.Hamburg initiative, evidently various other agencies and policy departments in Hamburg are involved. This might be due to the fact, that the senate office (Senatskanzlei Hamburg) has created a media department (Amt für Medien), integrating the responsibility for the media/IT industry cluster at highest level of regional administration (Senatskanzlei Hamburg 2011). This commendable approach, although undoubtably very complicated, seems to be in line with findings by Audio et al. (2007) at first glance, emphasising the need for new focus and sophistication to be introduced in policy making to nurture entrepreneurial potential and cross traditional limitations of policy silos. Concrete implementations of strategic measures in Hamburg unfortunately lack transparency to comprehensively assess the efficiency of the policy in this regard.

Throughout the regional innovation strategy there is strong emphasis on education as well as research and development (R&D) efforts with the specific objective to nurture commercialisation of research. Although background data and underlying motivations behind this aspiration cannot be found in official documents, this is in line with findings by Moutinho et al. (2015) who analyse the role of Regional Innovation Systems (RIS) for evidence of economic and employment growth through research & development. Factors such as knowledge spillovers, technological transference and new business formation might very well contribute to these objectives and could be attributed to some degree to the actors in the entrepreneurial ecosystem in Hamburg and measures by public entities. Still Moutinho et al. (2015) conclude that Regional Innovation Systems (RIS) might have severe side-effects if not managed in an integrated way, increased unemployment and slowed economic growth among others. University R&D investments are found to have potential to reduce unemployment, especially youth-unemployment, while government R&D investments have only small effect on economic growth and no significant impact on employment whatsoever.

Subsequently this calls for more investments in university research & development programs and potentially a shift away from traditional subsidies and incentives to use public funds more effectively. Since many subsidy programs are not managed regionally but on a federal level, they require new legislation. Although it is evident that some federal programs have limited effect on entrepreneurial growth, Hamburg's position towards these issues remains unclear. On a regional level however, the strategy seems to accentuate university research & development investment.

Acknowledging the fact that research & development (R&D) is not the only ingredient to innovation, the triple helix approach, developed by Etzkowitz, integrates the components university, industry and government with their interdependent relationships and functions and considers activities and factors such as technology adoption, organisational capacities, the role of individual entrepreneurs as well as means for networking, collaboration, conflict management and collaborative leadership (Ranga & Etzkowitz 2016). Subsequently "multi-sphere" (hybrid) institutes at the intersection of university, industry and government such as technology transfer offices, industry and university research labs, science parks and technology incubators etc. fulfil the necessary function to facilitate innovation towards economic growth. The importance of collaboration between industry and university is also addressed Hamburg's regional innovation strategy (BWVI Hamburg 2014), mentioning specific measures such as creating research & innovation parks, extending practise oriented R&D and increasing networks between research an industry stakeholders.

To sum up, Hamburg's policy towards entrepreneurship is in line with some very general research findings, although this seems to be rather coincidental than purposely planned. Many measures lack proper focus and orientation to be deemed considerate of issues raised by researchers Shane (2008, 2009), Morris et al. (2015), Audio et al. (2007), Autio & Rannikko (2016) and Brown & Mawson (2015). Although these researchers take opposing positions in many respects, a focus on one position or the other cannot be found in strategy documents and measures analysed. Still the City of Hamburg seems to actively pursue valid strategies in regard to Regional Innovation Systems (RIS) and is apparently aware of issues raised by Moutinho et al. (2015). In terms of a triple helix approach, Hamburg shows many promising measures and activities for a "balanced" triple model helix model as outlined by (Ranga & Etzkowitz 2016) with still ample room for future improvement.

4.3 Evaluating proposed metrics to track impact

In order to effectively manage the policy agenda and measure development within the entrepreneurial ecosystem, it is necessary to monitor general performance as well as individual measures and their implementation. To draw conclusions on activities' effectiveness it is necessary to not just report performance data but link data to concrete activities and impact within the entrepreneurial ecosystem. Among others, Autio et al. (2007) find that most common metrics used are new firm formations as well as firm deaths over a period of time. While recognising that most governments are unable to track firm growth effectively, they point out that absence of publicly reported performance data on high-growth entrepreneurship might lead to policy measures remaining ineffectively aligned to quantifiable outputs with no effect on entrepreneurial firm growth. This is substantiated by Ács et al. (2014) who also stipulate that lack of contextualization of any measurement might lead to erroneous policies.

The City of Hamburg also proposes metrics to track the measures outlined in the regional innovation strategy. These metrics mainly focus on financial performance data and are categorised as follows (BWVI Hamburg 2014):

- Research & Development expenditures, differentiated by university, industry and government sector in relation to the gross domestic product (GDP)
- Research & Development personal in total and differentiated by university, industry and government sector in relation to the working population
- Employment in research intensive industries and knowledge intensive services in relation to working population
- Third-party funds raised by Hamburg university professors, differential by fund providers (industry, foundations, etc.)
- Firm formation in research intensive industry and knowledge intensive services

Additionally, Hamburg aims to monitor success on an operational level through the Hamburgische Investitions- und Förderbank (IFB), tracking financial input and output variables, such as project costs or subsides paid and number of jobs or revenues created, as well as specific outcomes benefitting target audiences. Unfortunately, no details on how and in what intervals data will be obtained are available. Still Hamburg aims to monitor measures and activities on project basis, linking activities to specific outcomes in the entrepreneurial ecosystem in addition to tracking the de-facto standard metric of new firm formations.

To track development of high-growth startups, it would make more sense to track firms in their current stage of development by obtaining data on current phases within startups' lifecycles. Since the general goal is to stimulate economic growth and create jobs, it might be prudent to track if the percentage of startups reaching the growth stage increases over time or if the average time it takes firms to get there accelerates. This data might be hard or even impossible to gather through official data sources. Especially with potentially annual or even bigger intervals for many data points, it might also be very difficult to track the fast moving startup economy. Community reported data might be biased it could prove unsuitable. Still it would provide a deeper insight into the vibrancy and dynamics of the entrepreneurial ecosystem and might therefore be a compromise worth exploring

5. Conclusion

This case study explored the public policy agenda towards entrepreneurship in Hamburg, Germany. The study presents several insights into entrepreneurship policy in Hamburg and suggest multiple areas for improvement. Analysis of the regional innovation strategy reveals several disconnects between academic research on entrepreneurship policy and the practice in Hamburg. This is most evident in reviewing sources of information used in the strategy documents, use of jargon when using terms such as innovation or startup as well as in the vagueness of actions and metrics introduced. Despite strong focus on higher education and improvement of cooperation between government, industry and university prominently advertised, no academic input to policy agendas could be identified. Additionally, the proposed metrics might prove ineffective to monitor and more importantly manage public efforts to foster a prosperous development of the entrepreneurial ecosystem. With opportunities, business models and startups themselves changing rapidly, flexible policy instruments need to be able to track changes and adjust accordingly.

A disconnect between public policy makers and academic researchers might very well be a two-way street. The fact that increasing relevance of local universities is acknowledged but resources are not used when forming public policy, might call for a more structured exchange of knowledge between government and university. Local researchers can be more proactive to ensure current research is known within policy domains. Since policy making does not rely on scientific process, it calls for a collaborative approach to make scientific findings available and understandable and to protect policy makers from romantic views of innovation and entrepreneurship advertised by non-targeted research and media coverage. Further research might explore the policy formation process in greater detail, to better understand what drives the public policy discourse.

References

Ács, Z.J. & Mueller, P. (2008) „Employment effects of business dynamics: Mice, Gazelles and Elephants", *Small Business Economics*, 30(1), pp.85–100.

Ács, Z.J., Szerb, L. & Autio, E. (2014) "National Systems of Entrepreneurship: Measurement issues and policy implications", *Research Policy*, 43(3), pp.476–494.

Autio, E. (2005) "Global Entrepreneurship Monitor - 2005 Report on High- Expectation Entrepreneurship", *Global Entrepreneurship Monitor*. [online], https://www.gemconsortium.org/report/gem-2005-global-report.

Autio, E., Kronlund, M. & Kovalainen, A. (2007) "High-Growth SME Support Initiatives in Nine Countries: Analysis, Categorization, and Recommendations", *Finnish Ministry of Trade and Industry*, 2007(1), pp.1–92.

Autio, E. & Rannikko, H. (2016) "Retaining winners: Can policy boost high-growth entrepreneurship?", *Research Policy*, 45(1), pp.42–55.

BWVI Behörde für Wirtschaft, Verkehr und Innovation Hamburg (2010) "InnovationsAllianz Hamburg - Strategische Leitlinien", *hamburg.de*, [online], https://www.hamburg.de/contentblob/2325538/5e8c6994fae2f250644ecfa4fb6d393a/data/strategischen-leitlinien-der-innovationsallianz-hamburg.pdf.

BWVI Behörde für Wirtschaft, Verkehr und Innovation Hamburg (2014) "Regionale Innovationsstrategie 2020 der Freien und Hansestadt Hamburg", *hamburg.de*, [online], http://www.hamburg.de/contentblob/4612440/f4fbf213d2c3e9136e83337595f52821/data/regionale-innovationsstrategie-hamburg.pdf.

BWVI Behörde für Wirtschaft, Verkehr und Innovation Hamburg (2018) "Jahresbericht Der Hamburger Cluster 2017" *hamburg.de*, [online], https://www.hamburg.de/contentblob/11389662/de7a436e9a198e46d603d9e90c0ee53c/data/jahresbericht-der-hamburger-cluster-2017.pdf.

Brown, R. & Mawson, S. (2015) "Targeted support for high growth firms: Theoretical constraints, unintended consequences and future policy challenges", *Environment and Planning C: Government and Policy*, pp.1–21.

European Commission (2010) "Mitteilung der Kommision - Europa 2020", *europa.eu*, [online], https://ec.europa.eu/eu2020/pdf/COMPLET%20%20DE%20SG-2010-80021-06-00-DE-TRA-00.pdf.

Hamburg Chamber of Commerce (2016) "TOP funding programmes", *hk.de*, [online], https://www.hk24.de/en/produktmarken/startup/point-single- contact/top-funding-programmes/1168664.

Henrekson, M. & Johansson, D. (2009) "Gazelles as job creators: a survey and interpretation of the evidence", *Small Business Economics*, 35(2), pp.227–244.

IFB Hamburgische Investitions- und Förderbank (2014) "InnoRampUp", *innovationsstarter.com*, [online], https://www.ifbhh.de/fileadmin/pdf/IFB_Download/IFB_Foerderrichtlinien/FoeRi_InnoRampUp.pdf.

Metzger, G. (2015) "KfW Start-up Monitor 2015" *KfW Start-up Monitor*, 2015, pp.1– 11. [online] https://www.kfw.de/PDF/Download-Center/Konzernthemen/ Research/PDF-Dokumente-Gr%C3%BCndungsmonitor/Gr%C3%BCndungsmonitor-englische-Dateien/ Gr%C3%BCndungsmonitor-2015_EN.pdf.

Morris, M.H., Neumeyer, X. & Kuratko, D.F. (2015) "A portfolio perspective on entrepreneurship and economic development", *Small Business Economics*, 45(4), pp.1–16.

Moutinho, R. et al. (2015) "The Role of Regional Innovation Systems (RIS) in Translating R&D Investments into Economic and Employment Growth", *Journal of technology management & innovation*, 10(2), pp.9–23.

nextMedia.Hamburg (2016) "Startup Standort Hamburg", *nextmedia-hamburg.de*, [online], http://www.nextmedia-hamburg.de/fileadmin/user_upload/ Bilder_Seiten-Header/PDFs/Start-up-Standort-Hamburg.pdf.

Ranga, M. & Etzkowitz, H. (2013) "Triple Helix Systems: An Analytical Framework for Innovation Policy and Practice in the Knowledge Society", *Industry and Higher Education, 27(4), pp.237-262.*

Recke, M. P. (2016) "Hamburg's Entrepreneurial Ecosystem And The Next Media Initiative - Public Policy Towards Entrepreneurship", *haw-hamburg.de*, [online], http://users.informatik.haw/hamburg.de/~ubicomp/arbeiten/master/recke.pdf.

Recke, M. P. & Bliemel, M. J. (2017) "The City of Sydney's Tech Startups Action Plan: A Policy Review", Paper presented at ACERE - Australian Centre for Entrepreneurship Research Exchange Conference, Melbourne, VIC,
07 - 10 February 2017.

Recke, M. P. & Bliemel, M. J. (2018) "Policy Making Versus Policy Research: The Case of the City of Sydney's Tech Startups Action Plan", in *Economic Gardening - Entrepreneurship, Innovation and Small Business Ecosystems in Regional, Rural and International Development*, chapter 3. SEAANZ Annual Research Book Series, Tilde Publishing, pp. 58 - 79.

Senatskanzlei Hamburg (2011) "Medienexperte Carsten Brosda übernimmt Amt für Medien in Senatskanzlei", *hamburg.de*, [online], http://www.hamburg.de/ pressearchiv-fhh/2870970/pr-22-medien/.

Shane, S. (2008) *The Illusions of Entrepreneurship*, Yale University Press, New Haven & London.

Shane, S. (2009) "Why encouraging more people to become entrepreneurs is bad public policy", *Small Business Economics*, 33(2), pp.141–149.

Stam, E. et al., (2009) "High-Growth Entrepreneurs, Public Policies, and Economic Growth", In *Public Policies for Fostering Entrepreneurship: a European perspective*, Springer US, New York, pp. 91–110.

Application of Narrative Theory in Project Based Software Development Education

Moritz Philip Recke and Stefano Perna
University of Naples Federico II, Italy
moritzphilip.recke@unina.it
stefano.perna@unina.it
DOI: 10.34190/EIE.20.040

Abstract: University of Naples Federico II (Italy) utilises the Challenge Based Learning (CBL) methodology in its nine months formative education program focussing on software development for the Apple technology ecosystem offered for ~400 students per year. The collaborative and self-guided, inquiry-based learning method focuses on intrinsic motivation of learners that work on real world problems organised in projects (Challenges in CBL) with an experiential and progressive approach. The program is a guided immersion into reality that is entrepreneurial in nature, rather than just a simulation of hypothetical projects. In academic years prior 2019/2020, the overall program was designed as a sequence of independent Challenges, which was identified as an area for improvement. The need for an overarching connection between Challenges to better foster individual engagement in individual learning units prompted the introduction of narrative theory to design the learning experience for the future. Academic research illustrated benefits of storytelling for creating engaging learning experiences in higher education. Building on scientific findings, the authors present their educational experience design as a cohesive journey within a communal learning environment with a coherent and interconnected structure of learning Challenges to empower learners to take ownership of basic entrepreneurial skills as a set of tools to complete the program. As a result, the experience is designed with a narrative layer, representing the learners' journey with a classical monomyth dramaturgic sequence – the hero's journey – to drive student engagement, better interconnect between the sequence of Challenges and interweave individual and communal learning paths. Outcomes indicate further areas to be investigated to better support leaner autonomy and agency and to qualify the experience with narrative presence. Lastly, the authors present action points to develop this approach further into an emergent narrative system to manage and adapt the educational journey as it develops, rather than scripting it.

Keywords: narrative theory, challenge based learning, software development, experience design, entrepreneurship education

1. Introduction

The nine months formative training program offered at University of Naples Federico II (Italy) aimed at software development for the Apple technology ecosystem utilises the Challenged-Based-Learning (*CBL*) methodology as a framework for learning (Nichols & Cator 2008, Johnson et al. 2009, Johnson & Brown 2011). The program is collaborative in nature and relies on self-guided, inquiry-based learning while working on real-world - rather than hypothetical - problems in projects of different length and scope, called *Challenges* in *CBL*.

The programs' experiential orientation builds on critical thinking and caters to the notion that entrepreneurship requires a broad skillset (Chang & Rieple 2013, Dahlstrom & Talmage 2018) and is promoted experientially (Gibb 2002, Loué & Baronet 2012, Stuetzer et al. 2013, Kakouris 2015). The formative program aims to alter knowledge, skills and attitude but also learners' emotions and values during the course through learning by practice (Politis 2005). As illustrated by Chang & Rieple (2013), working on real world projects improves development of entrepreneurial skills. Entrepreneurial skills, categorised in (1) technical, (2) management, (3) entrepreneurship and (4) personal maturity according to Lichtenstein & Lyons (1996), can be broken down into subsets of which some are especially relevant here. A key technical skill identified in this model is being knowledgeable about new technologies, a cornerstone of the program aimed at software development. Key management skills identified in the approach are planning and organising, learning, problem solving as well as communication skills, all of which are deeply integrated into the program's daily practice. In regard to entrepreneurial skills, concept development, opportunity recognition and networking are relevant for learners to succeed. Lastly, in personal maturity skills identified in the approach, self-awareness, accountability, emotional coping and creativity are developed during the formative program. Subsequently, a large degree of entrepreneurial knowledge is gained from experience during the course, even though the direct aim is not entrepreneurship education but software development for the Apple technology ecosystem. As a highly entrepreneurial practice, the guided immersion into reality is differentiated from other learning frameworks by its strong emphasis on learners' engagement. The program's learning experience is driven by learners' intrinsic motivation to acquire knowledge required to complete the *Challenges*, which is represented in the *Engage* phase of the *CBL* process. In order to succeed, learners have to employ a highly entrepreneurial skillset to manage the complexity of their projects, identify opportunities for innovation and deliver demanding and applicable results - e.g. in form of digital software products with real market value - on tight deadlines. This is in line with Krueger's (2007) findings on experiential essence of entrepreneurial thinking.

In academic years prior 2019/2020, the overall program was designed as a sequence of independent *Challenges*, which was identified as an area for improvement. While learning goals followed a natural progression in difficulty over the year, the separation between *Challenges* turned out to be non-beneficial to learning outcomes. The need for an overarching connection between *Challenges* to better foster individual engagement in individual *Challenges* prompted the introduction of narrative theory to design the learning experience for the future. Storytelling was identified as a suitable tool to design the experience and drive engagement in an interconnected sequence of *Challenges* of different lengths and scope that feed different needs in terms of learning within the academic year. It also introduced elements of catharsis in the dramaturgic sequence that addresses learners' emotional states during the course's progression. The resulting narrative layer serves not just as toolset to design the program but is a contribution towards a new theory of experience in education. Aspects of "old" education systems are reinvented to support a new experiential approach where learning goals are achieved while learners engage with *Challenges* that are catered to them as narratively organised experiences rather than a sequence of learning steps.

To illustrate the applied concepts, the authors will present the relevance of storytelling in education and how underlying narrative theory has been utilised to develop a toolset to design the program's overall scope and sequence of the academic year 2019/2020 with a narrative layer and the classical monomyth structure of the hero's journey. The authors will then summarise findings from the new approach and lastly present implications and final remarks to further evolve the research.

2. Storytelling in education

The significance of storytelling in education has been shown repeatedly in academic research. It allows learners to emotionally engage with learning objectives, strengthen their comprehension and capacity to learn (Woodhouse 2001, Silbermann 2006, Jarret 2019). Furthermore, Skouge & Rao (2009) have shown that storytelling is well suited for inquiry-based and project-based learning, which is the main educational method within the formative program at hand through use of the CBL framework. Storytelling is also key in experiential learning, that is particularly aimed at engaging learners in its activities and hence requires experiences to be connected to subsequent experiences, according to Dewey (1938), the educational theorist who emphasised the relevance of experience, experimentation and purposeful learning for progressive education. The notion of knowledge being constructed through the transformation of experience is also supported in context of entrepreneurship education by Loué & Baronet (2012) in their attempt to introduce an entrepreneurial skills and competencies framework. Learning experiences have aesthetic qualities that need to be designed in order to create an immersive, coherent and complete result that learners engage with, respond to, influence and draws from (Parrish 2009). Storytelling can provide perceptual, emotional and motivational opportunities for learning according to Rowe et al. (2007) and supports understanding and knowledge with contextual structure. Key aesthetic qualities are intellectual and emotional tension, rhythm and sequence, which are directly connected to narrative sequences and patterns that can be employed in inquiry-based approaches to create tension, mystery and resolution (Parrish 2009) to qualify the experience with narrative presence that characterises the learners perceived relationship with the story (Rowe et al 2007). Therefore, narrative structure can be employed as a framework of representation that is natively and intuitively understood by anyone (Fiore et al. 2007) to describe key characteristics of learning experiences and can provide meaningful interpretations of stories learners live through (Woodhouse 2001). The cognitive process of organising experiences with narrative form can be utilised in active learning and allows the creation of interactive narratives, where learners can create or influence the dramaturgy through their actions (thereby creating meaningful consequences), immersing them into the world of the story (Riedl & Bulitko 2012). This approach has also been linked to problem-based and inquiry-based learning (Rowe et al. 2007, 2010, 2011).

It has been shown that academic findings substantiate the value of storytelling in education, especially in active learning environments such within the experiential education program discussed here. Building on theories of intrinsically motivating instruction (Malone 1981, Malone & Lepper 1987), a toolset for narratively driven experience design was developed by the authors to evolve the educational setup of the program aimed at software development for the Apple technology ecosystem. To illustrate the systematic approach towards employing it in a structured university program, a closer look at narrative theory will be provided.

3. Narratology and the monomyth dramaturgic sequence

Narrative Theory - also called Narratology - is building on the notion that people perceive complex relationships in forms of narrative structures (Polkinghorne 1988, Fludernik 2009) that connect cause-and-effect relationships to sequences of events (Bal 1946, Truby 2009). Three components in narrative theory can be distinguished, the narrative act of a narrator, narrative discourse as text and lastly the story that is told in the narrative (Fludernik 2009). The latter is most relevant in this context, as it allows the same story to be told in multiple ways. As a basic level of narrative, Russian Formalists coined the term fabula (fable) in the 1920s and 1930s to describe it as a source of different versions of the same story that can be manifested in different plots following the same structure (Propp 1968, Fludernik 2009), and drive suspense throughout the story as a sequences of events or actions that define the narrative.

Scholars in the field of Narratology identified recurring patterns behind a broad category of stories throughout different cultures and historical periods. One of the most acknowledged common patterns is the monomyth or Hero's Journey (Campbell 1949), a narrative archetype to which a vast majority of stories can be traced back. In its basic expression it involves a main character - the hero - who leaves his ordinary world to begin a journey during which he will face a crisis from which he will emerge victorious, then returning home deeply transformed. Monomyth theory was popularised by Campbell (1949) and then further explored by a long lineage of scholars (Vogler 1998, Bloom & Hobby 2009). Beyond academia it had huge impact on modern novelists and screenwriters (Voytilla & Vogler 1999, MacKey-Kallis 2001, Vogler 2017).

Most relevant for the context of this paper is the version of the monomyth proposed by Vogler (2017). This model slightly modifies the original schema -mainly aimed at analytical and comparative purposes - to turn it into an actionable template for screenwriters and is structured as follows: (1) Ordinary World: the Hero's world before the story begins, his everyday life, habits and behaviours; (2) Call To Adventure: The Hero receives a call to action that breaks his daily life and disrupts comforts of the ordinary world; (3) Refusal Of The Call: the Hero is confused, both curious and afraid to accept the challenge. Personal doubts push the hero to refuse the call; (4) Meeting The Mentor: a turning point where the hero needs some form of guidance. He meets a mentor figure who provides what he's missing to accept the call to adventure; (5) Crossing The Threshold: The hero finally commits to the adventure and enters the new world where he truly begins his quest, whether it be physical, spiritual or emotional; (6) Tests, Allies, Enemies: The hero encounters new challenges and tests, makes allies and enemies, and begins to learn the rules of the new world; (7) Approach To The Inmost Cave: The hero approaches the edge of a dangerous place - the cave - realising that he must undertake more preparation before taking the leap into the final trial; (8) Ordeal: The ordeal may be a danger or deep crisis. It is a critical moment in any story, in which the hero must die or appear to die so that he can be born again; (9) Reward: Having survived death, defeated the enemy, overcome his main challenge, the hero conquers the treasure and evolves into a new state, emerging from the battle as a stronger person; (10) The Road Back: The hero is not out of the woods yet. Now he must return home but there may still be some further hostile forces preventing him to return to the ordinary world; (11) Resurrection: The hero who has been in the inmost cave must be reborn and purified facing one last ordeal of death and resurrection before being ready to go back home; (12) Return With The Elixir: The hero returns to the ordinary world as a changed person. He brings back treasures or some form of new knowledge that could be useful to him or the community someday.

According to Vogler (2007), the 12 stages may also be organised in 3 main sections or Acts: Act 1, comprising stages from 1 to 5; Act 2, stages 6 to 9; Act 3, stages from 10 to 12. Narrative studies show that not all stages are necessarily contained in all stories, and that they may be assembled and deployed in different shapes. Anyway, the basic structure has been proven effective not only as an analytical tool for literary critics and comparative studies but also as a creative or compositional tool for writers in multiple fields (novels, movies, video games, public speaking) to craft a compelling storyline.

4. Narrative experience design

Benefits of applying narrative-like arcs and dramatic patterns to the design process of educational experiences, courses and classes have already been highlighted (Parrish 2009, Matthews 2018). In addition, tools and methods both from the field of experience design and narrative design - namely storyboarding, journey mapping and scripting - have been proposed as an expanded toolset for instructional designers and educators (Matthews 2018). In line with this approach, the authors adapted the monomyth narrative structure described above as a learning experience design tool for the program offered at University of Naples Federico II. The monomyth provided a well-established, solid but flexible, model for the organisation of sequences of learning units and activities along a narrative path. In particular the monomyth scheme - that has been reworked and adapted as a design canvas - was used to design the overall scope and sequence of the units of learning - Challenges in the context of the CBL framework used at the university. During the planning of the academic year 2019/2020, Challenges were sequenced not just according to a chronological juxtaposition of learning goals or to a logical movement from simple to complex, but rather in a way that would mainly trigger and articulate the level of engagement of learners with the purpose of fostering ownership and intrinsic motivation towards an autonomous and personalised exploration of learning goals and objectives of the program.

Following this approach, the program's first phase, or first Act - that encompasses stages of the monomyth from Ordinary World to Crossing The Threshold - was designed to function as the set-up and catalyst for a new experience of learning. The transition for learners from the Ordinary World of traditional education, highly structured curriculum and syllabus to a new model of learning based on Challenges, collaboration, ownership, creativity and self-regulation is planned as both exciting and uncomfortable. Early Challenges are designed as a Call To Adventure that trigger interests and curiosity while provoking some form of resistance in learners, that may experience, in Vogler's words, a Refusal of the Call. Following Challenges are then designed to function as catalysts for learners to immerse themselves into the new learning environment. Thanks to what in the monomyth is called Mentor Intervention, learners are encouraged to embrace failure and success and detach from their previous assumptions and expectations on the learning process. Specific Challenges are designed at this moment to let learners gain awareness about meaningful learning experiences and how learning objectives are achievable in context of the new educational framework. Learners are Crossing The Threshold as they build trust in their own learning capabilities. Solving real world Challenges and dealing with uncertainty and tight deadlines, learners start realising that they are acquiring a new set of hard and soft skills.

The second Act - that includes stages from Tests, Allies and Enemies to Reward - drives learners into the New World, where enhanced conflicts, new tensions, surprises and growing complication help maintaining and modulating learner engagement (Parrish 2009). More complex movements than simple linear progression are introduced through new *Challenges*, that are organised in a way that would provide turns, jumps, multiple paths, uphill and downhill inclines (Matthews 2018) following a multifaceted "physics of learner engagement" (Cates & Bishop 2003). Along this way, opportunities for learners to take agency in the learning process are increased and a high level of freedom on which part of the curriculum to explore is promoted. The road towards the program's main trial is set, but along the way learners will encounter new intermediate *Challenges* designed to let them face difficulties and moments of potential discomfort as they approach, in Vogler's terms, The Inmost Cave and The Ordeal. At this point in the academic year, the most important *Challenge* is placed, during which learners are encouraged to build upon what they learned in previous *Challenges* while deepening their skills and developing heightened levels of self-regulation and ownership.

The third Act - that goes from The Road Back to Return with the Elixir - is where a set of culminating events and experiences bring coherence to the entire process, justifying efforts taken to engage in the journey (Parrish 2009). Final pitches, reviews of projects with external stakeholders, portfolio showcases, are planned to enhance an effect of accomplishment. Multiple opportunities for retrospectives, self-assessment and reflective practices are embedded in the design of this part of the program to increase in learners' awareness of the journey they have undertaken.

5. Discussion and implications

The introduced approach employs narrative theory to design the experiential educational program aimed at software development at University of Naples Federico II and was applied for the academic year of 2019/2020. As a result, both learning goals and individual *Challenges* were introduced in a significantly more consistent and interconnected fashion that follows the outlined narrative structure. Beyond designing the overall academic year using the narrative layer, also individual *Challenges* have been designed with the narrative approach, creating an episodic sequence of narratives that drive leaner engagement and interconnect events within the learning environment.

In comparison to the previous unconnected sequence of *Challenges*, the new approach resulted in major improvements that can briefly be discussed. First, in contrast to previous course design where learners would explore topics in increasing depth over time, following a basic movement from simple to complex with logical relationship between topics (in line with concepts of spiral curriculum or elaboration theory), the new narrative approach follows not a conceptual-logical but a temporal and experiential scheme, which is in line with Matthews (2018) recommendations for sequencing learning experiences. This is further substantiated by Parrish (2009) who considers narrative dramatic organisation of experiences as the most engaging and effective sequence. Yet, there are some critical points to consider, as a narrative sequence does not guarantee that learners will experience the course as intended (Matthews 2018) and can therefore not be designed deterministically (Gray 2015). Rather, in context of narrative experiences, leaners have to be considered as co-authors of their experience. So secondly, the new narrative experience design of the program at hand gives considerable freedom and autonomy to learners to shape their path on their learning journey. In designing the narrative arc and characteristics of the environment on levels of the individual learning journey, *Challenge* group journey and communal journey, strong emphasis was given to fostering intrinsic motivation and engagement (Malone 1981, Malone & Lepper 1987) in the learners to induce the sense of ownership and agency. The inherent freedom of choice in designing specific learning paths became the central notion of the evolved learning experience. The new narrative experience design introduced is therefore in line with academic findings.

However, there is still room for further research. Most importantly, to support leaner autonomy and agency even better and ensuring that the narrative is being experienced in the intended way, more information about learners are needed. As pointed out by various scholars (Cates & Bishop 2003, Parrish 2014, Matthew 2018), deep empathetic understanding and analysis of the learners is required to understand how they will contribute to the experience and what decision they may take in order to qualify the experience with narrative presence in terms of Rowe et al. (2007). Subsequently, the faculty conducting the experiential education program needs to be equipped with appropriate sensors to better analyse and understand the learner's journey. To control the narrative, a systematic feedback loop for these sensors needs to be developed that evaluates the narrative progression qualified through appropriate measures to make adjustments on the narrative layer as they become necessary. To evolve this approach even further, the concept of emergent narratives can be explored. It is based on the notion that narratively driven experiences cannot just be authored or enacted in classical ways but can also emerge directly from the interactions between different protagonists or actors under specific conditions and create themselves from relationships between its elements (Louchart et at. 2004, Aylett 2006). In that sense, the experience is lived through and even more so driven by the learners, resulting in many enacted storylines rather than a single storyline that different learners need to conform to.

6. Conclusion

The authors have shown how narrative theory can be employed to construct a narrative layer for the design of the experiential education program aimed at software development for the Apple technology ecosystem at University of Naples Federico II. Results of the described approach include that through designing an overarching narrative and utilising the monomyth structure of the hero's journey, learning goals and *Challenges* are now an interconnected narrative sequence in the academic year 2019/2020, which is aimed at increasing perceived consistency and leaners' engagement. Within the context of entrepreneurship education, the paper contributes to academic research with highly relevant implications. The formative and experiential program requires learners to adopt key entrepreneurial skills relevant to any entrepreneurial endeavour in real world scenarios rather than learning abstract and theoretical concepts without application in practice. The narrative structure immerses learners deeper into the learning process and drives them to become more adaptable and eligible for potential entrepreneurial endeavours.

With results indicating that improved learning experience design is valid and in line with academic finding on narratively driven experiential education, further research could be aimed at developing this approach into a more systematic model, that is less pre-scripted and gives more control to learners in affecting progression of the narrative. The concept of emergent narratives could be used in designing a model to manage an educational experience affectively driven by learners that allows unscripted, emergent narratives for entrepreneurial education to emerge and empowers learners towards building entrepreneurial skills of ownership, growth mindset and self-learning as a complement to software development education they receive during the program.

Acknowledgements

This work was conducted at the Apple Developer Academy in Naples (Italy), operated in collaboration between University of Naples Federico II and Apple Inc., where the authors are faculty members.

References

Aylett, R. et al. (2006) "Unscripted narrative for affectively driven characters", *IEEE Computer Graphics and Applications*, Vol. 26, No. 3, pp. 42-52.

Bal, M. (2009) *Narratology - Introduction to the Theory of the Narrative,* Third Edition, University of Toronto Press, Toronto.

Bloom, H., & Hobby, B. (Eds.) (2009) *The Hero's Journey,* Infobase Publishing.

Campbell, J. (1949) *The Hero with a Thousand Faces,* (1st ed., 2nd ed. 1968, 3rd ed. 2008), Princeton University Press, New Jersey.

Cates, W.M. & Bishop, M.J. (2003) "Learner as Bobsled Operator: The Physics of Learner Engagement", *Journal of Educational Technology Systems*, Vol. 31, No. 3, pp. 291–305.

Chang, J. & Rieple, A. (2013) "Assessing students' entrepreneurial skills development in live projects", *Journal of Small Business and Enterprise Development*, Vol. 20, No. 1, pp. 225–241.

Dahlstrom, T.R. & Talmage, C.A. (2018) "Entrepreneurial skills for sustainable small business: An exploratory study of SCORE, with comparison", *Community Development*, Vol. 49. No. 4, pp. 450–468.

Dewey, J. (1938) *Experience And Education*, Reprint (1997), Touchstone, New York.

Fiore, S., Metcalf, D. & McDaniel, R. (2007) "Theoretical Foundations of Experiential Learning", In M. Silberman (Ed), *The Handbook of Experiential Learning,* John Wiley and Sons, San Francisco, pp. 33–58.

Fludernik, M. (2009) *An Introduction to Narratology*, Routledge, London.

Gibb, A. (2002) "In pursuit of a new 'enterprise' and "entrepreneurship" paradigm for learning: creative destruction, new values, new ways of doing things and new combinations of knowledge", *International Journal of Management Reviews*, Vol. 4, No. 3, pp. 233–269.

Gray, C.M. (2015) "Critiquing the Role of the Learner and Context in Aesthetic Learning Experiences", In B. Hokanson, G. Clinton, & M. W. Tracey (Eds.), *The Design of Learning Experience,* Springer, New York, pp. 199–213.

Jarrett, K. (2019) "Developing the art of storytelling as a pedagogical tool for academics", Articles from the 2018 University of Brighton Learning and Teaching Conference, Brighton, UK.

Johnson, L.F., Smith, R.S., Smythe, J.T., & Varon, R.K. (2009) "Challenge-based learning: An approach for our time, *The New Media Consortium.*

Johnson, L.F., & Brown, S. (2011) "Challenge based learning: The report from the implementation project", *The New Media Consortium.*

Kakouris, A. (2015) " Entrepreneurship pedagogies in lifelong learning: Emergence of criticality?", *Learning, Culture and Social Interaction*, Vol. 6, No. C, pp. 87–97.

Krueger Jr, N.F. (2007) "What lies beneath? The experiential essence of entrepreneurial thinking. Entrepreneurship", *Theory and Practice*, Vol. 31, No. 1, pp. 123-138.

Lichtenstein, G.A. & Lyons, T.S. (1996) *Incubating New Enterprise: A Guide to Successful Practice*, The Aspen Institute, Washington, DC.

Louchart, S. & Aylett, R. (2004) "Narrative theory and emergent interactive narrative", *Int. J. Continuing Engineering Education and Lifelong Learning*, Vol. 14, No. 6, pp. 506-518.

Loué, C. & Baronet, J. (2012) "Toward a new entrepreneurial skills and competencies framework: a qualitative and quantitative study", *International Journal of Entrepreneurship and Small Business*, Vol. 17, No. 4, pp. 455–477.

MacKey-Kallis, S. (2001) *The Hero and the Perennial Journey Home in American Film*, University of Pennsylvania Press, Philadelphia.

Malone, T.W. (1981) "Toward a theory of intrinsically motivating instruction", *Cognitive Science*, Vol. 5, No. 4, pp. 333–369.

Malone, T.W. & Lepper, M.R. (1987) "Making Learning Fun: A Taxonomy of Intrinsic Motivations for Learning", In R. E. Snow & M. J. Farr (Eds.), *Aptitude, learning, and instruction - Conative and affective process analyses*. Hillsdale, New Jersey, pp. 223–253.

Matthews, M.T. (2018) "Designing for Narrative-Like Learning Experiences", In B. Hokanson, G. Clinton, & K. Kaminski (Eds.), *Educational Technology and Narrative,* Springer, Cham, pp. 249–258.

Nichols, M., & Cator, K. (2008) "Challenge Based Learning", White Paper, Cupertino, California: Apple.

Parrish, P.E. (2009) "Aesthetic principles for instructional design", *Educational Technology Research and Development*, Vol. 57, No. 4, pp. 511–528.

Parrish, P. E. (2014) "Designing for the half-known world: Lessons for instructional designers from the craft of narrative fiction", In B. Hokanson & A. Gibbons (Eds.), *Design in educational technology: Design thinking, design process, and the design studio,* Springer, Cham, pp. 261–270.

Politis, D. (2005) "The process of entrepreneurial learning: A conceptual framework", *Entrepreneurship: Theory and Practice*, Vol. 29, No. 4, pp. 399–424.

Polkinghorne, D.E. (1988) *Narrative Knowing and the Human Sciences,*State, University of New York Press, Albany.

Propp, V. (1968) *Morphology of the Folktale,* Revised Edition, University of Texas Press, Houston.

Riedl, M.O. & Bulitko, V. (2013) "Interactive Narrative: An Intelligent Systems Approach" *AI Magazine*, Vol. 34, No. 1, pp. 67–67.

Rowe, J.P., McQuiggan, S.W. & Lester, J.C. (2007) "Narrative Presence in Intelligent Learning Environments", *AAAI Fall Symposium Intelligent Narrative Technologies*, pp. 127–134.

Rowe, J.P. et al. (2010) "Integrating Learning and Engagement in Narrative-Centered Learning Environments In Intelligent Tutoring Systems", In *Lecture Notes in Computer Scienc,* Springer, Berlin, Heidelberg, pp. 166–177.

Rowe, J., Shores, L., Mott, B., & Lester, J. (2011) "Integrating Learning, Problem Solving, and Engagement in Narrative-Centered Learning Environments", *International Journal of Artificial Intelligence in Education, Vol.* 21, No. 1–2, pp. 115– 133.

Silbermann, M. (2006) *Active Training - A Handbook of Techniques, Designs, Case Examples and Tips*, 3rd Edition, Pfeiffer, San Francisco.

Skouge, J.R. & Rao, K. (2009) "Digital Storytelling in Teacher Education: Creating Transformations through Narrative", *Educational Perspectives*, Vol. 42, No. 1-2, pp. 54-60.

Stuetzer, M. et al. (2013) "Where do entrepreneurial skills come from", *Applied Economics Letters*, Vol. 20, No. 12, pp. 1183–1186.

Truby, J. (2009) *The Anatomy of Story: 22 Steps to Becoming a Master Storyteller*, First Edition, Farrar, Straus & Giroux, New York.

Vogler, C. (1998) *The Writer's Journey: Mythic Structure For Writers,* Michael Wiese Productions, Studio City, CA.

Vogler, C. (2018) "Joseph Campbell Goes to the Movies: The Influence of the Hero's Journey in Film Narrative", *Journal of Genius and Eminence*, Vol. 9, pp.9–23.

Voytilla, S. & Vogler, C. (1999) *Myth & the Movies: Discovering the Myth Structure of 50 Unforgettable Films,* Michael Wiese Productions, Studio City, CA.

Woodhouse, H. (2011) "Storytelling in University Education: Emotion, Teachable Moments, and the Value of Life", *The Journal of Educational Thought (JET) / Revue De La Pensée Éducative*, Vol. 45, No. 3, pp. 211–238.

Entrepreneurial Capital of Individuals in Post-Socialist Poland in 1998 and 2018

Yevhen Revtiuk[1] and Olga Zelinska[2]
[1]Poznan University of Technology, Poznan, Poland
[2] Institute of Philosophy and Sociology, Polish Academy of Sciences, Warsaw, Poland
yevhen.revtiuk@put.poznan.pl
ozelinsk@sns.edu.pl
DOI: 1034190/EIE.20.095

Abstract: We investigate the impact of human capital, and its components -- family social capital and some aspects of cultural capital -- on entrepreneurial status in one socio-economic system, but at the different stages of its development from command to market. Using Polish Panel Survey (POLPAN) waves of 1998 and 2018 we study how different individual-level characteristics had impacted chances of entrepreneurial career in Poland under different conditions. In particular, we look at how human capital (operationalized as the level of education), social family capital (operationalized as father's occupation) and cultural capital characteristics (beliefs that characterize own responsibility values and the attitudes towards a strong state) impact the odds of an employed individual to engage in an entrepreneurial career. Our findings offer a nuanced view on how these different components of human capital impacted the odds of engagement in entrepreneurial activity in 1990ies and 2000s. While education and family social capital characteristics were significant and positive predictors of opening own business in the market economy, they did not turn significant in the transition period. The role of different aspects of cultural capital, at the same time, lacks clear interpretation and further research into the mechanisms how individual values and beliefs play out for entrepreneurship in both market and transition economies is required.

Keywords: entrepreneurial capital, human capital, social capital, cultural capital, market economy, transition economy, entrepreneurship, Poland

1. Introduction

Over the last century the researchers have paid a great attention to the phenomenon of entrepreneurship. The entrepreneur, being one of the main actors of innovation in a market economy (Gartner, 1990), uses the resources she or he has to construct new business processes aimed at new business opportunities (OECD, 1998), which leads to changes in social relations. The entrepreneurial capital is the main resource available at the disposal of the entrepreneur (Demartini and Paoloni, 2014; Erikson, 2002; Firkin, 2001 and others). Entrepreneurial capital of an individual consists of her or his individual human capital (Revtiuk and Malecka, 2019).

Human capital is a complex theoretical construct that emerged in economic theory to explain the link between investment in knowledge and skills of an individual and her or his subsequent reward (Becker, 1964; Schultz, 1961). Considering that investments in health, social connections or cultural habits have similar goals as investments in the acquisition of knowledge and skills, it is not sufficient to limit the study of human capital to the investment in education only. Therefore, we propose to consider individual components of human capital, namely social capital (Coleman, 1988) and cultural capital (Bourdieu, 2002) and their role in formation of individual entrepreneurial capital.

The role of human capital in the formation of entrepreneurial capital, the influence on the decision to open a business, the results of the entrepreneurial activity have been repeatedly investigated. In doing so, the researchers have interpreted the concept of human capital as investment in education, the number of years of study, acquired specific and general knowledge or skills (Unger et al., 2011). At the same time, social capital has been explored in terms of its impact on the success of the enterprise, namely the ability to access highly specialized human capital among individual social networks (Anderson and Miller, 2003) or through the use of family social capital (Hoffman, Hoelscher and Sorenson, 2006). The influence of the cultural characteristics on various aspects of entrepreneurial activity had also been studied (Hayton and Cacciotti, 2013), and the authors paid particular attention to the influence of different aspects of cultural capital (mostly at the national level) on entrepreneurial activity.

In this article we investigate the impact of human capital, family social capital and some aspects of cultural capital on entrepreneurial status in one socio-economic system, but at the different stages of its development from command to market. For this purpose, we investigate the example of Poland, a successful post-socialist country, which has moved from a systemic crisis and a collapse of the inefficient command-and-control economy in the late 1990ies, to a leader in economic development in Central Europe in the late 2000s. The beginning of economic reforms led to the revival of the entrepreneurial class in Poland, which played an important role in Poland's success story (McMillan and Woodruff, 2002). For example, by the end of 1989, more than 16,000 new businesses were registered (Wilson and Adams, 1994).

Studies of entrepreneurship in the post-socialist Poland take into account the impact of education and family history (Boruc, 2018), the role of social connections (Osborn and Słomczyński, 2005) and the level of parent-son inheritance of entrepreneur status (Domański, 2000) in choosing an entrepreneurial career. We add to the existing literature by exploring educational, social and cultural components of entrepreneurs' human capital in two different periods of Poland's development: transition economy in the late 1990ies and market economy ten years later. To test our prepositions, we use the results of the Polish Panel Survey (POLPAN), for 1998 and 2018 waves (Polish Panel Survey, 2020).

Researchers identify several significant obstacles to the development of entrepreneurship in Poland, including such factors traditional for transit countries as lack of equity to start a business, complicated legal system and inefficient institutions of public administration, low level of innovation in Polish companies, migration of young people to more developed EU countries (Rumiński, 2017). In Poland, the level of fear of failure is higher comparing to the other European countries and the status attributed to entrepreneurship is rather low (Zbierowski, 2014: 241).

2. Theory

There is no unified approach in the literature regarding the definition of the "entrepreneurship" and the "entrepreneur". Entrepreneurship definitions include: the entry of new firms, and the creation of high-growth firms (Hoffmann, 2007); the ability of individuals to create and develop innovative organizations that generate value (Gartner, 1990); or even competitive behaviors that drive the market process (Davidsson, 2016). In this article we will understand entrepreneurship as the ability of an individual (the entrepreneur) to pool resources for creating new business opportunities (OECD, 1998), or creating entrepreneurial capital.

Entrepreneurial capital is defined as a "multiplicative function of entrepreneurial competence and entrepreneurial commitment" (Erikson, 2002:275). It is considered a combination of human capital (entrepreneurial competence and behavior) and structural capital (entrepreneurial corporate culture and processes) (Demartini and Paoloni, 2014). Proponents of a resource-oriented approach suggest that this is the capital used for entrepreneurship (Firkin, 2001), or is necessary to start a business (Fletschner and Carter, 2008). Researchers pay a special attention to individual-specific resources, including the cognitive abilities of the individual entrepreneurs (Alvarez and Busenitz, 2001), which lead to formation of the entrepreneurial capital.

Human capital theory was originally developed to explain the relationship between investing in individual education (investment in human capital) (Becker, 1964) or other specific skills (Unger et al., 2011) and subsequent earnings of this individual. The proposal to consider human capital as a resource composed of individuals' knowledge, skills, abilities, and other characteristics (Ployhart and Moliterno, 2011) leads to the understanding of the concept of human capital, as consisting not only of the knowledge and skills of the individual (cognitive abilities), but also other characteristics that affect her or his ability to generate the added value, such as personal health (health capital) (Grossman, 2000), social skills and communication or social capital (Coleman, 1988), and cultural capital (Farkas, 2017). Elsewhere it was suggested to consider the human capital of an individual as consisting of the intellectual component, health capital, social capital, motivational capital and cultural capital (Revtiuk, 2015). Reference to the human capital theory further allows to introduce a category of individual entrepreneurial capital, which can be defined as a part of individual human capital which is used in the entrepreneurial process (Revtiuk and Malecka, 2019).

There is a vast research on the impact of human capital on entrepreneurial success in market economies. The value of human capital has a positive effect on the entrepreneurial success of an individual (Davidsson and Honig, 2003), especially by acquiring broader knowledge that an individual can use to find opportunities to start a new business (Lazear, 2005). Scholars highlight the impact of the specialized component of human capital (business education) (Unger et al., 2011), which makes human capital a key factor in entrepreneurship (Haber and Reichel,

2007). It should be noted that when studying the relationship between human capital and entrepreneurship, researchers focus more on the cognitive abilities of entrepreneurs, namely general or specific knowledge, entrepreneurial and managerial skills, experience (Unger et al., 2011). Thus, we are able to formulate the following hypothesis:

> *H 1.1. Individual's educational background is the significant and positive determinant of the entrepreneurial status in the market economy.*

The transition economy is characterized by a high level of uncertainty, which, in post-socialist countries, has been exacerbated by the emergence of many opportunities to start own business. Therefore, the availability of education, and especially education obtained in the socialist era, did not create an additional benefit for the individual (Manev, Gyoshev and Manolova, 2005). Thus, we can formulate the following hypothesis:

> *H 1.2. Individual's educational background is not a significant determinant of the entrepreneurial status in the transition economy.*

Social capital is an important factor in the formation of human capital within both the family and the immediate community (Coleman, 1988). Social capital impacts the economic activity both at the macro level (Coleman, 1990; Putnam, 1995) and at the micro level (Bourdieu, 2002). Considering the phenomenon of individual social capital (Yang, 2007), we should consider family or family capital as an important factor in forming this type of social capital in market economy (Hoffman, Hoelscher and Sorenson, 2016). On the one hand, family is one of the possible sources of capital needed for successful business (Chang et al., 2009). Family social capital forms the "incorporated cultural capital" of an individual who is socialized within the family in relation to particular styles, modes of representation, use of language, forms of social etiquette, confidence, and self-assurance (Bourdieu, 2002), which promotes the formation of individual social capital. In other words, people who are raised in families with higher social status are more likely to generate and use effective social capital to conduct business (Anderson and Miller, 2003). These considerations enabled us to formulate the following hypotheses:

> *H2.1. Family social capital is a significant and positive predictor of individual entrepreneurial status in market economy.*

On the other hand, during post-communist transition the societies are becoming more individualized (Swader, 2013). Under these new conditions traditional family ties may be losing their importance and individuals become more isolated in a society, starting new activities *tabula rasa*, regardless of origins and family connections. Thus, we can hypothesize that:

> *H2.2. Family social capital is not a significant predictor of individual entrepreneurial status in the transition economy.*

Cultural capital consists of the individual's institutionalized capital (e.g. occupational certificates, education diplomas and degrees), and the individual's incorporated capital (e.g. competencies, skills and habits contained in cultural values and behavioral routines) (Bourdieu, 2002:23). Cultural capital, and especially individual's incorporated capital, according to Bourdieu, influences the actions and the outcomes of the individual. In particular, personality, perception and ambitions are important factors for starting a business and developing it early on, when an entrepreneur lacks financial resources (Garnsey, 1998) or within the underdeveloped market infrastructure (Wdowiak et al., 2012). Given that hard work, initiative, responsibility are usually characteristic of entrepreneurs in advanced economies (Wdowiak et al., 2012), and favoritism, infantilism, and collective values that, in particular, lead to an exaggeration of the role of the state, will characterize the entrepreneurs of the transition economy to a greater extent, we can formulate the following groups of hypotheses:

> *H3.1. Responsibility values are a significant and positive predictor of individual entrepreneurial status in market economy.*
>
> *H3.2. Responsibility values are not significant predictor of individual entrepreneurial status in transition economy.*
>
> *and*
>
> *H3.3. Beliefs about the importance of the role of the state in social and economic life are a significant and positive predictor of entrepreneurial status in transition economy.*
>
> *H3.4. Beliefs about the importance of the role of the state in social and economic life are not a significant predictor of entrepreneurial status in market economy.*

3. Methodology

The study is based on the results of the POLPAN panel survey, the longest continuously run panel study in Central and Eastern Europe, carried out by the Institute of Philosophy and Sociology, Polish Academy of Sciences. Since it was initiated in socialist Poland in 1987-88, POLPAN reached the respondents in 5-year intervals. This panel study collects socio-demographic and socio-economic information of respondents and their families, as well as data on participants' various socio-political attitudes (Polish Panel Survey POLPAN, 2020). For this article, we used the results of the two waves of the POLPAN conducted in 1998 and 2018. The 1998 wave was the first after the painful but successful reforms of the economy in 1991-1993, and we expect the results of the survey to most accurately characterize entrepreneurship in the transition economy. In 2018 Poland ranked 37th in the Global Competitiveness Index and was a successful developed country and one of the leaders in Eastern Europe in terms of economic development. Considering the above, we expect the recently published survey results held in 2018 to reflect the opinions of the respondents in the market economy.

In particular, we used the information of the respondents who gave an affirmative answer regarding the presence of a permanent place of work, including those who conduct their own business. We created a dependent variable, which is the entrepreneurial status of the employed individual (1 = yes, 0 = no). To test the hypothesis on *educational background*, we looked at the question on the highest level of education obtained by the respondent, ranging from 1=elementary education only to 8=post-graduate studies completed.

The question of the occupation of the father at the age of the respondent at the time of the survey was used to assess *family social capital*. According to the answers of the respondents, three dummy variables were generated, which characterize three different spheres of family social capital, namely: (a) entrepreneurial (the father was an entrepreneur; 1 = yes, 0 = no); (b) higher managerial (father occupied high level officials' and managers' position; 1 = yes, 0 = no); and (c) manual worker (father occupied the position of a manual worker in elementary occupations, or unskilled worker in services and trade, or skilled manual worker or laborer in agriculture, forestry, and fishing; 1 = yes, 0 = no).

For the assessment of *cultural capital*, we used the questions which characterize the values and beliefs of the respondent. The first group of questions aimed at determining the respondent's beliefs about the factors that contribute to success. Namely, respondents were given a Likert scale from 1 to 5 (we reversed the original POLPAN scale and our variables range from "1=not at all important" to "5=very important") to assess (a) the importance of knowing the right people, (b) of hard work, (c) of coming from a rich family, and (d) of a good education for success in life. Using these categories, we operationalize own responsibility values as support of hard work and of educational attainment, and treat knowing the right people and rich family background as attribution to external factors.

The second block of questions is about the respondent's beliefs about the role of the state in the economic life. Respondents were asked to rate a range of statements on a scale of 1 to 5 (again, we reversed the original POLPAN scale into 1 = strongly disagree and 5 = strongly agree). We have selected 3 statements, namely: (a) The upper income limit that no one could exceed should be firmly established; (b) The state is responsible for reducing differences in people's incomes; and (c) The state should provide jobs for everyone who wants to work.

In the models we also controlled for age and gender (1=male; 2=female) of the respondents. Characteristics of the data used in the study for the 1998 and 2018 POLPAN waves are shown in Table 1.

4. Results

To test the hypotheses, we performed logistic regression analysis using SPSS software. As Table 2 demonstrates, the level of education of respondent failed to prove as statistically significant predictor of her entrepreneurial status in 1998, but was significant ten years later, in 2018, with education level increase associated with higher chances of becoming an entrepreneur by 1,2 times, all the rest equal. This may be explained by the fact that the mass privatization of enterprises in the 1990ies created the conditions for starting a business for a wide range of people, whereas in 2018 those with higher levels of human capital, operationalized through education, were more likely to engage in business. Thus, the hypothesis H1.1 that the higher levels of education would increase the chances of an individual to gain entrepreneurial status in market economy was confirmed. In the transition economy, as suggested by the H1.2 the impact of the level of education obtained on the entrepreneurial status was not significant.

The analysis of indicators characterizing the relationship between family social capital and entrepreneurial status demonstrates that entrepreneurial status of the respondent's father is statistically significant predictor of her or his entrepreneurial status in 2018, with the chance of becoming an entrepreneur for an individual with a "business history" within a family increased by 3,4 times, the rest equal. In the 1998, however, we failed to find this significant relationship. We also failed to find significant evidence that children of manual working fathers, as well as those of the high officials and managers are more or less likely to open own business, both in 1998 and in 2018. Thus, our hypothesis H 2.1 that family social capital, operationalized as entrepreneurial status of father, increases the chances of individual's entrepreneurial future in the market economy. The hypothesis H2.2 that family social capital would not be an important predictor of individual becoming an entrepreneur in the transition economy was also confirmed.

Considering the indicators that characterize cultural capital, we found that those who supported the idea that hard work pays off (and thus possessed high own responsibility values) were more likely to become an entrepreneur in 1998 (odds ratio = 1.26), but this indicator lost its predictive power in 2018. Instead, the more individual supported the statement that good education is important for success (which is also a responsibility value), the less likely she or he would engage in business in both 1998 and ten years later, but only 2018 results are statistically significant, the rest held equal. Both beliefs in importance of "knowing the right people" and "coming from wealthy family" turned insignificant for 1998 and 2018 models. Thus, our hypotheses H 3.1. and H3.2 had not received convincing confirmation.

Table 1: Descriptive statistics of the data used in the study

	1998					2018				
Variable	N	Min	Max	Mean	St.D.	N	Min	Max	Mean	St.D.
Enterprenuerial status	2135	.00	1.00	.0778	.26784	2077	.00	1.00	.0698	.2548
Level of education of respondent	2110	1	8	3.57	2.423	2161	1	8	4.66	2.427
Father's occupation at respondent's age:										
Manual worker	2135	.00	1.00	.3040	.46008	2161	.00	1.00	.2568	.43698
Entrepreneur	2135	.00	1.00	.0220	.14676	2161	.00	1.00	.0250	.15613
Managerial position	2135	.00	1.00	.0126	.11177	2161	.00	1.00	.0125	.11110
To what extent are some things important for achieving success in life?										
Knowing right people	1429	1.00	5.00	3.9538	.83639	2145	1.00	5.00	3.6289	.77285
Hard work	2094	1.00	5.00	3.254	1.0882	1749	1.00	5.00	3.8193	.89905
Coming from wealthy family	2091	1.00	5.00	2.833	1.1438	2117	1.00	5.00	2.8026	1.02646
Good education	2116	1.00	5.00	4.033	.83076	2146	1.00	5.00	3.8169	.82134
The upper income limit should be firmly established	2049	1.00	5.00	3.062	1.4957	2101	1.00	5.00	2.8710	1.35647
The state is responsible for reducing differences in incomes	2030	1.00	5.00	3.491	1.2602	2106	1.00	5.00	3.5484	1.12107
The state should provide jobs for everyone	2115	1.00	5.00	4.197	1.0819	2136	1.00	5.00	4.0037	1.08470
Age	2135	21	76	46.78	14.707	2161	21	95	50.34	20.439
Gender	2135	1.00	2.00	1.512	.49995	2161	1.00	2.00	1.5497	.49763
Valid N (listwise)	1258					1589				

Another block of indicators characterizes individuals' beliefs about the role of the state in regulating economic processes. First of all, greater support of (a) the establishment of upper income limit and (b) of the provision of jobs by the state, was a significant and negative predictor of entrepreneurial status in 1998 (OR, respectively, are .78 and .64), the rest equal. In 2018, however, these beliefs lost their predictive power. Support of the statement that the state is responsible for reducing differences in income was a significant and negative predictor of opening business in 2018 (OR=.78), all rest equal. In 1998 that same belief turned out to be insignificant. We note, at the same time, a change in sign in 1998. Given these results, we cannot confirm the hypotheses H3.3 and H3.4.

Table 2: Logistic regression of entrepreneurial status against the characteristics of human, social and cultural capital of individual in 1998 and 2018 Poland

	1998			2018		
	Coef.	S.E.	O.R.	Coef.	S.E.	O.R.
Level of education of respondent	.058	.047	1.059	.183*	.054	1.201
Father's occupation at respondent's age:						
Manual worker	-.353	.257	.702	.111	.226	1.117
Entrepreneur	.509	.578	1.663	1.245*	.398	3.472
Managerial position	.195	.633	1.215	-.460	.767	.631
To what extent are some things important for achieving success in life?						
Knowing right people	.065	.133	1.067	-.033	.137	.968
Hard work	.232**	.097	1.261	.162	.119	1.176
Coming from wealthy family	.124	.100	1.132	.108	.109	1.114
Good education	-.222	.125	.801	-.288**	.123	.750
Attitudes toward the state						
The upper income limit should be firmly established	-.233*	.086	.793	-.174	.093	.840
The state is responsible for reducing differences in incomes	.049	.095	1.050	-.247**	.095	.781
The state should provide jobs for everyone	-.439*	.090	.645	-.148	.092	.863
Control variables						
Age	-.008	.008	.992	.033*	.007	1.034
Gender	-.498**	.223	.608	-.906*	.221	.404
Constant	.206	.966	1.228	-1.789	.951	.167
Pseudo R2	0.153			0.145		
N	1252			1588		

**p<0.05 *p<0.01

Both age and gender, our control variables, are important predictors of entrepreneurial status in 1998 and in 2018. In both waves being a male is connected to higher chances of opening own business (OR are .6 for 1998 and .4 for 2018). Age is a positive and significant determinant of higher chances of opening business in 2018. In modern-day Poland each ten-year increase in age increases the chances of individual being entrepreneur by 3.4%, all other equal. We also note the negative sign for age in 1998, although this factor turned insignificant in the model. In the 1990ies Poland entrepreneurship might have attracted younger people, although this statement requires additional research.

Predictors analyzed for 1998 and 2018 models explain, respectively, 14 and 15% of likelihood of entrepreneurial status if an individual.

5. Conclusion and discussion

Formation of the entrepreneurial capital is critically dependent on the human capital of the individual. A broad interpretation of the definition of the human capital of an individual, which, unlike the traditional approach, in addition to knowledge and skills, includes her or his social capital and cultural capital, allows a comprehensive study of the relationship of human capital and entrepreneurship at the micro level. The proposed approach avoids concentrating on the role of social capital (Coleman, 1988) or cultural capital (Farkas, 2017) in shaping human capital, instead exploring the role of the entire productive capacity of the individual in generation of the added value. In our opinion, the ambiguous results obtained by researchers during the study of the importance of human capital in entrepreneurship (Unger et al., 2011) may be explained by little attention paid to the influences that generate social capital and cultural capital when using human capital in entrepreneurial activity.

Adding a layer of complexity, our research aimed at identifying the effects of human capital components on entrepreneurial status in two different types of economic systems – in transition and in market economy. The analysis of different periods of economic development in the same country demonstrated the fact that under different conditions individual entrepreneurial capital was formed on the basis of different characteristics of human capital. In 1998 the belief that hard work pays off was a significant predictor of opening own business, accompanied by a negative attitude towards a strong state (non-support of the upper income limit and general employment). Entrepreneurship attracted, first and foremost, young males (although the age factor lacks statistical significance). In 2018 the situation was different. Significant predictors of the entrepreneurial status were higher level of education, family entrepreneurial history, a belief that good education pays off, and support of state non-intervention in the economic life (state should not reduce differences in incomes). In late 2000s being a male remained a significant and positive predictor of engaging in business activity, but the age became significant and positive: additional years increased chances of becoming a businessperson.

Our results suggest that while formation of human (educational) and social family capital are relatively well-theorized, formation of cultural capital, of individual values and beliefs, and their role for entrepreneurship in market and transition economies lack clear interpretation. Furthermore, the mechanisms of influence of social and cultural capital under different economic conditions on the processes of entrepreneurship have to be explored in more detail.

The changes that occurred during the twenty years are the result of both the transformation of Poland from a transit to a market economy and the action of specific internal and external factors. These include increased migration of active youth to more developed countries as a result of Poland's EU accession. Lack of funds for starting own business, increasing competition in the domestic market, which requires additional knowledge, should also be considered while explaining the differences between 1998 and 2018. In our opinion, given the growing degree of Poland's integration into the European market, the identified trends will intensify in the future.

References

Anderson, A.R. and Miller, C.J. (2003) “Class matters”: Human and Social Capital in the Entrepreneurial Process”, *The Journal of Socio-Economics*, Vol 32, No. 1, pp. 17–36.

Becker, G.S. (1964) *Human Capital: A Theoretical and Empirical Analysis, with Special Reference to Education.* Chicago: University of Chicago Press.

Boruc, W. (2018) “Family, Friends, and Money - What Makes an Entrepreneur? Analysis of Data from Poland, 1993-2013”, *Polish Sociological Review*, Vol 1, pp. 47–60.

Bourdieu, P. (2002) *“The Forms of Capital”*, in Biggart, N. W. (ed.) *Readings in Economic Sociology*. Oxford, UK: Blackwell Publishers Ltd, pp. 280–291.

Chang, E.P.C., Memili, E., Chrisman, J.J., Kellermanns, F.W. and Chua, J.H. (2009) “Family Social Capital, Venture Preparedness, and Start-Up Decisions: A Study of Hispanic Entrepreneurs in New England”, *Family Business Review*, Vol 22, No.3, pp. 279–292.

Coleman, J.S. (1988) “Social Capital in the Creation of Human Capital”, *The American Journal of Sociology*, Vol 94, pp. 95–120.

Coleman, J.S. (1990) *Foundations of Social Theory*. Belknap Press of Harvard University Press.

Davidsson, P. (2016) *Researching entrepreneurship*. New York, NY: Springer Science+Business Media.

Davidsson, P. and Honig, B. (2003) “The role of social and human capital among nascent entrepreneurs”, *Journal of Business Venturing*, Vol 18, No. 3, pp. 301–331.

Demartini, P. and Paoloni, P. (2014) “Defining the Entrepreneurial Capital Construct”, *Chinese Business Review*, Vol 13, No. 11, pp. 668-680

Domański, H. (2000) *On the verge of convergence: social stratification in Eastern Europe*. Central European University Press.

Erikson, T. (2002) “Entrepreneurial capital: the emerging venture”s most important asset and competitive advantage”, *Journal of Business Venturing*, Vol 17, No. 3, pp. 275–290.

Farkas, G. (2017) *Human Capital or Cultural Capital?: Ethnicity and Poverty Groups in an Urban School*. District. Routledge.

Firkin, P. (2001) *Entrepreneurial Capital: A Resource-Based Conceptualisation of the Entrepreneurial Process*. working paper No. 7, Labour Market and Dynamics Research Programme Albany and Palmerston North.

Garnsey, E. (1998) “A Theory of the Early Growth of the Firm”, *Industrial and Corporate Change*, Vol 7, No.3, pp. 523–556.

Gartner, W.B. (1990) “What are we talking about when we talk about entrepreneurship?”, *Journal of Business Venturing*, Vol 5, No.1, pp. 15–28.

Grossman, M. (2000) “Chapter 7 - The Human Capital Model”, in Culyer, A. J. and Newhouse, J. P. (eds.) *Handbook of Health Economics. Handbook of Health Economics*. Elsevier, pp. 347–408.

Haber, S. and Reichel, A. (2007) “The cumulative nature of the entrepreneurial process: The contribution of human capital, planning and environment resources to small venture performance”, *Journal of Business Venturing*, Vol 22, No. 1, pp. 119–145.

Hoffman, J., Hoelscher, M. and Sorenson, R. (2006) “Achieving Sustained Competitive Advantage: A Family Capital Theory”, *Family Business Review*, Vol 19, No. 2, pp. 135–145.

Hoffmann, A.N. (2007) *“A rough guide to entrepreneurship policy”*, in *Handbook of Research on Entrepreneurship Policy*. Cheltenham, UK ; Northampton, MA: Edward Elgar, pp. 140–171.

Lazear, E.P. (2005) “Entrepreneurship”, *Journal of Labor Economics*, Vol 23, No. 4, pp. 649–680.

Manev, I.M., Gyoshev, B.S. and Manolova, T.S. (2005) "The role of human and social capital and entrepreneurial orientation for small business performance in a transitional economy", *International Journal of Entrepreneurship and Innovation Management*, Vol 5, No. 3–4, pp. 298–318.

McMillan, J. and Woodruff, C. (2002) "The Central Role of Entrepreneurs in Transition Economies", *Journal of Economic Perspectives*, 16(3), pp. 153–170.

OECD (1998) *Fostering entrepreneurship: The OECD jobs strategy*. Paris: Organization for Economic Cooperation and Development (OECD).

Osborn, E.A. and Słomczyński, K.M. (2005) *Open for business: the persistent entrepreneurial class in Poland.* IFiS Publishers.

Ployhart, R.E. and Moliterno, T.P. (2011) "Emergence of the Human Capital Resource: A Multilevel Model", *Academy of Management Review*, Vol 36, No.1, pp. 127-150.

Polish Panel Survey POLPAN (2020) *POLPAN: The Integrated Computer Database 1988-1993-1998-2003-2008-2013-2018* principal Investigator: Kazimierz M. Slomczynski, Director of Data Management and Software Development: Zbigniew Sawinski. Warsaw, PL: Polish Panel Survey POLPAN, Institute of Philosophy and Sociology, Polish Academy of Sciences.

Putnam, R.D. (1995) "Bowling Alone: America"s Declining Social Capital", *Journal of Democracy*, Vol 6, No.1, pp. 65–78.

Swader, Christopher S. (2013) *The Capitalist Personality: Face-to-Face Sociality and Economic Change in the Post-Communist World*, Routledge.

Revtiuk, Y. and Malecka, J. (2019) "The formation of entrepreneurial capital: Poland and Ukraine compared", in *ECIE 2019 14th European Conference on Innovation and Entrepreneurship. Academic Conferences and publishing limited*, pp. 862–870.

Rumiński, R. (2017) "*Toward Improving Entrepreneurship Development in Poland: Current Initiatives, Obstacles, and Possible Solutions*", in Sauka, A. and Chepurenko, A. (eds.) *Entrepreneurship in Transition Economies: Diversity, Trends, and Perspectives*. Springer International Publishing, pp. 187-207.

Schultz, T.W. (1961) "Investment in Human Capital", *The American Economic Review*, Vol 51, No. 1, pp. 1–17.

Unger, J.M., Rauch, A., Frese, M. and Rosenbusch, N. (2011) "Human capital and entrepreneurial success: A meta-analytical review", *Journal of Business Venturing*, Vol 26, No. 3, pp. 341–358.

Wdowiak, M.A., Schwarz, E.J., Breitenecker, R.J. and Wright, R.W. (2012) "Linking the cultural capital of the entrepreneur and early performance of new ventures: A cross-country comparison", *Journal of East European Management Studies*, Vol 17, No. 2, pp. 149–183.

Wilson, S. and Adams, A.V. (1994) *Self-Employment for the Unemployed: Experience in OECD and Transitional Economies*, World Bank Discussion Papers 243. World Bank.

Zbierowski, P. (2014) "*Entrepreneurship in Poland: Dynamics and Cross-Country Comparison*", in Hölscher, J. (ed.) *Poland and the Eurozone. Studies in Economic Transition*. London: Palgrave Macmillan UK, pp. 230–263.

Yang, K. (2007) "Individual Social Capital and Its Measurement in Social Surveys", *Survey Research Methods*, Vol 1, No.1, pp. 19–27.

Ревтюк [Revtiuk], Є. [Yevhen] (2015) *Концепція Управління Людським Капіталом Підприємств [The Concept of Human Capital Management at the Enterprises],* IFNUONG, Івано-Франківськ [Ivano-Frankivsk].

Knowledge and Innovation in MSE Companies in Transportation in Cascavel, Brazil

Marlon Ribeiro[1], Jefferson Staduto[1] and Knut Ingar Westeren[2]
[1]UNIOESTE, Campus Toledo, Toledo PR, Brazil
[2]Faculty of Social Sciences, Nord University, Levanger, Norway
marlonribeiro06@gmail.com
Jefferson.staduto@unioeste.br
knut.i.westeren@nord.no
DOI: 10.34190/EIE.20.023

Abstract: The micro and small enterprises (MSEs) have demonstrated fundamental importance for the functioning of all developed economies including BRICS countries like Brazil. According to OECD, they represented in 2016 close to 50% of all employment and 95% of the number of companies and they need higher investment in skills, innovation and tech to boost wages and productivity, (OECD, 2019). On this background we present a project where we analyze the innovation activities of 32 Micro and Small Enterprises (MSEs) in the logistics and transport sector in the city of Cascavel, Parana, Brazil, with special focus of the importance of knowledge transfer for the innovations. Cascavel is located on strategic place in Western Parana, an important Brazilian agribusiness region, in which logistics and transport sector has had key role in the competitiveness for trade. The empirical part of the project was based on data collection at two points in time – before and after an exchange of knowledge had taken place. This gave us the opportunity to study one of the key messages from the OECD – innovations need developments of skills – and we find that in most cases knowledge transfers has an effect on innovations via skill developments.

Keywords: innovations, knowledge transfers, micro and small enterprises, logistics, transportation

1. Introduction

We define Small and Medium sized Enterprises, or SMEs, as enterprises with up to 249 employees. We subsequently define Micro enterprises as firms with 1-9 employees and Small enterprises with 10-49 employees, forming the group we call MSEs. In 2016, SMEs accounted for 99% of all businesses and between 50% and 60% of value added in the OECD economic area, while the MSEs represented close to 50% of all employment and 95% of the number of all enterprises in the OECD area, OECD (2019). According to OECD, "MSEs are driving job growth, but need higher investment in skills, innovation and tech to boost wages and productivity.", OECD (2019, p. 5). Clearly, this group has demonstrated fundamental importance for the functioning of all developed economies including BRICS countries like Brazil.

In this project the aim is to study the relationships and linkages between knowledge and innovation in transportation sector and this raises several theoretical approaches. The first is that transport is a service sector and the innovation theory has to be adapted, considering that services (in the normal case) are produced and consumed at the same time. We will discuss the consequences of this further in the theory chapter. The second consideration is that innovations in transport are a multi-facetted feature. We have had a rapid and radical development in Information Technology Systems (ITS) in the transportation sector linked to the fundamental changes the Internet has brought like tracking systems and interactive maps. This has changed storage of goods for production from weeks to days/hours and thereby also reduced costs considerably.

The third consideration is about the technology and innovations of transportation vehicles, boats, planes and trains. The developments here are strongly influenced by environmental policies, plans and restrictions and we have seen innovative solutions here, like electric ferries transporting cars and people across fjords in Norway, that were inaccesible just a few years ago. The fourth consideration is the link between knowledge, technology, and innovations and here we have several examples revealing that new innovative initiatives and solutions demand higher skills and knowledge levels. It is mainly this perspective that is the focus of this article, but it is not possible to give a satisfactory treatment of this without being aware of the first three considerations.

To analyze innovation activities many methods and data collection procedures have been suggested. In this study we have considered different tools like the PINTEC (Brazilian's innovation research) questionnaire, the Berreyre model, and the Minnesota Innovation Survey methodology but chose The Innovation Radar because we found that the focus of this tool gave the best match to the innovations the companies emphasized. The

Innovation Radar also gave the most relevant framework for an analysis of links between knowledge transfers and innovations. The fundament of the project was based on data collection from two points in time – before and after an exchange of knowledge had taken place.

The research question in this article revolves around the analysis of how transfers of knowledge can influence innovations in the service sector by using transportation as the empirical case. The article will continue by looking at relevant theories of innovation and relationships to knowledge transfers. In the next part we will discuss different methodological procedures for operationalizing innovations and how to build our data into the model. The following section explores the results we find from the analyzed data and in the last section we give our final considerations and conclusions.

2. Theoretical background and literature review

Our way of looking at innovations starts, like most others, with Schumpeter (1934) and his ideas that (1) the development of the capitalist economy is based on a disequilibrium basis, (2) his definitions of innovations in five key elements where product, process and market innovations are the most important, and (3) the idea that "creative destruction" is the fundament for economic change. Schumpeter is looked at as contributing mainly to industrial innovative theory, but we must be aware that in his book "The Theory of Economic Development", Schumpeter (1934) he also spoke about innovations in the transport sector.

Schumpeter has been followed up by several writers like Freeman (1988) and Perez (1985) with emphasis on the importance of the endogenous nature of the innovative process. They underline the importance of the firm to develop their routines, not only in their company, but also in accordance with market structures, institutions and regions/nations.

Penrose (1959) and Nelson and Winter (2005) address the resource base and evolutionary logic as necessary to explain innovations in the capitalist economy. Dosi (1982, 1984) develops this further by emphasizing the learning process and the ability of the company to transfer knowledge as a part of the innovation process. Later developments, Westeren et al. (2018) show that an important part of the knowledge of the company is tacit and social, influenced by competitors, knowledge institutions and technological economic developments.

The study of innovations in the service sector increased in strength in the 1990's with founding work by Barras (1986), and Gallouj and Weistein (1997) , among others, introduced the concept of the "Reverse Product Cycle" as a characteristic innovation in services based on the observation that developments in services first started with improved efficiency, then improved quality and then new services based on innovative initiatives. Another approach was based on the fact that service production takes place in subsectors with very different production structures and market conditions. Physical services like transport, retail trade and hotels and restaurants have relatively low qualifications of labor, but we have seen large innovations based on advanced utilization of IT like in e. g. transport, which is the focus of this article. Another large group is called human services, where we have the health and social activities of both public and private sectors, education and research, the FIRE sectors (finance, insurance and real estate) and KIBS (knowledge intensive business services). It is often argued from a more systemic point of view that human services as an innovator itself and as an aide to innovations elsewhere, is one fundament for productivity of countries. The service part of Information technology; IT, is often singled out as a group of its own in the service sector, see Fagerberg, Mowery and Nelson (2005) and Hipp and Grupp (2005) but the success of most innovative actions in the service activities mentioned above is based on a productive integration from the IT services.

Service innovations come in a large variety because of great dispersion in products and processes and because service activities are to a large extent integrated with several other service and/or manufacturing activities. One fundamental characteristics of service production is that production and consumption take place within the same time frame. This means that the process and the product are linked together – the restaurant experience starts when you come inside the room, enjoy the smell from the grill, and see the bridge of sighs (in Venice) through the window. This example illustrates that innovations in services often are complex and evaluated (at least partly) through human experiences. In this project we deal with transportation which has a quite well-defined outcome, but innovations in transportation are often motivated to be productive for customers. Several writers like Djellal et al. (2003), Drejer (2004), Gallouj and Weinstein (1997) and Jensen and Westeren (2012) discuss how to establish a system of criteria to decide when an innovation can be defined as completed.

3. Road transportation and possibilities for innovations in Brazil

According to the National Transport Confederation in Brazil, CNT (2017), the distribution of total Brazilian cargo transport by method is roadways: 61.1%, railways: 21.2%, water transport: 13.1%, and air transport with 0.40%. The Brazilian economy is heavily dependent on processing of raw materials so an efficient transport system to secure supply chains is vital to the functioning of the Brazilian economy, IPEA (2016).

The transport services take place through both the companies' own fleet of transport operations and the contracting of carrier services which the logistics managers of the firms combine to reduce costs. The developments later years have favored the entry into the market of independent companies with specialized transport services, Bowersox, Closs and Cooper (2007) and IPEA (2016).

The need for innovation is present in several areas of transport companies and logistics operators. There are several activities capable of influencing the competitiveness of segments, such as the provision of services, organizational processes, marketing and market actions and supply chain. Actions include tasks for optimizing storage, separation, movement, and transportation operations. These innovations can be technological, linked to software and information technology, or simple tools for control and management (Ribeiro and Freitas, 2011).

The main innovations acquired or realized by service provider companies are related to warehouse management (production structure), transport management (types of services offered, fleet, freight, routes), planning of business resources (financial, human, quality, sales), inventory management, customer service, project/solution development and process control (Martins et al., 2011; Ribeiro and Freitas, 2011).

4. Methods to measure innovations

According to Fagerberg et al. (2007) and Westeren (2012) we have a debate on how the innovation concept shall be interpreted which again gives rise to discussions about how we generate methods for an evaluation of innovations in firms. We find a starting point for a definition of innovation in the Oslo Manual published by the OECD, which has been updated several times and the latest version now is OECD (2018).

The data collection in this work is based on Arroniz, Wolcott and Sawhney (2006) and is called The Innovation Radar. Its main feature is the idea of visualizing business innovation in defined dimensions. The tool's objective is to direct innovation actions in companies in order to reduce the waste of good business opportunities. Innovation Radar considered discussions with managers about fundamental efforts to maintain a cycle of innovation generation in these companies Arroniz, Wolcott and Sawhney (2006).

The Innovation Radar is an assessment tool for business innovations suitable for measuring the degree of innovation in small companies and is discussed and used in many connections, see e. g. Bachmann and Destefani (2008), Garcia (2008), Carvalho, et al. (2015) and Claudino (2015). According to Arroniz, Wolcott and Sawhney (2006) the innovation can be seen in 12 dimensions which correspond to four primary axes. Our model is extended with one more dimension:

<u>Definition of dimension:</u>
Offerings: Develop innovative new products or services.
Platform: Use common components or building blocks to create derivative offerings.
Solutions: Create integrated and customized offerings that solve end-to-end customer problems.
Customers: Discover unmet customer needs or identify underserved customer segments.
Customer Experience: Redesign customer interactions across all touch points and all moments of contact.
Value Capture: Redefine how company gets paid or create innovative new revenue streams.
Processes: Redesign core operating processes to improve efficiency and effectiveness.
Organization: Change form, function or activity scope of the firm.
Supply Chain: Think differently about sourcing and fulfillment.
Presence: Create new distribution channels or innovative points of presence, including the places where offerings can be bought or used by customers.
Networking: Create network-centric intelligent and integrated offerings.
Brand: Leverage a brand into new domains.
Innovative Ambience: The support received in the generation of business innovations.

5. Data collection and analysis

5.1 Introduction

This transportation sector is, in general, of great importance for the functioning of economic activities, in Brazil the transport segment accounted for 4.2% of GDP in 2015 with approximately 60% of cargo handling carried out by land routes (IPEA, 2017). Cascavel has a geographical position that stimulates entrepreneurship in the transportation sector. The city is located in the western region of the state of Paraná, in a roadway nucleus where the supply of grain and other agricultural products flows to the states of Santa Catarina, São Paulo, Mato Grosso do Sul and Mato Grosso, as well as to important coastal ports like Curitiba, and to other countries such as Paraguay and Argentina. This situation requires a continuous demand for trucks and services related to it. In 2017 the truck fleet associated with Cascavel numbered 8,130 vehicles, representing approximately 25% of the fleet in western Paraná (Schulze, 2013; IPARDES, 2018).

Logistics operators have great incentive for reducing transportation costs, as they generate economies of scale by sharing their capabilities and resources with multiple customers. However, this sector has challenges to innovation due to specific characteristics, such as low technology use and reduced range of services (Ribeiro and Ferreira, 2002).

Given the importance of the situation for regional development, this project will be focused on the development of innovative efforts by MSEs in the transport sector of the city of Cascavel-PR. The research question that forms the basis for data collection and analysis is:

What is the relevance of the transfer of knowledge in the generation of innovation in MSEs in the transport sector?

The choice of the transport sector for the study is centered around the hypothesis that SMEs have difficulties in absorbing knowledge and practicing it in business routines thereby hampering changes of routines that can be developed into innovations.

The research question can be divided in the following way:

- 1. What characterizes the innovative situation in a select number of participating MSEs before a process of knowledge transfers takes place?
- 2. How can we identify knowledge transfers within these firms?
- 3. How can we analyze the alteration of the innovative situation after the transfer of knowledge has taken place and has this transfer of knowledge changed the innovative performance of the firms?
- 4. How can we explain possible variations in innovative behavior between the firms?

5.2 Data collection and analysis

According to IPARDES (2018) there were a total of 615 SME enterprises registered in the transport sector in Cascavel-PR in the research period from 2015 to 2017. The sample studied comprised 32 MSEs registered in this category selected because they were willing to participate in the research project and because they were participants of the Local Innovation Agents (ALI) program. The ALI program was created by Brazilian Micro and Small Business Support Service (SEBRAE) and National Council for Scientific and Technological Development (CNPq) and it was centered on knowledge transfer and incentives for companies to improve in innovations (SEBRAE/CNPq, 2013).

The ALI program conducted a measurement of the level of innovation of the company when entering the program in May 2015, reflected in the first data collection, R1. During the program period the companies were encouraged to innovate using knowledge transfers from competent professionals as a part of the program. The firms' actions were monitored monthly by the program. After the period of implementation of knowledge transfers for improvements and innovations the companies did a second diagnosis in June 2016, measuring their developments, reflected in the second data collection, R2,. The 32 companies carried out 222 innovation actions between R1 and R2 covering all dimensions of the Innovation Radar. Figure 1 shows an overview of the distribution and frequency of activities.

In general, it is expected that the larger number of tasks performed during the transfer of knowledge, the larger possibility of implementing innovations. The measurement of innovation of the companies is done by using the Innovation Radar tool as earlier explained. Each dimension is given a score between one and five, five being the maximum degree of innovation that the company can achieve (Bachmann and Destefani, 2008) measured between the points of time R1 and R2. A paired Wilcoxon test was performed in order to analyze whether the transfer of knowledge had effect on innovations. The innovation scores at R1, Radar 1, is shown in Figure 1, and a comparison of the results from R1 to R2 (Radar 2) is shown in Figure 2. Figure 3 shows the innovative behavior of companies by dimensions of The Innovation Radar.

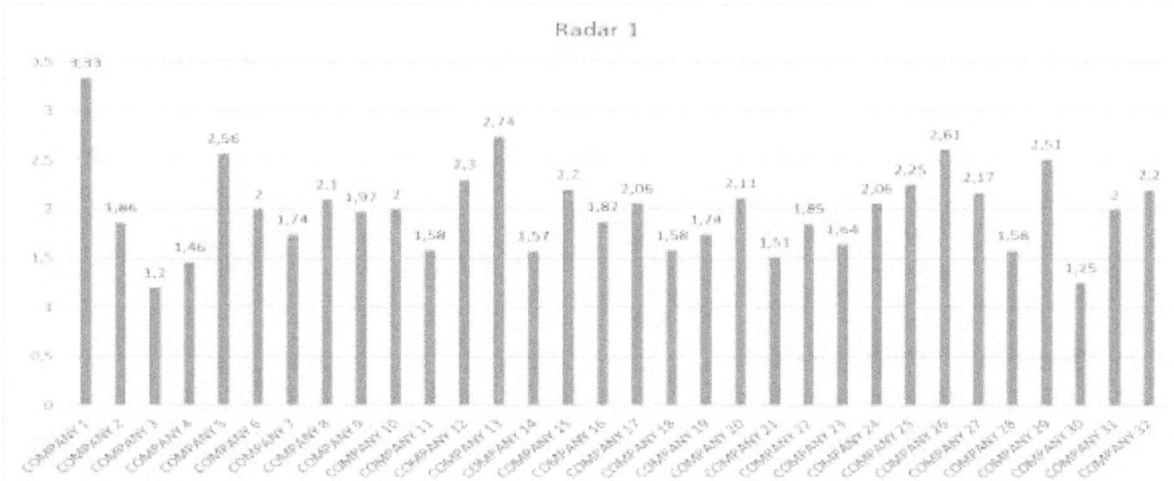

Source: Research data from the project.

Figure 1: Results of the innovative situation of the companies at the start of the project R1

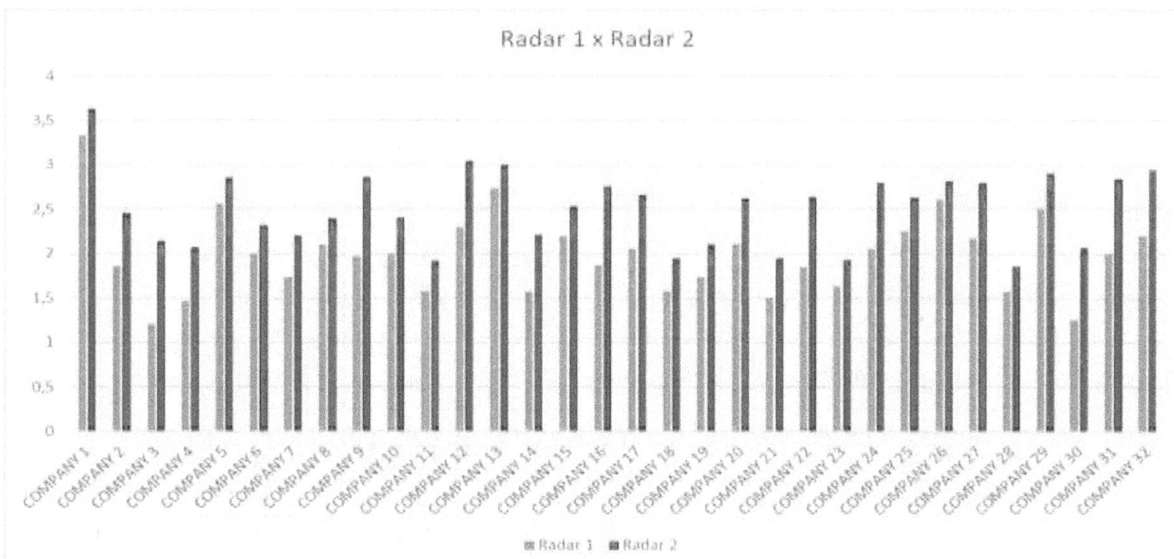

Source: Research data from the project.

Figure 2: Comparing the results of the innovative situation of the companies from R1 (May 2015) to R2 (June 2016)

The results are in line with Silva, Menezes Filho and Komatsu (2016) and show that the transport sector part of the services sector is not very innovative. Barbosa and Sousa (2011) consider that transport companies need to increase the degree of both internal competitiveness and external elements to innovate. Considering that a large percentage of the Brazilian fleet is owned by self-employed individuals with their own vehicles, this partly explains the low degree of innovation. Based on Figure 2 we observe that the transfer of knowledge has influenced the degree of innovation in all companies. However, it is important to highlight the differences, some firms are more impacted than others, indicating that the transfer of knowledge and the implementation of innovations are not homogeneous.

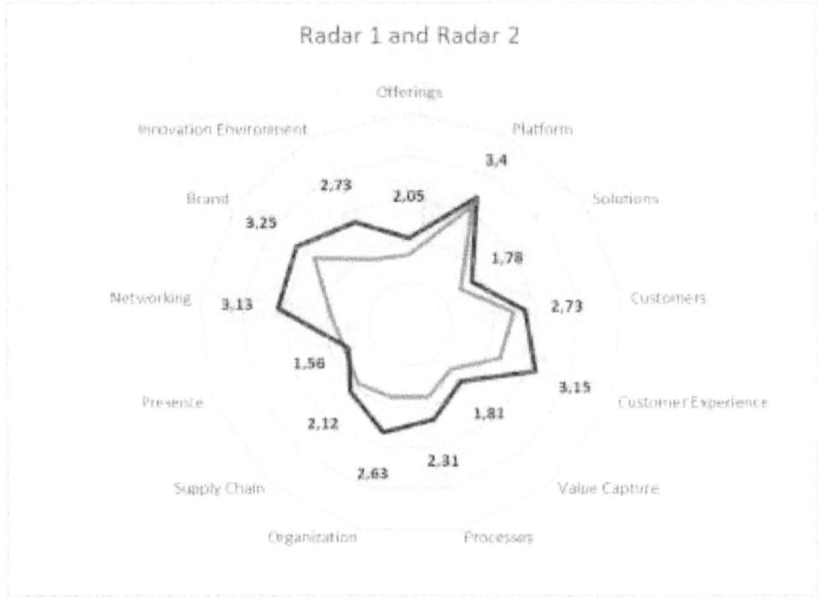

Source: Research data from the project.

Figure 3: Innovative behavior of companies by dimension of the Innovation Radar from R1 to R2

Positive changes occurred in almost all dimensions, see Figure 3. The exception was **Presence** which indicates that the companies did not create any new distribution channels or find new distribution places where offerings could be bought or used by customers. Also, the **Platform** dimension changed very little from R1 to R2. This means that the firms to a very small degree used common components or building blocks to create derivative offerings.

Table 1: Results of innovative behavior of the companies from R1 to R2

Dimension	Radar 1	Radar 2	Absolute change	Change in %
Offer	1,64	2,05	0,41	25,00
Platform	3,18	3,4	0,22	6,91
Solutions	1,46	1,78	0,32	21,91
Customers	2,45	2,73	0,28	11,42
Customer experience	2,25	3,15	0,90	40,00
Value capture	1,43	1,81	0,38	26,57
Processes	1,77	2,31	0,54	30,50
Organization	1,78	2,63	0,85	47,75
Supply chain	1,87	2,12	0,25	13,36
Presence	1,65	1,56	-0,09	-5,40
Network	1,88	3,13	1,25	66,48
Brand	2,75	3,25	0,5	18,18
Innovative Ambience	1,74	2,73	0,99	56,89
Global Innovation Degree (GID)	1,98	2,50	0,52	26,26

Source: Research data from the project.

Table 1 shows the variation of the degree of innovation between Radar 1 and Radar 2 and the changes were large in several dimensions. 7 dimensions had a variation of more than 25%. This also reinforces the notion of low innovative potential before the transfer of knowledge. The Global Innovation Degree (GID), representing the average of all dimensions, gives an absolute value of 2,50 and a change of 26,26%. In the literature about the Innovation Radar, Arroniz, Wolcott and Sawhney (2006) an average score of 3,0 is viewed as the level to characterize systemic innovation. Even though the change in percent from R1 to R2 is quite high, the situation for the group as a whole is still quite low in terms of innovative potential.

Table 2: Results from Wilcoxon test (Z Value) about variation of the degree of innovation between Radar 1 and Radar 2

Dimension	Z Value	Prob. Statistics	Significance
Offer	-3,310	0,0009	*
Platform	-1,710	0,0870	**
Solutions	-2,820	0,0048	*
Customers	-2,200	0,0200	*
Customer experience	-4,370	< 0,0001	*
Value capture	-2,470	0,0130	*
Processes	-4,180	< 0,0001	*
Organization	-4,560	< 0,0001	*
Supply chain	-2,000	0,0450	*
Presence	0,099	0,9211	**
Network	-3,640	0,0003	*
Brand	-2,920	0,0035	*
Innovative Ambience	-4,930	< 0.0001	*

*: Z value significant on 5% level (or better) **: Z value not significant on 5% level.

We chose a (non-parametric) Wilcoxon test to analyze dimensional averages because then we do not need to make any assumptions about the distributions of the results for the dimensions. Table 2 shows that we have significant results for 11 of 13 dimensions. This indicates that the ALI program to a reasonable degree fulfilled its objective to significantly improve the innovative activities of the companies from R1 to R2.

Regarding the dimension **Offererings** (Develop innovative new products or services), a study conducted by Barbosa and Sousa (2011) for 400 small transport companies showed that these companies do not feel encouraged to create transports that contribute to the diversification of services. For the **Customers** dimension (Discover unmet customer needs or identify underserved customer segments) the results converge with the analyses of Martins et al. (2011) and Barbosa and Souza (2011) who argue that transport companies prioritize the fields that generate greater satisfaction for consumers. With regard to the **Process** dimension the results are consistent with the fact that innovation in the service sector is closely associated with process innovation (Gallouj and Weinstein, 1997; Djellal and Gallouj, 2005; Lubeck et al., 2012). For the **Presence** dimension we observed that the transfer of knowledge did not influence the indexes of innovation yet the opposite was found for **Network** and **Brand**. The result for the **Presence** dimension was expected because this was the only dimension where the innovation index fell after the transfer of knowledge. This may be related to stable points of sale and the recession of the Paraná economy and the transportation sector specifically during the research period. For the dimension **Innovative Ambience** (The support received in the generation of business innovations), it is likely that the transfer of knowledge contributed by the ALI program and the relative low cost of implementation stimulated innovations, see Stal, Nohara and Chagas (2014).

6. Conclusions and suggestions for further research

This project has analyzed the influence of knowledge transfer on the degree of innovation in a group of 32 MSEs in the transport sector in the city of Cascavel-PR. The presentation of R1 data showed low innovative behavior of companies, only one was classified as occasional innovator with an index above 3, all the others had a low innovative potential according to our classification system. In general, the transfer of knowledge increased the index of innovation in all companies and in almost all dimensions. Based on the paired Wilcoxon test the transfer of knowledge was statistically significant for 11 of 13 dimensions.

Based on this work, it is concluded that it is valid for SMEs to seek knowledge and apply them in their business routines, and use this knowledge to change routines, which is a sound start for innovative actions. The project showed that the transfer of knowledge proved to be an effective way to increase the competitiveness of companies and create bases for supporting economic development. This also supports the view that an institutional apparatus is important in the innovative process of business development and this project contributed to the view that the objective of transferring knowledge in a concrete way can be achieved. Sometimes even the scarcity of innovations in small businesses is significant and quite simple and cheap activities can have a positive impact on the operation of the businesses and, consequently, on the market.

Continuous research is needed in this field – it is necessary to get a more detailed view on how the knowledge processes take place and how transfer of knowledge has both barriers and enablers inside firms, between firms and between firms and professional services providers. It is also therefore necessary to study larger samples of firms especially in the lower knowledge segments of the service sectors like transport, hotels and restaurants, and retail.

References

Arroniz, I, Wolcott, R.C. and Sawhney, M. (2006) "The 12 Different Ways for Companies to Innovate", *MIT Sloan Management Review*, Vol 47, No. 3, pp 75-81.

Bachmann, D.L. and Destefani, J.H. (2008) *Metodologia para Estimar o Grau de Inovação nas MPE*, Seminário Nacional de Parques Tecnológicos e Incubadoras de Empresas, Brazil, Aracaju.

Barbosa, E.D.S. and Sousa, C.V. (2011) *Infraestrutura Logística em Transporte Rodoviário de Carga Fracionada: um Estudo de Caso em uma Transportadora Mineira*, Paper read at XXXIth Encontro Nacional de Engenharia da Produção, Brazil, Belo Horizonte.

Barras, R. (1986) "Towards a theory of innovation in services", *Research Policy*, Vol 15, pp 161-173.

Bowersox, D. J., Closs, D. J. and Cooper, M. B. (2007) *Gestão da Cadeia de Suprimentos de Logística*, Elsevier, Rio de Janeiro.

Carvalho, G.D.G., et al. (2015) "Radar da Inovação como ferramenta para o alcance de vantagem competitiva para micro e pequenas empresas", *Revista de Administração e Inovação*, Vol 12, No. 4, pp 162-18.

Claudino, T.B. (2015) *Evolução, Facilitadores e Dificultadores da Inovação na Micro e Pequena Empresa: um Estudos dos Empreendimentos Participantes do Programa ALI em Picos – PI*, Federal University of Ceara, Post-Graduate in Management, Master's thesis, Fortaleza.

CNT. (2017) *Transporte Rodoviário: Desempenho do Setor, Infraestrutura e Investimentos*, CNT, Brasília.

Djellal, F. and Gallouj, F. (2005) "Mapping Innovation Dynamics in Hospitals", *Research Policy*, Vol 34, pp 817-835.

Djellal, F., et al. (2003) "Revising the definition of research and development in the light of the specificities of services", *Science and Public Polic*, Vol 30, No.6, pp 415–429.

Dosi, G. (1982) "Technological Paradigms and Technological Trajectories: a Suggested Interpretation of the Determinants and Directions of Technical Change", *Research Policy* 11, pp 147-162.

Dosi, G. (1984) *Technical Change and Industrial Transformation*, St. Martin's Press, New York.

Drejer, I. (2004) "Identifying Innovation in Surveys of Services: a Schumpeterian Perspective" *Research Policy*, Vol 33, pp 551–562.

Fagerberg, J.; Mowery, D.C. and Nelson, R.R. (Eds) (2005) *The Oxford handbook of innovation*, Oxford university press, Oxford, 2005.

Freeman, C (1988) *Introduction*, In Dosi, G. et al. (Orgs), *Technical Change and Economic Theory*, Pinter Publishers, London.

Gallouj, F. and Weinstein, O. (1997) "Innovation in Services", *Research policy*, Vol 26, No. 4-5, pp 537-556.

Hipp, Christiane and Grupp, Hariolf. (2005) "Innovation in The Service Sector: the Demand for Service-Specific Innovation Measurement Concepts and Typologies", *Research Policy* Vol 34 No.4, pp 517-535.

IPARDES. (2018) *Caderno Estatístico Município de Cascavel*, [online], IPARDES, Curitiba, http://www.ipardes.gov.br/cadernos/MontaCadPdf1.php?Municipio=85800

IPEA. (2016) *Logística e Transportes no Brasil: uma análise do programa de investimentos 2013-2017 em rodovias e ferrovias*, [online], IPEA, Rio de Janeiro, https://www.ipea.gov.br/portal/images/stories/PDFs/relatoriopesquisa/161026_relatorio_pesquisa_logistica_transportes_brasil.pdf

IPEA. (2017) *IPEA DATA*, [online], IPEA, Rio de janeiro, http://www.ipeadata.gov.br/Default.aspx

Jensen, H. S. and Westeren, K. I. (2013) *The role of public sector innovations in the knowledge economy*, In *Public Management in the Twenty-first Century*, pp 251-267, Universitetsforlaget, Oslo.

Lubeck, R.M., et al. (2012) "Inovação em Serviços de Transporte Público", *Revista Organizações em Contexto* Vol. 8, No. 15. pp 65-86.

Martins, R.S, et al. (2011) "Gestão dos Transportes Orientada para Clientes: Nível de Serviço Desejado e Percebido", *Revista de Administração Contemporânea*, Vol 15, No. 6, pp 1100-1119.

Nelson, R. R. and S. G. Winter (1982) *An Evolutionary Theory of Economic Change*, Belknap Press, Cambridge.

OECD (2019) *SME and Entrepreneurship Outlook 2019*, OECD Publishing, Paris.

OECD (2018) OSLO Manual: *Proposed Guidelines for Collecting And Interpreting Technological Innovation Data*, OECD, Paris.

Oliveira, M.R.G. et al. (2014) Mensurando a inovação por meio do grau de inovação setorial e do característico setorial de inovação", *Revista de Administração e Inovação*, Vol 11, No. 1, pp 114-137.

Penrose, E.T. (1959) *The theory of the growth of the firm*, John Wiley & Sons, New York.

Perez, C. (1985) "Microelectronics, long waves and world structural change: New perspectives for developing countries", *Journal World Development*, Vol 13, pp 441-463.

Ribeiro, P.C.C. and Ferreira, K.A. (2002*) Logística e Transportes: uma Discussão Sobre os Modais de Transporte e o Panorama Brasileiro*, Paper read at XXIIth Encontro Nacional de Engenharia de Produção, Brazil, Curitiba, October.

Ribeiro, P.C. and Freitas, R.M. (2011) *Logística e Transportes: uma Discussão sobre a Terceirização e os Prestadores de Serviços*, Paper read at XXXIth Encontro Nacional de Engenharia de Produção, Brazil, Belo Horizonte, October.

Schulze, C.A. (2013) "O Turismo de Negócios e Eventos em Cascavel (Paraná, Brasil): Oportunidade para Expansão e Consolidação do Segmento na Cidade", *Turismo & Sociedade* Vol. 6, No. 2, pp 345-363.

Schumpeter, J.A. [1934] (1997) *Theory of economic development*, Routledge, New York.

SEBRAE/CNPq. (2013) *Cadernos de Inovação em Pequenos Negócios: comércio e serviços*, [online], SEBRAE/CNPq, Brasília.

Silva, C. M., Menezes Filho, N. and Komatsu, B. (2016) Uma *abordagem sobre o setor de serviços na economia brasileira*, [online], Insper, São Paulo. https://www.insper.edu.br/wp-content/uploads/2018/09/Abordagem-sobre-Setor-Servicos-Economia-Brasileira.pdf

Stal, E., Nohara, J.J. and Chagas, M.F. (2014) "Os Conceitos da Inovação Aberta e o Desempenho de Empresas Brasileiras", *Revista de Administração e Inovação*, Vol 11, No. 2, pp 295-320.

Westeren, K.I. (2012) *Foundations of the Knowledge Economy*, Cheltenham: E. Elgar, Northampton.

Westeren, K.I. et al. (2018) *Competitiveness and Knowledge: An International Comparison of Traditional Firms*, Routledge, London.

Evaluating the Impact of Small and Medium Business on the Innovative Activity of Regions in Russia

Dmitrii Rodionov, Olga Nadezhina and Sergei Yalimov
Graduate School of Industrial Economics6Peter the Great St. Petersburg Polytechnic University (SPbPU), Russia
rodionov_dm@spbstu.ru
nadezhina_os@spbstu.ru
yalimov74@mail.ru
DOI: 10.34190/EIE.20.218

Abstract: This paper studies the dependence between the innovative activity of a region (evidence from federal districts of the Russian Federation) and the development indicators of small and medium business in this region. It was revealed that small and medium business (SMB) operates in a very competitive environment and therefore needs to get involved in innovative development. At the same time, however, it lacks enough financial means to generate innovations. In this research it was established which of the above properties of SMB is of primary importance for Russian enterprises, and areas for further research were formulated in order to learn about the dependence between the innovative activity of a region and the development indicators of its small and medium enterprises.

Keywords: innovations, innovative activity of a region, small and medium business

1. Introduction

Entrepreneurship is one of the key elements of a society's economic life. The innovation sphere is mostly responsible for the successful development of entrepreneurship, something which is especially true for small and medium business. At the same time The SME sector is a major contributor to technical innovation and new product developments (Ayandibu A. O., Houghton J. (2017).

Researchers from many countries pay attention to how various aspects of small and medium business influence the development of individual countries and areas (Ribeiro-Soriano D. 2017; Kubičkova L., Moravkova M., Tuzova M. et al. 2017; Hillary, R. (Ed.). 2017; Leonidou L. C., Christodoulides P., Kyrgidou 2017; Distanont A.,Khongmalai O. 2018; Demidenko D., Malevskaia-Malevich E., Dubolazova Y. 2018; Shinohara M., Fisher D. 2019). This highlights the relevance of this paper.

The study is aimed at learning how the development of SMB influences the innovative activity indicators at a federal districts level. To achieve this goal the following objectives were set:

- using a review of regulatory acts and studies conducted by foreign and Russian authors on the development of small and medium business in order to identify and substantiate both the factors and the resulting indicators used for modelling;
- to build an econometric model which can describe and evaluate the relationship between the coefficient of inventive activity in the regions of Russia and the headcount in small and medium enterprises;
- to determine areas for further research on the matter.

2. Theoretical framework and literature review

A small enterprise is a firm which is not dominant in its field while the proprietor is an independent owner who manages a small number of subordinates in comparison with other firms operating in the same industry. Medium enterprises are in between small and large companies. As a rule, a medium enterprise is one that is run by a manager who reports to the shareholders and which is within the upper limit of ultimate values set for small business.

Different countries have their own criteria for classifying companies as small and medium-sized businesses. In Russia, as in Europe, the segmentation of enterprises is carried out in accordance with the staff headcount either turnover. In Russia, the following limit values are set: ≥ 15 staff headcount with a turnover ≥ € 1.6 m (the conversion was made at the exchange rate on the date the relevant law was adopted) - micro-enterprises; ≥ 100 staff headcount with a turnover ≥ € 10.5 m - small enterprises, ≥ 250 staff headcount with a turnover ≥ € 26.2 m

- medium-sized enterprises. These criteria for Europe are the following: micro-enterprise - ≥ 10 staff headcount with a turnover ≥ € 2 m, small enterprises -≥ 10 staff headcount with a turnover ≥€ 10 m, medium-sized enterprises ≥ 250 staff headcount with a turnover ≥€ 50 m. Thus, it is possible to conclude that the criteria are mostly similar and the results of this study may be compared with other survey conducted in EU countries.

The activities of most small enterprises have a social burden and bring together socially vulnerable groups of the population (Konnikov, E.A., Konnikova, O.A., Negashev, D.S. et al (2018). Therefore, today, the role of small enterprises is to support the efforts that vulnerable groups of the population make in order to survive. Small and medium enterprises are a traditional and important part of the economy in virtually all countries, including industrially developed ones. It is natural that the development of small enterprises in various countries is specific in its own way due to historical traditions and to the role and place of small enterprises in the economy of a country. As a rule, it depends on the achieved level of concentration and industrialization of the economy and on the goals that small and medium business works towards in the current social and economic conditions. Small and medium business has a number of advantages, which are objective prerequisites for the important role that small business plays in the system of reproduction. These are (Peredera, Zh.S., Gritsenko, T.S., Teryaeva, A.S. 2018) increased flexibility and promptness in decision-making, receptiveness to innovations, fast adaptation to external impacts, quick financial turnover, and a high level of specialization in production and labour. At the same time the main constraints of SMMEs were customer dependency, skills and knowledge acquisition through training, poor learning attitude and networking because of their tradition of being insular and autonomous (Laforet S, Tann J ,2006). The place and role of SMB in the innovative development of the region is reflected in the article by Rudskaia I. (2017).

An integral part of any research is studying the factors influencing the variables under consideration. In particular, the author Pinkovetskaya, Yu.S. (2018) carried out research into the dependence of the production output (turnover) of small and medium enterprises on the level of investment in fixed capital and the amounts of the employees' salaries in these enterprises on the basis of official statistics for 82 regions of Russia (for 2016). The author proved that today the need for increasing the development rates of SMB in the Russian Federation is quite high, which brings up the question of determining the growth reserves of small and medium enterprises on the scale of every region of the country. Four business functions were developed (by types of enterprises) to show the dependence of SMB turnover on investments in fixed capital and employee salaries by Russian regions. As a result, the relationship between SMB turnovers and these factors was identified and, additionally, it was proven that the economy of the country's regions did not reach saturation with the products of SMB. Learning from the experience of Asian countries, it was suggested that in order to quickly increase the production output of SMB in Russia, it would be reasonable to ensure the simultaneous growth of volume in terms of both of the factors under consideration (i.e. investment in fixed capital and salary amounts). Increasing one of the factors of the production function improves the conditions for using the other. With a growth in production output in SMB the possibility of replacing one factor with the other is increasing. The factor of employee salaries in all production functions affects the turnover more that the factor of investment in fixed capital.

The other way to research the phenomenon is to analyze the programs of social support and innovation in the development of small and medium business such as was carried out in paper (Ruchkina, G., Melnichuk, M., Frumina, S., Mentel, G. 2017). It was revealed that the documents adopted in the Russian Federation to project and plan government support and innovations in the development of small and medium business lack consistency. They are not suitable for harmonization, and they contain various values for the same indicator and have no explanations or economic grounds for assumptions and deviations from the projections. This problem is one of the reasons why budget funds are used ineffectively, and it misleads potential users of the program documents. None of the federal subjects studied in the paper faces the objective of monitoring and supporting young entrepreneurs (individuals aged younger than 30). The authors of the paper highlight that the program documents should include not only the amount of financing of specific actions but also a detailed substantiation of the latter. Moreover, special attention should be drawn to the programs which have no orientation on a small-scale prospect of activity with an indicated timeframe. The authors Nikolova, L.V., Kuporov, J.J., Rodionov, D.G. (2015) conclude that there is a need to clarify and specify the objectives of the state programs as well as to determine the procedures for making them consistent with the priorities of economic development, innovations, and socioeconomic projections stipulated in the position papers and sectoral strategies.

In order to evaluate the opportunities for the development of small and medium enterprises in Russia, it is worth paying attention to the experience of other countries. Thus, for example, the authors Luo P., Song D. Chen B

(2020) present the results of the opportunities that they studied for developing small and medium business at the expense of government subsidies and through interaction between the banking and tax systems using the example of China. They paid special attention to two investment strategies and estimated the amount of losses that may be expected when establishing a partnership with state authorities. In particular, a model was created to implement investment and financial strategies to develop SMB. The model was built to consider such factors as the interrelation between banking and tax systems and the partnership between public and private sectors of the economy. Thus, in the opinion of the authors, the relationship of the banking and tax systems of the economy can be used as a tool for developing SMB, which can mitigate the problem of insufficient investment in times of market instability. Furthermore, in comparison to net private lending, the above factors also impact increasing the value of a firm. They also reduce the amount of financial leverage and the probability of bankruptcy of an organization. The study identified the structure of lending to SMB to be dependent on the amount of the tax rate, the distribution of investment costs, the credit multiplier and volatility.

Principally new solutions to the problem of developing small and medium business in the country are considered in paper Pletnev D., Barkhatov, V. (2016) from the position of the impact made by the managers of an organization on the performance of the enterprise. The methodology of this study is based on the analysis of the results of a survey in which about 250 executives of Russian companies took part. The survey was aimed at studying such topics as: the key success factors of an enterprise, barriers preventing business from developing successfully and the salary level of employees at the enterprise in comparison to the income of the top executive. According to the survey, an overwhelming majority of executives believe that employees, together with the professional and personal qualities of the company's owner, are a key success factor of small and medium business; there is a direct correlation between the level of remuneration and the success of SMB. The authors also found that the social responsibility of an executive positively influences the success of small and medium business; a relative optimum of remuneration was determined (from 20,000 to 25,000 rubles) as well as the difference in income (from 10 to 15 times), which can be necessary for an enterprise to operate successfully.

Kersten R., Harms J., Liket K. et al (2017). analyze the relationship between innovation at the level of firms and the external financing of small and medium enterprises. To conduct the research study, a series of 13,430 companies from Eastern European and Central Asian countries was used. The obtained results show how important it is that the government have a wider formalized financial system which is capable of taking care of entrepreneurs at different stages of the development of small firms. Official suppliers of financial services such as banks and micro-financial companies should expand their capabilities in servicing SMB so as to stimulate the growth of business. Formalizing the activity of informal financial institutions will not only facilitate access of SMB to financing, but it will also improve their own work, which, in turn, increases the availability of inexpensive financing for innovative SMB. The problem of financing SMB is also discussed in paper by Rodionov D.G., Nadezhina O.S., Titarenko D.S. (2016), whose authors carried out a systematic review and multidimensional meta-analysis of the existing measures to facilitate access to financial resources for SMB. The following results were obtained. Firstly, very few evaluations of the SMB financing programs use the same strict experimental methods that are applied in the research studies of micro-financing. Secondly, most of the evaluations of the SMB financing programs consider neither the side effects for other enterprises nor the impact on the employees. Thirdly, in the authors' opinion, the impact of SMB financing on capital investment, company productivity and employment in a supported firm is quite positive while the accumulated effect on profitability and salaries is insignificant. As a whole, it is still unclear to what extent SMB financing contributes to economic development and poverty reduction.

Moving on to a dynamic analysis of the development of small and medium business in Russia in terms of the stability of the economic environment depending on the economic cycles, the authors Levushkina, S.V., Eremenko, N.V. (2015) establish that every cycle of development of the SMB system has three stages: reaction to a crisis and birth; new cycle of development – 2-3 years; growth – 5-7 years; pre-crisis – 1-2 years. Small and medium enterprises react differently to crisis phenomena in the economy. The former react relatively quickly, while the latter are more inert. This circumstance ensures that the entire SMB system reacts more adequately to a crisis. On the one hand, actions take place immediately and, on the other, there is a robust conservatism aimed at keeping the system stable and balanced. It is also quite interesting that when a crisis in the SMB system is evaluated, such indicators are used as: 'the share of the employed in small and medium enterprises in the total number of the employed in the economy of the country' and 'the share of profitable enterprises', which are especially sensitive to crisis phenomena in the economy, particularly in small enterprises.

Thus, the literature review shows that there is a certain dependency between the indicator of innovative activity at the national level and the development indicators for small and medium business. On the one hand, the specifics of small and medium business precondition the fact that it exists in an extremely competitive environment and for this reason requires the involvement in innovative development, which is one of the ways of achieving competitive advantages on the market. On the other hand, SMB traditionally lacks money to generate innovation (Laforet S, Tann J (2006). These properties have a dual character and their antecedence in relation to each other has not been established so far.

In the context of this research study, the question should be answered about which of the above properties of SMB is of primary importance for Russian enterprises. This will be done by method of experiment.

3. Details experimental

3.1 Materials and method

To conduct the experiment, the panel data from the website of the Russian Federal State Statistics Service for the period from 2012 to 2019, differentiated by federal districts, was used.

When building the model, it is suggested to use as an indicator of the innovative activity level the indicator 'Coefficient of Inventive Activity (the number of national patent applications for inventions submitted in Russia and calculated per 10,000 people of the population)' (the projected one, estimated in units as the number of patent applications for inventions submitted in the country by Russian applicants (the indicator from the Rospatent annual report) / population x 10,000). This

As an indicator of the development level of SMB, the indicator 'Headcount in small and medium business enterprises (estimation)' is used (calculated as the number of people and reflecting the estimated headcount (excluding external part-timer workers) in small and medium enterprises (legal entities)). We suggest to use indicator because only human capital is the resource which generates ideas and permanent accumulate of all impulses which could lead to innovations (Lesáková, Ľ. (2009).

Based on this data an equation of simple pair regression was formed. The calculations were made using the software product Stata 14.

4. Results and discussion

Following the results of the correlation-regression analysis, equation (1) was obtained:

$$Y = 0.39 + 6.89E\text{-}07 * X \qquad (1)$$

where Y is the coefficient of inventive activity,

X is the headcount staff in small and medium enterprises.

The determination coefficient of the equation (normalized R-square) = 66.75%. Therefore, the dispersion of the dependent variable is by 2/3 explained by the dispersion of the independent variable. The correlation coefficient is 0.82, which is an indicator of a strong positive relation between the dependent and independent variables. The importance of F does not exceed the admissible threshold of 5%, which is an indicator of the importance of the regression model constructed.

Thus, the hypothesis about the impact of the development of SMB on the indicators of innovative activity at the national level can be considered to be partially proven. Undoubtedly, the dynamics of development of SMB is not the only indicator that determines the dynamics of innovative activity, but it definitely has a contribution.

This impact can be expressed quantitatively through an elasticity coefficient, which is 0.73 according to the results of the experiment. It can be interpreted in the following way. If the headcount in small and medium enterprises changes by 1%, the coefficient of inventive activity will change by 0.73%.

Despite the identified relation, the quality of this equation is quite different by the federal districts under consideration, which can be illustrated with a graph see Figure 1 (where 1 is the Central Federal District; 2 is the North-West Federal District; 3 is the South Federal District; 4 is the North Caucasus Federal District; 5 is the Privolzhsky Federal District; 6 is the Ural Federal District; 7 is the Siberian Federal District; 8 is the Far East Federal District)

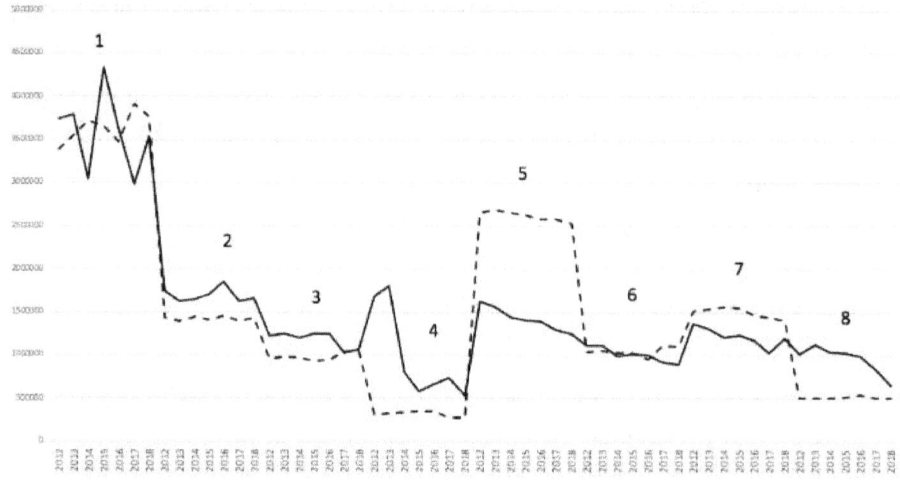

Figure 1: Differentiation of the quality of the regression equation by federal districts

As can be seen on the graph, the actual data (the dashed line in Figure 1) is differentially variable from the theoretical one (the solid line in Figure 1) depending on the federal district. The biggest deviations are inherent in the Privolzhsky and Far East Federal Districts, while the smallest ones are indicative for the Central and Ural Federal Districts.

Thus, it can be concluded that there is an impact of other factors, differentiated in the regional context. In particular, such factors can be: the presence or absence of fossils or other natural resources, a well-developed mining or manufacturing industry (large industrial complexes), advancement and specialization of the educational sector, religious features of the region's population and other factors.

5. Conclusions

It can be concluded that this research study discusses the issues of a relationship between a region's innovative activity and the development indicators of its small and medium enterprises. It was revealed that developing the SMB sector can mediate a growth in innovative activity, namely, an increment in the SMB sector by 1% makes the level of innovative activity go up by 0.73%. The result of this study

However, there are many other factors influencing innovative activity and some of them synergistically interact with the development of the SMB sector while others can have a reverse impact on SMB while simultaneously mediating the innovative development of a region. It is the main limitation of this study. Searching for and investigating these factors, their mathematical formalization as well as formalizing their impact on innovative activity (from a multi-dimensional point of view) is the subject of further research by the authors.

Acknowledgements

This research work was supported by the Academic Excellence Project 5- 100 proposed by Peter the Great St. Petersburg Polytechnic University

References

Ayandibu, A. O., & Houghton, J. (2017). *The role of Small and Medium Scale Enterprise in local economic development (LED).* Journal of Business and Retail Management Research, *11*(2).

Demidenko, D., Malevskaia-Malevich, E., Dubolazova, Y. (2018). *Optimization of the innovation process management at a manufacturing enterprise*. Advanced Science Letters, 24(9), 6308-6310.

Distanont, A., Khongmalai,O. (2018), *The role of innovation in creating a competitive advantage*, Kasetsart Journal of Social Sciences https://doi.org/10.1016/j.kjss.2018.07.009

Domingo Ribeiro-Soriano (2017) *Small business and entrepreneurship: their role in economic and social development.* Entrepreneurship & Regional Development, 29:1-2, 1-3, DOI: 10.1080/08985626.2016.1255438

Hillary, R. (Ed.). (2017). *Small and medium-sized enterprises and the environment: business imperatives.* Routledge.

Hewa Wellalage, Nirosha & Fernandez, Viviana (2019). *Innovation and SME finance: Evidence from developing countries.* International Review of Financial Analysis. 10.1016/j.irfa.2019.06.009.

Kersten, Renate & Harms, Job & Liket, Kellie & Maas, Karen (2017). *Small Firms, large Impact?* A systematic review of the SME Finance Literature. World Development. 10.1016/j.worlddev.2017.04.012.

Konnikov, E. A., Konnikova, O. A., Negashev, D. S., Novikova, A. V. (2018). *Sustainability of development of industrial enterprises depending on the level of their manufacturability.* In Proceedings of the 32nd International Business Information Management Association Conference (IBIMA) (pp. 4431-4444).

Kubíčková L. , Morávková M. , Tuzová M. , Nečas I. (2017). *The Role of Small and Medium-Sized Enterprises in the Development of Rural Areas.* Acta Universitatis Agriculturae et Silviculturae Mendelianae Brunensis, 65(6): 1987 – 1996.

Laforet S, Tann J (2006). *Innovative Characteristics of Small Manufacturing Firms.* J. Small Bus. Entrep. Dev., 13(3): 363-380

Leonidou, L. C., Christodoulides, P., Kyrgidou, L. P., & Palihawadana, D. (2017). *Internal drivers and performance consequences of small firm green business strategy: The moderating role of external forces.* Journal of business ethics, 140(3), 585-606.

Lesáková, Ľ. (2009). Innovations in Small and Medium Enterprises in Slovakia, 6(3), 23–34.

Levushkina, S.V., Eremenko, N.V. (2015). *Dynamic analysis of the development of small and medium enterprises.* Political Internet electronic scientific journal of the Kuban State Agrarian University, (107), 63-76.

Nikolova, L.V., Kuporov, J.J., Rodionov, D.G. (2015) *Risk management of innovation projects in the context of globalization. International Journal of Economics and Financial Issues,* 5, 3S, 68-72

Pengfei Luo, Dandan Song, Biao Chen (2020) *Investment and financing for SMEs with bank-tax interaction and public-private partnerships.* International Review of Economics & Finance, 65, 163-172.

Peredera, Zh.S., Gritsenko, T.S., Teryaeva, A.S. (2018) *Small and medium-sized businesses: definition criteria and role in the economy.* Bulletin of Eurasian Science, 6, https://esj.today/PDF/38ECVN618.pdf (free access).

Pinkovetskaya, Yu.S. (2018) *Factors affecting the turnover of small and medium-sized enterprises: an assessment based on data from Russian regions.* Ars Administrandi (The Art of Management), 10 (2), pp. 199–216.

Pletnev, D., Barkhatov, V. (2016) *Business Success of Small and Medium Sized Enterprises in Russia and Social Responsibility of Managers.* Social and Behavioral Sciences, 221, 185-193.

Rodionov, D.G., Nadezhina, O.S., Titarenko, D.S. (2016) *Development of a model of adaptive management of innovative activities of an enterprise.*Global Scientific Potential, 9 (66), 84-92

Rudskaia, I. (2017). *Regional innovation foresights: drivers and barriers for development*. In proceedings of the 30th international business information management association conference, IBIMA (pp. 889-903).

Ruchkina, G., Melnichuk, M., Frumina, S., & Mentel, G. (2017). *Small and medium enterprises in regional development and innovations.* Journal of International Studies, 10(4), 259-271

Shinohara, M., & Fisher, D. (2019). *The role of small industry in the process of economic growth* (Vol. 7). Walter de Gruyter GmbH & Co KG.

Entrepreneurial Universities Inclusive Perspective: Does it Trigger Social Innovation Process and Entrepreneurship?

Nibedita Saha[11] and Petr Sáha[1,2]
[1]University Institute, Tomas Bata University in Zlín, Czech Republic
[2]Centre of Polymer Systems, Tomas Bata University in Zlin, Czech Republic
nibedita@utb.cz
DOI: 10.34190/EIE.20.082

Abstract: This paper addressed an overview of the Entrepreneurial Universities Inclusive perspective in the era of globalization and socio-scientific innovation research. This conceptual paper builds a framework to explore and investigate the impression of entrepreneurial universities, enabling factors that foster social innovation and social entrepreneurship development in order to create and sustain social value. Moreover, this research intends to classify the style-the entrepreneurial universities are now recognizing their prominence as an incubator of a social innovation process that triggers the emergence of social entrepreneurship mindset. Since, the distinctive challenges of entrepreneurial universities are persistently pursuing new opportunities to swear out the university's mission; engaging in a process of continuous innovation, adaptation and learning that facilitate to run across the societal challenges and technological break. Therefore, this paper argues that it is important to understand the supports of entrepreneurial universities in the society that flows through the unique tacit knowledge in order to make an indispensable contribution to encouraging knowledge based urban development. Consequently, it activates the key driving forces of the social innovation process and its impact on the entrepreneurial innovation system, entrepreneurial skill development and social entrepreneurship. The main purpose of this paper is to exemplify, how does entrepreneurial development process can foster social innovation and social entrepreneurship. Thus, it mainly highlighted that it is important to understand the correlation of entrepreneurial universities empowering activities that deliberate innovation –driven economic growth, exceptional implicit knowledge that materializes the concept of social innovation process and contributes to support the Sustainable Development Goals (SDGs).

Keywords: entrepreneurial universities, knowledge-based innovation, social innovation, social entrepreneurship, sustainability

1. Introduction

Today's social dimensions of reforming Higher Educational institutions (HEIs), are numerous, multifaceted, and crucial, for promoting social innovation system and security. Regarding this debated issue there is a wide consent of the interruption between economic growth and well -being which is rapidly increasing day by day. At the same the emergence of entrepreneurial universities inclusive perspectives has become one of the main engines of social and economic growth nationally and internationally. Reacting to this vibrant condition of technological disruption as well as to meet the societal challenges, this paper discloses the prospective awareness of entrepreneurial university's strategic initiatives that enhances the role of social and institutional contexts in the social innovation process through academic spin-offs for scaling up innovation, resources and action to deliver the Sustainable Development Goals (SDGs) (Franco-Leal, 2020). Therefore, in order to discourse the economic development challenges, this paper tries to demonstrate the significance of entrepreneurial universities, comprehensive perspectives that have been perceived as an operational approach of promoting social innovation system and social entrepreneurship. Where, the idea of entrepreneurial ecosystems on the social innovation system has been viewed with the responsiveness of growing wide-ranging innovation, developmental universities, social business and social entrepreneurship to meet the challenges of internationalization.

In addition, this paper tries to emphasize on how entrepreneurial universities cope with the new challenges and diversities of the socioeconomic contexts. Such as: inclusiveness in higher education, inclusiveness in innovation, social innovation, inclusiveness in the university's developmental process, social development, and social entrepreneurship. Responding to this contextual matter, Carl (2020), exposed that the inclusive perspectives of entrepreneurial universities have great influence on the ongoing paradigm shift from the technological upbringing to social development process which links up the two emerging research fields of entrepreneurial ecosystems and social innovation through social business development that automatically initiating for social entrepreneurship development. Since 2007, Professor Dr. Muhammad Yunus started to trigger among academics and researchers for social innovation and social entrepreneurship development as a combined effort of community development (Yunus et al., 2012;2010); (Muktadir-Al-Mukit, et al., 2016).

[1](Corresponding Author)

Similarly, from the conceptual point of view, Păunescu et al, (2013) and Ciccarino et al., (2019) also expressed that one of the core characteristics of entrepreneurial universities driving force mainly regulates the social entrepreneurial behaviour of academic community members as well as enable managers to develop their dynamic capabilities. Which, comprehends a direct link between social responsibility, social innovation system and social entrepreneurship in higher education. On the other hand, it is also necessary to mention that through this developmental perspective of entrepreneurial ecosystems, the substantial knowledge is developed within universities and it acts as a significant facilitator for provincial economic growth and socioeconomic development, due to the spin-off of new, innovative initiatives that add value through knowledge creation and entrepreneurial discovery process (EDP) (Daniel et al, 2020); (Saha et al, 2020a).

Furthermore, this paper provides a review of the reasoning for entrepreneurial universities strategic and inclusive perceptions which, represent one of the most common policy approaches to address the tensions between localization and globalization. Where, this paper discusses about the significance of entrepreneurial universities inclusive perspectives and its impact on the social innovation system that enable creating new social structures, allow issues of justice, education, environmental protection, sustainability and/or community development. In short, the main aim of this paper is to resolve the strain of understanding about the influence of entrepreneurial university's innovative capabilities that trigger the key driving forces of the social innovation process, contribute to knowledge-based urban development process and enables higher educational institutes, business and policy-makers, to face the societal challenges as well as technological disruption. However, much of the research that investigated the relationships among entrepreneurial universities attitudes toward regional knowledge spill over and their dimensions has been conducted in entrepreneurial ecosystems. Additionally, there is a lack of research investigating both entrepreneurial universities inclusiveness and social innovation process. Therefore, it is worth to have discussion on entrepreneurial universities distinctive features, i.e. inclusiveness process that accelerate the social innovation process and entrepreneurship approach through developing and integrating explicit knowledge in order to achieve social value. Hence, this paper recognizes the consequence of entrepreneurial universities dynamic perspectives that distinctively stimulates the social innovation process and entrepreneurship approach in the era of the 21st century. It exemplifies a conceptual model of entrepreneurial university's initiatives, which encourage the social innovation process and its impact on the entrepreneurial innovation system.

1.1 Conceptual overview of entrepreneurial universities inclusive development and social innovation

To address the relevance of entrepreneurial universities inclusive development styles and social innovation practices, it is obligatory to emphasize that in the era of modernization and internationalization, entrepreneurial universities insights has progressively been acknowledged as a leading approach of socioeconomic development strategy. Where, it plays a dynamic role, especially in developing entrepreneurial ecosystems, social innovation process and social entrepreneurship development. Research show that nowadays the impression of this conceptual perception about entrepreneurial universities innovative and strategic capability has been comprehended as an excellent social and regional innovation as well as entrepreneurship development approach due to its value in realizing the entrepreneurial mindset creation process for managing regional growth. Continuing this discussion researcher Gibb (2012) pointed out that the conception of entrepreneurial universities inclusive perspectives and innovative strategy is nothing new approach towards socioeconomic and regional development. Rather, it is better to exemplify that the perception of the entrepreneurial university actually appeared during the phase of social and economic turbulence where, it enables HEIs and academics to cope up with the unwanted challenges and consequences. During this transition period, entrepreneurial universities were acting as a booster to inspire the impulse of internal organizational development of the university as well as to face the external influences on the university. Precisely, the conception of 'entrepreneurial university' can be described as a collective influence of *Adopting new knowledge, Improving existing knowledge and Developing innovative knowledge,* (AID) in the society in order to condense knowledge-based social innovation system. Apart from these the presence of entrepreneurial universities inclusiveness promotes innovation-driven societal growth to attain the prerequisites of its specific environmental impact that stimulate regional, social, and national economic development through an interchange of knowledge which is nowadays becoming greater impact in developing countries, especially the perception of academicians in entrepreneurial universities (Ahmad et al, 2018); (Saha et al, 2020a) (Saha et al, 2020b). Correspondingly, Hannon (2013) too specified that currently entrepreneurial universities perception in higher education institutes (HEI) has been recognized as a key enabling driving forces that reinforces innovation within the society and in regions too. Regarding this issue, several researchers have pointed out that entrepreneurial university approach empowers firms and higher education institutes (HEIs) to tackle as well as to face the economic, societal, and industrial turbulence.

On the other hand, in order to define the conceptual overview of 'Social Innovation', Stanford University's Centre for Social Innovation, mentioned that *"social innovation" can be defined as a practice that enable the process of developing and deploying effective solutions to face the social and environmental challenges in a very systematic manner in order to facilitate the progress of the society. Where, the collaborative effort of government, business, and the nonprofit organizations like entrepreneurial universities initiatives are required* (Clavier et. al., 2018, Stanford Centre for Social Innovation). Similarly, as pointed out by the European Commission's opinion that the perception of Social innovation has been emerged initially during the period between 2006 and 2014 in order to process and map up the policy tools that would be suitable for sustainable development goals (SDGs) including for example innovative education system, managing ageing, and healthcare system. But later on, this social innovation domain has been considered as one of the major novelties introduced by the Europe 2020 Strategy. Where, social innovation concept has been presented as a key area for facilitating and achieving Europe 2020's ambition, i.e. to promote smart, sustainable and inclusive growth (European Commission 2010a, 2010b,2010c, 2010d); (Sabato et al, 2015). Therefore, from the entrepreneurial universities inclusive social innovation point of view, researcher Brundenius et al (2017) emphasized in their book entitled: *"Universities, Inclusive Development and Social Innovation"* that actually entrepreneurial universities are capable to play a crucial role in inclusive development during the transition period in order to enhance and trigger the social innovation system and social entrepreneurship development. Which is one of the most important sectors for the inclusiveness of social innovation, i.e. promoting economic growth and demonstrate the ways in which universities can be the pioneers through their strategic initiatives in social responsibility and social innovation. More precisely, it can be said the role of entrepreneurial universities inclusive perspectives enhances the chances and possible opportunities for implementing social innovation, social entrepreneurship, as well as overall regional economic and social development.

1.2 Entrepreneurial universities inclusive perspectives and social innovation system

In order to discuss about the relationship between 'entrepreneurial universities inclusive outlooks' and 'social innovation system', it is necessary to mention that both the perceptions and their methodological approaches significantly inter-related due to their essential potentials that enhance innovation-led regional social as well as economic growth and entrepreneurial mind setup. It has been observed as the pillars of creating distinctive entrepreneurship and knowledge-driven social innovation center in the region that are associated with the regional development strategy. More comprehensively, it can be said that social innovation process and entrepreneurial universities strategic initiatives mainly focused on promoting social innovation system and social entrepreneurship development. As, currently both the conceptions have expanded an enormous drive in academic research, civic society dialogue and on the political agenda. Additionally, it is noteworthy, to specify that from the socioeconomic development point of view, both the perceptions have been admired by the policy makers, researchers, scientists, technocrats, industrialists and early career investigators, i.e. students' nationally and internationally due to its inclusive targets that fulfills the millennium development goals and sustainable development goals (UN millennium goals, 2015); (UN Sustainable Development Goals, 2016).

Continuing to this debated issue, on entrepreneurial universities role on sustainable development and societal development, Wakkee et al, (2019) has specified the way nowadays the entrepreneurial universities are functioning as a change agents for social reform as well as for regional economic development. According to their study research shows how entrepreneurial universities creativities and social innovation process can drive forward the regional sustainable development in developing countries, though earlier this inventiveness was not that much focused and mostly neglected. Therefore, from the institutional development and regional economic development perspectives point of view, it is complementary to highlight the key activities of entrepreneurial universities. Such as: entrepreneurial university plays a vibrant role in order to enhance the sustainable development change within the society as a whole; entrepreneurial university plays a stimulating role for developing as well as organising a sustainability vision among the civil society that accordingly becomes the driver of institutional change.

1.3 Entrepreneurial universities efforts to boost social entrepreneurship

To determine entrepreneurial universities efforts to social entrepreneurship, at first we need to discuss about what exactly mean by the social entrepreneurship? Which has recently become so popular among the policy-makers, particularly in Europe. In response to this question, European Commission (EC) (2013) emphasized that according to the Entrepreneurship 2020 Action Plan of EC, social entrepreneurship can be considered as a predetermined action plan and successive policy briefs that facilitate and encourage innovative universities for societal development. Even though, surprisingly universities are generally expected to generate some substantive contributions in order to persuade social entrepreneurship. But traditionally within the context of higher education there is almost no consideration has been observed where, these social innovation processes can function with social entrepreneurship (Cinar,2019). However, it is necessary designate that social entrepreneurship processes typically involve changes in social processes and organization, not necessarily in monetized settings. Therefore, it can be assumed that basically the social entrepreneurship perceptions have mainly benefited the poorer sections of the society that we're unable to provide formal returns to the university knowledge input.

Simultaneously, to confront the discussion, entrepreneurial university's role in boosting social entrepreneurship, Benneworth and Cunha (2015) indicated that entrepreneurial universities inclusive strategies basically create societal benefits that enable to meet the societal challenges through contemporary 'strategic', i.e. (competitive) university. In addition, entrepreneurial universities also encourage to engage with and stimulate (co-operative) social innovation processes. On the other hand, according to Bazan et al (2020) also emphasized on how the entrepreneurial university environment can create an atmosphere within the university's environment and support system (ESS) in order to influence the social entrepreneurial intention (SEI). Research shows that while considering the benefit of triggering social entrepreneurship perception, actually social entrepreneurs play an important role in the economic and social developments of the communities in which they operate, and consequently they start to encourage more students and more students to be engage in social entrepreneurial behaviour. Therefore, based on these systematic approaches of various researchers, it can be said that entrepreneurial universities basically play a very significant role which influence the impact of various motivational factors related to the university's entrepreneurial ecosystem in order to boost social entrepreneurship (Cunha et al, 2015) ;(Choi and Majumdar, 2014).

2. Research methodology

This research primarily discusses about the inclusive perceptions of entrepreneurial universities that mainly triggering the social innovation system in order to create an entrepreneurial environment that facilitates to develop social entrepreneurship mind set up within the entrepreneurial ecosystems'. This academic research particularly addressed the pragmatic knowledge (that gained from various researchers' apprehension of distinctive ideas, perceptions) based on logical approach. Which have been developed by conceptual understanding of social innovation and social entrepreneurship. Generally, inductive reasoning represents the degree of support in the sort of probabilistic reasoning and the underpinning of most debated scientific theories initiated on the contemporary approaches of social innovation system, social entrepreneurship and entrepreneurial universities inclusiveness.

Therefore, to understand the study within the limited time frame, this paper considers to demonstrate the accessibility and initiatives of entrepreneurial universities that influence on social entrepreneurship and create social awareness through social innovation process to meet the societal challenges and sustainable development goals (SDGs) and create regional economic value. The significance of linking regional, social, economic at national and international level - is one of the techniques of building regions, societies, organizations and academic institutions more innovative and competitive. Consequently, it has been observed that the creative and innovative regions development process has been always being attracted by the policy makers, researchers, technocrats and students to develop an entrepreneurial spirit. So, there is a vibrant role aimed entrepreneurial universities inclusive perceptions and social entrepreneurship initiatives (SEI) for sustainable development as well as to stimulate the regions entrepreneurial spirit of their staff members, students by contributing appropriate guidance and services in a comprehensible way that fulfil the present business prerequisites. Accordingly, the significance of this study shows entrepreneurial universities inventiveness is influential instruments to foster and develop a knowledge-based society that directly and indirectly enhances their competitiveness, social as well as regional innovation and progression due to their unique intrinsic competence.

3. Results and discussion

This study tries to investigate the prospective and convincing contribution of entrepreneurial universities as well as social innovation process that stimulate *Social entrepreneurship* and *involves* researchers and universities students for creating new products or services in order to meet the social as well as environmental needs. Where, these innovative products and/or services are made available within the existing market structures which can creates shared value, with the meaning that the organization, i.e. entrepreneurial universities can simultaneously generate some economic benefits as well as environmental and/or social benefits. According to the findings of evolutionary theory of entrepreneurial universities strategic initiatives and social innovation process have normally given a comparative insight to us about the conceptual aspects of both the entrepreneurial mind setup perspectives and social entrepreneurship development capabilities. Based on the conceptual perspective it has been observed that entrepreneurial universities intrinsic role on social entrepreneurship development are considered as an innovative process which occurs in social mission-driven organizations that mainly aimed to generate creative new solutions to fulfill the societal needs, by using a limited pool of human resources. Furthermore, it can be said that during this innovation –driven knowledge development process gradually lead to social transformation and value creation. Which show the key priorities of disruptive change and entrepreneurial universities contribution to trigger social innovation process and social entrepreneurship development that endure a big effect on sustainable development goals success and enhance competitive advantage.

Correspondingly, it is essential to remark that in this paper social innovation system and or social entrepreneurship initiatives (SEIs)) concept has been realized as the leading concept for formulating strategic goals and processes related to entrepreneurial universities inclusive targets , i.e. innovation –driven knowledge based society through capitalization of knowledge, interdependence with the industry and government, independence with another institutional spheres, hybrid organizational forms and renovation. Hence, it can be expected that during contemporary social transformation period entrepreneurial universities inclusive as well as strategic initiatives play a vibrant role essentially that overwhelmed to modern higher educational institutes (HEIs) initiatives and social organizations as well as regional organizations with the intention of motivating the innovative spirit of the regional staff members and universities students, by offering guidance and services in a comprehensible manner that articulated with the present business requisites. Consequently, to address the significance of entrepreneurial universities emergence, researcher Stolze (2020) also indicated that in order to respond the turmoil situation the occurrence of entrepreneurial spirit has been observed through the entrepreneurial university model, which enhances as a third mission to HEIs in order to contribute to economic, technological and social development. Accordingly, Giuliani (2018) also stressed that how the technological determinism and 'transformative change' frameworks also stimulate the appearance of social innovation system in order to cope up with the regulation of global capitalism needs which give rise to yet another generation for social entrepreneurship development and social innovation policies (Carmen et al, 2013).

3.1 The way of entrepreneurial universities contribution to trigger social innovation process and social entrepreneurship development

Concerning entrepreneurial universities inclusive perceptions and social innovation policies synergetic effect that trigger social entrepreneurship development, it is required to discuss the relation between both approaches, the way they are interconnected and inter-related for enhancing social entrepreneurship that is embedded in an entrepreneurial discovery process. Though, it is not a simple process to initiate as there is some constraint on the main social innovation process especially for generating information that identifies the restricted set of research and innovation priorities. Regarding this matter, from the social innovation's conceptualization point of view, Sinclair et al (2018) mentioned that essentially social innovation, can be considered as "distinctive and effective approach that emerged in response to meet the unwanted effects, i.e. social problems and needs that prompted and motivated by a social purpose. Alternatively, it can be said that this transition condition in reality enhances the social assets and capabilities" which is nowadays has become prominent in discussions of social policy reform across the world. Research shows that such inspired solutions will be able to relief, rejuvenate and recuperate the existing welfare services and create a social value.

Simultaneously, in order to justify the significance of *entrepreneurial universities inclusiveness* and *social innovation* priorities influence on social entrepreneurship development Borzaga and Bodini, (2012) pointed out that the purpose of creating and forming social innovation is not only to cope with radical technological change that acts as an emergent phenomenon of social entrepreneurship drive that creates an environment for finding an alternative solutions as well as to reduce the social gaps in the market and public sector. On the other hand, it also enables to identify the best potential ways to empower existing people's resources, human resources specifically from the underprivileged groups by activating their core competences and involving them in the innovative process. (Sinclair et al, 2018).

From the socioeconomic development and social entrepreneurship development point of view, several researchers have numerous opinion. Among them, Oganisjana et al (2017); (Oganisjana and Surikova, 2015); (Philips et al, 2015) explained that social innovation priority mainly encompasses with the development of *social capital, social cohesion, social inclusion*, which empower to face the systemic changes and societal transformation in order to carry out the sustainable development of the society. From the operational and innovative perspective point of view, it can be said that social innovation process largely supports the creation of new ideas for improving the well-being, welfare and quality of life for investing the entrepreneurial activities and expedite innovation –driven socio-economic growth.

However, more precisely, it can be said that even though initially entrepreneurial university representing as drivers for sustainable change through education and outreach programme. But ultimately, it has been observed that the role of entrepreneurial universities strategic inclusiveness such as-

- Eliciting to positive inspirations and identifies the firmness that highlight the need for social innovation);
- Enabling to draw insights and generate ideas through creative methods for social innovation);
- Empowering to sharpen the pioneering ideas by identifying the best possible ways of sustaining it in the longer term for social innovation)

are basically accentuating more than the traditional commercialization activities and notably in developing countries which, is one of the crucial aspects of triggering the social innovation system through systemic change.

Furthermore, the below mentioned Fig.1 also depicts the significance of entrepreneurial universities inclusiveness and its potential influences that trigger the social innovation system and social entrepreneurship development. The below mentioned Fig. 1 illustrate the three important elements of entrepreneurial universities, which were all arranged around the question of how entrepreneurial universities inclusive contribution enable to trigger social innovation process and social entrepreneurship development. Where, social innovation, social entrepreneurship and entrepreneurial universities inclusive perceptions facilitate encourage and expedite to cope up with the *societal challenges, social needs and systematic social change* that enhance the capacity to adopt the change and create social entrepreneurship a could be understood within the broad spectrum of entrepreneurial system that facilitate regions to compete successfully and foster innovation–led regional social growth that promotes entrepreneurial network spirit.

Consequently, Schröder and Krüger (2019) emphasized that nowadays one of the major issues of the new role of higher educational institutes (HEIs), i.e. entrepreneurial universities that enabling, exchanging, moderating and researching social innovation. From entrepreneurial universities inclusive perspective point of view, research shows how the inventive ways of social transformation focusing the emergent role of universities existing potentialities in order to set up a more innovation friendly environment. On other hand, to apprehend the relationship between entrepreneurial universities initiatives, social innovation system, social business and social entrepreneurship development, it can be said that all the approaches inter connection enable, encourage and empower students and graduates to be involve in the startup creation (Barbini et al., 2020). Where, they realize the significance of all societal sectors that integrating and fostering social innovations and social entrepreneurships for clarifying the prospective for enhancing innovative higher education system, entrepreneurial ecosystems.

As a result, it can be assumed that this conceptual study shows the way the entrepreneurial universities inclusive perceptions combines both the social innovation and social entrepreneurship as well as resource-based and positioning views of regional development in relationship with entrepreneurial university activity and social innovation process.

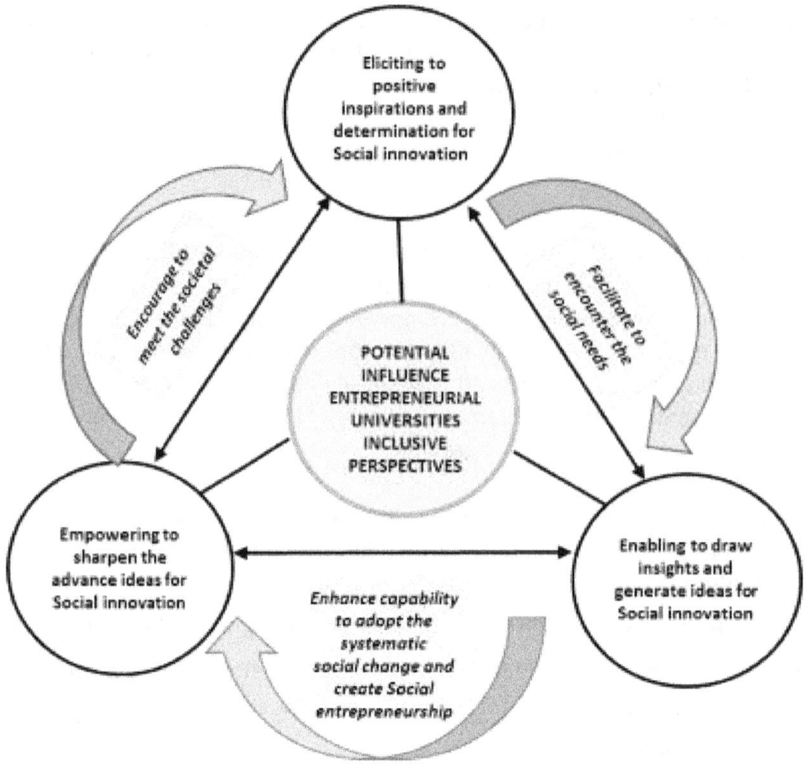

Figure 1: Thematic model of entrepreneurial universities potential inclusive perspectives influence on social innovation and social entrepreneurship development (own interpretation).

Concerning entrepreneurial universities inclusive initiatives this study mainly classifies and distinguish the following two important research propositions or RPs that facilitate us to get the target, interest and justification of doing this thematic research such as:

- RP1: Which states that entrepreneurial universities inclusive effect on social innovation and entrepreneurship development is considered as one of the major policy and process of creating social reformation, regional development, organizations and institutions more innovative and competitive. Thus, it can be said that *entrepreneurial universities inclusiveness and social innovation process plays a crucial role for enhancing millennium development goals and sustainable development goals as well as to trigger social enterprises through entrepreneurial spirit*, by providing requisite guidance and services in a rational way.
- RP2: It indicates that though entrepreneurial universities intrinsic role and social innovation policies combined effort has a synergistic effect on socio-economic development, but the implementation of regional development strategies dynamism also plays a dynamic role on entrepreneurial ecosystems, entrepreneurial discovery process(EDP) and smart inclusive innovation –driven growth oriented entrepreneurship spirit within the region.

Precisely, it can be assumed that the social innovation system and or social entrepreneurship initiatives (SEIs)) concept has been comprehended as the important conception for formulating strategic goals that has been taken in to consideration for further studies related to entrepreneurial universities inclusive factors, that provides an valuable insight into social entrepreneurship in practice and the challenges encountered by social entrepreneurs when starting up and developing their businesses.

4. Recommendations and conclusion

To conclude, it is noteworthy to mention that this conceptual thematic research precisely suggested that the connection between entrepreneurial universities strategic capabilities and social innovations emergence excludes the impediment in societal economic development. Linking to the question of entrepreneurial universities inclusive influence on societal reform and entrepreneurial spirit development, i.e. (social innovation and social entrepreneurship development). Precisely, this paper exposes that both entrepreneurial universities inclusiveness and social innovation poly play a significant role on enhancing social entrepreneurship development. Equally, it is significant to highlight that the role of entrepreneurial universities inclusive target mainly facilitates on fostering the social entrepreneurship development under certain conditions, for example during the period when *social entrepreneurs realize the urgency for deep understanding of the region especially when there arises some social issue, and its socio-political conditions. On the other hand, when* social entrepreneurs consider the necessity for the development of a particular segment of the society that eventually suffers from a social issue and they should need a good governance to develop entrepreneurial initiatives that mainly targeting for socio-economic development.

From the future research prospective point of view, this research recommended that social innovation system and or process contain some powerful instruments that encourage the researchers, policy makers, young generations innovative mind-set through proper leadership and governance, i.e. fostering industrial competitiveness, enhancing regional knowledge production within the region, through solving the problems that arise among the higher education institutions either for proper access to education or for enhancing quality of education. More precisely, this paper tries to reveal that entrepreneurial universities inclusive perceptions mainly focusing on creating an environment that will facilitate to ripen the desire of innovativeness through social innovation process that enable to become ambitious social entrepreneurs. Though, the main drive of the social entrepreneurship in higher education is considered to be the prime goal of solving the *social problems, but it has been observed that* determinants of social entrepreneurship in universities primarily plays a vital role on encouraging innovation–driven knowledge creation and exchange within the community, civil society, which quantifies the sustainable development goals through organizational change. Where, entrepreneurial discovery process and inclusive strategic approaches will allow individuals to learn not only about social entrepreneurship, but it will also empower and trigger undeveloped and unprivileged with their existing human resources within the region to develop an entrepreneurial mindset, entrepreneurial capabilities to rejuvenate their socio-economic value.

Acknowledgements

This work is supported by the institutional project entitled: "Process of implementing a Human Resources Strategy for Researchers (HRS4R)". Development of TBU research and development capacities in Zlín, Reg. No. CZ.02.2.69 / 0.0 / 0.0 / 16_028 / 0006243. It is conducted within the framework of COST Action CA 18236 "SHIINE". The first author is thankful to the Director of the University Institute for providing management support system (MSS) and infrastructure facility to carry out this contemporary research. Also, the first author dedicates this study to her only beloved son "Kanishka Binayak Saha" and her beloved father "Chittaranjan Saha".

References

Ahmad, N.H., Halim H.A., Ramayah, T., Popa, S., and Papa. A. (2018). The ecosystem of entrepreneurial university: the case of higher education in a developing country. *International Journal of Technology Management 78(*1–2), 52–69.

Barbini, F.M., Corsino, M., and Giuri, P. (2020). How do universities shape founding teams? Social proximity and informal mechanisms of knowledge transfer in student entrepreneurship. *The Journal of Technology Transfer, Springer,* 1-37. https://doi.org/10.1007/s10961-020-09799-1

Bazan, C., Gaultois, H., Shaikh, A., Gillespie, K., Frederick, S., Amjad, A., Yap, S., Finn, C., Rayner, J. and Belal, N. (2020). A systematic literature review of the influence of the university's environment and support system on the precursors of social entrepreneurial intention of students. *Journal of Innovation and Entrepreneurship 9*(4), 1-28. https://doi.org/10.1186/s13731-020-0116-9

Benneworth, P., & Cunha, J. (2015). Universities' contributions to social innovation: Reflections in theory & practice. European Journal of Innovation Management, 18(4), 508–527. doi:10.1108/EJIM-10-2013-0099

Borzaga, C., and Bodini, C. (2012). What to make of social innovation? Towards a framework for policy development. *EURICSE, Working Paper No. 036* /12. Trento: EURICSE.

Brundenius, C., Göransson, B., and Carvalho de Mello, J.M. (2017). Universities, Inclusive Development and Social Innovation: An International Perspective. eBook ISBN: 978-3-319-43700-2, pp-403, Springer International Publishing, Switzerland, DOI:10.1007/978-3-319-43700-2.

Carl, J. (2020). From technological to social innovation – the changing role of principal investigators within entrepreneurial ecosystems, *Journal of Management Development,1*(1), 1-14, https://doi.org/10.1108/JMD-09-2019-0406

Carmen, P., Denisa, D., Ramona, C., and Adina, F. (2013). Towards a Conceptualization of Social Entrepreneurship in Higher Education, *The International Journal of Management Science and Information Technology (IJMSIT),* ISSN1923-0273, NAISIT Publishers, Toronto, Iss. 10-(Dec), pp. 51-69

Cinar, R. (2019) Delving into social entrepreneurship in universities: is it legitimate yet?, *Regional Studies, Regional Science, 6*(1), 217-232, DOI:10.1080/21681376.2019.1583602.

Ciccarino, I. D. M., Malpelli, D. C., De Mello Moraes, A. B. G., and Nascimento, E. S. D. (2019). Social innovation and entrepreneurial process: application of typologies in start-ups of Yunus Social Business Brazil. *Cadernos EBAPE.BR, 17*(4), 1031-1047.

Choi, N., and Majumdar, S. (2014). Social entrepreneurship as an essentially contested concept: Opening a new avenue for systematic future research. *Journal of Business Venturing, 29*(3), 363–376. doi:10.1016/j.jbusvent.2013.05.001.

Clavier, Soule, Malhotra (2018). Social Innovation Insights by Stanford Business. May 18. www.gsb.stanford.ed,https://www.gsb.stanford.edu/faculty-research/centers-initiatives/csi/defining-social-innovation

Cunha, J., Benneworth, P., and Oliveira, P. (2015). Social entrepreneurship and social innovation: A conceptual distinction. *In Handbook of research on global competitive advantage through innovation and entrepreneurship* pp. 616–669. doi:10.4018/978-1-4666-8348-8.ch033

Daniel, A. D., Teixeira, A. A., and Preto, M. T. (2020). *Examining the Role of Entrepreneurial Universities in Regional Development.* IGI Global. http://doi:10.4018/978-1-7998-0174-0

European Commission. (2013). Entrepreneurship 2020 action plan: Reigniting the spirit of entrepreneurship in Europe. COM, 2012, 795. Final. Brussels, Belgium.

European Commission (2010a), Call for proposals for social experimentations, VP/2010/007, DG Employment, Social Affairs and Inclusion.

European Commission (2010b), Europe 2020. A strategy for smart, sustainable and inclusive growth, Communication from the Commission, Brussels 3.3.2010, COM (2010) 2020 final.

European Commission (2010c), Communication from the Commission to the European Parliament, the Council, the European Economic and Social Committee and the Committee of the Regions 'Europe 2020 Flagship Initiative Innovation Union' , SEC(2010) 1161 , COM/2010/0546 final, Brussels, 6.10.2010.

European Commission (2010d), The European Platform against Poverty and Social Exclusion: A European Framework for social and territorial cohesion, Communication from the Commission, COM (2010) 758.

Franco-Leal, N., Camelo-Ordaz, C., Dianez-Gonzalez, J.P., and Sousa-Ginel, E. (2020). The Role of Social and Institutional Contexts in Social Innovations of Spanish Academic Spinoffs. *Sustainability 12*(3), 906; https://doi.org/10.3390/su12030906.

Gibb, A. A. (2012) Exploring the Synergistic Potential in Entrepreneurial University Development: Towards the Building of a Strategic Framework. *Annals of Innovation & Entrepreneurship, 3,* 1-21.

Giuliani, E. (2018), Regulating global capitalism amid rampant corporate wrongdoing—reply to Three frames for innovation policy. *Research Policy, 47* (9), 1577-1582.

Hannon, D. P. (2013). Why is the entrepreneurial university important? *Journal of Innovation Management,1*(2), 10–17. doi:10.24840/2183-0606_001.002_0003

Muktadir-Al-Mukit, D., Ashraf, M. M., Rahman, S., and Amir Khasru, A.F. M. (2016). The Role of Social Business towards Development: Case Study of Bangladesh. *Australia and New Zealand Journal of Social Business, Environment and Sustainability*, *2*(2), 153-173.

Oganisjana, K., Svirina, A., Surikova, S., Grīnberga-Zālīte, G., and Kozlovskis, K. (2017). Engaging universities in social innovation research for understanding sustainability issues. *Entrepreneurship and Sustainability Issues, 5* (1), 9 - 22. http://doi.org/10.9770/jesi.2017.5.1(1)

Oganisjana, K., and Surikova, S. (2015). Social innovation in the promotion of sustainable development of the contemporary Latvian society. *Journal of Security and Sustainability Issues 5*(2), 249–258.

Păunescu, C., Drăgan, D., Cantaragiu, R., and Filculescu, A. (2013). Towards a Conceptualization of Social Entrepreneurship in Higher Education, *The International Journal of Management Science and Information Technology (IJMSIT), 10*(2), 51-69. ISSN 1923-0273, NAISIT Publishers, Toronto.

Phillips, W., Lee, H., Ghobadian, A., O'Regan, N., and James, P. (2015). Social innovation and social entrepreneurship: A systematic review. *Group & Organization Management 40*(3), 428–461. Sabato, S., Vanhercke, B. and Verschraegen, G. (2015). The EU framework for social innovation - Between entrepreneurship and policy experimentation, *ImPRovE Working Paper (15/21)* .

Saha, N., Sáha, T., & Sáha, P. (2020a). Entrepreneurial Universities' Strategic Role in Accelerated Innovation for Regional Growth. In Daniel, A. D., Teixeira, A. A., & Preto, M. T. (Ed.), *Examining the Role of Entrepreneurial Universities in Regional Development* (pp. 51-65). IGI Global. http://doi:10.4018/978-1-7998-0174-0.ch003

Saha, N., Sáha, T., & Sáha, P. (2020b). Entrepreneurial universities perception and regional innovation system: Do they really create an environment for regional economic development? *Journal of Entrepreneurship Education, 23*(2), 1-15.

Sinclair, S., Mazze,i M., Baglioni, S., and Roy, M.J. (2018). Social innovation, social enterprise, and local public services: Undertaking transformation? *Social Policy and Admin;* https://doi.org/10.1111/spol.12389

Schröder, A. and Krüger, D. (2019). Social Innovation as a Driver for New Educational Practices: Modernising, Repairing and Transforming the Education System. *Sustainability MDPI, Open Access Journal, 11*(4), 1-25.

Stolze, A. (2020). A meta-ethnography on HEIs' transformation into more entrepreneurial institutions: Towards an action-framework proposition. *Industry and Higher Education* 1–14. https://doi.org/10.1177%2F0950422220922677

United Nations The Sustainable Development Goals Report (2016). Retrieved from http://ggim.un.org/documents/The%20Sustainable%20Development%20Goals%20Report%202016.pdf

United Nations The Millennium Development Goals Report (2015). Retrieved from https://www.un.org/millenniumgoals/2015_MDG_Report/pdf/MDG%202015%20rev%20(July%201).pdf

Wakkee, I., Sijde, P., Vaupell, C., and Ghuman, K. (2019). The university's role in sustainable development: Activating entrepreneurial scholars as agents of change, *Technological Forecasting and Social Change, 141*, 195-205. https://doi.org/10.1016/j.techfore.2018.10.013

Yunus, M., Sibieude, T., and Lesueur, E. (2012). Social Business and big business: innovative, promising solutions to overcome poverty? *Field Actions Science Reports*, *4,* 68-74. Retrieved from: https://journals.openedition.org/factsreports/1574

Yunus,M., Moingeon, B., and Lehmann-Ortega, L. (2010), Building Social Business Models: Lessons from the Grameen Experience. *Long Range Planning, 43*, 308-325.

Yunus, M. (2007), Creating a World Without Poverty: Social Business and the Future of Capitalism, New York: Public Affairs.

Organizational Agility and Organizational Learning: Do They Accelerate Organizational Innovation and Competency?

Nibedita Saha[11], Tomas Sáha[1], Aleš Gregar[1] and Petr Sáha[1,2]
[1]University Institute, Tomas Bata University in Zlín, Czech Republic
[2]Centre of Polymer Systems, Tomas Bata University in Zlin, Czech Republic
nibedita@utb.cz
DOI: 10.34190/EIE.20.030

Abstract: This paper deliberates about the impact of Organizational Agility (OA) on Organizational learning (OL) strategy and innovative capability development process that enables organizations and business to face the challenges of technological disruption. It also determines the significant dynamic competence of OA that has a great influence on the organizational learning process. Basically, this paper demonstrates the distinctive features of OA and OL process that expedite business; to hasten their innovative capabilities through developing and integrating organizational knowledge and win today's dynamic business environment. The aim of this paper is to explore and investigate the perception of both organizational learning and organizational agility process that influence on linking disruptive technological innovation as a novel approach in order to accelerate organizational innovation and competency. It reveals the way organizational learning (i.e. human resources learning capabilities, strategies within the organization) and organizational agility (i.e. firm's quick adopting, adjusting and accepting capability with the changing environment) influence significantly disruptive technological innovation in order to enhance organizational competitiveness. In addition, this paper also determines the significant perceptions of organizational agility and its values on strategic HRM that reflects on sustainable organizational learning as well as technological innovation (i.e. knowledge development.). Essentially, this area of study is reflected as an active multidisciplinary research approach, where academicians, researchers, technocrats, engineers, management experts, policy makers and business analysts, and industrialists combine their knowledge in order to provide a better management system. On the other hand, it is necessary to mention that the implications of new emerging perspectives of organizational agility and organizational learning mostly enable firms to respond promptly and flexibly through organizational innovativeness and technological surveillance to cope up with the dynamic world.

Keywords: competency, disruptive technology, knowledge, organizational agility, organizational learning, organizational innovation

1. Introduction

The significance of organizational agility has been comprehensively with the impression of organizational knowledge and innovative capability development process that strived for in-creasing the competence of individual and organizational performance. Nowadays, the most promising and modern organizations are under great pressure to work in a dynamic environment, with continuously changing instable events, to invest their valued time and energy on creativity and knowledge sharing activities that deliver them to instant and reckonable advantage. Under these circumstances, competitiveness and innovation have become a burning topic of academic, business and managerial debates with regard to be agile and be able to sense and respond to market changes quickly and smoothly to maintain their effectiveness, i.e. organizational excellence. Wherever, organizational agility is accountable for high ability to adapt and adopt the unwanted changes in the marketplace and allocate resources, i.e. human resources to take advantage of that change. According to Dupont (2019), organizational agility can be considered as the ability of an organization that effectively immerses itself in its ecosystem, and facilitate organizations to keep pace with the technological, economic, societal and cultural challenges in an ever-changing environment. Similarly, Saha et. al, (2019a), (2019b) also emphasized that organizational learning as well as agile capacity of an organization is basically for rapid, continuous and systematic entrepreneurial innovation which gradually focused organizations to achieve their competitive advantage through organizational innovation and knowledge development). Consequently, it is necessary to mention that organizational agility can simplify firms' performance through reactive, proactive and innovative agility (Najrani 2016). On the other hand, in order to justify organizational agility and organizational learning's combined efforts several researchers stated that an organizational learning theory, mainly emphasizing the existing knowledge within the organization, i.e. exploitative and exploratory learning as well as which is vibrant for organizational innovation and knowledge development (Saha et al, 2016), (Liao et al, 2019).

[1](Corresponding Author)

Accordingly, Chan et al. (2019) emphasized that organization agility can be reflected as an eminent components of an organization that facilitate them to cope up with the disruptive innovation that empowers firms and organizations innovative capability. Where, it enables organizations to face the challenges of hypercompetitive market conditions as well as it stimulates to be agile in order to survive and sustain their competitive advantage. Correspondingly, Hamada and Yozgat (2017) also pointed out that both the approaches organizational agility and learning capability are the most fundamental elements that play a great role on organizational survival and organizational success during techno-logical disruption. Finally, the thematic approach of this paper persuades different approaches and models concerning organizational agility (OA), organizational learning (OL) and organizational competence development approach which includes organizational innovativeness and organizational growth that enable them to develop the attitude to competently respond to the dynamic world. This paper deliberates about the influence of Organizational Agility (OA) on Organizational learning (OL) and innovative capability development process that enables organizations and business to face the challenges of technological disruption. Primarily, this paper highlights the significance of organizational agility and organizational learning process as an identical approach for the organizations of the 21st century that enable business to accelerate organizational innovativeness. It represents a conceptual model that could be useful for integrating organizational knowledge and win today's dynamic business environment.

Furthermore, the consequence of this study shows that organizational agility inventiveness in addition to organizational learning perspectives are influential instruments to foster organizational knowledge-development process, effectiveness and organizational innovativeness due to their intrinsic competence. Finally, this paper proposed some research assumptions that the added value of this knowledge development process within the organization will accentuate the way HR specialists are involved in operational matters and are progressively observed as a source of competitive advantage in order to meet the global challenges. Although, it is quite difficult to enhance firms' sustainable growth quickly due to the urge of gradual expansion of the competitive marketplace and today's rapidly-changing business world and vice-versa. Conversely, it can be said that nowadays organizational research, (i.e. managerial and operational activities) deals with both the phases that are combined as well as inter- linked and focuses primarily on the following key elements, i.e. (innovation-oriented and technology-oriented).

1.1 Contextual issues of organizational learning and organizational agility

Continuing the discussion on organizational learning and organizational agility, it is necessary to highlight that these identical approaches progressively become more and more significant mainly for improving knowledge and innovation-driven organizational competitiveness in order to sustain competitive advantage in the world market. Regarding this sizzling topic on organizational agility and organizational learning strategy and their relationship different authors, academicians, management experts, industrialists, policy-makers, researchers and technologists have various opinions. Basically, nowadays the general conceptual background of these expressions such as: organizational learning, organizational agility and disruptive technologies that mainly relating the importance of organizational learning issues on disruptive technological innovation and organizational agility development. It is essentially to put an emphasis on the contemporary economic environment that facilitating organizations to accelerate their innovation policies to reverberate organizational or business competency. In another way, it can be said that the influence of organizational learning on organizational agility development really enables organizations and its initiatives on disrupting innovations (DI) and their characteristics as well as its effects. Additionally, it extends organizational learning and organizational agility combined effort on sustainable organizational performance development, i.e. innovativeness. According to Professor Clayton M. Christensen, the notion of 'Disruptive Technological Innovation' can be reflected as an innovation that primarily creates a novel market opportunity by connecting different set of values, strategies and norms that suddenly surpasses an existing market condition Bower (1995) and Christensen, (2006). Similarly, researcher Teece, Peteraf, and Leih, (2016) also stated that the concept of organizational agility emerged as a key business imperative in order to cope up with the rapid technological turmoil carried through disruptive technological innovation. Then again, research shows that due to the presence of organizational agility perception recently firms become more capable to take the advantages of technological disruption in order to create a market niche and expand their foothold in a hypercompetitive economy (Kane, Palmer, Phillips, and Kiron, 2015); (Lyytinen and Rose, 2004); (Sambamurthy, Bharadwaj, and Grover, 2003); (Chan et al, 2019).

On the other hand, from the organizational learning perception point of view, Zirak (2015) mentioned that the concept of organizational learning has emerged initially during 1970s. Since, then within the organizations it has been observed that spontaneous desire of individuals in order to develop their knowledge through learning within the organizations. As, they consider that it will enable them to survive in the long run by enabling their capabilities with the diversified tasks, technologies, and environments. Consequently, Khan and Wisner (2019) pointed out that organizations learning capability (i.e. external learning as well as and internal learning) enable organizations to be responsive and flexible to meet the unanticipated changes, but may not always influence positive impacts on a firm's performance(Jermsittiparserta and Wajeetongratanac, 2019). Therefore, it is necessary for organizations to work on developing new knowledge and innovation to enhance organizational performance as well as to create a learning-oriented firm. Equally, Noruzy et al. (2013) identified that organizational performance depends not only on organizational innovation and learning process, but also it depends on organizational knowledge management process. Alternatively, Saha et al. (2016) described that currently, the strategic part of HRM practices within the organization enlighten the success of the organizational performance. Moreover, it basically exists in developing positive attitudes of individuals, groups, and organizations which mainly put emphasis on enhancing individual competence as well organizational competence through organizational learning. Concerning organizational competency point of view, Rialti et al. (2020) emphasized that in order to keep pace with the dynamic business world, contemporary organisations nowadays intended to develop their organizational innovative capabilities, so that they can accomplish the competitive advantage.

1.2 Relationship between organizational agility and organizational learning as key drivers for enhancing organizational competitiveness

While addressing the relationship between 'organizational agility' and 'organizational learning' it is important to be emphasized that both approaches and their conceptual philosophies are closely related as they share various similarities in their justification. For example: (a) *The connection between organizational learning and organizational agility can only become valuable if there are some resources (i.e. human capital), some innovative system (technological up gradation) that can blow into the knowledge that has been created during this knowledge development process through research and technology;* (b) *On the other hand both the perceptions can provide the appropriate knowledge (expertise and organizational capability) in order to stimulate the innovation during the period of technological disruption that takes place and be implemented.*

Though, the two conceptions are not really comparable as there are significant differences within them. Since, organizational agility focuses specifically on innovation related intensive sectors whereas; the impression of organizational learning strategy applies to a wider set of sectors in organizational performance development. According to Saha et al. (2017a); (2017b) the effect of organisational agility (OA) on knowledge management (KM), enables organisations to survive and achieve their competitive advantage through developing and integrating the KM strategy and sustainable knowledge transfer capability. Basically, the main principle of organizational agility concept exemplifies a set of challenges, i.e. organizations responsiveness, adaptability and thrive in the changing environment through collaboration, iteration, experimentation and empowerment (Linda, 2018).

From the implementation perspective point of view, the below mentioned Figure.1 demonstrate how organizational learning and organizational agility empower organizations contribute to the development of organizational competitiveness. It shows how organizational agility strategy could be an influential instrument to foster sustainable organizational learning that allows and encourages to develop the level of organizational performance development through adaptability, accountability, openness and suppleness. Similarly, it can be said that the presence of organizational agilities attributes and priorities that positively *influence on organizational competitiveness* through stimulating *Organizational Knowledge; Organizational Skills, Organizational Abilities', i.e. Knowledge Skills & Abilities (KSAs)* within the organization in one way which leads to promote innovative capability and business growth due to their intrinsic competences.

Furthermore, Figure.1 also depicts the significance of organizational agility that facilitate firms to compete successfully due to its initiative on innovation system with the presence of organizational learning capability. Where it specially focuses on organizational technological growth that promotes effectiveness by enhancing organizational effectiveness and increasing organizational knowledge. Confirming this matter, Lu and Ramamurthy (2011), highlighted that basically organizational agility signifies an organizations capability to deal with unexpected challenges that enable them to adopt rapid and innovative responses. Then again, Hamada and Yozgatb (2017) also pointed out that both the approaches- organizational agility and learning capability are the most fundamental elements that play a great role on organizational survival and organizational success during technological disruption.

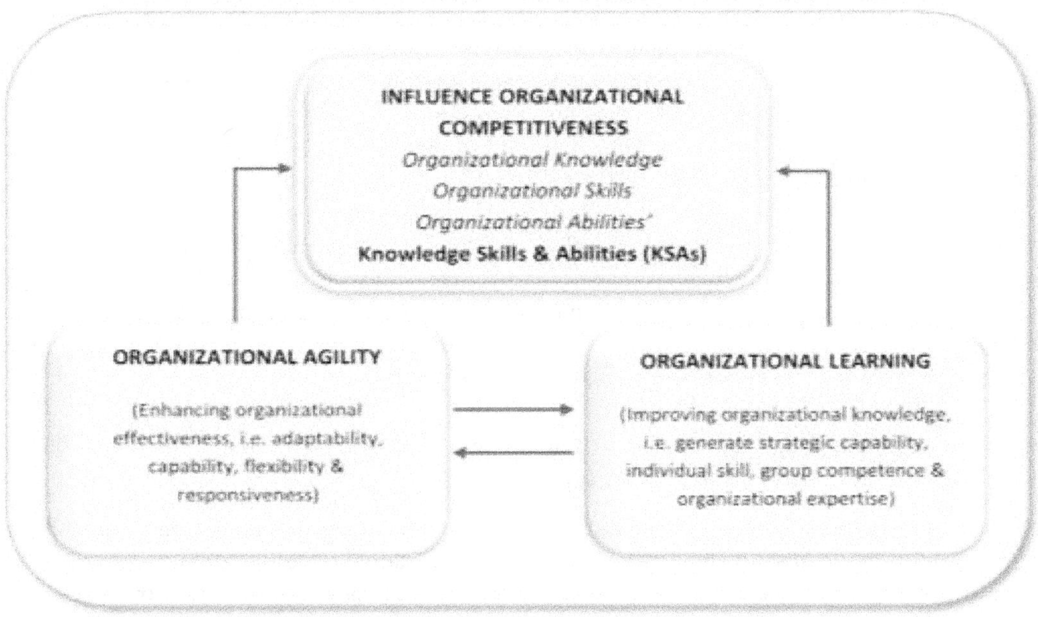

Figure 1: Relationship between organizational agility and organizational learning as key drivers for organizational competitiveness

2. Research methodology

This conceptual research predominantly articulated the amalgamation of both pragmatic evidence and inductive reasoning. Pragmatic evidence represents the methods of acquisition material and data (knowledge). Usually, inductive reasoning exhibits the degree of support in the sort of probabilistic reasoning and the groundwork of most scientific theories initiated on the contemporary approaches of organizational learning and organizational agility. This study mainly addressed the combination of both empirical evidence and inductive reasoning. Empirical argument depicts the methods of obtaining information and data (knowledge). Normally, inductive reasoning displays the degree of support in the sort of probabilistic reasoning and the foundation of most scientific theories founded on the contemporary approaches of organizational learning, agility and disruptive technological innovation.

Therefore, to understand the study within the limited time frame, the realistic phase of the knowledge about organizational agility and organizational learning capability has been done on the basis of different academic expert's, policy makers and management expert specialists opinion. Eventually, the outcomes of this study marked the development of disruptive technological initiatives and objectives of organizational learning strategies, connections between both the impressions (i.e. organizational learning and organizational agility) and their diverse priorities and characteristics that streamline the organizations technological growth and business, i.e. knowledge and innovation driven (entrepreneurial spirit and enhance 'Knowledge' for regional growth) organizational competitiveness. From global perspective point of view, organizational agility enables organizations to have prospective cooperation for potential competitive advantage.

3. Results and discussion

This study tries to investigate the prospective and convincing contribution of organizational agility as well as organizational learning priorities that stimulate organizational *knowledge and innovation capability*, that empower to gain some competitive advantages and enhance business' capacity. According to the findings of evolutionary theory of organizational learning and organizational agility process have normally given a comparative perception to us about the conceptual aspects of both the agile organizational perspectives and learning capabilities. Which show the key priorities of disruptive change and organizational development that sustain a big impact on organizational success and enhance competitive advantage.

Concerning this burning issue, it is required to accentuate that organizations innovative attitude creation is an integrated process based model of organizational learning capability and organizational agility perceptions that combines together with the technology intensive innovative learning capabilities. Equally, the challenging perception of organizational agility that has been steered in this study in order to explore the potential and its distinguishing features that enhances organizations' flexibility as well as capability and performance in relation to the implementation of organizational learning strategies through disruptive technological innovativeness (i.e. Know-what, know-why, know-how and know-who). On the other hand, from the organizational knowledge development process point of view, organizational learning can be considered as a novel approach to make changes and keep pace with the dynamically changing environment.

This impression highlights that organizational learning is a key factor in stimulating disruptive technological innovation and creativity within the organization. Therefore, the question of sustainable organizational learning and performance development becomes crucial elements in assessing and strengthening the overall development of organizational effectiveness. In order to justify, this perception of disruptive technological innovation, Schiavi and Behr (2018) specified that principally disruptive technological perception mainly influence organizations to replace their existing business models, strategies that enable them to adapt the new organizational structures that create organizational distinctive value.

3.1 The way of organizational agility and organizational learning influence on knowledge and innovation-driven organizational development

The encouraging synergetic influence of organizational agility and organizational learning capabilities (know-how) put emphasis on knowledge and innovation – driven organizational growth, i.e. (sustainable value creation process within the organization). In order to rationalize, Figure.2 illustrate whether the manifestation of organizational agility and organizational learning priorities, i.e. organizations' performance can really *influence on knowledge and innovation-driven organizational development i.e.* (the key drivers of organizational agility and Organizational learning) or not for achieving the competitive advantage; whether the distinctive features (organizational agility) and organizational learning capabilities can empower sustainable growth, social innovation and skills development support, and focus the development of innovation strategies or not; whether the organizational learning strategies (Organizational knowledge, Skills & Abilities –KSAs) can really incorporate its main novelties for enhancing organizational performance development, i.e. (technological innovation) or not.

In order to justify organizational agility and organizational learning's combined effort on organizational knowledge and capacity development, the below mentioned Figure.2 demonstrates different organizational learning phases within the organization, i.e. the priorities (individual skill, group competency and organizational expertise) relationships. This study investigates that different extents of human capital, i.e. human resources (HR) and social capital are indeed significantly influencing related to the level of organizational learning priorities. The conceptual aspects and determinant factors of both the organizational agility and organizational learning shows the key elements of organizational innovative capability development that empowers a firm's organizational competence to rapidly achieve their sustainable organizational success and enhance competitive advantage. To apprehend the significance of organizational agilities key attributes and organizational learning's key capabilities influence on disruptive technological innovation, several researchers' such as Baškarada and Koronios, (2018); Liao et al. (2019); Saha et al. (2019a) highlighted that both the approaches play a vital role on enhancing organizational knowledge development process during technological turbulence. Where, it exemplifies the best possible way an organization can meet their dynamic challenges through gaining knowledge, relationship development and presentation of knowledge, i.e. by sharing knowledge.

Furthermore, to identify the positive and negative effect of disruptive innovation within the organization, it can be said that disruptive innovations viewpoint is against the sustaining innovation which does not generate any new market rather it only facilitates to change the existing markets with higher value in association with organizational agility and organizational learning capability, which is vital for organizational development, i.e. sustainable competitive advantage. Regarding this matter, Michael Porter (1998) expresses in his 'Competitive Strategy' book that industry incumbents are always struggling in order to maintain their business with their existing customers, that influence their all existing resources, i.e. (Knowledge, skills, abilities and initiatives) in order to maintain their competitive position (Downes, and Nunes, 2013); (Minavand and Lorkojouri, 2013). On the other hand, Alegre et al (2012) also emphasized that recent study on organizations innovative capability, organisational learning process plays a great role that can deliver firms a challenging perspective with a basis to sustain their competitive advantage. While there is an evidence in research that organisational learning affects intensively in innovation in order to evaluate its impact in organisations.

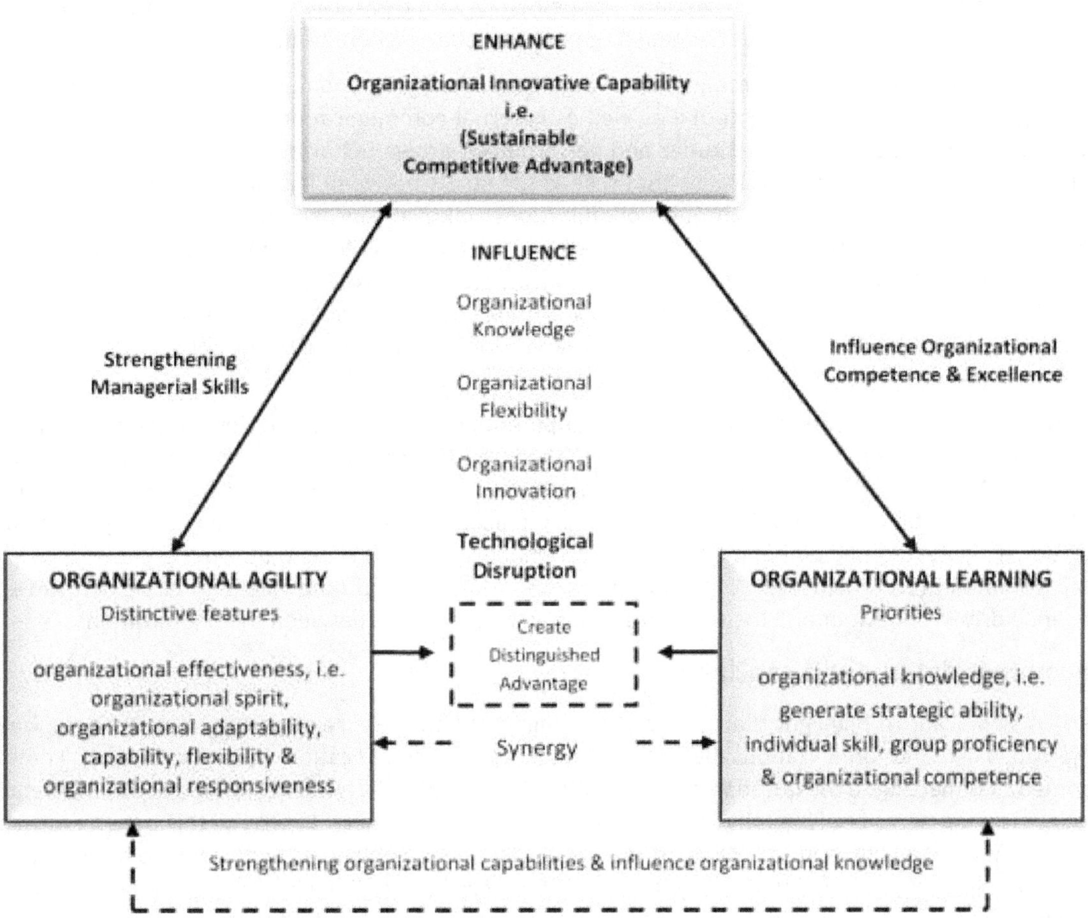

Figure 2: Thematic model of organizational agility and organizational learning influence on knowledge and innovation-driven organizational innovative capability

Simultaneously, in order to justify the significance of *organizational agility* attributes and *organizational learning* priorities influence on knowledge and innovation-driven organizational development Alexiou et al. (2019) also stated that the ability of an organization to cope with radical technological change is regarded to be heavily dependent on organizational capability, organizational knowledge development process and its driving forces that acts as an emergent phenomenon of organizational learning dynamism that creates an environment as the enabler of this combined relationship.

Therefore, it can be assumed that this study shows the way of innovation oriented organizations performance development capability with a higher impact on organisational learning capability tend to be more innovative and dynamic due to the presence organizational agility attributes.

Relating to the question of organizational agility and organizational learning strategies influence on knowledge and innovation, this study leads to recognize the following three important research propositions or RPs that enable us to comprehend the rationalization of this research intents such as:

- *RP1:* Which states that organizational agility and organizational learning are the key driving forces, priorities and stimulation of an organization to accelerate the organizational knowledge production system and its implementation, i.e. (to enrich organizational knowledge). In another way, it can be said that organizational learning can be considered as one of the main key elements of HR systems that creates value through organizational proficiency, i.e. (know-how, know-what, know-who and know-why) and individual employee's creativity.

- *RP2:* Which indicate that organizational agility along with the key enabling factors, i.e. organizations strategic HRM perspective enable organizations to improve their existing resources (Knowledge skills and abilities) in order to survive in the long-run as well as during the turbulence period. According to authors understanding basically organizational agility is the deliberated effort of an organization to enter in to the new market condition where, they can perform their work with pleasure as well as rapidly they can update themselves with the continuously changing fragmented global environment.
- *RP3:* Which expresses that the prominence of organizational agility and implementation of organizational learning activities that reduces internal as well as external communication activities, organizations work culture, and knowledge sharing attitudes and performance-driven behaviour and their expertise gaps and deficiencies between the organizations that relieve the stress between industrialization and globalization impact through Uniqueness, i.e.(through organizational innovativeness), Responsiveness, i.e. (through organizational awareness and openness cooperative development) Motivation, i.e. through organizational commitment and urge for progress) between organizations and firms where, organizational agility and organizational learning has a significant impact on disruptive technological innovation that nowadays become a crucial factor for the successful organizational capacity and knowledge development, i.e. sustainable competitive.

In a nutshell, from the organizational knowledge development perspective point of view, organizational learning can be considered as an opportunity to make changes and keep pace with the dynamically changing environment. This impression highlights that organizational learning is a key factor in stimulating disruptive technological innovation and creativity within the organization. On the other hand, the prominence of organizational agility and implementation of organizational learning activities that reduces internal as well as external communication activities, organizations work culture, and knowledge sharing attitudes and performance-driven behaviour and their expertise gaps and deficiencies between the organizations.

4. Recommendations and conclusion

Finally, it is significant to highlight that this research suggested that the relationship between organizational learning capability and organizations flexibility eliminates the complication in organizational knowledge development. Connecting to the question of organizational learning's influence on organizational excellence and knowledge development, i.e. (Organizational innovation and competency). Precisely, this paper exposes that both organizational agility and its decision-making agile strategy play a significant role on enhancing organizational learning capability as well as innovative capability. Equally, organizational learning and organizational agility play a significant role to boost organizational innovation to adopt, accommodate and adjust themselves in a recovering way as well as in an innovative manner through an integrated focus on organizational knowledge creation, technological up gradation and knowledge distribution, i.e. through sharing knowledge.

While addressing the key positive features of organizational learning proficiency and organizational agility attributes it determines some valuable understandings and recommendations such as: organizational agility concept is a flexible process of increasing organizational knowledge and competency; organizational learning capability actually encourages to anticipate the organizational knowledge development capability that mainly depends on its existing resource (human capital); To generate the greatest effort for organizational professional capability it ensures that organization has the skilled, promised, devoted and well-motivated employees to accomplish organizational innovative capability , i.e. sustainable competitive advantage. In addition, it is necessary to mention that this paper provides an understanding of the significance of organizational learning and its effect on the occurrence of disruptive technological innovation as a novel approach. Moreover, while doing this study authors were mainly focusing and excited to study the prominence of learning at the organizational level which occurs when the firms empower to create new knowledge (i.e. innovation) enable to develop an innovative way of understanding or insight rapidly during the period of technological turbulence, (i.e. agility) that facilitates either new knowledge creation or the improvement of existing ones, (i.e. the influence of disruptive technologies up gradation or technological surveillance). Essentially, it is to be noted that organizational learning, (i.e. human resources learning capabilities, strategies within the organization) organizational agility (i.e. firm's quick adopting, adjusting and accepting capability with the changing environment) and disruptive technological innovation are significantly inter-connected.

Apart from the above mentioned discussion, this paper also intends to offer some valuable perceptions from the practical perspective point of view, where the suggested propositions might be valued for the organizations that are assuming to anticipate themselves as a successful performance-oriented and innovation–driven organization. Wherever, they tried to accept the organizational agility concept along with organizational learning phases (exploitative and exploratory learning initiatives) in order to create organizational innovation and competency, i.e. (competitive advantage).

Acknowledgements

This work is supported by the institutional project entitled: "Process of implementing a Human Resources Strategy for Researchers (HRS4R)". Development of TBU research and development capacities in Zlín, Reg. No. CZ.02.2.69 / 0.0 / 0.0 / 16_028 / 0006243.The first author is thankful to the Director of the University Institute for providing management support system (MSS) and infrastructure facility to carry out this contemporary research. Also, the first author dedicates this study to her only beloved son "Kanishka Binayak Saha" and her beloved father "Chittaranjan Saha".

References

Alegre, J., Pla-Barber, J., Chiva, R. and Villar, C. (2012) Organisational learning capability, product innovation performance and export intensity, *Technology Analysis & Strategic Management, 24*(5),511-526, DOI: 10.1080/09537325.2012.674672.

Alexiou, A., Khanagha, S., and Schippers, M. C. (2019). Productive organizational energy mediates the impact of organizational structure on absorptive capacity. *Long Range Planning, 52*(2), 55-172, https://doi.org/10.1016/j.lrp.2018.02.001

Baškarada, S. and Koronios, A. (2018) The 5S organizational agility framework: a dynamic capabilities perspective. *International Journal of Organizational Analysis, 26* (2), 331-342.

Bower, J. and Christensen, C. M. (1995). Disruptive technologies: Catching the wave.*Harvard Business Review, 73* (1).

Chan, C. M. L., Teoh, S.Y., Yeow, A., and Pan, G. (2019). Agility in responding to disruptive digital innovation: Case study of an SME. *Information Systems Journal, 29*(2), 436-455.

Christensen, C. M. (2006). The ongoing process of building a theory of disruption. *Journal of Product Innovation Management, 23*(1), 39-55.

Downes, L., and Nunes, P.F (2013). Big-Bang disruption. Harvard business review.

Dupont, L. (2019). Agile innovation: Creating value in uncertain environments. *Journal of Innovation Economics & Management,* 1(28) 1-5. ISBN: 9782807392816.

Hamada, Z.M.M. and Yozgat, U. (2017). Does organizational agility affect organizational learning capability? Evidence from commercial banking. *Management Science Letters 7*, 407–422.

Jermsittiparserta, K. and Wajeetongratanac, P. (2019). The Role of Organizational Culture and It Competency in Determining the Supply Chain Agility in the Small and Medium-Size Enterprises. *International Journal of Innovation, Creativity and Change, 5*(2), 416-432.

Kane, G. C., Palmer, D., Phillips, A. N., and Kiron, D. (2015). Is your business ready for a digital future? *Sloan Management Review, 56,* 37–44.

Khan, H., and Wisner, J. D. (2019). "Supply Chain Integration, Learning, and Agility: Effects on Performance". *Journal of Operations and Supply Chain Management,* 12: 14-23.

Liao, S., Liu, Z. and Ma, C. (2019). Direct and configurational paths of open innovation and organisational agility to business model innovation in SMEs. *Technology Analysis & Strategic Management,* https://doi.org/10.1080/09537325.2019.1601693.

Linda Susan, H. (2018). Organizational effectiveness and agility. *Journal of Organizational Effectiveness-People and Performance, 5*(4), 302-313.

Lu, Y., and Ramamurthy, K. (2011). Understanding the link between information technology capability and organizational agility: An empirical examination. *MIS Quarterly, 35*(4), 931–954.

Lyytinen, K., and Rose, G. M. (2004). How agile is agile enough? Towards a theory of agility in software development. IFIP International Federation for Information Processing.

Minavand, H. and Lorkojouri, Z. (2013). The linkage between strategic human resource management, innovation and firm performance. *IOSR Journal of Business and Management (IOSR-JBM), 11*(2), 85-90.

Najrani, M. (2016). The endless opportunity of organizational agility. *Strategic Direction*, 32(3) 37 – 38.

Noruzy, A., Dalfard, V., Azhdari, B., Nazari-Shirkouhi, S., and Rezazadeh, A. (2013), Relations between transformational leadership, organizational learning, knowledge management, organizational innovation, and organizational performance: An empirical investigation of manufacturing firms, *The International Journal of Advanced Manufacturing Technology, 64* (5/8), pp. 1073-1085.

Porter, M.E. (1998). Competitive Strategy: Techniques for Analyzing Industries and Competitors *Chapter-16.* Free Press; 1st edition.

Rialti, R., Marzi, G., Caputo, A. and Mayah, K.A. (2020), "Achieving strategic flexibility in the era of big data: The importance of knowledge management and ambidexterity", Management Decision, Emerald Publishing Limited 0025-1747. https://doi.org/10.1108/MD-09-2019-1237.

Sambamurthy, V., Bharadwaj, A. S., and Grover, V. (2003). Shaping agility through digital options: Reconceptualizing the role of information technology in contemporary firms. *MIS Quarterly, 27,* 237–263.

Saha, N., Chatterjee, B., Gregar, A., and Sáha, P. (2016). The impact of SHRM on sustainable organizational learning and performance. *International Journal of Organizational Leadership, 5*(1), 63-75. http://dx.doi.org/10.33844/ijol.2016.60291

Saha, N., Gregar, A., Van der Heijden, B. I. and Sáha, P. (2019a). The Influence of SHRM and Organizational Agility: Do They Really Boost Organizational Performance? In Ç. Doğru (Ed.), Handbook of Research on Contemporary Approaches in Management and Organizational Strategy (pp. 62-83). Hershey, PA: IGI Global.

Saha, N., Sáha, T. & Sáha, P. (2019b). Organizational Agility and Strategic HRM: A Twin Perspective Strategy of Organizational Capacity and Knowledge Development. *Proceedings of the 33rd International Business Information Management Association Conference (IBIMA). Education Excellence and Innovation Management through Vision 2020*, 1181-1185. ISBN: 978-0- 9998551-2-6.

Saha, N., Gregar, A. and Sáha, P. (2017a). Organizational agility and HRM strategy: Do they really enhance firms 'competitiveness? *International Journal of Organizational Leadership 6*(3) 323-334. 10.33844/ijol.2017.60454

Saha, N., Gregar, A. and Sáha, P. (2017b). Organizational agility and KM strategy: Are they the effective tool for achieving sustainable organizational excellence? *New Trends and Issues Proceedings on Humanities and Social Sciences. 4*(10), 110–117. https://doi.org/10.18844/prosoc.v4i10.3084

Schiavi, G.S. and Behr, A. (2018) Emerging technologies and new business models: a review on disruptive business models. *Innovation & Management Review, 15*(4), 338-355.

Teece, D., Peteraf, M., and Leih, S. (2016). Dynamic capabilities and organizational agility: Risk, uncertainty, and strategy in the innovation economy. *California Management Review, 58,* 13–35.

Zirak, A. (2015). Implementation of learning organization components in Ardabil social security hospital. *International Journal of Organizational Leadership, 3*(4), 200–212.

Social Opportunities and Business Model Design: Evidence From Three Social Enterprises

Silvia Sanasi, Antonio Ghezzi and Andrea Rangone
Politecnico di Milano, Milan, Italy
Silvia.sanasi@polimi.it
Antonio1.ghezzi@polimi.it
Andrea.rangone@polimi.it
DOI: 10.34190/EIE.20.081

Abstract: The tremendous pressures of growing social needs pose relevant challenges for governments attempting to allocate resources to deal with deficiencies and failures. At the same time, non-profit organizations, facing rising costs, intense competition over grants and donations, and ever-growing social needs, are struggling to financially sustain their operations. Scholarly research on Social Enterprises has been growing, mainly dealing with Social Enterprises as entrepreneurial endeavors and peculiar types of business models. However, the growing number of Social Enterprises and their relevance within communities is calling for better use of established theories and models from the strategic management and entrepreneurship literatures within the domain of Social Enterprises. The present research aims at addressing the transition that leads Social Enterprises from the identification of the social opportunity to business model design. By means of a series of semi-structured interviews to entrepreneurs from three different Social Enterprises, we lay the foundation for a closer investigation on opportunities in Social Entrepreneurship. We distinguish two composing aspects of Social opportunities: a social aspect, and an economic aspect of the opportunity, the recognition of which does not necessarily happen simultaneously. We then relate this finding to the transition towards business model design and reveal that, while the social aspect is the driving force of the entrepreneur, the recognition of the economic aspect signals the moment of mobilization of the social entrepreneur. Finally, we find that different typologies of social enterprises experience the transition to business model design differently, depending on how intuitive or challenges is the identification and exploitation of the economic aspect of the opportunity. We thus contribute to scholarly theory on entrepreneurship and business models, by extending the discourse on social business model design and social opportunity recognition, as well as provide actionable guidelines to social entrepreneurs struggling with translating the social opportunities, they have recognized into sustainable business models.

Keywords: business model, entrepreneurship, opportunity theories, social enterprises

1. Introduction

The inability to adequately address social needs of all members of a society has been a shared concerned throughout human history, as well as the source of inspiration for various political theories and societal philosophical discussions originated from renowned thinkers such as Marx, Rousseau, Hegel, Schopenhauer, Nietzsche, Kierkegaard, Schumpeter (Koliopoulos et al., 2012). In modern history, pressing trends such as growing world population, social and economic inequities, lack of resources, climate change, and so on, the most severe of societal and environmental problems have been traditionally assigned to the state to deal with, in a centralized way. Although many leaps forward compared to the past century, in today's internationalized economy, under the tremendous pressure of social needs, governments have increasingly been failing to secure and allocate adequate resources to deal with all market deficiencies and failures, and even though regulation is present, the lack of responsibility from the private sector to deal with societal and environmental challenges makes this global endeavor an uneven game. Furthermore, more extreme and fundamental state- capacity deficiencies have made their appearance, such as the recent economic crisis and Covid-19, which brought entire national economies to their knees, leaving them unable to provide even the very essential to the disadvantaged, weak and poor.

At the same time, organizational entities specifically created to address social problems, the so-called non-profit organizations, in the face of rising costs, intense competition with other non-profits over grants and donations, and ever-growing social needs have been struggling more and more over the years to financially sustain their growing operations. These organizations, which for years have complemented the government work – wherever that fails to address a social need tolerably – have always operated in a regime of dependence by fundraising methods such as donations, public or private grants and engagement of volunteers instead of paid employees (Dees 1998). Thus, running short of one of the above sources inevitably mean that the social impact provided is diminished, creating a vicious loop of more and more underserved social needs.

All these social-value-creation entities are part of the so-called Social Sector, or otherwise called third sector, independent sector or citizen sector (Bornstein, 2004). The social sector is occupied with the creation and provision of products and services with social value. However, the strict distinctions between sectors have been collapsing more and more over the last decades, as citizens and organizations are seeking for innovative and more efficient ways to address the pressing social inadequacies (Dees & Anderson, 2003). The progressively unbalanced situational context has ignited a shift of thinking to reinvent the way social value is being created and offered, but more importantly, its sources and its contributors. Discussions about the role and responsibility of for-profit organizations and their shareholders in the societal challenges pie are becoming more and more frequent. Many executives have become keenly aware over the last decades of the potential of their business to do more than just business, in the presence of ever stronger societal expectations and often the predominant social interest of individual shareholders (Santos et al. 2015). More recently, Hart & Zingales (2017) have challenged the meaning of "shareholder's welfare" - both in their academic work and their Harvard Business Review article - arguing that solely economic return might not actually be the kind of return a shareholder is seeking, an idea also brought up almost a decade earlier by J. Dees & Anderson (2003). A fruit of this shift in cultural mindset, social entrepreneurship (SE) has emerged to address this variety of assumed-as-trivial questions, putting entrepreneurial activity in the portrait of social value creation.

Social entrepreneurs deploy traditional entrepreneurship knowledge and organizational theories to create sustainable solutions for social problems, thus combining economic and social value creation at the same time (Yunus et al., 2010).

Products of SE are the so-called Social Enterprises. Social Enterprises are organizations that pursue a clearly defined social mission while operating as traditional for-profit organizations in financial terms (Dorado, 2006). These businesses have various origins, such as non-profits evolving to include trading activities (Boschee, 1995), for-profits that adopt a social mission (Dees, 1998), or even cross-sector collaborations aiming at addressing social needs (Kanter, 1999). Furthermore, depending on the mix between social and economic value creation, they can also be mapped on a spectrum between purely philanthropic and purely commercial extremes (Dees, 1998), depending on the resources leveraged and the organizational structure they adopt. The sector of the economy that is constituted by these businesses is referred to as "Social Economy" (Sanasi et al., 2020).

Turning the attention to the phase of creation of those enterprises, studying the process through which these businesses are conceived and establish their operations proves valuable, since research might extract insights that would encourage more social entrepreneurs to move from opportunity identification to establishing an organization. Although the field of social entrepreneurial opportunities is not thoroughly explored in literature (Dorado, 2006), there is a wider consensus that social opportunities present some differences compared to traditional ones due to their residence in the social sector and the motivation of social entrepreneurs (Robinson, 2006).

At the borders of this transition between entrepreneurial opportunities and the establishment of a new organization lies the concepts of Business Model Design (BMD). If we consider the Business Model (BM) concept as the way firms create, deliver and capture value, then the BMD is the process of conceptualization of the BM (Amit & Zott, 2015; Sanasi et al., 2019).

There is little reference in the SE literature on how social businesses progress from opportunity identification to the design of their BM. This research seeks to address this gap in both theoretical and practical terms, through an empirical study of three young social enterprises, by leveraging a multiple case-study to draw insights and observations on how different real-life social businesses experience this transition.

The present research aims at addressing this transition from opportunity to BMD, by contributing in various aspects. First of all, we lay the foundation for a closer investigation on opportunities in SE, by distinguishing two composing aspects, a social aspect and an economic aspect of the opportunity, the recognition of which does not necessarily happen simultaneously. We, then, relate this finding to the transition towards the BMD and reveal that, while the social aspect is the driving force of the entrepreneur, the recognition of the economic aspect signals the moment of mobilization of the social entrepreneur. Finally, we found that different typologies of social enterprises - based on existing theory classifiers – experience the transition to BMD differently, depending on how intuitive or challenging is the identification and exploitation of the economic aspect of the opportunity. Along with those contributions, we also discuss other findings on social enterprises' social impact and BMs and investigate their validity in extant literature.

2. Theoretical background

When it comes to entrepreneurial opportunity and its connection to the formation of a Social Enterprise (SE), although for traditional ventures that connection is widely admitted, it cannot be safely generalized for SEs, thus leaving a gap for research (Dorado, 2006). Social entrepreneurial opportunities differ from traditional ones by definition, as the former inhibit the Social Sector (Cannatelli et al., 2012; Robinson, 2006).

Scott & Venkataraman (2000, p. 218) define Entrepreneurship as "...the scholarly examination of how, by whom, and with what effects opportunities to create future goods and services are discovered, evaluated, and exploited". This definition highlights the role of opportunity identification in the entrepreneurial process (Eckhardt & Shane, 2003) and the fact that the opportunity pursuit also includes the mobilization of others' resources (Stevenson & Gumpert, 1985).

Indeed, while strategic management addresses the search for competitive advantage as a main source to create wealth by efficiently allocating resources towards growth, entrepreneurship adopts an opportunity-seeking mindset that will foster future innovation to sustain growth in the long-run (Demil et al., 2015): on this intersection between strategy and entrepreneurship, the BM constitutes the practical link between the two areas, (Demil et al., 2015) and the operationalization of a firm's strategy (Casadesus-Masanell and Ricart, 2010; Cavallo et al., 2020).

The opportunity is the key constituent of entrepreneurship (Mair & Martí, 2006). There are two theoretical streams when it comes to entrepreneurial opportunity: the first, called *opportunity recognition* (Katz & Gartner, 1988; Scott & Venkataraman, 2000), perceives opportunities as an objective phenomenon, that exist independently from the entrepreneurs (Eckhardt & Shane, 2003); while the second, *opportunity creation* (Alvarez & Barney, 2007), suggests that opportunities may be created by the entrepreneurs and are therefore subjective phenomena. To connect BMs with entrepreneurship, Teece (2010) argues that entrepreneurial activity deals with generating hypotheses on what is valuable for customers and how the firm creates, delivers and captures value, i.e., the BM. Another important topic in the opportunity field is the one that deals with the capacity of the entrepreneur to identify opportunities. To that end, research suggests that the knowledge background and experience of the entrepreneur notably influences the capacity to discover opportunities (Cavallo et al., 2019; Shane, 2000), while other scholars argue that this observation also extends to other contextual factors (Robinson, 2006).

Several scholars agree that the essence of entrepreneurship lies in the design of effective BMs (Casadesus-Masanell & Ricart, 2010). In the context of management, the term "design" has been predominantly used to denote organizational structuring (or restructuring) in the firm (Crossan & Apaydin, 2010). Relevant studies identify the role of design as that of an analytical instrument to conceptualize value creation and value capture and allocate resources accordingly (Teece, 2010). As the BM is a system of interdependent activities spanning beyond the boundaries of the firm (Zott & Amit, 2010), BMD involves the conceptualization of the aforementioned boundary-spanning systems of activities, how they are interconnected and who are the parties that preform them (Amit & Zott, 2015; Ghezzi et al., 2020).

Venkataraman (1997, p. 133), wrote: "Entrepreneurship is particularly productive from a social welfare perspective when, in the process of pursuing selfish ends, entrepreneurs also enhance social wealth by creating new markets, new industries, new technology, new institutional forms, new jobs, and net increases in real productivity". This statement relates to the phenomenon of SE. Seelos and Mair (2005, p. 241) define SE as a function of the phenomenon of the increasing number of organizations "that have created models for efficiently catering to basic human needs that existing markets and institutions have failed to satisfy." Robinson (2006), under a perspective of how opportunities are identified and evaluated by social entrepreneurs and what are the differences with traditional entrepreneurship, defines SE as a process that includes identifying a social problem and its solution, evaluating the impact and potential BM to address it, and the creation of an entity that pursues the double- or triple-bottom line (Robinson, 2006).

Organizational products of the phenomenon of SE are the so-called Social Enterprises, defined as businesses "designed and operated just like a 'regular' business enterprise, with products, services, customers, markets, expenses and revenues. It is a no-loss, no-dividend, self-sustaining company that sells goods or services and repays investments to its owners, but whose primary purpose is to serve society and improve the lot of the poor." (Yunus et al., 2010).

On these premises, social businesses are classified as social profit maximizers which, at the same time, do repay the capital invested, in contrast to the non-profit organizations, even if they also have a social focus.

Even though the various entrepreneurial, organizational and strategic aspects of social enterprises are investigated by numerous scholars, the connection of opportunities and BMD is a widely unexplored field (Cannatelli et al., 2012). For this reason, in the present research we advance to explore the following research question: *How do social enterprises transition from opportunity identification to BMD?*

The development of theoretical models and frameworks will encourage new and ambitious entrepreneurs to navigate this uncharted field more easily, providing practical tools to increase the risk of success and relevant implications for BM theory in the field of SEs.

3. Method

We have selected a multiple-case study as a research method given the exploratory nature of our research question (Eisenhardt and Graebner, 2007): according to Yin (1984), multiple cases are more robust compared to single case studies, and while a single case would allow a number of observations, it would be hard to generalize them, or in general extract positions that may apply to other firms, other than the subject one (Meredith, 1998). The analysis encompassed a series of semi-structured interviews with selected informants, with the aim of understanding the transition from the recognition of a social entrepreneurial opportunity to BMD. The informants were treated as "knowledgeable agents", while the research is a mere carrier of the experiences reported by the informants (Gioia et al., 2013).

The identification of the research question and its theoretical grounding were not part of the communication with the informants to avoid introducing biases in their answers (Eisenhardt, 1989).

We selected three SEs through the following criteria:

- they primarily used commercial means to achieve a social or environmental mission (Santos et al., 2015); the social mission came as a first priority (Yunus et al., 2010);
- profits were not shared in dividends but reinvested to the company, although investors might be remunerated for their investment (Yunus et al., 2010).

In addition to the above requisites, we strived to select relatively young firms. The informants were founding members, so to have a recent and first-hand experience of the transition from opportunity to BMD. The companies identified will be described as *Janus*, *Vesta* and *Jupiter* to maintain anonymity.

The interviews were focused on gathering information regarding the process undergone by each of the SEs, from the moment the entrepreneur(s) recognized the opportunity, until they were a fully-functioning SE with a sustainable BM. Interviews questions were open, so to let the informants speak (e.g., "How did you understand your idea was valuable? How did you recognize this was the appropriate revenue model?").

The interviews were fully transcribed and analyzed through a two-step process. First, two independent researchers performed in-vivo coding by examining the themes emerging from the informants' words (Eisenhardt, 1989). Then, we compared the codes from each firm and iteratively built an inductive coding tree for each of the three firms (Gioia et al., 2013), seeking patterns and similarities across firms (Strauss & Corbin, 1998).

4. Results

Janus is a SE based in Geneva, Switzerland and Jordan, selling high-quality embroideries created by refugee women in the Jerash "Gaza" camp, Jordan. The company was founded in 2013. The key opportunity observation was that many of the adult women in the Jerash Gaza refugee camp were capable to leverage -or be taught to their long tradition of creating hand-made embroideries to produce quality products. Janus targeting at this unexploited pool of talent and guiding by its mission of social interest, evolved into a business of contemporary embroidery production, hand-made and by the highest quality of materials. Then, the products were sold into European Markets, through boutique shops and the company's e-commerce website.

Vesta was founded in 2014 by three undergraduate students in the University of Business and Economics of Athens, Greece, aiming to reduce the obstacle and facilitate access to blood units for those who need it, a long-standing problem of the Greek society. The original idea was born a couple of years earlier due to the medical condition of a family member of one of the founders that demanded very often blood transfusions. Alongside with the platform where individuals can seek or donate blood, it offers paid services to corporate clients that wish to organize blood donation events, thus internalizing the relevant costs the company would suffer to organize this event. In the years since its foundation, Vesta has served more than 12.000 people in need of blood. But, further to that, the company strives to impact the culture and insecurities around blood donating at a national level, which is believed to be the dominant obstacle towards a capable nation-wide blood distribution system.

Jupiter was founded in 2015 as a restaurant inside a prison in the outskirts of Milan, Italy. Despite its location, Jupiter is a normal restaurant open to the public, offering high-quality gourmet cuisine, but with one key difference; employees are prison inmates. This social restaurant was born with a mission to give more opportunities to detainees to build a strong curriculum to use upon the completion of their rehabilitation period, rather than decay in inactivity. At the same time the company aimed at reducing the social stigma that accompanies these people after their sentence, especially in a professional level. Among the achievements of Jupiter is the 250 detainees that make use of the law for an alternative sentence (compared to sentence in prison), a number that is equal to the total beneficiaries of the law in a national level.

5. Discussion

The first common pattern identified in all three companies analyzed was the composition of opportunities by two aspects: a social and a commercial/economic one. The first one related directly to the social need or market failure that the entrepreneur seeks to address. More specifically, all three companies started with the identification of a social problem and the subsequent identification of a disadvantaged group in need. However, the opportunity pursuit towards a venture that combines profit with purpose starts when the economic aspect of opportunity is also identified, to complement the initial idea an provide insight for financial sustainability that will support the social impact envisioned.

The research on the three companies shows that, even though the starting point and initial inspiration and intention is the social cause (Dacin et al., 2011; Santos, 2012; Yunus et al., 2010), the economic aspect may be recognized at a much later stage.

The research also brings to the surface other aspects of the opportunity and BMs in socially enterprises, that may appear or not in the extant literature, such as:

- The previous experience of the entrepreneur seems to have an influence on the entrepreneurial activity (Alvarez et al., 2012; Robinson, 2006; Shane, 2000)
- The intuition of the entrepreneurs, supported by intention, is a dominant factor of entrepreneurial process as well as during the BMD (Frankenberger & Sauer, 2019; Krueger et al., 2000; Schneckenberg et al., 2019).
- SEs adopt a stakeholder satisfaction perspective, in contrast to the shareholder satisfaction view in for-profit organizations (Macke et al., 2018; Porter & Kramer, 2011) and have higher propensity in partnership and collaboration establishment (Yunus et al., 2010). Collaboration with the local public sector is essential for SEs. In the absence of a good collaboration with the state, Ses face significant barriers to entry (Robinson, 2006) and obstacles to operate.

Each one of the three opportunities recognized by the three SEs appears to have two aspects, a social and an economic (or commercial). The entrepreneurial intention (Krueger et al., 2000) appears to have a social starting point, which means that the entrepreneurs are primarily motivated by the social cause, as also verified in the relevant literature (Santos, 2012; Yunus et al., 2010). However, the turning point that marks the opportunity pursuit is the identification of an economic aspect in the opportunity that will be able to guarantee the financial viability of the SE. More importantly, as it becomes evident through the evolution of Vesta's opportunity process, the phases of opportunity discovery and exploitation often overlap. This position is agreed by a number of scholars (e.g., Lehner & Kaniskas, 2012).

As Sitoh et al. (2014, p. 2) reason, since the size of the social problem usually 'far outstrips the resources available to address them (Austin et al., 2006, p. 371), the challenge of financial viability comes down to the design of a viable BM. The present research indicates that, while Bridging hybrids present a more linear transition process, coupling hybrids – where both beneficiaries and customers are external – may experience a more circular process of transition, where the opportunity and BMD overlap, as recognized in literature by George & Bock (2009).

Combining the concept of the social and economic aspects of an opportunity with the different BMD findings between coupling and bridging hybrids, a more general pattern emerges about the process of transition between opportunity and BMD.

Bridging hybrids (e.g., *Janus*, *Jupiter*) are a type of SE that appears in more traditional markets, where the economic aspect of the opportunity is easier to identify. Their beneficiaries are easier to manage, as they are usually integrated into the BM by default (Santos et al., 2015). Due to the intuitive recognition of the commercial aspect of the opportunity, the evolution of opportunities from recognition to exploitation is more linear and present less experimentation. The opportunity recognition resembles opportunity discovery rather than creation, as it is a more knowledge-driven process that allows for risk-based decision making (Alvarez & Barney, 2007). For this reason, the previous knowledge and experience of the entrepreneur play a more important role than intuition.

As described so far, the transition in Bridging hybrids appears to be more linear and the steps sequential, without extensive experimentation and pivoting. The entrepreneurial activity starts upon the search for the economic aspect of opportunity. Any activity before that stage, if any, could potentially relate to a nonprofit scheme. But the mobilization towards a SE initiative can only take place in the presence of an economic aspect in the opportunity.

Coupling hybrids (e.g., *Vesta*) may be the cause of the creation of new markets, and thus may relate to a novelty in the BM. The economic aspect may remain uncertain for a significant amount of time after the entrepreneur's mobilization. Beneficiaries are usually not integrated into the BM and need to be reached in ways similar to that of the customers. The identification of the economic aspect of the opportunity – which coincides the identification of customers that will appreciate the value proposition – is overlapping with the opportunity exploitation phase and the BMD in a 'forwards and backwards' fashion. The opportunity recognition resembles opportunity creation rather than discovery, as it is a more intuition-driven process that enables incremental, inductive, and intuitive decision making (Alvarez & Barney, 2007).

By comparing the transition process with that of bridging hybrids, we can observe the iterative and circular movement between BMD and the identification of the economic aspect of opportunity, which overlap (George & Bock, 2009).

6. Conclusions

At the beginning of the present work, we set out to investigate the transition from entrepreneurial opportunity to the BMD in the context of SEs. The contribution of this research lies in the investigation of this uncharted transition, which has not been systematically analyzed in the literature. To address this gap, an exploratory research was conducted as it is the most suited in case of study of an unexplored phenomenon. In doing so, this research provides various contributions. First, on the opportunity side for SEs, the case study reveals that two distinct aspects are involved, a social and an economic. This distinction, in return, provides useful insight on how and when the social entrepreneur decides to mobilize and how financial sustainability of the social mission can be achieved and designed in BM.

A second contribution is related to how different types of BM typologies in SE seem to experience the transition from opportunity to BMD. This analysis reveals that bridging hybrids associate themselves to more traditional markets, where the economic aspect of opportunity is more easily distinguishable and the transition to BMD is rather linear, whereas coupling hybrids appear to generate a new, unexplored market and thus the process of transition shows a circular, "forwards and backwards" movement between the identification of the economic aspect of the opportunity and the design of the BM.

The present research is not free of limitations. One of the greatest objective difficulties faced during this research was the identification of SEs that fulfill the literature criteria to be characterized as such. Also, we had the opportunity to elaborate and analyze three SEs with purely social missions. Future research may also include in the research ventures that also have an environmental mission and examine their particularities.

References

Alvarez, S.A. and Barney, J.B., 2007. Discovery and creation: Alternative theories of entrepreneurial action. Strategic entrepreneurship journal, 1(1-2).

Amit, R., & Zott, C. (2015). Crafting Business Architecture: the Antecedents of Business Model Design. Strategic Entrepreneurship Journal, 9(4).

Boschee, J. (1995). Social entrepreneurship: Some non-profits are not only thinking about the unthinkable, they're doing it – Running a profit. The Conference Board Magazine.

Cannatelli, B., Masi, A. G., & Molteni, M. (2012). Green Technology Implementation in Developing Countries: Opportunity Identification and Business Model Design, *Social Innovation*.

Cavallo, A., Ghezzi, A. and Balocco, R., 2019. Entrepreneurial ecosystem research: present debates and future directions. International Entrepreneurship and Management Journal, 15(4).

Cavallo, A., Sanasi, S., Ghezzi, A. and Rangone, A., 2020. Competitive Intelligence and Strategy formulation: connecting the dots. Competitiveness Review. In press.

Crossan, M. M., & Apaydin, M. (2010). A multi-dimensional framework of organizational innovation: A systematic review of the literature. Journal of Management Studies

Dorado, S. (2006). Social Entrepreneurial ventures: Different Values so different process of creations, no? Journal of Developmental Entrepreneurship, 11(4).

Eisenhardt, K. M. (1989). Building Theories from Case Study Research. Academy of Management Review

Frankenberger, K., & Sauer, R. (2019). Cognitive antecedents of business models: Exploring the link between attention and business model design over time. Long Range Planning, 52(3).

Ghezzi, A. (2012). Emerging business models and strategies for mobile platform providers: a reference framework. Info, 14(5).

Ghezzi, A., Sanasi, S., & Cavallo, A. (2020). Business Model Adaptation: Evidence of Lean Experimentation in Digital Startups. In Proceedings of the 53rd Hawaii International Conference on System Sciences.

Gioia, D. A., Corley, K. G., & Hamilton, A. L. (2012). Seeking Qualitative Rigor in Inductive Research: Notes on the Gioia Methodology. Organizational Research Methods, 16(1).

Glaser, B., & Strauss, A. (1967). The discovery of grounded theory: Strategies for Qualitative Research. In Aldine Publishing Company.

Grassl, W. (2012). Business Models of Social Enterprise: A Design Approach to Hybridity. ACRN Journal of Entrepreneurship Perspectives.

Hart, O., & Zingales, L. (2017b). Serving Shareholders Doesn't Mean Putting Profit Above All Else. Harvard Buisness Review.

Koliopoulos, Hatzivasiliou, Scholinakis, & Heliotis. (2012). History of the latest modern world: From 1815 until today.

Krueger, N. F., Reilly, M. D., & Carsrud, A. L. (2000). Competing models of entrepreneurial intentions. Journal of Business Venturing.

Mair, J., & Schoen, O. (2007). Successful social entrepreneurial business models in the context of developing economies. International Journal of Emerging Markets, 2(1), 54–68.

Meredith, (1989). Building operations management theory through case and field research. Journal of Operations Management, 16(4).

Porter, Michael E., & Kramer, M. R. (2011). Creating shared value. Harvard Business Review.

Robinson, J. (2006). Navigating social and institutional barriers to markets: How social entrepreneurs identify and evaluate opportunities, *Social Entrepreneurship*.

Sanasi, S., Ghezzi, A., Cavallo, A. and Rangone, A., (2019). Enacting business model change in digital startups: An exploratory multiple-case study. Proceedings of the European Conference on Innovation and Entrepreneurship, ECIE, 2, 936-942.

Sanasi, S., Ghezzi, A., Cavallo, A. and Rangone, A., (2020). Making sense of the sharing economy: a business model innovation perspective. Technology Analysis & Strategic Management.

Santos, F., Pache, A. C., & Birkholz, C. (2015). Making hybrids work: Aligning business models and organizational design for social enterprises. California Management Review, 57(3),

Scott, S., & Venkataraman, S. (2000). The promise of entrepreneurship as a field of research. Source: The Academy of Management Review, 25(1).

Seelos, C., & Mair, J. (2005). Social entrepreneurship: Creating new business models to serve the poor. Business Horizons, 48(3).

Shane, S. (2000). Prior Knowledge and the Discovery of Entrepreneurial Opportunities. Organization Science. Venkataraman, S. (1997a). The Distinctive Domain of Entrepreneurship Research. In Advances in entrepreneurship, firm emergence, and growth

Wilson, F., & Post, J. E. (2013). Business models for people, planet (& profits): exploring the phenomena of social business, a market-based approach to social value creation. Small Business Economics, 40(3).

Yunus, M., Moingeon, B. and Lehmann-Ortega, L., 2010. Building social business models: Lessons from the Grameen experience. Long range planning, 43(2-3).

Zott, C., Amit, R., & Massa, L. (2011). The business model: Recent developments and future research. Journal of Management.

Impacting Mindset and Innovation on Sustainability via Global Thematic Hackathon

Juha Saukkonen, Pavlos Tarasanski and Tapio Hämäläinen
School of Business JAMK University of Applied Sciences, Jyväskylä, Finland
juha.saukkonen@jamk.fi
pavlos.tarasanski@jamk.fi
m1858@student.jamk.fi
DOI: 10.34190/EIE.20.047

Abstract: Innovations related to social, economic and environmental grand challenges are common targets not only for societies as a whole, but also for the universities and business schools in them. This paper studies an example of how an intensive intervention via a local implementation of a global 3-day design hackathon (IFTP= Invent for the Planet) on global needs has impacted participants' understanding and motivation towards sustainability issues and solving them. The paper approaches the research objective by studying via a qualitative research approach the motivation letters that the participants submitted when applying for the event, learning outcome -report immediately after the event and their self-reported orientation to the issue area one month after the event. In addition, the views of the impacts were collected from the local facilitators and coaches to reflect their considerations to the views of the learners. The theory base of the paper discusses the approaches and models of behavioural change (nudging, planned behaviour, functional triad, etc.). The analysis offers insight on whether short-term interventions can have an effect on a sample that is already exposed and interested in the topic, since a course is a non-obligatory element of studies for all participants (from both business and engineering schools).

Keywords: innovation, globality, sustainability, social innovation, environmental innovation

1. Introduction

Integrating issues in sustainable development (SD) is a relevant topic in higher education today and, increasingly, higher education institutions (HEIs) attempt to take a role as promoting agents of SD principles (Ramos et al., 2015; Stough et al., 2018). The contribution of HEIs to the transition towards a more sustainable society can be divided into 1) creating knowledge that can be transferred to society, and, also, 2) preparing their students to take their future roles in a society needing sustainability (Stough et al., ibid.). Leal Filho et al. (2016) propose that, in order to address these two potential areas of impact, higher education institutions should find new ways and methods that cross the boundaries of curricula of disciplines and are project-based. Typically, a transdisciplinary approach has been embraced within the sciences (e.g. within engineering science), but crossing the boundaries between sciences such as technological and social sciences and humanities has been rarer (Tejedor et al., 2018).

Parallel to the growing volume of sustainability-addressing programmes and projects in HEIs, another phenomenon of fast-paced innovation events, a.k.a. hackathons, has emerged. A hackathon is an event (Kolog et al., 2016) where students and subject field specialists collaborate intensively in teams with the aim of creating and designing novel solutions to a given task within a limited time span. This type of learning is seen to be inquiry-based and student centric (Kienzler and Fontanesi, 2017), with the potential to stimulate and maintain students' interest in the subject area (Abdullah and Mtsweni, 2015).

The two phenomena of learning settings have -not surprisingly - occasionally merged. One implementation of an event with sustainable development content and hackathon process is Invent for the Planet (IFTP), developed at and facilitated by Texas A&M University, which reached more than 25 universities across continents and time zones in 2020.

This paper studies the motivations for and impacts of a sustainability-oriented global innovation event and more precisely one local implementation of it The units of analysis is thus the event and its impacts as perceived by the student participants pre- and post-event, as well as the viewpoints of the facilitators of the learning process.

To reach the abovementioned objectives, the research questions of the study were:

- What contextual and motivational factors make students to apply to a sustainability-oriented specific study unit?

- What is the knowledge that students self-assess to have gained from a team-based, sustainability-oriented intensive study arrangement?
- How does the learning support staff (facilitators and coaches) depict the potential outcomes of the study unit to various stakeholder groups/levels of impact?

2. Literature review

2.1 Theories on impacting behaviour

The issues related to environmental concerns and initiatives are available in width and depth. However, as Ölander and Thøgersen (2014) claim: "Information has not been proven a very successful means to promote voluntary behaviour change to protect the environment." One societal response to this difficulty would naturally be the establishment of norms as well as the punishments for breaking them. This, however, may require a sacrifice of motivation based on making a personal choice. In societies driven by "libertarian paternalism"the concept of *"nudging"* refers to steering individuals towards a decision without breaching their right of free choice (Cohen, 2013). The individual choices would then create "an informed consent" (ibid.).

An alternative approach in acting for behavioural change is that of "planned bahaviour", in which paradigm a central factor is the individual's intention to perform a given behaviour. Intentions are assumed to contain the motivational factors that influence a given behaviour; they indicate "how hard people are willing to try, of how much of an effort they are planning to exert, in order to perform the behaviour" (Ajzen, 1991). Thus, by affecting intentions the behaviour can be altered. However, not all intentions are carried out into action; some are abandoned, while others will be revised to make them fit to changing circumstances (Ajzen, 1985). To affect both intensions and their deployment into action, interventions are introduced. The achieved effects of interventions vary a lot from modest to strong – depending on both the context and type of interventions. As Steinmetz et al. (2016) state: To produce an intention to perform the behaviour, the intervention must target many facets such as behavioural, normative, and control beliefs that will determine the final behaviour of interest.

The concept of the functional triad was created by Fogg (1998) for a construct for improved persuasion. Persuasion attempts to steer others towards the adoption of some intended (by the persuader) behaviour via a reasoning process (Reardon, 1981). Fogg's original field of triad application was that of computer systems, but since the introduction the functional triad has been applied to various instances and areas of behavioural change, e.g. Robinson et al. (2017) for impacts of professional competences in health. As the name of the model hints, there are three elements that affect the persuasive capacity of a "system". The first dimension of the functional triad is its role as a tool. Tools deployed can provide information that enables improved decision-making (Xiao & Benbasat, 2007) and/or shapes mental models of individuals using the tools (Mutschler, 1990). The second triad role in impacting behaviour is media. As media, systems can create persuasive experiences, as symbolic media for presentation of information or as sensory media for experiencing the information. Thirdly, a system can be seen as a social actor with which people interact. The original Fogg's social actor role for a system was based on the "Computers as Social Actor" (CASA) approach (Reeves & Nass, 1996), which suggests that people attribute social characteristics to (computing) technologies when those are perceived to contain and reflect features associated with human (social) behaviour (Xu et al., 2018). Xu et al. (ibid) focused their study on the receiving end of the persuasive system. They perceived the functional triad on the following three outcomes: (1) persuading users to use a system, (2) persuading users to follow the proposal based on the outcomes of the system and (3) persuading users to recommend the system to others. In this last respect, the behavioural change is expected to be able to radiate outside the boundaries of the actors directly impacted by the triad.

The intervention being studied had, on the face of it, elements of nudging instead of norming, planned behaviour in its aim to turn intentions into action and a system with embedded structure, information and communication. The potential applicability of these three paradigms made the IFTP event a meaningful unit of analysis for the paper.

2.2 Impacting sustainability behaviour

Despite the widespread familiarity of challenges in sustainability, a low level of sustainability-enhancing behaviour may prevail (Marcell et al., 2004; Eagle et al., 2015). Pappas and Pappas (2015) claim that a truly successful stance on sustainability may lead to successful behaviours becoming personality characteristics. Their research indicates that students' desire for integrity and individual value consistency means that short interventions may precipitate a lasting change in behavior or values (ibid.). Findings by Whitley et al. (2018) indicate that one's values matter in environmental decision-making, but different values are associated with different behaviours. Those with altruistic values are more likely to engage in a range of sustainability behaviours than people with egocentric values. For those with the sustainability orientation, the Value-Belief-Norm (VBN) theory models the pathway between values and behaviour.

Godfrey and Feng (2017) remark that communicating sustainability challenges and solutions does not suffice when converting into sustainable practice. Consumption patterns did not change significantly as a result of the university-wide sustainability campaign, as the observed students opted for less sustainable choices due to time pressure and convenience (ibid.). The information-oriented structure commonly used in environmental education assumes that symbol-based knowledge directly leads to motivation and action, but it often fails to create a lasting impact on behaviour (Dutta and Chandrachekaran, 2018). Initiatives based on practices and actions in the world have been more successful in creating transformative behavioural changes (ibid.).

2.3 Contests and hackathons as methods of learning and behavioural change

Arranging learning opportunities in a competitive setting has been both practiced and studied extensively, to the point that as a method has been assigned its own name: Competition-Based Learning (CnBL). CnBL is a methodology where learning is achieved through participation in a competition, but the learning result is independent of success in such a competition (Johnson, Johnson and Stanne, 1985). CnBL can naturally be combined with other learning methodologies, like Project-based learning (PBL). Burguillo's (2010) empirical study on CnBL's impacts on learning indicated that "the use of friendly competitions provide a strong motivation that helps to increase the student performance." Among the advantages of the competitive learning approach, Burguillo (ibid.) cites interactivity, collaborative work inside the group, active participation, challenge vs. duties, and increased motivation for the students as they can explore their own topics.

Innovation competitions have also been used and discussed for industrial practice. MacCormack et al. (2013) from MIT Sloan School of Management suggest that the advantage of innovation competitions is in their ability to attract a variety of nontraditional solvers to the challenges. While (ibid.) nontraditional participants tend to perform worse than the traditional experts who work in an industry, competitions are able to induce greater variation, creating the possibilities that the "best" submissions with a novel angle will outperform the more traditional approaches.

One specific form of learning via competing is a hackathon, in which "participants will self-organize and develop meaningful projects through structured communications" (Duhring, 2014). This typically happens in a tight timeframe of two to three days. It is suggested that the benefits – for the organisers - of the pace and format include: accelerating early innovation, moving quickly from ideas to first prototypes and getting diverse people onboard (Frey and Luks, 2016), as well as the creation of common social knowledge and goals (Trainer et al., 2016). There might also be setbacks, since the very constrained format of the events, in time and methodology, may limit the contributions, causing them to often be similar and not so innovative (Rey, 2017). The motivations of and outcomes for the participants can be intangible or tangible. The first category includes the thrill of competing, the love of pastime, the passion for a cause and the potential reputational effect from participation and performance. On the tangible side, the winning/prize legitimizes the pursuit of a solution to the problem(s). Overall, a well-designed and well-mentored competition can help participants build skills and expertise. These "softer" motivations outweigh the financial incentives for many participants (MacCormack et al., 2013).

2.4 Invent For The Planet – the event under study

The overall aim of IFTP is to form teams based on similar interests in a global sustainability needs statement. The global facilitators for the event publish the needs statements (problems to which solutions are sought) to the facilitators for the orientation one week prior to the event and the facilitators pass them to the accepted students four days before the event, to allow them to make individual choices and team up (virtually) with peers interested in the same topic area. The teams then research the topic to come up with a plan and build a simple prototype within a 48 hours timeframe (TAMU, 2020).

The process then proceeds as follows (TAMU, ibid.): At the end of the 48-hour hackathon, each team presents their solution to a panel of local judges. Three teams are chosen for first, second and third place prizes. The first-place teams from each university will then have a week to perfect their presentation and submit a video that will be judged remotely by a global network of facilitators and narrowed down to a final five. Those five teams will visit the Texas A&M University final event to pitch their idea against each other, for a chance to be named the first-place winner overall.

The 14 needs statements in the 2020 IFTP event covered issues on all three basic pillars of sustainability: Environmental (e.g. the plastic pollution of oceans, bushfires), Economic (e.g. matching economic growth with energy sustainability) and Social (e.g. fake news, innovative parenting, coronavirus epidemic). The themes were further divided into subsections of Environment, Digital Technologies and Environment, Safety, Humanity, Aviation, Communications and Information Technology.

The five student teams of JAMK University of Applied Sciences worked on the following five needs statements:

- 1. Ocean trash heaps (environment)
- 2. Preventing injuries of distracted pedestrians (safety)
- 3. Australian bushfires (environment)
- 4. Waste management in aviation industry (aviation)
- 5. Seamless air travel (aviation)

3. Research method

The research method applied to this paper was of a qualitative and interpretive nature. The qualitative approach was chosen partly due to the amount of potential respondents: The 2020 implementation at the university consisted of 16 students across yearly cohorts and disciplines. The student body consisted of participants from seven nationalities, on top of which the six persons involved in facilitating the process and supporting the student teams consisted of three different nationalities. Thus, the small sample size would not have allowed a full scale of quantitative analysis with statistical significance. In addition, the cross-cultural and cross-disciplinary nature of the respondent pool could have led to differing interpretations of the respondents if subjected to a closed multiple-choice survey questionnaire. Instead, the participants wrote: 1) Short, open-ended motivation letters to support their application to the event one month prior to the event, 2) Reports of their learning outcomes immediately after the event, and 3) Assessments of potential impacts of the type of programmes they participated in to different stakeholders and layers (society, school, career, personal). The impact assessment was also sent to the event´s facilitators and coaches for comparison of the students' views. As the respondents were able to express themselves in their natural manner, the interpretation of their intended meanings was left to researchers, which is a basic tenet of qualitative (interpretivist) research.

The data collected was subjected to thematic content analysis. The themes were sourced from the prior-art literature on learning impacts, behavioural change and education for sustainability – added with themes arising from the data itself. Once the themes were defined, a vocabulary for each theme was created for use in content analysis, which aimed at recognising patterns of thought between respondents as well as disagreements within the respondent group and potential discrepancies between the student and the learning support group.

Table 1: An example of theme-vocabulary structure used in content analysis

Themes of Learning Outcomes	Words categorized to the theme
Collaboration	together, group, team, people, joint, cooperate, collaborate
Challenge	contest, competition, winning, needs, problems, challenge
Communication	presenting, sharing, showing, talking
Creativity	innovation, create, new, idea, solution, prototype
Crossculturality/-disciplinarity	diversity, different, studies, country, culture, international, (a)cross
Career	useful, future, work, career

The findings of the content analysis are presented in the results as word clouds for their communicativeness as well as summary tables. In addition, a graphical illustration showing the perceived benefits of such events for entrepreneurship – views from participants vs. facilitators – is shown.

4. Results

The motivation letters (16 pcs) that the students wrote as part of their individual application to this study unit (that belongs to the category of optional studies for all programmes at the university) were analysed for their content per team.

First, Figure 1 below offers an overview of the motivation letter contents in the form of a word cloud.

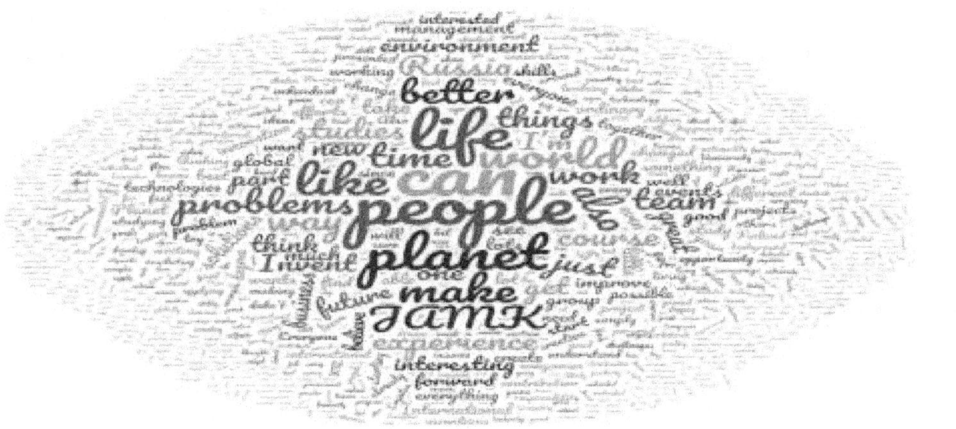

Figure 1: Overview of contents of pre-event motivation letters (word cloud)

Table 2 below summarises the most common themes in the motivation letters. The themes appear in the table in the order of their appearance in the individual motivation letters, i.e. if a theme was repeated in the same letter, the repetitions did not count for the analysis. The motivational issues were divided into two baskets: 1) Sources of motivation = which prior actions, attitudes and values were addressed 2) Orientation of the motivation = which usage value the respondent addresses to the event on offer.

Table 2: The most common themes in the pre-event motivation letters

Motivational Sources (context)	Motivational Orientation (utility)
teamwork	innovation process learning
issue importance	preparing for the future
values	cross-disciplinarity
earlier practice with the issue area	team process learning

Next, the self-reported learning outcomes (15 reports) were analysed. The assessments were done immediately post-event as a free-format text as part of study unit completion (not affecting the grading, which was pass/fail for the whole study unit). Figure 2 illustrates the content of reported learning outcomes as a word cloud.

Figure 2: Learning outcomes as a word cloud

Table 3 summarises the content of learning outcomes – assessment across themes.

Table 3: The themes of learning outcomes with examples of expression

Most common themes of Learning Outcomes	Density of theme vocabulary across 15 individual reports (the most common expression **highlighted**)
Collaboration	together (7), group (7), **team (14)**, people (12), joint (2), cooperated (1), collaborated (1)
Challenge	contest (1), competition (7), winning (9), **needs (12)**, problems (6), challenge (3)
Communication	**present (9)**, share (4), show (3), talk (6), discuss (3)
Creativity	innovation (5), create (10), new (10), **idea (14)**, solution (10), prototype (5)
Crossculturality/-disciplinarity	diversity (1), **different (8)**, studies (2), countries (3), cultures (5), international (3), (a)cross (3)
Career	useful (2), future (4), **work (6)**, career (3),

The models of affecting behaviour from the literature review were the additional lenses through which the content analysis of the process was conducted.

Table 4: Practices across the models of behavioural change

Behavioural Change type	Practices within the study unit/event
Nudging	inviting voluntariness asking for motivational context and learning reflection incentivising
Planned Behaviour	incentivising direction by needs statements pressure to make ideas into tangible solutions
Functional Triad	team process blueprint (tool) shared platform (media) the online network (social actor)

Lastly,.one month after the event the perceived benefits of contest-based and sustainability-oriented events (like the IFTP) was inquired from the facilitators (six people), and their views were reflected with those of the students (only two were within reach for immediate evaluation, as the approaching paper submission deadline was a major limiting factor for availability. The aim was to find out potential shared vs. diverging views between the two stakeholder groups. The layers of impact from individual to general benefits were: Individual personal benefit, Individual career benefit, School (University) level benefits, Societal benefits. Figure 3 below summarises the findings of that analysis.

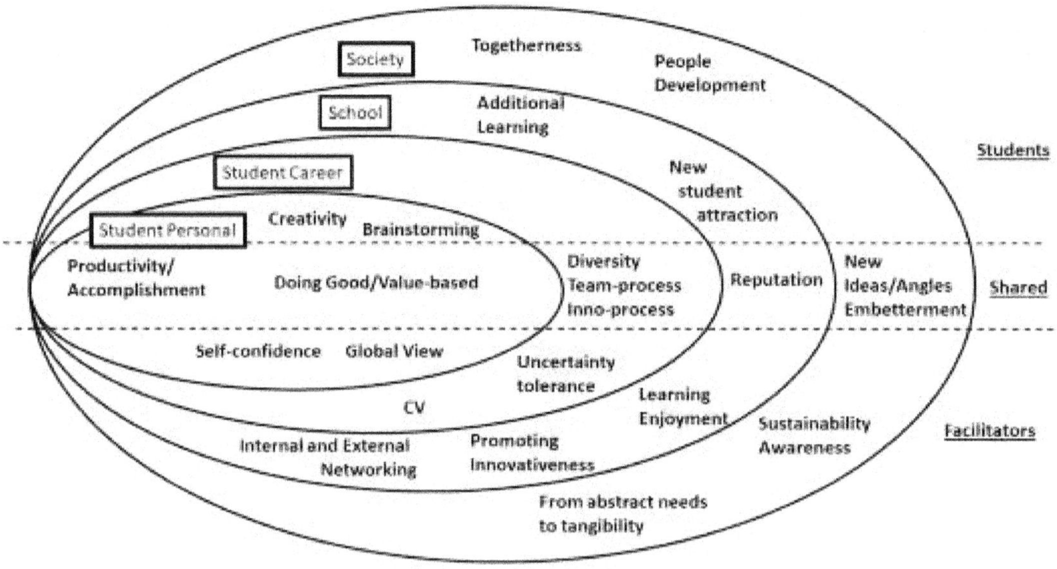

Figure 3: Perceived impacts across layers between facilitators and students

5. Conclusion

The overarching summary – derived from the expressions of learning outcomes of the themes – describing the sustainability-focused innovation event IFTP is that (see Chapter 4/Table 3 & Figure 3 for details) the event drew together people from different backgrounds to create and present as teams ideas based on true needs, and, while doing so, learn also skills for their future work. These longer-lasting effects contain the understanding of team and innovation processes in organisations. For the organizing parties the effects are in reputation and the increase in the quantity and quality of their relationships. On the one hand, the societal impacts are tied to the outcomes – new solutions to known problems. On the other hand, the benefits relate to belongingness and empowerment as well as the development of the future workforce. The ITFP implementation proved that it is possible to get early stage solutions in an intensive hackathon event, just as Haasnoot, Bouwer and Kwadijk (2017) commented on their environmental hackathon case:"the event proved it is possible to map within a short time frame the issues at hand, as well as potentially effective solutions". Haasnoot et al. also suggest that the format, when replicated for other problems, can be useful for decision-makers in search for quick but in-depth analysis of their long-term planning problems.

It is noticeable that the competitive nature (there were both local small-scale and global larger-scale awards) was not important as a motivator for participation, nor largely referred to in learning outcomes or perceived benefits. The role of competition and success in it was not highlighted as a personal motivator or outcome, nor was it seen as an important part of the contribution to any layers of impact. Thus, the finding of MacCormack et al. (2013) of a more meaningful role of soft values vs. competitive values got confirmed. In the corporate hackathon case reported by Nolte et al. (2018) the success as a proof of creativity was seen also as a career-enhancing outcome.In case of hackathons that combine corporate and student participants, this potential divergence of values and goals should be acted on by organizers. This is part of the pre-event preparation, importance of which (due to limited face-to-face time usable for forming and norming in teams) Trainer et al. (2016) highlight.

The facilitators did see the hackathon as a way of improving learning experience (via method), while students saw the contribution to learning be more in the way of impacting substance knowledge (additional learning). The student view echoes what Nolte et al. (2018) reported on impacts to individuals in a corporate hackathon. The participants in their study reported learning new substance skills (since they joined projects outside their normal working sphere) but also got inputs and insights outside to their own current work from the hackathon contents and way of working. Our results also support Briscoe and Mulligan (2014) findings from cross-analysis of multiple hackathons: Learning and networking are the most common reasons to attend, while social change and getting awarded follow (with a wide margin) in importance of motivators.

In relation to the topic area of the event, the students reported societal embetterment and values as their motivators as well as perceived benefits. The learning reports did not contain commentary of behavioural change on an individual level. The voluntary nature and strong and clear theme on sustainability hint that these kinds of events self-select people already oriented towards sustainability. In that sense, the effects on individuals are rather focused on maintaining and fortifying/amplifying sustainable behaviour. These civic-type of hackathons aiming at development of altruistic solutions and working for common good have their own rationale (Perng et al., 2018) and further study is needed to see if our results comply with other cases with similar civic orientation.

Based on the findings, it seems plausible to state that structured and networked events like IFTP can impact future behaviour in ways described in all three theoretical models presented: nudging, planned behavior and functional triad. Interestingly, the future behaviour that can be anticipated is more of the processual type: Participants reported the learnings of innovation and team processes as core takeaways, rather than the knowledge on the subject area. The voluntary nature of the programme may have self-selected those students with their values and behavioural base already resonating with the theme area of the event, and thus the foreseeable changes specifically in sustainability were not seen as important. The behavioural theories reviewed seem, in this setting, be more applicable to the behavioural change within the organising body, to whom the benefits perceived differ from the individual-level ones. In these studies the concept of learner should, perhaps,be the HEI responsible for arranging and facilitating the process. Exposure to sustainability hackathons may over time cause changes that the earlier research has adapted on an individual level. Another way of fortifying both the issue area knowledge and commitment would be a follow-up after hackathon event. Tools that document the progression at the hackathon would be helpful; This way the achieved but still incomplete new artifacts can be worked further in a distributed way after the hackathon, as Trainer et al. (2016) suggest.

The small yet comprehensive sample size and contextually (one university in Finland at one point of time) limited scope set limits to the generalizability of the findings. Hence, longitudinal studies following the participants and/or comparative studies between year-to-year-implementations and different locations (geographically and academically) would shed additional light on the impacts to innovations on sustainability via short-term interventions.

References

Abdullah, H. & Mtsweni, J. (2015). Stimulating and maintaining students' interest in Computer Science using the hackathon model. *The Independent Journal of Teaching and Learning*, *10*(1), 85-97.

Ajzen, I. (1985). From intentions to actions: A theory of planned behavior. In *Action control* (pp. 11-39). Springer, Berlin, Heidelberg.

Ajzen, I. (1991). The theory of planned behavior. *Organizational behavior and human decision processes*, *50*(2), 179-211.

Briscoe, G., & Mulligan, C. (2014). Digital innovation: The Hackathon phenomenon (CreativeWorks London Working Paper No. 6). London, England: Queen Mary University of London

Burguillo, J. C. (2010). Using game theory and competition-based learning to stimulate student motivation and performance. *Computers & education*, *55*(2), 566-575.

Cohen, S. (2013). Nudging and informed consent. *The American Journal of Bioethics*, *13*(6), 3-11.

Duhring, J. (2014). Project-based learning kickstart tips: Hackathon pedagogies as educational technology. In *VentureWell. Proceedings of Open, the Annual Conference* (p. 1). National Collegiate Inventors & Innovators Alliance.

Dutta, D. & Chandrasekharan, S. (2018). Doing to being: farming actions in a community coalesce into pro-environment motivations and values. *Environmental Education Research*, *24*(8), 1192-1210.

Eagle, L., Low, D., Case, P. & Vandommele, L. (2015). Attitudes of undergraduate business students toward sustainability issues. *International Journal of Sustainability in Higher Education*.

Fogg, B. J. (1998). Persuasive computers: Perspectives and research directions, Proceedings of CHI, ACM Press, 225–232.

Godfrey, D. M. & Feng, P. (2017). Communicating sustainability: student perceptions of a behavior change campaign. *International Journal of Sustainability in Higher Education*.

Johnson, R. T., Johnson, D. W. & Stanne, M. B. (1986). Comparison of computer-assisted cooperative, competitive, and individualistic learning. *American Educational Research Journal*, *23*(3), 382-392.

Kienzler, H. & Fontanesi, C. (2017). Learning through inquiry: A global health hackathon. *Teaching in Higher Education*, *22*(2), 129-142.

Kolog, E. A., Sutinen, E. & Nygren, E. (2016). Hackathon for learning digital theology in computer science. *International Journal of Modern Education and Computer Science*, *8*(6), 1.

Leal Filho, W., Shiel, C. & Paço, A. (2016). Implementing and operationalising integrative approaches to sustainability in higher education: the role of project-oriented learning. *Journal of cleaner Production*, *133*, 126-135.

MacCormack, A., Murray, F. & Wagner, E. (2013). Spurring innovation through competitions. *MIT Sloan Management Review*, *55*(1), 25.

Marcell, K., Agyeman, J. and Rappaport, A. (2004), "*Cooling the campus: experiences from a pilot study to reduce electricity use at Tufts University, USA, using social marketing methods*", *International Journal of Sustainability in Higher Education* , Vol. 5 No. 2, pp. 169-189.

Mutschler, E. (1990). Computer assisted decision making. Computers in Human Services, 6(4), 231–250.

Nolte, A., Pe-Than, E. P. P., Filippova, A., Bird, C., Scallen, S., & Herbsleb, J. D. (2018). You Hacked and Now What? - Exploring Outcomes of a Corporate Hackathon. *Proceedings of the ACM on Human-Computer Interaction*, *2*(CSCW), 1-23

Ölander, F. & Thøgersen, J. (2014). Informing versus nudging in environmental policy. *Journal of Consumer Policy*, *37*(3), 341-356.

Pappas, J. B. & Pappas, E. C. (2015). The Sustainable Personality: Values and Behaviors in Individual Sustainability. *International Journal of Higher Education*, *4*(1), 12-21.

Perng, S. Y., Kitchin, R., & Mac Donncha, D. (2018). Hackathons, entrepreneurial life and the making of smart cities. *Geoforum*, *97*, 189-197.

Ramos, T. B., Caeiro, S., Van Hoof, B., Lozano, R., Huisingh, D. & Ceulemans, K. (2015). Experiences from the implementation of sustainable development in higher education institutions: Environmental Management for Sustainable Universities. *Journal of Cleaner Production*, *106*, 3-10.

Reardon, K. (1981). Persuasion, theory and context. Beverly Hills, California: Sage Publications.

Reeves, B. & Nass, C. (1996). The media equation: How people treat computers, television, and new media like real people and places. New York: Cambridge University Press.

Rey, S. (2017, June). Museomix: lessons learned from an open creative hackathon in museums. Archives Ouvertes, Available online : https://hal.inria.fr/hal-01550565/document. Accessed 7.4.2020.

Robinson Jay, F., Ramos Duharte, D., Durand Rill, R., Mendoza Fonseca, N. L. & Masfarroll Rodríguez, M. (2017). The functional triad for the achievement of the socio-humanist competence in the professionals of the health. *Revista Información Científica*, *96*(6), 1111-1119.

Steinmetz, H., Knappstein, M., Ajzen, I., Schmidt, P. & Kabst, R. (2016). How effective are behavior change interventions based on the theory of planned behavior? *Zeitschrift für Psychologie*.

Stough, T., Ceulemans, K., Lambrechts, W. & Cappuyns, V. (2018). Assessing sustainability in higher education curricula: A critical reflection on validity issues. *Journal of Cleaner Production*, *172*, 4456-4466.

TAMU (Texas A&M University). (2020): What is invent for the planet? Available online: https://engineering.tamu.edu/student-life/aggies-invent/events/invent-for-the-planet/about.html Accessed 13.4.2020.

Tejedor, G., Segalàs, J. & Rosas-Casals, M. (2018). Transdisciplinarity in higher education for sustainability: How discourses are approached in engineering education. *Journal of cleaner production*, *175*, 29-37.

Trainer, E. H., Kalyanasundaram, A., Chaihirunkarn, C. & Herbsleb, J. D. (2016, February). How to hackathon: Socio-technical tradeoffs in brief, intensive collocation. In *proceedings of the 19th ACM conference on computer-supported cooperative work & social computing* (pp. 1118-1130).

Whitley, C. T., Takahashi, B., Zwickle, A., Besley, J. C. & Lertpratchya, A. P. (2018). Sustainability behaviors among college students: An application of the VBN theory. *Environmental education research*, *24*(2), 245-262.

Xiao, B. & Benbasat, I. (2007). E-commerce product recommendation agents: Use, characteristics, and impact. MIS Quarterly, 31(1), 137–209.

The Study of Relationship Between the Processes of Creating Technological and Marketing Innovations on the Example of Russia

Ravilya Sedunova and Oleg Golichenko
Central Economics and Mathematics Institute of Russian Academy of Sciences, Moscow, Russia
r.fakhrudinova@gmail.com
golichenko@ranbler.ru
DOI: 10.34190/EIE.20.173

Abstract: The purpose of the paper is to find an answer to the following questions: how the technological and marketing are innovation related, and to what extent is marketing innovation critical for the implementation of technological one? The study considers two possible types of relationship: complementarity and interdependence of these processes. The former type of relationship characterises the existence of the opportunity for the process interaction, and the latter one means its implementation. The concepts of the core and sub-core of the innovation process are used to find the answer to these questions. The set of enterprises involved in technological innovation is classified as a technology-innovative core; at the same time, the population of enterprises engaged in the marketing innovation shapes a marketing-innovative core. In turn, the enterprises that act simultaneously in both technological and marketing innovation form an innovative sub-core. The existence of a non-empty innovative sub-core means that complementarity of technological and marketing innovative processes takes place, i.e. there is room or potential for their interaction. If the potential is realised at least partially, we will consider the processes (or their corresponding activities) as interdependent. Those innovative active enterprises are forced to create marketing innovations promoting technological ones. In other words, to establish process interdependence, it is sufficient to demonstrate that marketing innovations contribute significantly greatly to promoting technologically new or significantly improved products. The investigation proves that for some Russian enterprises, these two just mentioned innovative processes are interconnected. The nature of such interconnection is investigated; namely, it finds out that marketing innovations are created and used to promote not well-known, but new for the market products. A comparative analysis of the strategies of using marketing innovations and their effectiveness for enterprises of Russian and foreign ownership is carried out.

Keywords: technological and marketing innovations, complementarity of processes, interaction of processes, promotion of technological innovations

1. Introduction

The term "innovation" traditionally refers to technological advances in new products or production processes. This approach dominated in the economic and management literature for a long time since Schumpeter's first work in 1934 (Schumpeter and Opie, 1961). With the formation and further development of innovation theory, the field of research expanded, in particular, with the addition "non-technological" types of innovation, i.e. marketing and organisational ones, began to be actively studied (OECD 2005, 2019).

The importance of the study of marketing innovation was emphasized in the 60s of the last century (Levitt, 1960). However, research related to this topic became widespread later in the 21st century. At the same time, it is worth noting that the studies of creating technological and marketing innovations are often unrelated in the literature. It can be justified if companies promote technologically new products mainly using standard marketing methods, but they prefer marketing innovations to expand sales of conventional products.

Nevertheless, according to economic practice, these types of innovation activities are often interrelated. In particular, a situation is possible when technological innovations, namely product innovations, may cause changes in marketing strategies requiring the creation and use of marketing innovations (Boer and During, 2001). Below we will try to find out, taking into account statistics, the answers for the questions:

Whether there is a significant relationship between the processes of creating technological and marketing innovations in Russia? How are the processes related? What is the structure of their links?

In doing so, we will adhere to the following outline. In the beginning, the concepts of complementarity and interconnection of the processes of creating technological and marketing innovations will be given in conjunction with the ideas of innovative cores and their sub-core. Then these terms are used to formulate and prove the necessary and sufficient conditions for the existence of the relationship between the processes of creating technological and marketing innovations. Finally, the strategies of the behaviour of enterprises which created technological and marketing innovations will be studied for Russian and foreign ownership.

2. The methodology of the study

The purpose of this study is to find answers to the questions mentioned above. The study considers two possible types of interrelationships between these processes to respond to the questions. These are complementarity and direct interaction. For determining the conditions under which these types of relationships occur, it is necessary to address the methodology of research of National innovation system (NIS), proposed in (Golichenko 2011, 2016). According to the methodology, it makes sense to distinguish a core of intensity for each innovation system process. The core is the minimal part of the production process on which it is concentrated. The part is located on various entities (organisations) whose activities are at least partially related to the considering processes. In other words, the core of intensity determines the set of resources available to the process at the given time. Therefore, it determines the current growth capacity of the process by involving unused core resources.

Since the two processes, the technological and marketing innovation ones, are the subject of the study, their intensity cores need to be considered below. The first of these cores relevant to the creation of technological innovations is called a technology-innovative core, and the second referred to generating marketing innovations is named a marketing-innovative core. The innovation cores of these processes determine the set of resources available to the innovation processes at the given time. In other words, they characterise the current growth potential of the innovation process (Golichenko, 2011).

The second notion actively used below is a sub-core of these innovation processes, which we call below the "innovative sub-core". Its carriers are the companies that are active simultaneously in the development of both technological and marketing innovations. In other words, the innovative sub-core represents the intersection of the innovative cores of the processes of creating technological and marketing innovations.

At the sub-core enterprises, the processes essentially supplement each other, i.e. they are complementary (Golichenko, 2014). The complementarity of processes means that there is room or potential for the interaction of these processes. If this potential is (at least partially) implemented, that is, activities to create technological and marketing innovations are interconnected (or interdependent), the corresponding processes will be called as conjugate ones.

The interconnection between the processes of creating technological and marketing innovations in enterprises, in particular, means that enterprises carrying out technological innovations are forced to develop marketing innovations for promoting technologically innovative products. The opposite is also possible when new marketing ideas generate the requirement for technological variations of the product.

Some studies are establishing the existence of a potential for interaction between technological and marketing innovation. In our terms, that means the non-emptiness of the sub-core. Among them, the article (Kijek, 2013), which analyses the innovative activity of industrial enterprises in Poland in 2008 – 2010. The regression analysis helps the author of the article to conclude that companies active in product innovation are more inclined to innovate in marketing. The research (Ilić et al., 2014) is also concerned to some extent, with an interaction potential of the processes of interest to us. In the article, the estimate based on a sample of 310 enterprises in Serbia shows that 73% of them used at least one type of non-technological innovation. In contrast, technological innovations took place for 61.5% of enterprises.

At the same time, it is worth noting that modern literature rarely highlights the issues of the interdependence of the processes. Among the studies in which these issues are addressed in some way, the research (Schubert, 2010) should be pointed out. Here, in particular, it is shown that when German firms are active in both technological and marketing innovations, their sales of innovative products are up. The fact indirectly indicates the presence of a conjugation effect of the processes of interest to us. Similar results can be found in the paper (Schmidt and Rammer 2013), which shows that in many firms that had technological innovations the utilisation of marketing innovations accompanies the increase in sales and reduction of innovation costs. The authors also conclude that the probability of creating technologically innovative products is higher in firms that use marketing innovations.

One of the disadvantages of current research in the field of marketing and technological innovation is the only use of micro-level data analysis. The statistics of groups of enterprises united by some attribute, for example, belonging to the same form of ownership or the same size class, are seldom studied. As a rule, no attempt is made to find out to what extent whether the potential for the interaction of processes is achieved. Moreover, finally, a sufficiently complete set of characteristics of the processes of innovation creation and dissemination processes is not taken into account.

And finally, the methodological framework just mentioned should also include the algorithm implemented in the next section. It is related to the study of the relationship between the two types of innovation and consists of two following steps. At the first one, we are looking for an area (sub-core) where either of the two types of innovation activities exists simultaneously. At the second step, we determine the sub-core and propose a hypothesis of the interconnection of these types of innovation activities for this area. To prove the hypothesis, we calculate some significant benchmarks characterising these innovation activities in the area. If the values of the corresponding indicators differ significantly for the sub-core and cores of two types of innovation activities, it means that there is a strong relationship between these types of innovation on the sub-core. If the changes are insignificant or absent at all, we can conclude that the two types of innovation are separated, and do not affect each other, i.e. they are not interconnected. Besides, if the hypothesis is correct, changes in benchmarks in one way or another have to reveal differences in the behaviour strategies of the enterprises under consideration.

3. Relationship between technological and marketing innovation in Russia

The issue of the relationship between creating technological and marketing innovations is relevant today. Usually, it is believed that marketing innovation accompanies technologically innovative products. However, in Russia, as shown in (Golichenko and Fakhrudinova, 2014, Gorodnikova et al, 2014,), marketing innovations have significantly smaller distribution than technological ones, i.e. a technology-innovative core is much larger than an innovative sub-core. Therefore, the question arises: are the processes of creating marketing and technological innovations connected on the sub-core or do they exist separately? In other words, it is necessary to confirm or refute the following hypothesis.

Hypothesis 1. There is an interdependence of the processes of creating technological and marketing innovations in Russia.

Necessary and sufficient conditions. The necessary condition for the interdependence of the processes, that is, the existence of their interaction, is their complementarity. The complementarity means that two sets have a non-empty intersection. One of the sets consists of the enterprises having carried out technological innovations, and the other contains companies having created marketing innovations. In other words, a necessary condition for the interrelation of processes is the non-emptiness of their innovative sub-core.

Before proceeding to formulate sufficient conditions for the existence of the interdependency, it is worth pointing out that there are two ways to divide the output of the enterprises of the sub-core.

On the one hand, it is worth taking into account that two disjoint parts compose the output of an enterprise. The first of them includes technologically innovative products (TIP), and the second is associated with products that are non-innovative technologically. On the other hand, the same output is a sum of two other unrelated parts, for one of which the marketing innovations (MI) are necessary to promote the output to the market, and for the other, they are not being used. It is easy to see that the following intersections of the output parts described above are possible.

- Marketing innovative products are a part of technologically innovative output (Figure 1).
- Marketing innovative products are part of both technologically innovative and non-innovative output (Figure 2).
- Marketing innovative products are part of conventional, technologically non-innovative products (Figure 3).

The fulfilment of 1) or 2) is a sufficient condition for the interdependence of technological and marketing innovation.

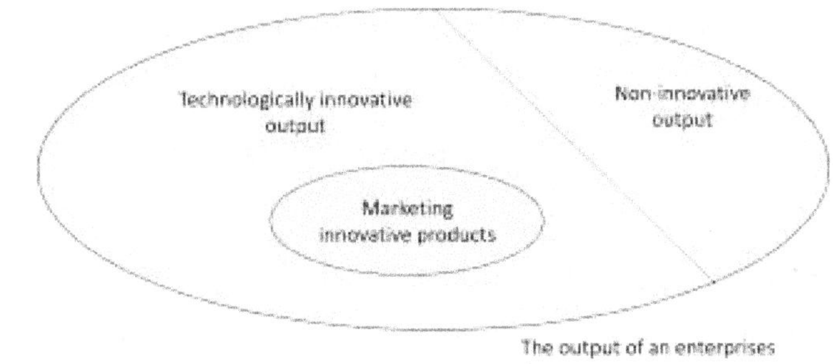

Figure 1: The interconnection of technological and marketing innovation (the use of marketing innovations to promote only technologically innovative products)

3.1 Proof of the interconnection between the processes.

For what follows, it is useful to introduce the notions of a "pure" technology-innovative core and a "pure" marketing-innovative core. To define such "pure" cores let us exclude the sub-core from the innovative cores mentioned above. Consequently, we get the two following types of pure cores:

- 1) "pure" technology-innovative core consisting of enterprises that only carried out technological innovations;
- 2) "pure" marketing-innovative core whose enterprises created merely marketing innovations.

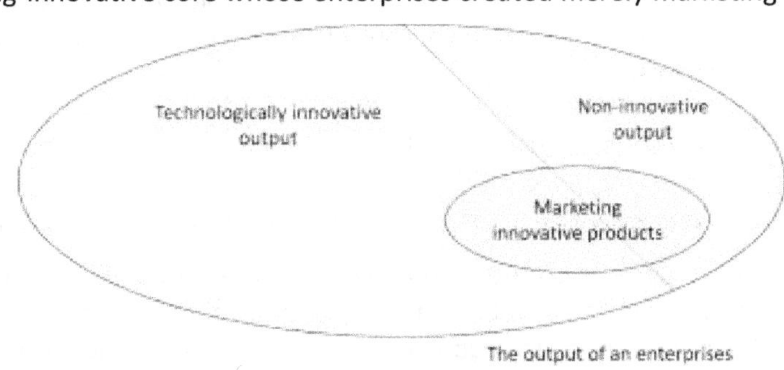

Figure 2: The interconnection of technological and marketing innovation (The use of marketing innovations to promote both technologically innovative and conventional, non-innovative products)

Below only "pure" cores are considered. Therefore, for the sake of simplicity, the attribute "pure" is omitted, that is, instead of the terms "pure technology-innovative core" and "pure marketing-innovative core", the expressions "technology-innovative core" and "marketing-innovative core" are respectively in use below. To prove the interdependence (or interconnection) of technological and marketing innovation, let us show that the necessary and sufficient conditions for it are met. As mentioned above, the necessary condition is the complementarity of the processes, that is, the non-emptiness of the innovative sub-core. The fact that the sub-core is not empty is proved by the data of Russian statistics (Form No. 4 - Innovation). According to these data, the sample of interest to us contains enterprises that simultaneously carried out technological and marketing innovations. For the period from 2013 to 2017, the number of such enterprises was 500-600 units. Further, enterprises that have carried out technological or marketing innovations will be denoted as TIE or MIE, respectively.

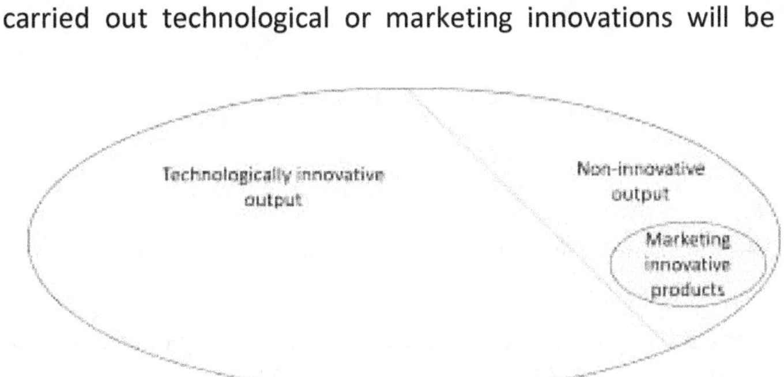

Figure 3: The lack of interconnection of technological and marketing innovation (The use of marketing innovations to promote only conventional, non-innovative products)

The fulfilment of sufficient conditions 1) and 2) (see Figures 1 and 2) can be proved by contradiction. To do this, let us assume that condition 3) is true and show the opposite. The proof consists in the analysis of transitions from each innovative core to the sub-core. If there are no significant shifts in the values of the control indicators for at least one of these transitions, it means that the processes we are interested in are not interdependent, i.e. condition 3) is satisfied.

As key control indicators are taken the following ones:

- 1. share of costs of product and process innovations in total costs for technological innovations;
- 2. cost-intensity of product innovation equal to the ratio of the costs of product innovation to the sales of technologically innovative products;
- 3. share of technologically radical, innovative products in total sales of technologically innovative output;
- 4. cost-intensity of marketing innovation equal to the ratio of the costs of the marketing innovations to the output sales increasing due to the marketing innovations.

The source of information for calculating all of these key control indicators is data from Russian statistics ("Form No.4 Innovation. Information on innovation activities of the organization").

Here and further technologically radical innovative products mean technologically innovative products that are new to the firm and the market. The indicators are considered in relation to enterprises of Russian and foreign ownership forms. Under the enterprises of foreign ownership in the Russian market, we mean the company with the participation of foreign ownership. In other words, the set of enterprises considering include both Russian-foreign and foreign-owned companies.

Let us proceed to the analysis of indicators just outlined.

3.1.1 The costs of product and process innovations in the total expenditure on technological innovations.

For Russian-owned enterprises belonging to the technological innovation core, almost three-quarters of the spending on technological innovation is accounted for product innovation and one-quarter is due to process innovations (see Figure 4). Nevertheless, for the sub-core of Russian property, the costs of product and process innovations are approximately equal. As far as foreign-owned enterprises are concerned, their transition from the technological innovation core to the sub-core cause a decrease in the share of costs for product innovations (from 37% to 27%) and an increase in the share of costs for process innovations (from 63% to 72%). Thus, regardless of the form of ownership, the shares for product and process innovations in total innovation expenditures are significantly changing while proceeding from the technological innovation core to the sub-core.

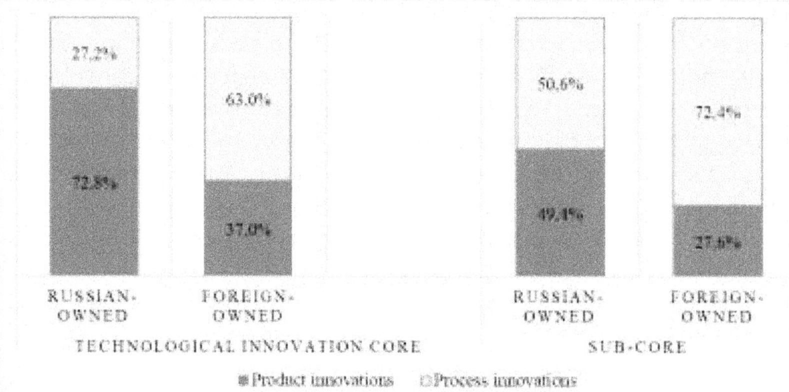

Source: Based on Russian statistics Database: Form No.4 Innovation. Information on innovation activities of the organization.

Figure 4: Ratio of costs for product and process innovation for various forms of ownership at the innovation core and sub-core, 2013-2017

3.1.2 Cost-intensity of product innovation

Cost-intensity of product innovation For Russian-owned firms of the technological and innovative core and sub-core, the cost-intensity of product innovation indicators are 19.6% and 63%, respectively (Figure5). Besides, for foreign-owned enterprises, the value of the cost intensity indicator, moving from a technology-innovative core to the sub-core, drops from 6.7% to 5.9%. The reasons for this difference in shifts in indicator values are investigated in the next section.

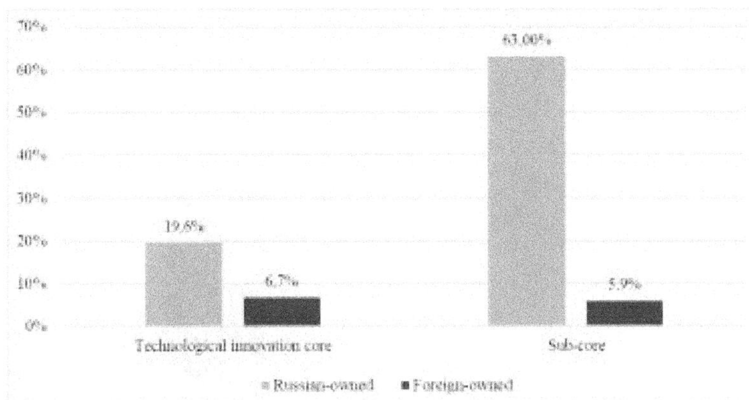

Source: Based on Russian statistics Database: Form No.4 Innovation. Information on innovation activities of the organization.

Figure 5: Cost-intensity of product innovation for various forms of ownership at the innovation core and sub-core, 2013-2017

3.1.3 New for the market, newly introduced and modernised products in the total volume of technological innovation output

For Russian-owned enterprises, the transition from a technologically innovative core to a sub-core significantly increases the share of new products for the market (1.7 times from 11.4% to 19.6%). The other two components of innovative output do not change so significantly (see Figure 6). A different dimension and magnitude of changes in the relevant indicators concerns enterprises of foreign ownership. For this form of ownership, the share of new products for the market decreases by two times (from 2.8% to 1.3%) after this transition. At the same time, the percentage of newly introduced or significantly technologically improved products in the sales increases 1.8 times (from 41.6% to 74.2%), and the share of modernised products decreases by 2.3 times (from 58.4% to 25.8%).

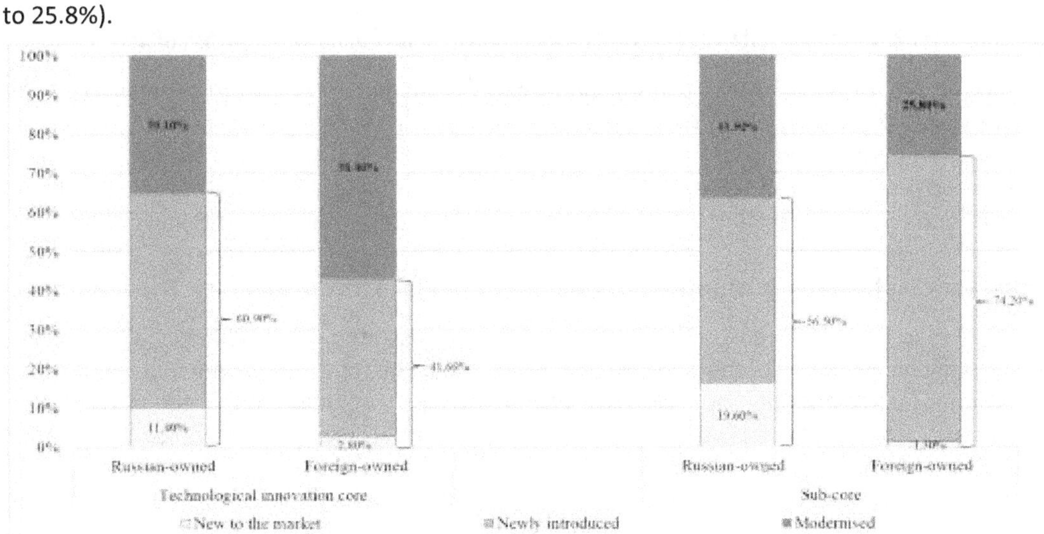

Source: Based on Russian statistics Database: Form No.4 Innovation. Information on innovation activities of the organization.

Figure 6: Ratios of new to the market, newly introduced and modernised innovative products, 2013-2017

Recapitulating the main points of the analysis of the three above-mentioned indicators, one can conclude that the economic activity of creating marketing innovations has a significant impact on the process of creating technological innovations. Moreover, the dimension of this influence depends significantly on whether the form of ownership is Russian or foreign.

3.1.4 Cost-intensity of marketing innovation.

The values of indicators of the cost-intensity at the pure marketing innovative core and sub-core differ significantly (Figure 7). When switching to the sub-core, MIEs of Russian ownership increase the cost of creating marketing innovations by 6.5 times (from 1.1% to 7.1%). Foreign-owned MIEs reduce their cost-intensity by two times (from 4.4% to 2.1%).

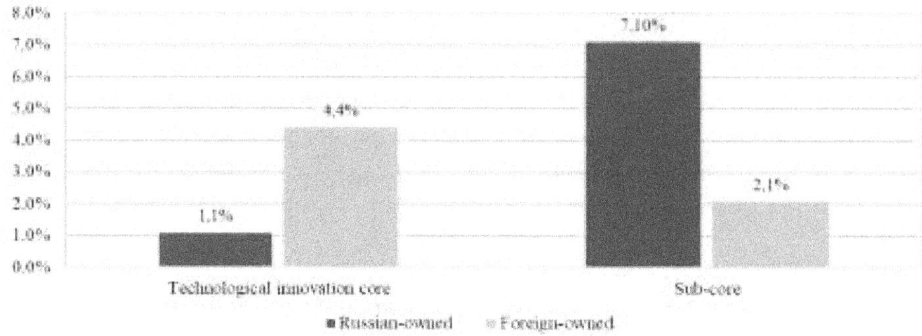

Source: Based on Russian statistics Database: Form No.4 Innovation. Information on innovation activities of the organization.

Figure 7: Cost-intensity of marketing innovation, 2013-2017

In other words, technological innovations have a considerable impact on the creation of marketing innovations at the sub-core. At the same time, the nature and depth of the impact depend largely on the type of ownership.

Summing up the results of the section, in accordance with the methodology section it is worthwhile to note that innovative processes in the field of marketing and technology are interdependent. Moreover, the interdependence works in both directions: the former ones affect the latter and vice versa. In other words, our assumption that technological and marketing innovations are not related to the sub-core is incorrect. It allows us to assert that sufficient conditions are met; that is, there is a correlation between the processes of creating technological and marketing innovations. Therefore, Hypothesis 1 is correct.

4. Behaviour strategies of enterprises depending on the forms of ownership

The distinctions in the relationships of the technological and marketing innovation for different forms of ownership was found above. This distinction stems from differences in the behaviour strategies of companies of the considered property forms. The first of these differences relates to the choice of the type of innovative products supported new marketing technologies. The second one is due to the choice of the type of market for which enterprises create marketing innovations to stimulate demand for their conventional products.

4.1 Strategy for creating and promoting product technological innovations on the market

First, let us recall that, the structure of expenditures on technological innovations changes, when moving from the technology-innovative core to the sub-core, changes for both forms of ownership, i.e. the share of expenditures on process innovations increases. Our research shows that this is due to the need to strengthen support to product innovation from process innovation. This structural shift is accompanied by a change in the costs-intensity of innovative products (see Figure 5). Moreover, these shifts are oppositely directed for the considered forms of ownership. If, for the Russian property, the costs-intensity increases from 19.6% to 63%, for foreign-owned enterprises, it decreases slightly: from 6.7% to 5.9%.

At the same time, it is not difficult to see that the cost-intensity of process innovations in both the technology-innovative core and sub-core is significantly higher for Russian-owned enterprises compared to enterprises of foreign owner-ship. This fact one can partly attribute to the greater efficiency of foreign-owned production. Also it is worth noting that switching from the innovative core to sub-core increases dramatically this gap. Indeed, according to the data shown in Figure 5, the cost-intensity of product innovation for Russian companies is almost three times higher than for companies with foreign participation on the technology-innovative core in 2013-2017; however, this ratio becomes equal to eleven times on the sub-core. The question arises: what explains this phenomenon?

To find the answer to this question, refer to the data in Figure 6. As it follows from them, there is a significant growth in the cost-intensity for Russian-owned enterprises, which can be explained by the increased complexity of product innovation, that is, the radicalisation of the process. Indeed, according to Figure 6, for Russian-owned enterprises, there is a sharp surge in the share of products of that are new to the market and, at the same time, technologically new or improved. The share increases from 11.4% (on the technology-innovative core) to 19.6% (on the sub-core). Market promotion of such "radically new products" requires the intensification of the processes of creating marketing innovations. Consequently, it is not surprising that, according to Figure 7, the cost-intensity of marketing innovation of Russian-owned enterprises is almost seven times higher on the sub-core than on the marketing-innovative core.

For foreign-owned enterprises, the picture is different: in passing to the sub-core, a decrease in the cost-intensity of product innovation is observed (see Figure 5). This drop is accompanied by a more than twofold decrease in the share of both "radically new" and modernized products (Figure 6). The decrease in the share of radically new products may cause a decrease in the cost-intensity of marketing innovation in approximately the same proportions.

Such peculiarities of behaviour of foreign-owned enterprises can be explained by the fact that they are more export-oriented, i.e. to world markets than Russian enterprises. Therefore, even radical new products of Russian-owned enterprises may not have sufficient market novelty for foreign markets. At the same time, another part of the production of foreign-owned enterprises classifying by Russian statistics as technologically new or significantly improved one, but not new to the (domestic) market of these enterprises, may turn out to have a significant novelty for the Russian market.

However, being already advanced in the foreign market, the production may not require deep marketing innovations for its promotion in the Russian market by foreign-owned enterprises. For them, a minor upgrade of already proven and well-established marketing methods may be sufficient to promote the production. It is relevant to the fact that of the low level of cost-intensity of marketing innovation of foreign-owned enterprises (it is more than three times lower than the corresponding value for Russian enterprises on the sub-core). Thus, for each of the two forms of ownership, the sub-core is more advanced in product innovation compared to the technology-innovative core. Enterprises of each form of ownership use marketing innovations to promote their radically new products. At the same time, enterprises of foreign ownership are in a better position than Russian enterprises, since promoting products new to the Russian market, but known to the world market, they can save on the cost of branding innovations.

4.2 Strategies for selecting areas of activity in marketing innovation

Enterprises involved in the process of creating marketing innovations face the problem of choosing the direction of the process organizing. The selection of the direction depends on the purpose of future use of these innovations. There are two main directions: 1) to conquest local markets of conventional (non-innovative) products 2) to promote a technologically new or significantly improved product to the local market.

To find out how this choice depends on the form of ownership, let us turn to the indicator of the cost-intensity of the marketing innovation. For each of the two property groups under consideration, we will consider the values of this indicator on a marketing-innovative core, whose enterprises do not participate in creating technological innovations, and on the innovation sub-core, whose companies are directly involved in both processes of creating technological and marketing innovations.

4.2.1 The market for traditional, non-innovative products

The use of marketing innovations to win a regional market of traditional products is relevant for enterprises of foreign ownership. It confirms the fact that for foreign-owned MIEs that are not involved in creating technological innovations, the cost-intensity of marketing innovation is four times higher than for Russian-owned enterprises (4.4% versus 1.1%, see fig.7). Such a significant difference is because the first group of enterprises loses out in the knowledge of the local market. This circumstance makes the enterprises of the group spend high expenditures on marketing innovations. These innovations allow them to attract more local consumers to purchase their products.

4.2.2 Market for innovative products

At the same time, if Russian-owned enterprises pass to the innovative sub-core, i.e. they create technological innovations along with marketing ones, the cost-intensity of marketing innovation increases by 6.5 times (from 1.1% to 7.1%, see fig.7). As mentioned above, the increased attention paid to the marketing innovation in the sub-core of Russian-owned enterprises because the marketing innovations contribute greatly to promoting radically new products to the market (technologically new or significantly improved and new to the market ones).

5. Conclusion

A theoretical scheme, which allows determining the presence or absence of interconnection of two innovative processes on the sub-core enterprises was proposed and implemented. The implementation of this scheme to industrial enterprises of the Russian Federation made it possible to establish the following.

Even though marketing innovations in Russia have a much smaller distribution area compared to technological ones, innovative processes in the field of marketing and technology are strongly related.

The necessary and sufficient conditions under which the strong links between the processes arise are determined. The requirements are quite logical and straightforward. So it was accepted that the necessary conditions should include the presence of a non-empty innovative sub-core, and as the most obvious and logical sufficient condition must be the fact that the output sold due to involving new methods of marketing must be at least in some part technologically innovative products.

However, although it is not hard to show the fulfilment of the necessary condition (complementarity of the processes), the situation with sufficient conditions is not so straightforward due to the lack of required data confirming the formulated statement directly.

Therefore, checking the sufficient condition, we assumed that it is met if there are substantial shifts in the values of the indicators characterising each of the innovative processes when switching from their innovation cores to sub-core.

Fixing these shifts for Russian and foreign-owned enterprises allows us to conclude that there is interdependence between innovation processes for creating technological and marketing innovations, that is, they are related for firms of two types of property. Moreover, the relationship works in both directions: the marketing innovation affects the parameters of technological innovation and vice versa.

At the same time, the difference in the direction and character of shifts in values of the indicators mentioned above of technological and marketing innovation shows the divergence in the behaviour strategies of companies of two ownership forms. The first difference is related to the type of innovative products whose distribution needs to be supported by marketing innovations. The second one is determined by the kind of market in which enterprises use marketing innovations stimulating demand for their products.

It is generally assumed in the literature that marketing innovation is a key driver of firm's innovation activity (Bartoloni, 2016). However, this is not always the case for Russian industrial enterprises. Speaking about the technologically innovative products supported by marketing innovations, it is worth noting that enterprises of each of the considered forms of ownership use marketing innovations to promote products that are radically new to the Russian market. However, foreign-owned enterprises are in a more favourable position compared to Russian enterprises. They can economize on marketing innovation when promoting products new to the Russian market, but known to the external market.

As for choosing the type of market for more intensive investment in marketing innovations, the market of non-innovative products seems to be the most relevant for foreign-owned enterprises. It confirms the fact that foreign-owned enterprises that are not involved in the creation of technological innovations, that is, the enterprises on the pure marketing-innovation core, have a cost-intensity of marketing innovation four times higher than Russian-owned enterprises.

Among the reasons for such differences, the degree of firms' orientation towards the export is the most attention-getting. The following measures can help smooth the differences. The first one is to create favourable conditions for the abroad economic activity of domestic enterprises. The second is to strengthen the competitive environment, stimulate the improvement of the quality of innovative products at local markets. The measures of the first dimension include the creation of preferential conditions for enterprises exporting innovative products, for example, through the state-level tax breaks or introducing preferential prices for some domestic production factors regulated by the government. The second dimension measures strengthening the competitive environment comprise reducing barriers for new players entering local markets. Participation in international trade and developing a competitive environment in the domestic market will generate incentives to improve the quality of technological innovations created by domestic enterprises and to activate the concurrent process of creating and applying marketing innovations.

References

Bartoloni, E. and Baussola, M. (2016) "Does Technological Innovation Undertaken Alone Have a Real Pivotal Role? Product and Marketing Innovation in Manufacturing Firms." *Economics of Innovation and New Technology* 25(2), pp. 91-113.

Boer, H. and During, W. (2001) "Innovation, What Innovation? A Comparison Between Product, Process and Organisational Innovation". *International Journal of Technology Management*, 22(1/2/3), pp.83-107.

Golichenko, O. (2011) *The Basic Factors for Development of the National Innovation System: Lessons for Russia* (in Russian with an abstract in English). Moscow: Nauka, Moscow

Golichenko, O. and Fakhrudinova, R. (2015) "The Role of Marketing as a Critical Process of Innovation". Civilizaciya znanij: rossijskie realii, pp 501-505.

Golichenko O. (2014) *"Methodological Bases of Research of National Innovation System Processes"*, Drukerovskijvestnik, Vol. 3, Novocherkassk: YuRGPU (NPI), pp. 22-36.

Golichenko O. (2016) "The National Innovation System." *Problems of Economic Transition* Vol. 58, 463-481

Gorodnikova, N. et al. (2017) *Indicators of Innovation Activity:2017,* NIU VSHE, Moscow.

Schumpeter J. A., Opie R. (1961), *The Theory of Economic Development: an Inquiry into Profits, Capital, Credit, Interest, and the Business Cycle*, Cambridge, MA : Harvard University Press.

Ilic, D., Ostojic, S. and Damnjanovic, N. (2014) "The Importance of Marketing Innovation in new Economy", *Singidunum Journal of Applied Sciences*, 11(1), pp.34-42.

Kijek, T. (2013) "An Empirical Analysis of the Relationship between Technological and Marketing Innovations: a Case of Polish Manufacturing Firms", *Acta Scientiarum Polonorum*, 12(2).

Levitt, T. (1960) "Growth and Profits through Planned Marketing Innovation", *Journal of Marketing*, 24(4), pp.1-8.

OECD (2005). *Oslo Manual: Guidelines for Collecting and Interpreting Innovation Data*. Paris: Committee for *Scientific and Technological Policy.*

OECD/Eurostat (2019) *Oslo Manual 2018: Guidelines for Collecting, Reporting and Using Data on Innovation, 4th Edition*, The Measurement of Scientific, Technological and Innovation Activities, OECD Publishing, Paris/Eurostat, Luxembourg.

Schmidt, T., & Rammer, C. (2006) "The Determinants and Effects of Technological and non Technological Innovations–Evidence from the German CIS IV", *Zentrum für Europäische Wirtschaftsforschung (ZEW),* Mannheim.

Schubert, T. (2010) "Marketing and Organisational Innovations in Entrepreneurial Innovation Processes and their Relation to Market Structure and Firm Characteristics", *Review of Industrial Organization*, 36(2), pp.189-212.

Innovation Through hub and Spoke Model: E-Commercializing Regional India's Handicraft Industry

Aman Sharma[1], Bhaskar Bhowmick[2] and Jayshree Patnaik[2]
[1]Department of Chemical Engineering, IIT Kharagpur, India
[2]Rajendra Misra School of Engineering Entrepreneurship, IIT Kharagpur, India
sharmaaman5598@iitkgp.ac.in
bhowmickb@gmail.com
jayshree_patnaik@iitkgp.ac.in
DOI: 10.34190/EIE.20.174

Abstract: Innovation serves a steppingstone for re-instigating growth in the indigenous industries of developing countries. One such sector which accounts for one of the largest employment generation opportunity in India is the handicraft sector. The informal sector, which includes handicrafts, has been described by the International Labour Organization (ILO) as a part of economic activity characterized by certain features like reliance on local available resources and skills, family ownership, small scale operations, labour intensity, traditional technology, skills generally acquired outside school system, unregulated and competitive markets. This study aims at understanding the challenges the Indian handicraft market is facing and highlighting the current practices adopted to tackle them. The handicraft sector today is faced with a lot of challenges ranging from unorganized marketing and inadequate market information to lack of support mechanism for product development. The study adopts a case-based methodology involving primary sources such as field interviews with the key stakeholders of the industry within North Indian region as well as secondary sources including publicly available information about competitive ventures and government interventions. The hub and spoke model is a significantly popular industry tool for dealing with the problems similar to the ones faced currently by the handicraft industry. A similar model was adopted and its compatibility within our problem statement was evaluated. Findings revolved around the fact that how incorporating a simple hub and spoke based model coupled with appropriate technological intervention could address the identified challenges. It also highlights how exchange of information through a digital marketplace can bring about sustainable change in an otherwise ailing industry. We conclude the paper with the proposal of a hub and spoke model custom-made for the North Indian sector, in an attempt to reinvigorate the regional handicraft business through innovative intervention.

Keywords: handicraft, sustainable employment generation, innovating digital marketplace, cluster units, e-commerce, hub and spoke model

1. Introduction

Handicrafts exports from India amounted to $105,302 million in 2011-12 which increased to $123,473 million in 2012-13, registering an annual growth rate of 14.71 percent (Indian Brand Equity Foundation, 2019). According to the World Bank report, there are about 9 - 10 million craft workers in India including part-timers. The craft accounts for 15-20 percent of the country's manufacturing workforce and contributes to 8 percent of manufacturing GDP.

Having realized the potential of the handicrafts industry and the kind of challenges it faces; a lot of minds have shifted their focus and recent efforts to make progress on both theoretical and application front. Scholars not only within India but across the world have proposed solutions to deal with the crisis one of India's most valuable possessions is struggling with. Putting the local handicraft business on the global map through *Glocalization* which opens doors for our not only global art forms to venture into India but also the other way around (Jha, 2010). The role of *e-tailing* (Kumari and Srivastava, 2016) and *e-business* (Bhattacharjee, 2012) were also recommended as remedies for boosting the industry. For today's tech savvy buyers, the online platform is the easiest way to find and shop for various handicrafts. Also, e-commerce is one of the most promising channels in today's marketing scenario for selling handicrafts. Government at both state and central levels are also taking active steps to support these initiatives and it, therefore, becomes imperative to understand and make sure that these policy reforms are in sync with the entrepreneurial effort being put in. We aim to understand the challenges and shortcomings in the handicraft industry, as well as, analyze if a possible solution can be derived from our fellow industries which had faced similar challenges in the past, especially considering the ease of information exchange in today's well connected world. Handicrafts is one of the largest sources of employment in India's indigenous industries, and therefore, if technology intervention can bring about sustainable change in this industry, it can potentially create a huge societal impact. The paper is further structured into 5 sections: *i)* Literature Review, *ii)* Methodology, *iii)* Discussion and i*v)* Conclusion.

2. Literature review

2.1 Significance of handicraft industry

Employment is the backbone of the rise or fall of any developing nation. India's diverse economy encompasses a wide range of industries, service sectors, categorized under private and public heads. However, none of these spectra of services have been able to generate as much employment opportunities as the indigenous sectors like agriculture. Agriculture sector is so far the leading job provider and facilitator. However, the allied sectors of agriculture like handicraft, handloom sector are also a prominent source of employment in developing countries as well as in developing countries, especially in India. These allied sectors of agriculture are categorized under the informal sector of economy in India and the workers working in agriculture and its allied sectors fall under the brand name informal workers according to International Labor Organization [ILO].

Herald (1992) elaborated in his study that in many developing nations, handicraft production is a major form of employment and in some countries, it constitutes a significant part of domestic as well as of the export economy. More specifically, artisans have been identified as the second largest sector of rural employment after agriculture not only in India but also in many countries of the world. Morris, Walter and Turok (1996) concluded that it is due to negligible start-up capital, flexible work hours, the ability to work at home and freedom to manage one's own business, handicraft production crosses all sectors of the modern global economy through preindustrial to industrial and post-industrial regime. Further in the study they said that artisan production has flourished because handicraft products offer distinct advantages such as income for those who have limited access to the cash economy and more importantly, unlike many other forms of labor, handicraft artisan can avail the benefit of degree of labor independence.

Suhail (2012) discussed various problems associated with exports of Indian handicrafts in terms of poor export incentives and credit facilities for start-up export houses. He suggested two-fold strategies for the government and exporters for promoting handicraft exports. The government should focus on setting up a transparent system, a supportive physical and economic infrastructure, market development and designing a policy framework. Barooah and Dedhia (2013) discussed the various socio-economic issues that are faced by women artisans in the handloom sector. They emphasized the fact that interventions in areas of design, technology, marketing and production; and information dissemination regarding Government policies are imperative to increase the sustainability of their profession. Creation of value-added products and product diversification can only justify the high value of handloom products which is labor intensive domain.

Raveendra, Rao and Harsha (2013) highlighted the plight of the handloom sector and the weavers engaged in the sector due to lack of sufficient marketing. It stressed the fact that due to lack of marketing; the weavers are still dependent on middlemen for selling their products and the market is being dominated by power-loom. The paper explores various marketing strategies and suggests a marketing mix that can improve the present scenario. Prashant (2014) underlined the various factors that govern the formation of Indian women consumer's attitude towards online shopping. The ease and convenience associated with online shopping is a key driver for women consumers. However, security issues, reliability in terms of product quality and authenticity and the traditional shopping experience of touch and feel which physical retail provide are deterrents that prohibit them from shopping online. Hence, online retailers should provide risk free and convenient shopping experience for the female consumers to take advantage of the growth in the e-commerce sector in India.

Veena (2014) explored the possibilities of using social media marketing for promoting handloom products. Social media marketing can help by driving the traffic to the websites selling handloom products, creating awareness, co-creating with consumers, establishing intimate relationships and providing information regarding consumers' psychographics and demographics. Kumari and Srivastava (2016) highlighted the opportunity right investments in e-tailing can bring to the handicraft sector. It also proposed the initiatives the government should take to improve the supply chain and payment gateway hurdles the retailers are currently facing. She also proposed the idea of launching convenient mobile apps for reaching more customers. Handicraft producers without much knowledge of the e-commerce platforms could tie-up with the e-commerce giants like Flipkart, SnapDeal, Amazon, Ebay etc.

2.2 Export landscape in the handicraft industry

The opportunity for Indian handicrafts in the global markets was observed when the Indian handicrafts exports crossed Rs 1220 cr in 1990-91 from merely 10 crores in mid-fifties (Vijayagopalan, 1993). Again, it increased to Rs 7157.64 crores in 1998-99 and Rs 9270.50 crores in 2000-01. Analysxing the growth rate information in Figure 1 reveals that apart from few dips in 2001-02 and 2007-09 the industry has shown an overall consistent progress.

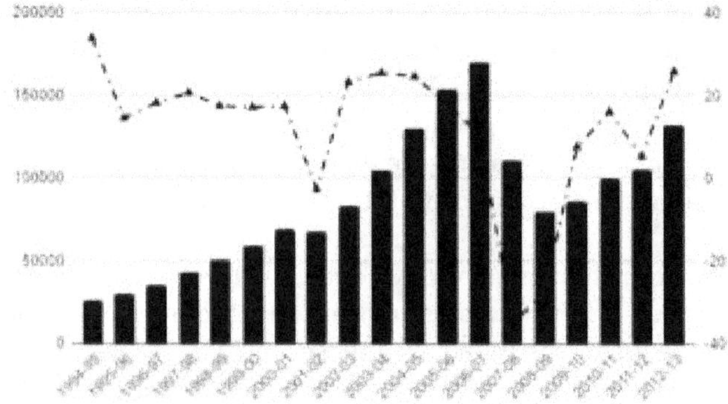

Figure 1: Export of Indian Handicrafts from 1994-95 to 2012-13 (in million $) (Source: International Journal of Business Quantitative Economics and Applied Management Research (2014))

2.3 Current market players

The gap between the artisan clusters in India and the potential market has been tried to be bridged by a lot of e-commerce players with different value propositions for each stakeholder. The flourishing of so many newly founded Indian startups in the handicraft industry is a clear indication of the anticipation of the upcoming market potential. Investors and philanthropists are constantly pouring into every possible effort to structure this largely unorganized sector. “An organization that combines social objectives with building a profitable venture will be of obvious interest to any investor,” pointed out Srikrishna Ramamoorthy, partner at Unitus Seed Fund, which has invested Rs 1 crore in Caravan Craft (Sudhanshu, 2006). Some of them include Fabindia.com, which is an Indian chain store retailing garments, furnishings, fabrics and ethnic products handmade by craftspeople across rural India. Fabindia sources its products from across India through 17 community-owned companies; a certain percentage of the shares of which are held by artisans and craftsperson. They are currently produced by over 40,000 artisans and craftspeople across India. The hand-crafted products also encourage good craftsmanship. However, Fabindia has increasingly been working on establishing itself as an exclusive brand only available in upper class urban metros regions. Moreover, Fabindia only markets itself through its independent stores in order to maintain its brand image, highly restricting its sales volumes. This in turn leads to higher exploitation of a limited set of artisans leading to low penetration rate in rural artisans. Fibre2fashion, a B2B supplier, is another example of modern efforts to revive and draw profits from this traditional industry. Fibre2fashion connects textile, apparel, fashion suppliers and buyers globally. However, it only fulfills wholesale demand and supply requirements. Craftsvilla is a more recent online market for handicrafts and jewelry. It directly connects buyers and sellers and has also integrated its sellers to its ERP software, allowing them access at all times. With an estimated artisan network of 4000, Craftsvilla’s modern approach of direct connection is widely gaining popularity among rural artisans. However, due to its highly restricted product portfolio, a lot of scope for penetration into rural networks still remains. A requirement for an umbrella brand which allows artisans to transparently sell their products directly to the consumers while at the same time provides them with marketing capabilities is much needed. The way taxi aggregation businesses like Uber and Ola have directly connected drivers and riders to successfully bridge the supply demand gap and at the same time empowered the stakeholders through its unanimous marketing presence is worth mentioning.

Based on the literature and practice review, the following research gaps were identified. Although, a lot of effort had been put into highlighting the ways to shape the current handicraft industry into a mould which fits into the evolving customer preferences, either through the introduction of e-tailing platforms, or by providing added marketing opportunities, however, little effort has been paid to utilizing the technology for the upliftment of the other major stakeholder in the business, the producers or the artisan. Apart from that, it has been registered in the past that businesses with suppliers spread across significantly large geographical area often run into supply chain hurdles and hence scaling up an e-tailing platform based business becomes quite challenging, an issue which had not been addressed so far in the context of handicraft industry.

3. Theoretical framework

3.1 Hub and spoke model

Formally defined, the hub and spoke model organization design is a model which arranges service delivery assets into a network consisting of an anchor establishment (hub) which offers a full array of services complemented by secondary establishments (spokes) which offer more limited and specific service arrays. The flexibility of the model makes it adaptable to any specific problem (Delphin, 2016). In this new era of Globalization, companies are growing exponentially and reaching new customers and markets daily. This approach is already being widely used in Aviation, Manufacturing, Logistics Business, Transportation and Healthcare. Delphin revisited the traditional hub and spoke model in his paper and highlighted its applicability in industry related scenario, the China-Brazil iron ore network. He also modelled the hub and spoke problem as a linear programming equation. One of the hubs was a port that received cargo from several supporting ports, called spokes, and then dispatched the cargo to another hub. Elrod and Fortenberry (2017) highlighted the application of the hub and spoke model in the healthcare industry. They claimed that this organization design model arranges service delivery assets into a network consisting of an anchor establishment (hub) which offers a full array of services, complemented by secondary establishments (spokes) which offer more limited service arrays, routing patients needing more intensive services to the hub for treatment. Hub-and-spoke networks afford many benefits for healthcare providers, but in order to capitalize fully, proper assembly is required. Figure 2 highlights the application in a localized region. The hub and spoke models have become more and more scalable with higher Internet penetration and enhanced communication abilities. The figure highlights the diagrammatic representation of the application of hub and spoke model in some of the most common industries. Some of the key benefits reaped by the application of these models include: i) consistency across operations ii) higher efficiencies iii) enhanced quality iv) more extensive market coverage v) improved agility.

4. Methodology

We have employed a Case Study Based Method. The observations are based on primary and secondary sources of data. Primary data comprised of field visits, interaction with various stakeholders including local artisans, vendors and representatives at various public outlets of local handicrafts. A case study-based approach is particularly well suited to new research areas or research areas for which existing theory seems inadequate. This type of work is highly complementary to incremental theory building from normal science research. The former is useful in early stages of research on a topic or when a fresh perspective is needed, whilst the latter is useful in later stages of knowledge (Eisenhardt, 1989). Secondary data included information regarding production processes, artisans and market related details included from various sources including Textile Ministry - Annual Report, UNDP, ILO, DGFT and others. Keeping the results of from primary and secondary research in notice and studying various industries which then faced similar challenges as the Indian handicraft industry today does, an analogy-based *Hub and Spoke Model* was carefully tailor-made for the Delhi-Moradabad region. The rationale behind choosing Moradabad region has been discussed in the later sub-section. The following sections briefly talk about the highlights of the hub and spoke model, the various successful spheres of its application and how can it be applied to the Indian handicraft sector.

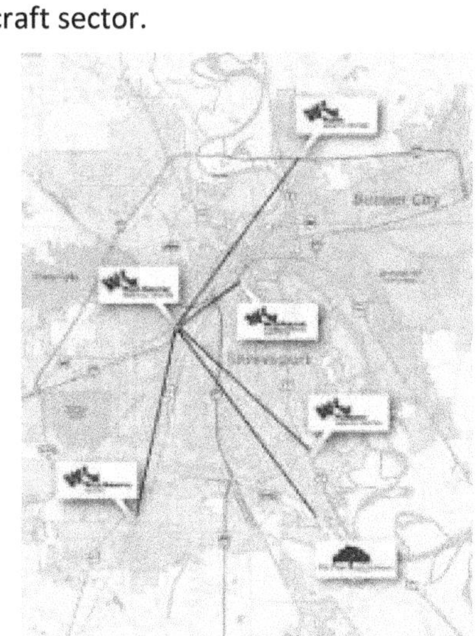

Figure 2: A map presenting Willis-Knighton Health System's hub-and-spoke network (Elrod, 2017)

4.1 A case study of the city Moradabad

We shift our focus to a region in UP - Moradabad also called "Petal Nagri" famous for its metalwork, particularly brass. Moradabad is famous for its handicrafts and is supported under the cluster development scheme. Moradabad city is the headquarters of Moradabad district (see Figure 3). Moradabad is located about 170 km (100 miles) from Southeast of Delhi on the banks of Ramganga, a tributary of the Ganges (Venkataramanaiah et al, 2011) Moradabad is famous for the production and supply of metal artifacts since the eighteenth century. Moradabad is well known for metal ware, particularly brass work and has made a mark in the world for handicrafts. The brassware is exported to countries such as the USA, Britain, Canada, Germany and the Middle East, Asia and many other countries in the world. Moradabad is popularly known as "Petal Nagri" or "Brass City". The brassware industry in Moradabad bloomed in the early 19th century and the British took the art to foreign markets Artisans from Benaras, Lucknow, Agra and many other places came to Moradabad. Local people learnt from the immigrating craftsmen and passed on the skills from one generation to another. A vast majority of the population of Moradabad city is dependent on handicrafts and most of the Artisans are not educated and they depend on the handicrafts industry as a source of employment and livelihood. It manufactures a wide variety of handicrafts for both domestic and overseas customers. Artisans from Benaras, Lucknow, Agra and many other places came to Moradabad. Local people learnt from the immigrating craftsmen and passed on the skills from one generation to another. A vast majority of the population of Moradabad city is dependent on handicrafts and most of the Artisans are not educated which makes them rely on handicrafts industry as a source of employment and livelihood. It manufactures a wide variety of handicrafts for both domestic and overseas customers.

4.2 Application in handicraft industry

The handicraft sector in northern India is largely unorganized and suffers from supply-demand gaps. Although a lot of effort has been made on the government's end to bring together all the essential resources at one place through cluster formation initiatives, still with low local market demand and insignificant market reach local artisans continue to struggle to make their ends meet. Moreover, the producers' whose crafts are able to reach the bigger markets after penetrating through multiple layers of intermediaries and middlemen are insulated from the profits made due to huge *margin- cuts* received by each of these unscrupulous distributors.

Table 1 represents a proposed set for location of hub and spokes. It includes a list of carefully chosen artisan clusters (spokes), each located at an accessible distance from the hub, New Delhi. The hub and spoke model is an attempt to unify various artforms in an umbrella brand and achieve higher transparency with the supply chain. Figure 3 shows the geographical location of the hub and spokes on a terrain map spanning across regions of Uttar Pradesh.

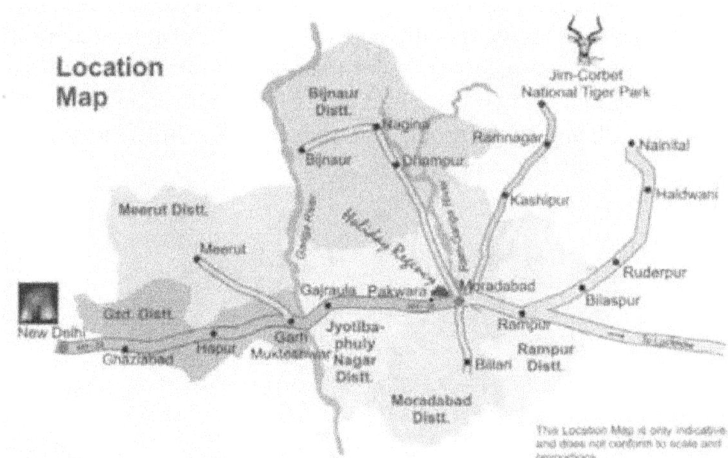

Figure 3: Moradabad location map

Table 1: Details of proposed local spokes located around the proposed hub: New Delhi (Source: Ministry of Textiles (Sudhanshu, 2006)

Spoke Number	Region	Artform / Handicraft famous for	Distance (Road Network)
1	Moradabad, UP	Brass, Copper and other metal ware; Zari Saree	170 km
2	Meerut, UP	Raffia based basket, furniture, trays and wall decorations	78 km
3	Aligarh, UP	Chickan embroidery, Taipchi, Pechni	190
4	Hisar, Haryana	Katoki Bel, Makaish, Marori Work	180 km
5	Sonipat, Haryana	Polyester fiber, fur, felt based toys	70 km
6	Faridabad, Haryana	Terracotta Products including lamps, pitchers	60 km

4.3 Hub

The proposed hub location is New Delhi since a lot of culturally rich clusters are located around Delhi and relative demand for consuming such goods in a metro city like Delhi ought to be higher, considering the significant tourism revenue. Within Delhi, a strategically chosen location like within Connaught Place or Rajiv Chowk could serve as the customer outlet. This outlet would serve as not only a hub for the handicrafts network but also as a hub for the local delivery network within Delhi. The presence of e-tailing in today's handicraft market is imperative. Thus, an outsourced or in-house delivery network would be required, which is where the centralized outlet or hub would come into play. Moreover, in a business like that of handicrafts which significantly depends on consumer preferences, a dynamic status of demanded goods should be globally accessible by both the producers i.e. the artisans and inventory managers. This dashboard would not only account for the orders made by online customers but also register the enquiries and sales made through the offline stores as updated by the respective store managers.

4.4 Spoke

Spokes would serve as the branches of trees outgrowing from the hubs. It is where the actual production work takes place. The currently suggested spokes (presented in Table 3) are carefully chosen government made cluster units where significant pooling of resources have already been done. With the right information of demand and a transparent profit system, these clusters can flourish even with their existing production capabilities. Location of these spokes were also chosen keeping in mind the existing road network so the transportation time between any hub and spoke is not more than four to five hours. An augmented outcome of the spokes is *vocational training* for enhancing skills or familiarizing artisans with new production technology as well as making them comfortable with interacting on the application-based platform, thus, making them more and more independent. Such workshops could also have skilled artisans from one spoke sharing their art form with artisans at the other spokes allowing rise of cross-cultural products. Evidence from the past suggests such products have very well been accepted by the consumers (Indian Brand Equity Foundation, 2019). Eventually, these spokes can branch out into smaller local artisan unions and serve as their hubs.

4.5 E-tailing platform

E-tailing or E-retailing refers to the selling and retail of goods electronically over the Internet. The term is short for "electronic retailing" and surfaced in the 1990s for being frequently used over the Internet. The e-tailing platform offers a wide variety of benefits highlighted in Table 2 as shown below.

Table 2: Benefits offered by online medium

For Customer	For Business
Comfort - Doorstep Delivery, Shopping on Click	**Outreach**: Target audience no longer bounded by physical reach
Discounts - Platform Integration allows discount coupons on a lot of other consumable goods	**Better Advertising**: Third party-based advertising services allow better identification of potential customers
Large Variety - Range of products offered by artisans from around 100km radius offered on a single click	**Core competencies**: With stores' sales being complimented by the e-tail platform, the artisans can focus on improving skills

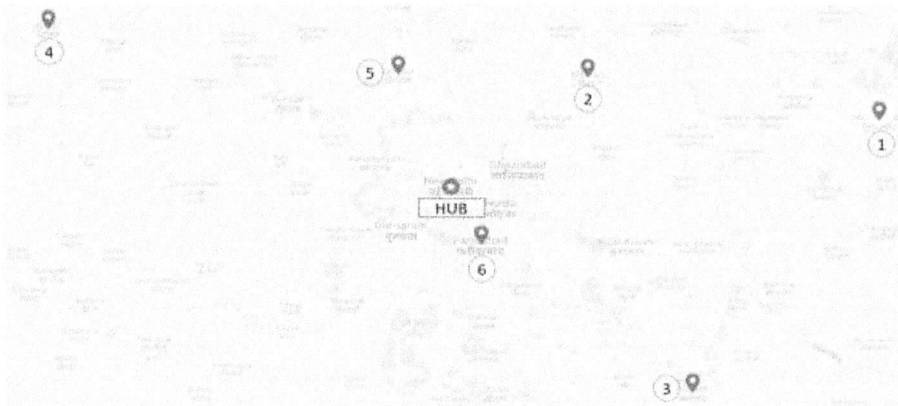

Figure 4: Geographical location of 1 hub and 6 spokes

5. Discussion

A lot of significant efforts have been put in the handicraft sector since the realization of its vast employment and export potential. People from different fields of expertise have proposed ideas of e-commercialization, e-tailing, supply chain optimization etc. in order for the sector to bloom. Policies put forward by the government also compliment the efforts of on ground revolutionaries like FabIndia and Craftsville. Over the past decade, the startup ecosystem in the handicraft industry has become populated with a number of such e-commerce players. A lot of these players are replicating the exact same business and operating model in different geographical regions. The handicraft industry is inherently a low investment and self-sustaining industry. However, practices like exclusive retail outlets, high income target audience, higher exploitation of a limited set of artisans are defeating its very purpose. They are creating higher entry barriers which most definitely are beneficial for the established players but is harmful for the industry. The survival of industry heavily depends on the welfare of the artisans. It should also be our prime objective to be able to reach out to as many artisans as possible and prove them their art can still be the source of their livelihood. Artisan families whose incoming generation is on the brink of dropping their family practice should be made aware of the significance their art holds. Therefore, as of now, startups should be employing an exploration based rather than exploitation-based model. A low investment, high outreach-based approach becomes imperative especially when the demand is particularly skewed in small urban regions. Technology has brought the world a lot closer and given the opportunity for various industries to connect the suppliers and buyers directly, e.g. in hotel (Oyo) and taxi (Uber, Ola) aggregation business. Layers of middlemen penetrating into supply chain has made the profits of these artisans hugely suffer and eventually entrapped them in debt cycles. Our proposed hub and spoke based model is a tailor knit to fit the demands of the handicraft industry. From bringing together artisans and artforms from cluster of regions on a single platform to connecting the artisans directly to the customers, the hub and spoke model has the potential to outperform the current practices in the industry. Below is an objective quantification of the advantages and possible shortcomings of the model.

5.1 Advantages

- *Transparency* - A lot of artisans are moving out of business because of not being able to reach enough customers, or if they do so, it is through multiple layers of which leaves them extremely low-profit margins. Hence trapping them in a vicious debt cycle. Dashboard for B2B and B2C price monitoring allows artisans to have a clear picture of what is the value of their goods but also understand what is it that consumers are willing to pay more for.
- *Skill Development* - A major loophole in today's businesses revolving around the handicraft industry is that they are too focused on the consumer leaving little or no incentive for the producers, i.e. our artisans. To pursue the next generation of artists to continue their family profession a little more than profit incentive is needed. The vocational training program serves the exact purpose, not only does it help the existing practitioners by teaching them the possible ways to improve and excel it also aims at making their next generation self-aware about the value of these artforms both culturally and economically.
- *Enhanced Customer Satisfaction* - With the boundary of physical inventory surpassed the customers can now surf through thousands of product categories, compare prices and be assured that they are being provided with the goods at a fair price, which is mostly the suspicion when people buy in local markets. In

addition to convenience at home, if they will, they can get a first-hand look of the product at the outlet located at the hub.

- *Higher Customer Reach* - E-tailing platform coupled with physical stores can surpass the customer reach offered by the existing platforms. Third party based targeted advertising also improves customer footfall and conversion rate.

5.2 Drawbacks

A lot of e-tailing platforms in the past haven't been able to scale up or attain as much success as they could have because of the following possible reasons:

- *Low level of trust within artisans* - As observed in the past, it takes time for artisans to build trust and get onboard on a platform. Considering the fact, that they have been enough exploited through multiple vendors and contractors in the past, it could be time-consuming to bring together various clusters. The management might also have to indulge in a price war initially until suitable trust has not been established.
- *Platform complications for artisans* - It is fair to assume that experience of the local artisans with application and dashboard-based interfaces would be minimal to zero. Thus, making them accustomed to the interface would also require time. The management can choose a cluster representative who can initially take care of the operations end.
- *Delayed Delivery* - Although the spokes are chosen carefully taking into account the availability of a fully developed road network, however, high road congestion is observed in the northern states which can thus sometimes lead to delayed delivery thus harming the customer retention. A well thought out inventory management approach would be required to tackle such issues.

5.3 Limitation of study

The study involved case study methodology particularly focusing on the artisans from the Moradabad region. As the artisan clusters expands from Moradabad to other regions, the artisan expectations can largely vary requiring to re-engineer the approach. Moreover, after a long history of exploitation by middlemen and some e-commerce players it is likely that the artisan unions would be highly skeptical about signing up anymore on such platforms. The study also assumed an outsourced delivery network, thus didn't get into the maintenance details. The question of whether the delivery network should be developed inhouse or outsourced depends on the financials and initial investment of the business.

6. Conclusion

The paper throws light upon some of the existing remedies for aiding the handicraft industry as well as points out the shortcomings of these remedies. It also highlights how the startup culture has evolved within the industry, and whether it is a healthy sign for the industry or an alarm for some artisan houses going out of business while another a smaller section ending up being highly exploited. Government's active involvement in devising strategies have also been praise-worthy. We've proposed a hub and spoke model which has, in the past, been proven very fruitful in various industries including healthcare, logistics and transportation, however, its application in the handicraft industry is unprecedented. With integration of all the stakeholders on a single digital platform, the problem of lack of transparency within the supply network can be dealt with ease. The real time case study of Delhi as hub and its nearing cluster units as spokes paints a clearer picture of the feasibility of the model. However, we aim to adopt an experimentation-based approach in order to further understand how well the approach is suited for the market. The hub and spoke model is not only a step toward solving the problems the industry has been struggling with for decades but also offers an opportunity of new business and employment generation.

References

Barooah N. and Dedhia E. (2013): Study of socio-economic status of women engaged in handloom weaving and measures for enhancing their sustainability. Colourage, Vol. 60 Issue 9, Page 29-33

Bissemb Celestin Delphin: Optimization of transportation networks: the double hub and spoke model; International Journal of Engineering and Innovative Technology (IJEIT) Volume 5, Issue 9, March 2016

Das Sudhanshu R.: Cultural life and economic growth. The Economic Times, 18th March 2006

Eisenhardt, K. M. (1989). Building theories from case study research. Academy of management review, 14(4), 532-550.

Gaitri Kumari, D. Abhya Ranjan Srivastava: Role of e-tailing in boosting the Indian Handicraft Industry, 2016.

Government of India: Annual Report of Ministry of Textiles 2006-07

Grag and Dhingra (2000): A Study of Perception of Quality of Work Life of Manpower in Handicraft Industry in India: A Conceptual Framework

Herald, 1992: World Crafts: A Celebration of Design and Skills. Oxfam, Cited in Seung-Eun and Littrell, 2003, p. 357

India Brand Equity Foundation (IBEF): Indian Handicrafts Industry and Exports - 2019, https://www.ibef.org/exports/handicrafts-industry-india.aspx

Iyer, K. S. (1999) Handicrafts of India and Its Artisans. Janapadham, 30

James K. Elrod and John Fortenberry Jr.- The hub-and-spoke organization design: an avenue for serving patients well, 2017.

Morris, Walter, F. and Turok, A. (1996) Handmade Money: Latin American Artisans in the Marketplace. Gebunden Oder Broschiert, ID: 9780827036994

Nadh Rayapati Raveendra, Rao P.Venkata and Harsha Vardhan B.M. (2013): HANDLOOM MARKET (Need For Market Assessment, Problems & Marketing Strategy)

Pradeep Kumar Jha: Indian Handicrafts in Glocalization Times: An analysis of Global-Local Dynamics. Interdisciplinary Description of Complex Systems 8(2), 119-137, 2010

Raman Prashant (2014): Factors influencing women consumers' buying behavior towards online shopping in India. Journal of Contemporary Management Research Vol. 8 Issue 2, Page 23-56

Sudip Bhattacharjee: E-business connecting handicrafts of Tripura to Globalization - An entrepreneurial opportunity. Zenith: International Journal of Business Economics and Management Research. Vol2 Issue 1, January 2012, ISSN 2249 8826

Suhail M.Ghouse: Indian Handicraft Industry : Problems and Strategies. International Journal of Management Research and Review. July 2012/ Volume 2/Issue 7/Article No-8/1183-1199

Veena (2014): Role of Social Media in Marketing of Handloom Products. International Journal of Science and Research (IJSR), Vol.3, Issue.7

Venkataramanaiah, S., & Kumar, N. G. (2011). Building competitiveness: a case of handicrafts manufacturing cluster units. Indore Management Journal, 3(2)

Vijayagopalan S.: Economic Status of Handicraft ARTISANS, NCAER, New Delhi, 1993

Innovation and Development: The Role of Social Innovation

Cristina Sousa and Maria de Fátima Ferreiro
Iscte Instituto universitário de Lisboa, DINÂMIA'CET, Lisbon, Portugal
cristina.sousa@iscte-iul.pt
maria.ferreiro@iscte-iul.pt
DOI: 10.34190/EIE.20.177

Abstract: The growing awareness of the destructive effects of technological innovation is reflected on the need to consider the need of other types of innovation in the analysis of development processes, particularly given the diversity/complexity of problems that characterize our societies: demographic trends, inequality, structural unemployment, knowledge intensification and globalization, and financialization. In this paper, we discuss the role of social innovation in economic development in the economics literature. We draw on the idea that social innovation entails a transformative and collaborative approach that can be part of the solution to the above-mentioned problem, propose an analytical framework and conduct a systematic literature review. The results show that this is still an underexplored topic in economics literature.

Keywords: social innovation, development, systematic literature review

1. Introduction

This paper sets out how researchers and economists are integrating the concept of social innovation in the study of economic development in contemporary societies.

Innovation is widely recognized, both among scholars and policy-makers, as an engine of wealth and prosperity, contributing to significant economic benefits in terms of competitiveness, growth and employment (Freeman, 1994; Verspagen, 2007). The acknowledgment of this fact has triggered, since the 1990s, the implementation of policies focused on high value-added activities (OECD 2003), and measures focused on investments in knowledge-intensive activities as the means of attaining sustained economic growth and creating high-skill, high paid jobs. This is namely the case of the EU strategy for smart, sustainable and inclusive growth.

Recently, the raising awareness of the destructive effects of technological innovation and the need to consider the role of other types of innovation in the analysis has started to be stressed by some scholars (Buenstorf et al, 2013; Pyka & Hanush, 2013). This paper advocate that, the role of social innovation needs to be considered in the analysis.

In fact, social innovation can be an important element in the development equation (Howaldt et al., 2016), mainly as a result of its distinctive features: its relation to social entrepreneurship; its relation with collective action; its collaborative, decentralized as distributed nature, often related to the prevalence of small-scale initiatives; and its effect on the empowerment of the civil society (Moulaert et al, 2013; Mulgan, 2006; Pika & Hanush, 2013). However, social innovation is largely ignored as a topic in economics and a little-recognized phenomenon (Gillwald, 2000 in Howaldt et al, 2016), a fact that is confirmed through the bibliometric analysis presented in this paper.

2. Growth and Innovation – an ambivalent relation

Innovation and technological progress are considered among the main drivers of development and economic prosperity. They have a positive influence on the competitiveness, growth and employment of firms, sectors and nations.

Accounting for this positive effect of innovation, after the 1980s, there was a policy shift in developed countries towards investments in innovation and a focus on high value-added activities (OECD 2003), leading to an increase of investments in knowledge-intensive activities as the means of attaining sustained economic growth and creating high-skill, high paid jobs.

This rationale is still present in current policy-making. However, some critical voices have begun to challenge this narrow perspective. For example, Lazonick and Mazzucato (2013), discussing the EC 2020 strategy for smart, sustainable and inclusive growth, argue that it requires an understanding of why periods characterized by plenty of smart investments in innovation, such as the 1990s were also periods in which inequality rose the fastest. The authors introduce three key characteristics of innovation - its uncertain, collective, and cumulative character – in the study of the relationship between innovation and inequality.

Some empirical evidence indicates that, in some cases, investing in innovation and moving up the value-chain is not sufficient to ensure long–term growth and reveal that higher rates of technological innovation are not necessarily related to higher prosperity. The evidence holds at the country (Dosi et al, 2006), regional (Fragkandreas, 2013) and sectoral (Ejermo et al, 2011) levels.

Some authors have also stressed the destructive effects of innovation (Buenstorf et al, 2013) and there is a growing awareness of the "dark-side of innovation" (Pyka & Hanush, 2013), related to job destruction and non-equitable distribution of wealth. Consequently, scholars increasingly consider the need of other types of innovation, besides new technologies, given the diversity/complexity of problems that characterize our societies, namely demographic trends, inequality, structural unemployment, knowledge intensification and globalization, and financialization (Lazonick & O'Sullivan, 2000; Mazzucato, 2013; Pyka & Hanush, 2013; Stiglitz, 2013).

This is the case of social innovation. Social innovation is a key aspect of the new innovation paradigm (Howaldt et al, 2016) which implies an innovation process that opens up to society, involves a broad and dynamic network of players and stakeholders, and where traditional roles disappear or lose their weight and new ones gain expression: citizens and customers are no longer seen as providing information about their needs; they are actively involved in the process of developing new products, services or models to solve problems (Rosted et al, 2009). In this sense, social innovation can be interpreted as a process of collective creation (Crozier & Friedberg, 1993 in Howaldt et al, 2016).

Social innovation is increasingly pointed out both by scholars and policy-makers as an important element in the development equation and in dealing with current problems and challenges (Howaldt et al., 2016), mainly as a result of its distinctive features: its relation to social entrepreneurship and therefore with agency; its relation with collective action; its collaborative nature; its decentralized and distributed nature, resembling a Hayekian process often related to the prevalence of small-scale initiatives; and its effect on the empowerment of the civil society (Moulaert et al, 2013; Mulgan, 2006; Pika & Hanush, 2013). This will be discussed in the next section of the paper.

3. Social innovation in the development equation

Human and socio-economic development goals constitute a central driver of social innovation (SI). In fact, the contribution of social innovation in terms of human needs satisfaction, inclusion and empowerment is at the core of some SI definitions. Moulaert & MacCallum (2019, p. 21), for instance, define SI as "*innovation in social relations* based on values of solidarity, reciprocity and association. Such values involve respect, empathy with diverse viewpoints and convictions, openness to diverse languages and modes of communication, tolerance and care".

The impact of SI in terms of improvement of human values and development constitutes an alternative to the centered vision on "economic growth, productivity and market-rational behaviour" (ibidem). Therefore, SI might encompass a vision that allows its conception as "a remedy to the negative social consequences (inequality, exclusion, marginalization) of growth-oriented innovation" involved in technology and entrepreneurship driven innovation literature prevailing until recently.

In addition to the analytical shift from "the exaggerated focus on technological innovation", research is also increasingly considering the social embeddedness of innovation. This approach was already present in Schumpeter's seminal work (1942), for whom social, organizational, and cultural structures were fundamental in innovation and entrepreneurship research. On the other hand, research is emphasizing the importance of SI in the emergence of other types of innovation as well as the social impact of technological innovation. In line with these approaches, Moulaert & MacCallum (2019, p. 26) refer that "literature on technological and economic innovation systems has (re)discovered the importance of SI for analyzing and materializing other forms of innovation, emphasizing the synergies between technological, social and organizational innovation, the relevance of the social impact of technological innovation (...) as well as the social impact of innovation strategies and policies".

The critical role of SI in innovation studies is materialized by its transformative power and, therefore, contribution to socio-economic and cultural development. Moulaert & MacCallum (2019) distinguish the following interconnected core principles in SI:

- needs satisfaction, neglected or exacerbated by the state/market apparatus.
- "new forms of ecological/institutional relations and polities.
- people's empowerment, "(especially marginalized people) to act-not only within the existent systems and modes of governance, but also towards transforming them". (ibidem).

Therefore, SI appears as a theoretical and empirical-based idea aiming change for a "fairer, more democratically inclusive world" (Moulaert & MacCallum, 2019).

Territorial development appears as an important research subject within SI studies (Estensoro, 2015; Moulaert, 2000, 2009; Moulaert & Nussbaumer, 2005; Moulaert et al, 2013; Bellemare, 2000; MacCallum et al, 2009; CRISES, 2003). Estensoro (2015) refers to a triple focus of SI within the territorial development perspective: satisfaction of basic stakeholder needs, empowerment of local actors, and the transformation of social and power relationships in communities (Estensoro, 2015). The interplay between different roles of SI in the case of territorial development is visible in the following words of Estensoro: "social innovation thus does not simply occur in a spatial context but involves changing the specific spatial relationships: that is, it is spatially negotiated and spatially embedded [...]. This transformation shows that specific contextual elements condition these processes [...] territorial development is related to the capacity of the territory to transform spatial relationships and to the embeddedness of relational assets and spatial proximity in networks. According to this explanation, territorial development will depend on the creation of networks in which the involved actors can transform their modes of relating to increase their control over these modes and their impact on development trajectories [...]. This means that social innovation is necessary for territorial development" (Estensoro, 2015, p.530).

The relation between social innovation and networks within specific territorial contexts was explored by Ferreiro & Sousa (2017), and Ferreiro et al. (2018). In fact, these studies discussed the use of the concept of social innovation in the response to problems affecting rural territories (e.g., desertification, aging) by exploring the links between social innovation and networks to identify the potentialities and challenges involved in the design of collective action to deal with these problems.

The transformative power of SI, as well as its context-based nature, was also considered by MacCallun (2009, p.12): "[...] social innovation involves, among others, the transformation of social relations in space, the reproduction of place-bound and spatially exchanged identities and culture, and the establishment of place-based and scale-related governance structures". This also means that social innovation is quite often either locally or regionally specific, or/and spatially negotiated between agents and institutions that have a strong territorial affiliation.

Therefore, we propose an analytical framework to conduct an analysis of the literature on social innovation and economic development, where the *social* appears as an element with different places (Table 1):

- Social as a type of innovation, *autonomous* or in combination with other types of innovation (e.g. technological, organizational)
- Social as a context of innovation (social embeddedness of innovation and innovation as a social process)
- Social as an impact of innovation

Table 1: SI and development – the analytical framework

SOCIAL AS CONTEXT	SOCIAL EMBEBEDNESS OF INNOVATION		
TYPES OF INNOVATION	TECHNOLOGICAL	TECHNOLOGICAL AND SOCIAL	SOCIAL
INNOVATION IMPACT	GROWTH, DEVELOPMENT	SOCIAL PROBLEMS (INEQUALITY, EXCLUSION, POVERTY, SOCIAL NEEDS) SOCIAL CHANGE, EMPOWERMENT	

4. Method

In order to detect how researchers, and economists in particular, are introducing social innovation in growth/development studies, a bibliometrics study and Systematic Literature Review (SLR) were conducted.

Bibliometrics is a quantitative analysis of the bibliographic references of a body of literature (Hawkins, 1977). It allows identifying the patterns of authorship and publication strategies (Lancaster, 1977), as well as the development of scientific fields (Calero-Medina & Noyons, 2008). The search procedures used for this analysis are described in Table 2.

Table 2: Bibliographic search procedures for the bibliometric analysis

Step	Decision	Comment / Result
Selection of the database	SCOPUS	Contains publications that are generally highly regarded by the academic community; large number of sources, providing broad coverage of the academic literature
Step 1	Search query: TITLE-ABS-KEY ("social innovation")	N = 3148
Step 2	Search query: TITLE-ABS-KEY ("social innovation") AND (LIMIT-TO(SUBJAREA "ECON"))	N = 604
Step 3	Search query: TITLE-ABS-KEY ("social innovation"AND ("economic growth" OR "economic development"))	N = 136

Source: Author's elaboration. Note: search performed on 23rd April 2020.

SLR is a way to summarize existing evidence, identify gaps and suggest some directions for future research. It enables us to "comprehensively identify, appraise and synthesize all relevant studies on a given topic" (Petticrew & Roberts 2006: 19). This approach requires scholars to provide explicit and rigorous criteria for searching, including, evaluating and synthesizing the literature. Decisions are noted down, leaving an audit trail, in order to assure its replication and transparency (Tranfield, et al, 2003). The search of the literature was performed on the SCOPUS database. The steps used for the search and selection of documents are presented in Table 3.

Table 3: Bibliographic search procedures for the SLR

Step	Decision	Result
Keyword search	Search query: TITLE-ABS-KEY ("social innovation"AND ("economic growth" OR "economic development"))	N = 136
Inclusion criteria	Subject area: Economics, Econometrics and Finance	N = 38
Inclusion criteria	Language: English	N = 29
Inclusion criteria	Publication type: journal article, conference paper or book chapter	N = 25
Scanning through title, abstract and keyword reading	Exclude 7 documents because they were out of scope	N = 18
Access check	2 book chapters were excluded because access to full text was not possible	N = 16

Source: Author's elaboration; Note: search performed on 23rd April 2020.

Therefore, the database used for the SLR has 16 documents: 13 journal articles and 3 book chapters. The SLR was organized in five structural dimensions: SI definition; research method adopted; empirical context the study; and the three dimensions in the analytical framework presented in Table 1 – the type of innovation; innovation as a social process (social embeddedness of innovation); and the impact of innovation.

5. Results

Figure 1 shows the evolution of the cumulative number of publications. The research on social innovation is rapidly increasing since 2009. However, only a small percentage of this research is being published in journals classified in the subject of "Economics" (Figures 1 and 2) and an even lower percentage is discussing the articulation between social innovation and economic development/growth (Figure 1).

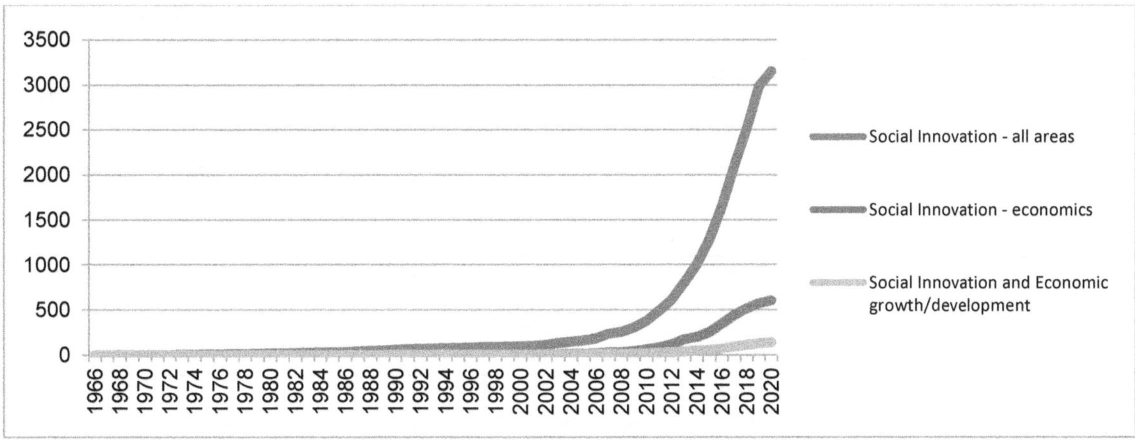

Figure 1: Evolution of the number of documents – cumulative values

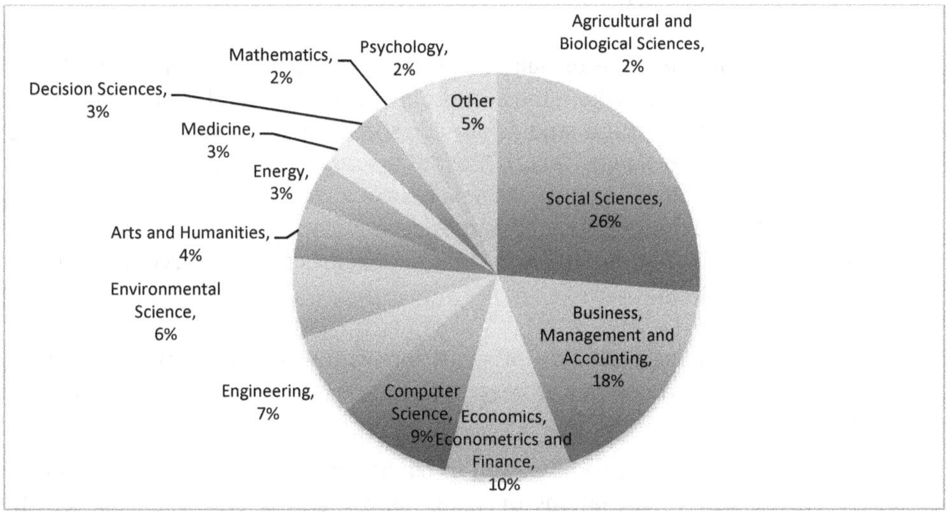

Figure 2: Subject area of documents on social innovation (N=3148)

Social innovation scholars are a global community: 169 authors affiliated in 160 different organizations from 97 countries. Table 3 shows the most cited documents on social innovation and economic growth/development reveals that most of them were published in the last 10 years and in journals that are not classified in the area of "economics".

Table 4: Top cited documents on SI and economic growth/development

Reference	Citations in SCOPUS	Citations in SCOPUS per year	Economics?
Winans, K., Kendall, A., & Deng, H. (2017). The history and current applications of the circular economy concept. *Renewable and Sustainable Energy Reviews, 68*, 825-833.	153	51	N
Moulaert, F., & Nussbaumer, J. (2005). The social region: beyond the territorial dynamics of the learning economy. *European urban and regional studies, 12*(1), 45-64.	111	7,4	N
Perrini, F., Vurro, C., & Costanzo, L. A. (2010). A process-based view of social entrepreneurship: From opportunity identification to scaling-up social change in the case of San Patrignano. *Entrepreneurship and regional development, 22*(6), 515-534.	98	9,8	Y
Ellström, P. E. (1998). The many meanings of occupational competence and qualification. In *Key qualifications in work and education* (pp. 39-50). Springer, Dordrecht.	38	2,6	N

Reference	Citations in SCOPUS	Citations in SCOPUS per year	Economics?
Quiggin, J. (2006). Blogs, wikis and creative innovation. *International journal of cultural studies*, *9*(4), 481-496.	32	2,3	N
Manning, S., & Roessler, D. (2014). The formation of cross-sector development partnerships: How bridging agents shape project agendas and longer-term alliances. *Journal of Business Ethics*, *123*(3), 527-547.	30	5	N
Draskovic, M., Milica, D., Mladen, I., & Chigisheva, O. (2017). Preference of institutional changes in social and economic development. *Journal of International Studies*, *10*(2).	28	9,3	Y
Fink, M., Lang, R., & Harms, R. (2013). Local responses to global technological change—contrasting restructuring practices in two rural communities in Austria. *Technological Forecasting and Social Change*, *80*(2), 243-252.	27	3,9	N
Ziegler, R. (2010). Innovations in doing and being: capability innovations at the intersection of Schumpeterian political economy and human development. *Journal of Social Entrepreneurship*, *1*(2), 255-272.	27	2,7	Y

Note: search performed on 23rd April 2020.

The SLR (based on the 16 studies identified as explained in table 3) reveals that around 40% of the studies have a theoretical, conceptual nature (Figure 3), where the authors are proposing new frameworks or models to study social innovation. Nonetheless, three of these studies provide some cases or examples to illustrate the use of the proposed framework (e.g. Heinze & Naegel, 2012). Most of the empirical studies adopt a qualitative method and use a case study approach, either focusing on one single case (e.g. Agostini et al., 2019) or comparing several cases (e.g. Pradel-Miquel, 2017). In these empirical studies several data collection techniques are employed, many times in combination, with an emphasis on in-depth semi-structured interviews and secondary data (reports, websites, databases, archives).

Several studies do not offer a working definition of social innovation. Ziegler (2010: 256) suggests its own definition "social innovation is the carrying out of new combinations of capabilities". The remaining draw on previously existing definitions, namely prosed by:

- Howaldt & Schwarz (2010, 2016): new combination or configuration of practices in areas of social action, prompted by certain actors or constellations of actors with the goal of better coping with needs and problems than is possible by use of existing practices. An innovation is therefore social to the extent that it varies social action and is socially accepted and diffused in society. This definition is used by Agostini et al (2019) and by Katelka et al. (2012)
- Stanford Center for Social Innovation (2009): novel solution to a social problem that is more effective, efficient, sustainable, or just than present solutions and for which the value created accrues primarily to society as a whole rather than private individuals. This definition is used by Prasad & Manimala (2018) and by Svensson & Bengtsson (2010)
- Phills, Deiglmeier & Miller (2008): novel solution to a social problem that is more effective, efficient, sustainable, or just than existing solutions and for which the value created accrues primarily to society as a whole rather than private individuals. This definition is used by Prasad & Manimala (2018) and by Scaffidi (2019)
- Moulaert, MacCallum, Medmood, & Hamdouch (2013): sets of practices linked to certain forms of social justice and the transformation of existing power relations. This definition is used by Pradel-Miquel (2017)
- Neumeier (2016): changes of attitudes, behaviour or perceptions of a group of people joined in a network of aligned interests that, in relation to the group's horizon of experiences, lead to new and improved ways of collaborative action within the group and beyond. This definition is used by Soma et al (2018)
- Mulgan, Tucker, Ali and Sanders (2007): innovative activities and services that are motivated by the goal of meeting a social need and that are predominantly developed and diffused through organisations whose primary purposes are social. This definition is used by Prasad & Manimala (2018).
- European Commission (2010): Social innovation is about new ideas that work to address pressing unmet needs. We simply describe it as innovations that are both social in their ends and in their means. Social

innovations are new ideas (products, services and models) that simultaneously meet social needs (more effectively than alternatives) and create new social relationships or collaborations. This definition is used by Heinze & Naegel (2012)

- Nelson & Sampat (2001): contains social technologies such as forms of division of labour and modes of coordination

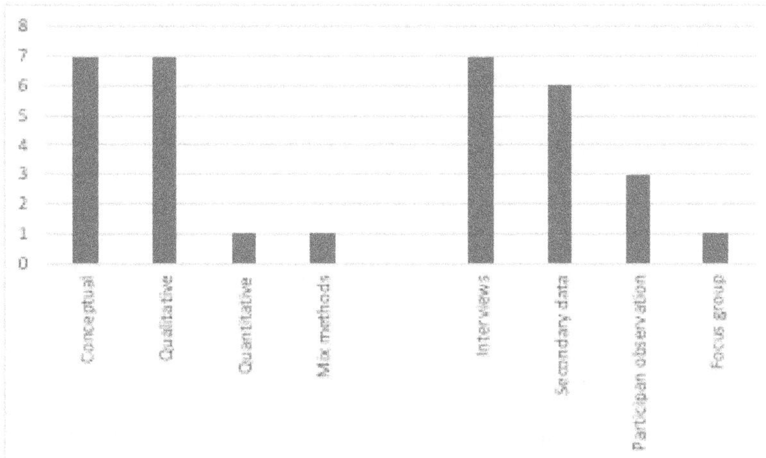

Figure 3: Research methods used in the studies

The studies cover a wide variety of social innovations in different contexts, both in developed (e.g. Heinze & Naegel 2012; Soma et al 2018) and developing countries (e.g. Kapoor 2019; Prasad & Manimala 2018). It is also possible to find studies addressing rural (e.g. Agostini et al 2019; Antonaras & Kostopoulos 2017; Kapoor, 2019) and urban contexts (e.g. Pradel-Miquel 2017), although there is a predominance of the first.

Considering the analytical framework presented in table 1 and starting with the types of innovations being considered, almost half of the studies (7 out of 16) are simultaneously considering technological and social innovations. This is particularly the case of conceptual papers proposing new frameworks or models that cover both types of innovation (e.g. Antonaras & Kostopoulos, 2017; Draskovic et al, 2017; Heinze & Naegel, 2012; Hepburn et al., 2014; Katelka et al. 2012). One study points the role of social innovation to fully exploit one technological innovation and thus to mitigate the effects of population aging (Heinze & Naegel 2012). But it is also the case of two empirical papers, one quantitative addressing the innovation capabilities of Asian firms that considers that covering "technological and social innovations which are more comprehensive and that expands the scope of the concept of innovations" (Singh & Gill, 2016: 113); and one that explores the benefits of social innovation approach for the blue growth strategy and that finds a conflicting relationship between technology and social innovation (Soma et al., 2018).

Only two studies explicitly mention the fact that it is necessary to consider that innovation takes place in social contexts – social embeddedness of innovation. Agostini et al (2019) state that "any social innovation initiative is both culturally and contextually dependent" (pp. 4) and that it is necessary to consider the social context (which is composed of institutions and structures) to understand social innovation processes. Pradel-Miquel (2017: 14) says that "creating spaces that foster social relations and trust, elements considered as a precondition for innovation". Additionally, other studies consider a local scale in the analysis of social innovation processes (e.g. Kapoor, 2019; Scaffidi 2019).

Regarding the innovation impact, the studies stress the role of social innovation in addressing several societal challenges (Figure 4), with emphasis on poverty (extreme, persistent), sustainability (balancing economic growth with the environment, resource scarcity), unemployment (youth, women) and aging, themes that predominate in the literature on social innovation in general.

Several studies point to the empowerment of actors as a result of social innovation related to its impact in terms of economic development. For example, Kapoor (2019) shows how a social innovation helped to empower the women in rural villages India and Agostini et al (2019) conclude that social innovation encourages social and economic empowerment. On the other hand, several studies mention the need for collaboration and collective action in order to implement and benefit from social innovation (e.g. Heinze & Naegel, 2012; Svensson & Bengtsson 2010).

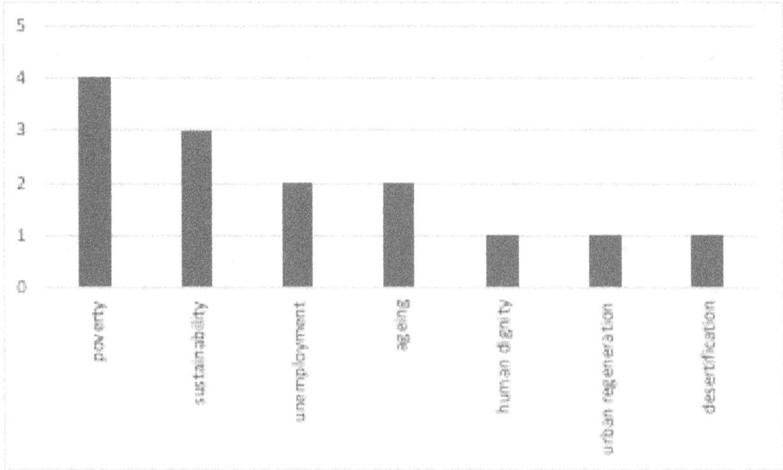

Figure 4: Societal problems considered in the studies

Only two studies explicitly mention that social change was the result of social innovation being implemented. Both studies were focusing on social entrepreneurship processes: Perini et al (2010: 529) highlight the "social value creation and the achievement of long-lasting social change" and Ziegler (2010: 256) shows that social entrepreneurs are "agents of social change".

6. Concluding remarks

Despite its importance, namely for the promotion of economic development and prosperity, our study shows that social innovation is still largely ignored as a topic in economics and a little-recognized phenomenon. In fact, despite the proliferation of studies on social innovation and the acknowledgment of its role in promoting the development of regions and countries and in dealing with current problems and challenges, there is a scarce number of studies published in the area of "economics".

This suggests that there is the need to go beyond the narrative "social innovation matters for economic development" and to stimulate scholars publishing in economic journals to study: the relationship between technological and social innovation in the development equation, to deeply understand its concrete impact on socio-economic development. Economists can further contribute to the conceptualization of social innovation and to the study of its impacts.

References

Agostini, M. R., Bitencourt, C. C., & Vieira, L. M. (2019). Social innovation in Mexican coffee production: filling 'institutional voids'. International Review of Applied Economics, 1-19.

Antonaras, A., & Kostopoulos, A. (2017). Stakeholder Agriculture: innovation from farm to store. In Driving agribusiness with technology innovations (pp. 125-147). IGI Global.

Bellemare, G. (2000). Innovation sociale et territoires, Presses de L´Université do Québec.

Buenstorf, G, Cantner, U, Hanusch, H, Lorenz, HW & Rahmeyer, F (2013) The two sides of innovation, Springer

Calero-Medina, C., & Noyons, E.C. (2008). Combining mapping and citation network analysis for a better understanding of the scientific development: The case of the absorptive capacity field. Journal of Informetrics, 2(4), 272-279.

Dosi, L, Llerena, P & Labini, MS (2006) The relationships between science, technologies and their industrial exploitation, Res Policy, 35:1450.

Draskovic, M., Milica, D., Mladen, I., & Chigisheva, O. (2017). Preference of institutional changes in social and economic development. Journal of International Studies, 10(2).

Ejermo, O, Kander, A & Henning, MS (2011) The R&D-growth paradox arises in fast-growing sectors, Res Policy, 40:664.

Estensoro, M. (2015). How can social innovation be facilitated? Experiences from an action research process in a local network. Systemic Practice and Action Research, 28(6), 527-545.

Fragkandreas, T (2013) When Innovation Does Not Pay Off: Introducing the European Regional Paradox, European Planning Studies, 21:2078

Ferreiro, M.F., & Sousa, C. (2017, September). Social innovation and Networks: Linkages and challenges. In European Conference on Innovation and Entrepreneurship (pp. 217-224). Academic Conferences International Limited.

Ferreiro, M.F., Sousa, C., & Lourenço, C. (2018). Social Innovation and Networks in Rural Territories: the case of EPAM. In 13th European Conference on Innovation and Entrepreneurship, ECIE 2018.

Freeman, C (1994) Innovation and growth, in: Dodgson, M & Rothwell, R (ed) The Handbook of Industrial Innovation, E Elgar.
Heinze, R. G., & Naegele, G. (2012). Social innovations in ageing societies. In Challenge Social Innovation (pp. 153-167). Springer, Berlin, Heidelberg.
Hepburn, C., Beinhocker, E., Farmer, J. D., & Teytelboym, A. (2014). Resilient and inclusive prosperity within planetary boundaries. China & World Economy, 22(5), 76-92.
Howaldt, J., Domanski, D., & Kaletka, C. (2016). Social Innovation: towards a new innovation paradigm. RAM. Revista de Administração Mackenzie, 17(6), 20-44.
Hawkins D.T. (1977). Unconventional uses of on-line Information retrieval Systems: on-line bibliometrics studies. Journal of the American Society for Information Science, 28(1), 13-18.
Kaletka, C., Kappler, K. E., Pelka, B., & de Querol, R. R. (2012). Challenges at the Intersection of Social Media and Social Innovation: a Manifesto. In Challenge Social Innovation (pp. 277-292). Springer, Berlin, Heidelberg.
Kapoor, S. (2019). Entrepreneurship for Economic and Social Empowerment of Women: A Case Study of a Self Help Credit Program in Nithari Village, Noida, India. Australasian Accounting, Business and Finance Journal, 13(2), 123-142.
Lancaster F.W. (1977). The measurement and evaluation of library Services. Washington D.C.: Information Resources Press.
Lazonick, W., & Mazzucato, M. (2013). The risk-reward nexus in the innovation-inequality relationship: who takes the risks? Who gets the rewards?. Industrial and Corporate Change, 22(4), 1093-1128.
Lazonick, W. & O'Sullivan, M. (2000) Maximising shareholder value: a new ideology for corporate governance, Economy and Society, 29 (1): 13-35.
MacCallum D, Moulaert F, Hillier J, Vicari Haddock S (2009)(eds) Social innovation and territorial development. Ashgate Publishing Ltd, Farnham
Mazzucato, M. (2013) Financing innovation: creative destruction vs destructive creation, Ind & Corporate Change, 22:851
Moulaert, F. (2000). Globalization and integrated area development in European cities. OUP Oxford.
Moulaert F (2009) Social innovation: institutionally embedded, territorially (re)produced. In: MacCallum D, Moulaert F, Hillier J, Vicari Haddock S (eds) Social innovation and territorial development. Ashgate Publishing Ltd, Farnham, pp 13–31
Moulaert, F., & MacCallum, D. (2019). Advanced introduction to social innovation. Edward Elgar Publishing.
Moulaert, F., MacCallum D. & Hillier J. (2013) Social innovation: intuition, precept, concept, theory and practice. In: Moulaert F, MacCallum D, Mehmood A, Hamdouch A (eds) The international handbook on social innovation. Collective action, social learning and transdisciplinary research. Edward Elgar, Cheltenham, pp 13–24.
Moulaert, F., & Nussbaumer, J. (2005). The social region: beyond the territorial dynamics of the learning economy. European urban and regional studies, 12(1), 45-64.
Mulgan, G. (2006). The process of social innovation. Innovations: technology, governance, globalization, 1(2), 145-162.
Mulgan, G., Tucker, S., Ali, R., & Sanders, B. (2007). Social innovation: what it is, why it matters and how it can be accelerated. Skoll Centre for Social Entrepreneurship Working Paper.
OECD (2003) The Sources of Economic Growth in OECD Countries, OECD.
Perrini, F., Vurro, C., & Costanzo, L. A. (2010). A process-based view of social entrepreneurship: From opportunity identification to scaling-up social change in the case of San Patrignano. Entrepreneurship and regional development, 22(6), 515-534.
Petticrew, M. & Roberts, H. (2006). Systematic reviews in the social sciences: a practical guide. Blackwell Publishing.
Pradel-Miquel, M. (2017). Kiezkulturnetz vs. Kreativquartier: Social innovation and economic development in two neighbourhoods of Berlin. City, culture and society, 8, 13-19.
Prasad, A., & Manimala, M. J. (2018). Circular Social Innovation: A New Paradigm for India's Sustainable Development. In Social Entrepreneurship and Sustainable Business Models (pp. 141-160). Palgrave Macmillan, Cham.
Pyka, A., & Hanusch, H. (2013). Social innovations in the perspective of Comprehensive Neo-Schumpeterian Economics. Social innovation–New forms of organization in knowledge-based societies, 29-43.
Singh, L., & Gill, A. (2016). Emergence of innovative manufacturing firms across Asian countries. Seoul Journal of Economics, 29, 113-149.
Rosted, J., Kjeldsen, C., Bisgaard, T., & Napier, G. (2009). New nature of innovation. Copenhagen: OECD.
Scaffidi, F. (2019). Soft power in recycling spaces: Exploring spatial impacts of regeneration and youth entrepreneurship in Southern Italy. Local Economy, 34(7), 632-656.
Soma, K., van den Burg, S. W., Hoefnagel, E. W., Stuiver, M., & van der Heide, C. M. (2018). Social innovation–A future pathway for Blue growth?. Marine Policy, 87, 363-370.
Stiglitz, J. (2013), The Price of Inequality. Norton: New York.
Svensson, P., & Bengtsson, L. (2010). Users' Influence in Social-service Innovations: Two Swedish Case Studies. Journal of Social Entrepreneurship, 1(2), 190-212.
Tranfield, D., Denyer, D. and Smart, P. (2003). Towards a methodology for developing evidenceinformed management knowledge by means of systematic review. British journal of management, 14(3), 207-222.
Verspagen, B. (2007) Innovation and economic growth theory: A Schumpeterian legacy and agenda, in: Malerba, F & Brusoni, S, Perspectives on Innovation, Cambridge U Press
Ziegler, R. (2010). Innovations in doing and being: capability innovations at the intersection of Schumpeterian political economy and human development. Journal of Social Entrepreneurship, 1(2), 255-272.

Towards a Blue Economy: The Influence of Policy Strategies in the Research and Technology Orientation of Portuguese Firms

Cristina Sousa[1], Margarida Fontes[2] and Oscarina Conceição[1,3]
[1]Iscte Instituto universitário de Lisboa, DINÂMIA'CET, Lisbon, Portugal
[2]LNEG - Laboratório Nacional de Energia e Geologia, Lisbon, Portugal
[3]IPCA, Barcelos, Portugal
cristina.sousa@iscte-iul.pt
margarida.fontes@lneg.pt
oconceicao@ipca.pt
DOI: 10.34190/EIE.20.150

Abstract: The "Blue Economy" was strategically identified as a driver of European growth, through the development of new competences and activities that enable a sustainable exploitation of ocean resources. Research and innovation policies oriented to the Blue Economy, at both European and country levels, can be described as attempts at "mission-oriented" policies, which seek to influence the direction of growth towards sustainable transformative change in the ocean area. The objective of this paper is to analyse the directions followed by the research and technological development (RTD) activities conducted by Portuguese firms in order to understand whether the strategies and policies aiming at the development of the Blue Economy are being effective in their endeavour of steering such development in certain directions, thus creating conditions for a sustainable transformation in ocean related areas. The results provide some evidence of the role being performed by RTD promoted by these policies towards a transformative change in ocean related activities. Particularly, they show that they are contributing to: i) the generation of new areas and the revitalisation of existing sectors, through the creation and exploitation of new technological opportunities; and ii) a sustainable use of resources and the mitigation of negative environmental effects created by previous activities. Moreover, the results show intense interaction between different types of organisations. Particularly, they show that new technology intensive firms and industries are working together with existing firms from traditional sectors to exploit the new opportunities and technologies. The evidence suggests processes of cross fertilisation and technological upgrading of traditional activities, through the interaction in the RTD projects funded by clearly targeted public policies.

Keywords: Blue economy, policy strategies, challenge-led policies, research & development, sectoral interactions, sustainability

1. Introduction

The "Blue Economy" was strategically identified as a driver of European growth, through the development of new competences and activities that enable a sustainable exploitation of ocean resources (EC, 2012). Strategies and policies were formulated to address this challenge, combining industrial growth objectives with sustainability concerns.

Research and innovation policies aiming at the development of the Blue Economy can be described as attempts at "mission-oriented" policies (Mazzucato, 2018a), which seek to influence the direction of growth towards sustainable transformative change in the ocean area. Policy initiatives such as the EU Blue Growth strategy (EC, 2012, 2019) or the Portuguese National Ocean Strategy 2013-2020 and Mar-Portugal Action Plan (RCM, 2014; DGPM, 2015), are examples of this mission-oriented approach. They present research and innovation activities as contributing to sustainable growth and job creation in the Blue Economy, through the development of emerging industries with growth potential, and the transformation of established industries with strong weight on European economies; and through a better understanding of the marine ecosystems and the protection and preservation of natural resources and the environment. These strategic objectives were translated into research and technology development (RTD) funding instruments, whose terms guide the activities of the actors engaged in ocean-related innovation activities.

The objective of this paper is to analyse the directions followed by the RTD activities conducted by Portuguese firms in the context of projects funded by national and European programmes, in order to understand whether the policies aiming at the development of the Blue Economy are being effective in their endeavour of steering such development in certain directions, thus creating conditions for a sustainable transformation in ocean-related areas. In particular the paper investigates whether there is some evidence that these policies are contributing to: i) generate new areas of activity and revitalise established ones; ii) ensure that these activities entail a sustainable use of natural resources and a lower environmental impact, or mitigate the negative effects of previous activity.

2. Literature review

The Blue Economy is a somewhat ambiguous concept that can be used in diverse and sometimes competing ways by different actors (Voyer et al, 2018; Silver et al, 2015). However one of its central tenets is the attempt to combine socio-economic development and sustainability concerns, when addressing on-going and future human activities related with the ocean (Voyer et al, 2018). In particular it contemplates the need to substantially transform the way ocean-related activities are conducted, in what concerns their content – e.g. upgrading existing industrial sectors or creating new ones; and their impacts on the natural resources and the environment – e.g. changing producer and consumer practices towards sustainability, introducing new actions focusing on environment protection. This transformation is a complex process that requires changes at different levels and the involvement of a variety of actors and institutions.

The nature and magnitude of these processes resounds with those described by the sustainability transitions literature, which addresses processes of transformation in the way key societal functions are fulfilled, describing them as complex, involving far reaching changes at technological, institutional, organizational and social levels (Markard et al, 2012). In addition, the preoccupation of combining sustainability with socio-economic development echoes recent issues raised by that literature, regarding the need to ensure that new sustainable technologies have a positive impact on the economy (Andersen et al., 2020). Sustainability transitions are often associated with processes of "creative destruction", i.e. processes through which new technologies challenge existing firms and technologies, making the technologies obsolete and forcing the firms to withdraw from the market (Kivimaa & Kern, 2016). However, as the "just transition" literature (McCauley & Heffron, 2018) points out, while technological change is essential for transition, not enough attention is paid to the negative impacts of the resulting "competence destroying innovation" on some existing activities, which have a strong weight in the economy of many countries and may have difficulties to adapt. Given the serious socio-economic effects that such "destruction" can have upon the regions/populations that depend on those activities, it is important to understand what types of transformative processes can contribute to mitigate those effects, including reconfiguring the affected activities. Recent research on the interaction of new sustainable technologies with the context in which they emerge, addressing the co-evolution between the new technologies and the established sectors (Fontes et al, 2019a; Steen & Weaver, 2017), is a step in that direction.

In this paper we argue that the Blue Economy concept and the associated "Blue Growth" strategies are a good setting to examine these issues. They address the ocean and ocean-related activities as a system and provide a context in which sustainable transformative changes can be enacted that favour creation and compensate for the effects of destruction. This is because they offer conditions for the interaction between previously unrelated activities, namely for the engagement of actors associated to emerging technologies (e.g. biotechnology, robotics, renewable energies) and actors associated to established activities (e.g. fisheries, shipbuilding, sea transportation) into acting – ideally in collaboration – towards the reconfiguration of existing activities and the creation of new ones; and into conducting their activities according to more sustainable attitudes regarding the use of ocean resources and the environment.

These types of transformation require the presence of a new type of innovation policies – challenge-led policies - which go beyond objectives of growth and competitiveness *per se* and seek to address major societal problems or challenges, by the means of research and innovation (Schot & Steinmueller, 2018; Mazzucato, 2018a). These policies aim to steering innovation and socio-economic impact in a particular direction, in order to achieve desirable transformative changes.

There are different approaches regarding the emphasis and design of these policies, which reflect different views on the innovation process (Diercks et al, 2019). One particularly influential approach has been that of the "mission-oriented" innovation policies, whose aim is turning grand societal challenges into concrete problems that can drive innovation across multiple sectors and actors (Mazzucato, 2018a; Foray et al, 2012). The formulation of clearly defined missions, focused on solving societal problems, enable governments to influence the direction of growth by "making strategic investments throughout the innovation chain and creating the potential for greater spillovers across multiple sectors, including low-tech sectors" (Mazzucato, 2018a: 806).

This approach inspired the European Commission in the formulation of European Union (EU) policies. It has namely influenced the formulation of the Framework Programme for Research and Innovation launched in 2014, the Horizon 2020 (2014–2020), in which broad societal challenges were combined with driving economic growth (Mazzucato, 2018b). Its influence extended to various EU member states, which have started to introduce changes in their innovation policies that reflected a challenge-led/mission-oriented perspective.

A mission-oriented approach equally appears to be behind the European "Blue Growth" strategy that defined the opportunities for marine and maritime sustainable growth (EC, 2012). In fact, the Blue Economy was identified as a driver of European growth, through the development of new competences and activities that "harness the untapped potential of Europe's oceans, seas and coasts for jobs" while simultaneously striving to "use the sea sustainably and respect potential environmental concerns given the fragile nature of the marine environment" (EC, 2012). Strategies and policies were defined to achieve these goals, targeting the broad variety of actors engaged in sea-related activities, both new and established. Research and innovation, aiming at the revitalisation of established sectors and the development of emerging industries, as well as at a better understanding of the marine environment and the requirements for its preservation, were regarded as key elements in these strategies. In the case of Portugal, the Blue Growth strategy influenced the National Ocean Strategy 2013-2020 and the Action Plan for the Sea (RCM; 2014; DGPM, 2015), which have similar goals and scope (Fontes et al, 2019b).

The European and country specific strategies and policies represent initial and often experimental attempts towards an implementation of the new type of innovation policies, still revealing many limitations (Diercks et al, 2019; Schot & Steinmueller, 2018). But in spite of that, they may have started providing a context that can favour the type of transformative change discussed above. Some features that can contribute to this include:

- Address societal problems, going beyond a focus on growth and competitiveness and including social and environmental goals.
- Formulate and support clear objectives that permit to coordinate the innovation efforts of a wide range of actors towards these broader goals.
- Favour the involvement of different types of actors (public and private), originating from a variety of domains of activity, including different industries (new, established, declining).
- Encourage different actors' co-engagement in experimenting with innovations that can contribute to a shared goal.

Against this background, the objective of this paper is to contribute to understand the extent to which the definition and early implementation of strategies for the development of a Blue Economy, is creating conditions for a sustainable transition in ocean-related domains. That is, to a systemic change that simultaneously: i) generates new areas of activity and revitalise established ones, contributing to create or maintain jobs and to the livelihood of populations that depend on the ocean; ii) ensures that these activities entail a sustainable use of natural resources and a lower environmental impact, or mitigate the negative effects of previous activity, contributing to the sustainability of oceans and coastal areas.

For that purpose, the analysis starts by identifying the areas defined in the European and Portuguese policies as composing the Blue Economy that are priority targets for policy action, and subsequently examines whether these policy objectives are influencing the directions followed by RTD activities conducted by Portuguese organisations, in the context of projects funded by European and national programmes.

In what concerns the identification of the target areas, a recent European document (EC, 2019) defines the Blue Economy as encompassing "all sectoral and cross-sectoral economic activities related to the oceans, seas and coasts", including "the closest direct and indirect support activities necessary for the sustainable functioning and development of these economic sectors" and comprising "emerging sectors and economic value based on natural capital and non-market goods and services". It also specifies the priority areas for action that are listed in Table 1, column 2.

As pointed out above, the Portuguese National Ocean Strategy 2013-2020 was strongly influenced by the European Blue Economy framework. Therefore, there is a strong overlap between the Blue Economy priority areas defined at European level and the Strategic Development Domains (SD) and Programme Areas defined in the Mar-Portugal Action Plan (DGPM, 2015), even if there are some differences in thematic aggregation and sectoral organisation, reflecting some country specificities. Table 1 compares and relates both approaches and also qualifies the areas as established or new. A more detailed description of the strategies and their translation in priority areas can be found in Fontes et al (2019b). Since the analysis focuses on the Portuguese organisations, the paper adopted the Portuguese version of the Blue Economy target areas, as listed in the first column of Table 1.

Table 1: Blue Economy priority areas in European and Portuguese strategic documents

PLAN MAR PORTUGAL (DGPM, 2015)	BLUE ECONOMY REPORT (EU, 2019)	Type
SD Governance		
Strategic thinking and action		
Education (ocean literacy)		N
Identity and culture		N
Protection & safeguard	Maritime Defence	N
SD System		
Ocean	Natural capital and ecosystem services	NC
Atmosphere	Natural capital and ecosystem services	NC
Integrated system	Natural capital and ecosystem services	NC
SD Natural resources: Living resources		
Fisheries and fishing industries	Marine living resources – Fisheries	E
Aquaculture	Marine living resources – Aquaculture	E
Marine biotechnology	Blue Bio economy	N
SD Natural resources: Non-living resources		
Marine mineral resources	Marine minerals & extraction of mineral, oil and gas	N&E
Marine energy	Blue energy	N
Infrastructure, uses and activities		
Ports, transport & logistics	Ports, warehousing & maritime transport	E
Recreation, sports and tourism	Coastal tourism	E
Shipbuilding	Shipbuilding & repair	E
Maritime works	(Ports, ... and) water projects	E

Legend: E-established sectors; N – new industries; NC – new areas/natural capital

Subsequently the paper analyses the projects funded in the Blue Economy areas, in order to understand whether there are indications that these policies are starting to have an impact upon the innovative behaviour of actors, in this case private companies. In particular it looks for evidence of:

- opportunities for interaction between firms from distinct sectors that potentially would not cross (Frenken & Janssen, 2019);
- emergence of new activities, which may still assume the form of new "niches", but can be the embryo of a new dynamics for the field (Smith & Raven, 2012);
- efforts towards a more sustainable behaviour, both in the way existing activities are performed and in the development of activities directed towards resource conservation or environmental stewardship and protection (Voyer et al, 2018)
- opportunities for the involvement of firms from sectors that have less tradition of research and innovation activities but operate in targeted application areas, leading them to engage in collective processes that may have a changing impact on their activities (Fontes et al, 2019a);
- processes of cooperation between firms and other organisations - public or from civil society - that manage/coordinate activities related to climate change, environment conservation, preservation of natural resources, that may improve the performance of these activities.

3. Methodology

The paper uses an exploratory approach, using a descriptive analysis – to characterise the activities and the actors – and social network analysis – to characterise the relations between the actors. Data analysis was conducted on two groups of RTD projects: 1) European projects funded by the Horizon 2020 with the participation of Portuguese firms; 2) projects funded by various operational programmes from the Portugal 2020 framework programme that involved Portuguese firms.

To identify the European funded projects, a search was conducted in the database provided by the Community Research and Development Information Service (CORDIS)[1], using a series of keywords related with the ocean and with sea-related activities and industrial sectors. As a result of this process we identified and collect data on 72 European funded projects

To identify the projects funded in Portugal, a search strategy similar to the one described above was conducted on several sources: the project database of the National Innovation Agency (ANI) and the lists of funded projects provided by the Portugal 2020 framework programme[2] and by the Fundo Azul programmes, which focuses on emerging domains [3]. Since the latter two only provide information on the project coordinator, online searches were necessary to identify the remaining participants. As a result of this process we identified and collect data on 96 Portuguese funded projects. After this data collection procedure, a new database was built for the 168 projects.

To capture the interactions between the organisations involved in the projects, a Social Network approach was used. Each project was considered a 2-mode network, where the projects are the events and the participants are the actors. Dyads between the Portuguese firms and the remaining project partners were reconstructed: it is considered that a Portuguese firm is tied to another organisation if they are/were participants in the same project. In this process the type of organisation, the industrial classification of Portuguese firms and the nationality of the partners (Portuguese vs. non-Portuguese) were considered. Network diagrams were prepared using the Netdraw software.

4. Results

In order to address the issues raised above, the data obtained was analysed with a view to answer to two sets of questions.

The first set of questions addresses the influence of the Blue Economy policy directions, as expressed in the priority domains/areas, in the RTD activities of Portuguese firms:

- Q1a: Are some strategic areas being privileged and others left behind?
- Q1b: In particular, are the RTD activities addressing both emerging areas and more established ones? Which is the balance between them? Which types of firms are addressing the different areas and with which types of partners?
- Q1c: Are RTD activities with firm involvement addressing sustainability concerns?

Table 2 presents the distribution of projects and respective funding by Blue Economy domain/area, showing the central position of research concerned with the exploitation of natural resources. The Living Resources domain has the highest number of projects (47.6%) and investment (37.3%). But projects targeting established areas such as fisheries and aquaculture have a relatively lower weight than those on the new area of marine biotechnology, which is the most important area in terms of projects (28.6%) and the second in investment (20.7%). The Non-living Resources domain is almost exclusively composed of projects in the Marine Energy area, since exploitation of marine mineral resources is underdeveloped in Portugal. Marine Energy is also the single area with the highest investment (24.9%), reflecting the capital-intensive nature of the projects.

Table 2 also shows that the System domain and the Infrastructure, Uses and Activities domain jointly occupy a second position, with similar weights in terms of number of projects (16.1% and 15.5%), although the former concentrates a higher investment (18.4% vs. 9.9%). The System domain is concerned with preserving and increasing the ocean natural capital and the projects focus either on knowledge development about the ocean ecosystem (Ocean area) or on modes of monitoring, risk assessment and conservation, to account for the effects of the diverse uses of the ocean (Integrated area). The Infrastructure, Uses and Activities domain encompasses research targeting sea-related industries. The relatively low investment is mostly concentrated in one area - Ports, transport & logistics. But there are also several projects developing technologies of a transversal nature that can be applied in a variety of marine-related sectors.

[1] CORDIS: https://cordis.europa.eu/projects

[2] Portugal 2020: https://www.portugal2020.pt; Fundo Azul: https://www.dgpm.mm.gov.pt/fundo-azul

[3] ANI: https://www.ani.pt/; Portugal2020: https://www.portugal2020.pt/content/lista-de-operacoes-aprovadas; Mar2020: http://www.mar2020.pt/;

Finally, the Governance domain, mostly concerned with state-related activities, has the lowest level of activity. But it is worth mentioning the weight of projects with firm participation in the Protection and Safeguard area.

Table 2: Number of projects and funding by Blue Economy target domain and area

Domain/Area	Type area	N projects	%	Funding	%
Governance		**12**	**7,1%**	**8.608.530,44 €**	**7,7%**
Strategic thinking and action	N	1	0,6%	1.386.616,25 €	1,2%
Education (ocean literacy)	N	0	0,0%	0,00 €	0,0%
Identity and culture	N	0	0,0%	0,00 €	0,0%
Protection & safeguard	N	11	6,5%	7.221.914,19 €	6,5%
System		**27**	**16,1%**	**20.469.780,27 €**	**18,4%**
Ocean	NC	13	7,7%	5.737.161,78 €	5,1%
Atmosphere	NC	0	0,0%	0,00 €	0,0%
Integrated	NC	14	8,3%	14.732.618,49 €	13,2%
Natural resources: Living resources		**80**	**47,6%**	**41.625.192,16 €**	**37,3%**
Fisheries and fishing industries	E	13	7,7%	3.217.909,33 €	2,9%
Aquaculture	E	20	11,9%	9.070.763,09 €	8,1%
Aquaculture & Fisheries	E	2	1,2%	6.720.518,13 €	6,0%
Marine biotechnology	N	45	26,8%	22.616.001,61 €	20,3%
Natural resources: Non-living resources		**23**	**13,7%**	**29.806.945,93 €**	**26,7%**
Marine mineral resources	N&E	3	1,8%	2.038.689,71 €	1,8%
Marine energy	N	20	11,9%	27.768.256,22 €	24,9%
Infrastructure, uses and activities		**26**	**15,5%**	**10.993.665,31 €**	**9,9%**
Ports, transport & logistics	E	12	7,1%	4.620.135,12 €	4,1%
Recreation, sports and tourism	E	0	0,0%	0,00 €	0,0%
Shipbuilding	E	3	1,8%	953.813,00 €	0,9%
Maritime works	E	4	2,4%	1.811.607,89 €	1,6%
Combination of activities (transversal)	N&E	7	4,2%	3.608.109,30 €	3,2%
Total		**168**	**100,0%**	**111.504.114,11 €**	**100,0%**

Legend: E-established sectors; N – new industries; NC – new areas/natural capital

The aggregation of information about the nature of the areas targeted, presented in Table 3, shows that, overall, there is a stronger focus on new areas and that, among these, RTD projects targeting new industries prevail over those on natural capital, which is not unexpected since we are analysing only projects with firm involvement. But there still are a substantial number of projects targeting established sectors, particularly among those funded by national programmes, as well as a few projects whose applications can encompass both new and established industries.

Table 3: Nature of areas targeted: new versus established

Nature of targeted area	Nº projects	%
New areas - new industries	76	45,2%
New areas - natural capital	22	13,1%
Established sectors	54	32,1%
Mixed targets	16	9,5%
Grand Total	**168**	**100,0%**

Going back to questions Q1a & Q1b, these results suggest that the strategy had some partial success in directing the focus of RTD activities towards industrial sectors that would be less likely to become involved in those types of activities. However, this effect is mostly concentrated in sectors related to the exploration of natural resources – fisheries and aquaculture - which are equally the target of several RTD projects in one of the new areas: marine biotechnology. These are sectors that have an important weight in the Portuguese economy (PWC, 2020) and whose upgrading can be potentiated this way. Other established sectors were much less able to become object of RTD activities, the only exception being the area of ports and marine transport. On the other hand the results reveal the importance of two emerging industries - marine biotechnology and marine renewable energies – in which the country had previously been building competences (Fontes, 2007; Sarmento et al, 2014) that the strategic focus contributed to further consolidate.

Regarding the type of firms that constitute the project team (Table 4), it should be noted that, in all domains, teams formed only by technology intensive firms predominate, being particularly dominant in the new areas.

Teams that bring together different types of firms (tech and non-tech) have a greater weight in the Non-living Resources domain (22%), namely in the marine energy area, and in the Living Resources domain (20%). The teams only composed of non-technology intensive firms, are mostly present in the Infrastructure, Uses and Activities domain (39%). In this domain, teams tend to be either exclusively composed of technology intensive firms (39%) or of non-technology firms (57%), the existence of partnerships between the two types being residual (4%).

Table 4: Type of firms and team composition by target domain and area (number of projects)

		Team		Type of Firm		
Domain/Area	**Type area**	**Only Firms**	**Firms & Other**	**Only Tech**	**Tech & Non-Tech**	**Only Non-Tech**
Governance		**5**	**7**	**9**	**2**	**1**
Strategic thinking and action	N	0	1	1	0	0
Protection & safeguard	N	5	6	8	2	1
System		**9**	**18**	**19**	**3**	**5**
Ocean	NC	1	12	7	2	4
Integrated	NC	8	6	12	1	1
Natural resources: Living resources		**38**	**42**	**48**	**16**	**16**
Fisheries and fishing industries	E	7	6	6	3	4
Aquaculture	E	6	14	12	5	3
Aquaculture & Fisheries	E	0	2	1	1	0
Marine biotechnology	N	25	20	29	7	9
Natural resources: Non-living resources		**6**	**17**	**15**	**5**	**3**
Marine energy	N	5	15	14	4	2
Marine mineral resources	N&E	1	2	1	1	1
Infrastructure, uses and activities		**11**	**15**	**15**	**1**	**10**
Ports, transport & logistics	E	2	10	7	1	4
Shipbuilding	E	2	1	2	0	1
Maritime works	E	3	1	1	0	3
Combination of activities	N&E	4	3	5	0	2
Total		**69**	**99**	**106**	**27**	**35**

Legend: E-established sectors; N – new industries; NC – new areas/natural capital

Considering the types of organizations that constitute the project teams (Table 4), we distinguished between teams only with firms and teams that involve partnerships between firms and other types of organizations. Table 4 shows that there is a balance between the two types of teams. Exceptions are the Non-living Resources domain and the System domain, in which partnerships between firms and other organizations prevail (respectively 74% and 67% of projects). Partnerships are more frequently with research organisations, but they can also involve public and other organisations, individually or in combination.

Finally, in what refers to sustainability concerns (Q1c), it was possible to identify 31 projects (18.5%) that focused on resource conservation or environmental stewardship and protection, the majority in the System domain, and a few in the Governance domain. However, there was also a substantial number of industrial development projects that explicitly included sustainability goals, concerning changes in the performance of the activities or impact mitigation actions.

The second set of questions inquires if the Blue Economy policy directions are creating opportunities for industrial change in marine and marine related areas, involving both new firms active in new areas and existing companies from established sectors, as well as transformative interactions between them, namely:

- Q2a: Are the RTD projects creating opportunities for interaction between firms from distinct sectors, enabling cross fertilisation?
- Q2b: In particular are they creating opportunities for the involvement of firms from application sectors that have less tradition of research and innovation activities, namely through collaboration with firms in emerging areas, which may subsequently induce upgrading processes in the former?
- Q2c: Are there some established sectors in which these processes are more active? Are there some new industries/firms that are driving these processes?

Figure 1 shows the network built from the relationships established by the Portuguese firms within the scope of the RTD projects. The network involves 964 organisations (231 Portuguese, 733 foreign) that are classified according to their type and, in the case of Portuguese companies, according to their 5-digit NACE code. The nodes in the network reflect this classification, represented by the colours in the diagram: red for firms, yellow for research organisations, blue for public organisations and green for other organisations. The size of the node is proportional to the number of organisation for each type of actor.

The network is composed of 609 dyads between the Portuguese firms and their project partners: the dashed lines represent ties that reflect collaborations in EU funded projects and the continuous lines represent ties that reflect collaborations in national funded projects.

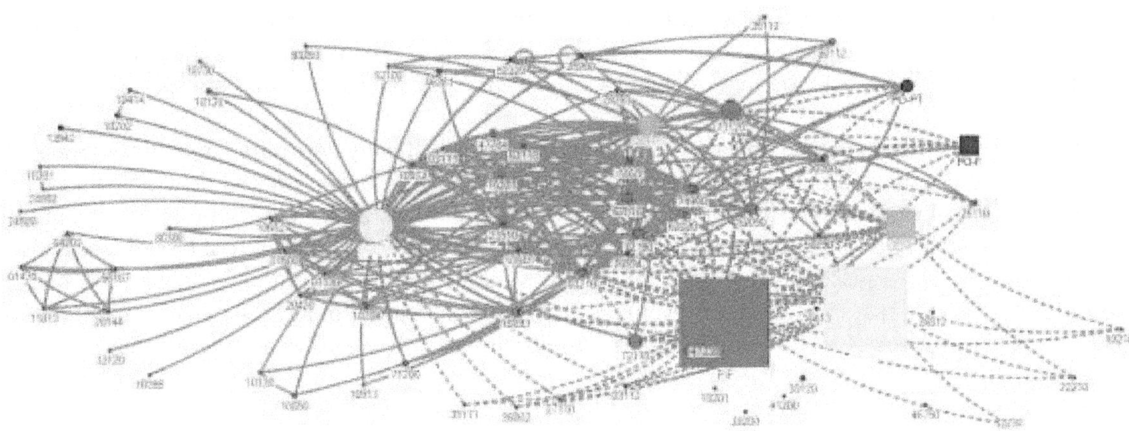

Figure 1: Relationships established by the Portuguese firms within the scope of the RTD projects

It is possible to conclude that the RTD projects are offering opportunities for collaboration between Portuguese industrial sectors and between them and other types of partners, with emphasis on foreign firms and research organisations, and national research organisations. This networks reflects the fact that a wide variety of industrial sectors are exploiting the new opportunities related to the Blue Economy, both in established activities related to ocean (e.g. ports and fisheries) or application activities (e.g. agrofood), and in new activities (e.g. biotech, R&D services, ICT). The network – which is a sole component quite dense since 12% of possible ties are active – also suggests the existence of opportunities that go beyond those associated with single projects: some firms – particularly from technology-intensive sectors - are active in several projects, both at EU and national levels and bridge several types of partners (including firms from different sectors).

To better capture the interaction between Portuguese firms from different sectors, we have isolated these firms from the above network, resulting on two different diagrams shown in Figure 2. In the left panel (a) all sectors are included while in the right panel (b) only non-technology (application sectors) are included. It is visible (panel a) that although some sectors only establish partnerships with non-industrial organisations, (appearing as isolates in the graph, while previously were connected), most sectors are interacting in these projects, in order to develop new opportunities, related to new technologies or to sustainability concerns. Therefore, we found some evidence of cross fertilisation between firms from different sectors (question 2a).

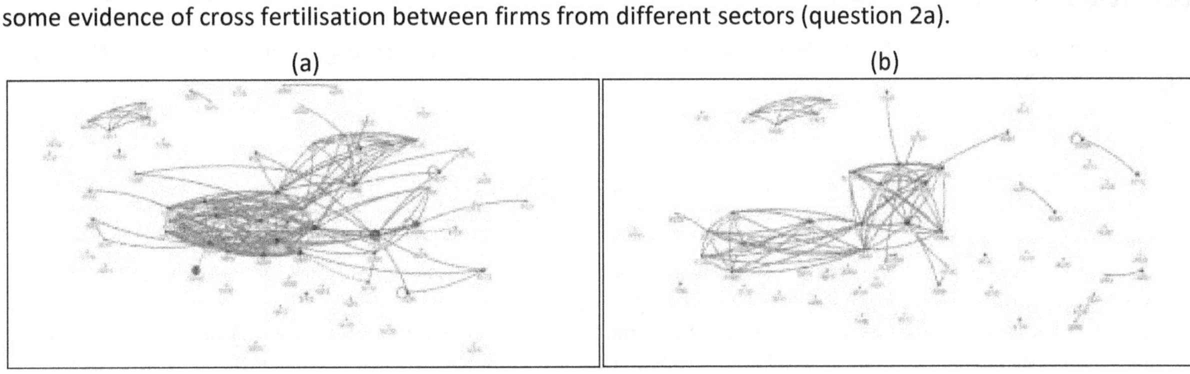

Figure 2: Relationships established between Portuguese firms within the scope of the RTD projects

Moreover, we find that these interactions involve both firms from application sectors, traditionally less involved in RTD activities and firms from new industries (more technology intensive). In panel (a) we see the existence of several sectors where these interactions occur: ports, fisheries, aquaculture, agrofood, metal products (question 2b). In panel (b) we see that if we remove from the network these more technology intensive industries (frequently positioned in industrial classifications such as engineering, technical consultancy, computing, scientific and professional activities, or research and development), it becomes much more fragmented, suggesting a role played by firms in these industries in driving the exploitation of the new opportunities related to the Blue Economy (question 2c).

5. Conclusion

This paper sets out to explore the effect of public policies aiming at the development of the Blue Economy on the direction of RTD activities conducted by Portuguese firms. It argues that the "Blue Growth" EU and Portuguese strategies and policies can be understood as an attempt to adopt a mission-oriented approach, contributing to: i) generate new areas of activity and revitalise established ones with impact on growth and job creation; ii) ensure that these activities are enabling a sustainable transformation in ocean-related activities.

The results provide some evidence towards a transformative role being performed by the RTD activities promoted by these policies, potentially leading to sustainable change in ocean related activities. Particularly, they show that RTD activities are contributing to: i) the generation of new areas (e.g. marine biotech or marine energy) and the revitalisation of existing sectors (e.g. fisheries and aquaculture and, to a less extent activities concerned with water transportation), through the creation and exploitation of new technological opportunities; and ii) to a sustainable use of resources and to the mitigation of negative environmental effects (which is the exclusive focus of several projects and also explicitly part of the goals of several industry-oriented projects).

Moreover, the results show intense interaction between different types of organisations, particularly different types of firms. We have found that new technology intensive firms and industries are often working together with existing firms from traditional sectors to exploit the new opportunities and technologies. A particularly interesting case is the interaction between a new science-based area that has been object of an important public investment in Portugal – biotechnology – and a set of established resource-based industries that have an important position in the Portuguese economy and a strong weight in the livelihood of some regions – fisheries, aquaculture, and sometimes also involving food processing. This is a good example of processes of cross-fertilisation and technological upgrading of traditional activities that can be promoted by clearly targeted challenge-led policies. This type of experience deserves a more in-depth examination, in order to offer policy insights into how to further encourage and uphold these virtuous transformational dynamics.

Overall, the results show that the Blue Economy policies are having some success in directing the activities of Portuguese firms towards some of the areas they define as priority, but also that some established areas are still being left behind, potentially requiring additional efforts. It is thus important for policymakers to take stock of the implications of this partial success, with a view to understand the conditions that explain the limited involvement of some sea-related sectors, as well as the lack of engagement of research-intensive companies in joint-activities with them.

Acknowledgements

This research was partly funded by *FCT - Fundação para a Ciência e a Tecnologia*, under project PTDC/GES-OUT/30559/2017-OceanTrans

References

Andersen, A.D., Steen, M., Mäkitie, T., Hanson, J., Thune, T.M., and Soppe, B. (2020). The role of inter-sectoral dynamics in sustainability transitions: A comment on the transitions research agenda. Environmental Innovation and Societal Transitions, 34, 348-351.

DGPM (2015). O Plano Mar Portugal – Anexo B - Actualização 2015, Direção-Geral de Política do Mar do Ministério do Mar. https://docs.wixstatic.com/ugd/eb00d2_7c89d6cb1c534720873df9c2cfa8d_14d.pdf.

EC (2012). Blue Growth opportunities for marine and maritime sustainable growth. Communication from the Commission to the European Parliament, the Council, the European Economic and Social Committee and the Committee of the Regions (COM/2012/0494 final). https://ec.europa.eu/maritimeaffairs/sites/ maritimeaffairs/files/docs/ publications/blue-growth_en.pdf.

EC (2019) The EU Blue Economy Report. 2019. Publications Office of the European Union. https://op.europa.eu/en/publication-detail/-/publication/676bbd4a-7dd9-11e9-9f05-01aa75ed71a1/language-en/format-PDF.

Fontes, M. (2007). Technological entrepreneurship and capability building in biotechnology, Technology Analysis and Strategic Management, 19(3), 351-367.

Fontes, M., Bento, N. and Andersen, A.D. (2019a). Unleashing the transformative potential of transitions: context, complementarities and competition, 10th International Sustainability Transitions Conference, June 23-26, Ottawa.

Fontes, M., Sousa, C. and Conceição, O. (2019b). Creating a Blue Economy: Research and innovation partnerships to accelerate the development of ocean-related industries. In Proceedings of International Scientific Conference on Innovations in Digital Economy (Article Nº 33). SPBPU IDE-2019.

Foray, D., Mowery, D.C., Nelson, R.R. (2012). Public R&D and social challenges: what lessons from mission R&D programs? Research Policy, 41(10), 1697–1702.

Janssen, M.J. and Frenken, K. (2019). Cross-specialisation policy: rationales and options for linking unrelated industries. Cambridge Journal of Regions, Economy and Society, 12(2), 195–212.

Kivimaa, P., Kern, F. (2016). Creative destruction or mere niche support? Innovation policy mixes for sustainability transitions. Research Policy, 45, 205-217.

Markard, J., Raven, R. and Truffer, B. (2012) Sustainability transitions: An emerging field of research and its prospects, Research Policy, 41, 955-967.

Mazzucato, M. (2018a). Mission-oriented innovation policies: challenges and opportunities. Industrial and Corporate Change, 27(5), 803–815.

Mazzucato, M. (2018b). Mission-Oriented Research & Innovation in the European Union. A problem-solving approach to fuel innovation-led growth. European Commission - Directorate-General for Research and Innovation, Luxembourg: Publications Office of the European Union.

McCauley, D. and Heffron, R. (2018). Just transition: Integrating climate, energy and environmental justice, Energy Policy, 119, 1-7.

PwC (2020). LEME – Barómetro PwC da Economia do Mar, Edição n.º 10 Portugal. https://www.pwc.pt/pt/publicacoes/leme/portugal/pwc-leme-2020.pdf

RCM (2014). Resolução do Conselho de Ministros nº 12/2014 – Estratégia Nacional para o Mar 2013-2020 (Nacional Ocean Strategy 2013-2020), Diário da República, 1.ª série, N.º 30, 12 de fevereiro de 2014.

Sarmento, A., Rocha, A.B. and Morais, T. (2014). Offshore Renewable Energy - Current Status. Future Perspectives For Portugal, INEGI, http://www.inegi.up.pt/publicacoes//livros/pdf/Offshore_Renewable_Energy.pdf.

Schot, J. and Steinmueller, E. (2018). Three frames for innovation policy R&D, systems of innovation and transformative change. Research Policy, 47(9), 1554-1567.

Silver, J. J., Gray, N. J., Campbell, L. M., Fairbanks, L. W., & Gruby, R. L. (2015). Blue economy and competing discourses in international oceans governance. The Journal of Environment & Development, 24(2), 135–160.

Smith, A. and Raven, B. (2012). What is protective space? Reconsidering niches in transitions to sustainability. Research Policy, 41, 1025-1036.

Steen, M. & Weaver, T. (2017). Incumbents' diversification and cross-sectorial energy industry dynamics. Research Policy, 46(6), 1071-1086.

Voyer, M., Quirk, G., McIlgorm, A. & Azmi, K. (2018). Shades of blue: what do competing interpretations of the Blue Economy mean for oceans governance? Journal of Environmental Policy & Planning, 20(5), 595-616.

Networking for Internationalization: Are Young Companies Different From Older Ones?

Cristina Sousa[1,2], Carla Lobo[2] and Carla Santos Pereira[2]
[1]Iscte Instituto universitário de Lisboa, Portugal
[2]Univ Portucalense, Research on Economics, Management and Information Technologies, Porto, Portugal
cristina.sousa@iscte-iul.pt
cadsa@upt.pt
carlasantos@upt.pt
DOI: 10.34190/EIE.20.203

Abstract: The internationalization process is complex, costly and uncertain. Existing theories stress the role of learning and knowledge and the role of networks in the acquisition of resources and information that affect the internationalization process. The "revised" Uppsalla model (Johanson and Vahlne 2009) incorporates relational networks, considering they have a strong impact on market selection, as well as on the identification of opportunities. The theory of International New Ventures (INV) emphasizes the importance of relational networks and vicarious learning as a way for companies to acquire knowledge about the external market. Some scholars consider that the participation in networks is particularly beneficial for younger and smaller firms. However, it is still unclear how the reliance on various network relationships potentially differs among younger and older ventures. This paper tackles this question by using a novel survey dataset of 238 Portuguese firms and a quantitative approach base on a descriptive and inferential analysis.

Keywords: internationalization, networking, young firms

1. Introduction

Currently, the expansion into international markets is vital for firms' growth, knowledge acquisition and access to new resources. But the internationalization process is complex, costly and uncertain (George, Wiklund, & Zahra, 2005). Given the importance of internationalization, a large body of research has examined numerous factors affecting it.

In the 1970s and 1980s the focus was on large, well-established multinational companies and the Uppsala model (Johanson & Vahlne, 1977) was widely used. Later, in a context of an increasing globalization of markets, scholars start to address the phenomenon of young and small international firms (McDougall & Oviatt, 2000). The Uppsala model was revisited (Johanson & Vahlne, 2009, 2011) and new approaches have emerged, namely the born global approach (Oviatt & McDougall, 1994, 1997, 2005) and the theory of International New Ventures.

All these new approaches stress the role of learning and knowledge and the role of networks in the acquisition of resources and information that affect the internationalization process. The "revised" Uppsalla model (Johanson & Vahlne 2009) incorporates relational networks, considering they have a strong impact on market selection, as well as on the identification of opportunities. The theory of International New Ventures (INV) emphasizes the importance of relational networks and vicarious learning as a way for companies to acquire knowledge about the external market, but also emphasizes congenital learning (experience and individual knowledge) as a way to recognize the importance of relational alliances and networks to the beginning of internationalization. The network approach emphasizes the use of the information acquired by the firm over a period of time and joining all the involved parties by establishing close relationships with customers, industry (including suppliers and distributors), regulatory and public agencies, as well as other market actors. Relationships are based on mutual trust, knowledge, and commitment between the firm and the aforementioned actors.

Despite the recognition of the importance of networks for the success of the process of internationalization of companies, the extant literature still misses to understand how the reliance on various network relationships potentially differs among younger and older companies. This paper tackles this question by assessing the differences between young and older companies in the reliance of different networks. With this aim it uses a novel, purposely collected, data set of 238 Portuguese firms and a quantitative approach base on a descriptive and inferential analysis.

2. Networks, social learning and internationalization

As mentioned above, internationalization theories are increasingly considering the role of networks for the success of internationalization processes. However, and with a few exceptions (e.g. Coviello, 2006), there is still a lack of studies including a detailed network analysis. Most studies either take the network as given, without analysing its configuration and structure (Bai & Johanson, 2017).

Several studies focus on access to resource and learning processes that happen through networks and partnerships and how this facilitates the internationalization process. Network literature acknowledges the role of networks in accessing a large set of resources, both tangible and intangible (Sousa & Fontes, 2012). Internationalization studies tend to focus on intangible resources, like information and knowledge. It is considered that managers may have limited information and limited capacity to collect it (i.e. inability to access, or unwillingness due to high costs). Social relations may act as facilitators in the process of information and knowledge gathering, namely when the company is entering new markets and there is the need to identify new business opportunities.

Several studies (e.g. Sarasvathy et al., 2014) argue that identifying opportunities is a driving force in internationalization, and observe and conceptualize the role of networks in identifying opportunity in firm internationalization (Holm, Johanson, & Kao, 2015; Galkina & Chetty, 2015). Networks also provide the founders of new ventures with new opportunities for enterprise and contribute to their entry into foreign markets and overcome the company's limited chance to benefit from foreign markets (Coviello, 2006; Ojala, 2009). According to Oviatt and McDougall, (1994) it seems that internationalization strategy is not merely uncertainty-reducing, but also opportunity-seeking. The network view says that opportunity development cannot take place in a vacuum. But rather it happens in a specific context, that is, within the firm's international network (Blankenburg Holm et al., 2015). In line with most conceptualizations of opportunity, a firm's knowledge is the critical element, and a firm with sophisticated knowledge about acting in a network is likely to pursue opportunities in different ways than an outsider firm with limited experience (Bai & Johanson, 2017).

Additionally, literature also suggests that, in the early internationalization of ventures, networks facilitate the access to the market knowledge and information, without which acquiring such knowledge would be costly and time-consuming (e.g. information about customer needs and market trends), identifying key clients, obtaining financial resources and supporting R&D activities (Bruneel, Yli-Renko, & Clarysse, 2010; Rezvani, Davari and Parvaneh, 2017; Vasilchenko & Morrish, 2011). Networks also enable companies to obtain initial credibility in new international markets (Vasilchenko & Morrish, 2011). Access to other resources (e.g. R&D facilities, production) is less studied. The above mentioned studies concluded that the greater the power (information, knowledge, financial resources, etc.) of people and firms in the network, the more information is granted them about new business opportunities, potential markets, etc. and more possibilities for them to make use of such information. As a result, new ventures can become internationalized in an early stage.

Acs and Terjesen (2007) proposed an intermediate model in which new ventures are internationalized through existing networks created by multinational companies and which act as facilitators of the internationalization process. Since these knowledge spillovers are local and the various markets have barriers to entry, using multinationals in this way is the most efficient method of internationalization (Alvarez & Molero, 2005).

Related to the access to knowledge and information, networks facilitate learning processes. According to De Clercq et al. (2012), vicarious learning (learning by observing others) plays a central role in the decision to internationalize the firm's operations early. The most common type of vicarious learning discussed in conceptual and empirical work involves learning with a network of partners. A central argument in these papers is that the presence or development of foreign contacts triggers opportunities for internationalization (e.g., Casillas, Moreno, Acedo & Gallego, 2009). Several authors, even without explicitly using the term "vicarious learning", clearly indicate learning "from observing others" as a mechanism that influences the beginning of internationalization decisions, either by imitating or working with others (Grosse & Fonseca, 2012), in a process that can be termed as social learning: learning related to interaction, observation and communication that occur in networks.

Another source of "vicarious" learning comes from observing other organizations that are not necessarily network partners. Fernhaber, McDougall & Oviatt (2007) have empirically investigated how the imitation of others by young companies can affect their own foreign market entry initiatives and argue that such companies, without their own routines or precise information about the nature of the business world, imitate the behaviours of others that are geographically closest. They conclude that the more nearby companies already internationalized, the more likely it is that an international solution will involve imitation and that the company will tend to internationalize early. Yet, and although much has been learned about the role of strategic alliances in the internationalization of new businesses, the existing literature focuses largely on foreign partnerships (e.g. Leiblein & Reuer, 2004; Oviatt & McDougall, 1995).

Another line of inquiry is focused on the type of relation that is built between the network partners. Network theory usually distinguishes between formal and informal relations and between strong and weak ties (Kontinen & Ojala, 2011; Ojala, 2009; Sousa, 2012; Vasilchenko & Morrish, 2011). Formal networks involve a codified agreement, a system of authority, distribution of competences, rights and duties and a conflict resolution device. They encompass subcontracting relationships, strategic alliances or participation in an industry-wide research consortium (Smith-Doerr & Powell, 2003). Informal networks are more spontaneously created, and are frequently associated with personal relationships (Coviello, 2006; Sousa, 2012). It was observed that many new companies have become internationalized as part of a network, where strategic alliances play a prominent role (Coviello, 2006; Coviello & Munro, 1997). Dependence on alliances is so critical that the term liability of outsidership has been used to describe the disadvantages of internationalization in the absence of an appropriate network (Johanson & Vahlne, 2009). Informal networks have been less frequently addressed by internationalization studies (Bruneel, Yli-Renko, & Clarysse, 2010).

Some scholars also distinguish or argue about what kind of connections is most useful to companies in their internationalization process. For example, Oviatt and McDougall (2005) theorize that in terms of accelerating the onset of internationalization, the most important source of "vicarious" external information comes from weak ties, because these ties efficiently eliminate redundant information.

Network theory also highlights the importance of considering the composition of the network, namely in terms of the type of actors/partners who make them. This literature stresses the importance of having a diversified network in terms of the type of partners, to avoid redundancy (Burt 2009) and increase the value of information and knowledge gained through networking (Nooteboom 1999; Baum et al. 2000). Some studies on internationalization have included several types of partners, namely companies in the supply or value chain, like suppliers, distributers and customers, and investors (Bruneel, Yli-Renko, & Clarysse, 2010). However, extant research usually does not analyse the importance of each of these partners for the achievement of the company's internationalization.

Extant literature also recognizes that the use of networks may vary with the type of company. Some scholars consider that the participation in networks is particularly beneficial for younger and smaller firms (Coviello & Munro, 1997; Harris & Wheeler, 2005; Sharma & Blomstermo, 2003; Styles et al., 2006). However, it is still unclear how the reliance on various network relationships potentially differs among younger and older ventures. Empirical studies tend to focus on the size of the company is the most studied aspect. They find that, given limited resources and market power, the internationalization process of SMEs differs significantly from the already-established multinationals (Paul, Parthasarathy & Gupta, 2017). SMEs, typically, rely heavily on their network relationships as they try to internationalize (Coviello & Munro, 1997; Coviello, 2006; Musteen, Datta, & Butts, 2014). Coviello and Munro (1997) found that the internationalization process of small software firms reflects an accelerated version of the stage model perspective, and is driven, facilitated, and inhibited by a set of formal and informal network relationships. It remains unclear how the reliance on various network relationships potentially differs among younger and older ventures.

This paper tackles this topic by assessing the differences between young and older companies in the reliance of different networks. In order to assess the existence of these differences, it considers several of the network dimensions highlighted in the network theory, but less explored by the internationalization studies: the type of relation (formal or informal), the resource that is being accessed and the type of partner.

3. Data and methods

Data collection was based on a questionnaire with 33 questions. The questionnaire was developed to study the enhancing factors of Portuguese business internationalization and assess the most frequent barriers and constraints in this process. It includes a set of questions, measured using five-point Likert scale ranging from: "not important" (1) to "extremely important" (5), that to understand the role of networks in achieving internationalization, namely by capturing the degree of importance attributed to:

- Formal network (e.g. formal relations with other companies) for the actual the internationalization of the company;
- Informal network (e.g. friends, family) for the actual the internationalization of the company;
- Partnerships with a specific type of partners for the realization of the internationalization of the company (consisting of 14 items – partner types)
- Partnerships established to obtain a specific type of resource (consisting of 10 items- resource types).

The questionnaire was sent to all companies registered in the AICEP database of Portuguese internationalized companies, by sending a link via e-mail and using the Google Forms tool. Between May 2019 and January 2020, a set of 238 valid answers were obtained. The questionnaire, before being online was submitted to the evaluation of experts and pre-tested in some firms.

The sample of 238 internationalized Portuguese companies that will be used in this research is composed of companies from different sectors (both from industry and services) and with different sizes. Considering the number of employees, the structure of the sample includes 36.1% micro firms, 40.3% small firms, 17.6% medium firms and 5.9% large firms.

Since this study aims to evaluate whether there are differences between young and older companies in their reliance of networks for their internationalization process, the founding year of the company was also considered. A new variable (young_old_firm) was created. Companies with 10 years or less were considered "young" and the remaining (those with more than 10 years) were considered "old". The 10-year threshold was already considered in other studies (e.g. Cloninger & Oviatt, 2007; LiPuma, 2012). Therefore, two groups of companies will be considered: young (60 companies) and old (178 companies).

Data collected were treated using IBM SPSS Statistics 26.0 software. The statistical analyses used for the data analysis (Maroco, 2018) were Descriptive Analysis (frequency analysis and descriptive statistics) and Inferential Analysis (Spearman's ordinal correlation, Mann-Whitney nonparametric test and Chi-square test for independent samples).

4. Results

We start the analysis of results by assessing whether the degree of importance attributed to formal and informal networks differs depending on whether the company is young or old we use non-parametric tests (the hypothesis of Normal distribution was not verified) and perform the Mann-Whitney statistical test, which is suitable for variables measured in an ordinal scale. Results show (Table 1) that, at a significance level of 5%, there is statistical evidence to reject the hypothesis that the degree of importance attributed both to formal and informal networks is identical in the 2 groups (young and old firms) (p-value=0.006<0.05 and p-value=0.008<0.05, respectively).

Table 1: Differences in the importance attributed to formal and informal networks for the actual the internationalization between young and old companies – Mann-Whitney non-parametric test

	Formal network	Informal network
Mann-Whitney U	4117,00	4156,00
Wilcoxon W	20048,000	20087,00
Z	-2,761	-2,650
Asymp. Sig. (2-tailed)	0,006	0,008

To determine the extent to which these differences are verified in the importance attributed to formal networks, we used the Chi-Square Independence Test (p-value=0.029<0.05). All conditions of applicability of the Chi-Square test were checked. The contingency table associated with this test (Table 2) allows us to conclude that there is a tendency for young companies to consider the formal contact network more important. It turns out that while only 14.6% of older companies consider the formal network of contacts extremely important, in young companies the equivalent percentage is 31.7%.

Table 2: Contingency table for formal network

		Old firms	Young firms	Total
Not important	Count	11	2	13
	% within Informal network	84,6%	15,4%	100,0%
	% within young or old firm	**6,2%**	**3,3%**	5,5%
Not very important	Count	19	6	25
	% within Informal network	76,0%	24,0%	100,0%
	% within young or old firm	**10,7%**	**10,0%**	10,5%
Important	Count	62	12	74
	% within Informal network	83,8%	16,2%	100,0%
	% within young or old firm	**34,8%**	**20,0%**	31,1%
Very important	Count	60	21	81
	% within Informal network	74,1%	25,9%	100,0%
	% within young or old firm	**33,7%**	**35,0%**	34,0%
Extremely important	Count	26	19	45
	% within Informal network	57,8%	42,2%	100,0%
	% within young or old firm	**14,6%**	**31,7%**	18,9%
Total	Count	178	60	238
	% within Informal network	74,8%	25,2%	100,0%
	% within young or old firm	100,0%	100,0%	100,0%

The same test was used to assess the extent to which these differences are verified in the importance attributed to informal networks. The results show (Table 3) that there is a tendency for younger companies to consider the informal network more important: while only 7.3% of older companies consider the informal network of contacts extremely important, in young companies the equivalent percentage is 20%.

Table 3: Contingency table for informal network

		Old firms	Young firms	Total
Not important	Count	23	6	29
	% within Informal network	79,3%	20,7%	100,0%
	% within young or old firm	**12,9%**	**10,0%**	12,2%
Not very important	Count	53	12	65
	% within Informal network	81,5%	18,5%	100,0%
	% within young or old firm	**29,8%**	**20,0%**	27,3%
Important	Count	60	16	76
	% within Informal network	78,9%	21,1%	100,0%
	% within young or old firm	**33,7%**	**26,7%**	31,9%
Very important	Count	29	14	43
	% within Informal network	67,4%	32,6%	100,0%
	% within young or old firm	**16,3%**	**23,3%**	18,1%
Extremely important	Count	13	12	25
	% within Informal network	52,0%	48,0%	100,0%
	% within young or old firm	**7,3%**	**20,0%**	10,5%
Total	Count	178	60	238
	% within Informal network	74,8%	25,2%	100,0%
	% within young or old firm	100,0%	100,0%	100,0%

Moreover, the results show that companies give more importance to formal networks than to informal contact networks, regardless of whether the company is young or old.

Regarding the type of partner to which companies assigned the greatest degrees of importance for the realization of their internationalization, the descriptive analysis (Table 4), taking into account the median value (the average is not a good measure, not only because in the variables in question are ordinal, but also because the coefficients of variation are high), allows us to conclude that the most important partner is (undoubtedly) "customers abroad". In the case of old companies, the median is 5, which indicates that this partner is considered extremely important; in the case of young companies the median is 4, meaning that it is considered very important. Both in young and old companies, other partners are considered important, namely: "national suppliers", "national customers", "competitors in the destination country" and "national government agencies".

Table 4: Descriptive statistics for the importance of each type of partners for the realization of the internationalization of the company

Type of partner	Old companies			Young companies		
	Mean	Median	Std. Deviation	Mean	Median	Std. Deviation
National suppliers	3.33	3.00	1.350	3.31	3.00	1.303
Suppliers abroad	2.51	2.00	1.318	2.60	2.00	1.432
National customers	2.79	3.00	1.236	2.54	3.00	1.264
Customers abroad	4.34	**5.00**	0.828	4.16	**4.00**	1.089
National competitors	2.39	2.00	1.183	2.29	2.00	1.043
Competitors abroad	3.09	3.00	1.285	3.14	3.00	1.290
National consultants	2.32	2.00	1.165	2.30	2.00	1.164
Consultants abroad	2.52	2.00	1.315	2.78	3.00	1.475
National universities and research centres	2.18	**2.00**	1.165	2.51	**3.00**	1.441
Universities and research centres abroad	1.95	2.00	1.102	2.23	2.00	1.389
National business associations	2.36	**2.00**	1.201	2.75	**3.00**	1.421
Business associations abroad	2.12	2.00	1.196	2.31	2.00	1.404
National government agencies	2.66	3.00	1.332	2.84	3.00	1.424
Government agencies abroad	2.21	2.00	1.257	2.39	2.00	1.473

In view of this descriptive analysis, there seem to be differences in the degrees of importance assigned to some types of partner, namely "costumers abroad", "national universities and research centres" and "national business associations". However, the Mann-Whitney test (Table 5) only corroborates the existence of significant differences, at a significance level of 10% (p-value=0.07<0.1) in the importance assigned to the partner "national business associations". Young companies tend to attach a greater degree of importance to this partner.

Table 5: Differences in the importance attribute to different types of partner for the actual the internationalization between young and old companies – Mann-Whitney non-parametric test

Type of partner	Mann-Whitney U	Wilcoxon W	Z	Asymp. Sig. (2-tailed)
National suppliers	5005.500	6775.500	-0.159	0.874
Suppliers abroad	3886.000	15667.000	-0.256	0.798
National customers	4463.000	6233.000	-1.299	0.194
Customers abroad	4279.500	5990.500	-0.817	0.414
National competitors	4773.000	6484.000	-0.375	0.708
Competitors abroad	4819.000	19525.000	-0.329	0.742
National consultants	4765.000	6418,000	-0.056	0.955
Consultants abroad	4370.500	18231.500	-1.071	0.284
National universities and research centres	4004.000	16565.000	-1.289	0.197
Universities and research centres abroad	4141.000	16544.000	-0.885	0.376
National business associations	4193.500	18389.500	-1.812	**0.070**
Business associations abroad	4497.000	17863.000	-0.577	0.564
National government agencies	4382.000	18747.000	-0.849	0.396
Government agencies abroad	4484.500	18014.500	-0.476	0.634

Finally, we analyze the degree of importance attributed to the partnerships established for each of the resources indicated, in terms of younger or older companies. Table 6 reveals that, both for young and old businesses, networks are considered very important for accessing "market information". In the case of young companies, the relationships established for accessing "distribution channels" and "credibility" are also considered very important, followed by (in the degree of importance attributed) accessing "information on possible partnerships".

Table 6: Descriptive statistics for the importance of networks to access each type of resource for the realization of the internationalization of the company

Type of resource	Old companies			Young companies		
	Mean	Median	Std. Deviation	Mean	Median	Std. Deviation
Scientific and technological knowledge	2.81	3.00	1.171	3.02	3.00	1.186
Market information	3.56	4.00	1.019	3.62	4.00	1.223
Information on funding and incentive systems	2.78	3.00	1.250	2.90	3.00	1.374

Type of resource	Old companies			Young companies		
	Mean	Median	Std. Deviation	Mean	Median	Std. Deviation
Information on possible partnerships	3.14	**3.00**	1.040	3.37	**3.50**	1.193
Information on the political and legal framework	3.02	3.00	1.099	3.27	3.00	1.326
Information on the macroeconomic and fiscal framework	2.92	3.00	1.104	3.02	3.00	1.295
Distribution channels	3.28	**3.00**	1.192	3.43	**4.00**	1.320
Production capacity	3.12	3.00	1.247	3.08	3.00	1.369
Counselling	2.89	3.00	1.122	3.02	3.00	1.200
Credibility	3.28	**3.00**	1.203	3.48	**4.00**	1.255

But to what extent is there a difference in the degree of importance attributed to the partnerships established for each of the resources indicated, in terms of younger or older companies? The Mann-Whitney test (Table 7) indicates that these differences do not seem to exist. We can only find a significant statistical difference, but at a significance level of 10% (p-value=0.099), for the "information on possible partnerships" feature. In this case it is concluded that the younger companies attach a slightly higher degree of importance to this resource.

Table 7: Differences in the importance attribute to networks to access different types of resources for the actual the internationalization between young and old companies – Mann-Whitney non-parametric test

Type of partner	Mann-Whitney U	Wilcoxon W	Z	Asymp. Sig. (2-tailed)
Scientific and technological knowledge	4784.500	20715.500	-1.242	0.214
Market information	4966.500	20897.500	-0.849	0.396
Information on funding and incentive systems	5085.500	21016.500	-0.566	0.572
Information on possible partnerships	4611.500	20542.500	-1.651	**0.099**
Information on the political and legal framework	4619.000	20550.000	-1.620	0.105
Information on the macroeconomic and fiscal framework	5040.500	20971.500	-0.671	0.502
Distribution channels	4857.000	20788.000	-1.082	0.279
Production capacity	5285.000	7115.000	-0.123	0.902
Counselling	5031.500	20962.500	-0.697	0.486
Credibility	4770.000	20701.000	-1.275	0.202

5. Conclusion

This paper set out to investigate the existence of differences between young and old companies in the importance they attach to networks for the implementation of their internationalization processes. To do this, it moves away from the aggregate view that most studies have in empirical studies and considers that networks are composed of different types of relationships and different types of actors and serve different purposes. Thus it distinguishes two types of relationships (formal and informal), 14 types of partners (not only companies in the supply/value chain but a broader set of actors, both in the origin country and abroad) and ten different types of resources that can be assessed through networking.

The results confirm the existence of statistical differences between young and old companies in two of the three dimensions of analysis. In terms of type of relationship, our research shows that young companies tend to attribute a greater degree of importance both to formal and informal relationships. This is in line with insights from previous research that have stressed that the participation in networks is particularly beneficial for the internationalization of younger companies, due to their lack of experience and resources (e.g Harris & Wheeler, 2005; Sharma & Blomstermo, 2003; Styles et al., 2006). Our study adds that this holds both for formal and informal networks. It also shows that formal relationships tend to be higher rated by all companies.

As stressed by previous research (e.g. Bruneel, Yli-Renko, & Clarysse, 2010) customers in the foreign markets are very important partners for the internationalization process. But our study as also found that partners in the home country are important to the internationalization process, not only at the level of the supply chain (suppliers and customers), but also governmental agencies. The results also suggest that young companies tend to attribute greater relevance to business associations in their home country, when compared to older companies. In the other types of partner, we did not find statistically significant differences between the two types of companies.

Finally, the results reveal that young companies consider networks more important to access information on possible partnerships, when compared to older companies. In the remaining types of resource, we did not find statistically significant differences between the two types of companies.

Acknowledgements

This work is supported by FEDER funds from COMPETE 2020 and Portuguese funds - PORTUGAL 2020. Project IEcPBI - Interactive Ecosystem for Portuguese Business Internationalization - POCI-01-0145-FEDER-032139"

References

Acs, Z., & Terjesen, S. (2007). Born locals: two avenues to internationalization. *JENA- economic research papers*, Friedrich-Schiller University and Max Planck Institute of Economics.

Alvarez, I., & Molero, J. (2005). Technology and the generation of international spillovers: an application to Spanish manufacturing firms . *Research Policy, vol. 34*, 1440-1452.

Bai, w. & Johanson, M. (2017). International opportunity networks. *Industrial Marketing Management.* http://dx.doi.org/10.1016/j.indmarman.2017.07004.

Baum, J. A., Calabrese, T., & Silverman, B. S. (2000). Don't go it alone: Alliance network composition and startups' performance in Canadian biotechnology. *Strategic Management Journal*, 21(3), 267-294.

Bruneel, J., Yli-Renko, H., & Clarysse, B. (2010). Learning from experience and learning from others: how congenital and interorganizational learning substitute for experiential learning in young firm internationalization. *Strategic Entrepreneurship Journal*, 4(2), 164-182.

Burt, R. S. (2009). *Structural holes: The social structure of competition*. Harvard university press.

Casillas, J., Moreno, A., Acedo, F., & Gallego, M. (2009). An integrative model of the role of knowledge in the internationalization process. *Journal of World Business, vol. 44, nº 3*, 311–322.

Cloninger, P.A., & Oviatt, B. (2007). Service content and the internationalization of young ventures: an empirical test. Entrepreneurship Theory and Practice, 31(2), 233-256.

Coviello, N. (2006). The network dynamics of international new ventures. *Journal of International Business Studies, vol. 37, nº 5* , 713-731.

Coviello, N., & Munro, H. J. (1997). Network relationships and the internationalization process of small software firms. *International Business Review, vol. 6, nº 4*, 361–386.

De Clercq, D., Sapienza, H., Yavuz, R., & Zhou, L. (2012). Learning and knowledge in early internationalization research: Past accomplishments and future directions. *Journal of Business Venturing, vol. 27*, 143–165.

Fernhaber, S., McDougall, P., & Oviatt, B. (2007). Exploring the role of industry structure in new venture internationalization. *Entrepreneurship Theory and Practice, vol. 31, nº 4*, 517–542.

Galkina, T. & Chetty, S. (2015). Effectuation and Networking of Internationalizing SMEs. *Management International Review, vol. 55, nº 5*. DOI: 10.1007/s11575-015-0251-x

George, G., Wiklund, J. & Zahra, S. (2005). Ownership and the Internationalization of Small Firms. *Journal of Management, vol 31, nº 2*, 210-233

Grosse, R., & Fonseca, A. (2012). Learning through imports in the internationalization process. *Journal of International Management, vol. 18, nº 4*, 366-378.

Harris, S., & Wheeler, C. (2005). Entrepreneurs' relationships for internationalization: functions, origins and strategies. *International business review*, 14(2), 187-207.

Holm, D.B., Johanson, M. & Kao, P. (2015). From outsider to insider: Opportunity development in foreign market networks, *Journal of International Entrepreneurship, vol. 13, nº 3*, 337-359.

Johanson, J., & Vahlne, J.-E. (1977). The Internationalization Process of the Firm: A Model of Knowledge Development and Increasing Foreign Market Commitments. *Journal of International Business Studies, vol.8*, 23-32.

Johanson, J., & Vahlne, J.-E. (2009). The Uppsala internationalization process model revisited: From liability of foreignness to liability of outsidership. *Journal of International Business Studies, vol. 40*, 1411-1431.

Johanson, J., & Vahlne, J.-E. (2011). Markets as networks: implications for strategy-making. *Journal of the Academy of Marketing Sciences, vol. 39*, 484-491.

Kontinen, T., & Ojala, A. (2011). Network ties in the international opportunity recognition of family SMEs. International Business Review, 20(4), 440-453.

Leiblein, M., & Reuer, J. (2004). Building a foreign sales base: the role of capabilities and alliances for entrepreneurial firms. *Journal of Business Venturing, vol. 19, nº 2*, 285–307.

LiPuma, J.A. (2012). Internationalization and the IPO performance of new ventures. *Journal of Business Research,* 65(7), 914-921.

McDougall, P., & Oviatt, B.M. (2000). International entrepreneurship: the intersection of two research paths. *Academy of Management Journal, vol. 43, nº 5*, 902–906.

Maroco, J. (2018). Análise Estatística com o SPSS, 7th ed; ReportNumber, Lda: Lisboa, Portugal.

Musteen, M., Datta, D.K., & Butts, M.M. (2014). Do International Networks and Foreign Market Knowledge Facilitate SME Internationalization? Evidence From the Czech Republic. *Entrepreneurship Theory and Practice*, 38(4), 749-774.

Nooteboom, B. (1999). Inter-Firm Alliances: Analysis and Design. Routledge, London.

Ojala, A. (2009). Internationalization of knowledge-intensive SMEs: The role of network relationships in the entry to a psychically distant market. *International Business Review*, 18(1), 50-59.

Oviatt, B.M., & McDougall, P.P. (1994). Toward a Theory of International New Ventures. *Journal of International Business Studies, vol. 25, nº 1*, 45-64.

Oviatt, B.M., & McDougall, P.P. (1995). Global start-ups: Entrepreneurs on a worldwide stage . *Academy of Management Executive, vol. 9, nº 2*, 30-43.

Oviatt, B.M., & McDougall, P.P. (1997). Challenges for internationalization process theory: The case of international new ventures. *Management International Review, vol. 37, nº 2*, 85-99.

Oviatt, B.M., & McDougall, P.P. (2005). Defining international entrepreneurship and modeling the speed of internationalization. *Entrepreneurship: Theory and Practice, vol. 29, nº 5* , 537–553.

Paul, J., Parthasarathy, S. & Gupta, P. (2017). Exporting challenges of SMEs: A review and future research agenda. *Journal of World Business, Elsevier, vol. 52, nº 3*, 327-342.

Rezvani, M., Davari, A., & Parvaneh, N. (2017). Identifying and Prioritizing the Contributory Factors to the Early Internationalization of International New Ventures in Halal Food Industry. *International Business Research, vol. 10, nº 6*, 189-198.

Sarasvathy, S., Kumar, K., York, J.G., & Bhagavatula, S. (2014). An effectual approach to international entrepreneurship: Overlaps, challenges, and provocative possibilities. *Entrepreneurship Theory and Practice, vol. 38, nº 1, 71-93.*

Sharma, D. D., & Blomstermo, A. (2003). The internationalization process of born globals: a network view. *International business review*, 12(6), 739-753.

Smith-Doerr, L. & Powell, W. (2003). Networks and economic life. In: Smelser, N., Swedberg, R. (Eds.), *The Handbook of Economic Sociology*. Princeton Univer- sity Press.

Sousa, C. (2012). Using social network analysis to study entrepreneurship: Methodological issues. In: Salavisa, I. & Fontes, M. (eds), *Social networks, Innovation and the Knowledge Economy* (pp. 89-106), London and NY, Routledge.

Sousa, C. & Fontes, M. (2012). Networks and Technological Entrepreneurship. In: Salavisa, I. & Fontes, M. (eds), *Social networks, Innovation and the Knowledge Economy* (pp. 69-88) London and NY, Routledge.

Styles, C., Loane, S., & Bell, J. (2006). Rapid internationalisation among entrepreneurial firms in Australia, Canada, Ireland and New Zealand. *International marketing review,* 23(5): 467-485.

Tamara, G. & Sylvie C. (2015). Effectuation and Networking of Internationalizing SMEs. Management International Review, vol. 55, nº 5. DOI: 10.1007/s11575-015-0251-x

Vasilchenko, E., & Morrish, S. (2011). The role of entrepreneurial networks in the exploration and exploitation of internationalization opportunities by information and communication technology firms. Journal of International Marketing, 19(4), 88-105.

Studying the Role of Proximity in Advancing Innovation Partnerships at the Dawn of Industry 4.0 era

Chryssi Stathaki, Apostolos Xenakis, Pantoleon Skayannis and George Stamoulis
University of Thessaly, Volos, Greece
hrstatha@uth.gr
axenakis@uth.gr
leonska@prd.uth.gr
georges@uth.gr
DOI: 10.34190/EIE.20.048

Abstract: The fourth Industrial revolution (a.k.a Industry 4.0 wave), presupposes the completion of digital business transformation. Industry 4.0 wave is based on cyber-physical production systems (CPS), aiming to connect the physical and digital production spaces. Under this framework, Industry 4.0 digital operations require the re-establishment of IT systems, in a way that human and machines are interconnected and interact in real-time, thus creating a more flexible, resource-efficient and optimal way of manufacturing. To this end, Industry 4.0 encompasses concepts that include Industrial Internet of Things (IIoT) and Artificial Intelligence (AI) in manufacturing, which promotes better smart production phases. Under the new digital framework of Industry 4.0, the role of proximity in advancing innovation partnerships and promoting efficient technology and knowledge transfer among the engaged partners, should be carefully examined. It becomes clear that stakeholders' coordination activities, which will ensure their efficient cooperation, continue to reflect issues of major importance and illustrate the value of proximity - in both physical and relative terms - in the newly defined innovation plane. One of the open theoretical challenges we attempt to tackle in the initial debate provided in our paper, concerns the possible functional transformation of proximity's spatial and non-spatial dimensions within this new digital Industry 4.0 framework, as well as the critical trade-offs that have to be made between the traditional (namely proximity) and the new technology-based approach (namely Industry 4.0) for the actors' effective coordination and cooperation. Towards this direction, we study the way proximity dimensions horizontally affect the new realm posed by Industry 4.0. Finally, given that the Industry 4.0 era of innovation cooperation gives rise to new issues, that is among others, cybersecurity and enhanced cognitive capabilities, we discuss the specific weight of each proximity dimension, and identify the need for certain dimensions to be developed amongst players compared to others that seem to rather diminish their significance.

Keywords: Industry 4.0, digital transformation, proximity, innovation, management of innovation, entrepreneurship

1. Introduction and related works

Innovation is now coming to the fore of the 4rth industrial era, either as a reinvigorating aspect of established productive procedures or as a force of radical or incremental change, setting new challenges and raising new policy issues. The new Industrial framework reflects the transformation that makes it possible to gather and analyze data across machines, enabling cyber-physical systems (CPS) cooperation with humans and, thus, more flexible and efficient processes enhancing production for higher quality goods at reduced costs (Lu, 2017). This manufacturing revolution will increase productivity, foster industrial growth and change economy production dynamics and competitiveness of companies and regions. Under this framework, Industry 4.0 digital operations require the re-establishment of IT systems, in a way that humans and machines interact real-time, creating a more digital-oriented way of manufacturing. For innovation partnerships to thrive under this new digital economy framework, proximity plays and important role (Boschma, 2005). However, both spatial and non-spatial proximity dimensions need to be carefully redefined and examined, in order to efficiently contribute to promoting technology and knowledge transfer among the engaged partners (Mattes, 2012).

In the 4th Industrial Revolution we move from the digitalized and Internet–based client–server model to ubiquitous computing and mobility, pervasive computing and analytics and combined digital and physical environments, with additional accelerators, such as advanced robotics, Artificial Intelligence (AI) and cognitive CPS, enabling automation and optimization in entirely new ways (Issa et. al 2017). The injection of AI methods into production, real–time data analytics and the involvement of autonomous smart machines (i.e. agents) have drastically changed the way actors work and cooperate, produce innovation and transfer knowledge. These new digital tools permit humans to technically control processes in a distant mode, yet many researchers may be skeptical as to how efficiently the lack of geographical proximity in businesses may work positively or not (Moodysson, 2007). The essence of Industry 4.0 is the digital–intensive transformation of manufacturing in a connected and autonomous environment of data, people, processes, services and IoT–enable CPS, as a way and means to realize smart industry and ecosystems of Industrial Innovation (Deloitte, 2015). Furthering, the inherent complexity of innovation turns space into a relational concept rather than a purely geographical one (Silvestre & Dalcol, 2009, Mattes, 2012). At the same time, heterogeneous innovation players (individuals, firms, universities, etc.), which are unevenly allocated in space, face the need to reduce their physical and relative distance and effectively communicate through trust-based relationships, shared values, common rules, shared competences, hierarchy, etc. (Bathelt et al., 2004, Asheim, et al., 2007), that is to establish a certain degree of proximity between them. The abovementioned findings highlighted the direct correlation between proximity and innovation, triggering the opening of proximity's black box for the identification of its overall contribution to innovative performance.

The debate on proximity and innovation regarding the promotion of innovative activity and the advancement of innovation collaborations, reflects a prominent concept in scientific literature. Innovation had been considered as a spatial and highly localized phenomenon in the past, cultivating a geographical bias in the explanation of innovativeness (Mattes, 2012). Hence, the assertion that "the more proximity there is (in a narrow spatial sense), the more interaction and innovation occur" reflected a common misleading consensus (Boschma, 2005, p. 62). This was the case until the French School of Proximity Dynamics made the first critical contribution to the field in the 1990s, by highlighting that proximity means more than just geography and identifying additional organizational elements (Torre & Gilly, 2000, Boschma, 2005, Moodysson & Jonsson, 2007). During the 20th century, further attempts were made by the academic community to investigate proximity in the light of a more complex perspective and, consequently, numerous proximity dimensions came into play. According to the contemporary, more sophisticated view developed, proximity comprises both spatial and non-spatial aspects, where the latter include laws, norms, culture, hierarchy, trust, etc.

This theoretical paper sets off from a short introduction regarding Industry 4.0 definition and the relation between proximity and innovation under the new framework posed, to explore the implications of proximity for this rising digitized production model. To this end, the identification of proximity dimensions emphasizes that it has to be taken into consideration in a broader and more elaborate view, so to redefine the involvement of proximity in advancing innovation partnerships. Following, in section 2, we provide a brief presentation regarding the Industry 4.0 framework, models and tools and highlight the criteria required for businesses to be Industry 4.0 compliant. In section 3, we attempt to summarize the most pertinent views on proximity dimensions and their contribution to innovation partnerships based on the scientific findings of the debate on the traditional proximity approach. We finally present our proposition regarding the redefinition of proximity's role in its five dimensions to the promotion of potential innovation partnerships, we investigate the specific weight and significance of each dimension and argue whether some certain dimensions necessarily need to be established and enhanced amongst stakeholders versus others that seem to rather diminish their significance. Our work attempts to shed light on the unexplored role of proximity and its entanglement in innovation potential under the new digitalized framework posed by Industry 4.0.

2. Industry 4.0 digital framework

The beginning of the 4th Industrial Revolution, a.k.a. Industry 4.0 wave, is based on CPS, aiming to connect the physical and the digital world of production. Therefore, Industry 4.0 digital operations require the completion of the industries' and businesses' digital transformation in a way that IT systems, machines and humans interact in real-time and create a more flexible, resource-efficient, customized and optimal way of manufacturing, i.e. the Smart Factory. To this end, the 4th Industrial Revolution encompasses concepts that include Industrial Internet of Things (IIoT), AI, Smart Production, Smart manufacturing, etc. Within the modular structured smart factories, CPS monitor physical processes, create a virtual copy of the physical world, and make optimal decentralized production decisions. With the use of IIoT, CPS communicate and cooperate with each other and with humans in real-time, either internally or across organizational services used by the value chain participants. Some of the components comprising Industry 4.0 digital trends are as follows: mobile devices, IoT devices and platforms, fog computing components, smart sensors, 3D printing components, Augmented Reality, wearables, big data analytics, AI prediction algorithms, etc.

2.1 Characteristics of Industry 4.0 digital framework

The rise of the new digital industrial technology requires a specific digital transformation that allows the real-time gathering and analysis of data across machines, enabling flexible and low-cost production processes. This manufacturing revolution will increase productivity, foster industrial growth and modify the workforce profile.

To this end, advanced digital tools will transform production. This technology is expected to modify traditional production relationships among suppliers, producers and customers, as well as between human–workers and production machines. Following, we present some of the technology trends, which account for the digital building blocks for Industry 4.0 (Figueredo et. al, 2007):

- *Big data Analytics:* refers to the collection and comprehensive evaluation of data from many different sources, production equipment and systems, as well as enterprise and customer-management systems, that will become standards for the support of real-time decision making
- *Industrial IoT:* refers to devices enriched by embedded computing that allows them to communicate and interact with centralized controllers as necessary.
- *Cybersecurity:* refers to the application of security communication protocols to protect critical industrial systems and manufacturing lines from cyber threats.
- *Cloud:* refers to production-related undertakings that require increased data sharing across sites and company boundaries. At the same time, new cloud technology protocols will achieve a reaction time of just several milliseconds. As a result, machine data and control applications will be easily deployed towards the cloud, enabling more data-driven services for production systems.
- *AI and Autonomous Robots:* refers to the use of interacting robots that safely collaborate side by side with humans and learn from them. These robots will cost less and have a greater range of capabilities than those used in manufacturing so far.

It is worth mentioning that Industry 4.0 is driven by digitalization and integration of vertical and horizontal value chains and the digitization of products and services. However, the implementation of Industry 4.0 related practices poses new challenges regarding IT security issues, sufficient human qualifications, surveillance, reliability of machine-to-machine (M2M) communications and adequate skill set that support the transition towards the 4th Industrial Revolution.

2.2 Criteria for Industry 4.0 business compliance

For the abovementioned building blocks to be adopted, industries pursuing to become Industrial 4.0-compliant may need to involve concrete technology design principles and goals as follows (Mueller, 2017):

- *Interconnection:* refers to the ability of machines, sensors, devices and workers to connect and communicate with each other via IIoT technologies.
- *Decentralized decisions:* refers to the ability of CPS to make real-time decisions without (or minimal) human intervention and perform their tasks as autonomously as possible.
- *CPS assistance:* refers to the ability of CPS to physically support human workers by conducting a range of tasks that are difficult, unpleasant, exhausting and potentially hazardous.

For Industry 4.0 compliance to be achieved, businesses need to define a digital transformation strategy. This means to develop new business models and operation forms that may be driven by technological innovations, such as AI, cloud data analytics, fog and edge computing, autonomous robots driven by machine learning techniques, cybersecurity models, wearables, IoT, big data, virtual and augmented reality, data collection and provisioning systems, etc. All these technological innovations demand more bandwidth and power-efficient connections. On top of that, cybersecurity solutions, such as BlockChain and smart contracts are necessary, especially in cases of high-volume transactions of crucial and sensitive personal data. The Industry 4.0 digital framework also requires adequate device interoperability, high efficiency and 100% uptime. Specifically, interoperability is technologically related to the heterogeneous components' connectivity and integration so to function harmoniously. Under this perspective, business compliance for Industry 4.0 describes the real–time communication of manufacturing and value chain creation, the intelligent horizontal and vertical networked systems, as well as smart factories that dynamically adapt to supply chain variations (PCW,2016).

The digital transformation strategy for Industry 4.0 compliance encompasses both a transformational management strategy and a business response to the autonomous production model mentioned before and, thus, the overall business strategy in innovation partnerships should include digital transformation policies. The objective of designing and applying such a transformation strategy that ensures Industry 4.0 compliance, is to guarantee that business models are adopted and realized in new technology investments (cloud data analytics, augmented reality, 3D printing applications, AI and machine learning algorithms, Cybersecurity and BlockChain, CPS, etc.) (Mueller, 2017).

3. Re-defying the role of proximity dimensions

All proximity dimensions refer to *"being close to something measured on a certain dimension"* (Knoben & Oerlemans, 2006, pp. 71-2) and are now perceived as tools for information sharing and knowledge transfer that may resolve the fundamental coordination issues among stakeholders and boost their innovative activity (Gertler, 2003). Yet these dimensions are not identical and each of them plays a specific role in the promotion of innovation, as analyzed below.

3.1 Spatial and non - spatial dimensions of proximity within the digital Industry 4.0 framework

The fivefold typology adopted here, as suggested by Boschma (2005) and Mattes (2012), focuses on the following dimensions: geographical, cognitive, organizational, social and institutional, as they represent a comprehensive account of all proximity aspects raised in the literature and capture all the barriers (spatial and non-spatial) that may hinder innovative performance.

- *Geographical proximity:* According to Kirrat and Lung (1999, p. 29) it refers to *"the positioning of agents within a predetermined spatial framework"*. Torre and Gilly (2000, p. 180) define it as *"both the economical, geographical separation of the individual or collective agents...and their position in an economic problem resolution process"*, and Torre and Rallet (2005, p. 49) as *"the kilometric distance that separates two units in geographical space"* weighted by the cost and time of transport and individual perceptions of distance. It is restrictively defined by Boschma as *"the spatial or physical distance between economic actors, both in absolute and relative meaning"* (Boschma, 2005, p. 69), by Moodysson and Jonsson (2007, p. 118) as *"the absolute and relative distance...affected by numerous factors such as mobility and associated with accessibility" and by Mattes as the "co-location of the involved actors"* (Mattes 2012, p. 1090).
- *Cognitive proximity*: According to Torre and Gilly (2000, p. 177) it represents *"communication and interactions between actors, which are essential to the establishment of codes and common languages, a process of interpretation of partial tacit knowledge, and the transformation of this knowledge into operational questions"*. According to Boschma (2005, p. 63) it is related to *"the capacity of actors or firms to absorb new knowledge...in order to communicate, understand and absorb it successfully"*. If accompanied by the intention to cooperate, split and absorb information, it facilitates interactive learning and innovation through common skills and expertise (Boschma, 2005, p. 63). Mattes (2012, pp. 1088-9) states that it refers to the actors' capacity to *"understand each other and use a common interpretative scheme"* based on shared experience and common apprehension.
- *Organizational proximity*: According to Blanc and Sierra (1999, p. 196) it refers to *"compatibility within a group...by encouraging or imposing connecting principles, i.e. a corporate culture, which will guide not merely choices but the concepts to be used in framing problems"*. Torre and Gilly (2000, pp. 177-180) state that *"actors close in organizational terms belong to the same space of relations...they are quite alike, they have the same reference space and share the same knowledge"*. It also denotes "the capacity to coordinate the exchange of complementary pieces of knowledge owned by a variety of actors within and between organizations" (Boschma, 2005, pp. 64-65), as well as *"the extent to which relations are shared in an organization arrangement...and the participants follow similar organizational logics"* (Mattes, 2012, p. 1089).
- *Social proximity:* As Boschma (2005, p. 66-7) points out *"relations between actors are socially embedded when they involve trust based on friendship, kinship and experience. The more socially embedded the relationships of a firm are, the more interactive learning, and the better its (innovative) performance"*. It also represents the outcome of shared personal characteristics, present or past interactions and *"a sense of familiarity between individual actors"* (Mattes, 2012, pp. 1089).
- *Institutional proximity*: According to Edquist and Johnson (1997, p. 46) it represents *"a set of common habits, routines, established practices, rules, or laws that regulate the relations and interactions between individuals and groups"*. Torre and Gilly (2000, p. 182) define it as the *"adhesion of agents to common space of representation, of patterns, and of rules of thought and action"*. According to Zeller (2004, p. 88) it refers to *"the institutional framework, such as legislative conditions, labor relations, business practices and rules, dominant workplace practices and the training system, that contribute to a cultural affinity". It also represents "common institutional rules of the game, a common language, shared habits and a law system"*

(Boschma, 2005, pp. 67-68), as well as to *"a complex combination of macro-level factors, that is hard institutional factors like laws and rules...and soft ones, that is, norms, values and routines"* (Mattes, 2012, p. 1089).

Table 1: The five dimensions of proximity presented in the paper and their significance based on the traditional proximity approach and the technology-oriented approach introduced here

		Significance	
Proximity dimension	Emphasis	when developed between actors based on the traditional proximity approach	when developed between actors based on the technology-oriented proximity approach
Geographical	Space	Co-location, interactions, easier transfer of knowledge, responses to problems, knowledge externalities	Less significant (due to the greater involvement of technology), still crucial for activities such as digital fabrication, 3D printing, etc.
Cognitive	Knowledge capabilities	Mutual understanding, effective communication, absorptive capacity	Further sophisticated knowledge base, higher skills, advanced capabilities, new problem-solving framework
Organizational	Control, hierarchy,	Coordination of actions, monitoring, hierarchy, ownership rights and rewards	Common elements of organizational culture, discouragement of unintended knowledge spillovers, monitoring of knowledge dissemination and access, cybersecurity
Social	Trust, interactions	Embedded social relations, trust, easier exchange of knowledge	Less significant (due to less physical interactions), personal interactions along and across industries and common strategies on industrial matters
Institutional	Framework	Common institutions and rules, coherence to laws, shared values and culture	Principal role, institutional convergence, cybersecurity, protection of intellectual property rights, coherence to hard and soft institutional settings, behavioral scope

Source: own elaboration

Following we elaborate Table 1 representing the impact of each proximity dimension when established between partners in innovation collaborations, based on the so far traditional approach of the proximity notion. Each dimension's significance presented here is distinct from the significance it acquires in the 'technology-based' proximity approach of Industry 4.0 context. In that way, we attempt to identify the differentiated contribution of proximity in innovation partnerships in Industry 4.0 era, allowing theoretical comparisons between the traditional and the technology-based approach to be made. More specifically:

- *Geographical proximity* always matters in the sense that distance is usually accompanied by linguistic, sociocultural, institutional and other constraints. This proximity type facilitates face to face interactions, knowledge exchange and problem-solving (Torre & Rallet, 2005). Stakeholders sharing the same geographical space may rapidly reap the benefits aroused from knowledge externalities with less effort or cost (Moodysson & Jonsson, 2007), yet the significance of this dimension has been intensely questioned, as it does not represent a prerequisite for learning and innovation to take place.
- *Cognitive proximity* between heterogeneous players guarantees they combine their complementary capabilities (Nooteboom, 2006) through a common perceptual scheme. Once developed, (new) knowledge can be identified, understood and processed by them successfully (Boschma, 2005).
- *Organizational proximity* assures alignment, coordination and hierarchy between innovation partners. It acts as the means for knowledge dissemination and information exchange, reducing transaction costs and attenuating economic relations' uncertainty. Its contribution is mostly strategic, as it ensures ownership rights and rewards for investments in new technological fields, preventing external players from accessing specific internal knowledge (Zeller, 2004).

- *Social proximity* indicates the formation of trust-based relationships that boost innovative capacity. Once established, it facilitates the actors' ability to learn from each other, interact and innovate within a framework of personal relations and interactive cooperation (Torre & Gilly, 2000).
- *Institutional proximity* guarantees coherence in respect of laws and values, as well as the development of a shared language that facilitates players' communication and boosts their innovation outcomes. Once established, players share the same institutional and behavioral environment, which catalytically affects their actions and their innovation potential (Boschma, 2005, Mattes, 2012).

3.2 Trade - offs among traditional and technology - based proximity approach

Industry 4.0 is strongly associated with the production system's structural change, posing new challenges, and raising complex cooperation-relevant issues. Stakeholders need to align with the new prerequisites aroused by the Industry 4.0 wave and engage the proximity notion in a more contemporary manner for the sake of novelty. The digital transformation of industries and businesses redefines the rules of the innovation game, alters the existing cooperation mechanisms, creates novel opportunities, and poses threats that need to be investigated. As such, the traditional cooperation practices are reformed and require the acquisition of modern or more sophisticated skills on behalf of the engaged actors, as analyzed in Section 2. Regardless of the production system's structural transformation, actors still need a coordination mechanism to cope with their distance in both physical and relative terms. That mechanism will determine the scope of their actions, ensure their effective communication, and boost their innovation capacity. This argument overemphasizes the advanced role of proximity, which, except for its traditional contribution to the overcoming of spatial and relative distance in innovation cooperation, it now acquires a more technology-based orientation. Technology and ICT systems offer opportunities for direct communication, administration, coordination, management, and organization with even greater potential than before. Nevertheless, the involvement of technological means (which certainly enrich the existing cooperation and coordination patterns, mostly in cases of distant collaborations in both spatial and non-spatial terms) may not always imply that advanced innovation outcomes or high-quality interactions between actors will take place. Furthermore, this new conditions framework also transforms each proximity dimension's explicit contribution to the promotion of innovativeness, as well as its specific weight regarding the innovation partnerships' outcomes, in the sense that some certain dimensions may be necessary to be established amongst players, whilst others may diminish their significance or become negligible after the first stages of an innovation project.

In Industry 4.0 context, collaboration strategy should build upon a deeper understanding of industry and innovation, covering the whole spectrum of activities across the value chain, as well as the new digital processes arising from this digital era of innovation cooperation. Therefore, each proximity dimension's role becomes subject to functional change, their specific weight is redefined and some trade-offs between the traditional and the technology-based proximity approach should be achieved so that actors catch up with the new digital realm and its requirements. Value chains expand across borders at a global scale and, thus, we should not discount the geographical dimension. Nevertheless, the spatial and non-spatial dimension come into some structural changes. In particular:

- Innovation literature findings agree that *geographical proximity* does not represent a prerequisite for learning and innovation to take place. In the case of Industry 4.0 wave, which is accompanied by the greater involvement of technology, its significance is further deemphasized, as the exploitation of technology means in collaborations (such as ICTs, IoT, AI, AR, etc.) may reduce or even eliminate geographical distance and boost the effective communication of the engaged partners even if they are distant. Nevertheless, some activities (such as digital fabrication, 3D printing, etc.) will still demand the geographical co-location of partners and the development of strong interpersonal relationships, introducing a new, more advanced role on behalf of the engaged actors (i.e. engineer).
- *Cognitive proximity*_amongst partners is anticipated to play a crucial and decisive role regarding the facilitation of innovation partnerships and the promotion of better innovation outcomes. Industry 4.0 compliance implies that actors develop a more sophisticated knowledge base along with higher skills, advanced capabilities in production capacity and management, and a new common problem-solving framework so to tackle the new cognitive requirements posed by Industry 4.0.
- *Organizational proximity's* contribution to innovation outcomes in Industry 4.0 framework is also advanced, in the sense that players should establish some common elements of organizational culture, such as values,

norms, ethics, etc., for the purpose of effective interactions and collaborations to be achieved. Despite the increasing entanglement of technology in cooperation, innovation partners still require the establishment of a control mechanism that coordinates their actions, discourages unintended knowledge spillovers and assures the development of strong personal ties. Organizational proximity amongst stakeholders in this digital framework will also guarantee the monitoring of knowledge dissemination and access, as well as the adoption of organizational arrangements that are commonly accepted to be beneficial for learning and innovation.

- *Social proximity's* role is believed to be less significant in the Industry 4.0 era. Socially embedded relationships will always matter and provide channels for knowledge diffusion. Nevertheless, the digital transformation of production systems will be accompanied by less physical interactions and fewer trust-based relationships, as technology means will compensate or even cover for the decrease or lack of face to face relations between the engaged actors. Still, there is scope for the establishment of social proximity amongst stakeholders, through the intensification of personal interactions along and across industries, and the development of certain strategies regarding interactions on industrial matters.
- *Institutional proximity* is anticipated to play a principal role in Industry 4.0 context, as it may ensure the institutional convergence of actors within this new digital innovation plane. As issues like cybersecurity emerge, this proximity aspect will guarantee the protection of intellectual property rights and the actors' coherence to hard (laws) and soft (norms, values, ethics) institutional settings. Except for the facilitation of good practices transfer, the establishment of institutional proximity amongst actors also determines the normative framework conditions of the innovation game and defines their behavioral scope.

4. Conclusion and future work

The 4rth Industrial Revolution is synonymous with the structural transformation of production systems, putting innovation and technological advancement at the heart of socio-economic development. Towards this direction, the entanglement of proximity in innovation should also move from the so far traditional perception of establishing the necessary prerequisites for the actors' effective coordination and collaboration, to a more technology-based approach. This novel perspective of proximity's role in innovation partnerships will assist actors to cope with the new cooperation conditions posed by Industry 4.0 wave, so to advance their innovation potential and eliminate -to some extent- distance-relevant barriers (spatial and non-spatial), through the redevelopment of their skills and competencies.

This paper presents a generic, theoretical framework triggered by the upcoming digital industrial transformations of Industry 4.0. To this end, without concentrating on a specific industrial sector and its stakeholders, we attempt to highlight the functional transformation of proximity dimensions' contribution to innovative performance as ensued from the additional criteria of this digitalization. Proximity is strongly context-oriented and, thus, its dimensions may reshape, emerge or disappear over time. Therefore, we attempt to identify the way proximity dimensions may contribute to better collaborations and advanced innovation outcomes within the Industry 4.0 era and the novel requirements it raises, rather than highlight which of them generally matters more for the promotion of innovation. As future work, we intend to focus on a specific business vertical and open a new debate circle on the specific weight of each dimension, given the assumption that the aspect of proximity required in innovation cooperation depends on the nature of the involved knowledge and the particular type of innovation each industry pursues.

References

Asheim, B., Coenen, L., and Vang, J. (2007) "Face-to-face, buzz, and knowledge bases: Sociospatial implications for learning, innovation, and innovation policy", *Environment and Planning C: Government and Policy*, **25** 655-670

Bathelt, H., Malmberg, A., and Maskell, P. (2004) "Clusters and knowledge: local buzz, global pipelines and the process of knowledge creation", *Progress in Human Geography, **28** (1) 31-56*

Blanc, H., and Sierra, C. (1999) "The Internationalization of R&D by multinationals: a trade-off between external and internal proximity", *Cambridge Journal of Economics*, **23** 187-206

Boschma, R. (2005) "Proximity and Innovation: A Critical Assessment", *Regional Studies*, **39** 61–74

Deloitte (2015) "Industry 4.0: Challenges and Solutions for the digital transformation and use of exponential technologies" [White Paper] https://www.pac.gr/bcm/uploads/industry-4-0-deloitte-study.pdf

Edquist, C. and Johnson, B. (1997) "Institutions and organizations in systems of innovation", in C. Edquist (Ed.) *Systems of Innovation: Technologies, Institutions and Organizations*, London: Pinter, 41–63

European Union Study for the ITRE Committee (2016), *Industry 4.0 Analytical Study*, Directorate General for Internal Policies, Policy Department A: Economic and Scientific Policy [White Paper] https://www.europarl.europa.eu/RegData/etudes/STUD/2016/570007/IPOL_STU(2016)570007_EN.pdf

Issa, A., A. Hatiboglu, Bildstein, A., and Bauernhansl, T. (2018) "Industrie 4.0 roadmap: Framework for digital transformation based on the concepts of capability maturity and alignment", *Elsevier Procedia CIRP,* **72** 973-978

Kirat, T., and Lung, Y. (1999) "Innovation and proximity. Territories as loci of collective learning processes", *European Urban and Regional Studies*, **6** 27-38

Knoben, J., and Oerlemans, L.A.G. (2006) "Proximity and interorganizational collaboration: a literature review", *International Journal of Management Reviews*, **6** (2), 71–89

Lu, Y. (2017) "Industry 4.0: A survey on technologies, applications and open research issues", *Elsevier Journal of Industrial Information Integration*, **6** (1) 1 – 10

Mattes, J. (2012) "Dimensions of Proximity and Knowledge Bases: Innovation between Spatial and Non-spatial Factors", *Regional Studies*, **46** (8) 1085–1099

Moodysson, J., and Jonsson, O. (2007) "Knowledge Collaboration and Proximity: The Spatial Organization of Biotech Innovation Projects", *Urban and Regional Studies*, **14** 115-131

Mueller, X., Chen., X., and Riedel, R. (2017) "Challenges and Requirements for the Application of Industry 4.0: A Special Insight with the Usage of Cyber-Physical System", *Chin. J. Mech. Eng.,* **30** 1050 – 1057

Nooteboom, B. (2006) "Learning and innovation in inter-organization relationships and networks", *Center Discussion Paper Series*, **39**, The Netherlands: Tilburg University. Available at http://ssrn.com/abstract=903754

Paci, A. (2018) "Strategic Note for a Digital Innovation Policy", *Proceedings of 3rd Int. Conf. on the Industry 4.0 Model for Advanced Manufacturing*, 5-7

PWC. (2016), "Industry 4.0: Building the digital enterprise" [White Paper] https://www.pwc.com/gx/en/industries/industries-4.0/landing-page/industry-4.0-building-your-digital-enterprise-april-2016.pdf

Silvestre, B. d., and Dalcol, P. R. (2009) "Geographical proximity and innovation: Evidences from the Campos Basin oil & gas industrial agglomeration —Brazil", *Science Direct*, **29** (8) 546–561

Torre, A., and Gilly, J.-P. (2000) "On the Analytical Dimension of Proximity Dynamics", *Regional Studies*, **34** (2) 169-180

Torre, A., and Rallet, A. (2005) "Proximity and Localization", *Regional Studies*, **39** (1) 47-59

Zeller, C. (2004) "North Atlantic Innovative Relations of Swiss Pharmaceuticals and the Proximities with Regional Biotech Arenas", *Economic Geography*, **80** (1) 83-111

Social Support in Migrant Entrepreneurship Before and During the Coronavirus Crisis

Nina Szczygiel[1,2], Carmina Nunes[1,3] and Dina Ramos[1,2]
[1]Research Unit on Governance, Competitiveness and Public Policies
[2]Department of Economics, Management, Industrial Engineering and Tourism, University of Aveiro, Portugal
[3]Águeda School of Technology and Management, University of Aveiro, Portugal
nina.szczygiel@ua.pt
carminanunes@ua.pt
dinaramos@ua.pt
DOI: 10.34190/EIE.20.222

Abstract: Successive waves of immigration have long shaped societies, cultures and traditions, and supported the growth and development of host economies. Immigrants are consumers, taxpayers, investors, job creators and entrepreneurs. However, immigrant communities, and immigrant entrepreneurs in particular, face distinctive challenges in regard to good understanding of the local context and local market, awareness of laws and regulations, networking, nuances of language and mentality, or cultural aspects of doing business. Each of these elements individually, and all of them together, may determine the success of a venture. Migration is a complex phenomenon that touches on a multiplicity of economic, social, psychological and security aspects. It is through social connections that individuals learn about migration destinations and evaluate the potential of migration. To migrants, who are often not equally equipped with human, financial, and cultural capital, social connections are a vehicle to mobilise resources in a person's social environment what is particularly relevant in migrants willing to establish and run a business. Social support that networks provide comes in different forms and can involve tangible assets, information, guidance, or motivation. Social support is an effective resource in reducing stress and promoting well-being. This paper aims to investigate the role and importance of social support for immigrant entrepreneurs in Portugal. It examines perceptions of informational, instrumental, appraisal and emotional support. The study explores the meaning of social support for immigrant business venturing before and during the coronavirus crisis. It seeks to understand how social support is activated in different situations. Findings suggest social support is one of key functions of social relationships, a mean of relevant business-related resources for immigrants and of utmost importance in major crisis situations such as the Covid-19 outbreak.

Keywords: migrant entrepreneurship, immigrant, social support, Covid-19

1. Introduction

People take decision to migrate for a variety of motives and every migrant has a story to tell. Migrations have been defining the structure of the world and of societies over the centuries. The receiving country business spirit is fuelled in large part by immigrants. The immigration-entrepreneurship association depends naturally on characteristics of sending and receiving countries, motivation and type of migration (Vandor and Franke, 2018) but evidence suggests that immigrants are more likely to enter entrepreneurship and create own employment than natives (Nazareno, Zhou and You, 2019) and that companies founded by immigrants grow faster and survive longer (Wood, 2018). However, upon arrival immigrants have an earnings disadvantage (Chiswick, 1978) and in developed countries are faced with limited job opportunities often struggling with career advancement (Bates, 2011). Entrepreneurship has been pointed out as a strategy that supports integration in that it expands social connections through the pursued business activity and helps migrant individuals become integrated into the host country economy (Sanders and Nee, 1996). Immigrants often lack social, financial and human capital specifically suited to the labour market of the receiving country and their social connections are a mechanism to mobilise resources in the social environment.

Mindful of the participation of immigrant communities in social, cultural and economic development and challenges encountered by foreign-born individuals when venturing into entrepreneurship, we focus the present research on social support in immigrant entrepreneurs and investigate perceived social support from the perspectives of routine and crisis support as suggested by Lin (1986). We analyse perceptions of support usually received and support received after the Covid-19 outbreak. The study addresses informational, instrumental, appraisal and emotional support as proposed by House (1987) and examines the importance of social support for immigrant entrepreneurs.

2. Importance of immigrants and migrant entrepreneurship to economies of receiving countries

Entrepreneurship is vital to economic, social, and technological development. Entrepreneurs are considered agents of growth and change (Galanti, 2018). With their ability to convey change to economic, technological, and organisational environments (Morrison, Rimmington, & Williams, 2011), they are hailed as "drivers of innovation" (Gartner, 1990).

Almost 10% of entrepreneurs in the European Union (EU) were born outside of their native country. From this number, around two thirds come from outside of the EU. Migrant entrepreneurship rates vary substantially across the EU, for instance, Poland registered 1% in 2016, whereas the rates in the UK and Cyprus reached almost 20% and 20.5% respectively (OECD/European Union, 2017). In Portugal, the rates of migrant entrepreneurship have been increasing in absolute as well as in relative terms. Migrants coming from China had the highest rates of entrepreneurship in 2011 (about 42%). Migrants deriving from Asian countries (especially from Bangladesh and Pakistan), the Americas (mainly from the USA and Brazil), and from England and Germany were also very alive in business venturing.

Migrants contribute to the social and economic development of both, sending and receiving countries. For sending countries, the resulting remittances can lead to increased income and improved education and healthcare. Receiving countries, with developed countries often on that end, may benefit through immigrant participation in the host economy (Noja et al, 2018). Immigrants are students, workers, consumers, taxpayers, savers, and entrepreneurs and investors (OECD/ILO, 2018). They support the advancement of wealth, stimulate economic growth and reinforce technological advancement. Foreign-born individuals are over-represented in patent applications, and in founders of high-tech and biotechnology companies (Wadhwa, Saxenian, Rissin, & Gere, 2007; Monti, Smith-Doerr, & MacQuaid, 2007). They also present higher than natives rates of business formation and business ownership (Fairlie, 2012) and are over-represented among small business owners (Fiscal Policy Institute, 2012), a sector that in developed economies accounts for 99% of the market (OECD, 2019).

3. Conceptual bases of social support

Social support concept aroused in late 1970s and it has been since then object of research interest in a range of contexts. The principal interest in social supports stems from its the relationship with psychological well-being and physical health (Dean and Lin, 1977). One of the very well-known approaches to social support is that of House (1981), who distinguished between four dimensions of social support: instrumental, informational, appraisal and emotional. Instrumental support is expressed in tangible aid and service. It may comprise material and financial resources provided to the individual. Informational support involves transmission of information in the form of advice, suggestions or recommendations. Emotional support is transmitted through empathy and understanding. In practice, it means creating a safe environment for a person to share their thoughts, feelings, and emotions. Appraisal support involves transmission of affirmation, reassurance, and encouragement. Other research works propose a three-dimensional model, found for example by MaloneBeach and Zarit (1995). Interestingly, a largely cited definition of social support of Cobb (1976) includes informational and emotional aspects of support but overlooks the instrumental dimension.

In this perspective, social support processes are defined as mechanisms through which support resources impact the person or "impinge on ego" (Lin, 1986, p. 340). Social support processes reflect the type (actual and perceived support) and temporal dimension of support (routine and crisis support) (Lin, 1986). Other studies discussed the difference between provided (real) and perceived (believed to be received if needed) social support. Perceived support has been found to be positively associated to social integration and well-being and negatively associated to stress and symptoms of anxiety (House, 1987; Hartley and Coffee, 2019), whereas received social support had limited effects (Hartley and Coffee, 2019).

4. Importance of social support to immigrant populations

Situations and events preceding the decision of migration determine the circumstances in which the process occurs. Potential pre-migration stressors are later replaced by stressors originating from the transition process and outcome. Post-migration stressors may comprise language barriers, difficulties with qualifications recognition, unemployment, discrimination and lack of social support (Kazemipur and Halli, 2001; Robert and Gilkinson, 2012), and can be extended over time. Social support is critical during the post-migration period to ease transition and adaptation and offers a buffering effect against stress and adverse life events. Simich et al (2005) suggest that social support is "most meaningful when it is enabling and comprehensive, satisfying needs and aspirations in all areas of a newcomer's life" (p. 256).

5. Research methodology

This research is part of the study on social support in foreign-born entrepreneurs. The present article reports on perceptions of social support before and during the coronavirus crisis. It adopts a four-dimensional model of social support as proposed by House (1987) and uses the classification of support processes by Lin (1986) to guide and organise the empirical work. The study aims to examine how immigrant entrepreneurs perceive social support available to them in the course of their entrepreneurial experience discriminating between the routine support and that thought to be received after the coronavirus outbreak. Departing from this research objective, a set of research questions was developed on the basis of evidence from the conducted literature review. The set of exploratory research questions served as a means to determine the main categories of analysis, which comprised the following: routine social support available to immigrant entrepreneurs and social support available to immigrant entrepreneurs after the Covid-19 outbreak. A full listing of categories and sub-categories of analysis is included in Table 1.

Table 1: Categories and sub-categories of analysis

	Category	Sub-category
1	Routine social support available to immigrant entrepreneurs	Perceived informational support Perceived instrumental support Perceived emotional support Perceived appraisal support
2	Social support available to immigrant entrepreneurs after the Covid-19 outbreak	Perceived informational support Perceived instrumental support Perceived emotional support Perceived appraisal support

The decision to start a business is driven by a variety of factors, in which personal characteristics are as relevant as external environment however, their relative importance depends on the situation and a person's psychological picture (Bauernschuster et al., 2009). For immigrant entrepreneurs, the surrounding institutional framework is oftentimes quite different from what they know from their country of origin. In this sense, entering entrepreneurship abroad can be related to additional challenges. The first research question is:

RQ1: What are the immigrant entrepreneurs' perceptions about usually received social support?

The coronavirus outbreak has dramatically changed the world we live in. A health crisis on this scale seems to be reordering societies and economies in a dramatic way. It has drastically transformed the way people work and communicate, changed consumer spending trends and affected many industries, sectors, branches of the economy worldwide. A survey conducted in March and April this year by Suomen Yrittäjät, the main organisation of Finnish enterprises, on the effects of coronavirus on immigrant entrepreneurs revealed that 92% experienced difficulties in operating their business and a fifth did not believe they would make it through the crisis. Moreover, 38% of the respondents said they had difficulties with coping and felt very bad (Yrittäjät, 2020). Entrepreneurs operating in the sectors most affected by the crisis and who did not speak fluently appeared to experience more difficulties (Abaday, 2020). The second research question inquires:

RQ2: What are the immigrant entrepreneurs' perceptions about social support received after the Covid-19 outbreak?

The research applied a qualitative methodology based on individual interviews with the purpose to get a deep understanding of the phenomenon under study. Interview is a technique which involves asking questions about a certain issue and is particularly useful for exploring the topic and getting the story behind the answer. It provides in-depth information about participants opinions and experiences. The main challenge in the use of interviews is to understand the meaning behind the interviewee' words (Kvale, 1996).

Data were collected with the use of asynchronous open-ended interviews conducted through email and online voice/chat platforms. Participants had to fulfil the following criteria: (a) be born outside of Portugal; (b) residing in Portugal for at least two years; and (c) be involved in developing and managing own business venture.

Participants were first contacted by a member of the research team through email or a social network site. The research team member presented the participant the scope of the study and inquired about the availability to collaborate and collected informed consent. Further interaction via email and voice/messaging service platforms reflected the process of managing and monitoring of the interview. The interview script that served as a foundation for carrying out the empirical study reflected the categories of analysis. Participants were ensured about the possibility to contact the research team in any study-related matter.

Data were collected in May and June 2020. Written and transcribed interviews were analysed with NVivo 12 Plus software (QSR International, 2020). Coding reflected the categories of analysis. Project references were associated to the nodes defined in the software. Two separate groups were created, routine and after Covid-19 outbreak, in which social support experiences were examined.

6. Results

6.1 Characteristics of the participants

All the seven participants were immigrant entrepreneurs and lived in Portugal. Participants' ages ranged from 36 to 58 years, five were female and two were male, all with at least secondary education and all in a relationship (registered or marriage) with children. Countries of origin of participants varied, three of them were originally from the three countries with the largest number of immigrants living in Portugal (Brazil, Cape Verde and Romania). Interviewees reported having lived in Portugal from 3 to 32 years and being active in business venturing from 2 to 22 years. Detailed socio-demographic information is presented in Table 2.

Table 2: Socio-demographic characteristics of the participants

ID	Gender	Age	Country of origin	Years in Portugal	Years in entrepreneurship	Main field of activity
1	F	45	Venezuela	8	8	Footwear production
2	M	49	Brazil	22	13	Car commerce
3	F	48	Cuba	24	22	Ballet instruction
4	M	36	Cape Verde	22	2	Software development/ Innovation
5	F	58	Finland	32	n.d.	Tourism
6	F	38	Poland	3	3	Tourism/events Blog/online
7	F	44	Romania	19	16	Translation/ Interpreting

In most cases, the decision to establish a business was made after having lived in Portugal for some time and gained awareness of the country, culture and market. The decision was driven by market demand or personal preferences and perceived as a contribution to improving the development of the country of origin as well as an obvious direction reflecting personal interests and passion.

6.2 Data analysis

The analysis of the interviews indicates that social support was recognised by all as an important facet of social connections namely in terms of suggestions, reassurance and a simple presence. Nevertheless, experiences of social support, both regular and after the Covid-19 outbreak, varied among the participants reflecting the diversity of expectations, needs and social environments.

6.2.1 Routine social support available to immigrant entrepreneurs

Performed data analysis indicated that the words most frequently used in that category were family and friends with the same number of references (12), support (9 references), work (7) and people (6). Figure 1 presents a cloud with most frequently mentioned expressions referring to regular support and support after the coronavirus outbreak.

The timespan in analysis was from the decision to enter entrepreneurship until the declaration of the state of emergency in Portugal caused by the Covid-19 pandemic. Participants, in general, highlighted the importance of familial, emotional and instrumental support. Familial support turned to be a general theme under which interviewees provided examples of attitudes and behaviours relevant in their entrepreneurship trajectory. Concrete situations of informational (business-related information, financial capital, suggestions), instrumental and emotional support were reported. Most of the participants recalled suggestions and critics, moral support and encouragement received from friends. Criticisms were recognised as opportunities to grow, *"to make me stronger, able to face any challenge"* (I3). I7 mentioned how friends used to talk to her to convince her she was able to do what she did not have the courage for. It was highlighted the importance of business-related networks in the process of integration and career development.

Figure 1: Cloud of most frequent expressions referring to routine social support and support experienced after the coronavirus outbreak

6.2.2 *Social support available to immigrant entrepreneurs after the Covid-19 outbreak*

Participants' focus changed as the analysis concentrated on the period after the coronavirus outbreak. In the post-pandemic scenario, the words most frequently used in the interviews were aid (9 references), support (8), friends (7), and family and financial (both 5 references) (see Figure 1).

The pandemic raised new challenges to immigrant entrepreneurs. Mandatory lockdown imposed by the government to slow down the spread of Covid-19 stopped almost all economic, social and cultural activity in the country. Sales slowed sharply at the height of the epidemic. As demand declined, business suffered from the reduction of revenues. All the participants agreed that the coronavirus crisis profoundly affected companies and people. Interviewees recalled the efforts to keep the business running: *" (...) even with the door closed to the public I managed to make enough sales to cover expenses"* (I2); *"I never stopped giving classes, some on-site other online"* (I3), but referred to sales drop, exceeding 80% (I7). Participants felt in general that their needs of support were different from those they usually had. Specific situations were brought up under the emotional and instrumental (including financial) support and complemented with government support. Government support was included because it was frequently mentioned in the interviews as companies sought support to pay salaries and resorted to the lay-off. Psychological and mental impact of the pandemic raised the need of emotional support, experienced in most cases from family and friends. To I6, that emotional support together with financial support were deeply appreciated as she was going through professional and personal difficulties: *"I was very lost when this pandemic started", "(...) I was having family problems"*. To a large extent, support needs were satisfied. However, as I7 refers: *"The need of compassion and affection seem to have increased, but I cannot say the same about the availability. The pandemic shook my confidence and my sense of security, as I think it happened to many other people"*.

6.2.3 *Cross-category analysis*

Comparative data analysis allowed examining the two social support scenarios altogether. References to support, family and friends represent three of four most used terms in routine and crisis support. In regular, day-to-day support, a reference to "business" stands out whereas the post-pandemic period reveals interviewees' interest in "financial support". There was indeed some need (in the case of three participants) to seek government support: *"suspension of payment of debts"* (I1, I5), *"support from the city council for the use of theatre to broadcast our shows"* (I3) as well as relying on kin and non-kin support to sustain the activity. All except from one participant pointed into economic impact of the coronavirus crisis referring in particular to sales. Support of family and/or friends was essential to these entrepreneurs in both analysed panoramas. before and after the Covid-19 outbreak: *"the person who encouraged me the most was my mother... and a few friends I have"* (ID7), *"I always had support of everyone (...) I have always been an optimist"* (I3).

7. Discussion and conclusion

Entrepreneurs and immigrant entrepreneurs in particular encounter a series of challenges of diverse nature during the entrepreneurial process. The aim of this study was to examine perceptions of immigrant entrepreneurs about social support received on a regular basis and after the coronavirus outbreak. Results suggest that family and friends are main sources of meaningful social support in both, usual and critical circumstances. These findings are in line with previous research. For example, Mustafa and Chen (2010) and Oliveira (2005) pointed out to family and friends as sources of financial capital and material resources, such as office space.

The analysis of interviews revealed that experiences of social support fell mainly in the categories of informational, instrumental and emotional support. Participants did not distinguish between emotional and appraisal support and these two constructs intertwined in their statements. This supports a three-dimensional structure of the social support proposed for instance by MaloneBeach and Zarit (1995). In another research, Hu, Su and Zhang (2019) investigated the role of family in social capital, human capital and emotional support in immigrant entrepreneurs and found that household composition had a buffering effect on stress and impact on behaviours. Individuals living with other family members were less likely to engage in unhealthy behaviours, such as smoking or drinking, used as a way to relieve stress, pressure and anxiety. Emotional and appraisal support was sought in a regular way and found to be of special importance in critical moments. Interviewees looked for advice, ideas and encouragement when starting the venture, in the case of personal or business-related problems, and in situations that might threaten the future of the company. With the impact on the global economy, putting at risk businesses, jobs and families, the coronavirus pandemic is one of such situations.

To the best of our knowledge, this is the first study that addresses social support in immigrant entrepreneurs examining two panoramas: the routine and the crisis support regarded as perceived to be received after the coronavirus outbreak. This is our modest contribution to the research on migrant entrepreneurship and social support.

Acknowledgements

This work was financially supported by the research unit on Governance, Competitiveness and Public Policy (UIDB/04058/2020), funded by national funds through FCT - Fundação para a Ciência e a Tecnologia.

References

Abaday, A. (2020) "Covid-19 hit immigrant entrepreneurs harder than native Finns", Foreigner.fi, 4 June 2020 [online]. Available at: https://www.foreigner.fi/articulo/guide-for-entre/survey-90-percent-of-immigrant-entrepreneurs-in-difficulty-due-to-covid19/20200604133304006246.html (Accessed: 9 June 2020).

Bates, T. (2011) "Minority Entrepreneurship", *Foundations and Trends in Entrepreneurship*, Vol 7, No. 3-4, pp 151-311, doi:http://dx.doi.org/10.1561/0300000036

Bauernschuster, S., Falck, O., Gold, R. and Heblich, S. (2009) *The Shadows of the Past: How Implicit Institutions Influence Entrepreneurship*, Friedrich Schiller University Jena and Max Planck Institute of Economics.

Chiswick, B. (1978) "The Effect of Americanization on the Earnings of Foreign-born Men", *Journal of Political Economy,* Vol 86, No. 5, pp 897-921, doi:https://doi.org/10.1086/260717

Cobb, S. (1976) "Social Support as a Moderator of Life Stress", *Psychosomatic Medicine,* Vol. 38, No. 5, pp. 300-314, doi:https://doi.org/10.1097/00006842-197609000-00003

Dean, A. and Lin, N. (1977) "The Stress-buffering Role of Social Support. Problems and Prospects for Systematic Investigation", *The Journal of Nervous and Mental Disease,* Vol 165, No. 6, pp 403-417, doi:10.1097/00005053-197712000-00006

Fairlie, R.W. (2012) *Immigrant Entrepreneurs and Small Business Owners, and their Access to Financial Capital,* SBA Office for Advocacy.

Fiscal Policy Institute (2012) *Immigrant Small Business Owners: A Significant and Growing Part of the Economy,* Fiscal Policy Institute. Available at: https://www.carnegie.org/publications/immigrant-small-business-owners-a-significant-and-growing-part-of-the-economy/ (Accessed 10 May 2020).

Galanti, M.T. (2018) "Enablers and Time: How Context Shapes Entrepreneurship in Institutional and Policy Change", in Bakir, D. and Jarvis, D.S. (eds.), *Institutional Entrepreneurship and Policy Change. Theoretical and Empirical Explorations*. Palgrave MacMillan, pp 41-61.

Hartley, C., and Coffee, P. (2019) "Perceived and Received Dimensional Support: Main and Stress-buffering Effects on Dimensions of Burnout", *Frontiers in Psychology,* Vol 10, p 1724, doi:10.3389/fpsyg.2019.01724

House, J.S. (1981) *Work Stress and Social Support,* Addison-Wesley, Reading.

House, J.S. (1987) "Social Support and Social Structure", *Sociological Forum,* Vol 2, No. 1, pp 135-146, doi:http://dx.doi.org/10.1007/BF01107897

Hu, M., Su, Y. and Zhang, H. (2019) "Migrant Entrepreneurship: The Family as Emotional Support, Capital and Human Capital", *Emerging Markets Finance and Trade* [online], doi:10.1080/1540496X.2019.1693364

Kazemipur, A. and Halli, S. (2001) "Immigrants and 'New Poverty:' The case of Canada", *International Migration Review,* Vol 35, No. 4, pp 1128-1156.

Kvale, S. (1996) *InterViews: An Introduction to Qualitative Research Interviewing,* Sage Publications.

Lin, N. (1986) "Epilogue: In Retrospect and Prospect", in Lin, N., Dean, A. and Ensel, W. (eds.), *Social Support, Life Events, and Depression*. Academic Press, pp 333-342.

MaloneBeach, E. and Zarit, S. (1995) "Dimensions of Social Support and Social Conflict as Predictors of Caregiver Depression", *International Psychogeriatrics,* Vol 7, No. 1, pp 25-38, doi:10.1017/S1041610295001827

Monti, D.J., Smith-Doerr, L. and MacQuaid, J. (2007) *Immigrant Entrepreneurs in the Massachusetts Biotechnology Industry*. The Immigrant Learning Center, Malden.

Morrison, A., Rimmington, M. and Williams, C. (2011) *Entrepreneurship in the Hospitality, Tourism and Leisure Industries*, Routledge.

Mustafa, M. and Chen, S. (2010) "The Strength of Family Networks in Transnational Immigrant Entrepreneurship", *Thunderbird International Business Review,* Vol 52, No. 2, pp 97-106, doi:https://doi.org/10.1002/tie.20317

Nazareno, J., Zhou, M. and You, T. (2019) "Global Dynamics of Immigrant Entrepreneurship: Changing Trends, Ethnonational Variations, and Reconceptualizations", *International Journal of Entrepreneurial Behavior & Research,* Vol 25, No. 5, pp 780-800, doi:https://doi.org/10.1108/IJEBR-03-2018-0141

Noja, G.G., Cristea, S.M., Yüksel, A., Pânzaru, C. and Drăcea, R.M. (2018) "Migrants' Role in Enhancing the Economic Development of Host Countries: Empirical Evidence from Europe", *Sustainability,* Vol 10, No. 3, p 894, doi:https://doi.org/10.3390/su10030894

OECD (2019) *OECD SME and Entrepreneurship Outlook 2019,* OECD Publishing, Paris.

OECD/European Union (2017) *The Missing Entrepreneurs 2017: Policies for Inclusive Entrepreneurship*, OECD Publishing, Paris, https://doi.org/10.1787/9789264283602-11-en

OECD/ILO (2018) *How Immigrants Contribute to Developing Countries' Economies,* OECD Publishing, Paris, doi:https://doi.org/10.1787/9789264288737-en

Oliveira, C.R. (2005) *Empresários de Origem Imigrante: Estratégias de Inserção Económica em Portugal,* ACIME, Porto.

QSR International. (2020). NVivo Qualitative Data Analysis Software [software]. Available at: https://www.qsrinternational.com/

Robert, A.-M. and Gilkinson, T. (2012) Mental Health and Well-being of Recent Immigrants in Canada: Evidence from the Longitudinal Survey of Immigrants to Canada, *Research and Evaluation*, Department of Citizenship and Immigration Canada [online]. Available at: https://novascotia.cmha.ca/wp-content/uploads/2020/01/mental-health.pdf (Accessed 24 May 2020).

Sanders, J.M. and Nee, V. (1996) "Immigrant Self-employment: The Family as Social Capital and the Value of Human Capital", *American Sociological Review,* Vol 61, No. 2, pp 231-249, doi:10.2307/2096333

Simich, L., Beiser, M., Stewart, M. and Mwakarimba, E. (2005) "Providing Social Support for Immigrants and Refugees in Canada: Challenges and Directions", *Journal of Immigrant Health,* Vol 7, No. 4, pp 259-268, doi:10.1007/s10903-005-5123-1

Vandor, P. and Franke, N. (2018) "Immigrant Entrepreneurship: Drivers, Economic Effects, and Policy Implications", in Globerman, S. and Clemens, J. (eds.), *Demographics and Entrepreneurship: Mitigating the Effects of an Aging Population.* Fraser Institute, pp 363-418.

Wadhwa, V., Saxenian, A., Rissin, B. and Gere, G. (2007) *America's New Immigrant Entrepreneurs,* Duke University.

Wood, J. (2018) Immigrants make good entrepreneurs. This study proves it, *World Economic Forum*, 18 November 2018 [online]. Available at: https://www.weforum.org/agenda/2018/11/immigrants-make-good-entrepreneurs-this-study-proves-it/ (Accessed: 10 June 2020).

Yrittäjät (2020) Survey: Around 90% of immigrant entrepreneurs in difficulty because of coronavirus, Suomen Yrittäjät, 4 June 2020 [online]. Available at: https://www.yrittajat.fi/en/news/628270-survey-around-90-immigrant-entrepreneurs-difficulty-because-coronavirus (Accessed: 8 June 2020).

Universal Language of Thoughts? Abstraction and Creativity

Gheorghe Teodorescu
International Institute for Integral Innovation, Meran, Italy
george_teodorescu@yahoo.de
DOI: 10.34190/EIE.20.018

Abstract: To see, you must close your eyes; to see beyond you must understand. As a mental process, Creativity has an abstract nature, meaning that no empiric perception is directly involved, not even words, which would bring semantic ballast. However, the relationship between the level of abstraction and the creative outcome has been largely neglected. Abstraction is not a homogenous block, but a nuanced entity. Our research considers five sublimation levels of abstraction: Paradigmatic, Pragmatic, Etiologic, Axiological and Archetypal and links them to the corresponding hierarchy of originated ideas: new Approaches, new Concepts, new Paradigms and new Formal Expressions (designs). The results show that: rising the abstraction level the number of ideas increases and reach a stronger originality and more seminal power, with a spectacular apex on the Archetypal level of abstraction. Therefore, we define the Etiologic level of abstraction as the threshold of new content. This perspective induces an efficient taxonomy of ideas, which enables the evaluation of the original mental outcome, introducing a hierarchy of ideas' quality, based on two criteria: disruptivity – degree of originality and seminality-aptitude of inspiring a bundle of subsequent ideas. This integrative theoretical approach facilitates the management of ideas and the navigation in the fluid mental outcome. In the paper we are describing an original methodology, which is facilitating the abstraction pathway to Archetypal Perspective and is illustrating the relationship between Abstraction levels, Speculation methods and the expected quality and quantity of original outcome.

Keywords: kenotomy, creativity, ideas management, levels of abstraction, archetypal perspective

1. Introduction

As a mental process, Creativity has an abstract nature, meaning that no empiric perception is directly involved, not even words, which bring semantic ballast and slow down the thinking process. However, the relationship between the level of abstraction and the creative outcome has been largely neglected, as well as her quality as a really universal platform of synergy, overcoming language, cultural and time frontiers.

The empiric perception and the associated terms and icons build together a solid roadblock of certitude, which the people generally are inclined to believe, it were the absolute truth.

That is more than a roadblock, it is a huge wall, obstructing any look beyond, hindering any creative attempt, reducing the effort to a cosmetic, epidermal intervention.

Before engaging the creative power, the wall of empiric impact must be penetrated, meaning in practice: the need to explore successively the paradigmatic, the pragmatic, the etiologic and the axiological levels of abstraction, aiming toward the apex understanding of archetypal perspective. The quest for the Archetypal Perspective is inducing a deep understanding of the addressed topic and the unexpected aspects of the context, defining in this way a larger and more complex reflection space.

In the paper we are describing the dedicated methodology, which is facilitating the abstraction pathway to Archetypal Perspective and illustrate the relationship between Abstraction levels, the Speculation methods and the ways for evaluating the resulted quality and quantity of original outcome.

Another aspect of our research is the universality of abstractly handling topics and the related effect of reticular synergy, that is emerging within multicultural creative teams.

This paper is reporting our practice with Master students' classes with multicultural backgrounds and different Bachelor majors.

2. Method

Abstraction is not an amorphous matter, but a structured entity. This structure is revealed by maieutic fathoming, interrogating repeatedly for the subsequent meaning, by climbing the abstraction's levels.

Our research considers five sublimation levels of abstraction: Paradigmatic, Pragmatic, Etiologic, Axiological and Archetypal and links them to the corresponding hierarchy of originated ideas: new Approaches, new Concepts, new Paradigms and new epidermal Expressions (designs).

Our method reveals the intimate relationship between awareness and creativity, as these stages are actually Levels of Awareness.

Paradigmatic Level –
Question: what is that?

The first layer behind the empirically perceived reality is the paradigm, the abstract solution, the semantic label, the term, stripped off all specific shape and material design, like the relationship sign-object by Peirce. (T.L Short, 2007)

This is a quite intuitive step, but a key one, for it is taking off the burden of the physical presence of existing. As an illustrative example we can consider the relationship between *This* Pen, as a real object and *The* Pen, as a paradigmatic term. (fig 1)

= A PEN, crayon, Bleistift, matita, μολύβι, 鉛筆

Figure 1: Ikon and language related terms

On this abstraction level, the icons take the place of words and allow a communication without words, overcoming the language gap, but only within a multilingual, but just within a paradigm-coherent civilization; by heterogeneous civilizations a symbol might have different significations or even none.

The abstraction on this basic level enables diversification by esthetics, aka: graphics and styling but no deeper creative achievement (Fig 2)

Figure 2: Superficial diversification on Empiric Level

This kind of creative intervention is superficial, but a low risk-low cost one and therefore preferred in the consume oriented mentality, as it is dissimulating visually some diversity, a colorful cozenage, for stimulating the shopper' instinct. (A.Pringle, 2017)

The creative challenge on is a dead-end street: *a pen is a pen*.
Pragmatic Level
Question: what is that for?

Even if the determinative question: "what is that?" liberates the terms from the material load of the related objects, the Paradigmatic level remains a para-abstract one. The paradigm is still a shadow of the material item.

Creative processes don't handle terms, ikons and even less their material projection.

Climbing higher, to pragmatic level, implies a real abstraction effort, fathoming the solution for discovering the driving need behind it. This might be and often is, much more than a material need, as a driving chain lays generally underneath: desires, longing, passion and even evergreen aspirations.

It is important to understand this complexity for avoiding a usual confusion, this is not about goals.

This interrogation step must be consistent with the pragmatism only: what could be done with a given paradigm?

Coming back to our pilot-example "pen ", the question "what is for?" gives rise to an array of answers, all of them converging into: *Making Signs*.

There is a highly inspiring question arising here: How can you make signs?

The answers are displaying a large array of solutions, far beyond the initially addressed term: "pen".

Larger the multiculturality of the team is, wider the spectrum of proposals and the level of novelty.(fig 3)

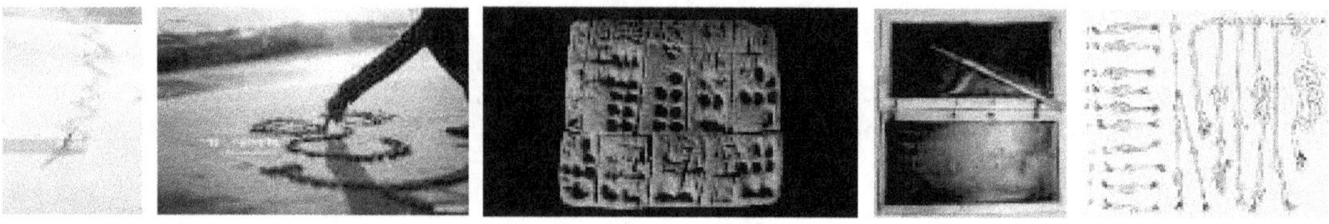

Figure 3: Making signs – diversity on pragmatic level

The real abstraction is seminal, therefore the challenge of a topic, that is free of substantive-terms, opens a highway to imagination and divergent thinking. An antithesis to (G.Gelade, 2009)

Etiologic Level
Question: why?

"Why?" the classic Socratic question of maieutic method ignites a deeper reflection about meaning and brings the reasons, which stay behind a concept, into clear consciousness. This etiologic quest makes transparent the causality of the addressed topic and reveals on the other hand the reach of analytic thinking and the mentality of participants. This higher level of abstraction relieves the load of materiality, technicalities and pragmatism from the thinking process and is ending up always in a colorful diversity of apparent reasons, which might be rich sources of inspiration, drifting the creativity process divergently into unexpected directions, a good start for heuristics.

These disparate opinions must be scrutinized one by one, which is an inspiring team experience and eventually integrated into in a coherent answer, that is corresponding to the ultimate etiologic level. This integration and the previous moderation might be done by a moderator with high abstraction aptitudes.

In our pilot-example, the sought-after reason for Making Signs is: *Recording Thoughts and Experiences.*

The speculation triggering question "How to record thoughts and experiences?" is opening a new realm of imagination far beyond trivial *Pens* and *Making Signs*, projecting the mental focus into the Conceptual Sphere, where human skills and handling procedures for "recording thoughts and experiences" display a large diversity of historical precedents, new technologic solutions, old, existing or potential ones. (Fig.4)

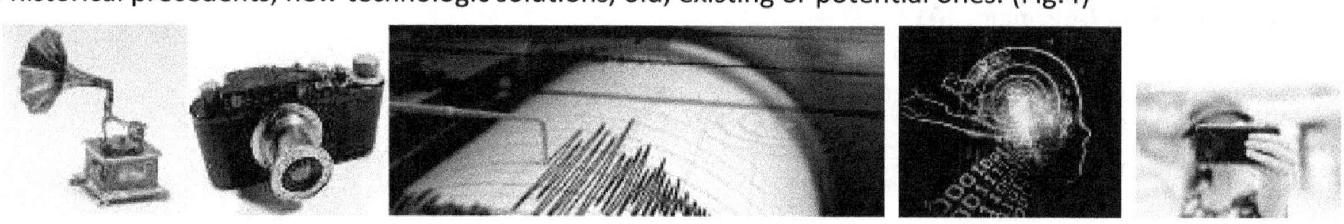

Figure4: Recording thoughts and experiences – conceptual creativity on etiologic level

The original outcome on Etiologic Level is exponentially richer, than the previous pragmatic options.

The Etiologic Level is *the first disruptive threshold*, the Conceptual one, as such the first one able to generate new content and therefore inspiring several divergent bundles of pragmatic solutions able to deliver substance for original start-ups, or even new industries.

There is a strong correlation between the addressed abstraction level and the entrepreneurship potential of the outcome. If *designs*, resulting from a paradigmatic start might improve the competitiveness as well as the *new solutions*, bred on the pragmatic one can do, new concepts bolster up a real, sustainable leadership, creating a hard to match handicap for the competitors.

Disruptive creativity is a matter of unexpected conceptual content, or fresh approaches therefore there is a nonsense to expect disruptive ideas, without reaching the Etiologic Level of Awareness.

Under the Etiologic *Level of Awareness,* the creative effort might deliver new solutions and new designs, but they are just expected outcome of consequent creativity, around extant items and solutions. (see fig 5)

Axiological Level
Question: Which aim, which way?

Bringing the reason to light on Etiologic Level rises the consequent question: which is the aim behind the reason? As in our example: if the reason for *Making Signs* is *Recording thoughts and experiences*, what is the aim for Recording?

Staying consistent with our example: the aim for Recording Thoughts and Experience is Defeating Time, an evergreen Aspiration of mankind.

The Axiological Level invites to a deeper reflection upon aims behind reasons, addressing potential attitudes and ethic aspects of the topic. This step nourishes inspiring discussions about different points of view, eventually outlining new Approaches, the highest level of Creativity.

The AL is *the second disruptive threshold*, the Approach one and delivers a cascade of seminal power, as Approaches generate bundles of Concepts, who initiate clusters of Solutions and eventually fascicles of designs.

There is a generic subsequence there between Approaches, Concepts, Solutions and Designs, with the Approaches at the peak of this descending order. (fig 5)

They are three relevant aspects here to notice:

- The level of abstraction generates the potential of the creative outcome
- The hierarchy of: Approaches, Concepts, Solutions and Designs is a backbone of a Taxonomy of Ideas.
- The Approaches are not just the peak of creative outcome, but generate an own world of subsequent Concepts, Solutions and Designs, making obsolete the trail of the previous approach, which is taking place of.

In terms of entrepreneurship, new Approaches might mean an industrial revolution, like the digital approach made obsolete the analog one.

In terms of mankind, a new Approach might induce a new culture, a new understanding of life and even a new civilization, like agriculture brought about sedentary life, after the nomadism of hunter-gatherer.

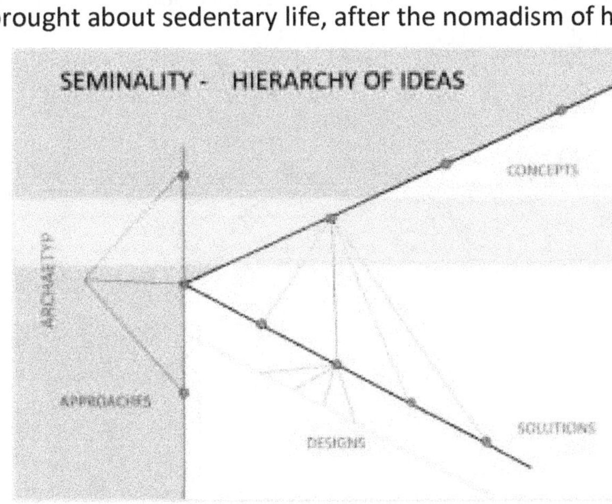

Figure 5: Hierarchy of creative outcome: approaches, concepts, solutions, designs

In order to illustrate the disruptive potential on Axiological level, enclosed we show an example of unexpected analogy related to our example: Paradigmatic: pen - Pragmatic: making signs -Etiologic: recording thoughts- Axiological: defeating time (fig 6)

Figure 6: Defeating time – approaches on axiological level

Archetypal Level
Question: which is the aspiration?

Arrived on the ultimate level of abstraction, the quest for the corresponding aspiration, that is laying behind an already defined aim, requires assessing it across the array of the seven Archetypes.

There is a generous cognitive experience there, discovering that the manifoldness is just an appearance, due to the empirical myopia, and that all the heterogeneity is converging in an apex of just seven terms.

Humanity developed for eons corresponding aspirations and projected them as attributes of super- human beings:

Omnipotence, Omniscience (pansophy), Ubiquity, Eternity, Autarchy, Uniqueness and Creation.

n.b. We understand here Creation as the *generative force of steady Change*, related to Aristoteles' entelechy (εντελεχεια).

After investigating thousands of topics with this Kenotomic methodology we found out, that behind any Aspiration there is one of the seven keystones, where the apparent multiformity is converging into: Mind, Freedom, Time, Space, Energy, Diversity and not least Change.

We have named them Archetypes, more in the spirit of the Greek etymology, that in the sense of CG Jung. (C.G.Jung, 1959) (fig.7) Archetypes, because they are the primordial (αρχικός) terms and fundamental building blocks of world awareness and because they are addressed since ever by the ultimate aspirations of humanity:

Mind-Omniscience, Autarchy-Freedom, Eternity-Time, Ubiquity-Space, Omnipotence-Energy, Uniqueness-Diversity and first of all, the Creativity-Change of the Universe.

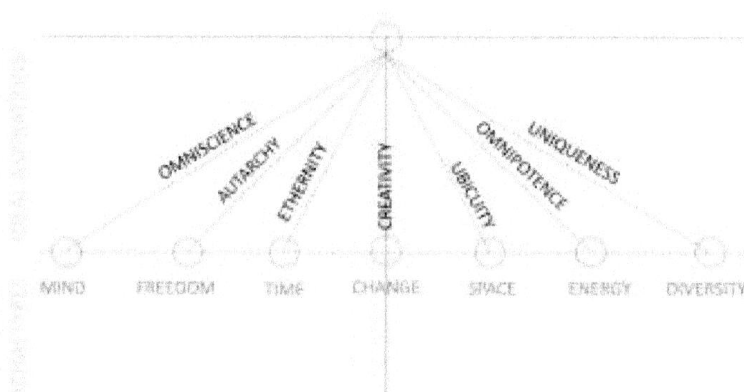

Figure 7: Dyads of archetypes/aspirations

The Archetypal level is invariable and offers the apex view, the *Archetypal Perspective*, which is facilitating the deep Awareness along the subsequent steps of investigation and stimulating generously both levels of disruptive creativity, the etiologic and axiological ones.

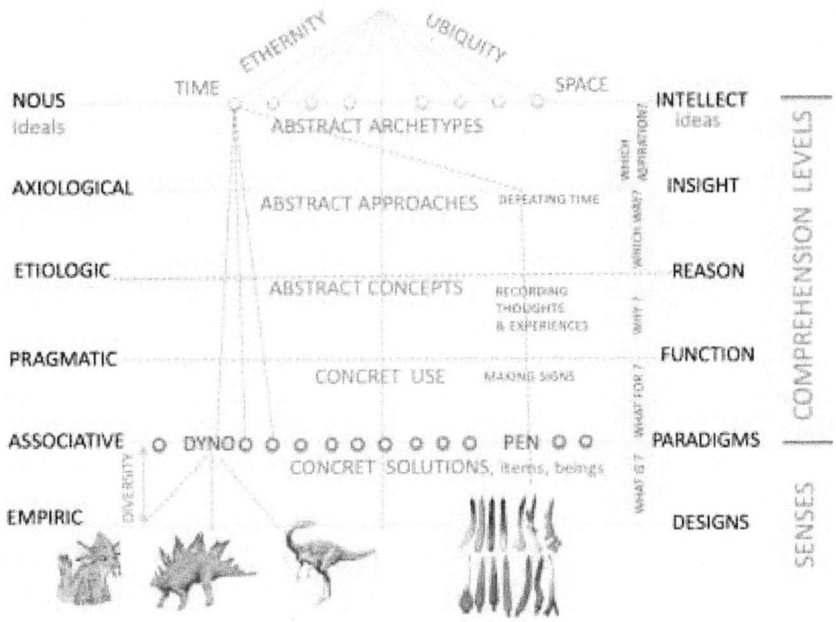

Figure 8: Archetypal Perspective, abstraction and creativity

It is a different creative deal, if you are getting, fully aware, downstream from the plateau Defeating Time to that of Recording Thoughts and Experiences and breeding there unexpected, disruptive concepts, as would be trying to imagine new ways of recording Thoughts and Experiences by climbing blindfolded from Making Signs plateau up. (Fig 8)

3. Results

The results show that rising the abstraction level the number and the quality of ideas increase in steps, winning a stronger originality and seminal power as the topic is getting sublimated from one abstraction level to the higher next.

We've found out, that the Axiological level of abstraction and the Etiologic one are the *thresholds of disruptive creativity,* plateaus suitable for generating respectively new Approaches and Concepts.

In order to find out the corresponding archetype to the addressed topic, a prerequisite is to reach the Archetypal Perspective. From this apex one might select the appropriate working plateau and to follow deliberately the creative process. As the result, the entire creativity process becomes more comprehensible and manageable and the outcome matches the set goal; this means: (fig 9 a)

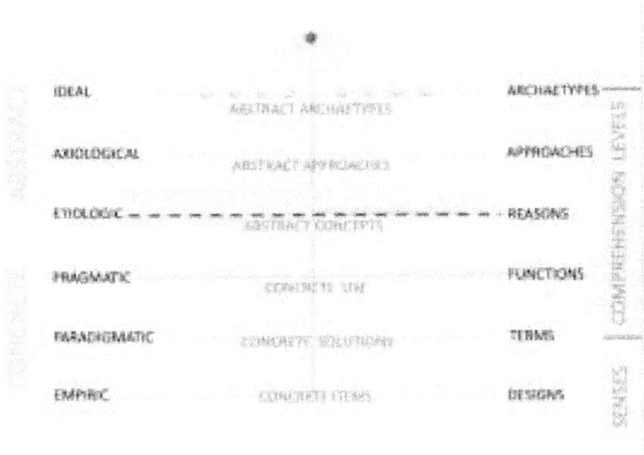

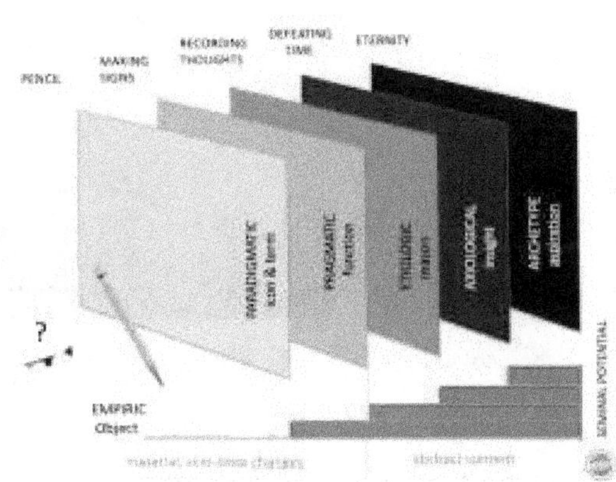

Figure 9a: Abstraction levels and outcome **Figure 9b:** Abstraction levels and seminality

- For a refreshment of looks, a redesign, the initiation plateau might be either the extant item, or the corresponding paradigm. The result is a firework of shapes and colors, a sensorial experience, due to artistic creativity, but lacking any content novelty.
- A functional upgrade, or even a new solution requires the Pragmatic Level of abstraction.

- However, the upgrades belong, as the previous redesigns too, to the modest competitiveness strategy for surviving in a crowded market, by avoiding the veritable, laborious and risky creative effort.
- A real creative Content, meaning a disruptive, new Concept, can't be expected under the Etiologic Level. This kind of seminal ideas are the substance for reaching the leadership and for starting up new enterprises.
- A new Concept generates a large cone of follow up solutions, from its seminal apex.
- A new Approach is a radical, staggering point of view or an attitude, able to shift the way of understanding and dealing with an aspect, a larger segment of a civilization or an entire culture.

The sedentary, agriculture-based civilization was an approach-shifting from the previous nomadic, hunting-gathering one.

Home working and automatization are shifting the approach of a company as a hub for employees.

Shared automated vehicles as urban, street equipment instead of ownership of cars would be another example in this respect.

In our pilot-example the Cloud and the life-monitoring by social media provide an all-over recording coverage of every moment of life for everyone, even if it happens often involuntarily, all the other recording devices are redundant and obsolete.

Creativity results in ideas of many kinds and relevance, this outcome can be measured by:

- -the *number* of generated ideas, the volume of generated ideas,
- -by *disruptivity*, the degree of originality of an idea, compared to extant ones. This type of ideas might be expected by the thresholds of Etiologic and Axiological levels of abstraction and
- -by *seminality*- the aptitude of an idea for inspiring a bundle of subsequent ideas. This is mainly a feature of Concepts and Approaches (Fig. 10)

These three criteria allow a sensible evaluation of creativity outcome, facilitating the creativity management.

The described kenotomial method of fathoming the abstract content on several levels of abstraction provides the ground for a spectacular increase of creative outcome and facilitates the management of ideas and the own navigation of those involved in creativity, in the fluid and heuristic mental process of ideation.

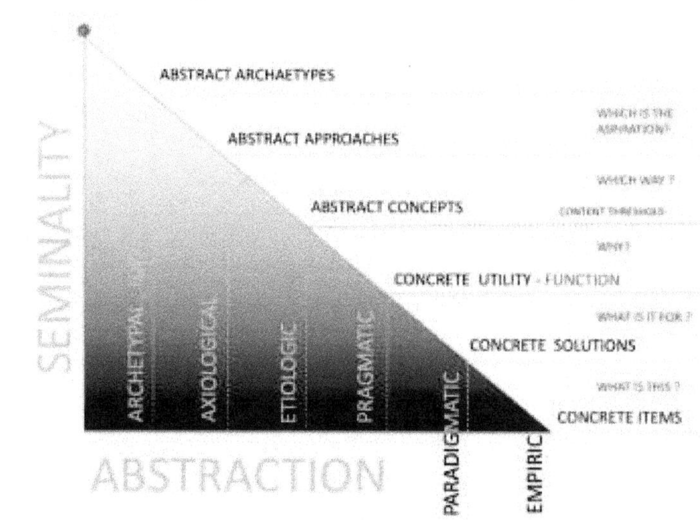

Figure 10: Seminality degrees and abstraction levels

4. Discussion

It is salient, that immaterial and even term-free questions are much more inspiring, than empiric and paradigmatic ones:

- How to make signs? vs. Make a "new" PEN!

- How to record thoughts and experiences? vs. How to make signs?
- How to defeat time? vs. Recording thoughts and Experiences.

Inputs related to senses, like visuals and even terms, are inhibitors of imagination and the related semantic is confusing and sluggish for the fathoming of a reality beyond the actual one.

The highest sequence of abstraction opens the *Archetypal Perspective,* the apex, where all possible Ideas, which are related to an *archetypal domain,* are converging into. (Fig.11) (G.Teodorescu, 2019)

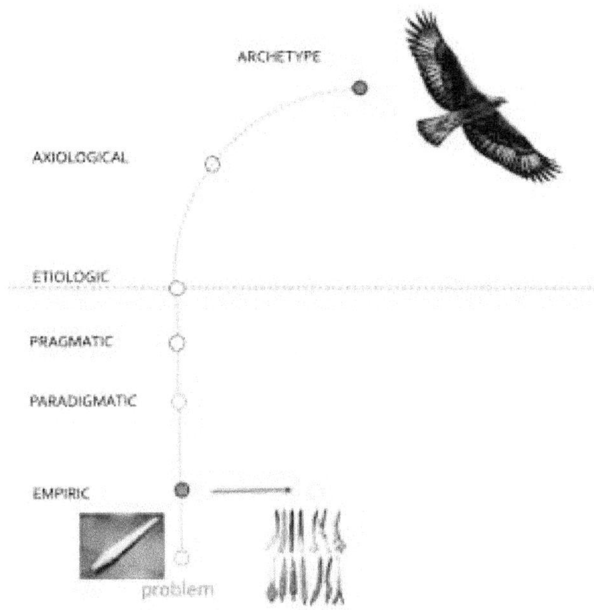

> Archetypal Perspective is transforming the creativity process in a transparent downward walk from the actual random upstream struggle.

Figure 11: Abstracting to archetypal perspective

Archetype as a reference is the guideline along the speculative steps from Archetype to Approach, then to concept and eventually to solution and designs (Fig 12)

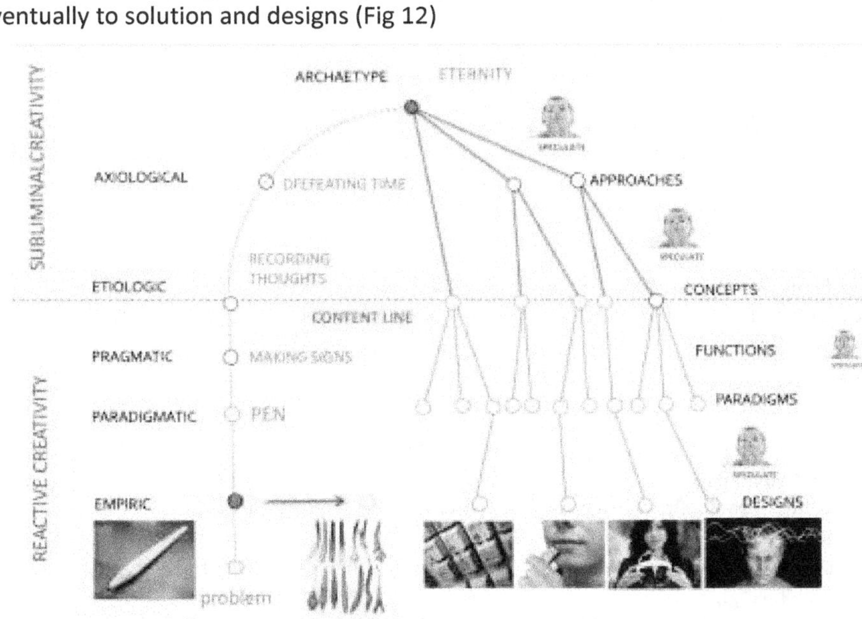

Figure 12: Kenotomial creative process

Our described, original method is the consequence of projecting the abstraction steps on the corresponding cognitive levels, making salient their relationship to the Abstract and Creative thinking and discovering the downward symmetry on the Creative phases of speculation, which inspired the reversibility into abstraction, as well as the referential role of the Archetype in this mental process. (ref 6), (A.Pringle, 2017)(R.Reiter, 2007)

The levels of Ideation Outcome, with their respective seminal and disruptive potential correspond harmoniously to their generative outgoing abstraction. (Fig.13)

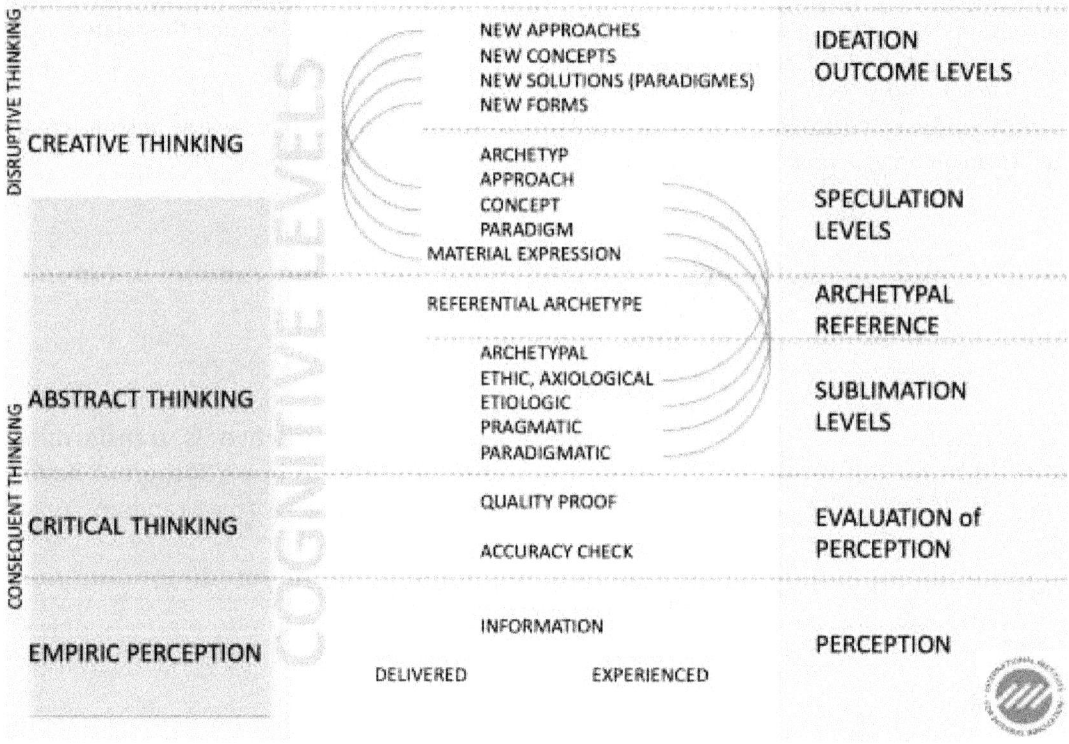

Figure 13: Abstract thinking and ideation

This method, which links creativity and abstraction, challenges the adopter's abstraction skills, but is rewarding him with a full awareness along the creative process and with a generous outcrop of ideas.

Furthermore, the method allows a fine planning in creativity management and delivers a procedure for evaluating the original mental outcome, by using the Taxonomy of Ideas and both criteria: seminality and disruptivity, additionally to the usual volume counting.

For the final, we need to mention a field observation by team working: -Starting a team work on an empiric, paradigmatic and even on the pragmatic level requires a semantical harmonizing of participants, especially if the attending people belong to dissimilar specialties and even more elaborate, if they have different cultural backgrounds. (P.Dennet, 2019)

If such a heterogenous team works on the Etiologic level or higher, they reach intuitively a common understanding, in a dialogue beyond words and ikons, like sharing a universal language of thoughts, a case of reticular synergy. Creativity and higher abstraction bridge minds together.

References

P.Dennett, Csikszentmihalyi meets Socrates: Fostering a sense of group flow to produce creative outcomes; Journal of Organizational Creativity, 2019

G. Gelade and Min Basadur, Creative Problem-Solving Style and Cognitive Work Demands

Proceedings of SIOP conference, New Orleans, 2009

Yu-Sein Lin, Fostering Creativity through Education—A Conceptual Framework of Creative Pedagogy, Creative Education 2011. Vol.2, No.3, 149-155

C.G. Jung, The Archetypes and The Collective Unconscious , 1959

E. Papaleontiou-Louca, Teaching for Creativity in Universities, 2014

Journal of Education and Human Development , Dec 2014., Vol 3, Nr 4.

A. Pringle, Shifting between modes of thought: a domain-general creative thinking skill? Proceedings International Conference on Knowledge, Information and Enterprise; Philadelphia USA, 2017; Creativity in Arts, Science and Technology Research Papers on Knowledge, Innovation and Enterprise Volume-IV,ISBN978-1-85924-276-6

R. Reiter, Anner Hermann, F. Yammarino, Creativity and Cognitive Processes, 2007

Univ. of Nebraska at Omaha, 2007

https://www.academia.edu/17013350/Creativity_and_cognitive_processes_Multi-level_linkages_between_individual_and_team_cognition

T-L- Short, Peirce's Theory of Signs, Cambridge Univ. Press, 2007, p.204, p.222

G. Teodorescu, Kenotomy , the Domain of Creative Thinking – 2019 https://www.dropbox.com/s/etwoshc2bfcudpa/ECIE19-Proceedings-Vol1-embedded.pdf?dl=0

G. Teodorescu, Kenotomy face to face with Artificial Intelligence – 2019 http://www.scholink.org/ojs/index.php/ape/article/view/2509

Sharing Innovation Activity Models in the Context of Open Innovation

Elena Tkachenko[1], Elena Rogova[2], Sergey Bodrunov[3], Alexander Karlik[1] and Vladimir Kokh[4]
[1]Saint Petersburg State University of Economics, Russia
[2]National Research University Higher School of Economics, Russia
[3]Institute for New Industrial Development, St. Petersburg, Russia
[5]Professionalaudit-consalting LLS
eletkachenko@ya.ru
erogova@hse.ru
inir@inir.ru
karlik1@mail.ru
profiaudit@ya.ru
DOI: 10.34190/EIE.20.199

Abstract: The study explores the models of sharing economy in open innovation environment that are implemented by companies. On the base of the survey of top managers of innovation companies from North-West of Russia, we identified four key sharing models: the sharing of laboratories and equipment, the sharing of highly qualified engineering teams and individual professionals, and the sharing of research and development based on open innovation systems. These models can be both independent and convergent. Over time, given the potential for digital platforms to advance innovation, sharing models could occupy the research and development niche and gradually displace traditional forms of innovation organization. To understand costs and benefits of using innovative resources sharing, we conducted the model analysis and received the indicator that characterizes the relative level of companies' losses related to innovative resources disintegration. Using the case of low temperature technologies project, we calculated the efficiency of using sharing innovative resources.

Keywords: open innovation, sharing economy, sharing innovative resources

1. Open innovation and the prerequisites for the concept of sharing innovative resources

World economic development is currently experiencing a deep penetration of digital technologies into all economic spheres. Digitalization is giving rise to the development of Industry 4.0. The change in the usual IT-based cooperation system is reducing the number of intermediaries and transforming global value chains. These processes occur under conditions of strong macroeconomic dynamics, and are characterized by a high degree of uncertainty. Today, many companies are actively implementing lean production, as high rates of change require austerity of financial resources. In this environment, innovation should, on the one hand, ensure the competitiveness of market participants, and on the other, be available taking into account the existing financial, human and physical constraints. From this position, the future of innovation is seen in the joint use of intangible assets and fixed assets for R&D implementation. In fact, it is a sharing model of the economy in the B2B sector. Using sharing models of innovation activity allows significantly accelerating the innovation cycle and reducing the costs for participants. The sharing economy has become an object of interest of a large number of researchers. Thus, 388 articles on the problems of development of sharing models published between 1978 and 2018 were analyzed in the review by Hossain (2020). The demand for research on the sharing economy indicates the growing role of this phenomenon in social and economic development.

The classical industrial system (absolutely dominated by industrial production) and the "service society" (where service industries supplant material production) are being replaced by a new second-generation industrial economy (the social structure based on it, that is, a new second-generation industrial society – NIS.2). The key provisions of the NIS.2 concept were developed by Bodrunov as part of a 10-year research conducted by the S.Y. Witte Institute for New Industrial Development (St. Petersburg) in the early 2000s (Bodrunov, 2016, 2018) . The provisions are formulated in a number of publications and presented at major economic forums in Russia and abroad.

The transformation of the economic model in the context of a new industrial society has triggered the emergence of new forms of cooperation, including those based on the open innovation concept. Our previous research was focused on the specifics of the integration processes developing as part of the current concept (Tkachenko et al, 2014).

The aim of this study is to identify the models of innovative resources sharing in the open environment and to develop the instruments of choosing the most efficient way of using scarce innovative resources based on the concept of sharing economy. The main methods of our study are observation, interview, information analysis and synthesis, as well as logical and mathematical simulation. The basic concept adopted in the study is the open innovation concept theory proposed by Chesbrough (2003). In the article "Open Innovation: The Next Decade" by West, Salter, Vanhaverbeke and Chesbrough (2014), 10 years of this approach were summarized. The authors confirmed the efficiency of this business model in the current conditions. The authors also identified several problems. Open innovation presents the problem of the interested parties' relationship within and outside the network. The problems of open innovation in the context of the SME's networks were studied by Lee et al. (2010), Drechsler and Natter (2012), Okatan (2012), Gnyawali and Srivastava (2013,) Tomlinson and Fai (2013). As noted by Rogo et al. (2014), open innovation efficiency is defined by several factors, including the level of development of legislation and availability of highly qualified personnel. These factors enable the interests of the network parties to be protected. Another problem is assessment of the efficiency of open innovation. Modern researchers suggest solving this problem within the framework of the value management concept (Wang et al., 2012; Rogo et al., 2014). We share this opinion and suggest assessing the efficiency of cooperation based on the changes in the value of the network intellectual capital.

The development of sharing services in Russia initially affected the C2C sector. The transaction volume of online sharing services operating in Russia in 2019 grew by 50% to RUB 770 billion. According to the RAEC and the TIAR Center, the C2C sales segment is the leader of the sharing economy with a volume of about RUB 566 billion. The most popular services are Avito, Yula and YouDo. For instance, Avito reports 120 transactions every minute on its website. Other notable segments of the Russian sharing economy include online labor exchanges (RUB 140 billion), car sharing (RUB 20.5 billion), and carpooling (search for travel companions, RUB 17.8 billion). Such an understanding of the essence of joint use models and sharing economics develops by Ciulli and Kolk (2019), and Curtis and Mont (2020). At that, we have identified a large layer of cooperation models that operate using the principles of resource sharing to achieve innovation activity goals. Analysis of the identified models enabled to classify them.

The remaining paper is structured as follows. We report the results of our survey and identify four innovative sharing models. After this, the model analysis of efficiency of innovative resources sharing is implemented. The next section contains the case analysis and the calculation of the efficiency based on the results of previous modeling. The final section is devoted to concluding remarks.

2. Identification of innovative sharing models. Company Research Results

To identify possible models of interaction, we conducted surveys of heads of innovative companies. The study was conducted in November - December 2019, respondents represent the North-West region of Russia. In total, 187 company executives took part in the study, but only 36 companies that have experience in implementing projects based on the principles of sharing innovative resources were selected for further analysis. The structure of companies on innovative activity is reflected in Fig. 1

Figure 1: The distribution of companies by the implementation of sharing innovation projects

Figure 2 presents the sector structure of companies participating in the survey and innovating on the principles of sharing innovative resources

Figure 2: The distribution of participating companies by the sector of economy

The main users of joint innovations are industrial companies - 44%, companies from the science and research sector - 15%, from the information communication sector - 12%, transport and transport infrastructure - 10%.

We have identified a wide range of views on joint innovation, and hypothesized the relationship between leadership education and the adoption of the concept of joint innovation. Figure 3 presents the attitude to joint innovations according to the type of education of the top manager

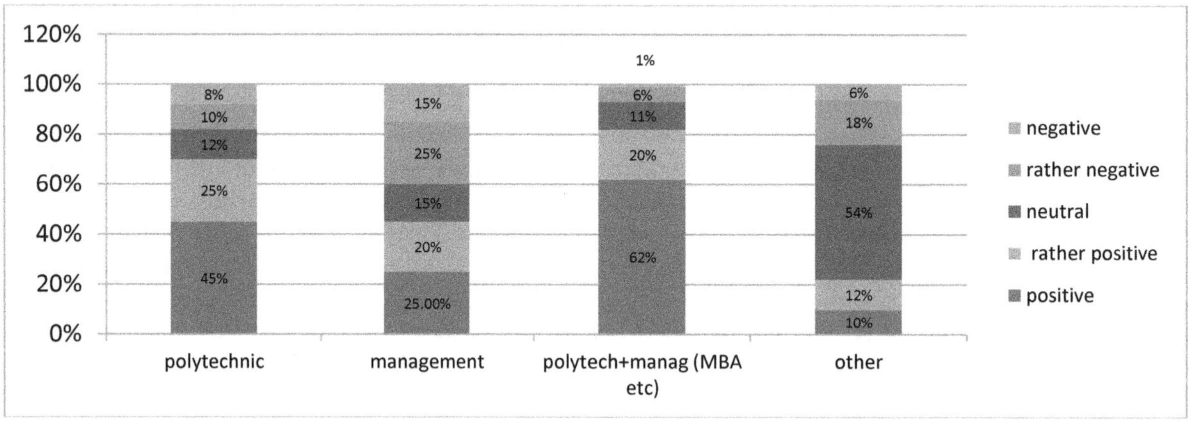

Figure 3: Attitudes to collaborative innovation depending on the type of education

We also researched the types of collaboration in joint innovation, which allowed us to identify the following models of sharing innovative resources:

- 1. Equipment sharing (process competence centers). The sharing of equipment allows to solve a set of problems faced by enterprises in the process of innovation and production of innovative products. These are such problems as the need to purchase high-precision equipment, 3D printers, laboratory equipment, etc. At the first stages of the development of equipment sharing centers, which we considered earlier in our 2014 work (Tkachenko & al., 2014), we were talking exclusively about specially created laboratory and production sites. Now this area has acquired the form of sharing of laboratory equipment and production facilities at existing enterprises, which solves the problem of optimal load of equipment and brings mutual benefit to all participants in this process, especially in conditions of unstable market situation with weakly determined demand. A similar model is described by Bouncken et al (2020)
- 2. Staff sharing. Given the shortage of highly qualified personnel and changes in the structure of employees, the sharing of personnel becomes an excellent solution for innovative companies. This ensures equal employment of staff, maintains a high level of motivation due to constant changes, new projects and new products, contributes to the growth of qualifications and the development of additional professional competencies. Initially, Staff sharing developed in construction as sharing construction workers, then there were companies that provided production personnel on the principles of outsourcing, now highly qualified personnel are used similarly.
- 3. Sharing engineering design teams (developer teams) is a special kind of Staff sharing, involving the sharing of engineering design teams (developer teams). Similar teams began to purposefully prepare in the Russian Federation, since last year, a project for the preparation of such teams started in St. Petersburg (Tkachenko et al., 2019). The key competencies of such participants are the skills of project management and implementation of projects in the field of engineering solutions and research and innovation projects. The

emergence of such teams is designed to solve the problem of a shortage of qualified project managers who understand the specifics of engineering projects and have practical project management skills in the innovation field.

- 4. Sharing ideas and process solutions. This type of sharing is a open innovation process. For example, based on the evaluation of the innovative backlog of large and medium-sized industrial companies in St. Petersburg, which was conducted by a group of researchers in 2006, more than 6000 promising technologies were identified that were under development. 10 years later, in 2016, according to the results of a repeated study, it was revealed that only 3% of them were brought to the stage of industrial use (Materials..., 2016) . Obviously, access to the base of promising developments for a wide range of innovators and developers would significantly expand the number of successful projects. Now platforms are developing to attract co-developers for promising innovative projects.

Figure 4 presented the results of the survey, reflecting the use of the listed models in joint innovative projects

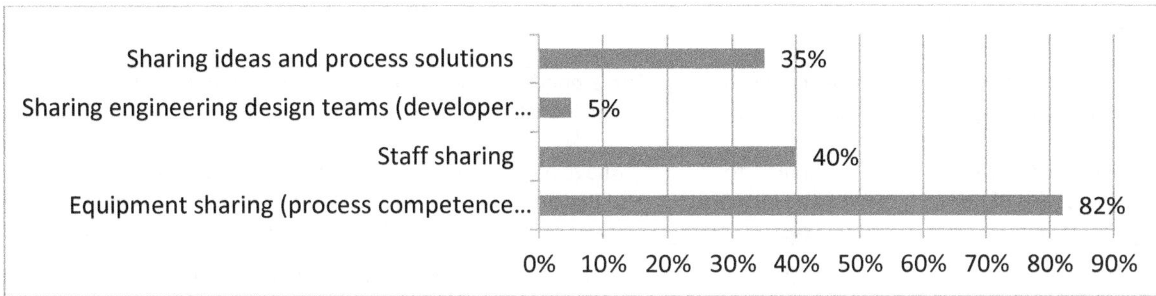

Figure 4: Using sharing models in innovative projects

Sharing engineering design teams (developer teams) remains the most popular area for joint innovations - 82% of companies participating in joint innovations use this model. In second place is Staff sharing, 40%, followed by Sharing ideas and process solutions - 35%. So far, engineering design teams (developer teams) has not been widely used - only 5%, but we believe this is due to the fact that this species has recently appeared and has not had time to establish itself as an effective form of joint innovation. We shall analyze the advantages and risks of the open innovation systems using sharing models.

The four innovative sharing models identified earlier based on a questionnaire survey conducted by company managers give us a varying assessment of the combined benefits (Table 1).

Table 1: Benefits of using sharing models

	Equipment sharing (process competence centers)	Staff sharing	Sharing engineering design teams (developer teams)	Sharing ideas and process solutions
Stage of use	Development work Laboratory tests Tests Specimens Production	R&D Development work production	R&D Development work Laboratory trials and tests Pilot production	All cycle stages
Advantages	30-60% reduction in costs associated with the acquisition of high-tech equipment, 30-40% reduction in equipment downtime, 30% reduction in costs associated with subcontracting	Attracting high-quality specialists, strengthening own personnel, improving the quality and speed of the development process, reducing the production cycle duration (by 10-20%)	Reducing the innovation cycle duration, reducing non-production losses, improving the quality of work due to "teamwork" by 10-20%	Reducing costs, reducing the innovation cycle duration, new areas of application of innovative solutions, technology transfer

As regards the risk level, the key risks are associated both with the general risks of the open innovation model and with the risks of the sharing participants' dishonesty. Table 2 shows the types and degree of risk associated with the use of sharing models.

Table 2 Types and degree of risk associated with the use of sharing models

Types of risk	Equipment sharing (process competence centers)	Staff sharing	Sharing engineering design teams (developer teams)	Sharing ideas and process solutions
Failure to achieve the innovation project goals due to failure to obtain the product with specified characteristics	Corresponds to market and industry level	Corresponds to market and industry level	Below market and industry level	Below market and industry level
Risks associated with product information leakage	n/a	High	High	Below market and industry level
Risks associated with the leakage of production secrets and know-how	N/a	High	High	Below market and industry level
Risks associated with project financial support	Corresponds to market and industry level	Corresponds to market and industry level	Below market and industry level	Below market and industry level
Risks associated with unlawful actions of third parties	Corresponds to market and industry level	Above market and industry level	Corresponds to market and industry level	Below market and industry level

After analyzing the losses and benefits for each model, we can conclude that cooperation is relevant in the particular case when the combined benefits are higher than the combined risks.

3. Model analysis of efficiency of innovative resources sharing. What is more profitable - integration or disintegration?

The overall economic efficiency of creating formal enterprise integration structures that are part of a single innovation and technology cycle (holdings) depends on several local effects, such as using the agreed transfer prices for work and services between cooperation stakeholders, concentrating financial resources allocated to scientific research and development, testing production processes and checking the quality and capacity of new business models, optimizing production volumes for the products for which small and medium-sized production volumes are not economically justified, ensuring the stability of the holding structure under bankruptcy situations in market conditions. For companies in cooperative networks that are not bound by formal cross-ownership relationships, the benefits include strategic and operational flexibility, which entails a higher level of production and information risk. To justify the integration effectiveness, we used a simple economic and mathematical modeling.

We shall consider the cost and pricing model for the final innovative product, the production of which requires the cooperation of the innovation cycle stakeholders. One of the main factors influencing the increase in the final product price is the number of developers and manufacturers engaged in the production process. Before turning to the costing and pricing model for the final innovative product in the holding structure, which involves interaction between organizationally independent innovation and production companies, we shall choose the pricing model. According to some researchers, such as Kapitonenko (1994), "given the nature of monopolism in the Russian industry and the current pricing models, it is natural to believe that each manufacturer of an innovative product in the conditions of free sale is guided by the principle of pricing at cost". According to this study, the use of other pricing models by no means contradicts the assumption that the competitive advantage will go to the manufacturer who brings the innovative product to the market with minimal costs allowing it to maximize profits and ensure the return on the innovation project under any pricing strategy.

Let $\sigma = (1 + \alpha)C$, where σ is the price, C is the net cost, α is the seller's expected rate of return.

A model analysis of the vertical integration advantages proposed by Kapitonenko (1994) considers the pricing of the final product in "corporate" (as defined by the author of the article) and disintegrated network structures. In this case, the target function is the price of the final product, and, based on the analysis logic, the minimum price increase is achieved in corporate structures rather than in disintegrated structures when passing through the innovation and process cycle stages. Let us follow the course of reasoning.

In the case of disintegration, the price at which the intermediate ("conversion") product is sold is part of the product cost at the next innovation cycle stage. Hence, the price of the final product in the event of associated production will be equal to:

$$\partial_n = \sum_{j=1}^{n} \prod_{i=1}^{n} (1 + \alpha_i) C_j^+ \quad (1)$$

where C_1^+ is the cost of the first intermediate product C_1, C_j^+ is the cost added at the jth stage of the production cycle.

In the particular event of equally profitable innovation cycle stages, this is inherent in industries engaged in innovative developments and delivering innovative products in the field of defense, where the profitability level is set as per the Russian federal law, when $\alpha_i = \alpha$, i = 1, n. Then Formula (1) takes the form:

$$\partial_n = \sum_{j=1}^{n} (1 + \alpha_i)^{n+1-j} C_j^+, \quad (2)$$

In a corporation, the price of the final product is calculated without considering the profitability of internal processes, and is determined by the formula:

$$P_n = (1 + \beta)(\sum_{j=1}^{n} C_j^+, \quad (3)$$

where β is the profitability of the entire production chain.

With equal profitability ($\alpha_i = \alpha = \beta$), the relative price increase due to disintegration will be

$$\Delta_n = \frac{\partial_n - P_n}{P_n} \quad (4)$$

Next, the model considered assumes that the contributions of all the innovation cycle links to the single net cost C are equal, that is: $C_j^+ = C / n$, j = 1, n. In this case, the price difference in the corporate structure and in the chain of disintegrated companies will be:

$$\partial_m - P_n = \frac{C(1+\alpha)}{n} [1 + (1 + \alpha)^1 + (1 + \alpha)^2 + \cdots (1 + \alpha)^{n-1} - n] \quad (5)$$

Hence, provided that $\alpha < 1$, we obtain the approximate equality:

$$\partial_m - P_n = \frac{C(1+\alpha)}{2} (n - 1)\alpha \quad (6)$$

Assuming that the corporate price is $P_n = C(1+\alpha)$, we are able to determine the relative price increase:

$$\Delta_n = \frac{(n-1)\alpha}{2} \quad (7).$$

Thus, the percentage price increase is proportional to the number of links n and profitability α. Given the restrictions introduced (that is, the assumption that the innovation cycle stages are equally profitable), the sequence Δ_n forms an arithmetic progression with a difference of $\alpha/2$. This means that an increase in the number of associated industries per unit leads to a relative increase in the product price, which is equal to ½ of the profitability.

However, as practice shows, long-term contractual relationships linking enterprises under a holding structure allow agreeing on the price level for research, development, project documentation and paperwork, components and semi-finished products so that the cost of the final product will be significantly lower than in disintegrated structures.

Let us assume that products manufactured by enterprises within a single process chain organized in the form of a holding are in steady demand at a certain market price level that is not influenced by individual manufacturers. In this case, the target function can be either lowering the net cost or raising the profitability of the final product, since the independent price level assumes that the lower the cost, the higher the profit, and, consequently, production profitability. In this case, the production cost of the final product for disintegrated enterprises will be equal to:

$$C' = C'_n + \sum_{j=1}^{n} \prod_{i=1}^{n} (1 + \varphi_i + k_j) C_j'^{+} \quad (8)$$

where ϕ_i is the pricing mark-up determined by the profitability requirements for the j-th enterprise, k_j is the commercial risk mark-up.

The production cost of the final product in the holding structure will be:

$$C^h = C'^h{}_n + \sum_{j=1}^{n} \prod_{i=1}^{n} (1 + \gamma_i) C_j^{h+} \ , \quad (9)$$

where γ_i is the pricing mark-up at the j-th stage of the process chain. By condition, $\phi_i > \gamma_i, k_j > 0$, which implies that $C' > C^h$.

With the market price level Z for the final product, the operating profit within the holding structure will be higher by Δ_p. In the particular case of equal contributions of all links in the innovation-process chain to the total cost:

$$\Delta_p = (n-1)(\gamma_i - \varphi_i - k_j) \quad (10)$$

Next, it is necessary to introduce a factor of different level of commercial risk in vertically integrated structures and innovative and process chains formed from independent enterprises. In this case, information risks associated with information leakage and disclosure of production secrets of an innovative product and its technical properties are not taken into account. For organizationally-disintegrated industries, the degree of probability that each link in the process chain will satisfy its need in the products of previous links is determined by several factors, including:

- availability of qualified personnel
- effectiveness of the project team
- level of supply and demand for the innovative product and the possibility of commercial use of products of incomplete phases of the innovation cycle;
- stability of relations between cooperation participants;
- consumer solvency level;
- scarcity of consumed resources, etc.

Naturally, within a corporation, in conditions of the complete dependence of research and production divisions on the administrative center, the probability of deviation from the given scale and terms of development is minimal, and is determined by the probability that each department will execute its part of the program. The probability also exists within the corporation that the innovative "intermediate product" will leak from the process chain. However, due to strategic management unity, the reliability level of the system will be significantly higher than in several disintegrated enterprises.

To obtain quantitative estimates, we shall consider the production process chain where each product i is used to produce the subsequent product (i + 1) with a certain expenditure coefficient $a_{i\,(i+1)}$. First, suppose that enterprises manufacturing semi-finished products are administratively independent. In this case, each i-th product has its own market R_i, the subjects of which are the supplier – the producer of product i S_i and the consumer of the product i – the producer of product (i + 1) – $S_{(i+1)}$:

$$S_1 \rightarrow R_1 \rightarrow S_2 \rightarrow R_2 \rightarrow \ldots \rightarrow S_{n-1} \rightarrow R_{n-1} \rightarrow S_n \rightarrow R_n, (12)$$

where n is the final product.

Market capacity $R_i - Vi$ may be greater or equal to the production requirement $S_{(i+1)}$ for product i. We denote the production need $S_{(i+1)}$ for the product i as $V_{i(i+1)}$. With V i? $V_{i(i+1)}$, a part of product i - E_i - leaves the manufacturing process system. As such, the market capacity V_i is equal to:

$$V_i = V_{i(i+1)} + E_i, \text{ for } i = 1, n\text{-}1. \qquad (13)$$

Let us consider the situation when the enterprise capacity - manufacturer S_i - M_{ij} - is less than the market capacity V_i. This is typical of industries with relatively developed competition between a significant number of enterprises producing the final product n with high monopolization of the production of semi-finished products. S_{nj} are the enterprises producing the final product (j = 1, k), and M_{nj} is the fashionability of each such enterprise. We assume that with the limited resource n-1, the volume of its acquisition U^{nj}_{n-1} by the j-th manufacturer of the finished products is proportional to the capacity M_{nj}:

$$U^{nj}_{n-1} = (M_{nj}/ M_n) * V_{(n-1)\,n}, \qquad (14)$$

where M_n is the total capacity of manufacturing enterprises of the final product n:

$$M_{n=\sum_{j=1}^{k} M_{nj}} (15)$$

Hence, the expected output of the final product n by the j-th enterprise will be:

$$Y_{nj} = U^{nj}_{n-1}/ a_{(n-1)n} = (M_{nj}/ M_n) * (V_{(n-1)\,n}/ a_{(n-1)n}) \text{ (16).}$$

Since, by condition, the market receives semi-finished products only from the innovation and process chain considered, then, by induction, $V_{1(2)} = V_1 - E_1$.

Obviously, due to limited resources, S_{nj} enterprises can produce the final product in the amount of Y_{nj}, which is less than M_nj. We assume that with the formal organization model of the production system, the integration effectiveness is determined similarly to the effectiveness of vertical integration within the production association, since the nature of relations within the holding guarantees that requirements of integrated enterprises for components and semi-finished products will be addressed first, and only the surplus will pass on to the external environment. Thus, defining Δ_{nj} as the difference between Y_{nj} and M_{nj}, we are able to evaluate the integration effectiveness from the viewpoint of the enterprise producing the final product, and, given the common strategic goals of enterprises within the holding structure, we are able to evaluate the effect for the entire holding:

$$\Delta_{nj} = M_{nj} - Y_{nj} = M_{nj} * \delta_n \text{, (17)}$$

where δ_n is a factor characterizing the relative underproduction or partial profit loss from the sale of the innovative product:

$$\delta_n = \left(1 - \frac{1}{M_n}\right)\left[\frac{V_1}{a_1} - \sum_{i=1}^{n-1} \frac{E_i}{a_i}\right] \text{ (18)}$$

Given the proportional distribution of resources, the characteristic δ_n will be the same for all enterprises producing the final product. The greater the value of δ_n, the greater the damage from the disintegration of the innovative process system.

4. Case-study of innovative sharing efficiency

Using the case study of project of development low temperature technologies (Sledge for Antarctica), we will examine the potential losses and benefits, taking into account the risks inherent in each model of innovation sharing. Table 3 presents the calculation results using the developed model.

The analysis showed that the maximum efficiency of the innovative project in this case will be achieved using Sharing ideas and process solutions, since the technologies being developed are universal and can be successfully applied in a wide variety of industries. If the company decides to use Equipment sharing (process centers), then the total effect will reach 125.551 million rubles. Thus, from the example of this analysis, it is possible to conclude that sharing is really effective in innovation, and the level of effect obtained will significantly depend on the industry and the type of innovative project.

Table 3: Calculate the cumulative effect of sharing innovation based on risks and benefits

	Number of companies participating in the innovation network, %*	Risk of information leakage per participant, %*	Risk of violation of obligations, %*	Technical risk of project completion%	Commercial risk of failure, %*	Expected economic effect (NPVi), bln rub (self-development)**	Expected benefit from Innovative Resource Sharing (NPVs) bln rub-	Expected losses from the risk of innovation sharing, bln rbl	Expected effect taking into account the sharing of innovative resources NPV bln rub
Equipment sharing (process competence centers)	5	0,5	0,1	4	10	85,772	12,22	5,14632	92,845
Staff sharing	3	2	1	8	10	85,772	1,8	5,832496	81,739
Sharing engineering design teams (developer teams)	5	2	1	8	5	85,772	4,3	7,204848	82,867
Sharing ideas and process solutions	8	0	1	8	10	85,772	24,3	8,405656	101,666

*based on the results of a survey of management and specialists of the company implementing the project

**from the business plan of the project, (self-development)

5. Conclusions

The rapid transformation of business models of innovation activity caused by the rapid formation of Industry 4.0 has resulted in the occurrence of new forms of industrial cooperation. Sharing, which had been initially seen as a form of new economic relations in the C2C sector, has demonstrated its effectiveness in the B2B sector. Sharing of resources – machine tools, equipment, production facilities, personnel, management teams and innovative ideas, gives a new impetus to the development of open innovation. Economic analysis (benefits-costs-risks) showed that the greatest efficiency for participants in innovative and process-related cooperation is provided by the sharing ideas and innovative solutions.

In this study, we aimed to identify the major types of innovative resources sharing used by companies, and to propose the approach to prove the efficiency of such sharing. These objectives were met, but the scope of the research is limited, so the evident direction of further study is to expand the scope of the survey. In the future, we plan to conduct a study of the relationship between the financial position of the company and the company participation in the innovative and industrial cooperation system based on the principles of sharing, which will justify the feasibility of using various forms of sharing in the innovation activity.

References

Bodrunov, S.D. (2018). From ZOO to NOO: Man, Society and Production in the Conditions of a New Technological Revolution. Voprosy Filosofii, 7, pp. 109-118. 10.31857/S0042874400002

Bodrunov, S.D. (2016). Re-industrialization: Socio-economic parameters of reintegrating production, science and education. 2016. pp. 20-28.

Bouncken, R., Ratzmann, M., Barwinski, R., Kraus, S. (2020) Coworking spaces: Empowerment for entrepreneurship and innovation in the digital and sharing economy. Journal of Business Research, 114, pp. 102-110

Chesbrough, H. (2003) Open Innovation: The New Imperative for Creating and Profiting from Technology. HBS Press.

Ciulli F., Kolk A. (2019) Incumbents and business model innovation for the sharingeconomy: Implications for sustainability. Journal of Cleaner Production, 214, pp. 995-1010. https://doi.org/10.1016/j.jclepro.2018.12.295

Curtis S.K., Mont O. (2020) Sharing economy business models for sustainability. Journal of Cleaner Production, 266, article 121519, https://doi.org/10.1016/j.jclepro.2020.121519

Drechsler, W., Natter, M. (2012). Understanding a firm's openness decisions in innovation. Journal of Business Research, 65 (3), pp. 438-445.

Gnyawali, D.R., Srivastava, M.K. (2013). Complementary effects of clusters and networks on firm innovation: A conceptual model. Journal of Engineering and Technology Management, 30 (1), pp. 1-20.

Hossain, M. (2020) Sharing economy: A comprehensive literature review. International Journal of Hospitality Management 87. Article 102470. https://doi.org/10.1016/j.ijhm.2020.102470

Kapitonenko. V.V. (1994) The advantages of vertical integration in the formation of organizational and production systems (model analysis), Russian Economic Journal, 10.

Lee, S., Park,G., Yoon, B., Park, J. (2010). Open innovation in SMEs— An intermediated network model. Research Policy, 39 (2), pp. 290-300

Martin C.J. Upham P., Budd L. (2015) Commercial orientation in grassroots social innovation: Insights from the sharing economy. Ecological Economics Volume, 118, pp. 240-251.

Materials of the study of innovative potential in the preparation of the concept of the development of the industrial complex of St. Petersburg (2016) , UNECON 2016

Okatan, K. (2012). Managing Knowledge for Innovation and Intra Networking: A Case Study. Procedia - Social and Behavioral Sciences, 62, pp. 59-63

Rogo F., Cricelli, L., Grimaldi M. (2014). Assessing the performance of open innovation practices: A case study of a community of innovation. Technology in Society, 38, pp. 60-80.

Tkachenko E., Rogova E., Bodrunov S. (2014). The Evolution of the Models of Knowledge Management within Networks: Cases of the Industrial and Construction Networks in St Petersburg. Proceedings of the 11th International Conference on Intellectual Capital, Knowledge Management And Organisational Learning ICICKM 2014 The University of Sydney Business School Australia 6-7 November 2014, pp 400-409

Tkachenko, E., Rogova, E., Bodrunov, S., Karlik, A. (2019). Application of KM techniques in the assessment competences in high-tech industries. Proceedings of the European Conference on Intellectual Capital, pp. 1023-1033.

Tomlinson, F.R., Fai, M.F. (2013). The nature of SME co-operation and innovation: A multi-scalar and multi-dimensional analysis. International Journal of Production Economics, 141 (1), pp. 316-326.

Wang Y., Vanhaverbeke, W., Roijakkers, N. (2012). Exploring the impact of open innovation on national systems of innovation — A theoretical analysis. Technological Forecasting and Social Change, 79(3), pp. 419–428.

West, J., Salter, A., Vanhaverbeke, W., Chesbrough H. (2014). Open innovation: The next decade. Research Policy, 43(5), pp. 805–811.

An Exploratory Study of Corporate Entrepreneurship in Latin America

Marcia Villasana[1] and Carlos Lozano[2]
[1]Tecnologico de Monterrey, Monterrey, Mexico
[2]Universidad de Santo Tomás, Bogotá, Colombia
marciavillasana@tec.mx
carloslozano@ustadistancia.edu.co
DOI: 10.34190/EIE.20.158

Abstract: Generating new products, services, or technologies may require drawing on available entrepreneurial human resources within the firm. Allowing an organizational climate in which employees engage as internal entrepreneurs can serve as a conduit for in-house generation of innovations. In order to sustain such innovative activity within a firm, corporate entrepreneurship integrates intentional and visible organizational conducts to engage employees in entrepreneurial behaviours that allow for revitalization and strategic renewal. In an understanding that an organizational climate influences employees´ behaviors, studies have found that certain organizational dimensions can increase employees' perceptions of organizational support that elicit their willingness to pursue entrepreneurial initiatives. In emerging and developing economies prevails a disparity on the capacity of firms to create an organizational climate that taps into the entrepreneurial behaviors of employees. In Latin America, even though many companies develop some type of innovation, the innovative performance of many firms lags significantly behind that of developed economies. The aim of this paper is to assess the perception of employees on five key dimensions in ten Latin American firms located in Colombia, Ecuador, Mexico, and Honduras from five different industries. To this end, the Corporate Entrepreneurship Climate Instrument (CECI) was applied to assess (1) top management support, (2) employee autonomy, (3) rewards/reinforcement, (4) time availability, and (5) organizational boundaries. Results from multivariate analysis show that the role of top managers within the company appears as one of the main inhibitors to entrepreneurial behaviour, highlighting the need for improving top management´s sensitivity to supporting entrepreneurial activity of employees. Findings also reveal that employees perceive a weakness of organizational resources and incentives to entrepreneurial behavior. The practical implication of this exploratory study is that as long as traditional managerial conducts are not transformed, entrepreneurial individuals will not flourish in detriment of higher innovative organizational performance.

Keywords: entrepreneurial activity, intrapreneurship, innovation strategy, management, organizational climate

1. Introduction

Entrepreneurial behaviour within organizations is considered important to detect and develop opportunities that may derive in achieving or maintaining competitive advantage (Hisrich and Kearney, 2014). As demonstrated by the 2008 worldwide economic downturn and later by the 2020 pandemic, hostile environments force organizations, large and small, to respond by engaging in entrepreneurial behaviours and pursue innovation as a means of survival. In calmer times, these behaviours can integrate to strategy as a path to higher levels of organizational performance (Kuratko, Hornsby and Hayton, 2015).

Corporate entrepreneurship is a conscious effort to promote entrepreneurial behaviours and practices within organizations; it refers to an over-arching strategy to create an internal environment to detect and exploit opportunities in pursuit of growth and sustainable advantage (Kuratko & Audretsch, 2013; Vadnjal, 2014). The literature suggests that certain environmental factors support an effective corporate entrepreneurship strategy to promote an internal entrepreneurial climate. Among these factors are the following: a top management with an entrepreneurial vision that supports innovative initiatives within the company; the autonomous behaviour of organizational members for discovery, evaluation, and exploitation of opportunities; and a reward system to incentivize risk-taking and pro-activeness (Bayarçelik and Özşahin, 2014; Calisto and Sarkar, 2017).

The purpose of this study is to explore the perceptions of employees in ten Latin American firms on the internal factors identified as key to promoting an entrepreneurial organizational climate. We aim to contribute to the literature of corporate entrepreneurship in emerging countries, where the innovative performance of many firms lags significantly behind that in developed economies. This paper comprises the following sections: Section two presents the theoretical background; section three addresses the methodology conducted; section four presents the main findings and discussion, and section five concludes with final comments and limitations to the study.

2. Theoretical framework

In this study, we adopt Kuratko, Morris & Covin´s (2010) definition of corporate entrepreneurship (herein CE), which entails the generation, development and implementation of new ideas within the organization. As the world becomes more complex, CE has come to be part of corporate strategy as a "vision-directed, organization-wide reliance on entrepreneurial behaviour that purposefully and continuously rejuvenates the organization and shapes the scope of its operations..." (Ireland, Kuratko and Morris, 2006, p. 10). Thus, at the centre of CE strategy is the individual: managerial and non-managerial employees become assets of the organization´s venture creation and strategic renewal activities (Gawke, Gorgievski and Bakker, 2017). Empowered, accountable, and autonomous employees become a critical resource for firms to leverage on their skills, competencies, and ability to think across the boundaries of organizational units to innovate through entrepreneurial behaviour (Blanka, 2019; Audretsch *et al.*, 2020). These individuals, defined as intrapreneurs, exert a tendency to engage beyond defined functions and roles to promote the interests of the company (Gasda, 2012; Buekens, 2014; Calisto and Sarkar, 2017). According to Gawke et al. (2017), employee intrapreneurship is an employee´s "agentic and anticipatory behaviours aimed at creating new businesses for the organization and enhancing an organization´s ability to react to internal and external advancements" (p. 89).

Studies have found that organizational internal conditions are important for innovative, risk-taking individuals (Alpkan *et al.*, 2010; Zakaria *et al.*, 2012; Neessen *et al.*, 2019). It is worth noting that in this paper we refer to employee intrapreneurship as those strategic, proactive work behaviours that "may enhance an organization´s ability to take risks and seize opportunities" (Gawke et al., 2019, p. 808). Since the focus is on behaviour, how to purposefully engage intrapreneurs must be part of an organization´s CE strategy.

2.1 Dimensions of corporate entrepreneurship

Corporate entrepreneurship is a top-down process that requires the effective adoption of specific practices (Falola *et al.*, 2018; Chebbi *et al.*, 2019). Research on intrapreneurship shows that certain organizational conditions are conducive of perceptions of confidence on competency, making employees be more innovative (Lin, 1998; Singh and Sarkar, 2012; Falola *et al.*, 2018; Mehmood *et al.*, 2019). Intrapreneurs may be found at all levels of the organization (Mustafa, Gavin and Hughes, 2018), and a suitable milieu includes the following five key internal organizational dimensions, which have been incorporated into the diagnostic tool Corporate Entrepreneurship Assessment Instrument (CEAI), later refined as the Corporate Entrepreneurship Climate Instrument (CECI) (Kuratko, Montagno and Hornsby, 1990; Hornsby, Kuratko, and Zahra, 2002).

Management support: The degree in which top managers promote and champion innovative ideas, and provide sufficient resources make employees be willing to undertake entrepreneurial initiatives (Kuratko, Hornsby and Covin, 2014; Neessen *et al.*, 2019). Employee proactiveness is recursively linked to management´s leadership style (Chebbi *et al.*, 2019; Felix, Aparicio and Urbano, 2019). Entrepreneurial leadership can inspire and empower individuals for idea generation and implementation (Kuratko, 2007; Leitch, Mcmullan and Harrison, 2013; Mehmood *et al.*, 2019) by seeking "novel and effective activities to employ and encourage others to discard the ineffective activities"(Gross, 2019, p. 21).

Work discretion: This is the extent to which management delegates authority and does not exercise excessive oversight, allowing latitude in decision-making. This dimension also relates to the autonomy and empowerment perceived by employees (Kirkman and Rosen, 1999; Kassa and Raju, 2015; Urban and Wood, 2017). Thus, when an employee´s esteem needs are satisfied, they will contribute to the achievement of organizational goals.

Rewards and reinforcement: The appropriate use of rewards must take into consideration how to enhance an individual´s willingness to assume risks inherent to entrepreneurial activity (Hornsby, Kuratko, and Zahra, 2002; Bayarçelik and Özşahin, 2014; Buekens, 2014; Kuratko, Hornsby and Covin, 2014).

Time availability: Time is considered as one of the resources to provide support to entrepreneurial efforts of employees. Work load can impact the level of energy, dedication and commitment to achieving short and long-term organizational goals (Kuratko et al, 2014; Kassa and Raju, 2015).

Organisational boundaries: The degree in which the organization manages uncertainty for employees (Kuratko et al, 2014) is defined by its type of organizational structure, which in turn impacts internal policy and procedural constraints (Kuratko, Hornsby and Covin, 2014; Orchard, Ribiere and Achtzehn, 2018). For intrapreneurship to flourish, it is vital that entrepreneurial initiatives are not constraint by hierarchical boundaries (Chebbi *et al.*, 2019).

3. Methodology

The entrepreneurial climate of ten Latin American firms located in Colombia, Ecuador, Mexico, and Honduras was analysed. The industries to which these firms correspond are retail (3), manufacturing (2) food (3), floriculture (1), and chemicals (1). Firm size ranged from small to large. The version of the Corporate Entrepreneurship Climate Instrument (CECI) by Morris, Kuratko and Covin (2010) was used to assess five dimensions that integrate factors that facilitate and promote innovative behaviour (Table 1). The instrument is integrated by 48 scaled questions, measured by using a five-point Likert scale from 1 (strongly disagree) to 5 (strongly agree). For details on the instrument refer to Morris et al (2010).

Table 1: Description of dimensions in the Corporate Entrepreneurship Climate Instrument (CECI)

Dimension	Item number
1. Top management support	1 - 19
2. Work discretion	20 – 29
3. Rewards/reinforcement	30 – 31
4. Time availability	36 – 41
5. Organizational boundaries	42 – 48

Source: Morris et al, 2010

The methodology follows the steps outlined by Kuratko et al (2010) to administer the instrument. Employees at different levels and departments of each organization (managerial 17%, production area 47%, commercial department 19%, finance department 12%, and technical area 1%) were asked to answer the questionnaire. For the medium and large firms in the study, purposeful sampling was applied for participant selection. As Patton (in Emmel, 2014) observes, purposeful sampling "must be selected to fit the purpose of the study, the resources available, the questions being asked, and constraints being faced" (p. 34). Managers heading the abovementioned areas aided in the respondent selection process by choosing employees to participate in the study. On average, there were 11 participants per firm, with Colombian firms having the largest number of respondents with an average of 19.

Regarding measures, as Morris et al (2010) state, this instrument aids in developing a company profile to identify areas that may require improvement to successfully benefit from initiatives in CE. The authors use mean values to measure the degree to which employees perceive each of the five dimensions within their firms. Higher mean scores are interpreted as higher levels of readiness to implement a CE strategy. For this study, multivariate regression was applied using Minitab Statistical Software to test the relationships between dependent and independent variables and to uncover correlations among items within the five dimensions.

4. Results and discussion

For Dimension 1, top management support, the mean score is 3.2. Correlational analysis indicates a strong relationship between item 18 ("There is considerable desire among people in the organization for generating new ideas without regard for crossing departmental or functional boundaries") and other variables in this dimension (Table 2). It is worth noting that mean scores per item are not higher than 3.3.

Table 2: Correlation matrix for the relationship between items in Dimension 2 Top management

ITEMS	I1	I2	I3	I4	I5	I6	I7	I8	I9	I10	I11	I12	I13	I14	I15	I16	I17	I18
I2	0.92	-																
I3	0.92	0.99	-															
I4	0.93	0.97	0.99	-														
I5	0.75	0.81	0.82	0.79	-													
I6	0.91	0.99	1.00	0.99	0.81	-												
I7	0.93	0.87	0.88	0.88	0.79	0.89	-											
I8	0.82	0.93	0.94	0.95	0.67	0.95	0.74	-										

ITEMS	I1	I2	I3	I4	I5	I6	I7	I8	I9	I10	I11	I12	I13	I14	I15	I16	I17	I18
I9	0.97	0.87	0.88	0.91	0.82	0.87	0.90	0.79	-									
I10	0.94	0.94	0.96	0.96	0.81	0.97	0.98	0.87	0.90	-								
I11	0.89	0.96	0.96	0.95	0.87	0.96	0.84	0.94	0.90	0.92	-							
I12	0.93	0.92	0.93	0.94	0.90	0.94	0.95	0.84	0.95	0.97	0.95	-						
I13	0.96	0.96	0.95	0.94	0.81	0.95	0.97	0.86	0.91	0.98	0.92	0.96	-					
I14	0.96	0.96	0.96	0.95	0.82	0.96	0.97	0.86	0.91	0.99	0.93	0.97	1.00	-				
I15	0.95	0.99	0.98	0.97	0.75	0.98	0.87	0.95	0.90	0.94	0.96	0.92	0.96	0.96	-			
I16	0.79	0.94	0.93	0.90	0.67	0.94	0.72	0.98	0.73	0.84	0.93	0.81	0.85	0.85	0.94	-		
I17	0.96	0.87	0.87	0.89	0.77	0.87	0.99	0.73	0.93	0.96	0.83	0.94	0.96	0.96	0.88	0.69	-	
I18	**0.97**	**0.97**	**0.96**	**0.94**	**0.83**	**0.95**	**0.95**	**0.83**	**0.92**	**0.97**	**0.92**	**0.95**	**0.99**	**0.99**	**0.95**	**0.83**	**0.96**	**-**
I19	0.74	0.90	0.90	0.89	0.76	0.91	0.66	0.96	0.76	0.80	0.95	0.82	0.79	0.80	0.90	0.96	0.64	0.78

For Dimension 2, work discretion, has a mean score of 3.4. For this dimension, correlational analysis indicates a moderate relationship between variables (Table 3). However, some variables show low scores. Items 20 ("I feel that I am own boss and do not have to double check all of my decisions with someone else") and 21 ("harsh criticism and punishment result from mistakes made on the job") show results of 0.66 and 0.57 respectively. These results suggest low levels of idea generation, and a moderate relationship between criticism in the job and developing new ideas.

Table 3: Correlation matrix for the relationship between items in Dimension 2 Work discretion

ITEMS	I20	I21	I22	I23	I24	I25	I26	I27	I28
I21	0.66	-							
I22	0.75	0.76	-						
I23	0.70	0.68	0.96	-					
I24	0.72	0.86	0.96	0.91	-				
I25	0.68	0.58	0.86	0.81	0.79	-			
I26	0.62	0.61	0.82	0.87	0.80	0.92	-		
I27	0.84	0.80	0.91	0.84	0.90	0.89	0.83	-	
I28	**0.66**	**0.57**	**0.85**	**0.81**	**0.80**	**1.00**	**0.92**	**0.88**	**-**
I29	0.66	0.82	0.74	0.63	0.79	0.85	0.78	0.87	0.85

Results for these two dimensions suggest a negative perception prevails among respondents on the extent to which the organization practices oversight, tolerates failure, and encourages experimentation. Scores show a low perception on the extent to which management champions new ideas and provides decision-making latitude. These results reflect findings in several studies on management style in Latin American companies, which reveal that the leadership style across the region is characterized as autocratic and paternalistic (Davila and Elvira, 2012; Castaño *et al.*, 2015). Davila and Elvira (2012) conducted a study on how cultural values impact the success and failure of Latin American organizations. Their findings show that new management techniques do not often fit with traditional corporate practices, and that employees tend to prefer senior management to make decisions. In another study led by Ogliastri, Altschul and Dorfman (1999), on organisational leadership across Latin American countries, findings reveal that for Mexico and Colombia, among other countries in the region, there is a strong preference for uncertainty avoidance, but at the same time managers wish for room for experimentation and innovation.

From Dimension1 and 2, the role of management appears as a large area of opportunity for Latin American companies. As Buekens (2014) states, individuals with entrepreneurial attitudes flourish when management empowers them. More than often, upper management plays a key role in articulating the entrepreneurial strategic vision, providing guidance and encouragement, and promoting structural changes that enable entrepreneurship within the organization (Buekens, 2014; Kuratko, Hornsby and Hayton, 2015; Jahanshahi, Nawaser and Brem, 2018; Kreiser *et al.*, 2019). In a systematic literature review on leadership styles and corporate entrepreneurship, Verma and Mehta (2020) explain that leadership, as the ability to give direction and motivate others, must move away from traditional styles and into positive leadership models. This type of attitude in top management is often a reflection of an organizational structure that allows wider spans of control and decentralisation (Srivastava and Agrawal, 2010).

Dimension 3, on rewards and reinforcement, shows a mean score of 4.0, the highest for all mean scores obtained. Values are higher for item 33 ("My supervisor will give me special recognition if my work performance is especially good"). Average correlation values for this dimension is 0.837. The results for this dimension suggest that the recognition of the organization´s leaders motivates individual effort (Table 4). However, the mean score for item 31 ("The rewards I receive are dependent upon my innovation on the job") is the lowest for all items. This is an indication that despite the perception that there are rewards, those aimed at innovative behaviours are not strongly promoted or are absent.

The purpose of a reward or incentives system is to recognize the worth of an employee to the organization (Hsieh and Chen, 2011; Marx, Reis Faleiros Soares and Barros, 2016). As a factor of an entrepreneurial climate, reward systems that incentivize innovation have a strong effect on entrepreneurial behaviours (Monsen, Patzelt and Saxton, 2010; Kuratko, Hornsby and Covin, 2014). According to Scheepers et al (2008), appropriate rewards and the availability of a supportive organizational structure contribute to employees perception of empowerment, accountability, autonomy, and higher levels of performance (Güngör, 2011; Hsieh and Chen, 2011). If managed properly, represents a powerful tool for implementing an organization´s competitive strategy (Hsieh and Chen, 2011). In a study on employee venture behaviour and strategic renewal behaviour, Gawke et al (2019) find that there is a strong relationship between reward sensitivity and employee intrapreneurship. In a study for Mexico, Galván Vela and Limón find a positive and significant relationship between the reward system to intrapreneurship and the perception of autonomy by employees (2017).

Table 4: Correlation matrix for the relationship between items in Dimension 3 Rewards/Reinforcement

ITEM	I30	I31	I32	I33	I34
I31	0.77	-			
I32	0.89	0.76	-		
I33	0.86	0.66	0.78	-	
I34	**0.89**	**0.80**	**0.93**	**0.73**	**-**
I35	0.78	0.69	0.84	0.46	0.88

The mean score for Dimension 4, time availability, is 3.2. The relationship between item 39 ("My job is structured so I have very little time to think about wider organizational problems") and items for this dimension denotes that daily workload limits employees to think about broader organizational issues (Table 5). For Dimension 5, organizational boundaries, the mean score is 3.7. Correlational analysis indicates a moderately strong relationship between item 47 ("My job description clearly specifies the standards of performance on which my job is evaluated") and other variables for this dimension (Table 6).

Table 5: Correlation matrix for the relationship between items in Dimension 4 Time availability

ITEM	I36	I37	I38	I39	I40
I37	0.61	-			
I38	0.72	0.83	-		
I39	**0.87**	**0.84**	**0.92**	**-**	
I40	0.76	0.71	0.78	0.74	-
I41	0.78	0.85	0.91	0.94	0.75

Table 6: Correlation matrix for the relationship between items in Dimension 5 Organizational boundaries

ITEM	I42	I43	I44	I45	I46	I47
I43	0.64	-				
I44	0.75	0.80	-			
I45	0.74	0.41	0.39	-		
I46	0.71	0.87	0.67	0.52	-	

ITEM	I42	I43	I44	I45	I46	I47
I47	**0.91**	**0.87**	**0.88**	**0.59**	**0.86**	-
I48	0.70	0.60	0.80	0.49	0.37	0.65

Time flexibility, with the right support from management, contributes to employee engagement and their ability to meet demands of work and explore opportunities for innovation (Richman *et al.*, 2008; Kuratko, Hornsby and Covin, 2014). Results for Dimensions 4 and 5 reflect findings in a study by Madero Gómez and Barboza (2015) on the relationship between flexible work arrangements and organizational practices, including innovation initiatives, at large firms located at the border between Mexico and California. They find that firms that apply flexible organizational practices have higher levels of employee satisfaction. In addition, their results show that there is a lack of support structures to innovation processes, and a need to implement more flexible practices to improve job satisfaction and creativity.

Findings for all five dimensions suggest that Dimension 1 is the most relevant dimension for the Latin American firms included in the study, accounting for 40.7% of total variance. Regarding the CE dimensions most significantly correlated to Dimension 1 we find that, firstly, Dimension 5 (organizational boundaries) on specific job description on performance standards (item 47) shows the highest scores (64.5%). Secondly, Dimension 3 Rewards/Reinforcement correlates the highest for special recognition from direct management (50.9%). The eigenanalysis values and coefficients matrix results are presented in Table 7, and the corresponding plotting of those values are presented in Figure 1.

Table 7: Eigen analysis of the correlation matrix loadings of the significant principal components

	PC1	PC2	PC3	PC4	PC5
I18 (There is considerable desire among people in the organization for generating new ideas without regard for crossing departmental or functional boundaries)	-0,11	-0,75	-0,08	0,12	-0,64
I28 (I have much autonomy on my job and am left on my own to do my own work)	-0,42	0,32	-0,66	-0,45	-0,30
I34 (My manager would tell his/her boss if my work was outstanding)	0,51	0,46	-0,21	0,49	-0,50
I39 (My job is structured so that I have very little time to think about wider organizational problems)	0,36	-0,36	-0,71	0,13	0,46
I47 (My job description clearly specifies the standards of performance on which my job is evaluated)	0,65	-0,08	0,12	-0,73	-0,18
Eigenvalue	2,04	1,63	0,95	0,23	0,14
Proportion (%)	0,40	0,3	0,19	0,05	0,02
Cumulative (%)	0,40	0,733	0,92	0,97	1,00

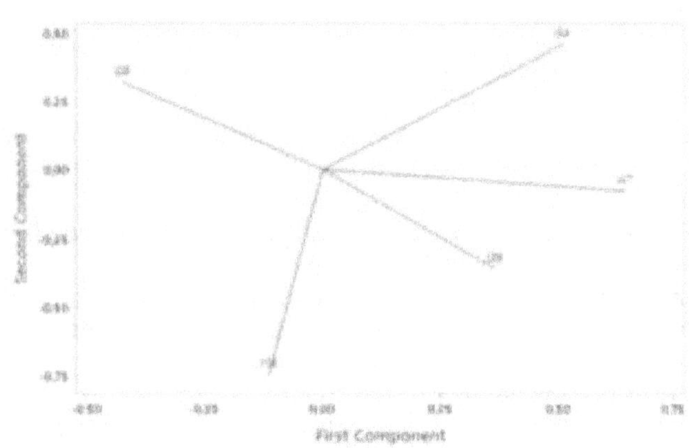

Figure 1: Component loading plot

5. Conclusion

This study explores the perceptions of employees on five internal organizational dimensions to supporting an entrepreneurial environment were analysed: management support; work discretion; rewards and reinforcement; time availability; and organizational boundaries. Although of exploratory nature, findings suggest that for organizations in Latin America, organizational boundaries, time availability, and work discretion may require reassessment, and even defy prevailing corporate practices. The management practices and style in Latin American organizations tend towards fostering a bureaucratic climate which stifles individual initiative (Lenartowicz and Johnson, 2002). The need for control that typically characterizes Latin-American managers limits employees' freedom to implement improved work methods and stiffles innovative ideas. Implementing a CE strategy requires a working environment that provides a supportive leadership and empowers employees, by reducing or eliminating hierarchical barriers and facilitating experimentation (Chebbi *et al.*, 2019).

A limitation is that results be contemplated considering the exploratory nature of the analysis, and sample size. In addition, there is a need to apply the instrument to additional firms and sectors in other countries in the region. Nonetheless, the findings highlight the relevance of seeing CE as a strategy, not only as isolated efforts within the organization, if companies in emerging economies want to seriously incorporate and benefit from their employees´ innovation and entrepreneurial initiatives.

References

Afshar Jahanshahi, A., Nawaser, K. and Brem, A. (2018) 'Corporate entrepreneurship strategy: an analysis of top management teams in SMEs', *Baltic Journal of Management*, 13(4), pp. 528–543.

Alpkan, L. *et al.* (2010) 'Organizational support for intrapreneurship and its interaction with human capital to enhance innovative performance', *Management Decision*, 48(5), pp. 732–755.

Audretsch, D. B. *et al.* (2020) 'Intrapreneurship and absorptive capacities: The dynamic effect of labor mobility', *Technovation*, in press.

Bayarçelik, E. B. and Özşahin, M. (2014) 'How Entrepreneurial Climate Effects Firm Performance?', *Procedia - Social and Behavioral Sciences*. Elsevier BV, 150, pp. 823–833.

Blanka, C. (2019) 'An individual-level perspective on intrapreneurship: a review and ways forward', *Review of Managerial Science*. Springer Verlag, pp. 919–961.

Buekens, W. (2014) 'Fostering Intrapreneurship: The Challenge for a New Game Leadership', *Procedia Economics and Finance*. Elsevier BV, 16, pp. 580–586.

Calisto, M. de L. and Sarkar, S. (2017) 'Organizations as biomes of entrepreneurial life: Towards a clarification of the corporate entrepreneurship process', *Journal of Business Research*, 70, pp. 44–54.

Castaño, N. *et al.* (2015) 'El Jefe: Differences in expected leadership behaviors across Latin American countries', *Journal of World Business*, 50(3), pp. 584–597.

Chebbi, H. *et al.* (2019) 'Focusing on internal stakeholders to enable the implementation of organizational change towards corporate entrepreneurship: A case study from France', *Journal of Business Research*. Available from https://www.sciencedirect.com/science/article/abs/pii/S0148296319303546

Davila, A. and Elvira, M. M. (2012) 'Humanistic leadership: Lessons from Latin America', *Journal of World Business*, 47(4), pp. 548–554.

Falola, H. *et al.* (2018) 'Employees' intrapreneurial engagement initiatives and its influence on organisational survival', *Business: Theory and Practice*, 19, pp. 9–16.

Felix, C., Aparicio, S. and Urbano, D. (2019) 'Leadership as a driver of entrepreneurship: an international exploratory study', *Journal of Small Business and Enterprise Development*, 26(3), pp. 397–420.

Galván Vela, E. and Limón, M. L. S. (2017) 'Autonomía y recompensas como factores organizacionales detonantes de la actividad intraemprendedora Autonomy and rewards as organizational factors triggering intrapreneurship', *Ciencias Adminstrativas Teoría y Praxis*, 2, pp. 237–249.

Gasda, J.-M. (2012) 'A Relational View on Intrapreneurial Behavior : A social cognitive Framework of employee´s individual level entrepreneurial behavior for the SME-context', in *57th World Conference of the International Council for Small Business (ICSB)*. Wellington, New Zealand: ICSB.

Gawke, J. C., Gorgievski, M. J. and Bakker, A. B. (2017) 'Employee intrapreneurship and work engagement: A latent change score approach', *Journal of Vocational Behavior*, 100, pp. 88–100.

Gawke, J. C., Gorgievski, M. J. and Bakker, A. B. (2019) 'Measuring intrapreneurship at the individual level: Development and validation of the Employee Intrapreneurship Scale (EIS)', *European Management Journal*, 37(6), pp. 806–817.

Gross, R. (2019) 'The nexus between followership and entrepreneurial leadership: A firm-level analysis', *Journal of Management Policy and Practice*, 20(5), pp. 18–27.

Güngör, P. (2011) 'The relationship between reward management system and employee performance with the mediating role of motivation: A quantitative study on global banks', *Procedia - Social and Behavioral Sciences*. Elsevier B.V., 24, pp. 1510–1520.

Hornsby, J., Kuratko, D., Zahra, S. A. (2002) 'Middle managers' perception ofthe internal environment for corporate entrepreneurship: assessing a measurement scale', *Journal of Business Venturing*, 9(2), pp. 253–273.

Hsieh, Y. H. and Chen, H. M. (2011) 'Strategic fit among business competitive strategy, human resource strategy, and reward system', *Academy of Strategic Management Journal*, 10(2), pp. 11–32.

Ireland, R. D., Kuratko, D. F. and Morris, M. H. (2006) 'A health audit for corporate entrepreneurship: Innovation at all levels: Part I', *Journal of Business Strategy*, 27(1), pp. 10–17.

Kassa, A. G. and Raju, R. S. (2015) 'Investigating the relationship between corporate entrepreneurship and employee engagement', *Journal of Entrepreneurship in Emerging Economies*, 7(2), pp. 148–167.

Kirkman, B. L. and Rosen, B. (1999) 'Beyond self-management: Antecedents and consequences of team empowerment', *Academy of Management Journal*, 42(1), pp. 58–74.

Kreiser, P. M., Kuratko, D., Covin, J., Ireland, R. and Hornsby, J. (2019) 'Corporate entrepreneurship strategy: extending our knowledge boundaries through configuration theory', *Small Business Economics,* 45(2), pp. 1-21.

Kuratko, D. F. (2007) *Entrepreneurial Leadership in the 21 st Century*, *Journal of Leadership and Organizational Studies,* 13(4), pp. 1-11.

Kuratko, D. F. and Audretsch, D. B. (2013) 'Clarifying the domains of corporate entrepreneurship', *International Entrepreneurship and Management Journal*, 9(3), pp. 323–335.

Kuratko, D. F., Hornsby, J. S. and Covin, J. G. (2014) 'Diagnosing a firm's internal environment for corporate entrepreneurship', *Business Horizons*, 57(1), pp. 37–47.

Kuratko, D. F., Hornsby, J. S. and Hayton, J. (2015) 'Corporate entrepreneurship: the innovative challenge for a new global economic reality', *Small Business Economics*. Kluwer Academic Publishers, 45(2), pp. 245–253.

Kuratko, D. F., Montagno, R. V and Hornsby, J. S. (1990) 'Developing an Intrapreneurial Assessment Instrument for an Effective Corporate Entrepreneurial Environment', *Strategic Management Journal*, 11, pp. 49–58.

Leitch, C. M., Mcmullan, C. and Harrison, R. T. (2013) 'The Development of Entrepreneurial Leadership: The Role of Human, Social and Institutional Capital', *British Journal of Management*, 24(3), pp. 347–366.

Lenartowicz, T. and Johnson, J. (2002) 'Comparing Managerial Values in Twelve Latin American Countries: An Exploratory Study', *Management International Review*, 42(3), pp. 279–307.

Lin, C. Y.-Y. (1998) 'The essence of empowerment: A conceptual model and a case illustration', *Preventing School Failure*, 7(2), pp. 223–238.

Madero Gómez, S. M. and Barboza, G. A. (2015) 'Interrelación de la cultura, flexibilidad laboral, alineación estratégica, innovación y rendimiento empresarial', *Contaduria y Administracion*. Universidad Nacional Autónoma de México, Facultad de Contaduría y Administración, 60(4), pp. 735–756.

Marx, R., Reis Faleiros Soares, J. P. and Barros, L. (2016) 'Variáveis de contexto organizacional a serem consideradas no projeto de sistemas de recompensas orientados à inovação de produtos', *Revista Brasileira de Gestao de Negocios*, 18(60), pp. 267–289.

Mehmood, M. S. *et al.* (2019) 'Impact of entrepreneurial leadership on Employee's innovative behavior: Mediating role of psychological empowerment', *ACM International Conference Proceeding Series*, pp. 223–229.

Monsen, E., Patzelt, H. and Saxton, T. (2010) 'Beyond simple utility: Incentive design and trade-offs for corporate employee-entrepreneurs', *Entrepreneurship: Theory and Practice*, 34(1), pp. 105–130.

Mustafa, M., Gavin, F. and Hughes, M. (2018) 'Contextual Determinants of Employee Entrepreneurial Behavior in Support of Corporate Entrepreneurship: A Systematic Review and Research Agenda', *Journal of Enterprising Culture*, 26(03), pp. 285–326.

Neessen, P. C. M. Caniëls, C.J., Vos, B. and de Jong, J. P. (2019) 'The intrapreneurial employee: toward an integrated model of intrapreneurship and research agenda', *International Entrepreneurship and Management Journal*. International Entrepreneurship and Management Journal, 15(2), pp. 545–571.

Ogliastri, E., Altschul, C. and Dorfman, P. W. (1999) 'Culture and Organizational Leadership in 10 Latin American Countries', *Academia: Revista Latinoamericana de Administración*, 22, pp. 29–57.

Orchard, S., Ribiere, V. and Achtzehn, D. (2018) 'The influence of the leader and led relationship on the intrapreneurship environment in UK SMEs', *Academy of Entrepreneurship Journal*, 24(3), pp. 1–20.

Richman, A. L. Civian, J. T., Shannon, L., Jeffrey Hill, E., and Brennan, R. T. (2008) 'The relationship of perceived flexibility, supportive work-life policies, and use of formal flexible arrangements and occasional flexibility to employee engagement and expected retention', *Community, Work and Family*, 11(2), pp. 183–197.

Singh, M. and Sarkar, A. (2012) 'The relationship between psychological empowerment and innovative behavior: A dimensional analysis with job involvement as mediator', *Journal of Personnel Psychology*, 11(3), pp. 127–137.

Srivastava, N. and Agrawal, A. (2010) 'Factors Supporting Corporate Entrepreneurship: An Exploratory Study', *Vision: The Journal of Business Perspective*, 14(3), pp. 163–171.

Urban, B. and Wood, E. (2017) 'The innovating firm as corporate entrepreneurship', *European Journal of Innovation Management*, 20(4), pp. 534–556.

Vadnjal, J. (2014) 'Innovative business growth strategy: Introduction of corporate entrepreneurship', *Actual Problems of Economics*, 157(7), pp. 304–314.

Verma, S. and Mehta, M. (2020) 'Effect of Leadership Styles on Corporate Entrepreneurship: A Critical Literature Review.', *Organization Development Journal*, 38(2), pp. 65–74. Available at: http://search.ebscohost.com/login.aspx?direct=true&db=bsu&AN=143053987&amp%0Alang=pt-pt&site=eds-live&authtype=sso.

Zakaria, Z., Shamsuddin, S., Othman, J. and Shahadan, M. (2012) 'The dimensions of corporate entrepreneurship and the performance of established organization', *ACRN Journal of Entrepreneurship Perspectives*, 1(2), pp. 111–131.

Student Entrepreneurial Identity Formation: The Role of Reflection

Birgitte Wraae[1] and Andreas Walmsley[2]
[1]Finance and Administration, UCL University College Denmark, Denmark
[2]International Centre for Transformational Entrepreneurship, Coventry University, UK
biwr@ucl.dk
ad3412@coventry.ac.uk
DOI: 10.34190/EIE.20.064

Abstract: The overall aim of this empirical paper is to contribute to the understanding of how students through video clips and narration develop their entrepreneurial identities. Literature on entrepreneurial identity development is regularly linked to either identity theory or social identity theory. Identity theory relates to the notion of roles that an individual assumes. In entrepreneurship education students are in a transition period between roles, i.e. role transformation from student to entrepreneur and/or professional. Furthermore, existing literature suggests how students can both develop and have an entrepreneurial identity while not necessarily starting up a business. Identity formation is further supported by the narrative the student creates with regard to their selves as the student engages in a form of dialogue with themselves but also with others as part of the entrepreneurial learning process. Upon this backdrop, this study proposes the following problem statement: "How can student self-insights assist with their entrepreneurial identity development journey?" To tackle this question, we analysed 51 student video clips after students had participated in an entrepreneurship course. Our findings support the theory of identity formation relating to the concept of roles: the self-reflective video clip as a form of assessment creates a means by which the students both raise their self-awareness and, crucially, construct their entrepreneurial identities. The results underline that students' entrepreneurial identities are formed in a social process and by what happens both inside and beyond the entrepreneurial classroom. These findings will be of interest to researchers and educators as it moves beyond a pure skills or competency approach of understanding the impact of entrepreneurship education.

Keywords: entrepreneurship education, student identity development, entrepreneurial identity formation, entrepreneurial career development, higher education

1. Introduction

Identity development is part of Higher Education, making sense of the question "Who am I?" including whom they are going to become (Nielsen & Gartner, 2017). However, only fairly recently has the link between identity development and entrepreneurship education (EE) gained research interest (Nielsen & Gartner, 2017). In fact, early notions of entrepreneurship being associated with personality traits (McClelland, 1961) which fundamentally cannot be learned, but are instead inherited, went against the grain not only of EE but also the notion of entrepreneurial identity development. Instead, today, EE is viewed as a driver for identity construction (Duane Ireland & Webb, 2007). Here we explore how self-reflective video-clips might assist students on their identity exploration and subsequent entrepreneurial identity development.

2. Entrepreneurship education and identity formation

It is widely accepted that EE can be viewed from several different approaches; "About," "For," "Through" and "Embedded" (Jamieson, 1984; Pittaway and Edwards, 2012). Teaching entrepreneurship is often recognised as a subject where students have to accomplish and develop both practical and conceptual skills in order to cope with the complexity that is part of the entrepreneurial process of starting up a new business (Balan and Metcalfe, 2012; Gibb, 2002). Moreover, the students are expected to develop certain personal qualities (Fayolle et al., 2006).

3. Stimulating identity formation through reflection

To begin with, we recognize that identity represents different concepts and approaches (P. Greene & Brush, 2018; Pratt et al., 2006) as well as being a "multidimensional, multifaceted and complex construct..." (Varelas, 2012, p. 1). However, 'messy' it seems, it is nevertheless vital to understand identity as this is a necessary component in understanding the development of students, including learning and teaching (Varelas, 2012).

More specifically, identity is of interest to researchers because behaviour is affected by one's identity in the sense that the individual seeks to achieve congruence between their identity(ies) and the behaviour they exhibit. Entrepreneurial identity relates in this sense also to motivation and "what moves entrepreneurial "dreamers" to action" (Farmer et al., 2011, p. 245). This focus on motivation and identity's role in fostering it is particularly relevant given the number of individuals who have intent but fail to engage in nascent start-up behaviour

(Bogatyreva et al., 2019). Here Farmer et al. (2011) confirmed what Hoang and Gimeno (2010:4) suggested, that developing an entrepreneurial identity may "guide and motivate goal-oriented behaviour, often to the extent that a possible role becomes an actual one." Thus, entrepreneurial intent is not just of academic interest, but has practical importance if the desire of EE is to foster business start-up. Developing the individual's entrepreneurial identity is a means of fostering entrepreneurship.

Studies that focus on identity in EE are no longer novel, and yet much of the focus has been on what the identity is, rather than how it has been shaped (Donnellon et al. 2014). At the outset we acknowledge that the formation of an entrepreneurial identity could be quite challenging as traditionally identities have been recognized as fairly stable. There are voices now however (Guichard, Pouyaud, de Calan, & Dumora, 2012) that suggest that with the fluidity of modern societies (Bauman, 2000; Giddens, 1991) individuals today assume numerous identities that are more malleable, particularly exposed to experiences. This speaks in favour of education providing a means of developing, via experiences, an individual's identity. This is compounded by the fact that young adults tend to find themselves at a stage of career exploration and identity development (Savickas, 2002) (at least more so that more mature individuals).

Moving on to how EE relates to identity development, it has been suggested that what happens in the entrepreneurial classroom, can function as a driver for identity formation (Duane Ireland and Webb, 2007). Here, entrepreneurial identity formation can be viewed as both a complex and reflective process where each students is trying to answer the "Who am I?" question (Harmeling, 2011; Ollila et al., 2012).

Identity formation is also frequently associated with role transition. Ashforth et al. (2000) argue that we all experience daily shifts in our social roles. As such, is it reasonable to assume that this role transformation is an incorporated part of the student's everyday life as well. From a helicopter perspective the educational setting is a place where such role transitions take place. Granted, the students take on the role as students. But, the role of being a student includes, in the classical conception, to prepare for class, show up for lectures, take on an active or passive attitude, attend the exam or hand in something and finally get their grade after the exam. Focusing on the entrepreneurial learning space which we comprehend as what happens both inside and outside the entrepreneurial classroom certain expectations are linked to being a student. Here, the entrepreneurship educator expects the students to take an active role in terms of taking a profound responsibility for their own learning while transforming their entrepreneurial development during the course or their entrepreneurial journey as a part of a given entrepreneurial course. Thus, the students' experienced learning forms their identities. Therefore, students' entrepreneurial development is strongly linked to identity construction (Brush and Gale, 2015). The role of being a student includes "identity capital" that defines the students themselves, and least how others define them in different contexts (Varelas, 2012).

According to Nielsen and Gartner (Nielsen and Gartner, 2017) students will sense multiple identities as a part of being a student, which means that alongside their student identity, they may also assume other identities including an entrepreneurial identity. The sense of being an entrepreneur is influenced when the students are confronted with several tasks in relation to the entrepreneurial process as a part of EE (Nielsen & Gartner, 2017). We could say that entrepreneurial identity develops through EE, i.e. adopting typical tasks associated with business start-up. In EE the students are being transformed during the course which affects the sense of self Nielsen & Gartner, 2017).

It is worth noting that there can be an element of conflicting identities developing in HE. Thus, students can experience the university" as a deterministic occupational structure that transforms students and makes them commit to a pre-defined, work-taker, identity" (Nielsen & Gartner, 2017, p. 148) and, as such not entirely entrepreneurial. However, the universities can act in the role of safe entrepreneurial identity development environments if they wish to do so which begs the questions: how do we make a "safe" educational environment for identity development for the students (Nielsen and Gartner, 2017)?

To better understand entrepreneurial identity formation, we have gathered different perspective on entrepreneurial identity formation presented in table 1.

Table 1: Perspectives on entrepreneurial identity formation

Quote	Authors
"...there are several possible constellations of meanings which may form the core of the entrepreneur's self-definition of the entrepreneurial role".	(Stanworth and Curran, 1976, p. 104)
"...entrepreneurial identity can be defined as a person's inclination to adopt a certain type of occupational entrepreneurial role."	(Vesalainen and Pihkala, 2000, p. 113)
"The idea is that EE will lead to entrepreneurship as a spontaneous (natural) behavior."	(Holmgren and From, 2005, p. 386)
"...being an entrepreneur allows an individual to have extraordinary control and input- when compared to more 'traditional' vocations- in their formulation of self-identity."	(Shepherd and Haynie, 2009, pp. 321–322)
"...an entrepreneurial identity has two elements, identity as 'what', the categorical identity; and personal identity, 'who', which serves to differentiate one from the other."	(Anderson and Warren, 2011, p. 592)
"...identity is central to meaning, motivation, decision-making, and other activities that can be seen as critical for entrepreneurial action."	(Ollila et al., 2012, p. 2)
"...entrepreneurship programmes can serve as arenas for identity construction.... The participants are active agents in the creation of meanings..."	(Hytti and Heinonen, 2013, p. 887)
"... they are continuously in the process of finding out if they are, would like to and have what it takes to become an entrepreneur while balancing their present student identity with a possible entrepreneurial identity."	(Thrane et al., 2016, p. 910)
"...entrepreneurial identity may be seen as the host of self-referential claims and actions that are associated with launching and running new organizations."	(Crosina, 2018, p. 105)

No doubt EE has the potential to assist in students' entrepreneurial identity formation. The students themselves must perceive their own entrepreneurial role, and how it balances with other identities. Moreover, the students develop their sense of identity in groups being a member of the entrepreneurial learning space. Students are therefore formed in a social process interacting with their educator, their student peers and what happens in the entrepreneurial learning space and at the educational facilities as well (Gergen, 2015; Kolb and Kolb, 2005; Nielsen and Gartner, 2017). But the students must also be able to look beyond the classroom and reflect on themselves in a future job-related perspective and how they will act either as entrepreneurs or intrapreneurs. Following this line of argument, we believe that EE acts as an 'opportunity arena' that allows each student both the space and opportunity to "become" someone. Thus, we derive:" Entrepreneurial identity formation is to give each student a sense of belonging. Student entrepreneurial identity is central to meaning, motivation, and decision-making. Entrepreneurship education can serve as arenas for entrepreneurial identity construction where the participants are active agents in the creation of meanings" (Donnellon et al., 2014; Ollila et al., 2012).

So, in order for students to develop their entrepreneurial development, reflection can act as the tool to do so:

"learning is developed into knowledge through reflecting on the experiences gained through actions taken" (Hägg and Kurczewska, 2016, p. 708). As such, reflection is a necessary tool in the EE tool box to heighten more in-depth learning and critical thinking (Murray et al., 2017). As Bourner (2003) argues, reflection can be enhanced by simply asking the right questions. While, that seems as an easy and realistic tool, it could be further argued that reflection could be incorporated as an assisting assessment tool (Wraae et al., 2018).

"Teachers are conceived as 'coaches' and 'developers' – while students are seen as individuals who actively construct their knowledge through their interaction with their educator(s) and peers." (Béchard and Grégoire, 2007, pp. 264–265). We therefore see a link between the entrepreneurial educational processes in EE reflection as a tool to stimulated students entrepreneurial identity formation as depicted in figure 1.

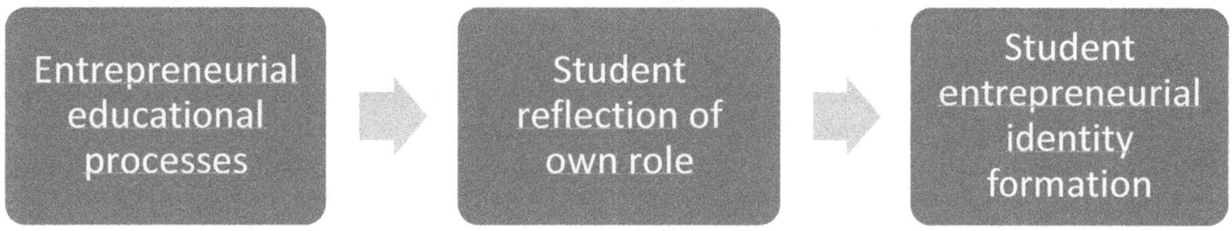

Source: Own depiction

Figure 1: The relationship between reflection in EE and identity formation

We will now move on to contribute to the understanding of the depicted relationship and how students through video clips and narration develop their entrepreneurial identities.

4. Methodology

To understand the identity formation of the students a qualitative study was chosen in the form of participatory storytelling (Gubrium and Harper, 2013). These stories took place via reflective video clips where students recounted stories of their own experiences and learning in an entre-/intrapreneurial perspective. We chose the narrative approach as this is known to support student reflection (Gubrium et al., 2014) that assist students in their identity formation and understanding (Hägg and Kurczewska, 2016).

The data were collected in spring 2017 in a Danish non-business class at a university of applied sciences. Students had chosen an elective unit containing innovation and entrepreneurship only. The teaching on this elective unit is planned and executed around "a transformative experience for the learner whereby not only knowledge but also skills, attitudes and identity are affected" (Svensson et al., 2017, p. 4). As a part of the exam, the students were instructed to create a short (2-3 minute) video clip where they talked about "Me as an entrepreneur or intrapreneur." The students had received both oral and written instruction for this task. The video clip was made individually and only the educator (at the same time educator and researcher) could see the clip. Although not formally graded, it was mandatory to hand in the video clip, which served as a precondition for access to an oral exam. Students could choose not to have their data included in the research project, although all students were happy to be included in the study (all data relating to the students' stories has been anonymized and students were informed of this prior to agreeing to participate). In total 58 students handed in a video clip with their stories.

As two students chose not to participate 56 individual video clips (N=56) were used in the research project. Since our overall research approach was both explorative and inductive so were our analytical approach as we let the data guide us (Saunders et al., 2012). Therefore, the video clips were not fully transcribed but instead we made summaries of each interview which were compiled alongside direct quotes where we felt these expressed an idea in a succinct, and meaningful form. An excel analysis scheme with key themes or criteria was created (Dana and Dana, 2005). We counted 17 different subjects, that the students talked about. We tried to categorise those into themes, for instance the entrepreneurial process, attitude towards becoming an entrepreneur before/after participation in the course and the meaning of family and upbringing and own role.

We acknowledge the danger of students providing what they deemed socially desirable responses, especially where they felt they might be able to please the educator (Blenker et al., 2014). However, most students seemed to be in their own world when they started talking so it reasonable to assume that not to be the case and the video-clip exercise was not tied to a graded assignment.

5. Results

Our first insight emerging from the videos and that we highlight here is students' unfamiliarity with the concepts of entrepreneurship and innovation, but their openness to them. Thus, for many of this group of students working with innovation and entrepreneurship appears remote. Nevertheless, many students have chosen the elective unit precisely because they acknowledge that the Danish public sector is under economic pressure and they acknowledge that the competences offered in the module are necessary for their own jobs but also for work more generally. Not surprisingly, it also emerged that many of the students chose the module for convenience reasons (e.g. it fit into their timetables, it was the most interesting of a range of options, their study group had chosen it etc.). As such, students enter the entrepreneurship classroom with different motives and backgrounds (Jones and Matlay, 2011; Neck and Greene, 2011).

Many video clips begin with an explanation of how each student perceives entrepreneurship and what it takes to become an entrepreneur. So, we witness the students' movement towards an understanding of entrepreneurship as both a concept (learning about entrepreneurship) and a possibility (learning for entrepreneurship). Students also describe which skills they believe are necessary to become an entrepreneur. Some students even discuss the 'born' or 'made' perspectives (Drucker, 2007; Nielsen et al., 2012) and how they acknowledge, that they probably are 'made' entrepreneurs as a result of participating in the course. This indeed refers to Gartner's (1985) conceptual model and how entrepreneurs are a product of situational conditioned dimensions. This links to students commenting how: "The surroundings have given me a drive" or "I need someone to trigger it". A few students, often those with an entrepreneurial family member, use the 'born' perspective to explain that entrepreneurship runs in the blood.

We believe that this introductory description in the video clips shows students building up a reflection on entrepreneurial formation. Later in the video clips we see, how students develop a sense of entrepreneurial identity. As such, we sense a development in their reflection on themselves in the entrepreneurial perspective.

It was interesting to note that in a society that extols enterprise and entrepreneurship, many students mentioned some reluctance towards entrepreneurship and an entrepreneurial career path before the elective course. However, all except one, talk about how becoming an entrepreneur could be an actual career path: "entrepreneurship is contagious" as one student says. Another student expresses how "The module has helped me to see how to reach the sky" while another has been surprised about how entrepreneurship education triggered something: "My mind got into gear".

Other students recognize, that while they might not be strictly entrepreneurial, they can see how entrepreneurship could be useful in an already existing organization as well: "I am definitely an intrapreneur". Many students mention intrapreneurship as a way to use their entrepreneurial skills in that setting. Also, for us, evidence that these reflections lead to identity formation.

The video clips showed an insight into how each student reflected on how the elective unit gave them a skill set, that they did not know they were able to use, but nevertheless did use. It is evident, that these reflections are happening while the students talk; the students transformation happened before our eyes viewing each video clip. Therefore, the video clip acts as a space for entrepreneurial identity formation (Svensson et al., 2017)

6. Discussion, conclusion and suggestions for further studies

The purpose with this paper was to answer the problem statement: "How can student self-insights assist students on their entrepreneurial identity development journey?" We have argued for a link between entrepreneurial educational processes, student reflection of own role – in this case video clips - and identity development as depicted in figure 1.

Overall, the reflective videos demonstrated a shift towards an entrepreneurial identity. As highlighted in the literature review, identities develop over time and thus we would not expect the students to throw existing identities as employees in the public sector entirely 'out of the window' and embrace wholesale an entrepreneurial identity. Nonetheless, we do recognize that for many students, the module could be the start of a journey of entrepreneurial identity formation. Surprisingly, to us, prior to undertaking the module students had not considered entrepreneurship as a career path and so the module served more as a means to raise awareness of entrepreneurship, than to strengthen existing positive attitudes towards it.

A further aspect that surprised us was students' chosen focus on whether it is possible to learn to become an entrepreneur. As entrepreneurship educators, this now feels something of an obsolete debate, and yet in the wider population the persistence of the notion that you are either born and entrepreneur or not could still be quite prevalent.

To counter the dated view of the possibility of learning to become and entrepreneur, students were aware of the wider societal discourses surrounding entrepreneurship, with application of this found within organisations (intrapreneurship) but also to individual's careers. Here then, this sample of public sector employees who might traditionally be regarded as having jobs at least at risk, did nonetheless acknowledge what academics have been writing about for at least two decades in terms of the fluidity of modern life (Bauman, 2000; Giddens, 1991), and within this careers (Arthur and Rousseau, 2001; Guichard et al., 2012; Hall, 2004).

With regard to recommendations for entrepreneurship educators, as a means to stimulating reflection with implications for identity formation we strongly recommend the use of reflective videos. Here we recognize the need to provide sufficient guidelines to permit in-depth reflection to occur. We also recognize that these guidelines should not be too restrictive. A balance must be sought between supporting reflection but without constraining it unnecessarily.

We also recommend firstly not to assume a 'level playing field' when it comes to students' awareness of entrepreneurship. Our cohort were not 'typical' beneficiaries of entrepreneurship education understood as youth on an undergraduate programme. Being more mature individuals, our assumption was a greater degree of familiarity with entrepreneurship and also having considered being an entrepreneur. Here though, many of the cohort appreciated the opportunity the programme had provided them to consider entrepreneurship as career option. Thus, student reflection empowers students to understand their own identity and identity creation. This includes students' awareness of the shift in their different identities; leaving something and moving towards something new is thus a transformation in student understanding of themselves.

Further studies could pursue entrepreneurial identity formation with non-standard cohorts such as ours. Further research could use video clips in a more extensive way (longer reflective videos, potentially even over a period of time) than ours (which was also a potential limitation of our study). There is even some scope for experimentation with different set up of video tasks and establishment of impacts on the individual. Overall, despite the growing literature on entrepreneurial identity, there is still much scope to examine how different educational tools can support it, and in our case, might act as a trigger for entrepreneurial identity development.

Finally, in lieu of the COVID-19 crisis and the educational processes going online, it would be highly relevant to investigate how or if online learning creates the same sense of identity formation than the traditional classroom? We suggest using video clips as the reflective tool to be able to identity differences.

References

Anderson, A.R., Warren, L. (2011) "The entrepreneur as hero and jester: Enacting the entrepreneurial discourse", International Small Business Journal 29, pp. 589–609.

Arthur, M., Rousseau, M., (2001) The Boundaryless Career: A New Employment Principle for a New Organizational Era, New Ed edition. ed. Oxford University Press USA, Oxford.

Ashforth, B.E., Kreiner, G.E., Fugate, M. (2000) "All in a Day's Work: Boundaries and Micro Role Transitions", The Academy of Management Review 25, pp. 472–491.

Balan, P., Metcalfe, M. (2012) "Identifying teaching methods that engage entrepreneurship students", Education + Training 54, pp. 368–384.

Bauman, Z. (2000) Liquid modernity. Polity Press ; Blackwell, Cambridge, UK : Malden, MA.

Béchard, J.-P., Grégoire, D. (2007) Archetypes of pedagogical innovation for entrepreneurship in higher education: model and illustrations, in: Fayolle, A. (Ed.), Handbook of Research in Entrepreneurship Education, Volume 1 A General Perspective. Edward Elgar, Cheltenham, UK ; Northampton, MA, p. 311.

Blenker, P., Trolle Elmholdt, S., Hedeboe Frederiksen, S., Korsgaard, S., Wagner, K. (2014) "Methods in entrepreneurship education research: a review and integrative framework", Education + Training 56, pp. 697–715.

Bogatyreva, K., Edelman, L.F., Manolova, T.S., Osiyevskyy, O., Shirokova, G. (2019), "When do entrepreneurial intentions lead to actions? The role of national culture", Journal of Business Research 96, 309–321.

Bourner, T., 2003. Assessing reflective learning. Education + Training 45, pp. 267–272.

Brush, C.G., Gale, M. (2015) Becoming Entrepreneurial: Constructing an Entrepreneurial Identity in Elective Entrepreneurship Courses, in: Crittenden, V.L., Esper, K., Slegers, R., Karst, N. (Eds.), Evolving Entrepreneurial Education: Innovation in the Babson Classroom. Emerald Group Publishing Limited, UK, pp. 305–322.
Crosina, E. (2018) On becoming an entrepreneur: unpacking entrepreneurial identity, in: Greene, P., Brush, C.G. (Eds.), A Research Agenda for Women and Entrepreneurship, Elgar Research Agendas. Edward Elgar Publishing.
Dana, L.P., Dana, T.E., (2005) "Expanding the scope of methodologies used in entrepreneurship research", International Journal of Entrepreneurship and Small Business 2, 79.
Donnellon, A., Ollila, S., Middleton, K.W. (2014) "Constructing entrepreneurial identity in entrepreneurship education", The International Journal of Management Education 12, pp. 490–499.
Drucker, P.F. (2007) Innovation and entrepreneurship. Practice and principles, Revised ed. ed, The classic Drucker collection. Elsevier/Butterworth-Heinemann, Amsterdam.
Duane Ireland, R., Webb, J.W. (2007) "A Cross-Disciplinary Exploration of Entrepreneurship Research", Journal of Management 33, pp. 891–927.
Farmer, S.M., Yao, X., Kung–Mcintyre, K. (2011) "The Behavioral Impact of Entrepreneur Identity Aspiration and Prior Entrepreneurial Experience", Entrepreneurship Theory and Practice 35, pp. 245–273.
Fayolle, A., Gailly, B., Lassas-Clerc, N. (2006) "Assessing the impact of entrepreneurship education programmes: a new methodology", Journal of European Industrial Training 30, pp. 701–720.
Gartner, W.B. (1985) "A Conceptual Framework for Describing the Phenomenon of New Venture Creation", The Academy of Management Review 10, 696.
Gergen, K.J. (2015) An Invitation to Social Construction, 3 edition. ed. Sage Publications Ltd, Los Angeles, CA.
Gibb, A. (2002) "In pursuit of a new 'enterprise' and 'entrepreneurship' paradigm for learning: creative destruction, new values, new ways of doing things and new combinations of knowledge", International Journal of Management Reviews 4, pp. 233–269.
Giddens, A. (1991) Modernity and Self-Identity: Self and Society in the Late Modern Age. Stanford University Press, Standford, CA.
Gubrium, A.C., Harper, K. (2013) Participatory Visual and Digital Methods, Developing Qualitative Inquiry. Routledge, New York.
Gubrium, A.C., Hill, A.L., Flicker, S. (2014) A situated practice of ethics for participatory visual and digital methods in public health research and practice: A focus on digital storytelling. American Journal of Public Health 104, pp. 1606–1614.
Guichard, J., Pouyaud, J., de Calan, C., Dumora, B. (2012) "Identity construction and career development interventions with emerging adults", Journal of Vocational Behavior 81, pp. 52–58.
Hägg, G., Kurczewska, A. (2016) "Connecting the dots: A discussion on key concepts in contemporary entrepreneurship education", Education + Training 58, pp. 700–714.
Hall, D.T. (2004) The protean career: A quarter-century journey. Journal of Vocational Behavior 65, 1–13.
Harmeling, S.S. (2011) "Re-storying an entrepreneurial identity: education, experience and self-narrative", Education + Training 53, pp. 741–749.
Holmgren, C., From, J. (2005) "Taylorism of the mind: entrepreneurship education from a perspective of educational research", European Educational Research Journal 4, pp. 382–390.
Hytti, U., Heinonen, J. (2013) "Heroic and humane entrepreneurs: identity work in entrepreneurship education", Education + Training 55, pp. 886–898.
Jamieson, I. (1984) Education for Enterprise, in: Watts, A.G., Moran, P. (Eds.), Education for Enterprise. CRAC, Ballinger, Cambridge.
Jones, C., Matlay, H. (2011) "Understanding the heterogeneity of entrepreneurship education: going beyond Gartner", Education + Training 53, pp. 692–703.
Kolb, A.Y., Kolb, D.A. (2005) "Learning Styles and Learning Spaces: Enhancing Experiential Learning in Higher Education", Academy of Management Learning & Education 4, pp. 193–212.
McClelland, D.C. (1961) The achieving society. Van Nostrand, New York.
Murray, E.L., Neck, H.M., Neck, D.C.P. (2017) Entrepreneurship: The Practice and Mindset, 1 edition. ed. SAGE Publications, Inc, Los Angeles.
Neck, H.M., Greene, P.G. (2011) "Entrepreneurship education: known worlds and new frontiers", Journal of Small Business Management 49, pp. 55–70.
Nielsen, S.L., Gartner, W.B. (2017) "Am I a student and/or entrepreneur? Multiple identities in student entrepreneurship", Education + Training 59, pp. 135–154.
Nielsen, S.L., Klyver, K., Evald, M.R. (2012) Entrepreneurship in Theory and Practice: Paradoxes in Play. Edward Elgar Publishing.
Ollila, S., Middleton, K.W., Donnellon, A. (2012) "Entrepreneurial Identity Construction – what does existing literature tell us?", Presented at the Institute of Small Business and Annual Entrepreneurship Conference, Ireland.
Pittaway, L., Edwards, C. (2012) "Assessment: examining practice in entrepreneurship education", Education + Training 54, pp. 778–800.
Saunders, M.N.K., Lewis, P., Thornhill, A. (2012) Research Methods for Business Students, 6 edition. ed. Financial Times/ Prentice Hall, Harlow, England ; New York.
Savickas, M.L. (2002) Career Construction: A Developmental Theory of Vocational Behavior, in: Brown, D., And Associates (Eds.), Career Choice and Development. Jossey-Bass, San Francisco, pp. 149–205.

Shepherd, D., Haynie, J.M. (2009) "Birds of a feather don't always flock together: Identity management in entrepreneurship", Journal of Business Venturing 24, pp. 316–337.

Stanworth, M.J.K., Curran, J. (1976) Growth and the Small Firm - an Alternative View. Journal of Management Studies 13, 95–110.

Svensson, O.H., Lundqvist, M., Middleton, K.W. (2017) "Transformative, Transactional and Transmissive Modes of Teaching in Action-based Entrepreneurial Education", Presented at the ECSB Entrepreneurship Education (3E) Conference, Cork Ireland, p. 15.

Thrane, C., Blenker, P., Korsgaard, S., Neergaard, H. (2016) "The promise of entrepreneurship education: Reconceptualizing the individual–opportunity nexus as a conceptual framework for entrepreneurship education", International Small Business Journal 34, pp. 905–924.

Varelas, M. (Ed.), (2012) Identity construction and science education research: learning, teaching and being in multiple contexts, Bold visions in educational research. Sense Publishers, Rotterdam Boston Taipei.

Vesalainen, J., Pihkala, T. (2000) "Entrepreneurial Identity, Intentions and the Effect of the Push-Factor", international Journal of Entrepreneurship 4, pp. 104–129.

Wraae, B., Tigerstedt, C., Kratzer, J. (2018) "Introducing Student Self-assessment as a New Assessment tool in Entrepreneurship Education", Journal of Higher Education Theory and Practice 18. pp. 86-101.

Developing Innovative Activity Management Tools as a way to Increase the Market Capitalization of an Industrial Enterprise

Andrey Zaytsev, Nikolay Dmitriev and Yuliya Asaturova
Peter the Great Saint-Petersburg Polytechnic University, Russian Federation
zajtsev.aa@spbstu.ru
ndmitriev1488@gmail.com
asaturova_yum@spbstu.ru
DOI: 10.34190/EIE.20.091

Abstract: The trends towards transformation of the world economy from a material sphere to a non-material one bring about the need to search for new opportunities for carrying out analysis of innovative activity in the context of how it influences the market value of an enterprise as one of the major indicators of successful business. Fast introduction of innovations in production, development of scientific and technical progress, unstable behavior of the stock market and growing international integration of business processes precondition the importance of developing the existing methods of assessment of efficiency of an industrial enterprise based on the dynamics of its capitalization, which considers the interests of many stakeholders. The authors believe that innovative activity is an integral factor of stable development from the strategic point of view at all levels of management. This research study analyzes the impact of increased innovative activity on the market value of an industrial enterprise with an aim of managing its dynamics. A logical chain for developing a strategy of capitalization management was built and the place of innovation management in it was defined. A mechanism was proposed for forming the market value through changing the innovation potential of an enterprise. Based on the performed analysis, some tools were selected to estimate the integral indicator of innovative development of an enterprise for its further use in a regression model to find out how it influences the capitalization and economic value added. This modelling helps to assess what impact innovative processes have on the total value and to develop guidelines for managing its dynamics. The practical relevance of the research study is in the ability to forecast the level of innovative activity for a certain period of time to ensure growth of the market value, and its possible reduction in case innovative activity is insufficient. Further research is planned to be aimed at testing the obtained model for concrete enterprises and some sectors of the economy.

Keywords: capitalization, market value, innovative activity, intellectual capital, economic value added, innovative activity, innovative development

1. Introduction

The market conditions in which economic agents operate are characterized by the presence of risk and considerable uncertainty. The key significance is attributed to such indicators as the value of an enterprise, its stability and dynamics of economic development. The above indicators are influenced by various externalities and internalities, which have to be studied to make economic activity as effective as possible in strategic prospect (Demidenko et al, 2018a).

The purpose of any enterprise is a steady growth, which enables stable operation. The relevance of this problem today is confirmed by an instable geopolitical situation, growing processes of globalization and international integration, presence of macroeconomic disproportions and other crisis phenomena. Even in case of economic stability, which is only possible in abstract terms, the matters related to a steady growth will be of high priority, since they are directly related to taking rational decisions, planning economic activity and selecting a long-term strategy.

The following factors make an impact on the steady growth and dynamics of the market value of industrial enterprises (Huseynov, 2013; Demidenko et al, 2018b), (Selentyeva et al., 2019):

- level of technological development of production processes;
- raw material base for production activity;
- structure of capital assets, degree of their use;
- degree of intellectualization of the enterprise and quality of human resources;
- diversification of production processes.

These factors depend on the activity of an enterprise. Without intensifying innovative activity, it is virtually impossible to achieve a steady growth. Innovations represent the most promising types of change and contribute a lot to maximizing the effect from economic activity.

Innovation is a result of a meaningful activity manifested as output of new products, services, technologies, forms and methods of management. They are the bottom line of an innovative process while the presence of novelty is determined and captured by consumers (Turgaev, 2013; Kichigin et al, 2019).

In this study, innovations are seen as a basic element of steady growth of an agent, and there is an assumption that they have a considerable impact on its market value.

Innovative activity in the time of geopolitical instability, which is common for many developing countries, including Russia, is especially difficult. Innovative developments in the Russian economy led to its integration into the world markets while many management models have not transformed to a full extent and non-market conditions do not allow us to use standardized criteria for performance assessment (Ivanov, Baranov, 2011; Balashova, Gromova, 2017).

The market value of industrial enterprises in developing countries is a lot lower than in the developed ones. It is not only due to the efficiency of production processes, but also to a high level of intellectual rent, which is an outcome of innovative development. Advancement on both developed and developing markets calls for substantial investment into intellectual elaborations, which, if used effectively, can considerably increase the market value (Akhmetshin et al, 2018; Degtereva et al, 2019, Kozlov et al, 2019).

In the Russian economy, industrial enterprises increase their profits due to monopolization of the market, incentives and tax deduction envisaged for companies with a large share of the state, and for the so-called "pseudo-public" companies, which are controlled by the state only legally, but in fact are a means of enrichment for those groups of people who are close to government bodies. Such a position is wrong and leads to little increase in capitalization, lower competitiveness of both an enterprise, and the sector on the global market, and it does not meet public interests, making social unrest grow. It has to be realized that an increase in the company value and its transfer to a long-term steady growth are primarily related to the implementation of investment projects aimed at modernization, technological upgrade and creation of product innovations.

The purpose of the research is to build a model for managing the market capitalization of an industrial enterprise through regulating innovative activity by means of mathematical simulation.

The following objectives have to be fulfilled:

- to analyze the existing research studies in market value management;
- to build a chain of capitalization management strategy and find out the place for management of innovative activity in it;
- to propose a mechanism for forming the market value based on the development of the innovation potential of the industrial enterprise;
- to find out the key indicators, showing the market capitalization of the enterprise;
- to form a model for assessing the level of innovative development of the industrial enterprise and determine the ways to find the general integral indicator of innovative activity;
- to present an algorithm for performing a correlation-regression analysis, considering innovative activity as a variable and market capitalization as a resulting indicator.

The subject of the research is a system of economic relations emerging when the market value of innovatively active enterprises is formed.

The scientific novelty of the study implies that a strategy is developed to manage the market value of industrial enterprises based on the regulation of their innovative activity.

The practical relevance of the work is in the authors' methodology, which can be used as a basis for drawing up guidelines for managing innovative development. The built model allows us to understand the nature of the value created by individual innovative components and regulate them to influence capitalization.

2. Methodological aspects of managing the market value of an enterprise

The essence and significance of the market value and how it is influenced by innovative activity was studied as early as in the previous century, for example, in works by D. Hay and D. Morris (1979). The researchers claimed that innovative interaction of a company with the environment lets it gain additional competitive advantages. Thus, introducing innovations can solve many important tasks, including financial ones, and ensure growth both in the asset value and the enterprise value.

V. Daskovsky and V. Kisilev (2011) consider enterprise value in terms of investment performance. In their opinion, there should be a rational correlation between the balance value of a company, which is a difference between the total value of assets and total liabilities, and the market value, which is the most probable price at which the company can be sold. Under such conditions, the goal of an enterprise is to make the market value exceed the balance one, and in order to achieve this, innovative activity has to be practiced.

T. Copeland, T. Koller and J. Murrin (1999) studied the processes of managing the value of an economic agent as a totality of innovative methods and processes aimed at maximizing the value of the company through focusing managerial decision-making on the most significant factors of adding value.

In the context of company value management, R.S. Kaplan and D.P. Norton (2001) defined the basic purpose of management as the owners' increased wealth through maximization of the market value, which calls for considerable investments in innovative development.

The views of the scientific community on management of an enterprise have transformed considerably over the last decades because new methods were introduced to organize and manage production processes and these methods are capable of adapting to the changing conditions of the external environment. One of the most important criteria of performance of business operations is the indicator of market value. For capitalization maximization in innovative economy, a logical chain for developing a capitalization management strategy has to be built. The authors' example of such a chain is illustrated in Figure 1.

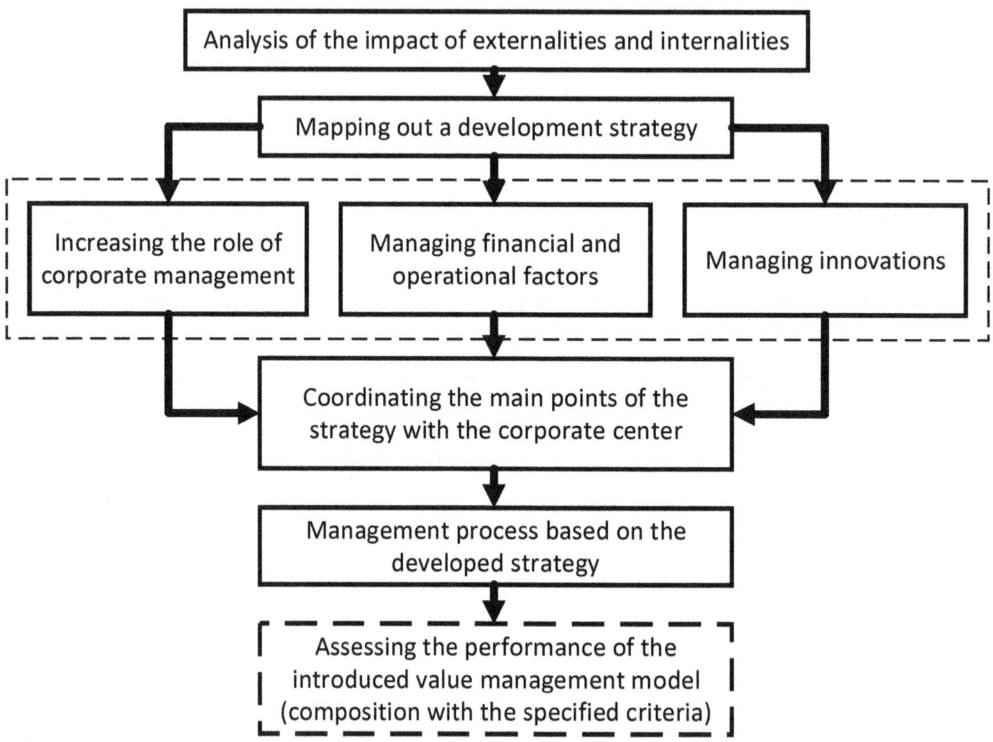

Source: Compiled by the authors based on (Huseynov, 2013; Turgaev, 2013; Demidenko et al, 2018b)

Figure 1: Logical chain for developing a capitalization management strategy

The suggested algorithm implies taking subsequent steps based on which the development strategy is mapped out thanks to improved corporate management, management of financial and operational factors and innovation management. Further research is planned to be aimed at analyzing the potential impact that other components have on market value management and their interaction including external factors related to government financial policy (Stetsyunich et al, 2019).

Market value can be increased using a number of ways. The main internality is rational distribution of cash flows. Effective organization of cash flow management in the enterprise is an important indicator of its "financial well-being", and a prerequisite that can ensure a high growth and achievement of high performance indicators (Gorbunova et al, 2019). These factors can be estimated and optimized. It is much more difficult to estimate externalities, which are related to innovative activity and depend on the investment policy of the entity (Nikolova et al, 2017; Krasyuk et al, 2018; Polyakova et al, 2019).

D.S. Demidenko et al (2018a; 2018b) studied capitalization management methods, considering digitalization processes and the need for innovative renewal of the economy. Considering the standpoints of the authors such as B.M. Huseynov (2013), S.N. Yashin, Y.S. Soldatova (2013a; 2013b), E.M. Kiseleva et al (2017), V.A. Dergaeva (2019), it can be concluded that innovation projects have a direct impact on the change in the value and represent a set of actions aimed at conducting R&D, production, organizational, financial and other work. Any innovation projects are investments. They require capital expenditure, and their implementation is connected to a long recuperation period and high risk, but, in the long run, they contribute to increased cash flows due to the realization of products at higher prices, reduced self-cost, and bigger competitiveness of the legal entity (Krasyuk et al, 2018).

So, a market value management mechanism relying on the use of the company innovation capital is proposed. This mechanism is illustrated in Figure 2.

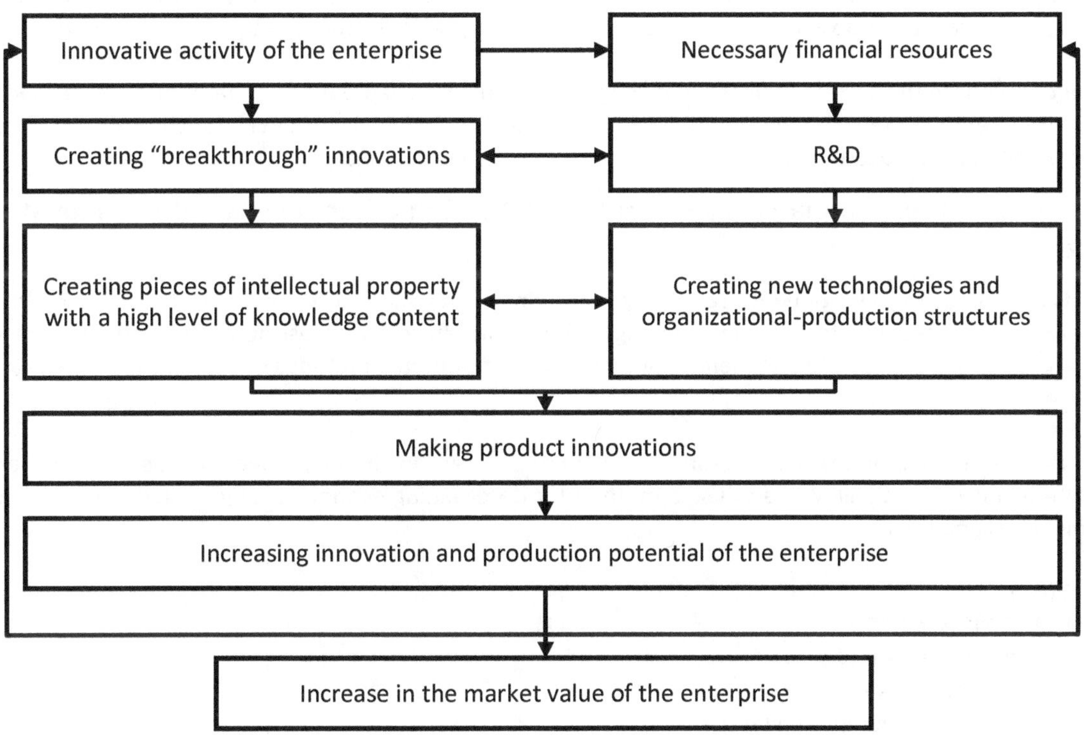

Source: compiled by the authors on the basis of (Ivanov, Baranov, 2011; Nikolova et al, 2017)

Figure 2: Market value formation mechanism based on the development of the enterprise's innovation capital

Intensification of innovative activity contributes to creating "breakthrough" innovations, whose principal distinction is the emergence of new pieces of intellectual property with a high level of knowledge content. Apart from innovations, R&D, production, marketing and other work has to be carried out, which increases financial costs. An enterprise focused on innovative activity has to ensure an increase in production potential (Kiseleva et al, 2017).

In the works by L. Cohen, K. Diether and C. Malloy (2013), innovative activity is considered to be a total capital aimed at development, or, in other words, innovation capital. Innovation capital is measured as a totality of expenses on R&D, staff retraining, transformation of the production system. The availability of innovation capital means that high quality products are being created and the living standard of the population is growing. It positively influences business and produces a social effect, which has a great significance for a steady growth in the developed countries.

J.K. Chen and I.S. Chen (2008) consider the following indicators of innovation capital:

- 1. RD / Sales is the ratio of total research and development costs to total sales of the enterprise. If there is no R&D data, it is recommended to use the average indicator for the sector.
- 2. EmpRate is the quantity of staff involved in innovative processes.
- 3. InnProdNew is the ratio of sales of products obtained as a result of innovative activity.
- 4. InnProdModif is the ratio of sales of modified and changed products (changed over the past 3 years).
- 5. PatentAppScaled is the number of patent claims adjusted for the average level of the year.

It can be concluded that innovations are a crucial indicator of a steady growth and market value increase in the digital economy, since they can form the prices of shares and make the asset value go up.

Considering the interaction of innovative activity and market value in the Russian context, it is worth noting that many sectors of the economy experience difficulties in forming the resources for innovative development and intensifying digitalization processes (Dmitriev, Zaytsev, 2019).

While innovative actions can be measured quantitatively, it is practically impossible to analyze the impact of an innovation project or a set of projects on the market value in quantitative terms. In order to develop a model of factor dependence it is proposed to determine the general integral indicator of innovative development.

Economic analysis in the system of financial management can be carried out using mathematical methods that allow us to determine numeric parameters (Morozova et al, 2017). In this research study it is proposed to use mathematical tools to build the model, namely, correlation-regression analysis.

3. Developing tools for managing market capitalization based on intensified innovative activity

Methods of innovation management used today in the time of digital transformation of the economy have to consider a lot of factors, for example, change in the structure of investments and the processes of intellectualization that need to be implemented. Thus, using traditional methods of capitalization management is not enough.

The market value of an industrial enterprise is estimated based on the economic analysis and principles of corporate finances, which allows us to use a method for determining economic value added (EVA), calculated by formulas (1) and (2):

$$EVA = IC\,(ROI - WACC), \quad (1)$$
$$EVA = NOPAT - IC \times WACC, \quad (2)$$

where IC is the investment capital;
ROI is the return on invested capital;
WACC is the weighted average capital cost;
NOPAT is the net operating profit after tax, but before interest is paid on the borrowed funds.

Economic value added reflects the economic profit an industrial enterprise gains from its operations. A universal appraisal of business based on this indicator characterizes the quality of managerial decisions and allows us to create models for managing this value (Brigham, Gapenski, 2017).

The value of the indicator determines the behavior of the legal entity's owners in relation to the organization of investment projects. Table 1 illustrates the essence of the EVA indicator for business.

Table 1: EVA content for business

EVA	Content
= 0	The market value of the enterprise is equal to the balance value of its net assets. The gain of the owners in case they invest into such an enterprise is 0.
> 0	The market value of the enterprise exceeds the balance value of its net assets. The enterprise is effective and the owners can yield additional profits from investments.
< 0	The market value of the enterprise is less than the balance value, which means that business is run ineffectively. The owners lose some of their capital as a result of no alternative return on investment.

Source: Compiled by the authors on the basis of (Yakubovich, 2005; Brigham, Gapenski, 2017)

In addition, the indicator can be decomposed and, thus, the effectiveness of individual business units can be assessed. The EVA indicator can be integrated in the system of control and motivation of the enterprise, which will have an impact on the objectivity of managerial decisions (Yakubovich, 2005). This fact means that the problem can be further investigated taking into account specific business units in the company.
The market value of the enterprise is in the following dependence:

$$V = f\,[IC, PV(EVA)], \qquad (3)$$

where V is the market value of the enterprise;
PV(EVA) is the present EVA.

It is assumed in the study that the EVA indicator can be referred to innovative activity. Using capitalization as a resulting indicator can bring about incorrect results, so it is suggested that 3 resulting indicators should be used to build a regression model and correlate the obtained data:

- 1. V is the market value indicator as a key factor in determining the efficiency of the economic agent;
- 2. EVA is the indicator of economic valued added as a factor of successful business and a target indicator for the enterprise;
- 3. EVA/V is the share of economic value added in the general market capitalization as the most important indicator.

When practical calculations of the model are made, it is necessary to build up the dynamics for every indicator (EVA; V; EVA/V), which is presented in Table 2, where: (y1; y2; y3; y4; ... yn) is the time period; (No.1; No.2; ... No.m) is a concrete enterprise; (x_{11}; x_{12}; x_{13}; x_{14}; ... x_{1n}) is the dynamics of indicators for enterprise No.1 (calculated for every enterprise).

Table 2: Example of EVA, V, EVA/V dynamics

(EVA, V, EVA/V)	y1	y2	y3	y4	yn
No.1	x_{11}	x_{12}	x_{13}	x_{14}	x_{1n}
No.2	x_{21}	x_{22}	x_{23}	x_{24}	x_{2n}
No.m	x_{31}	x_{32}	x_{33}	x_{34}	x_{mn}

Source: Compiled by the authors

After the economic meaning of the above indicators is defined, they have to be compared to the value of the investment development level of specific enterprises.

An enterprise is an investment and financial system, which today cannot be developed without innovative activity. The level of innovative development is measured using special indicators, which ensures a comprehensive approach to the analysis of investment activity in the innovative processes of an economic agent. Developing a methodology for assessing the innovative activity of individual enterprises is one of the elements of effective distribution of financial and labor resources, which is characterized by the following statements (Marginson, 2019; Zaytsev et al, 2019), (Demidenko and Dubolazova, 2019):

- weak investigation into innovative processes using traditional economic approaches;

- an increasing need for creating the structures of innovative process management in the development strategy;
- insufficient number of ways to assess the intellectual capital of the enterprise;
- inability to measure the precise efficiency of innovation projects introducing radical innovations and the lack of clear understanding of the long-term effects from their introduction into business units;
- lack of unambiguity in revealing the factors creating market value;
- need for considering the significance of risk in more detail.

It can be stated that today there is no single indicator capable of measuring the level of innovative development of an enterprise. Scientific literature suggests considering this indicator using a system (Yakubovich, 2005; Asaturova, Khvatova, 2018). Table 3 lists a system of indicators that can be used to measure the level of innovative development.

Table 3: Performance indicators of the innovative development level

No.	Name	Formula	Content
1	Capital renewal coefficient	*K1 = FCs / FCa,* FCs is the value of regained fixed assets; FCa is the annual average value of fixed assets.	The assessment of the enterprise's innovative development level has to consider its ability for new production.
2	Investment activity performance coefficient	*K2 = Ri / Rt,* Ri is the revenue from investment activity; Rt is the total revenue.	Investment activity is the main indicator of the ability for innovative development.
3	Coefficient of available pieces of intellectual property	*K3 = IA / FA,* IA is the value of intangible assets; FA is the fixed assets.	The advantage of any economic entity is in the use of intellectual resources, which determine the prospects of the enterprise.
4	Investment activity indicator	*K4 = (CP + Pita + FIlt) / FA,* CP is the construction in progress; Pita is the income-bearing investments in tangible assets; FIlt is the long-term financial investments; FA is the fixed assets	A totality of investments into innovative renewal through modifying and improving property and into other economic entities.
5	Coefficient of innovative development financing	*K5 = VIia / Ia,* VIia is the volume of investments into intangible assets; Ia is the total volume of investment.	Innovative development of the industrial enterprise cannot be insured without investing into intangible assets.

Source: Compiled by the authors on the basis of (Yakubovich, 2005; Brigham, Gapenski, 2017)

The coefficient of innovative development financing is especially important for the Russian economy, which is due to the low innovative activity of industrial enterprises (Yashin, Soldatova, 2013a; Yashin, Soldatova 2013b). The totality of the innovative development indicators have to be considered in dynamics. An example for one enterprise is considered in Table 4, where (y_1; y_2; y_3; y_4; ... y_n) is the time period; (K1; K2; K3; K4; K5) is a concrete coefficient; (z_{11}; z_{12}; z_{13}; z_{14}; ... z_{1n}) is the dynamics of the first coefficient (calculated for every coefficient).

Table 4: Example of dynamics of the indicators

Indicator	y_1	y_2	y_3	y_4	y_n
K1	z_{11}	z_{12}	z_{13}	z_{14}	z_{1n}
K2	z_{21}	z_{22}	z_{23}	z_{24}	z_{2n}
K3	z_{31}	z_{32}	z_{33}	z_{34}	z_{3n}
K4	z_{41}	z_{42}	z_{43}	z_{44}	z_{4n}
K5	z_{51}	z_{52}	z_{53}	z_{54}	z_{5n}

Source: Compiled by the authors

The next step is to introduce the general integral indicator. This can be done if the weight of every individual indicator is calculated. It is calculated by formula:

$\Sigma K_e = \Sigma z_{ije} * p_i$ (4)

where p_i is the weighted importance of the indicators;
z_{ije} is the value of the given coefficient;
i is the indicator number;
j is the time period;
e is the number of the enterprise.

The weight of every indicator is calculated using an expert method. In further research, the author's methodology will be proposed to calculate the weight of the indicators considering their significance in the context of the impact they have on the resulting indicators of business activity, such as market value.

In order to compare the assessment results of the innovative development level of various enterprises for a specific year, we suggest using a subsequence demonstrated in Table 5, where (K1; K2; K3; K4; K5) is a concrete coefficient; (ΣK) is the general integral indicator; (p_1; p_2; p_3; p_4; p_5) is the weight of the indicator with $p_1 + p_2 + p_3 + p_4 + p_5 = 1$; (No.1; No.2; ... No.m) is the specific enterprise; ($z_{1y\,1} * p_1$; $z_{2y\,1} * p_2$; $z_{3y\,1} * p_3$; $z_{4y\,1} * p_4$; $z_{5y\,1} * p_5$) is the assessment of innovative development level of the first enterprise for every individual indicator (calculated for every enterprise); ΣK_{1y} is the general integral indicator for the first enterprise (calculated for every enterprise), with $z_{1y\,1} * p_1 + z_{2y\,1} * p_2 + z_{3y\,1} * p_3 + z_{4y\,1} * p_4 + z_{5y\,1} * p_5 = \Sigma K_{1y}$.

Table 5: Example of the results of the estimated level of innovative development for various enterprises for a specific year

Indicator	Weight	No.1	No.2	No.3	No.n
K1	p_1	$z_{1y\,1} * p_1$	$z_{1y\,2} * p_1$	$z_{1y\,3} * p_1$	$z_{1y\,n} * p_1$
K2	p_2	$z_{2y\,1} * p_2$	$z_{2y\,2} * p_2$	$z_{2y\,3} * p_2$	$z_{2y\,n} * p_2$
K3	p_3	$z_{3y\,1} * p_3$	$z_{3y\,2} * p_3$	$z_{3y\,3} * p_3$	$z_{3y\,n} * p_3$
K4	p_4	$z_{4y\,1} * p_4$	$z_{4y\,2} * p_4$	$z_{4y\,3} * p_4$	$z_{4y\,n} * p_4$
K5	p_5	$z_{5y\,1} * p_5$	$z_{5y\,2} * p_5$	$z_{5y\,3} * p_5$	$z_{5y\,n} * p_5$
ΣK	1	ΣK_{1y}	ΣK_{2y}	ΣK_{3y}	ΣK_{ny}

Source: Compiled by the authors

In order to build the regression model, the dynamics of the indicators has to be understood. The weight of each indicator can be determined statically or estimated for every year. The dynamics of change of the general integral indicator for various industrial enterprises is presented in Table 6, where (№1; №2; ... №m) is the concrete enterprise; (y1; y2; y3; y4; ... yn) is the time period; (ΣK_{11}; ΣK_{12}; ΣK_{13}; ΣK_{14}; ΣK_{1n}) is the dynamics of ΣK indicators for enterprise No.1 (calculated for every enterprise).

Table 6: Example of the changing dynamics of the general integral indicator for various industrial enterprises

	y1	y2	y3	y4	yn
No.1	ΣK_{11}	ΣK_{12}	ΣK_{13}	ΣK_{14}	ΣK_{1n}
No.2	ΣK_{21}	ΣK_{22}	ΣK_{23}	ΣK_{24}	ΣK_{2n}
No.3	ΣK_{31}	ΣK_{32}	ΣK_{33}	ΣK_{34}	ΣK_{3n}
No.m	ΣK_{m1}	ΣK_{m2}	ΣK_{m3}	ΣK_{m4}	ΣK_{mn}

Source: Compiled by the authors

It is suggested using the obtained indicators for regression analysis. The data are transposed from the table where the dynamics of the general integral indicator is considered for various industrial enterprises and from the table with the dynamics of EVA, V, EVA/V indicators. Table 7 presents the data for carrying out the regression.

Table 7: Data for the regression model for a concrete enterprise

Year	Y (EVA; V; EVA/V)	X (ΣK)
y1	x_{11}	ΣK_{11}
y2	x_{12}	ΣK_{12}
y3	x_{13}	ΣK_{13}
y4	x_{14}	ΣK_{14}
yn	x_{1n}	ΣK_{1n}

Source: compiled by the authors
Then every indicator has to be calculated:

$$Y\,(EVA) = a_{eva} * X\,(\Sigma K), \quad (5)$$
$$Y\,(V) = a_{v} * X\,(\Sigma K), \quad (6)$$
$$Y\,(EVA/V) = a_{EVA/V} * X\,(\Sigma K), \quad (7)$$

where Y (EVA; V; EVA/V) is the resulting indicator;
a_{eva}; a_{v}; $a_{EVA/V}$ are the regression coefficients;
X (ΣK) is the independent variable in a form of integral indicator of innovative activity.
In the end, it is recommended to choose the resulting indicator with the highest determination coefficient.

4. In conclusion

Maintaining competitiveness at a high level is an essential development goal of an economic agent. It is necessary to expand the ways of increasing market capitalization as one of the main indicators of efficiency of the agent. Special attention in this context should be drawn to innovative ways of raising value.

Considering the Russian aspect, it should be noted that the national economy is relatively young, which results in big problems when foreign methods are applied to assess the efficiency of business activity. Innovative and intellectual components allow economic agents to operate effectively and make it possible to increase the living standard. The mechanism forming competitive advantages of the national economy is demonstrated in Figure 3.

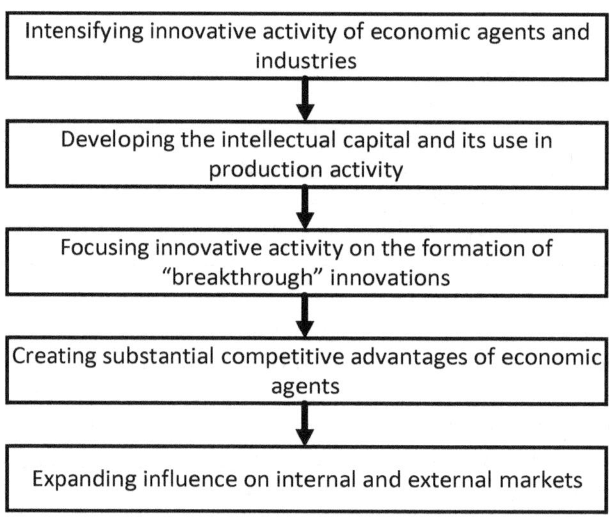

Source: Compiled by the authors on the basis of (Ivanov, Baranov, 2011; Balashova, Gromova, 2017)

Figure 3: Mechanism of competitive advantage formation for the national economy based on the growth of innovation potential of economic agents

Innovative activity has an impact on the creation of intellectual property, which brings additional profits and ensures growth in market value. A sufficient level of innovative activity results in superprofit, which is the evidence of intellectual rent (Degtereva et al, 2019). This stage is a necessary element of transformation of the current economy into the knowledge-driven economy, which should be considered in the formation of value.

Thus, this paper proposes some tools for managing market value by means of change in innovative activity. An integral indicator of innovative development was worked out. It depends on the processes in operational, investment and financial activities. Building a regression dependence allows us to manage such resulting indicators as economic value added and market value by making innovative processes more intense.

It is planned to focus further research on adapting the method to specific enterprises and sectors, to find out the dependences and consider the specifics of the industry. It is possible to take into account stress-inducing events in the modelling, which can create alternative options affecting the stability and the market value of the enterprise. This is why the topic has to be investigated in more detail in further research studies (Dmitriev, Zaytsev, 2019).

References

Akhmetshin, E.M., Ilyasov, R.H., Sverdlikova, E.A., Tagibova, A.A., Tolmachev, A.V. and Yumashev, A.V. (2018) *Promotion in emerging markets*, European Research Studies Journal, No 21, pp. 652-665.

Asaturova, Y. and Khvatova, T. (2018) *Innovative activity of enterprises under the condition of financial deficit*, In Proceedings of the 13th European Conference on Innovation and Entrepreneurship, Portugal: Aveiro, pp. 59-67.

Balashova, E.S. and Gromova, E.A. (2017) *Russian experience of integrating modern management models*, Espacios, No 38.

Brigham, U. and Gapenski, L. (2017) *Financial management*, Moscow: Book on Demand.

Chen, J.K. and Chen, I.S. (2008) *Indices for innovation in the R&D manufacturing using FAHP*, Journal of Global Business and Technology, No 2, pp. 42-53.

Cohen, L., Diether, K. and Malloy, C. (2013) *Misvaluing innovation*, Review of Financial Studies.

Copeland, T., Koller, T. and Murrin, J. (1999) *Valuation, measuring and managing the value of companies*, Moscow: Olympus-business.

Daskovsky, V. and Kisilev, V. (2011) *Improving the assessment of investment efficiency*, Management Consulting, No 3.

Degtereva, V., Zaytsev, A. and Dmitriev, N. (2019) *The development of the mathematical apparatus for calculation of the intellectual rent industrial enterprises to achieve innovation leadership*, Economic, and Academic Leadership, Czech Republic: Prague, No 14.

Demidenko, D.S., Kulibanova, V.V. and Maruta, V.G. (2018a) *Using the methods of the company's capitalization optimal management*, Proceedings of the 32nd International Business Information Management Association Conference, No 3, pp. 2144-2149.

Demidenko, D.S., Kulibanova, V.V. and Maruta, V.G. (2018b) *Using the principles of "digital economy" in assessing the company's capitalization*, Proceedings of the 31st International Business Information Management Association Conference, No 3, pp. 6087-6091.

Demidenko, D. S. and Dubolazova, Y. A. 2019. Drawing up an optimal investment program for innovative development of an enterprise, pp. 254–59, in Proceedings of the European Conference on Innovation and Entrepreneurship, ECIE

Dergaeva, V.A. (2019) *Assessment of the impact of innovative processes on the market value of a company. Advanced innovative developments*, Prospects and experience of use, problems of implementation in production, pp. 248-251.

Dmitriev, N. and Zaytsev, A. (2019) *Use of stress testing to increase the effectiveness of financial planning in the enterprise*, Digital Economy and Industry 4.0: New Challenges, SPb: Polytechnic Press, pp. 362-368. DOI: 10.18720/IEP/2019.1/55

Gorbunova, E.N., Zhovtenko, M.I. and Dmitriev, N.D. (2019) *Management of cash flows of the defense industry enterprise*, Modern Science, No 5, pp. 102-105.

Hay, D. and Morris, D. (1979) *Industrial Economics,* Theory and Evidence. Oxford: Oxford University Press.

Huseynov, B.M. (2013) *Improving management effectiveness in oil and gas companies*, Moscow: Institute of Economics of the Russian Academy of Sciences.

Ivanov, I. and Baranov, V. (2011) *Innovative development of Russia: Opportunities and prospects*, Moscow: Alpina Publisher.

Kaplan, R.S. and Norton, D.P. (2001) *The Strategy-focused Organization: How Balanced Scorecard Companies Thrive in the New Business Environment*, Boston: Harvard Business School Press.

Kichigin, O., Zaytsev and A., Korotkova, A. (2019) *Normative and dynamic tools for financial analysis and control of the enterprise in the digital economy,* SPBPU IDE-2019, Russia: St. Petersburg.

Kiseleva, E.M., Artemova, E.I., Litvinenko, I.L., Kirillova, T.V., Tupchienko, V.A. and Bing, W. (2017) *Implementation of innovative management in the actions of the business enterprise*, International Journal of Applied Business and Economic Research, No 15, pp. 231-242.

Kozlov, M., Zaytsev, A., Kichigin, O. (2019) Rental analysis of innovation component in resource productivity, IOP Conference Series: Materials Science and Engineering, vol. 497, 012064

Krasyuk, I.A., Kobeleva, A.A., Mikhailushkin, P.V., Terskay, G.A. and Chuvakhina, A.G. (2018) *Economic interests focusing as a basis of the formation of investment policy*, Espacios. No 39.

Marginson, S. (2019) *Limitations of human capital theory*, Studies in Higher Education, No 2, pp. 287-301, DOI: 10.1080/03075079.2017.1359823.

Morozova T.V., Polyanskaya T., Zasenko V.E., Zarubin V.I. and Verchenko Y.K. (2017) *Economic Analysis in the Financial Management System*, International Journal of Applied Business and Economic Research, No 15. pp. 117-124.

Nikolova, L.V., Malinin, A.M., Rodionov, D.G. and Velikova, M.D. (2017) *Performance management of innovation program at an industrial enterprise: An optimisation model*, Proceedings of the 30th International Business Information Management Association Conference, No 3, pp. 1033-1040.

Polyakova, A.G., Akhmetshin, E.M., Pavlyuk, A.V., and Meshkova, G.V. (2019) Investment appeal of a region and its impact on investment inflows, Entrepreneurship and Sustainability Issues, No 7(2), pp. 1089-1097. DOI: 10.9770/jesi.2019.7.2(21)

Selentyeva, T. N., Mikhel, E. A., and Mishura, L. G. 2019. Analysis of the company's activities as an open economic system in order to form a financial strategy, pp. 3727–31, in Proceedings of the 33rd International Business Information Management Association Conference, IBIMA 2019: Education Excellence and Innovation Management through Vision 2020.

Stetsyunich, Y., Busheneva, Y., and Zaytsev, A. (2019) Framing public financial policy: Transforming the classic concept in the time of digitalization, in ACM International Conference Proceeding Series.

Turgaev, S.A. (2013) *Assessing the impact of innovation on increasing the value of an organization*, Management Consulting, No 2.

Yakubovich, M.A. (2005) *Financial indicators of enterprises efficiency*, Project controls, 9, 36-39.

Yashin, S.N. and Soldatova, Y.S. (2013a) *An assessment of the innovation development stability of industrial enterprises*, Nizhny Novgorod: NSTU.

Yashin, S.N. and Soldatova, Y.S. (2013b) *Formation of an integrated assessment of the innovative development of enterprises*, Finance and credit, No 40, pp. 34-39.

Zaytsev, A., Rodionov, D., Dmitriev, N. and Kichigin, O. (2019) *Comparative analysis of results on application of methods of intellectual capital valuation*, Digital transformation on manufacturing, infrastructure and service», Russia: St. Petersburg.

PhD Research Papers

How can Organizations Harness the Intrapreneurial Capabilities of Their Engineers and Facilitate Innovation?

Maher Alzyadat, Bidyut Baruah and Anthony Ward
University of York, UK
msqa500@york.ac.uk
bidyut.baruah@york.ac.uk
tony.ward@york.ac.uk
DOI: 10.34190/EIE.20.176

Abstract: Intrapreneurship is considered as a contemporary concept to drive innovation inside an organization and achieve a competitive advantage in a complex and ever-changing business environment. Technology firms are particularly on the cutting edge not only to cope with the rapid changes in technology development but to lead the creation of innovative products and technological advancement. In such firms, engineers are expected to contribute significantly to the innovation process within organizations and bring real values to the marketplace. Technology firms are increasingly demanding their engineers to perform beyond their defined stereotypical responsibilities and operate actively as intrapreneurs. These organizations seek to promote intrapreneurship as a core business strategy and facilitate a supportive culture to enhance engineers' intrapreneurial behavior. However, researchers have not explored how engineers engage with intrapreneurship and how firms can develop the intrapreneurial capabilities of their engineers. The purpose of this paper is to explore how organizations can utilize engineers and drive their innovative initiatives so as to facilitate effective intrapreneurship. This study uses semi-structured interviews with engineers who are involved in innovative activities within their roles and work in different industrial sectors in the UK. The results indicate that engineers who are intrapreneurs show high motivation in their roles, demonstrate risk-taking in their strategies, and consider collaboration as a key approach for success. The findings re-emphasize the crucial role of engineers in providing alternative, valuable and robust solutions that shape the internal innovation of the company. Their proactive attitude towards organizational responsibilities and abilities to identify future opportunities are critical for sustaining innovation. Their intrapreneurial behavior depends on organizational factors and management support that shape their intrapreneurial attitudes and initiatives. The findings will help firms to get an understanding of the intrapreneurial potential of engineers and how to harness their capabilities by providing a supporting organizational framework.

Keywords: intrapreneurship, innovation, engineer, technology firms

1. Introduction

In today's dynamic, demanding, and fast-moving global economy, revolutionary changes and rapid diffusion of new technologies have placed increasing pressure on firms to generate continuous innovation to survive and stay ahead of the competition. Researchers increasingly consider intrapreneurship as a viable strategy for solving organizational complexity and gaining a competitive advantage that significantly influences the organizational renewal, profitability, growth, and overall performance of the firm (Baruah and Ward (2014), Falola et al (2018), Antoncic et al (2018)).

Many researchers view innovation and intrapreneurship as a vehicle to stimulate growth and development by utilizing the creative energy of employees. Zhao (2005) emphasizes that the essence of intrapreneurial efforts in an organization revolves around the innovative activities of the individual employees. The main source of innovation is to pursue an opportunity, and the basis of intrapreneurship is to recognize that opportunity and exploit it with a strong belief in its success (Heinonen and Korvela, 2003).

The organization is mainly responsible for creating an infrastructure that supports engineers and provides them the strategy, resources, and culture to empower their initiatives and make better use of their potential. Considering the main focus of intrapreneurship is about how employees could be encouraged to act in an intrapreneurial manner within the boundary of an organization, many definitions in the literature are based on this perspective. For instance, Mohanty (2006) observed that the concept of intrapreneurship is an essential approach for an organization to define specific strategies and action plans in order to incorporate significant employee contributions. Overall, this study considers intrapreneurship as an organization level process related to the organizational practices, strategies, and behaviors by which a firm seeks to innovate, develop new products, technologies and services, and foster more initiatives from their employees.

1.1 The multi-level construct of intrapreneurship and its influence on organizational success

Intrapreneurship is a multi-level concept that has been studied at the level of an employee, the team, and may take place at any level of the organization e.g. corporate, business division, functional, or project level (Zahra (1991), Blanka (2019)). Intrapreneurship can be developed in organizations regardless of their size (Antoncic and Hisrich, 2003).

There is growing empirical focus to study the different factors of intrapreneurship, their effect on organizational performance, and how the organization can stimulate and instill intrapreneurial attitudes among employees. In this regard, intrapreneurship is classified according to the level of the initiative as a "Top-down" process representing the organization, management, or firm-level and as a "bottom-up" process representing the individual or the employee level. This multi-level construct is commonly adopted by many authors such as Åmo and Kolvereid (2005), and Baruah and Ward (2015).

For this study, intrapreneurship success is a result of the interaction and correlation between both process layers and is a holistic approach. The final benefits will emerge when the different components integrate to transform the business towards the end goals. This complies with researchers such as Menzel et al (2007), who argued that the concept could be explained when the opportunity, intrapreneur, and organization are considered at the same time. Similarly, Neessen et al (2019) added that intrapreneurship is not merely an individual or an organizational behavior but is about a set of activities of an individual or an organization to get from point A to point B in time. Some of these studies, therefore, imply that intrapreneurship is an organizational process.

1.2 The interaction between employees and management to facilitate intrapreneurship

The center of any intrapreneurial activity is the intrapreneur themselves, who, according to Pinchot (1985), is a person who focuses on innovation and creativity and transforms a dream or an idea into a profitable venture by operating within the organizational environment. These intrapreneurs focus on developing ways of working and engaging effectively with organizational practices, processes, structures, or techniques. Intrapreneurial employees are proactive and action-oriented actors who show high confidence in their skills with a strong need to pursue their innovative ideas inside the realms of the organization (Åmo, 2010).

Several researchers have highlighted how employees can behave intrapreneurially only when the organizational frameworks have provisions and facilities to support them and their innovative initiatives. Thus, if engineers are given the platform and opportunities within their role to act more intrapreneurial, then this will be an added competitive bonus for the firm. Intrapreneurial behaviors of both individuals and organizations depend on the supportive cultural frameworks of the firm oriented towards stimulating innovation (Menzel et al., 2006). Zahra (1991) considers intrapreneurship to be a combination of both formal (Management level) and informal (employee level) activities aimed at creating new business in established companies through product and process innovations and market developments. Such organizations create a business culture that facilitates the innovation process in which intrapreneurship is embraced as a core practice and oriented towards the organizational objectives. In this sense, the management within an organization has a vital role to play in the two-way processes of intrapreneurship and to foster organizational and individual initiatives towards intrapreneurship. Management needs to support generating new ideas, establishing a structured screening system, giving freedom, rewarding the contributors, and providing effective leadership to achieve a consistent record of intrapreneurship (Rule and Irwin, 1988).

1.3 Engagement of engineers with intrapreneurship

Engineering is a crucial profession that acts as the backbone for many of technological firms. Engineers are often considered a strategic asset for their employers, and this segment of the labor force has to be carefully monitored and managed (Mignonac and Herrbach, 2003). Over the years, intrapreneurial engineers have brought in some of the most successful innovations like Gmail, new interactive features in Facebook, and Playstation. There are growing demands for engineers to play more consequential roles in all phases of the innovation process (Williamson et al., 2013), and act more intrapreneurially in their functions (Menzel et al., 2007). Such roles require knowledge, skills, and certain competencies that go well beyond those of regular engineers.

By the very nature of this profession, engineers are expected to follow strong engineering practices and are usually assumed to be good thinkers, planners, and designers. They have some of the advanced skills in analyzing and troubleshooting practical problems and provide critical solutions to complex engineering challenges. Engineers, by nature, are technically driven individuals who are oriented to find/ design solutions for technical problems. However, these classical functions are not sufficient in dealing with today's business challenges; the expectations are higher (Weissenberger-Eibl and Kugler, 2014). Engineers need to gain more comprehensive knowledge and build expertise outside the engineering domains and collaborate with other disciplines, and develop skills in effective communication, negotiation, creating value, dealing with challenges, resolving difficulties, and taking risks.

Some researchers like Menzel et al (2007) have highlighted the intrapreneurial capacity among engineers in high tech-firms and labeled them as "engineer-intrapreneurs", they particularly noted their interest in pursuing technological innovation within their organization. The continuous development and integration of technology in the current economic environment call for a more comprehensive contribution from engineers, especially in the ongoing technological evolution and market changes. Business, therefore, will need to tap into the intrapreneurial capabilities of their engineers so as to lead and enrich innovation to further enhance the company's competitive advantage.

1.4 Purpose of the study

From the literature review, it is evident that innovation and intrapreneurship play a significant role in any technology organization, and engineers here tend to make an essential contribution towards the innovation process. However, there are no substantial empirical researches that discuss the intrapreneurial capabilities within engineers and how they demonstrate innovation in their roles and is, therefore, one of the key research gaps in the fields of intrapreneurship and engineering. The purpose of this paper is to explore how organizations can utilize the capabilities of engineers and get them more involved with intrapreneurship. The paper will address the following questions:

- How do engineers engage with the innovation process within an organization, and what drives their motivation?
- What are the main intrapreneurial characteristics of engineers, and how can organizations support and successfully drive the innovative initiatives emerging from them?

2. Research methodology

This study is based on qualitative research using semi-structured interviews with engineers who actively engage in innovation-related activities within their roles. The qualitative research approach is an adequate method for obtaining rich and in-depth knowledge (Yin, 2017). This, therefore, signifies it as an appropriate approach for exploring the phenomenon of intrapreneurship in engineering contexts.

The sample of engineers has been selected from different engineering disciplines with varying roles and functions and with different years of work experience. All interviews were conducted using the same interview guide. Some of the questions in the interview guide centered around themes like motivation towards their roles, how they demonstrate innovation in their practice, and how they interact with the management during innovative activities. A semi-structured interviewing approach was followed as this allowed the researcher the flexibility to collect open-ended data, investigate participant thoughts, and delve deeper into their responses.

This paper uses interviews with 5 participants as a pilot study, which lasted approximately an hour. Each participant in this study has been assigned a specific code for the purpose of anonymity, as shown in Table 1. The following table shows the list of engineers with their industrial sectors, background, and role within their organization.

Table 1: Reference code for participants

Participant code	Industrial Sector	Educational Background	Current Role	Years of Experience
Participant 1	ICT	BSc Electrical Engineering	Network solution architect	16
Participant 2	Electronic industry	BSc Communication Engineering MSC in digital systems engineering	Verification engineer	13

Participant code	Industrial Sector	Educational Background	Current Role	Years of Experience
Participant 3	Media and TV	BSc in Electronic Engineering MSc in Music Technology	Project engineer	10
Participant 4	Food industry	BSc Mechanical Engineering	Process engineer	14
Participant 5	Music technology	BSc Electronic Engineering MSc Music Technology systems	R&D engineer	6

These variations in engineering backgrounds and industrial sectors among the participants were purposefully intended so as to reflect on engineers' engagement with innovation under different organizational setups and to give the researcher a broader context to investigate the phenomenon. The obtained data were processed and coded for emerging themes using Nvivo software, which is a qualitative data analysis software.

3. Analysis

The main contributions from the intrapreneurial activities of engineers are the proactive initiatives that are the main basis for creating innovative solutions, products, and services to transform their organization. All participants in this study find their role very challenging, and they consider innovation as a tool to resolve some of these challenges and add value to their company. One of the participants whose role is to provide innovative technologies to their food factory clients explains, *"innovation is absolutely at the heart of* everything we do here... even the maintenance of existing equipment".

Participant 1, who works as a network solution architect, engages in promoting innovative solutions to his clients, identifying their needs, proposing new products, and recommending improvement to exist products. He mentions, *"we are in this ICT world and all kinds of innovations are happening. The current trend in the company in order to promote automation, we identify areas where we can automate our daily tasks in which the project or the service can be quickly delivered and avoid any human or manual mistakes"*. Participant 2 is a verification engineer, and for him, innovation is very important in his role, and the business is based on innovative ideas that come from employees. Another participant who is a project engineer, summarizes *"innovation is basically what we are charged to do. So you could say that innovation is my entire role in short... we are charged with inventing the future for the company"*. Following the analysis of the interviews with these engineers, five key themes emerged which will be discussed in this paper:

- The high motivation among intrapreneurial engineers that influence their attitude toward innovation
- The willingness of intrapreneurial engineer to handle extra organizational responsibilities
- Risk-taking behavior and commitment towards the company strategy during innovative activities
- The proactiveness of intrapreneurial engineers to identify future opportunities
- Collaboration as a strategic attitude to promote innovation

Based on these main themes, the paper will now shed some light on how engineers interact with management and what organizational factors influence their intrapreneurial attitudes.

3.1 Motivation that drives intrapreneurial engineers' engagement with innovation

Motivation is the main driver for engineers to become intrapreneurs and to overcome the challenges in their route to pursue intrapreneurial ventures. They show a high level of confidence towards their professional roles with interest in the technical and non-technical responsibilities and duties they are assigned to. For instance, participant 1 says, *"I have a very good technical competence... and I can deliver what I promise. So this is the main reason that I stick to this role"*. Intrapreneurial engineers appreciate the technical strengths they have. What drives their motivation is that they are happy to speak the technical language that is aligned with their educational background and professional experience. From the interviews, it was clear that for intrapreneurial engineers, such drive brings satisfaction in their roles. This is supported by Chan et al (2017), who mentioned that intrapreneurs could be among employees who possess high intrapreneurial motivation in their roles to develop expertise, be a professional and lead and control, a concept they referred to as self-directed career motivation.

This intrapreneurial motivation among engineers pushes their ability to innovate as a step to fulfill their willingness to contribute not only to their firm success but also to create real values for their customers and people's lives. Such engineers have a vision and show commitment to achievement. Participant 3, for instance, highlights, *"One of the things that drive me is that I think there is a place where our organization can make things better for people. The thing that drives me is reinventing the company so that it can be useful for people in the 21st century... and I think without the work we are doing, the firm could very easily just disappear and fade into irrelevance"*. This motivation towards exploring new ideas and taking new challenges is what sets intrapreneurial engineers apart from the regular engineers. This motivation energizes them to create new business opportunities, take a risk, tackle challenges and difficulties, and implement innovative activities. Neessen et al (2019) explain how motivation, in addition to the satisfaction and the relationship with the organization, are the main factors that could influence the level of intention to behave intrapreneurially.

What also motivates intrapreneurial engineers is the level of freedom they experience in their roles. This allows them to experiment with things that they are passionate about, which could potentially add value to the company. Participant 2 comments on the freedom provided by the management *"we have the freedom to explore some new things, and we can decide which methodology to use... but the freedom of implementing our own ideas is what I like in my company, which motivates me to explore more"*. The management can let engineers work on what they are really good at to demonstrate their skills. However, this freedom needs to be monitored and guided in a way to make them more productive and meet organizational objectives effectively.

All participants in this study demonstrated a high level of satisfaction with their roles, which is why they showed no interest in pursuing their own businesses and become entrepreneurs. Their current organizations are giving them adequate support and opportunities to explore their ideas and innovation. Some preferred this idea of a safe haven. For example, Participant 4 explains, *"I like the comfort of operating within the safety net of a big company"*. This reaffirms how important it is for organizations to promote this supportive culture and is, therefore, the key to sustaining continuous innovation and retaining talented engineers within the organization.

3.2 Proactive approaches towards organizational responsibilities

In most of the organizations, engineers are usually assigned a specific title with a list of expected tasks and responsibilities associated with that role. However, intrapreneurial engineers have the tendency to go beyond their defined roles and job framework. They desire to spend time and effort outside their domain of expertise and accepting involvement with other activities, even if it is outside their level of competence. Participant 4 reflected on this tendency and said, *"I would never just operate within my own sphere just for the sake of not going the extra mile"*. This desire to go beyond defined organizational responsibilities signifies an intrapreneurial engineer.

Engineers who aspire to cross their functional borders will expand their knowledge and build new skills and competencies in new areas. It is a source of the learning process that will feed the innovative process with new ideas facilitating the implementation of innovation within the organization. Management in this process plays a significant role in supporting their engineers to develop skills and build expertise by exploring new areas out of their engineering core domain. Acknowledging this support, participant 2 explains, *"Even inside the organization ... we are given the opportunity to work on a totally different team on totally different new things. So once you feel like you are not learning much in this particular role, our company will provide an opportunity to explore other possible kinds of work. It could go into marketing to product management or engineering management... It gives us a wider picture of what we are actually into"*. This shows that management will need to go beyond their usual status quo if they want to nurture engineers. They might want to encourage employees to attend conferences, visit other sites, and collaborate with other departments to facilitate knowledge exchange and enrich the experience.

3.3 Some characteristics that signify intrapreneurial engineers within an organization

3.3.1 Risk-taking attitudes

Intrapreneurship is associated with newness and change and therefore has an element of risk associated with it. Risk-taking is, therefore, an important aspect that can be attributed to any engineer working on innovation and intrapreneurship. In this context, participant 2 discusses the importance of risk-taking attitude, *"without taking the risk, you will be very stagnant and may not be proceeding or progressing at all. In innovation or new ideas, the risk is in every step and part of a day to day work"*. Participant 1 similarly draws on one of his experiences. He highlights how he had to modernize an old system of hardware for a client that serves millions of customers. This solution he designed was the first to be implemented, and he was confident with the solution. This led to a series of discussions to convince the customer and to satisfy their requirements. In the interview, he noted how he was happy to take that big risk so as to provide a unique innovative solution.

Taking the risk, therefore, should be part of the freedom granted to engineers by the management to create and implement their ideas as explained by some of the participants. It should be incorporated with the general policy of the company and facilitate a culture that discourages risk-averse attitudes among engineers. It has to be noted that taking a risk in innovative activities may also lead to failure or unexpected results. This could lead to a loss of money and effort. Participants in this study feel that failure is reasonable and should be conceived as a part of the learning process. It can help in shaping the understanding of the ways to effectively implement such innovation and the experience to approach potential ideas or solutions in the future so as to avoid repeating such failures. This view is also emphasized by Menzel et al (2007), who note that engineers need to be supported for such failures.

In the interviews, participant 4 highlighted the importance of management support when engineers face failure and their positive attitudes towards learning from such failures. He explains further, *"we have got very strong support from our senior leadership team member... if we have put some technology in and that does not work and we are trying to work out what to do with it... they will be very decisive and supportive, and you never made to feel that is a black mark against your name".* This calls for an overall organizational culture that is receptive to innovation results, encourages risk-taking, and tolerates failure.

3.3.2 Commitment towards company strategies

The findings indicate that intrapreneurial engineers show a high commitment towards company vision, strategies, and firm values in their work. They are keen to contribute toward implementing the company strategy. In this regard, engineers aligned their creative ideas and innovative practices towards the overall objectives of the firm. Participant 1 highlighted how it is essential for engineers to keep the company strategy as the first priority by demonstrating the core values of the company in the primary tasks. In his case, these core values of the firm were related to *"delivering deliverables in a timely manner and in the proper quality".* This commitment to implementing the strategy defined at the organization and department level is the main driving force for him to incorporate the latest trend in technology service into his service delivery role.

Managers play a significant role in facilitating the overall company strategy to engineers. In this context, participants emphasized the role of managers to keep them updated with the latest business news and presenting the business targets and direction, which then drives the efforts from engineers to accomplish what is expected from them. According to Kuratko and Hornsby (1990), managers can generate a focused vision that could help in guiding the intrapreneurial energies of the organization. They should share and explain the innovation vision to their employees who could execute it. In this regard, engineers appreciate being involved in any new strategy and to be updated in the change of the current strategy that can direct their intrapreneurial intention to create more valuable innovation.

3.3.3 Following organizational rules and regulations

Engineers are generally very respectful of the company processes and ways of working. They tend to follow the instructions and rules in their innovative activities. As Participant 2 explains, *"We should always go through the company's advice, we should not be going behind their back, it is always good to be very transparent".* Some participants, however, preferred to evaluate the situations and discuss breaking some minor rules that are not critical to the business or attribute any risk to the process of innovation. In this context, participant 4 states, *"I look to make the best of the situation rather than to create waves".* Engineers interviewed generally adhere to current rules and regulations and would follow existing instructions as part of their commitment to the company. However, the attitude of engineers in this study to obey organizational rules and regulations is not consistent with the general behavior of intrapreneurs who, according to the literature, break and violate existing rules and traditions (De Jong and Wennekers, 2008).

3.3.4 Identifying future opportunities

Intrapreneurial engineers utilize their creativity by keeping eyes on future opportunities for their business. Participant 5, in his work for the development of the next release of a product, focused on long term research by scouting new technologies and new practices to bring new ideas that could keep their product at the forefront. He emphasizes the importance of scanning any academic and professional resources available, such as academic publications, online tutorials, and attending relevant conferences. For participant 1, his strategy for innovation is, *"I always look forward for the areas I can improve"*. Intrapreneurial engineers are, therefore, good at looking for any prospective future opportunities for innovation to keep their business ready for the next stage of technology development. Such proactive behavior, in addition to innovative practices related to the current business, is considered one of the success factors to maintain the business for future change. In this context, the supportive management actions, such as attending conferences and online tutorials related to the latest updates in the relevant areas of engineering and technology, are crucial for engineers to act proactively. Giving engineers the freedom to contact external industries and directly interact/liaise with customers can also speed up the process for talented engineers to identify future needs.

3.4 Strategic collaboration to promote innovation

Collaboration is an essential strategy that plays a major role in the innovation process, starting from idea creation to the final commercial outcome. According to the insights from all participants, innovation happens when people work together. Collaboration not only fosters innovation but can also deliver better qualities, save time, secure more resources for experimentation or result in new innovation. Participant 4 discusses his strategy to take his new idea forward, and on this note, he explains, *"the first thing I would do is probably discuss it amongst a little group of people I know and trust and who have strong skills"*. In his approach, peers can evaluate and validate the idea if it is 'feasible' or just a 'dream', or it is a 'daft' idea. Similarly, participant 3 describes the role of collaboration as an essential 'informal stage' before the idea formally can be escalated to management. His strategy is to start by building a 'technology demonstration' for the idea and demonstrating it to others, or by running workshops or sessions to spread the idea further to the broader community to develop the idea.

Intrapreneurial engineers are very active collaborators who give credit to their colleagues. For them, it is very important to consult with experts and stakeholders before initiating or embarking on any innovative work. They interact with other groups to bounce the idea off them, discuss and validate the initial idea, absorb inputs from qualified peers, and receive valuable feedback. The analysis shows that intrapreneurial engineers are open to combining their ideas with those of their peers, and this can potentially lead to greater concepts and pave a path for further opportunities. Collaboration is important for overcoming the difficulties encountered by engineers during the stages of innovation implementation. Consulting with others will provide valuable suggestions and recommendations; the engineer can analyze all these alternatives and find the right balance of solutions. Participant 1 cites an example that involved creating an innovative solution for a complex project to migrate subscribers database to the new hardware. He had to draw on effective collaboration with experts from cross-disciplinary departments such as R&D, who validated and developed his idea and helped with the implementation process. Without this active collaboration, it would have been difficult to process or validate this idea. For participant 4, collaboration is relationship-based, and having good connections cross-department and social interaction will facilitate getting support from peers.

According to Rule and Irwin (1988), the organization that promotes the approach of integrative team-building and collaborative problem-solving will facilitate the building of valuable and transferable skills that can be applied to intrapreneurial projects. Management can facilitate the collaborative and teamwork culture by organizing frequent sessions, workshop meetings, and social activities as a kind of knowledge sharing, where everyone has the freedom to present his/her ideas for further discussion.

4. Conclusion

Innovation and intrapreneurship play a significant role in any technology organization. This paper contributes to the literature by giving a comprehensive picture of intrapreneurship in engineering practices and the distinctive characteristics of engineers who are involved with innovation. Engineers with intrapreneurial capabilities and skills are self-motivated, collaborators who value teamwork and cooperation. They are generally risk-takers and proactive with their organizational responsibilities. They reflect a high commitment to the firm strategies and rules and focus on anticipating future opportunities. The intrapreneurial attitudes and skills should be encouraged among 21st century engineers so that organizations can successfully pursue and utilize their innovative activities and strengthen their competitive advantage. A preliminary study among 5 intrapreneurial engineers reflects the importance of the organization to understand and recognize the main attitudes and capabilities of their engineers toward innovation. Organizations should create a setup that encourages the initiatives from engineers and transforms their ideas into real opportunities that flourish the business. There is a high need to adopt intrapreneurship in technological firms and integrate it as part of the business strategy. Organizations with intrapreneurial engineers have an active human capital to nurture the business by feeding the innovative process with good ideas and initiatives. These can then lead to new products and solutions. Being a pilot study for a PhD project, the research analysis in this paper is limited to the selected 5 interviews. Future studies can look at a larger sample of engineers to further explore the phenomena. Also, through case studies, it might be worth investigating how organizations support their engineers' intrapreneurial capabilities.

References

Åmo, B. W. (2010). Corporate entrepreneurship and intrapreneurship related to innovation behaviour among employees. *International Journal of Entrepreneurial Venturing*, 2 (2), pp.144–158.

Åmo, B. W. and Kolvereid, L. (2005). Organizational Strategy, Individual Personality and Innovation Behavior. *Journal of Enterprising Culture*, 13 (01), pp.7–19.

Antoncic, B. and Hisrich, R. D. (2003). Clarifying the intrapreneurship concept. *Journal of Small Business and Enterprise Development*, 10 (1), pp.7–24.

Antoncic, J. A., Antoncic, B. and Li, Z. (2018). Creativity of the Entrepreneur, Intrapreneurship, and the Growth of Small and Medium-Sized Enterprises: Evidence from China. *Chinese Business Review*, 17 (7), pp.336–341.

Baruah, B. and Ward, A. (2014). Metamorphosis of intrapreneurship as an effective organizational strategy. *International Entrepreneurship and Management Journal,* 11 (4), pp.811–822.

Baruah, B. and Ward, A. (2015). ' X ' trapreneurship- a holistic approach to bring clarity in entrepreneurial research. *Voice of Research,* 4 (1), pp.65–72.

Blanka, C. (2019). An individual-level perspective on intrapreneurship: a review and ways forward. *Review of Managerial Science*, 13 (5), pp.919–961.

Chan, K.-Y. et al. (2017). Who Wants to Be an Intrapreneur? Relations between Employees' Entrepreneurial, Professional, and Leadership Career Motivations and Intrapreneurial Motivation in Organizations. *Frontiers in Psychology*, 8, pp.1–11.

Falola, H. O. et al. (2018). Employees' intrapreneurial engagement initiatives and its influence on organisational survival. *Business: Theory and Practice,* 19, pp.9–16.

Heinonen, J. and Korvela, K. (2003). *How about measuring intrapreneurship?*. In 33rd EISB Conference, Milan, Italy.

De Jong, J. and Wennekers, S. (2008). *Intrapreneurship conceptualizing entrepreneurial employee behaviour*. Scales Research Reports, H200802, Zoetermeer: EIM.

Kuratko, D. F. and Hornsby, J. S. (1990). Developing an Entrepreneurial Perspective in Contemporary. *Strategic Management Journal*, pp.1–15.

Menzel, H. C. et al. (2006). *Developing Characteristics of an Intrapreneurship-supportive Culture*. Netherlands: Eindhoven Centre for Innovation Studies.

Menzel, H. C., Aaltio, I. and Ulijn, J. M. (2007). On the way to creativity: Engineers as intrapreneurs in organizations. *Technovation*, 27 (12), pp.732–743.

Mignonac, K. and Herrbach, O. (2003). Managing individual career aspirations and corporate needs: A study of software engineers in France. *Journal of Engineering and Technology Management*, 20 (3), pp.205–230.

Mohanty, R. P. (2006). Intrapreneurial levers in cultivating value-innovative mental space in Indian corporations. *Vikalpa*, 31 (1), pp.99–105.

Neessen, P. C. M. et al. (2019). The intrapreneurial employee: toward an integrated model of intrapreneurship and research agenda. *International Entrepreneurship and Management Journal,* 15 (2), pp.545–571.

Pinchot, G. (1985). *Intrapreneuring: Why You Don't Have to Leave the Corporation to Become an Entrepreneur*. 1st ed. New York: Harper & Row publishers.

Rule, E. G. and Irwin, D. W. (1988). Fostering Intrapreneurship: The New Competitive Edge. *Journal of Business Strategy*, 9 (3), pp.44–47.

Weissenberger-Eibl, M. A. and Kugler, F. (2014). Innovation Engineering: The Skills Engineers Need to be Innovative. In: *Research in Competence-Based Management*. 7 (October 2014). pp.219–246.

Williamson, J. M., Lounsbury, J. W. and Han, L. D. (2013). Key personality traits of engineers for innovation and technology development. *Journal of Engineering and Technology Management*, 30 (2), pp.157–168.

Yin, R. k. (2017). *Case Study Research and Applications: Design and Methods*. Sixth Edit. Thousand Oaks, California: SAGE Publications.

Zahra, S. A. (1991). Predictors and financial outcomes of corporate entrepreneurship: An exploratory study. *Journal of Business Venturing*, 6 (4), pp.259–285.

Zhao, F. (2005). Exploring the synergy between entrepreneurship and innovation. *International Journal of Entrepreneurial Behavior & Research*, 11 (1), pp.25–41.

Socially Responsible Marketing as an Educational and Communication Tool of Modern Business in the Context of the Circular Economy

Natália Augustínová and Jaroslav Bednárik
University of Ss. Cyril and Methodius, Trnava, Slovakia
nataliaaugustinova@gmail.com
jaroslav.bednarik@ucm.sk
DOI: 10.34190/EIE.20.184

Abstract: The aim of this study is to point out the current issues at home and abroad, which is the concept of socially responsible marketing in the organization in the context of the circular economy. We can perceive this concept not only as a competitive advantage in the fight for customer or voluntary awareness, but also as a modern educational tool that has its place in the business. Commercial benefit for many companies is no longer the only goal; on the contrary, they also aim to eliminate the consequences of their own activities and to improve the life in which the entire society lives, including their customers. Logically linking social issues to the focus of your business may not be the easiest. Finding a way to communicate the issue as effectively as possible to the target audience is a significant effort, especially creative. In order to achieve a synergistic effect, it is important to use several communication tools, for example influencer marketing. In a practical example, we show how a topic can be addressed that should have an educational potential for the target audience and reach it in B2B and B2C markets. In order to achieve the stated goal of this document, we have prepared published findings and solutions of domestic and foreign authors concerning the researched issue, using the synthetic-analytical method, the inductive-deductive method.

Keywords: socially responsible marketing, education, influencer marketing, environment, campaign, circular economy

1. Introduction

Today's world faces many social, economic and environmental challenges. There is no greater responsibility, no higher duty of professional management than to gain the respect of the general public through objective participation in issues concerning society as a whole. (Abrams, 1951) On the other hand, organizations face another challenge, and that is the question of how to reach the target audience with such a serious problem as human impact on the environment. Finding a suitable way encounters public disinterest, information overload and thus generally more difficulties to attract the target audience. A brief description of the problem is not enough. It is necessary to look for more attractive ways to reach the audience. Addressing environmental issues is linked to public education. At first sight, educational content may not be attractive and may not interest the target group. It is necessary to find a way to educate the public in an attractive way. That is the beginning of problem solving. The aim of the study is to verify whether corporate social responsibility can also be interconnected with education. The secondary goal was to investigate the use of influencer marketing as the main form of communication in socially responsible marketing.

2. Literature review

2.1 Socially responsible business

Socially responsible marketing or thus corporate social responsibility is playing an increasingly important role in the business environment. In the literature, we encounter a certain plurality of opinions or inconsistency in the identifying and definition of this issue. In this work we proceed from the conceptual definition of corporate social responsibility, as in our opinion it is the closest to the researched issue and from our point of view it is a starting area.

Having a closer look at the CSR we can reflect on the benefits that this concept brings. We can perceive these benefits as a certain value. Chandler (2019) also points to this concept as a process of value creation. The authors Green and Peloza (2011) develop the idea of value. They claim that socially responsible activities within the concept can create three types of value for consumers: utilitarian, emotional and social. In addition, they point to the fact that this socially responsible behaviour represents a certain form of good behaviour. From the company's point of view, this behaviour is perceived positively, which can evoke a sense of pride and positive feelings among stakeholders. We can predict that this feeling of pride may be one of the prerequisites for the customer's future involvement in socially responsible activity. The mentioned good feeling will accompany them during the participation in the activity and will also influence their further participation or non-participation.

We can also perceive this value process as a way of education. Developing activities within the individual pillars can also represent a form of education for stakeholders. For example, dealing with environmental problems, pointing them out and coming up with solutions also represent a means of raising awareness of the issue. In our opinion, this spreading can also be understood as education about global issues that need to be communicated to the public and also to business entities. We see value in this type of education.

2.2 Environmental socially responsible business

In connection with the environmental pillar of the CSR, it is worth referring to an advertisement in The New York Times focusing on environmental activism, which also held Chandler's interest and is addressed in his publication. They called on society for environmental activism by saying: "*every decision we make has consequences. We choose what we put into our lakes and rivers. We choose what we release into the air we breathe. We choose what we put into our bodies and where we let our children run and play. We choose the world we live in, so make the right choices*." (Chandler, 2008) In fact, the environment in which we live is constantly exposed to the outcome of our activities, whether at the level of individualists or entire organizations. Environmental activism is no longer just a question of non-governmental or governmental organizations. This question is already becoming more and more common within the companies themselves, finding its place among the standard activities of the organization. Thanks to corporate social responsibility, we can also see more companies fulfilling their activities under the environmental pillar. Environmental activities are defined as initiatives that aim at minimizing the impact on natural resources and reducing negative environmental effects. (Hart, 1995; Bansal, 2005) This may include waste separation, the use of reusable materials, the search for ecological solutions within the company with minimal impact on the environment, and others.

Environmental protection is certainly a big area that has an increasing place in the functioning of society, which undoubtedly and rightfully belongs to it. The authors Chouinard and Stanley are advocates of the environmental surrounding and attach a significant role to it in business. According to them: "*our common destiny depends on nature, but she herself does not have a voice to hear, or at least not one we can hear. We can't sit down with her at the same table and ask her what she needs to make her function and what she cares about the most. Facing the silence of nature, we must respect the precautionary principle.*" (2014) This caution should accompany the company throughout its existence and be present in all its sectors. Caution is one of the manifestations of responsibility and conscious behaviour that should be characteristic of socially responsible behaviour. Responsibility begins with caution and anticipation of the consequences of our actions. That is why we highlight caution as one of the first steps towards protecting the environment and fighting for sustainability. Overall, it is an aspect which, in our view, is a sign of responsibility and respect for any activity, but it has an even more important place in the case of environmental protection.

2.3 Methodology

We have elaborated the theoretical part of the paper on the basis of domestic and foreign literature, while we have taken into account the topicality of sources and the content compliance with the topic set by us.

Subsequently, during the practical part, we obtained the necessary information from secondary sources in the form of press releases, web articles and various posts from social networks. In addition, this part was processed on the basis of primary sources. In April 2020, a research was conducted through an in-depth interview. This research was limited in time to the two weeks needed to collect all the necessary data from both parties, the client and the agency. The selection criterion was sufficient awareness of the person about the required activity of the company ZľavaDňa. It was necessary to cover the client's side as well as the agency's side, as the mentioned organization uses the services of the Divino PR agency. After careful consideration, the account responsible for the client on the agency's side was selected - Martina Kostúrková, who is also a team leader. On the client's side, a person was selected for the position of campaign manager - Barbora Hargašová. The in-depth interview was conducted exclusively in electronic form, as the conditions associated with the pandemic did not allow for personal contact. The conducted interviews followed the same structure. The aim of the interviews was to gain knowledge that could not be obtained from secondary sources. In terms of structure, the interviews focused on the following areas

- basic principles of corporate social responsibility of the subject ZľavaDňa
- campaign implementation
- campaign results and future activity direction

The data were recorded automatically, as the interviews were conducted on the basis of electronic – email – communication. Subsequently, the data were also processed with the data obtained from the secondary sources.

In addition, some data and information were obtained from the primary source, as the author herself participated in certain aspects of creating the campaign for ZľavaDňa.

In domestic conditions, we could observe a certain trend in the field of environmental social responsibility. In 2019, several campaigns were implemented aimed at environmental sustainability and responsibility. The campaign of the company ZľavaDňa was selected on the basis of success in terms of addressing the target audience as well as their commitment, use of creativity and choice of media.

Due to the limitation of the research only an in-depth interview in electronic form was usable. The reason was a pandemic and related measures. In addition, there were personnel changes on the part of the client and the agency, so some details could be misrepresented.

2.4 Case study

Chandler ponders the question – "*What is the place of a company within society*?". According to the author, it determines the future of humanity, the way we live, the way we integrate and whether we leave the planet habitable for future generations. It is important that these issues are addressed today and not adjourned. We can say that future steps depend on maintaining the current state. (Chandler, 2019) Similar thinking should be the standard in modern business if we want to preserve the natural heritage for future generations. Martin Rakovský, CEO of Zľavadňa, belongs to a similar-minded current of opinion. "*We are a Slovak company that has been operating in Slovakia for almost 10 years, and the basis of our business is travel. Therefore, we want to invest part of our profits back - to support Slovakia and our nature. We want to support such travelling, which will help the environment so that our children can also enjoy the beautiful nature,"* said Martin Rakovský, CEO of the company Zľavadňa. *(Hoscheková, 2019)*

ZlavaDna.sk was established in 2010 and since then it has been one of the stable companies on the Slovak collective shopping market. It belongs to the Creative Web group and operates several Internet portals. A significant breakthrough in 2013 was its inclusion in the ranking of the fastest growing technology companies in Central Europe, while the ranking was compiled by the international company Deloitte. In 2014, it had an admirable turnover of 23 mil Euros. The award of the Minister of Economy of the Slovak Republic for the most inspiring business story in 2018 also confirms that it is one of the major companies on the Slovak market. ZľavaDňa is a company operating in the B2B and B2C markets. It provides mediation of services and experiences for end consumers. These are mostly offers of services in the field of gastronomy, travel, health and beauty, sports and leisure activities and the automotive industry. (Kosturková, 2019)

Tourism is a sector of the economy that can generally have a significant impact on the environment. Hotels, as one of the main businesses in the sector, can help the country move towards a long-term strategy aimed at conserving natural resources and protecting the environment. In addition, for hotels themselves, environmental behaviour has a significant impact on their performance. (Molina-Azorín, et al, 2009) According to a survey of the company booking.com, up to 87% of travellers say they want to travel in a sustainable way, and almost 4 out of 10 say they can do so often or always. (Booking.com, 2018) We can state that tourism has a significant impact on the environment. On the other hand, we can also argue that tourism is significantly affected by the state of the environment, the natural heritage in a given location and similar aspects. Thus, not only is tourism changing the environment, but it is also largely dependent on it. It is therefore logical that organizations operating in this sector should carry out activities aimed at sustainability and nature protection. Their existence is significantly influenced by environmental factors.

It is important that companies operating in this sector contribute to the public good, especially in the field of environmental issues, as they are mostly very close to it. Tourism contributes to environmental pollution. The company ZľavaDňa also became aware of this fundamental problem. In addition to the established concept of corporate social responsibility, in 2019 it came up with an environmental activity in which it involved Slovaks. The concept represented the idea of responsible travel and wise usage, the #somvreckar (#imapickpocket) project. It was a form of education in the field of travel and waste management. Through the activity, the company tried to educate the public about the problem of waste in nature. In order for a society to be able to solve a certain problem, it must first be educated about it. In our opinion, education represents the beginning of the way to a solution. The idea was to clean nature, the environment in which we live, from the rubbish that irresponsible tourists leave in nature. Communicating such a serious topic needed a creative background to attract the attention of the target audience. The idea of #somvreckar was an attempt to steal the waste left by someone else in nature. A funny wordplay, it drew attention to thieves, pickpockets and at the same time the activity associated with garbage collection.

As the company provides services to customers mainly in the field of tourism and experiences, the activity was focused mainly on hotels and guest houses. More than 60 hotels took part in this activity and educated their visitors about the project at their receptions, while visitors could take biodegradable garbage bags for their walk or hike in nature. In the case of repeated implementation of the campaign, it would be appropriate to extend the activities to cottages and chalets. We can assume that mainly larger groups of young people use these forms of accommodation. Therefore, it could be interesting to extend this activity to more forms of accommodation, as the company also cooperates with these entities.

Figure 1: #somvreckar stand with biodegradable bag

It was important to address the target audience effectively and thus reach the target group in as many ways as possible. The use of influencer marketing also played a significant role in this campaign. The main ambassador is a well-known Slovak influencer – Radoslav Hoppej – Nie je túra bez Štúra (There is no hike without Štúr), which is one of the influencers focused on hiking, lifestyle, environmental issues and issues of a responsible approach to nature.

The Divino agency further developed the idea of "thieves". Sending creative packages is one of the standard activities in building good PR between the audience and the brand. In this case, they approached this activity differently. The mentioned ambassador distributed large packages tied with a beautiful ribbon to selected influencers, which represented a way to reach the target audience of the company ZľavaDňa. Influencer marketing is an effective form of marketing communication. In 2017, in general, up to 75% of marketers placed part of their marketing budget in influencer marketing, because according to surveys, up to 92% of consumers trust the recommendations of the individuals they follow, even though they do not know them personally. (Anonym, 2018) Influencers are no longer a suitable way to address a target audience with a topic from fashion, beauty or other consumer goods or another commodity. An era is coming when responsibilities and issues related to life in society are also communicated through influencer marketing. We appreciate the use of this form even on a topic such as waste collection. We have to say that this is not a seemingly attractive topic. This is absolutely all right. The ability and willingness of influencers to engage in such cooperation, with or without financial or non-financial compensation, speaks for itself as of a progress in this area. From our point of view, this fact also speaks of a shift in society. The topic of responsibility is becoming more and more present.

The ambassador distributed packages that were exceptionally not full of beautifully wrapped products that could be proudly presented on social networks. These huge gift boxes contained waste. There were food packaging, plastic bottles, glass and paper. Sending packages is a standard procedure within PR. Selected influencers are sent a package containing news from the client. In this way, the new product becomes known to the general public. Sending waste to bloggers is not such a standard procedure, which we consider a suitable form of addressing. We predict that it is difficult to find a person who assumes that a waste package will be sent to them. We consider this to be an attractive form, as the shock after the opening could be and also has been published on social networks. In addition, there was a message in the bottle that answered the questions that appeared in the minds of the influencers after the package was opened.

Figure 2: Radoslav Hoppej for ZľavaDňa

The account caring for the client ZľavaDňa stated that Radoslav: *"distributed garbage wrapped in gift boxes to twenty of the chosen influencers. Almost all of them decided to share the shock of opening the box on their social networks and thus support the #somVreckar campaign without claiming any compensation."* (Hoscheková, 2019)

Figure 3: Package for influencers

Among the selected personalities were influencers from the field of travel, lifestyle, fashion, but also mothers with children. At that time, stories depicting the opening of the gift box could be seen on their social networks. They all expected something positive, but they did not expect the company sending them a package with waste. *"Hi, have you ever realized what we humans give to nature? How does it feel to receive a gift in the form of garbage? What if nature gave it back to us ...?"* was the message in the bottle that accompanied the contents of the package. (Zľavadňa, 2019) We highlight the simplicity of the idea behind the campaign. In addition, the basic educational form was used here, with which most people grow up from an early age – don't do to others what you don't want them to do to you. In our opinion, the simplicity of the idea is one of the reasons of success. The complexity of the problem was presented by the client and the agency very easily and clearly.

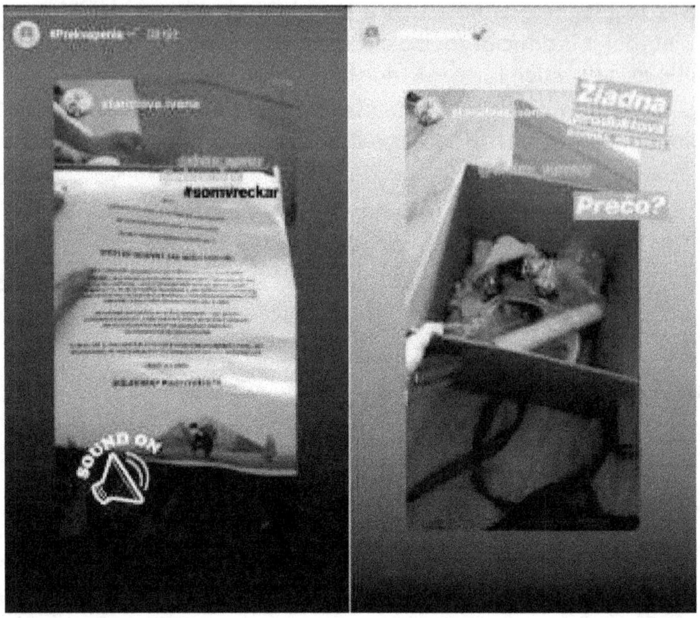

Figure 4: Reactions of the influencers for the packages

Thanks to these non-traditional packages the agency together with the client managed to reach over 70,000 people. And they received over 5,000 likes, 50 comments and 150 shares on Facebook. (Kosturkova,2019) Positive feedback also came from their partners who participated in this activity. The activity succeeded within the audience, both B2B and B2C. About halfway through the activity, reprints and other deliveries to hotels had to be made, as there was a decrease in materials that would inform about this activity within the given hotels. The public came with positive responses to the campaign and the company itself. *"Finally a super meaningful campaign. Very nice campaign. It is really important to address such a topic as well. Thumb up.; Let's protect our beautiful nature,"* customers reacted. (Kosturkova, 2019) In addition, photos of people who decided to clean their surroundings of garbage started to appear on social networks. They also boasted of what they had managed to "steal" from nature. *"The CEO of our biggest competitor – Zľavomat – also noticed this activity and shared it as well,"* said Hargašová (2020), ZľavaDňa campaign manager. Based on the above data, we can evaluate that this activity was perceived positively by the public, which could increase the perceived attractiveness of the company ZľavaDňa.

In addition, the campaign was associated with a contest in which, over the course of more than a month, the winners of € 100 vouchers were drawn every week which could be used on the zlavadna.sk portals. The condition was the publication of a photo of them "stealing" garbage from nature. During that time, the ambassador of this activity himself called on people to behave responsibly and published photos on social networks about how he travels responsibly and eliminates the amount of waste in nature.

In our opinion, it would be appropriate if some of the influencers to whom the packages were sent were also involved in this activity and continued to communicate it further. A more significant activity could have been made on the part of the selected influencers, which would keep the audience informed for the entire duration of the activity.

In addition, the organization ZľavaDňa tried to reach the target group by providing the opportunity to use the frames on the Facebook social network. The agency tried to support their motivation and feeling of a job well done with a graphic visual depicting a clean country with a campaign claim. They decided to use these positive visual elements, as they assumed that the visual with the waste might not be very attractive. Unfortunately, the organization did not provide information on the number of frames used.

Figure 5: #somVreckar in practice

Figure 6: #somvreckar frames

The campaign began as a project that was to have the potential to educate the public about responsible tourism and help the environment. Due to the approaching autumn, this activity had to be terminated as outdoor conditions no longer allowed continuing. However, the positive feedback led to the decision to continue in this activity again after the onset of warmer days in 2020. *"We are very happy for the participation and feedback we have received from people. Also, that we have inspired more people to keep our country clean. The campaign is coming to an end, but we still want to support this idea and we believe that people do the same. We have proved that we care about our country and have contributed to its protection," said the CEO of ZľavaDňa at the end of the activity*. In addition, they implemented this educational and environmental activity in internal conditions. *"Because our employees also liked this activity, we distributed a garbage bag to everyone so that they could also collect rubbish in their surroundings,"* said Hargašová. They managed to dispose of a black dump in one district of the capital. (Hargašová, 2020) We also appreciate the involvement of employees in the activity. We want to emphasize the fact that if corporate social responsibility is to be fully implemented, it is important that it comes from within the company, from the employees themselves. On the one hand, it stands on strong pillars and on the other hand, employees can communicate this activity to the external environment of the organization.

We can say that the campaign was positive not only by verbal feedback from the public and partners, but also by involving these entities in the collection of waste. Based on the statements of the account, the CEO of ZľavaDňa and the campaign manager, we can say that fulfilling their goal set before the campaign, drawing attention to the problem of waste accumulation and educating the target audience about responsible travelling was fulfilled. The disadvantage was the fact that no research was carried out after the end of the mentioned activity. We therefore rely on their internal results and their evaluation.

3. Discussion

According to our method, the company ZľavaDňa created the right concept, which educated about the environmental problem in a creative way. In a simple, easy-to-understand way, they pointed out the seriousness of the situation and created a classic principle – don't do to others what you don't want them to do to you. It is an idea that young children grow up with. The simplicity of this idea reached the target audience and educated them without unnecessarily complicated procedures. The standard procedure – sending products to influencers – who present the opening of wonderful products with expressions of enthusiasm on their profiles, was replaced by the agency with the shock that the brand sent them garbage. They communicated the mentioned idea in a simple and cheap way. At the same time, they educated the influencers themselves, who previously probably had not been involved in this environmental problem. We can assume that there may have been a certain shift in thinking that they will also communicate spontaneously.

We appreciate the creativity and simplicity of this activity. The problem-solving approach highlights awareness and progressive thinking that should be pursued by more than one company.

Based on the above, it can be stated that socially responsible business is not a separate subject, but rather a set of guiding principles and values, such as fairness, equality, tolerance, adequacy and responsibility, which are to be passed on with foresight. The CSR can also play a role in developing the skills needed to improve employment. As sustainable development skills are best gained through personal experience, we recommend that the learning process focus as much as possible on inclusive education, activities and motivation. Emphasis should be placed on creative thinking, innovation and long-term perspectives, and in particular on our responsibility to future generations.

4. Conclusion

The environment is constantly exposed to the influence of individualists, but also organizations. Fortunately, there are also influences that we do not consider negative in the context of the circular economy, on the contrary, they help to reduce waste in nature, either by collecting or using materials that are easier to decompose or reuse. These activities are often educational, as was the case with ZľavaDňa, which pointed to a serious problem the environment is facing. According to information from primary and secondary sources, we can assess that environmental corporate social responsibility was in this case combined and perceived as the education of society. In order to achieve a solution, it is necessary that the problem is explained and that the public is sufficiently informed, i.e. educated. We assume that this area needs even more detailed research, which would bring a more thorough and comprehensive view of the issue. In addition, ZľavaDňa found a constructive way of eliminating waste in nature, which it effectively linked to its business activities. We emphasize the logic of choosing a pillar and the very interconnectedness of the given activity to the company's activities. We consider this to be a manifestation of real awareness and responsibility within the company. In our opinion, in this way, the organization is able to communicate the activity more credibly and avoids possible doubts, either on the part of employees or the general public, if it focuses on the pillar of social responsibility that is closest to it. Organizations are increasingly integrating corporate social responsibility into their operations and carrying out activities that benefit society as a whole. It is important that multiple companies follow this trend, which is welcomed from the customer's point of view and they respond positively to it. However, it is a long-term activity that needs time, effort and the desire to change the functioning of the society in which we live.

The secondary goal was to find out how it is possible to communicate a given topic. We can say that the topic of waste separation is often communicated, but on the other hand often overlooked. Finding a creative solution is the basis for effectively addressing the target group. The catchy campaign slogan, along with the thieving visual, strengthened the power of the idea. We appreciate the use of influencer marketing as the main medium for communicating the topic at the beginning of the campaign. The company ZľavaDňa and the Divino agency focused significantly on social networks, while not forgetting traditional media such as printed materials and stands. The use of various frames in profile pictures is no longer just a form of entertainment and attractiveness of the user's profile picture, but various initiatives are communicated through it, reflecting the state of society and life in it. We highlight the use of this form. Overall, we can say that it is important to use a wide range of media. It is the media that may not appear to be the most effective that can help bring the required message to the target audience. We believe that standard media and methods used for commercial purposes represent new possibilities for communicating topics that affect the life of society as a whole, including environmental issues. We can say that topics that affect the life of the whole society are given more space.

Acknowledgements

This paper was created within the project VEGA no. 1/0078/18 entitled "Aspects of marketing communication in the management processes of the circular economy".

References

Abrams, F.W. (1951) "Management´s responsibilities in a complex world", Harvard Business Review, Vol 29, No. 3, pp 34.

Anonym. (2018) „Pravdy o influcencer marketingu" Stratégie, 2018, roč. XXIV, č. 9, s. 35.

Bansal, P. (2005) "Evolving sustainably: A longitudinal study of corporate sustainable development", *Strategic Management Journal*, Vol 26, No. 3, pp 197-218.

Booking.com. (2018) „Where Sustainable Travel in Headed in 2018" [online] https://globalnews.booking.com/where-sustainable-travel-is-headed-in-2018/

Chandler, D. (2008) *"Strategic CSR – Earthshare.org"*, [online] http://strategiccsr-sage.blogspot.com/2008/10/.

Chandler, D. (2019) *Strategic corporate social responsibility:Sustainable Value Creation*, SAGE Publications Ltd., London.

Chouinard, Y and Stanley. (2014) *Zodpovědná firma*, Peoplecomm, Praha

Green, T. and Peloza, J. (2011) "How does corporate social responsibility create value for consumers?", Journal of Consumer Research, Vol 28, No. 1, pp 48-56.

Hart, S.L. (1995) "A natural-resource-based view of the firm", Academy of Management Review, Vol 20, No. 4, pp 986-1014.

Hoscheková, S. (2019) "Unikátny projekt #somvreckar", [online] https://www.divino.sk/blog/somvreckar

Kosturková, M. (2019) "Kampaň končí, myšlienka zotrváva" tlačová správa

Molína-Azorín, J. F., et al. (2009) „Environmental practices and firm performance: An empirical analysis in the Spanish hotel industry", *Journal of Cleaner Production*, Vol 17, pp 516-524.

Zľavadňa. (2019) Odkaz vo fľaši.

Organization's Proactive Transformation Competence: Identification and Development

Gediminas Baublys
Department of Business, Faculty of Economics and Business Administration, Vilnius University, Vilnius, Lithuania
gediminas.baublys@ef.vu.lt
DOI: 10.34190/EIE.20.088

Abstract: For a long time considered to be a consequence of crises, systemic problems, or performance issues, today, organizational transformation is understood as the inevitable necessity to cope with environmental surprises, enhance creativity and resilience. In a volatile and disruptive modern environment, competitive advantage is momentary and unsustainable, rigid processes and traditional structures are insufficient for sustainable development and continuous innovation. Businesses must prepare for constant changes, embrace uncertainty and unpredictability. Moreover, to enable proactive identification of unexpected internal and external triggers that might lead to renewal and develop competence to respond to them appropriately, the whole organizational system must operate in an agile and creative way. The conducted literature review of published empirical research and theoretical articles and organizational transformation concept analysis demonstrates a gap in scientific knowledge. Scholars focus on organizational change, with little attention given to the development of transformability capabilities and business proactiveness. Transformation competence is a multilayered and complex construct, and new ways of academic thinking and research approaches are required to explore it. The paper aims to narrow the identified gap by answering the question, what set of characteristics, skills, competencies enhance organizational innovativeness, flexibility, and adaptability, enables capacity to initiate and successfully implement business transformations proactively? By developing a conceptual framework for proactive organizational transformation, linking existing research on elements of adaptability, agility, and resilience, discussing implications for empirical research methodology, this paper is a groundwork for further empirical research. Apart from that, it provides practical value by offering insights for organizational flexibility, resilience, and innovation capacity development.

Keywords: business transformation, innovativeness, organizational competence, resilience for transformation.

1. Introduction

Modern organizations operate in extreme velocity and highly unpredictable and uncertain environment. They must keep continuously increasing their pace to stay relevant. Businesses must refocus from targeting short term competitive advantage to continuous renewal for long term sustainability. Moreover, executives must direct and shape strategic reorientations while mediating between organizational inertia and the need for fundamental renewal when incremental changes fail to achieve a sustainable level of performance and acceleration.

Due to the volatile business landscape, the average tenure of companies narrows year by year and is forecasted to shrink further (Anthony et al. 2016). There are industries where companies may need to reinvent themselves every few years to keep up with changes in the markets (Bower and Paine 2017). However, organizations can achieve long-term sustainability if they develop resilience, competence, and ability to transform, continuously learn, adapt, and innovate.

Innovativeness and transformability require navigation between stability and unpredictability as a qualitatively different organizational state can be reached only at the point when the system is pressured from outside and inside. Navigate business at such paradoxical states to continually produce creativeness, and changeable behavior is a primary mission for executives. Whereas, for management scholars figuring out what interventions can increase innovative capacity and organizational longevity is one of the highest priorities.

Turbulent context changes how scholars view organizational evolution also. Little relevance and slow progress of current discoveries in the organizational change field raises many doubts that scholars and practitioners are stuck in the exploitation of well-known (By 2020). The apparent struggle for academics is the need to combine complexity science theory and research methods with more traditional organizational change research methodology to break through to new levels of phenomenon research. A growing knowledge of complexity science requires new ways of thinking and qualitatively different organizational transformation conceptualization.

This paper aims to expand scientific knowledge and serve for future explorations by answering the question: what set of capabilities, skills, characteristics, and competencies enhance organizational flexibility and adaptability, enables capacity to initiate and successfully implement business transformations proactively?

A literature review was conducted to get a holistic view of diverse perspectives and viewpoints in academic thinking concerning organizational transformation competence as a concept. Books, edited volumes, and journal articles were collected using several relevant keywords: transformation competence, transformation capabilities, capacity for transformation, transformation readiness, transformability. The material was evaluated and delimited by the relativeness of the problem addressed. Later it was analyzed to identify knowledge gaps and issues that scholars face in explaining the phenomenon. Moreover, identify opportunities for further studies and research.

Complexity and non-linear dynamic features of modern organizations were explored to understand better how interrelated concepts of organizational resilience, adaptability, and agility contribute to overall organizational transformation ability. Furthermore, to investigate what organizational elements scholars attribute to the construct. The presented theoretical insights, conclusions, and implications where drown from cited references.

This paper is structured as follows: in section two, the importance of proactivity in early identification and anticipation of transformation triggers is discussed. Section three provides an overview of previous research on concept configuration. Interactions of resilience, agility, and adaptation capabilities in competence development are highlighted next. In section five, the organizational transformation conceptual framework is developed and presented. Finally, in section six, implications for future-oriented conceptualization and research are given. The article ends with the most important conclusions.

2. The value of proactive identification of transformation triggers

Transformation is the least explained and the most complex type of change. It is a radical shift to a new state of being, altering the composition of operations and processes, structure, culture, and strategy. It sets the new strategic vision of the organization and involves a critical mass of stakeholders (Anderson and Anderson 2010).

For an exceedingly long time, in the minds of management scholars, it was a consequence of systemic crises, performance issues. For this reason, two opposite views have evolved from the case studies of business failures. On the one hand, a wide variety of scholars advocated for the punctuated equilibrium model of change (Tushman and Romanelli 1985; Gersick 1991; Greenwood and Hinings 1993). They argued that organizations evolve through long periods of stability that are punctuated by short, revolutionary moments when fundamental transformations happen. After each punctuation, organizations stabilize on a new equilibrium.

Conversely, other distinguished scientists supported the continuous transformation concept (Orlikowski 1996; Weick and Quinn 1999; Brown and Eisenhardt 1997; Eisenhardt and Bhatia 2017). They assumed that organizations must develop the ability to continuously change to ensure long-term survival in the disruptive and turbulent environment. They never settle to equilibrium, and one reconfiguration is followed by the other. Smaller changes may happen simultaneously in different parts of the organization, and they accumulate to the qualitative transformation of the whole company at the end.

There is only one strong consensus between academics and practitioners that the disruptions organizations face are enormous, and the ability to manage them is the core organizational competence as most of the strategic transformations fail to reach their initial objectives (Burnes 2005). One of the primary rationales for the high failure rate is the lack of proactivity in response to triggers with such a highly risky affair.

The inability to act timely significantly reduces the likelihood of success. When organizations are performing well, managers are reluctant to take significant risks. Consequently, organizations fail to prepare for plateau and decline in the evolution cycle. They rely on patterns and inertia instead of innovating and renewing on the peak of their performance. Later, when radical change is inevitable as performance issues arise or environmental jolts happen, organizations fight for survival rather than solve evolution challenges.

Scholars have generalized three main trigger categories: crises (problems), potential crises (threats, risks), opportunities (Kotter 1995; Paton and Mccalman 2008). However, there is an endless number of multilayered external and internal factors that can catalyze radical change (Paton and Mccalman 2008) that companies miss identifying.

Thus, the biggest challenge for business organizations in today's high-velocity environment and the pace of technological progress is to recognize threats and opportunities, not based on patterns, but to be able to look ahead, anticipate future trends and factors, analyze and measure their impact and potential consequences for the organization. It is essential to choose the right response.

3. The complexity of organizational configuration and dynamics

Complex and constant changes in the business environment, also accelerated technology advancement, have made scientists increasingly hesitant in support of the more traditional punctuated equilibrium model of organizational transformation (Orlikowski 1996). Scholars finally admitted that business transformation is constant recombination of both reactive modifications and proactive actions led by corporate goals and intentional managerial decisions rather than formed by unmanageable and unforeseen convergence periods (Weick and Quinn 1999). However, the studies of what makes more intelligent, robust, and prescient changes (Galunic and Weeks 2000) were rare and usually had substantial limitations.

Scholars started exploring the organizational transformation beyond the static conception of it with the assumption that organizations are dynamic systems and fundamentally change continuously, and the ability to manage this change is a critical capability for survival (Brown and Eisenhardt 1997). Before that, the organizational change concept was constructed on a linear understanding, when the process is composed of individual succeeding steps (Styhre 2002). With the recent rise of attention on complexity theory, the impossibility of prediction of non-linear systems was understood (Tsoukas 1998), and emergence, unpredictability, diversity, and adaptability irreversibly changed the understanding of organizations.

The organization itself emerges from quasi-stable structures through a continuously evolving agency of its members. It is an ever-mutating entity were even strict rules, hierarchies and structures are often ignored by actors whose actions highly depend on specific conditions and personal choices (Tsoukas and Chia 2002). Hence, change is a natural condition of organizational life, and leaders must be prepared to cope with the chaos and manage organizational complexity (Farazmand 2003) as responses to environmental and internal triggers are complex, multilayered rather than fixed. They are highly dependent on internal organizational assumptions and interpretations.

Organizations never settle to equilibrium (Eisenhardt and Bhatia 2017). Thus, the foundation of corporate action, the competence to transform lies in organizational design, and its complex network dynamics. However, to determine how to develop organizational transformation ability, the complex modern organization and how all its diverse capabilities, strategy, structure, culture, and processes interact and interrelate must be understood (Miller et al. 2009). Moreover, innovativeness, creativity, and transformability emerge only at the paradoxical state of stability and instability (Stacey 1995).

Therefore, the inability to deal with the dynamics of a multitude of self-interested actors interacting with each other dynamics is considered as the primary cause of organizational transformation failures (Janssen et al. 2015). The vital element of survival becomes the capability to operate with sufficient stability and retain the capacity for change (Stacey 2002). Otherwise, if an organization is too stable, nothing can change, if too chaotic, the system will be drowned by change (Lewin and Volberda 1999).

Furthermore, an organization as a complex system is the set of various interactions among its large number of constituent parts that act according to their particular context and limited knowledge of the whole system (Maguire 2011). Their interconnected actions form non-linear behavior, which is unpredictable from the viewpoint of its elements.

Every complex system is in continuous transformation by itself and the environment (Cilliers 2002). Therefore, to understand organizational transformation, "we badly need complex theories, which will take into account context, time, histories, process, meaning, politics, emergence, contingency, feedback, novelty, change" (Tsoukas 1998). Unfortunately, there is no single unified theory of complexity, but several different theories and concepts that have arisen from the natural science (Boisot 2011; Mitchell 2009; Cham and Johnson 2007;

Lawrence et al. 2006; Mitleton-Kelly 2003). There is also a noticeable distance between complexity science and organizational change research. Hence, it is the inevitable challenge to combine both if organizational science seeks to break through to new levels of organizational transformation research.

4. The components of dynamic organizational transformation competence configuration

The configuration of organizational elements must be analyzed in full scope with the evolution, and limitedness of predictability in mind. Components are situation, and company-specific and some of the attributes are related to individuals. Everything that is bounded inside the organization and affects its ability to reach goals is part of the organization's competence (Taatila 2004).

Furthermore, even a minor detail can have an impact on the organizational agility, innovation capabilities, and competence to respond to changes and the ability to recover from failures (Greising 1998). However, there is little scientific knowledge, how proactive business transformation can be facilitated by enhanced organizational transformation competence, how the capacity of it can be configured and sustained.

Nevertheless, the paradox of corporate system potential and capabilities ambiguity is evident. Organizations might share the same structure, have similar technologies and product portfolio, yet they might be extremely different when it comes to taking actions.

Beyond standardization and operational excellence, there is an action repertoire and intelligence not described in procedures that manifest in unexpected events and are individual to every organization (Weick et al. 2008). Proactive transformation requires scenario planning and assessment of alternative development trajectories, risks, and opportunities, the ability to uncover and manage unexpected events effectively. Therefore, organizations should learn how to self-organize and solve problems that never happened before, develop all-inclusive resilience and sensitivity to internal and external triggers and act in an agile way near to the problem, risk, or opportunity source.

Developed organizational transformation competence enables to establish a fundamentally new system when existing becomes untenable (Walker et al. 2004) and jump to different development course (Folke et al. 2010). It is the interpretation of unfamiliar situations, problem-solving creativity (Lengnick-Hall and Beck 2009), and the strength of innovativeness. The quality configuration of culture, social connections, structure, agility, and strategy (Wang and Ahmed 2007) helps cross the thresholds and create new, more stable territories (Folke et al. 2010) and reach long-term sustainability.

It is not an extraordinary feature, but rather an achievable condition. It emerges from conventional processes and structures when the organizational configuration is enabled with flexibility and reliable structural, cognitive, emotional connectivity. As a result, business resilience changes depending on the challenges it is facing (Sutcliffe and Vogus 2003) and enables the ability to cope with unexpected events, and to utilize on them proactively, to renew and transform in response.

Hence, it is essential to foster the system's flexibility, leaving room for improvised actions, and develop the skills of the actors as they fuel connections and reinforces a common perception of the environment. Reliable interconnectivity prevents failures, unleashes the potential to pursue new opportunities, positively affect future adaptability, and evolve competence after every change. Adequately developed, organizational transformation competence equips an organization with the repertoire of powerful routines and enables motivated choice between adaptation and robust transformation (Lengnick-Hall and Beck 2005).

Furthermore, organizational flexibility, creativity, and the quick selection and implementation of actions are the components of strategic agility (Mccann 2004; Jamrog et al. 2006), which allows quick selection of configuration alternatives of resources and capabilities, mobilization, complex problem solving, and prompt actions. It is inseparable from overall business transformation competence. When the environment is changing rapidly, and it is not possible to predict alterations, organizations must change the traditional rules to operate with experimentation, innovation, and agility. They have to decentralize, enable internal expert networks, project teams, empower people (Stacey 2007).

5. Proactive organizational transformation conceptual framework

Organizations have limited knowledge and must be ready to deal with unpredictability coming from outside and uncertainty inside. They adapt and transform in constant interaction with a dynamic environment that influences the development of the organizational system, as well as the transformation, reinforcement, and stabilization of patterns in it (Cilliers 2002). Business capabilities and competencies are not growing and not degrading gradually and consistently. With new emergent developments, changes are asymmetrical. The adaptive organizational system must aim to maintain dynamism, rather than sustain the development of specific elements.

Organizational fit with the environment it is operating, and the ability to attain and manage diverse resources to be capable of actively renewing itself, change behavior, expand internal knowledge and connections are critical for longevity (Merali and Allen 2011) and innovation capacity (Duchek et al. 2019). The environment selects out those who fail to reorient promptly and successfully. Thus, an organizational system and external complexity must correspond (Boisot and Mckelvey 2011). Adaptive capacity is in constant need to learn and develop in the face of new technologies, actions of competitors, legal regulations, and other environmental changes. Organizations should seek efficiency combined with agility and adaptability, leaving room for organizational slack, experimentation, and creativity rather than focus on operational efficiency maximization.

Organizations are unpredictable outcomes of interactions (according to the hierarchies and processes, but more often, despite them) between actors (Thietart and Forgues 2011; Hidalgo et al. 2011). Every organization is also a connection with other organizations and, in the end, acts as a node in a vast network of similar entities and institutions.

Thus, they must develop sensitivity, understanding of connections, environmental dynamics, and self-awareness. Create scenarios for internal and external triggers and anticipate their impact. Furthermore, configure internal elements: structure, culture, strategy, processes, with the evolution, and limitedness of predictability in mind rather than aim for stability. They have to be agile in motivated response to environmental changes and internal impulses as well as recovery from failures of configuration (Greising 1998).

Companies can coevolutionary adapt to the environment by continuously shaping configuration to keep a balance between flexibility and efficiency, enable improvisation, and ensure the capture of all opportunities (Eisenhardt and Piezunka 2011). This active adaptivity becomes part of organizational resilience and helps adjust to unpredicted environmental shocks without putting in jeopardy the whole system (Holling 2001). They should become qualitatively different after the transformation (Hazy 2011) and focus on future resilience rather than operational and effectiveness improvements.

Literature review findings convert to the conceptual framework, which presents the continuous adaptation cycle (Figure 1). Organizations must develop a keen sensitivity to unexpected external events and internal crises, track the strength of network connections, be open to signals that pass through the social links, proactively gather, decode, and share information. Planned actions must aim to increase resilience capacity around transformation target, simultaneously weakening existing configuration and breaking free from withholding inertia. Consequently, new conditions may enable new successive cycles of innovation and transformation.

Hence, the role of the leaders is to keep organizations on this continuous cycle and develop a culture of innovativeness, where improvisation and experimentation are the foundation. Raise the intelligence to deal with the problems and opportunities as near as possible to the source. They should foster dynamic and open connections to quickly and adequately transfer decision making if the local capacity to develop solutions is not enough.

Therefore, proactive transformation competence and rapid coevolution with the high-velocity environment are directly dependent on the dynamic configuration of organizational capabilities at each distinct stage. What discrete elements constitute the whole construct is the fundamental question for further studies and requires empirical research.

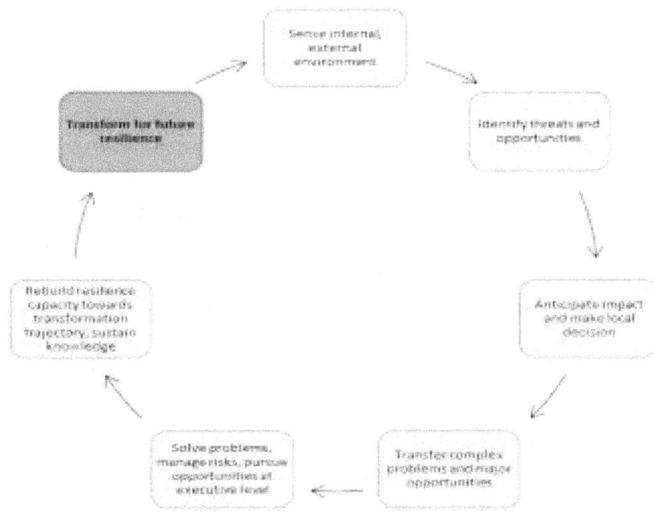

Figure 1: Organizational transformation and adaptation cycle (Prepared by the author)

6. Implications for proactive transformation competence research methodology

In order to gain considerable progress in organizational transformation competence development research, the dynamics and constituting elements of the fluctuating state of the firm and enablers of multilayered proactivity must be evaluated. Diverse aspects of the business characteristics must be addressed as it is dependent on various intricate factors and environment business operates. Overlaying elements of strategic agility and organizational resilience must also be assessed.

Literature review findings and current scientific knowledge provide stimulus to lead phenomenon research to postmodern thought style, the ontology of becoming, which accentuates the momentary, continually fluctuating, and emergent reality (Chia 1995). Postmodernism allows uncertainty, unknowns, and complexity attributes to scientific research and privileges action and movement. Exploration focus must be on changing dynamics rather than change itself (Weick and Quinn 1999).

Besides, complexity theory is valuable for potential research as it aims to explain how complex systems endure, adapt, and grow in chaotic conditions. It offers an advantage by not forcing to understand all parts of a complex organizational system (Baumann and Siggelkow 2011). There is no obligation to represent the global specification of a system's behavior. Instead, the focus is on local agents and interconnections of system elements. Thus, simulation experiments can uncover mechanisms of interdependencies.

The literature review has revealed, it is essential to be where change happens as initial impacts, and actors' initial responses provide especially rich data. These turning points may be unnoticeable for general linear methods, but with multi-method research can provide a vast amount of qualitative data. Thus, process apprehension through observational and qualitative data can be more valuable than variance explanation and verification of enduring relationships. Longitudinal and temporally sensitive methods are preferable, as the use of general linear methods is not sufficient to represent social reality (Meyer et al. 2005).

Organizations change qualitatively, not incrementally (Byrne 2011). Therefore, appropriate measurement is not a continuous ratio scale but nominal/categorical addressing non-linear and radical shifts in size, culture, effectiveness, and functions. The focus must be on organizational evolution, understanding patterns for the future, through theory testing, outcome anticipation, and performance evaluation. The multi-method approach is the most appropriate for complex organizational systems research (Eoyang 2011; Eisenhardt and Bhatia 2017).

Moreover, only a statistical explanation of variations between independent and dependent variables is often too narrowly focused on representing temporal events and order of fundamental corporate changes. Scholars must switch from transformation background and consequences explanation to exploring emergence, development, and termination of it (Van De Ven and Poole 2017) to explain how organizations can adapt, reconfigure, and manage resilience capacity for constant transformation and innovation.

7. Conclusions

Organizations are complex systems, and they change constantly. However, rigid structures and processes can prevent innovation and lock in inertia. Continuous learning, creativity, adaptation, and sustainable development require goal-directed senior management actions in response to internal and external triggers. Companies must identify and observe them, anticipate the impact. Business transformation may be a reactive response to reached adaptation limits or crises, as well as a proactive initiative in pursuit of opportunities and innovations. This paper has highlighted the importance of organizational readiness to cope with surprises and the capacity to effectively select and implement responses to both repeatable and unfamiliar events. Management must enable proactive transformation mechanisms in the repertoire of strategic actions and practices and configure organizational resilience capacity. While being the foundation of transformation competence, it not only enables qualitative transitions but also converts crises to strategic renewal and innovation opportunities.

However, despite many endeavors to apply different theoretical perspectives in the exploration of proactive transformation competence, there is a dearth of empirical investigations on understanding its constituting elements. Further research could expand scientific knowledge significantly and serve for future investigations in the organizational science field as well as add tangible, practical value for the business, providing insights into what interventions can increase innovativeness and longevity of organizations. Furthermore, to develop the organizational transformation competence research methodology and identify organizational multilayer proactivity enabling elements, an all-inclusive multi-method research design to measure diverse aspects of the business is mandatory. Hence, further researches should consider organizations as indivisible, firmly integrated systems to determine the attributes constituting organizational transformation competence and identify the rules of their configuration. Also, bear in mind culture, social connections, structure, agility, and strategy to understand how it can be managed and developed. Seek to provide insights on, and how in a high paced and turbulent environment, this dynamic and complex configuration can stay self-organizing and adaptable in response to constant external and internal changes.

References

Anderson, D. & Anderson, L. A. (2010). Beyond change management: How to achieve breakthrough results through conscious change leadership, John Wiley & Sons.

Anthony, S. D., Viguerie, S. P. & Waldeck, A. (2016). Corporate longevity: Turbulence ahead for large organizations. Strategy & Innovation, 14, 1-9.

Baumann, O. & Siggelkow, N. (2011). Complexity and competitive advantage. Handbook of complexity and management, 494-505.

Boisot, M. (2011). Knowledge management and complexity. The SAGE handbook of complexity and management, 436-453.

Boisot, M. & Mckelvey, B. (2011). Complexity and organization-environment relations: Revisiting Ashby's law of requisite variety. The Sage handbook of complexity and management, 279-298.

Bower, J. L. & Paine, L. S. (2017). The error at the heart of corporate leadership. HBR'S 10 MUST, 165.

Brown, S. L. & Eisenhardt, K. M. (1997). The art of continuous change: Linking complexity theory and time-paced evolution in relentlessly shifting organizations. Administrative science quarterly, 1-34.

Burnes, B. (2005). Complexity theories and organizational change. International journal of management reviews, 7, 73-90.

By, R. T. (2020). Organizational Change and Leadership: Out of the Quagmire. Journal of Change Management, 20, 1-6.

Byrne, D. S. (2011). Exploring organizational effectiveness: The value of complex realism as a frame of reference and systematic comparison as a method. The Sage handbook of complexity and management, 131-141.

Cham, K. & Johnson, J. (2007). Complexity theory: a science of cultural systems. M/C Journal, 10, 21-34.

Chia, R. (1995). From modern to postmodern organizational analysis. Organization Studies, 16, 579-604.

Cilliers, P. (2002). Complexity and postmodernism: Understanding complex systems, Routledge.

Duchek, S., Raetze, S. & Scheuch, I. (2019). The role of diversity in organizational resilience: a theoretical framework. Business Research, 1-37.

Eisenhardt, K. M. & Bhatia, M. M. (2017). Organizational complexity and computation. The Blackwell companion to organizations, 442-466.

Eisenhardt, K. M. & Piezunka, H. (2011). Complexity theory and corporate strategy. The SAGE handbook of complexity and management, 506-523.

Eoyang, G. (2011). Complexity and the dynamics of organizational change. The sage handbook of complexity and management, 317-332.

Farazmand, A. (2003). Chaos and Transformation Theories: A Theoretical Analysis with Implications for Organization Theory and Public Management. Public Organization Review, 3, 339-372.

Folke, C., Carpenter, S., Walker, B., Scheffer, M., Chapin, T. & Rockström, J. (2010). Resilience thinking: integrating resilience, adaptability, and transformability. Ecology and Society, 15.

Galunic, C. & Weeks, J. (2000). Intra organizational ecology, Citeseer.

Gersick, C. J. G. (1991). Revolutionary Change Theories: A Multilevel Exploration of the Punctuated Equilibrium Paradigm. The Academy of Management Review, 16, 10-36.
Greenwood, R. & Hinings, C. R. (1993). Understanding strategic change: The contribution of archetypes. Academy of Management Journal.
Greising, D. (1998). I'd like the world to buy a coke: the life and leadership of Roberto Goizueta, Wiley New York, NY.
Hazy, J. K. (2011). More than a metaphor: Complexity and the new rules of management. P. Allen, S. Maguire. & B. McKelvey., Sage handbook of complexity and Management, Los Angeles 524Y539, London, Sage.
Hidalgo, C., Allen, P., Maguire, S. & Mckelvey, B. (2011). The value in between: organizations as adapting and evolving networks. The SAGE Handbook of Complexity and Management. SAGE Publications, London.
Holling, C. S. (2001). Understanding the complexity of economic, ecological, and social systems. Ecosystems, 4, 390-405.
Jamrog, J. J., Mccann, J., Lee, J. M., Morrison, C. L., Selsky, J. W. & Vickers, M. (2006). Agility and resilience in the face of continuous change. American Management Association.
Janssen, M., Van Der Voort, H. & Van Veenstra, A. F. (2015). Failure of large transformation projects from the viewpoint of complex adaptive systems: Management principles for dealing with project dynamics. Information Systems Frontiers, 17, 15-29.
Kotter, J. P. (1995). Leading change: Why transformation efforts fail.
Lawrence, T. B., Suddaby, R., Clegg, S. R., Hardy, C., Lawrence, T. & Nord, W. R. (2006). The SAGE handbook of organization studies. Sage publications. London.
Lengnick-Hall, C. A. & Beck, T. E. (2005). Adaptive fit versus robust transformation: How organizations respond to environmental change. Journal of Management, 31, 738-757.
Lengnick-Hall, C. A. & Beck, T. E. (2009). Resilience capacity and strategic agility: Prerequisites for thriving in a dynamic environment, Citeseer.
Lewin, A. Y. & Volberda, H. W. (1999). Prolegomena on coevolution: A framework for research on strategy and new organizational forms. Organization Science, 10, 519-534.
Maguire, S. (2011). Constructing and appreciating complexity. The SAGE handbook of complexity and management, 79-92.
Mccann, J. (2004). Organizational effectiveness: Changing concepts for changing environments. People and Strategy, 27, 42.
Merali, Y. & Allen, P. (2011). Complexity and systems thinking. The SAGE handbook of complexity and management, 31-52.
Meyer, A. D., Gaba, V. & Colwell, K. A. (2005). Organizing far from equilibrium: Non-linear change in organizational fields. Organization Science, 16, 456-473.
Miller, D., Greenwood, R. & Prakash, R. (2009). What happened to organization theory? Journal of Management Inquiry, 18, 273-279.
Mitchell, M. (2009). Complexity: A guided tour, Oxford University Press.
Mitleton-Kelly, E. (2003). Ten principles of complexity and enabling infrastructures.
Orlikowski, W. J. (1996). Improvising organizational transformation over time: A situated change perspective. Information systems research, 7, 63-92.
Paton, R. A. & Mccalman, J. (2008). Change management: A guide to effective implementation, Sage.
Stacey, R. D. (1995). The science of complexity: An alternative perspective for strategic change processes. Strategic management journal, 16, 477-495.
Stacey, R. D. (2002). Complexity and management, Routledge.
Stacey, R. D. (2007). Strategic management and organisational dynamics: The challenge of complexity to ways of thinking about organisations, Pearson education.
Styhre, A. (2002). Non-linear change in organizations: organization change management informed by complexity theory. Leadership & Organization Development Journal, 23, 343-351.
Sutcliffe, K. M. & Vogus, T. J. (2003). Organizing for resilience. Positive organizational scholarship: Foundations of a new discipline, 94, 110.
Taatila, V. (2004). The concept of organizational competence: a foundational analysis, University of Jyväskylä.
Thietart, R.-A. & Forgues, B. (2011). Complexity science and organization. The sage handbook of complexity and management, 53-64.
Tsoukas, H. (1998). Introduction: chaos, complexity, and organization theory. Sage Publications Sage CA: Thousand Oaks, CA.
Tsoukas, H. & Chia, R. (2002). On Organizational Becoming: Rethinking Organizational Change.
Tushman, M. L. & Romanelli, E. (1985). Organizational evolution: A metamorphosis model of convergence and reorientation. Research in organizational behavior.
Van De Ven, A. H. & Poole, M. S. (2017). Field research methods. The Blackwell companion to organizations, 867-888.
Walker, B., Holling, C. S., Carpenter, S. & Kinzig, A. (2004). Resilience, adaptability, and transformability in social-ecological systems. Ecology and Society, 9.
Wang, C. L. & Ahmed, P. K. (2007). Dynamic capabilities: A review and research agenda. International journal of management reviews, 9, 31-51.
Weick, K. E. & Quinn, R. E. (1999). Organizational change and development. Annual review of psychology, 50, 361-386.
Weick, K. E., Sutcliffe, K. M. & Obstfeld, D. (2008). Organizing for high reliability: Processes of collective mindfulness. Crisis management, 3, 81-123.

Corporate Social Responsibility (CSR) as a Factor of Entrepreneurship Sustainable Development: Research in the Czech Republic

Jaroslava Blažková (Němcová)
Tomas Bata University in Zlín, Czech Republic
nemcova@utb.cz
DOI: 10.34190/EIE.20.144

Abstract: Corporate social responsibility is a voluntary approach based on ethical principles and structured management controls. These principals and controls are based on a variety of activities that an enterprise can choose from according to its orientation and on the requirements of the surroundings. The primary motivation for this approach is to remain sustainable, build a strong company culture and maintain the good name of the enterprise to attain a competitive advantage. These principals are usually fruitful, lead to better stability, attract new employees and open up new business opportunities. This is also proven in the research presented in this paper where CSR managers declare the most common reasons why CSR methodology implemented by a company are to build and maintain corporate values and gain a competitive advantage on the market. The first research phase was conducted using a questionnaire survey from June to September 2019 to map the current level of CSR implementation in large companies in the Czech Republic. A research panel of forty CSR managers completed fifteen open, matrix and scale questions. The purpose of the survey was to verify the research process methodology and identify trends in the area. The conclusions from the first research phase show interesting trends in the field of corporate social responsibility of enterprises in the Czech Republic and the mapping of the current level of CSR implementation in companies in the region. Interesting findings were made based on the research presented in the paper and these will serve as a base for further studies. One of the findings shows that very few companies have a clear methodology or a strategy for deciding the direction of CSR. Companies often act randomly or based on individual preferences so that CSR management in enterprises is not centralised with a clear focus but instead divided across different departments (HR, CEO´s office, marketing or sales department).

Keywords: corporate social responsibility, sustainable development, enterprise, corporate values, CSR, company culture

1. Introduction: The current situation in the CSR area

In a market economy awash with social networks, hoax and fake news and a lack of trust, companies face a challenging environment when presenting themselves. Paradoxically, the availability and excess of information coupled with the ease of reaching a company complicate the decision-making process within the framework of social responsibility. The basis of the sustainability of the CSR model is an elaborate integrated system of social responsibility rules, based on the specifics and uniqueness of a company, which is an indivisible part of company culture. Therefore, enterprises focus more on trustworthiness and maintaining their good name through a system of CSR activities. These trends can also be observed in large Czech enterprises.

1.1 The Czech Republic in the SDG Index and Dashboards 2019

There are different ways to compare the level of CSR and I chose this index as a measure because it compares a large number of states based on equal attributes of CSR. Even the Czech Republic, as a post-communist country, reached a very high position. The United Nations began tracking sustainable development goals (SDGs) in 2015 as a guideline to move towards a sustainable and equitable society. In 2019, the Czech Republic ranked seventh out of 162 countries evaluated under the SDG Index, just behind the Scandinavian countries and Germany. It reached a score of 81.9, which is above average worldwide and within a region where the average is 77.7 (Sustainable Development Report 2019). Based on a high SDG index level, the Czech Republic can be a good model as a country and using it as an example, can verify the effectiveness of CSR activities and measure their impact on sustainable business development.

1.2 Sustainable development

Sustainable development is regarded as the base for a CSR branch because the implementation of its principles into an enterprise should lead to sustainable development and maintain a company's value in the long term. In Bruthland´s (1987) point of view, sustainable development should meet the needs of the present generation without compromising the ability of future generations to meet their own needs. Hopking (2009) says: "Enough, for all, forever". These simple concepts provide the initial definition for the complexity of sustainable development and help to frame the global search for solutions to the social, economic, and environmental issues that threaten the planet. Forty-three years ago, Daly (1977) came up with some basic sustainable development principles, which surprisingly, have not dated.

- The consumption of renewable resources should never exceed the speed of renewal.
- Renewable resources should not be consumed faster than the substitution can be developed.
- Pollution intensity must not exceed environmental assimilation capacity.
- Part of the current technology should be invested in decreasing pollution, reducing waste and increasing the efficiency of the resources used.

WILLARD, 2012 describes sustainable strategies as something that gives companies a competitive advantage. Its business benefits are quantifiable and real. I would summarise this quote with the claim that sustainable development is an ongoing process for ensuring progress while preventing the destruction of the resources needed to keep our society productive.

2. Corporate social responsibility (CSR)

The theory of social responsibility dates back to its development since the second half of the 20th century, especially in the United States of America where its principles have existed a lot longer (patronage, philanthropy, etc.). CSR theories have permeated throughout Europe since the 1990s and CSR is considered an excellent tool to achieve sustainable development by offering a mutually beneficial strategy. In principle, CSR can be divided into two parts. The first area of responsibility is determined by law (equal opportunities and rights, occupational safety, protection of the employee, etc.) while the second part provides extensive creativity and opportunities and can lead to increasing an enterprise's value and business sustainability. Lee & Chen (2018) state that CSR enables companies to improve their performance while providing social benefits; Gangi (2020) points out in his study that the higher the CSR engagement then the lower the corporate risk of financial distress; LI, 2019 highlights that the impact of CSR on a firm's value is what gives all corporate stakeholders satisfactory returns under a value-centred approach and the rule of law; McBarnet (2007) refers to CSR as a market-driven complex of interactions between government, business and civil society, private law, state regulation and self-regulation at national and international levels.

In literature, the term CSR is often confronted with the concepts of business ethics. It is widely accepted that social responsibility is an applied set of rules of business ethics. This view is taken, for example, by Professor Dytrt (2017). In his insight study, Bangsa (2019) summarises the relationship between sustainable product attributes and consumer decision-making. The conclusions are not one-sided, although the study confirms some types of products are more likely to be chosen by consumers when they are sustainable. In her studies, Spodarczyk, 2017 and 2019 claims that some enterprises identify social responsibility as a tool to build company image and that social responsibility complements the value system that underlies their business. These are the activities that companies are undertaking to strengthen their reputation, support stability, build a corporate culture and increase employee loyalty.

2.1 Communication with stakeholder groups

Stakeholder groups usually rapidly influence and evaluate CSR activities and are the reason why CSR activities are implemented in an enterprise. In 1983, Freeman declared that in a corporation, a stakeholder is a member of a group without whose support the organisation would cease to exist. CSR must be an essential part of a communication strategy and should fulfil the mission and vision of the company. A high level of internal and external communication is essential. Arvidsson (2010) points out that from a management perspective, communication problems arise when determining how CSR information should be communicated to meet the stakeholders' information requirements. Due to an insufficiently established framework for CSR communication, e.g. Ellerup Nielsen and Thomsen (2007) argue that many companies are not ready for this task. Communication is half the success of CSR – Williams, 2015 invented the term "Truthsparency". Dang (2019) also confirms that pressure from stakeholders (e.g. governments, suppliers, consumers and local communities) has gradually driven business firms towards taking environmentally responsible action. While communicating sustainability, Ottman, 2011 recommends beginning the planning process by considering the challenges.

If stakeholders suffer from a lack of information about CSR project outputs, it is very difficult to defend the budget for these activities, as the benefits may be invisible to others if they have not been directly affected. Each project must be prepared and planned and have a long-term outlook. Kucharska, Kowalczyk (2019) pointed out that companies with short-term orientation are unlikely to ever implement CSR strategies that are strong enough to affect their reputation and support company performance. Ferro-Soto (2018) claims that stakeholder orientation also focuses on competitor actions, since this stakeholder group is of crucial importance in the marketing strategy design, which is highly relevant to their success in the marketplace. Therefore, the results are only seen in the long term and it greatly depends on the good relations with different stakeholders' groups in the whole process. It is necessary not only to understand what stakeholders want but also why they want it (Ferro-Soto, 2018). Only by identifying their needs and defining a "problem", can the right solution be found that will thus improve the company's reputation and, in the longer term, integrate the CSR principles into the company culture. “CSR has been proven to lead to greater loyalty among customers” (Marin, 2009). By implementing a corporate responsibility system, a company influences customer purchasing behaviour, so CSR activities should be conducted to meet the needs of customers as one of the major stakeholder groups.

2.2 What CSR brings to companies and does it pay off?

In the research presented, I also focus on the motivation of companies to use CSR tools. A key benefit of the CSR system is to assist the work-life balance of employees by improving working conditions, creating benefit systems and increasing employer loyalty. Corey (2016) insists that letting employees actively participate in a CSR project delivers results. While it is not possible for everyone to identify with projects equally, it is possible to reach a wider group of employees in this way. However, theorists and practitioners claim that corporate social responsibility is not just pure philanthropy and that socially responsible interventions should bring benefits to society and businesses. Żychlewicz (2017) comments that it is understandable that companies expect benefits from these activities. I view CSR as a comprehensive strategy that must help and support companies' goals, although it is equally important that it delivers the expected effect on the company.

The sustainable development of modern societies is based, among other things, on their social responsibility. This is due to a competitive environment and a less stable economic environment, where it is necessary to be a highly trustworthy company to maintain the value of the company (Baumann-Pauly, 2013). Company reputations are becoming more important than ever. Customers now push companies towards socially responsible behaviour and are fully aware that they have a choice of companies.

2.3 The CSR decision-making process

Due to the focus of the research, I address the issue of the decision-making process in the field of CSR in literary research. I am interested in the evaluation of projects from the position of the stakeholders, the evaluation of the success of projects and, in particular, I want to thoroughly investigate the basis of the information used for decision-making by the CSR manager responsible for evaluating the suitability of the project for the given business area.

Interesting findings were raised in the research by Toliver (2013), which addressed the measurement of socially responsible behaviour of the company through the company's value chain – e.g. a significant correlation was found between the satisfaction of the company's employees and the socially responsible behaviour of the company. Cheney, 2006 examines the decision-making process in CSR from the perspective of eight key areas of the so-called FPILEPAR (facts, parties – stakeholders, interests, laws, ethics, practicality, alternatives and rationalisation). At the end of the study, he adds: “The broader decision-making model will take more time and will cost some money, but it is very likely to pay off in the long run.”

Weber (2008) is engaged in the evaluation of the impact of CSR projects, after implementation, on the performance of the company according to indicators in the study for Philips. The evaluation includes quantitative data, such as the number of employees involved, the number of children supported, rate of increase in subsidies, media outputs and project costs. The author thus provides CSR managers with a suitable evaluation tool for assessing the impact of projects. The study by Rogers (2013) focuses on the decision-making model of one of the stakeholder group of investors evaluating the value of a company, where a strong positive correlation between the value of the company and a correctly implemented CSR system was also found. Rodrigo (2017) also confirms in his study that strategic CSR helps to generate an effectively committed workforce.

A challenge for each CSR manager arises when a company creates a CSR strategy and aims to focus on specific areas. Since budgets are usually precisely defined, companies must have systems to help them decide which direction of support and communication they should take. It is here that I found a research gap, which I would like to explore with my research. The literature deals with the decision-making processes of companies who are thinking about CSR but less often the effectiveness of decision-making from the practical point of view of a manager who is already following the principles, looking for the right areas of support, facing many variants and projects and has the complex task of what to choose to best support the goals and values of the company.

Proven and well-functioning methods of project cooperation within the framework of social responsibility are close cooperation with the non-profit sector and establishing partnerships with non-profit organisations. Non-profit organisations change the lives of disadvantaged people, who the state cannot take full care of, develop talent, fill up free time, help, cure and protect. They are closer to people, know their needs and can help them in better and cheaper ways. Over time, non-profit organisations have come to understand the market and are aware that companies want counter-service for their cooperation and support. This is where the non-profit world can cooperate with commerce in a unique synergy.

I believe, that based on the value chain of a company and NGO projects, a strong connection can be found based on the type of project that supports companies' values. The goal is to confirm this hypothesis in my research. The second aim is to create an evaluation tool that can be easily applied to simplify the decision-making process for supporting specific types of projects.

3. Research design and field of research

3.1 Research design

Based on the literature, interviews with CSR managers and participation in professional conferences, as well as my knowledge of the issue, a target group of respondents was approached regarding CSR decision-making in large companies in the Czech Republic. A pilot pre-survey was prepared, which was verified by ten respondents from the target group. The main reasons for this preparation were to obtain the correct information, verify the correctness of the wording of the questions, avoid any misunderstandings by the respondents and find out the time-consuming difficulties of completing the questionnaire.

The methods of data collection and the wording of some of the questions have been changed. The panel was comprised of four representatives from small or medium-sized companies and six from large companies. Based on the pilot and the subsequent analysis of the completed questionnaires and telephone calls with the respondents, I drew several conclusions.

Only CSR managers in companies could answer the questions correctly – in the case of the wrong person, the data must be removed from the resulting file. Marketers from small companies do not understand all concepts and either do not or only partially carry out activities related to social responsibility. Some questions needed to be reworded, which sometimes turned closed questions into semi-open ones. This was because the approaches to CSR are highly creative. After verifying the correctness of the methodology of the data collection and the modifications resulting from this pilot, an updated survey was launched.

Research project

3.2 Data collection

Data collection took place from June to September 2019 using electronic questionnaires. This form was chosen because of its flexibility and processing options in the managers' free time, for example, via mobile phone.

3.3 Data analysis

At this stage, I found that the statistical quantities express the frequency of the occurrence of the phenomenon of mean values as well as the habits of the individual companies in these areas. The choice of the method of analysis depends on the objective of the research and the method of obtaining data. I used Survio software to process the data, as well as Excel with advanced functions to determine the correlation and filtration of the selected data.

3.4 Processing and presentation of the final report

The results of the research were further sorted. I excluded responses from respondents who were not decision-makers in CSR (13 out of 55 questionnaires) or worked in a smaller than large company (7 out of 55 questionnaires) because the answers could be distorted. I processed data from forty respondents who matched the profile – the CSR manager of a large company. I have drawn preliminary conclusions from each area, which will be refined, and have a growing sample of respondents. The target number is eighty people (respondents) from the sample, which represents approximately half the total sample of CSR managers from large companies in the Czech Republic.

3.5 Techniques for measuring attitudes and obtaining information

The questions in the questionnaire were chosen to obtain the maximum range of information within the segment. In areas where trends in the industry are very much reflected, I have chosen evaluation scales to gain an idea of the industry's customs. The target was not to exceed fifteen minutes to finish the questionnaire.

4. Research – Current situation of CSR in large companies in the Czech Republic

Respondents were filtered by the first two questions focused on the size of the company and the personal responsibility of the respondents to keep the sample as relevant as possible.

The basic information about the companies involved in the research was:

4.1 Type of enterprise

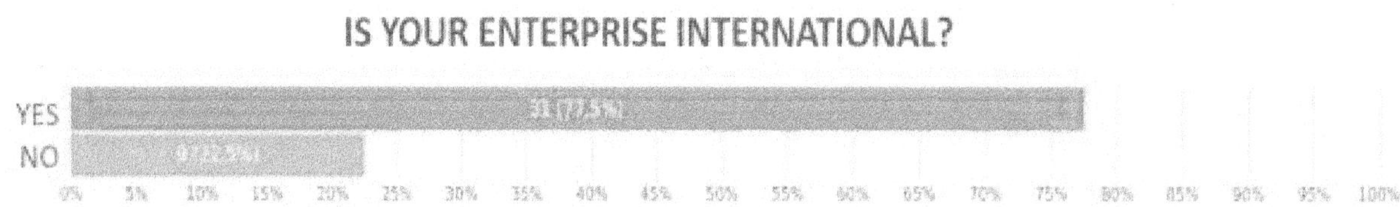

Figure 1: Source: Blažková, 2019, own research

Most large enterprises in the Czech Republic (77.5%) involved in the research were international, which shows that this trend (having a CSR position and principles in the structure) is often set by companies' headquarters abroad.

4.2 CSR budget

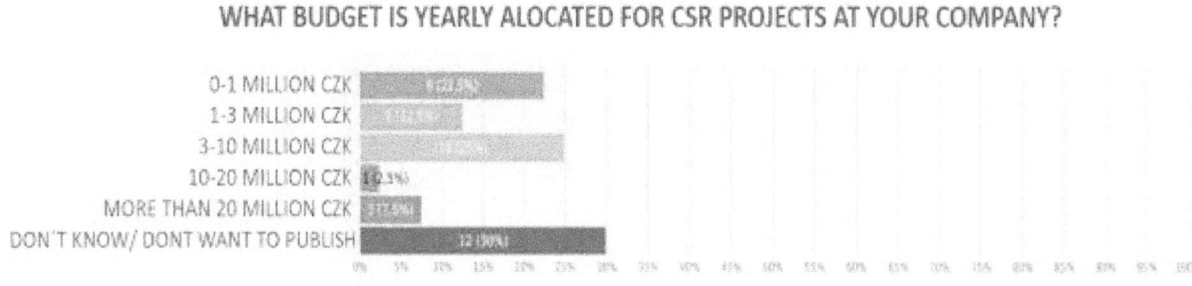

Figure 2: Source: Blažková, 2019, own research

The budget varies a lot although this may be influenced by different approaches to CSR budgeting, such as splitting CSR costs between different departments (HR, marketing, General manager's office etc.), which can influence this chart (Figure 2). Interesting information would also be, for example, to know what methodology the budget created is based on.

4.3 Decision-making process

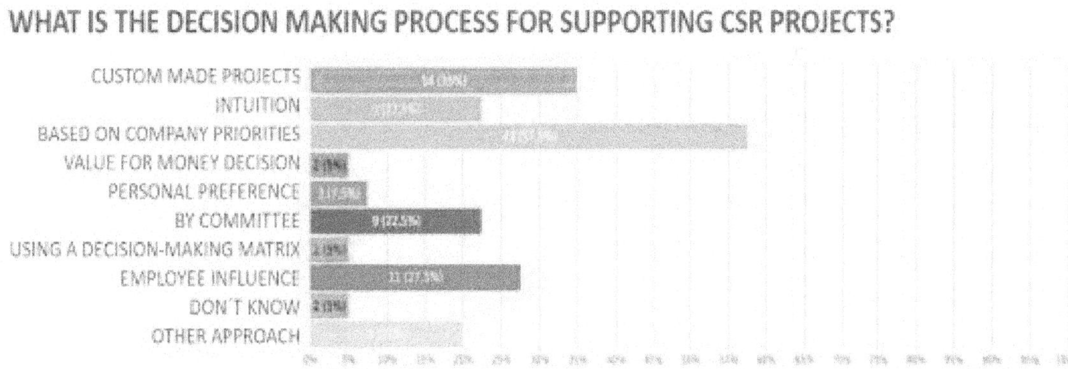

Figure 3: Source: Blažková, 2019, own research

The research significantly focuses on the decision-making process of the managers, which is influenced by different factors and brings many challenges. The chart (Figure 3) shows that most decisions are made based on some kind of strategy, although only 5% of the respondents answered that there is a decision-making matrix to help them decide.

4.4 Departments involved

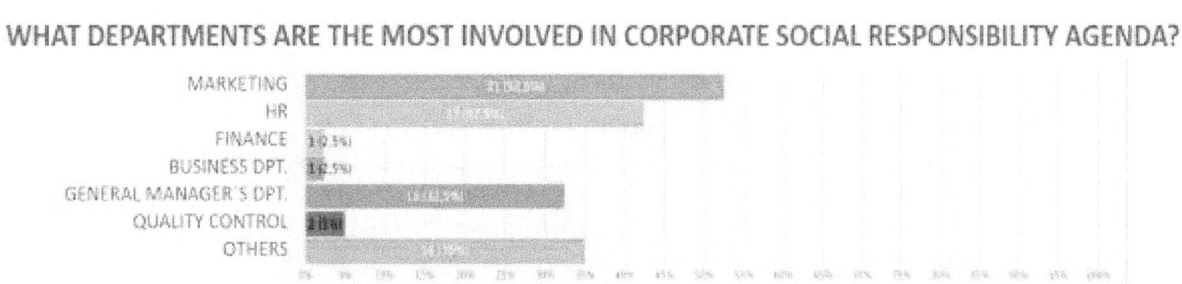

Figure 4: Source: Blažková, 2019, own research

This chart 9Figure 4) shows the diversity of CSR structures. Very few companies have a "CSR department". CSR tasks are split between Marketing, HR and the CEO's department.

4.5 Supported CSR projects

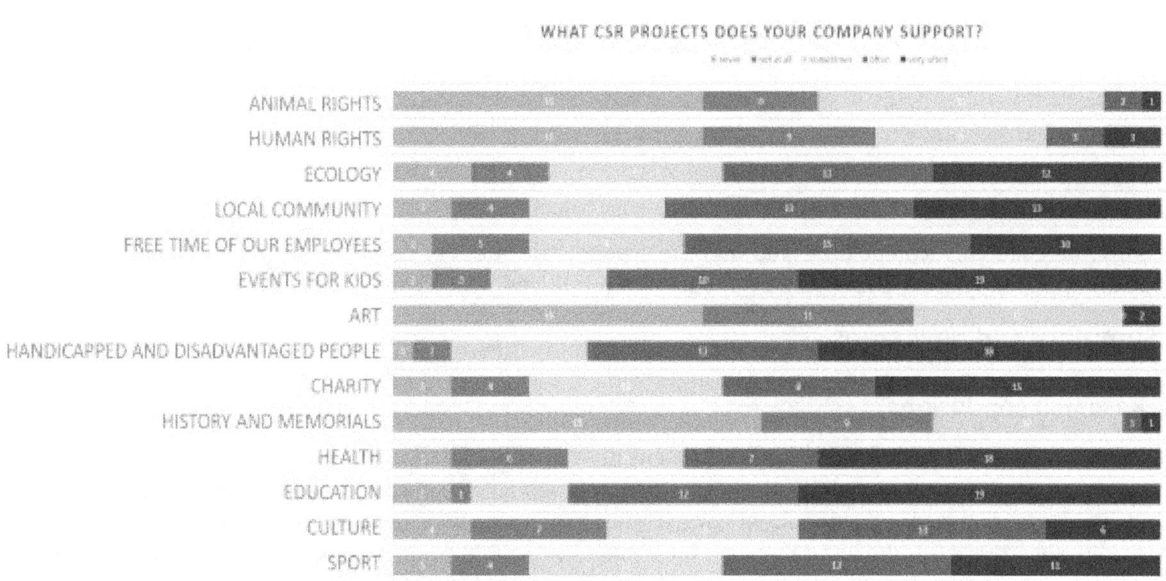

Figure 5: Source: Blažková, 2019, own research

This part of the research shows the most actively supported CSR projects in large companies from the sample. The most likely supported projects are those that help disabled and disadvantaged people, support education, events for children, health and general charity projects. This table (Figure 5) also serves as a base for comparing how supported projects are related to company values (future research).

4.6 Company values importance

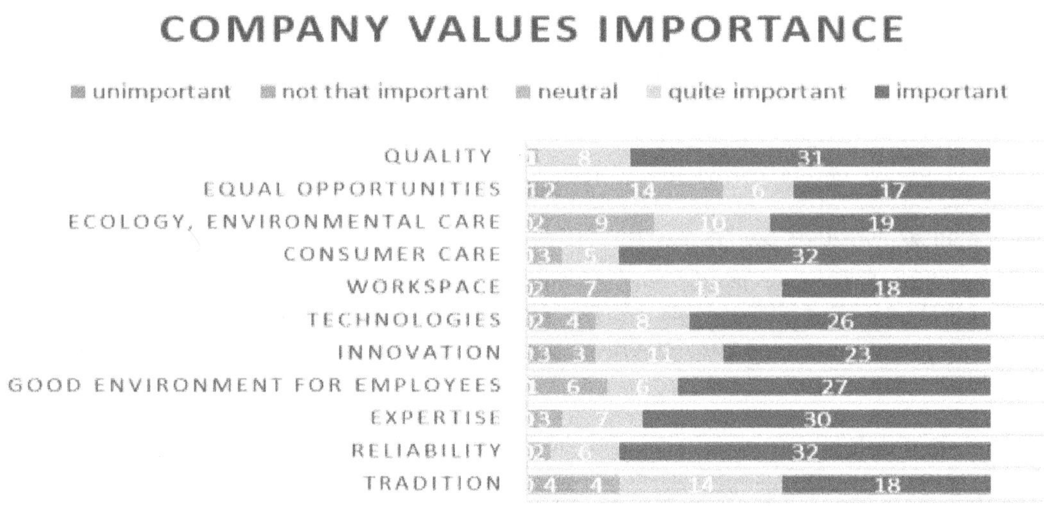

Figure 6: Source: Blažková, 2019, own research

This chart (Figure 6) shows the most important company values (reliability and consumer care stands on highest points followed by quality an expertise). It brings very important data for further research, which will compare the link between company values and supported projects.

4.7 Motivation for CSR activities

This research question was inspired by the Business Leaders Forum research conducted in 2004.

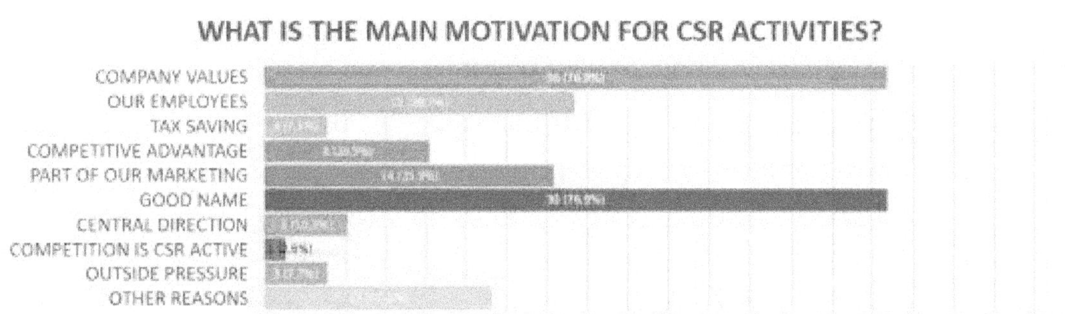

Figure 7: Source: Blažková, 2019, own research

Based on the research, it can be observed that the top CSR priorities are company values (77%) and reputation (good name) (77%). These are followed by support for employees (39 %) and marketing activities (36%).

5. Summary and next steps

5.1 Research conclusions

Although the research was based only on a representative sample of a target group (which is not much larger in the framework of the Czech Republic), the respondents were more than capable of describing strong trends in the industry because they are the people who most influence the development of Czech CSR. The research shows that even though there is quite a strong trend for implementing CSR principles in large companies in the Czech Republic, the approach in every firm is still very different and leadership and competence structure is not united. The lack of methodology (different names for CSR positions, competences and departments, different positions in companies' structures, no decision-making matrix) can also be observed. The following research findings show the increasing importance of CSR, which is caused by trends, the changing and unstable environment and recruitment motivation.

5.2 Most interesting findings

- 1. Most companies do not have a place in the company chart for a CSR manager; it is often designated as a part-time task for the HR Director/Marketing Manager/Managing Director.
- 2. CSR is perceived as an essential part of a company's reputation, its strategy and as a tool for building a good name.
- 3. In questions related to CSR, the respondents mentioned the HR department, marketing department and the CEO office in equal proportion as the departments that were involved.
- 4. Very few enterprises have a clear methodology or strategy for deciding what CSR direction to take. They often act randomly or based on individual preferences or go for "safe projects".
- 5. The most common reasons why CSR methodology is implemented by a company is to build and maintain corporate values and gain a competitive advantage on the market.
- 6. The most frequently supported projects are those that support children's events, education, disabled people, vulnerable and disadvantaged children and general charity projects.

Even the Czech Republic stands very high in SDG index chart, there is still much to improve in approach to CSR. The survey shows that there is a lack of CSR strategy in large Czech firms as this trend is still brand new. This survey will serve as a basis to establish the foundation for building a decision-making model, through which it will be possible to define the main weaknesses in the system.

5.3 Next steps

The first phase of the research showed interesting data, which needs to be analysed, structured and commented. To verify all information, the sample of the respondents needs to be extended. The second phase of research will be focused on enlarging the group of respondents to verify the findings made in the first phase. The last part of the planned research will contain a comparative analysis according to the specific values of the companies and the values linked to different supportive NGO projects. Finally, the conclusions will be specified to build a new decision-making system for CSR managers. In this system, I would like to connect company values to supported CSR projects to recommend the most efficient and useful cooperation to fulfil CSR strategy.

Acknowledgements

The author is grateful to the International Grant agency of FAME TBU, Grant. No. IGA/FaME/2018/010 for financial support.

References

Arvidsson, Susanne (2010) Communication of Corporate Social Responsibility: A Study of the Views of Management Teams in Large Companies. Journal of Business Ethics [online]. **96**(3), 339-354

Bangsa, Adjengdia Bunga a Bodo B. Schlegelmilch (2020) Linking sustainable product attributes and consumer decision-making: Insights from a systematic review. Journal of Cleaner Production [online], **245**.

Baumann-Pauly, Dorothée, Christopher Wickert, Laura J. Spence a Andreas Georg Scherer (2013) Organizing Corporate Social Responsibility in Small and Large Firms: Size Matters. Journal of Business Ethics [online]. 2013, 115(4), 693-705 [cit. 2019-04-04].

Blewitt, John (2008) Understanding sustainable development. London, UK: Earthscan

Bris, Petr, Jiri Svoboda a Hana Brisova (2013) The Growing Importance of the Practical Application of Corporate Social Responsibility in the Management of Companies in the Czech Republic. Journal of Competitiveness [online]. **5**(2), 124-138

Brundtland, Gro Harlem. (1987) UN world commission on environment and development. Our Common Future: World Commission on Environment and Development. 1. Oxford: Oxford University Press, 400 s.

Cohen, Daniel a Marcelo Soto (2007) Growth and human capital: good data, good results. Journal of Economic Growth [online]. 2007, **12**(1), 51-76

Cheney, Tim D. (2006) A Decision Making Model To Enhance Corporate Ethics / Business Ethics / Social Responsibility. Business Renaissance Quarterly [online]. Business Renaissance Institute, **1**(3), 15-20

Daly, Herman E. (1977) Steady-state economics: the economics of biophysical equilibrium and moral growth. San Francisco: W. H. Freeman

Dang, Van Thac, Nine Nguyen, Xiangzhi BU a Jamming Wang (2019) The Relationship between Corporate Environmental Responsibility and Firm Performance: A Moderated Mediation Model of Strategic Similarity and Organization Slack. Sustainability [online]. **11**(12)

Dytrt, Zdeněk, Pavla Staňková a Lucie Tomancová (2007). Manažerská etika: etika v managementu a podnikání. Zlín: Univerzita Tomáše Bati ve Zlíně

Ellerup Nielsen, A. a C. Thomsen (2007). Reporting CSR – What and How to Say It?. Corporate Communication: An International Journal. **12**(1), 25-40.

Ferro-Soto, Carlos, Luz Macías-Quintana a Paula Vázquez-Rodríguez (2018) Effect of Stakeholders-Oriented Behavior on the Performance of Sustainable Business. Sustainability [online]. 2018, 10(12)

Freeman, R. Edward a David L. Reed (1983) Stockholders and Stakeholders: A New Perspective on Corporate Governance. California Management Review [online]. **25**(3), 88-106

Gangi, Francesco, Antonio Meles, Stefano Monferrà a Mario Mustilli (2020) Does corporate social responsibility help the survivorship of SMEs and large firms? Global Finance Journal [online]., **43**(43)

Hopking, Charles (2009) Enough, for All, Forever: The Quest for a More Sustainable Future. Education Canada. 1. Canada: Canadian Education Association, **1**(1), 42-46.

Kucharska, Wioleta a Rafał Kowalczyk. How to achieve sustainability?-Employee's point of view on company's culture and CSR practice. Corporate Social Responsibility and Environmental Management [online]. 2019, **26**(2), 453-467

Li, Zhenghui, Gaoke Liao a Khaldoon Albitar (2019) Does corporate environmental responsibility engagement affect firm value? The mediating role of corporate innovation. Business Strategy and the Environment [online]. **29**(3), 1045-1055

Lee, L., & Chen, L. F. (2018). Boosting employee retention through CSR: A configurational analysis. Corporate Social Responsibility and Environmental Management, 1–13.

Lešingrová, Romana (2008) Baťova soustava řízení. 3. vyd. Uherské Hradiště: Romana Lešingrová

Lin-Hi, Nick a Igor Blumberg (2018) The Link Between (Not) Practicing CSR and Corporate Reputation: Psychological Foundations and Managerial Implications. Journal of Business Ethics [online]. **150**(1), 185-198

Marin, L., Ruiz, S., & Rubio, A. (2009). The role of identity salience in the effects of corporate social responsibility on consumer behavior. Journal of Business Ethics, P. Grover et al. International Journal of Information Management 48 (2019) 39–52

McBarnet, Doreen, Aurora Voiculescu a Tom Campbell (2009) The New corporate accountability: Corporate social responsibility and the Law. 2. New York: Cambridge University Press

Ottman, Jacquelin A.(2011) The new rules of green marketing: Strategies, Tools, and Inspiration for Sustainable Branding. 1. San Francisco: Berret-Koehler Publishers

Park, J., Lee, H., & Kim, C. (2014). Corporate social responsibilities, consumer trust and corporate reputation: South Korean consumers' perspectives. Journal of Business Research, 67(3), 295–302.

Pavlík, Marek a Martin Bělčík (2010) Společenská odpovědnost organizace: CSR v praxi a jak s ním dál. Praha: Grada, Management (Grada).

Poplawska, Jolanta, Ashraf Labib a Deborah M. Reed (2017) From vicious to virtuous circles: problem structuring for quantified decision making in operationalization of corporate social responsibility. Journal of the Operational Research Society [online]. **68**(3), 291-307

Rok, B. (2007) CSR to nie filantropia. Harvard Business Review Polska. (54), 92-93.

Rodgers, Waymond, Hiu Lam Choy a Andrés Guiral (2013) Do Investors Value a Firm's Commitment to Social Activities?. Journal of Business Ethics [online]. **114**(4), 607-623

Rodrigo, Pablo, Claudio Aqueveque a Ignacio J. Duran (2019) Do employees value strategic CSR? A tale of affective organizational commitment and its underlying mechanisms. Business Ethics: A European Review [online]. **28**(4), 459-475

Sachs, J., G. Schmidt-Traub, C. Kroll, G. Lafortune a G. Fuller (2019) - Sustainable development solutions network (SDSN). Sustainable development report 2019: Transformations to achieve the sustainable development goals [online]. New York: Bertelsmann Stiftung and Sustainable Development Solutions Network, 2019, **5.**(1), 478 s.. yearbook.

Spodarczyk, Edyta (2019) An attempt to determine the determinants of an effective impact of corporate social responsibility on consumer behaviour. A pilot study report. Management [online]., **23**(2), 64-79

Siegele, Linda a Halina Ward (2007). Corporate social responsibility: A step towards stronger involvement of business in MEA implementation?. Review of European Community and International Environmental Law. pp. 135-144

SULPHEY, M. (2017) Corporate Social Responsibility or Corporate Social Irresponsibility: where should be the focus?. Problems and Perspectives in Management [online], 15(4), 293-301

Sustainable Development Report (2019): Transformations to Achieve the Sustainable Development Goals. SDG index [online]. Sustainable Development Solutions Network, Available from: https://www.sdgindex.org/

Toliver, Adria Denise (2013) Measuring corporate social responsibility through organizational values: A scale validation study. Ann Arbor: The University of Texas at Arlington

Trnková, Jana (2004) SPOLEČENSKÁ ODPOVĚDNOST FIREM: kompletní průvodce tématem & závěry z průzkumu v ČR. Www.blf.cz: Business leaders Forum [online].

Urban, Jan (2014) Firemní kultura a identita. Praha: Ústav práva a právní vědy, Právo a management.

Wang, D. H. M., CHEN, P. H., YU, T. H. K., & Hsiao, C. Y. (2015). The effects of corporate social responsibility on brand equity and firm performance. Journal of Business Research, 68(11), 2232–2236.

Weber, Manuela (2008) The business case for corporate social responsibility: A company-level measurement approach for CSR. European Management Journal [online]. **26**(4), 247-261

Willard, Bob (2012) The New Sustainability Advantage: Seven business case benefits of a tripple bottom line. 2. Canada: New society publishers

Williams, E. Freya (2015) Green Giants: how smart companies turn sustainability into billion-dollar business. 1. New York: Amacom,

Żychlewicz, Maja. (2017) Corporate Social Responsibility in Large and Medium-sized Companies in Poland. Journal of Corporate Responsibility and Leadership [online]. **3**(1), 69-80

Innovative Entrepreneurial Companies in the Digital era: The Impact of Business Automation on International Development and Competitive Advantage

Alexandru Ilie Buzatu, Alexandra Cristina Dinu, Cristian Iulian Costache and Dragoș Tohănean
Academy of Economic Studies from Bucharest, Romania
alexilie.buzatu@gmail.com
alexandracristina.dinu@gmail.com
costache.cristi22@gmail.com
tohanean_dragos@yahoo.com
DOI: 10.34190/EIE.20.009

Abstract: In a global business world and highly competitive business environments, it is important for any industry to innovate continuously and to take advantage of all the new technologies brought by the new industrial revolution for automation and increase efficiency, be it process, people, promotion, technology or to transform the business itself. This objective can be achieved by developing an increase in knowledge and control of the operations, and of the determinants of innovation. This broader vision allows entrepreneurs to understand what products need to be redesigned, where automation should be used, and what technologies make sense for different activities. The major challenges for entrepreneurial companies are summed up by the fear of change and the use of new technologies, the lack of support from information technology, the lack of awareness of the value of digital solutions, and the change brought by these technologies. The author's past research suggests that innovation in technology capabilities, networking, social capabilities, and the capabilities for learning and development should be the priorities for sustainable business development and competitive advantage Entrepreneurs, or pioneers of the new business world, are considered main actors for industrial innovation growth and they contribute to the development of digital entrepreneurship and contribute to the increase of global competitiveness.

Keywords: innovative entrepreneurial businesses, competitive advantage, digital transformation, sustainability, business automation, international development

1. Introduction

Countries with stronger regulation on performance, that have time to develop an overall digital business environment, entrepreneurial businesses, support digital natives companies. The cornerstone of the entrepreneurial ecosystem analysis suggests business taxation and regulatory environment (McKinsey & Company, 2018).

Innovation for a sustainable business has received an increasing amount of attention from management, as innovation is increasingly recognized as an important means to contribute to sustainability. Innovation is a key element for the organizations and ensures the success of the business. Any research and development activity within the company is considered innovative. The more a company spends on R&D, the more it will develop and implement new innovations and become more competitive on the market (Costache and Buzatu, 2019).

Business sustainability drives a company to adopt management of innovation. The capabilities and competencies required to innovate for competitive purposes in sustainable business are: systems thinking, learning and developing, networking and social capabilities, integrating business, environmental, information and technology. (Costache and Buzatu, 2019).

One of the most important indicators that measures the innovation worldwide is the Global Innovation Index (GII). GII demonstrates the positive link between innovation performance and the level of development of an economy, measured in GDP per capita. High-income economies keep small countries in the shadow when we are speaking about the absolute performance in innovation (Costache and Buzatu, 2019).

Innovation linkages and public/private/academic partnerships are essential to innovation. Markets that are open to foreign trade and investment have the additional effect of exposing domestic firms to best practices around the globe, which is critical to innovation through knowledge absorption and diffusion as shown in GII 2019.

For digital entrepreneurs, security is very important and so governance of data and privacy rules are required. In the Digital Barometer, it is shown that the prevalence of technology, science, and quantitative skills, in a local economy is an important driver of performance on "digital skills and entrepreneurial education" (E&Y, 2018).

As companies strive to adapt and even survive, they are increasingly pursuing automation to improve corporate margins and more demanding customer expectations. Recent analyses show that the need for sustainability is not based on cost reduction but on the use of digital solutions and the use of automated systems to support innovation, and the use of these systems are job creators.

Digital transformation is the first step towards operational efficiency and transparency and repetitive process automation would bring more discipline and efficiency. It is important to find out what systems are appropriate, who wants to implement digital solutions, and discuss the challenges involved in transforming the business (Dumitrescu and Buzatu, 2020).

These solutions tend to provide only an incremental, cost-saving, and temporary advantage, as most companies work to improve core business. In order to improve the results and to be more efficient, the companies have to approach the automation differently, based on systems of analysis and thinking, focuses on growth and forces teams to consider customer experience (Wagner, M., 2017).

In highly competitive business environments, it is important for the industry to innovate continuously, be it process, people, promotion, technology or transform the business itself. This objective can be achieved by developing a better understanding and control of the activities, and of the determinants of innovation. This broader vision allows companies to see where automation should be used, what products need to be redesigned, and what technologies make sense for different activities (Schepers, 2017).

Digital infrastructure for international development is the standout sub pillar for the entrepreneurial digital business environment (Tohanean, et al., 2019).

2. Objectives

According to a survey done by the McKinsey & Company, 2018, (Figure no. 1) regarding implementing innovative digital tools, more than 80% of the people interviewed stated that their companies have made considerable efforts in this direction in the past years.

However, past research from McKinsey & Company shows that the success of these transformations has proven to be elusive, and less than a third of the companies who implemented digital tools actually succeeded in improving performance. Their survey shows that the rates of success vary depending on the company size: small to medium entrepreneurial companies with less than 100 employees are more likely to report a successful digital transformation (2.7 times more) than an organization with more employees (McKinsey & Company, 2018).

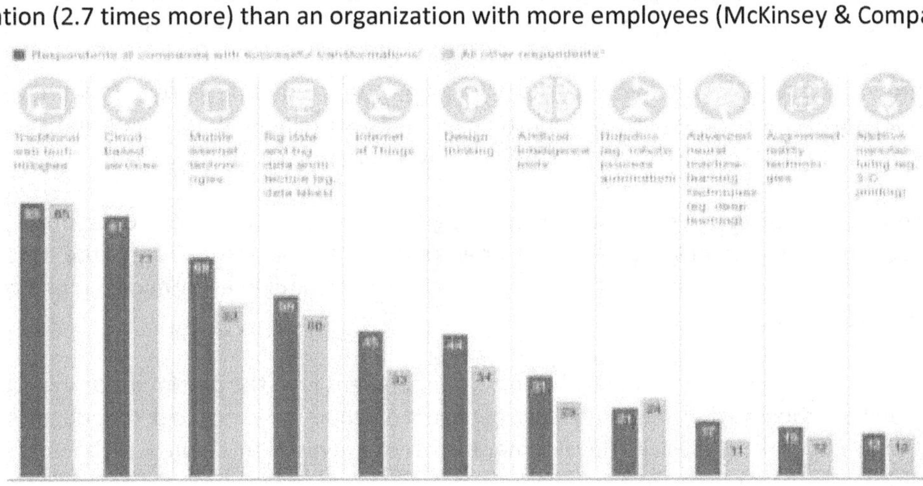

Source: McKinsey, 2018

Figure 1: Digital technologies, tools and methods currently used by organizations

Based on this report our objective is to verify in our business environment if the results maintain, to see the local knowledge and flexibility for the adoption of new digital instruments to gain efficiency and competitive advantage, regardless of the targeted department or internal process.

3. Methodology

The research paper is based on qualitative and quantitative research, which supports a thorough understanding of the researched situation and the use of new technologies in the development of a sustainable and internationally competitive business. The analysis is based on a review of the literature, empirical data are collected through self-inspection and specialized consulting companies that promote sustainable business development with the help of new tools brought by the new industrial revolution 4.0. Data are taken from very recent reports (2017-2019) by large consulting companies (E&Y, McKinsey, etc.), specialized journals, existing books in the fields of entrepreneurship, strategic management and business model innovation. The main sustainability goals (including the Digital Revolution and the use of new technologies) are discussed based on reference work provided by The World in 2050 (TWI2050, 2019).

This research paper defines and researches the concepts of Innovative Digital Tools and Sustainability, in the context of the Digital Revolution and the activity of sustainable development of international business.

Based on the research results of the literature and the information collected about companies in developed and emerging areas, we applied a series of questionnaires and interviews to verify and support these findings.

The results are used to understand what investments are needed to make the new digital instruments to improve the company's performance (gain a competitive advantage), to identify whether companies are implementing sustainable development and internationalization strategies.

To achieve the objectives of the research paper we apply a series of offline questionnaires with some of the local entrepreneurs, from technology-based companies and an online survey. A total of 92 respondents from the local business market answered a series of questions on adoption the new digital tools, innovation, knowledge of the concept of global competitiveness, investment in technology and other relevant topics, which shows the level of understanding for entrepreneurs for the use of digital tools to increase efficiency, discover weak processes, the level of digital knowledge for employees at all levels in the company in developing economies and allows us to monitor the innovative activities on entrepreneurial or international enterprises.

4. Literature review based on previous researched published

The entrepreneurial ecosystem in the EU region represents the backbone for the new and complex business world, with understanding upon adopting new technologies, a process to innovate, and to develop new business models. Entrepreneurs around the EU region bring an important contribution to economic development, speed in gaining foreign knowledge and develop innovative processes to increase efficiency (Buzatu, 2020).

There are two different business environments in the EU region, with major differences in adopting new digital tools, from developed countries and emerging countries, one with sustainable businesses and the other with great openness to adopt new technologies for competitive advantage (Buzatu, 2020).

When it comes to adoption of new technology, maintaining the constant adaptation to keep the paces with competition on adapting to new trends in technology, or accepting in the business strategy the digitalization as a new way - all companies need to open their doors to this approach, companies from developed countries or emerging one from the EU region.

The turbulent nature and continuously changing business environment is to the detriment of the acquisition of new technologies and open innovation. It is important that every company does not seek to reduce development costs, pursue optimization, and include in its development strategies investments in new technologies, software solutions, or robotic systems for repetitive processes.

The analysis of information flows within the companies indicates quite large differences in the business strategy for the digitalization. The differences are evident regardless of the digital tool or digital strategy we are talking about: cloud migration, integrated management solutions, suitability in digital paths, or automating repetitive processes within companies. The strategic approach to investing in digital solutions shows differences in knowledge and financial budgeting, depending on the size of the company.

Every company, regardless of its size, goes through changes aimed at developing the business in a sustainable way. The influence of competitiveness in a global market, as well as the development (optimization) of internal or external connections in an organization, can bring competitive advantage and create a framework for the development of sustainable business.

5. Quantitative analysis of investments in digital technologies, in order to improve the company's performance and gain a competitive advantage

Our survey outlines a higher interest (74,4 % of the involved companies) to strategic directions and international development. These companies want to develop the ability to maintain all their activities at a certain rate or level.

For developing sales in new markets, internationally, companies' activities toward sustainable development are supported by patenting, R&D equipment purchase and assisting in openness to new development in the internal processes. Our survey indicates 5 directions in which companies direct their investments: customer experience, business operations, decision making, innovation and competitive advantage.

According to a project requested by European Entrepreneurs CEA-PME and a study carried out through the DigitaliseSME pilot project (2020), the level of awareness of digitalization and the reasons why companies invest in technology is very high. Activities such as changing the business model, logistics management, general marketing, data management, acquiring new customers, or internal processes have changed significantly.

According to DigitaliseSME (2020), companies were asked where they feel they need digital solutions for optimization and what processes they want to digitize, see figure 2.

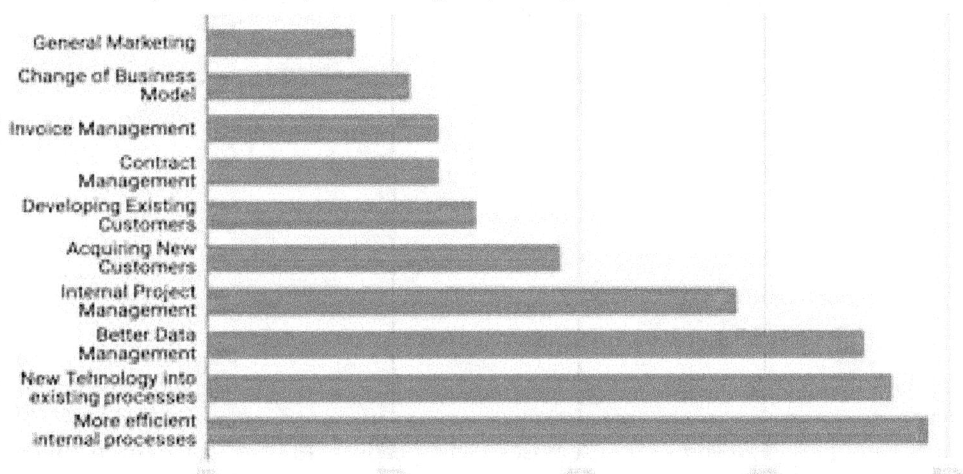

Source: DigitaliseSME, 2020

Figure 2: Internal processes needed to be improved with digital solutions

For a better implementation of digital tools, besides the knowledge of these tools, consulting companies need to transform and understand the challenges of companies, to speak their language, and to help their partners to develop self-help programs and knowledge. Even if they do not invest as much as big companies in digital tools SMEs (small and medium enterprises) are the motor of economic development, implementers of innovative activities, creators of technological knowledge, and technological changes. The key to these SMEs in this area is their agility and flexibility for effective adaptation and the presence of a sustainable strategy. For implementing sustainable growth programs and gaining competitive advantages the companies from developing countries should improve the usage of all resources available that lead to the creation of new business models, new efficient economy, or knowledge economy(Marquardt, et al., 2019).

To enable major business improvements, to increase customer experience, creating new business models or streamlining operations, companies need to use new digital technologies in a never stopping process, tools such as analytics, mobile or embedded devices. Digital assets result in digitalization of processes that goes beyond digitizing information, resources, and creating value and increasing revenues. The structure of the survey is presented below in terms of turnover, the number of employees, and the field of activity. The size of the companies interviewed according to the turnover is as follows: 25.6% (up to 0.2 million EUR), 14% (from 0.2 to 1 million EUR), 11.6% (from 1 to 4 million EUR), 9.3% (from 4-20 million EUR) and 39.5% (more than 20 million EUR). The size of the companies interviewed according to the number of employees is as follows: 30.2% (from 1 to 10 employees), 20.9% (from 11 to 50 employees), 9.3% (from 51 to 100 employees), and 39.5% (over 101 employees). The interviewed companies according to the field of activity are as follows: 2.2% (import/export), 14% (industrial production), 14% (retail/distribution), 16.3% (IT production: software and hardware), and 53.5% (other service areas).

The survey respondents understand that for sophistication in this approach, the use of process automation is a new capability for all but digital natives, and that varies accordingly, companies needed to develop more and more new skills and digital knowledge through their employees. Our survey strengthens McKinsey & Company report and you can see, in figure no. 3, that for an increase in competitiveness companies have a similar understanding and the two most important pillars for a competitive company are: 72,1% of them invest in employees and 65,1% invest in quality services for customers. Respondents were asked what they consider important to have a competitive advantage. The answer was one that admits previous research and defines as important pillars to gain a competitive advantage: performance-oriented employees(81.4%), products and services with added value to the customer(72.1%), and the development of standardized processes and procedures(58.1%), (see figure no.5).

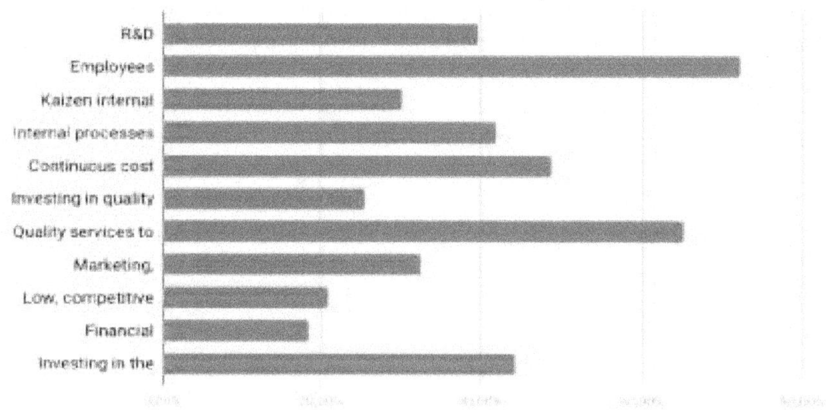

Source: Authors own creation, based on the survey

Figure 3: Investment strategy for increasing the competitiveness

Regarding sustainable development (figure no. 4) the opinion is split and entrepreneurs or managers believe that for sustainable development, mostly internationally, companies need to invest in the development of internal values for continuous improvement of processes and procedures (67,4%), standardization of processes and procedures (55,8%) and investments to create an innovative environment (55,8%).

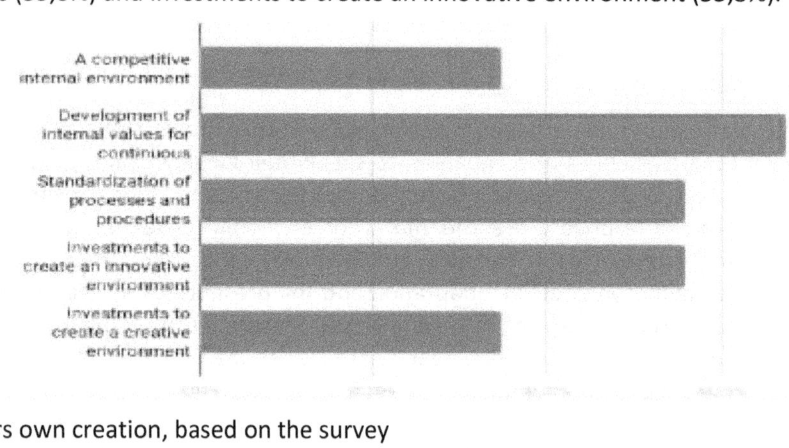

Source: Authors own creation, based on the survey

Figure 4: Strategy for sustainable business development

The survey identifies an increased interest in the digitalization of the internal processes and increases knowledge about the advantages brought by the new technologies. 62.8% of the respondents recognize the need for digitization and the importance of these tools for the efficiency and development of their companies. Besides digitalization, the survey emphasizes, in addition to the importance of digitalization, the importance of including international development in companies' strategy. Respondents(62.8%) acknowledge, for business development, the inclusion in their strategy of benefiting from globalization and thinking of international business, whether they are start-ups or established businesses. Comparing the importance shown for competitive advantage, respondents were asked what they consider important to develop sustainable international business. The answer was one that supports and maintains the trend of sustainability and competitiveness, and respondents place employees(83.7%) again as important for sustainable business and followed by investments in new technologies or research and development(41.9%).

The results of the survey were analyzed with a series of correlations and cross-tabulations, with strong results of connection between them. Correlated with the research objectives of this paper, the authors made a series of analyzes with the correlation between the questions related to the interests of competitive advantage, digital transformation, and business development.

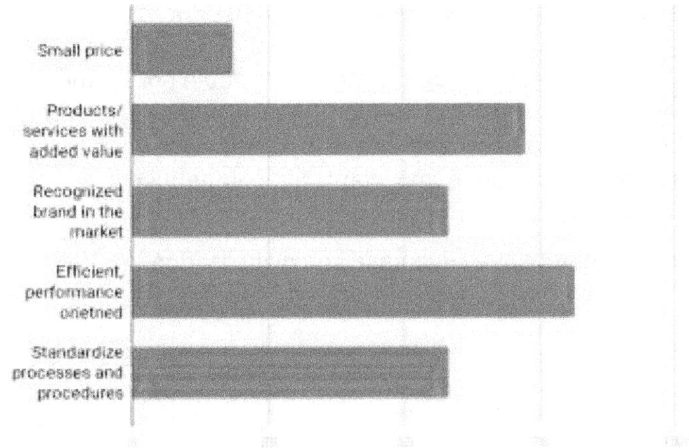

Source: Authors own creation, based on the survey

Figure 5: Importance of competitive advantage for the respondents

The authors analyze the connection between the impact on sustainable business development and investment in digitalization (see table no.1). The survey shows the paramount importance of employees and their influence on business development, whether we are talking about sustainability or flexibility in adopting new technologies. Respondents admit the importance of allocating resources for digitalization but using these technologies to develop and help employees, whether we are talking about knowledge development or operational support for high performance.

Table 1: Cross Tabulation between sustainable development strategy and investment in digitalization

		Sustainable development strategy				
		Financial availability	Employees	Op. efficiency	Marketing budget	R&D
Investment in digitalization	Count - yes, % within Investdigitaliz	18.1%	38.9%	15.3%	5.6%	22.2%
	Count - no, % within Investdigitaliz	12.0%	40.0%	28.0%	4.0%	16.0%
	Count % of Total	16.5%	39.2%	18.6%	5.2%	20.6%

Percentages and totals are based on responses

Source: Authors own creation, based on the survey

For a better understanding and implementation of new digital instruments, companies need to transform and embrace the challenges, changes and to develop self-help programs and knowledge. Information from the survey shows that companies understand that to enable major business improvements and support for international development, to create new business models, to increase customer experience, or perform operations, companies need to use new digital technologies in a never stopping investment in the process.

The research shows that high interest for digitalization and improvement is for companies over 100 Mil. Euro and a medium interest split between startup and medium companies. The respondents outline, for start-ups, the importance to include in the business strategy from the beginning the help of digital tools and to develop the businesses faster and deploy internationally much faster then established businesses. The respondents from companies over 100 Mil. Euro outlines the importance for optimization and to use robotics for automated solutions.

The analysis continues with a linkage between turnover and international development. The results show a high interest and include international development in their strategy for companies over 100 Mil. Euro. For companies from emerging countries the interest is high to go internationally and to develop products or services for developed regions and to be more competitive then the incumbent ones.

When it comes for gaining a competitive advantage strategy (see Table no. 2), the respondents who take into consideration the digitalization of their companies consider the main pillars for competitive advantage: efficient, performance-oriented employees and products/services with added value to the consumer, involving a higher price, which show that respondents consider important for competitive advantage the development of employees and a customer oriented strategy.

Table 2: Crosstabulation between competitive advantage and digitalization

		Digitalization		Total
		Yes	No	
Competitive Advantage	Small price	10	6	16
	Products/services with added value to the consumer, involving a higher price	50	18	68
	The brand recognized in the market	44	10	54
	Efficient, performance-oriented employees	52	22	74
	Standardized procedures and processes	40	10	50
Total		64	28	92

Percentages and totals are based on respondents.

Source: Authors own creation, based on the survey

The respondents who take into consideration the digitalization of their companies consider the main pillars for sustainable development: developing internal values of continuous improvement of processes and procedures, and standardization of processes and procedures, which show the high interest in stabilized operation and clear information flow.

In Table no. 3 the authors outline much stronger reasons that respondents consider for sustainable business development, adopting the new technologies and influence on the business activity the main pillar are employees, and the need to constantly improve their skills and knowledge.

Table 3: Crosstabulation between competitive advantage and digitalization

		Digitalization		Total
		Yes	No	
Competitive Advantage	Financial availability	24	8	32
	Employees	50	26	76
	Operational efficiency	20	16	36
	Marketing budget	8	2	10
	Investments in Research and Development	32	8	40
Total		64	28	92

Percentages and totals are based on respondents.

Source: Authors own creation, based on the survey

The authors have made a correlation to show the veracity of the answers, between turnover, digitalization, and international development and the results show moderate to strong relations in these cases (see table no. 4).

Table 4: Correlation between sustainable development strategy and investment in digitalization

		Turnover	International Development	Digitalization
Turnover	Pearson Correlation	1	-.404**	-.544**
	Sig. (2-tailed)		.000	.000
International Development	Pearson Correlation	-.404**	1	.109
	Sig. (2-tailed)	.000		.299
Digitalization	Pearson Correlation	-.544**	.109	1
	Sig. (2-tailed)	.000	.299	

6. Conclusions

An entrepreneurial company can develop sustainable and competitive international businesses if the country of incumbent has the ability to create an innovative and sustainable business environment. The company and the environment are linked together and they must develop and grow together for attraction in the region of new capabilities and develop knowledge to generate economic growth and by increasing levels of entrepreneurial activity and SME sector. The research studies done before and the literature review show a connection between strategic international development and innovation capacity on entrepreneurial companies. This connection can go on another level when talking about internationalization and development of new business models, and they need to be included as strategic and crucial competitiveness strategies for entrepreneurs and regional economies in the development stage, and developing business sophistication through digital adoption.

Our survey shows interesting results regarding developing sustainable international businesses and increasing knowledge about competitive development. The survey, based on the responses, discovered the main pillars to achieve competitive advantage and develop sustainable businesses in a globally connected business environment. The results support past research done by authors and specialized research magazines and consulting companies regarding the influence on the improvement of internal processes, the degree of digitization, and the development of competitive advantage through innovation and creativity. The respondents outline the importance of the digitalization process for gaining agility and flexibility, to see the investment process in these tools as a strategic one and to see IT as a partner in the business, that will bring stability especially for uncertainty and troubled times.

Based on the research presented in this paper, the authors recommend the following action for participating entities. Every company has digitization initiatives and digitalization of internal processes, knowledge, and skills that need to be cataloged and assessed. This transformation and challenges need to be considered as an opportunity, the transformation is not only a singular phase but also offers the opportunity to improve the operations and people's acceptance of the change.

The survey supports the idea for the digital tools for developing sustainable businesses and gaining competitive advantage. Important facts that are shown in the survey are the acknowledgment for developing employees and their influence on the sustainability of the business. Another interesting result is about the international business environment that is detrimental to open innovation, the battle for cost reduction, gaining competitive advantage, and the acquisition of new technologies. Transformation towards a sustainable future is possible, but the action is required from all stakeholders. Because everything is integrated into the connected world, the grand transformation requires a holistic perspective (TWI2050, 2019).

A possible future research direction for authors may be research among companies in terms of process automation in every department and to monitor what kind of instrument they use based on turnover and see the differences between start-ups, small-medium, and corporate companies to show the speed of deployment and the flexibility to change when they are in a process of go to market in an international environment. Also, a further research that covers a larger number of countries to analyze different models of business environment that puts into perspective the balance between the support for start-ups and market success regarding the SMEs sector.

Acknowledgements

This work was co-financed from the European Social Fund through Operational Programme Human Capital 2014-2020, project number POCU/380/6/13/125015 "Development of entrepreneurial skills for doctoral students and postdoctoral researchers in the field of economic sciences" sau Această lucrare a fost cofinanţată din Fondul Social European, prin Programul Operațional Capital Uman 2014-2020, proiect numărul POCU/380/6/13/125015 „Dezvoltarea abilităţilor antreprenoriale pentru doctoranzi şi postdoctoranzi în domeniul ştiinţelor economice."

References

Acs, Z. J., Szerb, L., Autio, E., Global Entrepreneurship Index 2016. *The Global Entrepreneurship and Development Institute*, Washington, USA

Bendor-Samuel, P., 2017. *The power of digital transformation in a data-driven world.* Available at: <https://www.forbes.com/sites/peterbendorsamuel/2017/07/21/the-power-of-digital-transformation-in-a-data-driven-world/#500b37aa3f2c> [Accessed 15 April 2020].

Bhattacharya, U., Hsu, P.-H., Yian, X. & Xu, Y., 2017. What affects Innovation More> Policy or Policy Uncertainty. *Cambridge University Press*, 52(5).

Biskupek, A., 2018. *Risk Management in IT Projects – Case Study.* TRENDS ECONOMICS AND MANAGEMENT, 32(2), pp. 21-34.

Choi, Woon G., Kang, T., Kim, Geun-Y. and Lee, B., 2017. *Global liquidity transmission to emerging market economies, and their policy responses.* Journal of International Economics, 109(C), pp.153-166.

Buzatu, A.I., 2020. International Growth Strategies for Digital Entrepreneurial Companies in Developing Countries from EU Region. *Junior Scientific Researcher Journal*, Bucharest.

Costache, I.C. and Buzatu, A.I., 2019. Innovation in Romanian companies – trends and patterns. *Proceedings of IBIMA 2019 International Conference.*

Dumitrescu, I.B., Buzatu, A.I., 2020. Sustainable Businesses Enhanced Through Digital Transformation and Artificial Intelligence in the Context of Industry 4.0. *Proceedings of BASIQ International Conference: New Trends in Sustainable Business and Consumption 2020, edited by Pamfilie, R., Dinu, V., Tachiciu, L., Plesea, D., Vasiliu, C.*

E&Y, 2018. *Growth Barometer Survey*. Available at: <https://www.ey.com/en_gl/growth/growth-barometer-2018> [Accessed 12 March 2020].

European Entrepreneurs CEA-PME, 2020. *DigitaliseSME (Digital Enablers in SMEs: Support for Digitalisation to Enhance SMEs' Capacity to Go International and Innovate)*. Available at: <http://www.cea-pme.com/cea-pme/cea-pme-projects/digitalisesme.html> [Accessed 15 April 2020].

Fred, D. and Forest, D., 2017. Strategic Management. Competitive Advantage Approach, 16th Edition. Pearson Education, London.

Ghazzawi, I. 2018. Organizational Turnaround: A Conceptual Framework and Research Agenda. *American Journal of Management*, 17(7), pp.10-24.

Global Innovation Index, 2019. Available at: <*https://www.globalinnovationindex.org/analysis-indicator*,> [Accessed 15 March 2020].

Kiehne, J. and Olaru, M., 2017. Implementing Industrie 4.0 strategies: Beyond technical innovations. Proceedings of BASIQ, Pages: 363-371.

Maier, D. Irmer S., J. Astrid F. & Maier, A., 2017. Development and Operationalization of a Model of Innovation Management System as Part of an Integrated Quality-Environment-Safety System. Amfiteatru Economic, Volume: 19, No. 44/2017, pp 302-314.

Marquardt, K., Olaru, M., Golowco, N. and Kiehne, J., 2018. Study on economic trends, drivers and developments of the 21th century. *Proceedings of BASIQ International Conference: New Trends in Sustainable Business and Consumption 2018, edited by Pamfilie, R., Dinu, V., Tachiciu, L., Plesea, D., Vasiliu, C.*, pp. 65-73.

McKinsey & Company., 2018. *Unlocking success in digital transformations*. Available at: <https://www.mckinsey.com/business-functions/organization/our-insights/unlocking-success-in-digital-transformations#> [Accessed 29 March 2020].

Meidell, A. K. K., 2017. How the enterprise risk management function influences decision-making in the organization- A field study of a large, global oil and gas company. The British Accounting Review, 49(1), pp. 39-55.

PWC, 2018. Fourth Industrial Revolution for the Earth / Harnessing Artificial Intelligence for the Earth. Available at: <https://www.pwc.com/gx/en/sustainability/assets/ai-for-the-earth-jan-2018.pdf> [Accessed 12 March 2020].

PWC, 2019. How CEOs can tap AI's full potential. Available at: <https://www.pwc.com/gx/en/issues/data-and-analytics/artificial-intelligence/how-ceos-can-tap-ai-full-potential.html> [Accessed 12 March 2020].

Schepers, S., 2017. The Risk Averse Society: A Risk for Innovation?. *Sustainability in Digital World,* pp. 21-36.

Tohanean, D. & Zainea, N. L., 2019. Entrepreneurial challenges through innovative business models – a sigma approach. *Emerging Trends in Marketing and Management*, IV(1).

Wagner, M., 2017. Entrepreneurship, Innovation, and Sustainability. *S.l.: Greenleaf Publishing Book.*

Startup Kernels: Towards a Teaching Framework for Fundamental Elements of new Ventures

Jeroen Coelen and Frido Smulders
Delft University of Technology, Delft, The Netherlands
j.coelen@tudelft.nl
f.e.h.m.smulders@tudelft.nl
DOI: 10.34190/EIE.20.200

Abstract: This paper contains a first step towards a holistic understanding of fundamental elements in startups. It develops the first version of a framework based on theory on startup failure and validated by analysing interviews. It sets out directions for further research on this topic as a PhD-project.

Keywords: entrepreneurship, education, startups, iterations, design, learning

1. Introduction

Entrepreneurship is considered something that can be taught and is aimed by European Union policy 'to be a basic feature in education systems' (European Union, 2006). The authors of this paper are educators of entrepreneurship. They don't teach 'about' or 'for' entrepreneurship, but follow the idea of education 'through' entrepreneurship (Nielsen & Gartner, 2017). Doing so, because law-like forms of knowledge are only scarcely available and therefore the appropriate mental model should be generated by the entrepreneurs themselves. This constructivist educational model is emphasised in Donald Schön's Reflective Practitioner (1983). In the author's course, entrepreneurs undergo experiential learning cycles as a basic didactic structure (Kolb, 1984) while building their startup from the ground up, ultimately to deliver value to customers (and other stakeholders). In line with constructive alignment (Biggs, 1999) we have chosen to tailor the educational model towards the entrepreneurial process being the learning goals of the course.

During the course students go through the very early stages of new organisation while considering multiple variations of the constituting parts, varying from a solid name to appropriate distribution channels, from the right pricing to the first target customer and from a value proposition to the startup's positioning in the value network. There are no predefined solutions for these parts, nor is it possible to capture upfront the myriad of things that need to be developed. In weekly coaching sessions, triggering questions force students to reflect on their considerations, decisions and framing related to their startup.

One could say that the design of startups show lots of similarities with the design of products. Dorst (1997) suggested that the accumulating knowledge of a design process not just contains the choices and motivations of the final design, but also the considerations of alternatives not chosen. Therefore, we've come to frame the entrepreneurial process in these early stages as the creation of a 'house of knowledge' that, like products, needs to be robust enough to become a viable business. Like the fundaments of a house the knowledge fundaments of a new company need to become robust. The fundamental elements that we envision form the ground structure of the emerging company and in this research refer be referred to as the 'kernels' of the company. It is built on the assumption that these elements will organically grow as the company matures and that a holistic model of the future company will go beyond the popular canvasses (Coes, 2014). This brings is to the main questions of this paper: What are the fundamental elements ('kernels') of a viable startup?

Another assumption is that by knowing these 'kernels', we will be able to increase the effectiveness and efficiency of our teaching. Students will take these fundamental elements earlier into account by front-loading them in the entrepreneurial journey (Thomke & Fujimoto, 2000).

2. Literature

A popular answer to the former question is the Business Model Canvas (BMC) (Osterwalder, 2005), which aims to capture the essence of a mature business. The BMC is discussed in the scientific discourse, however, studies on strengths and limitations are not too prevalent. We combined one of the few sources on its limitations with our personal teaching experience in order to highlight two limitations for the goal of our project.

Firstly, the BMC has a rather narrow focus. Literature shows that the canvas is a static snapshot that excludes 'external forces to a business model such as competition and market factors' (Coes, 2014). On top of that, relating to holism, it doesn't show in detail how for example the various inbound & outbound channels link the startup to an existing network of entities, nor has it notions of structural emptiness in said networks. We believe that the answers to the 'kernels' relate to a holistic view, drawing from structural holes theory by Burt (2009).

Secondly, in line with our educational experience, Coes highlights a limitation in the different levels of abstraction in elements of the canvas. For instance, 'Value Proposition' has one block and 'Key Resources' and 'Key Activities' have their own block, implying a different level of detail. We have noticed that this makes it hard for students to consider various optional solutions while they are constructing the fundaments of their individual 'house of knowledge'. Canvasses don't really provide such instructions. A popular way of working towards answers is the Lean Startup (Ries, 2007), with the idea of breaking down a startup into falsifiable hypothesis that can be validated in focused iterations. However, adoption of working with falsifiable hypothesis is low (Ghezzi, 2019).

3. Method

In order to develop this framework, the study first develops a thematic lens on fundamental elements in startups based on existing literature with failure as a focus. Here we draw from the idea that reasons for failure might point to fundamental elements not present within the canvasses. As startup failure can't be attributed to a single factor (Duschenau & Gartner, 1990), we drew up a list of many interacting factors from literature with a multifaceted analysis of startup failures. We then connect the lens to a set of experiential data from startups to see if the struggles from the startup trenches resonate with these topics of failure. Five papers, well cited, have been selected from Google Scholar together with one popular research report from a consultancy firm (Bruderl et al, 1992; Bruno & Leidecker, 1988; Duschenau & Gartner, 1990; Khelil, 2015; Zacharakis et al, 1999; CB Insights, 2019). The 86 factors that are mentioned in relation to failure have been brought back via clustering in XMind Zen to thematic clusters. It aims to form a first-stepping stone towards the 'kernels' beyond the Business Model Canvas, as the first research question dictates. This lens was subsequently applied to interviews among YES!Delft (a Delft incubator) startups that went over the tipping point of entering the market and followed entrepreneurship courses at the faculty of Industrial Design Engineering. The data includes two focused interviews over a four-year time span. One just after the course ended and one once embedded within the YES!Delft incubator. The interviews were held and transcribed by a former PhD-student with a slightly different purpose in mind. However, for the early stage of this new PhD-project we believe we could still use them to frame the research. Thus, the interviews were re-coded in Atlas TI Cloud with this new lens. For the purpose of this short PhD paper, data of two startups is used. Startup 1 is a SaaS company in the event industry and Startup 2 is an aerodynamic engineering studio.

4. Findings

4.1 Clustering

Figure 1 shows six dominant themes that arose from the clustering. Most startup failures factors can be contributed to human related issues.

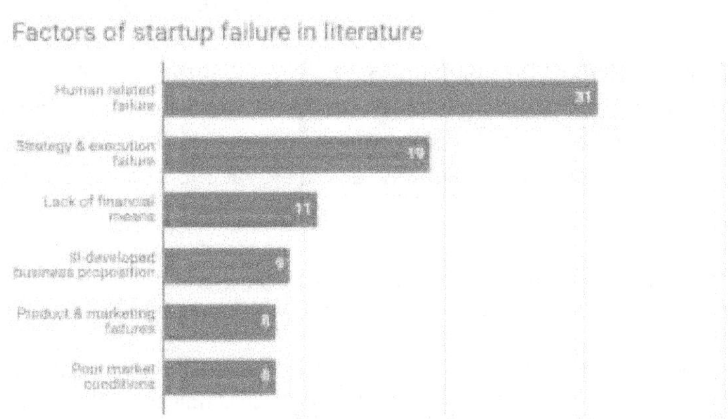

Figure 1: Factors per found cluster

4.2 Coding with the lens

All elements of the thematic clusters were found in the two interviews (Table 1). Like with factors for failure human related problems were the dominantly coded cluster. It makes sense that the second cluster, marketing and distribution issues, is found challenging during the startup situation. Positioning issues and looking for a 'structural hole' within the existing industrial fabric should receive such attention during the early phases. In addition to the thematic clusters we found issues related to processual activities and termed these: planned and unplanned iterations. Meaning, the interviewees explicitly pointed to experimental activities on one side (planned iterations) and unexpected events that caused them to alter their line of activities. We found that the unplanned iterations almost doubled the planned versions. In itself, the observation of iterations during the early phases support the designerly behaviour mentioned earlier. However, since unplanned iterations consume scarce resources it might be better to 'frontload' these in the form of planned (thought) experiments. It is better to stay on the wheel then to be surprised. We see here a clear relation of process and behaviour related elements to the dominant human related issues. Therefore, we will include these in our future research.

Table 1: Code counts per startup

	Startup 1	Startup 2	Total
Clusters			
Ill-designed products	7	3	10
Ill-designed propositions	4	7	11
Marketing/distribution issues	9	7	16
Human related problems	7	8	15
Lack of financial means	2	2	4
Strategy/execution fail	5	5	10
Iterations			
Planned iterations	3	3	6
Unplanned iterations	4	7	11

5. Discussion and next steps

Our first research aim was to start identifying the contours of what are startup 'kernels'. The six found clusters also arise in the interviews, highlighting a first stepping stone towards our goal. However, it seems that not all clusters have a similar weight. This disparity is two-fold. On one hand, not all clusters have a similar granularity. 'Human related problems' had far more related factors than for instance 'Ill-designed products', allowing for a better understanding of why a startup had multiple problems regarding that cluster. E.g., the 'ill-designed products' clusters stops at factors such 'Poor product design' (Zacharakis et al, 1999), we imagine there are deeper explanations. On the other hand, we find that both the clusters in terms of amount of factors and interviews in terms of amount of codes are skewed towards human related problems. This could suggest that for other themes not only literature has a limited vocabulary, but the entrepreneurs do too. Furthermore, the dominance of human related problems in literature is in stark contrast with the absence of any team related elements in the Business Model Canvas. Thus, underpinning our experience with limitations of the BMC.

This paper forms the beginning of a PhD-project and for that purpose the interviews were appropriate. Given the limitations, the six identified clusters emerged in the analysed interviews and seem to form a first stepping stone towards a framework of startup 'kernels'. The iterative nature of this early entrepreneurial phase provided us with yet another 'kernel' of building a new company: a processual and behavioural element.

References

Biggs, J. 1999. *Teaching for Quality Learning at University*, Buckingham: SRHE and Open University Press

Brüderl, J., Preisendörfer, P., & Ziegler, R., 1992. Survival chances of newly founded business organizations. *American sociological review*, pp.227-242.

Bruno, A.V. & Leidecker, J.K., 1988. Causes of new venture failure: 1960s vs. 1980s. *Business horizons*, 31(6), pp.51-56.

Burt, R.S., 2009. *Structural holes: The social structure of competition*. Harvard university press.

Coes, D.H., 2014. *Critically assessing the strengths and limitations of the Business Model Canvas*. Unpublished Master's thesis, University of Twente.

CB Insights. 2014. *The top 20 reasons startups fail*. Viewed on 6 January 2020. <https://[www.cbinsights.com/research/startup-failure-reasons-top>

Dorst, K., 1997. *Describing design: a comparison of paradigms.* Unpublished PhD thesis, Delft University of Technology.

Duchesneau, D.A. & Gartner, W.B., 1990. *A profile of new venture success and failure in an emerging industry. Journal of business venturing*, 5(5), pp.297-312.

European Union 2019. *Entrepreneurship education*, viewed May 13 2011. <https://ec.europa.eu/growth/smes/promoting-entrepreneurship/support/education_en>

Ghezzi, A., 2019. Digital startups and the adoption and implementation of Lean Startup Approaches: Effectuation, Bricolage and Opportunity Creation in practice. *Technological Forecasting and Social Change*.

Khelil, N., 2016. The many faces of entrepreneurial failure: Insights from an empirical taxonomy. *Journal of business venturing*, 31(1), pp.72-94.

Kolb, D.A. (1984). *Experiential learning*. Englewood Cliffs (NJ): Prentice-Hall.

Nielsen, S.L., & Gartner, W.B., 2017. Am I a student and/or entrepreneur? *Multiple identities in student entrepreneurship*. Education+ Training.

Osterwalder, A., Pigneur, Y., & Tucci, C.L., 2005. Clarifying business models: Origins, present, and future of the concept. *Communications of the association for Information Systems*, 16(1)

Ries, E., 2011. *The lean startup: How today's entrepreneurs use continuous innovation to create radically successful businesses*.

Schön, D. A. 1983. *The reflective practitioner: How professionals think in action*. New York: Basic Books.

Thomke, S., & Fujimoto, T. (2000). The effect of "Front-Loading" on product development performance. *Journal of Product Innovation Management*, 17 (2), 128-142.

Zacharakis, A.L., Meyer, G.D. , & DeCastro, J., 1999. Differing perceptions of new venture failure: a matched exploratory study of venture capitalists and entrepreneurs. *Journal of Small Business Management*, 37(3), p.1.

A Review of Performativity Shaping Innovation in the Fourth Industrial Revolution

Joan Edwards
School of Engineering, Waterford Institute of Technology, Ireland
joanxedwards@gmail.com
DOI: 10.34190.EIE.20.234

Abstract: The innovation process, which describes the activities that bring forth technological artefacts, entails a great degree of interaction amongst innovators, users, organizations, technologies, and markets. While it is understood that there is no single correct model of the innovation process, some models possess characteristics that have been applied widely – this relates particularly to those that describe the process as linear or unvariegated. There has been considerable development amongst models over time; however, the interwovenness of the technological, cognitive, and social influences in the process, are not explicitly addressed. These influences are crucial when discussing more recent innovations that relate to cyber-physical systems, artificial intelligence (AI), Internet of Things (Iot) or 3D printing. The mechanisms of the innovation process in the fourth industrial revolution are directed by iterative dialogue between innovators, users, technology, and an environment - in which communicative and cognitive elements of the innovation process continuously interact. Distinct from previous industrial revolutions, innovation in the fourth industrial revolution is motivated by several complex and overlapping activities that contribute to the development of a technological artefact's identity which inextricably links digital, physical, and biological worlds. This interrelationship indicates that a technology that arises from the process has the ability transform, alter, and ultimately configure the environment to which it joins – a phenomenon which can be described by using the concept of performativity. The aim of this paper is to investigate the elements inherent in the innovation processes of technologies developed in the fourth industrial revolution and to develop a conceptual model that better describes the intricacies of the system. To elucidate key features of the process, a review of innovation and science and technology studies (STS) literature is employed. A summary of the relationship between innovation models and previous industrial revolutions is proposed to highlight the increasing complexity of the innovation process as time goes on. The concept of performativity is introduced to illustrate how technologies evolve in a sociotechnical sphere.

Keywords: performativity, entanglement, innovation models, sociotechnical, fourth industrial revolution

1. Introduction

Industrial revolutions are characterised by the inventions and innovations that define them (Sae-Lim and Jermsittiparsert 2019). The first industrial revolution focused on technological developments in textile, manufacturing, and the steam engine; the second industrial revolution centred on technology associated with steel production, automotive, and electricity; the third industrial revolution saw advances in the field of telecommunication and electronics (Lee et al. 2018).

Models and methods for expressing the link between technology, industry, and society have been proposed (Meissner 2019) – with examples such as Kondratieff's cycles (Ferasso and Bergamaschi 2020), Moore's law (Holt 2016), technological determinism (Hallström 2020), and the social shaping of technology (Williams and Edge 1996). The models suggest the major changes that impact, and reorder economic and social systems correlate with developments in science and technology.

There have been several endeavours at modelling the dynamics inherent in the process of technological innovation (for example Rothwell, 1994; Tidd, Bessant and Pavitt, 2005). Yet, the fourth industrial revolution presents new challenges that highlight a more complex interpretation of the innovation process – in which substantive intricacies and interwovenness are inherent in the relationship between society and technology. It is distinct from the first three industrial revolutions, as it is characterised by the widespread application of cyber-physical systems (Liu and Xu 2017). In these systems, computing is used to fortify and increase the efficacy of traditionally physical approaches in order to achieve integration amongst virtual, mechanised, and physical worlds.

In the fourth industrial revolution, the influence of technology is not linear, but global and multifaceted. The question goes beyond how technology affects society, but also includes how society informs the development, scope, and diffusion of technological artefacts, as well as what factors contribute to the occurrence of these events. Models of innovation identify social factors and the use of feedback in the innovation process. This identification; however, does not explicitly address the entanglement of the material, cognitive, and social influences in the process. This necessitates an updated model of innovation that features a shift towards the intertwining and reciprocal entanglement of the social and the technological as related to the development and diffusion of technologies.

2. Background

In the classical Schumpeterian interpretation, innovation is defined as a major and irreversible change in the method of production of objects (Schumpeter 1934). These changes are inevitable, and their impacts are made visible through societal changes, market forces, and economic processes. According to this interpretation, innovation promotes some element of novelty amongst consumers, markets, materials or organisational paradigms (Carlile and Lakhani 2011). This definition of innovation suggests it is not specific to an exact technology or business process, but instead is an interactive process that links ideas, markets, and environments. Innovation is not merely invention, but instead incorporates the context in which an invention is applied (Häggström 2016); for a technological artefact to be truly innovative, it must address a need and interact with the market.

Early conceptualisations of the process from ideation to market, propose the path of innovation is straightforward and uncomplicated. Linear models of innovation present the process as having distinct sequential steps that are characterised by unidirectional, causative relationships, which tend not to extensively acknowledge feedback paths or social components. A range of linear models of innovation have been proposed in the literature (Rothwell 1994; Nacu and Avasilcai 2015) and suggest the innovation process starts with applied research and development, and is then followed by increased production, and widespread application (diffusion). This understanding of innovation is proposed in such models as Rothwell's (1994) first- and second-generation models of innovation. Rothwell provides a historic overview of innovation by describing that the complexity and integration in innovation models increases with each subsequent generation - as new practices emerge to adapt to changing contexts (Ortt and van der Duin 2008), as summarised in Table 1.

Table 1: Summary of Rothwell's five generations of innovation models

Model	Time (ca.)	Description
Technology Push (1st Generation)	1950	Simple linear sequential process Emphasis on R&D and science
Market Pull (2nd Generation)	1960	Simple linear sequential process More emphasis on social factors - communicative elements addressed
Coupling (3rd Generation)	1970	Interaction between different elements Feedback loops addressed
Functionally Integrated (4th Generation)	1980	Combination of push and pull - feedback and iteration The parallel lines model integration within firms - upstream with key suppliers and downstream with demanding and active customers Emphasis on linkages and alliances
System Integration & Network (SIN) (5th Generation)	1990	Recognised influence and communication of external and environment and the effective with the external environment Networking and continuous innovation

In the earlier generations, innovation is described as a relatively straight-forward activity. Advances in science, changes in technological systems, and shortened product lifecycles changed the pace and way in which previously distinct sequential activities, shifted events to parallel and concurrent activities (Minderhoud and Fraser 2005). More complex models recognise the dynamic integration and intersection of these activities. Such models emphasise bidirectional, cyclic, or spiral approaches to innovation, in which entities develop amongst lateral connections and repeat actions in order to establish roles for both human and non-human entities. Though these models address the positioning and timing of events in the innovation process, they do not necessarily focus on the dynamics and entanglement of social and material elements that are inherent in innovations that affect the fourth industrial revolution.

The characteristics of linear models of innovation can be seen in the development and diffusion of scientific inventions, particularly in the first and second industrial revolution, as outlined in Table 2. As time progresses the process of innovation moves away from the linear model and becomes more complex. Technologies become more entwined with society and help construct social realities; the process of innovation includes greater levels of feedback, iteration, and understanding of motivations for development.

Table 2: Description of industrial revolutions

Industrial Revolution	Technology	Impacted Industries
First (ca. 1760)	Steam-powered mechanisation	Textile, steel, railway infrastructure
Second (ca. 1860)	Internal combustion engine, assembly lines	Automotive vehicles, communications, electricity
Third (ca. 1960)	Automation technology, programmable logic controllers (PLCs), robotics, Internet	Electronics, telecommunications, synthetic materials, petrochemicals, information technology
Fourth (ca. 2010)	Information and communications technology (ICT), Internet of things (IoT), big data, smart devices, genetic engineering, 3D printing, artificial intelligence (AI)	Healthcare, banking and finance, aerospace, manufacturing, cyber-physical systems, cloud computing, cognitive computing

Source: Adapted from (Xu, David, and Kim, 2018)

The more complex a new technology is, the more challenging it is for society in terms of changing roles, and the less linear the route through idea-invention-marketization becomes (Rip, 2018). In these cases, the route to marketization requires a diverse and overlapping set of skills and knowledge to manage successfully. More recent models of technological innovation describe the process as a system greatly influenced by repetition and identity-shaping characteristics, in which feedback and sequential introductions of an invention incrementally lead to a finalised version of a product as well as a series of new ideas and concepts (Etzkowitz 2002).

Innovations, as they occurred in the first, second, and third industrial revolution, are represented by the models discussed in literature. These models; however, do not accurately depict the process for current technological innovations, because they do not highlight the identity-shaping elements in the process. There is an interconnectedness of user and technological artefacts, which focuses on the purposefulness and the directedness of technology while impacting the user and environment. Current technologies cannot be understood without identifying how that technology is embedded in its social context (Moldaschl 2010; Zizlavsky 2013). A model that explains the imbrication of social, cognitive, and material elements, and focuses on the of interlacing of users, tools, and actions would contribute to the discussion on the complex path of innovation in the fourth industrial revolution.

3. Methodology

The objective of this paper is to outline the characteristics of innovation in the fourth industrial revolution and to develop a conceptual model that highlights the dynamics of the involved elements. The contribution of this paper is the identification of the components that describe current technological innovations, in order to develop a more holistic understanding of what the process entails.

A qualitative research approach was adopted involving bibliographic and descriptive methods for the collection and distillation of relevant literature on technology, society, and innovation. A systematic literature review was conducted to synthesise information and identify elements to include in a conceptual model (Khan and Andersson 2011; Snyder 2019).

Peer-reviewed academic journal articles in the fields of innovation management, sociology, economics, science and technology studies, and design thinking were used as source material to acquire knowledge of the innovation process and its dynamics. Synthesis of gathered material was used to render a conceptual model of the dynamics of the innovation process.

4. Defining performativity

As technology progresses, it becomes apparent that the innovation process involves complex relationships between communicative and social factors – drawing attention to key elements, such as feedback, iteration, and routine. This interaction and weaving of the social, cognitive, and technological features can be discussed by using the concept of *performativity* (MacKenzie, Muniesa, and Siu 2007; Healy 2015).

Performativity expounds the idea that actions can construct an identity (Boldyrev 2020). Essentially, actions carried out into the world in a specific way, reformat and reorganise the phenomena they purport to describe (Healy 2015) – often bringing the world into line with theory (D'Adderio 2017). Users and tools are performative when they do more than describe a given reality, but also change the social reality they are describing. Constructing identity through routine and theoretical constructs is not merely guiding but contributes to actively shaping actual processes (Mäki 2013).

Originally stemming from the field of linguistics (Austin 1962), the discussion surrounding performativity has extended to several fields including economics (Çalışkan and Callon 2010), gender studies (Butler 1997), information systems (IS), (Orlikowski 2005; Kautz and Cecez-Kecmanovic 2014) and science and technology studies (STS) (Konrad and Böhle 2019). The concept recognises that there are multiple permutations for the development of elements within a performative relationship, and the path which distinct elements follow is contingent on the environment and factors that influence their development.

It is through the performed communicative and social actions of the user that the identity is constructed.

In relating these key features of the concept, performativity is then understood as the iterative and routine activities within a phenomenon (Barad, 2003) that construct an identity. The ability to act, emerges from within the relationships not from outside it; this association may be referred to as intra-action (instead of interaction), and the communication is not between elements that may be performative, but amongst the entities that make up the environment.

4.1 Performativity in the context of creating technology

Performativity denotes the ability to create a reality by enacting practice and prescribing function to artefacts, while considering the impact artefacts have on the development of the environment. According to Orlikowski and Scott (2005), the notion of performativity draws attention to how relations and boundaries between humans and technologies are not fixed but 'enacted in practice' (ibid. p. 462), as a technological artefact is a package of material properties presented in a socially recognisable form.

Non-human entities, such as technological artefacts, exercise agency, and promote performativity through the things they do, for which users cannot completely or directly control. Technology impacts the users, but users also impact the technology. In this way, coordinated human/social and material agencies both represent capacities for action, but they differ with respect to intentionality. Pickering (2001) offers an explanation of human and material agencies that illustrate this difference by suggesting social agency is part of a network that is coordinated and exercised by the forming and realisation of an entities' goals.

What a technology does can change depending on an environment or time. Function and material agency are a construct that depend, in part, on materiality, but are also contingent on one's perceptions of whether materiality allows or affords (Graver, 1991) the ability to achieve goals or hinder usage by placing constraints.

User's goals are formulated by their perceptions of what a technology can or cannot do, just as those perceptions are shaped by the user's desires; this alludes to expectations that are developed by the user that relate customer requirements to functional characteristics. Literature (Gibson 1977; Van Osch and Mendelson 2011) proposes affordances as a means of discussing this phenomenon and the sociomateriality within technological development. Both innovators and users approach materiality with diverse goals around which they perceive a technology as affording distinct possibilities for action. The perception and expectations of what functions an artefact affords can change based on whether users perceive that a technology affords or constrains their goals, and users make choices about how they will imbricate social and material agencies.

The flow of information is integral to the development of a performative innovation and to define the process is to recognise both the communicative and cognitive elements that describe it.

5. Model of performativity within technological innovation

A conceptual model of performativity within innovation was developed. The main components are outlined in Figure 1. The communicative elements of the process are feedback, iteration, and routine. Feedback has been recognised as critical part of the innovation process (Chesbrough, 2003; Kline & Rosenberg, 1986; Rothwell, 1994). Feedback is inherent throughout the process and all entities engage in levels or feedback. By repeating a practice (iteration) in a particular sequence (routine) an understanding and identity is created. In short, continued feedback promotes iteration, and iterations that repeatedly perform the same types of tasks with an end goal, signify routine.

This sequence of actions is repeated until the perceptible tasks or limitations of the artefact reach a terminus. This; however, is an oversimplification of the system, which does not describe the several means by which feedback is generated or the range of entities that may contribute to iterative development. Within the innovation process several actors, including researchers, academic institutions, financial bodies, social groups, engage to produce many iterations of a technological artefact. The interactions between these entities and the artefacts that may emerge are fundamental to the process of performativity. This can be further understood as the relationship is dictated by what the technological artefact offers as well as how the user and innovator may choose to use it, and what results from the interaction. The terms around 'what the artefact offers,' and how users 'choose to use it', highlight the role of affordances within the process.

The cognitive elements of the conceptual model are affordances, motivations, and expectation. Affordances are a sociomaterial construction (Van Osch and Mendelson, 2011) that represent the complex interactions between multiple social entities and material artefacts within a given environment. When a user interacts with an artefact, the user realises actions that they are able to perform because of the artefact. The affordances promote agency and the user is able to distinguish possibilities for action in the environment. An affordance is some possibility for action that is mutually specified by the user and the environment - affordances are explored.

Gaver (1991) provides a view on the nature of this exploration and describes nested and sequential affordances to illustrate the emergence of different affordances within singular evolving relationships. The implication is - design suggests the affordance, as distinct from the affordance suggesting an action. This adds to the view that knowledge is imbricated in the process of constructing the identity of a technological artefact.

Motivations are the reasons for acting or behaving in a distinct manner to garner feedback and promote movement within the innovation process; expectations are strong beliefs about the ways in which an artefact affects a user, market, or another artefact. Motivations and expectations are present for all agents within the innovation process but refine as the process goes through multiple iterations.

The conceptual model shows the bidirectional flow between the cognitive and communicative elements within innovation environment, as opposed to unidirectional information flows represented in linear models of innovation. The broken lines also indicate permeability that accommodates the free-flowing movement of information and encourages transformation.

The model depicts feedback continually happens between the technological artefact and the user. Repeated feedback and communication are part of an iterative process and create knowledge, both for the innovator and for the end-user. Routine is the mode by which this knowledge gains meaning. By repeating a practice (iteration) in a sequence (routine) an understanding and identity is created. Continued feedback promotes iteration and iterations that repeatedly perform the same types of tasks with an end goal, signify routine.

Additionally, when a user interacts with a technological artefact, the user realises actions that they are able to perform because of the artefact. The affordances promote agency and the user is able to distinguish possibilities for action in the environment; an affordance is some possibility for action that is mutually specified by the user and the environment.

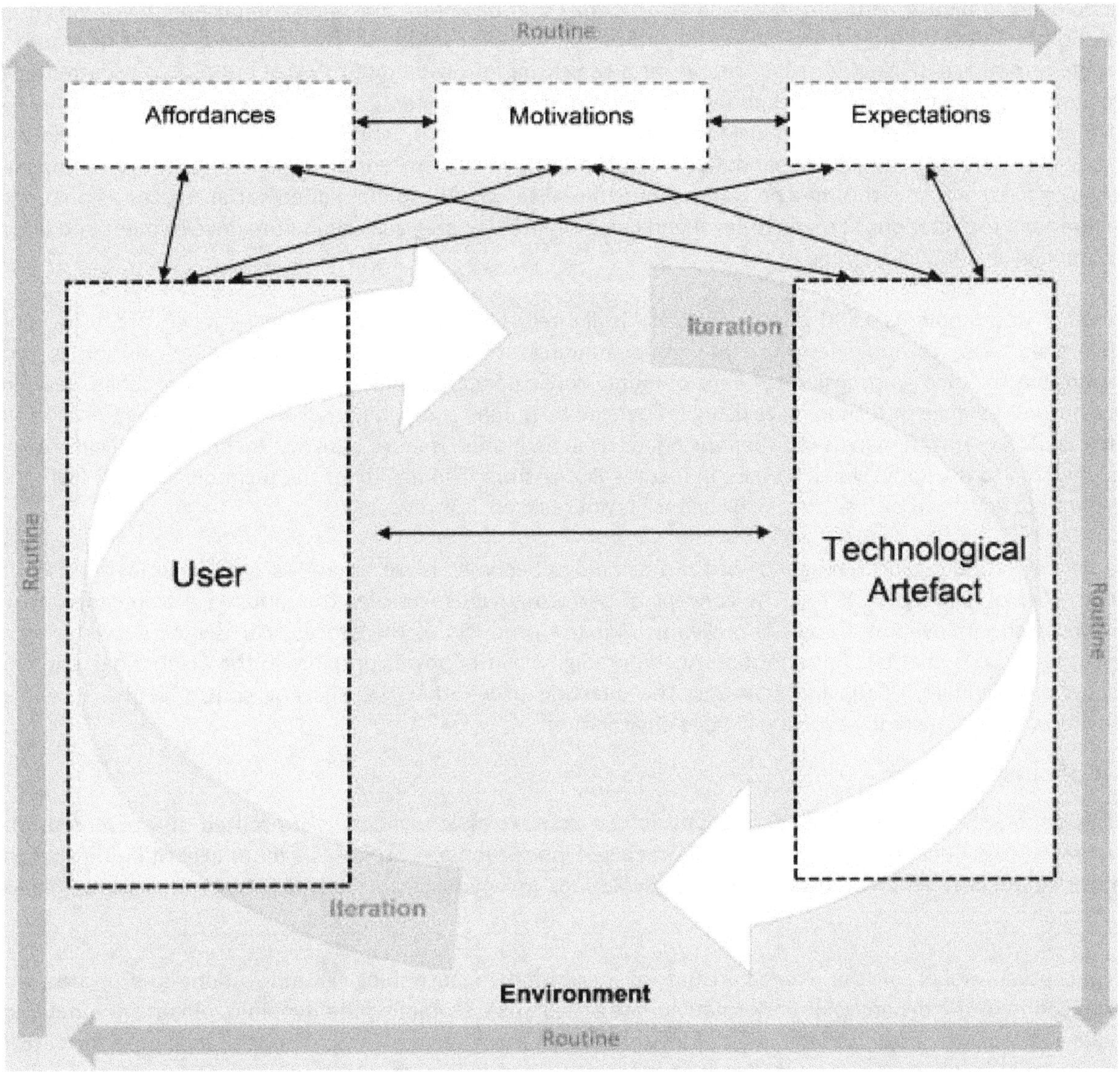

Figure 1: Conceptual model of performativity in the innovation process as related to technology

There are multiple permutations for the development of elements within a performative relationship, and the path which particular entities follow is contingent on the environment and factors that influence their development. In any distinct case, the users involved and the conditions must be appropriate to the invocation of the procedure. It is only by the actions carried out using a routine procedure, by appropriate users, under fitting conditions, that an identity is formed. This identity-shaping feature is performativity.

6. Discussion

Theories of technology have been applied extensively to earlier models of innovation. Such theories as technological determinism, social construction of technology, social shaping of technology have all been used to describe the phenomenon of technology impacting society or vice versa.

As technological determinism presumes that technology drives the development of social structures (Bimber, 1990), it is argued that within the theory the contribution of the human user becomes muddled and miniaturised. To assert that technology leads to inevitable change does not consider the impact of human agency within the growth of society. Conversely, approaches such as the social construction and social shaping of technology, challenge this perspective and illuminate the roles played by social factors in the development of technology. The methodology; however, does not guarantee comprehensiveness in discussing the innovation process and suffers from a propensity to minimise the participation of less influential social groups.

The conceptual model proposed in this research attempts to address the relationship between technology and society. The current industrial revolution is characterised by the application of information and communication technologies to industry and proposes holistic solutions that have real-time global implications – in which the evolution of industry differs from the previous three industrial revolutions. The technologies arising from the 'mangle of practice' (Pickering, 1993) represent a coalescing of digital and physical entities, in an attempt to transform the production of goods and services, but also transform user and innovator expectations. Collective social behaviour is fuelled by individual motivations and expectations, which inform the possibilities and uses for a new technology. The individual outlook highlights the issues present at the micro-level of developing a technology. Accordingly, this may be zoomed out to realise how these embedded social structures, influence activities and expectations at a macro-level and can ultimately strategically shape the development and use of a technology and industry.

With such developments as 3D printing, IoT, artificial intelligence, technological convergence, etc. It becomes visible that these technologies raise the understanding of how the fourth industrial revolution is both 'responsible for' and 'responsive to' development. For instance, predictive analytics and machine learning present the challenge of technologies being influenced by human users, but also, shape the understanding and customs of the same human users. The fourth industrial revolution is more than just technology-driven change; it is powered to disruptively impact core industries and sectors. The finality of the technological artefacts that arise are not governed by 'essence' – the agency is not realised, it is revealed.

The desire to understand the agency of the technology becomes more urgent as the technology slips from human control (Heidegger 1977). The concept of performativity reconciles the Janus face of technology, by purporting the innovation process is malleable and the products of the process can switch between being beneficial and detrimental. This confronts such paradigms as the power problem in the Collingridge dilemma (Liebert and Schmidt, 2010) and confronts the question of whether there is any control in the system of innovation, if it is constantly evolving with its environment.

7. Conclusion

In this paper, the concept of performativity in the context of innovation is presented and explored. This discussion takes a departure from simplified models of innovation and proposes a more explicit defining of the innovation process in the fourth industrial revolution, in which performativity frames the sociotechnical interaction.

A conceptual model of the characteristics of performative technological innovation is proposed and identification of the dynamics of performativity are articulated. Examining the dynamics of current innovation practices, the paper introduces the idea of affordances as a cognitive means of understanding performativity and highlights feedback, iteration, and routine as communicative factors in the innovation process.

As innovation management is increasingly burdened with uncertainty and complexity, understanding the projection of a technological artefact reduces the level of ambiguity associated with technological forecasting and makes technological alignment easier to achieve. Analysis of the performative characteristics of innovation and the subsequent development of a more refined model of the process can contribute to: better understanding of market trends and identification of more effective marketing actions, more refined strategic initiatives, greater success in new product development, and improved strategic navigation of the exploration–exploitation dilemma.

Acknowledgements

I would like to express my deep gratitude to Dr Jim Lawlor, my research supervisor, for his patient guidance, enthusiastic encouragement, and useful critiques of this research work.

References

Austin, J. L. (1962) How To Do Things with Words. Cambridge, Mass: Harvard University Press

Bandala, Argel. (2018). Preparing the Philippines for the Fourth Industrial Revolution: A Scoping Study.

Barad, K., 2003. Posthumanist performativity: Toward an understanding of how matter comes to matter. *Signs: Journal of women in culture and society*, 28(3), pp.801-831.

Bijker, W.E., 2009. Social Construction of Technology. *A Companion to the Philosophy of Technology*. JKB Olsen, SA Pedersen and VF Hendricks.

Boldyrev, I., 2020. Technology, society, and performativity: on a new book by Nicolas Brisset: Economics and performativity: exploring limits, theories and cases, London, Routledge, 2018, pp.300

Butler, J., 1997. Excitable Speech: A Politics of the Performative. New York and London: Routledge.

Çalışkan, K. and Callon, M., 2010. Economization, part 2: a research programme for the study of markets. *Economy and Society*, 39(1), pp.1-32.

Carlile, P.R. and Lakhani, K.R., 2011. Innovation and the Challenge of Novelty: The Novelty-Confirmation-Transformation Cycle in Software and Science. *Harvard Business School Technology & Operations Mgt* (No. 11-096). Unit Working Paper.

D'Adderio, L., 2017. Performativity and the innovation–replication dilemma. *In the Elgar companion to innovation and knowledge creation*. Edward Elgar Publishing.

Etzkowitz, H., 2002. Incubation of incubators: innovation as a triple helix of university-industry-government networks. *Science and Public Policy*, 29(2), pp.115-128.

Ferasso, M. and Bergamaschi, E.A., 2020. Kondratieff's Economic Waves and Future Scenarios Planning: an approach for organizations. *Technology Innovation Management Review*, 10(2), pp.51-61.

Gaver, W.W., 1991, March. Technology affordances. *In Proceedings of the SIGCHI conference on Human factors in computing systems* (pp. 79-84).

Gibson, J., 1977. The concept of affordances. Perceiving, acting, and knowing.

Häggström, O., 2016. Here be dragons: Science, technology and the future of humanity. Oxford University Press.

Hallström, J., 2020. Embodying the past, designing the future: technological determinism reconsidered in technology education. *International Journal of Technology and Design Education*, pp.1-15.

Healy, K., 2015. The performativity of networks. *European Journal of Sociology*, 56(02), pp.175-205.

Heidegger, M., 1977. The question concerning technology (pp. 3-35). New York: Harper & Row.

Holt, W.M., 2016. Moore's law: A path going forward. *IEEE International Solid-State Circuits Conference (ISSCC)* (pp. 8-13). IEEE.

Kautz, K. and Cecez-Kecmanovic, D., 2013, June. Sociomateriality and information systems success and failure. *In International Working Conference on Transfer and Diffusion of IT* (pp. 1-20). Springer, Berlin, Heidelberg.

Khan, S. and Andersson, K., 2011. A Design Methodology for Haptic Device. DS 68-4: *Proceedings of the 18th International Conference on Engineering Design (ICED 11)*, Impacting Society through Engineering Design, Vol.
4: Product and Systems Design, Lyngby/Copenhagen, Denmark, 15.-19.08. 2011 (pp. 288-298).

Konrad, K. and Böhle, K., 2019. Socio-technical futures and the governance of innovation processes—An introduction to the special issue. *Futures*, 109, pp.101-107.

Lee, M., Yun, J.J., Pyka, A., Won, D., Kodama, F., Schiuma, G., Park, H., Jeon, J., Park, K., Jung, K. and Yan, M.R., 2018. How to respond to the fourth industrial revolution, or the second information technology revolution? Dynamic new combinations between technology, market, and society through open innovation. *Journal of Open Innovation: Technology, Market, and Complexity*, 4(3), p.21.

Liebert, W. and Schmidt, J.C., 2010. Collingridge's dilemma and technoscience. Poiesis & Praxis, 7(1-2), pp.55-71.

Liu, Y. and Xu, X., 2017. Industry 4.0 and cloud manufacturing: A comparative analysis. Journal of *Manufacturing Science and Engineering*, 139(3).

Mäki, U., 2013. Performativity: Saving Austin from MacKenzie. *In EPSA11 perspectives and foundational problems in philosophy of science* (pp. 443-453). Springer, Cham.

Marti, E. and Gond, J.P., 2019. How do theories become self-fulfilling? Clarifying the process of Barnesian performativity. *Academy of Management Review*, 44(3), pp.686-694.

Meissner, D., 2019. Public-private partnership models for science, technology, and innovation cooperation. *Journal of the Knowledge Economy*, 10(4), pp.1341-1361.

Minderhoud, S. and Fraser, P., 2005. Shifting paradigms of product development in fast and dynamic markets. *Reliability Engineering & System Safety*, 88(2), pp.127-135.

Mody, C.C., 2006. Small, but determined: Technological determinism in nanoscience. *In Nanotechnology challenges: implications for philosophy, ethics and society* (pp. 95-130).

Moldaschl, M., 2010. Why innovation theories make no sense (No. 9/2010). *Papers and Preprints of the Department of Innovation Research and Sustainable Resource Management*.

Nacu, C.M. and Avasilcai, S., 2015. A model of technological innovation process. Gheorghe Asachi. Technical University of Iasi, Romani.

Orlikowski, W.J., 2005. Material works: Exploring the situated entanglement of technological performativity and human agency. *Scandinavian Journal of Information Systems,* 17(1), p.6.

Ortt, J.R. and van der Duin, P.A., 2008. The evolution of innovation management towards contextual innovation. *European journal of innovation management.*

Pickering, A., 1993. The mangle of practice: Agency and emergence in the sociology of science. *American journal of sociology*, 99(3), pp.559-589.

Pickering, A., 2001. Practice and posthumanism: Social theory and a history of agency. The practice turn in contemporary theory, pp.163-74.

Prisecaru, P. (2016). Challenges of the Fourth Industrial Revolution. *Knowledge Horizons. Economics,* 8(1), 57-62.

Rip, A., 2018. Processes of technological innovation in context–and their modulation. In Futures of Science and Technology in Society. Springer VS, Wiesbaden. (pp. 49-73).

Rothwell, R., 1994. Towards the fifth-generation innovation process. *International marketing review.*

Sae-Lim, P. and Jermsittiparsert, K., 2019. Is the fourth industrial revolution a panacea? Risks toward the fourth industrial revolution: Evidence in the thai economy. *International Journal of Innovation, Creativity and Change,* 5(2), pp.732-752.

Schumpeter, J.A. 1934. The Theory of Economic Development. *Harvard University Press* (originally published in German in 1911; reprinted by Transaction Publishers, New Brunswick, New Jersey in 1997).

Snyder, H., 2019. Literature review as a research methodology: An overview and guidelines. *Journal of Business Research*, 104, pp.333-339.

Tatnall, A. ed., 2010. Actor-Network Theory and Technology Innovation: Advancements and New Concepts: *Advancements and New Concepts. IGI Global.*

Tidd, J., Bessant, J., and Pavitt, K., 2005. Managing Innovation: Integrating Technological, Market and Organisational Change, 3rd edition, John Wiley and Sons Ltd.

Van Osch, W. and Mendelson, O., 2011. A typology of affordances: Untangling sociomaterial interactions through video analysis.

Williams, R. and Edge, D., 1996. The social shaping of technology. *Research policy*, 25(6), pp.865-899.

Xu, M., David, J.M. and Kim, S.H., 2018. The fourth industrial revolution: opportunities and challenges. *International journal of financial research*, 9(2), pp.90-95.

Žižlavský, O., 2013. Past, present and future of the innovation process. *International Journal of Engineering Business Management*, 5, p.47.

Wellbeing Program Implementation at a Fortune 500 Company: A Case Study

Alice Vo Edwards[1] and Arezou Harraf[2]
[1]The CEO Within, LLC, North Las Vegas, USA
[2]Learn and Evolve, LLC & Box Hill College, Kuwait City, Kuwait
alice@theceowithin.me
Dr.Harraf@learnandevolve.com
DOI: 10.34190/EIE.20.224

Abstract: In the wake of the COVID-19 pandemic, there is an increased acknowledgement of the importance of mental health in retaining a healthy and productive workforce. In the months following the pandemic, a number of prominent companies have begun offering wellbeing programs that go beyond physical health benefits that have been a stable employee benefit, to include other types of health benefits, including mental health supports. While it appears that the trend in offering workplace wellbeing programs is growing, is it sustainable? Those seeking to navigate this space and sell to corporate (B2B) customers will face stiff competition from other providers. Do we understand what organizations are expecting to gain from bringing these interventions into the workplace? Do they get what they expect? What are the challenges in bringing wellbeing programs into workplace settings? How can entrepreneurs and innovators increase the likelihood of success in retaining new corporate clients? How can we encourage clients to retain these services after short-term pandemic-related demand has passed? To provide insight to these questions, the authors will discuss and reflect upon a pre-COVID-19 implementation of a wellbeing program at a Fortune 500 Company. The case study will walk the reader through processes the authors and their client went through in implementing and evaluating a wellbeing program offered to employees at a Fortune 500 Company. This case study includes a summary of the process and challenges the startup company faced in implementing their program as a third-party provider of a wellbeing program to a large corporation. The case study also includes a summary of the program outcome, including quantitative program benefits identified and how these were obtained. Additional qualitative data further informs on aspects of the case study, including qualitative feedback from participants in the wellbeing programs and the hiring manager. Perspective from the startup entrepreneurial firm that developed and provided the wellbeing program is also included. In discussing the scenario to its conclusion, we provide a thoughtful discourse for consideration on how to leverage what was learned through this case study to improve product development and implementation for other entrepreneurs.

Keywords: workplace, health, wellbeing program, employee, product evaluation, COVID-19

1. Introduction

In recent years, there has been a growing movement to redefine our conception of employee health and wellbeing programs beyond provision of basics such as healthcare and paid time off. Newer definitions of wellbeing suggest that wellbeing is multidimensional and inclusive of many factors; these include physical, economic, social, developmental, emotional, psychological, life satisfaction, domain-specific satisfaction, and engaging activities and work (CDC, 2018). The COVID-19 pandemic supports this definition and has shown that workplace health and workplace productivity are inextricably linked. These relationships are not one-dimensional; nor are they fully physical. Many workers refused to go back to work when lockdowns were ended, not due to physically having an illness, but due to anxiety about whether the workplace would be safe or might expose them to COVID-19. The anxiety and other mental health issues that have arisen during the COVID-19 pandemic has increased our cultural awareness of the need to offer multidimensional workplace wellbeing support to employees (e.g. CDC, 2020).

Within this expanded understanding of wellbeing and how improving wellbeing can improve organizational performance, business leaders are rapidly considering and adopting a multitude of additional wellbeing course topics outside of the traditional mental and physical health model. Yet as companies race to show their support for employees and provide expanded health and wellbeing programming, researchers warn that in many cases wellbeing programs do not provide value equivalent to their cost (Goetzel et al., 2014). Programs used for wellbeing in the workplace often lack evidence that they correlate with other desired workplace outcome benefits (Bartlett et al., 2017). In addition to the many types of wellbeing factors and types of wellbeing programs, there is also no consistent mechanism for program delivery, leading to substantial inconsistencies in program efficacy (Tam & Yeung, 2018). Goetzel et al. (2014) evaluated 30 years of health and wellbeing programs and advised employers that if their only goal was to deliver clear monetary benefits, quickly, they were likely to be disappointed. Instead, Goetzel et al. (2014) advised organizations to identify their objectives and choose appropriate wellbeing program components that align with their goals as well as the types of metrics and timeframes that the organization wanted to deliver results within. Today, this advice is critical not just to companies in seeking to choose wellbeing programs, but also to the entrepreneurs and innovators seeking to meet this growing demand.

We suggest that, in order to improve the quality and efficacy of health and wellbeing program offerings, it is important for program developers to use similar strategies to those Goetzel et al. (2014) recommend. Innovators should employ research methods in piloting interventions, evaluating products, and designing product improvement plans. Not only does this type of rigorous internal study lead to increased program quality, it also moves a company on an upward path from having an evidence-informed product (i.e., one influenced by existing research, but with no proof of efficacy) towards building the evidence to become evidence-based (i.e., confirmed by high-level quantitative analysis as being effective). To guide further consideration of health and wellbeing program evaluation, this article presents a case study in which mixed-methods research and analysis was used to assist a wellbeing company in evaluating and reporting on the program benefits received by their Fortune 500 company client.

2. Approach to this study

While having more than 20 years' experience working in program development, implementation, and technical product development, over the past four years, the PI has increasingly focused her efforts on supporting programs that promote human thriving. This paper presents one project that can help health and wellbeing entrepreneurs better understand how to navigate the corporate (B2B) sales landscape. The case study will describe the aim of the project, the research methods employed, and the outcomes. Our direct client was the wellbeing provider (WBP) and their customer was a Fortune 500 company (Company). The identity of the Company may not be disclosed per the WBP's nondisclosure agreements. For this case, we were able to stay in contact with the WBP for more than a year past the end of the initial intervention and evaluation timeframe. Because of this, we are able to provide a longitudinal perspective on the outcomes experienced by the WBP. We then discuss our perspective on how other entrepreneurs might learn from or build upon this case study to improve outcomes for other health and wellbeing product and service providers.

3. Case study: A multidisciplinary workplace wellbeing program intervention performed for a Fortune 500 company client

The WBP was hired by a facilities manager for one region of the Company to provide wellbeing classes within the region the individual managed. The CEO actively marketed the WBP by being a thought leader in the workplace wellbeing space. As a thought leader, the CEO sought opportunities to educate and inspire organizations to conceptualize wellbeing outside of traditional concepts of physical health metrics. The CEO participated in multiple public speaking events, some of which were recorded and further shared online through platforms such as YouTube. This thought leadership-focused marketing resulted in being contacted by the client about providing the company's programs to them after the client heard the CEO speak at an event.

The WBP offered numerous activity topics spanning the multidimensional wellbeing model but allowed the Company to choose which activities they wanted to offer, based on the Company's perception of alignment with employee needs and organizational goals. The intervention consisted of offering live one-hour classes on each activity topic then supporting application of the learned material through wellness challenges. The wellness challenges were offered via email and website and were designed to encourage employees to work together on teams to achieve wellness goals.

The CEO contacted the PI to assist in evaluating the pilot program. The objectives of the project were to:

- Help the CEO understand what they were doing well and how to improve their pilot program, and
- Help the CEO demonstrate to their client how the pilot program provided positive benefits to encourage client retention beyond the initial pilot program.

4. Study design

4.1 Stage 1: Foundation research

During the foundation research stage, the PI worked with the CEO to understand the product offering and the CEO current understanding about how the intervention would benefit employee wellbeing. The PI also requested any anecdotal evidence the CEO may have received from prior product demonstrations. This information guided the selection and development of the research methods used. The literature review included academic and trade journals and articles as well as reference books on qualitative, quantitative, and mixed methods research, as well as survey development. These were synthesized into development of a pilot test utilizing mixed-methods explanatory sequential research design modified for its intended use in a commercial setting to assess the pilot test of the product to evaluate outcomes and inform future improvements.

4.2 Stage 2: Performing the pilot intervention

The first phase of the study included performing the in-person class component of the pilot intervention, while obtaining pre- post- data on how participant wellbeing was impacted, in the short term. Edwards (2017) developed a custom survey that included the Happiness Mini Survey (Edwards, 2016), a short pre- and post-wellbeing survey, along with additional open-ended questions for participant feedback.

The wellbeing classes were offered on three corporate campuses in a large metropolitan area in the United States during a two-month period. The client chose five classes: Stress: Taming the tigers: how to avoid chronic stress (Phillips, 2017), Meditation: Don't hate. Meditate (Jasso, 2017), Personal Finance: What you should have learned about money but never did (Bera, 2017), Interpersonal Relationships: The powerful language of the nervous system (Howard, 2017), and Communication and Presentation Skills: Empower Yourself: Present like a Pro (Zamcheck, 2017). The client sent emails to approximately 435 employees to invite them to participate in the classes. The wellbeing classes lasted one-hour. The company handed out the printed double-sided, one-page survey handout at the beginning of each class. Printed surveys were used for anonymity to encourage honest feedback. Participants were given time to complete the front, pre- survey portion at the start of each one-hour class, followed by a reminder to complete the post- survey on the back of the handout at the end of the class. Seventy-eight surveys were collected.

Participants were encouraged to go online to utilize the online components of the pilot intervention, which encouraged participation in additional classes, team activities with their peers, and provided health challenges and prompts to encourage ongoing self-awareness and increased social consciousness about health.

4.3 Stage 3: Mixed method data analysis from Stage 2 and additional qualitative data collection

At the conclusion of the program, initial analysis of participant survey responses was performed and used to develop a summary report for the Fortune 500 customer as well as a questionnaire for the manager. The questionnaire design was informed by the appreciative inquiry model for change management (Bushe, 2013). The appreciative inquiry model uses a focus on understanding what went well in order to build upon successes. The researchers interviewed the manager who had hired the company to better understand how results of the participant survey findings aligned with the manager's initial goals in starting the pilot program while also asking about secondary benefits the corporation had identified and attributed to implementation of the pilot program (Edwards & Harraf, 2018). Follow-up calls and emails were exchanged over an additional period of one year to better understand the long-term implications.

5. Findings and outcomes of the pilot study

Employees who completed the pre- and post- surveys demonstrated significantly improved wellbeing in a t-test analysis of four wellbeing traits measured (mental, physical, emotional, and stress). Overall, the greatest reduction was in the stress score, and the least reduction was in physical wellbeing (Edwards & Marcus, 2018). This was an expected result as the particular wellbeing activities offered did not specifically focus on physical wellbeing. One employee stated that "The Wellshift challenge was key for reducing stress levels by being grateful and valuing small things." Employees also felt that the classes were useful to them in ways that were practical and could be applied immediately. Said one employee regarding the class *Empower yourself: Present Like a Pro*, "I'll use it today on a career conversation talk I have. I'll use it every day in casual and formal presentations I have with customers :)." After taking the class *Financial Basics: What you should have learned in school but never did* which taught participants to create a *spending plan* and use the bucket method, rather than following traditional perspectives on creating a *budget*, another participant said they had learned not to combine student loans and that closing credit cards wasn't always a good thing, and stated an intent to start a spending plan and check their credit score. Another employee responded to the course *Taming the Tigers: How to avoid chronic stress* by stating that, "[it would help them] slow down, relax, and focus on proper responses."

One limitation encountered in the implementation of the intervention was marketing within the Company to the employees. All marketing of the class dates and times was required to be sent to employees through the Company contact, and the Company did not want the classes marketed in publicly visible areas due to their desire to limit the attendance to non-contractors. This significantly limited the WBC's ability to recruit participants. Another limitation was the corporate culture and perception that employees need to appear productive at all times. This influenced employee concerns about attending multiple sessions.

The secondary qualitative interviews and ongoing conversations with the manager who requested the program identified a number of expected and unexpected benefits that the manager attributed to the wellbeing program (see Figure 1). Evidence of these benefits include the manager having been told by the on-site cafe that there was a noticeable reduction in the number of sodas being consumed by employees and that employees were requesting healthier foods. The manager also received feedback from employees that the program positively impacted the employees' view of the organization. There were also noticeable changes in the organizational culture, with the manager stating that it seemed as if the workplace was a different environment now that employees were discussing their health openly and participating in cross-team collaborations on some of the challenges.

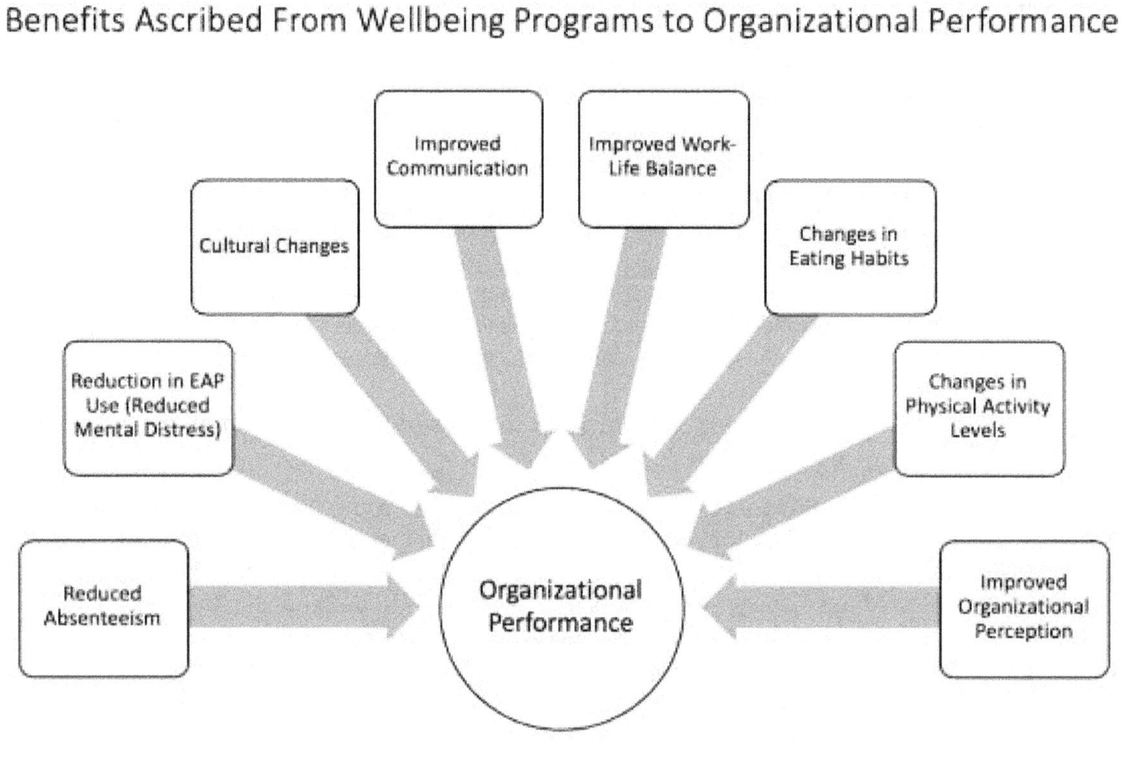

Figure 1: Benefits ascribed from wellbeing programs

While the facilities manager at the Company was eager to continue with the project after the pilot ended, the Company went through an internal restructuring period. During this, the budget and responsibility for employee wellbeing programs was removed from the local, state-level facility managers to instead be managed by a national, out of state department. The local, state-based contact the WBP had been working with did not have high enough connections to endorse the wellbeing program being continued by the new, national, out of state corporate officer. The program was not renewed after the pilot due to this organizational change.

6. Discussion

The use of multiple research methods in this mixed-method explanatory sequential design was undertaken by the authors in a corporate consultative capacity to assist the client in evaluating the pilot of their product. As this was not performed for academic research or a clinical trial, IRB oversight was not required, but similar care in the ethical handling of participant data was used. The instruments and methods of inquiry were informed by more than 30 years cumulative management and academic experience between the two authors. This section reflects upon relevant literature in the field by connecting it with the case study and future applications of elements included in this case by future researchers.

6.1 Reflection on the case study and use of explanatory sequential design

Using both quantitative and qualitative data collection, and both structured and unstructured interviews and follow-up methods allowed us to more clearly understand the challenges facing a wellbeing startup. It also clearly demonstrated the value explanatory sequential design offers to a researcher. By allowing us to develop further qualitative data based on the initial mixed methods data collected in the survey instrument, a more complete understanding of the benefits and challenges the organization faced emerged.

The Happiness Mini Survey (Edwards, 2016) pre- post- format was designed to encourage self-reflection. By allowing for increased metacognition, cognitive evaluation, and appreciation of the benefits received for the individual, it is intended to help the individual self-identify the course content value to their own wellbeing. This study format did not allow for longitudinal analysis of participants in regard to whether they continued to use or build on the skills learned in the classes taught. Longitudinal design is challenging within commercial product testing due to limited access to Client employees. Where possible, it is recommended that program evaluators seek to incorporate methods of capturing longitudinal data. For example, had our team been brought in earlier in the product development process, we may have been able to advocate for longitudinal data collection to be incorporated into the online component of the course.

6.2 Key takeaways from the case study for other wellbeing program innovators and entrepreneurs

There are several key takeaways to be learned from this case study that can assist the health and wellbeing-oriented entrepreneur in strategizing their own product development, marketing, and evaluation.

- *A Fortune 500 contract is not out of reach.* Despite the fact that the corporate restructuring kept the pilot program discussed in this case from being renewed, the case still highlights that such an achievement is possible even for a small startup. Entrepreneurs should understand that each corporation has multiple levels of administrative personnel with purchasing power. Additionally, this case demonstrates the need to be open-minded in considering who might wield the checkbook; in this example, it wasn't an executive from HR, but the facilities manager, who championed the product. While higher-ups may be needed for large-scale adoption, local staff often have authority to pay for small pilot program tests within their existing budgets.
- *Marketing matters.* In this case study, the CEO was an experienced marketer and used that expertise to obtain a contract with a Fortune 500 company. The CEO also successfully converted the facilities manager from simply a purchaser to an internal advocate for the product. Don't discount the importance of marketing experience and skill in getting your product sold.
- *Leverage external experts.* The CEO leveraged external consultant support to build and implement a system to develop and report on the program efficacy. The CEO also leveraged third-party experts to provide individual course content; this increased the quality and evidence-basis for each class without requiring significant time or resources or internal expertise.
- *Start gathering evidence to build your evidence-based model as soon as possible.* Spence (2015) warns that when it comes to wellbeing programs, "if you build it, they may not come." Highly effective wellbeing programs do not choose content offerings without strategically considering the needs of their particular workforce, what types of wellbeing programs may best meet their particular organizations' needs, and how the organization will be able to educate, implement, and encourage employees to make use of the program. This company came to us to assist in developing evidence for the effectiveness of their product while already under contract to deliver the pilot to the Fortune 500 Company and the facilities manager had already

chosen the courses. Earlier interaction with wellbeing experts would have allowed the CEO to develop the product and suggest which classes might be the most effective for the company, using an evidence-informed or evidence-based model.

- *Provide openings for unexpected learning.* In this case study, we obtained qualitative preliminary evidence that the impact on employee health might be measurable through quantitative tracking of food choices. This information suggested an interesting new avenue for future wellbeing researchers to quantitatively evaluate program outcomes: inventory or costs related to healthy vs. unhealthy food purchases. This knowledge was uncovered through our choice to use appreciative inquiry and interviews in addition to the quantitative pre- post- survey.
- *Ask client questions up-front to understand limitations that may impact your program's effectiveness.* It is recommended to discuss up-front any desired limitations on attendance and the related difficulties inherent in recruiting participants to open discussions of how marketing for the program will be addressed within those constraints. Each corporate culture poses unique challenges to effective program utilization. It is important to perform discovery prior to implementation with the client to understand what some of these challenges might be and how to work together to address them to optimize your program's effectiveness. In the case study example of a performance-oriented culture, one suggestion for overcoming this is to consider ways to educate managers in understanding how these courses contribute to overall employee performance and productivity. Encourage managers to provide verbal and written encouragement to employees to participate in the activities, most notably by setting the example and participating, themselves.

6.3 Where to start in gathering evidence and development metrics on program effectiveness

Recent collaborations between the Health Enhancement Research Organization, and Population Health Alliance (HERO-PHA) (2014) led to the recommendation of seven metrics for evaluating wellness programs: financial outcomes, health impact, participation, satisfaction, organizational support, productivity and performance, and value on investment (VOI). These seven metrics are a great place to start in identifying potential metrics for measuring the efficacy of your health or wellbeing intervention and its benefits (Figure 2).

Figure 2: Key metrics for workplace wellbeing advocated by HERO-PHA

The findings of our case study support these seven metrics, as participant and manager responses are aligned with these metrics and some outcomes tie to multiple metrics. For example, reduced EAP is linked to financial outcomes, health impact, organizational support, and productivity and performance. Until concrete data for a particular program is available, providers can elaborate on how their work ties to existing data that has been published on similar programs in their field. This can be supplemented by becoming thought leaders in educating organizational decision makers on the seven key workplace wellbeing metrics and especially highlighting the importance of considering value on investment and other metrics shown in Figure 2 rather than purely financial outcomes (return on investment; ROI).

Flynn and Brennan (2015) found that value on investment (sometimes referred to as return on value) may offer an even greater demonstration of the benefits that wellbeing programs offer than traditional return on investment statistics. Value on investment (VOI) is the value that is added which may not be quantifiable or may be difficult to measure. VOI is quantified through "a financial analysis that better reflects the broader savings potential of wellness programs, rather than an ROI measure designed to calculate revenue rather than savings" (Miller, 2015). In the case discussed here, reduced soda expenses would be a quantifiable return on investment, supported with data that the organization's accounting department could provide after the completion of a program due to secondary relationships between soda and obesity, along with obesity and workplace productivity (Barkin, Heerman, Warren, & Rennhoff (2010). On the other hand, the examples of increased collaboration between teams of different departments and requests for healthier versus less healthy foods would be considered return on value and would be harder to quantify. However, if considered in advance and with enough support from organizational partners in collecting and measuring data, appropriate measures could be put in place to track these types of outcomes prior to implementing the program.

7. Conclusion

In conclusion, we recommend that health innovators with wellbeing interventions or programs consider current and future use of program evaluation methods strategically. It is undoubtedly important to support organizations with health and wellbeing needs as part of COVID-19 response initiatives in the short term. While accomplishing this, we urge you to consider how to increase the sustainability of your programs. How are you validating the need for your product and services? We recommend incorporating metrics that can be used to demonstrate value, as well as how to improve buy-in at the purchaser level and transforming employee participants into "raving fans by considering "what's in it for me" from the perspective of each specific stakeholder audience. Once these stakeholder groups are identified, develop appropriate methods to track engagement, and evaluate impact. We hypothesize that entrepreneurs that rapidly move to be able to market their products as evidence-based will experience better performance compared to organizations that do not attain this status. Future research should investigate differences between companies that provide programs that are evidence based, compared to those without. Due to the known challenges and critiques regarding government and public policies on using evidence based programs (e.g., La Caze & Colyvan, 2019) further inquiry should be made into how to assist entrepreneurs and innovators who lack academic research background in developing programs in a way that can lead to attaining the status of being evidence-based.

Technology supported program delivery methods such as online and app-based methods provide great potential for scalability of program implementations especially during pandemics. However, research on the benefits of programs delivered online found mixed results due to challenges in gaining enough employee participation to achieve significant positive benefit (Abbott et al., 2009; Healy et. al, 2016). It is hoped that, with the increase in online wellbeing programs and remote employment spurred by the pandemic (Edwards, 2020), researchers will be able to gather larger data sets in order to re-address this issue with greater clarity. Looking forward, digital health technology provides an increased array of possibilities to support program developers in identifying wellbeing benefits quantitatively through the use of biometrics and other health data reporting mechanisms.

References

Abbott, J. A., Klein, B., Hamilton, C., & Rosenthal, A. J. (2009). The impact of online resilience training for sales managers on wellbeing and performance. *Sensoria: A Journal of Mind, Brain & Culture*, *5*(1), 89-95.

Barkin, S.L., Heerman, W.J., Warren, & Rennhoff, C. (2010). *Journal of Business Psychology 25,* 239-245. https://doi.org/10.1007/s10869-010-9166-5

Bartlett, L., Sanderson, K., Martin, A., Memish, K., & Otahal, P. (June, 2017). Workplace Mindfulness Training Outcomes By Intervention And Participant Characteristics: A Systematic Review And Meta-analysis [Conference: Abstract]. American Psychological Assocation (APA) . doi:10.1037/e506912017-001

Bera, S. (2017). Financial basics: What you should have learned about money but never did. Wellshift, Austin, TX.

Bushe, G.R. (2013) The appreciative inquiry model. In E.H. Kessler, (ed.) Encyclopedia of Management Theory, (Volume 1, pp. 41-44), Sage Publications, 2013.

CDC. (June 12, 2020). Coronavirus Disease 2019 (COVID-19): Coping with Stress. Retrieved from https://www.cdc.gov/coronavirus/2019-ncov/daily-life-coping/managing-stress-anxiety.html

CDC. (2018). Well-Being Concepts. *Health-Related Quality of Life (HRQOL).* Centers for Disease Control and Prevention. Retrieved on February 3, 2019 from https://www.cdc.gov/hrqol/wellbeing.htm#three.

Edwards, A. V. (2016). *Initial pre/post class wellbeing survey.* (Handout). Las-Vegas, NV: Lift Up Vegas.

Edwards, A.V. (2017). Revised *pre/post class wellbeing survey.* (Handout). Austin, TX: Wellshift.

Edwards, A.V. (June 4, 2020). Thriving at work: An updated outlook on the sector. Retrieved from http://www.alicevoedwards.com/musings/thriving-at-work-an-updated-outlook-on-the-sector/

Edwards, A. V. & Harraf, A. (2018). Employer Perspective on Wellness Programs: A qualitative Benefit Analysis At A Fortune 500 Company In the United States. (Presented at ISQOLS, June 2018).

Edwards, A.V. & Marcus, S. (2018) Employee Perceptions of Well-Being Programs. *Journal of Social, Behavioral, and Health Sciences, 12*(1), 7.

Flynn, J. & Brennan, M. (2015). Chapter 6: organizational support. *In* Health, Enhancement Research Organization, and Population Health Alliance (HERO-PHA). (2014). Program Measurement & Evaluation Guide: Core Metrics for Employee Health Management. *American journal of health promotion: AJHP*, 28(4).

Goetzel, R. Z., Henke, R. M., Tabrizi, M., Pelletier, K. R., Loeppke, R., Ballard, D. W., ... Metz, R. D. (2014). Do workplace health promotion (wellness) programs work? *Journal of Occupational and Environmental Medicine*, 56(9), 927–934. https://doi.org/10.1097/JOM.0000000000000276

Healy, G. N., Goode, A., Schultz, D., Lee, D., Leahy, B., Dunstan, D. W., ... & Eakin, E. G. (2016). The BeUpstanding Program™: Scaling up the Stand Up Australia Workplace Intervention for Translation into Practice. *AIMS public health*, *3*(2), 341.

Health, Enhancement Research Organization, and Population Health Alliance (HERO-PHA). (2014). Program Measurement & Evaluation Guide: Core Metrics for Employee Health Management. *American journal of health promotion: AJHP*, 28(4).

Howard, J. (2017). *The powerful language of the nervous system*. Wellshift, Austin, TX.

Jasso, J. *Don't hate. Meditate*. Wellshift, Austin, TX.

La Caze, A., & Colyvan, M. (2019). Evidence-based policy: Promises and challenges.

Miller, S. M. (2015). Metrics beyond ROI can capture your outcomes. Society for human resource management. Retrieved on December 11, 2018 from https://www.shrm.org/resourcesandtools/hr-topics/benefits/pages/wellness-metrics-beyond-roi.aspx.

Phillips, J. (2017). Taming the tigers: how to avoid chronic stress. Wellshift, Austin, TX.

Spence, G. B. (2015). Workplace wellbeing programs : If you build it they may NOT come ... because it's not what they really need! *International Journal of Wellbeing*, *5*(2), 109–124. https://doi.org/10.5502/ijw.v5i2.7.

Tam, G., & Yeung, M. P. (2018). A systematic review of the long-term effectiveness of work-based lifestyle interventions to tackle overweight and obesity. *Preventive medicine, 107*, 54-60.

Zamcheck, K. (2017). *Empower yourself: Present like a pro*. Wellshift, Austin, TX.

Charity and tax Planning in Socially Responsible Entrepreneurships in the Czech Republic

Blanka Jarolimova and Zuzana Tuckova
Tomas Bata University in Zlin, Czech Republic
jarolimova@utb.cz
tuckova@utb.cz
DOI: 10.34190/EIE.20.161

Abstract: Today, more and more companies in the Czech Republic are committed to the concept of sustainable business or corporate social responsibility (CSR). Charity donations belong among the most common areas in which companies invest in terms of socially responsible behaviour. However, some critics point out that responsible companies should primarily behave in a way that does not endanger their core business. Regardless, CSR has become a global theme, both academically and in practice, and a broad concept that addresses economic, environmental, and social dimensions of entrepreneurship. The environmental and social issues were dominant in the concept of sustainable business and CSR practices but recently, a lot of the discussion has targeted the companies' responsibility to pay taxes. Indeed, taxation is not a new dimension and, instead, should be seen as part of economic responsibility, as paying taxes into public finances is inherently part of how businesses contribute to society. Thus, socially responsible companies will play an important role in the development of communities and as leaders of social innovations. To achieve its economic objectives, entrepreneurship, to be responsible, must always obey the law. That does not mean that socially responsible companies need to pay more in taxes than required by the law. CSR activities should not create obstacles to the normal and appropriate tax planning. Yet, CSR can be perceived as to set some limits to and requirements for the tax planning activities, such as aggressive tax planning; these are steps taken by taxpayers which are in line with the tax requirements, but do not correspond with reasonable expectations of the stakeholders. The first section of the article contains scientific work, with the introductory part focused on a survey of the current state of the issue and the level of knowledge. The following part of the research will use secondary data available, namely from the Ministry of Finance of the Czech Republic, concerning charitable donations and their effect on the overall tax base and income tax to prove or disprove whether Czech companies use charitable donations as a mean of aggressive tax planning. In conclusion, the findings will be formulated and presented.

Keywords: charity, tax planning, income tax, tax allowances, corporate social responsibility

1. Introduction

The obligation to be socially responsible is referred as being over and above minimum requirements imposed on companies by formal legal rules (Commission of the European Communities, 2002). Corporate social responsibility (CSR) is a business approach that contributes to sustainable development by delivering economic, social and environmental benefits for all stakeholders. It can be also viewed as a self-regulating business model that helps a company become socially accountable. Based on Buhmann, Roseberry and Morsing (2011), since mid-1990s, the world has experienced increasing public attention to CSR and the impact of corporations on global welfare. Since then the challenge of how best to ensure the strategic business potential for individual business in assuming social responsibility has been heavily debated. For many years, however, the opponents of the CSR such as Friedman (1962, 1970) argued that social issues are not the interests of business, that purpose of business is purely business, and the responsibility of business is to increase its profits. Nevertheless, the extent of issues involved in CSR is expanding, CSR is not regarded as only involving social and environmental issues but also aiming at business operations such as accounting and tax policies. Stanford (2014) claims that responsible business offers a new and strategic approach to all aspects of an organization, allowing for returns at every level.

CSR requires a change in the focus of corporate responsibility from profit maximisation for shareholders within the law to responsibility to a broader range of stakeholders, involving protection of environment, ethical and legal obligations, community development as well as human rights (McBarnet, 2009). Stakeholder engagement is a core element of corporate responsibility practice and triple-bottom-line thinking (Cohen, 2010). Elkington's Triple Bottom Line model (1998) is an influential model that has helped share the corporate social responsibility agenda. It is a concept that encourages the assessment of overall business performance based on three important areas: Profit, People and Planet. It refers to three kinds of impact of a company – social, environmental and economic. Business should measure all three kinds of performance and be responsible to all stakeholders, not just the ones interested in the financial bottom line, as the overall sustainability of the business depends on meeting needs of all stakeholders. Sustainable organizations recognize that "profit" isn't contradictory to "people" or "planet." In other words, organizations cannot operate sustainably by focusing only on the financial outcome they create, as that is not what most stakeholders desire. Shareholders may provide the funds, but stakeholders influence the ability of the business to become successful.

From the beginning the CSR has been viewed as a voluntary concept; a voluntary link between social, economic and environmental considerations in the organization's business to meet the expectations of all categories of stakeholders as well as ensuring long-term prosperity. As stated by McBarnet (2009), from the start, "voluntary" CSR has been socially and economically driven.

CSR can be described as behaviour by businesses 'going beyond legal requirements' but it could be as well viewed as going against the law, as the legal duty of managers to owners, still embedded in many national legislations, should not been forgotten. After all, any business that strives to be 'sustainably' socially responsible, needs to be able to maintain profitable on a long-term basis. Thus, if justification for adhering to CSR is to increase shareholders' value, it cannot be assumed in conflict of demands. However, this is not always enough. Hereby, modern shareholders realize that there is more to business than profit and that there out to be other elements involved in the way business is done. As appointed by Carroll (1979), the social responsibility of business encompasses the economic, legal, ethical, and discretionary expectations that society has of organizations at a given point in time. Parker (2009) notes that ideally CSR includes compliance with business responsibilities but goes 'beyond compliance' in order to incorporate all dimensions of CSR. Campbell (2009) indicates that CSR activities are value-creating, because they strengthen a company's relationship with its key stakeholders, and thus CSR objectives are ultimately in a company's economic interests. Williams (2015) supports the idea by stating that addressing sustainability need not to be in conflict with delivering shareholder value, in fact sustainability and social good can drive it; sustainability is not where businesses spend their money but how they earn it, purpose of the business is beyond profit. Also (conversely), in the long term, environmentally unsustainable business practises have the potential to significantly damage the financial sustainability of business (Hopwood, Unerman and Fries, 2010).

When talking about giving and CSR, the role of institutional economics should not be forgotten. It is an economic perspective that attempts to extend economics by focusing on the institutions, i.e. social and legal norms and rules that underlie economic activity. Representatives of the theory, Marshal and Veblen, connected their work with the fundamental analysis of poverty in the late nineteenth century and the role of organized charity. Marshall (1961) saw charity as a necessity to solve the problems of the poor and suggested that the human spirit of helping others is based on an evolutionary-driven altruism gene. Veblen (1979) saw poverty as the necessary outcome of the market system of the capitalist economy and charity as a natural outgrowth of the system. Lately, there has been an increased interest in the role of shared values and in the sociological literatures surrounding such concepts as social capital, trust, community, and civil society (Knight, 1998). The role of government intervention is discussed as well; it understood that institutions matter, and that economists need to think hard about the ways in which institutions shape economic behaviour and outcomes (Rutheford, 2001).

2. Taxation as an element of CSR

Taxation is a means by which governments finance their expenditure by imposing charges on citizens and corporate entities. The main purpose of taxation is to accumulate funds for the functioning of the economy, provide public revenues to meet economic and social objectives, as well as distribute wealth. It is still discussed whether tax planning should be presented as a CSR element, even a separate dimension. Most agree that taxation should not be viewed as a new dimension, instead, should be part of economic responsibility. Factually, a call for transparency in tax reporting around the globe intensifies. Latterly, creative compliance, creative accounting and tax avoidance has become an issue regarding CSR. Companies are compelled to deal with the CSR pressure on the taxation issues. Information on amount of tax paid and tax planning policies have started to emerge in the CSR reports. To date, companies have largely advocated their right to minimize their tax, as long as it is within the limits of the law. And this opinion is still embedded in the minds of many managers and executives. However, the attention over legal compliance with the law has been shifting to compliance with the spirit of the law. The concept of CSR refers to the operations or actions of companies that are above or independent of the limits or minimum requirements set by legislation (Knuutinen, 2014). It is important that taxpayers recognize that their compliance with an acceptable and fair tax administration is fundamental to a stable economic system.

CFE Tax Advisers Europe stated in their report on CSR and taxation (CFE, 2016) that taxpayers should be free to adopt any tax planning strategy that is within the boundaries of the law. OECD Guidelines (Action Plan on Base Erosion and Profit Shifting, 2013) point out that complying with the spirit of law "does not require an enterprise to make payment in excess of the amount legally required". The study undertaken by Laguir et al (2015) indicates that companies enter tax avoiding activities based on the nature of the CSR activities it engages in, i.e. the higher the level of the social responsibility involvement, the lower the level of tax aggressiveness. That is supported by the idea that tax minimisation must be balanced against reputation risk minimisation and the maintenance of good relations with tax authorities (McBarnet, 2009). Tax planning often refers to the transactions of taxpayers which are not, per se, against the purpose of the tax law. Opposite, tax avoidance can be viewed and formulated as a global sustainability problem as it effectively dislocates social and environmental resources (Bird and Davis-Nozemack, 2018). However, where a line between acceptable behaviour and aggressive avoidance lies and who is going to set the standards, only remains to be seen.

Reputation counts more than ever that is why companies out to incorporate responsibility to tax planning into their overall sustainable strategy. From the CSR point of view, we could formulate, that aggressive tax planning are actions taken by taxpayers which are in the line of requirements of tax law, but which do not meet the reasonable and justified expectations and requirements of the stakeholders. Thus, the discussion is mainly about the purpose and real substance of the actions.

2.1 CSR reporting on tax

Payment of taxes is a major way for companies to support the communities where they operate. Yet too many businesses are unwilling to disclose how much, and where, they pay taxes. Since 1997 Global Responsibility Initiative (GRI) has pioneered sustainability reporting and came up with GRI 207 Tax Standard that challenges this status quo by outlining clear best practice for disclosure.

In 2017, the Global Sustainability Standards Board (GSSB, 2019), initiated a project to develop new disclosures related to tax and payments to governments, which will be considered for incorporation into the GRI Standards. Its aim is to help promote greater transparency on a reporting organization's approach to taxes. Making tax data more widely accessible will help build stakeholder trust and contribute to better-informed policy and investment decisions. Companies will report and disclose their information in the three areas, i.e. how the approach to tax is linked to the business and sustainable development strategies of the organization, how tax governance, control, and risk management are identified, managed, and monitored, in the third area a description of the approach to stakeholder engagement and management of concerns related to tax, and country-by-country reporting is reported. Public reporting on tax increases transparency and promotes trust and credibility in the tax practices of organizations and in the tax systems. It enables stakeholders to make informed judgments about an organization's tax positions. Tax transparency also informs public and supports the development of socially desirable tax policy. However, the standard will only come to an effect in 2021.

3. Charity as an element of CSR

3.1 Charity as a social element of CSR

McBaret (2009) implies that CSR is not philanthropy[1], contributing charitable donations from profits, but involves exercise of social responsibility in how profits are made. CSR is too often about how companies spend (or donate) the money they have earned elsewhere in their business (Williams, 2015). The purpose of business is to be a driving force for social, environmental and economic benefit (World Economic Forum, 2019). Firms donating additional resources to CSR activities can construct a more ethical work climate that encourages executives to control tax risk while lowering tax expenses. For firms with unsatisfactory performance, the ethical benefits of CSR could disappear, thus suggesting a relationship with firm performance (Lin et al, 2019).

Often, relationship between CSR and philanthropy is barely distinguishable from each other, even in some cases used interchangeably. Both are positive concepts designed to deliver corporate resources to the community the corporation serves, and the giving may also be aimed toward specific causes. It is only true when companies' interests to be involved in CSR is beyond simply giving money, when a business engages in a more committed

[1] the authors are aware of the different definitions of philanthropy and charity, but believe that for the purpose of this article, their mutual confusion will not matter

form of giving with clear objectives. Philanthropy is most often seen in the form of financial contributions, but it can also include time and resources. The concept behind philanthropy involves making an effort to drive social change. It's not only the charitable donations that can go toward any number of direct-giving scenarios. Philanthropy involves finding a long-term solution.

Based on Caroll (2016) motivation of companies to strive to do the ethically right things is driven by philanthropic their responsibilities. Carroll's pyramid of CSR includes economic, legal, ethical, and philanthropic components. According to this pyramidal construct, one of the most popular constructs of the CSR that has been used in literature and practice since 1979, a firm should maximize its profit, obey the law, be ethical, and be a good corporate citizen, whereas the philanthropic responsibilities are at the top of the pyramid (Carroll, 1991). Most companies feel compelled to give to charity. Only few have figured out how to do it well. There must be a convergence of interests between philanthropy and business. It is when corporate expenditure produces simultaneous social and economic gains that this convergence will occur. Thinking about corporate philanthropy in this way, you have to use CSR activities as part of your business model (Enquist, Edvardsson and Sebhatu, 2008).

3.2 Charity as an economic element of CSR

Companies are also encouraged to foster CSR indirectly for example through tax incentives or government procurement policies. The major tax policy instrument affecting giving is the charitable deduction allowed in the calculation of taxable income for taxpayers who itemize their deductions. As a result of this tax treatment, there are two major tax effects on giving: the tax liability affects the after-tax income from which taxpayers can make contributions and the deduction reduces the net price per dollar of contribution made. The econometric analysis of individual giving implies that the income tax has a strong effect on giving (Clotfelter, 1985).

Andrews (1972) argues that contributions are properly excluded from the income tax base because they constitute neither accumulation nor consumption. An alternative justification for the current charitable deduction is to view the deduction as an incentive by which the tax law encourages desirable behaviour. According to this view charitable giving is an item of discretionary spending that warrants an incentive. A deduction is only one of several forms such an incentive might take; a tax credit or some matching arrangements might be as good or better.

Attitudes towards taxes are often contradictory. On the one hand, taxes are like any other costs for a company, but on the other hand, they are an economic contribution to the society in which the business is conducted. It is in nature of the business to lower the cost as much as possible. Lin et al (2019) suggest that the influence of CSR on tax risk tends to disappear in the presence of firm profitability, unsatisfactory performance and financial constraints. A possible explanation is that good firm performance provides the economic resources for the development of CSR corporate culture that is manifested in activities such as job creation and community donations; further a lower tax burden does not necessarily create high tax risk; thus, increased tax savings and lower tax risk can coexist

4. Methods and data

In 2018, the Ministry of Industry and Trade of the Czech Republic (Ministry of Industry and Trade of the Czech Republic, 2018) published the results of the CSR on-line survey. In the spring 2019, the survey was followed by a study concerning relations between CSR and taxation in small companies in the Czech Republic (Jarolimova, Tuckova, 2019). Results of the study were in line with those of the survey. Both revealed, among other results, that undoubtfully tax issues are important part of a decision-making process in connection to CSR, that CSR activities should be enhanced by the government in some form of tax incentives, such as possibility to reduce tax or a tax base in case of charity giving or other philanthropy oriented activities, and lastly that regardless the social aspects of responsible behaviour, tax savings are on the list of reasons why companies take part in CSR. That raises questions whether motivation to CSR is necessarily a genuine concern and whether the primary purpose of charity giving aspiration in the Czech Republic is to reduce corporate income taxes or socially responsible behaviour that serves to the community and society?

Most Czech companies actively supporting a concept of CSR do not currently report on CSR in the field of taxation. However, previous researches revealed that companies in the Czech Republic, regardless the size, know and support an idea of CSR. Therefore, the research is based on publicly available secondary data retrieved from the materials of the Ministry of Finance of the Czech Republic, comprising all corporations reporting income tax. The ministry publishes annually, on its website, information summarizing data from all tax returns submitted by legal and natural persons. Figures from the years 2005 to 2018 presented in various divisions are available. Also, aggregate data comprising gift deductions are available for a period starting in the year of 2000. Data set was also acquired from the publication by Via Foundation in the Czech Republic (Nadace Via, 2018).

The research wants to build on the above-mentioned survey and the study and aims to explore whether Czech companies view charitable donations as a way to significantly reduce their taxes.

5. Result and discussion

Previous research has shown that Czech corporations, whether small or large, see socially responsible behaviour as their contribution the society and something they deserve to be rewarded for, for example by possibility to reduce their tax. Such thinking may be contributed to the fact that in the Czech Republic, the income tax act allows certain items to be deducted from a tax base and deduction of charitable donations is among them. This nevertheless is not the common practice only in the Czech Republic. In 1938 U.S. Congress gave the justification for deduction in its Congressional Report: "The exemption from taxation on money or property devoted to charitable and other purposes is based upon the theory that the Government is compensated for the loss of revenue by its relief from financial burden which would otherwise have to be met by appropriations from public funds, and by the benefits resulting from the promotion of the general welfare" (U.S. Congress, House of Representatives 1938).

Most EU countries also motivate taxpayers to charitable giving by using various tax-advantaged approaches in the form of various deductions from the tax base, tax credit or other compensations mainly in order to strive for longevity and sustainability of altruistic behaviour of taxpayers.

Carroll and Joulfaian (2005) analysed tax return data to determine whether firms make charitable contributions for the purpose of receiving a tax deduction. The results showed that corporate philanthropy declines with the tax price and rises with income and advertising. However, results from the data retrieved from the Ministry of Finance of the Czech Republic prove otherwise.

In the Czech Republic, the support is implemented through the deduction of the value of the charitable donation or contribution from the tax base with the fixed minimum and maximum limits[2]. Since 2014 the maximum limit is determined by 10% of the tax base when it doubled compare to 2013.

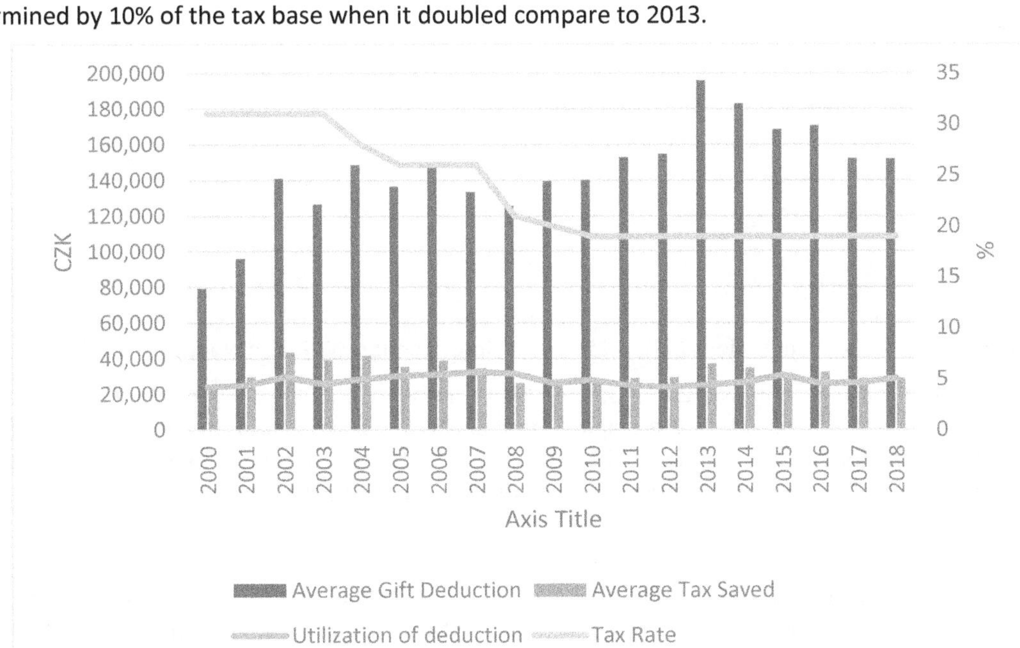

Figure 1: Development of the use of deduction of charity donations (MFCR and Nadace Via, 2019)

[2] §20 of Income Tax Act

If tax deductions on charitable donations and contributions should be an important factor considered in the company's decision-making process to provide a donation in order to reduce its own tax liability, should it be assumed that donations will reflect the level of tax rates. However, as shown in Figure 1, in the years when the corporate tax rate was above 30%, the average amount of deductions was the lowest, and conversely, in the period of the lowest 19% tax rate since 2010, the average amount of deductions gradually increased until 2013 and then started decreasing again regardless the fact the tax rate remained unchanged. Thus, it cannot be confirmed that the reduction of tax rate also reduces willingness of taxpayers to donate.

Donations were also not affected by the fact that the maximum limit for the deduction was doubled in 2014, exactly the opposite, average amount of donations show descending level and gradually returns to its original level. Studying macroeconomic conditions of the Czech Republic, it is more likely to attribute the increase in the volume of donations to the wave of solidarity due to the natural disaster of 2013 than to the willingness to donate more generally, irrespective the period of economic growth. Surprisingly, willingness to donate did not dramatically drop during the worldwide economic crisis in 2008 and 2009, from which it can be concluded that in the Czech Republic donors are mostly not influenced by economic or political aspects and donate regardless of these influences.

Although the average amount of donations has not been positively influenced by the increased limit for deduction, it is positive that number of companies reporting charitable donating increases as shown in Figure 2. Based on the assumptions of Knauer (1994) that legal entities always itemize the deduction of charitable donation in their tax returns, the deductions reflect the real situation. Therefore, if the deduction was reported by 5.1 % of legal entities in 2018 (Figure 1), there are only 5.1% of donors among corporations.

Figure 2: Development of gift deductions in relation to maximum limit (MFCR and Nadace Via, 2019)

The research showed that the set maximum deduction limit is enough. Though, the limitation of maximum can be counterproductive, as it basically tells the taxpayer to make sure not to contribute above the limit, because it will not be beneficial for him if he exceeds the upper limit. Despite responsible behaviour, approaches to altruistic behaviour are still influenced by the economic aspects of individual companies.

6. Conclusion

One of the triggers for the increased attention to tax and tax planning matters within CSR has been the financial and debt crisis in 2008 due to which public finances of many countries suffered. It is going to be interesting to see how the situation evolves with, yet another ongoing crisis caused by Covid-19. The process of social responsibility has been implemented in the mind set of many companies and their stakeholders. However, with less resources, it can be only guessed whether companies will be able to sustain their CSR activities, such as philanthropy and charity giving.

Even though taxation for long time stayed aside the interests of CSR, it is not seen as a completely new dimension and, instead, we can see it as part of economic responsibility. It is often said that philanthropy is charity with other people's money. Attacking CSR by attacking philanthropy could be seen as inappropriate as, as resulted from data, corporate donations and gifts currently amount to less than 1% per annum of pre-tax profits. The data also show that the average amount of the gift in relation to the size of the profit does not change with the size of the company.

Donation is always associated with expense, and a donor is faced with a decision to donate and lose funds that might be otherwise at his disposal. In return, the company gains tax savings that equal usual tax rate on the donated amount. In the current situation in the Czech Republic, deduction loses its effectiveness. If the state is to play an active role in supporting CSR activities, it should choose another form of support.

The data of the Ministry of Finance reveal that the reduction in taxes is not the primary purpose of Czech companies to donate, but rather the result of it. In the Czech environment, tax deductions resulting from charitable donations are not used to the maximum and thus it cannot be addressed as aggressive tax planning. This also corresponds with the results of the last year's survey that tax deductions are viewed rather as a reward for responsible behaviour.

In order to understand some other contexts, further research will need to examine the behaviour of entities in terms of their motivation, so that the conclusions that have been drawn from the data from tax returns can be verified.

Acknowledgements

The Authors are grateful to the International Grant Agency of FaME TBU, Grant No. IGA/FaME/2018/010 for financial support.

References

Andrews, W. (1972) "Personal Deductions in an Ideal Income Tax", *Harvard Law Review,* Vol 86, No 2, pp 309-385, [online], https://www.jstor.org/stable/1339894.

Bird, R. and Davis-Nozemack, K. (2018) "Tax avoidance as a sustainability problem ", *Journal of Business Ethics*, Vol 151, No 4, pp 1009-1025.

Buhmann, K., Roseberry, L. and Morsing, M. (2011) *Corporate Social and Human Rights Responsibilities, Global Legal and Management Perspectives,* Palgrave Macmillan, Hampshire.

Campbell, K. (2009) 'Disclosure law and market for corporate social responsibility', in McBarnet, D., Voiculescu, A., Campbell, T. (ed.). *The New Corporate Accountability, Corporate Social Responsibility and the Law,* Cambridge University Press, Cambridge, pp 241-278.

Carroll, A.B. (1979) "A three-dimensional Conceptual Model of Corporate Performance", *Academy of Management Review,* Vol 4, No 4, pp 497-505, [online], https://www.jstor.org/stable/pdf/257850.

Caroll, A.B. (1991) "The pyramid of corporate social responsibility: toward the moral management of organisational stakeholders", *Business Horizons*, Vol 34, No 4, pp 39-48.

Caroll, A.B. (2016) "Carroll's pyramid of CSR: taking another look", *International Journal of Corporate Social Responsibility*, Vol 1, No 3, pp 1-8.

Carroll, R. and Joulfaian, D. (2015) "Taxes and Corporate Giving to Charity", *Public Finance Review*, Vol 33, No 3, pp 300-317.

CFE observation on corporate social responsibility in taxation (2016), [online], KDPCR, www.kdpcr.cz/informace/aktuality/danove-novinky/navrh-stanoviska-fc-pac-ke-spolecenske-odpovednosti-firem.

Clotfelter, C.T. (1985) 'Charitable Giving Behavior and the Evaluation of Tax Policy', in Clotfelter (ed.). *Federal Tax Policy and Charitable Giving,* University of Chicago Press, pp 273-288.

Cohen, E. (2010) *CSR for HR,* Greenleaf Publishing, New York.

Commission of the European Communities (2002) *'Communication from the Commission Concerning Corporate Social Responsibility: A Business Contribution to Sustainable Development',* Com (2002) 347, [online], https://eur-lex.europa.eu/legal-content/EN/TXT/?uri=LEGISSUM%3An26034.

Elkington, J. (1998) "Accounting for the Triple Bottom Line", *Measuring Business Excellence*, Vol 2, No 3, pp 18-22, [online], https://doi.org/10.1108/eb025539.

Enquist, B., Edvardsson, B. and Petros Sebhatu, S. (2008), "Corporate Social Responsibility for Charity or for Service Business?", *Asian Journal on Quality*, Vol 9 No 1, pp 55-67, [online], https://doi.org/10.1108/15982688200800004.

Friedman, M. (1962) *Capitalism and freedom,* University of Chicago Press, Chicago.

Friedman, M. (2007) 'The Social Responsibility of Business Is to Increase Its Profits', in Zimmerli, W.C., Holzinger, M., Richter, K. (ed.). *Corporate Ethics and Corporate Governance,* Springer, Heidelberg, pp 173-178.

GSSB (2019) Global Sustainability Standards Board and GRI Standards, *GRI 207: Tax*, [online], https://www.globalreporting.org/.

Hopwood, A., Unerman, J. and Fries, J. (2010) 'Introduction to the Accounting for Sustainability Case Studies', in Hopwood, A., Unerman, J. and Fries, J. (ed.). *Accounting for Sustainability: practical insights,* Earthscan, New York, pp 1-26.

Jarolimova, B., Tuckova, Z. (2019) 'What Does "Corporate Social Responsibility" Mean in Taxation in Small Entrepreneurships?', in Liargovas, P., Kakouris, A. (ed.). *14th European Conference on Innovation and Entrepreneurship ECIE 2019,* Academic Conferences and Publishing International Limited, Reading, pp 1163-1169.

Knauer, N. J. (1994) "The Paradox of Corporate Giving: Tax Expenditures, the Nature of the Corporation, and the Social Construction of Charity ", *DePaul Law Review,* Vol 44, No 1, pp 1-28.

Knight, J. (1998) "The Bases of Cooperation: Social Norms and the Rule of Law", *Journal of Institutional and Theoretical Economics,* Vol 154, No 4, pp 754-63.

Knuutinen, R. (2014) "Corporate Social Responsibility, Taxation and Aggressive Tax Planning", *Nordic Tax Journal,* Vol 1, pp 36-75.

Laguir, I., Staglina, R. and Elbaz, J. (2015) "Does corporate social responsibility affect corporate tax aggressiveness?", *Journal of Cleaner Production*, Vol 107, pp 662-675.

Lin, X., Liu, M., So, S. and Yuen, D. (2019) "Corporate social responsibility, firm performance and tax risk", *Managerial Auditing Journal*, Vol 34 No 9, pp 1101-1130.

Marshall, A. (1961) *Principles of Economics,* 9th ed, Macmillan Company, London.

McBarnet, D. (2009) 'Corporate social responsibility beyond law, through law, for law; the new corporate accountability', in McBarnet, D., Voiculescu, A., Campbell, T. (ed.). *The New Corporate Accountability, Corporate Social Responsibility and the Law,* Cambridge University Press, Cambridge, pp 9-56.

Ministry of Industry and Trade (2018) *CSR survey for the needs of the Ministry of Industry and Trade of the Czech Republic,* [online], www.mpo.cz/cz/podnikani/spolecenska-odpovednost-organizaci/vyhodnoceni-dotaznikoveho-pruzkumu-csr--236623/.

Nadace Via (2018) *Vývoj soukromého dárcovství v ČR,* [online], https://www.nadacevia.cz/wp-content/uploads/2018/11/Nadace-Via_statistiky-soukromeho-darcovstvi-2016.pdf.

OECD (2013) *Action Plan on Base Erosion and Profit Shifting*, OECD Publishing, Paris.

Parker, C. (2009) 'Meta-regulation: legal accountability for corporate social responsibility', in McBarnet, D., Voiculescu, A., Campbell, T. (ed.). T*he New Corporate Accountability, Corporate Social Responsibility and the Law,* Cambridge University Press, Cambridge, pp 207-237.

Rutheford, M. (2001) "Institutional Economics: Then and Now", *Journal of Economic Perspectives,* Vol 15, No 3, pp 173–194.

Sanford, C. (2014) *The Responsible Business: remaining sustainability and success,* Jossey-Bass Pub., San Francisco.

U.S. Congress (1938) House of Representatives, [online], https://www.govinfo.gov/content/pkg/GPO-CRECB-1938-pt3-v83/pdf/GPO-CRECB-1938-pt3-v83-8-2.pdf, pp 2927-3006.

Veblen, T. (1979) *The Theory of the Leisure Class,* reprint 1899, Penguin Books, New York.

Williams, E.F. (2015) *Green giants: how smart companies turn sustainability into billion-dollar business,* American Management Association, New York.

World Economic Forum in Davos (2019) *The future of business? Purpose, not just profit,* [online], https://www.weforum.org/agenda/2019/01/why-businesses-must-be-driven-by-purpose-as-well-as-profits/.

An Exploratory Conceptual Model for Digital Entrepreneurs Within Entrepreneurial Ecosystems

Ekapong Jungcharoensukying, Joseph Feller, Brian O'Flaherty and Stephen Treacy
University College Cork, Ireland
117220715@umail.ucc.ie
jfeller@ucc.ie
bof@ucc.ie
Stephen.treacy@ucc.ie
DOI: 10.34190/EIE.20.221

Abstract: The entrepreneurial ecosystem is a well-known concept in supporting the creation and growth of entrepreneurs, driving the economy in a region. However, entrepreneurship is evolving, as more and more novel digital technologies are introduced into our lives. Accordingly, this paper focuses on digital entrepreneurs, who are defined as the entrepreneurs, who utilize innovation based on digital technology to create economic or social value by starting new ventures or transform existing ones (European Commission, 2015), and the relevant ecosystem that supports them. The change in the relationship between digital entrepreneurs and an entrepreneurial ecosystem, as they evolve towards digital products and customer engagement is the focus of this research. We reviewed the literature on the topic of digital entrepreneurs and entrepreneurial ecosystem using a concept-centric matrix, capturing 14 elements of an entrepreneurial ecosystem. These elements include networks, policy and government, professional and support services, capital services, human capital, culture, markets, knowledge sources, intermediaries, informal networks, leadership, physical infrastructure, engagement, and cooperative companies. The identified elements were then used to develop a conceptual framework, which will form the basis for the research strategy. This study sets out to establish the existence of these elements in the ecosystems and the extent of their usefulness. Therefore, this paper seeks to address the research gap of how digital entrepreneurs utilize each ecosystem element to understand their importance in the conceptual framework. We intend to conduct an exploratory quantitative research approach, gathering data from start-up digital entrepreneurs that are engaged in an entrepreneurial ecosystem, by using a data instrument derived from the conceptual framework. Then, we will analyze the data using descriptive and bi-variate statistical tools to uncover causal relations between the elements. The next phase of the research will involve case studies, where we plan to use the updated conceptual framework to undertake in-depth interviews to establish the context of digital entrepreneurial ecosystems.

Keywords: digital entrepreneur, entrepreneurial ecosystem, entrepreneurial process

1. Introduction

The success of famous entrepreneurs such as Bill Gates or Mark Zuckerberg has been inspired many younger generations to the entrepreneurship. Many tried to duplicate their success by studying characteristics of these entrepreneurs, however, the credits for their success are not from individual entrepreneurs alone, but also contributed to by external institutions that systematically support the creation and growth of their ventures (Radosevic & Yoruk, 2013). Entrepreneurial ecosystems are known to effectively and successfully support young startup entrepreneurs to set up their own business and further encouraging the progress of them (Robertson, Pitt, & Ferreira, 2020; van Rijnsoever, 2020). These entrepreneurs, who receive the offered supports from the ecosystem, are evidently more in number and more impactful to the economy comparing to other practices (Leffel & Agrawal, 2014). However, the way the new generation of entrepreneur works is slowly changing with more digital technologies become accessible. These so-called digital entrepreneurs work differently and can easily access alternative support structures on the internet similar to what an entrepreneurial ecosystem can offer. Unfortunately, there is a lack of evidence that explores how these changes can affect the entrepreneurial ecosystem (Elia, Margherita, & Passiante, 2020).

It is agreed that new digital innovations are crucial to economic growth and the entrepreneurs, who utilize them to establish a new venture or transform existing ones, not only make a profit for themselves but also vitalize the economy around them (Lindholm-Dahlstrand, Andersson, & Carlsson, 2019; Robertson et al., 2020; Tripathi, Seppänen, Boominathan, Oivo, & Liukkunen, 2019; van Rijnsoever, 2020). By producing innovative products, they strengthen their markets and by expansion, create job opportunities in their immediate area. There is evidence highlighting that entrepreneur's businesses can be responsible for job creation on a large scale (Tripathi, Oivo, Liukkunen, & Markkula, 2019). Therefore, encouraging new entrepreneurs and supporting the growth of existing ones has become an important issue to policymakers and academics seeking to further energize the economy for their cities or even nations. The entrepreneurial ecosystem is a well-recognized concept that aims to create an influential environment and gather a variety of support entities needed by entrepreneurs into a region (Robertson et al., 2020). Entrepreneurial ecosystems have become popularized by successful exemplars, including Silicon Valley and Boston's Route 128 (Du, Pan, Zhou, & Ouyang, 2018). Given the achievements of these cases, cities all around the world have been trying to replicate their success with an ecosystem of their own (Startup Genome, 2018). Therefore, the two main goals of entrepreneurial ecosystems are: (1) to enhance their regional economy, and (2) to facilitate the birth of new entrepreneurial ventures and the growth of the already established ones.

Within this environment, a community of inventors and innovators already operating within the ecosystem can offer ideas for new products or services to these new entrants, and in some cases, they may even help translate those ideas into business plans (Isenberg, 2011). After that, the universities or colleges which are usually stationed within the ecosystem's area can provide skilled workers or training for the new ventures. Similarly, venture capitalists or angel investors in the ecosystem can support them by funding the establishment of a new business or in a business expansion (Cohen, 2006). The vicinity of the ecosystem will also become the first market for those new firms' products (Stam, 2015). Moreover, the Government can also support them with beneficial policies to further their chances of survival (Spigel, 2017). Furthermore, the network among the actors within the ecosystem can fluidly guide the entrepreneurs from one service they needed to another along their entrepreneurial process (Bell-Masterson & Stangler, 2015). These supports undoubtedly help the entrepreneurs to achieve their goals which, in turn, help the ecosystem realize another goal that is stimulating its economy.

However, with the advance of digital technologies and the internet, information and support platforms became easier to access by the majority of people all around the world in this age of the 4th industrial revolution. The entrepreneurs are also changing in this new digital environment. Their ways of operations rely more on digital tools. And there are online platforms that offer supports similar to that offered by entrepreneurial ecosystems such as crowdsourcing where entrepreneurs can raise funding from the mass instead of capital services from venture capital or angel investors, online community platforms that offer consultation on business ideas, or online marketplaces that even more suits to digital products. Not only that, evidently, Hernández and González (2016) report that entrepreneurs found some supports, in an ecosystem, are not relevant to their business. Thus, it is time to reaffirm the usefulness of those supports offered by the entrepreneurial ecosystem in order to adapt to the changing demand of digital entrepreneurs.

In section 2, we explain our method of literature review and discuss the concept-centric matrix. Then, in section 3, we discuss the background of the entrepreneur, digital entrepreneur, the entrepreneurial ecosystem, and its support elements and their alternatives. Next, in section 4,

2. Methodology

This review explores the entrepreneurial ecosystem concept where digital technology is involved. We select the ScienceDirect database to explore as it offers a wide variety of journals. We used search phrases "entrepreneurial ecosystem" and "digital technology" to look between 2016-2020 with article type as "research article". However, it yields only 38 search results with only 6 related to the entrepreneurial ecosystem. Realizing that the search phrases are too narrow, we change search phrases to "entrepreneurial ecosystem" and "technology" instead while the other criteria remain the same. This time, the search yields 195 results.

After the search, the results are screened in detail to select only relevant papers. We exclude articles we determined unrelated to the entrepreneurial ecosystem. For example, an article with only the search phrase "technology" in its title but is not related to the entrepreneurial ecosystem at all. We also include a few papers, which even though there are no search phrases we used at all in the title, are related to the entrepreneurial ecosystem. After screening out irrelevant papers, there are 35 papers as the final results for our review.

2.1 The concept-centric matrix

Introduced by Webster and Watson (2002) to emphasize that literature review should be done in a concept-centric approach, not an author-centric approach. This matrix was designed to capture key concepts found in the selected literature without subjective bias. The captured concepts from literature can, then, be used to categorize the papers in a meaningful way that help define topic area such as theoretical issues or gaps in the literature.

We utilize the concept-centric matrix on the selected papers. Several themes of studies emerge, for example, topics that concern the survival of entrepreneurial ecosystems such as the sustainability (Neumeyer & Santos, 2018; Tiba, van Rijnsoever, & Hekkert, 2020; Znagui & Rahmouni, 2019), the resilience of entrepreneurial ecosystem (Roundy, Brockman, & Bradshaw, 2017), the revival of an inactive one (Ghazinoory, Sarkissian, Farhanchi, & Saghafi, 2020; Reynolds & Uygun, 2018; Roundy, 2019), or the exaptation caused by disruptive innovation (Beltagui, Rosli, & Candi, 2020). Some papers tackle the emergence of entrepreneurial ecosystems (Roundy, Bradshaw, & Brockman, 2018; Wiszniewski, 2019). Additionally, some papers studies in specific areas such as the roles of women and how they are treated in entrepreneurial ecosystems (Berger & Kuckertz, 2016; Lawson, 2019), the making of a green entrepreneurial ecosystem (Zhao, Shang, & Song, 2019), the education on the entrepreneurial ecosystem (Jha, 2018), or the digital entrepreneurship and entrepreneurial ecosystem (Chandna & Salimath, 2020; Elia et al., 2020; Han, Ruan, Wang, & Zhou, 2019). Meanwhile, Scaringella and Radziwon (2018) look back and compare the entrepreneurial ecosystem with similar concepts that come before. Moreover, the majority of papers concern about what and how to make a successful entrepreneurial ecosystem (Arenal et al., 2020; Dedehayir, Mäkinen, & Ortt, 2018; Feng et al., 2019; Fuster, Padilla-Meléndez, Lockett, & del-Águila-Obra, 2019; Kahle, Marcon, Ghezzi, & Frank, 2020; Kantis, Federico, & García, 2020; Kuckertz, 2019; Prencipe, Corsi, Rodríguez-Gulías, Fernandez, & Rodeiro-Pazos, 2020; Pustovrh, Rangus, & Drnovšek, 2020; Sarma & Sunny, 2017; Stephens, Butler, Garg, & Gibson, 2019; Sun, Zhang, Cao, Dong, & Cantwell, 2019; Tripathi, Oivo, et al., 2019; Tripathi, Seppänen, et al., 2019; van Rijnsoever, 2020; Xu, Wu, Minshall, & Zhou, 2018; Znagui & Rahmouni, 2019).

From the sample of papers analysed, there are only three papers among the selected that focus on digital entrepreneurs and only one of those that discuss how entrepreneurs turning into digital ones affect how their entrepreneurial process (Elia et al., 2020). Furthermore, none of them raises the implication of that change upon the elements that make a successful entrepreneurial ecosystem. Therefore, we intend to address this research gap that is how the change in the entrepreneurial process of digital entrepreneurs affects the supportive elements offered by the entrepreneurial ecosystem.

3. Literature review

In this section, we discuss entrepreneurship and digital entrepreneurship and their differences. After that, we explore the entrepreneurial process that happens during entrepreneurship. Then, we review the entrepreneurial ecosystem, the concept that is made to support entrepreneurship. And lastly, we consider the elements that make a successful entrepreneurial ecosystem.

3.1 Entrepreneurship and digital entrepreneurship

Entrepreneurship happened all the time in human history long before it was conceptualized (Casson & Casson, 2014). It has been defined and redefined many times over. Each time, more characteristics were added to it. In 1965, Joseph Alois Schumpeter (1965) defined entrepreneurship as "individuals who exploit market opportunity through technical and/or organizational innovation". In this definition, the first feature of entrepreneurship is specified which is they utilize innovation in pursuit of business opportunity. Later, Hébert and Link (1989) add that the entrepreneurs have to face many judgmental decision-making situations in their entrepreneurship. Then, Drucker (2014) suggests in his definition that entrepreneurship involves taking risks especially financial risk. To emphasize on taking risks characteristic, Stevenson (2000) gives his definition of entrepreneurship as "Entrepreneurship is the pursuit of opportunity beyond the resources you currently control." Additionally, Joseph A Schumpeter (2010) put in another feature of entrepreneur that entrepreneurship includes both those who create new ventures and who transform the existing ones with innovations. Moreover, Morris, Lewis, and Sexton (1994) propose that entrepreneurship is a process activity which means entrepreneurship is not simply characteristics of entrepreneurs but rather actions the happen over time in the entrepreneurial process. Therefore, entrepreneurship is a process of individuals utilizing innovation to take risks building new ventures, or transforming existing ones in order to exploit the market opportunity and have to face difficult decisions along the process.

Digital entrepreneur refers to entrepreneurs who are familiar with digital tools and online resources which make starting new ventures easier than ever (Rathee & Rajain, 2017). European Commission (2015) gives a definition of digital entrepreneurship as "Digital entrepreneurship embraces all new ventures and the transformation of existing businesses that drive economic and/or social value by creating and using novel digital technologies." Though it does not mention about taking risks and decision making, it is quite clear that the differences between digital entrepreneurs and traditional ones are the utilization of digital technologies that change the ways of business operations. Furthermore, Nambisan (2017) offers more characteristics that further distinguish them which is the outcomes, processes, and supports are less bounded in digital entrepreneurs' cases. The entrepreneurial outcomes refer to products or services which can be partially digitalized or fully digital. The partially digitized products may hold many functions and capabilities, and potentially the software within the products can be fixed or upgraded online. Even better, in case of fully digitized products, they have no physical restraint at all which means no need for stocking space and can reach out to customers all around the world at once. Next, the entrepreneurial process, which usually advances step by step, can now go in a parallel fashion. For example, traditionally, a firm starts doing business in the local market first, then, later on, expand to new areas until finally to new countries. With the help of the internet, digital entrepreneurs' products can be globalized through digital marketplaces at once. Finally, some entrepreneurial supports are not limited to locations which are the entrepreneurial ecosystems anymore.

3.2 Entrepreneurial process

As mentioned in the above subsection, Morris et al. (1994) insist that entrepreneurship should be viewed as a process, not just some attributes of the entrepreneurs. His definition expands our understanding of entrepreneurship from their characteristics to their actions overtime in their path of entrepreneurship (Anderson, 2000). This expansion will allow further understanding of how the entrepreneurial ecosystem support entrepreneurship by matching up each entrepreneurial process with ecosystem supports.

The entrepreneurial process was proposed by Ahmadi (2003) as 3 phases: (1) initiation phase where new entrepreneurs draw up product ideas and business plan, (2) establishment phase where ideas and plans are implemented into an actual business, and (3) growth phase where the business is stabled and expansion are planned and executed. This proposed process covers all the lifetime of entrepreneurship. However, another version with more details in-between phases by suggested by Ruef (2005). It focuses more on the activities in the entrepreneurial process as follows: (1) Initiation phase where founders commit themselves to entrepreneurial path, (2) Resource mobilization phase where founders prepare their business plan and procure funding, (3) Legal establishment phase where founders legalize their firm, (4) Social organization phase where founders recruit needed employees, and (5) Operational startup phase where the venture start its operation. Though this version expands the initiation and establishment phase of Ahmadi (2003) into 5 phases of activities, it overlooks the growth phase entirely. Moreover, Jones and Coviello (2005) expand the growth phase into 2 steps which are the growth phase and the internationalization or globalization phase as the 2 phases are on a different scale and should be treated differently.

Therefore, we combine and propose a working entrepreneurial process for our study as seven stages including (1) Initiation, (2) Resource mobilization, (3) Legal establishment, (4) Social organization, (5) Operational startup, (6) Growth, and (7) globalization.

3.3 Entrepreneurial ecosystem

There are many similar concepts that come before the entrepreneurial ecosystem such as environments for entrepreneurs or entrepreneurial systems. Evidently, however, the usage of the term entrepreneurial ecosystem has overtaken other concepts (Malecki, 2018). When the entrepreneurial ecosystem is still called an entrepreneurial system, Spilling (1996) defines it as "*The complexity and diversity of actors, roles, and environmental factors that interact to determine the entrepreneurial performance of a region or locality*." This definition suggests that as the ecosystem consists of actors with roles and environment factors who work together toward a goal, entrepreneurial performance, in a region. Later, Cohen (2006) suggests that "*Entrepreneurial ecosystems represent a diverse set of inter-dependent actors within a geographic region that influence the formation and eventual trajectory of the entire group of actors and potentially the economy as a whole. Entrepreneurial ecosystems evolve through a set of interdependent components which interact to generate new venture creation over time*." He expands that the ecosystem benefits, not only the entrepreneurs their main target but also the actors and that regional economy as Kuckertz (2019) suggest that a well-managed ecosystem should be. Furthermore, the definition emphasizes that the outcomes of the entrepreneurial ecosystem happen over time. It stresses that the supports offered by the entrepreneurial ecosystem are given to the entrepreneurs along the entrepreneurial process, not instantly happen. Then, Audretsch (2015) offers 3 distinct characteristics of the entrepreneurial ecosystem as (1) entrepreneurial ecosystem are bounded to a geographic location, (2) there can be many institutions, organizations, enterprises, or even individuals as members of the entrepreneurial ecosystem, and (3) to be considered a part of the ecosystem, an entity need to contribute toward entrepreneurial performance rather than being co-located only. Therefore, an entrepreneurial ecosystem is the gathering of many interdependent entities, no matter big or small, who contribute toward entrepreneurial performance over time in a region which, in turn, benefit those entities and regional economy.

3.4 Entrepreneurial ecosystem's elements

There are multiple attempts to conceptualize what makes a successful entrepreneurial ecosystem in terms of its attributes or elements. Cohen (2006) suggests 7 components that make a sustainable entrepreneurial ecosystem as (1) **informal network** which is the informal relationship of the entrepreneur such as family and friends, (2) **formal network** among the actors in an ecosystem, (3) **university** that provide training and innovation, (4) **government** who support entrepreneurs with policies, (5) **professional and support services** such as legal or accounting services, (6) **capital services** who provide funding for entrepreneurs, and (7) **talent pool** which is the sources of skilled employees for hire. This study signifies the importance of networks both formal and informal while putting the actors into a group of services they provide. Then Isenberg (2011) brings 2 more elements into academic attention which are, first, the **culture** that inspires individuals to take risks and become entrepreneurs, and, second, the **market** that is the first group of customers and, potentially is a social network that attracting more customers. Later, 4 more elements are introduced by Stam (2015) as (1) **leadership** which are successful entrepreneurs who are willing to inspire and support new entrepreneurs to settle in their ecosystem, (2) **intermediaries** which are mentors, who support new entrepreneurs by business knowledge and networks, such as accelerators or incubators, (3) **engagement** which is events that bring actors together and forming new networks, and (4) **companies** within the region who are willing to cooperate and support new entrepreneurs. Furthermore, Spigel (2017) suggests elements that make a successful entrepreneurial ecosystem and adds **physical infrastructure** to our conceptual framework. Among these studies, some elements are suggested by multiple scholars, however, the university element, first suggested by Cohen (2006), was argued by Stam (2015) that it should not be limited to university but refer to any sources of knowledge both public and private organizations. Therefore, 14 elements are identified from the literature as supportive elements that directly or indirectly facilitate the birth and growth of entrepreneurs. The definition for each element is shown in Table 1.

Table 1: Entrepreneurial ecosystem elements' definition

Elements	Working definitions
Ecosystem engagement	Stam (2015) suggests that holding a large number of community events within the ecosystem can raise the presence of the entrepreneurial ecosystem and continuously build more networks in the ecosystem. Such events are pitching day, hackathons, or boot camps. These activities create shared common intentions, patterns of thinking, and strengthen the association between actors (Roundy et al., 2018).
Formal network	This type of network is established as cooperation among organizations that are actors within the entrepreneurial ecosystem. With this network, each actor who gives support to entrepreneurs can guide them to the next supporting actors that the entrepreneurs need (Cohen, 2006). Additionally, this social network among actors and entrepreneurs means the sharing of knowledge and skills (Spigel, 2017).
Culture	The societal norms in the region that admire successful entrepreneurs, tolerate risks and mistakes, encourage ambition, invention, and wealth creation (Isenberg, 2011). Investing in cultural resources such as public arts or community gardens can attract entrepreneurs, actors, or even skilled workers to the region (Roundy, 2019).
Physical Infrastructure	This refers to communication infrastructure, transportation infrastructure, and availability of office space which will allow the creation and growth of new ventures (Spigel, 2017). Cities that become an innovation hub attract young entrepreneurs to them (Sarma & Sunny, 2017).
Market	Markets provide first customers with first feedbacks who then, provide access to more customers through social networks (Isenberg, 2011).
Government and Policies	This refers to the support given by the government, at any level, through programs or regulations. The support might be direct funding or policies that make the creation of new ventures easier (Spigel, 2017).
Leadership	Leadership refers to a group of successful entrepreneurs who give advice and inspiration to new entrepreneurs (Stam, 2015; Tiba et al., 2020).
Informal network	This element refers to the entrepreneur's own informal network that can be family, friends, colleagues, or even companies that the entrepreneur closely familiar with. This network can potentially provide advice or the first funding for establishing a new venture (Cohen, 2006).

Elements	Working definitions
Knowledge sources	The sources of knowledge such as universities generate new generations of entrepreneurs, knowledge spillovers through discussions, or even spin-off ventures using know-how from research (Prencipe et al., 2020; Spigel, 2017). Moreover, personnel from entrepreneurs' ventures can be trained for necessary skills by this actor (Cohen, 2006).
Professional and support services	Professional services are in demand even before the establishment of new ventures. Lawyers are the first service the entrepreneurs need to consult in order to patent their product or service, or legally start their business. After that, accounting, real estate, or insurance are the services that also support the entrepreneurs (Spigel, 2017). This also includes suppliers needed by entrepreneurs (Cohen, 2006).
Capital services	Access to funding from supportive venture capital, angel investors, or other forms of finance is critical to new ventures. Therefore, the density of these capital services should be high to provide access to funding to the entrepreneurs (Stam, 2015).
Talent pool	Ideally, an entrepreneurial ecosystem should have, at least, a source for all levels of employees in every area of expertise. The university is such a place and should be well-connect to the ecosystem network (Stam, 2015).
Intermediaries	Intermediaries are mentors and dealmakers who support entrepreneurs through advice on their product design or business plan. Then, they utilize the ecosystem network to guide the entrepreneurs to more support needed for each phase of entrepreneurship. These intermediaries are incubators, accelerators, or even those successful advisors who want to give back to the entrepreneurial ecosystem (Stam, 2015). These mentors also play an important role in building the ecosystem's network (van Rijnsoever, 2020).
Cooperative companies	Large companies in the ecosystem area should be encouraged to provide support programs to new startups (Stam, 2015).

4. Research strategy

We plan to conduct exploratory quantitative research based on our conceptual framework in order to understand the changes that occur upon the entrepreneurial process of digital entrepreneurs. The data will be gathered from the startup digital entrepreneurs who are participating or participated in an entrepreneurial ecosystem within the last 2 years to get accurate data that is not tainted by unreliable memory. Figure 1 shows the proposed conceptual framework.

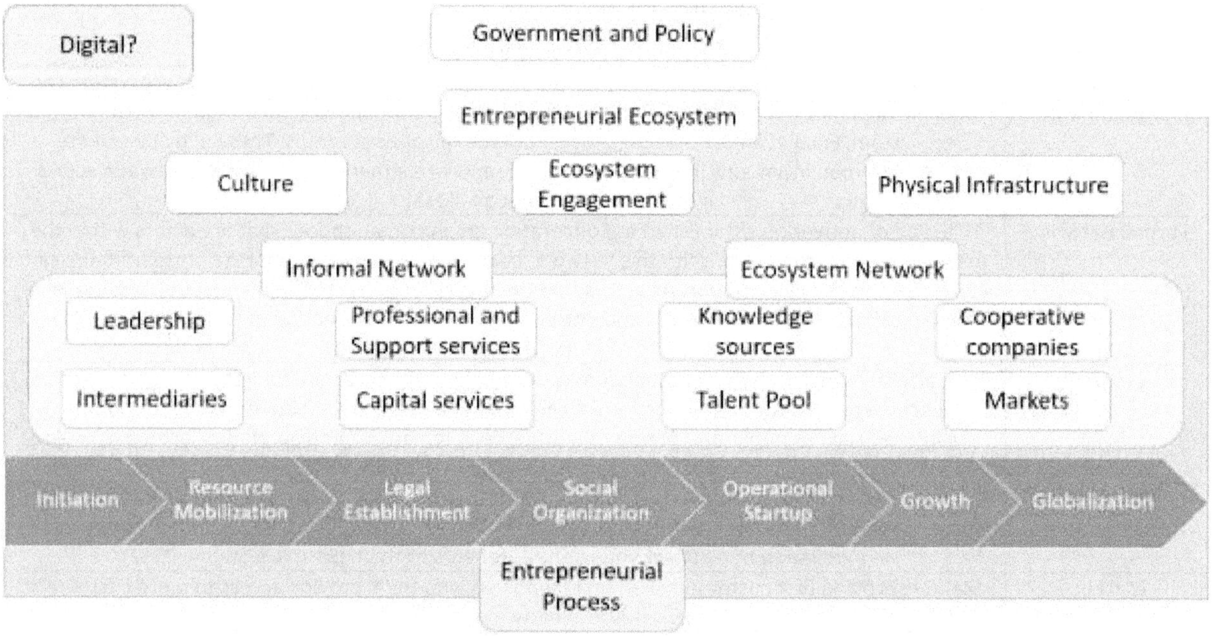

Figure 1: Conceptual framework on entrepreneurial ecosystem elements and entrepreneurial process

The theoretical framework we adopted is the assimilation of literature gathered and analyzed in the previous section. The entrepreneurial process is included in the conceptual framework because, as we define it in section 3.3, the entrepreneurial ecosystem enables improved entrepreneurial performance to startup that are members and the entrepreneurial process is the performance aspect of our conceptual framework. This conceptual framework will be our base in the forming of the structure for the data collection which we will attempt to confirm the existence of and the relationships between the elements of the digital ecosystem framework. Our objective is to gain an understanding of the role of digital entrepreneurs and their evolved entrepreneurial process within the entrepreneurial ecosystem.

Then, in the data analysis phase, we use descriptive and bi-variate statistical tools to discover summary and causal relations between the elements. After that, we plan to use the updated conceptual framework to undertake in-depth interviews to establish the context of digital entrepreneurial ecosystems

5. Discussion

We propose a conceptual framework that can show a digital entrepreneurial ecosystem's support elements and the entrepreneurial process. This conceptual framework will be the base of the next phase of this study in learning what are the changes in entrepreneurial processes in the context of the digital entrepreneur as well as the delivery of the ecosystem in a digital manner. Partial elements of the ecosystem may indeed become more digital with subsequent implications on the services the ecosystem offers. There exists an absence of literature focusing on the evolution of supportive elements within these digital entrepreneurial ecosystems. We believe that after adapting entrepreneurial processes caused by entrepreneurs turning digital as suggested by Elia et al. (2020), the ecosystems also have to adapt themselves to this situation. Multiple online crowdsourcing platforms have emerged that offer digital entrepreneurial supports, for example, "OpenIDEO" or "Idea Bounty" which offers a place for digital entrepreneurs to get ideas from the online community in the product design process. Another example involves the platform "ioby" that offers fundraising services for local environmental projects. These alternative digital capital services may reduce, to some degree, the importance of those more traditional elements of capital services, such as angel investors and venture capitalists. The way in which digital entrepreneurs engage with the digital and traditional ecosystem is a key element in this research study.

6. Conclusion

This study reviews the literature on the interlinked subjects of the digital entrepreneurial ecosystem and the digital entrepreneur. The concepts of an entrepreneurial ecosystem, as found, in the literature were reviewed and 14 support elements within entrepreneurial ecosystem were identified as ecosystem engagement, leadership, informal network, formal network, intermediaries, professional and support services, capital services, knowledge sources, talent pool, cooperative companies, culture, government and policies, physical infrastructure, and markets. These elements as well as the entrepreneurial process were incorporated to create a conceptual framework as a theoretical lens to explore the changes in the entrepreneurial processes of digital entrepreneurs and subsequently to the support elements of the entrepreneurial ecosystem. After that, we outline our research plan for the next phase of the study. This research study will contribute to knowledge by developing a better understanding of the digital entrepreneurial processes and the emerging digital entrepreneurial ecosystem capabilities.

References

Ahmadi, A. (2003). The entrepreneurial process: An institutional perspective. *rapport nr.: FE-reports*(2003-396).

Anderson, A. R. (2000). The protean entrepreneur: the entrepreneurial process as fitting self and circumstance. *Journal of Enterprising Culture, 8*(03), 201-234.

Arenal, A., Armuña, C., Feijoo, C., Ramos, S., Xu, Z., & Moreno, A. (2020). Innovation ecosystems theory revisited: The case of artificial intelligence in China. *Telecommunications Policy*, 101960.

Audretsch, D. B. (2015). *Everything in its place: Entrepreneurship and the strategic management of cities, regions, and states*: Oxford University Press.

Bell-Masterson, J., & Stangler, D. (2015). Measuring an entrepreneurial ecosystem. *Available at SSRN 2580336*.

Beltagui, A., Rosli, A., & Candi, M. (2020). Exaptation in a digital innovation ecosystem: The disruptive impacts of 3D printing. *Research policy, 49*(1), 103833.

Berger, E. S., & Kuckertz, A. (2016). Female entrepreneurship in startup ecosystems worldwide. *Journal of business research, 69*(11), 5163-5168.

Casson, M., & Casson, C. (2014). The history of entrepreneurship: Medieval origins of a modern phenomenon. *Business History, 56*(8), 1223-1242.

Chandna, V., & Salimath, M. S. (2020). When technology shapes community in the cultural and craft Industries: Understanding virtual entrepreneurship in online ecosystems. *Technovation, 92*, 102042.

Cohen, B. (2006). Sustainable valley entrepreneurial ecosystems. *Business Strategy and the Environment, 15*(1), 1-14.

Dedehayir, O., Mäkinen, S. J., & Ortt, J. R. (2018). Roles during innovation ecosystem genesis: A literature review. *Technological Forecasting and Social Change, 136*, 18-29.

Drucker, P. (2014). *Innovation and entrepreneurship*: Routledge.

Du, W., Pan, S. L., Zhou, N., & Ouyang, T. (2018). From a marketplace of electronics to a digital entrepreneurial ecosystem (DEE): The emergence of a meta-organization in Zhongguancun, China. *Information Systems Journal, 28*(6), 1158-1175.

Elia, G., Margherita, A., & Passiante, G. (2020). Digital entrepreneurship ecosystem: How digital technologies and collective intelligence are reshaping the entrepreneurial process. *Technological Forecasting and Social Change, 150*, 119791.

European Commission. (2015). *Digital Transformation of European Industry and Enterprises: A report of the Strategic Policy Forum on Digital Entrepreneurship*. Retrieved from http://ec.europa.eu/DocsRoom/documents/9462/attachments/1/translations/en/renditions/native

Feng, N., Fu, C., Wei, F., Peng, Z., Zhang, Q., & Zhang, K. H. (2019). The key role of dynamic capabilities in the evolutionary process for a startup to develop into an innovation ecosystem leader: An indepth case study. *Journal of Engineering and Technology Management, 54*, 81-96.

Fuster, E., Padilla-Meléndez, A., Lockett, N., & del-Águila-Obra, A. R. (2019). The emerging role of university spin-off companies in developing regional entrepreneurial university ecosystems: The case of Andalusia. *Technological Forecasting and Social Change, 141*, 219-231.

Ghazinoory, S., Sarkissian, A., Farhanchi, M., & Saghafi, F. (2020). Renewing a dysfunctional innovation ecosystem: The case of the Lalejin ceramics and pottery. *Technovation*, 102122.

Han, J., Ruan, Y., Wang, Y., & Zhou, H. (2019). Toward a complex adaptive system: The case of the Zhongguancun entrepreneurship ecosystem. *Journal of business research*.

Hébert, R. F., & Link, A. N. (1989). In search of the meaning of entrepreneurship. *Small Business Economics, 1*(1), 39-49.

Hernández, C., & González, D. (2016). Study of the start-up ecosystem in Lima, Peru: Collective case study. *Latin American Business Review, 17*(2), 115-137.

Isenberg, D. (2011). The entrepreneurship ecosystem strategy as a new paradigm for economic policy: Principles for cultivating entrepreneurship. *Presentation at the Institute of International and European Affairs*.

Jha, S. K. (2018). Entrepreneurial ecosystem in India: Taking stock and looking ahead. *IIMB management review, 30*(2), 179-188.

Jones, M. V., & Coviello, N. E. (2005). Internationalisation: conceptualising an entrepreneurial process of behaviour in time. *Journal of International Business Studies, 36*(3), 284-303.

Kahle, J. H., Marcon, É., Ghezzi, A., & Frank, A. G. (2020). Smart Products value creation in SMEs innovation ecosystems. *Technological Forecasting and Social Change, 156*, 120024.

Kantis, H. D., Federico, J. S., & García, S. I. (2020). Entrepreneurship policy and systemic conditions: Evidence-based implications and recommendations for emerging countries. *Socio-Economic Planning Sciences*, 100872.

Kuckertz, A. (2019). Let's take the entrepreneurial ecosystem metaphor seriously! *Journal of Business Venturing Insights, 11*, e00124.

Lawson, L. (2019). Women working in the Thai coloured gemstone industry: Insights from entrepreneurial ecosystems. *The Extractive Industries and Society, 6*(4), 1066-1074.

Leffel, C. H. A., & Agrawal, L. d. I. V. M. (2014). Accelerating collegiate entrepreneurship (ACE): The architecture of a university entrepreneurial ecosystem encompassing an intercollegiate venture experience. *Journal of Business & Entrepreneurship*, 95.

Lindholm-Dahlstrand, Å., Andersson, M., & Carlsson, B. (2019). Entrepreneurial experimentation: a key function in systems of innovation. *Small Business Economics, 53*(3), 591-610.

Malecki, E. J. (2018). Entrepreneurship and entrepreneurial ecosystems. *Geography Compass, 12*(3), e12359.

Morris, M. H., Lewis, P. S., & Sexton, D. L. (1994). Reconceptualizing entrepreneurship: an input-output perspective. *SAM Advanced Management Journal, 59*(1), 21.

Nambisan, S. (2017). Digital entrepreneurship: Toward a digital technology perspective of entrepreneurship. *Entrepreneurship Theory and Practice, 41*(6), 1029-1055.

Neumeyer, X., & Santos, S. C. (2018). Sustainable business models, venture typologies, and entrepreneurial ecosystems: A social network perspective. *Journal of cleaner production, 172*, 4565-4579.

Prencipe, A., Corsi, C., Rodríguez-Gulías, M. J., Fernandez, S., & Rodeiro-Pazos, D. (2020). Influence of the regional entrepreneurial ecosystem and its knowledge spillovers in developing successful university spin-offs. *Socio-Economic Planning Sciences*, 100814.

Pustovrh, A., Rangus, K., & Drnovšek, M. (2020). The role of open innovation in developing an entrepreneurial support ecosystem. *Technological Forecasting and Social Change, 152*, 119892.

Radosevic, S., & Yoruk, E. (2013). Entrepreneurial propensity of innovation systems: Theory, methodology and evidence. *Research policy, 42*(5), 1015-1038.

Rathee, R., & Rajain, M. P. (2017). ENTREPRENEURSHIP IN THE DIGITAL ERA. *Asia Pacific Journal of Research in Business Management, 8*(6).

Reynolds, E. B., & Uygun, Y. (2018). Strengthening advanced manufacturing innovation ecosystems: The case of Massachusetts. *Technological Forecasting and Social Change, 136*, 178-191.

Robertson, J., Pitt, L., & Ferreira, C. (2020). Entrepreneurial ecosystems and the public sector: A bibliographic analysis. *Socio-Economic Planning Sciences*, 100862.

Roundy, P. T. (2019). Back from the brink: The revitalization of inactive entrepreneurial ecosystems. *Journal of Business Venturing Insights, 12*, e00140.

Roundy, P. T., Bradshaw, M., & Brockman, B. K. (2018). The emergence of entrepreneurial ecosystems: A complex adaptive systems approach. *Journal of business research, 86*, 1-10.

Roundy, P. T., Brockman, B. K., & Bradshaw, M. (2017). The resilience of entrepreneurial ecosystems. *Journal of Business Venturing Insights, 8*, 99-104.

Ruef, M. (2005). Origins of organizations: The entrepreneurial process. *Research in the Sociology of Work, 15*, 63-100.

Sarma, S., & Sunny, S. A. (2017). Civic entrepreneurial ecosystems: Smart city emergence in Kansas City. *Business Horizons, 60*(6), 843-853.

Scaringella, L., & Radziwon, A. (2018). Innovation, entrepreneurial, knowledge, and business ecosystems: Old wine in new bottles? *Technological Forecasting and Social Change, 136*, 59-87.

Schumpeter, J. A. (1965). Economic Theory and Entrepreneurial History. In A. HG (Ed.), *Explorations in enterprise*. Cambridge, MA: Harvard University Press.

Schumpeter, J. A. (2010). *Capitalism, socialism and democracy*: routledge.

Spigel, B. (2017). The relational organization of entrepreneurial ecosystems. *Entrepreneurship Theory and Practice, 41*(1), 49-72.

Spilling, O. R. (1996). The entrepreneurial system: On entrepreneurship in the context of a mega-event. *Journal of business research, 36*(1), 91-103.

Stam, E. (2015). Entrepreneurial ecosystems and regional policy: a sympathetic critique. *European Planning Studies, 23*(9), 1759-1769.

Startup Genome. (2018). Global Startup Ecosystem Report 2018. Retrieved from https://startupgenome.com/reports/global-startup-ecosystem-report-gser-2018

Stephens, B., Butler, J. S., Garg, R., & Gibson, D. V. (2019). Austin, Boston, Silicon Valley, and New York: Case studies in the location choices of entrepreneurs in maintaining the Technopolis. *Technological Forecasting and Social Change, 146*, 267-280.

Stevenson, H. H. (2000). Why entrepreneurship has won. *Coleman White Paper*, 1-8.

Sun, S. L., Zhang, Y., Cao, Y., Dong, J., & Cantwell, J. (2019). Enriching innovation ecosystems: The role of government in a university science park. *Global Transitions, 1*, 104-119.

Tiba, S., van Rijnsoever, F., & Hekkert, M. P. (2020). The lighthouse effect: How successful entrepreneurs influence the sustainability-orientation of entrepreneurial ecosystems. *Journal of cleaner production*, 121616.

Tripathi, N., Oivo, M., Liukkunen, K., & Markkula, J. (2019). Startup ecosystem effect on minimum viable product development in software startups. *Information and Software Technology, 114*, 77-91.

Tripathi, N., Seppänen, P., Boominathan, G., Oivo, M., & Liukkunen, K. (2019). Insights into startup ecosystems through exploration of multi-vocal literature. *Information and Software Technology, 105*, 56-77.

van Rijnsoever, F. J. (2020). Meeting, mating, and intermediating: How incubators can overcome weak network problems in entrepreneurial ecosystems. *Research policy, 49*(1), 103884.

Webster, J., & Watson, R. T. (2002). Analyzing the past to prepare for the future: Writing a literature review. *MIS quarterly*, xiii-xxiii.

Wiszniewski, B. (2019). Building Polish space sector–from small islands of excellence to a national innovation ecosystem. *IFAC-PapersOnLine, 52*(8), 211-220.

Xu, G., Wu, Y., Minshall, T., & Zhou, Y. (2018). Exploring innovation ecosystems across science, technology, and business: A case of 3D printing in China. *Technological Forecasting and Social Change, 136*, 208-221.

Zhao, X., Shang, Y., & Song, M. (2019). Industrial structure distortion and urban ecological efficiency from the perspective of green entrepreneurial ecosystems. *Socio-Economic Planning Sciences*, 100757.

Znagui, Z., & Rahmouni, B. (2019). What ecosystem model to support the creation of social innovation technopoles? *Procedia Computer Science, 158*, 877-884.

A Study on the Factors Affecting the Performance of SMEs

Seok-Soo Kim and Hyoung-Yong Lee
Hansung University, Seoul, Korea
ssjm4475@gmail.com
leemit@yahoo.com
DOI: 10.34190/EIE.20.076

Abstract: To promote technology-based entrepreneurship, this paper examines the concept of entrepreneurship success factors and entrepreneurship competency that can increase the likelihood of a small business entrepreneur's business success. The impact on the related factors and the characteristics of the impact were analyzed to analyze the impacts on entrepreneurial competency and to confirm the correlation. To derive a solution to improve the business performance of start-ups, the following objectives were studied. First, the causal relationship was identified by analyzing the effect of the success variable on entrepreneurship on entrepreneurship competency and each on business performance. Second, the effect of success variables on business performance through the mediating effect of technology entrepreneurship was analyzed empirically. Third, we intend to empirically analyze the impact of entrepreneurship capabilities on business performance. Fourth, the control effect of how the factors affecting business performance are different and the degree of impact is different according to six industries, such as electricity / electronics, IT / SW, was verified and confirmed. The results of this study will be provided to the government policy makers and government support organizations to foster youth entrepreneurship, and even if they are founded, they will contribute to creating business results without failure by supplementing and strengthening the success factors for each industry sectors.

Keywords: technology-based entrepreneur, entrepreneur success factors, entrepreneurship capability, business performance, technology innovation capability, technical marketing capability

1. Introduction

In accordance with the policies to promote entrepreneurship in which poor entrepreneurship conditions are proactive, the components of entrepreneurs' ability to conduct entrepreneurship are identified, and the influence is evaluated to improve the ability and ability to improve the entrepreneurship success factors according to the characteristics of entrepreneurship and entrepreneurship conditions. Expanding business performance by linking the core competency of startups to successful startups has been expressed as an important task. Autio(1997), Kortum and Lerner(2001) found that the development of a new start-up company was lowered by barriers to entry into the start-up due to the development of ICT and the generalization and spread of crowd funding. He mentioned that technology-based start-ups or venture companies are already playing a major role in the national economic development while playing the role of a growth engine driving innovation in the industrial sector. In addition, Bollinger et al., (1983) stated a small number of people are established with innovative technology and business motives, and Cooper et al., (1986) mentioned R & D center or companies focusing on the use of new technical knowledge or knowledge, and Carland et al., (1984) defined as a company that achieves profit and growth objectives through the introduction of new technologies, new products and new production methods and new market development. In particular, in the classification according to the type of entrepreneurship classified by the Korea Small and Medium Business Administration and the Korea Entrepreneurship Incubation Association (2015), they are categorized into technical start-ups, venture start-ups, and general start-ups. It can be seen that the definitions are similar because the distinction is not clear.

2. Literature review

2.1 Success factors (independent variables)

As an independent variable, the sub-factors of the success variables of technology start-up were divided into four sub-factors: management ability, technology ability, technology commercialization ability, and exit strategy. For each sub-factor, detailed items were set and measured as follows.

2.1.1 Management ability

Chandler and Jansen (1992) and Chandler and Hanks (1994) have studied prior operational definitions of management competency in various fields. The management competence on management performance and financial performance was studied with leadership and entrepreneurship. Smith and Grimm (1987) have been trying to find such elements on the premise that the focus of the study will have different characteristics for successful managers. Based on prior research, management research was classified into four categories. The first is the study on manager's characteristics such as age, characteristics, education, and experience. The second is the study on personality characteristics such as achievement motivation, risk taking, and continuity.

2.1.2 Technical ability

In the study of Burgelman et al (2004), technological competence is regarded as an important result of innovation activities as well as a very important resource for promoting and supporting corporate innovation strategies and for sustainable success. Yam et al (2004) suggested seven kinds of corporate skills, such as learning competency, R & D competency, resource allocation competency, production competency, organizational competency, and strategic planning competency. Schoenecker and Swanson (2002) used R & D expenditures, patents, new product launches, and R & D investments as indicators of technological competence. Hiroyuki and Tsuyoshi (1992) presented technology as the most fundamental element of the company's core competencies.

2.1.3 Technology commercialization ability

According to a study by Nevens et al (1990), a multi-functional capability was developed, and finally, the chief executive officer was directly involved in the technology commercialization process. Technology commercialization ability is also divided into the concept of consultation and broadness. Booz, Allen and Hamilton (1982) addressed technology commercialization capabilities in the context of a new product development strategy, and firms that successfully entered the new product market went through a formal formulation process in the development process of new products and developed strategic plans in the long term. It was reported that systematic technological innovation ability and technology commercialization ability affect management performance by revealing the existence.

2.1.4 Exit strategy ability

Kogut, Shan, and Walker (1992) described that the business-to-business network acts as a company's competitiveness by allowing companies to pursue new alliances with trusted partners. This is because the competitiveness of the company is an important function directly related to performance. In addition, Gulati and Gargiulo (1999) stated that these network resources play a role in reducing the search cost required to find new investments, and that this helps to solve various information uncertainty problems.

2.2 Technology-based start-up capability (mediating variables)

2.2.1 Technology commercialization capability

According to a report by Booz, Allen and Hamilton (1982), companies that successfully introduced new products into the market by addressing their technology commercialization capabilities in the context of new product development strategies, went through a universally formal process in the new product development process and made strategic plans in the long term. By revealing that it was established, it was identified that systematic technological innovation ability and technical commercialization ability affect management performance. In a research by Chen (2008), incubator and VC support and technology commercialization effects were verified as a factor influencing the performance of new ventures in resource-based perspective (RBV). It was analyzed that the role of technology commercialization was highlighted.

2.2.2 Technology innovation capability

Burgelman and Wheelwright (2004) mentioned that technology innovation competency is a very important capability to drive the continuous growth of a company, and at the same time, it is a comprehensive company characteristic that promotes and supports technological innovation. Acs and Audretsch (1988) described that research on technological innovation creates competitiveness and management performance of a company through strategies or research and development that are difficult to mimic based on management resources possessed by a company. Westphal, Kim and Dahlman (1985) defined technological innovation competency as an ability not only to effectively utilize technical knowledge, but also to create new technologies based on it, which is a concept based on a technological perspective.

2.2.3 Technology marketing capability

According to a study by Carr (1994), the interpretation of the term technology marketing varies, but the National Technology Transfer Center (NTTC) has defined it extensively as a comprehensive effort to effectively transfer or trade the technology itself. Miller and Power (2005) analyzes the success or failure factors of technology development and reduces the importance of marketing. In other words, 20 ~ 40% of the technology is due to the defect of the technology itself, and the rest of Clugston CO. (1995) is due to the lack of marketing ability, especially in the case of high-tech products due to the lack of marketing ability He said that the ratio reached as high as 75%.

2.3 Business performance (independent variables)

2.3.1 Financial performance

Despite the diversity in the measurement of management performance and the selection of measurement indicators, profit performance growth is mainly used for empirical analysis. Quantitative methods and methods for measuring performance based on the quantitative values in financial statements are also used for measuring financial performance. Financial performance indicators show past management results, but have limitations in predicting future management performance. Kaplan and Norton (1996), one of the newly emerged performance indicators to respond to these problems, is the Balanced Scored Card (BSC). Instead, it suggested that the indicators were managed in a long-term and comprehensively balanced manner from four perspectives: financial perspective, customer perspective, internal process perspective, and learning and growth perspective.

2.3.2 Non-Financial performance

Epstein et al (1994) suggest that a positive image of a company has a significant impact on the business performance of investment decisions through research showing that investors prefer decisions based on ethical behavior of the company over short-term profits for non-financial performance. Alaa (1996) stated that the traditional method of measuring business performance mainly used financial indicators based on the financial point of view, but the recent method of measuring performance uses environmental performance and various non-financial performances based on corporate strategy.

2.3.3 Technical performance

According to Johannisson (1986), technology performance has a relatively large influence on technology and technology management competency production support, marketing competency research and development competency, and new product development competency, and has a great influence on market information as well as business performance. It is said that securing excellent technology is directly related to the growth or profits of venture companies, so it can act as a determinant of investment by venture capital or other investment companies.

3. Research model and hypothesis

Our research model, as shown in Figure 1, attempts to answer the following research questions.

- 1) To what extent are SME success variables and capabilities affecting business performance?
- 2) If a success variable affects performance, which one has a mediating effect?
- 3) Does the industry sector have a moderating effect on performance, or is there a difference in the moderating effect by industry?

The research model is summarized below.

- 1) The independent variable is the success variable and consists of four sub-factors, and the parameter is the start-up capability, has three sub-factors, and the three dependent variables.
- 2) Business performance consists of three sub-factors to empirically analyze each causal relationship and impact level.
- 3) It consists of verifying the differences in business performance impact using Data Group Analysis by industry and presenting the results.

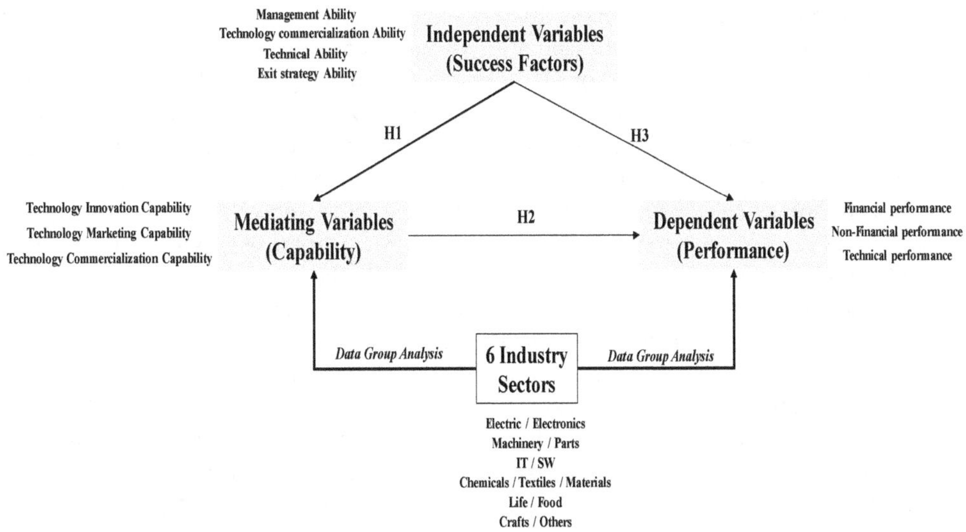

Figure 1: Conceptual research model

As one of the characteristics of this paper, the distinctive and unique point from previous studies was to verify the difference between the effect on entrepreneurship and business performance according to the six industries by Data Group Analysis. The overall structural study model of this study is shown in Figure 2. [Hypothesis H1] Success factors for entrepreneurship will positively affect technological entrepreneurship. [Hypothesis H2] Entrepreneurship capabilities will have a positive impact on technology performance. [Hypothesis H3] Success factors in entrepreneurship will positively affect technological performance. [Hypothesis H4] Industry variables will have a moderating effect on business performance.

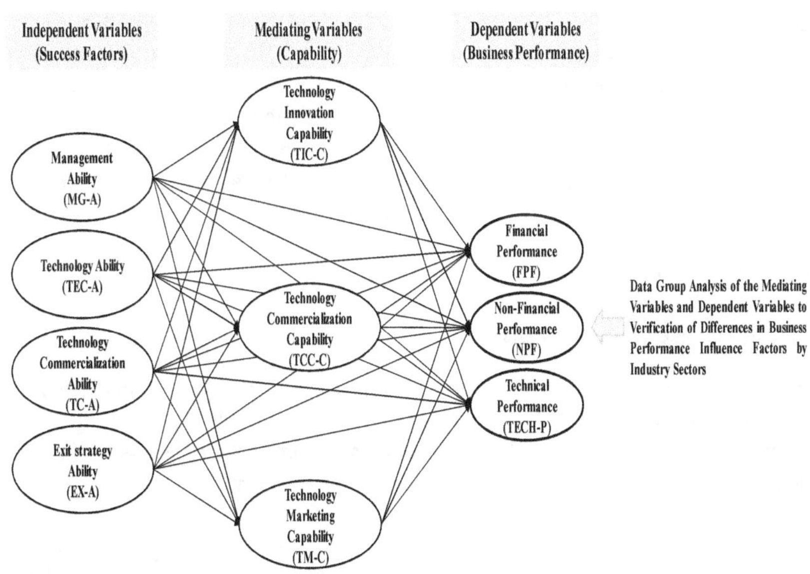

Figure 2: Final structural research model

3.1 Research method

The data was collected from 330 entrepreneur-based young entrepreneurs using the online questionnaire method. As a result of the survey, the questionnaire was collected from 205 people, and the recovery rate was 62%. Youth start-up entrepreneurs are less than 5 years after start-up, and the industry sector is 6 fields that are defined in Korean start-up company classification standards: electrical / electronics, machinery / parts, IT / SW, chemicals / textiles / materials, life / food, and crafts. / Other. The 5-point scale was used to measure the questionnaire. The collected data was verified and analyzed with SPSS 22 and Smart PLS 3.2.9 along with basic statistical analysis and measurement models and structural models. The model of this study is composed of a reflective measurement model composed of only reflective indicators. The collected data first analyzed the basic statistics using SPSS, and after removing the insignificant measurement indicators through factor analysis, the PLS Algorithm of Smart PLS 3.2.9 was used to verify the reliability and validity required for the evaluation of the reflective measurement model. By performing it, the reliability of internal consistency, concentration validity and discriminant validity were analyzed and evaluated. The internal consistency reliability was evaluated by Cronbach's Alpha, Dijkstra-Henseler's rho_A, and Composite Reliability (CR), and the centralized validity was evaluated by external placement, measurement variable reliability, and Average Variance Extracted (AVE). Hair et al (2017a) evaluated discriminant validity using Fornell-Larcker Criterion, Cross-Loadings. Cronbach's α, Dijkstra-Henseler's rho_A, Composite Reliability (CR) of internal consistency reliability evaluation are criteria for evaluating internal consistency reliability, and Average Variance Extracted (AVE) is a criterion for evaluating intensive validity. Fornell-Larcker Criterion, Cross Loadings, and HTMT are presented as criteria for determining discriminant validity in a reflective measurement model. Fornell-Larcker Criterion was used for the evaluation results and interpretation of the reflective measurement model for external placement, measurement variable reliability, AVE value, Cronbach's α, rho_A, Composite Reliability (CR) and discriminant validity. PLSE-SEM performs multi-collinearity, coefficient of determination (R2), effect size (f2), and predictive suitability (Q2) by performing bootstrapping and blindfolding to evaluate and hypothesize structural models. The significance of the path coefficient and the suitability of the model were evaluated by finally confirming that the structural model was a suitable model. Finally, by introducing industry-specific variables, the difference in influence by industry was confirmed, and by verifying the effect on the moderating effect on business performance as a dependent variable, it was confirmed that the model of this study was suitable and could be identified as having a moderating effect.

3.2 Characteristics of samples

In this study, the demographic characteristics of respondents to the survey showed that male and female males and females were 66.8% and 33.2%, respectively, with a high proportion of males. Looking at the industry, electricity / electronics 18.5%, machinery / parts 14.8%, IT / SW 17.6%, chemicals / textiles / materials / parts 17.6%, life / food 12.7%, crafts and other 19.0%. Looking at it, 32.2% under 2 ~ 3 years, 32.2% under 1 ~ 2 years were the most with 64.4% between 1 and 3 years, 23.4% under 3 ~ 5 years, 7.3% under 1 year, more than 5 years, 4.9%. Looking at the sales volume of the previous year, less than 0.1 million $ was 35.1%, followed by 32.2% from 0.1 million $ to 0.3 million $, 22.0% from 0.3 million $ to less than 0.5 million $, and less than 1 million $ from 0.5 million $ 9.3 %, More than 1 million $, 1.5%. Looking at the manufacturing method, outsourcing and in-house manufacturing accounted for the largest portion with 62.0%, outsourcing 22.9%, and 15.1%. Looking at the number of employees, less than 3 people were the most with 46.3%, 39.0 people with less than 6 people were 39.0%, 5 people with less than 10 people were 13.7%, and more than 10 people were 1.0%. By age, 40.0% were in their 30s, 38.5% in their 40s, 12.7% in their 50s and 8.8% in their 20s.

4. Result and discussion

4.1 Assessment of the measurement model

To evaluate the measurement model of the research model, PLS Algorithm of Smart PLS 3.2.9 was executed to analyze and evaluate internal consistency reliability, concentration validity, and discriminant validity. The reliability of internal consistency was evaluated by Cronbach's Alpha, Dijkstra-Henseler's rho_A, and Composite Reliability (CR). Table 1 shows the results of the PLS Algorithm execution.

Table 1: Evaluation results of reflective measurement models

Latent Variables	Convergent Validity			Internal Consistence Reliability			Discriminant Validity
	Outer Loadings	Measurement Variables Reliability	AVE	Cronbach's Alpha	Dijkstra-Henseler's rho_A	Composite Reliability (CR)	Cross Loadings
	>0.7	>0.5	>0.5	0.5~0.9	>0.7	0.5~0.9	
EX-A	0.951	0.905	0.905	0.895	0.896	0.950	Yes
FPF	0.933	0.870	0.870	0.851	0.851	0.931	Yes
MG-A	0.937	0.877	0.877	0.860	0.863	0.935	Yes
NPF	0.935	0.873	0.873	0.855	0.858	0.932	Yes
TCC-C	0.925	0.856	0.857	0.834	0.848	0.923	Yes
TC-A	0.912	0.831	0.831	0.797	0.801	0.908	Yes
TEC-A	0.914	0.835	0.835	0.901	0.903	0.938	Yes
TECH-P	0.940	0.883	0.883	0.867	0.867	0.938	Yes
TIC-C	0.924	0.854	0.854	0.829	0.832	0.921	Yes
TM-C	0.948	0.899	0.899	0.887	0.889	0.947	Yes

4.2 Assessment of the structural model

The average variance extracted value, which is another criterion for concentration validity, was also confirmed that all the measurement variables were above the threshold value of 0.5, as shown in Table 1. Fornell-Larcker Criterion and Cross Loadings are presented as criteria for determining discriminant validity in a reflective measurement model. Since the AVE square root of the diagonal line is greater than the correlation between the study variables below the diagonal line, it is evaluated that discriminant validity is secured between the study variables. Table 2 shows the results.

Table 2: Evaluation results of reflective measurement models (Fornell-Larcker Criterion)

	EX-A	FPF	MG-A	NPF	TCC-C	TC-A	TEC-A	TECH-P	TIC-C	TM-C
EX-A	0.952									
FPF	0.702	0.933								
MG-A	0.749	0.728	0.937							
NPF	0.756	0.849	0.769	0.935						
TCC-C	0.628	0.668	0.663	0.741	0.926					
TC-A	0.609	0.579	0.632	0.655	0.759	0.912				
TEC-A	0.704	0.673	0.641	0.742	0.637	0.633	0.914			
TECH-P	0.715	0.757	0.669	0.797	0.682	0.597	0.796	0.940		
TIC-C	0.654	0.699	0.670	0.734	0.750	0.709	0.695	0.684	0.924	
TM-C	0.609	0.695	0.616	0.706	0.608	0.568	0.701	0.765	0.656	0.948

The evaluation of the structural model can be considered as a procedure that finally confirms the research model designed and developed by the researcher and confirms that the structural model is a suitable model. When the structural model is identified as a suitable model, it is possible to perform hypothesis verification. For the evaluation of structural models in PLS-SEM, this study evaluated and evaluated multicollinearity, coefficient of determination (R2), effect size (f2), and predictive fit (Q2). Table 3 shows the results of confirming the internal VIF value by executing the PLS Algorithm to check the multicollinearity. If the Inner VIF Values between study variables are less than 5, it can be judged that there is no multicollinearity. As a result of the confirmation, it can be evaluated that there is no multicollinearity since all are less than 5. Table 4 shows the results of confirming the determination coefficient R2 by executing the PLS algorithm to evaluate the explanatory power of endogenous research variables. The effect size (f2) is used as the criterion for evaluating the relative impact of exogenous research variables (or predictors, independent variables) on endogenous research variables. If f2 is 0.02, it is evaluated as a small effect size, 0.15 as a medium effect size, and 0.35 as a large effect size. Table 5 shows the results of confirming the effect size (f2). Evaluate whether the structural model has predictive suitability for specific endogenous research variables. For this, the predictive suitability (Q2) is used. If the structural model has a Q2 greater than 0 for a specific endogenous research variable, it is evaluated that there is a predictive fit. Blindfolding of Smart PLS 3.2.9 was performed to confirm the results of Cross-Validated Redundancy, Q2 was evaluated, and the results are shown in Table 6.

Table 3: Inner VIF

Inner VIF	FPF	NPF	TCC-C	TECH-P	TIC-C	TM-C
EX-A	2.903	2.903	2.866	2.903	2.866	2.866
MG-A	2.839	2.839	2.618	2.839	2.618	2.618
TCC-C	3.189	3.189		3.189		
TC-A	2.780	2.780	1.979	2.780	1.979	1.979
TEC-A	2.884	2.884	2.322	2.884	2.322	2.322
TIC-C	3.158	3.158		3.158		
TM-C	2.318	2.318		2.318		

Table 4: R square

R^2	R Square	Adjusted R Square
FPF	0.681	0.669
NPF	0.767	0.759
TCC-C	0.648	0.640
TECH-P	0.757	0.749
TIC-C	0.637	0.630

Table 5: f2

f^2	FPF	NPF	TCC-C	TECH-P	TIC-C	TM-C
EX-A	0.030	0.052	0.006	0.039	0.009	0.004
MG-A	0.076	0.089	0.045	0.003	0.042	0.035
TCC-C	0.022	0.069		0.045		
TC-A	0.012	0.003	0.352	0.012	0.167	0.014
TEC-A	0.006	0.040	0.024	0.183	0.093	0.192
TIC-C	0.027	0.012		0.000		
TM-C	0.076	0.042		0.174		

Table 6: Q^2

Q^2	Q^2 (=1-SSE/SSO)
FPF	0.554
NPF	0.638
TECH-P	0.645
TIC-C	0.534
TM-C	0.467

4.3 Hypothesis verification result

Since the evaluation of the structural model has been confirmed, it is possible to conduct hypothesis verification through bootstrapping. The significance and suitability of the path coefficients are evaluated using the t-value calculated by performing bootstrapping. Through this, hypothesis verification was performed. The significance and suitability evaluation of the path coefficient were performed by Basic Bootstrapping of Smart PLS 3.2.9, and the t-value, p-value, and confidence interval required for hypothesis verification were verified at a significance level of .05. Table 7 shows the results.

Table 7: Hypothesis verification results

	Original Sample	Sample Mean	Standard Deviation	T statistics	P Value	Confidence Interval		Significance
	(O)	(M)	(STDEV)	(|O/STDEV|)		2.50%	97.50%	(p<0.05)
EX-A → NPF	0.188	0.192	0.090	2.084	**0.037**	0.012	0.367	**Accept**
MG-A → FPF	0.262	0.255	0.099	2.657	**0.008**	0.038	0.453	**Accept**
MG-A → NPF	0.242	0.239	0.088	2.749	**0.006**	0.070	0.410	**Accept**
MG-A → TIC-C	0.200	0.201	0.087	2.286	**0.022**	0.030	0.361	**Accept**
TCC-C → TECH-P	0.186	0.177	0.084	2.228	**0.026**	0.018	0.334	**Accept**
TC-A → TCC-C	0.496	0.499	0.072	6.839	**0.000**	0.350	0.629	**Accept**
TC-A → TIC-C	0.346	0.347	0.084	4.126	**0.000**	0.191	0.507	**Accept**
TEC-A → TECH-P	0.358	0.354	0.086	4.188	**0.000**	0.181	0.519	**Accept**
TEC-A → TIC-C	0.280	0.277	0.093	3.016	**0.003**	0.091	0.463	**Accept**
TEC-A → TM-C	0.449	0.440	0.122	3.692	**0.000**	0.193	0.665	**Accept**
TM-C → FPF	0.237	0.234	0.079	2.994	**0.003**	0.076	0.385	**Accept**
TM-C → NPF	0.150	0.146	0.071	2.116	**0.035**	0.007	0.286	**Accept**
TM-C → TECH-P	0.313	0.317	0.086	3.633	**0.000**	0.140	0.487	**Accept**

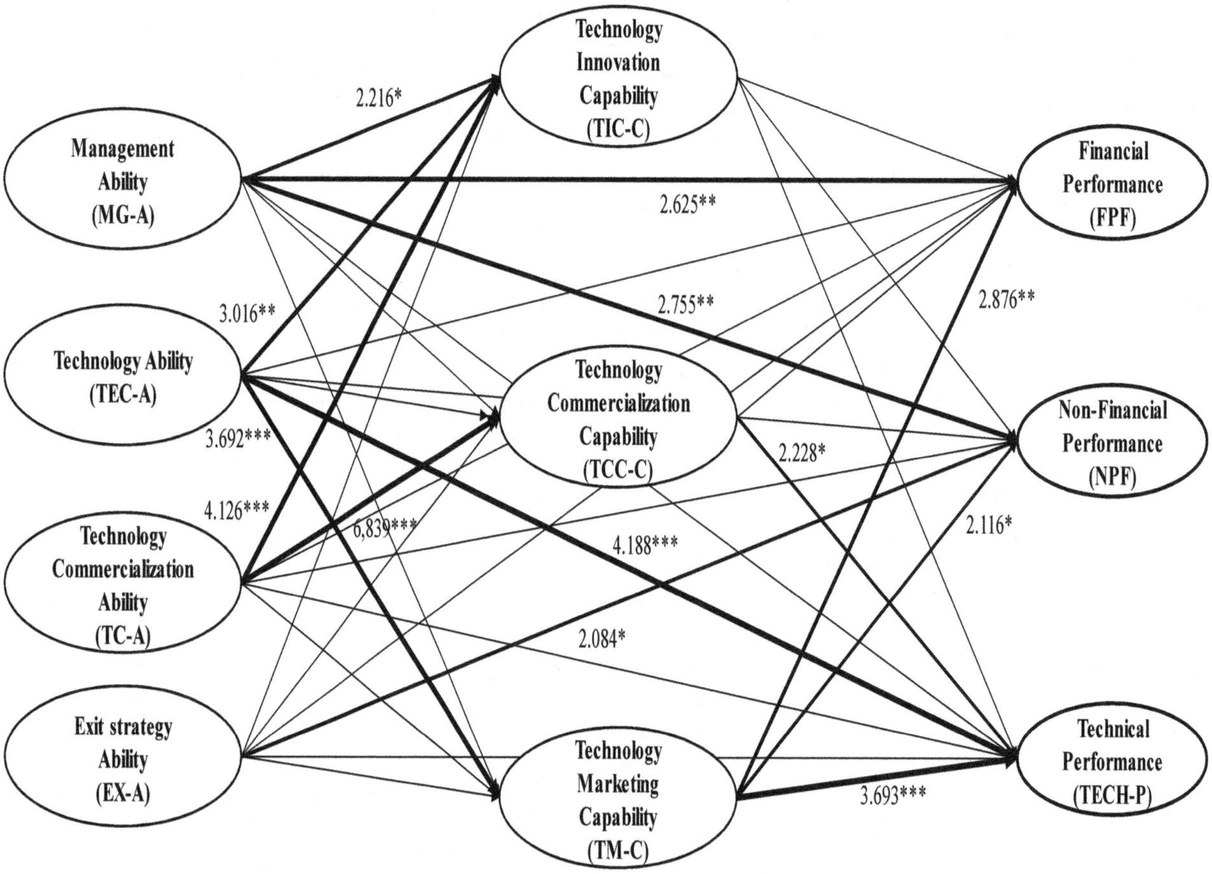

Figure 3: Hypothesis verification result (T-Value, P-Value)

4.4 Result of mediating effect

As a result of significant hypothesis verification of the effect of the startup ability as a parameter on the business performance as a dependent variable, bootstrapping was executed to confirm the specific indirect effect (parameter effect) of the startup ability as a parameter. Table 8 shows the results. The mediating effect was verified by checking the t-value, p-value, and confidence interval required for hypothesis verification at a significance level of .05.

As shown in Table 8, the mediating effect on the technical performance (TECH-P) showed a significant mediating effect by the technology commercialization ability (TC-A) mediating the technology commercialization capability

(TC-A) (T value 2. -69, P Value .039), and the technical ability (TEC-A) showed a significant mediating effect by mediating the technical marketing competency (TM-C) (T value 2.547, P Value .011). As for the mediating effect on financial performance, the technical competency (TEC-A) mediated the technical marketing competency (TM-C) and showed a significant mediating effect (T value 2.127, P Value .034).

Table 8: Special indirect effect (mediating effect)

	Original Sample	Sample Mean	Standard Deviation	T statistics	P Value	Confidence Interval		Significance
	(O)	(M)	(STDEV)	(|O/STDEV|)		2.50%	97.50%	(p<0.05)
TEC-A → TM-C → FPF	0.107	0.104	0.050	2.127	0.034	0.024	0.216	Accept
TC-A → TCC-C → TECH-P	0.092	0.088	0.045	2.069	0.039	0.009	0.178	Accept
TEC-A → TM-C → TECH-P	0.141	0.139	0.055	2.547	0.011	0.044	0.256	Accept

4.5 Differences in business performance by industry sectors

To confirm the difference in business performance and impact according to the industry, the difference between adjusted R2 and f2 values was compared and analyzed. The six industries have analyzed the CEO's business responding to the survey * Overall: Results obtained by analyzing the entire industry without distinction by industry ** DIV 1: electrical / electronics, ** DIV 2: machinery / parts, ** DIV 3 : IT / SW, ** DIV 4: chemicals / textiles / materials, ** DIV 5: life / food, ** DIV 6: Crafts / others. The adjusted R2 value was compared with the R2 value for 3 sub-factors and 3 sub-factors in the initial overall condition without distinction by industry, and the changes in R2 valuesafter analyzing the PLS Algorithm of 6 individual industries. In addition, the R2 value for the entrepreneurship capability as a parameter was also analyzed, and the results are shown in Table 9.

Table 9: Adjusted square result of business performance impact by industry sectors

R^2	Overall	DIV 1	DIV 2	DIV 3	DIV 4	DIV 5	DIV 6
	Adjusted R Square						
FPF	0.669	0.655	0.792	0.855	0.589	0.911	0.747
NPF	0.759	0.750	0.877	0.743	0.719	0.935	0.780
TCC-C	0.640	0.484	0.586	0.663	0.645	0.921	0.785
TECH-P	0.749	0.549	0.871	0.858	0.741	0.958	0.722
TIC-C	0.630	0.617	0.612	0.666	0.689	0.893	0.716
TM-C	0.538	0.590	0.711	0.723	0.421	0.585	0.471

Overall R2 for financial performance (FPF), non-financial performance (NFP), and technical performance (TECH-P) was .669, .759, and .749, respectively. DIV 1 decreased to .655, .750, .549, and DIV 4 also decreased to .589, .719, and .741. On the other hand, DIV5 increased significantly to .911, .935 and .958. DIV2 also increased significantly to .792, .877, and .871. DIV4 increased to .630, .729, and .903 only for TECH-P, and DIV5 increased significantly to .930, .952, and .959. It was confirmed that DIV6 increased to .860, .809, and .899. The results showed that DIV5 (life / food) contributed the most to the business performance, and DIV3 (IT / SW) increased the next. It was also confirmed that DIV2 and DIV6 increased.

5. Conclusion

The research on the impact of business performance according to the industrial sector presented in this paper was not conducted in the previous research and is considered to be a distinguishing characteristic of this paper. Providing research results to government policy makers and government support organizations to foster youth entrepreneurship will help contribute to creating business results without failure by supplementing and strengthening the success factors of each sector even when starting a business. In detail, it was checked whether there is a causal relationship between the degree of influence on the entrepreneurship success factor and the business performance of the entrepreneur's success factors. In addition, the entrepreneurship ability of small and medium-sized entrepreneurs was analyzed and verified to have a mediating effect on success factors and business performance. Electrical / electronics, machinery / parts, IT / SW, chemicals / textiles / materials, life / food, crafts / others We verified and confirmed how the factors affecting business performance differ according to the six industries and the degree of impact. First, as a result of the hypothesis verification on the measurement model 1) The significant variables influencing the financial performance (FPF), which are dependent variables, were the management capacity (MGC-A), which is an independent variable, and technical marketing capability (TM-C), which is a parameter. Non-financial performance (NPF) had significant influence on management capability (MGC-A) as an independent variable and technical marketing capability (TM-C) as an exit strategy (EX-A) parameter. The significant influence variables on the technical performance (TECH-P) were the independent variables, the technical capability (TEC-A), the parameters, the technical commercialization capability (TCC-C), and the technical marketing capability (TM-C). 2) As a success factor, which is an independent variable that significantly affects the parameters of entrepreneurship, the factors affecting technology innovation competency (TIC-C) are management competency (MG-A), technology competency (TEC-A), and technology commercialization capability (It was verified that it was TC-A), that the technology commercialization competency (TCC-C) influence factor was the technology commercialization capability (TC-A), and that the technology marketing competency (TM-C) influence factor was the technical capability (TEC-A). Second, the verification result of the mediating effect 1) One of the success factors, which is an independent variable, the technical competence (TEC-A) is based on the mediating effect of the technology marketing competency (TM-C), which is the start-up competency. (TECH-P), and 2) Technology commercialization ability (TC-A) was confirmed to affect technology performance (TECH-P) through the mediating effect of technology commercialization capability (TCC-C). Third, there are different factors affecting business performance according to six industries: electrical / electronics, machinery / parts, IT / SW, chemicals / fibers / materials, life / food, and crafts / other, and the degree of impact is somewhat different. As a result of verifying whether there is a change in the R2 value, it was found that, in particular, DIV 5 (life / food) showed the greatest increase in the R2 value for business performance. It is interpreted that life / food companies are most influenced by success factors and entrepreneurial competency to increase business performance. In the case of Life industry, it is difficult to succeed in business only with technological superiority. It is a very meaningful result by proving that it is an important factor that needs to improve technology marketing capabilities and technology commercialization capabilities. This result can be analyzed to apply in the same context to DIV 3 (IT / SW), which has significantly increased technical performance and financial performance. In the life / food industry, information technology industry, and software industry, socio-economically meaningful results that prove that entrepreneurship, entrepreneurship, and success factors must be continuously learned and applied to business to create business results The results of this study will be provided to the government policy makers for the promotion of youth entrepreneurs and the staff in charge of the government support organizations to create business and technical results without failure even when starting a business. This future research project can be divided into the following three categories. First, it is said that it is necessary to carry out further research on the subdivided technology field along with the materialization of the future technology field, and we intend to carry out future research as an advanced research subject following this study.

Second, to expand the scope of this research to include a wide range of start-up entrepreneurs, early entrepreneurs, re-challenged entrepreneurs, etc. As such, we intend to conduct future research. In addition, it aims to expand the youth entrepreneurs in countries around the world to perform national and industrial journeys.

Third, in the future, it is said that it is necessary to perform additional research by dividing the technical field into a whole frame and dividing it into manufacturing, non-manufacturing, IT, Industry 4.0, Smart Farm & Smart Factory, etc. We want to conduct research. Based on the above results, as a major research topic in the future, the government and industry will focus on digital transformation, digital entrepreneurship, digital innovation, data-driven innovation, new business models, new venture creation & technology ventures for start-up entrepreneurs from around the world. Through intensive cooperation with academics. Based on the results of the above research, cooperation with the government, industry, and academia under the theme "Research on Start-up Entrepreneurs and Digital Transformation, Digital Entrepreneurship, Digital Innovation, Data-Driven Innovation, New Business Models, New Venture Creation & Technology Ventures" Therefore, it will be conducted as a key research in the future.

References

Acs, Z. J., Audretsch, D. B. (1988) "Innovation in large and small firms: an empirical analysis", The American economic review, pp 678-690.

Alaa, N. (1996) "Solutions faibles d'équations paraboliques quasilinéaires avec données initiales mesures", In Annales mathématiques Blaise Pascal, Vol 3, No. 2, pp 1-15.

Autio, E. (1997) "New, technology-based firms in innovation networks symplectic and generative impacts", Research policy, Vol 26, No 3, pp 263-281.

Bailetti, T. (2012) "Technology entrepreneurship: overview, definition, and distinctive aspects", Technology Innovation Management Review, Vol 2, No 2, pp. 5-12.

Bollinger, L., Hope, K. and Utterback, J. M. (1983) "A review of literature and hypotheses on new technology-based firms", Research policy, Vol 12, No 1, pp 1-14.

Booz, Allen and Hamilton. (1982) New product management for the 1980s. New York: BA&H.

Burgelman, R. A., & Sayles, L. R. (2004) "Transforming invention into innovation: the conceptualization stage", Strategic Management of Technology and Innovation. McGraw-Hill, Boston, pp 682-690.

Burgelman, R. M., Wheelwright, M. S. (2004) "Integrating technology and strategy: A general management perspective", Strategic management of technology and innovation 208.

Carland, J. W., Hoy, F. and Boulton, W. R., & Carland, J. C. (1984) "Differentiating small business owners from entrepreneurs", Academy of Management Review, Vol 9, No 2, pp 354-359.

Carr RK. (1994) "Doing technology transfer in federal laboratories", From Lab to Market. Springer, Boston, MA, pp 61-87.

Castka, P., Balzarova, M. A. (2007) "A critical look on quality through CSR lenses: Key challenges stemming from the development of ISO 26000", International Journal of Quality and Reliability Management, Vol 24, No 7, pp 738-752.

Chandler, G. N., & Hanks, S. H. (1994) "Market attractiveness, resource-based capabilities, venture strategies, and venture performance", Journal of business venturing, Vol 9, No 4, pp 331-349.

Chandler, G. N., & Jansen, E. (1992) "The founder's self-assessed competence and venture performance", Journal of Business venturing, Vol 7, No 3, pp 223-236.

Clugston, C. O. (1995) "High-Tech demands own new-product plan", Electronic news, Vol 41, No 2094, pp 33-36.

Cooper, A. C., Willard, G. E. and Woo, C. Y. (1986) "Strategies of high performing new and small firms: A reexamination of the niche concept", Journal of Business Venturing, Vo 1, No 3, pp 247-260.

Dijkstra, T. K. (2010) "Latent variables and indices: Herman Wold's basic design and partial least squares", Handbook of partial least squares. Springer, Berlin, Heidelberg, pp 23-46.

Gulati, R., & Gargiulo, M. (1999) "Where do interorganizational networks come from?", American journal of sociology, Vol 104, No 5, pp 1439-1493.

Hadjimanolis, A. (2000) "A resource-based view of innovativeness in small firms", Technology analysis & Strategic management, Vol 12, No 2, pp 263-281.

Itami, H., & Numagami, T. (1992) "Dynamic interaction between strategy and technology", Strategic Management Journal, Vol 13, No S2, pp 119-135.

Johannisson, B. (1986) "Network strategies: management technology for entrepreneurship and change ", International small business journal, Vol 5, No 1, pp 19-30.

Kaplan, R. S., Norton, D. P. (1996) "Linking the balanced scorecard to strategy", California management review, Vol 39, No 1, pp 53-79.

Kogut, B., Shan, W., and Walker, G. (1992) "The make-or-cooperate decision in the context of an industry network", Networks and organizations, pp 348-65.

Lester, D. H. (1998) "Critical success factors for new product development", Research-Technology Management, Vol 41, No 1, pp 36-43.

McCutchen Jr, W. W, Swamidass, P. M. (1996) "Effect of R&D expenditures and funding strategies on the market value of biotech firms", Journal of Engineering and Technology, Vol 12, No 4, pp 287-299.

Miller, P., & Power, M. (2005) "Calculating corporate failure", Professional Competition and Professional Power. Routledge, pp 65-90.

Smith, K. G, Grimm, C. M. (1987) "Environmental variation, strategic change and firm performance: A study of railroad deregulation", Strategic Management Journal, Vol 8, No 4, pp 363-376.

Souitaris, V. (2002) "Technological trajectories as moderators of firm-level determinants of innovation" Research policy, Vol 31, No 6, pp 877-898.

Westphal, L., Kim, L., and Dahlman, C. J., Rosenberg, N, Frischtak, C. (1985) "International technology transfer: Concepts, measures, and comparisons", pp 167-221.

Wu, L. Y, Wang, C. J, and Chen, C. P, Pan, L. Y. (2008) "Internal Resources, External Network, and Competitiveness during the Growth Stage: A Study of Taiwanese High–Tech Ventures", Entrepreneurship theory and practice, Vol 32, No 3, pp 529-549.

Zahra, S. A, Nielsen, A. P. (2002) "Sources of capabilities, integration and technology commercialization", Strategic Management Journal, Vol 23, No 5, pp 377-398.p 377-398.

Supporting Microenterprises Growth and Innovation by Regional Partnership Model

Anneli Manninen[1] and Tarja Meristö[2]
[1]Estonian Business School, Tallin, Estonia
[2]Laurea University of Applied Sciences, Lohja, Finland
anneli.manninen@laurea.fi
tarja.meristo@laurea.fi
DOI: 10.34190/EIE.20.078

Abstract: Microenterprises are mostly unable to give enough thought for their future business development and innovation. Development Companies' task is to foster growth and development of individual enterprises. At the same time, students and teachers from the Universities of Applied Sciences (UAS) are so engaged in disciplinary content that more advanced skills for entrepreneurship may suffer. We have brought these parties together in order to study how to build a joint holistic co-creation framework. Pedagogical approach Learning by Developing (LbD) action model links learning to applied research, development projects and regional developing. Emphasis is in social interaction, knowledge and competence sharing, researching and problem solving. LbD enhances sharing knowledge, creativity and the contact network of the university with working life. In this study, three Regional Development Companies recruited 43 companies to participate training programme built by Laurea UAS. Simultaneously business field students integrating entrepreneurial competence into their programmes were engaged in the development work. All together 13 thesis and 16 development projects were carried out with enterprises. Student engagement gave microenterprises new perspective for customer and business surface evaluation in addition to entrepreneurial capabilities. The results reveal three different kind of approaches to partnership creation as well as their future development. Critical elements of the model are 1) Equality in partnerships, no sub-contractor roles; 2) Enabling synergy effects for the entrepreneurs to enable joint learning and value creation; 3) Realistic expectations from the students as stakeholding learners and; 4) Ability to meet the demands of rapidly changing environment. Our aim is to create a permanent engagement platform for matching microenterprises' needs with regional development companies' and university's resources and know how. Anticipating future needs and ability to change accordingly has to be built in this model.

Keywords: co-creation, entrepreneurial capabilities, innovation, microenterprises, partnership

1. Background

Regional development is dependent on attracting new enterprises and helping the existing enterprises to develop their businesses. Kurtz (2012) emphasizes the role of entrepreneur in creating innovation and growth. The focus of development and innovation funding has shifted towards small and medium sized enterprises (SMEs). However, in order to create growth there is a lack in number of SMEs in Finland. Thus, growth potential of micro and small enterprises (MSEs) is essential in order to enhance future growth.

Microenterprises are defined (European Commission 2017) as companies with annual headcount less than ten persons and annual turnover less than two million euros. Corresponding figures for small enterprises are 50 employees and ten million euros. In 2018, MSEs represented 93 percentage the companies' establishments in Finland and their share of the personnel was 63.9 % and 52.6 % of total turnover (Official Statistics of Finland 2020).

From the perspective of MSEs as drivers for regional development and welfare, we are building a model to enhance both the individual enterprises' as well as regional possibilities for innovation and growth. In order to do so, cooperation between the UAS and three regional development companies in the Uusimaa region was established. Development companies have wide access to the entrepreneurs in the region. They recruited 35 micro and seven small enterprises to take part in the development project, RADAR, financed by European Regional Development Fund. The initial idea of the model is in picture 1.

Innovation is important for the future survival and growth. At the same time, there exists huge potential for opportunities and growth in microenterprises. However, the lack of capabilities and other resources often inhibit the outburst of this potential. Is it possible, by cooperation of the regional agents and entrepreneurs to build a joint model to enhance innovation and growth? Moreover, what are the critical elements in this?

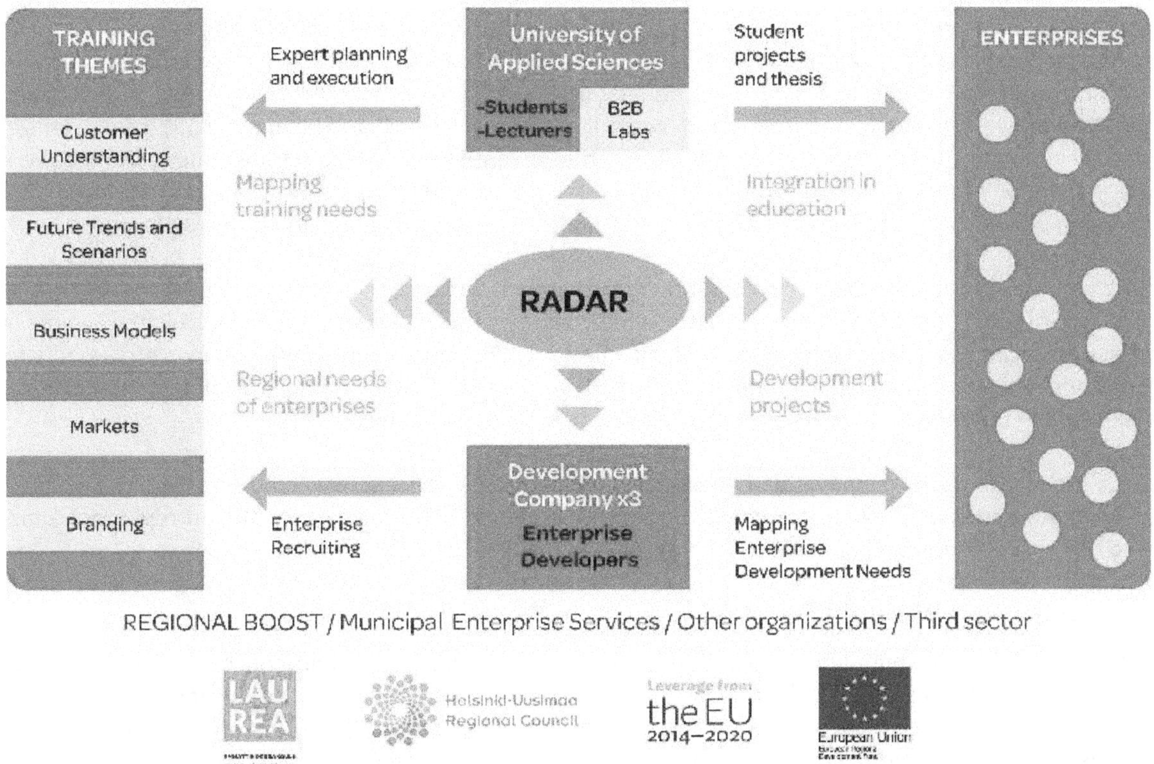

Figure 1: The initial RADAR model construction

We focus on the engagement model building by the main actors. Their interviews aim to discover the best possible future solution for MSEs as well. In addition, we include capability development and innovation as aspects of the regional effort.

2. Framework

The initial framework is based on traditional open innovation thinking where inwards and outward flow of information speeds up internal innovation process and exploration of new markets (Chesbrough Vanhaverbeke and West 2008). Open service innovation (Chesbrough 2011) and further value co-creation (Alam 2006), which has its roots in service design, recognizes service users as significant sources of innovation.

The regional innovation system consists of institutions whose interaction determines the production, diffusion and use of economically useful knowledge. In the cumulative process, innovations result from processes of learning, searching and exploring. In our study, the regional institutions are the regional development companies and the Laurea UAS and the means of knowledge diffusion is LbD action model. The training theme offering for the enterprises consists of five parts: customer understanding, future trends and scenarios, business models, markets and branding. In addition, there is coaching by the Enterprise Developers and development projects by the students.

The permanent action model, that is the final objective, consists of four processes: regional needs of the enterprises, development projects, mapping the training needs and integration in education. The whole model has to be co-created by the main actors and engagement by the stakeholding enterprises, experts and students.

2.1 Innovation and co-creation

Innovation according to Schumpeter (1934) is the main driver of competiveness and economic dynamics. It is divided into five types: new products, methods, market, sources or industry structures. Kahn (2018) introduces three aspects of innovation: innovation as an outcome, as a process and as a mindset. It has individual and cultural aspects. Innovation includes three parts: discover, develop and deliver.

Mason and Brown (2013) recommend a broad view on innovation by co-creation and opportunity recognition enhanced by market engagement. Growth is more a consequence of external environment than internal characteristics of a firm. Thus, external and relational aspects are mediating firm performance. Porter and Heppelmann (2015) predict a radical shift in company functions because of smart connected products. Customer relationships become continuous and open-ended. Intensive cooperation, new forms of cross-functional cooperation or even new functions are needed. According to Polaine Løvlie and Readon (2013), services have to change according to changing needs of people. It becomes essential to combine business models and design as well as innovation processes. In fact, over two-thirds of service innovations arise directly from user involvement (Alam 2006). Value co-creation has capacity to change individual services as well as service systems.

Ramaswamy and Ozcan (2014) regard co-creation as both means and ends in the cycle of outcomes. Interactions are the core of value creation as value is created and evolved jointly with stakeholding individuals. The process includes resources and skills of individuals and organizations. Platforms and agential actions are essential for making connecting and joint value creation possible. Transformative change entails a fundamental change in the mindset of individuals. Co-creative capability building is necessary as well.

Taking a broad approach to innovation is necessary in co-creation keeping in mind that MSEs' challenges are often concrete pieces of innovation process. Creating value and growth means that the entrepreneur aims to expand the firm to its full potential (Elert, Henrekson and Stenkula 2017).

2.1.1 Innovation in small enterprises

Chaston (2010) regards continuous innovation as one of the operational competence needed in delivering strategy. Limited resources of a small firm cause participation in a network important for innovation activities. Filippini, Güttel, and Nosella (2010) have concerned about SMEs' lack of slack resources for developing internal capabilities to observe the environment. Their studies indicate that establishment of social networks and development of trustful environment is prerequisite for absorbing knowledge from outside.

Nybakk (2009) wished to advance knowledge about the factors triggering creativity and innovation in small firms. He found out that entrepreneurial attitude influences innovativeness and performance of microenterprises. There is a positive link between networking and innovativeness as well as indirectly to growth.

Iturrioz, Aragón and Narvaiza (2015) identified drivers to foster the dynamics of shared innovation of SMEs. Safe environment required to share innovation projects is based on trust, reciprocity and long-term commitment. Operationalising the innovation strategy means creating new organisational structures to share the competencies to innovate as well. Innovation should be a common strategic aim for competitiveness in the network. There exists a need for intermediaries with greater resources and executive powers to attract agents for efficient cooperation. Improvements in social capital help to develop shared innovation strategies, reduce costs and risks and guarantee fairness.

Beckett and Chapman (2018) studied innovation in Australian manufacturing SMES. They recognized that continuous innovation depends on the business models and the individual entrepreneurial mindset of the managers and owners. These factors also influence the level and type of purposeful networking together with innovation orientation and vice versa.

There exist only few studies on innovation in microenterprises or MSEs (Tu, Hwang and Wong 2014, Faherty and Stephens 2016, Dunne et al. 2016, Gomes, Mendes and Constantino 2019). Recommended further studies should answer, whether current support structures, networks and clusters can be effectively tailored to the needs of microenterprises. Lahiri (2014) suggest value creation to be used to measure performance.

2.2 Entrepreneurship and entrepreneurial capabilities

Entrepreneurship is defined by Wiklund (1998) as "taking advantage of opportunities by novel combinations of resources in ways which have impact on the market". According to Elert, Henrekson and Stenkula (2017) entrepreneurship is the ability and willingness of individuals to discover and create new economic opportunities, introduce ideas into the market, and create value. Bessant and Tidd (2011) describe the entrepreneurial goal setting and its phases as recognizing the opportunity, finding resources, developing a venture and creating value.

There exists several approaches to capabilities needed in entrepreneurial activities. Miller (1983) developed a scale for measuring the dimensions of entrepreneurship called Entrepreneurial Orientation (EO). The three dimensions are innovation, risk-taking, and proactiveness. It has been the main tool for assessing SMEs' prerequisite for performance. Bradley and Marino (2011) claim that conceptual variation of EO hinders the accumulation of knowledge in the field. They suggest a family of constructs instead. Aminu (2009) considers entrepreneurial orientation to be an antecedent of dynamic capabilities (DCs). DCs facilitate the reconfiguration processes of the firms' existing resources to determine superior performance in unpredicted environments (Helfat et al. 2007). The dimensions of DC are sensing, seizing and managing threats and transforming. Both EO and DC derive from resource-based view.

Entrepreneurial capability (EC) is a distinct set of individual and organizational capabilities, skills and actions to exploit new business opportunities (Alijani 2013). Abdelgawad et al. (2013) highlight the role of EC in achieving and sustaining firm's competitive advantage. EC is anticipating and realizing forthcoming change. However, unlike other dynamic capabilities, the primary contribution of EC is to induce change into the environment to gain an advantage. EC is used to create opportunities, thus it expands the influence and actions of an enterprise beyond its own resources. The four dimensions of EC are sensing, selecting, shaping and synchronizing.

Individual opportunity-recognition processes are crucial for entrepreneurial activities (Shane 2003, Philips and Tracey 2007). They can also enhance learning, adaptation, renewal, and strategy formulation processes of any organizations (Zott and Amit 2007). Resources can be found through cooperation, partnerships and new business models. Moreover, capabilities can be enhanced by joint efforts and learning. In order to be able to induce change MSEs would need to join their forces.

Even though microenterprises form a huge potential for growth and innovation, there is a lack of research in this field. Existing research is mostly connected to different capabilities. Rasmussen and Nybakk (2016) have studied growth drivers in Norwegian micro firewood firms. They found out, that microenterprises differ in how they can configure and exploit their strategic resources. Customer orientation, innovativeness and tenacity were detected to have significant effect on growth. Asad et al. (2018) detected that the size of enterprises moderate the relationship between risk taking and performance, pro-activeness and performance as well as innovation and performance. They also identified both EO and innovation to be very important for improvement in performance of SMEs as well as microenterprises. Entrepreneurial orientation and innovation have been found to be higher in small enterprises than in microenterprises.

2.3 Partnerships

Partnerships are defined as an arrangement between two or more organizations for reaching a shared, where the benefits and risks can be shared (Bendell 2011). Strategic partnership aims to combine knowledge capital in order to gain significant strategic advantage (Ståhle and Laento 2000). Eddy and Amey (2015) describe strategic partnerships to be a conscious choice to achieve strategic objectives, specify priorities as well as support change in the partner organizations. Successful partnerships enable value creation, protect the partners' interests and facilitate change (De Mann 2013). The main requirement for selecting partners is to understand the needs of the customers.

Andersen (2008) describes partnerships as ideal modes of collaboration. The concept is defined by structural and binding collaboration, which includes equal influence, common development activities, dialogue-based collectivity and community as well as equality, trust and respect. Creating a partnership model has six basic questions (Ala-Mutka 2008): aim, competitive position, offering, revenue model, value network and capabilities. The answers help to create understanding of value creation. Partnerships between companies and public organizations aim at collaborative advantage (Huxman and Vangen 2004). Common basis for collaborative advantage are access to resources, shared risk, efficiency, coordination, learning and moral imperative. Strategic alliances are cooperative inter-firm agreements, which aim at creating competitive advantages for all parties involved (Das and Teng 2000). Alliances are formal relationship, which give enterprises access to the resources they need for innovation and growth.

In interaction with partners, entrepreneurs can access new information and knowledge or learn about new opportunities. Strategic alliances are a gateway to important external knowledge for SMEs (Shepherd and Patzelt 2018). They provide the access to new ideas and innovation (Dyer and Singh 1998) and knowledge about markets

(Anand, Glick and Manz 2002). According to Iturrioz, Aragón and Narvaiza (2015) SMEs need to open up for cooperation to develop sustainable cooperative advantage. Shared innovation is only achievable in specific social context. Intermediaries, such as education institutions are necessary for extracting value from the social resources as well as to enhance shared innovation among the companies.

Partnerships are important in this study for two reasons: First, the regional model and platforms are built together with several organisations. Second, the aim of the new model is to give microenterprises access to knowledge of other stakeholders as well. Studies on regional partnerships, which focus on shared value creation or regional business development and innovation, are rare.

3. Methodology

The research uses qualitative approach. Qualitative research is an iterative process between research ideas, theoretical concepts, research design, data collection, analysis and findings (Eriksson and Kovalainen 2011). The research question is defined how to build a regional cooperation model for enhancing microenterprises' growth. The main aim is to understand how the main actors define the regional framework for enhancing business development of microenterprises now and in the future.

3.1 Data collection

Theme interviews were used as the data collection method. According to Patton (2002) thematic interviews are an appropriate method for holistic information acquisition in qualitative research. It favours human beings as the means of information gathering. The themes list those topics, which are to be shed light on during the interview. The themes were gathered around the model and actors' roles anticipated benefits for different stakeholders. The interviewees were persons working in close connection to the participating enterprises. Interviews were recorded and transcripted.

3.2 Data analysis

Thematic interview content is easily dividable into themes (Tuomi and Sarajärvi 2009). The content is divided into categories using inductive reasoning. In practice, small phrases describing the phenomenon are gathered and classified. We looked for sentences describing the cooperation or different actors. Analysis of the interview content forms the basis for understanding, describing and modelling the phenomenon at hand.

The researchers categorized the original transcribed interviews independently. In the second phase, the main categories were agreed together. After that, the second level subcategories were jointly agreed. Main characteristics for the subcategory were selected from the sentences describing it. Limited scope unable showing examples of these sentences.

4. Findings

The findings are divided in two different interpretations. First, the classification of the interview data into different categories and subcategories is presented. Second, the different partnership approaches with example sentences will follow.

4.1 Categories for modelling

Main categories found by the analysis of the interview data are the following: shared identity, model building, enterprises, students and fields of knowledge. They are further divided into subcategories together with their short descriptions. The whole classification is shown in table 1.

Table 1: Categories, subcategories and their description

Main category	Subcategory	Description
Shared identity	Region	Cultural and geographical closeness, acquaintance and easiness
	Municipalities	Business promotion, developmental actions, financing, strategic choices
	Development companies UAS	Customer understanding, development projects, problem areas, co-creation, territory
Model building	Understanding each other	Consciousness, informal frequent cooperation, knowing each other, trust

Main category	Subcategory	Description
	Relevant development projects	Authenticity, practical applied science approach, learning possibilities
	Platforms and decisions needed	Contact persons, fees, experts, finding students
	Enablers	Management and municipalities commitment, contracts and plans, resources, partnership, network, processes, wider ecosystem, productization
Enterprises	Motivation	commitment, enthusiasm, networking
	Learning	Multidiciplinarity, difference, new areas of expertise, ideas and conversations, readiness for competence development, learning from others, wider thinking, further development of thinking and doing
	Capabilities development	Anticipating changes, ideation, mutual sparring, new solutions, business development, equal discussions
	Systematic approach	Individuality, emerging developmental needs, development path, resources, networking, mini ecosystems, other actors
Students	As a resource	Competence, tutoring, access, products
	Motivation	Benefit, being of use and help, own subject field
	Entrepreneurial understanding	Learning, transferable skills for entrepreneurship, orientation, mindset
Fields of Knowledge	Selling	Branding
	Customer understanding	Service design, mapping customer needs
	Marketing	Digital marketing, social media

4.2 Partnership approaches

Three main approaches for cooperation between the UAS and development companies were detected. They are subcontracting, developing joint offering and strategic partnership.

Subcontracting was identifiable by the partners: Development companies consider the student work as an independent part, which is useful anyway. UAS gains access to the development projects to use them fot their own educational purposes.

> *"All of these training themes are new for most of the companies. At least they gain readiness for developing their capabilities."*
>
> *"In a way we would have a channel for both direction. The enterprises need those development projects by the students, and the student need the jobs."*
>
> *"Development companies give leads to us, that is, in away suitable projects and cases are directed to Laurea."*

Joint offering is an approach where the productization of the development package is developed together:

> *"It is very difficult for small companies to engage time for thinking. I fancy this cooperation where we jointly operate at the enterprise interface to support them."*
>
> *"It really could be this kind of a package, a joint product."*

The strategic partnership approach was brought out when thinking the customer needs in the future. Joint process development would primarily optimize the content for customers:

> *"Even so that we would all see the whole picture and would be able to have impact on the contribution of other parties as well. This would be good to do. And kind of us to know, what this regional design is."*

5. In conclusion

Several public sector enterprises are together responsible for the regional model building. Primary focus was in their views on the process. Their experts and students participate in the value creation process. Entrepreneurs are stakeholding co-creators in their own as well as joint value creation.

Obviously, there is still huge variation in mindset from subcontracting to more strategic approach. Partnership closes to co-creation and joint value creation when focusing on enterprises' needs. Evolving technical, social, and organizational architectures together with several organizations is challenging. It requires joint mindset and capability ecosystem. Therefore, the first step should be to agree on the partnership approach.

Interviewees brought clearly out informal cooperation, which would hardly give an accessible and transparent solution. Therefore, we conclude that model building requires

- 1) Equality in partnerships, no sub-contractor roles;
- 2) Enabling synergy effects for the entrepreneurs to enable joint learning and value creation;
- 3) Realistic expectations from the students as stakeholding learner and not a consultant;
- 4) Ability to meet the demands of rapidly changing environment and capability ecosystem.

Value creation requires strategic partnership by the enabling organizations (De Man 2013), access to resources, shared risk, efficiency, coordination, learning and even moral imperative (Huxman and Vangen 2004). Structural binding collaboration includes equal influence, common development activities, dialogue-based community as well as equality, trust and respect (Andersen 2008). These cannot be attained by subcontracting model.

Anticipating changes, finding new solutions and business development were capabilities found further developed. Enterprises also found mutual sparring, learning from others and networking valuable for their learning and development. This is in line with both co-creation and EC approaches anticipating and realizing forthcoming change (Alijani 2013, Abdelgawad et al. 2013). Both are essential for innovation and growth of microenterprises and regions as well. Important fields of knowledge found were customer understanding, sales and marketing. This is in accordance with the findings of Mason and Brown (2013).

6. Theoretical and managerial implications

Co-creation framework is clearly adaptable for this action research type of work. The permanent engagement platform should able productive and meaningful interaction for collaborative innovation. Co-creation and joint innovation process appear to be the value creation system, which brings benefits for multiple stakeholders as well.

Guidelines and decisions are needed in order to bring the joint action model forward. Multi-stakeholder system is not easy to coordinate and needs clear set of roles especially when opening the network for wider group of entrepreneurs. Deepening joint customer understanding capabilities is highly important as well.

When the entrepreneurs, experts and students are stakeholders in value co-creation, unrealistic expectations are not justified. The main task in model development and management is to take care of equal and fair treatment of all parties. It must also enable flexible adaptation to the altering needs of the microenterprises in the region. It is clear that substantial changes are due in management. Orchestrating a joint co-creation effort is demanding not to speak about creating a joint mindset for all the stakeholders. Serving different industries would require administrating more specified flow of expertise.

Permanent engagement model is to change according to the altering customer needs. It should also be sustainable structure maintaining offering for MSEs in the region. This requires a lot from management systems and structures.

7. Limitations and future research

Some findings of this study may be useful for other districts, but on average different strategies apply and promote entrepreneurship and economic growth in different countries and clusters (Elert et al. 2017). The study is the first step in the regional co-creation model building and thus very limited in scope. In the future, we will study in more depth the experience and future expectations of the entrepreneurs as well as other stakeholders.

Specific needs of different fields of industry were not included because of the multi-field approach. Whether this approach is better for the innovation of the enterprises and region remains to be investigated. Different time perspectives and priorities of the participants are to be taken into account in further research as well. One could also study further the possibilities of collaborative networks in this shared innovation context.

References

Abdelgawad, S.G., Zahra, S.A., Svejenova S. and Sapienza, H.J. (2013) "Strategic leadership and entrepreneurial capability for game change", *Journal of Leadership and Organizational Studies*, Vol 20, No 4, pp 394–407.

Ala-Mutka, J. (2008) *Strategy Model*, Talentum Media, Helsinki.

Alam, I. (2006) "Removing the Fuzziness from the Fuzzy Front-End of Service Innovations Through Consumer Interactions", *Industrial Marketing Management*, Vol 35, pp 468–480.

Alijani S. (2013) "Entrepreneurial Capability and Leadership", In: Carayannis E.G. (Eds) *Encyclopedia of Creativity, Invention, Innovation and Entrepreneurship*, Springer, New York, pp 18–58.

Aminu, M.I. (2016) "Building Dynamic Capabilities through Entrepreneurial Orientation", *International Journal of Organizational & Business Excellence*, Vol.1, No 2, pp 1–14.

Anand, V., Glick, W.H. and Manz, C.C. (2002) "Thriving on the knowledge of outsiders: Tapping organizational social capital", *The Academy of Management Executive*, Vol 16, No. 1, pp 87–101.

Andersen, N.Å. (2008) *Partnerships: Machines of possibility*, The Policy Press, Bristol.

Asad, M., Shabbir, M. S., Salman, R., Haider, S. H. and Ahmad, I. (2018) "Do entrepreneurial orientation and size of enterprise influence the performance of micro and small enterprises? A study on mediating role of innovation", *Management Science Letters*, Vol 8, No. 10, pp 1015–1026.

Beckett, R.C. and Chapman, R.L. (2018) "Business model and innovation orientation in manufacturing SMES: An Australian multi-case study", *Journal of Innovation Management*, Vol 6, No. 1, pp 111–134.

Bendell, J. (2011) *Evolving Partnerships: A Guide to Working with Business for Greater Social Change*, Greenleaf Publishing, Sheffield.

Bessant, J. and Tidd, J. (2011) *Innovation and Entrepreneurship*, Wiley, Chichester.

Bradley, A.G. and Marino, L. (2011) "The Epistemology of Entrepreneurial Orientation: Conceptual Formation, Modelling, and Operationalization", *Entrepreneurship Theory and Practice*, Vol 35, No. 5, pp 989–1024.

Chaston, I. (2010) *Entrepreneurial Management in Small Firms*, Sage Publications, London.

Chesbrough, H.W. (2011) *Open services innovation: rethinking your business to grow and compete in a new era*, Jossey-Bass, San Francisco.

Chesbrough, H., Vanhaverbeke, W. and West, J. eds. (2008) *Open Innovation: Researching a New Paradigm*, Oxford University Press, New York

Das, T. K. and Teng, B. (2000) "A Resource-Based Theory of Strategic Alliances", Journal of Management, Vol 26 No. 1, pp 31–61.

De Man, A.-P. (2013) Alliance: Executive Guide to Designing Successful Strategic Partnerships, John Wiley &Sons, Chicester. pp. 21–22.

Dunne, T. C., Aaron, J. R., Mcdowell, W. C., Urban, D. J. and Geho, P. R. (2016) "The impact of leadership on small business innovativeness", *Journal of Business Research*, Vol 69, No. 11, pp 4876–4881.

Dyer, J.H. and Singh, H. 1998. The relational view: Cooperative Strategy and sources of interorganizational competitive advantage. The Academy of Management Review 23 (4), 1998, 660 – 679.

Eddy, P.L. and Amey, M.J. (2014) Creating Strategic Partnership: A Guide for Educational Institutions and Their Partners. Stylus Publishing, Sterling.

Elert, N., Henrekson, M. and Stenkula, M. (2017*) Institutional Reform for Innovation and Entrepreneurship*, Springer International Publishing, Cham.

Eriksson, P. and Kovalainen, A. (2011) Qualitative Methods in Business Research, SAGE Publications, London.

European Commission (2017) *User guide to SME Definition*. Publication Office of the European Commission.

Faherty, U, and Stephens, S. (2016) Innovation in micro enterprises: reality or fiction? *Journal of Small Business and Enterprise Development*, Vol 23, No. 2, pp 349–362.

Filippini, R., Güttel, W.H. and Nosella, A. (2010) "Enhancing Competences for Competitive Advantage", *Advances in Applied Business Strategy*, Vol 12, pp 63–86.

Gomes, R. R. M., Mendes, D. R. F. and Constantino, M. (2019) "Degree if Innovation in Micro-enterprises and Small Enterprises (MSE) of the Federal Dictrict (DF): A study of innovation radar" *Economia & Região*, Vol 6, No. 2, pp 157–169.

Helfat, C. Finkelstein, S. Mitchell, W. Peteraf, M. Singh, H. Teece, D. and Winter, S. (2007) *Dynamic Capabilities: Understanding Strategic Change in organization,* Blackwell Publishing, Oxford.

Huxham, C. and Vangen, S. (2004) Managing to Collaborate: The Theory and Practice of Collaborative Advantage, Routledge, Abingdon.

Iturrioz, C, Aragón, C. and Narvaiza, L. (2015) "How to foster shared innovation within SME' networks: Social capital and the role of intermediaries", *European Management Journal*, Vol 33, pp 104–115.

Kahn, K.B. (2018) "Understanding Innovation", *Business Horizons*, Vol 61, pp 453–460.

Kurtz, H.D. (2012) *Innovation, Knowledge and Growth: Adam Smith, Schumpeter and the moderns*, Routledge, London.

Lahiri, D. (2014) "Identifying 'anchor' micro-enterprises - an empirical study*", Journal of Small Business & Entrepreneurship,* Vol 27, No 1, pp 1–26.

Mason, C. and Brown, R. (2013) "Creating good public policy to support high-growth firms", *Small Business Economics*, Vol 40, No. 2, pp 211–225.

Miller, D. (1983) "The correlates of entrepreneurship in three types of firms", *Management Science*, Vol 29, No. 7, pp 770–791.

Nybakk, E. (2009) *Innovation and entrepreneurship in small firms: The influence of entrepreneurial attitudes, external relationships and learning orientation*, Department of Economics and Resource Management, Norwegian University of Life Sciences, Ås.

Official Statistics Finland (OSF) (2020) "Enterprises by industry and categories of personnel size 2013 – 2018", Statistics Finland, Helsinki, [database accessed 10.3.2020].

Patton, M.Q. (2002) *Qualitative Research & Evaluation Methods*, Sage Publications Inc., Thousand Oaks.

Phillips N. and Tracey P. (2007) "Opportunity recognition, entrepreneurial capabilities and bricolage: connecting institutional theory and entrepreneurship in strategic organization", *Strategic Organization*, Vol 5, No 3, pp 313–320.

Piperopoulos, P. G. 2011. *Entrepreneurship, Innovation and Business Clusters.* Ashgate Publising Ltd.

Polaine, A., Løvlie, L. and Readon, B. (2013) *Service Design From Insight to Implementation*, Rosenfeld Media, New York.

Porter, M.E. and Heppelmann, J.E. (2015) "How smart connected products are transforming companies", *Harvard Business Review*, October 2015, pp 97–114.

Ramaswamy, V. and Ozcan, K. (2014) *The Co-Creation Paradigm*, Stanford University Press, Stanford.

Rasmussen, C. and Nybakk, E. (2016) "Growth drivers in low technology micro firms", *International Journal of Entrepreneurship and Innovation Management,* Vol 20, No. 3-4, pp 258–277 .

Schumpeter, J.A. (1934) The theory of economic development: an inquiry into profits, capital, credit, interest and the business cycle, *Harvard Economic Studies*, Vol 46, Harvard College: Cambridge.

Shane, S.A. (2003) *A general theory of entrepreneurship: the individual-opportunity nexus*, Edward Elgar, Cheltenham.

Shepherd, D.A, and Patzelt, H. (2018) *Entrepreneurial Cognition, Exploring the Mindset of Entrepreneurs*, Palgrave Macmillan, Cham.

Ståhle, P. and Laento, K. (2000) *Strateginen kumppanuus – avain uudistumiskykyyn ja ylivoimaan. (Strategic Partnership – key for renewal and excellance),* WSOY, Helsinki.

Tu, C., Hwang, S. and Wong, J. (2014) "How does cooperation affect innovation in micro-enterprises? ", *Management Decision*, Vol 52, No. 8, pp 1390–1409.

Tuomi, J. and Sarajärvi, A. (2009) *Laadullinen tutkimus ja sisällönanalyysi. (Qualitative Research and Content Analysis*). Kustannusosakeyhtiö Tammi, Helsinki.

Wiklund, J. (1998) *Small Firm Growth and Performance: Entrepreneurship and Beyond*, Doctoral Thesis, Jönköping International Business School, Jönköping.

Zott, C., and Amit, R. (2007) "Business model design and the performance of entrepreneurial firms", *Organization Science*, Vol 18, No. 2, pp 181–199.

Exploration of the Role of Immigrant Entrepreneurs in Regional Entrepreneurial Food Ecosystems

Anna Murphy[1], Joe Bogue[2] and Brian O'Flaherty[3]
[1]Department of Biological Sciences, School of Science and Informatics, Cork Institute of Technology, Ireland
[2]Department of Food Business and Development, Cork University Business School, University College Cork, Ireland
[3]Department of Business Information Systems, Cork University Business School, University College Cork, Ireland
anna.murphy@cit.ie
J.Bogue@ucc.ie
b.oflaherty@ucc.ie
DOI: 10.34190/EIE/20.214

Abstract: Entrepreneurship is a key driver of economies through the creation of new opportunities and business ventures. Immigrant entrepreneurs have enriched global economies, particularly in high tech industries (Fairlie, 2008) and face numerous challenges in their host country. For small to medium sized enterprises, strategic networking in entrepreneurial ecosystems, creating rich resources, is vital to minimise these challenges (McAdam and Soetanto, 2018). These entrepreneurial ecosystems consist of interdependent actors and other factors integrated in a way that enables entrepreneurship within a particular region (Stam and Spigel, 2018). The objective of this research is to analyse the factors that contribute to the existence of entrepreneurial ecosystems in the Irish food industry and the types of networking immigrant food entrepreneurs participate in within these ecosystems. This methodology consisted of a quantitative empirical study using a questionnaire administered to immigrant food entrepreneurs in the Munster region of Ireland, selected through purposive sampling. The findings highlighted that these immigrant food entrepreneurs originated from 26 different countries, the majority founded their own business, with some businesses established over 40 years. The existence of different types of entrepreneurial food ecosystems and contrasting success factors are emerging in this research. The support of local farmer's markets and the community spirit with local producers leading to formal and informal networking for exchange knowledge and social engagement is vital for some immigrant food entrepreneurs, with support from entrepreneurial agencies driving the entrepreneurial ecosystem proving a greater importance for others. Entrepreneurial food ecosystems give immigrants, who do not have the same access to the employment market, an opportunity to make a living which was evident in this research where the immigrant food entrepreneurs demonstrated high levels of self-efficacy in terms of their contribution to local economies. Immigrants also enhance diversity in the food industry and give local consumers an opportunity to experience international and ethnic food experiences. This research provides a deeper understanding of immigrant entrepreneurs and their strategic networking and adds to research on how the model of entrepreneurial ecosystems can be utilised to measure the diversity and density of these networks.

Keywords: entrepreneurial ecosystems, immigrant entrepreneurs, entrepreneurship, food industry, networking

1. Introduction

This paper explores the role of immigrant entrepreneurs and how they network in regional entrepreneurial food ecosystems. Immigrant entrepreneurs have enriched global economies with reported evidence of significant socio-economic benefits by immigrants to international business incomes, employment and innovation through high levels of self-employment, particularly evident in technology, engineering and ICT sectors (Saxenian, 1999; Fairlie, 2008; Lofstrom, 2017; Drinkwater, 2018). The global food industry has also been heavily influenced by immigrant entrepreneurs resulting in a wide range of ethnic food choices available in all countries worldwide. This global food industry consists of a high proportion of small to medium sized enterprises (SMEs) which contributes widely to rural economies (McKitterick *et al.*, 2016). This paper is structured as follows. Firstly, literature on immigrant entrepreneurs, networks and entrepreneurial ecosystems will be reviewed. This is followed by the research objective and questions, the methodology, presentation of results, discussion of these results and a conclusion. This paper will conclude with the limitations of this research and suggestions for future research.

1.1 Immigrant entrepreneurs

Immigrant entrepreneurs are heterogeneous, often considered more heterogeneous that indigenous entrepreneurs and especially entrepreneurial (Lofstrom, 2017) partly due to their migration to a host country. However, their heterogeneity makes it more challenging for researchers and policy makers to understand how and why they engage in networks. Entrepreneurs possess varying characteristics that influence their entrepreneurial decisions, with education and prior work experience considered important determinants of self-employment (Altinay and Wang, 2011; Drinkwater, 2018). Altinay and Wang (2011, p. 685) reported that a third level education enhanced an entrepreneur's ability to *"synthesise the market intelligence"* leading to increased innovation. In contrast, however, Drinkwater (2018) argued that higher education created greater opportunities for immigrants in paid employment, reducing their rate of self-employment. Prior experience is reported to develop the intellectual framework of the entrepreneur, to help manage risk associated with entrepreneurial behaviour and discover more entrepreneurial opportunities (Altinay and Wang, 2011). Entrepreneurs face several barriers or challenges when establishing a business and additionally immigrants encounter extra challenges when they relocate to another country. These challenges include access to finance, often cited as the most significant barrier to entrepreneurship, lack of business connections, lack of trust, lack of knowledge of support agencies, lack of familiarity with the legal environment and a language barrier (McKitterick *et al.* 2016; Drinkwater, 2018). The impact of these challenges can be minimised through engagement of immigrant entrepreneurs with other actors via strategic networking.

1.2 Networks

To facilitate engagement between immigrant entrepreneurs and other actors, connections or relationships are necessary through networking, formally or informally, forming strong or weak ties (McAdam and Soetanto, 2018). Actors in networks vary from other business individuals, family members and formal entrepreneurial and state organisations. They assist entrepreneurs source resources, by exchanging information or incremental knowledge, access finance, increase trust and feelings of respect and reciprocity among members and reduce risk for the business (Saxenian, 1999; McKitterick *et al.* 2016). Identification of the correct agencies to obtain support from, and how to access these supports, was reported as problematic for entrepreneurs where *"a lack of cohesion or joined-up approach between institutional actors"* was described as a factor contributing to the uncertainty about appropriate agencies (McKitterick *et al.* 2016, p. 46).

To facilitate engagement with the relevant actors, strategic networking is important to ensure that there are no barriers that restricts resource flow. This is particularly important for SMEs, where they may lack the necessary competencies or skills to participate in a network and consequently fail to form strategic or dynamic networks to convert *"limited resources into rich resources"* (McAdam and Soetanto, 2018, p. 88). As entrepreneurs can behave in an *"adaptive way"*, they rely on their local environment where they interact through their various connections (Alvedalen and Boschma (2017, p. 893) which is important for immigrants when they set up and embed in a locality. Initially, social networking is an essential component to allow them to become part of the local structure and to identify opportunities, but formal business networks are necessary for immigrant entrepreneurs to grow and expand their business, through mentoring and growing contacts (Saxenian, 1999). Networking as a result is important on a regional basis with different actors involved on a formal or informal basis.

1.3 Entrepreneurial ecosystems

The elements of the entrepreneur, formal support institutions and networks can be combined together through their interdependency into an organised structure such as an entrepreneurial ecosystem which has been defined as *"a set of interdependent actors and factors coordinated in such a way that they enable productive entrepreneurship within a particular territory"* (Mason and Brown, 2014, p. 5). Stam and Spigel (2018, p. 409) reported that entrepreneurial ecosystems were intrinsically geographical in nature and focused on the *"cultures, institutions and networks"* that develop over time in specific regional areas, with the level and type of connectivity between actors determining the strength and success of entrepreneurial ecosystems. However, there are limitations or weaknesses in research on the concept of entrepreneurial ecosystems. Alvedalen and Boschma (2017, p. 894) stated that existing literature had not yet produced a detailed approach to networks that would help identify why some entrepreneurial ecosystems were successful through making those *"vital connections"* and suggested that the network literature could potentially enrich the concept of entrepreneurial ecosystems Stangler and Bell-Masterson (2015) similarly agreed that the analysis of networks would be beneficial in terms of tracking the connectivity of the different organisations in the network. Acs, Stam and Audretsch, (2017, p. 9) further suggested that added research was needed in areas of *"resourcing, network interactions, power relationships and cultural or social fit among actors within the entrepreneurial ecosystem"* and argued that the apparent heterogeneity among the actors made it difficult for policy makers to target specific areas for improvement.

The research objective of this paper is to determine if an entrepreneurial ecosystem is a valid perspective for understanding the experiences of immigrant food entrepreneurs. In Ireland, the agri-food sector is its largest indigenous industry, with revenues of €26 Billion in 2015 and consisting mainly of SMEs (DAFM, 2015). Traditionally, the food sector in Ireland consisted mainly of indigenous businesses but an increasing number have been established by immigrant entrepreneurs which is consistent with global trends where the rate of nascent or new business establishment is higher in foreign born than native born persons (Lofstrom, 2017). The entrepreneurial ecosystem lens has been applied extensively in research to study high-tech or high growth businesses but there is a gap in the literature in the application of this lens to smaller scaled enterprises. This creates an opportunity to research immigrant entrepreneurs and explore how they interact in regional food networks, to give a greater understanding of entrepreneurial ecosystems and to guide policy makers.

The study addresses the following research questions.

RQ1: How do the characteristics of immigrant entrepreneurs influence their networking with other actors in a regional area?
RQ2: How do immigrant entrepreneurs perceive their role and that of other actors in the context of an entrepreneurial ecosystem structure?

These research questions are addressed using the following methodology.

2. Methodology

This research adopted a quantitative approach involving a questionnaire administered to immigrant food entrepreneurs in the Munster region of Ireland, consisting of six counties, Cork, Kerry, Limerick, Clare, Waterford and Tipperary. Purposive sampling was utilised to select this geographical region due to its long history of food production (Patton, 2002). As no official directory of food producers existed for this region, the population sample of immigrant food producers was identified from varying sources including regional food organisations, Bord Bia (Irish Food Board) and farmers markets. From these sources, a population sample of over 170 immigrant food entrepreneurs was identified. These entrepreneurs were contacted to request their participation in the research study. Several of the entrepreneurs were no longer in operation, some did not respond to the request and a small number declined to participate due to time constraints.

A sample population agreed to participate in this study and a quantitative questionnaire was administered to 119 immigrant entrepreneurs at farmer's markets, food specific events and various food festivals in the Munster region. A total of 82 questionnaires were completed providing a 69% response rate. This quantitative approach was selected for the initial stage of this study to gain an understanding of how variables, that were identified in previous research on entrepreneurship and entrepreneurial ecosystems, influence how and why these immigrant food entrepreneurs' networked and participated in entrepreneurial ecosystems (Creswell and Creswell, 2018). This questionnaire was designed into thematic areas including characteristics of entrepreneurs, business establishment challenges, networking and entrepreneurial ecosystems. The self-administered questionnaire was administered offline, either directly to the entrepreneur at food events or farmer's markets or posted to increase the level of convenience for the respondents as many were under time constraints (Bryman, 2016). For the purpose of this research study, an immigrant food entrepreneur is defined as a first- or second-generation immigrant, who has established a food manufacturing business in the Munster region of Ireland. The quantitative data obtained from the questionnaires was coded and inputted into IBM SPSS Statistics 26 for statistical analysis and the qualitative data inputted into Microsoft Excel and was analysed thematically, corresponding to the research questions (Creswell and Creswell, 2018).

3. Results

3.1 Characteristics of immigrant entrepreneurs

As is outlined in Table 1, the immigrant food entrepreneurs in this study were heterogeneous in nature, with a broad age profile ranging from 18 to 65+ years, and an equal number of males and females. The majority (95.1%) founded their own food business and several had prior experience of running a business or being employed in another business, prior to establishing their existing business. Most of the food businesses (72%) were considered established businesses, being established for more than 4 years. There was a high number of female business owners for newly established businesses. In terms of education, 76.8% had attained a post-secondary qualification and 19.5% had attained a postgraduate degree. They originated from 26 countries and were located mainly in two counties of the Munster region. They produced a diverse range of food products and sold these products mainly at farmer's markets, food events and speciality food stores.

Table 1: Profile of Immigrant Food Entrepreneurs

Characteristic of Immigrant Entrepreneur (n = 82)	Percentage of Immigrant Entrepreneurs
Age of Entrepreneur	18-29 - 2.4%; 30-39 - 18.3%; 40-49 - 30.5%; 50-64 - 35.4%; 65+ - 9.8%
Formation of Business	Founder of own business (95.1%); took over established business (2.4%); took over family business (2.4%)
Time business established	Established business (>4 years) (72%); New Business (<4 years) (27%)
Gender	Male (48.8%); Female (47.6%); Both (1.2%); no reply (3.7%)
Country of Origin	UK (34.1%); France (11%); Germany (8.5%); Poland (6.1%); Italy (4.9%); Canada, America and Netherlands (3.7%); Australia (2.4%); remaining 17 countries (1.2% each)
County Location	Cork (56.1%); Limerick (1.22%); Kerry (19.51%); Clare (7.32%); Waterford (3.66%); Tipperary (6.1%); outside Munster but trading in Munster (4.88%)
Level of Education	Post-secondary (76.8%); Undergraduate degree (31.7%); Postgraduate degree (19.5%)
Prior work experience	Owned own business in home country (22%) and in Ireland before setting up current food business (16%); employed in a business in Ireland (56%)
Number of employees	No employees (37.8%); <10 employees (90.2%); < 50 employees (100%)
Income in previous year	<€100,000 (77.5%); <€2,000,000 (97.5%); >€2,000,001 (2.4%)

All these immigrant food entrepreneurs had established SMEs, with the majority (90.2%) considered micro enterprises, employing less than 10 staff and having a turnover less than €2,000,000, as seen in Table 1.

3.2 Networking

In relation to the importance of networking, over 63% of the immigrant entrepreneurs considered it important for their business. The heterogeneous engagement by these entrepreneurs in formal and informal networks was demonstrated by the diversity of actors they networked with. Informal networking with family, friends and local food producers and formal networking with entrepreneurship specific support agencies and regional specific food agencies were considered important for their business. Family members were valued in terms of business advice, finance and assisting sales and distribution. Most of the producers (78%) networked with indigenous or local producers and some networking was evident with food producers from their own and different nationalities. This networking with other producers occurred through various means, including in person and through social media, on a frequent basis where almost half (44%) networked once a week or more. Networking with other food producers was in response to different needs which ranged from social purposes to multiple business purposes that included sourcing of ingredients, knowledge exchange, mentoring and distribution.

In relation to networking with formal entrepreneurial and educational organisations, 24% of producers reported no networking, with time reported as the main constraint, followed by poor support and entrepreneurial agencies being too money focused. As is evident in Figure 1, Local Enterprise Offices (LEOs) (government organisations in Ireland, operating at regional level, to promote entrepreneurship and develop micro and small businesses), banks and county specific food support organisations were the main formal stakeholders the immigrant entrepreneurs networked with for business. Enterprise Ireland (a government organisation responsible for the development and growth of Irish enterprises in global markets) and Area Partnerships, regional business support organisations in Ireland, were the main organisations least engaged with for business support.

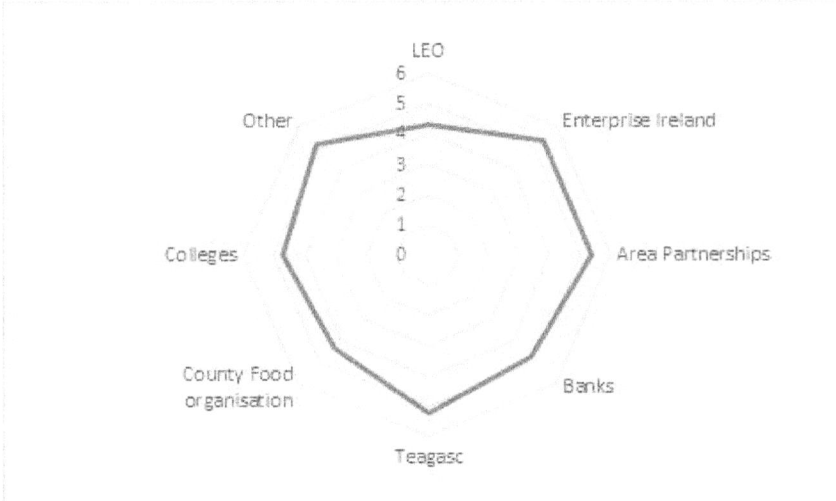

Figure 1: Mean frequency values for networking with formal support organisations

1 = most frequent (weekly); 5 = less than once a year; 6 = no networking

3.3 Entrepreneurial ecosystems

The majority of the immigrant food entrepreneurs (56%) stated they perceived an entrepreneurial ecosystem existed in their region. In term of geographical dispersion within the Munster region, most of the immigrant entrepreneurs located in Tipperary (100%), Waterford (100%) and Cork (66.7%) positively perceived the existence of an entrepreneurial ecosystem. The perceived presence of an entrepreneurial ecosystem was attributed to local food producers in some regions, for instance "great producers in our area", "multi-cultural artisan food production hotspot", "I am part of an artisan food culture in my region", " we have been strongly supported by other producers and the community", "we are lucky to have local food producers with great community spirit". Other attributing factors to the presence of an entrepreneurial ecosystem included farmer's markets and the presence and support of LEOs. A high proportion (67.1%) of the immigrant entrepreneurs sold their products at farmer's markets, which in part explained the importance of these as sales outlets for their food products. Of the immigrant entrepreneurs who agreed they perceived an entrepreneurial ecosystem existed, 90.9% agreed that an entrepreneurial spirit existed among food producers ($p<0.05$) which was particularly evident in Cork, Clare and Kerry. They were marginally more likely to attend formal networking events and a higher proportion (81.8%) knew what organisation to obtain business support from compared to those who did not know or only sometimes knew (18.2%) ($p<0.05$). In contrast, the immigrant entrepreneurs who did not perceive an entrepreneurial ecosystem existed cited reasons such as "programmes hard to reach" and "aware of its existence in other regions but not in mine".

With regards the immigrant's entrepreneurs' agreement with the level of support provided by formal support organisations, there was very strong evidence to show a relationship between perception of an entrepreneurial ecosystem and the support from financial and educational organisations ($p<0.05$) as is evident in figure 2. Entrepreneurial support organisations were also considered important. This correlated with findings on the frequency of networking with different agencies where banks and Area Partnerships were on average engaged with less than once a year as is evident in figure 1. In contrast, insufficient entrepreneurial resources and entrepreneurial and training programmes were perceived in some regions. The immigrant entrepreneurs who perceived a presence of an entrepreneurial ecosystem indicated a higher level of agreement overall with supports from formal organisations and the presence of resources and programmes in their regions than those who did not perceive an entrepreneurial ecosystem.

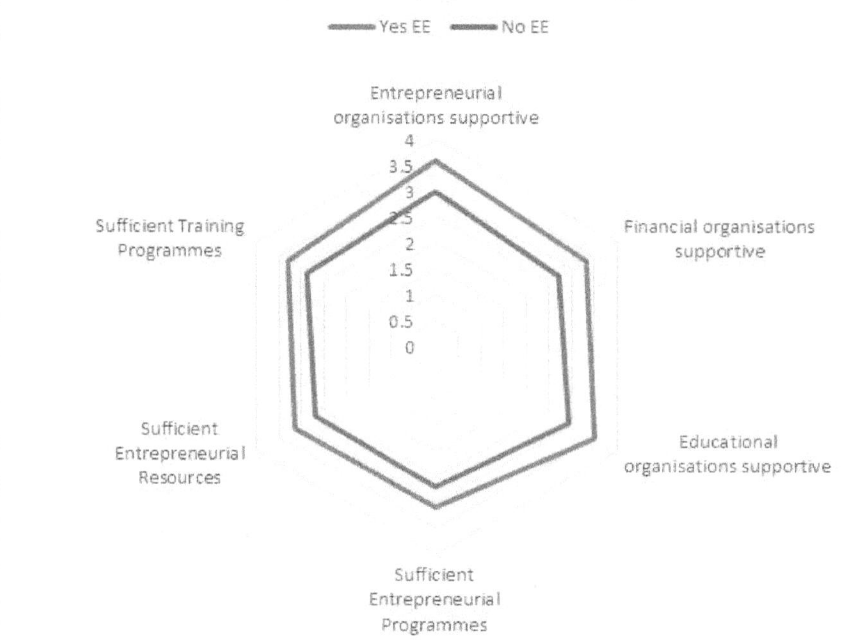

Figure 2: Mean values for immigrant entrepreneurs' agreement with support of formal actors in a region

1 = strongly disagree, 5 = strongly agree, Yes EE = perceived the presence of an entrepreneurial ecosystem in their region, No EE = did not perceive the presence of an entrepreneurial ecosystem in their region

4. Discussion

The findings from this quantitative study concurred with previous research on the heterogeneity of entrepreneurs, immigrants and entrepreneurial ecosystems (Acs, Stam and Audretsch, 2017; Drinkwater, 2018; Lofstrom, 2017) as outlined in Table 1. The characteristics of the immigrant food entrepreneurs supported findings on age of migrant entrepreneurs by Drinkwater (2018) but contrasted with findings from the Irish GEM Report (2018) who reported more younger entrepreneurs and a higher rate of self-employment rates in men. The education level of the immigrant food entrepreneurs concurred with reported education levels for entrepreneurs in Ireland (Fitzsimons and O'Gorman, 2019). The high level of education, further enhanced by 72.1% having upskilled since coming to Ireland, was beneficial to provide these immigrant entrepreneurs with an enhanced ability to adapt to new situations, increased their capacity for self-direction and broadened their knowledge base (Altinay and Wang, 2011). Of the immigrant entrepreneurs who perceived an entrepreneurial ecosystem in their region. In terms of the first research question, there was very strong evidence of a relationship between age and the importance of networking for their business, with the majority of immigrant entrepreneurs aged 40 or over, considering networking important for their business ($p=0.05$).

Their engagement in formal and informal networks demonstrated the importance of strong and weak ties formed with different actors (McAdam and Soetanto, 2018). The networking with both local producers and own or different nationalities demonstrated embeddedness by the immigrant entrepreneurs in their region, enabling them to become part of the local structure, to grow contacts and form information networks to create opportunities and exchange networks to access resources and reduce barriers (Alvedalen and Boschma (2017). The networking by these entrepreneurs for multiple purposes supports findings by McAdam and Soetanto, (2018) on the importance of networking for socio-economic benefits in a region, This is evident where a higher proportion (84.1%) of the immigrant entrepreneurs who perceived an entrepreneurial ecosystem existed agreed they had contributed to the local economy ($p<0.05$) compared to 50% of those who did not perceive an entrepreneurial ecosystem existed. However, the main barrier faced by the immigrant entrepreneurs was lack of finance with 78% using their personal finance as their main source of funding which agreed with findings by Drinkwater (2018) on ethnic entrepreneurs.

In terms of the second research question on perception of the role of actors in entrepreneurial ecosystems, these have been classified into "bottom up" and "bottom down" ecosystems (Mason and Brown, 2014). The local food producer and the community spirit created the connectivity in the ecosystem from the bottom up for some entrepreneurs and the LEOs and other support agencies from the top down for others. Even though, the entrepreneurial organisations were considered supportive, there was strong evidence of a relationship between the county the entrepreneur lived in and their agreement with the presence of entrepreneurial programmes and resources and training programmes ($p<0.05$) which Stangler and Bell-Masterson (2015) recommended were important indicators of connectivity in an entrepreneurial ecosystem.

5. Conclusion

The aim of this paper was to determine if an entrepreneurial ecosystem was a valid perspective for understanding the experiences of immigrant entrepreneurs. The literature demonstrated that the entrepreneurial ecosystems lens had been successfully utilised to explore the success of high-tech industries. This research has shown that it is also a valid research lens for exploring the role of heterogeneous immigrant entrepreneurs and small business development. These entrepreneurial ecosystems can be "bottom up" or "top down", which creates implications for policy makers in terms of promoting a community spirit among entrepreneurs in all regions, to grow entrepreneurial ecosystems from the bottom up as well as developing a top down approach. As the existence of entrepreneurial ecosystems has a significant impact on the presence of strategic stakeholders and the availability of resources and training for entrepreneurs within a specific geographical area, these top down initiatives need to be developed regionally. These initiatives are normally developed within a national policy framework and are not sufficiently focused on the specific requirements at a regional or local level. Further analysis of these entrepreneurial ecosystems is necessary to identify what connections and strategic networks are vital for their existence and development to facilitate their replication in other regions through entrepreneurial policies.

6. Future research

The main limitation of this research is that it is based on a small sample size and is limited to one regional area in one country. Future research creates opportunities to explore the presence of entrepreneurial ecosystems at regional levels in other countries. A deeper insight is needed on the causality of relations existing within entrepreneurial ecosystems and what factors have contributed to the emergence of these ecosystems. By using a case study approach, a more in depth understanding of the various actors and their entrepreneurial story at a local level would contribute to identifying the vital connections formed in these ecosystems.

References

Acs, Z.J., Stam, E. and Audretsch, D.B. (2017) The lineages of the entrepreneurial ecosystem approach. *Small Business Economics* **49,** 1-10

Alvedalen, J. and Boschma, R. (2017) A critical review of entrepreneurial ecosystems research: /towards a future research agenda. *European Planning Studies,* **25**(6) pp. 887-903.

Altinay, L. and Wang, C.L. (2011) The influence of an entrepreneur's socio-cultural characteristics on the entrepreneurial orientation of small firms. *Journal of Small Business and Enterprise Development*, **18**(4) pp. 673-694.

Creswell, J.W. and Creswell, J.D. (2018) *Research Design, Qualitative, Quantitative and Mixed Method Approaches*. 5th edition. SAGE Publications Inc. Thousand Oaks, California.

Department of Agriculture, Food and the Marine (DAFM) (2015). Food Wise 2025. A 10-year vision for the Irish Agri-Food Industry. [online] Available at https://www.agriculture.//.ie/foodwise2025/ [Accessed 4 August 2016]

Drinkwater, S. (2018) Migrant Entrepreneurship. In *the Sage Handbook of Small Business and Entrepreneurship*. (Blackburn, B., De Clecq, D. and Heinonen, J. eds), SAGE Publications, London, pp. 94-106.

Fairlie, R.W. (2008) Estimating the Contribution of Immigrant Business Owners to the U.S. Economy. *Small Business Research Summary,* No. 334.

Fitzsimons, P. and O'Gorman, C. (2019) *Entrepreneurship in Ireland (2018) Global Entrepreneurship Monitor (GEM)* [Online] Available at www.gemconsortium.org/report [Accessed 31 October 2019]

Lofstrom, M. (2017) Immigrant Entrepreneurship: Trends and Contributions. *Cato Journal,* **37**(3) pp. 503-522.

Mason, C. and Brown, R. (2014) *Entrepreneurial Ecosystems and growth orientated entrepreneurship. Paris: Final Report to OECD*. Available at: https://www.oecd.org/cfe/leed/Entrepreneurial-ecosystems.pdf [Accessed 15 June 2018]

McAdam, M. and Soetanto, D. (2018) Networks and Entrepreneurship. In *the Sage Handbook of Small Business and Entrepreneurship*. (Blackburn, B., De Clecq, D. and Heinonen, J. eds), SAGE Publications, London, pp. 74-93.

McKitterick, L., Quinn, B., McAdam, R. and Dunn, A. (2016) Innovation networks and the institutional actor-producer relationship in rural areas: The context of artisan food production. *Journal of Rural Studies.* **48** pp. 41-52.

Patton, M.Q. (2002), *Qualitative research and evaluation methods*. 3rd edition. Sage Publications, Thousand Oaks, California

Saxenian, A.L. (1999) *Silicon Valley's New Immigrant Entrepreneurs*. Public Policy Institute of California, USA

Stam, E. and Spigel, B. (2018) Entrepreneurial Ecosystems. In *the Sage Handbook of Small Business and Entrepreneurship*. (Blackburn, B., De Clecq, D. and Heinonen, J. eds), SAGE Publications, London, pp. 407-422.

Stangler, D. and Bell-Masterson, J. (2015) *Measuring an entrepreneurial ecosystem*. Kansas City: Kauffman Foundation

Present and Future in Family-Own Technology-Based Businesses in Romanian Book Publishing Industry

Gabriela Doina Stănciulescu and Cezar Scarlat
Doctoral School of Entrepreneurship, Business Engineering and Management, University Politehnica of Bucharest, Romania
stanciulescu.gabriela2na@yahoo.com
cezarscarlat@yahoo.com
DOI: 10.34190/EIE.20.099

Abstract: The book publishing industry in Romania is currently facing many challenges generated by the particular characteristics of the book market and the technological level, necessary to optimize the sectors of editorial production and distribution. The question that the paper focuses on is the following – "Is the Book Publishing Becoming a Technology-Based Industry?" The objective of this article is to analyse a certain technological characteristics of the editorial production and their influence on the quality, the efficiency, on the structure of the editorial costs and the potential of developing the sector in the future. At the same time, the analysis focuses on the technology used in the field, both in book publishing operations and in other functions (marketing, distribution, contracting etc.). The paper reviews the book market in Romania and its growth potential in future years. A number of issues are being pursued, such as the volume of Romanian book publishing market, the level and quality of market competition, customers, suppliers and substitution products. Also, the evolution impact of digital technology and Internet on the level of book publishing production and on the book market future in Romania is highlighted. The studies and statistics of the book market present difficulties due to the lack of transparency in the field, as well as due to the lack of systematic and in-depth information (studies and analyses) on the editorial activity. One thing is certain in the book publishing industry: the ownership is 100% Romanian. The close correlation between the students` instruction level as volume of general knowledge and skills and the number of books read is demonstrated as well. The conclusions of this paper provide the answer to the main question and the authors hope these will also be a warning, for the top decision and policy-makers, about the difficulties faced by the book publishing industry in the effort to promote the written book as a cultural support, with a major impact on the education and training of many generations.

Keywords: book publishing, technology-based industry, editorial field, family business, digital technology

1. Introduction

The article represents a brief overview of the publishing industry in Romania and of some problems facing the family business in this field. The article is part of the research for the accomplishment of the PhD thesis with the title "Research on Some Particularities of the Family-own Technology-Based Businesses".

At the foundation of the doctoral thesis are the questionnaires addressed to the leaders and successors of the family businesses in the Romanian publishing industry, as well as the brainstorming sessions regarding the ways of innovation, optimization and adaptation of the businesses to the current trends, but also of the ways of accelerating the succession process - an important factor in continuing the family business and in creating new visions for the future (Stănciulescu, Scarlat, 2019; Stănciulescu, Scarlat and Cojocea, 2019; Stănciulescu, Scarlat and Ganciu, 2019; Stănciulescu, Scarlat and Stroe, 2019). At present, the small number of data obtained allows only expressing qualitative conclusions about the particularities and specific problems pursued.

It is worth mentioning that, in Romania, the publishing industry is an area where no thorough research has been done on the needs and problems faced by companies in the digital age, where technology changes the support and presentation forms of the printed book.

2. Literature review

> *"The printed book has been since its invention by Gutenberg in the mid-15th century a unique product: more precisely, a mass product and an information medium, a work of art and a commodity, a symbol of knowledge and of prestige, a commercial product and a propaganda medium" (Eisenstein, 1983; Johns, 1998; Banou, 2017, p.2).*

From the beginning, book publishing was a special business because of the complex nature of the final product and due to the expectations and demands of the book consumers. The publishing industry combines in a unique form, characteristic of each historical period, the creative (Hartley *et al.*, 2013), artistic and informational side of book production, with the technological means at its disposal, with the financial and legislative aspects, in order to maintain and develop in a highly competitive environment (Cope, Phillips, 2014).

The book consumption appeared and developed in the background of meeting the needs of information and knowledge of the people, of their curiosity, expectations and desires for immediate access to new ideas and intellectual and cultural training values. These needs and expectations of the readers have not changed much over time, instead, the demands for quality, originality and forms of information presentation have increased, as well as the aesthetic value of books at an acceptable price. (Clark, Phillips, 2014; Banou, 2017)

The book price issue is extremely important because in the end the book will come as any commodity and compete with similar products on the market. The publishing value chain contains the added values in all stages of transforming the author's work up to the book sold to the reader.

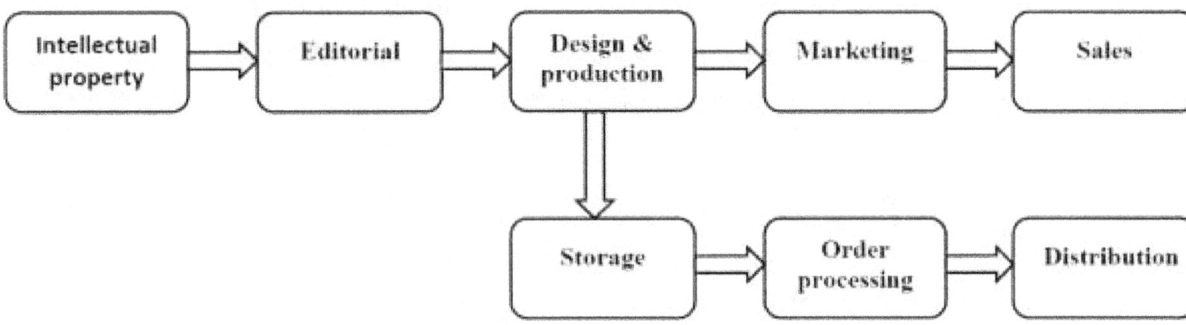

Figure 1: The publishing value chain (Amended from Cope and Phillips, 2014; Clark and Phillips, 2014)

The evolution of digital, information and communication technology in the last decades has brought important transformations in the publishing industry, greatly easing and accelerating certain stages of the production chain (Phillips, 2014).

If, until the '80s of the 20th century, the publishing activity was cumbersome and relatively slow, most of the stages being incorporated into a functional aggregate model, the emergence of digital technology of editing, storage and printing represented an important qualitative leap in the field. (Striphas, 2009; Banou, 2017). Thus, the transition from traditional typographies to offset printers (litho) and then to digital printing has greatly increased the profitability of publishers in the case of small prints and increased the quality and variety of printing, creating the framework for innovation in publishing, especially as an offer of aesthetic forms.

In the current period of globalization and accentuated digitalization, the publishing industry is facing major challenges. The main challenge comes from the technology evolution used in this field, which evolves much faster than the needs, expectations and ability to adapt the editorial output and even often the final beneficiary – the reader.

Another challenge is the wide variety of substitution products, digital books (eBooks, audio books) - all offered by the evolution of digital technology. This variety can cover a wide range of customised presentation methods of the same product (book) with very low costs.

The direction of publishing industry evolution has always been that of democratizing information, knowledge and taste, of fast access to friendly books with aesthetic value and accessible as a price. Digital technology has given a strong impetus in this regard, starting with the creative segment of the publishing industry (Hartley *et al.*, 2013; Clark, Phillips, 2014; Cope, Phillips, 2014; Banou, 2017) and continuing with the entire book production and marketing chain. This trend has led to the modification of the value chain (Thompson, 2012), reaching in many cases the highest wish of readers: immediate and free access to a wide range of books offered by various publishers and online bookstores. (Clark, Phillips, 2014; Ramrattan, Szenberg, 2016)

Exploiting the new capabilities available to the technology offers the publishing industry multiple opportunities to improve and diversify the offer in promotion, distribution and sale, as well as in direct interaction with readers or readers with authors (Greco, Milliot and Wharton, 2013; Michaels, 2015). An immediate opportunity for publishers is to offer readers, especially young people, editions for smartphones, iPads and computers through the use of multimedia, storytelling, gamification, through changes in content (serialization, short forms) and book aesthetics. (Cox, 2014; Striphas, 2009; Phillips, 2014)

Undoubtedly, the publishing industry is at a turning point and needs to quickly and effectively manage the new challenges and opportunities that it faces (Cox, 2014). These are obvious from the nature of the informational path from author to reader and should clarify certain trends such as:

- the future nature of reading and communication (Phillips, 2014; Michaels, 2015);
- the behavior of the reader (Clark, Phillips, 2014);
- new forms and supports for information (Cox, 2014; Phillips, 2014);
- building online communities of readers (Cox, 2014; Banou, 2017);
- developing new marketing and promotion strategies (Cope, Phillips, 2014; Phillips, 2014);
- involvement of the readers in the act of creation and production (Banou, 2017).

Phillips (2014) draws a parallel between the publishing industry and the music industry and, at the same time, emphasizes the impact of the Internet and technology on them. Countries such as the US, UK, Italy, Canada, Brazil, Sweden have taken drastic measures to combat free downloads, which is a copyright infringement. A solution was subsequently sought for the legal download of content such as iTunes and Spotify for music. Similar to the book industry, Amazon is one of the online platforms that offers e-book download service. The opportunities offered by digital technology to the publishing industry had to be offset by new legislative measures to protect intellectual property, measures similar to those in the music industry (Phillips, 2014).

In conclusion, the present and future of the publishing industry are closely related to the technological evolution, the needs and behaviour of readers.

3. The objective and methodology of research

The main objective of the article is to analyse the publishing industry from the perspective of publishing value chain and of the influence of information technology development on the components of the chain. Thus, the impact on the product quality and the role in the efficiency of the activity, as well as the reduction of the editorial costs, are essential elements of maintaining the companies in the book market. In this article, some aspects are pursued:

- Transforming the publishing activity into a technology-based industry;
- Opportunities offered by digital technology for self-publishing and small publishers and family publishers through the profitability of small prints and personalized books.
- The future development of the publishing industry will be closely linked to digital technology and communications, both for the written book and the electronic book, which will coexist for a long time.

The methodological approach is that of primary research conducted through interviews and questionnaires applied to leaders and successors of the family-own businesses in the publishing industry. In addition, we conducted secondary and empirical research of some surveys and studies conducted at national level, but we also performed the selection and interpretation of significant data for the objectives and aspects pursued in the article.

4. Circumstances and sources of information

The present study starts from the following circumstances regarding the existence of the challenges and opportunities faced by the publishing businesses in the context of the rapid development of information and communication technology:

- Stimulating and transforming businesses of the publishing industry into modern businesses based on new technologies in the digital field.
- Increasing the quality of the information and its aesthetic value by using the facilities offered by the new technologies and multimedia applications.
- Deep changes in the publishing value chain as a result of the use of the Internet, social networks and communications.

- Analysis of the transformations that have occurred in the behaviour of the reader and the publisher as a result of the access and use of the latest communications technologies.

The data sources used to produce the article are the interviews, the questionnaires applied to Romanian companies in the field and the studies carried out by national and international companies and organizations dealing with the analysis of the editorial phenomenon.

5. Results

5.1 Digital technology in the book publishing industry

The publishing industry over the last three decades has been strongly transformed, especially due to the evolution of information and communication technology. Thus, many of the stages of the production chain have undergone profound changes, simplified and acquired new facilities (possibilities) to increase the informative and aesthetic quality of the book, the production capacity, the efficiency of marketing, distribution and sales. All these have made important changes in the value chain of the editorial field. Publishers play an essential role in the book production cycle. The stages of production, promotion and marketing define a value chain because each stage adds value to the final product. A classic scheme of the value chain nowadays is shown in Figure 2.

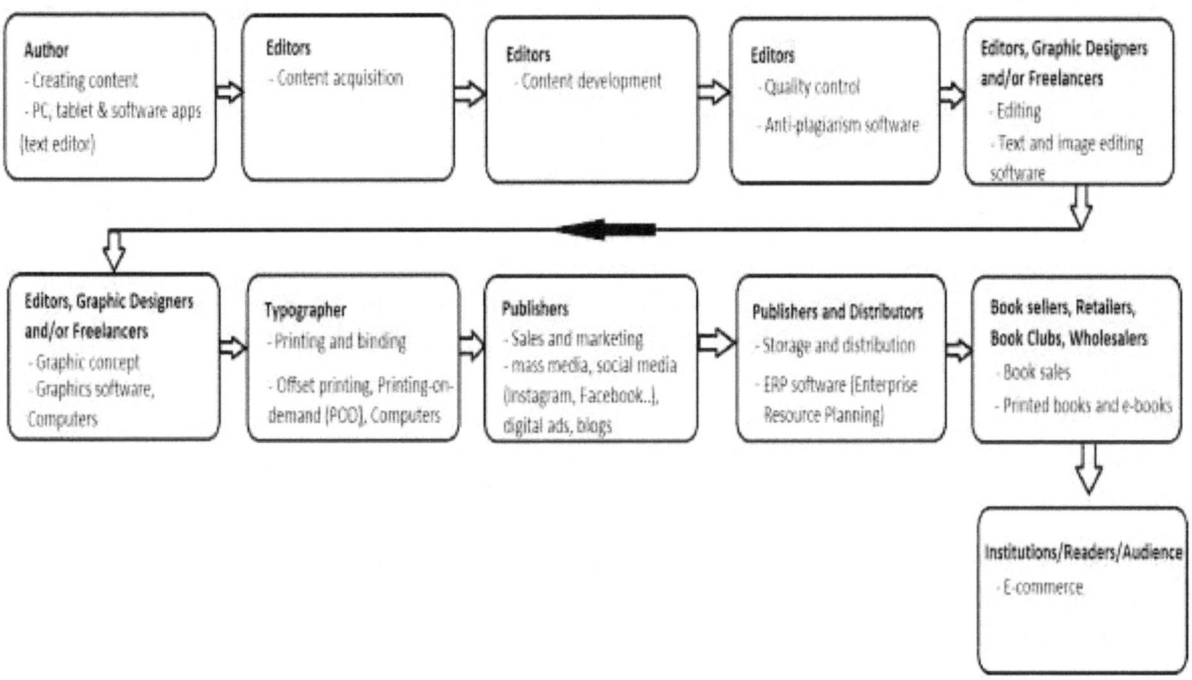

Figure 2: The publishing value chain nowadays (Amended from Thompson, 2012)

The first stage of the chain is the conception - the creation of the content and it is the author's responsibility. In the digital age, design work is done using computers that contain advanced writing programs (Microsoft Word, Open Office Writer, Notepad, WordPad, Google Drive, or other Windows Store applications for both iOS and Android.

Protecting content made in a "work day" by a writer can be easily accomplished by saving the document in computer memory or on external storage devices such as USB memory sticks, hard disk drives or by sending the content directly to the e-mail address (ex: JustWrite app). In conclusion, establishing the form and fixing the content of the author's creation is achieved through the use of digital technological capabilities.

Publishers purchase the content of the author's work, content that is subject to a process of verification, development and quality control in direct collaboration with the author. Content is sent to publishers via communications networks (e-mail) or physical media (USB Memory Stick), and processing and verification are performed by publishing through digital technology and specialized programs for content development, anti-plagiarism verification and quality control.

The final stage of text editing (to be printed), with the added graphics for pages and covers, is also accomplished with dedicated graphics and editing programs using digital technology (example: Adobe Photoshop, Illustrator, InDesign, Corel DRAW, GIMP, Inkscape, Pixlr etc.). This stage is carried out by the big publishers or is outsourced along with the printing stage - in the case of the small publishers.

The actual production of the book is done in typographies that perform both printing, as well as the production and binding operations of the covers. These operations are performed with the help of modern computer-controlled printers. They allow the creation of multiple formats of the same book, custom or luxury editions.

Upon exiting the typography, the book becomes a commodity and follows a route similar to other products to be sold: marketing, sales, storage and distribution. In each of these stages, the technological means specific to each process are used:

- means of transport;
- facilities offered by mass media, Internet, social media, electronic communications for marketing and advertising;
- spaces and means of storage and distribution.

All these operations are monitored, controlled and managed with the help of computers through special management programs - ERP (Enterprise Resource Planning) software. They assist business leaders in the publishing industry in the monitoring, control and integrated management of activities, processes and operations within companies. Thus, the components of the publishing value chain that involve the greatest financial and time resources can be identified, in order to find efficient solutions.

The electronic versions of the books are made by publishers in response to the opportunities offered by the development of technology and communications, of the changes brought by them among the readers as a new way of consuming the printed book. Because the e-book is heavily competed on smartphones by complex modes of information and entertainment, both the form of the book and its content had to be modified (updated) by including specific media processes (movies, photos, animations), gamification, serialization , short forms, augmented reality.

The insertion of multimedia elements (audio, video, photo) increases the content and aesthetic value of the forms shortened by electronic book, according to the old principle of Fred R. Barnard: "an image is worth a thousand words".

All these processes to increase the attractiveness and aesthetic value of electronic books represent directions exploited by the major publishers on the basis of new technologies and the software of graphic processing increasingly improved.

The entire modern publishing industry has developed and is based on information technology and communications technology. They have produced an important qualitative leap in advertising by improving the ways of presenting information and increasing the aesthetic value of books, both traditional and electronic.

The qualitative leap has occurred in several stages closely related to the development of digital technologies and the Internet.

- Mass production and distribution of books by a large number of authors, producers and publishers who have benefited from the new technologies of book printing and production. Thus, a multitude of small (family-own) companies appear that produce on a small scale and have a distribution capacity.
- After 1990, the development of the Internet and online commerce changed the way in which books were produced and marketed for readers connected to computer technology.
- The emergence of specialised peripherals for digital printing (around 2000) led to a third qualitative leap around small businesses and self-publishing, making small print runs cost-effective, as well as custom editions.
- The fourth jump was determined by the technological evolution in the field of small electronic displays, specialized iPads for reading (e-readers). This technology has shortened the value chain of the book by

eliminating paper as a traditional book support, printing, inventory, storage and distribution. The publishers, producers and distributors of books received a powerful blow, remaining on the market only those who have adapted their activity to the new trends in technology.

- The last level of organisation intervened with the development of smart technologies (smartphones, iPads etc.) that led to major changes in the behaviour of the reader and the publisher. Readers, busy and comfortable, want to read from the phone they always have on them and which also provides them with communication functions, access to various media channels, to social networks and to many other functions (maps, GPS, YouTube...). The publishers, in addition to the strong media competition on the reader's phone, must adapt the editorial output in an attractive way and in line with the readers' devices: short forms of books, serialization, gamification, use of multimedia and augmented reality technologies for increasing the artistic value of the book and defining a distinct identity of it.

Also, the use of digital technology, the Internet, social networks and communications has led to important changes in the value chain of publishing, even causing the authors to self-publish their works, using the facilities offered by the computer industry. Thus the value chain was shortened between authors and readers, they could take the link and exchange ideas and impressions without the publishers.

5.2 An overview of the book industry in Romania

The publishing industry, as an economic activity, generates a global value of approximately 114 billion euros in 2015, surpassing the entertainment, music and video games industry. The largest market share is held by publishers in the European Union, approximately 33%, followed by those in the U.S. by 26%. (Ceobanu, Despoiu, 2016; Ceobanu, Dinu and Cristea, 2017; Federation of European Publishers - FEP, 2017)

The global value of the book industry in Europe ranges from 22 to 24 billion euros to a volume of over 500,000 new titles published in 2016 (figure 3). The largest book markets in the world are (in order): US, China, Germany, Japan, the UK and France and together they accumulate about 60% of the world book market (sales) (Ceobanu, Despoiu, 2016). Europe, with a long tradition in book printing and publishing, owns 6-8 of the top 10 largest publishing groups in the world and the largest book fairs in the world: Frankfurt, London, Bologna, according to the President of the Federation of European Publishers - Henrique Mota (FEP, 2017).

The European demographic and linguistic diversity prints a great deal of advertising diversity, in 24 official languages and several tens of minority languages. European publishers represent a diverse and solid cultural sector, with high demands and satisfaction of the reader, as well as a large volume of book exports.

Figure 3: An overview of book publishing industry – Romania & Europe (Amended from Ceobanu, Dinu and Cristea, 2016; FEB, 2019; Forbes Romania, 2019)

In Romania, according to the National Institute for Cultural Research and Training (INCFC), the total number of publishers registered at the level of 2016 was 6175, of which only 1956 were active, these being distributed as in table 1:

Table 1: The distribution of active publishing houses in Romania, in 2016

The size of active publishers	Number of active publishers	Number of ISBNs published	Percentage
Small active publishers	752	10 - 30	38 %
Medium active publishers	787	20 - 230	40 %
Large active publishers	379	231 - 2230	20 %
Very large active publishers	38	> 2231	2 %

*active publishers = publishers who have requested ISBNs from the National Centre ISBN-ISSN-CIP, in the last 5 years

As a geographical distribution, most of the Romanian publishers are concentrated in the big university centres (table 2) and in the big cities with high population density and which concentrate many institutions.

Table 2: Distribution of publishers in the major university centres in Romania

No	City	Number of publishers					
		Registered	Active	Small	Medium	Large	Very large
1	Bucharest	3021	792	348	286	138	20
2	Cluj Napoca	341	136	40	61	32	3
3	Iaşi	336	92	27	31	30	4
4	Craiova	203	64	23	18	21	2
5	Timişoara	151	64	17	31	13	3

According to the data of the National Institute of Cultural Research and Training (INCFC) in 2017, the editorial activity in Romania can be summarized as follows:

- over 50% of publishers declare that they carry out activities other than book publishing. Almost half of these work within universities, cultural institutions, museums, county centres for promoting the traditional culture, ensuring the editing of specific materials for their activity.
- over 78% of the book production is intended for the general public and 28% is for the target audience.
- 30% of all publishers have their own printers and 70% outsourced this activity.
- 87% of publishers declare that they print the books in Romania.
- 58% of publishers work at the request of the beneficiaries (institutions, organisations, authors).
- 12% of publishers produced books in electronic format (e-books).
- 11% of publishers made book exports.
- 9% of publishers produced audio-books.

Therefore, the Romanian publishers hardly adapt to the current trend of electronic book production and only a small part of them make e-books and audio-books. The trend of e-books is increasing, reaching the level of 2019 at about 5% of total book production. The same rising trend is also evident in readers` searches for books and e-books on Google (Figure 4).

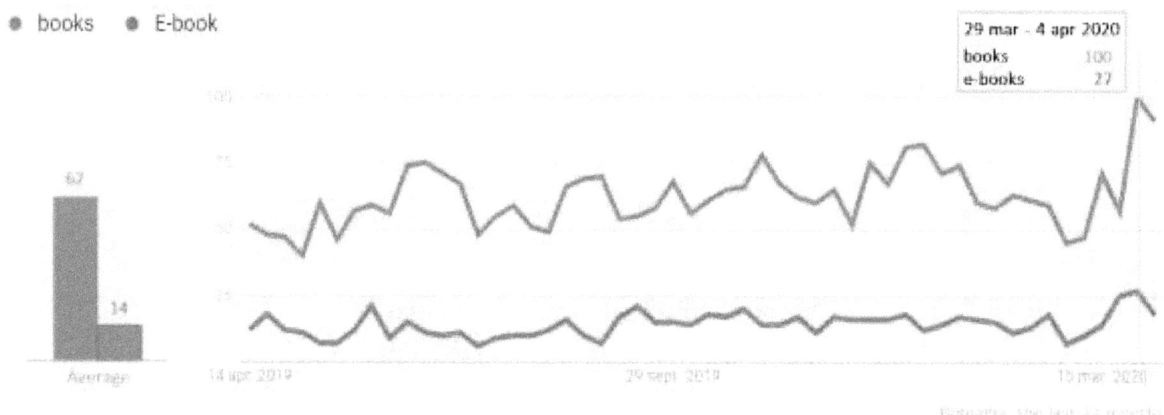

Figure 4: The evolution of Romanian book and e-book searches between 2019 and 2020 (Amended from Google Trends)

In the current period of transformation that the publishing industry is undergoing worldwide, due to the technological evolution and the readers` tastes, the field is facing a lack of medium and long-term strategy, as well as the indifference of the political factor for the publishers` support.

The publishing industry, being one of the essential supports of the national culture, must be the main objective of the Ministry of Culture. Because after 1989 the ministry did not have a coherent strategy to support the national culture and education due to the lack of funds allocated, its activity was limited to: organising national and international book fairs, preferential financing of cultural magazines, and book purchases for public libraries. Among the strategic objectives that Ministry of Culture has proposed in the last electoral cycles, this paper mentions:

- increasing the number of domains and titles published;
- support given to publishers for the distribution and sale of books;
- supporting new forms of editing (digital, audio).

The lack of long-term vision of the policy makers, the disinterest in the national culture, as well as the lack of a consistent budget allocated to the ministry for the materialization of the proposed objectives, made the publishing industry face major challenges. These are given by the technological changes in all the traditional stages of publication, distribution, sale and consumption of the book, as well as by the competition of the production of electronic book.

It should be emphasized the role that the school and family need to continue to play in maintaining the interest of students and young people for the written book, regardless of support, as a means of informing, educating and training them.

In conclusion, digital technology has had a major impact on the book publishing because new methods of presentation have been adopted regarding the aesthetics, format and support of the printed book, but also of the electronic book, by adapting it to all types of technological devices. Both the studies of the researches and the present article show that the two formats will coexist for a long time.

6. Conclusions, recommendations and limitations of the research

6.1 Conclusions

The publishing industry in Romania is 100% Romanian and has seen a visible progress in the last 3 years in terms of book purchases from both the classical and online bookstores. The vast majority of publishers are family businesses that have carried out the transfer of management and property to the second generation, much more prepared for the current period of transformations forced by the development of digital technology.

This article presents an updated overview of the Romanian book market and also answers the question "Is the book publishing becoming a technology-based industry?", thanks to the qualitative leaps in the publishing field determined by the technical-digital innovations.

The book market is undergoing a period of change determined by the technology evolution that has led to the industry restructuring in most stages of production, distribution, storage and sale. The facilities offered by digital technology and modern printers have enabled authors to self-publish, distribute and sell works. Some of the publishing houses that work within some institutions/organizations, carry out activities other than book publishing: research, advertising, symposiums, cultural events, marketing and consulting.

Publishers must respond to the challenges caused by changes in the field of e-book consumption. It competes on the same device (smartphone, computer, iPad) with mass media products, games, social networks and communication applications. The challenges come from the extremely fast pace in which the technology in the field evolves, from the changes of the readers' requirements regarding the content, the aesthetic value and the form of presentation of the book, but also from the political factor, unable to understand the direction of evolution of the book production and to come up with legislative measures to support this evolution.

6.2 Recommendations

- The publishers need to be much more transparent regarding the advertising activity (number of titles, print runs, publishing domains) so that the researchers in the field can make relevant analyses on the industry and its evolution trends.
- The own sites of the publishers can present semi-annual / annual situations of the sales of printed book and electronic book - on publishing domains, in order to increase the level of domain research.
- The publishers associations in Romania can carry out extensive marketing studies to find the most advantageous ways of distributing and selling the written book, as well as studies regarding the changes in the tastes of the Y Generation and the Millennials in terms of reading.
- The government (top policy makers in general), through the Ministry of Culture and the Ministry of Finance, must pay greater attention and substantial support to the national culture and the publishing industry in particular. The support aims to overcome the current stage of profound transformations in the field, but also to be able to participate effectively in the reform of the Romanian education and in the development of the interest for reading.

6.3 Limitations of the research

- The Romanian book market is not transparent in terms of turnover, number of titles and prints published.
- The number of studies on the publishing industry in Romania is very low and limited to editorial, financial, legislative and personnel aspects.
- The technological aspects of copyright, e-book and e-commerce are dealt with briefly.
- The disinterest and even the refusal of publishers to respond to requests for interviews or questionnaires regarding specific aspects of the editorial activity. (Ex. INCFC, when distributing 1360 questionnaires to as many publishers, obtained a response rate of 12%, *i.e.* 156 completed questionnaires.)
- The pandemic period interrupted the more-open, face-to-face interview sessions with the founders and their successors of the family businesses in the publishing industry in Romania.

References

Banou, C. (2017) Re-Inventing the Book: Challenges from the Past for the Publishing Industry. Chandos Publishing, Cambridge.

Ceobanu, I., Dinu, G.C. and Cristea, T. (2016) Study on the book market in Romania. INCFC, Bucureşti.

Ceobanu, I. and Despoiu, A.M. (2017) Study on the dynamics of publishing houses and publishing activity in Romania. INCFC, Bucureşti.

Clark, G. and Phillips, A. (2014) Inside Book Publishing. Fifth Edition, Routledge, Abingdon.

Cope, B. and Phillips, A. (2014) The Future of the Book in the Digital Age. Chandos Publishing, Oxford.

Cox, E.L. (2014) Designing books for tomorrow's readers: How Millennials consume content. Publishing Technology and Publishing Perspectives, New York. [online] https://www.ingenta.com/wp-content/uploads/2014/10/White-Paper-How-Millennials-Consume-Content.pdf

Eisenstein, E. (1983) The Printing Revolution in Early Modern Europe. Cambridge University Press, Cambridge.

Federation of European Publishers (2017) The Book Sector in Europe: Facts and Figures. FEP, Bruxelles.

Federation of European Publishers (2019) European Publishing Matters: the FEP Manifesto 2019. Bruxelles.

Forbes Romania (2019) The financial ranking of the most important publishers in Romania in 2018.

Greco, A., Milliot, J. and Wharton, R. (2013) The book Publishing Industry. Routledge, New York and London.

Hartley, J., Potts, J., Cunningham, S., Flew, T., Keane, M. and Banks, J. (2013) Key Concepts in Creative Industries. SAGE Publications, London.

Johns, A. (1998) The Nature of the Book. Print and Knowledge in the Making. The University of Chicago Press, Chicago and London.

Michaels, K. (2015) "The evolving challenges and opportunities in global publishing". Publishing Research Quarterly, Vol 31, p 1-8.

Phillips, A. (2014) Turning the page: The evolution of the book. Routledge, New York.

Ramrattan, L. and Szenberg, M. (2016) Revolutions in Book Publishing: The Effects of Digital Innovation on the Industry. Palgrave Macmillan, Hampshire.

Stănciulescu, G.D. & Scarlat. C. (2019) "An overview of the major factors blocking the development of family businesses in Romania". The 9th International Conference of Management and Industrial Engineering – ICMIE (2019): Management Perspectives in the Digital Transformation, Bucharest, Romania, pp 96-107.

Stănciulescu, G.D., Scarlat, C. and Cojocea, A. (2019) "Some Cultural Aspects Regarding the Management and Ownership Succession in Romanian Small, Family-owned, Businesses". In Youth and Women Entrepreneurship in Challenging International (Global) Business Environment, Bulgarian Association for Management Development and Entrepreneurship, Sofia, Bulgaria, pp 221-238.

Stănciulescu, G.D., Scarlat, C. and Ganciu, M.R. (2019) "The development tendencies of the family-own technology-based businesses in Romania". The 9th International Conference of Management and Industrial Engineering – ICMIE (2019): Management Perspectives in the Digital Transformation, Bucharest, Romania, pp 88-95.

Stănciulescu, G.D., Scarlat, C. and Stroe, S. (2019) "Specific Issues Faced by Romanian Family Businesses during the Succession Process". The 14th European Conference on Innovation and Entrepreneurship – ECIE (2019), Vol.2, Kalamata, Greece, pp 1013-1022.

Striphas, T. (2009) The Late Age of Print. Everyday Book Culture from Consumerism to Control. University of Columbia Press, New York, Chichester and West Sussex.

Thompson, J.B. (2012) Merchants of Culture. The Publishing Business in the Twenty-First Century. John Wiley & Sons, New Jersey.

Innovative Approaches in Marketing Communication in Sustainable Fashion Business

Marianna Urmínová and Alena Kusá
University of Ss. Cyril and Methodius, Trnava, Slovakia
urminova.m@gmail.com
alena.kusa@ucm.sk
DOI: 10.34190/EIE.20.183

Abstract: Sustainability and responsible entrepreneurship are now becoming the cornerstone of many successful companies at the present. Despite the growing awareness of environmental issues, we are constantly encountering an enormous scale of problems in the textile and fashion industry. It is undeniable that the textile and fashion industry is one of the oldest and largest industries in the world. It consumes a large amount of water in its processes compared to any other industry and releases enormous amounts of toxic chemicals into the environment. It is also considered to be the second most polluting industry in the world. The theoretical study consists of several parts. The first part is devoted to the processes of business in the field of sustainable fashion in the world and current forms of its communication towards consumers and it also focuses on pointing out the need of sustainability in the fashion industry in the processes of circular economy. The second part of the study focuses on secondary research in the field of sustainable marketing communication and on the analysis of opinions of several contemporary authors about the sustainability issue in the fashion industry. It is also focused on the analysis from several surveys in the field of marketing communication sustainable fashion and the effectiveness of its marketing tools. In general, sustainable fashion communications should be properly timed through several appropriate communication channels. We focus our attention mainly on social media. We focus on the efficiency and effectiveness of social networks, which have a significant impact on the environmental consumer behaviour. Based on the previous knowledge, the study concludes with the reader several innovative approaches and ways of communication of responsible business processes in the field of sustainable fashion. Innovative approaches and ways of communicating should be part of the education processes about the sustainability and responsible business of fashion companies. Based on the previous opinions and research, the study provides a general concept of recommendations that can be educationally established within responsible business processes of many companies operating in the fashion industry.

Keywords: sustainability fashion, circular fashion, sustainability communications, social media, education

1. Introduction

The 24th April 2013 was considered as one of the most tragic days in the history of fashion industry. More than 1,130 people died and more than 2,500 were badly injured in the collapse of Rana Plaza in Bangladesh. One day earlier, the factory with two illegal floors had been evacuated due to static equilibrium issues. On the day of the tragedy, the staff were forced to resume their work duties under the threat of losing their monthly wages. This day has been considered a breakthrough in the whole perception of the fashion industry all over the world - from the ethical, transparent as well as sustainable point of view.

Nowadays, the fashion industry is standing on the crossroads. The production machines and equipment are turning at a high pace and any corresponding impact and pollution generated by cheap, fast and unsustainable fashion are turning into a global-scale problem. Textile production is responsible for greenhouse emissions that are far bigger than worldwide transport resources. Toxic substances are discharged into the environment while polluting the nature or deteriorating health of not only producers, but also consumers. Fashion industry does not respect any limits of our planet as it primarily focuses on solving short-term economic problems. In light of the aforementioned, more and more movements, organisations, ethical or sustainable brands are being launched with endorsement of various celebrities or personalities. The communication itself has become an inseparable part of sustainability and fashion industry awareness. Marketing communication of sustainable brands and fashion businesses is the main precondition and tool promoting the change of thinking and modifying individual's buying behaviour. The modern digital era is powerful enough to channel communication towards individuals or consumers through various platforms - mass media, social media, websites, blogs or applications. Which of these platforms is the most effective? How to properly communicate sustainability in fashion? Can the properly developed marketing communication really lead to switch of consumer behaviour to the environmental one? Thanks to sustainable communication, businesses are trying to target the most individuals possible. Digital technologies enable them to do so on a both local and global level. Even though the transfer to more sustainable development may require substantial changes, these are especially individuals whose combined influence is eligible to change the world as a whole (Sherin, 2013).

2. Literature review: Circular fashion as a part of circular economy

As Abraham Lincoln, the American politician and lawyer, put it: "The best way how to protect future is to create it." That is exactly what developed societies or company executives and scientists are trying to achieve in their sustainable concepts or articles. Through their decisions, steps and opinions relating to circular economy and business, they are trying to protect the people across the planet. The circular economy concept was created in the late 70s (Geissdoerfer et al., 2016). In its principle, this idea took up with the justification that the circular economy should eliminate a negative environmental impact. However, the linear flow model prevailed, which caused serious environmental damage. The circular economy, in contrast to traditional recycling, focuses on business while placing emphasis on reuse of products, components, materials or recycling, repairing, renovation, modernisation as well as on solar and wind energy or biomass waste management (Korhonen et al., 2017). In his article, Rathinamoorthy defines the circular economy as the industrial system with an encouraging and regenerative design and objective. In other words, its main aim is to replace "the expiry of the product lifetime" by renewal, which can be defined as a certain shift towards exploitation of solar energy or elimination of toxic chemicals impairing the reusability of products and, thanks to its sustainable models, to focus on reduction and elimination of waste not only in the production process but also during the product life cycle (Rathinamoorthy, 2019). The fashion industry plays a key role on the way to sustainability and circular economy worldwide. It represents the industry with a huge environmental impact. It entails a rather long and complicated supply chain linked to extreme water and energy consumption, doubled by use of chemicals, water and air pollution or uncontrolled waste production (Jacometti, 2019). Compared with the past, the average number of wearing of a particular garment has been reduced and what is more, a huge amount of garment production has resulted in the market saturation. The fact is, however, that not all the goods that had been produced can really make their way to the market. Various sources point out that up to 20% of garments to have been produced were placed on the market but not purchased (Niinimäki, 2018). Extending the product usability period is one of the key questions of sustainable development. For instance, if we are able to double the period of use of garments, we will also be able to reduce the sources that are necessary for production by half while cutting the waste consumption accordingly (Stahel, 2017). According to Jacometti, the main precondition for establishment of the circular fashion is an average consumer driven by the consumption phenomenon to purchase lots of garments at relatively low prices. Constant changes in fashion often mean that the clothes that were purchased for one season usually end up in bins. In general, consumers tend to look at easily available and cheap garments as single-use goods (Jacometti, 2019). The main objective of the circular economy, as defined by Niinimäki, is to develop a more sustainable system with a closed circuit with the purpose of extending the period of use of garments; in addition, all materials should be recyclable in various rounds. Products should be designed to be incorporated into the system taking into consideration all their aspects: an original concept and usability for all cycles, materials for the system, assessment of waste as a precious source and eventually, the collection of all products after their use (Niinimäki, 2017). In its principle, the circular economy stands for one of the most strategic innovation fields in the future development of the textile and garment industry across Europe, or even further away (ETP Fibers Textiles Clothing, 2016). The clothing industry is becoming more and more linked to establishment of the circular economy in fashion, even though it is still in its infancy on the way to form more ethical and sustainable fashion future (European Sustainable Business Federation, 2019).

3. The sustainable fashion concept and its perception by consumers

Fashion is the language by means of which person's individuality demonstrates itself (Khandual, Pradhan 2018). Consumption in different product categories is influenced by a natural human desire to express one's own significance or identity. Both fashion and clothing enable consumers to create their own identity within certain social norms (Murray, 2002). Due to its significance, it can be assumed that those consumers who wish to be "fashionable" often prevail over those who promote ethics and sustainability in their buying behaviour. This paradox highlights the conflict between the consumer society and the desire to limit our consumption (McNeill, Moore, 2015). In their research, Bristwistle and Moore declare that this may be caused by insufficient knowledge of negative environmental impacts of the fashion industry (Bristwistle, Moore, 2007). Awareness of sustainable fashion is still in its infancy and therefore is not that popular as fast fashion trends. According to Khandual and Pradhan, the main disadvantage of ecological activities is a cost-efficiency factor. Sustainable fashion and clothing materials are much more expensive than conventional ones (Khandual, Pradhan, 2018). Environmental sustainability is nowadays regarded as a proper management programme. These days, various fashion brands see it as a top priority. Its main goal is to maximise benefits while minimising negative impacts (Khandual, Pradhan, 2018). In its principle, sustainable fashion as a part of the slowly growing industry is often seen as an antipode to fast fashion which represents cheap, mass production with a 14-day product life cycle and is often linked to "the products being thrown away" (Watson, Yan, 2013). According to Kin and Kang, sustainability can be defined as a business goal aiming to achieve a positive environmental, social and economic result (Kim, Kang, 2018). There is not just one framework to sustainability. Issues to be solved quickly and without any consideration tend to lead to unfavourable and unforeseeable effects elsewhere. In order to avoid such effects, it is necessary to bear in mind a product's impact on ecological, economic and social systems as well as on the whole product life cycle (Fletcher, 2013).

Yip declares that sustainable fashion also has a local / regional application, thus supporting not only the local community but also creating job opportunities while lowering transport costs (Yip, 2010). The main challenge of sustainable fashion is, however, consumers' behaviour as these are interested in cheap, but high-quality fashionable products that can satisfy their hunger for an exciting shopping experience. Despite the fact that customers are worried about sustainability, real consumption and buying behaviour does not reflect such tendency (Varmužová, 2019). Chan and Wong also agree with the opinions of Khandual and Pradhan as they think that fashionable consumers are interested in purchasing ecological or sustainable fashion, but on the other hand, are not willing to offer sacrifice, for example by paying a much higher price. They also declare that the relationship between the environmental thinking and environmental behaviour is closely linked to a price policy (Chan, Wong, 2012). When speaking about the perception of sustainable fashion by consumers, we mainly consult the research by Lai et other authors, which has shown some essential findings. According to this research, consumers are not quite aware of what sustainable fashion refers to and tend to distrust retailers selling sustainable clothes. In their opinion, sustainability is regarded as a short-term fashion which fails to maximise its potential. The findings of these research also demonstrate that it is necessary to permanently enhance awareness of what sustainable fashion represents, not only for businesses but for consumers as well. The main precondition for a shift in buying behaviour is communication of businesses towards those consumers who consider purchasing sustainable clothes. Market leaders including those fashion brands which offer a sustainable product range have to provide more information about their products and ensure easier accessibility for their consumers. The whole industry has to clearly show the sustainable fashion story which would help their clients grasp its characteristics and eliminate the current perception of fashion, which tends to be vague and full of improper interpretations (Lai et al., 2017).

4. Communication of sustainable fashion and the role of social media

Fashion needs to be one step ahead, the same as the communication strategy. Constantly changing trends force businesses to keep searching for new ways of communication with the wide public (Borboni, 2019). Bloggers and influencers occupy a key position in this modern world of digital technologies as they have a great influence on large groups of users. In general, sufficient information and communication in the field of sustainable fashion are crucial for each consumer (Shen et al., 2013). In order to promote sustainable clothes or brands, businesses use a number of equivalent denominations such as ecological, green, organic, sustainable, natural, etc. These equivalents can be found in their logos, products, labels or various forms of advertising or on company websites (Yan et al., 2012). In his paper, Yan states that these features often happen no to have specific significance as they do not provide their consumers with information about the production process or particular materials, which may generate certain insecurity and be off-putting in their subsequent purchase (Yan et al., 2012). Mohr, Eroğlu and Ellen were the first to introduce the phenomenon of scepticism in ecological marketing and expressed mistrust against environmental declarations that appear in the advertising (Mohr, Eroğlu, Ellen, 1998). They explain that this scepticism can be linked to a cognitive reaction that may differ according to the context and content provided and therefore can appear only under certain circumstances. Paco and Reis also stated that credibility of green advertising is generally regarded as relatively low. Consumers that wish to be sustainable and ecological assume that the information available is less consistent while the variety of labels, packaging and other environmental declarations tend to be confusing rather than informative (Paco, Reis, 2012). To remove consumers' scepticism against sustainable products and fashion, we should first focus on those ecological affirmations that are specific, clear, concise and promote specific advantages for a consumer (Fritzell, 2018).

With the growing Internet use, social media have become one of the strongest innovations of the 21st century (Strähle, Gräff, 2017). Even though many trends have sunk into oblivion lately, social media have not. Generally speaking, media are worldwide known and play a crucial role when gaining public endorsement for various sustainable initiatives (Kolandai-Matchett, 2009). Social media have substantially changed the way we communicate, cooperate, consume and create. They represent one of the most important transformational influences of information technologies in business, either within a company or far beyond. They have revolutionised the manners in which businesses penetrate the market and the society, create the new world of possibilities and challenges for all business aspects ranging from marketing of various operations until finance or human resources management (Sinan, 2013). According to Reiter et al. (2017), social media also enable development of virtual relationships that connect people on various levels. In his article, Diaz (2015) assumes that due to the digital age, exchange of information and values should be done online, ideally on social media platforms. The same applies to communication of sustainability in the fashion industry. Various companies use their own websites or annual reports to communicate sustainability efforts to the public. The modern interactive age and consumers that are hungry for information, combined with the current critical situation in the fashion industry, need to be provided information in the easiest way possible. Social media offer the space for sharing information across a specific community. Apart from being a tool for promoting sustainability issues, these can also serve as an effective source of communication of sustainability while enabling engagement of users into various related debates. The main reason why businesses use social media for communication with their users is their influence on consumers' trust. Proper feedback, high evaluation and positive comments all influence the level of trust and reduce the risk. This leads to greater motivation in product purchase (Strähle, Gräff, 2017). According to Tigrul and Gocer (2017), sustainable brands will be expected to communicate ecological messages through social media more regularly than less valuable brands.

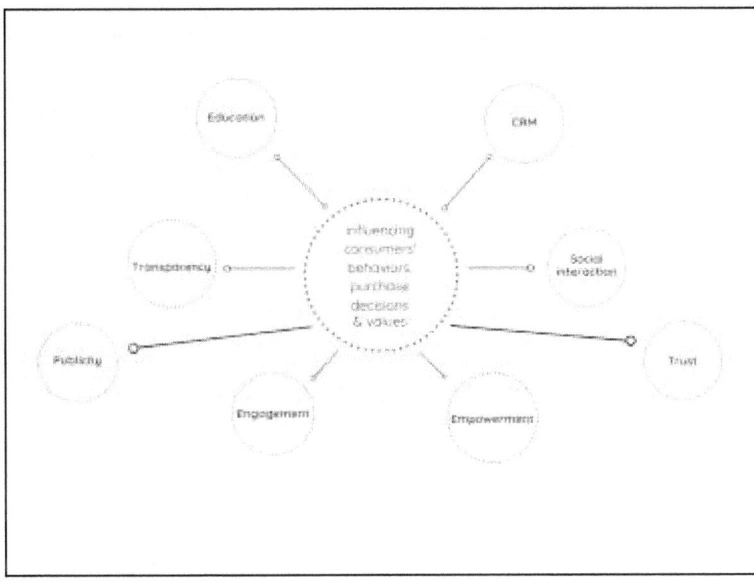

Figure 1: The role of social media within the sustainability concept. Own sources

5. Methodology

The main goal of our paper is to establish a general concept of innovative approaches and ways of communication of sustainable fashion based upon the analysis of three studies of selected authors. Information on this topic was mainly obtained from the articles in the scientific literature, databases and relevant book or Internet publications. The given theoretical knowledge was sorted according to its content and time relevance. When elaborating the study, various logical methods such as the content analysis, factual analysis, description, deduction or critical thinking were applied.

6. The results and the discussion

In this part of the paper, we focused on three scientific studies that have brought interesting conclusions in the field of communication of sustainability fashion.

In his article "Consumer attitudes ad communication in circular fashion", Vehmas et al. (2017) dealt with researching consumers' opinions and expectations in the field of circular fashion. In addition, the article also clarifies in what manner the recycling process in the circular fashion should be properly communicated towards consumers and potential customers. The main methodic consisted of online interviews which were carried out through the Owela platform. The findings point out that consumers require more visible and detailed information about the circular fashion. In their opinion, communication of sustainable fashion should be properly timed by means of various communication channels. Digital services should refer to a certain added value. The analysed study has a qualitative character and no quantitative information about consumer behaviour was obtained.

In his paper, the author is developing the question of the current standpoint and consumer behaviour in the field of sustainable fashion. Based upon the author's assumptions, the following facts have been drawn:

- the price is an ongoing and decisive factor in decision making about the product purchase,
- the issue of sustainable garments is too complicated for consumers,
- consumers are heterogeneous when it comes to ethical and value principles,
- consumers do not perceive clothes shopping as an altruistic step,
- sustainability is regarded as a minor problem worldwide,
- cultural differences may have an impact on how ethical fashion is perceived,
- if consumers recycle their clothes, they prefer second-hand garments to recycled textile waste,
- young consumers prefer swaps when it comes to environmental behaviour.

The key topic of the article is the communication of sustainable fashion. Based upon the author's assumptions, the following conclusions have been drawn:

- Insufficient awareness of sustainable fashion in caused by inappropriate media coverage,
- communication should be brief, include all realistic messages, should be delivered through a large media spectrum, be catchy and take various visual or non-verbal forms,
- celebrity endorsement in green product promotion,
- promotion and labelling of ordinary garments should emphasise the environmental damage that may be caused in comparison with ecological or sustainable alternatives.

As far as the research part of the work is concerned, the outcomes of the second research question are essential. The second question is: *How should the remanufacturing process be communicated to encourage consumers to choose circular garments?* (Vehmas et al, 2017)

Based upon the above mentioned research question and respondents' answers, the following general conclusions have been deduced:

- the message promoting sustainable fashion should be communicated in a neutral way so as the consumers do not get a feeling they had behaved wrong,
- sustainable fashion should be communicated through stories,
- according to the respondents, sustainable garments should be communicated as luxury clothes of our future, as a certain form of prestigious goods,
- it is recommended to use various web and media channels,
- communication should be courageous and large-spectrum, e.g. a small ecological project displayed on the company website may disappear in light of other information.

In their article "The Role of Social Media for a Sustainable Consumption", Strähle a Gräff (2017) primarily focus on the field of social media. The article is split into several chapters. Taking into account the assumptions of other authors, they first define key tasks of social media and their place within marketing communication as a part of a completely new and effective dialogue among consumers. Another part of the article focuses on the green target groups of social media users. According to the authors, the young represent the largest target audience from the group of green consumers. In this part of the article, they also recommend that businesses, companies or organisations should not focus their communication only on "a green consumer". Their attention should be paid to each single potential consumer with his / her needs individually understood and respected.

Despite a number of advantages, social sites and social media have to face several challenges that are so typical for the digital era. These include: fast changes, inter-cultural changes and various forms of consumer behaviour or the possibility to express consumers' negative opinions in comments etc. (Strähle, Gräff , 2017).

As far as the research is concerned, one of the chapters we would like to highlight focuses on the use of various digital platforms of social media by means of which sustainability can be effectively communicated. These newly established platforms include various mobile applications such as Giki enabling its users to scan a QR code of a selected product to help them find sustainable and healthy products in the supermarket. The main benefit of mobile apps is their quick availability or practicability. Blogs are another effective tool how to spread and enhance consumers' awareness. Blogs have a huge impact on behaviour of consumers as well as followers. Fashion and environmentally focused bloggers communicate their views and experience to a number of users who trust them. Apart from that, they keep sharing fashion news and advice and information about various environment-related topics their followers are interested in. What is more, they help co-create new trends such as a slow-fashion trend or second-hand fashion. Nowadays, Instagram has become the strongest platform and the most popular communication tool for Generation Y and Z. Environment-related Instagram accounts enable connection and sharing between sustainable blogs or ethical e-shops. The main goal of Instagram is to share and publish the visual content that, when properly set and maintained, has a great impact on enhancing consumers' awareness in this field. The last social platform we have selected are swaps and various communities specialising in clothes sharing. These communities belong to social innovations supporting a shift towards a more sustainable society and sustained development as such.

In his study and research, Fritzell (2018) focused on social media as a communication channel that fast fashion companies use for promotion of their own products. The author of the study used the qualitative research method by interviews with the selected respondents of Generation Y. These interesting findings confirm social media as a favourable communication tool of fast fashion companies, a kind of an antipode to former research into effective use of social media in this field.

Within the research, the author opted for the following research questions:

- How is Generation Y influenced by sustainable fashion advertising from fashion houses posted on social media?
- Does sustainable advertising of fast fashion houses on social media encourage Generation Y to purchase sustainable clothes? (Fritzell, 2018)

Based upon the results of this research, the author highlights some important factors related to behaviour of Generation Y on social sites and in the social media space. One of these is the fact that Generation Y is generally seen as a lazy generation, therefore businesses that want to communicate a message or information to this generation have to do so in an entertaining form as most of these users are online just to have fun. As the research shows, social media users prefer videos because they require less energy. That is why videos should be communicated in a funny form to avoid rolling their content. The author also says that Generation Y perceive sustainable garments as expensive and unattractive. It means that if promotion of sustainable advertising and garments wants to be successful, respondents' views and perception need to be changed. To do so, marketing of sustainable garments should be funny and modern while showing its customers there are other variants of sustainable garments than just white plain T-shirts. The last common thread of these respondents was wrong perception of sustainable garments due to incorrect information or improper labelling. The solution to this problem is to provide as much information as possible and enhance consumers' awareness of sustainability and innovations. Businesses should bring valuable information in a simple and concise message.

7. Conclusion

There have been so many natural disasters, but we are still not ready to learn a lesson. It is weird to see how we throw away the survival of the humankind only for our own comfort. People have doubts when they have to get used to new habits and they need lots of support to do so. Positive feedback through social media give them hope to carry on. In general, sustainability is a complicated issue for consumers and they tend to overlook it. Proper marketing communication plays a key role in this process. Fashion is also seen as a form of non-verbal communication by means of which people demonstrate their individuality. The research has shown that insufficient knowledge in the field of sustainable fashion is caused by poor media coverage, incorrect information and labelling of sustainable garments. Communication should be brief, concise and should deliver messages across the large media spectrum in attractive visual or non-verbal forms. It is also necessary for the messages to be communicated neutrally to avoid making a potential buyer guilty for his former non-ecological behaviour. A consumer needs to experience something strong and special. Celebrity endorsement and communication is essential from this point of view. Due to the fact that social media are primarily used by younger age groups, it is important to make sure messages are communicated in a funny form even if the environment is at stake. Social media are able to target large groups of young users who are online just to have fun. Videos are a perfect way how to communicate messages on social media as they require less energy. Other powerful social media tools include various mobile applications, blogs, Instagram, product swaps and communities dealing with clothes swap. In order for green promotion to be successful, consumers' behaviour and views have to change at first. For instance, Generation Y perceives sustainable garments as too expensive and non-attractive. The price is still a decisive factor when purchasing a sustainable product. If we want to change respondents' philosophy and perception, we have to boost their awareness in this field. The field of education might be the best place to start making a change we need to see in the world. Education plays a key role when establishing the sustainable fashion industry. Sustainable fashion is an added competence, not a key element of fashion education. Value systems and traditional designer skills have to be modified. Education in the field of sustainable industry needs to be incorporated not only into the curriculum of many designer schools, but also into primary, secondary schools and universities as a part of their environmental education. Today's world needs not only smart fashion businessmen, but also smart consumers that are willing to support this market with their buying behaviour.

Acknowledgements

This contribution is a partial result of the project VEGA 1/0078/18 Aspects of marketing communication in the management processes of the circular economy.

References

Birtwistle, G. and Moore, C. M. (2007) „Fashion clothing–where does it all end up?", International Journal of Retail & Distribution Management,Vol 35, No.3, pp. 210

Borboni. E. (2019) *Communication of Sustainability and EthicalIssues in Fashion: The Lombardy's Experience*, Fashion Communication in the Digital Age, Springer, Ascona.

ETP Fibres Textiles Clothing (2016) Towards a 4th Industrial Revolution of Textiles and Clothing –Strategic Innovation and Research Agenda for the European Textile and Clothing Industry, [online], http://www.textile-platform.eu.

European Sustainable Business Federation (2019) „Circular Fashion Advocacy: A strategy towards a circular fashion industry in Europe", [online], Ecopreneur.eu, https://ecopreneur.eu/wp-content/uploads/2019/03/EcoP-Circular-Fashion-Advocacy-Report-28-3-19.pdf

Finisterra do Paco, A. M., Reis, R. (2012) "Factors Affecting Skepticism Toward Green Advertising", *Journal of Advertising*, Vol 41, No. 4, pp. 147

FLETCHER, K. (2013) *Sustainable Fashion and Textiles: Design Journeys*, Routledge, London.

Fritzell, J. (2018) „#sustainable#fastfashion - A qualitative study investigating social media as a channel for fast fashion companies to advertise sustainability", [online], University of Borås, https://www.diva-portal.org/smash/get/diva2:1372260/FULLTEXT01.pdf.

Geissdoerfer, M. et al (2017) "The Circular Economy – A new sustainability paradigm?", Journal of Cleaner Production, Vol 143, No.1, pp. 18

Jacometti, V. (2019) „Circular Economy and Waste in the Fashion Industry", Law, Vol 8, No. 10, pp. 1

Khandual, A. and Pradhan, S. (2018) „Fashion Brands and Consumers Approach Towards Sustainable Fashion", Fast Fashion, Fashion Brands and Sustainable Consumption, Springer Nature Singapore Pte Ltd., pp. 45-52

Kim, J., Kang, S. and Lee, K.H. (2018) „How social capital impacts the purchase intention of sustainable fashion products", Journal of Business Research, pp. 1

Kolandai-Matchett, K (2009) "Mediated communication of "sustainable consumption" in the alternative media: a case study exploring a message framing strategy", International Journal of Consumer Studies, Vol 33, No. 2, pp. 113–125.

Korhonen, J., Honkasalo, A. and Seppälä, J. (2018) "Circular Economy: The Concept and its Limitations", Ecological Economics, Vol 143, No. 1, pp. 37

Lai, Z., Henniger, C.E. and Alevizou, P.J. (2017) „An Exploration of Consumers' Perceptions Towards Sustainable Fashion – A Qualitative Study in the UK", Sustainability in Fashion: A Cradle to Upcycle Approach, Springer International Publishing AG, pp. 81 -97

McNeill, L. and Moore, R. (2015) „ Sustainable fashion consumption and the fast fashion conundrum: fashionable consumers and attitudes to sustainability in clothing choice", International Journal of Consumer Studies, Vol 39, No. 3, pp. 212

Mohr, L. A., Eroğlu, D., & Ellen, P. S. (1998) "The development and testing of a measure of skepticism toward environmental claims in marketers' communications", *Journal of consumer affairs*, Vol *32,* No.1, pp. 30-55

Murray, J.B. (2002) The politics of consumption: a re-inquiry on Thompson and Haytko's (1997)" Speaking of Fashion", Journal of Consumer Research, Vol 29, No. 12, pp. 427

Niinimäki, K. (2018) *Circularity and Fashion*, Sustainable Fashion in a Circular Economy, Aalto University, pp. 15

*Niinimäki, K. (2017) „*Fashion in Circular Economy*", Sustainability in Fashion: A Cradle to Upcycle Approach, Springer International Publishing AG, pp. 152*

Rathinamoorthy, R. (2019) Circular Economy in Textiles and Apparel, The Textile Institute Book Series, Coimbator.

Reiter, L., McHaney, R. and Hiller Connell, K.Y. (2017) "Social media influence on purchase intentions: instrument validation", Int. J. Web Based Communities, Vol. 13, No. 1, pp. 59.

Shen, B. et al (2013) „Perception of fashion sustainability in online community", The Journal of The Textile Institute, Vol. 105, No. 9, pp. 971

Sherin, A. (2013) *Sustainable Thinking. Ethical Approaches to Design and Design Management*, Bloomsbury, New York.

Sinan, A., and Dellarocas, C., Godes, D. (2013) "Introduction to the special issue - Social media and business transformation: A framework for research", Information Systems Research, Vol 24, No.1, pp. 3–13

Stahel, W . (2017) "Preface", Baker-Brown, The re-use atlas, London, pp. 13–18

Strähle, J., and Gräff, Ch. (2017) *The Role of Social Media for a Sustainable Consumption*, Green Fashion Retail, Springer Series in Fashion Business, pp. 225–247

Tigrul, O.T., and Gocer, A. (2017) "Communicating Sustainability on Social Media: A study on leading turkish and global Brands in Turkey", International Journal of Marketing, Communication and New Media, Vol 5, No. 8, p. 10

Ting-yan, Ch. Ch. and Wong, W.Y. (2012) "The consumption side of sustainable fashion supply chain", Journal of Fashion Marketing and Management: An International Journal, Vol 16, No. 2 pp. 194.

Varmužová, A. (2019) "Marketingová komunikace jako nástroj pro prosadzení udržitelné módy", [online], Univerzita Tomáše Bati ve Zlíně, https://digilib.k.utb.cz/bitstream/handle/10563/45694/varmu%C5%BEov%C3%A1_2019_dp.pdf?sequence=1

Vehmas, K. et al (2017) „Consumer attitudes and communication in circular fashion", Journal of Fashion Marketing and Management: An International Journal, Vol 22, No. 3, pp. 286-300.

Watson, M. Z. and Yan, R. N. (2013) „An exploratory study of the decision processes of fast versus slow fashion consumers", Journal of Fashion Marketing and Management,Vol 17, No. 2, 141–159.

Yan et al (2012) „Marketing eco-fashion: The influence of brand name and message explicitness", Journal of Marketing Communications, Vol. 18, No. 2, pp. 152

Yip, D. (2010) „What does sustainable fashion mean to you?", [online], BC Living, http://www.bcliving.ca/style/what-does-sustainable-fashionmean- to-you

Start-Up-Specific Performance Indicator System for Flexible and Scalable Logistics

Nicole Vaskovits and Johannes Fottner
Technical University of Munich, Chair of Materials Handling, Material Flow, Logistics, Munich, Germany
nicole.vaskovits@tum.de
j.fottner@tum.de
DOI: 10.34190/EIE.20.079

Abstract: Technology-oriented start-ups often consider logistical challenges in a late development stage, when a lot of money, capacity and manpower have already been spent for special processes, inefficient storage of materials and/or unfavourable supplier contracts. The reason is that they often focus on product development and financing aspects, especially at the outset. Cross-cutting functions like logistics are not given much attention. Additionally, start-ups grow very fast. Hence the requirements in terms of logistics also change very fast without this being recognised. This can be prevented if start-ups use a performance indicator system for the logistics right from the beginning. With such a system, start-ups can monitor their logistics constantly and can respond to changes in good time. However, there are no recommendations for start-ups to design a performance indicator system for logistics. Existing approaches for established companies are mostly too complex and not useful for start-ups. In order to concentrate on their core competences, start-ups need an efficient performance indicator system that is easy to implement and use. Therefore, the aim of this research is to develop an easy and efficient performance indicator system for logistics, especially tailored to the requirements of technology-oriented start-ups, and which grows with them. A development model for technology-oriented start-ups is the basis for designing a start-up-specific performance indicator system for logistics. This model defines the development stages. The stages are described by indicators and characteristics, and the logistical challenges are allocated within each stage. To design the performance indicator system, the relevant performance indicators for each challenge are identified, in order to monitor the current situation. For this purpose, a literature review of performance indicators for established companies is undertaken. The identified indicators are analysed in order to find out if they fulfil the requirements of start-ups and if the required basic data is already available for start-ups in the corresponding phase. Based on this analysis, the final performance indicators are defined. The result of the research is a start-up-specific performance indicator system for logistics. This system recommends performance indicators to technology-oriented start-ups, which are easy to determine and monitor.

Keywords: performance indicator, logistics controlling, supply chain controlling, logistics, start-up, entrepreneurship

1. Introduction

Start-ups often do not care about logistics, especially at the outset and consider logistical challenges in a late development stage when a lot of money, capacity and manpower have already been spent for special processes, inefficient storage of materials and/or unfavourable supplier contracts. The reason is that they are founded on the basis of an innovative business idea, usually with a low seed capital (Alisch, Arentzen and Winter, 2004). Due to their high degree of innovation and the low seed capital they focus on product development, marketing and financing aspects, especially at the outset. Cross-cutting functions like logistics are not paid much attention. Another reason for neglecting logistics is that the founders and first employees are usually no logistics experts and have only a few or none experience in this field. Additionally, start-ups aim to scale up, and accordingly intend to grow their employee numbers and/or the markets they are operating in (Steigertahl and Mauer, 2018). Therefore, start-ups change very fast and the requirements in terms of logistics for start-ups also change very fast without this being recognised. The neglecting of logistics and the not recognizing of changes in logistics can be prevented if start-ups use a performance indicator system for logistics right from the outset. With such a system, they can monitor their logistics constantly and respond to changes in good time. However, there are no recommendations for start-ups to design a performance indicator system for logistics. There exist only guidelines for designing performance indicators for general controlling, without indicators for logistics. Existing approaches for established companies are mostly too complex and not useful for start-ups. In order to concentrate on their core competences, start-ups need an efficient performance indicator system that is easy to implement and use. Accordingly, the aim of this research is to develop an easy and efficient performance indicator system for logistics, which is especially tailored to the requirements of start-ups, and grows with them. This system should recommend performance indicators to technology-oriented start-ups, which are easy to determine and monitor. Since logistics is not relevant for all start-ups, this research focuses on start-ups operating in the sectors of industrial technology, production and hardware. In this paper, such companies are termed "technology-oriented start-ups".

2. Literature review

As shown in the introduction, start-ups differ greatly from established companies. They change very fast and are subject to many uncertainties. Therefore, they have particular requirements for designing a performance indicator system for logistics. Accordingly, it is necessary to define these requirements first. Existing approaches for established companies, which are identified by a literature review, can thus be discussed with regard to these requirements. By means of this discussion it will be highlighted if the existing approaches are usable for technology-oriented start-ups.

Diehm (2017) gives an overview of the requirements for general controlling in young companies. According to him, controlling has to be flexible and adaptable. Additionally, controlling for start-ups should include risk management, and should offer easy, reduced, clear and standardised controlling instruments without great scope for interpretation. Controlling also must take the knowledge level of the founder(s) into account. Finally, Diehm (2017) quote compatibility to the controlling requirements of the investors and the controlling of intangible assets as requirements for controlling in young companies. Some of these requirements also apply to a start-up-specific performance indicator system for logistics. The performance indicator system should not hinder the flexibility of start-ups, and should make opportunities and risks in logistics visible and measurable. In order to ensure rational decisions, the system should be standardised and clear. Additionally, the system must also be reduced to a few, easily manageable and yet meaningful performance indicators. Finally, the performance indicator system must be tailored to the information needs and knowledge level of the founder(s).

For established companies, there are much approaches to designing a performance indicator system for logistics. The first approaches are some guidelines from the Association of German Engineers. VDI 4400 introduces many logistic indicators for procurement (Verein Deutscher Ingenieure, 2001), for production (Verein Deutscher Ingenieure, 2004) and for distribution (Verein Deutscher Ingenieure, 2002). Additionally, VDI 4490 provides many operational-logistics key figures, from goods received to dispatch (Verein Deutscher Ingenieure, 2007). The recommended indicators provide an early warning system, and are standardised and clear. However, a start-up must select the right indicators from the wide range of those proposed. This is in opposition to the requirement that such indicators must be simple and limited in scope, and that the indicators must be oriented towards the knowledge level of the founder(s). Start-ups aim to concentrate on their key business and do not wish to spend a great amount of time finding out the right performance indicators. Another guideline from the Association of German Engineers, VDI 2525 (Verein Deutscher Ingenieure, 1999), provides practice-oriented characteristic values for logistics in small and medium-sized companies. In contrast to VDI 4400 and VDI 4490, this guideline concentrates on just nine indicators. Therefore, the guideline provides standardised, clear, simple and reduced performance indicators. However, the guidelines are not geared up to fast-changing start-ups.

In addition to the VDI guidelines, other authors have proposed performance indicator systems for logistics. Aichele (1997) gives many performance indicators for business-process analysis, and describes the meaning of each indicator. Amongst others, he names and describes 113 indicators for procurement, warehouse management and distribution. Sliwczynski (2016) describes the controlling processes in the supply chain and introduces 58 indicators for supply, production, distribution, inventory, warehouse and transportation controlling. Werner (2014) explains the essence and importance of supply-chain controlling, and introduces 82 indicators for procurement, warehousing, material provision, manufacturing, distribution and financing. Due to the wide range of indicators proposed by Aichele (1997), Sliwczynski (2016), and Werner (2014), these performance indicator systems are not useful for start-ups, as is also true of VDI 4400 and VDI 4490. Another approach is provided by Gladen (2014). He gives an overview of the entire corporate controlling process. He also responds to functional divisions such as logistics, and lists 16 indicators for the objective and the performance target of logistics. The proposed indicators are reduced, though only very roughly and not very clearly. Sucky & Asdecker (2016) describe logistics controlling and how to create a performance indicator system in general, but do not give concrete indicators. Syska (1990) only describes a method to design a company-specific performance indicator system for logistics: concrete indicators are also missing here. Wannenwetsch (2014) only provides fifteen examples of performance indicators for logistics. Therefore, a holistic view is not given here.

This discussion shows that existing approaches for established companies are not directly useful for technology-oriented start-ups. Most studies propose a wide range of indicators, or only give an overview how to design a performance indicator system for start-ups. Therefore, the approaches require an intensive familiarization with this topic. Requirements around the system's orientation towards the knowledge level of the founder(s), and that the indicators should be standardised, clear, simple and reduced, are not given. The only requirement which is fulfilled by all approaches is that they include an early warning system. The most suitable approach for start-ups is the VDI 2525. However, the indicators provided are not geared up to the development of a start-up. Over the course of their development, different indicators will become relevant. Therefore, the performance indicator system is not flexible and adoptable.

For start-ups, guidelines only exist for designing performance indicators for general controlling, without indicators for logistics. Diehm (2017), Georg (2019), Lycko & Mahlendorf (2017), Lüdtke (2017), Wittenberg (2006) provide guidelines for general controlling in start-ups. They give an insight as to how a start-up-specific performance indicator system in general could be designed, but do not consider indicators especially for logistics. The performance indicator systems mostly concentrate on financial and market issues, like working capital, profitability and market analysis.

Viewed holistically, there are no guidelines for start-ups for designing a performance indicator system especially for logistics, and approaches aimed at established companies are not directly useful for start-ups. This leads to the following research question, which will be answered herein: How should a start-up-specific performance indicator system be designed in order to enable technology-oriented start-ups to control their current logistic situation?

3. Objective and methodology

According to the research question, the aim of this research is to develop an easy and efficient performance indicator system for logistics, which is especially tailored to the requirements of technology-oriented start-ups, and grows alongside them. In order to enable flexible and scalable logistics, the system should focus on the development stages of a start-up. For each stage, a few and clear performance indicators should be defined for logistics, which enable start-ups to control their current logistics situation and to react in good time. The defined performance indicators should be easy to determine and monitor.

In order to achieve a focus on the development stages, a development model for technology-oriented start-ups has to be developed. This model defines the development stages, which are described by indicators and characteristics. For each stage it is also defined which conditions exist and which data are available. The development model, the conditions and available data are based on a literature review of existing development models for start-ups. A further precondition for defining relevant performance indicators is to know the logistical challenges, which come up at each stage. To identify these challenges, a literature review of the challenges faced by established companies was conducted. Based on the identified conditions, the relevant challenges seen at each stage were filtered and defined.

To design the performance indicator system, the relevant performance indicators for each challenge have to be identified in order to monitor the current situation. For this purpose, a literature review of performance indicators for established companies occurs. The identified indicators are analysed for whether they match the requirements of start-ups and the conditions of the given stage. Furthermore, it is analysed whether the required basic data is already available for start-ups at the corresponding stage. Based on this analysis, the final performance indicators can be defined.

4. Development stages of technology-oriented start-ups

4.1 Development model

In this research the development model of Hietschold and Fottner (2018) is used. This model is developed especially for technology-oriented start-ups, and takes their requirements into consideration. It combines the business development models of Ripsas and Tröger (2014), Blank (2013) and Schefczyk (2006) with the product development model of Cooper (1996). The model is shown in Figure 1.

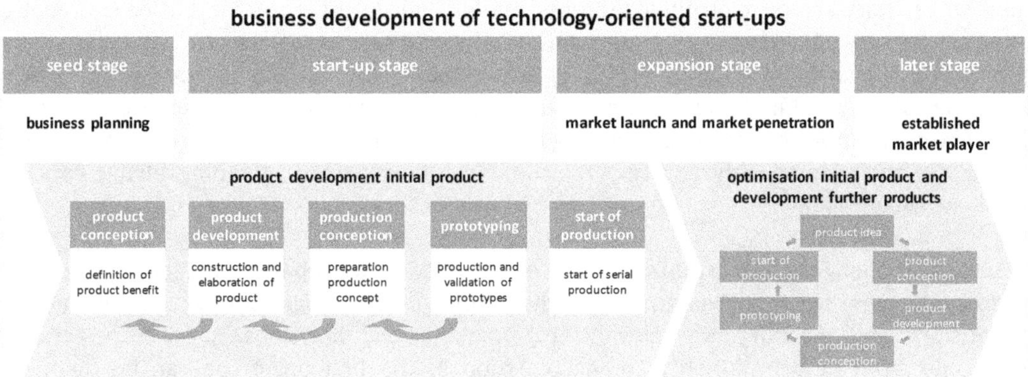

Figure 1: Development model of technology-oriented start-ups, based on Hietschold and Fottner (2018)

Each phase of this model is described by indicators, which help start-ups to allocate in one development phase. The indicators and their manifestations in each phase are shown in Figure 2.

BUSINESS DEVELOPMENT	seed stage	start-up stage			expansion stage	later stage
PRODUCT DEVELOPMENT	product conception	product development	production conception	prototyping	start of production	optimisation initial product and development further products
INDICATOR: sales / customer benefits	no sales	realisation of first sales and/or cutomer benefits			strong sales and/or customer growth	stable sales
INDICATOR: marketing and sales activities	first market anaysis, first customer contacts	development of a marketing and sales concept			intensive marketing efforts, expansion of the sales system	
INDICATOR: market uncertainty	very high	high			low	hardly noticeable
INDICATOR: technology readiness level	basic and technology research, formulating the technical concept, technical feasibility studies	analytical and experimental evidence of critical functions, experimental setup in the laboratory and in the operational environment			product launch and operations	qualified product, evidently successfully used in the market
INDICATOR: role of founder	personal handling of all activities	asuption of operational as well as strategic activities			assumption of strategic activities only	delegation of strategic activities
INDICATOR: standardisation	no processes exist, operations mainly take place for the first time	identification, standardisation and formalisation of processes			establishing standard processes	optimisation of standard processes, high efficiency of core processes
INDICATOR: organisational structures	no organisational structures exist	generating first organisational structures and hierarchy levels			building of departments	permanent organisational structures

Figure 2: Indicators to be allocated in one development phase, based on Hietschold and Fottner (2018)

This research focuses on the start-up stage and the expansion stage. At the seed stage, there are no relevant performance indicators, because there are no logistical challenges. In the later stages, a start-up is an established market player and does not change as fast as in the previous stages. Sales are stable and standardised processes and permanent organisational structures exist. Therefore, start-ups can rely on approaches aimed at established companies in this respect.

4.2 Conditions, data and logistical challenges at the start-up stage

The start-up stage is characterised by product development. The desired milestone for start-ups is a viable business model or product, and the market launch. The aim of start-ups at this stage is to convince first users or buyers of the benefit of their product, and to achieve an early validation of their business idea as efficiently as possible using the existing resources. They focus mostly on product development, sales and market research. technical problems must be solved with few financial resources. In the start-up stage, start-ups are mostly funded by the savings of the founders themselves, government grants or business angels. (Lüdtke, 2017)

At the seed stage, start-ups develop their business model. Mostly they use the business model canvas of Osterwalder and Pigneur (2011) and generate a business plan. These plans are also available at the start-up stage. Based on these plans, first assumptions for logistics can be made, like the potential product sales and the potential number of required materials. However, these data are still very vague and uncertain at this point. Start-ups have to get to know the market better in order to obtain reliable data. The business model and business plan will be revised and adapted in the course of the company's development. The only reliable data in this stage is the current available capital.

With regard to the challenges, the start-up stage has to be divided in two separate sub-stages. This is why, during the product development fewer challenges crop up than during prototyping. During product development, only strategic decisions and planning are relevant, e.g. make-or-buy decisions, supplier selection for core components, and strategic distribution planning. As soon as the first prototype can be built, operational challenges such as those involved in the installation and operation of a prototype warehouse should be considered. Additionally, as soon as it becomes apparent that the prototype complies with the customer requirements and that market launch is within reach, preparatory strategic activities for series production come to the fore, such as warehouse planning. Altogether, the challenges arising at the start-up stage are mostly strategic in nature. They are summarised and described in Table 1 and Table 2. The challenges do not occur temporarily in one stage, but come up for the first time either during product development or prototyping. Subsequently, they arise at regular intervals during the following stages.

Table 1: Logistical challenges at the start-up stage during product development

Logistical challenge	*Need*
Logistics-compatible product development	Reduction of logistics effort and logistics costs in later development phases
Make-or-buy decision	Focus on the core components of the product and core competencies of the start-up
Procurement market research	Getting an overview of potential suppliers for the required materials, and whether the procurement is economical
Material classification	Classification of materials according to economic aspects for identifying items that will have a significant impact on logistics effort and costs
Supplier selection for core components (A items)	Building of strategic partnerships already during product development
Strategic distribution planning	Definition of sales channels and distribution concepts

Table 2: Logistical challenges at the start-up stage during prototyping

Logistical challenge	*Need*
Change management	Use of components with current development status
Installation and operation of prototype warehouse	Storage of all necessary components in one place for an optimal overview
Definition of the procurement strategy	Selection of the most economical procurement strategy per material, such as the number of suppliers per material, local or global procurement or type of cooperation
Supplier selection (B and C items)	Selection of suitable suppliers for each material according to the individual conditions of a start-up
Material requirements planning	Determination of the future demand for materials according to time and quantity
Determination of the optimal procurement quantity	Quantity of material to be retrieved from the supplier in the event of a purchase order
Material inventory planning	Determination of stock levels required to fulfil customer orders, including reorder and safety stock levels
Warehouse planning and installation for series production	Dimensioning of the warehouse for sufficient storage capacity, selection of the most suitable warehouse technology, installation and implementation of the warehouse

4.3 Conditions, data and logistical challenges at the expansion stage

The expansion stage is characterised by the market launch and the expansion of sales. The milestone desired by start-ups is the substantial expansion of sales activities and the development of organisational structures (Lüdtke 2017). The aim of start-ups at this stage is to acquire their first customers and to optimise their product in cooperation with the customers (Lycko and Mahlendorf, 2017). Additionally a proof of the expandability of the business model takes place (Lüdtke, 2017). According to these aims, start-ups at this stage focus mostly on sales and product optimisation, and adapt and finalise their product to the requirements of the customer as quickly as possible (Lycko and Mahlendorf, 2017). At the expansion stage, start-ups are mostly funded by business angels and venture capital (Lüdtke, 2017).

Like in the start-up stage, the business model canvas and the business plan are available at the expansion stage. Accordingly, the plans can also be used at this stage for first assumptions. Because of the fact that start-ups now know their market a little better, the potential product sales and the potential amount of resources required can be estimated better, although they are still uncertain. In addition to the current available capital, a start-up knows the exact current customer demand at this point. Therefore, start-ups have an initial idea of the numbers involved, and which can be scaled.

At the expansion stage, due to the market launch and the start of serial production, operational challenges (e.g. operational purchasing and warehouse operation) arise in addition to the challenges of the start-up stage. The logistical challenges in the expansion stage are summarised and described in Table 3.

Table 3: Logistical challenges at the expansion stage

Logistical challenge	*Need*
Operational supplier management	Evaluation of the existing supplier relationships and improvement of collaborative activities
Operational purchasing	Creation and transmission of orders to the supplier, monitoring during the delivery period, invoice processing
Warehouse operation	Processing of the storage, rearrangement and removal activities, as well as the corresponding data repository
Operational dispatch	Order picking and packaging of the finished products for dispatch

5. Start-up-specific performance indicators for logistics

5.1 Performance indicators at the start-up stage

By considering which logistical challenges come up at the start-up stage during product development, it can be determined that indicators are not necessary in this stage. At this stage, only qualitative strategic decisions and planning are relevant. Therefore, quantitative indicators do not make any sense. During prototyping, some qualitative strategic challenges also arise, such as the definition of the procurement strategy and supplier selection. However, for the preparatory strategic activities for series production, quantitative decisions must be made. This concerns the challenges around material-requirements planning, the determination of the optimal procurement quantity, material-inventory planning and warehouse planning for series production. For these decisions, performance indicators are useful.

5.1.1 Indicator for material-requirements planning

For the material-requirements planning, it is necessary to define the **number of required materials per period**. This indicator is the basis for further planning like the material-inventory planning, and provides information on how much material has to be reordered and how much space is needed in the warehouse. Because start-ups can only rely on uncertain data, the amount of required materials can only be determined by a heuristic estimate from the potential number of customer orders. To ensure flexibility, start-ups should work on one-month time scales. Accordingly, the indicator should be re-assessed each month.

5.1.2 Indicator for the determination of the optimal procurement quantity

The determination of the **optimum order quantity** per material is necessary to define the economic quantity of material to be procured from the supplier in the case of a purchase order. Due to changes in customer demand, start-ups should use the least-unit-cost method. In this method, the optimal procurement quantity is the cumulative demand for the period up to the planning period for which minimum unit costs are expected. In order to react to changes, the indicator should be re-calculated each month.

5.1.3 Indicators for material-inventory planning

Material-inventory planning is used to determine the **inventory levels** required to fulfil customer orders. It also determines the associated **reorder level** and **the safety level** (Stich, Hering and Brosze 2013). The indicators are determined based on a replenishment strategy. The most suitable strategy for start-ups is to trigger the optimum order quantity when levels fall below the reorder level. Accordingly, the maximum inventory level results from the already calculated optimum order quantity and the reorder level. The reorder level is the sum of the safety level and the consumption during the replacement time. Overall, the following indicators are relevant for start-ups during the material inventory planning:

$$maximum\ inventory\ level = optimum\ order\ quantity + reorder\ level$$

$$reorder\ level = safety\ \ level + \ consumption\ during\ replacement\ time$$

Like the optimum order quantity, these indicators should also be re-calculated each month.

5.1.4 Indicator for warehouse planning and installation for series production

The purpose of warehouse planning is to define the inventory strategies and to dimension the warehouse for the **sufficient storage capacity**, which can be calculated using the already calculated maximum inventory level and a scale factor.

$$sufficient\ storage\ capacity = maximum\ inventory\ level \times scale\ factor$$

The scale factor takes the growth of a start-up into account. Every six months, a start-up should check whether the warehouse still has sufficient storage capacity.

5.2 Performance indicators at the expansion stage

5.2.1 Indicator for operational supplier management

Within the scope of the operational supplier management, the existing suppliers are evaluated. For this purpose, the suppliers are evaluated according to their performance. From this, possible consequences and measures for cooperation with the suppliers can be derived. In addition, regular monitoring and control of the suppliers can be carried out. (Weigel and Rücker, 2015).

For the evaluation of supplier performance, the indicator **deliver reliability** can be used. This indicator measures the availability of the delivered goods, and results from the number of satisfied order items and the total number of order items. The number of satisfied order items includes all satisfied items with regard to compliance with deadline, quantity and product quality. (Verein Deutscher Ingenieure, 2001)

$$deliver\ reliability = \frac{number\ of\ satisfied\ order\ items}{total\ number\ of\ order\ items}$$

5.2.2 Indicator for operational purchasing

Operational purchasing includes the generation of orders and their transmission to the supplier, and monitoring during the delivery period. For this purpose the **current inventory level** has to be checked constantly (ideally daily). As described in section 5.1.3 the optimum order quantity has to be triggered when the level falls below the reorder level. Accordingly the indicators **optimum order quantity** and **reorder level** are also relevant for operational purchasing.

5.2.3 Indicators for warehouse operation

Warehouse operation includes the storage, rearrangement and removal activities as well as the corresponding data repository. As described in the operational purchasing paragraph, it is necessary to know the current inventory level. This data should be gathered during warehouse operation. Additionally, checks can be made during operation as to whether the optimum order quantity and reorder level are correctly determined. The indicators **inventory range** and **storage costs per unit** can be used as a basis for this. They can be calculated as follows:

$$inventory\ range = \frac{inventory}{warehouse\ outgoings\ per\ unit\ of\ time}$$

(Verein Deutscher Ingenieure 1999)

$$storage\ costs\ per\ unit = \frac{space\ costs + operational\ costs + repair\ costs\ per\ period}{average\ number\ of\ units\ stored\ in\ the\ period}$$

(Verein Deutscher Ingenieure 1999)

5.2.4 Indicator or operational dispatch

The operational dispatch includes order-picking and the packaging of the finished products for dispatch, as well as the transportation of the products to the customer. Especially for start-ups, it is important that the customer receives the product in the correct quantity, time frame and quality. This can be measured by the indicator **deliver reliability**. The delivery dates and delivery quantities accepted by the customer and confirmed by the supplier are used as evaluation criteria. The indicator thus makes a statement about the fulfilment of assurances made to the customer. (Verein Deutscher Ingenieure, 2002)

Deliver reliability can be calculated as follows:

$$deliver\ reliability = \frac{number\ of\ satisfied\ customer\ order\ items}{number\ of\ customer\ order\ items}$$

6. Conclusion

The aim of this research was to develop an easy and efficient performance indicator system for logistics, which is especially tailored to the requirements of technology-oriented start-ups, and grows with them. In order to enable flexible and scalable logistics, the system should focus on the development stages of a start-up. For this purpose, the development model from Hietschold and Fottner (2018) was used. This model defines the development stages, which were used to allocate the logistical challenges of technology-oriented start-ups. For each challenge, maximum two clear performance indicators for logistics are defined according to the requirements of start-ups, and the conditions and the available data at the corresponding stage. These indicators enable start-ups to control their current logistics situation and react in good time. In future research, a validation of the developed system with several technology-oriented start-ups in different development stages will take place.

References

Aichele, C. (1997) *Kennzahlenbasierte Geschäftsprozeßanalyse,* Gabler Verlag, Wiesbaden.

Alisch, K., Arentzen, U. and Winter, E. (2004) *Gabler Wirtschaftslexikon,* Gabler, Wiesbaden.

Blank, S. (2013) *The four steps to the epiphany: Successful strategies for products that win,* K & S Ranch, Pescadero.

Cooper, R.G. (1996) "Overhauling the new product process", *Industrial Marketing Management*, Vol. 25, No. 6, pp 465–482.

Diehm, J. (2017) *Controlling in Start-up-Unternehmen. Praxisbuch für junge Unternehmen und Existenzgründungen,* Springer Gabler, Wiesbaden.

Georg, S. (2019) *Key Performance Indicators für junge Unternehmen: Die Steuerung von Start-ups anhand kritischer Erfolgsfaktoren,* Gabler, Wiesbaden.

Gladen, W. (2014) *Performance Measurement. Controlling mit Kennzahlen,* Springer Gabler, Wiesbaden.

Hietschold, N. and Fottner, J. (2018) „Beschaffung bei technologieorientierten Startups: Wie Startups beschaffungslogistische Aspekte von Beginn an berücksichtigen können", *ZWF*, Vol. 113, No. 1-2, pp 31-36.

Lüdtke, C. (2017) "Pragmatisch und flexibel: Controlling in der Frühphase", *Controlling & Management Review*, Vol. 61, No. 6, pp 34–40.

Lycko, M.A. and Mahlendorf, M.D. (2017) "Management-Control-Systeme in Start-ups", *Controlling & Management Review*, Vol. 61, No. 6, pp 24–33.

Osterwalder, A. and Pigneur, Y. (2011) *Business Model Generation. Ein Handbuch für Visionäre, Spielveränderer und Herausforderer,* Campus Verlag, Frankfurt am Main.

Ripsas, S. and Tröger S. (2014) *Deutscher Startup Monitor 2014,* KPMG in Deutschland, Berlin.

Schefczyk, M. (2006) *Finanzieren mit Venture Capital und Private Equity. Grundlagen für Investoren, Finanzintermediäre, Unternehmer und Wissenschaftler,* Schäffer-Poeschel, Stuttgart.

Sliwczynski, B. (2016) "Controlling Processes in the Supply Chain" in *Controlling Supply Chains. Theory and Practice,* eds Sliwiczynski, B. and Kolinski, A., Nova Science Publishers, New York, pp 71–115.

Steigertahl, L. and Mauer, R. (2018), *EU Startup Monitor,* Graz.

Stich, V., Hering, N. and Brosze, T. (2013) „Beschaffungslogistik" in *Logistikmanagement. Handbuch Produktion und Management,* eds Schuh, G. and Stich, V., Springer, Berlin, Heidelberg, pp 77–113.

Sucky, E. and Asdecker, B (2016) „Logistikcontrolling in der Unternehmenspraxis. Logistikcontrolling, Kennzahlen, Kennzahlensysteme, Retourenmanagement" in *Handbuch Controlling,* eds Becker, W. and Ulrich, P., Springer Fachmedien, Wiesbaden, pp. 141–158 [07 April 2020].

Syska, A. (1990) *Kennzahlen für die Logistik,* Springer, Berlin, Heidelberg.

Verein Deutscher Ingenieure (1999), *Praxisorientierte Logistikkennzahlen für kleine und mittelständische Unternehmen*, No. 2525.

Verein Deutscher Ingenieure (2001) *Logistikkennzahlen für die Beschaffung*, No. 4400 Blatt 1.

Verein Deutscher Ingenieure (2002) *Logistikkennzahlen für die Distribution*, No. 4400 Blatt 3.

Verein Deutscher Ingenieure (2004) *Logistikkennzahlen für die Produktion*, No. 4400 Blatt 2.

Verein Deutscher Ingenieure (2007) *Operative Logistikkennzahlen von Wareneingang bis Versand*, No. 4490.

Wannenwetsch, H. (2014), *Integrierte Materialwirtschaft, Logistik und Beschaffung,* Springer Vieweg, Berlin, Heidelberg.

Weigel, U. and Rücker, M. (2015) *Praxisguide Strategischer Einkauf. Know-how, Tools und Techniken für den globalen Beschaffer,* Springer Gabler, Wiesbaden.

Werner, H. (2014) *Kompakt Edition: Supply Chain Controlling. Grundlagen, Performance-Messung und Handlungsempfehlungen,* Springer Fachmedien Wiesbaden, Wiesbaden.

Wittenberg, V. (2006), *Controlling in jungen Unternehmen. Phasenpsezifische Controllingkonzeption für Unternehmen in der Gründungs- und Wachstumsphase,* DUV Deutscher Universitäts-Verlag, Wiesbaden.

Masters Research Papers

Intrapreneurial Activity Within the Hospitality Sector: Evidence From Ireland

Wayne Hand and Kate Johnston
School of Business and Humanities, Dundalk Institute of Technology, Ireland
handwayne@hotmail.co.uk
Kate.Johnston@dkit.ie
DOI: 10.34190/EIE.20.215

Abstract: In today's globally competitive environment, creativity and innovation are critical for organisational competitiveness. Intrapreneurship, typically defined where an individual or team act in an entrepreneurial manner within an organisation (Omotunde 2017; Burns 2015; Buekens 2014) has emerged as a new buzzword in organisations as diverse as Virgin, Google and Intel, driving innovation and competitiveness. Fostering intrapreneurship within organisations, while hugely beneficial, (Trott 2008 and Desouza 2011) can be problematic. Often it can be a delicate balance between environmental, internal organisational and managerial factors (Costello and Powers 2018). Research suggests that internal organisational conditions (Buekens, 2014; Desouza, 2011), organisational strategy (Perez-Uribe et al. 2018), business hierarchy and culture (Antoncic and Hisrich (2003), Kuratko et al. 2014) and crucially management support and tolerance of risk-taking (Alpkan et al. (2010) all play a critical role in creating and supporting an intrapreneurial culture. How different sectors manage the intrapreneurship process, most notably the healthcare, ICT, educational and banking industries (for example Lages et al (2016) and Benitez-Amado (2010) is now gaining increased attention. Intrapreneurship offers huge potential to service businesses, where continuous innovation in terms of service, customer experience and technology is critical to maintaining competitiveness within the sector (Backman, Klaesson and Oner (2017). The hospitality sector, a sector in the front line in terms of competition and technology disputing is a case in point. In Ireland alone, the hospitality sector generated some €7.6 billion in 2020 and is responsible for nearly 200,000 jobs, (ITIC 2020), equivalent to 8% of the working population. This research paper investigates intrapreneurship within the hospitality sector, by analysing interview data with industry experts along with survey data from 110 companies. The results suggest that while managers understand and perceive the sector as intrapreneurial, the reality in practice suggest a lack of time, management supports and rewards for employees. Intrapreneurship, where it happens, occurs organically. The paper closes with suggestions for policy initiatives and the role of support agencies.

Keywords: intrapreneurship, service sector, hospitality, Ireland

1. Research context

1.1 The history of intrapreneurship as an academic discipline

Any discussion on intrapreneurship necessitates some reference to the theory of entrepreneurship; a term first discussed term within the literature as early as the 1930s, when Schumpeter (1934) recognised the role of entrepreneurship to firm innovation and economic growth. The term intrapreneurship emerged from this literature and while the two terms share common themes (Blanka, 2019), intrapreneurship is still a relatively new concept.

The first reference to the term intrapreneurship was coined by Pinchot and Pinchot (1985) which they define as the actions of an individual or team that is acting in an entrepreneurial manner within an organisation, to serve the best interests of the organisation. According to Pinchot (1985), it is the intrapreneur, who is a key driver for innovation and competitive advantage for the firm. Since Pinchot's initial work, globalisation and the IT revolution has meant that increasingly service sector companies, large companies such as Intel, Microsoft, Google all recognise the critical role entrepreneurial employees play in the processes of innovation and competitiveness. Examples of intrapreneurship include the Post-It Note, Sony PlayStation, Gmail and the "Likes" now widely used by Facebook and other social media platforms. The latter was developed from the Facebook "hack-a-thons" in-house policy where engineers and coders were given time to create and develop new ideas.

1.2 A Definition of Intrapreneurship and the Intrapreneur

While no consistent definition exists within the literature, the term has become synonymous with innovative and creative organisations. In the context of this study, intrapreneurship is defined as "entrepreneurship within an existing business structure" (Naidu and Rao, 2008, p.161).

The intrapreneur is one of the central players in this debate – the person charged with generating ideas and thinking creatively. At one level, intrapreneurs have been viewed as having similar characteristics to entrepreneurs; they are strategically aware, creative, idea-driven, innovative, flexible, good networkers and take responsibility for developing innovative ideas to exploit those opportunities for the benefit of the organisation (Desouza 2011; Burns 2015; Kuratko et al. 2011). However, there are differences; the entrepreneur is seen as being driven by his or her success, while the success of the organisation drives the intrapreneur (Eilenberg 2012) and crucially, intrapreneurs work within the existing organisation structure; its existing resources, policies and bureaucracy (Baruah and Ward 2015).

1.3 A brief review of the current literature in Intrapreneurship

Numerous themes have emerged within the literature which are relevant to this study. First, understanding the dimensions of intrapreneurship and what does it mean to be intrapreneurial? Several authors argue that the term has three distinct dimensions, innovativeness, risk-taking and pro-activity (Kuratko et al. 2011; Covin and Slevin 1991; Miller, 1983). Subsequent work has added two further dimensions, autonomy and competitive aggressiveness consistent with a five-dimensional model (Lumpkin and Dess 1996; Wales 2015) suggesting that all these dimensions form the basis of measuring intrapreneurial activity.

Second, there is an almost universally accepted view that intrapreneurship has significant positive impacts on firm financial performance, (Lumpkin and Dees (1996), Zahra and Garvis 2000 and Antoncic and Hisrich 2003), an increase in innovativeness, (Kuratko et al. 2011; Covin and Slevin 1991; Miller, 1983) leading to new venture creation (Antoncic and Hisrich 2003) generating new opportunities, creating customer value and new business platforms within the organisation (De Jong and Wennekers 2008). Others cite the impact on competitive advantage (Block and MacMillan 2003; Trott 2008 and Desouza 2011) enabling access to new markets through product or service innovations (new venturing) (Antoncic and Hisrich (2003). Moreover, the intrapreneurial organisation have also been shown to lead to higher employee job satisfaction (Wood 2004).

Finally, much of the literature has centred on factors that stimulate intrapreneurship and understanding the barriers to Intrapreneurship. The research suggests that managing and fostering an intrapreneurial culture across the whole organisation can be problematic – suggesting the level of intrapreneurial activity within an organisation is a delicate balance between environmental, internal organisational and managerial factors (Costello and Powers 2018). The role of management is crucial. Management plays a key role, facilitating the allocation of resources and championing innovative ideas (Feyzbakhsh et al. 2008; Kuratko et al. 2014), fostering a culture of failure tolerance, (Custódio et al. (2017), ensuring flexibility and freedom to pursue their projects without bureaucratic barriers (Hisrich and Kearney 2012), opportunity (Parker 2011), and time (Kuratko et al. 2014). Moreover, rewards and incentives whether financial (Hellriegel et al. 1999) or non-financial (acknowledgement etc) (Scheepers 2011 and Kuratko 2017) are critical. Similarly, organisational design (Boon et al. 2013) favouring a decentralised structure is shown to foster intrapreneurial activity (Delic et al. 2016). Googles 20% rule, allows employees 20% of their work time to develop innovations in the workplace and is a prime example of intrapreneurship being supported in the workplace (Deloitte 2015).

1.4 The importance of Intrapreneurship within the hospitality industry

The impact of intrapreneurship and how different organisations and sectors foster or limit the intrapreneurship process has been the subject of growing interest among academics. Research has examined the healthcare, (Heinonen et al 2013) ICT (Benitez-Amado et al 2010), education (Bicknell et al. 2010) and financial sectors Lages et al (2016). Service sectors stand to particularly benefit. A case in point is the hospitality and tourism sectors. A hugely important sector (valued at $8.81 trillion), (Statista 2019), yet under increasing competition and disruption, in the form of innovative technology and reputation management. In Ireland, the hospitality sector is valued at €7.6bn and employs 180,000 (PWC 2020). A total of 71% of sectoral employment is outside of Dublin. The activities of the hospitality sector are crucial for regional and local economies (PWC,2020), and supports the larger tourism sector, which is Ireland's largest indigenous industry.

The arrival of Covid-19 for the Hospitality industry (Hotels, Restaurants and Pubs) has been close to catastrophic. The arrival of Covid-19 has created new problems for hospitality businesses. Social distancing guidelines will require businesses in the sector to think and operate differently. Innovation has been championed as a key to responding to these changes (Enz and Harrison 2010 and Mogelonsky 2016). Richard (2017) indicates that innovation in the hospitality industry is no longer a choice, customer demands mean that organisations must utilise open innovation to stay ahead of the competition and provide the best service for customers.

In the context of the above, this study seeks to examine the extent to which intrapreneurship exists within the hospitality sector. The objectives of the research are to establish the extent to which those working in the sector perceive the sector as intrapreneurial, to explore the extent to which intrapreneurship is actively supported and to identify what initiatives are required to support intrapreneurship.

2. Methods of data collection

The research adopts an exploratory research approach (Robinson, 2002), and combined a qualitative and quantitative research approach consisting of the in-depth interviews and survey. Semi-structured interviews were conducted with three key stakeholders; namely the CEO of The Restaurant Association of Ireland, a body representing over 2500 members, an academic who teaches /researches in the hospitality sector and a business consultant and adviser working with hospitality businesses. All interviews were recorded, transcribed and analysed to identify common themes.

The questions were structured to identify the following

- Identify if the term intrapreneurship was known within the industry
- Determine if hospitality businesses support, encourage and demonstrate intrapreneurial behaviour in Ireland
- Identify barriers that exist for intrapreneurship in hospitality businesses
- Get stakeholder recommendations as to how intrapreneurship can be supported in Ireland's hospitality businesses

Following these initial explanatory interviews, an online and paper-based survey was developed and using various email and social media platforms were circulated to various entrepreneurial groups throughout Ireland. The surveys were anonymous. The final number of responses was 127. The final survey consisted of 13 questions and was designed to establish a demographic and business profile of respondents, their attitudes and knowledge of intrapreneurship within the sector and challenges and barriers to supporting a more intrapreneurial culture.

3. Results

3.1 Results of the qualitative research – interview

The key insights drawn from the interview are summarised below.

- **#1:** All interviewees suggested that the terms were not well known, management may be familiar with the term.
- #2: All the stakeholders agreed that the concept of intrapreneurship is being practised within the industry but in an ad-hoc manner. *"It happens, but in an unstructured and organic way"* (Academic). However, this is dependent on the size and structure of the business. According to the business consultant, *"It depends on the owner, traditional family-run businesses wouldn't encourage this behaviour". This was echoed by the* academic, stating *"high levels of family-run businesses may not embrace this behaviour".*
- *#3: General agreement that* rewards were not the norm.
- #4: All stakeholders agreed that neither management support nor allowance for risk-taking was the norm in the industry. The academic states *"hospitality businesses would facilitate intrapreneurial behaviour if the benefits were made clear".*
- #5 Risk-taking within the sector is limited within the industry. The industry representative indicated that *"the industry is fairly generic; innovation is limited to the culinary sense".* The academic believes that hospitality businesses are *"reactive rather than proactive".*
- #6 Time is critical the academic stated that *"If intrapreneurship isn't given the time, it won't develop and this will limit the business".*
- **#7:** All stakeholders indicated that training and supports are key. The business consultant states *"management needs to start talking about the term and recognise the intrapreneur and support them,*

management can facilitate this behaviour for the benefit of the business. The consultant suggested that *"if policymakers start to talk about the term and educate people about what it means, companies will recognise it in staff"*

3.2 Results of the survey research

A total of 127 participants took part in the survey, 50% female, 50% male. The percentage age was <35 range (57%), 35-50 age range (35%), over 50+ (8%). In terms of their educational attainment levels, the majority had a degree or higher; some 56% had a degree with 23% holding a masters or postgraduate qualification; less than 5% had no formal qualification. According to the job role, some 33% were employees, while the majority (77%) were management. Most respondents (70%) had worked in the industry for over 5 years. Of the businesses involved, 47% were from the accommodation sector, 38% food and drink and 16% other. The size of the businesses reflects the business profile in Ireland generally. A total of 40% were small, and 35% medium (51-250 employees) and 17% had over 250 employees. Finally, most were established businesses, with 79% in business for 10+ years.

Respondents were initially asked the extent to which they were familiar with the term intrapreneurship. The majority had heard of the term intrapreneurship before the survey (84%), with over 47% fully aware of the term.

3.3 How intrapreneurial is the hospitality sector in Ireland

Several of the questions sought to examine the perception among managers in terms of how intrapreneurial they view their sector. Respondents were given a series of questions on a scale of 1-5 (1- strongly disagree to 5 strongly agree). A summary of the results is presented in Table 1 next.

Table 1: The degree to which you believe the following statements to be true about businesses which operate in the hospitality sector (n=83): Managers

Statements		**Neither Agree or Disagree %**	**Agree %**	**Strongly Disagree %**
Often take risks		25	40	14
Often develop innovative and creative new products or services		18	45	18
Are proactive and responsible for creating change in the industry		23	49	15
Often enter new markets by changing or adding to their products or services		21	51	11

A total of 83 mangers responded, just over half, 54% of respondents either "agreed" or "strongly agreed" that sector often took risks. Similarly, nearly two-thirds of managers (63%) "agreed" or "strongly agreed" that businesses in their sector are innovative in terms of new product development. There was also a positive perception among managers that the sector was proactive (64% agreed/strongly agreed) and innovative (62%). Overall, the results indicate that there is a strong belief among managers that the hospitality sector is intrapreneurial as measured by the three dimensions associated with intrapreneurship, innovativeness, risk-taking and pro-activity as noted by Kuratko et al. 2011, among others.

3.4 Do internal conditions limit or foster intrapreneurship in the sector?

The following section sought to assess to what extent factors such as management, time and rewards exist within the industry to foster or limit intrapreneurial activity.

Of the 110 respondents approx, two-thirds of respondents (65%) agreed employees were given sufficient time to come up with "new ideas and solutions for the business" and 68% felt they could "freely communicate across department and sections". Two conditions typically associated with intrapreneurship. However, supports in terms of reward and acknowledgement for intrapreneurial appear to be less prevalent in the industry. Nearly half disagreed that employees were rewarded with promotion for their ideas. Intrapreneurship occurs, but not in a structured, supported manner.

Table 2: Barriers and internal conditions for fostering intrapreneurship (n=110)

Statements		Disagree/ Strongly Disagree %	Unsure %	Agree/Strongly Agree %
Employees are given adequate time during work to be innovative and come up with new ideas and solutions for the business		42	21	37
Employees are actively encouraged by their manager/ supervisor to come up with new solutions and ideas for the business		21	14	65
Taking risks is an accepted part of my job		31	24	45
Employees often receive a financial reward for their ideas		55	26	19
Employees often receive promotion for their ideas		49	19	32
Rules and procedures limit my ability to be innovative and come up with new ideas		41	20	39
Employees can communicate freely across sections or departments		19	14	68

3.5 How to improve and foster a culture of intrapreneurship within the sector

Table 3: How to improve innovation and creativity in your workplace (n=110)

Top three Suggestions	Responses	Rank
More management support for the development of ideas	32%	1
Allocation of adequate time to come up with new ideas	29%	2
Being rewarded for my ideas	19%	3

The results suggest that the highest proportion (31.82% or 35) of the 110 respondents believe that more management support for idea development is required. Respondents also indicate that adequate time 29.09% (32) and being rewarded for their ideas 19.09% (21) would improve creativity and innovation.

The data was further analysed to identify any underlying trends within the data set. Some notable trends indicated that there is a link between business size and intrapreneurial behaviour, the results indicate larger businesses have a lower barrier and better environments for supporting and fostering intrapreneurial behaviour, this decreases with the size of the business.

4. Discussion and recommendations for future research

This study aimed to examine the extent to which intrapreneurship exists within the hospitality industry, the supports and barriers that are prevalent and to formulate some policy implications. The results of both survey data for approx. 110 businesses and interviews indicate that respondents believe Ireland's hospitality businesses demonstrate intrapreneurial behaviour. The results suggest that while intrapreneurship is encouraged (coming up with ideas and risk-taking), conditions that the literature consistently demonstrates that are crucial in creating a culture of intrapreneurship financial rewards, management support and time are not widely prevalent. Approximately 50% felt that employees did not receive financial rewards or promotion for their ideas. The evidence is consistent with a view that intrapreneurship exists but in an informal, ad hoc manner.

5. Implications for further research

For many small open economies such as Ireland, tourism and hospitality are crucial to the economy and social infrastructure. Fostering a culture of innovation and intrapreneurship is vital in ensuring the future health and success of the sector, particularly in the current economic climate. This is a small qualitative study but raises important issues around intrapreneurship for the hospitality industry in Ireland and potentially worldwide.

Further research would seek to expand this study using a larger data set, from both the managers' and the employees' perspective – two central players in the debate. A larger data set would be important, allowing for statistical analysis to explore firm-specific factors such as firm size, ownership, and management play in creating intrapreneurial behaviour.

There is also the issue of the role of management, particularly middle managers in driving intrapreneurial behaviour. Middle managers play a key role as conduits of change in motivating employees to be innovative but also, they have the authority and responsibility in terms of resources allocation – both time and money. A more in-depth study would better understand their role in fostering innovation and risk-taking. This could also provide important insights into the policy implications for training and supports at both a firm and industry level.

References

Alpkan, L., Bulut, C. & Gunday, G., (2010). Organizational support for intrapreneurship and its interaction with human capital to enhance innovative performance. *Management Decision,* 48(5), pp. 732-755.

Antoncic, B. & Hisrich, R. D., (2003). Clarifying the intrapreneurship concept. *JOURNAL OF SMALL BUSINESS AND ENTERPRISE DEVELOPMENT,* 10(1), pp. 7-24.

Baruah B, Ward A (2015) Metamorphosis of intrapreneurship as an effective organizational strategy. International Entrepreneurship Management Journal 11:pp. 811–822

Block, Z. & MacMillan, I. C., (2003). *Corporate Venturing: Creating New Businesses Within The Firm.* 3rd ed. USA: Harvard Business School Press.

Bobek, A. & Wickham, J., (2015). *Working Conditions in Ireland Project Employment in the Irish hospitality sector: A preliminary background report,* Dublin: TASC.

Boon, J., Van Der Klink, M. & Janssen, J., (2013). Fostering Intrapreneurial Competencies of Employees In The Education Sector. *International Journal of Training and Development,* 17(3), pp. 210-221.

Buekens, W., (2014). Fostering Intrapreneurship: The challenge for a new game leadership. *Procedia Economics and Finance,* 16(3), pp. 580-586.

Burns, P., (2015). *Corporate Entrepreneurship, Building an Entrepreneurial Organization.* UK: E-study Guides.

Benitez-Amado, J. Montes, F. and Perez-Arostegui M. (2010). Information technology-enabled intrapreneurship culture and firm performance. Industrial Management & Data Systems. 110(4) pp.:550-566

Chen, M.-H. & Cangahuala, G., (2010). *Corporate entrepreneurship environment and organizational performance in technology manufacturing sector.* Phuket, Portland International Conference on Management of Engineering & Technology (PICMET).

Costello, L. & Powers, M., (2018). *Developing In-House Digital Tools in Library Spaces.* USA: IGI Global.

Covin, J. G. & Slevin, D. P., (1991). A conceptual model of entrepreneurship as a firm behaviour. *Entrepreneurship: Theory and practice,* 16(1), pp. 7-25.

Custódio, C., Ferreira, M. A. & Matos, P., (2017). *Do General Managerial Skills Spur Innovation?,* Brussels: European Corporate Governance Institute.

Damanpour, F., (1991). Organizational Innovation: A Meta-Analysis of Effects of Determinants and Moderators. *The Academy of Management Journal,* 34(3), pp. 355-390.

Deloitte, (2015). Five Insights into Intrapreneurship, UK: Deloitte Digital.

De Jong, J. & Wennekers, S., (2008). *Intrapreneurship: conceptualizing entrepreneurial employee behaviour,* Zoetermeer: EIM Business and Policy Research.

Delic, A., Djonlagic, S. & Mešanović, M., (2016). The Role of the Process Organizational Structure in the Development of Intrapreneurship in Large Companies. *Our Economy,* 4(63), pp. 42-51.

Deloitte, (2015). *Five Insights into Intrapreneurship,* UK: Deloitte Digital.

Desouza, K. C., (2011). *Intrapreneurship: Managing Ideas Within Your Organization.* Toronto: Rotman-UTP Publishing.

Eilenberg, K., (2012). *The Business Intrapreneur: Profiles of Unsung Heroes of Corporate America.* USA: Lodestone Logic.

Enz, C. A. & Harrison, J. S., (2008). Innovation and Entrepreneurship in the Hospitality Industry. In: R. C. Wood & B. Brotherton, eds. *The SAGE Handbook of Hospitality Management.* London: Sage Publications, pp. 213-228.

Fayolle, A. & Kyrö, P., (2008). *The Dynamics Between Entrepreneurship, Environment and Education.* Cheltenham: Edward Elgar.

Feyzbakhsh, S.A., Sadeghi, R., & Shoraka, S (2008). A case study of intrapreneurship obstacles: The RAJA Passenger Train Company. Journal of Small Business and Entrepreneurship, 21 (2) 171-180, 251.

Finkle, T. A., (2012). Corporate Entrepreneurship and Innovation in Silicon Valley: The Case of Google, Inc. *Entrepreneurship Theory and Practice,* 36(4), pp. 863-887.

Hancer, M., Bulent-Ozturk, A. & Ayyildiz, T., (2009). Middle-level hotel managers' corporate entrepreneurial behaviour and risk-taking propensities: a case of Didim, Turkey. *Journal of Hospitality Marketing and Management,* 18(5), pp. 523-537.

Heinonen, J. & Korvela, K. M., (2003). *How About Measuring Intrapreneurship.* Milan, EISB Conference.

Hellriegel, D., Jackson, S. E. & Slocum, J. W., (1999). *Management.* 8th ed. United States of America: South-Western College Publications.

Hisrich, R. D., (2016). *International Entrepreneurship: Starting, Developing, and Managing a Global Venture.* 2nd ed. Singapore: Sage.

Hisrich, R. D. & Peters, M. P., (1998). *Entrepreneurship.* 4th ed. UK: McGraw-Hill.

Hisrich, R. & Kearney, C., (2012). *Corporate Entrepreneurship: How to Create a Thriving Entrepreneurial Spirit Throughout Your Company.* USA: Mcgraw Hill.

Hornsby, J. S., Naffziger, D. W., Kuratko, D. F. & Montagna, R. V., (1993). An Interactive Model of The Corporate Entrepreneurship Process. *Entrepreneurship Theory and Practice,* 17(2), pp. 29-37.

Hough, J., Nieman, G. & Nieuwenhuizen, C., (2003). *Entrepreneurship: A South African Perspective.* South Africa: Van Schaik Publishers.

ITIC, (2017). *ITIC.* [Online] Available at: http://www.itic.ie/YE17/index.html[Accessed 15 August 2018].

Kuratko, D. F. (2005) The Emergence of Entrepreneurship Education: Development, Trends, and Challenges', *Entrepreneurship Theory and Practice*, 29(5), pp. 577–597

Kuratko, D., (2009). *Entrepreneurship theory process practice.* 8th ed. USA: South-Western Cengage Learning.

Kuratko, D., (2017). *Entrepreneurship Theory, Process, Practice.* 10th ed. United States of America: Cengage Learning.

Lumpkin, G. T., (2007). Intrapreneurship and Innovation. In: J. R. Baum, M. Frese & R. Baron, eds. *The Psychology of Entrepreneurship.* Sussex: Lawrence Erlbaum Associates Inc, p. 237.

Lumpkin, G. T. & Dees, G. G., (1996). Clarifying the Entrepreneurial Orientation Construct and Linking It to Performance. *The Academy of Management Review, Vol. 21, No. 1 (Jan. 1996), pp. 135-172,* 21(1), pp. 135-172.

Miller, D., (1983). The Correlates of Entrepreneurship in Three Types of Firms. *Management Science,* 29(7), pp. 770-791.

Mogelonsky, L., (2016). *Hospitality New.* [Online] Available at: https://www.hospitalitynet.org/opinion/4075102.html[Accessed 15 August 2018].

Naidu, N. & Rao, T., (2008). *Management and Entrepreneurship.* New Delhi: I. K. International Publishing House.

Omotunde, A., (2017). *The Intrapreneur, Ignite Your Work Life.* UK: Pervium Consulting.

Parker, S. C., (2018). *The Economics of Entrepreneurship.* 2nd ed. Cambridge: Cambridge University Press.

Perez-Uribe, R., Salcedo-Perez, C. & Ocampo-Guzman, D., (2018). *Handbook of Research on Intrapreneurship and Organizational Sustainability in SME's.* United States of America: IGI Global.

Pinchot, G., (1985). *Intrapreneuring: Why You Don't Have to Leave the Corporation to Become an Entrepreneur.* Michigan: Harper & Row.

Pinchot, G. & Pellman, R., (1999). *Intrapreneuring in Action: A Handbook for Business Innovation.* United States of America: Berrett-Koehler.

Robson, C. (2002). Real World Research: A Resource for Social Scientists and Practitioner-Researchers (2nd ed.). Oxford: Blackwell Publishers Ltd.

Scheepers, R. d. V., (2011). Motivating Intrapreneurs: The Relevance of Rewards. *Industry and Higher Education,* 25(4), pp. 249-263.

Schumpeter, J., (1934). *The Theory of Economic Development.* Uk: Taylor and Francis.

Sherman, A., (2012). *Harvesting Intangible Assets: Uncover Hidden Revenue in Your Company's Intellectual Property.* USA: AMACOM.

Smith, L., Rees, P. & Murray, N., (2016). Turning entrepreneurs into intrapreneurs: Thomas Cook, a case-study. *Tourism Management,* 56(1), pp. 191-204.

Trott, P., (2008). *Innovation Management and New Product Development.* 4th ed. Harlow: Pearson Education.

Tucker, R. B., (2002). *Driving Growth Through Innovation.* San Francisco: Berrett-Koehler Publishers.

Wood, C. C., (2004). *Entrepreneurial Mindset In the Department of Defense (DoD) Organisations: Antecedents and Outcomes.* [Online] Available at: http://www.dtic.mil/dtic/tr/fulltext/u2/a423134.pdf [Accessed 29 June 2018].

Zahra, S. A. & Garvis, D. M., (2000). International corporate entrepreneurship and firm performance: The moderating effect of international environmental hostility. *Journal of Business Venturing,* 15(5), pp. 469-492.

Entrepreneurial Marketing in a Crowdfunding Campaign

Monika Ilves, Stefan Stumpp and Daniel Michelis
Hochschule Anhalt, Bernburg, Germany
ilves.mnk@gmail.com
Stumpp@hs-anhalt.de
Daniel.Michelis@hs-anhalt.de
DOI: 10.34190/EIE.20.051

Abstract: Based on a qualitative study, this paper provides recommendations for an online marketing strategy for a crowdfunding campaign. Whereas the introduction of an innovative product to a crowdfunding community, such as Kickstarter.com, requires less effort, the effort in marketing the product, which most likely does not even exist yet, is relatively high. In addition to the legal, personnel, and financial challenges, a major challenge is the missing knowledge that is needed to be able to communicate the product effectively. More flexible, innovative, and proactive marketing measures are recommended for crowdfunding campaigns in order to achieve the funding goal. The community at crowdfunding platforms is essential for a successful crowdfunding campaign. Social media acts as a catalyst to spread the campaign. Honest as well transparent communication is mandatory for a successful execution. Innovative business models are difficult in terms of promoting classical marketing measures. To explore successful crowdfunding marketing strategies, a qualitative study was conducted. The study includes campaigns completed in Germany, which were realized in the last 4 years. Only founders that have successfully conducted a crowdfunding campaign on the Kickstarter platform and delivered the product were interviewed. A total of five Co-founders of crowdfunding campaigns were interviewed, who received a funding of approximately 20,000 Euro to one million Euros. The results of the study could show the resources and the amount of expertise needed to successfully conduct a crowdfunding campaign at Kickstarter. The results of the study support the theoretical elaboration that crowdfunding campaigns of a certain scheme have to be prepared and that certain methods are advantageous for an online marketing strategy in founding companies. It is possible to run a crowdfunding campaign without any marketing knowledge, but the knowledge presented in this paper will help to address the right audience and make a campaign more successful. This paper is relevant for founding companies that want to conduct a crowdfunding campaign, but also for anyone who is struggling with classical marketing methods in crowdfunding projects.

Keywords: entrepreneurial marketing, crowdfunding, kickstarter, entrepreneurship, founder, crowdfunding campaign, online marketing

1. Introduction

The basic idea of marketing is the consistent orientation of the entire company to the needs of the market. In addition, marketing is an enterprise task whose most important challenges include the recognition of market changes and to identify opportunities for increasing benefits and to increase the benefits for customers in the long term (Gabler Wirtschaftslexikon, 2018). In traditional marketing, top-down segmentation is followed, in which customers are increasingly segmented and finally a target group is defined. On this basis, the established companies position their products and services. (Belz, 2009). In traditional marketing, customers are observed in order to initiate targeted product developments and to gain capital and market power. For this purpose, customer needs are researched with well-known marketing tools and existing resources are used (Gabler Wirtschaftslexikon, 2018).

Innovative business models are hard to promote with classical marketing strategies. Entrepreneurial marketing is linked in theory with the fields of business administration, entrepreneurship and innovation (Harms & Grichnik, 2007). Crowdfunding is used as a possible means of market entry or initial funding. Entrepreneurs are regarded as catalysts for the generation of ideas for innovative design and implementation of business models (Schumpeter J. A., 1952). Entrepreneurs, who are often founders of new businesses, have to make decisions despite a limited knowledge and experience in a certain field, as they are not knowledgeable in all areas, such as marketing. Likewise, entrepreneurs have often achieved only little or nothing in this field. They have hardly any market information about how well the product to be sold is developing (Amiri & Marimaei, 2012, p. 152). Over time, the understanding of Entrepreneurial Marketing as a form of marketing for start-up companies changed to an entrepreneurial-innovative strategy (Schmid, 2017). In contrast to the theory of traditional marketing, which assumes a foreseeable environment, the position of entrepreneurs and start-up companies is dominated by uncertainties in the market. In order to achieve a stable environment, there are broad and methodical solutions which, for resource reasons, are not suitable for start-up companies (Schmid, 2017).

The term "crowdfunding" (in German: Schwarmfinanzierungen[1]) was introduced by Michael Sullivan in 2006 (Röhreich, 2017). The advantage of start-up financing through online crowdfunding campaigns is the faster processing of financing in contrast to known alternatives such as the search for investors. Furthermore, it offers the opportunity to test the market for the product. To successfully enter the market on highly competitive platforms, such as Kickstarter with 15 million users, the founding company needs suitable marketing methods. The problem is that start-up companies often have neither the knowledge nor the resources for a marketing campaign.

This article presents the current research situation on entrepreneurship, entrepreneurial marketing and crowdfunding. After the basic understanding of the current research, a typical sequence of a crowdfunding campaign in a community is explained. Subsequently, the structure of the Master's thesis is shown and the results of the research are presented. In the last section an open discussion is encouraged.

2. Research to date

So far, the three research fields, Entrepreneurship, Entrepreneurial Marketing and Crowdfunding, have been researched with varying degrees of intensity or on the surface within their defined area or in combination with another research field. The understanding of the relevant research fields and consequently of the following definitions of terms is changing. The area of crowdfunding, separated from crowdsourcing or crowd investing, is hardly researched compared to the other fields. Crowdfunding is defined as the financing of projects or companies by means of a call for proposals from private individuals to a general public (Berger, Kuckertz and Der, 2015). Crowdfunding can be considered a two-sided market. An accessible platform brings together two interest groups, the capital seekers and the investors. On the platform they exchange information about the project and its conditions. The platform acts as a "trusted person" to ensure that an exchange of services is established. Crowdfunding platforms become more attractive the more funders are active on them and, conversely, the more investors (also known as communities) are active (Damiano & Li, 2007). Caillaud and Jullien (2003) call this a network effect (Caillaud & Jullien, 2003). In the field of entrepreneurship, entrepreneurs in the market economy are seen as innovators and inventors, who lead to disruptive effects in the economy with innovative solutions. The term 'entrepreneurship' has been examined in a number of ways by various researchers and authors worldwide. As a result, no standardized definition of the term has been adopted to date (Fritsch, 2019). For the current research between the fields, Schumpeter's definition is valid, since founding companies and individual founders usually use crowdfunding campaigns to solve an unsolved problem. The more recent definitions have been empirically supported in the research of Kilenthong et al (Kilenthong, Hills, Hultman, and Sclove, 2010). Research in the field of Entrepreneurial Marketing focused on understanding the relationships between start-up companies and their marketing with limited resources (Kraus, Eggers, Harms, & Hultmann, 2011). For the current empirical study it is important to highlight that Entrepreneurial Marketing represents an innovative and non-traditional market approach which start-up companies can benefit from, especially with regard to their agility. With entrepreneurial marketing, customers are integrated, not only "played" by communication and thus it is a useful tool for start-up companies with crowdfunding goals.

In each research field, research is conducted independently of each other, combining individual areas of entrepreneurship, crowdfunding and entrepreneurial marketing. The focus is on sub-areas such as the general scheme of crowdfunding carried out by entrepreneurs or their mindset in crowdfunding. Ahsen Bayraktar has evaluated the general idea of crowdfunding in 2019 (Başar & Durmaz, 2019). Lin Hu, Zhenhua Wu and Bin Gu (2020) looked at the different approaches of businesses to crowdfunding in this field. Moreover, there are different focus areas, which are dedicated to thematic, strategic, temporal or geographical issues. There are also a number of studies that deal with marketing approaches, but so far no previous study has looked at the importance of the community in crowdfunding campaigns from a marketing perspective and provided recommendations for entrepreneurs. Linda Telve (2017) examined the significance of certain marketing formats during a crowdfunding campaign and discovered that certain communicative activities such as the number of updates, Facebook shares and comments are more likely to achieve success than others. Yang Song, Hong Wu, Jingdong Ma, Naiji Lu (2019) researched the investment behaviour of donors from 2013 to 2017 in relation to the influences and interactive effects on the Chinese platform Zhongchou.cn. Annaleena Parhankangasa and Maija Renkob (2017) researched how language in a crowdfunding campaign impacts the success of fundraising. In the following report, the successful campaigns, their practical experiences and the resulting recommendations

1 In pool financing, a project is implemented by a large number of donors. (Bartelt, 2011).

for further action are highlighted and are of interest to all those who would like to successfully present their innovative ideas to the community on crowdfunding platforms.

3. Implementation of a crowdfunding campaign in a community

A crowdfunding campaign takes place in different stages (Lyons, 2017). The initial plan prepared by the project initiator includes a milestone plan, a target group analysis, the conceptual design for project communication and the press as well as public relations (Kickstarter, 2019). The multipliers, e.g. influencers, help to make the campaign better known and are part of the overall communication strategy. Once the campaign site has been built, support can be looked for in the form of people, e.g. from the initiator's personal environment. An important aspect of successful campaigns is the activation of the own community and reaching the new community. The social capital of the entrepreneur forms the basis of any interaction and refers to the entirety of the networks. This capital can be used positively within social media to create trusting relationships of exchange. The common language and a similar language scheme are developed through interacting with the network resulting in a stronger connection (Nahapiet & Ghoshal, 1998). Through the ties in a social network, resources and people can be mobilised (Lin, 2008). Depending on the extent of the social capital, the founding company can access information, finance or competencies (Klyver & Hindle, 2007). Ahlers claims that good networks provide entrepreneurs with important information and support. The larger and more active the network is, the more likely the entrepreneur will get assistance. (Ahlers, Cumming, & Günther, 2015). Entrepreneurs rely on the help of their social network to bring a campaign to a successful conclusion for the start-up company (Agrawal, 2015). Compared to offline-based networks, which have been used in the past to help people because of the trust and reputation, establishing a solid relationship with the supporter online is more difficult for the entrepreneur (Agrawal, 2015). The bonds between founder and supporter have an impact on the different phases of crowdfunding. A founder's strong connections, such as friends and acquaintances, are particularly helpful at the beginning of a crowdfunding campaign, as they "want to do something good for the founder" (Borst, 2018). For online communities, connections of "weak ties" are essential and can be used in a crowdfunding campaign to convince more people to support the product. In addition, there are the "latent ties" that are hidden in online communities (Ellison, 2011). The weak and latent links are looking for direct information in the social media and by including social media in crowdfunding campaigns, they can help to spread the information. (Borst, 2018). The press and existing supporters should be animated to recommend the campaign. Events and newsletters can also be used when appropriate. While the campaign is running, supporters can donate money via the crowdfunding platform and see how successful the campaign is (Harzer, 2011). It is helpful to create a common social identity among the group of supporters. The more a supporter can relate to the project, the more likely they are to share it with their own friends and acquaintances (Kromidha, 2016). If the crowdfunding campaign already has a group of supporters, it should continually stay in touch with them. Additionally, the founder can post updates on the platform, respond to and comment on supporters' comments and introduce Q&As. The more comments, i.e. interactions, the better the crowdfunding campaign will be (Mollick, 2014; Xu, 2018). Trust in particular is created by the shared values within a community (Zhao, 2017). The interaction rate can be used as an indicator for the success of a crowdfunding campaign. After the campaign is over, communication with supporters is recommended, as they are now more enthusiastic about the future product or project.

4. Research design

The objective of this thesis is to develop recommendations for an online marketing strategy for the implementation of a crowdfunding campaign. This online marketing strategy should be used as a guide for start-up companies that have no experience with online crowdfunding campaigns. Following the theoretical method of investigating research approaches to Entrepreneurial Marketing and Crowdfunding, qualitative interviews with executives of start-up companies were conducted in addition to best-practice examples at Kickstarter.com.

Throughout the research, the following questions were addressed:

- Which Entrepreneurial Marketing strategies are essential for a market entry of a start-up company and why?
- Which online marketing strategies are suitable for a crowdfunding campaign?
- Which best practice strategies have been implemented on Kickstarter so far?
- Which strategies, if any, have been implied by start-up companies to promote the product of a crowdfunding campaign online?

A qualified study was carried out in order to establish the recommended actions for a crowdfunding campaign. The expert interviews are intended to give an insight into the practice of a crowdfunding campaign of start-up companies and to identify which online marketing strategies and whether entrepreneurial marketing methods are already applied by companies in practice. Experts are identified as persons who have built up branch-specific knowledge through experience. They are considered to be experts because they still manage the company after one (or more) crowdfunding campaigns. The elaboration is based on the example of the platform "Kickstarter.com", but is also relevant for other platforms. For a comparison all successful Kickstarter campaigns of the last 4 years in Germany were contacted. Kickstarter campaigns that did not reach their own financing target were not included.

	Occupation	Campaign period	Received funding	Number of performed Campaigns
Mrs. A	Co-Founder[2] & CEO	May 2019	53.596 €	1
Mr. B	Co-Founder	June 2017, March 2019	131,107€ 86,242 €	2
Mr. C	Co-Founder	January 2016, May 2018	18,410 € 58,930 €	2
Mr. D	Co-Founder	March 2019	72,386 €	1
Mr. E	Co-Founder	June 2014, May 2016	179,399 US-Dollar 942,673 €	2
Mr. F	Co-Founder	January 2017, August 2019	49,362 € 34,403€	2

In order to be able to develop recommendations for further action as accurately as possible, the guideline interview was divided into different parts, with a total of 22 questions, in line with the course of a Kickstarter campaign. In order to examine the approaches taken by start-up companies when conducting Kickstarter campaigns, semi-structured interviews with different start-up companies were conducted. During these interviews, open questions are asked in order to find out the most accurate description of actions and strategic approach to crowdfunding. After three introductory questions, the first part of the interview will focus on the preparation for the Kickstarter campaign. The second part is about the fields of action during the campaign and the third part is about the time after the Kickstarter campaign. The after-work of a Kickstarter campaign plays a crucial role, so that there must be a constant exchange between campaign creators and donors, as the delivery of the product is usually still to be completed. The questionnaire is rounded off with a general assessment of the campaign.

The interviews of the six participants were made using Skype with a duration of about 45 minutes. Referring to the quality content analysis by Philipp Mayring, the guideline interviews were divided into different sections. Although Mayring's analysis follows a certain systematic approach, it has to be adjusted to the research question and has no fixed standard (Mayring, 2008). To ensure the credibility of this study, the same category system was used for all interviews. The following categories were created: campaign focus, target group, community building and communication, online marketing, multipliers, additional actions, negative opinions, workload.

5. Research findings

For a crowdfunding campaign, the campaign objectives range from financing through a distribution channel to marketing activities. As an entrepreneur and founder of a start-up, the people interviewed agreed that although they did not need a finished product for a crowdfunding campaign, they did need a precise target for the campaign. For the interviewees, this included testing the product, financing the production, communicating with early adopters or the campaign as a marketing measure. Ultimately, it is fundamental to define the goal of the campaign right from the start. This is followed by the definition of the target group on which the focus should be set (setting priorities through potential assessment), which also allows the platform to be determined. Finally, one starts to build and expand the community consisting of the target group.

2 A Co-Founder is the co-founder of a company.

After determining the key data for a crowdfunding campaign, the right way of approaching the community must be identified. To be noted is that without a defined target group, most crowdfunding campaigns cannot achieve the potential success because they are not communicated in a target-oriented way. In the same way, the channels used by the defined target group should be highlighted. For reasons of time and cost, broad communication via all existing channels is not recommended. When choosing target group-specific channels, priority should be given to the most important communication channels in order to use the limited resources of the founding companies efficiently. If the platform to use (e.g. Kickstarter) is unknown among the target group, more communication effort must be made to explain it.

When building a community, the founder can fall back on online marketing measures. The most effective method for the experts was to generate contact data, mainly e-mail addresses, of potential customers. A video, photo or other value-adding content can be used as a leading magnet. In most cases, the ad redirects to another landing page by showcasing the solution as a product. The result is the generation of many leads (several thousands). Costs of the ads should neither be too high nor too low, but should be appropriate for the industry, which is a valid indicator. Through research, the founders found suitable numbers for their own industry. Lead generation is the most time-consuming task before a campaign, next to the creation of the prototype or product. Additionally to the lead generation, the interaction with the current community can be increased by raffles, product reviews or the exchange of opinions. Most experts could manage four-digit amounts, but almost all of them would increase the marketing budget for the next campaign.

The future supporters of the campaign are the secure foothold of the campaign and have the right for transparent communication. As the campaign gets closer to the start, more communication is needed. In addition to the generally most used channel "Facebook", some crowdfounders, adjusted to the individual target group, have also used Twitter, Instagram, target group specific forums and the update and comment section of Kickstarter for marketing purposes. The interaction with the community will be continuously increased until the campaign starts. All marketing measures should be planned in detail for the first 48 hours after the campaign launch, so that cooperation partners, the own network, the acquired community and targeted media communicate together during this time. If the performance is good, there is the opportunity to receive further support from the platform. Before and after the start of the campaign, the experts worked together with various service providers in the marketing sector, where only one expert had good experiences. Well-known and named providers are Kickbooster, Jellop and Backercamp, among others, who help crowdfunding campaigns with online marketing at a variety of levels. When choosing a marketing agency, the founding team must be aware of the exact goal and method of payment. Many marketing agencies want to make profit-oriented deals, but these are not always profitable for the founding team. It's not recommended to take a deal in which the campaign is advertised in a specific Backer e-mails list, as these lists are not target group oriented enough. In the case of a follow-up campaign, the founder can address the already generated leads again, and this time integrate more of them by allowing them to give feedback on the future product. This email list, in the first and second campaign, can receive special discounts and promotions before the campaign to support in the first 48 hours.

The crowdfunding campaign and the subsequent product will benefit greatly from the engagement of supporters before, during and after the campaign. The supporters of a campaign are human capital and essential for the overall success of a campaign. As an active community of a crowdfunding platform such as Kickstarter, they not only have an interest in innovative ideas, but also have certain expectations of the campaign. Consequently, a campaign has to communicate transparently and clearly about developments throughout the entire period in order to appear trustworthy for support. By communicating transparently and clearly, supporters will also tolerate mistakes later on, such as supply problems. The more the supporter becomes enthusiastic and the more empathetic he/she feels, the more he/she is willing to intrinsically help the campaign. The closeness to the supporter is well caught up by asking for their opinion, which can be done by presenting a pre-Kickstarter page, but also by communicating while working on the product. Some campaigns have involved supporters in the design process. One campaign conducted a poll for another product during the current campaign and created the product during the campaign. This creates trust and commitment to the campaign.

The actively involved community is the initial catalyst for the first positive results at the beginning of a Kickstarter campaign. One of the campaigns studied used another way of promoting the campaign besides the 'Call to Action's' in the emails: the Kickbooster platform. Kickbooster helps founders achieve their crowdfunding goals through affiliate marketing with influencers as well as supporters. The principle of Kickbooster is a platform for better coordination of affiliate marketing (Kickbooster, 2019). In addition to other viral platforms, campaigns can cross-promote one another to promote each other through an update on their own campaign site. These cross promotions are most effective when they are undertaken with the same or similar target groups. For this purpose, there are agencies that provide this service for the founders, but the campaigns investigated reported an irregular arrangement of promotions that did not have the same target groups. Another multiplier is influencers who advertise the product through their own channels. In one campaign, this resulted in a long-term cooperation with specially designed products. With the help of multiplicators such as influencers or bloggers, further interactive initiatives such as prize draws can be strategically used.

In addition to the self-generated network and multipliers, media can help spread the campaign. After researching the journalists that are relevant to the topic, possibly around 100, they should be categorised and the top 30 of the most promising should be researched in more detail. For the most suitable journalists, it is essential to address them as personally as possible in order to attract attention. One campaign that was investigated, which mainly focused on journalists, received an article in the Mashable, a digital platform for news after two weeks of contact. Often a sample also helps to convince, but it is rare to find this before production. If the tactic is to get press releases during the campaign, the founder should be able to send out some product samples. If the founder is not successful with the methods explained above, he can start with less well-known journalists or people from the network. According to one campaign, press releases from the former university also helped to be discovered by the founder scene.

6. Discussion

The strategic approach of the Kickstarter campaigns examined takes up A. Schumperter's understanding of entrepreneurship. Thus, the founder begins in a section of the market and, after a successful campaign, scales to other target groups or sectors. The campaign is used to create and optimize a product in a user-centred manner. Strategically planned crowdfunding campaigns tailored to the target group offer great potential for a successful entry into the market economy as a start-up company. That ties in with the close relationship of the target group and crowdfunding community, which is again a unique aspect of the platforms. And inevitably it does confirm crowdfunding as a social environment that can use multiplier effects of an individual. Social capital in crowdfunding is very important and without the enthusiasm of the supporters no product can be realised. Almost all campaigns have had a follow-up campaign after a prior successful one, often with even greater funding.

Instead of using a traditional financial service provider, the founder bears a lower risk than when financing via a crowdfunding platform. The founders do not need to introduce a finished product to the market, but primarily the idea. If the idea does not reach a market, the product is not being produced. With the help of action-focused behaviour (see Effectuation by Sarasvathy), the founder plans the campaign using his own resources, watches out for possible partners to secure the campaign and then uses opportunities to disseminate it (Sarasvathy, 2001). An entrepreneurial mindset can help the founder to complete a successful campaign. The experts interviewed as part of this research did not have a marketing background prior to carrying out their first crowdfunding campaigns. The interviewees all stated that marketing background knowledge would have been an advantage for an even more successful campaign. The entrepreneurs independently acquired the knowledge for the respective campaign. It should be noted that professional marketing is advantageous for income scaling and can significantly increase the amount of financing.

Based on the findings of specialist literature, the analysis of the procedure of the two best practice crowdfunding campaigns as well as the expert interviews conducted specifically for this research project, recommendations for the use of crowdfunding platforms as a marketing and financing method are provided. For each campaign, a goal should be set, whether it is market entry and product validation or has a marketing motivation. In order for this objective to succeed, however, precise strategic preparation of the crowdfunding campaign is required. For communication, the target group should be defined and when choosing target group specific channels, the most important communication channels should be prioritized. Broad communication via all existing channels is not recommended, among other things for reasons of time and cost. Only a few, extremely innovative products, such as Pebble with the revolution of the watch market, can be lucky enough to be able to carry out a successful crowdfunding campaign despite an initially wrongly defined target group. As part of the lead-ad campaign, relevant contacts can be generated for the crowdfunding campaign. Among all interview partners, the extent of the right leads due to a lack of knowledge in marketing was not enough to make the campaign successful on its own. For a successful marketing campaign, basic marketing knowledge is important to activate the community and structure the first days of the campaign. In addition to your own marketing activities, cooperation with multipliers help to spread the campaign. The press also helped to generate attention for the interviewees. To maintain this attention requires several months of preparation.

The goal of this work was to provide basic recommendations for start-up companies that see crowdfunding as a solution to a problem (e.g. financing). Further in-depth research into detailed interaction measures during a crowdfunding campaign would expand this work. Likewise, in-depth interviews with more and more international experts are conceivable, since current research only relates to the campaigns in Germany. With regard to the development of communication on online platforms, is research into the change in communication in a longer period of time interesting. All these further researches could underline the result of this more practical research.

References

Agrawal, A. C. (2015). Crowdfunding: Geography, social networks, and the timing of investment decisions. Journal Economics and Management Strategy.

Ahlers, G., Cumming, D., & Günther, C. S. (2015). Signaling in Euity Crowdfunding . Entrepreneurship Theory and Practice.

Amiri, N. S., & Marimaei, M. R. (2012). Concept of Entrepreneurshipand Entrepreneurs Traits and Characteristics. Scholarly Journal of Business Administration.

Bartelt, D. (2011). Ersetzt Crowdfunding die öffentliche Kulturförderung? Wie kleine Projekte schon heute alternativ finanziert werden. . Politik und Kultur - Zeitschrift des deutschen Kulturrats , S. 20.

Başar, S. and Durmaz, A. (2019). Selected Issues on Current International Economics and Macroeconomics. [online] Google Books. Cambridge Scholars Publishing. Available at: https://books.google.de/books?hl=de&lr=&id=Axu7DwAAQBAJ&oi=fnd&pg=PA71&dq=Entrepreneurship.

Berger , Elisabeth S.C., Kuckertz, A. and Der, V. (2015). Crowdfunding: mehr als nur Kapitalbeschaffung - Wie Start-ups von der Vernetzung der Investoren... [online] ResearchGate. Available at: https://www.researchgate.net/publication/276285601_Crowdfunding_mehr_als_nur_Kapitalbeschaffung_-_Wie_Start-ups_von_der_Vernetzung_der_Investoren_profitieren_konnen.

Borst, I. M. (2018). From friendfunding to crowdfunding: Relevance of relationsships, social media, and platform activities to crowdfunding performance. New Media & Society.

Caillaud, B., & Jullien, B. (2003). Chicken & Egg: competition among inter-mediation service providers. Rand Journal of Economics, S. 309 - 328.

Damiano, E., & Li, H. (2007). COMPETING MATCHMAKING. Toronto: Universtiy of Toronto.

Ellison, N. B. (2011). Connection strategies: Social capital. New Media & Society.

Fritsch, M. (2019). Entrepreneurship. Berlin, Heidelberg: Springer Berlin Heidelberg.

Harms, R., & Grichnik, D. (2007). Zur Zukunft der deutschsprachigen Entrepreneurshipforschung – Strategien und thematische Schwerpunkte. Zeitschrift für KMU und Entrepreneurship 55, 266–275.

Harzer, A. (2011). Erfolgsfaktoren von Crowdfunding-Projekten. Dresden: Tyclipso.me.

Hornuf, L. and Schwienbacher, A. (2018). Market mechanisms and funding dynamics in equity crowdfunding. Journal of Corporate Finance, 50, pp.556–574.

Hu, L., Wu, Z. and Gu, B. (2020). Product-driven Entrepreneurs and Online Crowdfunding. [online] Available at: https://scholarspace.manoa.hawaii.edu/handle/10125/64474.

Kilenthong, P., Hills, G. E., Hultman, C., & Sclove, S. L. (2010). Entrepreneurial marketing practice: Systematic relationships with firm age, firm size and operators status. In U. Fueglistaller, T. Volery, & W. Weber, Strategic entrepreneurship – The promise for future entrepreneurship, family business and SME research? (S. 1-15). St. Gallen: Verlag KMU HSG.

Kickstarter. (Oktober 2019). Kickstarter: Handbook. Von https://www.kickstarter.com/help/handbook abgerufen am.

Klyver, K., & Hindle, K. (2007). The Role of Social Networks. At Different Stages of Business Formantion. Small Enterprise Research.

Kraus, S., Eggers, F., Harms, R. H., & Hultmann, C. (2011). Diskussionslinien der Entrepreneurial Marketing-Forschung: Ergebnisse einer Zitationsanalyse. Zeitschrift der Betriebswirtschaft, 81:27 - 58.

Kromidha, E. a. (2016). Social identity and signalling success factors in online crowdfunding. Entrepreneurship & Regional Developments.

Lin, N. (2008). A Network Theory of Social Capital. Von http://pro-classic.com/ethnicgv/SN/SC/paper-final-041605.pdf.

Lyons, S. (2017). The Five Phases of Crowdfunding Campaigns. [online] Available at: www.slideshare.net/StevenLyons4/the-five-phases-of-crowdfunding-campaigns.

Marketing. (2018, Februar 15). Gabler Wirtschaftslexikon. https://wirtschaftslexikon.gabler.de/definition/marketing-39435/version-262843

Mayring, P. (2000). Qualitative Inhaltsanalyse. In E. Uwe/Kardorff, & I. Steinke, Qualitative Forschung. Ein Handbuch. (S. S. 468 – 475). Reinbek bei Hamburg: Rowohlt.

Mollick, E. (2014). The dynamics of crowdfunding: An exploratory study. Journal of Business.

Nahapiet, J., & Ghoshal, S. (1998). Social Capital, Intellectual Capital, and the Organizational Advantage. The Academy of Management Review.

Parhankangas, A. and Renko, M. (2017), Linguistic style and crowdfunding success among social and commercial entrepreneurs. Journal of Business Venturing, 32(2), pp.215–236.

Röhreich, P.S./ S.G. (2017). AKADEMIE ONLINE – Crowdfunding – eine echte Alternative für Kapitalnachfrager und -anleger? [online] Available at: https://www.vwa-akademie-online.de/wissenschaft-und-praxis/crowdfunding-eine-echte-alternative-fuer-kapitalnachfrager-und-anleger/.

Sarasvathy, S. (2001). Causation and effectuation: Toward a theoretical shift from economic inevitability to entrepreneurial contingency. Academy of Management Review, 26, 243–263.

Schumpeter, J. A. (1952). Theorie der wirtschaftlichen Entwicklung. Volkswirtschaft. Leipzig: Duncker & Humblot.

Schmid, J. (2017). Entrepreneurial Marketing: Konzeption, Messung und Erfolgswirkung in wirtschaftlich krisenhaften Zeiten. Wiesbaden: Springe Fachmedien Wiesbaden.

Song, Y., Wu, H., Ma, J. and Lu, N. (2019), "Exploring the dynamic influences and interaction effects of signals on backers' investment in the crowdfunding market", Information Technology & People, Vol. 33 No. 2, pp. 792-812.

Telve, L. (n.d.). Building a successful crowdfunding campaign: what marketing factors do really matter for your project? [online] Available at: https://repositorio.ucp.pt/bitstream/10400.14/29177/1/152117005%20Linda%20Telve%20W.pdf.

Xu, J. J. (2018). Cheap Talk? The Impact of Lender-Borrower Communi-cation on Perr-to-Peer Lending Outcomes. Journal of Management Information Systems.

Zhao, Q. C.-D.-L.-C. (2017). Determinants of backers' funding intention in crowdfunding: Social exchange theory and regulatory focus. Telematics and Informatics.

Understanding the World of Crowdfunding in Driving Entrepreneurial Growth: A Case Study Analysis

Chun Yan Wang, Kate Johnston and Maeve Caraher
School of Business and Humanities at Dundalk Institute of Technology, Dundalk, Ireland
d00061619@student.dkit.ie
Kate.Johnston@dkit.ie
maeve.caraher@dkit.ie
DOI: 10.34190/EIE.20.112

Abstract: The case describes the challenges and opportunities the founder of an innovative cycling product experienced as he attempted to use crowdfunding as a platform to establish and grow his business idea. The case begins with a brief overview of how the entrepreneur came up with the idea and the journey from product concept to product launch. The decision to crowdfund the idea is explained and the challenges and opportunities in trying to navigate the crowdfunding arena are explored; from selecting a suitable crowdfunding platform to the launch and management of the final campaign. Despite the fact the campaign failed to raise the necessary funds, the media coverage from the crowdfunding campaign led to a number of significant business avenues, which ultimately helped launch the product onto the international market. The case examines these events and closes as the entrepreneur reflects on the lessons learnt from the experience and his advice going forward to anyone considering crowdfunding.

Keywords: crowdfunding, innovation, case study, entrepreneurship

1. Introduction

In the new global digital economy, crowdfunding has emerged as a powerful yet disruptive business model, transforming the financial landscape for entrepreneurs worldwide. Numerous continents and sectors as diverse as information technology, creative arts, social and community groups, have embraced this new funding source. Recent statistics suggest that in 2013, approximately US€5.1 billion (Massolution, 2013) was contributed in the form of crowdfunding. By 2015, this figure had increased to over US$ 34.2 billion. According to recent statistics from Technavio (2018), the global crowdfunding market size will grow to USD 89.72 billion during 2018-2022.

Within the last ten years there has been a significant growth in crowdfunding research. Studies have examined the role of crowdfunding as an alternative to traditional funding methods (Gedda et al, 2016; Roggan, 2015; Estrin et al, 2017), as a source of much needed capital and seed funding (Belleflamme et al, 2013; Baskerville and Cordery, 2014; Lehner, 2013; Schwienbacher and Larralde, 2010) particularly at the start-up stage (Sassoon and Duggal, 2015, Belleflamme and Lambert, 2014). Within this literature, research has also championed crowdfunding in terms of the non-financial benefits in the form of market validation and skills development for the entrepreneur.

A major challenge facing entrepreneurs moving into the crowdfunding space, is both the proliferation of crowdfunding platforms and the high failure rate. Research suggests that as of 2017, there are more than 2000 active platforms. (Galkiewicz and Galkiewicz, 2018). However, even more concerning is the fact that, success rates have relatively low with no evidence of rates improving over time. Research (Bidaux 2018) suggests that during the period 2015 -2016, success rates for Kickstarter, the industry leader, was 36% and 32% respectively. Success rates for Indiegogo, the second largest crowdfunding platform, as of 2015 was less than 10% (Zhao, Chen, Wang and Chen, 2017).

This case examines the challenges and opportunities as the founder of a start-up company attempts to navigate the world of crowdfunding. The case begins with brief introduction tracing how the entrepreneur came up with the idea and the entrepreneur's journey from the initial concept to product development. In 2018, having successfully market tested the product, the entrepreneur, Simon was faced with the challenge of raising €50,000 to fund production. The case examines the challenges in trying to secure funding as a start-up enterprise with an innovative product and the factors that drove the decision to crowdfund the idea. Preparing for the campaign and the challenges this presented and the impact unforeseen events had following the campaign launch are also examined. The case study closes with the lessons learnt as the entrepreneur reflects on the experience in an attempt to provide insights into how to successfully navigate this new funding arena. The case concludes with his final advice for anyone considering crowdfunding in the future.

2. Methodological approach employed

Case study research design is a widely adopted methodology in social science research (Harrison, Birks, Franklin and Mills, 2017). Typically, it involves an in-depth, multi-dimensional approach involving the use of multiple sources of data and methods (Merriam, 2009; Stake, 2006 and Yin, 2014) in an attempt to try and understand a particular issue in a real life setting. Numerous authors have examined the value and use of case study methodology, most notably Yin, (2014), Stake (2006), Green and Thorogood, (2009) and Stewart (2014).

For the purposes of this case the approach adopted was an instrumental case study approach. Consistent with the work of Stake (2006) and acknowledged by Crowe, Cresswell, Robertson, Huby, Avery and Sheikh (2011) the instrumental approach uses a particular case or event to allows the researcher to gain " a broader appreciation of an issue of phenomenon" (p.2). For the purposes of this case, the information was drawn from a variety of sources including in-depth interviews conducted with the entrepreneur over a period of several months, supplemented with information from the company social media pages, news articles and company website.

3. Introduction to the case

The only way to get ahead in a crisis as large as climate change is through pioneering innovation. In 2003 one budding entrepreneur, Simon Chan, moved to Ireland and with a strong interest in environmental issues. In 2005, he began pouring his passion and energy into developing a Super-bicycle: SuperWheel, one of the most important component for the SuperCycle project, one that converted human power (weight) into energy that was both efficient and environmentally friendly and thus the SuperWheel concept was born. Driven by a combination of passion and ingenuity, and with help from various colleges and enterprise agencies in the region, Simon spent over five years developing the technology behind this innovative idea. With the prototypes and product development completed, Simon was ready to commence production, but needed to secure finance for the project. In 2018 Simon entered the world of crowdfunding in an attempt to secure €50,000 funding.

4. Starting SuperWheel

In 2003, Simon moved to Ireland having spent the previous 20 year working in the UK. Originally from Hong Kong, Simon worked in the catering industry for most of his life. His decision to move to Ireland was driven in equal parts by his love of the country and by his perception of Ireland having a supportive entrepreneurial and innovative business culture, and he was convinced that Ireland would provide a very good environment in which he could explore and develop his innovative SuperCycle idea.

Deeply concerned about environmental issues and fascinated with "the power steering in his father's truck", he poured his passion and energy into making a Super bicycle. The main component of the SuperCycle – called SuperWheel - would be environmentally friendly and would give the user the ability to convert human power (weight) into energy that would improve cycling efficiency. It relies on an innovative technology entitled Weight to Energy Conversion Technology (WTECT). The secret of the SuperWheel is made up of two innovative mechanisms: the external springs and the internal drive. The combination of these two systems can generate additional energy to assist pedalling and provides the only alternative to electric power bicycles.

In 2010 through the Enterprise Ireland Innovation Voucher Scheme, Simon secured some initial research and development funding from Enterprise Ireland for the EasyPedal project. Three years later, after a chance encounter with an enterprise development adviser, Simon applied to the VITAL programme at Dundalk Institute of Technology (DkIT) which gave him his initial start into the world of entrepreneurship. Shortly after, he completed a licensing agreement on the EasyPedal with a County Down engineering company in 2015, who would eventually take a small shareholding in the SuperWheel project, to help drive the innovation and perfect the technology. At this stage links with industry and academia provided the much needed research and development that was crucial to get the innovative technology developed and market tested.

In 2016, supported by an Innovation Voucher awarded by Enterprise Ireland, the SuperWheel concept was developed by researchers in the School of Mechanical and Manufacturing Engineering in Dublin City University (DCU), the computerized evaluation confirmed that by using 10kg active weight, the system generated a moment ranging in the size of 7.3 to 7.8 Nm.

In 2016 and 2017, Simon enrolled on the New Frontiers programme phase 1 and phase 2. This programme is an entrepreneur development programme funded by Enterprise Ireland provided at the Regional Development

Centre (RDC), which is an incubation hub attached to Dundalk Institute of Technology. It was a crucial step in launching the 'SuperWheel' concept. With the help of Garett Duffy, the Enterprise Development Manager at the RDC, Simon spent the next few years understanding the business and marketing aspects of the business and developing and testing the project.

In July 2018 Simon had successfully market-tested the product and the feedback was overwhelmingly positive. With an award from Climate KIC Accelerator and the positive consumer feedback, Simon, and his small and enthusiastic team, decided to launch the first model the 700c model of SuperWheel that could be used on Roads and Trekking bikes. There are four members in the SuperWheel team in 2018: Simon Chan (CEO); Charlie Fegan (Co. Founder); Colleen Murray and Oisin Murphy (Marketing Promoters). To achieve their ambition, the company needed €50,000 to fund the first production run.

5. The challenge of accessing funding as a start-up

Accessing funding is a universal problem for entrepreneurs. Whether starting a business in Dublin, London, New York, or Brussels, securing funding is a major challenge, particularly when you have new innovative technology. In Ireland, despite having a really dynamic and supportive entrepreneurial culture, accessing funding can still be a major challenge. The funding sector for business in Ireland is problematic largely due to the fact that the three main banks - BoI, AIB and Ulster Bank - control approximately 95 percent of the funding market (FOR A, 2016). The remainder is catered for by enterprise support agencies as venture capitalist and business angel markets. Within the last ten years access to funding has certainly improved, but there are still major obstacles for many start-up companies.

For Simon entering the funding arena was a major challenge. He had successfully developed what he felt was a great product and positive market feedback from consumer tests meant that the next step was to commence production. However, trying to identify and secure funding to start manufacturing was far less certain. The most obvious path, the traditional funding sources from bank financing was not an option for Simon. According to Simon "If you are a limited company with a trading history and a business plan, bank funding is certainly an option, but in my case, as a start-up, the banks could not help me". This despite the fact that he was accepted in the Climate KIC Accelerator, which included a 10,000 euro grant. Simon recounted his meeting with his local bank: "Despite having emails confirming the acceptance of the Climate KIC Accelerator, the bank refused a 3000euro overdraft facility". He has since lost faith with the bank support.

Unfortunately for him, he is not alone. Citing friends who applied for loans from the bank and were put "under pressure to provide personal guarantees" he looked to go outside traditional funding sources.

From the outset, Simon was reluctant to approach venture capitalist (VCs) and business angels. Venture funding involves firms or individuals who provide capital, typically for a certain share of the start-up. Simon considered venture capitals but felt it was too risky "VCs often take a certain percentage of shares out of the company. It was too risky and you could lose control of the company". He felt that at this stage it was not the right move.

6. Entering the world of Crowdfunding

Crowdfunding is a term that has become a powerful yet disruptive force for entrepreneurs worldwide in accessing start-up funding. Typically it involves raising funding from the crowd often referred to as backers. Money can be raised by a large number of individuals (so called backers) who each typically contribute a small amount, usually via the internet online to help entrepreneurs (and community projects) access much needed findings outside the traditional financial system.

Over the last ten years, the hype concerning crowdfunding has led to a dramatic rise in the value of the industry and the number of projects funded. According to recent statistics from Technavio and Forbes (2018), the global crowdfunding market size will more than double in the next two years to USD 89.72 billion for 2022. In 2015, the industry was valued at US$ 34.2 billion. As for 2017, research suggests that there are more than 2000 active platforms (Galkiewicz and Galkiewicz, 2018). However, despite the growth in the crowdfunding space, success rates remain a major challenge. Research (Bidaux 2018) suggests that during the period 2015 -2016, success rates for Kickstarter, the industry leader, were 36% and 32% respectively. Success rates for Indiegogo, the second largest crowdfunding platform, as of 2015 was less than 10% (Zhao, Chen, Wang and Chen, 2017).

One of the biggest problems facing a start-up moving into the crowdfunding arena is to identify the most suitable platform for their product or company. As Simon acknowledges when "you go on social media everyone is talking about Kickstarter and Indigegogo, but this is becoming a very crowded market, there are so many companies now in this space... even InterTradeIreland (a cross-border Trade and Business Development Body, funded by the Department of Business, Enterprise and Innovation in Ireland (DBEI) and the Department for the Economy (DFE) in Northern Ireland) has started crowdfunding" . Trying to navigate this arena can be challenging and according to Simon "there are so many different types of crowdfunding available" it can be difficult to know which is most suitable to your particular product or concept. He further notes that Kickstater is "the biggest, but it is all or nothing ... if your target is 6,000 euro, and if over the crowdfunding period of four or five weeks, you do not reach your target, you get nothing". However, Indiegogo has more flexibility and this is what attracted Simon to this platform. "Indiegogo, they do flexible funding. If you set up 6,000 euro, if you only have 5,900 or 5,000 or a smaller amount, you still can take it". The other advantage according to Simon was the pre-order facility offered. He makes the point that "with pre-order, you do not have to sell equity in your company...you only sell the product". The pre-order facility gave him important information on potential sales which impacted on production costs. "Because we needed large batches of orders to start manufacturing, the pre-sale crowdfunding was the best option for us ...also the pre-order option enables you to get some money upfront, vital at this stage of the business".

7. Preparing for the Super Wheel Crowdfunding campaign: The pre-launch

There are considered three core elements to building a successful crowdfunding campaign: storytelling including developing video(s) to explain the product; setting up rewards; and engaging social networks such as Facebook and Twitter, (Li, Jarvenpaa and Pattan (2016) Successfully managing these core elements is a major challenge. According to Simon "It seems simple, but the difficulty faced by most entrepreneurs is that they do not have the time and skillsets" for this. As he mentioned it, there is significant time and energy involved before launching a crowdfunding campaign". Simon recounts the challenge of putting together the promotional videos, website which all play an important part in a campaign. According to Simon "your promotional video and website are your shop front so they need to be professional". Even putting together a short promotional video can be a challenge. Simon had no knowledge in video design. Initially he worked with some students from DKIT to produce a video which was a start. Eventfully he bought a high end camera and with the help of a professional in the area, put together a short three minute promotional video. But he had other serious concerns.

This was his first crowdfunding campaign and as the launch date approached, Simon was very aware that the marketing material and product information, so vital to the successful launch was not sufficient to attract the necessary backers. According to Simon " the Product design at the time was very basic, and lacked a convincing and wow factor". Plus there was a lack of pre-launch marketing campaign. According to Simon the marketing campaign should have started at least " a few months before the crowdfunding campaign".

In July, a serious accident soon after the pre-launch event held in DkIT caused a major disruption to the pre-launch crowdfunding campaign. An avid cycler, Simon was cycling close to College Green in Dublin, and had a serious accident, caused by a collision with a tram track. "I broke my arm in three places", Simon recounts and "I needed surgery" and "was off work for a while". In fact, Simon was off work "for several months". The impact of all this, was that the SuperWheel crowdfunding campaign on Indiegogo, which was initially set for September, was delayed to November, one of the worst time for crowdfunding campaign. With little pre-campaign preparation caused by the surgery after the accident, Simon had serious concerns for the upcoming campaign launch.

8. The launch

The crowdfunding campaign commenced on the 19th November and would run for four weeks. Within the first two weeks, Simon along with his team were very aware that the campaign would not raise the necessary funds. One of the problems he recounts was around the verification of the technology. According to Simon "the potential backers were sceptical about the technology, SuperWheel Weight To Energy Conversion Technology, was ground breaking technology" and "without a verified testing data from a respectable organization, we simply could not convince the backers". Like many entrepreneurs he was undeterred. "This was my first crowdfund so I had to embrace it, and to use it as an opportunity for free exposure".

As the crowdfunding campaign drew to a close, financially the campaign was not successful. "We have just approximately €2000 out from our target of 50,000.. ..it has to be a failed campaign". After the four weeks campaign, Simon refunded all the money raised on the campaign to his backers.

9. Lessons learnt

Looking back on the experience, Simon is overwhelmingly positive. Despite having not crowdfunded the money required to commence production, it was a turning point for the business. "There were huge benefits from the crowdfunding experience, the social media benefits were huge". Shortly after the crowdfunding launch, Simon's story was picked up by a number of global media sources including Yahoo Headlines news Japan and several global media platforms. This led to hundreds of news stories and videos worldwide, and this was the result of global exposure of the project during the crowdfunding campaign.

Getting this exposure made it easier to reach global marketing channels and markets. According to Simon "the crowdfunding campaign gave the product global exposure around the world. It also helped the product to gain licensing agreements in many countries" Within a matter of months, Simon was approached by a number of companies looking to sign licensing agreements with the company. In 2019 a French company, which sells and hires bicycles for the holiday market approached Simon to agree a licensing agreement. This was followed shortly with license agreements in Asia and North America. With a matter of months following the crowdfunding campaign, SuperWheel had signed licensing agreements in France, Japan, Hong Kong and Canada, and had secured the first 50 pre-sales orders to allow the first production and 30,000 euro investment to complete the Nation phase of the Patent application. These licensing agreements, orders and investment were all linked to the initial crowdfunding campaign.

Asked about the challenges in crowdfunding for entrepreneurs, according to Simon, "the first time you crowdfund, there are so many unknowns". At the outset, he believes that understanding the mind-set of the potential backers/funders is key. According to Simon "the people who support your product, they are not normal buyers. They are buying goods from you, because they are supporting your project, supporting your ideas". This is a fundamental difference between crowdfunding backers and normal customers. According to Simon, "building trust with the buyers, the backers is key". Building trust and making sure that the content you produce provides confidence to potential backers that you can produce the goods is a key aspect of the whole process. According to Simon you need to "show them your product, your team.... It is not just about getting the money". For him having secured a number of awards "helped build this credibility". This he considers all very important.

Simon also makes the point that not all projects should be crowdfunded. His advice is to "look at the types of crowdfunding out there and choose the one to suit your company - there is no one fits all". Simon makes the point that "most backers on crowdfunding are relatively young, in their mid-20s to mid-30s, early adopters, so it is important to understand your target market". Hence, different types of projects suit different types of crowdfunding platforms. "So you do need to do research to assess which one is most suitable for your project".

Asked about the potential risks and patent infringement, Simon is quick to advise "not to disclose your idea too early" and to "hold back on certain information". For Simon "the patent and copyright infringement was a major concern". Like many innovators, he has spent many years inventing a product, so initially it is best "to hold back certain information until you go to a later stage". Getting your patent application in place before you start your crowdfunding campaign is crucial here, particularly for new technology products. Simon commenced the patent application in 2017 and in Spring 2020, has just completed the National Phase of Patent application. According to Simon "is a long process, but one that is crucial".

One of the major challenges and learning from the experience was the skillset required around the marketing and promotional activities central prior to the crowdfunding campaign. Simon recounts his experience as a start-up, "you cant's afford to have a marketing company" and "you have to manage all the social media yourself, you constantly do updates by yourself and build a good portfolio and promotional video and introduce your product is a major step". Going forward he feels that more training and education on crowdfunding would be vital. "I do think in Ireland you should have One-Stop-Shop or at least have advisors specialists in this area". He also points to the need for more success stories of crowdfunding. This according to Simon would "encourage more people to do it. Looking at how other companies do on Kickstarter campaigns, that's how we learned things from them."

The other piece of advice from Simon is "Do not be afraid". Was he afraid of losing his reputation of not reaching the fundraising targets? For Simon, the worst thing is to "never try". Simon makes the point that "for entrepreneurs, we do not expect when we do everything that is needed to be successful. You go back to analyse what it went wrong and how to avoid the same mistake in the future". Simon is acutely aware that to successfully navigate the crowdfunding arena requires strong belief in your product and idea. He recounts the "colourful language" he received on some social media posts, and notes that you need to be "resilient". He views crowdfunding as an "adventure". Certainty for this entrepreneur it has been a success story. At the time of this case, the company has its first production, with Super-Wheel bicycles now on the road.

10. Conclusion and closing remarks

Within the last 10 years, crowdfunding has become a powerful but disruptive force within the financial landscape. According to Technavio (2018), the global crowdfunding market is currently a multibillion dollar industry, estimated to be grow to $89.72 billion by 2022. The mass appeal of crowdfunding is that it allows anyone who is willing to put their idea into the public domain to raise funds from anywhere in the world, via online platforms. For entrepreneurs, crowdfunding has become a game changer.

Despite the potential benefits, crowdfunding is not without its challenges and success rates remain a major challenge. This case examines the experience of one entrepreneur who attempted to crowdfund the money required to commence production of his innovative product. Due to an unforeseen accident the campaign was unsuccessful financially.

The key takeaways from this case can be summarized as follows. There is no doubt that entering the world of crowdfunding is challenging and takes time, determination and a specific skillset. In the words of this entrepreneur "there are so many unknowns". According to Simon, crowdfunding involves a huge "learning curve" and requires "considerable time, skills and commitment. It takes considerable time to build trust between backers, developing a good image of the product, promotional skills and to understand details of costs and components and manufacturing and the logistics process".

In terms of the key advice for anyone considering crowdfunding, this case highlights the importance of building trust with the backers and the marketing and communication skills required both at the pre and launch period. Simon also makes the point that crowdfunding requires a specific skillset in terms of communicating and managing all marketing communications such as social media updates associated with the campaign. For Simon, more education and training and the development of a one stop shop in terms of guidance for aspiring entrepreneurs would be a major step forward. Crowdfunding is not suitable for everyone and there is a need to understand the different crowdfunding platforms, due diligence and the importance of understanding the mind-set of potential backers.

Despite the challenges, for those willing to enter this dynamic environment, the gains can be significant. Although the campaign was not financially successful, the non-financial benefits in terms of the marketing exposure far surpassed the entrepreneur's expectations. According to Simon, "it was a major turning point for the business". The global media coverage resulting from the campaign led to hundreds of news stories and videos worldwide, which resulted in the company signing licensing agreements to sell the product in several countries. This was all due to the initial crowdfunding campaign.

When asked for one closing piece of advice for any entrepreneur considering crowdfunding, Simon remarks that "an entrepreneur must tackle opportunities and problems when managing positive or negative feedback. As a leader you must have the ability to take care of the product and achieve the results of which backers expect".

References

Baskerville, R. and Cordery, C., (2014) *"Crowdfunding: A Threat or Opportunity for University Research Funding?".* [Online] Available at: Available at SSRN: http://ssrn.com/abstract=2458638

Belleflamme, P., Lambert, T. and Schwienbacher, A., (2013). *"Crowdfunding: Tapping The Right Crowd".* [Online] Available at: Google Scholar

Belleflamme, P. and Lambert, T., 2014. *"Crowdfunding: Some Empirical Findings and Microeconomic Underpinnings".* [Online] Available at: Google Scholar

Bidauz, T. (2018) "Games and Crowdfunding in 2018" Gamasutra.com. http://gamastutra.com/blogs/thomasBidau/20190115/334360/Games_and_crowdfunding_in-2018.php.

Crowe, S., Cresswell, K., Robertson, A., Huby, G., Avery, A. and Sheikh, A., (2011). The case study approach. *BMC Medical Research Methodology,* p. 2.

Estrin, S., Gozman, D. and Khavul, S., 2017. *"The Evlution and Adoption of Equity Crowdfunding: Entrepreneur and Investor Entry Into A New Market".* [Online] Available at: Springer

Galkiewicz,D and Galkiewicz, M. (2018) "Crowdfunding Monitor 2018" [online} http://www.fh.kufstein.ac.at/content/download/3537648/file/crowdfundingmonitor_2018.pdf.

Gedda, D., Nilsson, B., Sathen, Z. and Soilen, K. S., 2016. Crowdfunding: finding the optimal platform for funders and entrepreneurs. *Technology Innovation Management Review,* 6(3), pp. 31-40.

Green, J. & Thorogood, N., (2009). *Qualitative Methods for Health Research.* 2 ed. Los Angeles: Sage.

Harrison, H., Birks, M., Franklin, R. & Mills, J., (2017). Case Study Research: Foundations and Methodological Orientations. *Forum: Qualitative Social Research,* 18(1).

Lehner, O. M., 2013. Crowdfunding social ventures; a model and research agenda. *Venture Capital: An International Journal of Entrepreneurial Finance ,* pp. 1-22.

Massolution, 2013. *The Crowdfunding Industry Report,* s.l.: s.n.

Merriam, S. B., 2009. *Qualitative research: A guide to design and implementation.* 2 ed. San Francisco: Jossey-Bass.

Roggan, J., 2015. *Motivation of German Entrepreneurs to Seek Equity via Crowdfunding: An Exploratory Study.* [Online] Available at: Google Scholar

Sassoon, D. and Duggal, S., 2015. *Crowdfunding: Insigths Into The Motives Taht Influence Entrepreneurs When Launching A Successful Campaign.* [Online] Available at: Google Scholar

Schwienbacher, A. and Larralde, B., (2010). *Crowdfunding of Small Entrepreneurial Ventures.* [Online] Available at: Google Scholar

Stake, R. E., (2006). *Multiple Case Study Analysis.* New York: Guilford

Stewart, A., (2014). Case study. In Jane Mills & Melanie Birks (Eds.), *Qualitative methodology: A practical guide* (pp.145-159). Thousand Oaks, CA: Sage.

Technavio Research Report. (2018)"Crowdfunding Market. Available online. https://www.technavio.com/talk-to-us?report=Global%20Crowdfunding%20Market%202018-2022&type=sample&src=report

Yin, R. K., (2014). *Case study research: Design and methods.* Los Angeles: Sage.

Zhao, C., Chen, C. D., Wang, J., and Chen. P. (2017) "Determinants of backers' funding intention in crowdfunding: Social exchange theory and regulatory focus" Telematics and Informatics, Vol 34, No 1, pp370-384.

Work in Progress Paper

Application of Radiant University-Wide Program Model in Entrepreneurship Education: A Case of University of Oradea in Romania

Anca Otilia Dodescu and Vasile Aurel Căuş
University of Oradea, Romania
otiliaanca.dodescu@gmail.com
relu.caus@gmail.com
DOI: 10.34190/EIE.20.179

Abstract: The project entitled: "Entrepreneur for the future" financed by the European Social Fund is implemented by University of Oradea, Romania from 2019-2021. The project addresses both the lack of entrepreneurship education opportunities outside the Economics Faculty and the decline in the rate of access, participation and graduation of the Bachelor's degree programmes, especially for rural area high school graduates, by increasing the attractiveness of the educational supply in terms of entrepreneurship correlated with improving the teachers' skills. The project provides integrated packages of training programmes and support services tailored to the specific needs of the target group: high school students, students and teachers. The entrepreneurial program for students is customized within the project in students' field of study following the "cross-campus entrepreneurship education" trends and "radiant university-wide programs in entrepreneurship education" approach. From the entrepreneurial education perspective, the main project results are three new educational offers: Entrepreneurship, Career Coaching and Life Skills customised in partnership with regional labor market partners on different non-economic fields of study: engineering, health, social sciences, mathematics and nature sciences, humanities and arts, where, traditionally, the offer of entrepreneurial education is poor or non-existent and a radiant university-wide program created as a replicable model. The project's contribution in entrepreneurial innovative learning and teaching in higher education is twofold. First, it is given by the particularization of the entrepreneurial program in 14 non-economic fields of studies and designing it tailored on local needs. Second, it is given by the integration of inclusive entrepreneurship approach, addressing simultaneously student's entrepreneurship, employability and social inclusion.

Keywords: inclusive entrepreneurship, student's entrepreneurship, entrepreneurship education model, radiant university-wide program, entrepreneurial innovative learning and teaching in higher education

1. Description of programme

The project named *"Entrepreneur for the future"* (AntreV) is a project co-financed by the Social European Fund, implemented in Romania (North-West Region, Bihor County) between 2019-2021, by the University of Oradea in partnership with Corporactive Consulting Ltd. The project aims to increase the number of students of the University of Oradea by stimulating the participation of students in undergraduate programmes, especially those in vulnerable categories, and by increasing the attractiveness of the educational supply, especially in terms of entrepreneurship, correlated with improving the teachers' skills. Potential participants must be potential undergraduate students (high school students), undergraduate students and teachers from non-economic fields of study from the University of Oradea. The project is addressed to an overall target group of 450 students (including 330 students from rural areas, students with special educational needs and disabilities, Roma people, non-traditional students and other disadvantaged groups), 84 teachers from the University of Oradea and 100 high school students from Bihor County, especially from the rural area. The project provides training programmes and support services tailored to the specific needs of the target group. The training programmes for students: Entrepreneurial Skills, Career Coaching and Life Skills - are customized within the project in students' field of study. The training programmes for teachers - Training for Trainers and Instructional Design - aims to improve teaching skills for design and teaching a customized study offer in their field of expertise. The support services packages meet the identified needs of the target group: professional counseling and personalized career guidance, educational assistance and financial support for students; workshops and counseling for the development of new customized educational offers in partnership with employers and correlated with the labor market needs for teachers; professional counseling and personalized career guidance and information services about undergraduate programmes for high school students.

2. Problem addressed

First of all, the project addresses the lack of entrepreneurship education programmes outside the Economics Faculty as well as the lack of personalised counseling and guidance services for students in various fields of study. Secondly, the project addresses the problem of decreasing the rate of access, participation and graduation of the Bachelor's degree programmes of the University of Oradea, including those belonging to vulnerable groups. The University of Oradea has been facing for the past five academic years a decline in the number of students enrolled in undergraduate programmes, to which is added a high risk of dropping out in the first year of study (the highest rate is 17.4% in 2015-2016 academic year). The explanation is the same as for all Romanian universities in the demographic decline, more pronounced in rural and small urban areas, but also in the progressive aggravation of the situation of high school graduates in rural areas which have become a vulnerable category with an accelerated risk of exclusion in recent five years.

3. Approach

Regarding the entrepreneurial program for students, the project follows the "cross-campus entrepreneurship education" trends (Welsh, 2014; Katz et al., 2014; Schneider, 2015) and "radiant university-wide programmes in entrepreneurship education" approach (Streeter, Jaquette and Hovis, 2002; Morris, Kuratko and Pryor, 2014) focused on the specific context of non-Economics students with entrepreneurship courses outside the Faculty of Economics. This approach is recognized as "extremely appealing to students, parents and alumni" (Streeter, Jaquette and Hovis, 2002) but more expensive and difficult to administer. These difficulties were overcome in our case by the meeting between the opportunity of a European financing and strong motivation for the university-wide focus of the University of Oradea which is in a stage of consolidation of its "third mission". The entrepreneurial program is located in 14 participating faculties covering all non-economic fields of study at the University of Oradea: engineering, health, social sciences, mathematics and natural sciences, humanities and arts. The administration of the program is coordinated at the university level by a team of highly experienced internal experts in entrepreneurship education and project management. The entrepreneurship course support is the result of AntreS project, a previous project of the University of Oradea addressed to female entrepreneurship, selected as an example of good practice (OECD&CE, 2013) and will be customized by areas of undergraduate study within the AntreV project. The team of experts includes a key-expert from each faculty certified in Entrepreneurial Competencies, who will be both employed and target group within the project, being first advised to customize on the field of bachelor study the entrepreneurship course support and configure it as an e-learning educational offer. The expert in entrepreneurship at the faculty level is seconded by 4-6 teachers, depending on the number of mentored students, who, similarly, will customize and teach Career Coaching and Life Skills courses. The course supports, in this case, are prepared by the Partner, a company with relevant experience in professional training at the regional level. The students' selection criterion is the average grade of the previous study year. After selection, students sign a contract which states they are committed to participate in aptitude testing, counselling and professional orientation, to attend all courses and to write a business plan. The students are trained in their faculty, in a specific context for their own major or field of study and develop their business plan related to this. After completing the entrepreneurial training, students can submit the business plan in a contest with cash prizes within the project. The evaluation and awarding of business plans are decided by a joint committee including representatives of the local business environment relevant to each field of study. Finally, students benefit from Career Coaching and Life Skills courses to increase employability in their field of study. At the end of the project, Entrepreneurship, Career Coaching and Life Skills will be introduced in the curricula of all undergraduate programmes of the University of Oradea as optional disciplines. These disciplines will be further taught by teachers trained through this project virtual or face to face depending on the decision of each faculty. The value added of this project in the field of entrepreneurial innovative learning and teaching in higher education is given by the particularization of both the theoretical part and the practical part of the entrepreneurial program in 14 various non-economic fields of studies with statistical data, concrete and relevant data about local and regional economy, examples of local entrepreneurs, role models, good practices etc. from the field of activity corresponding to the field of study; choosing the business idea in correspondence with regional smart specialization fields of activity and according to the specific needs of inclusive entrepreneurship target group - young people, students who do not have basic and specialized knowledge in the Economics or Business and who belong to a disadvantaged category (rural area, non-traditional students with socio-economic difficulties, people with disabilities, Roma people etc.); carrying out the practical part with the support of the employers for the validation of the business idea and the improvement of the business plan within those organisations with which the faculty that carries out the bachelor program has concluded practice collaboration agreements; the qualitative evaluation of the business plans by a joint commission of which the employers will be part, offering students not only the possibility of cash prizes but also internship or employment or even business plan financing opportunities in close connection with their field of study.

4. Results and future developments

Besides 100 high school students tested, counselled and career-oriented; 450 undergraduate students tested, counselled, career-oriented and trained in Entrepreneurship, Career Coaching and Life Skills to foster entrepreneurship and employability in their field of study; 84 teachers who have improved their teaching skills; 450 business plans and 3 new educational offers: Entrepreneurship, Career Coaching, Life Skills - realized and customized in 14 fields of study, the main project results is a radiant university-wide program created as a replicable model. The key to the success of this project is, in our opinion the integrated approach for training and support services packages tailored on specific target group needs. The challenge is to ensure the continuity of the project activities and its results after the completion of the European grant. The key institutional structures in this regard are the Student Entrepreneurship Society - which will manage, improve or adapt, even sale, the entrepreneurial program with the practical component developed through the project, for other fields of study, other target groups etc.; the Career Counselling and Services Center - which will manage and improve or adapt the integrated package of services, including personalized counselling and career guidance, developed through the project for the rest of the students of the University of Oradea and undergraduate candidates focusing on those belonging to disadvantaged categories, other target groups etc. and, finally, the Advisory Council for Public-Private Partnership - which will monitor and strengthen partnerships with employers created by the project to facilitate the student entrepreneurship and insertion on the labour market, as well as increasing the employability of all undergraduate students and graduates of the University of Oradea.

Acknowledgements

The project *"Entrepreneur for the future"*, is financed by the European Social Fund – Investing in People!, Human Capital Operational Programme, POCU/379/6/21/OS.6.7,6.9,6.10, **MySMIS Code: 124167**, Value: **7.282.442 lei** (approx. 1,500,000 Euros), Period of implementation: **24.05.2019 - 23.05.2021 (2 years)**, Coordinator: University of Oradea, Romania, Partner: Corporactive Consulting Ltd., website: **https://antrev.uoradea.ro/ro/**.

References

Katz, Jerome A., Roberts, Joseph, Strom, Robert et al. (2014) "Perspectives on the Development of Cross Campus Entrepreneurship Education", *Entrepreneurship Research Journal*, Vol. 4 (1), Special Issue, pp: 13-44.

Morris, Michael N., Kuratko, Donald F. and Pryor, Christopher G. (2014) "Building Blocks for the Development of University-Wide Entrepreneurship", *Entrepreneurship Research Journal*, Vol. 4 (1), Special Issue, pp: 45-68.

OECD/The European Commission (2013) "Romania: AntrES Women's School of Entrepreneurship", *The Missing Entrepreneurs: Policies for Inclusive Entrepreneurship in Europe,* OECD Publishing, pp. 228-230, [online], http://dx.doi.org/10.1787/9789264188167-en.

Schneider, Michael (2015) "Kauffman Campuses Initiative: A Study that Explores the Phenomenon of Cross-Campus Entrepreneurship", Dissertation In Higher Education Management, University of Pennsylvania,[online],https://www.bdmorganfdn.org/sites/default/files/editor/Schneider_Dissertation_Final_7-10_2015.pdf.

Streeter, Deborah H., Jaquette, John P. and Hovis, Kathryn Jr. (2002) "University-wide Entrepreneurship Education: Alternative Models and Current Trends", *Working Paper*, WP 2002-02, Department of Applied Economics and Management, Cornell University, Ithaca, New York.

Welsh, Diane H.B (2014) *Creative Cross-Disciplinary Entrepreneurship: A Practical Guide to a Cross Campus Program*, Palgrave-MacMillan.

From Entrepreneur to Undergraduate: Does the University Support or Constrain Student Entrepreneurs?

Peter McLuskie
Coventry University, UK
ab2893@coventry.ac.uk
DOI: 10.34190/EIE.20.067

Abstract: This paper focusses on an under researched area of research within the fields of enterprise education and the entrepreneurial start-up. Much of the scholarly focus around enterprise education and support within Higher Education (HE) institutions has been on the development of entrepreneurial identity, capability and intent leading to start-up (Nabi et al 2016). The role of the university is understood in terms of a potential ecosystem supporting and helping to generate entrepreneurial intent and start-ups in response to wider social and economic demands for entrepreneurial action. Arguably, within these discourses and policy literature, the student is assumed to be a blank slate who may have intent and potential but is, nevertheless, a novice with no prior experience. However, there has been little interest in students who begin their HE studies as entrepreneurs and business owners and who have already demonstrated entrepreneurial intent. These students with prior entrepreneurial experience (PEE) are a significant and growing constituency and are likely to have different development needs than students who have no or very limited practical experience of entrepreneurship. PEE students are the focus of this study which uses data drawn from annual surveys distributed at Coventry University over a 3-year period. These surveys identify a number of students who arrive at university with PEE and in many cases continue to run their venture during their studies. This data, which explores characteristics of these entrepreneur students, provides a first insight into this neglected aspect of entrepreneurship education and support. This paper will outline the results of the survey data and discuss the future direction of the research, which will include qualitative methods and interviews with student entrepreneurs. The aim is to begin establishing a focus and research agenda for a neglected area of enterprise education and business support.

Keywords: enterprise, education, entrepreneurial, intent, ecosystem

1. Theoretical background

This paper builds on research and policy formulation around university entrepreneurial ecosystems and enterprise education. The starting point here is that universities can provide an effective environment for supporting students towards entrepreneurial action, whether that be in the form of resources, such as financial support, or mind-set and skills development through enterprise education (Kautonen et al 2015). Many of these studies demonstrate a positive correlation between enterprise education and key indicators such as increased entrepreneurial intent, increased capability and growing entrepreneurial identity. However, there are also studies which indicate a negative impact from enterprise education (Nabi et al 2016).

Developing this theme of university support further, several scholars have explored the university as an eco-system: as a dynamic and networked set of resources rather than individual and isolated interventions (Isenberg 2010; Morris et al 2017). Several studies identify a range of resources that make up an effective university ecosystem, including the availability of enterprise education, engagement of alumni, incubators, prototype services, funding (Morris et al 2017). However, questions arise about the model of an appropriate ecosystem and whether a one-size all model will accommodate the diversity of student needs (Wright et al 2017).

A limited number of studies have begun to explore the differences between those students who are novices and those who come to university with PEE and the different needs and expectations of these different student groups. For example Morris et al (2017), claim that PEE can diminish the impact of enterprise education and that there can be a tension between the offerings of the university ecosystem and the needs of the student with prior experience. The authors conclude that there "remains a 'missing link' in the literature regarding the way previous business experience affects the impact university entrepreneurial activities have on venture creation by student entrepreneurs" (p.70).

A further issue relating to enterprise education and the university ecosystem is concerned with the apparent tensions between the student role and the role of the entrepreneur which are often understood to be conflicting identities that struggle to coexist (Hannon 2005). This topic has been addressed by Nielsen, & Gartner (2017) who go onto to explore the nuanced tensions that might be expected to emerge from the entrepreneur-student dynamic where different dominant identities might emerge in different contexts

It is the intention of this work in progress paper to begin to address these gaps in the literature and to explore the nature, scale and experience of students with PEE and their relationship to the university enterprise support ecosystem.

2. Methodology

The research design involved surveying students at a HE Institution during their induction period a week before formal teaching had commenced. The survey distribution was repeated over a 3 year period and captured data from first year undergraduates in 2016, 2017 and 2018. This strategy helps generate substantial data as well as helping to identify recurring and changing themes and historical patterns. The surveys generated substantial responses over the 3 year period, as indicated below, and in combination the 3 years add up to 5342 survey responses from students across all four university faculties. The timing of the survey is novel and aimed at capturing a moment in the student journey and allows this study to conduct further research to understand subsequent developments in the student journey as they enter their second and third years of study.

The survey asked students: 'Have you ever run your own business or been self-employed?' and 'Do you currently run your own business or are you self-employed?' In addition, students were asked to state gender and ethnicity and this was cross-tabulated with the other questions in the data analysis.

3. Data collection

The responses have been aggregated over the 3 year period

Have you ever run your own business or been self-employed?

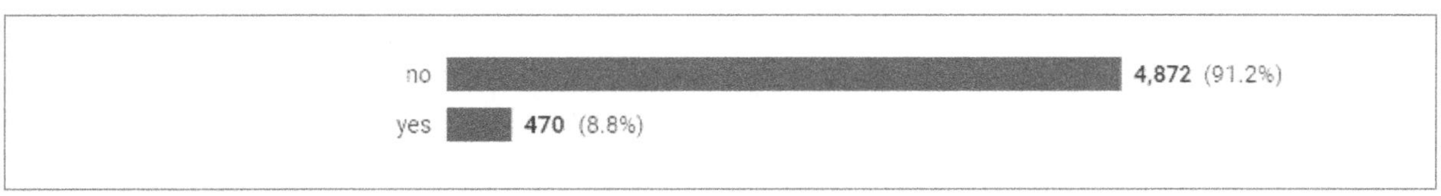

Figure 1: Over the 3 year period 8.8% of students, 470, stated they had run their own business or been self-employed

Do you currently run your own business or are you self employed?

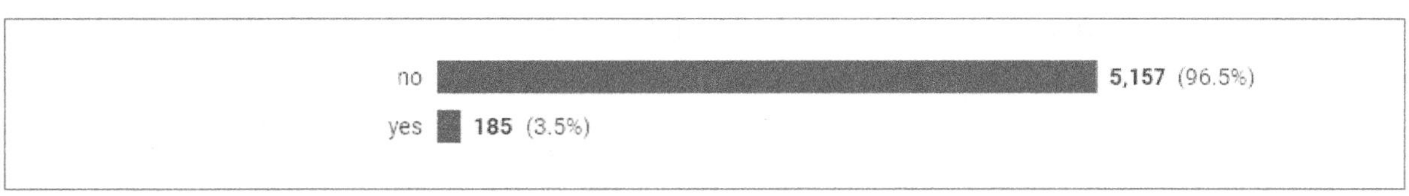

Figure 2: Over the 3 year period 3.5%, 185 students, stated that they are currently running a business or are self-employed

Have you ever run your own business or been self-employed?	Gender	
	Female	Male
no	93.74%	91.57%
yes	6.26%	8.43%
No answer	0.00%	0.00%

Figure 3: Shows the number of females v males who have previously run their own business or been self-employed

Do you currently run your own business or are you self employed?	Gender	
	Female	Male
no	97.60%	96.52%
yes	2.40%	3.48%
No answer	0.00%	0.00%

Figure 4: Shows the number of females v males who are currently running a business or are self-employed

Have you ever run your own business or been self-employed?	White - British	White - Irish	any other White background - please add	Mixed - White & Black Caribbean	Mixed - White & Black African	Mixed - White & Asian	any other Mixed back ground - please add	Asian /Asian British - Indian
no	94.36%	100.00%	89.05%	96.77%	88.24%	100.00%	80.00%	94.67%
yes	5.64%	0.00%	10.95%	3.23%	11.76%	0.00%	20.00%	5.33%

Figure 5: Have you ever run your own business or been self-employed by ethnicity

Asian /Asian British - Pakistani	Asian/Asian British - Bangladeshi	any other Asian background - please add	Black or Black British - Caribbean	Black or Black British - African	any other Black background - please add	Chinese	or other ethnic group - please add
98.78%	84.62%	98.77%	96.00%	97.06%	80.00%	96.23%	98.18%
1.22%	15.38%	1.23%	4.00%	2.94%	20.00%	3.77%	1.82%

Figure 6: Have you ever run your own business or been self-employed by ethnicity, continued

Do you currently run your own business or are you self employed?	White - British	White - Irish	any other White background - please add	Mixed - White & Black Caribbean	Mixed - White & Black African	Mixed - White & Asian	any other Mixed back ground - please add	Asian /Asian British - Indian
no	98.03%	100.00%	94.97%	100.00%	100.00%	100.00%	90.00%	97.33%
yes	1.97%	0.00%	5.03%	0.00%	0.00%	0.00%	10.00%	2.67%

Figure 7: Do you currently run your business or are you self-employed by ethnicity

Asian /Asian British - Pakistani	Asian/Asian British - Bangladeshi	any other Asian background - please add	Black or Black British - Caribbean	Black or Black British - African	any other Black background - please add	Chinese	or other ethnic group - please add
93.90%	84.62%	92.59%	92.00%	86.76%	80.00%	94.34%	96.36%
6.10%	15.38%	7.41%	8.00%	13.24%	20.00%	5.66%	3.64%

Figure 8: Do you currently run your business or are you self-employed by ethnicity, continued

The data can also be presented historically to demonstrate trends:

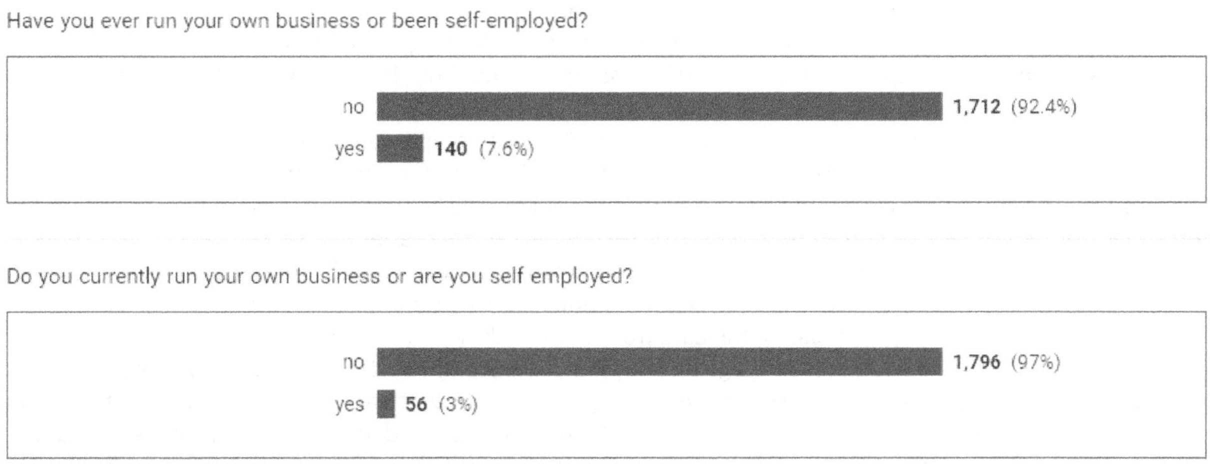

Figure 9: Shows response regarding PEE and current business in 2016

Figure 10: Shows response regarding PEE and current business in 2017

Figure 11: Shows response regarding PEE and current business in 2018

4. Discussion and implications

In terms of PPE, on average 8.8% of the sample reported that they had prior experience running a business while 3.5% continue to run a business on entry to HE. Over the 3 year period between 2016 – 2018 these figures rose from 7.6% to 9.9% (have you ever run a business or been self-employed) and 3% - 4% (do you currently run your own business or are you self-employed). These are small but significant figures when compared to other kinds of indicators. For example research from a 2016 study suggests that 6.6% of students, taken from a sample of undergraduate and postgraduates from several universities, were running their own business (Saridakis et al 2016). This represents only 2.6% more than the 4% who start university as business owners as indicated by the data collected here. It suggests that 60% of start-ups at university may have existed prior to the students entering the university ecosystem. In which case this raises questions about the net impact of university support.

In terms of gender and PEE, the data records that 2.4% females compared to 3.48% males currently run a business on entry into HE and 6.26% females compared to 8.43% report prior experience running a business. This balance is not surprising given the widely reported variance in start-up related to gender and prominence of male entrepreneurs, for example do Paço et al (2015). However, this variation of 26% is slight compared to other studies. For example, recent research has shown that women are only half as likely to start-up than men and that according to a survey only 5.6% of women compared to 11.2% of men had started a business, a difference of 50% (GEM 2017). Comparing the data from both studies would suggest that start up rate amongst females compared to males decreases with age and beyond graduation. The data on ethnicity and PEE reveals a number of trends. First, it can be seen that a significant group are Asian/Asian British, Bangladeshi, for whom just over 15% recorded previously running a business or being self-employed and the same figure recorded that they were currently running a business or are self-employed. This is closely followed by Black or Black British, African, 13.24% of whom recorded previous experience running and business and are currently still running their business. This could be compared to White - British of whom 5.64% have previously run a business or been self-employed which reduces to 1.97% who record currently run a business or are self-employed. A key insight here is that, not only are there ethnic variations in terms of PEE, but that some ethnic groups are more likely to continue running their business or self-employment as they become a student.

5. Conclusions and future plans

The study is a work in progress. It raises important questions regarding the journey and development of the student with PEE specifically in relation to their learning needs and how the university ecosystem might support rather than potentially constrain the students' entrepreneurial journey. More broadly, it raises questions about whether the current university ecosystem and research agenda on the development of entrepreneurial intent and start up is appropriate for this group and what a revised support framework might look like. The next stage will involve a shift to qualitative research methods to gain insights into the student entrepreneurial journey. Over the next two years, interviews will be conducted with the students with PEE to understand key questions. First, do the student enterprises thrive or stall during their HE studies? Second, what factors in the university ecosystem led their enterprises to stall/fail? Third, do different personal and social factors such as gender and ethnicity modify responses and do they reveal different needs and different journeys. Fourth, what can universities do differently to support students with PEE

References

GEM (2017) *Women's Entrepreneurship 2016/2017 Report,* viewed 3/6/20 available from https://www.gem-spain.com/wp-content/uploads/2015/03/gem-womens-2016-2017.pdf

Hannon, P. D. (2005) *Making the journey from student to entrepreneur: a review of the existing research into graduate entrepreneurship. Proceedings of the 14th Internationalizing Entrepreneurship Education and Training Conference*, Surrey, UK.

Isenberg, D. (2010) "How to Start an Entrepreneurial Revolution", Harvard Business Review, accessed 14/4/20 available from https:// hbr.org/2010/06/the-big-idea-how-to-start-an-entrepreneurial-revolution/ar/1

Kautonen, T. van Gelderen, M. Fink, M. (2015) "Robustness of the theory of planned behaviour in predicting entrepreneurial intentions and actions", Entrepreneurship Theory and Practice 39(3): 655-674

Morris, M. Shirokova, G. and Tsukanova, T. (2017) "Student entrepreneurship and the university ecosystem: a multi-country empirical exploration", European J. International Management, Vol. 11, No. 1

Nabi, G. and Liñán, F. and Fayolle, A. and Krueger, N. and Walmsley, A. (2016) "The Impact of Entrepreneurship Education in Higher Education: A Systematic Review and Research Agenda", Academy of Management: Learning and Education, 16 (2). pp. 277-299

Nielsen, S. & Gartner, B. (2017) "Am I a Student and/or Entrepreneur? Multiple Identities in Student Entrepreneurship", Education + Training , Vol. 59, No. 2, 2017, p. 135-154.

do Paço, A. Ferreira, J.M., Raposo, M. et al. (2015) "Entrepreneurial intentions: is education enough?" International Entrepreneurship and Management Journal March 2015, Volume 11, Issue 1, pp 57–75

Saridakis, G. Iskandarova, M. and Blackburn, R. (2016) "Student Entrepreneurship in Great Britain: Intentions and Activities", The British Report of the 2016 GUESSS Project, Small Business Research Centre, Kingston University, UK

Wright, W. Siegel, D. Mustar, P. (2017) "An emerging ecosystem for student start-ups", Journal of Technology Transfer, 42:909–922

Emerging Pedagogical Principles in Teachers' Training on Entrepreneurship Education: An Interdisciplinary Intervention

Katerina Sarri[1], Nikolaos Mouratoglou[2] and Stavroula Laspita[3]
[1]Department of Balkan, Slavic and Oriental Studies, University of Macedonia, Thessaloniki, Greece
[2]School of Philosophy and Education, Aristotle University of Thessaloniki, Greece
[3]School of Economics, Business Administration and Legal Studies, International Hellenic University, Thessaloniki, Greece
ksarri@uom.edu.gr
mpnikola@edlit.auth.gr
s.laspita@ihu.edu.gr
DOI: 10.34190/EIE.20.026

Abstract: The purpose of Entrepreneurship Education does not only relate to the establishment of a business, but also to the development of skills and attitudes that contribute to individuals' personal and professional growth. At the same time, the concept itself encompasses both the content, as well as the pedagogical and didactic methods. However, teachers/educators need to be properly trained beforehand in order to ensure that students' learning is delivered and facilitated effectively. In this respect, the present paper attempts to contribute to the wider dialogue regarding teachers' training in Entrepreneurship Education, by presenting an innovative training programme aimed at in-service teachers working in General Secondary Education and Vocational Education and Training. In specific, InnoGFEED constitutes a non-formal training programme, aligned with the European Commission's Directives on the need for innovation in teaching entrepreneurship that adopts an experiential approach drawing on learners' "indirect experience", namely, the use of films, documentaries and video games. The authors briefly describe the programme's rationale, along with the fundamental pedagogical principles based on which it has been developed such as the adoption of alternative, experiential and learner-centred approaches. The discussion contributes to the methodological considerations that need to be taken into account since the designing phase and proposes the "Re-C-Re" approach for selecting learning resources for EE programmes.

Keywords: entrepreneurship education, innovation, experiential learning, films, videogames, learning resources

1. Background

Entrepreneurs contribute significantly to the economic development of their countries by introducing new products and services that create jobs and improve people's lives (Ribeiro-Soriano, 2017). These promising outcomes have led many countries to invest in the promotion of Entrepreneurship Education (EE), while the European Commission (2006) further endorsed the development of entrepreneurial thinking through education. Since then, entrepreneurship has been acknowledged as one of the eight basic skills that should be cultivated based on the European policy on Lifelong Learning (European Commission, 2019a).

Despite the immediate response of Higher Education institutions, the provision of EE remains rather limited in primary and secondary education, as well as in vocational education and training (VET) (European Commission 2016). In this level of education, several questions on pedagogical aspects arose concerning the teaching methods used by teachers not trained in delivering education in entrepreneurship, learning objectives, as well as the content fragmentation and difficulties in evaluating learning outcomes (Mwasalwiba, 2010). Hence, this context has hindered the attempt to link EE to clear national policy objectives and contextualise it under a pedagogical framework, resulting in multiple diversified approaches with uncertain results.

According to Lackéus (2015), EE refers both to the content and to the pedagogical and didactic methods. In terms of content, it leads to specific knowledge such as the evaluation of ideas, different marketing strategies and the creation of business models. However, in terms of pedagogical and didactic methods it develops and enhances students' entrepreneurial behavior with a more practical orientation, encouraging them to act based on initiative and to feel and do things based on the knowledge and the experiences that they have gained (Sarri and Zikou, 2014). This second part partially reflects dimensions of Entrepreneurial Pedagogy that can be considered as the backbone of EE and in which learning theories are being translated into practice; it is manifested through the approaches, techniques, tools and methods that trainers and educators adopt in order to deliver entrepreneurial learning.

In more than half of the EU Member States there are very few or no guidelines for entrepreneurship teaching methods (European Commission, 2009). In addition, EE is rarely part of teachers' training at the University and is more common in the context of continuing professional development (European Commission, 2016). As a result, teachers in cooperation with external mentors, or through field visits (e.g. in companies), are expected to incorporate elements of entrepreneurship in their lessons without prior training and without methodologies linked to clear educational goals. Therefore, the need for teachers' training in entrepreneurship is (still) pivotal (Hytti and O' Gorman, 2004).

At a national level, the need to create an entrepreneurial culture from an early age in Greece is imperative mainly for two reasons. The first one relates to the economic downturn that the country has been facing in recent years and which has shrunken the entrepreneurial initiatives considered sustainable (Ioannidis and Giotopoulos, 2014). The second reason refers to the general attitude of the Greek society towards entrepreneurship and entrepreneurs; until recently, they were perceived and treated as "fraudsters" (Varsakelis et al, 2010). To tackle these challenges, the design and delivery of effective, appealing and efficient EE in Greece needs to be seriously considered. Even though several attempts have been made at different educational levels, the national educational and training policies and systems need to take further steps in order to establish an entrepreneurial culture. To address the issues raised above, the present paper discusses the emerging pedagogical principles in Entrepreneurship Education including not only the process of teachers' training, but also the pedagogical methodologies related to students' learning.

2. Methodology

The InnoGFEED (Innovation, Games Film, Entrepreneurship Education) proposed intervention program has been designed and is expected to be delivered by the University of Macedonia (Greece). It was deployed as a case study. The reasons for this selection derive from the fact that it is an output of a joint interdisciplinary collaboration of researchers and academics from the fields of Entrepreneurship Education, Adult Education, Pedagogy and Audio-visual Education. Additionally, it introduces an experiential approach in EE and it is expected to contribute to the development of a self-assessment tool for students in order to reflect on their entrepreneurial learning experiences. Therefore, the case study reflects the need for promoting innovation and assessing learning outcomes in EE.

3. The InnoGFEED intervention programme

The goals of the InnoGFEED project consist of the development of innovative experiential methods regarding EE, the cultivation of students' entrepreneurial culture attending general secondary schools and VET, as well as of training provision for in-service secondary teachers. The project's objectives include the:

- creation of a thematic library related to various topics of entrepreneurship, that will include national and international films and documentaries;
- creation of a thematic library with videogames related to the development of entrepreneurial skills;
- development of two toolkits –educational and methodological– that will assist teachers in practically applying the proposed methodology and teaching plans in their daily practice;
- creation of a community of practice in order collaboration and knowledge transfer to be enhanced;
- pilot-testing of the teaching plans in general secondary education and in VET;
- creation of the InnoGFEED innovation hub, where all the above-mentioned outputs will be uploaded for teachers in remote areas (i.e. islands, rural areas).

The overall methodology of the project includes four parts. The first one refers to the development of the educational material and includes the selection of the films, documentaries and videogames that will form the two thematic libraries. The authors formulated the "Re-C-Re" approach including three main criteria for selecting these resources:

- *relevance*: how/to what extent does the content of the resources relate to: a) entrepreneurship and/or innovation, b) the learners' needs and c) the wider societal needs and challenges?
- *contextualisation*: how/to what extent are the resources associated with a) the existing school curricula and b) other non-formal (extracurricular) learning trends?

- *reflection*: how/to what extent do the resources permit and promote a) individual and b) collective reflection?

The second part relates to the methodology that will be adopted during and after teachers' training. The learning theory of Andragogy has been considered to provide the most appropriate principles, as the learning process will be directly related to participants' daily lives and needs, considering their educational experience(s) (Knowles, 1973; Knowles et al, 2005) in the broader historical and sociocultural context (Brookfield, 1986). Moreover, a community of practice will be developed in the framework of the situated learning theory (Lave, 1988), a socio-cultural theory that perceives learning as an activity taking place in a specific social and cultural context, interacting with the social and natural context (Lave, 1991). This will allow the members to exchange best practices, ideas and concerns, establishing a support network and promoting the sense of belonging.

The third part includes the methodology of the learning process that will involve the ultimate beneficiaries, students attending general secondary education and/or VET. In specific, the learning process will follow Kolb's (1984) learning cycle, in which learning begins based on some experience and may lead to a more abstract generalisation level in the form of reflective learning. However, in terms of this experience, InnoGFEED will be based on learners' "indirect experience" (Jarvis, 2006) using films, documentaries and videogames, moving beyond the traditional approaches.

Finally, the teachers who will participate in the training will apply some of the proposed educational plans in their teaching practice with their students. To be able to assess the impact of the proposed intervention on their students, a self-assessment tool will be developed including quantitative and qualitative items based on the 15 entrepreneurial skills and the learning outcomes defined by the European Entrepreneurship Framework (Bacigalupo et al, 2016).

4. Conclusion

While there is extensive research on EE offered by universities, there is a paucity of research related to EE offered at earlier stages of learning (Rosique-Blasco et al, 2016), namely in secondary education. The InnoGFEED program attempts to fill this gap at a national level by providing learning through entrepreneurship and not learning about and for entrepreneurship (Lackéus, 2015).

Regarding, the practical pedagogical and methodological implications emerging from the present case study, the authors highlight the need of adopting an interdisciplinary approach since the designing phase of EE programs. This collaborative interdisciplinary approach provides several insights on which pedagogical theories and methodologies may better fit the purpose and learning objectives set in the learning content, in a realistic way. In addition, it contributes to generating ideas that combine different elements and that were not considered at an individual or a single-discipline level. Therefore, addressing interdisciplinarity at the stage of delivering the content is not enough.

Additionally, the learning theories and pedagogical principles underpinning such interventions should be in line with the learners' needs, the objectives, tools and techniques utilised, as well as with the assessment. This pedagogical continuum may better support the learning process denoting a holistic meaningful experience both for teachers/trainers/educators and students. In this way, challenges attained to teachers' resistance or assessment may be proactively tackled (Lackéus, 2015). Finally, the case study provides a practical reflection "approach" for selecting learning resources in EE, based on (and extending) the principles of learning through entrepreneurship.

The "Re-C-Re" approach reflects the need of taking a "break" and considering three fundamental factors before making a decision on which learning resources will be used in a learning process. The first factor refers to the resources' *relevance* concerning the learning content (in this case EE), the learner's needs, as well as the wider societal needs and challenges. The second factor is *contextualisation* acknowledging the need that the resources need to promote connectivity and interdisciplinarity both with curricular subjects (formal learning) and extracurricular (non-formal) learning trends, while the third factor refers to whether the learning resources permit and promote individual and collective *reflection*.

References

Bacigalupo, M., Kampylis, P., Punie, Y. and Van den Brande, G. (2016) *EntreComp: The Entrepreneurship Competence Framework*. Luxembourg: Publications Office of the European Union. https://doi.org/10.2791/593884

Brookfield, S. (1986) *Understanding and Facilitating Adult Learning*. San Francisco: Jossey-Bass.

European Commission (2006) *Oslo Agenda for Entrepreneurship Education in Europe*. https://ec.europa.eu/docsroom/documents/8968/attachments/1/translations/en/renditions/pdf

European Commission (2009) *Entrepreneurship in vocational education and training: final report of the expert group*. Brussels: European Commission, DG Enterprise and Industry. https://ec.europa.eu/docsroom/documents/10446/attachments/1/translations/en/renditions/native

European Commission (2016) *Entrepreneurship education at school in Europe. Eurydice Report.* Luxembourg: Publications Office of the European Union. https://eacea.ec.europa.eu/national-policies/eurydice/content/entrepreneurship-education-school-europe_en

European Commission (2019), *Key competences for lifelong learning*. Luxembourg: Publication Office of the European Union. https://op.europa.eu/en/publication-detail/-/publication/297a33c8-a1f3-11e9-9d01-01aa75ed71a1/language-en

Hytti, U. and O'Gorman, C. (2004) '"What is "enterprise education"? An analysis of the objectives and methods of enterprise education programmes in four European countries.", *Education + Training,* Vol. 46 No.1, pp.11–23. https://doi.org/10.1108/00400910410518188

Ioannidis, S. and Giotopoulos, I. (2014) *Entrepreneurship in Greece 2012-2013. Indications for recovery of small business*. Financial and Industrial Research Foundation.

Jarvis, P. (2006) *Towards a comprehensive theory of human learning*. Routledge.

Knowles, *M. (1973) The Adult Learner: A Neglected Species. American Society for Training and Development.* ERIC Document. https://files.eric.ed.gov/fulltext/ED084368.pdf

Knowles, M., Holton, E., and Swanson, R. (2005) *The adult learner: The definitive classic in adult education and human resource development* (6th ed.). Amsterdam; Boston: Elsevier.

Kolb, D. (1984) *Experiential learning: Experience as the source of learning and development*. Englewood Cliffs, NJ: Prentice-Hall.

Lackéus, M. (2015) "*Entrepreneurship in education: What, why, when, how.*", OECD Background Paper. https://www.oecd.org/cfe/leed/BGP_Entrepreneurship-in-Education.pdf

Lave, J. (1988) *Cognition in Practice: Mind, mathematics, and culture in everyday life*. Cambridge: Cambridge University Press.

Lave, J. (1991) Situating learning in communities of practice. In L.B., Resnick, J.M., Levine, S.D., Teasley (Eds). *Perspectives on Socially Shared Cognition*. Washington, DC: American Psychological Association, pp.63–82.

Mwasalwiba, E.S. (2010) "Entrepreneurship education: A review of its objectives, teaching Methods, and impact indicator", *Education + Training, 52*(1), pp.20–47. https://doi.org/10.1108/00400911011017663

Ribeiro-Soriano, D. (2017) "Small Business and Entrepreneurship: Their Role in Economic and Social Development." *Entrepreneurship and Regional Development,* Vol. 29 No. (1–3). https://doi.org/10.1080/08985626.2016.1255438

Rosique-Blasco, M., Madrid-Guijarro, A. and García-Pérez-de-Lema, D. (2016) "Entrepreneurial skills and socio-cultural factors: an empirical analysis in secondary education students", *Education + Training*, Vol. 58 No. (7/8). https://doi.org/10.1108/ET-06-2015-0054

Sarri, K. and Zikou E. (2014) "Entrepreneurship education: Why, What, How and when", *Journal of Educational Research*, Vol. 3, pp.50–63.

Varsakelis, N., Koutsoulianos, Chr., Zikou, E. (2010) *Local Government and Entrepreneurship, Policies for the Development of Entrepreneurship*. Thessaloniki: Public Benefit Municipal Enterprise for Social Welfare and Assistance of Kalamaria.

A Road to Empowerment: Social Media Usage by Women Entrepreneurs in China

Heidi Zihui Zhou and Kate Johnston
Dundalk Institute of Technology, Ireland
D00217099@student.dkit.ie
kate.johnston@dkit.ie
DOI: 10.34190/EIE.20.128

Abstract: Women's entrepreneurship is on the rise globally. In the past few years, 163 million women were starting businesses across 74 economies worldwide, while 111 million were running established businesses, according to the Global Entrepreneurship Monitor (GEM) 2018/19 Women's Report (GEM, 2019). Globally, the TEA (Total Entrepreneurial Activity) rate for women was 10.2% in 2019. Numerous studies throughout the world have consistently demonstrated the positive effect of women entrepreneurs on economic growth, job creation as well as social benefits, particularly for developing economies in the Middle East, Africa and Asia. (Cuberes and Teignier, 2015; Fetsch et al., 2015; Lewis et al., 2014; Hailemariam and Kroon, 2019). A point in case is China. The economy currently has the largest population in the world, with 1.4 billion people, of which 48.7 per cent are women (World Bank, 2019). However, up until recently, female entrepreneurs were mostly unheard of in China's business environment largely due to cultural barriers and the dominant male-focused society, as noted by Lai (2017). Interestingly, social media offers enormous potential in this regard. The benefits that online social networking, e-marketing campaigns have been well documented and validated (Ukpere et al., 2014). As such, social media platforms (WeChat and Weibo), offering huge potential with minimum cost and has the potential to empower Chinese female entrepreneurs globally. Using a sample of 60 female entrepreneurs in China, the study explores how social media use benefits women entrepreneurs in an emerging market. The research points to evidence that female entrepreneurs are embracing this new marketing channel with new impetus and this has resulted in more significant economic gains (through greater market and customers' access) along with a greater feeling of empowerment. The study also points to certain challenges and disadvantages and highlights the need for supports/training in the social media space.

Keywords: women entrepreneurship, economic development, social media, women entrepreneurs, support and training

1. Introduction

Over the last five years, China has experienced one of the fastest-growing economies with an annual GDP growth rate of 6.6%. (Trading Economics, 2019). Behind this economic growth, improvement in the entrepreneurial environment has led to a rise in female entrepreneurship (Gemconsortium.org, 2019) as a key component of this success.

The economic and social impact of female entrepreneurship is widely acknowledged (Tran, 2014; Kiyai et al., 2019 and GEM, 2019) leading to higher economic activity, job creation as well as social benefits, Hailemariam and Kroon, 2019; Genc and Öksüz, 2015). Research has shown that this is particularly important for developing economies in the Middle East, Africa and Asia. (Cuberes and Teignier, 2015; Fetsch et al., 2015; Lewis et al., 2014; Hailemariam and Kroon, 2019). China provides an interesting case in this regard. As one of the most populous countries in the world, currently 1.4 billion people, of which 48.7 per cent are women (worldbank.org, 2019). China is one where social media usage is among the highest rates in the world.

This study examines and undertakes a literature review of social media usage among female entrepreneurship in China, and explores the use, benefits and challenges social media (i.e. WeChat, Weibo) can offer to female entrepreneurs. Using survey data with 60 female entrepreneurs and four in-depth interviews, the results suggest that female entrepreneurs are embracing this new marketing channel leading to a range of benefits such as greater customer engagement and market opportunity. There are challenges suggesting a need for supports and training to maximise the potential of social media platforms for these entrepreneurs.

2. Female entrepreneurship

There is growing interest in the field of female entrepreneurship. According to the Global Women Entrepreneurship Report (GEM, 2019), rates for female entrepreneurship are on the rise and presents an exciting area of study. Female entrepreneurs are different from their male counterparts; their motivations for starting a business are different to that of men, (Buttner and Moore, 1997; Kepler and Shane, 2007; Robinson,

2001; Marlow et al., 2009) and they face unique barriers and challenges (Jennings and Brush, 2013). As such female entrepreneurship represents a separate but related area of study within the entrepreneurship literature.

3. Female entrepreneurship in China and the role of social media

Research in the field of female entrepreneurs in China is at an early stage. In 2015, MasterCard conducted a significant survey of women's entrepreneurship in China which showed that the Chinese Women's Pioneer Index scored 63.6 points in 2014, higher than the Asia-Pacific average (59.9). However, subsequent research into the number of Chinese female business owners' statistics in the past few years has shown no significant improvement. (ILO, 2018).

The potential of social media to drive entrepreneurship and economic development is a growing area of academic study (Whelan et al., 2013; Meredith, 2012; Schreck and Keim, 2013 and Peters et al., 2013). These studies cite greater customer reach (Meredith, 2012), information disclosure (Osatuyi, 2013) and greater customer engagement in the marketing communication process (Pentina et al., 2012 and Papasolomou & Melanthiou, 2012). How women entrepreneurs engage with this technology is a relatively new area. To date, researchers have examined social media usage among female entrepreneur in various settings (Genc and Okuz, 2015) and countries such as South Africa (Upkere et al., 2014), South Korea (Park and Sung, 2017) and Bangladesh in south Asia (Hossain and Rahman, 2018).

China provides an interesting case. China has among the highest social media usage in the world, from users "following" celebrities on Weibo, to consumers "linking" their favourite brands on WeChat (Chen et al., 2018). As of 2019, WeChat has reached over 650 million users, followed by Sina Weibo with 359.6 million (Cheung, 2019). Statistics on the monthly active users (MAU) of WeChat has reached 1.2 billion in the first quarter of 2020 (CIW Team, 2020).

In order to extend research in this area, this paper aims to investigate the use of social media (i.e. WeChat, Weibo) among the female entrepreneurship in China, covering both in Hong Kong and mainland China (where Facebook and Instagram are not available). Furthermore, this paper also aims to identify the benefits and challenges that social media can bring to these female entrepreneurs. The study seeks to explore what supports or training in the social media space that government can provide to female entrepreneurs to help them to build and grow profitable and sustainable businesses.

4. Methodology

The methodology adopted in this study, in line with the research objectives, have employed a mixed-method approach. Semi-structured interviews with four entrepreneurs and an online survey involved 60 female entrepreneurs were conducted. Due to the ongoing situation surrounding Covid-19, the authors were unable to go ahead with a face-to-face interview. Therefore, a phone interview approach was adopted.

5. Results

Interview data: Key insights

- 1. Benefits and use of social media in business: The four entrepreneurs used a variety of platforms, and all acknowledged the benefits of using this technology in terms of access to customers through engagement with customers, creating greater loyalty.
- 2. Challenges: The discussion centred on the struggle with the managing time spent on social media and the duplication of ideas - others can easily replicate any products. Many of the entrepreneurs acknowledged the increased competition, due to the easy access and user-friendly features of social media – it has become the go-to tool for many businesses. As a result, businesses have become more competitive.
- 3. Advice and plan for business development in the future: There was a clear discussion for a need to identify the business target audience and secondly clearly identifying which platforms are the most effective.

Survey results: Key insights documented

- Based on a survey of 60 respondents, analysis of the data reveal that most were young (two thirds (68%) under the age of 35 years) well educated (45% held a bachelor's degree, while 36.7% are found to have higher diploma certificates) and were in relatively new business (63% were in operation for less than three years). A range of sectors was covered in the survey.

- Use of social media among female entrepreneurs-The majority (88.3% have an active presence on social media (i.e., WeChat, Weibo, and Tick Tock).
- Motivations for using social media platforms-The motivations and benefits of using social media platforms for the entrepreneurs are varied and include being a cost-effective marketing tool (66%) contact with customers (86.8%) and grow sales domestically (51%). There was also general agreement that social media provides an opportunity to exploit new markets and customers (75%).
- The time involved and difficulties in building brand awareness through social media (i.e., Weibo and Instagram) were identified as the main challenges in using social media platforms. There is little evidence of a lack of knowledge in using social media technology (this may be due in part to the fact that most of the respondents were relatively young, under the age of 35 years. Fear of fraud or being deceived was viewed as a barrier).

6. Discussion and limitations and implications for further research

The results of this study suggest that female entrepreneurs who are doing businesses in China are embracing and utilising technology and using a variety of social media platforms. The entrepreneurs clearly acknowledge the benefits of this tool but are acutely aware of the challenges, time and utilising this technology more effectively are the two major challenges identified. Among a key concern cited in using social media is the increased competition due to widespread ease to which social media platform can be accessed.

The results of this study are based on a small sample. Hence, the need for caution in interpreting the results. The study clearly shows that social media platforms are a crucial feature of female entrepreneurs' business and marketing activities in China. Extending the study to a larger data set and undertaking some further statistical analysis to determine trends could be useful in further validating these results.

References

Buttner, E.H. and Moore, D.P. (1997). Women's organizational exodus to entrepreneurship: self-reported motivations and correlates with success. *Journal of small business management*, *35*, pp.34-46.

Chen, K., Xie, Y., Zhu, L. and Xu, Z. (2018). THE EFFECTIVENESS OF GLOBAL BRANDS SOCIAL MEDIA COMMUNICATION IN CHINA: EVIDENCE FROM WEIBO. *Global Fashion Management Conference*, 2018, pp.417-421.

Cheung, M. (2019). *China Social Network Users 2019.* [Online] Available at: https://www.emarketer.com/content/china-social-network-users-2019 [Accessed 26 May 2020].

CIW Team. (2020). *WeChat statistical highlights 2020*. [Online] Available at: https://www.chinainternetwatch.com/30201/wechat-stats-2019/ [Accessed 24 of May 2020].

Cuberes, J. and Teignier, A. (2015). Women and entrepreneurship: an alluring or luring option. *International Journal of Entrepreneurship and Small Business*, 25(3), p.351.

Fetsch, A., Wilhelmina, S., Oyelana, A. and Ibrahim, S. (2015). Challenges Faced by Women Entrepreneurs and Strategies Adopted by Women Entrepreneurs to Ensure Small Business Success in Nkonkobe Municipality, South Africa. *Journal of Economics*, 6(1), pp.37-49.

GEM. (2019). *GEM 2019 / 2020 GLOBAL REPORT.* [Online] Available at: https://www.gemconsortium.org/report/gem-2019-2020-global-report[Accessed 21 March 2020].

Gemconsortium.org (2019). *Global entrepreneurship monitor 2018/2019 report.* [Online] Available at: https://www.gemconsortium.org/report/gem-2018-2019-global-report [Accessed 19 October 2019].

Genç, M. and Öksüz, B. (2015). A fact or an illusion: Effective social media usage of female entrepreneurs. *Procedia-Social and Behavioral Sciences*, *195*, pp.293-300.

Hailemariam, A.T., Kroon, B., Van Engen, M. and Van Veldhoven, M. (2019). *Dreams and reality: autonomy support for women entrepreneurs in Ethiopia.* [Online] Available at: https://www.emerald.com/insight/content/doi/10.1108/EDI-10-2017-0230/full/html [Accessed 16 December 2019].

Hossain, M. and Rahman, M.F. (2018). Social Media and the Creation of Entrepreneurial Opportunity for Women. *Management*, *8*(4), pp.99-108.

International Labour Organization. （2018）. *International Labour Organization Report.* [Online] Available at :https://www.ilo.org/empent/Publications/WCMS_714125/lang--en/index.htm [Accessed 5 December 2019].

Jennings, J.E. and Brush, C.G. (2013). Research on women entrepreneurs: challenges to (and from) the broader entrepreneurship literature? *The Academy of Management Annals*, *7*(1), pp.663-715.

Keim, D. and Schreck, T. (2013). Visual Analysis of Social Media Data. *Computer*.

Kepler, E. and Shane, S. (2007). *Are male and female entrepreneurs really that different?* [Online] Available at: http://www.pw.seipa.edu.pl/s/p/artykuly/90/909/Female%20Entrepreneurs%20Different%20Shane%202007.pdf [Accessed 17 March 2020].

Kiyai, G., Namusonge, M. and Jagongo, A. (2019). Factors hindering the growth of women-owned micro and small enterprises: A case of microfinance borrowers in Makadara, Nairobi. *International Academic Journal of Economics and Finance*, *3*(3), pp.187-203.

Lai, J. (2017). The Rise of Female Entrepreneurs in China. [Online] Available at: https://www.henleyglobal.com/industry-news-details/the-rise-of-female-entrepreneurs-in-china/ [Accessed 8 January 2020].

Lewis, B., Md Yusoff, R. and Sadi, M. (2014). Women Entrepreneurs in Bahrain: Motivations and Barriers. *Jurnal Teknologi*, 64(2).

Marlow, S., Henry, C. and Carter, S. (2009). Exploring the Impact of Gender upon Women's Business Ownership. *International Small Business Journal: Researching Entrepreneurship*, 27(2), pp.139-148.

MasterCard Social Newsroom. (2015). *Women in Charge: Mastercard Index Reveals How Countries Are Progressing to Empower Women Entrepreneurs*. [Online] Available at:https://newsroom.mastercard.com/press-releases/women-in-charge-mastercard-index-reveals-how-countries-are-progressing-to-empower-women-entrepreneurs/ [Accessed 10 December 2019].

Meredith, M.J. (2012). Strategic communication and social media: An MBA course from a business communication perspective. *Business Communication Quarterly*, *75*(1), pp.89-95.

Osatuyi, B. (2013). Information sharing on social media sites. *Computers in Human Behavior,* 29(6), pp.2622-2631.

Park, J.Y., Sung, C.S. (2017). Does social media use influence entrepreneurial opportunity? A review of its moderating role. *Sustainability*, *9*(9), p.1593.

Peters, K., Chen, Y., Kaplan, A.M., Ognibeni, B. and Pauwels, K. (2013). *Social media metrics—A framework and guidelines for managing social media.* [Online] Available at: https://www.sciencedirect.com/science/article/pii/S109499681300042X?casa_token=xapBdBV4OVEAAAAA:Kly4gAImJnOJmPnh8SVtC-cCBOkhnbBQvEp7zrmBSVZRwlhhyljlpTk-40NFZ6WTrCANVp9qaw [Accessed 28 May 2020].

Papasolomou, I. and Melanthiou, Y. (2012). Social media: Marketing public relations' new best friend. *Journal of Promotion Management,* 18 (3), p. 319-328.

Pentina, I., Koh, A. C., & Le, T. T. (2012). Adoption of social networks marketing by SMEs: Exploring the role of social influences and experience in technology acceptance. *International Journal of Internet Marketing and Advertising,* 7(1), 65-82.

Robinson, S. (2001). Fast-growth women and men entrepreneurs take different paths toward business success. *Journal of European Industrial Training*, 25(8).

Trading Economics.(2019). *China GDP Annual Growth Rate*. [Online] Available at: https://tradingeconomics.com/china/gdp-growth-annual [Accessed 24 May 2020].

Tran, K. (2014). *The Impact of Digital Media on Female Entrepreneurship.* [Online] Available at:https://pressfoliosproduction.s3.amazonaws.com/uploads/story/story_pdf/106402/1064021413388007.pdf [Accessed 10 January 2020].

Ukpere, C.L., Slabbert, A.D. and Ukpere, W.I. (2014). *Rising trend in social media usage by women entrepreneurs across the globe to unlock their potentials for business success*. Mediterranean Journal of Social Sciences, 5(10), p.551.

Whelan, E., Golden, W. and Donnellan, B. (2013). Digitising the R&D social network: revisiting the technological gatekeeper. *Information Systems Journal*, *23*(3), pp.197-218.

World Bank.org (2019). *Overview*. [Online] Available at: https://www.worldbank.org/en/country/china/overview [Accessed 4 March 2020].

Late Submissions

The Impact of Financial Illiteracy on Entrepreneurship: Evidence From Bahrain

Noora Khalid Ali and Allam Hamdan
Ahlia University, Manama, Bahrain
Allamh3@hotmail.com
DOI: 10.34190/EIE.20.229

Abstract: Financial literacy is a key factor in entrepreneurship because entrepreneurship requires one make sound decisions and judgments based on a given situation. Understanding the impact of financial illiteracy on entrepreneurship has significance on a country's strategies for implementing financial education literacy in its population. The research incorporates a literature review and data collection in form of a questionnaire distributed to Bahraini entrepreneurs. 120 questionnaires were distributed, while only 108 were viable for the study. The researcher used IBM's Statistical Package for Social Sciences (SPSS) to analyze the data. The researcher conducted a Reliability Test, Normality Test, Correlation Test, and Regression Analysis. The results of the regression test allowed the researcher to accept the hypothesis that financial illiteracy has negative effect on entrepreneurship success, as entrepreneurs need to be financially literate in order to make reliable decisions and make sure their business is successful in the market. The research contributed to studies relating the impact of financial illiteracy and factors affecting entrepreneurship success, as well as filling the gap in knowledge regarding studies related to the research topic. The research is helpful to entrepreneurs to realize the importance of financial literally, and for organizations to assure their top decision makers have the required skills and knowledge to assure business success.

Keywords: financial literacy, entrepreneurship

1. Introduction

Financial literacy as defined by Klapper et al. (2015) is the ability to come up with informed judgments and decisions regarding how best to use and manage money. According to the US Financial Literacy and Education Commission (2007), financial literacy is defined as "the ability of coming up with informed judgments as well as taking effective actions when it comes to the management of current and future use of money". Basing on these two definitions, we can simply define financial illiteracy as the lack of the ability to come up with sound and informed judgments when it comes to managing money (Worthington, 2016). Basing on these definitions, we can also say that financial literacy is related to financial knowledge, skills and behavior.

Calcagno & Monticone (2015) observed that financial literacy affects us as individuals, our households, our financial institutions and even on a broader scope it affects the economy of a nation. Financial literacy instills in us skills and knowledge including; Mathematical literacy- which involves basic numeracy and comprehension skills; financial understanding – where an individual must understand the nature and forms of money and the consequences that comes with particular decisions; financial competence- this involves understanding the main features that a basic financial service has, the attitudes towards spending and saving money, basic understanding of financial records, being aware on the risks associated with given financial products and understanding the relationship that exists between risk and return.); and financial responsibility- the ability of an individual to come up with the appropriate and relevant personal life decision on financial issues, an understanding of consumer rights and responsibilities. Entrepreneurship involves coming up with a business idea the putting it into practice by creating a business and scaling it to generate profit. Clearly, financial illiteracy has a negative impact on entrepreneurship.

Financial literacy is a key factor in entrepreneurship because entrepreneurship requires one make sound decisions and judgments based on a given situation; be able to budget appropriately in order to meet expenditures, be able to identify the appropriate financial products or services that meets his/her needs etc. Entrepreneurial Success basically relates to achieving the goals and objective set by a particular business venture. According to Jones et al., (2018), entrepreneurial Success has different forms which can include business survival, profits made; the return on investment, sales growth, number of employed people, happiness in business operations, reputation of a business etc. This means that when we talk about entrepreneurial success, we actually refer to quite a number of things depending on an individual's perspective. The objective of this paper is to examine the impact of financial illiteracy on entrepreneurship.

1.1 Problem statement

The economy of countries within the Gulf, especially Bahrain, depends on natural resources, specifically petrol to maintain their economy. As the prices of fuel went down, Bahrain's national budget struggled along with the economy. The number of graduating individuals exceeds the amount of available vacancies in all fields in both the public and private sectors. With the increase of population and unemployment rates, individuals began to start their own businesses. The Government of Bahrain is now focusing on entrepreneurs and start-ups as a means of boosting the economy and increasing Gross Domestic Product (GDP) of the country while supporting new sources of income other than their focus on natural resources. The increase in entrepreneurship has helped the economy, as more people are self-employed and aid the economy. The research aims to fill the gap in knowledge in regard to the factors affecting entrepreneurs in Bahrain and leading them to shut down. The researcher wishes to seek solutions for the problem of businesses shutting down in Bahrain by realizing the effect of financial illiteracy of such outcome.

1.2 Research question

The research topic can be translated into two main research questions as follows:

1) *What is the impact of financial illiteracy on entrepreneurship success?*
2) *What is the role of the government in increasing financial literacy of entrepreneurs?*

The research sub-question is:

a) *What is the extent of effect of financial literacy on entrepreneurship success?*

1.3 Significance of the research

The study will have significance to;

- Entrepreneurs
- The government and financial institutions
- Training institutions
- Investors

Entrepreneurs will benefit from this research by realizing the importance of financial literacy in running a successful business. This will allow them more opportunities of growth and development.

The government and financial institutions will be able to come up with policies and programs that promote financial literacy in the struggle to reduce poverty. The government will also realize its role in increasing entrepreneurship skills and financial literacy through education. Financial institutions will also realize the importance of financial literacy and the effect of literacy on business decisions and processes, therefore promoting them to be more thorough in their hiring strategies and organizational structure.

This study will also have significance on training institutions because they will understand the significance of business and financial education on business success. This will see that the academicians of a particular nation established relevant curriculum to be taught in business schools that will lead to the actual success in the real word. Financial institutions will also be able to understand and rate the risk profile that comes with financially illiterate entrepreneurs as compared to the risk profile of literate entrepreneurs. Furthermore, Microfinance institutions and non-governmental institutions will determine whether or not should they build financial literacy capacity with the efforts of reducing poverty through entrepreneurship.

This study will be significant to investors due to the fact that it will also explore to understand the benefits that come with firms acquiring financial literacy. With proper financial management skills, firms will be able maximize their profits. Investors on the other hand, will also emphasize on the importance financial literacy because they will need to be able to properly understand financial reports of their firms, understand ways with which assets are allocated, the ratio of debt to quality that need to be used and the means with which profits can be further derived.

1.4 Nominal definitions

Financial literacy refers to the ability of an individual in understanding how money works along with the knowledge and skills to make financially responsible decisions.

Entrepreneurship is the process through which an individual of a group of people designs, establishes and runs a new business, often starting small and then gradually growing o form a larger business.

1.5 Summary

While entrepreneurship is a continually growing trend across world economies, starting and running a business requires more than just having an idea and capital. The management of resources is an essential skill that hopeful entrepreneurs must strive to gain. Understanding the impact of illiteracy on entrepreneurship will determine whether a government should put in place financial literacy programs in efforts to stimulate economic growth in the small and medium business enterprises. Therefore, this paper is motivated by the need to determine the impact of financial illiteracy on entrepreneurship.

Bahraini Entrepreneurs will be targeted to complete the questionnaire and collected necessary data for the analysis. The researcher aims to address the gap in knowledge regarding the role of financial illiteracy on business closures and understand the role of the government in increasing entrepreneur skills to stop such closures.

2. Literature theory and review

This part basically presents previous studies conducted in an attempt to understand the impact of financial illiteracy on entrepreneurship. The part also digs deeper to understand the concepts entrepreneurship and entrepreneurship success.

2.1 Theoretical review

For a long time, entrepreneurship has been perceived little more than an applied trade and not as an academic area of study. Many researchers have also failed to carry out studies on the impact of financial illiteracy on entrepreneurship because most people have always has the perception that even those who could not attend college could simply practice the concepts of entrepreneurship and start businesses. However, due to the deep impacts of financial illiteracy on entrepreneurship and its critical role in economic growth, many researchers have begun to carry out studies that aim to deepen their understanding on financial literacy and entrepreneurship. We will review some of the relevant concepts relevant to our study.

2.1.1 The knowledge spillover theory of entrepreneurship

Knowledge spillover can be seen as an exchange of ideas among individuals. Knowledge spillover comes from a stock of knowledge where a spillover effect has technological improvements on a neighbor through one's own innovation. Looking at the theory of knowledge spillover, we get to understand that the creation of new knowledge expands the set of technological opportunity. Entrepreneurial activity is not just a simple activity involving the arbitrage of opportunities but is an activity that calls for exploitation of intra-temporal knowledge spillovers. Using this theory, we will determine whether knowledge spillover affects an entrepreneur's success. This will in turn also help us to distinguish between financial literacy and economic knowledge.

2.1.2 The theory of planned behavior and financial literacy

While it is true that acquiring additional financial information can improve an individual's financial behavior, it is not automatically counted to do so. Most research indicates that there is no consistent behavior in individuals and households when it comes to their financial interests even when these people have accurate financial information. In most of the cases, financial education has always focused on enhancing knowledge, skills and attitudes that are related to a particular finance topic like management of money, savings etc. and not personal behavior. Using this theory, we will be able to understand the effect of financial literacy on the behavior of entrepreneurs and what this implies on entrepreneurial success.

2.1.3 Financial knowledge

Huston (2017) defines financial knowledge as the understanding of key financial terms as well as key financial concepts that are needed for our daily financial lives. Potrich et al. (2016) defines financial education as the ability needed to manage income, expenditure and savings is a safe manner. The Organization of Economic Co-Operation and Development (OECD, 2011) explains that financial knowledge helps in determining whether an individual is financial literate or not by simply asking questions revolving around simple and compound interest, inflation, and risk and return.

Huston (2017) explains that financial education is an important constituent when coming up with individual or financial decisions. The author argues that improved financial knowledge results to more responsible financial behavior thus effective financial decisions. Huston explains that individuals with higher level of knowledge usually engage in a number of best practices financial behaviors like having an adequate emergency fund, monitoring their credit reports, having insurance covers etc. The author therefore attempts to offer some solution to lack of financial knowledge (financial illiteracy). By having financial education in place, there will be improved knowledge and this will result in more effective financial decision-making. Huston urges policy makers, the financial service industry and educators to put numerous initiatives that will aid in combating low levels of financial knowledge. Financial education will improve the financial wellbeing of an individual and their ability to make better decisions needed for the success of entrepreneurship.

2.1.4 Financial literacy and behavior

Hilgert et al. (2003) conducted a nationwide survey on financial behavior and financial literacy. The authors formed a Financial Practices Index that they based on behavior in four variables; cash-flow management, credit management, savings, and investment practices. The authors then compared the results of this index with scores on financial literacy questions. It was found that individuals who were more financially literate had higher Financial Practices Index scores. This strongly indicated that financial knowledge is related to financial behavior.

2.1.5 Financial knowledge and profitability

According to Lusardi & Mitchell (2014) financial literacy forms a critical aspect in any decision making regardless of the subject matter. The authors even propose that financial literacy is needed to create some measure of financial competence when it comes to participation in the financial market and management of financial matters. The authors even conducted a survey on financial literacy in the US where they majored on examining the impacts of financial literacy on economic decision making. Their study can be concluded that financial knowledge is an investment in human capital which basically promotes accumulation of wealth.

The authors however argues that despite the fact that financial knowledge being important part in ensuring financial performance of both individuals and businesses, it is somehow still an insufficient factor in ensuring performance. These two researchers therefore tries to bring in another factor; psychological characteristics of an individual and not just financial knowledge alone. Psychological characteristics include parental influence and self-discipline. The authors conclude by saying that the amount of wealth of an individual depends on his/her acquisition of financial knowledge.

2.2 Churchill and Lewis model

In 1983, Churchill and Lewis suggested a five-stage model to understand entrepreneurial success. The five stages are existence, survival, success, and takeoff and resource maturity. The first stage of entrepreneurial venture is existence. In this stage, an enterprise will be seen to be struggling to establish its processes and even operates without a formal structure. At this stage, the business owner takes a close supervision and looks into each and every activity. The second stage is survival where the business can be seen to be growing and the entrepreneur feels begins to have desires to get more capital for expansion of the business. The entrepreneur tries to reach the breakeven point in order to adequate cash and meet day-to-day requirements of the business. In the third stage, success stage, the enterprise begins to earn profits. There is enough capital that can be used for further business opportunity. The fourth stage is the takeoff stage where the business focuses on further growth, expansion and even seeking new opportunities. The business becomes more formal in nature and its work becomes properly defined. The last stage is resource maturity stage where the firm graduates and becomes a company and focuses more on quality control, financial control, and creating a niche market.

The Churchill Lewis model is a clear indicator that when one is financially literate, he can be able to make the right choices as their business grows and become more complex. The key factors for attaining growth of business also includes individual's aspirations, goals, entrepreneurial skills and willingness to delegate. This therefore clearly indicates that financial literacy skills of a business owner, is the key factor that will lead to growth of the firm.

2.3 Conceptual framework

The conceptual framework illustrates the proposed relationship between the two variables in the study as follows:

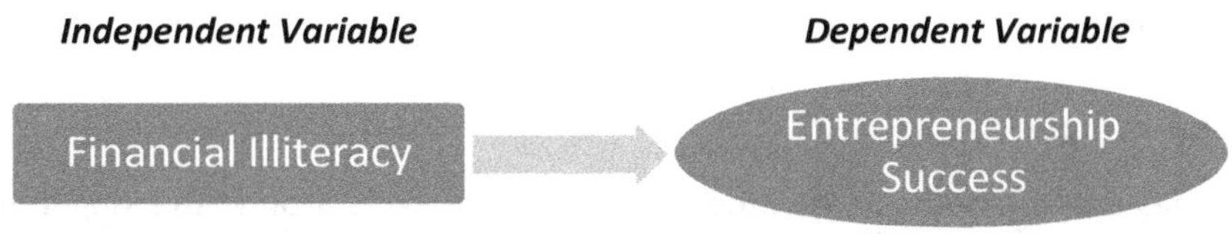

The independent variable is Financial Illiteracy, and the dependent variable is Entrepreneurship Success. The researcher aims at evaluating whether financial illiteracy has negative effect on entrepreneurship.

2.4 Research hypothesis

Financial literacy is a key factor in entrepreneurship because entrepreneurship requires sound decisions and judgments based on a given situation. Entrepreneurs should be able to budget appropriately in order to meet expenditures and identify the appropriate financial products or services that meets his needs, know how to manage the business to retain success. Entrepreneurial Success basically relates to achieving the goals and objective set by a business venture. Entrepreneurial success has different forms which can include business survival, profits made; the return on investment, sales growth, number of employed people, happiness in business operations, reputation of a business etc. This means that when we talk about entrepreneurial success, we refer to several things depending on an individual's perspective. The objective of this paper is to examine the impact of financial illiteracy on entrepreneurship. The hypothesis of the study is as follows:

H1: Financial Literacy adds to entrepreneurship failure.

H0: Financial Literacy does not add to entrepreneurship failure.

2.5 Scope of the study

From the reviews of the past studies, we can see entrepreneurship theory responding to the functions that entrepreneurs have to perform to be successful. From the studies we have reviewed, it is evident that financial illiteracy has a negative effect on entrepreneurship success. However, most researches done have always focused on the impact of financial literacy on entrepreneurship. Most researchers have focused more on the concept of entrepreneurship. There is no specific research that has ever focused on the impact of financial illiteracy on entrepreneurship. Therefore, in this paper, we will focus on establishing the possible relationship between these two variables (financial illiteracy and entrepreneurship) by asking a simple question: What is the impact of financial illiteracy to entrepreneurship success?

3. Research methodology

3.1 Introduction

This part focuses to look at the design and methodology that was applied while carrying out the study. The part focuses to look at the research design, variables and the location of the study, the targeted population sampling techniques and sample size, the research instruments, the validity and reliability of research instruments, data collection and the techniques used in the analysis of data.

3.2 Research design

Secondary data was collected through journal articles from past studies conducted by many authors in regard to financial illiteracy and entrepreneurship. Secondary data was used in the literature review to present background study related to the research topic. We looked at different literature sources. Basing on these previous studies, we were able to develop a structured questionnaire. The questionnaire is used to receive primary data for the research. The questionnaire contained 8 questions for each of the variables that are financial illiteracy and entrepreneurship success. The questionnaire is based on researching the problem of entrepreneurs closing in Bahrain and therefore evaluating whether financial illiteracy affects such outcome.

Data analysis was done using descriptive statistics where we used mean mode standard deviation and variance. In order to determine the statistical relationship between dependent and independent variable, the study used a simple regression analysis. Statistical Program for Social Sciences (SPSS version 23) was used to enable us obtain reliability, correlation, and regression analyses. The relationship between financial illiteracy and entrepreneurship was determined by analyzing the answers of the questions we had in the questionnaire. Each of the answers provided were scale from 1-5.

3.3 Population and sample

The population includes entrepreneurs in the different business markets around the Kingdom of Bahrain. The study adopted a criterion that selected sample entrepreneurs running small to medium business, or those with startups around the Kingdom. The study includes a population of all entrepreneurs owning small to medium businesses whether as a physical or virtual store. The population is of entrepreneurs is unknown as a large portion of them are not registered. The sample size the researcher wishes to target is 100 business owners.

3.4 Measurement of study variables

Independent Variable: This variable's variation doesn't depend on another. It is the variable that is controlled in the scientific experiment. The Independent variable in this study is financial illiteracy.

Dependent Variable: This variable depends on the value of another variable. This is what the researcher measures in the experiment and what is affected during the experiment as it 'depends' on the independent variable. The dependent variable in this study is entrepreneurship success.

3.5 Validity and reliability test

The validity of the questionnaire needs to be measured to verify that the questionnaire used is viable to address the research topic. A reliability analysis will be conducted to measure consistency of the questions against each other. Also, a normality test will be conducted in order to assure random distribution of the questionnaire to decrease degree of risk and bias.

4. Data analysis and discussion

This part presents the analysis of data gathered from respondents and the discussion of the hypothesis to be able to reach a conclusion regarding the effect of illiteracy on entrepreneurship success. The part includes a reliability and validity test, a normality test, a correlation test, and a regression analysis.

4.1 Result analysis

A total of 120 questionnaires were distributed. The researcher regathered 112 questionnaires, but only 108 were reliable to be used in the study as they were fully complete, therefore the response rate is 90%.

4.1.1 Descriptive analysis

Gender

Male	*Female*
45	63

Out of 108 respondents, 42% were male, while the other 58% were female entrepreneurs.

Age

18-25 years	*25-30 years*	*30-40 years*	*Above 40 years*
7	64	29	8

Out of 108 respondents, 7% were between 18 and 25 years, old, 59% were between 25 and 30 years old, 27% were between 30 and 40 years old, while the final 7% were above 40 years old.

Qualifications

High School Degree	*Diploma*	*Bachelor's Degree*	*Master's Degree*	*PhD*
1	3	79	21	4

Out of 108 respondents, 1% hold High School Degrees, 3% hold Diplomas, 73% hold Bachelor's Degrees, 19% hold Master's Degrees, and the final 4% hold PhDs.

How many years has your business been in the market?

Under 2 years	*2-6 years*	*6-10 years*	*Above 10 years*
35	53	13	7

Out of all businesses involved in the study, 32% have been operating for under 2 years, 49% have been operating for 2 to 6 years, 12% have been operating for 6 to 10 years, while the final 7% have been operating for over 10 years.

Was Business your field of study?

Yes	*No*
60	48

Out of 108 respondents, 56% studied in the field of business, while the other 44% did not.

Have you taken any courses or workshops in the field of business?

Yes	*No*
19	89

Out of 108 respondents, 18% took courses or workshops in the field of business, while the other 82% did not.

Are you planning on taking courses or workshops in the field of business?

Yes	*No*
37	71

Out of 108 respondents, 34% are planning on taking courses or workshops in the field of business, while the other 66% did not.

4.1.2 Reliability and validity test

A reliability test was used to test the validity of questions to measure whether there was bias and measuring the consistency of the questionnaire.

Reliability test for financial illiteracy

Table 1: Reliability statistics

Cronbach's Alpha	Cronbach's Alpha Based on Standardized Items	N of Items
.894	.896	8

Table 2: Inter-Item correlation matrix

	Q1	Q2	Q3	Q4	Q5	Q6	Q7	Q8
Q1	1.000	.806	.472	.517	.397	.470	.546	.468
Q2	.806	1.000	.537	.697	.476	.674	.648	.615
Q3	.472	.537	1.000	.608	.496	.359	.400	.337
Q4	.517	.697	.608	1.000	.465	.548	.632	.474
Q5	.397	.476	.496	.465	1.000	.638	.322	.376
Q6	.470	.674	.359	.548	.638	1.000	.386	.431
Q7	.546	.648	.400	.632	.322	.386	1.000	.696
Q8	.468	.615	.337	.474	.376	.431	.696	1.000

Table 3: Item-Total statistics

	Scale Mean if Item Deleted	Scale Variance if Item Deleted	Corrected Item-Total Correlation	Squared Multiple Correlation	Cronbach's Alpha if Item Deleted
Q1	25.731	47.133	.686	.678	.879
Q2	25.602	46.018	.858	.833	.863
Q3	25.435	48.828	.585	.475	.889
Q4	25.481	48.140	.743	.640	.875
Q5	25.102	50.111	.583	.508	.888
Q6	25.361	48.083	.645	.627	.883
Q7	25.491	47.561	.679	.632	.880
Q8	25.639	47.747	.629	.554	.885

Table 1 shows that Cronbach's Alpha for questions related to financial illiteracy is 0.894, therefore there is good internal consistency. Table 2 shows that the questions are well correlated (0.806 > 0.3, 0.472 > 0.3, 0.517 > 0.3, 0.397 > 0.3, 0.470 > 0.3, 0.546 > 0.3, 0.468 > 0.3). Table 3 shows that each question correlated well with others through their item-total correlation (0.686 > 0.5, 0.858 > 0.5, 0.585 > 0.5, 0.743 > 0.5, 0.583 > 0.5, 0.645 > 0.5, 0.679 > 0.5, 0.629 > 0.5).

Entrepreneurship

Table 4: Reliability statistics

Cronbach's Alpha	Cronbach's Alpha Based on Standardized Items	N of Items
.828	.835	8

Table 5: Inter-Item correlation matrix

	Q9	Q10	Q11	Q12	Q13	Q14	Q15	Q16
Q9	1.000	.605	.399	.476	.311	.408	.082	.163
Q10	.605	1.000	.562	.574	.345	.418	.321	.285
Q11	.399	.562	1.000	.545	.384	.399	.297	.303
Q12	.476	.574	.545	1.000	.451	.433	.348	.279
Q13	.311	.345	.384	.451	1.000	.385	.274	.375
Q14	.408	.418	.399	.433	.385	1.000	.384	.293
Q15	.082	.321	.297	.348	.274	.384	1.000	.729
Q16	.163	.285	.303	.279	.375	.293	.729	1.000

Table 6: Item-Total statistics

	Scale Mean if Item Deleted	Scale Variance if Item Deleted	Corrected Item-Total Correlation	Squared Multiple Correlation	Cronbach's Alpha if Item Deleted
Q9	27.056	29.530	.483	.458	.818
Q10	27.009	28.308	.647	.544	.796
Q11	27.093	29.150	.596	.418	.803
Q12	27.185	29.573	.651	.486	.798
Q13	27.731	28.460	.515	.318	.814
Q14	26.917	29.871	.565	.352	.807
Q15	27.389	28.464	.501	.612	.817
Q16	27.593	29.066	.518	.580	.813

Table 4 shows that Cronbach's Alpha for questions related to Entrepreneurship success is 0.8282, therefore there is good internal consistency. Table 5 shows that the questions are well correlated (0.605 > 0.3, 0.399 > 0.3, 0.476 > 0.3, 0.311 > 0.3, 0.408 > 0.3) except for questions 15 and 16 (0.082 < 0.3, 0.613 < 0.3). Table 6 shows that each question correlated well with others through their item-total correlation (0.483 > 0.5, 0.647 > 0.5, 0.596 > 0.5, 0.651 > 0.5, 0.515 > 0.5, 0.565 > 0.5, 0.501 > 0.5, 0.518 > 0.5). Though Questions 15 and 16 had low correlations, there is no statistical reason to remove them as Cronbach's Alpha would decrease if they were removed from the questionnaire as shown in Table 6.

4.1.3 Normality test

Normality Test for the Questionnaire

Table 7: Statistics

N	Valid	108
	Missing	0
Mean		60.2593
Median		62.0000
Mode		80.00
Std. Deviation		13.38249
Skewness		-.440
Kurtosis		-.223

Table 7 shows the values of the mean, median, mode, and standard deviation. The mean shows the average value in a data set. The median shows the middle score of the data set. The mode shows the data entry with the largest frequency in the set. While the standard deviation measures the variability and consistency of the sample. In the table provided, the values of the mean, median, and mode are greater than the value of the standard deviation, therefore the values are acceptable. Also, the values of the skewness and kurtosis are between -2 and +2, and are closer to zero and therefore accepted. The values of the skewness and kurtosis show that the sample distribution was normal for the questionnaire, therefore confirming random sampling.

4.1.4 Pearson's correlation

Table 8: Correlations

		FI	En
FI	Pearson Correlation	1	.841**
	Sig. (2-tailed)		.000
	N	108	108
En	Pearson Correlation	.841**	1
	Sig. (2-tailed)	.000	
	N	108	108
**. Correlation is significant at the 0.01 level (2-tailed).			

In Table 8, the results for Pearson's correlation test between the two variable of the study are presented. The results show a positive correlation between Financial Illiteracy and Entrepreneurship Success at a value of r=0.841. This shows that a significant portion of the independent variable that is financial illiteracy (FI) is seen through the portion in the dependent variable that is entrepreneurship success (En).

4.1.5 Regression analysis

A regression analysis is used to test the influence of the independent variable on the dependent variable, showing the relationship between the two variables. The results of the regression analysis are as follows:

Table 9: Model summary

Model	R	R Square	Adjusted R Square	Std. Error of the Estimate
1	.841[a]	.707	.704	3.31244
a. Predictors: (Constant), FI				

Table 10: ANOVA[a]

Model		Sum of Squares	df	Mean Square	F	Sig.
1	Regression	2799.857	1	2799.857	255.176	.000[b]
	Residual	1163.060	106	10.972		
	Total	3962.917	107			
a. Dependent Variable: En						
b. Predictors: (Constant), FI						

Table 11: Coefficients[a]

Model		Unstandardized Coefficients		Standardized Coefficients	t	Sig.
		B	Std. Error	Beta		
1	(Constant)	12.174	1.229		9.904	.000
	FI	.651	.041	.841	15.974	.000
a. Dependent Variable: En						

Table 9 shows the coefficient determination R^2 is .707, showing that 70.7% of the variation of the dependent variable is explained through the independent variable. This result is significant as seen in Table 10 as p-value = 0.000 < 0.01. Moreover, Table 11 shows that there is evidence that Financial Illiteracy has negative affect on Entrepreneurship Success. Therefore, the results show that Financial Illiteracy has negative effect on Entrepreneurship Success within the Kingdom of Bahrain.

4.2 Discussion of hypothesis

The researcher aimed at evaluating the relationship between financial illiteracy and entrepreneurship success. The researcher conducted a reliability test which showed Cronbach's Alpha rate of 0.894 for financial illiteracy and 0.828 for entrepreneurship success, therefore showing internal consistency between items as both values were higher than 0.7 therefore are considered optimal.

The normality test showed normal distribution as the values of skewness and kurtosis were closed to zero, therefore confirming random sampling. Also, the correlation test showed the correlation between the two variables is high at a value of 0.841.

The results of the regression analysis showed the rate of r=0.841 with a significance level of 0.000. the results of the regression test and acceptable and show that there is a strong relationship between the variables. The researcher therefore concludes that financial illiteracy has negative effect on entrepreneurship success, so H1 is accepted.

5. Conclusion

5.1 Introduction

This part presents the researcher's conclusion regarding the study. Also provided are the implications of the research, the limitations of the study, and opportunities for future research.

5.2 Summary and conclusion

The aim of the study was to determine whether there is a relationship between entrepreneurship success and the level of financial literacy or lack of. The researcher conducted different analyses in order to measure the relationship between the two variables. The researcher conducted a reliability and validity analysis to determine the internal consistency of questions in the survey. A normality test was also conducted to measure the sampling method and to assure that the researcher used a random sampling method in his research. Also, a correlation test was conducted to measure the correlation between the two variables to find the linear relationship between them. Finally, a regression analysis was used to measure the relationship between the two variables and to evaluate the portion of the dependent variable that changes based on changes on the independent variable. The study found that financial illiteracy effects the rate of entrepreneurship success.

From the findings of the research, it is evident that financial illiteracy impacts entrepreneurship success, as the more literate an entrepreneur is, the most chances he would achieve success in his business ventures. The majority of successful businesses are owned and operated by well-educated entrepreneurs that understand financial concepts. Business owners need to understand key financial concepts which include risk management, inflation and interest rates, time value for money, and other concepts related to the financial market. Financial illiteracy would negatively impact entrepreneurship success as there would be less effective decision making, and therefore less chances of success in the market.

Upon realizing the effect of financial illiteracy on the rate of success of businesses, the government needs to make sure that all business owners have basic financial education and literacy to increase their percentage of success in the market as those businesses aid greatly towards the economy of Bahrain. Financially literate entrepreneurs need to be diversified in their knowledge in order to stimulate growth of their business. Entrepreneurs also need to seek higher education and more detailed courses in order to increase their knowledge in their field, and know how to properly assess the market and the economy to make sound decisions for their success.

5.3 Implications of the study

The aim of the research was to investigate the influence of financial illiteracy on entrepreneurship success, and to address the gap in literature and lack of studies conducted within the Kingdom of Bahrain. the contribution of the research includes filling the gap in knowledge and literature, giving information that would benefit both individuals and organizations in their business operations. Entrepreneurs need to understand the important of financial literacy and how illiteracy may lead to the failure of their business. Also, organization needs to acknowledge such importance when hiring senior management as their financial literacy would influence their decision-making processes and organizational strategies. The research also contributed to literary content related to Ahlia University, and to studies conducted within Bahrain.

5.4 Limitations of the study

The researcher faced a number of limitations when completing the research. The first limitation is the time constraint as it limited the number of possible respondents, and also limits the scope of the study as there is no time for in-depth analysis, and no time to find more respondents to include in the population sample. Another constraint was regathering the questionnaires, as respondents needed a time to fill in their answers therefore not all questionnaires were regathered. Also, the study is limited to the Kingdom of Bahrain and therefore a comparison cannot be made with other countries to assess the influence of financial illiteracy on entrepreneurship success across regions.

5.5 Suggestions for future research

The study was limited within the Kingdom of Bahrain, therefore future research can include different countries to provide a comparison of the effect of financial illiteracy on entrepreneurship success. Also, the study can involve different factors in financial illiteracy and their effect on different aspects of entrepreneurship. More factors can be involved in the study to achieve more detailed results.

References

Allgood, S. and Walstad, W.B., 2016. The effects of perceived and actual financial literacy on financial behaviors. Economic inquiry, 54(1), pp.675-697.

Calcagno, R. and Monticone, C., 2015. Financial literacy and the demand for financial advice. Journal of Banking & Finance, 50, pp.363-380.

Charan, S., & Kishinchand, P. W. (2016). Finance for MIcro, small and medium- sized enterprises in india: sources and challenges. ADBI Working Paper, (409).

Churchill, N.C. & Lewis, V.L. (1983): The Five Stages of Small Business Growth. Harvard Business Review, 61(3),

Hilgert, M., Hogarth,J & Beverly ,S.(2003), Household Financial Management: The Connection between Knowledge and Behavior. Federal Reserve Bulletin.

Jones, R., Petrie, J. and Murrell, A., 2018. Measuring Impact While Making a Difference: A Financial Literacy Service-Learning Project as Participatory Action Research. Journal of Service-Learning in Higher Education, 8.

Klapper, L., Lusardi, A. and Van Oudheusden, P., 2015. Financial literacy around the world. Standard & Poor's Ratings Services Global Financial Literacy Survey., Access mode: http://media. mhfi. com/documents/2015-Finlit_paper_17_F3_SINGLES. pdf.

OECD. (2013). Advancing National Strategies for Financial Education.

U.S. Financial Literacy and Education Commission 2007, 'Taking Ownership of the Future: The National Strategy for Financial Literacy', http://www.mymoney.gov/pdfs/add07strategy.pdf

Worthington, A.C., 2016. Financial literacy and financial literacy programmes in Australia. In Financial Literacy and the Limits of Financial Decision-Making (pp. 281-301). Palgrave Macmillan, Cham.

Contribution of Diaspora to Entrepreneurship in the Arab World

Amer Al-Roubaie[1], Adel Sarea, [1]Muneer Al Mubarak[2] and Allam Hamdan
[1]College of Business and Finance, Accounting and Economics department, Ahlia University, Kingdom of Bahrain
[2]College of Business and Finance, Management and Marketing department, Ahlia University, Kingdom of Bahrain
allamh3@hotmail.com
DOI: 10.34190/EIE.20.227

Abstract: The contribution of the private sector to the national output in the Arab world is relatively small compared to other regions in the rest of the world. Over the last several decades, economic development in most Arab countries has been shaped by public expenditures giving the public sector a substantial leverage over economic growth and job creation. Recent regional and global trends highlight the need for greater participation of private enterprises in the new economy driven by innovation, skills and knowledge. Governments in the region seem to take notice of these new changes and began to initiate policies and introduce regulations so that to encourage entrepreneurship and benefit from the creativity and contribution of the private sector to the new economy. Diaspora represents an impotent human capital asset that countries in Arab region can be utilized to enhance local capabilities and speed up the process of socio-economic transformation. Closely working with local enterprises the diaspora can become an effective channel for transferring technical and managerial skills so that to increase the domestic capabilities to diversify productivity, create linkages and enhance global competitiveness. There are millions of diaspora from Arab origin who currently engaged in productive activities across nations their contribution can provide incentive and support for integrating Arab economies into the digital world. The main purpose of this paper is to examine the potential and contribution of diaspora to the current state of development in the Arab world. Most enterprises in Arab countries are still lacking to some of the basic managerial and technical skills to meet the current challenges facing the region. The new digital economy underscores the importance of knowledge transfer and innovation in building capacity for digital society. Creating appropriate business environment could encourage entrepreneurship, including young people and women, to participate in the new economy. The paper highlights the importance of global linkages, including the contribution of diaspora, to the development in the Arab world.

Keywords: diaspora, entrepreneurship, the Arab world

1. Introduction

Entrepreneurship plays an important role in the development of the economy not only through knowledge creation and innovation, but also through collaboration and partnership. The new economy is driven by ideas and critical thinking that require scientific research, human capital assets and adequate skills to strengthen the fundamentals for knowledge creation and innovation diffusion. Responding to the challenges of the new economy entail countries to improve the quality of education, build sound institutions, and invest in Information and Communications Technology (ICTs).

Private enterprises contribution to development underscores the importance of knowledge sharing, skills transfer and economic diversification. In the Arab world, the private sector could have substantial impact on economic transformation by strengthening the economy capabilities to foster economic growth and participate in the digital economy. In recent years, globalization has been offering new opportunities, especially for developing countries, to participate in the global economy and gain access to external financial, technical and managerial resources. The Arab world needs to cultivate the benefit of globalization by deepening integration into the global markets and acquiring knowledge and information for development.

Diaspora members represent millions of nationals living outside their countries seeking better economic opportunities and appropriate business environment to cultivate their tacit knowledge and contribute to development. Cooptation and collaboration with diaspora could facilitate knowledge transfer and encourage domestic entrepreneurship to participate in market activities. Government in the Arab region should initiate policies and introduce regulations that encourage diaspora members to take more active role in the development of the economy.

The main purpose of this paper is to examine the contribution of diaspora members to development in the Arab world. Private enterprises in most Arab countries are still lacking to some of the basic managerial and technical skills to meet the current challenges facing the region. The new digital economy underscores the importance of vocational skills, social networks and ICTs infrastructure for building knowledge society. Creating appropriate business environment encourages entrepreneurship and provides new opportunities for young people to participate in the new economy. The paper highlights the importance of global linkages, including the contribution of diaspora members to development in the Arab world. Private enterprises are among the key drivers of the new economy so that to promote change through knowledge sharing and economic diversification.

2. Entrepreneurship

During the last several decades, the contribution of the private sector to development in most Arab countries has been relatively small compared to that of the public sector. Contribution of the private sector was reduced to providing services and producing traditional goods for domestic use. Industrialization did not take place due to the duality of the economic structure as well as to low incentives for production of manufactured goods. The state, especially in the Gulf region, used oil revenues to import capital goods and consumer products with little attention paid for producing these goods at home. Under such circumstances, local firms were not able to fully participate in market activities and equally compete due to government subsidies and the influence of family business on project financing and access to government services.

An entrepreneur is defined as an "individual who identifies opportunities in the market place, allocates resources, and creates value. Entrepreneurship –the act of being an entrepreneur, - implies the capacity and willingness to undertake conception, organization, and management of a productive new venture, accepting all attendant risks and seeking profit as a reward. In economics, entrepreneurship is sometimes considered a factor of production, at par with land, labour, natural resources, and capital." (UNCTAD, 2012, P. 1) Supporting entrepreneurship requires the formulation of an effective national strategy capable of improving access to finance, creating suitable business environment, promoting awareness and networking, enhancing education and skills development, and facilitating knowledge acquisition and technology transfer.

Entrepreneurship makes considerable contribution to wealth accumulation, job creation, investment allocation and productivity growth. Tacit knowledge and creativity are important elements that motivate entrepreneurs to work hard and contribute to market activities. They make decisions to start business and employ people so that to increase productivity and support national development. However, compared to the rest of the world regions, entrepreneurship in the Arab world remains underdeveloped contributing small share to the total output in these countries. "The Arab world entrepreneurship ecosystems are underdeveloped and require a concerted effort on behalf of policymakers to address the significant gaps that are hindering existing and potential entrepreneurs." (World Economic Forum, 2018, P. Xvii)

Entrepreneurship increases the economy capabilities to produce knowledge and support innovation. In particular, the developing countries can benefit from entrepreneurship to alleviate poverty, redistribute income, improve skills and diversify output. In the new economy, entrepreneurship could facilitate rapid economic transformation to close the knowledge gap and speed up the process of integration into the digital economy.

The Fourth Industrial Revolution, driven by new technologies, is expected to have serious socio-economic consequences generating structural unemployment and changing the labor market requirements. Small and Medium Enterprises (SMEs) contribute to the new economy, driven by the Fourth Industrial Revolution, by increasing the economy ability to deepen integration into the global markets and gain access to finance, skills and information. Similarly, access to global trade stimulates domestic entrepreneurship by allowing local firms to compete in new markets which facilitate the transfer of technology and skills that can be used not only to promote innovation, but also to develop indigenous technologies and encourage entrepreneurship. "The swiftly spreading Fourth Industrial Revolution-a dramatic change that involves a range of new technologies that are fusing the physical, digital, and biological worlds, impacting all disciplines, economies, and industries-provides new opportunities that can support growth. In this context, entrepreneurship and diversification will be key to enabling Arab societies to thrive and prosper in the coming decades." (World Economic Forum, 2018, P. V)

Formulating policies to encourage diaspora entrepreneurship can become an effective strategy for development in the Arab world. People around the world are becoming connected through the internet and other social networks. Such connectivity eases many of the barriers for diaspora entrepreneurship to move freely and engage in productive activities across a wide range of geographical locations. The experience of India and Chana with their diaspora can be a good model for development in Arab countries. Arab diaspora, particularly in Western countries, can contribute to their national economies through knowledge sharing and information dissemination. Not only such partnership encourages entrepreneurship and stimulate production linkages, but also provides new opportunities for local entrepreneurs to gain access to wider geographical locations so that to benefit from various foreign markets. FDI is another vehicle for global integration which the diaspora can drive for promoting internationalization.

Bridging the digital gap is necessary for domestic entrepreneurs to avoid exclusion in the global markets. Digital technologies encourage entrepreneurs to participate in the Global Value Chains (GVCs) which enhance the economy ability to compete by producing goods and services for the global markets. Collaboration and joint projects with the diaspora members stimulate linkages and provide new opportunities for entrepreneurship to engage in both local and global investment activities. "SMEs contribute significantly to Gross Domestic Product (GDP) and to private sector employment in the MENA region, yet often lack access to the type of investment and financial services that they need to start-up, operate and grow." (World Bank Group, 2012, P. 2)

3. Arab Diasporas

Diaspora can help their countries of origin by transferring skills, knowledge and money as well as create new business opportunities which encourage entrepreneurship, foster economic growth and support development. Diaspora members represent important human capital assets which can be mobilized for knowledge transfer and innovation dissemination. There is a large number of highly skilled people living and working in several western countries. It is estimated that 20 million people from MENA region live outside the region. Among these people are professionals representing important human capital assets which can be mobilized to increase local capabilities and support entrepreneurship. Building partnership with the diaspora could bring new business opportunities by channeling financial capital and transferring technology urgently needed to close the technological gap and speed up the process of global integration. No doubt, benefit from diaspora members will have positive impact on development which many Arab countries are in dire need to foster economic growth and create jobs for the newcomers. The 'MENA diaspora' can also provide a partnership support for fostering entrepreneurship and enhancing global competitiveness. Globally, the region is among the least connected regions to benefit from globalization and therefore, mobilization of diaspora could stimulate trade and encourage FDI inflows. "The MENA diaspora can transfer money and skills; enhance trade, investment, and business opportunities, improve the social contract; and help alleviate the refugee crisis. " (World Bank Group, 2016, P. xii)

Compared to several other regions in the world, the contribution of the private sector in the Arab world is relatively low to respond to the current challenges driven by the Fourth Industrial Revolution. Lack of financing and inadequate business environment have weakened the ability of local firms to gain access to trade, FDI, skills, knowledge and information. In recent decades, globalization has provided countries, particularly the developing ones, new opportunities to participate in the global markets and benefit from the new economy. Global linkages strengthen diaspora contribution by improving collaboration and partnership with local enterprises. For national governments, diaspora represents important capital assets which can be utilized not only to gain access to global markets, but also to promote entrepreneurship and foster economic growth. Arab countries should realize the potential contribution of diaspora and make efforts to increase their engagements with local entrepreneurs and participate to the development. In addition, diaspora could introduce new thinking and employ different methods which assist policy makers to construct strategies and formulate policies more applicable for development. In the case of natural disasters, wars and political instability, for example, diaspora members can provide support and assistance to ease the impact of these circumstances on the stability of the country.

Gaining access to diaspora services could overcome some of the challenges facing local entrepreneurs by having diaspora to fill in the financial, technical and managerial gaps. Local enterprises usually face barriers to internationalization which reduce incentives for entrepreneurship to participate and compete in international markets. Perhaps, the most important cited problem is the high cost of the internationalization process including adaptation of products to foreign markets, translation of documents, purchasing legal consulting services, and high financial risk. (OECD (2007) In addition, several other external barriers may hinder efforts of entrepreneurship from having access to global markets including inadequate financing, low skills, product standards, laws and regulations and inadequate access to the internet. Such barriers can be eased through collaboration and cooperation with the diaspora so that local firms benefit from the know-how and expertise of the diaspora members.

Entrepreneurial capabilities are crucial for building productive capacity and fostering innovation. Productive capacity is defined as "the productive resources, entrepreneurial capabilities and production linkages which together determine the capacity of a country to produce goods and services and enable it to grow and develop." (UNCTAD, 2018, P. 8) The Least developed Countries Report.) In this age of global access, engagement of entrepreneurship with diasporas allow local firms to utilize resources effectively so that to improve technological learning, knowledge sharing and output diversification. Building bridges through the internet and ICTs increase local capabilities to make better use of productive resources to expand the production possibility frontier and improve global competitiveness. Access to regional and global markets will have a major impact on productivity, profitability, performance and survival of entrepreneurship. The geographical locations of diaspora provide valuable linguistic, cultural, legal, managerial and technical support for entrepreneurs to penetrate into foreign markets and participate in global trade.

In this age of global interdependence, easy access to global business reduces the cost of doing business and unleashes new entrepreneurial opportunities, especially for youth, women and underprivileged groups in society. By limiting the participation of youth in the new economy could discourage rapid transformation and reduce the economy capabilities to speed up the process of technological learning and innovation. However, harnessing entrepreneurship for economic change requires public policies and government support to improve local firm's capabilities not only to maximize their contribution, but also stimulate growth and sustain development. Entrepreneurship policies should be integrated into the national economic strategy to ensure that the contribution of local firms will be in line with development objectives. In the new digital economy, the government must support local firms to enhance their technological capabilities by increasing skill requirements and training to encourage innovative activities and develop appropriate technologies for local development.

Another important contribution of diaspora to the national development is the transfer of remittances into the sending countries. "Over the past three decades, labour migration has contributed to regional development via the transfer of income from rich to poor countries. The remittances of foreign workers have directly and indirectly provided incentives for investment in the receiving countries by stimulating aggregate demand and improving the country's capacity to import some of the essential capital goods for economic and social development. These remittances have also helped the local governments to improve their financial status and have increased funding for important public services such as health and education." (Amer Al-Roubaie, P. 80) According to the World Bank, remittances flows to developing countries reached to $529 billion in 2017 representing a substantial amount of transfer of hard currencies which can be utilized for investment in the new economy. The flows to MENA region accounted for $62 billion in 2018 and are expected to increase to $66 billion in 2020. For example, in 2018 Egypt earned $28.9 billion from its diaspora whereas Morocco earned $7.4 billion or 6.2 percent of the country's national output from its diaspora. (World Bank Group, 2019)

4. Conclusion

The discussion in this paper focuses on the relationship between diaspora members and entrepreneurship in the Arab world. Diaspora contributes positively to development by encouraging entrepreneurship, creating jobs, diversifying output and enhancing the ability of the economy to compete in the global markets. Worldwide, migrants are engaged in various productive activities including scientific research, knowledge creation, product development and innovation. Harnessing diaspora expertise and skills bridge the scientific and technological gaps in the sending countries providing local entrepreneurs with low cost services and incentives to participate in market activities.

The paper examines the potential that diaspora members can contribute to entrepreneurship, economic diversification and innovation dissemination in the Arab world. It is estimated that there are more than 20 million nationals of Arab origin living abroad, mainly in Western countries. Collaboration, Joint ventures and partnerships with members of the diaspora strengthen the economic capabilities to generate linkages, deepen global integration, sustain growth and participate in the Fourth Industrial Revolution. Governments in the region must encourage partnership and collaboration with diaspora in order to increase the economy reediness by acquiring skills, sharing knowledge and diffusing information. The internet and social networks are offering new opportunities for developing countries to participate in the global economy and benefit from globalization. Participation in the Global Value Chains (GVCs) facilitates the transfer of financial, technical and managerial resources for development. GVCs enhance the country capabilities to promote industrialization and diversify output. In the Arab world, currently there is tendency to restructure the economic system and reduce dependency on the energy sector. Most countries in the region are adapting new strategies aiming at using knowledge and innovation to strengthen participation in the digital economy and benefit from the Fourth Industrial Revolution.

Building ICTs capacity is critical for mobilization of diaspora services and deepening integration into the global markets. The internet has become a powerful tool for knowledge transfer and information diffusion. Local entrepreneurs can make use of e-services to broaden access to trade, finance and technology so that to enhance local capabilities and stimulate investment. In this regard, governments in the region must invest in ICTs to improve participation and support entrepreneurship. Broadening the economic base entails the support and contribution of both local and foreign players. Working closely with diaspora members could help these countries speeding the process of economic diversification and deepening integration into the 21st century economy.

References

Amer Al-Roubaie, (2005), Labor Movement in the Middle East: A Regional Perspective, in Usuki Akira, Omar Farouk Bajunid and Yamagishi Tomoko (eds.) Population Movement beyond the Middle East: Migration, Diaspora, and Network (2005), The Japan Center for Area Studies, Osaka)

OECD, (2007) The Role of SMEs and Entrepreneurship in OECD Economies http://dx.doi.org/10.1787/9789264009257-3-en

UNCTAD, Entrepreneurship Policy Framework and Implementation Guidance (2012) https://unctad.org/en/PublicationsLibrary/diaeed2012d1_en.pdf)

UNCTAD (2018) The Least Developed Countries Report, Entrepreneurship for Structural Transformation. https://unctad.org/en/PublicationsLibrary/ldcr2018overview_en.pdf

World Bank Group Arab World Diaspora's Strong Attachment to Home could Play Role in Regional Development (March, 28 2017) https://www.worldbank.org/en/news/feature/2017/03/28/arab-world-diaspora-s-strong-attachment-to-home-could-play-role-in-regional-development

World Economic Forum, (2018) Arab World Competitiveness Report https://www.weforum.org/reports/arab-world-competitiveness-report-2018

World Bank Group, (2012) SMEs for Job Creation in the Arab World http://documents.worldbank.org/curated/en/687631468110059492/pdf/715510WP0Box370r0Job0Creation0Final.pdf

World Bank Group, (2016) Mobilizing the Middle East and North Africa Diaspora for Economic Integration and Entrepreneurship https://www.worldbank.org/en/region/mena/publication/mobilizing-the-middle-east-and-north-africa-diaspora-for-economic-integration-and-entrepreneurship

World Bank Group, (2019) Migration and Remittances https://www.knomad.org/sites/default/files/2019-04/Migrationanddevelopmentbrief31.pdf

The Role of "FinTech" on Banking Performance

Salman Fadhul[1] and Allam Hamdan[2]
[1]College of Business, Manama, Bahrain
[2]Ahlia University, Manama, Bahrain
Salman.sjf@gmail.com
allamh3@hotmail.com
DOI: 10.34190/EIE.20.230

Abstract: The aim of the study generally is to explore the FinTech factors affecting banking performance in the kingdom of Bahrain. FinTech has a multi-dimension scope that missing in the traditional financial industry with the ability to alter the world's financial expectations and reality. Countries worldwide racing in this field to be the leader of this massive industry with the aim of continues development and progress, investing in FinTech's R&D will determine the leaders and winners of this industry. The aim of this paper is to explore the importance and the impact of FinTech on Bahrain's Banking sectors and to examine to what level the FinTech industry growth has reached since its inception. During 2018 only Bahrain we able to raise more than 100 million dollars in funding FinTech development, which represent a huge amount compared to Bahrain's GDB. In addition, regulators contributed efforts in providing a free space for investors and creators to test their products before applying it in the real market, which gives investors a good idea to project the cost and profit of operating in the region's FinTech industry, resulting in gaining investors trust in Bah- rain economy. However, a huge challenge facing Bahrain FinTech industry with a long way to master it, which raise an important question, will Bahrain be a leader or a follower in this industry?

Keywords: FinTech, innovation, performance, banking, financial industry

1. Introduction

The era of FinTech revolution has begun. FinTech is a portmanteau of Finance and Technology. The term FinTech originated from the Financial Services Technology Consortium, which first initiated by Citigroup in the early 1990s (Schueffel, 2016). FinTech refers to a new financial model, the financial innovation of the technology, which takes the technology as the carrier and provides financial services such as settlement, financial management, and financing through online settlement, mobile payment, cloud computing and other emerging scientific and technological means (Schueffel, 2016). S&P Analysts believe that FinTech could have a tremendous impact on the financial industry worldwide, causing a mega transformation in traditional financial products and services. According to KPMG report (2019), the global investment in FinTech in compression with the previous year indicate a growth rate of 120% in 2018 to reach 111.8 billion dollars in 2018. Due to the rapid growth of FinTech funding's value have led the Fintech firm's population and deals to increase as well. Therefore, the technological innovation development strategy and corresponding mechanism process should be established to gradually form a new competitive advantage.

1.1 Finance industry in Bahrain

Bahrain is the home for more than 400 financial institutions, delineating a verity of international, regional and local firms, incorporate the broad dimension of Islamic and conventional financial markets and institutions, consist of finance companies, whole- sale and retail banks, insurance companies and brokers, mutual funds, money changers, and investment advisors (eGovernment, 2018). In addition, the financial industry in Bahrain regulated by the CBB which is the sole regulator. Since 2017 the financial industry registered a total of 14,093 workforces, 66% of them Bahraini nationals and 34% foreign nationals (CBB, 2018). The open market economy and its alliance with international measure powered by creditable regulation has contributed and opened the gates for the growth of the financial sector. According to the Central Bank of Bahrain, the current GDP of Bahrain reached 34.5 billion dollars in 2017, resulting in a 3.8 per- cent growth rate over the past year. Furthermore, the statistic stated that the contribution from the financial industry to the GDP represent 16.7%, a significant factor in boosting Bahrain economic development.

Hence, the high number of the financial institution located in the kingdom of Bahrain allowed the financial industry to become the largest employer in the country and the most important part of its economy.

1.2 FinTech investments figures

Vision 2030 of Bahrain is a comprehensive economic strategic plan focusing on the growth and development of Bahrain entire economy (eGovernment, 2019). FinTech is a major player in 2030 vision to strategically assist Bahrain to become the nursery of technological advancement in the region. The year of 2018 illustrated Bahrain ability in launching and growing the largest FinTech hub in MENA partnering with international FinTech firms (EDB, 2019), combining Islamic and conventional compliant FinTech solution. Startup Bahrain (2018) reported the total number of firms involved in FinTech since its inception reached more than 75 firms, along with big names in FinTech industry such as Benefit, NEC, AFS, Eazy, Paytabs and PIE, with a vital force in raising fund of more than 100 million dollars under "AL WAHA" fund of fund to invest in FinTech in 2018. According to a survey conducted by Bahrain FinTech bay in 2018 indicate the FinTech development in Bahrain facing challenges on three levels. The result shown 60.2% believe one of the challenges is achieving scale and reach, which means Bahrain have to increase the effort to internationalized the local firms. Next outcome talent recruitment by 50.3%, this illustrated the awareness shortage in Bahrain workforce regarding the future of FinTech. Furthermore, the survey has shown funding comes in the third place in the challenges facing FinTech development by 49.3%, even though Bahrain raised a huge amount of fund towards FinTech, yet new advanced technology requires extra investment in order to keep up with the interna- tional fast development of FinTech.

1.3 Statement of problem

According to Economic development board released figures regarding FinTech funding, the kingdom of Bahrain is aiming to put Bahrain on the developed FinTech's map. In fact, Bahrain is pushing forward to be the leader of the FinTech industry in the region. However, setting the objectives high will be associated with advantages and dis- advantages. Considering the size of Bahrain market could act as barrier facing the progress of developing the FinTech sector, also could lead to a tense competition among banking and FinTech sectors. While competition increasing rapidly in FinTech application, it raised an area of concern for banking sectors, how will this situation affect their performance in general. In contrast, it could lead to a great collaboration that boosts the growth of FinTech products, yet unclear path needs to be charted. Is FinTech and Banking friends or foes?

1.4 Significant and implication

Nowadays, banks in Bahrain are facing great challenges in the implementation and the determination of FinTech applications that could assist in enhancing their performance. Though out the years, a variety of researches been applied on an international level regarding FinTech implementation in the banking sector, some of the researches in countries such as US, UK, and

China acknowledged factors of FinTech that contribute to the enhancement of banking performance dramatically, therefore increasing the bank's actual profits. Nevertheless, this paper seeking to assist banks in Bahrain identifying the factors that lead to enhancement and improvement of banking performance. In addition, to measure the impact of each FinTech factor selected, the benefit, there- fore, to focus on increasing the competitive edge in the banking sector.

Experience (Vives, 2017), the late adoption of FinTech by GCC countries may cause the cost of it to become higher, but still may boost the economic development and at- tract more foreign investors. The study will discuss the effect of Finch on banking performance in Bahrain, and state some factors that have a major role in assisting the banking's sector overall performance.

To shed the light on this subject in a scientific path, the rest of the paper will be co-ordinated as follow; section two is the literature review, followed by discerption of re- search method and design, next to that presenting data analysis, and finally providing summary and conclusion.

2. Literature review

2.1 Segments of FinTech

Firms in the FinTech sector can be segmented into four major segments based on their idiosyncratic financial model, segments include Asset Management, Payments, Financing, and other FinTech (Dorfleitner, 2017).

Indeed, with the development of the new market demands and needs makes the traditional ways of financing unable to adapt and satisfy those needs. Corporate financing was the only source of reliance for the capital market for decades, requiring a guarantee from a third-party institution, leading to a delay in financing operations and cost increment. Now, looming crowdfunding and credit factoring (subsegments) enormously de-creased the cost of a firm's financing and shortened a number of needless operations (Gozman et al., 2018). With the extensive upgrading of information technology, gradually replacing the old way of traditional payments by alternative methods, online payment and smartphones payment (Gomber et al., 2018). Businesses thrive to add new methods for payments with the intention to ease and smooth consumer's transactions to increase their sales. Mobile payment is the trend of the century, Specifically, in small and medium payment's scope. In addition, the progress of Blockchain and cryptocurrencies could potentially remove banks from being intermediaries in financial transactions. Furthermore, the asset management umbrella consists of social trading, roboadvise, and personal financial management. Likewise, FinTech in asset management pro- vides a variety of financial services to business and individuals. Last of all, other FinTech can be divided into InsurTech and RegTech subsegments that cannot fit the traditional financial functions.

The areas of application of new technologies

Bahrain's FinTech industry established the infrastructure for phenomenal growth (EDB, 2017), the fixable and advanced telecoms industry and MENA's wide ICT structure has assisted in the creation of a dynamic platform to assemble on. Meanwhile, the FinTech application in fields in particular e-commerce, digital services, transaction security, and payments systems, thus strengthened the financial industry's cohesion. Some of the major FinTech application in Bahrain namely Electronic Fund Transfer System (EFTS) a system by benefit in which function as an interconnection between all banks in Bahrain to facilitate fund transfers and bill payments, along with other solutions such as BCTS, POS, Internet Banking, Mobile Bill Payments. Moreover, Crowdfunding to support entrepreneurs in Bahrain specifically in P2B lending under supervised AML rules (CBB, 2018). One of the big FinTech transformation in the kingdom launching E-Wallet, that allows consumers to execute payments and collections via smart phone's app through credit & debit cards, up until 2018 firms in Bahrain launched 4 E-wallet namely b-wallet, Benefit pay, Max wallet, and viva cash. Further- more, the endless innovative movement towards FinTech is yet at the start line in Bah- rain, with projected projects that will be available by 2020 including e-KYC, e-taxation, chatbot, FinTech for SME lending, VTM, and seamless payments.

Acknowledging the reliance on oil put the country in a perilous position, which makes it excessively essential to explore diversified resources (Miller & Epstein, 2013). Nevertheless, based on the facts stated previously, the kingdom of Bahrain is expected to play an indispensable role in accelerating FinTech industry growth in the MENA region. Bahrain's FinTech growth due to a clear vision from the decision makers, FinTech been given a high priority rate in focusing on the transformation of the financial industry, resulting in boosting and supporting Bahrain's total economy. However, the Fintech Industry in Bahrain appears relatively small compared to other countries, yet, notable efforts been made toward financial technology development. Likewise, the ease of regulation encouraged foreign investors to select Bahrain as their FinTech investment destination. While extensive progress made in Bahrain's FinTech, yet the new technology application area is limited in comparison with the global progress in FinTech performance. Indeed, researches have a tremendous impact in developing the FinTech industry, despite FinTech firms' effort toward it still, the industry is facing a shortage on this matter. In fact, among the total number of firms applying FinTech products and ser- vices, there are only a few firms that actually contribute to the development of the FinTech industry and widen its applications.

2.2 Regulators and other players

The future success of financial technology cannot happen without effective innovative regulation (Treleaven, 2015), regulation and governance have a huge impact on where industry is headed and how far it could go, regulators obligated to have full understanding of FinTech function and development, as it is crucial to set the rules and regulation (Wang et al., 2017). As stated previously, the financial industry in the kingdom of Bah- rain has a sole regulator, which make FinTech function under the regulatory umbrella of the Central Bank of Bahrain. Regulatory sandbox one of the most important CBB's contributions toward FinTech innovation and attracting FinTech firms to expand and advance their business in MENA region in 2017, the sandbox is a framework to facilitate innovative products, services, and business model testing without bearing the financial consequences (CBB, 2018).In addition, establishing FinTech & innovation unit by the CBB in 2017 as a part of their contribution to the financial digital transformation, resulting in enhancement of the financial service provided to corporates and individuals, by providing a competent regulatory framework in line with FinTech requirements. Although innovative FinTech has a positive impact on the capital market, yet is associated with a huge risk requiring up to date regulation in order to support the Fintech development. In order for the CBB to effectively reduce the risk, CBB entertained other innovative regulatory such as regulatory technology (RegTech). In fact, the central bank of Bahrain initiated regulatory framework pertaining to legal data usage and management, cybersecurity, vigorous compliance, and regulatory reporting. Besides, the incensement of the partnership under the supervision of CBB between financial institutions, FinTech, and the regulator (CBB, 2018) was an effective effort toward developing regulation to support FinTech operations in Bahrain. In summary, Bahrain set regulation to protect and support FinTech investors along with a reasonable requirement for firms licensing.

FinTech and Banking relationship

Now, finance and technology have a greater blend, can better improve the efficiency of financial services, financial technology has become a link between the two. Financial technology companies are characterized by low cost, easy access, flexible operation, in line with the current economic development requirements. Therefore, in the competition with technology financial companies, banks are often at a disadvantage, bringing great pressure to banks. Traditional banks have great advantages in capital risk management and control, and they also involve a wider range of customers.

The banks in the GCC anticipate FinTech have low-level effect in the short term, yet concerns about some business might be affected in the medium and long-term, how- ever, the banking's sector recognizes the future opportunities involved and considering the FinTech companies as a potential partner in the future (EY, 2017).

3. Conclusion

Hence, the enormous funding towards FinTech development clarifies the importance of it in changing the global financial industry, which indeed will have an impact on other industries as well as the global economy. Although FinTech developed rapidly, yet still facing big challenges in some fields including artificial intelligence, big data, blockchain, and cloud computing. However, the kingdom of Bahrain should focus on enhancing the application area of FinTech through collaboration with firms operating in advance FinTech countries such as US, China, UK, etc. Bring in FinTech experts, on one hand, will result in increasing the speed of developing the industry, on the other hand, will increase the expertise of Bahraini workforce's talent. In addition, the education system is one of the factors that could determine the future of the FinTech sector, therefore, FinTech material should be taught in all universities in Bahrain with more focus on the practical parts of it. To develop a sustainable FinTech industry, extra effort should be contributed from the legal field in the country, through supporting and issuing clear policies protecting firms and consumer rights and increase the FinTech regulation awareness. Last of all, the corporation between GCC countries and their united vision towards the future will fuel and boost the FinTech industry in the region.

References

Dorfleitner, G., Hornuf, L., Schmitt, M., & Weber, M. (2017). The FinTech Market in Germany. FinTech in Germany,13-46.

EY (2017). Banking in emerging markets GCC fintech play, report, Decem- ber.

Gomber, P., Kauffman, R. J., Parker, C., & Weber, B. W. (2018). On the Fintech Revolution: Interpreting the Forces of Innovation, Disruption, and Transformation in Financial Services. Journal of Management Information Systems, 35(1), 220–265.

Gozman, D., Liebenau, J., & Mangan, J. (2018). The Innovation Mecha- nisms of Fintech Start-Ups: Insights from SWIFT's Innotribe Competition. Journal of Management Information Systems, 35(1), 145–179.

Kingdom of Bahrain - eGovernment Portal. (2018, February). Retrieved March, 2019, from https://www.bahrain.bh

Luying Wang, Yiyang Lu, Jiasi Liu, & Qiang Gong. (2017). FinTech, Infor- mation Disclosure and Regulation. Proceedings of the New York State Eco- nomics Association, 10, 44–60.

Middle East's perfect Launchpad for startups. (2018). Retrieved March, 2019, from https://startupbahrain.com/

Miller, M., & Epstein, S. (2013). Teaching Applied Macro in Emergent Econ- omies: Lessons from Bahrain. Journal of Teaching in International Busi- ness, 24(2), 138–149.

Schueffel, P. M. (2016). Taming the Beast: A Scientific Definition of Fintech. SSRN Electronic Journal.

The Pulse of FinTech. (2019, February 13). Retrieved March, 2019, from https://assets.kpmg/xx/en/home.html

The Central Bank of Bahrain. (2018). Retrieved March, 2019, from https://www.cbb.gov.bh/

The Economic Development Board. (2019). Retrieved March, 2019, from https://bahrainedb.com/

Treleaven, Philip. (2015). Financial Regulation of Fintech. Journal of Finan- cial Perspectives, Vol. 3, No. 3, 2015.

Vives, X. (2017). The Impact of Fintech on Banking. EUROPEAN ECONOMY, 2, 97-105.

Structured Analysis of Methodologies for the Assessment of the Technological Capability of RTOs: Using a Method Engineering Approach

Fabian Hecklau[1], Florian Kidschun[1], Holger Kohl[2] and Sokol Tominaj[1]
[1]Fraunhofer IPK, Division Corporate Management, Berlin, Germany
[2]Technical University of Berlin, Department Sustainable Corporate Development, Berlin, Germany
fabian.hecklau@ipk.fraunhofer.de
florian.kidschun@ipk.fraunhofer.de
holger.kohl@tu-berlin.de
sokol.tominaj@ipk.fraunhofer.de
DOI: 10.34190/EIE.20.029

Abstract: New state-of-the-art technologies in evolving markets enable organizations to lead the competition and gain advantages over their competitors. The constantly changing technological developments and market demands not only affect industrial companies but also Research and Technology Organizations (RTOs). As RTOs are situated between universities and organizations that pursue fundamental research on the one hand, and business entities on the other, they are strongly influenced by changing economical environments. Hence, to generate value for their customers, RTOs need to use state-of-the-art technologies in order to be able to provide high-quality products and services to their customers. In consequence, regular analysis and assessment of the technological capability of RTOs is an important strategy to ensure progress and success. In previous research work a generic process model for the structured analysis of methods used in the context of the technological capability of Research and Technology Organizations has been developed. Therefore, method engineering approaches have been used as a basis to create a holistic model that can be used as a structured approach for the analysis of methodologies. Building on this, this paper uses the approach to analyze different methodologies. The generic process model of method engineering will be applied to analyze existing methodologies for the assessment of technological capabilities of RTOs in a structured way. Therefore, a literature review is conducted to identify existing methodologies in the context of the technological capabilities of organizations with a special interest in RTOs. Furthermore, the identified methodologies are assessed using the method engineering approach. In a final step, limitations and further developments of methodologies for the assessment of technological capabilities are discussed.

Keywords: method engineering, method development, capability methodologies, research and technology organizations, RTO, technological capability

1. Introduction

In a continuously fluctuating, dynamic environment, organizations in all areas must adapt quickly to changes, such as the digital transformation, in order to ensure their sustainable development and growth. Furthermore, the capability of generating and using new technologies effectively and efficiently has a direct impact on the organization's competitiveness and long-term success. Organizations with a high technological capability are able to achieve greater differentiation through more innovative products and to increase efficiency or reduce costs through process innovation.

Moreover, an advancing liberalization of markets intensifies competition not only for regular businesses, but also for Research and Technology Organizations (RTOs) that cooperate with these businesses. RTOs are facing the challenge of shorter innovation cycles, while at the same time the demand for advanced and market-ready product and process solutions is rising.

In order to be successful, RTOs have to pursue technical solutions that eventually lead to state-of-the-art products and services. It is therefore necessary for RTOs to use technological resources and therefore acquire or maintain technological capabilities that make it possible to achieve the aforementioned technical solutions, which ultimately end in high-quality and innovative products. Hence, sustainable success and a competitive edge are the result of technological capabilities that are optimally cultivated and used. (Wang et al. 2008)

Subsequently, RTOs have to be able to analyze and assess their technological capability, given that an advanced technological capability is imperative for their competitiveness. A tool or method that assesses the technological capability of RTOs in an objective and practical way, while being suitable to the special requirements of RTOs, is needed. While several other authors have previously developed models for the assessment of technological capability in organizations, there is yet to be developed a method that fully meets the specific requirements of RTOs. Therefore, in this paper, existing methodologies will be analyzed and reviewed.

Within a previous paper of the authors (see (Hecklau et al. 2020)) a literature review has been conducted that gives an overview of different method engineering approaches, that have been used to create a generic process model. This method engineering process model is described in chapter 2 and is used for the structured analysis of technology capability methodologies in this paper.

A specific method that evaluates the technological capability of RTOs in an objective and practical way, while being suitable to the unique requirements of RTOs, has not been developed so far. While several authors or institutions such as Javier Garcia-Arreola with the *Technology Effectiveness Audit Model* or Phaal et al. with *Technology Management Process Assessment* have previously developed models for the assessment of technological capability in organizations, there is yet to be developed a method that fully meets the specific requirements of RTOs. (Phaal et al. 2001; Garcia-Arreola 1996) As a basis for the development of a methodology for the assessment of the technological capability of RTOs, the aforementioned approaches will be analyzed in chapter 3.

2. Method engineering as structured approach for the analysis of methods

In a previous paper (see (Hecklau et al. 2020)) a literature review has been conducted that gives an overview about different method engineering approaches, which mainly originate from the application in software development projects. As these identified approaches build the basis for a generic process model, which will be used for the structured analysis of RTO capability methodologies, this paper focuses on the specificities of RTOs and not on the requirements of software development projects.

According to Gutzwiller, methods can be classified according to the principles of method engineering using the following five building blocks: meta model, results, techniques, activities and roles. (Gutzwiller 1994)

The *meta model* describes the structuring of the results of a method using a holistic data model. A method defines a procedure in the form of *activities.* Activities are structured and can be broken down into several sub-activities ('activity structure') as well as put into a sequence that defines which activities take place before or after a certain activity. The structured arrangement of the activities and the determination of a certain sequence among themselves form the procedural model. Therewith, activities generate or use one or more results. *Techniques* support the generation of results with the help of various tools, such as databases. All results are summarized in a documentation model. *Results* capture the concept and represent decisions and illustrate information and their interrelations. They can be structured complex-forming, i.e. they can be broken down into their components. The initiators or the executing instances of activities are called *roles* and thus describe the persons or organizational units associated with the execution of the method. (Gutzwiller 1994)

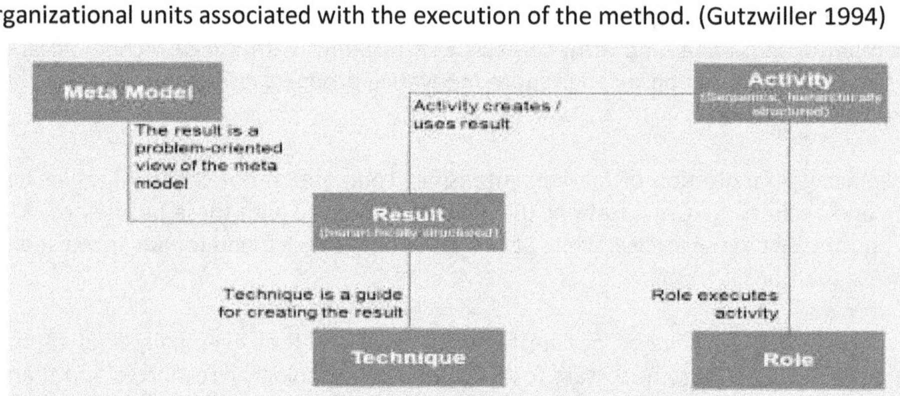

Figure 1: Components of the method description in method engineering (Edited based on (Gutzwiller 1994))

The elements of method description are suitable for the structured analysis of existing methods. Therefore, the elements are used in the following chapter to analyze methodologies for the assessment of the technological capability of organizations.

3. Analysis of methodologies for the assessment of the technological capability of RTOs

In this chapter, the described method engineering approach is used to analyze different methodologies for the analysis and assessment of the technological capability of organizations. Therefore, the elements of method description are used to structure the analysis (see Figure 1: Components of the method description in method engineering (Edited based on (Gutzwiller 1994)) above):

- Role
- Activity
- Technique
- Result
- Meta Model

The following methodologies will be analyzed:

- Technology Management Process Assessment (Phaal et al. 2001)
- Technology Effectiveness Audit Model (Garcia-Arreola 1996)
- Model for Technological Capability Assessment in R&D Organizations (Mohammad et al. 2010)

3.1 Technology Management Process Assessment (Phaal et al. 2001)

The *Technology Management Process Assessment* by Phaal et al. is a top-down assessment model that analyzes and evaluates technology management practices in a business unit. (Phaal et al. 2001) The methodology is based on the five-process model of Gregory: (1) Identification, (2) Selection, (3) Acquisition, (4) Exploitation and (5) Protection. (Gregory 1995)

The methodology has been developed and tested in the context of an "action research approach", which allows the investigation of business systems through a process of active intervention (i.e. collaborative participation). The primary aim of this practical approach is to support communication, decision-making processes and action in companies, which requires close collaboration with industry. (Phaal et al. 2001) A further specification of the methodology, according to the method description approach of Gutzwiller as described in chapter 2 is elaborated in the following.

3.1.1 Role

A variety of employees of the organization participate in the application of this methodology, which is carried out in three workshops. In the application example by Phaal et al., where a high-volume manufacturer (approx. 50,000 different components) from the UK is being evaluated, senior managers from different business divisions, such as product development, supply processes, marketing, quality and technology areas take part in the workshops to support the assessment. That way, knowledge from all areas of the organization is bundled. The workshops are led by a moderator and also supported by an internal assessment "champion", who is not explained in more detail. (Phaal et al. 2001)

3.1.2 Activity

The assessment procedure consists of the following three workshop-based stages:

- 1. Strategic overview;
- 2. Process overview;
- 3. Process investigation

The outcome of the methodology is the identification of improvement potentials in specific technology-business areas. Figure 3 displays the procedural steps of the methodology.

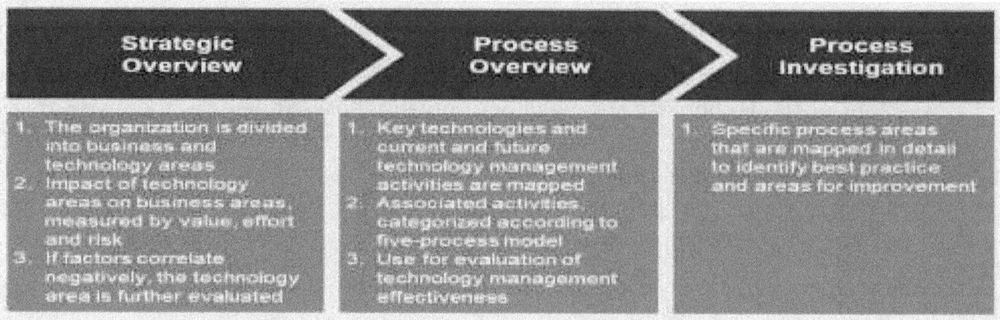

Figure 2: Technology Management Process Assessment – procedural steps of the methodology (Phaal et al. 2001)

In the first stage, the "Strategic overview", the business is divided into business and technology areas. In a session of discussion and brainstorming, the participants agree on the different business segments. The segmentation process is intended to generate a healthy dialogue between the various functions within the company and to create an interface between corporate strategy and technology management (de Wet 1996). Thereafter, the impact of each technology area on each business area is estimated by the participants, regarding value, effort and risk. These parameters (value, effort and risk) are defined as:

- *Value*: "What level of competitive advantage does each technology area provide for each business area?"
- *Effort*: "What level of effort is being directed at each technology area for the benefit of each business area?"
- *Risk*: "What level of risk is associated with realizing the competitive advantage of each technology area for each business area?"

Each of the business-technology relationships is assessed by a 4-point Likert-Scale (Likert 1932): high (H), medium (M), low (L), or not significant (-), according to their estimated value, effort and risk. Naturally, these parameters correlate. If there is a mismatch in a business-technology relationship, a debate regarding the cause of the mismatch is started. Hence, following the discussion about the results of the strategic overview, points of interest are chosen, which need further investigation in the next stage due to their poor outcome.

In the second stage, the "Process overview", the critical technology area is decomposed into its key technologies. Further, internal and external dependencies of these key technologies are elaborated, with special regards to the business areas they are related to. Then, recent events and activities that are associated with the identified technologies are listed and classified according to Gregory's five process-model (Gregory 1995). The activities are also structured into their time of happening. This step is followed by an assessment of the activities in the five-process-model. Therefore, the elaborated activities are assessed using the three components of a generic systems model, namely inputs, process and outputs. Thus, the participants rank the activities on scale from 1 (strongly disagree) to 5 (strongly agree) with respect to the following statements:

- *Inputs:* "The requirement for this activity was always clearly defined".
- *Process:* "The activity was always well managed".
- *Outputs:* "The results for this activity were always exploited".

Subsequently, the processes are further subdivided into sub-categories. Identification, selection and protection processes are for example split into reactive and proactive types. Further subdivisions are made to go into detail of the roots and causes of problems.

In the third stage, the "Process investigation", participants go into detail on areas identified in the second step. Hence, the processes are mapped and compared to other generic process models of the same type. This induces a rich debate among participants, questioning the hows and whys of the process activities. Strengths and weaknesses of the process are discovered and are the basis for learnings and improvements.

3.1.3 Technique

The process includes a series of moderated workshops based on group discussions and open critical debate. This allows the knowledge of several employees from different areas to be incorporated into the process models. Gregory's five-process model provides a framework for the workshops. A detailed workbook, which contains various procedures and guidelines, serves as an aid. This includes questionnaires and ranking activities as well as the creation of time-based activity diagrams and process mapping.

It is also recommended to have feedback sessions after each workshop to link operational and strategic views and to enable the transfer of results to other technology and business units.

3.1.4 Results

The primary goal of this methodology is to support communication, decision-making processes and actions within a company. These are achieved through various discussions and debates between the different business units in the workshops and generate value, since they help to combine the organization's strategy and technology management. (de Wet 1996)

After the "Strategic Overview" stage evaluates the impact of the technologies on the company, the "Process Overview" and "Investigation" stages provide detailed insights into the activities of technology management. In Phaal's application example, the acquisition processes of the selected technologies were compared with a generic process model for technology acquisition. This included the development of new products as well as the acquisition of a company for a recovery action. In group discussions, the strengths and potential weaknesses of the individual areas were identified with regard to the generic technology management processes. As a direct result, the functions of the processes and the respective technology management, as well as the connection to the business units, are better understood, so that decisions can be made on technological (and financial) feasibility.

3.1.5 Meta model

A meta model of the underlying methodology in a broad sense is Gregory's five process-model as a framework that is used to structure the technology management activities according to the five following steps:

- 1. *Identification* of potentially relevant technologies
- 2. *Selection* of appropriate technologies, that should be used in the organization
- 3. *Acquisition* and assimilation of the selected technologies
- 4. *Exploitation* of technologies to generate value
- 5. *Protection* of knowledge and expertise embedded in usage of products and/or manufacturing systems

Gregory's framework is a generic model that encompasses all activities in a company. It is often closely linked to the processes of innovation and new product development.

A rough summary of the activities in the individual process steps is shown in the following figure:

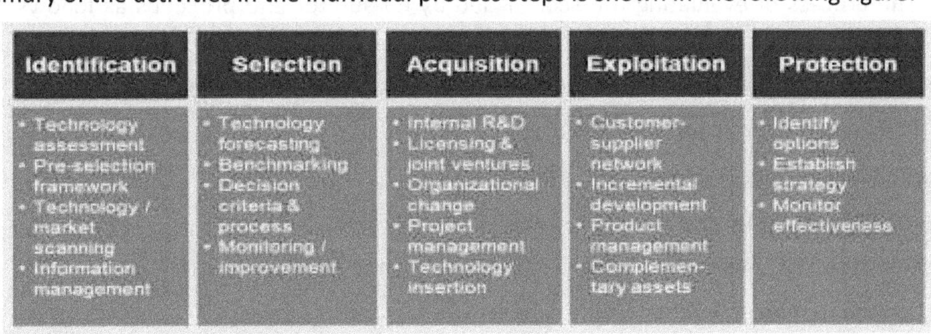

Figure 3: Gregory's five process model (Gregory 1995)

3.1.6 Critical analysis

The methodology is a quite generic approach that can be used in different organizations to assess technology management processes. It consists of a series of moderated workshops based on a detailed workbook with procedures and guidelines. However, it serves more as a self-assessment tool, which is conditionally suitable for an objective assessment of technology management in an organization.

The Strategic Overview stage considers the impact of current technologies on current business units. Nevertheless, to support strategic planning, it is also necessary to include a future perspective, which is not considered here.

Moreover, this approach is completely qualitative. It does not analyze hard factors and technology content, but rather the functions as well as strengths and weaknesses of technology management to develop key technologies. It is therefore only of limited use for the assessment of technological resources and capabilities.

3.2 Technology Effectiveness Audit Model (Garcia-Arreola 1996)

The *Technology Effectiveness Audit Model* by Garcia-Arreola provides an approach to evaluate the technological capabilities of a company. This strategic tool supports the user to identify a gap between the existing and desired technological situation. By applying this methodology, the results can encourage further technological developments. Considering technologically relevant aspects such as approach, methods, strategies, plans, goals and policies, the methodology attempts to generate entrepreneurial and organizational knowledge. It aims to:

- 1. Determine current technological status,
- 2. Stress areas of opportunity,
- 3. Take advantage of the organization's strong capabilities. (Garcia-Arreola 1996)

3.2.1 Role

The roles in the audit are clearly divided. The participants consist of internal company representatives, such as employers and employees, who have to follow a specific questionnaire and classify their answers into a rating scale. The auditor initiates, leads and evaluates the survey. To do this, it is essential that the performing evaluator disposes of a comprehensive knowledge of processes, assets and other resources of the company. When conducting audits, the auditor may identify weak or non-existing linkages to business strategies, a narrow focus on innovation, the inability to measure efficiency and a lack of communication between layers. By exposing these deficiencies in corporate planning, further precautions can be taken by decision-makers. (Garcia-Arreola 1996; Dolinšek et al. 2007)

3.2.2 Activity

The methodology provides a quantitative scoring form to be filled in by participants of the company under investigation. Employers and employees answer a questionnaire covering twenty technology assessment areas. The respondents categorize their answers into a five-point Likert scale. A score of 5 is outstanding, 4 is good, 3 is average, 2 is below average, and 1 is poor (Khalil 2000). After the survey is completed, all answers and their numerical counterparts are added together to give a mean value that represents a general technology status of the company. The process of evaluating the score is led by an auditor and proceeds as follows (Khalil 2000; Garcia-Arreola 1996):

- 1. Analyze the internal technological products and processes to identify core competencies.
- 2. Pinpoint external and basic technologies.
- 3. Identify technological gaps and scope for action.
- 4. Investigate the science push and market pull.
- 5. Establish both factors (Science Push/Market Pull) in the innovation process.
- 6. Check the time to market/implementation time.
- 7. Control the R&D strategy. Is the strategy consistent with Science Push/Market Pull?
- 8. Check for overlaps in core technologies, R&D and marketing.
- 9. Monitor progress and improvement in production and execution.
- 10. Evaluate partnerships and cooperation. Do they fit into the overall strategy?
- 11. Analyze the knowledge management organization. How does the company ensure that acquired knowledge is recorded and passed on?

- 12. Analyze the corporate structure. Is it flexible? How does the communication between all levels take place?

3.2.3 Technique

The methodology can be described as a diagnostic tool with limitations in the applicability. Thus, it requires specific skills and techniques to ensure a reliable result based on further strategic technology planning. In addition to the roles and activities (as described in 3.2.1 and 3.2.2), the methodology requires a defined procedure and application. The assessment process uses an evaluation form that is carried out by internal experts or auditors using a five-level Likert scale. The aim of the questionnaire is to provide a quantitative measure that allows auditors to gain insights into the technological performance of the organization. (Štrukelj and Dolinšek 2011). With the help of the checklist and the result of the survey, in which 20 assessment areas are reviewed, the auditor can draw comprehensive conclusions on the six main categories. Accordingly, it can provide indications for improvements and strategic adjustments. (Garcia-Arreola 1996)

3.2.4 Result

The methodology's aim is to result in a quantitative technology assessment. Each answer of the given questionnaire is added and results in a score from which information about the technological status of the company and its management capabilities can be obtained. Apart from a numerical result, the methodology does not provide explicit recommendations for action. It does, however, offer a starting point for highlighting the strengths and weaknesses of the organisation, which can lead to further knowledge and insights. In order to guarantee a consistent result, the assessment procedure can be repeated after a reasonable period of time. Whereas the auditors have to focus on the company's performance results and progress. Once it is not satisfactory, a strategic change should be considered. (Garcia-Arreola 1996) The *Technology Effectiveness Audit Model* and its results could be an important diagnostic tool for monitoring the progress and effectiveness of technological development and implementation. In addition, it provides an overall assessment of the company's competitive environment and enables the auditor to identify and targeted use of important options for action. Ideally, the self-assessment leads to continuous improvement and technological development. (Khalil 2000)

3.2.5 Meta model

The *Technology Effectiveness Audit Model* comprises a three-level model. The first level is divided into six categories that are of interest in assessing the technological position of the organization: technological environment, technologies categorization, markets and competitors, innovation process, value-added functions, acquisition and exploitation of technology. At the second level, 20 assessment areas enroll a closer look on each category. Finally, the areas unfold into 43 assessment elements that form the third level. The methodology allows a more specific analysis by going deeper into each level and revealing the technological position of a chosen organization. The process model is shown in the following figure. (Garcia-Arreola 1996; Khalil 2000)

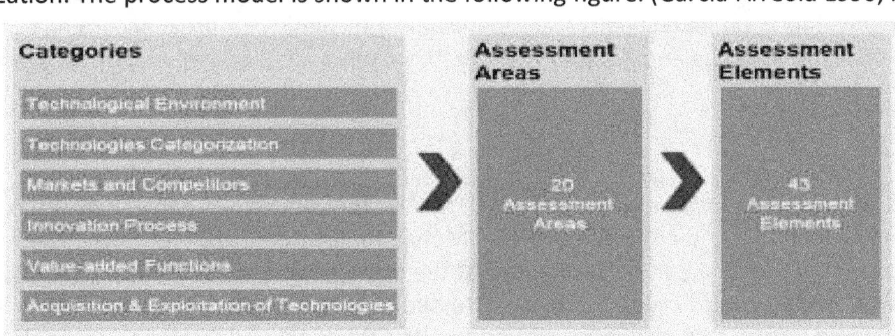

Figure 4: Process model of the technology effectiveness audit model (Garcia-Arreola 1996; Khalil 2000)

3.2.6 Critical analysis

The methodology provides a useful starting point for obtaining a general overview of the technological status of the company. Nevertheless, it has some shortcomings in its applicability: On the one hand, multiple categories (e.g. markets and competitors), assessment areas and elements (e.g. market pull, entrepreneurship) are not directly related to technology. Thus, it goes beyond a mere assessment of technological capability, which could lead to a too complex process in a large organization, and also focuses on aspects of strategic management issues. On the other hand, the methodology does not define how exactly the auditors are required to rate the performance for the assessment areas or elements. Hence, the rating is highly subjective and could differ for a single organization if different auditors apply the methodology. Thus, it is not possible to compare the results of different auditors in different organizations. It also does not describe the practical measures resulting from the assessment achieved by the methodology. Consequently, the auditors do not receive any guidance on how to proceed once the assessment is completed. In addition, the organization's assessment scale is not a purely quantitative assessment, as there is no detailed description of the numbers used for the assessment. Since 1 = poor and 5 = outstanding, the auditors could also use different numbers for these qualitative determinations. Subsequently, this could result in inconsistencies, as these indexing numbers are not quantitative determinations but rather numerical representations of qualitative determinations (Štrukelj and Dolinšek 2011).

Finally, the assessment model seems to be complex and therefore has limitations in the application of larger organizations, as the effort would be too high. Moreover, the methodological approach does not allow a precise derivation from it and no instructions for action.

3.3 Model for technological capability assessment in R&D centers (Mohammad et al. 2010)

Mohammad et al. developed a model for the assessment of the technological performance of R&D centers with the main focus on the development of technologies. Despite some limitations, this model is considered to be the most promising approach for the purposes of this paper, as it is the only one focusing on R&D organizations with their specific requirements.

3.3.1 Role

In the description of the model by Mohammad et al. it is not clear, which roles are involved in the assessment process. However, it can be assumed that several roles exist, since the technological skills are evaluated separately. It can also be assumed that an expert is involved who uses the model to assess the technological capabilities of the R&D organization.

3.3.2 Activity

In this model, the four core capabilities (see 3.3.5, meta-model) are to be evaluated using macro and micro indicators. Each technological capability should be assessed separately. For the evaluation of the capabilities Mohammad et al. suggest using a scoring table that allows the assessment of each capability with an individual indicator. This indicator can be rated with a number between 1 (very poor) and 5 (very good). Subsequently, the points achieved per indicator are added up and set in relation to the maximum number of points that could be achieved. In a weighting table, the indicators are then assigned relative weightings. As a result, a final score is calculated for each type of the four capabilities by multiplying the result of the scoring and weighting table. (Mohammad et al. 2010) The final step is to define a scale for the final evaluations which, together with the assessments, is needed to evaluate technological capability in a technological area. According to Mohammad et al. these three tables enable the auditors to identify the causes of weak, mediocre or good capabilities. (Mohammad et al. 2010)

3.3.3 Technique

Mohammad et al. describe two basic evaluation tools. The first tool is a scoring table, which serves to evaluate the technological capability in a technological area. (Mohammad et al. 2010) Although this is not explicitly described by Mohammad et al., it can be assumed that the scoring table contains four main aspects. The first column contains the technological capability to be assessed. In the second column follow the indicators that need to be evaluated. After the evaluation is made, the third column assesses the achieved score of technological capability for each indicator. Finally, a column with the result follows. This is a relative value from the achieved and the maximum score. In addition to the scoring table, Mohammad et al. describe a weighting table in which relative weightings are assigned to the indicators to be assessed. (Mohammad et al. 2010)

3.3.4 Results

The results of the methodology are a qualitative or semi-quantitative analysis of the organization's technological capability, operationalized in the four technological areas and their indicators. The outputs of the process are the scoring table, the scoring table combined with weights for the indicators and the scale for the final scores.

(Mohammad et al. 2010) There is no explanation about further results, such as hints for the next steps, action planning or a guideline for future improvements of the technological capability of the R&D organization.

3.3.5 Meta model

The model assesses technological capabilities on the macro and micro level. The macro level within the methodology comprises criteria that are common among innovation organizations, such as:

- The position of innovation in the organization,
- Knowledge management and importance of knowledge acquisition,
- The position of innovation in developing strategies,
- Learning,
- Team working,
- Training.

These criteria are the basis for the analysis of "innovation culture in the organization". (Mohammad et al. 2010)

On the micro level the technological performance is assessed. For this purpose, Mohammad et al. describe four core capabilities that need to be evaluated. Each of these core capabilities will be assessed separately:

- Capability of internal development of technologies,
- Capability of technology development via cooperative R&D,
- Capability of performing basic researches,
- Capability of presenting consultation services to industry. (Mohammad et al. 2010)

There are 6 groups of indicators identified for the evaluation of these core capabilities:

- Human resource indicators,
- Equipment,
- Knowledge management and communication indicators,
- Management indicators,
- Marketing and sales indicators,
- Achievements indicators. (Mohammad et al. 2010)

The following Figure 5 summarizes the meta model of the methodology of Mohammad et al. for the assessment of the technological capability in R&D organizations.

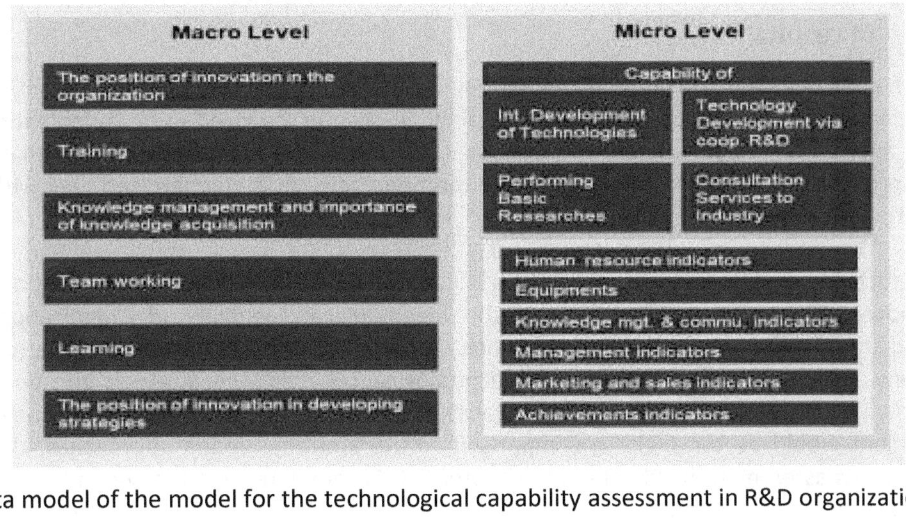

Figure 5: Meta model of the model for the technological capability assessment in R&D organizations

3.3.6 Critical analysis

The technology audit model of Mohammad et al. is not a general model for assessing the technological performance of companies but focuses solely on technology development in R&D centers.

For the assessment of the technological performance of such R&D centers, the authors consider all factors that can have a certain influence on an organization. There is no restriction to essential elements of technological performance. This has the effect of avoiding the arbitrary selection or exclusion of factors, but makes the model more complex, which makes it more difficult to achieve a reasonable cost-benefit ratio. In addition, this contradicts the assumption that the model should follow practical evaluation criteria, such as simplicity, speed and ease, rather than theoretical aspects of technological performance.

Furthermore, the evaluation at the macro level does not aim at a direct assessment of technological performance, but rather at the analysis of the innovation culture. The indicators at this level are very abstract, as they assess issues common to all innovative organizations. However, this very generic level contradicts the fact that the model was designed specifically for R&D organizations and not for other (innovative) organizations. It also remains unclear what kind of questions can in principle be derived to operationalize these abstract indicators.

Moreover, the model does not reveal the extent to which the macro level is linked to the micro level and the relationship between the results of these levels. Therefore, the question arises as to why the model consists of different levels, whereby the assessment of technological performance is only carried out in one of these levels.

Furthermore, it is not clear whether the micro level only presupposes R&D centers involved in all four main groups of activities mentioned above, or whether R&D centers involved in only some of them can also be assessed. It is clear, however, that research organizations that only carry out basic research cannot be assessed according to this model, as it requires organizational units that develop technologies.

The micro-level indicators used to assess technological performance do not relate directly to the technologies themselves. Here, a more general assessment of an organization's performance (e.g. managerial, educational, financial, equipment, communication, marketing, sales) is made. There is also an inconsistency in the assessment of these indicators: qualitative determinations (from very weak to very good) are evaluated quantitatively (from 1 to 5). However, the model does not indicate how the evaluation process should be carried out. Furthermore, the calculation of the proposed total score by weighting and numerous mathematical operations is prone to errors: on the one hand, it is not clear according to which criteria the weighting is carried out. On the other hand, mathematical operations with qualitative determinations or their index numbers (quantitative determinations) are not possible or do not make sense. Moreover, the total number merely indicates that an R&D center is weak or good, but not what the reasons for this are. (Štrukelj and Dolinšek 2011)

4. Discussion of results

In a first step, an approach based on method engineering for the analysis of methodologies has been described. Especially the elements of method description as explained in chapter 2 proved to be suitable for the detailed and structured analysis of the assessment methodologies in chapter 3. It could be shown, that the method engineering approach allows the examination of the methodologies in a standardized way with benefits in understanding the methods and the differences.

Based on the structured analysis of the four methods in chapter 3, it could be shown that most of the methods are valuable approaches for the assessment of the technological capability of organizations. However, weaknesses and shortcomings were also found in each method. The model of Garcia-Arreola (chapter 3.2) is considering many aspects that are broader as the technological capability, i.e. strategic questions concerning market demands. Therefore, this model is not practical as it is very complex and the effort for the application in larger organizations would be too high. In comparison to the aforementioned approaches, the technology management process assessment by Phaal et al. (chapter 3.1) is completely qualitative and does not consider hard factors and technology content.

When regarding the special requirements of research and technology organizations only the method of Mohammad et al. (chapter 3.3) is focusing on this special target group, which is of particular interest in this paper. Nevertheless, this model has several weaknesses as i.e. the focus on the innovation culture rather than the focus on technological capability.

As a result, it can be stated, that all of the methodologies contribute to the discussion on how to analyze and assess the technological capability of RTOs, but no analyzed methodologies fully meet the specific requirements of RTOs.

5. Outlook

As described above, none of the mentioned methods are fully applicable for the analysis and assessment of the technological capability of RTOs. Therefore, the need for the creation of a new methodology for the analysis and assessment of the technological capability of RTOs could be pointed out within this paper. Further research work of the authors will focus on the creation of a methodology that fully meets specific requirements. The results will then be used to create a new method for the assessment of the technological capability of RTOs.

In a critical review, a limitation of this paper is the limited number of the considered approaches. In order to extend the base of considered methods, further approaches need to be identified and analyzed. The results of further research work need to be integrated into the final approach of this paper. The research in this paper as well as the mentioned future research is partly supported by the European Commission through the H2020 project EPIC - Centre of Excellence in Production Informatics and Control under grant No. 739592.

References

de Wet, Gideon (1996): Corporate strategy and technology management: Creating the interface. In: Management of technology V. Technology management in a changing world. Proceedings of the Fifth International Conference on Management of Technology; Official conference of the International Association for Management of Technology; February 27 - March 1, 1996, Miami, Florida, USA. With assistance of Robert M. Mason, Louis A. Lefebvre, Tarek. M. Khalil. Oxford: Elsevier Advanced Technology.

Dolinšek, S.; Janeš, A.; Čosić, P.; Ekinović, S. (2007): Development of the technology audit model. In Proceedings of the 8th International Conference of the Faculty of Management Koper, 20th-24th November 2007, Congress Centre Bernardin. Portorož, Slovenia, 2007.

Garcia-Arreola, J. (1996): Technology Effectiveness Audit Model (TEAM): A Framework for Technology Auditing. Dissertation. University of Miami, Miami, FL.

Gregory, M. J. (1995): Technology management- a process approach. In Proceedings of the Institution of Mechanical Engineers (Vol. 209), pp. 347–356.

Gutzwiller, Thomas A. (1994): Das CC RIM-Referenzmodell für den Entwurf von betrieblichen, transaktionsorientierten Informationssystemen. Heidelberg: Physica-Verl. (Betriebs- und Wirtschaftsinformatik, 54).

Hecklau, Fabian; Kidschun, Florian; Kohl, Holger; Tominaj, Sokol (2020): Generic Process Model for the Structured Analysis of Methods. A Method Engineering Approach for the Analysis of RTO Capability Methodologies. In Manuel Au-Yong Oliveira, Carlos Costa (Eds.): Proceedings of the 19th European Conference on Research Methodology for Business and Management Studies (ECRM): Academic Conferences and Publishing International (ACPI).

Khalil, Tarek. M. (2000): Management of Technology: The Key to Competitiveness and Wealth Creation. US: Irwin Mcgraw-Hill.

Likert, R. (1932): A Technique for the Measurement of Attitudes. In Archives of psychology 140 (22), pp. 5–55.

Mohammad, A. P.; Razaee, S.; Shayegh, F.; Torabi, F. (2010): A Model for Technological Capability Assessment in R&D Centers. Proceedings of the 14th international Oil, Gas & Petrochemical Congress.

Phaal, R.; Farrukh, C.J.P.; Probert, D. R. (2001): Technology management process assessment. A case study. In Int Jrnl of Op & Prod Mnagemnt 21 (8), pp. 1116–1132. DOI: 10.1108/EUM0000000005588.

Štrukelj, Peter; Dolinšek, Slavki (2011): Towards A New Comprehensive Technology Audit Model. Edited by Faculty of Management. University of Primorska. Koper, Slovenia.

Wang, Chun-hsien; Lu, Iuan-yuan; Chen, Chie-bein (2008): Evaluating firm technological innovation capability under uncertainty. In Technovation 28 (6), pp. 349–363. DOI: 10.1016/j.technovation.2007.10.007.

Entrepreneurial Opportunities and Challenges in Emerging Economic

Marwa Naqi[1] and Allam Hamdan[2]
[1]King Hamad University Hospital, Bahrain
[2]Ahlia University, Manama, Bahrain
allamh3@hotmail.com
DOI: 10.34190/EIE.20.228

Abstract: What do entrepreneurial openings see like? How do firms find and misuse these openings to form esteem and maintain competitive advantage? This paper audits the key administration and business enterprise literary works to distinguish the nature and character of entrepreneurial openings and the entrepreneurial procedures that firm utilize to commercialize these openings. The social cognitive school contends that entrepreneurial openings exist as a result of natural uncertainty and social assets accessible to translate and characterize these openings. At last, the social political school stresses the part of arrange and political structures in characterizing entrepreneurial openings. We coordinate these points of view to offer a way to move forward understanding of the opportunity creation and misuse prepare. The methodology used in this research is literature review and data collected via questionnaire among different people involved in business and whether they are involved in a business or about to start a business. The findings we have come up with the questionnaire verifies that leaders in entrepreneur's world facing different challenges, environments and cultures may play an important role in bringing positive impact, and act as an effective team player in order to achieve the desired goals and objectives. Sometime recently business visionaries can construct a comprehensive set of procedures, they must to begin with set up commerce objectives and targets. Which deliver them target to point for and give a premise for assessing their company's execution.

Keywords: entrepreneurial, opportunities, emerging, economic, data, collected, financial, development

1. Introduction

When financial development and advancement is considered in an authentic viewpoint, the part of business visionary comes into more honed center. Enterprise shows up as an individual quality which empowers certain people to create choices with far-reaching results. With the advantage of insight into the past of history specialist can see that certain individuals where were right at a time when for all intents and purposes everybody else was off-base. By acting in unexpected way from other individuals, and accomplishing victory in doing so. Their illustration caused other individuals to alter their intellect, and treatment changed the course of history. The centrality of entrepreneur lies within the reality, firstly that he could be an ordinary. What subsequently is required isn't so much a hypothesis of the victory of business model as a hypothesis of the disappointment of those around him. The substance of the hypothesis of business visionary isn't so much the realization of victory as the clarification of disappointment.

It may be said very categorically that at the show there's no built up financial hypothesis of the business person. The subject has been surrendered by financial matters to sociologist, clinician and political researcher. In fact, all the social science have a hypothesis of the business person but for financial matters.

There are two primary reasons why there's no financial hypothesis of the business visionary. The primary lies within the exceptionally extraordinary presumptions about access to information which are certain in other financial matters that is within the neoclassical school of economic thought. Basic neoclassical models accept that everybody incorporates a free get to all the data key require to require choices.

Besides, the Austrian school of financial matters which takes the business visionary more genuinely is committed to extraordinary subjectivism a philosophical angle which makes a prescient hypothesis of the business visionary outlandish. They contend that anybody who has the sort of data essential to anticipate the behavior of business person incorporates a solid motivating force to halt theorizing and ended up a business visionary him-self.

Moreover, they propose that by entering the framework himself, the scholar might produce a behavioral reaction which would distort his possess expectation of entrepreneurial disappointments. The contention moreover comes up short to recognize that numerous financial lows reflects the total behavior of people. Which it may be conceivable to foresee the behavior of business people indeed in the event of that it is outlandish to anticipate the person behavior of anyone of them. In any case, the failure to anticipate person behavior depends vitally on the nonappearance of boundaries to section into enterprise.

As we might see, there are regularly critical obstructions and in this case the fruitful scholar has no opportunity to demonstrate his forecasts. As a result it may indeed be conceivable be to foresee the abuse of particular entrepreneurial openings. At long last, indeed is inconceivable, it may still be attainable to create a regenerative hypothesis of entrepreneurship that is a hypothesis that can be tried, with the good thing that hand locate, on chronicled information.

In this way indeed on the off chance that a prescient hypothesis cannot be created, it is still conceivable to have a testable one.

In any case the generalization is variable in that it gives different speculation with respect to family foundation, individual qualities and the trade strategies of the business visionary. The reality that those theory are esteem stacked does not matter, so long as they are respected as it were as working speculation and not as explanations of observational consistency. The generalization is valuable as an enunciation of the see that there is a relationship between different individual characteristics and entrepreneurial action. It serves to coordinate the scholar attention to drive, in case conceivable, relations between perceptible individual characteristics and the level of entrepreneurial movement.

2. Define an entrepreneurial

A business person is somebody who takes a judgmental choices around the coordination of rare asset. In guideline, the business visionary may be an organizer in a communist economy, or indeed a cleric or a lord in a conventional society. In spite of the fact that, business person is distinguished with private venture in a advertise economy.

2.1 Define mission, vision and value

Vision is based on entrepreneur's value. Explaining how an entrepreneurs values are the nucleus around which a company grows, author and consultant Ken Blanchard says. "Winning companies first emphasize values-the values that you, as the business owner, have about your customers, quality, ethics integrity, social responsibility, growth, stability, innovation and flexibility. Managing by values not by profits is a powerful process. "Successful entrepreneurs build their business around a set of three or six core values that might range from respect for the individual and innovation to creating satisfied customers and making the world a better place. Indeed, truly entrepreneurs see their company's primary purpose as more than just "making money". (The Foundation of Entrepreneurship)

2.2 The demand for active decision making

Having defined the function of entrepreneur, it must now be established that this function is not completely trivial. This segment appears that business is a continuous work instead of a once for all, or conceivably discontinues movement.

There will be a request for entrepreneurial administrations as long as openings for coordination exist. Openings will exist as long as unused data is getting to be accessible, within the light of which existing allotment of assets shows up wasteful. The unused data maybe a net expansion to the stock of information, within the since of disclosure of something around which individuals were already uninformed, or a substitution for out of date information. The former case is exemplified by scientific breakthroughs, successful prospecting for minerals. Updating of knowledge will occur so long as unpredictable disturbances affect the state of world. It is not necessary to assume that the actual opportunities which occur should be unpredictable to the economic agents themselves. Otherwise agents could plan ahead with just as much certainty as if things were to remain unchanged. All coordination could be organized in the present to be implemented automatically in the future. In this way whereas there would be strongly entrepreneurial action within the current period there would be none at all in the future periods.

3. Literature review

3.1 The role of entrepreneurship in economic growth and development Research into economic

Improvement features a long history. Since Adam Smith's (2003) (unique work distributed in 1776) seminal work, the riches of countries, a few speculations have contributed to the clarification of financial improvement. Within the writing, financial advancement is considered a complex and multifaceted handle that incorporates intuitive among distinctive planned objectives and arrangements over time in a particular nations (Dang and Pheng, 2015).

This prepare of financial improvement may require auxiliary changes driving to a generally higher development direction on diverse social, social political frameworks and regulation levels. Hence, the concept of financial advancement goes past the definition of financial development (GDP, GNP or GNI) per capita, as the idle is considered one of the measurements of improvements (Naudé, 2010; Dang and Pheng, 2015). In any case, Dang and Pheng (2015) contended that financial improvement target seem not be accomplished without understanding the sources of financial development as the nation needs asset to achieve other long-term objectives. In line with this contention, distinctive thinks about created hypothetical models by advertising conceivable clarifications of how business enterprise can contribute to financial development (Minniti and Lévesque, 2010; Sautet, 2013). In addition, impressive sum of observational considers have the part of business in financial development (e.g., Audretsch and Keilbach, 2004a, b, 2005, 2008; Acs et al., 2018a). Moreover, Audretsch and Keilbach (2004a) examined the affiliation between diverse measures of business enterprise capital and territorial financial execution, measured as per-capita wage for Germany. In this respect, business enterprise capital is characterized as"those component affecting and forming an economy's milieu of specialists in such a way as to be conducive to the creation of modern firms" (Audretsch and Keilbach, 2004a, p. 419). Additionally, Audretsch and Keilbach (2004b) have proposed extending Solow's (1956) show of the generation work to incorporate business capital for financial development.

3.2 The divergent effects of entrepreneurship on economic growth

Although entrepreneurship has been commonly recognized as a key driver to economic growth and development, the relationship between entrepreneurship and 32 economic development has attracted conflicting interpretations from different stages of economic development. Moreover, some studies found that there is a u-shaped relationship between entrepreneurship and the level of economic development (Sternberg and Wennekers, 2005; Wennekers et al., 2005; Thurik, 2009). For example, Wennekers et al. (2005) conducted an empirical study to examine the determinants of entrepreneurship and macro-level of nations by using GEM data from 36 countries for the year 2002. Specifically, opportunity-based nascent entrepreneurial activity has a U-shaped relationship with economic development. When the country develops economically, the entrepreneurial activity decreases. The authors found that entrepreneurship ha a vital role in predicting and explaining the economic performance of countries. However, the impact of entrepreneurship on economic growth is more significant in developed economies rather than emerging economies. Therefore, Valliere and Peterson (2009) suggested that emerging economies should priorities their economic development policies on bringing gazelle firms (i.e., fast-growing firms) into the formal economy to increase productive entrepreneurship and economic growth. Recently, Chowdhury et al. (2015b) analyzed the data from 44 countries during 2001 to 2005. The previous discussion showed that entrepreneurship could play a different role under the stage of economic development and the quality of the institutional environment. In addition, emerging economies that are in the innovation-driven stage most likely have higher rates of export-oriented entrepreneurship than emerging economies located in lower stages (De Clercq et al., 2008). Therefore, it is critical for emerging economies to promote innovation in order to reach technological frontier, and consequently a knowledge based economy that is particular to the innovation-driven stage (Acs and Amorós, 2008).

4. Entrepreneurship education and enterprise system

Literature highlights a significant extend of quality of ponders overviewed and it is evident from these thinks about that the observational inquire about education for business enterprise is still within the exploratory arrange. In this regard, Filion (1994) suggests that "high school is the foremost determinant level within the improvement of youthful people's entrepreneurial potential". The related writing is checked on to analyze the four key measurements of business enterprise instruction.

Comes about from a study conducted by Hood and Youthful (1993) of 100 chief officials in entrepreneurial firms demonstrates that promoting is the foremost imperative content area, administration is the foremost basic aptitude and inventiveness is the foremost critical of the attitude zones. Respondents from the overview conducted by Hood and Youthful (1993) moreover accepted that whereas identity characteristics are troublesome to impact, the tremendous share of information required by business people can be instructed. These comes about give a premise for planning enterprise courses and programs. Knight (1991) is one to bargain with this substance. He proposes a system and strategy for instructing business that incorporates the taking after components: opportunity distinguishing poor, methodology improvement, asset procurement and execution. Knight (1991) propose that these components of enterprise apply at the gather, organization, industry and society levels as well as at the person level, which a system for instructing ought to be amplified to incorporates these dimensions.

4.1 Descriptive demographic

Demographic	Answer	Frequency	Percent %
How Old are you?	under 18	1	2%
	18 - 24	13	28%
	25 - 34	26	55%
	35 - 44	3	6%
	45 - 54	2	4%
	55 - 64	2	4%
	Total	47	99%
Are you involved with entrepreneurial or about to start a business?	Yes	17	36%
	No	30	64%
	Total	47	100%
Entrepreneurship should develop a clear vision and translate it to a meaningful mission statement.	Strongly Agree	28	60%
	Agree	17	36%
	Neither agree or disagree	2	4%
	Disagree	0	0%
	Strongly Disagree	0	0%
	Total	47	100%
Successful entrepreneurs introduce new ideas, products and services that solve a problem or fill a need.	Strongly Agree	33	72%
	Agree	11	24%
	Neither agree or disagree	2	4%
	Disagree	0	0%
	Strongly Disagree	0	0%
	Total	46	100%
The rapid pace of change shaping the economy also is placing new demand on leaders, Technology is changing the ways in which people work, the ways in which the various parts of an organization operate and interconnect.	Strongly Agree	5	11%
	Agree	9	20%
	Neither agree or disagree	11	24%
	Disagree	11	24%
	Strongly Disagree	10	22%
	Total	46	101%

Demographic	Answer	Frequency	Percent %
Effective leaders exhibit certain behaviors: Leaders should not provide financial rewards to encourage top performance among their people.	Strongly Agree	5	11%
	Agree	9	20%
	Neither agree or disagree	11	24%
	Disagree	11	24%
	Strongly Disagree	10	22%
	Total	46	101%
Effective leaders exhibit certain behaviors: Leaders should not encourage risk taking in their companies, when employees try something innovative and it fails they resort to punishment.	Strongly Agree	5	11%
	Agree	9	20%
	Neither agree or disagree	5	11%
	Disagree	15	33%
	Strongly Disagree	12	26%
	Total	46	101%
Effective leaders exhibit certain behaviors: rather than punish workers who take risks and fail, effective leaders are willing to accept failure as a natural part of innovation and creativity.	Strongly Agree	23	50%
	Agree	15	33%
	Neither agree or disagree	7	15%
	Disagree	1	2%
	Strongly Disagree	0	0%
	Total	46	100%
Effective leaders exhibit certain behaviors: one of the most important tool a leader can have is a sense of humor. Without it, work can become dull and unexciting for everyone.	Strongly Agree	17	37%
	Agree	12	26%
	Neither agree or disagree	14	30%
	Disagree	3	7%
	Strongly Disagree	0	0%
	Total	46	100%
Coronavirus have affected the global economy in a bad way.	Strongly Agree	25	53%
	Agree	14	30%
	Neither agree or disagree	5	11%
	Disagree	2	4%
	Strongly Disagree	1	2%
	Total	47	100%

The result of first question which is asking about participants "Age", shows that most of the survey participants are aged between 25 - 34 years old (55%) of the total sample population, the second Majority are participants aged between 18-24 (28%), then between 35-44 (6%), between 45-54 (4%), between 55-64 (4%), and finally under 18 (2%).

The Majority of participants are involved with entrepreneurial were not about to start a business with (64%), than (17%) involved with entrepreneurial about to start a business.

Most of participants the participants with (24%) were neither agreed or disagreed that effective leaders should not provide financial rewards to encourage top performance among their people.

The Survey showed that most participants with (33%) were disagree as leaders should not encourage risk taking in their companies, when employees try something innovative and it fails they resort to punishment, However, participants comes in the second place with (26%) and they are strongly disagree as leaders should not encourage risk taking in their companies. In the third place, came participants with (20%) agree as leaders should not encourage risk taking in their companies, then neither agree or disagree with (11%) and finally agreed with (11%).

The findings shows the majority of participants with (50%) strongly agreed rather than punish workers who take risks and fail, effective leaders are willing to accept failure as a natural part of innovation and creativity. Secondly, participants agreed with (33%). After that participants with (15%) Neither agree nor disagree and Finally Participants with (2%) disagree. Most of the participants strongly agree that effective leaders should have a sense of humor with (37%), then participants agree with (26%). In the third place, came neither agree nor disagree with (30%) and finally other disagree with (7%). From the table, we can see that most of participants have agreed that coronavirus had a negative impact on the global economy which shows (53%). Participants who agree comes in the second place with (30%), then comes participants how neither agree nor disagree with (11%), after that who disagree with (4%) and finally who strongly disagree with (2%).

5. Conclusion

Given that entrepreneurship is a key driver to economic growth and development through job creation, innovation and prosperity, the primary aim and contribution of this thesis was to study the impact of institutional dynamics on the development of entrepreneurial activity in the context of emerging economies. Education and training, access to credit and technology absorption on the rates of entrepreneurial activity. Moreover, this previous relationship may vary under the level of development of a particular emerging economy. Therefore, there is a continuous need to understand the institutional determinants that encourage entrepreneurial activity in emerging economies located at different stages of development theoretically, empirically and from a policy viewpoint. In short, this study confirmed the effective entrepreneurial behavior with different characteristics ad confirmed that the dynamic of institution will not have the same effects on entrepreneurs in emerging economies that might be expected in developed countries, as suggested by the literature (Bruton et al., 2009; Hoskisson et al., 2011; Pathak et al., 2016). The results indicated that institutions might have different, even negative effects of, access to credit and technology used by new start-ups in emerging economies. This could go a long way towards explaining the conflicting findings of the interaction effect of institutions on entrepreneurship found in the existing literature (Dutta and Sobel, 2016).

References

Acemoglu, D., Gallego, F. & Robinson, J.A. (2014). Institutions, human capital and development, Annual Review of Economics, *6*(1), 875-912.

Acs, Z.J. & Amorós, J.E. (2008). Entrepreneurship and competitiveness dynamics in Latin America, Small Business Economics, *31*(3), 305-322. Acs

Acs, Z.J., Audretsch, D.B., Braunerhjelm, P. & Carlsson, B. (2012). Growth and entrepreneurship, Small Business Economics, *39*(2), 289-300.

Acs, Z.J., Autio, E. & Szerb, L. (2014a). National systems of entrepreneurship: measurement issues and policy implications, Research Policy, *43*(3), 476-494.

Acs, Z.J. & Correa, P.G. (2014). Identifying the obstacles to high-Impact entrepreneurship in Latin America and the Caribbean, The World Bank, 1-32.

Acs, Z.J., Szerb, L. & Autio, E. (2016). The Global Entrepreneurship and Development Index 2016, The Global Entrepreneurship and Development Institute, Washington, DC, 88.

Aparicio, S., Urbano, D. & Audretsch, D. (2016). Institutional factors, opportunity entrepreneurship and economic growth: Panel data evidence, Technological Forecasting and Social Change, *102*(C), 45-61.

Audretsch, D.B. & Keilbach, M. (2004b). Entrepreneurship capital and economic performance, Regional Studies, *38*(8), 949-959.

Audretsch, D.B. & Keilbach, M. (2005). Entrepreneurship capital and regional growth, The Annals of Regional Science, *39*(3), 457-469.

Audretsch, D.B. & Keilbach, M. (2007). The localisation of entrepreneurship capital: evidence from Germany, Papers in Regional Science, *86*(3), 351-365.

Audretsch, D.B. & Keilbach, M. (2008). Resolving the knowledge paradox: Knowledge-spillover entrepreneurship and economic growth, Research Policy, *37*(10), 1697-1705.

Acs, Z.J., Audretsch, D.B., Braunerhjelm, P. & Carlsson, B. (2012). Growth and entrepreneurship, Small Business Economics, *39*(2), 289-300.

Belitski, M., Chowdhury, F. & Desai, S. (2016). Taxes, corruption, and entry, Small Business Economics, *47*(1), 201-216.

Bosma, N.S., Stam, F.C. & Wennekers, A.R.M. (2010). Intrapreneurship: An international study, EIM Research Report Intrapreneurship, 9, 1-29.

Bowen, H.P. & De Clercq, D. (2008). Institutional context and the allocation of entrepreneurial efforts, Journal of International Business Studies, *39*(4), 747-767.

Bruton, G.D., Ahlstrom, D. & Obloj, K. (2008). Entrepreneurship in emerging economies: Where are we today and where the research should go in the future, Entrepreneurship Theory and Practice, *32*(1), 1-14.

Bruton, G.D., Ahlstrom, D. & Puky, T. (2009). Institutional differences and the development of entrepreneurial ventures: A comparison of the venture capital industries in Latin America and Asia, Journal of International Business Studies, *40*(5), 762-778.

Bruton, G.D., Ahlstrom, D. & Li, H.L. (2010). Institutional theory and entrepreneurship: where are we now and where do we need to move in the future?, Entrepreneurship theory and practice, *34*(3), 421-440.

Carlos Díaz Casero, J., Almodóvar González, M., de la Cruz Sánchez Escobedo, M., Coduras Martinez, A. & Hernández Mogollón, R. (2013). Institutional 191 variables, entrepreneurial activity and economic development, Management Decision, *51*(2), 281-305.

Chowdhury, F., Terjesen, S. & Audretsch, D. (2015b). Varieties of entrepreneurship: institutional drivers across entrepreneurial activity and country, European Journal of Law and Economics, *40*(1), 121-148.

Dang, G. & Pheng, L.S. (2015). Theories of economic development, in Dang, G. and Pheng, L.S. (Eds), Infrastructure Investments in Developing Economies, Springer, Singapore, 11-26.

De Clercq, D., Hessels, J. & van Stel, A. (2008). New ventures' export orientation: outcome and source of knowledge spillovers, Small Business Economics, *31*(3), 283-303.

Djankov, S., La Porta, R., Lopez-de-Silanes, F. & Shleifer, A. (2002). The regulation of entry, The Quarterly Journal of Economics, *117*(1), 1-37.

Dutta, N. & Sobel, R. (2016). Does corruption ever help entrepreneurship? Small Business Economics, 47(1), 179-199.

Hoskisson, R.E., Eden, L., Lau, C.M. & Wright, M. (2000). Strategy in emerging economies, Academy of management journal, *43*(3), 249-267.

Klapper, L., Laeven, L. & Rajan, R. (2006). Entry regulation as a barrier to entrepreneurship, Journal of financial economics, *82*(3), 591-629.

Kuckertz, A., Berger, E.S. & Mpeqa, A. (2016). The more the merrier? Economic freedom and entrepreneurial activity, Journal of Business Research, *69*(4), 12881293.

Leitch, C.M. & Harrison, R.T. (1999). "A process model for entrepreneurship education and development", Journal of Entrepreneurial Behavior & Research, *5*(3), pp. 83-102.

Méndez-Picazo, M.T., Galindo-Martín, M.Á. & Ribeiro-Soriano, D. (2012). Governance, entrepreneurship and economic growth, Entrepreneurship and Regional Development, *24*(9-10), 865-877.

Minniti, M. & Lévesque, M. (2010). Entrepreneurial types and economic growth, Journal of Business Venturing, *25*(3), 305-314.

Naudé, W. (2010), Entrepreneurship, developing countries, and development economics: new approaches and insights, Small Business Economics, *34*(1), 1-12.

Noseleit, F. (2013). Entrepreneurship, structural change, and economic growth, Journal of Evolutionary Economics, *23*(4), 735-766.

Pathak, S., Xavier-Oliveira, E. & Laplume, A.O. (2016). Technology use and availability in entrepreneurship: informal economy as moderator of institutions in emerging economies, The Journal of Technology Transfer, *41*(3), 506-529.

Porter, M., Sachs, J. & McArthur, J. (2001). Executive summary: competitiveness and stages of economic development, The Global Competitiveness Report, 20012002, New York, NY, 16-25.

Romer, P.M. (1990), Endogenous technological change, Journal of Political Economy, *98*(5, Part 2), S71-S102.

Sautet, F. (2013). Local and systemic entrepreneurship: Solving the puzzle of entrepreneurship and economic development, Entrepreneurship Theory and Practice, *37*(2), 387-402.

Schumpeter, J.A. (1947). The creative response in economic history, The journal of economic history, *7*(2), 149-159.

Schwab, K. & Sala-i-Martín, X. (2014). Insight report: the Global Competitiveness Report 2014-2015, World Economic Forum, Geneva.

Sternberg, R. & Wennekers, S. (2005). Determinants and effects of new business creation using Global Entrepreneurship Monitor data, Small Business Economics, *24*(3), 193-203.

Urbano, D., Aparicio, S. & Audretsch, D. (2018). Twenty-five years of research on institutions, entrepreneurship, and economic growth: what has been learned?, Small Business Economics, 1-29, https://doi.org/10.1007/s11187-018-0038-0.

Turró, A., Urbano, D. & Peris-Ortiz, M. (2014). Culture and innovation: The moderating effect of cultural values on corporate entrepreneurship, Technological Forecasting and Social Change, 88, 360-369.

European-Wide ICT Entrepreneurship Education in Action

Brian O'Flaherty[1], Diego Alonso Caceres[2], Pedro Sanchez Palma[2] and Katerina Pramatari[3]
[1]Cork University Business School, University College Cork, Ireland
[2]Universidad Politécnica de Cartagena, Spain
[3]Athens University of Economics and Business, Greece
b.oflaherty@ucc.ie
diego.alonso@upct.es
Pedro.Sanchez@upct.es
k.pramatari@aueb.gr
DOI: 10.34190/EIE.20.154

Abstract: EUXCEL, a Trans-European technology entrepreneurship education initiative funded by the European Union, has demonstrated that creating cross-border collaboration between Europe's young ICT entrepreneurs is an achievable policy objective. The literature in this paper explores the importance of Entrepreneurship Education, the concept of European Nationalism and Born Global firms. This paper then outlines the context of EUXCEL, an international entrepreneurship programme, describing the key outcomes and education process, highlighting lessons learned and suggests key policy features that can make borderless entrepreneurship the norm rather than the exception. The research question is 'How can trans-regional entrepreneurship, with multi-nationality founders, be enabled and supported?' The findings of the paper identifies internationalisation and Pan-European collaboration as key outcomes of participants. This paper demonstrates that European-wide cross-border entrepreneurship education is an achievable outcome that has the potential to revolutionise the European entrepreneurial culture and push the boundaries of what is possible. Sharing the first-hand experiences of this project will be of interest to entrepreneurship educationalist, practitioners and policy makers.

Keywords: European wide ICT entrepreneurship education

1. Introduction

This paper explores the emergence of international entrepreneurship in the ICT field and the key empirical focus on this paper is an international case study of ICT entrepreneurship. The justification for this case stems from findings of a survey of start-up profiles in European incubators. The single nationality of a large number of companies in incubators across Europe is problematic and the case describes a European wide ICT entrepreneurship initiative that attempts to address this issue. The paper outlines the outcome of a multi-national European wide entrepreneurship, which is a Horizon 2020 project, funded by the European Commission. The implications of single nationalities of European start-ups is explored in the context of the tension between nationalism and a European wide identity. The paper concludes with a summary of the lessons learned for the ICT community from a European wide ICT entrepreneurship initiative.

2. Entrepreneurial ecosystems

Spilling, (1996) characterises the entrepreneurial system as "a complexity and diversity of actors, roles, and environmental factors that interact to determine the entrepreneurial performance of a region or locality". There seems to be a tendency to think of entrepreneurship as an individual activity (Pennings, 1982, as cited by Spilling, 1996). However, effective entrepreneurship requires a great deal more than a single individual. Van de Ven (1993) argues that the study of entrepreneurship is lacking if it focuses solely on the individual entrepreneur and if it treats social, economic and political factors as external demographic statistics.

Entrepreneurial systems (Spilling, 1996) consists of all economic actors and environmental factors existing in a geographical area and that the quality of this system are determined by the amount of actors who have both entrepreneurial experience and potential. The author also highlights the importance of the elements that interact within this system and argues that the development of an entrepreneurial community requires infrastructure and public institutions in addition to the development of a number of businesses. Entrepreneurial processes take place within the existing sociocultural and economic structures and entrepreneurial activity grows from the knowledge, competence and role models that are ingrained in these cultures (Spilling, 1996).

Entrepreneurial ecosystems evolve through a set of inter-dependant components which seek to generate new venture creation over time (Van de Ven, 1993). The relationship between components is complex and their interaction can have an impact on a region's overall economic development (Neck et al., 2004). Neck et al. (2004)

examined the interaction of these components by conducting semi-structured interviews and qualitative analysis to identify the elements of the entrepreneurial ecosystem in Boulder, Colorado, USA which led to the creation of an area of dense high-technology entrepreneurial activity. The findings indicated that these elements consisted of incubator organizations, spin-offs, informal and formal networks, the physical infrastructure, and the culture of the region. One key component of any potential entrepreneurial eco-system is entrepreneurship education. This study considers how the facilitation of a European wide ecosystem can support start-ups.

2.1 The need for entrepreneurship education

The World Economic Forum (2009) report on Entrepreneurship Education called "Educating the Next Wave of Entrepreneurs" consolidates existing knowledge of entrepreneurship education so that it may be shared and new approaches can be developed. Specifically, it identifies opportunities and challenges in entrepreneurship in higher education. It was found that education plays a significant role in whether students will become entrepreneurial in that the greater the exposure to entrepreneurship and innovation, the higher the likelihood that the student will become entrepreneurial. The need for embedding Entrepreneurship in schools is highlighted by Eurydice (2016). In 2014 a taskforce was set up by the Irish government to review initiatives aimed at cultivating an entrepreneurial ecosystem in Ireland. Specifically, the report outlines an initiative to create a national education strategy for entrepreneurship at all levels of the education system, thus supporting the potential of entrepreneurship education to encourage students to develop an entrepreneurial mind-set (DJEI, 2014). Such thinking is supported by studies confirming entrepreneurship education raises the entrepreneurial intentions of students (Rasmussen and Sorheim, 2006). Furthermore, Souitaris et al (2007) argue entrepreneurship programmes raise student entrepreneurial intention, citing inspiration as the programmes' most influential benefit.

Wennberg et al., (2011) propose that there are two paths to knowledge intensive entrepreneurship based on university knowledge. These are the direct path 'where individuals first study, then work at universities and subsequently spin off their business directly from the university' and the second path is represented by 'university graduates who pursue careers in private industry and spin off their companies from that context'. For this paper we distinguish between 1) direct as staff and researcher within the university and 2) indirect as student involvement, in academic entrepreneurship activities. This distinction is also used in this paper to structure a broad discussion on the applicability of academic entrepreneurship to a broad range of stakeholders in the ICT community.

2.2 Nationalism and a European identity

The large proportion of single nationality start-ups in European incubators is an interesting finding and this may be indication of a broader issue, namely the tensions or general interplay between being nationalistic and expression a broader European identity. Are they mutually exclusive or can they co-exist? The European Union is undergoing a number of major crises at the moment, which includes the refugee situation, scenarios where national agendas are in conflict with the European one and a perceived failure of European governance and the outcome of the UK referendum, and more recently reopening businesses after the COVID pandeminc (Striessnig, and Lutz, 2016). A European Identity is related to 'a shared consciousness of belonging to an economic and political space defined by capitalism, social welfare, liberal democracy, respect for human rights, freedom and the rule of law, prosperity and progress' (Guibernau, 201).

Empirical studies indicate that European population continues to become more European minded despite continuing economic and political challenges (Striessnig, and Lutz, 2016). A sense of European Identity is related to age, as older Europeans tend to have a single national identity, but younger cohorts are socialised in a way that decreases their association with solely national identities and increases their association with multiple identities (Striessnig, and Lutz, 2016). In future, as younger more European minded cohorts take the place of older nationalistic citizen, could lead to a significant change in the prevalence of a European Identity (Striessnig, and Lutz, 2016). A 'European identity' is also presented as a 'non-emotional identity', which is in sharp contrast with traditional forms of national identity associated with intense nationalistic feelings (Guibernau, 2011). The ultimate goal of this engagement is to produce truly European enterprises that are internationalised and grow quickly from a very early stage. The next section discusses such enterprises.

2.3 From born global to born European

The distinguishing characteristic of International New Ventures/Born Globals (INVs/BGs) is that they have foreign sales from the outset, or very quickly afterwards (Hennart 2013). Hennart (2013) describes Born Global enterprises as Accidental Internationalists. Born Globals were categorised by Rennie (1993) as one of two types of exporting enterprises. The first was domestic based. These enterprises focused on building a sustainable base in their home markets before turning to exportation as a means of growth. However, they retained their focus on the domestic market with exports averaging only 20% of their total sales. The average age of these enterprises was 27 years. Rennie (1993) categorised the second type of exporting enterprise as the born global enterprise. These enterprises began exporting on average 2 years after foundation and achieved 76% of total sales through exports.

Born Global Enterprises developed as a result of a number of changes. Firstly, consumer preferences changed significantly in the 1970s and 1980s, moving towards demand for increasingly specialised products, providing niche opportunities for small enterprises. Secondly, the advent of electronic process technology allowed SME's to compete with larger enterprises on cost and quality. Thirdly, smaller enterprises were better equipped to make changes reflecting consumer tastes and finally, updates in communication technology enabled enterprises of any size to manage their business systems even when they extend beyond their own boundaries (Rennie, 1993).

This case study reflects on the concept of a European-wide Ecosystem. Having outlined the challenges of a European identity and the emergence of highly internationalised companies called 'Born Globals', the next section explores the experiences of an international ICT entrepreneurship initiative.

3. International entrepreneurship case study

This paper highlights the outcomes of a survey of start-ups in incubators across Europe, the findings of which was used to shape a European Entrepreneurship project. This European-wide entrepreneurship education initiative involved 6 summer schools per year over a two-year period. EUXCEL was extended by 6 months, in order to support the start-ups that were formed in the previous two years. The survey findings highlight the single nationality nature of start-up in incubators across Europe. This fact undermines the potential of developing a European entrepreneurship culture and making 'Born European' start-ups the norm. The tension between nationalism and a European Identity, and 'Born-European' start-ups is also explored. Key outcomes of the case includes findings relating to the development of individual entrepreneurial networks, international impact and Pan-European collaboration.

3.1 Survey of current practice

The EUXCEL consortium circulated a brief survey to the enterprises in European Incubators, associated with the project consortium, with 54 enterprises responses. The survey set out to establish the following: the number of ICT enterprises in incubators, how long ICT enterprises developed their technology before entering the incubator, the nationalities of the founders and the international orientation of the enterprises. Specifically, what is currently happening in EU incubators and how can the EUXCEL proposal make a profound difference to ICT entrepreneurship in Europe.

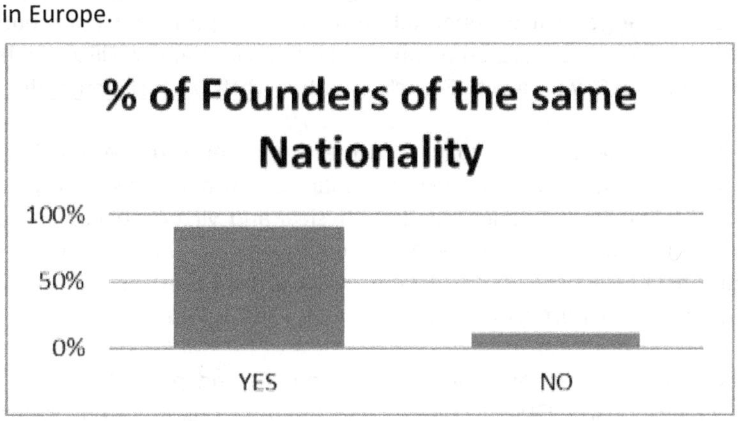

Figure 1: % of founders of the same nationality in the sample of EU incubators

These results revealed that there was on average two founders in each responding enterprise. Two respondents had five founders, the highest, and ten enterprises had one founder only. The average enterprise size was between 2-3 founders. Forty-four percent of enterprises surveyed were incubating in Germany, 11% in Ireland, 24% in Spain, 2% in Belgium, 13% in Poland and 4% in Greece. One enterprise listed three locations as the incubation country, Finland, Russia and Spain. Ninety-one percent (see figure 1) of respondents stated that all enterprise founders were of the same nationality.

Of those enterprises with founders of a single nationality, 41% were German, 11% were Irish, 22% were Spanish, 4% were Greek, 11% were Polish and 2% were French. Nine percent of enterprises had founders of different nationalities which included British, Turkish, Italian, Russian, Baltic, Belgium and Greek. Eighty-three percent 3% of enterprises surveyed operated within the ICT sector. The other non-ICT industry sectors included automotive, health care, education and food. Enterprises developed their technology for an average of 15 months prior to incubation and six enterprises developed the technology while in incubation. Twenty-two percent 22% of enterprises focussed on a city-wide market, 20% on state/regional market, 39% on a country wide market, 33% on a European market and 52% on the global market. Enterprises offered their product in two languages on average. However, three enterprises offered their products in five languages.

From the sample size, the status quo in incubators across Europe was that the majority of enterprises had 2 to 3 founders, who were, in general, all of the same nationality. Over 85% of enterprises in incubators were in the ICT sector, which has significant implications for the IS discipline, as many of the graduates from IS programmes progress to found start-ups. The average development time of ICT technology before teams enter an incubator is on average 15 months. The EUXCEL consortium sets out to differentiate the grant proposal by focusing on higher quality enterprise development, adopting a European wide training and collaborative focus, while recognising the characteristics of existing enterprises in incubators, such as the time required to build an ICT product. Many organisations in the ecosystem focus on brief entrepreneurial experiences, such as, a start-up weekend, which do not produce many high-performance start-ups and cannot possibly develop an actual product. They do inspire participants to start an entrepreneurial journey. The initiative described in this case study will addresses the single nationality challenge and considers the high-quality support required to produce Born European enterprises and how European ICT entrepreneurship can be enhanced. The fact that start-ups across Europe are being founding by single nationality teams raises an important issue, regarding nationalism and a European entrepreneurship identity. The next section will explore background concepts concerning nationalism and the relationship with European identity. How can these concepts enhance a European-wide entrepreneurship initiative?

3.2 Cultivating born European enterprises

The authors of this paper have successfully secured a funding for a Horizon 2020 funded Project, called EUXCEL, which set out to establish ICT entrepreneurship education initiatives and spaces across Europe. The consortium consists of Universities and incubators in Germany, Denmark, Poland, Spain, Greece and Ireland and the focus of the project is to develop more ICT entrepreneurs.

Europe does have a challenge as a growing gap has emerged between the needs of employers and the skills of employees. Europe is not fostering an entrepreneurial spirit. 'Many aspiring entrepreneurs simply leave Europe to seek their fortunes elsewhere. There are an estimated 50,000 Germans in Silicon Valley, and an estimated 500 start-ups in the San Francisco Bay area with French founders' (http://start-upmanifesto.eu/).

This entrepreneurship programme sets out to train ICT entrepreneurs to be 'incubator ready' and this is informed by research into current practice in incubators across Europe. This entrepreneurship programme developed a network of ICT entrepreneurship creative physical and virtual spaces and coordinate European-wide intensive entrepreneurial action training events called 'Start-up Summer schools' between consortia members with multi-nationality teams. EUXCEL attempted to cultivate internationalised companies from the beginning, which has parallels with 'born global' ventures.

The programme cultivated a European entrepreneurial mind-set and piloted a 'Born European Enterprise' annual event. It engaged with nearly 250 ICT students per annum using an intensive training package over 4 months, starting with the 'start-up Summer schools', continuing with virtual support via an EU Virtual Incubator and culminating with the best teams competing in a 'Born European Enterprise Challenge'. A key element of the programme is student exchange as well as staff exchange, which will enable cross-fertilisation. The ICT teams have opportunities to pursue their new ventures in a number of European incubators, within the consortia.

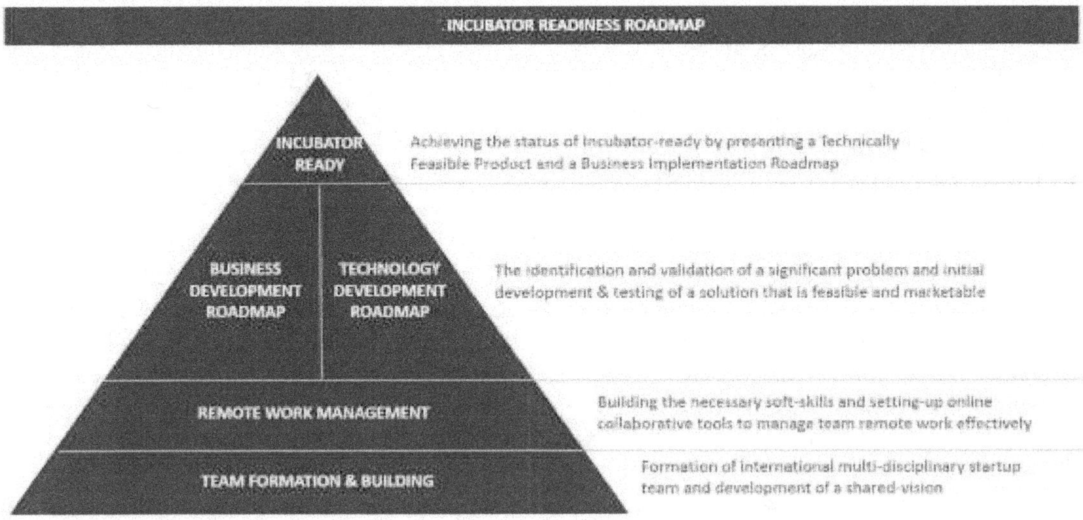

Figure 2: The EUXCEL incubator readiness roadmap

Six five-day start-up summer schools were hosted in each of the partner countries between June and July in 2015 and 2016, with 42 applicants per start-up summer school To ensure as diverse, expansive and inclusive a range of European countries as possible, it was agreed that each of the six summer schools would include 5 participants from each of the 5 visiting (i.e. non-hosting) partner countries (5x5), 8 candidates from the host country and 9 'other' participants to be selected from EU countries outside of the 6 partner countries. The incubator readiness road map adopted is outlined in Figure 2 and the initial step involved forming international teams with at least 3 nationalities in each team.

In total, once selections and applicant availability details finalised, 239 aspiring young entrepreneurs from across 25 European countries participated in the summer schools as scheduled. To maximise the internationalisation element and to ensure as much cross-border learning as possible, all EUXCEL partners had at least one representative present at each of the six summer schools and where feasible incorporated the inclusion of wider institutional staff from across technology and entrepreneurship domains to maximise institutional learning and the development and strengthening of cross European entrepreneurship networks.

The interactive EU Virtual Incubator (software) was made available online from May 2015 in advance of start-up summer schools commencement in June 2015. The platform provided a range of resources and support tools to guide and assist teams during their start-up summer school and in the succeeding virtual incubation phase as they further develop, test and validate the initially conceptualized idea (end-point of the start-up scrum) in several cycles of iteration, by applying prototyping and business modelling techniques, taking into account the inter-regional nature of the entrepreneurs within start-up teams. The platform was based on Moodle and provided a repository for all EUXCEL related resources. It also enabled mass communication with all participants in the summer schools and the whole project.

The 2015 Challenge Final was held in November 2015. Following a thorough short-listing process, the 12 highest ranked teams using the incubator-readiness score card from across the six summer schools and the 56 participants on these teams were selected to pitch to the Challenge Final Judging Panel which included four partner nominated investors from across the European tech start-up scouting and investment space, two nominated representatives leading global technology companies. A 150+ audience from across the investor, tech industries, start-up/entrepreneurial agencies landscape in addition to media and fellow tech entrepreneurs attended the Challenge Final event facilitating excellent networking and relationship development opportunities for the start-up finalists presenting at the showcase exhibition and awards ceremony and for the EUXCEL consortium itself.

Through the work carried out to date, EUXCEL has demonstrated that creating cross-border entrepreneurial collaboration is an achievable policy objective. In year two of the project, 187 participants were chosen from 436 applications, drawn from 18 countries. Of the selected participants, 29.1% were female, significantly higher than the EU37 average of 19% female entrepreneurial representation in ICT, while 70.9% were male. For 133 participants, this programme represented the first occasion on which they had created a start-up. For 104 participants it was the first time that they had developed a business plan. For 88 participants this programme was the first occasion on which they had pitched a business idea. Participants were assigned to each of the six start-up summer schools on the basis of skillset and interest complementarity, and 36 multinational start-up teams were created at the summer schools. Task completion rate for the virtual phase of the programme was 95.1%, indicating a very high level of engagement with the virtual incubation platform and mentorship programme. An assessment of EUXCEL impact with respect to 7 core entrepreneurial skills was conducted. The skills assessed included start-up management skills relevant to this setting (e.g. developing a start-up with a European-wide team), market research (e.g. end user analysis), and product testing (e.g. user validation). Measured against a baseline taken at the outset of the programme, the analysis found that participation had a highly significant positive impact on each of the 7 practical skills assessed. Across the overall skillset measured, we observed improvement in 86% of participants. This compares well with the impact of programmes such as Erasmus for Young Entrepreneurs which has had a skills development impact on 60% of participating new entrepreneurs' management skills and on 40% of participants' marketing skills. Of particular relevance to the programme is the finding that 79% of its participants indicated greater confidence in their knowledge of start-up development with a European-wide team, which is a promising outcome.

3.3 Development of the entrepreneurial individual networks

During applicant pre-screening, potential participants were asked to indicate their "willingness to locate to another European country to start a business". Responses indicated that for a large majority **(77%)** of both the applicant (613) and participant pool (245), moving to another member state for entrepreneurial purposes was either favourable (24% of participants) or very favourable (53%). However, the actual experience of working in an entrepreneurial initiative in a different country held by the participants, or the experience of working with other nationalities, was minimal. This is consistent with the survey carried about the EUXCEL consortium in developing the initial proposal, which found that 91% of its respondent incubated enterprises had a management team compose of just one nationality.

The EUXCEL consortium addressed this absence of European-wide entrepreneurial networks in a number of ways. Firstly, 100% of participants founded a new start up with entrepreneurs from at least two different countries. A number of teams had as many as four different nationalities represented. Secondly, 80% of participants travelled to a different EU member state for the summer school phase of the programme, establishing contacts with both the resident staff of the consortium partner hosting each scrum, as well as with the international mentoring team assembled for each event.

In analysing individual network growth, 72.7% of respondents to a post-programme survey issued in February 2016 identified international entrepreneurial teamwork as a key learning outcome of their participation in the programme and 70.5% of respondents felt that their entrepreneurial network had been improved as a result of their participation in the programme.

3.4 International impact

In order to test the international impact, a measure for the international entrepreneurial social capital (IESC) held by participants was issued at the beginning and end of the programme. For this purpose, the resource generator instrument, a measure of the social resources available to individuals, was adapted (Van Der Gaag and Snijders 2005). Participants were asked to consider their access to a range of entrepreneurial resources, and then to indicate whether they first had access, whether they had access to such resources in their own country only, or if they also had access to those resources in another country. The full list of resources participants were asked to consider are provided in Table 1.

Having gathered responses from participants at both the beginning and the end of the programme, statistical analysis using a t-test was employed to test for the impact of the programme on the internationality of participant entrepreneurial networks. A statistically significant difference in the scores at the outset (M=1.31, SD=.44) and at the end (M=1.45, SD=.40) of the programme (t=3.775, p<.001). These results indicate that the programme did in fact have a statistically significant impact on the international entrepreneurial network of its participants, a central aim of the programme. These findings are reinforced by the testimonies of the participants themselves.

> *"All of a sudden I have people in all these countries I can turn to...It makes you feel so much more confident about what you can do" (Jonathan, Germany)*
>
> *"I know not that if I need a back-end architect in Greece, I can go to Stathis. If I need a front-end guy in Germany I can go to Rui. Having those options changes what's possible for you as an entrepreneur." (Tom, United Kingdom).*

Table 1: Social resources available to participants

Entrepreneurial Resource	Question
Financing Expertise	Someone who knows about the different sources of finance available for start-ups
Financing Expertise	Knows how to manage a company's finances
Financial Expertise	Can give advice on approaching venture capitalists
Legal Expertise	Can give advice on the legal requirements you would face as a business owner
Legal Expertise	Knows about the legal process of setting up a company
Management Expertise	Has run their own business
Management Expertise	Can give advice on how to organise a new business
Product Development Expertise	Knows how to match technologies to people's needs
Product Development Expertise	Can give advice on how to design a technical product for the marketplace

3.5 Pan-European collaboration

A number of further measures were taken several months after the conclusion of the programme in order to assess the impact of the programme on the Pan-European collaborative networks of participants. The results of these measures are presented in the table 2.

Table 2 During the EUXCEL programme, I learned most about

Identifying a New Business Idea	21.6%
Evaluating Business Ideas	30.7%
Validating an Idea in the Market	13.6%
Building a Business Model	11.4%
International Entrepreneurial Teamwork	72.7%
Pitching/Self-Presentation	22.7%
Other	6.8%

Firstly, participants were asked to report their key areas of learning during the programme. Respondents were asked to indicate the two areas within which they had learned most. Responses indicated that 72.7% of participants identified international entrepreneurial teamwork as one of the areas where they experienced their greatest learning, the largest area of learning by a margin of over 40%.

4. Discussion

At the conclusion of the 2016 cycle, 19 multi-nationality teams aspired to develop their start-ups to market readiness and commence commercial activity. This indicates that opportunity, and not a single nationality mind-set is the primary barrier to co-founder matchmaking across regional borders. The programme's virtual support structure has provided the opportunity for its participants to develop their multi-nationality projects to this point. However, these teams faced a new set of challenges in transitioning from the pre-incubation educational context of this programme, to physical incubation and commercial activity. Withdrawal of support at this crucial point in their lifecycle greatly heightens the risks of collaboration breakdown, due to the challenges of cross-regional entrepreneurial development in this difficult next step. Based on learnings from this project, the consortium has identified five specific pitfalls which may lead to the termination of cross-national start-up projects at this point:

- 1. Lack of a structured roadmap to market readiness in an international setting
- 2. Lack of dedicated mentorship support and structured feedback at a critical phase in the start-up lifecycle
- 3. Due to their geographical distribution, the teams must re-orientate from the educational setting to commercial operating structure in the absence of close incubation support.
- 4. Lack of a network which will connect the teams to new business partners
- 5. Lack of technical support in the development of their minimum viable product (MVP).

The dynamic entrepreneurship culture envisioned in EUXCEL is best represented in Pan-European founding teams that integrate young entrepreneurs from different cultures, countries, and disciplines. Within this programme, such teams were brought into existence. However, the absence of structures that will sustain their existence reflect the shortcomings in the connectivity of the European entrepreneurial ecosystem. Based on the potential to contribute to policy in this space, to build upon expert reviewer recommendations, and to fully capitalise on EUXCEL outcomes, the consortium proposed a 6-month extension to support the transition of its multi-nationality start-ups to market readiness. The consortium believe that this step is critical in consolidating the impact and long-term legacy of this project.

5. Conclusion

What are the major lessons one can draw from our analysis and case example presented regarding the encouragement of European-wide ICT entrepreneurship education. In posing this question of the relationship between IS and academic entrepreneurship, the presumption is that the case example and discussion presented are at least somewhat emblematic of the variety of IS academic entrepreneurship initiatives at other universities and capture the diversity of practices. This case demonstrates that teams of multi-national ICT professionals can come together and create 'Born-European' start-ups with the right support and mentoring. Distributed teams once socialised, can advance a start-up in a virtual manner.

We propose future research should be conducted to extend our research agenda to other countries in order to reflect on the frequency of such academic entrepreneurship practices emerging from IS disciplines. We shed light on the nature of IS entrepreneurship education and outline how there is a natural synergy between the discipline of IS and Entrepreneurship. We outlined a European-wide case that implemented an entrepreneurship teaching strategies and supports to encourage student entrepreneurship. We argue the significance of student entrepreneurship for the creation of world-changing ideas to be created and implemented. Thus, we argue IS and Entrepreneurship deserves future research and debate as our research agenda presented in the paper showcases an area which is ripe to discover.

Finally, the European entrepreneurship initiative demonstrates that a systematic educational programme can produce strong start-ups that continue long after the programme completion. A support ecosystem is required to facilitate the continuation of the early stage companies. There are clear policy implications for Europe, as this initiative demonstrated that 'Born European' companies can be created and mechanism that facilitate multi-national co-founders to come together are required to enhance an 'openness to Europe' mentality and ultimately create a European entrepreneurship identity.

Acknowledgements

EUXCEL was funded from the European Union's Horizon 2020 Research and Innovation Programme under Grant Agreement No 644801. Details are available at http://www.euxcel.eu

References

DJEI, (2014) Department of Jobs, Enterprise and Innovation. Entrepreneurship in Ireland–Strengthening the

Eurydice (2016). Entrepreneurship Education at School in Europe. Eurydice Report. Luxembourg: Publications Office of the European Union.

Guibernau, M. (2011). Prospects for a European identity. *International Journal of Politics, Culture, and Society*, *24*(1-2), 31-43.

Hennart, J. F. (2014) 'The Accidental Internationalists: A Theory of Born Globals', Entrepreneurship Theory and Practice, 38(1), 117-135.

Neck, H, Meyer, G, Cohen, B, & Corbett, A 2004. 'An Entrepreneurial System View of New Venture Creation', Journal of Small Business Management, 42, 2, pp. 190-208, Business Source Complete, EBSCOhost, viewed 9 March 2014.

Rasmussen, E. A., & Sørheim, R. 2006. Action-based entrepreneurship education. Technovation, 26(2), 185-194

Rennie, M.,W. (1993) 'Born global', Mckinsey Quarterly, 4, pp. 45-52, Business Source Complete, EBSCOhost, viewed 25 March 2014.

Spilling, O. R. (1996). 'The Entrepreneurial System: On Entrepreneurship in the Context of a Mega-Event', Journal of Business Research, 36, 1, pp. 91-103, Business Source Complete, EBSCOhost, viewed 17 March 2014

Striessnig, E. and Lutz, W. (2016), Demographic Strengthening of European Identity. Population and Development Review, 42: 305–311.

Van de Venn, H. 1993. The development of an infrastructure for entrepreneurship. Journal of Business venturing, 8(3), 211-230.

Van der Gaag, M. P. J., & Snijders, T. A. B. (2005). The Resource Generator: measurement of individual social capital with concrete items. *Social Networks, 27,* 1–29.

World Economic Forum. 2009. "Educating the Next Wave of Entrepreneurs - Unlocking entrepreneurial capabilities to meet the global challenges of the 21st Century", Switzerland: WEF. [pdf] Available at: <http://www.weforum.org/pdf/GEI/2009/Entrepreneurship_Education_Report.pdf > [Accessed 19 March 2014]

Literature Review: Impact Assessment of Research and Technology Organizations

Florian Kidschun, Fabian Hecklau, Holger Kohl and Berrak Sarikaya
Fraunhofer IPK, Berlin, Germany
florian.kidschun@ipk.fraunhofer.de
fabian.hecklau@ipk.fraunhofer.de
holger.kohl@tu-berlin.de
berrak.sarikaya@ipk.fraunhofer.de
DOI: 10.34190/EIE.20.122

Abstract: Due to their ability to bridge the gap between knowledge created by basic research and market requirements, Research and Technology Organizations (RTOs) play a major role in countries' innovation systems. Their R&D results should lead to innovations, which in turn generate the economic output of public investment in research and development. Moreover, they should support the foundation of new companies and industrial innovations. Given the continuing pressures of growing challenges, such as the digital transformation with its significant impact on organizations of all sectors, the changing behavior of customers and the rise of new business models, there is a higher demand for evaluating the actual contribution of RTOs in national innovation systems. It becomes essential for policy makers to gain a transparent insight into relevant and comprehensive performance metrics showing the impact of RTOs from a micro- and macroeconomic perspective. This is complemented by the increase of interest and funding in research and innovation in both public and private sectors. Governments and other clients seek to determine the value of their investments in applied R&D. Simply stating assumptions of achieving a positive impact is not enough anymore, RTOs must provide robust evidence that this impact is actually being accomplished by their research and innovation activities. Yet, the definition of impact and its operationalization in specific performance indicators seem to differ across literature. Against this background, this contribution aims to review impact assessment studies to address the challenge of a missing standard of impact assessment methods for RTOs. Therefore, existing impact studies of RTOs are to be analyzed and compared according to their overall approaches, frameworks and metrics. Therewith, possible limitations among the different assessment strands will be identified. Moreover, further methodological development possibilities for the impact assessment of RTOs will be discussed.

Keywords: Impact Assessment, Research & Technology Organizations, Performance Measurement, Innovation Performance, Innovation Measurement

1. Introduction

Technological and scientific enhancements (Acemoglu, Akcigit and Kerr, 2016) as well as rapid innovations (Pradhan et al., 2017) are the long-run vehicles for economic growth and sustainable prosperity in our highly competitive and fast changing global economy and society. Hence, innovation evolved into a new imperative in the centre of agendas of almost any policy makers in our world. According to Oxford Economics (2008) Research and Technology Organisations /RTOs) are becoming major actors in addressing these processes. Their operations range from providing basic research, R&D services, and products to different clients from a variety of fields, such as the industry, public organizations, or other administrations. This positions RTOs in a distinct way; they act as intermediaries between academia and industry whilst having strong relationships with the government. (Akrich and Miller, 2007).

Against this background, it comes as no surprise that many countries are counting on RTOs by considering them in their long-term strategies, especially concerning global challenges such as the Sustainable Development Goals (SDGs) of the United Nations. Countries all over the world have pledged to "build resilient infrastructure, promote inclusive and sustainable industrialization and foster innovation" (SDG9; U, 2020), meaning in particular to grow the number of researchers and substantially increase the public and private expenditures on R&D by 2030. According to the UNESO Institute for Statistics (2020) expenditures for Research and Development (R&D) has globally hit as good as US$ 1.7 trillion, while 10 countries cover 80% of funding. In this context, national targets for public funding on R&D has been set by many countries. For instance, one of the five key targets in the Europe 2020 strategy (2010) was to dedicate 3.00% of GDP to R&D funding. In 2017, the expenditure on R&D was situated at 2.06% (Eurostat, 2019). Germany's government and industry alone has achieved that target in the same year by spending 99.6 billion euros on R&D, which is an equivalent to 3.04% of the GDP (Federal Ministry of Education and Research, 2018).

In the light of these significant amounts of public funding for research organizations, the essentiality of comprehensible, comparable, and practical metrics for measuring the concrete impact and outputs of policy makers' public funding of research and innovation seems unambiguous.

Yet, the meaning of "impact" appears indefinite, or even vague as a concept to be assessed. The Oxford Dictionary says impact is generally "the action of one object coming forcibly into contact with one another; a marked effect or influence. The Research Impact Statement of the University of York defines impact in the context of research as follows: "... when the knowledge generated by our research contributes to, benefits and influences society, culture, our environment and the economy" (2016). Similarly, the Australian Research Council defines impact in a scientific manner, namely as "the demonstrable contribution that research makes to the economy, society, environment and culture beyond the contribution to academic research" (2017). The Methods Lab, an action-learning collaboration between the Overseas Development Institute (ODI), BetterEveluation (BE) and the Australian Development of Foreign Affairs and Trade (DFAT) published a report to get an understanding of the dimensionality of "impact" (2016). Certainly, their analysis indicate that impact happens to be multi-dimensional; how it is defined can depend on various factors, such as the authors of the evaluation, the project or the organization assessing the impact, or the stakeholders which are addressed with the impact evaluation.

Cheah and Yu (2016) compared diverse studies making this inconsistency issue (respecting the use of definition, metrics, theoretical and methodological approaches) roughly detectable. They outlined the different metrics, or theoretical and methodological approaches at the centre of the studies, which indicate the overall impact dimension: Impact as academic spin-offs (Colombo et al., 2010), impact as contribution to employment and income by the Lancaster University (Armstrong, 1993), impact as the licensed inventions from academic research of United States Universities (Carlsson and Fridh, 2002), impact as knowledge transfer in forms of publications, number of conferences, or any other exchange of information (Nelson, 2009), impact as the number of patents (Fischer and Varga, 2003), or impact as the intensity of technological transfer in partnership with companies (Bach and Llerena, 2007). In other words, a variety of perspectives on the term "impact" can be distinguished.

Yet, the focus of interest in Cheah and Yu's mentioned analysis (2016) laid on public research in and from universities. As a result, in this study, the literature review of impact assessment methods will be concentrated on four studies of Research and Technology Organizations (RTOs) in particular. Especially, because the fragmentation of literature in the R&D field can make it also problematic for policy makers to gain a fully comprehension about the value of their public funding for RTOs in specific. The increased need of monitoring and managing performance, showing accountability to government and society, and justification of expenditures for policy makers (Penfield et al., 2014) make it therefore also important to dig deeper into this issue with the slightly shifted focus on specifically RTOs.

This paper, therefore, aims to address this issue by reviewing impact studies which will be presented in the next chapters. Consequently, the result is expected to be an analysis of the different impact definitions, frameworks, methodologies, metrics, and finally, limitations.

2. Overview of Four Studies on Impact Assessment of Research & Technology Organizations

2.1 The Impact of Fraunhofer Gesellschaft on the German Innovation System 2016

The Fraunhofer-Institute for System and Innovation Research (ISI) conducted a survey itself on the Impact of the Fraunhofer-Gesellschaft on the German Innovation System in 2016. The researchers evaluated the multi-dimensionality of Fraunhofer's contributions with a systemic perspective. Hence, they have chosen a three-step approach to make them verifiable and quantifiable:

First, an *innovation-economic* analysis was used to demonstrate the role of Fraunhofer in the development of technology lines. Meyer-Krahmer and Dreher (2004) have proposed an ideal-typical model with the aim of a general description and classification of technology cycles and their stages. This ideal-typical model was subsequently transferred to real technological developments. In addition to document analyses of annual reports and other publications of the Fraunhofer-Gesellschaft, interviews with selected representatives from headquarters and selected institute directors were used as a starting point for identifying the technology lines in which Fraunhofer has made a special contribution over the past years. It was possible to identify lines of technology in which Fraunhofer has contributed significantly to the strong position and international competitiveness of German industry and Germany as a location for innovation. Besides, the impact of Fraunhofer is also reflected in scientific publications and patents. The generation, diffusion and application of scientific knowledge is of crucial importance for further technological activities and key elements of the scientific performance of national innovation systems (Moed et al., 2004; van Raan, 1988). In contrast, patents or their application or grant serve as a central indicator for assessing the technological performance of companies, technology fields and innovation systems in general. As an output indicator for research and development performance they serve to measure innovation potential and competitiveness (Freeman 1982; Grupp, 1998). Overall, the findings of the analysis present that Fraunhofer-Gesellschaft is currently responsible for 1.1% of all transnational patent applications in Germany. This is a considerable share, since the lion's share of all patent applications originates from companies. According to a study of Dornbusch et. Al. (2013) and Dornbusch & Neuhäusler (2015) Public research institutions are responsible for only about 2.1% of all applications from Germany. Although Fraunhofer only provides about 22% of the total scientific staff in public institutions in Germany (ibid, 2015), the organization achieves a share of about 52% of all patent applications of non-university research institutions.

Second, a *microeconomic* analysis was devoted to the structures and effects of cooperation between companies and Fraunhofer, i.e. the direct customer benefits of Fraunhofer research. In particular, the characteristics of companies that cooperate frequently with Fraunhofer were examined. For example, the question was whether the companies under consideration are more likely to serve end customers / consumer markets or to act as suppliers or intermediate manufacturers. In addition, it was also examined what direct benefit the respective cooperation partner of Fraunhofer has and whether product or market innovations are created. It was also investigated whether Fraunhofer's partners also benefit from the cooperation in terms of their financial performance. The basis for these analyses was the German survey of the European Manufacturing Survey, which was carried out in Germany by Fraunhofer ISI under the title "Modernization of Production (short: PI- Survey)". Two successive methods were applied. On the one hand, these are logit regressions for estimating the relationship between a cooperation with Fraunhofer and various dependent variables for measuring the innovation performance of companies and their cooperation intensity. Secondly, the models were again estimated on the basis of a matched-pair approach, in which the companies cooperating with the Fraunhofer-Gesellschaft are directly compared with "twin companies". The findings imply that for innovative companies, companies with a complex product portfolio and especially for small and medium-sized enterprises (SMEs), such cooperation with Fraunhofer are of particular importance. While there is no empirical evidence of a direct effect of cooperation with Fraunhofer on key financial figures for large companies, a significantly positive effect on operating income and EBIT (earnings before tax) could be found as evident for small and medium-sized companies. Partners in collaborative projects generally award Fraunhofer a direct research contract within three years of project completion. Furthermore, the analysis additionally showed that Fraunhofer Institutes have measurable economic effects on the respective metropolitan region in which they are located. These effects are particularly large when the economic return ratio is high.

Third, a *macroeconomic* analysis was conducted to explore Fraunhofer's contribution to the economy as a whole and to the regional economy in Germany. On this basis, estimates of Fraunhofer's economic, fiscal and employment effects could be made. The core indicators of the individual Fraunhofer Institutes were aggregated from the Fraunhofer SIGMA database at regional level (NUTS 3) and combined with regional economic data provided by the Federal Statistical Office (DESTATIS). Subsequently, panel data econometrics methods were used to identify the systematic relationships between regional Fraunhofer activity and regional economic core variables, whereby the researchers first concentrated on descriptive analyses and in the first multivariate step on the effects on GDP per capital. They presented the observable effects on broad economic core indicators, in particular technology development (patents per capita), labor productivity and the unemployment rate. The results of this analysis imply that in 2014, Fraunhofer (on the basis of approximately 1.1 billion € national project revenues) contributed about 20.1 billion € to the German gross domestic product (ratio about 1:18.3). In other words, this results in estimated additional tax revenues for the federal, state and local governments of about 4.1 billion €, with about 1.1 billion € of public financing.

2.2 The impact of the innovation, research and technology sector on the UK economy of Oxford Economics 2014

The Association for Innovation, Research and Technology Organisations (AIRTO) commissioned an independent study of the impact of the innovation, research and technology (IRT) sector on UK's economy (Oxford Economics,

2014) in 2012 and 2013. The study included 56 companies with AIRTO membership in the report's analysis, with the aim of examining the standard economic impact, the wider benefits of the IRT sector and an evaluation of six hypotheses related to the performance of the IRT sector. In this study, "impact" is therefore defined as an "comprehensive understanding of the sector's core impacts (including the impact of the sector itself, its supply chain impacts and wage-consumption impacts) as well as its extended impacts (such as spill-over returns to R&D, increased UK investment attractiveness, and an improved skills base)" (ibid, p. 1).

The standard economic impact was broken down to (1) the gross value added on UK economy, (2) employment rate, and (3) tax receipts. Moreover, the impact on the economy was categorized by the scholars in three types of expenditures: (1) direct impacts of IRT members' operational expenditure on trainings, consultancy, knowledge transfer, etc., (2) indirect impacts as a result of IRT organisations' expenditure on goods and services in the supply chain in the UK, and (3) induced impacts that result from IRT employees expenditure of their salary on goods and services in the UK.

To gather relevant data for the analysis the researchers collected financial statements as well as survey responses from the 56 AIRTO members in order to investigate the employment, gross value added and tax contributions to the IRT sector. Afterwards an individualized impact model of the UK economy was developed to screen the synergy-effects in the IRT sector's supply chain and additionally impacts of employee wages. Finally, Oxford Economics' leading research was used to combine them with AIRTO members' survey responses in an effort to measure wider impacts, for instance R&D spill-overs or human/knowledge capital improvements for the UK workplace. The results indicated that the turnover in the IRT sector in 2012/13 to be £6.9 billion, while having employed 57,200 people and having paid an estimated £6.9 billion in tax. When it comes to supply chain and wage-consumption impacts the results show that the IRT sector have contributed £7.6 billion to gross value added, to have supported 140,100 jobs and to have supported £2.9 billion in tax revenue. In addition, the results indicate that spill-over effects on the wider economy of the R&D activity in the sector alone were approximately at GBP 9,8 billion, while the study also demonstrates the IRT sectors' contribution to "difficult-to-quantify" effects connecting to inter alia attractiveness of investment or development of competences to be at around GBP 14.5-18.5 billion. As a result, the whole impact of the IRT sector to the UK economy is estimated at £32-36 billion, which is comparable to 2.3-2.6% of total UK gross value added in 2012/13.

2.3 Economic Footprint Study – Impact of 9 RTOs in 2016 of the European Association of Research and Technology Organisations 2016

In 2016 the European Association of Research and Technology Organizations (EARTO) conducted a meta-study specifically drawing attention to the economic impact of nine Research and Technology Organizations (RTOs), which were representing at that time one third of the EARTO members considering the workforce and the revenue. The economic contribution of the following RTOs were examined: The Austrian Institute of Technology (AIT), The French Alternative Energies and Atomic Energy Commission (CEA), The Danish Technology Institute (DTI), The Fraunhofer Institute (DE), The Belgian Interuniversity Microelectronics Centre (imec), The Norwegian Research Institute Stiftelsen for industriell og teknisk forskning (Sintef), The Spanish Research and Technology Centre (Tecnalia), Netherlands Organization for Applied Scientific Research (TNO) and The Technical Research Centre in Finland (VTT). Together, the group of RTOs represented a good mix of the RTO landscape, as they comprised either smaller or larger transnational organizations.

The aim of this study was to close the data gap and offer a robust observation of the economic impact in the EU Research and Innovation landscape. With this intention, EARTO commissioned this study to IDEA Consult, which in return estimated the economic footprint of the nine active EARTO members mentioned above. However, in this study other dimensions of impact (for instance, social or environmental) were not covered. Impact is understood by the authors as an economic effect resulting of different 'events' (e.g. project, product, process, policy development and/or implementation etc.). Economic impact analysis, on the other hand, is defined as an assessment of the changes which can be observed in case this 'event' occurs and what would have happened if not (counterfactual). Generally, the authors conducted monetary output indicators, such as in- or decrease in revenues.

In the underlying study, the focus of interest laid on two types of activities:
First, the RTOs economic advantage of key activities through expenditures and employment: Specifically, human capital, contract research, new business start-ups & spin-offs, and direct, indirect and induced expenditure effects. Second, the RTOs economic advantage of knowledge transfer and conversion. To measure the final

economic impact, IDEA consult designed an analytical framework which comprised the direct, indirect, induced and fiscal and parafiscal effects of those research activities. Direct economic effects contain employment, value added and output of the RTO, whereas indirect economic effects contain the supply of goods and services which in turn generate additional employment and demand for EU companies. Induced economic effects, on the other hand, are created through both direct and indirect spending activities on goods and services, which generate upstream turnover and employment. And all of these types of economic impacts lead to dynamics that generate fiscal and parafiscal effects for governments. The methodology for the measurement of each of these impacts was designed as follows:

1. Direct economic effects: The data employed was delivered by the RTOs and merged with a web and document analysis.
2. Indirect economic effects: Analysis of provided purchase and invoice data of the nine RTOs as well as EU sectoral averages for ratios like value added or employment. Furthermore, input-output tables from Eurostat were used in order to calculate upstream effects.
3. Induced economic effects: Average ratios of the European wide economy were the basis as IDEA consult didn't have precise insights of expenditures. The figures of direct and indirect effects were added and multiplied with the average figures of the sectors where RTOs had direct and indirect influence on employment.
4. Fiscal and parafiscal effects: Under consideration were three pillars, namely labor taxes, corporate taxes, and value added (CAT). Among others, they were based on data of labor for the EU (average implicit tax rate – ITR). These include personal income taxes as well as social security figures. Gross salaries of RTOs and suppliers from Eurostat were added to the ITR. Different NACE codes from Eurostat served as data basis for the turnover rate (corporate taxes).

The result of their analysis imply that the activities of RTOs created a total of 284,000 jobs, which is an equivalent to 35.8 billion euro. In other words, for each position in RTOs, there were four other jobs in different sectors in the European economy created. Above that, the total value added of the nine RTOs investigated amounted 16.8 billion euro, while core activities, contract research, and start-up activities generated up to 6.7 billion euro of fiscal return. In addition, the study found that every euro in investments in RTOs resulted in almost three euros in return to the national governments.

2.4 Social Balance Embrapa 2018

Another approach to impact assessment is offered by Embrapa (2019), the Brazilian Agricultural Research Corporation, a state-owned research organization affiliated to the Brazilian Ministry of Agriculture. After conducting, since 2001, an exclusively quantitative impact analysis of its implemented actions, Embrapa expanded and evolved its impact assessment in 2018 into a more structured and multiperspective methodology, based on its own upstream model named Ambitec-Agro (Social Impact and Agro-Technological Innovation Assessment System). As a result, the assessment of each of Embrapa's implemented technology or biological variety includes, apart from the widely known economic, social and environmental dimensions, a fourth dimension named "institutional development".

Concerning the organization's overall performance, the assessment of the economic impact in Brazilian economy is twofold. First, using the well-established Internal Rate of Return (IRR), it estimates a return of 37,6%. Second, it proposes the proportion of 1 (organization's net operational revenue) to 12 (generated social profit) – the latter including the economic impact of its created technologies and plant varieties. Regarding the social dimension, the impact appears, for instance, in terms of new jobs created through Embrapa's technologies (69,936 in 2018), but also the payment of taxes and non-compulsory social benefits as an employer (e.g. public and private pension, education and childcare, healthcare and work safety, etc.). The environmental real is considered regarding four aspects: reach, efficiency, contribution to environmental preservation and contribution to recovery of natural habitats (Magalhães et al., 2004). The newly included dimension "institutional development" differs from the other three by addressing the impact not from the perspective of external partners that adopt the technology or the broader society, but the Embrapa units that develop them. This dimension comprises four aspects, namely relational capacity, scientific-technological capacity, organizational capacity and R&D outcomes. These dimensions are measured according to eight different criteria and further broken down in 45 KPIs. Finally, the report highlights other aspects of Embrapa's impact such as its influence in the formulation of public policies, the total number of project outcomes and publications in scientific outlets, as well as the acknowledgement from society in the form of awards and honors.

3. Comparison

Table 1: Deductive and Qualitative Analysis: Similarities & Differences

	Social Balance, Embrapa 2018	**Economic Footprint Study, EARTO 2016**	**The Impact of Fraunhofer Research, Fraunhofer Gesellschaft 2016**	**The impact of the innovation, research and technology sector on the UK economy, Oxford Economics 2014**
Focus	Multi-perspective assessment of Embrapa's contribution to Brazilian society as a whole.	Economic impact assessment of 9 RTOs in the EU Research and Innovation landscape.	Assessment of Fraunhofer's contribution to the German science and innovation system.	Quantification of total economic contribution of the innovation, research and technology sector in UK
Objective	Systematically demonstrate and quantify Embrapa's contributions to the Brazilian society as a whole, as well as to its own institutional development.	Closing data gap in order to achieve objective and robust observations on economic contributions of RTOs in EU economy.	Systematically demonstrate and quantify Fraunhofer's contributions to the success of Germany as a location for business and innovation.	Discussing and quantifying the economic impact of the IRT sector on the UK economy in 2012/13.
Impact Definition	Impact as a set of multidimensional contributions to society. These contributions can be performed directly to society via own project outcomes as their consequences in the economic, social, environmental and Institutional realms, as well as indirectly via contribution to the formulation of public policies.	Impact as economic contribution on the EU economy through effects of spending, effects of RTOs daily activities and effects of knowledge transfer as well as conversion through a selected number of channels.	Impact as a systemic contribution to the German science and innovation system, divided into: - The innovation economic perspective (mostly technological impact) - The microeconomic perspective (effects from synergies between Fraunhofer and customers due to relations and cooperations) - The macroeconomic perspective (focusing on the monetary economic contribution).	Impact as a total economic contribution to the IRT sector, including 'core' economic effects and 'wider' economic effects, as well as benefits of the IRT sector.
Framework	The framework utilized comprises three dimensions from the perspective of adopting actors (economic, social, and environmental) and one from the perspective of the organization itself and its partners (institutional). Additionally, the study quantifies the number of concrete outcomes, the impact in the formulation of public policies, as well as the public acknowledgement through awards and honors.	Cost-based analysis of direct economic impact, indirect economic impact, induced economic impact, and fiscal & parafiscal impact. Additionally, technological spillover effects were measured (knowledge transfer through contract research, spinoffs and outflow of research staff).	A systemic perspective was chosen: - An innovation-economic analysis demonstrates the role of Fraunhofer in the development of technology lines - A microeconomic analysis is devoted to the structures and effects of cooperation between companies and Fraunhofer, i.e. the direct customer benefits of Fraunhofer's research - A macroeconomic analysis examines Fraunhofer's economic contribution to the overall and regional economy in Germany.	A wholesome perspective on economic impact was chosen: The direct economic impact, which was measured across three indicators (gross value added, employment ate and tax receipts), the indirect and induced economic impact, which was measured using an input-output modelling, and finally wider impacts, such as spillover benefits or knowledge transfer.
Methodology	Quantitative data analysis at project and organization levels by means of a set of KPIs associated to the aforementioned dimensions, as well as qualitative analysis of impact in public policies.	Input-output approach, combined with micro-data collected from nine EARO members participating in this study.	Qualitative interviews with selected representatives from headquarters and selected institute directors were used as a starting point for the innovation economic perspective, a descriptive analysis and several multivariate models were used to measure microeconomic effects and internal databases from individual Fraunhofer institutes combined with regional economic data served as the basis for the macro-economic perspective.	Three tools served as the basis for the assessment: A financial statement analysis (data from IRT organizations, including survey responses), a customized impact model (Input-Output modelling), and a detailed survey of the participating members, which were combined with the leading research from Oxford Economics.
Results	The main results demonstrate that, in 2018: - Each Real (R$) invested in the organization's operation generated 12,16 Real of social profit - The Internal Rate of Return (IRR) was 37,6% - The implemented technologies generated 69,936 new jobs - The organization's activity generated a total of 3.389 concrete outcomes.	Aggregated economic effects show: - 284,000 created jobs - € 35.8 billion in revenue - € 18.8 billion value added - € 6.7 billion in fiscal and parafiscal return to governments - One job in an RTO creates four jobs elsewhere in Europe - For € 1 invested in RTOs, € 3 flew back to governments in 2016.	For example, in the fields of laser technology, material sciences, and renewable energy, the German industry and innovation system benefits greatly from Fraunhofer for their international competitiveness. Furthermore, companies cooperating with Fraunhofer are more likely to launch new products and the majority (80%) of SMEs would collaborate with Fraunhofer again. Besides, companies' revenue climb by an average of 9%. In terms of effects on GDP, every euro of public investment to Fraunhofer generates four euros in return in form of higher tax revenues.	Aggregated economic impacts show: - £7.6 billion in gross value added - 140,100 jobs created - £2.9 billion in tax receipts - Private and spillover benefits at £9.8 billion - Investment attractiveness in the UK and skills development valued between £14.5-18.5 billion - All together Oxford Economics assumes the impact to be in the range of £32-36 billion, which is an equivalent to 2.3-2.6% of total UK gross value added in 2012/13.
Limitations	The high complexity of the study hinders its comprehensibility, since the final report does not go deep in the description of the structure and actual components of the framework. Therefore, the possibility to replicate or adapt the study for other settings is not given. Moreover, the role of certain KPIs mentioned in the study to the organization's impact is not clearly explained, for instance when it comes to the scientific production.	Since the study is based on the micro-data provided by the 9 RTOs, it cannot be guaranteed that the data is always complete, qualitatively correct or consistent. For instance, Data for value added and life cycle information on spin-offs weren't provided in two cases and investment shares were absent in one case.	Technologically successful customers often have no interest in disclosing their cooperation with Fraunhofer due to safety of competition-sensible information. Moreover, even in the event of disclosure, it is difficult to separate Fraunhofer's contribution from that of the customer (especially with process-oriented solutions). After all, an impact assessment can only ever be as good as the data on which it is based.	The dependency of the provided data by participating members of the study could be a problem when it comes to quality and completeness. Also, since the study concentrates solely on economic effects, social aspects as well as other influencing factors are ignored, which could have, in fact, additional impact on the economy in UK.

All four organizations show a different access to the focus of their studies. They differ in terms of their impact specialization, their target group, or their depth. While Embrapa (2018) decides to take a wider, multi-perspective look on impact on the society, EARTO (2016) and Oxford Economics (2014) are particularly interested in the economic impact in specific, except they differ in their national or international spectrum. Fraunhofer Gesellschaft, on the other hand, decided to focus on the science and innovation system, which, needless to say, influences their understanding and operationalization of impact, which will be outlined further below.

When it comes to the objective, any of the studies, aim to provide evidence, objectively quantify, or systematically categorize their understanding of impact. But in terms of the definition of impact, there can be differences observed, indeed. When comparing the four impact assessment studies, the first striking characteristic is the broad variety of the understanding of "impact". What contribution an organization makes to which area of society or the economy is a highly individual and subjective process, as it seems. Roughly speaking, it can be observed that the spectrum ranges from a systemic holistic approach (Embrapa, 2018 / Fraunhofer Gesellschaft, 2018) to a focused atomistic approach (EARTO, 2016 / Oxford Economics, 2014). However, if a deeper look is taken into the details, the scope of the definitions also differs. While Embrapa's Social Balance Study (2018) focuses specifically on society as the object of investigation (social dimension), the Fraunhofer Society's study (2016) concentrates on the German innovation and science system (technological-economic dimension). The Economic Footprint Study by EARTO (2016) and the Impact Study by Oxford Economics (2014) both focus on the specific economic contributions of RTOs, which in most cases consist of monetary and quantifiable indicators - except that the EARTO study deals with the entire European innovation system and the Oxford study with the innovation, science and technology sector in particular.

Consequently, these two studies show similarities in their frameworks. Both differentiate economic impact into direct, indirect, induced contributions and ultimately broader impacts, such as spillover effects or knowledge transfer. However, the studies, which underly a holistic approach (Embrapa, 2018 / Fraunhofer Gesellschaft, 2016) show differences in their frameworks. For example, Embrapa (2018) combines an institutional dimension (the inner perspective of the impact of the organization itself) with the economic, social and environmental dimensions (the outer perspective of the impact of the organization on the society). The Fraunhofer Gesellschaft (2016), then again, developed its own framework, which takes the science and innovation system into account. This results in a subdivision of impact into an innovation-economic, micro-economic and macro-economic perspective on the German innovation system.

What all studies have in common is that they all aim to make their own contributions to society or the economy quantifiable, comparable and comprehensible. Likewise, a form of quantitative content analysis (descriptive data analysis or mathematical analysis of content from various databases) or qualitative research (interviews or surveys) is a component of the evaluation. If the focus is on social, innovation-economic or ecological effects that cannot be directly quantified, qualitative methods are used or recommended by almost all studies, such as interviews, qualitative content analysis, or surveys. While the Fraunhofer Gesellschaft (2016) relies on qualitative interviews with representatives of headquarters and other selected institutes to evaluate technological competitiveness, Embrapa (2018) uses qualitative analysis to determine the impact in public policies. For economic-monetary effects, various quantitative methods are taken into account. For example, the two economic-focused studies by EARTO (2016) and Oxford Economics (2014) used both input-output modelling based on available data on revenues and expenditures of RTOs. The Fraunhofer Gesellschaft (2016), among other things, lean on different descriptive analysis and multivariate mathematical models to assess economic impact.

The results of most studies show that especially the indicators "jobs generated" and different shapes of return on investment (distinction between social profit (Embrapa, 2018), effects on the gross domestic product (Fraunhofer Gesellschaft, 2016), or taxes (EARTO, 2016)), and different spillover effects (e.g. knowledge transfer, skills development, attractiveness of the sector or industry) are seen as core effects on society or the economy. For example, the results of Oxford Economics (2014) imply that the investment attractiveness in the UK economy and the skills development was valued between £14.5-18.5 billion in 2014 due to the RTO activities and, therefore, contributions. The Economic Footprint Study of EARTO (2016), besides, took collaborative contract research and spin-off activities as a basis for spillover effects to evaluate economic leverage effects, such as the total number of created jobs, the value added in the European Economy or fiscal and parafiscal return to governments in 2016. They summarized those spill-over effects with core economic activities, and in this way, coming to their total aggregated economic impact values. In its results, the study of the Fraunhofer Gesellschaft (2016) dives deeper into more detail about the direct effects of cooperation with its customers (how many new products are launched and how many of the customers would cooperate with Fraunhofer again in the future) and summarizes which divisions contribute most to the success and competitiveness of the industry and the German innovation system (such as laser technology, material sciences, and renewable energy). Embrapa (2018), lastly, points further to the generated Internal Rate of Return (IRR), how many concrete projects have been realized and how many awards and other honors they have received on an institutional level.

Of course, all studies present implications. First and foremost, the comparability depends highly on transparency and comprehensibility of the framework, methodology, different KPI's and structure behind the study. This applies to all studies. Especially this is not given in the impact study of Embrapa (2018), which makes it difficult to adapt the study for different contexts. The Economic Footprint Study (2016) and Oxford Economics, furthermore, focused solely on economic factors, which, in fact, are important indicators for impact studies since they reflect objective and quantifiable data. But in this case, the quality and the source of the data influences the results. In the EARTO Study (2016), for example, in two cases information for value added and life cycle in spin-off's weren't given. Additionally, it is worth to discuss the extent to which social factors play another key role in impact assessments, since they can have additional effects on the economy. When it comes to the study of Fraunhofer Gesellschaft (2016) they outlined that it can be challenging to get information of the customers, since in some cases there exist non-disclosure agreements or their lack of interest due to competition-sensible information. Furthermore, even in events of successful disclosure of data, it could be complicated to separate the contributions to the final result from both sides, Fraunhofer Gesellschaft and customer.

4. Conclusion

The objective of this contribution was to provide an overview of impact assessment studies, including impact definitions, frameworks, methodologies, and limitations. By doing so, the paper offered insight into the importance of impact evaluations when it comes to showing credibility, effectiveness and accountability, since RTO's depend on investments both from policy makers and the industry. In this way, a number of ways on how impact of RTOs can be assessed, together with limitations which can occur, were presented. In order to gain an understanding of the impact of organizational activities, RTOs use different assessment methods, which address different impact dimensions.

Against this background, this impact assessment paper synthetized a few detailed studies of RTOs around the world that investigated whether their activities contributed objectively to the national innovation system, economy, society, or the environment. First, the chosen studies were consolidated and analyzed regarding their objective, definition of impact, framework, methodology, results and limitations. Second, the studies were compared based on the parameters mentioned above. And third, similarities and differences were identified and therewith opportunities and gaps for future research in this area.

The studies which were analyzed in this paper clearly imply that the impact assessment scope differ from organization to organization, and from context to context. In some cases, impact is associated with economic contributions alone, in other cases also with social and environmental effects. Up until now, there is still no consensus on how to define, operationalize and measure impact in the research and technology sector and consequently no standard that can be adapted in different fields and is accepted in different industries. These findings may suggest, that every RTO has unique synergies, processes, activities, customers, or disciplines, which makes it comprehensible why there are so many multifaceted techniques for measuring impact. Take academia; "impact" is generally associated with knowledge-related contributions to a specific area of discipline in the public research field, while companies in the private sector understand "impact" more from an economic perspective, like how much taxes they pay, or how many products they sell.

References

Acemoglu, D. et. al. (2016). Innovation network. *Proceedings of the National Academy of Sciences*, *113*(41), 11483-11488.

Akrich, M. and Miller, R. (2007). The Future of Key Research Actors in The European Research Area. Luxembourg: Office for Official Publications of the European Communities.

Armstrong, H. (1993). The local income and employment impact of Lancaster University. Urban Stud 30:1653–1668

Arnold, E. et. al. (2010). Impacts of European RTOs: A Study of Social and Economic Impacts of Research and Technology Organizations. A Report to EARTO, technopolis Group.

Australian Research Council. (2017). Engagement and impact assessment pilot 2017. [PDF]. Available at: https://www.arc.gov.au/file/5946/download?token=chR9gwjD

Austrian Cooperative Research (FFG). (2011). FFG – Wirkungsmonitoring 2010, [online] https://www.ffg.at/sites/default/files/wirkungsmonitoring2010.pdf.

Bach, L. and Llerena, P. (2007). Indicators of higher-education institutes and public-research organizations technology transfer activities: insights from France. Sci Public Policy 34(10):709–721

Behlau, L. (2012). Strategic Management of a Contract Research Organization - The Fraunhofer Model, Munich: Fraunhofer.

BMBF. (2020). Research and Innovation - BMBF's Data Portal. [online] Data Portal of Federal Ministry of Education and Research - BMBF. Available at: https://www.datenportal.bmbf.de/portal/en/research.html

Carlsson, B. and Fridh, AC. (2002). Technology transfer in United States universities: a survey and statistical analysis. J Evol Econ 12:199–232

Cheah, S., Yu, C. (2016). Assessing economic impact of research and innovation originating from public research institutions and universities—case of Singapore PRIs. Triple Helix 3, 6. https://doi.org/10.1186/s40604-016-0037-6

Colombo, M. et. a. (2010). An empirical analysis. J Technol Transf 35(1):113–140

Dornbusch, F. et. al. (2013). Identification of university- based patents: A new large-scale approach, Research Evaluation, 22, 52-63.

EARTO, European Association of Research and Technology Organization. (2015). Knowing your innovation ecosystem actors: data on European RTOs. Available at: https://www.earto.eu/about-rtos/

Ec.europa.eu. (2020). R & D Expenditure - Statistics Explained. [online] Available at: https://ec.europa.eu/eurostat/statistics-explained/index.php/R_%26_D_expenditure

Economic and Social Research Council. (2020). What Is Impact? -[online] Esrc.ukri.org. Available at: https://esrc.ukri.org/research/impact-toolkit/what-is-impact/

European Commission and RISE. (2015). Value of Research: Policy Paper by The Research, Innovation, And Science Policy Experts (RISE). [ebook] Brussels: European Commission. Available at: https://ec.europa.eu/futurium/en/system/files/ged/60_-_rise-value_of_research-june15_1.pdf

European Commission. (2010). Europe 2020: A European Strategy for Smart, Sustainable And Inclusive Growth. [PDF] Brussels: European Commission. Available at: https://ec.europa.eu/eu2020/pdf/COMPLET%20EN%20BARROSO%20%20%20007%20-%20Europe%202020%20-%20EN%20version.pdf

Fischer, MM. and Varga, A. (2003). Spatial knowledge spillovers and university research: evidence from Austria. Ann Reg Sci 37:303–22

Fraunhofer-Gesellschaft (2011). Strategic Management of a Contract Research Organization - The Fraunhofer Model. München: Fraunhofer.

Freeman, C. (1982). The Economics of Industrial Innovation. London: Pinter Publishers.

Frietsch, R. et. al. (2016). Der Beitrag der Fraunhofer-Gesellschaft zum Deutschen Innovationssystem, Fraunhofer ISI, [online] https://www.fraunhofer.de/en/research/range-of-services/impact-of-fraunhofer-research.html.

Guthrie, S. et. al. (2013). Measuring research - A guide to

Hearn, S. and Buffardi, A.L. (2016). 'What is impact?'. A Methods Lab publication. London: Overseas

IDEA Consult. (2016). Economic Footprint Of 9 European RTOs in 2015-2016. [online] Brussels: EARTO – European Association of Research and Technology Organisations. Available at: <https://www.earto.eu/wp-content/uploads/EARTO-Economic-Footprint-Study-Impact-of-9-RTOs-in-2015-2016-Final-Report.pdf> [Accessed 27 March 2020].

Meyer-Krahmer, F. and Dreher, C. (2004). Neuere Betrachtungen zur Technikzyklen und Implikationen für die Fraunhofer-Gesellschaft. (2004). In: Spath, D.: Forschungs- und Technologiemanagement. Potenziale nutzen - Zukunft gestalten. München: Hanser.

Modrego, A. et al. (2009). "Hacia una medida de la contribución de los Centros Tecnológicos (CTs) españoles a la mejora de la competitividad de las empresas.", FEDIT – DOSSIER.

Moed, H.F. et. al. (2004). Handbook of Quantitative Science and Technology Research. The Use of Publications and Patent Statistics in Studies of S&T Systems. Dordrecht: Kluwer Academic Publisher.

Nelson, AJ. (2009). Measuring knowledge spillovers: what patents, licenses and publications reveal about innovation diffusion. Res Policy 38:994–1005

Netherlands Organization for Applied Scientific Research (2006). Effectmeeting TNO Cofinancieringsprogramma, internal document.

Oxford Economics. (2014). The impact of the innovation, research and technology sector on the UK economy, [online] https://www.oxfordeconomics.com/recent-releases/the-impact-of-the-innovation-research-and-technology-sector-on-the-uk-economy.

Oxford Economics. Study of The Impact of The Intermediate Research And Technology Sector On The UK Economy. (2008). [PDF]. Available at: http://www.airto.co.uk/wp-content/uploads/2015/08/oxfordeconomics.pdf

Penfield, T. et. al. (2014) Assessment, evaluations, and definitions of research impact: a review. Res Eval 23:21–32

Pradhan, R. et. al. (2017). Does innovation promote economic growth? Evidence from European countries. Journal of Innovation and Entrepreneurship, 6.

research evaluation frameworks and tools. Report MG-1217-AAMC. RAND Europe

Rogers, E. (1995). Diffusion of Innovations, Fourth Edition, 4. Aufl., Amsterdam, Nederland: Amsterdam University Press.

United Nations Sustainable Development. (2020). Infrastructure and Industrialization - United Nations Sustainable Development. (2020) [online] Available at: https://www.un.org/sustainabledevelopment/infrastructure-industrialization/

York.ac.uk. (2020). What Is Research Impact? - Staff Home, The University Of York. [online] Available at: https://www.york.ac.uk/staff/research/research-impact/impact-definition/

Dialectics of the Renewable Energy Market

Evgeniy A. Konnikov[1], Olga A. Konnikova[2], Yulia A. Dubolazova[1] and Ruslan D. Mansurov[1]
[1]Peter the Great St. Petersburg Polytechnic University (SPbPU), Russia
[2]St. Petersburg State University of Economics, Russia
konnikov.evgeniy@gmail.com
olga.a.konnikova@gmail.com
julia005@mail.ru
wozen@yandex.ru
DOI: 10.34190/EIE.20.068

Abstract: The subject of the research in the article is scientific-theoretical, organizational-economic, legal, labour and social problems of sharing economy. Anthropogenic pollution is considered to be one of the most important global problems of our time. Worldwide industrial development, widespread use of combustible minerals as energy sources leads to the accumulation of greenhouse gases in the atmosphere. This process contributes to mass climate changes. The Paris Climate Agreement, signed by 175 countries, is the evidence that the vast majority of countries in the world are aware of the scale of the problem and are ready to make efforts to limit global temperature growth. One of the ways to achieve the goals of the Paris Agreement is a low-emission development direction: switching to energy from renewable sources. Technological development makes such energy more widely used, accessible to a wide range of consumers, but growth rate of energy consumption from renewable energy sources is still insufficient. Also, investments in renewable energy show disappointing dynamics in recent years. If these trends continue, the achievement of global goals is at high risk. In this regard, the purpose of this study is to identify factors affecting investments in renewable energy and to propose methods that contribute to the growth of investments. Based on the results of regression analysis, the authors came to the conclusion that the nature of the renewable energy market is rather dialectic. The results of this study may be useful to national governments, international organizations, which aim to increase investments in renewable energy to stimulate the development of this energy sector.

Keywords: renewable energy market, market development dialectic, wind power generation, solar power generation, investment in renewable energy

1. Introduction

One of the most important problems our days is anthropogenic pollution of the environment. The development of industry, the widespread use of combustible minerals as energy sources leads to the accumulation of greenhouse gases in the atmosphere. This process contributes to the development of another global problem: climate change. The Paris Climate Agreement, which was signed by 175 countries, is evidence that the vast majority of countries in the world are aware of the scale of the problem and are ready to make efforts to limit global temperature growth to 1.5 ° C. One way to achieve the goals of the Paris Agreement is to bring financial flows towards a low-emission development direction.

One way to reduce emissions is to switch to energy from renewable sources. With the development of technology, such energy is becoming more widely used, becoming more accessible to a wide range of consumers, but the rate of growth of energy consumption from renewable energy sources is still insufficient to achieve the goals set by the Paris Agreement.

In this regard, the purpose of this study is to identify factors affecting investments in renewable energy and the proposal of impact methods that contribute to the growth of investments.

In this regard, the purpose of this study is to identify factors affecting investments in renewable energy and the proposal of impact methods that contribute to the growth of investments.

As part of the study, the following tasks were set:

- analyze the theoretical basis, study the specifics of investments in the renewable energy market;
- to formulate a research methodology;
- implement a methodology and obtain an econometric result (a model describing the nature and strength of the relationship between endogenous and exogenous variables);
- to analyse the simulation results;

- formulate recommendations on how to influence investments in renewable energy to stimulate the development of this market.

The object of this study is the renewable energy market and its specifics. The subject matter is the factors affecting the volume of investments in green energy.

The results of the study may be useful to governments and international organizations aimed at bringing financial flows towards a development characterized by low emissions.

2. Statement and description of the research problem

First of all, a study of the theoretical basis for the formation of the primary complex of factors that can influence the volume of investment should be carried out. (Chebotareva et al., 2019) noted that over the past few years, the volume of investments aimed at developing new capacities in renewable energy sources exceeds the amount of financing of traditional energy. In this regard, the relevance of studying the motives that drive investors in financing renewable energy projects is growing. The authors emphasize state support and the price at which the produced energy can be sold as two main factors that are fundamental in assessing the attractiveness of projects affecting the volume of investment. It is noted that the main indicator determining investment attractiveness is the level of stability and predictability of public policy. Based on the results of studying the structure of sources of world investment, it turned out that the growth of the renewable energy market is not ensured by state financing of the sector, but by private investment. Other researches also believe that it is worth exploring primarily market factors that affect the volume of investment in renewable energy (Rodionov et al., 2018).

Otherwise, in (Global Trends in Renewable Energy Investment, 2019) is noted that over the past decade, the cost of energy generated by the sun and wind has decreased significantly. Cost reduction can potentially attract new investors, as this helps to reduce risks associated with long payback periods for renewable energy projects due to high capital intensity. It is noted that renewable energy technologies require a high level of capital costs, however, in the case of solar and wind energy, maintenance costs are relatively low. This leads to the fact that solar and wind energy is becoming cheaper than the energy obtained by coal in a number of countries. This factor is the main driver for the growth of solar module installations for generating electricity, which allows this technology to confidently lead among other types of alternative energy. (Khabachev et al., 2018) note that, despite the low cost of solar energy, solar panels operate in the range of 11-35% of potential power (depending on illumination), while combustible minerals can produce full power at any time of the day and under any conditions. This allows to conclude that the power level of renewable energy generation plants should be taken into account when identifying factors affecting the volume of investments in renewable energy projects. (Lebedev et al., 2018) noted that there is a lag between making the final investment decision (when the cash flow is fixed) and between the commissioning of this facility. In the case of solar panels, the lag is from 3 to 6 months, in the case of land-based wind generators it is 1 year, and for coastal (offshore) wind generators, geothermal stations and bioenergy, the lag is from 2 to 4 years. In this regard, authors of the current paper consider to first of all take into account indicators of solar and wind energy generation that are potentially capable of influencing the investment attractiveness of renewable energy projects. This will allow the most reliable study of the relationship between such indicators as the total capacity of solar installations, the total capacity of land and coastal (offshore) wind generators and the level of investment in renewable energy. Moreover, (Rodionov et al., 2017) note a significant impact on the level of investment by the simultaneous launch of a number of large-scale projects. So, after the launch of a relatively high number of high-power coastal (offshore) power plants in one year, there may be less growth in investments (or a decrease in the overall level of investments) in the next year. Solar energy (solar PV) and ground-based wind generators (onshore wind) are the cheapest in terms of capital costs, other technologies are much more expensive. The authors note that if it had not been for recent years' investments in renewable energy, the level of carbon dioxide emissions would have been higher by 15% in 2018.

At another point, (Akhmedov, 2018) discusses mechanisms to support the development of renewable sources. The author provides the main mechanisms for supporting renewable projects, such as the use of feed-in-premium and feed-in-tariff, unhindered connection to technological networks as a generating source, and subsidizing the costs of acquiring equipment for generating energy from renewable sources. However, (Sushko et al., 2017) consider an assessment of the application of preferential tariffs and subsidies at the global level will not allow reliable conclusions. In addition, it is noted that changes are taking place in the policy of state support for the new energy sector, the support mechanism is moving to market conditions by auctions and tenders that helps to reduce the final cost of energy and contributes to the growth of investments in renewable energy sources. The ability to compete with traditional energy increases the investment attractiveness of renewable energy projects and, therefore, it is necessary to take into account scientific and technological progress as a factor affecting investments in renewable energy sources. (Balashova & Gromova, 2017).

(Sedash, 2016) by analyzing world experience notes that the following tools are used to stimulate investments in renewable energy: preferential tax rates (or tax exemptions), soft loans, subsidies for special tariffs for electricity from renewable energy sources, subsidies for producers, grants. Despite these factors have a certain impact on the volume of investments, their reliable quantitative assessment is difficult (Bekbaev et al., 2019).

It is also reported that high levels of subsidies allocated by the state for the development of renewable energy can lead to the deindustrialization of the country, and there is a tendency to move from measures of strict state regulation of renewable energy sources to market instruments to stimulate their development. Such a trend allows to abandon the study of the relationship between the level of investment in renewable energy and public policy and focus on market drivers of investment growth in this area (Rodionov & Rudskaia, 2018).

These include the total cost of using various types of renewable energy (the cost of technology), the total capacity of already installed systems, and others. Exploring the reasons for a significant decrease in investments in renewable energy in the EU, Sedash identifies a technological breakthrough that has led to cheaper production, technologies and equipment for wind and solar power plants. The author notes the tendency to simultaneously combine in government programs the goals of both renewable energy growth and energy efficiency and energy saving. This opinion drew our attention to factors that could reflect the level of technology in the field of energy efficiency and energy conservation. Due to the dependence of renewable energy on external conditions (light, wind force, tides, etc.), lithium-ion batteries are used to accumulate the generated electricity. The charge accumulated during the high activity of the generator is gradually consumed during the period when the installation power drops, which significantly increases energy efficiency. Based on this, we believe that the price of lithium and its production volumes can also affect the level of investment in renewable energy.

In (Renewables 2019 Global Status Report, 2019) it is noted that renewable energy investments focus primarily on solar-related technologies because of the relatively lower overall cost of generating such type of energy.

The authors, exploring the reason for the double reduction of solar energy investments in China in 2018, note a change in the state preferential tariff policy. In addition, there has been a decline in investments in solar energy in India due to increased uncertainty in import tariffs and exchange rates. In general, the decrease in the global level of investments in solar energy in 2018 is explained by experts as a result of a reduction in investments in solar energy in China (as in the leading country in the use of renewable energy sources) and the consequences of a reduction in capital costs for projects related to solar panels. Considering bioenergy, the authors note that most of the investments were allocated for R&D.

(Zogo et al., 2017) report that, due to the high investment costs at the initial stage of the implementation of renewable energy projects, financing is often carried out under the public-private scheme partnership. The authors attribute this to the fact that governments experience difficulties in independently financing such projects that require large investments. The government concludes long-term contracts with private investors to guarantee incentives or other support measures over a period of time. At the same time, the authors believe that the use of renewable energy is a source of social benefits such as improving the environment, the quality of medical and educational services. We believe that private investment and market mechanisms can more efficiently stimulate the development of renewable energy, while creating a win-win environment where some get cheap energy, and the entire population of the Earth gets the opportunity to have a less detrimental effect on the environment. Based on this, we believe that we should focus on factors that influence the volume of investments within the framework of the market mechanism, while not taking into account government participation.

At another point, (Bushukina, 2019) draws attention to the fact that there are a number of financial risks and barriers in financing renewable energy projects, while the main factor that creates these risks and barriers is the high cost of renewable energy projects. Agreeing with the author, we assume that the cost of renewable energy projects is one of the key factors affecting the level of investment in this area. It is also noted that a shift in the structure of investments towards solar energy, and the factors causing this shift include a reduction in the cost of production of solar panels and an increase in their productivity (Nikolova et al., 2017). In our opinion, this is achieved mainly through the development of solar energy technologies, therefore, in our study we will assess how the level of technology development affects the volume of investments in renewable energy sources.

Further research by Bushukina states that with a high level of capital investment in the construction of renewable energy stations, their operating costs are low. In our opinion, this is reflected in the LCOE indicator (levelized cost of electricity). The relatively low cost of electricity generation is achieved due to low operating costs over a long period of time. The low cost of electricity contributes to an increase in demand for such energy, which, in turn, attracts investors. Therefore, it is worth exploring the impact of LCOE on investment in renewable energy (Zaychenko et al., 2018). Bushukina notes that the governments stimulate this industry by developing support programs and various state structures, however, the current trend in European countries is the rejection of a significant part of state support for renewable energy projects due to the growing competitiveness of renewable energy power plants. The author notes that the reason for the slow development of renewable energy in the Russian Federation is an imperfect technological base, which in turn is the result of a lack of sufficient investment in R&D.

(Zhai & Lee, 2019) explore the reasons for the decline in renewable energy investments in 2018. The authors believe one of the main factors to be the reduction in the cost of installing solar and wind electricity generators. This leads to the fact that launching projects of the same level of capacity requires less investment. Taking into account the opinion of the authors, we believe that the power of installed solar or wind energy sources can affect the level of investment in renewable energy, so this indicator should be considered in our study.

(Pernik & Slen, 2018) draw attention to the fact that the technological breakthrough has allowed to open up significant economies of scale available with renewable energy sources. Among the main drivers of alternative energy growth, the authors highlight the reduction in the cost of energy production from renewable energy sources, global electrification and the introduction of restrictions on the volume of carbon dioxide emissions into the atmosphere. In addition, there is a shift in investments from fossil fuels towards renewables, as well as an increase in the demand for "clean energy" both in corporate sector and among households.

Summarizing Literature review section, it is worth saying that the level of investment in renewable energy is a comprehensive indicator that depends on many factors, both quantitative and qualitative. A literature review revealed a number of quantitative variables potentially affecting investments that can be reliably interpreted when studying dependencies at the global level. In addition, it helped to conclude that it is necessary to focus on the energy generated by the sun and wind, since these two types of renewable energy, having a low cost, attract the vast majority of investments in the industry. Despite the significant influence exerted by state policy and the support in the form of subsidies and benefits, we considered it inappropriate to take into account such factors for several reasons. Firstly, a reliable quantitative assessment of these factors is difficult.

Secondly, the interpretation of these indicators at the global level may be erroneous in view of the fact that the policies pursued by different countries to support the generation of energy from renewable sources differ. Thirdly, there is a tendency towards a transition from measures of state regulation of renewable energy sources to market instruments to stimulate their development. In our opinion, this trend allows to abandon the study of the relationship between the level of investment in renewable energy and public policy and focus on market drivers of investment growth in this area.

3. The methodological basis of the research

The methodology of this study is based on the classical methodology of regression analysis. The relationships between time series are investigated. The first stage involves the determination of endogenous and exogenous variables of the future regression model. Since the study is conducted at a global level, all variables reflect aggregate values around the world. The authors limited themselves to this time period for the reason indicated below, when introducing the variable "Number of patents". New investments in renewable energy (hereinafter "Investments") are the subject of ongoing research, therefore, this indicator will act as an endogenous variable.

Additional areas of research are the study of the impact of investments on the production of electricity from renewable sources (hereinafter referred to as "Production") and on the share of energy consumption generated from renewable sources in the total volume of consumption (hereinafter "Share of consumption"). A study of these relationships will allow us to conclude whether it is possible to influence the Production and the Share of consumption by changing the level of Investments. Production and consumption share also play the role of endogenous variables. The independent variables were indicators that will be considered later.

The following variables are indicators reflecting the total capacity of installed solar and wind energy generators. There are two types of renewable energy sources, for three reasons: 1) low cost of electricity produced; 2) because of this, wide popularity and prevalence (solar panels are the leaders in terms of investment among all other types of renewable energy sources); 3) as a result of an increase in the efficiency of solar or wind turbines, a lower level of investment is required to launch the same level of projects, which increases the availability of renewable energy technologies, and hence investment attractiveness.

In our opinion, the deterioration of air quality contributes to increased attention to the problems of air pollution and global warming. Consider the amount of carbon dioxide emissions into the atmosphere (hereinafter "CO_2 Emissions") as one of the factors affecting the level of investment in renewable energy. The final set of variables is presented in table 1.

Table 1: Endogenous and exogenous variables

№	Variable	Variable type	Symbol	Units
1.	Investment	Endogenous	Y	billion $
2.	Aggregate transactions	Exogenous	X_1	billion $
3.	Number of patents	Exogenous	X_2	pcs
4.	Google trends. Renewable energy	Exogenous	X_3	pcs
5.	Google trends. Solar Panel	Exogenous	X_4	pcs
6.	Google trends. Onshore wind	Exogenous	X_5	pcs
7.	Google trends. Small wind turbine	Exogenous	X_6	pcs
8.	Production	Endogenous	Z	TWh
9.	Power of solar cells	Exogenous	X_7	MW
10.	The cost of the solar panel module	Exogenous	X_8	USD / kW
11.	Power of solar panel	Exogenous	X_9	MW
12.	Power of wind generators	Exogenous	X_{10}	MW
13.	Share of consumption	Endogenous	Q	%
14.	N.V. total installation cost	Exogenous	X_{11}	USD / kW
15.	N.V. LCOE	Exogenous	X_{12}	USD / kW
16.	P.V. share of power	Exogenous	X_{13}	%
17.	N.V. total installation cost	Exogenous	X_{14}	USD / kW
18.	P.V. LCOE	Exogenous	X_{15}	USD / kW
19.	P.V. share of power	Exogenous	X_{16}	%
20.	P.V. Turbine size	Exogenous	X_{17}	MW
21.	Emissions CO^2	Exogenous	X_{18}	mln. tons

The structure of relations between these factors can be represented as a conceptual model (Figure 1).

All exogenous variables included in the study have an impact on Investments. Investments, in turn, affect the Production and Share of Consumption, as they are a necessary resource for the development of technologies and the spread of renewable energy. The power of solar cells, solar panels and wind generators, in addition to influencing Investments, also affects Production with a Share of Consumption, since these indicators characterize the efficiency of electricity generators and their potential ability to satisfy energy demand. Based on the results of the study, we will adjust the model, leaving only significant relationships.

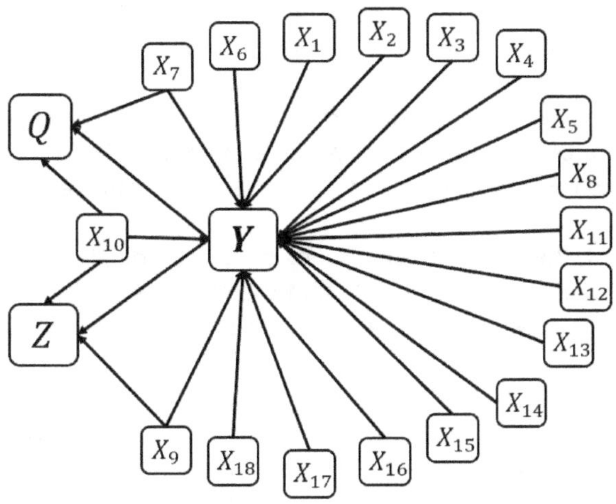

Figure 1: Theoretical conceptual model

The factors we are considering will be added to the regression model to further explore the relationships between regressors and dependent variables. The study of the influence of factors on dependent variables is carried out in isolation: when building a model with one endogenous variable, the other two endogenous variables, along with the others, act as exogenous. In total, three models will be built and there will be one endogenous variable in every model. The central model, the purpose of the study, describes how various factors influence the Investment. Models reflecting the influence of various factors on Production and Share of Consumption are secondary to this study.

When conducting a regression analysis, you should verify the significance and reliability of the model obtained as a result of the study. The characteristics that allow us to conclude about the quality of the model are:

- The significance level of the model. This indicator is set by the researcher depending on the type of study and the expected results. The significance level of the model reflects the probability of the model to make a mistake, we take the significance level not exceeding 0.1, i.e. 10%.
- Coefficient of determination. This criterion allows us to estimate the proportion of variance explained by factors. The normalized R2 in our study is taken at a level not lower than 80% so that the model can be considered effective
- P-level. This indicator reflects the probability with which the null hypothesis can be erroneously rejected (that the exogenous variable does not have a significant effect on the endogenous). Since the significance level of the model was set to at least 0.1, then the p-level for each of the regressors should not exceed 10%.
- The approximation error allows us to assess the quality of the resulting model and reflects the average relative deviation of the calculated values from the actual ones.

4. Research results

According to the results of processing statistical data, the following model was obtained:

$$Y = 422{,}7496 + 0{,}0055X_2 + 0{,}0012X_7 + 0{,}0601X_8 - 0.2901X_{11} - 382{,}4192X_{16}$$

Y - investment (billion dollars);
X_2- the number of patents;
X_7 - power of solar cells (MW);
X_8 - the cost of the solar panel module (USD / kW);
X_{11} - N.V. total installation cost (USD / kW);
X_{16} - P.V. share of power (%).

This model allows us to describe 98% of the variance (normalized R2 = 98.09%), while, on average, the calculated values deviate from the actual by 6% (approximation error of 6.17%), which is acceptable in such regression models. The resulting model is significant because with a confidence level of 90% specified in the methodology, the F-significance is 1.10 * E-06. The P-level of each of the regressors also does not exceed 6%, which corresponds to a given level of confidence in the model (with it, the p-level should not exceed 10%).

These characteristics indicate that the constructed model describes the relationships arising between the regressors and the dependent variable with the necessary accuracy.

In accordance with our methodology, a number of factors were excluded from it to obtain the final form of the model. Among them are statistics on search queries in Google Trends, N.V. LCOE, P.V., LCOE, P.V. Size, Aggregate Transactions, P.V. The total cost of the installation, N.V. Percentage of capacity, Emissions CO_2.

Given the quality indicators of the constructed model and, accordingly, the high approximation of the calculated values to the actual ones, we can conclude that the model is significant. This allows you to move on to the next stage to research how Investments affect the Consumption Share and how they affect Production.

To study the relationship between the Share of Consumption (as an endogenous variable) and Investments (as an exogenous variable), two models were constructed. The first model is the paired regression model. Despite the fact that the model turned out to be significant, Investments described only 47% of the variance.

The second model is a multiple regression model, in which, in addition to Investments, factors from Table 1 were added as exogenous variables. In accordance with our methodology, insignificant regressors were excluded from the model. As a result, this model is significant and describes 98% of the variance. It is worth noting that there are no Investments among the regressors. This implies the following: despite the fact that investments, if we consider them separately, have a certain impact on the Consumption share, other factors more effectively describe the variance (this is confirmed by the second model), which means that the influence of Investments on the Consumption Share can be neglected.

Similarly, factors affecting Production were identified. The model of paired regression of Production and Investment turned out to be significant, while describing 75% of the variance, which is slightly lower than the satisfactory level established in our study. In turn, from the significant model of multiple regression that initially included the factors from Table 1, and in the final iteration explaining 99% of the variance, Investments were excluded. It turns out that, as in the case of the Share of Consumption, there are other factors that describe the variance more efficiently than the Investments, therefore the relationship between Production and Investment is not significant

As a result, a new conceptual model was constructed (Figure 2), reflecting the relationships identified as a result of the construction of regression models. Non-significant factors were excluded from this model in accordance with our methodology.

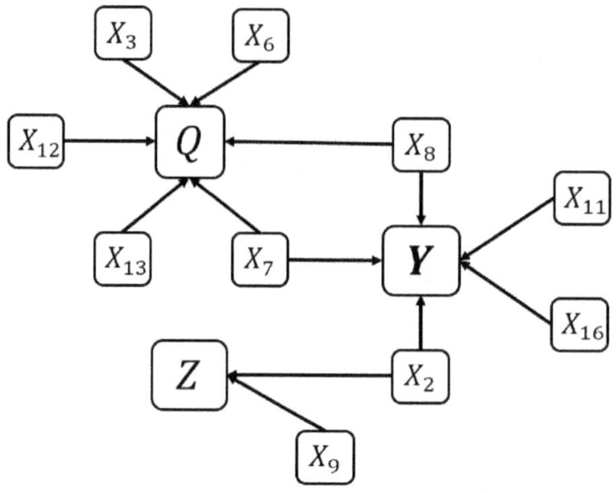

Figure 2: New conceptual model

Having identified the factors affecting the Investments, we evaluate the degree of influence of each of the regressors included in the final iteration of the main regression model, in which the Investments act as the endogenous variable.

After calculating the coefficient of elasticity for each factor and constructing a histogram of these values, it was possible to draw the following conclusions. The greatest impact on the volume of investments in renewable energy is exerted by the total cost of installing ground-based wind generators and the number of patents filed. At the same time, an increase in the number of patents filed leads to a significant increase in investments, and the most effective driver for increasing investments in renewable energy is to reduce the total cost of installing ground-based wind electricity generators. So, with an increase in the number of patents filed by 1% of the average value and a simultaneous reduction in the total cost of installing wind generators by 1% of the average value, the growth in investment will average 3.17%.

According to the results of our study, the most rational steps to increase the level of Investments are to stimulate the growth of the number of patents and to help create the conditions under which the total cost of installing ground-based wind generators will decrease.

The number of patents filed directly depends on the demand for renewable energy technologies and on grants (financing) allocated for the development of this field. It is important to identify the importance of "green energy" in terms of the global goals of humanity and the direct benefits of using renewable energy for companies and households. This will create the demand for energy from renewable energy sources, which, in turn, will allow attracting a larger amount of financing, which will not only become an incentive for scientists, but also provide an opportunity to develop more technological and energy-efficient solutions.

5. Discussion of the study results

After calculating the coefficient of elasticity for each factor and constructing a histogram of these values, it was possible to draw the following conclusions. The greatest impact on the volume of investments in renewable energy is exerted by the total cost of installing ground-based wind generators and the number of patents filed.

At the same time, an increase in the number of patents filed leads to a significant increase in investments, and the most effective driver for increasing investments in renewable energy is to reduce the total cost of installing ground-based wind electricity generators. So, with an increase in the number of patents filed by 1% of the average value and a simultaneous reduction in the total cost of installing wind generators by 1% of the average value, the growth in investment will average 3.17%.

According to the results of our study, the most rational steps to increase the level of Investments are to stimulate the growth of the number of patents and to help create the conditions under which the total cost of installing ground-based wind generators will decrease.

The number of patents filed directly depends on the demand for renewable energy technologies and on grants (financing) allocated for the development of this field. It is important to identify the importance of "green energy" in terms of the global goals of humanity and the direct benefits of using renewable energy for companies and households. This will create the demand for energy from renewable energy sources, which, in turn, will allow attracting a larger amount of financing, which will not only become an incentive for scientists, but also provide an opportunity to develop more technological and energy-efficient solutions.

6. Conclusion

In the framework of the study, regression models were built, the central model was an equation describing the nature of the influence of a number of factors on investments in renewable energy. The influence of each of the factors was assessed and a scenario analysis of sensitivity was carried out: the effect of changing the values of the regressors by 1% in the direction conducive to the growth of investments over three years was calculated. As a result of this change in values, the total cumulative investment volume grew by 1.7%.

The results of this study may be useful to national governments, international organizations, which aim to increase investment in renewable energy to stimulate the development of this energy sector.

Analysing the results, we came to the following conclusion: there is a dialectic of the renewable energy market. A prerequisite for increasing investment in green energy is the influx of investment into this market as a means to develop technology. Indirect methods of influence, such as stimulating a conscious demand for "green energy", will give a greater impetus to the development of this industry, the growth of Investments, and will provide access to a new level in a shorter time.

Acknowledgement

This research work was supported by the Academic Excellence Project 5 100 proposed by Peter the Great St. Petersburg Polytechnic University

References

Akhmedov, V.S. "World experience in investing in alternative energy", Publishing House of Tomsk State University of Architecture and Civil Engineering. 2018 (in Russian)

Balashova, E.S., Gromova, E.A. (2017) "Norwegian experience as a promising measure for the Russian energy system development", International Journal of Energy Economics and Policy, Vol. 7 N 3 pp. 31-35

Bekbaev, A.B., Shakenov, K.B., Titkov, V.V. (2019) "Analysis of the roof of an autonomous house for efficient use of wind energy", EAI Endorsed Transactions on Energy Web, Vol. 19 N 21

Bushukina, V.I. "Financing of investment projects in the field of renewable energy", Vestnik YuUrGU. Seriya "Energetika" [Bulletin of SUSU. Series "Energy"]. 2019. Vol. 19, No. 1. P. 50–57. DOI: 10.14529 / power190106 (in Russian)

Chebotareva, G.S., Strielkovsky V., Blaginin, V.A. "Renewable energy market: development and profitability of companies", Upravlenets [Manager]. 2019. Vol. 10. No. 3. P. 58-69. DOI: 10.29141 / 2218-5003-2019-10-3-6 (in Russian)

Global trends in Renewable Energy Investment 2019. Frankfurt School-UNEP Centre/BNEF. 2019.

Khabachev, L.D., Plotkina, U.I., Bugaeva, T.M., Yurkova, A.B. (2018), "Assessment of systemic effects from integration of distributed generation facilities into regional energy systems", 2017 6th International Conference on Reliability, Infocom Technologies and Optimization: Trends and Future Directions, ICRITO 2017, pp. 188-193

Lebedev, O.T., Mokeeva, T.V., Rodionov, D.G. (2018) "Matrix structures of science and technology innovations development and implementation trajectory", Proceedings of the 31st International Business Information Management Association Conference, pp. 1759-1768

Nikolova, L.V., Rodionov, D.G., Afanasyeva, N.V. (2017). "Impact of globalization on innovation project risks estimation", European Research Studies Journal, Vol 20 №2, pp 396-410

Pernick, R., Slen, E. "Clean Energy & Smart Grid Infrastructure". Nasdaq Global Information Services. 2018.

Renewables 2019 Global Status Report. REN21. 2019.

Rodionov, D.G., Konnikov, E.A., Konnikova, O.A. (2018) "Approaches to ensuring the sustainability of industrial enterprises of different technological levels", Journal of Social Sciences Research, Special Issue 3, pp. 277-282

Rodionov, D., Rudskaia, I. (2018) "Problems of infrastructural development of "industry 4.0" in Russia on sibur experience", Proceedings of the 32nd International Business Information Management Association Conference, pp. 3534-3544

Rodionov, D., Rudskaia, I., Degtereva, V. (2017) "Regional foresight as a technology for development of the regional innovation system", Proceedings of the 29th International Business Information Management Association Conference, pp. 2699-2705

Sedash, T.N. "Renewable energy sources: investment promotion in Russia and abroad", Rossijskij vneshneekonomicheskij vestnik [Russian Foreign Economic Bulletin]. 2016. No. 5. P. 50-56 (in Russian)

Sushko, O.P., Kaznin, A.A., Babkin, A.V., Bogdanov, D.A. (2017) "Economic Evaluation of the Information Security Levels Achieved by Electric Energy Providers in North Arctic Region", IOP Conference Series: Earth and Environmental Science, Vol. 90 N 1

Zhai, Y., Lee, Y. "Investment in renewable energy is slowing down", World Economic Forum in collaboration with Asian Development Bank. 2019. URL: https://www.weforum.org/agenda/2019/09/global-renewable-energy-investment-slowing-down-worry/

Zaychenko, I., Gutman, S., Kalinina, O. (2018) "Adjustment of Energy Strategy of Russia to Specific Nature of Far North: Analytic Hierarchy Process", Advances in Intelligent Systems and Computing, Vol. 692 pp. 453-462

Zogo, B., Cedrick, E. & Long, W. "Investment Motivation in Renewable Energy: A PPP Approach", Energy Procedia. Volume 115. June 2017. Pages 229-238. DOI: 10.1016/j.egypro.2017.05.021

www.ingramcontent.com/pod-product-compliance
Lightning Source LLC
LaVergne TN
LVHW060209210926
848481LV00008B/2678